CHORAL MUSIC IN PRINT

1976 SUPPLEMENT

Edited By:

Thomas R. Nardone

MUSICDATA, INC.

Philadelphia, 1976

Published volumes from the "Music-In-Print" series:

Vol.   I: Sacred Choral Music In Print
Vol. II: Secular Choral Music In Print
       1976 Supplement To Choral Music In Print
Vol. III: Organ Music In Print

International Standard Book Number: 0-88478-007-4

Library of Congress Catalog Card Number: 73-87918

Manufactured in the United States of America by Port City Press

Musicdata, Inc.
18 West Chelten Avenue
Philadelphia, Pennsylvania 19144

Contents

Preface

Musicdata, Inc. has produced a computerized system which is used to standardize titles of music into a concise bibliographic form in an attempt to provide comprehensive and current listings of music in print. Our Music-In-Print series, which began with the publication of *Choral Music In Print Vols. I & II* in 1974 followed by *Organ Music In Print* in 1975, is growing in its coverage of the different areas of music for performance and its comprehensive international outreach. One can readily see the expansion since our earliest editions by comparing the publisher listings in this supplement against that of *Choral Music In Print Vol. I.* Musicdata has achieved this increase in publisher information through constant direct correspondence with music publishers throughout the world.

This supplement to *Choral Music In Print* is a complete supplement to both Vols. I & II and serves as the first supplement in the Music-In-Print series. The book is divided into two complete alphabetical listings: sacred and secular. This breakdown follows the pattern used for the first edition of *Choral Music In Print.* The publisher list follows the secular choral music editions and is the most complete version to date.

The contents of the supplement is largely composed of music from publishers who were not listed in the first edition. There are also many new works from those music publishers who were already a part of our series. We have also included editions which were inadvertently omitted by us in the first edition. This supplement does not include corrections of typographical or other errors which were passed through into the 1974 edition. All errors of this nature will be attended to upon the publication of a completely revised second edition.

Many people expressed their opinions about *Choral Music In Print* either in reviews or directly to the publisher. I am grateful for the many people who voiced their feelings and appreciation for what we have started, and hope that all publications stemming from this are equally well received. It would be very difficult to mention all the people who wrote to us and about us but I would like to thank two people for their extraordinary assistance; they are Joseph Boonin and Richard Bloesch. Mr. Boonin scoured our publisher listing and provided a list of changes which were necessary to update the list. Publishers and their agents change very often and it is very difficult to keep track of their frequent shifting. Mr. Bloesch reviewed our book in RQ, an American Library Association periodical, and stated that we had omitted a large number of foreign publishers. Through further correspondence with him it was revealed that we had contacted most of the publishers he had been referring to. I say contacted because most of them never sent any materials or responded whatsoever to our requests. Our policy is to keep requesting materials until we receive some answer in reference to a publisher's music editions in print. With Mr. Bloesch's cooperation we were able to contact and obtain materials from several foreign publishers whose works were new to our series, greatly increasing the scope of our supplement and the size of the book itself. Any publisher who has not been contacted by us may send catalogs directly to Musicdata for future inclusion.

Overall thanks are due to the publishers who did a good job of providing lists of new sacred and secular choral editions. I am especially grateful to those publishers who did some extra work by checking our 1974 edition for the complete listings of their works; this is important for both parties involved. We will strive to maintain our pleasant association with the music publishers and to continue listing their editions in a clear and concise manner.

Special mention should be made of our "Publisher's Advertisements" section which is noticeably larger in this supplement. We are pleased to see this type of a response and see it as an enrichment of the Music-In-Print series. Please browse through these pages and keep these publishers in mind when ordering choral music. Most of these publishers represent a large number of other publishers and all are interested in the advancement of choral music in performance.

The following people on our staff have made this supplement possible: Our coders and proofreaders were Stephen C. Fisher, Joanne S. Godeck, Nancy K. Nardone, Anne Marie Regan and Suzanne M. Sharrock. Our teletypist was Corlette Mosley. Computer programming and processing were done by Mark Resnick. Final typing and collating of the supplement were done by Anne Marie Regan and Mary Ann Resnick.

Philadelphia, Pa.
February, 1976

Thomas R. Nardone

Guide to Use

GENERAL ARRANGEMENT

Within each catalog from the "Music-In-Print" series the user will find a comprehensive listing of the works of music publishers throughout the world. The arrangement of this listing is a single alphabetic interfiling of composers' names, titles of works, and cross references. The title under the composer's name serves as the focus for major information on each composition. In the absence of a composer the title in the main list is the focal point.

For each title there are two types of information: a) generic information about the composition and b) specific information pertaining to the editions which are in print. Included in the generic information category are the uniform title of the composition, a structured title for the work (e.g., Cantata 140), a thematic catalog number or opus and number designation, the larger source from which the work was taken, and remarks. The remarks are a series of codes or abbreviations giving information on the seasonal or other usage of the piece, the type of music, and the national origin and century for folk or anonymous pieces. (These codes also make it possible to retrieve, from the data base developed for the "Music-In-Print" series, specialized listings of music for particular seasons, types, etc.)

Following the generic information about the piece is the information about the individual editions. This information includes the arranger, the published title of the edition if different from the uniform title, the language of the text, instrumentation required for performance, a difficulty rating assigned for the edition by the publisher, the format of the publication, publisher, publisher's number, price, and information on the availability of music for rental or the availability of orchestral parts.

Following is a typical entry under a composer:

(All examples in this Guide are taken from Vol. I: *Sacred Choral Music In Print*)

AHLE, JOHANN RUDOLPH (1625-1673)
Furchtet Euch Nicht *Xmas, cant
(Lillehaug, L.) "Be Not Afraid" [Eng/Ger]
dbl cor,cont,4trom sc CONCORDIA 97-6407
$1.50, cor pts CONCORDIA 97-6430 $.40,
ipa   (A316)

In this entry, the title, "Furchtet Euch Nicht" is shown in the section for the composer, Johann Rudolph Ahle. "Xmas" and "cant" are remark codes indicating that the piece is a cantata appropriate for Christmas use. (The asterisk before Xmas merely serves to set off the remarks from the title.) The piece has only one edition, arranged by L. Lillehaug. The English title is "Be Not Afraid." The text is in English and German. The piece is scored for double chorus, continuo and four trombones. Both score and choral parts may be obtained from Concordia at the prices shown. 97-6407 and 97-6430 are the publisher's order numbers. The code "ipa" indicates that instrumental parts are available, but we have not undertaken to list the prices of these.

SACRED-SECULAR DESIGNATIONS

With few exceptions, we have relied upon the sacred-secular distinctions made for us by the publishers. Where publishers have not made the distinction, for the purpose of this index we have taken music with a scriptural text or which is appropriate for religious usage or church service to be sacred.

SEQUENCE NUMBERS

An alphanumeric number, appearing on the right margin, has been assigned to each edition represented in this catalog. These are for the purpose of easing identification and location when corrections are made in our updating service.

PRICES

We can give no assurances of the accuracy of stated prices. The prices of editions have been increasing steadily over the last few years, yet we have thought it helpful to give the user a U.S. dollar figure, where available, for comparative purposes. The publishers should be consulted directly for current prices.

CROSS REFERENCES

In order to provide the user with as many points of access as possible, the "Music-In-Print" series has been heavily cross-referenced. For example, the piece by Ahle, illustrated above, may be located under either its German or English title in the main alphabet, as well as under the composer. Therefore, the following cross references exist in the main alphabet:

FURCHTET EUCH NICHT see Ahle, Johann Rudolph

and

BE NOT AFRAID see Ahle, Johann Rudolph, Furchtet Euch Nicht

and in addition, the following cross reference will be found under the composer's name:

Be Not Afraid *see Furchtet Euch Nicht

s.p.	separately published	Swed	Swedish	UL	partially listed
Sab	Sabbath	SWV	Schütz-Werke-Verzeichnis	unis	unison
sac	sacred			unis cor	unison chorus
sc	score	T	tenor	US	United States
Scot	Scottish	tamb	tambourine		
sec	secular	Thanks	Thanksgiving	vcl	violoncello
Septua	Septuagesima	Thomas	Thomas organ	vla	viola
Sexa	Sexagesima	timp	timpani	vln	violin
Slav	Slavic	treb cor	treble chorus	voc pt	vocal part
So Am	South American	treb inst	treble instruments	voc sc	vocal score
Span	Spanish	Trin	Trinity		
speak cor	speaking chorus	trom	trombone	wom cor	women's chorus
spir	spiritual	trp	trumpet	Wurlitzer	Wurlitzer organ
sr cor	senior chorus				
study sc	study score	U	unlisted	Xmas	Christmas

SACRED CHORAL MUSIC

ADORAMUS TE, CHRISTE see Gasparini,
   Quirino

ADORAMUS TE, CHRISTE see Lassus, Roland
   de (Orlandus)

ADORATE DEUM see Heftrich, Wilhelm

ADORATION see Billings, William

ADORE THE CHILD OF BETHLEHEM *Xmas,
   anthem/carol,Fr
   cor CHORISTERS R-1 $.15 contains
   also: Chime Music   (A44)

ADORNA THALAMUM see Scarlatti,
   Alessandro

ADORNA THALAMUM TUUM, SION see Lassus,
   Roland de (Orlandus)

ADORO TE see Kempter, Karl

ADVENT see Kutzer, Ernst

ADVENT see Egebjer, Lars

ADVENT CANTATA see Stout, Alan

ADVENT CAROL see Wood, Dale

ADVENT CAROL, AN see Paviour, Paul

ADVENT I see Genzmer, Harald

ADVENT II see Genzmer, Harald

ADVENT LULLABY, AN see Young, Gordon

ADVENT RESPONSORY, AN see Bryant

ADVENT: THREE VIEWS see Parker, Alice

ADVENTI ENEK see Kodaly, Zoltan

ADVENTLIED "LASS DEN HEILAND EIN" see
   Nentwig, W.

ADVENTS MASS SONGS NO. 2 see Zouhar,
   Zdenek, Roraty C. 2

ADVENTS- UND WEIHNACHTSGESANGE see
   Zoll, Paul

ADVENTS- UND WEIHNACHTSKANTATEN *CC7L,
   Adv/Xmas,cant
   mix cor,inst BOHM s.p. contains works
   by: Herold; Jochum; Kutzer;
   Lemacher and others   (A45)

ADVENTS- UND WEIHNACHTSMUSIK see
   Taubert, Karl Heinz

ADVENTSKANTATE see Schweizer, Rolf

ADVERSITY
   see Four Folk Songs From Abroad

AEOLIAN COLLECTION OF ANTHEMS, BOOK I
   see Lutkin, Peter Christian

AEOLIAN COLLECTION OF ANTHEMS, BOOK II
   see Lutkin, Peter Christian

AEOLIAN COLLECTION OF ANTHEMS, BOOK III
   *CC13U
   (Nolte, Ewald V.) 1-2pt treb cor
   FITZSIMONS $.60   (A46)

AEOLIAN COLLECTION OF ANTHEMS, BOOK IV
   see Scholin, C. Albert

AETERNA CHRISTI MUNERA see Palestrina,
   Giovanni

AETERNE REX see Benkert, Lorenz

AETERNE REX see Dantonello, Josef

AETERNE REX see Erhard, Karl

AETERNE REX see Kromolicki, Joseph

AETERNE REX see Lemacher, Heinrich

AETERNE REX see Lipp, Alban

AETERNE REX see Messner, Joseph

AETERNE REX see Welcker, Max

AETERNE REX ALTISSIME see Rehmann, Th.

AETERNE REX ALTISSIME see Schroeder,
   Hermann

AFFERENTUR REGI see Bruckner, Anton

AFRICAN CAROL
   (Wetzler, Robert) SATB/SAB,fl,bvl,
   drums,fing.cym. ART MAST 1026 $.40
                                 (A47)

AFRICAN EASTER see Silver

AFTERNOON ON A HILL see Whitecotton,
   Shirley

AGAIN THE TIME OF THE SAVIOR'S BIRTH
   see Caldwell, Mary [Elizabeth]

AGAZZARI, AGOSTINO (1578-1640)
   Ave Virgo Gratiosa *mot
   (Beichert, Eugen) 3pt wom cor,acap/
   org (easy) sc SCHOTTS C 34 479
   s.p.   (A48)

AGELESS THOU ART see Bryson

AGENDE see Hufschmidt, Wolfgang

AGER, LAURENCE
   Rising Again, The
   unis ASHDOWN U98   (A49)

AGINCOURT see Dyson, George

AGNUS DEI see Baudrier, Yves

AGNUS DEI see Des Prez, Josquin

AGNUS DEI see Dumont, [Henri]

AGNUS DEI see Dvorak, Antonin

AGNUS DEI see Faure, Gabriel-Urbain

AGNUS DEI see Hall, William D.

AGNUS DEI see Haydn, (Johann) Michael

AGNUS DEI see Lassus, Roland de
   (Orlandus)

AGNUS DEI see Lotti, Antonio

AGNUS DEI see Monteverdi, Claudio

AGNUS DEI see Palestrina, Giovanni

AGNUS DEI see Pierson, Henry Hugo

AGNUS DEI see Praetorius, Michael

AGNUS DEI see Spencer, Williametta

AGNUS DEI see Victoria, Tomas Luis de

AGNUS DEI see Williamson, Malcolm

AGNUS DEI "ES SUCHT DAS LAMM" see
   Fortner, Wolfgang

AH, DEAREST JESUS see Harris

AH HELPLESS WRETCH see Ravenscroft,
   Thomas

AH, HOLY JESU *Easter
   (Bissell, Keith W.) SATB (med easy)
   WATERLOO $.35   (A50)

AH HOLY JESU see Bach, Johann Sebastian

AH, HOLY JESUS see Cruger, Johann

AH KNOW DE LORD see Clements, John

AH KNOW DE LORD HIS HANDS ON ME *spir
   (Clements, John) "Ich Weiss Die Hande
   Gottes Uber Mir" [Eng] mix cor,pno
   (med easy) sc SCHOTTS SL 5158 s.p.
                                 (A51)

AH LORD, SINCE I AM WHOLLY THINE see
   Bach, Johann Sebastian

AH, LORD, WHO HAST CREATED ALL see
   Schutz, Heinrich

AH MY DEAR ANGRY LORD see Wills, Arthur

AHAVAT OLAM see Helfman, Max

AHLEN, DAVID
   Garningar Utan Karlek Aro Intet Varda
   4pt mix cor ERIKS 2 s.p.   (A52)

   Tiden, Ar Fullbordad *Bibl
   4pt mix cor ERIKS 20 s.p.   (A53)

AHLEN, WALDEMAR
   Julafton
   4pt mix cor ERIKS 3 s.p.   (A54)

AHLWEN
   He The Pearly Gates Will Open
   *anthem/gospel
   (Johnson, Norman) SATB oct SINGSPIR
   ZJP-8025 $.30   (A55)
   (Mercer, W. Elmo) SATB,acap oct
   BENSON S4383 $.25   (A56)

AHNFELT, O.
   Day By Day *anthem
   (Johnson, Norman) SATB oct SINGSPIR
   ZJP-7350 $.30   (A57)

AHRENS, JOSEPH (1904-   )
   Ave Maria, Du Ros' Ohn Alle Dorn
   *Xmas
   mix cor (med easy) sc SCHOTTS
   C 38 003 s.p.   (A58)

   Drei Weihnachtliche Liedsatze *Xmas
   mix cor (med easy) sc SCHOTTS
   C 38 004 s.p.
   contains: In Trinitatis Speculum
   "Der Spiegel Der
   Dreifaltigkeit"; Kindelein Im
   Stall; Kindelein Zart   (A59)

   In Trinitatis Speculum "Der Spiegel
   Der Dreifaltigkeit"
   see Drei Weihnachtliche Liedsatze

   Jesu, Jesu Komm Zu Mir
   SATB,acap (med) MULLER MS73   (A60)

   Kindelein Im Stall
   see Drei Weihnachtliche Liedsatze

   Kindelein Zart
   see Drei Weihnachtliche Liedsatze

   Missa Dorica
   2pt jr cor,org (med easy) sc
   SCHOTTS C 37 464 s.p., cor pts
   SCHOTTS C 37 464A s.p.   (A61)

AH'S NOT AFEARED OF JESUS see LaCheur,
   Rex

AIBLINGER, JOHANN KASPAR (1779-1867)
   Jubilate Deo
   [Lat] SATTB,acap sc,cor pts BOHM
   s.p.   (A62)

   Veni Sancte Spiritus
   [Lat] 4pt mix cor,acap BOHM s.p.
                                 (A63)

AICHINGER, GREGOR (1564-1628)
   Ave Regina Coelorum
   [Lat] 4pt mix cor,acap sc,cor pts
   BOHM s.p.   (A64)

   Cantiones Ecclesiasticae *CCU
   (Hettrick, William E.) cor,cont bds
   A-R ED $9.95   (A65)

   Meine Seele Lobe Den Herren Mein
   *Fest
   mix cor,acap BOHM s.p.   (A66)

   O Sacrum Convivium
   [Lat] SATTB,acap sc,cor pts BOHM
   s.p.   (A67)

   Pange Lingua
   [Lat] SATTB sc,cor pts BOHM s.p.
                                 (A68)

   Ubi Est Abel? *anthem
   (Proulx, R.) "Where Is Now Abel?"
   SAB (med) GIA GI854 $.40   (A69)

   Where Is Now Abel? *see Ubi Est
   Abel?

AIN'A THAT GOOD NEWS see Dawson,
   William Levi

AINGER
   God Is Working His Purpose Out
   (composed with Buffaloe, James)
   *anthem
   SATB (easy) oct BROADMAN 4554-64
   $.30   (A70)

AIN'T DAT GOOD NEWS! *anthem/gospel
   (Johnson, Norman) SATB oct SINGSPIR
   ZJP-8106 $.30   (A71)

AKERS, DORIS
   Lead Me, Guide Me
   SSA BIG3 $.40   (A72)
   SATB BIG3 $.50   (A73)

   Sweet, Sweet Spirit
   (Krogstad, Bob) SATB oct GOSPEL
   05 TM 0159 $.40   (A74)

AL LA RU see Schroth, G.

AL-LE-LU! see McNair, Jacqueline Hanna

ALAS, AND DID MY SAVIOR BLEED *anthem
   (Turner) SATB oct BROADMAN 4554-98
   $.30   (A75)

ALAS, AND DID MY SAVIOR BLEED see Watts

ALAS! AND DID MY SAVIOUR BLEED
   *Easter,anthem
   (Bartlett) SATB FINE ARTS CM 1009
   $.30   (A76)

ALAS, AND DID MY SAVIOUR BLEED see
   Work, John [Wesley]

ALAS FOR THE DAY see Parris, Robert

ALAS, MY SAVIOR DIED see Williams,
   David H.

ALAS, THAT I OFFENDED EVER see Hooper,
Edmund

ALAS, THEY HAVE TAKEN THE LORD see
Morley, Thomas, Eheu Sustulerunt
Dominum

ALBERT, HEINRICH (1604-1651)
Gott Des Himmels Und Der Erden
SSATB (contains also: Wohl Dem, Der
Nicht Den Weg Des Frevlers Wahlt)
SCHWEIZER. SK 59.03-4 s.p. see
also MUSIKBEILAGE ZUM
"EVANGELISCHEN KIRCHENCHOR 1959"
(A77)
Lobet Gott In Seinem Heiligthum
SSATB SCHWEIZER. SK 63.01 s.p. see
also MUSIKBEILAGE ZUM
"EVANGELISCHEN KIRCHENCHOR 1963"
(A78)

ALBERT, JOHANN
There's Love In The Air
(Bock, Fred) SATB,acap (easy)
GENTRY G-259 $.30   (A79)

ALBINONI, TOMASO (1671-1750)
Magnificat
(Schroder, Felix) [Lat] 4pt mix
cor,SATB soli,org,2vln,bvl,opt
vla&bvl&trp&trom (med easy) min
sc SCHOTTS ETP 1074 s.p., ipa
(A80)

ALBRIGHT, WILLIAM H.
Alleluia Super-Round, An
8pt,opt inst (med) oct ELKAN-V
362-03180 $.40   (A81)

Father, We Thank Thee
unis/cong,solo,pno/org,opt inst
(easy) oct ELKAN-V 362-03179 $.30
(A82)

ALCORN, JEANIE
All Because Of His Love
(Smith, Herb) SATB oct GOSPEL
05 TM 0146 $.20   (A83)

ALDER
Nisi Domine
4pt,acap voc pt HENN 613 s.p. (A84)

Veni Electa Mea
4pt,acap voc pt HENN 615 s.p. (A85)

ALDERSGATE PRAYER see Werle, Floyd
Edwards

ALFORD
He Is Alive *see Thomas

ALL BECAUSE OF GOD'S AMAZING GRACE see
Adams, Steven R.

ALL BECAUSE OF HIS LOVE see Alcorn,
Jeanie

ALL BREATHING LIFE see Bach, Johann
Sebastian

ALL CREATURES OF OUR GOD AND KING
(Rutter) SATB,inst (easy) cor pts
OXFORD 40.029-40 $.45, ipa, ipr see
from Two Hymns Of Praise   (A86)

ALL DAY LONG MY HEART KEEPS SINGING see
Dunlop, Merrill

ALL FLESH IS GRASS see Bliem

ALL FOR JESUS see James, Mary

ALL GLORY BE TO GOD ON HIGH
see Three Hymns Of Praise

ALL GLORY BE TO GOD ON HIGH see
Rotermund, Melvin

ALL GLORY, LAUD AND HONOR see Durhan

ALL GLORY, LAUD AND HONOR see Peek,
Richard

ALL GLORY, LAUD AND HONOR see Teschner

ALL GLORY, LOVE AND POWER TO THEE see
Beethoven, Ludwig van

ALL GLORY, PRAISE, AND MAJESTY see
Bach, Johann Sebastian

ALL GLORY TO JESUS see Peterson, John
W.

ALL GOD'S CHILDREN see Gaither, William
J. (Bill)

ALL GOD'S CHILDREN ARE SINGING TONIGHT
see Wild, Eric

ALL GOD'S PEOPLE see Hughes, Robert J.

ALL GOOD GIFTS AROUND US see
Southbridge, James

ALL HAIL THAT FESTIVE DAY see Rogers,
Sharon Elery

ALL HAIL THE POWER OF JESUS' NAME see
Eller

ALL HAIL THE POWER OF JESUS' NAME see
Holden, [Oliver]

ALL HAIL THE POWER OF JESUS' NAME see
Thompson

ALL HAIL THE QUEEN see Willan, Healey

ALL HEAVEN ON HIGH REJOICES see Coggin

ALL I CAN GIVE IS MYSELF see Gagliardi,
George

ALL I HAVE BELONGS TO JESUS see Kirby

ALL I NEED see Johnson

ALL I NEED see Jones, C.P.

ALL MEN ARE GRASS see Berger, Jean

ALL MERCIFUL SAVIOUR see Bechler

ALL MY HEART THIS NIGHT REJOICES
see Merry Christmas

ALL MY HEART THIS NIGHT REJOICES see
Cornell, Garry A.

ALL MY HEART THIS NIGHT REJOICES see
Ebeling, Johann Georg

ALL MY HEART THIS NIGHT REJOICES see
Lutkin, Peter Christian

ALL MY HEART THIS NIGHT REJOICES see
Rogers, Sharon Elery

ALL MY HEART THIS NIGHT REJOICES see
Sowerby, Leo

ALL MY HEART THIS NIGHT REJOICES see
Williams, David H.

ALL NATURE'S WORKS HIS PRAISE DECLARE
see Butler

ALL NATURE'S WORKS HIS PRAISE DECLARE
see Herbek, Raymond H.

ALL NIGHT, ALL DAY see McNair,
Jacqueline Hanna

ALL OF ME see Grady

ALL OF ME see Lister, Mosie

ALL ON A CHRISTMAS DAY see Pulsifer,
Thomas R.

ALL PEOPLE THAT ON EARTH DO DWELL see
Arbatsky, [Yury]

ALL PEOPLE THAT ON EARTH DO DWELL see
Bourgeois, Loys (Louis)

ALL PEOPLE THAT ON EARTH DO DWELL see
Lawes, William

ALL PEOPLE THAT ON EARTH DO DWELL see
Roberts

ALL POOR MEN AND HUMBLE see
Christiansen, Paul

ALL POOR MEN AND HUMBLE see Kirby, L.M.
Jr.

ALL PRAISE AND THANKS TO GOD see
Pachelbel, Johann

ALL PRAISE TO THEE see Burroughs

ALL PRAISE TO THEE ETERNAL GOD see
Barrett, Arthur T.

ALL THAT THRILLS MY SOUL see Harris

ALL THE ANGELS SING A SONG see McNair,
Jacqueline Hanna

ALL THE ENDS OF THE EARTH HAVE SEEN see
Arbatsky, [Yury]

ALL THE WAY see Kleiman, Richard

ALL THE WAY FROM NAZARETH see Van
Hulse, Camil

ALL THE WAY MY SAVIOUR LEADS ME see
Bartlett

ALL THE WAY MY SAVIOUR LEADS ME see
Lowry, Robert

ALL THE WORLD IS GOD'S OWN FIELD
*anthem,Welsh
(Lovelace, Austin C.) 1-2pt WORD
CS-2695 $.35   (A87)

ALL THE WORLD WORSHIPS THEE see Handel,
George Frideric

ALL THEY THAT WAIT UPON THEE see Hilse,
W.

ALL THINGS see Wink

ALL THINGS ARE THINE see Wetzler,
Robert

ALL THINGS BRIGHT AND BEAUTIFUL
(McCabe, M.) unis,org GRAY CMR 3323
$.30   (A88)

ALL THINGS BRIGHT AND BEAUTIFUL see
Red, Buryl

ALL THINGS BRIGHT AND BEAUTIFUL see
Thomas, C.

ALL THINGS WORK TOGETHER FOR GOOD see
Glarum, L. Stanley

ALL THIS NIGHT see Case, J.

ALL THIS TIME see Walton

ALL THIS TIME THIS SONG IS BEST see
Constantino, Joseph

ALL-TIME FAVORITES FOR THE CHOIR NO. 1
*CCUL
(VanHorn, Charles) cor SINGSPIR 4281
$1.95   (A89)

ALL-TIME FAVORITES FOR THE CHOIR NO. 2
*CCUL
(VanHorn, Charles) cor SINGSPIR 4301
$1.95   (A90)

ALL-TIME FAVORITES FOR THE CHOIR NO. 3
*CCUL
(VanHorn, Charles) cor SINGSPIR 4302
$1.95   (A91)

ALL TOGETHER SING see Davis

ALL WE LIKE SHEEP see Burroughs

ALL WHO LOVE AND SERVE YOUR CITY see
Thiman, Eric Harding

ALL YE NATIONS PRAISE THE LORD see
Mozart, Wolfgang Amadeus

ALLA TRINITA
4pt mix cor LIENAU
MUSICA SACRA, NR. 56 sc s.p., cor
pts s.p.   (A92)

ALLAS OGON VANTA PA DIG, HERRE see
Schutz, Heinrich

ALLE WELT SPRINGE see Backer, Hans

ALLEGRI, GREGORIO (ca. 1582-1652)
Incipit Lamentatio
4pt mix cor LIENAU
MUSICA SACRA, NR. 49 cor pts
s.p., sc s.p.   (A93)

ALLEIN GOTT IN DER HOH' SEI EHR see
Praetorius, Michael

ALLEIN GOTT IN DER HOH SEI EHR see
Schroter, Leonhard

ALLEIN GOTT IN DER HOH SEI EHR see
Zipp, Friedrich

ALLEIN ZU DIR, HERR JESU CHRIST see
Kukuck, Felicitas

ALLELU! REJOICE AND SING! see Wilhelm

ALLELUIA see Bernabei

ALLELUIA see Butler

ALLELUIA see Diemente, Edward

ALLELUIA see Ein Frolich Gesang

ALLELUIA! see Hughes, Robert J.

ALLELUIA see James, Will

ALLELUIA see Johnston, Richard

ALLELUIA see Kam, Dennis

ALLELUIA see Lekberg, Sven

ALLELUIA see Pergolesi, Giovanni
Battista

ALLELUIA see Pinkham, Daniel

ALLELUIA see Ultan, Lloyd

ALLELUIA see Whitecotton, Shirley

ALLELUIA see Wigglesworth, Frank

ALLELUIA! ALLELUIA! *Easter,anthem
(Ehret, Walter) SATB,org,opt 3trp
(easy) GIA G1890 $.45   (A94)
(Rogers) 1-2pt jr cor oct LILLENAS

BACH, JOHANN SEBASTIAN (cont'd.)

CHBL 272 s.p.   (B18)

Ah Holy Jesu
  (Bissell, Keith W.) SATB (med easy)
  WATERLOO $.35   (B19)

Ah Lord, Since I Am Wholly Thine
  (Miles) SATB (med) FITZSIMONS 2096
  $.25   (B20)

All Breathing Life
  (White) SATB oct SCHMITT 1450 $.45
                                       (B21)

All Glory, Praise, And Majesty (from
  Cantata 106)
  (Chandler, H.) [Eng/Ger] SATB,pno
  oct NATIONAL WHC-30 $.45   (B22)

At The Lamb's High Feast We Sing
  see Four Easter Chorales

Auf Meinen Lieben Gott
  see Musikbeilage Zum "Evangelischen
  Kirchenchor 1968"

Aus Tiefer Not (from Cantata No. 38)
  SATB,cont sc HANSSLER HE 1.543 s.p.
                                       (B23)
  SATB,cont EGTVED MK15, 17 s.p.
                                       (B24)

Awake My Heart With Gladness *anthem
  (Davies) SATB,opt acap (easy)
  OXFORD 43.457 $.30   (B25)

Babe Is Born In Bethlehem, A
  (Rowley) mix cor BANKS MUS YS 1150
  $.20   (B26)

Beim Letzten Abendmahle
  see Erytraeus, Gottfried,
  Erschienen Ist Der Herrlich Tag

Bleed And Break Thou Loving Heart
  (from St. Matthew Passion)
  (Hall, W.D.) [Eng] SATB,pno/org/
  hpsd,opt 2fl oct NATIONAL WHC-2
  $.35   (B27)

Blessed Christ Is Risen Today, The
  *Easter,anthem/chorale
  see Four Easter Chorales
  (Lee, J.) SA (easy) GIA G1800 $.25
                                       (B28)

Break Forth, O Beauteous Light
  (Pitcher) SSA WILLIS 9660 $.35
                                       (B29)

Cantata 78 *see Jesu, Der Du Meine
  Seele

Cantata 176 *see Es Ist Ein Trotzig
  Und Verzagt Ding

Christ Jesus Lay In Death's Strong
  Bands
  see Four Easter Chorales

Christ Reigneth Still
  see Two Sacred Songs

Come And Thank Him *anthem
  (Davies) SS/SA (easy) OXFORD 44.231
  $.65   (B30)

Come Unto Me
  (Hall) SATB GALAXY 1.0592.1 $.35
                                       (B31)
  (Rasley, John M.) SATB oct SINGSPIR
  ZJP-7365 $.35   (B32)

Communion Chorales, Set II *CC6U
  (Miles, R.H.) SATB (med) FITZSIMONS
  2092 $.30   (B33)

Complete Works. Bach-Gesellschaft
  Edition *sac/sec,CCU
  (Rust, William, Rietz, J.;
  Hauptmann, M.; Becker, C.F.;
  Kroll, F.; Doerffel, A.; Naumann,
  E; Von Waldersee; Kretzchmar, H.)
  microfiche UNIV.MUS.ED.
  originally published as 47
  volumes in 61 bindings, Leipzig,
  1851-1899, and 1926. $310.00
                                       (B34)

Der Geist Hilft Unsrer Schwachheit
  Auf *S.226
  SATB&SATB,cont,opt 8inst sc
  HANSSLER 31.226 s.p.   (B35)

Die Choralsatze Der Johannespassion
  (from Johannespassion) CC11L
  SATB,cont,opt strings&winds CARUS
  CV 40.109 s.p.   (B36)

Dir, Dir Jehova Will Ich Singen
  *S.299
  mix cor (med easy) sc SCHOTTS
  CHBL 273 s.p.   (B37)
  SATB HANSSLER 6.322 s.p. contains
  also: Hassler, Hans Leo, Im
  Kuhlen Mai (SATB&SATB); Metzger,
  Hans-Arnold, Vater Unser Im
  Himmelreich (SATB)   (B38)

BACH, JOHANN SEBASTIAN (cont'd.)

Dir, Dir Jehovah Will Ich Singen
  SATB EGTVED MK4, 16 s.p.   (B39)

Dir, Jesu, Gottes Sohn, Sei Preis
  *S.421
  SATB HANSSLER 6.319 s.p. contains
  also: Schutz, Heinrich, Singet
  Mit Frueden Unserm Gott, SWV 178
                                       (B40)

Dreiundvierzig Vierstimmige Satze Zu
  Kirchenliedern *CC43U
  SATB LANDES LKB 1 s.p.   (B41)

Du Friedefurst, Herr Jesu Christ
  SATB EGTVED KB118 s.p.   (B42)

Durch Dein Gefangnis, Gottes Sohn
  (from Johannespassion)
  SATB,cont CARUS CV 40.403 s.p.
  contains also: In Meines Herzens
  Grunde (SATB,cont)   (B43)

Es Ist Ein Trotzig Und Verzagt Ding
  (Cantata 176) S.176, Trin,cant
  [Ger] SATB,SATB soli,2ob,strings,
  cont,org,opt bsn, oboe da caccia
  or English horn (med) s.p., ipa
  min sc BAREN. TP190, cor pts
  BAREN. BA5128, voc sc BAREN.
  BA5128A   (B44)

Final Chorus From The St. Matthew
  Passion *see Schlusschor Aus Der
  Matthauspassion

For Me To Live Is Jesus
  see Six Chorales Harmonized By
  Johann Sebastian Bach

Forget Me Not
  (Kinsman, F.) SATB BOURNE
  B218289-358 $.50   (B45)

Fount Of Every Blessing
  (Kinsman, F.) SATB BOURNE
  B230557-358 $.50   (B46)

Four Advent Chorales *CC4U,Adv,
  anthem
  (Lee, J.) SATB (easy) GIA G1877
  $.50   (B47)

Four Easter Chorales *Easter,anthem/
  chorale
  (Lee, J.) (med easy) oct GIA G1583
  $.50
  contains: At The Lamb's High
  Feast We Sing; Blessed Christ
  Is Risen Today, The; Christ
  Jesus Lay In Death's Strong
  Bands; Let Hymns Of Joy To
  Grief Succeed   (B48)

Freut Euch Und Jubiliert *S.243b
  SSAT/SSAB,cont,vln,opt 2ob&bsn&vla&
  vln CARUS CV 40.111 s.p.   (B49)

From Darkest Tomb Now Turn Away
  (Kinsman, F.) SATB BOURNE
  B218263-358 $.50   (B50)

From Heaven Glowing
  (Kinsman, F.) SATB BOURNE
  B218225-358 $.50   (B51)

From Heaven On High *anthem
  SATB oct CHANTRY CLA 6815 $.30
                                       (B52)

Gelobet Sei Der Herr *Fest
  mix cor,acap BOHM s.p.   (B53)

Gelobet Seist Du, Jesu Christ
  SATB DOBLINGER 213-214 s.p.
  contains also: Praetorius,
  Michael, Im Frieden Dein   (B54)

Gloria In Excelsis Deo *S.243c
  SSATB,opt cont EGTVED MK7, 1 s.p.
                                       (B55)
  SSATB,cont,vln,opt 2ob&bsn&vla&vln
  CARUS CV 40.112 s.p.   (B56)

God Is Life
  (Davis) SATB GALAXY 1.1833.1 $.30
                                       (B57)

God Liveth Still
  see Two Sacred Songs

God Of Mercy *anthem
  (Ehret, Walter) SAB AUGSBURG
  11-1698 $.35   (B58)

Gottlob, Es Geht Nunmehr Zu Ende
  men cor,acap TONOS 5634 s.p.   (B59)

Grant Us To Do With Zeal
  see Two Bach Chorales

Hear The Joyful News *Xmas
  (Kernochan) SATB/SAAB GALAXY
  1.2174.1 $.40   (B60)

BACH, JOHANN SEBASTIAN (cont'd.)

Herr Christ, Der Einig Gotts Sohn
  see Musikbeilage Zum "Evangelischen
  Kirchenchor 1968"

Herrscher Uber Tod Und Leben
  SATB,cont EGTVED MK3, 13 s.p.   (B61)

Holy Spirit Source Of Gladness
  *Easter/Pent
  (Wetzler) SATB,acap ART MAST 109
  $.30   (B62)

I Stand Before My God
  (Kinsman, F.) SATB BOURNE
  B218263-358 $.50   (B63)

Ich Will Den Namen Gottes Loben (from
  Cantata No. 142)
  SATB,org EGTVED KB124 s.p.   (B64)

If Thou But Suffer God To Guide Thee
  see Two Bach Chorales

In Faith I Quiet Wait
  (Protheroe) SATB (easy) FITZSIMONS
  2036 $.20   (B65)

In Meines Herzens Grunde (from
  Johannespassion)
  see Bach, Johann Sebastian, Durch
  Dein Gefangnis, Gottes Sohn

Je Veux Rester En Paix
  (Barblan) 4pt,acap voc pt HENN 183
  s.p.   (B66)

Jesu, Der Du Meine Seele (Cantata 78)
  S.78, cant
  [Eng/Ger] SATB,SATB soli,orch (med
  diff) cor pts BAREN. BA5139, voc
  sc BAREN. BA5139A, min sc BAREN.
  TP80   (B67)

Jesu, Geh Voran
  see Zwei Trauungschorale

Jesu, Meine Freude *see Cruger,
  Johann

Jesu, Nun Sei Gepreiset
  SATB,org,3trp,timp KING,R MFB 611
  cor pts $.20, cmplt ed $1.00
                                       (B68)

Jesu, Priceless Treasure
  (Hufstader, Robert) SSATB SCHIRM.G
  2913 $1.50   (B69)

Jesus All Min Gladje Bliver *see
  Jesus Bleibet Meine Freude

Jesus Bleibet Meine Freude (from
  Cantata No. 147) chorale
  see Bach, Johann Sebastian, Wohl
  Mir, Dass Ich Jesum Habe
  SATB,org,opt inst cor pts EGTVED
  MK2, 1 s.p., ipa   (B70)
  "Jesus All Min Gladje Bliver" 4pt
  mix cor ERIKS 100 s.p.   (B71)

Jesus, Redeemer Unchanging
  (Kinsman, F.) SATB BOURNE
  B230821-358 $.50   (B72)

King Of All Heavens (from Christmas
  Oratorio) Xmas
  (Harris) SATB,opt trp&timp PRO ART
  2787 $.40   (B73)

Komm, Susser Tod!
  (Klink, Waldemar) mix cor (med
  easy) sc SCHOTTS CHBL 261 s.p.
                                       (B74)

Kommt, Seelen, Dieser Tag
  (Klink, Waldemar) mix cor (easy) sc
  SCHOTTS CHBL 275 s.p.   (B75)

Lent And Easter Chorales *CCU
  (Hansen) SATB oct SCHMITT 1447 $.40
                                       (B76)

Let Hymns Of Joy To Grief Succeed
  *anthem/chorale
  see Four Easter Chorales
  (Lee, J.) SA (easy) GIA G1799 $.25
                                       (B77)

Liebster Jesu, Wir Sind Hier
  see Musikbeilage Zum "Evangelischen
  Kirchenchor 1968"

Little Hosanna, A (from English
  Suites No. 2) anthem
  (Shull, June; Zumwalt, Betty) cor
  CHORISTERS R-8 $.15   (B78)

Live Your Life For Him *anthem
  (Davies) SATB,opt acap (easy)
  OXFORD 43.456 $.25   (B79)

Lob, Ehr', Und Preis Sei Gott (from
  Cantata No. 192)
  SAB,strings sc,cor pts EGTVED
  MK8, 18 s.p., ipa   (B80)

BACH, JOHANN SEBASTIAN (cont'd.)

Lobe Den Herren
  SATB,org EGTVED KB101 s.p.   (B81)

Lobgesang (from Weihnachts-Oratorium)
  Xmas
  SATB,org/harmonium sc,cor pts
  PELIKAN PE190   (B82)

Lobpreiset All
  SATB DOBLINGER S 203 s.p.   (B83)

Lofty Cedars (from Cantata 150)
  (Dawson, E.) [Eng/Ger] SAB/STB,pno/
  org/strings oct NATIONAL WHC-43
  $.35   (B84)

Lord As Thou Willest
  (Kinsman, F.) SATB BOURNE
  B218247-358 $.50   (B85)

Lord How Bounteous Is Thy Kindness
  SATB BOURNE B230532-358 $.50   (B86)

Lord Of Light
  (Sateren) SATB,acap ART MAST 123
  $.30   (B87)

Louons Le Dieu Puissant
  4pt,acap voc pt HENN 282 s.p. (B88)

Magnificat
  (Schering, Arnold) SSATB,soli,2fl,
  2ob,bsn,3trp,strings,timp (med)
  min sc SCHOTTS ETP 964 s.p.   (B89)

Markus-Passion *S.247
  SATB,SAT soli,2ob,strings,cont,
  English horn, optional 2 lutes
  voc sc HANSSLER 10.209 s.p.   (B90)

Matthaus-Passion
  (Elgar; Atkins) "Passion Of Our
  Lord According To St. Matthew,
  The" SATB,SATB soli,2fl,2ob,bsn,
  org,cembalo,strings,2orch voc sc
  NOVELLO rental   (B91)
  (Griffiths; Young; Darlow) "Passion
  Of Our Lord According To St.
  Matthew, The" SATB,SATB soli,2fl,
  2ob,bsn,org,cembalo,strings,2orch
  voc sc NOVELLO rental   (B92)

Matthaus-Passion (Neue Bach Ausgabe)
  *Psntd
  "St. Matthew Passion" [Ger] SATB&
  SATB,SSATTBB soli,orch sc BAREN.
  BA5038, voc sc BAREN. BA5038A,
  min sc BAREN. TP196   (B93)

Meinen Jesum Lass Ich Nicht (from
  Cantata No. 157)
  SATB&opt SA HANSSLER 6.321 s.p.
  contains also: Kurig, Hans-
  Hermann, Dein Ist Das Jahr, Dein
  Ist Die Zeit (SATB/SSATB); Kurig,
  Hans-Hermann, Lobet Den Herren,
  Alle, Die Ihn Ehren (SATB/SSATB);
  Kurig, Hans-Hermann, Meinen Jesum
  Lass Ich Nicht (SA); Salieri,
  Antonio, Herbei, Ihr Bruder (3pt)
                                 (B94)

Musikbeilage Zum "Evangelischen
  Kirchenchor 1968"
  SATB SCHWEIZER. SK 68.01-2 s.p.
  contains: Auf Meinen Lieben Gott;
  Herr Christ, Der Einig Gotts
  Sohn; Liebster Jesu, Wir Sind
  Hier; Uns Ist Ein Kindlein Heut
  Geborn   (B95)

My Heart Ever Faithful
  (Lutkin) unis (diff) FITZSIMONS
  5013 $.20   (B96)

My Weary Eyes I Close In God's Dear
  Name So Blest
  see Six Chorales Harmonized By
  Johann Sebastian Bach

Now Let Every Tongue Adore Thee
  (Pitcher) SSA WILLIS 9661 $.35
                                 (B97)

Now Thank We All Our God (from
  Cantata 79)
  (Bevan, Gwilym) SATB,band (med
  easy) cor pts WATERLOO $.40, ipr
                                 (B98)

Nun Danket Alle Gott
  see Bach, Johann Sebastian, Wenn
  Ich Einmal Soll Scheiden

Nun Ruhen Alle Walder
  see Bach, Johann Sebastian, Wach
  Auf, Mein Herz Und Singe

O Be Glad, My Soul, Be Cheerful
  see Six Chorales Harmonized By
  Johann Sebastian Bach

O Lord, Thou Hast Formed My Every
  Part
  see Two Bach Chorales

BACH, JOHANN SEBASTIAN (cont'd.)

O Thou Who Camest From Above
  see Two Bach Chorales

Oh, How Blest Are Ye Whose Toils Are
  Ended
  see Six Chorales Harmonized By
  Johann Sebastian Bach

Passion Of Our Lord According To St.
  John, The
  (Atkins) SATB,SATB soli,2fl,2horn,
  org,cembalo,strings, oboe d'amore
  voc sc NOVELLO rental   (B99)

Passion Of Our Lord According To St.
  Matthew, The *see Matthaus-
  Passion

Passionschoral "Der Leib Zwar In Der
  Erden" (from Komm, Du Susse
  Todestunde) Psntd,chorale
  [Eng/Ger] 4pt mix cor,org,strings,S
  rec,T rec (easy) sc SCHOTTS
  SL 6538 s.p., ipa   (B100)

Pecheurs Sor La Calvaire
  4pt,acap voc pt HENN 257 s.p. (B101)

Praise Him
  (Barrie) SAB SCHIRM.G LG51722 $.35
                                 (B102)

Prayer For Peace, A
  (Miles) SATB,T solo (med)
  FITZSIMONS 2097 $.25   (B103)

Preis Und Dank Sei Unserm Gott (from
  Osteroratorium) Easter
  SATB,org sc,cor pts PELIKAN PE180
                                 (B104)

Prepare Thyself, Zion
  see THREE CHRISTMAS SONGS WITH
  SYNTHESIZER ACCOMPANIMENT

Rest Thou Contented
  (Kinsman, F.) SATB BOURNE
  B218271-358 $.50   (B105)

St. Matthew Passion *see Matthaus-
  Passion (Neue Bach-Ausgabe)

Sanctus (from Mass In B-Minor)
  [Lat] SSAATB (diff) FITZSIMONS 2029
  $.30   (B106)

Sanctus In D *Sanctus
  (Steinitz) SATB,inst (med diff)
  OXFORD 46.514 $1.15, ipr   (B107)

Schlusschor Aus Der Matthauspassion
  (from Matthauspassion) Psntd
  "Final Chorus From The St. Matthew
  Passion" SATB,org sc,cor pts
  PELIKAN PE130   (B108)

Sheep May Safely Graze *sac/sec,
  Xmas,fr
  (Brown, F.E.) 3pt ALLANS 834 (B109)
  (Davis) SATB GALAXY 1.1278.1 $.35
                                 (B110)
  (Davis) SAB GALAXY 1.2297.1 $.35
                                 (B111)
  (Davis) SA GALAXY 1.1280.1 $.30
                                 (B112)
  (Lefebvre) TTBB GALAXY 1.1320.1
  $.30   (B113)

Shine Ye Stars In Highest Heaven
  (Kinsman, F.) SATB BOURNE
  B218280-358 $.50   (B114)

Singet Dem Herrn Ein Neues Lied
  SATB&SATB,cont,opt 8inst sc
  HANSSLER 31.225 s.p.   (B115)

Six Bach Chorales *CC6U,chorale
  (Hudson; Jaocbson) 4pt men cor
  CURWEN 50826 s.p.   (B116)

Six Chorales Harmonized By Johann
  Sebastian Bach
  (Buszin) SATB SCHMITT 1701 $.35
  contains: For Me To Live Is
  Jesus; My Weary Eyes I Close In
  God's Dear Name So Blest; O Be
  Glad, My Soul, Be Cheerful; Oh,
  How Blest Are Ye Whose Toils
  Are Ended; Soar, My Soul, To
  God On High; Will Of God Is
  Always Best, The   (B117)

Soar, My Soul, To God On High
  see Six Chorales Harmonized By
  Johann Sebastian Bach

Ten Chorales *CC10U,anthem
  (Lee, J.) SATB (easy) GIA G1810
  $1.00   (B118)

This Day To Us A Child Is Born *see
  Uns Ist Ein Kindlein Heut Geborn

Three Chorales (from St. Matthew
  Passion) CC3U,chorale
  (Carlton) SATB,acap oct BOOSEY 5146

BACH, JOHANN SEBASTIAN (cont'd.)

  $.30   (B119)

Thy Way, Not Mine, O Lord *anthem/
  hymn
  (Roff, Joseph) SATB,pno/org
  SHATTINGER 403 $.25   (B120)

Twelve Songs From Schemellis
  Gesangbuch *CC12U
  (Gore, Richard T.) unis jr cor/2pt
  jr cor,opt solo CHANTRY CHC 563
  $.80   (B121)

Two Bach Chorales *Xmas
  (Carlton) SATB oct BOOSEY 5411 $.30
  contains: Grant Us To Do With
  Zeal; If Thou But Suffer God To
  Guide Thee   (B122)

Two Bach Chorales *chorale
  (Barrie) SATB,acap oct LAWSON 821
  $.25
  contains: O Lord, Thou Hast
  Formed My Every Part; O Thou
  Who Camest From Above   (B123)

Two Chorales (from Christmas
  Oratorio) CC2U,Xmas,chorale
  (Bevan, G.) SATB (med easy)
  WATERLOO $.35   (B124)

Two Easter Chorales *CCU
  (Miles) SATB (easy) FITZSIMONS 2099
  $.25   (B125)

Two Sacred Songs
  2pt ENOCH T.P.126 s.p.
  contains: Christ Reigneth Still;
  God Liveth Still   (B126)

Uns Ist Ein Kindlein Heut Geborn
  see Musikbeilage Zum "Evangelischen
  Kirchenchor 1968"
  (Talmadge) "This Day To Us A Child
  Is Born" SSAA BRODT HC 5 $.26
                                 (B127)

Vijf Koralen En Slotkoor Uit De
  Matthaus Passion (from
  Matthauspassion) CC6U,Psntd
  (De Wolff) unis,pno/harmonium HEER
  1109 s.p.   (B128)

A Vocal Companion To Bach's
  Orgelbuchlein, Book Three
  (composed with Emery, Walter J.)
  *CCU,chorale
  SATB NOVELLO s.p.   (B129)

Vom Himmel Hoch, Da Komm Ich Her
  *S.243a
  SATB,opt org CARUS CV 40.110 s.p.
                                 (B130)

Wach Auf, Mein Herz Und Singe
  mix cor (med easy) sc SCHOTTS
  CHBL 307A-B s.p. contains also:
  Nun Ruhen Alle Walder   (B131)

Wachet Auf, Ruft Uns Die Stimme (from
  Cantata No. 140) ECY
  mix cor (med) sc SCHOTTS CHBL 312
  s.p.   (B132)
  SATB EGTVED KB158 s.p.   (B133)

We Hurry With Tired, Unfaltering
  Footsteps (from Cantata 78) sec
  SA GALAXY 1.0904.1 $.45   (B134)

Weihnachten Mit Johann Sebastian Bach
  *CCU,Xmas
  (Jode, Fritz) SATB/SSATB,kbd (med)
  sc SCHOTTS ED. 4133 s.p.   (B135)

Weihnachtschorale Aus Dem
  Weihnachtsoratorium (from
  Weihnachtsoratorium) CCU,Xmas,
  chorale
  SATB,acap/org (med) BAREN. BA6230
                                 (B136)

Wenn Ich Einmal Soll Scheiden (from
  Matthauspassion)
  mix cor (med easy) sc SCHOTTS
  CHBL 373 s.p. contains also: Nun
  Danket Alle Gott   (B137)
  SATB EGTVED KB83 s.p.   (B138)

Wer Nun Den Lieben Gott Lasst Walten
  see Zwei Trauungschorale

Will Of God Is Always Best, The
  see Six Chorales Harmonized By
  Johann Sebastian Bach

Wohl Mir, Dass Ich Jesum Habe (from
  Cantata No. 147)
  SATB,cont,orch voc sc CARUS
  CV 40.108 s.p. contains also:
  Jesus Bleibet Meine Freude   (B139)

Zion Hears The Watchmen's Voices
  (Rutter) SATB,inst (easy) OXFORD
  84.212 $.45   (B140)

BE GLAD see Fritschel, James

BE GLAD AND REJOICE see Van Hulse,
Camil

BE GLAD THEN AMERICA see La Montaine,
John

BE JOYFUL! see Brandon, George

BE MERCIFUL UNTO ME see Silvester,
Frederick

BE MERRY, YE PEOPLE *Xmas
(Ehret, Walter) SATB,pno (easy)
GENTRY G-245 $.40   (B276)

BE NOT AFRAID see Mana-Zucca, Mme.

BE NOT AFRAID see Mendelssohn-
Bartholdy, Felix

BE NOT DECEIVED see Hegenbart, Alex F.

BE PEACE ON EARTH see Crotch, William

BE STILL AND KNOW THAT I AM GOD see
Wetherill

BE STILL, MY SOUL see Sibelius, Jean

BE STILL, MY SOUL, AND LISTEN see
Welch, Ray

BE STRONG IN THE LORD see Matthews,
Thomas

BE THOU EXALTED see Handel, George
Frideric

BE THOU MY VISION *anthem/hymn,Ir
(Ehret, Walter) SATB oct LILLENAS
AN-2418 $.30   (B277)
(Johnson, Norman) SATB oct SINGSPIR
ZJP-7331 $.30   (B278)

BE WELCOME, O EMANUEL see Westra, Evert

BE WITH US, LORD, WE PRAY see
Rosenberg, Wolf

BE YE JOYFUL see Sateren, Leland
Bernhard

BEAL
Brother, Show Us The Way
BarBar&2camb CAMBIATA C97444 (B279)

Thanks Be To God *anthem
2pt FINE ARTS CM 1102 $.30   (B280)

BEAMS OF GENTLE LIGHT see Holmes,
Robert

BEARD
I Got The Rhythm
SATB oct SCHMITT 8507 $.40   (B281)

I Sing For The Joy
SATB oct SCHMITT 8506 $.40   (B282)

BEATA ES see Lemacher, Heinrich

BEATA ES VIRGO MARIA see Gabrieli,
Giovanni

BEATA MORTUI see Mendelssohn-Bartholdy,
Felix

BEATA VISCERA see Egk, Werner

BEATITUDE I: BLESSED ARE THE POOR IN
SPIRIT see Rottura, Joseph James

BEATITUDE II: BLESSED ARE THEY THAT
MOURN see Rottura, Joseph James

BEATITUDE III: BLESSED ARE THE MEEK see
Rottura, Joseph James

BEATITUDE V: BLESSED ARE THE MERCIFUL
see Rottura, Joseph James

BEATITUDES see Ridout, Alan

BEATITUDES, THE see Ballou, Esther W.

BEATITUDES, THE see Bliss, Sir Arthur

BEATITUDES, THE see Buettell

BEATITUDES, THE see Ford, Virgil T.

BEATITUDES, THE see Gore, Richard T.

BEATITUDES, THE see Hays, Peggy
McAllister

BEATITUDES, THE see Holman, Derek

BEATITUDES, THE see Hufschmidt,
Wolfgang, Seligpreisungen

BEATITUDES, THE see Peterson, John W.

BEATITUDES, THE see Rohwer, Jens, Die
Seligpreisungen

BEATITUDES, THE see Schweizer, Rolf,
Die Seligpreisungen

BEATITUDES, THE see Sinzheimer, Max

BEATITUDES, THE see Van Hulse, Camil

BEATITUDES, THE see Wommack, Chris

BEATITUDES FOR SMALLER CHILDREN see
Hays, Peggy McAllister

BEATTIE, HERBERT
Holy, Holy, Holy
see Six Choral Settings From The
Bible, Group II

Six Choral Settings From The Bible,
Group II *Bibl
SATB,acap/opt org oct LAWSON 551
$.25
contains: Holy, Holy, Holy;
Truly, My Soul   (B283)

Truly, My Soul
see Six Choral Settings From The
Bible, Group II

BEATUS HOMO see Weis, Flemming

BEATUS HOMO INVENIT see Villa-Lobos,
Heitor

BEATUS VIR see Carissimi, Giacomo

BEATUS VIR see Galuppi, Baldassare

BEATUS VIR see Lotti, Antonio

BEATUS VIR see Monteverdi, Claudio

BEATUS VIR see Perti, Giacomo Antonio

BEATUS VIR see Victoria, Tomas Luis de

BEATUS VIR see Vivaldi, Antonio

BEAUDROT
Praise The Lord! Ye Heavens Adore
Him!
SATB PRO ART 2768 $.35   (B284)

BEAUMONT, ADRIAN (1937-   )
Long, Long Ago
SSAA,acap ROBERTON 75021 s.p.
(B285)

BEAUMONT HYMN TUNES see Beaumont, Rev.
Geoffrey

BEAUMONT, REV. GEOFFREY
Beaumont Hymn Tunes *CCU
unis BELWIN $1.00   (B286)

Three Hymn Tunes *CC3U,hymn
SATB oct PAXTON P85385 s.p. (B287)

BEAUTY OF GOD, THE *CCUL
(Burroughs, Bob) wom cor,opt fl
BROADMAN 4523-07 $1.50   (B288)

BEAUVERD
Trois Chants De Noel *CC3U,Xmas
cor (easy) sc HENN 687 s.p. (B289)

BECAUSE HE FIRST LOVED US see Mueller

BECAUSE HE LIVES see Gaither, William
J. (Bill)

BECAUSE HE LIVES see Gaither, William
J. (Bill)

BECAUSE HE LIVES *CCUL
(Huff, Ronn) cor BENSON B0772 $1.95
stereo recording, tapes, and-or
accompaniment tape also available;
for book-record sets available,
contact publisher   (B290)

BECAUSE HE LOVES US ALL see
Whitecotton, Shirley

BECHLER
All Merciful Saviour
(Kroeger) [Ger/Eng] SATB oct
MORAVIAN 5880 $.45   (B291)

It Is Our God *see Kroeger, Karl

Kroeger, Karl
"It Is Our God" SATB,org,2horn,
strings (med) FISCHER,C CM 7849
s.p., ipr   (B292)

BECHLER, JOHANN CHRISTIAN (1784-1857)
Praises, Thanks And Adoration
(Pfohl) mix cor BRODT 105 $.25
(B293)

BECK, CONRAD (1901-   )
Es Kommt Ein Schiff Geladen
mix cor (med diff) sc SCHOTTS
C 32 657 s.p.   (B294)

BECK, JOHN NESS (1930-   )
Have Ye Not Known?
SATB,pno (med) BECKEN BP 1008 $.40
(B295)

Hymn For David
SATB SCHIRM.G B11993 $.40   (B296)

In Heavenly Love *Gen/Thanks
unis,org/pno,fl/rec&gtr CHORISTERS
A-94 $.30   (B297)

Once In David's Royal City *Xmas,
anthem
SATB oct SACRED S-177 $.35   (B298)

Once In Royal David's City *Xmas,
carol
SATB oct SACRED S-177 $.35   (B299)

Psalm 67
SATB SCHIRM.G B11991 $.40   (B300)

Shepherds, The *Xmas,cant
SATB SCHIRM.G B2953 $1.50   (B301)

Sing Unto Him *Gen/Thanks
2pt CHORISTERS A-52 $.25   (B302)

Song Of Moses
SATB SCHIRM.G B11992 $.40   (B303)

Thou Art God!
SATB&cong&opt jr cor,5brass&hndbl
(med easy) BECKEN BP 1005 $.50
(B304)

Who Shall Separate Us?
SATB,org ART MAST 261 $.35   (B305)

BECK, THEODORE
Seven Anthems For Treble Choirs
*CC7L
1-3pt treb cor,opt inst CONCORDIA
97-5218 $1.50   (B306)

Seven Anthems For Treble Choirs, Set
II *CC7L,Xmas/Easter
treb cor,opt inst CONCORDIA 97-5163
$1.90   (B307)

Songs For Christmas *CC8L
2-3pt treb cor,opt inst CONCORDIA
97-5156 $1.00   (B308)

BECKER
Wo Du Hingehst *Op.60
LIENAU sc s.p., cor pts s.p. (B309)

BECKER, JOHN J. (1886-1961)
Mass In Unison Or Two Parts
1-2pt,acap AM.COMP.AL. $3.58 (B310)

Missa Symphonica
TTBB,acap AM.COMP.AL. $3.85 (B311)

Nunc, Sancti, Nobis, Spiritus
SATB,acap AM.COMP.AL. $.55   (B312)

BECKWITH, JOHN (1927-   )
Sharon Fragments
SATB (med diff) WATERLOO $1.15
(B313)

BED NAR MORKRET TATNAR see Soderholm,
Valdemar

BEDNARCHUK, BRUCE
God's Land
SATB,pno,opt bvl ART MAST 1032 $.40
(B314)

BEEBE
And They Shall Beat Their Swords Into
Plowshares
unis,pno/org,opt bvl&gtr WARNER
CD0793 $.60   (B315)

Psalm 24 *see Who Shall Ascend

Who Shall Ascend (Psalm 24)
(easy) FISCHER,C CM 7863 $.40
(B316)

BEEBE, EDWARD J.
Psalm I *anthem,Contemp
SATB,org oct CHANTRY COA 549 $.20
(B317)
Who Has Believed *anthem,Contemp
SATB oct CHANTRY COA 6328 $.18
(B318)

BEEBE, HANK
Earth Is The Lord's, The
unis (easy) FISCHER,C CM 7820 $.30
(B319)

BEECROFT, NORMA
Living Flame Of Love
SATB (diff) WATERLOO $.75   (B320)

BEERS
Peace Carol *Xmas
(Ehret, Walter) SATB WARNER
WB-360 187   (B321)

BEETHOVEN, LUDWIG VAN (1770-1827)
All Glory, Love And Power To Thee
(Douglas) SAB PRO ART 2769 $.35
(B322)

Born Again
(Glazer) SATB (Scarborough hymn)
WARNER WB-358 187   (B323)

BEETHOVEN, LUDWIG VAN (cont'd.)

Complete Works *sac/sec,CCU
(Adler, Guido; Bagge, Selmar;
David, Ferdinand; Espagne, Franz;
Manoycewski, Eusebius; Nottebohm,
Gustav; Reinecke, Carl; Richter,
E.F.; Rietz, Julius) microfiche
UNIV.MUS.ED. $170.00 originally
published as 25 volumes, Leipzig,
1862-1888.   (B324)

Die Ehre Gottes In Der Natur "Die
Himmel Ruhmen"
(Lutz, Wilhelm) 4pt mix cor,acap/
pno/4horn,2trp,3trom,tuba cor pts
SCHOTTS C 39 646 s.p., voc sc
SCHOTTS C 38 165A s.p., ipa
                                  (B325)

(Lutz, Wilhelm) men cor,acap/pno/
org&4horn&2trp&3trom&tuba sc
SCHOTTS C 38 165-01 s.p., cor pts
SCHOTTS C 31 870 s.p.   (B326)

(Wagner, Franz) 4pt mix cor/3pt jr
cor,acap/pno/org,3vln,vcl,bvl,
timp sc SCHOTTS C 39 515 s.p.,
cor pts SCHOTTS C 39 518 s.p.,
ipa   (B327)

(Wagner, Franz) 3pt jr cor,acap/
pno/org&3vln&vcl&bvl&timp (med
easy) cor pts SCHOTTS C 39 517
s.p., ipa   (B328)

Die Vesper "Hort Vom Strand Ein
Vesper Singen"
(Haas, Joseph) men cor sc SCHOTTS
C 31 874 s.p.   (B329)

Every Child Stand Up And Sing
*anthem
(Shull, Jane; Zumwalt, Betty) cor
CHORISTERS R-12 $.15   (B330)

Gottes Macht Und Vorsehung "Gott Ist
Mein Lied"
(Haas, Joseph) men cor SCHOTTS
C 31 871 s.p.   (B331)

Hallelujah (from Mount Of Olives)
mix cor BANKS MUS YS 269 $.55
                                  (B332)
(Knudson) SATB,band ART MAST 1013
$.40, ipa   (B333)

Heavens Declare The Glory Of God, The
(Lutkin) SAB (easy) FITZSIMONS 6007
$.20   (B334)

Hymne An Die Nacht "Heil'ge Nacht, O
Giesse Du"
(Heim, Ignaz; Haas, Joseph) men cor
sc SCHOTTS C 31 873 s.p. (B335)

Hymnus *see Kyrie

Joyful, Joyful, We Adore Thee (from
Ninth Symphony) Thanks,anthem
(Johnson, Norman) SATB oct SINGSPIR
ZJP-7257 $.30   (B336)
(Lutkin) SA (med) FITZSIMONS 5011
$.25   (B337)
(Rasley, John M.) SATB (easy) oct
SINGSPIR ZJP-6019 $.25   (B338)

Kyrie (from Messe C-Dur)
(Chandler, H.) "Hymnus" [Lat] SATB,
SATB soli,pno oct NATIONAL WHC 34
$.35   (B339)

Messe In C-Dur *Op.86, Mass
[Lat] SATB,SATB soli,orch (C maj,
diff) min sc SCHOTTS ETP 996 s.p.
                                  (B340)

Missa Solemnis *Op.123, Mass
[Lat] SATB,SATB soli,orch (diff)
min sc SCHOTTS ETP 951 s.p.
                                  (B341)

Six Cantiques *CC6U
[Fr] cor LEMOINE 429 s.p.   (B342)

BEFIEHL DEM HERRN see Wiedermann,
Bedrich

BEFIEHL DU DEINE WEGE see Gesius,
Bartholomaus

BEFORE JEHOVAH'S AWFUL THRONE see Madan

BEGIN, MY TONGUE, SOME HEAVENLY THEME
see Greatorex, Thomas

BEGINNINGS see Courtney, Ragan

BEGINNINGS-A PRAISE CONCERT see Red,
Buryl

BEGLUCKT IST see Killmayer, Wilhelm

BEHOLD A MIGHTY PRELATE see MacNutt,
Walter

BEHOLD A MIGHTY PROPHET see Hallock,
Peter

BEHOLD A SILLY TENDER BABE see Roe

BEHOLD A STRANGER see Hegenbart, Alex
F.

BEHOLD! A STRANGER see Williams, David
H.

BEHOLD, BLESS YE THE LORD see Van
Hulse, Camil

BEHOLD, GOD IS MY SALVATION see Sitton,
Carl

BEHOLD, HE COMETH! see Kirk

BEHOLD HE IS MY SALVATION see Selby,
William

BEHOLD HOW GOOD see Pulsifer, Thomas R.

BEHOLD HOW GOOD AND JOYFUL A THING see
Vann

BEHOLD, I BRING YOU GLAD TIDINGS see
Gibbons, Orlando

BEHOLD, I BUILD A HOUSE see Wyner,
Yehudi

BEHOLD, LET US LOVE see Graham

BEHOLD MY SERVANT see Rochberg, George

BEHOLD NOW, BLESS THE LORD see Proulx,
Richard

BEHOLD NOW, PRAISE THE LORD see Powell,
Robert J.

BEHOLD THAT STAR-RISE UP SHEPHERDS ON
FOLLER
(Hudson, Hazel) 2pt ASHDOWN EA379
                                  (B343)
BEHOLD, THE FIELD IS WHITE, ALREADY TO
HARVEST see Bender, Jan

BEHOLD THE GLORIES OF THE LAMB see
Billings, William

BEHOLD THE GLORY OF THE LAMB see Dean,
T.W.

BEHOLD THE KING OF GLORY see Carlson,
J. Bert

BEHOLD THE LAMB OF GOD see Bass, Claude
L.

BEHOLD THE LAMB OF GOD see Bridges

BEHOLD THE LAMB OF GOD see Handel,
George Frideric

BEHOLD THE LAMB OF GOD see Littleton,
Bill J.

BEHOLD THE LORD SHALL COME see Schroth,
G.

BEHOLD, THE LORD'S HAND see Van Hulse,
Camil

BEHOLD THE MAN see Owens, Jimmy

BEHOLD THE SAVIOR OF MANKIND *Easter/
Lent,folk
(Ehret) SATB oct LILLENAS AN-2402
$.30   (B344)

BEHOLD THE SAVIOR OF MANKIND see
Welsey, Burrough

BEHOLD THE TABERNACLE OF GOD see
Bissell, Keith W.

BEHOLD, THE TABERNACLE OF GOD see
Joubert, John

BEHOLD THE TABERNACLE OF GOD see
Matthews, Thomas

BEHOLD, THOU SHALT CONCEIVE see Gallus,
Jacobus, Ecce Concipies

BEHOLD WHAT LOVE see Hegenbart, Alex F.

BEHOLD, WHAT MANNER OF LOVE see Mueller

BEHOLD, WHAT MANNER OF LOVE see Roff,
Joseph

BEHOLD, YOU ARE CHARMING see Des Prez,
Josquin, Ecce Tu Pulchra Es

BEHOLD YOUR GOD see Adler, Samuel

BEHOLD YOUR KING *Lent
cor ROYAL s.p.   (B345)

BEHOLD YOUR KING see Peterson, John W.

BEHOLDING THEE, LORD JESUS see Rasley,
John M.

BEI DER KRIPPE see Zahner, Bruno

BEIM LETZTEN ABENDMAHLE see Bach,
Johann Sebastian

BEIN, WILHELM
Sancta Maria, Ora Pro Nobis
[Lat] 4pt mix cor,acap BOHM s.p.
                                  (B346)

BELCHER, SUPPLY (1751-1836)
Blow Ye The Trumpet
(Van Camp, Leonard) cor,opt pno/org
(easy) FISCHER,C CM 7935 $.40
                                  (B347)
While Shepherds Watched Their Flocks
*Xmas,carol
(Van Camp, Leonard) cor FISCHER,C
CM 7936 $.40   (B348)

BELIEVE *CCUL
(Johnson, Derric) cor BENSON B0169
$1.95 stereo recording, tapes, and-
or accompaniment tape also
available; for book-record sets
available, contact publisher (B349)

BELIEVE ALSO IN ME see Boozer, Pat

BELIEVING SOULS, REJOICE AND SING see
Landon, Stewart

BELL, ROBERT H.
Magnificat *Magnif/Nunc
SATB (med easy) WATERLOO $.35
contains also: Nunc Dimittis
                                  (B350)
Nunc Dimittis
see Bell, Robert H., Magnificat

BELL' AMFITRIT ALTERA see Lassus,
Roland de (Orlandus)

BELL CAROL *Xmas
(Brandon, George) SA (easy) WATERLOO
$.40   (B351)

BELL CAROL see Thiman, Eric Harding

BELL CAROL, THE see Wichman

BELL HORSES see Copley

BELL NOEL see Frey, Richard

BELLERMANN, SANGERFAHRT
Mein Herz Dichtet Ein Feines Lied
*Op.33
mix cor,pno LIENAU sc s.p., cor pts
s.p.   (B352)

Zwei Gesange Fur Trauungen *Op.43,
CC2U,funeral
LIENAU sc s.p., cor pts s.p. (B353)

BELLO, TAVARES
Christmas Blessing (composed with
Filipe, Jaime) *Xmas
[Eng/Port] SSA,org/pno SHATTINGER
301 $.40   (B354)

BELLS OF BETHLEHEM see Brusey

BELLS OF BETHLEHEM, THE see Slaney,
Ivor

BELLS OF CHRISTMAS see Walton, K.

BELLS OF CHRISTMAS, THE see Croswell

BELLS ON CHRISTMAS DAY, THE see Wilson

BELLS RING OUT AT CHRISTMAS, THE see
Williams, A.

BELOVED, LET US LOVE see Lovelace,
Austin C.

BELOVED LET US LOVE ONE ANOTHER
(Etherington) SATB (med easy)
WATERLOO $.30   (B355)

BELOVED, LET US LOVE ONE ANOTHER see
Corina, John

BELOVED, LET US LOVE ONE ANOTHER see
Mueller

BELOVED, LET US LOVE ONE ANOTHER see
Peterson, John W.

BELYEA, W.H.
Invitatory Carol
SATB HARRIS $.35   (B356)

Nativity Tale *Xmas
SATB HARRIS $.35   (B357)

BENCINI, PIETRO PAOLO
Jesu Redemptor Omnium *cant
mix cor,S solo,cont sc BIELER DK 9
s.p., cor pts BIELER s.p. (B358)

BENDER, JAN (1909-   )
Alleluia! Christ Our Passover
    *Easter
    SSAB,acap (med) oct CONCORDIA
    98-2207 $.30   (B359)

Angel Hosts Rejoiced With Mirth
    *anthem,Contemp
    SATB oct CHANTRY COA 7352 $.35
                              (B360)

Baptismal Cantata *cant
    SATB,S solo,inst CHANTRY COC 735
    $1.25, ipa   (B361)

Behold, The Field Is White, Already
    To Harvest *Harv
    SA WHITE HARV. CHO 741 $.35 (B362)

Creation, The *Op.50,No.1
    dbl cor,soli,acap CHANTRY COA 7557
    $1.00   (B363)

He Shall Be Called A Nazarene
    see Three Prophecies

He Who Is Not With Me Is Against Me
    *Gen/Lent
    SA/TB oct CONCORDIA 98-2058 $.30
                              (B364)

How Lovely Shines The Morning Star
    SATB (chorale concertato) cor pts
    CONCORDIA 98-2260 $.60, sc
    CONCORDIA 98-2211 $3.40, ipa
                              (B365)

If God Were Not Upon Our Side
    *anthem,Contemp
    SATB oct CHANTRY COA 7349 $.25
                              (B366)

Mass In A *liturg
    SATB&opt cong CHANTRY LIT 693 $1.00
                              (B367)

Music For Reformation Day *cant,
    Contemp
    2pt mix cor,S solo,inst CHANTRY
    COC 672 $2.00, ipa   (B368)

O Konig Aller Ehren
    SAT/SAB (contains also: Sonne Der
    Gerechtigkeit) SCHWEIZER.
    SK 56.06 s.p. see also
    MUSIKBEILAGE ZUM "EVANGELISCHEN
    KIRCHENCHOR 1956"   (B369)

Out Of Egypt
    see Three Prophecies

Passion According To Saint Mark, The
    SATB,T solo,kbd CHANTRY PAS 632
    $2.00   (B370)

Peace Be With You
    SA/TB (med) oct CONCORDIA 98-2086
    $.30   (B371)

Psalm 84 *anthem,Contemp
    SSA,S solo,kbd oct CHANTRY COA 6836
    $.40   (B372)

Quempas Nuc Angelorum, The *anthem,
    Contemp
    SAB oct CHANTRY COA 65 $.15 (B373)

Sonne Der Gerechtigkeit
    SAT/SAB (contains also: O Konig
    Aller Ehren) SCHWEIZER. SK 56.06
    s.p. see also MUSIKBEILAGE ZUM
    "EVANGELISCHEN KIRCHENCHOR 1956"
                              (B374)

Three Prophecies
    SA/TB (med) oct CONCORDIA 98-2133
    $.30 New Year
    contains: He Shall Be Called A
    Nazarene; Out Of Egypt; Voice
    Was Heard In Ramah, A   (B375)

Unless One Is Born Anew
    SA/TB (med) oct CONCORDIA 98-2056
    $.35   (B376)

Voice Was Heard In Ramah, A
    see Three Prophecies

Weary Of All Trumpeting *hymn
    SATB CHANTRY HS 721 $.10   (B377)

When The Counselor Comes
    SA/TB (med) oct CONCORDIA 98-2055
    $.30   (B378)

You Wicked Servant
    SA/TB (med) oct CONCORDIA 98-2085
    $.40   (B379)

BENDITA SABEDORIA see Villa-Lobos,
    Heitor

BENDL, KAREL (1838-1897)
Christmas Eve *see Stedry Den

Stedry Den *cant
    "Christmas Eve" [Czech] mix cor,
    soli,2fl,2ob,2clar,2bsn,6horn,
    2trp,3trom,tuba,timp,perc,harp,
    strings CZECH s.p.   (B380)

BENEATH THE CROSS OF JESUS see Clephane

BENEATH THE FORMS OF RITE see Lovelace,
    Austin C.

BENEATH THE ROMAN EAGLE see Lovelace,
    Austin C.

BENEDIC ANIMA MEA see Saunders, Neil

BENEDIC DOMINO see Holmboe, Vagn

BENEDICAM DOMINUM, QUI TRIBUIT MIHI
    INTELLECTUM see Lassus, Roland de
    (Orlandus)

BENEDICAMUS DOMINO see Anonymous

BENEDICITE see Ridout, Alan

BENEDICTA ET VENERABILIS ES see
    Schutky, F.J.

BENEDICTIO NUPTIALIS see Felciano,
    Richard

BENEDICTION see Weigl, Vally

BENEDICTUS see Dantonello, Josef

BENEDICTUS see Dvorak, Antonin

BENEDICTUS see Haydn, (Franz) Joseph

BENEDICTUS see Palestrina, Giovanni

BENEDICTUS see Stoker, Richard

BENEDICTUS see Wassmer, Berthold

BENEDICTUS ES DOMINE see Diggle, Roland

BENEDICTUS ES, DOMINE see Peek, Richard

BENEDICTUS ES, DOMINE see Schubert,
    Franz (Peter)

BENEDICTUS ES, DOMINE see Sowerby, Leo

BENEDICTUS ES, DOMINE, DOCE ME
    JUSTIFICATIONES TUAS see Lassus,
    Roland de (Orlandus)

BENEDICTUS, QUI VENIT see Lassus,
    Roland de (Orlandus)

BENEDICTUS SIT DEUS see Mozart,
    Wolfgang Amadeus

BENHAM, ASAHEL (1757-1805)
Redemption Anthem
    (Bennett, Lawrence) SATB,acap
    BROUDE BR. $.45   (B381)

BENJAMIN, THOMAS E.
Adoramus Te
    "We Adore Thee" [Lat/Eng] SATB AMP
    A-681 $.35   (B382)

Laudate Dominum
    [Lat] SATB,acap FOSTER MF142 $.50
                              (B383)
We Adore Thee *see Adoramus Te

BENKERT, LORENZ
Aeterne Rex
    see Hymnen Fur Die Prozession Am
    Fronleichnamstag

Hymnen Fur Die Prozession Am
    Fronleichnamstag
    [Lat] 4pt mix cor,org/2horn&2trp&
    2trom sc,cor pts BOHM s.p., ipa
    contains: Aeterne Rex, Op.14,
    No.4; Pange Lingua, Op.14,No.5;
    Sacris Solemniis, Op.14,No.1;
    Salutis Humanae Sator, Op.14,
    No.3; Verbum Supernum, Op.14,
    No.2   (B384)

Pange Lingua
    see Hymnen Fur Die Prozession Am
    Fronleichnamstag

Sacris Solemniis
    see Hymnen Fur Die Prozession Am
    Fronleichnamstag

Salutis Humanae Sator
    see Hymnen Fur Die Prozession Am
    Fronleichnamstag

Verbum Supernum
    see Hymnen Fur Die Prozession Am
    Fronleichnamstag

BENNARD, GEORGE (1873-1958)
Het Ruw-Houten Kruis *Psntd
    unis,pno/harmonium/electric HEER
    279 s.p.   (B385)

Old Rugged Cross, The *anthem
    (Brown, Charles F.) SATB WORD
    CS-2577 $.30 see from OLD RUGGED
    CROSS, THE   (B386)
    (Wilson) SATB oct LORENZ 4450 $.35

BENNARD, GEORGE (cont'd.)

                              (B387)
BENNETT
    Prayer For My Parents *see Spicer

BENNETT, F. ROY
    Welcome The Christ Child *CC7U,Xmas,
    carol
    unis jr cor ASHDOWN   (B388)

BENNETT, ROY C. (1947-   )
Little White Donkey *Palm
    (Ehret, Walter) SATB,pno oct REGENT
    R-119 $.30   (B389)

BENNETT, SIR WILLIAM STERNDALE
    (1816-1875)
God Is A Spirit
    mix cor BANKS MUS YS 326 $.20
                              (B390)

BENSON
    Marriage Hymn, A *Marriage
    (Griffiths) SSAA ALLANS 471 (B391)

BENZLER, FRITZ GUSTAV (1903-   )
Christ Ist Erstanden *Easter
    [Ger] 3pt mix cor,acap MERSEBURG
    EM308 contains also: Heut
    Triumphiert Gottes Sohn   (B392)

Heut Triumphiert Gottes Sohn
    see Benzler, Fritz Gustav, Christ
    Ist Erstanden

BEPPI see Roff, Joseph

BERBERICH, LUDWIG
Messe In F-Dur *Mass
    [Lat] SSATBB,acap (F maj) sc,cor
    pts BOHM s.p.   (B393)

BERCEUSE DE NOEL *Xmas
    cor JOBERT s.p. see also Douze
    Cantiques De Fetes   (B394)

BERCHEM, JACOBUS DE
O Jesu Christe
    4pt,acap voc pt HENN 315 s.p.
                              (B395)

BERG, GOTTFRID
Ack, Herre Jesu, Hor Min Rost
    4pt mix cor ERIKS 30 s.p. (B396)

Det Ar En Ros Utsprungen *Xmas
    SABar ERIKS 64 s.p.   (B397)

Lyssna, Herre, Till Mit Bejande
    (Psalm 86)
    4pt mix cor ERIKS 37 s.p. (B398)

Nu Stige Jublets Ton
    SABar ERIKS 67 s.p.   (B399)

O Du Saliga
    SABar ERIKS 61 s.p.   (B400)

O Gud Sum Horer Allas Rost
    4pt mix cor ERIKS 39 s.p. (B401)

Psalm 86 *see Lyssna, Herre, Till
    Mit Bejande

Ringen, I Klockor
    SABar ERIKS 62 s.p.   (B402)

Si, Natten Flyr
    SABar ERIKS 63 s.p.   (B403)

Varldens Fralsare Kom Har
    SAB ERIKS 66 s.p.   (B404)

BERGER
Psalm 86
    SATB SHAWNEE A5684 $.45   (B405)

BERGER, JEAN (1909-   )
All Men Are Grass
    cor (med diff) FISCHER,C CM 7930
    $.45   (B406)

Build A Little Fence Of Trust
    *anthem
    SATB AUGSBURG 11-0955 $.35 (B407)

Cherry Tree Carol *Xmas
    SATB,kbd,fl,bvl,2perc, dancers sc
    AUGSBURG 11-9094 $2.50, ipa
                              (B408)

If A Man Die
    SATB,acap (med) FISCHER,C CM 7809
    $.30   (B409)

Man Born Of Woman
    cor (med diff) FISCHER,C CM 7929
    $.40   (B410)

Of Life
    SATB (med) FISCHER,C 0 4951 $2.50
                              (B411)

Parable Of The Sower *Bibl
    SATB (med) FISCHER,C CM 7810 $.40
                              (B412)

Pater Noster
    SATB,opt kbd BOONIN B 209 $.50
                              (B413)

BERGER, JEAN (cont'd.)

This Is The Covenant *anthem
SATB,org AUGSBURG 11-1677 $.40
(B414)

Thou Alone Art Israel's Shield
*anthem
SATB AUGSBURG 11-1714 $.30 (B415)

BERGGREEN
One There Is Above All Others *hymn
(Berglund) SATB oct LILLENAS
AN-6038 $.30 (B416)

BERGHOLZ
Wer Unter Dem Schirm Des
Allerhochsten Sitzt *mot
SATB HANSSLER 1.517 s.p. (B417)

BERGHORN, ALFRED
Adoramus Te
see Vier Passionsmotetten

Alleluja-Chor "Terra Tremuit" *Op.17
[Lat] 4-6pt mix cor,acap BOHM s.p.
(B418)

Ave Maria *Op.59b
[Lat] 4pt mix cor,acap BOHM s.p.
(B419)

Deutsche Liedmesse "Herr, Zeig Mir
Deine Wege" *Mass
[Ger] jr cor/wom cor&cong,org BOHM
sc s.p., cor pts s.p. (B420)

Haec Dies *Op.64
[Lat] 4pt mix cor,acap sc,cor pts
BOHM s.p. (B421)

Messe Zu Ehren Des Heiligen Joseph
*Op.73, Mass
[Lat] 4pt mix cor,acap sc,cor pts
BOHM s.p. (B422)

O Bone Jesu
see Vier Passionsmotetten

O Vos Omnes
see Vier Passionsmotetten

Popule Meus
see Vier Passionsmotetten

Soli Deo Honor Et Gloria *Op.72
[Lat] 4pt mix cor,org sc,cor pts
BOHM s.p. (B423)

Tantum Ergo *Op.21a
[Lat] 4-6pt mix cor,acap BOHM s.p.
(B424)

Vier Passionsmotetten *Psntd,mot
[Lat] 4pt mix cor,acap sc,cor pts
BOHM s.p.
contains: Adoramus Te, Op.79,
No.2; O Bone Jesu, Op.79,No.4;
O Vos Omnes, Op.79,No.3; Popule
Meus, Op.79,No.1 (B425)

Was Mein Gott Will
see Zwei Lieder Des Vertrauens

Wer Nur Den Lieben Gott Lasst Walten
see Zwei Lieder Des Vertrauens

Zwei Lieder Des Vertrauens *Fest
mix cor,acap BOHM s.p.
contains: Was Mein Gott Will,
Op.78,No.1; Wer Nur Den Lieben
Gott Lasst Walten, Op.78,No.2
(B426)

BERGLUND
Credo *anthem
SATB oct LILLENAS AN-6021 $.60
(B427)

BERICHT VON DER GEBURT JESU see Buchsel

BERKELEY, LENNOX (1903-)
Three Latin Motets *CC3U,mot
[Lat] SSATB,opt pno CHESTER
JWC 8895 s.p. (B428)

BERLIOZ, HECTOR (1803-1869)
Die Kindheit Christi *see L'Enfance
Du Christ

Hector Berlioz Works *sac/sec,CCU
(Malherbe, Charles; Weingartner,
Fleix) microfiche UNIV.MUS.ED.
$115.00 originally published as
20 volumes in 18 bindings.
Leipzig, 1900-1907. (B429)

L'enfance Du Christ *Op.25, ora
cor,soli,orch HENN s.p. (B430)
"Die Kindheit Christi" [Eng/Fr/Ger]
SATB,MezTTBarBarBB soli,orch
(diff) min sc SCHOTTS ETP 1092
s.p. (B431)

Requiem *Op.5, funeral/Req
SSAATTBB,T solo,orch (diff) min sc
SCHOTTS ETP 1091 s.p. (B432)
[Lat] cor,T solo,orch,brass min sc
EULENBURG 1091 s.p. (B433)

BERMAN, JUDITH M.
And Thou Shalt Love *see V'ahavta

V'ahavta
"And Thou Shalt Love" [Eng] cor,
cantor TRANSCON. TCL 629 $.75
(B434)

BERNABEI
Alleluia
(Wiley) SATB,acap PRO ART 2781 $.35
(B435)

BERNABEI, GIUSEPPE ANTONIO (1649-1732)
O Sacrum Convivium
see HYMNEN UND MOTETTEN ALTER
MEISTER HEFT 3

BERNARDI, STEFFANO (ca. 1576-1636)
Il Bianco E Dolce Cigno *Mass
[Lat] 4pt mix cor,acap sc,cor pts
BOHM s.p. (B436)

Praeparate Corda Vestra *Mass
[Lat] 4pt mix cor,acap sc,cor pts
BOHM s.p. (B437)

BERNHARD
As The Deer Cries For Flowing Water
(Streetman) SATB SCHIRM.G LG51706
$.50 (B438)

Habe Deine Lust An Dem Herrn
(Streetman) SATB SCHIRM.G LG51830
$.60 (B439)

Hear Our Prayer, O God
(Streetman) SATB SCHIRM.G LG51792
$.60 (B440)

Hear Our Prayer, Oh Lord *see Lieber
Herre Gott

Lieber Herre Gott *Xmas
(Streetman) "Hear Our Prayer, Oh
Lord" SATB SCHIRM.G LG51792 $.60
(B441)

Missa Durch Adam's Fall
(Streetman) "Missa Through Adam's
Fall" SATB SCHIRM.G LG51791 $1.50
(B442)

Missa Through Adam's Fall *see Missa
Durch Adam's Fall

BERNHARD, CHRISTOPH (1627-1692)
Jauchzet Dem Herrn, Alle Welt
*concerto
SS,2vln,cont (med) sc,cor pts
BAREN. BA835 s.p., ipa (B443)

BERNSTEIN, LEONARD (1918-)
Almighty Father (from Mass)
TTBB SCHIRM.G A11975 $.25 (B444)

Chichester Psalms
SATB (first movement) SCHIRM.G
A12000 $.60 (B445)

Gloria Tibi (from Mass)
SA,T solo SCHIRM.G 11964 $.30
(B446)
SATB SCHIRM.G A11964 $.30 (B447)

Sanctus (from Mass) Sanctus
SATB SCHIRM.G A11973 $.35 (B448)

BERT, HENRI
Noel
2pt mix cor/4pt mix cor GRAS s.p.
(B449)

BERUHMTES "LIBERA" see Zaininger, B.

BESIG
Carol For Christmas, A
SSATBB,acap PRO ART 2792 $.35
(B450)

BESINNA NU OCH MINNS see Ravenscroft,
Thomas

BESINNA NU OCH MINNS see Remember Thou
O Man

BESTOW THY LIGHT UPON US see Pasquet,
Jean

BETHANY, O PEACEFUL HABITATION see
Sorenson

BETHEL
Galilee, Bright Galilee *see Sherwin

BETHLEHEM
see At The Manger

BETHLEHEM see Cobine, Al

BETHLEHEM see Trojan, Vaclav, Betlem

BETHLEHEM OF NOBLEST CITIES see
Hurford, Peter

BETHLEHEM, THE CHOSEN see Graham,
Robert

BETLEM see Trojan, Vaclav

BETTERIDGE, LESLIE
Three Anthems *CC3U,anthem
SATB (med diff) WATERLOO $.50
(B451)

BETTINELLI, BRUNO (1913-)
Laudi Del 1200
mix cor,SMez soli,strings,harp sc
CARISH 20754 s.p. (B452)

Sono Una Creatura *cant
cor,orch sc RICORDI-ENG 131879
(B453)

BEULAH LAND see Sweney

BEVAN, GWILYM
Easter Carol, An *Easter,Introit
SATB (easy) WATERLOO $.35 see from
Six Introits (B454)

In Memoriam
SATB (med easy) WATERLOO $.35
(B455)

Magnificat *Magnif/Nunc
SATB (med easy) WATERLOO $.35
contains also: Nunc Dimittis
(B456)

Nunc Dimittis
see Bevan, Gwilym, Magnificat

Six Introits *see Easter Carol, An
(B457)

Six Introits, An Easter Carol And A
Baptismal Motet *CC8U,carol/
Introit/mot
SATB (med easy) WATERLOO $.35
(B458)

Versicles, Responses And Lord's
Prayer *CCU,cor-resp
SATB (easy) WATERLOO $.40 (B459)

BEYOND A DREAM see Yantis, David

BEZANSON, PHILIP
Dies Domini Magnus
"Great Day Of The Lord, The" SATB,
2horn,2trp,2trom,tuba,3timp
AM.COMP.AL. $6.60 (B460)

Great Day Of The Lord, The *see Dies
Domini Magnus

BIBER, HEINRICH IGNAZ FRANZ VON
(1644-1704)
Darkness Was Over All *see Tenebrae
Factae Sunt

Tenebrae Factae Sunt *Easter
(Pauly) "Darkness Was Over All"
SATB SCHIRM.G 11934 $.30 (B461)

BIBLISCHE MOTETTEN FUR DAS KIRCHENJAHR,
BAND 1 *CCU,Adv/Xmas/Epiph,Bibl/
mot
SATB/SAATB,acap/cont (med) cloth,
cmplt ed BAREN. BA5473 (B462)

BIBLISCHE MOTETTEN FUR DAS KIRCHENJAHR,
BAND 1, HEFT 1: FUNF SATZE FUR DEN
WEIHNACHTSFESTKREIS *CC5U,Xmas,
Bibl/mot
SATB/SSATB (med easy) BAREN. BA6223
contains works by Briegel, Wolfgang
Carl; Raselius, Andreas (B463)

BIBLISCHE MOTETTEN FUR DAS KIRCHENJAHR,
BAND 1, HEFT 2: FUNF SATZE ZU
STEPHANSTAG, ALTJAHRSABEND, UND
EPIPHANIASZEIT *CC5U,Epiph,Bibl/
mot
SATB/SSATB/SSAB (med easy) BAREN.
BA6224 contains works by:
Christenius, Johann;Michael,
Tobias; Vulpius, Melchior;
Raselius, Andreas; Dressler, Gallus
(B464)

BIBLISCHE MOTETTEN FUR DAS KIRCHENJAHR,
BAND 2 *CCU,Asc/Easter/Holywk/
Lent/Palm/Pent/Psntd/Trin,Bibl/mot
SATB/SAATB,acap/cont (med) cloth,
cmplt ed BAREN. BA5474 (B465)

BIBLISCHE MOTETTEN FUR DAS KIRCHENJAHR,
BAND 2, HEFT 3: ACHT SATZE FUR DIE
ZEIT VOM TAG DER DARSTELLUNG DES
HERRN BIS PFINGSTMONTAG *CC8U,Asc/
Easter/Holywk/Lent/Palm/Pent/Psntd,
Bibl/mot
SATB/SAATB/SSATB (med easy) BAREN.
BA6229 (B466)

BIBLISCHE MOTETTEN FUR DAS KIRCHENJAHR,
BAND II see Christenius, Johann

BIEBL, FRANZ (1906-)
Auf Haltet Euer Herz Bereit
see Schieri, Fritz, Es Flog Ein
Taublein

Auf, Zundet Eure Herzen An
see Zwei Adventslieder

Der Advents-Stern
see Zwei Adventslieder

BLESS THE LORD, O MY SOUL see Peterson, John W.

BLESS THIS HOUSE see Brahe, May H.

BLESS THOU THE LORD see Pulkingham, B.C.

BLESS YAHWEH, MY SOUL see Arnatt, Ronald

BLESSED ARE ALL THEY see Gibbons, Orlando

BLESSED ARE THE PEOPLE see Latrobe, Christian I.

BLESSED ARE THEY see Glarum, L. Stanley

BLESSED ARE THEY THAT MOURN see Hodgson, H.

BLESSED ART THOU see Diggle, Roland, Benedictus Es Domine

BLESSED ART THOU, LORD GOD OF OUR FATHERS see Clarke, F.R.C.

BLESSED ART THOU, O LORD see Pasquet, Jean

BLESSED ART THOU, O LORD GOD OF OUR FATHERS see Peek, Richard, Benedictus Es, Domine

BLESSED ASSURANCE *anthem
  (Powers) SATB oct BROADMAN 4540-88
  $.30   (B601)

BLESSED ASSURANCE see Hughes

BLESSED ASSURANCE see Knapp, (Mrs.) Joseph F.

BLESSED BE THAT MAID MARY see Maria Of The Cross, Sister

BLESSED BE THE DAY THAT I BEGAN A PILGRIM FOR TO BE see Moore, J. Chris

BLESSED BE THE FATHER see Christiansen, Paul

BLESSED BE THE GOD AND FATHER see Brandon, G.

BLESSED BE THE GOD AND FATHER see Wesley, S.S.

BLESSED BE THE LORD see Roff, Joseph

BLESSED BE THE LORD, WHO SCHOOLS ME see Hruby, Delores

BLESSED BE THE NAME see Hudson, Richard

BLESSED BE THOU see Roff, Joseph

BLESSED BE THOU; LORD GOD OUR FATHER see Fischer, Irwin

BLESSED CALVARY see Latham, L.

BLESSED CHRIST IS RISEN TODAY, THE see Bach, Johann Sebastian

BLESSED CITY, HEAVENLY SALEM see Bairstow, Edward Cuthbert

BLESSED HOPE, THE see Peterson, John W.

BLESSED HOUR OF PRAYER see Huggins, Richard

BLESSED IS HE see Haydn, (Franz) Joseph, Benedictus

BLESSED IS HE WHO WALKS NOT IN THE PATHS OF GODLESSNESS see Schutz, Heinrich

BLESSED IS THE MAN see Buffaloe, James

BLESSED IS THE MAN see Butler, Eugene

BLESSED IS THE MAN see Clarke, Henry Leland

BLESSED IS THE MAN see Vycpalek, Ladislav

BLESSED IS THE MAN THAT TRUSTETH IN THE LORD see Hovhaness, Alan

BLESSED MAN, THE see Pierce, Christine

BLESSED MARY TO THE TEMPLE WENT see Buszin

BLESSED MORN, THE see Dean, T.W.

BLESSED QUIETNESS see Boalt, S.

BLESSED QUIETNESS see Ferguson

BLESSED REDEEMER
  see He Lives!

BLESSED REDEEMER see Christensen

BLESSED THE CHILDREN see Cobine, Al

BLESSED VIRGIN, THE see Egk, Werner, Beata Viscera

BLESSING see Sleeth, Natalie

BLESSING AND GLORY see Jackson, Francis

BLESSING AND HONOR, PRAISE AND LOVE see Brahms, Johannes

BLESSING AND HONOUR see Palestrina, Giovanni

BLESSINGS OF MARY, THE *Adv/Xmas
  (Johnson) SATB oct LILLENAS AN-5016
  $.25   (B602)

BLEST ARE THE PURE IN HEART see Eaton, Richard S.

BLEST ARE THEY see Brahms, Johannes

BLEST BE THE TIE see Fawcett

BLIEM
  All Flesh Is Grass
  SATB SCHIRM.G LG51788 $.35   (B603)

BLISS
  My Redeemer (composed with Mc Granahan)
  (Mercer, W. Elmo) SATB BENSON S4218
  $.35   (B604)

BLISS, PAUL
  Hallelujah, What A Savior! *Easter, anthem
  (Wyrtzen, Don) SATB oct SINGSPIR
  ZJP-3543 $.30   (B605)

  Hallelujah, What A Saviour! *Easter
  (Crabtree, R.) SATB oct GOSPEL
  05 TM 0205 $.20   (B606)

  Hold The Fort
  (Crabtree, R.) SATB oct GOSPEL
  05 TM 0127 $.25   (B607)

  It Is Well With My Soul *anthem/gospel
  (Rasley, John M.) SATB oct SINGSPIR
  ZJP-8105 $.30   (B608)

  Wonderful Words Of Life
  (Yoder, David) SATB oct GOSPEL
  05 TM 0106 $.20   (B609)

BLISS, SIR ARTHUR (1891-   )
  Beatitudes, The *cant
  SATB,ST soli,2fl,2pic,2ob,2clar,
  2bsn,4horn,2trp,3trom,tuba,timp,
  perc,2harp,org,strings voc sc
  NOVELLO rental   (B610)

  Golden Cantata
  SATB,T solo,3fl,2ob,2clar,2bsn,
  4horn,3trp,3trom,tuba,timp,perc,
  harp,org,strings,celeste voc sc
  glockenspiel, celeste voc sc
  NOVELLO rental   (B611)

  Mary Of Magdala
  SATB,ABar soli,2fl,pic,2ob,clar,
  bsn,2horn,2trp,timp,perc,harp,
  strings voc sc NOVELLO rental
                                    (B612)

  Shield Of Faith *cant
  SATB,SBar soli,org voc sc NOVELLO
  s.p.   (B613)

  World Is Charged With The Grandeur Of God, The *cant
  SATB,2fl,3trp,4trom voc sc NOVELLO
  rental   (B614)

BLOCH, ERNEST (1880-1959)
  Sacred Service
  "Servizio Sacro" mix cor,Bar solo,
  4fl,3ob,3clar,3bsn,4horn,3trp,
  3trom,tuba,harp,perc,timp,
  celeste voc sc CARISH 21744 s.p.
                                    (B615)
  Servizio Sacro *see Sacred Service

BLOM
  He The Pearly Gates Will Open *see Ahlwen

BLOW GABRIEL! I'M GOIN' UP *spir
  (Williams, P.A.) TTBB BRODT 538 $.18
                                    (B616)

BLOW YE THE TRUMPET see Belcher, Supply

BLOW YE THE TRUMPET, BLOW see Edson

BLUM, ROBERT (1900-   )
  Kantate *Bibl/cant
  mix cor,strings MODERN s.p., rental
                                    (B617)

  Trias *CCU
  men cor,Bar/B solo,orch HUG Psalms
  150, 146, 117   (B618)

BOALT, S.
  Blessed Quietness *folk
  (Wyrtzen, Don) SATB oct SINGSPIR
  ZJP-5042 $.25   (B619)

BOAT OF JADE see Graham

BOCK, FRED (1939-   )
  Grateful Heart, A
  2pt,pno (very easy) GENTRY G-293
  $.35   (B620)

  I Sing The Greatness Of Our God
  cor BRIDGE Z 0120   (B621)

  Joy To The World, The Lord Is Coming
  cor BRIDGE Z 0180   (B622)

  Lord, We Thank You
  1-2pt,pno (very easy) GENTRY G-292
  $.30   (B623)

  Meditation On "Passion Chorale" *anthem
  SATB oct SACRED S-167 $.35   (B624)

  Never Quite The Same *Xmas/Easter
  SATB,pno (med) GENTRY G-260 $.50
                                    (B625)

  Sing Forth His Praise, He Reigneth! *anthem
  SATB WORD CS-663 $.25   (B626)

  Sleep, Holy Child *Xmas
  SATB&jr cor,pno GENTRY G-274 $.40
                                    (B627)

  Two Responses For Beginning And
  Ending Worship *see White, Rex

BOHEMIAN HYMN, THE see Goossen, Frederic

BOHM, GEORG (1661-1733)
  Das Himmelreich Ist Gleich Einem Konige
  SSATB,B solo,cont,strings
  SCHWEIZER. SK 120 sc s.p., cor
  pts s.p., ipa   (B628)

BOHME, FRANZ MAGNUS (1827-1898)
  Grabgesang "Ach, Was Ist Das Leben Doch So Schwer"
  (Humperdinck, Engelbert) men cor sc
  SCHOTTS CHBL 123 s.p.   (B629)

BOLAND, CLAY A.
  Mary Gentle Mother Of Mine (composed with O'Keefe, Walter)
  SATB CHAPLET 2000 $.25   (B630)

BOLLBACH
  Ring The Bells *Xmas,anthem
  (DeCou, Harold) SATB oct SINGSPIR
  ZJP-3000 $.30   (B631)
  (Rasley, John M.) SA&opt TB (easy)
  oct SINGSPIR ZJP-3040 $.25 (B632)

BOLTON *hymn
  (Lindsley) TTBB,acap (easy) OXFORD
  94.103 see from Five Early American
  Hymn Tunes   (B633)

BOLZ, HARRIETT
  Sweet Jesus
  SAB,pno/org (med) BECKEN BP 1006
  $.40   (B634)

BON see Johansen, Sven-Erik

BON, WILLEM FREDERIK (1940-   )
  Missa Brevis *Op.25
  mix cor,fl,pic,ob,clar,bsn,horn,
  trp,trom,tuba DONEMUS   (B635)

BOND OF LOVE, THE see Skillings, Otis

BONONCINI, ANTONIO MARIA (1677-1726)
  Stabat Mater
  SATB,SATB soli,org,strings voc sc
  NOVELLO rental   (B636)
  (Smith, Peter) SATB,SATB soli,
  strings,cont voc sc NOVELLO s.p.
                                    (B637)

BONZORNO MADONNA see Scandello

BOOK OF CANONS, A see Wolff, Harald

BOOK OF RESPONSES see Fuller

BOOKS OF THE NEW TESTAMENT see Hays, Peggy McAllister

BOOKS OF THE OLD TESTAMENT see Hays, Peggy McAllister

BOONE
Three Motets *CC3U,mot
SATB,acap oct SALABERT-US $3.00
(B638)

BOOTH
Cross Is Not Greater, The *Easter
(Krogstad, Bob) SATB oct GOSPEL
05 TM 0312 $.35   (B639)

BOOZER
In Heavenly Love *anthem
SATB,2treb inst,org oct MCAFEE
M1033 $.35   (B640)

Mary's Lullaby *Xmas,anthem
SATB oct MCAFEE M1057 $.35   (B641)

BOOZER, PAT
Believe Also In Me *hymn
SATB,opt hndbl oct LILLENAS AN-6039
$.30   (B642)

Christmas Carol, A *Adv/Xmas
SAATBB,hndbl oct LILLENAS AN-3859
$.35   (B643)

Christmas Offering, A
1-2pt jr cor,opt hndbl oct LILLENAS
AN-4030 $.30   (B644)

Come, Sound His Praise Abroad *hymn
SATB/unis jr cor oct LILLENAS
AN-3871 $.30   (B645)

Lord, Thou Art My Shepherd *anthem
SATBB oct LILLENAS AN-6022 $.30
(B646)

O Thou In Whose Presence *hymn
SATB oct LILLENAS AN-2420 $.30
(B647)

Oh, My Lord, Your Light Divine
unis jr cor,opt fl oct LILLENAS
AN-4042 $.25   (B648)

Who? God!
2pt jr cor, rhythm instruments oct
LILLENAS AN-4038 $.30   (B649)

BORGE, NORMAN
I Found The Lord *Contemp
(Walters, Bob) jr cor,fl/vln oct
GOSPEL 05 TM 0155 $.35   (B650)

BORN A KING see Peterson, John W.

BORN A KING see Peterson, John W.

BORN AGAIN see Beethoven, Ludwig van

BORN ANEW THIS DAY see Roff, Joseph

BORN IN A MANGER *Xmas,folk,Ir
(Hughes, Robert J.) SA/SATB (easy)
oct LORENZ A557 $.30   (B651)

BORN IN A MANGER see Hughes

BORN IN A STABLE see Thygerson, Robert
J.

BORN IS HE, THE CHILD DIVINE *Xmas,
carol,Fr
(Ehret, Walter) 2pt jr cor,opt bells,
tamb oct LILLENAS AN-4035 $.30
(B652)

BORN IS LITTLE JESUS see Pelz, Walter
L.

BOROWSKI, FELIX (1872-1956)
Angels Of Light
SATB (easy) FITZSIMONS 2038 $.25
(B653)

SA (easy) FITZSIMONS 5007 $.25
(B654)

BORRIS, SIEGFRIED (1906-   )
Ein Feste Burg Is Unser Gott
see Borris, Siegfried, Ein Feste
Burg Ist Unser Gott

Ein Feste Burg Ist Unser Gott
SAT/SAB/SA,treb inst,opt bass inst
HANSSLER 14.201 s.p. contains
also: Ein Feste Burg Is Unser
Gott (SAT/SAB/2pt,opt treb inst&
bass inst)   (B655)

Nun Lasst Uns Den Leib Begraben
SAT/SAB HANSSLER 14.174 s.p. (B656)

BORTH, STEVEN
Great Controversy, The *CC13U,pop
(Johnson, Paul) SATB,pno (med) oct
GENTRY G-620 $3.50   (B657)

Long Ago In Bethlehem (from Great
Controversy, The) Xmas
(Johnson, Paul) SATB,acap/pno (med)
GENTRY G-271 $.40   (B658)

BORTNIANSKY, DIMITRI STEPANOVITCH
(1751-1825)
Adoramus Te *see Dos Togno

Dos Togno
"Adoramus Te" 4pt mix cor LIENAU
MUSICA SACRA, NR. 14 cor pts

BORTNIANSKY, DIMITRI STEPANOVITCH
(cont'd.)

s.p., sc s.p.   (B659)

Doxologie: Gloria In Excelsis
"Ehre Sei Gott" 4pt mix cor LIENAU
MUSICA SACRA, NR. 37 sc s.p., cor
pts s.p.   (B660)

Ehre Sei Gott *see Doxologie: Gloria
In Excelsis

Hymn Of Praise
SSA (easy) WATERLOO $.30   (B661)

Ich Bete An Die Macht Der Liebe
(Koenig, F.) men cor,acap TONOS
3007 s.p.   (B662)
(Poos, Heinrich) men cor sc SCHOTTS
CHBL 197 s.p.   (B663)
(Siegel, F. J.) men cor,acap TONOS
3003 s.p.   (B664)

Russian Vesper Hymn
(Soderstrom) SSAATTBB (easy)
FITZSIMONS 1048 $.25   (B665)

Vesper Hymn
see Cauntlet, For All Thy Care

BOSOM OF ABRAHAM see Brooks, Ted

BOSSI, MARCO ENRICO (1861-1925)
Inno Di Gloria *Op.76
mix cor,3fl,2ob,2clar,2bsn,4horn,
6trp,5trom,tuba,harp,timp,perc,
bells CARISH rental   (B666)

Tota Pulchra *Op.96
mix cor,harp,strings CARISH rental
(B667)

BOSSI, RENZO (1883-1965)
Messa Da Requiem *Op.34, funeral
mix cor,org,3fl,3ob,2clar,2bsn,
4horn,3trp,2trom,tuba,timp,perc,
harp,bells, celeste CARISH rental
(B668)

BOSSLER, KURT (1911-   )
Ach Gott Und Herr, Wie Gross Und
Schwer
SAT/SAB/SA,treb inst,opt bass inst
HANSSLER 14.168 s.p.   (B669)

Christ Unser Herr Zum Jordan Kam
SAT/SAB,opt treb inst/bass inst
HANSSLER 14.146 s.p.   (B670)

THE BOSTON HANDEL AND HAYDN SOCIETY
COLLECTION OF CHURCH MUSIC *CCU,
19th cent
(Mason, Lowell) DA CAPO
ISBN 0-306-77315-5 LC 77-171078
$18.50 contains works by: Haydn;
Handel; Beethoven; Mozart;and
others   (B671)

BOTTESINI, GIOVANNI (1821-1889)
Messa Da Requiem *funeral
(Gallini) cor,SSATB soli,orch voc
sc ZERBONI 7535 s.p.   (B672)

BOTTOME
Comforter Has Come, The
(Kirkpatrick; McLellan) SATB oct
GOSPEL 05 TM 0134 $.35   (B673)

BOUD, RON
It's Gotta Happen Within *anthem/
folk
2pt oct SINGSPIR ZJP-5065 $.35
(B674)

BOUGHT WITH A PRICE see Miles

BOUND FOR CANAAN *anthem/gospel
(Rasley, John M.) SATB oct SINGSPIR
ZJP 8141 $.30   (B675)

BOUND FOR CANAAN'S LAND *spir
(Moore) SATB WARNER W-3653 $.40
(B676)

BOURGEOIS, LOYS (LOUIS) (ca. 1510-1561)
All People That On Earth Do Dwell
*Thanks,anthem
(Johnson, Norman) SSATB oct
SINGSPIR ZJP-7255 $.25   (B677)

Darkening Light
see Two Evening Hymns

O Bread Of Life From Heaven (composed
with Goudimel, Claude)
SATB oct CONCORDIA 98-2241 $.25
(B678)

O Gladsome Light
see Two Evening Hymns

Old Hundredth *anthem
(Carmichael, Ralph) SATB,2trp,2trom
LEXICON CS-2506 $.35, ipa see
from NOW HEAR THIS   (B679)

Two Evening Hymns *Eve,hymn
(Simkins, C.F.) TTBB,acap (very
easy) oct OXFORD 41.021 $.20
contains: Darkening Light; O

BOURGEOIS, LOYS (LOUIS) (cont'd.)

Gladsome Light   (B680)

BOUSTEAD, A.
Mary Stuart's Prayer
SA EMI   (B681)
SSA EMI s.p.   (B682)
SATB EMI s.p.   (B683)

BOUZIGNAC, GUILLAUME
Jubilate Deo "Omnis Terra, Servite
Domino"
SATTB,acap sc SCHOTTS C 42 232 s.p.
(B684)

BOW DOWN THINE EAR see Clark, Henry A.

BOW DOWN THINE EAR see Douglas

BOW DOWN THINE EAR see Franck, Cesar,
Domine Non Secundum

BOW DOWN THINE EAR, O LORD see Hayes

BOWEN
I Will Praise Thee, O Lord *anthem
SATB oct HERITAGE H124 $.35 (B685)

BOWERS-BROADBENT, CHRISTOPHER
Two Short Motets *CC2U,mot
SATB STAINER 3.0742.1 $.50   (B686)

BOWIE, WILLIAM
Faith *anthem
SATB (med diff) OXFORD 42.353 $.35
(B687)

Welcome, Happy Morning *Easter
SATB (med diff) OXFORD 42.351 $.60
(B688)

BOWLES
Christ, The Newborn King *anthem
SATB WORD CS-2697 $.35   (B689)

Prayer For Serenity
SATB PRO ART 2816 $.35   (B690)

BOWMAN
Lamb, The *see Blake

BOWMAN, CARL
Festival Of Praise *Te Deum
SATB,org (med) oct GENTRY G-210
$1.00   (B691)

BOY CHILD OF MARY see Lovelace, Austin
C.

BOY WAS BORN, A see Kirby, L.M. Jr.

BOY WAS BORN, A see Weelkes, Thomas

BOY WAS BORN IN BETHLEHEM, A see
Prentice, Fred

BOYAJIAN, GLORIA
Let The Whole Creation Cry Glory
*anthem
SATB,SBar soli,org,opt 2trp&2horn&
trom WORLD CA-2412-8 $.75   (B692)

BOYCE, WILLIAM (1710-1779)
By The Waters Of Babylon
(Young, Percy) [Eng] SATB,SATB
soli,org BROUDE BR. $.75 see from
MUSIC OF THE GREAT CHURCHES VOL.
V: ST. PAUL'S CATHEDRAL, LONDON
(B693)

King Shall Rejoice, The (from Two
Anthems For The Georgian Court)
(Van Nice, John R.) cor bds A-R ED
$9.95   (B694)

Lord, Thou Hast Been Our Refuge
(Bevan) SATB,AT soli,inst OXFORD
ipr   (B695)

Souls Of The Righteous (from Two
Anthems For The Georgian Court)
(Van Nice, John R.) cor bds A-R ED
$9.95   (B696)

BOYD
When The Terms Of Peace Are Made
SATB SCHIRM.G 11963 $.40   (B697)

BOYD, JACK
Evening Shade
see Three Frontier Hymns

Holy Manna
see Three Frontier Hymns

Jerusalem
see Three Frontier Hymns

Three Frontier Hymns *hymn
SATB,acap oct KERBY 6404C $.35
contains: Evening Shade; Holy
Manna; Jerusalem   (B698)

BOYD, JEANNE
Descants On Eight Hymns *CC8U
SATB (easy) FITZSIMONS 2073 $.30
(B699)

C

CA, BERGERS, ASSEMBLONS-NOUS *Xmas
(McLaulay, Wm.) SATB (easy) WATERLOO
$.35　　　　　　　　　　　　　　　(C1)

CABENA, BARRIE
Introit For The New Year *Introit
SATB,T/B solo (med) OXFORD 02.059
$.30　　　　　　　　　　　　　　　(C2)

Joseph Dearest, Joseph Mine *Xmas,
carol
unis (easy) OXFORD 02.002 $.25 (C3)

Jubilate Deo
unis (med) OXFORD 02.003 $.40　(C4)

Let Your Light So Shine Before Men
SATB WATERLOO $.60　　　　　　　(C5)

Loving Shepherd Of Thy Sheep
unis (easy) OXFORD 02.004 $.25　(C6)

O Lord Of Life
unis (med) OXFORD 02.005 $.20　(C7)

Psalm 150
2pt/SATB (med) OXFORD 02.021 $.35
　　　　　　　　　　　　　　　　　(C8)

Te Deum *Te Deum
cong/unis (easy) sc OXFORD 02.012
$2.00, cor pts OXFORD 02.013 $.15
　　　　　　　　　　　　　　　　　(C9)

Twelve Benediction Amens *CC12U
2-8pt (med easy) OXFORD 02.022 $.30
　　　　　　　　　　　　　　　　　(C10)

CABEZON, ANTONIO DE (1510-1566)
Hispaniae Schola Musica Sacra Vol.
III: Antonius A Cabezon, 1895
*CCU
(Pedrell, F.) cor pap JOHNSON
$12.00 contains also: Vol. IV:
Cabezon, 1895　　　　　　　　　(C11)

Hispaniae Schola Musica Sacra Vol.
IV: Antonius A Cabezon, 1895
*CCU
(Pedrell, F.) cor pap JOHNSON
$12.00 contains also: Vol. III:
Cabezon, 1895　　　　　　　　　(C12)

Hispaniae Schola Musica Sacra Vol.
VII: Antonius A Cabezon, 1897
*CCU
(Pedrell, F.) cor pap JOHNSON
$12.00 contains also: Vol. VIII:
Antonius A Cabezon, 1898　　　(C13)

Hispaniae Schola Musica Sacra Vol.
VIII: Antonius A Cabezon, 1898
*CCU
(Pedrell, F.) cor pap JOHNSON
$12.00 contains also: Antonius A
Cabezon, 1897　　　　　　　　　(C14)

Jesu Christe, Gottes Lamm
see MUSIKBEILAGE ZUM "EVANGELISCHEN
KIRCHENCHOR 1963"

CABRA MASS see Illing, Robert

CACAVAS, JOHN (1930-　　)
Miracle Of Bethlehem *Xmas
(Becker) SATB BELWIN 2303 $.40
　　　　　　　　　　　　　　　　　(C15)
(Becker) SSA BELWIN 2304 $.40 (C16)

CADWALLADER, ANN
Come, Follow Me *anthem/folk
SATB,pno/gtr (easy) GIA G1773 $.45
　　　　　　　　　　　　　　　　　(C17)

My Beloved Spoke *Bibl/folk
unis,pno/gtr GIA G1784 $.30　(C18)

My Lover And My Master *anthem/folk/
hymn
unis,pno/gtr (easy) GIA G1779 $.25
　　　　　　　　　　　　　　　　　(C19)

CAIN, NOBLE (1896-　　)
King And The Star, The *Xmas,cant
SA/SAB,orch (easy) FITZSIMONS voc
sc $.60, sc rental　　　　　　(C20)

CALDARA, ANTONIO (1670-1736)
Have Mercy, Lord *Lent
(Wetzler) SATB,acap ART MAST 148
$.40　　　　　　　　　　　　　　(C21)

Lauda Anima Mea *Fest
[Lat] cor,soli,2vln,org,vcl,bvl,opt
3trom sc,cor pts BOHM s.p., ipa
　　　　　　　　　　　　　　　　　(C22)

Six Canons For The Church Year
*CC6U,canon
(Heiberg) SSA/SSAA,acap oct MCA
s.p.　　　　　　　　　　　　　　(C23)

CALDBECK
Peace, Perfect Peace *anthem
(Berglund) SATB oct LILLENAS
AN-6030 $.30　　　　　　　　　　(C24)

CALDWELL
Celebrate The Risen Christ *Easter,
anthem
1-2pt (med easy) oct BROADMAN
4560-28 $.35　　　　　　　　　　(C25)

Circle Of Love, A *anthem
1-2pt oct BROADMAN 4560-29 $.35
　　　　　　　　　　　　　　　　　(C26)

Cloud *anthem
1-2pt oct BROADMAN 4560-30 $.35
　　　　　　　　　　　　　　　　　(C27)

Let The Trumpet Sound *anthem
unis,opt inst oct BROADMAN 4560-33
$.35　　　　　　　　　　　　　　(C28)

Lord Of The Loving Heart *anthem
2pt oct BROADMAN 4558-63 $.30 (C29)

Lullaby Carol *Xmas,anthem/carol
SATB oct BROADMAN 4560-31 $.35
　　　　　　　　　　　　　　　　　(C30)

O Sing For Joy *anthem
1-2pt oct BROADMAN 4560-32 $.35
　　　　　　　　　　　　　　　　　(C31)

On Christmas Day In The Morning
*Xmas,anthem
unis,hndbl (med) oct BROADMAN
4558-03 $.30　　　　　　　　　　(C32)

Sing To God *anthem
2pt (easy) oct BROADMAN 4558-14
$.30　　　　　　　　　　　　　　(C33)

Year's At The Spring *anthem
unis oct BROADMAN 4557-08 $.30
　　　　　　　　　　　　　　　　　(C34)

CALDWELL, MARY [ELIZABETH] (1909-　)
Again The Time Of The Savior's Birth
*Xmas
2pt,pno (very easy) PRESSER G-280
$.40　　　　　　　　　　　　　　(C35)

Calm And Lovely *see Schubert, Franz
(Peter)

Christus Resurrexit *Easter
SATB,org (med) GENTRY G-220 $.40
　　　　　　　　　　　　　　　　　(C36)

Freedom Song, The *cant
1-2pt BROADMAN 4511-03 $1.50　(C37)
SATB BROADMAN 4510-05 $1.75　(C38)

Let Us Follow Him *Easter,cant
jr cor BROADMAN 4515-03 $1.00 (C39)

O Love That Wilt Not Let Me Go
2pt mix cor TRIUNE TUM 105 $.35 see
also LET THE WORLD SING　　　(C40)

Of Prayer And Praise
SATB,org/pno (med) FISCHER,C
CM 7924 $.45　　　　　　　　　　(C41)

Of Time And Eternity *Easter,cant
SATB BROADMAN 4514-07 $2.00　(C42)

Palm Sunday, A.D. 33 *Palm
cor (med) FISCHER,C CM 7858 $.40
　　　　　　　　　　　　　　　　　(C43)

Road To Bethlehem, The *Xmas,cant
jr cor,Bar solo,pno,timpa,bells,perc
BROADMAN 4513-05 $1.25　　　　(C44)

Simon, Called Peter
unis,pno (easy) GENTRY G-224 $.40
　　　　　　　　　　　　　　　　　(C45)

Song Is A Gift To God, A
2-3pt jr cor (easy) FISCHER,C
CM 7874 $.35　　　　　　　　　　(C46)

Spring Prayer
unis,pno (very easy) GENTRY G-291
$.35　　　　　　　　　　　　　　(C47)

CALEGARI, ANTONIO (1757-1828)
Pange Lingua-Tantum Ergo
see HYMNEN UND MOTETTEN ALTER
MEISTER HEFT 1

CALENDAR SONG, THE see Jordahl

CALIFORNIANS SING NO. 2 see Skillings,
Otis

CALIFORNIANS SING TODAY *CC10UL
(Skillings, Otis) cor,pno,bvl,gtr
LILLENAS MB-283 $1.95　　　　(C48)

CALIGAVERUNT see Welcker, Max

CALIGAVERUNT OCULI MEI see Ingegneri,
Marco Antonio

CALL, THE see Fischer, Irwin

CALL, THE see Furnivall, Anthony C.

CALL, THE see Whitecotton, Shirley

CALL OF GOD, THE see Burroughs, Bob

CALL OF ISAIAH see Pinkham, Daniel

CALL TO WORSHIP *CCU,cor-resp
(Johnson, Norman) cor (med diff)
SINGSPIR 5027 $1.50　　　　　(C49)

CALL TO WORSHIP see Canning, Thomas

CALLING see Peterson, John W.

CALLS TO PRAYER, PRAISE, BENEDICTION
see Yarrington, John

CALM AND LOVELY see Schubert, Franz
(Peter)

CALM WAS THE NIGHT see Hill, Harry

CALVARY see Cossetto, Emil

CALVARY see Culross, David

CALVARY LOVE see Hughes

CALVARY'S MOUNTAIN see Allen, Lanny

CALVI, LORENZO
Victimae Paschali Laudes *mot
4pt mix cor,cont BIELER DM 3 sc
s.p., cor pts s.p.　　　　　　(C50)

CALVIN
Great Is The Lord *anthem
SATB FINE ARTS CM 1053 $.35　(C51)

Psalm 1 *anthem
SATB FINE ARTS CM 1051 $.35　(C52)

CALVISIUS, SETHUS (1556-1615)
Der Herr Ist Mein Getreuer Hirt
SAT/SAB (contains also: Nun Lob,
Mein Seel, Den Herren) SCHWEIZER.
SK 58.03-4 s.p.
MUSIKBEILAGE ZUM "EVANGELISCHEN
KIRCHENCHOR 1958"　　　　　　(C53)

Gloria In Excelsis *Xmas
(Ehret, Walter) "Glory To God Upon
High" SSATBB,acap (med diff)
PRESSER 312-41085 $.40　　　(C54)

Glory To God Upon High *see Gloria
In Excelsis

Joseph, Joseph, Dearest One *see
Joseph, Lieber Joseph Mein

Joseph, Lieber Joseph Mein
(Young, Percy) "Joseph, Joseph,
Dearest One" [Ger/Lat/Eng]
SSATB,acap BROUDE BR. $.65 see
from MUSIC OF THE GREAT CHURCHES
VOL. IV: ST. THOMAS' CHURCH,
LEIPZIG　　　　　　　　　　　　(C55)

Tricinien *CC22L
SAT/SAB HANSSLER 4.020 s.p.　(C56)

Weihnachtslied V.J. 1557 *Xmas
6pt mix cor LIENAU
MUSICA SACRA, NR.59 sc s.p., cor
pts s.p.　　　　　　　　　　　　(C57)

CAMBRIDGE *hymn
(Lindsley) TTBB,acap (easy) OXFORD
94.103 see from Five Early American
Hymn Tunes　　　　　　　　　　(C58)

CAMIDGE, MATTHEW (1758-1844)
Sanctus
SSA (med easy) WATERLOO $.30
contains also: This Joyful
Eastertide (Fenwick, Roy G.)
　　　　　　　　　　　　　　　　　(C59)

CAMMAROTA, CARLO (1905-　　)
Psalm 67 *see Salmo XLVII

Salmo XLVII (Psalm 67)
mix cor sc CARISH 21666 s.p. (C60)

CAMP, MABEL JOHNSTON
That Beautiful Name *Xmas,anthem/
gospel
(DeCou, Harold) SATB oct SINGSPIR
ZJP-3012 $.30　　　　　　　　　(C61)

CAMPBELL
And Can It Be? *Commun/Gd.Fri.,
anthem
(Johnson, Norman) SSATB oct
SINGSPIR ZJP-7259 $.30　　　(C62)

Love Held Him To The Cross *see
Brown

CAMPBELL, B.
Jesus, Use Me (composed with
Campbell, J.)
(Collins, Hope) SATB oct GOSPEL
05 TM 0174 $.25　　　　　　　　(C63)

CAMPBELL, J.
Jesus, Use Me *see Campbell, B.

CAMPBELL, SYDNEY S.
God Is Gone Up
see Three Introits And Two Chants

Righteous Shall Be Had In Everlasting
Remembrance, The
see Three Introits And Two Chants

This Is The Day
see Three Introits And Two Chants

Three Introits And Two Chants *ASD/
Asc/Easter,anthem
mix cor oct NOVELLO 50.0335.00 s.p.
contains: God Is Gone Up;
Righteous Shall Be Had In
Everlasting Remembrance, The;
This Is The Day   (C64)

CAMPBELL-WATSON, FRANK (1898-   )
In You, O Lord, Have I Put My Trust
SATB SUMMY A-5963 $.40   (C65)

Rejoice In The Lord, Always *Adv
SATB,org GRAY CMR 3320 $.30   (C66)

CAMPIAN, THOMAS (1567-1620)
Four Devotional Songs *CC4U
(Bergdolt, Kenneth) SATB,opt kbd&
gtr, and lute (med diff) DEAN
CMC-103 $1.85 lute songs intended
for multiple ways of performance
                                   (C67)

CAMPRA, ANDRE (1660-1744)
Easter Praise *Easter
(Wetzler, Robert) SATB,org/3trp,
2trom,tuba ART MAST 262 $.35
                                   (C68)

Song Of Praise To God, A
(Ehret, Walter) SATB,pno GENTRY
G-222 $.35   (C69)

CAN ANYBODY TELL ME? see Carlson, J.
Bert

CAN I SEE ANOTHER'S WOE see Marshall

CAN YOU NOT SEE OUR GOD see Handel,
George Frideric

CANAAN see Anonymous

CANADIAN PRAYER, A see Hains, S.B.

CANITE JESU NOSTRO see Buxtehude,
Dietrich

CANNING, THOMAS
Anthem
SATB,S solo,3trp,3trom,strings
AM.COMP.AL. sc $5.50, voc pt
$2.20   (C70)

Call To Worship (from Hope College
Service)
SATB,acap AM.COMP.AL. $.28   (C71)

Christmas Greeting, A *canon
SSAA,acap AM.COMP.AL. $1.10   (C72)

Covenant Hymn
SATB,acap AM.COMP.AL. $.35   (C73)

God Is My Strong Salvation *anthem
SATB,harp AM.COMP.AL. sc $3.85,
ipa, voc pt $3.30   (C74)

Hymn For Our Nation, A
SATB,3trp,3trom,tuba,3timp,perc
AM.COMP.AL. sc $7.70, ipa, voc pt
$3.30   (C75)

My Soul Thirsteth For God (from Hope
College Service)
SSA,acap AM.COMP.AL. $4.40   (C76)

O God, Our Lord, Thy Holy Word
SATB,2horn,2trp,2trom,strings
AM.COMP.AL. sc $7.15, voc pt
$1.65   (C77)

Offering Of Carols And Rounds, An
SATB,3trp,2trom,perc AM.COMP.AL. sc
$6.60, ipa, voc pt $3.30   (C78)

Psalm 1
SATB,ob sc AM.COMP.AL. $4.40, ipa
                                   (C79)

Rogation Hymn
SATB,2trp,2trom AM.COMP.AL. sc
$6.60, ipa, voc sc $6.88, voc pt
$1.65   (C80)

Seven-Fold Amen (from Hope College
Service)
SATB,acap AM.COMP.AL. $.28   (C81)

Shepherds Carol, The
SSATB/SSAA,acap AM.COMP.AL. sc
$5.50, min sc $4.40   (C82)

CANNING, THOMAS (cont'd.)

Temptation Of Jesus, The
TTBB,narrator,2horn,2trp,3trom,
tuba,perc AM.COMP.AL. sc $13.20,
ipa, voc sc $2.20, voc pt $1.65
                                   (C83)

Trumpets On The Tower
SSAATTBB,2trp,2trom AM.COMP.AL. sc
$7.15, ipa, voc pt $3.30   (C84)

Wisdom Hath Builded Her House
SSA,acap AM.COMP.AL. $4.95   (C85)

CANNON
O Lord, Grant Us Thy Mercy (composed
with Peninger) *anthem
SATB (easy) oct BROADMAN 4554-44
$.30   (C86)

CANON IN FOUR VOICES see Stout, Alan

CANON OF PRAISE, A see Sleeth, Natalie

CANONIC RESPONSES *CCU
(Van Camp, Leonard) eq voices (very
easy) FOSTER MF203 $.30 contains
works by: Martini, Padre;
Praetorius, Christoph; Tallis,
Thomas   (C87)

CAN'T STAY AWAY *spir
(Shaw, Ruby) SATB,acap (easy)
FITZSIMONS 2072 $.25   (C88)

CAN'T YOU HEAR? see Price

CAN'T YOU HEAR WHAT MY LORD SAID?
*spir
(Ehret) SAB oct LILLENAS AN-3864 $.30
                                   (C89)

CAN'T YOU HEAR WHAT MY LORD SAID see
Ehret, Walter

CANTABO DOMINO SEMPER see Praetorius,
Michael

CANTATA ANGLICA IN HONOREM THADDAEI
FRATRIS DOMINI see Jenni, Donald

CANTATA CORPUS CHRISTI see Jillett,
David

CANTATA DOMINO see Naylor, Bernard

CANTATA FOR CITY, NATION, WORLD see
Bassett, Leslie

CANTATA FOR EASTER see Effinger

CANTATA FOR EASTER see Gardner

CANTATA ON "SAINT ANNE" see Gore,
Richard T.

CANTATA: POEMS OF WAR RESISTANCE see
Rovics, Howard

CANTATE DE LA PASSION see Mozart,
Wolfgang Amadeus

CANTATE DOMINE see Hassler, Hans Leo

CANTATE DOMINO *Xmas,Contemp
SATB VANGUARD V566 $.35 see from Come
To Bethlehem   (C90)

CANTATE DOMINO see Dumont, [Henri]

CANTATE DOMINO see Hassler, Hans Leo

CANTATE DOMINO see Kraft, Karl

CANTATE DOMINO see Kreutz, Robert E.

CANTATE DOMINO see Pitoni, Giuseppe
Ottavio

CANTATE DOMINO see Seckinger, Konrad

CANTATE DOMINO *CC202U,hymn
unis BAREN.
BA4994; ISBN 3-7618-0500-4 in 25
languages   (C91)

CANTATE DOMINO, CANTATE NOVUM see
Buxtehude, Dietrich

CANTATE SING TO THE LORD see Goemanne,
Noel

CANTATIBUS ORGANIS see Liszt, Franz

CANTI SPIRITUALI D'ISRAELE *CCU
(Veneziani, V.) cor BONGIOVANI 2468
s.p.   (C92)

CANTIBUS ORGANICIS see Gombert, Nicolas

CANTICA NOVA see Philipp, Franz

CANTICLE see Schramm

CANTICLE FOR MODERN MAN see Langston,
Paul

CANTICLE OF PRAISE see Anthony, Dick

CANTICLE OF ZACHARY, THE see Felciano,
Richard, Antiphon And Benedictus

CANTICLES OF THE VIRGIN MARY see Hurd,
Michael

CANTICUM B. SIMEONIS "HERR, NUN LASSEST
DU DEINEN DIENER" see Schutz,
Heinrich

CANTICUM NOVUM see Mills, Charles

CANTIO SACRA DE ANNUNTIATIONE B. MARIAE
VIRGINIS see Buissons, M. des

CANTIO SACRA DE NATIVITATE B. MARIAE
VIRGINIS see Prenner, Georg

CANTIO SACRA DE VISITATIONE B. MARIAE
VIRGINIS see Roy, S. de

CANTIONES ECCLESIASTICAE see Aichinger,
Gregor

CANTIONES SACRAE see Lemacher, Heinrich

CANTIONES SACRAE DE CONCEPTIONE B.
MARIAE VIRGINIS *CCU,BVM
4-5pt mix cor DOBLINGER TH 31 sc
s.p., voc pt s.p. contains works
by: Prenner, G.; Formellis, G.
                                   (C93)

CANTIONES SACRAE DE CORPORE CHRISTI
*CCU,Corpus
4-6pt mix cor DOBLINGER TH 35 sc
s.p., voc pt s.p. contains works
by: Prenner, G.; Loys, J.;
Buissons, M. des   (C94)

CANTIQUE DE MARIAGE *Marriage
cor JOBERT s.p. see also Douze
Nouveaux Cantiques De Fetes   (C95)

CANTIQUE DE NOEL see Adam, Adolphe-
Charles

CANTIQUE DE NOEL see Polignac, Armande
de

CANTIQUE DE PAQUES see Honegger, Arthur

CANTIQUES A L'UNISSON see Montillet

CANTIQUES DE ROSSI see Rossi, Salomone

CANTO IV see Zender, Hans

CANTO V see Zender, Hans

CANTUAL *CC130L
(Schauerte, Gustav) [Lat/Ger] mix
cor,acap/org BOHM cloth s.p., voc
pt s.p. contains works by: Handl;
Hassler; Marenzio; Eberlin;
Bruckner; Siegl; Haas and others
                                   (C96)

CANTUS FIRMI see Oertzen, Rudolf von

CANTUS FIRMI see Oertzen, Rudolf von

CANTUS FIRMI see Oertzen, Rudolf von

CANTUS FIRMI see Oertzen, Rudolf von

CANZONE A BALLO see Pratella, Francesco
Balilla

CANZONE DEL SONNO see Pratella,
Francesco Balilla

CANZONEN-MESSE see Limbacher, Fridolin

CANZONI HEFT 1 see Hoffmann, Ernst
Theodor Amadeus

CANZONI HEFT 2 see Hoffmann, Ernst
Theodor Amadeus

CANZONI HEFT 3: SALVE REGINA see
Hoffmann, Ernst Theodor Amadeus

CAPERS
Bridegroom Is Coming, The
(Eleiott; Adams, Glenn) SATB oct
GOSPEL 05 TM 0427 $.40   (C97)

It Can't Be Much Longer
(Eleiott; Adams, Glenn) SATB oct
GOSPEL 05 TM 0424 $.35   (C98)

CAPRICORNUS, SAMEUEL (1628-1665)
Mein Gott Und Herr *concerto
SSB,2vln,cont (med) sc,voc sc
BAREN. BA6226 s.p., ipa   (C99)

CARIBBEAN CAROL
(Verrall, Pamela) unis EMI   (C100)

CARILLON see Briel, Marie

CARISSIMI, GIACOMO (1605?-1674)
Annunciate Gentes *mot
[Lat] SSATB,SATB soli,cont sc,cor
pts EGTVED OCIII s.p.   (C101)

Beatus Vir *anthem
(Seymour) SATB OXFORD   (C102)

Jephte *see Jephthah

Jephthah
(Beat, Janet) "Jephte" SSSATB,SATB
soli,opt vln&vcl&bvl,org voc sc
NOVELLO s.p., ipr   (C103)
(Contino, Fiora) "Jephte" cor,soli,
cont DEAN CMC-107 s.p.   (C104)

Jephte *see Jephthah

Jonah *ora
(Pilgrim) SSAATTBB,SATB soli,inst
(med diff) OXFORD 46.177 $4.25
                              (C105)

Jubilemus Omnes Et Cantemus *cant
"Lasst Uns Alle Preisen Und
Lobsingen" [Lat/Ger] SSB,cont
(med) sc BAREN. BA6225 s.p., ipa
                              (C106)

Lasst Uns Alle Preisen Und Lobsingen
*see Jubilemus Omnes Et Cantemus

Sancta Et Individua Trinitas *cant
SA,cont,2vln sc HANSSLER 10.273
s.p.   (C107)

CARLIER
In Memoriam
4pt mix cor GRAS s.p.   (C108)

CARLSON, GORDON
Communion Meditations *anthem
SATB,opt B solo AUGSBURG 11-1711
$.30   (C109)

He Came Among Us *anthem
SATB,B solo AUGSBURG 11-0417 $.40
                              (C110)

Jesus, Refuge Of The Weary *anthem
SATB&cong,org AUGSBURG 11-1699 $.40
                              (C111)

O Day Full Of Grace *anthem
SATB AUGSBURG 11-1653 $.40   (C112)

Wake, Awake *anthem
SATB,bvl AUGSBURG 11-0548 $.45
                              (C113)

CARLSON, J. BERT
Behold The King Of Glory *Palm
SATB,drums ART MAST 236 $.35 (C114)

Can Anybody Tell Me? *Adv/Xmas
SATB,acap ART MAST 166 $.30   (C115)

Cradle God, O Heart
SATB ART MAST 274 $.35   (C116)

Let The World Rejoice *Adv/Xmas
SATB,acap ART MAST 192 $.30   (C117)

Sabbath Day Was By, The *Easter,
anthem,Contemp
SATB,org (easy) oct CHANTRY
COA 6938 $.25   (C118)

CARLTON
O Sleep, Thou Babe So Holy *Xmas,
anthem
SATB oct BROADMAN 4551-78 $.30
                              (C119)

CARMICHAEL, RALPH
God Can See Us (from Natural High)
anthem
SATB LEXICON CS-2610 $.35 contains
also: I Can See God (unis,opt
solo); God Doesn't See Us Through
The Flowers (SATB,solo)   (C120)

God Doesn't See Us Through The
Flowers (from Natural High)
see Carmichael, Ralph, God Can See
Us

I Can See God (from Natural High)
see Carmichael, Ralph, God Can See
Us

I Have No Right (from Natural High)
anthem
SATB,solo LEXICON CS-2609 $.40
contains also: Someone Loved Me
First; What Gives You The Right
                              (C121)

I Just Lost (from Cross And The
Switchblade) anthem
SATB LEXICON CS-2510 $.30   (C122)

I'm Here, God's Here, Now We Can
Start *see Kaiser, Kurt

Love (from Cross And The Switchblade)
anthem
SATB,2trp,2trom LEXICON CS-2511
$.35, ipa   (C123)

CARMICHAEL, RALPH (cont'd.)
Miracle Of Faith, The *anthem
TTBB/SATB LEXICON CS-2605 $.35
                              (C124)

My Little World *anthem
SATB,solo LEXICON CS-2612 $.35 see
from NATURAL HIGH   (C125)

Natural High *anthem
SATB LEXICON CS-2608 $.35 see from
NATURAL HIGH   (C126)

Quiet Place, A *anthem
SATB LEXICON CS-2622 $.30   (C127)

Reach Out To Jesus *anthem
SATB LEXICON CS-2623 $.35   (C128)

Searching Questions *anthem
SATB LEXICON CS-2607 $.35 see from
NATURAL HIGH   (C129)

Season Of The Long Rains *anthem
SATB LEXICON CS-2626 $.30   (C130)

Someone Loved Me First (from Natural
High)
see Carmichael, Ralph, I Have No
Right

Something Good Is Going To Happen To
You *anthem
SATB,solo LEXICON CS-2621 $.35
                              (C131)

What Gives You The Right (from
Natural High)
see Carmichael, Ralph, I Have No
Right

When I Think Of The Cross *anthem
1-2pt LEXICON CS-2611 $.35 see from
NATURAL HIGH   (C132)

Where Is It? (from Cross And The
Switchblade) anthem
2-3pt,2trp,2trom LEXICON CS-2509
$.30, ipa   (C133)

CARMINA CHROMATICO see Lassus, Roland
de (Orlandus)

CARMONY, BRYAN M.
Wonderful Christmastime *Xmas
cor,solo&narrator LILLENAS MC-244
$.60   (C134)

CARNEY, DAVID
Angel Gabriel, The
SATB,pno/gtr/harp SCHIRM.EC 2775
                              (C135)

Child Is Born, A
SATB,pno/gtr/harp SCHIRM.EC 2774
                              (C136)

CAROL CHOIR SINGS, THE *CCU
1-2pt jr cor BROADMAN 4526-01 $1.25
                              (C137)

CAROL FOR ALL SEASONS see Whitecotton,
Shirley

CAROL FOR CHRISTMAS see Jackson

CAROL FOR CHRISTMAS, A see Besig

CAROL FOR MARY see Whitter

CAROL FOR NEW YEAR'S DAY see Pinkham,
Daniel

CAROL FOR OUR TIME, A see Wienandt,
Elwyn A.

CAROL FOR PENTECOST see Hunnicutt, Judy

CAROL OF ADORATION, A see Pettman,
Edgar

CAROL OF CHRISTMAS see Peterson, John
W.

CAROL OF JOY (ALERIA) see Zgodava,
Richard A.

CAROL OF LOVE see Lorenz, Ellen Jane

CAROL OF PRAISE see Rasley, John M.

CAROL OF THANKSGIVING see Wetzler,
Robert

CAROL OF THE BAGPIPERS *Xmas,anthem
(Rasley, John M.) SATB oct SINGSPIR
ZJP-3045 $.30   (C138)

CAROL OF THE BIRDS see Malin, Don

CAROL OF THE EASTER VICTORY see Kirby

CAROL OF THE FISHERMEN see Sleeth,
Natalie

CAROL OF THE FRIENDLY BEAST *Xmas
(Simpson, John) unis EMI   (C139)

CAROL OF THE HOLY CHILD *Adv/Xmas,
folk,Aus
(Caldwell) SATB oct LILLENAS AN-6013
$.30   (C140)

CAROL OF THE ITALIAN PIPERS see
Zgodava, Richard A.

CAROL OF THE LITTLE KING see Fogg, Eric

CAROL OF THE NATIVITY see Godden,
Reginald

CAROL OF THE NEW PRINCE see Sitton,
Carl

CAROL OF THE ROSE see Thompson, Randall

CAROL OF THE SMALL CHILD see Runyan

CAROL OF THE SUN see Blake, Leonard

CAROL OF THE TREE see Hovdesven, E.A.

CAROL OF THE TREES see Copes, V. Earle

CAROL ON ST. STEPHEN see Davies, Peter
Maxwell

CAROL (THE FIRST NOEL) see Cory, George

CAROL "TO A BABY" *Xmas,carol
(Davies) SS/SA (easy) OXFORD 82.097
$.25   (C141)
(Davies) SSA,acap (easy) OXFORD
83.082 $.30   (C142)

CAROL TO THE KING see Newbold, David

CAROLINE TE DEUM see Handel, George
Frideric

CAROLS BY CANDLELIGHT see Hawkins,
Floyd W.

CAROLS FOR CHOIRS, BOOK 2 *CCU,Xmas,
carol
(Willcocks; Rutter) SATB (easy/med)
OXFORD pap $3.50, bds $5.00   (C143)

CAROLS OF KING DAVID see Williamson,
Malcolm

CAROLS TO PLAY AND SING see Parker,
Alice

CARPENTER
Sing We Merrily *anthem
SSATB,acap (med diff) OXFORD 43.478
$.50   (C144)

CARPENTRAS
Lamentations For Maundy Thursday Part
1 *Easter
AATB STAINER 3.0869.1 $.75   (C145)

CARR
Old Book And The Old Faith, The
*anthem/gospel
(DeCou, Harold) SATB oct SINGSPIR
ZJP-8110 $.30   (C146)

CARRARD
Nuit De Noel *Xmas
mix cor,acap HENN 747 s.p.   (C147)
4pt mix cor,acap sc HENN 747 s.p.
                              (C148)

CARRAZ
Acclamations Carolingiennes
4pt,acap voc pt HENN 556 s.p.
                              (C149)

Hymne
4pt,acap HENN 289 s.p. sc, voc pt
                              (C150)

Messe Franciscaine
4pt mix cor,pno/org HENN 458 s.p.
sc, voc pt   (C151)

Messe Gaudeamus
4pt mix cor,acap voc pt HENN 312
s.p.   (C152)

Musiques De Noel (composed with
Maeder) *CCU,Xmas
4pt mix cor,acap sc HENN 749 s.p.
                              (C153)

Noels En Sucre D'orgue *CCU,Xmas
cor (easy) HENN 365 s.p. sc, voc pt
                              (C154)

O Gloriosa Dominum
3pt,acap voc pt HENN 307 s.p.
                              (C155)

Priere Litanique
4pt,acap HENN 288 s.p. sc, voc pt
                              (C156)

Salut
4pt,acap voc pt HENN 208 s.p.
                              (C157)

CARRILLO
Messe A Jean XXIII
3pt men cor,acap JOBERT s.p. (C158)

CARROLL, J. ROBERT
Seven French Noels *CC7L,Xmas,
anthem,Fr
TTBB (easy) GIA G1746 $1.00 (C159)

CARTER
O Come, Let Us Sing *anthem
SATB oct BROADMAN 4545-94 $.30
(C160)

Of The Father's Love Begotten
*anthem
SATB oct BROADMAN 4545-79 $.30
(C161)

Psalm 23 *anthem
SSA oct HERITAGE H6010 $.35 (C162)

Psalm 100
SATB WALTON 2932 $.40 (C163)

CARTER, JOHN
Gloria *anthem
SSATB AUGSBURG 11-0546 $.35 (C164)

Hosanna To The Son Of David *Palm
SATB&jr cor ART MAST 271 $.40
(C165)

O Come And Mourn With Me Awhile
*Lent
SATB ART MAST 254 $.30 (C166)

Psalm 140 *anthem
dbl cor AUGSBURG 11-3014 $.10
(C167)

Through The Eyes Of A Child *anthem
mix cor HERITAGE H125 $.40 (C168)

CARTER, SYDNEY
Lord Of The Dance
unis GALAXY 1.2538.1 $.25 (C169)

CARTWRIGHT
Ship Ahoy!
(Towner; Collins, Hope) SATB oct
GOSPEL 05 TM 0200 $.20 (C170)

CASCIOLINI, CLAUDIO (ca. 1650- ?)
Lo, Angels' Bread *Commun,anthem
(Lee, J.) SA/TB (easy) GIA G1837
$.30 (C171)

Missa Brevis *Mass
[Eng] SATB WHITE,ERN $.25 (C172)

Panis Angelicus
see HYMNEN UND MOTETTEN ALTER
MEISTER HEFT 3

Sacris Solemniis
see HYMNEN UND MOTETTEN ALTER
MEISTER HEFT 3

CASE, J.
All This Night *Xmas
SATB,org,trp GRAY CMR 3319 $.30
(C173)

CASEBOW
Through The Wilderness *folk
(Schubert) SATB oct LILLENAS
AN-5036 $.30 (C174)

CASHMORE, DONALD (1926-)
This Child Behold
SATB,SATB soli,strings voc sc
NOVELLO rental (C175)

CASSLER, G. WINSTON
Earth To Ashes *anthem
SATB,kbd AUGSBURG 11-1716 $.25
(C176)

Easter Glory *anthem
SATB&cong,org,opt trp AUGSBURG
11-1688 $.35 (C177)

Infant Christus *Xmas,anthem
SATB,S solo AUGSBURG 11-1737 $.45
(C178)

CAST THY BURDEN UPON THE LORD see Bass,
Claude L.

CAST THY BURDEN UPON THE LORD see
Mendelssohn-Bartholdy, Felix

CASTIGLIONI, NICCOLO (1932-)
Anthem
[It] mix cor,pno,harmonium,3fl,3ob,
3clar,3bsn,3horn,3trp,3trom,
strings,perc,timp,celeste (diff)
sc SCHOTTS rental, ipr (C179)

CATES
Go Where The People Are *see
Seabough, Ed.

Jesus, My Everything *anthem
SATB (easy) oct BROADMAN 4554-48
$.30 (C180)

To The Ends Of The Earth *see
Seabough, Ed.

CATES, BILL
Common Cup, The
cor (music drama) BROADMAN 4516-07
$2.95 (C181)

CATES, BILL (cont'd.)

Encounter *see Seabough, Ed.

Joy
SATB,soli&narrator BROADMAN 4518-08
$2.95 (C182)

CAUNTLET
For All Thy Care
(Hill, Harry) SSA (easy) WATERLOO
$.30 contains also: Bortniansky,
Dimitri Stepanovitch, Vesper Hymn
(C183)

CAURROY, EUSTACHE DU
Rise From Your Bed Of Hay *Xmas
(Couper, A.B.) [Eng/Fr] SATB,acap
(med diff) PRESSER 312-41079 $.50
(C184)

CAVALLI, FRANCESCO
see CAVALLI, (PIETRO) FRANCESCO

CAVALLI, (PIETRO) FRANCESCO (1602-1676)
Ave Maris Stella
see Three Hymns

Deus Tuorum Militum
see Three Hymns

Iste Confessor
see Three Hymns

Missa Pro Defunctis *funeral
(Bussi) cor,inst/orch ZERBONI 7671
s.p. (C185)

Three Hymns *hymn
(Leppard, Raymond) [Lat] FABER
rental
contains: Ave Maris Stella (TTB,
cont,2vln,opt 2vla); Deus
Tuorum Militum (TTB,cont,2vln,
opt 2vla); Iste Confessor (SS/
TT,cont,2vln,opt 2vla) (C186)

CAVIEZAL, P. ADELGOTT
Anima Christi, Sanctifica Me
[Lat] 4pt mix cor,acap sc,cor pts
BOHM s.p. (C187)

CAWSTON, NANCY
Harvest Fields, The
(Rose, Steven) SATB oct GOSPEL
05 TM 0367 $.35 (C188)

CELEBRATE! see Burroughs, Bob

CELEBRATE see Tyler

CELEBRATE! see Wyrtzen, Don

CELEBRATE LIFE see Courtney, Ragan

CELEBRATE THE LORD see Jordahl

CELEBRATE THE RISEN CHRIST see Caldwell

CELEBRATION *CCUL,Fest
(Huff, Ronn) cor,opt orch BENSON
B0182 $1.98, ipa stereo recording,
tape, and-or book-record sets
available, contact publisher (C189)

CELEBRATION II *CCUL,Fest
(Huff, Ronn) cor,opt orch BENSON
B0183 $1.98, ipa stereo recording,
tape, and-or book-record sets
available, contact publisher (C190)

CELEBRATION OF HOPE, A see Skillings,
Otis

CELEBRATION OF PRAISE see Skillings,
Otis

CELEBRATION OF PRESENCE, PRAYER AND
PRAISE see Peloquin, C. Alexander

CELEBRATION OF UNITY see Hebble, Robert

CELEBRATION SONGS FOR CHOIR see
Wyrtzen, Don

CELESTIAL COUNTRY, THE see Ives,
Charles

CELTIC HYMN see Roberton, Hugh
Stevenson

CELTIC REQUIEM see Taverner, John

CEREROLS, JOAN (1618-1676)
O Lord Jesus Christ, Our Master
(Peek) mix cor BRODT 545 $.28
(C191)
CERNO DEI NATUM see Lassus, Roland de
(Orlandus)

CESKA VANOCNI MSE "HEJ MISTRE" see
Ryba, Jan Jakub Simon

CHADWICK, GEORGE WHITEFIELD (1854-1931)
Hark, Hark My Soul
SATB HARRIS $.35 (C192)

CHAILLEY, JACQUES (1910-)
Le P'tit Quinquin
4pt mix cor GRAS s.p. (C193)

CHAMBERS, H.A.
Now Thank We All Our God
mix cor LESLIE 4006 $.30 (C194)

CHANGING NIGHT, THE see Le Fleming,
Christopher (Kaye)

CHANNELS ONLY see Gibbs

CHANSON NOEL
(Thorpe, Raymond) SATB,acap EMI s.p.
(C195)

CHANT A LA VIERGE see Decha, Abbe

CHANT DE PAQUES ET PENTECOTE see
Praetorius, Michael

CHANT POUR LE JOUR DES MORTS ET DE LA
TOUSSAINT see Gagnebin, Henri

CHANTICLEER see Gardner

CHANUKAH STORY see Adler

CHAPLIN
I Have Come From The Darkness
(composed with Lyall) *anthem
SATB (easy) oct BROADMAN 4537-78
$.30 (C196)

CHAPMAN
Christ Is The Flower Within My Heart
*anthem
SATB (med diff) OXFORD 42.364 $.50
(C197)

Our Great Saviour
(Prichard; Krogstad, Bob) SATB oct
GOSPEL 05 TM 0133 $.35 (C198)

CHARIOT OF CLOUDS see Peterson, John W.

CHARON "NOVITE CHARON IMPERIOSUM" see
Reutter, Hermann

CHARPENTIER, MARC-ANTOINE (1634?-1704)
Extremum Dei Judicium *ora
[Lat] SATB,B solo,2vln,opt 2trp,
cont sc,cor pts EGTVED OCVI s.p.
(C199)

Judicium Salomonis *ora
(Hitchcock, H. Wiley) cor bds A-R
ED $9.95 (C200)

Mass *Mass
(De Nys) SSAATTBB,inst (med diff)
voc sc OXFORD 46.168 $13.00, cor
pts OXFORD 46.169 $3.15, ipr
(C201)

Messe De Minuit *Xmas,Mass
"Midnight Mass For Christmas Eve"
[Lat] SATB,SSATB soli,3vln,opt
2fl,cont sc,cor pts EGTVED KB50
s.p., ipa (C202)

Midnight Mass For Christmas Eve *see
Messe De Minuit

CHASS, BLANCHE
Hanukah Lights
SATB FOSTER MF679 $.35 (C203)

CHASSANG
D'ou Venez-Vous? *Xmas
4pt mix cor,acap HENN 410 s.p. sc,
voc pt (C204)

Quem Vidisti Pastores
4pt,acap HENN 410 s.p. sc, voc pt
(C205)

CHATELAIN
Messe Saint Germain
4pt mix cor,pno/org HENN 521 s.p.
sc, voc pt (C206)

CHATHAM
My Jesus Wept *Easter,anthem
SATB (easy) oct BROADMAN 4554-47
$.30 (C207)

CHEMIN-PETIT, HANS (1902-)
Straf Mich Nicht In Deinem Zorn
SAT/SAB HANSSLER 14.176 s.p.
contains also: Linke, Norbert,
Straf Micht Nicht In Deinem Zorn
(1-2pt,opt treb inst&bass inst)
(C208)

CHENOWETH, WILBUR (1899-)
God Of Comfort
SATB SCHIRM.G LG51855 $.40 (C209)

CHERRY FLOWER see Graham

CHERRY TREE CAROL *Adv/Xmas
(Johnson, Mark) SATB,acap ART MAST
267 $.30 (C210)

CHERRY TREE CAROL see Berger, Jean

CHERRY TREE CAROL see Wilson, Charles
M.

CHERRY TREE CAROL, THE
   (Willcocks) SATB,acap (easy) OXFORD
   84.197 $.30   (C211)

CHERUB CHOIR NO. 1 *CCUL
   jr cor SINGSPIR 5030 $1.25   (C212)

CHERUB CHOIR NO. 2 *CCUL
   jr cor SINGSPIR 5031 $1.25   (C213)

CHERUB CHOIR NO. 3 *CCUL
   jr cor SINGSPIR 5032 $1.25   (C214)

CHERUBIM SONG see Young, Gordon

CHERUBINI, LUIGI (1760-1842)
   Lacrymosa (from Requiem In C Minor)
   (Glass; Di Pietto) SATB SCHIRM.G
   LG51853 $.45   (C215)

   Lamb Of God, For Sinners Slain
   *Lent,anthem
   (Ehret, Walter) SATB (easy) GIA
   G1847 $.40   (C216)

   Like As A Father *Gen/Thanks,canon
   (Lovelace, Austin C.) 3pt,org/pno
   CHORISTERS A-156 $.40   (C217)

   Marcia Corale (from Ronda)
   see RACCOLTA CORALE LIBRO III

   Messa In La Maggiore *Mass
   (Ballola, Carli) cor,orch voc sc
   ZERBONI 7900 s.p.   (C218)

   Musique Religieuse *CCU
   FORNI s.p.   (C219)

   Pie Jesu (from Requiem In C Minor)
   funeral
   (Hall, W.D.) [Lat] SATB,pno oct
   NATIONAL WHC-46 $.40   (C220)

   Requiem
   (Luck, Rudolf) 4pt men cor,orch pap
   SCHOTTS ETP 992 s.p.   (C221)

   Requiem In C-Moll *Req
   4pt mix cor,orch (C min,med) min sc
   SCHOTTS ETP 993 s.p.   (C222)

CHERUBINISCHE GESANGE see Krietsch,
   Georg

CHESTER see Billings, William

CHICHESTER PSALMS see Bernstein,
   Leonard

CHILD
   O Praise The Lord
   (Wienandt) SATB SCHIRM.G LG51667
   $.50   (C223)

CHILD IN A MANGER SLEEPING, A *Adv/
   Xmas,carol,Span
   (Ehret) SAB,fl oct LILLENAS AN-3855
   $.35   (C224)

CHILD IN THE MANGER *Xmas
   (Bock, Fred) SAB,fl GENTRY G-278 $.40
                                        (C225)
   (Duson, D.) SSAA,acap oct SOMERSET
   AD 1987 $.30   (C226)

CHILD IS BORN, A see Carney, David

CHILD IS BORN, A see Moorse, Peter

CHILD IS BORN, A see Williams, David H.

CHILD IS BORN IN BETHLEHEM, A
   see Two Carols

CHILD IS BORN IN BETHLEHEM, A see Kuntz

CHILD IS BORN IN BETHLEHEM, A see
   Schalk, Carl

CHILD IS BORN IN BETHLEHEM, A see
   Scheidt, Samuel

CHILD IS BORN IN BETHLEHEM, A see
   Sinzheimer, Max

CHILD IS BORN TO US, A see Davye

CHILD OF GOD see Ehret, Walter

CHILD OF MORNING see Winter, Sister
   Miriam Therese

CHILD OF OUR TIME, A see Tippett,
   Michael

CHILD OF THE KING, A see Sumner

CHILD THIS DAY IS BORN, A see Arnold,
   Corliss

CHILDING SLEPT, A see Thiman, Eric
   Harding

CHILDREN, GO WHERE I SEND THEE
   (Trant) SSAA (easy) OXFORD 83.081
   $.35   (C227)

CHILDREN OF BETHLEHEM, THE see Davis,
   Katherine K.

CHILDREN OF GOD, THE see Flandorf, W.

CHILDREN OF JERUSALEM see Ehret, Walter

CHILDREN, OF THE HEAVENLY FATHER
   *anthem
   see Christ, Whose Glory Fills The
   Skies
   (Johnson, Norman) SSATB/SSATTBB oct
   SINGSPIR ZJP-7358 $.30   (C228)
   (Krogstad, Bob) SATB oct GOSPEL
   05 TM 0307 $.30   (C229)

CHILDREN OF THE HEAVENLY KING
   (Grieb, Herbert) SATB&jr cor (easy)
   FITZSIMONS 2189 $.25   (C230)

CHILDREN OF THE HEAVENLY KING see
   Whitecotton, Shirley

CHILDREN OF THE HEBREWS see Palestrina,
   Giovanni

CHILDREN'S CAROLS FOR IMPROVISATION see
   Thoren, Nancy

CHILDREN'S CHRISTMAS FESTIVAL see
   Mendoza

CHILDREN'S HYMN see Binkerd, Gordon

CHILDREN'S NATIVITY PLAY FOR RHYTHMIC
   MOVEMENT see Martin, D.

CHILDREN'S UNISON CHOIR NO. 1 *CCUL
   unis jr cor SINGSPIR 5793 $1.25
                                        (C231)

CHILDREN'S UNISON CHOIR NO. 2 *CCUL
   unis jr cor SINGSPIR 5798 $1.25
                                        (C232)

CHILDREN'S UNISON CHOIR NO. 3 *CCUL
   unis jr cor SINGSPIR 5800 $1.25
                                        (C233)

CHILDREN'S UNISON CHOIR NO. 4 *CCUL
   unis jr cor oct SINGSPIR 5893 $1.25
                                        (C234)

CHILDS, BARNEY (1926-   )
   Heal Me, O Lord
   SATB,pno,trom sc AM.COMP.AL. $4.95,
   ipa   (C235)

   This Is The Praise Of Created Things
   mix cor,ob AM.COMP.AL. sc $4.95,
   voc pt $2.75   (C236)

CHILD'S GRACE, A see Kennedy

CHILD'S MESSAGE OF EASTER, A see Rains,
   Dorothy Best

CHILD'S PRAYER see Coulthard, Jean

CHILD'S PRAYER, A see Pfautsch, Lloyd

CHILD'S PRAYER TO THE SHEPHERD see
   France, William E.

CHIME MUSIC
   see Adore The Child Of Bethlehem

CHIME OF EASTER TIME, THE see Burke,
   John

CHOIR FAVORITES NO. 1 *CCUL
   SATB SINGSPIR 5101 $1.75   (C237)

CHOIR FAVORITES NO. 2 *CCUL
   SATB SINGSPIR 5102 $1.75   (C238)

CHOIR FAVORITES NO. 3 *CCUL
   SATB SINGSPIR 5103 $1.75   (C239)

CHOIR FAVORITES NO. 4 *CCUL
   SATB SINGSPIR 5104 $1.75   (C240)

CHOIR FAVORITES NO. 5 *CCUL
   SATB SINGSPIR 5105 $1.75   (C241)

CHOIR FAVORITES NO. 6 *CCUL
   SATB SINGSPIR 5106 $1.75   (C242)

CHOIR HANDBELL PROCESSIONAL see Ivey,
   Robert

CHOIR IMPACT *CC14UL
   (Mercer, W. Elmo) cor BENSON B0950
   $1.50   (C243)

CHOIR MELODIES *CC11UL
   cor (easy/med) GOSPEL 05 TM 4863
   $1.00 contains arrangements by:
   McLellan, Cyril; Collins, Hope;
   Ferrin, Paul; Yoder, Dave; Larsen,
   L.B.; Loes, Harry Dixon and others
                                        (C244)
CHOIR MELODIES, NO. 2 *CC10L
   SATB GOSPEL s.p. contains works by:
   White, Clyde; Flaten, Becky;
   Livingston, Hugh; Cox, Randy;

   Krogstad, Bob and others   (C245)

CHOIR PRAISE *CC10L
   (Mickelson, Paul) cor,opt orch GOSPEL
   05 TM 0559 $1.95, ipa recording,
   cassette, or trax also available
                                        (C246)

CHOIR SING! NO. 4 *CC10UL
   (Mickelson, Paul) cor LILLENAS MB-304
   $1.50   (C247)

CHOIR SPECIALS *CCUL
   (Berntsen, W.R.) cor SINGSPIR 5592
   $1.50   (C248)

CHOIR SPECIALS see Hughes, Robert J.

CHOISY
   Petit Mystere De Noel *Xmas
   cor (easy) sc HENN 683 s.p.   (C249)

   Six Noels Premiere Serie *CCU
   wom cor,acap HENN 276 s.p.   (C250)

   Six Noels Premiere Serie *CCU,Xmas
   wom cor,pno (easy) HENN 424 s.p.
   sc, voc pt   (C251)

   Six Noels Deuxieme Serie *CCU,Xmas
   wom cor,pno (easy) HENN 599 s.p.
   sc, voc pt   (C252)

   Six Noels Duexieme Serie *CCU,Xmas
   wom cor,acap HENN 600 s.p.   (C253)

THE CHORAL ART, VOL. II see Leaf

CHORAL BENEDICTIONS see Parthun, Paul

CHORAL CALLS TO WORSHIP see Fuller

CHORAL CARILLON see Williams

CHORAL COLLECTION, THE *CCUL,gospel/
   hymn
   (Hughes, Robert J.) cor SINGSPIR
   ZD-5477 $.60   (C254)

CHORAL HYMNS see Ortlund, Anne

CHORAL MASTERWORKS *CC7L
   SATB PRO ART 358 $1.25   (C255)

CHORAL MEDITATION ON "THERE'S AN OLD,
   OLD PATH", A
   (Rider, D.G.) SATB/unis,narrator
   WHITE HARV. CHO 721 $.35   (C256)

CHORAL-MESSE IN F see Bruckner, Anton

CHORAL MUSIC FOR WORSHIP *CC18L
   (Hilty, Everett Jay) 2-6pt PRUETT
   $3.95 contains trilogies consisting
   of an Introit, Prayer Collect,
   Extroit.Contains Works By: Hilty,
   E.J.; Praetorius; Tscesnokov;
   Schutz; Palestrina and others
                                        (C257)

CHORAL PREFACE AND BENEDICTION, A see
   Gore, Richard T.

THE CHORAL REPERTORY - BLUE BOOK *sac/
   sec,CCU
   (Bradley) SATB SCHIRM.G 2970 $4.00
                                        (C258)

THE CHORAL REPERTORY - RED BOOK *sac/
   sec,CCU
   (Bradley) SATB SCHIRM.G 2969 $4.00
                                        (C259)

CHORAL RESPONSES see Van Hulse, Camil

CHORAL STYLINGS *CCUL,hymn
   (Schrader, Jack) SATB,pno SINGSPIR
   ZD-5473 $1.50   (C260)

CHORAL VARIATIONS see Hively, Wells

CHORALBUCH see Pepping, Ernst

CHORALCREDO I see Goller, Fritz

CHORALCREDO III see Goller, Fritz

CHORALE AND ALLELUIA see Parrish, Mary
   Kay

CHORALE CANTATA see Wenzel, Eberhard

CHORALES FOR ADVENT see Schalk, Carl

CHORALES FOR CHRISTMAS AND EPIPHANY see
   Schalk, Carl

CHORALFANTASIE "AUS TIEFER NOT" see
   Hessenberg, Kurt

CHORALMESSE see Woll, Erna

CHORALSUITE TEIL I see Pepping, Ernst

CHORALSUITE TEIL II see Pepping, Ernst

CHORALSUITE TEIL III see Pepping, Ernst

CHORBAJIAN, JOHN (1936-   )
When David Heard That His Son Was
Slain
SATB SCHIRM.G 11997 $.35   (C261)

CHORBUCH 1968 *CC81U
SAT/SAB,org cloth SCHWEIZER. SK 169
s.p.   (C262)

CHORBUCH ZUM KIRCHENJAHR *CC98U,16-
18th cent
(Steichele, Paul) mix cor BOHM s.p.
(C263)

CHORE DER PASSION NACH DEM HEILIGEN
JOHANNES see Kromolicki, Joseph

CHORHEFT 1 "WEIHNACHT" *CC13U,Xmas
SATB SCHWEIZER. SK 149 s.p. contains
works by: Burck; Cruger; Freundt;
Herman; Osiander; Praetorius (C264)

CHORHEFT I-2 FUR DAS KIRCHENJAHR
*CC42U
SATB LANDES LKB 3 s.p. contains works
by: Bach; Cruger; Hassler;
Praetorius; Schein; and others
(C265)

CHORHEFT ZUM BADISCHEN
LANDESKIRCHENGESANGSTAG *CC14U
SAT/SAB/SATB/dbl cor LANDES LKB 2
s.p. contains works by: Bach;
Cabezon; Micheelsen; Vulpius and
others   (C266)

CHORSINGBLATT ZUM SCHUL-
REFORMATIONSGOTTESDIENST *CCU
[Ger] wom cor/treb cor MERSEBURG
EM304; mix cor MERSEBURG EM305
(C267)

CHORUS CHOIR VOICES NO. 8 *CCUL
SATB LILLENAS MB-247 $1.50   (C268)

CHORUS MELODIES, NO. 1 *CC113U,gospel
jr cor BENSON B0190 $.50   (C269)

CHORUS MELODIES, NO. 2 *CC144U,hymn
BENSON B0200 $.75   (C270)

CHORUSES FROM THE MESSIAH see Handel,
George Frideric

CHRIST AROSE see Lowry, Robert

CHRIST BECAME OBEDIENT see Anerio,
Felice

CHRIST BECAME OBEDIENT EVEN UNTO DEATH
see Anerio, Felice, Christus Factus
Est

CHRIST BECAME OBEDIENT FOR US UNTO
DEATH see Lee, J.

CHRIST CHILD, THE see Lovelace, Austin
C.

CHRIST CHILD SLEEPS, THE see DeShantz,
Louis M.

CHRIST CHILD'S LULLABY, THE see Diggle,
Roland

CHRIST DER IST ERSTANDEN see Bruck,
Arnold von

CHRIST FOR THE WORLD see Paviour, Paul

CHRIST FUHR GEN HIMMEL see Praetorius,
Michael

CHRIST HAS NO HANDS BUT OUR HANDS see
Mallory

CHRIST HATH A GARDEN see Willan, Healey

CHRIST IS ARISEN see Hassler, Hans Leo

CHRIST IS BORN see Bartlett

CHRIST IS BORN, ALLELUIA see Newbury,
Kent A.

CHRIST IS BORN TODAY see Burroughs, Bob

CHRIST IS BORN TODAY see Elder, Dorothy
Kosanke

CHRIST IS BORN TODAY see Pulsifer,
Thomas R.

CHRIST IS MADE THE SURE FOUNDATION see
Price, Milburn

CHRIST IS OUR CORNERSTONE see Fox,
George

CHRIST IS RISEN see Christus Ist
Auferstanden

CHRIST IS RISEN see Elvey, George Job

CHRIST IS RISEN! see Neander

CHRIST IS RISEN! see Williams

CHRIST IS RISEN AGAIN (SECOND PART) see
Bateson, Thomas

CHRIST IS RISEN, ALLELUIA! see Young,
Gordon

CHRIST IS RISEN FROM THE DEAD *Easter
(Bissell, Keith W.) SATB (med diff)
WATERLOO $.40   (C271)

CHRIST IS RISEN FROM THE DEAD see Fox,
George

CHRIST IS RISEN FRON THE DEAD see
Dunlop, Merrill

CHRIST IS RISEN INDEED see Hampton

CHRIST IS RISEN, RISEN INDEED see
Wetzler, Robert

CHRIST IS RISEN TODAY see Lora, Antonio

CHRIST IS THE ANSWER see Gunn

CHRIST IS THE FLOWER WITHIN MY HEART
see Chapman

CHRIST IS THE KING see Peek, Richard

CHRIST IST ERSTANDEN see Benzler, Fritz
Gustav

CHRIST IST ERSTANDEN see Kramer,
Gotthold

CHRIST IST ERSTANDEN see Pepping, Ernst

CHRIST IST ERSTANDEN see Pfluger, Hans
Georg

CHRIST IST ERSTANDEN see Schubert,
Franz (Peter)

CHRIST IST ERSTANDEN see Schutz,
Heinrich

CHRIST IST GEBOREN see Deutschmann,
Gerhard

CHRIST JESUS LAY IN DEATH'S STRONG
BANDS see Bach, Johann Sebastian

CHRIST JESUS, LORD AND KING see Lowe,
Helenclair

CHRIST KEEP US ALL see Holman, Derek

CHRIST-KONIG-MESSE see Haas, Joseph

CHRIST LAG IN TODESBANDEN see Cruger,
Johann

CHRIST LAG IN TODESBANDEN see Rohr,
Elli

CHRIST LIVES IN ME see Bartlett, Gene

CHRIST LIVES THROUGH ME! see Peterson,
John W.

CHRIST LIVETH IN ME see Mc Granahan

CHRIST LIVING IN ME see Kirby

CHRIST MY BELOVED see Palmer, Catherine

CHRIST OF BETHLEHEM, THE see Hafso

CHRIST OUR LIGHT AND LIFE see Englert,
Eugene

CHRIST, OUR LORD, IS ARISEN see Gallus,
Jacobus

CHRIST, OUR LORD, IS RISEN! see Van
Hulse, Camil

CHRIST OUR PASSOVER see Bales, Gerald

CHRIST OUR PASSOVER see Goss, John

CHRIST OUR SACRIFICE IS BORN see
Williams, D.

CHRIST REIGNETH STILL see Bach, Johann
Sebastian

CHRIST RETURNETH see Mc Granahan

CHRIST RISING AGAIN see Byrd, William

CHRIST RISING AGAIN see Tye,
Christopher

CHRIST ROSE FROM THE DEAD see Kverno,
Trond, Krist Sto Opp Av Dode

CHRIST THE LORD see Warner

CHRIST THE LORD IS BORN see Smith

CHRIST THE LORD IS BORN see Smith, Lani

CHRIST THE LORD IS RISEN see Atkinson,
Thelma

CHRIST THE LORD IS RISEN! see Bruck,
Arnold von, Christ Der Ist
Erstanden

CHRIST THE LORD IS RISEN AGAIN see
Rutter

CHRIST THE LORD IS RISEN TODAY
*Easter,anthem
(DeCou, Harold) SA/TB (easy) oct
SINGSPIR $.35   (C272)
(Peterson, John W.) SSATB,opt 3trp
oct SINGSPIR ZJP-3517 $.30   (C273)

CHRIST THE LORD IS RISEN TODAY see
Davidica, Lyra

CHRIST THE LORD IS RISEN TODAY see
Littleton, Bill J.

CHRIST THE LORD IS RISEN TODAY see
Monk, William Henry

CHRIST THE LORD IS RISEN TODAY see
Weber, Dennis

CHRIST THE LORD IS RISEN TODAY see
Wesley, Charles

CHRIST THE LORD TO US IS BORN
see Three Christmas Songs With
Synthesizer Accompaniment

CHRIST, THE NEWBORN KING see Bowles

CHRIST THE SURE FOUNDATION see Kirk,
Theron W.

CHRIST, THOU LAMB OF GOD see Lenel,
Ludwig

CHRIST UNSER HERR ZUM JORDAN KAM see
Bossler, Kurt

CHRIST WAS A PRETTY BABE see Fargo,
Milford

CHRIST WAS BORN see Broughton

CHRIST, WE DO ALL ADORE THEE see
Dubois, Theodore, Adoramus Te,
Christe

CHRIST WENT UP INTO THE HILLS ALONE see
Bitgood, Roberta

CHRIST, WHOSE GLORY FILLS THE SKIES
*anthem
(Alma) SSA FINE ARTS TR 103 $.30
contains also: Children, Of The
Heavenly Father (Alma); Somebody's
Knockin' (Littleton, Bill J.)
(Easter)   (C274)

CHRISTCHILD'S LULLABY see Weigl, Vally

CHRISTE, DU BEISTAND DEINER
KREUZGEMEINE see Baudach, Ulrich

CHRISTE, DU BIST DER HELLE TAG see
Vulpius, Melchior

CHRISTE, DU LAMM GOTTES see Hessenberg,
Kurt

CHRISTE, EINIGER TROST UND DU HOCHSTE
ZUVERSICHT see Staden, Johann

CHRISTENIUS, JOHANN
Biblische Motetten Fur Das
Kirchenjahr, Band II *see Ich
Bin Der Weg   (C275)

Ich Bin Der Weg *Bibl/mot
SATB,acap (easy) BAREN. BA6317 s.p.
see from Biblische Motetten Fur
Das Kirchenjahr, Band II   (C276)

CHRISTENSEN
Blessed Redeemer (composed with Loes)
*Easter/Gen
(Mercer, W. Elmo) SSATB oct BENSON
S4050 $.20   (C277)

CHRISTIAN MEN, REJOICE see Littleton,
Bill J.

CHRISTIANS AWAKE *Xmas
(Hamilton, H.C.) SATB (med easy)
WATERLOO $.30   (C278)

CHRISTIANS GATHER, DAY IS BREAKING see
Leaf, Robert

CHRISTIAN'S PRAYER, THE see Sparling,
William

CHRISTIANSEN
Festive Procession
SATB oct SCHMITT 1936 $.40   (C279)

CHRISTIANSEN, P.
  O Holy Night *Xmas
    SATB oct SCHMITT 932 $.45   (C280)

CHRISTIANSEN, PATRICIA
  Gift Of Love, A
    SATB,acap oct NATIONAL WHC-22 $.35
                                   (C281)

CHRISTIANSEN, PAUL
  All Poor Men And Humble *anthem
    SATB,opt solo AUGSBURG 11-1744 $.35
                                   (C282)

  Blessed Be The Father
    SATB,acap ART MAST 200 $.35   (C283)

  Everlasting Mercy
    SATB,acap ART MAST 151 $.30   (C284)

  Thy Kingdom Come On Earth *anthem
    SATBB,narrator,kbd AUGSBURG 11-1666
    $.35   (C285)

CHRISTKINDL KUMEDI see Bresgen, Cesar

CHRISTKONIGSMESSE see Gauss, Otto

CHRISTKONIGSMESSE see Peissner, Karl

CHRISTMAS
  Rejoice And Be Glad *anthem
    SAB,inst (easy) oct BROADMAN
    4551-51 $.30   (C286)

CHRISTMAS see Mendelssohn-Bartholdy,
  Felix, Weihnachten

CHRISTMAS ALLELUYA see Bayco, Fredric

CHRISTMAS BALLAD see Winter, Sister
  Miriam Therese

CHRISTMAS BALLAD, A see Read

CHRISTMAS BELLS see Mourant, Walter

CHRISTMAS BELLS ARE RINGING see
  Burroughs, Bob

CHRISTMAS BLESSING see Bello, Tavares

CHRISTMAS BOLERO, A see Hamil

CHRISTMAS BRINGS JOY *Xmas,carol,Norw
  (Pasquet, Jean) SA,pno (very easy)
    ELKAN-V 362-03187 $.40   (C287)

CHRISTMAS BRINGS JOY see Weyse

CHRISTMAS CALL TO WORSHIP, A see
  Fettke, Tom

CHRISTMAS CANON, A see Bacon, Ernst

CHRISTMAS CANTATA see Lubeck,
  Vincentius

CHRISTMAS CANTATA, A see Bush, Geoffrey

CHRISTMAS CANTATA (SINFONIA SACRA) see
  Pinkham, Daniel

CHRISTMAS CAROL, A see Boozer, Pat

CHRISTMAS CAROL MASS see Jirim,
  Frantisek, Vanocni Koledova Mse

CHRISTMAS CAROL SEQUENCE, A see Thiman,
  Eric Harding

CHRISTMAS CAROLER, THE *sac/sec,CC32L
  (Cookson, Frank B.) cor FITZSIMONS
    $.40   (C288)

CHRISTMAS CAROLS *CCU,Xmas,carol
  (Malin) 1-2pt oct BELWIN 64291 $.40
                                   (C289)

CHRISTMAS CAROLS *CCU,Xmas,carol
  (Massey, V.; Massey, J.) SATB ALLANS
    133 s.p.   (C290)

CHRISTMAS CAROLS see Fogg, Eric

CHRISTMAS CAROLS FOR CHILDREN *CC36UL,
  Xmas
  (Peterson, John W.) jr cor SINGSPIR
    5805 $.60   (C291)

CHRISTMAS CELEBRATION *Xmas,cant
  (Carmichael, Ralph) cor LEXICON 37695
    $2.95   (C292)

CHRISTMAS CHILD see McGlohan

CHRISTMAS CHILD see McGlohon, Loonis

CHRISTMAS CHILD see Rocherolle

CHRISTMAS CHOIR MELODIES *carol
  cmplt ed GOSPEL 05 TM 0311 $.75
    contains: Hark! The Herald Angels
    Sing (Collins, Hope) (SATB); How
    Far Is It To Bethlehem?
    (Krogstad, Bob) (SSATB,pno/harp,
    fl/vln,bvl) (orchestration
    available for this selection); O
    Little Town Of Bethlehem (Smith,

Harold J.) (jr cor); What Child
    Is This (Herb Smith) (SAB) (C293)

THE CHRISTMAS CHOIR NO. 1 *CCUL,Xmas
  (Peterson, John W.) SATB SINGSPIR
    5949 $1.00   (C294)

THE CHRISTMAS CHOIR NO. 2 *CCU,Xmas
  (Rasley, John) SATB SINGSPIR 5890
    $1.50   (C295)

CHRISTMAS CHORALE see Kenins, Talivadis

CHRISTMAS COLLAGE FOR SHEEP, SHEPHERDS,
  AND ANGELS see Young, Carlton R.

CHRISTMAS COMES ANEW *Xmas,anthem/
  carol,Fr
  (Ehret, Walter) SAB,org,opt perc
    (easy) GIA G1852 $.40   (C296)

CHRISTMAS CONCERT, A see Wilson, Roger
  C.

CHRISTMAS-CYCLE see Monnikendam, Marius

CHRISTMAS DAY IS COME *carol,Ir
  (Rice, M.R.) mix cor,brass BRODT 568
    $.20, ipa   (C297)

CHRISTMAS ENSEMBLE *CCU,Xmas
  (DeCou, Harold; Johnson, Norman) SSA&
    TTBB SINGSPIR 5764 $1.50   (C298)

CHRISTMAS EVE see Bendl, Karel, Stedry
  Den

CHRISTMAS EVE see Rice, M.R.

CHRISTMAS FESTIVAL see Emig, Lois Myers

CHRISTMAS FESTIVAL, A see Skillings,
  Otis

CHRISTMAS FOLK SONG, A *Xmas
  (Fettke) unis jr cor oct LILLENAS
    AN-4041 $.25   (C299)

CHRISTMAS FOLKSONG, A see Rishel, R.

CHRISTMAS GARLAND *Xmas
  (Johnston, R.) cor WATERLOO $1.00
                                   (C300)

CHRISTMAS GARLAND, A see Dyson, George

CHRISTMAS GREETING, A see Canning,
  Thomas

CHRISTMAS HAIKU see Olson

CHRISTMAS HYMN see Gardner

CHRISTMAS HYMNS AND ROUNDS see Gore,
  Richard T.

CHRISTMAS IN HOLLAND see Kemp, Helen

CHRISTMAS IN THE HOLY LAND see Weigl,
  Vally

CHRISTMAS IN YOUR HEART see Wommack,
  Chris

CHRISTMAS IS A TIME FOR LOVING see
  Wild, Eric

CHRISTMAS JOURNEY, THE see Verrall,
  Pamela

CHRISTMAS KIND OF NIGHT, A see Scheidt,
  Patricia

CHRISTMAS KINGS, THE see Young, Gordon

CHRISTMAS LONG AGO see Swanson, Howard

CHRISTMAS LULLABY see Hill, Harry

CHRISTMAS LULLABY, A see Schubert,
  Franz (Peter)

CHRISTMAS MADRIGAL, A see Felciano,
  Richard

CHRISTMAS MASS see Kagerer, Chr. Lor.,
  Weihnachtsmesse In G

CHRISTMAS MEDLEY
  see There Is A Song

CHRISTMAS MESSAGE see Klusmeier, R.T.A.

CHRISTMAS MORN see Morgan, Hilda

CHRISTMAS MORNING *Xmas,carol,Pol
  (Welch, John) SATB STUDIO V752 $.30
                                   (C301)

CHRISTMAS MOSAIC, A see Lamb

CHRISTMAS MOTET *Xmas,anthem/mot
  (Young) SAB/SATB,hndbl (easy) oct
    BROADMAN 4554-40 $.30   (C302)

CHRISTMAS MUSIC FROM COLONIAL AMERICA
  *CCU,Xmas
  (Van Camp, Leonard) cor GALAXY

1.2586.1 $2.50   (C303)

CHRISTMAS NIGHT see James, D.

CHRISTMAS NIGHT see Raph

CHRISTMAS OFFERING, A see Boozer, Pat

CHRISTMAS OFFERING, A see Kubik, Gail

CHRISTMAS ORATORIO, THE see Van Hulse,
  Camil

CHRISTMAS PRAYER *Xmas,Contemp
  SATB VANGUARD V559 $.35 see from Come
    To Bethlehem   (C304)

CHRISTMAS PROCESSIONAL see Proulx,
  Richard

CHRISTMAS RING, A see Soderwall

CHRISTMAS SONG, A see Hunter, Ralph

CHRISTMAS SONGS AND ROUNDS see Gore,
  Richard T.

CHRISTMAS SPIRIT, THE see Fox, Baynard

CHRISTMAS SPIRITUAL COLLECTION *Xmas
  (Walker, David) jr cor,inst CONCORDIA
    97-5204 $1.00
    contains: Little Cradle Rocks
    Tonight In Glory, The; Mary Had A
    Baby; O Mary, Where Is Your
    Baby?; Rise Up, Shepherd, And
    Follow; Spiritual Quodlibet For
    Christmas, A   (C305)

CHRISTMAS STORY see DeCou, Harold

CHRISTMAS STORY, THE see Billings,
  William

CHRISTMAS STORY, THE see Keetman,
  Gunild

CHRISTMAS TIME see Roff, Joseph

CHRISTMAS TIME AT THE PILGRIM INN see
  Lewis

CHRISTMAS TRIAD, A see Thiman, Eric
  Harding

CHRISTMAS TRIPTYCH, A see Elder,
  Dorothy Kosanke

CHRISTNACHT see Haas, Joseph

CHRISTO CANAMUS PRINCIPI see Sigmund,
  Oskar

CHRIST'S ADVENT see Walker, Jack

CHRIST'S BIRTHDAY see Montgomery, Bruce

CHRIST'S CAROL see Vale, Charles

CHRIST'S LULLABY *Xmas
  (Fearing, R.) SSA (easy) WATERLOO
    $.30   (C306)

CHRISTUM WIR SOLLEN LOBEN see Pepping,
  Ernst

CHRISTUS DER IST MEIN LEBEN see
  Vulpius, Melchior

CHRISTUS, DER UNS SELIG MACHT see
  Oertzen, Rudolf von

CHRISTUS FACTUS EST see Anerio, Felice

CHRISTUS FACTUS EST see Bruckner, Anton

CHRISTUS FACTUS EST see Haydn, (Johann)
  Michael

CHRISTUS FACTUS EST see Petrassi,
  Goffredo

CHRISTUS FACTUS EST (1844) see
  Bruckner, Anton

CHRISTUS FACTUS EST (1869) see
  Bruckner, Anton

CHRISTUS GLORIOSUS see Bamer, Alfred

CHRISTUS IST AUFERSTANDEN
  "Christ Is Risen" see Four Easter
  Chorales

CHRISTUS IST FUR UNS GESTORBEN see
  Lechner, Leonhard

CHRISTUS LICHT DER WELT "NACHT UND
  FINSTERNIS" see Willms, Franz

CHRISTUS REGNAT see Rehmann, Th.

CHRISTUS RESURGENS see Johnson

CHRISTUS RESURREXIT see Caldwell, Mary [Elizabeth]

CHRISTUS SPRICHT: WER MICH LIEBT see Baudach, Ulrich

CHRISTUS VICTOR see Roe, Betty

CHURCH AND RADIO CHOIR, THE *CC14U
(McLellan, Cyril) cor BENSON B0220
$1.00 (C307)

CHURCH BELLS AND FISHERMEN see Fargo, Milford

CHURCH IS SINGING AGAIN, THE
(Carmichael, Ralph) cor LEXICON 37657
$1.95
contains: Deliverance Medley; Light
Medley; Love Medley; Singing
Medley; Spirit Medley; Walking
Medley (C308)

CHURCH, O LORD, IS THINE, THE see Johnson, Norman

CHURCH OF THE LIVING GOD see Hughes

CHURCH OF THE LIVING GOD see Hughes, Robert J.

CHURCH TRIUMPHANT, THE see Nelson

CHURCH'S ONE FOUNDATION, THE *CC12L
(Mann, Johnny) cor LEXICON 37698
$1.95 (C309)

CHURCH'S ONE FOUNDATION, THE see Wesley, Samuel Sebastian Jr.

CHURCH'S ONE FOUNDATION, THE see Wesley, Samuel Sr.

CICHY, SIEGFRIED
Marienmesse *see Messe In A-Moll

Messe In A-Moll *Op.4, Mass
"Marienmesse" [Lat] 4pt mix cor,org
(A min) sc,cor pts BOHM s.p. (C310)

CIMAROSA, DOMENICO (1749-1801)
Missa Pro Defunctio *see Requiem

Requiem *funeral
"Missa Pro Defunctio" cor,soli,orch
voc sc EULENBURG GM188 s.p., sc
EULENBURG 10087 s.p., ipr (C311)

CIRCLE OF LOVE, A see Caldwell

CITY OF GOD see Langston, Paul

CITY OF GOLD see Cohron

CITY OF OUR GOD, THE see Avery, S.R.

CLAFLIN, AVERY (1898-)
He Shall Be Great *Adv,anthem
7pt mix cor,org AM.COMP.AL. $7.70
(C312)

Mary Of Nazareth, Pts 1 And 2
7pt,org AM.COMP.AL. $63.80 (C313)

Mary Of Nazareth, Pt 3
7pt,org AM.COMP.AL. $8.25 (C314)

Mary Of Nazareth, Pt 4
7pt,org AM.COMP.AL. $9.90 (C315)

Narrative And Chorale (from Mary Of
Nazareth)
SSATB,narrator,acap AM.COMP.AL.
$4.40 (C316)

Saul Of Taurus *cant
SSAATTBB,org AM.COMP.AL. $38.50
(C317)

CLAIM HIM LORD see Billingsley

CLAP HANDS ALL PEOPLE, SHOUT FOR JOY
see Harris

CLAP HAPPY PSALM see Ridenour, Joe

CLAP YOUR HANDS see Roberts

CLAP YOUR HANDS AND SHOUT WITH JOY
*anthem
(Graham) unis oct BROADMAN 4558-66
$.30 (C318)

CLAP YOUR HANDS, CHILDREN see Kerrick, Mary Ellen

CLAP YOUR HANDS, STAMP YOUR FEET see Nelson, Ronald A.

CLAP YOUR HANDS YE PEOPLES see
Buxtehude, Dietrich, Frohlocket Mit
Handen Alle Volker

CLAPP, DONALD
O God Unseen
SATB,acap (med easy) GENTRY G-248
$.35 (C319)

CLARK
Happy Is The Man Who Finds Wisdom
SATB SCHIRM.G LG51679 $.30 (C320)

O That My Head Were Water
SATB SCHIRM.G LG51698 $.35 (C321)

CLARK, EUGENE L.
Greatest Story Yet Untold, The *cant
SATB,solo,narrator SINGSPIR 5991
$1.25 (C322)

Last Commandment, The *cant
SATB,solo,narrator SINGSPIR 6003
$1.25 (C323)

Let The Earth Hear His Voice *cant
SATB,solo,narrator SINGSPIR 5995
$1.25 (C324)

CLARK, HENRY A.
Alleluia Christ Is Risen *Easter,
anthem
SATB LESLIE 4111 $.30 (C325)

Bow Down Thine Ear
SATB HARRIS $.35 (C326)

Breathe On Me, Breath Of God
SAB HARRIS $.30 (C327)

Come Holy Ghost
SATB HARRIS $.35 (C328)

Come Unto Me
SATB HARRIS $.35 (C329)

He Is Risen
mix cor LESLIE 4108 $.45 (C330)

I Will Praise The Name
SATB HARRIS $.35 (C331)

Let Thy Merciful Ears
SATB HARRIS $.35 (C332)

Praise To God, Immortal Praise
mix cor LESLIE 4109 $.45 (C333)

CLARK, K.
Shepherd's Star, The *Xmas,carol
SATB,T solo,acap FISCHER,J
FEC 10127 $.35 (C334)

CLARKE, F.R.C.
Blessed Art Thou, Lord God Of Our
Fathers *Fest
SATB,inst WATERLOO $.50, ipr (C335)

Father We Praise Thee
unis (med easy) WATERLOO $.30
(C336)

Hail Our Monarch *Easter
SATB (med) WATERLOO $.40 (C337)

Hail, Thou Source Of Every Blessing
SATB (med easy) WATERLOO $.40
(C338)

Let Every Soul Be Subject
SATB (med) WATERLOO $.40 (C339)

Lord Of All Hopefulness, Lord Of All
Joy
SA (easy) WATERLOO $.35 (C340)

Lord Of Our Life
unis (med easy) WATERLOO $.35
(C341)

Missa Brevis
unis (easy) WATERLOO $.40 (C342)

O Father On Our Festal Day
SATB (easy) WATERLOO $.50 (C343)

O Sing A New Song To The Lord
SATB (med diff) WATERLOO $.50
(C344)

With Joy We Go Up To The House Of The
Lord
SATB (med easy) WATERLOO $.35
(C345)

CLARKE, HENRY LELAND (1907-)
Above Our Western Earth *Xmas,anthem
SATB,pno AM.COMP.AL. $3.30 (C346)

Blessed Is The Man
SATB,acap AM.COMP.AL. $2.20 (C347)

Confitemini Domino
SATB,org AM.COMP.AL. $2.75 (C348)

Dona Nobis Pacem
TTBB,acap AM.COMP.AL. $1.10 (C349)

Eternal Spirit Of Truth And Love
SSAA/SATB,acap AM.COMP.AL. $3.30
(C350)

Gloria
[Eng/Fr/Span/Russ/Chin] SATB,pno/
org AM.COMP.AL. $3.58 (C351)
[Chin/Fr/Eng/Russ/Span] SATB,SAB
soli,vln,3fl,2ob,2clar,2bsn,
4horn,2trp,2trom,tuba,timp,perc,
harp,strings, bass trombone sc
AM.COMP.AL. $6.60 (C352)

CLARKE, HENRY LELAND (cont'd.)

Hope Of The World, The
SATB,acap AM.COMP.AL. $2.00 (C353)

In Praise Of Peace
SA,pno AM.COMP.AL. $3.30 (C354)

It Came Upon The Midnight Clear
1-2pt,pno AM.COMP.AL. $3.30 (C355)

Kyrie From The Mass For All Men
SB,soli,pno,org,perc sc AM.COMP.AL.
$2.75 (C356)

May Creatures All Abound
SATB,acap AM.COMP.AL. $2.20 (C357)

Now Abideth Faith, Hope, Love
SATB,acap AM.COMP.AL. $.55 (C358)

Restore Our Eyes
SATB,acap AM.COMP.AL. $.55 (C359)

Think On These Things
SATB,pno/org AM.COMP.AL. $2.20 (C360)

CLASSIC CHORALES, CAROLS AND HYMNS
*CC20L
(Ford; Hadley) SATB/unis,opt band PRO
ART 776 $1.50 (C361)

CLASSICS BY SCHUBERT *CC9UL
(Schubert, Myra) cor,pno LILLENAS
MB-319 $1.50 (C362)

CLATTERBUCK
Deep Down In My Heart *anthem/gospel
(Johnson, Norman) SATB oct SINGSPIR
ZJP-8104 $.30 (C363)

CLAYBERG, RICHARD P.
Missa Orbis Factor
SATB,org (easy) FOSTER MF149 $.40
(C364)

CLAYTON, NORMAN
For All My Sin *anthem
(Roe, Gloria) SATB WORD CS-2264
$.25 (C365)

Some Sweet Day
(Ferrin, Paul) SATB oct GOSPEL
05 TM 0218 $.30 (C366)

CLEANSING WAVE, THE see Knapp, (Mrs.)
Joseph F.

CLEMENS, JACOBUS (ca. 1510-ca. 1556)
Dona Nobis Pacem *canon
(Van Camp, L.) SSATB,acap oct
SOMERSET SP 723 $.35 (C367)

CLEMENS NON PAPA
see CLEMENS, JACOBUS

CLEMENTS
He Leadeth Me *anthem
SATB oct BROADMAN 4540-75 $.30
(C368)

CLEMENTS, JOHN (1910-)
Ah Know De Lord
SATB SCHOTT 11305 s.p. (C369)

CLEPHANE
Beneath The Cross Of Jesus
(Maker; Collins, Hope) SATB oct
GOSPEL 05 TM 0212 $.20 (C370)

CLERAMBAULT, LOUIS-NICOLAS (1676-1749)
L'Histoire De La Femme Adultere *ora
(Foster, Donald) [Lat] cor,soli,
cont,strings voc sc DEAN CMC-104
$4.50 (C371)

CLIFF BARROWS AND THE YOUNG CHURCH
SINGERS SINGIN' A NEW SONG *CC10L
(Kaiser, Kurt; Brown, Charles F.) jr
cor WORD 37705 $2.50 (C372)

THE CLIFF BARROWS CHOIR NO. 1 *CCU
cor SINGSPIR 5843 $1.50 (C373)

THE CLIFF BARROWS CHOIR NO. 2 *CCUL,
gospel/hymn
cor SINGSPIR 5838 $1.50 (C374)

THE CLIFF BARROWS CHOIR NO. 3 *CCUL,
gospel/hymn
cor SINGSPIR 5856 $1.50 (C375)

CLIFF BARROWS PRESENTS EXCITING SONGS
ON THE WAY *CC22L
(Carmichael, Ralph) cor LEXICON 37637
$1.95 (C376)

CLOISTER HYMN see Schumann, Requiem
Aeternam

CLOKEY, JOSEPH WADDELL (1890-1960)
Short Anthems, Set I *CCU
SATB (med) FITZSIMONS 2126 $.35
(C377)

Short Anthems, Set II *CCU
SATB (med) FITZSIMONS 2127 $.35
(C378)

CLOKEY, JOSEPH WADDELL (cont'd.)

Short Anthems, Set III *CCU
SATB (med) FITZSIMONS 2128 $.35
(C379)

CLOSE TO THEE see Moore, Rick

CLOSE TO THEE see Vail, Silas J.

CLOSE TO YOUR MOTHER see Tate

CLOSER TO JESUS see Fox, Baynard

CLOSER WALK, A *gospel/medley
(Nelson) SATB,trom oct LILLENAS
AN-1690 $.35   (C380)

CLOSSET
Noel
4pt mix cor HENN 902 s.p.   (C381)

CLOUD see Caldwell

CLOUDS see Graham

CLUTE
O Love Of God Most Full (composed
with Cole) *anthem
2pt (easy) oct BROADMAN 4540-49
$.30   (C382)

COATES
How Far Is It To Bethlehem
SA/TB SHAWNEE E160 $.35   (C383)

I Found Him (In A Quiet Place)
SSATB oct BENSON S4133 $.35   (C384)

COBBLER'S GUEST, THE see Pooley, Fred

COBINE, AL
Bethlehem
SATB,opt fl/bells, opt vibes (med)
FISCHER,C PC 1001   (C385)

Blessed The Children *Xmas
SATB STUDIO V742 $.45   (C386)

Little Christmas Star *Xmas
SSAA STUDIO V744 $.45   (C387)

Oh Lord, Help Us Live Each Day
*anthem
SATB STUDIO V716 $.40   (C388)

Sing Noel *Xmas
SATB STUDIO V743 $.45   (C389)

COELI ENARRANT see Sayve

COENEN, HANS (1911-   )
Die Weihnachtsgeschichte *Xmas
jr cor,solo,inst BOHM sc s.p., cor
pts s.p., ipa   (C390)

Geheiligte Zeit *CC20U,Fest
cor,inst sc,cor pts BOHM s.p.
(C391)

Kleine Hirtenmusik Zur Weihnacht
*Xmas
2pt jr cor,2S rec,A rec,2perc
PELIKAN PE916   (C392)

COGGIN
All Heaven On High Rejoices *anthem
SATB oct BROADMAN 4545-73 $.30
(C393)

Resurrection Fanfare *see Weisse

Three Short Anthems Of Praise *CC3U,
anthem
SAB SHAWNEE D5231 $.40   (C394)

COHEN
Ballad Of The Lion And The Lamb, The
*see Sutton, Nancy

COHRON
City Of Gold
(Mercer, W. Elmo) SATB oct BENSON
S4057 $.30   (C395)

COKE-JEPHCOTT, NORMAN
Awake, Awake To Love And Work!
SATB (med) FITZSIMONS 2172 $.25
(C396)

Manger Of Bethlehem Cradles A King,
The
SATB (med) FITZSIMONS 2163 $.25
(C397)

COLBORN, ARTHUR G.
Now Is Christ Risen
mix cor BANKS MUS YS 808 $.25
(C398)

COLD AND LONELY NIGHT see Johnson, Paul

COLE
He's Coming Back *gospel
(Roberts) SSATB oct LILLENAS
AT-1125 $.30   (C399)

O Love Of God Most Full *see Clute

Singing For Jesus *anthem
1-2pt,opt fing.cym.,opt hndbl oct
BROADMAN 4560-27 $.35   (C400)

COLE (cont'd.)

We Are Children Of The King *see
Wills

COLE, LETHA
Jesus *Easter,cant
unis BROADMAN 4515-06 $1.50 (C401)

COLE, WILLIAM
What Child Is This
see SIX CHRISTMAS CAROLS

COLEMAN, JACK
Zack, Junior *cant
cor LEXICON 37636 $1.95   (C402)

COLEMAN'S SONGS FOR MEN *CC196U
men cor BROADMAN 4522-01 $2.00 (C403)

COLLECTED ANTHEMS see Weelkes, Thomas

COLLECTED EDITION see Mendelssohn-
Bartholdy, Felix

COLLECTED EDITION see Mozart, Wolfgang
Amadeus

COLLECTED WORKS see Liszt, Franz

COLLECTED WORKS see Schein, Johann
Hermann

COLLECTED WORKS see Schutz, Heinrich

COLLECTED WORKS see Sweelinck, Jan
Pieterszoon

COLLECTED WORKS OF WILLIAM BYRD, VOL.
1, THREE MASSES AND CANTIONES
SACRAE see Byrd, William

COLLECTED WORKS OF WILLIAM BYRD, VOL. 2
CANTIONES SACRAE (1589) see Byrd,
William

COLLECTED WORKS OF WILLIAM BYRD, VOL.
3, CANTIONES SACRAE (1591) see
Byrd, William

COLLECTED WORKS OF WILLIAM BYRD, VOL.
12, PSALMS, SONETS AND SONGS (1588)
see Byrd, William

COLLECTED WORKS OF WILLIAM BYRD, VOL.
13, SONGS OF SUNDRIE NATURES see
Byrd, William

COLLECTED WORKS OF WILLIAM BYRD, VOL.
14, PSALMS, SONGS AND SONETS (1611)
see Byrd, William

COLLECTED WORKS OF WILLIAM BYRD, VOL.
15, CONSORT SONGS see Byrd, William

COLLECTED WORKS OF WILLIAM BYRD, VOL.
16, CONSORT MUSIC see Byrd, William

COLLECTED WORKS. SERIES 2: SACRED WORKS
NO. 1 see Donizetti, Gaetano

COLLECTION OF SEVEN TWO-PART SONGS
*CC7UL
(Sturman, Paul) cor EMI   (C404)

COLLINS
As He Walks With Me *gospel
SATB oct LILLENAS AT-1106 $.30
(C405)

Come, Thou Fount Of Every Blessing
*see Robinson

Give Thanks And Sing *hymn
SATB oct LILLENAS AT-1136 $.30
(C406)

One Way *anthem
SA/SAB (easy) oct BROADMAN 4551-47
$.30   (C407)

Praise Thee, Lord *folk
SSBar&camb,pno,opt bvl&drums&gtr
CAMBIATA L17553 $.40   (C408)

Song To Sing, A *gospel
SAB oct LILLENAS AT-1104 $.30
(C409)

We Sing With Grace In Our Hearts
*Proces
SSBar&camb,pno CAMBIATA C117449
$.35   (C410)

COLLINS, HOPE
Let Not Your Heart Be Troubled
SATB oct GOSPEL 05 TM 0468 $.25
(C411)

COLOM
Weary Marching Up The Calvary Road
*Gd.Fri.,anthem
(Johnson, Norman) SATB oct SINGSPIR
ZJP-3511 $.25   (C412)

COLONNA, GIOVANNI PAOLO (1637-1695)
Messe A Nove Voci Concertata Con
Stromenti
(Schnoebelen, Anne) dbl cor,soli,
strings (diff) bds A-R ED $9.95

COLONNA, GIOVANNI PAOLO (cont'd.)

(C413)

COLUMBIA see Ingalls, Jeremiah

COLUMBINI
Laudate Dominum *cant
SSAATTBB,STT/SAT soli,cont,strings
HANSSLER 10.276 sc s.p., cor pts
s.p.   (C414)

COLUMBUS THEME see Yahres, Samuel C.,
Adelante! (Sail On!)

COME ALL YE FRIENDS OF LYON *Xmas
(Bampton) SAB (easy) FITZSIMONS 6012
$.25   (C415)

COME AND BEHOLD see Keller

COME AND DINE see Widmeyer

COME AND GATHER, LITTLE CHILDREN see
Wihtol, A.A.

COME AND MOURN WITH ME AWHILE see Faber

COME AND PRAISE see Krogstad, Bob

COME AND PRAISE THE LORD WITH JOY see
Hruby, Delores

COME AND THANK HIM see Bach, Johann
Sebastian

COME, CHILDREN, LIFT YOUR VOICES see
Burroughs

COME CHILDREN, WITH SINGING see Umer
Uwa Golibe

COME, CHRISTIANS, JOIN TO SING *anthem
(DeCou, Harold) SATB oct SINGSPIR
ZJP-7250 $.30   (C416)

COME, CHRISTIANS, JOIN TO SING see
Englert, Eugene

COME, CHRISTIANS, JOIN TO SING see
Thomas, C.

COME, COME YE SAINTS see Roy, Fred

COME DOWN, LORD see Winter, Sister
Miriam Therese

COME DOWN, O LOVE DIVINE see Fettke,
Tom

COME DOWN, O LOVE DIVINE see Nelson,
Havelock

COME, FOLLOW ME see Cadwallader, Ann

COME GLAD HEARTS see Mozart, Wolfgang
Amadeus

COME, GO WITH ME TO BETHLEHEM see
Parks, Joe E.

COME, GO WITH ME TO THAT LAND
(Goemanne, N.) SATB,SATB soli,acap
oct SOMERSET SP 726 $.45   (C417)

COME HEAR THE WONDERFUL TIDINGS see
Thygerson, Robert J.

COME, HEAVY SOULS see Burroughs, Bob

COME HITHER, CHILD AND REST see
Lekberg, Sven

COME HITHER, YE CHILDREN see Cram,
James D.

COME HOLY GHOST *Pent,anthem/hymn
(Goemanne, N.) SATB&cong,org,trp
(easy) GIA G1896 $.40   (C418)

COME HOLY GHOST see Blackmer, Elmer F.

COME HOLY GHOST see Clark, Henry A.

COME, HOLY GHOST, CREATOR BLEST see
Walter (Walther), Johann

COME HOLY GHOST, ETERNAL GOD see
Naylor, Bernard

COME, HOLY LIGHT, GUIDE DIVINE see
Handel, George Frideric

COME, HOLY SPIRIT see Gaither, William
J. (Bill)

COME HOLY SPIRIT see Littleton, Bill J.

COME HOLY SPIRIT see Peterson, John W.

COME HOLY SPIRIT see Street

COME, HOLY SPIRIT, HEAVENLY DOVE see
Watts

COME HOLY SPIRIT, HEAV'NLY DOVE see Cooper, Rose Marie

COME, JESUS, COME see Wetzler, Robert

COME LET US ADORE HIM see Vandre, Carl W.

COME, LET US GO see Pulsifer, Thomas R.

COME LET US JOIN OUR CHEERFUL SONGS see Kimball

COME LET US SING
(Caldwell, Mary E.) SATB,org (med easy) oct GENTRY G-219 $.40   (C419)

COME, LET US SING JOYFULLY see Hallock, Peter

COME, LET US SING TO THE LORD see Williams, David H.

COME, LET US SING TO THE LORD see Wyrtzen, Don

COME, LET US TUNE OUR LOFTIEST SONG see Burroughs, Bob

COME LET US TUNE OUR LOFTIEST SONG see Corina, John

COME, LET US TUNE OUR LOFTIEST SONG see Lutkin, Peter Christian

COME, LET'S REJOICE see Amner, John

COME LORD JESUS see Jordahl

COME LOVELY AND SOOTHING DEATH see Goossen, Frederic

COME, MAGNIFY THE LORD see Couperin, Francois

COME, MY WAY, MY TRUTH, MY LIFE see Kent, F.J.

COME, MY WAY, MY TRUTH, MY LIFE see Powell

COME, O COME see Cromie, Marguerite Biggs

COME, O COME LIFE'S DELIGHT see Willan, Healey

COME, O CREATOR SPIRIT, COME see Noble, Thomas Tertius

COME, O JESUS see Cornell, Garry A.

COME O THE SPIRIT see Dailey, William

COME O THOU TRAVELLER see Noble, Thomas Tertius

COME ON AND SING NOEL *Xmas,anthem (Reynolds) SATB (easy) oct BROADMAN 4565-22 $.35   (C420)

COME ON DOWN see Hayford

COME ON KNEES see Williams, David H.

COME PRAISE THE LORD see Amner, John

COME, PRAISE THE LORD see Couperin, Francois

COME REST IN ME see Wild, Eric

COME, RISEN LORD see Lovelace, Austin C.

COME, SAYS JESUS' SACRED VOICE see Barbauld

COME SEE THE WONDERS see Billings, William

COME SHEPHERDS, ONE AND ALL see Kommt's Her Ihr Hirten

COME, SING A SONG UNTO THE LORD see Ayers, David

COME, SING TO THE GLORY OF THE LORD (Wild, Eric) SATB,pno BERANDOL BER1228 $.50   (C421)

COME, SING TO THE LORD see Cooper, Lowell

COME, SOUND HIS PRAISE ABROAD *anthem (Brandon) SAT/SAB FINE ARTS CM 1116 $.30   (C422)

COME, SOUND HIS PRAISE ABROAD see Boozer, Pat

COME, SOUND HIS PRAISE ABROAD see Burroughs, Bob

COME, TAKE MY YOKE see Wetzler, Robert

COME, THOU ALMIGHTY KING *anthem (Cram, James D.) SATB FINE ARTS CM 1001 $.35   (C423)

COME, THOU ALMIGHTY KING see Burroughs

COME, THOU ALMIGHTY KING see Giardini, Felice de'

COME THOU ALMIGHTY KING see Hill

COME, THOU ALMIGHTY KING see Lovelace, Austin C.

COME, THOU ALMIGHTY KING see Mickelson, Paul

COME THOU ALMIGHTY KING see Newberry, Kent

COME THOU FOUNT (from Nettleton) anthem (Young, Gordon) SATB WORD CS-2660 $.25   (C424)

COME, THOU FOUNT see Robinson

COME, THOU FOUNT see Wyeth, John

COME THOU FOUNT OF EVERY BLESSING *anthem (Cram, James D.) 2pt FINE ARTS CM 1013 $.30   (C425)

COME, THOU FOUNT OF EVERY BLESSING see Robinson

COME, THOU FOUNT OF EVERY BLESSING see Wyeth, John

COME, THOU LONG-EXPECTED JESUS see Leaf, Robert

COME, THOU REDEEMER see Six Christmas Hymns

COME, THOU SPIRIT EVERLASTING see Vivaldi, Antonio

COME TO BETHLEHEM *Xmas,Contemp SATB VANGUARD V560 $.35 see from Come To Bethlehem   (C426)

COME TO BETHLEHEM *see Asleep To The World; Cantate Domino; Christmas Prayer; Come To Bethlehem; Glory To God In Heaven; Hallelujah! Hallelujah!; How Could There Be A Fairer One?; Jesus Christ, The Holy Infant; Lord, Give Us Lasting Faith; Lord Of Lords, King Of Kings; Mary, Mary, Pray For Us; Star In The East   (C427)

COME TO ME see Dvorak, Antonin

COME TO ME, ALL WHO LABOR see Hruby, Delores

COME TO ME, ALL WHO LABOR see Purifoy, John

COME TO THE CELEBRATION see Page

COME TO THE SAVIOR see Taylor

COME TO THE SAVIOR NOW see Parks

COME TOGETHER *see Owens, Carol, Freely, Freely; Owens, Jimmy, God So Loved The World; Owens, Jimmy, Holy, Holy   (C428)

COME TOGETHER see Owens, Carol

COME TOGETHER see Owens, Jimmy

COME UNTO HIM see Handel, George Frideric

COME UNTO ME *Easter,anthem (Daniels) SATB FINE ARTS CM 1052 $.30   (C429)

COME UNTO ME see Atkinson, Thelma

COME UNTO ME see Bach, Johann Sebastian

COME UNTO ME see Clark, Henry A.

COME UNTO ME, YE WEARY *anthem (Alma) 1-2pt FINE ARTS CM 1008 $.30   (C430)

COME WE THAT LOVE THE LORD see Littleton, Bill J.

COME, WE THAT LOVE THE LORD see Williams, Aaron

COME, YAHWEH, COME see Graham, Robert Virgil

COME, YE BLESSED ONES OF MY FATHER see Scheidt, Samuel, Kommt Her, Ihr Gesegneten Meines Vaters

COME YE BRAVE AND COME YE STRONG see Blakley, D. Duane

COME, YE DISCONSOLATE see Roff, Joseph

COME, YE DISCONSOLATE see Silvester, Frederick

COME, YE DISCONSOLATE see Webbe, Samuel

COME, YE FAITHFUL, RAISE THE STRAIN *Easter,anthem (Rasley, John M.) SATB oct SINGSPIR ZJP-3528 $.30   (C431)

COME, YE FAITHFUL, RAISE THE STRAIN see Ayers, Jacob S.

COME, YE FAITHFUL, RAISE THE STRAIN see Damascus

COME, YE PEOPLE see Van Hulse, Camil

COME, YE SINNERS, POOR AND NEEDY (from Sacred Harp, The, 1844) anthem/ folk/hymn,US (Ehret, Walter) SATB WORD CS-2703 $.35   (C432)
(Wood) SATB (easy) oct BROADMAN 4534-64 $.30   (C433)

COME, YE THANKFUL PEOPLE, COME see Elvey, George Job

COME, YOUR HEARTS AND VOICES RAISING (Douglas) SSA,opt ob PRO ART 2756 $.35   (C434)

COME YOUR HEARTS AND VOICES RAISING see Ehret, Walter

COMFORT, O LORD see Crotch, William

COMFORTER HAS COME, THE see Bottome

COMIN' BACK TO THE LORD see Wilson

COMING CHILD, THE see Sinzheimer, Max

COMING OF OUR KING, THE see Twelve Christmas Carols: Set 2

COMING OF THE LORD, THE see Lovelace, Austin C.

COMMAND THINE ANGEL THAT HE COME see Buxtehude, Dietrich

COMMISSION see Hall

COMMIT THOU ALL THY GRIEFS see Cousins, M. Thomas

COMMON CUP, THE see Cates, Bill

COMMUNION see Robison

COMMUNION ANTHEM see McAfee

COMMUNION CHORALES, SET II see Bach, Johann Sebastian

COMMUNION HYMN see Morgan, Hilda

COMMUNION MEDITATION see Baker

COMMUNION MEDITATIONS see Carlson, Gordon

COMMUNION RITE see Peloquin, C. Alexander

COMMUNION SERVICE see Darst, W. Glenn

COMMUNION SERVICE see Lovelace, Austin C.

COMMUNION SERVICE see Matthews, Thomas

COMMUNION SERVICE see Pinkham, Daniel

COMMUNION SERVICE (ADAPTED FOR ROMAN CATHOLIC USAGE) see Merbecke, John

COMMUNION SERVICE IN C see Mathias, William

COMMUNION SERVICE IN C see Stanford, Charles Villiers

COMMUNION SERVICE IN E see Walker, Robert

COMMUNION SERVICE IN E-FLAT see Weatherseed, John .J.

COMMUNION SERVICE IN G MINOR see Grant, W. Parks

COMMUNION SERVICE (SERIES II) see Ridout, Godfrey

COMMUNION SERVICE (SERIES III) see Dearnley

COMMUNION SERVICE (SERIES III) see
Jackson

COMMUNION SERVICE (SERIES III) see
Kelly

COMMUNION SERVICE (SERIES III) see
Rutter

COMMUNIONMUSIK see Nilsson, Torsten

COMMUNITY MASS see Markaitis, Fr. Bruno

COMPLETE CHURCH MUSIC VOL. 1 *CCU
(Humfrey) cor STAINER 3.8934.8 $26.00
(C435)

COMPLETE CHURCH MUSIC VOL. 2 *CCU
(Humfrey) cor STAINER 3.8935.8 $25.00
(C436)

COMPLETE HOLY WEEK SERVICES see Bauman,
W.A.

COMPLETE PSALMS see Dowland, John

COMPLETE WORKS see Beethoven, Ludwig
van

COMPLETE WORKS see Brahms, Johannes

COMPLETE WORKS see Lassus, Roland de
(Orlandus)

COMPLETE WORKS see Rameau, Jean-
Philippe

COMPLETE WORKS see Schumann, Robert
(Alexander)

COMPLETE WORKS see Glinka, Mikhail
Ivanovitch

COMPLETE WORKS see Schubert, Franz
(Peter)

COMPLETE WORKS see Dunstable, John

COMPLETE WORKS. BACH-GESELLSCHAFT
EDITION see Bach, Johann Sebastian

THE COMPLETE WORKS OF JOHANN WALTER
VOL. I: GEISTLICHES GESANGBUCHLEIN
PART I see Walter (Walther), Johann

THE COMPLETE WORKS OF JOHANN WALTER
VOL. II: GEISTLICHES GESANGBUCHLEIN
PART II see Walter (Walther),
Johann

THE COMPLETE WORKS OF JOHANN WALTER
VOL. III: GEISTLICHES
GESANGBUCHLEIN PART III see Walter
(Walther), Johann

THE COMPLETE WORKS OF JOHANN WALTER
VOL. IV: CANTIONES SEPTEM VOCUM AND
MAGNIFICAT OCTO TONORUM see Walter
(Walther), Johann

CONCERT see Anonymous

CONCERT MUSIC NO. 2 see Karlins, M.
William

CONCERTO SPIRITUALE see Ghedini,
Giorgio Federico

CONCORD CANTATA, A see Thompson,
Randall

CONFIRMA HOC see Filke, Max

CONFIRMA HOC see Gauss, Otto

CONFIRMA HOC see Gruber, Joseph

CONFIRMA HOC see Lemacher, Heinrich

CONFITEMINI DOMINO see Clarke, Henry
Leland

CONFITEOR see Pouwels, Jan

CONFLICT OF THE AGES, THE see Morris

CONFORTAMINI ET IAM NOLITE TIMERE see
Lassus, Roland de (Orlandus)

CONKEY, ITHAMAR (1815-1867)
In The Cross Of Christ I Glory
*Gd.Fri.,anthem
(Burkwall, Eldon) SATB oct SINGSPIR
ZJP-7302 $.25
(C437)

CONNOLLY, JUSTIN [RIVEAGH] (1933-   )
Te Deum *Op.21
cor&cong,org voc sc NOVELLO rental
(C438)

CONNOLLY, RICHARD
Go Teach All Nations *Mass
cong,org,opt 2trp&2trom&perc EMI sc
s.p., cor pts s.p.
(C439)

Hail O Queen
SSA EMI s.p.
(C440)

CONQUEROR, THE see Ramquist, Grace

CONSECRATION A LA SAINTE-VIERGE *BVM
cor JOBERT s.p. see also Douze
Nouveaux Cantiques De Fetes (C441)

CONSERVA, FILI MI see Weis, Flemming

CONSIDER THE LILIES see Young, Gordon

CONSIDER THE PRICE HE PAID see
Peterson, John W.

CONSTANTINO, JOSEPH
All This Time This Song Is Best
SATB BOURNE B223941-358 $.50 (C442)

CONSTRUE MY MEANING see Farnaby, Giles

CONTENTMENT see Williams

CONTENTMENT IN HIS LOVE see Dunlop,
Merrill

CONVERSE, CHARLES CROZAT (1832-1918)
What A Friend We Have In Jesus
*anthem
(Kaiser, Kurt) SATB WORD CS-2668
$.35 see also HE LIVES (C443)
(Lee, John) SATB WORD CS-2637 $.35
(C444)
(Wyrtzen, Don) SA/TB (easy) oct
SINGSPIR ZJP-6033 $.35 (C445)

CONVERTENTUR SEDENTES see Mozart,
Wolfgang Amadeus

COOK, D.F.
Puer Natus *Xmas
SATB (med) WATERLOO $.40 (C446)

COOPER
Psalm 150 *anthem
1-2pt oct BROADMAN 4557-10 $.30
(C447)

COOPER, LOWELL
Come, Sing To The Lord
1-2pt,kbd,opt gtr&bvl oct HOPE
CF 172 $.35 (C448)

COOPER, ROSE MARIE (1937-   )
Come Holy Spirit, Heav'nly Dove
see Three Anthems For Junior Choir

For You A Child Is Born
see Three Anthems For Junior Choir

O Word Of God Incarnate
see Three Anthems For Junior Choir

Psalm 146
mix cor BRODT 633 $.25 (C449)

Three Anthems For Junior Choir
*Xmas/Gen/Pent,anthem
unis/SA/jr cor,kbd (med easy) oct
CONCORDIA 98-1898 $.30
contains: Come Holy Spirit,
Heav'nly Dove; For You A Child
Is Born; O Word Of God
Incarnate (C450)

COPE
Holy Spirit, Be My Guide *hymn
(Mickelson, Paul) SSATB oct
LILLENAS AN-2419 $.25 (C451)

Jolly Wat *cant
SATB,inst (med diff) OXFORD 46.163
$1.30, ipr (C452)

COPE, CECIL
Quid Petis, O Fili
SATB THOMP.G s.p. (C453)

COPERARIO, GIOVANNI (ca. 1575-1626)
I'll Lie Me Down To Sleep In Peace
SATTB STAINER 3.0736.1 $.60
contains also: O Lord How Do My
Woes Increase (C454)

O Lord How Do My Woes Increase
see Coperario, Giovanni, I'll Lie
Me Down To Sleep In Peace

COPES, V. EARLE
Carol Of The Trees
see Three Carols For Juniors

Harvest Carol
see Three Carols For Juniors

Mary's Lullaby
see Three Carols For Juniors

Three Carols For Juniors *CC3U,carol
unis oct KERBY 814 $.25 (C455)

Three Carols For Juniors *carol
unis oct BERANDOL 81471 $.25
contains: Carol Of The Trees;
Harvest Carol (Thanks); Mary's
Lullaby (Xmas) (C456)

COPLEY
Bell Horses
see Three Songs

Robin Red Breast
see Three Songs

Three Songs *sac/sec
unis,pno LENGNICK s.p.
contains: Bell Horses; Robin Red
Breast; Who Slept That Night In
Bethlehem (C457)

Who Slept That Night In Bethlehem
see Three Songs

COR MEUM see Lassus, Roland de
(Orlandus)

CORIGLIANO, JOHN (1938-   )
L'Invitation Au Voyage
SATB SCHIRM.G 11978 $.35 (C458)

CORINA, JOHN
Beloved, Let Us Love One Another
SATB oct BENSON S4040 $.30 (C459)

Come Let Us Tune Our Loftiest Song
SATB oct BENSON S4060 $.30 (C460)

Easter Fanfare Anthem
SATB,brass,orch BENSON S4080 $.30,
ipa (C461)

Infant Holy *Xmas
unis,bells BENSON S4150 $.20 (C462)
SATB BENSON S4160 $.25 (C463)

Is It Nothing To You? *Lent,cant
(Huff, Ronn) SATB,pno/org,opt
winds/brass BENSON B0450 $1.50,
ipa (C464)

O Holy Child Of Love *Xmas
unis BENSON S4230 $.25 (C465)

CORINTHIANS ON LOVE see McAfee

CORNELIUS
Kings, The
(Davies) SSATB,opt acap (med easy)
OXFORD 84.228 $.25 (C466)

CORNELIUS, PETER (1824-1874)
Absolve Domine
(Scriba, H.) 4pt mix cor BREITKOPF-
W CHB 4956 s.p. (C467)

Ach, Wie Nichtig, Ach, Wie Fluchtig
*Op.9,No.1
TTBBB/4pt men cor,A solo,acap sc
SCHOTTS C 38 536 s.p., voc pt
SCHOTTS C 38 531 01-05 (C468)

Mitten Wir Im Leben Sind *Op.9,No.3
sc SCHOTTS CHBL 34 s.p. (C469)
(Scriba, H.) 4pt mix cor BREITKOPF-
W CHB 4957 s.p. (C470)

Requiem Aeternam *Req
[Lat] mix cor (easy) sc SCHOTTS
CHBL 321 s.p. (C471)

Seele, Vergiss Sie Nicht *Req
[Ger/Eng] 6pt mix cor,acap
BREITKOPF-W CHB 4955 s.p. (C472)

CORNELL
Wonderful Peace
(Cooper; McLellan) SATB oct GOSPEL
05 TM 0113 $.20 (C473)

CORNELL, GARRY A.
All My Heart This Night Rejoices
*Adv/Xmas
1-2pt ART MAST 256 $.35 (C474)
SATB ART MAST 138 $.40 (C475)

Angels' Song, The *Xmas,anthem
SA/cong,kbd,opt gtr, C inst
AUGSBURG 11-0317 $.40 (C476)

Bread, In Mercy Broken *Commun
SATB ART MAST 229 $.35 (C477)

Come, O Jesus *Lent
SATB/unis/2pt ART MAST 211 $.45
(C478)

Happening At Bethlehem, The *Xmas
SATB,bvl,drums,gtr ART MAST 212
$.50, ipa (C479)

Joy Dawns Again *Easter/Pent
2pt ART MAST 180 $.40 (C480)

Let The Bright Red Berries Glow
*Xmas
2pt ART MAST 157 $.40 (C481)

Lord Of All Being
SATB&opt cong,org,brass,timp ART
MAST 263 $.50 (C482)

Manger Of Bethlehem, The *Xmas
SATB/unis/2pt ART MAST 174 $.40
(C483)

CORNELL, GARRY A. (cont'd.)

My Lord, My Brother
1-2pt mix cor,opt kbd,gtr,perc oct
AGAPE AG 7160 $.40   (C484)

No Place Drives Him Away
SATB ART MAST 218 $.40   (C485)

Who Would Be A Shepherd Boy? *Adv/
Xmas
unis ART MAST 201 $.40   (C486)

CORNYSH, WILLIAM
Magnificat
SATBB STAINER 3.0865.1 $.75 (C487)

Woefully Array'd
SATB STAINER 3.0540.1 $.60 (C488)

CORSI, GIUSEPPE (fl. 1659-1681)
Adoramus Te
(Watson) TTBB BRODT NC 1 $.26
(C489)

CORTECCIA, FRANCESCO BERNARDO
(1504-1571)
Eleven Works To Latin Texts *CC11U
(McKinley, Ann) cor bds A-R ED
$9.95   (C490)

CORUM
Peace In Our Time (composed with
Price) *anthem
SATB (easy) oct BROADMAN 4551-39
$.30   (C491)

CORY, GEORGE
Carol (The First Noel) *Xmas
SATB,acap GENERAL 736CH $.50 (C492)

COSSETTO, EMIL (1918-   )
Calvary
see Passion Spirituals

Golgatha *Psntd
[Ger] men cor,acap sc,cor pts TONOS
3451 s.p.   (C493)

Hammering
see Passion Spirituals

Passion Spirituals
[Eng] men cor sc SCHOTTS C 43 511
s.p.
contains: Calvary; Hammering
(C494)

COSTANTINI, ALESSANDRO (fl. ca. 1616)
Pastores Loquebantur *Xmas,mot
[Lat] TTB/mix cor,org sc SCHOTTS
C 34 491 s.p., cor pts SCHOTTS
C 34 492 s.p.   (C495)

COTHRAM, J.
Planted Wheat *anthem/folk,Heb
SATB,treb inst, woodblock (easy)
GIA G1774 $.25   (C496)

COULD IT BE see Lanier, Gary

COULTHARD, JEAN (1908-   )
Child's Prayer
unis/SA (easy) OXFORD 02.008 $.20
(C497)

Lullaby For Christmas *Xmas
unis&desc (easy) OXFORD 02.006 $.35
(C498)

Star Shown Down, A *Xmas
unis/SA (easy) OXFORD 02.007 $.25
(C499)

COUNT YOUR BLESSINGS *CC11UL,gospel
(Ehret, Walter) SATB LILLENAS MB-349
$1.95   (C500)

COUNTRY-WESTERN CHOIR, THE *CCUL,
gospel
(Peterson, John W.) SATB SINGSPIR
5865 $1.95   (C501)

THE COUNTRY-WESTERN CHOIR NO. 2 *CCUL,
gospel
cor SINGSPIR 5872 $1.95   (C502)

COUPERIN, FRANCOIS (1668-1733)
Come, Magnify The Lord
(Jewell) SA (med) oct CONCORDIA
98-2179 $.50   (C503)

Come, Praise The Lord
(Jewell) SAB (med) oct CONCORDIA
98-2164 $.50   (C504)

Hymn Of Praise, A *anthem
(Jewell, Kenneth W.) SAB,pno/org,
2vln WORLD CA-2411-7 $.45 (C505)

Jubilemus *mot
[Lat] SAB,2inst,cont EGTVED MS6B9
s.p.   (C506)

O Praise The Lord With One Accord
(Jewell) SAB oct CONCORDIA 98-2226
$.45   (C507)

COURTNEY, RAGAN
Beginnings *see Glorious In
Holiness; Jesus, Gentle Lamb;
Peace Like A River   (C508)

Beginnings-A Praise Concert *see
Red, Buryl

Celebrate Life (composed with Red,
Buryl)
cor,narrator,inst BROADMAN 4518-06
$3.50, ipa   (C509)

Ecclesiastes 4:11 (composed with
Red, Buryl) *anthem
SATB oct BROADMAN 4565-29 $.35
(C510)

Glorious In Holiness (composed with
Red, Buryl)
2pt mix cor TRIUNE TUM 118 $.40 see
from Beginnings   (C511)

In Remembrance (composed with Red,
Buryl) *anthem
SATB oct BROADMAN 4565-35 $.50
(C512)

Jesus, Gentle Lamb (composed with
Red, Buryl)
2pt mix cor TRIUNE TUM 117 $.40 see
from Beginnings   (C513)

Peace Like A River (composed with
Red, Buryl)
2pt mix cor TRIUNE TUM 116 $.40 see
from Beginnings   (C514)

Prayer For Peace (composed with Red,
Buryl) *anthem
SATB oct BROADMAN 4565-33 $.35
(C515)

There Is A Great Joy Coming (composed
with Red, Buryl) *anthem
SATB oct BROADMAN 4565-34 $.50
(C516)

Truth Shall Make You Free, The
(composed with Red, Buryl)
*anthem
SATB oct BROADMAN 4565-36 $.35
(C517)

COUSINS, M. THOMAS (1914-   )
And The Word Was Made Flesh
mix cor BRODT 613 $.35   (C518)

Commit Thou All Thy Griefs
mix cor BRODT 505 $.20   (C519)

Credo
mix cor BRODT 611 $.25   (C520)

Eternal God Is Thy Refuge, The
mix cor BRODT 559 $.26   (C521)

Glorious Everlasting
mix cor,opt brass/orch BRODT 504
$.35, ipr   (C522)

Hark The Sound Of Holy Voices
mix cor BRODT 510 $.24   (C523)

Holy Father, Pure And Gracious
mix cor BRODT 596 $.20   (C524)

Hymn To Truth, A
mix cor BRODT 626 $.25   (C525)
SSAA BRODT WC 4 $.26   (C526)

Invocation
mix cor BRODT BC 1 $.30   (C527)

Lord Is In His Holy Temple, The
mix cor BRODT 511 $.25   (C528)

Miserere Mei, Deus
mix cor BRODT 597 $.20   (C529)

O Clap Your Hands
mix cor BRODT 527 $.45   (C530)

Praise The Lord! Ye Heavens Adore Him
mix cor BRODT 517 $.24   (C531)

Rejoice In The Lord Alway
mix cor,opt orch BRODT 591 $.50,
ipr   (C532)

Sanctus
mix cor BRODT 509 $.20   (C533)

COVENANT HYMN see Canning, Thomas

COVENANT OF PEACE see Zaninelli, Luigi

COVENANT OF THE RAINBOW see Crosse

COVENTRY CAROL see Currie, Randolph

COVENTRY CAROL see Ferris, William

COVENTRY CAROL *Xmas,Eng
(Terry, Richard) SATB EMI s.p.
contains also: Coventry Carol
(Routley, Eric)   (C534)

COVENTRY CAROL
see Coventry Carol

COWAN, MARIE
God Bless Australia
(Snr, L. Kean) ALLANS 843 (C535)

COWEN
Three Kings Once Lived *Xmas
(Calahan) SATB&opt unis,opt med
solo (easy) FITZSIMONS 2108 $.20
(C536)

COWPER, WILLIAM
Sometimes A Light
(Marshall) SATB,opt pno&bvl,opt gtr
(easy) FISCHER,C CM 7890 $.35
(C537)

COX
Nowell! Heap On More Wood
SATB,inst (med diff) OXFORD 84.199
$.45, ipa   (C538)

COZENS, JOHN
Six Christmas Carols *CC6U,Xmas,
carol
SATB THOMP.G G-527 s.p.   (C539)

CRADLE, THE *Xmas,carol,Aus
(Houkom) SATB oct SCHMITT $.40 (C540)

CRADLE, THE see Hinton

CRADLE CAROL, A see Preus

CRADLE GOD, O HEART see Carlson, J.
Bert

CRADLE IN A MANGER see Kirby

CRADLE IN BETHLEHEM, A see Stock, Larry

CRADLE SONG see Grimes, Gordon

CRADLE SONG see Le Fleming, Christopher
(Kaye)

CRADLED IN HAY *Xmas
(Hill, Harry) SATB (med easy)
WATERLOO $.30   (C541)

CRAM
Favor And Good Understanding *anthem
SATB oct BROADMAN 4545-81 $.30
(C542)

Jesus Bids Us Shine *see Miller

Lord Is My Light, The *anthem
2pt (easy) oct BROADMAN 4545-64
$.30   (C543)

Lord, Our Lord *anthem
SATB oct BROADMAN 4545-86 $.30
(C544)

My Redeemer *anthem
SATB oct BROADMAN 4540-74 $.30
(C545)

Place Of Joy And Peace, A *anthem
SATB oct BROADMAN 4545-72 $.30
(C546)

Praise God In His Holiness *anthem
SATB oct BROADMAN 4565-50 $.50
(C547)

Psalm Of Praise, A *anthem
SATB (easy) oct BROADMAN 4554-50
$.30   (C548)

Redeemed *see Crowby

CRAM, JAMES D. (1931-1974)
Come Hither, Ye Children *Xmas,
anthem
2pt, opt triangle FINE ARTS CM 1089
$.30   (C549)

In The Bleak Midwinter *Xmas,anthem
SSA,pno,opt tamb FINE ARTS TR 106
$.35   (C550)

Long Life And Peace
see Three Proverbs

Mercy And Truth
see Three Proverbs

Oh, Bless The Lord *anthem
SATB,kbd AUGSBURG 11-0659 $.30
(C551)

Three Prayers From The Ark
SSA,acap FISCHER,C CM 7811 $.30
(C552)

Three Proverbs *anthem
SA,fl WORD CS-2698 $.40
contains: Long Life And Peace;
Mercy And Truth; Trust In The
Lord   (C553)

Trust In The Lord
see Three Proverbs

CRANE, LOR.
Glory Be To The Father
SATB,org BROUDE,A 730 $.50 (C554)

CRAPPIUS, ANDREAS
Da Pacem Domine *mot
SSSATB,opt inst MOSELER MOR44 s.p.
contains also: Erhalt Uns, Herr,
Bei Deinem Wort; Verleih Und
Frieden   (C555)

CRAPPIUS, ANDREAS (cont'd.)

Erhalt Uns, Herr, Bei Deinem Wort
see Crappius, Andreas, Da Pacem
Domine

Verleih Und Frieden
see Crappius, Andreas, Da Pacem
Domine

CRAWFORD
Ash Wednesday
SATB,SBar soli (diff) OXFORD rental
(C556)

Psalm 98
TBB,pno/5brass (med diff) sc OXFORD
94.102 $.70, ipa (C557)

CRAWLEY
Glory Be
see Sir Gawain Carols

Jesu Almighty
see Sir Gawain Carols

Make We Mirth
see Sir Gawain Carols

Sir Gawain Carols *Xmas,carol
SATB (med diff) OXFORD 84.241 $.45
contains: Glory Be; Jesu
Almighty; Make We Mirth (C558)

CREATE IN ME A CLEAN HEART see Barnes,
Marshall

CREATE IN ME A CLEAN HEART see
Burroughs, Bob

CREATE IN ME A CLEAN HEART see LaCheur,
Rex

CREATE IN ME A CLEAN HEART, O GOD see
Willan, Healey

CREATE IN ME A CLEAN HEART WILLING see
Yantis, David

CREATION, THE see Bender, Jan

CREATION JAZZ see Arch, Gwyn

CREATION MASS IN B FLAT MAJOR see
Haydn, (Franz) Joseph

CREATOR GOD, WE GIVE YOU THANKS see
Burroughs

CREATOR OF THE STARS OF NIGHT *Adv
(Pasquet, Jean) SA,pno (very easy)
oct ELKAN-V 362-03170 $.30 (C559)

CREATOR OF THE STARS OF NIGHT see
Darst, W. Glenn

CREATOR OF THE STARS OF NIGHT see
Newbury, Kent A.

CREATOR SPIRIT see Waters, Charles F.

CREDO see Berglund

CREDO see Cousins, M. Thomas

CREDO see Donizetti, Gaetano

CREDO see Dvorak, Antonin

CREDO see Marshall, Jane M.

CREDO see Palestrina, Giovanni

CREDO see Savelli, M.A.

CREDO see Vivaldi, Antonio

CREDO IV VOCUM see Isaac, Heinrich

CREDO MASS see Mozart, Wolfgang Amadeus

CREED see Hampton, Calvin

CREED see Palestrina, Giovanni

CRIVELLI, GIOVANNI BATTISTA (? -1682)
Ut Flos, Ut Rosa
(Roche) SS/TT (med easy) OXFORD
44.081 $.50 (C560)

CROCE
Exaudi Deus
(Klein) "Oh, Hear Me, Lord God"
SATB SCHIRM.G 11985 $.30 (C561)

Oh, Hear Me, Lord God *see Exaudi
Deus

CROCE, GIOVANNI (ca. 1560-1609)
Hore, O Herr, Das Gebet Deiner
Gemeinde *mot
(Kronberg, Gerhard) [Ger] mix cor
cor pts BOHM 25 s.p. see from
MOTETTEN ALTER MEISTER (C562)

CROCE, GIOVANNI (cont'd.)

O Sacrum Convivium
see HYMNEN UND MOTETTEN ALTER
MEISTER HEFT 2

Voce Mea Ad Dominum Clamavi
[Lat] 4pt mix cor,acap BOHM s.p.
(C563)

CROFT, COLBERT
He Just Loved Me More And More
(composed with Croft, Joyce)
*anthem
SATB WORD CS-2640 $.30 (C564)

CROFT, JOYCE
He Just Loved Me More And More *see
Croft, Colbert

CROFT, WILLIAM (1678-1727)
Music Of The Great Churches Vol. VI:
Westminster Abbey, London *see
We Will Rejoice (C565)

O God, Our Help In Ages Past *anthem
(Bolks, Dick) SATB oct SINGSPIR
ZJP-7240 $.30 (C566)

We Praise Thee, O God
(Follett) SAB,opt 2trp PRO ART 2771
$.35 (C567)
(Plott) TTBB BRODT DC 4 $.24 (C568)

We Will Rejoice
(Young, Percy) [Eng] SATB,ATB soli,
org BROUDE BR. $.90 see from
Music Of The Great Churches Vol.
VI: Westminster Abbey, London
(C569)

CROLEY, RANDELL
Midnight Kyrie
SATB,acap BOONIN B 177 $.40 (C570)

CROMIE, MARGUERITE BIGGS
Come, O Come *Adv/Xmas
2 eq voices/dbl cor,pno/org (very
easy) PRESSER 312-41077 $.40
(C571)

Lord's Prayer, The
unis,solo,org/pno/gtr PRESSER
312-41083 $.30 (C572)

Mass In Honor Of The Queen Of Angels
SATB&cong,org PRESSER 312-41081
$.50 (C573)

Quid Retribuam
"What Return Shall I Make?" [Eng/
Lat] SSAATB,acap (easy) PRESSER
312-41082 $.40 (C574)

What Return Shall I Make? *see Quid
Retribuam

CROSBY
Like Thee *see Billingsley

Will Jesus Find Us Watching?
(Doane; McLellan) SATB oct GOSPEL
05 TM 0203 $.20 (C575)

CROSBY, F.
Saved By Grace
(Stebbins, G.; Cope, Paul) SATB oct
GOSPEL 05 TM 0152 $.20 (C576)

Savior, More Than Life To Me
(composed with Faircloth)
*anthem
SATB (easy) oct BROADMAN 4540-36
$.30 (C577)

CROSS, THE *Easter,anthem
(Lovan) SATB (easy) oct BROADMAN
4532-56 $.30 (C578)

CROSS IS NOT GREATER, THE see Booth

CROSS, LINDA
Fifth Psalm, The (Psalm 5) (composed
with Brown, Charles F.) anthem
SAB WORD CS-2603 $.30 (C579)

Psalm 5 *see Fifth Psalm, The

CROSS WAS HIS OWN, THE see Fettke, Tom

CROSSE
Covenant Of The Rainbow
SATB,inst (diff) sc OXFORD 46.165
$7.35, ipr, cor pts OXFORD 46.166
$1.50 (C580)

CROSSING THE BAR
(Hill, Harry) SATB (easy) WATERLOO
$.35 (C581)

CROSSING THE BAR see Ives, Charles

CROSWELL
Bells Of Christmas, The (composed
with Thomas)
(Newman) SATB WARNER E-109 187 $.50
(C582)

CROTCH, WILLIAM (1775-1847)
Be Peace On Earth
mix cor BANKS MUS YS 437 $.20
(C583)
(Ley) SS/SA BANKS MUS YS 1504 $.25
(C584)

Comfort, O Lord *anthem
(Davies) SS/SA (easy) OXFORD 44.228
$.25 (C585)

CROUCH, ANDRAE
Bless His Holy Name *anthem
SATB LEXICON CS-2624 $.30 (C586)

I'm Gonna Keep On Singin' *CC9L
cor LEXICON 37528 $1.95
see also: I'm Gonna Keep On
Singin' (C587)

I'm Gonna Keep On Singin' *anthem
SATB LEXICON CS-2706 $.35 see also
I'm Gonna Keep On Singin' (C588)

I've Got Confidence (from Cross And
The Switchblade) anthem
SATB,soli LEXICON CS-2507 $.35
(C589)

Just Andrae *CC11L
jr cor LEXICON 37553 $1.95 (C590)

My Tribute *anthem
SATB,solo LEXICON CS-2625 $.35
(C591)

Take Me Back *CC10UL
jr cor LEXICON 37675 $1.95 (C592)

CROUCH, LETHA
Alleluia, Angels Sing *see Leach,
Bill F.

Sing Christmas *Xmas,cant
jr cor,kbd,inst BROADMAN 4513-13
$1.50 (C593)

CROWBY
More Like Jesus Would I Be (composed
with McClard) *anthem
SATB oct BROADMAN 4540-87 $.30
(C594)

Redeemed (composed with Kirkpatrick;
Cram) *anthem
SATB (easy) oct BROADMAN 4545-69
$.30 (C595)

CROWN HIM WITH MANY CROWNS *anthem
(Goemanne, Noel) SAB,org,opt trp
(easy) GIA G1892 $.30 (C596)

CROWN HIM WITH MANY CROWNS see Elvey,
George Job

CROWN THE SAVIOUR, KING OF KINGS see
Hughes

CRUCIFIXION *spir
(Siegler, W.) men cor,acap TONOS 2388
s.p. (C597)

CRUCIFIXION, THE see Stainer, John

CRUCIFIXUS see Lotti, Antonio

CRUCIFIXUS see Palestrina, Giovanni

CRUCIFIXUS (DIE SIEBEN WORTE DES
ERLOSERS) see Simon, Hermann

CRUFT, ADRIAN (1921-   )
Passiontide Carol
SATB,A solo,timp,vcl,strings voc sc
NOVELLO rental (C598)

Te Deum
SATB,perc,org,strings voc sc
NOVELLO rental (C599)

CRUGER, JOHANN (1598-1662)
Ah, Holy Jesus
(Pfohl) mix cor BRODT 208 $.30
(C600)

Christ Lag In Todesbanden
see MUSIKBEILAGE ZUM "EVANGELISCHEN
KIRCHENCHOR 1963"

Jesu, Meine Freude (composed with
Bach, Johann Sebastian)
"Jesu, Priceless Treasure" SATB
(easy) FITZSIMONS 2051 $.20
(C601)
(Talmadge) "Jesus, Joy And
Treasure" SSAA BRODT HC 4 $.22
(C602)

Jesu, Priceless Treasure *see Jesu,
Meine Freude

Jesus, Joy And Treasure *see Jesu,
Meine Freude

Komm, Heiliger Geist
SATB,opt 2treb inst SCHWEIZER.
SK61.04 s.p. see also
MUSIKBEILAGE ZUM "EVANGELISCHEN
KIRCHENCHOR 1961" (C603)

CRUGER, JOHANN (cont'd.)

Lobet Den Herren Alle
men cor,acap TONOS 5629 s.p. (C604)

Lobet Den Herren, Alle, Die Ih Ehren
see Blank, August, Nun Saget Dank
Und Lobt Den Herren

Mein Hoffnung, Trost Und Zuversicht
SAT/SAB SCHWEIZER. SK 68.08 s.p.
see also MUSIKBEILAGE ZUM
"EVANGELISCHEN KIRCHENCHOR 1968"
(C605)

Now Thank We All Our God *Thanks,
anthem
(DeCou, Harold) SATB oct SINGSPIR
ZJP-3205 $.25 (C606)
(Rasley, John M.) SATB oct SINGSPIR
ZJP-7284 $.30 (C607)

Nun Danket All
see Unuberwindlich Starker Held

Nun Danket All Und Bringet Ehr
men cor,acap TONOS 5605 s.p. (C608)

Nun Danket Alle Gott
men cor,acap TONOS 5603 s.p. (C609)

O Lord, I Sing With Lips And Heart
*anthem
(Ehret, Walter) SATB WORD CS-661
$.25 (C610)

CRUICKSHANK, R.
He Is There
SATB,acap BERANDOL DC10 $.50 (C611)

Little People's Prayer
unis,pno BERANDOL DC9 $.35 (C612)

CRUSADE CHOIR *CCUL
(Reese, Jim) SATB SINGSPIR ZD-5474
$1.95 (C613)

CRUSADE CHOIR, VOL. I *CC14UL
(Mercer, W. Elmo) cor,opt brass
BENSON B0245 $1.50, ipa stereo
recording, tape, and-or book-record
sets available, contact publisher
(C614)

CRUSADE CHOIR, VOL. II *CCUL
(Mercer, W. Elmo) cor,opt brass
BENSON B0246 $1.50, ipa stereo
recording, tape, and-or book-record
sets available, contact publisher
(C615)

CRUSADE CHOIR, VOL. III *CCU
(Mercer, W. Elmo) cor,opt brass
BENSON B0247 $2.00, ipa stereo
recording, tape, and-or book-record
sets available, contact publisher
(C616)

CRUSADE MEDLEYS see Gaither, William J.
(Bill)

CRUSADERS FOR CHRIST see Naylor, Eric

CRUSADER'S HYMN
(Wick, Fred) TTBB oct SCHMITT W146
$.30 (C617)
(Wick, Fred) SAB oct SCHMITT W222
$.30 (C618)
(Wick, Fred) SATB oct SCHMITT W246
$.30 (C619)
(Wick, Fred) SSA oct SCHMITT W300
$.30 (C620)

CRUX AVE see Ketterer, Ernst

CRUX FIDELIS see Blaschke, Paul

CRY OF THE PERSECUTED, THE see Grant,
W. Parks

CUI, CESAR ANTONOVITCH (1835-1918)
Angelic Bread Of Heaven *Commun,
anthem
(Schroth, G.) SATB (easy) GIA G1878
$.30 (C621)

CULROSS, DAVID
Calvary *anthem
SATB oct SINGSPIR ZJP-8209 $.35
(C622)

CUMMINGS, EVA J.
Biography Of Christ *Easter
cor,narrator LILLENAS ME-4 $.50
(C623)

CUNDELL, EDRIC (1893-1960)
Hymn To Providence *Op.25
SATB,2fl,2ob,2clar,2bsn,4horn,2trp,
3trom,tuba,perc,strings voc sc
NOVELLO rental (C624)

CUNNINGHAM, ARTHUR
Sunday Stone *Easter
SATB,pno/org (med) PRESSER
312-41053 $.50 (C625)

CUNTIPOTENS see Maeder

CURRIE, RANDOLPH
Bless The Lord O My Soul
SATB,Bar solo,org,opt clar (med)
BECKEN BP 1003 $.40 (C626)

Brethren, We Have Met To Worship
*Gen/Thanks
2pt,pno/org,opt hndbl, or
glockenspiel CHORISTERS A-130
$.35 (C627)

Coventry Carol *Xmas,carol
2pt/SATB/SAB, inst (very easy)
BECKEN BP 1007 $.40 (C628)

His Peace
unis,pno/org DEAN CE-104 $.40
(C629)

Hymn Of Consecration *anthem
SATB MCAFEE M1086 $.40 (C630)

Out Of The Depths I Cry (Psalm 130)
SAB/SATB,org DEAN CE-103 $.40
(C631)

Psalm 130 *see Out Of The Depths I
Cry

To Everything There Is A Season
SATB&speak cor MCAFEE M1077 $.50
(C632)

CURTWRIGHT CAROLEE
Listen, Shepherds, Listen
see Two Christmas Songs For Younger
Children

Sleep, Little Baby Jesus
see Two Christmas Songs For Younger
Children

Two Christmas Songs For Younger
Children *Xmas
unis CHORISTERS A-58 $.25
contains: Listen, Shepherds,
Listen; Sleep, Little Baby
Jesus (C633)

CUSHING
Hiding In Thee (composed with Sankey,
I.)
(Young) 2pt oct BENSON S4134 $.35
(C634)

Ring The Bells Of Heavens
(Root; Collins, Hope) SATB oct
GOSPEL 05 TM 0148 $.20 (C635)

CUSTODI ME see Stout, Alan

CUSTODI ME, DOMINE see Lassus, Roland
de (Orlandus)

CZAJOWSKI, MICHAEL
Psalm 134
SATB STANDARD A44MX1 $.50 (C636)

CZECH CHRISTMAS MASS "HEY MASTER" see
Ryba, Jan Jakub Simon, Ceska
Vanocni Mse "Hej Mistre"

CZECH LULLABY CAROL
(Jenkins, Joseph W.) SSA,pno/winds&
strings GALAXY 1.2364.1 $.30 (C637)

CZECH REQUIEM see Vycpalek, Ladislav

D

DA DIE ZEIT ERFULLET WAR see Liebhold

DA JESUS AN DEM KREUZE STUND see
Hoyoul, Balduin

DA PACEM DOMINE see Crappius, Andreas

DAAR IST PLAATS BIJ HET KRUIS
mix cor sc HEER 2128 s.p. (D1)

DAHLGREN, HANS-ERIK
Gloria Patri
mix cor MUSIKK (D2)

O, Guds Lamm
mix cor MUSIKK (D3)

DAHROUGE
I Know Where I'm Goin' (composed with
Holiday, Mickey) *folk
(Johnson, Norman) SAB/SATB oct
SINGSPIR ZJP-5000 $.30 (D4)

DAILEY, WILLIAM
Come O The Spirit *anthem
SATB WORD (D5)

Hem Of His Robe, The *anthem
SATB LEXICON CS-2662 $.25 (D6)

I'm Gonna Be Free
SATB,kbd oct HOPE HO 1808 $.40 (D7)

Jesus Christ Is The Same *anthem
SATB WORD CS-2670 $.40 (D8)

Prayer *anthem
unis WORD CS-2679 $.30 (D9)

Shout It Everywhere *anthem
SATB WORD CS-2661 $.35 (D10)

DALBY, MARTIN (1942-   )
Missa Fi-Fi
ST/SAT CHESTER JWC 8886 s.p. (D11)

DALE, MERVYN
At Calvary's Cross
see Three Sacred Songs

From Ties Of Bondage
see Three Sacred Songs

In Courts Above
see Three Sacred Songs

Three Sacred Songs
SATB ENOCH EC333 s.p.
contains: At Calvary's Cross;
From Ties Of Bondage; In Courts
Above (D12)

DALLA VECCHIA, WOLFANGO
Lauda Alla Madonna
cor ZANIBON 5298 s.p. (D13)

DALTON, LARRY
Sing Around The World *CC10L
cor LEXICON 37697 $1.95 (D14)

DAMASCUS
Come, Ye Faithful, Raise The Strain
(composed with Price) *anthem
3pt oct BROADMAN 4554-83 $.30 (D15)

D'ANA, FRANCESO
O Thou Who Art All-Wise *Lent
(Ehret, Walter) SATB,acap (med)
PRESSER 312-41063 $.40 (D16)

DANCE THE HORAH
(Frackenpohl, Arthur) SATB CHARTER
CO30207 (D17)

DANCING DAY *CCU,carol
(Rutter) SSA,inst OXFORD s.p., ipa
(D18)

DANIEL *spir
(Miller, J.) SATB GALAXY 1.1610.1
$.45 (D19)

DANIEL! see Wood, Dale

DANIELS, BOB
Only Lord, The *anthem
unis,kbd,opt fl,gtr AUGSBURG
11-3009 $.10 (D20)

DANIELSON, DAVIS G.
Secret Place Of God, The *anthem
SATB oct SINGSPIR ZJP-7323 $.30
(D21)

DANK see Lemacher, Heinrich

DANK SAGEN WIR ALLE see Osiander, Lucas

DANK U O HEER see Pronk, Arie

DANKET DEM HERREN ALLE ZEIT see Staden,
Johann

DANKET DEM HERREN, SCHOPFER ALLER DINGE
see Herzogenberg, Heinrich von

DANKET DEM HERRN! see Herold, J.

DANKET DEM HERRN see Wiedermann,
Bedrich

DANKET GOTT, DENN ER IST GUT see
Planyavsky, Peter

DANKLIED see Handel, George Frideric

DANNER
My Faith Has Found A Resting Place
(composed with Edmunds) *anthem
SATB,opt vln (easy) oct BROADMAN
4540-66 $.30   (D22)

DANNIEBELLE *CC10L
(Danniebelle) cor LEXICON 37674 $1.95
                                  (D23)

DANSE UNE ETABLE OBSCURE *Xmas
(McCauley) SATB (easy) WATERLOO $.30
                                  (D24)

DANTONELLO, JOSEF
Adeste Fideles *Xmas
[Lat] 4pt mix cor,acap sc,cor pts
BOHM s.p.   (D25)

Aeterne Rex
see Lobgesange Zur
Fronleichnamsprozession

Benedictus *funeral
[Lat] 4pt mix cor,acap sc,cor pts
BOHM s.p.   (D26)

Deutsche Advent-Messe "O Heiland
Reiss Die Himmel Auf" *Op.38,
Adv,Mass
BOHM sc s.p., cor pts s.p.   (D27)

Liedmesse Zur Weihnacht *Op.40,
Xmas,Mass
cor&cong,soli,org,2vln sc,cor pts
BOHM s.p., ipa   (D28)

Lobgesange Zur
Fronleichnamsprozession
[Lat] 4pt mix cor,opt 5brass sc,cor
pts BOHM s.p., ipa
contains: Aeterne Rex, Op.24b,
No.4; Pange Lingua, Op.24b,
No.5; Sacris Solemniis, Op.24b,
No.1; Salutis Humanae Sator,
Op.24b,No.3; Verbum Supernum,
Op.24b,No.2   (D29)

Missa Brevis In F-Dur *Op.47, Mass
"Missa In Honorem St. Elizabeth"
[Lat] 4pt mix cor,strings,org (F
maj) sc,cor pts BOHM s.p., ipa
                                  (D30)
"Missa In Honorem St. Elizabeth"
[Lat] 4pt mix cor,org (F maj) sc,
cor pts BOHM s.p.   (D31)

Missa In Honorem St. Elizabeth *see
Missa Brevis In F-Dur

Pange Lingua
see Lobgesange Zur
Fronleichnamsprozession

Sacris Solemniis
see Lobgesange Zur
Fronleichnamsprozession

Salutis Humanae Sator
see Lobgesange Zur
Fronleichnamsprozession

Verbum Supernum
see Lobgesange Zur
Fronleichnamsprozession

DANZA SACRA DEI FIORI E DELL'INCENSO
see Pratella, Francesco Balilla

DAR SJONGO TRE ANGLAR see Olson, Daniel

DARE
Angel's Song, The
SA/TB SHAWNEE E5174 $.35   (D32)

DARE, ELKANAH KELSEY (1782-1826)
Babylonian Captivity
see THREE SONGS OF TRIBULATION

Wilmington *Xmas,anthem
(Bennett, Lawrence) STTB,acap
BROUDE BR. $.40   (D33)

DARIOLI
Ascendi Deus
4pt,acap voc pt HENN 266 s.p.   (D34)

DARK-LIGHT see Wyrtzen, Don

DARKENING LIGHT see Bourgeois, Loys
(Louis)

DARKNESS WAS O'ER THE EARTH see
Victoria, Tomas Luis de, Tenebrae
Factae Sunt

DARKNESS WAS OVER ALL see Biber,
Heinrich Ignaz Franz von, Tenebrae
Factae Sunt

DARKNESS WAS OVER ALL see Poulenc,
Francis, Tenebrae Factae Sunt

DARMSTADT, HANS (1943-   )
Blankeneser Chor Heft I *CCU
mix cor cor pts GERIG HG 1153 (D35)

DARNTON, C.
Break Forth Into Joy
mix cor BANKS MUS YS 28 $.30   (D36)

DARST, W. GLENN (1896-   )
Awake, My Soul
SATB (med) FITZSIMONS 2111 $.25
                                  (D37)

Communion Service
SATB (D maj,easy) FITZSIMONS 7003
$.25   (D38)

Creator Of The Stars Of Night *Adv
SATB (med) FITZSIMONS 2161 $.25
                                  (D39)

Look From Thy Sphere Of Endless Day
SATB,SBar soli (med) FITZSIMONS
2164 $.20   (D40)

Lord God Of Hosts
SATB (med) FITZSIMONS 2112 $.25
                                  (D41)

Now In The Days Of Youth
SA,org GRAY CMR 3312 $.30   (D42)

Peace In Our Time, O Lord
SATB (easy) FITZSIMONS 2110 $.25
                                  (D43)

Rise, Crowned With Light
SATB,org,trp GRAY CMR 3316 $.35
                                  (D44)

Shepherd Of Israel *Lent,Bibl
SATB (med) FITZSIMONS 2166 $.25
                                  (D45)

Ye Watchers And Ye Holy Ones
SAB,org GRAY CMR 3343 $.30   (D46)

DARWALL, JOHN (1731-1789)
Join All The Glorious Names *anthem
(Wyrtzen, D.) SATB oct SINGSPIR
ZJP-7341 $.30   (D47)

Rejoice! The Lord Is King! *Palm,
anthem
(Berntsen, William B.) SSATB oct
SINGSPIR ZJP-7206 $.30   (D48)

DAS ALTE JAHR VERGANGEN IST see
Brunner, Adolf

DAS ALTE JAHR VERGANGEN IST see
Steuerlein, Johann

DAS ANDERE FEUERBEWAHREN "WOHLAUF, WIR
WOLLENS WECKEN" see Schnellinger

DAS BLUT JESU see Bach, Johann Michael

DAS BLUT JESU CHRISTI MACHET UNS REIN
see Schutz, Heinrich

DAS CHRISTKINDELSPIEL see Reusch, Fritz

DAS DREIFACHE GLORIA see Bresgen, Cesar

DAS GANZE WELTRUND see Killmayer,
Wilhelm

DAS GLEICHNIS VOM BARMHERZIGEN
SAMARITER "MEISTER, WAS MUSS ICH
TUN" see Reutter, Hermann

DAS GLEICHNIS VOM REICHEN NARREN, "SEHT
ZU UND HUTET EUCH VOR DER GEIZ" see
Eglin, Arthur

DAS GLEICHNIS VOM SAMANN "HORET ZU" see
Reutter, Hermann

DAS GLEICHNIS VON DEN TORICHTEN UND
KLUGEN JUNGFRAUEN "DAS HIMMELREICH
WIRD SEIN" see Reutter, Hermann

DAS GLEICHNIS VON DEN ZEHN JUNGFRAUEN
"DANN WIRD DAS HIMMELREICH GLEICH
SEIN" see Lohr, Ina

DAS GOTTESJAHR see Wenzel, Eberhard

DAS GRADUALLIED, TEIL 1 see Reda,
Siegfried

DAS GROSSE HALLELUJAH "EHRE SEI DEM
HOCHERHAB'NEN" see Schubert, Franz
(Peter)

DAS GROSSE SALZBURGER ALLELUJA see
Doppelbauer, Josef Friedrich

DAS HEIL DER WELT see Schroeder,
Hermann

DAS HIMMELREICH IST GLEICH EINEM KONIGE
see Bohm, Georg

DAS HOHELIED DER LIEBE see Trubel,
Gerhard

DAS HOHELIED SALOMONIS see Lechner,
Leonhard

DAS IST EIN BOSES DING see Pepping,
Ernst

DAS IST EIN KOSTLICH DING see Poos,
Heinrich

DAS JAHR HEBT AN see Rothschuh, Franz

DAS KINDLEIN LIEGET DA see Mutter,
Gerbert

DAS LEBENSBUCH GOTTES see Haas, Joseph

DAS LIED DES LAMMES see Mattheson,
Johann

DAS NEUE KURRENDEHEFT *CCU,mot
(Anger, Erhard) jr cor,inst
HOFMEISTER DVFM7932 s.p.   (D49)

DAS NEUGEBORNE KINDELEIN see Vulpius,
Melchior

DAS REICH DER HIMMEL "DIE HERREN DER
WELT KOMMEN UND GEHEN" see Eglin,
Arthur

DAS SAGT, DER AMEN HEISST see
Hessenberg, Kurt

DAS SCHERFLEIN DER WITWE see David,
Johann Nepomuk

DAS SCHULCHOR BAND II *CC77L
mix cor SCHOTTS ED. 5402 s.p.
contains works by:Bach; Distler;
Genzmer; Pepping; Rohwer; Vulpius
and others   (D50)

DAS VATER UNSER see Krause, Theodor

DAS VOLK, SO IM FINSTERN WANDELT see
Buchsel

DAS WEIHNACHTSKONZERT I *CC12L,Adv/
Xmas
(Mohler, Philipp) men cor SCHOTTS
ED. 4056 s.p. contains works by:
Rein; Lang; Haas; Klink; Praetorius
and others   (D51)

DAS WEIHNACHTSKONZERT II *CC12L,Adv/
Xmas
mix cor SCHOTTS ED. 4359 s.p.
contains works by: Rein; Lang;
Haas; Praetorius and others   (D52)

DAS WILL ICH MIR ZU HERZEN NEHMEN see
Zipp, Friedrich

DAS WORT GEHT VON DEM VATER AUS see
Petzold, Rudolf

DAS WORT VOM KREUZ see Schweizer, Rolf

DAS WORT WARD FLEISCH see
Hammerschmidt, Andreas

DAUERMANN, STUART
Arm Of The Lord, The (composed with
Spradlin) *folk
SATB/jr cor oct LILLENAS AN-5094
$.45   (D53)

Make Ready *folk
SATB/jr cor oct LILLENAS AN-5093
$.45   (D54)

DAUGHTER OF ZION see Denton, James

DAVID see Burroughs, Bob

DAVID AND GOLIATH see Detweiler, Alan

DAVID AND GOLIATH see Wood, Dale

DAVID JAZZ, THE see Robinson, Edwin
Meade

DAVID, JOHANN NEPOMUK (1895-   )
Das Scherflein Der Witwe *evang/mot
4pt mix cor,acap cor pts CHB-3076
s.p. see from Sechs
Evangelienmotetten   (D55)

Der Barmherzige Samariter *evang/mot
4pt mix cor,acap cor pts CHB-3077
see from Sechs Evangelienmotetten
                                  (D56)

DAVID, JOHANN NEPOMUK (cont'd.)

Der Pharisaer Und Der Zollner
*evang/mot
4pt mix cor,opt SS soli,acap cor
pts CHB-3071 s.p. see from Sechs
Evangelienmotetten   (D57)

Die Ehebrecherin *evang/mot
5pt mix cor,acap cor pts CHB-3073
s.p. see from Sechs
Evangelienmotetten   (D58)

Die Zwei Blinden *evang/mot
4pt mix cor,acap cor pts CHB-3078
s.p. see from Sechs
Evangelienmotetten   (D59)

Komm, Heiliger Geist, Herre Gott
dbl cor,orch cor pts BREITKOPF-W
CHB 3587 s.p., ipr   (D60)

Lasset Die Kindlein Zu Mir Kommen
*evang/mot
4pt mix cor,acap cor pts CHB-3072
s.p. see from Sechs
Evangelienmotetten   (D61)

Messe *Op.67
4pt treb cor cor pts BREITKOPF-W
CHB 3557 s.p.   (D62)

Sechs Evangelienmotetten *see Das
Scherflein Der Witwe; Der
Barmherzige Samariter; Der
Pharisaer Und Der Zollner; Die
Ehebrecherin; Die Zwei Blinden;
Lasset Die Kindlein Zu Mir Kommen
                                      (D63)

DAVID, THOMAS [CHRISTIAN] (1925-   )
Mir Ist Gegeben Alle Gewalt
see Zwei Deutsche Motetten

Wahrlich, Ich Sage Euch: Ihr Werdet
Weinen Und Heulen
see Zwei Deutsche Motetten

Zwei Deutsche Motetten *Trin,mot
[Ger] SSAATTBB,acap (med diff)
BAREN. BA 3933 $2.50
contains: Mir Ist Gegeben Alle
Gewalt; Wahrlich, Ich Sage
Euch: Ihr Werdet Weinen Und
Heulen   (D64)

DAVID WEPT FOR SLAIN ABSALOM see
Hovhaness, Alan

DAVIDICA, LYRA
Christ The Lord Is Risen Today
*Easter,anthem
(Johnson, Norman) SATB&opt cor oct
SINGSPIR ZA-4604 $.40   (D65)

DAVIDS DANKLIED see Gardonyi, Zsolt

DAVID'S HOTSHOT SLINGSHOT see Graham,
Robert

DAVID'S LAMENTATION see Pfautsch, Lloyd

DAVIDSON
Give Thanks Unto The Lord *see
Sanders

Morning Star *see Scheffler, J.J.

We Are Not Alone *see Sanders

DAVIDSON, CHARLES (1929-   )
Bar'chu, Ahavat Olam, Sh'ma
[Heb] mix cor,cantor TRANSCON.
TCL 669 $.60   (D66)

DAVIES, HENRY WALFORD (1869-1941)
O Little Town Of Bethlehem *Xmas,
carol
SATB EMI s.p. contains also: Lang,
C.S., I Saw Three Ships   (D67)

DAVIES, I.R.
O God Of Earth And Altar
mix cor BANKS MUS YS 1247 $.20
                                   (D68)

DAVIES, PETER MAXWELL (1934-   )
Alleluia, Pro Virgine Maria (from O
Magnum Mysterium)
SATB,acap SCHOTT 11274 s.p. see
also Four Carols   (D69)

Alma Redemptoris Mater
4 eq voices SCHOTT 11268 s.p. see
from Four Christmas Carols   (D70)

Carol On St. Stephen
SATB SCHOTT 11269 s.p. see from
Four Christmas Carols   (D71)

Fader Of Heven, The (from O Magnum
Mysterium)
SA,acap SCHOTT 11275 s.p. see also
Four Carols   (D72)

Four Carols (from O Magnum Mysterium)
SATB,acap SCHOTT 11276 s.p.
contains & see also: Alleluia,

DAVIES, PETER MAXWELL (cont'd.)
Pro Virgine Maria (from O
Magnum Mysterium); Fader Of
Heven, The (from O Magnum
Mysterium); Haylle, Comly And
Clene (from O Magnum
Mysterium); O Magnum Mysterium
(from O Magnum Mysterium)   (D73)

Four Christmas Carols *see Alma
Redemptoris Mater; Carol On St.
Stephen; Jesus Autem Hodie;
Nowell   (D74)

Haylle, Comly And Clene (from O
Magnum Mysterium)
SATB,acap SCHOTT 11273 s.p. see
also Four Carols   (D75)

Jesus Autem Hodie
SATB SCHOTT 11270 s.p. see from
Four Christmas Carols   (D76)

Lord's Prayer, The
SATB SCHOTT 11277 s.p.   (D77)

Nowell
SATB SCHOTT 11271 s.p. see from
Four Christmas Carols   (D78)

O Magnum Mysterium (from O Magnum
Mysterium)
S&SA&SATB,acap SCHOTT 11272 s.p.
see also Four Carols   (D79)

Te Lucis Ante Terminum
SATB,winds,gtr, glockenspiel sc
SCHOTT 10817B s.p., cor pts
SCHOTT 10817A s.p.   (D80)

DAVIS
All Together Sing *anthem
2pt oct BROADMAN 4558-68 $.30   (D81)

Ascensions
WALTON M127 $1.00   (D82)

Praise The Lord Who Reigns Above
*anthem
1-2pt,opt trp (easy) oct BROADMAN
4562-07 $.30   (D83)

Song Of The Magi *Adv/Xmas
SATB oct LILLENAS AN-6031 $.30
                                   (D84)

Stand Up And Sing
SABar&camb,pno/org,opt trp CAMBIATA
C97319 $.35   (D85)

DAVIS, D. EVAN
Holy Lord Our Grateful Prayer Now
Hear
SATB (med easy) WATERLOO $.40 (D86)

DAVIS, KATHERINE K. (1892-   )
Amazing Grace
SATB GALAXY 1.2569.1 $.35   (D87)

Children Of Bethlehem, The *Xmas,
cant
2pt jr cor,narrator,kbd,opt fl&perc
BROADMAN 4513-12 $1.60   (D88)

Joy Has Filled The Sky
SATB&desc,org,hndbl BELWIN 2308
$.40   (D89)

Land We Hold So Dear, The
SATB,kbd,opt fl&ob&trp&rec BELWIN
2316 $.30   (D90)

Lord All Glorious, Lord Victorious
SATB&opt unis jr cor,opt S solo
GALAXY 1.2357.1 $.30   (D91)

Love Is Born *Adv/Xmas
SATB ART MAST 203 $.40   (D92)

Tale Of Glory *Easter
SAB WARNER WB-320 184 $.40   (D93)

Who Is Jesus? *Easter,cant
1-2pt jr cor,solo&narrator,kbd
BROADMAN 4515-08 $1.50   (D94)

Who Was The Man *Gen/Thanks
unis CHORISTERS A-110 $.35   (D95)

DAVISON, M.T.
Jesus, Jesus, Rest Your Head
SSA PARAGON 1032 $.35   (D96)

DAVYE
Child Is Born To Us, A
SSA AMP A-689 $1.25   (D97)

Missa Brevis
SATB AMP A-714 $1.50   (D98)

DAWE
Hymn To The Trinity *anthem
SATB,acap (easy) OXFORD 43.454 $.25
                                   (D99)

DAWN CAROL see Williamson, Malcolm

DAWN OF GLORY, THE see Latrobe,
Christian I.

DAWN OF REDEEMING GRACE see Graham,
Robert

DAWSON, ANTHONY
O Christ Who Holds The Open Gate
SATB (med easy) WATERLOO $.40
                                   (D100)

O Give Thanks Unto The Lord
SA (easy) WATERLOO $.40   (D101)

O How Amiable
SATB (med) WATERLOO $.50   (D102)

DAWSON, WILLIAM LEVI (1898-   )
Ain'a That Good News
SSAA TUSKEGEE T140 $.40   (D103)

DAY BY DAY see Ahnfelt, O.

DAY BY DAY WE MAGNIFY THEE see Grimes,
Travis

DAY FOR SINGING, A see Reynolds,
William Jensen

DAY OF LIBERATION, THE see Skillings,
Otis

DAY OF MIRACLES, THE see Lister, Mosie

DAY OF PENTECOST see Sateren, Leland
Bernhard

DAY OF RESURRECTION, THE *Easter/Lent,
16th cent
(Ehret) SAB,trp oct LILLENAS AN-2399
$.30   (D104)

DAY OF RESURRECTION, THE see Brandon,
George

DAY OF RESURRECTION, THE see Haydn,
(Franz) Joseph

DAY OF RESURRECTION, THE see Matthews,
Thomas

DAY OF RESURRECTION, THE see Willan,
Healey

DAY OF WRATH, THAT DREADFUL DAY , THE
see Latrobe, Christian I., Dies
Irae

DAY, PEGGY
Gentle Father
(Martindale, James A.) 1-2pt LESLIE
2049   (D105)

DAY YOU MEET THE LORD, THE see Wild,
Eric

DE DEER IS MIJN HERDER
mix cor sc HEER 2883 s.p.   (D106)

DE HEILIGE NACHT see Gerretson

DE HEILIGE STAD see Adams, Stephen,
Holy City, The

DE KONING
Als Christus Vandaag Werd Geboren
(Pronk, A.) mix cor HEER 1537
                                   (D107)

Ik Weet Dat Mijn Verlosser Leeft
*Easter
(Pronk, A.) mix cor HEER 1536 s.p.
                                   (D108)

Israel
(Pronk, A.) mix cor HEER 1534
                                   (D109)

Jahwe, O God Der Goden
(Pronk, A.) mix cor HEER 1533
                                   (D110)

O Heilig Godslam
(Pronk, A.) mix cor HEER 1532
                                   (D111)

Sh'ma Yisroayl
(Pronk, A.) mix cor HEER 1530
                                   (D112)

Veertig Dagen, Veertig Nachten
(Pronk, A.) mix cor HEER 1531
                                   (D113)

DE LAMARTER, ERIC (1880-1953)
How Lovely Are Thy Dwellings *Bibl
SSATBB,A solo (diff) FITZSIMONS
2077 $.25   (D114)

DE PILGRIMS BIJ HET KRUIS *Psntd
Bar,pno/harmonium HEER 77 s.p. (D115)

DE PROFUNDIS see Edler, Robert

DE PROFUNDIS see Hoffmann, Ernst
Theodor Amadeus

DE PROFUNDIS see Krieger, Fritz

DE PROFUNDIS see Salieri, Antonio

DE PROFUNDIS see Spranger, Jorg

DE PROFUNDIS see Wehle, Gerhard
Furchtegott

DE PROFUNDIS CLAMAVI see Morley, Thomas

DE SOM KJENNER DITT NAVN see Strand,
Ragnvald

DE STER VAN BETHLEHEM see Adams

DE VIRGIN MARY *spir
(Arch, Gwyn) SSA EMI   (D116)

DE VREEMDELING VAN GALILEA see Morris

DEALE
O Men From The Fields
SATB,acap (med easy) OXFORD 84.237
$.30   (D117)

DEAN
Just Over In The Gloryland *gospel
(Lister, Mosie) SATB oct LILLENAS
AL-1035 $.30   (D118)

DEAN, T.W.
Behold The Glory Of The Lamb *ora
mix cor,AT soli BROADMAN 4510-01
$2.50   (D119)

Blessed Morn, The *Xmas,cant
unis jr cor&opt desc,med solo/
narrator BROADMAN 4513-04 $1.00
(D120)

DEANE
How Great And Marvelous Is My Lord
*anthem
SATB (easy) oct BROADMAN 4551-53
$.30   (D121)

Thou, O Christ Of Calvary *see More

DEAR CHRISTIANS, ONE AND ALL, NOW
REJOICE see Rotermund, Melvin

DEAR INNSBRUCK, I MUST LEAVE YOU
(Pitcher) SSA WILLIS 9663 $.25 (D122)

DEAR LITTLE JESUS see Hill, Harry

DEAR LITTLE JESUS see Tarner, Evelyn F.

DEAR LITTLE STRANGER see Hill, Harry

DEAR LORD AND FATHER
(Whittier; Brandon, G.) SATB (med
easy) WATERLOO $.35   (D123)

DEAR LORD AND FATHER see Pottle, Sam

DEAREST LORD, TO THEE I PRAY see Lowe,
Helenclair

DEARNLEY
Communion Service (Series III)
(composed with Wicks)
unis&SATB (med easy) voc sc OXFORD
40.027 $.45, cor pts OXFORD
40.040 $.55   (D124)

DEATH OF GOD, THE see Holloway

DECHA, ABBE
Chant A La Vierge
2pt mix cor/4pt mix cor GRAS s.p.
(D125)

DECK THE HALLS
(McKelvey, James) SATB,acap FOSTER
MF605 $.35   (D126)

DECLARE HIS GLORY see Peterson, John W.

DECLARE, O HEAVENS, THE LORD OF SPACE
*anthem
1-2pt,trp,tamb,perc BROADMAN 4560-24
$.35 see from Four Festive Anthems
For Children's Voices   (D127)

DECLARE, O HEAVENS, THE LORD OF SPACE
see Butler

DECOU, HAROLD
Christmas Story *Adv,anthem
SATB oct SINGSPIR ZJP-3049 $.30
(D128)

God's Love Gift *Xmas,cant
SATB,narrator,SAT soli,fl,ob,3trp,
3trom,horn,2vln,vla,vcl,bvl,harp,
perc,timp,gtr SINGSPIR 4369
$1.95, ipa   (D129)

Lord, We Thank Thee *Thanks,anthem
SATB oct SINGSPIR ZJP-3108 $.25
(D130)

May God Bless You And Keep You
*anthem/gospel
SATB oct SINGSPIR ZJP-8206 $.30
(D131)

No Tears Tomorrw *anthem
SATB oct SINGSPIR ZJP-8220 $.35
(D132)

DEDICATION see Gerschefski, Edwin

DEDICATORY ANTHEM, A see Martin,
Gilbert M.

DEEP DOWN IN MY HEART see Clatterbuck

DEEP PEACE see Posegate, Maxcine W.

DEEP RIVER *spir
see Funf Spirituals
(Lees, Heath) SSAA,acap ROBERTON
75033 s.p.   (D133)
(Roberton, Hugh S.) SATB,acap (easy)
FITZSIMONS 1035 $.20   (D134)

DEEP RIVER see Nosse

DEEP RIVER see Petersen, Rolf

DEEP WAS THE SILENCE *Xmas,anthem
(Rasley, John M.) SATB oct SINGSPIR
ZJP-3027 $.25   (D135)

DEEPER AND DEEPER see Smith

DEEPER, DEEPER see Jones

DEERING, RICHARD (ca. 1580-ca. 1629)
Quem Vidisti Pastores *Xmas
(Biester) TTBB SCHIRM.G LG51758
$.75   (D136)

DEGEN, J.
Freu Dich, Du Himmelskonigin
see Degen, J., Konigin Im
Himmelreich

Konigin Im Himmelreich
SATB DOBLINGER S 217-218 s.p.
contains also: Freu Dich, Du
Himmelskonigin   (D137)

DEIHL, W.H.
Jesu, Jesu, Most And Least
mix cor BRODT 507 $.20   (D138)

Oh Lord Our God, We Humbly Pray
SAATB,acap (easy) FITZSIMONS 2078
$.20   (D139)

DEIN IST DAS JAHR, DEIN IST DIE ZEIT
see Kurig, Hans-Hermann

DEIN SOHN, O GOTT, DU TROST DER FROMMEN
see Briegel, Wolfgang Carl

DEIN WORT, HERR, IST MIR EIN LICHT AUF
DEM WEG see Staden, Johann

DE LA RUE, PIERRE (1460-1518)
Wir Danken Dir, O Gottes Lamm
SATB (contains also: Danket Dem
Herren Alle Zeit) SCHWEIZER.
SK 51.04 s.p. see also
MUSIKBEILAGE ZUM "EVANGELISCHEN
KIRCHENCHOR 1951"   (D140)

DELAYE
Jesu Est Ne Parmi Les Fleurs *Xmas
cor (easy) sc HENN 197 s.p.   (D141)
4pt mix cor,acap sc HENN 478 s.p.
(D142)

Nos Petits Souliers *Xmas
cor (easy) sc HENN 009 s.p.   (D143)

O Joyeux Noel *Xmas
cor (easy) sc HENN 460 s.p.   (D144)

DELIA, SISTER
With Music And Song *see Duchesne,
Sister

DELIVER ME see Faure, Gabriel-Urbain,
Libera Me

DELIVER US, GOOD LORD see Tye,
Christopher

DELIVERANCE MEDLEY
see Church Is Singing Again, The

DELMONTE, PAULINE
Forever Wider Than The Sky *Gen/
Thanks
unis/SATB CHORISTERS A-147 $.40
(D145)

He Is Coming *Palm
unis,org/pno,inst CHORISTERS A-142
$.35   (D146)

Stars Are For Those Who Lift Their
Eyes *Xmas
unis/SA,pno/harp,opt vcl CHORISTERS
A-117 $.35   (D147)

Within A Manger Harsh With Hay *Xmas
unis/SA CHORISTERS A-80 $.30 (D148)

DELSINNE, ABBE
Le P'tit Quinquin
5pt mix cor GRAS s.p.   (D149)

DEM ALLGEGENWARTIGEN see Sutermeister,
Heinrich

DEMONE, RICHARD
O Come, O Come Emmanuel
SATB/SAB,opt fl/rec/ob/clar,org
MCAFEE M1091 $.40   (D150)

Wondrous Love *folk/hymn,US
SATB,acap/inst MCAFEE M1092 $.40
(D151)

DEMUTH, NORMAN (1898-1968)
Holly And The Ivy *Xmas
SATB STAINER 3.0762.1 $.40   (D152)

DEN DIE HIRTEN LOBETEN SEHRE see Kern

DEN DIE HIRTEN LOBETEN SEHRE see
Pepping, Ernst

DEN DIE HIRTEN LOBETEN SEHRE see
Praetorius, Michael

DEN DIE HIRTEN LOBTEN see Praetorius,
Michael, Quem Pastores Laudavere

DEN ENDE SANNA GLADJE, SOM JAG VET see
Schutz, Heinrich, Jauchzet Gott
Alle Lande Sehr

DEN GEBOREN HAT EIN MAGD *Xmas,carol/
folk
(Bausznern, D. von) [Ger] 4pt men cor
MERSEBURG EM9042   (D153)

DEN GEBOREN HAT EINE MAGD see Kelling,
Hajo

DEN GEFALLENEN "UNTER DEN KREUZEN" see
Weber, Bernhard

DEN MENSCHEN FRIED UND WOHLGEFALL
*CC9U,Xmas
3-4pt mix cor MOSELER HEFT23 s.p.
contains works by: Vom Brandt,
Jobst; Biebl, Franz; Lerich,
Rudolf; Sommer, Johannes; Koerppen,
Alfred; Klein, Karl Heinz   (D154)

DEN SIGNADE DAG see Lindberg, Oskar
[Fredrik]

DEN SOM HOR MINA ORD see Forsberg,
Roland

DEN TOTEN "FREI VON MENSCHLICHEN
GEBOTEN" see Knab, Armin

DEN TOTEN: "SELIG SIND DES HIMMELS
ERBEN" see Bleier, P.

DENKMAELER DER TONKUNST IN OESTERREICH
*sac/sec,CCU
microfiche UNION ESP. editors
include: Haber; Rietsch; Bezecny;
Wolf, Johannes; Nettl, Paul;
Webern, Albert Von and others.
Originally published as 83 volumes
in 79 bindings. $495.00   (D155)

DENKMAELER DEUTSCHER TONKUNST *sac/
sec,CCU
(Musikgeschichtlichen Kommission;
Moser, Hans Joachim; Crosby Jr., C.
Russel) microfiche UNION ESP. 65
volumes, includes original
Breitkopf and Haertel edition of
1892-1931 with critical revisions
by Akademische Druckund
Verlagsantalt, Graz, 1957-1961.
$425.00   (D156)

DENNE AR MIN ENFODDE SON see Schonberg,
Stig Gustav

DENNOCH BLEIBE ICH STETS AN DIR see
Lohr, Ina

DENTON, JAMES
Daughter Of Zion *Adv/Gen,anthem
SATB (med easy) oct LORENZ B229
$.35   (D157)

I Believe In God *anthem
SATB oct LORENZ B223 $.35   (D158)

I Saw The Cross Of Jesus *Easter,
anthem
SATB oct LORENZ B228 $.35   (D159)

Jesus Saves *anthem
SATB (med easy) oct LORENZ B237
$.35   (D160)

Long Time Ago *Xmas,anthem
SAB oct LORENZ 7421 $.35   (D161)

O Christ, Why Should A Manger Be?
*Xmas,anthem
SATB oct LORENZ C355 $.35   (D162)

O God, Thou Hast The Dawn Of Life
*Easter,anthem
SATB oct LORENZ B211 $.35   (D163)

When God Is The Honored Guest *Gen,
anthem
SATB,med solo (med diff, mother's
day) oct LORENZ C362 $.35   (D164)

DENTON, JAMES (cont'd.)

When There's Love At Home
SATB (mother's day) oct LORENZ B213
$.35   (D165)

DEO DICAMUS GRATIAS see Homilius,
Gottfried August

DEO GRACIAS see Mc Cray, James

DER 100. PSALM see Reger, Max

DER ADVENTS-STERN see Biebl, Franz

DER BARMHERZIGE SAMARITER see David,
Johann Nepomuk

DER BARMHERZIGE SAMARITER see
Hufschmidt, Wolfgang

DER BLINDE BETTLER see Kretzschmar,
Gunther

DER DRITTE PSALM see Hess, Reimund

DER DU BIST DREI IN EINIGKEIT see
Pepping, Ernst

DER DU DEN MENSCH SCHUFST see
Killmayer, Wilhelm

DER DU DIE ZEIT IN HANDEN HAST see
Lambertz, Johann Sebastian

DER DU DIE ZEIT IN HANDEN HAST see
Marx, Karl

DER ENGEL BRINGT WAHREN BERICHT see
Burck, Joachim

DER ENGEL LOBGESANG "AUF DEM FELDE
SANGEN ENGEL" see Brendel,
Engelbert

DER ERSTE PSALM "O DU MEIN GOTT" see
Schoenberg, Arnold, Modern Psalm
Facsimile

DER EUCH BERUFT IST TREU see Rothschuh,
Fritz

DER GEIST DES HERRN ERFULLT DAS ALL see
Planyavsky, Peter

DER GEIST HILFT UNSRER SCHWACHHEIT AUF
see Bach, Johann Sebastian

DER GERECHTE KOMMT UM see Kuhnau,
Johann, Tristis Est Anima Mea

DER GERECHTE, OB ER GLEICH see Bach,
Johann Christian

DER GERECHTEN SEELEN SIND IN GOTTES
HAND see Zipp, Friedrich

DER HEIDEN HEILAND KOMM HER see
Pepping, Ernst

DER HEILGEN GEISTES GNADE GROSS see
Praetorius, Michael

DER HEILIG GEIST VOM HIMMEL KAM see
Praetorius, Michael

DER HERR, DER EWIGE GOTT see Schwarz-
Schilling, Reinhard

DER HERR, DER IST MEIN HIRT see Schein,
Johann Hermann

DER HERR HAT SEINEN ENGELN BEFOHLEN see
Mendelssohn-Bartholdy, Felix

DER HERR IST ALLMACHTIG see Seib,
Valentin

DER HERR IST GROSS IN SEINER MACHT see
Haydn, (Franz) Joseph

DER HERR IST KONIG see Burkhard Willy

DER HERR IST KONIG UBERALL see Schutz,
Heinrich

DER HERR IST MEIN GETREUER HIRT see
Calvisius, Sethus

DER HERR IST MEIN GETREUER HIRT see
Marx, Karl

DER HERR IST MEIN HIRT see
Hammerschmidt, Andreas

DER HERR IST MEIN HIRT see Klein,
Bernhard

DER HERR IST MEIN HIRT see Schutz,
Heinrich

DER HERR IST MEIN LICHT UND MEIN HEIL
see Kretzschmar, Gunther

DER HERR IST MEIN LICHT UND MEIN HEIL
see Ruppel, Paul Ernst

DER HERR IST MEINE STARKE see Fussan,
Werner

DER HERR KENNET DEN WEG DER GERECHTEN
see Othmayr, Kaspar

DER MENSCHEN HOFFART MUSS VERGEHEN see
Hennig, Walter

DER MESSIAS see Handel, George Frideric

DER MESSIAS (HALLISCHE HANDEL-AUSGABE)
see Handel, George Frideric,
Messiah

DER MESSIAS (NEUE MOZART-AUSGABE) see
Handel, George Frideric, Messiah

DER MORGENSTERN IST AUFGEDRUNGEN see
Zipp, Friedrich

DER MORGENSTERN IST AUFGEGANGEN *16th
cent
(Knab, Armin) jr cor (med easy) sc
SCHOTTS CHBL 550A-B s.p. contains
also: Weiss Mir Ein Blumlein Blaue
(D166)

DER MORGENSTERN IST AUFGEGANGEN see
Rein, Walter

DER NAME "VIELLEICHT, DASS HEISENBERG
WIRKLICH" see Eglin, Arthur

DER PHARISAER UND DER ZOLLNER see
David, Johann Nepomuk

DER PURPURGLANZ DER MORGENFRUHE see
Killmayer, Wilhelm

DER SABBAT VON GOTT IST DRUM G'MACHT
see Staden, Johann

DER SAMARITANER see Kretzschmar,
Gunther

DER SCHLAF IST DREIERLEI see Krietsch,
Georg

DER SCHULCHOR BAND VI: MOTETTEN
*CC46L,mot
(Kraus, Egon) mix cor SCHOTTS
ED. 5406 s.p. contains works by:
Bialas; Brahms; Hassler;
Palestrina; Reger; Verdi and others
(D167)

DER SOHN, DER WIEDER HEIMKEHRTE see
Schmidt-Mannheim, Hans

DER SONNENGESANG DES HEILIGEN
FRANZISKUS see Lang, Hans

DER STERN see Taubert, Karl Heinz

DER STERN see Kaufmann, Otto

DER STERN VON BETHLEHEM see
Rheinberger, Josef

DER TAG IST HIN see Kaminski, Heinrich

DER TAG IST HIN, DIE SONNE GEHET NIEDER
see Kaminski, Heinrich

DER TOD see Rau, Christoph

DER TOD IST VERSCHLUNGEN IN DEN SIEG
see Studer, Hans

DER TOD JESU see Graun, Karl Heinrich

DER VERDUNER ALTAR see Stekl, Konrad

DER WACHE VOGEL see Killmayer, Wilhelm

DER WEIHNACHTS-SINGKREIS *CCU,Xmas
1-4pt PELIKAN   (D168)

DERBY, RICHARD
Adoramus Te And Ressurexi
SATB SCHIRM.G LG51739 $.50   (D169)

DES HERRN WORT BLEIBT IN EWIGKEIT see
Anonymous

DESCANTS FOR CHOIRS see Johnson, Norman

DESCANTS ON EIGHT HYMNS see Boyd,
Jeanne

DESCANTS ON FAMILIAR HYMNS see Lutkin,
Peter Christian

DESCANTS ON TEN HYMNS see Boyd, Jeanne

DESCH, RUDOLF (1911-   )
Komm, O Geist
men cor,acap TONOS 5691 s.p. (D170)

DESERT SHALL BLOOM LIKE A ROSE, THE see
Lister, Mosie

DESHANTZ, LOUIS M.
Christ Child Sleeps, The *Xmas
SSA,acap (med easy) oct ELKAN-V
362-03168 $.30   (D171)

DESHUSSES
Messe En Fa
mix cor,org (F maj) HENN 839 s.p.
sc, voc pt   (D172)

DES PREZ, JOSQUIN (ca. 1450-1521)
Absalom Fili Mi
SATB,trp,2horn,trom KING,R MFB 605
cor pts $.20, cmplt ed $1.50
(D173)
Agnus Dei (from Missa Hercules) Agnus
SATB,acap SALABERT-US $1.00   (D174)
Ave Maria
SATB,acap SALABERT-US $.75   (D175)

Behold, You Are Charming *see Ecce
Tu Pulchra Es

Ecce Tu Pulchra Es
(Klein) "Behold, You Are Charming"
SATB SCHIRM.G 11988 $.40   (D176)

Et Incarnatus Est (from Pange Lingua)
see Lassus, Roland de (Orlandus),
Agnus Dei

Gloria (from Missa Hercules) Gloria
SATB,acap SALABERT-US $.75   (D177)

Hosanna (from Missa Pange Lingua)
[Lat] SATB,acap BROUDE BR. $.30
(D178)
In Pace
[Lat] SAB,acap EGTVED MK14, 10 s.p.
(D179)
Kyrie (from Missa Pange Lingua) Kyrie
[Lat] SATB,acap BROUDE BR. $.40
(D180)
SATB,acap SALABERT-US $.60   (D181)

O Heilige Dreifaltigkeit
(Klink, Waldemar) men cor sc
SCHOTTS CHBL 50 s.p.   (D182)

Sanctus - Benedictus (from Missa
Hercules) Sanctus
SATB,acap SALABERT-US $.75   (D183)

Tu Solus, Qui Facis Mirabilia
(Hunter) SATB AMP N-36 $.40   (D184)

DESTINY see Parks, Joe E.

DET AR EN ROS UTSPRUNGEN see Berg,
Gottfrid

DET AR EN ROS UTSPRUNGEN see
Praetorius, Michael, Es Ist Ein Ros
Entsprungen

DET STAR ETT TRAD PA MIN FADERS GARD
see Olson, Daniel

DETTIGEN TE DEUM see Handel, George
Frideric

DETWEILER, ALAN
David And Goliath
SATB,soli,inst voc sc NOVELLO s.p.,
ipr   (D185)

DEUS GENITOR ALME see Kutzer, Ernst

DEUS IN ADJUTORIUM see Senft

DEUS MISERATUR NOSTRI see Pederson,
Mogens

DEUS MISEREATUR see Naylor, Bernard

DEUS MISEREATUR NOSTRI see Schutz,
Heinrich

DEUS, QUI BEATUM MARCUM see Gabrieli,
Giovanni

DEUS TUORUM MILITUM see Cavalli,
(Pietro) Francesco

DEUS TUORUM MILITUM see Monteverdi,
Claudio

DEUS, VENERUNT GENTES see Dulichius,
Philippus

DEUTSCHE ADVENT-MESSE "O HEILAND REISS
DIE HIMMEL AUF" see Dantonello,
Josef

DEUTSCHE ADVENTSGESANGE see Lemacher,
Heinrich

DEUTSCHE BAUERNMESSE *folk/Mass
cor,org HIEBER s.p.   (D186)

DEUTSCHE CHORALMESSE see Hahn, L.

DEUTSCHE CHORALMESSE see Pepping, Ernst

DEUTSCHE CHORALMESSE see Trubel, Gerhard

DEUTSCHE FESTSINGMESSE NACH KIRCHENLIEDERN see Mutter, Gerbert

DEUTSCHE JUGENDMESSE see Schmalz, Paul

DEUTSCHE KIRCHENLIEDER see Praetorius, Michael

DEUTSCHE KORNELIUS-MESSE see Hoffmann, Bernhard

DEUTSCHE LIEDMESSE "HERR, ZEIG MIR DEINE WEGE" see Berghorn, Alfred

DEUTSCHE LITURGISCHE BEGRABNISGESANGE see Menschik, W.

DEUTSCHE MESSE see Ebner, Hans

DEUTSCHE MESSE see Fritz, Richard

DEUTSCHE MESSE see Haydn, (Johann) Michael

DEUTSCHE MESSE see Hoss, Franz

DEUTSCHE MESSE see Mixa, Franz

DEUTSCHE MESSE see Schubert, Franz (Peter)

DEUTSCHE MESSE see Wenzel, Eberhard

DEUTSCHE MESSE see Zillinger, Erwin

DEUTSCHE MESSE "EHRE SEI GOTT" see Mayer, Alfonso

DEUTSCHE MESSE "KYRIE GOTT VATER IN EWIGKEIT" see Pepping, Ernst

DEUTSCHE MESSE "LOBET DEN HERREN" see Federl, A.

DEUTSCHE MESSE MIT GEMEINDERUFEN see Quack, Erhard

DEUTSCHE MESSE "WOHIN SOLL ICH MICH WENDEN" see Schubert, Franz (Peter)

DEUTSCHE MESSE ZUM EHREN DES HEILIGEN JOHANNES BOSCO see Hierdies, W.

DEUTSCHE MESSGESANGE see Trapp, Willy

DEUTSCHE MOTETTE see Strauss, Richard

DEUTSCHE ORDINARIUMS-MESSE see Schieri, Fritz

DEUTSCHE SEELENMESSE see Welcker, Max, Herr, Lass Sie Ruhn Im Frieden

DEUTSCHE SINGMESSE see Kronberg, G.

DEUTSCHE SINGMESSE "ZU DIR, O GOTT, ERHEBEN WIR" see Frommlet, Franz

DEUTSCHE SPRUCHE VON LEBEN UND TOD see Lechner, Leonhard

DEUTSCHE TOTENMESSE see Bresgen, Cesar

DEUTSCHE TOTENMESSE see Kraft, Karl

DEUTSCHE VOLKSMESSE see Hoss, Franz

DEUTSCHE WEIHNACHTSMESSE see Haas, Joseph

DEUTSCHES HOCHAMT see Erhard, Karl

DEUTSCHES LIEDPROPRIUM NACH DEM EINHEITSGESANGBUCH *CCU
(Erhard, Karl) [Ger] 3pt mix cor BOHM s.p. (D187)

DEUTSCHES ORDINARIUM "CHRISTUS UNSER LICHT" see Monter, Josef

DEUTSCHES REQUIEM see Hoss, Franz

DEUTSCHES TE DEUM see Brugk, Hans Melchoir

DEUTSCHES TE DEUM see Schroeder, Hermann

DEUTSCHMANN, GERHARD
  Christ Ist Geboren
    see Europaische Weihnachtslieder

  Die Krippe Im Stall
    see Europaische Weihnachtslieder

  Europaische Weihnachtslieder *Xmas, Eur
    3-4 eq voices sc BOHM s.p.
     contains: Christ Ist Geboren; Die Krippe Im Stall; Grunet Felder; In Einem Kripplein (D188)

DEUTSCHMANN, GERHARD (cont'd.)
  Grunet Felder
    see Europaische Weihnachtslieder

  In Einem Kripplein
    see Europaische Weihnachtslieder

  O Du Frohliche *Xmas
    cor BOHM s.p. (D189)

  Stille Nacht, Heilige Nacht *Xmas
    cor BOHM s.p. (D190)

  Weihnachtsmusik *Xmas
    unis jr cor,pno/org,strings,3rec, trp BOHM s.p. (D191)

DEUX NOELS FRANCAIS QUINZIEME SIECLE
*CC2U,Xmas,15th cent
(Caraz) 4pt mix cor, acap sc HENN 544 s.p. (D192)

DE VICTORIA, TOMAS LUIS
see VICTORIA, TOMAS LUIS DE

DEXTERA DOMINI see Dietrich, J.H.

DEXTERA DOMINI see Rottmanner, Eduard

DEXTERA DOMINI FECIT VIRTUTEM see Lassus, Roland de (Orlandus)

DEXTERAM TUAM see Villa-Lobos, Heitor

DEY CAN'T COTCH ME TO BURY ME see Rider-Meyer, L.

DIABELLI, ANTON (1781-1858)
  Pastoral-Messe In F *Op.147, Mass
    [Lat] 4pt mix cor,soli,fl,2clar/ 2ob,2bsn,2trp,strings,timp,org sc,cor pts BOHM s.p., ipa (D193)

  Virgo Maria Beata Es *hymn
    [Lat] 4pt mix cor,org/fl&strings& org sc,cor pts BOHM s.p., ipa (D194)

DIAGOLO PER LA PASCUA see Stout, Alan

DIALOGUE see Karlen, Robert

DIAMENT, ABRAHAM
  Ashira La'adonai
    SATB,acap ISR.PUB.AG. s.p. (D195)

  Ata Kidashta
    SATB,acap ISR.PUB.AG. s.p. (D196)

  Hand Of The Diligent, The
    SA,solo,pno ISR.PUB.AG. s.p. (D197)

  Hariu Le'elohim (Psalm 66)
    SA,pno ISR.PUB.AG. s.p. (D198)

  He That Tilleth *canon
    SATB ISR.PUB.AG. s.p. (D199)

  Lekda Dodi *Psalm
    SATB,acap ISR.PUB.AG. s.p. (D200)

  Psalm 66 *see Hariu Le'elohim

  Seven Pillars
    SAT,pno ISR.PUB.AG. s.p. (D201)

  Shalom Aleikhem
    SATB,acap ISR.PUB.AG. s.p. (D202)

  Thoughts
    SA,pno ISR.PUB.AG. s.p. (D203)

  Yehalelu
    SATB,solo,pno ISR.PUB.AG. s.p.
     contains also: Yom-Tov (D204)

  Yom-Tov
    see Diament, Abraham, Yehalelu

DIC NOBIS, MARIA see Philipp, Franz

DICH LIEBT MEIN HERZ, O HERR see Goudimel, Claude

DICKS, ERNEST A.
  Lord's Prayer, The
    SATB HARRIS $.35 (D205)

  Prayer Of Thanksgiving
    SA HARRIS $.25 (D206)
    SATB HARRIS $.35 (D207)

DID YOU HEAR THE ANGELS SING? see Perera, Ronald

DID YOU HEAR THE SHEPHERDS SAY?
(Ehret, Walter) SAB,opt vcl VOLKWEIN VB-742 $.40 (D208)

DIDN'T HE SHINE! see McDill

DIDN'T MY LORD DELIVER DANIEL? *spir
(Springfield) BarBar&2camb CAMBIATA S97445 (D209)

DIDN'T MY LORD DELIVER DANIEL see Petersen, Rolf

DIE AUFERSTEHUNG UND HIMMELFAHRT JESU see Bach, Karl Philipp Emanuel

DIE AUFERSTEHUNGS-HISTORIE see Schutz, Heinrich

DIE CHOR-ANTWORTEN ZU DEN PASSIONEN see Suriano, Francesco

DIE CHORALSATZE DER JOHANNESPASSION see Bach, Johann Sebastian

DIE EHEBRECHERIN see David, Johann Nepomuk

DIE EHRE GOTTES IN DER NATUR "DIE HIMMEL RUHMEN" see Beethoven, Ludwig van

DIE ENGEL UND DIE HIRTEN
  see Drei Altbohmische Weihnachtslieder

DIE ENGEL UND DIE HIRTEN see Riedel, Karl

DIE ENTSCHLAFENEN "EINEN VERGANGLICHEN TAG" see Fortner, Wolfgang

DIE FINSTERNIS VERGEHT see Zillinger, Erwin

DIE FURCHT DES HERREN IST DER WEISHEIT ANFANG see Schutz, Heinrich

DIE GANZE WELT, HERR JESU CHRIST see Gippenbusch, Jakob

DIE GESCHICHTE VON DANIEL UND DEN LOWEN IN DER GRUBE see Wenzel, Eberhard

DIE GOTTSELIGKEIT IST ZU ALLEN DINGEN NUTZE see Schutz, Heinrich

DIE GULDNE SONNE see Pepping, Ernst

DIE HEILING DREI KONIG see Lang, Hans

DIE HELLE SONN see Lau, Heinz

DIE HELLE SONN see Vulpius, Melchior

DIE HELLE SONN LEUCHT JETZT HERFUR see Diener, Theodor

DIE HIMMEL ERZAHLEN see Haydn, (Franz) Joseph

DIE JAHRESZEITEN see Haydn, (Franz) Joseph

DIE JAKOBSLEITER see Schoenberg, Arnold

DIE JUNGFRAU MARIA see Burthel, Jakob

DIE KINDHEIT CHRISTI see Berlioz, Hector, L'Enfance Du Christ

DIE KRIPPE IM STALL see Deutschmann, Gerhard

DIE LIEBE SONNE see Kaminski, Heinrich

DIE LIEBE, WENN SIE NEU see Krietsch, Georg

DIE LINIEN DES LEBENS SIND VERSCHIEDEN see Haas, Joseph

DIE MIT TRANEN SAEN see Schutz, Heinrich

DIE NACHT IST KOMMEN see Hessenberg, Kurt

DIE NACHT IST VORGEDRUNGEN see Oertzen, Rudolf von

DIE OFFERTORIEN DER HAUPTFESTE DES KIRCHENJAHRES see Pranschke, Johannes

DIE PASSION DES MENSCHENSOHNS see Koll, Fritz

DIE PFINGSTGESCHICHTE see Fortner, Wolfgang

DIE PROPRIUMS-GESANGE ZU MARIA HIMMELFAHRT see Lemacher, Heinrich

DIE REDE DES PAULUS AN DIE ATHENER see Gerhard

DIE RUCKKEHR DES VERLORENEN SOHNES see Reutter, Hermann

DIE SEELEN DER GERECHTEN see Goller, Fritz

DIE SELIGEN see Haas, Joseph

DIE SELIGPREISUNGEN see Hindermann, Walter Felix

DIE SELIGPREISUNGEN see Rohwer, Jens

DIE SELIGPREISUNGEN see Schweizer, Rolf

DIE SELIGPREISUNGEN see Trubel, Gerhard

DIE SIEBEN LETZTEN WORTE UNSERES ERLOSERS AM KREUZE see Haydn, (Franz) Joseph

DIE SIEBEN WORTE JESU CHRISTI see Schutz, Heinrich

DIE SONN HOCH AN DEN HIMMEL STEHT see Hessenberg, Kurt

DIE SONNE IST GESUNKEN see Biebl, Franz

DIE STECHPALM UND DER EFEU *Xmas, carol/folk
   (Biebl, F.) [Ger] 4pt men cor
   MERSEBURG EM9044   (D210)

DIE STILLE LEBEN see Grosse-Schware, Hermann

DIE STUND IST UNS VERBORGN see Vulpius, Melchior

DIE TOTEN RUHN IN GOTT "HALTET NICHT FEST DIE TRAUER" see Zipp, Friedrich

DIE VESPER "HORT VOM STRAND EIN VESPER SINGEN" see Beethoven, Ludwig van

DIE VIER CHORAL-CREDO see Welcker, Max

DIE WEIHNACHTS-BOTSCHAFT see Simon, Hermann

DIE WEIHNACHTSGESCHICHTE see Barth, Hans Joachim

DIE WEIHNACHTSGESCHICHTE see Coenen, Hans

DIE WEIHNACHTSGESCHICHTE see Keetman, Gunild

DIE WEIHNACHTSGESCHICHTE see Langhans, Herbert

DIE WEIHNACHTSGESCHICHTE see Rienecker

DIE WEIHNACHTSGESCHICHTE see Schroeder, Hermann

DIE ZWEI BLINDEN see David, Johann Nepomuk

DIEMENTE, EDWARD
   Alleluia
   SAB,electronic tape GRAY GCCS 22
   $.30   (D211)

DIEMER, EMMA LOU (1927-   )
   Jesus, Lover Of My Soul
   2pt mix cor TRIUNE TUM 111 $.35 see
   also LET THE WORLD SING   (D212)

   Prophecy, The
   SSAA,acap oct BOOSEY 5882 $.70
                                        (D213)

   Sing, O Heavens
   cor,acap (med) FISCHER,C CM 7928
   $.40   (D214)

DIENER, THEODOR (1908-   )
   Alles Was Odem Hat, Lobe De Herrn
   (Psalm 146)
   men cor,2trp,2trom,timp HUG see
   from Two Psalms   (D215)

   Die Helle Sonn Leucht Jetzt Herfur
   SATB&cong,org SCHWEIZER. SK 61.01-2
   s.p. see also MUSIKBEILAGE ZUM
   "EVANGELISCHEN KIRCHENCHOR 1961"
                                        (D216)

   Ein Feste Burg Ist Unser Gott
   see MUSIKBEILAGE ZUM "EVANGELISCHEN
   KIRCHENCHOR 1959"

   Ich Sag Dir Dank, Gott Vater Gut
   SAT/SAB/SB/SATB SCHWEIZER. SK 62.04
   s.p. see also MUSIKBEILAGE ZUM
   "EVANGELISCHEN KIRCHENCHOR 1962"
                                        (D217)

   Lobet Den Herrn In Seinem Heiligtum
   men cor,2trp,2trom,timp HUG see
   from Two Psalms   (D218)

   O Leib, Gebrochen Mir Zu Gut
   SATB (contains also: Es Ist
   Gewisslich An Der Zeit;So Fuhrst
   Du Doch Recht Selig, Herr, Die
   Deinen) SCHWEIZER. SK 54.01-2
   s.p. see also MUSIKBEILAGE ZUM
   "EVANGELISCHEN KIRCHENCHOR 1954"
                                        (D219)

   O Wie Sehr Lieblich Sind
   SATB (contains also: Ich Singe Dir
   Mit Herz Und Mund) SCHWEIZER.

DIENER, THEODOR (cont'd.)
   SK 68.04 s.p. see also
   MUSIKBEILAGE ZUM "EVANGELISCHEN
   KIRCHENCHOR 1968"   (D220)

   Psalm 47 *see Singt Mit Froher Stimm

   Psalm 146 *see Alles Was Odem Hat, Lobe De Herrn

   Singt Mit Froher Stimm (Psalm 47)
   SAT/SAB/SATB,org SCHWEIZER. SK 159
   s.p.   (D221)

   Two Psalms *see Alles Was Odem Hat,
   Lobe De Herrn (Psalm 146); Lobet
   Den Herrn In Seinem Heiligtum
                                        (D222)

DIES DOMINI MAGNUS see Bezanson, Philip

DIES IRAE see Latrobe, Christian I.

DIES IRAE see Lotti, Antonio

DIES IRAE see Toni, Alceo

DIES IST DER TAG, DEN DER HERR MACHT see Kretzschmar, Gunther

DIES JAHR HABEN WIR AUCH ERLEBT see Anonymous

DIES SANCTIFICATUS see Palestrina, Giovanni

DIES UNUS see Kelterborn, Rudolf

DIETRICH, FRITZ (1905-1945)
   Ascendit Deus *Op.42, Asc,Offer
   [Lat] 4pt mix cor,org sc,cor pts
   BOHM s.p.   (D223)

   Ave Maria *Op.7,No.1
   [Lat] 4pt mix cor,org sc,cor pts
   BOHM s.p.   (D224)

   Inimicitias Ponam *Op.80a, BVM,Offer
   [Lat] 4pt mix cor,org sc,cor pts
   BOHM s.p.   (D225)

DIETRICH, J.H.
   Dextera Domini *Op.14b, Holywk
   [Lat] SSATTBB,acap sc,cor pts BOHM
   s.p.   (D226)

   Gloria In Excelsis Deo *Op.78, Mass
   [Lat] 4pt mix cor,org sc,cor pts
   BOHM s.p.   (D227)

   Messe Zu Ehren Der Allerseligsten
   Jungfrau Maria *Op.20, Mass
   [Lat] 4pt mix cor,org sc,cor pts
   BOHM s.p.   (D228)

   Messe Zu Ehren Des Heiliges Kreuzes
   *Op.15, Mass
   [Lat] 4pt mix cor,org,opt 2trp,
   trom,horn cor pts BOHM s.p., ipa
                                        (D229)

   O Crux, Benedicta *Op.52, Psntd
   [Lat] 8pt mix cor,acap sc,cor pts
   BOHM s.p.   (D230)

   O Salutaris Hostia *Op.8
   [Lat] SSATTBB,acap sc,cor pts BOHM
   s.p.   (D231)

   Panis Angelicus *Op.14a
   [Lat] SSATTBB,acap sc,cor pts BOHM
   s.p.   (D232)

   Regina Coeli Laetare *Op.49, Easter
   [Lat] 4pt mix cor,acap sc,cor pts
   BOHM s.p.   (D233)

DIETSCHMANN
   He's On His Way (composed with
   Meyers)
   (Huff, Ronn) SATB oct BENSON S4386
   $.35   (D234)

DIETTERICH, PHILIP R.
   Psalm 23
   2pt mix cor&cong,pno/org oct AGAPE
   AG 7164 $.45   (D235)

DIFFERENT DRUM, A see Mueller

DIFFUSA EST GRATIA see Lemacher, Heinrich

DIGGLE, ROLAND (1887-1954)
   Benedictus Es Domine
   "Blessed Art Thou" SSATB (med)
   FITZSIMONS 2059 $.25   (D236)

   Blessed Art Thou *see Benedictus Es
   Domine

   Christ Child's Lullaby, The *Xmas
   1-2pt treb cor (med) FITZSIMONS
   5015 $.20   (D237)

DIGNUS EST AGNUS see Williamson, Malcolm

DIJK, JAN VAN (1918-   )
   By The Rivers Of Babylon (Psalm 137)
   wom cor,org,2fl,ob,bsn,horn,trp,
   strings,perc,alto saxophone
   DONEMUS   (D238)

   Psalm 137 *see By The Rivers Of
   Babylon

DI LASSO, ORLANDO
   see LASSUS, ROLAND DE (ORLANDUS)

DIMENSIONS IN MUSIC *CCUL,Xmas/Easter
   (Wyrtzen, Don) SATB,1-3 soli,inst oct
   SINGSPIR 5672 $1.95   (D239)

DING! DONG! MERRILY ON HIGH see Wood, Charles

DIR, DIR JEHOVA WILL ICH SINGEN see Bach, Johann Sebastian

DIR, DIR JEHOVA, WILL ICH SINGEN see Werner

DIR, DIR JEHOVAH WILL ICH SINGEN see Bach, Johann Sebastian

DIR, JESU, GOTTES SOHN, SEI PREIS see Bach, Johann Sebastian

DIRECT US, O LORD see Matthews, Thomas

DIRIGE NOS, DOMINE, IN VERITATE TUA see Lassus, Roland de (Orlandus)

DIRKSEN
   Annunciation Story, The
   SATB SHAWNEE A5609 $.40   (D240)

   Song Of Mary At The Manger *Xmas
   SSAATTBB,acap (med diff) OXFORD
   94.329   (D241)

DISCIPLESHIP see Kirby

DISCOVERY see Skillings, Otis

DISCOVERY see Wyrtzen, Don

DISMISSAL see Stout, Alan

DISMISSAL, THE see Green, Philip

DISPERSIT, DEDIT PAUPERIBUS see Zimmer, Jan

DISTLER, HUGO (1908-1942)
   Es Ist Ein Ros Entsprungen
   SATB SCHWEIZER. SK 63.02 s.p. see
   also MUSIKBEILAGE ZUM
   "EVANGELISCHEN KIRCHENCHOR 1963"
                                        (D242)

   For God So Loved The World
   SAB oct CONCORDIA 98-2239 $.30
                                        (D243)

   Gott Sei Dank Durch Alle Welt
   SAT/SAB (contains also: Wie Schon
   Leuchtet Der Morgenstern; Warum
   Sollt Ich Mich Denn Gramen)
   SCHWEIZER. SK 69.01-2 s.p. see
   also MUSIKBEILAGE ZUM
   "EVANGELISCHEN KIRCHENCHOR 1969"
                                        (D244)

   Lobe Den Herren
   (Stone, Kurt) "Praise Ye The Lord"
   [Eng/Ger] SATB,acap BOONIN B 134
   $.50   (D245)

   Our Lord Is Risen With Flag Unfurled
   SAB oct CONCORDIA 98-2242 $.25
                                        (D246)

   Praise Ye The Lord *see Lobe Den
   Herren

   Sing, Ye, The Lord A New-Made Song
   *see Singet Dem Herrn Ein Neues
   Lied

   Singet Dem Herrn Ein Neues Lied
   *Op.12,No.1
   (Richter, Clifford G.) "Sing, Ye,
   The Lord A New-Made Song" [Eng/
   Ger] SATB,acap BOONIN B 243 $1.50
                                        (D247)

   Was Mein Gott Will, Das Gscheh
   Allzeit
   SAT/SAB SCHWEIZER. SK 66.03 s.p.
   see also MUSIKBEILAGE ZUM
   "EVANGELISCHEN KIRCHENCHOR 1966"
                                        (D248)

   Wie Schon Leuchtet Der Morgenstern
   SAT/SAB (contains also: Gott Sei
   Dank Durch Alle Welt; Warum Sollt
   Ich Mich Denn Gramen) SCHWEIZER.
   SK 69.01-2 s.p. see also
   MUSIKBEILAGE ZUM "EVANGELISCHEN
   KIRCHENCHOR 1969"   (D249)

DITTENHAVER, S.L.
    Light Of The Lonely Pilgrim's Heart
        SA BRODT 570 $.22   (D250)

    Trust In The Lord
        unis BRODT 608 $.22   (D251)
        mix cor BRODT 634 $.30   (D252)

DIVERSI DIVERSA ORANT see Gombert,
    Nicolas

DIVES AND LAZARUS see Byrt, John C.

DIVINE PRIORITY, THE see Wyrtzen, Don

DIXIT see Lotti, Antonio

DIXIT DOMINUS see Eberlin, Johann Ernst

DIXIT DOMINUS see Pergolesi, Giovanni
    Battista

DIXIT MARIA AD ANGELUM see Hassler,
    Hans Leo

DIXITQUE FIAT see Pezzati, Romano

DO DON'T TOUCH *spir
    (Thomas) SATB,acap oct LILLENAS
        AN-7002 $.35   (D253)

DO GOD'S WILL see Hegenbart, Alex F.

DO, LORD see Tanis

DO YOU HAVE AN EMPTY HEART? see Fiscus

DO YOU HEAR WHAT I HEAR see Regney,
    Noel

DO YOU KNOW? see Nichols

DO YOU KNOW WHAT TIME IT IS? see
    Reynolds, William Jensen

DO YOU KNOWN MY JESUS? see Ellis

DO YOU LOVE MY LORD? *anthem
    (Littleton, Bill J.) 2pt FINE ARTS
        CM 1075 $.30   (D254)

DO YOU WANT PEACE? see Matthews

DOANE, [WILLIAM HOWARD] (1832-1915)
    More Love To Thee *anthem/gospel
    (Rasley, Hohn M.) SATB oct SINGSPIR
        ZJP-8094 $.30   (D255)

    Rescue The Perishing *anthem/gospel
    (Mayfield, Larry) SATB oct SINGSPIR
        ZJP-8152 $.25   (D256)

    To God Be The Glory *anthem
    (Rasley, John M.) SATB (easy) oct
        SINGSPIR ZJP-6021 $.30   (D257)

    To The Work *anthem/gospel
    (Heacock, Harry) SATB oct SINGSPIR
        ZJP-8020 $.30   (D258)

DOBIAS, VACLAV (1909-   )
    Kdoz Jste Bozi Bojovnici
    "Oh Warriors Of God" [Czech] men
        cor,Bar solo,2fl,ob,2clar,bsn,
        3horn,3trp,2trom,tuba,timp,perc,
        strings CZECH s.p.   (D259)

    Oh Warriors Of God *see Kdoz Jste
        Bozi Bojovnici

DODD
    New Day!, A *anthem/gospel
    (Johnson, Norman) SATB oct SINGSPIR
        ZJP-8165 $.30   (D260)

DOEBLER, CURT
    Ave Maria
        [Lat] 4pt mix cor,acap BOHM s.p.
                                             (D261)
    Domine Non Sum Dignus *Commun
        [Lat] 4pt mix cor,acap BOHM s.p.
                                             (D262)
    Ego Sum Pastor Bonus *Easter
        [Lat] 4pt mix cor,acap BOHM s.p.
                                             (D263)
    Gott Ist Die Liebe *Fest
        3pt BOHM s.p.   (D264)

    Lauda Anima Mea, Dominum *Fest
        [Lat] 4pt mix cor,acap BOHM s.p.
                                             (D265)
    Morgenglanz Der Ewigkeit *Fest
        3pt BOHM s.p.   (D266)

    O Crux Ave *Psntd
        [Lat] 4pt mix cor,acap BOHM s.p.
                                             (D267)
    O Salutaris Hostia *Commun,mot
        [Lat] 4pt mix cor,acap BOHM s.p.
                                             (D268)
    Postula A Me *Offer
        [Lat] 4pt mix cor,acap BOHM s.p.
                                             (D269)
    Stabat Mater *Psntd
        [Lat] 4pt mix cor,acap BOHM s.p.
                                             (D270)

DOEBLER, CURT (cont'd.)

    Veni, Sanctificator *Offer
        [Lat] 4pt mix cor,acap BOHM s.p.
                                             (D271)

DOGWOOD CROSS, THE see Landon, Stewart

DOLOROSA ET LACRIMABILIS see Lendvai,
    Erwin

DOLU KOPCEM K BETLEMU see Drazan, Josef

DOMINE, AD ADIUVANDUM ME FESTINA see
    Vivaldi, Antonio

DOMINE, CONVERTERE ET ERIPE ANIMAM MEAM
    see Lassus, Roland de (Orlandus)

DOMINE DEUS see Ammann, Benno

DOMINE DEUS see Franck, Cesar

DOMINE EXAUDI ORATIONEM MEAM see
    Gabrieli

DOMINE EXAUDI ORATIONEM MEAM see
    Gabrieli, Giovanni

DOMINE, EXAUDI ORATIONEM MEAM see
    Lassus, Roland de (Orlandus)

DOMINE, FAC MECUM MISERICORDIAM TUAM
    see Lassus, Roland de (Orlandus)

DOMINE, IN AUXILIUM MEUM RESPICE see
    Lassus, Roland de (Orlandus)

DOMINE JESU CHRISTE see Willaert,
    Adrian

DOMINE, LABIA MEA APERIES see Lassus,
    Roland de (Orlandus)

DOMINE NE LONGE see Stout, Alan

DOMINE NON SECUNDUM see Franck, Cesar

DOMINE NON SUM DIGNUS see Doebler, Curt

DOMINE, NON SUM DIGNUS see Victoria,
    Tomas Luis de

DOMINE QUID MULTIPICAVIT see Vannius

DOMINE, REFUGIUM FACTUS ES see
    Scarlatti, Alessandro

DOMINICA DE PASSIONE see Eben, Petr

DOMINICA IV IN QUADRAGESIMA see Eben,
    Petr

DOMINO CANTICUM NOVUM see Philipp,
    Franz

DOMUS MEA see Ammann, Benno

DONA NOBIS PACEM
    (Foster) 3pt,inst (easy) sc OXFORD
        40.025 $2.55, cor pts OXFORD 40.026
        $.25   (D272)

DONA NOBIS PACEM see Clarke, Henry
    Leland

DONA NOBIS PACEM see Clemens, Jacobus

DONA NOBIS PACEM see Holliger, Heinz

DONA NOBIS PACEM see Mutter, Gerbert

DONAHUE, ROBERT
    Jesus Was A Baby *Xmas
        SATB,acap (med easy) ELKAN-V
        362-03181 $.50   (D273)

DONATI
    Non Vos Relinquam Orphanos *anthem
    (Roche) SSA/TTB (med) OXFORD 40.024
        $.40   (D274)

DONATO, ANTHONY (1909-   )
    God Be Merciful (Psalm 67)
        SATB,acap OPUS 3-01 $.45   (D275)

    Psalm 67 *see God Be Merciful

DONIZETTI, GAETANO (1797-1848)
    Collected Works. Series 2: Sacred
        Works No. 1 *see Messa Di
        Requiem   (D276)

    Credo
        cor,soli,2fl,2ob,2clar,2bsn,2horn,
        2trp,2trom,strings,timp BRUZZI
        S.V.-063 s.p.   (D277)

    Messa Di Requiem
        SATB,soli,org voc sc BROUDE,A
        $15.00 see from Collected Works.
        Series 2: Sacred Works No. 1   (D278)

    Miserere
        cor,7 soli,orch voc sc EULENBURG
        GM219 s.p., sc EULENBURG 10102
        s.p., ipr   (D279)

DON'T-A YOU JUDGE see Smith

DON'T KNOCK (JUST WALK RIGHT IN) see
    Staples

DON'T LET THE SONG GO OUT OF YOUR HEART
    see Peterson, John W.

DON'T TAKE MY CROSS AWAY see Rambo,
    Dottie

DON'T YOU HEAR THE LAMBS A-CRYIN'
    *spir
    (Brown) SATB oct LILLENAS AN-7009
        $.30   (D280)

DOOR, THE see Peninger, David

DOOR'T STERRELICHT IN PRAAL EN PRACHT
    see Pronk, Arie

DOPPELBAUER, JOSEF FRIEDRICH
    (1918-   )
    Das Grosse Salzburger Alleluja
        SATB DOBLINGER G 733 s.p.   (D281)

DORMI JESU see Leigh, Eric

DORMI JESU see Lemacher, Heinrich

DORNROSCHEN see Biebl, Franz

DORS MA COLOMBE *Xmas
    (McCauley, Wm.) SATB (med easy)
        WATERLOO $.35   (D282)

DORT OBEN VOM BERGE see Zipp, Friedrich

DOS CANCIONES SAFARDIES see Rodrigo

DOS TOGNO see Bortniansky, Dimitri
    Stepanovitch

DOST THOU IN A MANGER LIE? see Tarry

DOST THOU IN A MANGER LIE see Wise,
    Gerald J.

D'OU VENEZ-VOUS? see Chassang

DOUDNEY
    Master Hath Come, The (composed with
        Warford) *anthem
        SATB oct BROADMAN 4562-43 $.35
                                             (D283)

DOUGLAS
    Bow Down Thine Ear
        SATB PRO ART 2793 $.35   (D284)

DOUZE CANTIQUES DE FETES
    cor JOBERT s.p.
        contains & see also: Au Sacre
        Coeur; Berceuse De Noel;
        L'Ascension; L'Assomption; Le
        Jour Des Morts; Le Nom De Marie;
        L'Eucharistie; Maternite De
        Marie; Paques; Pentecote; Priere
        A L'Enfant Jesus; Saint Joseph
                                             (D285)
DOUZE NOUVEAUX CANTIQUES DE FETES
    cor JOBERT s.p.
        contains & see also: A L'Immaculee-
        Conception; A Ste-Therese De
        L'Enfant-Jesus; Action De Graces;
        Au Saint-Esprit; Cantique De
        Mariage; Consecration A La
        Sainte-Vierge; Pour La
        Confirmation; Pour La Premiere
        Communion ; Pour La Premiere
        Communion ; Pour La Toussaint;
        Pour Le Jour Des Rameaux;
        Renouvellement Des Promesses Du
        Bapteme   (D286)

DOWLAND, JOHN (1563-1626)
    Complete Psalms *CCU,Psalm
    (Poulton) SATB STAINER 3.1100.1
        $3.75   (D287)

    Heart That's Broken And Contrite, An
        SATB STAINER 3.0771.1 $.75 contains
        also: I Shame At Mine
        Unworthiness   (D288)

    I Shame At Mine Unworthiness
        see Dowland, John, Heart That's
        Broken And Contrite, An

    In Prayer Together
        "O Lord, Consider My Distress" see
        Seven Hymn Tunes, Part 1

    Lord In Thy Wrath *see O Help Us,
        Lord

    Lute Lullaby, A
        see Byrd, William, Sing We, Then
        Merrily

    O God Of Bethel
        "O Lord, Of Whom I Do Depend" see
        Seven Hymn Tunes, Part 1

    O Help Us, Lord
        "Lord In Thy Wrath" see Seven Hymn
        Tunes, Part 1

DOWLAND, JOHN (cont'd.)

O Lord, Consider My Distress *see In
Prayer Together

O Lord, Of Whom I Do Depend *see O
God Of Bethel

O Lord, Turn Not Away
see Seven Hymn Tunes, Part 1

Seven Hymn Tunes, Part 1
SATB,acap (med) OXFORD 43.239 $.55
contains: In Prayer Together, "O
Lord, Consider My Distress"; O
God Of Bethel, "O Lord, Of Whom
I Do Depend"; O Help Us, Lord,
"Lord In Thy Wrath"; O Lord,
Turn Not Away   (D289)

DOWLING, ERIC
Great And Marvelous Are Thy Works
SATB (med) WATERLOO $.60   (D290)

DOWN BY THE RIVERSIDE
(Wild, Eric) SATB,pno BERANDOL
BER1681 $.50   (D291)

DOWN IN YON FOREST
see Eight Christmas Carols: Set 2

DOWN THE HILL TO BETHLEHEM see Drazan,
Josef, Dolu Kopcem K Betlemu

DOXOLOGIE: GLORIA IN EXCELSIS see
Bortniansky, Dimitri Stepanovitch

DOXOLOGY: AMEN, PRAISE YE THE LORD see
Hasse

DRAUMKVEDET see Neilsen, Ludvig

DRAYTON
Ecce Ancilli Domini *anthem
SATB (med) OXFORD 42.368 $.45
                                   (D292)
Lord Behold Us *anthem
unis (easy) OXFORD 45.067 $.30
                                   (D293)
My Soul, There Is A Country *anthem
SATB OXFORD A 308   (D294)

DRAYTON, PAUL
Easter Day *Easter
SSATTBB,acap GRAY CMR 3328 $.35
                                   (D295)
Lift Up Your Heads, Great Gates *Asc
2pt GRAY CMR 3300 $.35   (D296)

Now Glad Of Heart Be Every One!
*Easter,carol
SATB,org NOVELLO MW 41 s.p.   (D297)

What Sweeter Music Can We Bring
*Xmas
SATB,org FISCHER,J FEC 10105 $.35
                                   (D298)

DRAZAN, JOSEF (1909-   )
Dolu Kopcem K Betlemu *Xmas,cant
"Down The Hill To Bethlehem"
[Czech] jr cor&mix cor,2fl,2ob,
2clar,2bsn,2horn,timp,org,strings
CZECH s.p.   (D299)

Down The Hill To Bethlehem *see Dolu
Kopcem K Betlemu

DREAM THING ON BIBLICAL EPISODES see
London, Edwin

DREI ADVENTSLIEDER see Weinreich,
Waltraut

DREI ADVENTSLIEDER see Mullich, Hermann

DREI ALTBOHMISCHE WEIHNACHTSLIEDER
*Xmas,Boh
(Riedel, K.) SATB,acap s.p. cor pts
BREITKOPF-L PB-2476, voc pt
BREITKOPF-L CHB-1403
contains: Die Engel Und Die Hirten;
Freu Dich, Erd' Und Sternenzelt;
Lasst Alle Gott Uns Loben (D300)

DREI ALTBOHMISCHE WEIHNACTSLIEDER see
Riedel, Karl

DREI BEERDIGUNGSGESANGE *Rembrnc
(Seidel, F.) cor sc,cor pts BOHM s.p.
contains: Graun, Karl Heinrich,
Auferstehen Wirst Du; Handel,
George Frideric, Wenn Christus,
Der Herr; Vulpius, Melchior, Die
Stund Ist Uns Verborgn   (D301)

DREI BIBLISCHE SZENEN see Schutz,
Heinrich

DREI EVANGELIEN-MOTETTEN see Pepping,
Ernst

DREI FEST-PANGE-LINGUA see Kagerer,
Chr. Lor.

DREI GEISTLICHE CHORE see Fortner,
Wolfgang

DREI GEISTLICHE CHORE see Krenek, Ernst

DREI GLEICHNISSE AUS DEM NEUEN
TESTAMENT see Reutter, Hermann

DREI GRABLIEDER see Frey, Carl

DREI HYMNEN see Genzmer, Harald

DREI HYMNISCHE GESANGE see Weber,
Bernhard

DREI KLEINE PASSIONSMOTETTEN NACH
ALTBOHMISCHEN GESANGEN see Hanus,
Jan

DREI LIEDER see Lang, Hans

DREI MOTETTEN see Succo

DREI MOTETTEN see Wiedermann, Bedrich

DREI MOTETTEN see Hohlfeld, Christoph

DREI PASSIONSMOTETTEN see Brautigam,
Volker

DREI PAULUS-MOTETTEN see Werner

DREI PSALMEN see Weiss, Manfred

DREI TANTUM ERGO see Schubert, Franz
(Peter)

DREI VENI CREATOR see Mutter, Gerbert

DREI WEIHNACHTLICHE LIEDSATZE see
Ahrens, Joseph

DREI WEIHNACHTSCHORE see Zipp,
Friedrich

DREI WEIHNACHTSGESANGE see Mullich,
Hermann

DREI WEIHNACHTSLIEDER see Schroeder,
Hermann

DREIKONIGSKANTATE see Lemacher,
Heinrich, Proprium "In Epiphania
Domini"

DREISTIMMIGE KIRCHENLIEDSATZE see
Praetorius, Michael

DREISTIMMIGE MOTETTEN UND LIEDSATZE
ZEITGENOSISSCHER KOMPONISTEN *CCU,
mot,Contemp
3-4pt mix cor&opt treb cor&opt cong,
acap/inst (med easy) BAREN. BA6420
                                   (D302)
DREIUNDVIERZIG VIERSTIMMIGE SATZE ZU
KIRCHENLIEDERN see Bach, Johann
Sebastian

DRESE
Jesu, Geh Voran
(Hollfelder, W.) men cor,acap TONOS
5658 s.p.   (D303)

Jesus Still Lead On *anthem
(Rasley, John M.) SATB oct SINGSPIR
ZJP-7268 $.30   (D304)

DRESSLER, GALLUS (1533-1585)
Lobet Den Herren, Alle Heiden
mix cor (med easy) sc SCHOTTS
C 43 535 s.p. contains also:
Osiander, Lucas, Gelobet Seist
Du, Jesu Christ   (D305)

DRIESSLER, JOHANNES (1921-   )
O Mensch, Bewein Dein Sunde Gross
SAT/SAB (contains also: Des Heilgen
Geistes Gnade Gross) SCHWEIZER.
SK 58.06 s.p. see also
MUSIKBEILAGE ZUM "EVANGELISCHEN
KIRCHENCHOR 1958"   (D306)

DRIFTING see Stanphill

DRITTE MESSE IN ES see Faist, Anton

DRITTE SINGMESSE "HERR, WIR KOMMEN
SCHULDBELADEN" see Faist, Anton

DRIZGA, EDUARD (1944-   )
Mala Mulier *cant
[Czech/Lat] mix cor,soli,3fl,2ob,
2clar,2bsn,4horn,3trp,3trom,tuba,
perc,2pno, celeste, xylophone
CZECH s.p.   (D307)

DROBISH, DOUGLAS
Tree, The
(Bock, Fred) SATB,pno (med diff)
GENTRY G-199 $.40   (D308)

DROP DROP SLOW TEARS
(Fox, George) SATB (med diff)
WATERLOO $.35   (D309)

DROP, DROP, SLOW TEARS see Young, P.

DRY BONES *spir
(Field, Robert) SAB,pno (med easy)
PRESSER 312-41058 $.50   (D310)
(Schubert) SATB oct LILLENAS AN-3863
$.40   (D311)

DU BIST'S DEM RUHM UND EHRE GEBUHRET
see Haydn, (Franz) Joseph

DU FRIEDEFURST, HERR JESU CHRIST see
Bach, Johann Sebastian

DU GABST, O HERR see Schubert, Franz
(Peter)

DU HAST GEDULDET see Biebl, Franz

DU HAST, O JESULEIN, KEIN BETT see
Liebhold

DU NARR, DIESE NACHT see Manicke,
Dietrich

DU SOLLST GOTT, DEINEN HERRN, LIEBEN
see Franck, Melchior

DUBOIS, THEODORE (1837-1924)
Adoramus Te, Christe
(Hansen) "Christ, We Do All Adore
Thee" SATB oct SCHMITT 5911 $.40
                                   (D312)
Christ, We Do All Adore Thee *see
Adoramus Te, Christe

DUCHESNE, SISTER
With Music And Song (composed with
Delia, Sister) *CCU,hymn
cong,org/gtr EMI   (D313)

DUCIS, BENEDICTUS (ca. 1490-1544)
Aus Tiefer Not Schrei Ich Zu Dir
SAT/SAB (contains also: Nun
Jauchzet, All Ihr Frommen; Allein
Gott In Der Hoh Sei Ehr)
SCHWEIZER. SK 53.01-2 s.p. see
also MUSIKBEILAGE ZUM
"EVANGELISCHEN KIRCHENCHOR 1953"
                                   (D314)
Nun Freut Euch, Lieben Christeng'mein
SATB,acap (med easy) sc SCHOTTS
C 37 377 s.p. contains also:
Eccard, Johannes, In Dieser
Osterlichen Zeit (SATB,acap);
Eccard, Johannes, Nun Freut Euch,
Liebe Christeng'mein (SSATB,acap)
                                   (D315)
SATB (contains also: Lobt Gott Mit
Schall) SCHWEIZER. SK 57.01-2
s.p. see also MUSIKBEILAGE ZUM
"EVANGELISCHEN KIRCHENCHOR 1957"
                                   (D316)

DUE CANTI NATAIZI
(Malatesta, Gianni) 4pt men cor
ZANIBON 5427 s.p.
contains: Natale E Amore; Puer
Natus   (D317)

DUE CANTICHE RELIGIOSE see Toni, Alceo

DUE MOTETTI see Veretti, Antonio

DUE SALMI IN MEMORIA DI ALFREDO CASELLA
see Mortari, Virgilio

DUFAY, GUILLAUME (ca. 1400-1474)
Ave Regina Coelorum
4pt,acap voc pt HENN 901 s.p.
                                   (D318)
Missa Caput *Mass,Renais
(Planchart, Alejandro E.) cor bds
A-R ED $9.95 contains also:
Obrecht, Jacob, Missa Caput;
Ockeghem, Johannes, Missa Caput
                                   (D319)

DUIS, ERNST (1896-1967)
Alte Weihnachtliche Lieder *CCU,Xmas
2-3pt mix cor,acap/kbd (easy) sc
SCHOTTS B 166 s.p.   (D320)

DULICHIUS, PHILIPPUS (1562-1631)
Deus, Venerunt Gentes *mot
SSAT&AATB HANSSLER 1.505 s.p.
                                   (D321)
Omnes Gentes Plaudite Maibus *mot
SATB&SATB HANSSLER 1.504 s.p.
                                   (D322)
Omnes Gentes Plaudite Manibus *mot
SATB&SATB HANSSLER 1.504 s.p.
                                   (D323)

DUM MEDITOR QUONDAM see Lassus, Roland
de (Orlandus)

DUM TRANSISSET SABATUM see Taverner,
John

DUMONT, [HENRI] (1610-1684)
Agnus Dei
(Selen, E.) 3-5pt mix cor ERIKS 52
s.p.   (D324)

Cantate Domino
(Selen, E.) 4pt mix cor ERIKS 165
s.p.   (D325)

DUMONT, [HENRI] (cont'd.)

Kyrie
(Selen, E.) 5pt mix cor,opt soli
ERIKS 60 s.p.   (D326)

Magnificat Du Premier Ton
(Selen, E.) 4pt mix cor ERIKS 158
s.p.   (D327)

Media Vita In Morte Sumus
(Selen, E.) "Mitt I Var Levnad Av
Doden Fangna" 4pt mix cor ERIKS
169 s.p.   (D328)

Mitt I Var Levnad Av Doden Fangna
*see Media Vita In Morte Sumus

DUNAJEWSKY, A. (1843-1911)
Israelitische Tempel Compositionen
*CC30U,Sab-Eve/Sab-Morn
mix cor,solo SAC.MUS.PR. S.M.P. 18
$10.00   (D329)

DUNFORD, BENJAMIN
Te Deum Laudamus
mix cor BRODT 569 $.45   (D330)

We Come To Meet Thee Lord
SATB,acap FISCHER,J FEC 10114 $.30
(D331)

DUNHAM, ARTHUR
O Come, Let Us Sing
SATB,B solo (diff) FITZSIMONS 2001
$.25   (D332)

DUNLOP, MERRILL
All Day Long My Heart Keeps Singing
*anthem/gospel
(DeCou, Harold) SATB oct SINGSPIR
ZJP-8182 $.30   (D333)

Amen! Hallelujah! *anthem/gospel
(DeCou, Harold) SATB oct SINGSPIR
ZJP-8176 $.30   (D334)

Christ Is Risen Fron The Dead
*Easter,anthem
(DeCou, Harold) SATB oct SINGSPIR
ZJP-3515 $.30   (D335)

Contentment In His Love *anthem/
gospel
(DeCou, Harold) SATB oct SINGSPIR
ZJP-8077 $.30   (D336)

He Was Wounded For Our Trangressions
*anthem
(Mickelson, P.) SATB oct SINGSPIR
ZJP-8197 $.30   (D337)

I Believe That Jesus Died For Me
*Easter,anthem/gospel
SATB oct SINGSPIR ZJP-8173 $.25
(D338)

Lord, I Want A Diadem! *anthem/
gospel
(Johnson, Norman) SAB oct SINGSPIR
ZJP-8056 $.25   (D339)

My Sins Are Blotted Out I Know
*anthem/gospel
(Carmichael, Ralph) SATB oct
SINGSPIR ZJP-8012 $.30   (D340)
(Ferrin, Paul) SATB oct SINGSPIR
ZJP-8084 $.25   (D341)

Ye Shall Know The Truth *anthem/
gospel
SATB oct SINGSPIR ZJP-8170 $.25
(D342)

DUNSTABLE, JOHN (ca. 1385-1453)
Complete Works *sac/sec,CCU
cor GALAXY AMS 9.0002.08 $27.50
(D343)

Magnificat Secundi Toni *Magnif
(Pernye) wom cor/men cor/mix cor,
acap oct EULENBURG 10072 s.p.
(D344)

DUO CANTICA see Lvoff

DURANTE, FRANCESCO (1684-1755)
Misericordias Domini In Aeternum
Cantabo *mot
SATB&SATB (two motets) HANSSLER
1.507 s.p.   (D345)

DURCH DEIN GEFANGNIS, GOTTES SOHN see
Bach, Johann Sebastian

DURHAN
All Glory, Laud And Honor *Easter/
Lent,hymn
(Fettke) SATB,brass oct LILLENAS
AN-6033 $.35   (D346)

DURRETT
Pass It On *folk
(Kerrick) SATB/jr cor oct LILLENAS
AN-5092 $.30   (D347)

DUSON, DEDE
New Silent Night, A *Xmas
SATB,acap oct AGAPE AG 7186 $.30
(D348)

DUSSEK, JOHANN LADISLAUS (1760-1812)
Two Carols *CC2U,Xmas,carol
SA BOOSEY-CAN s.p.   (D349)

DUSTY ROAD, THE see Klevdal, T.

DVORAK, ANTONIN (1841-1904)
Agnus Dei
see Dvorak, Antonin, Sanctus

Benedictus
see Dvorak, Antonin, Sanctus

Come To Me *Commun/Lent,anthem
(Hughes) SATB oct LORENZ B231 $.35
(D350)
(Hughes, Robert J.) SATB (med easy)
oct LORENZ B231 $.35   (D351)

Credo (from Orgelmesse D-Dur) Credo
SATB,SATB soli,org CARUS CV40.100-3
s.p.   (D352)

Gloria (from Orgelmesse D-Dur) Gloria
SATB,SATB soli,org CARUS
CV 40.100-2 s.p.   (D353)

Kyrie (from Orgelmesse D-Dur) Kyrie
SATB,SATB soli,org CARUS
CV 40.100-1 s.p.   (D354)

Mass In D Major *Op.86, Mass
[Lat] mix cor,2ob,2bsn,3horn,2trp,
3trom,timp,org,strings SUPRAPHON
s.p.   (D355)
"Orgelmesse D-Dur" SATB,SATB soli,
org CARUS CV 40.100 s.p.   (D356)

Orgelmesse D-Dur *see Mass In D
Major

Psalm 149 *Op.79
[Czech/Eng/Ger] mix cor,2fl,2ob,
2clar,2bsn,4horn,2trp,3trom,tuba,
timp,org,strings SUPRAPHON s.p.
(D357)

Requiem *Op.89, cant
[Lat] mix cor,SATB soli,3fl,3ob,
3clar,3bsn,4horn,4trp,3trom,tuba,
org,perc,strings SUPRAPHON s.p.
(D358)

Saint Ludmila *Op.71, ora
[Czech/Eng/Ger] mix cor,soli,2fl,
3ob,3clar,3bsn,4horn,3trp,3trom,
tuba,timp,perc,harp,org,strings
SUPRAPHON s.p.   (D359)

Sanctus *Allelu/Bene/Sanctus
SATB,SATB soli,org CARUS
CV 40.100-4 s.p. contains also:
Benedictus; Agnus Dei   (D360)

Stabat Mater *Op.58, cant
[Lat] mix cor,SATB soli,2fl,3ob,
2clar,2bsn,4horn,2trp,3trom,tuba,
timp,org,strings SUPRAPHON s.p.
(D361)

Te Deum
SATB SCHIRM.G 2960 $2.00   (D362)

Te Deum Laudamus *Op.103
[Lat] mix cor,soli,2fl,3ob,2clar,
2bsn,4horn,2trp,3trom,tuba,timp,
perc,strings SUPRAPHON s.p.
(D363)

DWELLING IN BEULAH LAND see Milano, R.

DYKES
Eternal Father, Strong To Save
*anthem
(Burroughs) SATB,brass oct LILLENAS
AN-2385 $.30   (D364)

DYKES, JOHN BACCHUS (1823-1876)
Lead, Kindly Light *hymn
(Lister, Mosie) SATB oct LILLENAS
AL-1040 $.30   (D365)

DYSON, GEORGE (1883-1964)
Agincourt
SATB,SATB soli,2fl,2ob,2clar,2bsn,
4horn,3trp,3trom,tuba,timp,perc,
harp,strings voc sc NOVELLO
rental   (D366)

Christmas Garland, A
SSA,Mez solo,strings voc sc NOVELLO
rental   (D367)

Hierusalem
SATB,S solo,strings,opt harp,org
voc sc NOVELLO rental   (D368)

Nebuchadnezzar
SATB,TBar soli,3fl,pic,3ob,3clar,
3bsn,4horn,3trp,3trom,tuba,timp,
perc,harp,org,strings voc sc
NOVELLO rental   (D369)

Three Choral Hymns *CC3U,hymn
SATB,SATB soli,strings voc sc
NOVELLO rental   (D370)

Three Songs Of Praise *CC3U
SATB,SATB soli,2trp,3trom,timp,
strings voc sc NOVELLO rental

DYSON, GEORGE (cont'd.)

(D371)

E

EACH FAMILY THINE OWN see Eichorn, Hermene Warlick

EACH STEP I TAKE see Mercer, W. Elmo

EACH STEP OF THE WAY see Harper, Redd

EAGLE, M. ROSALYN
Jesus Of Nazareth *Easter
cor&jr cor,narrator LILLENAS ME-223
$.60   (E1)

EARLS, PAUL
Brevis Mass
SATB,SSAAT soli,org,perc SCHIRM.EC
2751 s.p., ipr   (E2)

EARLY AMERICAN ANTHEM BOOK, THE *CCU,
anthem,US
(Davis, Katherine K.) SATB,kbd GALAXY
1.2587.1 $2.25   (E3)

EARLY AMERICAN CHRISTMAS TRIPTYCH, AN
see Read

EARLY AMERICAN FOLK HYMNS - SPIRITUALS
*CC14UL,anthem/folk/hymn/spir,US
(Wells, Dorothy) unis/SAB/SB/SA
LORENZ $1.95   (E4)

EARLY EASTER MORNING see Weigl, Karl

EARLY IN THE MORNING see Van Iderstine,
A.P.

EARTH IS THE LORD'S see Lovelace,
Austin C.

EARTH IS THE LORD'S, THE see Beebe,
Hank

EARTH IS THE LORD'S, THE see Pierne,
Paul

EARTH IS THE LORD'S, THE see Pratt, G.

EARTH TO ASHES see Cassler, G. Winston

EARTH TODAY GREETS ITS LORD
see As With Gladness Men Of Old

EARTH WILL SING, THE see Hauge

EARTH WITH JOY CONFESSES see Lovelace,
Austin C.

EASTER ALLELUIA, AN see Butler

EASTER ALLELUIA, AN see Peterson, John
W.

EASTER ALLELUYA, AN see Pasquet, Jean

EASTER CAROL *Easter
(Fearing, John) SSA (easy) WATERLOO
$.30   (E5)

EASTER CAROL see Ives, Charles

EASTER CAROL see Pinkham, Daniel

EASTER CAROL see Powell, Robert J.

EASTER CAROL see Van Hulse, Camil

EASTER CAROL see Williams, David H.

EASTER CAROL, AN see Bevan, Gwilym

EASTER CAROLS NEW AND OLD *CC68U,
Easter
mix cor LILLENAS ME-8 $1.00   (E6)

EASTER CHIME see Young

EASTER CHOIR, THE *CCUL,Easter/Holywk/
Palm
(Rasley, John M.) SATB SINGSPIR 5330
$1.50   (E7)

EASTER DAWN see Saar, Louis Victor

EASTER DAY see Drayton, Paul

EASTER DAY see Rose, Michael

EASTER EPISODES see Wilkinson

EASTER FANFARE see Van Iderstine, A.P.

EASTER FANFARE ANTHEM see Corina, John

EASTER FESTIVAL, AN see Rogers

EASTER GLORY see Cassler, G. Winston

EASTER HYMN see Melleci, Adelmo

EASTER HYMN see Rasley, John M.

EASTER JOY see Hafso

EASTER JOY see Osterfreude

EASTER MORNING see Weigl, Vally, Soli
Deo Gloria

EASTER NARRATIVE see Jennings, Kenneth
L.

EASTER PRAISE see Campra, Andre

EASTER REJOICING, AN see Parker, Alice

EASTER SEQUENCE see Leighton, Kenneth

EASTER SONG see Herring, Anne

EASTER SONG see Peterson, John W.

EASTER SONG see Vantine

EASTER SONG see Wild, Eric

EASTER SONG see Williams, David

EASTER SONG OF PRAISE, AN see Riemann,
H.

EASTER SONG OF THE PASCHAL LAMB see
Brandon, George

EASY ANTHEMS FOR CHILDREN'S VOICES
*CCU,anthem
jr cor (easy) BROADMAN 4526-07 $1.25
(E8)

EASY DOES IT *CCU
(McClard, LeRoy) jr cor/sr cor
BROADMAN 4520-24 $1.50   (E9)

EASY RESPONSES FROM EARLY AMERICA
*CCU,cor-resp
(Van Camp, Leonard) SATB oct SCHMITT
8071 $.50   (E10)

EASY SONGS FOR MEN'S CHORUS *CC10U
(Hall, O.D.) 1-2pt men cor,kbd
BROADMAN 4522-12 $2.25   (E11)

EATON, RICHARD S.
Blest Are The Pure In Heart
SATB (med) WATERLOO $.40   (E12)

EBELING, JOHANN GEORG (1637-1676)
All My Heart This Night Rejoices
*Xmas
(Locklair, D.) SATB,org FISCHER,J
FEC 10117 $.35   (E13)

Warum Sollt Ich Mich Denn Gramen
SATB,opt 2treb inst (contains also:
Gott Sei Dank Durch Alle Welt;
Wie Schon Leuchtet Der
Morgenstern) SCHWEIZER.
SK 69.01-2 s.p. see also
MUSIKBEILAGE ZUM "EVANGELISCHEN
KIRCHENCHOR 1969"   (E14)

Zeuch Ein Zu Deinen Toren
SATB,2treb inst (contains also:
Lobet Den Herren, Alle Heiden)
SCHWEIZER. SK 63.07 s.p. see also
MUSIKBEILAGE ZUM "EVANGELISCHEN
KIRCHENCHOR 1963"   (E15)

EBEN, PETR (1929-   )
Dominica De Passione *Psntd
[Lat/Ger] unis,org (med) cmplt ed
BAREN. BA6250 BA6254 s.p. see
from Liturgische Gesange   (E16)

Dominica IV In Quadragesima *Lent
[Lat/Ger] unis,org (med) cmplt ed
BAREN. BA6250 BA6253 s.p. see
from Liturgische Gesange   (E17)

Festum Omnium Sanctorum *ASD
[Lat/Ger] unis,org (med) cmplt ed
BAREN. BA6250 BA6260 s.p. see
from Liturgische Gesange   (E18)

Festum Sacratissimi Cordis Jesu
[Lat/Ger] unis,org (med, Sacred
Heart of Jesus) cmplt ed BAREN.
BA6250 BA6257 s.p. see from
Liturgische Gesange   (E19)

In Ascensione Domine *Asc
[Lat/Ger] unis,org (med) cmplt ed
BAREN. BA6250 BA6255 s.p. see
from Liturgische Gesange   (E20)

In Conceptione Immaculata B.M.V.
*BVM
[Lat/Ger] unis,org (med) cmplt ed
BAREN. BA6250 BA6251 s.p. see
from Liturgische Gesange   (E21)

In Festo Corporis Christi *Corpus
[Lat/Ger] unis,org (med) cmplt ed
BAREN. BA6250 BA6256 s.p. see
from Liturgische Gesange   (E22)

EBEN, PETR (cont'd.)

In Festo D.N. Jesu Christi Regis
[Lat/Ger] unis,org (med, Christ The
King) cmplt ed BAREN. BA6250
BA6259 s.p. see from Liturgische
Gesange   (E23)

In Praesentatione Domine
[Lat/Ger] unis,org (med, Candlemas)
cmplt ed BAREN. BA6250 BA6252
s.p. see from Liturgische Gesange
(E24)

Liturgische Gesange *see Dominica De
Passione; Dominica IV In
Quadragesima; Festum Omnium
Sanctorum; Festum Sacratissimi
Cordis Jesu; In Ascensione
Domine; In Conceptione Immaculata
B.M.V.; In Festo Corporis
Christi; In Festo D.N. Jesu
Christi Regis; In Praesentatione
Domine; Theresiae A Jesu Infante
(E25)

Theresiae A Jesu Infante
[Lat/Ger] unis,org (med) cmplt ed
BAREN. BA6250 BA6258 s.p. see
from Liturgische Gesange   (E26)

EBERLE, KARL
Requiem Und Libera *Op.26
[Lat] SA&opt TB,org sc,cor pts BOHM
s.p.   (E27)

EBERLIN, JOHANN ERNST (1702-1762)
Dixit Dominus
see Eberlin, Johann Ernst, Te Deum

Magnificat
see Eberlin, Johann Ernst, Te Deum

People Know Thee
(Hilton, Arthur) SATB,acap MERCURY
352-00471 $.40   (E28)

Te Deum
(Pauly, Reinhard G.) cor,orch bds
A-R ED $9.95 contains also: Dixit
Dominus; Magnificat   (E29)

EBNER, HANS
Deutsche Messe *Op.141, Mass
[Ger] 4pt mix cor,org sc,cor pts
PELIKAN PE939   (E30)

ECCARD, JOHANNES (1553-1611)
Anbetung Der Weisen "Aus Jakobs Stamm
Ein Stern So Klar"
SSATB SCHWEIZER. SK 139 s.p.   (E31)

Ich Steh An Deiner Krippe Hier
SSATB SCHWEIZER. SK 60.03 s.p. see
also MUSIKBEILAGE ZUM
"EVANGELISCHEN KIRCHENCHOR 1960"
(E32)

In Dieser Osterlichen Zeit
see Ducis, Benedictus, Nun Freut
Euch, Lieben Christeng'mein

In Dulci Jubilo
SATTB,acap (med easy) sc SCHOTTS
C 38 069C s.p. contains also:
Raselius, Andreas, Nun Komm, Der
Heiden Heiland (SSATB,acap) (E33)

Mag Ich Ungluck Nit Widerstahn *mot
SATB LAUDINELLA LR 139 s.p.   (E34)

Nun Freut Euch, Liebe Christeng'mein
see Ducis, Benedictus, Nun Freut
Euch, Lieben Christeng'mein

O Lamm Gottes
5pt mix cor LIENAU
MUSICA SACRA, NR. 25 cor pts
s.p., sc s.p.   (E35)

Two Sacred Songs *CC2U
[Ger] 5-6pt PETERS 4881 $.50   (E36)

Verleih Uns Frieden Gnadiglich
SATTB DOBLINGER S 206 s.p.   (E37)

When To The Temple Mary Went
(Bevan, G.) SATB (med easy)
WATERLOO $.30   (E38)

ECCE, AGNUS DEI see Stout, Alan

ECCE ANCILLI DOMINI see Drayton

ECCE CONCIPIES see Gallus, Jacobus

ECCE DIES, NIGRAS see Lassus, Roland de
(Orlandus)

ECCE DIES VENIET see Lassus, Roland de
(Orlandus)

ECCE HOMO see Reda, Siegfried

ECCE NUNC BENEDICITE DOMINUM see
Victoria, Tomas Luis de

ECCE QUOMODO MORITUM JUSTIS see Gallus,
Jacobus

ECCE, QUOMODO MORITUR see Gallus,
Jacobus

ECCE SACERDOS see Bruckner, Anton

ECCE SACERDOS see Erhard, Karl

ECCE SACERDOS see Gruber, Joseph

ECCE SACERDOS see Hilber

ECCE SACERDOS see Hunecke, Wilhelm

ECCE SACERDOS see Kromolicki, Joseph

ECCE SACERDOS see Lampart, Karl

ECCE SACERDOS see Messner, Joseph

ECCE SACERDOS see Trapp, Willy

ECCE SACERDOS see Weirich, August

ECCE SACERDOS see Weis-Ostborn, Rudolf
von

ECCE SACERDOS MAGNUS see Haas, Joseph

ECCE SACERDOS MAGNUS see Jenni, Donald

ECCE TU PULCHRA ES see Des Prez,
Josquin

ECCE VIRGO see Isaac, Heinrich

ECCE VIRGO CONCIPIET see Rehmann, Th.

ECCLESIASTES 4:11 see Courtney, Ragan

ECHO CAROL *Xmas,carol
(Cromie, Marguerite Biggs) 3 eq
voices/3 cor,opt pno (very easy)
PRESSER 312-41078 $.40   (E39)

ECLOGUE, ENCOMIUM AND EVOCATION see
Bassett, Leslie

EDGAR
God, Who Touchest Earth With Beauty
(composed with Butler) *anthem
unis (easy) oct BROADMAN 4558-23
$.30   (E40)

EDLER, ROBERT
De Profundis
men cor,2trp,2horn,2trom,tuba,timp
sc,cor pts TONOS 4928 s.p., ipa
                               (E41)

EDMUNDS
My Faith Has Found A Resting Place
*see Danner

EDSON
Blow Ye The Trumpet, Blow *anthem
(Burroughs) SATB,trp oct LILLENAS
AN-6019 $.35   (E42)

EDWARDS, P.M.H.
I Sing Of A Maiden
mix cor LESLIE 4096 $.30   (E43)

EENS BREEKT IN MIJ HET ZILV'REN KOORD
mix cor sc HEER 2802 s.p.   (E44)

EFFINGER
Cantata For Easter *Easter,cant
SATB SCHIRM.G 2849 $1.50   (E45)

EFFINGER, CECIL (1914-   )
This We Believe
mix cor,2 soli BROADMAN 4519-06
$4.50   (E46)

EGEBJER, LARS
Advent
4pt mix cor ERIKS 12 s.p.   (E47)

"Till Frojd Forutan Ande" *cant
4pt mix cor,orch voc sc ERIKS 6
s.p., cor pts ERIKS 7 s.p., ipa
                               (E48)

EGENER
Lord's Prayer
SATB (med easy) WATERLOO $.30 (E49)

EGIDI
Psalm 84 *Op.6
LIENAU sc s.p., cor pts s.p.   (E50)

EGK, WERNER (1901-   )
Alleluia Let Us Sing *see Alleluia
Psallat

Alleluia Psallat *mot
"Alleluia Let Us Sing" [Eng/Lat]
SMezA/TBarB (med) sc SCHOTTS
SL 5225 s.p.   (E51)

Angelus Ad Virginem *Xmas
[Eng/Lat] 3-6pt mix cor,acap/inst
(med easy) sc SCHOTTS SL 39 955
s.p.   (E52)

EGK, WERNER (cont'd.)

Beata Viscera *Xmas
"Blessed Virgin, The" [Eng/Lat]
ATB/TTB (med easy) sc SCHOTTS
SL 5226 s.p.   (E53)

Blessed Virgin, The *see Beata
Viscera

EGLIN, ARTHUR (1932-   )
Das Gleichnis Vom Reichen Narren,
"Seht Zu Und Hutet Euch Vor Dem
Geiz"
SATB,opt org/brass LAUDINELLA
LR 101 s.p.   (E54)

Das Reich Der Himmel "Die Herren Der
Welt Kommen Und Gehen"
3pt&SATB,kbd LAUDINELLA LR 129 s.p.
contains also: Der Name
"Vielleicht, Dass Heisenberg
Wirklich" (SSA&cong,bass inst)
                               (E55)

Der Name "Vielleicht, Dass Heisenberg
Wirklich"
see Eglin, Arthur, Das Reich Der
Himmel "Die Herren Der Welt
Kommen Und Gehen"

Ich Schau Nach Jenen Bergen Fern
(Psalm 121)
SAT/SAB/SATB,2trp,2trom SCHWEIZER.
SK 160 s.p.   (E56)

Nun Saget Dank Und Lobt Den Herren
SATB&SATB/1-2pt,opt org/brass/treb
inst LAUDINELLA LR 39 s.p.   (E57)

Psalm 121 *see Ich Schau Nach Jenen
Bergen Fern

Sonne Der Gerechtigkeit
SSATB/SATB/ATB/SSAB/SS/unis,2trp,
trom LAUDINELLA LR 6 s.p.   (E58)

Wer Unter Dem Schirm Des Hochsten
Sitzt
SATB&SAT/SAB,opt inst LAUDINELLA
LR 83 s.p.   (E59)

Wohl Dem, Der Nicht Den Weg Des
Frevlers Wahlt
SAT/SAB/SS/SB,opt trp,trom
(contains also: Gott Des Himmels
Und Der Erden) SCHWEIZER.
SK 59.03-4 s.p. see also
MUSIKBEILAGE ZUM "EVANGELISCHEN
KIRCHENCHOR 1959"   (E60)

Zwei Jesusgebete *CC2U
unis,solo,org,opt treb inst
LAUDINELLA LR 143 s.p.   (E61)

EGO SUM PASTOR BONUS see Doebler, Curt

EGO SUM PASTOR BONUS see Frommlet,
Franz

EGYNEMUKAROK see Szabo, [Ferenc]

EHEU SUSTULERUNT DOMINUM see Morley,
Thomas

EHR' SEI DEM VATER, SOHN UND GEIST see
Strauss-Konig, Richard

EHRE SEI DEM VATER see Kronberg, G.

EHRE SEI DEM VATER see Schutz, Heinrich

EHRE SEI GOTT see Bortniansky, Dimitri
Stepanovitch, Doxologie: Gloria In
Excelsis

EHRE SEI GOTT BAND I *CC246U
2-5 eq voices,opt inst HANSSLER 2.029
s.p. contains works by: Bach;
Franck; Handel; Praetorius; Schutz;
Vulpius; and others   (E62)

EHRE SEI GOTT IN DER HOHE see Hunecke,
Wilhelm

EHRE SEI GOTT IN DER HOHE see
Zimmermann, Heinz Werner

EHRE SIE GOTT IN DER HOHE see Schubert,
Franz (Peter)

EHRET, WALTER (1918-   )
Amen *Xmas
SATB RICHMOND MI-90 $.35   (E63)

Anthems For Children's Voices *CCU,
Xmas/Easter/Gen,anthem
1-2pt jr cor,opt fl,trp,inst
BROADMAN 4560-39 $1.75   (E64)

Can't You Hear What My Lord Said
*anthem
SATB (easy) oct BROADMAN 4545-66
$.30   (E65)

EHRET, WALTER (cont'd.)

Child Of God
SAB SHAWNEE D186 $.35   (E66)
TTBB SHAWNEE C240 $.35   (E67)

Children Of Jerusalem
SA/TB SHAWNEE E5170 $.35   (E68)

Come Your Hearts And Voices Raising
SA/TB SHAWNEE E5173 $.30   (E69)

God Is Wisdom, God Is Love
SATB SHAWNEE A5670 $.30   (E70)

How Small Art Thou, How Weak And
Helpless *Xmas,anthem
2pt,opt fl FINE ARTS CM 1113 $.35 (E71)

In Bethlehem Is Born A King *anthem
SAB,kbd,opt vcl AUGSBURG 11-1708
$.40   (E72)

Mary Is Rocking Her Babe
SA/TB SHAWNEE E5172 $.30   (E73)

Old Ark's A Moverin', The *spir
SSA&opt camb CAMBIATA S97204 $.40
                               (E74)
SABar&opt camb CAMBIATA 597205 $.40
                               (E75)

Shepherds Rejoice Lift Up Your Eyes
SAB SHAWNEE D5223 $.35   (E76)

Sing We All Now Alleluia *Easter,
anthem
SATB,2trp,2trom BROADMAN 4563-03
$.50   (E77)
SATB,brass oct BROADMAN 4563-03
$.50   (E78)

This Day Our Lord Is Born *Xmas,
anthem
SA,pno,opt fl AUGSBURG 11-0316 $.35
                               (E79)

Thy Blessing, Lord, Grant Unto Me
*anthem
SAB oct BROADMAN 4551-75 $.30 (E80)

To Us A Child Of Royal Birth
SAB SHAWNEE $.35   (E81)

Who's The Little Baby *Xmas
SATB RICHMOND MI-88 $.35   (E82)

EICHORN, HERMENE WARLICK (1906-   )
Each Family Thine Own
mix cor BRODT 531 $.20   (E83)

I Know
mix cor BRODT 551 $.22   (E84)

In A Stable Heavenly Bright
mix cor BRODT 552 $.22   (E85)

Master Of Eager Youth
unis BRODT 528 $.25   (E86)

So Let Me Live
SSA BRODT 580 $.26   (E87)

EIDSVOOG
He Is Born *Xmas
SSA oct SCHMITT 2904 $.40   (E88)

EIGHT BURGUNDIAN CAROLS *CC8U,Xmas,
carol,Fr
(Bartholomew, M.) SATB GALAXY
1.1684.1 $1.25   (E89)

EIGHT CHRISTMAS CAROLS: SET 1 *Xmas,
carol
(Rutter) SATB,inst (easy) OXFORD
48.008 $1.20, ipr
contains: Angel Tidings; Il Est Ne;
In Dulci Jubilo; Of The Father's
Love Begotten   (E90)

EIGHT CHRISTMAS CAROLS: SET 2 *Xmas,
carol
(Rutter) SATB,inst (easy) OXFORD
48.009 $1.20
contains: Down In Yon Forest; I Saw
Three Ships; Quelle Est Cette
Odeur?; Twelve Days Of Christmas
                               (E91)

EIGHT FOLKSONGS AND SPIRITUALS *CC8U,
anthem
(Johnson, David N.) TBB,opt gtr
AUGSBURG 11-1718 $.45   (E92)

EIGHT FOR CHRISTMAS *sac/sec,CC8U,
Xmas,carol,Fr
(Ratcliffe, Desmond) SATB NOVELLO
s.p.   (E93)

EIGHT TRADITIONAL ENGLISH CAROLS
*CC8L,carol,Eng
(Vaughan Williams, Ralph) unis&SATB
GALAXY   (E94)

EIGHTEEN LENTEN MOTETS (TENEBRAE
RESPONSORIA) see Victoria, Tomas
Luis de

EILERS, JOYCE ELAINE
My Lord
3pt LEONARD-US 08545500 $.50   (E95)

Silent Night *Xmas,carol
SATB MCAFEE M1089 $.40   (E96)

Thy Will Be Done
mix cor,Bar solo,pno HERITAGE H131
$.35   (E97)

EIN DANKLIED SEI DEM HERRN see Woss,
Josef Venantius von

EIN DEUTSCHES GLORIA "SING DEM HERRN
EIN LIED" see Haas, Joseph

EIN DEUTSCHES REQUIEM see Brahms,
Johannes

EIN FESTE BURG IS UNSER GOTT see
Borris, Siegfried

EIN FESTE BURG IST UNSER GOTT see
Diener, Theodor

EIN FESTE BURG IST UNSER GOTT see
Praetorius, Michael

EIN FESTE BURG IST UNSER GOTT see
Schutz, Heinrich

EIN FESTE BURG IST UNSER GOTT see
Borris, Siegfried

EIN FROLICH GESANG *anthem/folk
"Alleluia" see Four Easter Chorales
(Mercer, W. Elmo) "Alleluia!" SATB
oct BENSON S4016 $.30   (E98)
(Mickelson, P.) "Alleluia!" SATB
oct SINGSPIR ZJP-8195 $.30   (E99)
(Parks) "Alleluia" 2pt oct BROADMAN
4551-00 $.30   (E100)
(Wilson, J.F.) "Alleluia" SSA,pno,fl/
ob oct HOPE CF 179 $.40 contains
also: God Is So Good (SSA) (Afr)
(E101)
(Wyrtzen, Don) "Alleluia!" SATB oct
SINGSPIR ZJP-5052 $.30   (E102)

EIN HAUS VOLL GLORIE SCHAUET see
Govert, Willibald

EIN JEGLICHES HAT SEINE ZEIT see
Pepping, Ernst

EIN KIND GEBORN ZU BETHLEHEM *Xmas,
carol/folk
(Bausznern, D. von) [Ger] 4pt men cor
MERSEBURG EM9059   (E103)
(Biebl, F.) [Ger] 5pt men cor
MERSEBURG EM 9041   (E104)

EIN KIND IST UNS GEBOREN see Miller,
Franz R.

EIN KIND IST UNS GEBOREN see Seckinger,
Konrad

EIN KLEINES CHRISTKIND see Bausznern,
Dietrich von

EIN LAMMLEIN GEHT UND TRAGT DIE SCHULD
see Lohr, Ina

EIN LIEBLICH ENGELSPIEL see Rein,
Walter

EIN LOB- UND DANKLIED "O GROSSER GOTT,
DICH LOBEN WIR" see Haydn, (Johann)
Michael

EIN LOBLIED see Schmid, Walter

EIN TAG, DER SAGT'S DEM ANDERN see
Etti, Karl

EIN TRAUM IST UNSER LEBEN see Grosse-
Schware, Hermann

EINARSSON, SIGFUS
Two Hymns *CC2U,hymn
mix cor,org/pno ICELAND s.p. (E105)

EINE DEUTSCHE LIEDMESSE see Fortner,
Wolfgang

EINE KLEINE WEIL see Frey, Carl

EINE VIELZAHL *CC9L,Xmas
mix cor,inst BOHM s.p. contains works
by: Bach; Handel; Hollfelder, ;
Kutzer   (E106)

EINS BITT ICH VOM HERREN see Hartmann,
Heinrich

EINSTIMMIGES REQUIEM UND LIBERA see
Mayer, Alfonso

EKLOF, EINAR (1886-1954)
Lovsang
4pt mix cor ERIKS 341 s.p.   (E107)
men cor ERIKS 341 s.p.   (E108)

EKSTASE "GOTT, DEINE HIMMEL" see Weber,
Bernhard

EL MOLE RACHAMIN see Holde, Arthur

EL REY QUE MUNCHO MADRUGA see Rodrigo

ELAINE, SISTER M. (GENTEMANN)
Mass In D *Mass
SA,org GIA G1932 $1.00   (E109)

ELCKERLYC-EVERYMAN see Monnikendam,
Marius

ELDER, DOROTHY KOSANKE
Christ Is Born Today
see Christmas Triptych, A

Christmas Triptych, A *Xmas
1-2pt, Orff Instruments CHORISTERS
A-90 $.30
contains: Christ Is Born Today
(anthem); Gloria In Excelsis
Deo (Introit); What Can I Give
Him? (CC,anthem/cor-resp/
prayer)   (E110)

Gloria In Excelsis Deo
see Christmas Triptych, A

Sing We A Glad Noel *Adv/Xmas
unis,fl,bells, glockenspiel ART
MAST 242 $.35   (E111)

What Can I Give Him?
see Christmas Triptych, A

ELDRIDGE, GUY H. (1904-   )
Hymn To God The Father
SATB,acap ROBERTON 85015 s.p.
(E112)

Strengthen All Thy Servants
mix cor CRAMER $.25   (E113)
SATB,org CRAMER A21   (E114)

ELEAZER see Foxx, Charles

ELEGERUNT APOSTOLI see Kromolicki,
Joseph

ELEGERUNT APOSTOLI see Lauterbach,
Lorenz

ELEIOTT, MAX
He Came, He'll Come Again
(Krogstad, Bob) SATB,opt 2fl&ob&
2clar&2horn&3trp&3trom&3vln&vla&
vcl&bvl&timp&2perc&harp voc sc
GOSPEL 05 TM 0353 $.35, sc GOSPEL
05 TM 0354 $15.00   (E115)

He Lives *see Krogstad, Bob

Rejoice (composed with Krogstad, Bob)
*Xmas,cant,Contemp
SATB/SSATB,pno,fl, or C inst (easy,
recording or tape also available)
cor pts GOSPEL 05 TM 0474 $1.75
(E116)
SATB/SSATB,2fl,ob,2clar,2horn,3trp,
3trom,timp,3vln.vla.vcl.bvl,
2perc,harp (easy, recording or
tape also available) sc GOSPEL
ipr   (E117)

ELEVEN MOTETS see Rogier, Philippe

ELEVEN WORKS TO LATIN TEXTS see
Corteccia, Francesco Bernardo

ELGAR, EDWARD (1857-1934)
Apostles, The *Op.49
SATB,SATBBB soli,3fl,3ob,3clar,
3bsn,4horn,3trp,3trom,timp,
perc,2harp,org,strings voc sc
NOVELLO rental   (E118)

Banner Of Saint George
SATB,opt S solo,2fl,pic,2ob,2clar,
2bsn,4horn,3trp,3trom,tuba,timp,
perc,org,strings voc sc NOVELLO
rental   (E119)

Give Unto The Lord (Psalm 29) Op.74
SATB,SATB soli,2fl,2ob,2clar,2bsn,
4horn,2trp,3trom,timp,perc,
harp,org,strings voc sc NOVELLO
rental   (E120)

Great Is The Lord (Psalm 48) Op.67
SATB,B solo,2fl,2ob,2clar,3bsn,
4horn,2trp,3trom,tuba,timp,org,
strings voc sc NOVELLO rental
(E121)

Prologue (from Apostles, The)
SATB,SATB soli,2fl,3ob,3clar,3bsn,
4horn,3trp,3trom,tuba,timp,perc,
2harp,strings voc sc NOVELLO
rental   (E122)

Psalm 29 *see Give Unto The Lord

Psalm 48 *see Great Is The Lord

ELGAR, EDWARD (cont'd.)

Te Deum And Benedictus In F *Op.34
SATB,2fl,2ob,2clar,3bsn,4horn,3trp,
3trom,tuba,timp,perc,org,strings
voc sc NOVELLO rental   (E123)

ELIAS see Mendelssohn-Bartholdy, Felix

ELIASON
Name I Highly Treasure, A *gospel
(Widen) SATB oct LILLENAS AN-1697
$.35   (E124)

ELIJAH! see Wood, Dale

ELIOT
Alleluia! Alleluia! *Easter,anthem
SATB oct LORENZ B226 $.35   (E125)

ELLENBERGER, LORETTA
Lo, I Am With You Always *anthem
(Wilson, J.F.) SATB oct HOPE CF 176
$.40   (E126)

ELLER
All Hail The Power Of Jesus' Name
*anthem
(Schubert) SATB oct LILLENAS
AN-2377 $.35   (E127)

ELLIS
Do You Known My Jesus? (composed with
Lakey) *gospel
(Mickelson, Paul) SSATB oct
LILLENAS AN-1704 $.30   (E128)

Where There Is Love *gospel
SATB oct LILLENAS AN-1667 $.25
(E129)

ELLIS, JAMES
Let Me Touch Him *gospel
(Owens) SATB oct LILLENAS AN-1659
$.35   (E130)

ELLSTROM, EVA E.
His Harbor
see Two Songs Of Praise

Lord Hold My Hand
see Two Songs Of Praise

Two Songs Of Praise
SATB CHAPLET 2005 $.25
contains: His Harbor; Lord Hold
My Hand   (E131)

ELMORE, ROBERT [HALL] (1913-   )
My Soul, Awake! *anthem
SATB WORD CS-338 $.30   (E132)

See, My Soul *anthem
SATB WORD CS-319 $.30   (E133)

What Offering Shall I Bring? *Adv/
Xmas
1-2pt ART MAST 195 $.30   (E134)

ELRICH, DWIGHT
Songs Of Redemption *CC8UL
SATB BROADMAN 4520-18 $1.50   (E135)

ELVEY, GEORGE JOB (1816-1893)
Arise, Shine, For Thy Light Is Come
*Xmas/Gen
(Lutkin) SAB (easy) FITZSIMONS 6010
$.20   (E136)

Christ Is Risen
mix cor BANKS MUS YS 109 $.20
(E137)

Come, Ye Thankful People, Come
*Thanks,anthem
(Anthony, Dick) SATB oct SINGSPIR
ZJP-3101 $.30   (E138)

Crown Him With Many Crowns *Easter,
anthem
(Wyrtzen, Don) SATB oct SINGSPIR
ZJP-3549 $.35   (E139)

Harvest Carol *Thanks
(Schubert) SATB,trp oct LILLENAS
AN-2381 $.40   (E140)

We Wait For Thy Loving Kindness
SS (med easy) OXFORD 44.427 $.45
(E141)

EMBODIED WORD, THE see Pennington,
Chester

EMERGENCY ANTHEM BOOK, THE *CCU
(Hughes, Robert J.) unis/SA/SAB
(easy) LORENZ $1.95   (E142)

EMERY, WALTER J. (1909-1974)
A Vocal Companion To Bach's
Orgelbuchlein, Book Three *see
Bach, Johann Sebastian

EMIG
People Carol, The
SATB SHAWNEE A5688 $.30   (E143)

EMIG, LOIS MYERS
Christmas Festival *Xmas,anthem
unis&unis&unis&unis,opt hndbl oct
SACRED S-6505 $.40   (E144)

EMITTE SPIRITUM see Holler, Karl

EMITTE SPIRITUM TUUM see Schutky, F.J.

EMMANUEL see Batozynski, Larry

EMPTY CAVE, THE see Neff, James

EMPTY HANDS see Fettke, Tom

EN DYR KLENOD, EN KLAR OCH REN see
Bjarnegard, Gustaf

EN DYR KLENOD, EN KLAR OCH REN see
Hassler, Hans Leo

EN ENDA ROST see Soderholm, Valdemar

EN HERRDAG I HOJDEN see Holm, Gunnar

EN HUNDRA ATTA OG FYRTIO PSALMEN UR
PSALTAREN see Robertson, Karl-Olof

EN NATT SOM LYSTE see Hemberg, Eskil

ENATUS EST EMANUEL see Praetorius,
Michael

ENATUS EST EMMANUEL see Praetorius,
Michael

ENCOUNTER see Seabough, Ed.

ENEBERG, GALE (GAIL)
Happy Song, A *Contemp
(Walters, Bob) jr cor oct GOSPEL
05 TM 0158 $.35   (E145)

It's A Young World! *folk
2pt oct SINGSPIR ZJP-5033 $.30
(E146)

Love For Life *folk
(Johnson, Norman) SAB/SATB oct
SINGSPIR ZJP-5007 $.30   (E147)

Peace In Your World *folk
2pt oct SINGSPIR ZJP-5009 $.25
(E148)

ENGEL HABEN HIMMELSLIEDER see
Schroeder, Hermann

ENGEL-TERZETT "HEBE DEINE AUGEN AUF"
see Mendelssohn-Bartholdy, Felix

ENGELHART, F.X.
Veni Creator Spiritus
see Faist, Anton, Veni Creator
Spiritus

ENGLERT, EUGENE
Alleluia! Let The Holy Anthem Rise
*anthem
SATB,chimes,bells/hndbl AUGSBURG
11-1673 $.40   (E149)

Christ Our Light And Life *anthem
SATB,kbd AUGSBURG 11-1750 $.40
(E150)

Come, Christians, Join To Sing
*anthem
SATB (easy) GIA G1840 $.40   (E151)

King Of Love My Shepherd Is, The
*anthem
SATB (easy) GIA G1842 $.40   (E152)

Lord, From Your Cross, Look Upon Us
*Lent,anthem
SATB,acap (easy) GIA G1841 $.40
(E153)

Rejoice, You Pure In Heart *anthem
SATB (easy) GIA G1843 $.40   (E154)

We Sing Excelsis Deo
SATB SHAWNEE A5686 $.35   (E155)

ENGLISH
I Heard The Voice Of Jesus *anthem
(Ralston) 1-2pt oct LILLENAS
AN-6004 $.30   (E156)

ENGLISH MASS, AN see Howells, Herbert
Norman

ENGLISH UNISON MASS (ST. FRANCIS
XAVIER) see Jillett, David

ENTER HIS SANCTUARY SINGING see Hopson,
Hal H.

ENTRUST THY CARES UPON HIM see
Altnikol, Johann Christoph

ENTWISLE
Sweeter Than All *gospel
(Mickelson, Paul) SATB oct LILLENAS
AN-1710 $.25   (E157)

EPILOGUE see Suk, Josef

EPILOGUE "NON NOBIS DOMINE" see
Tippett, Michael

EPIPHANIAS see Zelter, Carl Friedrich

EPIPHANIAS: DIE HEILIGEN DREI KONIGE
see Zelter, Carl Friedrich

EPIPHANY ALLELUIAS see Weaver

EPITAPH FOR THIS WORLD AND TIME see
Hamilton, Iain

EPSTEIN, ALVIN
L'adonai Ha-Arets (Psalm 24)
[Heb] mix cor TRANSCON. TCL 661
$1.00   (E158)

Psalm 24 *see L'adonai Ha-Arets

ER IST ZONNESCHIJN
mix cor sc HEER 2483 s.p.   (E159)

ERBACH, CHRISTIAN (1573-1635)
Regina Coeli
[Lat/Ger] 4pt mix cor,acap BOHM
s.p.   (E160)

ERBARM DICH, HERRE GOTT see Staden,
Johann

ERDE SINGE see Kronberg, G.

ERDE SINGE! see Ophoven, Hermann

ERE ZIJ GOD *Xmas
unis,pno/harmonium HEER 268 s.p.
(E161)

ERFREUE DICH, ERDE see Buxtehude,
Dietrich

ERHALT UNS, HERR, BEI DEINEM WORT see
Crappius, Andreas

ERHALT UNS HERR BEI DEINEM WORT see
Pepping, Ernst

ERHALT UNS, HERR, BEI DEINEM WORT see
Zillinger, Erwin

ERHARD, KARL
Acht Alleluja-Kanons *CC8U,canon
[Lat] 3-4 eq voices/3-4pt mix cor
BOHM s.p.   (E162)

Aeterne Rex
see Erhard, Karl, Gesange Zur
Prozession Am Fronleichnamsfest
see Gesange Zur Prozession Am
Heiligen Fronleichnamsfest

Deutsches Hochamt *Mass
[Ger] mix cor BOHM sc s.p., cor pts
s.p.   (E163)

Ecce Sacerdos
[Lat] 1-4pt,org,2trp,2trom, 2tenor
horns sc,cor pts BOHM s.p., ipa
(E164)

Festliche Messe In C *Mass
[Lat] 4pt mix cor,org/2trp,2trom
sc,cor pts BOHM s.p., ipa (E165)

Gesange Zur Prozession Am
Fronleichnamsfest
[Lat] 4pt mix cor,opt 2trp&2trom
sc,cor pts BOHM s.p., ipa
contains also: Sacris Solemniis;
Verbum Supernum; Salutis Humanae
Sator; Aeterne Rex; Pange Lingua
(E166)

Gesange Zur Prozession Am Heiligen
Fronleichnamsfest
[Lat] 4pt mix cor,opt 2trp&2trom
sc,cor pts BOHM s.p., ipa
contains: Aeterne Rex; Pange
Lingua; Sacris Solemniis;
Salutis Hymanae Sator; Verbum
Supernum   (E167)

Lied Zur Heiligen Nacht "Also Lasst
Uns Wieder Singen" *Xmas
men cor BOHM s.p.   (E168)

Messe In D *Mass
[Lat] 4pt mix cor,org sc,cor pts
BOHM s.p.   (E169)

Messe In E *Mass
[Lat] 4pt mix cor,org sc,cor pts
BOHM s.p.   (E170)

Pange Lingua
see Erhard, Karl, Gesange Zur
Prozession Am Fronleichnamsfest
see Gesange Zur Prozession Am
Heiligen Fronleichnamsfest

Requiem Und Libera
[Lat] 4pt mix cor,acap sc,cor pts
BOHM s.p.   (E171)
[Lat] 1-4pt mix cor,org/2trp&2trom/
org&2trp&2trom sc,cor pts BOHM
s.p., ipa   (E172)
[Lat] 2pt mix cor,org sc,cor pts
BOHM s.p.   (E173)

ERHARD, KARL (cont'd.)

Sacris Solemniis
see Erhard, Karl, Gesange Zur
Prozession Am Fronleichnamsfest
see Gesange Zur Prozession Am
Heiligen Fronleichnamsfest

Salutis Humanae Sator
see Erhard, Karl, Gesange Zur
Prozession Am Fronleichnamsfest

Salutis Hymanae Sator
see Gesange Zur Prozession Am
Heiligen Fronleichnamsfest

Stabat Mater *Psntd
[Lat] cor,S solo,org,fl/ob/clar/vln
sc,cor pts BOHM s.p., ipa   (E174)

Verbum Supernum
see Erhard, Karl, Gesange Zur
Prozession Am Fronleichnamsfest
see Gesange Zur Prozession Am
Heiligen Fronleichnamsfest

ERHARDT
Exalting Season, The
unis/SA (easy) OXFORD 82.094 $.25
(E175)

ERHORE MICH see Schulz, H.

ERICKSON, JOHN
Of The Father's Love Begotten *Gen/
Thanks
unis,hndbl CHORISTERS A-150 $.30
(E176)

ERK
Himmelsknabe
see Zwei Weihnachtsliedlein

Stille Nacht
see Zwei Weihnachtsliedlein

Zwei Weihnachtsliedlein *Xmas
5pt mix cor LIENAU sc s.p., cor pts
s.p.
contains: Himmelsknabe; Stille
Nacht   (E177)

ERNTE DES LEBENS see Ruppel, Paul Ernst

ERRETTE, HERR, MICH VON DEN BOSEN see
Le Jeune, Claude

ERSCHEINEN IST DER HERRLICH TAG see
Oertzen, Rudolf von

ERSCHIENEN IST DER HERRLICH TAG see
Erytraeus, Gottfried

ERSTANDEN IST DER HEILIG CHRIST see
Raselius, Andreas

ERYTRAEUS, GOTTFRIED (1560-1617)
Erschienen Ist Der Herrlich Tag
SATB DOBLINGER S 215-216 s.p.
contains also: Bach, Johann
Sebastian, Beim Letzten
Abendmahle   (E178)

Mitten Wir Im Leben Sind
men cor,acap TONOS 5611 s.p. (E179)

Nun Bitten Wir Den Heiligen Geist
SATB DOBLINGER S 207 s.p.   (E180)
SATB (contains also: Wohlauf, Ihr
Christen, Freuet Ich) SCHWEIZER.
SK 53.05 s.p. see also
MUSIKBEILAGE ZUM "EVANGELISCHEN
KIRCHENCHOR 1953"   (E181)

ES BEGAB SICH see Gebhard, Ludwig

ES BLUHEN DIE MAIEN see Reusch, Fritz

ES BLUHEN DIE MAIEN see Zoll, Paul

ES BLUHEN DREI ROSEN see Zoll, Paul

ES FAND DIE SEELE HEIM see Kutzer,
Ernst

ES FLOG EIN TAUBLEIN see Schieri, Fritz

ES FLOG EIN TAUBLEIN WEISSE see Zipp,
Friedrich

ES FLOG EIN TAUBLIEN WEISSE see
Lemacher, Heinrich

ES GINGEN ZWEEN MENSCHEN see Schutz,
Heinrich

ES HAT SICH HALT EROFFNET *Adv/Xmas
(Bauernfeind, Hans) wom cor,acap oct
DOBLINGER s.p. see also In Dulci
Jubilo   (E182)

ES IST DAS HEIL UNS KOMMEN HER see
Brahms, Johannes

ES IST DAS HEIL UNS KOMMEN HER see
Brahms, Johannes, Es Ist Das Heil
Uns Kommen Her

ES IST DAS HEIL UNS KOMMEN HER see
     Vulpius, Melchior

ES IST EIN FREUD DEM HERZEN MEIN see
     Schutz, Heinrich

ES IST EIN KOSTLICH DING see Michel,
     Paul-Baudouin

ES IST EIN ROS ENTSPRUNGEN see Trexler,
     Georg

ES IST EIN ROS ENTSPRUNGEN *Adv/Xmas
     see In Dulci Jubilo
     (Bauernfeind, Hans) wom cor,acap oct
     DOBLINGER s.p. see also In Dulci
     Jubilo   (E183)

ES IST EIN ROS' ENTSPRUNGEN see Backer,
     Hans

ES IST EIN ROS ENTSPRUNGEN see Bresgen,
     Cesar

ES IST EIN ROS ENTSPRUNGEN see Distler,
     Hugo

ES IST EIN ROS ENTSPRUNGEN see
     Hufschmidt, Wolfgang

ES IST EIN ROS ENTSPRUNGEN see Motte,
     Diether de la

ES IST EIN ROS ENTSPRUNGEN see Oertzen,
     Rudolf von

ES IST EIN ROS ENTSPRUNGEN see
     Praetorius, Michael

ES IST EIN ROS ENTSPRUNGEN see Vulpius,
     Melchior

ES IST EIN TROTZIG UND VERZAGT DING see
     Bach, Johann Sebastian

ES IST GEWISSLICH AN DER ZEIT see
     Studer, Hans

ES IST VOLLBRACHT see Kaminski,
     Heinrich

ES KAM EIN ENGEL VOM HOHEN HIMMEL see
     Hollfelder, Waldram

ES KOMMT EIN SCHIFF, GELADEN
     (Herrmann, H.) men cor,acap TONOS
     5624 s.p.   (E184)
     (Merhof) men cor,acap TONOS 5635 s.p.
                                   (E185)
     (Mittergradnegger, G.) men cor,acap
     TONOS 5646 s.p.   (E186)

ES KOMMT EIN SCHIFF GELADEN see Beck,
     Conrad

ES KOMMT EIN SCHIFF, GELADEN see Haus,
     Karl

ES KOMMT EIN SCHIFF, GELADEN see
     Mullich, Hermann

ES KOMMT EIN SCHIFF, GELADEN see
     Oertzen, Rudolf von

ES KOMMT EIN SCHIFF, GELADEN see
     Schweizer, Rolf

ES MUSSEN SICH FREUEN UND FROHLICH SEIN
     see Niedt, Friedrich Ehrhardt

ES SINGT WOHL EIN VOGLEIN see
     Brautigam, Helmut

ES STEHT EIN LIND IM HIMMELREICH see
     Zoll, Paul

ES SUNGEN DREI ENGEL see Goller, Fritz

ES SUNGEN DREI ENGEL EINEN SUSSEN
     GESANG see Rein, Walter

ES WARD EIN STERN ENTZUNDET see Weber,
     Bernhard

ES WIRD SCHO GLEI DUMPA *Adv/Xmas
     (Bauernfeind, Hans) wom cor,acap oct
     DOBLINGER s.p. see also In Dulci
     Jubilo   (E187)

ES WIRD SCHON GLEICH DUNKEL see Schmid,
     Alfons

ES WIRD SCHON GLEICH DUNKEL see
     Schroeder, Hermann

ES WOLLE GOTT UNS GNADIG SEIN see
     Barbe, Helmut

ES WOLLE GOTT UNS GNADIG SEIN see Reda,
     Siegfried

ESCHER, P.
     Herr Unser Gott, Du Bist Erhaben Uber
     Himmel Und Erde *prayer
     SATB SCHWEIZER. SK 170 s.p. (E188)

ESKELIN
     Let's Pray For America
     (McLellan) SATB oct GOSPEL
     05 TM 0313 $.40   (E189)

ESPECIALLY FOR CHILDREN *CCUL
     (Powell, Rick) jr cor&cor BENSON
     B0226 $2.50 stereo recording, tape,
     and-or book-record sets available,
     contact publisher   (E190)

EST SILENTIUM IN CAELO see Pezzati,
     Romano

ESTERHAZY, PAL (1635-1713)
     Ascendit Deus In Jubilo *cant/Psalm
     [Lat/Ger] SATB,2trp,cont (med) sc,
     cor pts BAREN. BA6402 s.p., ipa
     see from Harmonia Caelestis, Heft
     2   (E191)

     Harmonia Caelestis, Heft 2 *see
     Ascendit Deus In Jubilo   (E192)

     Weihnachtskantaten (from Harmonia
     Caelestis, Heft 1) CC10U,Xmas,
     cant
     [Lat/Ger] S/SS,2fl/2rec,strings,
     cont,opt harp, SATB chorus in no.
     1 (med easy) sc,voc sc BAREN.
     BA6401 s.p., ipa   (E193)

ESTHER see Moreau, Jean-Baptiste

L'ESTOCART, PASCHAL DE (1539-1584)
     Ich Erhebe Mein Gemute (Psalm 25)
     SATB SCHWEIZER. SK 117 s.p. (E194)

     Psalm 25 *see Ich Erhebe Mein Gemute

ESURIENTES IMPLEVIT see Vivaldi,
     Antonio

ET FACTA EST LUX see Jacobsen,
     Katherine

ET INCARNATUS EST see Des Prez, Josquin

ET UDELT HJERTE see Strand, Ragnvald

ETERNAL see Bartlett

ETERNAL FATHER, STRONG TO SAVE see
     Dykes

ETERNAL GOD see Burroughs, Bob

ETERNAL GOD IS THY REFUGE, THE see
     Cousins, M. Thomas

ETERNAL LIGHT see Sermisy, Claude de,
     Lux Aeterna

ETERNAL MYTH see Zrno, Felix, Vecna Baj

ETERNAL REWARD see Azevedo, Lex de

ETERNAL RULER see Butler, Eugene

ETERNAL RULER OF THE CEASELESS ROUND
     see Harris, D.S.

ETERNAL SPIRIT OF TRUTH AND LOVE see
     Clarke, Henry Leland

ETERNAL VOICES see Janson, T.

ETT, KASPAR (1788-1847)
     Attollite Portas
     [Lat] 4pt mix cor,org,fl,2clar,2ob,
     2bsn,2horn,3trp,3trom,strings,
     timp sc,cor pts BOHM s.p., ipa
                                   (E195)
     Haec Dies *Easter,Gradual
     [Lat] mix cor,org/2clar&2horn&2trp&
     trom&strings&timp sc,cor pts BOHM
     s.p., ipa   (E196)

     Laudate Dominum
     [Lat] 4pt mix cor,acap BOHM s.p.
                                   (E197)

     Libera Zum Requiem In Es
     [Lat] 4pt mix cor,acap sc,cor pts
     BOHM s.p.   (E198)

     Missa De Profundis *Req
     [Lat] 4pt mix cor,opt 3trp,trom (E
     flat maj) sc,cor pts BOHM s.p.,
     ipa   (E199)

     Pange Lingua
     [Lat] 4pt mix cor/unis,org BOHM
     s.p.   (E200)

     Requiem In C-Moll
     [Lat] 4pt mix cor,org (C min) sc,
     cor pts BOHM s.p.   (E201)

     Zwolf Lateinische Kirchengesange
     *CC12L
     [Lat] 4pt mix cor,acap/org sc,cor
     pts BOHM s.p.   (E202)

ETTI, KARL (1912-   )
     Ein Tag, Der Sagt's Dem Andern (from
     Artaban)
     8pt mix cor DOBLINGER G 674 s.p.
                                   (E203)

EUROPAISCHE WEIHNACHTSLIEDER see
     Deutschmann, Gerhard

EVANGELIE see Rosseau, Norbert

EVANGELISM ARRANGEMENTS NO. 1 *CCUL
     (Souther, Billy) cor SINGSPIR 4000
     $1.50   (E204)

EVANGELISM ARRANGEMENTS NO. 2 *CCUL
     (Souther, Billy) cor SINGSPIR 4191
     $1.50   (E205)

EVANGELISTIC CHOIR, THE *CC23U,evang
     cor (easy) BROADMAN 4520-14 $.75
                                   (E206)

EVANGELIUM see Mayer, Harry

EVANS
     Twenty-One Service Responses *CC21U,
     cor-resp
     SATB WARNER G1651 187 $1.40 (E207)

EVEILLE-TOI see Binet

EVEN SO, LORD JESUS see Gaither,
     William J. (Bill)

EVEN SO, LORD JESUS, COME see Gaither,
     William J. (Bill)

EVENING COLLECT, AN see Miller, R.B.

EVENING HYMN see Handel, George
     Frideric

EVENING PRAYER see Isaacson, Michael,
     Hashkivenu

EVENING SERVICE IN G see Paviour, Paul

EVENING SHADE see Boyd, Jack

EVENING SHADE see Walker, William

EVENSEN, GLENN
     Thine Forever *anthem
     SATB,opt SB soli AUGSBURG 11-1683
     $.25   (E208)

EVERETT, ASA B.
     Footsteps Of Jesus
     (Buffaloe, James) SATB,pno
     SHATTINGER 404 $.25   (E209)

EVERLASTING MERCY see Christiansen,
     Paul

EVERY BLESSING WE ENJOY
     (Brandon, George) unis/SA WILLIS 9989
     $.25   (E210)

EVERY CHILD STAND UP AND SING see
     Beethoven, Ludwig van

EVERY DAY IS A BETTER DAY see Bartlett

EVERY GOOD AND PERFECT GIFT see Sisler,
     Hampson A.

EVERY TIME I FEEL THE SPIRIT *anthem/
     gospel
     see Five Negro Spirituals
     see Vier Negro-Spirituals
     (Johnson, Norman) SATB oct SINGSPIR
     ZJP-8188 $.25   (E211)

EVERY TIME I FEEL THE SPIRIT see
     Peninger

EVERY TIME I THINK ABOUT JESUS see
     Fleming, Larry L.

EVERY WAY, DAY BY DAY see Thygerson,
     Robert J.

EVERYBODY NEEDS SOMEBODY see Gibson

EVERYTIME I FEEL *spir
     (Becker, H.-G.) men cor,pno TONOS
     2397 s.p.   (E212)

EVERYWHERE AND ALWAYS see Holiday,
     Mickey

EVETT, ROBERT (1922-   )
     Last Supper, The
     TTBB,TBB soli,hpsd,fl,ob sc
     AM.COMP.AL. $8.80   (E213)

EWIGES LICHT LEUCHTE IHNEN see Goller,
     Fritz

EXALTATION, AN see Klein, Lothar

EXALTING SEASON, THE see Erhardt

EXAUDI DEUS see Croce

EXAUDI DEUS ORATIONEM MEAM see
    Gabrieli, Giovanni

EXAUDI, DEUS, ORATIONEM MEAM see
    Lassus, Roland de (Orlandus)

EXAUDI, DOMINE, VOCEM MEAM see Schwarz-
    Schilling, Reinhard

EXAUDI NOS ERHORE UNS "HERR, GIB UNS
    HELLE AUGEN" see Wittmer, Eberhard
    Ludwig

EXCELL
    Since I Have Been Redeemed (composed
        with Butler) *anthem
        SATB (easy) oct BROADMAN 4540-68
        $.30   (E214)

EXPANDI MANUS MEAS AD TE see Lassus,
    Roland de (Orlandus)

EXPLODE WITH JOY see Rohlig, Harald

EXSPECTA DOMINUM see Stout, Alan

EXSPECTANS EXSPECTAVI DOMINUM see
    Lassus, Roland de (Orlandus)

EXSPECTANS EXSPECTAVI DOMINUM see
    Lemacher, Heinrich

EXSULTATE DEO see Kremer, Karl

EXSULTET see Schroeder

EXSULTET see Schutz, Heinrich

EXTREMUM DEI JUDICIUM see Charpentier,
    Marc-Antoine

EXULTATE DEO see Najera, Edmund

EXULTATE DEO see Scarlatti, Alessandro

EXULTET COELUM LAUDIBUS see Paynter,
    John P.

EYBLER, JOSEPH (1765-1846)
    Jubilate Deo *Fest
        [Lat] 4pt mix cor,2trp,strings,org,
        opt 2ob&2clar&2bsn&2horn&timp sc,
        cor pts BOHM s.p., ipa   (E215)
        mix cor,org,orch sc,cor pts BOHM
        s.p., ipa   (E216)

    Omnes De Saba *Epiph
        [Lat] 4pt mix cor,org,2ob,2bsn,
        2horn,2trp,strings,timp sc,cor
        pts BOHM s.p., ipa contains also:
        Reges Tharsis   (E217)

    Reges Tharsis
        see Eybler, Joseph, Omnes De Saba

    Terra Tremuit *Easter,Offer
        [Lat] 4pt mix cor,2ob,2bsn,2trp,
        2trom,strings,org,timp sc,cor pts
        BOHM s.p., ipa   (E218)

EYES OF ALL, THE see Schroth, G.

EYES OF ALL HOPE IN THEE, THE see
    Felciano, Richard

F

FABER
    Come And Mourn With Me Awhile
        (composed with Ford) *anthem
        SATB oct BROADMAN 4545-84 $.30 (F1)

FABRICIUS
    Ich Weiss, Dass Mein Erloser Lebet
        *mot
        SATTB HANSSLER 1.587 s.p.   (F2)

FACE TO FACE - SAVED BY GRACE see
    White, Ernie

FACTUS EST DOMINUS FIRMAMENTUM MEUM see
    Lassus, Roland de (Orlandus)

FACTUS EST REPENTE see Montillet

FADER OF HEVEN, THE see Davies, Peter
    Maxwell

FAHRE FORT see Preisenhammer

FAIR MOON HATH ASCENDED, THE see Schulz

FAIRCHILD
    What Wondrous Sacred Love (composed
        with Paris) *anthem
        SATB (easy) oct BROADMAN 4540-70
        $.30   (F3)

FAIRCLOTH
    I Belive In Almighty God *see
        Sanders

    Kevin's Carol *Xmas,anthem/carol
        unis oct BROADMAN 4557-29 $.30 (F4)

    Nearer, Still Nearer *see Morris

    Savior, More Than Life To Me *see
        Crosby, F.

FAIREST, LORD JESUS *anthem
    (Mann, Johnny) SATB LEXICON   (F5)
    (Rasley, John M.) SATB oct SINGSPIR
        ZJP-7253 $.30   (F6)

FAIST, ANTON
    Alma Redemptoris Mater
        see Vier Marianische Antiphonen

    Ave Maria *Op.15
        [Lat] 4pt mix cor,org/2clar&2horn&
        strings sc,cor pts BOHM s.p., ipa
                                       (F7)

    Ave Regina Coelorum
        see Vier Marianische Antiphonen

    Dritte Messe In Es *Op.8, Mass
        [Lat] 4pt mix cor,org/fl,2clar,
        2horn,2trp,trom,strings,opt timp
        (E flat maj) sc,cor pts BOHM
        s.p., ipa   (F8)

    Dritte Singmesse "Herr, Wir Kommen
        Schuldbeladen" *Op.55a, Mass
        [Ger] men cor BOHM sc s.p., cor pts
        s.p.   (F9)

    Funf Tantum Ergo *Op.48,No.1-5
        [Lat] 4pt mix cor,org/fl&2clar&
        2horn&2trp&trom&strings&timp sc,
        cor pts BOHM s.p., ipa   (F10)

    Funfte Messe In F *Op.16, Mass
        [Lat] 4pt mix cor,org/fl&2clar&
        2horn&2trp&trom&strings&opt timp
        sc,cor pts BOHM s.p., ipa   (F11)

    Libera *Op.12b
        [Lat] 4pt mix cor,org,opt 2trp,
        2trom sc,cor pts BOHM s.p., ipa
                                      (F12)

    Missa Septima In A *Op.30, Mass
        [Lat] 4pt mix cor,org/fl&2clar&
        2horn&2trp&trom&strings&timp sc,
        cor pts BOHM s.p., ipa   (F13)

    Neunte Messe In B *Op.50, Mass
        [Lat] 4pt mix cor,org/fl&ob&2clar&
        2horn&2trp&trom&strings&timp sc,
        cor pts BOHM s.p., ipa   (F14)

    Regina Coeli
        see Vier Marianische Antiphonen

    Requiem In C-Moll *Op.12
        [Lat] 4pt mix cor,org,1-2trp,2trom
        (C min) sc,cor pts BOHM s.p., ipa
                                      (F15)

    Salve Regina
        see Vier Marianische Antiphonen

    Veni Creator Spiritus
        [Lat] 4pt mix cor,inst sc,cor pts
        BOHM s.p. contains also:
        Engelhart, F.X., Veni Creator

FAIST, ANTON (cont'd.)

    Spiritus; Welcker, Max, Veni
    Creator Spiritus   (F16)

    Vier Marianische Antiphonen
        [Lat] 4pt mix cor,org sc,cor pts
        BOHM s.p.
        contains: Alma Redemptoris Mater,
        Op.2,No.1; Ave Regina Coelorum,
        Op.2,No.2; Regina Coeli, Op.2,
        No.3; Salve Regina, Op.2,No.4
                                      (F17)

FAITH see Bowie, William

FAITH see Newbury, Kent A.

FAITH AND CONFIDENCE see Holde, Arthur

FAITH, HOPE AND LOVE see Peloquin, C.
    Alexander

FAITH OF OUR FATHERS see Hemy, [Henri
    Frederick]

FAITH, TEARS AND RESURRECTION see
    Fasig, Bill

FALCKE
    Karfreitagsgesang *Op.3, Gd.Fri.
        mix cor,pno LIENAU voc sc s.p., cor
        pts s.p.   (F18)

    Trauungsgesang *Op.2,No.2, funeral
        LIENAU sc s.p., cor pts s.p. (F19)

FALCON, THE see Rutter

FAMILIAR HYMNS FOR MEN *CC31L,hymn
    (Reynolds, William Jensen) men cor
    CENTURY PR $.75   (F20)

FAMILIAR HYMNS FOR WOMEN *CC30L,hymn
    (Reynolds, William Jensen) wom cor
    CENTURY PR $.75   (F21)

FAMILY CHRIST MASS, A see Fargo,
    Milford

FAMILY OF GOD, THE *CC8L
    SATB TRIUNE TUO 100 $2.50 contains
    works by: Red, Buryl; Brown,
    Charles F.; Burroughs, Bob;
    McKinley, David; Hawthorne, Grace;
    Seabough, Ed
    see also: Hawthorne, Family Of God,
    The   (F22)

FAMILY OF GOD, THE see Gaither, William
    J. (Bill)

FAMILY OF GOD, THE see Hawthorne

FANFARE see Burroughs, Bob

FANFARE see Whitecotton, Shirley

FANFARE AND ALLELUIA FOR EASTER see
    Whitecotton, Shirley

FANFARE FOR AN INFANT KING see Smith,
    Stanley

FANFARE FOR EASTER MORNING see Young

FANFARE FOR THE KING see McNair,
    Jacqueline Hanna

FANFARE FOR THE SEASONS see Moore

FANFARE WITH ALLELUIAS see Young

FANFARE WITH ALLELUIAS see Young,
    Phillip M.

FANTASIA ON THE OLD ONE HUNDRED FOURTH
    PSALM TUNE see Vaughan Williams,
    Ralph

FANTASY OF CAROLS, A *CC12UL,Xmas,
    carol
    (Thomas, C. Edward) SATB LILLENAS
    MC-27 $1.25   (F23)

FAR IT WAS TO BETHLEHEM see Van Hulse,
    Camil

FAR SHINING NAMES FROM AGE TO AGE (ST.
    NICOLAS)
    see Two Hymns

FARE YOU WELL *anthem/spir
    (Ehret) SAT/SAB FINE ARTS EP 53 $.35
                                      (F24)
    (Moore) SATB WARNER W-3419 $.40   (F25)

FARGO, MILFORD
    Christ Was A Pretty Babe (from Family
        Christ Mass, A) Xmas
        SA KENDOR $.45   (F26)
        SSA KENDOR $.45   (F27)
        SAB KENDOR $.45   (F28)
        SATB KENDOR $.45   (F29)

FARGO, MILFORD (cont'd.)

Church Bells And Fishermen (from
Family Christ Mass, A) Xmas
SA,opt pic&chimes KENDOR $.35 (F30)
SSA,opt pic&chimes KENDOR $.35
(F31)
SAB,opt pic&chimes KENDOR $.35
(F32)
SATB,opt pic&chimes KENDOR $.35
(F33)

Family Christ Mass, A *Xmas/Gen/
Psntd,Mass
SATB&opt 2pt jr cor&opt SAB,pno/
org,opt inst KENDOR $7.50, ipa
(F34)

How Many Christmases? (from Family
Christ Mass, A) Xmas
SATB KENDOR $.35 (F35)
SAB KENDOR $.35 (F36)
SSA KENDOR $.35 (F37)
SA KENDOR $.30 (F38)

Lord Of Children (from Family Christ
Mass, A) Xmas
SA KENDOR $.30 (F39)

Spirit Bears Witness, The (from
Family Christ Mass, A) Xmas
SA KENDOR $.30 (F40)

FARLEY
He Doth Care
(Murray; Smith, Herb) SATB oct
GOSPEL 05 TM 0126 $.20 (F41)

FARNABY, GILES (ca. 1560-1640)
Construe My Meaning
(Shipp) SATB SCHIRM.G LG51719 $.40
(F42)

FARRANT, RICHARD (ca. 1530-1581)
Hide Not Thou Thy Face From Us, O
Lord *Gen/Lent
(Wolff) TTBB (med) oct CONCORDIA
98-2201 $.30 (F43)

Lord For Thy Tender Mercies
SATB HARRIS HC 4050 $.30 (F44)

Lord, For Thy Tender Mercies Sake
mix cor BANKS MUS YS 160 $.20 (F45)

Te Deum
SATB,opt acap (med diff) OXFORD
43.021 $1.65 (F46)

FARRIER, WALTER
Psalm 150
SATB BOURNE B224238-358 $.65 (F47)

FASIG, BILL
Faith, Tears And Resurrection
*Easter,cant
SATB SINGSPIR ZD-5879 $1.95 (F48)

FAST
Alleluia To The Lord Of Being
SATB SCHIRM.G 11937 $.40 (F49)

FATHER, HEAR OUR SONG OF PRAISE
(Schroeder) SA oct SCHMITT 2907 $.40
(F50)

FATHER, I WILL OBEY see Andrews, C.T.

FATHER IN HEAVEN WE THANK THEE see
Thomas, C.

FATHER OF COMPASSION see Graham, Robert

FATHER OF HEAVEN see Walmisley, Thomas
Attwood

FATHER THE HOUR IS COME see Wild, Eric

FATHER WE PRAISE THEE see Clarke,
F.R.C.

FATHER, WE PRAISE THEE see Peek,
Richard

FATHER, WE THANK THEE see Albright,
William H.

FATSCHER, RICHARD
Veni Creator
[Lat] 4pt mix cor,acap BOHM s.p.
(F51)

FAURE, GABRIEL-URBAIN (1845-1924)
Agnus Dei (from Requiem) Lent
"Lamb Of God" SATTBB (med)
FITZSIMONS 2134 $.25 (F52)
(Stevens) "Lamb Of God" SATB ART
MAST 111 $.40 (F53)

Deliver Me *see Libera Me

Grant Them Rest Eternal (from
Requiem)
[Lat/Eng] SATTBB (med) FITZSIMONS
2147 $.25 (F54)

Holy, Holy, Holy *see Sanctus

In Paradise *see In Paradisum

FAURE, GABRIEL-URBAIN (cont'd.)

In Paradisum (from Requiem)
"In Paradise" SATB (med) FITZSIMONS
2133 $.30 (F55)

Introit And Kyrie (from Requiem)
[Lat/Eng] SATTBB (med) FITZSIMONS
2147 $.25 (F56)

Lamb Of God *see Agnus Dei

Lead Us Unto Life *Lent
(Wetzler) SATB ART MAST 159 $.35 (F57)

Libera Me
"Deliver Me" SATB,Bar solo (med)
FITZSIMONS 2135 $.35 (F58)

Offertorium (from Requiem)
"Offertory" SATB,Bar solo (med)
FITZSIMONS 2136 $.25 (F59)

Offertory *see Offertorium

Requiem *Lent/Palm,funeral/Req
cor,soli,orch min sc EULENBURG 1096
s.p. (F60)
(Evans, Mack) [Lat/Eng] cor,SBar
soli,org,2fl,2clar,2bsn,4horn,
4trp,3trom,strings,timp,harp
FITZSIMONS voc sc $1.25, cor pts
$.60, sc ipa, ipr,

Sanctus (from Requiem)
SA (med) FITZSIMONS 5017 $.25 (F61)
SATTBB (med) FITZSIMONS 2119 $.25
(F62)
"Holy, Holy, Holy" SATB (med)
FITZSIMONS 2119 $.30 (F63)

FAURE, JEAN-BAPTIST
Palms, The *Easter,anthem
SATB HARRIS HC 4051 $.35 (F64)
(Lyall) SATB (easy) oct BROADMAN
4538-11 $.30 (F65)

FAVOR AND GOOD UNDERSTANDING see Cram

FAVORITE CHOIR ARRANGEMENTS NO. 1
*CCUL
cor SINGSPIR 5427 $1.50 (F66)

FAVORITE CHOIR ARRANGEMENTS NO. 2
*CCUL
(Van Horn, Charles) cor SINGSPIR 5465
$1.50 (F67)

FAVORITE CHOIR MELODIES *CC27UL,Bibl/
gospel/spir
cor (easy) GOSPEL 05 TM 0489 $1.00
(F68)

FAVORITE HYMNS OF EARLY AMERICA *CC9U
(Van Camp, Leonard) SATB,opt acap
DEAN CD-103 $2.00 (F69)

FAVORITE PROPHETIC SONGS FOR THE CHOIR
*CCUL
(Wyrtzen, Don) cor SINGSPIR 5666
$1.95 (F70)

FAVORITE SPIRITUALS NO. 1 *CCUL,spir
(Johnson, Norman) cor SINGSPIR 5593
$1.25 (F71)

FAVORITE SPIRITUALS NO. 2 *CCUL,spir
(DeCou, Harold; Johnson, Norman) cor
SINGSPIR 5792 $1.25 (F72)

FAWCETT
Blest Be The Tie (composed with
Lange) *anthem
SATB oct BROADMAN 4540-93 $.30
(F73)

FEAR NOT YE, O ISRAEL see Buck, Dudley

FEAR YE NOT: HE IS RISEN! see
Goldsworthy, William Arthur

FEARHEILEY
Help Me Be Me (composed with Krause)
*anthem
SATB (easy) oct BROADMAN 4554-68
$.30 (F74)

FEAST OF JOY see Pelz, Walter L.

FEAST OF LIGHTS, A see Silver

FEATHERSTONE
My Jesus, I Love Thee (composed with
Lanier) *anthem
SATB (easy) oct BROADMAN 4545-29
$.30 (F75)

FEDERL, A.
Deutsche Messe "Lobet Den Herren"
*CC8L,Mass
[Ger] mix cor BOHM sc s.p., cor pts
s.p. (F76)

FEED US NOW, O SON OF GOD see Allen,
Peter

FEEL THE SPIRIT MOVING see Fischer,
William Gustavus

FEIERLICHES HOCHAMT IN B see Haydn,
(Franz) Joseph, Heiligmesse

FEIERLICHES PANGE LINGUA see Mutter,
Gerbert

FELCIANO, RICHARD (1930-   )
Antiphon And Benedictus (from Songs
For Darkness And Light)
"Canticle Of Zachary, The" unis,org
SCHIRM.EC 2805 (F77)

As The Hind Longs For The Running
Waters
SSA SCHIRM.EC 2803 see from Songs
For Darkness And Light (F78)

Benedictio Nuptialis *Marriage
"Just Man Shall Flourish, The"
unis,org SCHIRM.EC 2818 (F79)

Canticle Of Zachary, The *see
Antiphon And Benedictus

Christmas Madrigal, A
SATB,pno,brass,perc SCHIRM.EC 2905
s.p., ipr (F80)

Eyes Of All Hope In Thee, The
SATB SCHIRM.EC 2918 (F81)

Give Ear, O Heavens
SSA SCHIRM.EC 2803 see from Songs
For Darkness And Light (F82)

Give Thanks To The Lord (from Songs
For Darkness And Light)
unis,org SCHIRM.EC 2804 (F83)

I Will Sing To The Lord
SSA SCHIRM.EC 2803 see from Songs
For Darkness And Light (F84)

Just Man Shall Flourish, The *see
Benedictio Nuptialis

Lullaby On "Von Himmel Hoch" *Xmas
unis treb cor,org/4strings/strings
SCHIRM.EC 2811 s.p., ipr (F85)

My Friend Had A Vineyard
SSA SCHIRM.EC 2803 see from Songs
For Darkness And Light (F86)

Praise The Lord In His Sanctuary
(Psalm 150)
SATB,org SCHIRM.EC 2799 see from
Songs For Darkness And Light
(F87)

Psalm 150 *see Praise The Lord In
His Sanctuary

Pshelley's Psalm
SATB SCHIRM.EC 2920 (F88)

Signs
SATB,electronic tape, filmstrips sc
SCHIRM.EC 2927 s.p., ipa (F89)

Songs For Darkness And Light *see
Praise The Lord In His Sanctuary
(Psalm 150) (F90)

Songs For Darkness And Light *see As
The Hind Longs For The Running
Waters; Give Ear, O Heavens; I
Will Sing To The Lord; My Friend
Had A Vineyard (F91)

Two Hymns To Howl By *CC2U,round
4pt treb cor SCHIRM.EC 2806 (F92)

FELDMAN, JAMES
Song Of Peace *Bibl
SATB,pno/harp FOSTER MF134 $.50,
ipa (F93)

FENNELLEY, BRIAN
Festive Psalm
SATB,narrator,org,electronic tape
AM.COMP.AL. $3.85 (F94)

Psalm 13
SSATBB,2trp,2trom AM.COMP.AL. $3.85
(F95)

FERGUSON
Bless The Lord
SATB SCHIRM.G LG 51697 $.40 (F96)

Blessed Quietness
(Marshall; Smith, Harold) SAB oct
GOSPEL 05 TM 0101 $.20 (F97)

On The Twenty-Third Psalm *hymn
SATB oct LILLENAS AN-2415 $.30
(F98)

This Day, A Christmas Fanfare *Adv/
Xmas
SATB,brass oct LILLENAS AN-3866
$.30 (F99)

FERGUSON, BARRY
  Good Christian Men, Rejoice And Sing!
    *Easter,carol
    SATB,org NOVELLO MT 1571 s.p.
                                    (F100)

FERIA SEXTA IN PARASCEVE see
  Kromolicki, Joseph

FERRIN
  Take My Life And Let It Be *gospel
    SATB oct LILLENAS AN-1694 $.30
                                    (F101)

  There Is Joy In My Soul *gospel
    SATB oct LILLENAS AN-1672 $.30
                                    (F102)

FERRIS, WILLIAM
  Coventry Carol *Xmas
    SATB,2fl,org GRAY CMR 3327 $.35
                                    (F103)

  Gentle Mary *Xmas
    2pt mix cor GRAY CMR 3311 $.30
                                    (F104)

FERTILE GROUND see Landgrave, Phillip

FEST- UND GEDENKSPRUCHE see Brahms,
  Johannes

FESTAL SONG see Stanton

FESTIVAL EUCHARIST, A see Proulx,
  Richard

FESTIVAL HYMN see Spinney, Montague

FESTIVAL MASS see Gelineau, [Joseph]

FESTIVAL MASS, A see Swenson

FESTIVAL OF PRAISE see Bowman, Carl

FESTIVAL PROCESSION see Knox, Charles

FESTIVAL PSALM, A see Watson, Walter

FESTIVAL SERVICE BOOK 7 *CCU,
  meditation
  cor ROYAL s.p.   (F105)

FESTIVE HYMN TO WORSHIP see Brown

FESTIVE PROCESSION see Christiansen

FESTIVE PSALM see Fennelley, Brian

FESTLICHE HYMNE "SINGE, O SINGE DICH"
  see Wittmer, Eberhard Ludwig

FESTLICHE KANTATE see Haass, Walter

FESTLICHE MESSE IN C see Erhard, Karl

FESTMESSE ZU EHREN DER GEBURT UNSERES
  HERRN JESU CHRISTI see Koch, Karl

FESTSPRUCH "MACHET DIE TORE WEIT" see
  Rothschuh, Franz

FESTUM OMNIUM SANCTORUM see Eben, Petr

FESTUM SACRATISSIMI CORDIS JESU see
  Eben, Petr

FETLER, PAUL
  Glory Be To God
    SATB,acap ART MAST 172 $.40 (F106)

FETTKE, TOM
  At The Name Of Jesus *anthem
    SATB,brass oct LILLENAS AN-2409
    $.35   (F107)

  Babe Of Bethlehem, The *Adv/Xmas
    SATB oct LILLENAS AT-C105 $.35
                                    (F108)

  Christmas Call To Worship, A *Adv/
    Xmas
    SATB,opt 3trp,2trom oct LILLENAS
    AT-C107 $.30   (F109)

  Come Down, O Love Divine *anthem
    SATB oct LILLENAS AN-6025 $.30
                                    (F110)

  Cross Was His Own, The *Easter/Lent,
    gospel
    SATB oct LILLENAS AT-1129 $.30
                                    (F111)

  Empty Hands *gospel
    SSATB/SSA,opt inst oct LILLENAS
    AT-1109 $.30   (F112)

  Gospel Of Peace, The *gospel
    SATB oct LILLENAS AT-1132 $.30
                                    (F113)

  Joy Has Come Down *Adv/Xmas
    SATB oct LILLENAS AN-3869 $.35
                                    (F114)

  Love, Joy, Peace *Xmas,cant
    SATB LILLENAS MC-26 $1.50 (F115)

  Master's Touch, The *hymn
    SSATB oct LILLENAS AN-6036 $.30
                                    (F116)

  My God, How Wonderful Thou Art
    *anthem
    SATB oct LILLENAS AN-6018 $.30
                                    (F117)

FETTKE, TOM (cont'd.)

  O Blessed Holy Spirit *hymn
    SATB oct LILLENAS AT-1135 $.30
                                    (F118)

  O Lord *anthem
    SATB oct LILLENAS AN-6017 $.30
                                    (F119)

  Sense Of Him, A *gospel
    SATB oct LILLENAS AT-1128 $.30
                                    (F120)

  Thanks *hymn
    SATB oct LILLENAS AT-1127 $.30
                                    (F121)

FIDELIA see Lewer

FIEBIG
  Herz Und Herz Vereint Zusammen
    SAT/SAB/SA,opt treb inst&bass inst
    HANSSLER 14.217 s.p.   (F122)

FIEBIG, KURT (1908-   )
  Hallelujah! Let Praises Ring *cant,
    Contemp
    SAATB,inst CHANTRY COC 714 $.45,
    ipa   (F123)

  Jesus Christus, Unser Heiland, Der
    Von Uns Den Gotteszorn Wandt
    SAT/SAB,opt treb inst&bass inst
    (two settings) HANSSLER 14.154
    s.p.   (F124)

  Lobe Den Herren, Den Machtigen Konig
    Der Ehren
    SAT/SAB/2pt,opt treb inst&bass inst
    (two settings) HANSSLER 14.234
    s.p.   (F125)

FIERCE RAGE THE TEMPEST see McRae,
  James

FIERCE WAS THE WILD BILLOW see Noble,
  Thomas Tertius

FIFTH PSALM, THE see Cross, Linda

FIGH
  One Way *anthem
    SATB oct BROADMAN 4562-41 $.35
                                    (F126)

FIGHT IS ON, THE see Morris

FIGHT THE GOOD FIGHT see Johnson,
  Norman

FIGHT THE GOOD FIGHT see Monsell

FILI ME see Weis, Flemming

FILIPE, JAIME
  Christmas Blessing *see Bello,
    Tavares

FILKE, MAX (1855-1911)
  Angelus Domini *Op.70b,No.2
    see Filke, Max, Terra Tremuit

  Ascendit Deus *Op.70d,No.1, Asc/
    Corpus,Offer
    [Lat] 4pt mix cor,org/orch sc,cor
    pts BOHM s.p., ipa contains also:
    Sacerdotes Domini, Op.70d,No.2
                                    (F127)
  Confirma Hoc *Op.70c,No.1, Pent/
    Whitsun,Offer
    [Lat] 4pt mix cor,org/orch sc,cor
    pts BOHM s.p., ipa contains also:
    Intonuit De Coelo, Op.70c,No.2
                                    (F128)
  Intonuit De Coelo *Op.70c,No.2
    see Filke, Max, Confirma Hoc

  Messe In G In Honorem St. Caroli
    Borromaei *Op.80c, Mass
    [Lat] unis sc,cor pts BOHM s.p.
                                    (F129)
  Missa In F Zu Ehren Der Heiligen
    Hedwig *Op.122, Mass
    [Lat] 4pt mix cor,org/2clar&2horn&
    2trp&2trom&strings&timp sc,cor
    pts BOHM s.p., ipa   (F130)
  Missa In G-Dur In Honorem St. Caroli
    Borromaei *Op.80, Mass
    [Lat] SAB&opt T,org,opt fl&2horn&
    2trp&2trom&2clar/2ob&opt timp (G
    maj) sc,cor pts BOHM s.p., ipa
                                    (F131)
  Missa In Honorem Beatae Mariae
    Virginis In D-Moll *Op.47, Mass
    [Lat] 4pt mix cor,2ob/2clar,2horn,
    2trp,2trom,strings,timp,opt org
    (D min) sc,cor pts BOHM s.p., ipa
                                    (F132)
  Missa Solemnis In D "Oriens Ex Alto"
    *Op.106, Mass
    [Lat] 4pt mix cor,fl,2ob/2clar,
    2horn,strings sc,cor pts BOHM
    s.p., ipa   (F133)
    [Lat] 4pt mix cor,fl,2ob/2clar,
    2bsn,2horn,strings sc,cor pts
    BOHM s.p., ipa   (F134)
    [Lat] 4pt mix cor,fl,2ob/2clar,
    2bsn,2horn,2trp,trom,strings,timp
    sc,cor pts BOHM s.p., ipa (F135)

FILKE, MAX (cont'd.)

  Reges Tharsis *Op.70a,No.2
    see Filke, Max, Tui Sunt Coeli

  Sacerdotes Domini *Op.70d,No.2
    see Filke, Max, Ascendit Deus

  Tantum Ergo *Op.79,No.5
    [Lat] 4pt mix cor,org sc,cor pts
    BOHM s.p.   (F136)

  Terra Tremuit *Op.70b,No.1, Easter,
    Offer
    [Lat] 4pt mix cor,org/orch sc,cor
    pts BOHM s.p., ipa contains also:
    Angelus Domini, Op.70b,No.2
                                    (F137)
  Tui Sunt Coeli *Op.70a,No.1, Xmas/
    Epiph,Offer
    [Lat] 4pt mix cor,org/2horn,2trp,
    2trom,strings,2ob/2clar,timp,opt
    2bsn sc,cor pts BOHM s.p., ipa
    contains also: Reges Tharsis,
    Op.70a,No.2   (F138)

FILL MY LIFE, O LORD see Allen, Lanny

FILL THE EARTH WITH LOVE see Fischer,
  William Gustavus

FILL THE POTS WITH WATER *Contemp
  SATB VANGUARD V551 $.35 see from Go
  Tell Everyone   (F139)

FILLMORE, JAMES H. (1849-1941)
  I Am Resolved *anthem/gospel
    (Johnson, Norman) SATB oct SINGSPIR
    ZJP-8095 $.30   (F140)

  I Know That My Redeemer Liveth
    *Easter,anthem
    (Rasley, John M.) SATB oct SINGSPIR
    ZJP-3525 $.25   (F141)

FINAL CHORUS FROM THE ST. MATTHEW
  PASSION see Bach, Johann Sebastian,
  Schlusschor Aus Der Matthauspassion

FINALE! *CC10L,Xmas/Thanks
  (Carmichael, Ralph) cor LEXICON 37656
  $1.95   (F142)

FINDERS, KEEPERS see Smith, Eddie

FINK, MICHAEL
  Tell Out Magnificat *Xmas
    SATB STANDARD A47MX3 $.50   (F143)

FINLAY, KENNETH
  Our Blest Redeemer
    mix cor BANKS MUS YS 1278 $.25
                                    (F144)

FINLEY
  Fight The Good Fight *see Monsell

FIRE OF LOVE, THE see Roff, Joseph

FIRST CHRISTMAS MORNING see Hains, S.B.

FIRST CORINTHIANS NO. 13
  (McRae, William) SATB CHARTER PO10205
                                    (F145)

FIRST CRITICAL EDITION see Palestrina,
  Giovanni

FIRST EASTER DAWN, THE see Noble,
  Thomas Tertius

FIRST NOWELL, THE *Xmas
  see Four Christmas Carols
  (Kaplan) SATB SCHIRM.G LG 51715 $.30
                                    (F146)

FIRST NOWELL, THE see Murray, Margaret

FIRST THING I DO EVERY MORNING, THE
  see There Is A Song

FISCHER
  Still Life *CC10L
    1-2pt LEXICON 37679 $1.95   (F147)

FISCHER, I.
  Sussex Carol *Xmas
    SSA (diff) FITZSIMONS 3071 $.20
                                    (F148)

FISCHER, IRWIN
  Blessed Be Thou; Lord God Our Father
    SATB,pno AM.COMP.AL. $2.75   (F149)

  Call, The
    SATB,pno/org AM.COMP.AL. $4.40 (F150)
    SATB,pno/org/2horn&2trp&2trom&tuba
    sc AM.COMP.AL. $4.40   (F151)

FISCHER, JOHN
  New Covenant, The *cant
    cor LEXICON 37703 $2.95   (F152)

FISCHER, L.
  Sussex Carol *Xmas
    SSATB (med) FITZSIMONS 2118 $.25
                                    (F153)

FISCHER, THEO
Grabhymnus *funeral
men cor,acap TONOS 5659 s.p. (F154)

FISCHER, WALTER (1930-   )
Mein Schonste Zier
SAT/SAB (contains also: Also Hat
Gott Die Welt Geliebt) SCHWEIZER.
SK 67.04 s.p. see also
MUSIKBEILAGE ZUM "EVANGELISCHEN
KIRCHENCHOR 1967"   (F155)

FISCHER, WILLIAM GUSTAVUS (1835-1912)
Feel The Spirit Moving *gospel
unis CIMINO $.50   (F156)

Fill The Earth With Love *gospel
unis CIMINO $.50   (F157)

I Love To Tell The Story *anthem/
gospel
(Johnson, Norman) SSATB oct
SINGSPIR ZJP-8032 $.25   (F158)

Inner Peace Song *gospel
unis CIMINO $.50   (F159)

Message Of Joy *gospel
unis CIMINO $.50   (F160)

Prayer Is A Wonderful Thing, A
*gospel
unis CIMINO $.50   (F161)

Rose Colored Glasses *gospel
unis CIMINO $.50   (F162)

Set My Spirit Free *gospel
unis CIMINO $.50   (F163)

Speak Out *gospel
unis CIMINO $.50   (F164)

Testify *gospel
unis CIMINO $.50   (F165)

There Is A Way *gospel
unis CIMINO $.50   (F166)

FISCUS
Do You Have An Empty Heart? *anthem
SATB oct LORENZ B219 $.35 (F167)

FISER, LUBOS (1935-   )
Requiem
[Lat] mix cor&mix cor,SBar soli,
3fl,3ob,3clar,3bsn,3horn,3trp,
3trom,timp,strings SUPRAPHON s.p.
(F168)

Vanocni *CCU,Xmas,carol
[Czech] mix cor,STBar soli,2fl,2ob,
2clar,2bsn,3horn,3trp,2trom,perc,
harp,org,strings,celeste CZECH
s.p.   (F169)

FISHERS OF MEN see Moore

FITCH, DONALD
Glory To God *anthem
SAB,org WORLD CA-4014-7 $.45 (F170)

FIVE ANTHEMS FOR TODAY *anthem
cor ROYAL s.p.
contains: Gibbs, Alan, I Will Lift
Up Mine Eyes; Hurd, Michael, It
Is A Good Thing To Give Thanks;
Jackson, Francis, Blessing And
Glory; Mawby, Colin, Thee We
Adore; Wills, Arthur, Ah My Dear
Angry Lord   (F171)

FIVE CAROLS FOR CHRISTMAS see La Berge,
N.J.

FIVE CHORAL RESPONSES see Peterson,
P.W.

FIVE CHRISTMAS SONGS FROM JAPAN see
Graham, Robert Virgil

FIVE EARLY AMERICAN HYMN TUNES *see
Bolton; Cambridge; Orleans;
Tennessee; Williamstown   (F172)

FIVE LITTLE SONGS FOR YOUNG PEOPLE see
Martin, Gilbert M.

FIVE MOTETS see Jeppesen, Knud

FIVE MOUNTAINS TO CLIMB see McCall,
Harlo [E.]

FIVE NEGRO SPIRITUALS *spir
(Ducander, Sten) men cor,fl,gtr oct
FAZER s.p.
contains: By An' By; Every Time I
Feel The Spirit; Go Down, Moses;
Listen To Lambs; Nobody Knows The
Trouble I've Seen   (F173)

FIVE NEGRO SPIRITUALS see Tippett,
Michael

FIVE PSALM FRAGMENTS see Stanton, R.

FIVE PSALMS OF PRAISE AND THE
RESPONSORIUM FROM THE "BECKER
PSALTER" see Schutz, Heinrich

FIVE SEQUENCES FOR THE VIRGIN MARY see
Anonymous

FIVE SETTINGS OF TEXTS BY THOMAS
TIPLADY see Lovelace, Austin C.

FIVE SETTINGS OF TEXTS BY THOMAS
TIPLADY see Lovelace, Austin C.

FLAG TO FOLLOW, A see Peterson, John W.

FLAME FOR THEE, A see Tolladay, David

FLANDORF, W.
Children Of God, The *Xmas
SATB,Bar solo (easy) FITZSIMONS
2084 $.20   (F174)

FLEISHER, SIMI
I Will Lift Up Mine Eyes *Gen/Thanks
unis,fl CHORISTERS A-96 $.30 (F175)

FLEMING, LARRY L.
Every Time I Think About Jesus
*anthem
SATB AUGSBURG 11-0539 $.30 (F176)

Give Me Jesus *anthem
SATB AUGSBURG 11-0540 $.35 (F177)

Ride On, King Jesus *anthem
SATB,S solo AUGSBURG 11-0541 $.25
(F178)

FLEMING, ROBERT
Mass Of St. Thomas *Mass
SATB (med easy) WATERLOO $.40
(F179)

FLEMISH CAROL
(Hutter) SATB (easy) OXFORD 84.213
$.25   (F180)

FLEMMING, FREDERICH
Praise Ye The Triune God *CC8L
(Krogstad, Bob) SATB,opt pno&2fl&
ob&3trp&2trom&2vln&vla&vcl&bvl&
perc&timp&harp oct GOSPEL
05 TM 0138 $.35, ipa recording
and trax also available   (F181)

Praise Ye The Triune God! *anthem
(DeCou, Harold) SATB oct SINGSPIR
ZJP-7319 $.30   (F182)

FLETCHER
Sacred Cantata No. 1 "O Childe Swete"
*cant
SATB,org,opt inst,4brass GENERAL
WDS GC25 $1.50, ipa   (F183)

FLETCHER, H. GRANT
By The Waters Of Babylon *anthem
SSA,S solo,pno WORLD CA-4013-3 $.80
(F184)

FLETCHER, PERCY EASTMAN (1879-1932)
Passion Of Christ, The
SATB,SATB soli,2fl,2ob,3clar,bsn,
2horn,2trp,trom,timp,org,strings
voc sc NOVELLO rental   (F185)

FLEUVE PROFOND *spir
(Robillard) 4pt men cor/4pt mix cor
GRAS s.p.   (F186)

FLORIA, CAM
Apostle, The *cant
(Azevedo, Lex de) cor,2vln,2trp,
2trom,horn,fl,clar,gtr,bvl,kbd,
drums LEXICON 37650 $2.95, ipa
(F187)

He That Overcomes *anthem
SATB,brass LEXICON CS-2614 $.35 see
from IT'S GETTING LATE (F188)

Share *cant
cor,2trp,2trom,horn,fl,perc LEXICON
37687 $2.95, ipa   (F189)

FLORILEGIUM CANTUUM SACRORUM *CC52L,
mot
(Kromolicki, J.) [Lat] 4pt mix cor
BOHM sc s.p., voc pt s.p. contains
works by: Rosselli; Anerio;
Palestrina; Schubert; Haydn; Lassus
and others   (F190)

FLOWER
Price Paid For Me, The *Easter
(Williamson; Pappadopoulos) SATB
oct GOSPEL 05 TM 0167 $.25 (F191)

FLUTE GLORIA *Fr
(Young, Gordon) SATB,pno,fl (easy)
oct ELKAN-V 362-03158 $.35 (F192)

FLY, DOVE see Heilakka

FODD AR SASOM SKRIFTEN SAGT see
Soderholm, Valdemar

FOERSTER, JOSEF BOHUSLAV (1859-1951)
Te Deum Laudamus *Op.146, ora
mix cor,2fl,2ob,2clar,2bsn,4horn,
3trp,3trom,tuba,timp,harp,org,
strings CZECH s.p.   (F193)

FOGG, ERIC (1903-1939)
Carol Of The Little King
see Christmas Carols

Christmas Carols *Xmas,carol
SA/SATB/TTBB BOSWORTH s.p.
contains: Carol Of The Little
King; Jesukin   (F194)

Jesukin
see Christmas Carols

FOLK CELEBRATION *CCUL,Contemp
(Bock, Fred) cor cmplt ed SINGSPIR
4355 $1.50, min sc SINGSPIR 4356
$.95   (F195)

FOLK GLORIA see Johnson, David N.

FOLK HYMNS WITH GUITAR see Browne,
Sister Deirdre

FOLLOW AFTER HIM see Rogers, Ethel
Trench

FOLLOW, I WILL FOLLOW THEE see Brown

FOLLOW JESUS see Lee

FOLLOW JESUS *CCUL
(Huff, Ronn) cor BENSON B0244 $1.95
stereo recording, tape, and-or
book-record sets available, contact
publisher   (F196)

FOLLOW ME see Hegenbart, Alex F.

FOLLOW ME see Liljestrand, Paul

FOLLOW ON see Litherland, Donna

FOLLOW ON see Lowry, Robert

FOLLOW THE STAR see Kennedy

FOLLOWING THE STAR *Xmas
(Black, Charles) SATB&jr cor,S solo
(easy) FITZSIMONS 2190 $.20 (F197)
(Black, Charles) SA,S solo (easy)
FITZSIMONS 5021 $.20 (F198)

FOLPRECHT, ZDENEK (1909-1961)
Resurrection *see Vrkriseni

Vrkriseni *Op.4
"Resurrection" mix cor,Bar solo,
3fl,3ob,3clar,3bsn,6horn,3trp,
3trom,tuba,timp,perc,2harp,pno,
org,strings CZECH s.p. (F199)

FOOL HATH SAID IN HIS HEART, THE see
Hovhaness, Alan

FOOL'S WISDOM see Alwyn

FOOT WASHING SONG, THE see Brown, S.L.

FOOTSTEPS OF JESUS see Everett, Asa B.

FOOTSTEPS OF JESUS see Landon

FOOTSTEPS OF JESUS see Slade

FOR A SMALL MOMENT see Yeakle, Thomas

FOR ALL MY SIN see Clayton, Norman

FOR ALL THE BLESSINGS OF THE YEAR
*anthem
(Cram, James D.) SATB&opt jr cor,opt
solo FINE ARTS CM 1007 $.30 (F200)

FOR ALL THY CARE see Gauntlet

FOR BY GRACE see Wyrtzen, Don

FOR GOD IS LOVE see Roff, Joseph

FOR GOD SO LOVED THE WORLD see Distler,
Hugo

FOR GOD SO LOVED THE WORLD see Hays,
Peggy McAllister

FOR GOD SO LOVED THE WORLD see Schutz,
Heinrich

FOR HARD THINGS see Marshall, Jane M.

FOR ME *anthem
(Reynolds) SATB oct BROADMAN 4562-33
$.35   (F201)

FOR ME TO LIVE IS JESUS see Bach,
Johann Sebastian

FOR SINGING MEN NO. 1 *CC13UL
(Lister, Mosie) 2pt (easy) LILLENAS
MB-243 $1.50   (F202)

FOR SINGING MEN NO. 2 *CC13UL
(Lister, Mosie) men cor LILLENAS
MB-334 $1.50   (F203)

FOR SION LAMENTATION MAKE see Handel,
George Frideric

FOR THE BEAUTY OF THE EARTH *anthem
(Goemanne, Noel) SAB&cong,org,opt
2trp (easy) GIA G1904 $.40   (F204)
(Red, Buryl) SATB oct BROADMAN
4565-38 $.35   (F205)

FOR THE BEAUTY OF THE EARTH see
Brydson, J.

FOR THE BEAUTY OF THE EARTH see Huff,
Ronn

FOR THE BEAUTY OF THE EARTH see Kocher

FOR THE BEAUTY OF THE EARTH see Kocher,
[Conrad]

FOR THE BEAUTY OF THE EARTH see
Pierpoint

FOR THE BEAUTY OF THE EARTH see Red,
Buryl

FOR THE BLESSINGS OF THE FIELD see
Wetzler, Robert

FOR THE LIVING OF THESE DAYS see
Blakley

FOR THE LOVE OF OTHERS
(Easterling, R.B.) 2-4pt mix cor
BROADMAN 4528-01 $1.50   (F206)

FOR THE MOUNTAINS SHALL DEPART see
Powell, Robert J.

FOR THIS WAS I BORN see Sleeth, Natalie

FOR THOSE WHO BELIEVE see Adams, Steven
R.

FOR UNTO US A CHILD IS BORN see Handel,
George Frideric

FOR YOU see Billingsley

FOR YOU A CHILD IS BORN see Cooper,
Rose Marie

FOR YOU I AM PRAYING see Williams

FORCUCCI, SAMUEL L.
Alleluia And Chorale (from Child Of
Wonder)
SATB, piano-four hands AMP A-685
$.35   (F207)

FORD
Alleluia! He Has Risen *Easter,
anthem
SAB/SA/unis oct LORENZ 7842 $.30
(F208)

Come And Mourn With Me Awhile *see
Faber

I Will Give Peace
SAB PRO ART 2825 $.35   (F209)
SSA PRO ART 2829 $.35   (F210)

FORD, FAITH DELL
Voice Of Triumph *Easter
cor,narrator LILLENAS ME-220 $.60
(F211)

FORD, OLIVE ELIZABETH
I Didn't Know *Contemp
jr cor oct GOSPEL 05 TM 0154 $.35
(F212)

Love Of Christ, The
SATB oct GOSPEL 05 TM 0105 $.20
(F213)

Thanks Be To God *Easter,Bibl/cant
SATB,pno&org (med diff,
demonstration cassette available
on loan) GOSPEL 05 TM 0472 $1.95
(F214)

SATB,2fl,2ob,2clar,2horn,3trp,
3trom,tuba,3vln,vla,vcl,bvl,timp,
perc,harp, 2 alto saxophones, 2
tenor saxophones, 2 baritone
horns (med diff, demonstration
cassette available on loan) sc
GOSPEL ipr   (F215)

Theme Of My Song, The *Xmas,Bibl/
cant
SATB,opt 2fl&2ob&2clar&2bsn&horn&
3trp&2trom&tuba&2vln&vla&vcl&bvl&
perc&harp (easy, recording also
available) voc sc GOSPEL
05 TM 0471 $1.75, sc GOSPEL ipr
(F216)

FORD, VIRGIL T.
Beatitudes, The
SATB BROADMAN 4562-27 $.35 see from
Sermon On The Plain, The   (F217)

Have You Not Known? *anthem
SATB (easy) oct BROADMAN 4554-58
$.30   (F218)

FORD, VIRGIL T. (cont'd.)
Hearers And Doers Of The Word
*anthem
SATB oct BROADMAN 4562-22 $.35
(F219)
SATB BROADMAN 4562-22 $.35 see from
Sermon On The Plain, The   (F220)

If You Seek, You Will Find *anthem
SATB (easy) oct BROADMAN 4554-54
$.30   (F221)

Let The Heavens Rejoice
mix cor BRODT 609 $.26   (F222)

Most Gracious God
mix cor BRODT 606 $.22   (F223)

On Judging
SATB BROADMAN 4562-24 $.35 see from
Sermon On The Plain, The   (F224)

On Love Of One's Enemies
SATB BROADMAN 4562-25 $.35 see from
Sermon On The Plain, The   (F225)

Sermon On The Plain, The *see
Beatitudes, The; Hearers And
Doers Of The Word; On Judging; On
Love Of One's Enemies; Test Of
Goodness, A; Woes, The   (F226)

Taste And See
2pt jr cor,org/pno GRAY CMR 3339
$.30   (F227)

Test Of Goodness, A
SATB BROADMAN 4562-23 $.35 see from
Sermon On The Plain, The   (F228)

Woes, The
SATB BROADMAN 4562-26 $.35 see from
Sermon On The Plain, The   (F229)

FOREVER IS A LONG, LONG TIME see Jensen

FOREVER TOGETHER WITH HIM see Peterson,
Pamela

FOREVER WIDER THAN THE SKY see
Delmonte, Pauline

FORGET ME NOT see Bach, Johann
Sebastian

FORGIVE MY LITTLE FAITH see Wild, Eric

FORGIVENESS see Whittier

FORNEROD
Messe Septieme Ton
4pt mix cor,pno/org/acap HENN 724
s.p. sc, voc pt   (F230)

Messe Solennelle
mix cor,soli,orch,org HENN 809 s.p.
(F231)

FORSBERG, ROLAND
Den Som Hor Mina Ord *Bibl
4pt mix cor ERIKS 335 s.p.   (F232)

Massa
2desc,fl,opt vln/vla sc ERIKS 259
s.p., ipa   (F233)

FORSCHEN NACH GOTT see Kreutzer,
Konradin

FORSTER, PETER
Ave Maria *Op.10,No.3
[Lat] 4pt mix cor,acap BOHM s.p.
(F234)

Pange Lingua
[Lat] 4pt mix cor,acap BOHM s.p.
contains also: Tantum Ergo (F235)

Tantum Ergo
see Forster, Peter, Pange Lingua

FORTH IN THY NAME see Young, Gordon

FORTH THE CONQUEROR HAS GONE see Wood,
Dale

FORTH TO THE NEW YEAR! see Young,
Gordon

FORTH WE GO TO BETHLEHEM *Xmas,anthem
(Ehret) SATB (med) oct BROADMAN
4561-40 $.30   (F236)

FORTITUDO MEA see Thybo, Leif

FORTNER, WOLFGANG (1907-   )
Agnus Dei "Es Sucht Das Lamm"
mix cor (diff) sc SCHOTTS C 33 571
s.p. see from Drei Geistliche
Chore   (F237)

Die Entschlafenen "Einen
Verganglichen Tag"
TBB,acap sc SCHOTTS C 33 746 s.p.
(F238)

FORTNER, WOLFGANG (cont'd.)
Die Pfingstgeschichte *Pent/Whitsun,
ora
SSATBB,T solo,org,ob,bsn,trp,trom,
strings, English horn (diff) sc
SCHOTTS rental, ipr, min sc
SCHOTTS ED. 5039 s.p.   (F239)

Drei Geistliche Chore *see Agnus Dei
"Es Sucht Das Lamm"; Geistliches
Lied "Der Mensch Lebt Und
Bestehet"; Gott Ist Unsre
Zuversicht (Psalm 46)   (F240)

Eine Deutsche Liedmesse *Mass
SSATB,acap (med diff) sc SCHOTTS
ED. 2928 s.p.   (F241)

Geistliches Lied "Der Mensch Lebt Und
Bestehet"
SSAATB,acap (diff) sc SCHOTTS
C 33 570 s.p. see from Drei
Geistliche Chore   (F242)

Gott Ist Unsre Zuversicht (Psalm 46)
SSAATB,acap (diff) sc SCHOTTS
C 33 572 s.p. see from Drei
Geistliche Chore   (F243)

Herr, Bleibe Bei Uns! *CCU,Eve
mix cor,org/cembalo,strings (med)
sc,cor pts SCHOTTS ED. 4219 s.p.,
ipa   (F244)

Jauchzet Dem Herrn Alle Welt (Psalm
100) Bibl
5pt mix cor,3horn,2trp,2trom (med)
sc SCHOTTS C 40 915 s.p., ipa
(F245)

Psalm 46 *see Gott Ist Unsre
Zuversicht

Psalm 100 *see Jauchzet Dem Herrn
Alle Welt

FORTY DAYS AND FORTY NIGHTS *Lent
(Overley) SA/SSA (diff) FITZSIMONS
3080 $.25   (F246)

FORTY DAYS TO EASTER *CCU,Easter,
anthem
SATB LORENZ $1.95   (F247)

FOSS, LUKAS (1922-   )
Baruch Hagever
see Lamdeni

Lamdeni *Isr
[Heb] cor, mandolin, glockenspiel,
or xylophone; 2vibraphones or any
plucked instrument; 2 guitars or
2 marimbas or one of each
SALABERT-US $5.00
contains: Baruch Hagever (TTBB,
solo,6inst); Mi Al Har Horev
(SATB,SMezATBarB soli,6inst);
Wa-Eda Mah (SA,SSAA soli,
mandolin or vibraphone or
plucked inst)   (F248)

Mi Al Har Horev
see Lamdeni

Wa-Eda Mah
see Lamdeni

FOSTER, STEPHEN (1826-1864)
Stephen Foster Suite *CCU
(Sjoberg, Per-Anders) SATB NORDISKA
NMS 6417 s.p.   (F249)

FOUNT OF EVERY BLESSING see Bach,
Johann Sebastian

FOUR ADVENT CHORALES see Bach, Johann
Sebastian

FOUR ANTHEMS see Pratt, G.

FOUR ANTHEMS FOR CHILDREN see Walton,
K.

FOUR CAROLS see Gardner

FOUR CAROLS see Paviour, Paul

FOUR CAROLS see Davies, Peter Maxwell

FOUR CELTIC CHRISTMAS CAROLS *CC4U,
Xmas,carol
(Gomer) SATB SCHIRM.G 2945 $1.00
(F250)

FOUR CHORAL MEDITATIONS FOR LENT see
Andrews, C.T.

FOUR CHORALES see Mendelssohn-
Bartholdy, Felix

FOUR CHORALES FROM "THE CRUCIFIXION"
see Stainer, John

FOUR CHRISTMAS CAROLS see Murray,
Margaret

FOUR CHRISTMAS CAROLS see Davies, Peter
Maxwell

FOUR CHRISTMAS CAROLS
(Murray) unis, Orff instruments
SCHOTT 10857 s.p.
contains: First Nowell, The; In
Dulci Jubilo; O Little Town Of
Bethlehem; Past Three O'Clock
(F251)

FOUR CHRISTMAS MOTETS see Zimmermann,
Heinz Werner

FOUR DEVOTIONAL SONGS see Campian,
Thomas

FOUR EASTER CHORALES *Easter,chorale,
Ger
(Deis) 4pt mix cor oct SCHIRM.G 8063
$.25
contains: Christus Ist
Auferstanden, "Christ Is Risen"
(17th cent); Ein Frolich Gesang,
"Alleluia" (17th cent);
Osterfreude, "Easter Joy" (15th
cent); Von Den Heiligen Wunden,
"Lament And Weep" (17th cent)
(F252)

FOUR EASTER CHORALES see Bach, Johann
Sebastian

FOUR FESTIVE ANTHEMS FOR CHILDREN'S
VOICES *see Declare, O Heavens,
The Lord Of Space; Oh, The Joy Of
It!; Singing For Jesus; Voices
United To Sing God's Praise (F253)

FOUR FOLK HYMNS FROM WYETH'S REPOSITORY
(Bennett, Lawrence) BROUDE BR. $.45
contains: Anonymous, Animation (SB,
acap); Anonymous, Concert (TB,
acap); Anonymous, Springhill (SB,
acap); Robison, Communion (SB,
acap) (F254)

FOUR FOLK SONGS FROM ABROAD *folk
(Shaw) SSA,acap (med) OXFORD 44.232
$1.10
contains: Adversity (Hung); Harvest
Home (Finn); Winter (Slav); Youth
(Slav) (F255)

FOUR FREEDOMS, THE see Mann, Johnny

FOUR HYMN INTROITS see France, William
E.

FOUR HYMNS FOR WEDDINGS see Andrews,
C.T.

FOUR MOTETS see Hovhaness, Alan

FOUR MOTETS see Palestrina, Giovanni

FOUR PASTORAL SONGS see Whitecotton,
Shirley

FOUR PSALMS see Schutz, Heinrich

FOUR RESPONSES see Hennagin, Michael

FOUR SERVICE ROUNDS see Krapf, Gerhard

FOUR SERVICES FOR CHRISTMAS *CCUL,Xmas
(Ramquist, Grace) mix cor LILLENAS
MC-248 $1.00 (F256)

FOUR SONGS FOR MALE VOICES see Zelter,
Carl Friedrich

FOURTEEN LITURGICAL WORKS see Nanini
(Nanino), Giovanni Maria

FOURTEEN RESPONSES, BENEDICTION, AND
AMENS see Harris

FOURTEEN STATIONS OF THE CROSS, THE see
Liszt, Franz, Via Crucis

FOURTH SHEPHERD, THE see Whitecotton,
Shirley

FOX, BAYNARD
Amazing Grace, How Can It Be *CC11U,
gospel
SATB,pno,inst (med) GENTRY G-632
$2.50 (F257)

Christmas Spirit, The *Xmas,pop
(Marsh, Don) SATB,pno (easy) GENTRY
G-250 $.40 (F258)

Closer To Jesus
(Keene, Tom) SATB,pno (med easy)
oct GENTRY G-242 $.40 (F259)

I Have A Friend, His Name Is Jesus
(Keene, Tom) SATB,pno (med easy)
oct GENTRY G-244 $.40 (F260)

I Wonder Why He Should Love Me
(Keene, Tom) SATB,pno (easy) oct
GENTRY G-241 $.40 (F261)

FOX, BAYNARD (cont'd.)
I'll Tell The World
cor BRIDGE Z 0577 (F262)
(Bock, Fred) TTBB,pno (med easy)
GENTRY G-229 $.40 (F263)
(Ehret, Walter) SAB,pno (med easy)
GENTRY G-257 $.40 (F264)

I'll Tell The World That I'm A
Christian
(Huff, R.) cor BRIDGE Z 1089 (F265)

Well Done, Thou Good And Faithful
Servant
(Keene, Tom) SATB,pno (easy) oct
GENTRY G-243 $.40 (F266)

FOX, GEORGE
Christ Is Our Cornerstone
SATB (med easy) WATERLOO $.40
(F267)

Christ Is Risen From The Dead
*Easter
SATB (med diff) WATERLOO $.40
(F268)

In The Lord's Atoning Grief
SATB (med diff) WATERLOO $.50
(F269)

O Lord We Beseech Thee
SATB (med diff) WATERLOO $.35
(F270)

FOX, LUACINE CLARK
There Came A Star *Xmas,cant
SATB&wom cor&speak cor,SAT soli
(easy) LORENZ $1.95 (F271)

FOXX, CHARLES
Eleazer
(Simon, William) SSA BIG3 $.50
(F272)
(Simon, William) SATB BIG3 $.50
(F273)

FRACKENPOHL, ARTHUR (1924-   )
As Joseph Was A Walking *Xmas
SATB STANDARD A43MX3 $.50 (F274)

Bless The Lord, My Soul *Easter/Gen
SATB STANDARD A46MX4 $.50 (F275)

O Give Thanks Unto The Lord
SATB STANDARD A45MX1 $.50 (F276)

Shepherds, Rejoice
TTBB,3horn,3trom,tuba, Baritone
Horn KING,R MFB 612 cor pts $.35,
cmplt ed $2.00 (F277)

FRAGRANT THE PRAYER see Lekberg, Sven

FRANCE, WILLIAM E.
Child's Prayer To The Shepherd
SA HARRIS HC 2002 $.25 (F278)

Four Hymn Introits *CC4U,hymn/
Introit
SATB (med easy) WATERLOO $.60
(F279)

Hear Us, Holy Jesus
SA HARRIS $.25 (F280)

Jesus, Tender Shepherd
unis HARRIS $.25 (F281)

Lord Jesus Think On Me
SATB (easy) WATERLOO $.30 (F282)

Lord Of All Power And Might
SATB HARRIS $.35 (F283)

Loving Shepherd Of Thy Sheep
SA HARRIS $.25 (F284)

Midwinter Carol *Xmas
SATB (med) WATERLOO $.35 (F285)

Most Glorious Lord Of Lyfe *Easter
SATB (med diff) WATERLOO $.35
(F286)
SATB (med diff) WATERLOO $.35
(F287)

O Lord Support Me
SATB HARRIS $.35 (F288)

FRANCK
In Den Armen Dein, O Herr Jesu
Christe
SSATB LAUDINELLA LR 119 s.p. (F289)

Lobet Den Herren, Denn Er Ist Sehr
Freundlich
SATB&SATB SCHWEIZER. SK 142 s.p.
(F290)

Lobet Den Herrn In Seinem Heiligtum
SATBB&SB, opt org LAUDINELLA
LR 41-42 s.p. (F291)

Vater Unser Im Himmelreich
SATB LAUDINELLA LR 13 s.p. (F292)

Was Mein Gott Will, Das Gscheh
Allzeit
SAAB&SATB LAUDINELLA LR 103 s.p.
(F293)

FRANCK, CESAR (1822-1890)
At The Cradle *Xmas,anthem
SA oct LORENZ 5402 $.35 (F294)

Bow Down Thine Ear *see Domine Non
Secundum

Domine Deus
(Calahan) "Merciful Father" [Lat/
Eng] SATB (diff) FITZSIMONS 2150
$.25 (F295)

Domine Non Secundum *Lent
(Sowerby) "Bow Down Thine Ear"
[Lat/Eng] SATB,T solo (med)
FITZSIMONS 2058 $.25 (F296)

Merciful Father *see Domine Deus

O Lord Most Holy
SATB HARRIS HC 4053 $.35 (F297)
(O'Neill, C.) TTBB (med easy)
WATERLOO $.40 (F298)

Praise The Lord *Easter/Gen
(Sowerby) SATB,STB soli (med)
FITZSIMONS 2045 $.35 (F299)

Psalm 18 *see Thee Will I Love

Thee Will I Love (Psalm 18) anthem
(Holz, William W.) SATB oct SACRED
S-168 $.35 (F300)

FRANCK, J.
Lord, Whose Passion Didst Reveal
*Lent
(Sateren) SATB,acap ART MAST 208
$.30 (F301)

O Breath Of Life *anthem
(Burkwall, Eldon) SSATB oct
SINGSPIR ZJP-7339 $.25 (F302)

FRANCK, MELCHIOR (ca. 1579-1639)
Also Hat Gott Die Welt Geliebt
SATB (contains also: Mein Schonste
Zier) SCHWEIZER. SK 67.04 s.p.
see also MUSIKBEILAGE ZUM
"EVANGELISCHEN KIRCHENCHOR 1967"
(F303)

Aus Tiefer Not
SATBB DOBLINGER S 201 s.p. (F304)

Du Sollst Gott, Deinen Herrn, Lieben
SATB SCHWEIZER. SK 53.06 s.p. see
also MUSIKBEILAGE ZUM
"EVANGELISCHEN KIRCHENCHOR 1953"
(F305)

Herr Jesu, Der Du Bist Fur Mich
SATB SCHWEIZER. SK 61.03 s.p. see
also MUSIKBEILAGE ZUM
"EVANGELISCHEN KIRCHENCHOR 1961"
(F306)

Ich Danke Dir, Herr Jesu Christ
SATB (contains also: Ich Weiss,
Dass Mein Erloser Lebt)
SCHWEIZER. SK 57.03-4 s.p. see
also MUSIKBEILAGE ZUM
"EVANGELISCHEN KIRCHENCHOR 1957"
(F307)

Jesus, Thou Tender Little One
(Ehret, W.) SATTB BROUDE,A 772 $.50
(F308)

Unser Leben Wahret Siebzig Jahr
*funeral/mot
SSATTB MOSELER MOR42 s.p. (F309)

Wenn Ich In Todesnoten Bin
see Hassler, Hans Leo, Wenn Ich
Einmal Soll Scheiden

FRANCO, JOHAN (1908-   )
As The Prophets Foretold *Easter,
cant
SATB,TB soli,3trp,2trom, carillon
sc AM.COMP.AL. $13.75 (F310)

Gloria
SATB,pno/org AM.COMP.AL. $2.75
(F311)

Hymn To The Heart Of Jesus
SATB,pno AM.COMP.AL. sc $4.95, voc
pt $2.75 (F312)

My Soul Has Wings
SATB,pno AM.COMP.AL. $1.65 (F313)

Mysterious Presence, Source Of All
SSAATTBB,pno/org AM.COMP.AL. $3.30
(F314)

Prince And The Prophecy, The
cor,soli,pno AM.COMP.AL. $5.50
(F315)

Psalm 98
SATB,harp sc AM.COMP.AL. $3.85, ipa
(F316)

Psalm 126
cor,T/Mez solo,org AM.COMP.AL. sc
$3.85, voc pt $1.10 (F317)

Psalm And Alleluia
TBB,acap AM.COMP.AL. $2.20 (F318)

FRANCO, JOHAN (cont'd.)

Romans By Saint Paul
SATB, carillon sc AM.COMP.AL. $6.00
(F319)

Song Of Life, The
SATB,pno AM.COMP.AL. $3.30   (F320)

Star Of Love
SATB,acap AM.COMP.AL. $1.10   (F321)

Stars Look Down, The
SATBB&boy cor,soli,2fl,2ob,2clar,
2bsn,3horn,3trp,2trom,timp,harp,
strings voc sc AM.COMP.AL. $19.80
(F322)

Two Anthems *CC2U,anthem
SATB,acap AM.COMP.AL. $2.75   (F323)

FRANKISCHE WEIHNACHTSLIEDER see Lang,
Hans

FRANKLIN
In A Cave *Xmas,anthem
(DeCou, Harold) SATB,opt fl oct
SINGSPIR ZJP-3001 $.30   (F324)

FRASER
Our Blest Redeemer *anthem
SATB,acap (easy) OXFORD 43.468 $.20
(F325)

FRED ETTERLATER JEG DERE see Nystedt,
Knut

FREE AT LAST *anthem
(Burroughs) SATB,T solo FINE ARTS
CM 1064 $.30   (F326)

FREE SPIRIT *CC11UL
(Huff, Ronn) cor BENSON B0232 $1.95
stereo recording, tapes, and-or
accompaniment tape also available;
for book-record sets available,
contact publisher   (F327)

FREED, ISADORE (1900-1960)
Prophecy Of Micah, The *ora
mix cor,3 soli,orch/org SAC.MUS.PR.
voc sc $1.75, sc rental, ipr
(F328)

FREEDOM PROCLAMATION see La Montaine,
John

FREEDOM SONG, THE see Caldwell, Mary
[Elizabeth]

FREELY, FREELY see Owens, Carol

FREEPEOPLE SING *CC10UL,Contemp
(Johnson, Paul) cor,pno,bvl,gtr
LILLENAS MB-323 $1.95   (F329)

FREI, JOSEPH (1872-1945)
Missa *Op.96
4pt mix cor,pno/org HENN 737 s.p.
sc, voc pt   (F330)

FRENCH, JACOB (1754-1817)
Two Hymns Tunes *CC2U
(Mason) oct WORD CS-361 $.30 (F331)

FRESCOBALDI, GIROLAMO (1583-1643)
Messa A Otto Sopra L'aria Della
Monica *Mass
(Mischiati) cor,2org ZERBONI 7883
s.p.   (F332)

Messa A Otto Sopra L'aria Di Fiorenza
*Mass
(Mischiati) cor,2org ZERBONI 7894
s.p.   (F333)

FRET NOT WHEN DOUBTS AND FEARS ASSAIL
see Handel, George Frideric

FREU DICH, DU HIMMELSKONIGIN see Degen,
J.

FREU DICH, DU WERTE CHRISTENHEIT see
Pepping, Ernst

FREU DICH, ERD' UND STERNENZELT *Xmas,
carol/folk
see Drei Altbohmische
Weihnachtslieder
(Biebl, F.) [Ger] 4pt men cor
MERSEBURG EM9056   (F334)

FREU DICH ERD UND STERNENZELT see
Riedel, Karl

FREU DICH, ERD UND STERNENZELT see
Schmider

FREU DICH, ERD UND STERNENZELT see
Schroeder, Hermann

FREU DICH, HEILIGE CHRISTENHEIT see
Pepping, Ernst

FREU DICH, MARIA see Lotti, Antonio

FREUDE, FREUDE, GROSSE FREUDE see
Hammerschmidt, Andreas

FREUDE IM ADVENT see Mullich, Hermann

FREUE DICH, DU TOCHTER SION see
Hammerschmidt, Andreas

FREUET EUCH DES HERRN UND SEID FROHLICH
see Fussan, Werner

FREUET EUCH IM HERRN ALLEWEGE see
Kretzschmar, Gunther

FREUET EUCH IM HERRN ALLEZEIT see
Briegel, Wolfgang Carl

FREUET EUCH IN DEM HERRN ALLEWEGE see
Schaper, Heinz-Christian

FREUET EUCH IN DEM HERRN ALLEWEGE see
Schweizer, Rolf

FREUET EUCH IN DEM HERRN ALLEZEIT see
Schmidt, C.

FREUET EUCH ZUR STUND *Xmas,carol/folk
(Riethmuller, H.) [Ger] 4pt men cor
MERSEBURG EM9054   (F335)

FREUND, SOLLN WIR ALLESAMT WIE IMMER
EINES SCHREI'N see Haas, Joseph

FREUNDT, CORNELIUS (1535-1591)
Sehr Grosse Ding Hat Gott Getan
SATB SCHWEIZER. SK 161 s.p. (F336)

FREUT EUCH ALLE, WEIHNACHTSLIEDERSPIEL
see Stern, Alfred

FREUT EUCH IHR HIRTEN ALL see
Seckinger, Konrad

FREUT EUCH, IHR LIEBEN CHRISTEN see
Schroder, Laurentio

FREUT EUCH, IHR LIEBEN CHRISTEN see
Schroter, Leonhard

FREUT EUCH, IHR LIEBEN CHRISTEN ALL see
Gesius, Bartholomaus

FREUT EUCH, 'SIST WEINACHT! see
Brautigam, Helmut

FREUT EUCH UND JUBILIERT see Bach,
Johann Sebastian

FREY, CARL
Drei Grablieder *Rembrnc
2-3pt sc,cor pts BOHM s.p.
contains: Eine Kleine Weil,
Op.27b,No.3; Grablied "Du Hast
Geduldet", Op.27b,No.1; Trost
Am Grabe "O Weinet Nicht",
Op.27b,No.1   (F337)

Eine Kleine Weil
see Drei Grablieder

Grablied "Du Hast Geduldet"
see Drei Grablieder

Messe In Es Uber "Fest Soll Mein
Taufbund" *Op.33, Mass
[Lat] 4pt mix cor,acap (E flat maj)
sc,cor pts BOHM s.p.   (F338)

Messe Zu Ehren Der Gottlichen
Vorsehung *Op.25, Mass
[Lat] 4pt mix cor,acap sc,cor pts
BOHM s.p.   (F339)

O Sacrum Convivium *Op.21, Mass
[Lat] 4pt mix cor,acap sc,cor pts
BOHM s.p.   (F340)

Tantum Ergo *Op.2
[Lat] SSATTBB,acap sc,cor pts BOHM
s.p.   (F341)

Trost Am Grabe "O Weinet Nicht"
see Drei Grablieder

Veni Creator *Op.3,No.1
[Lat] SSATTBB,acap sc,cor pts BOHM
s.p.   (F342)

FREY, RICHARD
Bell Noel *Xmas
SATB,org,hndbl FISCHER,J FEC 10123
$.40   (F343)

Hosanna In The Highest! *Palm
SATB,acap ART MAST 177 $.30 (F344)

Warmness Of Joy, The
SATB,org,inst BELWIN $1.50   (F345)

FRIED SCHAFF, O HERR, DURCH EINE EHR
see Schede, Paul

FRIEDENMESSE see Rohr, Hugo

FRIEND MEDLEY
see Mini-Musicals

FRIEND OF THE FATHER see Harris, Ron

FRIENDLY BEASTS, THE *Xmas,anthem/
carol,Fr
SATB oct LORENZ 8874 $.35
(Ehret, Walter) SA,org,opt 2fl (easy)
GIA G1889 $.40   (F347)

FRIENDLY PEOPLE see Milo, Phil

FRIENDSHIP WITH JESUS see Ludgate

FRINK
I Want To Thank You *anthem
unis (easy) oct BROADMAN 4551-69
$.30   (F348)

In Love He Came *anthem
SATB (easy) oct BROADMAN 4540-45
$.30   (F349)

Sing Jesus *folk
SATB oct LILLENAS AN-5067 $.30
(F350)

FRISCH, AL
As Joseph Was A-Walking *Xmas
(Ehret, Walter) SATB,pno oct REGENT
R-115 $.30   (F351)

FRISCH AUF IN GOTTES NAMEN see Rein,
Walter

FRITSCHEL, JAMES
Be Glad *anthem
SSAATTBB AUGSBURG 11-0549 $.40
(F352)

FRITZ, RICHARD
Deutsche Messe *Mass
mix cor,org KRENN 1.29   (F353)

FROHLOCKET MIT HANDEN ALLE VOLKER see
Buxtehude, Dietrich

FROM ALL THAT DWELL BELOW THE SKIES
see Three Hymns Of Praise

FROM ALL THAT DWELL BELOW THE SKIES see
Rasley, John M.

FROM ALL THAT DWELL BELOW THE SKIES see
Rider, Dale G.

FROM ALL THAT DWELL BELOW THE SKIES see
Williams, David H.

FROM ALL WHO DWELL BENEATH THE SKIES
*Proces
(Roff, Joseph) SATB LITURGICAL $.50
see also Twelve Hymns   (F354)

FROM DARKEST TOMB NOW TURN AWAY see
Bach, Johann Sebastian

FROM DISCORD TO SONG see Schwab

FROM EAST TO WEST see Goodman, Joseph

FROM EAST TO WEST see Rutter

FROM EVERLASTING TO EVERLASTING see
Bissell, Keith W.

FROM EV'RY STORMY WIND see Hastings

FROM GOD TO EVERYONE see Whittemore

FROM HEAVEN ABOVE see Glarum

FROM HEAVEN ABOVE see Johnson, S.

FROM HEAVEN GLOWING see Bach, Johann
Sebastian

FROM HEAVEN HIGH I COME TO EARTH see
Baumgartner, H. Leroy

FROM HEAVEN ON HIGH see Bach, Johann
Sebastian

FROM HEAV'N AND STARS DESCENDED
(Werle, F.) SATB BOURNE B231084-358
$.45   (F355)

FROM THE STAR TO THE CROSS see
Bartlett, Gene

FROM THEE ALL SKILL AND SCIENCE FLOW
see Peek, Richard

FROM TIES OF BONDAGE see Dale, Mervyn

FROM WHOM ALL BLESSINGS FLOW
SATB CIMINO $.50   (F356)

FROMM, HERBERT (1905-   )
Yom Zeh L'yisrael
[Heb] mix cor,cantor TRANSCON.
TCL 664 $.60   (F357)

FROMMLET, FRANZ (1901-   )
Ad Te, Domine, Levavi *Mass
[Lat] 4pt mix cor,acap sc,cor pts
BOHM s.p.   (F358)

FROMMLET, FRANZ (cont'd.)

Deutsche Singmesse "Zu Dir, O Gott,
Erheben Wir" *Mass
[Ger] men cor BOHM sc s.p., cor pts
s.p.   (F359)

Ego Sum Pastor Bonus
[Lat] 4pt mix cor,acap BOHM s.p.
(F360)

FRONLEICHNAMS-MESSE see Lemacher,
Heinrich

FRUIT OF THE SPIRIT IS LOVE, THE see
Geisler

FUGER
Good Christian Men, Rejoice Again
*see Wir Christenleut Habn
Jetzund Freud

Wir Christenleut Habn Jetzund Freud
(Bach; Talmadge) "Good Christian
Men, Rejoice Again" SSAA BRODT
HC 6 $.24   (F361)

FULLER
Book Of Responses *CCUL,cor-resp
SATB PRO ART 259 $.85   (F362)

Choral Calls To Worship *CC7L
SATB PRO ART 698 $1.00   (F363)

FULLER SEMINARY MEN'S CHORUS SINGING
JOYFULLY *CC10L
(Carmichael, Ralph) TTBB LEXICON
37635 $1.95   (F364)

FUM, FUM, FUM
(Parker, Alice) SATB,pno/org/orch
(easy/med) cor pts FISCHER,C
CM 7842 $.30 see also Seven
Christmas Carols   (F365)

FUNF EUCHARISTISCHE HYMNEN FUR DIE
PROZESSION AM FRONLEICHNAMSTAG see
Kromolicki, Joseph

FUNF GRABGESANGE see Backer, Hans

FUNF HYMNEN see Kutzer, Ernst

FUNF KANONS AUS GLAREANS DODEKACHORDON
see Meyer

FUNF KURZE UND LEICHT AUSFUHRBARE PANGE
LINGUA see Piechler, Arthur

FUNF LITURGISCHE GESANGE see Scharf

FUNF MADRIGALE UBER DIE ALTE EPISTEL
ZUM FUNFSTE SONNTAG NACH EPIPHANIAS
see Reda, Siegfried

FUNF PANGE LINGUA see Kromolicki,
Joseph

FUNF PSALMEN see Ammann, Benno

FUNF ROSEN "FUNF ROSEN GING ICH
BRECHEN" see Lang, Hans

FUNF SPIRITUALS *spir
(Mammel, A.) men cor,pno cmplt ed,sc,
cor pts TONOS 2390 s.p.
contains: By An' By; Deep River; My
Lord, What A Morning; Roll,
Jordan; Swing Low   (F366)

FUNF TANTUM ERGO see Faist, Anton

FUNF WEIHNACHTSLIEDER see Schroeder,
Hermann

FUNFTE MESSE IN F see Faist, Anton

FUNFUNDZWANZIG GEISTLICHE LIEDER see
Burkhart, Franz

FUN'N'EASY, VOL. I "WHERE THE SPIRIT OF
THE LORD IS" *CCU
(Johnson, Derric) cor (easy) BENSON
B0241 $1.95 stereo recording,
tapes, and-or accompaniment tape
also available; for book-record
sets available, contact publisher
(F367)

FUN'N'EASY, VOL. II "H-A-P-P-I-N-E-S-S"
*CCU
(Johnson, Derric) cor BENSON B0242
$1.95 stereo recording, tapes, and-
or accompaniment tape also
available; for book-record sets
available, contact publisher (F368)

FUR WEIHNACHT see Reimann

FURCHTE DICH NICHT see Baudach, Ulrich

FURCHTET EUCH NICHT see Hammerschmidt,
Andreas

FURCHTET EUCH NICHT see Raselius,
Andreas

FURCHTET EUCH NICHT, ICH VERKUNDIGE
EUCH see Topff, Johann

FURER
Gebet Des Niklaus Von Der Flue "Mein
Herr Und Mein Gott"
SATB SCHWEIZER. SK 164 s.p. (F369)

FURNIVALL, ANTHONY C.
Call, The
SATB STANDARD A41MX1 $.50   (F370)

I Am The Way
SATB STANDARD A42MX1 $.50   (F371)

FURWAHR, ES IST EIN KOSTLICH DING see
Schein, Johann Hermann

FUSSAN, WERNER (1913-   )
Der Herr Ist Meine Starke *mot
mix cor (med) sc SCHOTTS C 39 685
s.p. see from Vier Kleine
Motetten   (F372)

Freuet Euch Des Herrn Und Seid
Frohlich *mot
mix cor (med) sc SCHOTTS C 39 682
s.p. see from Vier Kleine
Motetten   (F373)

Ich Bin Das Licht Der Welt *mot
mix cor (med) sc SCHOTTS C 39 684
s.p. see from Vier Kleine
Motetten   (F374)

Vier Kleine Motetten *see Der Herr
Ist Meine Starke; Freuet Euch Des
Herrn Und Seid Frohlich; Ich Bin
Das Licht Der Welt; Was Betrubst
Du Dich, Meine Seele   (F375)

Was Betrubst Du Dich, Meine Seele
*mot
mix cor (med) sc SCHOTTS C 39 683
s.p. see from Vier Kleine
Motetten   (F376)

FUX, JOHANN JOSEPH (1660-1741)
Ave Maria
(Young, Percy) "O Hail, Mary" [Lat/
Eng] SATB,acap BROUDE BR. $.50
see from Music Of The Great
Churches Vol. I: St. Stephen's
Cathedral, Vienna   (F377)

Missa In C *Mass
SATB,SATB soli,cont,4trp,strings,
timp HANSSLER 10.275 sc s.p., cor
pts s.p.   (F378)

Music Of The Great Churches Vol. I:
St. Stephen's Cathedral, Vienna
*see Ave Maria, "O Hail, Mary"
(F379)

O Hail, Mary *see Ave Maria

FYRA MOTETTER FOR ROSTER OCH ORGEL
4pt mix cor ERIKS
contains & see also: Schonberg,
Stig Gustav, Denne Ar Min Enfodde
Son; Schonberg, Stig Gustav, Om I
Icke Omvanden Eder; Schonberg,
Stig Gustav, Ty Var Tva Eller Tre
Aro Forsamlade; Schonberg, Stig
Gustav, Vart Rike Som Har Kommit
I Strid   (F380)

G

GABRIEL
Higher Ground *Easter/Gen,gospel
(Hall) TB,pno/org oct BENSON S4135
$.25   (G1)
(Linn) SATB,soli,brass,strings,perc
oct LILLENAS AT-1126 $.45   (G2)

Just When I Need Him Most *gospel
(Whitsett) SATB oct LILLENAS
AN-1688 $.30   (G3)

GABRIEL, SR., CHARLES H. (1856-1932)
Send The Light *anthem/gospel
(DeCou, Harold) SA oct SINGSPIR
ZJP-2005 $.30   (G4)
(Johnson, Norman) SSATB oct
SINGSPIR ZJP-8081 $.30   (G5)

GABRIELI
Domine Exaudi Orationem Meam *mot
SAAT&TBBB HANSSLER 1.523 s.p.   (G6)

Maria Magdalene
[Lat] ATTB RICORDI-ENG BA10088 s.p.
(G7)

Messe Brevis
4pt mix cor,acap voc pt HENN 350
s.p.   (G8)

Plaudite
(Jorgenson; Wolfe) 3 cor SCHIRM.G
11895 $.60   (G9)

Timor Et Tremor Venerunt Super Me
*mot
SATBBB HANSSLER 1.506 s.p.   (G10)

GABRIELI, ANDREA (1510-1586)
Maria Magdalene Et Altera Maria
(Young, Percy) "Scarce Had The
Daystar Risen" [Lat/Eng] SATB,
acap BROUDE BR. $.40 see from
MUSIC OF THE GREAT CHURCHES VOL.
II: ST. MARK'S CATHEDRAL, VENICE
(G11)

Musiche Di Chiesa Da Cinque A Sedici
Voci *CCU
5-6pt OLSCHKI s.p.   (G12)

Scarce Had The Daystar Risen *see
Maria Magdalene Et Altera Maria

GABRIELI, GIOVANNI (1557-1612)
Beata Es Virgo Maria
6pt mix cor BONGIOVANI 2343 s.p.
see also Quattro Symphoniae
Sacrae   (G13)

Deus, Qui Beatum Marcum *No.4 (from
Symphoniae Sacrae)
(Hindemith, Paul) SATTB/SATTB,acap
(med) sc SCHOTTS C 40 413 s.p.
(G14)

Domine Exaudi Orationem Meam
dbl cor BONGIOVANI 2342 s.p. see
also Quattro Symphoniae Sacrae
(G15)

Exaudi Deus Orationem Meam *mot
TTBBBBB HANSSLER 1.489 s.p.   (G16)

Hodie Christus Natus Est *Xmas,
concerto
SSSAT&ATBBB,opt inst sc MOSELER
s.p., ipa   (G17)

In Eccelesiis
(Nielsen, R.) dbl cor,2ob,2bsn,
2horn,2trp,2vla,2vcl,bvl CARISH
rental contains also: Jubilate
Deo; Virtute Magna   (G18)

In Ecclesiis *No.26 (from Symphoniae
Sacrae) mot
(Hudson, Frederick) SATB/SATB,org,
3trp,3trom (med) min sc SCHOTTS
ETP 1061 s.p.   (G19)
(Stevens) SABarB/SATBar soli,3ob/
3trp,3trom voc sc NOVELLO rental
(G20)

Jam Non Dicam Vos Servos *mot
SATB&SATB,opt inst MOSELER MOR41
s.p.   (G21)

Jubilate Deo
see Gabrieli, Giovanni, In
Eccelesiis
dbl cor BONGIOVANI 2345 s.p. see
also Quattro Symphoniae Sacrae
(G22)

Judica Me *No.6 (from Symphoniae
Sacrae)
(Hindemith, Paul) ATTBB/SSAAB,acap
(med) sc SCHOTTS C 40 416 s.p.
(G23)

Magnificat *No.53 (from Symphoniae
Sacrae)
(Hindemith, Paul) SAAB/ATBB/TBBB,
acap (med) sc SCHOTTS C 40 496

GABRIELI, GIOVANNI (cont'd.)

s.p.   (G24)

Nunc Dimittis *No.58 (from
  Symphoniae Sacrae)
  (Hindemith, Paul) SSAAT/STTB/ATTBB,
  acap (med) sc SCHOTTS C 40 502
  s.p.   (G25)

O Quam Suavis
  dbl cor BONGIOVANI 2344 s.p. see
  also Quattro Symphoniae Sacrae
                                              (G26)

Omnes Gentes Plaudite *No.61 (from
  Symphoniae Sacrae)
  (Hindemith, Paul) SAAT/ATBB/ATTB/
  STTB,acap (med) sc SCHOTTS
  C 40 505 s.p.   (G27)

Quattro Symphoniae Sacrae
  cmplt ed BONGIOVANI 2341 s.p.
  contains & see also: Beata Es
  Virgo Maria; Domine Exaudi
  Orationem Meam; Jubilate Deo; O
  Quam Suavis   (G28)

Surrexit Christus
  (Nielsen, R.) 3pt mix cor,2trp,
  4trom,2vln/vla,cembalo CARISH
  rental   (G29)

Suscipe Clementissime Deus
  (Nielsen, R.) 6pt mix cor,2bsn,
  2horn,vcl,bvl CARISH rental (G30)

Virtute Magna *No.49 (from
  Symphoniae Sacrae)
  see Gabrieli, Giovanni, In
  Eccelesiis
  (Hindemith, Paul) STBBBB/SATTBB,
  acap (med) sc SCHOTTS C 43 529
  s.p.   (G31)

GABRIEL'S MESSAGE
  see At The Manger
  see Twelve Christmas Carols: Set 2

GABRIEL'S MESSAGE see Pettman, Edgar

GADSCH, HERBERT (1913-   )
  Jesus Ist Kommen
  3pt wom cor/3pt treb cor,ST soli,
  org sc,cor pts MERSEBURG EM461
                                              (G32)

Kommt Her, Des Konigs Aufgebot
  SAT/SAB/SB/SA,opt treb inst&bass
  inst HANSSLER 14.224 s.p.   (G33)

Nun Sich Der Tag Geendet Hat
  SAT/SAB (contains also: Nun Danket
  Gott, Erhebt Und Preiset)
  SCHWEIZER. SK 62.05-6 s.p. see
  also MUSIKBEILAGE ZUM
  "EVANGELISCHEN KIRCHENCHOR 1962"
                                              (G34)

Wo Gott Zum Haus Nicht Gibt Sein
  Gunst
  SAT/SAB/SA,opt treb inst&bass inst
  HANSSLER 14.194 s.p.   (G35)

GADWOOD, GARY
  He Came Singing Love
  SATB SCHIRM.G LG51784 $.40   (G36)

GAFORIO, FRANCHINO (1451-1522)
  Missa Carneval *Mass
  (Hammar) SATB SCHIRM.G LG 51709
  $1.75   (G37)

GAGLIARDI, GEORGE
  All I Can Give Is Myself *anthem
  1-2pt,opt gtr FINE ARTS EP 43 $.35
                                              (G38)

Bless My Soul *anthem
  SATB FINE ARTS EP 24 $.35   (G39)

I Would Be True *anthem
  (Cram, James D.) 1-2pt,opt gtr FINE
  ARTS EP 44 $.35   (G40)

Man Of Galilee, A *anthem
  SAT/SAB FINE ARTS EP 42 $.35 (G41)

New Kind Of Dream, A
  (Cram, James D.) mix cor,pno,gtr (a
  Christian musical) FINE ARTS
  M22869 $1.50   (G42)

Open My Eyes *anthem
  (Cram, James D.) SATB FINE ARTS
  EP 34 $.35   (G43)

Psalm Of Praise, A *anthem
  SATB,opt gtr FINE ARTS CM 1057 $.35
                                              (G44)

GAGNEBIN, HENRI (1886-   )
  Chant Pour Le Jour Des Morts Et De La
  Toussaint *cant
  cor,soli,orch HENN s.p.   (G45)

Les Splendeurs De La Creation *ora
  mix cor,soli,orch HENN 913 s.p.
                                              (G46)

GAGNEBIN, HENRI (cont'd.)

Messe Latine *see Mix, Org

Mix, Org
  "Messe Latine" mix cor HENN 923
  s.p. sc, voc pt   (G47)

Requiem Des Vanites Du Monde
  mix cor,soli,orch,org HENN 637 s.p.
                                              (G48)

Saint Francois D'Assise *ora
  mix cor,soli,orch,org HENN 658 s.p.
                                              (G49)

GAITHER, GLORIA
  Crusade Medleys *see Gaither,
  William J. (Bill)

Let's Just Praise The Lord *see
  Gaither, William J. (Bill)

Something Beautiful No. 1 *see
  Gaither, William J. (Bill)

Something Beautiful No. 2 *see
  Gaither, William J. (Bill)

GAITHER, WILLIAM J. (BILL)
  All God's Children *anthem
  SATB oct SINGSPIR ZBG-1005 $.50
                                              (G50)

Because He Lives *CC10UL
  (Powell, R.) 2pt sc BROADMAN
  4520-38 $2.25   (G51)

Because He Lives *anthem
  SATB oct SINGSPIR ZBG-1004 $.50
                                              (G52)

Come, Holy Spirit *Gen/Pent,anthem/
  gospel
  SATB (easy) oct LORENZ B247 $.35
                                              (G53)
  SATB oct SINGSPIR ZBG-1010 $.50
                                              (G54)

Crusade Medleys (composed with
  Gaither, Gloria) *CC18U,medley
  (Mercer, W. Elmo) cor BENSON B0298
  $2.50 stereo recording, tape,
  and-or book-record sets
  available, contact publisher
                                              (G55)

Even So, Lord Jesus *anthem
  SATB oct SINGSPIR ZBG-1012 $.50
                                              (G56)

Even So, Lord Jesus, Come *anthem/
  gospel
  SATB (easy) oct LORENZ B250 $.30
                                              (G57)

Family Of God, The *anthem
  SATB oct SINGSPIR ZBG-1008 $.50
                                              (G58)

Gentle Shepherd *anthem/gospel
  SATB,narrator,inst (easy) oct
  LORENZ B246 $.30   (G59)

Get All Excited *CCUL
  (Owens, Jimmy) cor BENSON B0771
  $1.95 stereo recording, tapes,
  and-or accompaniment tape also
  available; for book-record sets
  available, contact publisher
                                              (G60)

Get All Excited *anthem
  SATB oct SINGSPIR ZBG-1009 $.50
                                              (G61)

He Touched Me *anthem
  SATB oct SINGSPIR ZBG-1000 $.50
                                              (G62)

I Will Serve Thee *anthem/gospel
  SATB (easy/med easy) oct LORENZ
  B243 $.30   (G63)

In The Upper Room *Gen/Psntd,anthem/
  gospel
  SATB (easy) oct LORENZ B248 $.35
                                              (G64)

Jesus Is Lord Of All *anthem/gospel
  SATB (easy/med easy) oct LORENZ
  B242 $.35   (G65)

King Is Coming, The *anthem
  SATB oct SINGSPIR ZBG-1001 $.50
                                              (G66)

Let's Just Praise The Lord (composed
  with Gaither, Gloria) *CCUL
  (Mercer, W. Elmo) BENSON B0453
  $1.60 stereo recording, 8-track
  tape, stereo cassette,
  accompaniment tapes, and spiral
  edition also available from
  publisher   (G67)

Lovest Thou Me? *anthem/gospel
  SATB (easy) oct LORENZ B249 $.35
                                              (G68)

My Faith Still Holds *anthem
  SATB oct SINGSPIR ZBG-1004 $.50
                                              (G69)

Redeeming Love *anthem/gospel
  SATB (easy/med easy) oct LORENZ
  B241 $.35   (G70)

Resurrection Morning *anthem
  SATB oct SINGSPIR ZBG-1002 $.50
                                              (G71)

GAITHER, WILLIAM J. (BILL) (cont'd.)

Something Beautiful *anthem
  SATB oct SINGSPIR ZBG-1006 $.50
                                              (G72)

Something Beautiful No. 1 (composed
  with Gaither, Gloria) *CCUL
  (Powell, Rick) cor SINGSPIR 4020
  $2.50   (G73)

Something Beautiful No. 2 (composed
  with Gaither, Gloria) *CCUL
  (Powell, Rick) cor SINGSPIR 4021
  $2.50   (G74)

Something Worth Living For *anthem/
  gospel
  SATB,med solo (easy) oct LORENZ
  B245 $.35   (G75)

Spirit Of Jesus Is In This Place, The
  *anthem
  SATB oct SINGSPIR ZBG-1011 $.50
                                              (G76)

There's Something About That Name
  *anthem
  SATB oct SINGSPIR ZBG-1003 $.50
                                              (G77)

They That Sow In Tears *anthem/
  gospel
  SATB (easy) oct LORENZ B244 $.35
                                              (G78)

GALILEE, BRIGHT GALILEE see Sherwin

GALLERY CAROL see Gardner

GALLICULUS, JOHANN
  Magnificat Quinti Toni *Xmas,Magnif
  SATB,acap (incorporates German
  Christmas carols) MOSELER MOR156
  s.p.   (G79)

GALLOWAY
  Savior, Teach Me Day By Day *see
  Leeson

GALLUS, JACOBUS (1550-1591)
  At Jesus' Holy Name *see In Nomine
  Jesu

Behold, Thou Shalt Conceive *see
  Ecce Concipies

Christ, Our Lord, Is Arisen *Easter
  (Wienandt, E.) SATB,acap FISCHER,J
  FEC 10104 $.30   (G80)

Ecce Concipies
  (Simkins) "Behold, Thou Shalt
  Conceive" SATB,acap oct CONCORDIA
  98-2244 $.50   (G81)

Ecce Quomodo Moritum Justis *anthem/
  funeral
  SATB,acap (easy) OXFORD 43.474 $.25
                                              (G82)

Ecce, Quomodo Moritur *Holywk,
  funeral
  [Lat] 4pt mix cor,acap sc,cor pts
  BOHM s.p.   (G83)

Hodie Christus Natus Est *Xmas
  (Harris) SSATTB SCHIRM.G LG 51695
  $.30   (G84)

Hodie Nobis Coelorum Rex *Xmas
  (Hines) "This Is The Day" dbl cor
  oct CONCORDIA 98-2219 $.65 (G85)

In Nomine Jesu *anthem
  (Herter, J.) "At Jesus' Holy Name"
  [Lat/Eng] SATB (easy) GIA G1860
  $.45   (G86)

Laus Et Perennis Gloria *mot
  [Lat] SATB&SATB,acap EGTVED MK14, 9
  s.p.   (G87)

Mirabile Mysterium
  (McKelvy, James) SATBB,acap FOSTER
  MF145 $.40   (G88)

Missa Super Levavi Oculos Meos
  (Snizkovy, Jitka) [Lat] mix cor,
  acap CZECH s.p.   (G89)

O Salutaris Hostia
  4pt mix cor LIENAU
  MUSICA SACRA, NR. 23 cor pts
  s.p., sc s.p.   (G90)

Omnes De Saba Venient *anthem
  (Parker) SATTB,acap OXFORD A 302
                                              (G91)

Siehe, Dein Konig Kommt
  SATB (contains also: Singet Dem
  Herrn Ein Neues Lied, Denn Er Tut
  Grosse Wunder) SCHWEIZER.
  SK 58.01-2 s.p. see also
  MUSIKBEILAGE ZUM "EVANGELISCHEN
  KIRCHENCHOR 1958"   (G92)

This Is The Day *see Hodie Nobis
  Coelorum Rex

GALUPPI, BALDASSARE (1706-1785)
Beatus Vir (Psalm 112)
SATB,2ob,2horn,org,strings voc sc
BROUDE,A $5.60, ipr   (G93)

Psalm 112 *see Beatus Vir

GAMBOLD
Bring Us, O Lord, Closer To Thee
(Kroeger) SATB,S solo oct BOOSEY
5859 $.50   (G94)

GAMMAL FABODPSALM *folk/Psalm
(Kjell, Erik) "Old Alpine Psalm" mix
cor NORDISKA NMS 6526 s.p.   (G95)

GANSCHOW, T.F.
Sleep, Holy Babe *Xmas
SSAATTBB,A solo,acap (med)
FITZSIMONS 2042 $.25   (G96)

GARDEN AND THE SEPULCHRE, THE see
Protheroe, Daniel

GARDINER
Jesus, Thy Blood And Righteousness
*Commun,anthem
(Carmichael, Ralph) SATB oct
SINGSPIR ZJP-7229 $.25   (G97)

GARDNER
Balulalow *Xmas,carol
SA/SATB (med) OXFORD 84.217 $.35
see from Four Carols   (G98)

Cantata For Easter *Easter,cant
SATB,inst (med diff, also available
on rental) OXFORD 46.179 $9.50,
ipr   (G99)

Chanticleer *Xmas,carol
SA/SATB (med) OXFORD 84.216 $.35
see from Four Carols   (G100)

Christmas Hymn *Xmas
SATB (diff) OXFORD 84.215 $.55
                                (G101)

Four Carols *see Balulalow;
Chanticleer; Gallery Carol;
Remember   (G102)

Gallery Carol *Xmas,carol
SA/SATB (med) OXFORD 84.219 $.45
see from Four Carols   (G103)

Remember *Xmas,carol
SA/SATB (med) OXFORD 84.218 $.55
see from Four Carols   (G104)

GARDNER, INGRID N.
Lenten Meditation, A *Lent
unis&2pt CHORISTERS A-111 $.35
                                (G105)

Prayer For Lent, A *Lent
unis CHORISTERS A-128 $.30   (G106)

GARDONYI, ZSOLT
Davids Danklied *Bibl
SATB,Bar solo,2trp,trom,org (med)
sc,cor pts BAREN. BA5434 s.p.,
ipa   (G107)

GARLAND, HUGH
Two Christmas Carols (First Set)
*CC2U,Xmas,carol
mix cor LESLIE 4056 $.30   (G108)

GARNIER
Messe St. Nicolas De Flue
4pt mix cor,pno/org HENN 582 s.p.
sc, voc pt   (G109)

GARNINGAR UTAN KARLEK ARO INTET VARDA
see Ahlen, David

GASPARINI, QUIRINO (1749-1770)
Adoramus Te, Christe *mot
4pt mix cor,cont BIELER DM 2 sc
s.p., cor pts s.p.   (G110)

GASSMAN, CLARK
Gloria *anthem
SATB LEXICON CS-2658 $.45 see from
In Christ There Is No East Or
West   (G111)

In Christ There Is No East Or West
*see Gloria   (G112)

Step Into The Sunshine *see Thank
You For Doing It So Well   (G113)

Thank You For Doing It So Well
*anthem
2pt LEXICON CS-2573 $.30 see from
Step Into The Sunshine   (G114)

Word Was Made Music, The *cant
cor LEXICON 37699 $2.95   (G115)

GAST
Wir Ruhmen Uns Allein Des Kreuzes
unis,org sc HANSSLER 12.218 s.p.
                                (G116)

GASTOLDI
In Thee Is Gladness
(Schalk) SATB oct CONCORDIA 98-2229
$.40   (G117)

GASTORIUS, SEVERIUS
Was Gott Tut, Das Ist Wohlgetan
(Sellentin) men cor,acap TONOS 5631
s.p.   (G118)

GATE OF THE YEAR, THE see Walker, M.

GATHER ROUND AND PRAISE THE LORD see
Wild, Eric

GAUDE TERRA TENEBROSA see Anonymous

GAUDE, VIRGO GLORIOSA see Palestrina,
Giovanni

GAUDEAMUS IGITUR
see Sanctus

GAUDENS GAUDEBO see Lechthaler, Josef

GAUDETE see Ohrwall

GAUL, HARVEY BARTLET (1881-1945)
Ancient Moravian Christmas Carol
*sec,Xmas
SA GALAXY 1.1314.1 $.30   (G119)

Tennessee Mountain Psalm
SATB GALAXY 1.0748.1 $.30   (G120)

GAULTNEY
My Lord Is Near Me All The Time
*anthem
SATB (easy) oct BROADMAN 4535-47
$.30   (G121)

GAUNTLETT, [HENRY JOHN] (1805-1876)
Jezus Onze Grote Koning *Xmas
mix cor oct HEER 1521 s.p.   (G122)

GAUSS, OTTO
Assumpta Est *Op.104, Fest
[Lat] 4pt mix cor,acap sc,cor pts
BOHM s.p.   (G123)

Ave Verum Corpus *Op.231, Psntd,mot
[Lat] 4pt mix cor,acap BOHM s.p.
                                (G124)

Christkonigsmesse *Op.118, Mass
[Lat] unis sc,cor pts BOHM s.p.
                                (G125)

Confirma Hoc *Op.103, Whitsun,Offer
[Lat] 4pt mix cor,acap sc,cor pts
BOHM s.p.   (G126)

Messe Zu Ehren Der Heiligen Cacilia
*Op.81, Mass
[Lat] 4pt mix cor,acap sc,cor pts
BOHM s.p.   (G127)

Messe Zu Ehren Des Heiligen
Bonifatius *Op.198, Mass
[Lat] 4pt mix cor,acap sc,cor pts
BOHM s.p.   (G128)

Predigt- Und Segensgesange, Op. 26,
Heft 1: 3 Veni Creator *CC3U
[Lat] 4pt mix cor,acap sc,cor pts
BOHM s.p.   (G129)

Predigt- Und Segensgesange, Op. 26,
Heft 2: 4 Pange Lingua *CC4U
[Lat] mix cor,acap/org sc,cor pts
BOHM s.p.   (G130)

Terra Tremuit *Op.102, Easter,Offer
[Lat] 4pt mix cor,acap sc,cor pts
BOHM s.p.   (G131)

Tui Sunt Coeli *Op.101, Xmas,Offer
[Lat] 4pt mix cor,acap sc,cor pts
BOHM s.p.   (G132)

GAVAZZENI, GIANANDREA (1909-   )
Interludio (from Canti Per
Sant'Alessandro)
unis wom cor,3fl,3ob,2clar,3bsn,
4horn,3trp,3trom,tuba,timp,perc,
harp,pno CARISH rental   (G133)

GAVITT
I'm So Happy! *anthem/gospel
(Johnson, Norman) SA/TB oct
SINGSPIR ZJP-8086 $.30   (G134)

GAY
Nous Etions Trois Bergerettes *Xmas
4pt mix cor,acap sc HENN 719 s.p.
                                (G135)

GEBET see Simon, Hermann

GEBET DES NIKLAUS VON DER FLUE "MEIN
HERR UND MEIN GOTT" see Furer

GEBET IM ZWANZIGSTE JAHRHUNDERT "HERR,
DER DU DIE WEIHE DES LEBENS
SCHENKST" see Wolters, Karl-Heinz

GEBET "LEIH AUS DEINES HIMMELS HOHEN"
see Gluck, Christoph Willibald
Ritter von

GEBETE UND GESANGE see Nowakowsky,
David

GEBHARD
It Was For Our Iniquities
(Kroeger) [Ger/Eng] SATB oct
MORAVIAN 5852 $.50   . (G136)

GEBHARD, LUDWIG (1907-   )
Es Begab Sich *Op.35, Xmas,cant
eq voices/mix cor,narrator,soli,
inst (med easy) sc,cor pts
SCHOTTS ED. 5767 s.p., ipa   (G137)

GEBOREN IST DER IMMANUEL see
Praetorius, Michael

GEBOREN IST EMMANUEL see Brendel,
Engelbert

GEBORGENHEIT see Lemacher, Heinrich

GEBORN IST UNS EIN KINDELEIN *Xmas,
17th cent
(Knab, Armin) jr cor/wom cor (med
easy) sc SCHOTTS CHBL 520 s.p.
                                (G138)

GEBORN IST UNS IMMANUEL see Praetorius,
Michael, Enatus Est Emanuel

GEDENKE AN DEINEN SCHOPFER see Pepping,
Ernst

GEH HIN, MOSES see Petersen, Rolf, Go
Down Moses

GEHEILIGTE ZEIT see Coenen, Hans

GEIBEL
Sleep, My Little Jesus *Adv/Xmas
(Ehret, Walter) SA,opt fl oct
LILLENAS AN-3876 $.30   (G139)

GEISEL, GUSTAV
Mein Schonste Zier
SAT/SAB,SBar soli,org,2vln,opt vcl
cor pts HANSSLER s.p., ipa   (G140)

GEISLER
Fruit Of The Spirit Is Love, The
(Kroeger) [Ger/Eng] SATB,org,fl oct
MORAVIAN 5892 $.50   (G141)

Ode For Children's Day *cant
(Gombosi) 2pt treb cor,opt strings
(med) FISCHER,C CM 7846 $.40, ipr
                                (G142)

GEISTLICHE CHORMUSIK FOLGE 7: BITTE UM
VERTRAUEN (S 161-180) *CC20U
SATB cmplt ed DOBLINGER 43 508 s.p.
                                (G143)

GEISTLICHE CHORMUSIK FOLGE 9:
PSALMLIEDER (S 181-187, 189-192,
194-200) *CC18U,Psalm
SATB cmplt ed DOBLINGER 43 510 s.p.
                                (G144)

GEISTLICHE GESANGE see Hug, Emil

GEISTLICHE GESANGE-HEFTSAMMLUNG *CCU
men cor,acap TONOS 4605 s.p.   (G145)

GEISTLICHE HYMNEN UND GESANGE see
Killmayer, Wilhelm

GEISTLICHE LIEDER see Lahusen,
Christian

GEISTLICHE LIEDSATZE see Vento, Ivo de

GEISTLICHE ZWEIGESANGE, BAND 2: SPRUCH-
BICINIEN *CC65U
2 eq voices,acap/inst (med easy)
BAREN. BA3470   (G146)

GEISTLICHES LIED "DER MENSCH LEBT UND
BESTEHET" see Fortner, Wolfgang

GEISTLICHES LIEDERHEFT FUR MANNERCHOR
*CCU,hymn
men cor KROMPHOLZ s.p.   (G147)

GELINEAU, [JOSEPH] (1920-   )
Festival Mass
unis&cong/mix cor&cong,org BOOSEY
5922 cor pts $.45, sc $2.50
                                (G148)

GELOBET SEI DER HERR see Bach, Johann
Sebastian

GELOBET SEI DER HERR see Oertzen,
Rudolf von

GELOBET SEIST DU, JESU CHRIST see
Hammerschmidt, Andreas

GELOBET SEIST DU, JESU CHRIST see Heer,
Emil

GELOBET SEIST DU, JESU CHRIST see
Hennig, Walter

GELOBET SEIST DU, JESU CHRIST see
Oertzen, Rudolf von

GELOBET SEIST DU, JESU CHRIST see
   Osiander, Lucas

GELOBET, SEIST DU, JESU CHRIST see
   Pepping, Ernst

GELOBET SEIST DU, JESU CHRIST see
   Seckinger, Konrad

GELOBT SEI GOTT IM HOCHSTEN THRON see
   Oertzen, Rudolf von

GELOBT SEI GOTT IM HOCHSTEN THRON see
   Studer, Hans

GELOBT SEI GOTT IM HOCHSTEN THRON see
   Vulpius, Melchior

GELOBT SEIST DU, JESU CHRIST see Bach,
   Johann Sebastian

GEMEINSAME KIRCHENLIEDER *CCU
   unis MERSEBURG
   ISBN 3-87537-008-2 EM383   (G149)

GEN HIMMEL AUFGEFAHREN IST see Oertzen,
   Rudolf von

GEN HIMMEL FAHRT DER HERRE CHRIST see
   Burck, Joachim

GENE BARTLETT REVIVAL CHOIR BOOK, THE
   *CCUL,evang
   (Bartlett, Gene) SATB (very easy)
   BROADMAN 4520-19 $1.50   (G150)

THE GENE BARTLETT REVIVAL CHOIR BOOK,
   NO. 2 *CCUL,evang
   (Bartlett, G.) SATB (easy) BROADMAN
   4520-29 $1.50   (G151)

GENESIS see Williamson, Malcolm

GENESIS 4 see Newlin, Dika

GENESIS 21:6 see London, Edwin

GENNINGS
   In Bethlehem *Xmas
   SATB oct SCHMITT 8068 $.30   (G152)

GENTLE AS MORNING *CC10L
   (Kerr, Anita) SATB WORD 37707 $2.50
                                 (G153)

GENTLE FATHER see Day, Peggy

GENTLE JESUS, HOLY SAVIOUR see Jennings

GENTLE LIKE YOU
   see He Lives!

GENTLE LIKE YOU see Brown, Charles F.

GENTLE MARY see Ferris, William

GENTLE MARY see Harris

GENTLE MARY KNEW see Lovelace, Austin
   C.

GENTLE SHEPHERD see Gaither, William J.
   (Bill)

GENTLY MARY LAID HER CHILD see
   Rotermund, Melvin

GENZMER, HARALD (1909-   )
   Advent I
   see Drei Hymnen

   Advent II
   see Drei Hymnen

   Drei Hymnen *Adv/Xmas
   mix cor,SABar soli,2fl,2ob,2bsn,
   2horn,2trp,strings,timp (diff) sc
   SCHOTTS rental, ipr
   contains: Advent I; Advent II;
   Weihnacht   (G154)

   Messe In E *Mass
   SSATBB,SABar soli,2fl,2ob,bsn,
   2horn,2trp,trom,strings,timp (med
   diff) sc SCHOTTS rental, ipr
                                 (G155)
   Weihnacht
   see Drei Hymnen

GEORGE, EARL (1924-   )
   Infant Joy
   see Songs Of Innocence

   Introduction
   see Songs Of Innocence

   Lamb, The
   see Songs Of Innocence

   Laughing Song
   see Songs Of Innocence

   Shepherd, The
   see Songs Of Innocence

GEORGE, EARL (cont'd.)

   Songs Of Innocence *sac/sec
   SATB SUMMY $2.50
   contains: Infant Joy;
   Introduction; Lamb, The;
   Laughing Song; Shepherd, The
                                 (G156)

GEORGE FRIEDRICH HANDEL'S WORKS see
   Handel, George Frideric

GEORGE, GRAHAM (1912-   )
   Stir Up We Beseech Thee
   SATB HARRIS HC 4065 $.60   (G157)

GEPREISEN SEI DIE HEIL'GE NACHT see
   Burthel, Jakob

GERHARD
   Die Rede Des Paulus An Die Athener
   *cant
   SATB,B solo,2fl,trp,trom,strings,
   timp,harp,pno HANSSLER 10.243
   rental   (G158)

GERIG
   Lord, Make Us Instruments Of Thy
   Peace
   SATB oct SCHMITT 7046 $.35   (G159)

   On The Cross Of Calvary *Easter/Lent
   (Bock, Fred) SSAATTBB oct LILLENAS
   AN-1689 $.30   (G160)

GEROVITSCH, ELIEZER (1844-1913)
   Shire T'filoh *CCU,Fest/Rosh Ha-
   Shanah/Sab-Morn/Yom Kippur
   mix cor,cantor SAC.MUS.PR.
   S.M.P. 2-3 $15.00 three volumes,
   bound in two books   (G161)

   Shirej Simroh *CCU,Fest/Rosh Ha-
   Shanah/Sab-Morn/Yom Kippur
   mix cor,cantor SAC.MUS.PR.
   S.M.P. 4-5 $15.00 three volumes,
   bound in two books   (G162)

GERRETSON
   De Heilige Nacht *Xmas,cant
   mix cor/unis,pno/harmonium HEER 134
   s.p.   (G163)

   Golgotha *Psntd
   Mez/Bar,pno/harmonium HEER 103 s.p.
                                 (G164)

   In Efrata's Velden *Xmas
   mix cor/unis,pno/harmonium HEER 142
   s.p.   (G165)

GERSCHEFSKI, EDWIN (1909-   )
   Dedication *Op.36,No.3
   SSA,acap AM.COMP.AL. $3.30   (G166)

   Lord's Controversy With His People,
   The *Op.34,No.1b, cant
   men cor,T solo,orch sc AM.COMP.AL.
   $9.90   (G167)
   SSA,Bar solo,fl,ob,clar,bsn,2horn,
   trp,trom,timp,perc,harp,strings
   sc AM.COMP.AL. $11.00   (G168)

   Psalm 100
   SATB,acap AM.COMP.AL. $7.70   (G169)

   There Is A Man On The Cross *Op.34,
   No.2
   SATB,A solo,org AM.COMP.AL. sc
   $3.03, cor pts $1.10   (G170)
   SATB,A solo,org,2fl,2ob,2clar,
   2horn,2trp,2trom,perc,strings sc
   AM.COMP.AL. $6.05   (G171)

GESANGE ZUR PROZESSION AM
   FRONLEICHNAMSFEST see Erhard, Karl

GESANGE ZUR PROZESSION AM HEILIGEN
   FRONLEICHNAMSFEST see Erhard, Karl

GESIUS, BARTHOLOMAUS (ca. 1555-1613)
   Befiehl Du Deine Wege
   (Herrmann, H.) men cor,acap TONOS
   5644 s.p.   (G172)
   (Wiese, G.) men cor,acap TONOS 5622
   s.p.   (G173)

   Freut Euch, Ihr Lieben Christen All
   SATB (contains also: Ehre Sei Dem
   Vater) SCHWEIZER. SK 72.01-2 s.p.
   see also MUSIKBEILAGE ZUM
   "EVANGELISCHEN KIRCHENCHOR 1972"
                                 (G174)

   Nun Jauchzet, All Ihr Frommen
   SATB (contains also: Aus Tiefer Not
   Schrei Ich Zu Dir; Allein Gott In
   Der Hoh Sei Ehr) SCHWEIZER.
   SK 53.01-2 s.p. see also
   MUSIKBEILAGE ZUM "EVANGELISCHEN
   KIRCHENCHOR 1953"   (G175)

GESUALDO, DON CARLO (ca. 1560-1613)
   O Vos Omnes
   [Lat] SSATB,acap EGTVED MK11, 8
   s.p.   (G176)

GET ALL EXCITED see Gaither, William J.
   (Bill)

GET ALL EXCITED see Gaither, William J.
   (Bill)

GET IN TOUCH WITH THE SAVIOUR see Lee

GET READY see Mayfield, Larry

GETHSEMANE see Graham, Robert Virgil

GETHSEMANE see Steel, Christopher
   [Charles]

GETTING TO KNOW GOD see Golden, Nolan

GEVAERT, FRANCOIS AUGUSTE (1828-1908)
   Hymne De L'Office Du Soir
   "Vesper Hymn" SSA BRODT HC 3 $.28
                                 (G177)
   Vesper Hymn *see Hymne De L'Office
   Du Soir

GHEDINI, GIORGIO FEDERICO (1892-1965)
   Concerto Spirituale
   SS,pno,horn,2trp,strings,timp (med
   diff) sc SCHOTTS ESZ 5227 s.p.,
   voc sc SCHOTTS ESZ 4246 s.p., ipr
                                 (G178)

GIARDINI, FELICE DE' (1716-1796)
   Come, Thou Almighty King *anthem
   (Johnson, Norman) SATB oct SINGSPIR
   ZJP-3201 $.25   (G179)

GIB DICH ZUFRIEDEN UND SEI STILLE see
   Pepping, Ernst

GIB UNS LEBEN see Gottschick,
   Friedemann

GIBBONS, ORLANDO (1583-1625)
   Almighty God Who By Thy Son
   SAATB STAINER 3.0808.1 $.75   (G180)

   As On The Night Before This Blessed
   Morn *Xmas
   SATB,acap (easy) oct CONCORDIA
   98-1756 $.25   (G181)

   Behold, I Bring You Glad Tidings
   *Xmas,anthem
   SAATB,SSATB soli,org EGTVED KB31
   s.p.   (G182)

   Blessed Are All They
   SAATB STAINER 3.0807.1 $1.00 (G183)

   Glorious And Powerful God
   SAATB STAINER 3.0776.1 $1.00 (G184)

   Go, Labor On!
   (Clokey) SATB&jr cor (easy)
   FITZSIMONS 2138 $.25   (G185)

   Jesu, Grant Me This I Pray
   (Bairstow) mix cor BANKS MUS
   YS 1000 $.20   (G186)

   Magnificat *Magnif
   [Eng] SATB,acap EGTVED MK5, 8 s.p.
                                 (G187)

   O Come, Let Us Sing Unto The Lord
   *see Venite, Exultemus

   O God The King Of Glory
   (McCullough) SATB SCHIRM.G LG51787
   $.45   (G188)

   O Lord, Increase My Faith
   SATB,acap EGTVED MK6, 7 s.p. (G189)

   See, The Word Is Incarnate
   SSAATB STAINER 3.0758.1 $.75 (G190)

   This Is The Record Of John
   SATTB,T solo,cont EGTVED MK4, 17
   s.p.   (G191)

   Thou, The Central Orb
   SAATB STAINER 3.0817.1 $.75   (G192)

   Venite, Exultemus
   (Simkins) "O Come, Let Us Sing Unto
   The Lord" SATB,acap oct CONCORDIA
   98-2233 $.80   (G193)

GIBBS
   At The Manger *Xmas
   SATB,acap oct BOOSEY 1820 $.30
                                 (G194)

   Channels Only *anthem
   (Peterson, John W.) SATB oct
   SINGSPIR ZJP-7223 $.25   (G195)
   (Rasley, John M.) SA&opt TB (easy)
   oct SINGSPIR ZJP-6004 $.30   (G196)

GIBBS, ALAN
   I Will Lift Up Mine Eyes
   see FIVE ANTHEMS FOR TODAY

   Sing Ye To The Lord
   SATB STAINER 3.0783.1 $.40   (G197)

GIBSON
  Everybody Needs Somebody (composed
    with Krause)
    unis oct BENSON S4098 $.30   (G198)

  Hey God, I Really Love You (composed
    with Krause)
    unis oct BENSON S4132 $.30   (G199)

GIDEON, MIRIAM (1906-   )
  Adon Olom
    SATB,pno/org AM.COMP.AL. $2.75
                                  (G200)

    SATB,pno/org/ob&trp&strings
    AM.COMP.AL. sc $6.05, voc pt
    $1.38   (G201)

  Habitable Earth, The *cant
    SATB,SATB soli,pno/org,ob sc
    AM.COMP.AL. $12.10   (G202)

  Sacred Service *Psalm
    [Heb] SATB,SATB soli,org,fl,ob,bsn,
    trp,vla,vcl sc AM.COMP.AL.
    $11.00, ipa   (G203)

GIFT IS GIVEN, THE see Mathews

GIFT OF LIFE, THE see Burroughs

GIFT OF LIGHT, A see Wescott, Steve

GIFT OF LOVE see Moore, Michael

GIFT OF LOVE, A see Christiansen,
  Patricia

GIFT OF LOVE, THE see Hughes, Robert J.

A GIFT OF MADRIGALS AND MOTETS VOL. II
  *sac/sec,CC30U,madrigal/mot,16th
  cent
  (Slim, H. Colin) mix cor pap UNIV.CH
  ISBN:0-226-76272-6 $7.50   (G204)

A GIFT OF MADRIGALS AND MOTETS VOLS. I
  & II *sac/sec,CC30U,madrigal/mot,
  16th cent
  (Slim, H. Colin) cmplt ed,cloth
  UNIV.CH ISBN:0-226-76271-8 $37.50
  Vol. I Contains Artistic And
  Historical Background   (G205)

GIFT OF NEW SIGHT, THE see Klusmeier,
  R.T.A.

GIFT OUTRIGHT, THE see Thompson,
  Randall

GIFT TO BE SIMPLE, THE see Wood, Dale

GIFTS WE SHALL BRING *Xmas,anthem/
  carol,Span
  (Ehret, Walter) SAB (easy) GIA G1848
  $.40   (G206)

GILBERT
  Jacob's Ladder
    unis&SSA (easy) OXFORD 83.086 $.50
                                  (G207)
  Praise To The Lord
    SATB (med easy) OXFORD 42.371 $.50
                                  (G208)
    SS (med easy) OXFORD 82.106 $.50
                                  (G209)

GILLES, JEAN (1669-1705)
  Requiem Aeternam (from Messe De
    Morts) funeral
    (Dawson, E.; Guinaldo, N.) [Lat]
    SATBB,org/pno oct NATIONAL WHC-40
    $.30   (G210)

GILLETTE, JAMES ROBERT (1886-   )
  Three Anthems For Junior Choir
    *CC3U,anthem
    (med) ABINGDON APM-243 $.40 (G211)

GILLIS, DON
  Nazarene, The
    cor,soli&narrator sc BROADMAN
    4516-01 $4.95, cor pts BROADMAN
    4516-02 $1.50   (G212)

GILMORE, P.
  He Leadeth Me
    (Bradbury; Collins, Hope) SATB oct
    GOSPEL 05 TM 0204 $.20   (G213)

GILMOUR
  He Brought Me Out *anthem/gospel
    (Kirk, Jerry) SATB oct SINGSPIR
    ZJP-8137 $.25   (G214)

GINGRICH, I.
  Thou Didst Leave Thy Throne
    SATB (med) FITZSIMONS 2016 $.25
                                  (G215)

GIORDANI, TOMMASO (1730-1806)
  Trauungsgesang "Herr Du Und Gott"
    (Lechner, Lothar) mix cor (easy) sc
    SCHOTTS CHBL 301 s.p.   (G216)
    (Lechner, Lothar) men cor sc
    SCHOTTS C 37 874 s.p.   (G217)

GIORDANO
  Thanks Be To Thee
    (Goldman) SATB SCHIRM.G LG51744
    $.35   (G218)

GIORGI, GIOVANNI
  Laetentur Coeli *mot
    4pt mix cor,cont BIELER DM 1 sc
    s.p., cor pts s.p.   (G219)

GIPPENBUSCH, JAKOB (1612-1664)
  Die Ganze Welt, Herr Jesu Christ
    SATB,cont (contains also: Wenn Wir
    In Hochsten Noten Sein)
    SCHWEIZER. SK 66.04 s.p. see also
    MUSIKBEILAGE ZUM "EVANGELISCHEN
    KIRCHENCHOR 1966"   (G220)

GIROTTO, ALMERIGO
  Messa
    dbl cor,org ZANIBON 5460 s.p.
                                  (G221)

GIVE A CUP OF WATER see Turner

GIVE A CUP OF WATER see Turner, Lee

GIVE ALMES OF THY GOODS see Tallis,
  Thomas

GIVE EAR, O HEAVENS see Felciano,
  Richard

GIVE EAR, O LORD see Butler, Eugene

GIVE HIM THE GLORY see Hoffman

GIVE HIM YOUR HAND see Kirk

GIVE JESUS A CHANCE see Harrell, Jan

GIVE ME A VISION see Terrell

GIVE ME JESUS
  (Hairston, J.; Wilson, H.R.) SATB
    BOURNE B230672-357 $.45   (G222)

GIVE ME JESUS see Fleming, Larry L.

GIVE ME THE LOVE see Butler

GIVE OF YOUR BEST TO THE MASTER see
  Grose

GIVE THANKS AND SING see Collins

GIVE THANKS TO GOD see Peterson, John
  W.

GIVE THANKS TO THE LORD see Felciano,
  Richard

GIVE THANKS TO THE LORD see Wapen,
  Francis A.

GIVE THANKS UNTO THE LORD see Sanders

GIVE THE LORD A CHANCE see Reynolds,
  William Jensen

GIVE TO OUR GOD IMMORTAL PRAISE see
  Hurlbutt, Patricia E.

GIVE TO THE WINDS THY FEARS see Wesley

GIVE UNTO THE LORD see Elgar, Edward

GIVE YOUR HEART TO JESUS CHRIST see
  Perkins

GIVE YOUR LIFE TO THE LORD see Wild,
  Eric

GLAD AND BLITHE see Anonymous

GLAD, DIG, DU KRISTI BRUD see
  Bjarnegard, Gustaf

GLAD SONG see Mitchell, David L.

GLAD SOUNDS OF CHRISTIANS see Leaf,
  Robert

GLAD TIDINGS! GLAD TIDINGS! see
  Brandon, George

GLARUM
  From Heaven Above
    SATB SCHIRM.G LG51835 $.35   (G223)

GLARUM, L. STANLEY (1908-   )
  All Things Work Together For Good
    SATB (easy) FITZSIMONS 2209 $.20
                                  (G224)
  Ask And Ye Shall Receive
    SATB (easy) FITZSIMONS 2207 $.25
                                  (G225)
  Blessed Are They *Bibl
    SATB,acap (easy) FITZSIMONS 2156
    $.25   (G226)
  I Will Praise Thee
    SATB,acap (med) FITZSIMONS 2196
    $.20   (G227)

GLARUM, L. STANLEY (cont'd.)

  In Thee, O Lord *Bibl
    SATB,acap (easy) FITZSIMONS 2158
    $.20   (G228)

  Seek Ye First The Kingdom
    SATB (med) FITZSIMONS 2210 $.25
                                  (G229)
    SA (easy) FITZSIMONS 5027 $.25
                                  (G230)
  Trust In The Lord *Bibl
    SATB,acap (easy) FITZSIMONS 2162
    $.25   (G231)

GLASER, CARL G.
  O For A Thousand Tongues *anthem
    (Johnson, Norman) SATB oct SINGSPIR
    ZJP-7271 $.30   (G232)
    (Soderstrom) SSAATTBB,acap (med)
    FITZSIMONS 2062 $.25   (G233)
    (Soderstrom) TTTTBBBB,acap (med)
    FITZSIMONS 4053 $.25   (G234)

GLAUBE IST DER SEELE LEBEN see
  Gumpelzhaimer, Adam

GLEICHNIS VOM UNKRAUT ZWISCHEN DEM
  WEIZEN "DAS HIMMELREICH IST GLEICH
  EINEM MENSCH" see Pepping, Ernst

GLEICHNIS VON DER KONIGLICHEN HOCHZEIT
  "SAGET DEN GASTEN see Pepping,
  Ernst

GLINKA, MIKHAIL IVANOVITCH (1804-1857)
  Complete Works *sac/sec,CCU
    (Schwartz, Boris) [Russ/Eng]
    microfiche UNION ESP. 18 volumes
    in 23 bindings. $250.00   (G235)

GLORIA see Brown

GLORIA see Carter, John

GLORIA see Clarke, Henry Leland

GLORIA see Des Prez, Josquin

GLORIA see Dvorak, Antonin

GLORIA see Franco, Johan

GLORIA see Gassman, Clark

GLORIA see Haydn, (Franz) Joseph

GLORIA see Hoffmann, Ernst Theodor
  Amadeus

GLORIA see Hunkins, A.B.

GLORIA see Jenni, Donald

GLORIA see Mathias, William

GLORIA see Monteverdi, Claudio

GLORIA see Patterson, Paul

GLORIA see Peloquin, C. Alexander

GLORIA see Peters, William C.

GLORIA see Power

GLORIA see Rutter

GLORIA see Ryba, Jan Jakub Simon

GLORIA see Vivaldi, Antonio

GLORIA see Washburn

GLORIA see Zimmermann, Heinz Werner

GLORIA AND ALLELUIA see Lekberg

GLORIA "ENGEL, STEIGT ZUR ERDE NIEDER"
  see Trapp, Willy

GLORIA FOR THE KING OF GLORY see
  Pulkingham, B.C.

GLORIA IN EXCELSIS *Xmas
  SATB CIMINO $.40   (G236)
  (Hamilton, H.C.) SATB (med easy)
    WATERLOO $.30   (G237)

GLORIA IN EXCELSIS see Calvisius,
  Sethus

GLORIA IN EXCELSIS see Mozart, Wolfgang
  Amadeus

GLORIA IN EXCELSIS see Stanford,
  Charles Villiers

GLORIA IN EXCELSIS see Vivaldi, Antonio

GLORIA IN EXCELSIS DEO *Xmas
  (Bissell, Keith W.) TTBB (med diff)
    WATERLOO $.35   (G238)

GLORIA IN EXCELSIS DEO see Bach, Johann
Sebastian

GLORIA IN EXCELSIS DEO see Dietrich,
J.H.

GLORIA IN EXCELSIS DEO see Elder,
Dorothy Kosanke

GLORIA IN EXCELSIS DEO see Mozart,
Wolfgang Amadeus

GLORIA IN EXCELSIS DEO see Owens

GLORIA IN EXCELSIS DEO see Staden,
Johann

GLORIA IN EXCELSIS - PRAISE THE LORD
see White, Louie L.

GLORIA, LAUS ET HONOR see Stout, Alan

GLORIA PATRI *Contemp
(Pitts, Clay) SATB VANGUARD V575 $.30
see from Let Trumpets Sound (G239)

GLORIA PATRI see Dahlgren, Hans-Erik

GLORIA PATRI DOMINO see Palestrina,
Giovanni

GLORIA-SANCTUS-BENEDICTUS see Arnatt,
Ronald

GLORIA SEI DIR GESUNGEN *Xmas,folk,Fr
(Ophoven, H.) men cor,acap TONOS 2098
s.p.   (G240)

GLORIA TIBI see Bernstein, Leonard

GLORIA TIBI DOMINE see Welcker, Max

GLORIEZANG ('K ZAL EENS MIJN HEILAND)
mix cor sc HEER 2568 s.p.   (G241)

GLORIOUS AND POWERFUL GOD see Gibbons,
Orlando

GLORIOUS AND POWERFUL GOD see Stanford,
Charles Villiers

GLORIOUS CHURCH, A see Hudson, Richard

GLORIOUS EASTER DAY see Lush, Ron

GLORIOUS EVERLASTING see Cousins, M.
Thomas

GLORIOUS IN HOLINESS see Courtney,
Ragan

GLORIOUS IS THY NAME *anthem
(Angell) SATB oct BROADMAN 4562-35
$.35   (G242)

GLORIOUS STAR IS BEAMING, A *Xmas
(Hardwicke) SATB PRO ART 2847 $.40
                                   (G243)

GLORIOUS THINGS OF THEE ARE SPOKEN see
Ayers, Jacob S.

GLORIOUS THINGS OF THEE ARE SPOKEN see
Haydn, (Franz) Joseph

GLORIOUS THINGS OF THEE ARE SPOKEN see
Williams

GLORY *CC8U,folk
cor,pno/gtr GIA G1816 $2.00   (G244)

GLORY (from Freedom Country)
SATB WALTON 3064 $.40   (G245)

GLORY AND HONOR see Hegenbart, Alex F.

GLORY BE see Crawley

GLORY BE TO GOD see Fetler, Paul

GLORY BE TO GOD see York, Daniel
Stanley

GLORY BE TO GOD ON HIGH see Green,
Philip

GLORY BE TO HIM see Peter, Johann
Friedrich

GLORY BE TO THE FATHER see Crane, Lor.

GLORY, HALLELUJAH TO THE LAMB! see
Jones

GLORY OF CHRISTMAS, THE see King

GLORY OF EASTER, THE see Peterson, John
W.

GLORY OF OUR KING, THE see Lovelace,
Austin C.

GLORY OF THE FATHER, THE see Hovland,
Egil

GLORY OF THIS DAY, THE see Moe, Daniel

GLORY TO GOD see Neufeld, Rick

GLORY TO GOD see Adler

GLORY TO GOD see Fitch, Donald

GLORY TO GOD see Handel, George
Frideric

GLORY TO GOD see Haydn, (Franz) Joseph,
Gloria

GLORY TO GOD see Hooper, William L.

GLORY TO GOD IN HEAVEN *Xmas,Contemp
SATB VANGUARD V570 $.35 see from Come
To Bethlehem   (G246)

GLORY TO GOD IN THE HIGHEST see Gregor

GLORY TO GOD IN THE HIGHEST see Haydn,
(Franz) Joseph, Gloria

GLORY TO GOD IN THE HIGHEST see
Pergolesi, Giovanni Battista

GLORY TO GOD IN THE HIGHEST, GLORY see
White

GLORY TO GOD IN THE HIGHEST, GLORY see
White, Edward L.

GLORY TO GOD THE CREATOR see Parris,
Herman M.

GLORY TO GOD, THE SAVIOUR, KING see
Keller

GLORY TO GOD UPON HIGH see Calvisius,
Sethus, Gloria In Excelsis

GLORY TO GOD WE SING! see Skoog

GLORY TO HIS NAME see Bartlett

GLORY TO THE LAMB *Easter,cant/spir
(Johnson, Norman) SATB,Bar solo,org,
opt pno SINGSPIR 4269 $1.50 (G247)

GLUCK
Round The Lord In Glory Seated
(Miller) SATB SHAWNEE A5669 $.35
                                   (G248)

GLUCK, CHRISTOPH WILLIBALD RITTER VON
(1714-1787)
Gebet "Leih Aus Deines Himmels Hohen"
(from Iphigenie In Tauris) prayer
(Klink, Waldemar) jr cor (easy) sc
SCHOTTS CHBL 514 s.p.   (G249)

GO AND TELL see Plunkett, Bonnie

GO CONGREGATION, GO see Antes, John

GO-DAY, SIRE CHRISTEMAS see Kellam

GO DOWN, MOSES *anthem/spir
see Five Negro Spirituals
(Kennedy, M. ; Cadwallader, A.) 2pt
mix cor,pno/gtr GIA G1770 $.30
                                   (G250)
(Weber, Bernhard) [Eng] mix cor (med
easy) sc SCHOTTS CHBL 413 s.p.
                                   (G251)

GO DOWN MOSES see Petersen, Rolf

GO IN PEACE see Lovelace, Austin C.

GO LABOR ON see Blankenship, Mark

GO, LABOR ON! see Gibbons, Orlando

GO NOT FAR FROM ME, O GOD see
Zingarelli, Nicola Antonio

GO TEACH ALL NATIONS see Connolly,
Richard

GO TELL EVERYONE *Contemp
SATB VANGUARD V549 $.35 see from Go
Tell Everyone   (G252)

GO TELL EVERYONE *see Baker Woman,
The; Fill The Pots With Water; Go
Tell Everyone; It's Dark, Mary; Let
Trumpets Sound; Lower Your Eyes;
Peter And John   (G253)

GO TELL IT ON THE MOUNTAIN *sac/sec,
Xmas,anthem/spir
(DeCou, Harold) SATB oct SINGSPIR
ZJP-3029 $.25   (G254)
(Jackson, D.) SAB oct GOSPEL
05 TM 0172 $.35   (G255)
(Springfield) SSBar&camb,opt drums&
gtr CAMBIATA S117325 $.40   (G256)
(Work, J.W.) SATB GALAXY 1.1532.1
$.40   (G257)
(Work, J.W.) SA GALAXY 1.1960.1 $.30
                                   (G258)
(Work, J.W.) SSA GALAXY 1.1753.1 $.50
                                   (G259)
(Work, J.W.) TTBB,acap GALAXY
1.1583.1 $.35   (G260)

GO TELL IT ON THE MOUNTAIN see Loboda,
S.

GO, TELL IT ON THE MOUNTAINS *Xmas,
spir
(Huntley, F.) TTBB,acap (easy)
FITZSIMONS 4067 $.20   (G261)
(Soderstrom, Emil) SATB,acap (med)
FITZSIMONS 2114 $.25   (G262)

GO TELL THE UNTOLD MILLIONS see
Peterson, John W.

GO TO DARK GETHSEMANE see Miles,
Russell Hancock

GO TO GALILEE
CHAPPELL 0087403-3743 $1.00 (G263)

GO WHERE THE PEOPLE ARE see Seabough,
Ed.

GO YE INTO ALL THE WORLD see Butler,
Eugene

GO YE THEREFORE see Hancock, Gerre

GOD AND COUNTRY *CC9UL
(Skillings, Otis) mix cor cmplt ed
LILLENAS MB-324 $1.95   (G264)

GOD BE IN MY HEAD see Lovelace, Austin
C.

GOD BE IN MY HEAD see Matthews, Thomas

GOD BE IN MY HEAD see Ritchey, Lawrence

GOD BE IN MY HEAD see Rutter

GOD BE MERCIFUL see Donato, Anthony

GOD BE MERCIFUL UNTO US
(Bissell, K.W.) SATB (med diff)
WATERLOO $.40   (G265)

GOD BE MERCIFUL UNTO US see Hovhaness,
Alan

GOD BE MERCIFUL UNTO US see Schutz,
Heinrich, Deus Misereatur Nostri

GOD BE MERCIFUL UNTO US see Watson,
Ruth

GOD BLESS AUSTRALIA see Cowan, Marie

GOD BLESS THIS HOUSE see Smith, Julia

GOD CAN SEE US see Carmichael, Ralph

GOD CREATED see Ridenour, Joe

GOD, CREATOR see Hunnicutt, Judy

GOD DOESN'T SEE US THROUGH THE FLOWERS
see Carmichael, Ralph

GOD DOTH NOT SLUMBER NOR SLEEP see
Rasley, John M.

GOD GAVE HIM LIFE AGAIN! see Wilhelm

GOD GIVES HIS PEOPLE STRENGTH see
Winter, Sister Miriam Therese

GOD HAS GONE UP see Goode, J.

GOD IS A FIRE OF LOVE see Temple,
Sebastian

GOD IS A SPIRIT see Bennett, Sir
William Sterndale

GOD IS ALIVE! see Artman

GOD IS ALWAYS NEAR see Kemp, Helen

GOD IS GONE UP see Campbell, Sydney S.

GOD IS GONE UP see Rutter

GOD IS GONE UP see Young

GOD IS HERE LET'S CELEBRATE see Brandt,
Jobst vom

GOD IS HERE RIGHT NOW see Kaiser, Kurt

GOD IS IN EVERY TOMORROW see Wild, Eric

GOD IS IN HIS HOLY PLACE see Peloquin,
C. Alexander

GOD IS JUST A PRAYER AWAY see Watters,
William T.

GOD IS LIFE see Bach, Johann Sebastian

GOD IS LOVE see Ramseth, Betty Ann

GOD IS MY SHEPHERD see Young

GOD IS MY SONG see Ringwald, [Roy]

GOD IS MY STRONG SALVATION see Canning, Thomas

GOD IS MY STRONG SALVATION see Mueller

GOD IS NOW see Wright, Alberta Childs

GOD IS OUR ETERNAL REFUGE see Parks, Joe E.

GOD IS OUR HOPE see Grieb, Herbert [C.]

GOD IS OUR REFUGE see Mozart, Wolfgang Amadeus

GOD IS OUR REFUGE see Squire, Fred

GOD IS OUR REFUGE AND OUR STRENGTH see Tipton

GOD IS OUR REFUGE AND STRENGTH see Pool, K.

GOD IS SO GOOD
see Alleluia

GOD IS SO WONDERFUL *CC9UL
(Ferrin, Paul) cor BENSON B0960 $1.50
(G266)

GOD IS WISDOM, GOD IS LOVE see Ehret, Walter

GOD IS WORKING HIS PURPOSE OUT see Ainger

GOD KNOWS ALL ABOUT TOMORROW see Peterson, John W.

GOD LEADS US ALONG *cant
(Mercer, W. Elmo) cor BENSON B0779
$1.50   (G267)

GOD LIVES! see Hughes

GOD LIVES IN LOVE
see Three Peace And Brotherhood Canons

GOD LIVETH STILL see Bach, Johann Sebastian

GOD LOVES see Landgrave, Phillip

GOD LOVES ME see Mercer, W. Elmo

GOD MADE THESE FOR US TO LOVE see Turner

GOD MAKES A MIRACLE see Mickelson, Paul

GOD-MAN, THE see Wyrtzen, Don

GOD MOVES IN A MYSTERIOUS WAY see Greatorex, Thomas

GOD MOVES IN A MYSTERIOUS WAY see Roberts

GOD MY FATHER see Thomas, C.

GOD NEVER CHANGES see Skillings, Otis

GOD OF ABRAHAM PRAISE, THE
(Krone, B.) SAB KJOS 5739 $.35 (G268)
(Overley, Henry) SATB (easy)
FITZSIMONS 2188 $.25   (G269)

GOD OF ABRAHAM PRAISE, THE see Goemanne, Noel

GOD OF ABRAHAM PRAISE, THE see Mourant, Walter

GOD OF ABRAHAM PRAISE, THE see Schroth, Gerhard

GOD OF COMFORT see Chenoweth, Wilbur

GOD OF COMPASSION see Wilson, Keith E.

GOD OF CONCRETE see Lovelace, Austin C.

GOD OF EARTH AND PLANETS see Leaf, Robert

GOD OF EVERLASTING GLORY see Peterson, John W.

GOD OF GRACE AND GOD OF GLORY see Hughes

GOD OF GRACE AND GOD OF GLORY see Langston, Paul

GOD OF GREAT AND GOD OF SMALL see Sleeth, Natalie

GOD OF LOVE, THE see Marshall

GOD OF MERCY see Bach, Johann Sebastian

GOD OF OUR COUNTRY see Nagel

GOD OF OUR FATHERS
(Smith, C.T.) SATB WINGERT s.p.
(G270)

GOD OF OUR FATHERS see Warren

GOD OF OUR FATHERS see Warren, George William

GOD OF OUR LIFE see Purday, Charles Henry

GOD OUR FATHER see Hokanson, Margrethe

GOD PLACED HIS HAND ON MINE see Rhea, Raymond

GOD PUT HIS HAND ON MY SHOULDER see Peterson, John W.

GOD REST YE MERRY GENTLEMEN
(Parker, Alice) SATB,pno/org/orch
(easy/med) cor pts FISCHER,C
CM 7839 $.40, ipr see also Seven
Christmas Carols   (G271)
(Sharpe, E.) SA CRAMER $.25   (G272)

GOD REST YE MERRY GENTLEMEN see Lovelace, Austin C.

GOD REST YOU MERRY
(Willan) TTBB,acap (easy) OXFORD
94.101 $.15 see from Two Christmas
Carols   (G273)

GOD REST YOU MERRY, GENTLEMEN *Xmas,
anthem/carol
(Burroughs) SATB (easy) oct BROADMAN
4561-93 $.35   (G274)
(DeCou, Harold) SATB oct SINGSPIR
ZJP-3017 $.30   (G275)
(Lenel, L.; Plott) TTBB BRODT DC 8
$.24   (G276)
(MacNutt, Walter) SATB (med easy)
WATERLOO $.40   (G277)
(Nickel, Don) SATB (med diff)
WATERLOO $.40   (G278)

GOD SAID "I LOVE YOU" see Reese

GOD SAID IT see Adams, Steven R.

GOD SAVE THE QUEEN
(Bissell, Keith W.) SAB (med easy)
WATERLOO $.30   (G279)

GOD SAVE THE QUEEN see MacMillan, Ernest Campbell

GOD SO LOVED THE WORLD see Bruckner, Anton

GOD SO LOVED THE WORLD see Owens, Jimmy

GOD SO LOVED THE WORLD see Scheidt, Samuel, Sic Deus Dilexit Mundum

GOD SO LOVED THE WORLD see Stainer, John

GOD SO LOVED THE WORLD see Vick

GOD SPEAKS see Butler

GOD THAT WAS REAL see Wyrtzen, Don

GOD, THE LORD, SENT A MESSENGER see Anerio, Felice, Angelus Autem Domini Descendit

GOD, THE OMNIPOTENT see Lwoff

GOD, THE SOURCE OF LIGHT AND BEAUTY see Rider, Twila R.

GOD WAITS FOR YOU see Landgrave, Phillip

GOD WAS IN JESUS see Herbst, Johannes

GOD WHO MADE THE EARTH see Allen, Lanny

GOD WHO MADE THE EARTH see Thiman, Eric Harding

GOD, WHO MADE THE EARTH see Thomas, C.

GOD, WHO TOUCHEST EARTH WITH BEAUTY see Edgar

GOD WHO TOUCHEST EARTH WITH BEAUTY see McNair, Jacqueline Hanna

GOD WHO TOUCHEST EARTH WITH BEAUTY see Parrish, Mary Kay

GOD WITH US! EMMANUEL see Young, Phillip M.

GODDEN, REGINALD
Carol Of The Nativity *Xmas
SATB (med) WATERLOO $.35   (G280)

GODLY AND THE UNGODLY
(Harwood-Jones, H.F.) SATB (med easy)
WATERLOO $.30   (G281)

GOD'S ALIVE see Mahnke, Allan

GOD'S CHOIR IN THE SKIES see Overholt, R.

GOD'S ETERNAL PLAN see Miles, Russell Hancock

GOD'S FINAL CALL see Peterson, John W.

GOD'S GIFT see Burroughs, Bob

GOD'S GIFT see Vick

GOD'S GIFT OF LOVE
(Krone, B.) SSB/SSAB KJOS 5741 $.35
(G282)

GOD'S GONNA SET THIS WORLD ON FIRE see Red, Buryl

GOD'S GRACE IS ENOUGH FOR ME see Bartlett

GOD'S GRACE IS ENOUGH FOR ME see Bartlett, Gene

GOD'S GRANDEUR see Paynter, John P.

GOD'S LAND see Bednarchuk, Bruce

GOD'S LARK AT MORNING see Jordan, Alice

GOD'S LOVE GIFT see DeCou, Harold

GOD'S MERCY see Kodaly, Zoltan

GOD'S MIGHT RECALL, YE PEOPLE ALL
(Greyson, N.) SATB BOURNE B230839-358
$.50   (G283)

GOD'S MIGHTY STYLE
SATB UP WITH 6512 $.40   (G284)

GOD'S PEOPLE see Kaiser, Kurt

GOD'S PROMISE see Adler

GOD'S SON THIS DAY TO US IS BORN see Praetorius, Michael, Enatus Est Emmanuel

GOD'S WONDERFUL PEOPLE (LANNY WOLFE'S CHOIR BOOK) *CCU
(Powell, Rick) cor BENSON B0796 $2.50
(G285)

GOD'S WORD IN THEIR HEARTS see Butler, Eugene

GOD'S WORD SHALL STAND see Van Horn

GOEMANNE, NOEL
Cantate Sing To The Lord
SATB (easy) FOSTER MF147 $.40
(G286)
God Of Abraham Praise, The *anthem
2 eq voices/SAB/SATB,org,ob/fl
(easy/med) GIA G1830 $.40 (G287)

Magnificat *Magnif
"Mary's Canticle" [Eng/Lat] mix
cor,solo&narrator,org/pno oct
AGAPE AG 7159 $.45   (G288)

Mary's Canticle *see Magnificat

Missa Hosanna
treb cor,soli,acap FOSTER MF906
$.90   (G289)

Mit Freuden Zart *anthem
"Sing Praise To God" SATB/cong,org,
trp (easy) GIA G1833 $.40 (G290)

Praise The Lord
SATB,opt org,opt brass&timp SUMMY
M-5949 $.85   (G291)

Sanctus (from Missa Hosanna)
SSAA,acap FOSTER MF907 $.30 (G292)

Second Mass For Two Voices *Mass
2pt&cong,fl,vcl/org (med) GIA G1814
$1.00   (G293)

Sing Praise To God *see Mit Freuden Zart

GOETZE, ARTHUR A.
Hear Us, Holy Jesus *Lent
SATB,opt S solo,org ART MAST 132
$.30   (G294)

GOING TO BETHLEHEM see Hegenbart, Alex F.

GOLD, INCENSE AND MYRRH see Winter, Sister Miriam Therese

GOLDE, WALTER (1887-1910)
I Will Lift Up Mine Eyes
mix cor BRODT 522 $.30   (G295)

GOLDEN BREAKS THE DAWN see Graham

GOLDEN CANTATA see Bliss, Sir Arthur

GOLDEN CAROL *Xmas
(MacNutt, Walter) SATB (med easy)
WATERLOO $.40   (G296)
(McKelvy, James) TTBB (easy) FOSTER
MF1001 $.30   (G297)

GOLDEN CAROL OF THE THREE MAGI, THE
see Two Carols

GOLDEN HARPS see Reynolds, William
Jensen

GOLDEN LEGEND, A see Arch, Gwyn

GOLDEN, NOLAN
Getting To Know God
(McLellan, Cyril) SATB oct GOSPEL
05 TM 0135 $.35   (G298)

Melody
(Johnson, Paul) SATB oct GOSPEL
05 TM 0164 $.25   (G299)

GOLDEN RULE, THE see Mana-Zucca, Mme.

GOLDEN SEQUENCE, THE see Hamilton, Iain

GOLDMAN
Oh, May The Words
SATB SCHIRM.G LG51842 $.30   (G300)

GOLDSWORTHY, WILLIAM ARTHUR (1878-   )
Fear Ye Not: He Is Risen! *Easter,
Bibl
SATB (med) FITZSIMONS 2173 $.30
(G301)

O Little Lamb
SSA (easy) FITZSIMONS 3077 $.20 (G302)
SATB (med) FITZSIMONS 2085 $.20 (G303)

Out Of The Deep *Gen/Lent,Bibl
SATB (med) FITZSIMONS 2168 $.25
(G304)

GOLGATHA see Barbe, Helmut

GOLGATHA see Cossetto, Emil

GOLGOTHA see Gerretson

GOLGOTHA see Graham, Robert

GOLLER, FRITZ (1914-   )
Choralcredo I
[Lat] 3pt mix cor,solo,opt org sc,
cor pts BOHM s.p. contains also:
Choralcredo III   (G305)

Choralcredo III
see Goller, Fritz, Choralcredo I

Die Seelen Der Gerechten
see Totengeleit

Es Sungen Drei Engel *Xmas,Mass
[Lat] SABar,org,opt 2vln&vcl sc,cor
pts BOHM s.p., ipa   (G306)

Ewiges Licht Leuchte Ihnen
see Totengeleit

In Paradisum "Es Mogen Engel Dich
Geleiten"
see Totengeleit

Maria Aufgenommen Ist *cant
4-5pt mix cor&cong,org,opt 4brass
BOHM sc s.p., cor pts s.p. (G307)

Marien-Messe "Gruss Dir, Fraue"
*Mass
[Ger] 2 eq voices,org sc,cor pts
BOHM s.p.   (G308)

Pange Lingua
[Lat] 4pt mix cor,acap BOHM s.p.
(G309)

Proprium Der Messe Vom Allerheiligste
Altarsakrament *CCU
[Lat] 4-6pt mix cor,acap sc,cor pts
BOHM s.p.   (G310)

Requiem In F
[Lat] SABar,org (with Libera) sc,
cor pts BOHM s.p.   (G311)

St. Michaels-Messe *Mass
[Lat] 4pt mix cor,org,opt 2clar&
2horn&2trp&trom&strings&timp sc,
cor pts BOHM s.p., ipa   (G312)

Selig, Die Reinen Herzens Sind
see Totengeleit

Totengeleit *Rembrnc
3 eq voices sc,cor pts BOHM s.p.
contains: Die Seelen Der
Gerechten; Ewiges Licht Leuchte
Ihnen; In Paradisum "Es Mogen
Engel Dich Geleiten"; Selig,
Die Reinen Herzens Sind   (G313)

Totengeleit *CC4U,Rembrnc
[Ger] cor sc,cor pts BOHM s.p.
(G314)

GOLLER, VINZENZ
Leichtes Requiem *Op.27
[Lat] SAB&opt T/1-2pt,org,opt 2trp&
2trom sc,cor pts BOHM s.p., ipa
(G315)

Missa Simplex *Op.91, Mass
[Lat] SAB&opt T,org/harmonium sc,
cor pts BOHM s.p.   (G316)

Requiem *Op.10b
[Lat] 4pt mix cor,org sc,cor pts
BOHM s.p.   (G317)

GOMBERT, NICOLAS (ca. 1490-1550)
Angelus Domini
(Maniates, Rika) SATB (med diff)
WATERLOO $.60   (G318)

Ave Maria *BVM
(Maniates, Rika) SATB (med diff)
WATERLOO $.60   (G319)

Cantibus Organicis
(Maniates, Rika) SATB (med diff)
WATERLOO $1.00   (G320)

Diversi Diversa Orant
(Maniates, Rika) SATB (med diff)
WATERLOO $.75   (G321)

In Illo Tempore Loquente Jesu *mot
SATTBB,acap (med) sc SCHOTTS
ETP 991 s.p. contains also:
Monteverdi, Claudio, Messe No. 1
In C (mix cor) (Mass)   (G322)

Quam Pulchra Est
(Maniates, Rika) SATB (med diff)
WATERLOO $.60   (G323)

GONNA LOSE MY BURDENS see Mercer, W.
Elmo

GOOD
Take A Step
SSATB oct BENSON S4260 $.20   (G324)

GOOD-BY, WORLD, GOOD-BY see Lister,
Mosie

GOOD-BYE, WORLD, GOOD-BYE see Lister,
Mosie

GOOD CHEER see Hamilton

GOOD CHRISTIAN FOLK, REJOICE *Xmas/
Gen,cant
(Blakley, Duane) 1-2pt jr cor,kbd,
hpsd,2fl,vln,vla,vcl/bsn BROADMAN
4513-09 $1.50, ipa   (G325)

GOOD CHRISTIAN MEN, REJOICE *Xmas,
anthem/carol
see Three Christmas Carol Anthems
(Clark, Henry A.) mix cor LESLIE 4110
$.30   (G326)
(Johnson, Norman) SATB oct SINGSPIR
ZJP-3006 $.25   (G327)
(Parker, Alice) SATB,pno/org/orch
(easy/med) cor pts FISCHER,C
CM 7840 $.40, ipr see also Seven
Christmas Carols   (G328)

GOOD CHRISTIAN MEN, REJOICE AGAIN see
Fuger, Wir Christenleut Habn
Jetzund Freud

GOOD CHRISTIAN MEN, REJOICE AND SING!
see Ferguson, Barry

GOOD CHRISTIAN MEN, REJOICE AND SING
see Vulpius, Melchior

GOOD FRIDAY see Hovland, Egil,
Langfredag

GOOD FRIDAY see Holst, Gustav

GOOD FRIDAY MEDITATION see King

GOOD KING WENCESLAS see Hill, Harry

GOOD KING WENCESLAUS *sac/sec,Xmas
(Bergmann) unis,pno,strings,perc,rec
SCHOTT RS23 cmplt ed s.p., sc s.p.,
ipa   (G329)

GOOD LIFE!, THE see Peterson, John W.

GOOD LIFE, THE see Red, Buryl

GOOD MORNING, LORD see Salsbury, Sonny

GOOD NEWS see Leaf, Robert

GOOD NEWS *folk
(Oldenburg, Bob) cor,gtr BROADMAN
4518-01 $2.95   (G330)

GOOD NEWS! see Pelz, Walter L.

GOOD NEWS FROM HEAVEN see Littleton,
Bill J.

GOOD SAMARITAN, THE see Hufschmidt,
Wolfgang, Der Barmherzige Samariter

GOODE, GEORGE
O For A Closer Walk With God
unis CRAMER $.25   (G331)

GOODE, J.
God Has Gone Up
SATB,org GRAY CMR 3332 $.30   (G332)

GOODMAN, JOSEPH
Angelus Ad Virginem
see Two Carols For Christmas

Babe In Bethlehem's Manger Laid, The
*carol,Eng
SATB,perc sc BROUDE,A $1.00 (G333)

From East To West *Xmas
SATB WHITE,ERN $.30   (G334)

Missa Brevis *Mass
[Eng] unis,org WHITE,ERN $.50
(G335)

On Christmas Night All Christians
Sing *carol,Eng
2pt mix cor,perc sc BROUDE,A $.65
(G336)

Quem Pastores
see Two Carols For Christmas

St. Luke's Mass *Mass
[Eng] SATB,acap (diff) WHITE,ERN
$.85   (G337)

Two Carols For Christmas *Xmas
2pt, triangle GRAY CMR 3341 $.30
contains: Angelus Ad Virginem;
Quem Pastores   (G338)

When The Lord Drew Nigh *Easter/Lent
SATB WHITE,ERN $.40   (G339)

GOODNIGHT, GOD BLESS YOU
(Wild, Eric) SATB,pno BERANDOL
BER1229 $.50   (G340)

GOODWIN, DAISY
I'm Alive! *Easter,Contemp
(Krogstad, Bob) jr cor oct GOSPEL
05 TM 0344 $.35   (G341)

GOOSSEN, FREDERIC
American Meditations *see Bohemian
Hymn, The; Come Lovely And
Soothing Death; It Is No Dream Of
Mine; Man's Life Is Like A Rose;
Only God   (G342)

Bohemian Hymn, The *sac/sec
SA PEER $.40 see from American
Meditations   (G343)

Come Lovely And Soothing Death *sac/
sec
SSA PEER $.60 see from American
Meditations   (G344)

It Is No Dream Of Mine *sac/sec
SSA PEER $.40 see from American
Meditations   (G345)

Man's Life Is Like A Rose *sac/sec
SSA PEER $.40 see from American
Meditations   (G346)

Only God *sac/sec
SSA PEER $.40 see from American
Meditations   (G347)

GORCZYCKI, GREGOR GERVASIUS
(ca. 1664-1734)
Ave Maria
(Herter, Joseph A.) [Lat] TTBB GIA
G1971 $.30   (G348)

GORDON, ADONIRAM J.
My Jesus, I Love Thee *anthem
(Smith, Lani) SATB (med easy) oct
LORENZ B239 $.35   (G349)

GORDON, JOHN
Three Christmas Chorales *CC3U
SSA EMI s.p.   (G350)

GORDON, PHILIP (1894-   )
Masters In This Hall
SATB BOURNE B216242-358 $.50 (G351)

GORE, RICHARD T.
Beatitudes, The *anthem,Contemp
SATB,acap oct CHANTRY COA 512 $.24
(G352)

Bring Us, O Lord God
SATB,org CHANTRY COA 7455 $.30
(G353)

Cantata On "Saint Anne"
SATB,SBar soli,org CHANTRY COC 746
$.75   (G354)

Choral Preface And Benediction, A
*anthem,Contemp
SATB,acap oct CHANTRY COA 6015 $.10
(G355)

GORE, RICHARD T. (cont'd.)

Christmas Hymns And Rounds *CCU,
Xmas,round
cor CHANTRY COA 5912 $.35   (G356)

Christmas Songs And Rounds *CC3UL,
Xmas,anthem,Contemp
SATB oct CHANTRY COA 5912 $.35
(G357)

Hundredth Psalm, The (Psalm 100)
anthem,Contemp
SATB,org (easy) oct CHANTRY
COA 6014 $.25   (G358)

I Sing Of A Maiden *anthem,Contemp
SATB,acap oct CHANTRY COA 534 $.16
(G359)

Introits And Graduals For The Church
Year I *CCU,liturg
SATB,opt solo CHANTRY LIT 621 $3.50
(G360)

Introits And Graduals II Section I
*CCU,liturg
CHANTRY LIT 739 $.40   (G361)

Introits For Lent And Easter *CCU,
Easter/Lent,liturg
mix cor CHANTRY LIT 621EX $.50
(G362)

Moon Her Light Is Showing, The *Eve/
Gen,anthem,Contemp
SATB,acap (easy) oct CHANTRY
COA 6834 $.30   (G363)

New Commandment, A *anthem,Contemp
SATB,org oct CHANTRY COA 5911 $.24
(G364)

O Lord, Support Us *anthem,Contemp
SATB,acap oct CHANTRY COA 513 $.15
(G365)

Prayer Of Saint Francis, The
*anthem,Contemp
SATB,acap (med easy) oct CHANTRY
COA 6624 $.20   (G366)

Psalm 100 *see Hundredth Psalm, The

Seven French Noels On Daquin Carols
*CC7U,Xmas,Fr
unis jr cor&desc,opt solo CHANTRY
CHC 675 $1.00   (G367)

Three Songs For Lent And Easter *see
Lenel, Ludwig

With Joy We Come *Easter,anthem/
hymn,Contemp
unis&2pt oct CHANTRY COA 6833 $.25
(G368)

GOSPEL ACCLAMATION VERSES see Pross, D.

GOSPEL CHOIR CLASSICS NO. 1 *CCUL,
gospel
cor SINGSPIR 5195 $1.25   (G369)

GOSPEL CHOIR CLASSICS NO. 2 *CCUL,
gospel
cor SINGSPIR 5196 $1.25   (G370)

GOSPEL CHOIR CLASSICS NO. 3 *CCUL.
gospel
cor SINGSPIR 5197 $1.25   (G371)

GOSPEL CHOIR FAVORITES *CCUL,gospel
(DeCou, Harold) cor SINGSPIR 5660
$1.50   (G372)

GOSPEL CHOIR-NASHVILLE STYLE, VOL. I
*CCUL
(Mercer, W. Elmo) cor BENSON B0234
$1.50 stereo recording, tapes, and-
or accompaniment tape also
available; for book-record sets
available, contact publisher (G373)

GOSPEL CHOIR-NASHVILLE STYLE, VOL. II
*CCUL
(Mercer, W. Elmo) cor BENSON B0237
$1.50   (G374)

GOSPEL CHOIR-NASHVILLE STYLE, VOL. III
*CCUL
(Mercer, W. Elmo) cor BENSON B0239
$1.95   (G375)

GOSPEL CHOIR SELECTIONS *CC16U,anthem
(Bock, Fred) mix cor LILLENAS MB-307
$1.50   (G376)

GOSPEL FAVORITES FOR THE SMALL CHURCH
CHOIR *CCU,gospel
(Rasley, John) cor SINGSPIR 5210
SINGSPIR 5210 $1.50   (G377)

GOSPEL OF PEACE, THE see Fettke, Tom

GOSPEL SING! *CCU
(Raymer, Elwyn) jr cor/sr cor
BROADMAN 4520-17 $1.50   (G378)

GOSPEL SONG ANTHEMS NO. 6 *CCU,anthem/
gospel
SATB/SA LORENZ $1.95   (G379)

GOSPEL SONG OF JESUS see Lanier

GOSPEL TRAIN *spir
(Johnson) SA,inst OXFORD T108 ipa
(G380)

GOSS, JOHN (1800-1880)
Christ Our Passover
mix cor BANKS MUS YS 104 $.20
(G381)

I Will Magnify Thee, O Lord
mix cor BANKS MUS YS 137 $.25
(G382)

If We Believe That Jesus Died
*anthem
(Wood, Dale) SATB WORD CS-327 $.30
(G383)

O Saviour Of The World
mix cor BANKS MUS YS 403 $.20
(G384)

SATB (easy) FITZSIMONS 2050 $.20
(G385)

Praise! *anthem
(Johnson, N.) SATB oct SINGSPIR
ZJP-7359 $.30   (G386)

Praise, My Soul, The King Of Heaven
*anthem
(Mickelson, Paul) SATB oct SINGSPIR
ZJP-7306 $.30   (G387)

Who Is On The Lord's Side? *anthem
(Peterson, John W.) SATB oct
SINGSPIR ZJP-3202 $.30   (G388)

GOSSE, BARRY
This Joyful Eastertide *Easter
SATB (med easy) WATERLOO $.40
(G389)

GOT ANY RIVERS *medley
(Huff, Ronn) SATB oct BENSON S4123
$.35   (G390)

GOTT ABER KANN MACHEN see Zimmermann,
Heinz Werner

GOTT, DER HERR, IST SONN UND SCHILD see
Spar, Otto

GOTT DER WELTSCHOPFER see Schubert,
Franz (Peter)

GOTT DES HIMMELS UND DER ERDEN see
Albert, Heinrich

GOTT, HEILIGER SCHOPFER ALLER STERN see
Lemacher, Heinrich

GOTT IM UNGEWITTER see Schubert, Franz
(Peter)

GOTT IST DIE EW'GE SONN see Haas,
Joseph

GOTT IST DIE LIEBE see Doebler, Curt

GOTT IST DIE LIEBE see Haas, Joseph

GOTT IST DIE LIEBE see Wiedermann,
Bedrich

GOTT IST GEGENWARTIG see Burkhard Willy

GOTT IST IN MIR DAS FEUER "DIE WELT IST
MIR ZU ENG" see Lang, Hans

GOTT IST LIEBE see Zipp, Friedrich

GOTT IST MEIN HIRT see Schubert, Franz
(Peter)

GOTT IST MEIN TROST see Vento, Ivo de

GOTT IST UNSERE ZUVERSICHT UND STARKE
see Zipp, Friedrich

GOTT IST UNSRE ZUVERSICHT see Fortner,
Wolfgang

GOTT IST UNSRE ZUVERSICHT see
Zimmermann, Heinz Werner

GOTT, MEIN GOTT, IM MORGENLICHT WACH
ICH AUF ZU DIR see Strauss-Konig,
Richard

GOTT SEI DANK DURCH ALLE WELT see
Distler, Hugo

GOTT SEI GELOBET UND GEBENEDEIET see
Hassler, Hans Leo

GOTT SEI GELOBET UND GEBENEDEIET see
Osiander, Lucas

GOTT SEI GELOBET UND GEBENEDEIET see
Rohwer, Jens

GOTT, SEI MIR GNADIG see Zeutschner

GOTT SIND DIE WEGE GLEICH see Krietsch,
Georg

GOTT VATER, SENDE DEINEN GEIST see
Studer, Hans

GOTTES LOB ZUR NACHT see Kronberg, G.

GOTTES MACHT UND VORSEHUNG "GOTT IST
MEIN LIED" see Beethoven, Ludwig
van

GOTTES SOHN IST KOMMEN see Praetorius,
Michael

GOTTESLOB "LOBT IHN, DEN HERRN" see
Haas, Joseph

GOTTLIEB, JACK (1930-   )
Three Candle Blessings *CC3U
[Heb] SATB,solo TRANSCON. TCL 668
$1.00   (G391)

Verses From Psalm 118
[Eng/Heb] mix cor TRANSCON. TCL 667
$.75   (G392)

GOTTLOB, ES GEHT NUNMEHR ZU ENDE see
Bach, Johann Sebastian

GOTTSCHICK, FRIEDEMANN (1928-   )
Gib Uns Leben *cant
SATB&cong,narrator,2trp,2trom sc
HANSSLER HE 10.322 s.p.   (G393)

Wohlauf, Die Ihr Hungrig Seid
SAT/SAB,opt bass inst HANSSLER
14.155 s.p.   (G394)

GOUDEN HARPEN RUISEN
mix cor sc HEER 2720 s.p.   (G395)

GOUDIMEL, CLAUDE (ca. 1505-1572)
Dich Liebt Mein Herz, O Herr (Psalm
18)
SATB SCHWEIZER. SK 102 s.p. (G396)

Herr, Erhore Meine Klagen
SATB SCHWEIZER. SK 52.06 s.p. see
also MUSIKBEILAGE ZUM
"EVANGELISCHEN KIRCHENCHOR 1952"
(G397)

Hodie Nobis Coelorum Rex *Xmas,mot
[Lat/Ger] SATB,acap MOSELER MOR172
s.p.   (G398)

O Bread Of Life From Heaven *see
Bourgeois, Loys (Louis)

O Hochster, Deine Gutigkeit (Psalm
36)
SATB SCHWEIZER. SK 103 s.p. (G399)

O Seht, Wie Schon Und Lieblich Ist's
(Psalm 133)
SATB SCHWEIZER. SK 65.06 s.p. see
also MUSIKBEILAGE ZUM
"EVANGELISCHEN KIRCHENCHOR 1965"
(G400)

Psalm 18 *see Dich Liebt Mein Herz,
O Herr

Psalm 36 *see O Hochster, Deine
Gutigkeit

Psalm 113 *see Singt Halleluja

Psalm 133 *see O Seht, Wie Schon Und
Lieblich Ist's

Singet Hocherfreut
men cor,acap TONOS 5636 s.p. (G401)

Singt Halleluja (Psalm 113)
SATB (contains also: Herr, Hore
Doch Auf Meine Rede) SCHWEIZER.
SK 64.07-8 s.p. see also
MUSIKBEILAGE ZUM "EVANGELISCHEN
KIRCHENCHOR 1964"   (G402)

Singt, Singt Dem Herren Neue Lieder
SATB (contains also: Gelobet Seist
Du, Jesu Christ) SCHWEIZER.
SK 72.04-5 s.p. see also
MUSIKBEILAGE ZUM "EVANGELISCHEN
KIRCHENCHOR 1972"   (G403)

GOULD
Onward Christian Soldiers
(Sullivan;McLellan) SATB oct GOSPEL
05 TM 0170 $.30   (G404)

GOUNOD, CHARLES FRANCOIS (1818-1893)
By Babylon's Wave
mix cor BANKS MUS YS 204 $.30
(G405)

Jesus, Word Of God Incarnate
(Coggin) SAB KJOS 5743 $.35 (G406)

Magnificat
(Townsend, D.) [Lat] SATB,org
BROUDE,A 771 $.75   (G407)

Nazareth
mix cor BANKS MUS YS 298 $.25
(G408)

O Divine Redeemer *anthem
(Keely) SATB (med) oct BROADMAN
4534-15 $.30   (G409)

GOUNOD, CHARLES FRANCOIS (cont'd.)

Sanctus (from Communion Service In G)
(Ganschow) SSAATTBB (easy)
FITZSIMONS 2048 $.20　　　　(G410)

Send Out Thy Light
mix cor BANKS MUS YS 328 $.25
(G411)

Unfold Ye Portals (from Redemption,
The)
SATTBB (med) FITZSIMONS 2040 $.25
(G412)

GOVERT, WILLIBALD
Adeste Fideles　*Xmas,hymn
[Lat] mix cor&cong,org sc,cor pts
BOHM s.p.　　　　　　　　(G413)

Ein Haus Voll Glorie Schauet　*Fest
mix cor&unis,org sc,cor pts BOHM
s.p.　　　　　　　　　　(G414)

Pange Lingua
[Lat] 4pt mix cor,acap sc,cor pts
BOHM s.p.　　　　　　　(G415)

Sanctus　*Fest
[Lat] 4-8pt mix cor BOHM s.p.
(G416)

Verbum Supernam　*hymn
[Lat] 4pt mix cor,acap sc,cor pts
BOHM s.p.　　　　　　　(G417)

GRAAP, LOTHAR (1933-　)
Wenn Der Herr Die Gefangenen Zions
Erlosen Wird
4pt mix cor,acap MERSEBURG EM468
(G418)

GRABGESANG "ACH, WAS IST DAS LEBEN DOCH
SO SCHWER" see Bohme, Franz Magnus

GRABGESANG "WENN WIR IN HOCHSTEN NOTEN
SEIN see Breinl, A.

GRABHYMNUS see Fischer, Theo

GRABLIED "DU HAST GEDULDET" see Frey,
Carl

GRACE　*Easter/Gen,gospel/medley
(Jeffrey; Grammer) 2pt oct BENSON
S4387 $.35　　　　　　　(G419)
(Skillings, Otis) SATB oct LILLENAS
AT-1112 $.40　　　　　　(G420)

GRACE OF LOVING, THE
(Wild, Eric) SATB,pno BERANDOL
BER1240 $.50　　　　　　(G421)

GRACE TO YOU see Blankenship, Mark

GRACIOUS SPIRIT, DWELL WITHIN ME
*anthem
(Nichols) SATB oct BROADMAN 4562-38
$.35　　　　　　　　　(G422)

GRACIOUS SPIRIT, LOVE DIVINE see Young

GRADUAL FOR EASTER see Stout, Alan

GRADUALE UND OFFERTORIUM IN FESTO JESU
CHRISTI REGIS see Gruber, Joseph

GRADY
All Of Me　*anthem
SATB FINE ARTS EP 45 $.35　(G423)

Sing We Joyously　*Xmas,anthem
SATB,opt bvl&gtr FINE ARTS CM 1097
$.35　　　　　　　　　(G424)

GRAF, DORIS
Story Of Jesus, The　*Easter,cant
jr cor,narrator,fl/vln,2trp
LILLENAS ME-34 $1.00　　(G425)

GRAHAM
Behold, Let Us Love　*anthem
2pt oct BROADMAN 4554-74 $.30
(G426)
Boat Of Jade　*anthem
1-2pt oct BROADMAN 4560-21 $.35
(G427)
Cherry Flower　*anthem
1-2pt oct BROADMAN 4560-22 $.35
(G428)
Clouds　*anthem
1-2pt oct BROADMAN 4560-23 $.35
(G429)
Golden Breaks The Dawn　*anthem
2pt oct BROADMAN 4558-31 $.30
(G430)
Have Faith In God (composed with
Reeves, J. Flaxington)
see Two Songs Of Faith

He Comes In The Lord's Name　*Easter,
anthem
2pt (easy) oct BROADMAN 4558-34
$.30　　　　　　　　　(G431)
He Is My Father　*anthem
2pt (easy) oct BROADMAN 4554-67
$.30　　　　　　　　　(G432)

GRAHAM (cont'd.)

Hill Of The Cross (composed with
Reeves, J. Flaxington)
TTBB CHAPLET 2001 $.25　　(G433)

Let The Beauty Of The Lord　*anthem
1-2pt oct BROADMAN 4560-44 $.50
(G434)

Praise To God　*see Barbauld

Shout To God With Shouts Of Joy
*Xmas,anthem
2pt (easy) oct BROADMAN 4558-47
$.30　　　　　　　　　(G435)

Sing Praises To God　*anthem
SAB (easy) oct BROADMAN 4554-61
$.30　　　　　　　　　(G436)

Though You Go Far　*anthem
1-2pt oct BROADMAN 4560-43 $.35
(G437)

Thy Robe Of Righteousness (composed
with Reeves, J. Flaxington)
see Two Songs Of Faith

Two Songs Of Faith (composed with
Reeves, J. Flaxington)
SATB CHAPLET 2003 $.25
contains: Have Faith In God; Thy
Robe Of Righteousness　(G438)

GRAHAM, JEANA
Journey To Bethlehem (composed with
Graham, Robert)　*Xmas,cant
jr cor&opt SATB/jr cor&opt TTB/jr
cor&opt TTBB,hndbl BROADMAN
4513-07 $1.50　　　　　(G439)

GRAHAM, ROBERT
Bethlehem, The Chosen　*Xmas,cant
2pt SACRED $1.95　　　　(G440)

David's Hotshot Slingshot
1-2pt,narrator,kbd sc BROADMAN
4518-11 $1.98　　　　　(G441)

Dawn Of Redeeming Grace　*Xmas,cant
SATB,narrator,inst BROADMAN 4512-01
$1.25　　　　　　　　　(G442)

Father Of Compassion　*Gen,anthem
unis BROADMAN 4560-52 $.40　(G443)

Golgotha　*Easter,cant
SATB BROADMAN 4514-02 $1.25　(G444)

Jonah's Tale Of A Whale
1-2pt jr cor,narrator BROADMAN
4518-10 $1.95　　　　　(G445)

Journey To Bethlehem　*see Graham,
Jeana

Lo! A Star　*Xmas,cant
jr cor BROADMAN 4513-01 $1.00
(G446)
Lord Emmanuel, The　*Xmas,cant
jr cor/sr cor BROADMAN 4512-04
$1.25　　　　　　　　　(G447)

Praise The Lord　*anthem
cor BROADMAN 4560-51 $.40　(G448)

Sing Joy!　*Xmas,anthem
SA oct SACRED S-5400 $.35　(G449)

Sower And The Seed, The　*Easter,cant
cor BROADMAN 4515-01 $1.00　(G450)

Within A Little Stable　*Xmas,cant
3pt jr cor BROADMAN 4513-03 $1.00
(G451)
GRAHAM, ROBERT VIRGIL (1912-　)
Alleluia! Christ Is Born　*Adv/Xmas
SATB ART MAST 140 $.40　　(G452)

Barefoot School　*cant
2pt jr cor/SA,narrator,S solo,pno,
inst CHORISTERS D-2 $1.50　(G453)

Come, Yahweh, Come
2pt ART MAST 231 $.40　　(G454)

Five Christmas Songs From Japan
*CC5U,Xmas,Jap
1-2pt, Orff Instruments CHORISTERS
A-105 $.60　　　　　　(G455)

Gethsemane　*Lent
SATB ART MAST 135 $.40　　(G456)

Green The Weeping Willow Tree　*Lent
2pt ART MAST 179 $.40　　(G457)

Have You Seen Three Kings?　*Xmas
2pt ART MAST 217 $.35　　(G458)

Little Jesus
see Two Songs Of Bethlehem

Loving Shepherd
SAB,org ART MAST 133 $.40　(G459)

GRAHAM, ROBERT VIRGIL (cont'd.)

Must Jesus Bear The Cross Alone?
*Lent
SATB ART MAST 188 $.30　　(G460)

Now I Know
see Two Songs Of Bethlehem

Two Songs Of Bethlehem　*CC2U
SATB&unis,org KERBY 813 $.40 (G461)

Two Songs Of Bethlehem
unis oct KERBY 80978 $.40
contains: Little Jesus; Now I
Know　　　　　　　　(G462)

GRAND DIEU, NOTRE SEIGNEUR, COMBIEN ICI
TON NOM A GRAND HONEUR see Le
Jeune, Claude

GRANDI, ALESSANDRO (?　-1630)
Peace Descends Today From Heaven
SA,kbd FOSTER MF 803 $.40　(G463)

GRANT, DON
Were You There!　*Easter,cant
SATB,narrator (med diff) SINGSPIR
4014 $1.95　　　　　　(G464)

GRANT, W. PARKS
Communion Service In G Minor　*Op.19
unis,org AM.COMP.AL. $4.40　(G465)

Cry Of The Persecuted, The (from
Op37, No2)
SATB,acap AM.COMP.AL. $3.30　(G466)

Lines From The Magnificat　*Op.37,
No.1
SATB,acap AM.COMP.AL. $3.30　(G467)

GRANT PEACE, WE PRAY see Mendelssohn-
Bartholdy, Felix

GRANT THEM REST ETERNAL see Faure,
Gabriel-Urbain

GRANT UNDERSTANDING see Stanton

GRANT US TO DO WITH ZEAL see Bach,
Johann Sebastian

GRAPE
Jesus Paid It All　*anthem
(Rasley, J.M.) SATB oct SINGSPIR
ZJP-7361 $.35　　　　　(G468)

GRATEFUL HEART, A see Bock, Fred

GRAU, P. THEODOR
Lauretanische Fest-Litanei　*Op.43
[Lat] cor,soli,org sc,cor pts BOHM
s.p.　　　　　　　　　(G469)

Missa Brevis De Requiem　*Op.52
[Lat] 4pt mix cor,org sc,cor pts
BOHM s.p.　　　　　　　(G470)

Missa Brevissima Dominicalis In
Honorem Sancti Francisci De
Assisi　*Op.45, Mass
[Lat] 4pt mix cor,org sc,cor pts
BOHM s.p.　　　　　　　(G471)

Missa Brevissima II In Honorem Beatae
Mariae Virgini　*Op.51, Mass
"Muttergottes-Messe" [Lat] 4pt mix
cor,org sc,cor pts BOHM s.p.
(G472)
Muttergottes-Messe　*see Missa
Brevissima II In Honorem Beatae
Mariae Virgini

Tu Es Petrus　*Op.37, Fest
[Lat] 4pt mix cor,org,opt 2trp&
2trom&timp sc,cor pts BOHM s.p.,
ipa　　　　　　　　　(G473)

Vierzehn Pange Lingua　*Op.54,No.1-7,
CC7U
[Lat] mix cor,acap sc,cor pts BOHM
s.p.　　　　　　　　　(G474)

Vierzehn Pange Lingua　*Op.54,No.8-
14, CC7U
[Lat] mix cor,org sc,cor pts BOHM
s.p.　　　　　　　　　(G475)

GRAUN, KARL HEINRICH (1703-1759)
Auferstehen Wirst Du
see DREI BEERDIGUNGSGESANGE

Der Tod Jesu　*cant
4pt mix cor,SATB soli,org,2fl,2ob,
2bsn,strings,timp voc sc
BREITKOPF-W EB 6748 s.p., cor pts
BREITKOPF-W CHB 3638 s.p., ipr
(G476)
GRAVES, F.
He Was Nailed To The Cross　*Easter
(Ferrin, P.) SATB oct GOSPEL
05 TM 0217 $.20　　　　(G477)

GREAT AND MARVELLOUS see Haydn, (Franz) Joseph

GREAT AND MARVELOUS ARE THY WORKS see Dowling, Eric

GREAT AND MIGHTY WONDER, A see Vick

GREAT AND MIGHTY WONDER, THE see Martin, Gilbert M.

GREAT COMMANDMENT, THE see Marshall

GREAT COMMISSION, THE see Ingram, Bill

GREAT CONTROVERSY, THE see Borth, Steven

GREAT DAY *spir
(Owens) SATB oct LILLENAS AN-3848 $.30 (G478)

GREAT DAY OF THE LORD, THE see Bezanson, Philip, Dies Domini Magnus

GREAT GLAD TIDINGS TELL, THE see Blakley, D. Duane

GREAT GOD, HOW FRAIL A THING IS MAN see Billings, William

GREAT GOD OF WONDERS see Peterson, John W.

GREAT IS THE GLORY OF THE LORD see Peterson, John W.

GREAT IS THE LORD! see Burroughs, Bob

GREAT IS THE LORD see Calvin

GREAT IS THE LORD see Elgar, Edward

GREAT IS THE LORD see Lawson, J.A.

GREAT IS THE LORD see Schutz, Heinrich

GREAT IS THE LORD see Whitcomb

GREAT JEHOVAH, HEAR THY CHILDREN'S PRAYER see Slauson, Loyal

GREAT PHYSICIAN, THE *anthem
(Burroughs) SSA FINE ARTS TR 104 $.30 contains also: Whiter Than Snow (G479)
(Cram, James D.) SATB FINE ARTS CM 1101 $.35 (G480)

GREAT PHYSICIAN, THE see Stockton, John H.

GREAT THE NAME OF CHRIST OUR LORD see Pekiel, Bertlomiej, Magnum Nomen Domini

GREATER IS HE THAT IS IN ME see Wolfe

GREATER LOVE see Ringwald, [Roy]

GREATEST OF THESE IS LOVE see Ridout, Alan

GREATEST STORY YET UNTOLD, THE see Clark, Eugene L.

GREATOREX, THOMAS (1758-1831)
Begin, My Tongue, Some Heavenly Theme *anthem
(Peterson, John W.) SATB oct SINGSPIR ZJP-7236 $.25 (G481)

God Moves In A Mysterious Way *anthem
(Gerig) SATB oct LILLENAS AN-2359 $.30 (G482)

GREEN
Suffer Little Children
(Cacavas) SATB BELWIN 2309 $.40 (G483)
(Cacavas) SA BELWIN 2310 $.40 (G484)

GREEN, JAMES
Processional Carol *Xmas
dbl cor CHORISTERS A-134 $.40 (G485)

GREEN, PHILIP
Dismissal, The
SATB BOURNE B223669-358 $.40 (G486)

Glory Be To God On High
SATB BOURNE B223644-358 $.85 (G487)

Holy, Holy, Holy Lord, God Of Hosts
SATB BOURNE B223636-358 $.50 (G488)

I Believe In One God
SATB BOURNE B215970-358 $1.25 (G489)

Introit *Introit
SATB BOURNE B217950-359 $.50 (G490)

GREEN, PHILIP (cont'd.)

Kyrie *Kyrie
"Lord Have Mercy" SATB BOURNE B217984 $.30 (G491)

Lamb Of God
SATB BOURNE B216135-358 $.50 (G492)

Lord Be With You
SATB BOURNE B223651-358 $.60 (G493)

Lord Have Mercy *see Kyrie

Our Father *see Pater Noster

Pater Noster
"Our Father" SATB BOURNE B223628-358 $.50 (G494)

GREEN, R.
Jesus, So Lowly *Lent
SATB,acap GRAY CMR 3299 $.30 (G495)

GREEN THE WEEPING WILLOW TREE see Graham, Robert Virgil

GREENE, MAURICE (1695-1775)
Hear My Prayer
(Young, Percy) [Eng] SATB,ATB soli, org BROUDE BR. $.70 see from MUSIC OF THE GREAT CHURCHES VOL. V: ST. PAUL'S CATHEDRAL, LONDON (G496)

O Clap Your Hands
(Simkins) SSATB oct CONCORDIA 98-2224 $.70 (G497)

GREENHILL, HAROLD
Angels From The Realms Of Glory
mix cor BANKS MUS YS 1202 $.30 (G498)

GREETING SONG, THE see Herrick

GREETINGS ON ST. JOHN'S DAY see Kodaly, Zoltan

GREGOR
Glory To God In The Highest
SATB oct BOOSEY 5861 $.45 (G499)

GREGOR, [CHRISTIAN FRIEDRICH] (1723-1801)
Hosanna
(Pfohl) SA BRODT 200 $.25 (G500)

Hosianna, O Blessed Is He Who Comes *anthem
cor CHORISTERS R-2 $.15 (G501)

O Had I Been There And Shared, Lord
(Pfohl) mix cor BRODT 107 $.22 (G502)

O Jesus, My Shepherd
(Nolte) SA,opt inst BRODT 1009 $.45, ipr (G503)

O Shepherd Of Israel
(Latrobe; Nolte) SA BRODT 1005 $.25 (G504)

GREINER, ALLEN
Preces And Responses
SATB,acap oct PRESSER 312-41001 $.35 (G505)

GRESSUS MEOS DIRIGE SECUNDUM ELOQUIUM TUUM see Lassus, Roland de (Orlandus)

GRETCHANINOV, ALEXANDER TIKHONOVITCH (1864-1956)
Vouchsafe, O Lord
SATB GALAXY 1.1356.1 $.35 (G506)

GRIEB, HERBERT [C.] (1898-)
God Is Our Hope *Bibl
SATTBB (med) FITZSIMONS 2185 $.25 (G507)

Haste Thee, O God *Bibl
SATB (med) FITZSIMONS 2181 $.25 (G508)

There's A Wideness In God's Mercy
SA (easy) FITZSIMONS 5022 $.25 (G509)

We Will Carol Joyfully *Easter
desc (easy) FITZSIMONS 5020 $.20 (G510)

GRIEG, EDVARD HAGERUP (1843-1907)
Jesu, Tender Saviour
(Ganschow) SSAATTBB,acap (med) FITZSIMONS 2052 $.25 (G511)

GRIESBACHER, PETER (1864-1933)
Mater Admirabilis *Op.86, Mass
[Lat] 4pt mix cor,org/fl&2clar& 2horn&2trp&trom&strings&timp sc, cor pts BOHM s.p., ipa (G512)

Missa Dominicalis *Op.140, Mass
[Lat] 4pt mix cor,org/harmonium sc, cor pts BOHM s.p. (G513)

Stella Maris *Op.141, Mass
[Lat] 4pt mix cor,org/fl&2clar& 2horn&trom&strings&org sc,cor pts BOHM s.p., ipa (G514)

GRIESBACHER, PETER (cont'd.)

Veni Creator Spiritus *Op.141d
[Lat] 4pt mix cor,org sc,cor pts BOHM s.p. (G515)

GRIFFITH
Mountain Of The Lord
SATB SCHIRM.G R11981 $.30 (G516)

GRIFFITHS, VERNON (1894-)
Ode Of Thanksgiving, An
SATB,strings,opt timp voc sc NOVELLO rental (G517)

GRIMES
Jesus Gives Me A Song *anthem/gospel
(DeCou, Harold) SATB oct SINGSPIR ZJP-8045 $.25 (G518)

What Shall I Give Thee, Master? *anthem
(Schubert) SATB oct LILLENAS AN-1687 $.30 (G519)

GRIMES, GORDON
Cradle Song
see Pettman, Edgar, Gabriel's Message

Shepherd's Cradle Song *Xmas
SATB EMI s.p. (G520)

Sleep, My Saviour, Sleep (composed with Pettman, Edgar)
see Pearsall, Robert Lucas de, In Dulci Jubilo

GRIMES, TRAVIS
Day By Day We Magnify Thee
SA BRODT 631 $.25 (G521)

Praise Be Thine, O Jesu
SA BRODT 636 $.20 (G522)

There Is A Green Hill Far Away
SA BRODT 635 $.20 (G523)

GRIMM, CARL HUGO (1890-)
It Came To Pass In Shushan *Bibl/ cant
SATB,narrator,STBar soli WILLIS $2.00 (G524)

GRIMM, JURGEN (1927-)
Mein Gott, Ich Danke Dir
SAT/SAB/SATB SCHWEIZER. SK 64.06 s.p. see also MUSIKBEILAGE ZUM "EVANGELISCHEN KIRCHENCHOR 1964" (G525)

Nun Schlagt Die Stunde Mitternacht
SAT/SAB/SATB (contains also: Es Ist Ein Freud Dem Herzen Mein; Aus Meines Herzens Grunde) SCHWEIZER. SK 64.01-2 s.p. see also MUSIKBEILAGE ZUM "EVANGELISCHEN KIRCHENCHOR 1964" (G526)

GRITTON, ERIC
How Far Is It To Bethlehem? *Xmas
unis STAINER 3.0775.1 $.40 (G527)

Welcome Yule *Xmas
unis STAINER 3.0572.1 $.40 (G528)

GROSE
Give Of Your Best To The Master
(Barnard; Collins, Hope) SAB oct GOSPEL 05 TM 0165 $.25 (G529)

GROSS FREUD *Xmas,carol/folk
(Biebl, F.) [Ger] 4pt men cor MERSEBURG EM9045 (G530)

GROSSE-SCHWARE, HERMANN (1931-)
Die Stille Leben
see Zwei Deutsche Motetten

Ein Traum Ist Unser Leben
see Zwei Deutsche Motetten

Zwei Deutsche Motetten *mot
men cor,acap TONGER s.p. contains also: Die Stille Leben; Ein Traum Ist Unser Leben (G531)

GROSSER GOTT, DU LIEBST ERBARMEN see Ruppel, Paul Ernst

GROSSER GOTT, WIR LOBEN DICH see Hoss, Franz

GROTE, GOTTFRIED
Silent Night! Holy Night! *anthem, Contemp
[Eng/Ger] SATB oct CHANTRY COA 6319 $.10 (G532)

GRUBER, FRANZ XAVER (1787-1863)
Holy Night, Silent Night *see Stille Nacht, Heilige Nacht

Silent Night *see Stille Nacht, Heilige Nacht

GRUBER, FRANZ XAVER (cont'd.)

Silent Night! Holy Night! *see
Stille Nacht, Heilige Nacht

Stille Nacht, Heilige Nacht *Xmas,
anthem
(Chapman) "Silent Night" SATB (med
easy) OXFORD 84.221 $.35   (G533)
(DeCou, Harold) "Silent Night! Holy
Night!" SATB oct SINGSPIR
ZJP-3041 $.30   (G534)
(Grimes) "Holy Night, Silent Night"
SATB EMI s.p.   (G535)
(Haydn, Michael; White, Ernest
Franklin) "Silent Night" SATB
WHITE,ERN $.30   (G536)
(Mohr; Track, Gerhard) "Silent
Night, Holy Night" mix cor,soli,
org,opt orch,gtr AUGSBURG 11-9390
$.50   (G537)

GRUBER, JOSEPH
Angelus Domini *Op.85b,No.2
see Gruber, Joseph, Terra Tremuit

Ascendit Deus *Op.85c,No.1, Asc/
Pent/Whitsun,Offer
[Lat] 4pt mix cor,org/orch sc,cor
pts BOHM s.p., ipr contains also:
Confirma Hoc, Op.85c,No.2 (G538)

Confirma Hoc *Op.85c,No.2
see Gruber, Joseph, Ascendit Deus

Ecce Sacerdos *Op.149,No.1
[Lat] 4pt mix cor,org sc,cor pts
BOHM s.p. contains also: Veni,
Sancte Spiritus, Op.149,No.2
(G539)

Graduale Und Offertorium In Festo
Jesu Christi Regis *Op.340
[Lat] 4pt mix cor,org sc,cor pts
BOHM s.p.   (G540)

Herz-Jesu-Festmesse *Op.213, Mass
[Lat] 4pt mix cor,org,2ob/2clar,
2horn,strings,opt 2trp&trom&timp
sc,cor pts BOHM s.p.   (G541)

Kurze Und Leichte Pastoralmesse In G
*Op.45, Mass
[Lat] 4pt mix cor,fl,2clar,2horn,
strings,org,opt trp,trom,timp sc,
cor pts BOHM s.p., ipa   (G542)

Mater Dolorosa *Op.51, Mass
[Lat] 4pt mix cor,org/strings,
2horn,org (E flat maj) sc,cor pts
BOHM s.p., ipa   (G543)

Missa De Nativitate Domini Nostri
Jesu Christi *Op.92, Mass
[Lat] 4pt mix cor,org/fl&2clar&
2horn&2trp&trom&strings&timp&org
sc,cor pts BOHM s.p., ipa (G544)

Missa Pro Defunctis *Op.179
[Lat] SAB,org sc,cor pts BOHM s.p.
(G545)

Primiz-Messe In Es *Op.249a, Mass
[Lat] 4pt mix cor,org/brass/winds
(E flat maj) sc,cor pts BOHM
s.p., ipa   (G546)

Reges Tharsis *Op.85a,No.2
see Gruber, Joseph, Tui Sunt Coeli

Requiem In C-Moll *Op.21
[Lat] SAB&opt T,org/2vln&vcl&bvl&
org&opt 2horn (C min) sc,cor pts
BOHM s.p., ipa   (G547)

Requiem In D-Moll *Op.20
[Lat] 4pt mix cor,org/2vln&vcl&bvl&
org&opt 2horn (D min) sc,cor pts
BOHM s.p., ipa   (G548)

St. Agnes-Messe *Op.62, Mass
[Lat] SAB&opt T,opt org sc,cor pts
BOHM s.p.   (G549)
[Lat] SAB&opt T,opt org sc,cor pts
BOHM s.p.   (G550)

St. Leopolds-Messe *Op.65, Mass
[Lat] SAB&opt T,org sc,cor pts BOHM
s.p.   (G551)

St. Mathias-Messe *Op.220, Mass
[Lat] 1-2pt,org/harmonium sc,cor
pts BOHM s.p.   (G552)

St. Paulus-Messe *Op.215b, Mass
[Lat] SAB&opt T,org,strings,opt
2horn sc,cor pts BOHM s.p., ipa
(G553)

Terra Tremuit *Op.85b,No.1, Easter,
Offer
[Lat] 4pt mix cor,org/orch sc,cor
pts BOHM s.p., ipa contains also:
Angelus Domini, Op.85b,No.2
(G554)

Tui Sunt Coeli *Op.85a,No.1, Xmas/
Epiph,Offer
[Lat] 4pt mix cor,org/2clar,2horn,
2trp,trom,strings,timp sc,cor pts

GRUBER, JOSEPH (cont'd.)

BOHM s.p., ipa contains also:
Reges Tharsis, Op.85a,No.2 (G555)

Veni, Sancte Spiritus *Op.149,No.2
see Gruber, Joseph, Ecce Sacerdos

Vier Pange Lingua *Op.177,No.1-4,
CC4U
[Lat] 4pt mix cor,org/fl&2clar&
2horn&2trp&trom&strings&timp sc,
cor pts BOHM s.p., ipa   (G556)

Zwei Libera *Op.26, CC2U
[Lat] SAB&opt T,org sc,cor pts BOHM
s.p.   (G557)

GRUM
Victory Ahead! *anthem/gospel
(Smith, Herb) SATB oct SINGSPIR
ZJP-8088 $.30   (G558)

GRUNAUER, I.
Verherrlich Gott In Eurem Leibe
*Mass
[Ger] 2pt&cong,opt solo,org,opt
3trp BOHM sc s.p., cor pts s.p.,
ipa   (G559)

GRUNDY, S.K.
I Found Joy *anthem
SATB WORD   (G560)

GRUNET FELDER see Deutschmann, Gerhard

GRUSSWORTE DER APOKALYPSE DES HEILIGEN
JOHANNES "DAS IST DIE OFFENBARUNG
VON GOTT" see Herrmann, Hugo

GUARNIERI, CAMARGO MOZART (1907-   )
Ave Maria *anti/Greg
[Lat] SATB,acap BROUDE BR. $.30
(G561)

GUD, NAR DU TIL OPPBRUDD KALLER see
Olsen, Sparre

GUERRERO, FRANCISCO (1528-1599)
Hispaniae Schola Musica Sacra Vol.
II: Franciscus Guerrero, 1894
*CCU
(Pedrell, F.) cor pap JOHNSON
$12.00 contains also: Vol. I:
Morales, 1894   (G562)

GUERRINI, GUIDO (1890-1965)
La Citta Beata *cant
wom cor,Bar solo,3fl,3ob,2clar,
3bsn,2horn,2trp,timp,bells,harp,
pno,org CARISH rental   (G563)

La Citta Perduta *cant
mix cor,MezB soli,3fl,3ob,2clar,
3bsn,4horn,3trp,3trom,tuba,timp,
perc,harp,pno,org CARISH rental
(G564)

GUEST, DOUGLAS
Wedding Responses (For The Marriage
Of H.R.H. The Princess Anne And
Captain Mark Phillips In
Westminster Abbey, 14 November,
1973) *Marriage
SATB,acap (easy) OXFORD 43.486 $.30
(G565)

GUIDE ME, O THOU GREAT JEHOVAH *anthem
(Rose) SATB&desc FINE ARTS EW 1018
$.35   (G566)

GUIDE ME, O THOU GREAT JEHOVAH see
Mozart, Wolfgang Amadeus, Ave Verum

GUIDE ME, O THOU GREAT JEHOVAH see
Young, Gordon

GUMPELZHAIMER, ADAM
Glaube Ist Der Seele Leben *canon
men cor sc SCHOTTS CHBL 54A-B s.p.
contains also: Isaac, Heinrich,
Innsbruck, Ich Muss Dich Lassen
(G567)

Herr Gott, Himmlischer Vater
see O Herr Jesu Christe

Ich Ruf Zu Dir, Herr Jesu Christ
see O Herr Jesu Christe

Lobt Gott Getrost Mit Singen
mix cor (med easy) sc SCHOTTS
C 38 069A s.p.   (G568)

Neue Deutsche Geistliche Lieder
*CC27L
SAT/SAB HANSSLER 4.019 s.p. (G569)

O Herr Jesu Christe *canon
SSATB LAUDINELLA LR 133 s.p.
contains: Herr Gott, Himmlischer
Vater; Ich Ruf Zu Dir, Herr
Jesu Christ; O Herr, Nimm Von
Mir; Vater Unser Im
Himmelreich; Wir Danken Dir,
Herr Gott Vater   (G570)

O Herr, Nimm Von Mir
see O Herr Jesu Christe

GUMPELZHAIMER, ADAM (cont'd.)

Vater Unser Im Himmelreich
see O Herr Jesu Christe

Wenn Mein Stundlein Vorhanden Ist
*mot
(Holle, Hugo) mix cor (med easy) sc
SCHOTTS C 32 831 s.p.   (G571)

Wir Danken Dir, Herr Gott Vater
see O Herr Jesu Christe

GUNN
Christ Is The Answer *anthem
SATB (easy) oct BROADMAN 4551-48
$.30   (G572)

GUNSENHEIMER, GUSTAV (1934-   )
Halt Im Gedachtnis Jesum Christ
see Jesus Und Der Unglaubige Thomas

Jesu, Gib Gesunde Augen
see Jesus Und Der Unglaubige Thomas

Jesu, Hilf Siegen
see Jesus Und Der Unglaubige Thomas

Jesus Und Der Unglaubige Thomas
HANSSLER 7.170 s.p.
contains: Halt Im Gedachtnis
Jesum Christ (SATB,S solo);
Jesu, Gib Gesunde Augen (SATB);
Jesu, Hilf Siegen (SATB); Und
Stehe, Die Junger Sassen
Beisammen (SSATBB)   (G573)

Und Stehe, Die Junger Sassen
Beisammen
see Jesus Und Der Unglaubige Thomas

GUSTAFSON, DWIGHT
House Of Our Lord, The *Ded,anthem
SATB oct SACRED S-176 $.35 (G574)

GUT IST ES, ZU PREISEN DEN HERREN see
Biener, G.

GUTE NACHT, O SCHONSTES JESULEIN see
Kuntz, Michael

GYRING, ELIZABETH
Kyrie, Sanctus, Agnus Dei And Gloria
SATB,org AM.COMP.AL. $3.85 (G575)

H

HAAN, RAYMOND
I Will Lift Up Mine Eyes
SATB,org ART MAST 259 $.35   (H1)

Keeper Of Israel, The
SATB ART MAST 268 $.35   (H2)

Psalm 23
SATB,org oct SCHMITT 6010 $.40 (H3)

HAAS, JOSEPH (1879-1960)
Christ-Konig-Messe *Op.88, Mass
unis men cor,org/strings&brass voc
sc SCHOTTS ED. 3290 s.p., ipa
(H4)

Christnacht *Op.85, Xmas
mix cor&jr cor/wom cor,narrator&
SSATBarB soli,pno,fl,2clar,horn,
strings (med easy) sc SCHOTTS
ED. 3311 s.p., voc sc,voc pt
SCHOTTS ED. 3270 s.p., ipa   (H5)

Das Lebensbuch Gottes *Op.87, ora
wom cor&opt mix cor,SA soli,org/
pno/fl,2clar,2horn,trp,trom,
strings,timp (med) voc sc,voc pt
SCHOTTS ED. 3282 s.p., ipa   (H6)

Deutsche Weihnachtsmesse *Op.105,
Xmas,Mass
unis mix cor,org/fl&clar&horn&
strings (easy) voc sc,voc pt
SCHOTTS ED. 4475 s.p., ipa   (H7)

Die Linien Des Lebens Sind
Verschieden
see Zwei Geistliche Motetten

Die Seligen *Op.106,No.1-8 (from
Bergpredict Oratorium) CC8L
mix cor&men cor&wom cor&jr cor,SBar
soli,org,2fl,2ob,2clar,2bsn,
4horn,2trp,3trom,tuba,strings,
perc,timp (med) voc sc,cor pts
SCHOTTS ED. 4921 s.p., ipr   (H8)

Ecce Sacerdos Magnus *Op.80a, hymn
[Ger/Lat] unis wom cor,org/brass
(easy) voc sc SCHOTTS ED 3255
s.p., ipa   (H9)

Ein Deutsches Gloria "Sing Dem Herrn
Ein Lied" *Op.86
4pt mix cor&4pt mix cor,acap (med)
sc,cor pts SCHOTTS ED. 4228 s.p.
(H10)

Freund, Solln Wir Allesamt Wie Immer
Eines Schrei'n *Op.75,No.1, mot
mix cor (med) sc SCHOTTS C 32 024
s.p., voc pt SCHOTTS C 32 024A-B
s.p. see from Kanonische Motetten
(H11)

Gott Ist Die Ew'ge Sonn *Op.75,No.2,
mot
mix cor (med) sc SCHOTTS C 32 025
s.p. see from Kanonische Motetten
(H12)

Gott Ist Die Liebe *Op.72 (from
Deutsche Vesper)
mix cor (med) sc SCHOTTS C 31 816F
s.p.   (H13)

Gotteslob "Lobt Ihn, Den Herrn"
*Op.104, hymn
4pt mix cor/4pt men cor/3pt jr cor/
3pt wom cor&unis jr cor,acap
(med) sc SCHOTTS C 38 767 s.p.,
voc pt SCHOTTS C 38 768A-D s.p.,
cor pts SCHOTTS C 38 770-769 s.p.
(H14)

Kanonische Motetten *see Freund,
Solln Wir Allesamt Wie Immer
Eines Schrei'n, Op.75,No.1; Gott
Ist Die Ew'ge Sonn, Op.75,No.2
(H15)

Lob Der Freundschaft *Op.109, hymn
mix cor&wom cor&jr cor,pno/org,fl,
clar,horn,strings,perc,timp
(easy) sc,cor pts SCHOTTS
ED. 4988 s.p., ipa   (H16)

Marianische Kantate *Op.112, cant
1-2pt wom cor,SA soli,org/harmonium
(med easy) sc,cor pts SCHOTTS
ED. 5174 s.p.   (H17)

Mensch, Steh Still Und Furcht Mich
see Zwei Geistliche Motetten

Munchner Liebfrauen-Messe *Op.96,
Mass
unis men cor,org/strings&brass voc
sc SCHOTTS ED. 3900 s.p., ipa
(H18)

Schillerhymne *Op.107, hymn
mix cor,Bar solo,2fl,2ob,2clar,
2bsn,4horn,2trp,3trom,strings,
perc,timp (med) voc sc,cor pts

HAAS, JOSEPH (cont'd.)

SCHOTTS ED. 4771 s.p., ipr   (H19)

Sechs Krippenlieder *Op.49, CC6U,
Xmas,cradle
jr cor,opt solo,pno BOHM sc s.p.,
cor pts s.p.   (H20)

Speyerer Domfestmesse *Op.80, cant
4pt men cor,org/strings&brass voc
sc SCHOTTS ED. 3239 s.p., cor pts
SCHOTTS C 39 772 s.p., ipa   (H21)

Trauungsgesang "Lobet Den Herrn"
jr cor/wom cor (med) sc SCHOTTS
CHBL 546 s.p.   (H22)

Vom Himmel Hoch Da Komm Ich Her
men cor sc SCHOTTS CHBL 126A-B s.p.
contains also: Lang, Hans, In
Dulci Jubilo (TTB,acap)   (H23)

Zwei Geistliche Motetten
SCHOTTS s.p.
contains: Die Linien Des Lebens
Sind Verschieden, Op.79,No.2
(men cor,Bar solo); Mensch,
Steh Still Und Furcht Mich,
Op.79,No.1 (men cor)   (H24)

HAASS, WALTER
Festliche Kantate
mix cor,orch sc GERIG HG 259 (H25)

HABE DEINE LUST AN DEM HERRN see
Bernhard

HABITABLE EARTH, THE see Gideon, Miriam

HAEC DIES see Berghorn, Alfred

HAEC DIES see Ett, Kaspar

HAEC DIES see Palestrina, Giovanni

HAENNI, CH.
Messe Notre Dame De La Confiance
4pt mix cor,acap voc pt HENN 210
s.p.   (H26)

HAFNER, JOHANNES
Summe Deus *Op.8, Mass
[Lat] 4pt mix cor,soli,org/2clar,
2horn,2trom,strings,org sc,cor
pts BOHM s.p., ipr   (H27)

HAFSO
Christ Of Bethlehem, The
SATB KJOS 5904 $.40   (H28)

Easter Joy
SAB KJOS 5738 $.40   (H29)

Love Is Patient And Kind
SATB KJOS 5915 $.35   (H30)

We, His Children
SA KJOS 6133 $.35   (H31)

HAGEN, FRANCIS FLORENTINE (1815-1907)
Morning Star, The
(Pfohl) mix cor BRODT 204 $.20
(H32)

HAHN, L.
Deutsche Choralmesse *Mass
[Ger] unis&cong,solo,org,opt 2trp,
2trom,tuba BOHM sc s.p., cor pts
s.p., ipa   (H33)

HAIL, GLADDENING LIGHT see Langlois,
H.G.

HAIL GLADDENING LIGHT see Swann, Donald

HAIL, GLORIOUS KING! see Peterson, John
W.

HAIL MARY see Illing, Robert

HAIL MARY see Senator, Ronald

HAIL O GOD INCARNATE see Willan,
Healey, Ave Verum Corpus

HAIL O QUEEN see Connolly, Richard

HAIL OUR MONARCH see Clarke, F.R.C.

HAIL, QUEEN OF HEAVEN, REJOICE see
Lotti, Antonio

HAIL! SACRED MUSIC, HAIL! see Billings,
William

HAIL THE DAY THAT SEES HIM RISE see
James, Will

HAIL THE HOLY INFANT *Xmas
(Douglas) SATB,opt 2trp&2trom PRO ART
2755 $.40   (H34)

HAIL THE KING OF HEAVEN *Xmas,Pol
(Ehret, Walter) SABar&opt camb,pno,
opt 2trp (med easy) CAMBIATA U97441
$.35   (H35)

HAIL, THOU ONCE-DESPISED JESUS see
Peterson, John W.

HAIL, THOU SOURCE OF EVERY BLESSING see
Clarke, F.R.C.

HAIL TO THE BRIGHTNESS! see Mason,
Lowell

HAIL TO THE KING! see Peterson, John W.

HAIL TO THE LORD'S ANOINTED *Adv/Palm,
anthem
(Johnson, Norman) SATB oct SINGSPIR
ZJP-7286 $.30   (H36)

HAINS, S.B.
Canadian Prayer, A
SATB,acap BERANDOL BER 1669 $.50
(H37)

First Christmas Morning (composed
with Wild, Eric) *Xmas
SATB (med easy) WATERLOO $.40 (H38)

HAIRSTON, JESTER (1901-   )
Oh, Holy Lord
SSAA BOURNE B202901-354 $.40 (H39)

HALELUYAH, CHRIST IS RISEN see Wihtol,
A.A.

HALEVY, [JACQUES-FRANCOIS-FROMENTAL-
ELIE] (1799-1862)
Yigdal
mix cor oct SAC.MUS.PR. 305 $.40
(H40)

HALFFTER, RODOLFO (1900-   )
Pregon Para Una Pascua Pobre *Easter
mix cor,orch sc PEER $9.00, ipr
(H41)

HALL
Commission *anthem
unis&desc (easy) oct BROADMAN
4554-25 $.30   (H42)

Jesus, Savior, Pilot Me *anthem
SATB oct BROADMAN 4554-72 $.30
(H43)

HALL, WILLIAM D.
Agnus Dei *Agnus
[Lat] SATB,S solo,acap oct NATIONAL
WHC-9 $.35   (H44)

Introits And Responses *CC10L,cor-
resp/Introit
SATB,org oct NATIONAL WHC-18 $.35
(H45)

Magnificat *Magnif
[Lat] SATB,S solo,pno,2horn,2trp,
2trom oct NATIONAL WHC-6 $.50,
ipa   (H46)

HALLELUIAH see Nelhybel, Vaclav

HALLELUJA see Handel, George Frideric

HALLELUJA see Handel, George Frideric,
Hallelujah

HALLELUJA, DIES IST DER TAG, DEN DER
HERR MACHT see Izschoppe, Eberhart

HALLELUJAH!
(Krogstad, Bob) SATB/SSATTB oct
GOSPEL 05 TM 0356 $.35   (H47)

HALLELUJAH see Beethoven, Ludwig van

HALLELUJAH see Butler

HALLELUJAH see Handel, George Frideric

HALLELUJAH see Nelhybel, Vaclav

HALLELUJAH see Reynolds, William Jensen

HALLELUJAH, AMEN see Handel, George
Frideric

HALLELUJAH, CHRIST AROSE see Hyllberg,
Ruth

HALLELUJAH FOR THE CROSS! see Mc
Granahan

HALLELUJAH FOR THE CROSS see Peterson,
John W.

HALLELUJAH! GREAT AND MARV'LOUS ARE THY
WORKS *hymn
(Brandon, G.) SATB GIA G1950 $.40
(H48)

HALLELUJAH! HALLELUJAH! *Xmas,Contemp
SATB VANGUARD V561 $.35 see from Come
To Bethlehem   (H49)

HALLELUJAH HIS BLOOD AVAILS FOR ME see
Owens, Jimmy

HALLELUJAH! JESUS IS LORD! see
Armstrong, Mimi

HALLELUJAH, JESUS LIVES! see Lindeman

HALLELUJAH! LET PRAISES RING see
    Fiebig, Kurt

HALLELUJAH, PRAISE THE LORD see
    Thygerson, Robert J.

HALLELUJAH SIDE, THE *CC10L
    (Schubert, Myra) SATB (easy) GOSPEL
    s.p.   (H50)

HALLELUJAH! WE SHALL RISE! see Thomas

HALLELUJAH, WE SHALL RISE see Thomas,
    J.

HALLELUJAH, WHAT A SAVIOR! see Bliss,
    Paul

HALLELUJAH, WHAT A SAVIOR see Butler,
    A.L.

HALLELUJAH! WHAT A SAVIOR! see
    Peterson, John W.

HALLELUJAH, WHAT A SAVIOUR! see Bliss,
    Paul

HALLETT, JOHN C.
    Take The Message
        SATB oct GOSPEL 05 TM 0317 $.30
                                 (H51)

HALLETTE
    Bless The Lord, O My Soul *anthem
        SATB oct BROADMAN 4540-89 $.30
                                 (H52)

    Glory Of Christmas, The *see King

HALLOCK, PETER
    Behold A Mighty Prophet
        SATB WALTON 2199 $.40   (H53)

    Come, Let Us Sing Joyfully
        SATB WALTON 2195 $.40   (H54)

HALLOWED DAY, A see Hannahs, Roger

HALLOWED MANGER, THE see Pitfield,
    Thomas Baron

HALT IM GEDACHTNIS JESUM CHRIST see
    Gunsenheimer, Gustav

HAMBRAEUS, BENGT (1928-   )
    Motetum Archangeli Michaelis *mot
        4pt mix cor,org ERIKS 162 s.p.
                                 (H55)

HAMIL
    Christmas Bolero, A *Xmas
        SATB SCHIRM.G LG51848 $.40   (H56)

HAMILTON
    Good Cheer
        SS (easy) OXFORD 82.105 $.55 (H57)

HAMILTON, H.C.
    Vesper Hymn
        SATB (easy) WATERLOO $.30   (H58)

HAMILTON, IAIN (1922-   )
    Epitaph For This World And Time
        3 cor,3org (diff) PRESSER 412-41057
        $4.00   (H59)

    Golden Sequence, The
        unis,org PRESSER 312-41036 $.50
                                 (H60)

    Te Deum
        SATB,winds,brass,perc PRESSER
        412-41060 $2.25, ipr   (H61)

HAMMACK, BOBBY
    I Want You *cant
        jr cor LEXICON 37689 $1.95   (H62)

    Sam (composed with Adair, Tom) *cant
        jr cor LEXICON 37632 $1.95   (H63)

HAMMERING see Cossetto, Emil

HAMMERSCHMIDT, ANDREAS (1612-1675)
    Also Hat Gott Die Welt Geliebet
        SSATTB,opt cont sc HANSSLER
        HE 1.595 s.p.   (H64)

    Das Wort Ward Fleisch
        SSATTB,opt cont sc HANSSLER
        HE 1.593 s.p.   (H65)

    Der Herr Ist Mein Hirt
        SSB,cont sc HANSSLER HE 1.590 s.p.
                                 (H66)

    Freude, Freude, Grosse Freude
        SSATTB,opt cont sc HANSSLER
        HE 1.592 s.p.   (H67)

    Freue Dich, Du Tochter Sion
        *concerto
        SATB,T solo,2inst,cont sc,cor pts
        EGTVED MS15B13 s.p., ipa   (H68)

    Furchtet Euch Nicht *Xmas,concerto
        SS/TT,cont sc HANSSLER HE 5.173
        s.p.   (H69)
        SATB,S solo,2inst,cont sc,cor pts
        EGTVED MS16B12 s.p., ipa   (H70)

HAMMERSCHMIDT, ANDREAS (cont'd.)
    Gelobet Seist Du, Jesu Christ
        *concerto
        T,2trp,4trom,opt cont (easy) sc,cor
        pts BAREN. BA5435 s.p., ipa (H71)

    Himmel Und Erde Vergehen
        SSATB,cont sc HANSSLER HE 1.597
        s.p.   (H72)

    Jauchzet Dem Herren, Alle Welt
        SSATTB,opt cont sc HANSSLER
        HE 1.594 s.p.   (H73)

    Lift Up Your Heads, Ye Gates *Xmas
        (Field, Robert) SSATBB,kbd/acap/
        brass (med) PRESSER 312-41080
        $.40   (H74)

    Lobet Den Herren, Meine Seele
        SS/TT,cont sc HANSSLER HE 5.174
        s.p.   (H75)

    Meine Seele Erhebt Den Herren
        SSATTB,cont sc HANSSLER HE 1.596
        s.p.   (H76)

    My Soul, Now Bless Thy Maker! *see
        Nun Lob, Mein Seel, Den Herren

    Nun Lob, Mein Seel, Den Herren
        (Mueller, Harold) "My Soul, Now
        Bless Thy Maker!" [Ger/Eng] unis,
        opt S solo,cont,brass sc
        CONCORDIA 97-5044 $3.00, ipa, cor
        pts CONCORDIA 97-5173 $.30 (H77)

    Truly, Truly, I Say To You *see
        Wahrlich, Ich Sage Euch

    Verleih Uns Frieden Gnadiglich
        SS/TT,cont sc HANSSLER HE 5.175
        s.p.   (H78)

    Wahrlich, Ich Sage Euch
        (Mueller, Harold) "Truly, Truly, I
        Say To You" SSATB,B solo,cont,
        2treb inst sc CONCORDIA 97-5164
        $1.75, ipa   (H79)

    Wer Walzet Uns Den Stein *Easter,
        cant
        (Mueller, Harold) "Who Rolls Away
        The Stone?" SSATB,B solo,org,
        2treb inst/2fl/2ob/2bsn/2vln/
        2rec,vcl/bvl CONCORDIA 97-5166
        $1.50, ipa   (H80)

    Who Rolls Away The Stone? *see Wer
        Walzet Uns Den Stein

    Wie Bin Ich Doch So Herzlich Froh
        SATB&TTBB,opt cont sc HANSSLER
        HE 1.591 s.p.   (H81)

HAMPTON
    Christ Is Risen Indeed *Easter,
        anthem
        SATB,acap oct MCAFEE M1036 $.40
                                 (H82)

    Lord, Speak To Me *anthem
        SATB oct MCAFEE M1043 $.40   (H83)

    This Is The Day *anthem
        cor,org,perc oct MCAFEE M1046 $.40
                                 (H84)

    Touch A Hand, Make A Friend *see
        Banks

HAMPTON, CALVIN
    Creed (from Mass For The New Rite)
        cong&opt SATB GIA G1959 $.50 (H85)

    Joyful! Joyful! *anthem
        SATB,electronic tape MCAFEE M1081
        $.40, ipa   (H86)

    Three Hymn Tunes *CC3U,hymn/liturg
        cor CONCORDIA 98-5143 $1.50 (H87)

HANCOCK, E.W.
    Babe Is Born, A *Xmas
        SATB/TTBB,org/bells GRAY CMR 3325
        $.30   (H88)

HANCOCK, GERRE
    Go Ye Therefore
        SATB&unis,4brass GRAY CMR 3331 $.30
                                 (H89)

    Infant Holy, Infant Lowly *Xmas
        SATB,org GRAY CMR 3334 $.30 (H90)

    Kindle The Gift Of God
        SATB,org GRAY CMR 3314 $.30 (H91)

HAND, COLIN (1929-   )
    O Be Joyful In The Lord (Psalm 100)
        SATB ASHDOWN EC349   (H92)

    Psalm 100 *see O Be Joyful In The
        Lord

    Stabat Mater
        SSA,2fl,2ob,2clar,bsn,2horn,timp
        voc sc NOVELLO rental   (H93)

HAND ME DOWN MY SILVER TRUMPET *anthem
(Burroughs) SATB,opt 3trp&2trom FINE
ARTS EP 30 $.35   (H94)

HAND OF THE DILIGENT, THE see Diament,
Abraham

HANDEL, GEORGE FRIDERIC (1685-1759)
    All The World Worships Thee (from
        Dettingen Te Deum)
        (Dawson, E.) SATB,org/pno oct
        NATIONAL WHC-42 $.40   (H95)

    Amen (from Messiah) Xmas
        (Ehret, Walter) SATB,pno (med)
        PRESSER 312-41065 $.50   (H96)

    And The Glory Of The Lord (from
        Messiah) Xmas/Gen
        mix cor BANKS MUS YS 210 $.40 (H97)
        SATB (med easy) WATERLOO $.40 (H98)
        (White) SATB oct SCHMITT 1451 $.45
                                 (H99)

    Be Thou Exalted
        (Douglas) SATB PRO ART 2810 $.35 (H100)

    Behold The Lamb Of God (from Messiah)
        Gd.Fri.,anthem
        (Beal) SABar&camb,pno CAMBIATA
        M17427 $.35   (H101)
        (Johnson, Norman) SATB oct SINGSPIR
        ZJP-3519 $.30   (H102)

    Can You Not See Our God
        (Pfohl) mix cor BRODT 108 $.25
                               (H103)

    Caroline Te Deum *Te Deum
        SATB,ATB soli,orch sc,cor pts
        EGTVED KB100 s.p., ipa   (H104)

    Choruses From The Messiah *CCUL,
        Xmas/Easter,cant
        (Johnson, Norman) SATB SINGSPIR
        5955 $1.95   (H105)

    Come, Holy Light, Guide Divine (from
        Judas Maccabaeus)
        (Wiley) SATB PRO ART 2817 $.35
                               (H106)
        (Wiley) SAB PRO ART 2820 $.35
                               (H107)

    Come Unto Him (from Messiah) Xmas/Gen
        (Protheroe) SSA (easy) FITZSIMONS
        5004 $.20   (H108)

    Danklied (from La Resurrezione) Fest
        3pt jr cor/3pt wom cor,org/pno,treb
        inst BOHM s.p.   (H109)

    Der Messias *Xmas,ora
        (Priestman, Brian) [Eng/Ger] SATB,
        SATB soli,cont,orch (med diff)
        min sc SCHOTTS ETP 956 s.p.
                               (H110)

    Der Messias (Hallische Handel-
        Ausgabe) *see Messiah

    Der Messias (Neue Mozart-Ausgabe)
        *see Messiah

    Dettigen Te Deum
        (Emery) SATB,SATB soli,2ob,2bsn,
        3trp,timp,strings voc sc NOVELLO
        rental   (H111)

    Evening Hymn *anthem
        (Lethbridge) SATB (easy) OXFORD
        42.386 $.30   (H112)

    For Sion Lamentation Make
        (Dawson, E.; Guinaldo, N.) SATB,
        org/pno oct NATIONAL WHC-39 $.35
                               (H113)

    For Unto Us A Child Is Born (from
        Messiah)
        SATB HARRIS HC 4006 $.40   (H114)

    Fret Not When Doubts And Fears Assail
        (Preston) SATB SHAWNEE A5690 $.35
                               (H115)

    George Friedrich Handel's Works
        *sac/sec,CCU
        microfiche UNION ESP. edition of
        the Deutschen
        Haendelgesellschaft.Edited by
        Friedrich Chrysander, 1858-1894.
        96 volumes and 6 supplements.
        $375.00   (H116)

    Glory To God (from Messiah)
        SATB HARRIS HC 4046 $.35   (H117)

    Halleluja (from Messiah) Xmas/Easter
        (Meinberg, Karl) 3pt jr cor/3pt wom
        cor,org,strings (med easy) sc
        SCHOTTS C 39 397 s.p., cor pts
        SCHOTTS C 39 400 s.p., ipa (H118)

    Halleluja *see Hallelujah

    Hallelujah (from Messiah) Xmas/
        Easter/Fest,anthem
        SATB,cont,orch voc sc CARUS
        CV 40.107 s.p., ipa   (H119)
        SATB (med diff) WATERLOO $.40
                               (H120)

HANDEL, GEORGE FRIDERIC (cont'd.)

SATB HARRIS HC 4009 $.35   (H121)
mix cor BANKS MUS YS 135 $.40
                               (H122)
"Halleluja" 3pt,org/pno,opt strings
BOHM sc s.p., cor pts s.p., ipa
                               (H123)
(Herrmann, Willy) "Halleluja" mix
cor,pno,3vln,vcl,opt org/
harmonium (med easy) sc SCHOTTS
C 39 397 s.p., voc pt SCHOTTS
C 39 399A-D s.p., ipa   (H124)
(Johnson, Norman) SATB oct SINGSPIR
ZJP-3538 $.35   (H125)
(Richison) SSBar&camb CAMBIATA
M97317 $.40   (H126)
(White) SATB oct SCHMITT 1452 $.45
                               (H127)

Hallelujah, Amen (from Judas
Maccabeas)
(Taylor) SS&camb&opt Bar CAMBIATA
M17312 $.35   (H128)

How Beautiful Are The Feet (from
Messiah) Xmas
(Kingsbury, John) SATB,pno/org
(med) PRESSER 312-41064 $.60   (H129)

How Excellent Thy Name (from Saul)
SATB,synthesizer/pno MCAFEE M1073
$.45, ipa   (H130)

Ich Will Singen Von Der Gnade Des
Herrn Ewiglich *Fest,anthem
(Bleier, Paul) mix cor,S/T solo,
strings,kbd sc,cor pts BOHM s.p.,
ipa   (H131)

Jesus, Lord Of All Creation
(Habash, John M.) SSA BIG3 $.40
                               (H132)
(Habash, John M.) SATB BIG3 $.40
                               (H133)
(Habash, John M.) SAB BIG3 $.40
                               (H134)
(Habash, John M.) SA/TB BIG3 $.40
                               (H135)

Largo
"Prayer, A" mix cor BANKS MUS
YS 380 $.20   (H136)

Life Indeed *see Questo E Il Cielo

Messiah *K.572, Xmas/Easter/Gen,
cant/ora
(Johnson, Norman) SATB,soli
(abridged edition) SINGSPIR 5595
$1.95   (H137)
(Mozart, W.A.) "Der Messias (Neue
Mozart-Ausgabe)" SSATB,SSATB
soli,orch cloth BAREN. s.p.,
cmplt ed BAREN. BA4529 rental
                               (H138)
(Shaw) SATB,SATB soli,2ob,2bsn,
2trp,strings voc sc NOVELLO
rental   (H139)
(Tobin, John) "Der Messias
(Hallische Handel-Ausgabe)" [Eng/
Ger] SSATB,SAATB soli,orch s.p.,
ipr sc BAREN. DA4012, voc sc
BAREN. BA4012A   (H140)

Music From "Semele"
(Blower) SSA,opt T solo,strings voc
sc NOVELLO rental   (H141)

O My Soul, Bless God The Father
(Wiley) SAB PRO ART 2765 $.35
                               (H142)
O Praise The Lord With One Consent
(Neuen) SATB SCHIRM.G LG51801 $.75
                               (H143)
O Sacred Head, Now Wounded
unis,S solo oct CONCORDIA 98-2237
$.40   (H144)
O Sing Unto The Lord *Easter/Epiph/
Gen
(Peek) SAB,ob (med) oct CONCORDIA
98-2200 $.35   (H145)

Praise The Lord
(Hopson) SAB SHAWNEE D5225 $.35
                               (H146)
Prayer, A *see Largo

Questo E Il Cielo (from Alcina)
(Wilson, J.F.) "Life Indeed" [Eng]
unis oct HOPE A 475 $.30   (H147)

Seht, Er Kommt Mit Preis Gekront!
(from Judas Maccabeas) Xmas
jr cor/wom cor (easy) sc SCHOTTS
CHBL 513 s.p. contains also:
Tochter Zion, Freue Dich!   (H148)

Since By Man Came Death *Easter
SATB (med easy) WATERLOO $.35
                               (H149)
Surely, He Hath Borne Our Griefs
(from Messiah) Psntd
"Wahrlich, Er Trug Unsre Qual"
SATB,org sc,cor pts PELIKAN
PE 195   (H150)
(Beal) SABar&camb CAMBIATA M97201

HANDEL, GEORGE FRIDERIC (cont'd.)

$.35   (H151)

Swell The Full Chorus
SATB,orch GALAXY 1 2144.1 sc
rental, ipr, cor pts $.35   (H152)

Thanks Be To Thee
SATB GALAXY 1.1228.1 $.30   (H153)
(Lefebvre) TTBB GALAXY 1.1222.1
$.30   (H154)
(Lefebvre) SAB GALAXY 1.1272.1 $.30
                               (H155)
(Lefebvre) SSA GALAXY 1.1288.1 $.30
                               (H156)
(Wiley) SSA PRO ART 2827 $.35
                               (H157)
(Wiley) SAB PRO ART 2823 $.35
                               (H158)
Thine Is The Glory *Easter,anthem
(Montgomery, K.) SATB/SA oct
SINGSPIR ZJP-3545 $.35   (H159)

Thine Own To Be *anthem
(Brault, Elizabeth) cor CHORISTERS
R-5 $.15   (H160)

Tochter Zion, Freue Dich! *Xmas
see Handel, George Frideric, Seht,
Er Kommt Mit Preis Gekront!
cor BOHM s.p.   (H161)
SATB,SSA/TTB soli,cont,orch CARUS
CV 40.101 sc s.p., voc sc s.p.,
ipa   (H162)

Unto Us A Child Is Born
(Shaw) SA,trp/clar,strings voc sc
NOVELLO rental   (H163)

Utrecht Jubilate, The
(Haverkampf) SSAATTBB&opt AAB,pno
AMP A-686 $1.75   (H164)

Utrecht Te Deum
(Shaw) SATB,ATB soli,fl,2ob,bsn,
2trp,strings voc sc NOVELLO
rental   (H165)

Wahrlich, Er Trug Unsre Qual *see
Surely, He Hath Borne Our Griefs

Wash Me Thoroughly From My Wickedness
(Plott) TB BRODT DC 7 $.25   (H166)

We Praise Thee, O God *see Croft,
William

Wenn Christus, Der Herr
see DREI BEERDIGUNGSGESANGE

Worthy Is The Lamb (from Messiah)
Bibl
mix cor BANKS MUS YS 266 $.30
                               (H167)
SATB (diff) FITZSIMONS 2030 $.25
                               (H168)
Zadok The Priest
mix cor BANKS MUS YS 370 $.70
                               (H169)
SATB HARRIS HC 4054 $.75   (H170)

HANDL, JACOB
see GALLUS, JACOBUS

HANEBECK, HUGO RUDOLF
Missa Dorica *Op.38, Mass
[Lat] 4pt mix cor,acap sc,cor pts
BOHM s.p.   (H171)

HANEROT HALALU
(Chass, Blanche) SAB (easy) FOSTER
MF678 $.40   (H172)
(Chass, Blanche) SA (easy) FOSTER
MF877 $.30   (H173)
(Chass, Blanche) TBB (easy) FOSTER
MF1077 $.40   (H174)
(Freed; Nolley) SATB oct SCHMITT 1214
$.40   (H175)

HANKEY
I Love To Tell The Story (composed
with Butler) *anthem
unis oct BROADMAN 4558-65 $.30
                               (H176)

HANNAHS, ROGER
Hallowed Day, A *Xmas,mot
SSA AMP A-698 $.35 see from Two
Christmas Motets   (H177)

Two Christmas Motets *see Hallowed
Day, A; When All The World   (H178)

When All The World *Xmas,mot
SSA AMP A-697 $.35 see from Two
Christmas Motets   (H179)

HANSON
Psalm 121
see Two Psalms

Psalm 150
see Two Psalms

HANSON (cont'd.)

Two Psalms *anthem
SATB oct FISCHER,C O-4806 $.60
contains: Psalm 121; Psalm 150
                               (H180)

HANUKAH LIGHTS see Chass, Blanche

HANUS, JAN (1915-   )
Drei Kleine Passionsmotetten Nach
Altbohmischen Gesangen *Op.65,
No.1a, CC3U,Psntd,mot
treb cor,4rec/org MERSEBURG EM180
                               (H181)

HAPPENING AT BETHLEHEM, THE see
Cornell, Garry A.

HAPPENING NOW! see Oldenburg, Bob

HAPPINESS IS INSIDE OF YOU see Vance,
Margaret Shelley

HAPPINESS IS THE LORD see Stanphill,
Ira F.

HAPPY AM I! see Holiday, Mickey

HAPPY BEATITUDES, THE see McElrath

HAPPY BIRTHDAY, BABY JESUS
see Sunshine And Snowflakes

HAPPY DAY CHOIR BOOK *CC10UL
(Bock, Fred) SATB,pno (med easy)
GENTRY G-656 $2.50   (H182)

HAPPY GOSPEL CHOIR *CC10UL
(Ehret, Walter) SA&opt Bar cmplt ed
LILLENAS MB-363 $1.50   (H183)

HAPPY IS THE MAN WHO FINDS WISDOM see
Clark

HAPPY JUBILEE, THE see Pace

HAPPY SONG, A see Eneberg, Gale (Gail)

HAPPY TIME SONGS NO. 1 *CC75UL
jr cor SINGSPIR 5500 $1.00   (H184)

HAPPY TIME SONGS NO. 2 *CC41UL
jr cor SINGSPIR 5501 $1.00   (H185)

HARDER, OTTO
Ave Maria
[Lat] 4pt mix cor,opt S solo,org
sc,cor pts BOHM s.p.   (H186)

HARDWICKE
When The Lord Cry Holy *anthem
SA oct HERITAGE H5011 $.35   (H187)

HARE
Thou, O God, Art Praised In Zion
SATB (med) OXFORD 42.377 $.55 (H188)

HARIU LE'ELOHIM see Diament, Abraham

HARK! BETHLEHEM
see Polish Christmas Carols

HARK, HARK MY SOUL see Chadwick, George
Whitefield

HARK, HARK MY SOUL see Smart, Henry
Thomas

HARK HOW ALL THE WELKIN RINGS see Roe

HARK! IN THE DARKNESS
see Polish Christmas Carols

HARK! TEN THOUSAND HARPS AND VOICES see
Mason, Lowell

HARK THE GLAD SOUND *Xmas
(Fox, George) SATB (med) WATERLOO
$.60   (H189)

HARK! THE GLAD SOUND! see Krogstad, Bob

HARK! THE HERALD ANGELS SING
see Christmas Choir Melodies

HARK, THE HERALD ANGELS SING see
Mendelssohn-Bartholdy, Felix

HARK THE SOUND OF HOLY VOICES see
Cousins, M. Thomas

HARK, THE VOICE OF JESUS CALLING see
Landgrave, Phillip

HARK! WHAT MEAN THOSE HOLY VOICES see
Wyton, Alec

HARK, YE PEOPLE, CHRIST IS RISEN! see
Hayes

HARKEN, STAY CLOSE TO HIM see Peter,
Johann Friedrich

HARLIG AR JORDEN see Olson, Daniel

HARMON, B.
He'll Be There
(Collins, Hope) SATB oct GOSPEL
05 TM 0215 $.20   (H190)

HARMONIA CAELESTIS, HEFT 2 see
Esterhazy, Pal

HAROLD DECOU PRESENTS CHORAL PRAISES
*CCUL
(DeCou, Harold) SATB SINGSPIR 4274
$1.00   (H191)

HARPER
Psalm 150 *anthem
2pt (med easy) OXFORD E 135 (H192)

HARPER, REDD (1903-   )
Back To The Prairies And Other
Country Songs *CCUL
SATB/1-2pt oct SINGSPIR 4063 $1.50
(H193)

Each Step Of The Way *anthem
(Krogstad, Bob) SA/TB (easy) oct
SINGSPIR ZJP-6034 $.35   (H194)

HARRELL, JAN
Give Jesus A Chance *anthem
SATB WORD CS-2574 $.30 see also
MUSIC FOR THE YOUNG CHURCH,
VOLUME I   (H195)

Reflection Of God, A *anthem
SATB WORD CS-2677 $.35   (H196)

HARRER
Mein Herz Ist Bereit
(Harris) "My Heart Sings With Joy"
SATB PRO ART 2840 $.40   (H197)
(Harris) "My Heart Sings With Joy"
SAB PRO ART 2836 $.35   (H198)

My Heart Sings With Joy *see Mein
Herz Ist Bereit

HARRHY, EDITH
Ring Bells Ring
unis HARRIS HC 1011 $.35   (H199)

HARRINGTON, KARL P.
There's A Song In The Air *Xmas,
anthem
(Johnson, Norman) SATB oct SINGSPIR
ZJP-3005 $.25   (H200)

HARRIS
Ah, Dearest Jesus *Xmas
SATB,acap PRO ART 2845 $.35 (H201)

All That Thrills My Soul (composed
with Lyall) *anthem
SATB (easy) oct BROADMAN 4538-91
$.30   (H202)

Clap Hands All People, Shout For Joy
SATB KJOS 5916 $.40   (H203)

Fourteen Responses, Benediction, And
Amens *CC14L
SATB PRO ART 1412 $1.00   (H204)

Gentle Mary *Xmas
SATB PRO ART 2832 $.35   (H205)

He That Is Down Needs Fear No Fall
*anthem
SSA (easy) OXFORD 44.082 $.35
(H206)

I Said To The Man Who Stood At The
Gate *anthem
TTBB,acap (easy) OXFORD 41.026 $.25
(H207)

Joyfully Sing We His Praise!
2pt PRO ART 2819 $.35   (H208)

O Love That Casts Out Fear
SATB KJOS 5917 $.35   (H209)

Our Day Of Praise Is Done *anthem
SSATB (easy) OXFORD 42.375 $.35
(H210)

Sing We Noel
SATB KJOS 5907 $.40   (H211)

HARRIS, D.
Spread, Thou Mighty Word
SATB,SBar soli,org GRAY CMR 3308
$.35   (H212)

HARRIS, D.S.
Eternal Ruler Of The Ceaseless Round
SATB,org GRAY CMR 3329 $.35 (H213)

Holy Banquet, The *Commun
SATB,Bar solo,org GRAY CMR 3309
$.30   (H214)

O Love Of God *Commun/Gen
SATB,org GRAY CMR 3307 $.30 (H215)

HARRIS, RON
Anticipation *anthem
SATB WORD   (H216)

HARRIS, RON (cont'd.)
Friend Of The Father *CCU,anthem
(Brown, Charles F.) SATB LEXICON
(H217)

I've Got Jesus In My Heart
SATB,pno (easy) GENTRY G-252 $.45
(H218)

HARRISON
I Want To Bloom Where I'm Planted
*anthem
SATB/SA (easy) oct SINGSPIR
ZJP-6025 $.35   (H219)

HARRISON, LOU (1917-   )
Mass *Mass
mix cor,trp,strings,harp PEER sc
$8.00, cor pts $.60, ipr   (H220)

HART
I Will Arise (composed with
Billingsley) *anthem
SATB oct BROADMAN 4562-40 $.35
(H221)
SATB (easy) oct BROADMAN 4554-49
$.30   (H222)

HARTMANN, HEINRICH (? -1616)
Eins Bitt Ich Vom Herren
SSATB (contains also: Hilf, A Und
O, Anfang Und Ende) SCHWEIZER.
SK 62.07-8 s.p. see also
MUSIKBEILAGE ZUM "EVANGELISCHEN
KIRCHENCHOR 1962"   (H223)

HARTSOUGH, L.
I Hear Thy Welcome Voice *anthem
(Medema, Ken) SATB WORD CS-2692
$.40   (H224)

HARVEST CAROL see Copes, V. Earle

HARVEST CAROL see Elvey, George Job

HARVEST CELEBRATION *see Heritage
Medley   (H225)

HARVEST FIELDS, THE see Cawston, Nancy

HARVEST HOME
see Four Folk Songs From Abroad

HARVEST TIME AGAIN see Archer, Darrell
V.

HARVEST TIME OF LOVE see Jensen, Wilma

HARWOOD, BASIL (1859-1949)
As By The Streams Of Babylon
SATB,S solo,2fl,pic,2ob,2clar,2bsn,
4horn,2trp,3trom,tuba,timp,perc,
harp,strings, English horn voc sc
NOVELLO rental   (H226)

HARWOOD-JONES, H.F.
Rise Up O Men Of God
SATB (med easy) WATERLOO $.40
(H227)

HAS SORROW THY YOUNG DAYS SHADED? see
Parke, Dorothy

HASHKIVENU see Isaacson, Michael

HASHKIVENU see Nowakowsky, David

HASKINS, WILLIAM
Since The Savior Found Me *anthem/
gospel
(DeCou, Harold) SATB oct SINGSPIR
ZJP-8021 $.30   (H228)

HASSE
Doxology: Amen, Praise Ye The Lord
(Kroeger) cor (med) FISCHER,C
CM 7879 $.35   (H229)

HASSE, JOHANN ADOLPH (1699-1783)
Miserere
wom cor,orch HENN s.p.   (H230)

HASSE, O.
Just To Feel Thy Presence Near Me
SATB (med) FITZSIMONS 2024 $.20
(H231)

HASSLER, HANS LEO (1564-1612)
And The World Became Flesh *see
Verbum Caro Factus Est

Cantate Domine
(Neuen) SATB SCHIRM.G LG51849 $.40
(H232)

Cantate Domino
[Lat] SATB,acap EGTVED MK8, 2 s.p.
(H233)

Christ Is Arisen *Easter
(Coggin, Elwood) SSA,pno (easy) oct
ELKAN-V 362-03159 $.30   (H234)
(Coggin, Elwood) SAB,pno (easy) oct
ELKAN-V 362-03160 $.30   (H235)

Dixit Maria Ad Angelum *BVM
[Lat] SATB,acap EGTVED MK2, 18 s.p.
(H236)

En Dyr Klenod, En Klar Och Ren
4pt mix cor ERIKS 47 s.p. (H237)

HASSLER, HANS LEO (cont'd.)
Gott Sei Gelobet Und Gebenedeiet
SATB DOBLINGER S 204 s.p. (H238)

Herr, Wie Lang Wilt Vergessen Mein
(Psalm 13)
SATB SCHWEIZER. SK 109 s.p. (H239)

Im Kuhlen Mai
see Bach, Johann Sebastian, Dir,
Dir, Jehova, Will Ich Singen

Kirchengesange *CC32U
SATB/SAATB,acap (easy) sc BAREN.
BA6221   (H240)

Missa Secunda *Mass
[Eng] SATB,acap WHITE,ERN $.50
(H241)

Missa Tertia *Mass
[Lat] 4pt mix cor,acap sc,cor pts
BOHM s.p.   (H242)

O Sacred Head, Now Wounded *Gd.Fri.,
anthem
(Johnson, Norman) SATB oct SINGSPIR
ZJP-3510 $.25   (H243)
(Peterson, John W.) SATB oct
SINGSPIR ZJP-3512 $.25   (H244)

Psalm 13 *see Herr, Wie Lang Wilt
Vergessen Mein

Singet Ein Neues Lied
SATB (contains also Herr Jesu Mein,
Sollst Doch Mein Trost)
SCHWEIZER. SK 55.05-6 s.p. see
also MUSIKBEILAGE ZUM
"EVANGELISCHEN KIRCHENCHOR 1955"
(H245)

Verbum Caro Factus Est
(Klein) "And The World Became
Flesh" SATB SCHIRM.G 11989 $.35
(H246)

Wenn Ich Einmal Soll Scheiden
(Bach, J. S.) men cor,acap TONOS
5612 s.p. contains also: Franck,
Melchior, Wenn Ich In Todesnoten
Bin   (H247)

Wenn Mein Stundlein Vorhanden Ist
[Ger] RICORDI-ENG BA 9831 s.p. (H248)

HAST THOU FORSAKEN ME see Nottingham

HAST THOU NOT KNOWN see Pflueger, Carl

HASTE THEE, O GOD see Grieb, Herbert
[C.]

HASTE THEE, O GOD see Shepherd

HASTEN SHEPHERDS ON
(Pablo, Juan) 2pt,S solo,pno/org,opt
gtr, opt. claves and maracas
FREDONIA see from Three Puerto
Rican Carols   (H249)

HASTINGS
From Ev'ry Stormy Wind *hymn
(Ehret, Walter) SATB oct LILLENAS
AN-2407 $.30   (H250)

Hiding In The Rock Of Ages *see
Sankey, I.

HATCH, OWEN A.
Let All The Earth Be Glad *Gen/
Thanks
SAB CHORISTERS A-100 $.40 (H251)

Rejoice And Sing *Easter
unis CHORISTERS A-68 $.30 (H252)

HATHCOCK
I Present You To Jesus *gospel
(Schubert) SATB oct LILLENAS
AN-1666 $.30   (H253)

HATTON
Jesus Shall Reign *see Watts

HATTON, JOHN [LIPTROT] (1809-1886)
Jesus Shall Reign *Palm,anthem
(Soderstrom) SSAATTBB,acap (med)
FITZSIMONS 2120 $.25   (H254)
(Williams, David E.) SATB oct
SINGSPIR ZJP-7237 $.25   (H255)

HAUBLER, ERNST
Jauchzet Gott, Alle Lande (Psalm 66)
Bibl/mot
4-6pt mix cor HIEBER sc s.p., voc
pt s.p.   (H256)

Psalm 66 *see Jauchzet Gott, Alle
Lande

HAUGE
Earth Will Sing, The *anthem
(Linn) SATB,brass oct LILLENAS
AT-1090 $.35   (H257)
(Schubert) SATB oct LILLENAS
AN-1665 $.30   (H258)

HAUGLAND, A.O.
Holy Spirit, Truth Divine
mix cor BRODT 602 $.25   (H259)

HAUS, KARL (1928-   )
Es Kommt Ein Schiff, Geladen *Adv
3pt BOHM s.p.   (H260)

Hort Eine Helle Stimm Erklingt
*Xmas,cant
2 eq voices/2pt mix cor,strings,
winds sc,cor pts PELIKAN PE929
(H261)

Im Stall Bei Esel, Schaf Und Rind
*Xmas,Fr
mix cor (easy) sc SCHOTTS CHBL 415
s.p.   (H262)
jr cor (easy) sc SCHOTTS CHBL 601
s.p.   (H263)

O Freude Uber Freude *Xmas
1-2pt jr cor,narrator,pno/2vln&vcl
BOHM sc s.p., cor pts s.p., ipa
(H264)

HAVE A LITTLE TALK WITH THE LORD see
Peterson, John W.

HAVE FAITH AND KEEP ON MOVIN' see
Lister, Mosie

HAVE FAITH IN GOD see Graham

HAVE FAITH IN GOD! see Peterson, John
W.

HAVE I DONE MY BEST FOR JESUS? see
Storrs, H.

HAVE MERCY see Pulsiter, Thomas R.

HAVE MERCY, LORD see Caldara, Antonio

HAVE MERCY ON ME see Tomkins, Thomas

HAVE MERCY, ON US, LORD see Lawes,
William

HAVE MERCY UPON ME O GOD see Bateson,
Thomas

HAVE NO FEAR, LITTLE FLOCK see
Zimmermann, Heinz Werner

HAVE THINE OWN WAY see Kirby, Charles

HAVE THINE OWN WAY, LORD see Smith

HAVE YE NOT KNOWN? see Beck, John Ness

HAVE YOU ANY ROOM FOR JESUS? *Xmas
(Huff, Ronn) SATB BENSON S4122 $.35
(H265)

HAVE YOU EVER FELT A GLOW?
(Wild, Eric) SATB,pno BERANDOL
BER1242 $.50   (H266)

HAVE YOU NOT KNOWN? see Ford, Virgil T.

HAVE YOU SEEN THREE KINGS? see Graham,
Robert Virgil

HAVERGAL
Welcome, Happy Morning! *Easter,
anthem
(DeCou, Harold) SATB oct SINGSPIR
ZJP-3513 $.25   (H267)

HAWKINS, FLOYD W. (1904-   )
Carols By Candlelight *Xmas
cor,narrator LILLENAS MC-3 $.25
(H268)

HAWTHORNE
Family Of God, The (composed with
McKinley)
(Red, Buryl) SATB TRIUNE TUM 113
$.35 see also FAMILY OF GOD, THE
(H269)

HAWTHORNE, GRACE
It's Cool In The Furnace *see Red,
Buryl

HAYDN, (FRANZ) JOSEPH (1732-1809)
Ave Regina Coelorum
[Lat] cor,S solo,org,2vln,bvl sc,
cor pts BOHM s.p., ipa   (H270)

Benedictus *Bene
(Ehret) "Blessed Is He" SSA WALTON
5032 $.35   (H271)

Blessed Is He *see Benedictus

Creation Mass In B Flat Major
(Landon) SATB SCHIRM.G 2943 $5.00
(H272)

Day Of Resurrection, The *Easter,
anthem
(Yungton, Al) SATB,opt 3trp oct
SINGSPIR ZJP-3506 $.25   (H273)

Der Herr Ist Gross In Seiner Macht
(from Die Schopfung)
(Gerster, Ottmar) jr cor/wom cor
(med easy) sc SCHOTTS CHBL 541
s.p.   (H274)

HAYDN, (FRANZ) JOSEPH (cont'd.)
Die Himmel Erzahlen (from Die
Schopfung) Fest
3pt,pno,opt strings&harmonium BOHM
sc s.p., cor pts s.p., ipa (H275)

Die Jahreszeiten *ora
SATB,STB soli,2fl,2ob,2clar,3bsn,
4horn,2trp,3trom,strings,
timp (med) min sc SCHOTTS ETP 987
s.p.   (H276)

Die Sieben Letzen Worte Unseres
Erlosers Am Kreuze *Psntd,ora
(Fodor, A.) cor,4 soli,orch sc
EULENBURG 10098 s.p.   (H277)

Du Bist's Dem Ruhm Und Ehre Gebuhret
*Xmas,Offer
"Tui Sunt Coeli" [Lat] cor,opt org,
strings sc,cor pts BOHM s.p., ipa
(H278)

Feierliches Hochamt In B *see
Heiligmesse

Gloria (from Heiligmesse) anthem/
Gloria
(Coggin, Elwood) "Glory To God In
The Highest" [Eng/Lat] SAB,pno/
org WORLD CA-2132-7 $.75   (H279)
(Coggin, Elwood) "Glory To God In
The Highest" [Eng/Lat] SSA,org/
pno WORLD CA-2130-3 $.75   (H280)
(Coggin, Elwood) "Glory To God In
The Highest" [Eng/Lat] SATB,org/
pno WORLD CA-2131-8 $.75   (H281)
(Ehret) "Glory To God" SSA WALTON
5034 $.35   (H282)
(Ehret, Walter) "Unto The Lord In
Heav'n" [Eng/Lat] SATB,kbd BOONIN
B 187 $.45   (H283)

Glorious Things Of Thee Are Spoken
*anthem
(DeCou, Harold) SATB oct SINGSPIR
ZJP-7254 $.30   (H284)

Glory To God *see Gloria

Glory To God In The Highest *see
Gloria

Great And Marvellous
(Dicks) mix cor BANKS MUS YS 716
$.55   (H285)

Heavens Are Telling, The (from
Creation, The)
SATB HARRIS HC 4013 $.35   (H286)

Heiligmesse *Mass
"Feierliches Hochamt In B" [Lat]
4pt mix cor,soli,org,2ob/2clar,
2bsn,2trp,strings,timp (B flat
maj) sc,cor pts BOHM s.p., ipa
(H287)

Hochamt In B *see Schopfungsmesse

Holy, Holy, Holy *see Sanctus

In Nomine Jesu
"Litany In B-Flat" SATB SCHIRM.G
2942 $2.50   (H288)

Kleine Orgelsolomesse *see Missa
Brevis In Honorem Sti. Joannis De
Deo In B

Kleine Orgelsolomesse *see Missa
Brevis Sti. Joannis De Deo

Kyrie (from Missa Brevis Sancti
Johannis De Deo) anthem/Kyrie
(Ehret) "Lord Have Mercy On Us" SSA
WALTON 5033 $.35   (H289)
(Ehret, Walter) "Lord, Have Mercy"
SATB,kbd AUGSBURG 11-1689 $.40
(H290)
(Harris) SATB PRO ART 2783 $.35
(H291)
(Talmadge) "Lord, Have Mercy Upon
Us" SSAA BRODT HC 1 $.32   (H292)

Litany In B-Flat *see In Nomine Jesu

Lord, Have Mercy *see Kyrie

Lord Have Mercy On Us *see Kyrie

Lord, Have Mercy Upon Us *see Kyrie

Lord, We Pray Thee
(Noble) mix cor BANKS MUS YS 505
$.20   (H293)

Mariazeller Messe In C *Mass
[Lat] 4pt mix cor,soli,org,2trp,
strings,timp,opt 2ob&2bsn sc,cor
pts BOHM s.p., ipa   (H294)

Marvelous Work (from Creation, The)
(Davis) SSA GALAXY 1.1950.1 $.30
(H295)

HAYDN, (FRANZ) JOSEPH (cont'd.)
Missa Brevis In Honorem Sti. Joannis
De Deo In B *Mass
"Kleine Orgelsolomesse" [Lat] men
cor,org,2vla,bvl (B flat maj)
BOHM sc s.p., cor pts s.p., ipa
(H296)

Missa Brevis Sancti Joannis De Deo
*Mass
(Landon) SATB,org SCHIRM.G 2923
$1.50   (H297)

Missa Brevis Sti. Joannis De Deo
*Mass
"Kleine Orgelsolomesse" [Lat] 4pt
mix cor,soli,org,2vln/2vla,bvl (B
flat maj) sc,cor pts BOHM s.p.,
ipa   (H298)
(Jochum, Otto) "Kleine
Orgelsolomesse" 3pt wom cor/3pt
jr cor,org,2vln,opt vla (B
flat maj) BOHM sc s.p., cor pts
s.p., ipa   (H299)

Missa In Angustiis C-Dur *Mass
SATB,SATB soli,orch (C maj,med) min
sc SCHOTTS ETP 995 s.p.   (H300)

Missa In G In Honorem Sti. Nicolai
*Mass
[Lat] 4pt mix cor,soli,org,strings,
opt 2ob&2horn&2trp&timp sc,cor
pts BOHM s.p., ipa   (H301)

Missa In Tempore Belli *Mass
"Pauken-Messe In C" [Lat] 4pt mix
cor,soli,org,fl,2ob/2clar,2bsn,
2horn,2trp,strings,timp sc,cor
pts BOHM s.p., ipa   (H302)

Non Nobis Domine *Fest
[Lat] 4pt mix cor,org sc,cor pts
BOHM s.p.   (H303)

O Jesu (O Maria) Te Invocamus *Fest
[Lat] 4pt mix cor,org/2trp,2vln,
2ob/2clar,timp,org sc,cor pts
BOHM s.p., ipa   (H304)

O Worship The King *anthem
SSA (easy) WATERLOO $.30   (H305)
(Mayfield, Larry) SATB oct SINGSPIR
ZJP-7304 $.30   (H306)

Pauken-Messe In C *see Missa In
Tempore Belli

Salus Et Gloria *Fest
[Lat] 4pt mix cor,org,2vln,vcl,trp,
timp,opt bvl sc,cor pts BOHM
s.p., ipa   (H307)

Salve Regina In Es
[Lat] 4pt mix cor,org,strings (E
flat maj) sc,cor pts BOHM s.p.,
ipa   (H308)

Sanctus (from Mass No. 3 In D - The
Nelson) Sanctus
(Devan, G.) TTBB (mcd diff)
WATERLOO $.40   (H309)
(Ehret) "Holy, Holy, Holy" SSA
WALTON 5031 $.35   (H310)
(Hilton, Arthur) "Holy, Holy, Holy"
[Eng/Lat] SSA,pno/org MERCURY
352-00468 $.35   (H311)
(Hilton, Arthur) "Holy, Holy, Holy"
[Eng/Lat] SATB,pno/org MERCURY
352-00469 $.35   (H312)

Schopfungsmesse *Mass
"Hochamt In B" [Lat] 4pt mix cor,
soli,org,2ob,2clar,2bsn,2horn,
2trp,strings,timp (B flat maj)
sc,cor pts BOHM s.p., ipa   (H313)

Theresien-Messe *Mass
[Lat] 4pt mix cor,soli,org,2trp,
strings,timp,opt 2clar (B flat
maj) sc,cor pts BOHM s.p., ipa
(H314)

Tui Sunt Coeli *see Du Bist's Dem
Ruhm Und Ehre Gebuhret

Unto The Lord In Heav'n *see Gloria

Ye Servants Of God *Palm,anthem
(DeCou, Harold) SATB oct SINGSPIR
ZJP-7239 $.25   (H315)

HAYDN, (JOHANN) MICHAEL (1737-1806)
Agnus Dei *Easter
(Hines) SATB SCHIRM.G LG51823 $.40
(H316)

Ave Maria
[Lat] 4pt mix cor,S solo,org,2vln,
bvl sc,cor pts BOHM s.p., ipa
(H317)

Ave Regina Coelorum
[Lat] 4pt mix cor,org,2vln,bvl,opt
2trp sc,cor pts BOHM s.p., ipa
(H318)

Christus Factus Est
see Zwei Propriumsgesange Fur Den
Grundonnerstag

HAYDN, (JOHANN) MICHAEL (cont'd.)

Deutsche Messe *Mass
  (Haas, Joseph) 2pt jr cor/2pt wom
  cor,org (easy) sc SCHOTTS
  ED. 5150 s.p.   (H319)

Ein Lob- Und Danklied "O Grosser
  Gott, Dich Loben Wir"
  (Schmid, Otto) 4pt men cor/mix cor/
  jr cor,pno/pno&fl&3vln&vcl&bvl&
  opt org&opt harmonium sc SCHOTTS
  C 39 902 s.p., voc pt SCHOTTS
  C 39 903-01-04 s.p.   (H320)
  (Schmid, Otto) 3pt jr cor/3pt wom
  cor,pno/pno&fl&3vln&vcl&bvl&opt
  org&opt harmonium (med easy) cor
  pts SCHOTTS C 39 905 s.p., ipa   (H321)

Herr, Grosser Gott, Dich Loben Wir
  *Fest,Te Deum
  [Ger] mix cor,org,2trp sc,cor pts
  BOHM s.p., ipa   (H322)

Hier Liegt Vor Deiner Majestat
  2pt wom cor,soli,2horn,bvl,org
  DOBLINGER sc s.p., cor pts s.p.,
  ipa   (H323)

Holy, Holy, Holy (from Missa Sub
  Titulo)
  (Ehret, Walter) [Eng/Lat] SSA,pno/
  org (easy) oct ELKAN-V 362-03195
  $.40   (H324)

Hymne An Gott
  men cor,acap TONOS 6331 s.p. (H325)

Jesu Redemptor Omnium
  [Lat] 4pt mix cor,acap sc,cor pts
  BOHM s.p.   (H326)

Laudate Pueri *Fest
  [Lat] SAT/SAB,org,2vln sc,cor pts
  BOHM s.p., ipa   (H327)

Lord, Have Mercy On Us (from Missa
  Sub Titulo)
  (Ehret, Walter) [Eng/Lat] SSA,pno/
  org (med easy) oct ELKAN-V
  362-03196 $.40   (H328)

Missa In Tempore Adventus Et
  Quadragesimae *Mass
  [Lat] 4pt mix cor,org (D min,
  contains a Gloria and a second Et
  Incarnatus Est by Josef Eybler)
  sc,cor pts BOHM s.p.   (H329)

Nos Autem
  see Zwei Propriumsgesange Fur Den
  Grundonnerstag

O Worship The King
  (Pool) mix cor BRODT 600 $.25
                                         (H330)

On Mount Of Olives
  (Hilton, Arthur) [Eng/Lat] SATB,opt
  org MERCURY 352-00467 $.35 (H331)

Salve Regina
  [Lat] 4pt mix cor,acap (B flat maj)
  sc,cor pts BOHM s.p.   (H332)

Sancti Dei *Fest
  [Lat] 4pt mix cor,acap BOHM s.p.
                                         (H333)

Te Deum *Te Deum
  mix cor,soli,org,orch HUG   (H334)

Te Deum In C
  (Pauly, Reinhard G.) cor bds A-R ED
  $8.95   (H335)

Tenebrae Factae Sunt *Holywk
  [Lat] SATB EGTVED MS8B2 s.p. (H336)

Tenebrae Factae Sunt *Holywk
  [Lat] 4pt mix cor,acap (E flat maj)
  BOHM s.p.   (H337)

Tenebrae Factae Sunt
  [Lat] 4pt mix cor,acap sc,cor pts
  BOHM s.p.   (H338)

Zwei Propriumsgesange Fur Den
  Grundonnerstag *Holywk
  [Lat] 4pt mix cor,acap sc,cor pts
  BOHM s.p.
  contains: Christus Factus Est;
    Nos Autem   (H339)

HAYES
  Bow Down Thine Ear, O Lord *anthem
  SATB,2S (med diff) OXFORD 42.374
  $1.35   (H340)

  Hark, Ye People, Christ Is Risen!
  (composed with Peninger)
  *Easter,anthem
  SATB (easy) oct BROADMAN 4551-62
  $.30   (H341)

HAYFORD
  Come On Down (composed with Stone)
  (Mercer, W. Elmo) SSATB oct BENSON
  S4061 $.45   (H342)

  What Will Your Answer Be? *folk
  (Skillings, Otis) SATB oct LILLENAS
  AN-5039 $.30   (H343)

HAYLLE, COMLY AND CLENE see Davies,
  Peter Maxwell

HAYS
  Lily Of The Valley, The *anthem/
  gospel
  (Mickelson, Paul) SATB oct SINGSPIR
  ZJP-8122 $.30   (H344)

HAYS, PEGGY MCALLISTER
  Beatitudes, The
  see Singing God's Word For
  Childrens Voices Book 2

  Beatitudes For Smaller Children
  see Singing God's Word For
  Childrens Voices Book 1

  Books Of The New Testament
  see Singing God's Word For
  Childrens Voices Book 2

  Books Of The Old Testament
  see Singing God's Word For
  Childrens Voices Book 3

  Bring Ye All The Tithes
  see Singing God's Word For
  Childrens Voices Book 3

  For God So Loved The World
  see Singing God's Word For
  Childrens Voices Book 3

  Lord's Prayer, The
  see Singing God's Word For
  Childrens Voices Book 1

  Seven Days Of Creation
  see Singing God's Word For
  Childrens Voices Book 1

  Singing God's Word For Childrens
  Voices Book 1 *anthem
  jr cor CENTURY PR $.35
    contains: Beatitudes For Smaller
    Children; Lord's Prayer, The;
    Seven Days Of Creation; Twelve
    Apostles, The   (H345)

  Singing God's Word For Childrens
  Voices Book 2 *anthem
  jr cor CENTURY PR $.35
    contains: Beatitudes, The; Books
    Of The New Testament; Twelve
    Apostles, The; Twelve Tribes,
    The; Twenty-Third Psalm (H346)

  Singing God's Word For Childrens
  Voices Book 3 *anthem
  jr cor CENTURY PR $.35
    contains: Books Of The Old
    Testament; Bring Ye All The
    Tithes; For God So Loved The
    World; Ten Commandments; Twelve
    Disciples Interesting Facts And
    Occupations   (H347)

  Ten Commandments
  see Singing God's Word For
  Childrens Voices Book 3

  Twelve Apostles, The
  see Singing God's Word For
  Childrens Voices Book 2
  see Singing God's Word For
  Childrens Voices Book 1

  Twelve Disciples Interesting Facts
  And Occupations
  see Singing God's Word For
  Childrens Voices Book 3

  Twelve Tribes, The
  see Singing God's Word For
  Childrens Voices Book 2

  Twenty-Third Psalm
  see Singing God's Word For
  Childrens Voices Book 2

HAYWOOD
  Jesus, The Son Of God
  (Johnson, Lois) SATB oct GOSPEL
  05 TM 0209 $.20   (H348)

HAYWOOD, G.
  I See A Crimson Stream *Easter
  (McLellan, Cyril) SATB oct GOSPEL
  05 TM 0103 $.25   (H349)

HAYWOOD, L.B.
  Lead, Kindly Light
  mix cor BRODT 532 $.24   (H350)

HE BROUGHT ME OUT see Gilmour

HE CALLS ME SON see Zilch, Margot

HE CAME AMONG US see Carlson, Gordon

HE CAME, HE COMES see Landgrave,
  Phillip

HE CAME, HE'LL COME AGAIN see Eleiott,
  Max

HE CAME SINGING LOVE see Gadwood, Gary

HE COMES see Winter, Sister Miriam
  Therese

HE COMES! HE COMES! see Wetzler, Robert

HE COMES IN THE LORD'S NAME see Graham

HE DIED FOR ME see Landgrave, Phillip

HE DIED FOR US see Owens

HE DOTH CARE see Farley

HE FED THEM WITH MOST PRECIOUS WHEAT
  see Tye, Christopher

HE GIVES LIGHT see Wild, Eric

HE GIVETH MORE GRACE see Mitchell

HE HAS SURELY BORNE OUR SORROW see
  Lister, Mosie

HE HATH FILLED THE HUNGRY see Vivaldi,
  Antonio, Esurientes Implevit

HE HIDETH MY SOUL see Kirkpatrick,
  William J.

HE HOLDS THE WORLDS TOGETHER see
  Skillings, Otis

HE IS ALIVE see Thomas

HE IS BORN see Eidsvoog

HE IS BORN see Higdon, George

HE IS BORN see Il Est Ne

HE IS COMING *Easter,anthem
  (Cram, James D.) SATB FINE ARTS
  CM 1060 $.35   (H351)

HE IS COMING see Delmonte, Pauline

HE IS DESPISED AND REJECTED see
  Martini, Giambattista

HE IS LORD *medley
  (Johnson, P.) SATB oct BENSON S4124
  $.40   (H352)

HE IS MY FATHER see Graham

HE IS MY ROCK see McCall, Harlo [E.]

HE IS RISEN see Clark, Henry A.

HE IS RISEN see Jennings, Kenneth L.

HE IS RISEN! see Peterson, John W.

HE IS RISEN! HE IS RISEN! see Burroughs

HE IS SLEEPING IN A MANGER
  see Polish Christmas Carols

HE IS SO GREAT see Lawson

HE IS THE DELIGHT OF OUR DAYS see
  McNair, Jacqueline Hanna

HE IS THE KING OF GLORY see Newbury,
  Kent A.

HE IS THE TENDER SHEPHERD see
  Mendelssohn-Bartholdy, Felix

HE IS THERE see Burnham

HE IS THERE see Cruickshank, R.

HE JUST LOVED ME MORE AND MORE see
  Croft, Colbert

HE JUSTLY CLAIMS A SONG FROM ME *CCU,
  anthem/chorale/folk/hymn/round/spir
  (Walker, David S.) treb cor CONCORDIA
  97-5208 $2.75   (H353)

HE KNOWS JUST WHAT I NEED see Lister,
  Mosie

HE KNOWS WHAT HE'S DOIN' ALL THE TIME
  see Stanphill, Ira F.

HE LEADETH ME see Clements

HE LEADETH ME see Gilmore, P.

HE LEADETH ME - I HAVE DECIDED
*gospel/medley
(Stanislaw) SATB oct LILLENAS AN-1655
$.30 (H354)

HE LEADS US ON *anthem
(Cram, James D.) SATB FINE ARTS
EW 1016 $.30 (H355)

HE LIVED THE GOOD LIFE see Wilson,
Richard

HE LIVES! *gospel
(Kaiser, Kurt; Brown, Charles F.) cor
RODEHEAVER 37641 $1.00
contains: Abide With Me; Blessed
Redeemer; Gentle Like You; He
Lives; Jesus, I Am Resting; What
A Friend We Have In Jesus
see also: Ackley, A.H., He Lives;
Brown, Charles F., Gentle Like
You; Converse, Charles Crozat,
What A Friend We Have In Jesus;
Mountain, James, Jesus, I Am
Resting (H356)

HE LIVES
see He Lives!

HE LIVES see Ackley, A.H.

HE LIVES see Krogstad, Bob

HE LOVES YOU, MY FRIEND! see Wyrtzen,
Don

HE LOVINGLY GUARDS EVERY FOOTSTEP see
Peterson, John W.

HE REMEMBERS ME see Roberts

HE RODE ON A DONKEY see Wilson, F.

HE SHALL BE CALLED A NAZARENE see
Bender, Jan

HE SHALL BE CALLED WONDERFUL see
Wilson, John F.

HE SHALL BE GREAT see Claflin, Avery

HE SHALL COME DOWN see Ortlund, Anne

HE SHALL RULE FROM SEA TO SEA see
Burroughs, Bob

HE TAUGHT ME THERE see Olson, D.

HE THAT DESCENDED MAN TO BE see Amner,
John

HE THAT IS DOWN NEEDS FEAR NO FALL see
Harris

HE THAT OVERCOMES see Floria, Cam

HE THAT SHALL ENDURE TO THE END see
Mendelssohn-Bartholdy, Felix

HE THAT TILLETH see Diament, Abraham

HE THE PEARLY GATES WILL OPEN see
Ahlwen

HE TOUCHED ME see Gaither, William J.
(Bill)

HE TURNED THE WATER INTO WINE see
Stearman

HE WALKED THAT LONELY ROAD see Turner

HE WAS NAILED TO THE CROSS see Graves,
F.

HE WAS WOUNDED FOR OUR TRANGRESSIONS
see Dunlop, Merrill

HE WAS WOUNDED FOR OUR TRANSGRESSIONS
see Byrd, William

HE WAS WOUNDED FOR OUR TRANSGRESSIONS
see Peterson, John W.

HE WATCHING OVER ISRAEL see
Mendelssohn-Bartholdy, Felix

HE WHO IS NOT WITH ME IS AGAINST ME see
Bender, Jan

HE WHOM JOYOUS SHEPHERDS PRAISED *Adv/
Xmas
(Rickard, Jeffrey) SATB ART MAST 163
$.40 (H357)

HE WHOM JOYOUS SHEPHERDS PRAISED see
Anderson, Paul L.

HE WORE A CROWN OF THORNS see Hyllberg,
Ruth

HEAL ME, O LORD see Childs, Barney

HEAL ME, O LORD see Roff, Joseph

HEALER OF BROKEN HEARTS see Stiffler,
Georgia

HEALEY, DEREK
O God Of Truth *anthem/hymn
SSA,org THOMP.G $.40 (H358)

There Is One Body
mix cor,org/synthesizer/electronic
tape THOMP.G $.40 (H359)

HEALING LOVE OF JESUS, THE see
Peterson, John W.

HEAR, HEAR, O YE NATIONS see Hosmer

HEAR ME, O LORD see Schulz, H., Erhore
Mich

HEAR ME, O LORD see Schutz, Heinrich

HEAR MY PRAYER see Greene, Maurice

HEAR MY PRAYER see Mendelssohn-
Bartholdy, Felix

HEAR MY PRAYER see Pergolesi, Giovanni
Battista

HEAR MY PRAYER see Walters, John

HEAR MY PRAYER see Willis

HEAR MY PRAYER, O LORD see Archangelsky

HEAR MY PRAYER, O LORD see
Archangelsky, Alexander

HEAR MY PRAYER, O LORD see Byrd,
William

HEAR MY PRAYER, O LORD see Kroeger

HEAR MY PRAYER, O LORD see Van Hulse,
Camil

HEAR MY PRAYER, O MY GOD see Jeppesen,
Knud

HEAR, O THOU SHEPHERD OF ISRAEL see
Ierley, Merritt

HEAR OUR PRAYER, O GOD see Bernhard

HEAR OUR PRAYER, OH LORD see Bernhard,
Lieber Herre Gott

HEAR THE JOYFUL NEWS see Bach, Johann
Sebastian

HEAR THE PRAYER, O OUR GOD see Batten,
Adrian

HEAR THIS see Ker

HEAR US! see Ballou, Esther W.

HEAR US, HOLY JESUS see France, William
E.

HEAR US, HOLY JESUS see Goetze, Arthur
A.

HEAR US, O LORD see Obrecht, Jacob,
Parce, Domine

HEAR YE, ALL YE PEOPLES see Weigl,
Vally

HEAR YE! BE JOYFUL! see McNair,
Jacqueline Hanna

HEAR YE HIM see Hughes, Robert J.

HEAR YE! JESUS IS THE LAMB OF GOD see
Homilius, Gottfried August, Siehe,
Das Ist Gottes Lamm

HEARERS AND DOERS OF THE WORD see Ford,
Virgil T.

HEART OF AMERICA, THE see Skillings,
Otis

HEART OF LOVE, A see Wyrtzen, Don

HEART THAT'S BROKEN AND CONTRITE, AN
see Dowland, John

HEART'S ADORATION see Marcello

HEAVEN see Hovhaness, Alan

HEAVEN CAME DOWN AND GLORY FILLED MY
SOUL see Peterson, John W.

HEAVEN IN MY HEART see Parsons

HEAVEN MEDLEY
(Mercer, W. Elmo) SATB oct BENSON
S4130 $.35 (H360)

HEAVENLY SUNLIGHT *CC10L,gospel
SATB TRIUNE TUO 103 $2.50; TTBB
TRIUNE TUO 102 $2.50
see also: Heavenly Sunlight;

Redeemed (H361)

HEAVENLY SUNLIGHT
(Red, Buryl) SATB TRIUNE TUM 101 $.35
see also Heavenly Sunlight (H362)

HEAVENS ARE TELLING, THE see Haydn,
(Franz) Joseph

HEAVENS ARE TELLING, THE see Schutz,
Heinrich

HEAVENS DECLARE, THE see Billings,
William

HEAVENS DECLARE THE GLORY OF GOD, THE
see Beethoven, Ludwig van

HEAVENS DECLARE YOUR GLORY, THE see
Powell, Robert

HEBBLE
And Rejoice *see Polistina

Jesus, Lord, We Look To Thee
SATB SHAWNEE A5694 $.35 (H363)

HEBBLE, ROBERT
Celebration Of Unity
SATB,org (med) GIA G1748 $1.25
(H364)

HEBE DEINE AUGEN AUF see Mendelssohn-
Bartholdy, Felix

HEBER
Holy, Holy, Holy
(Dykes; Smith, Herb) SATB oct
GOSPEL 05 TM 0149 $.25 (H365)

HECTOR BERLIOZ WORKS see Berlioz,
Hector

HEER, EMIL (1926-)
Brich An, Du Schones Morgenlicht
unis&SATB (contains also: Die
Finsternis Vergeht) SCHWEIZER.
SK 68.03 s.p. see also
MUSIKBEILAGE ZUM "EVANGELISCHEN
KIRCHENCHOR 1968" (H366)

Gelobet Seist Du, Jesu Christ
unis/SAT/SAB/SA/SATB,org SCHWEIZER.
SK 62.01-2 s.p. see also
MUSIKBEILAGE ZUM "EVANGELISCHEN
KIRCHENCHOR 1962" (H367)

Jauchzet Dem Herren, Alle Lande
(Psalm 100)
SATB SCHWEIZER. SK 152 s.p. (H368)

Kommet Ihr Hirten *Xmas,cant
4 eq voices/4pt mix cor,A rec/fl,
2vln,cont sc,cor pts PELIKAN
PE762 s.p., ipa (H369)

Lobe Den Herren, Den Machtigen Konig
Der Ehren
unis/SAT/SAB/2pt,org SCHWEIZER.
SK 70.06-7 s.p. see also
MUSIKBEILAGE ZUM "EVANGELISCHEN
KIRCHENCHOR 1970" (H370)

Mein Ganzes Herz Erhebet Dich (Psalm
138)
SAT/SAB SCHWEIZER. SK 55.01 s.p.
see also MUSIKBEILAGE ZUM
"EVANGELISCHEN KIRCHENCHOR 1955"
(H371)

Psalm 98 *see Singet Dem Herrn Ein
Neues Lied

Psalm 100 *see Jauchzet Dem Herren,
Alle Lande

Psalm 138 *see Mein Ganzes Herz
Erhebet Dich

Singet Dem Herrn Ein Neues Lied
(Psalm 98)
SATB SCHWEIZER. SK 166 s.p. (H372)

Singt Dem Herrn Ein Neues Lied
SA,org SCHWEIZER. SK 168 s.p.
contains also: Kukuck, Felicitas,
Ich Singe Dir Mit Herz Und Mund
(SSA); Stern, Hermann, Alles, Was
Odem Hat, Lobe Den Herrn (3pt)
(H373)

Wachet Auf, Ruft Uns Die Stimme
SATB,org SCHWEIZER. SK 59.05-6 s.p.
see also MUSIKBEILAGE ZUM
"EVANGELISCHEN KIRCHENCHOR 1959"
(H374)

Wie Schon Leuchtet Der Morgenstern
SATB,org,ob,vln,vcl SCHWEIZER.
SK 157 sc s.p., cor pts s.p., ipa
(H375)

HEER IN DE HEMEL! see Hemy, [Henri
Frederick]

HEER, JOH DE
O Heiland, Reiss Die Himmel Auf
SATB,S solo,org,strings SCHWEIZER.
SK 143 sc s.p., cor pts s.p., ipa
(H376)

HEER, JOH DE (cont'd.)

Twee Kerstliederen *CC3U,Xmas
mix cor/unis,pno/harmonium HEER 401
s.p.   (H377)

HEER, WEES MIJN GIDS
mix cor sc HEER 2569 s.p.   (H378)

HEFT AAN, HEFT AAN EEN LUIDE ZANG
*Xmas
mix cor sc HEER 1517 s.p.   (H379)

HEFTRICH, WILHELM
Adorate Deum *Mass
[Lat] SABar,org sc,cor pts BOHM
s.p.   (H380)

Kleine Messe *Op.20, Mass
[Lat] SAT/SAB,acap (without Credo)
sc,cor pts BOHM s.p.   (H381)

Muttergottes-Messe *Op.16, Mass
[Lat] 4pt mix cor,acap sc,cor pts
BOHM s.p.   (H382)

Pange Lingua
see Heftrich, Wilhelm, Veni Creator

Salus Autem Justorum *Fest
[Lat] 4pt mix cor,acap sc,cor pts
BOHM s.p.   (H383)

Salve Sancta Parens *Mass
[Lat] 4pt mix cor,acap sc,cor pts
BOHM s.p.   (H384)

Terribilis Est Locus Iste *Ded/Fest
[Lat] 4pt mix cor,acap sc,cor pts
BOHM s.p.   (H385)

Veni Creator
[Lat] SABar,org sc,cor pts BOHM
s.p. contains also: Pange Lingua
(H386)

HEGARTY, DAVID H.
Jesus, Jesus, Rest Your Head *Xmas,
anthem
SATB oct LORENZ B230 $.30   (H387)

Redeemer Shall Come, The *Adv,anthem
SA/SATB (easy) oct LORENZ A558 $.30
(H388)

HEGENBART, ALEX F.
Be Not Deceived
mix cor BRODT 560 $.26   (H389)

Behold A Stranger
mix cor BRODT 624 $.25   (H390)

Behold What Love
mix cor BRODT 621 $.25   (H391)

Do God's Will
mix cor BRODT 625 $.25   (H392)

Follow Me
mix cor BRODT 561 $.26   (H393)

Glory And Honor
mix cor BRODT 562 $.26   (H394)

Going To Bethlehem
mix cor BRODT 581 $.22   (H395)

I Am The Door *anthem
SAB oct BROADMAN 4540-77 $.30
(H396)

Psalm Of Life *anthem
SATB (easy) oct BROADMAN 4545-63
$.30   (H397)

Simeon's Prayer
mix cor BRODT 534 $.26   (H398)

HEILAKKA
Fly, Dove
SATB GENERAL WDS GC 61 $.40 (H399)

HEILIG see Mendelssohn-Bartholdy, Felix

HEILIG, HEILIG IST GOTT see Bach,
Wilhelm Friedemann

HEILIG, HELIG see Schubert, Franz
(Peter)

HEILIG IS GOTT see Bach, Karl Philipp
Emanuel

HEILIGE NACHT see Schultz

HEILIGMESSE see Haydn, (Franz) Joseph

HEILIGSTE NACHT see Ludwig, Eduard

HEILLER, ANTON (1923-   )
Nicht Knechte, Sondern Freunde Nenn'
Ich Euch
SATB DOBLINGER G 734 s.p.   (H400)

Passionsmusik
jr cor,org DOBLINGER 64 604 cor pts
s.p., voc sc s.p.   (H401)

HEILNER, IRWIN
Romans 14.19
2pt,acap AM.COMP.AL. $.38   (H402)

HEINS
Where Our Lord May Go *Adv,anthem
(Lorenz, Ellen Jane) SATB oct
SINGSPIR ZJP-7285 $.30   (H403)

HEISS, HERMANN (1897-1966)
Missa *Mass
mix cor,AT soli,electronic tape
MODERN s.p., rental   (H404)

HELAS, MON DIEU see Le Jeune, Claude

HELD, WILBUR
His Are The Thousand Sparkling Rills
*anthem
SATB,org AUGSBURG 11-1720 $.35
(H405)

HELDER, BARTHOLOMAEUS (1585-1635)
Herr Jesu Mein, Sollst Doch Mein
Trost
SATB (contains also: Singet Ein
Neues Lied) SCHWEIZER. SK 55.05-6
s.p. see also MUSIKBEILAGE ZUM
"EVANGELISCHEN KIRCHENCHOR 1955"
(H406)

O Treuer Gott Im Himmelsthron
SATB (contains also: Was Main Gott
Will, Das Gscheh Allzeit)
SCHWEIZER. SK 56.04 s.p. see also
MUSIKBEILAGE ZUM "EVANGELISCHEN
KIRCHENCHOR 1956"   (H407)

HELDMAN, KEITH
See The Shepherds Dancing *Xmas
SATB,fl/ob (med) GENTRY G-299 $.40
(H408)

HELFMAN, MAX (1901-1963)
Ahavat Olam
(Gottlieb, Jack) [Heb] cor,cantor
TRANSCON. TCL 678 $1.00   (H409)

Kedusha
(Gottlieb, Jack) [Heb] cor,cantor
TRANSCON. TCL 679 $.75   (H410)

HELFT, GOTTES GUTE PREISEN see Pidoux,
Pierre

HE'LL BE THERE see Harmon, B.

HE'LL BREAK THROUGH THE BLUE see
Wyrtzen, Don

HELL MORGONSTJARNA, MILD OCH REN see
Schelle, Johann Hermann

HELLO, WORLD! see Red, Buryl

HELMSCHROTT, ROBERT M.
Missa Brevis In D-Moll *Mass
[Lat] 4pt mix cor,acap (D min) sc,
cor pts BOHM s.p.   (H411)

Unisono-Messe *Mass
[Ger] unis&cong,solo,opt org BOHM
sc s.p., cor pts s.p.   (H412)

HELP, LORD; FOR THE GODLY MAN CEASETH
see Hovhaness, Alan

HELP ME BE ME see Fearheiley

HELP SOMEBODY TODAY
(Mercer, W. Elmo) SATB,acap oct
BENSON S4131 $.25   (H413)

HEM OF HIS ROBE, THE see Dailey,
William

HEMBERG, ESKIL
En Natt Som Lyste *cant
mix cor,S solo,inst ERIKS 86 s.p.
(H414)

Jag Ar Rosten Av En Som Ropar
*Bibl
4pt mix cor ERIKS 23 s.p.   (H415)

Jerusalem, Hav Upp Din Rost
3pt mix cor ERIKS 24 s.p.   (H416)

Maria Pa Barnet Aktar
SABar ERIKS 68 s.p.   (H417)

Mig Ar Given All Makt *Bibl
4pt mix cor ERIKS 21 s.p.   (H418)

Och Jag Sag Den Heliga Staden
3pt mix cor ERIKS 22 s.p.   (H419)

Paradis *cant
mix cor,narrator,T solo,org,
4strings ERIKS 45 s.p.   (H420)

Se, Vi Ga Upp Till Jerusalem
4pt mix cor ERIKS 25 s.p.   (H421)

HEMMERLE, J.
Allons Ensemble A Bethleem *Xmas
4pt mix cor,acap sc HENN 794 s.p.
(H422)

Recueil De Motets *CCU,mot
4pt,acap sc HENN 398 s.p.   (H423)

HEMY, [HENRI FREDERICK] (1818-1888)
Faith Of Our Fathers *anthem
(DeCou, Harold) SSATB oct SINGSPIR
ZJP-7356 $.35   (H424)
(Johnson, Norman) SA&opt TB (easy)
oct SINGSPIR ZJP-6005 $.30   (H425)
(Mann, Johnny) SATB LEXICON   (H426)

Heer In De Hemel!
mix cor sc HEER 1524 s.p.   (H427)

HENFORTH, T.W.
Sheffield Cathedral Descants *CCU
mix cor BANKS MUS YS 953 $.45
(H428)

Sheffield Cathedral Descants (Second
Set) *CCU
mix cor BANKS MUS YS 1099 $.45
(H429)

HENKING, BERNHARD (1897-   )
Alles Ist Euer
SAT/SAB SCHWEIZER. SK 69.07 s.p.
see also MUSIKBEILAGE ZUM
"EVANGELISCHEN KIRCHENCHOR 1969"
(H430)

Sorget Nicht Fur Euer Leben
SATB SCHWEIZER. SK 163 s.p.   (H431)

HENNAGIN, MICHAEL
Four Responses *CC4U
SATB WALTON 2809 $.35   (H432)

HENNIG, WALTER (1903-1967)
Der Menschen Hoffart Muss Vergehen
4-6pt mix cor MERSEBURG EM496
(H433)

Gelobet Seist Du, Jesu Christ
SATB (contains also: Singt, Singt
Dem Herren Neue Lieder)
SCHWEIZER. SK 72.04-5 s.p. see
also MUSIKBEILAGE ZUM
"EVANGELISCHEN KIRCHENCHOR 1972"
(H434)

HERALDS OF CHRIST see Johnson, Norman

HERBECK
Let All Mortal Flesh Keep Silence
*anthem
SATB oct BROADMAN 4562-47 $.40
(H435)

HERBEI, IHR BRUDER see Salieri, Antonio

HERBEI, O IHR GLAUBIGEN *Xmas,carol/
folk
(Biebl, F.) [Ger] 4pt men cor
MERSEBURG EM9052   (H436)

HERBEK, RAYMOND H.
All Nature's Works His Praise Declare
unis,org FISCHER,J FEC 10107 $.30
(H437)

HERBST, JOHANNES (1735-1812)
God Was In Jesus
(Kroeger) SATB,pno/org oct BOOSEY
5851 $.45   (H438)

Listen All Who Enter These Portals
(Kroeger) [Ger/Eng] SATB oct
MORAVIAN 5889 $.55   (H439)

Lord, Our Mighty Sov'reign, The
(Kroeger) [Ger/Eng] SATB oct
MORAVIAN 5863 $.55   (H440)

Sing Praises To The Lord
(Kroeger) [Ger/Eng] SATB,pno/org
oct MORAVIAN 5850 $.50   (H441)

Surely He Has Borne Our Sorrows
(Kroeger) [Ger/Eng] SATB oct
MORAVIAN 5890 $.50   (H442)

Thy Name Is Known Unto Him
(Kroeger) [Ger/Eng] SATB oct
MORAVIAN 5862 $.50   (H443)

To Us A Child Is Born
(Pfohl) mix cor BRODT 109 $.32
(H444)

HERBST, JOHANNES ANDREAS (1588-1666)
Singet Frisch Und Wohlgemut
SSATB SCHWEIZER. SK 138 s.p. (H445)

HERE AM I see Parks, Joe E.

HERE COMES JESUS *anthem/folk
(Mayfield, L.) SSATB oct SINGSPIR
ZJP-5068 $.35   (H446)

HERE COMES THE SON see Johnson, Paul

HERE COMES THE SON see Johnson, Paul

HERE IS A SONG see Billings, William

HERE IS MY LIFE see Bartlett

HERE, O LORD, THY SERVANTS GATHER see
Peek, Richard

HERE WE COME A-WASSAILING
see Twelve Christmas Carols: Set 1

HEREFORD CAROL *carol
(Thorpe, Raymond) SATB,acap EMI s.p.
(H447)

HERE'S ONE *CC10L,anthem
   TTBB FINE ARTS CLML-3-72 $1.95
   contains compositions and
   arrangements by: Butler; Gagliardi;
   Littleton, Bill J.; Cram; Bartlett;
   Burroughs; Spence   (H448)

HERE'S ONE *anthem/spir
   (Bartlett) SATB,med solo FINE ARTS
   CM 1066 $.30   (H449)
   (Burroughs, Bob) SATB WORD CS-2685
   $.35   (H450)

HERITAGE MEDLEY *anthem
   (Carmichael, Ralph) SATB LEXICON
   CS-2701 $.60 see from Harvest
   Celebration   (H451)

HERITAGE OF FOLK ANTHEMS, A *CCUL
   (Rasley, John M.) SATB SINGSPIR 5833
   $1.00 based on Early American hymns
                                (H452)

HERITAGE OF SPIRITUALS, A *CCU,spir,US
   (Fox, F.; Miller, J.; Work, J.) SATB
   GALAXY 1.2593.1 $2.50   (H453)

HERMANN, NIKOLAUS (ca. 1480-1561)
   Lobt Gott, Ihr Christen
   (Schaefers, A.) men cor,acap TONOS
   5625 s.p.   (H454)

   Wir Singen Dir, Immanuel *Xmas
   (Zipp, Friedrich) 4pt jr cor/4pt
   wom cor (easy) sc SCHOTTS
   CHBL 567A-B s.p. contains also:
   Praetorius, Michael, Es Ist Ein
   Ros Entsprungen   (H455)

HEROLD, J.
   Danket Dem Herrn! *Fest,cant
   mix cor&cong,opt solo,opt org/
   harmonium sc,cor pts BOHM s.p. (H456)

HERR, BLEIBE BEI UNS! see Fortner,
   Wolfgang

HERR CHRIST, DER EINIG GOTTS SOHN see
   Bach, Johann Sebastian

HERR CHRISTE KOMM IN UNSRE NOT see
   Weber, Ludwig

HERR CHRISTE, TREUER HEILAND WERT see
   Pepping, Ernst

HERR, DEINE GUTE see Schweizer, Rolf

HERR, DEINEN TOD VERKUNDEN WIR see
   Ruppel, Paul Ernst

HERR, DU WOLLST GNAD UND SEGEN see
   Schop

HERR, ERBARME DICH see Seckinger,
   Konrad

HERR, ERHORE MEINE KLAGEN see Goudimel,
   Claude

HERR, ES IST ZEIT see Wittmer, Eberhard
   Ludwig

HERR, FUR DEIN WORT SEI HOCH GEPREIST
   see Hessenberg, Kurt

HERR, GIB FRIEDEN see Lederer, F.

HERR GOTT, DICH LOBEN WIR see Peter,
   Johann Friedrich

HERR GOTT, DICH LOBEN WIR see Poos,
   Heinrich

HERR, GOTT, DU BIST UNSRE ZUFLUCHT FUR
   UND FUR see Lohr, Ina

HERR GOTT, HIMMLISCHER VATER see
   Gumpelzhaimer, Adam

HERR GOTT VATER, WIR PREISEN DICH see
   Vulpius, Melchior

HERR, GROSSER GOTT, DICH LOBEN WIR see
   Haydn, (Johann) Michael

HERR, HORE DOCH AUF MEINE REDE see
   Hindermann, Walter Felix

HERR JESU CHRIST, DICH ZU UNS WEND see
   Rohwer, Jens

HERR JESU CHRIST, DU HOCHSTES GUT see
   Werner

HERR JESU CHRIST, WAHR MENSCH UND GOTT
   see Zeuner, Martin

HERR JESU CHRISTE, MEIN GETREUER HIRTE
   see Marx, Karl

HERR JESU, DER DU BIST FUR MICH see
   Franck, Melchior

HERR JESU MEIN, SOLLST DOCH MEIN TROST
   see Helder, Bartholomaeus

HERR JESUS CHRIST, UNSER GOTT see
   Lassus, Roland de (Orlandus)

HERR, LASS SIE RUHN IM FRIEDEN see
   Welcker, Max

HERR, LASSE MICH DABEI SEIN see O When
   The Saints

HERR, MEIN GOTT, NIMM MEIN SEEL GNADIG
   ZU DIR see Staden, Johann

HERR, MEIN GOTT, WIE GROSS SIND DEINE
   WUNDER see Schibler, Armin

HERR, NEIGE DEINE OHREN see
   Kretzschmar, Gunther

HERR, NUN HEB DEN WAGEN SELB see
   Muller-Zurich, Paul

HERR, NUN LASSEST DU DEINEN DIENER see
   Leisring, Volkmar

HERR, SCHICKE, WAS DU WILLT see
   Hunecke, Wilhelm

HERR, SPRICH DEIN EWIGS WORT
   see Tod Und Ewigkeit

HERR UNSER GOTT, DU BIST ERHABEN UBER
   HIMMEL UND ERDE see Escher, P.

HERR, UNSER HERRSCHER see Neuber

HERR, UNSER HERRSCHER see Staden,
   Johann

HERR, WENN ICH NUR DICH HABE see
   Schutz, Heinrich

HERR, WER FESTEN HERZENS IST see
   Baudach, Ulrich

HERR, WIE LANG WILT DU MEIN SO GAR
   VERGESSEN? see Schutz, Heinrich

HERR, WIE LANG WILT VERGESSEN MEIN see
   Hassler, Hans Leo

HERR, WIE SIND DEINE WERKE SO GROSS UND
   VIEL see Schweizer, Rolf

HERR, WIR RUFEN DICH see Rohwer, Jens

HERRE, JAG HAR HORT DIN STAMMA see
   Johansen, Sven-Erik

HERRE, VEM FAR BO I DIN HYDDA? see
   Nystroem, Gosta

HERRICK
   Greeting Song, The *anthem
   SATB oct BROADMAN 4551-82 $.30
                                (H457)

HERRING, ANNE
   Easter Song *Easter,anthem
   SAT/SATB WORD CS-2689 $.35   (H458)

HERRING, W.B.
   O Bethlehem, How Still The Night
   mix cor BRODT 533 $.28   (H459)

HERRLIJK KLONK HET LIED DER ENG'LEN
   mix cor sc HEER 2070 s.p.   (H460)

HERRMANN, HUGO (1896-1967)
   Ave Maris Stella
   see Vier Lateinische Hymnen

   Grussworte Der Apokalypse Des
   Heiligen Johannes "Das Ist Die
   Offenbarung Von Gott" *Bibl
   [Ger] SSATB,Bar solo (med diff) sc
   SCHOTTS C 38 729 s.p., voc pt
   SCHOTTS C 38 730A-E s.p.   (H461)

   Loblied "Nun Wollen Wir Den Schopfer
   Droben"
   1-4pt mix cor,pno/2trp,2horn,trom,
   tuba (easy) voc sc SCHOTTS
   C 37 764 s.p., cor pts SCHOTTS
   C 37 765 s.p., ipa   (H462)

   Missa Brevis *Op.68, Mass
   [Lat] SABar,acap sc,cor pts BOHM
   s.p.   (H463)

   O Salutaris Hostia
   see Vier Lateinische Hymnen

   Pange Lingua
   see Vier Lateinische Hymnen

   Vexilla Regis
   see Vier Lateinische Hymnen

   Vier Lateinische Hymnen *hymn,Lat
   [Lat] 4pt mix cor,acap sc,cor pts
   BOHM s.p.
   contains: Ave Maris Stella,
   Op.33b,No.3; O Salutaris
   Hostia, Op.33b,No.1; Pange
   Lingua, Op.33b,No.2; Vexilla
   Regis, Op.33b,No.4   (H464)

HERRSCHER UBER TOD UND LEBEN see Bach,
   Johann Sebastian

HERTER, J.
   Two Motets From The Kancjonaxy
   Staniateckie *CC2U,Xmas,anthem/
   mot
   [Eng/Lat] SATB,acap (easy) GIA
   G1829 $.40   (H465)

HERZ-JESU-FESTMESSE see Gruber, Joseph

HERZ-JESU-MESSE see Hug, Emil

HERZ-JESU-MESSE see Lohle, A.

HERZ UND HERZ VEREINT ZUSAMMEN see
   Fiebig

HERZLIEBSTER JESU see Pepping, Ernst

HERZOGENBERG, HEINRICH VON (1843-1900)
   Danket Dem Herren, Schopfer Aller
   Dinge
   SATB SCHWEIZER, SK 70.4-5 s.p. see
   also MUSIKBEILAGE ZUM
   "EVANGELISCHEN KIRCHENCHOR 1970"
                                (H466)

   Kommt Her Zu Mir, Spricht Gottes Sohn
   SATB,acap (easy) BAREN. BA6318
                                (H467)

   Vier Choralmotetten *Op.102, CC4U,
   mot
   SATB,acap (med) BAREN. 19309 s.p.
                                (H468)

HE'S AND SHE'S *CCUL
   (Johnson, Derric) SSAA&TTBB BENSON
   B0243 $1.95 stereo recording,
   tapes, and-or accompaniment tape
   also available; for book-record
   sets available, contact publisher
                                (H469)

HE'S BACK see Skillings, Otis

HE'S COMING BACK see Cole

HE'S FILLING UP HEAVEN WITH SINNERS see
   Peterson, John W.

HE'S GOD'S GREAT LOVE see LaRowe

HE'S GOT THE WHOLE WORLD
   see Vier Negro-Spirituals
   (Zimmergren) men cor ERIKS 314 s.p.
                                (H470)

HE'S GOT THE WHOLE WORLD IN HIS HANDS
   *Gen,anthem/spir
   (Ferrin, Paul) SATB oct GOSPEL
   05 TM 0201 $.20   (H471)
   (Martin, Gilbert M.) SAB (med diff)
   oct LORENZ 7424 $.35   (H472)
   (Mickelson, P.) SATB oct SINGSPIR
   ZJP-8198 $.30   (H473)
   (Reynolds, William Jensen) mix cor/
   men cor CENTURY PR $.20   (H474)
   (Schubert) SATB oct LILLENAS AN-3862
   $.30   (H475)

HE'S GOT THE WHOLE WORLD IN HIS HANDS
   see Higgins, Charles

HE'S GOT THE WHOLE WORLD IN HIS HANDS
   see Martin, Gilbert M.

HE'S ON HIS WAY *CCU
   (Huff, Ronn) cor BENSON B0231 $1.95
   stereo recording, tapes, and-or
   accompaniment tape also available;
   for book-record sets available,
   contact publisher   (H476)

HE'S ON HIS WAY see Dietschmann

HE'S ON HIS WAY! see McCall, Harlo [E.]

HE'S THE LILY OF THE VALLEY *spir
   (Hansen) SSAB oct SCHMITT 928 $.35
                                (H477)

HESS, J.
   Psalm 108 *folk
   unis oct SINGSPIR ZJP-5045 $.30
                                (H478)

HESS, REIMUND (1935-   )
   Der Dritte Psalm (Psalm 30)
   4pt mix cor,org sc BREITKOPF-W
   PB 4986 s.p., cor pts BREITKOPF-W
   CHB 5092 s.p.   (H479)

   Psalm 30 *see Der Dritte Psalm

HESSENBERG, KURT (1908-   )
   Ach Bleib Bei Uns, Herr Jesu Christ
   see Vier Geistliche Lieder Durch
   Die Tageszeiten

   Choralfantasie "Aus Tiefer Not"
   see Psalmen-Triptychon

   Christe, Du Lamm Gottes *Op.37,No.2,
   mot
   SSATB (med easy) sc SCHOTTS
   C 37 421 s.p. see from Zwei
   Motetten   (H480)

HESSENBERG, KURT (cont'd.)

Das Sagt, Der Amen Heisst *Op.46,
  mot
  SSAT&ATBB (med) sc,cor pts SCHOTTS
  ED. 4242 s.p.   (H481)

Die Nacht Ist Kommen
  see Vier Geistliche Lieder Durch
  Die Tageszeiten

Die Sonn Hoch An Den Himmel Steht
  see Vier Geistliche Lieder Durch
  Die Tageszeiten

Herr, Fur Dein Wort Sei Hoch Gepreist
  SATB (contains also: Das Neugeborne
  Kindelin) SCHWEIZER. SK 57.05
  s.p. see also MUSIKBEILAGE ZUM
  "EVANGELISCHEN KIRCHENCHOR 1957"
                                 (H482)
Joseph, Lieber Joseph Mein *Xmas
  2pt jr cor&3pt men cor sc SCHOTTS
  C 40 652 s.p. see from Zwei
  Weihnachtslieder   (H483)

Maria Durch Ein Dornwald Ging *Xmas
  2pt jr cor&3pt men cor sc SCHOTTS
  C 40 653 s.p. see from Zwei
  Weihnachtslieder   (H484)

Mit Segen Mog Ich Heut Aufstehn
  see Vier Geistliche Lieder Durch
  Die Tageszeiten

Nun Jauchzt Dem Herren, Alle Welt
  SATB (contains also: Da Jesus An
  Dem Kreuze Stund) SCHWEIZER.
  SK 58.05 s.p. see also
  MUSIKBEILAGE ZUM "EVANGELISCHEN
  KIRCHENCHOR 1958"   (H485)

O Herr, Mache Mich Zum Werkzeug
  *Op.37,No.1, mot
  SSATBB,acap (med easy) sc SCHOTTS
  C 37 176 s.p. see from Zwei
  Motetten   (H486)

Psalm 8 "Herr, Unser Herrscher"
  see Psalmen-Triptychon

Psalm 26 *see Wenn Der Herr Die
  Gefangenen Zions Erlosen Wird

Psalm "Vater Unser"
  see Psalmen-Triptychon

Psalmen-Triptychon *Op.36, Bibl
  SATB&SATB,SBar soli,2fl,2ob,3clar,
  3bsn,4horn,2trp,3trom,strings,
  perc,timp (med diff) sc SCHOTTS
  rental, ipr
    contains: Choralfantasie "Aus
    Tiefer Not"; Psalm 8 "Herr,
    Unser Herrscher"; Psalm "Vater
    Unser"   (H487)

Vier Geistliche Lieder Durch Die
  Tageszeiten *Op.41
  mix cor (med) sc SCHOTTS C 37 422
  s.p.
    contains: Ach Bleib Bei Uns, Herr
    Jesu Christ; Die Nacht Ist
    Kommen; Die Sonn Hoch An Den
    Himmel Steht; Mit Segen Mog Ich
    Heut Aufstehn   (H488)

Weihnachtsgeschichte *Op.54, Xmas
  4pt mix cor,STB soli,strings,opt A
  rec&cembalo (med) sc,cor pts
  SCHOTTS ED. 77 s.p., ipa   (H489)

Weihnachtskantate *Op.27, Xmas,cant
  6pt mix cor,SA soli,org,fl,ob,clar,
  bsn,2horn,trp,strings,timp,
  English horn (med) voc sc,cor pts
  SCHOTTS ED. 3897 s.p., ipa (H490)

Wenn Der Herr Die Gefangenen Zions
  Erlosen Wird (Psalm 26) Op.87,
  mot
  SSATBB,acap (med diff) sc SCHOTTS
  C 43 141 s.p.   (H491)

Zwei Motetten *see Christe, Du Lamm
  Gottes, Op.37,No.2; O Herr, Mache
  Mich Zum Werkzeug, Op.37,No.1
                                 (H492)
Zwei Weihnachtslieder *see Joseph,
  Lieber Joseph Mein; Maria Durch
  Ein Dornwald Ging   (H493)

HET IS VOLBRACHT see Lienden, Van

HET RUW-HOUTEN KRUIS see Bennard,
  George

HET VLEESGEWORDEN WOORD see Wolff, H.
  de

HEUSSENSTAMM, GEORGE
  My Soul Is Exceeding Sorrowful
  SSATB ART MAST 173 $.40   (H494)

HEUT KAM EIN ENGEL *Xmas,carol/folk
  (Riethmuller, H.) [Ger] 4pt men cor
  MERSEBURG EM9055   (H495)

HEUT TRIUMPHIERT GOTTES SOHN see
  Benzler, Fritz Gustav

HEUTE IST CHRISTUS DER HERR GEBOREN see
  Schutz, Heinrich

HEWITT
  When We All Get To Heaven (composed
  with Wilson)
  (Mercer, W. Elmo) SATB oct BENSON
  S4366 $.35   (H496)

HEWITT-JONES, TONY (1926-   )
  Two Canticles *CC2U
  SATB,SBar soli,2fl,pic,ob,3-4clar,
  2horn,3-4trp,3-4trom,opt tuba,
  timp,perc,org,strings, euphonium
  voc sc NOVELLO rental   (H497)

HEY GOD, I REALLY LOVE YOU see Gibson

HIC HOMO SUM see Lidl, Vaclav

HICKS, MARJORIE KISBEY
  Word Was Made Flesh
  unis (med easy) WATERLOO $.30
                                 (H498)
HIDE NOT THOU THY FACE FROM US, O LORD
  see Farrant, Richard

HIDING IN THE ROCK OF AGES see Sankey,
  I.

HIDING IN THEE see Cushing

HIDING PLACE, THE see Leech, Bryan

HIER LIEGT VOR DEINER MAJESTAT see
  Haydn, (Johann) Michael

HIERDIES, W.
  Deutsche Messe Zum Ehren Des Heiligen
  Johannes Bosco *Mass
  [Ger] unis&cong,org (without Credo)
  BOHM sc s.p., cor pts s.p. (H499)

HIERUSALEM see Dyson, George

HIGDON, GEORGE
  He Is Born
  SATB WILLIS 9898 $.25   (H500)
  SSA WILLIS 9902 $.25   (H501)

HIGGINS, CHARLES
  He's Got The Whole World In His Hands
  *Gen/Thanks,spir
  8pt,T solo CHORISTERS A-98 $.35
                                 (H502)
HIGH ABOVE THE STARS OF HEAVEN see
  Johansen, Sven-Erik, Mit Liv Har Du
  Tant Hogt Ovan Himmelens Stjarnor

HIGHER GROUND see Gabriel

HIGHER HANDS see Peterson, John W.

HILARITER, ALLELUIA see Sinzheimer, Max

HILBER
  Ecce Sacerdos
  4pt,acap HENN 587 s.p. sc, voc pt
                                 (H503)
HILES, [HENRY] (1826-1904)
  Shadows Of The Evening *anthem
  (Mann, Johnny) SATB LEXICON (H504)

HILF, A UND O, ANFANG UND ENDE see Le
  Jeune, Claude

HILF, HERR GOTT, HILF IN DIESER NOT see
  Muller-Zurich, Paul

HILL
  Come Thou Almighty King *anthem
  unis&desc oct BROADMAN 4558-55 $.30
                                 (H505)
  Praise *anthem
  SATB oct BROADMAN 4554-88 $.30
                                 (H506)
  Sion's Daughter *carol
  SATB (easy) OXFORD 42.976 $.25
                                 (H507)
HILL, HARRY
  Bright Shone A Star
  see Hill, Harry, Out On A Hillside

  Calm Was The Night *Xmas
  SATB (easy) WATERLOO $.30   (H508)

  Christmas Lullaby *Xmas
  unis WATERLOO $.30   (H509)

  Dear Little Jesus *Xmas
  SATB (easy) WATERLOO $.30   (H510)

  Dear Little Stranger *Xmas
  unis (easy) WATERLOO $.30   (H511)

  Good King Wenceslas *Xmas
  SSA (med easy) WATERLOO $.30 (H512)

HILL, HARRY (cont'd.)

  In Bethlehem *Xmas
  SATB (med easy) WATERLOO $.30
                                 (H513)
  Late One Night *Xmas
  SATB (easy) WATERLOO $.35   (H514)

  Let Us Break Bread *Commun
  SATB (med easy) WATERLOO $.40
                                 (H515)
  Out On A Hillside *Xmas
  unis (easy) WATERLOO $.30 contains
  also: Bright Shone A Star   (H516)

  Psalm 23
  SSA (easy) WATERLOO $.35   (H517)

  Virgin's Cradle Song (composed with
  Lake, Ruth) *Xmas
  SSA (med easy) WATERLOO $.35 (H518)

  Whence O Shepherd Maiden *Xmas
  SSA (med easy) WATERLOO $.30 (H519)

HILL OF THE CROSS see Graham

HILLERT, RICHARD
  Passion According To St. John, The
  *Psntd
  SATB,solo/soli sc CONCORDIA 97-5209
  $2.00, cor pts CONCORDIA 97-5210
  $.60   (H520)

HILLS AWAKE TO SINGING, THE see
  Wilhelm, Patricia M.

HILSE, W.
  All They That Wait Upon Thee *Adv/
  Gen
  SATB,acap GRAY CMR 3322 $.35 (H521)

HILTON, JOHN (THE YOUNGER) (1599-1657)
  Lord, For Thy Tender Mercies' Sake
  *anthem
  SATB oct CHANTRY CLA 587 $.20
                                 (H522)
  Lord, For Thy Tender Mercy's Sake
  see Weelkes, Thomas, Let Thy
  Merciful Ears

HILTY
  Built On The Rock
  unis,solo (easy) OXFORD 94.504 $.30
                                 (H523)
  Lord's Prayer, The
  unis OXFORD 96.202 $.20   (H524)

  You Are The Temple
  SA (very easy) OXFORD 94.405 (H525)

HIMMEL, FRIEDRICH HEINRICH (1765-1814)
  Incline Thine Ear To Me
  mix cor BANKS MUS YS 112 $.20
                                 (H526)
  (Lutkin) SAB,B solo (easy)
  FITZSIMONS 6006 $.20   (H527)

HIMMEL UND ERDE VERGEHEN see
  Hammerschmidt, Andreas

HIMMEL UND ERDE WERDEN VERGEHEN see
  Micheelsen, Hans-Friedrich

HIMMELSKNABE see Erk

HINDERMANN, WALTER FELIX (1931-   )
  Die Seligpreisungen
  unis,narrator,org,perc LAUDINELLA
  LR 121 s.p.   (H528)

  Herr, Hore Doch Auf Meine Rede (Psalm
  5)
  SATB/unis/SB/SAT/SAB,org,opt 2trp,
  trom (contains also: Singt
  Halleluja) SCHWEIZER. SK 64.07-8
  s.p. see also MUSIKBEILAGE ZUM
  "EVANGELISCHEN KIRCHENCHOR 1964"
                                 (H529)
  Nun Danket Alle Gott
  unis,S rec,A rec,B rec,trp,strings
  LAUDINELLA LR 40 s.p.   (H530)

  Psalm 1 *see Selig Der Mensch, Der
  Den Parolen Der Partei Nicht
  Folgt

  Psalm 5 *see Herr, Hore Doch Auf
  Meine Rede

  Selig Der Mensch, Der Den Parolen Der
  Partei Nicht Folgt (Psalm 1)
  SAT/SAB,trp,bvl LAUDINELLA LR 75
  s.p.   (H531)

HINE, STUART
  How Great Thou Art
  (Bock, F.) cor BRIDGE Z 0161 (H532)

HINS, S.B.
  My Sweet Jesus
  (Wild, Eric) SATB (med easy)
  WATERLOO $.40   (H533)

HINTON
Cradle, The
unis,inst (easy) OXFORD 81.138 $.40
(H534)

HINUNTER IST DER SONNE SCHEIN see
Vulpius, Melchior

HIRTENLIED IM ADVENT "WINTERZEIT,
SCHONSTE ZEIT" see Siegl, Otto

HIRTENWEIHNACHT see Mullich, Hermann

HIRTH, HERMANN
Ostern *Easter
men cor,acap TONOS s.p. (H535)

HIS ARE THE THOUSAND SPARKLING RILLS
see Held, Wilbur

HIS GENTLE LOOK see Red, Buryl

HIS GRACE IS SUFFICIENT FOR ME see
Lister, Mosie

HIS HARBOR see Ellstrom, Eva E.

HIS LOVE IS ENDLESS see Jones, Richmond

HIS LOVE IS WONDERFUL TO ME see White,
P.

HIS LOVING KINDNESS LASTS FOREVER see
Wild, Eric

HIS MATCHLESS WORTH see Mozart,
Wolfgang Amadeus

HIS NAME IS JESUS see Whittemore

HIS NAME IS LOVE *anthem/carol/folk
(Sergisson) SATB oct SINGSPIR
ZJP-5067 $.35 (H536)

HIS NAME SHALL BE CALLED see Burpo,
Ruby E.

HIS OWN see Heynolds, Isham E.

HIS PEACE see Currie, Randolph

HIS SAVING GRACE PROCLAIM see Hooper,
William L.

HIS SHEEP AM I see Johnson, Orien

HIS TRUTH IS MARCHING ON see Steffe,
William

HIS WAY WITH THEE see Nusbaum, Cyrus S.

HIS YOKE IS EASY see Hudson, Richard

HISPANIAE SCHOLA MUSICA SACRA VOL. I:
CHRISTOPHORUS MORALES, 1894 see
Morales, Cristobal de

HISPANIAE SCHOLA MUSICA SACRA VOL. II:
FRANCISCUS GUERRERO, 1894 see
Guerrero, Francisco

HISPANIAE SCHOLA MUSICA SACRA VOL. III:
ANTONIUS A CABEZON, 1895 see
Cabezon, Antonio de

HISPANIAE SCHOLA MUSICA SACRA VOL. IV:
ANTONIUS A CABEZON, 1895 see
Cabezon, Antonio de

HISPANIAE SCHOLA MUSICA SACRA VOL. V:
JOANNES GINESIUS PEREZ, 1896 see
Perez, Joannes Ginesius

HISPANIAE SCHOLA MUSICA SACRA VOL. VI:
PSALMODIA MODULATA (VULGO
FABORDONES) A DIVERSIIS AUCTORIBUS,
1897 *CCU
(Pedrell, F.) cor pap JOHNSON $12.00
contains also: Vol. V: Joannes
Ginesius Perez, 1896 (H537)

HISPANIAE SCHOLA MUSICA SACRA VOL. VII:
ANTONIUS A CABEZON, 1897 see
Cabezon, Antonio de

HISPANIAE SCHOLA MUSICA SACRA VOL.
VIII: ANTONIUS A CABEZON, 1898 see
Cabezon, Antonio de

HISPANIAE SCHOLA MUSICA SACRA VOLS. I-
VIII, BARCELONA 1894-1898 *CCU
(Pedrell, F.) cor JOHNSON cmplt ed,
cloth $60.00, cmplt ed,pap $45.00
contains works by: Morales,
Christophorus; Guerrero,
Franciscus; Cabezon, Antonius;
Perez, Johannes Ginesius (H538)

HISTORIA DER AUFERSTEHUNG JESU CHRISTI
see Schutz, Heinrich

HISTORIE DER VERKUNDIGUNG see Vogt,
Hans

HISTORY OF THE FLOOD see Lord

HITCHCOCK, G.
Sleep, My Little One *Xmas
SATB EMI s.p. contains also:
Brahms, Johannes, St. Luke's
Carol (H539)

HIVELY, WELLS
Choral Variations
dbl cor,2pno AM.COMP.AL. $7.15
(H540)

Last Invocation, The *hymn
SATB,acap AM.COMP.AL. $.55 (H541)

HJELMBORG, BJORN
Vom Himmel Hoch Da Komm Ich Her
*Xmas,cant
SATB,org sc,cor pts EGTVED MK105
s.p. (H542)

HO! EVERYONE THAT IS THIRSTY see Meyer

HO! EVERYONE THAT THIRSTETH see
Pulkingham, B.C.

HOCH VOM HIMMEL KOMM ICH HER see
Weismann, Wilhelm

HOCHAMT IN B see Haydn, (Franz) Joseph,
Schopfungsmesse

HOCHZEITSGESANG "HERR, SEGNE, DIE SICH
HEUT VERBINDEN" see Kutzer, Ernst

HOCKEY, OLIVE
There Came Wise Men *see Babcock,
Rowena

HODDER
Thy Word Is Like A Garden *anthem
(Galloway) SATB oct BROADMAN
4551-84 $.30 (H543)

HODDINOTT, ALUN (1929-)
Out Of The Deep
SATB,acap (diff) OXFORD 43.477
$1.15 (H544)

Puer Natus
SSAATTBB/SSAA/TTBB (easy) OXFORD
84.229 $.45 (H545)

Tree Of Life, The
SATB,inst (diff) OXFORD 46.180
$12.75, ipr (H546)
SATB,inst (diff) OXFORD rental (H547)

HODGSON, H.
Atonement At Golgotha *cant
cor BRODT $2.00 (H548)

Blessed Are They That Mourn
mix cor BRODT 549 $.32 (H549)

HODIE CHRISTUS NATUS EST see Aston,
Peter

HODIE CHRISTUS NATUS EST see Gabrieli,
Giovanni

HODIE CHRISTUS NATUS EST see Gallus,
Jacobus

HODIE CHRISTUS NATUS EST see Kayser,
Leif

HODIE CHRISTUS NATUS EST see Kempter,
Karl

HODIE CHRISTUS NATUS EST see Sayve

HODIE CHRISTUS NATUS EST see Schutz,
Heinrich

HODIE CHRISTUS NATUS EST see Sweelinck,
Jan Pieterszoon

HODIE NOBIS COELORUM REX see Gallus,
Jacobus

HODIE NOBIS COELORUM REX see Goudimel,
Claude

HODIE SALVATOR APPARUIT see Brown,
Christopher

HOE GROOT ZIJT GIJ!
mix cor sc HEER 3008 s.p. (H550)

HOFER, FRANZ
Messe Zu Ehren Der Allerseligsten
Jungfrau Maria *Op.59, Mass
[Lat] SAB/SAT/2-3 eq voices,org sc,
cor pts BOHM s.p. (H551)

HOFFER, PAUL MARX (1895-1949)
Weihnachtskantate *Op.38, Xmas,cant
4pt mix cor&4pt mix cor,pno,3vln,
vcl,opt clar&trp (med easy) sc,
voc sc SCHOTTS ED. 5130 s.p., ipa
(H552)

HOFFMAN
Give Him The Glory *anthem/gospel
(Johnson, Norman) SATB oct SINGSPIR
ZJP-8050 $.30 (H553)

HOFFMAN (cont'd.)
Is Your All On The Altar?
(Mercer, W. Elmo) SATB oct BENSON
S4159 $.35 (H554)

What A Wonderful Savior! *Commun,
anthem
(DeCou, Harold) SATB oct SINGSPIR
ZJP-7225 $.25 (H555)

HOFFMAN, T.
Nine Japanese Haiku *CC9U
mix cor BRODT 637 $.75 (H556)

HOFFMANN, BERNHARD
Deutsche Kornelius-Messe *Mass
[Ger] cor,opt solo,org BOHM sc
s.p., cor pts s.p. (H557)

Messe Zu Ehren Der Heiligen Barbara
*Mass
[Lat] SABar,acap (without Credo)
sc,cor pts BOHM s.p. (H558)

Messe Zu Ehren Der Unbefleckten
Empfangnis Mariens *Mass
[Lat] 4pt mix cor,acap sc,cor pts
BOHM s.p. (H559)

Messe Zu Ehren Des Heiligen Georg
*Mass
[Lat] 4pt mix cor,acap sc,cor pts
BOHM s.p. (H560)

Zwei Pange Lingua *CC2U
[Lat] SAB BOHM s.p. (H561)

HOFFMANN, ERNST THEODOR AMADEUS
(1776-1822)
Ave Maria
see Canzoni Heft 1

Canzoni Heft 1
4pt,acap BREITKOPF-W CHB 4893 s.p.
contains: Ave Maria; De Profundis
(H562)

Canzoni Heft 2
4pt,acap BREITKOPF-W CHB 4894 s.p.
contains: Gloria; O Sanctissima;
Salve Redemptor (H563)

Canzoni Heft 3: Salve Regina
4pt,acap BREITKOPF-W CHB 4895 s.p.
(H564)

De Profundis
see Canzoni Heft 1

Gloria
see Canzoni Heft 2

O Sanctissima
see Canzoni Heft 2

Salve Redemptor
see Canzoni Heft 2

HOFMAYER, KARL
Veni Creator *Op.20a, Pent/Whitsun
[Lat] 4pt mix cor,acap BOHM s.p.
contains also: Wassmer, Berthold,
Veni Creator, Op.21a (H565)

HOHLFELD, CHRISTOPH (1922-)
Drei Motetten *CC3U,mot
4-5pt mix cor,acap MERSEBURG EM463
(H566)

HOIBY, LEE (1926-)
At The Round Earth's Imagined Corners
SATB,org GRAY CMR 3303 $.35 (H567)

HOKANSON, MARGRETHE (1893-)
God Our Father
SATB (easy) FITZSIMONS 2151 $.20
(H568)

HOLBEN, LARRY
Buildin' (composed with Tewson, Bill)
*CC10L
cor LEXICON 37672 $1.95 (H569)

Building (composed with Tewson, Bill)
*CCU,anthem
SATB LEXICON (H570)

Let Love Live (composed with Tewson,
Bill) *CC8L
cor LEXICON 37623 $1.95 (H571)

HOLBROOK, PETER WILLIAM
Thanks Be To God
unis ART MAST 224 $.40 (H572)

HOLD ON see Simpson, Eugene

HOLD OUT YOUR LIGHT! *anthem/gospel
(Johnson, Norman) SATB oct SINGSPIR
ZJP-8089 $.25 (H573)

HOLD THE FORT see Bliss, Paul

HOLDE, ARTHUR (1885-1962)
Adonoy, Moh Odom (from Memorial
Service)
[Eng/Heb] TRANSCON. TCL 265 $.75
contains also: What Is Man?; El
Mole Rachamin; Faith And

HOLDE, ARTHUR (cont'd.)

    Confidence   (H574)

    El Mole Rachamin (from Memorial
      Service)
      see Holde, Arthur, Adonoy, Moh Odom

    Faith And Confidence (from Memorial
      Service)
      see Holde, Arthur, Adonoy, Moh Odom

    What Is Man? (from Memorial Service)
      see Holde, Arthur, Adonoy, Moh Odom

HOLDEN, [OLIVER] (1765-1844)
    All Hail The Power Of Jesus' Name
      *Palm,anthem
      (Dean; Green) SATB oct SINGSPIR
        ZA-4453 $.25   (H575)
      (DeCou, Harold) SATB oct SINGSPIR
        ZJP-3204 $.30   (H576)
      (Hess, J.) SSATB oct SINGSPIR
        ZJP-7345 $.30   (H577)

    Early American Christmas Triptych, An
      *see Read

HOLIDAY, MICKEY
    Everywhere And Always *anthem
      (Johnson, Norman) SAB/SATB oct
      SINGSPIR ZJP-5004 $.25 (H578)

    Happy Am I! *folk
      SSATB oct SINGSPIR ZJP-5021 $.25
                    (H579)

    I Know Where I'm Goin' *see Dahrouge

    It's Yours For The Asking *folk
      (Johnson, Norman) SSAB oct SINGSPIR
      ZJP-5005 $.25   (H580)

HOLLAND, KENNETH
    To Us Is Born A Little Child
      *anthem,Contemp
      SATB oct CHANTRY COA 5913 $.18
                    (H581)

HOLLER, KARL (1907-   )
    Emitte Spiritum *Pent/Whitsun,
      Gradual
      [Lat] 4pt mix cor,org sc,cor pts
      BOHM s.p.   (H582)

HOLLFELDER, WALDRAM (1924-   )
    Es Kam Ein Engel Vom Hohen Himmel
      *Xmas
      men cor BOHM s.p.   (H583)

    Ich Bin Die Auferstehung
      4-6pt mix cor MERSEBURG EM454
                    (H584)

    Jesu, Geh Voran
      men cor,acap TONOS 5658 s.p. (H585)

    Lobt Gott, Ihr Christen *Adv/Xmas
      2pt BOHM s.p.   (H586)

    Missa In D-Moll *Mass
      [Lat] SABar,acap (D min) sc,cor pts
      BOHM s.p.   (H587)

HOLLIGER, HEINZ (1939-   )
    Dona Nobis Pacem
      SSSAAATTTBBB,acap (diff) sc SCHOTTS
      rental   (H588)

    Psalm
      mix cor,acap (diff) sc SCHOTTS
      ED. 6487 s.p.   (H589)

HOLLOWAY
    Death Of God, The
      SATB,soli,inst (diff) OXFORD rental
                    (H590)

HOLLY AND THE IVY *Xmas,carol,Eng
    SSA GALAXY 1.0594.1 $.35 (H591)

HOLLY AND THE IVY see Demuth, Norman

HOLLY AND THE IVY see Nieman, Alfred

HOLLY AND THE IVY, THE
    see Three Christmas Carol Anthems

HOLLY AND THE IVY, THE see Vance,
    Margaret Shelley

HOLM, GUNNAR
    En Herrdag I Hojden
      SABar ERIKS 91 s.p.   (H592)

    I Dina Helgons Spar *Eng
      4pt mix cor ERIKS 334 s.p. (H593)

    I Himmelen, I Himmelen
      SATB&anti cor ERIKS 92 s.p. (H594)

    Koraldiskantater Del 1-4 *CCU
      4pt mix cor ERIKS 201 s.p. four
        parts, sold separately (H595)

    Varen Icke Forskrackta
      4pt mix cor ERIKS 90 s.p. (H596)

HOLMAN, DEREK
    Beatitudes, The
      SATB THOMP.G $.35   (H597)

    Christ Keep Us All *carol
      mix cor,2 high soli THOMP.G $.40
                    (H598)

    Mass Of St. Thomas *Mass
      SATB (diff) WATERLOO $.60 (H599)

    Niagara Mass, The
      cong&opt SATB THOMP.G voc pt $.30,
      cor pts $.45   (H600)

HOLMBOE, VAGN (1909-   )
    Benedic Domino
      [Lat] SSATBB,acap EGTVED KB21 s.p.
                    (H601)

HOLMES, ROBERT
    Beams Of Gentle Light
      SATB (easy) FOSTER MF676 $.40
                    (H602)

      SA (easy) FOSTER MF876 $.30 (H603)

HOLST, GUSTAV (1874-1934)
    Babe Is Born, A *Xmas
      SATB (med) oct CONCORDIA 98-2181
      $.30   (H604)

    Good Friday
      TTBB,pno/org oct BOOSEY 5923 $.40
      see from Six Choruses For Male
      Voices   (H605)

    How Mighty Are The Sabbaths
      TTBB,pno/org oct BOOSEY 5925 $.45
      see from Six Choruses For Male
      Voices   (H606)

    In The Bleak Mid-Winter *Xmas
      SATB EMI s.p.   (H607)

    Intercession
      TTBB,pno/org oct BOOSEY 5924 $.45
      see from Six Choruses For Male
      Voices   (H608)

    Jesu, Thou The Virgin-Born *Xmas
      SATB (med) oct CONCORDIA 98-2183
      $.30   (H609)

    Now Let Us Sing *Xmas
      SATB (med) oct CONCORDIA 98-2182
      $.40   (H610)

    Six Choruses For Male Voices *see
      Good Friday ; How Mighty Are The
      Sabbaths; Intercession (H611)

HOLY ART THOU, O GOD! *anthem
    (Rasley, John M.) SATB oct SINGSPIR
    ZJP-7332 $.25   (H612)

HOLY BANQUET, THE see Harris, D.S.

HOLY BIRTH, THE see Wadely, F.W.

HOLY BIRTH, THE see Young, Gordon

HOLY CHILD, THE *Xmas
    (Hruby) SAB,opt fl PRO ART 2830 $.35
                    (H613)
    (Hruby) SSA,opt fl PRO ART 2801 $.35
                    (H614)

HOLY CHILD, THE see Anderson, [William
    H.]

HOLY CHILD SLEEPS see Rogers, Sharon
    Elery

HOLY CITY
    SSA CIMINO $.40   (H615)
    SATB CIMINO $.40   (H616)

HOLY CITY, THE see Adams, Stephen

HOLY DAWN, THE see Rubbra, Edmund

HOLY DAY HOLLY CAROL *Xmas,carol
    (Lefebvre, C.) SSA GALAXY 1.1010.1
    $.40   (H617)
    (Lefebvre, C.) SATB GALAXY 1.0596.1
    $.35   (H618)

HOLY FATHER see Mendoza, Michael, Santo

HOLY FATHER, PURE AND GRACIOUS see
    Cousins, M. Thomas

HOLY GOD, WE PRAISE THY NAME *anthem
    (Goemanne, Noel) SAB/SATB&cong,org,
    opt 1-2trp (easy) GIA G1903 $.35
                    (H619)
    (Johnson, Norman) SATB oct SINGSPIR
    ZJP-7337 $.25   (H620)

HOLY, HOLY see Owens, Jimmy

HOLY, HOLY see Palestrina, Giovanni

HOLY, HOLY, HOLY *Proces
    (Roff, Joseph) SATB LITURGICAL $.50
    see also Twelve Hymns (H621)

HOLY, HOLY, HOLY see Bach

HOLY, HOLY, HOLY see Beattie, Herbert

HOLY, HOLY, HOLY see Faure, Gabriel-
    Urbain, Sanctus

HOLY, HOLY, HOLY see Haydn, (Franz)
    Joseph, Sanctus

HOLY, HOLY, HOLY see Haydn, (Johann)
    Michael

HOLY, HOLY, HOLY see Heber

HOLY, HOLY, HOLY! see Johnson, Norman

HOLY, HOLY, HOLY see Liszt, Franz

HOLY, HOLY, HOLY see Mendelssohn-
    Bartholdy, Felix, Heilig

HOLY, HOLY, HOLY see Monteverdi,
    Claudio, Sanctus

HOLY, HOLY, HOLY LORD, GOD OF HOSTS see
    Green, Philip

HOLY IS THE LORD see Baber, John

HOLY IS THE LORD! see Bradbury, William
    Batchelder

HOLY IS THE LORD see Schubert, Franz
    (Peter)

HOLY, LORD OF HOSTS see Young

HOLY LORD OUR GRATEFUL PRAYER NOW HEAR
    see Davis, D. Evan

HOLY MANNA (from Southern Harmony)
    (Carter, John) SATB,acap DEAN CD-102
    $.50   (H622)

HOLY MANNA see Boyd, Jack

HOLY MANNA see Walker, William

HOLY MOUNTAIN, THE see Joubert, John

HOLY NIGHT, SILENT NIGHT see Gruber,
    Franz Xaver, Stille Nacht, Heilige
    Nacht

HOLY REDEEMER see Mozart, Wolfgang
    Amadeus, Sancta Maria

HOLY SPIRIT
    (Sweetman, Paul W.) SSA (med easy)
    WATERLOO $.35   (H623)

HOLY SPIRIT, BE MY GUIDE see Cope

HOLY SPIRIT BREATHE ON ME *anthem
    (Angell) SATB oct BROADMAN 4562-32
    $.35   (H624)

HOLY SPIRIT, FAITHFUL GUIDE see Hutson

HOLY SPIRIT, FLAME OF GOD see Pierce,
    Christine

HOLY SPIRIT, LIKE THE SPRING see
    Lovelace, Austin C.

HOLY SPIRIT, NOW OUT-POURED see
    Peterson, John W.

HOLY SPIRIT SOURCE OF GLADNESS see
    Bach, Johann Sebastian

HOLY SPIRIT, TRUTH DIVINE see Haugland,
    A.O.

HOMECOMING, THE see Roe, Christopher

HOMILIUS, GOTTFRIED AUGUST (1714-1785)
    Ave Maris Stella
      see Two Latin Fragments

    Deo Dicamus Gratias
      see Two Latin Fragments

    Hear Ye! Jesus Is The Lamb Of God
      *see Siehe, Das Ist Gottes Lamm

    Music Of The Great Churches VIII:
      Holy Cross Church, Dresden *see
      Siehe, Das Ist Gottes Lamm, "Hear
      Ye! Jesus Is The Lamb Of God"
                    (H625)

    See Now The Lamb Of God
      SATB oct CONCORDIA 98-2235 $.25
                    (H626)

    Siehe, Das Ist Gottes Lamm
      (Young, Percy) "Hear Ye! Jesus Is
      The Lamb Of God" [Eng/Ger] SATB&
      SATB,acap BROUDE BR. $.65 see
      from Music Of The Great Churches
      VIII: Holy Cross Church, Dresden
                    (H627)

    Two Latin Fragments
      (Salas) SATB WALTON 2974 $.40
        contains: Ave Maris Stella; Deo
        Dicamus Gratias (H628)

HOMO NATUS EX MULIERE see Wilbye

HONE, KARL-HEINZ (1924-)
Wir Gehn Dahin
TTBarBB,acap sc SCHOTTS C 38 666
s.p., voc pt SCHOTTS
C 38 667-01-05 s.p.   (H629)

HONEGGER, ARTHUR (1892-1955)
Alleluia! Christ Is Reborn *see
Cantique De Paques

Cantique De Paques *Easter
"Alleluia! Christ Is Reborn" [Fr/
Eng] SSA,SSA soli,org voc sc
SALABERT-US $1.25   (H630)
"Alleluia! Christ Is Reborn" [Fr/
Eng] SSA,SSA soli,orch sc
SALABERT-US rental   (H631)

HOOPER
There Is No Love *see Littlewood

When Christ Was Born Of Mary Free
*Xmas,anthem
SATB oct BROADMAN 4545-97 $.30
(H632)

HOOPER, EDMUND (ca. 1553-1621)
Alas, That I Offended Ever
see Three Short Introits

O Lord, Upon Thee Do I Call
see Three Short Introits

Three Short Introits
(Morehan, J.) GRAY CMR 3340 $.30
contains: Alas, That I Offended
Ever (SATB); O Lord, Upon Thee
Do I Call (SATB); Wellspring Of
Bounty (SSAATB)   (H633)

Wellspring Of Bounty
see Three Short Introits

HOOPER, WILLIAM L.
Glory To God
3SDar&camb,pno (med easy) CAMBIATA
C97439 $.40   (H634)

His Saving Grace Proclaim *Xmas,cant
jr cor/sr cor BROADMAN 4512-03
$1.00   (H635)

HOOVER
Three Carols *CC3U,carol
2pt oct FISCHER,C CM-7787 $.35
(H636)

HOPE COLLINS SPECIAL CHOIR MELODIES
*CCUL,Contemp
(Collins, Hope) cor (easy) GOSPEL
05 TM 0495 $1.00   (H637)

HOPE OF THE WORLD see Wolff, S.
Drummond

HOPE OF THE WORLD, THE see Clarke,
Henry Leland

HOPKINS
'Til The Whole World Knows *folk
(Skillings, Otis) SATB/jr cor oct
LILLENAS AN-5089 $.30   (H638)

HOPKINS, JAMES F.
I To The Hills Will Lift Mine Eyes
(Psalm 121)
SATB,acap OPUS 3-03 $.35   (H639)

Psalm 121 *see I To The Hills Will
Lift Mine Eyes

Psalm 150
SATB,org OPUS 3-04 $.50   (H640)

Under The Sun
2-6pt,org OPUS 3-05 $.35   (H641)

HOPSON
Make Me An Instrument Of Thy Peace
*anthem
1-2pt oct BROADMAN 4560-41 $.35
(H642)
Psalm Of Thanksgiving, A *anthem
SAB (easy) oct BROADMAN 4562-29
$.35   (H643)

HOPSON, HAL H.
Enter His Sanctuary Singing *Gen/
Proces/Thanks,Introit
dbl cor,org,4brass cmplt ed
CHORISTERS A-107 $.60, CHORISTERS
A-107C $.25   (H644)

Keep A Joyful Song Ringing In Your
Heart *Gen/Thanks
unis CHORISTERS A-136 $.40   (H645)

Litany Of Celebration
unis,pno GENTRY G-239 $.30   (H646)

Lord Is My Strength And My Song, The
*Gen/Thanks
unis,bells,drums,tamb,opt gtr,
autoharp CHORISTERS A-101 $.30
(H647)

HOPSON, HAL H. (cont'd.)
Night For Dancing, A *Xmas,cant
cor,solo,pno/org CHORISTERS A-155
$.65   (H648)

O Praise The Lord Who Made All Beauty
*Gen/Thanks
unis,pno/org/hpsd CHORISTERS A-143
$.40   (H649)

St. Paul's Letter On Love
SATB&speak cor,narrator,acap (med)
GENTRY G-270 $.35   (H650)

Star, A Song, A *Adv/Xmas
unis,pno CHORISTERS A-167 $.45
(H651)

HOR AUF, MEIN HERZ, IN DEINER HAST see
Zipp, Friedrich

HORAK, V. (1801-1891)
Missa Pastoralis (composed with
Stecker, Karel) *cant
[Lat] mix cor,fl,2clar,2horn,2trp,
trom,timp,strings CZECH s.p.
(H652)

HORE, O HERR, DAS GEBET DEINER GEMEINDE
see Croce, Giovanni

HORE UNS HERR see Trapp, Willy

HORMAN, JOHN D.
Jesus Christ Is Risen Today,
Halleluyah *Easter
unis&2pt CHORISTERS A-129 $.30
(H653)
Selkirk Prayer *anthem
cor CHORISTERS R-13 $.15   (H654)

Walk Softly *Gen/Thanks
unis&desc,pno/org,opt hndbl
CHORISTERS A-165 $.40   (H655)

We Thank Thee Father *Gen/Thanks
unis&desc CHORISTERS A-148 $.35
(H656)

Yonder Lies A Boy *anthem
cor CHORISTERS R-7 $.15   (H657)

HORSLEY, WALTER S.
One Hundred Per Cent Chance Of Rain
*Gen/Thanks,cant
unis&2pt,pno,fl,bvl,perc (jazz) sc
CHORISTERS A-120 $4.95, cor pts
CHORISTERS A-120C $.65   (H658)

HORT DER ENGEL HELLE LIEDER *Xmas,
carol/folk
(Biebl, F.) [Ger] 4pt men cor
MERSEBURG EM9048   (H659)

HORT DER ENGEL JUBELLIEDER *Xmas,folk,
Fr
(Becker, H.-G.) [Ger] men cor,acap
TONOS 2099 s.p.   (H660)

HORT EINE HELLE STIMM ERKLINGT see
Haus, Karl

HORT IHR DAS HELLE KLINGEN? *CC9L,
Xmas,Eur
(Kronberg, Gerhard) mix cor,acap BOHM
s.p.   (H661)

HORT IHR DIE ENGEL SINGEN see Kuntz,
Michael

HORT ZU UND SEID GETROST NUN see
Schroter, Leonhard

HOSANNA *anthem
(Red, Buryl) 1-2pt,opt inst oct
BROADMAN 4558-48 $.30   (H662)

HOSANNA see Des Prez, Josquin

HOSANNA see Gregor, [Christian
Friedrich]

HOSANNA see Leinbach, E.W.

HOSANNA! see Peterson, John W.

HOSANNA! *CCU
(Burroughs, Bob) men cor BROADMAN
4522-11 $1.50   (H663)

HOSANNA: A FOLK COMMUNION SERVICE see
Johnson, David N.

HOSANNA! BLESSED IS THAT COMES! see
Burroughs

HOSANNA! HALLELUJAH! see Azevedo, Lex
de

HOSANNA IN EXCELSIS see Kuntz, Michael

HOSANNA IN THE HIGHEST! see Frey,
Richard

HOSANNA IN THE HIGHEST! see Martin,
Gilbert M.

HOSANNA IN THE HIGHEST see Palestrina,
Giovanni

HOSANNA, KING OF ISRAEL see Stanley,
John

HOSANNA, LOUD HOSANNA see Wolff, S.
Drummond

HOSANNA TO THE LIVING LORD! see Maunder

HOSANNA TO THE SON OF DAVID see Carter,
John

HOSANNA TO THE SON OF DAVID see
Penhorwood, Edwin

HOSANNA TODAY! see Ydstie

HOSANNA WE SING see Rains, Dorothy Best

HOSIANNA see Vogler

HOSIANNA DEM SOHNE DAVIDS see Tunder,
Franz

HOSIANNA, O BLESSED IS HE WHO COMES see
Gregor, [Christian Friedrich]

HOSMER
Hear, Hear, O Ye Nations (composed
with Tipton) *anthem
SATB (easy) oct BROADMAN 4554-57
$.30   (H664)

HOSPODINE POMILUJ NY see Janacek, Leos

HOSPODINE, POMILUJ NY see Vlach-
Vruticky, Josef

HOSS, FRANZ
Deutsche Messe *Op.32, Mass
[Ger] mix cor (without Credo) BOHM
sc s.p., cor pts s.p.   (H665)

Deutsche Volksmesse *Op.30, Mass
[Ger] mix cor&cong,org/brass BOHM
sc s.p., cor pts s.p., ipa (H666)

Deutsches Requiem *Op.26, Req
[Ger] 1-4pt mix cor,acap/org sc,cor
pts BOHM s.p.   (H667)

Grosser Gott, Wir Loben Dich *Fest
mix cor&unis,org,opt brass BOHM
s.p.   (H668)

Messe Zu Ehren Des Heiligen Bruders
Konrad *Op.5, Mass
[Lat] 4pt mix cor,acap sc,cor pts
BOHM s.p.   (H669)

Messe Zu Ehren Des Heiligen Papstes
Pius X *Op.10, Mass
[Lat] 4pt mix cor,acap sc,cor pts
BOHM s.p.   (H670)

Missa Brevis Zu Ehren Des Heiligen
Franz Von Assisi *Op.20, Mass
[Lat] 4pt mix cor,acap sc,cor pts
BOHM s.p.   (H671)

Missa Sancta Maria *Op.1, Mass
[Lat] 4pt mix cor,acap sc,cor pts
BOHM s.p.   (H672)

Zwei Tantum Ergo *Op.9a, CC2U
[Lat] 4pt mix cor,acap BOHM s.p.
(H673)

HOSTIAS see Mozart, Wolfgang Amadeus

HOUKOM
Lo, How A Rose E'er Blooming *Xmas
SATB/SAB,fl/ob oct CONCORDIA
98-2216 $.35   (H674)

HOUSE
Soon We Will Be Free
KJOS 6116 $.35   (H675)

HOUSE OF OUR LORD, THE see Gustafson,
Dwight

HOUSE OF THE LORD, THE see Kirby

HOUSIEAUX, G.
Vivat Flamand
2pt mix cor GRAS s.p.   (H676)

HOVDESVEN, E.A. (1893-)
Carol Of The Tree *Xmas,anthem/carol
SATB oct LORENZ 7843 $.30   (H677)

HOVHANESS, ALAN (1911-)
Blessed Is The Man That Trusteth In
The Lord *No.1
SATB AMP A-691 $.40 see from Four
Motets   (H678)

David Wept For Slain Absalom
*Op.246,No.1
SSATBB,opt org PETERS P66448 (H679)

Fool Hath Said In His Heart, The
*No.4
SATB AMP A-694 $.35 see from Four

HOVHANESS, ALAN (cont'd.)

   Motets   (H680)

   Four Motets *see Blessed Is The Man
     That Trusteth In The Lord, No.1;
     Fool Hath Said In His Heart, The,
     No.4; Help, Lord; For The Godly
     Man Ceaseth, No.2; Lord Who Shall
     Abide In Thy Tabernacle?, No.3
                    (H681)

   God Be Merciful Unto Us *Op.259,
     Bibl
     unis,opt A/Bar solo RONGWEN $.50
     see from Three Motets   (H682)

   Heaven *Op.246,No.3, anthem
     SATB PETERS P66509   (H683)

   Help, Lord; For The Godly Man Ceaseth
     *No.2
     SATB AMP A-692 $.35 see from Four
     Motets   (H684)

   In The Lord I Put My Trust
     see Two Songs Of Faith

   Lord Is In His Holy Temple, The
     see Two Songs Of Faith

   Lord Who Shall Abide In Thy
     Tabernacle? *No.3
     SATB AMP A-693 $.40 see from Four
     Motets   (H685)

   Peace Be Multiplied *Op.259, Bibl
     SATB,acap RONGWEN $.35 see from
     Three Motets   (H686)

   Three Motets *see God Be Merciful
     Unto Us, Op.259; Peace Be
     Multiplied, Op.259; Wisdom,
     Op.259   (H687)

   Two Songs Of Faith
     SATB,acap BELWIN OCT 2312 $.35
     contains: In The Lord I Put My
     Trust; Lord Is In His Holy
     Temple, The   (H688)

   Way Of Jesus, The *Op.279
     SATB&Bar,STB soli,3fl,2ob,2clar,
     2bsn,4horn,3trp,3trom,tuba,timp,
     4perc,harp,3gtr,strings BROUDE,A
     sc rental, cor pts rental, ipr
                    (H689)

   Wisdom *Op.259, Bibl
     SATB,acap RONGWEN $.35 see from
     Three Motets   (H690)

   Word Of Our God Shall Stand Forever,
     The *Op.246,No.2, Bene/Bibl
     SSATBB,opt org PETERS P66507 (H691)

HOVLAND, EGIL
   Glory Of The Father, The
     SATB WALTON 2973 $.40   (H692)

   Good Friday *see Langfredag

   Langfredag
     "Good Friday" 2pt&speak cor,fl,org
     NORSK NMO 8764, 8764 B s.p.
                    (H693)

   Saul
     mix cor,org NORSK NMO 8754 s.p.
                    (H694)

   To Gammeltestamentlige Sange *CC2U,
     Bibl
     cor,S solo,fl,org NORSK NMO 8729
     s.p.   (H695)

HOW
   Jesus, Name Of Wondrous Love
     (composed with Wilcoxon) *anthem
     SATB (easy) oct BROADMAN 4551-36
     $.30   (H696)

HOW ARE THE MIGHTY FALLEN see Ramsey,
   Robert

HOW BEAUTIFUL ARE THE FEET see Handel,
   George Frideric

HOW BLEST ARE THEY see Proulx, Richard

HOW CAN I THANK THE LORD see Wild, Eric

HOW COULD THERE BE A FAIRER ONE?
   *Xmas,Contemp
   SATB VANGUARD V567 $.35 see from Come
   To Bethlehem   (H697)

HOW EXCELLENT IS THY NAME see Butler,
   Eugene

HOW EXCELLENT THY NAME see Burroughs

HOW EXCELLENT THY NAME see Handel,
   George Frideric

HOW FAR IS IT TO BETHLEHEM?
   see Christmas Choir Melodies

HOW FAR IS IT TO BETHLEHEM see Coates

HOW FAR IS IT TO BETHLEHEM? see
   Gritton, Eric

HOW FAR IS IT TO BETHLEHEM? see Lapo,
   Cecil E.

HOW FIRM A FOUNDATION *Gen,anthem/
   folk,US
   (Anderson, Paul Louis) SSATB,S solo,
     acap BOONIN B 186 $.50   (H698)
   (Dean, T.W.) SATB (easy) oct BROADMAN
     4561-01 $.30   (H699)
   (DeCou, Harold) SATB oct SINGSPIR
     ZJP-7300 $.30   (H700)
   (Peterson, J.W.) SSATB oct SINGSPIR
     ZJP-7362 $.35   (H701)
   (Skillings, Otis) SATB oct LILLENAS
     AN-2392 $.30   (H702)
   (Smith, Lani) SA/SATB (easy) oct
     LORENZ A568 $.35   (H703)

HOW FIRM A FOUNDATION see Smith

HOW FIRM A FOUNDATION see Tyler

HOW GOOD AND JOYOUS
   see Three Peace And Brotherhood
   Canons

HOW GREAT see Reynolds, William Jensen

HOW GREAT AND MARVELOUS IS MY LORD see
   Deane

HOW GREAT IS YOUR NAME see Senator,
   Ronald

HOW GREAT THOU ART
   (Wild, Eric) SATB (med) WATERLOO $.60
                    (H704)

HOW GREAT THOU ART see Hine, Stuart

HOW I HAVE LONGED see Winter, Sister
   Miriam Therese

HOW JESUS STILLED THE STORM see Nelson,
   Ronald A.

HOW LONG WILL IT BE? see Peterson, John
   W.

HOW LONG WILT THOU FORGET ME see
   Lekberg, Sven

HOW LONG WILT THOU FORGET ME see Manor,
   Russell

HOW LONG WILT THOU FORGET ME? see
   Pflueger, Carl

HOW LOVELY ARE THE MESSENGERS see
   Mendelssohn

HOW LOVELY ARE THOSE DWELLINGS see
   Mendelssohn-Bartholdy, Felix

HOW LOVELY ARE THY DWELLINGS see De
   Lamarter, Eric

HOW LOVELY ARE THY DWELLINGS FAIR see
   Spohr, Ludwig (Louis)

HOW LOVELY ARE THY MESSENGERS see
   Mendelssohn-Bartholdy, Felix

HOW LOVELY IS THE HOUSE OF GOD see
   Bradford

HOW LOVELY IS THE HOUSE OF GOD see
   Young

HOW LOVELY IS THY DWELLING PLACE see
   Brahms, Johannes

HOW LOVELY IS THY DWELLING PLACE see
   Nordin, Dayton W.

HOW LOVELY IS THY DWELLING PLACE see
   Powell, Robert J.

HOW LOVELY IS YOUR DWELLING see
   Lovejoy, A.

HOW LOVELY SHINES THE MORNING STAR see
   Bender, Jan

HOW MANY CHRISTMASES? see Fargo,
   Milford

HOW MANY MILES TO BETHLEHEM? see
   Ingram, Bill

HOW MIGHTY ARE THE SABBATHS see Holst,
   Gustav

HOW PLEASANT ARE THY DWELLINGS see
   Brahms, Johannes

HOW SHALL I SING THAT MAJESTY see
   Lovelace, Austin C.

HOW SMALL ART THOU, HOW WEAK AND
   HELPLESS see Ehret, Walter

HOW STILL AND PEACEFUL see Tye,
   Christopher

HOW SWEET, HOW HEAVENLY IS THE SIGHT
   see Parks, Joe E.

HOW SWEET THE NAME OF JESUS SOUNDS
   *anthem
   (Cram, James D.) mix cor CENTURY PR
   $.20   (H705)

HOW SWEET THY DWELLINGS, LORD see
   Latrobe, Christian I.

HOWELLS, HERBERT NORMAN (1892-   )
   English Mass, An
     SATB,fl,ob,timp,perc,harp,strings
     voc sc NOVELLO rental   (H706)

   Hymnus Paradisi
     SATB,ST soli,2fl,opt pic,2ob,2clar,
     2bsn,4horn,3trp,3trom,tuba,timp,
     perc,harp,strings,opt pno,
     optional English horn, bass
     clarinet, contrabassoon, celeste
     voc sc NOVELLO rental   (H707)

   Missa Sabrinensis
     SATB,SATBar soli,2fl,3ob,3clar,
     3bsn,4horn,3trp,3trom,tuba,timp,
     harp,org,strings, pno or celeste
     voc sc NOVELLO rental   (H708)

   Stabat Mater
     SATB,T solo,3fl,3ob,3clar,3bsn,
     4horn,3trp,3trom,tuba,timp,perc,
     pno,harp,org,strings, celeste voc
     sc NOVELLO rental   (H709)

HOWL, MY SOUL see Winter, Sister Miriam
   Therese

HOYOUL, BALDUIN (1547-1594)
   Da Jesus An Dem Kreuze Stund
     SAT/SAB (contains also: Nun Jauchzt
     Dem Herren, Alle Welt) SCHWEIZER.
     SK 58.05 s.p. see also
     MUSIKBEILAGE ZUM "EVANGELISCHEN
     KIRCHENCHOR 1958"   (H710)

HREBIC
   In A Far Off Town (composed with
     Kucera) *Xmas,carol
     SATB CHAPLET 2004 $.25   (H711)

HRUBY, DELORES
   Blessed Be The Lord, Who Schools Me
     see Three Sacred Songs

   Come And Praise The Lord With Joy
     *Adv
     SATB,drums, triangle (med) oct
     CONCORDIA 98-2170 $.35   (H712)

   Come To Me, All Who Labor
     see Three Sacred Songs

   I Lift My Hands To The Lord Most High
     *Gen/Thanks
     unis,pno/org,fl,drums,fing.cym.,
     tamb, triangle CHORISTERS A-166
     $.45   (H713)

   I Saw Three Ships *Xmas
     unis,bells,fing.cym.,tamb,pno/org,
     triangle CHORISTERS A-154 $.45
                    (H714)

   Peaceable Kingdom, The
     see Three Sacred Songs

   Three Sacred Songs *Gen
     (easy) oct CONCORDIA 98-2098 $.35
     contains: Blessed Be The Lord,
     Who Schools Me (SA,kbd); Come
     To Me, All Who Labor (unis,
     kbd); Peaceable Kingdom, The
     (unis,kbd)   (H715)

   Your Holy Cross *Lent,anthem
     SAB/3 eq voices,org (easy) GIA
     G1894 $.40   (H716)

HUBER, HEINRICH
   Requiem Mit Libera *Op.21
     [Lat] 4pt mix cor,org sc,cor pts
     BOHM s.p.   (H717)

   Salve Regina Pacis *Op.25, Mass
     [Lat] 4pt mix cor,org,opt fl&2horn&
     strings&2ob/2clar&opt 2trp&trom&
     timp sc,cor pts BOHM s.p., ipa
                   (H718)

HUBER, KLAUS (1924-   )
   Kleine Deutsche Messe *Mass
     [Ger/Lat] 6-8pt mix cor&opt cong,
     opt org&vln&vla&vcl&harp&perc
     (med diff) BAREN. BA5420 (H719)
     [Ger/Lat] 6-8pt mix cor&opt cong,
     vln,vla,vcl,harp (med diff)
     BAREN. BA6080   (H720)

HUDSON, RICHARD (1924-   )
   At The Cross *see Watts

HUDSON, RICHARD (cont'd.)

Blessed Be The Name *anthem
(Johnson, Norman) SATB (easy) oct
SINGSPIR ZJP-6018 $.30   (H721)

Glorious Church, A *anthem/gospel
(DeCou, Harold) SATB oct SINGSPIR
ZJP-8048 $.30   (H722)
(Mercer, W. Elmo) SATB oct BENSON
S4002 $.35   (H723)

His Yoke Is Easy *anthem
(DeCou, Harold) SATB oct SINGSPIR
ZJP-7230 $.30   (H724)

Song Of Dedication, A (composed with
Peninger) *anthem
SAB (easy) oct BROADMAN 4554-52
$.30   (H725)

HUFF, RONN
For The Beauty Of The Earth
SATB oct BENSON S4099 $.35   (H726)

New World, A
SATB,brass,orch oct BENSON S4000
$.35, ipa   (H727)

Time Is Now, The
SATB,orch oct BENSON S4320 $.35,
ipa   (H728)

HUFSCHMIDT, WOLFGANG (1934-   )
Agende
4 cor,3 narrators,org,electronic
tape, 2 slide projectors, radio
(med diff) BAREN. BA6099 rental
(H729)

Beatitudes, The *see Seligpreisungen

Der Barmherzige Samariter
"Good Samaritan, The" 3-5pt mix
cor,narrator (med) BAREN. BA5428
(H730)

Es Ist Ein Ros Entsprungen *Xmas
SAB.acap (med) BAREN. BA6304 (H731)

Good Samaritan, The *see Der
Barmherzige Samariter

Kontrafaktur II Nach Der "Missa
Cuiusvis Toni" Von Johannes
Ockeghem
5 cor (diff) BAREN. BA6286   (H732)

Seligpreisungen
"Beatitudes, The" SATB,acap (med
diff) BAREN. BA6146   (H733)

Stephanus
SSAATTBB,S,3 narrators,org,
electronic tape, slide projector;
electronic oboe, cello, and
percussion (diff) BAREN. BA6082
rental   (H734)

Texte Uber Frieden
TTBB,2pno,2perc (diff) BAREN.
BA6118 rental   (H735)

Vater Unser Am 30 Juli 1968 *prayer
SATB,electronic tape (diff) BAREN.
BA6117   (H736)

HUG, EMIL
Geistliche Gesange *Op.70, CCU
[Lat] 4pt mix cor,acap sc,cor pts
BOHM s.p.   (H737)

Herz-Jesu-Messe *Op.63, Mass
[Lat] 4pt mix cor,acap sc,cor pts
BOHM s.p.   (H738)

Missa In Honorem Sancti Jose Josephi
*Op.47, Mass
[Lat] 4pt mix cor,acap sc,cor pts
BOHM s.p.   (H739)

Pange Lingua
see Hug, Emil, Veni Creator
Spiritus

Veni Creator Spiritus
[Lat] 4pt mix cor,acap sc,cor pts
BOHM s.p. contains also: Pange
Lingua   (H740)

HUGGINS, RICHARD
Blessed Hour Of Prayer *anthem
SATB WORD CS-2644 $.35   (H741)

HUGH
Son Of God Is Born For All, The
(Jones) 2pt (easy) OXFORD 82.107
$.45   (H742)

HUGH-JONES, LLIFON
Torches
(Beeson) OXFORD W 97   (H743)

HUGHES
Blessed Assurance *anthem
SATB oct LORENZ B107 $.35   (H744)

HUGHES (cont'd.)

Born In A Manger *Xmas,anthem
SATB oct LORENZ A557 $.30   (H745)

Calvary Love *Gd.Fri.,anthem/gospel
(DeCou, Harold) SATB oct SINGSPIR
ZJP-8158 $.30   (H746)

Church Of The Living God *anthem
SATB oct LORENZ C357 $.35   (H747)

Crown The Saviour, King Of Kings
*Easter/Lent
(Rogers) SATB,trp oct LILLENAS
AN-5061 $.35   (H748)

God Lives! *anthem
SATB oct LORENZ A551 $.30   (H749)

God Of Grace And God Of Glory
*anthem
(Burroughs) SATB,brass oct LILLENAS
AN-2378 $.35   (H750)

I Will Praise Thee *anthem
unis&opt A oct LORENZ 8631 $.35
(H751)

Jesus Died On Calvary's Mountain
*Easter,anthem
SATB oct LORENZ B233 $.35   (H752)

Jesus Shall Reign *anthem
SATB oct LORENZ B235 $.35   (H753)

Listen With An Open Mind *anthem
SB oct LORENZ 5768 $.35   (H754)

Love Your Brother *Xmas/Easter/Gen,
anthem
unis&opt A oct LORENZ 8633 $.30
(H755)

O The Deep, Deep Love Of Jesus
*anthem
SATB oct LORENZ 9999 $.35   (H756)

On This Blessed Easter Day *Easter,
anthem
SA&opt B oct LORENZ 7847 $.35
(H757)

Savior, I Long To Be *anthem
SATB oct LORENZ A550 $.35   (H758)

Sing To The Lord A New Song *anthem
SATB oct LORENZ B218 $.35   (H759)

Tambourines To Glory (composed with
Moore) *sac/sec
SATB,acap WARNER WB-321 187 $.35
(H760)

When Love Shines In *anthem
unis&opt A oct LORENZ 8632 $.30
(H761)

HUGHES, EDWARD
Magnificat
SATB STAINER 3.0867.1 $.50   (H762)

HUGHES, KENT
Jesus Merciful *Lent
SATB CHORISTERS A-131 $.35   (H763)

HUGHES, MIKI
Look To The Skies Above *anthem
SAB/SA/unis oct LORENZ 7426 $.35
(H764)
Wonder When He's Coming *Adv,anthem
SA/SB oct LORENZ 5771 $.35   (H765)

HUGHES, ROBERT J. (1916-   )
All God's People *cant
SATB,pno/inst (med easy) LORENZ
$2.95   (H766)

Alleluia! *anthem
SATB,S solo (med easy) oct LORENZ
B240 $.35   (H767)

Choir Specials *CCU,anthem
cor (easy) LORENZ $1.95   (H768)

Church Of The Living God *Gen,anthem
SATB (med diff) oct LORENZ C357
$.35   (H769)

Gift Of Love, The *anthem
SAB oct LORENZ 7848 $.30   (H770)

Hear Ye Him *Cnfrm/Commun/Gen,anthem
SATB (med diff, baccalaureate) oct
LORENZ C363 $.35   (H771)

Lo! God Is Here *Gen,anthem
SATB (med diff) oct LORENZ C359
$.35   (H772)

Love Of My Lord To Me, The *Gen,
anthem
SA/SATB (easy) oct LORENZ A565 $.35
(H773)

My Father Is With Me *Gen,anthem
SA/SATB (easy) oct LORENZ A563 $.35
(H774)

HUGHES, S.M. HOWARD
Psalms For Advent *CCU,Psalm
cong,cantor,org (easy) GIA G1905
$3.00   (H775)

HULTMAN
Thanks To God! *Thanks,anthem
(Johnson, Norman) SATB oct SINGSPIR
ZJP-3103 $.30   (H776)

HUMBLE PRIERE
cor JOBERT s.p.   (H777)

HUME, ALEXANDER
Hymns And Sacred Songs *CCU
cor cloth JOHNSON BO34 $14.00
reprint of the Waldegrave
edition, 1599   (H778)

HUNDREDTH PSALM, THE see Gore, Richard
T.

HUNECKE, WILHELM
Ecce Sacerdos *Op.42a
[Lat] 4pt mix cor,acap sc,cor pts
BOHM s.p.   (H779)

Ehre Sei Gott In Der Hohe *Op.50c,
Adv/Xmas
3 eq voices BOHM s.p.   (H780)
cor BOHM s.p.   (H781)

Herr, Schicke, Was Du Willt *Op.30c,
Fest
3pt BOHM s.p.   (H782)

Lauda Jerusalem (Psalm 147) Op.47,
No.2, Fest/Palm
[Lat] cor,solo,opt org BOHM s.p.
(H783)

O Bone Jesu
see Zwei Passions-Motetten

O Crux, Ave
see Zwei Passions-Motetten

Oremus Pro Pontifice *Op.28a
[Lat] 4pt mix cor,acap BOHM s.p.
(H784)

Psalm 147 *see Lauda Jerusalem

Sacerdos Et Pontifex *Op.28b
[Lat] 4pt mix cor,acap BOHM s.p.
(H785)

Ut Omnes Unum Sint *Op.52, Mass
[Lat] cor&cong,opt solo,org/
harmonium sc,cor pts BOHM s.p.
(H786)

Wie Schon Leucht Uns Der Morgenstern
*Op.46,No.4, Adv/Xmas
3 eq voices BOHM s.p.   (H787)

Zwei Pange Lingua Und Tantum Ergo
*Op.44a
[Lat] 4pt mix cor,acap BOHM s.p.
(H788)

Zwei Passions-Motetten *Psntd,mot
[Lat] 4pt mix cor,acap sc,cor pts
BOHM s.p.
contains: O Bone Jesu, Op.15,
No.1; O Crux, Ave, Op.15,No.2
(H789)

HUNGARIAN BOYS' EASTER CAROL *Easter,
carol,Hung
(Gaul, Harvey) SATB&jr cor GALAXY
1.1032.1 $.40   (H790)

HUNKINS, A.B.
Gloria
mix cor BRODT 622 $.45   (H791)

HUNNICUTT, JUDY
Carol For Pentecost *Pent,anthem
unis,kbd,opt rec AUGSBURG 11-1676
$.30   (H792)

God, Creator *anthem
mix cor,hndbl AUGSBURG 11-3011 $.10
(H793)

In Bethlehem Is Born *Xmas
SATB&unis,opt fl&org oct SCHMITT
15020 $.40   (H794)

In Praise To God *anthem
SSAATTBB,org,hndbl AUGSBURG 11-0652
$.30   (H795)

Our Father, By Whose Name *anthem
SA,kbd AUGSBURG 11-1710 $.30 (H796)

Three Seasonal Songs *CC3U,anthem
unis,kbd,fl, opt glockenspiel
AUGSBURG 11-0323 $.45   (H797)

HUNTER, DENISE JOAN
Savior! I've No One Else To Tell
SATB,pno OPUS 3-02 $.50   (H798)

HUNTER, HARRY A.
I Saw A Cross
see Two Inspiring Gospel Songs

In The Morning
see Two Inspiring Gospel Songs

HUNTER, HARRY A. (cont'd.)

Two Inspiring Gospel Songs
SATB CHAPLET 2002 $.25
contains: I Saw A Cross; In The
Morning   (H799)

HUNTER, RALPH
Christmas Song, A *Xmas
SATB MARKS MC 4627 $.40   (H800)

HUNTINGTON, RONALD M.
Thy Word Is A Lamp
SATB,org FOSTER MF143 $.45   (H801)

HURD, MICHAEL (1928-)
Canticles Of The Virgin Mary
SSA,strings voc sc NOVELLO rental
(H802)

SSA,fl,ob,clar,vcl voc sc NOVELLO
rental   (H803)

It Is A Good Thing To Give Thanks
see FIVE ANTHEMS FOR TODAY

Missa Brevis
SSA,strings voc sc NOVELLO rental
(H804)

HURFORD, PETER
Bethlehem Of Noblest Cities *Xmas
SATB (med) OXFORD 84.214 $.25
(H805)

Magdalen, Cease From Sobs And Sighs
SATB,acap (easy) OXFORD 84.195 $.30
(H806)

HURLBUTT, PATRICIA E.
Give To Our God Immortal Praise
SATB,acap oct HOPE A 477 $.30
(H807)

Seek After God
SATB,pno oct HOPE CF 177 $.45
(H808)

HURNIK, ILJA (1922-   )
News From Bethlehem, The *see Novina
Betlemska

Noe *Bibl/ora
[Czech] mix cor,ST soli,3fl,3ob,
3clar,3bsn,6horn,3trp,3trom,tuba,
timp,perc,harp,pno,strings CZECH
s.p.   (H809)

Novina Betlemska
"News From Bethlehem, The" [Czech]
jr cor,vcl,timp,perc CZECH s.p.
(H810)

HURON CAROL *Xmas
(Johnston, Richard) SATB (med diff)
WATERLOO $.50   (H811)

HURRY LORD! COME QUICKLY! see Pfautsch,
Lloyd

HURU SKON OCH HURU LJUV see Nystroem,
Gosta

HUS-REIMANN
Jesus, All Our Souls Inspire
see Hus-Reimann, Word Of God Which
Ne'er Shall Cease, The

Word Of God Which Ne'er Shall Cease,
The
(Pfohl) mix cor BRODT 201 $.16
contains also: Jesus, All Our
Souls Inspire   (H812)

HUSH-A-BYE BOY CHILD JESUS see Truax

HUSH, MY BABE see Thygerson, Robert J.

HUSH, MY BABE, LIE STILL AND SLUMBER
*Xmas
(Ehret, Walter) SAB,opt ob&fing.cym.
oct SCHMITT 5547 $.30   (H813)

HUSH NOW see Archer, Darrell V.

HUSH THEE TO SLEEP see Powell,
Frederick J.

HUTCHESON
Lament For A Lost Child
SATB WALTON 2921 $.40   (H814)

HUTET EUCH, DASS EURE HERZEN NICHT
BESCHWERET WERDEN see Schutz,
Heinrich

HUTHER, K.
Zum Jahresschluss "Nun Geht Das Jahr
Zu Ende" *Op.54
cor BOHM s.p.   (H815)

HUTSON
Holy Spirit, Faithful Guide
SATB SHAWNEE A5665 $.35   (H816)

HYDE, HERBERT E.
Let The Words Of My Mouth *Bibl
SSAATTBB,acap (med) FITZSIMONS 2025
$.25   (H817)

HYLLBERG, RUTH
Hallelujah, Christ Arose *Easter
SATB oct GOSPEL 05 TM 0466 $.25
(H818)

He Wore A Crown Of Thorns *Easter,
Bibl/cant
SATB,SSA soli, mixed quartet,
duets, solos (recording
available) GOSPEL 05 TM 0470
$1.25   (H819)

Unto Us A Child Is Born *Xmas
SATB oct GOSPEL 05 TM 0469 $.25
(H820)

HYMN ANTHEMS FOR THE JUNIOR CHOIR
*CCU,hymn
(Hokanson, Margrethe) 1-2pt jr cor
BROADMAN 4526-06 $1.25   (H821)

HYMN FOR DAVID see Beck, John Ness

HYMN FOR OUR NATION, A see Canning,
Thomas

HYMN FOR THE NATIVITY see Parris,
Robert

HYMN IN PRAISE OF GOD AND MAN, A see
McAfee, D.

HYMN OF ASPIRATION, A see McAfee, D.

HYMN OF CONSECRATION see Currie,
Randolph

HYMN OF JOY see James, Will

HYMN OF PEACE
(Kent, A.T) SATB (easy) WATERLOO $.30
(H822)

HYMN OF PRAISE see Bortniansky, Dimitri
Stepanovitch

HYMN OF PRAISE, A see Couperin,
Francois

HYMN OF PRAISE, A see McAfee, D.

HYMN OF SAINT TERESA see Martin,
Gilbert M.

HYMN OF SPRING see Langston, Paul

HYMN OF THANKS, A see Rolle

HYMN OF WORSHIP see Peterson, John W.

HYMN ON THE MORNING OF CHRIST'S
NATIVITY see Woollen, Russell

HYMN TO GOD THE FATHER see Eldridge,
Guy H.

HYMN TO PROVIDENCE see Cundell, Edric

HYMN TO SPRING see Jordan

HYMN TO THE HEART OF JESUS see Franco,
Johan

HYMN TO THE TRINITY see Dawe

HYMN TO THE TRINITY see Wood, Dale

HYMN TO TRUTH, A see Cousins, M. Thomas

HYMNE see Carraz

HYMNE see Mendelssohn-Bartholdy, Felix

HYMNE see Piechler, Arthur

HYMNE see Pomper, A.

HYMNE see Schubert, Franz (Peter)

HYMNE AN DEN UNENDLICHEN see Schubert,
Franz (Peter)

HYMNE AN DIE NACHT "HEIL'GE NACHT, O
GIESSE DU" see Beethoven, Ludwig
van

HYMNE AN GOTT see Haydn, (Johann)
Michael

HYMNE DE L'OFFICE DU SOIR see Gevaert,
Francois Auguste

HYMNEN FUR DIE PROZESSION AM
FRONLEICHNAMSFEST see Messner,
Joseph

HYMNEN FUR DIE PROZESSION AM
FRONLEICHNAMSTAG see Benkert,
Lorenz

HYMNEN UND MOTETTEN ALTER MEISTER HEFT
1
(Bauerle, Hermann) [Lat] 4pt mix cor,
acap sc,cor pts BOHM s.p.
contains: Calegari, Antonio, Pange
Lingua-Tantum Ergo; Pitoni,
Giuseppe Ottavio, Pange Lingua-
Tantum Ergo   (H823)

HYMNEN UND MOTETTEN ALTER MEISTER HEFT
2
(Bauerle, Hermann) [Lat] 4pt mix cor,
acap sc,cor pts BOHM s.p.
contains: Croce, Giovanni, O Sacrum
Convivium; Palestrina, Giovanni,
Adoramus Te; Viadana, Lodovico
Grossi da, Adoramus Te   (H824)

HYMNEN UND MOTETTEN ALTER MEISTER HEFT
3
(Bauerle, Hermann) [Lat] 4pt mix cor,
acap sc,cor pts BOHM s.p.
contains: Bernabei, Giuseppe
Antonio, O Sacrum Convivium;
Casciolini, Claudio, Panis
Angelicus; Casciolini, Claudio,
Sacris Solemniis; Victoria, Tomas
Luis de, Domine, Non Sum Dignus
(H825)

HYMNI AD PROCESSIONEM IN FESTO CORPORIS
CHRISTI see Schroeder, Hermann

HYMNS AND SACRED SONGS see Hume,
Alexander

HYMNS FOR CELEBRATION *CC28U,Commun
cor ROYAL s.p.   (H826)

HYMNS OF HERITAGE *CC9L,hymn,US
(Ehret, Walter) SATB,kbd WORD 37685
$1.95   (H827)

HYMNS THAT LIVE *CC10UL
(Bolks, Dick) mix cor cmplt ed
LILLENAS MB-362 $1.50   (H828)

HYMNUS see Beethoven, Ludwig van, Kyrie

HYMNUS see Rosenberg, Hilding

HYMNUS see Willems, Josef

HYMNUS CREATURAE "GROSS IST DER HERR"
see Wittmer, Eberhard Ludwig

HYMNUS "GLORIA, LAUS ET HONOR" see
Spranger, Jorg

HYMNUS: JAUCHZET DEM HERRN see Silcher,
Friedrich

HYMNUS PARADISI see Howells, Herbert
Norman

HYMNUS (PART 4) see Zimmermann, Heinz
Werner

HYMNUS SOIXANTE-HUIT see Prin, Yves

I

I AM A POOR WAYFARING STRANGER *spir
(Eklund, Stig) mix cor GEHRMANS
KRB439 (I1)

I AM BOUND FOR THE KINGDOM
(Dinwiddie, R.) SATB,acap oct HOPE
CH 662 $.35 (I2)

I AM BOUND FOR THE PROMISED LAND see
Stennet, S.

I AM COME INTO MY GARDEN see Billings,
William

I AM NOT ALONE TODAY see Shea

I AM NOT WORTHY see Bixler

I AM REDEEMED FOREVERMORE see Mercer,
W. Elmo

I AM RESOLVED see Fillmore, James H.

I AM THANKFUL TO BE AN AMERICAN see
Skillings, Otis

I AM THE BREAD OF LIFE see Schiavone,
John

I AM THE DOOR see Hegenbart, Alex F.

I AM THE GOOD SHEPHERD see Burroughs,
Bob

I AM THE GOOD SHEPHERD see Roff, Joseph

I AM THE LIGHT see Johnson, Ralph

I AM THE RESURRECTION see Burroughs,
Bob

I AM THE RESURRECTION AND THE LIFE! see
Peterson, John W.

I AM THE ROSE OF SHARON see Billings,
William

I AM THE WAY see Furnivall, Anthony C.

I AM THINE, O LORD see Butler, A.L.

I AM TRUSTING THEE, LORD JESUS see
Smith

I AM TRUSTING THEE, LORD JESUS see
Smith, Lani

I AM WEARY OF MY GROANING see Morley,
Thomas, Laboravi In Gamitu Meo

I AM WITH YOU see Roff, Joseph

I ASK NONE ELSE OF THEE see Matthews,
David

I BEEN 'BUKED *spir
(Roberts) SATB oct LILLENAS AN-7008
$.25 (I3)

I BELIEVE
(Skillings) SSAATTBB oct BENSON S4137
$.45 (I4)
(Young, C.) SATB oct HOPE HO 1801
$.45 (I5)

I BELIEVE see Bartlett

I BELIEVE IN GOD see Denton, James

I BELIEVE IN MIRACLES see Peterson,
John W.

I BELIEVE IN ONE GOD see Green, Philip

I BELIEVE THAT JESUS DIED FOR ME see
Dunlop, Merrill

I BELIEVE THAT MY REDEEMER LIVES see
Peloquin, C. Alexander

I BELIVE see Ringwald, [Roy]

I BELIVE IN ALMIGHTY GOD see Sanders

I CALL ON THE LORD see Mahnke, Allan

I CAN BUT LOVE see Presser, William

I CAN FEEL THE SAVIOUR'S HAND see
Watters, William T.

I CAN KNOW see Meilstrup, David G.

I CAN SEE GOD see Carmichael, Ralph

I CHARGE YOU, O YE DAUGHTERS OF
JERUSALEM see Billings, William

I COME TO THEE see Presser, William

I COME TO THEE, JESUS *Xmas
(Follett) 2pt,opt ob&bells&fing.cym.
PRO ART 2808 $.35 (I6)

I COME WITH JOY see Lovelace, Austin C.

I COULDN'T HEAR NOBODY PRAY *spir
(Dawson, William) SATB,S solo (med)
FITZSIMONS 2008 $.25 (I7)

I DARE NOT BE DEFEATED see Zilch,
Margot

I DID WAIT IN PATIENCE FOR THEE see
Schumann, Robert (Alexander)

I DIDN'T KNOW see Ford, Olive Elizabeth

I DINA HELGONS SPAR see Holm, Gunnar

I FOUND HIM (IN A QUIET PLACE) see
Coates

I FOUND IT ALL IN JESUS see Mercer, W.
Elmo

I FOUND JOY see Grundy, S.K.

I FOUND THE LORD see Borge, Norman

I GOT A HOME IN-A DAT ROCK
(Wild, Eric) SATB (med diff) WATERLOO
$.60 (I8)

I GOT A ROBE *spir
(Ohrwall) 4pt mix cor ERIKS 55 s.p.
(I9)

I GOT A SHOES *spir
(Arch, Gwyn) SSA EMI (I10)

I GOT THE RHYTHM see Beard

I HAVE A FRIEND, HIS NAME IS JESUS see
Fox, Baynard

I HAVE A PEACE IN MY HEART see Paris

I HAVE COME FROM THE DARKNESS see
Chaplin

I HAVE DECIDED TO FOLLOW JESUS
*anthem/gospel
(DeCou, Harold) SATB oct SINGSPIR
ZJP-8166 $.30 (I11)
(Reynolds) SATB (easy) oct BROADMAN
4535-09 $.30 (I12)

I HAVE FOUND A HIDING PLACE see Weigle

I HAVE HOPE see Rambo, Dottie

I HAVE NO RIGHT see Carmichael, Ralph

I HEAR MUSIC see Stromberg, V.

I HEAR THY WELCOME VOICE see Hartsough,
L.

I HEARD THE BELLS ON CHRISTMAS DAY see
Newbury, Kent A.

I HEARD THE VOICE OF JESUS *gospel,Eng
(Ralston) 1-2pt oct LILLENAS AN-6004
$.30 (I13)

I HEARD THE VOICE OF JESUS see English

I HEARD THE VOICE OF JESUS SAY
(Johnson) SSAATTBB oct BENSON S4138
$.35 (I14)

I HEARD TWO SOLDIERS TALKING see
Williams, David H.

I HELA NATUREN see Olson, Daniel

I HERRENS TJANARE, PRISEN GUD see
Mendelssohn-Bartholdy, Felix,
Laudate Pueri

I HERRENS UTVALGTE see Kverno, Trond

I HIMMELEN, I HIMMELEN see Holm, Gunnar

I HUNGER AND THIRST see Wills, Arthur

I JUST CAME TO TALK WITH YOU, LORD see
Rambo, Dottie

I JUST COME FROM THE FOUNTAIN *spir
(Moore) SATB WARNER W-3418 $.30 (I15)

I JUST LOST see Carmichael, Ralph

I KNOW see Eichorn, Hermene Warlick

I KNOW A NAME see Lillenas, Haldor

I KNOW HE HOLDETH ME see Parks, Joe E.

I KNOW MY GOD see Irwin, Lois

I KNOW NOT HOW *Adv/Xmas
(Brandon, George) SATB ART MAST 117
$.30 (I16)

I KNOW THAT MY REDEEMER LIVES *CCU,
funeral
cor GIA G1702A $.50, ipa contains
works by: Gelineau; Andrews;
LaManna; Batastini (I17)

I KNOW THAT MY REDEEMER LIVES *Easter/
Gen,anthem
(DeCou, Harold) unis oct SINGSPIR
ZJP-3500 $.25 (I18)

I KNOW THAT MY REDEEMER LIVETH see
Fillmore, James H.

I KNOW THAT MY REDEEMER LIVETH see
Peterson, John W.

I KNOW THE SECRET see Winter, Sister
Miriam Therese

I KNOW WHERE I'M GOIN' *gospel,Scot
(Fettke) 2pt oct LILLENAS AT-1130
$.30 (I19)

I KNOW WHERE I'M GOIN' see Dahrouge

I KNOW WHERE I'M GOING *anthem/folk
(Huff) SATB oct BENSON S4139 $.35
(I20)
(Moffatt, James) SAB oct LORENZ 7849
$.35 (I21)
(Wyrtzen, Don) SATB oct SINGSPIR
ZJP-3588 $.25 (I22)

I KNOW WHERE I'M GOING see Moffatt

I LEAVE YE PEACE see Nystedt, Knut,
Fred Etterlater Jeg Dere

I LIFT MY HANDS TO THE LORD MOST HIGH
see Hruby, Delores

I LONG FOR THY SALVATION see Newbury,
Kent A.

I LOVE HIM TOO MUCH (TO FAIL HIM NOW)
see Wolfe

I LOVE THE LORD, HIS STRENGTH IS MINE
(Psalm 18) Fest,Ir
(Peninger) SABar&camb,SA/ST soli
HARRIS C17314 $.30 (I23)

I LOVE THE LORD, HIS STRENGTH IS MINE
see Peninger, David

I LOVE THEE *anthem
(Cromie, Marguerite Biggs) SATB,pno,
opt bells, opt Celeste (med easy)
PRESSER 312-41023 $.35 (I24)
(Littleton, Bill J.) 2pt,opt hndbl
FINE ARTS CM 1076 $.30 (I25)
(Wyrtzen, Don) SATB oct SINGSPIR
ZJP-7333 $.30 (I26)

I LOVE THEE see Ingall

I LOVE THEE, MY LORD *anthem
(Burroughs) SSA FINE ARTS TR 100 $.30
contains also: My Faith Has Found A
Resting Place (I27)
(Wood, Dale) SATB,acap ART MAST 162
$.35 (I28)

I LOVE THY CHURCH, O GOD see Snyder,
Wesley

I LOVE THY KINGDOM, LORD see Williams

I LOVE TO TELL THE STORY see Fischer,
William Gustavus

I LOVE TO TELL THE STORY see Hankey

I MANENS LJUS, I STJARNORS SKEN
*carol,Eng
(Angerdahl, Lars) SABar ERIKS 301
s.p. (I29)

I MEANT TO DO MY WORK TODAY see
Whitecotton, Shirley

I MET MY MASTER see Wilson, Roger C.

I MUST SHOUT HIS PRAISE see Burroughs,
Bob

I MUST TELL JESUS see Roberts

I NEED THEE EVERY HOUR *anthem
(Littleton, Bill J.) SATB FINE ARTS
CM 1026 $.30 (I30)

I NEED THEE, PRECIOUS JESUS see Reid

I NEVER FELT SUCH LOVE IN MY SOUL
BEFORE *spir
(Ferguson) SATB oct LILLENAS AN-3856
$.30 (I31)

I PRESENT YOU TO JESUS see Hathcock

I SACRI MISTERI *Greg
(Dallavecchia, Wolfango) cor ZANIBON
5323 s.p. (I32)

I SAID TO THE MAN WHO STOOD AT THE GATE
see Harris

I SAW A CROSS see Hunter, Harry A.

I SAW A MAIDEN see Pettman, Edgar

I SAW A STABLE see Parker, Alice

I SAW THE CROSS OF JESUS *Gd.Fri.,
anthem
(Mayfield, Lawrence) SATB oct
SINGSPIR ZJP-3521 $.30 (I33)

I SAW THE CROSS OF JESUS see Denton,
James

I SAW THREE SHIPS *Xmas,carol
see Eight Christmas Carols: Set 2
(Avalos) 3pt PRO ART 2774 $.35 (I34)
(Mead, G.) SATB GALAXY 1.1712.1 $.35
(I35)
(Mead, George) TTBB&jr cor GALAXY
1.1722.1 $.35 (I36)
(Morgan, Hilda) SSA (med easy)
WATERLOO $.35 (I37)
(Willcocks) SATB,acap OXFORD 43.340
$.30 see from Three Christmas
Carols (I38)

I SAW THREE SHIPS see Hruby, Delores

I SAW THREE SHIPS see Lang, C.S.

I SAW THREE SHIPS see Morgan, Hilda

I SEE A CRIMSON STREAM see Haywood, G.

I SEE A DAY see Runyan

I SEE HIM see Oldenburg, Bob

I SHALL BE SATISFIED see Zilch, Margot

I SHALL GIVE THANKS UNTO GOD see Van
Wormer, G.

I SHAME AT MINE UNWORTHINESS see
Dowland, John

I SHOULD HAVE BEEN CRUCIFIED see Jensen

I SING A SONG OF THE SAINTS OF GOD see
Marshall, Jane M.

I SING FOR THE JOY see Beard

I SING OF A MAIDEN see Anonymous

I SING OF A MAIDEN see Edwards, P.M.H.

I SING OF A MAIDEN see Gore, Richard T.

I SING OF A MAIDEN see Le Fleming,
Christopher (Kaye)

I SING OF A MAIDEN see Matthews, Thomas

I SING OF A MAIDEN see Shaw

I SING OF JESUS, MY LORD see Pottenger

I SING OF THE BIRTH see Paviour, Paul

I SING OF THEE see Weigle

I SING THE BIRTH see Powell, Robert J.

I SING THE GREATNESS OF OUR GOD see
Bock, Fred

I SING THE MIGHTY POWER OF GOD
*Thanks,anthem
(Lundberg, John) SATB oct SINGSPIR
ZJP-7312 $.30 (I39)
(Skillings, Otis) SATB oct LILLENAS
AN-2390 $.30 (I40)

I SING THE MIGHTY POWER OF GOD see Vick

I SING THE MIGHTY POWER OF GOD see
Young, P.

I STAND BEFORE MY GOD see Bach, Johann
Sebastian

I SURRENDER ALL *anthem
(Bass) SATB,T solo FINE ARTS CM 1087
$.35 (I41)

I THANK YOU GOD see Tipton, C.

I, THE ANGEL, AM OF GOD *Fr
SATB EMI s.p. (I42)

I TO THE HILLS WILL LIFT MINE EYES see
Hopkins, James F.

I VAGHI FIORI see Palestrina, Giovanni

I WAIT FOR THEE see Presser, William

I WAITED FOR THE LORD see Mendelssohn-
Bartholdy, Felix

I WANDERED LONELY AS A CLOUD see
Whitecotton, Shirley

I WANT JESUS MORE THAN ANYTHING see
Marsh

I WANT JESUS TO WALK WITH ME *anthem/
spir
SATB (med easy) oct LORENZ B238 $.30
(I43)
(Burroughs, Bob) SATB WORD CS-2580
$.30 see from Old Rugged Cross, The
(I44)
(Cram, James D.) SATB,Bar solo FINE
ARTS CM 1065 $.30 (I45)

I WANT THE WORLD TO KNOW see Smith

I WANT TO BE READY *spir
(Mickelson) SATB oct LILLENAS AN-3849
$.30 (I46)

I WANT TO BE THERE see Peterson, John
W.

I WANT TO BLOOM WHERE I'M PLANTED see
Harrison

I WANT TO DIE EASY *spir
(Roberts) SATB oct LILLENAS AN-7007
$.25 (I47)

I WANT TO SERVE THE LORD see Low, James
L.

I WANT TO TELL YOU OF JESUS see Tipton

I WANT TO THANK YOU see Frink

I WANT YOU see Hammack, Bobby

I WAS GLAD see Parry, Charles Hubert
Hastings

I WAS GLAD WHEN THEY SAID UNTO ME see
Snogren

I WAS GLAD WHEN THEY SAID UNTO ME see
Young

I WILL ARISE *folk
(Buffaloe, James) SATB,pno/org (med)
SHATTINGER 406 $.25 (I48)

I WILL ARISE see Armstrong, Mimi

I WILL ARISE see Hart

I WILL ARISE see Lovelace, Austin C.

I WILL ARISE AND GO TO JESUS *anthem/
gospel
(Carter, John) SATB,acap DEAN CD-105
$.45 (I49)
(Mickelson, Paul) SATB oct SINGSPIR
ZJP-8120 $.30 (I50)

I WILL COME AGAIN see Rasley, John M.

I WILL EXTOL THEE see Butler

I WILL EXTOL THEE see Watson, Ruth

I WILL GIVE PEACE see Ford

I WILL GIVE THANKS see Butler, Eugene

I WILL GIVE THANKS see Lorenz, Ellen
Jane

I WILL GIVE THANKS see Matthews, Thomas

I WILL GIVE THANKS see Purcell, Henry

I WILL GIVE THANKS see Silvester,
Frederick

I WILL GREATLY REJOICE see McLaughlin,
Marian

I WILL HEARKEN
(Sweetman, Paul) SATB (med easy)
WATERLOO $.40 (I51)

I WILL LIFT UP MINE EYES see Archer,
Violet

I WILL LIFT UP MINE EYES see Fleisher,
Simi

I WILL LIFT UP MINE EYES see Gibbs,
Alan

I WILL LIFT UP MINE EYES see Golde,
Walter

I WILL LIFT UP MINE EYES see Haan,
Raymond

I WILL LIFT UP MINE EYES see Lutkin,
Peter Christian

I WILL LIFT UP MINE EYES see McAfee

I WILL LIFT UP MINE EYES see Matthews,
Thomas

I WILL LIFT UP MINE EYES see Pool,
Kenneth

I WILL LIFT UP MINE EYES see Rogers,
Sharon Elery

I WILL LIFT UP MINE EYES see Rutter

I WILL LIFT UP MINE EYES see
Williamson, Malcolm

I WILL MAGNIFY THEE, O LORD see Goss,
John

I WILL NOT LEAVE YOU COMFORTLESS see
Burroughs, Bob

I WILL POUR MY SPIRIT see Leaf, Robert

I WILL PRAISE THE LORD see Turner

I WILL PRAISE THE NAME see Clark, Henry
A.

I WILL PRAISE THEE *hymn
(Fettke) SATB oct LILLENAS AT-1131
$.30 (I52)

I WILL PRAISE THEE see Glarum, L.
Stanley

I WILL PRAISE THEE see Hughes

I WILL PRAISE THEE, GOD see Nystedt,
Knut, Jeg Vil Prise Deg, Gud

I WILL PRAISE THEE, O LORD see Bowen

I WILL PROCLAIM HIS NAME WITH A SONG
see Landgrave, Phillip

I WILL SERVE THEE see Gaither, William
J. (Bill)

I WILL SING ALLELUIA see Mechem, Kirke

I WILL SING OF THY MIGHT see Butler

I WILL SING THE WONDROUS STORY see
Prichard, [Rowland Hugh]

I WILL SING THE WONDROUS STORY see
Rowley

I WILL SING TO THE LORD see Felciano,
Richard

I WILL SING TO THE LORD see Neff, James

I WISH WE'D ALL BEEN READY see Norman

I WISH YOU ALL COULD KNOW HIM *CCUL
(Marsh, Don) cor BENSON B0643 $1.95
stereo recording, tapes, and-or
accompaniment tape also available;
for book-record sets available,
contact publisher (I53)

I WISH YOU ALL COULD KNOW HIM see
Johnson, P.

I WONDER IF IT'S HAPPENED YET TO YOU
see Wyrtzen, Don

I WONDER WHY HE SHOULD LOVE ME see Fox,
Baynard

I WOULD BE TRUE see Gagliardi, George

I WOULD BE TRUE see Peek, Joseph Yates

ICH ABER BIN ELEND see Brahms, Johannes

ICH BETE AN DIE MACHT DER LIEBE see
Bortniansky, Dimitri Stepanovitch

ICH BIN DAS LICHT DER WELT see Fussan,
Werner

ICH BIN DER WEG see Christenius, Johann

ICH BIN DIE AUFERSTEHUNG see
Hollfelder, Waldram

ICH BIN DIE AUFERSTEHUNG UND DAS LEBEN
see Schmider, Karl

ICH BIN DIE AUFERSTEHUNG UND DAS LEBEN
see Schutz, Heinrich

ICH BIN GETAUFT AUF DEINEN NAMEN see
Peter, Johann Friedrich

ICH BIN GETAUFT AUF DEINEN NAMEN see
Reger, Max

ICH BIN'S! QUO VADIS, HOMO? see Marks, Gunther

ICH DANKE DIR, HERR JESU CHRIST see Franck, Melchior

ICH ERHEBE MEIN GEMUTE see L'Estocart, Paschal de

ICH FREU MICH DES see Vulpius, Melchior

ICH FREUE MICH, DASS MAN MIR SAGT see Schutz, Heinrich

ICH HAB EINEN GUTEN KAMPF GEKAMPFET see Staden, Johann

ICH HEBE MEINE AUGEN AUF see Bausznern, Dietrich von

ICH HEBE MEINE AUGEN AUF ZU DEN BERGEN see Schutz, Heinrich

ICH LIEGE UND SCHLAFE GANZ MIT FRIEDEN see Bach, Johann Christoph Friedrich

ICH RUF ZU DIR see Vento, Ivo de

ICH RUF ZU DIR, HERR JESU CHRIST see Gumpelzhaimer, Adam

ICH RUF ZU DIR, HERR JESU CHRIST see Schutz, Heinrich

ICH SAG DIR DANK, GOTT VATER GUT see Diener, Theodor

ICH SCHAU NACH JENEN BERGEN FERN see Eglin, Arthur

ICH SCHREIE ZUM HERREN see Rab, Valentin

ICH SINGE DIR MIT HERZ UND MUND see Kukuck, Felicitas

ICH STEH AN DEINER KRIPPE HIER see Eccard, Johannes

ICH STEH AN DEINER KRIPPE HIER see Schein, Johann Hermann

ICH TRETE HIER HEREIN see Brautigam, Helmut

ICH WAR AUF DEM FELD see Kuntz, Michael

ICH WEISS, DASS MEIN ERLOSER see Bach, Johann Michael

ICH WEISS, DASS MEIN ERLOSER LEBET see Fabricius

ICH WEISS, DASS MEIN ERLOSER LEBT see Burck, Joachim

ICH WEISS DIE HANDE GOTTES UBER MIR see Ah Know De Lord His Hands On Me

ICH WEISS, MEIN GOTT, DASS ALL MEIN TUN see Kramer, Gotthold

ICH WERFE MEINE FREUDE WIE VOGEL AN DEN HIMMEL see Burgmann, J. Hartmut

ICH WILL ALLZEIT ERHEBEN DICH see Schutz, Heinrich

ICH WILL DEN HERREN LOBEN see Rein, Walter

ICH WILL DEN NAMEN GOTTES LOBEN see Bach, Johann Sebastian

ICH WILL DES HERREN GNAD LOBSINGEN see Praetorius, Michael

ICH WILL DICH PREISEN, MEIN GOTT see Schmider, Karl

ICH WILL MEIN GANZES LEBEN see Schutz, Heinrich

ICH WILL MEINEN GEIST AUSGIESSEN see Studer, Hans

ICH WILL SEHR HOCH ERHOHEN DICH see Schutz, Heinrich

ICH WILL SINGEN VON DER GNADE DES HERRN EWIGLICH see Handel, George Frideric

ICH WILL VON HERZEN DANKEN GOTT see Schutz, Heinrich

ICHTHUS see Reynolds, William Jensen

ICY DECEMBER, THE *Xmas,anthem (Track, Gerhard) SATB,org (med easy) GIA G1871 $.50   (I54)

IERLEY, MERRITT
Adam Lay Y Bounden
SATB (med) oct CONCORDIA 98-2209 $.30   (I55)

Hear, O Thou Shepherd Of Israel
SATB (med) oct CONCORDIA 98-2162 $.35   (I56)

IF A MAN DIE see Berger, Jean

IF CHILDREN RULED THE WORLD *Contemp (Pitts, Clay) SATB VANGUARD V578 $.35 see from Let Trumpets Sound   (I57)

IF GOD WERE NOT UPON OUR SIDE see Bender, Jan

IF HE BE GOD see Zilch, Margot

IF I GAINED THE WORLD see Olander

IF I HAD ALL THE WORLD'S MONEY see Armstrong, Mimi

IF I WERE A FIFER see McNair, Jacqueline Hanna

IF I'VE FORGOTTEN see Stanphill, Ira F.

IF MY PEOPLE see Owens, Jimmy

IF MY PEOPLE see Vanderslice, Ellen

IF MY PEOPLE WILL PRAY see Owens, Jimmy

IF THAT ISN'T LOVE see Rambo, Dottie

IF THE CHRIST SHOULD COME TO ME see Wilson

IF THOU BUT SUFFER GOD TO GUIDE THEE see Bach, Johann Sebastian

IF THOU BUT SUFFER GOD TO GUIDE THEE see Mueller

IF THOU BUT SUFFER GOD TO GUIDE THEE see Neumark, Georg

IF THOU BUT SUFFER GOD TO GUIDE THEE see Peninger

IF WE BELIEVE THAT JESUS DIED see Goss, John

IF WITH ALL YOUR HEARTS see Pasquet, Jean

IF YOU ABIDE see Lanier, Gary

IF YOU LOVE ME see Uphaus

IF YOU REALLY LOVE HIM see Blankenship, Mark

IF YOU RECEIVE MY WORDS see Nystedt, Knut

IF YOU SEEK, YOU WILL FIND see Ford, Virgil T.

IF YOU WOULD HEAR THE ANGELS SING see Williams, David H.

IHLEBAEK, GUTTORM O.
Kantormusik - For Ogsa Kristus Led "Precentor's Music - For Christ Also Suffered" unis NORSK NMO 8781 s.p.   (I58)

Precentor's Music - For Christ Also Suffered *see Kantormusik - For Ogsa Kristus Led

IHR GESTIRN, IHR HOHEN LUFTE see Kaminski, Heinrich

IHR HIRTEN, IHR HIRTEN see Taubert, Karl Heinz

IHR KNECHTE GOTTES ALLZUGLEICH see Le Jeune, Claude

IK WEET DAT MIJN VERLOSSER LEEFT see De Koning

IK WIL ZINGEN VAN MIJN HEILAND mix cor sc HEER 2567 s.p.   (I59)

IKOS see Terzakis, Dimitri

IL BIANCO E DOLCE CIGNO see Bernardi, Steffano

IL CANTICO DI FRATE SOLE - LAUDES CREATURARUM DI SANTO FRANCESCO see Pratella, Francesco Balilla

IL EST NE *Adv/Xmas,carol,Fr see Eight Christmas Carols: Set 1 (Fettke) "He Is Born" SSATB,acap oct LILLENAS AN-6042 $.30   (I60) (Kirk) "He Is Born" [Eng/Fr] SATB, fing.cym. PRO ART 2794 $.35   (I61)

IL EST NE, LE DEVIN ENFANT *Xmas (McCauley) SATB (med easy) WATERLOO $.35   (I62)

IL GIUDIZIO DI SALOMONE see Procaccini, T.

IL NATALE see Sinigaglia, Leone

I'LL BELIEVE FOREVERMORE see Squire, Fred

I'LL GO NOW see Peterson, John W.

I'LL HEAR THE TRUMPET SOUND *anthem (Burroughs) SATB,opt 3trp&2trom FINE ARTS CM 1067 $.35   (I63)

I'LL LIE ME DOWN TO SLEEP IN PEACE see Coperario, Giovanni

I'LL NEVER BE THE SAME AGAIN see Wyrtzen, Don

I'LL RAISE MY VOICE TO SING see Lyman, Ed.

I'LL TELL THE WORLD see Fox, Baynard

I'LL TELL THE WORLD THAT I'M A CHRISTIAN see Fox, Baynard

I'LL TRUST AND NEVER BE AFRAID see Price

I'LL TRUST AND NEVER BE AFRAID see Van Der Puy, D.

ILLING, ROBERT
Cabra Mass
EMI s.p.   (I64)

Hail Mary
SSA EMI s.p.   (I65)

Let All The World
unis EMI   (I66)

Light Of The Church
SSA EMI s.p.   (I67)

I'M A-GOIN' TO GLORY see Stanphill, Ira F.

I'M A GONNA WALK *anthem (Littleton, Bill J.) SATB,med solo FINE ARTS EP 23 $.30   (I68)

I'M A SOLDIER see Peterson, John W.

IM ADVENT see Mendelssohn-Bartholdy, Felix

I'M ALIVE! see Goodwin, Daisy

IM DUNKELN TRET ICH GERN HINAUS see Taubert, Karl Heinz

IM FRIEDEN DEIN see Praetorius, Michael

IM FRIEDEN DEIN, O HERRE MEIN see Linke, Norbert

IM GARTEN LEIDET CHRISTUS NOT see Burck, Joachim

I'M GONNA BE FREE see Dailey, William

I'M GONNA KEEP ON SINGIN' see Crouch, Andrae

I'M GONNA KEEP ON SINGIN' see Crouch, Andrae

I'M GONNA LET MY LOVE SHINE see Roesch

I'M GONNA SING *anthem (Douglas) 2pt FINE ARTS CM 1005 $.35   (I69)

I'M GONNA WALK WITH JESUS see Roberts

I'M HERE, GOD'S HERE, NOW WE CAN START see Kaiser, Kurt

I'M HERE, GOD'S HERE, NOW WE CAN START see Kaiser, Kurt

IM KUHLEN MAI see Hassler, Hans Leo

I'M NOT ALONE see Peterson, John W.

I'M OK, YOU'RE OK see Smith, G. Alan

I'M REACHING OUT see Wild, Eric

I'M SO GLAD *anthem (Grady) SAT/SAB FINE ARTS EP 51 $.30   (I70)

I'M SO GLAD TROUBLE DON'T LAST ALWAYS (McLin) SATB KJOS 5898 $.35   (I71)

I'M SO HAPPY! see Gavitt

I'M SO NEEDY, HOLY SPIRIT see Nelson

IM STALL BEI ESEL, SCHAF UND RIND see
    Haus, Karl

IM STALL IN DER KRIPPE *Xmas,carol/
    folk
    (Kammeier, H.) [Ger] 4pt men cor
    MERSEBURG EM9046   (I72)

I'M TROUBLED *anthem
    (Littleton, Bill J.) SATB,med solo
    FINE ARTS CM 1061 $.30   (I73)

I'M TROUBLED IN MIND see Lenel, Ludwig

IMMORTAL BABE see Van Dyke

IMMORTAL, INVISIBLE *anthem
    (DeCou, Harold) SATB oct SINGSPIR
    ZJP-7242 $.30   (I74)

IMMORTAL, INVISIBLE, GOD ONLY-WISE see
    Terry, Barbara

IMMORTAL LOVE, FOREVER FULL *anthem
    (Dean) SATB (easy) oct BROADMAN
    4561-02 $.30   (I75)

IMPART see Paulus, Stephen

IMPROPERIA see Palestrina, Giovanni

IMPROPERIUM see Lassus, Roland de
    (Orlandus)

IMPROPERIUM see Petrassi, Goffredo

IMPROPERIUM see Spranger, Jorg

IMPROPERIUM see Stout, Alan

IMPROPERIUM EXSPECTAVI see Palestrina,
    Giovanni

IMPROPERIUM EXSPECTAVIT COR MEUM see
    Lassus, Roland de (Orlandus)

IN A CAVE see Franklin

IN A FAR OFF TOWN see Hrebic

IN A LITTLE TOWN CALLED BETHLEHEM see
    Lanier

IN A SILENT WORLD see Lyman, Ed.

IN A STABLE HEAVENLY BRIGHT see
    Eichorn, Hermene Warlick

IN ADVENT see Mendelssohn-Bartholdy,
    Felix, Im Advent

IN ALL THE WORLD see Powell, Robert J.

IN ASCENSIONE DOMINE see Eben, Petr

IN BETHLEHEM *Xmas
    (Bissell, Keith W.) unis (easy)
    WATERLOO $.30   (I76)
    (Graham, Robert) 2pt ART MAST 194
    $.35   (I77)

IN BETHLEHEM see Gennings

IN BETHLEHEM see Hill, Harry

IN BETHLEHEM see Parker, Alice

IN BETHLEHEM IS BORN see Hunnicutt,
    Judy

IN BETHLEHEM IS BORN A KING see Ehret,
    Walter

IN BETHLEHEM, THAT FAIR CITY
    (Payne) SATB,acap (easy) OXFORD
    94.327 $.30   (I78)

IN BETHLEHEM THAT WONDROUS NIGHT see
    Williams, David H.

IN CHRIST THERE IS NO EAST OR WEST see
    Gassman, Clark

IN CHRIST THERE IS NO EAST OR WEST
    *anthem
    (Johnson, Norman) SATB oct SINGSPIR
    ZJP-7283 $.25   (I79)

IN CONCEPTIONE IMMACULATA B.M.V. see
    Eben, Petr

IN CONVERTENDO DOMINUS see Peeters,
    Flor

IN COURTS ABOVE see Dale, Mervyn

IN DARK GETHSEMANE see Peterson, John
    W.

IN DE HOF VAN GETHSEMANE see Jurgens,
    Jac.

IN DEN ARMEN DEIN, O HERR JESU CHRISTE
    see Franck

IN DEO SPERAVIT COR MEUM see Lendvai,
    Erwin

IN DER PASSIONZEIT see Mendelssohn-
    Bartholdy, Felix

IN DICH HAB ICH GEHOFFET, HERR see
    Poser, Hans

IN DIE NATIVITATIS see Smert, Richard

IN DIESER OSTERLICHEN ZEIT see Eccard,
    Johannes

IN DIR IST FREUDE see Stern, Hermann

IN DULCI JUBILO *Adv/Xmas
    see Eight Christmas Carols: Set 1
    see Four Christmas Carols
    see Six Carols For SAB And Piano
    (Bauernfeind, Hans) wom cor,acap oct
    DOBLINGER s.p. see also In Dulci
    Jubilo   (I80)
    (Kaplan) SATB SCHIRM.G LG51714 $.35
                                            (I81)
    (Rust) men cor,acap TONOS 5639 s.p.
    contains also: Es Ist Ein Ros
    Entsprungen   (I82)

IN DULCI JUBILO see Backer, Hans

IN DULCI JUBILO see Eccard, Johannes

IN DULCI JUBILO see Lang, Hans

IN DULCI JUBILO see Murray, Margaret

IN DULCI JUBILO see Najera, Edmund

IN DULCI JUBILO see Pearsall, Robert
    Lucas de

IN DULCI JUBILO see Praetorius, Michael

IN DULCI JUBILO see Mc Kinney, Howard
    B.

IN DULCI JUBILO *Adv/Xmas
    (Bauernfeind, Hans) wom cor,acap
    cmplt ed DOBLINGER s.p.
    contains & see also: Es Hat Sich
    Halt Eroffnet; Es Ist Ein Ros
    Entsprungen; Es Wird Scho Glei
    Dumpa; In Dulci Jubilo; Juch-He;
    Maria Durch Ein Dornwald Ging; O
    Heiland Reiss Die Himmel Auf;
    Susani; Und Unser Lieben Frauen;
    Uns Ist Geborn Ein Kindelein; Uns
    Kommt Ein Schiff Gefahren; Zu
    Bethlehem Geboren   (I83)

IN ECCELESIIS see Gabrieli, Giovanni

IN ECCLESIIS see Gabrieli, Giovanni

IN EFRATA'S VELDEN see Gerretson

IN EINEM KRIPPELEIN *Xmas,carol/folk
    (Kammeier, H.) [Ger] 4pt men cor
    MERSEBURG EM9057   (I84)

IN EINEM KRIPPLEIN see Deutschmann,
    Gerhard

IN EXCELSIS GLORIA DEO *Xmas
    (Pears, James R.) SSA (med easy)
    WATERLOO $.30   (I85)

IN FAITH I QUIET WAIT see Bach, Johann
    Sebastian

IN FESTO CORPORIS CHRISTI see Eben,
    Petr

IN FESTO D.N. JESU CHRISTI REGIS see
    Eben, Petr

IN FESTO ST. CRUCIS see Palestrina,
    Giovanni

IN GOD I TRUST see Robertson

IN GOD WE TRUST see Mana-Zucca, Mme.

IN GOD WE TRUST see Skillings, Otis

IN GOTTES NAMEN FANG ICH AN see
    Kronberg, G.

IN GOTTES NAMEN WIR ANFAHN see
    Rothschuh, Franz

IN HEAVENLY LOVE see Beck, John Ness

IN HEAVENLY LOVE see Boozer

IN HEAVENLY LOVE ABIDING see Blair

IN HEAVENLY LOVE ABIDING see Brahms,
    Johannes

IN HEAVENLY LOVE ABIDING see Burroughs,
    Bob

IN HIM ALL THINGS WERE CREATED see
    Newbury, Kent A.

IN HIM I ABIDE see Traver, James F.

IN HIS HANDS see Atkins, John G.

IN HORA ULTIMA see Lassus, Roland de
    (Orlandus)

IN HORA ULTIMA see Zimmer, Jan

IN ILLO TEMPORE LOQUENTE JESU see
    Gombert, Nicolas

IN JEDEM NEUGEBORNEN KIND "DU DENKST
    UND HAST'S NICHT AUSGEDACHT" see
    Taubert, Karl Heinz

IN JENER LETZTEN DER NACHTE see
    Bruckner, Anton

IN LORD'S ATONING GRIEF *Easter
    (Fox, George) SATB (med diff)
    WATERLOO $.50   (I86)

IN LOUD THANKSGIVING PRAISE see
    Montgomery

IN LOVE *CC12U,Contemp
    wom cor,gtr/inst VANGUARD V579 $2.50
                                            (I87)

IN LOVE HE CAME see Frink

IN LOVE WITH THE LOVER OF MY SOUL see
    Kerr

IN ME GRATIA see Lemacher, Heinrich

IN MEINES HERZENS GRUNDE see Bach,
    Johann Sebastian

IN MEMORIA see Vivaldi, Antonio

IN MEMORIAM see Bevan, Gwilym

IN MEMORIAM see Carlier

IN MEMORY OF THE SAVIOR'S LOVE see
    Peninger

IN MONTE OLIVETI see Lassus, Roland de
    (Orlandus)

IN MONTE OLIVETI see Palestrina,
    Giovanni

IN MY FATHER'S HOUSE see Johnson, Paul

IN MY FATHER'S HOUSE see Rosenberg,
    Wolf

IN MY GARDEN see Young

IN MY HEART see Peterson, John W.

IN MY HEART THERE RINGS A MELODY see
    Roth

IN MY NAME: LORD'S SUPPER MUSIC FOR
    UNISON CHOIR see Burroughs, Bob

IN NIGHT'S DEEP SILENCE *Xmas,anthem/
    carol,Pol
    (Herter, J.) SATB (easy) GIA G1859
    $.30   (I88)

IN NOMINE JESU see Gallus, Jacobus

IN NOMINE JESU see Haydn, (Franz)
    Joseph

IN PACE see Des Prez, Josquin

IN PACE IN IDIPSUM see Taverner, John

IN PARADISE see Faure, Gabriel-Urbain,
    In Paradisum

IN PARADISUM see Faure, Gabriel-Urbain

IN PARADISUM "ES MOGEN ENGEL DICH
    GELEITEN" see Goller, Fritz

IN PASSION WEEK see Mendelssohn-
    Bartholdy, Felix, In Der
    Passionzeit

IN PEACE AND JOY see Nordin, Dayton W.

IN PEACE AND JOY I NOW DEPART see
    Brahms, Johannes, Warum Ist Das
    Licht Gegeben Den Muhseligen

IN PETRA STABILITUS NON CONCUITOR see
    Kayser, Leif

IN PLEASANT PLACES see Peterson, John
    W.

IN PRAESENTATIONE DOMINE see Eben, Petr

IN PRAISE OF EASTER see Locklair, Dan

IN PRAISE OF MARY see Bush, Geoffrey

IN PRAISE OF MARY'S SON see Kurth, Burton L.

IN PRAISE OF PEACE see Clarke, Henry Leland

IN PRAISE TO GOD see Hunnicutt, Judy

IN PRAYER TOGETHER see Dowland, John

IN PRINCIPIO ERAT VERBUM see Stout, Alan

IN REMEMBRANCE see Courtney, Ragan

IN REMEMBRANCE OF HIM see Peninger

IN REMEMBRANCE OF ME see Parks, Joe E.

IN SEINER ORDNUNG see Weber

IN TE, DOMINE, SPERAVI see Schutz, Heinrich

IN TE SPERAVI see Spranger, Jorg

IN TE SPERAVI, DOMINE see Wassmer, Berthold

IN THE AGES TO COME see Zilch, Margot

IN THE ARMS OF SWEET DELIVERANCE see Lister, Mosie

IN THE BEGINNING see Wild, Eric

IN THE BEGINNING see Winter, Sister Miriam Therese

IN THE BEGINNING WAS THE WORD see Lockwood, Normand

IN THE BLEAK MID-WINTER
SATB CIMINO $.40   (I89)

IN THE BLEAK MID-WINTER see Holst, Gustav

IN THE BLEAK MIDWINTER see Cram, James D.

IN THE CHILL OF WINTERTIME see Young

IN THE COOL OF THE EVENING
(Bolks, Dick) SATB,pno (med easy)
GENTRY G-216 $.35   (I90)

IN THE CROSS OF CHRIST I GLORY see Conkey, Ithamar

IN THE FULNESS OF TIME see Reynolds, William Jensen

IN THE IMAGE OF GOD see Peterson, John W.

IN THE LAST DAYS! see Kirk

IN THE LORD I PUT MY TRUST see Hovhaness, Alan

IN THE LORD'S ATONING GRIEF see Fox, George

IN THE LORD'S NAME see Kirby

IN THE MANGER *Xmas,folk,Fr
(Branscombe) [Fr/Eng] SSA (med)
FITZSIMONS 3072 $.20   (I91)

IN THE MIDNIGHT HEAVENS *Xmas,folk, Span
(Ehret, Walter) SSA,pno (easy) GENTRY
G-246 $.40   (I92)

IN THE MORNING see Hunter, Harry A.

IN THE SILENCE OF PRAYER see McCormick, [Clifford]

IN THE SPIRIT see Wood, Jeff

IN THE SWEET BY AND BY see Webster

IN THE TOWN OF BETHLEHEM see Powell, Robert J.

IN THE UPPER ROOM see Gaither, William J. (Bill)

IN THEE IS GLADNESS
see Three Hymns Of Praise

IN THEE IS GLADNESS see Gastoldi

IN THEE, O LORD see Glarum, L. Stanley

IN THEE, O LORD see Rolle, Johann Heinrich

IN THEE, O LORD see Thompson, R.G.

IN THEE, O LORD, HAVE I TRUSTED
*anthem
(Ehret) SATB oct BROADMAN 4545-90
$.30   (I93)

IN THIS OLD TROUBLED WORLD see Peterson, John W.

IN THY WORD DO I HOPE see Pfohl, H.

IN TIME OF PESTILENCE see Rorem, Ned

IN TIMES LIKE THESE see Jones

IN TRINITATIS SPECULUM "DER SPIEGEL DER DREIFALTIGKEIT" see Ahrens, Joseph

IN VENERIS ANNIS see Lassus, Roland de (Orlandus)

IN VENISTE ENIM GRATIAM see Victoria, Tomas Luis de

IN YOU, O LORD, HAVE I PUT MY TRUST see Campbell-Watson, Frank

INCARNATIO see Johnson

INCARNATION, THE see La Rowe, Jane

INCIPIT LAMENTATIO see Allegri, Gregorio

INCLINE THINE EAR TO ME see Himmel, Friedrich Heinrich

INDES DER SCHLAF see Killmayer, Wilhelm

INFANT CHRISTUS see Cassler, G. Winston

INFANT HOLY *Xmas,anthem/carol,Pol
SATB EMI s p contains also: On The
Bethlehem Road   (I94)
(Wagner, D.) SATB BOURNE B231001-358
$.45   (I95)
(Young, C.) SAB/SATB,bvl,perc,opt
pno/org/gtr oct AGAPE AG 7183 $.40
                                      (I96)

INFANT HOLY see Corina, John

INFANT HOLY, INFANT LOWLY see Hancock, Gerre

INFANT HOLY, INFANT LOWLY see Quimby, J.S.

INFANT JOY see George, Earl

INFANT KING
see Twelve Christmas Carols: Set 1

INFANT KING, THE see Pettman, Edgar

INFANT MOST BLEST! *Xmas,carol,Ger
(Ehret, W.) SATB,pno,opt fl/inst oct
NATIONAL WHC-53 $.40   (I97)

INGALL
I Love Thee *anthem
(Dale) SATB oct LILLENAS AN-2389
$.30   (I98)

INGALLS, JEREMIAH
Columbia *sac/sec
(Bennett, Lawrence) TTB,acap BROUDE
BR. see from Two Songs Of
Mourning   (I99)

Lamentation *sac/sec
(Bennett, Lawrence) TTB,acap BROUDE
BR. see from Two Songs Of
Mourning   (I100)

Northfield
see THREE FUGING-TUNES

Pilgrim's Farewell
(Bennett, Lawrence) TTB,acap BROUDE
BR.   (I101)

Two Songs Of Mourning *see Columbia;
Lamentation   (I102)

INGEGNERI, MARCO ANTONIO (1545-1592)
Caligaverunt Oculi Mei *Easter
(Klein) "My Eyes Are Blinded By My
Weeping" SATB SCHIRM.G 11986 $.35
                                      (I103)
My Eyes Are Blinded By My Weeping
*see Caligaverunt Oculi Mei

INGRAM, BILL
Great Commission, The (composed with
Reynolds, William Jensen)
*anthem
SATB (easy) oct BROADMAN 4533-68
$.30   (I104)

How Many Miles To Bethlehem?
1-2pt jr cor oct LILLENAS AN-4032
$.30   (I105)

Risen And Returning *Easter,cant
1-2pt jr cor,opt fl LILLENAS ME-17
$1.00   (I106)

INGRAM, BILL (cont'd.)

Tell The Good News *Gen,cant
jr cor,narrator,pno LILLENAS MP-603
$1.00   (I107)

INGRESSUS (PART 1) see Zimmermann, Heinz Werner

INIMICITIAS PONAM see Dietrich, Fritz

INIMICITIAS PONAM see Lemacher, Heinrich

INIMICITIAS PONAM see Welcker, Max

INMITTEN DER NACHT see Backer, Hans

INMITTEN DER NACHT see Kutzer, Ernst

INMITTEN DER NACHT see Lang, Hans

INMITTEN DER NACHT see Zoll, Paul

INNER PEACE SONG see Fischer, William Gustavus

INNES, JOHN
Prince Of Peace *Xmas,cant
SATB,narrator,SATB soli SINGSPIR
ZM7001 $1.95   (I108)

INNO AL BENE see Pratella, Francesco Balilla

INNO ALLA BELLEZZA DELLA VITA see Pratella, Francesco Balilla

INNO ALLA CETRA
see Raccolta Corale Libro I

INNO ALLA PATRIA see Pratella, Francesco Balilla

INNO DEI PREMILITARI see Pratella, Francesco Balilla

INNO DI GLORIA see Bossi, Marco Enrico

INNOVATIVE CHOIR, THE *CC21UL,cor-
resp/hymn/Introit
(Gerig, Richard) cor&cong LILLENAS
MB-298 $1.25   (I109)

INNSBRUCK, ICH MUSS DICH LASSEN see Isaac, Heinrich

INTENDE VOCIS ORATIONIS MEAE see Lassus, Roland de (Orlandus)

INTERCESSION see Holst, Gustav

INTERLUDIO see Gavazzeni, Gianandrea

INTO THE WOODS MY MASTER WENT see Briel, Marie

INTO THIS WORLD OF SORROWS see Bayley, Robert Charlton

INTO THY HANDS, O LORD see Pasquet, Jean

INTONUIT DE COELO see Filke, Max

INTRODUCTION see George, Earl

INTRODUZIONE AL GLORIA see Vivaldi, Antonio

INTROIT see Green, Philip

INTROIT AND KYRIE see Faure, Gabriel-Urbain

INTROIT FOR THANKSGIVING DAY see Pinkham, Daniel

INTROIT FOR THE NEW YEAR see Cabena, Barrie

INTROITS AND GRADUALS FOR THE CHURCH YEAR I see Gore, Richard T.

INTROITS AND GRADUALS II SECTION I see Gore, Richard T.

INTROITS AND RESPONSES see Werle, Floyd Edwards

INTROITS AND RESPONSES see Hall, William D.

INTROITS FOR LENT AND EASTER see Gore, Richard T.

INTROITUS (HOMAGE TO TON DE LEEUW) see Vriend, Jan

INTROITUS PA PASKDAGEN see Soderholm, Valdemar

INVENI DAVID see Bruckner, Anton

INVENI DAVID see Lachner, Franz

INVICTUS see Martin, Gilbert M.

INVIOLATA see Lemacher, Heinrich

INVIOLATA-FUNF MARIENGESANGE see
   Lemacher, Heinrich

INVITATORY CAROL see Belyea, W.H.

INVOCATION see Cousins, M. Thomas

INVOCATION see Mana-Zucca, Mme.

IPSA DEUM VIDI see Lassus, Roland de
   (Orlandus)

IRELAND, JOHN (1879-1962)
   Adam Lay Ybounden
      SATB EMI s.p.   (I110)

   Vexilla Regis
      SATB,brass/org STAINER 3.0793.1
      $2.00   (I111)

IRRET EUCH NICHT, GOTT LASST SICH NICHT
   SPOTTEN see Werner

IRVINE
   Lord's My Sheperd, The *anthem
      (Carmichael, Ralph) SATB oct
      SINGSPIR ZJP-7238 $.30   (I112)

IRVING, GEORGE
   Psalm 27
      (Walters, Robert) SATB oct GOSPEL
      05 TM 0132 $.35   (I113)

IRWIN, LOIS
   I Know My God
      (Cope, Paul) SATB oct GOSPEL
      05 TM 0151 $.20   (I114)

IS A LIGHT SHINING *spir
   (Christiansen) SATB oct SCHMITT 15021
   $.35   (I115)

IS ANY AFFLICTED, LET HIM PRAY see
   Billings, William

IS GOD FOR US see Schutz, Heinrich

IS IT NOTHING TO YOU? see Corina, John

IS IT NOTHING TO YOU? see Pedrette

IS IT NOTHING TO YOU? see Victoria,
   Tomas Luis de, O Vos Omnes?

IS THAT THE LIGHTS OF HOME? see Rambo,
   Dottie

IS THERE A PARADE IN BETHLEHEM? see
   Young, Gordon

IS THERE A REASON WHY?
   SATB UP WITH 6511 $.40   (I116)

IS THERE REALLY A GOD? see Skillings,
   Otis

IS THERE REASON see Runyan

IS YOUR ALL ON THE ALTAR? see Hoffman

ISAAC
   Nu Vilar Hela Jorden (composed with
      Praetorius, Michael; Bach)
      4pt mix cor ERIKS 46 s.p.   (I117)

ISAAC, HEINRICH (ca. 1450-1517)
   Credo IV Vocum
      see Messen Teil 1

   Ecce Virgo *mot
      mix cor (med easy) sc SCHOTTS
      C 43 563 s.p. contains also:
      Rorate Coeli Desuper   (I118)

   Innsbruck, Ich Muss Dich Lassen
      see Gumpelzhaimer, Adam, Glaube Ist
         Der Seele Leben
      mix cor (med easy) sc SCHOTTS
      CHBL 364 s.p.   (I119)

   Messen Teil 1 *Mass
      mix cor (med diff) cloth SCHOTTS
      s.p.
         contains: Credo IV Vocum; Missa
         De Beata Virgine, IV Vocum (I);
         Missa De Beata Virgine, V Vocum
         (I); Missa De Beata Virgine, V
         Vocum (II); Missa De Beata
         Virgine, VI Vocum   (I120)

   Messen Teil 2 *Mass
      (med) cloth SCHOTTS BSS 43 176 s.p.
         contains: Missa Argentum Et Aurum
         (4pt mix cor); Missa La Mi La
         Sol-O Praeclara (4pt mix cor);
         Missa Salva Nos (4pt mix cor);
         Missa Virgo Prudentissima (6pt
         mix cor)   (I121)

ISAAC, HEINRICH (cont'd.)
   Missa Argentum Et Aurum
      see Messen Teil 2

   Missa De Beata Virgine, IV Vocum (I)
      see Messen Teil 1

   Missa De Beata Virgine, V Vocum (I)
      see Messen Teil 1

   Missa De Beata Virgine, V Vocum (II)
      see Messen Teil 1

   Missa De Beata Virgine, VI Vocum
      see Messen Teil 1

   Missa La Mi La Sol-O Praeclara
      see Messen Teil 2

   Missa Salva Nos
      see Messen Teil 2

   Missa Virgo Prudentissima
      see Messen Teil 2

   Rorate Coeli Desuper
      see Isaac, Heinrich, Ecce Virgo

ISAAC WATTS CONTEMPLATES THE CROSS see
   Work, John [Wesley]

ISAACSON, MICHAEL
   Avodat Amamit
      [Heb] cor,gtr (Folk Service)
      TRANSCON. TCL 390 $3.50   (I122)

   Evening Prayer *see Hashkivenu

   Hashkivenu
      "Evening Prayer" [Eng] mix cor
      TRANSCON. TCL 619 $.75   (I123)

ISELE, D.C.
   Mass For A Feast Day
      SAB/SATB&cong,org (easy) GIA G1869
      $1.25   (I124)

   Notre Dame Mass, The
      SATB&cong,cantor,org (easy) GIA
      G1908 $1.50   (I125)

ISN'T IT REASSURING? see Sleeth,
   Natalie

ISN'T IT STRANGE?
   (Wild, Eric) SATB,pno BERANDOL
   BER1682 $.50   (I126)

ISN'T THE LOVE OF JESUS SOMETHING
   WONDERFUL see Peterson, John W.

ISRAEL see De Koning

ISRAELITISCHE TEMPEL COMPOSITIONEN see
   Dunajewsky, A.

IST GOTT FUR UNS, WER MAG WIDER UNS
   SEIN? see Schutz, Heinrich

IST NICHT EPHRAIM? see Schutz, Heinrich

ISTE CONFESSOR see Cavalli, (Pietro)
   Francesco

ISTI SUNT see Palestrina, Giovanni

IT CAME TO PASS IN SHUSHAN see Grimm,
   Carl Hugo

IT CAME UPON THE MIDNIGHT CLEAR
   see Six Christmas Hymns
   (Sharpe, E.) SA CRAMER $.20   (I127)

IT CAME UPON THE MIDNIGHT CLEAR see
   Clarke, Henry Leland

IT CAME UPON THE MIDNIGHT CLEAR see
   Wesley

IT CAN'T BE MUCH LONGER see Capers

IT IS A GOOD THING TO GIVE THANKS see
   Hurd, Michael

IT IS A GOOD THING TO GIVE THANKS UNTO
   THE LORD see Bartlett

IT IS GLORY JUST TO WALK WITH HIM see
   Lillenas, Haldor

IT IS GOOD TO GIVE THANKS see Kirby

IT IS NO DREAM OF MINE see Goossen,
   Frederic

IT IS OUR GOD see Bechler, Kroeger,
   Karl

IT IS TRULY WONDERFUL *CCU
   (Krogstad, Bob) SATB GOSPEL s.p.
                                           (I128)

IT IS WELL WITH MY SOUL see Bliss, Paul

IT IS WELL WITH MY SOUL see Roberts

IT MAY BE TODAY see Bixler

IT SHALL FLOW LIKE A RIVER see Weston,
   David

IT TOOK A MIRACLE see Peterson, John W.

IT WAS A COLD AND LONELY NIGHT see
   Walker, Jack

IT WAS FOR OUR INIQUITIES see Gebhard

ITE AD JOSEPH see Pasquier

ITE AD JOSEPH see Welcker, Max

IT'S A GIFT TO BE SIMPLE
   (Wells, Tony) SATB,opt gtr&bvl&drums
   MCAFEE M1082 $.40   (I129)

IT'S A HAPPY DAY see Phieffer, Don

IT'S A LONG ROAD TO FREEDOM see Winter,
   Sister Miriam Therese

IT'S A WONDERFUL, WONDERFUL LIFE! see
   Peterson, John W.

IT'S A YOUNG WORLD! see Eneberg, Gale
   (Gail)

IT'S CHRISTMAS TIME AGAIN see Bartlette

IT'S COOL IN THE FURNACE see Red, Buryl

IT'S COOL IN THE FURNACE see Red, Buryl

IT'S DARK, MARY *Contemp
   (Cockett; O'Riorda; Hermann) SATB
   VANGUARD V555 $.35 see from Go Tell
   Everyone   (I130)

IT'S GETTING LATE *see Azevedo, Lex
   de, Hosanna! Hallelujah!; Floria,
   Cam, He That Overcomes   (I131)

IT'S GETTING LATE see Azevedo, Lex de

IT'S GETTING LATE see Floria, Cam

IT'S GOTTA HAPPEN WITHIN see Boud, Ron

IT'S IN MY HEART see Slater, A.

IT'S ME *spir
   (Huntley, F.) TTBB (easy) FITZSIMONS
   4030 $.20   (I132)

IT'S NOT AN EASY ROAD see Peterson,
   John W.

IT'S OUR WORLD see Kaiser, Kurt

IT'S YOURS FOR THE ASKING see Holiday,
   Mickey

IV MOTETS see Ammann, Benno

I'VE DANCED SO HARD
   see Six Songs

I'VE GOT A REASON TO SING see
   Skillings, Otis

I'VE GOT CONFIDENCE see Crouch, Andrae

I'VE GOT JESUS see Smith

I'VE GOT JESUS see Smith, Lani

I'VE GOT JESUS IN MY HEART see Harris,
   Ron

I'VE GOT PEACE LIKE A RIVER see Turner

I'VE GOT THE HOPE OF THE WORLD see
   Blakeley

IVES
   Nova, Nova
      SATB (med easy) OXFORD 84.232 $.50
                                           (I133)

IVES, CHARLES (1874-1954)
   Celestial Country, The *cant
      cor,SSAATTBB soli,org,trp,strings,
      timp, euphonium cor pts PEER
      $1.40   (I134)

   Crossing The Bar
      (Kirkpatrick) SATB AMP A-702 $.60
                                           (I135)

   Easter Carol *Easter,carol
      (Kirkpatrick) SATB AMP A-684 $1.25
                                           (I136)

   Turn Ye, Turn Ye
      (Kirkpatrick, John) SATB,org (med)
      oct MERCURY 352-00464 $.40   (I137)

IVEY, ROBERT
   Choir Handbell Processional *Proces,
      anthem
      cor CHORISTERS R-11 $.15   (I138)

J

JACKSON
Carol For Christmas
(Indihar) SA oct SCHMITT 2134   (J1)

Communion Service (Series III)
SATB (med diff) OXFORD 42.385 $1.00
(J2)

Touch A Hand, Make A Friend *see
Banks

JACKSON, FRANCIS
Blessing And Glory
see FIVE ANTHEMS FOR TODAY

Sing A New Song To The Lord *anthem
SATB,S solo,org NOVELLO NCM 37 s.p.
(J3)

JACKSON, STEPHEN
Sweet Was The Song
see SIX CHRISTMAS CAROLS

JACOB, DOM CLEMENT
Le Chemin De La Croix *CCU
cor,narrator,strings sc JOBERT s.p.
(J4)

JACOB, GORDON (1895-   )
Babe So Sweet *Xmas
SATB STAINER 3.0829.1 $.50   (J5)

JACOB'S LADDER see Gilbert

JACOBSEN, KATHERINE
Et Facta Est Lux
WALTON M132 $1.50   (J6)

JAESCHKE
Less Than The Least Of All Thy
Mercies
(Kroeger, Karl) 2pt treb cor
FISCHER,C CM 7878 $.35   (J7)

My Faith Is In Thee
(Pfohl) mix cor BRODT 103 $.26 (J8)

One Thing We Ask, O Lord
(Pfohl) mix cor BRODT 106 $.28 (J9)

**JAG AR ROSTEN AV EN SOM ROPAR see
Hemberg, Eskil**

JAG AR VARLDENS LJUS see Olson, Daniel

**JAG HAR ETT BLOMSTER KANNA LART see
Wideen, Ivar**

JAG LANGTAR AV ALLT HJARTA *folk
(Ohrwall) 4pt mix cor ERIKS 302 s.p.
(J10)

**JAG TACKAR DIG, MIN HOGSTE GUD see
Staden, Johann**

JAHWE, O GOD DER GODEN see De Koning

JAKES
Laughter In Bethlehem (composed with
Martin, Gilbert M.) *Xmas,anthem
SATB oct MCAFEE M1053 $.40   (J11)

**JAM MEA CERTA MANENT see Lassus, Roland
de (Orlandus)**

**JAM NON DICAM VOS SERVOS see Gabrieli,
Giovanni**

JAMES, D.
Christmas Night
SSAATB,acap (med) FITZSIMONS 2046
$.20   (J12)

Little Jesus Came To Town, The *Xmas
SSAATTBB,acap (med) FITZSIMONS 2053
$.20   (J13)

JAMES, DOROTHY (1901-   )
Mary's Lullaby *Xmas
4pt treb cor (diff) FITZSIMONS 3066
$.20   (J14)

JAMES, MARY
All For Jesus
(Ferrin, Paul) SATB oct GOSPEL
05 TM 0110 $.20   (J15)

JAMES, WILL (1896-   )
Alleluia
SATB,acap (easy) FITZSIMONS 2109
$.25   (J16)
SSA (easy) FITZSIMONS 3083 $.25
(J17)

Hail The Day That Sees Him Rise
*Easter
SSAATTBB,acap (med) FITZSIMONS 2169
$.25   (J18)

Hymn Of Joy
SSATTBB,A solo,acap (easy)
FITZSIMONS 2102 $.25   (J19)

JAMES, WILL (cont'd.)
Little Jesus Came To Town, The *Xmas
SSA (easy) FITZSIMONS 3064 $.20
(J20)

SATB (easy) FITZSIMONS 2144 $.25
(J21)

Prepare Ye The Way Of The Lord
SSATTBB,acap (easy) FITZSIMONS 2125
$.30   (J22)

Preserve My Soul, O God *Bibl
SATB,acap (easy) FITZSIMONS 2086
$.25   (J23)

Sing And Rejoice *Bibl
SSATTBB,acap (easy) FITZSIMONS 2079
$.25   (J24)

Song Of Praise, A *Gen/Thanks
SATB,acap (easy) FITZSIMONS 2115
$.25   (J25)

JANACEK, LEOS (1854-1928)
Hospodine Pomiluj Ny *cant
"Lord Have Mercy Upon Us" [Czech/
Ger] mix cor&mix cor,4 soli,org,
3trp,4trom,tuba,harp SUPRAPHON
s.p.   (J26)

Lord Have Mercy Upon Us *see
Hospodine Pomiluj Ny

Unfinished Mass, The
(Petrzelka, V.) [Lat] mix cor,soli,
2fl,2ob,2clar,2bsn,4horn,3trp,
3trom,tuba,timp,perc,harp,strings
SUPRAPHON s.p.   (J27)

Unvollendete Messe Es-Dur (Kyrie,
Credo, Agnus Dei) *Mass
SAIB,SATB soli,org (med) BAREN.
BA5421   (J28)

JANNEQUIN, CLEMENT (ca. 1475-ca. 1560)
Mass "La Bataille"
SATB,acap SALABERT-US $5.00   (J29)

JANSON, T.
Eternal Voices
SATB,solo,acap GRAY CCS 23 $.35
(J30)

**JATI BAO ALLUR HEIMUR HER see
Stefansson, Fjolnir**

JATON
Quatre-Vent Motets *CC24U,mot
4pt,acap HENN 402 s.p. sc, voc pt
(J31)

**JAUCHZ, ERD UND HIMMEL see Praetorius,
Michael**

**JAUCHZE, ALLE WELT, DEM HERREN see
Lang, Hans, Jubilate Deo**

**JAUCHZE, DU TOCHTER SION FSP see
Seckinger, Konrad**

**JAUCHZET, ALLE LANDE, GOTT ZU EHREN see
Zehner**

**JAUCHZET DEM HERREN, ALLE LANDE see
Heer, Emil**

**JAUCHZET DEM HERREN, ALLE WELT see
Hammerschmidt, Andreas**

**JAUCHZET DEM HERREN, ALLE WELT see
Schutz, Heinrich**

**JAUCHZET DEM HERREN, ALLE WELT see
Staden, Johann**

JAUCHZET DEM HERRN see Burkhard Willy

**JAUCHZET DEM HERRN, ALLE WELT see
Bernhard, Christoph**

**JAUCHZET DEM HERRN ALLE WELT see
Fortner, Wolfgang**

**JAUCHZET DEM HERRN ALLE WELT see
Mendelssohn-Bartholdy, Felix**

JAUCHZET, FROHLOCKT see Batten, Adrian

**JAUCHZET GOTT, ALLE LANDE see Haubler,
Ernst**

**JAUCHZET GOTT, ALLE LANDE see
Kromolicki, Joseph**

**JAUCHZET GOTT ALLE LANDE SEHR see
Schutz, Heinrich**

**JAUCHZET GOTT, DEM HERREN, ALLE WELT
see Zimmermann, Heinz Werner**

**JAUCHZET HELL, PREISET LAUT UNSERM
JESUM see Buxtehude, Dietrich,
Canite Jesu Nostro**

**JAUCHZET, IHR HIMMEL see Telemann,
Georg Philipp**

**JAUCHZT, ALLE LANDE, GOTT ZU EHREN see
Koch, Johannes H.E.**

JAZZELUIA see Kaufmann, Ronald

**JE VEUX RESTER EN PAIX see Bach, Johann
Sebastian**

JEEP
Ancient Of Days *anthem
(Pool, Kenneth) SATB oct SINGSPIR
ZCP-7224 $.25   (J32)

**JEG VIL PRISE DEG, GUD see Nystedt,
Knut**

JEHN
Kleine Osterkantate "Auferstanden
Heute" *Easter
SA,2treb inst, xylophone HANSSLER
12.228 s.p. contains also:
Kramer, Gotthold, Christ Ist
Erstanden (SA,bass inst,opt 2treb
inst)   (J33)

Singt Das Lied Der Freude Uber Gott
unis,fl, bass xylophone sc HANSSLER
12.229 s.p. contains also:
Kretzschmar, Gunther, Rufe Mich
An In Der Not (unis,2A rec,timp,
glockenspiel, metallophone,
xylophone)   (J34)

JENNI
Ad Te Levavi
SATB AMP A-708 $.40   (J35)

JENNI, DONALD
Ave Verum Corpus
SAT,acap AM.COMP.AL. $.55   (J36)

Cantata Anglica In Honorem Thaddaei
Fratris Domini
SATB,STB soli,fl,2ob,bsn,horn,trp,
trom, English horn AM.COMP.AL. sc
$7.70, ipa, voc pt $5.50   (J37)

Ecce Sacerdos Magnus
SATB,org AM.COMP.AL. $1.38   (J38)
SATB,acap AM.COMP.AL. $1.38   (J39)

Gloria
[Eng] SATB,acap AM.COMP.AL. $1.10
(J40)

Missa Brevis In Honore Sanctae
Julianae
2pt,acap AM.COMP.AL. $2.20   (J41)

On The Life Of Jesu *chorale
STB,acap AM.COMP.AL. $1.38   (J42)

Vox In Rama
SATB,acap AM.COMP.AL. $2.20   (J43)

JENNINGS
Gentle Jesus, Holy Saviour *Adv/Xmas
(Ehret) SATB oct LILLENAS AN-3877
$.30   (J44)

JENNINGS, KENNETH L.
Easter Narrative *anthem
SATB,org,fl AUGSBURG 11-1727 $.45
(J45)

He Is Risen *Easter,anthem
mix cor,opt org&inst AUGSBURG
11-1731 $.30   (J46)

Love Came Down At Christmas *Xmas,
anthem
SSAA AUGSBURG 11-1728 $.25   (J47)

JENNY, ALBERT (1912-   )
Messe SS Cordis Jesu
4pt mix cor,pno/org HENN 513 s.p.
sc, voc pt   (J48)

JENSEN
Forever Is A Long, Long Time
(Mercer, W. Elmo) SATB oct BENSON
S4102 $.30   (J49)

I Should Have Been Crucified
*Easter/Gen
(Mercer, W. Elmo) SSATB oct BENSON
S4379 $.35   (J50)

Redemption Draweth Nigh *gospel
(Fettke) SATB oct LILLENAS AT-1134
$.35   (J51)
(Huff, Ronn) SSATB oct BENSON S4259
$.30   (J52)
(Mercer, W. Elmo) SSATB oct BENSON
S4253 $.40   (J53)

JENSEN, DONALD F.
Susanni *Xmas
SATB&jr cor,opt hndbl CHORISTERS
A-61 $.40   (J54)

JENSEN, WILMA
Harvest Time Of Love *Xmas
unis,fl,hndbl,fing.cym.,gtr,org
CHORISTERS A-92 $.40   (J55)

JEPHTE see Carissimi, Giacomo, Jephthah

JEPHTHAH see Carissimi, Giacomo

JEPPESEN, KNUD (1892-1974)
    Five Motets *see Hear My Prayer, O
        My God (Psalm 55); O Lord, How
        Numerous Are My Foes (Psalm 3);
        One Thing Have I Desired Of The
        Lord (Psalm 27); Praise God, My
        Soul (Psalm 103); What Is A Man?
                                        (J56)
    Hear My Prayer, O My God (Psalm 55)
        SATB,acap BROUDE BR. $.35 see from
        Five Motets   (J57)

    O Lord, How Numerous Are My Foes
        (Psalm 3)
        SATB,acap BROUDE BR. $.35 see from
        Five Motets   (J58)

    One Thing Have I Desired Of The Lord
        (Psalm 27)
        SATB,acap BROUDE BR. $.35 see from
        Five Motets   (J59)

    Praise God, My Soul (Psalm 103)
        SATB,acap BROUDE BR. $.35 see from
        Five Motets   (J60)

    Psalm 3 *see O Lord, How Numerous
        Are My Foes

    Psalm 27 *see One Thing Have I
        Desired Of The Lord

    Psalm 55 *see Hear My Prayer, O My
        God

    Psalm 103 *see Praise God, My Soul

    What Is A Man?
        SATB,acap BROUDE BR. $.35 see from
        Five Motets   (J61)

JEPTHE see Carissimi, Giacomo, Jephthah

JEREMIAH'S CRY - OH MY STRICT LORD AND
    MASTER see Truhlar, Jan, Jeremiasuv
    Plac - O, Prisny Pane Muj

JEREMIASUV PLAC - O, PRISNY PANE MUJ
    see Truhlar, Jan

JERGENSON, DALE
    Lament Of Job
        SATB SCHIRM.G 12030 $.75   (J62)

JEROME, HOWARD W.
    Lord's Prayer, The *prayer
        SATB HARRIS $.35   (J63)

JEROME, PETER
    Seven Tunes For Twelve Psalms *CC7U,
        Gen/Thanks,Psalm
        unis/2pt,pno,opt hndbl/perc
        CHORISTERS A-115 $.55   (J64)

JERUSALEM see Blake

JERUSALEM see Boyd, Jack

JERUSALEM see Walker, William

JERUSALEM, HAV UPP DIN ROST see
    Hemberg, Eskil

JERUSALEM THE GOLDEN see Avery, S.R.

JERUZALEM, JERUZALEM see Pronk, Arie

JESOUS AHATONHIA *carol
    see Two Christmas Carols
    (Willan, Healey) SATB (Huron) HARRIS
    $.35   (J65)

JESOUS AHATONHIA see Read

JESU *anthem/medley
    (Skillings, Otis) SATB oct LILLENAS
    AT-1118 $.30   (J66)

JESU ALMIGHTY see Crawley

JESU CHRISTE, GOTTES LAMM see Cabezon,
    Antonio de

JESU, DER DU MEINE SEELE see Bach,
    Johann Sebastian

JESU DULCIS MEMORIA see Parris, Robert

JESU DULCIS MEMORIA see Victoria, Tomas
    Luis de

JESU DULCISSIME see Schutz, Heinrich

JESU EST NE PARMI LES FLEURS see Delaye

JESU, GEH VORAN see Bach, Johann
    Sebastian

JESU, GEH VORAN see Drese

JESU, GEH VORAN see Hollfelder, Waldram

JESU, GIB GESUNDE AUGEN see
    Gunsenheimer, Gustav

JESU, GRANT ME THIS I PRAY see Gibbons,
    Orlando

JESU, HILF SIEGEN see Gunsenheimer,
    Gustav

JESU, JESU KOMM ZU MIR see Ahrens,
    Joseph

JESU, JESU, MOST AND LEAST see Deihl,
    W.H.

JESU, MEINE FREUDE see Buxtehude,
    Dietrich

JESU, MEINE FREUDE see Cruger, Johann

JESU, MERCY, HOW MAY THIS BE? see
    Browne, John [Lewis]

JESU NACHTGESPRACH MIT NIKODEMUS "ES
    WAR ABER EIN MENSCH UNTER DEN
    PHARISAERN" see Reutter, Hermann

JESU NOSTRA REDEMPTIO see Kutzer, Ernst

JESU, NUN SEI GEPREISET see Bach,
    Johann Sebastian

JESU, PRICELESS TREASURE see Bach,
    Johann Sebastian

JESU, PRICELESS TREASURE see Cruger,
    Johann, Jesu, Meine Freude

JESU REDEMPTOR OMNIUM see Bencini,
    Pietro Paolo

JESU REDEMPTOR OMNIUM see Haydn,
    (Johann) Michael

JESU REX ADMIRABILIS see Palestrina,
    Giovanni

JESU, SON OF GOD see Waite

JESU, SON OF MARY see MacNutt, Walter

JESU SPES POENITENTIBUS see
    Schattenberg, Thomas

JESU, SPLENDOR PATRIS see Lemacher,
    Heinrich

JESU, TENDER SAVIOUR see Grieg, Edvard
    Hagerup

JESU, TENDER SHEPHERD see MacLennan,
    Robert

JESU, THOU THE VIRGIN-BORN see Holst,
    Gustav

JESU, WORD OF GOD INCARNATE see Mozart,
    Wolfgang Amadeus, Ave Verum

JESU, WORD OF GOD INCARNATE see Mozart,
    Wolfgang Amadeus, Ave Verum [2]

JESU, WORD OF GOD INCARNATE see
    Wilkinson, Charles A.

JESUKIN see Fogg, Eric

JESUS see Cole, Letha

JESUS see Wetzler, Robert

JESUS ALL MIN GLADJE BLIVER see Bach,
    Johann Sebastian, Jesus Bleibet
    Meine Freude

JESUS, ALL OUR SOULS INSPIRE see Hus-
    Reimann

JESUS, ALLELULA see Burroughs, Bob

JESUS AND ME see Stanphill, Ira F.

JESUS AND THE WOOLLY SHEEP see Newbury,
    Kent A.

JESUS AUTEM HODIE see Davies, Peter
    Maxwell

JESUS, BABE OF BETHLEHEM see Overley,
    Henry

JESUS BIDS US SHINE see Miller

JESUS BLEIBET MEINE FREUDE see Bach,
    Johann Sebastian

JESUS CALLS US *anthem
    (Brandon, George) SAB/SATB VOLKWEIN
    VB-743 $.30   (J67)
    (Williams) SATB oct BROADMAN 4551-94
    $.30   (J68)

JESUS CALLS US see Mueller

JESUS CALLS US see Wilson

JESUS CHILD see Race, Steve

JESUS CHILD see Rutter

JESUS CHRIST IS BORN TODAY see Butler,
    Eugene

JESUS CHRIST IS KING see Rains, Dorothy
    Best

JESUS CHRIST IS RISEN TODAY, HALLELUYAH
    see Horman, John D.

JESUS CHRIST IS THE SAME see Dailey,
    William

JESUS CHRIST IS THE SAME, YESTERDAY,
    TODAY AND FOREVER see Prussing,
    Stephen

JESUS CHRIST, THE CRUCIFIED *Easter,
    anthem
    (Bartlett) SSA FINE ARTS TR 105 $.30
    contains also: Leaning On The
    Everlasting Arms (Raper)   (J69)

JESUS CHRIST, THE HOLY INFANT *Xmas,
    Contemp
    SATB VANGUARD V568 $.35 see from Come
    To Bethlehem   (J70)

JESUS CHRIST WAS BORN THIS DAY see
    Traver, James Ferris

JESUS CHRISTUS, UNSER HEILAND, DER VON
    UNS DEN GOTTESZORN WANDT see
    Fiebig, Kurt

JESUS, DER RETTER IM SEESTRUM "UND
    SIEHE, DA GING EIN STURMWIND AUF
    DEN SEE NIEDER" see Strohbach,
    Siegfried

JESUS, DIE AUFERSTEHUNG UND DAS LEBEN
    "UND ES GESCHAH" see Strohbach,
    Siegfried

JESUS DIED ON CALVARY'S MOUNTAIN *ECY,
    anthem/folk,US
    (Hughes, Robert J.) SATB,med solo
    (med easy) oct LORENZ B233 $.35
                                      (J71)

JESUS DIED ON CALVARY'S MOUNTAIN see
    Hughes

JESUS DULCIS MEMORIA see Kutzer, Ernst

JESUS DULCIS MEMORIA see Victoria,
    Tomas Luis de

JESUS ER MITT HAP, MIN TROST see Nyhus,
    Rolf

JESUS, GENTLE LAMB see Courtney, Ragan

JESUS GIVES ME A SONG see Grimes

JESUS GIVES ME SWEET PEACE see
    Reynolds, William Jensen

JESUS GOES WITH ME WHEREVER I GO see
    Watters, William T.

JESUS HAS LIFTED ME see Williamson

JESUS (HE IS THE SON OF GOD) see Lee

JESUS HEILT EINEN GELAHMTEN "SIEHE, DA
    BRACHTEN SIE ZU JESUS EINEN
    GELAHMTEN" see Strohbach, Siegfried

JESUS, I AM RESTING
    see He Lives!

JESUS, I AM RESTING see Mountain, James

JESUS, I LONG FOR THY PRESENCE see
    Williams

JESUS! I LOVE HIM BEST see Skaggs, M.

JESUS, I LOVE THEE see Smith

JESUS IN THE MORNING *anthem
    (Burroughs, Bob) SATB WORD CS-2576
    $.30   (J72)

JESUS IN US HAS BEGUN see Lanier

JESUS IS A PRECIOUS NAME see Peterson,
    John W.

JESUS IS ALL THE WORLD TO ME see
    Thompson

JESUS IS CALLING see Sparling, William

JESUS IS COMING AGAIN see Peterson,
    John W.

JESUS IS COMING SOON see Parks

JESUS IS COMING! (THEME II) see
Peterson, John W.

JESUS IS HIS NAME see Mercer, W. Elmo

JESUS IS LORD! see Peninger

JESUS IS LORD OF ALL see Gaither,
William J. (Bill)

JESUS IS MIGHTY see Vandall

JESUS IS MY SHEPHERD
see There Is A Song

JESUS IS MY SHEPHERD see Munger, Oren

JESUS IS THE FRIEND OF SINNERS see
Peterson, John W.

JESUS IST KOMMEN see Gadsch, Herbert

JESUS IST KOMMEN, GRUND EWIGER FREUDE
see Oertzen, Rudolf von

JESUS, JESUS
(White, Herbert) SATB (med easy)
WATERLOO $.40   (J73)

JESUS! JESUS! see Owens

JESUS, JESUS, REST YOUR HEAD *Adv/
Xmas,anthem/folk,US
(Christiansen, Paul) SATB,acap ART
MAST 153 $.30   (J74)
(Fjerstad) 2pt oct SCHMITT 253 $.30
(J75)
(Hegarty, David H.) SATB,T/S solo
(med easy) oct LORENZ B230 $.30
(J76)

JESUS, JESUS, REST YOUR HEAD see
Davison, M.T.

JESUS, JESUS, REST YOUR HEAD see
Hegarty, David H

JESUS, JOY AND PLEASURE see Buxtehude,
Dietrich

JESUS, JOY AND TREASURE see Cruger,
Johann, Jesu, Meine Freude

JESUS, KEEP ME NEAR THE CROSS *anthem
(Raymer) SATB (easy) oct BROADMAN
4540-29 $.30   (J77)

JESUS, LEAD THOU ON see Brandon, George

JESUS LEBT, MIT IHM AUCH ICH see Reger,
Max

JESUS LED ME ALL THE WAY see Peterson,
John W.

JESUS LIVES *anthem
(Sider) SATB oct BROADMAN 4554-85
$.30   (J78)

JESUS, LORD OF ALL CREATION see Handel,
George Frideric

JESUS, LORD, WE LOOK TO THEE see Hebble

JESUS, LOVER OF MY SOUL see Diemer,
Emma Lou

JESUS, LOVER OF MY SOUL see Parry,
Charles Hubert Hastings

JESUS, LOVER OF MY SOUL see Smith

JESUS, LOVER OF MY SOUL see Wesley

JESUS LOVES EVEN ME *Easter/Gen
(Mercer, W. Elmo) SATB oct BENSON
S4158 $.30   (J79)

JESUS LOVES ME *anthem
(Littleton, Bill J.) SATB FINE ARTS
CM 1103 $.35   (J80)

JESUS LOVES ME see Bradbury

JESUS LOVES ME see Bradbury, William
Batchelder

JESUS LOVES ME see Burroughs, Bob

JESUS MAKES MY HEART REJOICE *hymn
(Dunford, B.) SATB,org (Moravian)
FISCHER,J FEC 10115 $.30   (J81)

JESUS MAKES MY HEART REJOICE see Pfohl,
J.C.

JESUS, MEINE ZUVERSICHT
men cor,acap TONOS 5618 s.p.   (J82)

JESUS MERCIFUL see Hughes, Kent

JESUS, MY EVERYTHING see Cates

JESUS, MY JOY see Wyrtzen, Don

JESUS MY LORD, MY LIFE, MY ALL see
Burroughs

JESUS, MY LOVE AND MY LIKING see
MacLennan, Robert

JESUS, NAME ALL NAMES ABOVE see Strom

JESUS, NAME OF WONDROUS LOVE see
Butler, Eugene

JESUS, NAME OF WONDROUS LOVE see How

JESUS! NAME OF WONDROUS LOVE! see
Lockwood, Normand

JESUS OF NAZARETH see Eagle, M. Rosalyn

JESUS ON THE WATERSIDE *spir
(Aschenbrenner) TTBB,acap (med)
FITZSIMONS 4044 $.25   (J83)

JESUS OUR LORD ON THIS DAY WAS BORN see
Schutz, Heinrich, Heute Ist
Christus Der Herr Geboren

JESUS, OUR LORD, WE ADORE THEE see
Mabry

JESUS, OUR SAVIOR *anthem
(Peninger) SATB oct BROADMAN 4545-95
$.30   (J84)

JESUS PAID IT ALL *anthem
(Mulloy) SATB oct BROADMAN 4540-85
$.30   (J85)

JESUS PAID IT ALL see Grape

JESUS, PRECIOUS JESUS see Blankenship,
Mark

JESUS! PRECIOUS NAME! see Billingsley

JESUS, REDEEMER UNCHANGING see Bach,
Johann Sebastian

JESUS, REFUGE OF THE WEARY see Carlson,
Gordon

JESUS SAID TO THE BLIND MAN see
Vulpius, Melchior, Jesus Sprach Zu
Dem Blinden

JESUS SAVES *anthem
(Angell) SATB FINE ARTS CM 1041 $.35
(J86)

JESUS SAVES see Denton, James

JESUS SAVES see Kirkpatrick

JESUS, SAVIOR, PILOT ME see Hall

JESUS SHALL REIGN *anthem
(Hughes, Robert J.) SATB&wom cor (med
easy) oct LORENZ B235 $.35   (J87)

JESUS SHALL REIGN see Hatton, John
[Liptrot]

JESUS SHALL REIGN see Hughes

JESUS SHALL REIGN see Mueller

JESUS SHALL REIGN see Watts

JESUS, SO LOWLY see Green, R.

JESUS, SOUL OF MY HEART'S DESIRE see
Moss, Cyril

JESUS SOURCE OF MY SALVATION see Bach

JESUS SPRACH ZU DEM BLINDEN see
Vulpius, Melchior

JESUS STILL LEAD ON see Drese

JESUS STORY, THE see Tigner, Marcy

JESUS STYLE SONGS, VOL. I, REVISED
*CCU
(Anderson, David L.C.) unis,gtr
AUGSBURG 11-9245 $2.00 keyboard
accompaniment edition available for
$4.95 (no. 11-9246)   (J88)

JESUS, TENDER SHEPHERD see France,
William E.

JESUS, THE HOPE see Skillings, Otis

JESUS THE KING PASSES BY see Peterson,
John W.

JESUS, THE SON OF GOD see Haywood

JESUS! THE VERY THOUGHT OF THEE
*Easter/Gen
(Johnson) SSATTB oct BENSON S4166
$.35   (J89)

JESUS, THE VERY THOUGHT OF THEE see
Rasley, John M.

JESUS, THE VERY THOUGHT OF THEE see
Wyrtzen, Don

JESUS, THOU JOY OF LOVING HEARTS see
Baker, Henry

JESUS, THOU JOY OF LOVING HEARTS see
Bass, Claude L.

JESUS, THOU TENDER LITTLE ONE see
Franck, Melchior

JESUS, THY BLOOD AND RIGHTEOUSNESS see
Gardiner

JESUS, THY BOUNDLESS LOVE see
Burroughs, Bob

JESUS TOOK MY SINS AWAY see Adams

JESUS TOOK THE CUP see Pelz, Walter L.

JESUS UND DER OBERZOLLNER ZACHAUS "UND
JESUS GING NACH JERICHO HINEIN" see
Strohbach, Siegfried

JESUS UND DER UNGLAUBIGE THOMAS see
Gunsenheimer, Gustav

JESUS UND DIE EHEBRECHERIN "DIE
PHARISAER UND SCHRIFTGELEHRTEN
BRACHTEN EINE FRAU HERBET" see
Strohbach, Siegfried

JESUS UND MARTHA "ES GESCHAH, ALS SIE
WANDERTEN" see Strohbach, Siegfried

JESUS UND NIKODEMUS "ES WAR ABER EIN
MENSCH" see Pepping, Ernst

JESUS, USE ME see Campbell, B.

JESUS WALKED THIS LONESOME VALLEY
*spir
see Two Spirituals For Chorus
(Dawson) mix cor WARNER G821 $.30
(J90)
(Dawson) SSA WARNER G823 $.30   (J91)
(Dawson) SSAA WARNER G1839 $.30 (J92)
(Dawson) men cor WARNER G822 $.30
(J93)

JESUS WALKED THIS LONESOME VALLEY see
Red, Buryl

JESUS WAS A BABY see Donahue, Robert

JESUS WAS HIS NAME see Johnson, Mark

JESUS, WHO DIED A WORLD TO SAVE see
Kimball

JESUS, WONDERFUL LORD! see White, P.

JESUS, WORD OF GOD INCARNATE see
Gounod, Charles Francois

JETZT FAHRN WIR UBERN SEE see Lang,
Hans

JEZUS ONZE GROTE KONING see Gauntlett,
[Henry John]

JEZUS, RUSTPUNT VAN MIJN HART
mix cor sc HEER 2581 s.p.   (J94)

JILLETT, DAVID
Cantata Corpus Christi *CCU
[Lat/Eng] SATB,soli,org EMI s.p.
(J95)

English Unison Mass (St. Francis
Xavier)
unis (with Gloria and Credo) EMI
s.p.   (J96)

Resurrection *mot
SATB EMI s.p.   (J97)

JIMMY OWENS AND THE COME TOGETHER
SINGERS TELL THE WORLD see Owens,
Jimmy

JIMMY OWENS IMPACT, THE *CC10UL
(Owens, Jimmy) cor BENSON B0438 $1.95
stereo recording, tapes, and-or
accompaniment tape also available;
for book-record sets available,
contact publisher   (J98)

JIRAK, KAREL BOLESLAV (1891-   )
Psalm 23 *see Psalm XXIII

Psalm XXIII (Psalm 23) Op.19
[Czech] mix cor,3fl,3ob,3clar,3bsn,
4horn,3trp,3trom,tuba,timp,perc,
harp,strings, celeste CZECH s.p.
(J99)

Requiem *Op.70
[Lat] mix cor,3fl,2ob,2clar,2bsn,
4horn,3trp,3trom,tuba,perc,timp,
harp,org,strings CZECH s.p.
(J100)

JIRASEK, IVO (1920-   )
    Stabat Mater
        mix cor&jr cor,4 soli,4horn,4trp,
        4trom,timp,perc,org CZECH s.p.
                                                (J101)

JIRIM, FRANTISEK (1837-1914)
    Christmas Carol Mass *see Vanocni
        Koledova Mse

    Vanocni Koledova Mse
        "Christmas Carol Mass" [Czech] mix
        cor,TB soli,fl,clar,2horn,2trp,
        trom,timp,strings CZECH s.p.
                                                (J102)

JOCHUM, OTTO (1898-1969)
    Alleluja-Chor "Haec Dies" *Op.16a,
        Easter
        [Lat] 4pt mix cor,org sc,cor pts
        BOHM s.p.   (J103)

    Lobgesang "Lobe Den Herrn, Meine
        Seele" *Op.103, Fest
        mix cor,orch sc,cor pts BOHM s.p.,
        ipa
        mix cor,pno,strings sc,cor pts BOHM
        s.p., ipa   (J105)
        mix cor,org sc,cor pts BOHM s.p.,
        ipa   (J106)

    Messe Zu Ehren Der Heiligen Felix Und
        Regula *Op.53, Mass
        [Lat] 4pt mix cor,acap sc,cor pts
        BOHM s.p.   (J107)

    Mundo Salus Redditur *Op.178,No.1,
        Adv/Xmas
        [Lat] 4pt mix cor,S solo sc,cor pts
        BOHM s.p.   (J108)

    Salve Regina *Op.52, Mass
        [Lat] 4pt mix cor,org sc,cor pts
        BOHM s.p.   (J109)

    Veni Creator Spiritus *hymn
        [Lat] 4-6pt mix cor,acap sc,cor pts
        BOHM s.p.   (J110)

JOHANNESPASSION 1737 see Telemann,
    Georg Philipp

JOHANSEN, SVEN-ERIK
    Bon
        4pt mix cor ERIKS 75 s.p.   (J111)

    Herre, Jag Har Hort Din Stamma
        3pt mix cor ERIKS 67 s.p.   (J112)

    High Above The Stars Of Heaven *see
        Mit Liv Har Du Tant Hogt Ovan
        Himmelens Stjarnor

    Kom Karlekens Ande
        mix cor GEHRMANS KRB456   (J113)

    Mit Liv Har Du Tant Hogt Ovan
        Himmelens Stjarnor
        "High Above The Stars Of Heaven"
        4pt mix cor NORDISKA NMS 6528
        s.p.   (J114)

    O Jesus, Du Som Vagen Ar
        mix cor GEHRMANS KRB 455 see from
        Tre Andliga Visor   (J115)

    O Lat Oss Guds Karlek Bevisa
        mix cor GEHRMANS KRB 455 see from
        Tre Andliga Visor   (J116)

    Tre Andliga Visor *see O Jesus, Du
        Som Vagen Ar; O Lat Oss Guds
        Karlek Bevisa; Var Stilla Min
        Sjal   (J117)

    Var Stilla Min Sjal
        mix cor GEHRMANS KRB 455 see from
        Tre Andliga Visor   (J118)

JOHN MCKAY CHOIR BOOK see McKay, John

JOHN RASLEY PRESENTS A CHORAL SAMPLER
    *CCUL
    cor SINGSPIR 4277 $1.50   (J119)

JOHN W. PETERSON ANTHEMS FOR SAB see
    Peterson, John W.

JOHN W. PETERSON'S FOLIO OF CHOIR
    FAVORITES NO. 1 see Peterson, John
    W.

JOHN W. PETERSON'S FOLIO OF CHOIR
    FAVORITES NO. 2 see Peterson, John
    W.

JOHN W. PETERSON'S FOLIO OF CHOIR
    FAVORITES NO. 3 see Peterson, John
    W.

JOHN W. PETERSON'S FOLIO OF GOSPEL
    CHOIR FAVORITES NO. 1 see Peterson,
    John W.

JOHN W. PETERSON'S FOLIO OF GOSPEL
    CHOIR FAVORITES NO. 2 see Peterson,
    John W.

JOHN W. PETERSON'S FOLIO OF GOSPEL
    CHOIR FAVORITES NO. 3 see Peterson,
    John W.

JOHNNY APPLESEED see Verrall, Pamela

JOHNSON
    All I Need *gospel
        (Skillings, Otis) SATB oct LILLENAS
        AN-5079 $.30   (J120)

    Christus Resurgens *Easter
        SATB,acap (diff) OXFORD 84.235
        $1.10   (J121)

    Incarnatio
        SSATB,acap (diff) OXFORD 84.227
        $.60   (J122)

    Love Theme *folk
        SATB oct LILLENAS AN-5072 $.35
                                        (J123)
        (Skillings, Otis) SATB/jr cor oct
        LILLENAS AN-5084 $.35   (J124)

    Mindful Of Me *folk
        SATB oct LILLENAS AN-5074 $.30
                                        (J125)

    Mountain Brook With Rushing Waters
        unis SHAWNEE FA5010 $.35   (J126)

    Take A Look At Jesus *folk
        SATB oct LILLENAS AN-5073 $.30
                                        (J127)

    Trust In The Lord *folk
        SATB oct LILLENAS AN-5066 $.30
                                        (J128)
        (Skillings, Otis) SATB/jr cor oct
        LILLENAS AN-5091 $.30   (J129)

JOHNSON, D.
    That Easter Day With Joy Was Bright
        unis,opt trp,timp,hndbl oct SCHMITT
        1886 $.45   (J130)

JOHNSON, DAVID N.
    Folk Gloria *CCU
        SAB,opt inst AUGSBURG 11-9183 $2.00
                                        (J131)
    Hosanna: A Folk Communion Service
        unis,kbd,opt inst sc AUGSBURG
        11-9227 $2.00, cor pts AUGSBURG
        11-9228 $.30   (J132)

    Lead On, O King Eternal *anthem
        SATB,org,opt trp AUGSBURG 11-1664
        $.35   (J133)

    O Love, How Deep *anthem
        unis,org,opt trp AUGSBURG 11-1671
        $.35   (J134)

    Saw Ye My Saviour *anthem
        unis,kbd,opt fl AUGSBURG 11-1732
        $.40   (J135)

    Set Free Within
        SATB,acap ART MAST 145 $.30   (J136)

    Souls Of The Righteous *anthem
        SATB,org AUGSBURG 11-1700 $.35
                                        (J137)
    To A Virgin Meek And Mild *anthem
        SAB,opt fl AUGSBURG 11-1667 $.30
                                        (J138)

JOHNSON, LOIS
    My Heart Sings Hosanna *Palm,anthem
        (Drevits, Jon) SSATB oct SINGSPIR
        ZJP-3526 $.25   (J139)

JOHNSON, MARK
    Jesus Was His Name *Adv/Xmas
        SATB,acap ART MAST 241 $.30   (J140)

    My Heart Is Ready
        unis ART MAST 258 $.30   (J141)

JOHNSON, NORMAN
    Church, O Lord, Is Thine, The
        SATB oct SINGSPIR ZJP-7367 $.35
                                        (J142)

    Descants For Choirs *CCU
        desc,opt vln/fl SINGSPIR 5544 $1.50
        coordinated with the Great Hymns
        Of The Faith hymnal   (J143)

    Fight The Good Fight *anthem
        SATB oct SINGSPIR ZJP-7275 $.25
                                        (J144)

    Heralds Of Christ *anthem
        SATB oct SINGSPIR ZJP-7235 $.25
                                        (J145)

    Holy, Holy, Holy! *anthem
        SATB oct SINGSPIR ZJP-7246 $.30
                                        (J146)

    Lord God, Our Thanks To Thee We Raise
        *anthem
        SATB (Church Anniversary) oct
        SINGSPIR ZJP-3105 $.30   (J147)

    Now Is Christ Risen *Easter,anthem
        SSATBB oct SINGSPIR ZJP-3547 $.35
                                        (J148)

    Ride On In Majesty! *Palm,anthem
        SATB oct SINGSPIR ZJP-3516 $.25
                                        (J149)

JOHNSON, NORMAN (cont'd.)
    Ride On, Ride On In Majesty *Palm,
        anthem
        dbl cor oct SINGSPIR ZA-4621 $.30
                                        (J150)

    Sing To The Lord Of Harvest *Thanks,
        anthem
        SATB oct SINGSPIR ZJP-3015 $.25
                                        (J151)

    This I Believe *anthem/gospel
        SATB oct SINGSPIR ZJP-8099 $.25
                                        (J152)

    Will It Be Soon? *Thanks,anthem
        SSATTBB oct SINGSPIR ZJP-8145 $.30
                                        (J153)

JOHNSON, ORIEN
    His Sheep Am I *anthem
        (Bolks, Dick) SATB WORD CS-2589
        $.30   (J154)

JOHNSON, P.
    I Wish You All Could Know Him
        (Huff, Ronn) SSATB oct BENSON S4374
        $.40   (J155)

JOHNSON, PAUL
    Cold And Lonely Night *anthem
        SATB WORD CS-2708 $.35 see from
        Here Comes The Son   (J156)

    Here Comes The Son *see Cold And
        Lonely Night   (J157)

    Here Comes The Son *cant
        cor WORD 37683 $2.95   (J158)

    In My Father's House
        cor BRIDGE Z 0200   (J159)

    Last Trumpet, The
        cor BRIDGE Z 249   (J160)

    Make Us One, Father *anthem
        SATB WORD   (J161)

    Paul Johnson Singers *CC10U
        cor,pno,bvl,gtr LILLENAS MB-269
        $1.95   (J162)

    Sacrifice Of Praise, A *Gen
        SATB,pno (med) GENTRY G-235 $.45
                                        (J163)
        cor BRIDGE Z 235   (J164)

    Sonlife *CC14U,pop
        jr cor/sr cor cmplt ed LILLENAS
        MB-360 $2.95   (J165)

    Spirit Of '76
        cor,pno LILLENAS MB-271 $2.95
                                        (J166)

    That The World May Know *anthem
        SATB WORD CS-2664 $.40 see from
        MUSIC FOR THE YOUNG CHURCH,
        VOLUME II   (J167)

    Trophy Of His Love, A
        cor BRIDGE Z 214   (J168)

    When I Trust The Savior
        cor BRIDGE Z 218   (J169)

JOHNSON, RALPH
    I Am The Light *anthem
        unis,kbd AUGSBURG 11-1679 $.30
                                        (J170)

    This Is The Day *anthem
        SATB,B solo,kbd,fl AUGSBURG 11-1690
        $.35   (J171)

JOHNSON, S.
    From Heaven Above
        SATB GENERAL WDS GC53 $.40   (J172)

    Passerby, The
        SATB GENERAL WDS GC63 $.35   (J173)

JOHNSON, WILLIAM
    Bosom Of Abraham *see Brooks, Ted

JOHNSTON
    One God *anthem
        SATB oct LORENZ B194 $.35   (J174)

JOHNSTON, BEN
    Kyrie (from Mass)
        SATB,org/trom,bvl,perc FOSTER
        MF 141A $.40   (J175)

    Mass
        SATB,bvl,drums,inst FOSTER MF141
        $3.00, ipa   (J176)

JOHNSTON, H.
    Merry Christmas *Xmas,anthem
        (LeBar, S.) SATB oct SINGSPIR
        ZJP-3046 $.35   (J177)

JOHNSTON, RICHARD
    Alleluia *Easter
        SSA (med diff) WATERLOO $.35 (J178)

JOIN ALL THE GLORIOUS NAMES see
    Darwall, John

JOIN HANDS, BROTHERS
(Wood, Dale) SATB,opt solo ART MAST
158 $.30 (J179)

JOLLY WAT see Cope

JONAH see Carissimi, Giacomo

JONAH see Wood, Dale

JONAH'S TALE OF A WHALE see Graham,
Robert

JONES
Deeper, Deeper (composed with Kelso)
*gospel
(Mickelson, Paul) SSATB oct
LILLENAS AN-1702 $.30 (J180)

Glory, Hallelujah To The Lamb!
*Easter,anthem/gospel
(Johnson, Norman) SATB oct SINGSPIR
ZJP-8171 $.30 (J181)

I Will Arise *see Hart

In Times Like These *anthem/gospel
(Anthony, Dick) SATB oct SINGSPIR
ZJP-8004 $.30 (J182)
(DeCou, Harold) SA&opt TB (easy)
oct SINGSPIR ZJP-6002 $.30 (J183)

Keep Christ In Christmas *Xmas,
anthem
(DeCou, Harold) SATB oct SINGSPIR
ZJP-3024 $.25 (J184)

Power In The Blood *anthem
SATB oct BROADMAN 4554-79 $.30
(J185)
There Is Power In The Blood *Easter/
Gen,folk
(Burroughs, Bob) SATB/jr cor,brass
oct LILLENAS AN-5088 $.35 (J186)
(Ferrin) SSATB oct BENSON S4350
$.20 (J187)

JONES, C.P.
All I Need
(Krogstad, Bob) SATB oct GOSPEL
05 TM 0310 $.35 (J188)

JONES, DANIEL (1912-)
St. Peter *ora
SATB,STB soli,2fl,pic,2ob,2clar,
2bsn,2horn,2trp,strings voc sc
NOVELLO rental (J189)

JONES, JR., S.
Oh Come Let Us Bow Down
mix cor BRODT 550 $.22 (J190)

JONES, MARJORIE
What Can I Give Him?
cor BRIDGE Z 0183 (J191)

JONES, RICHMOND
His Love Is Endless *folk
2pt oct SINGSPIR ZJP-5046 $.30
(J192)

Let Us Pray *folk
2pt oct SINGSPIR ZJP-5038 $.30
(J193)

JONES, ROBERT
What Shall I Render To The Lord
(Wolff) SATB oct CONCORDIA 98-2232
$.40 (J194)

JONES, ROBERT C.
Let There Be Light
SATB,org/5brass FOSTER MF146 $.45
(J195)

JORDAHL
Calendar Song, The
2pt KJOS 6134 $.35 (J196)

Celebrate The Lord
jr cor GENERAL WDS GC57 $.35 (J197)

Come Lord Jesus
SATB KJOS 5911 $.35 (J198)

Risen Today
SSA KJOS 6137 $.35 (J199)

JORDAN
Hymn To Spring *anthem
unis (easy) oct BROADMAN 4558-38
$.30 (J200)

JORDAN, ALICE
God's Lark At Morning
SSA (easy) FITZSIMONS 3082 $.20
(J201)

JOSEF A MARIE V BETLEME see Zelinka,
Jan Evangelista

JOSEPH AND MARY AT BETHLEHEM see
Zelinka, Jan Evangelista, Josef A
Marie V Betleme

JOSEPH AND THE AMAZING TECHNICOLOR
DREAMCOAT see Webber, Andrew Lloyd

JOSEPH AND THE ANGEL
see Two Christmas Carols

JOSEPH DEAREST, JOSEPH MINE *Xmas,
carol,Ger
(Ehret, Walter) SABar&camb,pno,opt
fing.cym. CAMBIATA U117326 $.40
(J202)
JOSEPH DEAREST, JOSEPH MINE see Cabena,
Barrie

JOSEPH, DU SOHN DAVID, FURCHTE DICH
NICHT see Schutz, Heinrich

JOSEPH FILI DAVID see Lachner, Franz

JOSEPH, JOSEPH, DEAREST ONE see
Calvisius, Sethus, Joseph, Lieber
Joseph Mein

JOSEPH, LIEBER JOSEPH MEIN *Xmas
(Hessenberg, Kurt) 2pt jr cor&TTB,
acap (med) sc SCHOTTS C 40 652 s.p.
see from Zwei Weihnachtslieder
(J203)
JOSEPH, LIEBER JOSEPH MEIN see
Calvisius, Sethus

JOSEPH, LIEBER JOSEPH MEIN see
Hessenberg, Kurt

JOSEPH, LIEBER JOSEPH MEIN see Reusch,
Fritz

JOSEPHS, WILFRED (1927-)
So She Went Into The Garden
3 eq voices,pno,opt rec NOVELLO
TRIOS 677 s.p. (J204)

JOSH'A FIT DE BATTLE OB JERICHO *spir
(Enders, H.) TTBB,acap (med)
FITZSIMONS 4057 $.25 (J205)

JOSHUA FIT DE BATTLE OF JERICHO
*anthem/spir
(Kennedy, M.; Cadwallader, A.) 2pt
mix cor,pno/gtr (easy) GIA G1772
$.30 (J206)

JOSHUA FIT DE BATTLE OF JERICO see
Petersen, Rolf

JOSHUA FIT THE BATTLE *spir
(Ohrwall) 4pt mix cor ERIKS 56 s.p.
(J207)

JOSHUA FIT THE BATTLE OF JERICHO
*anthem/gospel/spir
(Drevits, Jon) SATB oct SINGSPIR
ZJP-8043 $.30 (J208)

JOSHUA FOUGHT THE BATTLE OF JERICHO
*spir
2pt ASHDOWN EA377 (J209)

JOSHUA SCHLUG DIE SCHLACHT VON JERICHO
see Petersen, Rolf, Joshua Fit De
Battle Of Jerico

JOSQUIN
see DES PREZ, JOSQUIN

JOUBERT, JOHN (1927-)
Behold, The Tabernacle Of God
*anthem
SATB,org NOVELLO NCM 40 s.p. (J210)

Holy Mountain, The
SATB,2pno voc sc NOVELLO rental
(J211)
Martyrdom Of St. Alban, The *Op.59
SATB,TBar&narrator,fl,ob,clar,bsn,
horn,timp,perc,pno voc sc NOVELLO
rental (J212)

Raising Of Lazurus *Op.67
SATB,MezT soli,pic,3fl,3ob,3clar,
3bsn,4horn,4trp,4trom,tuba,timp,
perc,2harp,pno,strings voc sc
NOVELLO rental (J213)

Urbs Beata *cant
SATB,TBar soli,3fl,3ob,3clar,3bsn,
4horn,3trp,3trom,tuba,timp,perc,
harp,org,strings voc sc NOVELLO
rental (J214)

JOURNEY TO BETHLEHEM see Graham, Jeana

JOY see Cates, Bill

JOY see Mechem, Kirke

JOY DAWNS AGAIN see Cornell, Garry A.

JOY HAS COME DOWN see Fettke, Tom

JOY HAS FILLED THE SKY see Davis,
Katherine K.

JOY IS LIKE THE RAIN see Winter, Sister
Miriam Therese

JOY IS LIKE THE RAIN see Winter, Sister
Miriam Therese

JOY IS THE CENTER OF HIS WILL *anthem
SATB LEXICON CS-2586 $.35 (J215)

JOY OF HEAVEN, THE see Peterson, John
W.

JOY THAT DWELLS WITHIN US see Bach,
J.C., Unsers Herzens Freude

JOY THAT KNOWS NO BOUNDS *Xmas
(Springfield) S&camb/Bar CAMBIATA
L97438 $.35 (J216)

JOY TO THE WORLD see Burroughs, Bob

JOY TO THE WORLD see Lenel, Ludwig

JOY TO THE WORLD! see Mason, Lowell

JOY TO THE WORLD! see Peterson, John W.

JOY TO THE WORLD see Thiman, Eric
Harding

JOY TO THE WORLD - HALLELUJAH *anthem
(Carmichael, Ralph) SATB LEXICON
CS-2683 $.45 (J217)

JOY TO THE WORLD, THE LORD IS COMING
see Bock, Fred

JOYFUL ADVENT SONG, A see Kunkel, Carol
Lapo

JOYFUL! JOYFUL! see Hampton, Calvin

JOYFUL, JOYFUL WE ADORE THEE see
Beethoven, Ludwig van

JOYFUL NOISE see Powell, Rick

JOYFUL NOISE, A see Allen

JOYFULLY SING WE HIS PRAISE! see Harris

JOYOUS NEWS OF CHRISTMAS, THE see
Parks, Joe E.

JOYOUS PSALM, A see Butler, Eugene

JOYS OF LIFE, THE see Lovelace, Austin
C.

JUBELHYMNE see Koch, Martin

JUBILATE see Arnatt, Ronald

JUBILATE, AMEN! see Kjerulf, [Halfdan]

JUBILATE DEO *CCU,Greg
eq voices/unis,org GIA G1909 $.49,
ipa (J218)

JUBILATE DEO see Aiblinger, Johann
Kaspar

JUBILATE DEO see Bales, Gerald

JUBILATE DEO see Cabena, Barrie

JUBILATE DEO see Eybler, Joseph

JUBILATE DEO see Gabrieli, Giovanni

JUBILATE DEO see Koch, Karl

JUBILATE DEO see Lang, Hans

JUBILATE DEO see Lassus, Roland de
(Orlandus)

JUBILATE DEO see Peissner, Karl

JUBILATE DEO see Perrin, Ronald

JUBILATE DEO see Saunders, Neil

JUBILATE DEO see Walton

JUBILATE DEO see Weber, Bernhard

JUBILATE DEO see Wienand, Karl

JUBILATE DEO, OMNIS TERRA see Lassus,
Roland de (Orlandus)

JUBILATE DEO "OMNIS TERRA, SERVITE
DOMINO" see Bouzignac, Guillaume

JUBILATE IN D see Purcell, Henry

JUBILATE JAZZ see Sansom, Clive

JUBILAUMS-CHORHEFT *CC20U
SAT/SAB/SATB LANDES LKB 4 s.p.
contains works by: Forster;
Scheller; Weinreich; Weiss; and
others (J219)

JUBILEE! *CC10UL
(Skillings, Otis) cor LILLENAS MB-299
$1.95 (J220)

JUBILEE IS COME see Littleton, Bill J.

JUBILEE MASS see Lee, J.

JUBILEMUS see Couperin, Francois

JUBILEMUS OMNES ET CANTEMUS see
    Carissimi, Giacomo

JUCH-HE *Adv/Xmas
    (Bauernfeind, Hans) wom cor,acap oct
    DOBLINGER s.p. see also In Dulci
    Jubilo   (J221)

JUDA, HOCHGELOBTES LAND see Weber

JUDAS, MERCATOR PESSIMUS see Victoria,
    Tomas Luis de

JUDGMENT ANTHEM see Morgan, Justin

JUDICA ME see Gabrieli, Giovanni

JUDICIUM SALOMONIS see Charpentier,
    Marc-Antoine

JUL OG PASKE see Solberg, Per

JULAFTON see Ahlen, Waldemar

JUNGST
    While By My Sheep *Xmas
    (White) SATB oct SCHMITT 1448 $.40
             (J222)
JUNIOR CHOIR NO. 1 *CCUL
    1-2pt jr cor SINGSPIR 5445 $1.25
             (J223)
JUNIOR CHOIR NO. 2 *CCUL
    1-2pt jr cor SINGSPIR 5446 $1.25
             (J224)
JUNIOR CHOIR NO. 3 *CCUL
    1-2pt jr cor SINGSPIR 5447 $1.25
             (J225)
JUNIOR CHOIR NO. 4 *CCUL
    1-2pt jr cor SINGSPIR 5448 $1.25
             (J226)
JUNIOR CHOIR NO. 5 *CCUL
    1-2pt jr cor SINGSPIR 5444 $1.25
             (J227)
JUNIOR CHOIR NO. 6 *CCUL
    1-2pt jr cor SINGSPIR 5451 $1.25
             (J228)
JUNIOR CHOIR NO. 7 *CCU
    1-2pt jr cor SINGSPIR 5502 $1.25
             (J229)
THE JUNIOR CHOIR SINGS, NO. 1 *CCUL
    1-2pt jr cor BROADMAN 4526-02 $1.25
             (J230)
THE JUNIOR CHOIR SINGS, NO. 2 *CCUL
    1-2pt jr cor BROADMAN 4626-03 $1.25
             (J231)
THE JUNIOR CHOIR SINGS, NO. 3 *CCUL
    1-2pt jr cor BROADMAN 4526-04 $1.25
             (J232)
JURGENS, JAC.
    In De Hof Van Gethsemane *Psntd
    (Van Weelden, J.) unis,pno HEER
    1251 s.p.   (J233)

JUST A CLOSER WALK
    (Wilson, J.F.) SATB,kbd,opt bvl&drums
    oct HOPE 1809 $.40   (J234)

JUST A CLOSER WALK WITH THEE *anthem
    (Lojeski, Ed) SATB LEONARD-US
    08330750 $.50   (J235)
    (Lojeski, Ed) SSA LEONARD-US 08330752
    $.50   (J236)
    (Rasley, J.M.) SSATB oct SINGSPIR
    ZJP-8211 $.35   (J237)

JUST A WAYWARD LAMB see Ramon

JUST ANDRAE see Crouch, Andrae

JUST ANOTHER BABY? see Sleeth, Natalie

JUST AS I AM see Landgrave, Phillip

JUST AS I AM see Nicol

JUST AS I AM THINE OWN TO BE see
    Thiman, Eric Harding

JUST ASK HIM - LISTEN - RIGHT NOW -
    RECEIVE HIM NOW see Skillings, Otis

JUST LISTEN
    (Wild, Eric) SATB,pno BERANDOL
    BER1678 $.50   (J238)

JUST MAN SHALL FLOURISH, THE see
    Felciano, Richard, Benedictio
    Nuptialis

JUST ONE TOUCH
    (Smith, W.) SATB oct GOSPEL
    05 TM 0314 $.35   (J239)

JUST OVER IN THE GLORYLAND see Dean

JUST TO FEEL THY PRESENCE NEAR ME see
    Hasse, O.

JUST TO SEE HIM see Wilson, John F.

JUST WHEN I NEED HIM MOST see Gabriel

JUSTORUM ANIMAE see Salieri, Antonio

JUSTUM DEDUXIT DOMINUS see Mozart,
    Wolfgang Amadeus

JUSTUS UT PALMA see Mutter, Gerbert

K

KAELIN
    Messe Du Sacre
    4pt mix cor,pno/org HENN 354 s.p.
    sc, voc pt   (K1)

    Messe Pour La Paix
    4pt mix cor,acap voc pt HENN 376
    s.p.   (K2)

KAGERER, CHR. LOR.
    Christmas Mass *see Weihnachtsmesse
    In G

    Drei Fest-Pange-Lingua *Op.16,No.1-
    3, CC3U
    [Lat] 4pt mix cor,org/fl&2clar&
    2bsn&2horn&2trp&3trom&strings&
    timp sc,cor pts BOHM s.p., ipa
            (K3)
    Missa Brevis In Honorem St.
    Christophori *Op.15, Mass
    [Lat] mix cor,org sc,cor pts BOHM
    s.p.   (K4)

    Weihnachtsmesse In G *Op.51, Xmas,
    Mass
    "Christmas Mass" [Lat] mix cor,
    soli,org,fl,2clar,2horn,2trp,
    strings,timp sc,cor pts BOHM
    s.p., ipa   (K5)

KAIM, ADOLF
    Missa Sancta Anna *Op.8, Mass
    [Lat] 4pt mix cor,acap sc,cor pts
    BOHM s.p.   (K6)

KAISER, KURT
    God Is Here Right Now *anthem
    2pt LEXICON CS-2657 $.35 see from
    I'm Here, God's Here, Now We Can
    Start   (K7)

    God's People (composed with Brown,
    Charles F.) *cant
    SATB&cong,med solo,narrator,3trp,
    2trom WORD 37684 $2.50, ipa (K8)

    I'm Here, God's Here, Now We Can
    Start *see God Is Here Right Now
            (K9)

    I'm Here, God's Here, Now We Can
    Start (composed with Carmichael,
    Ralph) *cant
    cor,2trp,2trom LEXICON 37652 $2.95,
    ipa   (K10)

    It's Our World *anthem
    unis LEXICON CS-2606 $.35 see from
    NATURAL HIGH   (K11)

    Let All Things Praise The Lord
    SATB,org (med) FISCHER,C CM 7869
    $.35   (K12)

    Moment Of Truth, The *anthem
    SATB LEXICON CS-2613 $.35 see from
    NATURAL HIGH   (K13)

    Oh How He Loves You And Me *anthem
    SATB WORD   (K14)

    Our Father *anthem
    SAB WORD CS-2600 $.30 (K15)

    Reach Your Hand *anthem
    SA WORD CS-2572 $.30   (K16)

    Tell It To Jesus *anthem
    (Powell, Rick) SATB WORD CS-2681
    $.40 see from RICK POWELL CHOIR
    BOOK   (K17)

KALEIDOSCOPIC COLORS see Red, Buryl

KALNINS, JANIS (1904-   )
    Lord's Prayer, The *prayer
    SATB,acap HARRIS $.40 (K18)

    When Jesus Came To Birmingham
    SATB HARRIS $.35   (K19)

KAM, DENNIS
    Alleluia
    mix cor MEDIA 5115   (K20)

KAMEKE, ERNST-ULRICH VON (1926-   )
    Osterpsalm *Easter,Psalm
    SATB,acap (med diff) BAREN. BA5423
            (K21)

    Vaterunser
    mix cor&speak cor,4 soli BREITKOPF-
    W CHB 3698 s.p.   (K22)

KAMINSKI, HEINRICH (1886-1946)
    Aus Der Tiefe Rufe Ich, Herr (Psalm
    130) Op.1a, Bibl
    mix cor,S solo sc SCHOTTS C 30 879
    s.p.   (K23)

KAMINSKI, HEINRICH (cont'd.)

Der Tag Ist Hin
mix cor (med) sc SCHOTTS CHBL 251
s.p. (K24)

Der Tag Ist Hin, Die Sonne Gehet
Nieder
see Sechs Chorale

Die Liebe Sonne
see Sechs Chorale

Es Ist Vollbracht
see Sechs Chorale

Ihr Gestirn, Ihr Hohen Lufte
see Sechs Chorale

O Herre Gott *mot
SSAATTBB,opt org (med) sc,cor pts
SCHOTTS ED. 4195 s.p. (K25)

O Jesulein Suss
see Sechs Chorale

Psalm 130 *see Aus Der Tiefe Rufe
Ich, Herr

Sechs Chorale *chorale
SATB (med) sc SCHOTTS C 30 878
s.p., voc pt SCHOTTS C 30 878A-D
s.p.
contains: Der Tag Ist Hin, Die
Sonne Gehet Nieder; Die Liebe
Sonne; Es Ist Vollbracht; Ihr
Gestirn, Ihr Hohen Lufte; O
Jesulein Suss; Vergiss Mein
Nicht (K26)

Vergiss Mein Nicht
see Sechs Chorale

Vergiss Mein Nicht, Mein
Allerliebster Gott
mix cor (med) SCHOTTS CHBL 252 s.p.
(K27)

KANONISCHE MOTETTEN see Haas, Joseph

KANTATE see Blum, Robert

KANTATE-CHORHEFT 1966 *CC10U,Xmas,Eur
SAT/SAB&unis LANDES LKB 5 s.p.
contains works by: Stern; Weiss;
Schmidt-Mannheim; Zipp; and others
(K28)

KANTATE PART I: VENI CREATOR SPIRITUS
see Orff, Carl

KANTATE PART II: DER GUTE MENSCH see
Orff, Carl

KANTATE PART III: FREMDE SIND WIR see
Orff, Carl

KANTORMUSIK - FOR OGSA KRISTUS LED see
Ihlebaek, Guttorm O.

KAPP, R.S.
Lord Is My Shepherd, The
mix cor BRODT 503 $.25 (K29)

KARFREITAGSGESANG see Falcke

KARLEN, ROBERT (1923-)
Dialogue
cor,electronic tape ART MAST 175
$ 40 (K30)

Psalm 27 (Part I)
SATB,fl,fing cym,tamb, bongos,
triangle ART MAST 213 $.40 (K31)

Psalm 27 (Part III)
SATB,fl,perc ART MAST 160 $.40
(K32)

KARLINS, M. WILLIAM
Concert Music No. 2 *Psalm
mix cor,2fl,2ob,2clar,2bsn,4horn,
2trp,3trom,tuba,timp,harp,strings
AM.COMP.AL. sc $16.50, voc pt
$8.25 (K33)

KARLSEN, KJELL MORK
Krist La I Dodens Lenker *cant
cor&cong,winds,org sc NORSK
NMO 8751 A s.p. (K34)

Vil Du Mot Malet Renna
mix cor NORSK NMO 8740 s.p. (K35)

KATAWASSA see Terzakis, Dimitri

KAUFMANN, GEORG FRIEDRICH (1679-1735)
Now Thank We All Our God
(Peek) SA BRODT 576 $.20 (K36)

KAUFMANN, OTTO
Der Stern *CC15U,Xmas
2-3pt jr cor MOSELER s.p. (K37)

KAUFMANN, RONALD
Jazzeluia
SATB,pno,opt perc oct HOPE CF 182
$.45 (K38)

KAUFMANN, RONALD (cont'd.)

Sing A Joyful Song Of Christmas
*Xmas
SATB,pno, Bongo Drum, Wood Block
(med easy) ELKAN-V 362-03182 $.50
(K39)

KAYSER, LEIF (1919-)
Ave Maria *BVM
SSAA cmplt ed EGTVED MS8A1 s.p.
contains also: Regina Caeli
Letare (SA) (K40)

Hodie Christus Natus Est *Xmas
SATB,acap EGTVED MK9, 4 s.p. (K41)

In Petra Stabilitus Non Concuitor
SATB,acap EGTVED MK7, 4 s.p. (K42)

Messa III *Mass
SATB,opt strings sc,cor pts EGTVED
KB55 s.p., ipa (K43)

Pange Lingua *Corpus,hymn
SATB,acap EGTVED KB56 s.p. (K44)

Regina Caeli Letare
see Kayser, Leif, Ave Maria

Te Deum For Blandet Kor Og Orkester
"Te Deum For Mixed Chorus And
Orchestra" SATB,3fl,ob,3clar,
3bsn,4horn,2trp,2trom,timp,
perc SAMFUNDET voc sc s.p., cor
pts s.p., sc s.p., ipa (K45)

Te Deum For Mixed Chorus And
Orchestra *see Te Deum For
Blandet Kor Og Orkester

KDOZ JSTE BOZI BOJOVNICI see Dobias,
Vaclav

K'DUSHA see Richards, Stephen

KEDUSHA see Helfman, Max

KEEGAN, PATRICK
My Soul Shall Be Joyful *CC10U
cong,pno/gtr EMI (K46)

KEEP A JOYFUL SONG RINGING IN YOUR
HEART see Hopson, Hal H.

KEEP CHRIST IN CHRISTMAS see Jones

KEEP ON THE FIRING LINE
(Ferrin, Paul) SATB oct GOSPEL
05 TM 0108 $.25 (K47)

KEEP SINGIN' THAT LOVE SONG *CCUL
(Archers; Sisco, Bob) cor BENSON
B0173 $2.50 stereo recording, tape,
and-or book-record sets available,
contact publisher (K48)

KEEP WALKING see Roberts

KEEPER OF ISRAEL, THE see Haan, Raymond

KEESE, K
O Lord, How Excellent Thy Name
mix cor BRODT 556 $.26 (K49)

O Sing Unto The Lord A New Song
mix cor BRODT 623 $.25 (K50)

KEETMAN, GUNILD
Christmas Story, The *Xmas
[Eng] 1-3pt jr cor,narrator,8 soli,
inst (med easy) sc,cor pts
SCHOTTS ED. 5144 s.p., ipa (K51)

Die Weihnachtsgeschichte *Xmas
[Ger] 1-3pt jr cor,narrator,8 soli,
inst (med easy) sc,cor pts
SCHOTTS ED. 3565 s.p., ipa (K52)

KEIN HALMLEIN WACHST AUF ERDEN see
Bach, Wilhelm Friedemann

KEINER KANN MEINEN KUMMER VERSTEHN see
Petersen, Rolf, Nobody Knows De
Trouble I've Seen

KELLAM
And The Angel Came In Unto Mary
(med easy) OXFORD 42.342 $.25 (K53)

Go-Day, Sire Christemas *Xmas,carol
SATB (med) OXFORD 84.179 $.35 (K54)

KELLER
Come And Behold *anthem
(Christiansen, Paul) SATB AUGSBURG
11-3010 $.10 (K55)

Glory To God, The Saviour, King
*Xmas
(Cassler) SATB oct SCHMITT 8511
$.45 (K56)

KELLER, HOMER
Magnificat
SATB,pno AM.COMP.AL. $4.95 (K57)
SATB,2fl,2ob,2clar,2bsn,4horn,3trp,
4trom,tuba,timp,bvl AM.COMP.AL.
sc $8.25, voc sc $4.95 (K58)

KELLING, HAJO (1907-)
Den Geboren Hat Eine Magd *Adv/Xmas
3 eq voices BOHM s.p. (K59)

KELLNER, JOHANN PETER
O Sacred Head, Now Wounded
(Johnson; McCorkle) mix cor,inst
BRODT 1003 $.35, ipr (K60)

KELLY
Communion Service (Series III)
SATB (med) OXFORD 42.383 $1.00
(K61)

KELLY, BRYAN (1934-)
Let There Be Light
SATB,S&narrator,2fl,2ob,2clar,2bsn,
4horn,2trp,3trom,tuba,timp,perc,
pno,harp,strings voc sc NOVELLO
rental (K62)

Stabat Mater
SATB,SB soli,fl,ob,clar,bsn,2trp,
2horn,timp,perc,pno,strings voc
sc NOVELLO rental (K63)

Surrexit Hodie *cant
SATB,Bar solo,org,strings,opt timp&
perc voc sc NOVELLO rental (K64)

Tenebrae Nocturnes
SATB,T solo,timp,perc,pno,strings
voc sc NOVELLO rental (K65)

KELLY, ROBERT (1916-)
Torment Of Job, The *Op.36
men cor,narrator,pno,3trp,3trom,
perc AM.COMP.AL. ipa (K66)

KELSO
Deeper, Deeper *see Jones

KELTERBORN, RUDOLF (1931-)
Dies Unus *ora
[Lat] 6pt men cor,S solo (diff,
(fragment)) BAREN. BA6078 rental
(K67)

KEMP, HELEN
Christmas In Holland *Xmas/Gen/
Thanks
jr cor,narrator (chancel play)
CHORISTERS D-1 $1.00 (K68)

God Is Always Near *Gen/Thanks
1-2pt CHORISTERS A-31 $.25 (K69)

Ride On Now, O King! *Palm
unis&opt desc,opt vol&fing.cym.
CHORISTERS A-54 $.35 (K70)

Welcome, Dearest Jesus *Xmas
unis,opt hndbl/fing.cym., or
glockenspiel or metallophone
CHORISTERS A-64 $.35 (K71)

KEMP, JOHN
Procession Into The World (Alleluia!)
*Gen/Thanks
unis&cong,org,brass/hndbl,perc
CHORISTERS A-95 $.30 (K72)

KEMP, WALTER
Three Christmas Songs *CC3U,Xmas
unis (med easy) WATERLOO $.40 (K73)

KEMPTER, KARL (1819-1871)
Adoro Te *Op.65, Commun,hymn
[Lat] cor,org,opt 5strings sc,cor
pts BOHM s.p., ipa (K74)

Hodie Christus Natus Est *Op.25a,
Xmas,Gradual
[Lat] 4pt mix cor,4strings,opt fl&
2clar&2horn&2trp&timp sc,cor pts
BOHM s.p., ipa (K75)

Messe In D *Op.9, Mass
[Lat] 4pt mix cor,org,strings,opt
fl&2clar&2horn&2trp&timp sc,cor
pts BOHM s.p., ipa (K76)

Pastoral-Messe *Op.42b, Xmas,Mass
men cor,org/orch sc,cor pts BOHM
s.p., ipa (K77)

Pastoralmesse In G *Op.24, Mass
[Lat] 4pt mix cor,org/strings&org&
opt fl&2clar&2horn&2trp&timp sc,
cor pts BOHM s.p., ipa (K78)

KENINS, TALIVADIS (1919-)
Christmas Chorale *Xmas
SATB (med diff) WATERLOO $.40 (K79)

Piae Cantiones Novae
SATB (diff) WATERLOO $1.15 (K80)

Psalm 150
SATB (med diff) WATERLOO $.40 (K81)

KENNEDY
  Child's Grace, A *anthem
    cor,pno oct MCAFEE M1035 $.35 (K82)

  Follow The Star *Xmas
    SATB&opt jr cor,trp,timp FISCHER,C
    CM 7856 $.35   (K83)

  Peace
    (med) FISCHER,C CM 7883 $.35 (K84)

  Rise Up, Shepherd *Xmas,anthem
    SATB oct MCAFEE M1051 $.40   (K85)

  Set Me As A Seal *Bibl
    SSA (med) FISCHER,C CM 7884 $.35
                                  (K86)

KENNEDY, JAMES
  Let There Be Peace
    SATB,pno WEINBERGER s.p.   (K87)
    SA,pno WEINBERGER s.p.   (K88)

KENT
  Snow Lay On The Ground, The *Xmas
    SATB SCHIRM.G LG51782 $.35   (K89)

  While Shepherds Watched *Xmas
    SATB SCHIRM.G LG51781 $.40   (K90)

KENT, F.J.
  Come, My Way, My Truth, My Life
    SATB,org GRAY CMR 3298 $.30   (K91)

KER
  Hear This
    unis GENERAL WDS GC55 $.35   (K92)

KERLL, [JOHANN CASPAR] (1627-1693)
  Missa Superba
    (Giebler, Albert C.) cor bds A-R ED
    $9.95   (K93)

KERN
  Den Die Hirten Lobeten Sehre
    [Ger] unis treb cor&3pt mix cor,
    org,inst MERSEBURG EM181   (K94)

KERN, JEROME (1885-1945)
  Prefaces For The New Sacramentary
    *CCU
    cor GIA G1918 $10.00   (K95)

KERN, MATTHAIS (1921-   )
  Kommet, Ihr Hirten *Xmas
    SATB,kbd,fl/pic,strings,perc,
    English horn (ballet) sc MOSELER
    s.p., ipa   (K96)

KERR
  In Love With The Lover Of My Soul
    *anthem/gospel
    (Boersma, J.) SATB oct SINGSPIR
    ZJP-8192 $.30   (K97)

  Melody Divine *anthem/gospel
    (Boersma, J.) SATB oct SINGSPIR
    ZJP-8191 $.30   (K98)

KERR, E.
  Now Glad Of Heart By Everyone!
    *Easter
    SATB,org GRAY CMR 3301 $.35   (K99)

KERRICK, MARY ELLEN
  Clap Your Hands, Children *anthem
    SATB WORD   (K100)

KERSTCANTATE see Bahler, Adr. U.

KERSTCANTATE see Polman, Th.

KERSTLIED see Pomper, A.

KERSTLIEDERENBLAD *CC100U,Xmas,hymn
    HEER 9 s.p.   (K101)

KERSTLIEDJES VOOR HET JONGE VOLKE see
    Tierie, J.F.

KERSTZANG see Spoel, A.

KETTERER, ERNST
  Ave Maris Stella
    [Lat] 4pt mix cor,acap BOHM s.p.
                                 .(K102)

  Crux Ave *Psntd,mot
    [Lat] 4pt mix cor,acap BOHM s.p.
                                  (K103)

  O Salutaris Hostia *Commun,mot
    [Lat] 4pt mix cor,acap BOHM s.p.
                                  (K104)

  Pange Lingua I
    [Lat] 4pt mix cor,acap BOHM s.p.
    contains also: Pange Lingua II
                                  (K105)

  Pange Lingua II
    see Ketterer, Ernst, Pange Lingua I

  Veni Creator
    [Lat] 4pt mix cor,acap BOHM s.p.
                                  (K106)

KEVIN'S CAROL see Faircloth

KEY, FRANCIS SCOTT (1779-1843)
  Star-Spangled Banner, The
    (Skillings, Otis) SATB oct LILLENAS
    AN-3847 $.25   (K107)

KEYHOLE SONG BOOK , THE *CC17U,folk
    (easy) unis,gtr GIA G1720 $1.50;
    SATB,kbd/gtr GIA G1742 $3.00 (K108)

KI LEKACH TOV see Richards, Stephen

KIELER LIEBFRAUENMESSE see Lemacher,
    Heinrich

KILLMAYER, WILHELM (1927-   )
  Begluckt Ist
    see Geistliche Hymnen Und Gesange

  Das Ganze Weltrund
    see Geistliche Hymnen Und Gesange

  Der Du Den Mensch Schufst
    see Geistliche Hymnen Und Gesange

  Der Purpurglanz Der Morgenfruhe
    see Geistliche Hymnen Und Gesange

  Der Wache Vogel
    see Geistliche Hymnen Und Gesange

  Geistliche Hymnen Und Gesange
    3-6pt mix cor (diff) sc SCHOTTS
    C 41 320 s.p.
    contains: Begluckt Ist; Das Ganze
      Weltrund; Der Du Den Mensch
      Schufst; Der Purpurglanz Der
      Morgenfruhe; Der Wache Vogel;
      Indes Der Schlaf   (K109)

  Indes Der Schlaf
    see Geistliche Hymnen Und Gesange

  Laudatu I "Laudatu Si Mi Signore Per
    Quilli Ke Perdonano Per Lo Tuo"
    [It] SSAATTBB,opt inst (diff) sc
    SCHOTTS C 43 363 s.p.   (K110)

  Laudatu II "Laudatu Si Mi Signore Per
    Sora Nostra Morte Corporale"
    [It] SSAATTB,acap/org (diff) sc
    SCHOTTS C 43 364 s.p.   (K111)

KIMBALL
  Come Let Us Join Our Cheerful Songs
    see Two Early American Anthems

  Jesus, Who Died A World To Save
    see Two Early American Anthems

  Two Early American Anthems *anthem,
    US
    (Van Camp) SATB SCHIRM.G LG51862
    $.40
    contains: Come Let Us Join Our
      Cheerful Songs; Jesus, Who Died
      A World To Save   (K112)

KIND-JESU-MESSE see Schweitzer,
    Johannes

KIND VAN BETHLEHEM see Voila

KINDELEIN IM STALL see Ahrens, Joseph

KINDELEIN IM STALL "O JESULEIN" see
    Lang, Hans

KINDELEIN ZART see Ahrens, Joseph

KINDELEIN ZART see Schroeder, Hermann

KINDLE THE GIFT OF GOD see Hancock,
    Gerre

KINDLER, PAUL
  Schnabels Mittlere Stationen *Op.11,
    Corpus
    [Lat] 4pt mix cor,brass sc,cor pts
    BOHM s.p., ipa   (K113)

KING
  Glory Of Christmas, The (composed
    with Hallette) *Xmas,anthem
    SATB,solo (easy) oct BROADMAN
    4540-58 $.30   (K114)

  Good Friday Meditation *Gd.Fri.,
    anthem
    SATB oct LORENZ C352 $.30   (K115)

  Welcome Home Children
    (Huff, Ronn) SATB oct BENSON S4365
    $.30   (K116)

KING AND I, THE see Lister, Mosie

KING AND THE STAR, THE see Cain, Noble

KING INDEED, A see Parks, Joe E.

KING IS COMING, THE see Gaither,
    William J. (Bill)

KING JESUS IS A-LISTENIN' *spir
    (Kirby) SATB oct LILLENAS AN-3851
    $.30   (K117)

KING JESUS IS A-LISTENING *spir
    (Dawson, William) TTBB,acap (med)
    FITZSIMONS 4025 $.25   (K118)
    (Dawson, William) SSA (med)
    FITZSIMONS 3061 $.25   (K119)
    (Dawson, William L.) SATB,acap (med)
    FITZSIMONS 2004 $.25   (K120)

KING, LEW
  Proclaim His Great Love *anthem
    SATB WORD   (K121)

KING OF ALL HEAVENS see Bach, Johann
    Sebastian

KING OF GLORY see La Rowe, Jane

KING OF GLORY *CC11U,anthem
    cor NOVELLO s.p. cmplt ed, cor pts
    also available separately   (K122)

KING OF GLORY, KING OF PEACE see
    Sandresky, M.V.

KING OF GLORY see Kruspe, Glenn

KING OF KINGS *Easter,anthem
    (Douglas) SATB FINE ARTS CM 1030 $.35
                                 (K123)

KING OF KINGS see Protheroe, Daniel

KING OF KINGS, THE see Peterson, John
    W.

KING OF LOVE, THE see Nolte, Ewald
    Valentin

KING OF LOVE IS ON HIS WAY, THE see
    Verrall, Pamela

KING OF LOVE MY SHEPHERD IS, THE
    (Follett) 2pt PRO ART 2809 $.35
                                 (K124)

KING OF LOVE MY SHEPHERD IS, THE see
    Englert, Eugene

KING OF LOVE MY SHEPHERD IS, THE see
    Whitaker, P.

KING SHALL REJOICE, THE see Boyce,
    William

KING SHALL REJOICE, THE see MacMillan,
    Ernest Campbell

KING SOLOMON see Bantock, Granville

KINGS, THE see Cornelius

KINGSLEY, GERSHON
  Modim Anachnu Lach
    [Heb] mix cor,cantor TRANSCON.
    TCL 666 $.75   (K125)

  Shepherd Me Lord (composed with
    Rosenbaum, Samuel)
    SSA BOURNE B211573-354 $.60 (K126)
    SAB BOURNE B211573-356 $.60 (K127)
    2pt BOURNE 211573-352 $.60   (K128)

KIRBY
  All I Have Belongs To Jesus *anthem
    SATB (easy) oct BROADMAN 4551-54
    $.30   (K129)

  Carol Of The Easter Victory
    SATB SHAWNEE A5667 $.30   (K130)

  Christ Living In Me *gospel
    1-2pt oct LILLENAS AN-5055 $.25
                                 (K131)

  Cradle In A Manger
    SATB SHAWNEE A5685 $.35   (K132)

  Discipleship *gospel
    SATB oct LILLENAS AN-1691 $.30
                                 (K133)

  House Of The Lord, The *anthem
    2pt FINE ARTS CM 1083 $.30   (K134)

  In The Lord's Name *anthem
    SAT/SAB FINE ARTS CM 1109 $.35
                                 (K135)

  It Is Good To Give Thanks *anthem
    2pt FINE ARTS CM 1058 $.30   (K136)

  Let Me So Live *hymn
    SATB oct LILLENAS AN-1692 $.30
                                 (K137)

  Lord Of Lords And King Eternal
    SATB SHAWNEE A5674 $.35   (K138)

  Master's Pace, The
    SATB,opt gtr PRO ART 2853 $.35
                                 (K139)

  Praise The Lord With Song *anthem
    SAT/SAB FINE ARTS CM 1086 $.30
                                 (K140)

  Prince Of Peace Is Coming, The
    *Xmas,anthem
    (Cram, James D.) SAT/SAB,opt gtr
    FINE ARTS CM 1099 $.35   (K141)

  Prophecies Of Christmas, The *Xmas,
    cant
    unis,inst PRO ART 1445 $1.25 (K142)

KIRBY (cont'd.)

Psalm For Singing, A
2pt jr cor oct LILLENAS AN-4039
$.30 (K143)

Rejoice And Be Merry
SATB SHAWNEE A5692 $.35 (K144)

Youth's Prayer *anthem
SATB FINE ARTS EP 46 $.35 (K145)

KIRBY, CHARLES
Have Thine Own Way
2pt oct HOPE CH 663 $.40 (K146)

What Do All Of These Things Mean?
*Xmas,folk
SABar&camb,pno,bvl,gtr CAMBIATA
L117208 $.35 (K147)
(Rich) BarBar&2camb CAMBIATA L97443 (K148)

KIRBY, L.M. JR.
All Poor Men And Humble *Xmas
SATB,acap FISCHER,J FEC 10112 $.30 (K149)

Boy Was Born, A *Xmas
SATB,org/pno FISCHER,J FEC 10124
$.30 (K150)

KIRCHENGESANGE see Hassler, Hans Leo

KIRCHENLIEDER-HEFTSAMMLUNG *CCU
men cor,acap TONOS 4607 s.p. (K151)

KIRCHER, JOHANN
St. Canisius-Messe *Op.28, Mass
[Lat] 4pt mix cor,org/fl,2clar,
2horn,2trp,trom,strings,timp,org
sc,cor pts BOHM s.p., ipa (K152)

St. Martinus-Messe *Op 26, Mass
[Lat] 4pt mix cor,org sc,cor pts
BOHM s.p., ipa (K153)

KIRK
Antiphon (Psalm 105)
SATB,pno/org,opt bass,perc PRO ART
1271 $.85, ipa (K154)

Behold, He Cometh! *anthem
SAB,inst oct LILLENAS AN-1089 $.30,
ipa (K155)

Give Him Your Hand
SATB KJOS 5910 $.50 (K156)

In The Last Days! *anthem
SATB,2tamb oct LILLENAS AT-1103
$.35 (K157)

Let The People Praise Thee
SATB,opt trp oct SCHMITT 5910 $.40 (K158)

Praise The Lord
SATB,opt tamb PRO ART 2788 $.40 (K159)

Psalm 105 *see Antiphon

Rejoice
2pt PRO ART 2818 $.35 (K160)

Ye Shall Be Witnesses *anthem
SAB,inst oct LILLENAS AT-1101 $.30,
ipa (K161)

KIRK, THERON W. (1919-)
Christ The Sure Foundation
SATB RICHMOND MI-91 $.35 (K162)

O Shepherds Go Quickly *Xmas
SATB RICHMOND MI-96 $.35 (K163)

Sing, Rejoice
SATB,acap oct SOMERSET SP 724 $.35 (K164)

KIRKHAM, GAYLA
O That I Were An Angel
SSA PIONEER 1019 $.40 (K165)

KIRKLAND, TERRY
Prayer For America (from Sound Of
America, The) anthem
1-2pt,kbd BROADMAN 4560-55 $.35 (K166)

Sound Of America, The
1-2pt jr cor,narrator BROADMAN
4518-12 $2.25 (K167)

KIRKPATRICK
Away In A Manger *Xmas,anthem
(DeCou, Harold) SATB oct SINGSPIR
ZJP-3008 $.25 (K168)

Jesus Saves (composed with Peninger)
*anthem
SATB (easy) oct BROADMAN 4540-67
$.30 (K169)

Oh, Steal Away Softly To Jesus
*gospel
(Lister, Mosie) SATB oct LILLENAS
AL-1036 $.30 (K170)

KIRKPATRICK (cont'd.)

Redeemed *anthem/gospel
(Mercer, Elmo) SATB oct SINGSPIR
ZJP-8150 $.30 (K171)

Redeemed *see Crosby

We Have An Anchor *anthem/gospel
(Yungton, Al) SATB oct SINGSPIR
ZJP-8005 $.30 (K172)

When Love Shines In *anthem/gospel
(DeCou, Harold) SATB oct SINGSPIR
ZJP-8074 $.30 (K173)
(Mickelson, Paul) SSATB oct
LILLENAS AN-1714 $.30 (K174)

KIRKPATRICK, WILLIAM J.
He Hideth My Soul *anthem
(Warford, Hermon) SATB WORD CS-2604
$.35 (K175)

O To Be Like Thee *anthem
(Landon, Stewart) SA/SATB (easy)
oct LORENZ A 567 $.35 (K176)

'Tis So Sweet To Trust In Jesus
*anthem/gospel
(Bolks, Dick) SATB oct SINGSPIR
ZJP-8151 $.30 (K177)

KIRSCHKE, D.
Living Water *folk
(Krogstad, B.) SATB oct SINGSPIR
ZJP-5059 $.35 (K178)

Written In The Book Of Love *folk
(Krogstad, B.) SATB oct SINGSPIR
ZJP-5054 $.30 (K179)

KITCHEN
Broken Pieces *see Martin, Gilbert
M.

KITSON, CHARLES HERBERT (1874-1944)
As Pants The Hart
(Thomas) SATB (diff) FITZSIMONS
2204 $.35 (K180)

KITTLESON
On The Mountainside
SATB BOURNE B231019-358 $.50 (K181)

KJERULF, [HALFDAN] (1815-1868)
Jubilate, Amen!
SATB oct SCHMITT W138 $.30 (K182)

KLEIMAN, RICHARD
All The Way *anthem
(Allen, Lanny) SATB WORD CS-2641
$.35 see from Music For The Young
Church (K183)

Music For The Young Church *see All
The Way (K184)

KLEIN, BERNHARD (1793-1832)
Der Herr Ist Mein Hirt (Psalm 23)
men cor,acap TONOS 3008 s.p. (K185)

Psalm 23 *see Der Herr Ist Mein Hirt

KLEIN, LOTHAR (1932-)
Exaltation, An
SATB (med diff) WATERLOO $.50 (K186)

KLEINE DEUTSCHE MESSE see Huber, Klaus

KLEINE FESTMESSE ZU EHREN DER HEILIGEN
EUCHARISTIE UBER "LAUDA SION" see
Monter, Josef

KLEINE HIRTENKANTATE see Seckinger,
Konrad

KLEINE HIRTENMUSIK ZUR WEIHNACHT see
Coenen, Hans

KLEINE HOCHZEITSMOTETTE see Burkhart,
Franz

KLEINE MESSE see Heftrich, Wilhelm

KLEINE MUTTERGOTTESMESSE "AVE MARIA
ZART" see Spranger, Jorg

KLEINE ORGELSOLOMESSE see Haydn,
(Franz) Joseph, Missa Brevis In
Honorem Sti. Joannis De Deo In B

KLEINE ORGELSOLOMESSE see Haydn,
(Franz) Joseph, Missa Brevis Sti.
Joannis De Deo

KLEINE OSTERKANTATE "AUFERSTANDEN
HEUTE" see Jehn

KLEINE SCHWARZE PASSION see Koster,
Ernst, Little Negro Passion

KLEINE WEIHNACHTSLIEDER-KANTATE see
Woehl, Waldemar

KLEINER LIEDPSALTER see Wagner

KLEINES MAGNIFICAT see Buchsel

KLEVDAL, T.
Dusty Road, The *folk
(Blake, K.) SATB oct SINGSPIR
ZJP-5056 $.25 (K187)

KLIEWER, JONAH
My Song Is Love Unknown
SATB,pno (med easy) GENTRY G-296
$.30 (K188)

KLUMP, GEORGE E.
Lord Jesus Christ, Be Present Now
*anthem
unis sr cor/unis treb cor,org oct
NATIONAL WHC-29 $.35 (K189)

Psalm 120
SATB,S solo,org/pno oct NATIONAL
WHC-27 $.35 (K190)

KLUSMEIER, R.T.A.
Christmas Message
SATB HARRIS HC 4058 $.60 (K191)

Gift Of New Sight, The
SATB HARRIS HC 4059 $.60 (K192)

Lord Is My Shepherd, The
SATB HARRIS HC 4063 $.50 (K193)

Man Is Not Alone
SATB HARRIS HC 4064 $.40 (K194)

Parting Blessing, A
SATB HARRIS HC 4066 $.60 (K195)

Praise To The Lord *CC12U
cor, dance orchestra HARRIS $2.95 (K196)

KNAB, ARMIN (1881-1951)
Den Toten "Frei Von Menschlichen
Geboten"
men cor,acap sc SCHOTTS CHBL 33
s.p. (K197)
1-3pt men cor,inst sc SCHOTTS
C 37 859 s.p. (K198)

Weihnachtskantate *Xmas,cant
mix cor,opt narrator,SABBB soli,ob,
2horn,trp,strings,timp (med) voc
sc,cor pts SCHOTTS ED. 3278 s.p.,
ipa (K199)
mix cor,SA soli,org,bvl,vln (med)
voc sc SCHOTTS ED. 4039 s.p., ipa (K200)

KNAPP, (MRS.) JOSEPH F.
Blessed Assurance *anthem/gospel
(DeCou, Harold) SATB oct SINGSPIR
ZJP-8007 $.30 (K201)

Cleansing Wave, The *anthem/gospel
(DeCou, Harold) SATB oct SINGSPIR
ZJP-8080 $.30 (K202)

Open The Gates Of Temple *Easter/
Palm,anthem
(Johnson, Norman) SAB/SATB&unis/SA
oct SINGSPIR $.30 (K203)

KNIGHT OF BETHLEHEM, THE see Burroughs

KNOBEL, EWALD
Tantum Ergo
[Lat] 4pt mix cor,acap BOHM s.p. (K204)

KNOCK, KNOCK see Winter, Sister Miriam
Therese

KNOX, CHARLES
Festival Procession *Gen/Proces/
Thanks
unis&opt ATB,org,4brass sc
CHORISTERS A-114 $1.10, cor pts
CHORISTERS A-114C $.30 (K205)

Sing We To Our God Above *Gen/Thanks
1-3pt CHORISTERS A-91 $.35 (K206)

KNUDSEN
When Lights Are Lit On Christmas Eve
*Xmas,anthem
(Johnson, Norman) SATB oct SINGSPIR
ZJP-3028 $.25 (K207)

KNUTSEN, INGVAR
Ar An Min Rost Som Anglars Tunga
4pt mix cor ERIKS 332 s.p. (K208)

KOCH, HEINZ (1916-)
Wir Glauben All An Einen Gott
SATB (contains also Des Herrn Wort
Bleibt In Ewigkeit) SCHWEIZER.
SK 60.06 s.p. see also
MUSIKBEILAGE ZUM "EVANGELISCHEN
KIRCHENCHOR 1960" (K209)

KOCH, JOHANNES H.E. (1918-)
Jauchzt, Alle Lande, Gott Zu Ehren
SAT/SAB/SA,treb inst,opt bass inst
HANSSLER 14.181 s.p. (K210)

KOCH, JOHANNES H.E. (cont'd.)

   Lektion Uber Liebe *Bibl/cant
     SATB,Bar solo,org,2trp,2trom sc
     HANSSLER HE 10.321 s.p., ipa
                          (K211)

   Lobt Gott, Ihr Frommen Christen
     SAT/SAB/1-2pt,opt treb inst
     HANSSLER 14.202 s.p.   (K212)

   Nun Lasst Uns Gott Dem Herren
     SAT/SAB/SA,opt treb inst&bass inst
     (two settings) HANSSLER 14.227
     s.p.   (K213)

KOCH, KARL
   Festmesse Zu Ehren Der Geburt Unseres
     Herrn Jesu Christi *Op.7, Xmas,
     Mass
     "Mass For The Nativity" [Lat] 4pt
     mix cor,org/fl,ob,2clar,bsn,
     2horn,2trp,2trom,strings,timp sc,
     cor pts BOHM s.p., ipa   (K214)

   Jubilate Deo *Op.6,No.1, Fest
     [Lat] 4pt mix cor,org/fl&2clar&
     2horn&2trp&2trom&strings sc,cor
     pts BOHM s.p., ipa   (K215)

   Mass For The Nativity *see Festmesse
     Zu Ehren Der Geburt Unseres Herrn
     Jesu Christi

KOCH, MARKUS
   Missa In Honorem Sancti Isidori
     *Op.15, Mass
     [Lat] 4pt mix cor,org/fl&2clar&
     2horn&trom&strings&timp sc,cor
     pts BOHM s.p., ipa   (K216)

KOCH, MARTIN
   Jubelhymne *Op.76, Fest
     1-3pt wom cor/1-3pt jr cor,pno,opt
     4-5strings sc,cor pts BOHM s.p.,
     ipa   (K217)

KOCHER
   As With Gladness Men Of Old *Xmas,
     anthem
     (Johnson, Norman) SSATB oct
     SINGSPIR ZJP-3010 $.25   (K218)

   For The Beauty Of The Earth *anthem
     (Gerig) SATB,brass oct LILLENAS
     AN-2383 $.30   (K219)

KOCHER, [CONRAD] (1786-1872)
   For The Beauty Of The Earth *Thanks,
     anthem
     (DeCou, Harold) SATB oct SINGSPIR
     ZJP-3107 $.30   (K220)

KODALY, ZOLTAN (1882-1967)
   Adventi Enek
     mix cor BUDAPEST 7154 s.p. (K221)

   Ave Maria
     jr cor/wom cor BUDAPEST 6835 s.p.
                        (K222)

   God's Mercy
     (Russell-Smith) TBB,acap oct BOOSEY
     5877 $.40   (K223)

   Greetings On St. John's Day
     (Russell-Smith) SAB,acap oct BOOSEY
     5866 $.35   (K224)

KOENIG, FRANZ
   Requiem
     men cor,acap TONOS 3938 s.p. (K225)

KOHS, ELLIS B. (1916-   )
   Psalm 23
     SSAATTBB,SATB soli,acap AM.COMP.AL.
     $11.00   (K226)

   Psalm 25
     SATB,2fl,2ob,2clar,2bsn,2horn,2trp,
     2trom,strings AM.COMP.AL. sc
     $8.80, voc sc $6.60   (K227)

KOL NIDRE see Schoenberg, Arnold

KOL RINNAH see Lewandowski, Louis

KOLL, FRITZ
   Die Passion Des Menschensohns *Psntd
     "St. Luke Passion" 3-4pt mix cor,
     SBar soli,fl,strings,org
     MERSEBURG EM535   (K228)

   St. Luke Passion *see Die Passion
     Des Menschensohns

KOLTER
   Schmucke Dich, O Liebe Seele
     SAT/ASB HANSSLER 14.157 s.p.
     contains also: Peter, Johann
     Friedrich, Schmucke Dich, O Liebe
     Seele (SAT/SAB,treb inst,opt bass
     inst)   (K229)

KOM HAAST'LIJK, HERE JEZUS
   mix cor sc HEER 2214 s.p.   (K230)

KOM KARLEKENS ANDE see Johansen, Sven-
   Erik

KOMM, DER VOLKER HEILAND DU see
   Lemacher, Heinrich

KOMM, HEIL'GER GEIST see Scheck, Helmut

KOMM, HEILIGER GEIST see Cruger, Johann

KOMM, HEILIGER GEIST see Pfluger, Hans
   Georg

KOMM, HEILIGER GEIST, ERFULL DIE HERZEN
   see Werner

KOMM, HEILIGER GEIST, HERRE GOTT see
   David, Johann Nepomuk

KOMM HER, MIT FLEISS ZU SCHAUEN see
   Wenzel, Eberhard

KOMM, NACHTIGALL MEIN! see Lang, Hans

KOMM, NACHTIGALL MEIN! see Schroeder,
   Hermann

KOMM NUN, HOCHSTES FEST see Burgmann,
   J. Hartmut

KOMM, O GEIST see Desch, Rudolf

KOMM, SUSSER TOD! see Bach, Johann
   Sebastian

KOMMET HER ZU MIR ALLE see Michel,
   Josep

KOMMET IHR HIRTEN see Heer, Emil

KOMMET, IHR HIRTEN see Kern, Matthais

KOMMT ALL HEREIN, IHR ENGELEIN *Xmas,
   carol/folk
   (Marx, K.) [Ger] 4pt men cor
   MERSEBURG EM 9050   (K231)

KOMMT ALLE BEI NACHT see Taubert, Karl
   Heinz

KOMMT HER, DES KONIGS AUFGEBOT see
   Gadsch, Herbert

KOMMT HER, IHR GESEGNETEN MEINES VATERS
   see Scheidt, Samuel

KOMMT HER ZU MIR, SPRICHT GOTTES SOHN
   see Herzogenberg, Heinrich von

KOMMT HERZU see Liebhold

KOMMT, SEELEN, DIESER TAG see Bach,
   Johann Sebastian

KOMMT, SINGT DEM SCHONEN KINDELEIN! see
   Backer, Hans

KOMMT'S HER IHR HIRTEN *Xmas,anthem,
   Aus,16th cent
   (Theuring, G.) "Come Shepherds, One
   And All" [Eng/Ger] SATB,ST soli oct
   AGAPE AG 7188 $.40   (K232)

KOMMUNIONGESANG "KOMMT UND LASST UNS
   CHRISTUS EHREN" see Trapp, Willy

KONIG BIST DU, HERR! see Monter, Josef

KONIGIN IM HIMMELREICH see Degen, J.

KONIGIN IN GOTTES REICHEN see Piechler,
   Arthur

KONTRAFAKTUR II NACH DER "MISSA
   CUIUSVIS TONI" VON JOHANNES
   OCKEGHEM see Hufschmidt, Wolfgang

KONZERT IN FORM EINER TEUTSCHEN
   BEGRABNIS see Schutz, Heinrich

KORALDISKANTATER DEL 1-4 see Holm,
   Gunnar

KORALER FRAN SKANE *CCU
   (Rosenberg; Runback; Hjorth) 4pt mix
   cor ERIKS 172 s.p.   (K233)

KORTE, KARL (1928-   )
   May The Sun Bless Us
     TTBB,pno/brass SCHIRM.EC 2317 s.p.,
     ipr   (K234)

   Psalm 13
     SATB,electronic tape sc SCHIRM.EC
     2926 s.p., ipa   (K235)

   Sing Praises To The Lord
     mix cor BRODT 599 $.22   (K236)

KOSTER, ERNST (1900-   )
   Kleine Schwarze Passion *see Little
   Negro Passion

   Little Negro Passion
     "Kleine Schwarze Passion" [Eng/Ger]
     4-6pt mix cor,acap (med diff) sc,

KOSTER, ERNST (cont'd.)

     voc pt SCHOTTS ED.4858 s.p.
                         (K237)

KOX, HANS (1930-   )
   Trois Psaumes, Pour Le Temps Present
     *sac/sec,CC3U,Psalm
     mix cor,4 soli,2fl,2ob,2clar,2bsn,
     3horn,strings,perc,timp,
     xylophone DONEMUS   (K238)

KRAFT, KARL (1908-   )
   Augsburger Domfest-Messe *Op.100,
     Mass
     [Ger] mix cor&cong,opt solo,org,opt
     2trp&2trom&tuba BOHM sc s.p., cor
     pts s.p., ipa   (K239)

   Cantate Domino *Op.94, Mass
     [Lat] STB/ATB,org sc,cor pts BOHM
     s.p.   (K240)

   Deutsche Totenmesse *Req
     [Ger] SABar,acap sc,cor pts BOHM
     s.p.   (K241)
     [Ger] SA,org sc,cor pts BOHM s.p.
                        (K242)

   Kurze Und Leichte Messe In B *Op.68,
     Mass
     [Lat] 4pt mix cor,acap (B flat maj)
     sc,cor pts BOHM s.p.   (K243)

   Messe In G *Op.47, Mass
     [Lat] 4pt mix cor,org sc,cor pts
     BOHM s.p.   (K244)

   Missa De Sanctissima Trinitate
     *Op.86, Mass
     [Lat] 6pt mix cor,acap sc,cor pts
     BOHM s.p.   (K245)

   Missa Dominicalis *Op.74, Mass
     [Lat] mix cor/2 eq voices,org sc,
     cor pts BOHM s.p.   (K246)

   Missa Pro Defunctis *Op.95
     [Lat] SABar,opt org sc,cor pts BOHM
     s.p.   (K247)

   Missa Unisona *Op.97, Mass
     [Lat] unis,opt solo,org sc,cor pts
     BOHM s.p.   (K248)

   Psallite Deo *Op.87, Mass
     [Lat] 4pt mix cor,org sc,cor pts
     BOHM s.p.   (K249)

   Sanctae Crucis *Op.70, Mass
     [Lat] mix cor,org sc,cor pts BOHM
     s.p., ipa   (K250)

   Statuit *Op.92, Mass
     [Lat] 4pt mix cor,org/strings sc,
     cor pts BOHM s.p., ipa   (K251)

KRAFT, LEO (1922-   )
   Proverb Of Solomon, A
     SATB,pno GENERAL 761CH $.60 (K252)

KRAMER, GOTTHOLD
   Christ Ist Erstanden
     see Jehn, Kleine Osterkantate
     "Auferstanden Heute"

   Ich Weiss, Mein Gott, Dass All Mein
     Tun
     SA/jr cor,vcl,opt bvl, and
     metallophon HANSSLER 12.112 s.p.
     contains also: Kretzschmar,
     Gunther, Freuet Euch Im Herrn
     Allewege (SSA/jr cor); Michel,
     Josep, Vater Unser Im Himmelreich
     (SA/jr cor)   (K253)

KRAPF, GERHARD (1924-   )
   Four Service Rounds *CC4U,round
     cor CHANTRY CAR 731 $.25   (K254)

   Psalm 130 *anthem,Contemp
     SATB oct CHANTRY COA 7354   (K255)

   Seven Verses *anthem
     eq voices AUGSBURG 11-1751 $.40
                         (K256)

KRAUSE
   Everybody Needs Somebody *see Gibson

   Help Me Be Me *see Fearheiley

   Hey God, I Really Love You *see
   Gibson

KRAUSE, E.
   Lobe Den Herrn *Op.54, Marriage,cant
     LIENAU sc s.p., cor pts s.p. (K257)

KRAUSE, THEODOR (1833-1910)
   Das Vater Unser *Op.40
     LIENAU cor pts s.p. s.p.   (K258)

KRECOVICE MASS, THE see Suk, Josef,
   Krecovicka Mse

KRECOVICKA MSE see Suk, Josef

KREMER, KARL
  Exsultate Deo *Op.10, Mass
    [Lat] 4pt mix cor,org/fl,ob,clar,
    bsn,horn,2trp,3trom sc,cor pts
    BOHM s.p., ipr   (K259)

  Pange Lingua *Op.7,No.1
    [Lat] 4pt mix cor,org/2trp&2trom&
    tuba sc,cor pts BOHM s.p., ipa
    contains also: Tantum Ergo, Op.7,
    No.2   (K260)

  Tantum Ergo *Op.7,No.2
    see Kremer, Karl, Pange Lingua

KRENEK, ERNST (1900-   )
  Drei Geistliche Chore *see Oculi Mei
    Semper Ad Dominum; Psalmverse Zur
    Kommunion; Veni Sanctificator
                                    (K261)

  Messe "Gib Uns Frieden" *Mass
    SATB,SATB soli,orch (med diff)
    BAREN. BA6064 rental   (K262)

  Oculi Mei Semper Ad Dominum
    SABar (med easy) sc SCHOTTS
    C 39 419 s.p. see from Drei
    Geistliche Chore   (K263)

  Psalmverse Zur Kommunion
    SA/SATB (med easy) sc SCHOTTS
    C 39 420 s.p. see from Drei
    Geistliche Chore   (K264)

  Veni Sanctificator
    SABar (med easy) sc SCHOTTS
    C 39 559 s.p. see from Drei
    Geistliche Chore   (K265)

KRENN, FRANZ (1816-1897)
  Pastoral-Messe In D Zu Ehren Des
    Gottlichen Kindes *Op.6, Mass
    [Lat] 4pt mix cor,org/fl,2clar,
    2trp,strings,org sc,cor pts BOHM
    s.p., ipa   (K266)

KRETER, LEO
  Sound A Trumpet
    SATB,opt 2trp&trom GALAXY 1.2423.1
    $.40, ipa   (K267)

KRETZSCHMAR, GUNTHER (1929-   )
  Der Blinde Bettler
    jr cor,2 soli,gtr,opt org,cembalo
    sc HANSSLER 12.234 s.p.   (K268)

  Der Herr Ist Mein Licht Und Mein Heil
    SSA/jr cor,rec,timp, triangle,
    glockenspiel, metallophone, 2
    xylophone sc HANSSLER 12.226 s.p.
                                    (K269)

  Der Samaritaner
    jr cor,S rec,A rec,vcl/bvl,timp,
    glockenspiel, metallophone,
    xylophone sc HANSSLER 12.235 s.p.
                                    (K270)

  Dies Ist Der Tag, Den Der Herr Macht
    unis,opt solo,org sc HANSSLER
    12.223 s.p.   (K271)

  Freuet Euch Im Herrn Allewege
    see Kramer, Gotthold, Ich Weiss,
    Mein Gott, Dass All Mein Tun

  Herr, Neige Deine Ohren
    unis,org,2vln,vcl sc HANSSLER
    12.224 s.p.   (K272)

  Machet Die Tore Weit
    see Tzschoppe, Eberhart, Halleluja.
    Dies Ist Der Tag, Den Der Herr
    Macht

  Rufe Mich An In Der Not
    see Jehn, Singt Das Lied Der Freude
    Uber Gott

KREUTZ, ROBERT E.
  Cantate Domino *anthem
    "Sing To God" SATB,acap WORLD
    CA-4011-8 $.80   (K273)

  Mass Of Thanksgiving *Mass
    SATB/cong (easy) GIA G1794 $1.00
                                    (K274)

  Sing To God *see Cantate Domino

  To You, O Lord, I Lift My Soul
    *anthem
    SATB,org (easy) GIA G1879 $.35
                                    (K275)

KREUTZER, KONRADIN
  Forschen Nach Gott
    men cor,acap TONOS 6312 s.p. (K276)

KRIEG, FRANZ
  Weihnachtsmesse *Xmas,Mass
    [Lat] cor,soli,org,strings sc,cor
    pts BOHM s.p., ipa   (K277)

KRIEGER, FRITZ
  De Profundis
    [Lat] 4pt mix cor,acap BOHM s.p.
                                    (K278)

KRIEGER, FRITZ (cont'd.)
  Missa In Honorem Sanctissimi
    Salvatoris *Mass
    [Lat] 4-6pt mix cor,org sc,cor pts
    BOHM s.p.   (K279)

  O Sacrum Convivium *Commun,mot
    [Lat] SSATBB,acap BOHM s.p.   (K280)

  Oremus Pro Pontifice
    [Lat] SSATB,acap BOHM s.p.   (K281)

  Regnum Ejus *mot
    [Lat] 5-6pt mix cor,acap sc,cor pts
    BOHM s.p.   (K282)

KRIEGER, JOHANN PHILIPP (1649-1725)
  Nu Tackar Gud Allt Folk *see Nun
    Danket Alle Gott

  Nun Danket Alle Gott
    (Selen, E.) "Nu Tackar Gud Allt
    Folk" mix cor,cont,2vln ERIKS 167
    s.p.   (K283)

  Rufet Nicht Die Weisheit *cant
    SATB,STB soli,strings,cont sc,cor
    pts EGTVED KB115 s.p., ipa (K284)

KRIEKEN, VAN
  Onze Doden *Psntd
    mix cor/unis,pno/harmonium HEER 309
    s.p.   (K285)

KRIETSCH, GEORG (1904-1969)
  Cherubinische Gesange
    men cor,acap cmplt ed TONOS 4040
    s.p.
    contains: Der Schlaf Ist
    Dreierlei; Die Liebe, Wenn Sie
    Neu, Gott Sind Die Wege Gleich
                                    (K286)

  Der Schlaf Ist Dreierlei
    see Cherubinische Gesange

  Die Liebe, Wenn Sie Neu
    see Cherubinische Gesange

  Gott Sind Die Wege Gleich
    see Cherubinische Gesange

KRIPPENLIED see Weber, Bernhard

KRIPPENLIED "KOMMT HERBEI ZUR KRIPPE"
  see Weber, Bernhard

KRIST LA I DODENS LENKER see Karlsen,
  Kjell Mork

KRIST STO OPP AV DODE see Kverno, Trond

KRISTUS AR UPPSTANDEN see Bruck, Arnold
  von, Christ Der Ist Erstanden

KROEGER
  Hear My Prayer, O Lord
    SATB,acap oct BOOSEY 5905 $.70
                                    (K287)

KROEGER, KARL see Bechler

KROGSTAD, BOB
  Come And Praise *Easter,Contemp
    jr cor oct GOSPEL 05 TM 0156 $.40
                                    (K288)

  Hark! The Glad Sound! *Xmas,anthem
    SSATBB oct SINGSPIR ZJP-3048 $.35
                                    (K289)

  He Lives (composed with Eleiott, Max)
    *Easter,cant
    cor,brass SINGSPIR 5056 $1.95, ipa
                                    (K290)

  Praise The Lord, His Glories Show
    *anthem
    SATB oct SINGSPIR ZJP-7369 $.35
                                    (K291)

  Psalm 121 *anthem
    SATB,opt fl/vln oct SINGSPIR
    ZJP-7363 $.30   (K292)

  Rejoice *see Eleiott, Max

KROMOLICKI, JOSEPH (1882-1961)
  Aeterne Rex
    see Funf Eucharistische Hymnen Fur
    Die Prozession Am
    Fronleichnamstag

  Assumpta Est *Op.29,No.2, Offer
    [Lat] 4pt mix cor,org sc,cor pts
    BOHM s.p.   (K293)

  Ave Regina Coelorum
    see Zwei Lateinische Mariengesange

  Chore Der Passion Nach Dem Heiligen
    Johannes
    see Feria Sexta In Parasceve

  Ecce Sacerdos *Op.22
    [Lat] 4pt mix cor,org,opt 2trp&
    2trom sc,cor pts BOHM s.p., ipa
                                    (K294)

  Elegerunt Apostoli *Op.25,No.3,
    Offer
    [Lat] 4pt mix cor,org sc,cor pts

KROMOLICKI, JOSEPH (cont'd.)

  BOHM s.p.   (K295)

  Feria Sexta In Parasceve *Gd.Fri.
    [Lat] 4pt mix cor,acap sc,cor pts
    BOHM s.p.
    contains: Chore Der Passion Nach
    Dem Heiligen Johannes, Op.40,
    No.1; Popule Meus, Op.40,No.2;
    Vexilla Regis, Op.40,No.3
                                    (K296)

  Funf Eucharistische Hymnen Fur Die
    Prozession Am Fronleichnamstag
    *hymn
    [Lat] 4pt mix cor,2trp,2horn,2trom,
    tuba,opt timp sc,cor pts BOHM
    s.p., ipa
    contains: Aeterne Rex, Op.24a,
    No.4; Pange Lingua, Op.24a,
    No.5; Sacris Solemniis, Op.24a,
    No.1; Salutis Humanae Sator,
    Op.24a,No.3; Verbum Supernum,
    Op.24a,No.2   (K297)

  Funf Pange Lingua *Op.11, CC5U
    [Lat] 4-6pt mix cor,acap sc,cor pts
    BOHM s.p.   (K298)

  Jauchzet Gott, Alle Lande *Op.32,
    Fest,Psalm
    mix cor,S solo,org sc,cor pts BOHM
    s.p.   (K299)

  Laetentur Coeli *Op.25,No.1, Xmas,
    Offer
    [Lat] 4pt mix cor,org sc,cor pts
    BOHM s.p.   (K300)

  Messe In B-Moll *Op.9, Mass
    [Lat] 4pt mix cor,acap (B flat min)
    sc,cor pts BOHM s.p.   (K301)

  Missa Brevis In Es *Op.14, Mass
    [Lat] 4pt mix cor,acap (E flat maj)
    sc,cor pts BOHM s.p.   (K302)

  O Gloriosa Virginum
    see Zwei Lateinische Mariengesange

  Pange Lingua
    see Funf Eucharistische Hymnen Fur
    Die Prozession Am
    Fronleichnamstag

  Popule Meus
    see Feria Sexta In Parasceve

  Reges Tharsis *Op.25,No.4, Epiph,
    Offer
    [Lat] 4pt mix cor,org sc,cor pts
    BOHM s.p.   (K303)

  Sacris Solemniis
    see Funf Eucharistische Hymnen Fur
    Die Prozession Am
    Fronleichnamstag

  Salutis Humanae Sator
    see Funf Eucharistische Hymnen Fur
    Die Prozession Am
    Fronleichnamstag

  Te Deum *Op.43
    [Lat] 4pt mix cor,org,opt 2trp&
    2trom sc,cor pts BOHM s.p., ipa
                                    (K304)

  Tui Sunt Coeli *Op.25,No.2, Xmas,
    Offer
    [Lat] 4pt mix cor,org sc,cor pts
    BOHM s.p.   (K305)

  Verbum Supernum
    see Funf Eucharistische Hymnen Fur
    Die Prozession Am
    Fronleichnamstag

  Vexilla Regis
    see Feria Sexta In Parasceve

  Zwei Lateinische Mariengesange
    [Lat] 4pt mix cor,org/2trp,2trom
    sc,cor pts BOHM s.p., ipa
    contains: Ave Regina Coelorum,
    Op.57,No.1; O Gloriosa
    Virginum, Op.57,No.2   (K306)

  Zweite Festmesse In D In Honorem St.
    Sophiae *Mass
    [Lat] 4pt mix cor,org/org&brass/
    org&strings sc,cor pts BOHM s.p.,
    ipa   (K307)

KRONBERG, G.
  Deutsche Singmesse *Mass
    [Ger] 2pt,org/harmonium sc,cor pts
    BOHM s.p.   (K308)

  Ehre Sei Dem Vater
    see Weihe Des Tages

  Erde Singe *Fest
    3 eq voices BOHM s.p.   (K309)

KRONBERG, G. (cont'd.)

Gottes Lob Zur Nacht
    see Weihe Des Tages

In Gottes Namen Fang Ich An
    see Weihe Des Tages

Lobsinget Dem Herrn
    see Weihe Des Tages

Nun Singt Dem Herrn Ein Neues Lied
    *Fest
    3 eq voices BOHM s.p.   (K310)

Singt Dem Herrn Ein Neues Lied
    see Weihe Des Tages

Wahrlich, Hier Ist Das Haus Gottes
    *Fest
    5pt mix cor,acap BOHM s.p.   (K311)

Weihe Des Tages
    3 eq voices BOHM s.p.
    contains: Ehre Sei Dem Vater;
    Gottes Lob Zur Nacht; In Gottes
    Namen Fang Ich An; Lobsinget
    Dem Herrn; Singt Dem Herrn Ein
    Neues Lied   (K312)

KRONUNGSMESSE IN ES-DUR see Liszt,
Franz

KRUSPE, GLENN
King Of Glory   *CCU,anthem
    jr cor WATERLOO $1.50   (K313)

This New Christmas Carol   *Xmas
    SSA (med easy) WATERLOO $.40 (K314)

KUBIK, GAIL (1914-   )
Christmas Offering, A
    mix cor,SATTB soli,acap voc sc
    BOOSEY $1.00   (K315)

KUBIZEK, AUGUSTINIAN (1918-   )
Ave Maria   *Op.37a,No.1
    SATB DOBLINGER G700 s.p.   (K316)

Neue Messe   *Op.32
    mix cor,acap (med diff) sc,voc pt
    SCHOTTS ED.6577 s.p.   (K317)

Psalm 126   *Op.31,No.3b
    SATB DOBLINGER G 650 s.p.   (K318)

Salve Regina   *Op.37a,No.2
    SATB DOBLINGER G 701 s.p.   (K319)

KUBLER, EMIL (1909-   )
Mit Freuden Zart
    SATB/SAT/SAB SCHWEIZER. SK 62.03
    s.p. see also MUSIKBEILAGE ZUM
    "EVANGELISCHEN KIRCHENCHOR 1962"
                                 (K320)

KUCERA
In A Far Off Town   *see Hrebic

KUCKUCK, FELICITAS
Lied, Das Die Welt Umkreist   *CC24U,
    hymn
    MOSELER s.p.   (K321)

KUEHNHAUSEN, JOHANN GEORG (? -1714)
O Lamm Gottes, Unschuldig
    SATB,cont (contains also: Das Blut
    Jesu Christi) SCHWEIZER.
    SK 64.03-4 s.p. see also
    MUSIKBEILAGE ZUM "EVANGELISCHEN
    KIRCHENCHOR 1964"   (K322)

KUHNAU, JOHANN (1660-1722)
Der Gerechte Kommt Um   *see Tristis
    Est Anima Mea

Tristis Est Anima Mea
    (Bach, J. S.) "Der Gerechte Kommt
    Um" SSATB,cont,2ob,strings sc
    HANSSLER 35.001 s.p., ipa   (K323)

Wie Schon Leuchtet Der Morgenstern
    SATB,high solo,cont,2horn,2A rec,
    strings SCHWEIZER. SK 167 sc
    s.p., cor pts s.p., ipa   (K324)

KUHNHOLD
Am Osterfest   *Op.22,No.2, Easter
    LIENAU sc s.p., cor pts s.p. (K325)

Weihnachten   *Op.22,No.4, Xmas
    LIENAU sc s.p., cor pts s.p. (K326)

Weihnachtslied   *Op.22,No.5, Xmas
    LIENAU sc s.p., cor pts s.p. (K327)

KUKUCK, FELICITAS (1914-   )
Allein Zu Dir, Herr Jesu Christ
    SAT/SAB,opt S solo,opt treb inst
    HANSSLER 14.166 s.p.   (K328)

Ich Singe Dir Mit Herz Und Mund
    see Heer, Emil, Singt Dem Herrn Ein
    Neues Lied
    unis&SAT/SAB (contains also: O Wie
    Sehr Lieblich Sind) SCHWEIZER.
    SK 68.04 s.p. see also

KUKUCK, FELICITAS (cont'd.)

MUSIKBEILAGE ZUM "EVANGELISCHEN
    KIRCHENCHOR 1968"   (K329)

KUM BA YAH!   *folk
    see Vier Negro-Spirituals
    (Mayfield, L.) SAB/SSATBB oct
    SINGSPIR ZJP-5061 $.35   (K330)

KUNKEL, CAROL LAPO
Joyful Advent Song, A   *Adv,anthem
    CHORISTERS R-19 $.15   (K331)

KUNTZ
Child Is Born In Bethlehem, A
    SATB SHAWNEE A5691 $.35   (K332)

KUNTZ, MICHAEL
Auf, Ihr Hirtensleut
    see Zwei Weihnachtliche Chore

Gute Nacht, O Schonstes Jesulein
    *Xmas
    mix cor BOHM s.p. see from
    Weihnachtslieder Nach
    Ostdeutschen Weisen   (K333)

Hort Ihr Die Engel Singen
    see Zwei Weihnachtliche Chore

Hosanna In Excelsis   *Mass
    mix cor,S/T solo,org sc,cor pts
    BOHM s.p.   (K334)

Ich War Auf Dem Feld   *Xmas
    mix cor BOHM s.p. see from
    Weihnachtslieder Nach
    Ostdeutschen Weisen   (K335)

Laufet, Ihr Hirten   *Xmas
    mix cor BOHM s.p. see from
    Weihnachtslieder Nach
    Ostdeutschen Weisen   (K336)

O Schonste Morgenrot
    see Zwei Marienlieder

Sei Uns Willkommen, Herre Christ
    *Xmas,ora
    mix cor&jr cor,soli,pno,orch sc,cor
    pts BOHM s.p., ipa   (K337)

Weihnachtslieder Nach Ostdeutschen
    Weisen   *see Gute Nacht, O
    Schonstes Jesulein; Ich War Auf
    Dem Feld; Laufet, Ihr Hirten (K338)

Zu Dir, Maria, Kommen Wir
    see Zwei Marienlieder

Zwei Marienlieder   *Xmas
    mix cor sc,cor pts BOHM s.p.
    contains: O Schonste Morgenrot;
    Zu Dir, Maria, Kommen Wir
                                 (K339)

Zwei Pange Lingua   *CCU
    [Lat] 4pt mix cor,acap BOHM s.p.
                                 (K340)

Zwei Weihnachtliche Chore   *Xmas
    mix cor BOHM s.p.
    contains: Auf, Ihr Hirtensleut;
    Hort Ihr Die Engel Singen   (K341)

KUNZ, ALFRED
Sweet Child Of God
    TTBB (med diff) WATERLOO $.35
                                 (K342)

KUNZ, JACK
Visions Of Christmas   *Xmas
    SSA RICHMOND F-27 $.30   (K343)

KURIG, HANS-HERMANN (1914-   )
Dein Ist Das Jahr, Dein Ist Die Zeit
    see Bach, Johann Sebastian, Meinen
    Jesum Lass Ich Nicht

Lobet Den Herren, Alle, Die Ihn Ehren
    see Bach, Johann Sebastian, Meinen
    Jesum Lass Ich Nicht

Meinen Jesum Lass Ich Nicht
    see Bach, Johann Sebastian, Meinen
    Jesum Lass Ich Nicht

KURTH, BURTON L.
In Praise Of Mary's Son
    SSA LESLIE 3046 $.30   (K344)

Lord's My Shepherd, The
    (Crimond) SA LESLIE 2045 $.30
                                 (K345)

Praise To The Lord
    SSAA LESLIE 3043 $.30   (K346)

KURTH, DIETRICH
Maria Verkundigung   *BVM/Xmas,mot
    3-8pt mix cor,acap MOSELER LB489
    s.p.   (K347)

KURZE UND LEICHTE MESSE IN B see Kraft,
Karl

KURZE UND LEICHTE PASTORALMESSE IN G
see Gruber, Joseph

KUTZER, ERNST
Advent   *Op.54,No.1, CCU,Adv,Mass
    [Ger] mix cor&unis,org sc,cor pts
    BOHM s.p.   (K348)

Deus Genitor Alme   *Op.45, Mass
    [Lat] ST/AB&jr cor,solo,org sc,cor
    pts BOHM s.p., ipa   (K349)

Es Fand Die Seele Heim
    see Zwei Grablieder

Funf Hymnen   *hymn
    [Lat] 4pt mix cor,org/2trp&2trom,
    or 2 flugelhorns&tenor horn&
    baritone horn BOHM sc,cor pts BOHM
    s.p., ipa
    contains: Jesu Nostra Redemptio,
    Op.48,No.4; Jesus Dulcis
    Memoria, Op.48,No.5; Pange
    Lingua, Op.48,No.1; Sacris
    Solemniis, Op.48,No.2; Verbum
    Supernum, Op.49,No.3   (K350)

Hochzeitsgesang "Herr, Segne, Die
    Sich Heut Verbinden"   *Op.25,
    No.2b, Fest/Marriage
    3pt BOHM s.p.   (K351)

Inmitten Der Nacht   *Adv/Xmas,cant
    3pt wom cor/3pt jr cor&unis,2rec&
    vln/3vln BOHM sc s.p., cor pts
    s.p., ipa   (K352)

Jesu Nostra Redemptio
    see Funf Hymnen

Jesus Dulcis Memoria
    see Funf Hymnen

Lobe Den Herren   *Fest
    mix cor&unis,org/brass sc,cor pts
    BOHM s.p., ipa   (K353)

Messe In C   *Op.3,No.2, Mass
    [Lat] 4pt mix cor,acap sc,cor pts
    BOHM s.p.   (K354)

O Nimm Dich An Der Armen Seele
    see Zwei Grablieder

Pange Lingua
    see Funf Hymnen

Sacris Solemniis
    see Funf Hymnen

Verbum Supernum
    see Funf Hymnen

Weihnachtszeit   *Op.54,No.2, CCU,
    Xmas,Mass
    [Ger] mix cor&unis,org sc,cor pts
    BOHM s.p.   (K355)

Zwei Grablieder   *Rembrnc
    cor sc,cor pts BOHM s.p.
    contains: Es Fand Die Seele Heim,
    Op.27a,No.1; O Nimm Dich An Der
    Armen Seele, Op.27a,No.2   (K356)

KVANDAL, JOHAN
And This Is The Judgement   *see Og
    Dette Er Dommen

Og Dette Er Dommen
    "And This Is The Judgement" mix cor
    NORSK NMO 8583 s.p.   (K357)

Sandelig, Sandelig Sier Jeg Dig
    "Verily, Verily I Say Unto You" mix
    cor NORSK NMO 8584 s.p.   (K358)

Verily, Verily I Say Unto You   *see
    Sandelig, Sandelig Sier Jeg Dig

KVERNO, TROND
Christ Rose From The Dead   *see Krist
    Sto Opp Av Dode

I Herrens Utvalgte
    "Ye Select Of The Lord" mix cor
    NORSK NMO 8742 s.p.   (K359)

Krist Sto Opp Av Dode
    "Christ Rose From The Dead" mix cor
    NORSK NMO 8739 s.p.   (K360)

Ye Select Of The Lord   *see I Herrens
    Utvalgte

KYRIE (from Missa Luba) Kyrie
    (Haazen) SATB SCHIRM.G LG51803 $.40
                                 (K361)

KYRIE see Beethoven, Ludwig van

KYRIE see Des Prez, Josquin

KYRIE see Dumont, [Henri]

KYRIE see Dvorak, Antonin

KYRIE see Green, Philip

KYRIE see Haydn, (Franz) Joseph

KYRIE see Johnston, Ben

KYRIE see Mozart, Wolfgang Amadeus

KYRIE see Nystedt, Knut

KYRIE see Palestrina, Giovanni

KYRIE see Patterson, Paul

KYRIE see Schubert, Franz (Peter)

KYRIE see Vivaldi, Antonio

KYRIE [1] see Mozart, Wolfgang Amadeus

KYRIE [2] see Mozart, Wolfgang Amadeus

KYRIE AND GLORIA see Mozart, Wolfgang
Amadeus

KYRIE ELEISON see Mozart, Wolfgang
Amadeus

KYRIE ET GLORIA see Praetorius, Michael

KYRIE FROM THE MASS FOR ALL MEN see
Clarke, Henry Leland

KYRIE "LEROY" see Taverner, John

KYRIE, SANCTUS, AGNUS DEI AND GLORIA
see Gyring, Elizabeth

L

LA CITTA BEATA see Guerrini, Guido

LA CITTA PERDUTA see Guerrini, Guido

LA MORTA DI ABEL see Leo, Leonardo

LA PASTORELLA SI LEVA PER TEMPO
see Raccolta Corale Libro III

LA PIETA D'AVIGNON see Rosenthal,
Manuel

LA POLESANA
see Raccolta Corale Libro I

LAAT DE HEILAND STUURMAN ZIJN
mix cor sc HEER 2803 s.p.   (L1)

LA BERGE, N.J.
Five Carols For Christmas *CC5U,
Xmas,anthem/carol
SATB (easy) GIA G1898 $.75   (L2)

LABORAVI IN GAMITU MEO see Morley,
Thomas

LACHEUR, REX
Ah's Not Afeared Of Jesus
TTBB HARRIS HC 5002 $.40   (L3)

Create In Me A Clean Heart
SATB HARRIS HC 4062 $.40   (L4)

LACHNER, FRANZ (1803-1890)
Inveni David *Fest
[Lat] 4pt mix cor,acap sc,cor pts
BOHM s.p.   (L5)

Joseph Fili David
[Lat] SATBB,acap sc,cor pts BOHM
s.p.   (L6)

LACRYMOSA see Cherubini, Luigi

LADIES' QUARTETS *CC66UL
(Coleman, Robert) 4pt wom cor pap
BROADMAN 4523-01 $.50   (L7)

L'ADONAI HA-ARETS see Epstein, Alvin

LAETAMINI IN DOMINO see Lassus, Roland
de (Orlandus)

LAETATUS SUM see Vannius

LAETENTUR COELI see Lemacher, Heinrich

LAETENTUR COELI see Giorgi, Giovanni

LAETENTUR COELI see Kromolicki, Joseph

LAETENTUR COELI see Lemacher, Heinrich

LAETENTUR COELI see Spindler, Fritz

LAHUSEN, CHRISTIAN (1886-   )
Geistliche Lieder *CCU
unis,acap (easy) BAREN. BA4996 (L8)

Steht Auf Und Wacht
SATB (contains also: Geborn Ist Uns
Immanuel) SCHWEIZER. SK 65.02-3
s.p. see also MUSIKBEILAGE ZUM
"EVANGELISCHEN KIRCHENCHOR 1965"
(L9)

LAJARRIGE, MAX
Ave Verum Corpus
4pt mix cor ENOCH   (L10)

LAKE, RUTH
Virgin's Cradle Song *see Hill,
Harry

LAKEY
Do You Known My Jesus? *see Ellis

LALLOUETTE, J.F.
O Sacrum Conuivium *anthem
SA/TB oct MCAFEE M8015 $.35   (L11)

LAMB
Christmas Mosaic, A *Xmas,anthem
unis,opt org&hndbl oct MCAFEE M102
$.35   (L12)

Wash Your Hands You Sinners *anthem
SATB,opt brass FINE ARTS CM 1070
$.35   (L13)

LAMB, THE *Xmas
SATB CHAPPELL W020891-357 $.40 (L14)

LAMB, THE see Bassett, Leslie

LAMB, THE see Blake

LAMB, THE see George, Earl

LAMB, THE see Protheroe, Daniel

LAMB OF GOD see Faure, Gabriel-Urbain,
Agnus Dei

LAMB OF GOD see Green, Philip

LAMB OF GOD see Monteverdi, Claudio,
Agnus Dei

LAMB OF GOD see Praetorius, Michael,
Agnus Dei

LAMB OF GOD see Tallis, Thomas

LAMB OF GOD see Victoria, Tomas Luis
de, Agnus Dei

LAMB OF GOD, FOR SINNERS SLAIN see
Cherubini, Luigi

LAMB OF GOD MOST LOWLY see Young,
Gordon

LAMB OF GOD THOU SHALT REMAIN TOGETHER
see Mueller, G.G.

LAMB OF LOVE see Roff, Joseph

LAMBERTZ, JOHANN SEBASTIAN
Der Du Die Zeit In Handen Hast
SATB HANSSLER 6.320 s.p.   (L15)

LAMB'S HOLY FEAST, THE see Azevedo, Lex
de

LAMDENI see Foss, Lukas

LAMENT AND WEEP see Von Den Heiligen
Wunden

LAMENT FOR A LOST CHILD see Hutcheson

LAMENT OF DAVID, THE see Pinkham,
Daniel

LAMENT OF JOB see Jergenson, Dale

LAMENTATION see Anonymous

LAMENTATION see Ingalls, Jeremiah

LAMENTATION, THE see Lawes, William

LAMENTATION OF JEREMIAH see Ridout,
Alan

LAMENTATIONS FOR MAUNDY THURSDAY PART 1
see Carpentras

LAMENTATIONS OF JEREMIAH *Holywk
(Sweetman, P.A.) SAB (med easy)
WATERLOO $.40   (L16)

LAMENTATIONS OF JEREMIAH, THE see
Tallis, Thomas

LAMENTAZIONE FUNEBRE see Pratella,
Francesco Balllla

LAMMETUN, JOHN
Mitt Lys I Morke *CCU
mix cor NORSK NMO 8741 s.p.   (L17)

O Man, Thy Sin Is Great *see O
Menneske, Din Synd Er Stor

O Menneske, Din Synd Er Stor
"O Man, Thy Sin Is Great" mix cor
NORSK NMO 8748 s.p.   (L18)

LA MONTAINE, JOHN (1920-)
Be Glad Then America *Op.43, sac/sec
cor,4 soli,orch FREDONIA   (L19)

Freedom Proclamation *anthem
mix cor,2 soli,org,hndbl FREDONIA
(L20)

Nine Lessons Of Christmas, The
*Op.44
mix cor,narrator,2 soli,perc,harp
FREDONIA   (L21)

LAMPART, KARL
Ecce Sacerdos *Op.87,No.5
[Lat] 4pt mix cor,org/2trp&2horn&
2trom&tuba&org sc,cor pts BOHM
s.p., ipa   (L22)

Mater Dei *Op.110, Mass
[Lat] 4pt mix cor,opt org sc,cor
pts BOHM s.p.   (L23)

LAND OF OUR LOYALTY see Rogers

LAND OF OUR LOYALTY see Rogers, Lee

LAND OF SONG
see Now The Day Is Over

LAND WE HOLD SO DEAR, THE see Davis,
Katherine K.

LANDGRAVE, PHILLIP
Fertile Ground *anthem
SATB (easy) oct BROADMAN 4562-09
$.35   (L24)

God Loves *anthem
SATB WORD CS-2659 $.35   (L25)

God Waits For You *anthem
SATB oct BROADMAN 4562-37 $.35   (L26)

Hark, The Voice Of Jesus Calling
*anthem
SATB (easy) oct BROADMAN 4550-56
$.30   (L27)

He Came, He Comes *anthem
SATB oct BROADMAN 4565-41 $.35   (L28)

He Died For Me *anthem
SATB oct BROADMAN 4565-39 $.50   (L29)

I Will Proclaim His Name With A Song
*anthem
SATB (easy) oct BROADMAN 4562-10
$.35   (L30)

Just As I Am *anthem
SATB oct BROADMAN 4565-08 $.35   (L31)

Living In The Spirit
jr cor BROADMAN 4515-05 $1.75   (L32)

My Lord Cares *anthem
SATB (easy) oct BROADMAN 4562-12
$.35   (L33)

O Give Thanks
SATB (med) FISCHER,C CM 7837 $.40
(L34)

One Thing *anthem
SATB (easy) oct BROADMAN 4554-51
$.30   (L35)

Purpose
cor BROADMAN 4518-02 $2.95   (L36)

There Is No One Like My Jesus
*anthem
SATB WORD CS-2675 $.40   (L37)

When Jesus Comes *Xmas,cant
SATB sc BROADMAN 4512-19 $1.95
(L38)

Who Am I? *anthem
unis oct BROADMAN 4554-73 $.30   (L39)

Why Do I Do? *anthem
SATB (easy) oct BROADMAN 4562-15
$.35   (L40)

Wondrous Cross, The *anthem
SATB (easy) oct BROADMAN 4550-48
$.30   (L41)

LANDON
Footsteps Of Jesus *anthem
SATB oct LORENZ A548 $.35   (L42)

LANDON, STEWART
Believing Souls, Rejoice And Sing
*Easter,anthem
SATB oct LORENZ A552 $.35   (L43)

Dogwood Cross, The *Easter,anthem
SATB oct LORENZ A539 $.35   (L44)

Noel! *Xmas,anthem
SA/SATB (easy) oct LORENZ A556 $.35
(L45)
SATB oct LORENZ A556 $.35   (L46)

O To Be Like Thee *anthem
SATB oct LORENZ A567 $.35   (L47)

LANG, C.S.
I Saw Three Ships
see Davies, Henry Walford, O Little
Town Of Bethlehem

LANG, HANS (1897-1968)
Als Ich Bei Meinen Schafen Wacht'
*sec,Xmas,Fr
mix cor (easy) sc SCHOTTS C 34 841
s.p. see from Frankische
Weihnachtslieder   (L48)

Der Sonnengesang Des Heiligen
Franziskus *Op.52
4-6pt mix cor,3horn,3trp,3trom,
tuba,opt perc,timp (med) voc sc,
cor pts SCHOTTS ED. 4853 s.p.,
ipa   (L49)

Die Heiling Drei Konig *Xmas
2pt jr cor&4pt men cor,acap (easy)
sc SCHOTTS C 40 663 s.p.   (L50)

Drei Lieder *see Jetzt Fahrn Wir
Ubern See; Lob Des Schneiders;
Mein Christian "Wo Mag Denn Nur
Mein Christian Sein"   (L51)

Frankische Weihnachtslieder *see Als
Ich Bei Meinen Schafen Wacht';
Inmitten Der Nacht; Kindelein Im

LANG, HANS (cont'd.)
Stall "O Jesulein"; Komm,
Nachtigall Mein!; O
Freudenreicher Tag   (L52)

Funf Rosen "Funf Rosen Ging Ich
Brechen" *Op.19,No.4, Xmas
3pt wom cor/3pt men cor/mix cor,
acap sc SCHOTTS C 32 636 s.p. see
from Vier Weihnachtslieder   (L53)

Gott Ist In Mir Das Feuer "Die Welt
Ist Mir Zu Eng" *mot
TTTTBBBB,TT soli,acap sc SCHOTTS
C 33 607 s.p., voc pt SCHOTTS
C 33 608-01-04 s.p.   (L54)

In Dulci Jubilo *Op.51, Xmas,cant
see Haas, Joseph, Vom Himmel Hoch
Da Komm Ich Her
4-8pt mix cor&jr cor/wom cor,SBar
soli,pno,fl,ob,clar,strings,opt
horn (med easy) sc SCHOTTS
ED. 4388 s.p., voc sc,cor pts
SCHOTTS ED. 4240 s.p., ipa   (L55)

Inmitten Der Nacht *sec,Xmas,Fr
mix cor (easy) sc SCHOTTS C 34 839
s.p. see from Frankische
Weihnachtslieder   (L56)

Jauchze, Alle Welt, Dem Herren *see
Jubilate Deo

Jetzt Fahrn Wir Ubern See
2pt wom cor&4pt men cor,acap (easy)
sc SCHOTTS C 38 322 s.p. see from
Drei Lieder   (L57)

Jubilate Deo *Op.43,No.1, Xmas,mot
[Ger/Lat] unis jr cor&4pt wom cor/
4pt men cor,acap (med) sc SCHOTTS
C 33 914 s.p., cor pts SCHOTTS
C 33 915A-E s.p.   (L58)
"Jauchze, Alle Welt, Dem Herren"
[Lat/Ger] 4-5pt wom cor&unis jr
cor/4-5pt men cor&unis jr cor,
acap s.p. sc SCHOTTS C 33 914,
voc pt SCHOTTS C 33 917-01-07 see
from Zwei Motetten   (L59)

Kindelein Im Stall "O Jesulein"
*sec,Xmas,Fr
mix cor (easy) sc SCHOTTS C 34 833
s.p. see from Frankische
Weihnachtslieder   (L60)

Komm, Nachtigall Mein! *sec,Xmas,Fr
mix cor (easy) sc SCHOTTS C 34 835
s.p. see from Frankische
Weihnachtslieder   (L61)

Laudate Dominum *Op.43,No.2, mot
[Lat/Ger] unis jr cor&4pt wom cor/
4pt men cor,acap (med) sc SCHOTTS
C 33 916 s.p., cor pts SCHOTTS
C 33 917A-E s.p.   (L62)
"Singt Ein Loblied" [Lat/Ger] 4-5pt
wom cor&unis jr cor/4-5pt men
cor&unis jr cor,acap voc pt
SCHOTTS C 33 917-01-07 s.p. see
from Zwei Motetten   (L63)

Lob Des Schneiders
2pt wom cor&4pt men cor,acap (easy)
sc SCHOTTS C 38 320 s.p. see from
Drei Lieder   (L64)

Maria Konigin "O Wohl Die Koniginne"
*Op.19,No.2, Xmas
3pt wom cor/3pt men cor/mix cor,
acap sc SCHOTTS C 32 634 s.p. see
from Vier Weihnachtslieder   (L65)

Mein Christian "Wo Mag Denn Nur Mein
Christian Sein"
2pt wom cor&4pt men cor,acap (easy)
sc SCHOTTS C 38 321 s.p. see from
Drei Lieder   (L66)

O Frau Ob Aller Frauen Schar *Xmas,
hymn
3pt wom cor,3treb inst (med easy)
sc SCHOTTS C 34 737 s.p.   (L67)

O Freudenreicher Tag *sec,Xmas,Fr
mix cor (easy) sc SCHOTTS C 34 837
s.p. see from Frankische
Weihnachtslieder   (L68)

O Heiland, Reiss Die Himmel Auf (from
In Dulci Jubilo)
mix cor&unis jr cor,acap (med easy)
sc SCHOTTS C 40 654 s.p.   (L69)

Singt Ein Loblied *see Laudate
Dominum

Susani "Vom Himmel Hoch, Ihr Engel
Kommt" *Xmas
2pt jr cor&SSAATTBB,acap (easy) sc
SCHOTTS C 40 655 s.p.   (L70)

LANG, HANS (cont'd.)
Vier Weihnachtslieder *see Funf
Rosen "Funf Rosen Ging Ich
Brechen", Op.19,No.4; Maria
Konigin "O Wohl Die Koniginne",
Op.19,No.2; Weihnachtslicht "Nun
Ward Zu Trost Uns Allen", Op.19,
No.3; Zweig Von Bethlehem "O
Pilgerpaar, Mach Weit Die Tur",
Op.19,No.1   (L71)

Weihnachtslicht "Nun Ward Zu Trost
Uns Allen" *Op.19,No.3, Xmas
3pt wom cor/3pt men cor/mix cor,
acap sc SCHOTTS C 32 635 s.p. see
from Vier Weihnachtslieder   (L72)

Zwei Motetten *see Jubilate Deo,
"Jauchze, Alle Welt, Dem Herren",
Op.43,No.1; Laudate Dominum,
"Singt Ein Loblied", Op.43,No.2 (L73)

Zweig Von Bethlehem "O Pilgerpaar,
Mach Weit Die Tur" *Op.19,No.1,
Xmas
3pt wom cor/3pt men cor/mix cor,
acap sc SCHOTTS C 32 633 s.p. see
from Vier Weihnachtslieder   (L74)

LANGDON
Walk With Me *anthem
(McCall, Craig) SA/TB (easy) oct
SINGSPIR ZJP-6029 $.30   (L75)

LANGE
Blest Be The Tie *see Fawcett

LANGE, GREGOR (ca. 1540-1587)
Wenn Ich Nur Dich Hab, Herr, Allein
SAT/SAB SCHWEIZER. SK 65.08 s.p.
see also MUSIKBEILAGE ZUM
"EVANGELISCHEN KIRCHENCHOR 1965"
(L76)

LANGFREDAG see Hovland, Egil

LANGHANS, HERBERT
Die Weihnachtsgeschichte (composed
with Lau, Heinz) *Xmas
1-3 eq voices,fl/S rec&A rec,2perc,
vcl PELIKAN PE814   (L77)

LANGLAIS, JEAN (1907-   )
Messe Solenelle *Mass
SATB,org (med) sc,cor pts SCHOLA
(L78)

Missa In Simplicitate *Mass
[Eng] unis,org WHITE,ERN $.75   (L79)
unis,org/harmonium (med) sc,cor pts
SCHOLA   (L80)

LANGLEY, LEANNE
Most Unusual Champion, A *anthem
SB WORD CS-2592 $.30   (L81)

LANGLOIS, H.G.
Hail, Gladdening Light
SATB,acap HARRIS $.35   (L82)

LANGSTON, PAUL
Canticle For Modern Man *anthem
SATB BROADMAN 4565-57 $.40   (L83)

City Of God
mix cor BRODT 563 $.26   (L84)

God Of Grace And God Of Glory
mix cor BRODT 513 $.25   (L85)

Hymn Of Spring
mix cor BRODT 520 $.25   (L86)

LANGWIG
Prayer
(Frackenpohl, Arthur) SATB CHARTER
CO30206   (L87)

LANIER
Gospel Song Of Jesus *anthem
SATB oct BROADMAN 4540-90 $.30
(L88)

In A Little Town Called Bethlehem
*Xmas,anthem
SATB (easy) oct BROADMAN 4554-23
$.30   (L89)

Jesus In Us Has Begun *anthem
SATB oct BROADMAN 4540-98 $.30
(L90)

My Jesus, I Love Thee *see
Featherstone

Sing Praise Unto The Lord *anthem
SATB oct BROADMAN 4554-81 $.30
(L91)

LANIER, GARY
Could It Be *anthem
SATB WORD   (L92)

If You Abide *anthem
SATB WORD   (L93)

LAPO, CECIL E. (1910-   )
    How Far Is It To Bethlehem? *Xmas
    unis,pno/org/hndbl CHORISTERS A-127
    $.35   (L94)

    Mary's Carol *Xmas
    unis,fl,vcl,org CHORISTERS A-139
    $.35   (L95)

LAPP, HORACE
    O Lamb Of God
    SATB (med easy) WATERLOO $.40 (L96)

LARGO see Handel, George Frideric

LARK, THE see Billings, William

LAROWE
    He's God's Great Love *anthem
    SATB (easy) oct BROADMAN 4540-47
    $.30   (L97)

LA ROWE, JANE
    Alleluia, Alleluia! *anthem
    SATB oct SINGSPIR ZJP-7274 $.25
                                      (L98)

    Incarnation, The *Xmas,cant
    SATB,narrator SINGSPIR 5952 $1.50
                                      (L99)

    King Of Glory *Easter,cant
    SATB,narrator,SATBar soli SINGSPIR
    5990 $1.50   (L100)

LARSSON
    Missa Brevis *Mass
    SAB WALTON 2719 $.75   (L101)

L'ARTE MUSICALE IN ITALIA *sac/sec,
    CCU,14-18th cent
    (Torchi, Luigi) microfiche UNION ESP.
    $55.00 7 volumes   (L102)

L'ARTE MUSICALE IN ITALIA, VOL. I see
    Torchi

L'ARTE MUSICALE IN ITALIA, VOL. II see
    Torchi

LAS MORADAS see Balada, Leonardo

L'ASCENSION *Asc
    cor JOBERT s.p. see also Douze
    Cantiques De Fetes   (L103)

LASS DICH NUR NICHTS NICHT DAUREN see
    Brahms, Johannes

LASSET DIE KINDLEIN ZU MIR KOMMEN see
    David, Johann Nepomuk

LASSO, ORLANDO DI
    see LASSUS, ROLAND DE (ORLANDUS)

L'ASSOMPTION
    cor JOBERT s.p. see also Douze
    Cantiques De Fetes   (L104)

LASST ALLE GOTT UNS LOBEN
    see Drei Altbohmische
    Weihnachtslieder

LASST ALLE GOTT UNS LOBEN see Riedel,
    Karl

LASST UNS ALLE PREISEN UND LOBSINGEN
    see Carissimi, Giacomo, Jubilemus
    Omnes Et Cantemus

LASST UNS ERHEBEN HERZ UND STIMM see
    Sigmund, Oskar

LASST UNS TIEFGEBEUGI VEREHREN see
    Schmider, Karl

LASST VOR GOTTES THRON UNS TRETEN see
    Spranger, Jorg

LASSUS, ROLAND DE (ORLANDUS)
    (1532-1594)
    Adoramus Te, Christe *anthem
    SATB,acap (med diff) OXFORD 43.483
    $.25   (L105)

    Adorna Thalamum Tuum, Sion *mot
    SATB HANSSLER 1.571 s.p.   (L106)

    Agnus Dei (from Doulce Memoire)
    SATB HANSSLER 6.317 s.p. contains
    also: Des Prez, Josquin, Et
    Incarnatus Est (from Pange
    Lingua)   (L107)

    Audite Nova "Der Bau'r Von
    Eselkirchen"
    men cor sc SCHOTTS C 38 816 s.p.
                                      (L108)

    Bell' Amfitrit Altera *Mass
    [Lat] 4pt mix cor&4pt mix cor,acap
    sc,cor pts BOHM s.p.   (L109)

    Benedicam Dominum, Qui Tribuit Mihi
    Intellectum *mot
    SATB HANSSLER 1.573 s.p.   (L110)

LASSUS, ROLAND DE (ORLANDUS) (cont'd.)
    Benedictus Es, Domine, Doce Me
    Justificationes Tuas *mot
    SATB HANSSLER 1.576 s.p.   (L111)

    Benedictus, Qui Venit
    SA LAUDINELLA LR 123 s.p. contains
    also: Dirige Nos, Domine, In
    Veritate Tua; Expandi Manus Meas
    Ad Te; Laetamini In Domino (L112)

    Carmina Chromatico
    see Prophetiae Sybillarum, Heft 1

    Cerno Dei Natum
    see Prophetiae Sybillarum, Heft 4

    Complete Works *sac/sec,CCU
    (Haberl, F.X.; Sandberger, Adolf)
    microfiche UNIV.MUS.ED. $100.00
    Breitkopf and Haertel , 1894-1927
    in 21 volumes.   (L113)

    Confortamini Et Iam Nolite Timere
    *mot
    SATB HANSSLER 1.584 s.p.   (L114)

    Cor Meum
    see Two Psalms

    Custodi Me, Domine *mot
    SATB HANSSLER 1.575 s.p.   (L115)

    Dextera Domini Fecit Virtutem *mot
    SATB HANSSLER 1.570 s.p.   (L116)

    Dirige Nos, Domine, In Veritate Tua
    see Lassus, Roland de (Orlandus),
    Benedictus, Qui Venit

    Domine, Convertere Et Eripe Animam
    Meam *mot
    SATB HANSSLER 1.578 s.p.   (L117)

    Domine, Exaudi Orationem Meam *mot
    SATB HANSSLER 1.574 s.p.   (L118)

    Domine, Fac Mecum Misericordiam Tuam
    *mot
    SATB HANSSLER 1.577 s.p.   (L119)

    Domine, In Auxilium Meum Respice
    *mot
    SATB HANSSLER 1.583 s.p.   (L120)

    Domine, Labia Mea Aperies *mot
    SATB HANSSLER 1.581 s.p.   (L121)

    Dum Meditor Quondam
    see Prophetiae Sybillarum, Heft 3

    Ecce Dies, Nigras
    see Prophetiae Sybillarum, Heft 2

    Ecce Dies Veniet
    see Prophetiae Sybillarum, Heft 1

    Exaudi, Deus, Orationem Meam *mot
    SATB HANSSLER 1.585 s.p.   (L122)

    Expandi Manus Meas Ad Te
    see Lassus, Roland de (Orlandus),
    Benedictus, Qui Venit

    Exspectans Exspectavi Dominum *mot
    SATB HANSSLER 1.565 s.p.   (L123)

    Factus Est Dominus Firmamentum Meum
    *mot
    SATB,acap EGTVED KB68 s.p.   (L124)
    SATB HANSSLER 1.566 s.p.   (L125)

    Gressus Meos Dirige Secundum Eloquium
    Tuum *mot
    SATB HANSSLER 1.572 s.p.   (L126)

    Herr Jesus Christ, Unser Gott *mot
    (Kronberg, Gerhard) [Ger] mix cor
    cor pts BOHM 24 s.p. see from
    MOTETTEN ALTER MEISTER   (L127)

    Improperium *anthem
    SATB oct MCAFEE M1064 $.40   (L128)

    Improperium Exspectavit Cor Meum
    *mot
    SATB HANSSLER 1.567 s.p.   (L129)

    In Hora Ultima *mot
    (Harler, Alan) SSATBB,acap DEAN
    CA-104 $.50   (L130)

    In Monte Oliveti *Holywk/Psntd
    [Lat] SAATBB,acap sc,cor pts BOHM
    s.p.   (L131)

    In Veneris Annis
    see Prophetiae Sybillarum, Heft 2

    Intende Vocis Orationis Meae *mot
    SATB HANSSLER 1.579 s.p.   (L132)

    Ipsa Deum Vidi
    see Prophetiae Sybillarum, Heft 3

LASSUS, ROLAND DE (ORLANDUS) (cont'd.)
    Jam Mea Certa Manent
    see Prophetiae Sybillarum, Heft 3

    Jubilate Deo
    (Klein) "Sing To God" SATB SCHIRM.G
    11987 $.35   (L133)

    Jubilate Deo, Omnis Terra *mot
    SATB HANSSLER 1.586 s.p.   (L134)

    Laetamini In Domino
    see Lassus, Roland de (Orlandus),
    Benedictus, Qui Venit

    Miserere Mei
    men cor,acap TONOS 5614 s.p. (L135)

    Miserere Mei, Domine *mot
    TTBBB LIENAU MUSICA SACRA, NR. 47
    cor pts s.p., sc s.p.   (L136)
    SATB HANSSLER 1.569 s.p.   (L137)

    Musica Dei Donum Optimi *mot
    (Contino, Fiora) SSATTB,acap DEAN
    CA-105 $.50   (L138)

    Non Tarde Veniet
    see Prophetiae Sybillarum, Heft 2

    O Crux Ave *Psntd,mot
    [Lat] 6pt mix cor,acap sc,cor pts
    BOHM s.p.   (L139)

    O Lord Of Heaven
    (Wick, Fred) SATB oct SCHMITT W253
    $.30   (L140)
    (Wick, Fred) SSA oct SCHMITT W318
    $.30   (L141)

    Perfice Gressus Meos In Semitis Tuis
    *mot
    SATB HANSSLER 1.580 s.p.   (L142)

    Populum Humilem Salvum Facies, Domine
    *mot
    SATB HANSSLER 1.582 s.p.   (L143)

    Prophetiae Sybillarum, Heft 1 *Xmas,
    madrigal
    SATB,acap MOSELER MOR178 s.p.
    contains: Carmina Chromatico;
    Ecce Dies Veniet; Virgine Matre
    Satus   (L144)

    Prophetiae Sybillarum, Heft 2 *Xmas,
    madrigal
    SATB,acap MOSELER MOR179 s.p.
    contains: Ecce Dies, Nigras; In
    Veneris Annis; Non Tarde Veniet
                                      (L145)
    Prophetiae Sybillarum, Heft 3 *Xmas,
    madrigal
    SATB,acap MOSELER MOR180 s.p.
    contains: Dum Meditor Quondam;
    Ipsa Deum Vidi; Jam Mea Certa
    Manent   (L146)

    Prophetiae Sybillarum, Heft 4 *Xmas,
    madrigal
    SATB,acap MOSELER MOR181 s.p.
    contains: Cerno Dei Natum; Summus
    Erit Sub Carne; Verax Ipse
    Deus; Virginis Aeternum   (L147)

    Quem Vidistis, Pastores *Xmas
    (Ehret, Walter) "Whom, O Shepherds"
    [Eng/Lat] SSATB,acap (med)
    PRESSER 312-41086 $.50   (L148)

    Resonet In Laudibus *mot
    (Harler, Alan) SATBB,acap DEAN
    CA-107 $.50   (L149)

    Serve Bone *mot
    (McKelvy, James) SA,acap FOSTER
    MF801 $.30   (L150)

    Sing To God *see Jubilate Deo

    Stabat Mater *Psntd
    (Homolya) dbl cor oct EULENBURG
    10097 s.p.   (L151)

    Summus Erit Sub Carne
    see Prophetiae Sybillarum, Heft 4

    Super Flumina Babylonis *mot
    SATB HANSSLER 1.568 s.p.   (L152)

    Surrexit Pastor Bonus *Easter,mot
    [Lat] SSATB,acap sc,cor pts BOHM
    s.p.   (L153)

    Tristis Est Anima Mea *Holywk
    [Lat] SATBB,acap sc,cor pts BOHM
    s.p.   (L154)

    Tritt Auf Den Riegel Von Der Tur
    (Field, Robert) "Unlatch The Bolt
    That Locks The Door" [Eng/Ger]
    SSATB,acap (med) PRESSER
    312-41095 $.40   (L155)

LASSUS, ROLAND DE (ORLANDUS) (cont'd.)

Tu Exsurgens
see Two Psalms

Two Psalms *mot/Psalm
(Dawson, E.) SSA/TTB,acap oct
NATIONAL WHC-33 $.40
contains: Cor Meum; Tu Exsurgens
(L156)

Unlatch The Bolt That Locks The Door
*see Tritt Auf Den Riegel Von Der
Tur

Verax Ipse Deus
see Prophetiae Sybillarum, Heft 4

Vexilla Regis
[Lat] SAATBB,acap sc,cor pts BOHM
s.p.   (L157)

Virgine Matre Satus
see Prophetiae Sybillarum, Heft 1

Virginis Aeternum
see Prophetiae Sybillarum, Heft 4

Whom, O Shepherds *see Quem
Vidistis, Pastores

LAST COMMANDMENT, THE see Clark, Eugene
L.

LAST INVOCATION, THE see Hively, Wells

LAST MILE OF THE WAY, THE see Oatman

LAST SUPPER, THE see Evett, Robert

LAST SUPPER, THE see Thiman, Eric
Harding

LAST TRIP TO JERUSALEM see Wilson,
Richard

LAST TRUMPET, THE see Johnson, Paul

LAST WEEK, THE see Peterson, John W.

LASTER, JAMES
Lord, I Want To Be A Christian
*anthem
SSATBB AUGSBURG 11-1739 $.35 (L158)

LATE ONE NIGHT see Hill, Harry

LATEINISCHE HYMNEN see Lemacher,
Heinrich

LATHAM, L.
Blessed Calvary *Gd.Fri.,anthem/
gospel
(DeCou, Harold) SATB oct SINGSPIR
ZJP-8009 $.30   (L159)
(Krogstad, B.) SATB/SA (easy) oct
SINGSPIR ZJP-6024 $.35 (L160)

LATHBURY
Break Thou The Bread Of Life
(composed with Vick) *anthem
2pt,opt fl&gtr (easy) oct BROADMAN
4554-70 $.30   (L161)

LATIMER
Our Cares We Can Cast On Thee
SATB SCHIRM.G LG51729 $.45   (L162)

THE LATIN CHURCH MUSIC, VOL. I see Tye,
Christopher

THE LATIN CHURCH MUSIC, VOL. II see
Tye, Christopher

LATROBE, CHRISTIAN I.
Blessed Are The People
(Nolte) mix cor BRODT 1006 $.50
(L163)
(Pfohl) mix cor BRODT 207 $.35
(L164)

Dawn Of Glory, The *cant
cor,orch BRODT $3.50, ipr   (L165)

Day Of Wrath, That Dreadful Day , The
*see Dies Irae

Dies Irae *cant
"Day Of Wrath, That Dreadful Day ,
The" cor,orch BRODT $2.00, ipr
(L166)

How Sweet Thy Dwellings, Lord
(Nolte) ST/SS,opt inst BRODT 1007
$.35, ipr   (L167)

Lord Of Life! Now Sweetly Slumber
(Nolte) [Ger/Eng] SATB,TB soli oct
MORAVIAN 5815 $.45   (L168)

Psalm 51
mix cor,SATB soli,pno/org BOOSEY
voc sc $3.50, sc rental   (L169)

Was Ever Grief Like Thine
(Nolte) mix cor BRODT 1010 $.50
(L170)

LATROBE, CHRISTIAN I. (cont'd.)

We Praise Thee, O God!
(Nolte, Ewald V.) SATB,SATB soli
voc sc BOOSEY $1.00   (L171)

What Shall We Render Unto The Lord
(Nolte) mix cor BRODT 1011 $.30
(L172)

LAU, HEINZ
Die Helle Sonn
4pt mix cor,orch cor pts PELIKAN
PE913   (L173)

Die Weihnachtsgeschichte *see
Langhans, Herbert

LAUBER, GUSTAV (1864-1952)
Te Deum
mix cor,orch HENN s.p.   (L174)

LAUDA ALLA MADONNA see Dalla Vecchia,
Wolfango

LAUDA ANIMA MEA see Caldara, Antonio

LAUDA ANIMA MEA, DOMINUM see Doebler,
Curt

LAUDA JERUSALEM see Hunecke, Wilhelm

LAUDA JERUSALEM see Vivaldi, Antonio

LAUDA JERUSALEM DOMINUM see Muller,
A.M.

LAUDA SION see Steinert, Bernhard

LAUDA SION see Lipphardt, W.

LAUDA SION SALVATOREM see Buxtehude,
Dietrich

LAUDA SPIRTUALE see Panunzi, M.

LAUDAMUS TE see Vivaldi, Antonio

LAUDAMUS TE see Young, Gordon

LAUDATE DOMINUM
WALTON M134 $2.95   (L175)

LAUDATE DOMINUM see Benjamin, Thomas E.

LAUDATE DOMINUM see Bissell, Keith W.

LAUDATE DOMINUM see Columbini

LAUDATE DOMINUM see Ett, Kaspar

LAUDATE DOMINUM see Lang, Hans

LAUDATE DOMINUM see Lotti, Antonio

LAUDATE DOMINUM see Mills, Charles

LAUDATE DOMINUM see Monteverdi, Claudio

LAUDATE DOMINUM see Mozart, Wolfgang
Amadeus

LAUDATE DOMINUM see Praetorius, Michael

LAUDATE DOMINUM see Robillard

LAUDATE DOMINUM see Rovetta, Giovanni

LAUDATE DOMINUM see Trapp, Willy

LAUDATE DOMINUM see Weis, Flemming

LAUDATE PUERI see Haydn, (Johann)
Michael

LAUDATE PUERI see Lotti, Antonio

LAUDATE PUERI see Mendelssohn-
Bartholdy, Felix

LAUDATE PUERI see Mozart, Wolfgang
Amadeus

LAUDATE PUERI see Pergolesi, Giovanni
Battista

LAUDATU I "LAUDATU SI MI SIGNORE PER
QUILLI KE PERDONANO PER LO TUO" see
Killmayer, Wilhelm

LAUDATU II "LAUDATU SI MI SIGNORE PER
SORA NOSTRA MORTE CORPORALE" see
Killmayer, Wilhelm

LAUDES EVANGELI see Bucchi, Valentino

LAUDES FRANCISCI "TE SANCTISSIMUM" see
Reutter, Hermann

LAUDI see Lidholm, Ingvar

LAUDI ALLA VERGINE MARIA see Verdi,
Giuseppe

LAUDI DEL 1200 see Bettinelli, Bruno

LAUFET, IHR HIRTEN see Kuntz, Michael

LAUFET, IHR HIRTEN see Zipp, Friedrich

LAUGHING SONG see George, Earl

LAUGHTER IN BETHLEHEM see Jakes

LAUGHTER IN YOUR SOUL see Owens, Jamie

LAURETANISCHE FEST-LITANEI see Grau, P.
Theodor

LAUS CREATORUM see Brown

LAUS ET PERENNIS GLORIA see Gallus,
Jacobus

LAUSNARINN KONGUR KRISTE see
Stefansson, Fjolnir

LAUTERBACH, LORENZ
Elegerunt Apostoli *Offer
[Lat] 4pt mix cor,acap BOHM s.p.
(L176)

Macht Hoch Die Tur *Adv
cor BOHM s.p.   (L177)

Magnificat
[Lat] 4pt mix cor,acap BOHM s.p.
(L178)

Proprium Der Osternacht-Messe *CCU,
Easter,Greg
[Lat] mix cor,opt org sc,cor pts
BOHM s.p.   (L179)

Sonne Der Gerechtigkeit *Fest,cant
mix cor&cong,org BOHM s.p. (L180)

Terra Tremuit *Easter,Offer
[Lat] 4pt mix cor,org sc,cor pts
BOHM s.p.   (L181)

Tui Sunt Caeli *Xmas,Offer
[Lat] cor,solo BOHM s.p.   (L182)

LAUTESPIELENDER ENGEL "SPRICH MICH
NICHT AN!" see Weber, Bernhard

LAVRY, MARC (1903-1967)
Sabbath Eve Sacred Service
mix cor,cantor,org/orch SAC.MUS.PR.
voc sc $3.00, sc rental, ipr
(L183)

LAW
Early American Christmas Triptych, An
*see Read

LAW OF THE LORD, THE see Mathias,
William

LAWES, WILLIAM (1602-1645)
All People That On Earth Do Dwell
(Psalm 100)
cong,TB soli,org STAINER 3.0757.1
$.60   (L184)

Have Mercy, On Us, Lord (Psalm 67)
SATB STAINER 3.0764.1 $.75 contains
also: Lamentation, The   (L185)

Lamentation, The
see Lawes, William, Have Mercy, On
Us, Lord

Psalm 67 *see Have Mercy, On Us,
Lord

Psalm 100 *see All People That On
Earth Do Dwell

LAWRENCE, BURTON
They That Go Down To The Sea In Ships
*anthem
SATB oct SINGSPIR ZJP-7324 $.30
(L186)

LAWSON
He Is So Great *gospel
(Widen) SATB oct LILLENAS AN-1705
$.30   (L187)

LAWSON, J.A.
Great Is The Lord
mix cor BANKS MUS YS 960 $.25
(L188)

LAWSON, MALCOLM
Proud Maisie *sac/sec
SSA,acap CRAMER U49   (L189)

L'CHA ANU SHIRA see Steinberg, Ben

LE CHEMIN DE LA CROIX see Jacob, Dom
Clement

LE JOUR DES MORTS *Rembrnc
cor JOBERT s.p. see also Douze
Cantiques De Fetes   (L190)

LE NOM DE MARIE *BVM
cor JOBERT s.p. see also Douze
Cantiques De Fetes   (L191)

LE PIU BELLE MELODIE RELIGIOSE see
Vittadini

LE P'TIT QUINQUIN see Chailley, Jacques

LE P'TIT QUINQUIN see Delsinne, Abbe

LE SOMMEIL DE L'ENFANT JESUS see
Praetorius, Michael

LEACH, BILL F.
Alleluia, Angels Sing (composed with
Crouch, Letha) *Xmas,anthem
2pt (easy) oct BROADMAN 4558-44
$.30   (L192)

LEAD, KINDLY LIGHT see Dykes, John
Bacchus

LEAD, KINDLY LIGHT see Haywood, L.B.

LEAD ME BACK TO CALVARY see Pace

LEAD ME, GUIDE ME see Akers, Doris

LEAD ME LORD see Wesley, S.S.

LEAD ME, O LEAD ME see Peterson, John
W.

LEAD ME ON see Wilson, John F.

LEAD ON MEDLEY
(Mercer, W. Elmo) SATB oct BENSON
S4167 $.35   (L193)

LEAD ON, O KING ETERNAL see Johnson,
David N.

LEAD ON, O KING ETERNAL see Smart,
Henry Thomas

LEAD US, HEAVENLY FATHER see Procter,
R.E.

LEAD US UNTO LIFE see Faure, Gabriel-
Urbain

LEAF
The Choral Art, Vol. II *sac/sec,CCU
SATB SCHIRM.G LG51732 $3.50 (L194)

LEAF, ROBERT
Break Forth In Joyful Song
unis ART MAST 255 $.35   (L195)

Christians Gather, Day Is Breaking
unis ART MAST 171 $.30   (L196)

Come, Thou Long-Expected Jesus *Adv/
Xmas
SATB ART MAST 196 $.40   (L197)

Glad Sounds Of Christians
unis ART MAST 230 $.35   (L198)

God Of Earth And Planets *anthem
SA,kbd,opt fl AUGSBURG 11-0315 $.35
                               (L199)
Good News *CCU
unis/SA,opt inst AUGSBURG 11-9194
$2.50   (L200)

I Will Pour My Spirit *anthem
SATB,narrator,org AUGSBURG 11-1674
$.35   (L201)

Let Us Be Happy *anthem
SAB,org, opt triangle AUGSBURG
11-0661 $.40   (L202)

Let Us Look Up And Live *anthem
SATB,org,opt 1-2trp AUGSBURG
11-1680 $.40   (L203)

Like Bells At Evening *anthem
SATB,opt org AUGSBURG 11-1712 $.30
                               (L204)
On This Day Of Glory *anthem
SATB,org,3trp AUGSBURG 11-1717 $.45
                               (L205)
Such A Very Bright Star *Adv/Xmas
unis ART MAST 244 $.30   (L206)

That Easter Morn At Break Of Day
*anthem
SATB,org,opt trp AUGSBURG 11-1691
$.40   (L207)
This Is A Day For Rejoicing *Easter/
Pent
SATB,3trp ART MAST 235 $.45, ipa
                               (L208)
This Night Did God Become A Child
*Xmas,anthem
SATB,org,opt 2trp AUGSBURG 11-1685
$.40   (L209)

LEANING ON THE EVERLASTING ARMS
see Jesus Christ, The Crucified

LEANING ON THE EVERLASTING ARMS see
Showalter

LEAVE, THEN, THY FOOLISH RANGES see
Street

LEBEN BEGEHREN IST DER WELT TROST
ALLEIN see Marx, Karl

LECHNER, LEONHARD (ca. 1550-1606)
Christus Ist Fur Uns Gestorben
SSAT/SSAB SCHWEIZER. SK 64.05 s.p.
see also MUSIKBEILAGE ZUM
"EVANGELISCHEN KIRCHENCHOR 1964"
                               (L210)

Das Hohelied Salomonis
SATB,acap BAREN. BA253   (L211)

Deutsche Spruche Von Leben Und Tod
SATB,acap (med) BAREN. BA255   (L212)

O Tod, Du Bist Ein Bittre Gallen
*sec,mot
(Holle, Hugo) SATTB,acap (med) sc
SCHOTTS C 32 829-33 s.p., voc pt
SCHOTTS C 32 830A-E s.p.   (L213)

LECHTHALER, JOSEF (1891-1948)
Gaudens Gaudebo *Op.25, Mass
[Lat] 4pt mix cor,acap sc,cor pts
BOHM s.p.   (L214)

Missa "Patronus Eccelesiae" In D Zu
Ehren Des Heiliges Joseph *Op.9,
Mass
[Lat] SSATB,org,opt 2vln/5strings
sc,cor pts BOHM s.p., ipa   (L215)

LED MY LORD see Brown

LEDERER, F.
Herr, Gib Frieden
see Zwei Beerdigungslieder

Wann Mein Schifflein Sich Will Weden
see Zwei Beerdigungslieder

Zwei Beerdigungslieder *Rembrnc
3pt BOHM s.p.
contains: Herr, Gib Frieden; Wann
Mein Schifflein Sich Will Weden
                               (L216)

LEE
Follow Jesus
(Huff, Ronn) SATB oct BENSON S4097
$.35   (L217)

Get In Touch With The Saviour
(Huff, Ronn) SATB oct BENSON S4385
$.40   (L218)

Jesus (He Is The Son Of God)
(Mercer, W. Elmo) SATB oct BENSON
S4380 $.35   (L219)

Let Him In Today
(Huff, Ronn) SATB oct BENSON S4171
$.35   (L220)

LEE, J.
Christ Became Obedient For Us Unto
Death *Lent,anthem
SA (med easy) GIA G1801 $.25 (L221)

Jubilee Mass
SATB (easy) GIA G1831 $1.00   (L222)
SA (easy) GIA G1832 $1.00   (L223)

O King Of Might And Splendor *anthem
SA (easy) GIA G1836 $.30   (L224)

LEE, JOHN
Music For The Church, Volume II *see
Thine Be The Glory   (L225)

O Brother Man *anthem
SAB WORD CS-2699 $.40 see from
MUSIC FOR THE YOUNG CHURCH,
VOLUME II   (L226)

Thine Be The Glory *anthem
SATB WORD CS-2682 $.40 see from
Music For The Church, Volume II
                               (L227)

LEECH, BRYAN
Hiding Place, The
(Elrich, Dwight) SATB,pno (med
easy) oct GENTRY G-237 $.40
                               (L228)
No Longer A Baby *Xmas
(Sanborn, Jan) SATB,pno (med easy)
GENTRY G-297 $.40   (L229)

LEESON
Savior, Teach Me Day By Day (composed
with Galloway) *anthem
SATB oct BROADMAN 4551-97 $.30
                               (L230)

LEFEBVRE, CHANNING
We Greet You, Jesus
STTBB STAINER 3.0768.1 $.40 (L231)

LE FLEMING, CHRISTOPHER (KAYE)
(1908-   )
Changing Night, The
see Two Motets For Christmas

Cradle Song
see Two Motets For Christmas

LE FLEMING, CHRISTOPHER (KAYE)
(cont'd.)

I Sing Of A Maiden *Xmas,mot
SSATBB,acap ROBERTON 85019 s.p. see
from Three Motets For Christmas
                               (L232)
Three Motets For Christmas *see I
Sing Of A Maiden   (L233)

Two Motets For Christmas *Xmas,mot
SSATBB,acap ROBERTON 85014 s.p.
contains: Changing Night, The;
Cradle Song   (L234)

Valley Of Arun *Op.33
SATB,Bar solo,2fl,2ob,2clar,2bsn,
2horn,2trp,3trom,timp,perc,pno,
strings voc sc NOVELLO rental
                               (L235)

LEGEND OF SAINT DOROTA see Martinu,
Bohuslav, Legenda O Svate Dorote

LEGEND OF ST. PROKOP see Provaznik,
Anatol, Legenda O Sv. Prokopovi

LEGEND OF ST. ZITA, THE see Ostrcil,
Otakor, Legenda O Sv. Zite

LEGENDA O SV. PROKOPOVI see Provaznik,
Anatol

LEGENDA O SV. ZITE see Ostrcil, Otakor

LEGENDA O SVATE DOROTE see Martinu,
Bohuslav

LEHNER, WALTER
Tu Es Petrus
[Lat] 4pt mix cor,acap BOHM s.p.
                               (L236)

LEICHTES REQUIEM see Goller, Vinzenz

LEIGH, ERIC
Dormi Jesu
see Two Carols

Puer Natus
see Two Carols

Two Carols *Xmas,carol
SATB EMI s.p.
contains: Dormi Jesu; Puer Natus
                               (L237)

LEIGHTON, KENNETH (1929-   )
Easter Sequence *Easter
SSA,trp (med diff) sc OXFORD 46.157
$3.30, ipa, cor pts OXFORD 46.144
$.45   (L238)

Magnificat And Nunc Dimittis
*Magnif/Nunc
SATB (med diff, Second Service)
OXFORD 42.370 $1.50   (L239)

Of A Rose Is All My Song
SATB,acap (med diff) OXFORD 84.203
$.65   (L240)

Solus Ad Victimam *anthem
SATB (med) OXFORD 42.384 $.40
                               (L241)
Three Psalms *CC3U,Psalm
TTBarBB,acap NOVELLO NCM 34 s.p.
                               (L242)

LEINBACH, E.W.
Christ The Lord *see Warner

Hosanna
(McCorkle) mix cor,opt orch BRODT
1004 $.50, ipr
(Pfohl) mix cor BRODT 100 $.35
                               (L244)
Softly The Night Is Sleeping *see
Warner

LEISRING, VOLKMAR (1588-1637)
Herr, Nun Lasset Du Deinen Diener
SSATB LAUDINELLA LR 23 s.p. (L245)

Machet Die Tore Weit
SATB&SATB LAUDINELLA LR 141-142
s.p.   (L246)

Wahrlich, Ich Sage Euch:Ich Bin Die
Tur
SATB&SATB LAUDINELLA LR37 s.p.
                               (L247)
Wie Der Hirsch Schreit Nach Frischem
Wasser
SATB&SATB LAUDINELLA LR 63 s.p.
                               (L248)

LEITZ, DARWIN
Magnificat, The *anthem,Contemp
unis,bvl,gtr oct CHANTRY COA 6728
$.35, ipa   (L249)

Nunc Dimittis, The *anthem,Contemp
unis,gtr oct CHANTRY COA 6729 $.25,
ipa   (L250)

O Sing Unto The Lord *anthem,Contemp
2pt,bvl,gtr oct CHANTRY COA 7042
$.30, ipa   (L251)

LEITZ, DARWIN (cont'd.)

Venite Exultemus, The *anthem,
Contemp
unis,bvl,gtr oct CHANTRY COA 6835
$.30, ipa   (L252)

LE JEUNE, CLAUDE (1528-1600)
Auf, Auf, Mein Seel *see Sus, Sus
Mon Ame

Errette, Herr, Mich Von Den Bosen
(Psalm 140)
SATB (two settings) LAUDINELLA
LR 15 s.p. contains also: Ihr
Knechte Gottes Allzugleich (Psalm
134) (SATB); Nun Freut Euch In
Gott, Ihr Frommen (Psalm 33)
(SATB/SSATB,treb inst)   (L253)

Grand Dieu, Notre Seigneur, Combien
Ici Ton Nom A Grand Honeur (Psalm
8) mot
"O Gott, Du Unser Herr, Wie Gross
Ist Hier Auf Erden Deine Ehr!"
SATB sc HANSSLER HE 1.545 s.p.
see from Psalmvertonungen (L254)

Helas, Mon Dieu
(Gardiner) SSATB,acap (med diff)
OXFORD 84.202 $.75   (L255)

Hilf, A Und O, Anfang Und Ende
SSATB (contains also: Eins Bitt Ich
Vom Herren) SCHWEIZER. SK 62.07-8
s.p. see also MUSIKBEILAGE ZUM
"EVANGELISCHEN KIRCHENCHOR 1962"
(L256)

Ihr Knechte Gottes Allzugleich (Psalm
134)
see Le Jeune, Claude, Errette,
Herr, Mich Von Den Bosen

Nun Freut Euch In Gott, Ihr Frommen
(Psalm 33)
see Le Jeune, Claude, Errette,
Herr, Mich Von Den Bosen

O Gott, Du Unser Herr, Wie Gross Ist
Hier Auf Erden Deine Ehr! *see
Grand Dieu, Notre Seigneur,
Combien Ici Ton Nom A Grand
Honeur

O Herr, Mein Gott, Dein Zorn Hat Sich
Gewendet
SAATB SCHWEIZER. SK 165 s.p. (L257)

Psalm 8 *see Grand Dieu, Notre
Seigneur, Combien Ici Ton Nom A
Grand Honeur

Psalm 33 *see Nun Freut Euch In
Gott, Ihr Frommen

Psalm 104 *see Sus, Sus Mon Ame

Psalm 134 *see Ihr Knechte Gottes
Allzugleich

Psalm 140 *see Errette, Herr, Mich
Von Den Bosen

Psalmvertonungen *see Grand Dieu,
Notre Seigneur, Combien Ici Ton
Nom A Grand Honeur, "O Gott, Du
Unser Herr, Wie Gross Ist Hier
Auf Erden Deine Ehr!" (Psalm 8);
Sus, Sus Mon Ame, "Auf, Auf, Mein
Seel" (Psalm 104)   (L258)

Sus, Sus Mon Ame (Psalm 104) mot
"Auf, Auf, Mein Seel" SATTB sc
HANSSLER HE 1.546 s.p. see from
Psalmvertonungen   (L259)

LEKBERG
Gloria And Alleluia
SATB SCHIRM.G 11976 $.30   (L260)

LEKBERG, SVEN (1899-   )
Alleluia
SATB,acap BROUDE BR. $.45   (L261)

Come Hither, Child And Rest
SATB GALAXY 1.2287.1 $.30   (L262)

Fragrant The Prayer
SATB,acap BROUDE BR. $.35   (L263)

How Long Wilt Thou Forget Me (Psalm
13)
SATB GALAXY 1.2260.1 $.35   (L264)

Lord Is My Shepherd (Psalm 23)
SATB GALAXY 1.2257.1 $.35   (L265)

Psalm 13 *see How Long Wilt Thou
Forget Me

Psalm 23 *see Lord Is My Shepherd

LEKDA DODI see Diament, Abraham

LEKTION UBER LIEBE see Koch, Johannes
H.E.

LEMACHER, HEINRICH (1891-1966)
Aeterne Rex
see Prozessionsgesange Zum
Fronleichnamsfest

Amici Dei *Op.190, Mass
[Lat] 4pt mix cor&4pt mix cor,acap
sc,cor pts BOHM s.p.   (L266)

Ascendit Deus
see Per Annum, Op. 139, No 2

Attollite Portas *Op.83,No.5, Asc/
Easter/Fest
[Lat] SATBB,acap BOHM s.p. (L267)

Aus Dem Psalter *Bibl
3pt sc,cor pts BOHM s.p.
contains: Dank, Op.192a,No.5;
Geborgenheit, Op.192a,No.2;
Lob, Op.192a,No.4; Vertrauen,
Op.192a,No.1; Zuflucht,
Op.192a,No.3   (L268)

Ave Maria *Op.136,No.2, Mass
see Inviolata-Funf Mariengesange
see Virgo Mater
[Lat] 2pt treb cor/4pt mix cor,org/
harmonium sc,cor pts BOHM s.p.
(L269)

Beata Es
see Virgo Mater

Cantiones Sacrae *Op.171a,No.1-7,
CC7L,Fest
[Lat] SAB,acap sc,cor pts BOHM s.p.
(L270)

Confirma Hoc
see Per Annum, Op. 139, No 2

Dank
see Aus Dem Psalter

Deutsche Adventsgesange *Adv
4pt mix cor/mix cor&unis,org BOHM
sc s.p., cor pts s.p.
contains: Es Flog Ein Taublien
Weisse, Op.202,No.5; Gott,
Heiliger Schopfer Aller Stern,
Op.202,No.1; Komm, Der Volker
Heiland Du, Op.202,No.2; O
Heiland, Reiss Die Himmel Auf,
Op.202,No.3; Singt Auf, Lobt
Gott, Op.202,No.4   (L271)

Die Propriums-Gesange Zu Maria
Himmelfahrt *Op.136,No.1, CCU
[Lat] 2 eq voices/4pt mix cor,org/
harmonium sc,cor pts BOHM s.p.
(L272)

Diffusa Est Gratia
see Virgo Mater

Dormi Jesu
see Inviolata-Funf Mariengesange

Dreikonigskantate *see Proprium "In
Epiphania Domini"

Es Flog Ein Taublien Weisse
see Deutsche Adventsgesange

Exspectans Exspectavi Dominum
*Op.83,No.2, Fest
[Lat] 4pt mix cor,acap BOHM s.p.
(L273)

Fronleichnams-Messe *Op.2, Corpus,
Mass
[Lat] 4pt mix cor,acap sc,cor pts
BOHM s.p.   (L274)

Geborgenheit
see Aus Dem Psalter

Gott, Heiliger Schopfer Aller Stern
see Deutsche Adventsgesange

In Me Gratia
see Virgo Mater

Inimicitias Ponam
see Virgo Mater

Inviolata
see Inviolata-Funf Mariengesange

Inviolata-Funf Mariengesange
[Lat] sc,cor pts BOHM s.p.
contains: Ave Maria, Op.35,No.1
(4pt mix cor,acap); Dormi Jesu,
Op.35,No.3 (4-8pt mix cor,
acap); Inviolata, Op.35,No.3
(4pt mix cor,acap); Salve Mater
Salvatoris, Op.35,No.5 (6pt mix
cor,acap); Salve Virgo Nobilis,
Op.35,No.4 (4pt mix cor,acap)
(L275)

Jesu, Splendor Patris *Op.60, Mass
[Lat] SATBB,acap sc,cor pts BOHM
s.p.   (L276)

LEMACHER, HEINRICH (cont'd.)
Kieler Liebfrauenmesse *Op.99, Mass
[Lat] 2pt treb cor/4pt mix cor,org/
harmonium sc,cor pts BOHM s.p.
(L277)

Komm, Der Volker Heiland Du
see Deutsche Adventsgesange

Laetentur Coeli *Xmas
[Lat] 4pt mix cor,org sc,cor pts
BOHM s.p.
contains: Laetentur Coeli,
Op.203,No.1; Lux Fulgebit,
Op.203,No.2; Puer Natus Est,
Op.203,No.3; Viderunt Omnes,
Op.203,No.4   (L278)

Laetentur Coeli
see Laetentur Coeli

Lateinische Hymnen *hymn
[Lat] 4pt mix cor,org/2trp&horn&
trom&tuba sc,cor pts BOHM s.p.,
ipa
contains: O Quam Suavis Est,
Op.197,No.3; O Sacrum
Convivium, Op.197,No.1; Panis
Angelicus, Op.197,No.2; Rex
Pacificus, Op.197,No.4   (L279)

Lob
see Aus Dem Psalter

Locus Iste *Op.131, Mass
[Lat] 2 eq voices/4pt mix cor,org/
harmonium sc,cor pts BOHM s.p.
(L280)

Lux Fulgebit
see Laetentur Coeli

Magnificat *Op.136,No.3, Fest
[Lat] 2pt treb cor/4pt mix cor,org
sc,cor pts BOHM s.p.   (L281)

Manner Singen Zur Weihnacht *Op.173,
No.1-7, CC7L,Xmas,Mass
[Ger] men cor sc,cor pts BOHM s.p.
(L282)

Missa Cum Populo Activo *Op.196,
Mass
[Lat] cor&cong,opt soli,org/
harmonium sc,cor pts BOHM s.p.
(L283)

Missa In Honorem Sancti Michaelis
*Op.77, Mass
[Lat] 4pt mix cor,acap sc,cor pts
BOHM s.p.   (L284)

O Heiland, Reiss Die Himmel Auf
see Deutsche Adventsgesange

O Quam Suavis Est
see Lateinische Hymnen

O Sacrum Convivium
see Lateinische Hymnen

Omnia Instaurare In Christo *Op.150,
Mass
[Lat] 5pt mix cor,acap sc,cor pts
BOHM s.p.   (L285)

Pange Lingua
see Prozessionsgesange Zum
Fronleichnamsfest

Panis Angelicus
see Lateinische Hymnen

Per Annum, Op. 139, No 2 *Offer
[Lat] 2pt treb cor/4pt mix cor,org/
harmonium sc,cor pts BOHM s.p.
contains: Ascendit Deus (Asc);
Confirma Hoc (Pent/Whitsun);
Postula A Me (Christ The King);
Terra Tremuit (Easter); Tui
Sunt Coelii (Xmas)   (L286)

Postula A Me
see Per Annum, Op. 139, No 2

Proprium "In Epiphania Domini"
*Op.212, Xmas
"Dreikonigskantate" [Lat/Ger] 4pt
mix cor,acap&opt 2trp&2trom,org
sc,cor pts BOHM s.p., ipa (L287)

Prozessionsgesange Zum
Fronleichnamsfest *Op.139,No.1,
Corpus
[Lat] 4-5pt mix cor,opt 2trp&trom&
horn&tuba/org sc,cor pts BOHM
s.p., ipa
contains: Aeterne Rex; Pange
Lingua; Sacris Solemnis;
Salutis Humanae Sator; Verbum
Supernum   (L288)

Puer Natus Est
see Laetentur Coeli

Recordare, Virgo Mater
see Virgo Mater

LEMACHER, HEINRICH (cont'd.)

Regina Pacis *Op.100, Mass
[Lat] 4pt mix cor,org/fl&ob&clar&
bsn&2horn&3trp&3trom&tuba sc,cor
pts BOHM s.p., ipa   (L289)

Requiem Und Libera *Op.132
[Lat] 2pt treb cor/4pt mix cor,org/
harmonium sc,cor pts BOHM s.p.
(L290)

Rex Pacificus
see Lateinische Hymnen

Sacris Solemnis
see Prozessionsgesange Zum
Fronleichnamsfest

Salutis Humanae Sator
see Prozessionsgesange Zum
Fronleichnamsfest

Salve Mater Salvatoris
see Inviolata-Funf Mariengesange

Salve Virgo Nobilis
see Inviolata-Funf Mariengesange

Singt Auf, Lobt Gott
see Deutsche Adventsgesange

Tantum Ergo *Op.49,No.1
[Lat] 4pt mix cor,acap BOHM s.p.
(L291)

Te Deum *Op.140
[Lat] 4pt mix cor,org/3trp&2horn&
2trom&tuba sc,cor pts BOHM s.p.,
ipa   (L292)

Terra Tremuit
see Per Annum, Op. 139, No 2

Tui Sunt Coelii
see Per Annum, Op. 139, No 2

Verbum Supernum
see Prozessionsgesange Zum
Fronleichnamsfest

Vertrauen
see Aus Dem Psalter

Viderunt Omnes
see Laetentur Coeli

Vier Veni Creator *Op.216,No.1-4,
CC4U
[Lat] 4pt mix cor,org sc,cor pts
BOHM s.p.   (L293)

Virgo Mater *BVM,Offer
[Lat] SAB,acap sc,cor pts BOHM s.p.
contains: Ave Maria, Op.171b,
No.2; Beata Es, Op.171b,No.3;
Diffusa Est Gratia, Op.171b,
No.1; In Me Gratia, Op.171b,
No.6; Inimicitias Ponam,
Op.171b,No.5; Recordare, Virgo
Mater, Op.171b,No.4   (L294)

Zuflucht
see Aus Dem Psalter

LE MAISTRE, MATTHEUS (ca. 1505-1577)
Ach Gott, Du Liebster Vater Mein
*mot
SATB HANSSLER 1.470 s.p.   (L295)

Ach Gott, Erhalt Uns Bei Deinem Wort
*mot
SATB HANSSLER 1.472 s.p.   (L296)

Ach Gott, Vom Himmel Sieh Darein
*mot
SATB HANSSLER 1.467 s.p.   (L297)

Aus Tiefer Not Schrei Ich Zu Dir
*mot
SATB (two settings) HANSSLER 1.464
s.p.   (L298)

Vater Unser, Der Du Bist Im Himmel
*mot
SATB HANSSLER 1.462 s.p.   (L299)

Wir Glauben All An Einen Gott *mot
ATTB/SATB HANSSLER 1.468 s.p.
(L300)

Zu Gott Mein Trost Allein Ich Stell
*mot
SATB HANSSLER 1.469 s.p.   (L301)

LEMMEL, H.
Turn Yours Eyes Upon Jesus *anthem/
gospel
(Johnson, Norman) SATB oct SINGSPIR
ZJP-8183 $.30   (L302)

LENDVAI, ERWIN (1882-1949)
Dolorosa Et Lacrimabilis *Op.37,
No.13 (from Monumenta Gradualis)
wom cor sc SCHOTTS C 32 933-03 s.p.
see from Vier Geistliche Chore
(L303)

LENDVAI, ERWIN (cont'd.)

In Deo Speravit Cor Meum *Op.37,
No.14 (from Monumenta Gradualis)
wom cor sc SCHOTTS C 32 933-04 s.p.
see from Vier Geistliche Chore
(L304)

Ne Avertas Faciem Tuam *Op.37,No.12
(from Monumenta Gradualis)
wom cor sc SCHOTTS C 32 933-02 s.p.
see from Vier Geistliche Chore
(L305)

Unam Petii A Domino *Op.37,No.11
(from Monumenta Gradualis)
wom cor sc SCHOTTS C 32 933-01 s.p.
see from Vier Geistliche Chore
(L306)

Vier Geistliche Chore *see Dolorosa
Et Lacrimabilis, Op.37,No.13
(from Monumenta Gradualis); In
Deo Speravit Cor Meum, Op.37,
No.14 (from Monumenta Gradualis);
Ne Avertas Faciem Tuam, Op.37,
No.12 (from Monumenta Gradualis);
Unam Petii A Domino, Op.37,No.11
(from Monumenta Gradualis) (L307)

LENEL, LUDWIG
Christ, Thou Lamb Of God *anthem,
Contemp
SSAATTBB oct CHANTRY COA 535 $.15
(L308)

I'm Troubled In Mind *anthem,Contemp
SATTBB,S solo oct CHANTRY COA 6625
$.35   (L309)

Joy To The World *anthem,Contemp
SATB/dbl cor,inst oct CHANTRY
COA 6627 $.30, ipa   (L310)

O Christ, Who Art The Light And Day
*anthem,Contemp
SSATBB oct CHANTRY COA 537 $.20
(L311)

O Lord, Look Down From Heaven, Behold
*anthem,Contemp
SATBB oct CHANTRY COA 536 $.18
(L312)

Songs For Children's Voices *CCU
1-2pt jr cor CHANTRY CHC 491 $.50
(L313)

Three Songs For Lent And Easter
(composed with Gore, Richard T.)
*CC3U,Easter/Lent
jr cor CHANTRY CHC 706EX $.25
(L314)

L'ENFANCE DU CHRIST see Berlioz, Hector

LENGEND, A see Tchaikovsky, Piotr
Ilyitch

LENGTHEN THE CORDS AND STRENTHEN THE
STAKES see Peterson, John W.

LENT AND EASTER CHORALES see Bach,
Johann Sebastian

LENTEN MEDITATION, A see Gardner,
Ingrid N.

LENTEN PRAYER, A see Powell, Robert J.

LENZO
Send Out Thy Light
SATB SOUTHERN $.25   (L315)

LEO, LEONARDO (1694-1744)
La Morta Di Abel *ora
(Piccioli, G.) mix cor,soli,2ob,
2horn,cembalo,org sc CARISH 21447
rental, voc sc CARISH 21445 s.p.
(L316)

LEROY KYRIE, THE see Taverner, John

LES MAITRES MUSICIENS DE LA RENAISSANCE
FRANCAISE *sac/sec,CCU,16th cent
(Expert, Henry) microfiche UNION ESP.
$70.00 contains 23 volumes and the
Bibliographie Thematique.   (L317)

LES SPLENDEURS DE LA CREATION see
Gagnebin, Henri

LESS THAN THE LEAST OF ALL THY MERCIES
see Jaeschke

LET ALL MORTAL FLESH KEEP SILENCE
*Adv/Xmas,anthem
(Rasley, John M.) SSATB oct SINGSPIR
ZJP-7272 $.25   (L318)

LET ALL MORTAL FLESH KEEP SILENCE see
Bairstow, Edward Cuthbert

LET ALL MORTAL FLESH KEEP SILENCE see
Herbeck

LET ALL SOUNDING THINGS PRAISE THE LORD
see Reynolds, William Jensen

LET ALL THE EARTH BE GLAD see Hatch,
Owen A.

LET ALL THE HEATHEN WRITERS JOIN see
Billings, William

LET ALL THE WORLD see Illing, Robert

LET ALL THE WORLD see Lovelace, Austin
C.

LET ALL THE WORLD IN EVERY CORNER SING
(Hill, Harry) SATB (med easy)
WATERLOO $.30   (L319)

LET ALL THE WORLD IN EVERY CORNER SING
see Young, Carlton R.

LET ALL THE WORLD IN EVERY CORNER SING
see Young, Gordon

LET ALL THE WORLD IN EVERY CORNER SING
see Zaninelli, Luigi

LET ALL THE WORLD PRAISE THE LORD see
Vivaldi, Antonio

LET ALL THEM BE GLAD see Roff, Joseph

LET ALL THINGS PRAISE THE LORD see
Kaiser, Kurt

LET ALL TOGETHER PRAISE OUR GOD see
Smith

LET ALL WHO IN THIS KINGDOM LIVE see
Parks

LET CHRIST'S FREEDOM RING see Reynolds,
William Jensen

LET DOWN THE BARS, O DEATH see Weigl,
Vally

LET EVERY HEART REJOICE see Peterson,
John W.

LET EVERY SOUL BE SUBJECT see Clarke,
F.R.C.

LET FAITH BE MY SHIELD see Powell,
Robert J.

LET GOD BE AT HOME IN YOUR HEART see
Wild, Eric

LET HIM IN TODAY see Lee

LET HYMNS OF JOY TO GRIEF SUCCEED see
Bach, Johann Sebastian

LET LOVE LIVE see Holben, Larry

LET ME INTRODUCE YOU see Butler, D.

LET ME SO LIVE see Kirby

LET ME TELL YOU ABOUT JESUS see
Mayfield, Larry

LET ME TOUCH HIM see Ellis, James

LET MY LIGHT SHINE *CC40UL
(Marsh, Don) cor BENSON B0282 $1.95
stereo recording, tapes, and-or
accompaniment tape also available;
for book-record sets available,
contact publisher   (L320)

LET MY PRAYER COME UP see Purcell,
Henry

LET NOT THY KINDNESS WAIT see Lovelace,
Austin C.

LET NOT YOUR HEART BE TROUBLED see
Brahms, Johannes, Lass Dich Nur
Nichts Nicht Dauren

LET NOT YOUR HEART BE TROUBLED see
Collins, Hope

LET NOT YOUR HEART BE TROUBLED see
Young, Gordon

LET OUR JOYS BE KNOWN see Billingsley

LET THE BEAUTY OF THE LORD see Graham

LET THE BRIGHT RED BERRIES GLOW see
Cornell, Garry A.

LET THE EARTH HEAR HIS VOICE see Clark,
Eugene L.

LET THE EARTH RESOUND see Pekiel,
Bertlomiej, Resonet In Laudibus

LET THE FLOODS, CLAP THEIR HANDS see
Ludlow

LET THE HEART REJOICE see Brown,
Allanson G.Y.

LET THE HEAVENS PRAISE THY WONDERS! see
Warren, Elinor Remick

LET THE HEAVENS REJOICE see Ford,
Virgil T.

LET THE HEAVENS REJOICE see Wetzler, Robert

LET THE MOST BLESSED BE MY GUIDE see Moore, J. Chris

LET THE PEACE OF GOD see Roff, Joseph

LET THE PEOPLE PRAISE see Red, Buryl

LET THE PEOPLE PRAISE THEE see Kirk

LET THE SONG GO ROUND THE EARTH see Red, Buryl

LET THE TRUMPET SOUND see Caldwell

LET THE WHOLE CREATION CRY GLORY see Boyajian, Gloria

LET THE WHOLE WORLD KNOW! see Peterson, John W.

LET THE WORDS OF MY MOUTH see Hyde, Herbert E.

LET THE WORLD REJOICE see Carlson, J. Bert

LET THE WORLD SING *CC9L
  2pt mix cor TRIUNE TUO 101 $2.50
  contains works by: Burroughs, Bob;
  Butler, Eugene; Caldwell, Mary;
  Diemer, Emma Lou; Lovelace, Austin
  and others
  see also: Burroughs, Bob, Jesus,
  Thy Boundless Love; Butler,
  Eugene, At The Name Of Jesus;
  Caldwell, Mary [Elizabeth], O
  Love That Wilt Not Let Me Go;
  Diemer, Emma Lou, Jesus, Lover Of
  My Soul; Lovelace, Austin C., O
  Jesus, I Have Promised; Newbury,
  Kent A., O Master, Let Me Walk
  With Thee; Wetzler, Robert, All
  Things Are Thine; Young, Carlton
  R., Let All The World In Every
  Corner Sing; Young, Gordon, Guide
  Me, O Thou Great Jehovah   (L321)

LET THERE BE LIGHT see Butler

LET THERE BE LIGHT see Jones, Robert C.

LET THERE BE LIGHT see Kelly, Bryan

LET THERE BE PEACE see Kennedy, James

LET THY MERCIFUL EARS see Clark, Henry A.

LET THY MERCIFUL EARS see Moss, Cyril

LET THY MERCIFUL EARS see Weelkes, Thomas

LET THY MERCIFUL EARS, O LORD see Mudd

LET THY MERCIFUL EARS, O LORD see Weelkes, Thomas

LET THY MERCIFUL KINDNESS see Barnby, Sir Joseph

LET TRUMPETS SOUND   *Contemp
  (Cockett; Mayhem; Pitts) SATB
  VANGUARD V554 $.35 see from Go Tell
  Everyone   (L322)

LET TRUMPETS SOUND   *see Gloria Patri;
  If Children Ruled The World; Lord's
  Prayer, The; Twenty-Third Psalm,
  The (Psalm 23)   (L323)

LET US ALL BE GLAD see Ridout, Alan

LET US ALL BE ONE   *anthem
  (Brandon, G.) SATB,org GIA G1884 $.50
    (L324)

LET US ARISE AND SING see Young

LET US BE HAPPY see Leaf, Robert

LET US BREAK BREAD   *Commun,spir
  (Hill, Hilda) SSA (med easy) WATERLOO
  $.30   (L325)
  (Thomas) SATB,acap oct LILLENAS
  AN-7001 $.35   (L326)

LET US BREAK BREAD see Hill, Harry

LET US BREAK BREAD TOGETHER   *anthem/
  hymn/spir
  SA&opt B oct LORENZ 7844 $.35   (L327)
  (Goemanne, Noel) SATB GIA G1732 $.40
    (L328)
  (Hall, W.D.) SATTBB,acap oct NATIONAL
  WHC-4 $.35   (L329)

LET US BREAK BREAD TOGETHER see
  Armstrong, Mimi

LET US BREAK BREAD TOGETHER see Red,
  Buryl

LET US BREAK BREAD TOGETHER see Rogers

LET US EXALT HIM see Sisler, Hampson A.

LET US FOLLOW HIM see Caldwell, Mary
  [Elizabeth]

LET US GATHER see Waite

LET US GO NOW E'EN TO BETHLEHEM see
  Schnabel

LET US GO TO GOD'S HOUSE see Verdi,
  Ralph C.

LET US KEEP SILENCE see Martin, Gilbert
  M.

LET US LOOK UP AND LIVE see Leaf,
  Robert

LET US NOW OUR VOICES RAISE see
  Wennerberg, Gunnar

LET US NOW PRAISE FAMOUS MEN see
  Walker, M.

LET US PRAY see Jones, Richmond

LET US REJOICE, SING "ALLELUIA!" see
  Rider, Dale G.

LET US SING A NEW SONG UNTO THE LORD
  see Arwood

LET US SING THE NEW SONG see Wyatt

LET US WITH A GLADSOME MIND
  (Hill, Harry) SSA (easy) WATERLOO
  $.30 contains also: Purday, Charles
  Henry, Unto The Hills   (L330)

LET US WITH A GLADSOME MIND see Milton

LET US WITH A GLADSOME MIND see Ridout,
  Alan

LET US WITH A GLADSOME MIND see White,
  Herbert D.

LET US WITH GLADSOME MIND   *anthem
  (Ehret) SAB oct BROADMAN 4561-73 $.30
    (L331)

LET YOUR EYE BE TO THE LORD see Moe,
  Daniel

LET YOUR LIGHT SO SHINE BEFORE MEN see
  Cabena, Barrie

LET'S CELEBRATE EASTER! see Wyrtzen,
  Don

LET'S GO HOME see Staples

LET'S JUST PRAISE THE LORD see Gaither,
  William J. (Bill)

LET'S PRAY FOR AMERICA see Eskelin

LET'S TALK ABOUT JESUS MEDLEY
  (Mercer, W. Elmo) SATB oct BENSON
  S4169 $.35   (L332)

L'EUCHARISTIE
  cor JOBERT s.p. see also Douze
  Cantiques De Fetes   (L333)

LEUTERT
  Sollt Ich Meinem Gott Nicht Singen
  SSAA SCHWEIZER. SK 172 s.p.
  contains also: Nievergelt, Lobt
  Den Herren, Alle Heiden (SSA);
  Schmidt, C., Freuet Euch In Dem
  Herrn Allezeit (3pt); Schmidt,
  C., Steh Auf, Herr Gott (unis,
  treb inst)   (L334)

LEVAVI OCULOS MEOS AD MONTES see Weis,
  Flemming

LEWANDOWSKI, LOUIS (1821-1904)
  Kol Rinnah   *CCU,Fest/Rosh Ha-Shanah/
  Sab-Morn/Yom Kippur
  2pt,solo SAC.MUS.PR. S.M.P. 9
  $15.00 two volumes, bound in one
  book   (L335)

  Todah W'Simrah   *CCU,Gen
  SATB,solo,org SAC.MUS.PR.
  S.M.P. 10-12 $25.00 three
  volumes, bound in three books
    (L336)

LEWER
  Fidelia
  see THREE SONGS OF TRIBULATION

LEWIS
  Christmas Time At The Pilgrim Inn
  (Goudge) SATB,fl,bells,fing.cym.,
  tamb, triangle, sleigh-bells oct
  BOOSEY 5831 $.50   (L337)

  Six Choral Benedictions   *CC6U
  (Platt) SATB oct PLYMOUTH PCS-44
  $.25   (L338)

LEWIS, JOHN
  Tending Sheep   *Xmas
  SATB,acap (med) FITZSIMONS 2155
  $.25   (L339)

LEWKOVITCH
  Stabat Mater   *Easter
  SATB SCHIRM.G 11927 $.35   (L340)

L'HISTOIRE DE LA FEMME ADULTERE see
  Clerambault, Louis-Nicolas

LIBERA see Bruckner, Anton

LIBERA see Faist, Anton

LIBERA ANIMAS see Anerio, Felice

LIBERA ME see Anerio, Felice

LIBERA ME see Faure, Gabriel-Urbain

LIBERA ME DOMINE ET PONE ME see Byrd,
  William

LIBERA ZUM REQUIEM IN AS see Mitterer,
  Ignatius

LIBERA ZUM REQUIEM IN ES see Ett,
  Kaspar

LID OCH UMGALL see Lundell, Carl

LIDHOLM, INGVAR (1921-   )
  Laudi
  SATB WALTON 2718 $.60   (L341)

LIDL, VACLAV (1922-   )
  Hic Homo Sum   *cant
  [Lat] mix cor,T solo,pno,2perc
  CZECH s.p.   (L342)

LIEB NACHTIGALL, WACH AUF see
  Schroeder, Hermann

LIEBEN BRUDER, SCHICKET EUCH IN DIE
  ZEIT see Werner

LIEBER BRUDER, GEH MIT MIR
  see Alte Frankische Weihnachtslieder

LIEBER HERRE GOTT see Bernhard

LIEBHOLD (ca. 1725?)
  Da Die Zeit Erfullet War   *sec,Xmas,
  mot
  (Holle, Hugo) mix cor (med) sc
  SCHOTTS C 34 568 s.p.   (L343)

  Du Hast, O Jesulein, Kein Bett   *sec,
  Xmas,mot
  (Holle, Hugo) mix cor (med) sc
  SCHOTTS C 34 569 s.p.   (L344)

  Kommt Herzu   *sec,Xmas,mot
  (Holle, Hugo) mix cor (med) sc
  SCHOTTS C 34 570 s.p.   (L345)

  Uns Ist Ein Kind Geboren   *sec,Xmas,
  mot
  (Holle, Hugo) mix cor (med) sc
  SCHOTTS C 32 231 s.p., voc pt
  SCHOTTS C 32 231A-B s.p.   (L346)

LIEBSTER JESU, WIR SIND HIER see Bach,
  Johann Sebastian

LIEBSTER JESU, WIR SIND HIER, DICH UND
  DEIN WORT ANZUHOREN see Linke,
  Norbert

LIED, DAS DIE WELT UMKREIST see
  Kuckuck, Felicitas

LIED VAN DE NIEUWE HEMEL EN DE NIEUWE
  AARDE see Burg, Wim Ter

LIED ZUR HEILIGEN NACHT "ALSO LASST UNS
  WIEDER SINGEN" see Erhard, Karl

LIEDER AUS DEM "NUW GSANGBUCHLE"
  2-4pt mix cor SCHWEIZER. SK 171 s.p.
  contains works by: Ducis; Kotter;
  Senfl; and others
  contains: Psalm 13; Psalm 26; Psalm
  51; Psalm 71; Psalm 119   (L347)

LIEDERBUCH DES DEUTSCHEN SANGERBUNDES
  *sac/sec,CC107L
  mix cor SCHOTTS s.p. contains works
  by: Ahle; Bach; Hindemith; Neumark;
  Riedel; Staden and others   (L348)

LIEDMESSE ZUR WEIHNACHT see Dantonello,
  Josef

LIENDEN, VAN
  Het Is Volbracht   *Psntd
  mix cor/unis,pno/harmonium HEER 323
  s.p.   (L349)

LIFE see Skillings, Otis

LIFE ACTION SINGERS- "GOD'S CHURCH
  TRIUMPHANT"   *CCU
  (Marsh, Don) SATB BENSON B0435 $1.95

stereo recording, tapes, and-or
accompaniment tape also available;
for book-record sets available,
contact publisher   (L350)

LIFE ACTION SINGERS· "THEY CALL ME OLD-
FASHIONED" *CCU
(Marsh, Don) SATB BENSON B0436 $1.95
stereo recording, tapes, and-or
accompaniment tape also available;
for book-record sets available,
contact publisher   (L351)

LIFE IN JESUS see Stipe

LIFE INDEED see Handel, George
Frideric, Questo E Il Cielo

LIFE IS ABUNDANT see Blaylock

LIFE OF MOSES, THE see Weinberg, Jacob

LIFE VICTORIOUS see Sutter, W.J.

LIFT THINE EYES see Mendelssohn-
Bartholdy, Felix

LIFT UP OUR HEARTS, O KING OF KINGS see
Paulus, Stephen

LIFT UP YOUR EYES see Sutter, W.J.

LIFT UP YOUR HEADS see Amner, John

LIFT UP YOUR HEADS see Bateson, Thomas,
Attollite Portas

LIFT UP YOUR HEADS see Mathias, William

LIFT UP YOUR HEADS see Weissel

LIFT UP YOUR HEADS see Williams, David
H.

LIFT UP YOUR HEADS, GREAT GATES see
Drayton, Paul

LIFT UP YOUR HEADS, O YE GATES see
Ratzlaff, Paul

LIFT UP YOUR HEADS, O YE GATES see
Thompson, Robert B.

LIFT UP YOUR HEADS, O YE GATES see
Westra, Evert

LIFT UP YOUR HEADS, YE GATES see
Hammerschmidt, Andreas

LIFT UP YOUR HEADS, YE MIGHTY GATES see
Lundquist, Matthew Nathanael

LIFT UP YOUR HEADS *CCU,anthem
(Grimes, T.) unis WATERLOO $1.25
(L352)

LIFT UP YOUR OFFERINGS see Saint-Saens,
Camille

LIFT UP YOUR VOICE, YE CHRISTIAN FOLK
(LADYWELL)
see Two Hymns

LIGHT see Whitecotton, Shirley

LIGHT, A see Posegate

LIGHT MEDLEY *anthem
see Church Is Singing Again, The
(Carmichael, Ralph) SATB LEXICON
(L353)

LIGHT OF THE CHURCH see Illing, Robert

LIGHT OF THE LONELY PILGRIM'S HEART see
Dittenhaver, S.L.

LIGHT OF THE WORLD see Parks, Joe E.

LIGHT OF THE WORLD see Watson, L.W.

LIGHTSHINE see Red, Buryl

LIGNUM CRUCIS see Stout, Alan

LIKE A RIVER GLORIOUS see Mountain,
James

LIKE AS A FATHER see Cherubini, Luigi

LIKE BELLS AT EVENING see Leaf, Robert

LIKE THEE see Billingsley

LILJESTRAND, PAUL
Follow Me *cant
SATB,high solo&narrator (med)
SINGSPIR 4275 $1.50   (L354)

O Come To My Heart *Xmas,cant
SATB,high solo,med solo,narrator,
org/pno SINGSPIR 6010 $1.50
(L355)

LILLENAS, HALDOR
I Know A Name *gospel
(Widen) SAB oct LILLENAS AN-1707
$.30   (L356)

LILLENAS, HALDOR (cont'd.)

It Is Glory Just To Walk With Him
*anthem/gospel
(Johnson, Norman) SATB oct SINGSPIR
ZJP-8096 $.30   (L357)

Peace That Jesus Gives, The *gospel
(Ferrin) SATB oct LILLENAS AN-1654
$.30   (L358)

LILY OF THE VALLEY, THE see Hays

LILY OF THE VALLEY, THE see Smith

LILY OF THE VALLEY, THE see Smith, Lani

LIMBACHER, FRIDOLIN
Canzonen-Messe *Mass
[Ger] 4pt mix cor,org/4inst BOHM sc
s.p., cor pts s.p., ipa   (L359)

LINCKE, PAUL (1866-1946)
Aus Tiefer Not Schrei Ich Zu Dir
SAT/SAB/SA,opt treb inst&bass inst
HANSSLER 14.195 s.p. contains
also: Ruppel, Paul Ernst, Aus
Tiefer Not Schrei Ich Zu Dir
(SAT/SAB/SA,unis,treb inst,opt
bass inst)   (L360)

LINDBERG
Broken Heart I Gave, A
(Ferrin) SATB oct BENSON S4012 $.30
(L361)

Make Me Willing
(Mercer, W. Elmo) SATB oct BENSON
S4216 $.35   (L362)

LINDBERG, OSKAR [FREDRIK] (1887-1955)
Den Signade Dag
4pt mix cor ERIKS 77 s.p.   (L363)

LINDEMAN
Built On A Rock *anthem
(Rasley, John M.) SATB oct SINGSPIR
ZJP-7279 $.30   (L364)

Hallelujah, Jesus Lives! *Easter/
Lent
(Ehret) SAB,trp oct LILLENAS
AN-2400 $.30   (L365)

Salvation For Us Provideth
(Sateren) SATB,acap ART MAST 150
$.40   (L366)

LINDH, JODY W.
Psalm 47 *anthem
SATB,trp BROADMAN 4563-02 $.50
(L367)

LINES FROM THE MAGNIFICAT see Grant, W
Parks

LINKE, NORBERT (1933-   )
Im Frieden Dein, O Herre Mein
SAT/SAB,opt treb inst HANSSLER
14.165 s.p.   (L368)

Liebster Jesu, Wir Sind Hier, Dich
Und Dein Wort Anzuhoren
SAT/SAB,opt treb inst,bass inst
HANSSLER 14.127 s.p.   (L369)

O Glaubig Herz, Gebendei
SAT/SAB/1-2pt,treb inst,opt bass
inst HANSSLER 14.226 s.p.   (L370)

Straf Micht Nicht In Deinem Zorn
see Chemin-Petit, Hans, Straf Mich
Nicht In Deinem Zorn

L'INVITATION AU VOYAGE see Corigliano,
John

LIPP, ALBAN
Aeterne Rex
see Vier Gesange Und "Pange Lingua"
Zur Fronleichnamsprozession

Pange Lingua
see Vier Gesange Und "Pange Lingua"
Zur Fronleichnamsprozession

Requiem Mit Libera *Op.65
[Lat] SA&opt TB,org sc,cor pts BOHM
s.p.   (L371)

Sacris Solemnis
see Vier Gesange Und "Pange Lingua"
Zur Fronleichnamsprozession

St. Albans-Messe In C *Op.66, Mass
[Lat] SAB&opt T,2clar,2horn,2trp,
trom,strings,timp sc,cor pts BOHM
s.p., ipa   (L372)

Salutis Humanae Sator
see Vier Gesange Und "Pange Lingua"
Zur Fronleichnamsprozession

Schutzengel-Messe *Op.46, Mass
[Lat] 4pt mix cor,opt org/5brass
sc,cor pts BOHM s.p., ipa (L373)

LIPP, ALBAN (cont'd.)

Verbum Supernum
see Vier Gesange Und "Pange Lingua"
Zur Fronleichnamsprozession

Vier Gesange Und "Pange Lingua" Zur
Fronleichnamsprozession *Op.14
[Lat] 4pt mix cor,5brass sc,cor pts
BOHM s.p., ipa
contains: Aeterne Rex; Pange
Lingua; Sacris Solemnis;
Salutis Humanae Sator; Verbum
Supernum   (L374)

Zwei Libera *Op.29, CC2U
[Lat] 4pt mix cor,opt org sc,cor
pts BOHM s.p.   (L375)

LIPPHARDT, W.
Ave Maria, Dich Lobt Musica *CCU,BVM
SATB CHRIS 50853 s.p.   (L376)

Lauda Sion *CCU,Commun
SATB CHRIS 50856 s.p.   (L377)

LISTEN see Medema, Ken

LISTEN ALL WHO ENTER THESE PORTALS see
Herbst, Johannes

LISTEN, SHEPHERDS, LISTEN see
Curtwright Carolee

LISTEN TO LAMBS
see Five Negro Spirituals

LISTEN TO MY WORDS, LORD see Adler,
Samuel

LISTEN TO THE HEAVENLY SOUND see
McNair, Jacqueline Hanna

LISTEN TO THE LAMBS *spir
2pt ASHDOWN EA378   (L378)

LISTEN TO THE SOUND see Mercer, W. Elmo

LISTEN TO THE WIND see Riley

LISTEN WITH AN OPEN MIND see Hughes

LISTER, MOSIE
All Of Me *gospel
(Skillings, Otis) SATB oct LILLENAS
AN-1713 $.30   (L379)

At The Crossing *gospel
(Mickelson, Paul) SATB oct LILLENAS
AN-1699 $.25   (L380)

Day Of Miracles, The *gospel
SAB oct LILLENAS AL-1038 $.30
(L381)
(Schubert) SATB oct LILLENAS
AN-1673 $.30   (L382)

Desert Shall Bloom Like A Rose, The
*gospel
(Ferrin) SATB oct LILLENAS AN-1696
$.30   (L383)

Good-By, World, Good-By *gospel
(Schubert) 2pt/SATB oct LILLENAS
AN-1668 $.35   (L384)

Good-Bye, World, Good-Bye *gospel
(Widen) SATB oct LILLENAS AN-5078
$.35   (L385)

Have Faith And Keep On Movin' *spir
(Schubert) SATB oct LILLENAS
AN-5037 $.30   (L386)

He Has Surely Borne Our Sorrow
*gospel
(Skillings, Otis) SATB oct LILLENAS
AN-1683 $.30   (L387)

He Knows Just What I Need *gospel
(Owens) SATB oct LILLENAS AN-1658
$.35   (L388)

His Grace Is Sufficient For Me
*gospel
(Skillings, Otis) SATB oct LILLENAS
AN-1678 $.30   (L389)

In The Arms Of Sweet Deliverance
*gospel
(Linn) SATB,brass oct LILLENAS
AT-1091 $.35   (L390)
(Schubert) SSATB oct LILLENAS
AN-1671 $.30   (L391)
(Skillings, Otis) SATB oct LILLENAS
AN-1686 $.30   (L392)

King And I, The *gospel
(Collins) SATB oct LILLENAS AN-1679
$.30   (L393)

Seek Ye The Lord *anthem
SATB oct LILLENAS AL-1037 $.30
(L394)

LISTER, MOSIE (cont'd.)

Then I Met The Master *gospel
SATB oct LILLENAS AL-1034 $.30
                                    (L395)
(Widen) SATB oct LILLENAS AN-1709
$.30   (L396)

Where No One Stands Alone *gospel
(Widen) SATB oct LILLENAS AN-1711
$.30   (L397)

While Ages Roll *gospel
(Schubert) 2pt oct LILLENAS AN-1670
$.30   (L398)

LISZT, FRANZ (1811-1886)
Ave Maria
LIENAU sc s.p., cor pts s.p. (L399)

Cantatibus Organis
[Lat] SATB,S solo,org EGTVED MS8B11
s.p.   (L400)

Collected Works *sac/sec,CCU
(D'Albert, Busoni; Raabe, Peter;
Stradel, August; V. Da Motta, J.;
Kellermann, B.; Bartok, Bela;
Taubmann, Otto; Wolfrum, Philipp;
Stavenhagen, B.) microfiche
UNIV.MUS.ED. $150.00 originally
published as 34 volumes in 33
bindings by Breitkopf and
Haertal, Leipzig, 1907-1936
                                    (L401)
Fourteen Stations Of The Cross, The
*see Via Crucis

Holy, Holy, Holy (from Missa
Choralis)
(Ehret, Walter) [Eng/Lat] SATB,pno
oct ELKAN-V 362-03171 $.35 (L402)

Kronungsmesse In Es-Dur *Mass
[Lat] SATB&SATB&SATB&TTBB,SATB
soli,org,orch (E flat maj,med
diff) min sc SCHOTTS ETP 941 s.p.
                                    (L403)
Missa Choralis *Mass
[Lat] 4-8pt mix cor,org sc,cor pts
BOHM s.p.   (L404)
[Lat] SSAATBB,org min sc EULENBURG
1076 s.p.   (L405)

Missa Solemnis In D-Dur *Mass
4-8pt mix cor,SATB soli,org,orch (D
maj,med diff) min sc SCHOTTS
ETP 942 s.p.   (L406)

O Salutaris Hostia
see Liszt, Franz, Pater Noster

Pater Noster
SATB,acap EGTVED MS8B10 s.p.
contains also: O Salutaris Hostia
                                    (L407)
Requiem *funeral
(Darvas, Gabor) men cor,TTBB soli,
org,opt brass min sc EULENBURG
947 s.p.   (L408)

Tantum Ergo
[Lat] 4pt mix cor,org sc,cor pts
BOHM s.p.   (L409)

Tu Es Petrus *Fest
[Lat] 4pt mix cor,org/2fl&2ob&
2clar&2bsn&2horn&2trp&3trom&
strings&timp&org sc,cor pts BOHM
s.p., ipa   (L410)

Via Crucis *Psntd
(Sulyok) "Fourteen Stations Of The
Cross, The" [Ger/Lat] SATB,SSABar
soli,org/pno min sc EULENBURG
1082 s.p.   (L411)

Via Crucis (Der Kreuzweg) *Holywk
[Ger/Lat] mix cor,SATB soli,org/pno
s.p. sc BREITKOPF-W PB 1966, cor
pts BREITKOPF-W CHB 3588 (L412)

LITANIAE DE BEATA MARIA VIRGINE see
Mozart, Wolfgang Amadeus

LITANIAE LAURENTANAE see Salva, Tadeas

LITANIAE LAURETANAE see Mozart,
Wolfgang Amadeus, Litaniae De Beata
Maria Virgine

LITANIAE LAURETANAE D-DUR see Mozart,
Wolfgang Amadeus

LITANIE A LA VIERGE NOIR see Poulenc,
Francis

LITANIE DE VENERABILIS see Mozart,
Wolfgang Amadeus

LITANY IN B-FLAT see Haydn, (Franz)
Joseph, In Nomine Jesu

LITANY OF CELEBRATION see Hopson, Hal
H.

LITEN JULEKANTATE see Baden, Conrad

LITHERLAND, DONNA
Follow On *Gen,anthem,US
SA (med diff) oct LORENZ 5399 $.30
                                    (L413)
LITTLE CHILD ON THE STRAW see Lovelace,
Austin C.

LITTLE CHILUN *spir
(Beal, Loy) SABar&camb CAMBIATA
S17315 $.35   (L414)

LITTLE CHRISTMAS CANTATA see Baden,
Conrad, Liten Julekantate

LITTLE CHRISTMAS STAR see Cobine, Al

LITTLE CHURCH CHOIR, THE *CC10UL
(Carmichael, Ralph) 1-2pt/SATB WORD
37660 $1.95   (L415)

LITTLE CRADLE ROCKS TONIGHT IN GLORY,
THE *Xmas,spir
see Christmas Spiritual Collection
(Walker) jr cor, Orff inst (easy) oct
CONCORDIA 98-2139 $.40   (L416)

LITTLE DAVID, PLAY ON YOUR HARP
*anthem
(Cram) 2pt oct BROADMAN 4558-52 $.25
                                    (L417)
LITTLE GREY DONKEY see Sleeth, Natalie

LITTLE HOSANNA, A see Bach, Johann
Sebastian

LITTLE JESUS see Graham, Robert Virgil

LITTLE JESUS CAME TO TOWN, THE see
James, D.

LITTLE JESUS CAME TO TOWN, THE see
James, Will

LITTLE JESUS IN A MANGER LAY *Xmas,US
(Ehret) SATB oct CONCORDIA 98-2225
$.40   (L418)

LITTLE JESUS, SWEETLY SLEEP see
Sowerby, Leo

LITTLE KING'S CAROL, THE see Verrall,
Pamela

LITTLE LAMB see Artman

LITTLE LAMB see Simons, L.E.

LITTLE LORD JESUS see Slater, David D.

LITTLE NEGRO PASSION see Koster, Ernst

LITTLE PASSIONTIDE CANTATA, A ISATB,
ACAP see Payne, Anthony

LITTLE PEOPLE'S PRAYER see Cruickshank,
R.

LITTLE PRAYERS see Rorem, Ned

LITTLE SHEPHERD see Marriott, Michael
J.

LITTLE TOUCH OF HEAVEN, A see Watters,
Bob

LITTLE WHITE DONKEY see Bennett, Roy C.

LITTLETON, BILL J.
Alleluia! Alleluia! *Easter,anthem
unis,opt hndbl FINE ARTS CM 1079
$.30   (L419)

Behold The Lamb Of God *Easter,
anthem
SATB FINE ARTS CM 1040 $.35 (L420)

Christ The Lord Is Risen Today
*Easter,anthem
SATB FINE ARTS CM 1006 $.35 (L421)

Christian Men, Rejoice *Xmas,anthem
SATB FINE ARTS CM 1096 $.35 (L422)

Come Holy Spirit *anthem
SATB FINE ARTS CM 1024 $.35 (L423)

Come We That Love The Lord *anthem
1-2pt,opt hndbl FINE ARTS CM 1078
$.35   (L424)

Good News From Heaven *Xmas,anthem
unis,opt hndbl FINE ARTS CM 1077
$.30   (L425)

Jubilee Is Come *Easter,anthem/cant
SATB,inst sc FINE ARTS EC 100
$1.25, ipa   (L426)
SATB FINE ARTS CM 1021 $.35 (L427)

Love From The Heart *anthem
SATB,opt gtr FINE ARTS EP 36 $.35
                                    (L428)

LITTLETON, BILL J. (cont'd.)

One Way *anthem
SATB FINE ARTS EP 40 $.30   (L429)

Reach Out *see Bass, Claude L.

See Now The Lamb Of God *Easter,
anthem
SATB,MezBar soli FINE ARTS CM 1047
$.30   (L430)

Surely He Hath Born Our Griefs
*Easter,anthem
SATB FINE ARTS CM 1028 $.30 (L431)

Take Up Thy Cross The Saviour Said
*Easter,anthem
SATB FINE ARTS CM 1055 $.35 (L432)

This Is The Day *anthem
SATB FINE ARTS CM 1054 $.35 (L433)

Touch Of God, The *anthem
SATB,opt gtr FINE ARTS EP 52 $.30
                                    (L434)
Worthy Is The Lamb *Easter,anthem
dbl cor,inst FINE ARTS CM 1038
$.40, ipa   (L435)

LITTLEWOOD
There Is No Love (composed with
Hooper) *anthem
SATB oct BROADMAN 4554-90 $.30
                                    (L436)

LITURGICAL SONGS FOR THE CHURCH YEAR
see Neilsen, Ludvig

LITURGISCHE GESANGE see Eben, Petr

LITURGY OF THE EUCHARIST see Peloquin,
C. Alexander

LITURGY OF THE WORD see Peloquin, C.
Alexander

LIVE YOUR LIFE FOR HIM see Bach, Johann
Sebastian

LIVELY CHORUSES NO. 1 *CC71UL
jr cor SINGSPIR 5300 $.95   (L437)

LIVELY CHORUSES NO. 2 *CC56UL
jr cor SINGSPIR 5301 $.95   (L438)

LIVELY CHORUSES NO. 3 *CC48UL
jr cor SINGSPIR 5302 $.95   (L439)

LIVING BREAD see Sateren, Leland
Bernhard

LIVING FLAME OF LOVE see Beecroft,
Norma

LIVING HOPE, A see Skillings, Otis

LIVING IN A WEALTHY COUNTRY see
Williams

LIVING IN THE SPIRIT see Landgrave,
Phillip

LIVING WATER see Kirschke, D.

LIVINGSTON
Morning Trumpet, The *anthem
SATB WORD CS-2674 $.35   (L440)

Praise, My Soul, The King Of Heaven
*see Lyte

Sweetest Name I Know *see Bridgers

LLOYD, HENRY
O Christ! Thou Art Joy Alone *mot
SATB HARRIS $.30   (L441)

LO, A CHILD IS BORN TO US see Morales,
Cristobal de, Puer Natus Est Nobis

LO! A STAR see Graham, Robert

LO, ANGELS' BREAD see Casciolini,
Claudio

LO! GOD IS HERE! see Burroughs

LO! GOD IS HERE see Hughes, Robert J.

LO, GOD IS HERE see Rasley, John M.

LO, HE COMES WITH CLOUDS DESCENDING see
Owen

LO, HE COMES WITH CLOUDS DESCENDING see
Puer Nobis Nascitur

LO HOW A ROSE E'ER BLOOMING *Xmas
(Hill, Harry) SSA (easy) WATERLOO
$.30   (L442)

LO, HOW A ROSE E'ER BLOOMING see Houkom

LO, HOW A ROSE E'ER BLOOMING see
Praetorius, Michael, Es Ist Ein Ros
Entsprungen

LO, I AM WITH YOU ALWAYS see
Ellenberger, Loretta

LOB see Lemacher, Heinrich

LOB DER FREUNDSCHAFT see Haas, Joseph

LOB DES SCHNEIDERS see Lang, Hans

LOB, EHR SEI GOTT IM HOCHSTEN THRON see
Staden, Johann

LOB, EHR', UND PREIS SEI GOTT see Bach,
Johann Sebastian

LOB GOTT GETROST MEIN SINGEN see Marx,
Karl

LOB SEI DEM ALLMACHTIGEN GOTT see
Vulpius, Melchior

LOB UND EHR MIT STETEM DANKOPFER see
Pepping, Ernst

LOBE DEN HERREN *Proces,anthem
   (Goemanne, Noel) "Praise To The Lord"
   SATB/cong,org,opt 1-2trp (easy) GIA
   G1891 $.35   (L443)
   (Hokanson, Margrethe) "Praise To The
   Lord" SAB,opt trp (easy) FITZSIMONS
   6011 $.25   (L444)
   (Hokanson, Margrethe) "Praise To The
   Lord" SATB,opt trp (easy)
   FITZSIMONS 2195 $.25   (L445)
   (Newbury) "Praise To The Lord" SATB
   SCHIRM.G 11944 $.30   (L446)
   (Roff, Joseph) "Praise To The Lord"
   SATB LITURGICAL $.50 see also
   Twelve Hymns   (L447)

LOBE DEN HERREN see Bach, Johann
Sebastian

LOBE DEN HERREN see Distler, Hugo

LOBE DEN HERREN see Kutzer, Ernst

LOBE DEN HERREN see Trapp, Willy

LOBE DEN HERREN see Vierdanck, Johann

LOBE DEN HERREN, DEN MACHTIGEN KONIG
   men cor,acap TONOS 5602 s.p. (L448)

LOBE DEN HERREN, DEN MACHTIGEN KONIG
see Zipp, Friedrich

LOBE DEN HERREN, DEN MACHTIGEN KONIG
DER EHREN see Fiebig, Kurt

LOBE DEN HERREN, DEN MACHTIGEN KONIG
DER EHREN see Heer, Emil

LOBE DEN HERREN, MEINE SEELE see
Schutz, Heinrich

LOBE DEN HERREN, MEINE SEELE see
Wenzel, Eberhard

LOBE DEN HERRN see Krause, E.

LOBE DEN HERRN, MEINE SEELE see
Burkhard Willy

LOBET DEN HERREN ALLE see Cruger,
Johann

LOBET DEN HERREN, ALLE, DIE IH EHREN
see Cruger, Johann

LOBET DEN HERREN, ALLE, DIE IHN EHREN
see Kurig, Hans-Hermann

LOBET DEN HERREN, ALLE, DIE IHN EHREN
see Werner, Fritz

LOBET DEN HERREN, ALLE HEIDEN see
Dressler, Gallus

LOBET DEN HERREN, ALLE HEIDEN see
Praetorius, Michael

LOBET DEN HERREN, DENN ER IST SEHR
FREUNDLICH see Franck

LOBET DEN HERREN, MEINE SEELE see
Hammerschmidt, Andreas

LOBET DEN HERREN UND PREDIGT SEINEN
NAMEN see Staden, Johann

LOBET DEN HERRN, ALLE HEIDEN see
Telemann, Georg Philipp

LOBET DEN HERRN IN SEINEM HEILIGTUM see
Diener, Theodor

LOBET DEN HERRN IN SEINEM HEILIGTUM see
Franck

LOBET DEN NAMEN DES HERRN see
Schweizer, Rolf

LOBET GOTT IN SEINEM HEILIGTHUM see
Albert, Heinrich

LOBET GOTT, UNSERN HERRN ZEBAOTH see
Bach, Wilhelm Friedemann

LOBGESANG see Bach, Johann Sebastian

LOBGESANG DER BOHMISCHEN BRUDER see
Pepping, Ernst

LOBGESANG "LOBE DEN HERRN, MEINE SEELE"
see Jochum, Otto

LOBGESANGE ZUR FRONLEICHNAMSPROZESSION
see Dantonello, Josef

LOBLIED "NUN WOLLEN WIR DEN SCHOPFER
DROBEN" see Herrmann, Hugo

LOBODA, S.
   Go Tell It On The Mountain
   TTBB BRODT 516 $.22   (L449)

LOBPREISET ALL see Bach, Johann
Sebastian

LOBPREISET GOTT, UNSERN HERRN see
Anonymous

LOBSINGET DEM HERRN see Kronberg, G.

LOBSINGET GOTT see Staden, Johann

LOBSINGET, LOBSINGET see Seckinger,
Konrad

LOBT DEN HERREN, ALLE HEIDEN see
Nievergelt

LOBT DEN HERRN, IHR WESEN ALL see Zoll,
Paul

LOBT GOTT DEN HERREN IHR HEIDEN ALL see
Reda, Siegfried

LOBT GOTT DEN HERREN, IRH HEIDEN ALL
see Baudach, Ulrich

LOBT GOTT GETROST MIT SINGEN see
Gumpelzhaimer, Adam

LOBT GOTT, IHR CHRISTEN see Hermann,
Nikolaus

LOBT GOTT, IHR CHRISTEN see Hollfelder,
Waldram

LOBT GOTT, IHR CHRISTEN ALLE GLEICH see
Oertzen, Rudolf von

LOBT GOTT, IHR CHRISTEN ALLE GLEICH see
Pfluger, Hans Georg

LOBT GOTT, IHR CHRISTEN ALLZUGLEICH see
Schmider

LOBT GOTT, IHR FROMMEN CHRISTEN see
Koch, Johannes H.E.

LOBT GOTT MIT SCHALL see Schutz,
Heinrich

LOCKLAIR, DAN
   In Praise Of Easter *Easter,cant
   SATB,SB soli,org,4brass BELWIN
   $1.50   (L450)

   Prayer Of Supplication
   SATB,org FISCHER,J FEC 10126 $.35
                          (L451)
LOCKWOOD, NORMAND (1906-   )
   Alleluia, Christ Is Risen *Bibl
   SATB,acap RONGWEN $.70   (L452)

   At The Lamb's High Feast *Commun,
   anthem
   SATB oct SINGSPIR ZCS-4811 $.30
                          (L453)
   In The Beginning Was The Word *Xmas,
   anthem
   SATB,org AM.COMP.AL. $3.30 (L454)

   Jesus! Name Of Wondrous Love!
   SATB,acap AM.COMP.AL. $2.75 (L455)
   SATB,org AM.COMP.AL. $2.75 (L456)

   Magnificat
   cor,S solo,2fl,2ob,2clar,bsn,2horn,
   2trp,trom,tuba,timp,strings
   AM.COMP.AL. sc $14.85, voc pt
   $3.30   (L457)

   O Lamb Of God *Commun/Lent,anthem
   SATB oct SINGSPIR ZCS-4810 $.25
                          (L458)
   O Thou Who Through This Holy Week
   *Lent,anthem
   SATB oct SINGSPIR ZCS-4809 $.25
                          (L459)
   Service Music *anthem
   SATB oct SINGSPIR ZCS-4800 $.35
                          (L460)
LOCUS ISTE see Bruckner, Anton

LOCUS ISTE see Lemacher, Heinrich

LOCUS ISTE MIT ALLELUIA I UND II see
Ammann, Benno

LODATE DIO
   see Raccolta Corale Libro III

LOES
   Blessed Redeemer *see Christensen

LOES, [HARRY DIXON] (1892-1965)
   Love Found A Way *anthem/gospel
   (DeCou, Harold) SATB oct SINGSPIR
   ZJP-8003 $.30   (L461)

LOEWE, KARL GOTTFRIED (1796-1869)
   Pastorale
   (Johnson) mix cor BRODT 512 $.30
                          (L462)
LOFFLER, THOMAS TH.
   Terra Tremuit *Op.9a, Easter,Offer
   [Lat] 4pt mix cor,org sc,cor pts
   BOHM s.p.   (L463)

LOFTY CEDARS see Bach, Johann Sebastian

LOHLE, A.
   Herz-Jesu-Messe *Mass
   [Lat] 4pt mix cor,acap sc,cor pts
   BOHM s.p.   (L464)

   Marien-Messe *Mass
   [Lat] 4pt mix cor,acap sc,cor pts
   BOHM s.p.   (L465)

LOHMANN, A.
   Singet Dem Herrn Ein Neues Lied
   *cant
   SATB,org CHRIS 51401 s.p. (L466)

LOHR, INA (1903-   )
   Das Gleichnis Von Den Zehn Jungfrauen
   "Dann Wird Das Himmelreich Gleich
   Sein"
   SATB,trom,opt org LAUDINELLA LR 33
   s.p.   (L467)

   Dennoch Bleibe Ich Stets An Dir
   unis,kbd LAUDINELLA LR 127 s.p.
   contains also: Wohl Dem, Der Den
   Herren Furchtet (SS)   (L468)

   Ein Lammlein Geht Und Tragt Die
   Schuld
   SAT/SAB/SB,2vln,vcl,org LAUDINELLA
   LR2 s.p. contains also: O Lamm
   Gottes, Unschuldig (SAT/SAB)
                          (L469)
   Herr, Gott, Du Bist Unsre Zuflucht
   Fur Und Fur (Psalm 90) Bibl
   SATB LAUDINELLA LR 135 s.p. (L470)

   O Lamm Gottes, Unschuldig
   see Lohr, Ina, Ein Lammlein Geht
   Und Tragt Die Schuld

   Psalm 90 *see Herr, Gott, Du Bist
   Unsre Zuflucht Fur Und Fur

   Wie Herrlich Gibst Du, Herr, Dich Zu
   Erkennen
   SATB/unis,2treb inst,bass inst
   LAUDINELLA LR 46 s.p.   (L471)

   Wohl Dem, Der Den Herren Furchtet
   see Lohr, Ina, Dennoch Bleibe Ich
   Stets An Dir

LONDON, EDWIN
   Dream Thing On Biblical Episodes
   SSAA,38 soli,acap sc AGAPE AG 7162
   $1.00   (L472)

   Genesis 21:6
   SSSSAAAATTTTBBBB,org,5vln,vla,2vcl,
   bvl,fl,clar,bsn,trp sc AGAPE
   AG 7179 $.90   (L473)

   Sacred Hair
   SATB,org, combs BOONIN B 168 $.90
                          (L474)
LONELY ROAD! UP CALVARY'S WAY see
Mercer, W. Elmo

LONG AGO *Xmas
   (Kent, A.T.) SATB (easy) WATERLOO
   $.30   (L475)

LONG AGO IN BETHLEHEM see Barth, Steve

LONG AGO IN BETHLEHEM see Borth, Steven

LONG, B.
   World Is Filled With God's Music, The
   (Kemmerer, M.; Smith, Herb) SATB
   oct GOSPEL 05 TM 0143 $.20 (L476)

LONG LIFE AND PEACE see Cram, James D.

LONG, LONG AGO see Beaumont, Adrian

LONG TIME AGO see Denton, James

LONGFELLOW
One Holy Church Of God Appears
(composed with Peninger) *anthem
SATB (easy) oct BROADMAN 4545-61
$.30　　　　　　　　　　　　(L477)

LONSDALE see Anonymous

LOOK AND LIVE see Ogden

LOOK AND LIVE see Ogden, W.A.

LOOK AROUND THE WORLD see Ridenour, Joe

LOOK DOWN UPON YOUR CHILD see Artman

LOOK FOR HIM see Marsh, Donald T.

LOOK FOR ME! see Miles

LOOK FROM THY SPHERE OF ENDLESS DAY see
Darst, W. Glenn

LOOK INSIDE *CC10L
(Floria, Cam) cor LEXICON 37536 $1.95
(L478)
LOOK ON THE FIELDS see Brubaker

LOOK! SEE MY GOD! see Wyrtzen, Don

LOOK TO THE CROSS OF CHRIST see
Wilhelm, Patricia M.

LOOK TO THE LAMB OF GOD see Black,
James M.

LOOK TO THE SKIES ABOVE see Hughes,
Miki

LOOK UP AND SEE JESUS see Wyrtzen, Don

LOOK WITH FAVOR, O LORD see Lovejoy, A.

LOOK YE, HOW MY SERVANTS SHALL BE
FEASTING see Peter, Johann
Friedrich

LOOK YE SAINTS, THE SIGHT IS GLORIOUS
see Sinzheimer, Max

LOOK, YE SAINTS! THE SIGHT IS GLORIOUS
see Williams, David H.

LOOSEMORE, HENRY (? -1670)
Why Art Thou So Heavy, O My Soul?
(Morehen) SATB,opt acap (med)
OXFORD 43.459 $.30　　　　(L479)

LORA, ANTONIO
Christ Is Risen Today
SATB,pno AM.COMP.AL. $2.75　(L480)

Morn Of Praise
SATB,pno AM.COMP.AL. $2.75　(L481)

O Trinity Of Blessed Light
SATB,org AM.COMP.AL. $4.95　(L482)

LORD
History Of The Flood
SATB,narrator,inst (med diff) sc
OXFORD 46.172 $8.45, ipa, cor pts
OXFORD 46.173 $1.40　　　　(L483)

Most Glorious Lord Of Life *anthem
SATB (med) OXFORD 42.381 $.55
(L484)

Prayer For Peace *anthem
SATB,acap (med diff) OXFORD 43.470
$.30　　　　　　　　　　　　(L485)

LORD, ACCEPT THE GIFTS WE OFFER *Offer
(Roff, Joseph) SATB LITURGICAL $.50
see also Twelve Hymns　　　(L486)

LORD ALL GLORIOUS, LORD VICTORIOUS see
Davis, Katherine K.

LORD ARISE see Weelkes, Thomas

LORD AS THOU WILLEST see Bach, Johann
Sebastian

LORD AT FIRST see Willcocks, David

LORD, AT THY MERCY SEAT see Runyan

LORD BE WITH YOU see Green, Philip

LORD BEHOLD US see Drayton

LORD, COME LIVE AMONG US see McGlohon,
Loonis

LORD, CREATE IN ME A CLEAN HEART see
Schutz, Heinrich

LORD EMMANUEL, THE see Graham, Robert

LORD FOR THY TENDER MERCIES see
Farrant, Richard

LORD FOR THY TENDER MERCIES SAKE
(Hilton; Bevan, Gwilym) SATB (med
easy) WATERLOO $.35　　　　(L487)

LORD, FOR THY TENDER MERCIES SAKE see
Farrant, Richard

LORD, FOR THY TENDER MERCIES' SAKE see
Hilton, John (The Younger)

LORD, FOR THY TENDER MERCY'S SAKE see
Hilton, John (The Younger)

LORD, FROM YOUR CROSS, LOOK UPON US see
Englert, Eugene

LORD, GIVE US LASTING FAITH *Xmas,
Contemp
SATB VANGUARD V562 $.35 see from Come
To Bethlehem　　　　　　　　(L488)

LORD GIVE US PEACE see Tamblyn, B.L.

LORD, GOD I AM WEARY see Brahms,
Johannes, Ich Aber Bin Elend

LORD GOD IS A SUN AND SHIELD, THE see
Poos, Heinrich

LORD GOD OF HOSTS see Darst, W. Glenn

LORD GOD OF HOSTS see Purcell, Henry

LORD GOD, OUR THANKS TO THEE WE RAISE
see Johnson, Norman

LORD, GRANT US PEACE see Schutz,
Heinrich, Verleih Uns Frieden
Genadiglich

LORD HAVE MERCY see Green, Philip,
Kyrie

LORD, HAVE MERCY see Haydn, (Franz)
Joseph, Kyrie

LORD HAVE MERCY see O'Neal, Barry

LORD HAVE MERCY ON US see Haydn,
(Franz) Joseph, Kyrie

LORD, HAVE MERCY ON US see Haydn,
(Johann) Michael

LORD, HAVE MERCY UPON US see Bruckner,
Anton

LORD, HAVE MERCY UPON US see Haydn,
(Franz) Joseph, Kyrie

LORD HAVE MERCY UPON US see Janacek,
Leos, Hospodine Pomiluj Ny

LORD, HAVE MERCY UPON US see Purcell,
Henry

LORD, HE MADE THE EARTH AND SKY, THE
see Sleeth, Natalie

LORD, HERE AM I see Paulus, Stephen

LORD HOLD MY HAND see Ellstrom, Eva E.

LORD HOW BOUNTEOUS IS THY KINDNESS see
Bach, Johann Sebastian

LORD, HOW LONG WILT THOU BE ANGRY see
Purcell, Henry

LORD, HOW LONG WILT THOU FORGET ME? see
Brahms, Johannes

LORD, I BESEECH THEE see Bruckner,
Anton

LORD, I HEAR YOU SPEAK see Blaylock

LORD, I LOVE THE BEAUTY OF THY HOUSE
see Balazs, Frederic

LORD, I NEED YOU AGAIN TODAY see
Bradford

LORD, I WANT A DIADEM! see Dunlop,
Merrill

LORD, I WANT TO BE A CHRISTIAN *spir
(Thomas) SATB,acap oct LILLENAS
AN-7004 $.35　　　　　　　　(L489)

LORD, I WANT TO BE A CHRISTIAN see
Laster, James

LORD I WANT TO BE A CHRISTIAN see
McCain

LORD, I WANT TO BE A CHRISTIAN see
McGlohon, Loonis

LORD, I WANT TO BE A WITNESS see
Butler, A.L.

LORD, IN THEE DO I PUT MY TRUST see
Schutz, Heinrich, In Te, Domine,
Speravi

LORD IN THY WRATH see Dowland, John, O
Help Us, Lord

LORD IS AT WORK, THE see Posegate

LORD IS IN HIS HOLY TEMPLE, THE see
Cousins, M. Thomas

LORD IS IN HIS HOLY TEMPLE, THE see
Hovhaness, Alan

LORD IS KING, THE *anthem
(Johnson, Norman) SSATB oct SINGSPIR
ZJP-7209 $.25　　　　　　　　(L490)

LORD IS MY LIGHT, THE see Cram

LORD IS MY LIGHT, THE see Protheroe,
Daniel

LORD IS MY LIGHT, THE see Zimmermann,
Heinz Werner

LORD IS MY SHEPHERD see Lekberg, Sven

LORD IS MY SHEPHERD, THE
(Black, Charles) SA (easy) FITZSIMONS
5019 $.20　　　　　　　　　　(L491)

LORD IS MY SHEPHERD, THE see Black,
Charles

LORD IS MY SHEPHERD, THE see Kapp, R.S.

LORD IS MY SHEPHERD, THE see Klusmeier,
R.T.A.

LORD IS MY SHEPHERD, THE see Matthews,
Thomas

LORD IS MY SHEPHERD, THE see Mechem,
Kirke

LORD IS MY SHEPHERD, THE see Peninger,
David

LORD IS MY SHEPHERD, THE see Westra,
Evert

LORD IS MY SHEPHERD, THE see Wyrtzen,
Don

LORD IS MY STRENGTH AND MY SONG, THE
see Hopson, Hal H.

LORD IS MY STRENGTH AND MY SONG, THE
see Younger, John B.

LORD IS RIGHTEOUS, THE see
Shuttleworth, F.

LORD IS RISEN INDEED!, THE see
Billings, William

LORD JESUS BE NEAR ME see Sleeth,
Natalie

LORD JESUS CHRIST, BE PRESENT NOW see
Klump, George E.

LORD JESUS COME see Peloquin, C.
Alexander

LORD JESUS HAS A GARDEN
(Terri) SSA,opt hndbl SCHIRM.G
LG51733 $.40　　　　　　　　(L492)

LORD JESUS, THINK ON ME *Easter
(France, Wm.) SATB (easy) WATERLOO
$.30　　　　　　　　　　　　(L493)

LORD JESUS THINK ON ME see France,
William E.

LORD, LORD, LORD *spir
(Becker, H.-G.) men cor,pno TONOS
2396 s.p.　　　　　　　　　　(L494)

LORD, LORD, WE COME TO THEE see Port

LORD, MAKE ME AN INSTRUMENT OF THY
PEACE *anthem
unis oct BROADMAN 4554-93 $.30 (L495)

LORD, MAKE ME AN INSTRUMENT OF THY
PEACE see Mallette

LORD, MAKE US INSTRUMENTS OF THY PEACE
see Gerig

LORD MAKES ME HAPPY! see Butterworth

LORD MAKETH ME TO WHISTLE, THE see
McNair, Jacqueline Hanna

LORD, MAY WE FOLLOW see Bitgood

LORD, MY HOPE IS IN THEE see Schutz,
Heinrich

LORD MY PASTURE SHALL PREPARE, THE see
Billings, William

LORD NOW LET THY SERVANTS DEPART see
Lovelace, Austin C.

LORD, NOW LETTEST THOU THY SERVANT
DEPART see Purcell, Henry

LORD OF ALL BEING see Cornell, Garry A.

LORD OF ALL BEING, THRONED AFAR see Wehr, David A.

LORD OF ALL HOPEFULNESS, LORD OF ALL JOY see Clarke, F.R.C.

LORD OF ALL POWER AND MIGHT see France, William E.

LORD OF CHILDREN see Fargo, Milford

LORD OF LIFE see Mitchell, David L.

LORD OF LIFE! NOW SWEETLY SLUMBER see Latrobe, Christian I.

LORD OF LIGHT see Bach, Johann Sebastian

LORD OF LORDS AND KING ETERNAL see Kirby

LORD OF LORDS, KING OF KINGS *Xmas, Contemp
SATB VANGUARD V563 $.35 see from Come To Bethlehem   (L496)

LORD OF OUR LIFE see Burroughs

LORD OF OUR LIFE see Clarke, F.R.C.

LORD OF THE DANCE see Carter, Sydney

LORD OF THE LOVING HEART see Caldwell

LORD OMNIPOTENT IS KING, THE see Peninger

LORD OPEN MY EYES see Wild, Eric

LORD, OUR LORD see Cram

LORD, OUR MIGHTY SOV'REIGN, THE see Herbst, Johannes

LORD REIGNETH see Stein, Leon

LORD, SANCTIFY ME WHOLLY see Pasquet, Jean

LORD, SPEAK TO ME see Hampton

LORD, TEACH US HOLY JOY see Andrews, C.T.

LORD, THOU ART MY SHEPHERD see Boozer, Pat

LORD, THOU HAST BEEN OUR DWELLING PLACE see Bissell, Keith W.

LORD, THOU HAST BEEN OUR REFUGE see Boyce, William

LORD, TO THEE I MAKE MY MOAN see Weelkes, Thomas

LORD, WE ARE GLAD FOR THOSE WHO LAUGH see Wetzler, Robert

LORD, WE PRAY THEE see Haydn, (Franz) Joseph

LORD, WE THANK THEE see DeCou, Harold

LORD, WE THANK YOU see Bock, Fred

LORD, WHO AT CANA'S WEDDING FEAST see Andrews, C.T.

LORD WHO SHALL ABIDE IN THY TABERNACLE? see Hovhaness, Alan

LORD, WHOSE PASSION DIDST REVEAL see Franck, J.

LORD, YOU BEEN GOOD *anthem
(Cram, James D.) SATB,ST soli FINE ARTS CM 1107 $.35   (L497)

LORD, YOU HAVE THE WORDS see Proulx, Richard

LORD, YOUR GOD, WILL COME, THE see Westra, Evert

LORD'S CONTROVERSY WITH HIS PEOPLE, THE see Gerschefski, Edwin

LORD'S GONNA RAIN DOWN FIRE, THE *spir
(Jaeger, Richard) SSATTBB,acap (med) FITZSIMONS 2177 $.25   (L498)

LORD'S MY SHEPERD, THE see Irvine

LORD'S MY SHEPHERD, THE *anthem
(Gerig) SSATTBB oct LILLENAS AN-2205 $.30   (L499)

LORD'S MY SHEPHERD, THE see Kurth, Burton L.

LORD'S PRAYER see Egener

LORD'S PRAYER, THE see Butler

LORD'S PRAYER, THE see Cromie, Marguerite Biggs

LORD'S PRAYER, THE see Davies, Peter Maxwell

LORD'S PRAYER, THE see Dicks, Ernest A.

LORD'S PRAYER, THE see Hays, Peggy McAllister

LORD'S PRAYER, THE see Hilty

LORD'S PRAYER, THE see Jerome, Howard W.

LORD'S PRAYER, THE see Kalnins, Janis

LORD'S PRAYER, THE see Lovan

LORD'S PRAYER, THE see Lutkin, Peter Christian

LORD'S PRAYER, THE see McElrath

LORD'S PRAYER, THE see Moore, J. Chris

LORD'S PRAYER, THE see Pont

LORD'S PRAYER, THE see Rohwer, Jens, Unser Vater Im Himmel

LORD'S PRAYER, THE see Schaefer

LORD'S PRAYER, THE see Schutz, Heinrich

LORD'S PRAYER, THE see Sirola, [Bozidar]

LORD'S PRAYER, THE see Stone

LORD'S PRAYER, THE see Stralls, Arnold

LORD'S PRAYER, THE see Vater Unser

LORD'S PRAYER, THE see Verdi, Giuseppe, Pater Noster

LORD'S SUPPER, THE see Burroughs

LORENZ, ELLEN JANE (1907-   )
Carol Of Love *Xmas,cant
SATB (easy) BROADMAN 4512-08 $1.25   (L500)
I Will Give Thanks *Thanks,anthem
SATB oct SINGSPIR ZJP-3110 $.25   (L501)
Name Of Jesus, The *anthem/gospel
(Rasley, John M.) SATB oct SINGSPIR ZJP-8174 $.30   (L502)

Ring A Bell Of Joy *anthem
SATB,hndbl oct BROADMAN 4562-45 $.40   (L503)

LOS REYES MAGOS see Ramirez

LOST-BUT STILL HE LOVES YOU see Peterson, John W.

LOST IN THE NIGHT see Peterson, John W.

LOST MILLIONS STILL UNTOLD! see Martin, Bruce

LOTTI, ANTONIO (1667-1740)
Adoramus Te [1]
(Young, Percy) "We Adore You " [Lat/Eng] SATB,acap BROUDE BR. $.30 see from MUSIC OF THE GREAT CHURCHES VOL. II: ST. MARK'S CATHEDRAL, VENICE   (L504)

Adoramus Te [2]
(Young, Percy) "We Adore You " [Lat/Eng] SATB,acap BROUDE BR. $.40 see from MUSIC OF THE GREAT CHURCHES VOL. II: ST. MARK'S CATHEDRAL, VENICE   (L505)

Agnus Dei
(Opheim) SATB oct SCHMITT 1445 $.30   (L506)
Beatus Vir
(Piccioli, G.) 4pt mix cor sc CARISH 21711 rental   (L507)
Crucifixus
6pt mix cor LIENAU MUSICA SACRA, NR.7 cor pts s.p., sc s.p.   (L508)
Dies Irae
cor,soli,org,2ob,2trp sc CARISH 21698 s.p., cor pts CARISH 21707 rental, ipr   (L509)
Dixit
cor,soli,org,2ob,trp CARISH rental   (L510)

LOTTI, ANTONIO (cont'd.)
Freu Dich, Maria *mot
(Kronberg, Gerhard) [Ger] mix cor cor pts BOHM 26 s.p. see from MOTETTEN ALTER MEISTER   (L511)

Hail, Queen Of Heaven, Rejoice *ASD/BVM,anthem
(Lee, J.) SA (easy) GIA G1835 $.30   (L512)
Laudate Dominum
(Piccioli, G.) 4pt mix cor sc CARISH 21712 rental   (L513)
Laudate Pueri
3pt wom cor,strings sc CARISH 21691 s.p., ipr   (L514)
Magnificat
(Piccioli, G.) 4pt mix cor sc CARISH 21713 rental   (L515)
Messe
3pt mix cor,acap voc pt HENN 209 s.p.   (L516)
Miserere
(Piccioli, G.) 4pt mix cor sc CARISH 21714 rental   (L517)
Missa In F *Mass
[Lat] 4pt mix cor,acap sc,cor pts BOHM s.p.   (L518)
Regina Coeli *BVM/Easter
[Lat] 4pt mix cor,acap BOHM s.p.   (L519)
Vere Languores *Psnd,mot
[Ger/Lat] 4pt mix cor,acap sc,cor pts BOHM s.p.   (L520)

We Adore You *see Adoramus Te [1]

We Adore You *see Adoramus Te [2]

LOUONS LE DIEU PUISSANT see Bach, Johann Sebastian

LOVAD VARE HERREN see Olson, Daniel

LOVAN
Lord's Prayer, The *anthem
SATB (easy) oct BROADMAN 4554-35 $.30   (L521)

LOVE
cor,pno LILLENAS MB-267 $2.95   (L522)
(Wild, Eric) SATB,pno BERANDOL BER1677 $.50   (L523)

LOVE see Carmichael, Ralph

LOVE see Powell, Rick

LOVE CAME DOWN AT CHRISTMAS *Xmas
(Hassell, D.) SATB (med easy) WATERLOO $.35   (L524)

LOVE CAME DOWN AT CHRISTMAS see Jennings, Kenneth L.

LOVE CAME DOWN AT CHRISTMAS see Mc Cabe

LOVE CAME DOWN AT CHRISTMAS see Martin, Gilbert M.

LOVE CAME DOWN AT CHRISTMAS see Mitchell, David L.

LOVE CAME DOWN AT CHRISTMAS see Pettman, Edgar

LOVE CAME DOWN AT CHRISTMAS see Pinkham, Daniel

LOVE CAME DOWN AT CHRISTMAS see Rutter

LOVE CAME DOWN AT CHRISTMAS see Sowerby, Leo

LOVE CAME DOWN AT CHRISTMAS see Wetzler, Robert

LOVE CAME DOWN AT CHRISTMAS see Whikehart

LOVE CAME DOWN AT CHRISTMAS see Young, Robert H.

LOVE DIVINE see Wesley, Samuel Sr.

LOVE DIVINE ALL LOVE EXCELLING see Andrews, C.T.

LOVE DIVINE, ALL LOVES EXCELLING see Van Der Hoeck

LOVE FOR LIFE see Eneberg, Gale (Gail)

LOVE FOUND A WAY see Loes, [Harry Dixon]

LOVE FROM THE HEART see Littleton, Bill J.

LOVE GOD WITH YOUR HEART
see Three Peace And Brotherhood
Canons

LOVE HELD HIM TO THE CROSS see Brown

LOVE IS A MAN see Skillings, Otis

LOVE IS A SOUL THING see Skillings,
Otis

LOVE IS BORN see Davis, Katherine K.

LOVE IS COME AGAIN *Easter/Pent
(Erickson, John) SATB/SAB ART MAST
206 $.40   (L525)

LOVE IS PATIENT AND KIND see Hafso

LOVE, JOY, PEACE see Fettke, Tom

LOVE LIFTED ME see Parks

LOVE LIFTED ME see Rowe

LOVE LOOKS UPON THY FACE see Lovelace,
Austin C.

LOVE MEDLEY
see Church Is Singing Again, The
(Huff, Ronn) SSATTB oct BENSON S4213
$.35   (L526)

LOVE NOT THE WORLD see Blankenship,
Mark

LOVE OF CHRIST, THE see Ford, Olive
Elizabeth

LOVE OF JESUS SMILE ON YOU, THE see
Page, Sue Ellen

LOVE OF MY LORD TO ME, THE see Hughes,
Robert J.

LOVE ONE ANOTHER see Sleeth, Natalie

LOVE THE LORD see Vance, Margaret
Shelley

LOVE THEME see Johnson

LOVE TRANSCENDING see Peterson, John W.

LOVE US, OH LORD see Vlach-Vruticky,
Josef, Hospodine, Pomiluj Ny

LOVE WAS WHEN see Wyrtzen, Don

LOVE YOUR BROTHER see Hughes

LOVEJOY, A.
How Lovely Is Your Dwelling
SATB WILLIS 9873 $.25   (L527)

Look With Favor, O Lord
SATB WILLIS 9885 $.25   (L528)

LOVELACE, AUSTIN C. (1919-   )
As Joseph Was A-Walking
SATB,pno KERBY 11578-904 $.55
                                (L529)

Author Of Life Divine *Commun
SATB,acap (easy) FITZSIMONS 2165
$.20   (L530)

Awake, My Heart, With Gladness
*Easter
SATB,2treb inst (med) oct CONCORDIA
98-2173 $.35   (L531)

Beloved, Let Us Love
SATB,acap (easy) FITZSIMONS 2197
$.20   (L532)

Beneath The Forms Of Rite
mix cor BRODT 526 $.25   (L533)

Beneath The Roman Eagle
see Five Settings Of Texts By
Thomas Tiplady

Boy Child Of Mary *Xmas
unis/SATB CHORISTERS A-151 $.45
                                (L534)

Bread Of The World
SATB,acap (easy) FITZSIMONS 2160
$.20   (L535)

Breathe Into Our Souls
SATB,acap (easy) FITZSIMONS 2164
$.20   (L536)

Christ Child, The *Xmas
SATB oct SCHMITT 6236 $.40   (L537)

Come, Risen Lord *Commun,anthem
SATB oct AGAPE AG 7177 $.35   (L538)

Come, Thou Almighty King
mix cor BRODT 500 $.26   (L539)

Coming Of The Lord, The
MARKS MC 4606 $.30   (L540)

LOVELACE, AUSTIN C. (cont'd.)
Communion Service
unis (D min,easy) FITZSIMONS 7004
$.25   (L541)

Earth Is The Lord's *anthem
2pt mix cor,kbd AUGSBURG 11-1704
$.35   (L542)

Earth With Joy Confesses *Easter,
anthem
SAB oct SACRED S-7420 $.35   (L543)

Five Settings Of Texts By Thomas
Tiplady *CC5U
unis,kbd oct KERBY 6153 $.50   (L544)

Five Settings Of Texts By Thomas
Tiplady
unis oct KERBY 6153C $.50
contains: Beneath The Roman
Eagle; Holy Spirit, Like The
Spring; Joys Of Life, The; Let
Not Thy Kindness Wait; Song Of
Praise, A   (L545)

Gentle Mary Knew *Xmas
unis (med easy) WATERLOO $.30
                                (L546)

Glory Of Our King, The *anthem
SATB WORD CS-2583 $.25   (L547)

Go In Peace *anthem
SATB,kbd AUGSBURG 11-3012 $.10
                                (L548)

God Be In My Head
see Three Short Anthems

God Of Concrete *anthem
unis,kbd AUGSBURG 11-1695 $.30
                                (L549)

God Rest Ye Merry Gentlemen
SABar&camb CAMBIATA C117324 $.45
                                (L550)

Holy Spirit, Like The Spring
see Five Settings Of Texts By
Thomas Tiplady

How Shall I Sing That Majesty
*anthem
SAB oct SACRED S-7423 $.35   (L551)

I Come With Joy *anthem
unis,kbd AUGSBURG 11-1697 $.40
                                (L552)

I Will Arise *Gen,anthem
SAB oct SACRED S-7425 $.30   (L553)

Joys Of Life, The
see Five Settings Of Texts By
Thomas Tiplady

Let All The World
see Three Short Anthems

Let Not Thy Kindness Wait
see Five Settings Of Texts By
Thomas Tiplady

Little Child On The Straw *Xmas,
anthem
unis,kbd AUGSBURG 11-1738 $.30
                                (L554)

Lord Now Let Thy Servants Depart
see Three Short Anthems

Love Looks Upon Thy Face
SATB,opt acap (med) FISCHER,C
CM 7821 $.30   (L555)

Neighbors
SATB,org GRAY CMR 3337 $.30   (L556)

O Jesus, I Have Promised
2pt mix cor TRIUNE TUM 110 $.35 see
also LET THE WORLD SING   (L557)

On A Day When Men Were Counted
*Xmas,anthem
SAB oct SACRED S-7422 $.35   (L558)

Psalm 150 *see Wesley's Psalm 150

Risen Savior, The *Easter
unis,org,opt trp ART MAST 168 $.30
                                (L559)

Roundelay *Xmas
2pt mix cor,kbd oct HOPE A 478 $.35
                                (L560)

Sing Ye Praises *anthem
unis,kbd, rhythm inst AUGSBURG
11-0320 $.35   (L561)

Song Of Praise, A
see Five Settings Of Texts By
Thomas Tiplady

Song Of Saint Stephen
SATB&jr cor,org&bells/org/bells
KERBY 10498 $.55   (L562)

Song Of Saint Stephen, The
SATB&jr cor,org/hndbl KERBY
10498-954 $.55   (L563)

LOVELACE, AUSTIN C. (cont'd.)
Spirit Divine *Gen/Pent,anthem
SAB oct SACRED S-7426 $.35   (L564)

Stamp And Shout *sac/sec
unis jr cor KERBY 10771 $.30   (L565)

Still To Us Is Born Tonight *Xmas
unis CHORISTERS A-138 $.40   (L566)

Thou Shalt Know Him *Adv/Xmas
SATB,acap ART MAST 257 $.30   (L567)

Three Short Anthems *anthem
FISCHER,J 10077 $.35
contains: God Be In My Head
(SATB,org); Let All The World
(2pt mix cor); Lord Now Let Thy
Servants Depart (2pt mix cor)   (L568)

Throned Upon The Awful Tree *Easter,
anthem
SAB oct SACRED S-7421 $.35   (L569)

Time That Is Now, The *Gen/Thanks
unis,org/pno,fl,vcl, woodblocks
CHORISTERS A-121 $.35   (L570)

Tomorrow Christ Is Coming *anthem
2pt mix cor,kbd AUGSBURG 11-1665
$.35   (L571)

Walk Softly In Springtime *Gen/
Thanks
unis CHORISTERS A-108 $.30   (L572)

Wesley's Psalm 150 (Psalm 150) anthem
unis,brass BRODT 521 $.25, ipa
                                (L573)
SATB WORD CS-2680 $.40   (L574)

Who Can Behold *anthem
SATB,opt high solo&low solo
AUGSBURG 11-3001 $.10   (L575)

Winter Carol *Gen/Thanks
unis boy cor/unis girl cor
CHORISTERS A-76 $.35   (L576)

With Happy Voices Ringing
unis,opt kbd&hndbl GRAY CMR 3342
$.30   (L577)

World Itself Keeps Easter Day, The
*Easter,anthem
unis oct SINGSPIR ZCS-4766 $.25
                                (L578)

LOVELIEST NIGHTS *Xmas
(Brace) SA (easy) WATERLOO $.30
                                (L579)

LOVELY IS THE DARK BLUE SKY *Xmas
(Harris) SATB SCHIRM.G LG51740 $.35
                                (L580)

LOVELY MOTHER OF OUR SAVIOR see
Palestrina, Giovanni, Alma
Redemptoris Mater

LOVELY THE DAWNING see Youse, Glad
Robinson

LOVE'S A WORD see Bass, Claude L.

LOVE'S REDEEMING WORK IS DONE see
Powell, Robert

LOVEST THOU ME? see Gaither, William J.
(Bill)

LOVING see Reid, Robert A.

LOVING SHEPHERD see Graham, Robert
Virgil

LOVING SHEPHERD OF THY SHEEP see
Cabena, Barrie

LOVING SHEPHERD OF THY SHEEP see
France, William E.

LOVSANG see Eklof, Einar

LOW, JAMES L.
I Want To Serve The Lord *anthem
SA/unis oct LORENZ 5401 $.30   (L581)

LOWE, G.
Star Eternal, The
mix cor CRAMER $.30   (L582)

LOWE, HELENCLAIR
Christ Jesus, Lord And King *Lent
unis,fl,org/pno CHORISTERS A-158
$.40   (L583)

Dearest Lord, To Thee I Pray *Lent
unis CHORISTERS A-164 $.40   (L584)

LOWENSTERN, MATTHAUS APPELLES VON
(1594-1648)
Nun Preiset All Gottes Barmherzigkeit
(Schaefers, A.) men cor,acap TONOS
5606 s.p.   (L585)

LOWER YOUR EYES *Contemp
(Cockett; Mayhem; Hermann) SATB
VANGUARD V 552 $.35 see from Go
Tell Everyone   (L586)

LOWES
Thou And Thy Wondrous Deeds, O Lord
(Sweetman, Paul) SATB (med diff)
WATERLOO $.40   (L587)

LOWRY
Makes Me Want To Shout *anthem
unis oct BROADMAN 4558-60 $.28
                                 (L588)

When I Can Read My Title Clear
*anthem
(Medema, Ken) SATB WORD CS-2686
$.40   (L589)

LOWRY, ROBERT (1826-1899)
All The Way My Saviour Leads Me
*anthem
(Burroughs, Bob) SATB WORD CS-2634
$.25   (L590)
(Grant) SATB oct SINGSPIR ZA-4859
$.25   (L591)

Christ Arose *Easter,anthem
SATB oct SINGSPIR ZA-4602 $.25
                                 (L592)
(Collins, Hope) SATB oct GOSPEL
05 TM 0467 $.20   (L593)
(Johnson, Norman) SATB oct SINGSPIR
ZJP-3540 $.30   (L594)

Follow On *anthem/gospel
(DeCou, Harold) SATB oct SINGSPIR
ZJP-8029 $.25   (L595)

Shall We Gather At The River
*anthem/gospel
(DeCou, Harold) SATB oct SINGSPIR
ZJP-8109 $.30   (L596)

We're Marching To Zion *anthem/
gospel
(Ayero, David) SATB oct SINGSPIR
ZJP-8073 $.30   (L597)

When I Can Read My Title Clear
*anthem
(DeCou, Harold) SATB oct SINGSPIR
ZJP-7248 $.30   (L598)

LUBECK, VINCENTIUS (1654 1740)
Christmas Cantata *Xmas,cant
SS/SA, inst CHANTRY CLC 481 $.50,
ipa   (L599)

LUCIS LARGITOR SPLENDIDE see Siegl,
Otto

LUDGATE
Friendship With Jesus
(Kling, Roger) SATB oct GOSPEL
05 TM 0208 $.20   (L600)

LUDLOW
Let The Floods, Clap Their Hands
SATB SHAWNEE A5673 $.30   (L601)

LUDUS DE NATO INFANTE MIRIFICUS see
Orff, Carl

LUDWIG, EDUARD
Heiligste Nacht *Xmas,cant
cor,soli,orch BOHM s.p.   (L602)

LUETKEMAN, PAUL (ca. 1600?)
Nun Komm, Der Heiden Heiland
SATBB (contains also: Paduane Fur
Funf Instrumente) LAUDINELLA
LR 105 s.p.   (L603)

LUKAS, ZDENEK (1928-   )
Modlitba *Afr
"Prayer, The" [Czech] mix cor,org,
perc CZECH s.p.   (L604)

Prayer, The *see Modlitba

LULLABY see Mattson

LULLABY CAROL see Caldwell

LULLABY FOR CHRISTMAS see Coulthard,
Jean

LULLABY FOR CHRISTMAS NIGHT see Track

LULLABY, GENTLE WIND see Burrow

LULLABY ON "VON HIMMEL HOCH" see
Felciano, Richard

LULLAY, MY LIKING see Anonymous

LULLAY, MYN LYKYNG see Monelle, Raymond

LUMINA 1968-69 see Blake, David

LUNDELL, CARL
Lid Och Umgall *Bibl
4pt mix cor ERIKS 10 s.p.   (L605)

LUNDQUIST, MATTHEW NATHANAEL
(1884-1964)
Lift Up Your Heads, Ye Mighty Gates
SAATB,acap (easy) FITZSIMONS 2154
$.20   (L606)

LUNN, EDDIE
Happening Now! *see Oldenburg, Bob

LUPI, ROBERTO (1908-1971)
Psalm 56
cor,soli,3fl,3ob,3clar,3bsn,4horn,
3trp,3trom,tuba,timp,perc,bells,
harp,cembalo CARISH rental   (L607)

LUSH, CHARLES
Glorious Easter Day *see Lush, Ron

LUSH, RON
Glorious Easter Day (composed with
Lush, Charles) *Easter
4pt jr cor,narrator LILLENAS ME-13
$.60   (L608)

LUSH STEREO-PHONIC CHOIR *CC12UL
(Lush, Ron) dbl cor LILLENAS MB-286
$1.75   (L609)

LUTE BOOK LULLABY see Powell

LUTE LULLABY, A see Dowland, John

LUTHER, MARTIN (1483-1546)
Mighty Fortress Is Our God, A
*anthem
(Carmichael, Ralph) SATB oct
SINGSPIR ZJP-7219 $.30   (L610)
(Olds) SATB oct SCHMITT 1858 $.30
                                 (L611)
(Wick, Fred) TTBB oct SCHMITT W408
$.40   (L612)
(Wick, Fred) SATB oct SCHMITT W288
$.40   (L613)

LUTHERMESSE see Simon, Hermann

LUTKIN, PETER CHRISTIAN (1858-1931)
Above The Clear Blue Sky *Xmas/Gen,
canon
SA (easy) FITZSIMONS 5008 $.20
                                 (L614)
Aeolian Collection Of Anthems, Book I
*CC10U
SA FITZSIMONS $.60   (L615)

Aeolian Collection Of Anthems, Book
II *CC12U
SAB FITZSIMONS $.85   (L616)

All My Heart This Night Rejoices
*Xmas,mot
2pt,acap (diff) FITZSIMONS 2021
$.30   (L617)

Come, Let Us Tune Our Loftiest Song
SATB (easy) FITZSIMONS 2116 $.25
                                 (L618)
Descants On Familiar Hymns *CCU
SATB (easy) FITZSIMONS 2035 $.30
                                 (L619)
I Will Lift Up Mine Eyes *Bibl
SA (diff) FITZSIMONS 5010 $.20
                                 (L620)
Lord's Prayer, The
SATB (med) FITZSIMONS 2037 $.20
                                 (L621)
O Come, Let Us Sing Unto The Lord
SSAATTBB,acap (diff) FITZSIMONS
2026 $.30   (L622)

LUX AETERNA see Sermisy, Claude de

LUX FULGEBIT see Lemacher, Heinrich

LUX PERPETUA see Bozay, Attila

LVOFF
Duo Cantica
4pt mix cor LIENAU
MUSICA SACRA, NR. 30 cor pts
s.p., sc s.p.   (L623)

LWOFF
God, The Omnipotent *Thanks,anthem
(Lundberg, John) SATB oct SINGSPIR
ZJP-7307 $.25   (L624)

LYALL
All That Thrills My Soul *see Harris

I Have Come From The Darkness *see
Chaplin

Saviour's Name, The (composed with
Rudd) *anthem
SATB (easy) oct BROADMAN 4538-15
$.30   (L625)

LYFT NU DIN BLICK, DEN STUND AR NAR see
Angerdahl, Lars

LYMAN, ED.
I'll Raise My Voice To Sing
(Mercer, W. Elmo) SATB oct BENSON
S4147 $.30   (L626)

LYMAN, ED. (cont'd.)
In A Silent World *anthem
(DeCou, Harold) SATB WORD CS-2599
$.30   (L627)

LYNES
O Love Of God Most Full *anthem
SATB FINE ARTS CM 1022 $.30   (L628)

LYON
Winds Of Judea *Adv/Xmas
(Butler) SATB,acap ART MAST 182
$.30   (L629)

LYON, J.
Two Christmas Carols *CC2U,Xmas,
carol
mix cor LESLIE 4013 $.30   (L630)

LYRIC LITURGY see Peloquin, C.
Alexander

LYSSNA, HERRE, TILL MIT BEJANDE see
Berg, Gottfrid

LYTE
Praise, My Soul, The King Of Heaven
(composed with Livingston)
*anthem
SATB (easy) oct BROADMAN 4540-64
$.30   (L631)

M

M LA MORT DE SAINT-JOSEPH see
    Pergolesi, Giovanni Battista

MABRY
    Jesus, Our Lord, We Adore Thee
        *anthem
    SATB (easy) oct BROADMAN 4540-46
        $.30   (M1)

MCAFEE
    Communion Anthem *anthem
    cor,org oct MCAFEE M1040 $.35   (M2)

    Corinthians On Love *anthem
    SATB,acap oct MCAFEE M103 $.45 (M3)

    I Will Lift Up Mine Eyes *anthem
    unis,org oct MCAFEE M111 $.30   (M4)

    Near To The Heart Of God *anthem
    (Mayfield, Lawrence) SATB oct
        SINGSPIR ZJP-7334 $.30   (M5)

    Psalm 51 *anthem
    SATB,soli,org oct MCAFEE M1039 $.35
                                        (M6)

    Sing Praise To God *anthem
    unis,org/pno oct MCAFEE M101 $.35 (M7)

MCAFEE, D.
    Hymn In Praise Of God And Man, A
        (Psalm 8)
    see Three Psalm Hymns For Juniors

    Hymn Of Aspiration, A (Psalm 121)
    see Three Psalm Hymns For Juniors

    Hymn Of Praise, A (Psalm 120)
    see Three Psalm Hymns For Juniors

    Psalm 8 *see Hymn In Praise Of God
        And Man, A

    Psalm 120 *see Hymn Of Praise, A

    Psalm 121 *see Hymn Of Aspiration, A

    Three Psalm Hymns For Juniors *CC3U,
        hymn/Psalm
    unis,pno/org oct KERBY 6703 $.35
                                        (M8)
    Three Psalm Hymns For Juniors *hymn
    unis oct KERBY 6703C $.35
        contains: Hymn In Praise Of God
        And Man, A (Psalm 8); Hymn Of
        Aspiration, A (Psalm 121); Hymn
        Of Praise, A (Psalm 120)   (M9)

MC CABE
    Love Came Down At Christmas
    SATB oct SCHMITT 6234 $.40   (M10)

    Peace, Perfect Peace
    SATB/2 eq voices oct SCHMITT 6011
        $.40   (M11)

MC CABE, JOHN (1939-   )
    Upon The High Midnight *sac/sec,
        CC3U,Xmas
    SATB,SATB soli NOVELLO s.p.   (M12)

MCCABE, MICHAEL
    Praise Yet The Lord
    SATB (med) FISCHER,C CM 7818 $.35
                                       (M13)
    Prayer For Peace, A
    2pt/SATB/SAB ART MAST 238 $.40
                                       (M14)
    Ring Out Bells Of Christmas *Xmas
    2pt,bells ART MAST 252 $.40   (M15)

    Strengthen For Service, Lord
    unis,org GRAY CMR 3317 $.30   (M16)

    They Cast Their Nets
    2-4pt (easy) FISCHER,C CM 7817 $.30
                                       (M17)
    When The Child Of Mary Came *Xmas
    1-2pt (med) FITZSIMONS 2233 $.30
                                       (M18)

MCCAIN
    Lord I Want To Be A Christian
        *anthem
    SATB oct BROADMAN 4540-73 $.30
                                       (M19)

MCCALL, HARLO [E.] (1909-   )
    Five Mountains To Climb
    SATB BIG3 $.40   (M20)

    He Is My Rock
    SATB BIG3 $.40   (M21)

    He's On His Way!
    SATB BIG3 $.40   (M22)

MCCARTHY
    Saints! *anthem
    SATB oct MCAFEE M 1061 $.40   (M23)

MCCLARD
    More Like Jesus Would I Be *see
        Crowby

MCCLELLAN, ALBERT
    O Come, Modern Man (composed with
        Burroughs, Bob) *CC3U,anthem
    SATB,narrator BROADMAN 4519-03
        $1.25   (M24)

MCCLOHON
    Three Children's Songs *CC3U
    unis SHAWNEE F5007 $.35   (M25)

MCCLURE, VONNIE
    America, To Your Knees
    (Smith, Herb) SATB oct GOSPEL
        05 TM 0124 $.20   (M26)

MCCORMICK, [CLIFFORD]
    In The Silence Of Prayer *anthem
    SATB WORD CS-677 $.25   (M27)

MCCRARY, ALFRED
    Sunshine Day (composed with McCrary,
        Howard) *CC9L
    cor LEXICON 37559 $1.95   (M28)

MCCRARY, HOWARD
    Sunshine Day *see McCrary, Alfred

MC CRAY, JAMES
    Deo Gracias *Xmas
    SATB,acap BELWIN 2315 $.30   (M29)

MCDILL
    Didn't He Shine! (composed with
        Reynolds, William Jensen)
    (Huff, Ronn) SSATB oct BENSON S4065
        $.40   (M30)

MCELFRESH, CLAIR T.
    O Ye People *Commun,anthem
    SATB,org LUDWIG L1161 $.40   (M31)

MCELRATH
    Happy Beatitudes, The (composed with
        Butler) *anthem
    unis oct BROADMAN 4558-50 $.25
                                       (M32)
    Lord's Prayer, The (composed with
        Butler) *anthem
    2pt oct BROADMAN 4558-53 $.25 (M33)

MCFADDEN
    Thus Speaketh Christ
    SATB oct BENSON S4363 $.35   (M34)

MCFADDEN, GEORGE
    Bosom Of Abraham *see Brooks, Ted

MCGLOHAN
    Christmas Child *Xmas
    (Dedrick, A.) SAB KENDOR $.40 (M35)
    (Dedrick, A.) SSA KENDOR $.40 (M36)
    (Dedrick, A.) SATB KENDOR $.40
                                       (M37)
    Praise The Father Of Creation *Xmas
    (Wilder) 2pt wom cor KENDOR $.25
                                       (M38)
    (Wilder) SS KENDOR $.25   (M39)

    While I Am A Child *Xmas
    (Wilder) SS KENDOR $.25   (M40)
    (Wilder) 2pt wom cor KENDOR $.25
                                       (M41)

MCGLOHON, LOONIS
    Christmas Child *Xmas
    unis&2pt CHORISTERS A-157 $.30
                                       (M42)
    Lord, Come Live Among Us *anthem
    unis,pno CHORISTERS R-16 $.15 (M43)

    Lord, I Want To Be A Christian *Gen/
        Thanks,spir
    2pt,pno CHORISTERS A-104 $.35 (M44)

    Silent Night *Xmas
    unis,pno CHORISTERS A-126 $.35
                                       (M45)

MC GRANAHAN
    Bringing Back The King *anthem/
        gospel
    (DeCou, Harold) SATB oct SINGSPIR
        ZJP-8157 $.30   (M46)

    Christ Liveth In Me *anthem/gospel
    (Johnson, Norman) SATB oct SINGSPIR
        ZJP-8038 $.30   (M47)

    Christ Returneth *anthem/gospel
    (Mickelson, Paul) SATB oct SINGSPIR
        ZJP-8123 $.25   (M48)
    (Skillings, Otis) SATB oct LILLENAS
        AT-1087 $.30   (M49)

    Hallelujah For The Cross! *Easter/
        Gd.Fri.,anthem/gospel
    (Johnson, Norman) SSATB oct
        SINGSPIR ZJP-3505 $.25   (M50)

MC GRANAHAN (cont'd.)
    My Redeemer *see Bliss

    There Shall Be Showers Of Blessing
        *anthem/gospel
    (DeCou, Harold) SATB oct SINGSPIR
        ZJP-8027 $.25   (M51)

    Verily, Verily *anthem/gospel
    (Johnson, Norman) SATB oct SINGSPIR
        ZJP-8060 $.30   (M52)

MACHAUT, GUILLAUME DE (ca. 1300-1377)
    Messe De Notre Dame *Mass
    4pt oct EULENBURG 10103 s.p.   (M53)
    (Stevens) SATB,inst (diff) OXFORD
        46.184 $3.75, ipr   (M54)

MACHET DIE TORE WEIT see Kretzschmar,
    Gunther

MACHET DIE TORE WEIT see Leisring,
    Volkmar

MACHET DIE TORE WEIT see Schaper,
    Heinz-Christian

MACH'S MIT MIR see Backer, Hans

MACH'S MIT MIR, GOTT see Schein, Johann
    Hermann

MACHT HOCH DIE TUR see Lauterbach,
    Lorenz

MACHT HOCH DIE TUR, DIE TOR MACHT WEIT
    see Oertzen, Rudolf von

MACHT WEIT DIE PFORTEN see Rothschuh,
    Franz

MC KAY, DAVID PHARES
    Praise Him (Psalm 150) anthem
    SATB&SATB AUGSBURG 11-0648 $.35
                                       (M55)
    Psalm 150 *see Praise Him

MCKAY, JOHN
    John McKay Choir Book *CCUL,evang/
        gospel
    cor (med easy) SINGSPIR 5034 $1.50
                                       (M56)

MCKELVY, JAMES
    Acclamation (Psalm 95) Fest/Gen
    SATB,acap FOSTER MF154 $.35   (M57)

    Psalm 95 *see Acclamation

MCKINLEY
    Family Of God, The *see Hawthorne

MCKINNEY
    Place Your Hand (composed with
        Sutter) *anthem
    2pt oct BROADMAN 4551-87 $.30 (M58)

    Speak To My Heart (composed with
        Angell) *anthem
    SATB (easy) oct BROADMAN 4536-54
        $.30   (M59)

MC KINNEY, HOWARD B.
    In Dulci Jubilo *CCU,Xmas
    BELWIN $1.50   (M60)

MACKINTOSH
    Sing To The Lord A New Song
    SATB ALFRED 6339 $.50   (M61)

MCLAUGHLIN, MARIAN
    I Will Greatly Rejoice
    SSA,org FISCHER,J FEC 10118 $.35
                                       (M62)
    Sleep, Holy Jesus *Xmas
    2pt&opt cor CHORISTERS A-42 $.30
                                       (M63)

MAC LELLAN, GENE
    Put Your Hand In The Hand
    (Cobine, Al) SSA STUDIO V7112 $.45
                                       (M64)
    (Cobine, Al) SAB STUDIO V7113 $.45
                                       (M65)
    (Foust, Alan) SATB STUDIO V712 $.45
                                       (M66)

MACLENNAN, ROBERT
    Jesu, Tender Shepherd
    SA (easy) WATERLOO $.30   (M67)

    Jesus, My Love And My Liking
    SATB (med easy) WATERLOO $.30 (M68)

    O Lord My Babe Foretold *Xmas
    SATB (med) WATERLOO $.40   (M69)

MACMILLAN, ERNEST CAMPBELL (1893-1973)
    God Save The Queen
    cor,orch HARRIS $.30   (M70)

    King Shall Rejoice, The
    SATB HARRIS $.30   (M71)

MCNAIR, JACQUELINE HANNA
Al-Le-Lu! *Xmas,carol
2pt,pno/gtr,drums, Uli-uli,
Hawaiian feathered gourd
(Hawaiian) CHORISTERS A-89 $.40
(M72)

All Night, All Day *anthem
2pt oct BROADMAN 4557-40 $.30 (M73)

All The Angels Sing A Song *anthem
unis oct BROADMAN 4558-70 $.30
(M74)

Fanfare For The King *Xmas,cant
jr cor,S/T&narrator,opt inst
BROADMAN 4513-10 $1.50 (M75)

God Who Touchest Earth With Beauty
*anthem
1-2pt oct BROADMAN 4560-48 $.35
(M76)
1-2pt jr cor BROADMAN 4560-48 $.35
(M77)

He Is The Delight Of Our Days
1-2pt jr cor BROADMAN 4560-49 $.35
(M78)

Hear Ye! Be Joyful! *Xmas,cant
jr cor&sr cor BROADMAN 4512-07
$1.25 (M79)

If I Were A Fifer
1-2pt BROADMAN 4560-45 $.40 (M80)

Listen To The Heavenly Sound *anthem
2pt oct BROADMAN 4557-95 $.30 (M81)

Lord Maketh Me To Whistle, The
*anthem
1-2pt oct BROADMAN 4500-50 $.35
(M82)
1-2pt jr cor BROADMAN 4560-50 $.35
(M83)

Thousand Hosannas, A *Easter,cant
1-2pt,Bar&2 narrators,kbd BROADMAN
4515-07 $1.75 (M84)

Wo'll All Shout Together *anthem
unis oct BROADMAN 4557-66 $.30
(M85)

MCNAUGHTON, J.
When There's Love At Home *anthem
(McCall, C.) SATB (easy) oct
SINGSPIR ZJP-6014 $.25 (M86)

MACNUTT, WALTER
Behold A Mighty Prelate
SATB (med easy) WATERLOO $.30 (M87)

Jesu, Son Of Mary *Xmas
SATB (med easy) WATERLOO $.30 (M88)

Mass Of St. James *Mass
SATB (med) WATERLOO $.40 (M89)

Missa Brevis
SATB (med easy) WATERLOO $.40 (M90)

O Gladsome Light
SATB (med easy) WATERLOO $.30 (M91)

Short Mass Of Saint John The Baptist
unis (easy) WATERLOO $.30 (M92)

MCPHAIL
Psalm 150
mix cor/unis,pno/harmonium s.p. sc
HEER 102, cor pts HEER 102A (M93)

MCRAE, JAMES
Alleluia, Christ Is Risen
SATB HARRIS $.35 (M94)

Fierce Rage The Tempest
SATB HARRIS $.35 (M95)

MADAN
Before Jehovah's Awful Throne
(Brandon) SATB PRO ART 2831 $.45
(M96)

MAEDER
Cuntipotens *Mass
4pt mix cor,pno/org HENN 588 s.p.
sc, voc pt (M97)

Musiques De Noel *see Carraz

MAEGAARD JAN (1926-)
Sic Enim Amavit Deus Mundum *mot
SATB,trp,org EGTVED MK10, 8 s.p.
(M98)

MAEKELBERGHE, AUGUST [R.] (1909-)
Today Christ Is Risen *Easter,
anthem,Contemp
SATB,brass,perc oct CHANTRY
COA 5610 $.35, ipa (M99)

MAG ICH UNGLUCK NIT WIDERSTAHN see
Eccard, Johannes

MAGDALEN, CEASE FROM SOBS AND SIGHS see
Hurford, Peter

MAGNIFICAT see Albinoni, Tomaso

MAGNIFICAT see Bach, J.C.

MAGNIFICAT see Bach, Johann Sebastian

MAGNIFICAT see Bell, Robert H.

MAGNIFICAT see Bevan, Gwilym

MAGNIFICAT see Brixi, Simon

MAGNIFICAT see Bryant, Giles

MAGNIFICAT see Cornysh, William

MAGNIFICAT see Eberlin, Johann Ernst

MAGNIFICAT see Gabrieli, Giovanni

MAGNIFICAT see Gibbons, Orlando

MAGNIFICAT see Goemanne, Noel

MAGNIFICAT see Gounod, Charles Francois

MAGNIFICAT see Hall, William D.

MAGNIFICAT see Hughes, Edward

MAGNIFICAT see Keller, Homer

MAGNIFICAT see Lauterbach, Lorenz

MAGNIFICAT see Lemacher, Heinrich

MAGNIFICAT see Lockwood, Normand

MAGNIFICAT see Lotti, Antonio

MAGNIFICAT see Michna, Adam Vaclav

MAGNIFICAT see Monteverdi, Claudio

MAGNIFICAT see Mozart, Wolfgang Amadeus

MAGNIFICAT see Noble, Thomas Tertius

MAGNIFICAT see Petrassi, Goffredo

MAGNIFICAT see Pinelli, Giovanni
Batista

MAGNIFICAT see Purcell, Henry

MAGNIFICAT see Rehm, P. Otto

MAGNIFICAT see Russell

MAGNIFICAT see Vivaldi, Antonio

MAGNIFICAT, THE see Leitz, Darwin

MAGNIFICAT, THE see Schutz, Heinrich

MAGNIFICAT see Welcker, Max

MAGNIFICAT see Welcker, Max

MAGNIFICAT 1532 *Op.24,No.5
(Bender, Jan) SATB,kbd CHANTRY $.30
(M100)

MAGNIFICAT A SEI VOCI see Monteverdi,
Claudio

MAGNIFICAT AND NUNC DIMITTIS see Aston,
Peter

MAGNIFICAT AND NUNC DIMITTIS see
Leighton, Kenneth

MAGNIFICAT AND NUNC DIMITTIS see
Mathias, William

MAGNIFICAT AND NUNC DIMITTIS see
Weelkes

MAGNIFICAT AND NUNC DIMITTIS see Wills

MAGNIFICAT AND NUNC DIMITTIS see Wise

MAGNIFICAT AND NUNC DIMITTIS IN A MINOR
see Rowley, Alec

MAGNIFICAT AND NUNC DIMITTIS IN C MAJOR
see Stanford, Charles Villiers

MAGNIFICAT AND NUNC DIMITTIS IN G MAJOR
see Stanford, Charles Villiers

MAGNIFICAT ANIMA MEA DOMINUM see
Piechler, Arthur

MAGNIFICAT DU PREMIER TON see Dumont,
[Henri]

MAGNIFICAT IN G see Wintle

MAGNIFICAT (PART 5) see Zimmermann,
Heinz Werner

MAGNIFICAT QUINTI TONI see Galliculus,
Johann

MAGNIFICAT SECUNDI TONI see Dunstable,
John

MAGNUM NOMEN DOMINI see Pekiel,
Bertlomiej

MAHNKE, ALLAN
God's Alive *Easter/Pent
unis,pno,opt fing.cym. ART MAST 260
$.30 (M101)

I Call On The Lord
SATB,acap ART MAST 248 $.30 (M102)

Three Hymn-Carol Settings *CC3U,Adv/
Xmas/Gen
unis, Orff Instruments CHORISTERS
A-160 $.40 (M103)

We Praise You For The Sun *Gen/
Thanks
unis, opt Orff Instruments
CHORISTERS A-153 $.35 (M104)

MAINZER DOM-MESSE see Rohr, Hugo

MAISTRE, JAN (NASCO)
Passio D. n. J. Chr. Sec. Matthaeum
see OBERITALIENISCHE
FIGURALPASSIONEN

MAJOR CONGREGATIONAL RESPONSES AND
HYMNS, THE see Rothstein, Arnold

MAKE A JOYFUL NOISE see Blair

MAKE A JOYFUL NOISE see Brown

MAKE A JOYFUL NOISE see Williams, David
H.

MAKE A JOYFUL NOISE see Zimmermann,
Heinz Werner

MAKE A JOYFUL NOISE TO THE LORD see
Sindlinger, Maurine I.

MAKE A JOYFUL NOISE TO THE LORD see
Smith, G. Alan

MAKE A JOYFUL NOISE UNTO THE LORD see
Avshalomov, Jacob

MAKE A JOYFUL NOISE UNTO THE LORD see
Paynter, John P.

MAKE ME A BLESSING see Schuler, George
S.

MAKE ME AN INSTRUMENT OF THY PEACE see
Hopson

MAKE ME WILLING see Lindberg

MAKE READY see Dauermann, Stuart

MAKE US ONE, FATHER see Johnson, Paul

MAKE WE MIRTH see Crawley

MAKER OF THE STARS see Snyder

MAKES ME WANT TO SHOUT see Lowry

MAKING HAPPY NOISES see Ramseth, Betty
Ann

MALA MULIER see Drizga, Eduard

MALAN, H.A. CESAR (1787-1864)
Take My Life And Let It Be *anthem
(Johnson, Norman) SAB oct SINGSPIR
ZJP-2001 $.25 (M105)

MALATO ESTA EL HIJO DEL REY see Rodrigo

MALCOLM
Fool's Wisdom *see Alwyn

Rick Powell Choir Book *see Alwyn

MALCOLM SARGENT CAROL BOOK, A *CC11L,
Xmas
(Sargent) SATB,acap (med) OXFORD
48.031 $2.75 (M106)

MALIN, DON (1896-)
Carol Of The Birds *Xmas,carol,Fr
SATB GALAXY 1.1458.1 $.30 (M107)

MALLETTE
Lord, Make Me An Instrument Of Thy
Peace
SATB PRO ART 2849 $.35 (M108)

MALLORY
Christ Has No Hands But Our Hands
*anthem
SATB (easy) oct BROADMAN 4535-21
$.30 (M109)

MAMLOCK, URSULA
Psalm 1
mix cor,soli,pno AM.COMP.AL. $9.35
(M110)

MAN BORN OF WOMAN see Berger, Jean

MAN IS NOT ALONE see Klusmeier, R.T.A.

MAN OF GALILEE, A see Gagliardi, George

MARTIN, G.
And God Shall Wipe Away All Tears
SATB,org GRAY CMR 3324 $.35 (M164)

Morning Canticle, A
SATB,org/hpsd GRAY CMR 3336 $.35
(M165)

MARTIN, GILBERT M.
Above The Clear Blue Sky *anthem
2pt jr cor,pno/org,inst FISCHER,C
CM 7886 $.40   (M166)

And One Bright Star *Xmas,anthem
mix cor,fing.cym.,drums HERITAGE
H127 $.35   (M167)

Anthem For Communion, An *Commun,
anthem
SATB (med diff) oct LORENZ C365
$.35   (M168)

Broken Pieces (composed with Kitchen)
(Mercer, W. Elmo) SATB oct BENSON
S4055 $.30   (M169)

Dedicatory Anthem, A *anthem
SATB,acap oct SACRED S-169 $.35
(M170)

Five Little Songs For Young People
*CC5U,Gen/Thanks
unis&desc,gtr,inst CHORISTERS A-149
$.60   (M171)

Great And Mighty Wonder, The *Xmas,
anthem
SATB oct MCAFEE M1052 $.35 (M172)

He's Got The Whole World In His Hands
*anthem
SAB/SA/unis oct LORENZ 7424 $.35
(M173)

Hosanna In The Highest! *Easter,
anthem
SATB oct LORENZ B210 $.35 (M174)

Hymn Of Saint Teresa *anthem
cor,org oct MCAFEE M1038 $.35
(M175)

Invictus *anthem
SATB oct HERITAGE H110 $.40 (M176)

Laughter In Bethlehem *see Jakes

Let Us Keep Silence *anthem
SATB oct SACRED S-150 $.35 (M177)

Love Came Down At Christmas *Xmas,
anthem
SATB oct SACRED S-174 $.35 (M178)

More Things Are Wrought By Prayer
*anthem
SATB oct LORENZ C356 $.35 (M179)

My Anchor Holds
(Yoder, David; Towner) SATB oct
GOSPEL 05 TM 0214 $.20 (M180)

Newborn, The *Xmas/Easter,anthem
SATB oct SACRED S-165 $.35 (M181)

Passion Chorale, The *Easter,anthem
SA&opt B oct LORENZ 7846 $.35
(M182)

Poor World (Said I) *Xmas,anthem
SATB oct SACRED S-162 $.35 (M183)

To See The Lord *anthem
SB oct LORENZ 5770 $.35 (M184)

Water Is Wide, The *anthem
SATB oct LORENZ C361 $.35 (M185)

MARTINDALE, J.A.G.
Morning Prayer, A
SA LESLIE 2047 $.40 (M186)

MARTINI, GIAMBATTISTA (1706-1784)
He Is Despised And Rejected
(Coggin) mix cor BRODT 638 $.30 (M187)

MARTINO, DONALD (1931-   )
Seven Pious Pieces *CC7U
SATB SCHIRM.EC 2747 (M188)

MARTINU, BOHUSLAV (1890-1959)
Birth Of The Lord, The *see Narozeni
Pane

Legend Of Saint Dorota *see Legenda
O Svate Dorote

Legenda O Svate Dorote
"Legend Of Saint Dorota" [Czech]
mix cor,2ob,2clar,2bsn,2horn,
2trp,2trom,timp,perc,pno,strings
CZECH s.p. (M189)

Military Mass
[Czech/Eng/Fr/Ger] men cor,Bar
solo,2fl,2clar,3trp,2trom,timp,
perc,pno,harmonium SUPRAPHON s.p.
(M190)

Narozeni Pane
"Birth Of The Lord, The" [Czech]
wom cor&mix cor&jr cor,SMezBarB

MARTINU, BOHUSLAV (cont'd.)

soli,2fl,2ob,2bsn,4horn,trp,trom,
timp,perc CZECH s.p. (M191)

MARTYRDOM OF ST. ALBAN, THE see
Joubert, John

MARVELOUS WORK see Haydn, (Franz)
Joseph

MARX, AUGUST
Postula A Me *Offer
[Lat] 4pt mix cor,acap sc,cor pts
BOHM s.p. (M192)

MARX, KARL (1897-   )
Bis Hierher Hat Micht Gott Gebracht
SAT/SAB/2pt,opt 1-2treb inst
HANSSLER 14.236 s.p. (M193)

Der Du Die Zeit In Handen Hast
SA&unis men cor/SATB (easy) BAREN.
BA6309 (M194)

Der Herr Ist Mein Getreuer Hirt
SAT/SAB/SA,treb inst,opt bass inst
HANSSLER 14.178 s.p. (M195)

Herr Jesu Christe, Mein Getreuer
Hirte
SAT/SAB,opt treb inst HANSSLER
14.156 s.p. (M196)

Leben Begehren Ist Der Welt Trost
Allein *Op.15,No.1, sec,mot
mix cor (med diff) sc SCHOTTS
C 32 733 s.p. (M197)

Lob Gott Getrost Mein Singen
SAT/SAB/2pt,opt treb inst HANSSLER
14.205 s.p. (M198)

Nimm Von Uns, Herr, Du Treuer Gott
see MUSIKBEILAGE ZUM "EVANGELISCHEN
KIRCHENCHOR 1960

MARY see Wetzler, Robert

MARY AND A MARTHA
(Wild, Eric) SATB (med) WATERLOO $.60
(M199)

MARY GENTLE MOTHER OF MINE see Boland,
Clay A.

MARY HAD A BABY *Xmas,spir
see Christmas Spiritual Collection
(Biebl, Franz) [Eng/Ger] 4pt mix cor,
ST soli,acap (easy) sc SCHOTTS
C 43 217 s.p. see from Zwei
Weihnachtliche Spirituals (M200)
(Peninger, David) SA&camb&opt Bar,med
solo,acap CAMBIATA S117210 $.40
(M201)
(Walker) unis, Orff inst (easy) oct
CONCORDIA 98-2140 $.35 (M202)

MARY IS ROCKING HER BABE see Ehret,
Walter

MARY MAGDALENE see Steel, Christopher
[Charles]

MARY, MARY see Avery, Richard

MARY, MARY see Niles, John Jacob

MARY, MARY, PRAY FOR US *Xmas,Contemp
SATB VANGUARD V565 $.35 see from Come
To Bethlehem (M203)

MARY OF MAGDALA see Bliss, Sir Arthur

MARY OF NAZARETH, PTS 1 AND 2 see
Claflin, Avery

MARY OF NAZARETH, PT 3 see Claflin,
Avery

MARY OF NAZARETH, PT 4 see Claflin,
Avery

MARY STUART'S PRAYER see Boustead, A.

MARY THE ROSE see Pehkonen

MARY WALKED THROUGH A WOOD OF THORN see
Radcliffe

MARY WORE THREE LINKS OF CHAIN *Adv/
Xmas
(Christiansen, Larry) SATB,acap ART
MAST 137 $.30 (M204)

MARY'S CANTICLE see Goemanne, Noel,
Magnificat

MARY'S CAROL see Lapo, Cecil E.

MARY'S LULLABY see Boozer

MARY'S LULLABY see Copes, V. Earle

MARY'S LULLABY see James, Dorothy

MARY'S LULLABY see Regney, Noel

MARY'S NOWELL see Thiman, Eric Harding

MASON, LOWELL (1792-1872)
Hail To The Brightness! *anthem
(Mayfield, Larry) SATB oct SINGSPIR
ZJP-7321 $.25 (M205)

Hark! Ten Thousand Harps And Voices
*anthem
(DeCou, Harold) SATB oct SINGSPIR
ZJP-3203 $.30 (M206)

Joy To The World! *Adv/Xmas,anthem
(Johnson, Norman) SATB oct SINGSPIR
ZJP-3034 $.30 (M207)

Nearer My God To Thee *anthem
(Mann, Johnny) SATB LEXICON (M208)

O Could I Speak *hymn
(Ehret, Walter) SATB oct LILLENAS
AN-2410 $.30 (M209)

O Look To Golgotha *anthem
(Riedel) SATB AUGSBURG 11-1675 $.25
(M210)

O Praise The Lord (Psalm 117) anthem
(Brandon, G.) SATB (easy) GIA G1827
$.45 (M211)

Oh, For A Thousand Tongues *anthem
(Schubert) SATB,brass oct LILLENAS
AN-2395 $.35 (M212)

Psalm 117 *see O Praise The Lord

There Is A Fountain *anthem/gospel
(DeCou, Harold) SATB oct SINGSPIR
ZJP-8037 $.30 (M213)

MASS see Brumby

MASS see Burrell

MASS see Charpentier, Marc-Antoine

MASS see Harrison, Lou

MASS see Johnston, Ben

MASS see Stout, Alan

MASS see Woollen, Russell

MASS FOR A FEAST DAY see Isele, D.C.

MASS FOR ALL SEASONS, A see Andrews,
C.T.

MASS FOR CHRISTMAS see Wassmer,
Berthold, Weihnachtsmesse

MASS FOR FOUR MIXED VOICES see
Monteverdi, Claudio

MASS FOR PEACE see Maria Of The Cross,
Sister

MASS FOR SMALL CHORUS see Sims, Ezra

MASS FOR THE KING OF GLORY see
Pulkingham, B.C.

MASS FOR THE NATIVITY see Koch, Karl,
Festmesse Zu Ehren Der Geburt
Unseres Herrn Jesu Christi

MASS IN A see Bender, Jan

MASS IN D see Elaine, Sister M.
(Gentemann)

MASS IN D see Smyth, Ethel (Mary)

MASS IN D MAJOR see Dvorak, Antonin

MASS IN FIVE MOVEMENTS see Steel,
Christopher [Charles]

MASS IN HONOR OF ALL SAINTS see
Schiavone, John

MASS IN HONOR OF ST. JOHN VIANNEY see
Andrews, C.T.

MASS IN HONOR OF THE QUEEN OF ANGELS
see Cromie, Marguerite Biggs

MASS IN PRAISE OF GOD THE HOLY SPIRIT
see Schiavone, John

MASS IN PRAISE OF JESUS CHRIST THE
ETERNAL HIGH PRIEST see Schiavone,
John

MASS IN UNISON OR TWO PARTS see Becker,
John J.

MASS "LA BATAILLE" see Jannequin,
Clement

MASS OF RESURRECTION see Peloquin, C.
Alexander

MASS OF ST. JAMES see MacNutt, Walter

MASS OF ST. THOMAS see Bancroft, H. Hugh

MASS OF ST. THOMAS see Fleming, Robert

MASS OF ST. THOMAS see Holman, Derek

MASS OF THANKSGIVING see Kreutz, Robert E.

MASS OF THE BELLS see Peloquin, C. Alexander

MASSA see Forsberg, Roland

MASTER HATH COME, THE *anthem
    (Littleton, Bill J.) SATB FINE ARTS
    CM 1003 $.35   (M214)

MASTER HATH COME, THE see Doudney

MASTER OF EAGER YOUTH see Eichorn, Hermene Warlick

MASTER OF EAGER YOUTH see Powell

MASTER SLEEPS, THE see Smith, F.S. Breville

MASTERS IN THIS HALL
    (Parker, Alice) SATB,pno/org/orch
    (easy/med) cor pts FISCHER,C
    CM 7838 $.40, ipr see also Seven
    Christmas Carols   (M215)

MASTERS IN THIS HALL see Gordon, Philip

MASTERS IN THIS HALL see Powell, Wilfred

MASTERS IN THIS HALL see Willcocks, David

MASTER'S PACE, THE see Kirby

MASTER'S TOUCH, THE see Fettke, Tom

MASTER'S TOUCH, THE see Wyrtzen, Don

MASTIOLETTI
    Terribilis Est
    "Wie Schauervoll" TTB LIENAU
    MUSICA SACRA, NR. 42 sc s.p., cor
    pts s.p.   (M216)

    Wie Schauervoll *see Terribilis Est

MATCHLESS IN THY FORM - A CHRISTMAS
    CANTATA FROM COLONIAL AMERICA see
    Selby, William

MATER ADMIRABILIS see Griesbacher, Peter

MATER DEI see Lampart, Karl

MATER DOLOROSA see Gruber, Joseph

MATER ET FILIA see Orff, Carl

MATERNITE DE MARIE *BVM
    cor JOBERT s.p. see also Douze
    Cantiques De Fetes   (M217)

MATHEWS
    Gift Is Given, The *Xmas
    2pt oct SCHMITT 8074 $.40   (M218)

MATHIAS
    Palms Of Victory *Easter
    (Kling, Roger) SATB oct GOSPEL
    05 TM 0216 $.20   (M219)

MATHIAS, WILLIAM
    Alleluya Psallat *anthem
    SATB (med) OXFORD 42.387 $.70
                                      (M220)

    Ave Rex
    SATB,inst (diff) OXFORD 46.161
    $2.80, ipr   (M221)

    Babe Is Born!, A *Xmas
    SATB (diff) OXFORD 84.222 $.15
                                      (M222)

    Bless The Lord, O My Soul *anthem
    SATB (med diff) OXFORD 42.369 $.55
                                      (M223)

    Communion Service In C
    unis (med easy) voc sc OXFORD
    42.337 $1.75, cor pts OXFORD
    42.340 $.35   (M224)

    Gloria *Gloria
    TTBB (med diff) OXFORD 46.178 $1.35
                                      (M225)

    Law Of The Lord, The *anthem
    SATB,acap (med diff) OXFORD 43.485
    $.30   (M226)

    Lift Up Your Heads
    SATB (med) OXFORD 42.380 $.55
                                      (M227)

MATHIAS, WILLIAM (cont'd.)

    Magnificat And Nunc Dimittis
    *Magnif/Nunc
    SATB (med diff) OXFORD 42.375 $1.65
                                      (M228)

    O Salutaris Hostia *Commun/Gen
    TTBB,acap (med diff) OXFORD 85.018
    $.50   (M229)

    Psalm 150
    SATB,inst (med diff) OXFORD 46.159
    $1.70, ipr   (M230)

    Sir Christemas *Xmas,carol
    SATB (med) OXFORD 84.207 $.40
                                      (M231)

    Three Medieval Lyrics *CC3U,Mediev
    SATB,inst (med diff) OXFORD 46.154
    $4.10, ipr   (M232)

MATTHAUS-PASSION see Bach, Johann Sebastian

MATTHAUS-PASSION (NEUE BACH-AUSGABE)
    see Bach, Johann Sebastian

MATTHAUSPASSION see Schutz, Heinrich

MATTHES, RENE (1891-   )
    Ach Lieber Herr Im Hochsten Thron
    SAT/SAB (contains also: Der Herr
    Kennet Den Weg Der Gerechten)
    SCHWEIZER. SK 51.03 s.p. see also
    MUSIKBEILAGE ZUM "EVANGELISCHEN
    KIRCHENCHOR 1951"   (M233)

    Psalm 1 *see Wohl Dem, Der Nicht
    Wandelt Im Rat Der Gottlosen

    Wir Glauben All An Einen Gott
    wom cor/men cor/unis mix cor,org
    cor pts,sc PELIKAN PE191   (M234)

    Wohl Dem, Der Nicht Wandelt Im Rat
    Der Gottlosen (Psalm 1)
    SATB SCHWEIZER. SK 146 s.p.   (M235)

MATTHESON, JOHANN (1681-1764)
    Das Lied Des Lammes *Psntd
    (Cannon, Beekman C.) "Passion
    According To St. John, The" cor
    bds A-R ED $12.95   (M236)

    Passion According To St. John, The
    *see Das Lied Des Lammes

MATTHEWS
    As Seasons Surround Us
    unis treb cor KJOS 6143 $.35   (M237)

    Do You Want Peace? *anthem
    (DeCou, Harold) SATB oct SINGSPIR
    ZJP-8219 $.35   (M238)

    Praise Be To Jesus
    SATB WOLF GC54 $.35   (M239)

MATTHEWS, DAVID
    I Ask None Else Of Thee *anthem
    (Brown, Charles F.) SATB WORD
    CS-2595 $.30   (M240)

MATTHEWS, THOMAS
    Alleluia, Praise Ye The Lord
    SATB (med) FITZSIMONS 2219 $.25
                                      (M241)
    And I John, Saw The Holy City *Bibl
    SATB (med) FITZSIMONS 2216 $.25
                                      (M242)
    Be Strong In The Lord
    SATB (easy) FITZSIMONS 2132 $.20
                                      (M243)
    Behold The Tabernacle Of God
    SATB (med) FITZSIMONS 2228 $.30
                                      (M244)
    Communion Service
    SATB (G min,easy) FITZSIMONS 7002
    $.20   (M245)
    Day Of Resurrection, The *Easter
    SATB (easy) FITZSIMONS 2178 $.25
                                      (M246)
    Direct Us, O Lord
    SATB (easy) FITZSIMONS 2211 $.20
                                      (M247)
    God Be In My Head
    SATB,acap (easy) FITZSIMONS 2105
    $.20   (M248)
    I Sing Of A Maiden *Xmas
    SATB,acap (easy) FITZSIMONS 2191
    $.20   (M249)
    I Will Give Thanks
    SATB (easy) FITZSIMONS 2212 $.30
                                      (M250)
    I Will Lift Up Mine Eyes *Bibl
    SATB,acap (med) FITZSIMONS 2104
    $.20   (M251)
    Lord Is My Shepherd, The *Bibl
    SATB (med) FITZSIMONS 2137 $.25
                                      (M252)
    SSA (easy) FITZSIMONS 3084 $.30
                                      (M253)

MATTHEWS, THOMAS (cont'd.)

    SA (easy) FITZSIMONS 5026 $.25
                                      (M254)
    Missa De Sancto Luca *Commun
    unis (easy) FITZSIMONS 7005 $.30
                                      (M255)
    O Heavenly Father
    SATB,acap (easy) FITZSIMONS 2153
    $.20   (M256)
    O Praise God In His Sanctuary
    SATBB,acap (easy) FITZSIMONS 2124
    $.20   (M257)
    Praise The Lord, O My Soul *Bibl
    SATB (easy) FITZSIMONS 2226 $.30
                                      (M258)
    Rocking *Xmas
    SATB (easy) FITZSIMONS 2175 $.25
                                      (M259)
    Save Us, O Lord
    SATB,acap (diff) FITZSIMONS 2089
    $.20   (M260)
    Sing, Sing To The Lord *Bibl
    SATB (med) FITZSIMONS 2221 $.30
                                      (M261)
    Teach Me, O Lord *Bibl
    SATB (easy) FITZSIMONS 2234 $.30
                                      (M262)
    Thanks Be To God
    SATB (med) FITZSIMONS 2215 $.25
                                      (M263)
    Torches *Bibl
    SATB,acap (med) FITZSIMONS 2203
    $.20   (M264)
    Trumpeters And Singers Were As One,
    The
    SATB (med) FITZSIMONS 2167 $.25
                                      (M265)

MATTIOLI
    Messe Pax Et Bonum
    4pt mix cor,pno/org HENN 347 s.p.
    sc, voc pt   (M266)

MATTSON
    Lullaby *Xmas
    SATB oct SCHMITT 7045 $.40   (M267)

MAUL, WILLIAM
    Sacred Service *Sab-Eve
    [Heb] cor,orch TRANSCON. TCL 880
    $3.00, ipr   (M268)

MAUNDER
    Hosanna To The Living Lord!
    (Hadley) SATB PRO ART 2786 $.40
                                      (M269)

MAURICE, PIERRE (1868-1936)
    Angelus Du Soir
    mix cor,pno HENN 441 sc s.p., voc
    pt s.p.   (M270)

MAURON, FERNAND
    Missa Brevis *Mass
    [Lat] MezTB,acap (without Credo)
    sc,cor pts BOHM s.p.   (M271)

MAWBY, COLIN
    Thee We Adore
    see FIVE ANTHEMS FOR TODAY

MAY CAROL, A see Osgood, Muriel

MAY CREATURES ALL ABOUND see Clarke, Henry Leland

MAY GOD BLESS YOU AND KEEP YOU see DeCou, Harold

MAY I NEVER LOSE THE WONDER see Zilch, Margot

MAY JESUS CHRIST BE PRAISED see Barnby, Sir Joseph

MAY MAGNIFICAT see Paynter, John P.

MAY OUR GLAD SONGS ASCEND see Young

MAY THE GRACE OF CHRIST see Andrews, C.T.

MAY THE ROAD RISE TO MEET YOU see Turner

MAY THE SUN BLESS US see Korte, Karl

MAY THE WORDS see Ballou, Esther W.

MAY THY BLESSED SPIRIT see Tchesnokov, Pavel Grigorievitch

MAY THY HOLY SPIRIT see Roff, Joseph

MAYER, ALFONSO
    Deutsche Messe "Ehre Sei Gott" *Mass
    [Ger] mix cor,opt org BOHM sc s.p.,
    cor pts s.p.   (M272)

    Einstimmiges Requiem Und Libera
    [Lat] cor/cong,org sc,cor pts BOHM
    s.p.   (M273)

MAYER, ALFONSO (cont'd.)

Messe In G-Dur *Mass
[Lat] 2 eq voices/4pt mix cor,org
(G maj) sc,cor pts BOHM s.p.
(M274)

Vier Pange Lingua *CC4U
[Lat] 4pt mix cor,acap sc,cor pts
BOHM s.p. (M275)

MAYER, HARRY (1914-)
Evangelium
mix cor,5winds,strings DONEMUS
(M276)

MAYFIELD, LARRY
Get Ready *cant
cor,pno LILLENAS MC-28 $1.50 (M277)

Let Me Tell You About Jesus *folk
SATB/jr cor oct LILLENAS AN-5075
$.30 (M278)

We're Going To Sing *anthem/gospel
SATB oct SINGSPIR ZJP-8179 $.30
(M279)

MEANS, CLAUDE
O God Of Light
SATB,Bar solo (med) FITZSIMONS 2131
$.20 (M280)

MECHEM, KIRKE (1925-)
I Will Sing Alleluia
SATB,pno/org,fl, opt triangle and
temple blocks (easy) FISCHER,C
CM 7861 $.35 (M281)

Joy (from Children Of David, The)
SATB,Mez solo,org oct BOOSEY 5884
$.45 (M282)

Lord Is My Shepherd, The (Psalm 23)
mix cor (med easy) FISCHER,C
CM 7897 $.40 (M283)

Man Of My Own People (from Children
Of David, The)
SATB,Mez solo,org oct BOOSEY 5886
$.45 (M284)

Praise Him, Sun And Moon *Op.38
SSATBB,acap oct NATIONAL WHC-21
$.40 (M285)

Psalm (from Children Of David, The)
SATB,org oct BOOSEY 5883 $1.00
(M286)

Psalm 23 *see Lord Is My Shepherd,
The

Shepherd And His Love, The
SATB,pno,vla, piccolo sc SCHIRM.EC
2744 s.p., ipa (M287)

Song Of David (from Children Of
David, The)
SATB,org oct BOOSEY 5885 $.80
(M288)

MEDEMA, KEN
And This Is Love *anthem
(Powell, Rick) SATB WORD CS-2704
$.40 (M289)

Listen *CC10L
(Pursell, Bill) jr cor&cor WORD
37647 $2.50 (M290)

Moses *anthem
SATB WORD CS-2687 $.95 (M291)

Sing To The Lord *anthem
2pt WORD (M292)

Story-Tellin' Man, The *cant
jr cor WORD 37704 $1.95 (M293)

MEDIA VITA see Orff, Carl

MEDIA VITA IN MORTE SUMUS see Dumont,
[Henri]

MEDIEVAL CAROLS *sac/sec,CCU
(Stevens) cor (med) STAINER 3.8904.8
$20.00 (M294)

MEDIN, N. (1904-1969)
Alma Pax *cant
cor,Bar solo,3fl,3ob,3clar,3bsn,
4horn,3trp,3trom,tuba,timp,perc,
bells CARISH rental (M295)

MEDITATION ON "PASSION CHORALE" see
Bock, Fred

MEDITATIONS ON THE NATIVITY see Price,
Milburn

MEEK, KENNETH
Three Christmas Carols *CC3U,Xmas,
carol
mix cor LESLIE 4088 $.35 (M296)

MEERSTERN, ICH DICH GRUSSE see Reusch,
Fritz

MEET AMERICA'S WILLIAM BILLINGS see
Billings, William

MEETING IN THE AIR, THE see Williamson

MEILSTRUP, DAVID G.
I Can Know *anthem
SATB oct SINGSPIR ZJP-7326 $.30
(M297)

Where In The World *folk
(Marsh, Donald T.) SATB oct
SINGSPIR ZJP-5055 $.30 (M298)

Where Is Love Today? *folk
(Johnson, Norman) SA&opt TB oct
SINGSPIR ZJP-5001 $.30 (M299)

MEIN CHRISTIAN "WO MAG DENN NUR MEIN
CHRISTIAN SEIN" see Lang, Hans

MEIN FLEISCH IST WAHRHAFT EINE SPEISE
see Schmider, Karl

MEIN GANZES HERZ ERHEBET DICH see Heer,
Emil

MEIN GOTT, ICH DANKE DIR see Grimm,
Jurgen

MEIN GOTT, MEIN GOTT, VERLASSEN HAST DU
MICH see Sweelinck, Jan Pieterszoon

MEIN GOTT UND HERR see Capricornus,
Samueul

MEIN HEILAND, HERR see Schubert, Franz
(Peter)

MEIN HERZ DICHTET EIN FEINES LIED see
Bellermann, Sangerfahrt

MEIN HERZ IST BEREIT see Harrer

MEIN HERZ IST BEREIT see Vierdanck,
Johann

MEIN HERZ WILL ICH DIR SCHENKEN
see Alte Frankische Weihnachtslieder

MEIN HIMMLISCHER VATER see Othmayr,
Kaspar

MEIN HOFFNUNG, TROST UND ZUVERSICHT see
Cruger, Johann

MEIN SCHONSTE ZIER
(Schaefers, A.) men cor,acap TONOS
5623 s.p. (M300)

MEIN SCHONSTE ZIER see Fischer, Walter

MEIN SCHONSTE ZIER see Geisel, Gustav

MEIN SCHONSTE ZIER see Zipp, Friedrich

MEIN SEEL, O HERR, MUSS LOBEN DICH see
Zipp, Friedrich

MEIN SOHN, WARUM HAST DU UNS DAS GETAN?
see Schutz, Heinrich

MEIN ZUVERSICHT see Vento, Ivo de

MEINE SEELE ERHEBT DEN HERREN see
Hammerschmidt, Andreas

MEINE SEELE LOBE DEN HERREN MEIN see
Aichinger, Gregor

MEINEN JESUM LASS ICH NICHT see Bach,
Johann Sebastian

MEINEN JESUM LASS ICH NICHT see Kurig,
Hans-Hermann

MEISTER, G.
Adeste Fideles
4pt,acap voc pt HENN 287 s.p.
(M301)

Tui Sunt Coeli
4pt,acap HENN 286 s.p. sc, voc pt
(M302)

MELCHIZEDEK MASS FOR THE KING OF PEACE
see Pulkingham, B.C.

MELLECI, ADELMO
Easter Hymn *Easter,hymn
TTBB HARRIS $.35 (M303)
SATB HARRIS $.35 (M304)

MELODY see Golden, Nolan

MELODY DIVINE see Kerr

MEMORIAL ACCLAMATIONS I-IV see Roff,
Joseph

MEMORIAL SERVICE see Ancis, Solomon

MEN *CCUL
(Hall, O.D.Jr.) men cor BENSON B0495
$1.50 (M305)

MEN OF GOD, GO TAKE YOUR STATIONS see
Rider, Dale G.

MENDELSSOHN
How Lovely Are The Messengers
*anthem
(Lyall) 2pt (easy) oct BROADMAN
4558-49 $.25 (M306)

MENDELSSOHN-BARTHOLDY, FELIX
(1809-1847)
Above All Praise And All Majesty
*anthem
SSAATTBB,opt acap (med easy) OXFORD
43.458 $.55 (M307)

Be Not Afraid (from Elijah)
mix cor BANKS MUS YS 314 $.25
(M308)

Beata Mortui
(Himes) "O Blessed Are The Dead"
SATB SCHIRM.G LG51707 $.30 (M309)

Cast Thy Burden Upon The Lord (from
Elijah)
mix cor BANKS MUS YS 322 $.20
contains also: He That Shall
Endure To The End (M310)

Christmas *see Weihnachten

Collected Edition *sac/sec,CCU
(Rietz, Julius) microfiche UNION
ESP. $175.00 originally published
as 19 series in 36 bindings,
Leipzig, 1874- 1877. (M311)

Der Herr Hat Seinen Engeln Befohlen
(from Elias) Fest
mix cor,org sc,cor pts BOHM s.p.
(M312)

Elias *Op.70, Bibl/ora
SATB,SSAATTBB soli,2fl,2ob,2clar,
2bsn,4horn,2trp,3trom,tuba,
strings,timp (med) min sc SCHOTTS
ETP 989 s.p. (M313)

Engel-Terzett "Hebe Deine Augen Auf"
(from Elias) Fest
3pt,org/harmonium sc,cor pts BOHM
s.p. (M314)

Four Chorales (from Saint Paul) CC4U,
chorale
(Bevan, G.) SATB (med easy)
WATERLOO $.50 (M315)

Grant Peace, We Pray
(Schalk) SATB (med) oct CONCORDIA
98-2212 $.50 (M316)

Hark, The Herald Angels Sing *Xmas,
anthem
(DeCou, Harold) SATB,opt 3trp oct
SINGSPIR ZJP-3007 $.30 (M317)

He Is The Tender Shepherd
(Barrie) SATB SCHIRM.G LG51699 $.35
(M318)

He That Shall Endure To The End (from
Elijah)
see Mendelssohn-Bartholdy, Felix,
Cast Thy Burden Upon The Lord
SATB (med easy) WATERLOO $.30
(M319)

He Watching Over Israel (from Elijah)
SATB HARRIS HC 4016 $.30 (M320)

Hear My Prayer
mix cor BANKS MUS YS 300 $.80
(M321)

Hebe Deine Augen Auf (from Elijah)
jr cor/wom cor (easy) sc SCHOTTS
CHBL 509 s.p. (M322)

Heilig
(Klein) "Holy, Holy, Holy" dbl cor
SCHIRM.G 12005 $.40 (M323)

Holy, Holy, Holy *see Heilig

How Lovely Are Those Dwellings
*anthem
(Drevits, Jon) SATB oct SINGSPIR
ZJP-7227 $.25 (M324)

How Lovely Are Thy Messengers
SATB (med easy) WATERLOO $.50
(M325)

Hymne
mix cor,S solo,org cor pts
BREITKOPF-W CHB 4954 s.p. (M326)

I Herrens Tjanare, Prisen Gud *see
Laudate Pueri

I Waited For The Lord
mix cor BANKS MUS YS 188 $.30
(M327)

Im Advent *Adv
"In Advent" SATB WALTON 2259 $.40
(M328)

In Advent *see Im Advent

In Der Passionzeit *Psntd
"In Passion Week" SATB WALTON 2258
$.40 (M329)

MENDELSSOHN-BARTHOLDY, FELIX (cont'd.)

In Passion Week *see In Der
    Passionzeit

Jauchzet Dem Herrn Alle Welt
    SSAATTBB,acap EGTVED KB254 s.p.
                                    (M330)

Laudate Pueri
    (Angerdahl, Lars) "I Herrens
    Tjanare, Prisen Gud" wom cor/jr
    cor ERIKS 170 s.p.   (M331)

Lift Thine Eyes (from Elijah)
    (Bevan, Gwilym) SSA (med easy)
    WATERLOO $.30   (M332)
    (Kirby) SBar&camb&opt A,acap
    CAMBIATA M117322 $.35   (M333)

Now Be My Heart Inspired To Sing
    *anthem
    (Ehret, Walter) SATB WORD CS-660
    $.25   (M334)

O Blessed Are The Dead *see Beata
    Mortui

O Great Is The Depth
    mix cor BANKS MUS $.30   (M335)

O Rest In The Lord (from Elijah)
    (Moffatt) SATB (med) FITZSIMONS
    2208 $.25   (M336)

On Wings Of Song The Angels Come
    (Habash, John M.) SSA BIG3 $.50
                               (M337)
    (Habash, John M.) SATB BIG3 $.40
                               (M338)
    (Habash, John M.) SAB BIG3 $.50
                               (M339)
    (Habash, John M.) SA/TB BIG3 $.50
                               (M340)

Psalm 100
    (Hines) SATB,acap oct CONCORDIA
    98-2215 $.65   (M341)

Thanks Be To God (from Elijah)
    SATB (med) FITZSIMONS 2027 $.25
                               (M342)

Three Motets *Op.39, CC3U,mot
    [Ger/Lat] SSAA,SSAA soli,org/pno
    HINRICHSEN D397 voc pt s.p., voc
    sc s.p.   (M343)

Weihnachten
    "Christmas" SATB WALTON 2256 $.40
                               (M344)

Why Rage Fiercely The Heathens
    *anthem
    SATB&SATB AUGSBURG 11-0647 $.45
                               (M345)

MENDOZA
    Children's Christmas Festival
    (composed with Rimmer) *Xmas
    unis,inst (easy) sc OXFORD 01.021
    $2.80, cor pts OXFORD 01.022
    $1.00, ipa   (M346)

MENDOZA, MICHAEL
    Holy Father *see Santo

    Santo
    "Holy Father" [Span/Eng] SATB,acap
    oct SOMERSET JW 7780 $.35 (M347)

MENEGALI
    Ave Regina
    TTB LIENAU MUSICA SACRA, NR. 55 sc
    s.p., cor pts s.p.   (M348)

MENSCH, STEH STILL UND FURCHT MICH see
    Haas, Joseph

MENSCHIK, W.
    Deutsche Liturgische Begrabnisgesange
    *CCU,Rembrnc
    [Ger] 1-4pt mix cor,solo BOHM s.p.
                               (M349)

MERBECKE, JOHN (1510-1585)
    Communion Service (Adapted For Roman
    Catholic Usage) *Mass
    (Sumsion; Bergsagel) unis (easy)
    voc sc OXFORD 45.066 $1.00, cor
    pts OXFORD 45.040 $.25   (M350)

MERCER
    Way That He Loves, The *gospel
    (Linn) SATB,4vln oct LILLENAS
    AT-1093 $.30   (M351)

MERCER, W. ELMO
    Each Step I Take
    SATB oct BENSON S4070 $.30 (M352)

    God Loves Me
    (Ferrin) SATB oct BENSON S4117 $.30
                               (M353)

    Gonna Lose My Burdens
    SATB oct BENSON S4116 $.35 (M354)

    I Am Redeemed Forevermore
    SATB oct BENSON S4136 $.35 (M355)

MERCER, W. ELMO (cont'd.)

    I Found It All In Jesus
    SATB oct BENSON S4371 $.30 (M356)

    Jesus Is His Name
    (Ferrin) SSATB oct BENSON S4163
    $.30   (M357)

    Listen To The Sound
    SATB oct BENSON S4175 $.35 (M358)

    Lonely Road! Up Calvary's Way
    *Easter
    SSATB BENSON S4170 $.20   (M359)

    Nailing My Sins To His Cross
    SATB BENSON S4220 $.35   (M360)

    Song Was Born, A
    SSATB oct BENSON S4014 $.30 (M361)

    Story Unchanged, The *Xmas,cant
    (Huff, Ronn) SATB,soli BENSON B0785
    $1.25   (M362)

    That's What He Did For Me
    SATB oct BENSON S4280 $.20 (M363)

    Time Is Now, The
    SSATB oct BENSON S4340 $.30 (M364)

    Way That He Loves, The
    (Owens) SATB oct BENSON S4347 $.30
                               (M365)

MERCIFUL FATHER see Franck, Cesar,
    Domine Deus

MERCIFUL SAVIOR *Commun
    (Roff, Joseph) SATB LITURGICAL $.50
    see also Twelve Hymns   (M366)

MERCY see Mana-Zucca, Mme., Rachem

MERCY AND TRUTH see Cram, James D.

MERRILL
    Rise Up, O Men Of God (composed with
    Walter)
    (Young) 2pt oct BENSON S4382 $.35
                               (M367)

MERRILY ON HIGH *Xmas,anthem
    (Rasley, John M.) SSATB oct SINGSPIR
    ZJP-3018 $.25   (M368)

MERRY CHRISTMAS *Swed
    SATB EMI s.p. contains also: All My
    Heart This Night Rejoices (Ger)
                               (M369)

MERRY CHRISTMAS see Johnston, H.

MERRY CHRISTMAS see Patriquin, Donald

MESSA see Girotto, Almerigo

MESSA see Piccioni

MESSA A OTTO SOPRA L'ARIA DELLA MONICA
    see Frescobaldi, Girolamo

MESSA A OTTO SOPRA L'ARIA DI FIORENZA
    see Frescobaldi, Girolamo

MESSA DA REQUIEM see Bossi, Renzo

MESSA DA REQUIEM see Bottesini,
    Giovanni

MESSA DA REQUIEM see Sgambati, Giovanni

MESSA DA REQUIEM see Verdi, Giuseppe

MESSA DI REQUIEM see Donizetti, Gaetano

MESSA III see Kayser, Leif

MESSA IN LA MAGGIORE see Cherubini,
    Luigi

MESSAGE OF JOY see Fischer, William
    Gustavus

MESSE see David, Johann Nepomuk

MESSE see Lotti, Antonio

MESSE see Martin, Frank

MESSE see Plum, P.-J.-M.

MESSE A JEAN XXIII see Carrillo

MESSE A NOVE VOCI CONCERTATA CON
    STROMENTI see Colonna, Giovanni
    Paolo

MESSE BREVE (CUM GLORIA) see Montillet

MESSE BREVIS see Gabrieli

MESSE BREVIS see Palestrina, Giovanni

MESSE DANS LES MODES ANCIENS see Rabot

MESSE DE MINUIT see Charpentier, Marc-
    Antoine

MESSE DE NOTRE DAME see Machaut,
    Guillaume de

MESSE DOMINUM FIRMAMENTUM see Samson

MESSE DU SACRE see Kaelin

MESSE DULCIS DOMINA see Samson

MESSE ECCLESIA ORANS see Montillet

MESSE EN FA see Deshusses

MESSE EN FA LYDIEN see Montillet

MESSE EN MIB MAJEUR see Montillet

MESSE EN SOL MINEUR see Montillet

MESSE FACILIS see Boyer

MESSE FACILIS see Broquet, L.

MESSE FRANCISCAINE see Carraz

MESSE FUR DIE ADVENTS- UND FASTENZEIT
    see Spiess, Meinrad

MESSE FUR VERSTORBENE "HORE, HERR, AUF
    MEINE STIMME" see Metschnabel, Paul
    Joseph

MESSE GAUDEAMUS see Carraz

MESSE "GIB UNS FRIEDEN" see Krenek,
    Ernst

MESSE GREGORIENNE see Brun, Abbe F.

MESSE IN A see Messner, Joseph

MESSE IN A-MOLL see Cichy, Siegfried

MESSE IN B see Messner, Joseph

MESSE IN B see Schubert, Franz (Peter)

MESSE IN B-MOLL see Kromolicki, Joseph

MESSE IN C see Bruckner, Anton

MESSE IN C see Kutzer, Ernst

MESSE IN C-DUR see Beethoven, Ludwig
    van

MESSE IN C-DUR see Mozart, Wolfgang
    Amadeus, Missa Brevis

MESSE IN C-MOLL see Mozart, Wolfgang
    Amadeus

MESSE IN D see Erhard, Karl

MESSE IN D see Kempter, Karl

MESSE IN D see Nicolai, Otto

MESSE IN D see Pranschke, Johannes

MESSE IN D-MOLL see Bruckner, Anton

MESSE IN D-MOLL see Byrd, William

MESSE IN E see Biechteler, Sigismund

MESSE IN E see Erhard, Karl

MESSE IN E see Genzmer, Harald

MESSE IN ES see Siebzehnriebl, Franz X.

MESSE IN ES UBER "FEST SOLL MEIN
    TAUFBUND" see Frey, Carl

MESSE IN F see Scorra, Adolf

MESSE IN F-DUR see Berberich, Ludwig

MESSE IN F-DUR see Byrd, William

MESSE IN F-MOLL see Byrd, William

MESSE IN G see Kraft, Karl

MESSE IN G see Messner, Joseph

MESSE IN G see Rehm, P. Otto

MESSE IN G-DUR see Mayer, Alfonso

MESSE IN G-DUR see Schubert, Franz
    (Peter)

MESSE IN G IN HONOREM ST. CAROLI
    BORROMAEI see Filke, Max

MESSE LATINE see Gagnebin, Henri, Mix,
    Org

MESSE NO. 1 IN C see Monteverdi,
    Claudio

MESSE NO. 1 IN F-DUR see Pembaur, Karl
Maria

MESSE NO. 3 IN F-MOLL see Bruckner,
Anton

MESSE NO. 5 IN AS-DUR see Schubert,
Franz (Peter)

MESSE NO. 6 IN ES-DUR see Schubert,
Franz (Peter)

MESSE NOTRE DAME DE LA CONFIANCE see
Haenni, Ch.

MESSE O ADMIRABILE see Palestrina,
Giovanni

MESSE PAX ET BONUM see Mattioli

MESSE POUR LA PAIX see Kaelin

MESSE REGINA PACIS see Montillet

MESSE SAINT ANDRE see Marescotti

MESSE SAINT GERMAIN see Chatelain

MESSE SAINT-JOSPEH see Montillet

MESSE ST. NICOLAS DE FLUE see Garnier

MESSE SAINTE CECILE see Montillet

MESSE SEPTIEME TON see Fornerod

MESSE SOLENELLE see Langlais, Jean

MESSE SOLENNELLE see Fornerod

MESSE SS CORDIS JESU see Jenny, Albert

MESSE SURSUM CORDA see Muller

MESSE VINUM LAEFTIFICAT see Samson

MESSE VINUM LAETIFICAT see Samson

MESSE ZU EHREN DER ALLERSELIGSTEN
JUNGFRAU MARIA see Dietrich, J.H.

MESSE ZU EHREN DER ALLERSELIGSTEN
JUNGFRAU MARIA see Hofer, Franz

MESSE ZU EHREN DER GOTTLICHEN VORSEHUNG
see Frey, Carl

MESSE ZU EHREN DER HEILIGEN BARBARA see
Hoffmann, Bernhard

MESSE ZU EHREN DER HEILIGEN CACILIA see
Gauss, Otto

MESSE ZU EHREN DER HEILIGEN CACILIA see
Woss, Josef Venantius von

MESSE ZU EHREN DER HEILIGEN FELIX UND
REGULA see Jochum, Otto

MESSE ZU EHREN DER UNBEFLECKTEN
EMPFANGNIS MARIENS see Hoffmann,
Bernhard

MESSE ZU EHREN DES HEILIGEN BONIFATIUS
see Gauss, Otto

MESSE ZU EHREN DES HEILIGEN BRUDERS
KONRAD see Hoss, Franz

MESSE ZU EHREN DES HEILIGEN GEORG see
Hoffmann, Bernhard

MESSE ZU EHREN DES HEILIGEN JOSEPH see
Berghorn, Alfred

MESSE ZU EHREN DES HEILIGEN PAPSTES
PIUS X see Hoss, Franz

MESSE ZU EHREN DES HEILIGEN PETRUS see
Piechler, Arthur

MESSE ZU EHREN DES HEILIGEN ULRICH see
Bauer, Josef

MESSE ZU EHREN DES HEILIGES KREUZES see
Dietrich, J.H.

MESSE ZU EHREN DES HEILIGES PAPSTES
PIUS X see Rambold, Alois

MESSEN TEIL 1 see Isaac, Heinrich

MESSEN TEIL 2 see Isaac, Heinrich

MESSIAH see Handel, George Frideric

MESSITER, ARTHUR HENRY (1834-1916)
Rejoice, Ye Pure In Heart *Thanks,
anthem
(Johnson, Norman) SATB oct SINGSPIR
ZJP-7221 $.30   (M370)

MESSNER, JOSEPH (1893-   )
Aeterne Rex
see Hymnen Fur Die Prozession Am
Fronleichnamsfest

Ecce Sacerdos *Op.36b
[Lat] unis,org/2trp&2horn&2trom sc,
cor pts BOHM s.p., ipa   (M371)

Hymnen Fur Die Prozession Am
Fronleichnamsfest *hymn
[Lat] 4pt mix cor,2horn,2trp,2trom
sc,cor pts BOHM s.p., ipa
contains: Aeterne Rex, Op.25,
No.4; Pange Lingua, Op.25,No.5;
Sacris Solemniis, Op.25,No.1;
Salutis Humanae Sator, Op.25,
No.3; Verbum Supernum, Op.25,
No.2   (M372)

Marienmesse *Op.40, Mass
[Lat] cor,S solo,org/strings sc,cor
pts BOHM s.p., ipa   (M373)

Messe In A *Op.66, Mass
[Lat] 4pt mix cor,strings sc,cor
pts BOHM s.p., ipa   (M374)

Messe In B *Op.29, Mass
[Lat] cor,S solo,org/2trp&2trom&
2horn&org (B flat maj) sc,cor pts
BOHM s.p., ipa   (M375)

Messe In G *Op.46, Mass
[Lat] 4pt mix cor,org/fl&ob&2clar&
bsn&2horn&2trp&2trom&strings&timp
sc,cor pts BOHM s.p., ipr   (M376)

Pange Lingua
see Hymnen Fur Die Prozession Am
Fronleichnamsfest

Sacris Solemniis
see Hymnen Fur Die Prozession Am
Fronleichnamsfest

Salutis Humanae Sator
see Hymnen Fur Die Prozession Am
Fronleichnamsfest

Tu Es Petrus *Op.36,No.5, Fest
[Lat] 4-6pt mix cor,org/2horn&2trp&
2trom&timp sc,cor pts BOHM s.p.,
ipa   (M377)

Verbum Supernum
see Hymnen Fur Die Prozession Am
Fronleichnamsfest

METHINKS I SEE A HEAVENLY HOST see
Billings, William

METSCHNABEL, PAUL JOSEPH
Bist Du Es Der Da Kommen Soll
see Zwei Adventsgesange

Messe Fur Verstorbene "Hore, Herr,
Auf Meine Stimme" *Req
mix cor BOHM sc s.p., cor pts s.p.
(M378)

Wir Erwarten Unsern Heiland
see Zwei Adventsgesange

Zwei Adventsgesange *Adv
mix cor cor pts BOHM s.p.
contains: Bist Du Es Der Da
Kommen Soll; Wir Erwarten
Unsern Heiland   (M379)

METZGER, HANS-ARNOLD (1913-   )
Vater Unser Im Himmelreich
see Bach, Johann Sebastian, Dir,
Dir, Jehova, Will Ich Singen

MEYER
Funf Kanons Aus Glareans
Dodekachordon *CC5U,canon
2pt LAUDINELLA LR12 s.p.   (M380)

Ho! Everyone That Is Thirsty *anthem
(Johnson, N.) SSATB oct SINGSPIR
ZJP-8208 $.35   (M381)

MEYERBEER, GIACOMO (1791-1864)
Uvnucho Yomar
mix cor oct SAC.MUS.PR. 306 $.50
(M382)

MEYERS
He's On His Way *see Dietschmann

MI AL HAR HOREV see Foss, Lukas

MICHAELANGELO
Striving After God
(Moore) SATB WARNER W-3545 $.30
(M383)

MICHALOVE, PETER
Prayer
cong MEDIA 5116   (M384)

MICHEELSEN, HANS-FRIEDRICH (1902-1973)
Brich Uns, Herr, Das Brot
SA&opt TB,2treb inst,opt bass inst
(two settings) HANSSLER 14.162
s.p.   (M385)

MICHEELSEN, HANS-FRIEDRICH (cont'd.)

Himmel Und Erde Werden Vergehen
SAT/SAB SCHWEIZER. SK 69.06 s.p.
see also MUSIKBEILAGE ZUM
"EVANGELISCHEN KIRCHENCHOR 1969"
(M386)

O Christenheit, Sei Hocherfreut
SAT/SAB/SB/SA, opt treb inst (two
settings) HANSSLER 14.225 s.p.
(M387)

MICHEL, JOSEP (1928-   )
Kommet Her Zu Mir Alle
unis,opt Mez/Bar solo,org HANSSLER
HE 6.325 s.p. contains also:
Anonymous, Dies Jahr Haben Wir
Auch Erlebt (SATB)   (M388)

Vater Unser Im Himmelreich
see Kramer, Gotthold, Ich Weiss,
Mein Gott, Dass All Mein Tun

MICHEL, PAUL-BAUDOUIN
Es Ist Ein Kostlich Ding *CC10U,mot
[Ger] 2-6pt mix cor,acap MERSEBURG
EM238   (M389)

MICHELSON, PAUL
Miracle, The *Easter/Gen,cant
SATB oct SINGSPIR 4312 $1.95   (M390)

MICHNA, ADAM VACLAV (ca. 1600-1676)
Magnificat
[Lat] mix cor,org,4trom,vla,vcl,bvl
SUPRAPHON s.p.   (M391)

MICKELSON, PAUL
Come, Thou Almighty King *anthem
SATB oct SINGSPIR ZA-4446 $.30
(M392)

God Makes A Miracle *gospel
(Whitsett) SATB oct LILLENAS
AN-1676 $.30   (M393)

MIDNIGHT KYRIE see Croley, Randell

MIDNIGHT MASS FOR CHRISTMAS EVE see
Charpentier, Marc-Antoine, Messe De
Minuit

MIDNIGHT, SLEEPING BETHLEHEM see
Staton, Kenneth W.

MIDST THE DEEP SILENCE *Xmas
(Jennings) SATB,2fl oct SCHMITT 8504
$.45   (M394)

MIDWINTER CAROL see France, William E.

MIG AR GIVEN ALL MAKT see Hemberg,
Eskil

MIGHTY FORTRESS, A see Butler

MIGHTY FORTRESS IS OUR GOD, A see
Luther, Martin

MILANO, R.
Dwelling In Beulah Land
(Ferrin, Paul) SATB oct GOSPEL
05 IM 0129 $.35   (M395)

MILES
Bought With A Price *Easter
(Smith, Herb) SATB oct GOSPEL
05 TM 0102 $.20   (M396)

Look For Me! *anthem/gospel
(McLellan, Cyril A.) SSATB oct
SINGSPIR ZJP-8061 $.30   (M397)

MILES, RUSSELL HANCOCK
Go To Dark Gethsemane *Lent
SATB (easy) FITZSIMONS 2094 $.25
(M398)

God's Eternal Plan
SATB (med) FITZSIMONS 2076 $.25
(M399)

O Jesus, I Have Promised *Cnfrm/Gen
SATB (med) FITZSIMONS 2082 $.25
(M400)

Rise Up, O Men Of God!
SSAATTBB (easy) FITZSIMONS 2074
$.25   (M401)

There Is A Green Hill Far Away *Gen/
Lent
SATB (easy) FITZSIMONS 2093 $.25
(M402)

Woods And Every Sweet-Smelling Tree,
The *Bibl
SATB,A solo (easy) FITZSIMONS 2090
$.25   (M403)

MILGROVE
Bright And Joyful Is The Morn *Xmas
(Douglas) SATB,opt 2trp PRO ART
2811 $.35   (M404)

MILHAM, RICHARD
Searcher, The
(Burroughs, Bob) cor BROADMAN
4516-05 $2.50   (M405)

MILHAUD, DARIUS (1892-1974)
Promesse De Dieu *sec,CC4U,Bibl
[Lat] mix cor,acap (diff) sc
SCHOTTS ME 8067 s.p.   (M406)

Psalm 51
see Trois Psaumes De David

Psalm 114
see Trois Psaumes De David

Psalm 150
see Trois Psaumes De David

Trois Psaumes De David *sec,Bibl
[Lat] mix cor,acap (med) sc SCHOTTS
ME 6798 s.p.
contains: Psalm 51; Psalm 114;
Psalm 150   (M407)

MILITARY MASS see Martinu, Bohuslav

MILLER
Jesus Bids Us Shine (composed with
Cram) *anthem
SATB (easy) oct BROADMAN 4551-45
$.30   (M408)

Trumpeters And Singers Were As One,
The *anthem
SATB (easy) oct BROADMAN 4562-08
$.30   (M409)

When I Survey The Wondrous Cross
*Easter/Lent,hymn
(Ehret, Walter) SATB oct LILLENAS
AN-2412 $.30   (M410)

MILLER, ALMA GRACE
Bread Of The World *Commun,anthem
SATB oct SINGSPIR ZA-4273 $.20
(M411)

MILLER, FRANZ R.
Ein Kind Ist Uns Geboren *Xmas
men cor BOHM s.p.   (M412)

Unser Heiland Ist Geborn *Xmas
men cor BOHM s.p.   (M413)

Zu Dir O Herr, Erhebe Ich Meine Seele
*Bibl/mot
3pt mix cor cor pts BOHM s.p.
(M414)

MILLER, R.B.
Evening Collect, An
SATB,acap (easy) FITZSIMONS 2088
$.20   (M415)

MILLER, SARAH WALTON
David *see Burroughs, Bob

MILLER, THOMAS A.
Sing, All Ye People *Thanks,anthem
SATB oct SINGSPIR ZJP-7243 $.25
(M416)

MILLS, CHARLES (1914-   )
Canticum Novum
SATB,acap AM.COMP.AL. $.55 (M417)

Laudate Dominum
SATB,acap AM.COMP.AL. $.83 (M418)

O Christ Redeemer
SATB,acap AM.COMP.AL. $.55 (M419)

O Glorious Virgin
SATB,acap AM.COMP.AL. $.55 (M420)

O Holy Ghost In Kindly Flame
SATB,acap AM.COMP.AL. $.55 (M421)

Psalm 8
SATB,acap AM.COMP.AL. $.55 (M422)

Psalm 67
SATB,acap AM.COMP.AL. $.55 (M423)

Psalm 121
SATB,acap AM.COMP.AL. $.55 (M424)

Psalm 130
SATB,acap AM.COMP.AL. $.55 (M425)

To God The Merciful Father
SATB,acap AM.COMP.AL. $.55 (M426)

MILNER
Most Glorious Lord Of Life *anthem
SATB (med diff) OXFORD 42.352 $.35
(M427)

MILNER, ANTHONY (1925-   )
St. Francis *Op.8
SATB,T solo,2fl,pic,2ob,2clar,2bsn,
4horn,2trp,3trom,tuba,timp,
strings voc sc NOVELLO rental
(M428)

MILO, PHIL
Friendly People *Xmas,pop
(Metis, Frank) SATB,pno,opt bvl&gtr
(med easy) oct PRESSER 312-41047
$.35   (M429)

MILTON
Let Us With A Gladsome Mind (composed
with Roesch) *anthem
SATB oct BROADMAN 4554-96 $.30
(M430)

MINDFUL OF ME see Johnson

MINI-MUSICALS
(Carmichael, Ralph) cor LEXICON 37624
$1.95
contains: Bread Medley; Brother
Medley; Friend Medley; Praise
Medley; Shine Medley; Way Of The
Cross Medley, The   (M431)

MINOR
Bringing In The Sheaves *anthem/
gospel
(Johnson, Norman) SATB oct SINGSPIR
ZJP-8015 $.25   (M432)

MIR IST GEGEBEN ALLE GEWALT see David,
Thomas [Christian]

MIRABILE MYSTERIUM see Gallus, Jacobus

MIRACLE, THE see Michelson, Paul

MIRACLE OF BETHLEHEM see Cacavas, John

MIRACLE OF FAITH, THE see Carmichael,
Ralph

MIRACLE OF LOVE, A see Parks, Joe E.

MIRROR OF ST. ANNE, THE see Thompson,
Randall

MIRTH see Rose, Michael

MISERERE
see Tre Latinska Hymner

MISERERE see Donizetti, Gaetano

MISERERE see Hasse, Johann Adolph

MISERERE see Lotti, Antonio

MISERERE see Platti, Giovanni

MISERERE see Sipila, Eero

MISERERE MEI see Lassus, Roland de
(Orlandus)

MISERERE MEI, DEUS see Cousins, M.
Thomas

MISERERE MEI DOMINE see Byrd, William

MISERERE MEI, DOMINE see Lassus, Roland
de (Orlandus)

MISERERE NOSTRI, DOMINE see Palestrina,
Giovanni

MISERICORDIAS DOMINI see Mozart,
Wolfgang Amadeus

MISERICORDIAS DOMINI IN AETERNUM
CANTABO see Durante, Francesco

MISSA see Frei, Joseph

MISSA see Heiss, Hermann

MISSA see Straesser, Joep

MISSA A LA SAMBA see Peloquin, C.
Alexander

MISSA AD FUGAM see Palestrina, Giovanni

MISSA ARGENTUM ET AURUM see Isaac,
Heinrich

MISSA BARBARA IN D see Schmid, Heinrich
Kaspar

MISSA BREVIS see Bon, Willem Frederik

MISSA BREVIS see Casciolini, Claudio

MISSA BREVIS see Clarke, F.R.C.

MISSA BREVIS see Davye

MISSA BREVIS see Goodman, Joseph

MISSA BREVIS see Herrmann, Hugo

MISSA BREVIS see Hurd, Michael

MISSA BREVIS see Larsson

MISSA BREVIS see MacNutt, Walter

MISSA BREVIS see Mauron, Fernand

MISSA BREVIS see Mortari, Virgilio

MISSA BREVIS see Mozart, Wolfgang
Amadeus

MISSA BREVIS see Paviour, Paul

MISSA BREVIS see Peissner, Karl

MISSA BREVIS see Pranschke, Johannes

MISSA BREVIS see Preston

MISSA BREVIS see Rheinberger, Josef

MISSA BREVIS see Rorem, Ned

MISSA BREVIS see Sohner, Leo

MISSA BREVIS see Spencer, Williametta

MISSA BREVIS see Track, Gerhard

MISSA BREVIS see Ussachevsky, Vladimir

MISSA BREVIS DE REQUIEM see Grau, P.
Theodor

MISSA BREVIS IN B see Mozart, Wolfgang
Amadeus

MISSA BREVIS IN C see Mozart, Wolfgang
Amadeus

MISSA BREVIS IN D see Mozart, Wolfgang
Amadeus

MISSA BREVIS IN D-DUR see Mozart,
Wolfgang Amadeus

MISSA BREVIS IN D MINOR see Van Hulse,
Camil

MISSA BREVIS IN D-MOLL see Helmschrott,
Robert M.

MISSA BREVIS IN ES see Kromolicki,
Joseph

MISSA BREVIS IN F see Mozart, Wolfgang
Amadeus

MISSA BREVIS IN F-DUR see Dantonello,
Josef

MISSA BREVIS IN G see Mozart, Wolfgang
Amadeus

MISSA BREVIS IN HONORE SANCTAE JULIANAE
see Jenni, Donald

MISSA BREVIS IN HONOREM ST.
CHRISTOPHORI see Kagerer, Chr. Lor.

MISSA BREVIS IN HONOREM STI. JOANNIS DE
DEO IN B see Haydn, (Franz) Joseph

MISSA BREVIS "LAUDA SION SALVATOREM"
see Spranger, Jorg

MISSA BREVIS SANCTI JOANNIS DE DEO see
Haydn, (Franz) Joseph

MISSA BREVIS STI. JOANNIS DE DEO see
Haydn, (Franz) Joseph

MISSA BREVIS ZU EHREN DES HEILIGEN
FRANZ VON ASSISI see Hoss, Franz

MISSA BREVISSIMA DOMINICALIS IN HONOREM
SANCTI FRANCISCI DE ASSISI see
Grau, P. Theodor

MISSA BREVISSIMA II IN HONOREM BEATAE
MARIAE VIRGINI see Grau, P. Theodor

MISSA CAPUT see Dufay, Guillaume

MISSA CAPUT see Obrecht, Jacob

MISSA CAPUT see Ockeghem, Johannes

MISSA CARNEVAL see Gaforio, Franchino

MISSA CHORALIS see Liszt, Franz

MISSA CONCERTATE see Monnikendam,
Marius

MISSA CUM POPULO ACTIVO see Lemacher,
Heinrich

MISSA DA CAMERA see Naylor, Bernard

MISSA DA REQUIEM see Sutermeister,
Heinrich

MISSA DE BEATA VIRGINE, IV VOCUM (I)
see Isaac, Heinrich

MISSA DE BEATA VIRGINE, V VOCUM (I) see
Isaac, Heinrich

MISSA DE BEATA VIRGINE, V VOCUM (II)
see Isaac, Heinrich

MISSA DE BEATA VIRGINE, VI VOCUM see
Isaac, Heinrich

MISSA DE NATIVITATE DOMINI NOSTRI JESU CHRISTI see Gruber, Joseph

MISSA DE PROFUNDIS see Ett, Kaspar

MISSA DE SANCTISSIMA TRINITATE see Kraft, Karl

MISSA DE SANCTO LUCA see Matthews, Thomas

MISSA DOMINICALIS see Griesbacher, Peter

MISSA DOMINICALIS see Kraft, Karl

MISSA DORICA see Ahrens, Joseph

MISSA DORICA see Hanebeck, Hugo Rudolf

MISSA DURCH ADAM'S FALL see Bernhard

MISSA, [EDMOND JEAN LOUIS] (1861-1910)
Vierge Sainte
cor,pno/harmonium,opt vln JOBERT
s.p.   (M433)

MISSA FESTIVA see Pert

MISSA FI-FI see Dalby, Martin

MISSA FOR ARCHBISHOP COLLOREDO see Mozart, Wolfgang Amadeus

MISSA HOSANNA see Goemanne, Noel

MISSA HUMILITATIS see Siegl, Otto

MISSA IN ANGUSTIIS C-DUR see Haydn, (Franz) Joseph

MISSA IN C see Fux, Johann Joseph

MISSA IN D-MOLL see Hollfelder, Waldram

MISSA IN F see Lotti, Antonio

MISSA IN F ZU EHREN DER HEILIGEN HEDWIG see Filke, Max

MISSA IN G see Mittmann, Paul

MISSA IN G-DUR IN HONOREM ST. CAROLI BORROMAEI see Filke, Max

MISSA IN G IN HONOREM STI. NICOLAI see Haydn, (Franz) Joseph

MISSA IN HONOREM BEATAE MARIAE VIRGINIS IN D-MOLL see Filke, Max

MISSA IN HONOREM ST. ELIZABETH see Dantonello, Josef, Missa Brevis In F-Dur

MISSA IN HONOREM SANCTAE CRUCIS see Vetter, P. Pirmin

MISSA IN HONOREM SANCTI ISIDORI see Koch, Markus

MISSA IN HONOREM SANCTI JOSE JOSEPHI see Hug, Emil

MISSA IN HONOREM SANCTI MICHAELIS see Lemacher, Heinrich

MISSA IN HONOREM SANCTISSIMI SALVATORIS see Krieger, Fritz

MISSA IN HONOREM ST. ALBERTI MAGNI see Piechler, Arthur

MISSA IN HONOREM ST. THERESIAE AB INFANTE JESU see Refice, Licinio

MISSA IN HONOREM STAE. CLARAE ASSISIENSIS see Refice, Licinio

MISSA "IN ILLO TEMPORE" see Monteverdi, Claudio

MISSA IN SIMPLICITATE see Langlais, Jean

MISSA IN TEMPORE ADVENTUS ET QUADRAGESIMAE see Haydn, (Johann) Michael

MISSA IN TEMPORE BELLI see Haydn, (Franz) Joseph

MISSA INTEGRA see Brixi, Franz Xaver

MISSA LA MI LA SOL-O PRAECLARA see Isaac, Heinrich

MISSA OCTAVI TONI see Asola, Giovanni Matteo

MISSA ORBIS FACTOR see Clayberg, Richard P.

MISSA PARVA see Mutter, Gerbert

MISSA PARVA see Pranschke, Johannes

MISSA PASTORALIS see Brixi, Franz Xaver

MISSA PASTORALIS see Horak, V.

MISSA "PATRONUS ECCELESIAE" IN D ZU EHREN DES HEILIGES JOSEPH see Lechthaler, Josef

MISSA PETITE CAMUSETTE see Anonymous

MISSA PRO DEFUNCTIO see Cimarosa, Domenico, Requiem

MISSA PRO DEFUNCTIS see Cavalli, (Pietro) Francesco

MISSA PRO DEFUNCTIS see Gruber, Joseph

MISSA PRO DEFUNCTIS see Kraft, Karl

MISSA PRO DEFUNCTIS see Mitterer, Ignatius

MISSA PRO PACE see Overbeek, C. v.

MISSA ROMANA see Pergolesi, Giovanni Battista

MISSA SABRINENSIS see Howells, Herbert Norman

MISSA SALVA NOS see Isaac, Heinrich

MISSA SANCTA ANNA see Kaim, Adolf

MISSA SANCTA MARIA see Hoss, Franz

MISSA SECUNDA see Hassler, Hans Leo

MISSA SEPTIMA IN A see Faist, Anton

MISSA SERAPHICA see Sattner, Hugolin

MISSA SEXTI TONI see Porta, Costanzo

MISSA SIMPLEX see Goller, Vinzenz

MISSA SINE NOMINE see Palestrina, Giovanni

MISSA SOLEMNIS see Beethoven, Ludwig van

MISSA SOLEMNIS EX D see Brixi, Franz Xaver

MISSA SOLEMNIS IN C see Mozart, Wolfgang Amadeus

MISSA SOLEMNIS IN D-DUR see Liszt, Franz

MISSA SOLEMNIS IN D "ORIENS EX ALTO" see Filke, Max

MISSA SOLEMNIS IN HONOREM PURISSIMI CORDIS BEATAE MARIAE VIRGINIS see Weirich, August

MISSA SOLEMNIS "LAUDATE DOMINUM" see Wassmer, Berthold

MISSA SUPER LEVAVI OCULOS MEOS see Gallus, Jacobus

MISSA SUPER "PER SIGNUM CRUCIS" see Senfl, Ludwig

MISSA SUPERBA see Kerll, [Johann Caspar]

MISSA SYMPHONICA see Becker, John J.

MISSA TERTIA see Hassler, Hans Leo

MISSA THROUGH ADAM'S FALL see Bernhard, Missa Durch Adam's Fall

MISSA UNISONA see Kraft, Karl

MISSA VIRGO PRUDENTISSIMA see Isaac, Heinrich

MISSAE SUPER L'HOMME ARME see Obrecht, Jacob

MISSION MEDLEY
(White, Ernie) SATB oct GOSPEL
05 TM 0306 $.35   (M434)

MISTER SNOW'S SHOES see Ravosa

MIT ERNST, O MENSCHENKINDER see Zipp, Friedrich

MIT FREUDEN ZART see Goemanne, Noel

MIT FREUDEN ZART see Kubler, Emil

MIT FRIED UND FREUD FAHR ICH DAHIN see Pepping, Ernst

MIT FRIED UND FREUD ICH FAHR DAHIN see Walter (Walther), Johann

MIT KLINGENDEM SAITENSPIEL FROHLOCKEN WIR see Marenzio, Luca

MIT LIV HAR DU TANT HOGT OVAN HIMMELENS STJARNOR see Johansen, Sven-Erik

MIT SEGEN MOG ICH HEUT AUFSTEHN see Hessenberg, Kurt

MITCHELL
He Giveth More Grace *gospel
(Widen) SATB oct LILLENAS AN-1703
$.35   (M435)

MITCHELL, DAVID L.
Glad Song *anthem
SATB,org AUGSBURG 11-1670 $.35
                              (M436)
Lord Of Life (composed with Vitale, Gary) *anthem
SATB,org AUGSBURG 11-1701 $.45
                              (M437)
Love Came Down At Christmas *anthem
SATB,org,2fl,opt ob&horn AUGSBURG
11-1702 $.40   (M438)
On Wings Of Living Light *anthem
2pt mix cor,org,trp AUGSBURG
11-1703 $.40   (M439)

MITT I VAR LEVNAD AV DODEN FANGNA see Dumont, [Henri], Media Vita In Morte Sumus

MITT LYS I MORKE see Lammetun, John

MITTEN WIR IM LEBEN see Muller-Zurich, Paul

MITTEN WIR IM LEBEN SIND see Cornelius, Peter

MITTEN WIR IM LEBEN SIND see Erytraeus, Gottfried

MITTEN WIR IM LEBEN SIND see Pepping, Ernst

MITTEN WIR IM LEBEN SIND see Walter (Walther), Johann

MITTERER, IGNATIUS
Libera Zum Requiem In As
(Lampart, Karl) [Lat] 4pt mix cor,
org/4trom (A flat maj) sc,cor pts
BOHM s.p., ipa   (M440)
Missa Pro Defunctis
[Lat] 4pt mix cor,org/4trom sc,cor
pts BOHM s.p., ipa   (M441)

MITTLERE STATIONEN ZUR FRONLEICHNAMSPROZESSION see Schnabel, J.J.

MITTMANN, PAUL (1868-1920)
Missa In G *Op.140, Mass
[Lat] 4pt mix cor,org/strings,2ob/
2clar,2horn,2bsn,2trp,2trom,opt
timp sc,cor pts BOHM s.p., ipa
                              (M442)

MIX, ORG see Gagnebin, Henri

MIXA, FRANZ
Deutsche Messe *Mass
cor,soli,orch sc KRENN 1.37 s.p.
                              (M443)

MODERN PSALM FACSIMILE see Schoenberg, Arnold

MODIM ANACHNU LACH see Kingsley, Gershon

MODLITBA see Lukas, Zdenek

MOE, DANIEL
Glory Of This Day, The (from William Penn Reflections) anthem
SATB AUGSBURG 11-0542 $.30   (M444)
Let Your Eye Be To The Lord (from William Penn Reflections) anthem
SATB AUGSBURG 11-0544 $.30   (M445)
Man Of Integrity, A (from William Penn Reflections) anthem
SATB AUGSBURG 11-0545 $.30   (M446)
Whether Young Or Old (from William Penn Reflections) anthem
SATB AUGSBURG 11-0543 $.30   (M447)

MOFFATT
I Know Where I'm Going *anthem
SAB/SA/unis oct LORENZ 7849 $.35
                              (M448)
Peace Like A River *anthem
SATB oct LORENZ B236 $.35   (M449)

MOFFATT, RICHARD C. (1927-   )
Thy Word Is A Lamp Unto My Feet
*Bibl
SATB,acap (med) FITZSIMONS 2174
$.25   (M450)

MOHLER, PHILIPP (1908-   )
Ach, Wie Fluchtig, Ach, Wie Nichtig
*Op.15
men cor (choral variations) sc
SCHOTTS C 34 600 s.p., voc pt
SCHOTTS C 34 600-01-04 s.p.
(M451)

MOHR, DONALD F.
Most Holy Night *Xmas
SATB (med) FITZSIMONS 2227 $.25
(M452)

MOLLICONE, HENRY
Stabat Mater
SATB,ST soli,2fl,2ob,2clar,2bsn,
2horn,4perc,harp,3bvl, celeste sc
AM.COMP.AL. $16.50   (M453)

Te Deum
SATB,S solo,3fl,3ob,2clar,bsn,
4horn,2trp,3trom,tuba,perc,harp,
celeste AM.COMP.AL.   (M454)
wom cor,S solo,pno AM.COMP.AL.
$7.15   (M455)

MOMENT BY MOMENT see Whittle

MOMENT OF TRUTH, THE see Kaiser, Kurt

MONELLE, RAYMOND
Lullay, Myn Lykyng
SATB,S solo,acap ROBERTON 63011
s.p.   (M456)

MONK
New Song In The Morning *CCU,anthem
SATB LEXICON   (M457)

MONK, WILLIAM HENRY (1823-1889)
Abide With Me *anthem
(Mann, Johnny) SATB LEXICON (M458)

Christ The Lord Is Risen Today
*Easter
(Ehret, Walter) SATB,kbd,opt 3trp
(med easy) oct ELKAN-V 362-03174
$.50   (M459)

MONKLAND
Praise, O Praise Our God And King
*Thanks,hymn
(Ehret, Walter) SATB,trp oct
LILLENAS AN-2413 $.35   (M460)

MONNIKENDAM, MARIUS (1896-   )
Christmas-Cycle *sac/sec,CC6U,carol
mix cor,org DONEMUS   (M461)

Elckerlyc-Everyman *sac/sec
mix cor&boy cor,org,fl,ob,clar,bsn,
opt 2trp&2trom,strings,perc
DONEMUS s.p.   (M462)
men cor&boy cor,org,fl,ob,clar,bsn,
2trp,2trom,strings,perc DONEMUS
s.p.   (M463)

Missa Concertate
mix cor,pno,3fl,2ob,2clar,2bsn,
4horn,3trp,3trom,strings,perc,
timp,harp DONEMUS   (M464)

Via Sacra
boy cor&mix cor,org,perc DONEMUS
(M465)

MONSELL
Fight The Good Fight (composed with
Finley) *anthem
SATB oct BROADMAN 4554-89 $.30
(M466)

MONTER, JOSEF
Deutsches Ordinarium "Christus Unser
Licht"
[Ger] 3-6pt mix cor&cong,solo,org
BOHM sc s.p., cor pts s.p. (M467)

Kleine Festmesse Zu Ehren Der
Heiligen Eucharistie Uber "Lauda
Sion" *Mass
[Lat] 4pt mix cor,org sc,cor pts
BOHM s.p.   (M468)

Konig Bist Du, Herr! *Fest,Bibl/cant
mix cor,opt S/T solo,org/strings&
org sc,cor pts BOHM s.p., ipa
(M469)

Pilger In Der Welt *Req
[Ger] 3-4pt mix cor&cong,solo,org
sc,cor pts BOHM s.p.   (M470)

Zu Bethlehem Geboren *Xmas,cant
mix cor&unis,org BOHM s.p.   (M471)

MONTEVERDI, CLAUDIO (ca. 1567-1643)
Agnus Dei
(Ehret) "Lamb Of God" SATB SCHIRM.G
11995 $.35   (M472)

Angelus Ad Pastores Ait *Xmas,mot
[Lat] 3pt jr cor/3pt wom cor,acap
(med easy) sc SCHOTTS C 34 489
s.p.   (M473)

MONTEVERDI, CLAUDIO (cont'd.)
Beatus Vir
(Steele) SSATTB,vln,vla/trom,vcl,
bvl voc sc NOVELLO rental   (M474)

Deus Tuorum Militum
TTB,strings (med) OXFORD 41.028
$.25, ipa   (M475)

Gloria (from Messa A 4 Voci Da
Cappella)
[Lat] SATB (med) GIA G1868 $.60
(M476)

Holy, Holy, Holy *see Sanctus

Lamb Of God *see Agnus Dei

Laudate Dominum (Psalm 117) Easter,
cant
(Arnold, Denis) [Lat] SATB,SSTTB
soli,cont,2vln min sc SCHOTTS
ETP 1069 s.p., ipa   (M477)

Magnificat
(Stevens; Steele) dbl cor,soli,
4trom,org,strings voc sc NOVELLO
rental   (M478)

Magnificat A Sei Voci *Bibl
(Arnold, Denis) SSATTB,org (med)
min sc SCHOTTS ETP 1071 s.p. (M479)

Mass For Four Mixed Voices *Mass
[Lat] SATB GIA G1826 $1.50   (M480)

Messe No. 1 In C
see Gombert, Nicolas, In Illo
Tempore Loquente Jesu

Missa "In Illo Tempore"
[Lat] SATB,acap UNIVER. UE 13776NJ
(M481)

Psalm 117 *see Laudate Dominum

Sanctus
(Ehret) "Holy, Holy, Holy" [Eng/
Lat] SATB SCHIRM.G 11994 $.35
(M482)

Sonata Sopra Sancta Maria
unis,4trp,2trom, 2 Baritone Horns
KING,R MFB 607 cor pts $.15,
cmplt ed $7.00   (M483)

Vespers
(Stevens) dbl cor,soli,2fl,3ob,
2bsn,2trom,2rec,org,strings voc
sc NOVELLO rental   (M484)

MONTGOMERY
According To Thy Gracious Word
(composed with Starks) *anthem
SATB (easy) oct BROADMAN 4540-44
$.30   (M485)

In Loud Thanksgiving Praise (composed
with Newbury, Kent A.) *anthem
SATB (easy) oct BROADMAN 4545-58
$.30   (M486)

O Bless The Lord, My Soul! (composed
with Vick) *anthem
SAB oct BROADMAN 4551-91 $.30
(M487)

MONTGOMERY, BRUCE (1921-   )
Christ's Birthday *CCU,Xmas,carol
SATB,strings voc sc NOVELLO rental
(M488)

On The Resurrection Of Christ
*Easter
SATB,2fl,pic,2ob,2clar,2bsn,4horn,
3trp,3trom,tuba,timp,perc,harp,
strings voc sc NOVELLO rental
(M489)

Oxford Requiem, An *Req
SATB,2fl,pic,2ob,2clar,2bsn,4horn,
3trp,3trom,tuba,timp,perc,2harp,
strings voc sc NOVELLO rental
(M490)

MONTILLET
Audi Filia *Mass
4pt mix cor,pno/org HENN 609 s.p.
sc, voc pt   (M491)

Cantiques A L'unisson *CCU
unis,acap HENN 394 s.p. sc, voc pt
(M492)

Factus Est Repente
4pt,acap voc pt HENN 537 s.p.
(M493)

Messe Breve (Cum Gloria)
4pt mix cor,pno/org HENN 595 s.p.
sc, voc pt   (M494)

Messe Ecclesia Orans
4pt mix cor,pno/org HENN 610 s.p.
sc, voc pt   (M495)

Messe En Fa Lydien
4pt mix cor,pno/org HENN 345 s.p.
sc, voc pt   (M496)

Messe En Mib Majeur *Mass
4pt mix cor,acap (E flat maj) voc
pt HENN 342 s.p.   (M497)

MONTILLET (cont'd.)
Messe En Sol Mineur *Mass
4pt mix cor,acap (G min) voc pt
HENN 122 s.p.   (M498)

Messe Regina Pacis
2pt mix cor,pno/org HENN 383 s.p.
sc, voc pt   (M499)

Messe Saint-Jospeh
4pt mix cor,pno/org HENN 611 s.p.
sc, voc pt   (M500)

Messe Sainte Cecile
4pt mix cor,pno/org HENN 343 s.p.
sc, voc pt   (M501)

O Salutaris
4pt,acap HENN 201 s.p. sc, voc pt
(M502)

Regina Coeli
4pt,acap HENN 204 s.p. sc, voc pt
(M503)

Tantum Ergo
4pt,acap HENN 202 s.p. sc, voc pt
(M504)

Tu Es Sacerdos
4pt mix cor,pno/org HENN 203 s.p.
sc, voc pt   (M505)

MOODY, MICHAEL
Prayer For Courage, A *anthem
2pt AUGSBURG 11-3007 $.10   (M506)

MOON HER LIGHT IS SHOWING, THE see
Gore, Richard T.

MOORE
Burdens Are Lifted At Calvary
*anthem/gospel
(DeCou, Harold) SATB oct SINGSPIR
ZJP-8093 $.30   (M507)

Fanfare For The Seasons *Xmas/
Easter,anthem
SATB oct SACRED S-160 $.35   (M508)

Fishers Of Men *Gen,anthem
SATB oct SACRED S-148 $.35   (M509)

Sing Praise To God *anthem
SATB oct BROADMAN 4545-76 $.30
(M510)

Tambourines To Glory *see Hughes

Why? *Gd.Fri.,anthem
(Anthony, Dick) SATB oct SINGSPIR
ZJP-7212 $.30   (M511)

MOORE, J. CHRIS
Blessed Be The Day That I Began A
Pilgrim For To Be
see Two Songs From The Pilgrim's
Progress

Let The Most Blessed Be My Guide
see Two Songs From The Pilgrim's
Progress

Lord's Prayer, The *anthem,Contemp
cor oct CHANTRY COA 7350 $.30
(M512)

Two Songs From The Pilgrim's Progress
*anthem,Contemp
oct CHANTRY COA 7355 $.30
contains: Blessed Be The Day That
I Began A Pilgrim For To Be
(SATB,S solo); Let The Most
Blessed Be My Guide (SATB)
(M513)

MOORE, MICHAEL
Gift Of Love
SA,pno/gtr FOSTER MF 802 $.40
(M514)

MOORE, MOTHER B.M.
People Of God *CCU,hymn
cong,gtr EMI   (M515)

MOORE, P.
Angelus Ad Virginem *Xmas
SATB,org GRAY CMR 3304 $.30 (M516)

MOORE, RICK
Close To Thee
see Moore, Rick, My Faith Look Up
To Thee

My Faith Look Up To Thee
(White, Calvin) TTBB oct GOSPEL
05 TM 0348 $.35 contains also:
Close To Thee   (M517)

MOORE, W.
Brethren, We Have Met To Worship
*anthem
(Blakely) mix cor BRODT 603 $.30
(M518)
(Ehret) SATB oct LILLENAS AN-2397
$.30   (M519)

MOORSE, PETER
Child Is Born, A
see SIX CHRISTMAS CAROLS

MORALES, CRISTOBAL DE (ca. 1500-1553)
Hispaniae Schola Musica Sacra Vol. I:
Christophorus Morales, 1894 *CCU
(Pedrell, F.) cor pap JOHNSON
$12.00 contains also: Vol. II:
Guerrero, 1894   (M520)

Lo, A Child Is Born To Us *see Puer
Natus Est Nobis

My Transgressions *see Peccantem Me

Peccantem Me
(Ehret, Walter) "My Transgressions"
[Eng/Lat] SATB,acap (med) PRESSER
312-41068 $.40   (M521)

Puer Natus Est Nobis
"Lo, A Child Is Born To Us" [Lat/
Eng] SAB,acap BROUDE BR. $.40
(M522)

Quaeramus Cum Pastoribus *Mass
[Lat] 5pt mix cor/6pt mix cor,acap
sc,cor pts BOHM s.p.   (M523)

MORAVIAN CHORALES *CCU
(Pfohl, J.C.) cor BRODT $1.25   (M524)

MORE
Thou, O Christ Of Calvary (composed
with Deane) *anthem
SATB (easy) oct BROADMAN 4540-52
$.30   (M525)

MORE ABOUT JESUS
(Huff, Ronn) SATB oct BENSON S4217
$.35   (M526)

MORE ABOUT JESUS see Sweney, J.R.

MORE FOLK HYMNS OF EARLY AMERICA *CCU,
anthem/folk/hymn,US
SATB LORENZ $1.95   (M527)

MORE HYMNS FOR A NEW AGE *CCU,anthem/
hymn
SATB LORENZ $.95   (M528)

MORE LIKE JESUS *CCUL
(Burroughs, Bob) cor,4brass LILLENAS
MB-345 $1.95, ipa   (M529)

MORE LIKE JESUS see Sewell

MORE LIKE JESUS WOULD I BE see Crowby

MORE LOVE TO THEE *Easter/Gen,anthem
(Bartlett) SATB FINE ARTS EW 1014
$.30   (M530)
(Mercer, W. Elmo) SATB,acap oct
BENSON S4214 $.25   (M531)

MORE LOVE TO THEE see Burroughs, Bob

MORE LOVE TO THEE see Doane, [William
Howard]

MORE THAN RAIMENT see Petzold, Johannes

MORE THINGS ARE WROUGHT BY PRAYER see
Martin, Gilbert M.

MOREAU, JEAN-BAPTISTE (1656-1733)
Athalie
cor,soli,orch HENN s.p.   (M532)

Esther
cor,soli,orch HENN s.p.   (M533)

MORGAN, HILDA
Christmas Morn *Xmas
SSA (med easy) WATERLOO $.30 (M534)

Communion Hymn *Commun
SATB (med easy) WATERLOO $.30
(M535)

I Saw Three Ships *Xmas
SSA (med easy) WATERLOO $.30 (M536)

This Little Babe *Xmas
SATB (easy) WATERLOO $.30   (M537)

MORGAN, JUSTIN (1747-1798)
Judgment Anthem
(Bennett, Lawrence) SATB,acap
BROUDE BR.   (M538)

MORGENGLANZ DER EWIGKEIT see Doebler,
Curt

MORGENSTERN DER FINSTERN NACHT see
Rothschuh, Franz

MORLEY, THOMAS (1557-1602)
Alas, They Have Taken The Lord *see
Eheu Sustulerunt Dominum

De Profundis Clamavi
"Out Of The Deep" SATB STAINER
3.0760.1 $.60   (M539)

Eheu Sustulerunt Dominum
"Alas, They Have Taken The Lord"
SATB STAINER 3.0746.1 $.40 (M540)

MORLEY, THOMAS (cont'd.)

I Am Weary Of My Groaning *see
Laboravi In Gamitu Meo

Laboravi In Gamitu Meo
"I Am Weary Of My Groaning" SSAATB
STAINER 3.0743.1 $.60   (M541)

Out Of The Deep *see De Profundis
Clamavi

Sound Forth The Trumpet In Zion
*anthem
(Proulx, R.) SAB (easy) GIA G1867
$.30   (M542)

MORN OF PRAISE see Lora, Antonio

MORNING CANTICLE, A see Martin, G.

MORNING HAS BROKEN *Gen,anthem,Ir
(Martin, Gilbert M.) SATB (med diff)
oct LORENZ C360 $.35   (M543)
(Powell, Rick) SATB WORD CS-2587 $.30
(M544)

MORNING HYMN see Rhea, Raymond

MORNING PRAYER, A see Martindale,
J.A.G.

MORNING STAR see Scheffler, J.J.

MORNING STAR, THE see Hagen, Francis
Florentine

MORNING TRUMPET, THE see Burroughs, Bob

MORNING TRUMPET, THE see Livingston

MORNING TRUMPET, THE see White

MORRIS
Conflict Of The Ages, The *gospel
(Skillings, Otis) SATB oct LILLENAS
AN-1677 $.30   (M545)

De Vreemdeling Van Galilea
(De Wolff) mix cor,acap s.p. sc
HEER 484, cor pts HEER 484A   (M546)

Fight Is On, The *anthem/gospel
(Mayfield, Larry) SATB,opt 3trp oct
SINGSPIR ZJP-8042 $.30   (M547)

Nearer, Still Nearer (composed with
Faircloth) *anthem
SATB (easy) oct BROADMAN 4540-55
$.30   (M548)

'Tis Marvelous And Wonderful *gospel
(Mickelson) SSATB oct LILLENAS
AN-1712 $.30   (M549)

MORRISON, KENNETH L.
What A Joy *anthem
SATB WORD CS-2655 $.30   (M550)

MORS JANUA VITAE see Wilson, R. Barclay

MORS RESPONSURA-IN MEMORIAM FRATRIS
SPIRITUALIS JAN MUL see Strategier,
Herman

MORTARI, VIRGILIO (1902-   )
Due Salmi In Memoria Di Alfredo
Casella *CC2U
wom cor,S solo,fl,ob,clar,bsn,
2horn,harp,timp,perc sc CARISH
21800 rental, ipr   (M551)

Missa Brevis
SATB,acap cor pts ZANIBON 5459 s.p.
(M552)
Stabat Mater
2pt wom cor,horn,timp,pno,strings
sc CARISH 20972 s.p., voc sc
CARISH 21009 s.p.   (M553)

MORTON, DAVID
Mother's Secret, The *Xmas,anthem
SSA HERITAGE H6011 $.35   (M554)

MOSES see Medema, Ken

MOSES SMOTE THE WATER *spir
(Ohrwall) 4pt mix cor ERIKS 57 s.p.
(M555)
MOSS, CYRIL
Jesus, Soul Of My Heart's Desire
SATB HARRIS $.35   (M556)

Let Thy Merciful Ears *mot
SATB HARRIS $.35   (M557)

MOST GLORIOUS LORD OF LIFE see Lord

MOST GLORIOUS LORD OF LIFE see Milner

MOST GLORIOUS LORD OF LYFE see France,
William E.

MOST GRACIOUS GOD see Ford, Virgil T.

MOST HOLY NIGHT see Mohr, Donald F.

MOST UNUSUAL CHAMPION, A see Langley,
Leanne

MOTETS see Marescotti

MOTETTEN ALTER MEISTER *see Anonymous,
Lobpreiset Gott, Unsern Herrn;
Croce, Giovanni, Hore, O Herr, Das
Gebet Deiner Gemeinde; Lassus,
Roland de (Orlandus), Herr Jesus
Christ, Unser Gott; Lotti, Antonio,
Freu Dich, Maria; Marenzio, Luca,
Mit Klingendem Saitenspiel
Frohlocken Wir   (M558)

MOTETTEN ALTER MEISTER see Anonymous

MOTETTEN ALTER MEISTER see Croce,
Giovanni

MOTETTEN ALTER MEISTER see Lassus,
Roland de (Orlandus)

MOTETTEN ALTER MEISTER see Lotti,
Antonio

MOTETTEN ALTER MEISTER see Marenzio,
Luca

MOTETUM ARCHANGELI MICHAELIS see
Hambraeus, Bengt

MOTHER, AT YOUR FEET IS KNEELING see
Sister, S.C.

MOTHER'S SECRET, THE see Morton, David

MOTHER'S SONG, A see Obenshain, Kathryn
G.

MOTTE, DIETHER DE LA (1928-   )
Es Ist Ein Ros Entsprungen *Xmas,mot
2-3pt jr cor/2-3pt wom cor (med
easy) sc SCHOTTS CHBL 596 s.p.
(M559)

MOTTETTI PER LA PASSIONE see Petrassi,
Goffredo

MOUNTAIN BROOK WITH RUSHING WATERS see
Johnson

MOUNTAIN, JAMES
Jesus, I Am Resting *anthem
(Kaiser, Kurt) SATB WORD CS-2667
$.35 see also HE LIVES!   (M560)

Like A River Glorious *anthem
(Burroughs, Bob) SATB,pno (med
easy) PRESSER 312-41030 $.35   (M561)
(DeCou, Harold) SATB oct SINGSPIR
ZJP-7340 $.30   (M562)

MOUNTAIN OF THE LORD see Griffith

MOUNTAIN OF THE LORD, THE see Roff,
Joseph

MOURANT, WALTER
Antiphon For Easter *Easter
SATB&jr cor,B solo,pno AM.COMP.AL.
$1.38   (M563)

Bless The Lord, O My Soul
SATB,pno AM.COMP.AL. $1.38   (M564)

Christmas Bells *Xmas
SATB&jr cor,pno AM.COMP.AL. $3.30
(M565)

God Of Abraham Praise, The
SATB,band AM.COMP.AL. sc $4.95, voc
sc $3.58   (M566)

Psalm 1
SATB,A solo,org AM.COMP.AL. $3.30
(M567)

Psalm 29
SATB,pno/org AM.COMP.AL. $2.75   (M568)

Psalm 90
SATB,SAB soli,org AM.COMP.AL. $4.40
(M569)

Psalm 148
SATB,pno AM.COMP.AL. $3.30   (M570)

Revelations 7:12
SATB,acap AM.COMP.AL. $2.20   (M571)

MOUTON, JEAN (ca. 1470-1522)
Noel, Noel, Noel! *Xmas,mot
(Ehret, Walter) [Eng/Lat] SATB,acap
(med) PRESSER 312-41084 $.40   (M572)

MOVING WITH THE BROOKS *CC10L
(Gassman, Clark) jr cor LEXICON 37618
$1.95   (M573)

MOZART ANTHEM BOOK, VOL. I see Mozart,
Wolfgang Amadeus

MOZART ANTHEM BOOK, VOL. II see Mozart,
Wolfgang Amadeus

MOZART, LEOPOLD (1719-1787)
Parasti Mensam *mot
[Lat] cor,soli,org,2vln,bvl sc,cor
pts BOHM s.p., ipa   (M574)

MOZART, WOLFGANG AMADEUS (1756-1791)
Adoramus Te *K.327, mot
[Lat] 4pt mix cor,org sc,cor pts
BOHM s.p.   (M575)

All Ye Nations Praise The Lord
(Hadley) SATB PRO ART 2785 $.35
(M576)

Alma Dei Creatoris *K.277, mot
[Lat] cor,soli,org,2vln,bvl sc,cor
pts BOHM s.p., ipa   (M577)

Ave Maria *K.554
[Lat] 4pt mix cor,acap sc,cor pts
BOHM s.p.   (M578)

Ave Verum *K.618
SATB HARRIS HC 4014 $.30   (M579)
[Lat] mix cor,org,opt 4strings sc,
cor pts BOHM s.p., ipa   (M580)
[Lat] 4pt mix cor,acap BOHM s.p.
(M581)
"Jesu, Word Of God Incarnate" mix
cor BANKS MUS YS 410 $.20   (M582)
(Bevan, Gwilym) SATB (med easy)
WATERLOO $.35   (M583)
(Lutkin) "Guide Me, O Thou Great
Jehovah" SA (easy) FITZSIMONS
5005 $.20   (M584)
(Lyle, J.B.) SSBar&camb CAMBIATA
M17552 $.35   (M585)

Ave Verum [1]
"Very Savior, Hail Thee!" see
Mozart Anthem Book, Vol. II

Ave Verum [2]
"Jesu, Word Of God Incarnate" see
Mozart Anthem Book, Vol. II

Ave, Verum Corpus *anthem
[Lat/Eng] SATB oct CHANTRY CLA 609
$.20   (M586)

Benedictus Sit Deus *K.117, Trin
[Lat] 4pt mix cor,org,2vln,2vla,
bvl,2fl,2horn,2trp,timp sc,cor
pts BOHM s.p., ipa   (M587)

Cantate De La Passion *Psntd,cant
mix cor,orch HENN s.p.   (M588)

Collected Edition *sac/sec,CCU
microfiche UNION ESP. editors
include: Brahms, Johannes;
Espagne, Franz; Goldschmidt,
Otto; Joachim, Joseph and others.
Originally published as 24 series
in 67 bindings, Leipzig, 1876-
1907. $290.00   (M589)

Come Glad Hearts *anthem
(Kemp) cor,2vln,vcl/org CHORISTERS
R-14 $.15   (M590)

Convertentur Sedentes *K.177, Commun
[Lat] unis,soli,org,2vln,vla,2horn,
bvl sc,cor pts BOHM s.p., ipa
(M591)

Credo Mass *K.257
(Landon) SATB SCHIRM.G 2939 $2.50
(M592)

Gloria In Excelsis
SATB HARRIS HC 4034 $.45   (M593)

Gloria In Excelsis Deo (from Twelfth
Mass)
(Collins) SSBar&camb CAMBIATA
M97437 $.50   (M594)

God Is Our Refuge *anthem
SATB oct CHANTRY CLA 6712 $.20
(M595)

Guide Me, O Thou Great Jehovah *see
Ave Verum

His Matchless Worth *anthem
(DeCou, Harold) SATB oct SINGSPIR
ZJP-7234 $.30   (M596)

Holy Redeemer *see Sancta Maria

Hostias
(Dawson, E.) [Lat] SATB,pno/org oct
NATIONAL WHC-38 $.40   (M597)

Jesu, Word Of God Incarnate *see Ave
Verum

Jesu, Word Of God Incarnate *see Ave
Verum [2]

Justum Deduxit Dominus *K.326, Fest
[Lat] 4pt mix cor,org sc,cor pts
BOHM s.p.   (M598)

Kyrie *K.33, Kyrie
SATB,2vln,vcl EGTVED MS14B11 s.p.
(M599)

MOZART, WOLFGANG AMADEUS (cont'd.)

Kyrie [1]
see Mozart Anthem Book, Vol. II

Kyrie [2]
see Mozart Anthem Book, Vol. II

Kyrie And Gloria (from Missa Brevis,
K.115) Gloria/Kyrie
SATB EGTVED KB41 s.p.   (M600)

Kyrie Eleison
mix cor BANKS MUS YS 596 $.30
(M601)
(Wright) SSAA BRODT HC 7 $.24
(M602)

Laudate Dominum (from Vesperae
Solennes De Confessore) Fest
SSA (med) OXFORD 83.090 $.40 (M603)
3pt wom cor,S solo,org,2vln,bvl,opt
bsn/vcl sc,cor pts BOHM s.p., ipa
(M604)
[Lat] cor,S solo,2vln,bvl,org,opt
bsn/vcl sc,cor pts BOHM s.p., ipa
(M605)

Laudate Pueri (from Vesperae Solennes
De Confessore)
(Fuller-Maitland) SATB,pno AMP
A-683 $.35   (M606)

Litaniae De Beata Maria Virgine
*K.109
"Litaniae Lauretanae" [Lat] cor,
soli,org,2vln,vcl,bvl sc,cor pts
BOHM s.p., ipa   (M607)
(Klein) "Litaniae Lauretanae" SATB
SCHIRM.G 2964 $2.00   (M608)

Litaniae Lauretanae *see Litaniae De
Beata Maria Virgine

Litaniae Lauretanae D-Dur *K.195
SATB,SATB soli,org,2ob,2horn,
strings (med) min sc SCHOTTS
ETP 943 s.p.   (M609)

Litanie De Venerabilis
mix cor,orch HENN s.p.   (M610)

Magnificat
(Ehret, Walter) SATB,kbd (med diff)
PRESSER 312-41057 $.80   (M611)

Messe In C-Dur *see Missa Brevis

Messe In C-Moll *K.427, Mass
SATB,SATB soli,2ob,2bsn,2horn,2trp,
strings,timp (C min,med diff) min
sc SCHOTTS ETP 983 s.p.   (M612)

Misericordias Domini *K.222, Fest
[Lat] 4pt mix cor,org,2vln,bvl sc,
cor pts BOHM s.p., ipa   (M613)

Missa Brevis *K.317, Mass
"Messe In C-Dur" SATB,SATB soli,
2ob,bsn,2trp,2vln,bvl,timp (C
maj,med) min sc SCHOTTS ETP 971
s.p.   (M614)
"Messe In C-Dur" SATB,SATB soli,
2ob,2trp,2vln,bvl,timp (C maj,med
easy) min sc SCHOTTS ETP 944 s.p.
(M615)
(Landon, Robbins) "Organ Solo Mass"
SATB SCHIRM.G 2963 $2.50   (M616)
(Landon, Robbins) "Piccolomini
Mass" SATB SCHIRM.G 2961 $2.50
(M617)

Missa Brevis In B *K.275, Mass
[Lat] cor,soli,org,bvl,2vln,opt vla
(B flat maj) sc,cor pts BOHM
s.p., ipa   (M618)

Missa Brevis In C *K.259, Mass
"Orgelsolomesse" [Lat] cor,soli,
org,bvl,2trp,timp,2vln,opt vla
sc,cor pts BOHM s.p., ipa   (M619)

Missa Brevis In D *K.194, Mass
[Lat] cor,soli,org,bvl,opt 2vln,vla
sc,cor pts BOHM s.p., ipa   (M620)

Missa Brevis In D-Dur *K.194, Mass
SATB,SATB soli,org,2vln,bvl (D maj,
med easy) min sc SCHOTTS ETP 986
s.p.   (M621)
(Jochum, Otto) 3pt jr cor/3pt wom
cor,org,opt 2vln BOHM sc s.p.,
cor pts s.p., ipa   (M622)

Missa Brevis In F *K.192, Mass
[Lat] cor,soli,org,2vln,bvl sc,cor
pts BOHM s.p., ipa   (M623)

Missa Brevis In G *K.140, Mass
[Lat] cor,soli,org,2vln,bvl sc,cor
pts BOHM s.p., ipa   (M624)

Missa For Archbishop Colloredo
*K.337, Mass
(Landon) SATB SCHIRM.G 2916 $2.00
(M625)

Missa Solemnis In C *K.337, Mass
[Lat] cor,soli,org,2ob,2bsn,2trp,
3trom,2vln,vcl,bvl,timp sc,cor

MOZART, WOLFGANG AMADEUS (cont'd.)

pts BOHM s.p., ipa   (M626)

Mozart Anthem Book, Vol. I *CC8L,
anthem
(Boeringer, James) cor,acap,org,vcl
CONCORDIA 97-5230 $2.00, ipa
(M627)
Mozart Anthem Book, Vol. II *anthem
(Boeringer, James) cor,2vln,vla,vcl
CONCORDIA 97-5275 $2.50, ipa
contains: Ave Verum [1], "Very
Savior, Hail Thee!"; Ave Verum
[2], "Jesu, Word Of God
Incarnate"; Kyrie [1], K.33;
Kyrie [2], K.116; Sancta Maria,
"Holy Redeemer", K.273   (M628)

Organ Solo Mass *see Missa Brevis

Orgelsolomesse *see Missa Brevis In
C

Piccolomini Mass *see Missa Brevis

Praise Him Declare His Glory
(Coggin) SAB SHAWNEE D5227 $.35
(M629)

Praise Him, Ye Nations *Thanks,
anthem
(Coggin, Elwood) SATB oct SINGSPIR
ZJP-7310 $.30   (M630)

Psalm "De Profundis" *K.93
[Lat] 4pt mix cor,opt org sc,cor
pts BOHM s.p.   (M631)

Quaerite Primum Regnum Dei
(Smith, James G.) "Seek First The
Kingdom Of God" SATB,acap FOSTER
MF157 $.40   (M632)

Regina Coeli *K.276, Mass
SATB,SATB soli,org,2ob,2trp,2vln,
bvl,timp (D maj,med easy) min sc
SCHOTTS ETP 1083 s.p.   (M633)

Regina Coeli *see Regina Coeli

Regina Coeli *K.276, BVM
4pt mix cor,org,2ob,2trp,timp,
strings min sc EULENBURG 1083
s.p.   (M634)
"Regina Coeli" [Lat] cor,soli,org,
2vln,2ob,2trp,bvl,timp,cor pts
BOHM s.p., ipa   (M635)

Sancta Maria *K.273, Fest
"Holy Redeemer" see Mozart Anthem
Book, Vol. II
"Sancta Maria, Mater Dei" [Lat] 4pt
mix cor,org,2vln,vla,bvl sc,cor
pts BOHM s.p., ipa   (M636)

Sancta Maria, Mater Dei *see Sancta
Maria

Sanctus (from Missa Brevis In G
Major) Sanctus
(Kirk) SATB PRO ART 2851 $.35
(M637)

Seek First The Kingdom Of God *see
Quaerite Primum Regnum Dei

Sing A Song Of Merry Christmas *Xmas
(Ehret, Walter) SATB,pno (easy)
GENTRY G-283 $.45   (M638)

Tantum Ergo
see Zwei Tantum Ergo
see Zwei Tantum Ergo

Te Deum In C-Dur *K.141
[Lat] 4pt mix cor,org,2vln,bvl,opt
vla&2ob&2bsn&2trp&timp (C maj)
sc,cor pts BOHM s.p., ipa   (M639)

Veni Sancte Spiritus *K.47
[Lat] 4pt mix cor,org,2vln,vla,bvl,
2ob,2horn,2trp,timp sc,cor pts
BOHM s.p., ipa   (M640)

Very Savior, Hail Thee! *see Ave
Verum [1]

Vesperae De Dominica *see Vesperae
Solennes De Dominica

Vesperae Solennes De Dominica *K.321
SATB,SATB soli,pno/orch voc sc
SCHIRM.EC 2796 s.p., ipr   (M641)
"Vesperae De Dominica" [Lat] cor,
soli,org,2vln,vcl,bvl,2trp,timp,
opt bsn&3trom sc,cor pts BOHM
s.p., ipa   (M642)

Zwei Tantum Ergo
[Lat] 4pt mix cor,org,2vln,vla,bvl,
2trp,opt timp sc,cor pts BOHM
s.p., ipa
contains: Tantum Ergo, K.142 (B
flat maj); Tantum Ergo, K.191
(D maj)   (M643)

MUDD
Let Thy Merciful Ears, O Lord
SATB,acap (med, formerly attributed
to Weelkes) OXFORD 43.076 $.30
(M644)

MUELLER
Anthem Of Faith, An
SATB SCHIRM.G 12029 $.40   (M645)

Because He First Loved Us *anthem
SATB oct BROADMAN 4565-32 $.35
(M646)

Behold, What Manner Of Love *anthem
SAB (easy) oct BROADMAN 4540-60
$.30
SATB oct BROADMAN 4565-31 $.35
(M648)

Beloved, Let Us Love One Another
*anthem
SATB oct BROADMAN 4565-30 $.35
(M649)

Different Drum, A *folk
SATB oct LILLENAS AN-5045 $.35
(M650)

God Is My Strong Salvation *anthem
SATB oct BROADMAN 4565-51 $.35
(M651)

If Thou But Suffer God To Guide Thee
*anthem
SATB oct BROADMAN 4565-52 $.35
(M652)

Jesus Calls Us *anthem
SATB oct BROADMAN 4565-49 $.35
(M653)

Jesus Shall Reign *anthem
SATB oct BROADMAN 4565-47 $.35
(M654)

O Jesus, I Have Promised *anthem
SATB oct BROADMAN 4565-48 $.35
(M655)

Time For Everything, A *anthem
SATB oct BROADMAN 4565-46 $.50
(M656)

MUELLER, CARL F. (1892-   )
This Is My Father's World
SATB (easy) FISCHER,C CM 7914 $.40
(M657)

MUELLER, G.G.
Lamb Of God Thou Shalt Remain
Together
(Nolte) mix cor,opt inst BRODT 1008
$.45, ipr   (M658)

MULLER
I Have Found A Hiding Place *see
Weigle

I Sing Of Thee *see Weigle

Messe Sursum Corda
4pt mix cor,pno/org HENN 401 s.p.
sc, voc pt   (M659)

MULLER, A.M.
Lauda Jerusalem Dominum *Fest,Offer
[Lat] 4pt mix cor,acap sc,cor pts
BOHM s.p.   (M660)

Mysterium Fidei *Op.4, Mass
[Lat] 4pt mix cor,acap sc,cor pts
BOHM s.p.   (M661)

Veni Creator *Op.14a
[Lat] 4pt mix cor,acap BOHM s.p.
(M662)

MULLER-ZURICH, PAUL (1898-   )
Herr, Nun Heb Den Wagen Selb
SATB,org/3trp&2trom SCHWEIZER.
SK 148 sc s.p., cor pts s.p., ipa
(M663)

Hilf, Herr Gott, Hilf In Dieser Not
SATB SCHWEIZER. SK 147 s.p.   (M664)

Mitten Wir Im Leben
SATB SCHWEIZER. SK 107 s.p.   (M665)

MULLICH, HERMANN (1943-   )
Drei Adventslieder *Adv
3 eq voices BOHM s.p.
contains: Es Kommt Ein Schiff,
Geladen; Maria Durch Ein'
Dornwald Ging; O Heiland, Reiss
Die Himmel Auf   (M666)

Drei Weihnachtsgesange *Xmas
2 eq voices,soli,org/pno/4strings
BOHM sc s.p., cor pts s.p., ipa
contains: Freude Im Advent; Sanft
Neigt Sich Der Tag; Weihnacht
(M667)

Es Kommt Ein Schiff, Geladen
see Drei Adventslieder

Freude Im Advent
see Drei Weihnachtsgesange

Hirtenweihnacht *Xmas
2pt jr cor,soli, Orff instruments
BOHM sc s.p., cor pts s.p., ipa
(M668)

Maria Durch Ein' Dornwald Ging
see Drei Adventslieder

O Heiland, Reiss Die Himmel Auf
see Drei Adventslieder

MULLICH, HERMANN (cont'd.)

Sanft Neigt Sich Der Tag
see Drei Weihnachtsgesange

Weihnacht
see Drei Weihnachtsgesange

MULTAS NOVIT AMOR VIAS see Reutter,
Hermann

MUNCHNER LIEBFRAUEN-MESSE see Haas,
Joseph

MUNDO SALUS REDDITUR see Jochum, Otto

MUNDY, JOHN (? -1630)
Songs And Psalms Composed Into 3, 4,
And 5 Parts (1594) EM Vol. 35b
*CC28L
3-5pt STAINER 3.1936.1 $11.50
(M669)

MUNDY, WILLIAM (ca. 1529-1591)
Adhaesit Pavimento
SATBB STAINER 3.0748.1 $.60   (M670)

Adolescentulus Sum Ego
SSATBB STAINER 3.0749.1 $.75   (M671)

O Lord, The World's Saviour
(Simkins) SSAATTBB (diff) oct
CONCORDIA 98-2167 $.40   (M672)

MUNGER, OREN
Jesus Is My Shepherd
(Krogstad, Bob) SATB oct GOSPEL
(M673)

Vision, The
(Krogstad, Bob) SATB oct GOSPEL
05 TM 0318 $.35   (M674)

MURO, D.
O Be Joyful In The Lord
SATB,electronic tape GRAY GCCS 21
$.35   (M675)

MURRAY
Away In A Manger *Adv/Xmas
(Schubert) SATB oct LILLENAS
AN-3853 $.30   (M676)

Bless The Lord (All My Trials)
SATB oct SCHMITT 7047 $.40   (M677)

New Life Is Born *Xmas
SA oct SCHMITT 256 $.40   (M678)

Praise Him Today *Xmas
2pt oct SCHMITT 2135 $.40   (M679)

Tiny Little Baby Boy *Xmas
SATB oct SCHMITT 8069 $.30   (M680)

MURRAY, MARGARET (1921-   )
First Nowell, The
see Four Christmas Carols

Four Christmas Carols
[Eng] unis jr cor,rec,perc,
glockenspiel, xylophone (easy) sc
SCHOTTS ED. 10 057 s.p.
contains: First Nowell, The; In
Dulci Jubilo; O Little Town Of
Bethlehem; Waits   (M681)

In Dulci Jubilo
see Four Christmas Carols

O Little Town Of Bethlehem
see Four Christmas Carols

Waits
see Four Christmas Carols

MUSIC FOR COMMUNION *CC7L
1-2pt/SAB WHITE,ERN $1.25 contains
works by: Schroeder; De La Lande;
Noydon, Joseph; Marcello   (M682)

MUSIC FOR COURSES BOOK 4 *CCU,Easter,
cor-resp/hymn/Psalm
cor ROYAL s.p.   (M683)

MUSIC FOR COURSES BOOK 5 *CCU,Xmas,
cor-resp/hymn/Psalm
cor ROYAL s.p.   (M684)

MUSIC FOR COURSES BOOK 6 *CCU,Whitsun,
cor-resp/hymn/Psalm
cor ROYAL s.p.   (M685)

MUSIC FOR REFORMATION DAY see Bender,
Jan

MUSIC FOR THE CHURCH, VOLUME II see
Lee, John

MUSIC FOR THE EUCHARISTIC PRAYER
ACCLAMATIONS see Somary, Johannes

MUSIC FOR THE FUNERAL RITE see Roff,
Joseph

MUSIC FOR THE MESSIAH BOOK 1 *CCUL,Jew
(Dauermann, Stuart) cor cmplt ed
LILLENAS MB-368 $1.95   (M686)

MUSIC FOR THE MESSIAH BOOK 2 *CCUL,Jew
(Dauermann, Stuart) cor cmplt ed
LILLENAS MB-369 $1.95   (M687)

MUSIC FOR THE YOUNG CHURCH see Kleiman,
Richard

MUSIC FOR THE YOUNG CHURCH, VOLUME I
*CC10L
cor WORD 37614 $1.95
see also: Harrell, Jan, Give Jesus
A Chance   (M688)

MUSIC FOR THE YOUNG CHURCH, VOLUME II
*see Johnson, Paul, That The World
May Know; Lee, John, O Brother Man;
Wommack, Chris, Beatitudes, The
(M689)

MUSIC FOR THE YOUNG CHURCH, VOLUME II
see Johnson, Paul

MUSIC FOR THE YOUNG CHURCH, VOLUME II
see Lee, John

MUSIC FOR THE YOUNG CHURCH, VOLUME II
see Wommack, Chris

MUSIC FROM "SEMELE" see Handel, George
Frideric

MUSIC FROM WAY BACK WHEN *CCU,anthem
(Lyall, Max) 1-2pt,kbd BROADMAN
4526-11 $1.75 taken from music by
Bach; Mozart; Beethoven; and others
(M690)

MUSIC OF THE GREAT CHURCHES VIII: HOLY
CROSS CHURCH, DRESDEN see Homilius,
Gottfried August

MUSIC OF THE GREAT CHURCHES VOL. I: ST.
STEPHEN'S CATHEDRAL, VIENNA see
Fux, Johann Joseph

MUSIC OF THE GREAT CHURCHES VOL. II:
ST. MARK'S CATHEDRAL, VENICE *see
Gabrieli, Andrea, Maria Magdalene
Et Altera Maria, "Scarce Had The
Daystar Risen"; Lotti, Antonio,
Adoramus Te [1], "We Adore You ";
Lotti, Antonio, Adoramus Te [2],
"We Adore You "; Porta, Costanzo,
Vobis Datum Est, "You Are Given To
Know"   (M691)

MUSIC OF THE GREAT CHURCHES VOL. II:
ST. MARK'S CATHEDRAL, VENICE see
Gabrieli, Andrea

MUSIC OF THE GREAT CHURCHES VOL. II:
ST. MARK'S CATHEDRAL, VENICE see
Lotti, Antonio

MUSIC OF THE GREAT CHURCHES VOL. II:
ST. MARK'S CATHEDRAL, VENICE see
Porta, Costanzo

MUSIC OF THE GREAT CHURCHES VOL. III:
SANTA MARIA MAGGIORE, ROME see
Scarlatti, Alessandro

MUSIC OF THE GREAT CHURCHES VOL. IV:
ST. THOMAS' CHURCH, LEIPZIG *see
Calvisius, Sethus, Joseph, Lieber
Joseph Mein, "Joseph, Joseph,
Dearest One"; Schein, Johann
Hermann, Maria Magdalene Et Altera
Maria, "When Mary Magdalene" (M692)

MUSIC OF THE GREAT CHURCHES VOL. IV:
ST. THOMAS' CHURCH, LEIPZIG see
Calvisius, Sethus

MUSIC OF THE GREAT CHURCHES VOL. IV:
ST. THOMAS' CHURCH, LEIPZIG see
Schein, Johann Hermann

MUSIC OF THE GREAT CHURCHES VOL. V: ST.
PAUL'S CATHEDRAL, LONDON *see
Boyce, William, By The Waters Of
Babylon; Greene, Maurice, Hear My
Prayer   (M693)

MUSIC OF THE GREAT CHURCHES VOL. V: ST.
PAUL'S CATHEDRAL, LONDON see Boyce,
William

MUSIC OF THE GREAT CHURCHES VOL. V: ST.
PAUL'S CATHEDRAL, LONDON see
Greene, Maurice

MUSIC OF THE GREAT CHURCHES VOL. VI:
WESTMINSTER ABBEY, LONDON see
Croft, William

MUSIC OF THE GREAT CHURCHES VOL. VII:
ST. PETER'S BASILICA, ROME *see
Anerio, Felice, Angelus Autem
Domini Descendit, "God, The Lord,
Sent A Messenger"; Victoria, Tomas
Luis de, O Crux Ave, "O Hail!
Sacred Cross"   (M694)

MUSIC OF THE GREAT CHURCHES VOL. VII:
ST. PETER'S BASILICA, ROME see
Anerio, Felice

MUSIC OF THE GREAT CHURCHES VOL. VII:
ST. PETER'S BASILICA, ROME see
Victoria, Tomas Luis de

MUSICA DEI DONUM OPTIMI see Lassus,
Roland de (Orlandus)

MUSICHE DI CHIESA DA CINQUE A SEDICI
VOCI see Gabrieli, Andrea

MUSIKALISCHE EXEQUIEN see Schutz,
Heinrich

MUSIKALISCHE EXEQUIEN see Schutz,
Heinrich

MUSIKBEILAGE ZUM "EVANGELISCHEN
KIRCHENCHOR 1975" *CC7L
mix cor SCHWEIZER. SK 75.00 s.p.
contains works by: Telemann;
Gallus; Mendelssohn; Distler and
others   (M695)

MUSIKBEILAGE ZUM "EVANGELISCHEN
KIRCHENCHOR 1951" *CC8U
SAT/SAB/SATB SCHWEIZER. SK 51.00 s.p.
contains works by: Diener; Matthes;
Othmayr; Staden; and others
see also: de la Rue, Pierre, Wir
Danken Dir, O Gottes Lamm;
Matthes, Rene, Ach Lieber Herr Im
Hochsten Thron; Othmayr, Kaspar,
Der Herr Kennet Den Weg Der
Gerechten; Staden, Johann, Danket
Dem Herren Alle Zeit; Sweelinck,
Jan Pieterszoon, Mein Gott, Mein
Gott, Verlassen Hast Du Mich
(Psalm 22)   (M696)

MUSIKBEILAGE ZUM "EVANGELISCHEN
KIRCHENCHOR 1952"
SCHWEIZER. SK 52.00 s.p.
contains & see also: Briner, Wie
Selig Wer Im Glauben Nur;
Goudimel, Claude, Herr, Erhore
Meine Klagen; Zentner, Johannes,
Triumph! Triumph! Es Kommt Mit
Pracht   (M697)

MUSIKBEILAGE ZUM "EVANGELISCHEN
KIRCHENCHOR 1952" see Vulpius,
Melchior

MUSIKBEILAGE ZUM "EVANGELISCHEN
KIRCHENCHOR 1953"
SATB SCHWEIZER. SK 53.00 s.p.
contains & see also: Brandt, Jobst
vom, O Mensch, Bewein Dein Sunde
Gross; Ducis, Benedictus, Aus
Tiefer Not Schrei Ich Zu Dir;
Erytraeus, Gottfried, Nun Bitten
Wir Den Heiligen Geist; Franck,
Melchior, Du Sollst Gott, Deinen
Herrn, Lieben; Gesius,
Bartholomaus, Nun Jauchzet, All
Ihr Frommen; Praetorius, Michael,
Wohlauf, Ihr Christen, Freuet
Euch; Schroter, Leonhard, Allein
Gott In Der Hoh Sei Ehr   (M698)

MUSIKBEILAGE ZUM "EVANGELISCHEN
KIRCHENCHOR 1954"
SATB SCHWEIZER. SK 54.00 s.p.
contains & see also: Burck,
Joachim, Vom Olberge Zeucht
Daher; Diener, Theodor, O Leib,
Gebrochen Mir Zu Gut; Pepping,
Ernst, Wie Schon Leuchtet Der
Morgenstern; Studer, Hans, Es Ist
Gewisslich An Der Zeit; Studer,
Hans, So Fuhrst Du Doch Recht
Selig, Herr, Die Deinen; Vulpius,
Melchior, Uns Ist Ein Kind
Geboren; Widmer, Barmherziger,
Ewiger Gott   (M699)

MUSIKBEILAGE ZUM "EVANGELISCHEN
KIRCHENCHOR 1955"
SATB SCHWEIZER. SK 55.00 s.p.
contains & see also: Burck,
Joachim, Gen Himmel Fahrt Der
Herre Christ; Hassler, Hans Leo,
Singet Ein Neues Lied; Heer,
Emil, Mein Ganzes Herz Erhebet
Dich (Psalm 138); Helder,
Bartholomaeus, Herr Jesu Mein,
Sollst Doch Mein Trost   (M700)

MUSIKBEILAGE ZUM "EVANGELISCHEN
KIRCHENCHOR 1956" *CC10U
SATB/SAT/SAB SCHWEIZER. SK 56.00 s.p.
see also: Bender, Jan, O Konig
Aller Ehren; Bender, Jan, Sonne
Der Gerechtigkeit; Bruck, Arnold
von, Christ, Der Ist Erstanden;
Helder, Bartholomaeus, O Treuer
Gott Im Himmelsthron; Praetorius,
Michael, Gottes Sohn Ist Kommen;
Praetorius, Michael, Wir Danken
Dir, Herr Jesu Christ, Dass Du
Fur Uns Gestorben Bist; Schutz,
Heinrich, Ich Will Mein Ganzes
Leben; Sermisy, Claude de, Was
Mein Gott Will, Das Gscheh
Allzeit   (M701)

MUSIKBEILAGE ZUM "EVANGELISCHEN
KIRCHENCHOR 1957" *CC7U
SATB SCHWEIZER. SK 57.00 s.p.
see also: Brunner, Adolf, Das Alte
Jahr Vergangen Ist; Burck,
Joachim, Ich Weiss, Dass Mein
Erloser Lebt; Ducis, Benedictus,
Nun Freut Euch, Lieben
Christen'gmein; Franck, Melchior,
Ich Danke Dir, Herr Jesu Christ;
Hessenberg, Kurt, Herr, Fur Dein
Wort Sei Hoch Gepreist; Schutz,
Heinrich, Lobt Gott Mit Schall;
Vulpius, Melchior, Das Neugeborne
Kindelein   (M702)

MUSIKBEILAGE ZUM "EVANGELISCHEN
KIRCHENCHOR 1958"
SATB SCHWEIZER. SK 58.00 s.p.
contains & see also: Calvisius,
Sethus, Der Herr Ist Mein
Getreuer Hirt; Driessler,
Johannes, O Mensch, Bewein Dein
Sunde Gross; Gallus, Jacobus,
Siehe, Dein Konig Kommt;
Hessenberg, Kurt, Nun Jauchzt Dem
Herren, Alle Welt; Hoyoul,
Balduin, Da Jesus An Dem Kreuze
Stund; Praetorius, Michael, Der
Heilgen Geistes Gnade Gross;
Praetorius, Michael, Nun Lob,
Mein Seel, Den Herren; Schott,
Johann Georg, Singet Dem Herrn
Ein Neues Lied, Denn Er Tut
Grosse Wunder   (M703)

MUSIKBEILAGE ZUM "EVANGELISCHEN
KIRCHENCHOR 1959"
SATB SCHWEIZER. SK 59.00 s.p.
contains & see also: Albert,
Heinrich, Gott Des Himmels Und
Der Erden; Eglin, Arthur, Wohl
Dem, Der Nicht Den Weg Des
Frevlers Wahlt; Heer, Emil,
Wachet Auf, Ruft Uns Die Stimme
          (M704)

MUSIKBEILAGE ZUM "EVANGELISCHEN
KIRCHENCHOR 1959"
SCHWEIZER. SK 59.01-2 s.p.
contains: Diener, Theodor, Ein
Feste Burg Ist Unser Gott (SB);
Praetorius, Michael, Ein Feste
Burg Ist Unser Gott (SAT/SAB);
Schutz, Heinrich, Ein Feste Burg
Ist Unser Gott (SATB)   (M705)

MUSIKBEILAGE ZUM "EVANGELISCHEN
KIRCHENCHOR 1960" *CC8U
SATB SCHWEIZER. SK 60.00 s.p.
see also: Anonymous, Des Herrn Wort
Bleibt In Ewigkeit; Eccard,
Johannes, Ich Steh An Deiner
Krippe Hier; Koch, Heinz, Wir
Glauben All An Einen Gott;
Studer, Hans, Gelobt Sei Gott Im
Hochsten Thron   (M706)

MUSIKBEILAGE ZUM "EVANGELISCHEN
KIRCHENCHOR 1960"
SCHWEIZER. SK 60.04-5 s.p.
contains: Marx, Karl, Nimm Von Uns,
Herr, Du Treuer Gott (SAT/SAB);
Pidoux, Pierre, Wie Herrlich
Gibst Du, Herr, Dich Zu Erkennen
(SAT/SAB); Vulpius, Melchior,
Nimm Von Uns, Herr, Du Treuer
Gott (SATB); Walcha, Helmut, Nimm
Von Uns, Herr, Du Treuer Gott
(SS)   (M707)

MUSIKBEILAGE ZUM "EVANGELISCHEN
KIRCHENCHOR 1961" *CC6U
SATB SCHWEIZER. SK 61.00 s.p.
see also: Cruger, Johann, Komm,
Heiliger Geist; Diener, Theodor,
Die Helle Sonn Leucht Jetzt
Herfur; Franck, Melchior, Herr
Jesu, Der Du Bist Fur Mich;
Walter (Walther), Johann, Wach
Auf, Wach Auf, Du Christlich
Land; Werner, Fritz, Zeuch An Die
Macht, Du Arm Des Herrn   (M708)

MUSIKBEILAGE ZUM "EVANGELISCHEN
KIRCHENCHOR 1962" *CC7U
SATB SCHWEIZER. SK 62.00 s.p.
see also: Diener, Theodor, Ich Sag
Dir Dank, Gott Vater Gut; Gadsch,
Herbert, Nun Sich Der Tag Geendet
Hat; Hartmann, Heinrich, Eins
Bitt Ich Vom Herren; Heer, Emil,
Gelobet Seist Du, Jesu Christ;
Kubler, Emil, Mit Freuden Zart;
Le Jeune, Claude, Hilf, A Und O,
Anfang Und Ende; Studer, Hans,
Nun Danket Gott, Erhebt Und
Preiset   (M709)

MUSIKBEILAGE ZUM "EVANGELISCHEN
KIRCHENCHOR 1963"
SATB SCHWEIZER. SK 63.00 s.p.
contains & see also: Albert,
Heinrich, Lobet Gott In Seinem
Heiligthum; Distler, Hugo, Es Ist
Ein Ros Entsprungen; Ebeling,
Johann Georg, Zeuch Ein Zu Deinen

Toren; Praetorius, Michael, Lobet
Den Herren, Alle Heiden; Schutz,
Heinrich, Auf Dich, Herr, Trau
Ich Allezeit (Psalm 71); Schutz,
Heinrich, Ich Will Sehr Hoch
Erhohen Dich (Psalm 145);
Weismann, Wilhelm, Hoch Vom
Himmel Komm Ich Her   (M710)

MUSIKBEILAGE ZUM "EVANGELISCHEN
KIRCHENCHOR 1963"
SCHWEIZER. SK 63.05-6 s.p.
contains: Cabezon, Antonio de, Jesu
Christe, Gottes Lamm (SATB);
Cruger, Johann, Christ Lag In
Todesbanden (SATB, 2 treb inst);
Praetorius, Michael, Auf Dich,
Mein Herre Und Mein Gott (SATB);
Praetorius, Michael, Wir Wollen
Alle Frohlich Sein (SATB) (M711)

MUSIKBEILAGE ZUM "EVANGELISCHEN
KIRCHENCHOR 1964"
SATB SCHWEIZER. SK 64.00 s.p.
contains & see also: Goudimel,
Claude, Singt Halleluja (Psalm
113); Grimm, Jurgen, Mein Gott,
Ich Danke Dir; Grimm, Jurgen, Nun
Schlagt Die Stunde Mitternacht;
Hindermann, Walter Felix, Herr,
Hore Doch Auf Meine Rede (Psalm
5); Kuehnhausen, Johann Georg, O
Lamm Gottes, Unschuldig; Lechner,
Leonhard, Christus Ist Fur Uns
Gestorben; Schutz, Heinrich, Das
Blut Jesu Christi Machet Uns
Rein; Schutz, Heinrich, Es Ist
Ein Freud Dem Herzen Mein; Zipp,
Friedrich, Aus Meines Herzens
Grunde   (M712)

MUSIKBEILAGE ZUM "EVANGELISCHEN
KIRCHENCHOR 1965"
SATB SCHWEIZER. SK 65.00 s.p.
contains & see also: Goudimel,
Claude, O Seht, Wie Schon Und
Lieblich Ist's (Psalm 133);
Lahusen, Christian, Steht Auf Und
Wacht; Lange, Gregor, Wenn Ich
Nur Dich Hab, Herr, Allein;
Praetorius, Michael, Geborn Ist
Uns Immanuel; Schein, Johann
Hermann, Furwahr, Es Ist Ein
Kostlich Ding; Studer, Hans, Ich
Will Meinen Geist Ausgiessen;
Winer, Georg, Schaffe In Mir,
Gott, Ein Reines Herze (Psalm
51); Zeuner, Martin, Herr Jesu
Christ, Wahr Mensch Und Gott;
Zipp, Friedrich, Gott Ist Unsere
Zuversicht Und Starke (Psalm 64)
          (M713)

MUSIKBEILAGE ZUM "EVANGELISCHEN
KIRCHENCHOR 1966" *CC9U
SATB SCHWEIZER. SK 66.00 s.p.
see also: Distler, Hugo, Was Mein
Gott Will, Das Gscheh Allzeit;
Gippenbusch, Jakob, Die Ganze
Welt, Herr Jesu Christ;
Praetorius, Michael, Jauchz, Erd
Und Himmel; Serranus, Johann
Baptista, Wenn Wir In Hochsten
Noten Sein; Vulpius, Melchior,
Trachtet Am Ersten Nach Dem Reich
Gottes; Zipp, Friedrich, O
Heiland Reiss Die Himmel Auf
          (M714)

MUSIKBEILAGE ZUM "EVANGELISCHEN
KIRCHENCHOR 1967"
SATB SCHWEIZER. SK 67.00 s.p.
contains & see also: Fischer,
Walter, Mein Schonste Zier;
Franck, Melchior, Also Hat Gott
Die Welt Geliebt; Pidoux, Pierre,
Helft, Gottes Gute Preisen;
Praetorius, Michael, Wunderbarer
Gnadenthron; Ruppel, Paul Ernst,
Siehe, Dein Konig Kommt Zu Dir;
Schein, Johann Hermann, Der Herr,
Der Ist Mein Hirt; Studer, Hans,
O Christe, Wahrheit Und Leben;
Werner, Fritz, Lobet Den Herren,
Alle, Die Ihn Ehren; Zipp,
Friedrich, Allein Gott In Der Hoh
Sei Ehr   (M715)

MUSIKBEILAGE ZUM "EVANGELISCHEN
KIRCHENCHOR 1968"
SATB SCHWEIZER. SK 68.00 s.p.
contains & see also: Cruger,
Johann, Mein Hoffnung, Trost Und
Zuversicht; Diener, Theodor, O
Wie Sehr Lieblich Sind; Heer,
Emil, Brich An, Du Schones
Morgenlicht; Kukuck, Felicitas,
Ich Singe Dir Mit Herz Und Mund;
Raselius, Andreas, Erstanden Ist
Der Heilig Christ; Schein, Johann
Hermann, Nun Lob Den Herrn, O
Seele Mein; Studer, Hans, Gott
Vater, Sende Deinen Geist;
Studer, Hans, Siehe, Es Kommt Die
Zeit; Zillinger, Erwin, Die
Finsternis Vergeht   (M716)

MUSIKBEILAGE ZUM "EVANGELISCHEN
    KIRCHENCHOR 1968" see Bach, Johann
    Sebastian

MUSIKBEILAGE ZUM "EVANGELISCHEN
    KIRCHENCHOR 1969" *CC8U
    SATB SCHWEIZER. SK 69.00 s.p.
    see also: Distler, Hugo, Gott Sei
    Dank Durch Alle Welt; Distler,
    Hugo, Wie Schon Leuchtet Der
    Morgenstern; Ebeling, Johann
    Georg, Warum Sollt Ich Mich Denn
    Gramen; Henking, Bernhard, Alles
    Ist Euer; Micheelsen, Hans-
    Friedrich, Himmel Und Erde Werden
    Vergehen; Praetorius, Michael,
    Den Die Hirten Lobeten Sehre;
    Raselius, Andreas, Furchtet Euch
    Nicht; Stern, Hermann, In Dir Ist
    Freude   (M717)

MUSIKBEILAGE ZUM "EVANGELISCHEN
    KIRCHENCHOR 1970"
    SATB SCHWEIZER. SK 70.00 s.p.
    contains & see also: Heer, Emil,
    Lobe Den Herren, Den Machtigen
    Konig Der Ehren; Herzogenberg,
    Heinrich von, Danket Dem Herren,
    Schopfer Aller Dinge; Reger, Max,
    Ich Bin Getauft Auf Deinen Namen;
    Reger, Max, Jesus Lebt, Mit Ihm
    Auch Ich; Studer, Hans, Sollt Ich
    Meinem Gott Nicht Singen?;
    Telemann, Georg Philipp, Wenn
    Mich Die Sunden Kranken;
    Telemann, Georg Philipp, Wir
    Christenleut Habn Jetzund Freud;
    Werner, Fritz, Nun Danket Alle
    Gott   (M718)

MUSIKBEILAGE ZUM "EVANGELISCHEN
    KIRCHENCHOR 1971" *CC11U,mot
    2-4pt mix cor,org SCHWEIZER. SK 71.00
    s.p. contains works by: Diener;
    Kelterborn; Reichel; Studer and
    others   (M719)

MUSIKBEILAGE ZUM "EVANGELISCHEN
    KIRCHENCHOR 1972"
    SATB SCHWEIZER. SK 72.00 s.p.
    contains & see also: Gesius,
    Bartholomaus, Freut Euch, Ihr
    Lieben Christen All; Goudimel,
    Claude, Singt, Singt Dem Herren
    Neue Lieder; Hennig, Walter,
    Gelobet Seist Du, Jesu Christ;
    Ruppel, Paul Ernst, Herr, Deinen
    Tod Verkunden Wir; Schutz,
    Heinrich, Ehre Sei Dem Vater;
    Schutz, Heinrich, Ich Will Von
    Herzen Danken Gott (Psalm 111);
    Steuerlein, Johann, Das Alte Jahr
    Vergangen Ist; Zipp, Friedrich,
    Das Will Ich Mir Zu Herzen Nehmen
                                  (M720)

MUSIKBEILAGE ZUM "EVANGELISCHEN
    KIRCHENCHOR 1973" *CC7L
    mix cor,opt cont,treb inst SCHWEIZER.
    SK 73.00 s.p. contains works by:
    Bischoff; Helder; Marx; Zillinger
    and others   (M721)

MUSIKBEILAGE ZUM "EVANGELISCHEN
    KIRCHENCHOR 1975" *CC7L
    SATB SCHWEIZER. SK 74.00 s.p. (M722)

MUSIQUE RELIGIEUSE see Cherubini, Luigi

MUSIQUES DE NOEL see Carraz

MUST JESUS BEAR THE CROSS ALONE? see
    Graham, Robert Virgil

MUST JESUS BEAR THE CROSS ALONE see
    Turner

MUTTER, GERBERT
    Ad Te Levavi Animam Meam *Fest
    [Lat] 4pt mix cor,org sc,cor pts
        BOHM s.p.   (M723)

    Das Kindlein Lieget Da *Xmas
        cor BOHM s.p.   (M724)

    Deutsche Festsingmesse Nach
        Kirchenliedern *CC7L,Mass
    [Ger] mix cor BOHM sc s.p., cor pts
        s.p.   (M725)

    Dona Nobis Pacem *Mass
    [Lat] 4pt mix cor,org sc,cor pts
        BOHM s.p.   (M726)

    Drei Veni Creator *No.1-3, CC3U
    [Lat] 4pt mix cor,acap BOHM s.p.
        sold separately   (M727)

    Feierliches Pange Lingua
    [Lat] cor,org/2trp,2trom sc,cor pts
        BOHM s.p., ipa contains also:
        Tantum Ergo   (M728)

    Justus Ut Palma *Fest
    [Lat] 4pt mix cor,org sc,cor pts
        BOHM s.p.   (M729)

MUTTER, GERBERT (cont'd.)

    Missa Parva *Mass
    [Lat] 4pt mix cor,acap sc,cor pts
        BOHM s.p.   (M730)

    Spiritus Sanctus In Te Descendit,
        Maria *Adv/Fest
    [Lat] 4pt mix cor,org sc,cor pts
        BOHM s.p.   (M731)

    Stella Maris *Mass
    [Lat] 4pt mix cor,org/org&strings/
        fl&ob&2bsn&2horn&2trp&trom&
        strings sc,cor pts BOHM s.p., ipr
                                  (M732)

    Tantum Ergo
        see Mutter, Gerbert, Feierliches
        Pange Lingua

    Zwei Pange Lingua *No.1-2, CC2U
    [Lat] 4pt mix cor,acap BOHM s.p.
        sold separately   (M733)

MUTTERGOTTES-MESSE see Grau, P.
    Theodor, Missa Brevissima II In
    Honorem Beatae Mariae Virgini

MUTTERGOTTES-MESSE see Heftrich,
    Wilhelm

MY ALL IN ALL see Wyrtzen, Don

MY ANCHOR HOLDS see Martin, Gilbert M.

MY BELOVED SPOKE see Cadwallader, Ann

MY BEST FRIEND see Sewell

MY COUNTRY, 'TIS OF THEE *anthem
    (Krogstad, Bob) SSATTBB/SSATB oct
    SINGSPIR ZJP-7370 $.35   (M734)

MY EYES ARE BLINDED BY MY WEEPING see
    Ingegneri, Marco Antonio,
    Caligaverunt Oculi Mei

MY FAITH HAS FOUND A RESTING PLACE
    see I Love Thee, My Lord

MY FAITH HAS FOUND A RESTING PLACE see
    Danner

MY FAITH IS IN THEE see Jaeschke

MY FAITH LOOK UP TO THEE see Moore,
    Rick

MY FAITH SHOULD BE A HAPPY THING
    *anthem
    (Burroughs, Bob) 1-2pt oct BROADMAN
    4557-22 $.30   (M735)

MY FAITH STILL HOLDS see Gaither,
    William J. (Bill)

MY FATHER IS WITH ME see Hughes, Robert
    J.

MY FRIEND AND I
    see There Is A Song

MY FRIEND HAD A VINEYARD see Felciano,
    Richard

MY FRIEND JESUS see AuCoin

MY GOD AND I see Wihtol, A.A.

MY GOD, AND IS THY TABLE SPREAD see Van
    Der Hoeck

MY GOD, HOW WONDERFUL THOU ART *anthem
    (Rasley, John M.) SATB oct SINGSPIR
    ZJP-7264 $.30   (M736)

MY GOD, HOW WONDERFUL THOU ART see
    Fettke, Tom

MY GOD, I THANK THEE see Burroughs

MY HEART EVER FAITHFUL see Bach, Johann
    Sebastian

MY HEART FOR VERY JOY DOTH LEAP see
    Paviour, Paul

MY HEART IS READY see Johnson, Mark

MY HEART SINGS HOSANNA see Johnson,
    Lois

MY HEART SINGS WITH JOY see Harrer,
    Mein Herz Ist Bereit

MY HOPE OF GLORY see Skillings, Otis

MY JESUS, I LOVE THEE *anthem
    (Littleton, Bill J.) SATB FINE ARTS
    EW 1017 $.30   (M737)

MY JESUS, I LOVE THEE see Featherstone

MY JESUS, I LOVE THEE see Gordon,
    Adoniram J.

MY JESUS, I LOVE THEE see Rasley, John
    M.

MY JESUS, I LOVE THEE see Smith

MY JESUS WEPT see Chatham

MY JOURNEY HOME
    (Sateren, Leland) SATB,acap ART MAST
    156 $.30   (M738)

MY LIFE, MY ALL, I GIVE TO HIM see
    Parks

MY LITTLE WORLD see Carmichael, Ralph

MY LORD see Eilers, Joyce Elaine

MY LORD AND I see Wihtol, A.A.

MY LORD CARES see Landgrave, Phillip

MY LORD IS HENCE REMOVED see Amner,
    John

MY LORD IS NEAR ME ALL THE TIME see
    Gaultney

MY LORD, MY BROTHER see Cornell, Garry
    A.

MY LORD, MY GOD, MY ALL see Rasley,
    John M.

MY LORD, WHAT A MORNIN' *anthem
    (Dean) SATB (easy) oct BROADMAN
    4561-03 $.30   (M739)

MY LORD, WHAT A MORNING
    see Funf Spirituals
    (Siegler, W.) men cor,acap TONOS 2387
    s.p.   (M740)

MY LORD, WHAT A MOURNING *spir
    (Dawson, William) SSATTBB,acap (med)
    FITZSIMONS 2009 $.25   (M741)

MY LORD'S IN THE MOUNTAIN see Roberts

MY LOVER AND MY MASTER see Cadwallader,
    Ann

MY MEAT IS TO DO THE WILL OF HIM THAT
    SENT ME see Baumgartner, H. Leroy

MY PRAYER FOR AMERICA see Skillings,
    Otis

MY REDEEMER see Bliss

MY REDEEMER see Cram

MY SAVIOR FIRST OF ALL see Sweney

MY SHEEP HEAR MY VOICE see Brewer, R.H.

MY SHEPHERD see Martin, Bruce

MY SHEPHERD WILL SUPPLY MY NEED
    *anthem/hymn
    (Goemanne, Noel) SATB GIA G1738 $.35
                                  (M742)
    (Rasley, John M.) SATB oct SINGSPIR
    ZJP-7301 $.30   (M743)
    (Smith, C.T.) cor WINGERT s.p. (M744)
    (Tipton, Clyde) SATB,gtr, or autoharp
    DEAN CD-106 $.35   (M745)

MY SINGING IS A PRAYER see Preston

MY SINS ARE BLOTTED OUT I KNOW see
    Dunlop, Merrill

MY SINS ARE GONE see Vandall

MY SONG IS LOVE UNKNOWN see Kliewer,
    Jonah

MY SONG IS LOVE UNKNOWN see Schalk,
    Carl

MY SOUL, AWAKE! see Elmore, Robert
    [Hall]

MY SOUL DOTH MAGNIFY THE LORD see
    Pulkingham, B.C.

MY SOUL HAS WINGS see Franco, Johan

MY SOUL IS EXCEEDING SORROWFUL see
    Heussenstamm, George

MY SOUL, NOW BLESS THY MAKER! see
    Hammerschmidt, Andreas, Nun Lob,
    Mein Seel, Den Herren

MY SOUL SHALL BE JOYFUL see Keegan,
    Patrick

MY SOUL, THERE IS A COUNTRY see Drayton

MY SOUL THIRSTETH FOR GOD see Canning,
    Thomas

MY SWEET JESUS see Hins, S.B.

MY TASK see Ashford

MY TRANSGRESSIONS see Morales,
    Cristobal de, Peccantem Me

MY TRIBUTE see Crouch, Andrae

MY TRUST IS IN THEE see Bales, Gerald

MY WEARY EYES I CLOSE IN GOD'S DEAR
    NAME SO BLEST see Bach, Johann
    Sebastian

MY WORLD, YOUR WORLD see Blankenship,
    Mark

MYN LYKING
    see Two Christmas Carols

MYSTERIOUS PRESENCE, SOURCE OF ALL see
    Franco, Johan

MYSTERIUM FIDEI see Muller, A.M.

N

NACH DER WANDLUNG "AUF, GLAUBIGE
    SEELEN" see Trapp, Willy

NAGEL
    God Of Our Country
    cor&cong,inst (patriotic) oct
    LILLENAS AN-3875 $.45   (N1)

NAGEL, ROBERT
    Bread Of Life Together
    SA KJOS 6136 $.40   (N2)

NAIL-SCARRED HAND, THE *anthem
    (Bass) SATB oct BROADMAN 4554-94 $.30
                                     (N3)

NAILING MY SINS TO HIS CROSS see
    Mercer, W. Elmo

NAJERA, EDMUND
    Exultate Deo
    SATB SCHIRM.G 12011 $.40   (N4)

    In Dulci Jubilo *Xmas
    SATB SCHIRM.G 12012 $.45   (N5)

NAME I HIGHLY TREASURE, A see Eliason

NAME OF JESUS, THE *gospel
    (Skillings, Otis) SATB oct LILLENAS
    AT-1110 $.35   (N6)

NAME OF JESUS, THE see Lorenz, Ellen
    Jane

NAME OF JESUS, THE see Skillings, Otis

NAMEGIVERS, THE see Willcoxon, Larry

NANCE
    Alleluia, Amen *anthem
    SATB (easy) oct BROADMAN 4551-55
    $.30   (N7)

NANINI (NANINO), GIOVANNI MARIA
        (ca. 1545-1607)
    Fourteen Liturgical Works *CC14U
    (Schuler, Richard J.) cor bds A-R
    ED $9.95   (N8)

NAPRSTEK, GERHARD
    Orbis Factor *Mass
    [Lat] 2 eq voices/2pt mix cor,org
    (without Credo) sc,cor pts BOHM
    s.p.   (N9)

NAR DETTA FORGANGLIGA see Olson, Daniel

NAR NAR HJORTEN VATTENBACKEN see
    Soderholm, Valdemar

NAR VI I HOGSTA NODEN STA see Ritter,
    Christian

NAR VINTERMORKET KRING OSS STAR see
    Soderholm, Valdemar

NAROZENI PANE see Martinu, Bohuslav

NAROZENI PANE see Zelinka, Sr. Jan
    Evangelista

NARRATIVE AND CHORALE see Claflin,
    Avery

NATALE E AMORE
    see Due Canti Nataizi

NATIVITIE see O'Neal, Barry

NATIVITIE see Woollen, Russell

NATIVITY CAROL see Rutter

NATIVITY TALE see Belyea, W.H.

NATURAL HIGH *see Carmichael, Ralph,
    My Little World; Carmichael, Ralph,
    Natural High; Carmichael, Ralph,
    Searching Questions; Carmichael,
    Ralph, When I Think Of The Cross;
    Kaiser, Kurt, It's Our World;
    Kaiser, Kurt, Moment Of Truth, The
                                     (N10)

NATURAL HIGH see Carmichael, Ralph

NATURAL HIGH see Kaiser, Kurt

NATURAL HIGH see Carmichael, Ralph

NAUMBOURG, SAMUEL (1815-1880)
    Z'mirot Yisrael *CCU,Fest/Rosh Ha-
    Shanah/Sab-Morn/Yom Kippur
    mix cor/men cor,1-4 soli
    SAC.MUS.PR. S.M.P. 13-15 $25.00
    three volumes, bound in three
    books   (N11)

NAYLOR, BERNARD (1907-   )
    Annunciation, The
    SATB,ST soli,fl,clar,2horn,2trp,
    2trom,timp,harp,strings voc sc
    NOVELLO rental   (N12)

    Cantata Domino (Psalm 98)
    2pt treb cor,org ROBERTON 75031
    s.p.   (N13)

    Come Holy Ghost, Eternal God
    SATBB,org ROBERTON 85013 s.p. (N14)

    Deus Misereatur (Psalm 67)
    2pt treb cor,org ROBERTON 75032
    s.p.   (N15)

    Missa Da Camera
    SATB,4 soli,ob,clar,bsn,horn,
    strings voc sc NOVELLO rental
                                     (N16)

    Preces And Responses
    SSATB,acap (med) OXFORD 43.480 $.50
                                     (N17)

    Psalm 67 *see Deus Misereatur

    Psalm 98 *see Cantata Domino

    Ressurection, The *Easter
    SATB,SBarB soli,fl,ob,clar,bsn,
    horn,trp,trom,timp,pno,strings,
    cymbals voc sc NOVELLO rental
                                     (N18)

    Stabat Mater
    wom cor,2fl,2pic,2ob,2clar,2bsn,
    2horn,2trp,vln,vla,vcl voc sc
    NOVELLO rental   (N19)

NAYLOR, ERIC
    Crusaders For Christ
    SATB,acap HARRIS $.35   (N20)

NAZARENE, THE see Gillis, Don

NAZARETH see Gounod, Charles Francois

NAZARETH see Serieyx, Auguste

NE AVERTAS FACIEM TUAM see Lendvai,
    Erwin

NEALE
    Star, The Wise Men, The Child, The
    (composed with Newbury, Kent A.)
    *Xmas,anthem
    unis (easy) oct BROADMAN 4554-56
    $.30   (N21)

NEANDER
    Christ Is Risen! *Easter,anthem
    (Rasley, J.M.) SATB oct SINGSPIR
    ZJP-3548 $.35   (N22)

NEAR TO THE HEART OF GOD see McAfee

NEAR TO THY HEART see Peterson, John W.

NEARER MY GOD TO THEE see Mason, Lowell

NEARER, MY GOD, TO THEE see Street

NEARER, STILL NEARER see Morris

NEBUCHADNEZZAR see Dyson, George

NEEM MIJN LEVEN
    (De Wolff) mix cor s.p. sc HEER 1514,
    cor pts HEER 1514A   (N23)

NEFF, JAMES
    Empty Cave, The *Easter,anthem
    SSAAB AUGSBURG 11-1692 $.30 (N24)

    I Will Sing To The Lord *anthem
    2pt mix cor AUGSBURG 11-0653 $.30
                                     (N25)

    Shout For Joy Before The Lord
    *anthem
    SATB AUGSBURG 11-0655 $.40 (N26)

NEIDLINGER
    Birthday Of A King, The *Xmas,anthem
    (Johnson, Norman) SATB oct SINGSPIR
    ZJP-3004 $.25   (N27)

NEIGHBORS see Lovelace, Austin C.

NE'ILAH SERVICE see Nowakowsky, David,
    Schlussgebet

NEILSEN, LUDVIG
    Draumkvedet *liturg/ora
    SSA/SAB MUSIKK   (N28)

    Liturgical Songs For The Church Year
    *CCU,Gen,liturg
    2-4pt mix cor NORSK NMO 8749-3 s.p.
                                     (N29)

    Syng Lovsang For Gud, Alle Land
    cor,org NORSK NMO 8746 s.p.   (N30)

NEJEDLY, VIT (1912-1945)
    Vanocni Koledy *CCU,Xmas,carol
    [Czech] jr cor,2clar CZECH s.p.
                                     (N31)

NELHYBEL, VACLAV (1919-   )
Halleluiah
SATB,band KERBY 10278-994 $.75
(N32)

Hallelujah
cor,band (large full score in Helio
(on special order for $30.00))
cmplt ed KERBY 10234 $48.00, sc
KERBY 10233 $12.50, cor pts KERBY
10278 $.75, ipa   (N33)

NELSON
Church Triumphant, The *anthem
SATB,trp oct LILLENAS AN-2380 $.35
(N34)

I'm So Needy, Holy Spirit *gospel
2pt oct LILLENAS AN-1695 $.30 (N35)

Sing A New Song *folk
SSATB oct LILLENAS AN-5065 $.30
(N36)

Taking Chances *folk
SATB oct LILLENAS AN-5063 $.35
(N37)

NELSON, HAVELOCK
Come Down, O Love Divine *anthem
SSA,acap NOVELLO ELKIN 2775 s.p.
(N38)

NELSON, R.
Thy Truth Is Great
SATB,pno/org oct BOOSEY 5849 $.45
(N39)

NELSON, RONALD A.
Awake, My Soul *anthem
SAB,kbd AUGSBURG 11-0650 $.35 (N40)

Be Filled With The Spirit *anthem
SA,kbd AUGSBURG 11-1733 $.30 (N41)

Clap Your Hands, Stamp Your Feet
*anthem
unis,kbd AUGSBURG 11-0649 $.35
(N42)

How Jesus Stilled The Storm
see Nelson, Ronald A., Storm At Sea

Sanctify Them *Gen/Thanks
SA CHORISTERS A-162 $.40   (N43)

Season Of Tomorrow, The
SATB/unis jr cor/cong,org,fl,tamb,
Orff inst sc AUGSBURG 11-9374
$2.00, ipa   (N44)

Storm At Sea *anthem
CHORISTERS R-17 $.15 contains also:
How Jesus Stilled The Storm (N45)

Temples Of God *anthem
2pt mix cor&opt jr cor,opt solo
AUGSBURG 11-1696 $.35   (N46)

This Is The Feast Of Victory *anthem
SATB,org,opt trp AUGSBURG 11-1672
$.35   (N47)

We Know That Christ Is Raised
*anthem
unis,perc AUGSBURG 11-0318 $.30 (N48)

NENTWIG, W.
Adventlied "Lass Den Heiland Ein"
*Adv
3pt,acap/org BOHM s.p.   (N49)

NEUBER
Herr, Unser Herrscher
SSA/jr cor,org,3rec,bvl,
glockenspiel, xylophone,
metallophone, cymbals HANSSLER
12.512 s.p.   (N50)

NEUBERT, GOTTFRIED (1926-   )
O Jesu Christe, Wahres Licht *cant
SATB,S solo,org,3trp,2trom sc
HANSSLER 10.269 s.p.   (N51)

War Gott Nicht Mit Uns Diese Zeit
*cant
SAT/SAB,3trp,2trom sc HANSSLER
10.268 s.p.   (N52)

NEUE DEUTSCHE GEISTLICHE LIEDER see
Gumpelzhaimer, Adam

NEUE KRAFT see Burkhard Willy

NEUE MESSE see Kubizek, Augustinian

NEUES PSALMENBUCH *CCU
(Hucke, H.; Quack, E.; Schmidthus,
K.) SATB,org cmplt ed CHRIS
52167-68 s.p. contains works by:
Hummel, B.; Quack, E.; Schubert,
H.; Stingl, A.; Schieri, F.; Klein,
R.R.   (N53)

NEUFELD, RICK
Glory To God *CC2U,Introit
(Mayfield) SSATTB,brass oct
LILLENAS AN-6037 $.30   (N54)

NEUMARK, GEORG (1621-1681)
If Thou But Suffer God To Guide Thee
*Lent
(McAfee, Don) SATB ART MAST 149
$.35   (N55)

Wer Nur Den Lieben Gott Lasst Walten
men cor,acap TONOS 5608 s.p. (N56)

NEUNTE MESSE see Brosig, Moritz

NEUNTE MESSE IN B see Faist, Anton

NEVER IN A MILLION YEARS see Peterson,
John W.

NEVER QUITE THE SAME see Bock, Fred

NEVER WAS A CHILD SO LOVELY see Adler

NEVER WEATHER BEATEN SAIL see Russell,
Welford

NEW! see Martin, Bruce

NEW AND JOYFUL SONG OF PRAISE, A see
Staton, Kenneth W.

NEW BEGINNING, A see Blankenship, Mark

NEW COMMANDMENT, A see Gore, Richard T.

NEW COVENANT, THE see Fischer, John

NEW DAY!, A see Dodd

NEW DAY FOR AMERICA, A see Plunkett,
Bonnie

NEW GENERATION, THE see Turner

NEW KIND OF DREAM, A see Gagliardi,
George

NEW LIFE, THE see Riese

NEW LIFE IS BORN see Murray

NEW SILENT NIGHT, A see Duson, Dede

NEW SONG, A see Burroughs, Bob

NEW SONG, A see Tipton

NEW SONG IN THE MORNING see Monk

NEW SOUNDS IN SONG *CCUL
(Boalt, Steve) cor (easy) SINGSPIR
5665 $1.95   (N57)

NEW TOMORROW, A see Marsh, Donald T.

NEW WORLD, A see Huff, Ronn

NEW WORLD, A *CC9UL
(Huff, Ronn) cor BENSON B0233 $1.95
stereo recording, tape, and-or
book-record sets available, contact
publisher   (N58)

NEWBERRY, KENT
Come Thou Almighty King *anthem
SATB WORD   (N59)

NEWBOLD, DAVID
Carol To The King *Xmas,anthem
SATB (med) OXFORD 42.359 $.70 (N60)

NEWBORN, THE see Martin, Gilbert M.

NEWBURY, KENT A.
Almighty Reigns, The
SATB WALTON 2252 $.35   (N61)

Bless The Lord, O My Soul *anthem
SATB,pno/org WORLD CA-2315-8 $.45
(N62)

Christ Is Born, Alleluia *Xmas
SSA SCHIRM.G LG51809 $.40   (N63)

Creator Of The Stars Of Night
unis SHAWNEE FA5011 $.35   (N64)

Faith *anthem
SATB,pno/org WORLD CA-2310-8 $.40
(N65)

For The Beauty Of The Earth *see
Pierpoint

He Is The King Of Glory
SATB SHAWNEE A5672 $.35   (N66)

I Heard The Bells On Christmas Day
*Xmas
SATB RICHMOND MI-94 $.30   (N67)

I Long For Thy Salvation
SATB SCHIRM.G 11943 $.30   (N68)

In Him All Things Were Created
*anthem
SATB oct BROADMAN 4545-75 $.30
(N69)

In Loud Thanksgiving Praise *see
Montgomery

NEWBURY, KENT A. (cont'd.)

Jesus And The Woolly Sheep *Xmas
SATB,acap (easy) FITZSIMONS 2179
$.20   (N70)

Lift Up Your Heads *see Weissel

O Master, Let Me Walk With Thee
2pt mix cor TRIUNE TUM 108 $.35 see
also LET THE WORLD SING   (N71)

O Praise The Lord
SATB STANDARD A40MX1 $.50   (N72)

On This Rock *anthem
1-2pt,opt gtr&bvl (easy) oct
BROADMAN 4551-46 $.30   (N73)

Once At Ev'ry Gate
SATB RICHMOND MI-87 $.45   (N74)

Palm Sunday Procession *Easter/Palm
SATB SCHIRM.G 11946 $.35   (N75)

Psalm 93
SATB STANDARD A39MX1 $.50   (N76)

Seek Ye The Lord *anthem
SATB oct BROADMAN 4554-84 $.30
(N77)

Send Forth Thy Spirit O Lord
SATB SCHIRM.G 11998 $.35   (N78)

Star, The Wise Men, The Child, The
*see Neale

Thou Art My God *anthem
SATB,pno/org,opt 2trp WORLD
CA-2316-8 $.75   (N79)

NEWLIN, DIKA (1923-   )
Genesis 4
2pt mix cor,org,3horn sc
AM.COMP.AL. $.55   (N80)

This Is The Record Of John
SSATTB,AT soli,brass,org sc
AM.COMP.AL. $1.10   (N81)

NEWMAN, D.
Treasure Of Calvary *anthem
(McCall, C.) SATB (easy) oct
SINGSPIR ZJP-6015 $.25   (N82)

NEWS FROM BETHLEHEM, THE see Hurnik,
Ilja, Novina Betlemska

NEWTON
Amazing Grace (composed with Turner)
*anthem
SATB (easy) oct BROADMAN 4545-52
$.30   (N83)

NEWTON, JOHN
Amazing Grace
(Collins, Hope) SATB oct GOSPEL
05 TM 0147 $.20   (N84)

NIAGARA MASS, THE see Holman, Derek

NICHOL, H. ERNEST
We've A Story To Tell To The Nations
*anthem/gospel
(Leader; DeCou) SATB oct SINGSPIR
ZJP-8014 $.25   (N85)

NICHOLS
Do You Know? *anthem
unis&desc oct BROADMAN 4557-93 $.30
(N86)

NICHOLSON
Try Jesus, Man Of Galilee *Easter/
Gen
(Mercer, W. Elmo) SATB oct BENSON
S4362 $.30   (N87)

NICHT KNECHTE, SONDERN FREUNDE NENN'
ICH EUCH see Heiller, Anton

NICOL
Just As I Am *gospel
(Widen) SATB oct LILLENAS AN-5082
$.35   (N88)

NICOLAI, OTTO (1810-1849)
Messe In D *Mass
cor,soli,pno/org/strings&org/2clar&
2bsn&2horn&2trp&strings&timp BOHM
sc s.p., ipa, cor pts s.p.   (N89)

Pater Noster *mot
dbl cor cor pts BIELER DM 5 s.p.
(N90)

NICOLSON
When Jesus Sat At Meat
SATB,inst (med) OXFORD 42.233 $.85,
ipr   (N91)

NIEDERLANDISCHES DANKGEBET "WIR TRETEN
ZUM BETEN VOR GOTT" see Zipp,
Friedrich

NIEDT, FRIEDRICH EHRHARDT (1674-1717)
Es Mussen Sich Freuen Und Frohlich
Sein *Xmas,mot
(Holle, Hugo) mix cor (med) sc
SCHOTTS C 32 232 s.p., voc pt
SCHOTTS C 32 232A s.p.   (N92)

NIELSEN, CARL (1865-1931)
Three Motets *Op.55, CC3U,mot
[Lat] SATB HANSEN-DEN s.p.   (N93)

NIEMAN, ALFRED (1913-   )
Holly And The Ivy *Xmas
SATB STAINER 3.0754.1 $.35   (N94)

NIEVERGELT
Lobt Den Herren, Alle Heiden
see Leutert, Sollt Ich Meinem Gott
Nicht Singen

NIGHT FOR DANCING, A see Hopson, Hal H.

NIGHT OF MIRACLES see Peterson, John W.

NIGHT SO DARK AND HOUR SO LATE see
Wihtol, A.A.

NIGHT THE ANGELS SANG, THE see
Peterson, John W.

NIGHT THE CHRIST CHILD CAME, THE see
Peninger, David

NIGHT WAS STILL see White, Herbert D.

NIKIPROWETZKY
Numinis Sacra
mix cor,T solo,org,perc JOBERT s.p.
(N95)

NILES, JOHN JACOB (1892-   )
Mary, Mary *Xmas
SATB (easy) FOSTER MF512 $.40 (N96)

NILSSON, TORSTEN (1920-   )
Communionmusik *CCU,Commun
mix cor/cong cor pts NORDISKA
NMS 6391 s.p.   (N97)

NIMM VON UNS, HERR, DU TREUER GOTT see
Marx, Karl

NIMM VON UNS, HERR, DU TREUER GOTT see
Vulpius, Melchior

NIMM VON UNS, HERR, DU TREUER GOTT see
Walcha, Helmut

NINE CALLS TO WORSHIP see Procter, R.E.

NINE JAPANESE HAIKU see Hoffman, T.

NINE LESSONS OF CHRISTMAS, THE see La
Montaine, John

NINE NEGRO SPIRITUALS *CC9U
(Heading, Noel) 2-3pt treb cor EMI
(N98)

NISI DOMINE see Alder

NNO *Xmas,carol,Afr
(Ekwueme) "Welcome" SATB SCHIRM.G
LG51824 $.45   (N99)

NO GREATER LOVE see Peterson, John W.

NO HASSLE see Burroughs, Bob

NO LONELY DAY *CCUL
(Wyrtzen, Don; Walvoord, John) jr cor
SINGSPIR 4504 $1.50   (N100)

NO LONELY DAY see Wyrtzen, Don

NO LONGER A BABY see Leech, Bryan

NO LONGER ALONE see Winter, Sister
Miriam Therese

NO LOV'LIER COUNTRYSIDE *folk,Ger
(Welch, John) SATB STUDIO V751 $.30
(N101)

NO MORE DEATH see Peterson, John W.

NO, NOT ONE *anthem
(Coates) SATB oct BENSON S4225 $.35
(N102)
(Warford) SATB (easy) oct BROADMAN
4545-32 $.30   (N103)

NO PLACE DRIVES HIM AWAY see Cornell,
Garry A.

NO ROOM IN THE INN *Xmas,anthem
(Johnson, Norman) SATB oct SINGSPIR
ZJP-3030 $.25   (N104)

NO TEARS HAVE WE TO SHED see Weil

NO TEARS TOMORRW see DeCou, Harold

NO TIME! see Wyrtzen, Don

NOAH see Wright, Alberta Childs

NOBLE, THOMAS TERTIUS (1867-1953)
Come, O Creator Spirit, Come
mix cor BANKS MUS YS 499 $.25
(N105)
Come O Thou Traveller
mix cor BANKS MUS YS 497 $.20
(N106)
Fierce Was The Wild Billow
(Nordin) TTBB,acap (med) FITZSIMONS
4036 $.20   (N107)
First Easter Dawn, The *Easter
mix cor BANKS MUS YS 1044 $.25
(N108)
Magnificat *Magnif/Nunc
mix cor BANKS MUS YS 487 $.80
contains also: Nunc Dimittis
(N109)
Nunc Dimittis
see Noble, Thomas Tertius,
Magnificat
Office Of The Holy Communion, The
mix cor BANKS MUS YS 1071 $1.10
(N110)
Souls Of The Righteous
mix cor BANKS MUS YS 492 $.20
(N111)
Te Deum *Te Deum
mix cor BANKS MUS YS 486 $.80
(N112)

NOBODY KNOWS *spir
(Driessen, Rene) TTBB sc BROGNEAUX
s.p.   (N113)

NOBODY KNOWS DE TROUBLE I'VE SEEN see
Petersen, Rolf

NOBODY KNOWS THE TROUBLE I'VE SEEN
*spir
see Five Negro Spirituals
(Collins) SSBar&camb,opt pno (med
easy) CAMBIATA S97320 $.40   (N114)
(Ohrwall) 4pt mix cor ERIKS 58 s.p.
(N115)
(Wild, Eric; Waters, Deanna) SATB
(med easy) WATERLOO $.40   (N116)

NOE see Hurnik, Ilja

NOEL see Bert, Henri

NOEL see Burroughs, Bob

NOEL see Closset

NOEL! see Landon, Stewart

NOEL see Spoel, A., Kerstzang

NOEL see Warner, P.

NOEL see Young, Gordon

NOEL, CHANTONS, NOEL see Arma, Paul

NOEL DIALOGUE see Roger

NOEL, NOEL, A BOY IS BORN see Sleeth,
Natalie

NOEL, NOEL, NOEL! see Mouton, Jean

NOEL NOUVELET *Xmas
see Twelve Christmas Carols: Set 2
(Fearing, John) SSA (easy) WATERLOO
$.30   (N117)

NOEL NOUVELET see Shaw, Ruby

NOEL NOUVELET see Van Hulse, Camil

NOEL PASTORAL see Praetorius, Michael

NOELS *CCU,Xmas,carol
(Oberndorfer, Max; Oberndorfer, Anne)
mix cor,acap FITZSIMONS cloth
$2.95, cor pts $1.00   (N118)

NOELS ANCIENS see Paychere

NOELS BOURGUIGNON *CCU,Xmas
(Carraz) 4pt mix cor,acap sc HENN 746
s.p.   (N119)

NOELS EN SUCRE D'ORGUE see Carraz

NOLTE, EWALD VALENTIN (1909-   )
King Of Love, The
SA (easy) FITZSIMONS 5025 $.25
(N120)

NON NOBIS, DOMINE see Byrd, William

NON NOBIS DOMINE see Haydn, (Franz)
Joseph

NON PAPA, JACOBUS CLEMENS
see CLEMENS, JACOBUS

NON SECUNDUM PECCATA NOSTRA see
Philipp, Franz

NON TARDE VENIET see Lassus, Roland de
(Orlandus)

NON VOS RELINQUAM ORPHANOS see Donati

NONE OTHER LAMB *Easter
(Bissell, Keith W.) SATB (med diff)
WATERLOO $.40   (N121)

NONE OTHER LAMB see Ayers, Jacob S.

NONE OTHER LAMB see Bissell, Keith W.

NONE OTHER LAMB see Whitecotton,
Shirley

NOPS, MARJORY
Oh Hurry Hurry To Bethlehem *Xmas
SATB EMI s.p.   (N122)
Shepherds In The Fields *Xmas
SATB EMI s.p.   (N123)
There Was A Maid *Xmas
SATB EMI   (N124)

NORDHALM, IB
Offer, Op.34 *CC6U
mix cor HANSEN-DEN WH 29010 s.p.
(N125)

NORDIN, DAYTON W.
How Lovely Is Thy Dwelling Place
*Bibl
SATB (med) FITZSIMONS 2225 $.25
(N126)
In Peace And Joy *Nunc
SATB (easy) FITZSIMONS 2229 $.25
(N127)
Now, My Soul, Thy Voice Upraising
*Lent
SATB (easy) FITZSIMONS 2230 $.25
(N128)

NORMAN
I Wish We'd All Been Ready
SATB oct BENSON S4145 $.35   (N129)
Sweet, Sweet Song Of Salvation
SATB oct BENSON S4255 $.35   (N130)

NORMAN JOHNSON PRESENTS CHORAL CONCEPTS
*CC11UL
(Johnson, Norman) SATB SINGSPIR 4273
$1.00   (N131)

NORMAN, LUCILLE
That Precious Scarred Hand *Easter
(Smith, Herb) SATB oct GOSPEL
05 TM 0179 $.20   (N132)

NORTHFIELD see Ingalls, Jeremiah

NOS AUTEM see Haydn, (Johann) Michael

NOS PETITS SOULIERS see Delaye

NOSSE
Deep River *anthem
SATB (easy) oct BROADMAN 4540-65
$.30   (N133)

NOSTALGIA *CC10L,gospel
(Pursell, Bill) cor RODEHEAVER 37654
$1.95   (N134)

NOT TO THE HILLS see Peterson, John W.

NOTE OF GOLDEN SONG, A see Saar, Louis
Victor

NOTES OF ASSURANCE *CC8UL,anthem
(Johnson, Derric) cor LILLENAS MB-310
$1.50   (N135)

NOTHING BETWEEN see Tindley

NOTRE DAME MASS, THE see Isele, D.C.

NOTTINGHAM
Hast Thou Forsaken Me *Lent
(Glarum) SATB oct SCHMITT 931 $.45
(N136)

NOUS ETIONS TROIS BERGERETTES see Gay

NOVA, NOVA see Ives

NOVA, NOVA, AVE FIT EX EVA see Spencer,
Williametta

NOVAK, JAN (1921-   )
Testamentum
mix cor,4horn MODERN s.p.   (N137)
Tres Cantiones *CC3U
[Lat] mix cor,acap CZECH s.p. (N138)

NOVELLO, VINCENT (1781-1861)
O Come, All Ye Faithful
mix cor BANKS MUS YS 523 $.25 (N139)

NOVINA BETLEMSKA see Hurnik, Ilja

NOW A NEW SONG see Pethel, James

NOW ABIDETH FAITH, HOPE, LOVE see
Clarke, Henry Leland

NOW BE MY HEART INSPIRED TO SING see
Mendelssohn-Bartholdy, Felix

NOW BEHOLD TO THEE I CRY, O LORD see
  Schutz, Heinrich, Quoniam Ad Te
  Clambo, Domine

NOW FOR A TUNE OF LOFTY PRAISE see
  Work, John [Wesley]

NOW GLAD OF HEART BE EVERY ONE! see
  Drayton, Paul

NOW GLAD OF HEART BY EVERYONE! see
  Kerr, E.

NOW HEAR IT AGAIN! see Burroughs, Bob

NOW HEAR THIS *see Bourgeois, Loys
  (Louis), Old Hundredth; Wesley,
  Charles, Christ The Lord Is Risen
  Today   (N140)

NOW HEAR THIS see Bourgeois, Loys
  (Louis)

NOW HEAR THIS see Wesley, Charles

NOW I KNOW see Graham, Robert Virgil

NOW IN A MANGER SLEEPING *Xmas,carol,
  It
  (Field, Robert) SA,pno (easy) oct
  PRESSER 312-41041 $.35   (N141)

NOW IN THE DAYS OF YOUTH see Darst, W.
  Glenn

NOW IS CHRIST RISEN see Colborn, Arthur
  G.

NOW IS CHRIST RISEN see Johnson, Norman

NOW IS CHRIST RISEN see Rasley, John M.

NOW IS CHRIST RISEN see Younger, John
  B.

NOW ISRAEL MAY SAY
  (Brandon, G.) SAB (easy) WATERLOO
  $.40   (N142)

NOW IT IS CHRISTMAS TIME *folk,Swed
  (Pooler, M.) TBB BRODT 639 $.30
                                (N143)

NOW LET EVERY TONGUE ADORE THEE see
  Bach, Johann Sebastian

NOW LET US PRAISE see Red, Buryl

NOW LET US PRAISE see Red, Buryl

NOW LET US SING see Holst, Gustav

NOW MAKE WE MIRTHE, BOOK 1 *CCU,12-
  14th cent
  (Harrison) unis men cor,acap (med
  easy) OXFORD 48.023 $2.25   (N144)

NOW MAKE WE MIRTHE, BOOK 2 *CCU,Eng,
  14-15th cent
  (Harrison) 2-3pt,acap (med) OXFORD
  48.024 $3.00   (N145)

NOW MAKE WE MIRTHE, BOOK 3 *CCU,15-
  16th cent
  (Harrison) SATB,acap (med) OXFORD
  48.025 $3.00   (N146)

NOW, MY SOUL, THY VOICE UPRAISING see
  Nordin, Dayton W.

NOW PROCLAIM HIS BIRTH IN SONG see
  Preuss, Arthur

NOW SHALL ALL MY INWARD JOYS ABOUND see
  Billings, William

NOW SHALL MY HEAD BE LIFTED HIGH see
  Billings, William

NOW SING, ALL SAINTS! see Peterson,
  John W.

NOW SING NOW *sac/sec,CCU
  (MacKenzie, Robert) cor,opt gtr
  BENSON B0488 $1.95   (N147)

NOW SING PRAISE *CC10UL
  (Huff, Ronn) cor BENSON B0980 $1.50
                                (N148)

NOW SOUNDS see Wyrtzen, Don

NOW THANK WE ALL OUR GOD *anthem
  (Ehret) SATB (easy) oct BROADMAN
  4561-94 $.35   (N149)
  (Rutter) SATB,inst (easy) cor pts
  OXFORD 40.028-40 $.30, ipa, ipr see
  from Two Hymns Of Praise   (N150)

NOW THANK WE ALL OUR GOD see Bach,
  Johann Sebastian

NOW THANK WE ALL OUR GOD see Chambers,
  H.A.

NOW THANK WE ALL OUR GOD see Cruger,
  Johann

NOW THANK WE ALL OUR GOD see Kaufmann,
  Georg Friedrich

NOW THANK WE ALL OUR GOD see Pachelbel,
  Johann

NOW THAT THE DAYLIGHT FILLS THE SKY see
  Thomas, C.

NOW THE DAY IS OVER
  (Baring-Gould, S.) SSA (easy)
  WATERLOO $.30 contains also: Land
  Of Song (Wagner)   (N151)

NOW THE DAY IS OVER see Barnby, Sir
  Joseph

NOW THE DAY IS OVER see Barney

NOW THE HOLLY see Toplis

NOW THE HOLLY BEARS A BERRY *carol
  (Talmadge, A.S.) SSAA BRODT HC 2 $.28
                                (N152)

NOW THE HOLLY BEARS A BERRY see
  Anonymous

NOW THRICE WELCOME CHRISTMAS see Parry,
  W.H.

NOW TO THE KING OF ALL WORLDS see
  Zimmermann, Heinz Werner

NOW WALK WITH GOD see Skillings, Otis

NOW WE SING OF CHRISTMAS *carol,Fr
  (Ermey, William) SATB,acap DEAN
  CF-102 $.45   (N153)
  (Ermey, William) TTBB,acap DEAN
  CF-103 $.45   (N154)

NOWAK, LIONEL (1911-   )
  Psalm Of David, A
  mix cor,acap AM.COMP.AL. $3.30
                                (N155)

NOWAKOWSKY, DAVID (1848-1921)
  Gebete Und Gesange *CC16U,Sab-Eve
  cor,solo,acap/org SAC.MUS.PR.
  S.M.P. 22 $6.00   (N156)

  Hashkivenu
  (Helfman, Max) mix cor oct
  SAC.MUS.PR. 312 $.50   (N157)

  Ne'ilah Service *see Schlussgebet

  Ono Tovo
  mix cor oct SAC.MUS.PR. 303 $.70
                                (N158)

  Schlussgebet
  "Ne'ilah Service" mix cor,cantor&
  solo SAC.MUS.PR. S.M.P. 23 $4.00
                                (N159)

  Un'Saneh Tokef
  mix cor oct SAC.MUS.PR. 304 $1.15
                                (N160)

  V'chach Hoyoh Omeir
  (Helfman, Max) mix cor oct
  SAC.MUS.PR. 313 $.45   (N161)

NOWELL see Davies, Peter Maxwell

NOWELL! HEAP ON MORE WOOD see Cox

NU SAMLAR GUD I SIN HAND see Pergament,
  Moses

NU STIGE JUBLETS TON see Berg, Gottfrid

NU TACKAR GUD ALLT FOLK see Krieger,
  Johann Philipp, Nun Danket Alle
  Gott

NU VILAR HELA JORDEN see Isaac

NUCIUS, JOHANNES (ca. 1556-1620)
  Angelus Ad Pastores Ait *Xmas,mot
  SATTB,acap MOSELER MOR174 s.p.
                                (N162)

NUIT DE NOEL see Carrard

NUMINIS SACRA see Nikiprowetzky

NUN BITTEN WIR DEN HEILIGEN GEIST
  (Wiese, G.) men cor,acap TONOS 5627
  s.p.   (N163)

NUN BITTEN WIR DEN HEILIGEN GEIST see
  Erytraeus, Gottfried

NUN BITTEN WIR DEN HEILIGEN GEIST see
  Pepping, Ernst

NUN BITTEN WIR DEN HEILIGEN GEIST see
  Selle, Thomas

NUN DANKET ALL see Cruger, Johann

NUN DANKET ALL see Seckinger, Konrad

NUN DANKET ALL UND BRINGET EHR see
  Cruger, Johann

NUN DANKET ALLE GOTT see Bach, Johann
  Sebastian

NUN DANKET ALLE GOTT see Cruger, Johann

NUN DANKET ALLE GOTT see Hindermann,
  Walter Felix

NUN DANKET ALLE GOTT see Krieger,
  Johann Philipp

NUN DANKET ALLE GOTT see Pachelbel,
  Johann

NUN DANKET ALLE GOTT see Poser, Hans

NUN DANKET ALLE GOTT see Wagner

NUN DANKET ALLE GOTT see Werner, Fritz

NUN DANKET ALLE GOTT see Zipp,
  Friedrich

NUN DANKET GOTT, ERHEBT UND PREISET see
  Studer, Hans

NUN DEN TAG DES TAGS VERDROSS see
  Taubert, Karl Heinz

NUN FREUT EUCH IN GOTT, IHR FROMMEN see
  Le Jeune, Claude

NUN FREUT EUCH, LIEBE CHRISTENG'MEIN
  see Eccard, Johannes

NUN FREUT EUCH, LIEBEN CHRISTEN GMEIN
  see Brandt, Jobst vom

NUN FREUT EUCH, LIEBEN CHRISTENG'MEIN
  see Ducis, Benedictus

NUN HOSIANNA, DAVIDS SOHN see Staden,
  Johann

NUN JAUCHZET, ALL IHR FROMMEN see
  Gesius, Bartholomaus

NUN JAUCHZET DEM HERREN, ALLE WELT see
  Schmider, Karl

NUN JAUCHZT DEM HERREN, ALLE WELT see
  Hessenberg, Kurt

NUN JAUCHZT DEM HERREN, ALLE WELT see
  Zipp, Friedrich

NUN KOMM, DEN HEIDEN HEILAND see
  Wieser, Lukas

NUN KOMM, DER HEIDEN HEILAND see
  Luetkeman, Paul

NUN KOMM, DER HEIDEN HEILAND see
  Raselius, Andreas

NUN KOMM, DER HEIDEN HEILAND see
  Schutz, Heinrich

NUN LASST UNS DEN LEIB BEGRABEN see
  Backer, Hans

NUN LASST UNS DEN LEIB BEGRABEN see
  Borris, Siegfried

NUN LASST UNS GEHN UND TRETEN see
  Oertzen, Rudolf von

NUN LASST UNS GOTT see Manicke,
  Dietrich

NUN LASST UNS GOTT DEM HERREN see Koch,
  Johannes H.E.

NUN LASST UNS MIT DER ENGEL SCHAR see
  Stobaeus, Johann

NUN LOB DEN HERRN, O SEELE MEIN see
  Schein, Johann Hermann

NUN LOB, MEIN SEEL, DEN HERREN see
  Hammerschmidt, Andreas

NUN LOB, MEIN SEEL, DEN HERREN see
  Praetorius, Michael

NUN LOB, MEIN SEEL, DEN HERREN see
  Walliser, Christoph Thomas

NUN PREISET ALL GOTTES BARMHERZIGKEIT
  see Lowenstern, Matthaus Appelles
  von

NUN PREISET ALLE see Manicke, Dietrich

NUN RUHEN ALLE WALDER see Bach, Johann
  Sebastian

NUN SAGET DANK UND LOBT DEN HERREN see
  Blank, August

NUN SAGET DANK UND LOBT DEN HERREN see
  Eglin, Arthur

NUN SCHLAGT DIE STUNDE MITTERNACHT see
  Grimm, Jurgen

NUN SEI UNS WILLKOMMEN see Burthel,
  Jakob

NUN SICH DER TAG GEENDET HAT see
    Gadsch, Herbert

NUN SICH DER TAG GEENDET HAT see
    Pepping, Ernst

NUN SINGET UND SEID FROH see Oertzen,
    Rudolf von

NUN SINGT DEM HERRN EIN NEUES LIED see
    Kronberg, G.

NUNC ANGELORUM see Praetorius, Michael

NUNC DIMITTIS see Bell, Robert H.

NUNC DIMITTIS see Bevan, Gwilym

NUNC DIMITTIS see Bryant, Giles

NUNC DIMITTIS see Gabrieli, Giovanni

NUNC DIMITTIS see Noble, Thomas Tertius

NUNC DIMITTIS see Sluss, Robert

NUNC DIMITTIS see Stout, Alan

NUNC DIMITTIS see Wyton, Alec

NUNC DIMITTIS, THE see Leitz, Darwin

NUNC, SANCTI, NOBIS, SPIRITUS see
    Becker, John J.

NUSBAUM, CYRUS S.
    His Way With Thee
    (Krogstad, Bob) SATB oct GOSPEL
                                        (N164)

NUSSBAUMER, JOSEPH
    Acht Pange Lingua Und Tantum Ergo
    *Op.17, CC8U
    [Lat] mix cor,acap sc,cor pts BOHM
    s.p.   (N165)

NUT TREE, THE see Pitcher

NYHUS, ROLF
    Jesus Er Mitt Hap, Min Trost
    mix cor MUSIKK contains also: O
        Herre Krist, Ga Ikke Bort; O
        Herre Krist, Dig Til Oss Vend;
        Se, Solens Skjonne Lys Og Prakt
                                        (N166)
    O Herre Krist, Dig Til Oss Vend
        see Nyhus, Rolf, Jesus Er Mitt Hap,
        Min Trost

    O Herre Krist, Ga Ikke Bort
        see Nyhus, Rolf, Jesus Er Mitt Hap,
        Min Trost

    Se, Solens Skjonne Lys Og Prakt
        see Nyhus, Rolf, Jesus Er Mitt Hap,
        Min Trost

NYSTEDT, KNUT (1915-   )
    Audi (from Lucis Creator Optime)
    SATB AMP A-713 $.40   (N167)

    Fred Etterlater Jeg Dere
    "I Leave Ye Peace" mix cor NORSK
    NMO 8581 s.p.   (N168)

    I Leave Ye Peace *see Fred
        Etterlater Jeg Dere

    I Will Praise Thee, God *see Jeg Vil
        Prise Deg, Gud

    If You Receive My Words
    SSAATTBB AUGSBURG 11-9214 $.60
                                        (N169)
    Jeg Vil Prise Deg, Gud
    "I Will Praise Thee, God" mix cor
    NORSK NO 8582 s.p.   (N170)

    Kyrie (from Thanksgiving Mass, A)
        Kyrie
    SATB WALTON 2972 $.40   (N171)

    Psalm 77
    SATB WALTON 2923 $.50   (N172)

    Sa Sier Gud
    "Thus Sayeth God" mix cor NORSK
    NMO 8580 s.p.   (N173)

    Song Of Praise *anthem
    SSAATB,tamb, claves AUGSBURG
    11-0656 $.35   (N174)

    Thus Sayeth God *see Sa Sier Gud

NYSTROEM, GOSTA (1890-1966)
    Herre, Vem Far Bo I Din Hydda? (Psalm
        15)
    4pt mix cor ERIKS 28 s.p.   (N175)

    Huru Skon Och Huru Ljuv
    4pt mix cor ERIKS 44 s.p.   (N176)

    Psalm 15 *see Herre, Vem Far Bo I
        Din Hydda?

NYSTROEM, GOSTA (cont'd.)

    Sag Mig Du
    4pt mix cor ERIKS 43 s.p.   (N177)

O

O ABSALOM
    (Sweetman, P.W.) SAB (easy) WATERLOO
    $.30   (O1)

O ALTITUDO see Stout, Alan

O BE GLAD, MY SOUL, BE CHEERFUL see
    Bach, Johann Sebastian

O BE JOYFUL see Arnatt, Ronald,
    Jubilate

O BE JOYFUL IN THE LORD see Bancroft,
    H. Hugh

O BE JOYFUL IN THE LORD see Hand, Colin

O BE JOYFUL IN THE LORD see Muro, D.

O BE JOYFUL IN THE LORD see Severin,
    Leone

O BE JOYFUL IN THE LORD see Thiman,
    Eric Harding

O BE JOYFUL IN THE LORD see Wienand,
    Karl, Jubilate Deo

O BEATA INCENDIUM see Schattenberg,
    Thomas

O BETHLEHEM, HOW STILL THE NIGHT see
    Herring, W.B.

O BLESS THE LORD, MY SOUL! see
    Montgomery

O BLESSED ARE THE DEAD see Mendelssohn-
    Bartholdy, Felix, Beata Mortui

O BLESSED CHILD
    see Six Songs

O BLESSED HOLY SPIRIT see Fettke, Tom

O BLESSED HOLY TRINITY see Wolff, S.
    Drummond

O BONE JESU see Allmendinger, Carl

O BONE JESU see Berghorn, Alfred

O BONE JESU see Brahms, Johannes

O BONE JESU see Hunecke, Wilhelm

O BONE JESU see Palestrina, Giovanni

O BREAD OF LIFE FROM HEAVEN see
    Bourgeois, Loys (Louis)

O BREATH OF LIFE see Franck, J.

O BROTHER MAN see Lee, John

O BROTHER MAN see Robertson, Leroy

O BROTHER MAN see Wetzler, Robert

O CHRIST REDEEMER see Mills, Charles

O CHRIST! THOU ART JOY ALONE see Lloyd,
    Henry

O CHRIST, WHO ART THE LIGHT AND DAY see
    Lenel, Ludwig

O CHRIST WHO HOLDS THE OPEN GATE see
    Dawson, Anthony

O CHRIST, WHY SHOULD A MANGER BE? see
    Denton, James

O CHRISTE, WAHRHEIT UND LEBEN see
    Studer, Hans

O CHRISTENHEIT, SEI HOCHERFREUT see
    Micheelsen, Hans-Friedrich

O CHURCH OF GOD, REACH UP, REACH OUT!
    see Butler, Eugene

O CLAP YOUR HANDS see Cousins, M.
    Thomas

O CLAP YOUR HANDS see Greene, Maurice

O CLAP YOUR HANDS see Rutter

O CLAP YOUR HANDS see Van Iderstine,
    A.P.

O CLAP YOUR HANDS see Young

O COME ALL YE FAITHFUL *Adv/Xmas,
    anthem
    see Six Carols For SAB And Piano
    (Kunz, Jack) TTBB RICHMOND MA-6 $.30

(Linn) SATB&jr cor&cong,brass oct
LILLENAS AN-3870 $.40 (O2)
(Red) SATB&unis oct BROADMAN 4538-00
$.30 (O3)
(O4)

O COME, ALL YE FAITHFUL see Novello,
Vincent

O COME, ALL YE FAITHFUL see Wade

O COME, ALL YE FAITHFUL see Wolff, S.
Drummond

O COME ALL YE PEOPLE see Burroughs

O COME AND MOURN WITH ME AWHILE see
Carter, John

O COME, EMMANUEL
(Parker, Alice) SATB,pno/org/orch
(easy/med) cor pts FISCHER,C
CM 7841 $.35 see also Seven
Christmas Carols (O5)

O COME, LET US SING see Zettervall,
Howard

O COME, LET US SING *Thanks,anthem
(Engel, Thomas) SATB oct SINGSPIR
ZJP-7258 $.30 (O6)

O COME, LET US SING see Carter

O COME, LET US SING see Dunham, Arthur

O COME, LET US SING see Root

O COME, LET US SING UNTO THE LORD see
Gibbons, Orlando, Venite, Exultemus

O COME, LET US SING UNTO THE LORD see
Lutkin, Peter Christian

O COME LET US SING *CCU,anthem
(Bissell, K.W.) jr cor WATERLOO $1.75
(O7)

O COME, LET US WORSHIP see Black,
Charles

O COME, MODERN MAN see McClellan,
Albert

O COME, O COME, EMMANUEL *Adv/Xmas,
anthem
see Six Christmas Hymns
(Hilty) 1-2pt (easy) OXFORD 94.003
$.25 (O8)
(Johnson, Norman) SATB oct SINGSPIR
ZJP-3003 $.25 (O9)
(Johnson, Norman) SATB oct SINGSPIR
ZJP-3003 $.25 (O10)

O COME, O COME EMMANUEL see DeMone,
Richard

O COME, O COME, IMMANUEL *Adv
see Twelve Christmas Carols: Set 1
(Rutter) SATB,acap OXFORD 84.194 $.45
(O11)

O COME TO MY HEART see Liljestrand,
Paul

O COME YE SERVANTS OF THE LORD see Tye,
Christopher

O COULD I SPEAK see Mason, Lowell

O CRUX AVE see Doebler, Curt

O CRUX, AVE see Hunecke, Wilhelm

O CRUX AVE see Lassus, Roland de
(Orlandus)

O CRUX AVE see Victoria, Tomas Luis de

O CRUX, BENEDICTA see Dietrich, J.H.

O CRUX. O JESU CHRIST see Palestrina,
Giovanni

O DASS DOCH BALD DEIN FEUER BRENNTE see
Weiss, Ewald

O DASS ICH TAUSEND ZUNGEN HATTE see
Peter, Johann Friedrich

O DAY FULL OF GRACE see Carlson, Gordon

O DAY OF REST AND GLADNESS *anthem
(DeCou, Harold) SATB oct SINGSPIR
ZJP-7261 $.30 (O12)

O DEAREST, JESU see Sowerby, Leo

O DEAREST LORD see Roff, Joseph

O DEUS, EGO AMO TE see Rorem, Ned

O DIVINE REDEEMER see Gounod, Charles
Francois

O DOMINE JESU CHRISTE see Victoria,
Tomas Luis de

O DU FROHLICHE see Deutschmann, Gerhard

O DU FROHLICHE WEIHNACHTSZEIT see
Pfluger, Hans Georg

O DU SALIGA see Berg, Gottfrid

O ENGEL REIN see Wassmer, Berthold

O ERD, SCHLAG AUS see Schweizer, Rolf

O ESCA VIATORUM see Schmid, Alfons

O FATHER ON OUR FESTAL DAY see Clarke,
F.R.C.

O FOR A CLOSER WALK WITH GOD see Goode,
George

O FOR A THOUSAND TONGUES see Glaser,
Carl G.

O FOR A THOUSAND TONGUES see Ward,
Samuel A.

O FRAU OB ALLER FRAUEN SCHAR see Lang,
Hans

O FREUDE UBER FREUDE see Haus, Karl

O FREUDENREICHER TAG
see Alte Frankische Weihnachtslieder

O FREUDENREICHER TAG see Lang, Hans

O FROHER TAG! see Trapp, Willy

O GIVE ME A SOAPBOX see Wyrtzen, Don

O GIVE THANKS see Butler, Eugene

O GIVE THANKS see Landgrave, Phillip

O GIVE THANKS! see Ratzlaff, Paul

O GIVE THANKS see Willis, Richard
Storrs

O GIVE THANKS TO THE LORD see Track,
Gerhard

O GIVE THANKS UNTO THE LORD see Dawson,
Anthony

O GIVE THANKS UNTO THE LORD see
Frackenpohl, Arthur

O GIVE THANKS UNTO THE LORD see Smith

O GIVE THANKS UNTO THE LORD see Smith,
Lani

O GLADSOME LIGHT *Easter
(MacNutt, Walter) SATB (med easy)
WATERLOO $.30 (O13)

O GLADSOME LIGHT see Bourgeois, Loys
(Louis)

O GLADSOME LIGHT see MacNutt, Walter

O GLAUBIG HERZ, GEBENDEI see Linke,
Norbert

O GLORIOSA DOMINUM see Carraz

O GLORIOSA DOMINUM see Palestrina,
Giovanni

O GLORIOSA VIRGINUM see Kromolicki,
Joseph

O GLORIOUS LOVE see Peterson, John W.

O GLORIOUS RESURRECTION DAY! see
Peterson, John W.

O GLORIOUS VIRGIN see Mills, Charles

O GOD, ACCEPT MY HEART see Bridges

O GOD, ALMIGHTY FATHER *Reces
(Roff, Joseph) SATB LITURGICAL $.50
see also Twelve Hymns (O14)

O GOD, LET PEOPLE PRAISE THEE *Ger
(Coggin, Elwood) 2pt treb cor,pno/org
(easy) PRESSER 312-41033 $.35 (O15)

O GOD, MY HEART IS FIXED see Van Hulse,
Camil

O GOD OF BETHEL see Dowland, John

O GOD OF EARTH AND ALTAR see Davies,
I.R.

O GOD OF LIFE see Palestrina, Giovanni,
Panis Angelicus

O GOD OF LIGHT see Means, Claude

O GOD OF LOVE AND KINDNESS see Wild,
Eric

O GOD OF LOVE, O KING OF PEACE see Vick

O GOD OF TRUTH see Healey, Derek

O GOD, OUR HELP IN AGES PAST see Croft,
William

O GOD, OUR HELP IN AGES PAST see Young

O GOD, OUR LORD, THY HOLY WORD see
Canning, Thomas

O GOD THE KING OF GLORY see Gibbons,
Orlando

O GOD, THE KING OF GLORY see Powell,
Robert J.

O GOD, THOU HAST THE DAWN OF LIFE see
Denton, James

O GOD UNSEEN see Clapp, Donald

O GOD, WE THANK THEE see Barnes, Edward
Shippen

O GOD, WHOSE BLESSED SON see Thomas, C.

O GOD WHOSE MIGHTY WISDOM see Brandon,
George

O GOTT, DU UNSER HERR, WIE GROSS IST
HIER AUF ERDEN DEINE EHR! see Le
Jeune, Claude, Grand Dieu, Notre
Seigneur, Combien Ici Ton Nom A
Grand Honeur

O GREAT IS THE DEPTH see Mendelssohn-
Bartholdy, Felix

O GUD, SOM ALLT MED VISHET STYR see
Soderholm, Valdemar

O GUD SUM HORER ALLAS ROST see Berg,
Gottfrid

O, GUDS LAMM see Dahlgren, Hans-Erik

O HAD I BEEN THERE AND SHARED, LORD see
Gregor, [Christian Friedrich]

O HAIL, MARY see Fux, Johann Joseph,
Ave Maria

O HAIL! SACRED CROSS see Victoria,
Tomas Luis de, O Crux Ave

O HALLELUJAH *anthem
(Riddle) SATB FINE ARTS CM 1043 $.35
(O16)

O HAPPY DAY see Butler, A.L.

O HAPPY DAY see Rimbault, Edward
Francis

O HARKEN UNTO GOD see Reece, T.R.

O HAUPT VOLL BLUT UND WUNDEN see
Pepping, Ernst

O HAUPT VOLL BLUT UND WUNDEN see
Pfluger, Hans Georg

O HEAVENLY BEAUTY see Younger, John B.

O HEAVENLY FATHER see Matthews, Thomas

O HEILAND REISS DIE HIMMEL AUF *Adv/
Xmas
(Bauernfeind, Hans) wom cor,acap
(contains also: Und Unser Lieben
Frauen) oct DOBLINGER s.p. see also
In Dulci Jubilo (O17)

O HEILAND, REISS DIE HIMMEL AUF see
Brahms, Johannes

O HEILAND, REISS DIE HIMMEL AUF see
Brahms, Johannes, O Heiland, Reiss
Die Himmel Auf

O HEILAND, REISS DIE HIMMEL AUF see
Heer, Joh De

O HEILAND, REISS DIE HIMMEL AUF see
Lang, Hans

O HEILAND, REISS DIE HIMMEL AUF see
Lemacher, Heinrich

O HEILAND, REISS DIE HIMMEL AUF see
Mullich, Hermann

O HEILAND, REISS DIE HIMMEL AUF see
Oertzen, Rudolf von

O HEILAND, REISS DIE HIMMEL AUF see
Pfluger, Hans Georg

O HEILAND REISS DIE HIMMEL AUF see
Rein, Walter

O HEILAND, REISS DIE HIMMEL AUF see
Schweizer, Rolf

O HEILAND REISS DIE HIMMEL AUF see
Zipp, Friedrich

O HEILIG GODSLAM see De Koning

O HEILIGE DREIFALTIGKEIT see Des Prez,
Josquin

O HEILIGER GEIST, KEHR BEI UNS SEIN see
Oertzen, Rudolf von

O HEILIGER GEIST, O HEILIGER GOTT see
Oertzen, Rudolf von

O HELP, JESUS, SON OF GOD see Schutz,
Heinrich

O HELP US, LORD see Dowland, John

O HERR JESU CHRISTE see Gumpelzhaimer,
Adam

O HERR, MACHE MICH ZUM WERKZEUG see
Hessenberg, Kurt

O HERR, MEIN GOTT, DEIN ZORN HAT SICH
GEWENDET see Le Jeune, Claude

O HERR, NIMM VON MIR see Gumpelzhaimer,
Adam

O HERRE GOTT see Kaminski, Heinrich

O HERRE GOTT IM HIMMELREICH see Staden,
Johann

O HERRE KRIST, DIG TIL OSS VEND see
Nyhus, Rolf

O HERRE KRIST, GA IKKE BORT see Nyhus,
Rolf

O HOCHSTER, DEINE GUTIGKEIT see
Goudimel, Claude

O HOLY CHILD OF LOVE see Corina, John

O HOLY CITY SEEN OF JOHN *anthem
(Ralston) unis oct LILLENAS AN-6027
$.30   (O18)

O HOLY GHOST IN KINDLY FLAME see Mills,
Charles

O HOLY NIGHT see Adam, Adolphe-Charles,
Cantique De Noel

O HOLY NIGHT see Christiansen, P.

O HOLY SAVIOUR *anthem
(Wyrtzen, Don) SATB oct SINGSPIR
ZJP-7295 $.30   (O19)

O HOLY SPIRIT see Bissell, Keith W.

O HOLY SPIRIT see White, Calvin

O HOW AMIABLE see Dawson, Anthony

O HOW AMIABLE see Mana-Zucca, Mme.

O HOW HAPPY ARE THEY see Wesley

O HOW I LOVE JESUS *anthem
(Rasley, J.M.) SSATB oct SINGSPIR
ZJP-8216 $.35   (O20)

O HOW SHALL I RECEIVE THEE *Adv/Palm,
anthem
(Ehret, Walter) SATB,org (easy) GIA
G1888 $.40   (O21)

O; HUR SALLA AR NI EJ, NI FROMMA see
Reger, Max

O JERUSALEM THAT BRINGEST GOOD TIDINGS
see Protheroe, Daniel

O JESU, BLESSED LORD
(France, Wm.) SATB (med easy)
WATERLOO $.30   (O22)

O JESU CHRISTE see Berchem, Jacobus de

O JESU CHRISTE, WAHRES LICHT see
Neubert, Gottfried

O JESU KRIST, DIG TILL OSS VAND see
Vulpius, Melchior

O JESU MEEK see Ravenscroft, Thomas

O JESU (O MARIA) TE INVOCAMUS see
Haydn, (Franz) Joseph

O JESU SUSS, WER DEIN GEDENKT see
Schutz, Heinrich

O JESULEIN, O GOTTESSOHN
see Alte Frankische Weihnachtslieder

O JESULEIN, O GOTTESSOHN see Backer,
Hans

O JESULEIN SUSS see Kaminski, Heinrich

O JESULEIN ZART see Weber, Bernhard

O JESULEIN ZART see Zoll, Paul

O JESUS, CRUCIFIED FOR MAN see Pasquet,
Jean

O JESUS, DU SOM VAGEN AR see Johansen,
Sven-Erik

O JESUS, I HAVE PROMISED see Lovelace,
Austin C.

O JESUS, I HAVE PROMISED see Miles,
Russell Hancock

O JESUS, I HAVE PROMISED see Mueller

O JESUS MY SAVIOUR see Bass, Claude L.

O JESUS, MY SHEPHERD see Gregor,
[Christian Friedrich]

O JESUS, NOW HERE WITH US see Andrews,
C.T.

O JESUS, THOU SON OF GOD see Schutz,
Heinrich

O JESUS, WE ADORE THEE *Commun
(Roff, Joseph) SATB LITURGICAL $.50
see also Twelve Hymns   (O23)

O JOYEUX NOEL see Delaye

O JOYFUL MORN see Wagner, Richard

O JOYOUS ASSEMBLED ONES see Victoria,
Tomas Luis de, O Sacrum Convivium

O KIND, O WAHRER GOTTESSOHN see Weber,
Bernhard

O KING OF KINGS see Watson, Ruth

O KING OF MIGHT AND SPLENDOR *Offer
(Roff, Joseph) SATB LITURGICAL $.50
see also Twelve Hymns   (O24)

O KING OF MIGHT AND SPLENDOR see Lee,
J.

O KINGLY LOVE see Schalk, Carl

O KOMM, O KOMM, EMANUEL see Rothschuh,
Franz

O KONIG ALLER EHREN see Bender, Jan

O KONIG JESU CHRISTE see Wenzel,
Eberhard

O LAMB OF GOD *Easter
(Lapp, Horace) SATB (med easy)
WATERLOO $.40   (O25)

O LAMB OF GOD see Lapp, Horace

O LAMB OF GOD see Lockwood, Normand

O LAMM GOTTES see Eccard, Johannes

O LAMM GOTTES, UNSCHULDIG see
Kuehnhausen, Johann Georg

O LAMM GOTTES, UNSCHULDIG see Lohr, Ina

O LAMM GOTTES, UNSCHULDIG see
Planyavsky, Peter

O LAT OSS GUDS KARLEK BEVISA see
Johansen, Sven-Erik

O LEAVE YOUR SHEEP *Xmas,folk
(Lamb, Gordon H.) SATB STANDARD
C621MX3 $.50   (O26)

O LEIB, GEBROCHEN MIR ZU GUT see
Diener, Theodor

O LIEBER HERRE GOTT, WECKE UNS AUF see
Schulz, H.

O LIEBER HERRE GOTT, WECKE UNS AUF see
Schutz, Heinrich

O LITTLE LAMB see Goldsworthy, William
Arthur

O LITTLE TOWN OF BETHLEHEM
see Christmas Choir Melodies
see Four Christmas Carols

O LITTLE TOWN OF BETHLEHEM see Davies,
Henry Walford

O LITTLE TOWN OF BETHLEHEM see Murray,
Margaret

O LITTLE TOWN OF BETHLEHEM see Redner,
Lewis [Henry]

O LOOK TO GOLGOTHA see Mason, Lowell

O LORD see Fettke, Tom

O LORD AND MASTER OF US ALL see
Southbridge, James

O LORD, ATTEND UNTO MY CRY see
Sweelinck, Jan Pieterszoon

O LORD, BOW DOWN THINE EAR see
Palestrina, Giovanni

O LORD, CONSIDER MY DISTRESS see
Dowland, John, In Prayer Together

O LORD FROM WHOM ALL GOOD THINGS DO
COME see Bales, [Richard]

O LORD, GRANT US THY MERCY see Cannon

O LORD, HOW DO MY WOES INCREASE see
Coperario, Giovanni

O LORD, HOW EXCELLENT IS THY NAME see
Staton

O LORD, HOW EXCELLENT THY NAME see
Keese, K.

O LORD, HOW NUMEROUS ARE MY FOES see
Jeppesen, Knud

O LORD HOW SWEET IT IS
(Plant) SATB (med easy) WATERLOO $.30
(O27)

O LORD, I SING WITH LIPS AND HEART see
Cruger, Johann

O LORD, I WILL PRAISE THEE see Roff,
Joseph

O LORD, INCREASE MY FAITH see Gibbons,
Orlando

O LORD JESUS CHRIST, OUR MASTER see
Cererols, Joan

O LORD, LOOK DOWN FROM HEAVEN, BEHOLD
see Lenel, Ludwig

O LORD MOST HIGH, WITH ALL MY HEART see
Track, Gerhard

O LORD MOST HOLY see Franck, Cesar

O LORD MY BABE FORETOLD see MacLennan,
Robert

O LORD, MY INMOST HEART AND THOUGHT see
Peninger

O LORD OF HEAVEN see Burroughs

O LORD OF HEAVEN see Lassus, Roland de
(Orlandus)

O LORD OF LIFE see Cabena, Barrie

O LORD OF WHOM I DO DEPEND see Amner,
John

O LORD, OF WHOM I DO DEPEND see
Dowland, John, O God Of Bethel

O LORD, OUR GOD see Weerbecke, Gaspar
van

O LORD, OUR HEAVENLY KING see Baini,
Giuseppe

O LORD, SEND OUT THY LIGHT see Pasquet,
Jean

O LORD SUPPORT ME see France, William
E.

O LORD, SUPPORT US see Gore, Richard T.

O LORD, THE WORLD'S SAVIOUR see Mundy,
William

O LORD, THOU HAST FORMED MY EVERY PART
see Bach, Johann Sebastian

O LORD, THOU HAST SEARCHED ME see
Butler, Eugene

O LORD THOU HAST SEARCHED ME AND KNOWN
ME see Archer, Violet

O LORD THY WORD ENDURETH see Tye,
Christopher

O LORD, TURN NOT AWAY see Dowland, John

O LORD, UPON THEE DO I CALL see Hooper,
Edmund

O LORD WE BESEECH THEE see Fox, George

O LORD WHO SHALL ABIDE see Park, Chai
Hoon

O LOVE DIVINE see Protheroe, Daniel

O LOVE, HOW DEEP see Johnson, David N.

O LOVE OF GOD see Harris, D.S.

O LOVE OF GOD MOST FULL see Clute

O LOVE OF GOD MOST FULL see Lynes

O LOVE THAT CASTS OUT FEAR see Harris

O LOVE THAT WILT NOT LET ME GO see
   Caldwell, Mary [Elizabeth]

O LOVE THAT WILT NOT LET ME GO see
   Peace, Albert Lister

O LOVING JESUS see Andrews, C.T.

O LUX BEATA TRINITAS see Walter
   (Walther), Johann

O MAGNUM MYSTERIUM see Davies, Peter
   Maxwell

O MAGNUM MYSTERIUM see Page, Robert E.

O MAGNUM MYSTERIUM see Scarlatti,
   Alessandro

O MAKE A JOYFUL NOISE TO GOD see Roesch

O MAN, THY SIN IS GREAT see Lammetun,
   John, O Menneske, Din Synd Er Stor

O MARIA, SEI GEGRUSST see Planyavsky,
   Peter

O MARY DON'T YOU WEEP
   (Wild, Eric) SATB (med easy) WATERLOO
   $.60   (O28)

O MARY, WHERE IS YOUR BABY? *Xmas,spir
   see Christmas Spiritual Collection
   (Walker) 1-2pt, Orff inst (easy) oct
   CONCORDIA 98-2142 $.35   (O29)

O MASTER, LET ME WALK WITH THEE see
   Brandon, George

O MASTER, LET ME WALK WITH THEE see
   Newbury, Kent A.

O MASTER OF THE LOVING HEART *anthem
   (Burroughs, Bob) 2pt oct BROADMAN
   4558-67 $.30   (O30)

O MEN FROM THE FIELDS see Deale

O MEN OF GOD, ARISE *anthem/medley
   (Schubert) SATB oct LILLENAS AN-2387
   $.35   (O31)

O MENNESKE, DIN SYND ER STOR see
   Lammetun, John

O MENSCH, BEWEIN DEIN SUNDE GROSS see
   Brandt, Jobst vom

O MENSCH, BEWEIN DEIN SUNDE GROSS see
   Driessler, Johannes

O MENSCH, BEWEIN DEIN SUNDE GROSS see
   Oertzen, Rudolf von

O MENSCH BEWEIN DEIN SUNDE GROSS see
   Pepping, Ernst

O MIGHTY GOD, WHEN I BEHOLD THE WONDER
   *anthem
   (DeCou, Harold) SATB oct SINGSPIR
   ZJP-7293 $.30   (O32)

O MY DEAR HEART see Vulpius, Melchior

O MY SOUL, BLESS GOD THE FATHER see
   Handel, George Frideric

O NADENS SOL OG SETE see Schein, Johann
   Hermann

O NIMM DICH AN DER ARMEN SEELE see
   Kutzer, Ernst

O PERFECT LIFE OF LOVE see Powell, R.

O PERFECT LIFE OF LOVE see Wetzler,
   Robert

O PERFECT LOVE see Andrews, C.T.

O PRAISE GOD IN HIS SANCTUARY see
   Matthews, Thomas

O PRAISE GOD (UNIVERSAL PRAISE) see
   Billings, William

O PRAISE THE LORD see Child

O PRAISE THE LORD see Mason, Lowell

O PRAISE THE LORD see Newbury, Kent A.

O PRAISE THE LORD! see Owens

O PRAISE THE LORD see Parks

O PRAISE THE LORD OF HEAVEN see
   Billings, William

O PRAISE THE LORD OF HEAVEN see Pratt,
   G.

O PRAISE THE LORD WHO MADE ALL BEAUTY
   see Hopson, Hal H.

O PRAISE THE LORD WITH ONE ACCORD see
   Couperin, Francois

O PRAISE THE LORD WITH ONE CONSENT see
   Handel, George Frideric

O PRAISE THE LORD, YE CHILDREN see
   Powell, Robert J.

O PRAISE YE THE LORD see Wood

O QUAM SUAVIS see Gabrieli, Giovanni

O QUAM SUAVIS EST see Lemacher,
   Heinrich

O QUANTA IN COELIS LAETITIA EXUBERAT
   see Buchner, Philipp Friedrich

O REGEM COELI see Victoria, Tomas Luis
   de

O REST IN THE LORD see Mendelssohn-
   Bartholdy, Felix

O REX GLORIAE see Marenzio, Luca

O SACRED HEAD, NOW WOUNDED see Handel,
   George Frideric

O SACRED HEAD, NOW WOUNDED see Hassler,
   Hans Leo

O SACRED HEAD, NOW WOUNDED see Kellner,
   Johann Peter

O SACRUM CONUIVIUM see Lallouette, J.F.

O SACRUM CONVIVIUM see Aichinger,
   Gregor

O SACRUM CONVIVIUM see Bernabei,
   Giuseppe Antonio

O SACRUM CONVIVIUM see Croce, Giovanni

O SACRUM CONVIVIUM see Frey, Carl

O SACRUM CONVIVIUM see Krieger, Fritz

O SACRUM CONVIVIUM see Lemacher,
   Heinrich

O SACRUM CONVIVIUM see Schwarz-
   Schilling, Reinhard

O SACRUM CONVIVIUM see Tallis, Thomas

O SACRUM CONVIVIUM see Victoria, Tomas
   Luis de

O SALUTARIS see Anerio, Felice

O SALUTARIS see Montillet

O SALUTARIS HOSTIA see Dietrich, J.H.

O SALUTARIS HOSTIA see Doebler, Curt

O SALUTARIS HOSTIA see Gallus, Jacobus

O SALUTARIS HOSTIA see Herrmann, Hugo

O SALUTARIS HOSTIA see Ketterer, Ernst

O SALUTARIS HOSTIA see Liszt, Franz

O SALUTARIS HOSTIA see Mathias, William

O SALUTARIS HOSTIA see Schmid, Alfons

O SALUTARIS HOSTIA see Schumann, Robert
   (Alexander)

O SALUTARIS HOSTIA see Weber, Norbert

O SANCTISSIMA
   (Beethoven; Boyd) SAB SCHIRM.G
   LG51761 $.35   (O33)

O SANCTISSIMA see Hoffmann, Ernst
   Theodor Amadeus

O SAVIOR, OPEN HEAVEN WIDE see Brahms,
   Johannes, O Heiland, Reiss Die
   Himmel Auf

O SAVIOUR OF THE WORLD see Goss, John

O SCHLAFE LIEBLICHER JESU see
   Schroeder, Hermann

O SCHONSTE MORGENROT see Kuntz, Michael

O SEED OF GOD IN HUMANKIND see Weigl,
   Vally

O SEHT, WIE SCHON UND LIEBLICH IST'S
   see Goudimel, Claude

O SHEPHERD OF ISRAEL see Gregor,
   [Christian Friedrich]

O SHEPHERDS GO QUICKLY see Kirk, Theron
   W.

O SING A NEW SONG TO THE LORD see
   Clarke, F.R.C.

O SING A SONG OF BETHLEHEM see
   Burroughs

O SING FOR JOY see Caldwell

O SING UNTO THE LORD see Archer, Violet

O SING UNTO THE LORD see Handel, George
   Frideric

O SING UNTO THE LORD see Leitz, Darwin

O SING UNTO THE LORD see Pratt, G.

O SING UNTO THE LORD see Purcell, Henry

O SING UNTO THE LORD see Smith

O SING UNTO THE LORD see Wirick, E.

O SING UNTO THE LORD see Zimmermann,
   Heinz Werner

O SING UNTO THE LORD A NEW SONG see
   Koooo, K.

O SING UNTO THE LORD A NEW SONG see
   Pool, K.

O SINNER MAN *spir
   (Suerte) SS&camb&opt Bar,S solo,acap
   CAMBIATA S17430 $.40   (O34)

O SLEEP, THOU BABE SO HOLY see Carlton

O SONS AND DAUGHTERS see Pasquet, Jean

O SPIRIT OF JESUS see Sutter

O STAR OF BETHLEHEM see Willis, Kathe

O SUSSER JESU CHRIST, WER AN DICH RECHT
   GEDENKET see Schutz, Heinrich

O SWEET JESU see Binkerd, Gordon

O THAT I HAD A THOUSAND VOICES see
   Wood, Dale

O THAT I WERE AN ANGEL see Kirkham,
   Gayla

O THAT MY HEAD WERE WATER see Clark

O THE DEEP, DEEP LOVE OF JESUS see
   Hughes

O THOU BELOVED GOD see Schulz, H., O
   Lieber Herre Gott, Wecke Uns Auf

O THOU BY WHOM WE COME TO GOD see
   Peninger, David

O THOU GREAT FRIEND see Brandon

O THOU HEAVEN-SENT CHILD *Xmas,carol,
   It
   (Ehret, Walter) SA,pno (very easy)
   ELKAN-V 362-03189 $.40   (O35)
   (Ehret, Walter) SSA,pno (very easy)
   ELKAN-V 362-03190 $.40   (O36)

O THOU IN WHOSE PRESENCE *anthem
   (Ehret, Walter) SATB WORD   (O37)
   (Rasley, John M.) SATB oct SINGSPIR
   ZJP-7316 $.30   (O38)
   (Riddle) SATB FINE ARTS CM 1037 $.30
                                           (O39)

O THOU IN WHOSE PRESENCE see Boozer,
   Pat

O THOU IN WHOSE PRESENCE see Williams

O THOU STAR see Reynolds, William
   Jensen

O THOU TO WHOSE ALL-SEARCHING SIGHT see
   Butler

O THOU WHO ART ALL-WISE see D'Ana,
   Franceso

O THOU WHO CAMEST FROM ABOVE see
   Atkinson

O THOU WHO CAMEST FROM ABOVE see Bach,
   Johann Sebastian

O THOU WHO THROUGH THIS HOLY WEEK see
Lockwood, Normand

O TO BE LIKE THEE see Kirkpatrick,
William J.

O TO BE LIKE THEE see Landon, Stewart

O TOD, DU BIST EIN BITTRE GALLEN see
Lechner, Leonhard

O TREUER GOTT IM HIMMELSTHRON see
Helder, Bartholomaeus

O TRINITY OF BLESSED LIGHT see Lora,
Antonio

O VOS OMNES see Berghorn, Alfred

O VOS OMNES see Gesualdo, Don Carlo

O VOS OMNES? see Victoria, Tomas Luis
de

O WALY WALY
(Hare) SATB,acap (easy) OXFORD 84.181
$.20   (O40)

O WELT, SIEH HIER DEIN LEBEN see
Oertzen, Rudolf von

O WHAT A HAPPENING see Winter, Sister
Miriam Therese

O WHAT GRACE! see Peterson, John W.

O WHEN THE SAINTS *spir
(Desch, Rudolf) "Herr, Lasse Mich
Dabei Sein" [Ger/Eng] men cor sc
SCHOTTS C 43 183 s.p.   (O41)
(Desch, Rudolf) "Herr, Lasse Mich
Dabei Sein" [Eng/Ger] mix cor (med)
sc SCHOTTS C 43 598 s.p.   (O42)

O WIE SEHR LIEBLICH SIND see Diener,
Theodor

O WIE SELIG see Backer, Hans

O WONDROUS TYPE see Petrich, Roger

O WORD OF GOD INCARNATE see Cooper,
Rose Marie

O WORSHIP THE KING see Haydn, (Franz)
Joseph

O WORSHIP THE KING see Haydn, (Johann)
Michael

O WUNDERSCHON IST GOTTES ERDE see
Schlemm, Gustav Adolf

O YE PEOPLE see McElfresh, Clair T.

OATMAN
Last Mile Of The Way, The (composed
with Marks)
(Ferrin) SSATB oct BENSON S4300
$.20   (O43)

OB ICH SCHON ARM UND ELEND BIN see
Vento, Ivo de

OBENSHAIN, KATHRYN G.
Mother's Song, A *anthem
SA (mother's day) oct LORENZ 5400
$.35   (O44)
SA/unis oct LORENZ 5400 $.35   (O45)

OBERITALIENISCHE FIGURALPASSIONEN
(Schmitz, Arnold) (med) cloth SCHOTTS
s.p.
contains: Asola, Giovanni Matteo,
Passio In Die Parasceves (SATB);
Maistre, Jan (Nasco), Passio D.
n. J. Chr. Sec. Matthaeum
(SATTBB); Mantua, Jachet von,
Passio Die Veneris (SATTB); Rore,
Cipriano de, Passio D. n. J. Chr.
Sec. Joannem (SAATBB)   (O46)

OBEY THE SPIRIT OF THE LORD
(De Cormier) SATB SCHIRM.G LG51619
$.60   (O47)

OBGLEICH DIE WELT see Vento, Ivo de

OBRECHT, JACOB (ca. 1430-1505)
Alleluja *fugue
(Ehret, Walter) SATB (med) GIA
G1845 $.40   (O48)

Hear Us, O Lord *see Parce, Domine

Missa Caput *Mass
see Dufay, Guillaume, Missa Caput
(Darvas) 6pt mix cor oct EULENBURG
10099 s.p.   (O49)

Missae Super L'homme Arme
(Darvas, Gabor) mix cor BUDAPEST
6439 s.p.   (O50)

OBRECHT, JACOB (cont'd.)

Parce, Domine
(Proulx, Richard) "Hear Us, O Lord"
[Eng/Lat] SAB (med easy) GIA
G1900 $.40   (O51)

O'BYRNE, E.M.
Manger Carol, The
SSA BRODT 574 $.20   (O52)

OCH JAG SAG DEN HELIGA STADEN see
Hemberg, Eskil

OCH ORDET VART KOTT see Olson, Daniel

OCKEGHEM, JOHANNES (ca. 1430-1495)
Missa Caput
see Dufay, Guillaume, Missa Caput

Salve Regina
(Hunter) SATB AMP N-34 $.75   (O53)

OCULI MEI SEMPER AD DOMINUM see Krenek,
Ernst

ODE FOR CHILDREN'S DAY see Geisler

ODE OF THANKSGIVING, AN see Griffiths,
Vernon

O'ER THE STONE
(Arch, Gwyn) SSA EMI   (O54)

OERTZEN, RUDOLF VON (1910-   )
Ach Gott, Vom Himmel Sieh Darein
SAT/SAB/SA,opt treb inst&bass inst
HANSSLER 14.177 s.p.   (O55)

Aus Tiefer Not Schrei Ich Zu Dir
HANSSLER 19.616 s.p. contains also:
Wachet Auf, Ruft Uns Die Stimme   (O56)

Cantus Firmi
SATB,kbd,treb inst,bvl,perc
HANSSLER 19.606 s.p.
contains: Es Kommt Ein Schiff,
Geladen; O Heiland, Reiss Die
Himmel Auf   (O57)

Cantus Firmi
SATB,kbd,treb inst,bvl,perc
HANSSLER 19.607 s.p.
contains: Macht Hoch Die Tur, Die
Tor Macht Weit; Wie Soll Ich
Dich Empfangen   (O58)

Cantus Firmi
SATB,kbd,treb inst,bvl,perc
HANSSLER 19.608 s.p.
contains: Die Nacht Ist
Vorgedrungen; Lobt Gott, Ihr
Christen Alle Gleich   (O59)

Cantus Firmi
SATB,kbd,treb inst,bvl,perc
HANSSLER 19.609 s.p.
contains: Es Ist Ein Ros
Entsprungen; Gelobet Seist Du,
Jesu Christ   (O60)

Christus, Der Uns Selig Macht
HANSSLER 19.612 s.p. contains also:
O Welt, Sieh Hier Dein Leben   (O61)

Die Nacht Ist Vorgedrungen
see Cantus Firmi

Erscheinen Ist Der Herrlich Tag
see Oertzen, Rudolf von, Gelobt Sei
Gott Im Hochsten Thron

Es Ist Ein Ros Entsprungen
see Cantus Firmi

Es Kommt Ein Schiff, Geladen
see Cantus Firmi

Gelobet Sei Der Herr
see Oertzen, Rudolf von, O Heiliger
Geist, O Heiliger Gott

Gelobet Seist Du, Jesu Christ
see Cantus Firmi

Gelobt Sei Gott Im Hochsten Thron
HANSSLER 19.613 s.p. contains also:
Erscheinen Ist Der Herrlich Tag   (O62)

Gen Himmel Aufgefahren Ist
HANSSLER 19.614 s.p. contains also:
O Heiliger Geist, Kehr Bei Uns
Sein   (O63)

Jesus Ist Kommen, Grund Ewiger Freude
HANSSLER 19.611 s.p. contains also:
O Mensch, Bewein Dein Sunde Gross   (O64)

Lobt Gott, Ihr Christen Alle Gleich
see Cantus Firmi

Macht Hoch Die Tur, Die Tor Macht
Weit
see Cantus Firmi

OERTZEN, RUDOLF VON (cont'd.)

Nun Lasst Uns Gehn Und Treten
see Oertzen, Rudolf von, Nun Singet
Und Seid Froh

Nun Singet Und Seid Froh
HANSSLER 19.610 s.p. contains also:
Nun Lasst Uns Gehn Und Treten   (O65)

O Heiland, Reiss Die Himmel Auf
see Cantus Firmi

O Heiliger Geist, Kehr Bei Uns Sein
see Oertzen, Rudolf von, Gen Himmel
Aufgefahren Ist

O Heiliger Geist, O Heiliger Gott
HANSSLER 19.615 s.p. contains also:
Gelobet Sei Der Herr   (O66)

O Mensch, Bewein Dein Sunde Gross
see Oertzen, Rudolf von, Jesus Ist
Kommen, Grund Ewiger Freude

O Welt, Sieh Hier Dein Leben
see Oertzen, Rudolf von, Christus,
Der Uns Selig Macht

Wachet Auf, Ruft Uns Die Stimme
see Oertzen, Rudolf von, Aus Tiefer
Not Schrei Ich Zu Dir

Wie Soll Ich Dich Empfangen
see Cantus Firmi

OF A ROSE IS ALL MY SONG see Leighton,
Kenneth

OF LIFE see Berger, Jean

OF PRAYER AND PRAISE see Caldwell, Mary
[Elizabeth]

OF SINGING see Marshall, Jane M.

OF THE FATHER'S LOVE BEGOTTEN
see Eight Christmas Carols: Set 1

OF THE FATHER'S LOVE BEGOTTEN see
Carter

OF THE FATHER'S LOVE BEGOTTEN see
Erickson, John

OF TIME AND ETERNITY see Caldwell, Mary
[Elizabeth]

OFFER, OP.34 see Nordhalm, Ib

OFFERING OF CAROLS AND ROUNDS, AN see
Canning, Thomas

OFFERTORIUM see Faure, Gabriel-Urbain

OFFERTORY see Faure, Gabriel-Urbain,
Offertorium

OFFICE OF THE HOLY COMMUNION, THE see
Noble, Thomas Tertius

OG DETTE ER DOMMEN see Kvandal, Johan

OGDEN
Look And Live *anthem/gospel
(Peterson, John W.) SATB oct
SINGSPIR ZJP-8026 $.30   (O67)

OGDEN, W.A.
Look And Live
(Kling, Roger) SATB oct GOSPEL
05 TM 0112 $.20   (O68)

Where He Leads I'll Follow *anthem/
gospel
(DeCou, Harold) SATB oct SINGSPIR
ZJP-8047 $.30   (O69)

OH, BLESS THE LORD see Cram, James D.

OH COME LET US BOW DOWN see Jones, Jr.,
S.

OH, FOR A THOUSAND TONGUES see Mason,
Lowell

OH, HEAR ME, LORD GOD see Croce, Exaudi
Deus

OH, HE'S A WONDERFUL SAVIOR see
Peterson, John W.

OH, HOLY LORD *spir
(Zimmergren) 4pt mix cor ERIKS 317
s.p.   (O70)

OH, HOLY LORD see Hairston, Jester

OH! HOW BEAUTIFUL THE SKY
see Two Carols

OH, HOW BLEST ARE YE WHOSE TOILS ARE
ENDED see Bach, Johann Sebastian

OH HOW GREAT IS THY GOODNESS see
Palmer, Peggy Spenser

OH HOW HE LOVES YOU AND ME see Kaiser,
Kurt

OH, HOW I LOVE JESUS
(Krogstad, Bob) SAB oct GOSPEL
05 TM 0347 $.35   (O71)

OH, HOW I LOVE JESUS see Brown

OH HURRY HURRY TO BETHLEHEM see Nops,
Marjory

OH JERUSALEM see Tiffault

OH, LITTLE STAR see Simons, L.E.

OH LORD, HELP US LIVE EACH DAY see
Cobine, Al

OH LORD OUR GOD, WE HUMBLY PRAY see
Deihl, W.H.

OH, LOVING JESUS see Brahms, Johannes,
O Bone Jesu

OH, MAY THE WORDS see Goldman

OH, MY LORD, YOUR LIGHT DIVINE see
Boozer, Pat

OH MY SOUL! WHAT LOVE see Allen, Lanny

OH, PERFECT TEACHER see Wild, Eric

OH, POOR LITTLE JESUS *Xmas,spir
(Field, Robert) SATB,pno (easy) oct
PRESSER 312-41038 $.35   (O72)
(Field, Robert) SSA,pno (easy) oct
PRESSER 312-41039 $.35   (O73)

OH, STEAL AWAY SOFTLY TO JESUS see
Kirkpatrick

OH, TAKE THE WORD see Plunkett, Bonnie

OH, THANK THE LORD
(Krogstad, Bob) SATB oct GOSPEL
05 TM 0137 $.30   (O74)

OH, THE JOY OF IT! *anthem
1-2pt jr cor,opt perc BROADMAN
4560-25 $.35 see from Four Festive
Anthems For Children's Voices (O75)

OH, THE JOY OF IT see Red, Buryl

OH WARRIORS OF GOD see Dobias, Vaclav,
Kdoz Jste Bozi Bojovnici

OH! WASN'T DAT A WIDE RIBBER *spir
(Zimmergren) 4pt mix cor ERIKS 315
s.p.   (O76)

OH, WHAT A DAY see Schuler, George S.

O'HARA, GEOFFREY (1882-1967)
One World *see Bratton, John W.

Take My Life, Oh Lord
mix cor BRODT 515 $.28   (O77)

OHRWALL
Gaudete
WALTON SK100 $1.50   (O78)

O'KEEFE, WALTER
Mary Gentle Mother Of Mine *see
Boland, Clay A.

OLANDER
If I Gained The World (composed with
Starr) *anthem
unis/2pt oct BROADMAN 4540-99 $.30
                                         (O79)

OLD ALPINE PSALM see Gammal Fabodpsalm

OLD ARK'S A MOVERIN', THE see Ehret,
Walter

OLD BOOK AND THE OLD FAITH, THE see
Carr

OLD CAROLS FOR YOUNG MEN *CC17L
(Lefebvre, Channing) TBB GALAXY
1.1520.1 $.75   (O80)

OLD-FASHIONED MEETING, THE *CC10L,
gospel
(Bartlett, Gene) cor WORD 37682 $1.95
                                         (O81)

OLD-FASHIONED MEETING, THE see Buffum

OLD GAELIC PRAYER see Whitaker

OLD HUNDREDTH see Bourgeois, Loys
(Louis)

OLD HUNDREDTH PSALM TUNE, THE see
Vaughan Williams, Ralph

OLD JORDAN see Smith

OLD RUGGED CROSS, THE *see I Want
Jesus To Walk With Me; Bennard,
George, Old Rugged Cross, The;
Webster, In The Sweet By And By
                                         (O82)

OLD RUGGED CROSS, THE see Bennard,
George

OLD RUGGED CROSS, THE see Webster

OLD RUGGED CROSS, THE see Bennard,
George

OLD SONGS, THE *CCU
(Red, Buryl) cor BROADMAN 4520-30
$1.50   (O83)

OLD TIME POWER see Tillman

OLD TIME RELIGION *anthem
(Jeffrey) SATB,acap oct BENSON S4242
$.25   (O84)
(Woodward; Burroughs) SATB,bvl, opt
snare drum FINE ARTS EP 25 $.35
                                         (O85)

OLD-TIME RELIGION, THE *anthem/gospel
(Shepard, Bob) SATB oct SINGSPIR
ZJP-8071 $.30   (O86)

OLD TIME RELIGION, THE see Young,
Gordon

OLD YEAR NOW AWAY IS FLED, THE
(Peek, R.) SATB,org GRAY CMR 3338
$.30   (O87)

OLDENBURG, BOB
Happening Now! (composed with Lunn,
Eddie)
cor BROADMAN 4518-03 $2.95   (O88)

I See Him *anthem
(Allen, Lanny) SATB WORD CS-2588
$.30   (O89)

Song Of Life, A *Easter,cant
SATB BROADMAN 4514-05 $1.50   (O90)

Worship Now Our God (composed with
Allen) *anthem
SATB (easy) oct BROADMAN 4554-17
$.30   (O91)

OLDROYD, GEORGE (1886-1951)
Spiritual Rhapsody 'Jhesu Christ
Saint Mary's Sone'
SATB,T solo,2fl,3ob,2clar,2bsn,
2trp,2trom,timp,perc,hpsd,harp,
strings voc sc NOVELLO rental
                                         (O92)

OLIVET see Protheroe, Daniel

OLSEN, SPARRE (1903-   )
Gud, Nar Du Til Oppbrudd Kaller
SSA/SAB MUSIKK   (O93)

OLSON
Christmas Haiku *Xmas
SATB SCHIRM.G LG51687 $.30   (O94)

OLSON, D.
He Taught Me There
(Smith, Herb) SAB oct GOSPEL
05 TM 0173 $.20   (O95)

OLSON, DANIEL (1898-   )
Dar Sjongo Tre Anglar
SABar ERIKS 72 s.p.   (O96)

Det Star Ett Trad Pa Min Faders Gard
SABar ERIKS 88 s.p.   (O97)

Harlig Ar Jorden
SABar ERIKS 73 s.p.   (O98)

I Hela Naturen
SABar ERIKS 89 s.p.   (O99)

Jag Ar Varldens Ljus *Bibl
SABar ERIKS 345 s.p.   (O100)

Lovad Vare Herren *Psalm
3pt mix cor,solo ERIKS 13 s.p.
                                         (O101)

Nar Detta Forgangliga *Bibl
SABar ERIKS 346 s.p.   (O102)

Och Ordet Vart Kott *Bibl
SABar ERIKS 347 s.p.   (O103)

Om Icke Vetekornet *Bibl
4pt mix cor ERIKS 342 s.p.   (O104)

Vad I Bedjen Fadern Om *Bibl
3pt mix cor ERIKS 84 s.p. (O105)
wom cor&opt jr cor ERIKS 84 s.p.
                                         (O106)

OM DAGEN VID MITT ARBETE *folk
(Ohrwall) 4pt mix cor ERIKS 71 s.p.
                                         (O107)

OM I ICKE OMVANDEN EDER see Schonberg,
Stig Gustav

OM ICKE VETEKORNET see Olson, Daniel

OMNES DE SABA see Eybler, Joseph

OMNES DE SABA VENIENT see Gallus,
Jacobus

OMNES GENTES PLAUDITE see Gabrieli,
Giovanni

OMNES GENTES PLAUDITE MAIBUS see
Dulichius, Philippus

OMNES GENTES PLAUDITE MANIBUS see
Dulichius, Philippus

OMNIA INSTAURARE IN CHRISTO see
Lemacher, Heinrich

ON A DAY WHEN MEN WERE COUNTED see
Lovelace, Austin C.

ON A RUGGED HILL see Whitford, Keith

ON A RUGGED HILL see Whitford

ON A WINTER NIGHT see Patterson, Joy F.

ON ALL THE EARTH THY SPIRIT POUR *hymn
SATB GIA G1953 $.40   (O108)

ON BELIEF see Wyrtzen, Don

ON CHRISTMAS DAY IN THE MORNING see
Caldwell

ON CHRISTMAS EVE THERE CAME AN ANGEL
(Ehret, Walter) SATB oct SCHMITT 1885
$.45   (O109)

ON CHRISTMAS MORN see Peninger

ON CHRISTMAS NIGHT
see Three Christmas Songs With
Synthesizer Accompaniment

ON CHRISTMAS NIGHT see Vaughan
Williams, Ralph

ON CHRISTMAS NIGHT ALL CHRISTIANS SING
see Goodman, Joseph

ON JORDAN'S STORMY BANKS *anthem
(Cram, James D.) SATB FINE ARTS
CM 1027 $.30   (O110)

ON JORDAN'S STORMY BANKS see Smith

ON JUDGING see Ford, Virgil T.

ON LOVE OF ONE'S ENEMIES see Ford,
Virgil T.

ON MA JOURNEY *spir
(Thomas) SATB,acap oct LILLENAS
AN-7006 $.30   (O111)

ON MOUNT OF OLIVES see Haydn, (Johann)
Michael

ON MY HEART IMPRINT THINE IMAGE see
Rotermund, Melvin

ON THAT HOLY MIDNIGHT
(Pablo, Juan) 2pt,S solo,pno/org,opt
gtr, opt. claves and maracas
FREDONIA see from Three Puerto
Rican Carols   (O112)

ON THE BETHLEHEM ROAD
see Infant Holy

ON THE CROSS OF CALVARY see Gerig

ON THE EXISTENCE OF GOD see Smith,
Leland

ON THE LIFE OF JESU see Jenni, Donald

ON THE MOUNT OF OLIVES see Bruckner,
Anton

ON THE MOUNTAINSIDE see Kittleson

ON THE NATIVITY OF CHRIST see Butler,
Eugene

ON THE RESURRECTION OF CHRIST see
Montgomery, Bruce

ON THE TWENTY-THIRD PSALM see Ferguson

ON THE WOOD HIS ARMS OUTSTRETCHED see
Vulpius, Melchior

ON THIS BLESSED EASTER DAY see Hughes

ON THIS DAY, CHRIST THE LORD WAS BORN
see Schutz, Heinrich, Hodie
Christus Natus Est

ON THIS DAY GOD GAVE US CHRIST see
Powell

ON THIS DAY, O BEAUTIFUL MOTHER see Van
Hulse, Camil

ON THIS DAY OF GLORY see Leaf, Robert

ON THIS ROCK see Newbury, Kent A.

ON WINGS OF LIVING LIGHT see Mitchell, David L.

ON WINGS OF SONG THE ANGELS COME see Mendelssohn-Bartholdy, Felix

ONCE AT EV'RY GATE see Newbury, Kent A.

ONCE, BY GALILEE see Burroughs, Bob

ONCE IN DAVID'S ROYAL CITY see Beck, John Ness

ONCE IN ROYAL DAVID'S CITY
　　see Babe Is Born, I Wys, A
　　see Six Carols For SAB And Piano
　　see Six Christmas Hymns
　　(Preston) SAB SHAWNEE D5230 $.35
　　　　　　　　　　　　　　　　(O113)

ONCE IN ROYAL DAVID'S CITY see Beck, John Ness

ONCE MORE, MY SOUL　*anthem
　　(Price) SATB oct BROADMAN 4545-85
　　$.30　　　　　　　　　　　　(O114)

ONCE MORE, MY SOUL see Billings, William

ONE GOD see Johnston

ONE HOLY CHURCH OF GOD APPEARS see Longfellow

ONE HUNDRED PER CENT CHANCE OF RAIN see Horsley, Walter S.

ONE THERE IS ABOVE ALL OTHERS see Berggreen

ONE THING see Landgrave, Phillip

ONE THING HAVE I DESIRED OF THE LORD see Jeppesen, Knud

ONE THING I ASK OF THE LORD see Schutz, Heinrich

ONE THING WE ASK, O LORD see Jaeschke

ONE TOUCH see Plunkett, Bonnie

ONE WAY see Collins

ONE WAY see Figh

ONE WAY see Littleton, Bill J.

ONE WORLD see Bratton, John W.

ONE WORLD, ONE LORD, ONE WITNESS see Red, Buryl

ONE WORLD, ONE LORD, ONE WITNESS see Reynolds, William Jensen

O'NEAL, BARRY
　　Lord Have Mercy
　　SATB AMP A-687 $.35　　　　(O115)

　　Nativitie
　　SATB AMP A-688 $.45　　　　(O116)

ONLY A MANGER see Parrish, Mary Kay

ONLY A PRAYER AWAY see Rasley, John M.

ONLY GOD see Goossen, Frederic

ONLY JESUS CAN SATISFY YOUR SOUL see Wolfe

ONLY LORD, THE see Daniels, Bob

ONLY TRUST HIM　*anthem
　　(Mercer, W. Elmo) SATB oct BENSON
　　S4249 $.35　　　　　　　　　(O117)
　　(Reynolds) SATB oct BROADMAN 4540-82
　　$.30　　　　　　　　　　　　(O118)

ONLY TRUST HIM see Stockton

ONO TOVO see Nowakowsky, David

ONS GETSEMANE see Pomper, A.

ONWARD CHRISTIAN SOLDIERS see Gould

ONWARD, CHRISTIAN SOLDIERS see Sullivan

ONZE DODEN see Krieken, van

OPEN MY EYES see Gagliardi, George

OPEN THE GATES OF TEMPLE see Knapp, (Mrs.) Joseph F.

OPEN YOUR SPIRITUAL EYES see Salsbury, Ron

OPHOVEN, HERMANN (1914-　　　)
　　Acht Grabgesange　*CC8U
　　4pt mix cor,opt 2trom, 2 tenorhorns
　　BOHM s.p.　　　　　　　　　(O119)

　　Adoramus Te　*Psntd,mot
　　[Lat] 4pt mix cor,acap BOHM s.p.
　　　　　　　　　　　　　　　　(O120)

　　Erde Singe!　*Fest
　　mix cor&opt unis,acap/org BOHM
　　s.p., ipa　　　　　　　　　(O121)

　　Pange Lingua
　　[Lat] 4pt mix cor,acap BOHM s.p.
　　contains also: Tantum Ergo (O122)

　　Tantum Ergo
　　see Ophoven, Hermann, Pange Lingua
　　[Lat] 4pt mix cor,acap BOHM s.p.
　　　　　　　　　　　　　　　　(O123)

OR CHE SI OSCURA IL CIEL see Rossini, Gioacchino

ORA ET LABORA see Spranger, Jorg

ORATORIO PATRIS CONDREN: O JESU VIVENS IN MARIA see Rorem, Ned

ORBIS FACTOR see Naprstek, Gerhard

OREMUS PRO PONTIFICE see Hunecke, Wilhelm

OREMUS PRO PONTIFICE see Krieger, Fritz

ORFF, CARL (1895-　　　)
　　Kantate Part I: Veni Creator Spiritus
　　*cant
　　4-6pt mix cor,2-3pno,perc sc,cor
　　pts SCHOTTS ED. 6020 s.p., ipa
　　　　　　　　　　　　　　　　(O124)

　　Kantate Part II: Der Gute Mensch
　　*cant
　　8pt mix cor,2-3pno,perc sc,cor pts
　　SCHOTTS ED. 6021 s.p., ipa (O125)

　　Kantate Part III: Fremde Sind Wir
　　*cant
　　mix cor,2pno sc,cor pts SCHOTTS
　　ED. 6022 s.p.　　　　　　　(O126)

　　Ludus De Nato Infante Mirificus
　　*Xmas
　　mix cor,soli,orch (med easy) sc
　　SCHOTTS rental, ipr　　　　(O127)

　　Mater Et Filia
　　see Zwei Geistliche Chorsatze

　　Media Vita
　　see Zwei Geistliche Chorsatze

　　Zwei Geistliche Chorsatze
　　jr cor (med) sc SCHOTTS C 42 403
　　s.p.
　　contains: Mater Et Filia; Media
　　Vita　　　　　　　　　　　　(O128)

ORGAN SOLO MASS see Mozart, Wolfgang Amadeus, Missa Brevis

ORGELMESSE D-DUR see Dvorak, Antonin, Mass In D Major

ORGELSOLOMESSE see Mozart, Wolfgang Amadeus, Missa Brevis In C

ORLEANS　*hymn
　　(Lindsley) TTBB,acap (easy) OXFORD
　　94.103 see from Five Early American
　　Hymn Tunes　　　　　　　　　(O129)

ORR
　　Sing Aloud Unto God　*anthem
　　SATB (med diff) OXFORD 42.347 $.50
　　　　　　　　　　　　　　　　(O130)

ORTLUND, ANNE
　　Choral Hymns　*CCU
　　(Johnson, Norman) SATB SINGSPIR
　　5275 $.50　　　　　　　　　(O131)

　　He Shall Come Down　*anthem
　　SSATB oct SINGSPIR ZJP-7343 $.30
　　　　　　　　　　　　　　　　(O132)

　　Think Of It, Lord!　*folk
　　SATB oct SINGSPIR ZJP-5048 $.25
　　　　　　　　　　　　　　　　(O133)

　　Trusting Jesus　*anthem
　　SATB oct SINGSPIR ZJP-7353 $.25
　　　　　　　　　　　　　　　　(O134)

OS IUSTI see Bruckner, Anton

OS JUSTI see Bruckner, Anton

OSANNA FILIO DAVID see Stout, Alan

OSGOOD, MURIEL
　　May Carol, A　*anthem
　　cor CHORISTERS R-3 $.15　　(O135)

OSIANDER, LUCAS (1534-1604)
　　Dank Sagen Wir Alle
　　SATB SCHWEIZER. SK 125 s.p.
　　contains also: Gott Sei Gelobet
　　Und Gebenedeiet　　　　　　(O136)

OSIANDER, LUCAS (cont'd.)

　　Gelobet Seist Du, Jesu Christ
　　see Dressler, Gallus, Lobet Den
　　Herren, Alle Heiden

　　Gott Sei Gelobet Und Gebenedeiet
　　see Osiander, Lucas, Dank Sagen Wir
　　Alle

OSTERFREUDE
　　"Easter Joy" see Four Easter Chorales

OSTERLIED see Ruppel, Paul Ernst

OSTERN see Hirth, Hermann

OSTERPSALM see Kameke, Ernst-Ulrich von

OSTRCIL, OTAKOR (1879-1935)
　　Legend Of St. Zita, The　*see Legenda
　　O Sv. Zite

　　Legenda O Sv. Zite　*cant
　　"Legend Of St. Zita, The" [Czech]
　　mix cor,ST soli,3fl,3ob,3clar,
　　3bsn,4horn,3trp,3trom,tuba,timp,
　　perc,2harp,org,strings, celeste,
　　xylophone CZECH s.p.　　　(O137)

OTHMAYR, KASPAR (1515-1553)
　　Der Herr Kennet Den Weg Der Gerechten
　　SA (contains also: Ach Lieber Herr
　　Im Hochsten Thron) SCHWEIZER.
　　SK 51.04 s.p. see also
　　MUSIKBEILAGE ZUM "EVANGELISCHEN
　　KIRCHENCHOR 1951"　　　　　(O138)

　　Mein Himmlischer Vater　*mot
　　SATTB HANSSLER 1.538 s.p.　(O139)

OU S'EN VONT CES GAIS BERGERS TYRLE,
TYRLOW, TYRLE, TYRLOW
　　see Two Christmas Carols

OUCHTERLONY, DAVID
　　Anthems, Introits And Descants For
　　Youth Choirs　*CCU,anthem/Introit
　　jr cor HARRIS $1.25　　　　(O140)

OUR BLEST REDEEMER see Finlay, Kenneth

OUR BLEST REDEEMER see Fraser

OUR CARES WE CAN CAST ON THEE see Latimer

OUR CHRIST TODAY FROM DEATH HATH SPRUNG see Peek, Richard

OUR DAY OF PRAISE IS DONE see Harris

OUR FATHER see Green, Philip, Pater Noster

OUR FATHER see Kaiser, Kurt

OUR FATHER see Senator, Ronald

OUR FATHER see Whitaker

OUR FATHER see Young, Carlton R.

OUR FATHER, BY WHOSE NAME see Hunnicutt, Judy

OUR FATHER WHICH ART IN HEAVEN see Russell, Welford

OUR GLORIOUS KING see Van Hulse, Camil

OUR GREAT SAVIOR see Prichard, [Rowland Hugh]

OUR GREAT SAVIOUR
　　see There Is A Song

OUR GREAT SAVIOUR see Chapman

OUR HOME IN GLORY see Williamson

OUR HOUSE see Price, Florence B.

OUR LORD IN MAJESTY DOTH REIGN see Preston

OUR LORD IS RISEN WITH FLAG UNFURLED see Distler, Hugo

OUR RELIGIOUS HERITAGE IN SONG see Thygerson, Robert J.

OUR SACRED HONOR see Yahres, Samuel C.

OUR SACRIFICE OF PRAISE see Wyrtzen, Don

OUR SHRINE, OUR SHRINE see Slater, David D.

OUT IN THE FIELDS see Protheroe, Daniel

OUT IN THE FIELDS WITH GOD see Whitecotton, Shirley

OUT OF EGYPT see Bender, Jan

OUT OF THE DEEP see Goldsworthy,
William Arthur

OUT OF THE DEEP see Hoddinott, Alun

OUT OF THE DEEP see Morley, Thomas, De
Profundis Clamavi

OUT OF THE DEPTHS see Bassett, Leslie

OUT OF THE DEPTHS see Track, Gerhard

OUT OF THE DEPTHS I CRY see Currie,
Randolph

OUT OF THE ORIENT CRYSTAL SKIES see
Zgodava, Richard A.

OUT ON A HILLSIDE see Hill, Harry

OUTREACH *CC11UL
(Mercer, W. Elmo) cor BENSON B0489
$1.50   (O141)

OVENS
Wounded For Me *Easter,anthem
(DeCou, Harold) SATB oct SINGSPIR
ZJP-3535 $.30   (O142)

OVER IN BETHLEHEM
see Sunshine And Snowflakes

OVER IN BETH'LEM TOWN see Ridenour, Joe

OVER THE SUNSET MOUNTAINS see Peterson,
John W.

OVERBEEK, C. V.
Missa Pro Pace
2 eq voices,pno/org HENN 720A s.p.
sc, voc pt   (O143)
2pt mix cor,pno/org HENN 720 s.p.
sc, voc pt   (O144)

OVERHOLT, R.
God's Choir In The Skies
(McLellan, Cyril) SATB oct GOSPEL
05 TM 0135 $.35   (O145)

OVERLEY, HENRY
Jesus, Babe Of Bethlehem *Xmas
SATBB (easy) FITZSIMONS 2146 $.25
                                          (O146)
Psalm Of Thanksgiving, A *Thanks
SSATTBB,acap (diff) FITZSIMONS 2143
$.30   (O147)

Rejoice And Be Merry *Xmas
SATB (diff) FITZSIMONS 2157 $.30
                                          (O148)

OWEN
Lo, He Comes With Clouds Descending
*Adv
(Overley) SATBB,A solo (med)
FITZSIMONS 2145 $.25   (O149)

Praise To Thee, Thou Great Creator
*Thanks,hymn
(Ehret, Walter) SATB,trp oct
LILLENAS AN-2398 $.35   (O150)

Welcome, Yule *Xmas,carol
SATB,acap (med) OXFORD 84.243 $.30
                                          (O151)

OWEN, WILLIAM
Praise To Thee, Thou Great Creator
(Ehret, Walter) SATB,opt 3trp oct
LILLENAS AN-2398 $.35   (O152)

OWENS
Gloria In Excelsis Deo *Xmas,anthem
SATB (easy) oct BROADMAN 4551-61
$.30   (O153)

He Died For Us *Easter/Lent,folk
SATB oct LILLENAS AN-5058 $.30
                                          (O154)
SATB oct LILLENAS AN-5058 $.30
                                          (O155)
Jesus! Jesus! *folk
SAB oct LILLENAS AN-5033 $.30
                                          (O156)
Just Ask Him - Listen - Right Now -
Receive Him Now *see Skillings,
Otis

O Praise The Lord! *anthem
(Collins) SATB oct LILLENAS AT-1105
$.30   (O157)

'Twas On A Cold And Wintry Night
*Adv/Xmas
SATB oct LILLENAS AN-3873 $.35
                                          (O158)

OWENS, CAROL
Freely, Freely *anthem
2pt,solo LEXICON CS-2618 $.30 see
from COME TOGETHER   (O159)

If My People *see Owens, Jimmy

OWENS, FREDERICK
Choral Benedictions *see Parthun,
Paul

OWENS, JAMIE
Laughter In Your Soul *CC10L
(Owens, Jimmy) jr cor LEXICON 37659
$1.95   (O160)

OWENS, JIMMY
Behold The Man
SATB LEXICON CS-2702 $.35   (O161)

Christmas Festival, A *see
Skillings, Otis

God So Loved The World *anthem
SATB LEXICON CS-2619 $.35 see from
COME TOGETHER   (O162)

Hallelujah His Blood Avails For Me
(from Come Together) anthem
3pt,solo LEXICON CS-2620 $.35
                                          (O163)
Holy, Holy *anthem
SATB LEXICON CS-2617 $.30 see from
COME TOGETHER   (O164)

If My People (composed with Owens,
Carol) *cant
cor&cong&speak cor LEXICON 37702
$2.95   (O165)

If My People Will Pray *anthem
SATB LEXICON CS-2631 $.40 see also
TELL THE WORLD   (O166)

Jimmy Owens And The Come Together
Singers Tell The World *CC10L
jr cor LEXICON 37643 $1.95   (O167)

OXFORD BOOK OF CAROLS, THE *CCU
(Vaughan Williams; Dearmer; Shaw)
unis/SATB (easy) pap OXFORD 48.035
$4.65   (O168)

OXFORD REQUIEM, AN see Montgomery,
Bruce

P

PAASLIEDERENBLAD *CC100U,Easter
HEER 11 s.p.   (P1)

PACE
Happy Jubilee, The *gospel
(Skillings, Otis) SATB oct LILLENAS
AN-1680 $.30   (P2)

Lead Me Back To Calvary *Easter
(Smith) SATB oct GOSPEL 05 TM 0144
$.25   (P3)

PACE, MILLIE
Serve Him With All Your Heart
(Larsen, L.B.) SATB oct GOSPEL
05 TM 0219 $.25   (P4)

PACHELBEL, JOHANN (1653-1706)
All Praise And Thanks To God
(Lovelace) mix cor,brass BRODT 523
$.25, ipr   (P5)

Now Thank We All Our God
(Lovelace) mix cor BRODT 524 $.30
                                          (P6)

Nun Danket Alle Gott
SATB,org,2trp,horn,trom KING,R
MFB 604 cor pts $.50, cmplt ed
$7.00   (P7)

Psalm Fantasia *anthem
(Johnson) SATB oct LILLENAS AN-6010
$.35   (P8)

Singet Dem Herrn Ein Neues Lied
SATB&SATB SCHWEIZER. SK 128 s.p.
                                          (P9)

PAEAN OF PRAISE see Rasley, John M.

PAFFENDORF, P. ALEXANDER
Regina Coeli *BVM/Easter
[Lat] SSATB,acap sc,cor pts BOHM
s.p.   (P10)

PAGE
Come To The Celebration *anthem
1-2pt,opt drums&bvl&rec&gtr oct
BROADMAN 4560-40 $.35   (P11)

Trusting Jesus
(Sankey; McLellan) SATB oct GOSPEL
05 TM 0130 $.25   (P12)

PAGE, ROBERT E.
O Magnum Mysterium (from Three
Motets)
SATB,Mez solo STANDARD A5MX1 $.40
                                          (P13)
Quem Vidistis Pastores? (from Three
Motets)
SSA&TTB&SATB STANDARD A4MX1 $.50
                                          (P14)
Venite Exsultemus Domino (from Three
Motets)
SSA&TTB&SATB STANDARD A6MX1 $.50
                                          (P15)

PAGE, SUE ELLEN
Love Of Jesus Smile On You, The
*Xmas
SATB,fing.cym.,gtr,rec CHORISTERS
A-97 $.35   (P16)

Shepherds Play Your Melody *Xmas
2 eq voices,hpsd/pno&2rec
CHORISTERS A-77 $.30   (P17)

Sing Alleluia!
see Two Songs By Suzie

Two Songs By Suzie *Gen/Thanks
unis,inst CHORISTERS A-60 $.35
contains: Sing Alleluia!;
Wondrous Love   (P18)

Wondrous Love
see Two Songs By Suzie

PAGETTE
Shepherd Boy, The
(Sandison) SS EMI   (P19)

PAIX SUR LA TERRE see Binet

PALESTRINA, GIOVANNI (1525-1594)
Ad Te Levavi Oculos Meos
see Four Motets

Adoramus Te
see HYMNEN UND MOTETTEN ALTER
MEISTER HEFT 2

Aeterna Christi Munera *Mass
SATB,acap (med diff) OXFORD 43.466
$.65   (P20)

Agnus Dei
6pt mix cor LIENAU
MUSICA SACRA, NR. 19 sc s.p., cor

PALESTRINA, GIOVANNI (cont'd.)

    pts s.p.   (P21)

Alma Redemptoris Mater
(Klein) "Lovely Mother Of Our
Savior" SATB SCHIRM.G 12001 $.35
(P22)

Arise, Shine, For Thy Light Is Come
(Smith) mix cor BANKS MUS YS 1069
$.25   (P23)

Ave Regina Coelorum
see Four Motets

Benedictus
see Palestrina, Giovanni, Pleni
Sunt Coeli
[Eng] SATB WHITE,ERN $.35   (P24)

Blessing And Honour
(Smith) mix cor BANKS MUS YS 900
$.20   (P25)

Children Of The Hebrews *Easter
(Bevan, Gwilym) SATB (med easy)
WATERLOO $.30   (P26)

Credo (from Messe Brevis)
4pt mix cor,acap voc pt HENN 242
s.p.   (P27)

Creed (from Aeterna Christi Munera)
Commun
SATB,acap (med diff) OXFORD 43.467
$.35   (P28)

Crucifixus (from Missa Papae
Marcelli)
mix cor LIENAU MUSICA SACRA, NR. 20
sc s.p., cor pts s.p.   (P29)

Dies Sanctificatus
SATB,acap EGTVED MK6, 5 s.p.   (P30)
(Thorsen) [Lat] SATB,acap oct
NATIONAL WHC-64 $.40   (P31)

First Critical Edition *sac/sec,CCU
(De Witt, Theodor; Rauch, J.N.;
Espagne, Franz; Commer, Fr.;
Haberl, Fr. X.) microfiche UNION
ESP. $240.00 33 volumes published
at Leipzig, 1862-1907.   (P32)

Four Motets *mot
cmplt ed EGTVED OCII s.p.
contains: Ad Te Levavi Oculos
Meos (SATB,acap) (first part;
second part is Miserere Nostri,
Domine); Ave Regina Coelorum
(SSSA,acap) (BVM, first part;
second part is Gaude, Virgo
Gloriosa); Gaude, Virgo
Gloriosa (SSSA,acap) (BVM,
second part of Ave Regina
Coelorum); Isti Sunt (SATB,
acap); Miserere Nostri, Domine
(SATB,acap) (second part of Ad
Te Levavi Oculos Meos); Quae
Est Ista (SSATB)   (P33)

Gaude, Virgo Gloriosa
see Four Motets

Gloria Patri Domino *Fest,mot
[Lat] SATBB,acap sc,cor pts BOHM
s.p.   (P34)

Haec Dies *anthem
(Parker) SSATTB,acap (med) OXFORD
43.481 $.30   (P35)

Holy, Holy
(Smith) mix cor BANKS MUS YS 977
$.25   (P36)

Hosanna In The Highest *Easter/Lent
(Coggin) SAB oct SCHMITT 5548 $.40
(P37)

I Vaghi Fiori *madrigal
[It] SATB,acap EGTVED KB217 s.p.
(P38)

Improperia
dbl cor LIENAU MUSICA SACRA, NR. 15
sc s.p., cor pts s.p.   (P39)

Improperium Exspectavi *Palm,Offer
[Lat] SSATB,acap sc,cor pts BOHM
s.p.   (P40)

In Festo St. Crucis
4pt mix cor LIENAU
MUSICA SACRA, NR.16 sc s.p., cor
pts s.p.   (P41)

In Monte Oliveti *Lent
(Niven) SATB oct SCHMITT 1660 $.30
(P42)

Isti Sunt
see Four Motets

Jesu Rex Admirabilis
see Zwei Christkonigsgesange

PALESTRINA, GIOVANNI (cont'd.)

Kyrie
4pt mix cor LIENAU
MUSICA SACRA, NR.17 sc s.p., cor
pts s.p.   (P43)

Lovely Mother Of Our Savior *see
Alma Redemptoris Mater

Messe Brevis
4pt mix cor,acap voc pt HENN 241
s.p.   (P44)

Messe O Admirabile
5pt mix cor,acap voc pt HENN 227
s.p.   (P45)

Miserere Nostri, Domine
see Four Motets

Missa Ad Fugam *Mass
[Lat] 4pt mix cor,acap sc,cor pts
BOHM s.p.   (P46)

Missa Sine Nomine *Mass
[Lat] SSATTB,acap sc,cor pts BOHM
s.p.   (P47)

O Bone Jesu *Holywk
4pt,acap voc pt HENN 318 s.p. (P48)
[Lat] 4pt mix cor,acap BOHM s.p.
(P49)

O Crux. O Jesu Christ
5pt mix cor LIENAU
MUSICA SACRA, NR. 22 cor pts
s.p., sc s.p.   (P50)

O Gloriosa Dominum
4pt,acap voc pt HENN 319 s.p. (P51)

O God Of Life *see Panis Angelicus

O Lord, Bow Down Thine Ear
(Smith) mix cor BANKS MUS YS 893
$.20   (P52)

Panis Angelicus
(Ehret, Walter) "O God Of Life"
[Eng/Lat] SATB,acap (med) PRESSER
312-41066 $.40   (P53)

Pleni Sunt Coeli *Bene
SAB,acap EGTVED MS7B2 s.p. contains
also: Benedictus; Rex Virtutis
(P54)

Popule Meus *Gd.Fri.
[Lat/Ger] 4pt mix cor,acap BOHM
s.p.   (P55)

Pueri Hebraeorum *Palm
[Lat] 4pt mix cor,acap sc,cor pts
BOHM s.p.   (P56)

Quae Est Ista
see Four Motets

Rex Virtutis
see Palestrina, Giovanni, Pleni
Sunt Coeli
see Zwei Christkonigsgesange

Sanctus
6pt mix cor LIENAU
MUSICA SACRA, NR.18 cor pts s.p.,
sc s.p.   (P57)

Seek Ye The Lord
(Smith) mix cor BANKS MUS YS 1034
$.20   (P58)

Sicut Cervus *mot
4pt mix cor LIENAU
MUSICA SACRA, NR. 21 sc s.p., cor
pts s.p.   (P59)
SATB,acap (first part; second part
is Sitivit Anima Mea) EGTVED KB65
s.p.   (P60)

Sitivit Anima Mea *mot
SATB,acap (second part of Sicut
Cervus) EGTVED KB207 s.p.   (P61)

Soave Fia Il Morir *madrigal
[It] SSATB,acap EGTVED KB256 s.p.
(P62)

Strife Is O'er, The *Easter,anthem
(Johnson, Norman) SATB oct SINGSPIR
ZJP-3524 $.30   (P63)

Two Settings Of Palestrina's Missa
Papae Marcelli *CC2U
(Anerio, Francesco; Soriano,
Francesco) SSAATTBB bds A-R ED
$9.95   (P64)

Vier Tantum Ergo *see Victoria,
Tomas Luis de

We Adore You, O Christ *Lent,anthem
(Lee, J.) SA (easy) GIA G1838 $.30
(P65)

Zwei Christkonigsgesange
[Lat] 4pt mix cor,acap sc,cor pts
BOHM s.p.
contains: Jesu Rex Admirabilis;

PALESTRINA, GIOVANNI (cont'd.)

    Rex Virtutis   (P66)

PALKOVSKY, OLDRICH (1907-   )
Pastorely Ceske Vanocni *CCU,Xmas
[Czech] mix cor,soli,2fl,2clar,
2horn,2trp,tuba,org,strings CZECH
s.p.   (P67)

PALM SUNDAY, A.D. 33 see Caldwell, Mary
[Elizabeth]

PALM SUNDAY PROCESSION see Newbury,
Kent A.

PALM SUNDAY PROCESSION see Wyton, Alec

PALMER, CATHERINE
Christ My Beloved
SATB (med diff) WATERLOO $.35 (P68)

PALMER, PEGGY SPENSER
Oh How Great Is Thy Goodness
SA CRAMER $.50   (P69)

This Is The Day Which The Lord Hath
Made
SA CRAMER $.40   (P70)

PALMS, THE see Faure, Jean-Baptist

PALMS OF VICTORY see Mathias

PANGE LINGUA see Aichinger, Gregor

PANGE LINGUA see Benkert, Lorenz

PANGE LINGUA see Dantonello, Josef

PANGE LINGUA see Erhard, Karl

PANGE LINGUA see Ett, Kaspar

PANGE LINGUA see Forster, Peter

PANGE LINGUA see Goller, Fritz

PANGE LINGUA see Govert, Willibald

PANGE LINGUA see Heftrich, Wilhelm

PANGE LINGUA see Herrmann, Hugo

PANGE LINGUA see Hug, Emil

PANGE LINGUA see Kayser, Leif

PANGE LINGUA see Kremer, Karl

PANGE LINGUA see Kromolicki, Joseph

PANGE LINGUA see Kutzer, Ernst

PANGE LINGUA see Lemacher, Heinrich

PANGE LINGUA see Lipp, Alban

PANGE LINGUA see Messner, Joseph

PANGE LINGUA see Ophoven, Hermann

PANGE LINGUA see Peissner, Karl

PANGE LINGUA see Ridout, Godfrey

PANGE LINGUA see Schroeder, Hermann

PANGE LINGUA see Strauss-Konig, Richard

PANGE LINGUA see Trapp, Willy

PANGE LINGUA see Waldbroel, Wilhelm

PANGE LINGUA see Wassmer, Berthold

PANGE LINGUA see Williamson, Malcolm

PANGE LINGUA see Zubrod, Friedrich

PANGE LINGUA see Piechler, Arthur

PANGE LINGUA see Piechler, Arthur

PANGE LINGUA see Piechler, Arthur

PANGE LINGUA see Piechler, Arthur

PANGE LINGUA see Piechler, Arthur

PANGE LINGUA I see Ketterer, Ernst

PANGE LINGUA II see Ketterer, Ernst

PANGE LINGUA-TANTUM ERGO see Calegari,
Antonio

PANGE LINGUA-TANTUM ERGO see Pitoni,
Giuseppe Ottavio

PANIS ANGELICUS see Casciolini, Claudio

PANIS ANGELICUS see Dietrich, J.H.

PANIS ANGELICUS see Lemacher, Heinrich

PANIS ANGELICUS see Palestrina, Giovanni

PANIS ANGELICUS see Roff, Joseph

PANUNZI, M. (1907-   )
Lauda Spirtuale
cor,S solo,3fl,3ob,3clar,3bsn,
4horn,3trp,3trom,tuba,timp,perc,
2harp,pno,strings CARISH rental
(P71)

PAPINEAU-COUTURE, JEAN (1916-   )
Psalm 150
SATB,acap min sc BERANDOL $8.00
(P72)

PAQUES *Easter
cor JOBERT s.p. see also Douze
Cantiques De Fetes   (P73)

PARABLE OF THE SOWER see Berger, Jean

PARADIS see Hemberg, Eskil

PARASTI MENSAM see Mozart, Leopold

PARCE, DOMINE see Obrecht, Jacob

PARIS
I Have A Peace In My Heart *gospel
(Schubert) SATB oct LILLENAS
AN-1656 $.30   (P74)

Please Stop Running Away From God
*gospel
(Mickelson, Paul) SATB,solo oct
LILLENAS AN-1708 $.30   (P75)

This Old World Will Never Be The Same
*gospel
(Schubert) SATB oct LILLENAS
AN-1664 $.30   (P76)

What Wondrous Sacred Love *see
Fairchild

PARISH MASS see Rottura, Joseph James

PARK, CHAI HOON
O Lord Who Shall Abide
SATB HARRIS HC 4060 $.60   (P77)

PARKE, DOROTHY
Has Sorrow Thy Young Days Shaded?
*sac/sec
SA CRAMER C76   (P78)

PARKER
Prayer
dbl cor SCHIRM.G LG51737 $.30 (P79)

PARKER, ALICE (1925-   )
Advent: Three Views
SATB&SA&unis jr cor,org SCHIRM.EC
2935   (P80)

Brotherly Love *canon
2-5 eq voices SCHIRM.EC 2818 (P81)

Carols To Play And Sing *see I Saw A
Stable; In Bethlehem; Shrill
Chanticleer   (P82)

Easter Rejoicing, An
SATB,SATB soli,pno/harp,org,perc
voc sc SCHIRM.EC 2798 s.p., ipa
(P83)

I Saw A Stable
SATB,org,perc SCHIRM.EC 2780 see
from Carols To Play And Sing
(P84)

In Bethlehem
SATB,org,perc SCHIRM.EC 2779 see
from Carols To Play And Sing
(P85)

Sermon From The Mountain, A
SATB,SATB soli,org&perc&gtr/orch
SCHIRM.EC 2766 s.p., ipr   (P86)

Shrill Chanticleer
SATB,org,perc SCHIRM.EC 2781 see
from Carols To Play And Sing
(P87)

PARKS
Come To The Savior Now *gospel
SATB oct LILLENAS AN-1662 $.30
(P88)

Jesus Is Coming Soon *gospel
SATB oct LILLENAS AN-1661 $.25
(P89)

Let All Who In This Kingdom Live
*anthem
SATB oct BROADMAN 4554-80 $.30
(P90)

Love Lifted Me *anthem
SATB (easy) oct BROADMAN 4540-54
$.30   (P91)

My Life, My All, I Give To Him
*anthem
SATB (easy) oct BROADMAN 4554-62
$.30   (P92)

PARKS (cont'd.)
O Praise The Lord *anthem
SATB (easy) oct BROADMAN 4540-59
$.30   (P93)

Rejoice, O Earth *Adv/Xmas
SATB oct LILLENAS AN-3874 $.30
(P94)

Sing Alleluia, Jesus Is Risen
*Easter,anthem
2pt oct BROADMAN 4551-85 $.30 (P95)

Take His Name *anthem
SATB (easy) oct BROADMAN 4551-37
$.30   (P96)

Very Friend I Need, The *anthem
SATB (easy) oct BROADMAN 4551-52
$.30   (P97)

What Love Is This *anthem
SATB (easy) oct BROADMAN 4540-48
$.30   (P98)

Who Shall Abide *anthem
SATB (easy) oct BROADMAN 4540-61
$.30   (P99)

You've Got To Live Your Religion
*spir
SATB oct LILLENAS AN-3861 $.25
(P100)

PARKS, JOE E.
Away Over In The Gloryland *anthem/
gospel
SATB oct SINGSPIR ZJP-8164 $.30
(P101)

Come, Go With Me To Bethlehem *Xmas
unis&2pt CHORISTERS A-119 $.35
(P102)

Destiny *folk
(Johnson, Norman) SATB oct SINGSPIR
ZJP-3589 $.25   (P103)

God Is Our Eternal Refuge *Thanks,
anthem
SATB oct SINGSPIR ZJP-7309 $.25
(P104)

Here Am I *anthem
SA&opt TB (easy) oct SINGSPIR
ZJP-6000 $.30   (P105)

How Sweet, How Heavenly Is The Sight
*anthem
SATB (easy) oct SINGSPIR ZJP-6020
$.30   (P106)

I Know He Holdeth Me *anthem/gospel
SATB oct SINGSPIR ZJP-8167 $.30
(P107)

In Remembrance Of Me *Commun,anthem
SATB oct SINGSPIR ZJP-7347 $.50
(P108)

Joyous News Of Christmas, The *Xmas,
cant
SATB,narrator SINGSPIR 5055 $1.50
(P109)

King Indeed, A *Xmas,anthem
SA&opt TB (easy) oct SINGSPIR
ZJP-3039 $.30   (P110)

Light Of The World *cant
mix cor,solo,gtr SINGSPIR 4292
$1.50   (P111)

Miracle Of Love, A *Easter,cant
SATB,SATB soli BROADMAN 4514-08
$1.50   (P112)

Praise The Lord, Ye Congregation
*anthem
SATB oct SINGSPIR ZJP-7265 $.25
(P113)

Rejoice, O Earth *Xmas,cant
SATB LILLENAS MC-29 $1.50   (P114)

Song Was Born, A *Xmas,cant
SATB,soli oct SINGSPIR 4455 $1.95
(P115)

PARRIS, HERMAN M. (1903-   )
Glory To God The Creator
SATB PARAGON 1033 $.30   (P116)

PARRIS, ROBERT (1924-   )
Alas For The Day
SATB,T solo,2fl,2ob,2clar,2bsn,
2horn,trp,trom,timp,strings
AM.COMP.AL. sc $17.60, voc sc
$9.35   (P117)

Hymn For The Nativity
SATB,3trp,3trom,tuba,3timp,perc
AM.COMP.AL. sc $13.20, ipa, voc
pt $5.50   (P118)

Jesu Dulcis Memoria
SATB,acap AM.COMP.AL. $4.40 (P119)

Reflections On Immortality *cant
SATB,2horn,2trp,trom,3timp,perc,
bass trombone AM.COMP.AL. sc
$13.20, ipa, voc pt $7.70 (P120)

PARRISH, MARY KAY
America, Our Country
1-2pt BROADMAN 4560-54 $.40 (P121)

Chorale And Alleluia *anthem
SATB FINE ARTS CM 1084 $.35 (P122)

God Who Touchest Earth With Beauty
*anthem
2pt oct BROADMAN 4558-62 $.30
(P123)

Only A Manger *Xmas,anthem
2pt oct BROADMAN 4558-69 $.30
(P124)

PARRY, CHARLES HUBERT HASTINGS
(1848-1918)
I Was Glad *anthem
(Jacob,) SATB,2fl,2ob,2clar,2bsn,
4horn,8trp,3trom,tuba,timp,perc,
harp,org,strings voc sc NOVELLO
rental   (P125)

Jesus, Lover Of My Soul *anthem
(Berglund) SSAATTBB oct LILLENAS
AN-6026 $.30   (P126)

Riding Into Bethlehem
unis,rec (easy) OXFORD 81.148 $.35,
ipa   (P127)

PARRY, W.H.
Now Thrice Welcome Christmas *Xmas
unis EMI   (P128)

Spacious Firmament, The
mix cor BANKS MUS YS 1496 $.25
(P129)

PARSONS
Ave Maria *anthem
SATBB,acap (med diff) OXFORD 43.484
$.85   (P130)

Heaven In My Heart *anthem/gospel
(Johnson, Norman) SATB oct SINGSPIR
ZJP-8040 $.30   (P131)

PARTHUN, PAUL
Choral Benedictions (composed with
Owens, Frederick) *anthem
SATB AUGSBURG 11-1678 $.25 (P132)

PARTING BLESSING, A see Klusmeier,
R.T.A.

PASQUET, JEAN (1896-   )
Bestow Thy Light Upon Us
see Two Short Anthems

Blessed Art Thou, O Lord
SATB,acap (easy) FITZSIMONS 2198
$.20   (P133)

Easter Alleluya, An
SATB,S solo (med) FITZSIMONS 2194
$.25   (P134)

If With All Your Hearts
SATB (med) FITZSIMONS 2199 $.25
(P135)

Into Thy Hands, O Lord
SATB (easy) FITZSIMONS 2205 $.20
(P136)

Lord, Sanctify Me Wholly
SATB,acap (easy) FITZSIMONS 2182
$.25   (P137)

O Jesus, Crucified For Man *Gd.Fri.
SA,pno/org (very easy) oct ELKAN-V
362-03166 $.30   (P138)

O Lord, Send Out Thy Light
see Two Short Anthems

O Sons And Daughters *Easter
SATB,org GRAY CMR 3297 $.30 (P139)

That Easter Day *Easter
SA,pno/org (very easy) oct ELKAN-V
362-03165 $.30   (P140)

Two Short Anthems
SATB oct GRAY GCMR 2980 $.30
contains: Bestow Thy Light Upon
Us; O Lord, Send Out Thy Light
(P141)

When Jesus Into Sion Rode *Easter
SA,pno/org (very easy) oct ELKAN-V
362-03164 $.35   (P142)

PASQUIER
Ite Ad Joseph
4pt,acap voc pt HENN 211 s.p.
(P143)

PASS IT ON see Durrett

PASSED THRU THE WATERS see Avery,
Richard

PASSERBY, THE see Johnson, S.

PASSIO D. N. J. CHR. SEC. JOANNEM see
Rore, Cipriano de

PASSIO D. N. J. CHR. SEC. MATTHAEUM see
Maistre, Jan (Nasco)

PASSIO D.N. JESU CHRISTI SECUNDUM
    JOHANNEM see Scarlatti, Alessandro

PASSIO DIE VENERIS see Mantua, Jachet
    von

PASSIO IN DIE PARASCEVES see Asola,
    Giovanni Matteo

PASSION, THE see Warren, Raymond

PASSION ACCORDING TO ST. JOHN, THE see
    Hillert, Richard

PASSION ACCORDING TO ST. JOHN, THE see
    Mattheson, Johann, Das Lied Des
    Lammes

PASSION ACCORDING TO ST. JOHN, THE see
    Scarlatti, Alessandro, Passio D.N.
    Jesu Christi Secundum Johannem

PASSION ACCORDING TO SAINT JOHN, THE
    see Schutz, Heinrich

PASSION ACCORDING TO ST. JOHN, THE see
    Victoria, Tomas Luis de

PASSION ACCORDING TO SAINT MARK, THE
    see Bender, Jan

PASSION ACCORDING TO SAINT. LUKE see
    Bissell, Keith W.

PASSION AND RESURRECTION OF OUR LORD,
    THE see Billings, William

PASSION CHORALE, THE see Martin,
    Gilbert M.

PASSION MUSIC ON THE SEVEN WORDS OF
    JESUS CHRIST ON THE CROSS see
    Pfleger, Augustin, Passionsmusik
    Uber Die Sieben Worte Jesu Christ
    Am Kreuz

PASSION OF CHRIST, THE see Fletcher,
    Percy Eastman

PASSION OF OUR LORD ACCORDING TO ST.
    JOHN, THE see Bach, Johann
    Sebastian

PASSION OF OUR LORD ACCORDING TO ST.
    MATTHEW, THE see Bach, Johann
    Sebastian, Matthaus-Passion

PASSION SPIRITUALS see Cossetto, Emil

PASSIONMUSIK UBER DIE SIEBEN WORTE JESU
    CHRIST AM KREUZ see Pfleger,
    Augustin

PASSIONS-KANTATE see Biersack, Anton

PASSIONSCHORAL "DER LEIB ZWAR IN DER
    ERDEN" see Bach, Johann Sebastian

PASSIONSMUSIK see Heiller, Anton

PASSIONTIDE CAROL see Cruft, Adrian

PAST THREE A CLOCK
    see Twelve Christmas Carols: Set 2

PAST THREE O'CLOCK
    see Four Christmas Carols

PAST THREE O'CLOCK see Wood, Charles

PASTORAL-MESSE see Kempter, Karl

PASTORAL-MESSE IN D ZU EHREN DES
    GOTTLICHEN KINDES see Krenn, Franz

PASTORAL-MESSE IN F see Diabelli, Anton

PASTORALE see Loewe, Karl Gottfried

PASTORALMESSE IN G see Kempter, Karl

PASTORELY CESKE VANOCNI see Palkovsky,
    Oldrich

PASTORES LOQUEBANTUR see Anerio, Felice

PASTORES LOQUEBANTUR see Costantini,
    Alessandro

PATER NOSTER see Berger, Jean

PATER NOSTER see Green, Philip

PATER NOSTER see Liszt, Franz

PATER NOSTER see Nicolai, Otto

PATER NOSTER see Praetorius,
    Heironymous

PATER NOSTER see Schwarz-Schilling,
    Reinhard

PATER NOSTER see Verdi, Giuseppe

PATER, SI NON POTEST see Stout, Alan

PATRIQUIN, DONALD
    Merry Christmas *Xmas
        SATB (easy) WATERLOO $.30   (P144)

PATTERSON, JOY F.
    On A Winter Night *anthem
        CHORISTERS R-15 $.15   (P145)

PATTERSON, PAUL
    Gloria
        cor,pno sc WEINBERGER $6.00   (P146)

    Kyrie
        cor,pno sc WEINBERGER $2.50   (P147)

PAUKEN-MESSE IN C see Haydn, (Franz)
    Joseph, Missa In Tempore Belli

PAUL FERRIN'S SPECIAL CHOIR MELODIES,
    BOOK NO. 1 *CC12UL,gospel/hymn
    (Ferrin, Paul) cor,pno/org GOSPEL
    05 TM 0493 $1.00 recording also
    available   (P148)

PAUL FERRIN'S SPECIAL CHOIR MELODIES,
    BOOK NO. 2 *CC12UL,gospel/hymn
    (Ferrin, Paul) cor,pno/org GOSPEL
    05 TM 0494 $1.50   (P149)

PAUL JOHNSON SINGERS see Johnson, Paul

PAUL MICKELSON'S CHORAL ARRANGEMENTS
    *CCUL
    (Mickelson, Paul) cor SINGSPIR 4315
    $1.50   (P150)

PAULSEN, A.
    Thou Art, O God, The Life And Light
        SATB (easy) FITZSIMONS 2014 $.25
                                       (P151)

PAULUS, STEPHEN
    Alleluia! Christ Is Risen *Easter
        SATB ART MAST 250 $.30   (P152)

    At The Tomb *Lent
        SATB,acap ART MAST 239 $.30   (P153)

    Impart
        2pt ART MAST 1027 $.40   (P154)

    Lift Up Our Hearts, O King Of Kings
        1-2pt ART MAST 204 $.35   (P155)

    Lord, Here Am I
        SATB ART MAST 219 $.35   (P156)

    Snow Had Fallen; Christ Was Born
        *Adv/Xmas
        SATB ART MAST 226 $.40   (P157)

    Song In The Air, A *Adv/Xmas
        unis ART MAST 272 $.30   (P158)

    Underneath A Star *Adv/Xmas
        SATB ART MAST 251 $.35   (P159)

PAVIOUR, PAUL
    Advent Carol, An
        see Four Carols

    And Is There Care In Heaven *mot
        cor,acap RICORDI-ENG SD s.p.   (P160)

    Christ For The World
        2pt treb cor,org RICORDI-ENG SD
        s.p.   (P161)

    Evening Service In G
        unis/SATB,org EMI s.p.   (P162)

    Four Carols
        RICORDI-ENG SD s.p.
        contains: Advent Carol, An
        (unis); I Sing Of The Birth
        (SATB); My Heart For Very Joy
        Doth Leap (SATB); Welcome Yule
        (SATB)   (P163)

    I Sing Of The Birth
        see Four Carols

    Missa Brevis
        unis/SATB,org (Anglican) EMI s.p.
                                       (P164)

    My Heart For Very Joy Doth Leap
        see Four Carols

    Welcome Yule
        see Four Carols

PAYCHERE
    Noels Anciens *CCU,Xmas
        wom cor,acap (easy) sc HENN 705
        s.p.   (P165)

PAYNE, ANTHONY
    Little Passiontide Cantata, A Isatb,
        Acap *Psntd
        cor NOVELLO MT 1583 s.p.   (P166)

    Phoenix Mass
        mix cor,3trp,3trom CHESTER JWC 8900
        s.p.   (P167)

PAYNTER, JOHN P.
    Exultet Coelum Laudibus
        SATB,ST soli,inst (med) OXFORD
        84.168 $.40, ipa   (P168)

    God's Grandeur
        voc sc OXFORD   (P169)

    Make A Joyful Noise Unto The Lord
        SATB,acap (med diff) OXFORD 84.187
        $.35   (P170)

    May Magnificat
        SATB,acap (diff) OXFORD 46.181
        $1.90   (P171)

    Rose, The
        SATB,acap (med diff) OXFORD 84.192
        $.50   (P172)

    There Is No Rose *Xmas,carol
        any voices (med easy) OXFORD 40.021
        $.35   (P173)

PEACE see Kennedy

PEACE see Stringfield, Lamar

PEACE, ALBERT LISTER (1844-1912)
    O Love That Wilt Not Let Me Go
        *anthem
        (Collins) SATB oct LILLENAS AN-2386
        $.25   (P174)
        (Rasley, John M.) SATB oct SINGSPIR
        ZJP-7315 $.30   (P175)

PEACE BE MULTIPLIED see Hovhaness, Alan

PEACE BE MULTIPLIED see Ultan, Lloyd

PEACE BE WITH YOU see Bender, Jan

PEACE BE WITH YOU see Wetzler, Robert

PEACE CAROL see Beers

PEACE DESCENDS TODAY FROM HEAVEN see
    Grandi, Alessandro

PEACE FOR THE TAKING see Burroughs, Bob

PEACE I LEAVE WITH YOU see Burroughs,
    Bob

PEACE I LEAVE WITH YOU see Schinhan,
    J.P.

PEACE IN OUR TIME see Burroughs, Bob

PEACE IN OUR TIME see Corum

PEACE IN OUR TIME, O LORD see Darst, W.
    Glenn

PEACE IN YOUR WORLD see Eneberg, Gale
    (Gail)

PEACE LIKE A RIVER *anthem/spir
    (Moffatt, James) SATB (med easy) oct
    LORENZ B236 $.35   (P176)

PEACE LIKE A RIVER see Courtney, Ragan

PEACE LIKE A RIVER see Moffatt

PEACE ON EARTH see Peek, Richard

PEACE ON EARTH see Verrall, Pamela

PEACE ON EARTH see Wetzler, Robert

PEACE, PERFECT PEACE see Caldbeck

PEACE, PERFECT PEACE see Mc Cabe

PEACE, SWEET PEACE see Turner

PEACE THAT JESUS GIVES, THE see
    Lillenas, Haldor

PEACE TO ALL WHO ENTER HERE see Wild,
    Eric

PEACE UPON EARTH see Winter, Sister
    Miriam Therese

PEACEABLE KINGDOM, THE see Hruby,
    Delores

PEACEFUL WAS THE NIGHT see Butler,
    Eugene

PEARCE
    When He Shall Come *anthem
        (Johnson, Norman) SATB oct SINGSPIR
        ZJP-7294 $.25   (P177)

    When I See The Face Of Jesus *anthem
        (Johnson, Norman) SA/TB (easy) oct
        SINGSPIR ZJP-6027 $.35   (P178)

PEARS
    When Christ Was Born *Xmas
        SATB (med easy) WATERLOO $.30
                                       (P179)

PEARS, JAMES R.
When Christ Was Born *Xmas
    SSA (med easy) WATERLOO $.40 (P180)

PEARSALL, ROBERT LUCAS DE (1795-1856)
In Dulci Jubilo *Xmas
    SATB EMI s.p. contains also:
    Grimes, Gordon, Sleep, My
    Saviour, Sleep (composed with
    Pettman, Edgar)   (P181)

Sing We
    (Opheim) SATB oct SCHMITT 1212 $.30
                            (P182)

PECCANTEM ME see Morales, Cristobal de

PECCANTEM ME QUOTIDIE see Byrd, William

PECHEURS SOR LA CALVAIRE see Bach,
Johann Sebastian

PEDERSON, MOGENS (ca. 1580-1623)
Ad Te Levavi Oculos Meos
    SSATB,acap EGTVED MK13, 18 s.p.
                            (P183)

Deus Miseratur Nostri
    SSATB,acap EGTVED MK5, 1 s.p.
                            (P184)

Sanctus *Sanctus
    SATBB,acap EGTVED KB26 s.p. (P185)

PEDRETTE
Is It Nothing To You? *Easter
    SATB SCHIRM.G 11926 $.25   (P186)

PEEK, B.L.
Thou Art The Way
    mix cor BRODT 575 $.26   (P187)

PEEK, JOSEPH YATES
I Would Be True *anthem
    (DeCou, Harold) SA oct SINGSPIR
    ZJP-2003 $.25   (P188)

PEEK, RICHARD
All Glory, Laud And Honor *Palm
    unis CHORISTERS A-140 $.30 (P189)

Benedictus Es, Domine
    "Blessed Art Thou, O Lord God Of
    Our Fathers" mix cor BRODT 530
    $.32   (P190)

Blessed Art Thou, O Lord God Of Our
    Fathers *see Benedictus Es,
    Domine

Christ Is The King
    mix cor BRODT 539 $.20   (P191)

Father, We Praise Thee
    mix cor BRODT 519 $.24   (P192)

From Thee All Skill And Science Flow
    mix cor BRODT 607 $.26   (P193)

Here, O Lord, Thy Servants Gather
    *Gen/Thanks
    SATB,org,pno, Tam Tam CHORISTERS
    A-106 $.35   (P194)

Our Christ Today From Death Hath
    Sprung
    mix cor BRODT 525 $.26   (P195)

Peace On Earth *Xmas
    unis,pno/org, Tam Tam CHORISTERS
    A-125 $.35   (P196)

Saint Stephen
    cor BRODT $1.80   (P197)

PEETERS, FLOR (1903-   )
In Convertendo Dominus (Psalm 125)
    "When God The Lord" SATB SUMMY
    M-2479 $1.00   (P198)

Psalm 125 *see In Convertendo
    Dominus

To Bethlehem *cant
    2 eq voices,solo,org SUMMY $1.95
                            (P199)

When God The Lord *see In
    Convertendo Dominus

PEHKONEN
Mary The Rose
    SATB,acap (easy) OXFORD 84.176 $.30
                            (P200)

PEISSNER, KARL
Christkonigsmesse *Mass
    [Lat] 4pt mix cor,org sc,cor pts
    BOHM s.p.   (P201)

Jubilate Deo *Fest
    [Lat] mix cor&unis jr cor,org sc,
    cor pts BOHM s.p., ipa   (P202)

Missa Brevis *Mass
    [Lat] 4pt mix cor,opt org sc,cor
    pts BOHM s.p.   (P203)

Pange Lingua
    [Lat] 4pt mix cor,acap BOHM s.p.
                            (P204)

PEKIEL, BERTLOMIEJ (? -ca. 1670)
Great The Name Of Christ Our Lord
    *see Magnum Nomen Domini

Let The Earth Resound *see Resonet
    In Laudibus

Magnum Nomen Domini
    (Herter, Joseph A.) "Great The Name
    Of Christ Our Lord" [Eng/Lat]
    SATB (easy) GIA G1791 $.40 (P205)

Resonet In Laudibus
    (Herter, Joseph A.) "Let The Earth
    Resound" [Eng/Lat] SATB (easy)
    GIA G1792 $.40   (P206)

PELICAN, THE see Thompson, Randall

PELOQUIN, C. ALEXANDER
Alleluia! In All Things! *anthem
    2 eq voices/2pt mix cor,org,opt
    inst (easy) GIA G1822 $1.50
                            (P207)

Celebration Of Presence, Prayer And
    Praise *Ded
    cor GIA   (P208)

Communion Rite (from Lyric Liturgy)
    SATB&cong,solo,org,opt timp (easy)
    GIA G1866 $.45   (P209)

Faith, Hope And Love (from Lyric
    Liturgy) Commun,anthem
    SATB&opt cong,cantor,org (easy) GIA
    G1893 $.60   (P210)

Gloria (from Lyric Liturgy) Gloria
    SATB&cong,org,opt 3trp&2trom&bvl&
    timp&tamb (med easy) GIA G1865
    $.60   (P211)
    SATB&cong,org,opt brass GIA G1926
    $.90   (P212)

God Is In His Holy Place (from
    Celebration Of Presence, Prayer
    And Praise) Proces
    SATB&cong,org,opt brass,timp GIA
    G1924 $.75   (P213)

I Believe That My Redeemer Lives
    *Easter,anthem
    SA/SAA (med easy) GIA G1805 $.35
                            (P214)

Liturgy Of The Eucharist (from Lyric
    Liturgy)
    SATB&cong,cantor,org,opt brass,
    perc,bvl (easy) GIA G1882 $.50
                            (P215)

Liturgy Of The Word (from Lyric
    Liturgy)
    SATB&cong,cantor,org (easy) GIA
    G1881 $.75   (P216)

Lord Jesus Come (from Lyric Liturgy)
    anthem
    SATB&cong,cantor,org,brass,bvl,opt
    timp (med easy) GIA G1880 $.75
                            (P217)

Lyric Liturgy *CCU,Commun
    SATB&cong,cantor,org,brass,timp
    (easy) GIA G1907 $3.00   (P218)

Mass Of Resurrection *Easter
    SATB/cong,opt cantor GIA G1786
    $1.50   (P219)

Mass Of The Bells
    SATB&cong,opt cantor (med easy) GIA
    G1808 $1.00   (P220)

Missa A La Samba
    2-3 eq voices,opt trp,bvl, bongos
    (med) GIA G1581 $1.25, ipa (P221)
    unis,opt trp,bvl, bongos (med) GIA
    G1580 $1.25, ipa   (P222)
    SATB,opt trp,bvl, bongos (med) GIA
    G1582 $1.25, ipa   (P223)

Penitential Rite And Liturgy Of The
    Word (from Lyric Liturgy)
    SATB&cong,cantor,org GIA G1881 $.75
                            (P224)

Prayer
    cor,org GIA G1925 $.40   (P225)

Prayer For Us, A
    cor&cong,narrator,solo,org,opt
    brass,timp,bells voc sc GIA G1982
    $1.00, ipa   (P226)

Prayer Of St. Francis *anthem
    SATB,acap (easy) GIA G1823 $.45
                            (P227)

Psalm 100 *see Psalm One Hundred

Psalm One Hundred (Psalm 100) anthem/
    Bibl
    SATB,org,opt 4brass,bvl,perc (med)
    GIA G1861 $1.50   (P228)

Receive The Holy Spirit *Cnfrm/Pent,
    anthem
    SATB&cong,opt cantor,org (easy) GIA
    G1895 $.50   (P229)

PELOQUIN, C. ALEXANDER (cont'd.)
Song Of Daniel
    SATB&opt cong,cantor,org,2trp,
    2trom,timp (med easy) GIA G1185
    $1.00   (P230)
    TTBB&opt cong,cantor,org,2trp,
    2trom,timp (med easy) GIA G1158
    $1.00   (P231)

Songs Of Israel *CC12U,Psalm
    SATB&cong,cantor,org,opt brass,perc
    GIA G1666 $3.50   (P232)

PELZ, WALTER L. (1926-   )
Born Is Little Jesus
    SA,pno, Orff instruments oct
    SCHMITT 254 $.30   (P233)

Embodied Word, The *see Pennington,
    Chester

Feast Of Joy
    SATB,org,3trp,2trom,timp sc
    AUGSBURG 11-9116 $1.75, voc sc
    AUGSBURG 11-9117 $.45, ipa (P234)

Good News! *Adv/Xmas
    SATB,fl, glockenspiel ART MAST 215
    $.35   (P235)

Jesus Took The Cup *Commun
    SATB ART MAST 216 $.35   (P236)

Splendor Is Coming
    SATB ART MAST 247 $.35   (P237)

PEMBAUR, KARL MARIA (1876-1939)
Messe No. 1 In F-Dur *Op.10b, Mass
    [Lat] 4pt mix cor,org&
    opt 2ob&2clar&2horn&2trp sc,cor
    pts BOHM s.p., ipa   (P238)

PENDERECKI, KRZYSZTOF (1933-   )
Auferstehung
    mix cor&mix cor&jr cor,SATBB soli,
    orch sc SCHOTTS rental   (P239)

Utrenja
    mix cor&mix cor,SATBB soli,orch
    (diff) min sc SCHOTTS ED. 6314
    s.p., sc SCHOTTS rental, ipr
                            (P240)

PENHORWOOD, EDWIN
Hosanna To The Son Of David
    SATB,SSS soli,org,bvl (med)
    FISCHER,C CM 7902 $.50   (P241)

PENINGER
Bless The Father, O My Soul *anthem
    SATB (med) oct BROADMAN 4562-16
    $.35   (P242)

Every Time I Feel The Spirit *anthem
    SAB oct BROADMAN 4551-73 $.30
                            (P243)

Hark, Ye People, Christ Is Risen!
    *see Hayes

If Thou But Suffer God To Guide Thee
    *anthem
    SATB (med) oct BROADMAN 4562-18
    $.35   (P244)

In Memory Of The Savior's Love
    *anthem
    SATB oct SACRED S-152 $.40 (P245)

In Remembrance Of Him *Commun,anthem
    SATB oct BROADMAN 4519-01 $.35
                            (P246)

Jesus Is Lord! *anthem
    SATB (easy) oct BROADMAN 4562-31
    $.35   (P247)

Jesus Saves *see Kirkpatrick

Lord Omnipotent Is King, The *anthem
    SATB oct BROADMAN 4551-76 $.30
                            (P248)

O God, Accept My Heart *see Bridges

O How Happy Are They *see Wesley

O Lord, Grant Us Thy Mercy *see
    Cannon

O Lord, My Inmost Heart And Thought
    *anthem
    SATB oct BROADMAN 4551-89 $.30
                            (P249)

On Christmas Morn *CC4U,Adv/Xmas,
    chorale
    SATB oct LILLENAS AN-3852 $.35
                            (P250)

One Holy Church Of God Appears *see
    Longfellow

Song Of Dedication, A *see Hudson,
    Richard

What A Friend We Have In Jesus
    *anthem
    SATB oct BROADMAN 4540-76 $.30
                            (P251)

PENINGER (cont'd.)

What The World Needs *anthem
SAB (easy) oct BROADMAN 4554-65
$.30   (P252)

When I Survey The Wondrous Cross
*anthem
SAB oct SACRED S-7424 $.35   (P253)

PENINGER, DAVID
Door, The (composed with Treadwell,
William)
SAB,4 soli,pno (med easy, Music
Drama) PRESSER 412-41058 $1.95
                                        (P254)

I Love The Lord, His Strength Is Mine
SABar&camb,pno CAMBIATA C17314 $.35
                                        (P255)

Lord Is My Shepherd, The
mix cor BRODT 518 $.26   (P256)

Night The Christ Child Came, The
*anthem
SATB WORD CS-2651 $.30   (P257)

O Thou By Whom We Come To God
SABar&camb,pno/org CAMBIATA C17554
$.35   (P258)

PENITENTIAL RITE AND LITURGY OF THE
WORD see Peloquin, C. Alexander

PENNINGTON, CHESTER
Embodied Word, The (composed with
Pelz, Walter L.)
SATB,SSA&narrator,pno,org,fl,2perc
cmplt ed AUGSBURG 11-9180 $2.00,
ipa   (P259)

PENTECOTE *Pent
cor JOBERT s.p. see also Douze
Cantiques De Fetes   (P260)

PEOPLE CAROL, THE see Emig

PEOPLE EVERYWHERE NEED PEOPLE see
Skillings, Otis

PEOPLE KNOW THEE see Eberlin, Johann
Ernst

PEOPLE LOOK EAST see Bissell, Keith W.

PEOPLE OF GOD, THE see Butler, Eugene

PEOPLE OF GOD see Moore, Mother B.M.

PEOPLE TO PEOPLE see Reynolds, William
Jensen

PEPPING, ERNST (1901-   )
Ach Wie Fluchtig, Ach Wie Nichtig
SSATB&SSAATTBB,acap (diff) sc
SCHOTTS C 32 477 s.p. see from
Choralsuite Teil III   (P261)

An Wasserflussen Babylons
(Mahrenholz, Christian) SATB sc
SCHOTTS C 32 963 s.p. see from
Choralbuch   (P262)

Aus Hartem Weh
(Mahrenholz, Christian) SSATB sc
SCHOTTS C 32 968 s.p. see from
Choralbuch   (P263)

Aus Tiefer Not
(Mahrenholz, Christian) SATB sc
SCHOTTS C 33 028 s.p. see from
Choralbuch   (P264)

Choralbuch *see An Wasserflussen
Babylons; Aus Hartem Weh; Aus
Tiefer Not; Christ Ist Erstanden;
Christum Wir Sollen Loben; Der Du
Bist Drei In Einigkeit; Der
Heiden Heiland Komm Her; Erhalt
Uns Herr Bei Deinem Wort; Freu
Dich, Du Werte Christenheit; Freu
Dich, Heilige Christenheit;
Gelobet, Seist Du, Jesu Christ;
Gib Dich Zufrieden Und Sei
Stille; Herr Christe, Treuer
Heiland Wert; Mit Fried Und Freud
Fahr Ich Dahin; O Haupt Voll Blut
Und Wunden; O Mensch Bewein Dein
Sunde Gross; Vater Unser Im
Himmelreich; Wie Schon Leuchtet
Der Morgenstern   (P265)

Choralsuite Teil I *CCU
8pt mix cor&4pt mix cor,acap (diff)
sc SCHOTTS C 32 473 s.p.   (P266)

Choralsuite Teil II *see Christ Ist
Erstanden; Den Die Hirten Lobeten
Sehre; Herzliebster Jesu   (P267)

Choralsuite Teil III *see Ach Wie
Fluchtig, Ach Wie Nichtig; Die
Guldne Sonne; Nun Sich Der Tag
Geendet Hat   (P268)

PEPPING, ERNST (cont'd.)

Christ Ist Erstanden
SSATB (diff) sc SCHOTTS C 32 475
s.p. see from Choralsuite Teil II
                                        (P269)
(Mahrenholz, Christian) SATBB sc
SCHOTTS C 32 969 s.p. see from
Choralbuch   (P270)

Christum Wir Sollen Loben
(Mahrenholz, Christian) SATB sc
SCHOTTS C 32 970 s.p. see from
Choralbuch   (P271)

Das Ist Ein Boses Ding
see Prediger-Motette

Den Die Hirten Lobeten Sehre
SAB&SSATTB (diff) sc SCHOTTS
C 32 474 s.p. see from
Choralsuite Teil II   (P272)

Der Du Bist Drei In Einigkeit
(Mahrenholz, Christian) SSATBB sc
SCHOTTS C 33 035 s.p. see from
Choralbuch   (P273)

Der Heiden Heiland Komm Her
(Mahrenholz, Christian) SATBB sc
SCHOTTS C 32 971 s.p. see from
Choralbuch   (P274)

Deutsche Choralmesse *Mass
SSATBB,acap (med diff) sc SCHOTTS
ED. 3241 s.p.   (P275)

Deutsche Messe "Kyrie Gott Vater In
Ewigkeit"
SSATBB,acap sc SCHOTTS ED. 3546
s.p.   (P276)

Die Guldne Sonne
SSATB,acap (diff) sc SCHOTTS
C 32 478 s.p. see from
Choralsuite Teil III   (P277)

Drei Evangelien-Motetten *see
Gleichnis Vom Unkraut Zwischen
Dem Weizen "Das Himmelreich Ist
Gleich Einem Mensch"; Gleichnis
Von Der Koniglichen Hochzeit
"Saget Den Gasten; Jesus Und
Nikodemus "Es War Aber Ein
Mensch"   (P278)

Ein Jegliches Hat Seine Zeit
see Prediger-Motette

Erhalt Uns Herr Bei Deinem Wort
(Mahrenholz, Christian) SATBB sc
SCHOTTS C 33 032 s.p. see from
Choralbuch   (P279)

Freu Dich, Du Werte Christenheit
(Mahrenholz, Christian) SATB sc
SCHOTTS C 33 029 s.p. see from
Choralbuch   (P280)

Freu Dich, Heilige Christenheit
(Mahrenholz, Christian) SATBB sc
SCHOTTS C 33 033 s.p. see from
Choralbuch   (P281)

Gedenke An Deinen Schopfer
see Prediger-Motette

Gelobet, Seist Du, Jesu Christ
(Mahrenholz, Christian) SATB sc
SCHOTTS C 32 972 s.p. see from
Choralbuch   (P282)

Gib Dich Zufrieden Und Sei Stille
(Mahrenholz, Christian) SATBB sc
SCHOTTS C 32 964 s.p. see from
Choralbuch   (P283)

Gleichnis Vom Unkraut Zwischen Dem
Weizen "Das Himmelreich Ist
Gleich Einem Mensch" *evang/mot
mix cor (med) sc SCHOTTS C 35 565
s.p. see from Drei Evangelien-
Motetten   (P284)

Gleichnis Von Der Koniglichen
Hochzeit "Saget Den Gasten
*evang/mot
SSATTB (med) sc SCHOTTS C 35 566
s.p. see from Drei Evangelien-
Motetten   (P285)

Herr Christe, Treuer Heiland Wert
(Mahrenholz, Christian) SATB sc
SCHOTTS C 32 973 s.p. see from
Choralbuch   (P286)

Herzliebster Jesu
SATB&SATB,acap (diff) sc SCHOTTS
C 32 476 s.p. see from
Choralsuite Teil II   (P287)

Jesus Und Nikodemus "Es War Aber Ein
Mensch" *evang/mot
mix cor (med) sc SCHOTTS C 35 567
s.p. see from Drei Evangelien-
Motetten   (P288)

PEPPING, ERNST (cont'd.)

Lob Und Ehr Mit Stetem Dankopfer
see Lobgesang Der Bohmischen Bruder

Lobgesang Der Bohmischen Bruder
SATBB,acap (med) sc SCHOTTS
C 40 547 s.p.
contains: Lob Und Ehr Mit Stetem
Dankopfer; Wer Kann Dir, Herre;
Wer Mag Dich, Herre Gott (P289)

Mit Fried Und Freud Fahr Ich Dahin
(Mahrenholz, Christian) SATBB sc
SCHOTTS C 32 975 s.p. see from
Choralbuch   (P290)

Mitten Wir Im Leben Sind
TBarBB sc SCHOTTS CHBL 110 s.p.
                                        (P291)

Nun Bitten Wir Den Heiligen Geist
(from Deutschen Choralmesse No.
1)
SSATBarB (med) sc SCHOTTS C 32 603A
s.p.   (P292)

Nun Sich Der Tag Geendet Hat
SSSSAAATTTBB,acap (diff) sc SCHOTTS
C 32 479 s.p. see from
Choralsuite Teil III   (P293)

O Haupt Voll Blut Und Wunden
(Mahrenholz, Christian) SATB sc
SCHOTTS C 32 961 s.p. see from
Choralbuch   (P294)

O Mensch Bewein Dein Sunde Gross
(Mahrenholz, Christian) ATB&SSB sc
SCHOTTS C 32 976 s.p. see from
Choralbuch   (P295)

Prediger-Motette *mot
mix cor (med) sc SCHOTTS C 35 359
s.p.
contains: Das Ist Ein Boses Ding;
Ein Jegliches Hat Seine Zeit;
Gedenke An Deinen Schopfer
                                        (P296)

Spandauer Chorbuch Band I *CC50L
(Grote, Gottfried) 2-6pt mix cor
cloth SCHOTTS ED. 5211 s.p.
                                        (P297)

Spandauer Chorbuch Band II *CC60L,
Gen
(Grote, Gottfried) 2-6pt mix cor
cloth SCHOTTS ED. 5212 s.p.
                                        (P298)

Spandauer Chorbuch Band III *CC50L,
Gen
(Grote, Gottfried) 2-6pt mix cor
cloth SCHOTTS ED. 5213 s.p.
                                        (P299)

Spandauer Chorbuch Band IV *CC30L,
Gen
(Grote, Gottfried) 2-6pt mix cor
cloth SCHOTTS ED. 5214 s.p.
                                        (P300)

Uns Ist Ein Kind Geboren *Xmas,mot
mix cor (med) sc SCHOTTS C 34 927
s.p.   (P301)

Vater Unser Im Himmelreich
(Mahrenholz, Christian) SSATBB sc
SCHOTTS C 32 965 s.p. see from
Choralbuch   (P302)

Wer Kann Dir, Herre
see Lobgesang Der Bohmischen Bruder

Wer Mag Dich, Herre Gott
see Lobgesang Der Bohmischen Bruder

Wie Schon Leuchtet Der Morgenstern
SATB (contains also: Barmherziger,
Ewiger Gott) SCHWEIZER.
SK 54.05-6 s.p. see also
MUSIKBEILAGE ZUM "EVANGELISCHEN
KIRCHENCHOR 1954"   (P303)
(Mahrenholz, Christian) SATB sc
SCHOTTS C 32 958 s.p. see from
Choralbuch   (P304)

PER ANNUM, OP. 139, NO 2 see Lemacher,
Heinrich

PER LIGNUM SERVI FACTI SUMUS see Stout,
Alan

PER OMNIA SAECULA see Pranschke,
Johannes

PERERA, RONALD (1941-   )
Did You Hear The Angels Sing?
SATB,S solo,org SCHIRM.EC 2914
                                        (P305)

PEREZ, JOANNES GINESIUS
Hispaniae Schola Musica Sacra Vol. V:
Joannes Ginesius Perez, 1896
*CCU
(Pedrell, F.) cor pap JOHNSON
$12.00 contains also: Vol. VI:
Psalmodia Modulata (Vulgo
Fabordones) A Diversiis
Auctoribus, 1897   (P306)

PERFICE GRESSUS MEOS IN SEMITIS TUIS
see Lassus, Roland de (Orlandus)

PERGAMENT, MOSES (1893-)
Nu Samlar Gud I Sin Hand
SSAATTBB ERIKS 18 s.p.   (P307)

PERGOLESI, GIOVANNI BATTISTA
(1710-1736)
Alleluia
SATB WALTON 6033 $.40   (P308)

Dixit Dominus (Psalm 109)
dbl cor,solo,2orch voc sc EULENBURG
GM170 s.p., sc EULENBURG 10085
s.p., ipr   (P309)

Glory To God In The Highest *Xmas,
anthem
(Collins) SA/SAB (easy) oct
BROADMAN 4551-58 $.30   (P310)

Hear My Prayer
see Two Psalms

Laudate Pueri (Psalm 112)
cor,S solo,orch voc sc EULENBURG
GM171 s.p., sc EULENBURG 10084
s.p., ipr   (P311)

M La Mort De Saint-Joseph *ora
cor,soli,orch HENN s.p.   (P312)

Missa Romana *Mass
dbl cor,soli,2orch voc sc EULENBURG
GM172 s.p., sc EULENBURG 10083
s.p., ipr   (P313)

Psalm 109 *see Dixit Dominus

Psalm 112 *see Laudate Pueri

Remember Thy Congregation
see Two Psalms

Salve Regina
mix cor,orch HENN s.p.   (P314)

Two Psalms *Psalm
(Suchoff) SATB oct FOX PS118 $.35
contains: Hear My Prayer;
Remember Thy Congregation
                               (P315)

PERKINS
Give Your Heart To Jesus Christ
1-2pt jr cor oct LILLENAS AN-4033
$.30   (P316)

PERRIN, RONALD
Alleluya Sing To Jesus
unis (easy) FISCHER,C CM 7830 $.35
                               (P317)

Jubilate Deo
unis (easy) FISCHER,C CM 7829 $.30
                               (P318)

PERRY, JULIA
Ye, Who Seek The Truth
SATB GALAXY 1.1901.1 $.30   (P319)

PERT
Missa Festiva *Commun,Mass
SA,inst OXFORD 46.183 $3.00, ipr
                               (P320)

PERTI, GIACOMO ANTONIO (1661-1756)
Adoramus Te
(Klein) "We Adore Thee" SATB
SCHIRM.G 12002 $.30   (P321)

Beatus Vir (Psalm 112)
(Berger) SATB SCHIRM.G LG51764 $.75
                               (P322)

Psalm 112 *see Beatus Vir

We Adore Thee *see Adoramus Te

We Adore You, O Jesus
(Coggin) SAB KJOS 5742 $.35   (P323)

PERVIGILIUM VENERIS see Austin,
Frederick

PETER AND JOHN *Contemp
(Stewart; Pitts) SATB VANGUARD V553
$.35 see from Go Tell Everyone
                               (P324)

PETER, JOHANN FRIEDRICH (1746-1813)
Glory Be To Him
(McCorkle) mix cor BRODT 1001 $.40
                               (P325)

Harken, Stay Close To Him
(Kroeger, Karl) [Ger/Eng] 2 eq
voices (med easy) FISCHER,C
CM 7915 $.40   (P326)

Herr Gott, Dich Loben Wir
SAT/SAB&cong/SATB&SATB,org HANSSLER
14.137 s.p.   (P327)

Ich Bin Getauft Auf Deinen Namen
SAT/SAB,opt treb inst HANSSLER
14.152 s.p.   (P328)

Look Ye, How My Servants Shall Be
Feasting
(Kroeger) [Ger/Eng] SATB,S solo oct
MORAVIAN 5864 $.55   (P329)

PETER, JOHANN FRIEDRICH (cont'd.)
O Dass Ich Tausend Zungen Hatte
SAT/SAB/2pt,opt 1-2treb inst
HANSSLER 14.238 s.p.   (P330)

Praise The Lord, O My Soul
(Kroeger) SATB oct BOOSEY 5891 $.50
                               (P331)

Schmucke Dich, O Liebe Seele
see Kolter, Schmucke Dich, O Liebe
Seele

Sonne Der Gerechtigkeit
SAT/SAB/2pt,opt S solo,treb inst,
opt bass inst HANSSLER 14.218
s.p.   (P332)

PETERS, WILLIAM C.
Gloria (from Mass No. 1 In C Major)
[Lat] SATB,opt soli,pno BOONIN
B 193 $.60   (P333)

PETERSEN, ROLF (1923-)
Deep River
"Tiefe Fluten" see Spirituals For
All Heft II

Didn't My Lord Deliver Daniel
"Warum Rettet' Denn Gott Nur
Daniel" see Spirituals For All
Heft I

Geh Hin, Moses *see Go Down Moses

Go Down Moses
"Geh Hin, Moses" see Spirituals For
All Heft II

Joshua Fit De Battle Of Jerico
"Joshua Schlug Die Schlacht Von
Jericho" see Spirituals For All
Heft II

Joshua Schlug Die Schlacht Von
Jericho *see Joshua Fit De
Battle Of Jerico

Keiner Kann Meinen Kummer Verstehn
*see Nobody Knows De Trouble I've
Seen

Nobody Knows De Trouble I've Seen
"Keiner Kann Meinen Kummer
Verstehn" see Spirituals For All
Heft I

Spirituals For All Heft I *spir
[Eng/Ger] mix cor,pno,opt bvl,gtr
(med easy) sc,cor pts SCHOTTS
ED. 5926 s.p., ipa
contains: Didn't My Lord Deliver
Daniel, "Warum Rettet' Denn
Gott Nur Daniel"; Nobody Knows
De Trouble I've Seen, "Keiner
Kann Meinen Kummer Verstehn";
Swing Low, Sweet Chariot, "Trag
Mich Auf Sanften Schwingen"
                               (P334)

Spirituals For All Heft II *spir
[Eng/Ger] mix cor,pno,opt bvl,gtr
(med easy) sc,cor pts SCHOTTS
ED. 5927 s.p., ipa
contains: Deep River, "Tiefe
Fluten"; Go Down Moses, "Geh
Hin, Moses"; Joshua Fit De
Battle Of Jerico, "Joshua
Schlug Die Schlacht Von
Jericho"   (P335)

Swing Low, Sweet Chariot
"Trag Mich Auf Sanften Schwingen"
see Spirituals For All Heft I

Tiefe Fluten *see Deep River

Trag Mich Auf Sanften Schwingen *see
Swing Low, Sweet Chariot

Warum Rettet' Denn Gott Nur Daniel
*see Didn't My Lord Deliver
Daniel

PETERSON, JOHN W.
Above All Else *anthem/gospel
(Carmichael, Ralph) SATB oct
SINGSPIR ZJP-8010 $.30   (P336)
(Johnson, Norman) SAB oct SINGSPIR
ZJP-8054 $.25   (P337)

All Glory To Jesus *anthem
(Mickelson, P.) SATB oct SINGSPIR
ZJP-8196 $.30   (P338)

Angels Worship God In Heaven *anthem
SATB oct SINGSPIR ZJP-7330 $.25
                               (P339)

Answer, The *anthem/gospel
SATB oct SINGSPIR ZJP-8148 $.25
                               (P340)

As For Me And My House *anthem
SATB oct SINGSPIR ZJP-7241 $.30
                               (P341)

Beatitudes, The *anthem
SATB oct SINGSPIR ZJP-7215 $.30
                               (P342)

PETERSON, JOHN W. (cont'd.)
Behold Your King *Easter,cant
SAB,narrator,STBar soli SINGSPIR
5997 $1.95   (P343)
SATB,narrator,STBar soli SINGSPIR
5980 $1.95   (P344)
SA,narrator,STBar soli SINGSPIR
5957 $1.95   (P345)

Beloved, Let Us Love One Another
*Commun,anthem
SATB oct SINGSPIR ZJP-3200 $.30
                               (P346)

Bless The Lord, O My Soul *Thanks,
anthem
SATB oct SINGSPIR ZJP-7203 $.30
                               (P347)

Blessed Hope, The
SATB oct SINGSPIR ZJP-7371 $.35
                               (P348)

Born A King *Xmas,cant
SSA,narrator,SATBar soli,3trp,
3trom,perc,timp SINGSPIR 5966
$1.95   (P349)
SAB,narrator,SATBar soli,3trp,
3trom,perc,timp SINGSPIR 5982
$1.95   (P350)
SATB,narrator,SATBar soli,3trp,
3trom,perc,timp SINGSPIR 5981
$1.95   (P351)

Born A King (from Born A King) Xmas,
anthem
SATB oct SINGSPIR ZJP-3016 $.30
                               (P352)

But Now Is Christ Risen *Easter,
anthem
SATB,opt 3trp oct SINGSPIR ZJP-3508
$.30   (P353)

Calling *anthem/gospel
(DeCou, Harold) SATB,3trp,3trom,opt
bvl&gtr&perc&timp oct SINGSPIR
ZJP-5454 $.40   (P354)
(DeCou, Harold) SATB,3trp,3trom,opt
bvl&gtr&perc&timp oct SINGSPIR
ZJP-5462 $1.00 contains also:
Black, When The Roll Is Called Up
Yonder (DeCou, Harold); Peterson,
John W., So Send I You   (P355)

Carol Of Christmas *Xmas,cant
SATB,narrator,SATBar soli,3trp,
3trom,perc,timp SINGSPIR 5999
$1.95   (P356)
SSA,narrator,SATBar soli,3trp,
3trom,perc,timp SINGSPIR 6011
$1.95   (P357)
SAB,narrator,SATBar soli,3trp,
3trom,perc,timp SINGSPIR 5969
$1.95   (P358)

Chariot Of Clouds *anthem
SATB oct SINGSPIR ZJP-8213 $.35
                               (P359)

Christ Lives Through Me! *anthem/
gospel
SATB oct SINGSPIR ZJP-8160 $.30
                               (P360)

Come, Holy Spirit *anthem/gospel
SATB oct SINGSPIR ZJP-8101 $.30
                               (P361)

Consider The Price He Paid *anthem
SATB (easy) oct SINGSPIR ZJP-6016
$.25   (P362)

Declare His Glory *anthem
SATB oct SINGSPIR ZJP-7244 $.30
                               (P363)

Don't Let The Song Go Out Of Your
Heart *anthem/gospel
SATB oct SINGSPIR ZJP-8147 $.25
                               (P364)

Easter Alleluia, An *Easter,anthem
SATB oct SINGSPIR ZJP-3504 $.30
                               (P365)

Easter Song *Easter,cant
SAB,narrator,soli,inst/pno/org/
hndbl SINGSPIR 6008 $1.95, ipa
                               (P366)
SATB,narrator,soli,inst/pno/org/
hndbl SINGSPIR 6007 $1.95, ipa
                               (P367)
SSA,narrator,soli,inst/pno/org/
hndbl SINGSPIR 6009 $1.95, ipa
                               (P368)

Flag To Follow, A *anthem/gospel
SATB,opt brass&perc oct SINGSPIR
ZJP-8059 $.25   (P369)

Give Thanks To God *Thanks,anthem
SATB oct SINGSPIR ZJP-3109 $.30
                               (P370)

Glory Of Easter, The *Easter,cant
SAB,narrator,SATBar soli,3trp,
3trom,perc,timp SINGSPIR 5983
$1.95, ipa   (P371)
SATB,narrator,SATBar soli,3trp,
3trom,perc,timp SINGSPIR 5993
$1.95, ipa   (P372)
SA,narrator,SATBar soli,3trp,3trom,
perc,timp SINGSPIR 5963 $1.95,
ipa   (P373)

PETERSON, JOHN W. (cont'd.)

Go Tell The Untold Millions *anthem/
gospel
(Carmichael, Ralph) SATB oct
SINGSPIR ZJP-8034 $.30   (P374)

God Knows All About Tomorrow
*anthem/gospel
SATB oct SINGSPIR ZJP-8097 $.30
     (P375)

God Of Everlasting Glory *anthem
(Wyrtzen, Don) SATB oct SINGSPIR
ZJP-7349 $.30   (P376)

God Put His Hand On My Shoulder
*anthem/gospel
SATB oct SINGSPIR ZJP-8072 $.30
     (P377)

God's Final Call *anthem/gospel
(Anthony, Dick) SATB oct SINGSPIR
ZJP-8001 $.30   (P378)

Good Life!, The *anthem/gospel
SATB oct SINGSPIR ZJP-8154 $.35
     (P379)

Great God Of Wonders *Thanks,anthem
SATB oct SINGSPIR ZJP-7245 $.30
     (P380)

Great Is The Glory Of The Lord
*anthem
SATB oct SINGSPIR ZJP-7282 $.30
     (P381)

Hail, Glorious King! *Easter,cant
SATB,narrator,SATBar soli,3trp,
4trom,perc,timp SINGSPIR 5996
$1.95, ipa   (P382)
SSA,narrator,SATBar soli,3trp,
4trom,perc,timp SINGSPIR 5964
$1.95, ipa   (P383)
SAB,narrator,SATBar soli,3trp,
4trom,perc,timp SINGSPIR 5958
$1.95, ipa   (P384)

Hail, Thou Once-Despised Jesus
*anthem
SATB oct SINGSPIR ZJP-7262 $.30
     (P385)

Hail To The King! *Easter,anthem
SATB oct SINGSPIR ZJP-3552 $.40
     (P386)

Hallelujah For The Cross *Easter,
cant
SAB,narrator,STBar soli,3trp,3trom,
perc,timp SINGSPIR 5959 $1.95,
ipa   (P387)
SATB,narrator,STBar soli,3trp,
3trom,perc,timp SINGSPIR 5960
$1.95, ipa   (P388)
SSA,narrator,STBar soli,3trp,3trom,
perc,timp SINGSPIR 6004 $1.95,
ipa   (P389)

Hallelujah! What A Savior! *Easter,
cant
SATB,narrator,STBar soli (easy)
SINGSPIR 5978 $1.95   (P390)
SA,narrator,STBar soli (easy)
SINGSPIR 5998 $1.95   (P391)
SAB,narrator,STBar soli (easy)
SINGSPIR 5989 $1.95   (P392)
[Span] SATB,narrator,STBar soli
(easy) SINGSPIR 5988 $1.50 (P393)

Have A Little Talk With The Lord
*anthem/gospel
(Erb, Clayton) SATB oct SINGSPIR
ZJP-8115 $.30   (P394)

Have Faith In God! *anthem
SATB oct SINGSPIR ZJP-7252 $.30
     (P395)

He Is Risen! *Easter,anthem
SATB oct SINGSPIR ZJP-3544 $.25
     (P396)

He Lovingly Guards Every Footstep
*anthem/gospel
SATB oct SINGSPIR ZJP-8146 $.30
     (P397)

He Was Wounded For Our Transgressions
*Easter,anthem
SATB oct SINGSPIR ZJP-3550 $.40
     (P398)

Healing Love Of Jesus, The *anthem/
gospel
SATB oct SINGSPIR ZJP-8111 $.25
     (P399)

Heaven Came Down And Glory Filled My
Soul *anthem/gospel
(DeCou, Harold) SATB oct SINGSPIR
ZJP-8017 $.30   (P400)

He's Filling Up Heaven With Sinners
*anthem/gospel
SATB oct SINGSPIR ZJP-8130 $.25
     (P401)

Higher Hands *anthem/gospel
SATB oct SINGSPIR ZJP-8049 $.30
     (P402)
SAB oct SINGSPIR ZJP-8052 $.25
     (P403)

Holy Spirit, Now Out-Poured *anthem
(DeCou, Harold) SATB oct SINGSPIR
ZJP-7220 $.25   (P404)

PETERSON, JOHN W. (cont'd.)

Hosanna! *Palm,anthem
SATB oct SINGSPIR ZJP-3507 $.25
     (P405)

How Long Will It Be? *anthem/gospel
SATB,opt 3trp,perc,timp oct
SINGSPIR ZJP-8062 $.30   (P406)

Hymn Of Worship *anthem
SATB oct SINGSPIR ZJP-7348 $.25
     (P407)

I Am The Resurrection And The Life!
*Easter,anthem
SATB oct SINGSPIR ZJP-3539 $.30
     (P408)

I Believe In Miracles *anthem/gospel
(Anthony, Dick) SATB oct SINGSPIR
ZJP-8023 $.30   (P409)
(Johnson, Norman) SA/TB (easy) oct
SINGSPIR ZJP-6030 $.35   (P410)

I Know That My Redeemer Liveth
*Easter,anthem
SATB oct SINGSPIR ZJP-3534 $.30
     (P411)

I Want To Be There *anthem/gospel
SATB oct SINGSPIR ZJP-8069 $.25
     (P412)

I'll Go Now *anthem/gospel
SAB oct SINGSPIR ZJP-8053 $.25
     (P413)
SSATB oct SINGSPIR ZJP-8041 $.25
     (P414)

I'm A Soldier *anthem/gospel
(DeCou, Harold) SA/TB (easy) oct
SINGSPIR ZJP-6028 $.35   (P415)
(Mayfield, Larry) SATB oct SINGSPIR
ZJP-8116 $.30   (P416)

I'm Not Alone *anthem/gospel
(DeCou, Harold) SATB oct SINGSPIR
ZJP-8011 $.30   (P417)

In Dark Gethsemane *Gd.Fri.,anthem
SATB oct SINGSPIR ZJP-3520 $.25
     (P418)

In My Heart *anthem/gospel
SATB oct SINGSPIR ZJP-8103 $.30
     (P419)

In Pleasant Places *anthem/gospel
SATB oct SINGSPIR ZJP-7355 $.35
     (P420)

In The Image Of God *anthem/gospel
(Mickelson, Paul) SSATTBB oct
SINGSPIR ZJP-8129 $.30   (P421)

In This Old Troubled World *anthem/
gospel
SATB oct SINGSPIR ZJP-8078 $.30
     (P422)

Isn't The Love Of Jesus Something
Wonderful *anthem/gospel
(Parks, R.) SATB oct SINGSPIR
ZJP-8184 $.30   (P423)

It Took A Miracle *anthem
(Hedgren) SATB oct SINGSPIR ZA-4392
$.25   (P424)

It's A Wonderful, Wonderful Life!
*anthem/gospel
SATB oct SINGSPIR ZJP-8161 $.30
     (P425)

It's Not An Easy Road *anthem/gospel
(DeCou, Harold) SATB oct SINGSPIR
ZJP-8019 $.30   (P426)

Jesus Is A Precious Name *anthem/
gospel
SATB oct SINGSPIR ZJP-8102 $.30
     (P427)

Jesus Is Coming Again *anthem/gospel
(DeCou, Harold) SATB oct SINGSPIR
ZJP-8008 $.30   (P428)
(Mickelson, Paul) SATB oct SINGSPIR
ZJP-8139 $.30   (P429)

Jesus Is Coming! (Theme II) *anthem
SATB oct SINGSPIR ZJP 8212 $.35
     (P430)

Jesus Is The Friend Of Sinners
*anthem/gospel
SATB oct SINGSPIR ZJP-8128 $.25
     (P431)

Jesus Led Me All The Way *anthem/
gospel
(Yungton; Peterson; DeCou) SATB oct
SINGSPIR ZJP-8024 $.30   (P432)

Jesus The King Passes By *Palm,
anthem
SATB oct SINGSPIR ZJP-3533 $.35
     (P433)

John W. Peterson Anthems For SAB
*CCUL
SAB SINGSPIR 5867 $1.95   (P434)

John W. Peterson's Folio Of Choir
Favorites No. 1 *CCUL,anthem
cor SINGSPIR 5815 $1.50   (P435)

John W. Peterson's Folio Of Choir
Favorites No. 2 *CCUL,anthem
cor SINGSPIR 5834 $1.50   (P436)

PETERSON, JOHN W. (cont'd.)

John W. Peterson's Folio Of Choir
Favorites No. 3 *CCU,anthem
cor SINGSPIR 5837 $1.50   (P437)

John W. Peterson's Folio Of Gospel
Choir Favorites No. 1 *CCUL
cor SINGSPIR 5816 $1.50   (P438)

John W. Peterson's Folio Of Gospel
Choir Favorites No. 2 *CCUL
cor SINGSPIR 5835 $1.50   (P439)

John W. Peterson's Folio Of Gospel
Choir Favorites No. 3 *CCU
cor SINGSPIR 5868 $1.50   (P440)

Joy Of Heaven, The *folk
SATB oct SINGSPIR ZJP-5053 $.30
     (P441)

Joy To The World! *Xmas,cant
SAB,STBar soli,3trp,3trom,perc,timp
SINGSPIR 5945, $1.95, ipa   (P442)
SATB,STBar soli,3trp,3trom,perc,
timp SINGSPIR 5944 $1.95, ipa
     (P443)
SSA,STBar soli,3trp,3trom,perc,timp
SINGSPIR 6012 $1.95, ipa   (P444)

King Of Kings, The *Xmas,cant
SATB,soli SINGSPIR 4294 $1.95
     (P445)

Last Week, The *Easter,cant
SATB,narrator,soli,pno,hpsd,2fl,ob,
horn,3trp,2trom,2vln,vla,vcl,bvl,
perc,drums, English horn,celeste
SINGSPIR 5884 $2.50, ipa   (P446)

Lead Me, O Lead Me *anthem
SATB oct SINGSPIR ZJP-8217 $.30
     (P447)

Lengthen The Cords And Strenthen The
Stakes *anthem/gospel
SATB oct SINGSPIR ZJP-8039 $.30
     (P448)

Let Every Heart Rejoice *Thanks,
anthem
SATB oct SINGSPIR ZJP-7210 $.25
     (P449)

Let The Whole World Know! *anthem/
folk/gospel
SATB oct SINGSPIR ZJP-8063 $.30
     (P450)
(Peterson Sisters) SAB/SATB oct
SINGSPIR ZJP-5002 $.30   (P451)

Lost-But Still He Loves You *folk
(Wyrtzen, Don) SATB oct SINGSPIR
ZJP-5027 $.30   (P452)

Lost In The Night *anthem/gospel
SATB oct SINGSPIR ZJP-8092 $.30
     (P453)

Love Transcending *Xmas,cant
SAB,narrator,SATBar soli,3trp,
4trom,perc,timp (easy) SINGSPIR
5974 $1.95, ipa   (P454)
SATB,narrator,SATBar soli,3trp,
4trom,perc,timp (easy) SINGSPIR
5975 $1.95, ipa   (P455)
SA,narrator,SATBar soli,3trp,4trom,
perc,timp (easy) SINGSPIR 5954
$1.95, ipa   (P456)

Near To Thy Heart *anthem
(DeCou, Harold) SATB oct SINGSPIR
ZJP-7204 $.25   (P457)

Never In A Million Years *anthem/
gospel
SATB oct SINGSPIR ZJP-8079 $.25
     (P458)

Night Of Miracles *Xmas,cant
SATB,narrator,STBar soli,3trp&
2trom&timp/3trp&3trom&fl&clar&
horn&3vln&vla&vcl&perc&timp
SINGSPIR 5976 $1.95, ipa   (P459)
[Span] SATB,narrator,STBar soli,
3trp&2trom&timp/3trp&3trom&fl&
clar&horn&3vln&vla&vcl&bvl&perc&
timp SINGSPIR 5956 $1.50, ipa
     (P460)
SA,narrator,STBar soli,3trp&2trom&
timp/trp&3trom&fl&clar&horn&3vln&
vla&vcl&bvl&perc&timp SINGSPIR
5971 $1.95, ipa   (P461)
SAB,narrator,STBar soli,3trp&2trom&
timp/3trp&3trom&fl&clar&horn&
3vln&vla&vcl&bvl&perc&timp
SINGSPIR 5972 $1.95, ipa   (P462)

Night The Angels Sang, The *Xmas,
cant
SATB,med solo,narrator (easy)
SINGSPIR 5987 $1.95   (P463)
SA,med solo,narrator (easy)
SINGSPIR 5986 $1.95   (P464)
SAB,med solo,narrator (easy)
SINGSPIR 5968 $1.95   (P465)

No Greater Love *Easter,cant
SATB,narrator,SATBar soli,3trp&
4trom&perc&timp/3trp&4trom&3vln&
vla&vcl&bvl&perc&timp SINGSPIR
5977 $2.50, ipa   (P466)

PETERSON, JOHN W. (cont'd.)

SSA,narrator,SATBar soli,3trp&
  4trom&perc&timp/3trp4trom&3vln&
  vla&vcl&bvl&perc&timp SINGSPIR
  5984 $2.50, ipa   (P467)
SAB,narrator,SATBar soli,3trp&
  4trom&perc&timp/3trp4trom&3vln&
  vla&vcl&bvl&perc&timp SINGSPIR
  5992 $2.50, ipa   (P468)

No More Death *anthem/gospel
  SATB oct SINGSPIR ZJP-8155 $.35
                                      (P469)
Not To The Hills *anthem
  SATB oct SINGSPIR ZJP-7342 $.30
                                      (P470)
Now Sing, All Saints! *Easter,anthem
  SATB oct SINGSPIR ZJP-3530 $.30
                                      (P471)
O Glorious Love *anthem/gospel
  SATB oct SINGSPIR ZJP-8098 $.25
                                      (P472)
O Glorious Resurrection Day!
  *Easter,anthem
  SATB oct SINGSPIR ZJP:3523 $.30
                                      (P473)
O What Grace! *anthem
  SATB (easy) oct SINGSPIR ZJP-6017
  $.25   (P474)
Oh, He's A Wonderful Savior *anthem/
  gospel
  (Carmichael, Ralph) SATB oct
  SINGSPIR ZJP-8044 $.30   (P475)
Over The Sunset Mountains *anthem/
  gospel
  SATB oct SINGSPIR ZJP-8046 $.25
                                      (P476)
Praise Him Now *anthem
  SATB oct SINGSPIR ZJP-7273 $.25
                                      (P477)
Praise Our God *anthem
  (Colber; Johnson) SATB oct SINGSPIR
  ZJP-7218 $.25   (P478)
Really Live! *folk
  2pt oct SINGSPIR ZJP-5036 $.30
                                      (P479)
Rise Up And Sing Praise *anthem
  SATB oct SINGSPIR ZJP-7266 $.30
                                      (P480)
Send Thy Holy Breadth *anthem
  SATB oct SINGSPIR ZJP-7205 $.25
                                      (P481)
Shepherd Of Love *anthem/gospel
  SATB oct SINGSPIR ZJP-8127 $.25
                                      (P482)
Since We All Believe In Jesus
  *anthem
  SATB oct SINGSPIR ZJP-8221 $.30
                                      (P483)
So I Send You *cant
  SSA,narrator,soli,3trp,3trom,perc,
  timp SINGSPIR 6005 $1.95, ipa
                                      (P484)
  SATB,narrator,soli,3trp,3trom,perc,
  timp SINGSPIR 6002 $1.95, ipa
                                      (P485)
  SAB,soli,narrator,3trp,3trom,perc,
  timp SINGSPIR 6006 $1.95, ipa
                                      (P486)
So Send I You *anthem/gospel
  see Peterson, John W., Calling
  SATB,3trp,3trom,opt bvl&gtr&perc&
  timp oct SINGSPIR ZJP-5461 $.40
                                      (P487)
Solid Rock, The *folk
  2pt oct SINGSPIR ZJP-5029 $.25
                                      (P488)
Someone *anthem/gospel
  (DeCou, Harold) SATB oct SINGSPIR
  ZJP-8030 $.25   (P489)
Song Unending, A *Xmas,cant
  SATB,narrator,SATBar soli,3trp,
  3trom,perc,timp SINGSPIR 5979
  $1.95, ipa   (P490)
  SAB,narrator,SATBar soli,3trp,
  3trom,perc,timp SINGSPIR 5953
  $1.95, ipa   (P491)
  SA,narrator,SATBar soli,3trp,3trom,
  perc,timp SINGSPIR 5961 $1.95,
  ipa   (P492)
Sound Of Singing, The *cant
  SATB,soli,3trp,3trom,perc,timp
  SINGSPIR 5994 $1.95, ipa (P493)
  SA,soli,3trp,3trom,perc,timp
  SINGSPIR 5965 $1.95, ipa (P494)
  SAB,soli,3trp,3trom,perc,timp
  SINGSPIR 5962 $1.95, ipa (P495)
Springs Of Living Water *anthem/
  gospel
  (Johnson; DeCou) SATB oct SINGSPIR
  ZJP-8006 $.30   (P496)
Stand Up And Bless The Lord *anthem
  SATB oct SINGSPIR ZJP-7233 $.25
                                      (P497)
Steal Away *anthem/gospel
  SATB oct SINGSPIR ZJP-8169 $.30
                                      (P498)

PETERSON, JOHN W. (cont'd.)

Story Of Christmas, The *Xmas,cant
  SATB,narrator,SATBar soli,3trp&
  perc&timp/3trp&3trom&fl&clar&
  horn&3vln&vla&vcl&bvl&perc&timp
  SINGSPIR 5943 $1.95, ipa (P499)
  SAB,narrator,SATBar soli,3trp&
  3trom&perc&timp/3trp&3trom&fl&
  clar&horn&3vln&vla&vcl&bvl&perc&
  timp SINGSPIR 5881 $1.95, ipa
                                      (P500)
  SA,narrator,SATBar soli,3trp&3trom&
  perc&timp/3trp&3trom&fl&clar&
  horn&3vln&vla&vcl&bvl&perc&timp
  SINGSPIR 5882 $1.95, ipa (P501)
Surely Goodness And Mercy (composed
  with Smith, Alfred B.) *anthem/
  gospel
  SATB (Crusade Edition) oct SINGSPIR
  ZJP-8016 $.25   (P502)
  (Carmichael, Ralph) SATB oct
  SINGSPIR ZJP-8022 $.30   (P503)
  (DeCou, Harold) SAB oct SINGSPIR
  ZJP-8058 $.30   (P504)
Take My Life And Let It Be *folk
  SATB oct SINGSPIR ZJP-5017 $.25
                                      (P505)
  (Wyrtzen, Don) SATB oct SINGSPIR
  ZJP-5051 $.25   (P506)
Take Time To Pray *anthem/gospel
  SATB oct SINGSPIR ZJP-8117 $.25
                                      (P507)
Take Up Your Cross And Follow Me
  *anthem/gospel
  SATB oct SINGSPIR ZJP-8156 $.30
                                      (P508)
Teach Me To Love *anthem
  SATB oct SINGSPIR ZJP-8051 $.30
                                      (P509)
Tell The Good News *anthem/gospel
  SSATB oct SINGSPIR ZJP-8068 $.30
                                      (P510)
Then The Lord Stood By Me! *anthem
  SATB oct SINGSPIR ZJP-8207 $.40
                                      (P511)
There Is No Greater Love *anthem/
  gospel
  (DeCou, Harold) SATB (easy) oct
  SINGSPIR ZJP-6012 $.30   (P512)
  (Draper, James) SAB oct SINGSPIR
  ZJP-8018 $.25   (P513)
  (Mickelson, P.) SATB oct SINGSPIR
  ZJP-8193 $.30   (P514)
There Is No Room *Xmas,anthem
  SATB oct SINGSPIR ZJP-3050 $.35
                                      (P515)
There's A New Song In My Heart
  *anthem/gospel
  SATB oct SINGSPIR ZJP-8035 $.25
                                      (P516)
Think On These Things *anthem
  SATB oct SINGSPIR ZJP-7247 $.25
                                      (P517)
This Is The Day That The Lord Hath
  Made *anthem
  SATB oct SINGSPIR ZJP-7202 $.30
                                      (P518)
We Magnify Our Father God *anthem
  SATB oct SINGSPIR ZJP-7213 $.25
                                      (P519)
We Thank Thee *Thanks,anthem
  (DeCou, Harold) SATB oct SINGSPIR
  ZJP-3106 $.30   (P520)
What Grace Is This! *anthem/gospel
  (Mickelson, Paul) SATB oct SINGSPIR
  ZJP-8121 $.30   (P521)
When I Remember *Gd.Fri.,anthem/
  gospel
  (DeCou, Harold) SATB oct SINGSPIR
  ZJP-8091 $.30   (P522)
Where Is He? *Xmas,anthem
  SA oct SINGSPIR ZJP-2004 $.25
                                      (P523)
Who's Going To Walk That Road With
  Me? *anthem/gospel
  SATB oct SINGSPIR ZJP-8178 $.25
                                      (P524)
Will You Be Ready? *folk
  (Wyrtzen, Don) SATB oct SINGSPIR
  ZJP-5044 $.30   (P525)
Wings Of Prayer *anthem/gospel
  (DeCou, Harold) SATB oct SINGSPIR
  ZJP-8175 $.30   (P526)
Wise Men Still Seek Him *Xmas,anthem
  SATB oct SINGSPIR ZJP-3037 $.30
                                      (P527)
With A Holy Hush *anthem
  SATB oct SINGSPIR ZJP-7277 $.25
                                      (P528)
Wonder Of Christmas, The *Xmas,cant
  SATB,narrator,SATBar soli,3trp,
  3trom,perc,timp SINGSPIR 5973
  $1.95, ipa   (P529)
  SAB,narrator,SATBar soli,3trp,
  3trom,perc,timp SINGSPIR 5970
  $1.95, ipa   (P530)

PETERSON, JOHN W. (cont'd.)

SSA,narrator,SATBar soli,3trp,
  3trom,perc,timp SINGSPIR 5967
  $1.95, ipa   (P531)
Wonder Of Wonders *Xmas,anthem
  SATB oct SINGSPIR ZJP-3038 $.30
                                      (P532)
Wonderful Is Jesus! *anthem
  SATB oct SINGSPIR ZJP-7357 $.35
                                      (P533)
PETERSON, P.W.
Five Choral Responses *CC5U,cor-resp
  mix cor BRODT 1 $.20   (P534)
PETERSON, PAMELA
Forever Together With Him *folk
  (Wyrtzen, Don) SATB oct SINGSPIR
  ZJP-5034 $.25   (P535)
Where Is This Old World A-Goin'?
  *folk
  (Peterson Sisters) SAB/SATB oct
  SINGSPIR ZJP-5003 $.30   (P536)
PETHEL, JAMES
Now A New Song *Xmas,anthem
  SATB (easy) oct BROADMAN 4545-40
  $.30   (P537)
PETIT MYSTERE DE NOEL see Choisy
PETRASSI, GOFFREDO (1904-   )
Christus Factus Est
  see Mottetti Per La Passione
Improperium
  see Mottetti Per La Passione
Magnificat
  cor,S solo,pno/orch voc sc RICORDI-
  ENG 124988 s.p.   (P538)
Mottetti Per La Passione *Psntd,mot
  SATTB/SATBarB,acap (diff) sc
  SCHOTTS SZ 6533 s.p.
  contains: Christus Factus Est;
  Improperium; Tenebrae Factae
  Sunt; Tristis Est Anima Mea
                                      (P539)
Psalm 9 *see Salmo IX
Salmo IX (Psalm 9)
  cor,pno/orch voc sc RICORDI-ENG
  123983 s.p.   (P540)
Tenebrae Factae Sunt
  see Mottetti Per La Passione
Tristis Est Anima Mea
  see Mottetti Per La Passione
PETRICH, ROGER
O Wondrous Type
  SATB,acap (easy) OXFORD 94.328 $.40
                                      (P541)
PETTMAN, EDGAR
Carol Of Adoration, A
  see Pettman, Edgar, I Saw A Maiden
Gabriel's Message
  SA EMI   (P542)
  SATB EMI s.p. contains also:
  Grimes, Gordon, Cradle Song
                                      (P543)
I Saw A Maiden *Xmas
  SATB EMI s.p. contains also: Carol
  Of Adoration, A   (P544)
  SA EMI   (P545)
Infant King, The *Xmas
  SA EMI   (P546)
  SATB EMI s.p.   (P547)
Love Came Down At Christmas *Xmas
  SATB EMI s.p. contains also: When
  The Crimson Sun Had Set   (P548)
Sleep, My Saviour, Sleep *see
  Grimes, Gordon
When The Crimson Sun Had Set
  see Pettman, Edgar, Love Came Down
  At Christmas
Wherefore This Great Joy
  SATB EMI s.p. contains also: With
  Praises Abounding   (P549)
With Praises Abounding
  see Pettman, Edgar, Wherefore This
  Great Joy
PETZOLD, JOHANNES
Ach Bleib Mit Deiner Gnade
  SAT/SAB/1-2pt,opt vcl&treb inst
  HANSSLER 14.208 s.p.   (P550)
More Than Raiment *anthem
  SATB AUGSBURG 11-1682 $.30 (P551)

PETZOLD, RUDOLF (1908-   )
  Das Wort Geht Von Dem Vater Aus
    SAT/SAB,treb inst,opt bass inst
    HANSSLER 14.161 s.p.   (P552)

PEZZATI, ROMANO (1939-   )
  Dixitque Fiat
    men cor,acap ZERBONI 7619 s.p.
                                    (P553)

  Est Silentium In Caelo
    men cor,acap ZERBONI 7045 s.p.
                                    (P554)

  Psalm 43 *see Salmo 43

  Salmo 43 (Psalm 43)
    cor,acap ZERBONI 7327 s.p.   (P555)

  Viditque Quod Esset Bonum
    men cor,acap ZERBONI 7618 s.p.
                                    (P556)

PFANNSCHMIDT
  Trauungesang: Uber Deinem Haupte
    *Op.19, funeral
    mix cor LIENAU sc s.p., cor pts
    s.p.   (P557)

PFAUTSCH, LLOYD (1921-   )
  Annunciation
    SSA SCHIRM.G LG51627 $.35   (P558)

  Child's Prayer, A *Gen/Thanks
    unis,hndbl CHORISTERS A-27 $.30
                                    (P559)

  David's Lamentation
    SATB SCHIRM.G LG51800 $.30   (P560)

  Hurry Lord! Come Quickly!
    SATB,kbd,bvl,opt gtr oct AGAPE
    AG 7169 $.40   (P561)

  Prayer
    SATB SCHIRM.G LG51856 $.30   (P562)

  Six Anthems For Junior Choir *CC6U,
    anthem
    SA&jr cor/unis ABINGDON APM-368
    $.60   (P563)

PFLEGER, AUGUSTIN (ca. 1670)
  Passion Music On The Seven Words Of
    Jesus Christ On The Cross *see
    Passionmusik Uber Die Sieben
    Worte Jesu Christ Am Kreuz

  Passionmusik Uber Die Sieben Worte
    Jesu Christ Am Kreuz *Psntd
    "Passion Music On The Seven Words
    Of Jesus Christ On The Cross"
    SATB,SATB soli,cont,inst voc sc
    SCHIRM.EC 2721 s.p., ipa   (P564)

PFLUEGER, CARL
  Hast Thou Not Known
    mix cor BANKS MUS YS 646 $.30
                                    (P565)

  How Long Wilt Thou Forget Me?
    SATB WILLIS 7005H $.20   (P566)
    SA/unis WILLIS 7007H $.20   (P567)
    SSA WILLIS 7006H $.20   (P568)

PFLUGER, HANS GEORG (1944-   )
  Christ Ist Erstanden
    SATB,high solo,org CARUS CV 40.105
    s.p.   (P569)

  Komm, Heiliger Geist
    SATB,org CARUS CV 40.106 s.p.
                                    (P570)

  Lobt Gott, Ihr Christen Alle Gleich
    SATB,org CARUS CV 40.104 s.p.
                                    (P571)

  O Du Frohliche Weihnachtszeit *CC5U,
    Xmas
    1-4pt,pno/org,opt inst CARUS
    CV 40.405 s.p.   (P572)

  O Haupt Voll Blut Und Wunden
    SATB,org CARUS CV 40.102 s.p.
                                    (P573)

  O Heiland, Reiss Die Himmel Auf
    SATB,Bar solo,org CARUS CV 40.103
    s.p.   (P574)

PFOHL, H.
  In Thy Word Do I Hope
    TTBB BRODT 628 $.25   (P575)

PFOHL, J.C.
  Jesus Makes My Heart Rejoice
    mix cor BRODT 202 $.20   (P576)

  Three Responses *CC3U,cor-resp
    mix cor BRODT 110 $.22   (P577)

PHIEFFER, DON
  It's A Happy Day
    (Keene, Tom) SA/TB,pno (med easy)
    GENTRY G-226 $.35   (P578)

PHILIPP, FRANZ
  Auferstehung *see Dic Nobis, Maria

  Busse *see Non Secundum Peccata
    Nostra

PHILIPP, FRANZ (cont'd.)
  Cantica Nova *mot
    [Lat] 4pt mix cor,acap sc,cor pts
    BOHM s.p.
    contains: Dic Nobis, Maria,
    "Auferstehung", Op.98,No.2;
    Domino Canticum Novum,
    "Vollendung", Op.98,No.3; Non
    Secundum Peccata Nostra,
    "Busse", Op.98,No.1   (P579)

  Dic Nobis, Maria
    "Auferstehung" see Cantica Nova

  Domino Canticum Novum
    "Vollendung" see Cantica Nova

  Non Secundum Peccata Nostra
    "Busse" see Cantica Nova

  Vollendung *see Domino Canticum
    Novum

PHILIPS, PETER (1561-1628)
  Surgens Jesu
    (Hall, W.D.) [Eng/Lat] SSATB,acap
    oct NATIONAL WHC-32 $.35   (P580)

PHILLIPS, JOHN C. (1921-   )
  World Rejoice *CCU,carol
    wom cor,perc,pno,2vln,vla,vcl voc
    sc NOVELLO rental   (P581)

PHOENIX MASS see Payne, Anthony

PIAE CANTIONES NOVAE see Kenins,
  Talivadis

PICCIONI
  Messa
    4pt,org sc RICORDI-ENG 131922 s.p.
                                    (P582)

PICCOLOMINI MASS see Mozart, Wolfgang
  Amadeus, Missa Brevis

PICKELL
  Special Star, A *Xmas
    2pt, opt. triangle PRO ART 2761
    $.35   (P583)

PIDOUX, PIERRE (1905-   )
  Helft, Gottes Gute Preisen
    SSATB (contains also: Siehe, Dein
    Konig Kommt Zu Dir; Der Herr, Der
    Ist Mein Hirt) SCHWEIZER.
    SK 67.02 s.p. see also
    MUSIKBEILAGE ZUM "EVANGELISCHEN
    KIRCHENCHOR 1967"   (P584)

  Wie Herrlich Gibst Du, Herr, Dich Zu
    Erkennen
    see MUSIKBEILAGE ZUM "EVANGELISCHEN
    KIRCHENCHOR 1960

PIE JESU see Cherubini, Luigi

PIECHLER, ARTHUR (1896-1974)
  Funf Kurze Und Leicht Ausfuhrbare
    Pange Lingua
    [Lat] sc,cor pts BOHM s.p., ipa
    contains: Pange Lingua , Op.52,
    No.1 (4pt,org/2clar&2horn&2trp&
    strings&opt 2trom); Pange
    Lingua , Op.52,No.2 (4pt,org/
    2trp&2trom); Pange Lingua ,
    Op.52,No.3 (4pt,opt org/
    strings); Pange Lingua , Op.52,
    No.4 (4pt,org); Pange Lingua ,
    Op.52,No.5 (4pt,org)   (P585)

  Hymne *Op.32
    men cor,acap/pno/orch sc SCHOTTS
    rental, ipr   (P586)

  Konigin In Gottes Reichen
    SSATBB,acap (med) sc SCHOTTS
    C 38 853 s.p.   (P587)

  Magnificat Anima Mea Dominum *Magnif
    mix cor,S solo,acap/org (diff) sc
    SCHOTTS C 43 430 s.p.   (P588)

  Messe Zu Ehren Des Heiligen Petrus
    *Mass
    [Ger] mix cor&cong,org sc,cor pts
    BOHM s.p.   (P589)

  Missa In Honorem St. Alberti Magni
    *Op.35, Mass
    [Lat] cor,soli,org,1-2clar,strings,
    2horn,2trp,opt bsn&2trom&timp sc,
    cor pts BOHM s.p., ipa   (P590)

  Pange Lingua
    see Funf Kurze Und Leicht
    Ausfuhrbare Pange Lingua

  Pange Lingua
    see Funf Kurze Und Leicht
    Ausfuhrbare Pange Lingua

  Pange Lingua
    see Funf Kurze Und Leicht
    Ausfuhrbare Pange Lingua

PIECHLER, ARTHUR (cont'd.)
  Pange Lingua
    see Funf Kurze Und Leicht
    Ausfuhrbare Pange Lingua

  Pange Lingua
    see Funf Kurze Und Leicht
    Ausfuhrbare Pange Lingua

  Rex Pacificus *Op.50, Mass
    [Lat] 4pt mix cor,org/2clar&2trp&
    2horn&strings&opt 2trom&tuba&timp
    sc,cor pts BOHM s.p., ipa   (P591)

  St. Franziskus-Messe *Op.53, Mass
    [Lat] 4pt mix cor,org,opt 2vln&bvl
    sc,cor pts BOHM s.p., ipa   (P592)

  Salve Regina *Op.40
    [Ger/Lat] 4pt mix cor,acap sc,cor
    pts BOHM s.p.   (P593)

  Sursum Corda *hymn
    [Eng/Ger] 4-8pt mix cor,SATB soli,
    org,fl,2ob,clar,2bsn,2horn,2trp,
    2trom,strings,perc,timp,harp,
    celeste (med) sc SCHOTTS rental,
    ipr   (P594)

  Weltenhoffnung, Milde, Susse
    4-6pt mix cor,soli (med) sc SCHOTTS
    C 38 854 s.p.   (P595)

PIERCE, CHRISTINE
  America, Return To God
    (Smith, Herb) SATB oct GOSPEL
    05 TM 0125 $.20   (P596)

  Blessed Man, The
    SATB oct GOSPEL 05 TM 0460 $.50
                                    (P597)

  Holy Spirit, Flame Of God
    (Smith, Herb) SATB oct GOSPEL
    05 TM 0145 $.25   (P598)

PIERNE, PAUL (1874-1950)
  Earth Is The Lord's, The (Psalm 24)
    Fest/Palm,anthem
    (Brunelle, Philip) SATB,Bar solo,
    org voc sc SALABERT-US $.75
                                    (P599)
    (Brunelle, Philip) SATB,Bar solo,
    3trp,2trom,opt timp sc SALABERT-
    US $10.00   (P600)

  Psalm 24 *see Earth Is The Lord's,
    The

PIERPOINT
  For The Beauty Of The Earth (composed
    with Newbury, Kent A.) *anthem
    SATB oct BROADMAN 4551-83 $.30
                                    (P601)

PIERSON, HENRY HUGO (1815-1873)
  Agnus Dei
    SATB,org NOVELLO MT 1570 s.p.
                                    (P602)

PIKE, HARRY HALE
  When Christ Was Born *Xmas
    SATB,S solo (easy) FITZSIMONS 2066
    $.25   (P603)

  When Morning Gilds The Sky
    SATB (easy) FITZSIMONS 2061 $.25
                                    (P604)

PIKET, FREDERICK (1903-1974)
  Adonai Malach
    [Heb] mix cor,cantor TRANSCON.
    TCL 662 $.50   (P605)

PILGER IN DER WELT see Monter, Josef

PILGRIM SONG see Winter, Sister Miriam
  Therese

PILGRIMS' CHORUS see Wagner, Richard

PILGRIM'S FAREWELL see Ingalls,
  Jeremiah

PINELLI, GIOVANNI BATISTA (1544-1587)
  Magnificat
    (Reuning, Daniel G.) SATB GIA G1914
    $.60   (P606)

PINKHAM, DANIEL (1923-   )
  Alleluia
    SATB,soli SCHIRM.EC 2954   (P607)

  Angelus Ad Pastores Ait
    SSAA,4trp,3trom,opt tuba KING,R
    MFB 614 cor pts $.30, cmplt ed
    $2.50   (P608)

  Ave Verum Corpus
    SATB SCHIRM.EC 2945   (P609)

  Call Of Isaiah
    SATB/men cor/wom cor,org,electronic
    tape SCHIRM.EC 2911 s.p., ipa
                                    (P610)

  Carol For New Year's Day
    SATB SCHIRM.EC 2952   (P611)

PINKHAM, DANIEL (cont'd.)

Christmas Cantata (Sinfonia Sacra)
SATB&SATB,4trp,4trom,opt horn,
Baritone Horn KING,R MFB 602 cor
pts $.75, cmplt ed $4.00   (P612)

Communion Service
SATB,acap AM.COMP.AL. $1.10   (P613)

Easter Carol
SATB SCHIRM.EC 2955   (P614)

Introit For Thanksgiving Day
unis,org AM.COMP.AL. $.55   (P615)

Lament Of David, The
cor,electronic tape sc SCHIRM.EC
2939 s.p., ipa   (P616)

Love Came Down At Christmas
SATB SCHIRM.EC 2953   (P617)

Seven Last Words Of Christ On The
Cross, The *Psntd
SATB,TBarB soli,org,electronic tape
sc SCHIRM.EC 2907 s.p., ipa   (P618)

Sheepheard's Song, The
SATB,S solo,opt electronic tape sc
SCHIRM.EC 2913 s.p., ipa   (P619)

Te Deum
SA/TB,org,3trp KING,R MFB 613 cor
pts $.30, cmplt ed $1.50   (P620)

PISK, PAUL AMADEUS (1893-   )
Prophecy Of Zechariah, The
SATB,pno/org AM.COMP.AL. $3.85
(P621)

PITCHER
Nut Tree, The
SSA WILLIS 9976 $.60   (P622)

Praise God In Nature
SATB WILLIS 9975 $.75   (P623)

PITFIELD, THOMAS BARON (1903-   )
Hallowed Manger, The *cant
mix cor CRAMER $2.15   (P624)

Two Short Litanies *CC2U
mix cor CRAMER $.30   (P625)

PITONI, GIUSEPPE OTTAVIO (1657-1743)
Cantate Domino
(Lee, John; Mitchell, Bob) [Eng/
Lat] SATB GIA G1949 $.40   (P626)

Pange Lingua-Tantum Ergo
see HYMNEN UND MOTETTEN ALTER
MEISTER HEFT 1

PIZARRO
Fair Moon Hath Ascended, The *see
Schulz

PIZZETTI, ILDEBRANDO (1880-1968)
Santa Uliva *CC7L
cor,S solo,3fl,3ob,2clar,3bsn,
4horn,3trp,3trom,tuba,timp,perc,
harp,org sc CARISH 17119 s.p.
Seven Concert Pieces In Mixed
Combinations   (P627)

PLACE OF JOY AND PEACE, A see Cram

PLACE YOUR HAND see McKinney

PLANTED WHEAT see Cothram, J.

PLANYAVSKY, PETER (1947-   )
Danket Gott, Denn Er Ist Gut
3-4pt mix cor DOBLINGER KL27 s.p.
(P628)

Der Geist Des Herrn Erfullt Das All
3-4pt mix cor DOBLINGER KL 28 s.p.
(P629)

O Lamm Gottes, Unschuldig
3-4pt mix cor DOBLINGER KL 29 s.p.
(P630)

O Maria, Sei Gegrusst
3-4pt mix cor DOBLINGER KL 30 s.p.
(P631)

Wir Weihn Der Erde Gaben
3-4pt mix cor DOBLINGER KL 26 s.p.
(P632)

Zu Dir, O Gott, Erheben Wir
3-4pt mix cor DOBLINGER KL 25 s.p.
(P633)

PLAS, MICHEL VAN DER
Lied Van De Nieuwe Hemel En De Nieuwe
Aarde *see Burg, Wim Ter

PLATTI, GIOVANNI (1690-1763)
Miserere
(Lupi, R.) cor,soli,org,ob,strings
sc CARISH 21794 s.p., cor pts
CARISH 21795 rental, ipr, voc sc
CARISH 21797 s.p.   (P634)

PLATTS, KENNETH
Shepherd's Carol, A
2pt ASHDOWN EA376   (P635)

PLAUDITE see Gabrieli

PLEADING SAVIOUR *anthem
(Littleton, Bill J.) SATB FINE ARTS
CM 1069 $.35   (P636)

PLEASE STOP RUNNING AWAY FROM GOD see
Paris

PLEASURE IT IS see Thackray

PLENI SUNT COELI see Palestrina,
Giovanni

PLUM, P.-J.-M.
Messe
3 eq voices,pno/org HENN 734 s.p.
sc, voc pt   (P637)

PLUMTREE
Rejoice, Rejoice, Ye Pure In Heart
*anthem
SATB oct BROADMAN 4545-78 $.30
(P638)

PLUNKETT, BONNIE
Go And Tell
(Walters, Robert) SATB oct GOSPEL
05 TM 0136 $.30   (P639)

New Day For America, A
(Walters; Bow; Shows, John) SATB,
opt band voc sc GOSPEL 05 TM 0131
$.30, sc GOSPEL 05 TM 0338 $3.50
(P640)

Oh, Take The Word
(Walters, Bob) SATB oct GOSPEL
05 TM 0139 $.35   (P641)

One Touch
(Krogstad, Bob) SATB,narrator oct
GOSPEL 05 TM 0364 $.35   (P642)

What Christmas Means To Me *Xmas
(Swaim, Winnie) SATB oct GOSPEL
05 TM 0369 $.35   (P643)

PO' LIL' JESUS *Adv/Xmas
(Van Iderstine, A.P.) SATB,acap ART
MAST 227 $.35   (P644)

POLIGNAC, ARMANDE DE (1876-1962)
Cantique De Noel *Xmas
4pt mix cor,acap sc HENN 1020 s.p.
(P645)

POLISH CHRISTMAS CAROLS *Xmas
(Geer, E.) SSA&SSA,acap SCHIRM.EC 852
$.50
contains: Hark! Bethlehem; Hark! In
The Darkness; He Is Sleeping In A
Manger; Sleep, Thou, My Jewel;
When The Saviour Christ Is Born
(P646)

POLISH CHRISTMAS CAROLS *CCU,Xmas,
carol,Pol
(Michalski; Malin) [Eng/Pol] SA MARKS
$.85   (P647)

POLISTINA
And Rejoice (composed with Hebble)
*Xmas,anthem
SATB oct HERITAGE H117 $.35   (P648)

POLMAN, TH.
Kerstcantate *Xmas,cant
3pt wom cor HEER 46 s.p.   (P649)

POLOLANIK, ZDENEK (1935-   )
Sir-Har-Sirim *Bibl/ora
"Song Of Songs, The" [Heb] mix cor,
3 soli,2fl,2ob,3clar,2bsn,4horn,
3trp,3trom,timp,perc,2harp,pno,
strings, celeste, vibraphone
CZECH s.p.   (P650)

Song Of Songs, The *see Sir-Har-
Sirim

POLYCHORAL MOTETS: FIVE MOTETS FOR
THREE CHOIRS *CC5U,mot,16-17th
cent
(Gable, Frederick K.) 3 cor bds A-R
ED $9.95   (P651)

POLYCHORAL MOTETS: SIX MOTETS FOR TWO
CHOIRS *CC6U,mot,16-17th cent
(Gable, Frederick K.) dbl cor bds A-R
ED $9.95   (P652)

POMPER, A.
Hymne *hymn
men cor sc HEER 337 s.p.   (P653)

Kerstlied *Xmas
unis,pno/harmonium HEER 338 s.p.
(P654)

Ons Getsemane *Psntd
unis,pno/harmonium HEER 341 s.p.
(P655)

PONT
Lord's Prayer, The
unis,inst (easy) sc OXFORD 40.019
$2.50, ipa, cor pts OXFORD 40.020
$.35   (P656)

POOL, K.
God Is Our Refuge And Strength
mix cor BRODT 564 $.35   (P657)

O Sing Unto The Lord A New Song
mix cor BRODT 533 $.26   (P658)

POOL, KENNETH
I Will Lift Up Mine Eyes *anthem
SATB oct SINGSPIR ZJP-7308 $.30
(P659)

POOLEY, FRED
Cobbler's Guest, The (composed with
Pooley, Lorraine) *Xmas
mix cor,narrator (drama) LILLENAS
MC-246 $.75   (P660)

POOLEY, LORRAINE
Cobbler's Guest, The *see Pooley,
Fred

POOR WORLD (SAID I) see Martin, Gilbert
M.

POORMAN, JEANNE R.
Trumpet Shall Sound, The
(Rose, Steven) SATB oct GOSPEL
05 TM 0288 $.35   (P661)

POOS, HEINRICH (1928-   )
Das Ist Ein Kostlich Ding (Psalm 92)
SSAA&2pt treb cor,acap (med) BAREN.
BA6319   (P662)

Herr Gott, Dich Loben Wir
5pt mix cor MERSEBURG EM530   (P663)

Lord God Is A Sun And Shield, The
*anthem,Contemp
SATB oct CHANTRY COA 6730 $.35
(P664)

Psalm 92 *see Das Ist Ein Kostlich
Ding

Psalm 98 *see Singet Dem Herrn Ein
Neues Lied

Singet Dem Herrn Ein Neues Lied
(Psalm 98)
men cor sc SCHOTTS C 43 106 s.p.,
voc pt SCHOTTS C 43 107-01;02
(P665)

Tut Mir Auf Die Schone Pforte
SAT/SAB,opt 3inst&kbd HANSSLER
14.129 s.p.   (P666)

Zu Bethlehem Geboren *Xmas
jr cor/wom cor (easy) sc SCHOTTS
CHBL 594 s.p.   (P667)

POPE
Alleluia, Now May We Mirthes Make
SATB,acap (med) OXFORD 84.234 $.30
(P668)

POPOLO CHE SOGNA E POPOLO CHE BURLA
see Raccolta Corale Libro II

POPULE MEUS see Anerio, Felice

POPULE MEUS see Berghorn, Alfred

POPULE MEUS see Kromolicki, Joseph

POPULE MEUS see Palestrina, Giovanni

POPULE MEUS see Victoria, Tomas Luis de

POPULUM HUMILEM SALVUM FACIES, DOMINE
see Lassus, Roland de (Orlandus)

PORT
Lord, Lord, We Come To Thee *anthem
SATB oct LILLENAS AN-6024 $.30
(P669)

PORTA, COSTANZO (1529-1601)
Missa Sexti Toni *Mass
(Lueger, P. Wilhelm) [Lat] 4pt mix
cor,acap sc,cor pts BOHM s.p.
(P670)

Vobis Datum Est
(Young, Percy) "You Are Given To
Know" [Lat/Eng] SATB,acap BROUDE
BR. $.45 see from MUSIC OF THE
GREAT CHURCHES VOL. II: ST.
MARK'S CATHEDRAL, VENICE   (P671)

You Are Given To Know *see Vobis
Datum Est

PORTER
Psalm 100 *anthem
SATB (easy) oct BROADMAN 4537-65
$.30   (P672)

PORTRAITS OF THE SAVIOUR *Easter
(Young, Letta J.) cor,2 narrators
LILLENAS ME-15 $.50   (P673)

POSEGATE
Light, A
SATB SHAWNEE A5662 $.35   (P674)

Lord Is At Work, The *anthem
SATB (easy) oct BROADMAN 4545-55
$.30   (P675)

POSEGATE (cont'd.)

Return Of The Wise Men
SATB SHAWNEE A5659 $.35   (P676)

So Fragile *anthem
SATB oct BROADMAN 4545-92 $.30
(P677)

POSEGATE, MAXCINE W.
Deep Peace
SATB,acap oct HOPE A 473 $.30
(P678)

POSER, HANS (1917-1970)
In Dich Hab Ich Gehoffet, Herr
SAT/SAB/SA,treb inst,opt bass inst
HANSSLER 14.179 s.p.   (P679)

Nun Danket Alle Gott
SAT/SAB/SA,opt bass inst HANSSLER
14.228 s.p. contains also:
Wagner, Nun Danket Alle Gott
(SAT/SAB/2pt,opt 2treb inst)
(P680)

Preis, Lob, Und Dank Sei Gott Dem
Herren
SAT/SAB/SA,opt bass inst HANSSLER
14.206 s.p.   (P681)

POSTULA A ME see Doebler, Curt

POSTULA A ME see Lemacher, Heinrich

POSTULA A ME see Marx, August

POTE, ALLEN
Sing For Joy *Gen/Thanks
SATB,pno,fl/vln CHORISTERS A-161
$.50   (P682)

POTTENGER
I Sing Of Jesus, My Lord *gospel
SATB oct LILLENAS AN-1663 $.30
(P683)

POTTER'S VESSEL, THE see Zilch, Margot

POTTLE, SAM (1934-   )
Dear Lord And Father
SATB,opt band TRIGON TGM 102 $.35
(P684)

POULENC, FRANCIS (1899-1963)
Ave Verum Corpus
[Lat/Eng] SSA,acap SALABERT-US $.45
(P685)

Darkness Was Over All *see Tenebrae
Factae Sunt

Litanie A La Vierge Noir
[Eng] 3pt wom cor,org WHITE,ERN
$.75   (P686)

Quatre Petites Prieres De Saint
Francois D'Assise *CC4U,prayer
[Fr/Eng] TBarBarB,acap SALABERT-US
$.90   (P687)

Tenebrae Factae Sunt (from Sept
Repons Des Tenebres) Gd.Fri.
"Darkness Was Over All" [Lat/Eng]
SATB,S solo,org SALABERT-US $.50
(P688)

POUR LA CONFIRMATION *Cnfrm
cor JOBERT s.p. see also Douze
Nouveaux Cantiques De Fetes (P689)

POUR LA PREMIERE COMMUNION
cor JOBERT s.p. see also Douze
Nouveaux Cantiques De Fetes (P690)

POUR LA PREMIERE COMMUNION
cor JOBERT s.p. see also Douze
Nouveaux Cantiques De Fetes (P691)

POUR LA TOUSSAINT *ASD
cor JOBERT s.p. see also Douze
Nouveaux Cantiques De Fetes (P692)

POUR LE JOUR DES RAMEAUX *Palm
cor JOBERT s.p. see also Douze
Nouveaux Cantiques De Fetes (P693)

POUWELS, JAN (1898-   )
Confiteor (Psalm 31)
mix cor,A solo,vln,2fl,2ob,2clar,
2bsn,4horn,2trp,2trom,tuba,
strings,perc,timp DONEMUS (P694)

Psalm 31 *see Confiteor

POWELL
At The Name Of Jesus *anthem
SATB FINE ARTS CM 1073 $.30 (P695)

Come, My Way, My Truth, My Life
*anthem
SATB,3trp oct BROADMAN 4554-76 $.30
(P696)

Give To The Winds Thy Fears *see
Wesley

Lute Book Lullaby *Xmas,anthem
SATB oct BROADMAN 4554-78 $.30
(P697)

Master Of Eager Youth *anthem
2pt FINE ARTS CM 1044 $.30 (P698)

POWELL (cont'd.)

On This Day God Gave Us Christ
*anthem
SATB,brass oct BROADMAN 4563-05
$.50   (P699)

POWELL, FREDERICK J.
Hush Thee To Sleep
SATB EMI s.p.   (P700)

POWELL, R.
O Perfect Life Of Love *Lent
SATB,acap GRAY CMR 3302 $.30 (P701)

POWELL, RICK
Joyful Noise *anthem
SATB WORD CS-2691 $.40 see from
RICK POWELL CHOIR BOOK   (P702)

Love (composed with Powell, Sylvia)
(Bock, Fred) SATB,narrator,
electronic tape (very easy)
GENTRY G-277 $.35   (P703)

POWELL, ROBERT
Heavens Declare Your Glory, The
(easy) FISCHER,C CM 7915 $.40 (P704)

Love's Redeeming Work Is Done
SAB (easy) FISCHER,C CM 7824 $.35
(P705)

Sing All The Earth
SAB (easy) FISCHER,C CM 7822 $.35
(P706)

POWELL, ROBERT J.
Author Of Life *Commun,anthem
(Smith, G.A.) SATB,acap oct AGAPE
AG 7184 $.30   (P707)

Behold Now, Praise The Lord *Bibl
SA (diff) FITZSIMONS 5023 $.20
(P708)

Easter Carol *Easter
unis CHORISTERS A-86 $.35   (P709)

For The Mountains Shall Depart
SATB,acap (easy) FITZSIMONS 2201
$.20   (P710)

How Lovely Is Thy Dwelling Place
*Gen/Thanks
SAB CHORISTERS A-113 $.40   (P711)

I Sing The Birth *Xmas
SATB,acap ART MAST 221 $.30 (P712)

In All The World *anthem
SA, Orff inst AUGSBURG 11-0319 $.35
(P713)

In The Town Of Bethlehem *Xmas
unis,pno/org CHORISTERS A-169 $.35
(P714)

Lenten Prayer, A *Lent
unis,fl,org/pno CHORISTERS A-159
$.40   (P715)

Let Faith Be My Shield *Gen/Thanks
1-2pt CHORISTERS A-141 $.40   (P716)

O God, The King Of Glory
SATB,acap (easy) FITZSIMONS 2200
$.20   (P717)

O Praise The Lord, Ye Children
*Palm,canon
3pt,org/pno CHORISTERS A-163 $.40
(P718)

So Small A Boy *Xmas
unis CHORISTERS A-123 $.35 (P719)

POWELL, SYLVIA
Love *see Powell, Rick

POWELL, WILFRED
Masters In This Hall
SAB HARRIS HC 3001 $.35   (P720)

POWER
Gloria *Gloria
(Bent) TTBB,acap (diff) OXFORD
87.009 $.45   (P721)

POWER IN THE BLOOD
(Red, Buryl) SATB TRIUNE TUM 103 $.35
see also Victory In Jesus   (P722)

POWER IN THE BLOOD see Jones

POZDRO, JOHN
They That Go Down To The Sea In Ships
SATB SCHIRM.G LG51705 $.45   (P723)

PRAEPARATE CORDA VESTRA see Bernardi,
Steffano

PRAETORIUS, HEIRONYMOUS (1560-1629)
Pater Noster
SSAATBBB LAUDINELLA LR 111 s.p.
(P724)

PRAETORIUS, JAKOB (1586-1651)
Wachet Auf, Ruft Uns Die Stimme
SATB DOBLINGER S 202 s.p.   (P725)

PRAETORIUS, MICHAEL (1571-1621)
Agnus Dei
(Ehret, W.) "Lamb Of God" [Eng/Lat]
SSAT&ATBB,acap oct NATIONAL
WHC-67 $.35   (P726)

Allein Gott In Der Hoh' Sei Ehr
*chorale
3-8pt (med) BAREN. BA4398   (P727)

Auf Dich, Mein Herre Und Mein Gott
see MUSIKBEILAGE ZUM "EVANGELISCHEN
KIRCHENCHOR 1963"

Cantabo Domino Semper *concerto
2-6pt,cont sc,cor pts EGTVED
MS17B14 s.p.   (P728)

Chant De Paques Et Pentecote
*Easter/Pent
4pt,acap voc pt HENN 243 s.p.
(P729)

Christ Fuhr Gen Himmel
ST/SSB LAUDINELLA LR 3 s.p. (P730)

Den Die Hirten Lobeten Sehre
unis&SATB SCHWEIZER. SK 69.03 s.p.
see also MUSIKBEILAGE ZUM
"EVANGELISCHEN KIRCHENCHOR 1969"
(P731)

Den Die Hirten Lobten *see Quem
Pastores Laudavere

Der Heilgen Geistes Gnade Gross
SATB (contains also: O Mensch,
Bewein Dein Sunde Gross)
SCHWEIZER. SK 58.06 s.p. see also
MUSIKBEILAGE ZUM "EVANGELISCHEN
KIRCHENCHOR 1958"   (P732)

Der Heilig Geist Vom Himmel Kam
*Whitsun,mot
(Holle, Hugo) mix cor (med easy) sc
SCHOTTS C 32 810 s.p.   (P733)

Det Ar En Ros Utsprungen *see Es Ist
Ein Ros Entsprungen

Deutsche Kirchenlieder (from Musae
Sioniae) CC53L
SATB HANSSLER HE 4.004 s.p. (P734)

Dreistimmige Kirchenliedsatze *CC41L
SAT/SAB HANSSLER HE 4.003 s.p.
(P735)

Ein Feste Burg Ist Unser Gott
see MUSIKBEILAGE ZUM "EVANGELISCHEN
KIRCHENCHOR 1959"

Enatus Est Emanuel *Xmas
"Geborn Ist Uns Immanuel" SATB (two
settings; contains also: Steht
Auf Und Wacht) SCHWEIZER.
SK 65.02-3 s.p. see also
MUSIKBEILAGE ZUM "EVANGELISCHEN
KIRCHENCHOR 1965"   (P736)
"Geborn Ist Uns Immanuel" SATB
CARUS CV 40.402 s.p.   (P737)

Enatus Est Emmanuel *Xmas
(Hilton, Arthur) "God's Son This
Day To Us Is Born" [Eng/Ger] SAB,
acap/kbd/strings/winds/rec (easy)
oct MERCURY 352-00465 $.35 (P738)
(Hilton, Arthur) "God's Son This
Day To Us Is Born" [Eng/Ger] SSA,
acap/kbd/strings/winds/rec (easy)
oct MERCURY 352-00466 $.35 (P739)

Es Ist Ein Ros Entsprungen *Xmas
see Hermann, Nikolaus, Wir Singen
Dir, Immanuel
"Det Ar En Ros Utsprungen" 4pt mix
cor ERIKS 15 s.p.   (P740)
"Lo, How A Rose E'er Blooming" SATB
HARRIS HC 4047 $.30   (P741)
(Koenig, F.) men cor,acap TONOS 151
s.p.   (P742)
(Lang, Hans) men cor sc SCHOTTS
CHBL 125A, B s.p. contains also:
Vulpius, Melchior, Es Ist Ein Ros
Entsprungen (canon)   (P743)
(White) "Lo, How A Rose E'er
Blooming" SATB oct SCHMITT 1449
$.35   (P744)

Geboren Ist Der Immanuel
mix cor sc LIENAU s.p.   (P745)

Geborn Ist Uns Immanuel *see Enatus
Est Emanuel

God's Son This Day To Us Is Born
*see Enatus Est Emmanuel

Gottes Sohn Ist Kommen
SATB (contains also: Wir Danken
Dir, Herr Jesu Christ, Dass Du
Fur Uns Gestorben Bist)
SCHWEIZER. SK 56.01 s.p. see also
MUSIKBEILAGE ZUM "EVANGELISCHEN
KIRCHENCHOR 1956"   (P746)

Ich Will Des Herren Gnad Lobsingen
*mot
SATB&SATB HANSSLER 1.544 s.p.

PRAETORIUS, MICHAEL (cont'd.)

(P747)

Im Frieden Dein
see Bach, Johann Sebastian, Gelobt
Seist Du, Jesu Christ

In Dulci Jubilo *Xmas,mot
jr cor/wom cor (med easy) sc
SCHOTTS CHBL 593 s.p.   (P748)
SATB,2trp,2trom,horn KING,R MFB 606
cor pts $.30, cmplt ed $2.50
(P749)

Jauchz, Erd Und Himmel
SAT/SAB (contains also: O Heiland,
Reiss Die Himmel Auf) SCHWEIZER.
SK 66.02 s.p. see also
MUSIKBEILAGE ZUM "EVANGELISCHEN
KIRCHENCHOR 1966"   (P750)

Kyrie Et Gloria *Gloria/Kyrie/Mass
[Lat/Ger] 4pt mix cor,acap (med)
BAREN. BA4399   (P751)

Lamb Of God *see Agnus Dei

Laudate Dominum *concerto
2-6pt,cont sc,cor pts EGTVED MS18B6
s.p.   (P752)

Le Sommeil De L'enfant Jesus *Xmas
4pt mix cor,acap sc HENN 086 s.p.
(P753)

Lo, How A Rose E'er Blooming *see Es
Ist Ein Ros Entsprungen

Lobet Den Herren, Alle Heiden
SATB (contains also: Zeuch Ein Zu
Deinen Toren) SCHWEIZER. SK 63.07
s.p. see also MUSIKBEILAGE ZUM
"EVANGELISCHEN KIRCHENCHOR 1963"
(P754)

Maria Zart *BVM
men cor,acap TONOS 5637 s.p. (P755)

Noel Pastoral *Xmas
4pt mix cor,acap sc HENN 195 s.p.
(P756)

Nu Vilar Hela Jorden *see Isaac

Nun Lob, Mein Seel, Den Herren
SATB (contains also: Der Herr Ist
Mein Getreuer Hirt) SCHWEIZER.
SK 58.03-4 s.p. see also
MUSIKBEILAGE ZUM "EVANGELISCHEN
KIRCHENCHOR 1958"   (P757)

Nunc Angelorum *anthem
SATB oct CHANTRY CLA 503 $.12
(P758)

Praise Ye The Lord *Gen
(Ehret, Walter) [Eng/Lat] SATB,acap
(easy) PRESSER 312-41067 $.40
(P759)

Psallite
"Singt Und Klingt" [Ger/Lat] mix
cor (easy) sc SCHOTTS C 38 069B
s.p.   (P760)
(Greyson, N.) SAB BOURNE
B231068-356 $.45   (P761)

Quem Pastores Laudavere
"Den Die Hirten Lobten" mix cor
(easy) sc SCHOTTS C 38 069D s.p.
(P762)

Se, Morgonstjarnan Stralar Ater
4pt mix cor ERIKS 54 s.p.   (P763)

Singt, Ihr Lieben Christen All
SSATB,SS soli,cont,opt 2treb inst
SCHWEIZER. SK 124 sc s.p., cor
pts s.p., ipa   (P764)

Singt Und Klingt *see Psallite

Thirteen Amens (And Alleluias)
*CC13U
(Reuning, D.) 4-5pt mix cor GIA
G1915 $.75   (P765)

Three Christmas Carols (from Musae
Sioniae Vol. IX) CC3U,Xmas
(Tortolano, William) 3 eq voices
GIA G1944 $.50   (P766)

Vom Himmel Hoch, Da Komm Ich Her
SSA&opt men cor,cont,opt org/
strings SCHWEIZER. SK 119 sc
s.p., cor pts s.p., ipa   (P767)

Wir Danken Dir, Herr Jesu Christ,
Dass Du Fur Uns Gestorben Bist
SATB (contains also: Gottes Sohn
Ist Kommen) SCHWEIZER. SK 56.01
s.p. see also MUSIKBEILAGE ZUM
"EVANGELISCHEN KIRCHENCHOR 1956"
(P768)

Wir Wollen Alle Frohlich Sein
see MUSIKBEILAGE ZUM "EVANGELISCHEN
KIRCHENCHOR 1963"

Wohlauf, Ihr Christen, Freuet Euch
SATB (contains also: Nun Bitten Wir
Den Heiligen Geist) SCHWEIZER.
SK 53.05 s.p. see also
MUSIKBEILAGE ZUM "EVANGELISCHEN

PRAETORIUS, MICHAEL (cont'd.)

KIRCHENCHOR 1953"   (P769)

Wunderbarer Gnadenthron
SAT/SAB (contains also: O Christe,
Wahreit Und Leben) SCHWEIZER.
SK 67.03 s.p. see also
MUSIKBEILAGE ZUM "EVANGELISCHEN
KIRCHENCHOR 1967"   (P770)

PRAISE! see Goss, John

PRAISE see Hill

PRAISE see Roberts, C.

PRAISE AND LAUD AND HONOR see Till,
Johann Christian

PRAISE BE THINE, O JESU see Grimes,
Travis

PRAISE BE TO JESUS see Matthews

PRAISE FOR THIS DAY see Wetzler, Robert

PRAISE GOD AND SING *CCU,cor-resp
(Reynolds, Wm. J.) mix cor BROADMAN
4528-02 $1.25   (P771)

PRAISE GOD, I'M FREE see Allen

PRAISE GOD IN HIGHEST HEAVEN see Butler

PRAISE GOD IN HIS HOLINESS see Cram

PRAISE GOD IN NATURE see Pitcher

PRAISE GOD, MY SOUL see Jeppesen, Knud

PRAISE GOD, THE LORD see Burroughs, Bob

PRAISE GOD WITH A SHOUT see Price,
Milburn

PRAISE GOD WITH LOUD SONGS see Snell,
Frederick

PRAISE GOD YE SERVANTS OF THE LORD see
Roesch

PRAISE GOD YE SONS OF EARTH see Young,
Phillip M.

PRAISE HIM see Bach, Johann Sebastian

PRAISE HIM see Mc Kay, David Phares

PRAISE HIM! see Wyrtzen, Don

PRAISE HIM DECLARE HIS GLORY see
Mozart, Wolfgang Amadeus

PRAISE HIM IN THE MORNING *anthem/folk
(Wyrtzen, Don) SATB oct SINGSPIR
ZJP-5062 $.35   (P772)

PRAISE HIM NOW see Peterson, John W.

PRAISE HIM, O SERVANTS OF GOD see
Zimmermann, Heinz Werner

PRAISE HIM, SUN AND MOON see Mechem,
Kirke

PRAISE HIM TODAY see Murray

PRAISE HIM, YE NATIONS see Mozart,
Wolfgang Amadeus

PRAISE IS DUE TO THEE, O GOD see Butler

PRAISE MEDLEY
see Mini-Musicals

PRAISE, MY SOUL, THE KING OF HEAVEN
*anthem
(Brandon, G.) SATB,org (easy) GIA
G1885 $.40   (P773)

PRAISE, MY SOUL, THE KING OF HEAVEN see
Goss, John

PRAISE, MY SOUL, THE KING OF HEAVEN see
Lyte

PRAISE, O PRAISE OUR GOD AND KING see
Baker

PRAISE, O PRAISE OUR GOD AND KING see
Monkland

PRAISE OUR GOD see Peterson, John W.

PRAISE THE FATHER OF CREATION see
McGlohan

PRAISE THE LORD *CC62U,folk/hymn
(Wuerffel, Theodore) cor,opt gtr
CONCORDIA 97-5193 $1.50   (P774)

PRAISE THE LORD see Adams, John T.

PRAISE THE LORD see Adler

PRAISE THE LORD see Franck, Cesar

PRAISE THE LORD see Goemanne, Noel

PRAISE THE LORD see Graham, Robert

PRAISE THE LORD see Handel, George
Frideric

PRAISE THE LORD see Kirk

PRAISE THE LORD see Zimmermann, Heinz
Werner

PRAISE THE LORD! *CC3U,Psalm
(Van Camp, Leonard) unis, or any
combination of voices (easy) FOSTER
MF155 $.40 contains works by:
Billings, William; Belcher, Supply;
Kimball, Jacob Jr.   (P775)

PRAISE THE LORD, ALL YE NATIONS see
Roman, Johan Helmich

PRAISE THE LORD, ALLELUIA! see Watson,
Walter

PRAISE THE LORD, FOR HE IS GOOD see
Manz, Paul

PRAISE THE LORD, HIS GLORIES SHOW see
Krogstad, Bob

PRAISE THE LORD IN HIS SANCTUARY see
Felciano, Richard

PRAISE THE LORD, O JERUSALEM see
Purcell, Henry

PRAISE THE LORD, O MY SOUL see
Matthews, Thomas

PRAISE THE LORD, O MY SOUL see Peter,
Johann Friedrich

PRAISE THE LORD, SING ALLELUIA see
Smith, Claude T.

PRAISE THE LORD WHO REIGNS ABOVE see
Davis

PRAISE THE LORD WITH GLADNESS
SATB,acap PRO ART 2815 $.45   (P776)

PRAISE THE LORD WITH SONG see Kirby

PRAISE THE LORD, YE CONGREGATION see
Parks, Joe E.

PRAISE THE LORD! YE HEAVENS ADORE HIM!
see Beaudrot

PRAISE THE LORD! YE HEAVENS ADORE HIM
see Cousins, M. Thomas

PRAISE THE LORD: YOU HEAVENS ADORE HIM
*Reces
(Roff, Joseph) SATB LITURGICAL $.50
see also Twelve Hymns   (P777)

PRAISE THEE, LORD see Collins

PRAISE TO GOD see Barbauld

PRAISE TO GOD, IMMORTAL PRAISE see
Clark, Henry A.

PRAISE TO LORD GOD see Van Wormer, G.

PRAISE TO THE LORD see Gilbert

PRAISE TO THE LORD see Kurth, Burton L.

PRAISE TO THE LORD see Lobe Den Herren

PRAISE TO THE LORD see Manz, Paul

PRAISE TO THE LORD see Wolff, S.
Drummond

PRAISE TO THE LORD see Klusmeier,
R.T.A.

PRAISE TO THE LORD GOD see Schutz,
Heinrich, Lobe Den Herren, Meine
Seele

PRAISE TO THE LORD, THE ALMIGHTY
*anthem
(Cram, James D.) unis CENTURY PR $.20
(P778)

PRAISE TO THE VICTIM OF EASTER see
Victoria, Tomas Luis de, Victimae
Paschali Laudes

PRAISE TO THEE, THOU GREAT CREATOR see
Owen

PRAISE TO THEE, THOU GREAT CREATOR see
Owen, William

PRAISE WE THE NAME OF GOD see Bach

PRESTON
Missa Brevis *Commun,Mass
SATB,inst (med diff) OXFORD 42.355
$1.00, ipr (P800)

My Singing Is A Prayer (composed with
Williams) *anthem
unis&desc oct BROADMAN 4557-15 $.30
(P801)

Our Lord In Majesty Doth Reign
SATB SHAWNEE 5680 $.40 (P802)

Sleep Little Jesus
SAB SHAWNEE D5232 $.35 (P803)
SSA SHAWNEE B5159 $.35 (P804)
SAB SHAWNEE E168 $.35 (P805)

There Is No Rose *Xmas,carol
SATB,acap (med) OXFORD 84.223 $.35
(P806)

PREUS
Cradle Carol, A *Xmas
SA,opt fl oct SCHMITT 2589 $.30 (P807)

PREUSS, ARTHUR
Now Proclaim His Birth In Song
*Xmas,carol
SATB,acap oct SACRED S-175 $.35
(P808)

PRICE
Can't You Hear? *anthem
SATB oct LORENZ A546 $.35 (P809)

Come, Ye Faithful, Raise The Strain
*see Damascus

I'll Trust And Never Be Afraid
*anthem/folk
(Johnson, Paul) SATB oct SINGSPIR
ZJP-5066 $.35 (P810)

Peace In Our Time *see Corum

Shepherds And Angels *carol
SSA (med easy) OXFORD 46.162 $1.80
(P811)

Take Up Thy Cross *anthem
SATB oct LORENZ A560 $.30 (P812)

This Is My Father's World *anthem
SATB oct LORENZ A564 $.30 (P813)

PRICE, FLORENCE B. (1888-1953)
And That's The Truth *anthem/cant
jr cor LEXICON (P814)

Bright New World (from Cross And The
Switchblade) anthem
(Carmichael, Ralph) SATB,2trp,2trom
LEXICON CS-2508 $.40, ipa (P815)

Our House *cant
jr cor LEXICON 37651 $1.95 (P816)

PRICE, MILBURN
Christ Is Made The Sure Foundation
*Fest
SATB,pno/3trp&2trom (easy) FISCHER,
C CM 7926 $.40 (P817)

Meditations On The Nativity *Xmas
SATB&audience BROADMAN 4512-16
$1.75 (P818)

Praise God With A Shout
SATB (med) FISCHER,C CM 7815 $.35
(P819)

PRICE PAID FOR ME, THE see Flower

PRICHARD, [ROWLAND HUGH] (1811-1887)
Alleluia! Alleluia! *Easter,anthem
(DeCou, Harold) SATB,opt 3trp&trom
oct SINGSPIR ZJP-3502 $.25 (P820)

Alleluia, Sing To Jesus *Easter,
anthem
(Pasquet, Jean) SATB&cong&desc,org,
brass (easy) PRESSER 312-41054
$.50 (P821)
(Richardson) SAB (easy) oct
BROADMAN 4540-20 $.30 (P822)

I Will Sing The Wondrous Story
*anthem
(Johnson, Norman) SATB oct SINGSPIR
ZJP-7364 $.35 (P823)

Our Great Savior *anthem/gospel
(Berglund) SATB oct LILLENAS
AN-6028 $.35 (P824)
(Linn) SSATTBB,brass oct LILLENAS
AT-1092 $.35 (P825)
(Uphaus) SATB oct LILLENAS AN-2384
$.30 (P826)

PRIERE A L'ENFANT JESUS *Xmas
cor JOBERT s.p. see also Douze
Cantiques De Fetes (P827)

PRIERE LITANIQUE see Carraz

PRIERE POUR DEMANDER UNE ETOILE see
Veretti, Antonio

PRIMIZ-MESSE IN ES see Gruber, Joseph

PRIN, YVES
Hymnus Soixante-Huit *ora
cor,soli,orch RIDEAU s.p. (P828)

PRINCE AND THE PROPHECY, THE see
Franco, Johan

PRINCE OF PEACE see Innes, John

PRINCE OF PEACE IS COMING, THE see
Kirby

PRINCIPES PERSECUTI see Zimmer, Jan

PRINCIPIUM SAPIENTIAE see Villa-Lobos,
Heitor

PROCACCINI, T. (1934-)
Il Giudizio Di Salomone *cant
cor,soli,3fl,2ob,3clar,2bsn,4horn,
3trp,3trom,tuba,timp,perc CARISH
rental (P829)

PROCESSION INTO THE WORLD (ALLELUIA!)
see Kemp, John

PROCESSIONAL CAROL see Green, James

PROCESSIONAL PSALM see Proulx, Richard

PROCLAIM HIS GREAT LOVE see King, Lew

PROCTER, LELAND
Three Songs Of Service *CC3U
SATB,acap AM.COMP.AL. $3.58 (P830)

PROCTER, R.E.
Lead Us, Heavenly Father
mix cor BRODT 557 $.24 (P831)

Nine Calls To Worship *CC9U
mix cor BRODT 508 $.28 (P832)

PROLOGUE see Elgar, Edward

PROMESSE DE DIEU see Milhaud, Darius

PROMISE OF GOD'S LOVE, THE see Butler,
Eugene

PROMISE OF LOVE, THE see Snyder, George
B.

PROMISED LAND, THE
(Harris) SATB PRO ART 2759 $.40
(P833)

PROMISED LAND, THE see Arch, Gwyn

PROMISED ONE, THE see Smith

PRONK, ARIE
Als Er Eens God Was
mix cor HEER 1527 (P834)

Dank U O Heer
mix cor sc HEER 1522 s.p. (P835)

Door't Sterrelicht In Praal En Pracht
*Xmas
mix cor HEER 1526 s.p. (P836)

Jeruzalem, Jeruzalem
mix cor HEER 1535 (P837)

Sjalom' Voor Israel
mix cor sc HEER 1525 s.p. (P838)

Ziet Gij De Sterre Schijnen *Xmas
mix cor sc HEER 1519 s.p. (P839)

PROPHECIES OF CHRISTMAS, THE see Kirby

PROPHECY, THE see Diemer, Emma Lou

PROPHECY OF MICAH, THE see Freed,
Isadore

PROPHECY OF ZECHARIAH, THE see Pisk,
Paul Amadeus

PROPHETIAE SYBILLARUM, HEFT 1 see
Lassus, Roland de (Orlandus)

PROPHETIAE SYBILLARUM, HEFT 2 see
Lassus, Roland de (Orlandus)

PROPHETIAE SYBILLARUM, HEFT 3 see
Lassus, Roland de (Orlandus)

PROPHETIAE SYBILLARUM, HEFT 4 see
Lassus, Roland de (Orlandus)

PROPRIUM DER MESSE VOM ALLERHEILIGSTE
ALTARSAKRAMENT see Goller, Fritz

PROPRIUM DER OSTERNACHT-MESSE see
Lauterbach, Lorenz

PROPRIUM "IN EPIPHANIA DOMINI" see
Lemacher, Heinrich

PROPRIUM MISSAE IN DIE "PUER NATUS EST"
see Woll, Erna

PROPRIUMGESANGE FUR DAS KIRCHWEIHFEST
"TERRIBILIS EST LOCUS ISTE" see
Spranger, Jorg

PROPRIUMSLIEDER ZUR MESSFEIER IN DER
WEIHNACHTSZEIT see Trapp, Willy

PROPTER VERITATEM see Zimmer, Jan

PROSS, D.
Gospel Acclamation Verses *CCU
SATB&cong,org GIA G1652 $3.00, ipa
(P840)

PROTHEROE, DANIEL (1866-1934)
Garden And The Sepulchre, The
*Easter,cant
mix cor,ST/ABar soli (med easy)
FITZSIMONS $.60 (P841)

King Of Kings *Bibl/cant/hymn
mix cor,SATB soli,orch FITZSIMONS
voc sc $.90, sc rental (P842)

Lamb, The
SA (med) FITZSIMONS 5002 $.25 (P843)

Lord Is My Light, The *Bibl
SA (easy) FITZSIMONS 5001 $.25 (P844)

O Jerusalem That Bringest Good
Tidings *Xmas/Gen
SATB (easy) FITZSIMONS 2003 $.20
(P845)

O Love Divine
SATB,acap (easy) FITZSIMONS 2011
$.20 (P846)

Olivet *Lent,Bibl/cant/hymn
mix cor,STBar soli,orch (med)
FITZSIMONS voc sc $.90, sc rental
(P847)

Out In The Fields
SAB (easy) FITZSIMONS 6004 $.20
(P848)
TTBB (med) FITZSIMONS 4013 $.20
(P849)

There Shall Be Night No More *Bibl
SATB,acap (med) FITZSIMONS 2006
$.20 (P850)

Walking With The Master
SATB,A/Bar solo (easy) FITZSIMONS
2010 $.20 (P851)

PROUD MAISIE see Lawson, Malcolm

PROULX, RICHARD
Behold Now, Bless The Lord (Psalm
134) anthem/Bibl
2pt mix cor/2 eq voices,6hndbl GIA
G1821 $.35 (P852)

Christmas Processional *Xmas,anthem
2pt,cantor,4hndbl (easy) GIA G1708
$.25 (P853)

Festival Eucharist, A *Commun
SATB&cong,brass,perc GIA G1960
$1.25, ipa (P854)

How Blest Are They *anthem
unis,org,fl AUGSBURG 11-0654 $.35
(P855)

Lord, You Have The Words (Psalm 18)
Bibl
SB&cong,4perc,4hndbl GIA G1804 $.35
(P856)

Praise Ye The Lord, Ye Children
*anthem
unis,hndbl AUGSBURG 11-0322 $.25
(P857)

Processional Psalm *anthem
2 eq voices/2pt mix cor&cong,
cantor,4hndbl (easy) GIA G1750
$.30 (P858)

Psalm 18 *see Lord, You Have The
Words

Psalm 134 *see Behold Now, Bless The
Lord

Song Of Isaiah
2pt,2hndbl,tamb, triangle ART MAST
189 $.40 (P859)

Song Of The Three Young Men *anthem
1-2pt&cong,cantor,org,opt perc
(easy) GIA G1863 $.40 (P860)

Te Deum Laudamus *anthem
SATB,B solo,org,tamb,hndbl AUGSBURG
11-1729 $.45 (P861)

PROVAZNIK, ANATOL (1887-1950)
Legend Of St. Prokop *see Legenda O
Sv. Prokopovi

Legenda O Sv. Prokopovi
"Legend Of St. Prokop" [Czech] mix
cor,Bar solo,3fl,2ob,2clar,3bsn,
4horn,3trp,3trom,tuba,timp,perc,
harp,org,strings, celeste CZECH
s.p. (P862)

PROVERB, A see Wink

PROVERB OF SOLOMON, A see Kraft, Leo

PROVERBIA see Rebner, Wolfgang

PROZESSIONSGESANGE ZUM
FRONLEICHNAMSFEST see Lemacher,
Heinrich

PRUSSING, STEPHEN
Jesus Christ Is The Same, Yesterday,
Today And Forever
SATB,pno GENTRY G-240 $.40   (P863)

PSALLITE see Praetorius, Michael

PSALLITE DEO see Kraft, Karl

PSALLITE "SINGT UND KLINGT" see
Anonymous

PSALM see Holliger, Heinz

PSALM see Mechem, Kirke

PSALM 1 see Butler, Eugene, Blessed Is
The Man

PSALM 1 see Calvin

PSALM 1 see Canning, Thomas

PSALM 1 see Hindermann, Walter Felix,
Selig Der Mensch, Der Den Parolen
Der Partei Nicht Folgt

PSALM 1 see Mamlock, Ursula

PSALM 1 see Matthes, Rene, Wohl Dem,
Der Nicht Wandelt Im Rat Der
Gottlosen

PSALM 1 see Mourant, Walter

PSALM 1 see Schoenberg, Arnold, Modern
Psalm Facsimile

PSALM 1 see Schutz, Heinrich, Wohl Dem,
Der Nicht Wandelt Im Rat Der
Gottlosen

PSALM 2 see Succo

PSALM 3 see Jeppesen, Knud, O Lord, How
Numerous Are My Foes

PSALM 5 see Cross, Linda, Fifth Psalm,
The

PSALM 5 see Hindermann, Walter Felix,
Herr, Hore Doch Auf Meine Rede

PSALM 6 see Schutz, Heinrich, Ach Herr,
Straf Mich Nicht In Deinem Zorn

PSALM 8 see Baer, Psalm VIII

PSALM 8 see Burroughs, Bob

PSALM 8 see Le Jeune, Claude, Grand
Dieu, Notre Seigneur, Combien Ici
Ton Nom A Grand Honeur

PSALM 8 see McAfee, D., Hymn In Praise
Of God And Man, A

PSALM 8 see Mills, Charles

PSALM 8 see Staden, Johann, Herr, Unser
Herrscher

PSALM 8 "HERR, UNSER HERRSCHER" see
Hessenberg, Kurt

PSALM 9 see Petrassi, Goffredo, Salmo
IX

PSALM 9 see Strand, Ragnvald, De Som
Kjenner Ditt Navn

PSALM 13
see Lieder Aus Dem "Nuw Gsangbuchle"

PSALM 13 see Brahms, Johannes, Lord,
How Long Wilt Thou Forget Me?

PSALM 13 see Fennelley, Brian

PSALM 13 see Hassler, Hans Leo, Herr,
Wie Lang Wilt Vergessen Mein

PSALM 13 see Korte, Karl

PSALM 13 see Lekberg, Sven, How Long
Wilt Thou Forget Me

PSALM 13 see Zimmermann, Heinz Werner

PSALM 15 see Nystroem, Gosta, Herre,
Vem Far Bo I Din Hydda?

PSALM 18 see Franck, Cesar, Thee Will I
Love

PSALM 18 see Goudimel, Claude, Dich
Liebt Mein Herz, O Herr

PSALM 18 see Proulx, Richard, Lord, You
Have The Words

PSALM 21 see Schmidt, Christfried

PSALM 22 see Reda, Siegfried, Ecce Homo

PSALM 22 see Sweelinck, Jan
Pieterszoon, Mein Gott, Mein Gott,
Verlassen Hast Du Mich

PSALM 23 (from Bay Psalm Book)
(Beeson) SATB,acap (med diff) OXFORD
94.324 $.35   (P864)
(Hill, Harry) SATB (easy) WATERLOO
$.35   (P865)

PSALM 23 see Bass, Claude L.

PSALM 23 see Binkerd, Gordon

PSALM 23 see Carter

PSALM 23 see Dietterich, Philip R.

PSALM 23 see Haan, Raymond

PSALM 23 see Hill, Harry

PSALM 23 see Jirak, Karel Boleslav,
Psalm XXIII

PSALM 23 see Klein, Bernhard, Der Herr
Ist Mein Hirt

PSALM 23 see Kohs, Ellis B.

PSALM 23 see Lekberg, Sven, Lord Is My
Shepherd

PSALM 23 see Marsh, Twenty-Third Psalm,
The

PSALM 23 see Marshall, God Of Love, The

PSALM 23 see Mechem, Kirke, Lord Is My
Shepherd, The

PSALM 23 see Rozsa, Miklos, Twenty-
Third Psalm, The

PSALM 23 see Schubert, Franz (Peter),
Gott Ist Mein Hirt

PSALM 23 see Schutz, Heinrich, Der Herr
Ist Mein Hirt

PSALM 23 see Yahres, Samuel C., Psalm
Beautiful, The

PSALM 24 see Beebe, Who Shall Ascend

PSALM 24 see Epstein, Alvin, L'adonai
Ha-Arets

PSALM 24 see Pierne, Paul, Earth Is The
Lord's, The

PSALM 24 see Rhea, Arthur D.

PSALM 25 see Balazs, Frederic, Lord, I
Love The Beauty Of Thy House

PSALM 25 see L'Estocart, Paschal de,
Ich Erhebe Mein Gemute

PSALM 25 see Kohs, Ellis B.

PSALM 26
see Lieder Aus Dem "Nuw Gsangbuchle"

PSALM 26 see Hessenberg, Kurt, Wenn Der
Herr Die Gefangenen Zions Erlosen
Wird

PSALM 27 see Irving, George

PSALM 27 see Jeppesen, Knud, One Thing
Have I Desired Of The Lord

PSALM 27 see Zimmermann, Heinz Werner,
Lord Is My Light, The

PSALM 27 (PART I) see Karlen, Robert

PSALM 27 (PART III) see Karlen, Robert

PSALM 29 see Elgar, Edward, Give Unto
The Lord

PSALM 29 see Mourant, Walter

PSALM 30 see Hess, Reimund, Der Dritte
Psalm

PSALM 30 see Sinzheimer, Max, Song Of
Dedication

PSALM 30 see Tapel, Joseph

PSALM 30 see Tarry

PSALM 31 see Pouwels, Jan, Confiteor

PSALM 31 see Waters

PSALM 33 see Le Jeune, Claude, Nun
Freut Euch In Gott, Ihr Frommen

PSALM 34 see Rein, Walter, Ich Will Den
Herren Loben

PSALM 36 see Goudimel, Claude, O
Hochster, Deine Gutigkeit

PSALM 40 see Adler

PSALM 43 see Pezzati, Romano, Salmo 43

PSALM 46 see Fortner, Wolfgang, Gott
Ist Unsre Zuversicht

PSALM 46 see Zimmermann, Heinz Werner,
Psalm (Part 3)

PSALM 47 (from Bay Psalm Book)
(Beeson) SATB,acap (med diff) OXFORD
94.323 $.35   (P866)

PSALM 47 see Diener, Theodor, Singt Mit
Froher Stimm

PSALM 47 see Lindh, Jody W.

PSALM 48 see Elgar, Edward, Great Is
The Lord

PSALM 51
see Lieder Aus Dem "Nuw Gsangbuchle"

PSALM 51 see Latrobe, Christian I.

PSALM 51 see McAfee

PSALM 51 see Milhaud, Darius

PSALM 51 see Sipila, Eero, Miserere

PSALM 51 see Winer, Georg, Schaffe In
Mir, Gott, Ein Reines Herze

PSALM 55 see Jeppesen, Knud, Hear My
Prayer, O My God

PSALM 56 see Lupi, Roberto

PSALM 57 see Blazek, Vilem, Zalm 57

PSALM 62 see Strauss-Konig, Richard,
Gott, Mein Gott, Im Morgenlicht
Wach Ich Auf Zu Dir

PSALM 64 see Zipp, Friedrich, Gott Ist
Unsere Zuversicht Und Starke

PSALM 66 see Diament, Abraham, Hariu
Le'elohim

PSALM 66 see Haubler, Ernst, Jauchzet
Gott, Alle Lande

PSALM 66 see Slater, Richard W.

PSALM 67 see Beck, John Ness

PSALM 67 see Cammarota, Carlo, Salmo
XLVII

PSALM 67 see Donato, Anthony, God Be
Merciful

PSALM 67 see Lawes, William, Have
Mercy, On Us, Lord

PSALM 67 see Mills, Charles

PSALM 67 see Naylor, Bernard, Deus
Misereatur

PSALM 67 see Wenzel, Eberhard

PSALM 67 see Zimmermann, Heinz Werner

PSALM 71
see Lieder Aus Dem "Nuw Gsangbuchle"

PSALM 71 see Schutz, Heinrich, Auf
Dich, Herr, Trau Ich Allezeit

PSALM 77 see Nystedt, Knut

PSALM 84 see Bender, Jan

PSALM 84 see Egidi

PSALM 86 see Berg, Gottfrid, Lyssna,
Herre, Till Mit Bejande

PSALM 86 see Berger

PSALM 86 see Strand, Ragnvald, Et Udelt
Hjerte

PSALM 90 see Lohr, Ina, Herr, Gott, Du
Bist Unsre Zuflucht Fur Und Fur

PSALM 90 see Mourant, Walter

PSALM 90 see Weber, Bernhard, Jubilate Deo

PSALM 92 see Poos, Heinrich, Das Ist Ein Kostlich Ding

PSALM 92 see Soderholm, Valdemar, Sjungen Och Spelen Till Herrens Ara

PSALM 93 see Burkhard Willy, Der Herr Ist Konig

PSALM 93 see Newbury, Kent A.

PSALM 93 see Sturman, Paul

PSALM 95 see McKelvy, James, Acclamation

PSALM 98 see Crawford

PSALM 98 see Franco, Johan

PSALM 98 see Heer, Emil, Singet Dem Herrn Ein Neues Lied

PSALM 98 see Naylor, Bernard, Cantata Domino

PSALM 98 see Poos, Heinrich, Singet Dem Herrn Ein Neues Lied

PSALM 98 see Schutz, Heinrich, Singet Dem Herrn Ein Neues Lied

PSALM 99 see Ammann, Benno

PSALM 100 see Avshalomov, Jacob, Make A Joyful Noise Unto The Lord

PSALM 100 see Blake, Kevin

PSALM 100 see Carter

PSALM 100 see Fortner, Wolfgang, Jauchzet Dem Herrn Alle Welt

PSALM 100 see Gerschefski, Edwin

PSALM 100 see Gore, Richard T., Hundredth Psalm, The

PSALM 100 see Hand, Colin, O Be Joyful In The Lord

PSALM 100 see Heer, Emil, Jauchzet Dem Herren, Alle Lande

PSALM 100 see Lawes, William, All People That On Earth Do Dwell

PSALM 100 see Mendelssohn-Bartholdy, Felix

PSALM 100 see Peloquin, C. Alexander, Psalm One Hundred

PSALM 100 see Porter

PSALM 100 see Reger, Max, Der 100. Psalm

PSALM 100 see Rijp, A.W.

PSALM 100 see Rogers, Diane E.

PSALM 100 see Schutz, Heinrich, Jauchzet Dem Herren, Alle Welt

PSALM 100 see Schweizer, Rolf, Schlagt Froh In Die Hande

PSALM 100 see Staden, Johann, Jauchzet Dem Herren, Alle Welt

PSALM 103 see Jeppesen, Knud, Praise God, My Soul

PSALM 103 see Pulkingham, B.C., Bless Thou The Lord

PSALM 103 see Strategier, Herman, Psaume CIII

PSALM 103 see Wenzel, Eberhard

PSALM 104 see Le Jeune, Claude, Sus, Sus Mon Ame

PSALM 104 see Saunders, Neil, Benedic Anima Mea

PSALM 105 see Kirk, Antiphon

PSALM 108 see Hess, J.

PSALM 109 see Pergolesi, Giovanni Battista, Dixit Dominus

PSALM 111 see Schutz, Heinrich, Ich Will Von Herzen Danken Gott

PSALM 112 see Galuppi, Baldassare, Beatus Vir

PSALM 112 see Pergolesi, Giovanni Battista, Laudate Pueri

PSALM 112 see Perti, Giacomo Antonio, Beatus Vir

PSALM 112 see Vivaldi, Antonio, Beatus Vir

PSALM 113 see Goudimel, Claude, Singt Halleluja

PSALM 113 see Zimmermann, Heinz Werner, Praise The Lord

PSALM 114 see Milhaud, Darius

PSALM 116 see Weiss

PSALM 117 see Ames, William

PSALM 117 see Mason, Lowell, O Praise The Lord

PSALM 117 see Monteverdi, Claudio, Laudate Dominum

PSALM 117 see Roman, Johan Helmich, Praise The Lord, All Ye Nations

PSALM 117 see Zimmermann, Heinz Werner

PSALM 118 see Weiss

PSALM 118 see Zimmermann, Heinz Werner, Psalm (Part 2)

PSALM 119
    see Lieder Aus Dem "Nuw Gsangbuchle"

PSALM 120 see Klump, George E.

PSALM 120 see McAfee, D., Hymn Of Praise, A

PSALM 121 see Ammann, Benno

PSALM 121 see Bausznern, Dietrich von, Ich Hebe Meine Augen Auf

PSALM 121 see Eglin, Arthur, Ich Schau Nach Jenen Bergen Fern

PSALM 121 see Hanson

PSALM 121 see Hopkins, James F., I To The Hills Will Lift Mine Eyes

PSALM 121 see Krogstad, Bob

PSALM 121 see McAfee, D., Hymn Of Aspiration, A

PSALM 121 see Mills, Charles

PSALM 121 see Schutz, Heinrich, Ich Hebe Meine Augen Auf Zu Den Bergen

PSALM 121 see Verdi, Ralph C., Let Us Go To God's House

PSALM 121 see Vick

PSALM 121 see Walker, M.

PSALM 121 see Williamson, Malcolm, I Will Lift Up Mine Eyes

PSALM 122 see Ammann, Benno

PSALM 122 see Schutz, Heinrich, Ich Freue Mich, Dass Man Mir Sagt

PSALM 123 see Bassett, Leslie

PSALM 125 see Ammann, Benno

PSALM 125 see Peeters, Flor, In Convertendo Dominus

PSALM 125 see Smit

PSALM 125 see Zimmermann, Heinz Werner, Those Who Trust In The Lord

PSALM 126 see Franco, Johan

PSALM 126 see Kubizek, Augustinian

PSALM 126 see Schutz, Heinrich, Die Mit Tranen Saen

PSALM 126 see Succo

PSALM 126 see Tapel, Joseph

PSALM 126 see Vendler, Bohumil, Zalm 126

PSALM 127 see Schutz, Heinrich, Wo Der Herr Nicht Das Haus Bauet

PSALM 128 see Schutz, Heinrich, Wohl Dem, Der Den Herren Furchtet

PSALM 128 see Wetzler, Robert

PSALM 129 see Salieri, Antonio, De Profundis

PSALM 130 *cant
    2-4pt mix cor,strings/rec/org
    (assembled from works of Scheidt;
    Bach, J. S.; Schutz; and others)
    PELIKAN PE730   (P867)

PSALM 130 see Ammann, Benno

PSALM 130 see Currie, Randolph, Out Of The Depths I Cry

PSALM 130 see Kaminski, Heinrich, Aus Der Tiefe Rufe Ich, Herr

PSALM 130 see Krapf, Gerhard

PSALM 130 see Mills, Charles

PSALM 130 see Weigl, Vally

PSALM 130 see Wenzel, Eberhard

PSALM 130 see Wyton, Alec

PSALM 131 (from Bay Psalm Book)
    (Beeson) SATB,acap (med diff) OXFORD
    94.322 $.25   (P868)

PSALM 133 see Goudimel, Claude, O Seht, Wie Schon Und Lieblich Ist's

PSALM 134 see Czajowski, Michael

PSALM 134 see Le Jeune, Claude, Ihr Knechte Gottes Allzugleich

PSALM 134 see Proulx, Richard, Behold Now, Bless The Lord

PSALM 134 see Sweeney, J. Albert

PSALM 136 see Sanders, Give Thanks Unto The Lord

PSALM 137 see Braal, Andries de, Aan Babels Stromen

PSALM 137 see Dijk, Jan van, By The Rivers Of Babylon

PSALM 138 see Heer, Emil, Mein Ganzes Herz Erhebet Dich

PSALM 138 see Sweelinck, Jan Pieterszoon

PSALM 140 see Carter, John

PSALM 140 see Le Jeune, Claude, Errette, Herr, Mich Von Den Bosen

PSALM 143 see Wyner, Yehudi

PSALM 145 see Schutz, Heinrich, Allas Ogon Vanta Pa Dig, Herre

PSALM 145 see Schutz, Heinrich, Ich Will Allzeit Erheben Dich

PSALM 145 see Schutz, Heinrich, Ich Will Sehr Hoch Erhohen Dich

PSALM 146 see Cooper, Rose Marie

PSALM 146 see Diener, Theodor, Alles Was Odem Hat, Lobe De Herrn

PSALM 147 see Hunecke, Wilhelm, Lauda Jerusalem

PSALM 147 see Vivaldi, Antonio, Lauda Jerusalem

PSALM 148 see Mourant, Walter

PSALM 148 see Zimmermann, Heinz Werner

PSALM 149 see Dvorak, Antonin

PSALM 150
    (Archer, Violet) SATB (med easy)
    WATERLOO $.35   (P869)

PSALM 150 see Bruckner, Anton

PSALM 150 see Cabena, Barrie

PSALM 150 see Cooper

PSALM 150 see Farrier, Walter

PSALM 150 see Felciano, Richard, Praise The Lord In His Sanctuary

PSALM 150 see Hanson

QUITTEZ, PASTEURS
see Twelve Christmas Carols: Set 1

QUONIAM AD TE CLAMABO, DOMINE see
Schutz, Heinrich

Q

QUACK, ERHARD (1904-   )
Deutsche Messe Mit Gemeinderufen
*Mass
SSAA&cong/TTBB&cong,org cor pts
CHRIS 50745 s.p.   (Q1)
SATB,org cor pts CHRIS 50744 s.p.
(Q2)
SATB,org sc CHRIS 50743 s.p.   (Q3)

QUAE EST ISTA see Palestrina, Giovanni

QUAERAMUS CUM PASTORIBUS see Morales,
Cristobal de

QUAERITE PRIMUM REGNUM DEI see Mozart,
Wolfgang Amadeus

QUAM PULCHRA EST see Gombert, Nicolas

QUANDO COR NOSTRUM VISITAS see
Schattenberg, Thomas

QUANDO VEDRO DI QUESTO MORTAL VELO
see Raccolta Corale Libro I

QUATRE NOELS SAVOYSIENS CAHIER 1 *CCU,
Xmas
(Marescotti) 4pt mix cor,acap sc HENN
299 s.p.   (Q4)

QUATRE NOELS SAVOYSIENS CAHIER 2 *CCU,
Xmas
(Marescotti) 4pt mix cor,acap sc HENN
560 s.p.   (Q5)

QUATRE PETITES PRIERES DE SAINT
FRANCOIS D'ASSISE see Poulenc,
Francis

QUATRE-VENT MOTETS see Jaton

QUATTRO PEZZI SACRI see Verdi, Giuseppe

QUATTRO SYMPHONIAE SACRAE see Gabrieli,
Giovanni

QUEEN OF MERCY see Rubbra, Edmund

QUELLE EST CETTE ODEUR?
see Eight Christmas Carols: Set 2

QUELLE EST CETTE ODEUR AGREABLE
(Willcocks) SATB (med easy) OXFORD
84.209 $.25   (Q6)

QUEM PASTORES
see Six Songs

QUEM PASTORES see Goodman, Joseph

QUEM PASTORES LAUDAVERE
(Rutter) SATB (med easy) OXFORD
84.211 $.25   (Q7)

QUEM PASTORES LAUDAVERE see Praetorius,
Michael

QUEM VIDISTI PASTORES see Chassang

QUEM VIDISTI PASTORES see Deering,
Richard

QUEM VIDISTIS, PASTORES see Lassus,
Roland de (Orlandus)

QUEM VIDISTIS PASTORES? see Page,
Robert E.

QUEM VIDISTIS PASTORES see Rychnovsky,
Jiri

QUEM VIDISTIS PASTORES? see Victoria,
Tomas Luis de

QUEMPAS CAROL, THE *13th cent
unis jr cor CHANTRY CHC 502 $.12 (Q8)

QUEMPAS NUC ANGELORUM, THE see Bender,
Jan

QUESTO E IL CIELO see Handel, George
Frideric

QUID PETIS, O FILI see Cope, Cecil

QUID RETRIBUAM see Cromie, Marguerite
Biggs

QUIET HEART, A see Bass, Claude L.

QUIET PLACE, A see Carmichael, Ralph

QUIMBY, J.S.
Infant Holy, Infant Lowly
mix cor BRODT 506 $.20   (Q9)

R

RAB, VALENTIN (ca. 1548?)
Ich Schreie Zum Herren *mot
SATB HANSSLER 1.518 s.p.   (R1)

RABOT
Messe Dans Les Modes Anciens
3pt mix cor,acap voc pt HENN 353
s.p.   (R2)

Salut
4pt,acap voc pt HENN 538 s.p.   (R3)

Salve Regina D'Einsiedeln
4pt,acap voc pt HENN 542 s.p.   (R4)

RACCOLTA CORALE LIBRO I *sac/sec
unis,pno BONGIOVANI 1512 s.p.
contains: Inno Alla Cetra; La
Polesana; Quando Vedro Di Questo
Mortal Velo (16th cent);
Pratella, Francesco Balilla,
Canzone A Ballo; Pratella,
Francesco Balilla, Preghiera;
Pratella, Francesco Balilla,
Tempo Di Marcia   (R5)

RACCOLTA CORALE LIBRO II *sac/sec
1-2pt,pno BONGIOVANI 1513 s.p.
contains: Popolo Che Sogna E Popolo
Che Burla; Signor, Ti Benedico
(16th cent); Pratella, Francesco
Balilla, Inno Al Bene; Pratella,
Francesco Balilla, Inno Alla
Bellezza Della Vita; Pratella,
Francesco Balilla, Inno Alla
Patria; Pratella, Francesco
Balilla, Inno Dei Premilitari
(R6)

RACCOLTA CORALE LIBRO III
BONGIOVANI 1514 s.p.
contains:
La Pastorella Si Leva Per Tempo
(It,16th cent);
Lodate Dio (mix cor,pno) (16th
cent);
Signor, Per La Tua Fe (mix cor,
pno) (16th cent);
Cherubini, Luigi, Marcia Corale
(from Ronda) (mix cor,acap);
Pratella, Francesco Balilla,
Canzone Del Sonno (mix cor,
acap);
Rossini, Gioacchino, Or Che Si
Oscura Il Ciel (SSTBB,pno)
(canon)   (R7)

RACCOLTA CORALE LIBRO IV see Pratella,
Francesco Balilla

RACCOLTA DI COMPOSIZIONI SACRE E
PROFANE *sac/sec,CCU
(Furgeri, B. Maria) mix cor,acap
BONGIOVANI 2437 s.p.   (R8)

RACE, STEVE
Jesus Child
see SIX CHRISTMAS CAROLS

RACHEM see Mana-Zucca, Mme.

RADCLIFFE
Mary Walked Through A Wood Of Thorn
SATB,acap (med diff) OXFORD 84.180
$.20   (R9)

RADIANT LIGHT
(Christiansen, Paul) SATB,acap ART
MAST 228 $.30   (R10)

RAINS, DOROTHY BEST
Child's Message Of Easter, A
*Easter,cant
SSA&unis,4 narrators (med easy)
SINGSPIR 4010 $1.00   (R11)

Hosanna We Sing *Easter,anthem
unis oct SINGSPIR ZA-4641 $.25
(R12)

Jesus Christ Is King *Easter,anthem
unis&desc oct SINGSPIR ZA-4642 $.25
(R13)

Shadow Scenes Of The Savior's Birth
*Xmas,cant
unis&speak cor,opt fl/vln SINGSPIR
4001 $1.00   (R14)

RAISING OF LAZURUS see Joubert, John

RALSTON
Star Is Shining, A *Adv/Xmas
SATB oct LILLENAS AN-6035 $.30
(R15)

RAMBO, DOTTIE
Don't Take My Cross Away
(Mercer, W. Elmo) SATB oct BENSON
S4067 $.25   (R16)

RAMBO, DOTTIE (cont'd.)

I Have Hope
(Mercer, W. Elmo) SATB oct BENSON
S4143 $.30   (R17)

I Just Came To Talk With You, Lord
(Mercer, W. Elmo) SATB oct BENSON
S4141 $.35   (R18)

If That Isn't Love *Easter/Gen
(Mercer, W. Elmo) SATB oct BENSON
S4148 $.30   (R19)

Is That The Lights Of Home?
(Mercer, W. Elmo) SATB oct BENSON
S4162 $.25   (R20)

Remind Me, Dear Lord
(Mercer, W. Elmo) SATB oct BENSON
S4257 $.35   (R21)

Sing Faith And Hope, Vol. I *CC8L
(Lane, Harold) cor BENSON B0821
$1.95 stereo recording, tapes,
and-or accompaniment tape also
available; for book-record sets
available, contact publisher
                              (R22)

Sing Faith And Hope, Vol. II *CC9L
(Mercer, W. Elmo) cor BENSON B0822
$1.95 stereo recording, tapes,
and-or accompaniment tape also
available; for book-record sets
available, contact publisher
                              (R23)

RAMBOLD, ALOIS
Messe Zu Ehren Des Heiliges Papstes
Pius X *Mass
[Lat] 4pt mix cor,acap sc,cor pts
BOHM s.p.   (R24)

RAMEAU, JEAN-PHILIPPE (1683-1764)
Complete Works *sac/sec,CCU
(Saint-Saens, Camille; Malherbe,
Ch.; Emmanuel, M.; Teneo, M.)
microfiche UNION ESP. $220.00
originally published in 18
volumes, A. Durand, Paris 1895-
1913.   (R25)

RAMIREZ
Los Reyes Magos (from Navidad
Nuestra) Xmas
"Three Kings, The" SATB SCHIRM.G
LG51748 $.35   (R26)

Three Kings, The *see Los Reyes
Magos

RAMON
Just A Wayward Lamb *anthem/gospel
(DeCou, Harold) SATB oct SINGSPIR
ZJP-8143 $.30   (R27)

RAMQUIST, GRACE
Conqueror, The *Easter
cor,2 narrators LILLENAS ME-6 $.50
                              (R28)

We Seek Only Jesus *Easter
cor,2 narrators,solo LILLENAS
ME-222 $.50   (R29)

RAMSETH, BETTY ANN
God Is Love *anthem
2pt treb cor,fl, Orff inst AUGSBURG
11-0321 $.30   (R30)

Making Happy Noises *CCU
1-2pt,inst AUGSBURG 11-9280 $1.25
                              (R31)

Prepare Ye The Way *CCU,canon
cor,inst AUGSBURG 11-9365 $.80
                              (R32)

RAMSEY
Teach Me Thy Way, O Lord *hymn
(Hawkins) SATB oct LILLENAS AN-2422
$.30   (R33)

RAMSEY, ROBERT (ca. 1595- ?)
How Are The Mighty Fallen
SSATTB STAINER 3.0737.1 $.60 (R34)

RAMSFIELD, JEROME
Thou Wilt Keep Him In Perfect Peace
*Bibl
SATB,acap (med) FITZSIMONS 2186
$.25   (R35)

RANEY, SUE
Sue Raney's People Tree *CC10L
(Carmichael, Ralph) cor LEXICON
37549 $1.95   (R36)

RAPH
Christmas Night *Xmas
SATB,opt trp,opt horn,opt gtr,opt
drums SCHIRM.G 11945 $.40   (R37)

RAPHAEL, GUNTHER (1903-1960)
Maria Sat In Cattle Stall *anthem,
Contemp
SATB,inst oct CHANTRY COA 548 $.30,
ipa   (R38)

RASELIUS, ANDREAS (ca. 1563-1602)
Erstanden Ist Der Heilig Christ
SSATB (nun lob den herrn, o seele
mein) SCHWEIZER. SK 68.05-6 s.p.
see also MUSIKBEILAGE ZUM
"EVANGELISCHEN KIRCHENCHOR 1968"
                              (R39)

Furchtet Euch Nicht
SSATB SCHWEIZER. SK 69.04-5 s.p.
see also MUSIKBEILAGE ZUM
"EVANGELISCHEN KIRCHENCHOR 1969"
                              (R40)

Nun Komm, Der Heiden Heiland
see Eccard, Johannes, In Dulci
Jubilo

RASLEY
What Think Ye Of Christ? *Easter,
anthem
SATB oct LORENZ C358 $.35   (R41)

RASLEY, JOHN M. (1913-   )
Beholding Thee, Lord Jesus *anthem/
gospel
SATB oct SINGSPIR ZJP-8113 $.25
                              (R42)

Carol Of Praise *Xmas/Gen,anthem
SATB oct SINGSPIR ZJP-3026 $.25
                              (R43)

Easter Hymn *Easter,anthem
SATB oct SINGSPIR ZJP-3541 $.30
                              (R44)

From All That Dwell Below The Skies
*Thanks,anthem
SATB oct SINGSPIR ZJP-7360 $.25
                              (R45)

God Doth Not Slumber Nor Sleep
*anthem/gospel
SATB oct SINGSPIR ZJP-8172 $.25
                              (R46)

I Will Come Again *cant
SATB (easy) SINGSPIR 5664 $1.50
                              (R47)

Jesus, The Very Thought Of Thee
*anthem
SATB oct SINGSPIR ZJP-7320 $.25
                              (R48)

Lo, God Is Here *anthem
SATB oct SINGSPIR ZJP-7297 $.30
                              (R49)

My Jesus, I Love Thee *anthem
SATB oct SINGSPIR ZJP-7351 $.30
                              (R50)

My Lord, My God, My All *anthem
SATB oct SINGSPIR ZJP-7338 $.30
                              (R51)

Now Is Christ Risen *Easter,cant
cor SINGSPIR 5057 $1.95   (R52)

Only A Prayer Away *anthem
SA&opt TB (easy) oct SINGSPIR
ZPJ-6011 $.25   (R53)

Paean Of Praise *anthem
SATB (Church Anniversary) oct
SINGSPIR ZJP-7336 $.30   (R54)

Song Of Praise *anthem
SATB oct SINGSPIR ZJP-7281 $.30
                              (R55)

There'll Always Be A Christmas
*Xmas,cant
SATB (easy) SINGSPIR 4291 $1.50
                              (R56)

RATZLAFF, PAUL
Lift Up Your Heads, O Ye Gates
*Palm,anthem
SATB oct SINGSPIR ZJP-3514 $.25
                              (R57)

O Give Thanks! *Thanks,anthem
SATB oct SINGSPIR ZJP-3112 $.30
                              (R58)

RAU, CHRISTOPH
Der Tod
men cor,acap TONOS 5663 s.p. (R59)

RAVENSCROFT, THOMAS (1593-1635)
Ah Helpless Wretch
see Two Sacred Pieces

Besinna Nu Och Minns
4pt mix cor ERIKS 349 s.p.   (R60)
(Angerdahl, Lars;Widegard) wom cor/
jr cor ERIKS 351 s.p.   (R61)
(Angerdahl; Widegard) SABar ERIKS
359 s.p.   (R62)

O Jesu Meek
see Two Sacred Pieces

Two Sacred Pieces
SATB,inst (med) OXFORD 42.360 $.65,
ipr
contains: Ah Helpless Wretch; O
Jesu Meek   (R63)

RAVOSA
Mister Snow's Shoes
(Coates) SATB SHAWNEE A1266 $.35
                              (R64)

REACH OUT see Bass, Claude L.

REACH OUT see Thygerson, Robert J.

REACH OUT AND TOUCH see Skillings, Otis

REACH OUT TO JESUS see Carmichael,
Ralph

REACH YOUR HAND see Kaiser, Kurt

REACHING PEOPLE see Reynolds, William
Jensen

READ
Christmas Ballad, A *Xmas
SATB SCHIRM.G LG51815 $.45   (R65)

Early American Christmas Triptych, An
(composed with Holden, [Oliver];
Law) *CC3U,anthem
(Van Camp, Leonard) SATB AUGSBURG
11-1723 $.45   (R66)

Jesous Ahatonhia *Xmas
"T'was In The Moon Of Winterland"
SATB SCHIRM.G LG51847 $.45   (R67)

T'was In The Moon Of Winterland *see
Jesous Ahatonhia

READ, DANIEL (1757-1836)
Take Up Thy Cross *Gen,anthem/hymn,
US
(Price, Benton) SA/SATB (easy) oct
LORENZ A560 $.30   (R68)

READING
Preces And Responses
SATB,acap (med) OXFORD 43.479 $.30
                              (R69)

REAL LIFE LOVE see Burroughs, Bob

REALLY LIVE *CCUL,Contemp
(Wyrtzen, Don) jr cor SINGSPIR 4351
$1.95   (R70)

REALLY LIVE! see Peterson, John W.

REASON FOR SINGING, A see Ayers, David

REBNER, WOLFGANG
Proverbia
mix cor,2fl,2ob,3clar,2bsn,3trp,
3horn,3trom,perc,strings,pno,
saxophone, bass clarinet MODERN
s.p., rental   (R71)

RECEIVE THE HOLY SPIRIT see Peloquin,
C. Alexander

RECESSIONAL see Willan, Healey

RECONCILIATION see Red, Buryl

RECORDARE, VIRGO MATER see Lemacher,
Heinrich

RECUEIL DE MOTETS see Hemmerle, J.

RED
Up And Get Us Gone (composed with
Reynolds, William Jensen)
*anthem
SATB (easy) oct BROADMAN 4565-12
$.35   (R72)

RED, BURYL
All Things Bright And Beautiful
*anthem
1-2pt,opt inst oct BROADMAN 4560-42
$.35   (R73)

Beginnings *see Courtney, Ragan

Beginnings-A Praise Concert (composed
with Courtney, Ragan)
cor,narrator,pno,org,perc TRIUNE
TUO 105 $2.95, ipa   (R74)

Celebrate Life *see Courtney, Ragan

Ecclesiastes 4:11 *see Courtney,
Ragan

For The Beauty Of The Earth *anthem
1-2pt oct BROADMAN 4560-36 $.35
                              (R75)

Glorious In Holiness *see Courtney,
Ragan

God's Gonna Set This World On Fire
*anthem
SATB oct BROADMAN 4565-53 $.50
                              (R76)

Good Life, The *anthem
SATB WORD CS-2567 $.30 see from
Lightshine   (R77)

Hello, World!
SATB,kbd,opt gtr BROADMAN 4518-05
$2.95   (R78)

Here Is My Life *see Bartlett

His Gentle Look *anthem
SATB (easy) oct BROADMAN 4565-10
$.35   (R79)

RED, BURYL (cont'd.)

In Remembrance *see Courtney, Ragan

It's Cool In The Furnace *see Let The People Praise (R80)

It's Cool In The Furnace (composed with Hawthorne, Grace) *cant 1-2pt/speak cor,inst,perc WORD 37626 $1.95 (R81)

Jesus, Gentle Lamb *see Courtney, Ragan

Jesus Walked This Lonesome Valley *anthem SATB oct BROADMAN 4565-54 $.35 (R82)

Kaleidoscopic Colors *anthem SATB oct BROADMAN 4565-18 $.35 (R83)

Let The People Praise *anthem unis/3pt WORD CS-2602 $.30 see from It's Cool In The Furnace (R84)

Let The Song Go Round The Earth *anthem unis (med) oct BROADMAN 4536-94 $.30 (R85)

Let Us Break Bread Together *Commun, anthem SATB oct BROADMAN 4565-55 $.35 (R86)

Lightshine *see Good Life, The (R87)

Now Let Us Praise *anthem unis (easy) oct BROADMAN 4558-11 $.30 (R88)

Now Let Us Praise *CCU jr cor,kbd,inst BROADMAN 4527-01 $1.25 (R89)

Oh, The Joy Of It *anthem 1-2pt,opt perc oct BROADMAN 4560-25 $.35 (R90)

One World, One Lord, One Witness (composed with Reynolds, William Jensen) *anthem SATB (easy) oct BROADMAN 4565-11 $.35 (R91)

Peace Like A River *see Courtney, Ragan

Praise Ye The Lord *anthem unis oct BROADMAN 4560-18 $.20 (R92)

Prayer For Peace *see Courtney, Ragan

Psalm For Today SATB,kbd,electronic tape BROADMAN 4565-28 $.50 (R93)

Reconciliation SATB,soli&2 narrators (music drama) BROADMAN 4516-08 $2.95 (R94)

Rhyme, A Riddle, A Song, A *CCU, anthem unis jr cor,kbd,inst BROADMAN 4526-10 $1.50 (R95)

Silent Night, Holy Night *Xmas, anthem 1-2pt oct BROADMAN 4560-37 $.35 (R96)

Tell Man Of God *anthem SATB oct BROADMAN 4565-03 $.35 (R97)

There Is A Great Joy Coming *see Courtney, Ragan

This Is My Father's World *anthem 1-2pt oct BROADMAN 4560-38 $.35 (R98)

Truth Shall Make You Free, The *see Courtney, Ragan

REDA, SIEGFRIED (1916-1968) Das Graduallied, Teil 1 *see Es Wolle Gott Uns Gnadig Sein; Lobt Gott Den Herren Ihr Heiden All (R99)

Ecce Homo (Psalm 22) Psntd,mot SATB,acap (med) BAREN. BA2527 (R100)

Es Wolle Gott Uns Gnadig Sein *liturg SATB,acap (easy) BAREN. BA3078 s.p. see from Das Graduallied, Teil 1 (R101)

Funf Madrigale Uber Die Alte Epistel Zum Funfste Sonntag Nach Epiphanias *CC5U,madrigal SATB,acap (med diff) BAREN. BA5422 (R102)

Lobt Gott Den Herren Ihr Heiden All *liturg SATB,acap (easy) BAREN. BA3073 s.p. see from Das Graduallied, Teil 1 (R103)

REDA, SIEGFRIED (cont'd.)

Psalm 22 *see Ecce Homo

REDEEMED (Red, Buryl) SATB TRIUNE TUM 102 $.35 see also Heavenly Sunlight (R104)

REDEEMED see Butler

REDEEMED see Crowby

REDEEMED see Kirkpatrick

REDEEMER, THE see Shaw, Martin

REDEEMER SHALL COME, THE see Hegarty, David H.

REDEEMING LOVE see Gaither, William J. (Bill)

REDEMPTION ANTHEM see Benham, Asahel

REDEMPTION DRAWETH NIGH see Jensen

REDEMPTION DRAWETH NIGH (GORDON JENSEN CHOIR BOOK) *CCU (Mercer, W. Elmo) cor BENSON B0277 $2.50 stereo recording, tapes, and- or accompaniment tape also available; for book-record sets available, contact publisher (R105)

REDNER, LEWIS [HENRY] (1831-1908) O Little Town Of Bethlehem *Xmas, anthem (DeCou, Harold) SATB oct SINGSPIR ZJP-3044 $.30 (R106) (Hess, John J.) SSAATTBB oct SINGSPIR ZJP-3035 $.30 (R107)

REECE, I.H. O Harken Unto God SATB HARRIS $.30 (R108)

REESE God Said "I Love You" *anthem (Rasley, J.M.) SA/TB (easy) oct SINGSPIR ZJP-6032 $.35 (R109)

REEVES, J. FLAXINGTON Have Faith In God *see Graham

Hill Of The Cross *see Graham

Thy Robe Of Righteousness *see Graham

Two Songs Of Faith *see Graham

REFICE, LICINIO (1883-1954) Missa In Honorem St. Theresiae Ab Infante Jesu *Mass [Lat] 4pt mix cor,org sc,cor pts BOHM s.p. (R110)

Missa In Honorem Stae. Clarae Assisiensis *Mass [Lat] 4pt mix cor,org sc,cor pts BOHM s.p. (R111)

REFLECTION OF GOD, A see Harrell, Jan

REFLECTIONS ON DEATH see Billings, William

REFLECTIONS ON IMMORTALITY see Parris, Robert

RE'GENERATION-...BEAUTIFUL *CC10L, gospel (Johnson, Derric) cor WORD 37625 $1.95 (R112)

RE'GENERATION SONGS NO. 2 *CCUL (Johnson, Derric) cor,pno LILLENAS MB-266 $1.95 (R113)

REGER, MAX (1873-1916) Der 100. Psalm (Psalm 100) Op.106 (Hindemith, Paul) [Eng/Ger] cor, org,orch min sc EULENBURG 968 s.p. (R114)

Ich Bin Getauft Auf Deinen Namen SATB (contains also: Jesus Lebt, Mit Ihm Auch Ich) SCHWEIZER. SK 70.03 s.p. see also MUSIKBEILAGE ZUM "EVANGELISCHEN KIRCHENCHOR 1970" (R115)

Jesus Lebt, Mit Ihm Auch Ich SATB (contains also: Ich Bin Getauft Auf Deinen Namen) SCHWEIZER. SK 70.03 s.p. see also MUSIKBEILAGE ZUM "EVANGELISCHEN KIRCHENCHOR 1970" (R116)

O; Hur Salla Ar Ni Ej, Ni Fromma *cant [Swed] 4pt mix cor cor pts ERIKS 85 s.p., ipa (R117)

REGER, MAX (cont'd.)

Psalm 100 *see Der 100. Psalm

Responsory For Reformation Day, "Forever, O Lord" *anthem, Contemp SATB oct CHANTRY LIT 715 $.25 (R118)

REGES THARSIS see Eybler, Joseph

REGES THARSIS see Filke, Max

REGES THARSIS see Gruber, Joseph

REGES THARSIS see Kromolicki, Joseph

REGINA CAELI LETARE see Kayser, Leif

REGINA COELI see Erbach, Christian

REGINA COELI see Faist, Anton

REGINA COELI see Lotti, Antonio

REGINA COELI see Montillet

REGINA COELI see Mozart, Wolfgang Amadeus

REGINA COELI see Mozart, Wolfgang Amadeus, Regina Coeli

REGINA COELI see Paffendorf, P. Alexander

REGINA COELI see Strauss-Konig, Richard

REGINA COELI see Mozart, Wolfgang Amadeus

REGINA COELI LAETARE see Dietrich, J.H.

REGINA COELI LAETARE see Schubert, Ferdinand

REGINA COELI, LAETARE see Siegl, Otto

REGINA COELI LAETARE see Willan, Healey

REGINA PACIS see Lemacher, Heinrich

REGNEY, NOEL Do You Hear What I Hear (composed with Shayne, Gloria) *Xmas (Ehret, Walter) SATB,pno oct REGENT E-100 $.35 (R119)

Mary's Lullaby *Xmas (Ehret, Walter) SATB,pno oct REGENT R-111 $.30 (R120)

Three Wise Men, Wise Men Three (composed with Shayne, Gloria) *Xmas (Ehret, Walter) SATB,pno,drums, tamb, opt. triangle oct REGENT R-105 $.25 (R121)

REGNUM EJUS see Krieger, Fritz

REHM, P. OTTO Magnificat [Lat] 4-8pt mix cor,acap sc,cor pts BOHM s.p. (R122)

Messe In G *Mass [Lat] 4pt mix cor,acap (without Credo) sc,cor pts BOHM s.p. (R123)

Salve Regina [Lat] 4pt mix cor,acap sc,cor pts BOHM s.p. (R124)

Zwei Pange Lingua *CC2U [Lat] 4pt mix cor,acap sc,cor pts BOHM s.p. (R125)

REHMANN, TH. Aeterne Rex Altissime *Op.12,No.3, Asc/Easter [Lat] 4pt mix cor,acap BOHM s.p. (R126)

Christus Regnat *Op.12,No.5 [Lat] 4pt mix cor,acap BOHM s.p. (R127)

Ecce Virgo Concipiet *Op.12,No.2, Xmas [Lat] 4pt mix cor,acap BOHM s.p. (R128)

Spiritus Domini Replevit *Op.12, No.4, Pent/Whitsun [Lat] 4pt mix cor,acap BOHM s.p. (R129)

Surge, Illuminare Jerusalem *Op.12, No.1, Adv/Epiph,mot [Lat] STBB,acap BOHM s.p. (R130)

REICHEL, BERNARD (1901-   ) Singet Dem Herrn Ein Neues Lied 5pt mix cor,acap MERSEBURG EM477 (R131)

REID
    I Need Thee, Precious Jesus (composed
        with Whitfield) *anthem
        SATB oct BROADMAN 4562-39 $.35
                                        (R132)
REID, ROBERT A.
    Loving *anthem
        SAB WORD CS-2630 $.30   (R133)

REIMANN
    Fur Weihnacht *Op.22,No.1, Xmas,mot
        mix cor LIENAU sc s.p., cor pts
        s.p.   (R134)

REIN, WALTER (1893-1955)
    Der Morgenstern Ist Aufgegangen
        TTB,acap sc SCHOTTS CHBL 168 s.p.
                                        (R135)
    Ein Lieblich Engelspiel
        3 eq voices/3pt jr cor/3pt wom cor,
        2vln,vcl,pno sc,cor pts PELIKAN
        PE349 s.p., ipa   (R136)

    Es Sungen Drei Engel Einen Sussen
        Gesang *mot
        SSATTB,acap sc SCHOTTS C 38 415
        s.p.   (R137)

    Frisch Auf In Gottes Namen
        jr cor/wom cor (med easy) sc
        SCHOTTS CHBL 548 s.p.   (R138)

    Ich Will Den Herren Loben (Psalm 34)
        3 eq voices,strings sc,cor pts
        PELIKAN PE306 s.p., ipa   (R139)

    O Heiland Reiss Die Himmel Auf
        men cor sc SCHOTTS CHBL 91 s.p.
                                        (R140)
    Psalm 34 *see Ich Will Den Herren
        Loben

REJOICE see Eleiott, Max

REJOICE see Kirk

REJOICE! see Skillings, Otis

REJOICE see Watson, Walter

REJOICE ALL YE BELIEVERS see Butler,
    Eugene

REJOICE AND BE GLAD see Christmas

REJOICE AND BE MERRY *Xmas,carol
    (Brewer,R.H.) SSA BRODT 572 $.22
                                        (R141)
    (Coggin) SATB PRO ART 2805 $.35
                                        (R142)
REJOICE AND BE MERRY see Butler

REJOICE AND BE MERRY see Kirby

REJOICE AND BE MERRY see Overley, Henry

REJOICE AND SING *CCU
    SAB,kbd,opt inst AUGSBURG 11-9370
    $2.00 contains works by: Pelz,
    Walter; Carlson, Gordon; Proulx,
    Richard; Nelson, Ronald A.; Held,
    Wilbur; Leaf, Robert; Englert,
    Eugene   (R143)

REJOICE AND SING see Hatch, Owen A.

REJOICE! FOR WE ARE SAVED see Taranto

REJOICE IN THE LORD see Purcell, Henry

REJOICE IN THE LORD see Steffani,
    Agostino

REJOICE IN THE LORD ALWAY see Cousins,
    M. Thomas

REJOICE IN THE LORD ALWAY see Westra,
    Evert

REJOICE IN THE LORD, ALWAYS see
    Campbell-Watson, Frank

REJOICE, O BLESSED CREATION see Track,
    Gerhard

REJOICE, O EARTH see Parks

REJOICE, O EARTH see Parks, Joe E.

REJOICE! REJOICE! see Zimmerman, James

REJOICE, REJOICE, YE PURE IN HEART see
    Plumtree

REJOICE, SALVATION NOW IS NEAR see Van
    Hulse, Camil

REJOICE, SING OUT, BE HAPPY *US
    (Quesnel, Steven) SAB,pno,opt perc
    (med easy) PRESSER G-273 $.45
                                        (R144)
REJOICE! THE LORD IS KING! see Darwall,
    John

REJOICE, THE LORD IS KING see Vick

REJOICE, THE LORD IS KING! see Vidal,
    D. De

REJOICE! THE SAVIOR IS BORN see
    Wetzler, Robert

REJOICE, THOU LAMB'S BELOVED BRIDE see
    Till, Johann Christian

REJOICE TODAY WITH ONE ACCORD see
    Bissell, Keith W.

REJOICE WITH HEART AND VOICE see Byrd,
    William

REJOICE, YE PURE IN HEART see Messiter,
    Arthur Henry

REJOICE, YE SHINING WORLDS ON HIGH see
    Billings, William

REJOICE, YOU PURE IN HEART see Englert,
    Eugene

RELIGIOUS SONG *CCU
    (Sjoberg, Per-Anders) SATB NORDISKA
    NMS 6418 s.p.   (R145)

REMEMBER see Gardner

REMEMBER HE LOVES YOU see Turner

REMEMBER THOU O MAN
    (Aangerdal, Lars) "Besinna Nu Och
    Minns" SAB ERIKS 351 s.p.   (R146)
    (Aangerdal, Lars) "Besinna Nu Och
    Minns" wom cor ERIKS 353 s.p.
                                        (R147)
    (Aangerdal, Lars) "Besinna Nu Och
    Minns" SATB ERIKS 352 s.p.   (R148)

REMEMBER THY CONGREGATION see
    Pergolesi, Giovanni Battista

REMEMBER YOUR CREATOR see Adler, Samuel

REMIND ME, DEAR LORD see Rambo, Dottie

REMONDI, R.
    We Adore You, O Lord Jesus Christ
        *anthem
        (Lee, J.) SA (easy) GIA G1802 $.25
                                        (R149)
RENDELL, GLADYS
    Some Day
        (Smith, Herb) SATB oct GOSPEL
        05 TM 0150 $.20   (R150)

RENEW THY CHURCH see Burroughs, Bob

RENOUVELLEMENT DES PROMESSES DU BAPTEME
    cor JOBERT s.p. see also Douze
    Nouveaux Cantiques De Fetes   (R151)

REQUIEM see Berlioz, Hector

REQUIEM see Brahms, Johannes, Ein
    Deutsches Requiem

REQUIEM see Cherubini, Luigi

REQUIEM see Cimarosa, Domenico

REQUIEM see Dvorak, Antonin

REQUIEM see Faure, Gabriel-Urbain

REQUIEM see Fiser, Lubos

REQUIEM see Goller, Vinzenz

REQUIEM see Jirak, Karel Boleslav

REQUIEM see Koenig, Franz

REQUIEM see Liszt, Franz

REQUIEM see Stekl, Konrad

REQUIEM see Verdi, Giuseppe

REQUIEM see Wassmer, Berthold

REQUIEM see Welcker, Max

REQUIEM 1968 see Schidlowsky, Leon

REQUIEM AETERNAM see Cornelius, Peter

REQUIEM AETERNAM see Gilles, Jean

REQUIEM AETERNAM see Schumann

REQUIEM DES VANITES DU MONDE see
    Gagnebin, Henri

REQUIEM IN C-MOLL see Cherubini, Luigi

REQUIEM IN C-MOLL see Ett, Kaspar

REQUIEM IN C-MOLL see Faist, Anton

REQUIEM IN C-MOLL see Gruber, Joseph

REQUIEM IN D-MOLL see Gruber, Joseph

REQUIEM IN F see Goller, Fritz

REQUIEM MIT LIBERA see Huber, Heinrich

REQUIEM MIT LIBERA see Lipp, Alban

REQUIEM MIT LIBERA see Welcker, Max

REQUIEM UND LIBERA see Eberle, Karl

REQUIEM UND LIBERA see Erhard, Karl

REQUIEM UND LIBERA see Lemacher,
    Heinrich

REQUIEM UND LIBERA IN D-MOLL see
    Spranger, Jorg

RESCUE THE PERISHING see Doane,
    [William Howard]

RESONEMUS LAUDIBUS
    (Willcocks) SATB (med) OXFORD 84.210
    $.45   (R152)

RESONET IN LAUDIBUS see Lassus, Roland
    de (Orlandus)

RESONET IN LAUDIBUS see Pekiel,
    Bertlomiej

RESPONSE TO THE PSALMS see Schutz,
    Heinrich

RESPONSES, "SERVICE MUSIC FOR THE
    CHURCH" see Barnes, Marshall

RESPONSORIES FOR THE CHURCH YEAR see
    Wenzel, Eberhard

RESPONSORY FOR LENT, "HE WAS BROUGHT AS
    A LAMB" see Wenzel, Eberhard

RESPONSORY FOR REFORMATION see Wenzel,
    Eberhard

RESPONSORY FOR REFORMATION DAY see
    Wenzel, Eberhard

RESPONSORY FOR REFORMATION DAY,
    "FOREVER, O LORD" see Reger, Max

RESPONSORY IN TIME OF WAR, A see
    Willan, Healey

RESSURECTION, THE see Naylor, Bernard

RESSURECTION SONG see Butler

RESSURECTION STORY, THE see Almand,
    Claude

REST THOU CONTENTED see Bach, Johann
    Sebastian

RESTORE OUR EYES see Clarke, Henry
    Leland

RESURRECTION see Folprecht, Zdenek,
    Vrkriseni

RESURRECTION see Jillett, David

RESURRECTION, THE see Wilson, Richard

RESURRECTION ALLELUIA *Easter,anthem
    (DeCou, Harold) SATB oct SINGSPIR
    ZJP-3542 $.30   (R153)

RESURRECTION FANFARE see Weisse

RESURRECTION MORNING see Gaither,
    William J. (Bill)

RETURN OF THE WISE MEN see Posegate

REULAND, JACQUES (1918-   )
    Psalmen-Rondeel
        mix cor,org,4trp DONEMUS   (R154)

REUSCH, FRITZ (1896-1970)
    Das Christkindelspiel *Xmas
        jr cor,2-3inst (easy) sc SCHOTTS
        B 113 s.p.   (R155)

    Es Bluhen Die Maien *Adv/Xmas
        3pt BOHM s.p.   (R156)

    Joseph, Lieber Joseph Mein *Adv/Xmas
        3pt BOHM s.p.   (R157)

    Maria Durch Ein' Dornwald Ging
        see Zwei Adventliche Marienlieder

    Meerstern, Ich Dich Grusse
        see Zwei Adventliche Marienlieder

    Zwei Adventliche Marienlieder *Adv
        3pt BOHM s.p.
        contains: Maria Durch Ein'
        Dornwald Ging; Meerstern, Ich
        Dich Grusse   (R158)

REUTTER, HERMANN (1900-   )
Charon "Novite Charon Imperiosum"
mix cor (med diff) sc SCHOTTS
C 41 167 s.p. see from Tres
Laudes   (R159)

Das Gleichnis Vom Barmherzigen
Samariter "Meister, Was Muss Ich
Tun" *Bibl
mix cor (med diff) sc SCHOTTS
C 40 228 s.p. see from Drei
Gleichnisse Aus Dem Neuen
Testament   (R160)

Das Gleichnis Vom Samann "Horet Zu"
*Bibl
mix cor (med diff) sc SCHOTTS
C 40 226 s.p. see from Drei
Gleichnisse Aus Dem Neuen
Testament   (R161)

Das Gleichnis Von Den Torichten Und
Klugen Jungfrauen "Das
Himmelreich Wird Sein" *Bibl
mix cor (med diff) sc SCHOTTS
C 40 227 s.p. see from Drei
Gleichnisse Aus Dem Neuen
Testament   (R162)

Die Ruckkehr Des Verlorenen Sohnes
*Op.34, ora
mix cor,MezTBarBarB soli,pno,2fl,
2ob,2clar,2bsn,2horn,2trp,
strings,perc,timp, saxophone
(med) sc SCHOTTS rental, ipr
                              (R163)

Drei Gleichnisse Aus Dem Neuen
Testament *see Das Gleichnis Vom
Barmherzigen Samariter "Meister,
Was Muss Ich Tun"; Das Gleichnis
Vom Samann "Horet Zu"; Das
Gleichnis Von Den Torichten Und
Klugen Jungfrauen "Das
Himmelreich Wird Sein"   (R164)

Jesu Nachtgesprach Mit Nikodemus "Es
War Aber Ein Mensch Unter Den
Pharisaern" *mot
3pt men cor/3pt jr cor/3pt wom cor,
acap sc SCHOTTS C 42 544 s.p.
                              (R165)

Laudes Francisci "Te Sanctissimum"
mix cor (med diff) sc SCHOTTS
C 41 174 s.p. see from Tres
Laudes   (R166)

Multas Novit Amor Vias
mix cor (med diff) sc SCHOTTS
C 41 166 s.p. see from Tres
Laudes   (R167)

Tres Laudes *see Charon "Novite
Charon Imperiosum"; Laudes
Francisci "Te Sanctissimum";
Multas Novit Amor Vias   (R168)

Weihnachts-Kantilene *Xmas
mix cor,med solo,pno/org (med) sc,
cor pts SCHOTTS ED. 5903 s.p.,
voc sc SCHOTTS ED. 4487 s.p.
                              (R169)

REVELATION see Blankenship, Mark

REVELATIONS 7:12 see Mourant, Walter

REVERSE PATERNOSTER see Werle, Floyd
Edwards

REVIVAL *gospel/medley
(Skillings, Otis) SATB oct LILLENAS
AT-1114 $.40   (R170)

REVIVALTIME GOSPEL FAVORITES, BOOK NO.
1 *CC11L
(McLellan, Cyril) cor GOSPEL
05 TM 0560 $1.25   (R171)

REVIVALTIME GOSPEL FAVORITES, BOOK NO.
2 *CC12L
(McLellan, Cyril) cor GOSPEL
05 TM 0561 $1.25   (R172)

REVIVALTIME GOSPEL FAVORITES, BOOK NO.
3 *CC10L,medley
(McLellan, Cyril) cor,pno GOSPEL
05 TM 0562 $1.50   (R173)

REX PACIFICUS see Lemacher, Heinrich

REX PACIFICUS see Piechler, Arthur

REX VIRTUTIS see Palestrina, Giovanni

REYNOLDS, ISHAM E.
His Own *anthem
(Reynolds, William Jensen) mix cor
CENTURY PR $.20   (R174)

REYNOLDS, WILLIAM JENSEN (1920-   )
Day For Singing, A *anthem
unis oct BROADMAN 4558-39 $.30
                              (R175)

Didn't He Shine! *see McDill

REYNOLDS, WILLIAM JENSEN (cont'd.)
Do You Know What Time It Is? *anthem
1-2pt (easy) oct BROADMAN 4554-06
$.30   (R176)

Give The Lord A Chance *anthem
SATB oct BROADMAN 4565-44 $.35
                              (R177)

Golden Harps *anthem
SATB oct BROADMAN 4565-06 $.35
                              (R178)

Great Commission, The *see Ingram,
Bill

Hallelujah *anthem
SATB oct BROADMAN 4565-20 $.35
                              (R179)

Here Is My Life *see Bartlett

How Great *anthem
SATB,opt 3trp&2trom&tuba&perc
(easy) BROADMAN 4565-24 $.35
                              (R180)

I Believe *see Bartlett

Ichthus *cant
SATB BROADMAN 4510-04 $2.00 (R181)

In The Fulness Of Time *Xmas,anthem
SATB (med) oct BROADMAN 4565-19
$.35   (R182)

Jesus Gives Me Sweet Peace (from
Reaching People)
SATB BROADMAN 4565-45 $.35   (R183)

Let All Sounding Things Praise The
Lord *anthem
unis oct BROADMAN 4550-50 $.30
                              (R184)

Let Christ's Freedom Ring *anthem
SATB BROADMAN 4565-59 $.40   (R185)

O Thou Star *Xmas,anthem
SATB,opt fl/rec oct BROADMAN
4551-81 $.30   (R186)

One World, One Lord, One Witness
(Red, Buryl) SATB&SATB,opt gtr&bvl&
drums (easy) oct BROADMAN 4565-11
$.35, ipa   (R187)

One World, One Lord, One Witness
*see Red, Buryl

People To People *anthem
SATB oct BROADMAN 4565-26 $.35
                              (R188)

Reaching People
cor BROADMAN 4516-06 $2.50   (R189)

Share His Love (from Reaching People)
SATB BROADMAN 4565-43 $.35   (R190)

Sing A Joyful Song, Believers
*anthem
SATB oct BROADMAN 4565-07 $.35
                              (R191)

There Is A Name
SATB,acap (med) FISCHER,C CM 7813
$.30   (R192)

Up And Get Us Gone *see Red

We Have To Find A Way (composed with
Seabough, Ed.) *anthem
SATB oct BROADMAN 4565-21 $.35
                              (R193)

RHEA, ARTHUR D.
Psalm 24 *anthem,Contemp
cor oct CHANTRY COA 7245 $.40 (R194)

RHEA, RAYMOND (1910-   )
God Placed His Hand On Mine
SSAATTBB,acap (easy) FITZSIMONS
2075 $.20   (R195)

Morning Hymn
SSAATTBB,acap (med) FITZSIMONS 2142
$.25   (R196)

RHEINBERGER, JOSEF (1839-1901)
Angelis Suis Deus Mandavit *Op.140,
No.5, Fest
[Lat/Ger] cor,Bar solo,org sc,cor
pts BOHM s.p.   (R197)

Der Stern Von Bethlehem *Op.164,
Xmas,cant
mix cor,orch FORBERG voc sc s.p.,
voc pt s.p., ipr   (R198)

Missa Brevis *Op.83
mix cor FORBERG sc s.p., voc pt
s.p.   (R199)

Salve Regina *Op.107,No.4
mix cor FORBERG sc s.p., voc pt
s.p.   (R200)

Shepherd, Lead Me
(Miles) SATB (med) FITZSIMONS 2103
$.25   (R201)

RHEINBERGER, JOSEF (cont'd.)
Terra Tremuit *Easter,Offer
[Lat] 4pt mix cor&4pt mix cor,acap
sc,cor pts BOHM s.p.   (R202)

Trinitatis Messe *Op.117, Mass
mix cor FORBERG sc s.p., voc pt
s.p.   (R203)

RHYME, A RIDDLE, A SONG, A see Red,
Buryl

RICE, M.R.
Christmas Eve
mix cor BRODT 554 $.20   (R204)

RICE, TIM
Joseph And The Amazing Technicolor
Dreamcoat *see Webber, Andrew
Lloyd

RICHARDS, STEPHEN
K'dusha
[Heb] 2pt,cantor TRANSCON. TCL 700
$.75   (R205)

Ki Lekach Tov *Simchat Torah
[Heb] unis,cantor TRANSCON. TCL 396
$2.50   (R206)

RICK POWELL CHOIR BOOK *see Alwyn,
Fool's Wisdom; Kaiser, Kurt, Tell
It To Jesus; Powell, Rick, Joyful
Noise   (R207)

RICK POWELL CHOIR BOOK see Alwyn

RICK POWELL CHOIR BOOK see Kaiser, Kurt

RICK POWELL CHOIR BOOK see Powell, Rick

THE RICK POWELL CHOIR BOOK VOLUME I
*CC12L
(Powell, Rick) jr cor,electronic
tape, small pop group WORD 37648
$2.50   (R208)

THE RICK POWELL CHOIR BOOK VOLUME II
*CC11L
(Powell, Rick) SATB,synthesizer WORD
37706 $2.50   (R209)

RICKARD, JEFFREY
When Christ Was Born *Adv/Xmas
SATB,acap ART MAST 155 $.30 (R210)

RIDE ON! see Broughton

RIDE ON IN MAJESTY! see Johnson, Norman

RIDE ON, KING JESUS! *Easter,anthem
(Johnson, Norman) SATB oct SINGSPIR
ZJP-3546 $.35   (R211)

RIDE ON, KING JESUS see Fleming, Larry
L.

RIDE ON NOW, O KING! see Kemp, Helen

RIDE ON, RIDE ON IN MAJESTY see
Johnson, Norman

RIDE ON! RIDE ON IN MAJESTY see
Silvester, Frederick

RIDE THE CHARIOT *spir
(Melton) SABar&camb,acap CAMBIATA
S117450 $.35   (R212)

RIDENOUR, JOE
Clap Happy Psalm *anthem
cor CHORISTERS R-4 $.15 contains
also: God Created   (R213)

God Created
see Ridenour, Joe, Clap Happy Psalm

Look Around The World *anthem
cor CHORISTERS R-9 $.15   (R214)

Over In Beth'lem Town *Xmas
SATB oct HOPE CF 173 $.35   (R215)

Song Of Praise *Gen/Thanks
unis,org,fing.cym.,tamb, solo
instrument CHORISTERS A-71 $.30
                              (R216)

RIDER, DALE G.
From All That Dwell Below The Skies
unis/SATB WHITE HARV. CHO 754 $.30
                              (R217)

Let Us Rejoice, Sing "Alleluia!"
SATB WHITE HARV. CHO 732 $.35
                              (R218)

Men Of God, Go Take Your Stations
unis WHITE HARV. CHO 733 $.15
                              (R219)

RIDER-MEYER, L.
Dey Can't Cotch Me To Bury Me *sac/
sec,spir
SATB (med) FITZSIMONS 1001 $.25
                              (R220)

RIDER, TWILA R.
  God, The Source Of Light And Beauty
    SATB WHITE HARV. CHO 753 $.35
                                        (R221)

RIDING INTO BETHLEHEM see Parry,
  Charles Hubert Hastings

RIDOUT, ALAN (1934-   )
  Beatitudes *sec
    SA STAINER 3.0741.1 $.40   (R222)

  Benedicite
    SATB STAINER 3.0868.1 $.50   (R223)

  Greatest Of These Is Love
    SATB STAINER 3.0756.1 $.40   (R224)

  Lamentation Of Jeremiah
    SATB STAINER 3.0738.1 $.60   (R225)

  Let Us All Be Glad
    SATB STAINER 3.0774.1 $.40   (R226)

  Let Us With A Gladsome Mind
    SATB GALAXY 1.5077.1 $.40   (R227)

  Preces And Responses *CCU
    SSA STAINER 3.0866.1 $.50   (R228)

  St. John Passion *Easter
    unis STAINER 3.0766.1 $1.00   (R229)

RIDOUT, GODFREY (1918-   )
  Communion Service (Series II)
    unis&SATB (easy) voc sc OXFORD
    40.018 $1.00, cor pts OXFORD
    40.040 $.45   (R230)

  Pange Lingua *Corpus
    SATB,orch cor pts WATERLOO $1.00,
    ipr   (R231)

  Two Christmas Carols *CC2U,Xmas
    SSA (med easy) WATERLOO $.30 (R232)

RIEDEL, KARL (1827-1888)
  Die Engel Und Die Hirten
    see Drei Altbohmische
    Weihnactslieder

  Drei Altbohmische Weihnactslieder
    *Xmas,Boh
    4pt mix cor,acap cor pts BREITKOPF-
    W PB-2476 s.p.
      contains: Die Engel Und Die
      Hirten; Freu Dich Erd Und
      Sternenzelt; Lasst Alle Gott
      Uns Loben   (R233)

  Freu Dich Erd Und Sternenzelt
    see Drei Altbohmische
    Weihnactslieder

  Lasst Alle Gott Uns Loben
    see Drei Altbohmische
    Weihnactslieder

RIEMANN, H.
  Easter Song Of Praise, An
    (Dicks) mix cor BANKS MUS YS 545
    $.25   (R234)

RIENECKER
  Die Weihnachtsgeschichte *Op.3,
    Xmas,cant
    SA&unis men cor&cong,STB soli,org
    sc HANSSLER 10.294 s.p.   (R235)

RIESE
  New Life, The *anthem
    SAB oct LORENZ 7422 $.35   (R236)

RIGHTEOUS SHALL BE HAD IN EVERLASTING
  REMEMBRANCE, THE see Campbell,
  Sydney S.

RIJP, A.W.
  Psalm 100
    cor pts HEER 347A s.p.   (R237)

RIJST OOP, RIJST OOP VOOR JEZUS
  mix cor sc HEER 2205 s.p.   (R238)

RILEY
  Listen To The Wind *anthem
    unis (easy) oct BROADMAN 4545-65
    $.30   (R239)

RIMBAULT, EDWARD FRANCIS (1816-1876)
  O Happy Day *anthem/gospel
    (DeCou, Harold) SATB oct SINGSPIR
    ZJP-8118 $.30   (R240)

RIMMER
  Children's Christmas Festival *see
    Mendoza

RINCK, JOHANN CHRISTIAN HEIN.
    (1770-1846)
  Selig Sind Des Himmels Erben
    *Rembrnc
    cor sc,cor pts BOHM s.p.   (R241)

RINEHART
  Blade Of Grass, A *Xmas
    (Plank) SSAATTBB KENDOR $.40 (R242)

RING A BELL OF JOY see Lorenz, Ellen
  Jane

RING, BELLS, O RING see Snogren

RING BELLS RING see Harrhy, Edith

RING OUT BELLS OF CHRISTMAS see McCabe,
  Michael

RING OUT YE CRYSTAL SPHERES see Vaughan
  Williams, Ralph

RING, RING THE CHRISTMAS BELLS see
  Bunch

RING THE BELLS see Bollbach

RING THE BELLS OF HEAVENS see Cushing

RING THE BELLS; WATCH THE SKY see
  Butler, Eugene

RING, YE BELLS see Williams

RINGEN, I KLOCKOR see Berg, Gottfrid

RINGWALD, [ROY] (1910-   )
  God Is My Song
    SSA SHAWNEE B387 $.35   (R243)
    SA/TB SHAWNEE E144 $.35   (R244)
    SAB SHAWNEE D183 $.35   (R245)
    TTBB SHAWNEE C238 $.35   (R246)

  Greater Love
    SATB SHAWNEE A5663 $.35   (R247)

  I Belive
    (Tucker) SSA (quodlibet with Bach-
    Gounod "Ave Maria") SHAWNEE B400
    $.40   (R248)

  Turn Back O Man
    SATB SHAWNEE A1281 $.35   (R249)

RISE, CROWNED WITH LIGHT see Darst, W.
  Glenn

RISE FROM YOUR BED OF HAY see Caurroy,
  Eustache du

RISE, SHINE *anthem/gospel
  (Ehret, Walter) SATB WORD   (R250)
  (Littleton, Bill J.) SATB,med solo
    FINE ARTS CM 1063 $.30   (R251)
  (Lundberg, John W.) SATB oct SINGSPIR
    ZJP-8065 $.30   (R252)

RISE UP AND SING PRAISE see Peterson,
  John W.

RISE UP, O CHURCH! *anthem
  (Skillings, Otis) SAB,inst oct
    LILLENAS AT-1102 $.40, ipa   (R253)

RISE UP O MEN OF GOD see Harwood-Jones,
  H.F.

RISE UP, O MEN OF GOD see Merrill

RISE UP, O MEN OF GOD! see Miles,
  Russell Hancock

RISE UP, SHEPHERD see Kennedy

RISE UP, SHEPHERD, AN' FOLLER *Xmas,
  spir
  (Soderstrom, E.) SATB (med)
    FITZSIMONS 2117 $.25   (R254)

RISE UP, SHEPHERD AN' FOLLER see
  Routley, Eric

RISE UP, SHEPHERD, AND FOLLOW *Xmas,
  spir
    see Christmas Spiritual Collection
    (Walker) unis,solo, Orff inst (easy)
    oct CONCORDIA 98-2141 $.25   (R255)

RISEN AND RETURNING see Ingram, Bill

RISEN SAVIOR, THE see Lovelace, Austin
  C.

RISEN TODAY see Jordahl

RISHEL, R.
  Christmas Folksong, A
    SATB (easy) FITZSIMONS 2065 $.20
                                  (R256)

RISING AGAIN, THE see Ager, Laurence

RITCHEY, LAWRENCE
  God Be In My Head
    SAB (med easy) WATERLOO $.30 (R257)

  Twelve Unison Anthems *CC12U,anthem
    unis WATERLOO $1.25   (R258)

RITTER, CHRISTIAN (ca. 1640-ca. 1720)
  Nar Vi I Hogsta Noden Sta
    (Sellen, E.) mix cor,cont,inst
    ERIKS 166 s.p.   (R259)

  Tre Bibelsprak Om Guds Ord *CC3U
    mix cor,solo,org ERIKS 164 s.p.
                                  (R260)

  Ur Sakarias Lovsang
    mix cor,org ERIKS 163 s.p.   (R261)

ROAD TO BETHLEHEM, THE see Caldwell,
  Mary [Elizabeth]

ROAD TO EMMAUS see Burlison, Mabel Lee

ROBERTON, HUGH STEVENSON (1874-1952)
  Celtic Hymn *hymn
    TTBB,acap ROBERTON 50716 s.p.
                                  (R262)

ROBERTS
  All People That On Earth Do Dwell
    *anthem
    SATB (easy) oct BROADMAN 4562-28
    $.35   (R263)

  Am I A Soldier Of The Cross *anthem
    SATB FINE ARTS EP 29 $.35   (R264)

  At Even When The Sun Was Set *anthem
    SATB FINE ARTS CM 1091 $.30   (R265)

  Clap Your Hands *anthem
    SATB (easy) oct BROADMAN 4561-69
    $.25   (R266)

  God Moves In A Mysterious Way
    *anthem
    SATB (med easy) oct BROADMAN
    4538-93 $.30   (R267)

  He Remembers Me *gospel
    SSATB oct LILLENAS AT-1111 $.30 (R268)

  I Must Tell Jesus *anthem
    SATB (easy) oct BROADMAN 4550-25
    $.30   (R269)

  I'm Gonna Walk With Jesus *anthem
    unis (easy) oct BROADMAN 4558-12
    $.25   (R270)

  It Is Well With My Soul *anthem
    SATB (easy) oct BROADMAN 4545-03
    $.30   (R271)

  Keep Walking *gospel
    SSATB oct LILLENAS AT-1117 $.30
                                  (R272)

  My Lord's In The Mountain *anthem
    SATB (easy) oct BROADMAN 4550-69
    $.30   (R273)

  Time Almost Gone *gospel
    SSATB oct LILLENAS AT-1119 $.30
                                  (R274)

  To The Promised Land *gospel
    SATB oct LILLENAS AT-1115 $.30
                                  (R275)

  Who? *gospel
    SATB oct LILLENAS AT-1123 $.30
                                  (R276)

ROBERTS, C.
  Praise
    (Clodforwn) mix cor BANKS MUS
    YS 970 $.25   (R277)

ROBERTS, J. VARLEY
  Seek Ye The Lord
    (Lutkin) SAB,S/T solo (easy)
    FITZSIMONS 6008 $.25   (R278)

ROBERTS, V.
  Arise, Shine, For Thy Light Is Come
    mix cor BANKS MUS YS 134 $.25
                                  (R279)

ROBERTSON
  In God I Trust
    SS oct BENSON S4149 $.30   (R280)

  Ring, Ring The Christmas Bells *see
    Bunch

  To Be A People *anthem
    SATB oct BROADMAN 4551-99 $.30
                                  (R281)

ROBERTSON, KARL-OLOF
  En Hundra Atta Og Fyrtio Psalmen Ur
    Psaltaren *CC148U
    mix cor&wom cor/mix cor&girl cor,
    SBar soli,org,horn,strings ERIKS
    145 voc sc s.p., cor pts s.p.,
    ipa   (R282)

ROBERTSON, LEROY (1896-   )
  O Brother Man
    SATB GALAXY 1.2316.1 $.30   (R283)

ROBILLARD
  Laudate Dominum
    4pt men cor/4pt mix cor GRAS s.p.
                                  (R284)

  Tantum Ergo
    4pt men cor/4pt mix cor GRAS s.p.
                                  (R285)

ROBIN RED BREAST see Copley

ROBINSON
   Come, Thou Fount
     (Wyeth; Kling, Roger) SATB oct
     GOSPEL 05 TM 0176 $.20   (R286)

   Come, Thou Fount Of Every Blessing
     (composed with Collins) *anthem
     SA (easy) oct BROADMAN 4551-66 $.30
                      (R287)

   Yesterday, Today, And Tomorrow
     *anthem
     SATB oct BROADMAN 4545-80 $.30
                      (R288)

ROBINSON, EDWIN MEADE
   David Jazz, The (composed with
     Burnett, Michael) *Bibl
     cor EMI   (R289)

ROBISON
   Communion
     see FOUR FOLK HYMNS FROM WYETH'S
     REPOSITORY

ROCHBERG, GEORGE (1918-   )
   Behold My Servant *Gen
     SATB,acap PRESSER 312-41062 $.95
                      (R290)

ROCHEROLLE
   Christmas Child
     SSA WARNER WB-357 183 $.60   (R291)
     unis WARNER WB-357 180 $.60   (R292)
     SAB WARNER WB-357 187 $.60   (R293)

ROCK 'N' SOUL *CCU,spir
   (Red, Buryl) 2-4pt mix cor BROADMAN
   4520-28 $2.25   (R294)

ROCKING *Xmas,folk
   (Czajkowski, Michael) SATB STANDARD
   C624MX3 $.50   (R295)

ROCKING see Arnatt, Ronald

ROCKING see Matthews, Thomas

RODRIGO
   Dos Canciones Safardies
     mix cor UNION ESP. 21736 s.p.
       contains: El Rey Que Muncho
       Madruga; Malato Esta El Hijo
       Del Rey   (R296)

   El Rey Que Muncho Madruga
     see Dos Canciones Safardies

   Malato Esta El Hijo Del Rey
     see Dos Canciones Safardies

ROE
   Behold A Silly Tender Babe *Xmas
     SA (med easy) OXFORD 82.100 $.25
                      (R297)

   Hark How All The Welkin Rings
     SS (easy) OXFORD 82.099 $.25 (R298)

ROE, BETTY (1930-   )
   Christus Victor *cant
     SATB,ABar,narrator,ob,clar,horn,
     trp,timp,perc,gtr voc sc NOVELLO
     rental   (R299)

ROE, CHRISTOPHER
   Homecoming, The
     see SIX CHRISTMAS CAROLS

ROESCH
   At Christmas Time
     SA/TB SHAWNEE E5169 $.35   (R300)

   I'm Gonna Let My Love Shine *anthem
     SB oct LORENZ 5767 $.35   (R301)

   Let Us With A Gladsome Mind *see
     Milton

   O Make A Joyful Noise To God *anthem
     SATB oct BROADMAN 4545-93 $.30
                      (R302)

   Praise God Ye Servants Of The Lord
     SATB SHAWNEE A5682 $.30   (R303)

   Praises Be
     SA/TB SHAWNEE E152 $.40   (R304)

   We've Got A Lot To Live For *anthem
     SA/unis oct LORENZ 5398 $.35 (R305)

ROFF, JOSEPH
   Behold, What Manner Of Love
     mix cor BRODT 584 $.28   (R306)

   Beppi
     1-2 eq voices VOLKWEIN VB-741 $.40
                      (R307)

   Blessed Be The Lord
     SATB,acap (easy) FITZSIMONS 2193
     $.25   (R308)

   Blessed Be Thou *anthem
     SATB FINE ARTS CM 1049 $.35 (R309)

   Born Anew This Day
     mix cor/2 eq voices,org/pno
     FISCHER,J FEC 10119 $.30   (R310)

ROFF, JOSEPH (cont'd.)
   Christmas Time *Xmas
     SA RICHMOND SA-7 $.30   (R311)

   Come, Ye Disconsolate
     SATB (easy) FITZSIMONS 2224 $.30
                      (R312)

   Fire Of Love, The *anthem
     SATB,org (easy) GIA G1886 $.40
                      (R313)

   For God Is Love *Xmas/Easter/Gen
     SATB (med) FITZSIMONS 2231 $.30
                      (R314)

   Heal Me, O Lord
     mix cor BRODT 614 $.25   (R315)

   I Am The Good Shepherd *anthem
     SATB FINE ARTS CM 1094 $.35 (R316)

   I Am With You *anthem
     SATB oct SINGSPIR ZJP-7311 $.30
                      (R317)

   Lamb Of Love *Lent,anthem
     SATB oct SINGSPIR ZCS-4761 $.25
                      (R318)

   Let All Them Be Glad
     SATB (med) FITZSIMONS 2129 $.20
                      (R319)

   Let The Peace Of God *anthem
     SATB,org/pno WORLD CA-4012-8 (R320)

   May Thy Holy Spirit
     SATB,acap (med) FITZSIMONS 2130
     $.20   (R321)

   Memorial Acclamations I-IV *CCU,
     Rembrnc
     SATB&cong,org GIA G1546 $.30 (R322)

   Mountain Of The Lord, The *anthem
     SATB FINE ARTS CM 1092 $.35 (R323)

   Music For The Funeral Rite *CCU,
     funeral
     unis,org GIA G1717 $1.25   (R324)

   O Dearest Lord *Lent,anthem
     SATB oct SINGSPIR ZCS-4765 $.25
                      (R325)

   O Lord, I Will Praise Thee
     SATB (easy) FITZSIMONS 2202 $.25
                      (R326)

   Panis Angelicus
     SATB (med easy) WATERLOO $.35
                      (R327)

   Season Of Joy, Alleluia
     SSA VOLKWEIN VB-745 $.40   (R328)

   Seasonal Responsorial Psalms *CC13U,
     Psalm
     cong&opt SATB,cantor,org GIA G1744
     $2.00   (R329)

   Take Up Thy Cross *Gen/Lent
     SATB (easy) FITZSIMONS 2223 $.30
                      (R330)

   Turn Thee Unto Me *Bibl
     SATB (easy) FITZSIMONS 2217 $.25
                      (R331)

   Upon Easter Day *Easter,anthem
     SATB,org (easy) GIA G1887 $.40
                      (R332)

   We Adore Thee, O Christ *Lent,anthem
     SATB oct SINGSPIR ZCS-4795 $.30
                      (R333)

   Welcome All Wonders In One Sight
     SATB SHAWNEE A5687 $.35   (R334)

ROGATION HYMN see Canning, Thomas

ROGER
   Noel Dialogue *Xmas
     4pt mix cor,acap sc HENN 748 s.p.
                      (R335)

ROGERS
   Easter Festival, An *Easter
     SATB,opt brass&timp (a complete
     service) oct MCAFEE M1044 $.80
                      (R336)

   Land Of Our Loyalty *anthem
     SATB oct LORENZ A562 $.35   (R337)

   Let Us Break Bread Together *anthem
     SAB,pno/org oct MCAFEE M161 $.35
                      (R338)

   Sing Out - Jesus Lives!
     2pt jr cor oct LILLENAS AN-4029
     $.25   (R339)

   Song Of The Seasons, A *anthem
     (Schubert) SATB,fl oct LILLENAS
     AN-3840 $.30   (R340)

ROGERS, DIANE E.
   Psalm 100
     SSA PIONEER 1018 $.40   (R341)

ROGERS, ETHEL TRENCH
   Follow After Him *Xmas/Easter/Gen,
     cant
     jr cor,pno,opt fl&drums LILLENAS
     MP-602 $1.00   (R342)

ROGERS, LEE
   Land Of Our Loyalty *anthem/prayer,
     US
     SA/SATB (easy) oct LORENZ A562 $.35
                      (R343)

ROGERS, SHARON ELERY
   All Hail That Festive Day
     SATB BOURNE B223701-358 $.50 (R344)

   All My Heart This Night Rejoices
     *Xmas
     SATB GALAXY 1.2222.1 $.30   (R345)

   Holy Child Sleeps *Xmas
     SATB GALAXY 1.2288.1 $.30   (R346)

   I Will Lift Up Mine Eyes
     SATB BOURNE B218297-358 $.50 (R347)

ROGIER, PHILIPPE (1562-1596)
   Eleven Motets *CC11U,mot
     (Wagner, Lavern J.) cor bds A-R ED
     $9.95   (R348)

ROHLIG, HARALD (1914-   )
   Explode With Joy *CC12L
     cor CONCORDIA 97-5165 $1.50 (R349)

ROHR, ELLI (1915-   )
   Christ Lag In Todesbanden
     unis,2treb inst,1-2bass inst
     LAUDINELLA LR 26 s.p.   (R350)

ROHR, HUGO (1866-1937)
   Friedenmesse *Mass
     SATB&cong,org sc CHRIS 50658 s.p.
                      (R351)

     SSAA&cong/TTBB&cong,org cor pts
     CHRIS 50660 s.p.   (R352)
     SATB&cong,org cor pts CHRIS 50659
     s.p.   (R353)

   Mainzer Dom-Messe *Mass
     SATB&cong,org sc CHRIS 50650 s.p.
                      (R354)
     SSAA&cong/TTBB&cong,org cor pts
     CHRIS 50652 s.p.   (R355)
     SATB&cong,org cor pts CHRIS 50651
     s.p.   (R356)

   St. Alban-Messe *Mass
     SATB&cong,org cor pts CHRIS 50655
     s.p.   (R357)
     SSAA&cong/TTBB&cong,org cor pts
     CHRIS 50656 s.p.   (R358)
     SATB&cong,org sc CHRIS 50654 s.p.
                      (R359)

   St. Hildegard-Messe *Mass
     SSAA&cong/TTBB&cong,org cor pts
     CHRIS 50665 s.p.   (R360)
     SATB&cong,org sc CHRIS 50663 s.p.
                      (R361)
     SATB&cong,org cor pts CHRIS 50664
     s.p.   (R362)

ROHWER, JENS (1914-   )
   Beatitudes, The *see Die
     Seligpreisungen

   Die Seligpreisungen
     "Beatitudes, The" unis&cong,org/
     inst (easy) BAREN. BA6313 (R363)

   Gott Sei Gelobet Und Gebenedeiet
     SAT/SAB,opt bass inst HANSSLER
     14.163 s.p.   (R364)

   Herr Jesu Christ, Dich Zu Uns Wend
     SAT/SAB,opt bass inst HANSSLER
     14.126 s.p.   (R365)

   Herr, Wir Rufen Dich *hymn
     MOSELER unis s.p.; cor,org s.p.
                      (R366)

   Lord's Prayer, The *see Unser Vater
     Im Himmel

   Unser Vater Im Himmel *prayer
     "Lord's Prayer, The" [Ger] SATB&
     cong,org/inst MOSELER LB496 s.p.
                      (R367)

ROLL, JORDAN
   see Funf Spirituals

ROLL, JORDAN ROLL *spir
   (Johnson, Lois) SATB oct GOSPEL
   05 TM 0115 $.20   (R368)
   (Thomas) SATB,acap oct LILLENAS
   AN-7003 $.30   (R369)

ROLLE
   Hymn Of Thanks, A
     (Harris) SSA SCHIRM.G LG51827 $.60
                      (R370)

ROLLE, JOHANN HEINRICH (1716-1785)
   In Thee, O Lord
     (Pfohl) mix cor BRODT 205 $.26
                      (R371)

ROLLED AWAY (REVISITED) *folk
   (Wyrtzen, Don) 2pt oct SINGSPIR
   ZJP-5040 $.30   (R372)

ROMAN, JOHAN HELMICH (1694-1758)
Praise The Lord, All Ye Nations
(Psalm 117)
(Wolff, S. Drummond) SATB,cont,
2vln,vla,vcl sc CONCORDIA 97-5160
$1.85, ipa, voc sc CONCORDIA
97-5206 $1.00   (R373)

Psalm 117 *see Praise The Lord, All
Ye Nations

ROMANS 14.19 see Heilner, Irwin

ROMANS BY SAINT PAUL see Franco, Johan

ROOKE, PAT
Creation Jazz *see Arch, Gwyn

Golden Legend, A *see Arch, Gwyn

Promised Land, The *see Arch, Gwyn

That's The Spirit *see Arch, Gwyn

ROOM AT THE CROSS FOR YOU see
Stanphill, Ira F.

ROOM IN THE IN see Armstrong, Mimi

ROOT
O Come, Let Us Sing
(Harris) SATB PRO ART 2814 $.40
(R374)

RORATE CAELI see Bamer, Alfred

RORATE COELI DESUPER see Isaac,
Heinrich

RORATY C. 2 see Zouhar, Zdenek

RORE, CIPRIANO DE (1516-1565)
Passio D. n. J. Chr. Sec. Joannem
see OBERITALIENISCHE
FIGURALPASSIONEN

ROREM, NED (1923-   )
In Time Of Pestilence
SATB,acap oct BOOSEY 5888 $.45
(R375)

Little Prayers
mix cor,SBar soli,acap sc BOOSEY
$1.00   (R376)

Missa Brevis
SATB,acap oct BOOSEY 5894 $1.00
(R377)

O Deus, Ego Amo Te
see Three Motets

Oratorio Patris Condren: O Jesu
Vivens In Maria
see Three Motets

Praises For The Nativity
mix cor,SATB soli,org sc BOOSEY
$1.50   (R378)

Thee, God
see Three Motets

Three Motets *Xmas,mot
SATB,org oct BOOSEY 5881 $1.00
contains: O Deus, Ego Amo Te;
Oratorio Patris Condren: O Jesu
Vivens In Maria; Thee, God
(R379)

Three Prayers *CC3U
SATB,acap oct BOOSEY 5912 $.40
(R380)

ROSE, THE see Paynter, John P.

ROSE, THE see Tomlins, Greta

ROSE COLORED GLASSES see Fischer,
William Gustavus

ROSE, MICHAEL (1916-   )
Easter Day
wom cor/boy cor,org NOVELLO
CHORISTER SERIES 130 s.p.   (R381)

Mirth *anthem
wom cor/boy cor,org NOVELLO NCM 38
s.p.   (R382)

ROSE OF BETHLEHEM see Verrall, Pamela

ROSE OF LOVE, THE *Adv/Xmas
(Christiansen, Paul) SATB,acap ART
MAST 186 $.30   (R383)

ROSE OF SHARON, THE see Billings,
William

ROSENBAUM, SAMUEL (1919-   )
Shepherd Me Lord *see Kingsley,
Gershon

ROSENBERG, HILDING (1892-   )
Hymnus
jr cor&dbl cor,org ERIKS 141 s.p.
(R384)

ROSENBERG, WOLF
Be With Us, Lord, We Pray
see Testament Of Faith, A

In My Father's House
see Testament Of Faith, A

Testament Of Faith, A *anthem
(McCormick, Clifford) SATB,acap
WORD CS-676 $.25
contains: Be With Us, Lord, We
Pray; In My Father's House
(R385)

ROSENTHAL, MANUEL (1904-   )
La Pieta D'Avignon *CC6U,prayer
4pt mix cor,pno JOBERT s.p.   (R386)

Trois Pieces Liturgiques *CC3U
cor,pno/org/harmonium JOBERT sc
s.p., cor pts s.p.   (R387)

ROSETTI, STEFANO (fl. ca. 1750)
Sacrae Cantiones *CCU,mot/Psalm
(Skei, Allan B.) 5pt bds A-R ED
$9.95   (R388)

ROSSEAU, NORBERT
Evangelie *Op.1,No.65
cor,soli,acap CBDM   (R389)

ROSSELLINI, RENZO (1908-   )
Una Poesia Di Natale
[It] cor,orch sc RICORDI-ENG 131970
s.p.   (R390)

ROSSI, SALOMONE (ca. 1570-ca. 1630)
Cantiques De Rossi *CCU,hymn/Psalm
3-8pt SAC.MUS.PR. S.M.P. 16-17
$15.00 three volumes, bound in
two books   (R391)

ROSSINI, GIOACCHINO (1792-1868)
Or Che Si Oscura Il Ciel
see RACCOLTA CORALE LIBRO III

Sanctus
(Chandler, H.) [Lat] SATB,acap oct
NATIONAL WHC-37 $.35   (R392)

ROTERMUND, MELVIN
All Glory Be To God On High
unis,inst oct CONCORDIA 98-2231
$.35   (R393)

Dear Christians, One And All, Now
Rejoice *Xmas
unis,org/fl&bvl, and glockenspiel
(easy) oct CONCORDIA 98-2198
$.30, ipa   (R394)

Gently Mary Laid Her Child *Xmas
unis/SATB,opt fl&timp/opt timp, and
glockenspiel oct CONCORDIA
98-2230 $.35   (R395)

On My Heart Imprint Thine Image
*Lent
unis,fl,opt ob,vcl/bvl (easy) oct
CONCORDIA 98-2180 $.25   (R396)

Salvation Unto Us Has Come
unis,org/kbd,fl,bvl, glockenspiel
(easy) oct CONCORDIA 98-2199
$.30, ipa   (R397)

ROTH
In My Heart There Rings A Melody
(Coates) SATB oct BENSON S4151 $.35
(R398)

ROTHSCHUH, FRANZ (1921-   )
Als Ich Bei Meinen Schafen Wacht
*Adv/Xmas
3pt jr cor,S/A solo BOHM s.p.
(R399)

Das Jahr Hebt An
cor BOHM s.p.   (R400)

Festspruch "Machet Die Tore Weit"
*Adv
SSATB,acap (med) sc SCHOTTS
C 38 963 s.p.   (R401)

In Gottes Namen Wir Anfahn
see Zwei Lieder Zum Geburtstag Oder
Zu Neujahr

Macht Weit Die Pforten *Adv
cor sc BOHM s.p.   (R402)

Morgenstern Der Finstern Nacht *Adv/
Xmas
3 eq voices BOHM s.p.   (R403)

O Komm, O Komm, Emanuel *Adv
cor BOHM s.p.   (R404)

Uns Ist Ein Kindelein Geboren Im
Stall *Adv/Xmas
3 eq voices BOHM s.p.   (R405)

Wir Wunschen Heut
see Zwei Lieder Zum Geburtstag Oder
Zu Neujahr

ROTHSCHUH, FRANZ (cont'd.)
Zur Hausweihe "Du Liessest Uns Dieses
Werk Vollbringen"
3pt BOHM s.p.   (R406)

Zwei Lieder Zum Geburtstag Oder Zu
Neujahr *Fest
3 eq voices BOHM s.p.
contains: In Gottes Namen Wir
Anfahn; Wir Wunschen Heut
(R407)

ROTHSCHUH, FRITZ (1921-   )
Der Euch Beruft Ist Treu *mot
4pt mix cor,A solo,acap (med) sc
SCHOTTS C 42 240 s.p.   (R408)

Stabat Mater *Op.31
[Lat/Ger] 4pt mix cor,acap BOHM
s.p.   (R409)

ROTHSTEIN, ARNOLD
Major Congregational Responses And
Hymns, The *CCU
[Heb] cor TRANSCON. TCL 374 $2.50
(R410)

ROTTMANNER, EDUARD
Dextera Domini *Holywk
[Lat] 4pt mix cor,acap sc,cor pts
BOHM s.p.   (R411)

ROTTURA, JOSEPH JAMES (1929-   )
Beatitude I: Blessed Are The Poor In
Spirit *Bibl
SATB ALLOWAY A-102   (R412)

Beatitude II: Blessed Are They That
Mourn
SATB ALLOWAY A-103   (R413)

Beatitude III: Blessed Are The Meek
SATB ALLOWAY A-104   (R414)

Beatitude V: Blessed Are The Merciful
TTBB ALLOWAY A-107   (R415)

Parish Mass
unis/SATB/SATB&unis (edition no.
110 is for concert use) ALLOWAY
A-109, A-110   (R416)

ROUND THE LORD IN GLORY SEATED see
Gluck

ROUNDELAY see Lovelace, Austin C.

ROUTLEY, ERIC
Rise Up, Shepherd An' Foller *Xmas
SATB EMI s.p.   (R417)

Three Antiphonal Canticles *CC3U,
anti
SATB&cong/dbl cor,org NOVELLO MW 24
s.p.   (R418)

ROVETTA, GIOVANNI
Laudate Dominum
(Steele) SSTTB/SATTB/SAATB,cont,
org,2vln voc sc NOVELLO rental
(R419)

ROVICS, HOWARD
Cantata: Poems Of War Resistance
*sac/sec
cor,S,narrator,pno,2ob,2trp,vcl,
perc, tenor saxophone sc
AM.COMP.AL. $12.10   (R420)

ROWE
Love Lifted Me (composed with Smith)
(Allen, L.) SATB oct BENSON S4209
$.35   (R421)
(Mercer, W. Elmo) SAT oct BENSON
S4210 $.30   (R422)
(Reynolds) SATB oct BENSON S4211
$.35   (R423)
(Stevens) SATB oct BENSON S4212
$.35   (R424)

ROWLEY
I Will Sing The Wondrous Story
(composed with Wilcoxon) *anthem
SATB (easy) oct BROADMAN 4551-49
$.30   (R425)

ROWLEY, ALEC (1892-1958)
Magnificat And Nunc Dimittis In A
Minor
mix cor BANKS MUS YS 836 $.40
(R426)

When God Came A-Visiting
mix cor BANKS MUS YS 988 $.20
(R427)

When The Whole Heart Of Man
mix cor BANKS MUS YS 837 $.25
(R428)

ROXOLOGY see Blackwell, John

ROY, FRED
Come, Come Ye Saints
TTBB HARRIS $.35   (R429)

ROY, S. DE
Cantio Sacra De Visitatione B. Mariae
Virginis *BVM
5pt mix cor DOBLINGER TH 30 sc
s.p., voc pt s.p.   (R430)

ROZSA, MIKLOS (1907-   )
Psalm 23 *see Twenty-Third Psalm,
The

To Everything There Is A Season
*Op.21, Bibl/mot
SATB,opt org AMP A-690 $1.50 (R431)

Twenty-Third Psalm, The (Psalm 23)
SATB,acap BROUDE BR. $.90   (R432)

RUBBRA, EDMUND (1901-   )
Holy Dawn, The
see SIX CHRISTMAS CAROLS

Prayer To Jesus
see Three Hymn Tunes

Queen Of Mercy
see Three Hymn Tunes

That Virgin's Child Most Meek
see Three Hymn Tunes

Three Hymn Tunes *hymn
SATB,acap LENGNICK s.p.
contains: Prayer To Jesus,
Op.114,No.1; Queen Of Mercy,
Op.114,No.3; That Virgin's
Child Most Meek, Op.114,No.2
(R433)

RUDD
Saviour's Name, The *see Lyall

RUF IM ADVENT see Schroeder, Hermann

RUFE MICH AN IN DER NOT see
Kretzschmar, Gunther

RUFET NICHT DIE WEISHEIT see Krieger,
Johann Philipp

RUFFO, [VINCENZO] (1510-1587)
Adoramus Te *Psntd,mot
[Lat] 4pt mix cor,acap sc,cor pts
BOHM s.p.   (R434)

Salve Regina
[Lat] 4pt mix cor,acap BOHM s.p.
(R435)

RUFT ES AUS IN ALLE WELT see Telemann,
Georg Philipp

RULISON, CONSTANCE
This Is The Day *Xmas
unis WHITE,ERN $.25   (R436)

RUNYAN
Carol Of The Small Child *Xmas,
anthem
SATB FINE ARTS CM 1098 $.35 (R437)
2pt FINE ARTS CM 1112 $.35   (R438)

I See A Day *anthem
(Riddle) SATB FINE ARTS EP 31 $.35
(R439)
Is There Reason *anthem
(Riddle) SAT/SAB,opt gtr FINE ARTS
EP 26 $.35   (R440)

Lord, At Thy Mercy Seat *anthem
(Cram, James D.) SATB FINE ARTS
CM 1108 $.35   (R441)

Sing Noel *Xmas,anthem
SATB,opt gtr FINE ARTS CM 1082 $.30
(R442)

RUPPEL, PAUL ERNST (1913-   )
Aus Tiefer Not Schrei Ich Zu Dir
see Lincke, Paul, Aus Tiefer Not
Schrei Ich Zu Dir

Der Herr Ist Mein Licht Und Mein Heil
SA/jr cor,org,fl sc HANSSLER 12.222
s.p.   (R443)

Ernte Des Lebens
3-4pt mix cor,T solo,acap (med)
BAREN. BA6310 contains also:
Osterlied (3-4pt mix cor&cong&
unis,opt T solo,acap) (Easter,
easy)   (R444)

Grosser Gott, Du Liebst Erbarmen
SAT/SAB/SA,opt 1-2treb inst
HANSSLER 14.180 s.p.   (R445)

Herr, Deinen Tod Verkunden Wir
SAT/SAB (contains also: Das Will
Ich Mir Zu Herzen Nehmen)
SCHWEIZER. SK 72.07-8 s.p. see
also MUSIKBEILAGE ZUM
"EVANGELISCHEN KIRCHENCHOR 1972"
(R446)
Osterlied
see Ruppel, Paul Ernst, Ernte Des
Lebens

Siehe, Dein Konig Kommt Zu Dir
SAAT/SAAB (contains also: Helft,
Gottes Gute Preisen; Der Herr,
Der Ist Mein Hirt) SCHWEIZER.
SK 67.02 s.p. see also
MUSIKBEILAGE ZUM "EVANGELISCHEN
KIRCHENCHOR 1967"   (R447)

RUPPEL, PAUL ERNST (cont'd.)

Wunderbarer Konig
SAT/SAB/SA,opt 1-2treb inst
HANSSLER 14.235 s.p.   (R448)

RUSSELL
Magnificat
SATB SCHIRM.G 12009 $.40   (R449)
SATB SCHIRM.G 12009 $.40   (R450)

RUSSELL, OLIVE NELSON
What Are Those Bells?
SATB,pno/org,hndbl,gtr GENTRY
G -247 $.40   (R451)

RUSSELL, WELFORD
Never Weather Beaten Sail
SATB (easy) WATERLOO $.40   (R452)

Our Father Which Art In Heaven
SATB (med easy) WATERLOO $.35
(R453)
RUSSIAN VESPER HYMN see Bortniansky,
Dimitri Stepanovitch

RUST, FRIEDRICH WILHELM (1739-1796)
Am See Tiberius *Op.12
mix cor,S/A solo,pno LIENAU sc
s.p., cor pts s.p.   (R454)

RUSTHOI
When We See Christ *anthem/gospel
(Mickelson, Paul) SATB oct SINGSPIR
ZJP-8140 $.35   (R455)

RUTTER
Christ The Lord Is Risen Again
*Easter,anthem
SATB (easy) OXFORD 42.362 $.40
(R456)
Communion Service (Series III)
unis&SATB (easy) voc sc OXFORD
40.022 $.70, cor pts OXFORD
40.040 $.30   (R457)

Falcon, The
SATB,inst (med diff) OXFORD 46.160
$3.25   (R458)

From East To West
SATB,acap (easy) OXFORD 84.225 $.35
(R459)
Gloria *Gloria
SATB,inst (med) OXFORD   (R460)

God Be In My Head
SATB,acap (easy) OXFORD 94.326 $.25
(R461)
God Is Gone Up
see Rutter, O Clap Your Hands

I Will Lift Up Mine Eyes
SATB,inst OXFORD   (R462)

Jesus Child
SATB,inst OXFORD ipr   (R463)

Love Came Down At Christmas
SATB (easy) OXFORD 84.224 $.25
(R464)
Nativity Carol *Xmas,carol
SATB,inst (easy) OXFORD 84.169
$.25, ipr   (R465)
SSA,inst (easy) OXFORD 83.091 $.30
(R466)
O Clap Your Hands *anthem
SATB (easy) OXFORD 42.378 $.40
contains also: God Is Gone Up
(R467)
Praise Ye The Lord
SATB (easy) OXFORD 42.357 $.40
(R468)
Preces And Responses
TTBB,acap (med) OXFORD 41.027 $.30
(R469)
Shepherd's Pipe Carol *Xmas,carol
SATB,inst (easy) OXFORD 84.167 $.50
(R470)
SSAA,inst (easy) OXFORD 83.076 $.50
(R471)
SSAA,inst (easy) sc OXFORD 77.876
$5.00, ipa   (R472)
unis,inst (easy) OXFORD 81.133
$.40, ipr   (R473)
unis,inst (very easy) OXFORD 81.141
$.25, ipr   (R474)

Sing We To This Merry Company *Xmas,
carol
SATB (med easy) OXFORD 84.236 $.30
(R475)
Star Carol, The *Xmas,carol
SATB,acap (med easy) OXFORD 84.233
$.40   (R476)

RYBA, JAN JAKUB SIMON (1765-1815)
Ceska Vanocni Mse "Hej Mistre"
"Czech Christmas Mass "Hey Master""
[Czech] mix cor,soli,fl,2ob,tuba,
2horn,2trp,3trom,timp,strings
CZECH s.p.   (R477)

Czech Christmas Mass "Hey Master"
*see Ceska Vanocni Mse "Hej
Mistre"

RYBA, JAN JAKUB SIMON (cont'd.)

Gloria *Gloria
3pt mix cor,2S rec,2A rec,strings,
pno, glockenspiel sc,cor pts
PELIKAN PE940 s.p., ipa   (R478)

RYCHNOVSKY, JIRI (? -1616)
Quem Vidistis Pastores
(Snizlova, Jitky) [Lat] mix cor
CZECH s.p.   (R479)

S

S.A.T.B. BOOK I *CCU,anthem
(Leupold, U.S.) SATB WATERLOO $1.50
(S1)

S.A.T.B. BOOK II *CCU,anthem
(Leupold, U.S.) SATB WATERLOO $1.50
(S2)

SA SIER GUD see Nystedt, Knut

SAAR, LOUIS VICTOR (1868-1937)
Easter Dawn
SSAATTBB (med) FITZSIMONS 2018 $.20
(S3)

Note Of Golden Song, A
SSA (med) FITZSIMONS 3020 $.25 (S4)
TTBB (diff) FITZSIMONS 4022 $.20
(S5)
dbl cor,opt 4 soli,acap (med)
FITZSIMONS 1038 $.25   (S6)
SATB (med) FITZSIMONS 1011 $.25
(S7)

SAB CHOIR BOOK, THE *CC15U
(Ehret, Walter) SAB BROADMAN 4521-01
$1.25   (S8)

SABBATH DAY WAS BY, THE see Carlson, J.
Bert

SABBATH EVE SACRED SERVICE see Lavry,
Marc

SACERDOS ET PONTIFEX see Hunecke,
Wilhelm

SACERDOTES DOMINI see Byrd, William

SACERDOTES DOMINI see Filke, Max

SACERDOTES DOMINI see Spranger, Jorg

SACRAE CANTIONES see Rosetti, Stefano

SACRED AND SECULAR SONGS FOR THREE
VOICES, VOL. I see Turnhout, Gerard
de

SACRED AND SECULAR SONGS FOR THREE
VOICES, VOL. II see Turnhout,
Gerard de

SACRED CANTATA NO. 1 "O CHILDE SWETE"
see Fletcher

SACRED HAIR see London, Edwin

SACRED SERVICE see Bloch, Ernest

SACRED SERVICE see Gideon, Miriam

SACRED SERVICE see Maul, William

SACRED VERSES see Taylor, Clifford

SACRIFICE OF PRAISE, A see Johnson,
Paul

SACRIS SOLEMNIIS see Benkert, Lorenz

SACRIS SOLEMNIIS see Casciolini,
Claudio

SACRIS SOLEMNIIS see Dantonello, Josef

SACRIS SOLEMNIIS see Erhard, Karl

SACRIS SOLEMNIIS see Kromolicki, Joseph

SACRIS SOLEMNIIS see Kutzer, Ernst

SACRIS SOLEMNIIS see Messner, Joseph

SACRIS SOLEMNIIS see Schroeder, Hermann

SACRIS SOLEMNIIS see Welcker, Max

SACRIS SOLEMNIS see Lemacher, Heinrich

SACRIS SOLEMNIS see Lipp, Alban

SAFE IN THY MANGER *Xmas
(Douglas) 2pt,opt fl PRO ART 2789
$.35   (S9)

SAG MIG DU see Nystroem, Gosta

SAGE MEIN VOLK see Victoria, Tomas Luis
de, Popule Meus

ST. AGNES-MESSE see Gruber, Joseph

ST. ALBAN-MESSE see Rohr, Hugo

ST. ALBANS-MESSE IN C see Lipp, Alban

ST. BLASIUS-MESSE see Wassmer, Berthold

ST. CANISIUS-MESSE see Kircher, Johann

ST. FRANCIS see Milner, Anthony

SAINT FRANCOIS D'ASSISE see Gagnebin,
Henri

ST. FRANZISKUS-MESSE see Piechler,
Arthur

ST. FRANZISKUS-MESSE see Wassmer,
Berthold

ST. HEINRICHSMESSE see Schmid, K.N.

ST. HILDEGARD-MESSE see Rohr, Hugo

ST. JOHN PASSION see Ridout, Alan

SAINT JOSEPH
cor JOBERT s.p. see also Douze
Cantiques De Fetes   (S10)

ST. LEOPOLDS-MESSE see Gruber, Joseph

SAINT LUDMILA see Dvorak, Antonin

ST. LUDWIGS-MESSE see Zangl, Ludwig

SAINT LUKE see Vycpalek, Ladislav,
Svaty Lukas

ST. LUKE PASSION see Koll, Fritz, Die
Passion Des Menschensohns

ST. LUKE'S CAROL see Brahms, Johannes

ST. LUKE'S MASS see Goodman, Joseph

ST. MARK PASSION see Badings, Henk

ST. MARTINUS-MESSE see Kircher, Johann

ST. MATHIAS-MESSE see Gruber, Joseph

ST. MATTHEW PASSION see Bach, Johann
Sebastian, Matthaus-Passion (Neue
Bach-Ausgabe)

ST. MATTHEW PASSION see Schutz,
Heinrich

ST. MEINRADSMESSE see Wassmer, Berthold

ST. MICHAELS-MESSE see Goller, Fritz

ST. MICHAELSMESSE see Wassmer, Berthold

SAINT-NICOLAS see Ammann, Benno

ST. PAUL see Zelter, Carl Friedrich

ST. PAUL'S LETTER ON LOVE see Hopson,
Hal H.

ST. PAULUS-MESSE see Gruber, Joseph

ST. PETER see Jones, Daniel

SAINT-SAENS, CAMILLE (1835-1921)
Lift Up Your Offerings (from
Christmas Oratorio) Xmas
(Kaplan) SATB SCHIRM.G LG51717 $.30
(S11)
(Kaplan) SATB SCHIRM.G LG 51711
$.30   (S12)

Praise Ye The Mighty God *anthem
(Penninger) SAAB (easy) oct
BROADMAN 4551-59 $.30   (S13)

SAINT STEPHEN see Peek, Richard

SAINTS! see McCarthy

SALIERI, ANTONIO (1750-1825)
De Profundis (Psalm 129)
[Lat] 4pt mix cor,org/vla&bvl&bsn&
org sc,cor pts BOHM s.p., ipa
(S14)

Herbei, Ihr Bruder
see Bach, Johann Sebastian, Meinen
Jesum Lass Ich Nicht

Justorum Animae *Fest,Offer
[Lat] 4pt mix cor,org,2vln,vla,vcl,
bvl,2ob,bsn,2trom sc,cor pts BOHM
s.p., ipa   (S15)

Psalm 129 *see De Profundis

SALMO 43 see Pezzati, Romano

SALMO IX see Petrassi, Goffredo

SALMO XLVII see Cammarota, Carlo

SALSBURY, RON
Open Your Spiritual Eyes *anthem
SAB WORD CS-2653 $.30   (S16)

SALSBURY, SONNY
Backpacker's Pocketbook *CCU,anthem
SATB WORD   (S17)

Backpacker's Suite *CCU,anthem
SATB WORD   (S18)

SALSBURY, SONNY (cont'd.)
Good Morning, Lord *CC13L
cor WORD 37629 $1.95   (S19)

SALUS AUTEM JUSTORUM see Heftrich,
Wilhelm

SALUS ET GLORIA see Haydn, (Franz)
Joseph

SALUT see Carraz

SALUT see Rabot

SALUTIS HUMANAE SATOR see Benkert,
Lorenz

SALUTIS HUMANAE SATOR see Dantonello,
Josef

SALUTIS HUMANAE SATOR see Erhard, Karl

SALUTIS HUMANAE SATOR see Kromolicki,
Joseph

SALUTIS HUMANAE SATOR see Lemacher,
Heinrich

SALUTIS HUMANAE SATOR see Lipp, Alban

SALUTIS HUMANAE SATOR see Messner,
Joseph

SALUTIS HUMANAE SATOR see Schroeder,
Hermann

SALUTIS HUMANAE SATOR see Welcker, Max

SALUTIS HYMANAE SATOR see Erhard, Karl

SALVA, TADEAS (1937-   )
Litaniae Laurentanae
mix cor SLOV.HUD.FOND s.p. (S20)

SALVATION FOR US PROVIDETH see Lindeman

SALVATION UNTO US HAS COME see
Rotermund, Melvin

SALVATOR MUNDI see Stout, Alan

SALVE MATER SALVATORIS see Lemacher,
Heinrich

SALVE REDEMPTOR see Hoffmann, Ernst
Theodor Amadeus

SALVE REGINA see Byrd, William

SALVE REGINA see Faist, Anton

SALVE REGINA see Haydn, (Johann)
Michael

SALVE REGINA see Jochum, Otto

SALVE REGINA see Kubizek, Augustinian

SALVE REGINA see Ockeghem, Johannes

SALVE REGINA see Pergolesi, Giovanni
Battista

SALVE REGINA see Piechler, Arthur

SALVE REGINA see Rehm, P. Otto

SALVE REGINA see Rheinberger, Josef

SALVE REGINA see Ruffo, [Vincenzo]

SALVE REGINA see Schubert, Franz
(Peter)

SALVE REGINA D'EINSIEDELN see Rabot

SALVE REGINA IN ES see Haydn, (Franz)
Joseph

SALVE REGINA PACIS see Huber, Heinrich

SALVE SANCTA PARENS see Heftrich,
Wilhelm

SALVE VIRGO NOBILIS see Lemacher,
Heinrich

SALZBURG MASS see Track, Gerhard, Missa
Brevis

SAM see Hammack, Bobby

SAMMIS
Trust And Obey (composed with
Williams) *anthem
SATB (easy) oct BROADMAN 4540-51
$.30   (S21)

SAMSON
Messe Dominum Firmamentum
2pt mix cor,pno/org HENN 739 s.p.
sc, voc pt   (S22)

SAMSON (cont'd.)

Messe Dulcis Domina
3 eq voices,pno/org HENN 738 s.p.
sc, voc pt   (S23)

Messe Vinum Laeftificat
2pt mix cor,pno/org HENN 323 s.p.
sc, voc pt   (S24)

Messe Vinum Laetificat
2 eq voices,pno/org HENN 113 s.p.
sc, voc pt   (S25)

SAMUEL! see Butler, Eugene

SAMUEL WAS A FRIEND OF GOD see Butler,
A.L.

SANCTA ET INDIVIDUA TRINITAS see
Carissimi, Giacomo

SANCTA MARIA see Mozart, Wolfgang
Amadeus

SANCTA MARIA see Schweitzer, Johannes

SANCTA MARIA, MATER DEI see Mozart,
Wolfgang Amadeus, Sancta Maria

SANCTA MARIA, ORA PRO NOBIS see Bein,
Wilhelm

SANCTAE CRUCIS see Kraft, Karl

SANCTAE DEI GENITRIX see Wassmer,
Berthold

SANCTI DEI see Haydn, (Johann) Michael

SANCTIFY THEM see Nelson, Ronald A.

SANCTUS
(Perrin, Harvey) SATB (easy) WATERLOO
$.30 contains also: Gaudeamus
Igitur   (S26)

SANCTUS see Anerio, Felice

SANCTUS see Bach, Johann Sebastian

SANCTUS see Bernstein, Leonard

SANCTUS see Camidge, Matthew

SANCTUS see Cousins, M. Thomas

SANCTUS see Dvorak, Antonin

SANCTUS see Faure, Gabriel-Urbain

SANCTUS see Goemanne, Noel

SANCTUS see Gounod, Charles Francois

SANCTUS see Govert, Willibald

SANCTUS see Haydn, (Franz) Joseph

SANCTUS see Monteverdi, Claudio

SANCTUS see Mozart, Wolfgang Amadeus

SANCTUS see Palestrina, Giovanni

SANCTUS see Pederson, Mogens

SANCTUS see Rossini, Gioacchino

SANCTUS see Schvedov, Constantine

SANCTUS see Verdi, Giuseppe

SANCTUS - BENEDICTUS see Des Prez,
Josquin

SANCTUS: HEILIG, HEILIG see Silcher,
Friedrich

SANCTUS "HEILIG IST DER HERR" see
Schubert, Franz (Peter)

SANCTUS IN D see Bach, Johann Sebastian

SANDALS see Wyrtzen, Don

SANDELIG, SANDELIG SIER JEG DIG see
Kvandal, Johan

SANDERS
Give Thanks Unto The Lord (Psalm 136)
(composed with Davidson)
SATB ALFRED 6805 $.50   (S27)

I Belive In Almighty God (composed
with Faircloth) *anthem
SATB (easy) oct BROADMAN 4540-57
$.30   (S28)

Psalm 136 *see Give Thanks Unto The
Lord

We Are Not Alone (composed with
Davidson)
SAB/SATB (jazz-rock) ALFRED 6804
$.50   (S29)

SANDRESKY, M.V.
King Of Glory, King Of Peace
unis BRODT 544 $.22   (S30)

SANFT NEIGT SICH DER TAG see Mullich,
Hermann

SANKEY, I.
Hiding In The Rock Of Ages (composed
with Hastings) *anthem
(DeCou, Harold) SATB oct SINGSPIR
ZA-4383 $.35   (S31)

Hiding In Thee *see Cushing

Trusting Jesus *anthem/gospel
(Bunzel, Claude) SATB oct SINGSPIR
ZJP-8134 $.30   (S32)

Under His Wings *gospel
(Ehret, Walter) SATB oct LILLENAS
AN-1693 $.30   (S33)

SANS DAY CAROL
see Twelve Christmas Carols: Set 2

SANS DAY CAROL see Arnatt, Ronald

SANSOM, CLIVE
Jubilate Jazz
SATB,pno/gtr&bvl, and bongos or any
instrumental combination (med)
FISCHER,C PT 2767 $.40, ipa (S34)

SANTA ULIVA see Pizzetti, Ildebrando

SANTO see Mendoza, Michael

SAPIENTIA FORIS PREDICAT see Villa-
Lobos, Heitor

SATEREN, LELAND BERNHARD (1913-   )
As A Flower Of The Field *Lent
(Hoffman) SATB,acap ART MAST 181
$.40   (S35)

Be Ye Joyful *anthem
SATB AUGSBURG 11-1746 $.40   (S36)

Day Of Pentecost *Pent,anthem
SSAATTBB AUGSBURG 11-3501 $.60
(S37)

Living Bread *anthem
SATB AUGSBURG 11-1735 $.30   (S38)

Sing Alleluia, Jesus Lives *Easter,
anthem
SATB oct SACRED S-166 $.35   (S39)

To God Will We Sing
SATB,inst ART MAST 125 $.40   (S40)

SATTNER, HUGOLIN
Missa Seraphica *Mass
[Lat] 4pt mix cor,org/fl&2clar&bsn&
2horn&2trp&2trom&strings&opt timp
sc,cor pts BOHM s.p., ipr (S41)

SAUL see Hovland, Egil

SAUL OF TAURUS see Claflin, Avery

SAUNDERS, NEIL (1918-   )
Benedic Anima Mea (Psalm 104)
SATB,ST soli,org ROBERTON 85026
s.p.   (S42)

Jubilate Deo
SSATB,SBar soli,brass ROBERTON
85027 s.p.   (S43)

Psalm 104 *see Benedic Anima Mea

SAVE ME, O GOD see Van Hulse, Camil

SAVE US, O LORD see Matthews, Thomas

SAVED BY GRACE see Crosby, F.

SAVED, SAVED! see Scholfield

SAVED, SAVED, SAVED *cant
(Skillings, Otis) cor BENSON B0775
$1.50   (S44)

SAVELLI, M.A. (1920-   )
Credo
cor,T solo,3fl,3ob,3clar,3bsn,
4horn,3trp,3trom,tuba,timp,perc,
harp,cembalo,org CARISH rental
(S45)

SAVIOR, HELP US TO PROCLAIM see
Burroughs, Bob

SAVIOR, I LONG TO BE see Hughes

SAVIOR IS WAITING, THE *CCU,anthem
(Carmichael, Ralph) SATB LEXICON
(S46)

SAVIOR! I'VE NO ONE ELSE TO TELL see
Hunter, Denise Joan

SAVIOR, LIKE A SHEPHERD LEAD US see
Bradbury, William Batchelder

SAVIOR, LIKE A SHEPHERD LEAD US see
Trupp

SAVIOR, MORE THAN LIFE TO ME see
Crosby, F.

SAVIOR, TEACH ME DAY BY DAY see Leeson

SAVIOUR, HEAR US, WE PRAY see Brahms,
Johannes

SAVIOUR, LIKE A SHEPHERD LEAD US
(Johnson) SSAA oct BENSON S4258 $.30
(S47)

(Tipton, Clyde) SATB&opt treb cor,opt
solo,kbd DEAN CE-101 $.40   (S48)

SAVIOUR, LIKE A SHEPHERD LEAD US see
Bradbury, William Batchelder

SAVIOUR, LIKE A SHEPHERD LEAD US see
Thrupp

SAVIOUR TEACH ME DAY BY DAY see Butler,
A.L.

SAVIOUR TEACH ME DAY BY DAY see Thiman,
Eric Harding

SAVIOUR, TEACH ME, DAY BY DAY see
Thomas, C.

SAVIOUR WHILE MY HEART IS TENDER see
Butler, A.L.

SAVIOURS LOVE see Vaughan Williams,
Ralph

SAVIOUR'S NAME, THE see Lyall

SAW YE MY SAVIOUR see Johnson, David N.

SAY NOUGHT THE STRUGGLE see Willan,
Healey

SAY YES TO LIFE see Butler

SAYVE
Coeli Enarrant *mot
SSAATB,3trp,3trom MOSELER MOR167
s.p.   (S49)

Hodie Christus Natus Est *Xmas,mot
SATB&SATBB,inst MOSELER MOR166 s.p.
(S50)

SCANDELLO
Bonzorno Madonna
[It] SATB RICORDI-ENG BA10370 s.p.
(S51)

SCARCE HAD THE DAYSTAR RISEN see
Gabrieli, Andrea, Maria Magdalene
Et Altera Maria

SCARLATTI
Alleluia, Praise God *anthem
(Coggin, Elwood) SATB AUGSBURG
11-1693 $.40   (S52)

SCARLATTI, ALESSANDRO (1660-1725)
Adorna Thalamum
(Young, Percy) "Prepare Now Your
Finest Chamber" [Lat/Eng] SATB,
acap BROUDE BR. $.65 see from
Music Of The Great Churches Vol.
III: Santa Maria Maggiore, Rome
(S53)

Audi Filia
(Steele) SSATB,SSA soli,2ob,opt
bsn,org,strings voc sc NOVELLO
rental   (S54)

Domine, Refugium Factus Es *mot
5pt mix cor cor pts BIELER DM 4
s.p.   (S55)

Exultate Deo
SATB EGTVED KB103 s.p.   (S56)
[Lat] 4pt mix cor,acap BOHM s.p.
(S57)

Music Of The Great Churches Vol. III:
Santa Maria Maggiore, Rome *see
Adorna Thalamum, "Prepare Now
Your Finest Chamber"   (S58)

O Magnum Mysterium *mot
dbl cor cor pts BIELER DM 7 s.p.
(S59)

Passio D.N. Jesu Christi Secundum
Johannem *Psntd
(Hanley, Edwin) "Passion According
To St. John, The" cor bds A-R ED
$8.95   (S60)

Passion According To St. John, The
*see Passio D.N. Jesu Christi
Secundum Johannem

Prepare Now Your Finest Chamber *see
Adorna Thalamum

Sing Aloud With Gladness *Gen,
anthem,Class
cor ROYAL 252 s.p.   (S61)

SCHAEFER
Lord's Prayer, The
(Luboff, Norman) SATB CHARTER 3069
(S62)

SCHAFFE IN MIR, GOTT, EIN REINES HERZ
see Brahms, Johannes

SCHAFFE IN MIR, GOTT, EIN REINES HERZE
see Winer, Georg

SCHALK, CARL
Child Is Born In Bethlehem, A
*anthem
SATB,opt fl/rec AUGSBURG 11-1707
$.30   (S63)

Chorales For Advent *CCU,Adv,chorale
unis&SAB,1-3inst AUGSBURG 11-9134
$.60   (S64)

Chorales For Christmas And Epiphany
*CCU,Xmas/Epiph,chorale
unis/SAB,org,2-3inst AUGSBURG
11-9143 $.60   (S65)

My Song Is Love Unknown
2pt mix cor oct CONCORDIA 98-2236
$.30   (S66)

O Kingly Love
SATB,brass,timp (choraleconcertato)
sc CONCORDIA 97-5097 $.60, ipa,
cor pts CONCORDIA 97-5098 $.40
(S67)

Psalms For The Church Year *CCU,
Psalm
cong&opt cor,opt cantor,kbd cor pts
AUGSBURG 11-9360 $.60, ipa (S68)

Sing, My Tongue, How Glorious Battle
unis,opt inst oct CONCORDIA 98-2240
$.25   (S69)

There Through Endless Ranks Of Angels
*anthem
SATB,org AUGSBURG 11-1742 $.40
(S70)

Thy Strong Word
SATB,2-3trp (chorale concertato)
cor pts CONCORDIA 97-5234 $.40,
sc CONCORDIA 97-5167 $2.50, ipa
(S71)

SCHAPER, HEINZ-CHRISTIAN (1927-   )
Freuet Euch In Dem Herrn Allewege
see Zwei Adventsmotetten

Machet Die Tore Weit
see Zwei Adventsmotetten

Zwei Adventsmotetten *Adv,mot
6pt mix cor,acap MERSEBURG EM480
s.p.
contains: Freuet Euch In Dem
Herrn Allewege; Machet Die Tore
Weit   (S72)

SCHARF
Funf Liturgische Gesange *Op.10,
CC5U
8pt mix cor LIENAU sc s.p., cor pts
s.p.   (S73)

Zwei Geistliche Gesange *Op.11, CC2U
8pt mix cor LIENAU sc s.p., cor pts
s.p.   (S74)

SCHATTENBERG, THOMAS
Jesu Spes Poenitentibus
see Three Hymns

O Beata Incendium
see Three Hymns

Quando Cor Nostrum Visitas
see Three Hymns

Three Hymns *hymn
[Lat] 4pt mix cor,acap SMF5428 s.p.
contains: Jesu Spes
Poenitentibus; O Beata
Incendium; Quando Cor Nostrum
Visitas   (S75)

SCHECK, HELMUT
Komm, Heil'ger Geist
4pt mix cor,opt org cor pts BOHM
s.p.   (S76)

SCHEDE, PAUL
Fried Schaff, O Herr, Durch Eine Ehr
*mot
SATTB HANSSLER 1.458 s.p.   (S77)

SCHEFFLER, J.J.
Morning Star (composed with Davidson)
*anthem
2pt (easy) oct BROADMAN 4558-40
$.30   (S78)

SCHEIDT, PATRICIA
Christmas Kind Of Night, A *Xmas
SA RICHMOND SA-8 $.30   (S79)

SCHEIDT, SAMUEL (1587-1654)
Child Is Born In Bethlehem, A *Xmas
SSA,acap (med) OXFORD 83.085 $.30
(S80)

(Davis) SATB,acap (med) OXFORD
84.193 $.25   (S81)

Child Is Born In Bethlehem, A *Xmas
(Kaplan) SATB SCHIRM.G LG51716 $.25
(S82)

Come, Ye Blessed Ones Of My Father
*see Kommt Her, Ihr Gesegneten
Meines Vaters

God So Loved The World *see Sic Deus
Dilexit Mundum

Kommt Her, Ihr Gesegneten Meines
Vaters
(Steinitz, Paul) "Come, Ye Blessed
Ones Of My Father" SATTB,cont,opt
inst sc NOVELLO s.p.   (S83)

Sic Deus Dilexit Mundum
(Schmeltekopf, Gary) "God So Loved
The World" [Eng/Lat] SATB,org,
2trp,2trom (med) GIA G1819 $.75,
ipa   (S84)

Thou Art My God And Father *see Weil
Du Mein Gott Und Vater Bist

Weil Du Mein Gott Und Vater Bist
(Luce) "Thou Art My God And Father"
SA BRODT WC 2 $.24   (S85)

SCHEIN, JOHANN HERMANN (1586-1630)
Collected Works *sac/sec,CCU
(Pruefer, Arthur) microfiche UNION
ESP. $65.00 7 volumes, originally
published at Leipzig, 1901-1923.
(S86)

Der Herr, Der Ist Mein Hirt
SATB,cont (contains also: Helft,
Gottes Gute Preisen; Siehe, Dein
Konig Kommt Zu Dir) SCHWEIZER.
SK 67.02 s.p. see also
MUSIKBEILAGE ZUM "EVANGELISCHEN
KIRCHENCHOR 1967"   (S87)

Furwahr, Es Ist Ein Kostlich Ding
SATB,cont (contains also: Herr Jesu
Christ, Wahr Mensch Und Gott)
SCHWEIZER. SK 65.01 s.p. see also
MUSIKBEILAGE ZUM "EVANGELISCHEN
KIRCHENCHOR 1965"   (S88)

Ich Steh An Deiner Krippe Hier
SATB DOBLINGER S 205 s.p.   (S89)

Mach's Mit Mir, Gott
men cor,acap TONOS 5615 s.p. (S90)

Maria Magdalene Et Altera Maria
(Young, Percy) "When Mary
Magdalene" [Lat/Eng] SSATB,acap
BROUDE BR. $.60 see from MUSIC OF
THE GREAT CHURCHES VOL. IV: ST.
THOMAS' CHURCH, LEIPZIG   (S91)

Nun Lob Den Herrn, O Seele Mein
SATB,cont (contains also: Erstanden
Ist Der Heilig Christ) SCHWEIZER.
SK 68.05-6 s.p. see also
MUSIKBEILAGE ZUM "EVANGELISCHEN
KIRCHENCHOR 1968"   (S92)

O Nadens Sol Og Sete
SS,inst,cont NORSK NMO 8743 s.p.
(S93)

Vil Du Mot Malet Renna
"Wilt Thou Run To The Goal" mix cor
NORSK NMO 8740 s.p.   (S94)

Wenn Wir In Hochsten Noten Sein
*Rembrnc
cor BOHM s.p.   (S95)

When Mary Magdalene *see Maria
Magdalene Et Altera Maria

Wie Schon Leuchtet
SATB DOBLINGER S 208 s.p.   (S96)

Wilt Thou Run To The Goal *see Vil
Du Mot Malet Renna

SCHELLE, JOHANN HERMANN (1648-1701)
Hell Morgonstjarna, Mild Och Ren
4pt mix cor ERIKS 9 s.p.   (S97)

Vom Himmel Hoch *Xmas
(Wanek Friedrich) SSATB,ST soli,
cont,2ob,strings,opt 2trp,3trom
(med easy) sc,cor pts SCHOTTS
ED. 5744 s.p., ipa   (S98)

SCHIAVONE, JOHN
I Am The Bread Of Life *Commun,
anthem
SA/TB (easy) GIA G1855 $.40   (S99)

Mass In Honor Of All Saints *Mass
SAB&cong,org GIA G1929 $1.25 (S100)

SCHIAVONE, JOHN (cont'd.)

Mass In Praise Of God The Holy Spirit
*Mass
SATB&cong,org (med easy) GIA G1764
$1.25   (S101)

Mass In Praise Of Jesus Christ The
Eternal High Priest *Mass
SA/TB (med easy) GIA G1856 $1.25
(S102)

SAB (med easy) GIA G1857 $1.25
(S103)

SCHIBLER, ARMIN (1920-   )
Herr, Mein Gott, Wie Gross Sind Deine
Wunder
SATB SCHWEIZER. SK 122 s.p. (S104)

SCHIDLOWSKY, LEON (1931-   )
Requiem 1968
[Lat] SSSAAATTTBBB (diff) sc
SCHOTTS AV 49 s.p.   (S105)

SCHIERI, FRITZ (1922-   )
Deutsche Ordinariums-Messe
SATB&cong,org cor pts CHRIS 51646
s.p.   (S106)
SSAA&cong/TTBB&cong,org cor pts
CHRIS 51647 s.p.   (S107)

Es Flog Ein Taublein
[Ger] 4pt mix cor,acap MERSEBURG
SM76 contains also: Biebl, Franz,
Auf Haltet Euer Herz Bereit;
Biebl, Franz, Die Sonne Ist
Gesunken   (S108)

SCHILLERHYMNE see Haas, Joseph

SCHINHAN, J.P.
Peace I Leave With You
mix cor BRODT 578 $.26   (S109)

SCHIR ZION see Sulzer, Salomon

SCHIRE BETH ADONAI see Weintraub,
Hirsch A.

SCHLAF, MEIN KINDELEIN *Xmas,carol/
folk
(Biebl, F.) [Ger] 4pt men cor
MERSEBURG EM9060   (S110)

SCHLAGT FROH IN DIE HANDE see
Schweizer, Rolf

SCHLEMM, GUSTAV ADOLF
O Wunderschon Ist Gottes Erde
men cor,acap TONOS 4054 s.p. (S111)

SCHLUSSCHOR AUS DER MATTHAUSPASSION see
Bach, Johann Sebastian

SCHLUSSGEBET see Nowakowsky, David

SCHLUSSLIED "NUN JAUCHZET ALL" see
Trapp, Willy

SCHMALZ, PAUL (1904-   )
Deutsche Jugendmesse
jr cor,org HUG   (S112)

SCHMID, ALFONS
Es Wird Schon Gleich Dunkel *Xmas
3pt mix cor,opt inst BOHM s.p.
(S113)

O Esca Viatorum
see Zwei Eucharistische Gesange

O Salutaris Hostia
see Zwei Eucharistische Gesange

Zwei Eucharistische Gesange
[Lat] BOHM s.p.
contains: O Esca Viatorum, Op.7,
No.2 (4pt mix cor,acap); O
Salutaris Hostia, Op.7,No.1
(4pt mix cor,org)   (S114)

SCHMID, HEINRICH KASPAR (1874-1953)
Missa Barbara In D *Op.88, Mass
[Lat] 4pt mix cor,org sc,cor pts
BOHM s.p.   (S115)

SCHMID, K.N.
St. Heinrichsmesse *Mass
[Ger] 3 eq voices&cong,org sc,cor
pts BOHM s.p.   (S116)
[Ger] unis&cong,opt org (without
Credo) BOHM sc s.p., cor pts s.p.
(S117)

SCHMID, WALTER (1906-   )
Ein Loblied
men cor,ST soli,org HUG   (S118)

SCHMIDER
Freu Dich, Erd Und Sternenzelt
SA,kbd LAUDINELLA LR 132 s.p.
contains also: Lobt Gott, Ihr
Christen Allzugleich (SA/unis,
kbd,2treb inst)   (S119)

Lobt Gott, Ihr Christen Allzugleich
see Schmider, Freu Dich, Erd Und
Sternenzelt

SCHMIDER, KARL
  Aller Augen Warten
    see Vier Eucharistische Gesange

  Ich Bin Die Auferstehung Und Das
    Leben *Rembrnc
    cor BOHM s.p.   (S120)

  Ich Will Dich Preisen, Mein Gott
    [Ger] mix cor&cong,2trp,2trom,opt
    org BOHM sc s.p., cor pts s.p.,
    ipa   (S121)

  Lasst Uns Tiefgebeugt Verehren
    see Vier Eucharistische Gesange

  Mein Fleisch Ist Wahrhaft Eine Speise
    see Vier Eucharistische Gesange

  Nun Jauchzet Dem Herren, Alle Welt
    *Fest
    mix cor,acap BOHM s.p.   (S122)

  Sooft Ihr Esset Von Diesem Brot
    see Vier Eucharistische Gesange

  Vier Eucharistische Gesange *Commun
    mix cor cor pts BOHM s.p.
      contains: Aller Augen Warten;
      Lasst Uns Tiefgebeugt Verehren;
      Mein Fleisch Ist Wahrhaft Eine
      Speise; Sooft Ihr Esset Von
      Diesem Brot   (S123)

SCHMIDT, C.
  Freuet Euch In Dem Herrn Allezeit
    see Leutert, Sollt Ich Meinem Gott
    Nicht Singen

  Steh Auf, Herr Gott
    see Leutert, Sollt Ich Meinem Gott
    Nicht Singen

SCHMIDT, CHRISTFRIED (1932-   )
  Psalm 21
    [Ger] mix cor,SBar soli,org,2fl,
    2clar,2trp,2trom,2perc,2vla,2vcl
    cor pts MOECK 5119 s.p.   (S124)

SCHMIDT-MANNHEIM, HANS (1931-   )
  Der Sohn, Der Wieder Heimkehrte
    SS/jr cor&cong,narrator,solo,kbd,2S
    rec,A rec/B rec,timp,
    metallophone, xylophone,
    glockenspiel HANSSLER 12.514 s.p.
                                         (S125)

SCHMUCKE DICH, O LIEBE SEELE see Kolter

SCHMUCKE DICH, O LIEBE SEELE see Peter,
  Johann Friedrich

SCHNABEL
  Let Us Go Now E'en To Bethlehem
    *Adv/Xmas
    (Ralston) SATB,fl,vln oct LILLENAS
    AT-6006 $.35   (S126)

SCHNABEL, J.J.
  Mittlere Stationen Zur
    Fronleichnamsprozession *CCU
    [Lat] 4pt mix cor,brass sc,cor pts
    BOHM s.p., ipa   (S127)

  Transeamus Usque Bethlehem *Xmas
    [Lat] mix cor,org/strings,2fl,
    2clar/2ob,2horn,trom,org sc,cor
    pts BOHM s.p., ipa   (S128)
    [Ger/Lat] 2pt wom cor&opt unis men
    cor,pno sc,cor pts BOHM s.p.
                                         (S129)
    [Ger/Lat] 4pt men cor,B solo,org/
    orch sc,cor pts BOHM s.p.   (S130)
    [Ger/Lat] 3pt men cor,S solo,org/
    orch sc,cor pts BOHM s.p.   (S131)
    [Ger/Lat] mix cor,B solo,org,orch
    sc,cor pts BOHM s.p.   (S132)

SCHNABELS MITTLERE STATIONEN see
  Kindler, Paul

SCHNELLINGER
  Das Andere Feuerbewahren "Wohlauf,
    Wir Wollens Wecken"
    SATBB LAUDINELLA LR 125 s.p. (S133)

SCHOENBERG, ARNOLD (1874-1951)
  Der Erste Psalm "O Du Mein Gott"
    *see Modern Psalm Facsimile

  Die Jakobsleiter *Op.22,No.4, ora
    cor,orch BELMONT rental   (S134)

  Kol Nidre *Op.39
    [Eng] mix cor,narrator,2fl,ob,
    3clar,bsn,2horn,2trp,2trom,tuba,
    strings,perc,timp (diff) sc
    SCHOTTS rental   (S135)

  Modern Psalm Facsimile (Psalm 1)
    Op.50c, Bibl
    cor,narrator,orch bds BELMONT
    $45.00, ipr   (S136)
    "Der Erste Psalm "O Du Mein Gott""
    mix cor,narrator,3fl,3ob,3clar,
    2bsn,2horn,2trp,trom,strings, tam
    tam (diff) sc SCHOTTS rental

SCHOENBERG, ARNOLD (cont'd.)
                                         (S137)
  Psalm 1 *see Der Erste Psalm "O Du
    Mein Gott"

SCHOLA CANTORUM, VOL. I *sac/sec,CCU,
  chorale/mot,15-16th cent
  [Eng/Fr/Ger/Lat/It] BOOSEY $1.75
    contains works by: Agricola; Di
    Lasso; Friedrich; Morley; Fux,
    J.J.; Obrecht, J. and others (S138)

SCHOLA CANTORUM, VOL. II *sac/sec,CCU,
  chorale/mot,15-16th cent
  [Eng/Fr/Ger/Lat/It] BOOSEY $1.75
    contains works by: Agricola; Di
    Lasso; Friedrich; Morley; Fux,
    J.J.; Obrecht, J. and others (S139)

SCHOLA CANTORUM, VOL. III *sac/sec,
  CCU,chorale/mot,15-16th cent
  [Eng/Fr/Ger/Lat/It] BOOSEY $1.75
    contains works by: Agricola; Di
    Lasso; Friedrich; Morley; Fux,
    J.J.; Obrecht, J. and others (S140)

SCHOLA CANTORUM, VOL. IV *sac/sec,CCU,
  chorale/mot,15-16th cent
  [Eng/Fr/Ger/Lat/It] BOOSEY $1.75
    contains works by: Agricola; Di
    Lasso; Friedrich; Morley; Fux,
    J.J.; Obrecht, J. and others (S141)

SCHOLFIELD
  Saved, Saved! *anthem/gospel
    (Carmichael, Ralph) SATB oct
    SINGSPIR ZJP-8028 $.30   (S142)

SCHOLIN, C. ALBERT (1896-1958)
  Aeolian Collection Of Anthems, Book
    IV *CC8U,Fest/Gen
    jr cor&sr cor FITZSIMONS $.85
                                        (S143)

SCHOLTERS
  They'll Know We Are Christians By Our
    Love
    (Bock) cor BRIDGE Z 0133   (S144)

SCHOLTES, P.
  They'll Know We Are Christians *folk
    (Ades) SATB SHAWNEE A1301 $.45
                                        (S145)
    (Krogstad, B.) SATB oct SINGSPIR
    ZJP-5057 $.30   (S146)

SCHONBERG, STIG GUSTAV
  A Bereden Vag For Herran
    4pt mix cor ERIKS 192A s.p. (S147)

  Denne Ar Min Enfodde Son *Bibl
    4pt mix cor ERIKS 96 s.p. see also
    FYRA MOTETTER FOR ROSTER OCH
    ORGEL   (S148)

  Om I Icke Omvanden Eder *Bibl
    4pt mix cor ERIKS 94 s.p. see also
    FYRA MOTETTER FOR ROSTER OCH
    ORGEL   (S149)

  Ty Var Tva Eller Tre Aro Forsamlade
    *Bibl
    4pt mix cor ERIKS 93 s.p. see also
    FYRA MOTETTER FOR ROSTER OCH
    ORGEL   (S150)

  Vart Rike Som Har Kommit I Strid
    *Bibl
    4pt mix cor ERIKS 93 s.p. see also
    FYRA MOTETTER FOR ROSTER OCH
    ORGEL   (S151)

SCHONSTES KINDLEIN see Schroeder,
  Hermann

SCHOP
  Herr, Du Wollst Gnad Und Segen
    men cor,acap TONOS 5607 s.p. (S152)

SCHOPFUNGSMESSE see Haydn, (Franz)
  Joseph

SCHOTT, JOHANN GEORG (ca. 1600?)
  Singet Dem Herrn Ein Neues Lied, Denn
    Er Tut Grosse Wunder
    SATB (contains also: Siehe, Dein
    Konig Kommt) SCHWEIZER.
    SK 58.01-2 s.p. see also
    MUSIKBEILAGE ZUM "EVANGELISCHEN
    KIRCHENCHOR 1958"   (S153)

SCHOTT'S CHORBUCH BAND II *sac/sec,
  CC27L
  (Lang, Hans) 4pt men cor SCHOTTS
    ED. 4052 s.p. contains works by:
    Isaac; Caldara; Praetorius; Knab;
    Schutz and others   (S154)

SCHRAMM
  Canticle *anthem
    SATB,opt inst (aleatory) oct MCAFEE
    M105 $.40   (S155)

SCHRODER, LAURENTIO
  Freut Euch, Ihr Lieben Christen
    (Koenig, F.) men cor,acap TONOS
    5643 s.p.   (S156)

SCHROEDER
  Exsultet *CC67U,mot
    [Lat] SATB,acap PETERS WM37 $12.50
                                       (S157)

SCHROEDER, HERMANN (1904-   )
  Aeterne Rex Altissime
    see Hymni Ad Processionem In Festo
    Corporis Christi

  Als Ich Bei Meinen Schafen Wacht
    *Xmas
    2pt jr cor&4pt men cor,acap sc
    SCHOTTS C 42 417 s.p. see from
    Funf Weihnachtslieder   (S158)

  Ave Maria, Gratia Plena
    wom cor/jr cor (med easy) sc
    SCHOTTS CHBL 542 s.p.   (S159)

  Das Heil Der Welt
    see Drei Weihnachtslieder

  Deutsches Te Deum
    SATB,org sc CHRIS 50735 s.p., cor
    pts CHRIS 50737 s.p.   (S160)

  Die Weihnachtsgeschichte *Xmas
    2pt jr cor,solo,opt 2inst (easy)
    sc,cor pts SCHOTTS B 132 s.p.,
    ipa   (S161)

  Drei Weihnachtslieder *Xmas
    mix cor (easy) sc SCHOTTS C 35 732
    s.p.
      contains: Das Heil Der Welt;
      Schonstes Kindlein; Susani "Vom
      Himmel Hoch"   (S162)

  Engel Haben Himmelslieder *Xmas
    2pt jr cor&4pt men cor,acap sc
    SCHOTTS C 42 415 s.p. see from
    Funf Weihnachtslieder   (S163)

  Es Wird Schon Gleich Dunkel
    see Sechs Weihnachtslieder

  Freu Dich, Erd Und Sternenzelt *Xmas
    2pt jr cor&4pt men cor,acap sc
    SCHOTTS C 42 416 s.p. see from
    Funf Weihnachtslieder   (S164)

  Funf Weihnachtslieder *see Als Ich
    Bei Meinen Schafen Wacht; Engel
    Haben Himmelslieder; Freu Dich,
    Erd Und Sternenzelt; Vom Himmel
    Hoch, O Engel Kommt; Zu Bethlehem
    Geboren   (S165)

  Hymni Ad Processionem In Festo
    Corporis Christi
    2pt wom cor,org/2trp,3trom,2horn,
    tuba, 2 tenor horns (med easy)
    voc sc,voc pt SCHOTTS
    C 34 057, C 34 058-01;02 s.p.
      contains: Aeterne Rex Altissime;
      Pange Lingua; Sacris Solemniis,
      Salutis Humanae Sator; Verbum
      Supernum   (S166)

  Kindelein Zart
    see Sechs Weihnachtslieder

  Komm, Nachtigall Mein!
    see Sechs Weihnachtslieder

  Lieb Nachtigall, Wach Auf
    see Sechs Weihnachtslieder

  Maria Durch Ein Dornwald Ging *Adv
    [Ger] 4pt mix cor,acap MERSEBURG
    SM77 contains also: Ruf Im Advent
                                       (S167)

  O Schlafe Lieblicher Jesu
    see Sechs Weihnachtslieder

  Pange Lingua
    see Hymni Ad Processionem In Festo
    Corporis Christi

  Ruf Im Advent
    see Schroeder, Hermann, Maria Durch
    Ein Dornwald Ging

  Sacris Solemniis
    see Hymni Ad Processionem In Festo
    Corporis Christi

  Salutis Humanae Sator
    see Hymni Ad Processionem In Festo
    Corporis Christi

  Schonstes Kindlein
    see Drei Weihnachtslieder

  Sechs Weihnachtslieder *Xmas
    2pt jr cor/2pt wom cor,pno/org (med
    easy) sc,cor pts SCHOTTS ED. 3887
    s.p.
      contains: Es Wird Schon Gleich
      Dunkel; Kindelein Zart; Komm,
      Nachtigall Mein!; Lieb

SCHROEDER, HERMANN (cont'd.)

Nachtigall, Wach Auf; O Schlafe
Lieblicher Jesu; Susani (S168)

Susani
see Sechs Weihnachtslieder

Susani "Vom Himmel Hoch"
see Drei Weihnachtslieder

Tantum Ergo *Op.14
unis/unis jr cor/unis wom cor,org
(easy) voc sc SCHOTTS C 33 437
s.p., voc pt SCHOTTS C 33 438
s.p. (S169)

Trierer Dom-Messe *Mass
SATB,org,opt 2trp&2trom&2horn&tuba
CHRIS 50730-34 s.p. (S170)

Uns Kommt Ein Schiff Gefahren
*CC20L,Xmas
jr cor,rec/pno&vln/rec&vln&vcl sc
SCHOTTS B 145 s.p., ipa (S171)

Verbum Supernum
see Hymni Ad Processionem In Festo
Corporis Christi

Vom Himmel Hoch, O Engel Kommt *Xmas
2pt jr cor&4pt men cor,acap sc
SCHOTTS C 42 418 s.p. see from
Funf Weihnachtslieder (S172)

Zu Bethlehem Geboren *Xmas
2pt jr cor&4pt men cor,acap sc
SCHOTTS C 42 419 s.p. see from
Funf Weihnachtslieder (S173)

SCHROETER
Vier Weihnachtsliedlein *CC4U,Xmas
4-8pt mix cor LIENAU
MUSICA SACRA, NR.11 sc s.p., cor
pts s.p. (S174)

SCHROTER, LEONHARD (ca. 1540-1600)
Allein Gott In Der Hoh Sei Ehr
SATB (contains also: Aus Tiefer Not
Schrei Ich Zu Dir; Nun Jauchzet,
All Ihr Frommen) SCHWEIZER.
SK 53.01-2 s.p. see also
MUSIKBEILAGE ZUM "EVANGELISCHEN
KIRCHENCHOR 1953" (S175)
men cor,acap TONOS 5604 s.p. (S176)

Freut Euch, Ihr Lieben Christen
*Xmas
mix cor (easy) sc SCHOTTS CHBL 329
s.p. (S177)
SATB SCHWEIZER. SK 108 s.p. (S178)

Hort Zu Und Seid Getrost Nun
SATB SCHWEIZER. SK 140 s.p. (S179)

SCHROTH, G.
Al La Ru
SATB,org FISCHER,J FEC 10121 $.35
(S180)

Behold The Lord Shall Come *Adv/Gen
SATB,org FISCHER,J FEC 10122 $.35
(S181)

Eyes Of All, The
SATB,org FISCHER,J FEC 10111 $.35
(S182)

SCHROTH, GERHARD
God Of Abraham Praise, The
SATB WINGERT s.p. (S183)

Sun Has Gone Down, The
SATB WINGERT s.p. (S184)

SCHUBERT
Vrede Zij Ulieden *Psntd
mix cor/unis,pno/harmonium HEER 205
s.p. (S185)

SCHUBERT, FERDINAND (1794-1859)
Regina Coeli Laetare *Easter
[Lat] cor,soli,org/strings,2ob/
2clar,2trp,timp sc,cor pts BOHM
s.p., ipa (S186)

SCHUBERT, FRANZ (PETER) (1797-1828)
Ave Maria
(Brown) mix cor CRAMER $.50 (S187)

Benedictus Es, Domine *Op.150, Fest,
Gradual
"Preiset Gott, Den Herrn" mix cor,
org,orch sc,cor pts BOHM s.p.,
ipa (S188)

Calm And Lovely (composed with
Caldwell, Mary [Elizabeth])
cor,org (easy) FISCHER,C CM 7873
$.35 (S189)

Christ Ist Erstanden
SATB EGTVED KB198 s.p. (S190)

Christmas Lullaby, A
(Goldman) SSA SCHIRM.G LG 51804
$.40 (S191)

SCHUBERT, FRANZ (PETER) (cont'd.)

Complete Works *sac/sec,CCU
(Brahms, Johannes; Bruell, Ignaz;
Door, Anton; Epstein, Julius;
Fuchs, J.N.; Gaensbacher, J.;
Hellmesberger, J.; Mandyczewski,
Eusebius) microfiche UNION ESP.
$185.00 21 series in 33 bindings,
Leipzig, 1884-1897. (S192)

Das Grosse Hallelujah "Ehre Sei Dem
Hocherhab'nen"
3pt wom cor,pno (med easy) sc
SCHOTTS C 41 870 s.p., cor pts
SCHOTTS C 41 871 s.p. (S193)

Deutsche Messe *Mass
men cor,acap TONOS 4363 s.p. (S194)
(Haas, Joseph) 1-2pt jr cor/1-2pt
wom cor,org,orch (easy) voc sc,
cor pts SCHOTTS ED. 3883 s.p.,
ipa (S195)

Deutsche Messe "Wohin Soll Ich Mich
Wenden" *Mass
[Ger] mix cor,acap BOHM sc s.p.,
cor pts s.p. (S196)

Drei Tantum Ergo *Op.45,No.1-3
[Lat] 4pt mix cor,org,2fl,2clar,
2ob,2bsn,2horn,2trp,2trom,
strings,timp sc,cor pts BOHM
s.p., ipa (S197)

Du Gabst, O Herr (from Deutsche
Messe) Xmas
men cor,acap TONOS 4386 s.p. (S198)

Ehre Sie Gott In Der Hohe (from
Deutsche Messe)
men cor,acap TONOS 4375 s.p. (S199)

Gott Der Weltschopfer
mix cor,pno cor pts BREITKOPF-W
CHB 5101 s.p. (S200)
SATB,pno EGTVED KB126 s.p. (S201)

Gott Im Ungewitter
mix cor,pno cor pts BREITKOPF-W
CHB 5100 s.p. (S202)

Gott Ist Mein Hirt (Psalm 23) Op.132,
Bibl
men cor,pno sc,cor pts TONOS 4253
s.p. (S203)
(Gotze-Kohler) 4pt men cor,pno sc
SCHOTTS C 39 512 s.p., voc pt
SCHOTTS C 39 513-01-04 (S204)

Heilig, Helig *Sanctus
men cor,acap TONOS 4374 s.p. (S205)

Holy Is The Lord *anthem
(Gregory) SATB (easy) oct BROADMAN
4535-04 $.30 (S206)

Hymne
8pt men cor,soli,brass cor pts
BREITKOPF-W CHB 3589 s.p., ipr
(S207)

Hymne An Den Unendlichen
mix cor,pno cor pts BREITKOPF-W
CHB 5102 s.p. (S208)

Kyrie
(Chandler, H.) [Lat] SATB,pno oct
NATIONAL WHC-35 $.35 (S209)

Mein Heiland, Herr (from Deutsche
Messe)
men cor,acap TONOS 4387 s.p. (S210)

Messe In B *Op.141, Mass
[Lat] cor,soli,org,2ob,2bsn,2trp,
strings,timp (B flat maj) sc,cor
pts BOHM s.p., ipa (S211)

Messe In G-Dur *Mass
[Lat] 4pt mix cor,org/strings&org&
opt 2trp&timp,cor pts BOHM
s.p., ipa (S212)
3pt wom cor,org,2vln,vla,bvl,opt
2trp,timp (G maj) BOHM sc s.p.,
cor pts s.p., ipa (S213)

Messe No. 5 In As-Dur *Mass
SSAATTBB,SATB soli,orch (A flat
maj,med diff) min sc SCHOTTS
ETP 974 s.p. (S214)

Messe No. 6 In Es-Dur *Mass
SATB,SATB soli,orch (E flat maj,med
diff) min sc SCHOTTS ETP 970 s.p.
(S215)

Preiset Gott, Den Herrn *see
Benedictus Es, Domine

Psalm 23 *see Gott Ist Mein Hirt

Salve Regina *BVM
[Lat] 4pt mix cor,acap BOHM s.p.
(S216)
men cor,pno sc,cor pts TONOS 4261
s.p. (S217)

SCHUBERT, FRANZ (PETER) (cont'd.)

Sanctus "Heilig Ist Der Herr" (from
Deutschen Messe)
(Herbeck, Johann) men cor sc
SCHOTTS CHBL 27 s.p. (S218)

Selig Durch Die Liebe
men cor,acap TONOS 4379 s.p. (S219)

Stabat Mater
[Lat/Ger] 4pt mix cor,org,opt
strings sc,cor pts BOHM s.p., ipa
(S220)

Tov L'Hodos
mix cor oct SAC.MUS.PR. 307 $.65
(S221)

With Thee Is Peace
(Mansfield) SSA CRAMER $.25 (S222)
(Mansfield) SA CRAMER $.25 (S223)

Wohin Soll Ich Mich Wenden? (from
Deutschen Messe)
(Klink, Waldemar) men cor sc
SCHOTTS CHBL 26 s.p. (S224)

Zum Sanctus
(Kaplan) SATB SCHIRM.G LG 51850
$.40 (S225)

SCHULER, GEORGE S.
Make Me A Blessing *anthem
(Reynolds, William Jensen) mix cor
CENTURY PR $.20 (S226)

Oh, What A Day *anthem
(Boersma, James) SATB WORD CS-2324
$.35 (S227)

SCHULTZ
Heilige Nacht *Op.243,No.1
mix cor LIENAU sc s.p., cor pts
s.p. (S228)

Weihnachtslied *Op.243,No.2, Xmas
mix cor LIENAU sc s.p., cor pts
s.p. (S229)

SCHULZ
Fair Moon Hath Ascended, The
(composed with Pizarro)
mix cor BRODT 585 $.20 (S230)

SCHULZ, H.
Erhore Mich
(Ehret) "Hear Me, O Lord" mix cor
BRODT 565 $.26 (S231)

Hear Me, O Lord *see Erhore Mich

O Lieber Herre Gott, Wecke Uns Auf
(Ehret) "O Thou Beloved God" mix
cor BRODT 566 $.28 (S232)

O Thou Beloved God *see O Lieber
Herre Gott, Wecke Uns Auf

SCHULZ, JOH. ABRAHAM PETER (1747-1800)
Thou Child Divine
(McCorkle) mix cor BRODT 1000 $.35
(S233)
(Pfohl) mix cor BRODT 206 $.32
(S234)

SCHUMANN
Cloister Hymn *see Requiem Aeternam

Requiem Aeternam
(Boyd) "Cloister Hymn" SATB
SCHIRM.G LG 51651 $.30 (S235)

SCHUMANN, ROBERT (ALEXANDER)
(1810-1856)
Complete Works *sac/sec,CCU
(Schumann, Clara; Brahms, Johannes)
microfiche UNION ESP. published
in 14 series, Leipzig, 1879-1893
(S236)

I Did Wait In Patience For Thee
(Prussing, Stephen H.) SATB,acap
(easy) GENTRY G-4015 $.30 (S237)

O Salutaris Hostia
[Lat] cor,SBar soli,org/strings&fl&
ob&clar&bsn&horn sc,cor pts BOHM
s.p., ipa (S238)

SCHURMAN, RALPH
Tidings O'er The Hilltops *Xmas,cant
(Huff, Ronn) SATB&2pt&unis BENSON
B0790 $.50 (S239)

SCHUTKY, F.J.
Benedicta Et Venerabilis Es *Op.6,
Gradual
[Lat] SSATTBB,acap sc,cor pts BOHM
s.p. (S240)

Emitte Spiritum Tuum *Op.8, Pent/
Whitsun,Gradual
[Lat] SSATTBB,acap sc,cor pts BOHM
s.p. (S241)

SCHUTZ, HEINRICH (1585-1672)
Ach Herr, Straf Mich Nicht In Deinem
Zorn (Psalm 6) SWV 24
SATB&SATB,cont,opt 8inst sc
HANSSLER 20.024 s.p.   (S242)

Ah, Lord, Who Hast Created All *Adv/
Xmas
(Sateren) SATBB,acap ART MAST 202
$.40   (S243)

Allas Ogon Vanta Pa Dig, Herre (Psalm
145)
4pt mix cor ERIKS 49 s.p.   (S244)

Also Hat Gott Die Welt Geliebt
SATTB EGTVED MK13, 13 s.p.   (S245)

Auf Dich, Herr, Trau Ich Allezeit
(Psalm 71)
SATB,cont (contains also: Ich Will
Sehr Hoch Erhohen Dich)
SCHWEIZER. SK 63.08 s.p. see also
MUSIKBEILAGE ZUM "EVANGELISCHEN
KIRCHENCHOR 1963"   (S246)

Ausgewahlte Geistliche Chorsatze
*CCU
4-8pt,acap/cont (med easy) BAREN.
BA6222   (S247)

Birth Of Our Lord And Saviour, Jesus
Christ (from Christmas Story,
The) Xmas
(Mendel) SATB SCHIRM.G 12019 $.45
                              (S248)

Blessed Is He Who Walks Not In The
Paths Of Godlessness
(Agey) SA BRODT WC 1 $.32   (S249)

Canticum B. Simeonis "Herr, Nun
Lassest Du Deinen Diener"
see Musikalische Exequien

Christ Ist Erstanden *SWV 70, cant
SATB&SATB,SAT soli,4trom,cont, 4
violas da gamba (med) sc,cor pts
BAREN. BA5917 s.p., ipa   (S250)

Collected Works *sac/sec,CCU
(Spitta, Philipp; Schering, Arnold;
Spitta, Heinrich) [Ger/Lat/It]
microfiche UNION ESP $90.00
originally published as 18
volumes, Leipzig, Breitkopf and
Haertel, 1885-1927.   (S251)

Das Blut Jesu Christi Machet Uns Rein
*SWV 298
SAT/SAB,cont (contains works: O
Lamm Gottes, Unschuldig)
SCHWEIZER. SK 64.03-4 s.p. see
also MUSIKBEILAGE ZUM
"EVANGELISCHEN KIRCHENCHOR 1964"
                              (S252)
SSB,cont sc HANSSLER 20.298 s.p.
                              (S253)

Den Ende Sanna Gladje, Som Jag Vet
*see Jauchzet Gott Alle Lande
Sehr

Der Herr Ist Konig Uberall *Fest
mix cor,acap BOHM s.p.   (S254)

Der Herr Ist Mein Hirt (Psalm 23) SWV
33
SATB&SATB&opt SATB,cont,opt 4-8inst
HANSSLER 20.033 s.p.   (S255)

Deus Misereatur Nostri
(Klein) "God Be Merciful Unto Us"
SATB SCHIRM.G 11969 $.30   (S256)

Die Auferstehungs-Historie *SWV 50
SSATTB/SATB&SATB,ATTTB soli,cont,
12inst sc,cor pts HANSSLER 20.050
s.p., ipa   (S257)

Die Furcht Des Herren Ist Der
Weisheit Anfang *SWV 318
TT/SS,cont sc HANSSLER 20.318 s.p.
                              (S258)

Die Gottseligkeit Ist Zu Allen Dingen
Nutze *SWV 299
SSB,cont sc HANSSLER 20.299 s.p.
                              (S259)

Die Mit Tranen Saen (Psalm 126) SWV
42, mot
SATBB&SATBB,inst,cont (med) sc,cor
pts BAREN. BA5918 s.p., ipa   (S260)

Die Sieben Worte Jesu Christi *SWV
478, Psntd
(Stein, Fritz) SATTB,SATTB soli,
org,2vln,2vla (med) min sc
SCHOTTS ETP 977 s.p., voc sc
SCHOTTS PC 17 s.p., ipa   (S261)

Drei Biblische Szenen *Bibl
(Hqnlein, A.) voc sc,voc pt
BREITKOPF-W EB-1634, CHB-438A-C
s.p.
contains: Es Gingen Zween
Menschen (4pt mix cor,TB soli,
org/pno); Mein Sohn, Warum Hast
Du Uns Das Getan? (4pt mix cor,

SCHUTZ, HEINRICH (cont'd.)
SAB soli,cont,2vln); Weib, Was
Weinest Du? (4pt mix cor,org/
pno)   (S262)

Ehre Sei Dem Vater
SATB,cont (contains also: Freut
Euch, Ihr Lieben Christen All)
SCHWEIZER. SK 72.01-2 s.p. see
also MUSIKBEILAGE ZUM
"EVANGELISCHEN KIRCHENCHOR 1972"
                              (S263)

Ein Feste Burg Ist Unser Gott
see MUSIKBEILAGE ZUM "EVANGELISCHEN
KIRCHENCHOR 1959"

Es Gingen Zween Menschen
see Drei Biblische Szenen

Es Ist Ein Freud Dem Herzen Mein
SATB,cont (contains also: Nun
Schlagt Die Stunde Mitternacht;
Aus Meines Herzens Grunde)
SCHWEIZER. SK 64.01-2 s.p. see
also MUSIKBEILAGE ZUM
"EVANGELISCHEN KIRCHENCHOR 1964"
                              (S264)

Exsultet *CC67U,Gen,mot
3-5pt mix cor,opt org MULLER
SM 1890 s.p.   (S265)

Five Psalms Of Praise And The
Responsorium From The "Becker
Psalter" *CC5U,Psalm
(Reuning, Daniel G.) [Eng/Ger] SATB
GIA G1790 $.60   (S266)

For God So Loved The World *anthem
SATTB oct CHANTRY CLA 6713 $.25
                              (S267)

Four Psalms *CC4U,anthem
SATB oct CHANTRY CLA 598 $.25
                              (S268)

God Be Merciful Unto Us *see Deus
Misereatur Nostri

Great Is The Lord *anthem
2pt,pno/org oct MCAFEE M157 $.35
                              (S269)

Hear Me, O Lord *anthem
2pt,pno/org oct MCAFEE M159 $.35
                              (S270)

Heavens Are Telling, The *anthem
SSATTB&SSA oct CHANTRY CLA 7216
                              (S271)

Herr, Wenn Ich Nur Dich Habe
see Musikalische Exequien

Herr, Wie Lang Wilt Du Mein So Gar
Vergessen? *SWV 416
SSATTB&opt ATT/ATTB,cont,2-6inst sc
HANSSLER 20.416 s.p., ipa   (S272)

Heute Ist Christus Der Herr Geboren
*Xmas,concerto
SSAB,cont sc,voc sc EGTVED MK13, 12
s.p.   (S273)
(Klein) "Jesus Our Lord On This Day
Was Born" SATB SCHIRM.G 11970
$.40   (3274)

Historia Der Auferstehung Jesu
Christi *ora
(Stein, Fritz) SSATTB/SATB&SATB,
soli,cont,org,3vla (med) min sc
SCHOTTS ETP 980 s.p.   (S275)

Hodie Christus Natus Est *Xmas
(Klein) "On This Day, Christ The
Lord Was Born" SATB SCHIRM.G
11972 $.45   (S276)

Hutet Euch, Dass Eure Herzen Nicht
Beschweret Werden *SWV 413
SSATTB,cont,2inst sc HANSSLER
20.413 s.p., ipa   (S277)

Ich Bin Die Auferstehung Und Das
Leben
TTB/SSB,cont sc HANSSLER 20.324
s.p.   (S278)

Ich Freue Mich, Dass Man Mir Sagt
(Psalm 122) SWV 26
SATB,acap BAREN. BA6321 contains
also: Ich Will Allzeit Erheben
Dich (Psalm 145) SWV 250   (S279)

Ich Hebe Meine Augen Auf Zu Den
Bergen (Psalm 121) SWV 399
ATB&opt SATB,cont,opt 6inst sc
HANSSLER 20.399 s.p.   (S280)

Ich Ruf Zu Dir, Herr Jesu Christ
*SWV 326
SSST/SSSB,cont sc HANSSLER 20.326
s.p.   (S281)

Ich Will Allzeit Erheben Dich (Psalm
145) SWV 250
see Schutz, Heinrich, Ich Freue
Mich, Dass Man Mir Sagt

SCHUTZ, HEINRICH (cont'd.)
Ich Will Mein Ganzes Leben
SATB (contains also: Christ, Der
Ist Erstanden) SCHWEIZER.
SK 56.02-3 s.p. see also
MUSIKBEILAGE ZUM "EVANGELISCHEN
KIRCHENCHOR 1956"   (S282)

Ich Will Sehr Hoch Erhohen Dich
(Psalm 145)
SATB,cont (contains also: Auf Dich,
Herr, Trau Ich Allezeit)
SCHWEIZER. SK 63.08 s.p. see also
MUSIKBEILAGE ZUM "EVANGELISCHEN
KIRCHENCHOR 1963"   (S283)

Ich Will Von Herzen Danken Gott
(Psalm 111)
SATB,cont SCHWEIZER. SK 72.03 s.p.
see also MUSIKBEILAGE ZUM
"EVANGELISCHEN KIRCHENCHOR 1972"
                              (S284)

In Te, Domine, Speravi
(Klein) "Lord, In Thee Do I Put My
Trust" SATB SCHIRM.G 11971 $.35
                              (S285)

Is God For Us *SWV 329, anthem
[Eng/Ger] SATB oct CHANTRY CLA 492
$.35   (S286)

Ist Gott Fur Uns, Wer Mag Wider Uns
Sein? *SWV 329
SATB,cont sc HANSSLER 20.329 s.p.
                              (S287)

Ist Nicht Ephraim?
(Steinitz) SATB,inst (med diff) voc
sc OXFORD 46.170 $4.15, ipr, cor
pts OXFORD 46.171 $.75   (S288)

Jauchzet Dem Herren, Alle Welt (Psalm
100) SWV 47
SSATB&ST&SSATB,cont,opt 8inst sc
HANSSLER 20.047 s.p.   (S289)
SATB&SATB SCHWEIZER. SK 145 s.p.
                              (S290)

Jauchzet Gott Alle Lande Sehr
"Den Ende Sanna Gladje, Som Jag
Vet" 4pt mix cor ERIKS 343 s.p.
                              (S291)

Jesu Dulcissime
6pt (med) BAREN. BA6228   (S292)

Jesus Our Lord On This Day Was Born
*see Heute Ist Christus Der Herr
Geboren

Joseph, Du Sohn David, Furchte Dich
Nicht
SST/SSB,cont sc HANSSLER 20.323
s.p.   (S293)

Konzert In Form Einer Teutschen
Begrabnis
see Musikalische Exequien

Lobe Den Herren, Meine Seele *SWV
39, anthem
"Praise To The Lord God" 2pt,pno/
org oct MCAFEE M155 $.35   (S294)
(Ehret, Walter) "Praise Ye The
Lord, My Soul" [Eng/Ger] 2pt mix
cor,T solo,org/pno,opt brass
PRESSER 312-41056 $1.25, ipa
                              (S295)

Lobt Gott Mit Schall
SATB (contains also: Nun Freut
Euch, Lieben Christen Gmein)
SCHWEIZER. SK 57.01-2 s.p. see
also MUSIKBEILAGE ZUM
"EVANGELISCHEN KIRCHENCHOR 1957"
                              (S296)
SATB EGTVED MK13, 4 s.p.   (S297)

Lord, Create In Me A Clean Heart
*anthem
2pt,pno/org oct MCAFEE M158 $.35
                              (S298)

Lord, Grant Us Peace *see Verleih
Uns Frieden Genadiglich

Lord, In Thee Do I Put My Trust *see
In Te, Domine, Speravi

Lord, My Hope Is In Thee *anthem
2pt,pno/org oct MCAFEE M160 $.35
                              (S299)

Lord's Prayer, The *anthem
SATB oct CHANTRY CLA 504 $.15
                              (S300)

Magnificat, The *anthem
SATB oct CHANTRY CLA 6611 $.40
                              (S301)

Matthauspassion *SWV 479
SATTB/SSATTTB&SATB,TB soli cor pts
HANSSLER 20.479 s.p.   (S302)

Mein Sohn, Warum Hast Du Uns Das
Getan? *SWV 401
see Drei Biblische Szenen
SATB,SSB soli,cont,opt 6inst sc
HANSSLER 20.401 s.p.   (S303)

Musikalische Exequien *mot/Req
(Schumann, G.) dbl cor,soli,org voc
sc,sc,voc pt BREITKOPF-L

SCHUTZ, HEINRICH (cont'd.)

EB-4181, EB-2731, CHB-2578 s.p.
contains: Canticum B. Simeonis
"Herr, Nun Lassest Du Deinen
Diener"; Herr, Wenn Ich Nur
Dich Habe; Konzert In Form
Einer Teutschen Begrabnis
(S304)

Musikalische Exequien *SWV 279-281,
CC3U,ECY
(Schoneich, Friedrich) [Ger] 6-8pt
mix cor,cont (med diff) BAREN.
BA 250 sc $7.75, cor pts $5.60,
ipa   (S305)

Now Behold To Thee I Cry, O Lord
*see Quoniam Ad Te Clamabo,
Domine

Nun Komm, Der Heiden Heiland *SWV
301
SSBB,cont sc HANSSLER 20.301 s.p.
(S306)

O Help, Jesus, Son Of God *anthem
SATB oct CHANTRY CLA 575 $.20
(S307)

O Jesu Suss, Wer Dein Gedenkt *SWV
406
SSTT,cont,2inst sc HANSSLER 20.406
s.p., ipa   (S308)

O Jesus, Thou Son Of God *anthem
2pt,pno/org oct MCAFEE M156 $.35
(S309)

O Lieber Herre Gott, Wecke Uns Auf
*SWV 287
SS/TT,cont sc HANSSLER 20.287 s.p.
(S310)

O Susser Jesu Christ, Wer An Dich
Recht Gedenket *SWV 405
SSAT&opt SATB,cont,opt 6inst sc
HANSSLER 20.405 s.p., ipa (S311)

On This Day, Christ The Lord Was Born
*see Hodie Christus Natus Est

One Thing I Ask Of The Lord *anthem
2pt,pno/org oct MCAFEE M154 $.35
(S312)

Passion According To Saint John, The
*SWV 481
SATB,T solo,acap CHANTRY PAS 621
$1.25   (S313)

Praise To The Lord God *see Lobe Den
Herren, Meine Seele

Praise Ye The Lord *anthem
2pt,pno/org oct MCAFEE M153 $.35
(S314)

Praise The Lord, My Soul *see
Lobe Den Herren, Meine Seele

Psalm 1 *see Wohl Dem, Der Nicht
Wandelt Im Rat Der Gottlosen

Psalm 6 *see Ach Herr, Straf Mich
Nicht In Deinem Zorn

Psalm 23 *see Der Herr Ist Mein Hirt

Psalm 71 *see Auf Dich, Herr, Trau
Ich Allezeit

Psalm 98 *see Singet Dem Herrn Ein
Neues Lied

Psalm 100 *see Jauchzet Dem Herren,
Alle Welt

Psalm 111 *see Ich Will Von Herzen
Danken Gott

Psalm 121 *see Ich Hebe Meine Augen
Auf Zu Den Bergen

Psalm 122 *see Ich Freue Mich, Dass
Man Mir Sagt

Psalm 126 *see Die Mit Tranen Saen

Psalm 127 *see Wo Der Herr Nicht Das
Haus Bauet

Psalm 128 *see Wohl Dem, Der Den
Herren Furchtet

Psalm 145 *see Ich Will Allzeit
Erheben Dich

Psalm 150
SATB&SATB,cont,4trp,3trom,horn
KING,R MFB 601 cor pts $1.00,
cmplt ed $5.00   (S315)

Quoniam Ad Te Clamabo, Domine
(Klein) "Now Behold To Thee I Cry,
O Lord" SATB SCHIRM.G 11967 $.30
(S316)

Response To The Psalms *anthem
SATB oct CHANTRY CLA 6310 $.10
(S317)

St. Matthew Passion *SWV 479
mix cor,soli voc sc NORSK NMO 8752
s.p.   (S318)

SCHUTZ, HEINRICH (cont'd.)

Selig Sind Die Toten *mot
SSATTB,acap (med) sc SCHOTTS
C 32 829-33 s.p., voc pt SCHOTTS
C 32 833A-F s.p.   (S319)

Seven Penitential Psalms From The
"Becker Psalter" *CC7U,Psalm
(Reuning, Daniel G.) [Eng/Ger] SATB
GIA G1912 $.75   (S320)

Siehe, Dieser Wird Gesetzt Zu Einem
Fall *SWV 410
SSATB,cont,2inst sc HANSSLER 20.410
s.p.   (S321)

Siehe, Mein Fursprecher Ist Im Himmel
*SWV 304
SATB,cont sc HANSSLER 20.304 s.p.
(S322)

Singet Dem Herrn Ein Neues Lied
(Psalm 98) SWV 35
men cor,acap TONOS 5601 s.p. (S323)
SATB&SATB,cont,opt 8inst sc,cor pts
HANSSLER 20.035 s.p., ipa (S324)

Singet Mit Frueden Unserm Gott *SWV
178
see Bach, Johann Sebastian, Dir,
Jesu, Gottes Sohn, Sei Preis

Thrice Holy Lord *anthem
(Hardwicke) SATB oct SACRED S-155
$.35   (S325)

Thy Love Brings Joy *anthem
(Coggin, Elwood) SATB AUGSBURG
11-1694 $.35   (S326)

Vater Unser, Der Du Bist Im Himmel
*SWV 411
SSTTB/SATTB&opt SATB,cont,opt 6inst
sc HANSSLER 20.411 s.p., ipa
(S327)

Verleih Uns Frieden Genadiglich
(Klein) "Lord, Grant Us Peace" 5pt
mix cor SCHIRM.G 12003 $.35
(S328)

Vine Most Surely I Am, The *anthem
SSATTB oct CHANTRY CLA 6714 $.35
(S329)

Was Betrubst Du Dich, Meine Seele?
*SWV 335
SSATB,cont sc HANSSLER 20.335 s.p.
(S330)

Was Mein Gott Will, Das G'scheh'
Allzeit
2pt,inst s.p. sc NORSK NMO 8753 A,
cor pts NORSK NMO 8753 B (S331)

We Thank Thee, Lord *see Wir Danken,
Herr Gott

Weib, Was Weinest Du?
see Drei Biblische Szenen

Who Shall Separate Us *anthem
[Eng/Ger] SATB oct CHANTRY CLA 491
$.35   (S332)

Wir Danken, Herr Gott
(Biester) "We Thank Thee, Lord"
SATB SCHIRM.G LG51780 $.35 (S333)

Wo Der Herr Nicht Das Haus Bauet
(Psalm 127) SWV 400
SSB&opt SATB,cont,opt 6inst sc
HANSSLER 20.400 s.p.   (S334)

Wohl Dem, Der Den Herren Furchtet
(Psalm 128) SWV 30
SSAT&ATBB,cont,opt 8inst sc
HANSSLER 20.030 s.p.   (S335)

Wohl Dem, Der Nicht Wandelt Im Rat
Der Gottlosen (Psalm 1) SWV 28
SSAT&ATTB/SSAT&ATBB,cont,opt 8inst
sc HANSSLER 20.028 s.p.   (S336)

Wohl Denen, Die Da Wandeln
men cor,acap TONOS 5621 s.p. (S337)

SCHUTZENGEL-MESSE see Lipp, Alban

SCHVEDOV, CONSTANTINE (1889-   )
Sanctus
(Lovelace) mix cor BRODT 567 $.20
(S338)

We Sing To Thee *Gen
(Ehret, Walter) SATB,acap (med)
DITSON 332-40121 $.30   (S339)

SCHWAB
From Discord To Song *gospel
(Nelson) SATB oct LILLENAS AN-5076
$.30   (S340)

SCHWARZ-SCHILLING, REINHARD (1904-   )
Der Herr, Der Ewige Gott
see Schwarz-Schilling, Reinhard,
Vater Unser

Exaudi, Domine, Vocem Meam *CC4U,
mot/Psalm
SATB,acap (med) BAREN. BA5427

SCHWARZ-SCHILLING, REINHARD (cont'd.)
(S341)

O Sacrum Convivium *mot
[Lat] 4pt mix cor,acap BOHM s.p.
(S342)

Pater Noster *Gen
[Lat] SSATB,acap BOHM s.p. (S343)

Vater Unser *mot/prayer
[Eng/Ger] SATB,acap BAREN. BA5429
contains also: Der Herr, Der
Ewige Gott (SAATB,acap) (med)
(S344)

SCHWEIGT FEIN STILL see Weber, Bernhard

SCHWEITZER, JOHANNES
Kind-Jesu-Messe *Op.26, Mass
[Lat] SA&opt TB,org sc,cor pts BOHM
s.p.   (S345)

Sancta Maria
[Lat] SATTBB,acap BOHM s.p. (S346)

SCHWEIZER, ROLF (1936-   )
Adventskantate *Adv,cant/carol
treb cor,fl,ob,strings,org
MERSEBURG EM184   (S347)

Beatitudes, The *see Die
Seligpreisungen

Das Wort Vom Kreuz
SAT/SAB/SAAT/SAAB HANSSLER
HE 19.451 s.p.   (S348)

Die Seligpreisungen
"Beatitudes, The" SATB,cont (med)
BAREN. BA6318   (S349)

Es Kommt Ein Schiff, Geladen (from
Adventskantate)
see Schweizer, Rolf, O Heiland,
Reiss Die Himmel Auf

Freuet Euch In Dem Herrn Allewege
SATB,kbd,trom,bvl, 2 saxophones sc
HANSSLER 19.517 s.p.   (S350)

Herr, Deine Gute
SAT/SAB,3trp,2trom HANSSLER
HE 6.326 s.p.   (S351)

Herr, Wie Sind Deine Werke So Gross
Und Viel
1-2pt,org sc HANSSLER 12.225 s.p.
(S352)

Lobet Den Namen Des Herrn
SATB,org (med) BAREN. BA6320 (S353)

O Erd, Schlag Aus (from
Adventskantate)
see Schweizer, Rolf, O Heiland,
Reiss Die Himmel Auf

O Heiland, Reiss Die Himmel Auf (from
Adventskantate) Adv,carol
treb cor,fl,ob,strings,org
MERSEBURG s.p. contains also:

Psalm 100 *see O Erd, Schlag
AusSchlagt Froh In Die Hande

Schlagt Froh In Die Hande (Psalm 100)
SSA/jr cor,2rec,perc,timp,vcl,
glockenspiel, metallophone,
xylophone sc HANSSLER 12.513 s.p.
(S354)

Wie Soll Ich Dich Empfangen (from
Adventskantate)
see Schweizer, Rolf, O Heiland,
Reiss Die Himmel Auf

Zehn Psalmspruche *CC10U
3-4pt mix cor,org (med) BAREN.
BA5424   (S355)

SCORRA, ADOLF
Messe In F *Op.2, Mass
[Lat] 4pt mix cor,acap sc,cor pts
BOHM s.p.   (S356)

SE, MORGONSTJARNAN STRALAR ATER see
Praetorius, Michael

SE, SOLENS SKJONNE LYS OG PRAKT see
Nyhus, Rolf

SE, VI GA UPP TILL JERUSALEM see
Hemberg, Eskil

SEABOUGH, ED.
Call Of God, The *see Burroughs, Bob

Encounter (composed with Cates, Bill)
cor BROADMAN 4518-07 $2.00 (S357)

Go Where The People Are (composed
with Cates) *anthem
SATB oct BROADMAN 4565-40 $.35
(S358)

To The Ends Of The Earth (composed
with Cates) *anthem
unis oct BROADMAN 4565-56 $.35
(S359)

SEABOUGH, ED. (cont'd.)

We Have To Find A Way *see Reynolds,
William Jensen

SEAGARD, JOHN
Shepherds' Adoration *Xmas,anthem
SSATBB AUGSBURG 11-1730 $.35 (S360)

SEARCHER, THE see Milham, Richard

SEARCHING QUESTIONS see Carmichael,
Ralph

SEASON OF JOY, ALLELUIA see Roff,
Joseph

SEASON OF THE LONG RAINS see
Carmichael, Ralph

SEASON OF TOMORROW, THE see Nelson,
Ronald A.

SEASONAL RESPONSORIAL PSALMS see Roff,
Joseph

SEASONS see Winter, Sister Miriam
Therese

SEASONS OF RAPTURE see Wyrtzen, Don

SEASONS OF TIME see Adler, Samuel

SECHS CHORALE see Kaminski, Heinrich

SECHS EVANGELIENMOTETTEN see David,
Johann Nepomuk

SECHS EVANGELIENMOTETTEN see Strohbach,
Siegfried

SECHS GEISTLICHE LIEDER NACH GEDICHTEN
VON EICHENDORFF see Wolf, Hugo

SECHS KRIPPENLIEDER see Haas, Joseph

SECHS NEUE LIEDER see Zimmermann, Heinz
Werner

SECHS TANTUM ERGO HEFT 1 see Bruckner,
Anton

SECHS TANTUM ERGO HEFT 2 see Bruckner,
Anton

SECHS WEIHNACHTSLIEDER see Schroeder,
Hermann

SECKINGER, KONRAD (1935-   )
Cantate Domino *Mass
[Lat] SABar (without Credo) sc,cor
pts BOHM s.p.   (S361)

Ein Kind Ist Uns Geboren *Xmas,Mass
[Ger] mix cor,acap sc BOHM s.p.
(S362)
Freut Euch Ihr Hirten All
see Zwei Weihnachtslieder

Gelobet Seist Du, Jesu Christ *Xmas,
Mass
[Ger] mix cor&cong,org,ob,strings,
perc BOHM sc s.p., cor pts s.p.
(S363)
Herr, Erbarme Dich
[Ger] mix cor,org BOHM sc s.p., cor
pts s.p.   (S364)

Jauchze, Du Tochter Sion Fsp *Xmas
mix cor,S solo BOHM see from
Zwischengesange Fur Die
Weihnachtszeit   (S365)

Kleine Hirtenkantate
jr cor/wom cor,2vln,2fl,treb inst
sc,cor pts BOHM s.p., ipa (S366)

Lobsinget, Lobsinget
see Zwei Weihnachtslieder

Nun Danket All *Fest,cant
mix cor&unis,org BOHM s.p., ipa
(S367)
Seht, Ich Verkundige Grosse Freude
*Xmas
mix cor,S solo BOHM s.p. see from
Zwischengesange Fur Die
Weihnachtszeit   (S368)

Terra Tremuit *Easter,Offer
[Lat] 4pt mix cor,acap BOHM s.p.
(S369)
Uns Kommt Ein Schiff Gefahren *Adv
mix cor&opt cong,org/fl&strings sc,
cor pts BOHM s.p., ipa (S370)

Wir Ruhmen Dich Und Danken Dir *Mass
[Ger] mix cor&cong,high solo,org,
trp BOHM sc s.p., ipa, cor pts
s.p.   (S371)

Zwei Weihnachtslieder *Xmas
cor BOHM s.p.
contains: Freut Euch Ihr Hirten
All; Lobsinget, Lobsinget
(S372)

SECKINGER, KONRAD (cont'd.)
Zwischengesange Fur Die
Weihnachtszeit *see Jauchze, Du
Tochter Sion Fsp; Seht, Ich
Verkundige Grosse Freude (S373)

SECOND MASS FOR TWO VOICES see
Goemanne, Noel

SECOND MOTET BOOK, A *CC16L,mot
(Thomas, Paul) cor,inst CONCORDIA
97-5205 $2.25, ipa contains works
by: Redford; Brahms; Nanino;
Vivaldi; Schuetz; Mozart; Wesley
and others   (S374)

SECRET, THE see Sena, Tony

SECRET PLACE OF GOD, THE see Danielson,
Davis G.

SEDER, E.S.
And I Saw A New Heaven
SATB,SBar soli (med) FITZSIMONS
2039 $.25   (S375)

SEE FATHER, THY BELOVED SON see
Atkinson

SEE, MY SOUL see Elmore, Robert [Hall]

SEE NOW THE LAMB OF GOD see Homilius,
Gottfried August

SEE NOW THE LAMB OF GOD see Littleton,
Bill J.

SEE THE SHEPHERDS DANCING see Heldman,
Keith

SEE, THE WORD IS INCARNATE see Gibbons,
Orlando

SEEING WE ALSO see Sowerby, Leo

SEEK AFTER GOD see Hurlbutt, Patricia
E.

SEEK FIRST THE KINGDOM OF GOD see
Mozart, Wolfgang Amadeus, Quaerite
Primum Regnum Dei

SEEK THE LORD see Blakley, D. Duane

SEEK YE FIRST THE KINGDOM see Glarum,
L. Stanley

SEEK YE THE LORD see Lister, Mosie

SEEK YE THE LORD see Newbury, Kent A.

SEEK YE THE LORD see Palestrina,
Giovanni

SEEK YE THE LORD see Roberts, J. Varley

SEEK YE THE LORD see Southbridge, James

SEELE, VERGISS SIE NICHT see Cornelius,
Peter

SEELE, VERGISS SIE NICHT see Wittmer,
Eberhard Ludwig

SEHR GROSSE DING HAT GOTT GETAN see
Freundt, Cornelius

SEHT, ER KOMMT MIT PREIS GEKRONT! see
Handel, George Frideric

SEHT, ICH VERKUNDIGE GROSSE FREUDE see
Seckinger, Konrad

SEI GEGRUSST, MARIA see Wulz, Helmut

SEI GETROST UND UNVERZAGT see Baumann,
Max

SEI LOB UND EHR DEM HOCHSTEN GUT see
Preisenhammer

SEI NUN WIEDER ZUFRIEDEN, MEINE SEELE
see Staden, Johann

SEI UNS WILLKOMMEN, HERRE CHRIST see
Kuntz, Michael

SEIB, VALENTIN
Der Herr Ist Allmachtig
men cor,acap sc,cor pts TONOS 4019
s.p.   (S376)

SEID BARMHERZIG! see Tremmel, M.

SELBY, WILLIAM
Behold He Is My Salvation
SATB SCHIRM.EC 2755   (S377)

Matchless In Thy Form - A Christmas
Cantata From Colonial America
*Xmas
(McKay, David P.) ATB,ST soli,org
CONCORDIA 97-5094 $.85   (S378)

SELECTED CHORUSES FOR SATB *sac/sec,
CCU
SATB SCHIRM.G LG51496 $3.00   (S379)

SELECTIONS FOR THE REVIVAL CHOIR, NO. 1
*CCU,evang
(Sims, W. Hines) cor BROADMAN 4520-02
$.75   (S380)

SELECTIONS FOR THE REVIVAL CHOIR, NO. 2
*CCU,evang
(Sims, W. Hines) cor BROADMAN 4520-03
$.75   (S381)

SELECTIONS FOR THE REVIVAL CHOIR, NO. 3
*CCU,evang
(Sims, W. Hines) cor BROADMAN 4520-04
$.75   (S382)

SELECTIONS FOR THE REVIVAL CHOIR, NO. 4
*CCU,evang
(Sims, W. Hines) cor BROADMAN 4520-05
$.75   (S383)

SELIG DER MENSCH, DER DEN PAROLEN DER
PARTEI NICHT FOLGT see Hindermann,
Walter Felix

SELIG, DIE IN DEM HERREN STERBEN see
Brahms, Johannes

SELIG, DIE REINEN HERZENS SIND see
Goller, Fritz

SELIG DURCH DIE LIEBE see Schubert,
Franz (Peter)

SELIG SIND DES HIMMELS ERBEN see Rinck,
Johann Christian Hein.

SELIG SIND DIE TOTEN see Schutz,
Heinrich

SELIG SIND DIE TOTEN see Spohr

SELIGPREISUNGEN see Hufschmidt,
Wolfgang

SELKIRK PRAYER see Horman, John D.

SELLE, THOMAS (1599-1663)
Nun Bitten Wir Den Heiligen Geist
SATB,strings,cont sc,cor pts EGTVED
MK11, 9 s.p., ipa   (S384)

SELLERS, R.
Wonderful Jesus
(McLellan, Cyril) SATB oct GOSPEL
05 TM 0202 $.20   (S385)

SENA, TONY
Secret, The
(Ehret, Walter) SATB,pno,opt inst
(med easy) GENTRY G-258 $.50
(S386)

SENATOR, RONALD
Hail Mary
SATB EMI s.p. contains also: Our
Father   (S387)

How Great Is Your Name
unis,pno,vln,perc (Psalms 8, 43,
46) sc EMI s.p.   (S388)

Our Father
see Senator, Ronald, Hail Mary

SEND FORTH THY SPIRIT O LORD see
Newbury, Kent A.

SEND FORTH YOUR LIGHT see Verdi, Ralph
C.

SEND OUT THY LIGHT see Gounod, Charles
Francois

SEND OUT THY LIGHT see Lenzo

SEND THE LIGHT see Gabriel, Sr.,
Charles H.

SEND THY HOLY BREADTH see Peterson,
John W.

SENFL, LUDWIG (ca. 1490-1543)
Missa Super "Per Signum Crucis"
*Mass
[Lat] 4pt mix cor,acap sc,cor pts
BOHM s.p.   (S389)

SENFT
Deus In Adjutorium
4pt,acap voc pt HENN 552 s.p.
(S390)

SENSE OF HIM, A see Fettke, Tom

SERIEYX, AUGUSTE (1865-1949)
Nazareth
wom cor&jr cor,soli,orch HENN 340
s.p.   (S391)

SERMISY, CLAUDE DE (ca. 1490-1562)
Eternal Light *see Lux Aeterna

SERMISY, CLAUDE DE (cont'd.)

Lux Aeterna
(Luce) "Eternal Light" TTBB BRODT
NC 2 $.24   (S392)

Was Mein Gott Will, Das Gscheh
Allzeit
SATB (contains also: O Treuer Gott
Im Himmelsthron) SCHWEIZER.
SK 56.04 s.p. see also
MUSIKBEILAGE ZUM "EVANGELISCHEN
KIRCHENCHOR 1956"   (S393)

SERMON FROM THE MOUNTAIN, A see Parker,
Alice

SERMON ON THE PLAIN, THE see Ford,
Virgil T.

SERRANUS, JOHANN BAPTISTA (1540-1600)
Wenn Wir In Hochsten Noten Sein
SSATB (contains also: Die Ganze
Welt, Herr Jesu Christ)
SCHWEIZER. SK 66.04 s.p. see also
MUSIKBEILAGE ZUM "EVANGELISCHEN
KIRCHENCHOR 1956"   (S394)

SERVE BONE see Lassus, Roland de
(Orlandus)

SERVE HIM WITH ALL YOUR HEART see Pace,
Millie

SERVE THE LORD WITH GLADNESS *anthem
(Cram) SATB oct BROADMAN 4545-91 $.30
(S395)

SERVICE MUSIC see Lockwood, Normand

SERVIZIO SACRO see Bloch, Ernest,
Sacred Service

SET FREE WITHIN see Johnson, David N.

SET ME AS A SEAL see Kennedy

SET ME FREE, O LORD MY GOD see Byrd,
William, Libera Me Domine Et Pone
Me

SET MY SPIRIT FREE see Fischer, William
Gustavus

SETTE CANTI PENITENZIALI see Veretti,
Antonio

SETTEN, J.W. VAN
Wij Zien In De Kribbe Het Kindje
*Xmas,cant
unis,pno/harmonium HEER 147 s.p.
(S396)

SEVEN ANTHEMS FOR TREBLE CHOIRS see
Beck, Theodore

SEVEN ANTHEMS FOR TREBLE CHOIRS, SET II
see Beck, Theodore

SEVEN CHRISTMAS CAROLS *CC7L,Xmas,
carol
(Parker, Alice) SATB,pno/org/orch
(easy/med) sc FISCHER,C rental
see also: Away In A Manger; Fum,
Fum, Fum; God Rest Ye Merry
Gentlemen; Good Christian Men,
Rejoice; Masters In This Hall; O
Come, Emmanuel; So Blest A Sight
(S397)

SEVEN DAYS OF CREATION see Hays, Peggy
McAllister

SEVEN-FOLD AMEN see Canning, Thomas

SEVEN FRENCH NOELS see Carroll, J.
Robert

SEVEN FRENCH NOELS ON DAQUIN CAROLS see
Gore, Richard T.

SEVEN HYMN TUNES, PART 1 see Dowland,
John

SEVEN JOYS OF MARY
(McKelvy, James) SATB (easy) FOSTER
MF514 $.30   (S398)

SEVEN LAST WORDS OF CHRIST ON THE
CROSS, THE see Pinkham, Daniel

SEVEN PENITENTIAL PSALMS FROM THE
"BECKER PSALTER" see Schutz,
Heinrich

SEVEN PILLARS see Diament, Abraham

SEVEN PIOUS PIECES see Martino, Donald

SEVEN PSALMS FOR CONTEMPORARY LIVING
see Burroughs

SEVEN TUNES FOR TWELVE PSALMS see
Jerome, Peter

SEVEN VERSES see Krapf, Gerhard

SEVENTY-SIX TO SEVENTY-SIX - A STUDY OF
TWO CENTURIES OF SACRED MUSIC IN
AMERICA *CCU,anthem/folk/hymn,US
(Lorenz, Ellen Jane) cor LORENZ $4.95
(S399)

SEVERIN, LEONE
O Be Joyful In The Lord *Bibl
SATB (med) FITZSIMONS 2184 $.25
(S400)

SEWELL
More Like Jesus *folk
SATB/jr cor oct LILLENAS AN-5090 $.40
(S401)

My Best Friend *folk
SATB/jr cor oct LILLENAS AN-5085 $.30
(S402)

SGAMBATI, GIOVANNI (1841-1914)
Messa Da Requiem *Req
mix cor,Bar solo,org,2fl,2ob,3clar,
2bsn,4horn,3trp,3trom,tuba,
strings,perc,3timp,harp (med) sc
SCHOTTS rental, ipr   (S403)

SHADOW SCENES OF THE SAVIOR'S BIRTH see
Rains, Dorothy Best

SHADOWS OF THE EVENING see Hiles,
[Henry]

SHAFFER, JEANNE
Man Went Forth To Die, A *Easter,
anthem
SATB (easy) oct BROADMAN 4550-11 $.30
(S404)

Sing Noel *Xmas,cant
SATB,opt narrator BROADMAN 4512-02 $1.25
(S405)

SHAHAR AVAKESHKHA see Wohlberg, Max

SHAKER WORSHIP SERVICE, A
(Terri) TTBB/SSA/SA SCHIRM.G LG51731 $2.00
(S406)

SHALL WE GATHER AT THE RIVER *anthem
(Lyall) SATB (easy) oct BROADMAN 4538-04 $.30
(S407)

SHALL WE GATHER AT THE RIVER see Lowry,
Robert

SHALOM ALEIKHEM see Diament, Abraham

SHARE see Burroughs, Bob

SHARE see Floria, Cam

SHARE HIS LOVE see Reynolds, William
Jensen

SHARE THE SONG *CCUL
(Mercer, W. Elmo) cor,org/pno BENSON B0577 $2.95
(S408)

SHARE THE WORD *CCU
(Reynolds, Wm. J.) cor (easy)
BROADMAN 4520-23 $2.00   (S409)

SHARON FRAGMENTS see Beckwith, John

SHARPE, EVELYN
Turn Ye To Me
SA CRAMER $.20   (S410)

SHAW
I Sing Of A Maiden
(Price) SATB,acap (easy) OXFORD
94.325 $.30   (S411)

SHAW, MARTIN (1875-1958)
Redeemer, The *Easter
mix cor,orch STAINER 3.0842.1 $2.00, ipr
(S412)

SHAW, RUBY
Noel Nouvelet *Xmas
SSAATTBB (diff) FITZSIMONS 2083 $.30
(S413)

SHAYNE, GLORIA
Do You Hear What I Hear *see Regney,
Noel

Three Wise Men, Wise Men Three *see
Regney, Noel

SHEA
I Am Not Alone Today *anthem
SB oct LORENZ 5769 $.35   (S414)

SHEAFFER
Balm In Gilead *anthem
SATB oct BROADMAN 4532-19 $.30   (S415)

SHEELES
Spacious Firmament, The
(Clokey) SATB&jr cor (med)
FITZSIMONS 2141 $.25   (S416)

SHEEP MAY SAFELY GRAZE see Bach, Johann
Sebastian

SHEEPHEARD'S SONG, THE see Pinkham,
Daniel

SHEFFIELD CATHEDRAL DESCANTS see
Henforth, T.W.

SHEFFIELD CATHEDRAL DESCANTS (SECOND
SET) see Henforth, T.W.

SHENANDOAH HYMN *anthem
(Silver) 1-2pt,pno oct MCAFEE M8002 $.35
(S417)

SHEPHERD
Haste Thee, O God
(Buck) SATB,opt acap (med) OXFORD
43.256 $.40   (S418)

SHEPHERD, THE see George, Earl

SHEPHERD AND HIS LOVE, THE see Mechem,
Kirke

SHEPHERD BOY, THE see Pagette

SHEPHERD, LEAD ME see Rheinberger,
Josef

SHEPHERD ME LORD see Kingsley, Gershon

SHEPHERD OF ISRAEL see Darst, W. Glenn

SHEPHERD OF LOVE see Peterson, John W.

SHEPHERD OF SOULS see Wilson, Roger C.

SHEPHERD OF TENDER YOUTH see Strimple,
N.

SHEPHERD OF WILLING YOUTH *anthem
(Hokanson) 2pt oct BROADMAN 4557-33 $.25
(S419)

SHEPHERD PSALM, THE see Brown

SHEPHERD, SHEPHERD
(Wild, Eric) SATB,pno BERANDOL
BER1680 $.50   (S420)

SHEPHERD SONG, THE see Watters, Bob

SHEPHERDS, THE *CCU,carol/folk,Span
(Hudson, Hazel) cor,inst ASHDOWN
SGMS.8   (S421)

SHEPHERDS, THE see Beck, John Ness

SHEPHERDS' ADORATION see Seagard, John

SHEPHERDS AND ANGELS see Price

SHEPHERDS, ARISE AND LEAVE YOUR SHEEP
see Young, Gordon

SHEPHERDS' CAROL see Billings, William

SHEPHERD'S CAROL, A see Platts, Kenneth

SHEPHERDS CAROL, THE see Canning,
Thomas

SHEPHERDS COME A-RUNNING see Wetzler,
Robert

SHEPHERD'S CRADLE SONG see Grimes,
Gordon

SHEPHERDS' GLORY, THE see Butler,
Eugene

SHEPHERDS IN THE FIELD ABIDING *Xmas
(Bissell, K.W.) SSA (med easy)
WATERLOO $.35   (S422)

SHEPHERDS IN THE FIELDS see Nops,
Marjory

SHEPHERDS IN THE FIELDS A-WATCHING
*Xmas
(Douglas) 2pt,opt bells PRO ART 2757 $.35
(S423)

SHEPHERDS' NOEL
see Twelve Christmas Carols: Set 1

SHEPHERD'S PIPE CAROL see Rutter

SHEPHERDS PLAY YOUR MELODY see Page,
Sue Ellen

SHEPHERDS, REJOICE see Frackenpohl,
Arthur

SHEPHERDS REJOICE LIFT UP YOUR EYES see
Ehret, Walter

SHEPHERDS! SHAKE OFF YOUR DROWSY SLEEP
see Stainer, John

SHEPHERD'S STAR, THE see Clark, K.

SHEPHERDS' STORY, THE see Thiman, Eric
Harding

SHEPPARD, FRANKLIN L. (1852-1930)
This Is My Father's World *anthem
(Johnson, Norman) SATB oct SINGSPIR
ZJP-7211 $.25   (S424)
(Johnson, Norman) SSAATTBB oct
SINGSPIR ZJP-7344 $.25   (S425)

SHERWIN
Galilee, Bright Galilee (composed
with Bethel) *anthem
SATB (easy) oct BROADMAN 4545-71
$.30   (S426)

SHERWIN, WILLIAM F.
Sound The Battle Cry
(Yoder, David) SATB,orch/4-6brass
oct GOSPEL 05 TM 0109 $.25, ipa
(S427)

SHIELD OF FAITH see Bliss, Sir Arthur

SHINE MEDLEY
see Mini-Musicals

SHINE UPON OUR MINDS see Simons, L.E.

SHINE YE STARS IN HIGHEST HEAVEN see
Bach, Johann Sebastian

SHIP AHOY! see Cartwright

SHIRE T'FILOH see Gerovitsch, Eliezer

SHIREJ SIMROH see Gerovitsch, Eliezer

SH'MA, V'AHAVTA, MI CHAMOCHA see Adler,
Samuel

SH'MA YISROAYL see De Koning

SHORT ANTHEMS, SET I see Clokey, Joseph
Waddell

SHORT ANTHEMS, SET II see Clokey,
Joseph Waddell

SHORT ANTHEMS, SET III see Clokey,
Joseph Waddell

SHORT MASS see Burgon, Geoffrey

SHORT MASS, A see Wigglesworth, Frank

SHORT MASS OF SAINT JOHN THE BAPTIST
see MacNutt, Walter

SHORT MUSIC DRAMAS FOR CHILDREN see
Billingsley, Derrell

SHOUT AND SING see Smith

SHOUT FOR JOY BEFORE THE LORD see Neff,
James

SHOUT IT EVERYWHERE see Dailey, William

SHOUT THE GLAD TIDINGS see Thomas

SHOUT TO GOD WITH SHOUTS OF JOY
*anthem
(Graham) 2pt oct BROADMAN 4558-47
$.30   (S428)

SHOUT TO GOD WITH SHOUTS OF JOY see
Graham

SHOWALTER
Leaning On The Everlasting Arms
*anthem/folk/gospel
(Drevits, Jon) SATB oct SINGSPIR
ZJP-8114 $.25   (S429)
(Hess, John J.) SSATB oct SINGSPIR
ZJP-5031 $.30   (S430)

SHOWERS OF BLESSING see Whittle

SHRILL CHANTICLEER see Parker, Alice

SHUTTLEWORTH, F.
Lord Is Righteous, The
unis LESLIE 4053 $.20   (S431)

SI, NATTEN FLYR see Berg, Gottfrid

SIBELIUS, JEAN (1865-1957)
Be Still, My Soul *anthem
(DeCou, Harold) SATB oct SINGSPIR
ZJP-7287 $.30   (S432)

SIC DEUS DILEXIT MUNDUM see Scheidt,
Samuel

SIC ENIM AMAVIT DEUS MUNDUM see
Maegaard Jan

SICUT CERVUS see Palestrina, Giovanni

SIDE BY SIDE see Wood, Jeff

SIE KREUZIGTEN DEN HERRN see They
Crucified My Lord

SIEBZEHNRIEBL, FRANZ X.
Messe In Es *Op.4, Mass
[Lat] 4pt mix cor,org (E flat maj)
sc,cor pts BOHM s.p.   (S433)

SIEGL, OTTO (1896-   )
Hirtenlied Im Advent "Winterzeit,
Schonste Zeit" *Adv
cor BOHM s.p.   (S434)

Lucis Largitor Splendide *hymn
[Lat/Ger] 4pt mix cor,acap BOHM
s.p.   (S435)

Missa Humilitatis *Mass
[Lat] 4pt mix cor,org,opt strings&
2horn sc,cor pts BOHM s.p., ipa (S436)

Regina Coeli, Laetare *BVM/Easter
[Lat] 4pt mix cor,acap BOHM s.p. (S437)

Tu Es Petrus
[Lat] 4pt mix cor,opt org/orch sc,
cor pts BOHM s.p., ipa   (S438)

SIEH, WIE DAS KINDELEIN *Xmas,carol/
folk
(Marx, K.) [Ger] 4pt men cor
MERSEBURG EM9049   (S439)

SIEHE, DAS IST GOTTES LAMM see
Homilius, Gottfried August

SIEHE, DEIN KONIG KOMMT see Gallus,
Jacobus

SIEHE, DEIN KONIG KOMMT ZU DIR see
Ruppel, Paul Ernst

SIEHE, DIESER WIRD GESETZT ZU EINEM
FALL see Schutz, Heinrich

SIEHE, ES KOMMT DIE ZEIT see Studer,
Hans

SIEHE, MEIN FURSPRECHER IST IM HIMMEL
see Schutz, Heinrich

SIGMUND, OSKAR
Christo Canamus Principi *Mass
[Lat] 4pt mix cor,acap (without
Credo) so,cor pts BOHM s.p.   (S440)

Lasst Uns Erheben Herz Und Stimm
*Fest
mix cor,acap BOHM s.p.   (S441)

SIGNOR, PER LA TUA FE
see Raccolta Corale Libro III

SIGNOR, TI BENEDICO
see Raccolta Corale Libro II

SIGNS see Felciano, Richard

SILCHER, FRIEDRICH (1789-1860)
Hymnus: Jauchzet Dem Herrn *hymn
men cor,acap TONOS 5312 s.p. (S442)

Sanctus: Heilig, Heilig *Sanctus
men cor,acap TONOS 4324 s.p. (S443)

So Nimm Denn Meine Hande
3pt wom cor,org/harmonium sc,cor
pts BOHM s.p.   (S444)

Weihnachtsmotette *Xmas,mot
mix cor voc pt BRATFISCH GB3255
s.p.   (S445)

SILENT NIGHT *Xmas
(Lefebvre, C.) SATB GALAXY 1.0979.1
$.30 contains also: Adeste Fideles
(S446)
(Pears, James R.) SSA&desc (med easy)
WATERLOO $.35   (S447)

SILENT NIGHT see Baker

SILENT NIGHT see Eilers, Joyce Elaine

SILENT NIGHT see Gruber, Franz Xaver,
Stille Nacht, Heilige Nacht

SILENT NIGHT see McGlohon, Loonis

SILENT NIGHT, HOLY NIGHT *Xmas
(Kinyon) SA,opt band ALFRED 6814 $.30
(S448)
(Red, Buryl) 2pt jr cor (easy)
BROADMAN 4560-37 $.35   (S449)

SILENT NIGHT! HOLY NIGHT! see Grote,
Gottfried

SILENT NIGHT! HOLY NIGHT! see Gruber,
Franz Xaver, Stille Nacht, Heilige
Nacht

SILENT NIGHT, HOLY NIGHT see Red, Buryl

SILENT THE NIGHT see Winter, Sister
Miriam Therese

SILK
Sing And Rejoice *anthem
SATB (med diff) OXFORD 42.361 $.60
(S450)

SILVER
African Easter *Easter,anthem
cor,pno,opt inst oct MCAFEE M1037
$.40   (S451)

Feast Of Lights, A *anthem
1-2pt oct MCAFEE M8009 $.35   (S452)

SILVESTER, FREDERICK
Be Merciful Unto Me
SATB HARRIS $.35   (S453)

Come, Ye Disconsolate
SATB HARRIS $.35   (S454)

I Will Give Thanks
SATB HARRIS $.35   (S455)

Ride On! Ride On In Majesty
SATB HARRIS $.35   (S456)

Softly Now The Light Of Day
SATB HARRIS $.35   (S457)

SIMEON'S PRAYER see Hegenbart, Alex F.

SIMKINS, C.F.
Upon My Lap My Sovereign Sits
SATB EMI s.p.   (S458)

SIMON, CALLED PETER see Caldwell, Mary
[Elizabeth]

SIMON, HERMANN
Crucifixus (Die Sieben Worte Des
Erlosers)
4pt mix cor,SBar soli,org,opt orch
RIES   (S459)

Die Weihnachts-Botschaft *Xmas
4pt mix cor,S solo,org,strings RIES
(S460)

Gebet (from Luthermesse)
mix cor voc sc RIES s.p.   (S461)

Luthermesse *Mass
4-5pt,ABar soli cor pts RIES rental
(S462)

SIMONS, L.E.
Little Lamb
SSA BRODT WC 6 $.24   (S463)

Oh, Little Star
SA BRODT 617 $.25   (S464)

Shine Upon Our Minds
SA BRODT 586 $.20   (S465)

SIMONS, NETTY
Sing, O Daughter Of Zion
SATB,A&B soli,acap AM.COMP.AL.
$9.90   (S466)

SIMPLE BIRTH, THE *Xmas
(Kirk) SATB,acap,opt rec/fl PRO ART
2760 $.35   (S467)

SIMPLE SONGS FOR TODDLERS NO. 1
*CC43UL
jr cor SINGSPIR 5572 $.75   (S468)

SIMPLE SONGS FOR TODDLERS NO. 2
*CC42UL
jr cor SINGSPIR 5573 $.75   (S469)

SIMPLE SONGS FOR TODDLERS NO. 3
*CC40UL
jr cor SINGSPIR 5574 $.75   (S470)

SIMPLE SONGS FOR TODDLERS NO. 4
*CC51UL
jr cor SINGSPIR 5630 $.75   (S471)

SIMPSON
Come, Holy Spirit, Heavenly Dove
*see Watts

SIMPSON, EUGENE
Hold On
SSATTBB BOURNE B223610-358 $.60
(S472)

SIMPSON, JOHN
This New Christmas Carol
unis EMI   (S473)

SIMS, EZRA (1928-   )
Mass For Small Chorus
cor,acap AM.COMP.AL. $8.80   (S474)

What God Is Like To Him I Serve?
SATB,acap AM.COMP.AL. $2.20   (S475)

SINCE BY MAN CAME DEATH see Handel,
George Frideric

SINCE I HAVE BEEN REDEEMED see Excell

SINCE THE SAVIOR FOUND ME see Haskins,
William

SINCE WE ALL BELIEVE IN JESUS see
Peterson, John W.

SINDLINGER, MAURINE I.
Make A Joyful Noise To The Lord
*Gen/Thanks
unis,opt fl/rec CHORISTERS A-47
$.25   (S476)

SING A JOYFUL SONG, BELIEVERS see
Reynolds, William Jensen

SING A JOYFUL SONG OF CHRISTMAS see
Kaufmann, Ronald

SING A LULLABY FOR JESUS see Verrall,
Pamela

SING A NEW SONG see Nelson

SING A NEW SONG see Watson, Walter

SING A NEW SONG TO THE LORD see Archer,
Violet

SING A NEW SONG TO THE LORD see
Jackson, Francis

SING A NEW SONG UNTO THE LORD see
Thygerson, Robert J.

SING A SONG OF JOY see Marshall

SING A SONG OF MERRY CHRISTMAS see
Mozart, Wolfgang Amadeus

SING A SONG OF PRAISE see Stainer, John

SING ALL THE EARTH see Powell, Robert

SING, ALL YE PEOPLE see Miller, Thomas
A.

SING ALLELUIA see Angell

SING ALLELUIA! see Page, Sue Ellen

SING ALLELUIA see Wink

SING ALLELUIA see Young, Gordon

SING ALLELUIA, JESUS IS RISEN see Parks

SING ALLELUIA, JESUS LIVES see Sateren,
Leland Bernhard

SING ALLELUYA FORTH see Willan, Healey

SING ALOUD UNTO GOD see Orr

SING ALOUD UNTO GOD OUR STRENGTH see
Webb, E.

SING ALOUD WITH GLADNESS see Scarlatti,
Alessandro

SING AND REJOICE see James, Will

SING AND REJOICE see Silk

SING AND REJOICE see Young

SING AROUND THE WORLD see Dalton, Larry

SING, BROTHER, SING *CC6U,medley
(Skillings, Otis) cor LILLENAS MB-322
$1.95   (S477)

SING, BROTHER, SING *gospel/medley
(Skillings, Otis) SATB oct LILLENAS
AT-1116 $.45   (S478)

SING CAROLS GAY! see Butler, Eugene

SING CHRISTMAS see Crouch, Letha

SING FAITH AND HOPE, VOL. I see Rambo,
Dottie

SING FAITH AND HOPE, VOL. II see Rambo,
Dottie

SING FOR JOY see Pote, Allen

SING FOR JOY *CC12U,anthem
(Leach, Bill F.) jr cor BROADMAN
4526-09 $1.50 contains works by:
Burroughs; Red; Bass; Caldwell;
Young and others   (S479)

SING FORTH HIS PRAISE, HE REIGNETH! see
Bock, Fred

SING GOD'S PRAISE see Angell, Warren M.

SING HIS PRAISES NO. 1 *CCUL
(Till, Lee Roy) SATB SINGSPIR 5060
$1.50   (S480)

SING HIS PRAISES NO. 2 *CCUL
(Till, Lee Roy) SATB SINGSPIR 5768
$1.50   (S481)

SING HOSANNA IN THE HIGHEST see Butler,
Eugene

SING JESUS see Frink

SING JOY! see Graham, Robert

SING JOYFULLY *CCU,anthem/hymn
(Hooper, Wm. L.) SAB/SATB BROADMAN
4520-15 $1.25   (S482)

SING! MAKE A JOYFUL SOUND NO. 1 *CCUL,
evang
(Souther, Billy) cor (easy/med diff)
SINGSPIR 5491 $1.75   (S483)

SING! MAKE A JOYFUL SOUND NO. 2 *CCUL,
evang
(Souther, Billy) cor (easy/med diff)
SINGSPIR 5490 $1.75   (S484)

SING! MAKE A JOYFUL SOUND NO. 3 *CCUL,
evang
(Souther, Billy) cor (easy/med diff)
SINGSPIR 5492 $1.75   (S485)

SING! MAKE A JOYFUL SOUND NO. 4 *CCUL
cor oct SINGSPIR 5510 $1.75 (S486)

SING, MEN AND ANGELS, SING see Butler,
Eugene

SING MEN! NO. 1 *CCUL
4pt men cor SINGSPIR 5061 $1.75
                             (S487)

SING MEN! NO. 2 *CCUL
4pt men cor SINGSPIR 5062 $1.75
                             (S488)

SING MEN! NO. 3 *CCUL
4pt men cor SINGSPIR 5063 $1.75
                             (S489)

SING MEN! NO. 4 *CCUL
4pt men cor SINGSPIR 5064 $1.75
                             (S490)

SING MEN! NO. 5 *CCUL
4pt men cor SINGSPIR 5065 $1.75
                             (S491)

SING MEN! NO. 6 *CCUL
4pt men cor SINGSPIR 5066 $1.75
                             (S492)

SING MORNING STARS
see Two Christmas Carols

SING, MY TONGUE, HOW GLORIOUS BATTLE
see Schalk, Carl

SING NOEL see Cobine, Al

SING NOEL see Runyan

SING NOEL see Shaffer, Jeanne

SING NOW *CC16UL
(Skillings, Otis) cor LILLENAS MB-309
$1.95   (S493)

SING NOW NO. 2 *CC16UL
(Skillings, Otis) cor (easy) cmplt ed
LILLENAS MB-366 $1.95   (S494)

SING, O DAUGHTER OF ZION see Ames,
William

SING, O DAUGHTER OF ZION see Simons,
Netty

SING, O HEAVENS see Diemer, Emma Lou

SING, O HEAV'NS see Amner, John

SING OF BIRTH see Winter, Sister Miriam
Therese

SING OF HIM *CCUL
(Terry, Lindsay) cor BENSON B0970
$1.50   (S495)

SING OUT - JESUS LIVES! see Rogers

SING! PRAISE! REJOICE! see Allen, Lanny

SING PRAISE TO GOD! *Thanks,anthem
(Johnson, Norman) SATB oct SINGSPIR
ZJP-7207 $.30   (S496)

SING PRAISE TO GOD see Goemanne, Noel,
Mit Freuden Zart

SING PRAISE TO GOD see McAfee

SING PRAISE TO GOD see Moore

SING PRAISE TO GOD, THE ALMIGHTY *Russ
(Whitford, H.) SAB,org oct HOPE A 474
$.35   (S497)

SING PRAISE UNTO THE LORD see Lanier

SING PRAISES see Billings, William

SING PRAISES *CC20U
(Ehret, Walter) 3-4pt jr cor BROADMAN
4520-11 $1.25   (S498)

SING PRAISES, NO. 2 *CCU,anthem
(Ehret, Walter) 3-4pt BROADMAN
4520-12 $1.25   (S499)

SING PRAISES TO GOD see Graham

SING PRAISES TO THE LORD see Herbst,
Johannes

SING PRAISES TO THE LORD see Korte,
Karl

SING, REJOICE see Kirk, Theron W.

SING, SING, EV'RYONE SING
(Wild, Eric) SATB,pno BERANDOL
BER1230 $.35   (S500)

SING, SING, SING *CC109U
jr cor BENSON B0580 $1.00   (S501)

SING, SING TO THE LORD see Matthews,
Thomas

SING TO GOD see Caldwell

SING TO GOD see Kreutz, Robert E.,
Cantate Domino

SING TO GOD see Lassus, Roland de
(Orlandus), Jubilate Deo

SING TO GOD A JOYFUL SONG see Young

SING TO HIS NAME FOR HE IS GRACIOUS see
Butler, Eugene

SING TO OUR GOD *anthem
(Butler) SAB,trp oct LILLENAS AN-6020
$.35   (S502)

SING TO THE LORD see Medema, Ken

SING TO THE LORD see Sweelinck, Jan
Pieterszoon

SING TO THE LORD A NEW MADE SONG see
Billings, William

SING TO THE LORD A NEW SONG see Hughes

SING TO THE LORD A NEW SONG see
MacKintosh

SING TO THE LORD A NEW SONG see
Williams, David H.

SING TO THE LORD JEHOVAH'S NAME see
Billings, William

SING TO THE LORD OF HARVEST see Brewer,
R.H.

SING TO THE LORD OF HARVEST see
Johnson, Norman

SING TO THE LORD OF HARVEST see
Marshall

SING TO THE LORD OF HARVEST see
Steuerlein, Johann

SING TO THE LORD WITH CHEERFUL VOICE
see Young

SING UNISON! *CCU
(Thompson, J.W.) unis&opt desc
BROADMAN 4524-01 $1.25   (S503)

SING UNTO GOD see Purcell, Henry

SING UNTO HIM see Beck, John Ness

SING UNTO THE LORD see Smith, Stanley

SING UNTO THE LORD A NEW SONG see
Stern, Theodore

SING UNTO THE LORD A NEW SONG see
Young, Gordon

SING WE see Pearsall, Robert Lucas de

SING WE A GLAD NOEL see Elder, Dorothy
Kosanke

SING WE ALL NOEL see Wolff

SING WE ALL NOW ALLELUIA see Ehret,
Walter

SING WE JOYOUSLY see Grady

SING WE MERRILY see Carpenter

SING WE MERRILY see Symons

SING WE MERRILY UNTO GOD see Byrd,
William

SING WE NOEL *Xmas
(Ellison, Glenn) SATB (easy)
FITZSIMONS 2152 $.25   (S504)
(Ellison, Glenn) SSA (easy)
FITZSIMONS 3081 $.25   (S505)

SING WE NOEL see Harris

SING WE, THEN MERRILY see Byrd, William

SING WE TO OUR GOD ABOVE see Knox,
Charles

SING WE TO THIS MERRY COMPANY see
Rutter

SING WE WITH A MERRY HEART see Wetzler,
Robert

SING WITH MARCY *CC40UL
(Tigner, Marcy) jr cor SINGSPIR 5455
$1.00   (S506)

SING WITH THE JOY THE SAVIOR'S GLORY
*Commun
(Roff, Joseph) SATB LITURGICAL $.50
see also Twelve Hymns   (S507)

SING YE PRAISES see Lovelace, Austin C.

SING YE, SING NOEL see Wetzler, Robert

SING, YE, THE LORD A NEW-MADE SONG see
Distler, Hugo, Singet Dem Herrn Ein
Neues Lied

SING YE TO OUR LORD see Byrd, William

SING YE TO THE LORD see Gibbs, Alan

SINGE, O SINGE see Sturmer, Bruno

SINGEN WIR MIT FROHLICHKEIT see Trapp,
Willy

SINGET DEM HERRN HEFT 7 *CC17U,mot
SAT/SAB/SATB,cont HANSSLER 2.052 s.p.
contains works by: Schutz; Abel;
Ochs; Stolte; and others   (S508)

SINGET DEM HERRN, HEFT 8 *CC18U
SAT/SAB/SATB,inst HANSSLER 2.055 s.p.
contains works by: Bach; Cruger;
Gumpelzhaimer; Ruppel; and others
                                        (S509)

SINGET DEM HERRN EIN NEUES LIED see
Bach, Johann Sebastian

SINGET DEM HERRN EIN NEUES LIED see
Distler, Hugo

SINGET DEM HERRN EIN NEUES LIED see
Heer, Emil

SINGET DEM HERRN EIN NEUES LIED see
Lohmann, A.

SINGET DEM HERRN EIN NEUES LIED see
Pachelbel, Johann

SINGET DEM HERRN EIN NEUES LIED see
Poos, Heinrich

SINGET DEM HERRN EIN NEUES LIED see
Reichel, Bernard

SINGET DEM HERRN EIN NEUES LIED see
Schutz, Heinrich

SINGET DEM HERRN EIN NEUES LIED see
Zimmermann, Heinz Werner

SINGET DEM HERRN EIN NEUES LIED, DENN
ER TUT GROSSE WUNDER see Schott,
Johann Georg

SINGET EIN NEUES LIED see Hassler, Hans
Leo

SINGET FRISCH UND WOHLGEMUT see Herbst,
Johannes Andreas

SINGET FRISCH UND WOHLGEMUT see Zipp,
Friedrich

SINGET HOCHERFREUT see Goudimel, Claude

SINGET MIT FRUEDEN UNSERM GOTT see
Schutz, Heinrich

SINGING CHURCHMEN, THE *CC11L
(Carmichael, Ralph) TTBB LEXICON
37640 $1.95   (S510)

SINGING CHURCHMEN, NO. 1 *CCU,hymn
(Reynolds, W.J.) 4pt men cor BROADMAN
4522-06 $1.25   (S511)

SINGING CHURCHMEN, NO. 2 *CCU,hymn
(Reynolds, W.J.) 4pt men cor BROADMAN
4522-07 $1.25   (S512)

SINGING CHURCHMEN, NO. 3 *CCU,hymn
(Reynolds, W.J.) 4pt men cor BROADMAN
4522-08 $1.25   (S513)

SINGING FOR JESUS *anthem
1-2pt jr cor,opt fing.cym.&hndbl
BROADMAN 4560-27 $.35 see from Four
Festive Anthems For Children's
Voices   (S514)

SINGING FOR JESUS see Blakley

SINGING FOR JESUS see Cole

SINGING GOD'S WORD FOR CHILDRENS VOICES
BOOK 1 see Hays, Peggy McAllister

SINGING GOD'S WORD FOR CHILDRENS VOICES
BOOK 2 see Hays, Peggy McAllister

SINGING GOD'S WORD FOR CHILDRENS VOICES
BOOK 3 see Hays, Peggy McAllister

SINGING IN SEVEN PARTS *CCUL
(DeCou, Harold) 7pt SINGSPIR 5038
$1.75   (S515)

SINGING JOY *CC147U,anthem/gospel
(Benson, John T.) jr cor,solo cmplt
ed LILLENAS MB-192 $1.50   (S516)

SINGING JOY *CC178U
BENSON B0590 $1.50   (S517)

SINGING MEDLEY
see Church Is Singing Again, The

SINGING MEN *CCUL
(Peterson, John W.) 4pt men cor
SINGSPIR 4321 $1.50   (S518)

SINGING MEN, NO. 1 *CC49UL
men cor BENSON B0600 $1.00   (S519)

SINGING MEN, NO. 2 *CC51UL
(Mercer, W. Elmo) 4pt men cor BENSON
B0610 $1.00   (S520)

SINGING SAB NO. 2 *CCUL
(Boersma, James) SAB voc sc WORD
10078 $1.00   (S521)

SINGING THREE PARTS *CC26UL
(Mercer, W. Elmo) SAB BENSON B0620
$1.00   (S522)

SINGING THROUGH THE YEAR see Marshall,
Jane M.

SINGKANONS see Trust, Heinz-Ewald

SINGSPIRATION NO. 1 *CC91UL
cor SINGSPIR 5001 $1.25   (S523)

SINGSPIRATION NO. 2 *CC112UL
cor SINGSPIR 5002 $1.25   (S524)

SINGSPIRATION NO. 3 *CC106UL
cor SINGSPIR 5003 $1.25   (S525)

SINGSPIRATION NO. 4 *CC108UL
cor SINGSPIR 5004 $1.25   (S526)

SINGSPIRATION NO. 5 *CC78UL
cor SINGSPIR 5005 $1.25   (S527)

SINGSPIRATION NO. 6 *CC71UL
cor SINGSPIR 5006 $1.25   (S528)

SINGSPIRATION NO. 7 *CC51UL
cor SINGSPIR 5007 $1.25   (S529)

SINGSPIRATION NO. 8 *CC67UL
cor SINGSPIR 5008 $1.25   (S530)

SINGSPIRATION NO. 9 *CC41UL
cor SINGSPIR 5009 $1.25   (S531)

SINGSPIRATION NO. 10 *CC41UL
cor SINGSPIR 5010 $1.25   (S532)

SINGSPIRATION NO. 11 *CC47UL
cor SINGSPIR 5011 $1.25   (S533)

SINGSPIRATION NO. 12 *CCU
cor SINGSPIR 5012 $1.25   (S534)

SINGT AUF, LOBT GOTT see Lemacher,
Heinrich

SINGT DAS LIED DER FREUDE UBER GOTT see
Jehn

SINGT DEM HERRN EIN NEUES LIED see
Heer, Emil

SINGT DEM HERRN EIN NEUES LIED see
Kronberg, G.

SINGT EIN LOBLIED see Lang, Hans,
Laudate Dominum

SINGT HALLELUJA see Goudimel, Claude

SINGT, IHR LIEBEN CHRISTEN ALL see
Praetorius, Michael

SINGT LOB UND DANK *CCU
(Klause, Eugen) [Ger] 1-3pt wom cor&
unis men cor BAREN. EM 358 s.p.
                                        (S535)

SINGT MIT FROHER STIMM see Diener,
Theodor

SINGT, SINGT DEM HERREN NEUE LIEDER see
Goudimel, Claude

SINGT UND KLINGT see Praetorius,
Michael, Psallite

SINIGAGLIA, LEONE (1868-1944)
Il Natale *Op.6
4pt mix cor,2fl,2ob,2clar,2bsn,
2horn,2trp,timp,perc CARISH
rental   (S536)

SINNER MAN *spir
(Roberts) SATB,ST soli,acap,opt perc
oct LAWSON 51571 $.35   (S537)

SINNER, YOU CAN'T WALK MY PATH *spir
(Moore) SATB WARNER W-3546 $.35
                                        (S538)

SINNER YOU KNOW *anthem
(Bass) SATB,med solo FINE ARTS
CM 1062 $.35   (S539)

SINZHEIMER, MAX
Beatitudes, The *Bibl
mix cor,high solo/med solo,pno/org
PETERS P66308   (S540)

Child Is Born In Bethlehem, A
FLAMMER A 5258 $.25   (S541)

Coming Child, The *Adv/Xmas
2pt mix cor,kbd (med easy) oct
CONCORDIA 98-1961 $.30   (S542)

Hilariter, Alleluia *Xmas
SATB&opt jr cor,opt solo oct AGAPE
F 937 $.30   (S543)

Look Ye Saints, The Sight Is Glorious
*anthem/hymn
SATB,org/pno PETERS 6699 $.25
                                        (S544)

Psalm 30 *see Song Of Dedication

Song Of Dedication (Psalm 30)
SATB oct PRESSER MC483 $.30   (S545)

Song Of Mary, The
unis sr cor,solo,opt ob,clar,bsn,
bells (med) oct AUGSBURG 11-1662
$.60   (S546)

To Share The Cross
oct AGAPE A 409 $.30   (S547)

SION'S DAUGHTER *carol
SATB (easy) OXFORD 08.087 $.15 (S548)

SION'S DAUGHTER see Hill

SIPILA, EERO (1918-1972)
Miserere (Psalm 51) mot
[Lat] SATB,acap oct FAZER s.p.
                                        (S549)

Psalm 51 *see Miserere

Super Flumina Babylonis *Bibl/mot
[Lat] mix cor oct FAZER s.p. (S550)

SIR CHRISTEMAS see Mathias, William

SIR GAWAIN CAROLS see Crawley

SIR-HAR-SIRIM see Pololanik, Zdenek

SIRACH
And Now Bless The God Of All
(composed with Wilson)
SATB (med diff) WATERLOO $.40 (S551)

SIROLA, [BOZIDAR] (1889-1956)
Lord's Prayer, The *prayer
SAATTBB,Bar solo,acap AMP A159 $.25
                                        (S552)

SISLER, HAMPSON A.
Every Good And Perfect Gift *anthem
men&wom cor,org/pno WORLD
CA-2117-5 $.45   (S553)

Let Us Exalt Him *anthem
SATB,org,opt trp&perc WORLD
CA-2115-8 $.75   (S554)

SISTER, S.C.
Mother, At Your Feet Is Kneeling
(Walton) SA oct MCA s.p.   (S555)

SIT DOWN, SERVANT, SIT DOWN *spir
(Clark) SATB,acap oct BOOSEY 5067
$.30   (S556)

SITIVIT ANIMA MEA see Palestrina,
Giovanni

SITTLER, JEAN
Spirit Of The Lord, The *anthem
unis,gtr AUGSBURG 11-3006 $.10
                                        (S557)

That Christmas Long Ago *Xmas
SATB SCHMITT 1744 $.25   (S558)

SITTON, CARL
Behold, God Is My Salvation
SATB GALAXY 1.2307.1 $.35   (S559)

Carol Of The New Prince *Xmas
SATB GALAXY 1.2203.1 $.35   (S560)

SITTON, CARL (cont'd.)

Song Of Praise
SATB GALAXY 1.2195.1 $.30   (S561)

SIX AFRO-AMERICAN CAROLS FOR CHRISTMAS
*CC6U,Xmas,carol,Afr/US
(Clark) SATB MARKS 4587 $.40   (S562)

SIX AFRO-AMERICAN CAROLS FOR EASTER
*CC6U,Easter,carol,Afr/US
(Clark) SATB MARKS 4600 $.40   (S563)

SIX AMENS AND A COMMUNION SERVICE see
Bawden, Clarence

SIX ANTHEMS FOR JUNIOR CHOIR see
Pfautsch, Lloyd

SIX ANTHEMS FOR JUNIOR VOICES AND
HANDBELLS see Butler, Eugene

SIX ANTHEMS WITH BRASS see Zettervall,
Howard

SIX BACH CHORALES see Bach, Johann
Sebastian

SIX CANONS FOR THE CHURCH YEAR see
Caldara, Antonio

SIX CANTIQUES see Beethoven, Ludwig van

SIX CAROLS FOR SAB AND PIANO *Xmas,
carol
(Woodgate) SAB (med easy) OXFORD
42.157 $.60
contains: Angels From The Realms;
In Dulci Jubilo; O Come All Ye
Faithful; Once In Royal David's
City; Sussex Carol; While
Shepherds   (S564)

SIX CHORAL BENEDICTIONS see Lewis

SIX CHORAL SETTINGS FROM THE BIBLE,
GROUP II see Beattie, Herbert

SIX CHORALES HARMONIZED BY JOHANN
SEBASTIAN BACH see Bach, Johann
Sebastian

SIX CHORUSES FOR MALE VOICES see Holst,
Gustav

SIX CHRISTMAS CAROLS see Cozens, John

SIX CHRISTMAS CAROLS *Xmas,carol
LENGNICK s.p.
contains: Cole, William, What Child
Is This (mix cor,acap); Jackson,
Stephen, Sweet Was The Song (mix
cor,acap); Moorse, Peter, Child
Is Born, A (mix cor,acap); Race,
Steve, Jesus Child (mix cor);
Roe, Christopher, Homecoming, The
(mix cor); Rubbra, Edmund, Holy
Dawn, The (mix cor,acap)   (S565)

SIX CHRISTMAS CAROLS FROM EUROPE *sac/
sec,CC6U
(Bell) unis,rec,tamb,glockenspiel,
xylophone, triangle, cymbals, woodblock RICORDI-ENG LD588 sc s.p.,
cor pts s.p., ipa, cmplt ed s.p.
                     (S566)

SIX CHRISTMAS HYMNS *Xmas,hymn
(Willcocks) SATB,inst (med easy)
OXFORD 48.032 $1.00, ipr
contains: As With Gladness; Come,
Thou Redeemer; It Came Upon The
Midnight Clear; O Come, O Come,
Emmanuel; Once In Royal David's
City; While Shepherds Watched
Their Flocks By Night   (S567)

SIX CHRISTMAS SONGS *sac/sec,CC6U,Xmas
(Norlin, L.; Peterman, W.) TBB,opt
gtr&bvl&perc SUMMY $2.95   (S568)

SIX HYMN INTROITS see Tapscott, Carl

SIX INTROITS see Bevan, Gwilym

SIX INTROITS, AN EASTER CAROL AND A
BAPTISMAL MOTET see Bevan, Gwilym

SIX LOVE SONG WALTZES see Brahms,
Johannes

SIX NOELS PREMIERE SERIE see Choisy

SIX NOELS PREMIERE SERIE see Choisy

SIX NOELS DEUXIEME SERIE see Choisy

SIX NOELS DUEXIEME SERIE see Choisy

SIX SONGS
(Bissell, Keith) SA PEER $.75
contains: At The Gate Of Heaven;
I've Danced So Hard; O Blessed
Child; Quem Pastores; Spring; Ye
Sons And Daughters Of The King
                     (S569)

SIX SONGS *CC6U,Pol,17th cent
mix cor,acap POLSKIE FMAXXX s.p.
                     (S570)

SIXTEEN HYMNS AND PROCESSIONALS see
Williamson, Malcolm

SIXTEEN LITURGICAL WORKS see Asola,
Giovanni Matteo

SIXTEEN SINGING MEN *CCUL
(Peterson, John W.) 4pt men cor,pno
SINGSPIR 5458 $1.50   (S571)

SIXTEENTH-CENTURY BICINIA: A COMPLETE
EDITION OF MUNICH, BAYERISCHE
STAATSBIBLIOTHEK, MUS. MS. 260,
VOL. I *sac/sec,CCU
(Bellingham, Bruce; Evans, Edward G.
Jr.) cor bds A-R ED $9.95   (S572)

SIXTEENTH-CENTURY BICINIA: A COMPLETE
EDITION OF MUNICH, BAYERISCHE
STAATSBIBLIOTHEK, MUS. MS. 260,
VOL. II *sac/sec,CCU
(Bellingham, Bruce; Evans, Edward G.
Jr.) cor bds A-R ED $9.95   (S573)

SJALOM' VOOR ISRAEL see Pronk, Arie

SJUNGANDE KYRKA see Anonymous

SJUNGEN OCH SPELEN TILL HERRENS ARA see
Soderholm, Valdemar

SKAGGS, M.
Jesus! I Love Him Best
(Larsen, L.B.) SATB oct GOSPEL
05 TM 0169 $.25   (S574)

SKILES
Battle Hymn
SATB,brass oct LILLENAS MB-005 $.75
                     (S575)

SKILJAS VI MA FRAN VANNER OCH FRANDER
see Soderholm, Valdemar

SKILLINGS, OTIS
Alleluia Praise Chorus *gospel
SB oct LILLENAS AN-1674 $.30 (S576)

Bond Of Love, The *gospel
(Bock, Fred) 2pt oct LILLENAS
AN-5046 $.25   (S577)
(Bock, Fred) SATB oct LILLENAS
AN-5050 $.30   (S578)

Californians Sing No. 2 *CC9UL
cor,pno LILLENAS MB-314 $1.95
                     (S579)

Celebration Of Hope, A
cor,pno LILLENAS MB-303 $2.95
                     (S580)

Celebration Of Praise *anthem
SATB oct LILLENAS AN-2396 $.40
                     (S581)

Christmas Festival, A (composed with
Owens, Jimmy) *Xmas,cant
SATB LILLENAS MC-24 $1.95 (S582)

Day Of Liberation, The *gospel
SATB oct LILLENAS AN-5064 $.30
                     (S583)

Discovery
cor,soli,pno LILLENAS MB-337 $1.95
                     (S584)

God Never Changes *folk
SATB oct LILLENAS AN-5048 $.30
                     (S585)

He Holds The Worlds Together *gospel
SAATB oct LILLENAS AN-2393 $.30
                     (S586)

Heart Of America, The
SSATB oct LILLENAS AN-3845 $.30
                     (S587)

He's Back *gospel
SATB oct LILLENAS AT-1094 $.30
                     (S588)

I Am Thankful To Be An American
SSATB oct LILLENAS AN-3843 $.50
                     (S589)

In God We Trust
SATB oct LILLENAS AN-3841 $.25
                     (S590)

Is There Really A God? *gospel
SATB oct LILLENAS AN-5038 $.30
                     (S591)

I've Got A Reason To Sing *gospel
(Linn) SATB,strings,brass oct
LILLENAS AT-1096 $.35   (S592)

Jesus, The Hope *gospel
SATB oct LILLENAS AN-1675 $.25
                     (S593)

Just Ask Him - Listen - Right Now -
Receive Him Now (composed with
Owens) *gospel
SATB oct LILLENAS AN-5004 $.35
                     (S594)

Life
cor,pno LILLENAS MB-105 $2.95
                     (S595)
(Hall, O.D.) SAB,pno LILLENAS
MB-339 $2.95   (S596)

SKILLINGS, OTIS (cont'd.)

Living Hope, A *anthem
SATB oct LILLENAS AN-1681 $.30
                     (S597)

Love Is A Man *folk
2pt oct LILLENAS AN-5053 $.30
                     (S598)

Love Is A Soul Thing *folk
SATB oct LILLENAS AN-5049 $.30
                     (S599)

My Hope Of Glory *folk
SATB oct LILLENAS AN-5062 $.30
                     (S600)

My Prayer For America
SSATTB oct LILLENAS AN-3842 $.25
                     (S601)

Name Of Jesus, The *gospel/medley
SATB oct LILLENAS AT-1110 $.35
                     (S602)

Now Walk With God *gospel
SAB oct LILLENAS AN-5059 $.30
                     (S603)

People Everywhere Need People
ST oct LILLENAS AN-3844 $.30 (S604)

Praise Ye The Lord, The Almighty
*folk
SATB oct LILLENAS AN-5071 $.30
                     (S605)

Reach Out And Touch *folk
SATB oct LILLENAS AN-5052 $.30
                     (S606)
2pt oct LILLENAS AN-5056 $.30
                     (S607)

Rejoice! *Xmas,cant
cor,opt soli,opt inst LILLENAS
MC-25 $1.50   (S608)

Song Of Praise *anthem
SATB oct LILLENAS AN-2391 $.35
                     (S609)

Thank You, Lord *folk
SATB oct LILLENAS AN-5051 $.30
                     (S610)

There's Only One Solution *folk
SSATB oct LILLENAS AN-5042 $.35
                     (S611)

This Is The Hope *anthem
SATB oct LILLENAS AN-1684 $.30
                     (S612)

Today *folk
SATB oct LILLENAS AN-5070 $.35
                     (S613)

We Need More Love
SSATB oct LILLENAS AN-3846 $.40
                     (S614)

Your Invitation *gospel
STB/SAB oct LILLENAS AN-5040 $.25
                     (S615)

SKOOG
Glory To God We Sing! *Xmas,anthem
(Johnson, Norman) SATB oct SINGSPIR
ZJP-3033 $.30   (S616)

SKY CAN STILL REMEMBER, THE see Brooks

SLADE
Footsteps Of Jesus (composed with
Turner) *anthem
SATB oct BROADMAN 4540-95 $.30
                     (S617)

We Will Follow *see Billingsley

SLANEY, IVOR
Bells Of Bethlehem, The *Xmas
(Newman, Richard) SATB,pno oct
REGENT R-107 $.25   (S618)

SLATER, A.
It's In My Heart
(Collins, Hope) SATB oct GOSPEL
05 TM 0175 $.20   (S619)

SLATER, DAVID D.
Little Lord Jesus
SA HARRIS $.25   (S620)
SATB HARRIS $.35   (S621)
SSA HARRIS $.30   (S622)

Our Shrine, Our Shrine
SATB HARRIS $.35   (S623)

Prayer Of Thanksgiving *prayer,Dut
SATB HARRIS $.35   (S624)

SLATER, RICHARD W.
Psalm 66 *anthem
SATB,org AUGSBURG 11-0660 $.45
                     (S625)

Song Of Mary And Jesus, A *Xmas,
anthem
SATB,fl,fing.cym. WORLD CA-4026-8
$.45   (S626)

SLAUSON, LOYAL
Great Jehovah, Hear Thy Children's
Prayer *anthem
SATB oct SINGSPIR ZJP-7322 $.30
                     (S627)

Marching To Zion *anthem/gospel
SATB oct SINGSPIR ZJP-8149 $.30
                     (S628)

SLEEP, BABY, SLEEP see Wilhelm,
Patricia M.

SLEEP, HOLY BABE see Ganschow, T.F.

SLEEP, HOLY CHILD see Bock, Fred

SLEEP, HOLY JESUS see McLaughlin,
Marian

SLEEP, LITTLE BABY JESUS see Curtwright
Carolee

SLEEP LITTLE JESUS see Preston

SLEEP, MY CHILD, JESUS *Adv/Xmas,
carol,Pol
(Brown) SATBB oct LILLENAS AN-3860
$.30   (S629)

SLEEP, MY JESUS, SLEEP *Xmas
(Coggin) SATB PRO ART 2804 $.35
                                        (S630)

SLEEP, MY LITTLE JESUS see Geibel

SLEEP, MY LITTLE ONE see Hitchcock, G.

SLEEP, MY SAVIOR, SLEEP *Xmas,anthem
(Rasley, John M.) SATB oct SINGSPIR
ZJP-3043 $.25   (S631)

SLEEP, MY SAVIOUR, SLEEP
(Caldwell, Mary E.) SAB,org (easy)
oct GENTRY G-221 $.35   (S632)

SLEEP, MY SAVIOUR, SLEEP see Grimes,
Gordon

SLEEP OF THE INFANT PRINCE *Xmas,
anthem
(Farrell) SAAB/SATB (easy) oct
BROADMAN 4551-60 $.30   (S633)

SLEEP, THOU, MY JEWEL
see Polish Christmas Carols

SLEEP WELL, THOU LOVELY HEAVENLY BABE
*Xmas,anthem/carol,Ger
(Ehret, Walter) SA,org/vcl (easy) GIA
G1850 $.35   (S634)

SLEETH, NATALIE
Amen, So Be It
2pt (easy) FISCHER,C CM 7807 $.35
                                        (S635)

Blessing *Gen/Thanks
unis,pno/org,opt fl CHORISTERS
A-145 $.45   (S636)

Canon Of Praise, A *Gen/Thanks,canon
3pt treb cor/SAB,opt hndbl
CHORISTERS A-79 $.45, ipa   (S637)

Carol Of The Fishermen
2pt ART MAST 249 $.40   (S638)

For This Was I Born *Easter,anthem
SAB (easy) oct BROADMAN 4554-24
$.30   (S639)

God Of Great And God Of Small
unis (easy) FISCHER,C CM 7808 $.30
                                        (S640)

Isn't It Reassuring?
2pt FISCHER,C CM 7828 $.35   (S641)

Just Another Baby? *anthem
unis (easy) oct BROADMAN 4558-36
$.30   (S642)

Little Grey Donkey *Palm
unis,kbd,ob, sandblock, woodblock
CHORISTERS A-84 $.35   (S643)

Lord, He Made The Earth And Sky, The
2pt ART MAST 232 $.35   (S644)

Lord Jesus Be Near Me
unis,pno/org,opt clar/vcl (easy)
FISCHER,C CM 7928 $.40   (S645)

Love One Another
1-2pt oct HOPE A 480 $.35   (S646)

Noel, Noel, A Boy Is Born *Xmas
2pt ART MAST 223 $.45   (S647)

They All Lived Long Ago *anthem
unis (easy) oct BROADMAN 4558-24
$.30   (S648)

We Had A Share *Lent
2pt ART MAST 234 $.40   (S649)

SLUSS, ROBERT
Nunc Dimittis
(Trepp, J.M.) SATB LEONARD-US
08575500 $.50   (S650)

SMART
Song Of Praise, A *anthem
2pt,opt inst oct BROADMAN 4558-61
$.30   (S651)

SMART, HENRY THOMAS (1813-1879)
Angels, From The Realms Of Glory
*Xmas,anthem
(DeCou, Harold) SATB oct SINGSPIR
ZJP-3042 $.30   (S652)

SMART, HENRY THOMAS (cont'd.)
Hark, Hark My Soul *anthem
(Mann, Johnny) SATB LEXICON (S653)

Lead On, O King Eternal *anthem
(Johnson, Norman) SATB (easy) oct
SINGSPIR ZJP-6013 $.30   (S654)
(Rasley, John M.) SSATB oct
SINGSPIR ZJP-7251 $.30   (S655)

SMERT, RICHARD
In Die Nativitatis *Xmas
unis STAINER 3.0803.1 $.35   (S656)

SMILIN' MORE EVERYDAY *CCUL
(Krogstad, Bob) jr cor oct SINGSPIR
5013 $1.95   (S657)

SMIT
Psalm 125
(Wesselink) mix cor HEER 1529
                                        (S658)

SMITH
Christ The Lord Is Born *Xmas,anthem
SAB oct LORENZ 7428 $.35   (S659)

Deeper And Deeper *anthem
(Bolks, Dick) SATB oct SINGSPIR
ZJP-7305 $.30   (S660)

Don't-A You Judge
(Nelson) SATB oct SCHMITT 667 $.40   (S661)

Have Thine Own Way, Lord *anthem
SATB oct LORENZ B221 $.35   (S662)

How Firm A Foundation *anthem
SATB oct LORENZ A568 $.35   (S663)

I Am Trusting Thee, Lord Jesus
*anthem
SATB oct LORENZ B234 $.35   (S664)

I Want The World To Know *gospel
(Mickelson, Paul) SSATB oct
LILLENAS AN-1706 $.30   (S665)
(Skillings, Otis) SATB oct LILLENAS
AN-1657 $.25   (S666)

I've Got Jesus *anthem
SATB oct LORENZ B232 $.35   (S667)
unis oct LORENZ 8875 $.30   (S668)

Jesus, I Love Thee *anthem
(Williams, David E.) SATB oct
SINGSPIR ZJP-7280 $.25   (S669)

Jesus, Lover Of My Soul *anthem
SATB oct LORENZ A547 $.35   (S670)

Let All Together Praise Our God
*Xmas,anthem
SATB oct LORENZ A541 $.35   (S671)

Lily Of The Valley, The *anthem
SATB oct LORENZ A566 $.35   (S672)

Love Lifted Me *see Rowe

My Jesus, I Love Thee *anthem
SATB oct LORENZ B239 $.35   (S673)

O Give Thanks Unto The Lord *anthem
SATB oct LORENZ B225 $.35   (S674)
SAB/SA/unis oct LORENZ 7425 $.35
                                        (S675)

O Sing Unto The Lord *anthem
SATB oct BROADMAN 4545-83 $.30
                                        (S676)

Old Jordan *anthem
SAB oct LORENZ 7423 $.30   (S677)

On Jordan's Stormy Banks *anthem
SATB oct LORENZ A549 $.35   (S678)

Promised One, The *Xmas,anthem
SATB oct LORENZ B215 $.35   (S679)

Shout And Sing *anthem
SATB,brass (easy) oct BROADMAN
4545-46 $.30   (S680)

Spend A Little Time *folk
(Skillings, Otis) SATB oct LILLENAS
AN-5043 $.30   (S681)

To Zion Jesus Came *Easter,anthem
SATB oct LORENZ A553 $.35   (S682)

Why Was I Born? *folk
(Skillings, Otis) 2pt oct LILLENAS
AN-5044 $.30   (S683)

SMITH, ALFRED B.
Surely Goodness And Mercy *see
Peterson, John W.

SMITH, CLAUDE T.
Praise The Lord, Sing Alleluia
SATB WINGERT s.p.   (S684)

This Is The Will Of Our God
SATB WINGERT s.p.   (S685)

SMITH, EDDIE
Finders, Keepers
(Skillings, Otis) jr cor (musical)
cmplt ed LILLENAS MB-347 $1.50
                                        (S686)

SMITH, F.S. BREVILLE
Master Sleeps, The
mix cor BRODT 540 $.18   (S687)

SMITH, G. ALAN
I'm OK, You're OK
SATB,pno,opt gtr oct AGAPE AG 7167
$.40   (S688)

Make A Joyful Noise To The Lord
*Gen/Thanks,anthem
SATB,pno,opt gtr, claves oct HOPE
CF 175 $.40   (S689)

Two Prayers *Gen/Marriage
unis,pno/gtr/pno&gtr oct HOPE
CF 183 $.35   (S690)

SMITH, HAROLD
Song Of The Angels (composed with
Smith, Jean) *Xmas,Bibl/cant
SATB,SSA&S soli,pno (easy) GOSPEL
05 TM 0465 $.65   (S691)

SMITH, HERB
Praise Ye The Lord! *Thanks,anthem
SATB oct SINGSPIR ZJP-7335 $.30   (S692)

SMITH, JEAN
Song Of The Angels *see Smith,
Harold

SMITH, JULIA (1911-   )
God Bless This House
SATB,pno (med easy) JRB JRB-20 $.35
                                        (S693)

SMITH, LANI
Christ The Lord Is Born *Xmas,
anthem/carol
SAB oct LORENZ 7428 $.35   (S694)

I Am Trusting Thee, Lord Jesus *Gen,
anthem/hymn
SATB&wom cor&men cor (med easy) oct
LORENZ B234 $.35   (S695)

I've Got Jesus *Gen,anthem
unis (med diff) oct LORENZ 8875
$.30   (S696)
SATB (med easy) oct LORENZ B232
$.35   (S697)

Lily Of The Valley, The *anthem/
gospel
SA/SATB,opt S/T solo (easy) oct
LORENZ A566 $.35   (S698)

O Give Thanks Unto The Lord *Gen/
Harv/Thanks,pop
SAB,inst oct LORENZ 7425 $.35
                                        (S699)

SMITH, LELAND (1925-   )
On The Existence Of God
SATB,soli,2fl,2ob,2clar,2bsn,horn,
trp,trom,tuba,timp,perc,pno,
strings AM.COMP.AL.   (S700)

Two Motets *CC2U,mot
SATB,acap AM.COMP.AL. $1.10   (S701)

SMITH, STANLEY
Fanfare For An Infant King *Xmas
2pt CHORISTERS A-93 $.30   (S702)

Prayer For Children *Gen/Thanks
unis,rec CHORISTERS A-88 $.30
                                        (S703)

Sing Unto The Lord *Gen/Thanks
unis,opt perc CHORISTERS A-70 $.30
                                        (S704)

SMITH, TEDD
There's A Quiet Understanding
(Wilson, J.F) SSA/SSAA oct HOPE
CF 178 $.35   (S705)

SMYTH, ETHEL (MARY) (1858-1944)
Mass In D
SATB,SATB soli,2fl,pic,2ob,2clar,
3bsn,4horn,2trp,3trom,tuba,timp,
perc,strings, English horn voc sc
NOVELLO rental   (S706)

SNELL, FREDERICK
Praise God With Loud Songs *anthem
SATB&cong,org AUGSBURG 11-3008 $.10
                                        (S707)

SNOGREN, FREDERICK
I Was Glad When They Said Unto Me
*anthem
(Rasley, John M.) SA&opt TB (easy)
oct SINGSPIR ZJP-6009 $.30 (S708)

Ring, Bells, O Ring *Xmas,anthem
(Johnson, Norman) SATB oct SINGSPIR
ZJP-3013 $.25   (S709)

SNOW HAD FALLEN; CHRIST WAS BORN see
Paulus, Stephen

SNOW LAY ON THE GROUND, THE *Xmas,
  anthem/carol
  (Cram, James D.) mix cor CENTURY PR
  $.20   (S710)

SNOW LAY ON THE GROUND, THE see Kent

SNYDER
  Maker Of The Stars
  2pt jr cor oct LILLENAS AN-4037
  $.25   (S711)

SNYDER, GEORGE B.
  Promise Of Love, The *Xmas,cant
  (Huff, Ronn) SATB,narrator BENSON
  B0491 $1.50   (S712)

SNYDER, WESLEY
  I Love Thy Church, O God
  SATB STANDARD A50MX5 $.50   (S713)

SO BLEST A SIGHT
  (Parker, Alice) SATB,pno/org/orch
  (easy/med) cor pts FISCHER,C
  CM 7843 $.30 see also Seven
  Christmas Carols   (S714)

SO FRAGILE see Posegate

SO FUHRST DU DOCH RECHT SELIG, HERR,
  DIE DEINEN see Studer, Hans

SO GREAT A GIFT see Thomas, Daniel B.

SO I SEND YOU see Peterson, John W.

SO LET ME LIVE see Eichorn, Hermene
  Warlick

SO LET ME LIVE see Wyrtzen, Don

SO NIMM DENN MEINE HANDE see Silcher,
  Friedrich

SO SEND I YOU see Peterson, John W.

SO SHE WENT INTO THE GARDEN see
  Josephs, Wilfred

SO SMALL A BOY see Powell, Robert J.

SO SPRICHT DER HERR: ICH WILL DICH
  UNTERWEISEN see Studer, Hans

SOAR, MY SOUL, TO GOD ON HIGH see Bach,
  Johann Sebastian

SOAVE FIA IL MORIR see Palestrina,
  Giovanni

SODERHOLM, VALDEMAR (1909-   )
  Bed Nar Morkret Tatnar
  3pt mix cor ERIKS 321 s.p.   (S715)

  En Enda Rost
  4pt mix cor ERIKS 324 s.p.   (S716)

  Fodd Ar Sasom Skriften Sagt
  SABar ERIKS 69 s.p.   (S717)

  Introitus Pa Paskdagen *Easter,
  Introit
  4pt mix cor ERIKS 318 s.p.   (S718)

  Nar Nar Hjorten Vattenbacken
  4pt mix cor ERIKS 322 s.p.   (S719)

  Nar Vintermorket Kring Oss Star
  wom cor/jr cor ERIKS 5 s.p.   (S720)

  O Gud, Som Allt Med Vishet Styr
  wom cor/jr cor ERIKS 4 s.p.   (S721)

  Psalm 92 *see Sjungen Och Spelen
  Till Herrens Ara

  Sjungen Och Spelen Till Herrens Ara
  (Psalm 92)
  4pt mix cor ERIKS 29 s.p.   (S722)

  Skiljas Vi Ma Fran Vanner Och Frander
  4pt mix cor ERIKS 303 s.p.   (S723)

  Vi Miste Tron Pa Tingen
  4pt mix cor ERIKS 323 s.p.   (S724)

SODERWALL
  Christmas Ring, A *Xmas
  SATB RICHMOND MI-97 $.30   (S725)

SOFTLY AND TENDERLY see Thompson

SOFTLY NOW THE LIGHT OF DAY see
  Silvester, Frederick

SOFTLY THE NIGHT IS SLEEPING see Warner

SOFTLY THE STARS WERE SHINING see
  Torovsky

SOHNER, LEO (1889-   )
  Missa Brevis
  2-3pt jr cor/2-3pt wom cor/2-3pt
  men cor,org (med) sc SCHOTTS
  C 34 271 s.p., cor pts SCHOTTS
  C 34 272 s.p.   (S726)

SOLBERG, PER
  Jul Og Paske
  SSA/SAB MUSIKK   (S727)

SOLI DEO GLORIA *CCU
  cor OUVRIERES s.p.   (S728)

SOLI DEO GLORIA see Weigl, Vally

SOLI DEO HONOR ET GLORIA see Berghorn,
  Alfred

SOLID ROCK, THE *anthem
  (Cram, James D.) SATB FINE ARTS
  CM 1012 $.35   (S729)

SOLID ROCK, THE see Peterson, John W.

SOLLT ICH MEINEM GOTT NICHT SINGEN see
  Leutert

SOLLT ICH MEINEM GOTT NICHT SINGEN? see
  Studer, Hans

SOLLT ICH MEINEM GOTT NICHT SINGEN see
  Wiemer, Wolfgang

SOLLTE DENN DAS SCHWERE LEIDEN see
  Stobaeus, Johann

SOLUS AD VICTIMAM see Leighton, Kenneth

SOMARY, JOHANNES
  As The Hart Longs For The Running
  Waters
  SATB GALAXY 1.2476.1 $.25   (S730)

  Music For The Eucharistic Prayer
  Acclamations
  SATB&opt cong (med) GIA G1766 $.35
                                    (S731)

SOME DAY see Rendell, Gladys

SOME SWEET DAY see Clayton, Norman

SOMEBODY'S KNOCKIN'
  see Christ, Whose Glory Fills The
  Skies

SOMEBODY'S KNOCKIN' AT YOUR DOOR *spir
  (Lefebvre, C.) TTBB GALAXY 1.1624.1
  $.30   (S732)

SOMEBODY'S KNOCKING
  see Vier Negro-Spirituals

SOMEONE see Peterson, John W.

SOMEONE LOVED ME FIRST see Carmichael,
  Ralph

SOMERSET WASSAIL see Toplis

SOMETHING BEAUTIFUL see Gaither,
  William J. (Bill)

SOMETHING BEAUTIFUL NO. 1 see Gaither,
  William J. (Bill)

SOMETHING BEAUTIFUL NO. 2 see Gaither,
  William J. (Bill)

SOMETHING FOR JESUS see Ayers, Jacob S.

SOMETHING GOOD IS GOING TO HAPPEN TO
  YOU see Carmichael, Ralph

SOMETHING SPECIAL, VOL. I *CCUL,gospel
  (Mercer, W. Elmo) cor BENSON B0645
  $1.50   (S733)

SOMETHING SPECIAL, VOL. II *CCUL
  (Mercer, W. Elmo) cor BENSON B0646
  $1.50   (S734)

SOMETHING WONDERFUL see Butler, A.L.

SOMETHING WORTH LIVING FOR see Gaither,
  William J. (Bill)

SOMETIMES A LIGHT see Cowper, William

SOMETIMES I FEEL LIKE A MOTHERLESS
  CHILD *spir
  (Ohrwall) 4pt mix cor ERIKS 59 s.p.
                                    (S735)
  (Thomas) SATB,acap oct LILLENAS
  AN-7005 $.30   (S736)
  (Wild, Eric) SATB (med easy) WATERLOO
  $.35   (S737)

SOMMEIL DE L'ENFANT JESUS *Xmas
  (McCauley, Wm.) SATB (easy) WATERLOO
  $.30   (S738)

SON OF ASSISI see Verrall, Pamela

SON OF GOD IS BORN FOR ALL, THE see
  Hugh

SON OF GOD, THE SON OF MAN, THE see
  Turner

SON OF MAN see Brown, Charles F.

SONATA SOPRA SANCTA MARIA see
  Monteverdi, Claudio

SONG IN THE AIR, A *anthem
  (Lovelace, Austin C.) SATB WORD
  CS-2694 $.35   (S739)

SONG IN THE AIR, A see Paulus, Stephen

SONG IN THE FIERY FURNACE
  (Brandon, George) SATB (med easy)
  WATERLOO $.40   (S740)

SONG IS A GIFT TO GOD, A see Caldwell,
  Mary [Elizabeth]

SONG OF AFFIRMATION see Butler

SONG OF DANIEL see Peloquin, C.
  Alexander

SONG OF DAVID see Mechem, Kirke

SONG OF DEBORAH see Staton, Kenneth W.

SONG OF DEDICATION see Sinzheimer, Max

SONG OF DEDICATION, A see Hudson,
  Richard

SONG OF GLORY see Winter, Sister Miriam
  Therese

SONG OF ISAIAH see Proulx, Richard

SONG OF LIFE see Walker, M.

SONG OF LIFE, A see Oldenburg, Bob

SONG OF LIFE, THE see Franco, Johan

SONG OF LITTLE JESUS, THE see Thomas

SONG OF MARY, THE see Sinzheimer, Max

SONG OF MARY AND JESUS, A see Slater,
  Richard W.

SONG OF MARY AT THE MANGER see Dirksen

SONG OF MARY MAGDALENA
  (Terri) SSA,opt hndbl SCHIRM.G
  LG51734 $.35   (S741)

SONG OF MOSES see Beck, John Ness

SONG OF MOSES, THE see Pulkingham, B.C.

SONG OF PEACE see Feldman, James

SONG OF PRAISE see Nystedt, Knut

SONG OF PRAISE see Rasley, John M.

SONG OF PRAISE see Ridenour, Joe

SONG OF PRAISE see Sitton, Carl

SONG OF PRAISE see Skillings, Otis

SONG OF PRAISE, A see James, Will

SONG OF PRAISE, A see Lovelace, Austin
  C.

SONG OF PRAISE, A see Smart

SONG OF PRAISE, A see Tipton

SONG OF PRAISE AND PRAYER see Binkerd,
  Gordon, Children's Hymn

SONG OF PRAISE AND THANKSGIVING see
  Vleugel, Cornelius

SONG OF PRAISE TO CANADA, A see Brown,
  Allanson G.Y.

SONG OF PRAISE TO GOD, A see Campra,
  Andre

SONG OF SAINT STEPHEN see Lovelace,
  Austin C.

SONG OF SAINT STEPHEN, THE see
  Lovelace, Austin C.

SONG OF SONGS, THE see Pololanik,
  Zdenek, Sir-Har-Sirim

SONG OF THANKSGIVING
  (Bevan, G.) SA (med diff) WATERLOO
  $.35   (S742)

SONG OF THE ANGELS see Smith, Harold

SONG OF THE BELLS see Verrall, Pamela

SONG OF THE MAGI see Davis

SONG OF THE SEASONS, A see Rogers

SONG OF THE SHEPHERDS see Marshall,
  Paul A.

SONG OF THE SHEPHERDS see Ydstie

SONG OF THE SOUL SET FREE, THE *CC9L, gospel
(McLellan, Cyril) cor WORD 37649 $1.95 (S743)

SONG OF THE THREE YOUNG MEN see Proulx, Richard

SONG OF THE UPPER ROOM
(Brandon, George) 1-2pt ART MAST 225 $.30 (S744)

SONG TO SING, A see Collins

SONG UNENDING, A see Peterson, John W.

SONG WAS BORN, A see Mercer, W. Elmo

SONG WAS BORN, A see Parks, Joe E.

SONGS AND PSALMS COMPOSED INTO 3, 4, AND 5 PARTS (1594) EM VOL. 35B see Mundy, John

SONGS FOR CHILDREN'S VOICES see Lenel, Ludwig

SONGS FOR CHRISTMAS see Beck, Theodore

SONGS FOR CHRISTMAS *CC46U, Xmas, hymn
(Reynolds, Wm. J.) cor BROADMAN 4501-05 $.85 (S745)

SONGS FOR DARKNESS AND LIGHT see Felciano, Richard

SONGS FOR DARKNESS AND LIGHT see Felciano, Richard

SONGS FOR MEN NO. 1 *CCUL
(Anthony, Dick) men cor SINGSPIR 5436 $1.25 (S746)

SONGS FOR MEN NO. 2 *CCUL
(Anthony, Dick) men cor/mix cor SINGSPIR 5437 $1.25 (S747)

SONGS FOR MEN NO. 3 *CCUL
(Anthony, Dick) men cor/mix cor SINGSPIR 5438 $1.25 (S748)

SONGS FOR NAOMI see Burnett

SONGS FOR THE JUNIOR SCHOOL see Browne, Sister Deirdre

SONGS FOR TODAY K-1 *sac/sec, CCU
(Johnston, Richard) jr cor WATERLOO $4.95 (S749)

SONGS FOR TODAY VOLUME II *sac/sec, CCU
(Johnston, Richard) jr cor WATERLOO $2.25 (S750)

SONGS FOR TODAY VOLUME III *sac/sec, CCU
(Johnston, Richard) jr cor WATERLOO $2.25 (S751)

SONGS FOR TODAY VOLUME IV *sac/sec, CCU
(Johnston, Richard) jr cor WATERLOO $2.25 (S752)

SONGS FOR TODAY VOLUME V *sac/sec, CCU
(Johnston, Richard) jr cor WATERLOO $2.25 (S753)

SONGS FOR TODAY VOLUME VI *sac/sec, CCU
(Johnston, Richard) jr cor WATERLOO $2.25 (S754)

SONGS FOR TODAY VOLUME VII *sac/sec, CCU
(Johnston, Richard) jr cor WATERLOO $2.25 (S755)

SONGS FOR TODAY VOLUME VIII *sac/sec, CCU
(Johnston, Richard) jr cor WATERLOO $2.25 (S756)

SONGS FOR TODAY VOLUME IX *sac/sec, CCU
(Johnston, Richard) jr cor WATERLOO $2.25 (S757)

SONGS OF INNOCENCE see George, Earl

SONGS OF ISRAEL see Peloquin, C. Alexander

SONGS OF JESUS *CC9U, carol
(Terri) SSA SCHIRM.G LG51799 $3.00 (S758)

SONGS OF REDEMPTION see Elrich, Dwight

SONGS OF SALVATION, NO. 1 *CCU, gospel
(Reynolds, W.J.) cor BROADMAN 4520-06 $.75 (S759)

SONGS OF SALVATION, NO. 2 *CCU, gospel
(Reynolds, W.J.) cor BROADMAN 4520-07 $.75 (S760)

SONGS OF SALVATION, NO. 3 *CCU, gospel
(Reynolds, W.J.) cor BROADMAN 4520-08 $.75 (S761)

SONGS OF THE FAITH *CC64U, gospel
(Sims, W.H.; Reynolds, W.J.) cor (easy/med) BROADMAN 4520-09 $1.25 (S762)

SONGS OF THE GOSPEL *CCU, gospel
(Sims, W.H.; Reynolds, W.H.) cor BROADMAN 4520-10 $1.25 (S763)

SONGS OF THE OLD-TIME FAITH *CC175U, hymn
BENSON B0540 $1.00 (S764)

SONGS TO SEE AND SING *CCU
(Carlson, Adelle) cor BROADMAN 4506-04 $.85 (S765)

SONGS YOU'VE ALWAYS WANTED TO SING *CCUL
(Red, Buryl) cor/cong BROADMAN 4520-31 $1.75 (S766)

SONGSTER FAVORITES *CCUL, gospel
(Johnson, Norman) cor SINGSPIR 5439 $.50 (S767)

SONLIFE see Johnson, Paul

SONLIGHT *CC10L
(Crouch, Andrae) cor LEXICON 37634 $1.95 (S768)

SONNE DER GERECHTIGKEIT see Bender, Jan

SONNE DER GERECHTIGKEIT see Eglin, Arthur

SONNE DER GERECHTIGKEIT see Lauterbach, Lorenz

SONNE DER GERECHTIGKEIT see Peter, Johann Friedrich

SONNENHYMNE DES ECHNATON "ANBETUNG DEM GOTT" see Sturmer, Bruno

SONO UNA CREATURA see Bettinelli, Bruno

SOOFT IHR ESSET VON DIESEM BROT see Schmider, Karl

SOON WE WILL BE FREE see House

SORENSON
Bethany, O Peaceful Habitation
(Pfohl) mix cor BRODT 102 $.18 (S769)

SORGER, FRANZ
Vier Pange Lingua *CC4U
[Lat] 4pt mix cor, acap sc, cor pts BOHM s.p. (S770)

SORGET NICHT FUR EUER LEBEN see Henking, Bernhard

SORIANO, FRANCESCO (ALSO SURIANO)
see SURIANO, FRANCESCO

SOUL OF CHRIST
(Clokey) SATB&jr cor (med) FITZSIMONS 2140 $.25 (S771)

SOULS OF THE RIGHTEOUS
(Betts, Lorne) SATB (med diff) WATERLOO $.40 (S772)

SOULS OF THE RIGHTEOUS see Boyce, William

SOULS OF THE RIGHTEOUS see Johnson, David N.

SOULS OF THE RIGHTEOUS see Noble, Thomas Tertius

SOUND A TRUMPET see Kreter, Leo

SOUND FORTH THE TRUMPET IN ZION see Morley, Thomas

SOUND GENERATION "GOD'S LOVE" *CCUL
(Coates, John) cor BENSON B0643 $1.95 stereo recording, tapes, and-or accompaniment tape also available; for book-record sets available, contact publisher (S773)

SOUND OF AMERICA, THE see Kirkland, Terry

SOUND OF MUSIC, THE see Zilch, Margot

SOUND OF SINGING, THE see Peterson, John W.

SOUND THE BATTLE CRY see Sherwin, William F.

SOUNDS OF CELEBRATION NO. 1 *CCUL
(Wyrtzen, Don) jr cor SINGSPIR 5769 $1.95 (S774)

SOUNDS OF MAJESTY *CCUL
(Raymer, Elwyn) men cor BROADMAN 4522-09 $1.50 (S775)

SOUNDS OF THE CENTURYMEN *CCU, gospel
(Red, Buryl) men cor BROADMAN 4522-10 $1.50 (S776)

SOUTHBRIDGE, JAMES
All Good Gifts Around Us *anthem
SATB oct LORENZ B224 $.35 (S777)

O Lord And Master Of Us All *anthem
SATB oct LORENZ B222 $.30 (S778)

Seek Ye The Lord *Gen, anthem
SATB, med solo (med diff) oct LORENZ C364 $.35 (S779)

SOWER AND THE SEED, THE see Graham, Robert

SOWERBY, LEO (1895-)
All My Heart This Night Rejoices *Xmas
SATB (med) FITZSIMONS 2220 $.25 (S780)

Benedictus Es, Domine
unis (med) FITZSIMONS 7001 $.50 (S781)

Little Jesus, Sweetly Sleep *Xmas
unis (easy) FITZSIMONS 5018 $.20 (S782)

Love Came Down At Christmas
SSA (easy) FITZSIMONS 3046 $.20 (S783)
SATB (easy) FITZSIMONS 2054 $.25 (S784)

O Dearest, Jesu *Xmas, mot
SATB (diff) FITZSIMONS 2012 $.30 (S785)

Seeing We Also *Bibl, mot
SATB, acap (diff) FITZSIMONS 2159 $.50 (S786)

Te Deum Laudamus
SSATB (med) FITZSIMONS 2057 $.50 (S787)

There Comes A Ship A'Sailing
SATB (med) FITZSIMONS 2176 $.25 (S788)

SPACIOUS FIRMAMENT, THE see Parry, W.H.

SPACIOUS FIRMAMENT, THE see Sheeles

SPANDAUER CHORBUCH BAND I see Pepping, Ernst

SPANDAUER CHORBUCH BAND II see Pepping, Ernst

SPANDAUER CHORBUCH BAND III see Pepping, Ernst

SPANDAUER CHORBUCH BAND IV see Pepping, Ernst

SPAR, OTTO (1909-)
Gott, Der Herr, Ist Sonn Und Schild
[Ger] 5pt mix cor MERSEBURG EM182 (S789)

SPARLING, WILLIAM
Christian's Prayer, The
cor BRIDGE Z 7300 (S790)

Jesus Is Calling
cor BRIDGE Z 7302 (S791)

SPEAK, LORD, FOR THY SERVANT HEARETH see Stucky, Steven

SPEAK OUT see Fischer, William Gustavus

SPEAK TO ME, WIND see Winter, Sister Miriam Therese

SPEAK TO MY HEART see McKinney

SPECIAL CHOIR MELODIES *CC20UL, gospel
(McLellan, Cyril) cor GOSPEL 05 TM 4862 $1.00 (S792)

SPECIAL CHOIR MELODIES NO. 2 *CC16UL, gospel
(McLellan, Cyril) cor (easy) GOSPEL 05 TM 4861 $1.00 (S793)

SPECIAL SAB CHOIR MELODIES *CC11UL, gospel
(McLellan, Cyril) cor GOSPEL 05 TM 0496 $1.00 (S794)

SPECIAL STAR, A see Pickell

SPECIALS ARRANGED FOR MALE VOICES NO. 2 *CCUL
men cor SINGSPIR 4180 $1.50 (S795)

SPENCER, WILLIAMETTA
Agnus Dei (from Missa Brevis)
SATB, acap FOSTER MF140E $.30 (S796)

Missa Brevis
SATB, acap FOSTER MF140 $2.50 (S797)

SPENCER, WILLIAMETTA (cont'd.)

Nova, Nova, Ave Fit Ex Eva *Adv
[Eng] SSA,acap oct NATIONAL WHC-14
$.40   (S798)
[Eng] SATB,acap oct NATIONAL WHC-13
$.40   (S799)

SPEND A LITTLE TIME see Smith

SPEYERER DOMFESTMESSE see Haas, Joseph

SPICER
Prayer For My Parents (composed with
Bennett) *anthem
unis (easy) oct BROADMAN 4558-51
$.30   (S800)

SPIESS, MEINRAD (1683-1761)
Messe Fur Die Advents- Und Fastenzeit
*Adv,Mass
[Lat] 4pt mix cor,acap (without
Gloria) sc,cor pts BOHM s.p.
(S801)

SPINDLER, FRITZ (1817-1905)
Laetentur Coeli *Xmas,Offer
[Lat] 4pt mix cor,acap BOHM s.p.
(S802)

SPINNEY, MONTAGUE
Festival Hymn *Gen/Thanks
unis&4pt,org,trp CHORISTERS A-116
$.35   (S803)

SPIRIT BEARS WITNESS, THE see Fargo,
Milford

SPIRIT DIVINE see Lovelace, Austin C.

SPIRIT FILLED SONGS *CC212U,gospel/
hymn
BENSON B0760 $1.25   (S804)

SPIRIT MEDLEY
see Church Is Singing Again, The

SPIRIT OF '76 see Johnson, Paul

SPIRIT OF GOD see Winter, Sister Miriam
Therese

SPIRIT OF JESUS IS IN THIS PLACE, THE
see Gaither, William J. (Bill)

SPIRIT OF OUR FATHER, THE see Andersen,
Dorothy S.

SPIRIT OF THE LORD, THE see Sittler,
Jean

SPIRITUAL MEDLEY *Easter/Gen
(Jeffrey; Mercer, W. Elmo) SATB,acap
oct BENSON S4256 $.25   (S805)

SPIRITUAL-MESSE see Biebl, Franz

SPIRITUAL QUODLIBET FOR CHRISTMAS, A
see Christmas Spiritual Collection

SPIRITUAL RHAPSODY 'JHESU CHRIST SAINT
MARY'S SONE' see Oldroyd, George

SPIRITUAL SING OUT *medley/spir
(Skillings, Otis) SATB oct LILLENAS
AT-1120 $.50   (S806)

SPIRITUALS FOR ALL HEFT I see Petersen,
Rolf

SPIRITUALS FOR ALL HEFT II see
Petersen, Rolf

SPIRITUS DOMINI REPLEVIT see Rehmann,
Th.

SPIRITUS SANCTUS IN TE DESCENDIT, MARIA
see Mutter, Gerbert

SPLENDOR IS COMING see Pelz, Walter L.

SPOEL, A.
Kerstzang *Op.20, Xmas
"Noel" [Fr/Dut] mix cor,pno/
harmonium s.p. sc HEER 493B, cor
pts HEER 493A   (S807)

Noel *see Kerstzang

SPOHR
Selig Sind Die Toten
(Ketterer, E.) men cor,acap TONOS
5645 s.p.   (S808)

SPOHR, LUDWIG (LOUIS) (1784-1859)
As Pants The Hart
mix cor BANKS MUS YS 111 $.25
(S809)

How Lovely Are Thy Dwellings Fair
mix cor BANKS MUS YS 426 $.25
(S810)

SPONSUS
(Smolden) 2pt (med, eleventh century
mystery drama) OXFORD 46.176 $5.35
(S811)

SPRADLIN
Arm Of The Lord, The *see Dauermann,
Stuart

SPRANGER, JORG
Ave Maria
[Lat] SAT&opt B,acap BOHM s.p.
(S812)

De Profundis *ECY,Offer
[Lat] 4pt mix cor,acap BOHM s.p.
(S813)

Hymnus "Gloria, Laus Et Honor" *Palm
[Lat/Ger] 4pt mix cor,acap BOHM
s.p.   (S814)

Improperium *Palm
[Lat] 4pt mix cor,acap BOHM s.p.
(S815)

In Te Speravi
[Lat] 4pt mix cor,acap BOHM s.p.
(S816)

Kleine Muttergottesmesse "Ave Maria
Zart" *Mass
[Lat] SAT/SAB,org sc,cor pts BOHM
s.p.   (S817)

Lasst Vor Gottes Thron Uns Treten
*Mass
[Ger] 2 eq voices,org/harmonium sc,
cor pts BOHM s.p.   (S818)
[Ger] SABar&opt T BOHM sc s.p., cor
pts s.p.   (S819)

Maria Durch Ein' Dornwald Ging *Adv
mix cor/men cor,A/Bar solo BOHM
s.p.   (S820)

Missa Brevis "Lauda Sion Salvatorem"
*Mass
[Lat] 4pt mix cor,org,opt 2trp,
trom, tenor horn sc,cor pts BOHM
s.p., ipa   (S821)

Ora Et Labora *Mass
[Lat] SAB/SAT,acap sc,cor pts BOHM
s.p.   (S822)

Propriumgesange Fur Das Kirchweihfest
"Terribilis Est Locus Iste"
[Lat] 4pt mix cor,acap sc,cor pts
BOHM s.p.   (S823)

Requiem Und Libera In D-Moll
[Lat] SABar&opt T,org (D min) sc,
cor pts BOHM s.p.   (S824)

Sacerdotes Domini
[Lat] SAB&opt T,acap BOHM s.p.
(S825)

Venite, Filii *Fest
[Lat] 4pt mix cor,acap BOHM s.p.
(S826)

Von Seinem Ew'gen Festen Thron *Xmas
jr cor&mix cor,opt solo BOHM s.p.
(S827)

SPREAD, THOU MIGHTY WORD see Harris, D.

SPRING
see Six Songs

SPRING CAROL
(Ritchey, Lawrence) SATB (med easy)
WATERLOO $.35   (S828)

SPRING PRAYER see Caldwell, Mary
[Elizabeth]

SPRINGHILL see Anonymous

SPRINGS OF LIVING WATER see Peterson,
John W.

SPUR US ON TO DO THY WILL see Wilhelm

SPUR US ON TO DO THY WILL see Wilhelm,
Patricia M.

SPURGEON
Young Child's Carol, The *Xmas,carol
(Evans) SATB EMI s.p.   (S829)

SQUIRE, FRED
God Is Our Refuge *anthem
(Smith, Herb) SATB oct GOSPEL
05 TM 0228 $.25   (S830)

I'll Believe Forevermore
(Smith, Herb) SATB oct GOSPEL
05 TM 0177 $.20   (S831)

STABAT MATER see Blaha-Mikes, Zaboj

STABAT MATER see Bononcini, Antonio
Maria

STABAT MATER see Doebler, Curt

STABAT MATER see Dvorak, Antonin

STABAT MATER see Erhard, Karl

STABAT MATER see Hand, Colin

STABAT MATER see Howells, Herbert
Norman

STABAT MATER see Jirasek, Ivo

STABAT MATER see Kelly, Bryan

STABAT MATER see Lassus, Roland de
(Orlandus)

STABAT MATER see Lewkovitch

STABAT MATER see Mollicone, Henry

STABAT MATER see Mortari, Virgilio

STABAT MATER see Naylor, Bernard

STABAT MATER see Rothschuh, Fritz

STABAT MATER see Schubert, Franz
(Peter)

STABAT MATER see Toni, Alceo

STABAT MATER see Tuma, Frantisek Ignaz
Antonin

STABAT MATER DOLOROSA see Wassmer,
Berthold

STABAT MATER IN F-MOLL see Vanhal, Fr.
Krititel

STABILE III, "AVE MARIA" see Wilson,
Donald M.

STABLE BARE, A see Verrall, Pamela

STADEN, JOHANN (1581-1634)
Auf Dich, Herr, Hab Ich Gehoffet
see Staden, Johann, Sei Nun Wieder
Zufrieden, Meine Seele

Christe, Einiger Trost Und Du Hochste
Zuversicht *mot
SSAT/SSAB HANSSLER 1.559 s.p.
(S832)

Danket Dem Herren Alle Zeit
SAT/SAB (contains also: Wir Danken
Dir, O Gottes Lamm) SCHWEIZER.
SK 51.04 s.p. see also
MUSIKBEILAGE ZUM "EVANGELISCHEN
KIRCHENCHOR 1951"   (S833)

Dein Wort, Herr, Ist Mir Ein Licht
Auf Dem Weg *mot
SAT HANSSLER 1.562 s.p. contains
also: Herr, Mein Gott, Nimm Mein
Seel Gnadig Zu Dir (SSAT/SSAB)
(S834)

Der Sabbat Von Gott Ist Drum G'macht
*mot
SSAT/SSAB HANSSLER 1.555 s.p.
(S835)

Erbarm Dich, Herre Gott *mot
SSAT/SSAB HANSSLER 1.561 s.p.
(S836)

Gloria In Excelsis Deo *mot
SSAT/SSAB HANSSLER 1.554 s.p.
(S837)

Herr, Mein Gott, Nimm Mein Seel
Gnadig Zu Dir
see Staden, Johann, Dein Wort,
Herr, Ist Mir Ein Licht Auf Dem
Weg

Herr, Unser Herrscher (Psalm 8) mot
SAT HANSSLER 1.556 s.p.   (S838)

Ich Hab Einen Guten Kampf Gekampfet
*mot
SSAT/SSAB HANSSLER 1.552 s.p.
(S839)

Jag Tackar Dig, Min Hogste Gud
4pt mix cor ERIKS 16 s.p.   (S840)

Jauchzet Dem Herren, Alle Welt (Psalm
100) mot
SAT HANSSLER 1.553 s.p.   (S841)

Lob, Ehr Sei Gott Im Hochsten Thron
*mot
SSAT/SSAB HANSSLER 1.548 s.p.
(S842)

Lobet Den Herren Und Predigt Seinen
Namen *mot
SAT/SAB HANSSLER 1.551 s.p.   (S843)

Lobsinget Gott *mot
SSAT/SSAB HANSSLER 1.550 s.p.
(S844)

Nun Hosianna, Davids Sohn *mot
SSAT/SSAB HANSSLER 1.549 s.p.
(S845)

O Herre Gott Im Himmelreich *mot
SAT HANSSLER 1.557 s.p. contains
also: Vater Unser, Der Du Bist Im
Himmel (SAT/SAB)   (S846)

Psalm 8 *see Herr, Unser Herrscher

Psalm 100 *see Jauchzet Dem Herren,
Alle Welt

Sei Nun Wieder Zufrieden, Meine Seele
*mot
SSAT/SSAB HANSSLER 1.560 s.p.
contains also: Auf Dich, Herr,

STADEN, JOHANN (cont'd.)

Hab Ich Gehoffet (SSAT/SSAB)
(S847)

Vater Unser, Der Du Bist Im Himmel
see Staden, Johann, O Herre Gott Im
Himmelreich

Zwei Der Seraphinen Riefen Und
Sprachen *mot
SSAT/SSAB HANSSLER 1.563 s.p.
(S848)

STAINER, JOHN (1840-1901)
Crucifixion, The *Easter,cant
SATB (simplified edition) SINGSPIR
5808 $1.50   (S849)

Four Chorales From "The Crucifixion"
*CC4U,Easter/Lent
(Berglund) SATB oct SCHMITT 1928
$.35   (S850)

God So Loved The World
SATB HARRIS HC 4052 $.35   (S851)

Shepherds! Shake Off Your Drowsy
Sleep *Xmas
SATB EMI s.p. contains also: Terry,
Richard Runciman, What Is This
Fragrance   (S852)

Sing A Song Of Praise
mix cor BANKS MUS YS 268 $.25
(S853)

STAMP AND SHOUT see Lovelace, Austin C.

STAND UP AND BLESS THE LORD *anthem
(Douglas) SATB FINE ARTS EW 1015 $.30
(S854)

STAND UP AND BLESS THE LORD see
Peterson, John W.

STAND UP AND BLESS THE LORD see
Williams, David

STAND UP AND SING *CCUL
(Musto, Steve) cor SINGSPIR 4062
$1.95   (S855)

STAND UP AND SING see Davis

STAND UP FOR JESUS see Brandon, George

STAND UP FOR JESUS see Webb, George
James

STANDING IN THE NEED OF PRAYER *spir
(Arch, Gwyn) SSA EMI   (S856)
(Kirby) SATB oct LILLENAS AN-3850
$.30   (S857)

STANDING ON THE PROMISES *anthem
(Allen) SATB,Bar solo FINE ARTS EP 28
$.35   (S858)

STANFORD, CHARLES VILLIERS (1852-1924)
Communion Service In C
SATB STAINER 3.0715.1 $1.25   (S859)

Gloria In Excelsis
SATB STAINER 3.0632.1 $1.25   (S860)

Glorious And Powerful God
SATB STAINER 3.0712.1 $.50   (S861)

Magnificat And Nunc Dimittis In C
Major
SATB STAINER 3.0812.1 $1.00   (S862)

Magnificat And Nunc Dimittis In G
Major
SATB STAINER 3.0713.1 $1.25   (S863)

STANGE, MAX (1856-1932)
Wo Der Herr Sein Haus *Op.12
mix cor LIENAU sc s.p., cor pts
s.p.   (S864)

STANLEY, JOHN (1713-1786)
Hosanna, King Of Israel *anthem
SAB WORD CS-2672 $.35   (S865)

STANPHILL
Drifting *anthem/gospel
(Ferrin, Paul) SATB oct SINGSPIR
ZJP-8159 $.25   (S866)

STANPHILL, IRA F.
Happiness Is The Lord *anthem/gospel
SATB oct SINGSPIR ZJP-8075 $.25
(S867)

He Knows What He's Doin' All The Time
*anthem/gospel
(DeCou, Harold) SATB oct SINGSPIR
ZJP-8087 $.25   (S868)

If I've Forgotten *anthem
(McCall, Craig) SA&opt TB (easy)
oct SINGSPIR ZJP-6006 $.25   (S869)

I'm A-Goin' To Glory *anthem
(Ferrin, Paul) SATB oct SINGSPIR
ZJP-8218 $.35   (S870)

STANPHILL, IRA F. (cont'd.)

Jesus And Me *anthem/gospel
(DeCou, Harold) SATB oct SINGSPIR
ZJP-8100 $.30   (S871)

Mansion Over The Hilltop *anthem/
gospel
(Johnson, Norman) SATB oct SINGSPIR
ZJP-8083 $.25   (S872)

Room At The Cross For You *anthem/
gospel
(DeCou, Harold) SATB oct SINGSPIR
ZJP-8064 $.30   (S873)

We'll Talk It Over *anthem/gospel
(Johnson, Norman) SATB oct SINGSPIR
ZJP-8076 $.25   (S874)

Yesterday's Gone *anthem/gospel
(Johnson, Norman) SATB oct SINGSPIR
ZJP-8181 $.30   (S875)

You Can Have A Song In Your Heart
*anthem/gospel
(Johnson, Norman) SATB oct SINGSPIR
ZJP-8144 $.25   (S876)

STANTON
Festal Song
SATTBB SCHIRM.G LG51654 $.45 (S877)

Grant Understanding
SSAATTBB SCHIRM.G LG51653 $.30
(S878)

STANTON, R.
Five Psalm Fragments *CC5U
SATB,soli,acap GRAY CMR 3330 $.35
(S879)

STAPLES
Don't Knock (Just Walk Right In)
(composed with Westbrook)
(Sanford) SATB,opt perc WARNER
WB-309 187 $.60   (S880)

Let's Go Home
(Sanford) SATB,opt perc WARNER
WB-310 187 $.50   (S881)

Pray On
(Sanford) SATB,opt perc WARNER
WB-311 187 $.40   (S882)

STAR, A *Xmas,anthem
(Track, Gerhard) SATB,org (med easy)
GIA G1874 $.50   (S883)

STAR, A see Whitecotton, Shirley

STAR, A SONG, A see Hopson, Hal H.

STAR CAROL, THE see Rutter

STAR CAROL, THE see Verrall, Pamela

STAR ETERNAL, THE see Lowe, G.

STAR FOR MARIA, A see Verrall, Pamela

STAR IN THE EAST *Xmas,Contemp
SATB VANGUARD V564 $.35 see from Come
To Bethlehem   (S884)

STAR IS SHINING, A see Ralston

STAR OF LOVE see Franco, Johan

STAR SHININ' OVER BETHLEHEM *Xmas
(Kirk) SATB oct SCHMITT 8505 $.40
(S885)

STAR SHOWN DOWN, A see Coulthard, Jean

STAR-SPANGLED BANNER, THE see Key,
Francis Scott

STAR, THE WISE MEN, THE CHILD, THE see
Neale

STARKS
According To Thy Gracious Word *see
Montgomery

Arise, O Youth Of God *anthem
SATB oct BROADMAN 4554-75 $.30
(S886)

STARNBERG
Bairische Singmesse *see Zellner,
Hans

STARR
Be Eager To Give *anthem
SATB oct BROADMAN 4551-92 $.30
(S887)

If I Gained The World *see Olander

STARS ARE FOR THOSE WHO LIFT THEIR EYES
see Delmonte, Pauline

STARS LOOK DOWN, THE see Franco, Johan

STATON
O Lord, How Excellent Is Thy Name
*anthem
unis (easy) oct BROADMAN 4551-65
$.30   (S888)

STATON, KENNETH W.
Midnight, Sleeping Bethlehem *Xmas,
anthem
2 eq voices,opt fing.cym. AUGSBURG
11-1715 $.30   (S889)

New And Joyful Song Of Praise, A
*Gen/Thanks
unis CHORISTERS A-132 $.35   (S890)

Song Of Deborah
SSAA STANDARD A38F1 $.50   (S891)

There's A Wideness In God's Mercy
*anthem
2pt mix cor,kbd AUGSBURG 11-1684
$.30   (S892)

STATUIT see Kraft, Karl

STEAD
'Tis So Sweet To Trust In Jesus
(composed with Allen) *anthem
SATB,soli oct BROADMAN 4540-96 $.30
(S893)

STEAL AWAY *spir
(Wick, Fred) TTBB oct SCHMITT W181
$.40   (S894)

STEAL AWAY see Peterson, John W.

STEARMAN
He Turned The Water Into Wine
*gospel
(Skillings, Otis) SATB oct LILLENAS
AN-5080 $.25   (S895)

STECKER, KAREL (1861-1918)
Missa Pastoralis *see Horak, V.

STEDRY DEN see Bendl, Karel

STEEL, CHRISTOPHER [CHARLES]
(1939-   )
Gethsemane
SA,3fl,ob,3clar,2trp,strings,opt
timp&perc&2harp&hvl voc sc
NOVELLO rental   (S896)

Mary Magdalene *Op.29
SSA,fl,ob,clar,opt bsn,perc,2vcl,
glockenspiel voc sc NOVELLO
rental   (S897)

Mass In Five Movements *Op.17, Mass
SATB,ST soli,2fl,pic,2ob,2clar,
2bsn,4horn,2trp,3trom,tuba,timp,
perc,pno,harp,strings,celeste,
vibraphone voc sc NOVELLO rental
(S898)

STEFANSSON, FJOLNIR (1930-   )
Jati Bao Allur Heimur Her
see Three Songs From The Icelandic
Gradual

Lausnarinn Kongur Kriste
see Three Songs From The Icelandic
Gradual

Svo Vitt Um Heim Sem Solin Fer
see Three Songs From The Icelandic
Gradual

Three Songs From The Icelandic
Gradual
[ICELANDIC] ICELAND s.p.
contains: Jati Bao Allur Heimur
Her (ST); Lausnarinn Kongur
Kriste (SAB); Svo Vitt Um Heim
Sem Solin Fer (SAT)   (S899)

STEFFANI, AGOSTINO (1654-1728)
Rejoice In The Lord
SAB oct CONCORDIA 98-2217 $.55
(S900)

STEFFE, WILLIAM
Battle Hymn Of The Republic
(Burroughs) SATB,brass,drums oct
LILLENAS AN-3854 $.40   (S901)
(Loes; Paterson) SATB,3trp oct
GOSPEL 05 TM 0207 $.20   (S902)

His Truth Is Marching On *folk
(Johnson) SATB oct LILLENAS AN-5069
$.40   (S903)

STEH AUF, HERR GOTT see Schmidt, C.

STEHT AUF UND WACHT see Lahusen,
Christian

STEIN, LEON
Lord Reigneth
wom cor,T solo,pno/org,2fl,2ob,
2clar,2bsn,3horn,2trp,2trom,timp,
strings AM.COMP.AL. sc $2.20, voc
sc $8.25   (S904)

STEINBERG, BEN
L'cha Anu Shira *Sab-Eve
[Heb] cor TRANSCON. TCL 869 $4.00
(S905)

STEINERT, BERNHARD
  Lauda Sion
    see Zwei Sakramentsgesange

  Tantum Ergo
    see Zwei Sakramentsgesange

  Veni Creator Spiritus *Op.5,No.3
    [Lat] 4pt mix cor,acap sc,cor pts
    BOHM s.p.   (S906)

  Zwei Sakramentsgesange
    [Lat] 4pt mix cor,acap sc,cor pts
    BOHM s.p.
      contains: Lauda Sion, Op.19,No.1;
      Tantum Ergo, Op.19,No.2 (S907)

STEKL, KONRAD
  Der Verduner Altar *Op.58
    cor,soli,org/orch KRENN 1.30 voc sc
    s.p., cor pts s.p.   (S908)

  Requiem *Op.45, funeral
    8pt mix cor,soli,pno/orch voc sc
    KRENN 1.6   (S909)

STELLA MARIS see Griesbacher, Peter

STELLA MARIS see Mutter, Gerbert

STENNET, S.
  I Am Bound For The Promised Land
    (McLellan, Cyril) SATB oct GOSPEL
    05 TM 0107 $.25   (S910)

STEP INTO THE SUNSHINE see Gassman,
  Clark

STEPHANUS see Hufschmidt, Wolfgang

STEPHEN see Wyton

STEPHEN BEING FULL OF THE HOLY GHOST
  see Tomkins, Thomas

STEPHEN FOSTER SUITE see Foster,
  Stephen

STEPPING IN THE LIGHT *anthem
  (Allen) SATB FINE ARTS EP 32 $.40
               (S911)

STERN, ALFRED (1901-   )
  Freut Euch Alle,
    Weihnachtsliederspiel (composed
    with Stern, Klara) *Xmas,carol
    1-2 eq voices,S rec,A rec,vln,gtr,
    perc PELIKAN PE705   (S912)

STERN, HERMANN (1912-   )
  Alles, Was Odem Hat, Lobe Den Herrn
    see Heer, Emil, Singt Dem Herrn Ein
    Neues Lied

  In Dir Ist Freude
    unis&SAT/SAB SCHWEIZER. SK 69.08
    s.p. see also MUSIKBEILAGE ZUM
    "EVANGELISCHEN KIRCHENCHOR 1969"
               (S913)

STERN, KLARA
  Freut Euch Alle,
    Weihnachtsliederspiel *see
    Stern, Alfred

STERN, THEODORE
  Sing Unto The Lord A New Song
    *anthem
    SATB,org AUGSBURG 11-0657 $.45
               (S914)

STEUERLEIN, JOHANN (1546-1613)
  Das Alte Jahr Vergangen Ist
    SSAT/SSAB SCHWEIZER. SK 72.06 s.p.
    see also MUSIKBEILAGE ZUM
    "EVANGELISCHEN KIRCHENCHOR 1972"
               (S915)
  Sing To The Lord Of Harvest *Thanks,
    anthem
    (Ayers, Jacob S.) SATB oct SINGSPIR
    ZJP-3111 $.35   (S916)

STEVENS, HALSEY (1908-   )
  Three Hymns *CC3U
    SATB,pno/acap AM.COMP.AL. $3.30
               (S917)

STEWART, ROBERT [PRESCOTT] (1825-1894)
  Amen
    SATB,acap AM.COMP.AL. $1.10 (S918)

  Amen (Gaudete Populi)
    SATB,org AM.COMP.AL. $3.30 (S919)

STICHIRON see Terzakis, Dimitri

STIFFLER, GEORGIA
  Healer Of Broken Hearts *gospel
    (Bolks, Dick) SATB,pno (easy)
    GENTRY G-217 $.40   (S920)

STILL LIFE see Fischer

STILL, STILL *Xmas,anthem
  (Track, Gerhard) SATB,org (med easy)
    GIA G1873 $.50   (S921)

STILL, STILL, STILL *Xmas
  (Eilers, Joyce) SSA LEONARD-US
    08547300 $.50   (S922)

STILL TO US IS BORN TONIGHT see
  Lovelace, Austin C.

STILLA NATT, HELIGA NATT *Xmas
  (Berg, Gottfrid) SABar ERIKS 65 s.p. (S923)

STILLE NACHT
  see Twelve Christmas Carols: Set 1

STILLE NACHT see Erk

STILLE NACHT, EN TWEE ANDERE
  KERTSLIEDEREN *CC4U,Xmas
  unis,pno/harmonium HEER 266 s.p.
               (S924)

STILLE NACHT, HEILIGE NACHT *Op.13c,
  Xmas
  (Muller, A.M.) mix cor,orch sc,cor
    pts BOHM s.p., ipa   (S925)

STILLE NACHT, HEILIGE NACHT see
  Deutschmann, Gerhard

STILLE NACHT, HEILIGE NACHT see Gruber,
  Franz Xaver

STIPE
  Life In Jesus
    (Coates) SATB oct BENSON S4172 $.35
               (S926)

STIR UP WE BESEECH THEE see George,
  Graham

STOBAEUS, JOHANN (1580-1646)
  Nun Lasst Uns Mit Der Engel Schar
    SSATB SCHWEIZER. SK 141 s.p. (S927)

  Sollte Denn Das Schwere Leiden
    *Easter
    SST&TTBB/SSA&TTBB,opt inst
    LAUDINELLA LR 73 s.p.   (S928)

STOCK, LARRY (1896-   )
  Cradle In Bethlehem, A *Xmas,carol,
    Eng
    (Bock, Fred) SATB,pno (med easy)
    GENTRY G-264 $.40   (S929)

STOCKTON
  Glory To His Name *see Bartlett

  Only Trust Him *anthem/gospel
    (Collins, Hope) SATB oct GOSPEL
    05 TM 0210 $.20   (S930)
    (Rasley, John M.) SSATB oct
    SINGSPIR ZJP-8085 $.30 (S931)

STOCKTON, JOHN H.
  Great Physician, The *anthem
    (Burroughs, Bob) SATB WORD CS-2635
    $.30   (S932)

STOKER, RICHARD (1938-   )
  Benedictus
    SATB,orch ASHDOWN EC353 ipr (S933)

STONE
  Come On Down *see Hayford

  Lord's Prayer, The
    (Greening) SATB,acap (easy) OXFORD
    43.487 $.30   (S934)

STOOKEY
  Very Last Day (composed with Yarrow)
    (Siltman) TTB WARNER CT0412 $.40
               (S935)

STORM AT SEA see Nelson, Ronald A.

STORRS, H.
  Have I Done My Best For Jesus?
    *anthem/gospel
    (DeCou, Harold) SATB oct SINGSPIR
    ZJP-8189 $.30   (S936)

STORY OF CHRISTMAS, THE see Peterson,
  John W.

STORY OF JESUS, THE see Graf, Doris

STORY-TELLIN' MAN, THE see Medema, Ken

STORY UNCHANGED, THE see Mercer, W.
  Elmo

STOUT, ALAN (1932-   )
  Adoramus Te *Op.68,No.2, Gd.Fri.,mot
    SATB,org/strings,perc AM.COMP.AL.
    sc $2.75, ipa, voc pt $1.10
               (S937)

  Advent Cantata *Op.54, Adv,cant
    SATB,T solo,org,opt vcl sc
    AM.COMP.AL. $5.50, ipa   (S938)

  Ave Maria *Op.71a
    3pt,opt strings sc AM.COMP.AL.
    $2.75, ipa   (S939)
    SATB,acap AM.COMP.AL. $2.75 (S940)
    TB,org AM.COMP.AL. $.55   (S941)
    TB,acap AM.COMP.AL. $.55   (S942)

  Canon In Four Voices *Op.44b, canon
    cor,inst sc AM.COMP.AL. $1.38
               (S943)

STOUT, ALAN (cont'd.)
  Custodi Me *Op.68,No.3
    SATB,cantor,strings/org sc
    AM.COMP.AL. $.83, ipa contains
    also: Lignum Crucis, Op.68,No.4
               (S944)

  Diagolo Per La Pascua
    cor,SATB soli,harp,2vln,2vla,2vcl,
    bvl AM.COMP.AL. sc $8.25, ipa,
    voc pt $5.50   (S945)

  Dismissal *Op.44d
    cor,cantor,org AM.COMP.AL. $.28
               (S946)

  Domine Ne Longe *Op.68, mot
    men cor,T/Bar solo,org,strings sc
    AM.COMP.AL. $1.10, ipa   (S947)

  Ecce, Agnus Dei *Op.68,No.8
    SSATBB,org/strings sc AM.COMP.AL.
    $.55, ipa   (S948)

  Exspecta Dominum *Op.68,No.6
    SATB,perc/strings sc AM.COMP.AL.
    $2.75, ipa   (S949)

  Gloria, Laus Et Honor
    SATB,horn,2trom,bsn,org,4vln,2vla,
    2vcl,bvl sc AM.COMP.AL. $2.75
               (S950)

  Gradual For Easter *Op.44c, Easter,
    Gradual
    cor,cantor,org AM.COMP.AL. $1.38
               (S951)

  Improperium *Op.68,No.14, mot
    TTBB,org,6strings AM.COMP.AL. sc
    $3.30, ipa, voc pt $1.10 (S952)

  In Principio Erat Verbum *Op.44, mot
    SSAATTBB,strings,opt org sc
    AM.COMP.AL. $5.50   (S953)

  Lignum Crucis *Op.68,No.4
    see Stout, Alan, Custodi Me

  Mass *Op.25,No.2
    SATB,SATB soli,org,opt ob&bsn&perc&
    strings, English horn sc
    AM.COMP.AL. $11.55, ipa (S954)

  Nunc Dimittis *Op.5a
    SATB,fl,org,strings, cymbals
    AM.COMP.AL. sc $4.40, voc sc
    $4.40, voc pt $.55   (S955)

  O Altitudo *Bibl
    wom cor,S solo,fl,inst sc PETERS
    P66544 s.p., ipa, voc sc PETERS
    P66544A s.p.   (S956)

  Osanna Filio David *Op.68,No.16
    6pt mix cor,org,bsn,horn,2trp,
    3trom,perc,4vln,2vla,2vcl,bvl
    AM.COMP.AL. sc $3.85, voc pt
    $2.75   (S957)

  Pater, Si Non Potest *Op.68,No.17,
    Palm
    [Lat] men cor,harp,2vln,vla,2vcl,
    bvl, celeste, tam-tam AM.COMP.AL.
    sc $1.38, voc pt $.55 (S958)

  Per Lignum Servi Facti Sumus *Op.68,
    No.7, Gd.Fri.
    [Lat] SATB,harp,strings AM.COMP.AL.
    sc $3.30, voc pt $2.75 (S959)

  Pueri Hebraorum *mot
    cor,perc,harp,4strings sc
    AM.COMP.AL. $2.75, ipa (S960)

  Salvator Mundi *Op.68,No.1, Gd.Fri.,
    mot
    SATB,org/strings sc AM.COMP.AL.
    $1.10, ipa   (S961)
    mix cor,opt org AM.COMP.AL. $.55
               (S962)

  Two Motets *Op.68,No.12-13, CC2U,mot
    SATB,org,perc,strings AM.COMP.AL.
    sc $1.10, voc pt $1.10   (S963)

STRAESSER, JOEP (1934-   )
  Missa
    mix cor,winds DONEMUS   (S964)

STRAF MICH NICHT IN DEINEM ZORN see
  Chemin-Petit, Hans

STRAF MICHT NICHT IN DEINEM ZORN see
  Linke, Norbert

STRALLS, ARNOLD
  Lord's Prayer, The
    (Nowak, Jerry) SATB,pno,opt fl,
    drums,gtr, electric bass sc BIG
    BELL $3.00 $.50   (S965)
    (Nowak, Jerry) SAB,pno,opt fl,
    drums,gtr, electric bass sc BIG
    BELL $3.00 $.50   (S966)
    (Nowak, Jerry) SSA,pno,opt fl,
    drums,gtr, electric bass sc BIG
    BELL $3.00 $.50   (S967)
    (Nowak, Jerry) SA,pno,opt fl,drums,
    gtr, electric bass sc BIG BELL
    $3.00 $.50   (S968)

STRAND, RAGNVALD
De Som Kjenner Ditt Navn (Psalm 9)
SSA/SAB MUSIKK (S969)

Et Udelt Hjerte (Psalm 86)
SSA/SAB MUSIKK (S970)

Psalm 9 *see De Som Kjenner Ditt
Navn

Psalm 86 *see Et Udelt Hjerte

STRANGER IN THE STRAW see Blackley

STRATEGIER, HERMAN (1912-)
Mors Responsura-In Memoriam Fratris
Spiritualis Jan Mul
mix cor,SA soli,2fl,3ob,2clar,2bsn,
2horn,2trp,2trom,strings,perc,
timp DONEMUS (S971)

Psalm 103 *see Psaume CIII

Psaume CIII (Psalm 103)
cor,S solo,fl,ob,2clar,bsn,2horn,
strings,perc,harp, celesta
DONEMUS (S972)

STRAUSS, RICHARD (1864-1949)
Deutsche Motette *Op.62, mot
[Eng/Ger] SSSSAAAATTTTBBBB,SATB
soli,acap (diff) sc SCHOTTS
rental (S973)

STRAUSS-KONIG, RICHARD
Ave Maria
[Lat] 4pt mix cor,acap BOHM s.p.
(S974)

Ehr' Sei Dem Vater, Sohn Und Geist
*Fest
mix cor,acap BOHM s.p. (S975)

Gott, Mein Gott, Im Morgenlicht Wach
Ich Auf Zu Dir (Psalm 62)
1-3pt jr cor,inst BOHM s.p. (S976)

Pange Lingua
[Lat] 4pt mix cor,acap BOHM s.p.
contains also: Tantum Ergo (S977)

Psalm 62 *see Gott, Mein Gott, Im
Morgenlicht Wach Ich Auf Zu Dir

Regina Coeli
[Lat] 4pt mix cor,acap BOHM s.p.
(S978)

Tantum Ergo
see Strauss-Konig, Richard, Pange
Lingua

Veni Creator
[Lat] 4pt mix cor,acap BOHM s.p.
(S979)

STRAVINSKY, IGOR (1882-1972)
Babel *Bibl/cant
[Eng/Ger] 1-9pt men cor,3fl,2ob,
3clar,3bsn,4horn,3trp,3trom,
strings,timp,3harp voc sc,cor pts
SCHOTTS ED. 4342 s.p., ipa (S980)

STREET
Come Holy Spirit
SATB SCHIRM.G 12020 $.45 (S981)

Leave, Then, Thy Foolish Ranges
SATB SCHIRM.G 12021 $.40 (S982)

Nearer, My God, To Thee
SATB SCHIRM.G 12022 $.45 (S983)

STRENGTHEN ALL THY SERVANTS see
Eldridge, Guy H.

STRENGTHEN FOR SERVICE, LORD see
McCabe, Michael

STRICKEN, SMITTEN, AND AFFLICTED *Lent
(Olander) SAB oct SCHMITT 5545 $.40
(S984)

STRIFE IS O'ER, THE see Palestrina,
Giovanni

STRIMPLE, N.
Shepherd Of Tender Youth
SATB,org FISCHER,J FEC 10106 $.30
(S985)

STRINGFIELD, LAMAR (1897-1959)
Peace
cor,orch BRODT $1.25, ipr (S986)

STRIVING AFTER GOD see Michaelangelo

STROHBACH, SIEGFRIED (1929-)
Bild Und Gleichnis *Bibl/mot
6pt cor pts BREITKOPF-W CHB 3639
s.p. (S987)

Jesus, Der Retter Im Seesturm "Und
Siehe, Da Ging Ein Sturmwind Auf
Den See Nieder" *evang/mot
4-6pt mix cor,acap cor pts
BREITKOPF-W CHB-3054 s.p. see
also Sechs Evangelienmotetten
(S988)

STROHBACH, SIEGFRIED (cont'd.)

Jesus, Die Auferstehung Und Das Leben
"Und Es Geschah" *evang/mot
4-6pt mix cor,acap cor pts
BREITKOPF-W CHB-3059 s.p. see
also Sechs Evangelienmotetten
(S989)

Jesus Heilt Einen Gelahmten "Siehe,
Da Brachten Sie Zu Jesus Einen
Gelahmten" *evang/mot
4-6pt mix cor,acap cor pts
BREITKOPF-W CHB-3057 s.p. see
also Sechs Evangelienmotetten
(S990)

Jesus Und Der Oberzollner Zachaus
"Und Jesus Ging Nach Jericho
Hinein" *evang/mot
4-6pt mix cor,acap cor pts
BREITKOPF-W CHB-3056 s.p. see
also Sechs Evangelienmotetten
(S991)

Jesus Und Die Ehebrecherin "Die
Pharisaer Und Schriftgelehrten
Brachten Eine Frau Herbet"
*evang/mot
4-6pt mix cor,acap cor pts
BREITKOPF-W CHB-3058 s.p. see
also Sechs Evangelienmotetten
(S992)

Jesus Und Martha "Es Geschah, Als Sie
Wanderten" *evang/mot
4-6pt mix cor,acap cor pts
BREITKOPF-W CHB-3055 s.p. see
also Sechs Evangelienmotetten
(S993)

Sechs Evangelienmotetten *evang/mot
4-6pt mix cor,acap BREITKOPF-W
contains & see also: Jesus, Der
Retter Im Seesturm "Und Siehe,
Da Ging Ein Sturmwind Auf Den
See Nieder"; Jesus, Die
Auferstehung Und Das Leben "Und
Es Geschah"; Jesus Heilt Einen
Gelahmten "Siehe, Da Brachten
Sie Zu Jesus Einen Gelahmten";
Jesus Und Der Oberzollner
Zachaus "Und Jesus Ging Nach
Jericho Hinein"; Jesus Und Die
Ehebrecherin "Die Pharisaer Und
Schriftgelehrten Brachten Eine
Frau Herbet"; Jesus Und Martha
"Es Geschah, Als Sie Wanderten"
(S994)

STROM
Jesus, Name All Names Above
*Gd.Fri.,anthem
(Berglund) SATB oct LILLENAS
AN-6029 $.30 (S995)
(Rasley, John M.) SATB oct SINGSPIR
ZJP-3532 $.30 (S996)

STROMBERG, V.
I Hear Music *anthem/gospel
SATB oct SINGSPIR ZJP-8180 $.30
(S997)

STUCKY, STEVEN
Speak, Lord, For Thy Servant Heareth
*anthem
SATB WORD CS-2585 $.30 (S998)

STUDER, HANS (1911-)
Auf Dich Hab Ich Gehoffet, Herr
1-2pt/SAT/SAB,org SCHWEIZER. SK 158
s.p. (S999)

Der Tod Ist Verschlungen In Den Sieg
SATB SCHWEIZER. SK 156 s.p. (S1000)

Es Ist Gewisslich An Der Zeit
SATB (contains also: O Leib,
Gebrochen Mir Zu Gut; So Fuhrst
Du Doch Recht Selig, Herr, Die
Deinen) SCHWEIZER. SK 54.01-2
s.p. see also MUSIKBEILAGE ZUM
"EVANGELISCHEN KIRCHENCHOR 1954"
(S1001)
Gelobt Sei Gott Im Hochsten Thron
unis/SAT/SAB/SATB,org SCHWEIZER.
SK 60.01-2 s.p. see also
MUSIKBEILAGE ZUM "EVANGELISCHEN
KIRCHENCHOR 1960" (S1002)

Gott Vater, Sende Deinen Geist
SAT/SAB (contains also: Siehe, Es
Kommt Die Zeit) SCHWEIZER.
SK 68.07 s.p. see also
MUSIKBEILAGE ZUM "EVANGELISCHEN
KIRCHENCHOR 1968" (S1003)

Ich Will Meinen Geist Ausgiessen
SAT/SAB SCHWEIZER. SK 65.04 s.p.
see also MUSIKBEILAGE ZUM
"EVANGELISCHEN KIRCHENCHOR 1965"
(S1004)
Nun Danket Gott, Erhebt Und Preiset
SATB/SAT/SAB/2pt (contains also:
Nun Sich Der Tag Geendet Hat)
SCHWEIZER. SK 62.05-6 s.p. see
also MUSIKBEILAGE ZUM
"EVANGELISCHEN KIRCHENCHOR 1962"
(S1005)
O Christe, Wahrheit Und Leben
SAT/SAB (contains also: Wunderbarer
Gnadenthron) SCHWEIZER. SK 67.03
s.p. see also MUSIKBEILAGE ZUM

STUDER, HANS (cont'd.)

"EVANGELISCHEN KIRCHENCHOR 1967"
(S1006)
Siehe, Es Kommt Die Zeit
SATB,org (gott vater, sende deinen
geist) SCHWEIZER. SK 68.07 s.p.
see also MUSIKBEILAGE ZUM
"EVANGELISCHEN KIRCHENCHOR 1968"
(S1007)
So Fuhrst Du Doch Recht Selig, Herr,
Die Deinen
SAT/SAB (contains also: O Leib,
Gebrochen Mir Zu Gut; Es Ist
Gewisslich An Der Zeit)
SCHWEIZER. SK 54.01-2 s.p. see
also MUSIKBEILAGE ZUM
"EVANGELISCHEN KIRCHENCHOR 1954"
(S1008)
So Spricht Der Herr: Ich Will Dich
Unterweisen
SATB SCHWEIZER. SK 144 s.p. (S1009)

Sollt Ich Meinem Gott Nicht Singen?
2pt (contains also: Wenn Mich Die
Sunden Kranken; Wir Christenleut
Habn Jetzund Freud) SCHWEIZER.
SK 70.01-2 s.p. see also
MUSIKBEILAGE ZUM "EVANGELISCHEN
KIRCHENCHOR 1970" (S1010)

STURMAN, PAUL
Psalm 93
SATB,orch EMI s.p. (S1011)

STURMER, BRUNO (1892-1958)
Cantata 7 *see Sonnenhymne Des
Echnaton "Anbetung Dem Gott"

Singe, O Singe
men cor sc SCHOTTS 38 155 s.p., voc
pt SCHOTTS C 38 166-01-04 s.p.
(S1012)
Sonnenhymne Des Echnaton "Anbetung
Dem Gott" (Cantata 7) cant
men cor,pno,2horn,3trp,2trom,tuba,
perc voc sc,cor pts SCHOTTS
ED. 5761 s.p., ipr, sc SCHOTTS
rental (S1013)

STYRI MOTETA see Zimmer, Jan

SUB UMBRA ILLIUS see Ziegelmeier, M.

SUCCO
Drei Motetten *Op.7, CC3U
mix cor LIENAU sc s.p., cor pts
s.p. (S1014)

Psalm 2 *Op.21
8pt mix cor,pno LIENAU sc s.p., cor
pts s.p. (S1015)

Psalm 126 *Op.24
8pt mix cor,pno LIENAU sc s.p., cor
pts s.p. (S1016)

Zwei Motetten *Op.9, CC2U
8pt mix cor LIENAU sc s.p., cor pts
s.p. (S1017)

SUCH A VERY BRIGHT STAR see Leaf,
Robert

SUCHON, EUGEN (1908-)
Zalm Zeme Podkarpatskej *cant
mix cor,T solo,orch SLOV.HUD.FOND
s.p. (S1018)

SUCHY, FRANTISEK (1902-)
At Gethsemane *see V Getsemane

V Getsemane *Op.7, ora
"At Gethsemane" [Czech] mix cor,
TBar soli,3fl,3ob,3clar,3bsn,
4horn,2trp,3trom,tuba,timp,perc,
strings CZECH s.p. (S1019)

SUE RANEY'S PEOPLE TREE see Raney, Sue

SUFFER LITTLE CHILDREN see Green

SUFFERING AND THE RESURRECTION see
Burghauser, Jarmil, Utrpeni A
Vzkriseni

SUK, JOSEF (1874-1935)
Epilogue *Op.37, Bibl
[Czech/Ger] mix cor&mix cor,SBarB
soli,4fl,4ob,4clar,4bsn,6horn,
3trp,3trom,tuba,timp,perc,harp,
strings SUPRAPHON s.p. (S1020)

Krecovice Mass, The *see Krecovicka
Mse

Krecovicka Mse
"Krecovice Mass, The" [Lat] mix
cor,soli,org,strings,timp CZECH
s.p. (S1021)

SULLIVAN
Onward, Christian Soldiers *anthem
(DeCou, Harold) SATB oct SINGSPIR
ZJP-7366 $.35 (S1022)
(O'Neill, Charles) SATB (med diff)

SULLIVAN (cont'd.)

WATERLOO $.40   (S1023)

SULZER, SALOMON (1804-1890)
Schir Zion *CCU,Fest/Hanakkah/
Marriage/Purim/Rosh Ha-Shanah/
Sab-Morn/Tishah be-Av/Yom Kippur,
Psalm
mix cor,cantor,acap/org SAC.MUS.PR.
S.M.P. 6-8 $25.00 five volumes,
bound in three books   (S1024)

SUMME DEUS see Hafner, Johannes

SUMMER PSALM see Wirsen

SUMMUS ERIT SUB CARNE see Lassus,
Roland de (Orlandus)

SUMNER
Child Of The King, A *anthem/gospel
(Yungton, Al) SATB oct SINGSPIR
ZJP-8133 $.30   (S1025)

SUN HAS GONE DOWN, THE see Schroth,
Gerhard

SUN IS ON THE LAND AND SEA, THE see
Burroughs, Bob

SUN OF MY SOUL *anthem
(Berglund) SSAATTBB oct LILLENAS
AN-6023 $.30   (S1026)

SUNDAY CHOIR *CCUL
(Huff, Ronn) cor SINGSPIR ZD-5472
$1.50   (S1027)

SUNDAY STONE see Cunningham, Arthur

SUNLIGHT see Weeden

SUNSHINE AND SNOWFLAKES *Xmas
(Gassman, Clark) jr cor LEXICON 37653
$1.95
contains: Happy Birthday, Baby
Jesus; Over In Bethlehem;
Sunshine Christmas, A; Very First
Christmas, The; Where's
Christmas; Wise Men Still Adore
Him   (S1028)

SUNSHINE CHOIR NO. 1 *CC23UL
1-2pt jr cor SINGSPIR 5520 $1.25
(S1029)

SUNSHINE CHOIR NO. 2 *CC29UL
1-2pt jr cor SINGSPIR 5523 $1.25
(S1030)

SUNSHINE CHRISTMAS, A
see Sunshine And Snowflakes

SUNSHINE DAY see McCrary, Alfred

SUNSHINE IN MY SOUL *CC8UL,gospel
(Turner, Lee) SATB,pno BROADMAN
4520-36 $1.95   (S1031)

SUNSHINE IN MY SOUL *CC8L
(Turner, Lee) jr cor/sr cor sc
BROADMAN 4520-36 $1.95   (S1032)

SUNSHINE IN MY SOUL see Sweney

SUPER FLUMINA BABYLONIS see Lassus,
Roland de (Orlandus)

SUPER FLUMINA BABYLONIS see Sipila,
Eero

SURELY GOODNESS AND MERCY see Peterson,
John W.

SURELY HE HAS BORNE OUR SORROWS see
Herbst, Johannes

SURELY HE HATH BORN OUR GRIEFS see
Littleton, Bill J.

SURELY HE HATH BORNE OUR GRIEFS see
Handel, George Frideric

SURGE, ILLUMINARE JERUSALEM see
Rehmann, Th.

SURGENS JESU see Philips, Peter

SURIANO, FRANCESCO (1549-1621)
Alma Redemptoris Mater
(Lee, John; Mitchell, Bob) [Eng/
Lat] SATB GIA G1948 $.40 (S1033)

Ave Regina Caelorum
(Harris) SATB,acap PRO ART 2782
$.35   (S1034)

Die Chor-Antworten Zu Den Passionen
*CCU,Gd.Fri./Palm
[Lat] 4pt mix cor,acap sc,cor pts
BOHM s.p.   (S1035)

SURREXIT CHRISTUS see Gabrieli,
Giovanni

SURREXIT DOMINUS see Bresgen, Cesar

SURREXIT HODIE see Kelly, Bryan

SURREXIT PASTOR BONUS see Lassus,
Roland de (Orlandus)

SURSUM CORDA see Piechler, Arthur

SURSUM CORDA see Welcker, Max

SUS, SUS MON AME see Le Jeune, Claude

SUSANI *Adv/Xmas
(Bauernfeind, Hans) wom cor,acap oct
DOBLINGER s.p. see also In Dulci
Jubilo   (S1036)

SUSANI see Schroeder, Hermann

SUSANI "VOM HIMMEL HOCH" see Schroeder,
Hermann

SUSANI "VOM HIMMEL HOCH, IHR ENGEL
KOMMT" see Lang, Hans

SUSANNI *Xmas,carol,Ger
(Field, Robert) SSA,pno oct PRESSER
312-41043 $.40   (S1037)

SUSANNI see Jensen, Donald F.

SUSCIPE CLEMENTISSIME DEUS see
Gabrieli, Giovanni

SUSSEX CAROL *Adv/Xmas
see Six Carols For SAB And Piano
(Wood, Dale) SATB,harp ART MAST 139
$.40, ipa   (S1038)

SUSSEX CAROL see Fischer, I.

SUSSEX CAROL see Fischer, L.

SUSSMAYR, FRANZ XAVIER (1766-1803)
Ave Verum Corpus
mix cor,org,orch HUG   (S1039)

SUTERMEISTER, HEINRICH (1910-   )
Cantata 3 *see Dem Allgegenwartigen

Dem Allgegenwartigen (Cantata 3) cant
mix cor,SBar soli,2fl,2ob,
2clar,2bsn,4horn,3trp,3trom,tuba,
strings,harp,perc,timp (med) voc
sc,cor pts SCHOTTS ED. 4790 s.p.,
ipr   (S1040)

Missa Da Requiem *Req
[Lat] mix cor,SBar soli,pno,3fl,
2ob,2clar,3bsn,4horn,3trp,3trom,
tuba,strings,timp,harp, English
horn, bass clarinet (med) voc sc
SCHOTTS ED. 4516 s.p., min sc
SCHOTTS ED. 5012 s.p., ipr
(S1041)

SUTTER
O Spirit Of Jesus *anthem
SATB FINE ARTS CM 1002 $.30 (S1042)

Place Your Hand *see McKinney

SUTTER, W.J.
Life Victorious
mix cor BRODT 548 $.28   (S1043)

Lift Up Your Eyes *anthem
SATB WORD CS-2673 $.35   (S1044)

SUTTON, NANCY
Ballad Of The Lion And The Lamb, The
(composed with Cohen) *anthem
SATB,pno oct MCAFEE M1042 $.35
(S1045)

SVATY LUKAS see Vycpalek, Ladislav

SVO VITT UM HEIM SEM SOLIN FER see
Stefansson, Fjolnir

SWANN, DONALD (1923-   )
Hail Gladdening Light
SATB,gtr,bvl GALAXY 1.2479.1 $.30
(S1046)

SWANSON, HOWARD (1909-   )
Christmas Long Ago *Xmas,anthem
(Drevits, Jon) SATB oct SINGSPIR
ZJP-3021 $.25   (S1047)

SWAYZEE, T.W.
America Bless God
SATB,Bar solo,opt 3trp FRANTON
$.40, ipa   (S1048)

SWEELINCK, JAN PIETERSZOON (1562-1621)
Collected Works *sac/sec,CCU
(Sieffert, Max; Gehrmann, Hermann)
[Dut/Ger/Fr] microfiche UNION
ESP. $60.00 originally published
as 12 volumes, Leipzig, 1894-
1901.   (S1049)

Hodie Christus Natus Est *Xmas
5pt mix cor,acap sc HENN 084 s.p.
(S1050)

SWEELINCK, JAN PIETERSZOON (cont'd.)

Mein Gott, Mein Gott, Verlassen Hast
Du Mich (Psalm 22)
SATB SCHWEIZER. SK 51.05-6 s.p. see
also MUSIKBEILAGE ZUM
"EVANGELISCHEN KIRCHENCHOR 1951"
(S1051)

O Lord, Attend Unto My Cry
SATB,acap (med) oct CONCORDIA
98-2202 $.35   (S1052)

Psalm 22 *see Mein Gott, Mein Gott,
Verlassen Hast Du Mich

Psalm 138
(Peek) mix cor BRODT 558 $.28
(S1053)

Sing To The Lord
(Colton) SATB oct CONCORDIA 98-2222
$.60   (S1054)

Unto Thee We Give Our Thanks *Gen/
Thanks
SATB (diff) oct CONCORDIA 98-2210
$.40   (S1055)

Venite Exsultemus Domino
SSATB EGTVED MK10, 9 s.p. (S1056)

SWEENEY, J. ALBERT
Psalm 134
SATB GALAXY 1.1853.1 $.30 (S1057)

SWEET ARE THE THOUGHTS see Amner, John

SWEET CHILD OF GOD *Xmas
(Kunz, Alfred) TTBB (med diff)
WATERLOO $.35   (S1058)
(Kunz, Alfred) SATB (med diff)
WATERLOO $.35   (S1059)

SWEET CHILD OF GOD see Kunz, Alfred

SWEET FELLOWSHIP *CCU,evang
(Widen, Svante) SAB cmplt ed LILLENAS
MB-346 $1.95   (S1060)

SWEET IS THY MERCY LORD see Barnby, Sir
Joseph

SWEET JESU , KING OF BLISS see Archer,
Frederick

SWEET JESUS see Bolz, Harriett

SWEET LITTLE JESUS BABY *Xmas,spir
(Ehret, Walter) SATB,pno MCAFEE M1079
$.40   (S1061)

SWEET MUSIC see Wilson

SWEET, SWEET SONG OF SALVATION see
Norman

SWEET, SWEET SPIRIT see Akers, Doris

SWEET WAS THE SONG
(Hugh; Jones) SSA&opt S,opt S solo
(med easy) OXFORD 83.093 $.30
(S1062)

SWEET WAS THE SONG see Jackson, Stephen

SWEETER THAN ALL see Entwisle

SWEETEST NAME I KNOW see Bridgers

SWELL THE FULL CHORUS see Handel,
George Frideric

SWENEY
Beulah Land *anthem/gospel
(McLellan, Cyril A.) SSATB oct
SINGSPIR ZJP-8070 $.30   (S1063)

My Savior First Of All *gospel
(Whitsett) SATB oct LILLENAS
AN-1685 $.30   (S1064)

Sunshine In My Soul *anthem/gospel
(Mayfield, Larry) SATB oct SINGSPIR
ZJP-8136 $.30   (S1065)
(Smith, Wesley) SATB oct GOSPEL
05 TM 0349 $.35   (S1066)

SWENEY, J.R.
More About Jesus
(Larsen, L.B.) SATB oct GOSPEL
05 TM 0357 $.30   (S1067)

SWENSON
Festival Mass, A
SATB,1-2pno/org/hpsd,opt trp&
drums (med) cor pts FISCHER,C
0 4897 $1.50   (S1068)

SWENSON, WARREN
What Child Is This? *Xmas
SATB GALAXY 1.2474.1 $.20 (S1069)

SWING DOWN, CHARIOT *spir
(Ehret) SATB oct LILLENAS AN-3865
$.30   (S1070)

SWING LOW
see Funf Spirituals
(Siegler, W.) men cor,acap TONOS 2386
s.p.   (S1071)

SWING LOW, SWEET CHARIOT *spir
(Arch, Gwyn) SSA EMI   (S1072)
(Kirby) SATBar&opt camb,pno (easy)
CAMBIATA S17555 $.40   (S1073)

SWING LOW, SWEET CHARIOT see Petersen,
Rolf

SYKES
Thank You, Lord *Thanks,anthem/
gospel
(DeCou, Harold) SATB oct SINGSPIR
ZJP-3102 $.30   (S1074)

SYMONS
Sing We Merrily *anthem
SS (med easy) OXFORD 44.079 $.25
(S1075)

SYMPHONIA SACRA see Wuorinen, Charles

SYNG LOVSANG FOR GUD, ALLE LAND see
Neilsen, Ludvig

SZABO, [FERENC] (1902-1969)
Egynemukarok *CCU
eq voices BUDAPEST 6891 s.p.   (S1076)

T

TAFT, J.M.
Prayer Of St. Francis
mix cor,opt orch BRODT 612 $.40,
ipr   (T1)

TAKE A LOOK AT JESUS see Johnson

TAKE A STEP see Good

TAKE, BELIEVE see Wetzler, Robert

TAKE COURAGE see Winter, Sister Miriam
Therese

TAKE HIS NAME see Parks

TAKE ME AS I AM see Burroughs, Bob

TAKE ME BACK see Crouch, Andrae

TAKE MY HEART, O FATHER see
Blankenship, Mark

TAKE MY LIFE see Blankenship, Mark

TAKE MY LIFE AND LET IT BE see Ferrin

TAKE MY LIFE AND LET IT BE see Malan,
H.A. Cesar

TAKE MY LIFE AND LET IT BE see
Peterson, John W.

TAKE MY LIFE, OH LORD see O'Hara,
Geoffrey

TAKE THE MESSAGE see Hallett, John C.

TAKE TIME TO PRAY see Peterson, John W.

TAKE UP THY CROSS see Price

TAKE UP THY CROSS see Read, Daniel

TAKE UP THY CROSS see Roff, Joseph

TAKE UP THY CROSS THE SAVIOUR SAID see
Littleton, Bill J.

TAKE UP YOUR CROSS AND FOLLOW ME see
Peterson, John W.

TAKE US, O LORD see Andrews, C.T.

TAKING CHANCES see Nelson

TALE OF GLORY see Davis, Katherine K.

TALK ABOUT A CHILD THAT DO LOVE JESUS
*spir
(Dawson, William) SATTBB,S solo (med)
FITZSIMONS 2015 $.25   (T2)

TALK ABOUT LOVE *CCUL
(Skillings, Otis) cor,pno LILLENAS
MB-338 $1.95   (T3)

TALK ABOUT LOVE see Zeller

TALLIS, THOMAS (ca. 1505-1585)
Awake, My Soul, And With The Sun
*canon
(Lutkin) SA (easy) FITZSIMONS 5006
$.20   (T4)

Give Almes Of Thy Goods
SATB (med easy) OXFORD 43.217 $.50
(T5)
Lamb Of God
(Ehret, Walter) [Eng/Lat] SATB,acap
(med) PRESSER 312-41069 $.50 (T6)

Lamentations Of Jeremiah, The
(Brett) ATTBB,acap (med diff)
OXFORD 46.156 $3.60   (T7)

O Sacrum Convivium
SAATB,opt acap (med diff, formerly
'I Call And Cry') OXFORD 43.218
$.35   (T8)

This Is My Commandment
AATB,opt acap (med) OXFORD 41.025
$.30   (T9)

TAMBLYN, B.L.
Lord Give Us Peace
SATB HARRIS $.35   (T10)

TAMBLYN, WILLIAM
Antiphons And Psalm 150 *CCUL
SATB,org oct BOOSEY 5823 $.40 (T11)

You Are Peter
SATB,org/brass oct BOOSEY 5824
$.40, ipa   (T12)

TAMBOURINE NOEL see Young, Gordon

TAMBOURINES TO GLORY see Hughes

TANIS
Do, Lord
SATB,acap PRO ART 2795 $.40   (T13)

TANTUM ERGO see Berghorn, Alfred

TANTUM ERGO see Filke, Max

TANTUM ERGO see Forster, Peter

TANTUM ERGO see Frey, Carl

TANTUM ERGO see Knobel, Ewald

TANTUM ERGO see Kremer, Karl

TANTUM ERGO see Lemacher, Heinrich

TANTUM ERGO see Liszt, Franz

TANTUM ERGO see Montillet

TANTUM ERGO see Mozart, Wolfgang
Amadeus

TANTUM ERGO see Mutter, Gerbert

TANTUM ERGO see Ophoven, Hermann

TANTUM ERGO see Robillard

TANTUM ERGO see Schroeder, Hermann

TANTUM ERGO see Steinert, Bernhard

TANTUM ERGO see Strauss-Konig, Richard

TANTUM ERGO see Trapp, Willy

TANTUM ERGO see Victoria, Tomas Luis de

TANTUM ERGO see Volgyfy, Hans

TANTUM ERGO see Waldbroel, Wilhelm

TANTUM ERGO see Wassmer, Berthold

TANTUM ERGO see Williamson, Malcolm

TANTUM ERGO (1843) see Bruckner, Anton

TAPEL, JOSEPH
Psalm 30
see Two Psalms Of Dedication

Psalm 126
see Two Psalms Of Dedication

Two Psalms Of Dedication
mix cor oct SAC.MUS.PR. 308 $1.25
contains: Psalm 30; Psalm 126
(T14)
TAPSCOTT, CARL
Six Hymn Introits *CC6U,Introit
SATB (easy) WATERLOO $.90   (T15)

TARANTO
Rejoice! For We Are Saved
SATB PRO ART 2855 $.35   (T16)

TARNER, EVELYN F.
Dear Little Jesus *Xmas
unis oct LORENZ 8876 $.30   (T17)

TARP, SVEND ERIK (1908-   )
Te Deum *Te Deum
WALTON M129 $2.00   (T18)

TARRY
Dost Thou In A Manger Lie? *Adv/Xmas
SATB oct LILLENAS AN-3872 $.30
(T19)

Psalm 30 *Bibl/hymn
SATB oct LILLENAS AN-6041 $.30
(T20)

TASTE AND SEE see Ford, Virgil T.

TATE
Close To Your Mother
SA/TB (easy) OXFORD 82.095 $.30
(T21)
TAUBERT, KARL HEINZ
Advents- Und Weihnachtsmusik *CCU,
Adv/Xmas
3pt voc sc RIES s.p.   (T22)

Der Stern
mix cor TONGER s.p.
contains: Ihr Hirten, Ihr Hirten;
Im Dunkeln Tret Ich Gern
Hinaus; In Jedem Neugebornen
Kind "Du Denkst Und Hast's
Nicht Ausgedacht"; Kommt Alle
Bei Nacht; Nun Den Tag Des Tags
Verdross; Wir Haben Ein
Kindelein Geseh'n "Die Luft Ist
Noch Voller Geton"   (T23)

Ihr Hirten, Ihr Hirten
see Der Stern

TAUBERT, KARL HEINZ (cont'd.)

Im Dunkeln Tret Ich Gern Hinaus
see Der Stern

In Jedem Neugebornen Kind "Du Denkst
Und Hast's Nicht Ausgedacht"
see Der Stern

Kommt Alle Bei Nacht
see Der Stern

Nun Den Tag Des Tags Verdross
see Der Stern

Wir Haben Ein Kindelein Geseh'n "Die
Luft Ist Noch Voller Geton"
see Der Stern

TAVERNER, JOHN
Audivi Vocem
SSAA,acap STAINER 3.0763 $.50 (T24)

Celtic Requiem
jr cor&cor,S solo,orch sc CHESTER
JWC 8894 s.p., ipr   (T25)

Dum Transisset Sabatum
(Brett) SATBB,acap OXFORD   (T26)

In Pace In Idipsum
ATTB STAINER 3.0740.1 $.75   (T27)

Kyrie "Leroy"
(Crabtree, Phillip) SATB,acap (med)
DEAN CA-101 $.40   (T28)

Leroy Kyrie, The
SATB,acap (med) OXFORD 43.461 $.50
                               (T29)

TAYLOR
Come To The Savior *anthem
SATB oct BROADMAN 4540-94 $.30
                               (T30)

TAYLOR, CLIFFORD
Sacred Verses
SATB,SB soli,2fl,2ob,3clar,3bsn,
4horn,2trp,3trom,tuba,timp,3perc,
harp,strings sc AM.COMP.AL.
$24.20   (T31)
SATB,pno/org AM.COMP.AL. $13.20
                               (T32)

TCHAIKOVSKY, PIOTR ILYITCH (1840-1893)
Lengend, A *Xmas
(Cookson) SATB,acap (easy)
FITZSIMONS 2068 $.20   (T33)

TCHESNOKOV, PAVEL GRIGORIEVITCH
(1877-1944)
May Thy Blessed Spirit
(Cookson) TTBB,acap (easy)
FITZSIMONS 4062 $.25   (T34)

TE DEUM see Burkhard Willy

TE DEUM see Bush, Geoffrey

TE DEUM see Cabena, Barrie

TE DEUM see Connolly, Justin [Riveagh]

TE DEUM see Cruft, Adrian

TE DEUM see Dvorak, Antonin

TE DEUM see Eberlin, Johann Ernst

TE DEUM see Farrant, Richard

TE DEUM see Hamilton, Iain

TE DEUM see Haydn, (Johann) Michael

TE DEUM see Kromolicki, Joseph

TE DEUM see Lauber, Gustav

TE DEUM see Lemacher, Heinrich

TE DEUM see Mollicone, Henry

TE DEUM see Noble, Thomas Tertius

TE DEUM see Pinkham, Daniel

TE DEUM see Tarp, Svend Erik

TE DEUM AND BENEDICTUS IN F see Elgar,
Edward

TE DEUM FOR BLANDET KOR OG ORKESTER see
Kayser, Leif

TE DEUM FOR MIXED CHORUS AND ORCHESTRA
see Kayser, Leif, Te Deum For
Blandet Kor Og Orkester

TE DEUM IN C see Haydn, (Johann)
Michael

TE DEUM IN C-DUR see Mozart, Wolfgang
Amadeus

TE DEUM IN D see Bach, Johann Christian

TE DEUM IN D see Purcell, Henry

TE DEUM LAUDAMUS see Bales, Gerald

TE DEUM LAUDAMUS see Dunford, Benjamin

TE DEUM LAUDAMUS see Dvorak, Antonin

TE DEUM LAUDAMUS see Foerster, Josef
Bohuslav

TE DEUM LAUDAMUS see Proulx, Richard

TE DEUM LAUDAMUS see Sowerby, Leo

TE LUCIS ANTE TERMINUM see Davies,
Peter Maxwell

TEACH ME HOW TO LOOK *CCU
unis BELWIN $1.25   (T35)

TEACH ME O LORD see Attwood

TEACH ME, O LORD see Matthews, Thomas

TEACH ME THY WAY, O LORD see Ramsey

TEACH ME TO LOVE see Peterson, John W.

TEEN CHOIR *CCUL
(Krogstad, Bob) SAB SINGSPIR 5260
$1.50   (T36)

TEENAGE CHOIR NO. 1 *CCUL
SAB SINGSPIR 5588 $1.25   (T37)

TEENAGE CHOIR NO. 2 *CCUL
SAB SINGSPIR 5583 $1.25   (T38)

TEENAGE CHOIR NO. 3 *CCUL
SAB SINGSPIR 5579 $1.25   (T39)

TEENAGE CHOIR NO. 4 *CCUL
SAB SINGSPIR 5578 $1.25   (T40)

TELEMANN, GEORG PHILIPP (1681-1767)
Jauchzet, Ihr Himmel *cant
SA/SAB,SA soli,cont,strings
HANSSLER 10.253 sc s.p., cor pts
s.p., ipa   (T41)

Johannespassion 1737 *Psntd
voc sc EULENBURG GM242 s.p.   (T42)

Lobet Den Herrn, Alle Heiden
SS/SA&opt men cor,cont,2vln,opt
vla&3trp&timp sc HANSSLER 39.103
s.p.   (T43)

Ruft Es Aus In Alle Welt *Xmas,cant
SATB,SATB soli,3trp,timp,strings,
cont sc,cor pts BAREN. BA3468
                               (T44)
Wenn Mich Die Sunden Kranken
SATB,cont (contains also: Sollt Ich
Meinem Gott Nicht Singen?; Wir
Christenleut Habn Jetzund Freud)
SCHWEIZER. SK 70.01-2 s.p. see
also MUSIKBEILAGE ZUM
"EVANGELISCHEN KIRCHENCHOR 1970"
                               (T45)
Wider Die Falschen Propheten *cant
(Bergmann) [Eng/Ger] cor min sc
EULENBURG 1072 s.p.   (T46)
(Bergmann, Walter) [Eng/Ger] SAB,
SAB soli,cont,2vln,opt vla (easy)
min sc SCHOTTS ETP 1072 s.p., ipa
                               (T47)
Wir Christenleut Habn Jetzund Freud
SATB,cont (contains also: Sollt Ich
Meinem Gott Nicht Singen?; Wenn
Mich Die Sunden Kranken)
SCHWEIZER. SK 70.01-2 s.p. see
also MUSIKBEILAGE ZUM
"EVANGELISCHEN KIRCHENCHOR 1970"
                               (T48)

TELL IT TO JESUS see Kaiser, Kurt

TELL MAN OF GOD see Red, Buryl

TELL OUT MAGNIFICAT see Fink, Michael

TELL THE GOOD NEWS see Ingram, Bill

TELL THE GOOD NEWS see Peterson, John
W.

TELL THE WHOLE WORLD NOW see White,
Ernie

TELL THE WORLD *CC6UL,gospel/medley
(Skillings, Otis) cor cmplt ed
LILLENAS MB-320 $1.95
see also: Owens, Jimmy, If My
People Will Pray   (T49)

TEMPLE see Woollen, Russell

TEMPLE, SEBASTIAN
And The Waters Keep On Running
Through My Mind *CCU
SATB,pno/org,gtr GIA G1628 $2.50
                               (T50)

God Is A Fire Of Love *CCU,Pent
SATB,pno/org,gtr GIA G1630 $2.00
                               (T51)

TEMPLE UNTO GOD, A see Zilch, Margot

TEMPLES OF GOD see Nelson, Ronald A.

TEMPO DI MARCIA see Pratella, Francesco
Balilla

TEMPTATION OF JESUS, THE see Canning,
Thomas

TEN CHORALES see Bach, Johann Sebastian

TEN COMMANDMENTS see Hays, Peggy
McAllister

TEN COMMANDMENTS, THE see Brown,
Shirley

TEN COMMUNION HYMNS FOR TWO-VOICE
CHOIRS see Andrews, C.T.

TEN LEPERS see Winter, Sister Miriam
Therese

TEN WORSHIP RESPONSES see Warkentin

TENDING SHEEP see Lewis, John

TENEBRAE FACTAE SUNT see Biber,
Heinrich Ignaz Franz von

TENEBRAE FACTAE SUNT see Haydn,
(Johann) Michael

TENEBRAE FACTAE SUNT see Petrassi,
Goffredo

TENEBRAE FACTAE SUNT see Poulenc,
Francis

TENEBRAE FACTAE SUNT see Victoria,
Tomas Luis de

TENEBRAE FACTAE SUNT see Haydn,
(Johann) Michael

TENEBRAE FACTAE SUNT see Haydn,
(Johann) Michael

TENEBRAE NOCTURNES see Kelly, Bryan

TENNESSEE *hymn
(Lindsley) TTBB,acap (easy) OXFORD
94.103 see from Five Early American
Hymn Tunes   (T52)

TENNESSEE MOUNTAIN PSALM see Gaul,
Harvey Bartlet

TERRA TREMUIT see Eybler, Joseph

TERRA TREMUIT see Filke, Max

TERRA TREMUIT see Gauss, Otto

TERRA TREMUIT see Gruber, Joseph

TERRA TREMUIT see Lauterbach, Lorenz

TERRA TREMUIT see Lemacher, Heinrich

TERRA TREMUIT see Loffler, Thomas Th.

TERRA TREMUIT see Rheinberger, Josef

TERRA TREMUIT see Seckinger, Konrad

TERRELL
Every Day Is A Better Day *see
Bartlett

Give Me A Vision *anthem
SATB oct BROADMAN 4550-02 $.30
                               (T53)

TERRI
Around The Year In Rounds *sac/sec,
CCU,round
cor SCHIRM.G LG51746 $2.00   (T54)

TERRIBILIS EST see Ammann, Benno

TERRIBILIS EST see Mastioletti

TERRIBILIS EST LOCUS ISTE see Heftrich,
Wilhelm

TERRY, BARBARA
Immortal, Invisible, God Only-Wise
*anthem,Contemp
SATB,gtr oct CHANTRY COA 7043 $.25,
ipa   (T55)

TERRY, RICHARD RUNCIMAN (1865-1938)
What Is This Fragrance
see Stainer, John, Shepherds! Shake
Off Your Drowsy Sleep

TERZAKIS, DIMITRI (1938-   )
Ikos
[Greek/Ger] SSAATTBB,acap (diff)
BAREN. BA5425 contains also:
Katawassa (SSATTBar,acap)   (T56)

Katawassa
see Terzakis, Dimitri, Ikos

TERZAKIS, DIMITRI (cont'd.)

Stichiron
[Greek] SATB,ob,clar,horn,trom,
tuba,perc (diff) BAREN. BA6095
rental   (T57)

TESCHNER
All Glory, Laud And Honor *Palm,
anthem
(DeCou, Harold) SATB oct SINGSPIR
ZJP-3522 $.25   (T58)

TESORIERO, GAETANO
Ave Maria
SSA EMI s.p.   (T59)

TEST OF GOODNESS, A see Ford, Virgil T.

TESTAMENT OF FAITH, A see Rosenberg,
Wolf

TESTAMENTUM see Novak, Jan

TESTIFY see Fischer, William Gustavus

TEWSON, BILL
Buildin' *see Holben, Larry

Building *see Holben, Larry

Let Love Live *see Holben, Larry

TEXTE UBER FRIEDEN see Hufschmidt,
Wolfgang

THACKRAY
Pleasure It Is *anthem
unis (easy) OXFORD 45.068 $.25
(T60)

THANK YOU FOR DOING IT SO WELL see
Gassman, Clark

THANK YOU, LORD see Burgess, Dan

THANK YOU, LORD see Skillings, Otis

THANK YOU, LORD see Sykes

THANKS see Fettke, Tom

THANKS BE TO GOD see Beal

THANKS BE TO GOD see Ford, Olive
Elizabeth

THANKS BE TO GOD see Holbrook, Peter
William

THANKS BE TO GOD see Matthews, Thomas

THANKS BE TO GOD see Mendelssohn-
Bartholdy, Felix

THANKS BE TO THEE see Giordano

THANKS BE TO THEE see Handel, George
Frideric

THANKS TO GOD! see Hultman

THANKS WE GIVE see Wood, Dale

THANKSGIVING HYMN see Thiman, Eric
Harding

THANKSGIVING SERVICE, A *CC11U,Thanks,
anthem
(Fleming, Launa B.; Peterson, J.W.;
DeCou, H.; Johnson, N.; Rasley, M.)
SATB,6 narrators oct SINGSPIR $1.95
(T61)

THAT BEAUTIFUL NAME see Camp, Mabel
Johnston

THAT CHRISTMAS LONG AGO see Sittler,
Jean

THAT EASTER DAY see Pasquet, Jean

THAT EASTER DAY WITH JOY WAS BRIGHT see
Johnson, D.

THAT EASTER MORN AT BREAK OF DAY see
Leaf, Robert

THAT PRECIOUS SCARRED HAND see Norman,
Lucille

THAT SWEET STORY *CC11L,anthem
SSA FINE ARTS CLTR-2-72 $1.95
contains compositions and
arrangements by: Cram; Littleton,
Bill J.; Gagliardi; Alma;
Blankenship; Burroughs; Bartlett;
Grady   (T62)

THAT SWEET STORY OF OLD see
Blankenship, Mark

THAT THE WORLD MAY KNOW *CC10L,gospel
(Johnson, Paul) cor WORD 37667 $1.95
(T63)

THAT THE WORLD MAY KNOW see Johnson,
Paul

THAT VIRGIN'S CHILD MOST MEEK see
Rubbra, Edmund

THAT WE MAY SHOW THY LOVE see Young

THAT'S THE SPIRIT see Arch, Gwyn

THAT'S WHAT HE DID FOR ME see Mercer,
W. Elmo

THAT'S WORTH EVERYTHING *CCUL
(Huff, Ronn) cor BENSON B0769 $2.50
stereo recording, tapes, and-or
accompaniment tape also available;
for book-record sets available,
contact publisher   (T64)

THEE, GOD see Rorem, Ned

THEE WE ADORE see Mawby, Colin

THEE WILL I LOVE see Franck, Cesar

THEME see Yahres, Samuel C.

THEME OF MY SONG, THE see Ford, Olive
Elizabeth

THEN I MET THE MASTER see Lister, Mosie

THEN THE LORD STOOD BY ME! see
Peterson, John W.

THEOPHANE, SISTER M. (HYTREK)
When In Every Season
SATB,solo,org oct AGAPE AG 7163
$.35   (T65)

THERE CAME A MAN see Williams, J.J.

THERE CAME A STAR see Fox, Luacine
Clark

THERE CAME WISE MEN see Babcock, Rowena

THERE COMES A SHIP A'SAILING see
Sowerby, Leo

THERE IS A BALM IN GILEAD *spir
(Davis, Frederick) SATB,acap (med)
GENTRY G-234 $.40   (T66)
(Pooler, M.) mix cor BRODT 640 $.30
(T67)
THERE IS A FOUNTAIN see Mason, Lowell

THERE IS A GOD
TTBB GIA G1482 $.40   (T68)
SATB GIA G1483 $.40   (T69)
SA/TB GIA G1484 $.40   (T70)

THERE IS A GREAT JOY COMING see
Courtney, Ragan

THERE IS A GREEN HILL FAR AWAY see
Grimes, Travis

THERE IS A GREEN HILL FAR AWAY see
Miles, Russell Hancock

THERE IS A GREEN HILL FAR AWAY see
Younger, John B.

THERE IS A LAND OF PURE DELIGHT see
Thomas, C.

THERE IS A MAN ON THE CROSS see
Gerschefski, Edwin

THERE IS A NAME see Reynolds, William
Jensen

THERE IS A SONG *Contemp
(Krogstad, Bob) jr cor GOSPEL
05 TM 0565 $1.00 record and
songbook available for $3.00
contains: Christmas Medley; First
Thing I Do Every Morning, The;
Jesus Is My Shepherd; My Friend
And I; Our Great Saviour; There
Is A Song   (T71)

THERE IS A SONG
see There Is A Song

THERE IS A TIME FOR EVERYTHING
(Wild, Eric) SATB,pno BERANDOL
BER1683 $.75   (T72)

THERE IS A WAY see Fischer, William
Gustavus

THERE IS JOY IN MY SOUL see Ferrin

THERE IS NO GREATER LOVE see Peterson,
John W.

THERE IS NO LOVE see Littlewood

THERE IS NO ONE LIKE MY JESUS see
Landgrave, Phillip

THERE IS NO ROOM see Peterson, John W.

THERE IS NO ROSE see Paynter, John P.

THERE IS NO ROSE see Preston

THERE IS ONE BODY see Healey, Derek

THERE IS POWER IN THE BLOOD see Jones

THERE SHALL BE NIGHT NO MORE see
Protheroe, Daniel

THERE SHALL BE SHOWERS OF BLESSING see
Mc Granahan

THERE THROUGH ENDLESS RANKS OF ANGELS
see Schalk, Carl

THERE WAS A MAID see Nops, Marjory

THERE'LL ALWAYS BE A CHRISTMAS see
Rasley, John M.

THERE'S A DIFFERENCE see Watters, Bob

THERE'S A LAND THAT IS FAIRER THAN DAY
*anthem
(Gagliardi) SATB oct BROADMAN 4540-84
$.30   (T73)

THERE'S A NARROW ROAD see Allen

THERE'S A NEW SONG IN MY HEART see
Peterson, John W.

THERE'S A QUIET UNDERSTANDING see
Smith, Tedd

THERE'S A SONG IN THE AIR *Xmas,anthem
(Young) SATB oct BROADMAN 4539-00
$.30   (T74)

THERE'S A SONG IN THE AIR see
Harrington, Karl P.

THERE'S A WIDENESS IN GOD'S MERCY
(Brandon, George) SAB (med easy)
WATERLOO $.35   (T75)

THERE'S A WIDENESS IN GOD'S MERCY see
Grieb, Herbert [C.]

THERE'S A WIDENESS IN GOD'S MERCY see
Staton, Kenneth W.

THERE'S A WIDENESS IN GOD'S MERCY see
Tourjee, Lizzie S.

THERE'S LOVE IN THE AIR see Albert,
Johann

THERE'S ONLY ONE SOLUTION see
Skillings, Otis

THERE'S SOMETHING ABOUT THAT NAME see
Gaither, William J. (Bill)

THERESIAE A JESU INFANTE see Eben, Petr

THERESIEN-MESSE see Haydn, (Franz)
Joseph

THEY ALL LIVED LONG AGO see Sleeth,
Natalie

THEY ALL SANG "JESUS" see Turner, Lee

THEY BLAZED A PATHWAY TO THE MOON see
Burke, John

THEY CAST THEIR NETS see McCabe,
Michael

THEY CRUCIFIED MY LORD *Psntd,spir
(Biebl, Franz) "Sie Kreuzigten Den
Herrn" [Ger] 4pt mix cor,T/B solo
BOHM s.p.   (T76)

THEY SHALL MOUNT UP WITH WINGS see
Weatherseed, John .J.

THEY THAT GO DOWN TO THE SEA IN SHIPS
see Lawrence, Burton

THEY THAT GO DOWN TO THE SEA IN SHIPS
see Pozdro, John

THEY THAT SOW IN TEARS see Gaither,
William J. (Bill)

THEY'LL KNOW WE ARE CHRISTIANS see
Scholtes, P.

THEY'LL KNOW WE ARE CHRISTIANS BY OUR
LOVE see Scholters

THEY'LL KNOW WE ARE CHRISTIANS BY OUR
LOVE *CC11UL
(Huff, Ronn) cor BENSON B0787 $1.95
stereo recording, tapes, and-or
accompaniment tape also available;
for book-record sets available,
contact publisher   (T77)

THIMAN, ERIC HARDING (1900-   )
All Who Love And Serve Your City
*anthem
SATB,org NOVELLO MT 1574 s.p. (T78)

THIMAN, ERIC HARDING (cont'd.)

Bell Carol
SATB EMI s.p.   (T79)

Childing Slept, A *Xmas
SATB EMI s.p.   (T80)

Christmas Carol Sequence, A *Xmas
SATB,strings voc sc NOVELLO rental
(T81)

Christmas Triad, A *Xmas
SATB,2fl,2ob,2clar,2bsn,4horn,2trp,
3trom,timp,org,strings, cymbals
voc sc NOVELLO rental   (T82)

God Who Made The Earth
SA (easy) WATERLOO $.30   (T83)

Joy To The World *Adv/Xmas
unis (med easy) WATERLOO $.35 (T84)
SATB,org GRAY CMR 3335 $.30 (T85)

Just As I Am Thine Own To Be
SA (med easy) WATERLOO $.35   (T86)

Last Supper, The
SATB,SBar soli,fl,ob,clar,bsn,horn,
timp,org,strings voc sc NOVELLO
rental   (T87)

Mary's Nowell *Xmas
SATB SCHIRM.G 11958 $.30   (T88)

O Be Joyful In The Lord
mix cor BANKS MUS YS 1253 $.25
(T89)

Saviour Teach Me Day By Day
SA (med easy) WATERLOO $.40   (T90)

Shepherds' Story, The *Xmas
SATB,pno/org SCHIRM.G R11999 $.35
(T91)
SATB,pno/orch CURWEN 80910 s.p.
(T92)

Thanksgiving Hymn
SATB STAINER 3.0830.1 $.50   (T93)

Three Introits *CC3U
SATB,acap GRAY CMR 3306 $.30 (T94)

Three Ships, The *Xmas
SATB,opt org/pno,strings voc sc
NOVELLO rental   (T95)

Wondrous Love *anthem
SATB (easy) oct BROADMAN 4561-30
$.30   (T96)

THINE BE THE GLORY see Lee, John

THINE FOREVER see Evensen, Glenn

THINE IS THE GLORY see Handel, George
Frideric

THINE OWN TO BE see Handel, George
Frideric

THINK OF IT, LORD! see Ortlund, Anne

THINK ON THESE THINGS see Clarke, Henry
Leland

THINK ON THESE THINGS see Peterson,
John W.

THIRTEEN AMENS (AND ALLELUIAS) see
Praetorius, Michael

THIRTEEN ANTHEMS see Tomkins, Thomas

THIRTY-FIVE CONDUCTUS FOR TWO AND THREE
VOICES *CC35U,Mediev
(Knapp, Janet) 2-3pt bds A-R ED $8.95
(T97)

THIS CHILD BEHOLD see Cashmore, Donald

THIS CHRISTMAS DAY see Burroughs, Bob

THIS DAY A CHILD IS BORN see
Zimmermann, Heinz Werner

THIS DAY, A CHRISTMAS FANFARE see
Ferguson

THIS DAY CHRIST WAS BORN see Bateson,
Thomas

THIS DAY OUR LORD IS BORN see Ehret,
Walter

THIS DAY TO US A CHILD IS BORN see
Bach, Johann Sebastian, Uns Ist Ein
Kindlein Heut Geborn

THIS DAY WE WELCOME A LITTLE CHILD
*Xmas,anthem/carol,Dut
(Ehret, Walter) SA,org,opt 2fl (easy)
GIA G1851 $.35   (T98)

THIS ENDERS NIGHT *Xmas
(McKelvy, James) SATB (easy) FOSTER
MF 513 $.30   (T99)

THIS HAPPY EASTER DAY
see Two Easter Carols

THIS I BELIEVE see Johnson, Norman

THIS IS A DAY FOR REJOICING see Leaf,
Robert

THIS IS JUST WHAT HEAVEN MEANS TO ME
(Mercer, W. Elmo) SATB oct BENSON
S4360 $.25   (T100)

THIS IS MY AMERICA see Bass, Claude L.

THIS IS MY COMMANDMENT see Tallis,
Thomas

THIS IS MY FATHER'S WORLD *Gen,anthem
(Price, Benton) SA/SATB (easy) oct
LORENZ A564 $.30   (T101)
(Red, Buryl) 2pt jr cor (easy)
BROADMAN 4560-38 $.35   (T102)
(Tipton, Clyde) SATB,pno/org DEAN
CE-105 $.40   (T103)

THIS IS MY FATHER'S WORLD see Mueller,
Carl F.

THIS IS MY FATHER'S WORLD see Price

THIS IS MY FATHER'S WORLD see Red,
Buryl

THIS IS MY FATHER'S WORLD see Sheppard,
Franklin L.

THIS IS THE BIRTHDAY OF THE LORD *Xmas
(Douglas) SSA PRO ART 2846 $.40
(T104)

THIS IS THE COVENANT see Berger, Jean

THIS IS THE DAY see Campbell, Sydney S.

THIS IS THE DAY see Gallus, Jacobus,
Hodie Nobis Coelorum Rex

THIS IS THE DAY see Hampton

THIS IS THE DAY see Johnson, Ralph

THIS IS THE DAY see Littleton, Bill J.

THIS IS THE DAY see Rulison, Constance

THIS IS THE DAY OF VICT'RY *Easter/
Lent
(Ehret) SAB oct LILLENAS AN-2401 $.35
(T105)

THIS IS THE DAY THAT THE LORD HATH MADE
see Peterson, John W.

THIS IS THE DAY WHICH THE LORD HATH
MADE see Palmer, Peggy Spenser

THIS IS THE FEAST OF VICTORY see
Nelson, Ronald A.

THIS IS THE HOPE see Skillings, Otis

THIS IS THE LORD see Binckes

THIS IS THE MESSAGE see Butler

THIS IS THE PRAISE OF CREATED THINGS
see Childs, Barney

THIS IS THE RECORD OF JOHN see Gibbons,
Orlando

THIS IS THE RECORD OF JOHN see Newlin,
Dika

THIS IS THE WILL OF OUR GOD see Smith,
Claude T.

THIS IS WHY I WANT TO GO see York, C.

THIS JOYFUL EASTER-TIDE *Easter,Dut
(Fearing, J.) mix cor LESLIE 4104
$.35   (T106)

THIS JOYFUL EASTERTIDE *Easter
see Camidge, Matthew, Sanctus
(Fenwick, Roy) SSA (med easy)
WATERLOO $.30   (T107)

THIS JOYFUL EASTERTIDE see Gosse, Barry

THIS JOYFUL EASTERTIDE see Wolff, S.
Drummond

THIS LAND. . . OUR LAND! *CCUL
(Johnson, Derric) cor BENSON B0812
$1.95 stereo recording,tapes, and-
or accompaniment tape also
available; for book-record sets
available, contact publisher (T108)

THIS LITTLE BABE see Morgan, Hilda

THIS LITTLE LIGHT OF MINE *anthem
(Cram, James D.) SATB FINE ARTS
CM 1111 $.40   (T109)
(Powell) SATB&jr cor oct BENSON S4361
$.35   (T110)

THIS MOST GLORIOUS DAY see Track,
Gerhard

THIS NEW CHRISTMAS CAROL see Kruspe,
Glenn

THIS NEW CHRISTMAS CAROL see Simpson,
John

THIS NEW DAY see Blackley

THIS NIGHT DID GOD BECOME A CHILD see
Leaf, Robert

THIS OL' HAMMER see Work, John [Wesley]

THIS OLD WORLD WILL NEVER BE THE SAME
see Paris

THIS TRAIN
(Arch, Gwyn) SSA EMI   (T111)

THIS WE BELIEVE see Effinger, Cecil

THIS WORLD OUTSIDE see Wyrtzen, Don

THOMAS
Bells Of Christmas, The *see
Croswell

Hallelujah! We Shall Rise! *anthem/
gospel
(DeCou, Harold) SATB oct SINGSPIR
ZJP-8067 $.25   (T112)

He Is Alive (composed with Alford)
*Easter
SATB BENSON S4120 $.30   (T113)

Shout The Glad Tidings
SATB,brass,perc (med) OXFORD 94.211
s.p., ipa   (T114)

Song Of Little Jesus, The *Xmas
(Parry; Davis) unis (easy) OXFORD
81.149 $.30   (T115)

THOMAS, C.
All Things Bright And Beautiful
unis BRODT 632 $.20   (T116)

Come, Christians, Join To Sing
unis BRODT 629 $.20   (T117)

Father In Heaven We Thank Thee
SA BRODT 535 $.20   (T118)

God My Father
unis BRODT 536 $.20   (T119)

God, Who Made The Earth
unis BRODT 541 $.18   (T120)

Now That The Daylight Fills The Sky
SA BRODT 587 $.20   (T121)

O God, Whose Blessed Son
mix cor BRODT 537 $.20   (T122)

Saviour, Teach Me, Day By Day
unis BRODT 542 $.20   (T123)

There Is A Land Of Pure Delight
mix cor BRODT 555 $.26   (T124)

Twelve Choral Responses *CC12U,cor-
resp
mix cor BRODT 543 $.25   (T125)

THOMAS, DANIEL B.
So Great A Gift *Xmas,cant
(Johnson, Norman) SATB,SATBar soli
SINGSPIR 5985 $1.50   (T126)

THOMAS, J.
Hallelujah, We Shall Rise *Easter
(Kling, R.) SATB oct GOSPEL
05 TM 0128 $.25   (T127)

THOMAS LUDOVICI VICTORIA ABULENSIS
OPERA OMNIA (COMPLETE WORKS) see
Victoria, Tomas Luis de

THOMPSON
All Hail The Power Of Jesus' Name
*anthem
SATB oct LORENZ 9911 $.40   (T128)

Jesus Is All The World To Me *gospel
(Skillings) SATB oct LILLENAS
AN-5083 $.30   (T129)

Softly And Tenderly
(Yoder, David) SATB oct GOSPEL
05 TM 0111 $.20   (T130)

THOMPSON, R.G.
Bread Of The World
mix cor BANKS MUS YS 1063 $.20
(T131)

In Thee, O Lord
mix cor BANKS MUS YS 577 $.25   (T132)

THOMPSON, RANDALL (1899-   )
Carol Of The Rose (from Place Of The
Blest, The)
SSAA,pno/orch SCHIRM.EC 2800 s.p.,
ipr   (T133)

Concord Cantata, A
SATB SCHIRM.EC 3003   (T134)

Gift Outright, The
SATB SCHIRM.EC 3015   (T135)

Mirror Of St. Anne, The
SATB SCHIRM.EC 2921   (T136)

Pelican, The (from Place Of The
Blest, The)
SSAA,pno/orch SCHIRM.EC 2801 s.p.,
ipr   (T137)

THOMPSON, ROBERT B.
Lift Up Your Heads, O Ye Gates
*Palm,anthem
SATB oct SINGSPIR ZJP-3527 $.30
(T138)

THOREN, NANCY
Children's Carols For Improvisation
*CCU,Xmas
unis,kbd, Orff inst AUGSBURG
11-9115 $1.25   (T139)

THOSE WHO TRUST IN THE LORD see
Zimmermann, Heinz Werner

THOU ALONE ART ISRAEL'S SHIELD see
Berger, Jean

THOU AND THY WONDROUS DEEDS, O LORD see
Lowes

THOU ART GOD! see Beck, John Ness

THOU ART MY GOD see Newbury, Kent A.

THOU ART MY GOD AND FATHER see Scheidt,
Samuel, Weil Du Mein Gott Und Vater
Bist

THOU ART, O GOD, THE LIFE AND LIGHT see
Paulsen, A.

THOU ART THE WAY see Peek, B.L.

THOU ART THE WAY see Weigl, Vally

THOU ART THE WAY see Willis, Richard
Storrs

THOU CHILD DIVINE see Schulz, Joh.
Abraham Peter

THOU DIDST LEAVE THY THRONE see
Gingrich, I.

THOU HALLOWED CHOSEN MORN OF PRAISE
*anthem
see Two Easter Carols
(Ehret) SATB oct BROADMAN 4545-82
$.30   (T140)

THOU KNOWEST LORD see Purcell, Henry

THOU KNOWEST, LORD, THE SECRETS OF OUR
HEARTS see Purcell, Henry

THOU LOVELY, HEAVENLY BABE *Xmas,
carol,Ger
(Ehret, W.) SATB,acap,opt fl/rec oct
NATIONAL WHC-50 $.40   (T141)

THOU, O CHRIST OF CALVARY see More

THOU, O GOD, ART PRAISED IN ZION see
Hare

THOU, O LORD, ART GREAT AND RIGHTEOUS
see Bruckner, Anton

THOU SHALT KNOW HIM see Lovelace,
Austin C.

THOU, THE CENTRAL ORB see Gibbons,
Orlando

THOU WILT KEEP HIM IN PERFECT PEACE see
Ramsfield, Jerome

THOU WILT KEEP HIM IN PERFECT PEACE see
Walker, Robert

THOU WILT KEEP HIM IN PERFECT PEACE see
Wesley, S.S.

THOUGH YOU GO FAR see Graham

THOUGHTS see Diament, Abraham

THOUSAND HOSANNAS, A see McNair,
Jacqueline Hanna

THREE AMERICAN HYMN-TUNES see Burke,
John

THREE ANTHEMS see Betteridge, Leslie

THREE ANTHEMS FOR JUNIOR CHOIR see
Cooper, Rose Marie

THREE ANTHEMS FOR JUNIOR CHOIR see
Gillette, James Robert

THREE ANTHEMS OF COMMITMENT see Young

THREE ANTIPHONAL CANTICLES see Routley,
Eric

THREE BILLINGS CANONS see Billings,
William

THREE CANDLE BLESSINGS see Gottlieb,
Jack

THREE CAROLS see Hoover

THREE CAROLS see Arnatt, Ronald

THREE CAROLS FOR COMMUNION *CC3U,
Commun,carol
(Ritchey, L.) SATB (med) WATERLOO
$.40   (T142)

THREE CAROLS FOR JUNIORS see Copes, V.
Earle

THREE CAROLS FOR JUNIORS see Copes, V.
Earle

THREE CAROLS FOR YOUNG VOICES see Wood,
Dale

THREE CHILDREN'S SONGS see McClohon

THREE CHORAL HYMNS see Vaughan
Williams, Ralph

THREE CHORAL HYMNS see Vaughan
Williams, Ralph

THREE CHORAL HYMNS see Dyson, George

THREE CHORALES see Bach, Johann
Sebastian

THREE CHORALES see Brahms, Johannes

THREE CHRISTMAS CAROL ANTHEMS *Xmas,
anthem
(Roesch, R.A.) SAB BROADMAN 4521-02
$1.00
contains: Good Christian Men,
Rejoice; Holly And The Ivy, The;
T'was In The Moon Of Wintertime
(T143)

THREE CHRISTMAS CAROLS see Meek,
Kenneth

THREE CHRISTMAS CAROLS *see I Saw
Three Ships   (T144)

THREE CHRISTMAS CAROLS see Anonymous

THREE CHRISTMAS CAROLS *CC3U,Xmas
(Brough, G.) SSA (med easy) WATERLOO
$.30   (T145)

THREE CHRISTMAS CAROLS see Whear, Paul
William

THREE CHRISTMAS CAROLS see Praetorius,
Michael

THREE CHRISTMAS CHORALES see Gordon,
John

THREE CHRISTMAS SONGS see Kemp, Walter

THREE CHRISTMAS SONGS WITH SYNTHESIZER
ACCOMPANIMENT
unis,synthesizer cor pts CONCORDIA
98-2234 $.30, ipa
contains: Christ The Lord To Us Is
Born (Schultz) (Boh); On
Christmas Night (Vaughan
Williams, Ralph) (Eng); Bach,
Johann Sebastian, Prepare
Thyself, Zion (Schultz)   (T146)

THREE CONTEMPORARY ANTHEMS see
Pulsifer, Thomas R.

THREE FRONTIER HYMNS *CC3U,hymn
(Boyd, J.) SATB oct KERBY 6404 $.35
(T147)

THREE FRONTIER HYMNS see Walker,
William

THREE FRONTIER HYMNS see Boyd, Jack

THREE FUGING-TUNES
(Bennett, Lawrence) BROUDE BR. $.40
contains: Anonymous, Canaan (SATB,
acap); Anonymous, Lonsdale (TTB,
acap); Ingalls, Jeremiah,
Northfield (SATB,acap)   (T148)

THREE HOLY KINGS, THE
(Pablo, Juan) 2pt,S solo,pno/org,opt
gtr, opt. claves and maracas
FREDONIA see from Three Puerto
Rican Carols   (T149)

THREE HYMN-CAROL SETTINGS see Mahnke,
Allan

THREE HYMN TUNES see Hampton, Calvin

THREE HYMN TUNES see Beaumont, Rev.
Geoffrey

THREE HYMN TUNES see Rubbra, Edmund

THREE HYMNS see Cavalli, (Pietro)
Francesco

THREE HYMNS see Stevens, Halsey

THREE HYMNS see Schattenberg, Thomas

THREE HYMNS OF PRAISE
SATB&SATB,org,brass oct CONCORDIA
97-5290 $.60, ipa
contains: All Glory Be To God On
High; From All That Dwell Below
The Skies; In Thee Is Gladness
(T150)

THREE INTROITS see Thiman, Eric Harding

THREE INTROITS AND TWO CHANTS see
Campbell, Sydney S.

THREE KINGS, THE see Ramirez, Los Reyes
Magos

THREE KINGS ARE HERE see Verkouteran,
Adrian

THREE KINGS ONCE LIVED see Cowen

THREE LATIN MOTETS see Berkeley, Lennox

THREE LITTLE CAROLS see Wood, Dale

THREE MEDIEVAL LYRICS see Mathias,
William

THREE MOTETS see Hovhaness, Alan

THREE MOTETS see Baur, Jurg

THREE MOTETS see Victoria, Tomas Luis
de

THREE MOTETS see Boone

THREE MOTETS see Rorem, Ned

THREE MOTETS see Victoria, Tomas Luis
de

THREE MOTETS see Weis, Flemming

THREE MOTETS see Mendelssohn-Bartholdy,
Felix

THREE MOTETS see Nielsen, Carl

THREE MOTETS FOR CHRISTMAS see Le
Fleming, Christopher (Kaye)

THREE MOTETS FROM SAINT JOHN see
Baumgartner, H Leroy

THREE PART CHOIR NO. 1 *CCUL
(Peterson, John W.) SAB SINGSPIR 5813
$1.25   (T151)

THREE PART CHOIR NO. 2 *CCUL
(Peterson, John W.) SAB SINGSPIR 5830
$1.25   (T152)

THREE PART CHOIR NO. 3 *CCUL
(Peterson, John W.) SAB SINGSPIR 5829
$1.25   (T153)

THREE PART CHOIR NO. 4 *CCUL
(Peterson, John W.) SAB SINGSPIR 4286
$1.25   (T154)

THREE PART CHRISTMAS CHOIR, THE *CCUL,
Xmas
(Peterson, John W.) SAB SINGSPIR 5932
$1.25   (T155)

THREE-PART SONGS FOR WOMEN see Wilson,
Juanita

THREE PEACE AND BROTHERHOOD CANONS
*anthem
cor CHORISTERS R-6 $.15
contains: God Lives In Love (folk,
Heb); How Good And Joyous (folk,
Isr); Love God With Your Heart
(folk)   (T156)

THREE PRAYERS see Rorem, Ned

THREE PRAYERS FROM THE ARK see Cram,
James D.

THREE PRINCES *Xmas
(Bissell, Keith W.) SATB (med diff)
WATERLOO $.40   (T157)

THREE PROPHECIES see Bender, Jan

THREE PROVERBS see Cram, James D.

THREE PSALM HYMNS FOR JUNIORS see McAfee, D.

THREE PSALM HYMNS FOR JUNIORS see McAfee, D.

THREE PSALMS see Leighton, Kenneth

THREE PSALMS see White, Richard

THREE PUERTO RICAN CAROLS *see Hasten Shepherds On; On That Holy Midnight; Three Holy Kings, The   (T158)

THREE RESPONSES see Pfohl, J.C.

THREE SACRED SONGS see Hruby, Delores

THREE SACRED SONGS see Dale, Mervyn

THREE SEASONAL SONGS see Hunnicutt, Judy

THREE SHIPS, THE see Thiman, Eric Harding

THREE SHORT ANTHEMS see Lovelace, Austin C.

THREE SHORT ANTHEMS see Purcell, Henry

THREE SHORT ANTHEMS OF PRAISE see Coggin

THREE SHORT INTROITS see Baker, Richard C.

THREE SHORT INTROITS see Hooper, Edmund

THREE SONGS see Copley

THREE SONGS FOR LENT AND EASTER see Lenel, Ludwig

THREE SONGS FROM THE ICELANDIC GRADUAL see Stefansson, Fjolnir

THREE SONGS OF PRAISE see Dyson, George

THREE SONGS OF SERVICE see Procter, Leland

THREE SONGS OF TRIBULATION (Bennett, Lawrence) BROUDE BR. $.50 contains: Anonymous, Lamentation (SATB,acap); Dare, Elkanah Kelsey, Babylonian Captivity (SATB,acap); Lewer, Fidelia (TTB, acap)   (T159)

THREE WISE MEN, WISE MEN THREE see Regney, Noel

THRICE HOLY LORD see Schutz, Heinrich

THRONED UPON THE AWFUL TREE see Lovelace, Austin C.

THROUGH MIDNIGHT SILENCE *Xmas (Hardwicke) SAB,opt ob PRO ART 2807 $.35   (T160)

THROUGH THE EYES OF A CHILD see Carter, John

THROUGH THE WILDERNESS see Casebow

THROW OUT THE LIFELINE see Ufford, Edward S.

THRUPP
Saviour, Like A Shepherd Lead Us (Bradbury; Williams, David) SATB oct GOSPEL 05 TM 0213 $.20 (T161)

THUS SAITH THE HIGH, THE LOFTY ONE see Billings, William

THUS SAYETH GOD see Nystedt, Knut, Sa Sier Gud

THUS SINGS THE HEAV'NLY CHOIR see Amner, John

THUS SPEAKETH CHRIST see McFadden

THY BLESSING, LORD, GRANT UNTO ME see Ehret, Walter

THY HAND, O GOD, HAS GUIDED *Finn (Coggin, Elwood) SATB,org/pno (med easy) PRESSER 312-41028 $.35 (T162)

THY KINGDOM COME ON EARTH see Christiansen, Paul

THY LITTLE ONES DEAR LORD ARE WE *Xmas,anthem (Track, Gerhard) SATB,org (easy) GIA G1876 $.50   (T163)

THY LOVE BRINGS JOY see Schutz, Heinrich

THY NAME IS KNOWN UNTO HIM see Herbst, Johannes

THY PRAISE WE SING see Wetzler, Robert

THY ROBE OF RIGHTEOUSNESS see Graham

THY STRONG WORD see Schalk, Carl

THY TRUTH IS GREAT see Nelson, R.

THY WAY, NOT MINE, O LORD see Bach, Johann Sebastian

THY WILL BE DONE see Eilers, Joyce Elaine

THY WILL BE DONE see Mana-Zucca, Mme.

THY WORD HAVE I HID IN MY HEART see Bartlett

THY WORD IS A LAMP see Buffaloe, James

THY WORD IS A LAMP see Huntington, Ronald M.

THY WORD IS A LAMP UNTO MY FEET see Moffatt, Richard C.

THY WORD IS LIKE A GARDEN see Hodder

THY WORTHINESS IS ALL OUR SONG (Brandon, George) 2pt WILLIS 9988 $.25   (T164)

THYBO, LEIF
Fortitudo Mea [Lat] SSAATB,acap EGTVED KB114 s.p.   (T165)

THYGERSON, ROBERT J.
Born In A Stable *Xmas,anthem SATB oct SACRED S-178 $.35 (T166)

Come Hear The Wonderful Tidings *Xmas SATB RICHMOND MI-95 $.40 (T167)

Every Way, Day By Day *anthem SATB oct HERITAGE H106 $.40 (T168)

Hallelujah, Praise The Lord *anthem SATB oct HERITAGE H122 $.40 (T169)

Hush, My Babe *Xmas,anthem SATB oct SACRED S-154 $.35 (T170)

Our Religious Heritage In Song *CCU, anthem cor HERITAGE $1.95 (T171)

Reach Out SATB oct SCHMITT 1215 $.40 (T172)

Sing A New Song Unto The Lord *anthem SATB oct SACRED S-147 $.35 (T173)

Wasn't That A Mighty Day! *Xmas, anthem mix cor HERITAGE H129 $.35 (T174)

TIDEN, AR FULLBORDAD see Ahlen, David

TIDINGS FROM HEAVEN see Tidings So Wonderful

TIDINGS O'ER THE HILLTOPS see Schurman, Ralph

TIDINGS SO WONDERFUL *Xmas (Ehret, Walter) SATB oct GOSPEL 05 TM 0352 $.40 contains also: Tidings From Heaven (T175)

TIEFE FLUTEN see Petersen, Rolf, Deep River

TIERIE, J.F.
Kerstliedjes Voor Het Jonge Volke *CCU,Xmas,hymn unis,pno/harmonium HEER 146 s.p.   (T176)

TIFFAULT
Oh Jerusalem SATB PRO ART 2799 $.35 (T177)

TIGNER, MARCY
Jesus Story, The *cant jr cor,narrator LEXICON 37633 $1.95   (T178)

'TIL THE WHOLE WORLD KNOWS see Hopkins

"TILL FROJD FORUTAN ANDE" see Egebjer, Lars

TILL HE COME see Burroughs, Bob

TILL HE COMES see Wyrtzen, Don

TILL, JOHANN CHRISTIAN (1762-1844)
Praise And Laud And Honor (Kroeger, Karl) SATB (med easy) FISCHER,C CM 7899 $.40 (T179)

TILL, JOHANN CHRISTIAN (cont'd.)

Rejoice, Thou Lamb's Beloved Bride (Kroeger) [Ger/Eng] SATB oct MORAVIAN 5860 $.50   (T180)

TILLMAN
Old Time Power (McLellan, Cyril) SATB oct GOSPEL 05 TM 0134 $.35   (T181)

TIME ALMOST GONE see Roberts

TIME FOR EVERYTHING, A see Mueller

TIME IS NOW, THE see Huff, Ronn

TIME IS NOW, THE see Mercer, W. Elmo

TIME OF SALVATION, THE *CC24U (Cox, Jr., W.A.) cor BROADMAN 4520-27 $1.25   (T182)

TIME THAT IS NOW, THE see Lovelace, Austin C.

TIMOR ET TREMOR VENERUNT SUPER ME see Gabrieli

TINDLEY
Nothing Between *anthem/gospel (Shepard, Bob) SATB oct SINGSPIR ZJP-8132 $.30   (T183)

TINY LITTLE BABY BOY see Murray

TIPPETT, MICHAEL (1905-)
Child Of Our Time, A *ora SATB,SATB soli,orch min sc SCHOTT 10899 s.p.   (T184)

Epilogue "Non Nobis Domine" [Lat] 4pt mix cor,pno (med) sc SCHOTTS ED. 10 912 s.p. (T185)

Five Negro Spirituals (from Child Of Our Time, A) CC5U,spir SATB SCHOTT 10585 s.p. (T186)

Vision Of St. Augustine, The *cant cor,Bar solo,orch min sc SCHOTT 10897 s.p.   (T187)

TIPTON
God Is Our Refuge And Our Strength *anthem SAB (easy) oct BROADMAN 4551-57 $.30   (T188)

Hear, Hear, O Ye Nations *see Hosmer

I Want To Tell You Of Jesus *gospel (Kirby) SATB oct LILLENAS AT-1095 $.30   (T189)

New Song, A *anthem 2pt (easy) oct BROADMAN 4554-36 $.30   (T190)

Song Of Praise, A *anthem SATB (easy) oct BROADMAN 4562-30 $.35   (T191)

TIPTON, C.
I Thank You God SSAA,org,fl,hndbl FISCHER,J FEC 10125 $.35   (T192)

'TIS MARVELOUS AND WONDERFUL see Morris

'TIS SO SWEET TO TRUST IN JESUS see Kirkpatrick, William J.

'TIS SO SWEET TO TRUST IN JESUS see Stead

TO A VIRGIN MEEK AND MILD see Two Carols

TO A VIRGIN MEEK AND MILD see Johnson, David N.

TO BE A PEOPLE see Robertson

TO BE WHAT YOU WANT ME TO BE see Wyrtzen, Don

TO BETHLEHEM see Away In A Manger

TO BETHLEHEM see Peeters, Flor

TO EVERY THING THERE IS A SEASON see Pulsifer, Thomas R.

TO EVERYTHING THERE IS A SEASON see Currie, Randolph

TO EVERYTHING THERE IS A SEASON see Rozsa, Miklos

TO GAMMELTESTAMENTLIGE SANGE see Hovland, Egil

TO GOD AND COUNTRY LET US SING see
Young, Gordon

TO GOD BE THE GLORY see Doane, [William Howard]

TO GOD. . .GLORY *CC10UL,gospel
(Skillings, Otis) cor cmplt ed
LILLENAS MB-364 $1.95   (T193)

TO GOD THE MERCIFUL FATHER see Mills,
Charles

TO GOD WILL WE SING see Sateren, Leland
Bernhard

TO JESUS CHRIST OUR SOVEREIGN KING
*Reces,anthem
(Goemanne, Noel) SAB&cong,org,opt 1-
2trp (easy) GIA G1901 $.40   (T194)
(Roff, Joseph) SATB LITURGICAL $.50
see also Twelve Hymns   (T195)

TO JESUS OUR TRIUMPHANT KING *Easter,
anthem/hymn
(Roff, Joseph) SATB,pno/org
SHATTINGER 408 $.30   (T196)

TO KNOW GOD IS TO LOVE AGAIN see Wild,
Eric

TO RAISE A GRATEFUL SONG
(Brandon) SAB PRO ART 2802 $.35
(T197)

TO SEE THE LORD see Martin, Gilbert M.

TO SHARE THE CROSS see Sinzheimer, Max

TO THE ENDS OF THE EARTH see Seabough,
Ed.

TO THE PASCHAL VICTIM see Victoria,
Tomas Luis de

TO THE PROMISED LAND see Roberts

TO THE WORK see Doane, [William Howard]

TO US A CHILD IS BORN see Herbst,
Johannes

TO US A CHILD OF ROYAL BIRTH see Ehret,
Walter

TO US IS BORN A LITTLE CHILD see
Holland, Kenneth

TO US SALVATION NOW IS COME see Brahms,
Johannes, Es Ist Das Heil Uns
Kommen Her

TO YOU I LIFT MY SOUL see Track,
Gerhard

TO YOU, O LORD, I LIFT MY SOUL see
Kreutz, Robert E.

TO ZION see Weigl, Vally

TO ZION JESUS CAME see Smith

TOCHTER ZION, FREUE DICH! see Handel,
George Frideric

TOD UND EWIGKEIT *funeral
(Bausznern, D. Von) men cor,acap
TONOS 5641 s.p.
contains: Herr, Sprich Dein Ewigs
Wort; Wenn Wir In Hochsten Noten
(T198)

TODAH W'SIMRAH see Lewandowski, Louis

TODAY see Skillings, Otis

TODAY CHRIST IS RISEN see Maekelberghe,
August [R.]

TOGETHER NOW WE PRAISE THE LORD see
Burroughs, Bob

TOLLADAY, DAVID
Flame For Thee, A
SATB oct GOSPEL 05 TM 0206 $.20
(T199)

TOMKINS, THOMAS (ca. 1572-1656)
Almighty God, Whose Praise This Day
SSAATB STAINER 3.0767.1 $.50 (T200)

Have Mercy On Me (from Musica Deo
Sacra-1968)
(Proulx, Richard) SAB GIA G1899
$.40   (T201)

Stephen Being Full Of The Holy Ghost
SSAATBB STAINER 3.0765.1 $.50 (T202)

Thirteen Anthems *CC13U,anthem
(Cavanaugh, Robert W.) cor bds A-R
ED $9.95   (T203)

TOMLINS, GRETA
Rose, The *sac/sec
SSA CRAMER C74   (T204)

TOMORROW CHRIST IS COMING see Lovelace,
Austin C.

TOMORROW SHALL BE MY DANCING DAY
*anthem
(Ashfield) SATB,acap (med) OXFORD
84.204 $.30   (T205)
(Fissinger, Edwin) SATB,drums,tamb,
triangle WORLD CA-2448-8 $.75
(T206)
(Willcocks; Russell) unis (easy)
OXFORD 81.147 $.35   (T207)

TONI, ALCEO (1884-1969)
Dies Irae
see Due Cantiche Religiose

Due Cantiche Religiose
CARISH rental
contains: Dies Irae (cor,SMezT
soli,3fl,2ob,2clar,3bsn,4horn,
3trp,4trom,tuba,timp); Stabat
Mater (mix cor,SBar soli)
(T208)

Preghiera
see Tre Salmi

Stabat Mater
see Due Cantiche Religiose

Tramonto
see Tre Salmi

Tre Salmi *Psalm
cor,soli,3fl,3ob,2clar,3bsn,4horn,
2trp,3trom,tuba,timp,harp CARISH
rental
contains: Preghiera; Tramonto;
Veglia Funebre   (T209)

Veglia Funebre
see Tre Salmi

TOP SONGS FOR MEN *CCUL
(Peterson, John W.) men cor,pno
SINGSPIR 5831 $1.25   (T210)

TOPFF, JOHANN (fl. ca. 1700)
Furchtet Euch Nicht, Ich Verkundige
Euch *Xmas,mot
(Holle, Hugo) SSATB,acap (med) sc
SCHOTTS C 32 230 s.p., cor pts
SCHOTTS C 32 230A-B s.p.   (T211)

TOPLIS
Angel Gabriel, The
unis RICORDI-ENG LD607 s.p.   (T212)

Now The Holly
2-3pt RICORDI-ENG LD608 s.p.   (T213)

Somerset Wassail
2-3pt RICORDI-ENG LD609 s.p.   (T214)

TORCHES see Hugh-Jones, Llifon

TORCHES see Matthews, Thomas

TORCHI
l'arte Musicale In Italia, Vol. I
*sac/sec,CCU,14-16th cent
mix cor RICORDI-ENG 101366 s.p.
(T215)
L'arte Musicale In Italia, Vol. II
*sac/sec,CCU,16th cent
mix cor RICORDI-ENG 101409 s.p.
(T216)

TORMENT OF JOB, THE see Kelly, Robert

TOROVSKY
Softly The Stars Were Shining *Xmas
SATB oct SCHMITT 927 $.35   (T217)

TOTA PULCHRA see Bossi, Marco Enrico

TOTA PULCHRA see Bruckner, Anton

TOTENGELEIT see Goller, Fritz

TOTENGELEIT see Goller, Fritz

TOUCH A HAND, MAKE A FRIEND see Banks

TOUCH ME, LORD JESUS *anthem
(Bass) SATB oct BROADMAN 4562-34 $.35
(T218)

TOUCH OF FAITH see Baker

TOUCH OF GOD, THE see Littleton, Bill
J.

TOURJEE, LIZZIE S. (1858-1913)
There's A Wideness In God's Mercy
*anthem
(Johnson, Norman) SATB oct SINGSPIR
ZJP-7217 $.25   (T219)

TOUT LE CIEL RELUIT *Xmas
(McCauley) SATB (med easy) WATERLOO
$.30   (T220)

TOV L'HODOS see Schubert, Franz (Peter)

TOWNER
At Calvary *anthem/gospel
(Peterson, John W.) SATB oct
SINGSPIR ZJP-8002 $.30   (T221)

TOWNER, DANIEL B.
Anywhere With Jesus *anthem
(DeCou, Harold) SATB/SA (easy) oct
SINGSPIR ZJP-6023 $.35   (T222)

TRACHTET AM ERSTEN NACH DEM REICH
GOTTES see Vulpius, Melchior

TRACK
Lullaby For Christmas Night
SATB oct SCHMITT 923 $.35   (T223)

Usher In The Season *Xmas
SATB SCHIRM.G LG51832 $.40   (T224)

TRACK, GERHARD (1934-   )
Missa Brevis *Mass
"Salzburg Mass" [Eng/Lat] SAB,soli
(med) GIA G1834 $1.00   (T225)

O Give Thanks To The Lord *anthem
2pt mix cor/2pt treb cor&opt unis,
opt solo,org AUGSBURG 11-0651
$.30   (T226)

O Lord Most High, With All My Heart
*anthem
SATB (easy) GIA G1825 $.40   (T227)

Out Of The Depths
(Lojeski, Ed) SATB LEONARD-US
08556500 $.50   (T228)

Rejoice, O Blessed Creation
(Lojeski, Ed) SATB LEONARD-US
08556900 $.50   (T229)

Salzburg Mass *see Missa Brevis

This Most Glorious Day
(Strobbel) SATB LEONARD-US 08557500
$.50   (T230)

To You I Lift My Soul
(Lojeski, Ed) SATB LEONARD-US
08557700 $.50   (T231)

We Sing Now At Christmas *anthem
SATB,S solo AUGSBURG 11-1706 $.35
(T232)

Ye Sons And Daughters *Easter,anthem
SATB,org,opt 3trp (easy) GIA G1862
$.45   (T233)

TRAG MICH AUF SANFTEN SCHWINGEN see
Petersen, Rolf, Swing Low, Sweet
Chariot

TRAMONTO see Toni, Alceo

TRANSEAMUS USQUE BETHLEHEM see
Schnabel, J.J.

TRAPP, WILLY
Brich An, Du Schones Morgenlicht
*Xmas
cor BOHM s.p.   (T234)

Deutsche Messgesange *Mass
[Ger] mix cor,org,2horn,2trp,opt
tuba, baritone horn BOHM sc s.p.,
cor pts s.p., ipa   (T235)

Ecce Sacerdos
[Lat] 4pt mix cor,org sc,cor pts
BOHM s.p. contains also: Tu Es
Sacerdos   (T236)

Gloria "Engel, Steigt Zur Erde
Nieder" *Xmas
men cor BOHM s.p.   (T237)

Hore Uns Herr *Mass
[Ger] cong,org (based on
spirituals) sc,cor pts BOHM s.p.
(T238)
[Ger] men cor (based on spirituals)
cor pts BOHM s.p.   (T239)
[Ger] wom cor,org/gtr (based on
spirituals) sc,cor pts BOHM s.p.
(T240)
[Ger] mix cor (based on spirituals)
cor pts BOHM s.p.   (T241)

Kommuniongesang "Kommt Und Lasst Uns
Christus Ehren"
see Propriumslieder Zur Messfeier
In Der Weihnachtszeit

Laudate Dominum *Fest,mot
[Lat] 4pt mix cor,acap BOHM s.p.
(T242)

Lobe Den Herren
3pt wom cor/3pt jr cor BOHM s.p.
(T243)

Nach Der Wandlung "Auf, Glaubige
Seelen"
see Propriumslieder Zur Messfeier
In Der Weihnachtszeit

TRAPP, WILLY (cont'd.)

O Froher Tag!
[Ger] mix cor,acap BOHM sc s.p.,
cor pts s.p.   (T244)

Pange Lingua
[Lat] 4pt mix cor,acap BOHM s.p.
contains also: Tantum Ergo (T245)

Propriumslieder Zur Messfeier In Der
Weihnachtszeit *Xmas
[Ger] mix cor,acap BOHM sc s.p.,
cor pts s.p.
contains: Kommuniongesang "Kommt
Und Lasst Uns Christus Ehren";
Nach Der Wandlung "Auf,
Glaubige Seelen"; Schlusslied
"Nun Jauchzet All"; Zum Eingang
"Dies Ist Der Tag"; Zur
Gabenbereitung "Kommet, Ihr
Hirten"; Zwischengesang "Freu
Dich, Erd Und Sternenzelt"
(T246)

Schlusslied "Nun Jauchzet All"
see Propriumslieder Zur Messfeier
In Der Weihnachtszeit

Singen Wir Mit Frohlichkeit *Xmas
cor BOHM s.p.   (T247)

Tantum Ergo
see Trapp, Willy, Pange Lingua

Tu Es Sacerdos
see Trapp, Willy, Ecce Sacerdos

Zum Eingang "Dies Ist Der Tag"
see Propriumslieder Zur Messfeier
In Der Weihnachtszeit

Zur Gabenbereitung "Kommet, Ihr
Hirten"
see Propriumslieder Zur Messfeier
In Der Weihnachtszeit

Zwischengesang "Freu Dich, Erd Und
Sternenzelt"
see Propriumslieder Zur Messfeier
In Der Weihnachtszeit

TRAUUNGESANG: UBER DEINEM HAUPTE see
Pfannschmidt

TRAUUNGSGESANG see Falcke

TRAUUNGSGESANG "HERR DU UND GOTT" see
Giordani, Tommaso

TRAUUNGSGESANG "LOBET DEN HERRN" see
Haas, Joseph

TRAVER, JAMES F.
In Him I Abide
SA (easy) FITZSIMONS 5024 $.20
(T248)
SATB (easy) FITZSIMONS 2213 $.25
(T249)

TRAVER, JAMES FERRIS
Ballad Of The Christ Child, The
*Xmas
SATB,org/pno FISCHER,J CMR 2895
$.25   (T250)

Jesus Christ Was Born This Day *Xmas
SATB,acap GRAY CMR 3070 $.25 (T251)

When Jesus Was A Tiny Babe *Xmas,
anthem
CHORISTERS R-18 $.15   (T252)

TRE ANDLIGA VISOR see Johansen, Sven-
Erik

TRE BIBELSPRAK OM GUDS ORD see Ritter,
Christian

TRE LATINSKA HYMNER
(Berg, Gottfrid) 4pt mix cor ERIKS
330 s.p.
contains: Ave Maria; Miserere; Veni
Creator Spiritus   (T253)

TRE MOTETTI see Mannino, Franco

TRE SALMI see Toni, Alceo

TREADWELL, WILLIAM
Door, The *see Peninger, David

TREASURE OF CALVARY see Newman, D.

TREASURES IN HEAVEN see Blanchard

TREASURES IN HEAVEN see Burroughs, Bob

TREBLE CHOIR, THE *CCU,anthem
(Lyall, Max) SSA/SSAA BROADMAN
4523-06 $1.25   (T254)

TREE, THE see Drobish, Douglas

TREE OF LIFE, THE see Hoddinott, Alun

TREMMEL, M.
Seid Barmherzig! *Op.32, Fest
mix cor,org sc,cor pts BOHM s.p.
(T255)

TRES CANTIONES see Novak, Jan

TRES LAUDES see Reutter, Hermann

TREXLER, GEORG (1903-   )
Es Ist Ein Ros Entsprungen *CC4U,
Xmas,mot
mix cor,acap BREITKOPF-L PB 3960
s.p.   (T256)

TRIA CARMINA PASCHALIA see Argento,
Dominick

TRIAS see Blum, Robert

TRICINIEN see Calvisius, Sethus

TRIERER DOM-MESSE see Schroeder,
Hermann

TRILOGY OF PRAISE see Wetzler

TRINITATIS MESSE see Rheinberger, Josef

TRINKLER, ULRICH
Ave Maria
[Lat] 4pt mix cor,opt S solo,org,
opt vln sc,cor pts BOHM s.p., ipa
(T257)

TRISTIS EST ANIMA MEA see Kuhnau,
Johann

TRISTIS EST ANIMA MEA see Lassus,
Roland de (Orlandus)

TRISTIS EST ANIMA MEA see Petrassi,
Goffredo

TRITT AUF DEN RIEGEL VON DER TUR see
Lassus, Roland de (Orlandus)

TRIUMPH! TRIUMPH! ES KOMMT MIT PRACHT
see Zentner, Johannes

TROIS CHANTS DE NOEL see Beauverd

TROIS MOTETS see Vuataz

TROIS NOELS FRANCAIS *CC3U,Xmas
(Delor) 4pt mix cor,acap sc HENN 795
s.p.   (T258)

TROIS PIECES LITURGIQUES see Rosenthal,
Manuel

TROIS PSAUMES DE DAVID see Milhaud,
Darius

TROIS PSAUMES, POUR LE TEMPS PRESENT
see Kox, Hans

TROJAN, VACLAV (1907-   )
Bethlehem *see Betlem

Betlem *Xmas,cant/carol
"Bethlehem" [Czech] jr cor,soli,fl,
2ob,2clar,bsn,2horn,timp,harp,
strings CZECH s.p.   (T259)

TROPHY OF HIS LOVE, A see Johnson, Paul

TROST AM GRABE "O WEINET NICHT" see
Frey, Carl

TRUAX
Hush-A-Bye Boy Child Jesus *Xmas
(Stewart) SATB KENDOR $.35   (T260)

TRUBEL, GERHARD (1917-   )
Das Hohelied Der Liebe *cant
SATB,narrator,bvl,cembalo,
vibraphone HANSSLER 10.312 rental
(T261)
Deutsche Choralmesse *Mass
SATB,acap HANSSLER 10.311 rental
(T262)
Die Seligpreisungen *cant
SATB,narrator,ST soli,bvl,cembalo
HANSSLER 10.310 rental   (T263)

TRUE FREEDOM see Burroughs, Bob

TRUHLAR, JAN (1928-   )
Jeremiah's Cry - Oh My Strict Lord
And Master *see Jeremiasuv Plac
- O, Prisny Pane Muj

Jeremiasuv Plac - O, Prisny Pane Muj
*cant
"Jeremiah's Cry - Oh My Strict Lord
And Master" [Czech] mix cor,ABar
soli,2fl,2ob,2clar,2bsn,2horn,
2trp,trom,timp,perc,strings CZECH
s.p.   (T264)

TRULY, MY SOUL see Beattie, Herbert

TRULY OUR SAVIOR SUFFERED see Victoria,
Tomas Luis de, Vere Languores

TRULY THE SON OF GOD see Willingham,
Gloria

TRULY, TRULY, I SAY TO YOU see
Hammerschmidt, Andreas, Wahrlich,
Ich Sage Euch

TRUMPET SHALL SOUND, THE see Poorman,
Jeanne R.

TRUMPETERS AND SINGERS WERE AS ONE, THE
see Matthews, Thomas

TRUMPETERS AND SINGERS WERE AS ONE, THE
see Miller

TRUMPETS ON THE TOWER see Canning,
Thomas

TRUPP
Savior, Like A Shepherd Lead Us
(composed with Brown) *anthem
unis (easy) oct BROADMAN 4558-35
$.30   (T265)

TRUST AND OBEY see Sammis

TRUST, HEINZ-EWALD (1928-   )
Singkanons *CCU,canon
cor HANSSLER 25.007 s.p.   (T266)

TRUST IN THE LORD see Brandon, George

TRUST IN THE LORD see Cram, James D.

TRUST IN THE LORD see Dittenhaver, S.L.

TRUST IN THE LORD see Glarum, L.
Stanley

TRUST IN THE LORD see Johnson

TRUST IN THE LORD see Valdivieso,
Rosanne B.

TRUST JESUS AND LIVE see Blankenship,
Mark

TRUSTING JESUS see Ortlund, Anne

TRUSTING JESUS see Page

TRUSTING JESUS see Sankey, I.

TRUTH SENT FROM ABOVE see Vaughan
Williams, Ralph

TRUTH SHALL MAKE YOU FREE, THE see
Courtney, Ragan

TRY JESUS, MAN OF GALILEE see Nicholson

TRYING TO MAKE HEAVEN MY HOME *spir
(Peninger, David) SAB HERITAGE H7002
$.35   (T267)

TSCHESNOKOFF, PAUL
see TCHESNOKOV, PAVEL GRIGORIEVITCH

TU ES PETRUS see Grau, P. Theodor

TU ES PETRUS see Lehner, Walter

TU ES PETRUS see Liszt, Franz

TU ES PETRUS see Messner, Joseph

TU ES PETRUS see Siegl, Otto

TU ES PETRUS see Waldbroel, Wilhelm

TU ES SACERDOS see Montillet

TU ES SACERDOS see Trapp, Willy

TU EXSURGENS see Lassus, Roland de
(Orlandus)

TU SOLUS, QUI FACIS MIRABILIA see Des
Prez, Josquin

TUI SUNT CAELI see Lauterbach, Lorenz

TUI SUNT COELI see Filke, Max

TUI SUNT COELI see Gauss, Otto

TUI SUNT COELI see Gruber, Joseph

TUI SUNT COELI see Haydn, (Franz)
Joseph, Du Bist's Dem Ruhm Und Ehre
Gebuhret

TUI SUNT COELI see Kromolicki, Joseph

TUI SUNT COELI see Meister, G.

TUI SUNT COELII see Lemacher, Heinrich

TUMA, FRANTISEK IGNAZ ANTONIN
(1704-1774)
Stabat Mater
[Lat] mix cor,org CZECH s.p. (T268)

TUNDER, FRANZ (1614-1667)
Hosianna Dem Sohne Davids *cant
SSATB,cont,strings HANSSLER 10.047
sc s.p., cor pts s.p., ipa (T269)

TURN BACK O MAN see Ringwald, [Roy]

TURN IT OVER TO JESUS, HE CARES see
Yantis, David

TURN OUR CAPTIVITY, O LORD see Bateson,
Thomas

TURN THEE UNTO ME see Roff, Joseph

TURN YE TO ME see Sharpe, Evelyn

TURN YE, TURN YE see Ives, Charles

TURN YOURS EYES UPON JESUS see Lemmel,
H.

TURNER
Amazing Grace *see Newton

Are You The One? *anthem
SATB oct BROADMAN 4554-97 $.30
(T270)

Come, Holy Spirit, Heavenly Dove
*see Watts

Footsteps Of Jesus *see Slade

Give A Cup Of Water *anthem
SAB oct BROADMAN 4565-58 $.40
(T271)

God Made These For Us To Love
SA oct BENSON S4118 $.30 (T272)

He Walked That Lonely Road *Easter/
Gen
SATB oct BENSON S4126 $.30 (T273)

I Will Praise The Lord
SATB oct BENSON S4373 $.35 (T274)

I've Got Peace Like A River *anthem
SATB (easy) oct BROADMAN 4540-50
$.30 (T275)

May The Road Rise To Meet You
*anthem
unis oct BROADMAN 4554-77 $.30
(T276)

Must Jesus Bear The Cross Alone
*anthem
unis oct BROADMAN 4540-78 $.30
(T277)

New Generation, The
2pt oct BENSON S4310 $.30 (T278)

Peace, Sweet Peace
1-2pt,pno,opt fl oct BENSON S4375
$.35 (T279)

Remember He Loves You
SATB oct BENSON S4376 $.35 (T280)

Son Of God, The Son Of Man, The
*anthem
SATB oct BROADMAN 4554-91 $.30
(T281)

Who Moved? *see Blanchard

TURNER, DIANE
Give A Cup Of Water *see Turner, Lee

They All Sang "Jesus" *see Turner,
Lee

TURNER, LEE
Give A Cup Of Water (composed with
Turner, Diane) *anthem
SAB BROADMAN 4565-58 $.40 (T282)

They All Sang "Jesus" (composed with
Turner, Diane) *anthem
SATB&treb cor WORD CS-2690 $.40
(T283)

Your Life Has A Plan *anthem
1-2pt WORD CS-2684 $.30 (T284)

TURNHOUT, GERARD DE (1520-1580)
Sacred And Secular Songs For Three
Voices, Vol. I *sac/sec,CCU
(Wagner, Lavern J.) 3pt bds A-R ED
$9.95 (T285)

Sacred And Secular Songs For Three
Voices, Vol. II *sac/sec,CCU
(Wagner, Lavern J.) 3pt bds A-R ED
$9.95 (T286)

TUT MIR AUF DIE SCHONE PFORTE see Poos,
Heinrich

'TWAS IN THE MOON OF WINTER-TIME see
Van Hulse, Camil

T'WAS IN THE MOON OF WINTERLAND see
Read, Jesous Ahatonhia

T'WAS IN THE MOON OF WINTERTIME *Xmas,
anthem/carol/folk,Fr
see Three Christmas Carol Anthems
SATB (Canadian) EMI s.p. (T287)

(Ehret, Walter) SAB,pno/org,opt ob,
perc (easy) GIA G1849 $.40 (T288)

'TWAS IN THE MOON OF WINTERTIME see
Younger, John B.

'TWAS ON A COLD AND WINTRY NIGHT see
Owens

TWEE KERSTLIEDEREN see Heer, Joh De

TWEE PINKSTERLIEDEREN see Brucken Fock,
van

TWELVE APOSTLES, THE see Hays, Peggy
McAllister

TWELVE BENEDICTION AMENS see Cabena,
Barrie

TWELVE CHORAL RESPONSES see Thomas, C.

TWELVE CHRISTMAS CAROLS: SET 1 *Xmas,
carol
(Rutter) SATB,inst (easy) OXFORD
48.026 $2.20, ipr
contains: Here We Come A-
Wassailing; Infant King; O Come,
O Come, Immanuel; Quittez,
Pasteurs; Shepherds' Noel; Stille
Nacht (T289)

TWELVE CHRISTMAS CAROLS: SET 2
(Rutter) SATB,inst (easy) OXFORD
48.027 $2.20, ipr
contains: Away In A Manger; Coming
Of Our King, The; Gabriel's
Message; Noel Nouvelet; Past
Three A Clock; Sans Day Carol
(T290)

TWELVE DAYS OF CHRISTMAS
see Eight Christmas Carols: Set 2

TWELVE DISCIPLES INTERESTING FACTS AND
OCCUPATIONS see Hays, Peggy
McAllister

TWELVE HYMNS
(Roff, Joseph) SATB cmplt ed
LITURGICAL $5.00
contains & see also: Accept,
Almighty Father; From All Who
Dwell Beneath The Skies; Holy,
Holy, Holy; Lord, Accept The
Gifts We Offer, Merciful Savior;
O God, Almighty Father; O Jesus,
We Adore Thee; O King Of Might
And Splendor; Praise The Lord:
You Heavens Adore Him; Praise To
The Lord; Sing With The Joy The
Savior's Glory; To Jesus Christ,
Our Sovereign King (T291)

TWELVE SONGS FROM SCHEMELLIS GESANGBUCH
see Bach, Johann Sebastian

TWELVE TRADITIONAL CAROLS FROM
HEREFORDSHIRE *CC12L,carol,Eng
(Vaughan Williams, Ralph) SATB/unis
GALAXY 1.5034.1 $1.25 (T292)

TWELVE TRIBES, THE see Hays, Peggy
McAllister

TWELVE UNISON ANTHEMS see Ritchey,
Lawrence

TWENTY-FIVE CAROLS WITH GUITAR, BOOK 1
*CC25U,Xmas,carol
(Stickley) unis,gtr (easy) OXFORD
36.008 $2.00, ipa (T293)

TWENTY-FIVE CAROLS WITH GUITAR, BOOK 2
*CC25U,Xmas,carol
(Stickley) unis,gtr (easy) OXFORD
36.009 $2.00, ipa (T294)

TWENTY-ONE SERVICE RESPONSES see Evans

TWENTY-THIRD PSALM see Hays, Peggy
McAllister

TWENTY-THIRD PSALM, THE (Psalm 23) Ger,
Contemp
(Pitts, Clay) SATB VANGUARD V576 $.35
see from Let Trumpets Sound (T295)
(Taylor, Noxie) SS&camb/SSA/SABar&
camb,pno CAMBIATA U17556 $.35
(T296)

TWENTY-THIRD PSALM, THE see Marsh

TWENTY-THIRD PSALM, THE see Rozsa,
Miklos

TWENTY-THIRD PSALM - AN INTERPRETATION
see Waterman, Frances

TWO ANGELS see Victoria, Tomas Luis de

TWO ANTHEMS see Franco, Johan

TWO ANTHEMS FOR CHILDREN see Walton, K.

TWO BACH CHORALES see Bach, Johann
Sebastian

TWO BACH CHORALES see Bach, Johann
Sebastian

TWO CANTICLES see Hewitt-Jones, Tony

TWO CAROLS *Xmas,carol
(Willan, H.) SATB,kbd (easy) oct
CONCORDIA 98-1581 $.25
contains: Oh! How Beautiful The Sky
(Dan); To A Virgin Meek And Mild
(Span) (T297)

TWO CAROLS see Leigh, Eric

TWO CAROLS *carol
(Miller, M.R.) (easy) oct GIA G1044
$.40
contains: Child Is Born In
Bethlehem, A; Golden Carol Of The
Three Magi, The (T298)

TWO CAROLS see Waite

TWO CAROLS see Dussek, Johann Ladislaus

TWO CAROLS FOR CHRISTMAS see Goodman,
Joseph

TWO CHORALES see Bach, Johann Sebastian

TWO CHRISTMAS CAROLS see Ridout,
Godfrey

TWO CHRISTMAS CAROLS see Arnatt, Ronald

TWO CHRISTMAS CAROLS see Anderson,
[William H.]

TWO CHRISTMAS CAROLS see Lyon, J.

TWO CHRISTMAS CAROLS *Xmas,carol
(Mills) 3pt wom cor oct CURWEN 11169
$.20
contains: Joseph And The Angel; Myn
Lyking (T299)

TWO CHRISTMAS CAROLS *see God Rest You
Merry (T300)

TWO CHRISTMAS CAROLS
(Willan, Healey) SSAA,acap HARRIS
$.30
contains: Jesous Ahatonhia (Huron);
Ou S'en Vont Ces Gais Bergers
Tyrle, Tyrlow, Tyrle, Tyrlow
(T301)

TWO CHRISTMAS CAROLS *Xmas,carol
(Lyon, James) SATB oct LESLIE 4013
s.p.
contains: Away In A Manger; Sing
Morning Stars (T302)

TWO CHRISTMAS CAROLS (FIRST SET) see
Garland, Hugh

TWO CHRISTMAS CAROLS (SECOND SET) see
Anderson, [William H.]

TWO CHRISTMAS CAROLS, SET I see
Bancroft, H. Hugh

TWO CHRISTMAS CAROLS, SET II see
Bancroft, H. Hugh

TWO CHRISTMAS CAROLS (THIRD SET) see
Anderson, [William H.]

TWO CHRISTMAS MOTETS see Hannahs, Roger

TWO CHRISTMAS SONGS FOR YOUNGER
CHILDREN see Curtwright, Carolee

TWO EARLY AMERICAN ANTHEMS see Kimball

TWO EASTER CAROLS *Easter,anthem/
carol,Dut
(Chambers, H.A.) mix cor oct NOVELLO
40.1188.00 s.p.
contains: This Happy Easter Day;
Thou Hallowed Chosen Morn Of
Praise (T303)

TWO EASTER CAROLS see Ward, Arthur

TWO EASTER CAROLS see Brown, Allanson
G.Y.

TWO EASTER CHORALES see Bach, Johann
Sebastian

TWO EVENING HYMNS see Bourgeois, Loys
(Louis)

TWO FANFARE ANTHEMS OF PRAISE *CCU,
anthem
(Betteridge, L.) SATB (med easy)
WATERLOO $.60 (T304)

TWO HYMNS *hymn
oct ROYAL 314 s.p.
contains: Far Shining Names From
Age To Age (St. Nicolas); Lift Up
Your Voice, Ye Christian Folk
(Ladywell) (T305)

TWO HYMNS see Einarsson, Sigfus

TWO HYMNS IN HONOR OF ST. THOMAS MORE see Andrews, C.T.

TWO HYMNS OF PRAISE *see All Creatures Of Our God And King; Now Thank We All Our God   (T306)

TWO HYMNS TO HOWL BY see Felciano, Richard

TWO HYMNS TUNES see French, Jacob

TWO INSPIRING GOSPEL SONGS see Hunter, Harry A.

TWO INTROITS see Atkinson

TWO JUNIOR CHOIR ANTHEMS see White

TWO LATIN FRAGMENTS see Homilius, Gottfried August

TWO MOTETS see Amner, John

TWO MOTETS see Zimmermann, Heinz Werner

TWO MOTETS see Stout, Alan

TWO MOTETS see Smith, Leland

TWO MOTETS see Williamson, Malcolm

TWO MOTETS FOR CHRISTMAS see Le Fleming, Christopher (Kaye)

TWO MOTETS FROM THE KANCJONAXY STANIATECKIE see Herter, J.

TWO PART STYLINGS NO. 2 *CC11UL (Nelson, Jerry) 2pt cmplt ed LILLENAS MB-357 $1.50   (T307)

TWO PRAYERS see Smith, G. Alan

TWO PSALMS see Hanson

TWO PSALMS see Pergolesi, Giovanni Battista

TWO PSALMS see Lassus, Roland de (Orlandus)

TWO PSALMS see Diener, Theodor

TWO PSALMS OF DEDICATION see Tapel, Joseph

TWO RELIGIOUS CHORUSES OF OUR TIME see Weigl, Karl

TWO RESPONSES FOR BEGINNING AND ENDING WORSHIP see White, Rex

TWO SACRED PIECES see Ravenscroft, Thomas

TWO SACRED SONGS see Brahms, Johannes

TWO SACRED SONGS see Eccard, Johannes

TWO SACRED SONGS see Bach, Johann Sebastian

TWO SETTINGS OF PALESTRINA'S MISSA PAPAE MARCELLI see Palestrina, Giovanni

TWO SHORT ANTHEMS see Billings, William

TWO SHORT ANTHEMS see Pasquet, Jean

TWO SHORT LITANIES see Pitfield, Thomas Baron

TWO SHORT MOTETS see Bowers-Broadbent, Christopher

TWO SONGS BY SUZIE see Page, Sue Ellen

TWO SONGS FOR CHRISTMAS see Anonymous

TWO SONGS FROM THE PILGRIM'S PROGRESS see Moore, J. Chris

TWO SONGS OF BETHLEHEM see Graham, Robert Virgil

TWO SONGS OF BETHLEHEM see Graham, Robert Virgil

TWO SONGS OF FAITH see Hovhaness, Alan

TWO SONGS OF FAITH see Graham

TWO SONGS OF MOURNING see Ingalls, Jeremiah

TWO SONGS OF PRAISE see Ellstrom, Eva E.

TWO SPIRITUALS FOR CHORUS *spir (Dawson, William) TTBB WARNER R-3518 $.50
    contains: Jesus Walked This

Lonesome Valley; You Got To Reap Just What You Sow   (T308)

TWO SWINGING PSALMS see Williams, David H.

TY VAR TVA ELLER TRE ARO FORSAMLADE see Schonberg, Stig Gustav

TYE, CHRISTOPHER (ca. 1497-1572)
Christ Rising Again *anthem
    (Langden) SATTBB,acap (med) OXFORD
    43.469 $.65   (T309)

Deliver Us, Good Lord *anthem
    (LeHuray) SATB,acap (med easy)
    OXFORD 43.455 $.35   (T310)

He Fed Them With Most Precious Wheat
    *Commun,anthem
    (Lee, J.) SATB (easy) GIA G1906
    $.30   (T311)

How Still And Peaceful
    see Weelkes, Thomas, Let Thy
    Merciful Ears

The Latin Church Music, Vol. I *CCU
    (Satterfield, John) cor bds A-R ED
    $9.95   (T312)

The Latin Church Music, Vol. II *CCU
    (Satterfield, John) cor bds A-R ED
    $9.95   (T313)

O Come Ye Servants Of The Lord
    (Bevan, G.) SATB (med easy)
    WATERLOO $.30   (T314)

O Lord Thy Word Endureth
    mix cor BANKS MUS YS 1018 $.20   (T315)

TYLER
Bread Of The World *anthem
    unis oct BROADMAN 4551-72 $.30
                                           (T316)

Celebrate
    SATB PARKS PC811 $.35   (T317)

How Firm A Foundation *anthem
    SAB (easy) oct BROADMAN 4540-69
    $.30   (T318)

What Wondrous Love *anthem
    SAB (easy) oct BROADMAN 4551-70
    $.30   (T319)

TZSCHOPPE, EBERHART
Halleluja. Dies Ist Der Tag, Den Der
    Herr Macht
    SSA/jr cor,vcl,drums, metallophone,
    xylophone, triangle sc HANSSLER
    12.227 s.p. contains also:
    Kretzschmar, Gunther, Machet Die
    Tore Weit (1-2pt,rec,
    glockenspiel, metallophone,
    xylophone)   (T320)

U

UBI EST ABEL? see Aichinger, Gregor

UFFORD, EDWARD S.
Throw Out The Lifeline *anthem/
    gospel
    (Mickelson, Paul) SATB oct SINGSPIR
    ZJP-8126 $.30   (U1)

ULTAN, LLOYD
Alleluia
    SATB,org,horn,2trp,2trom,4timp sc
    AM.COMP.AL. $6.60, ipa   (U2)

Peace Be Multiplied
    SATB,acap AM.COMP.AL. $2.20   (U3)

UMER UWA GOLIBE *Xmas,carol,Afr
    (Ekwueme) "Come Children, With
    Singing" SSA SCHIRM.G LG51806 $.40
                                           (U4)

UNA POESIA DI NATALE see Rossellini, Renzo

UNAM PETII A DOMINO see Lendvai, Erwin

UNBOUNDED GRACE see Wyrtzen, Don

UND DAS WORT WARD FLEISCH see Zimmermann, Heinz Werner

UND STEHE, DIE JUNGER SASSEN BEISAMMEN see Gunsenheimer, Gustav

UND UNSER LIEBEN FRAUEN *Adv/Xmas
    (Bauernfeind, Hans) wom cor,acap
    (contains also: O Heiland, Reiss
    Die Himmel Auf) oct DOBLINGER s.p.
    see also In Dulci Jubilo   (U5)

UNDER HIS WINGS see Sankey, I.

UNDER THE SUN see Hopkins, James F.

UNDERNEATH A STAR see Paulus, Stephen

UNFINISIHED MASS, THE see Janacek, Leos

UNFOLD YE PORTALS see Gounod, Charles Francois

UNISONO-MESSE see Helmschrott, Robert M.

UNIVERSITY CAROL BOOK *CCU,carol/hymn/
    liturg
    4pt (easy) EMI   (U6)

UNIVERSITY CAROL BOOKLETS
    cor EMI series of 50 eight-page
    booklets. Includes carols from 20
    countries. Simple arrangements for
    SATB, ATB, 1PT, SS, SSA, SSAA are
    available   (U7)

UNLATCH THE BOLT THAT LOCKS THE DOOR
    see Lassus, Roland de (Orlandus),
    Tritt Auf Den Riegel Von Der Tur

UNLESS ONE IS BORN ANEW see Bender, Jan

UNS IST EIN KIND GEBOREN see Liebhold

UNS IST EIN KIND GEBOREN see Pepping, Ernst

UNS IST EIN KIND GEBOREN see Vulpius, Melchior

UNS IST EIN KIND GEBOREN see Zimmermann, Heinz Werner

UNS IST EIN KINDELEIN GEBOREN IM STALL
    see Rothschuh, Franz

UNS IST EIN KINDLEIN HEUT GEBORN see Bach, Johann Sebastian

UNS IST GEBORN EIN KINDELEIN *Adv/Xmas
    (Bauernfeind, Hans) wom cor,acap oct
    DOBLINGER s.p. see also In Dulci
    Jubilo   (U8)

UNS KOMMT EIN SCHIFF GEFAHREN see Schroeder, Hermann

UNS KOMMT EIN SCHIFF GEFAHREN *Adv/
    Xmas
    (Bauernfeind, Hans) wom cor,acap
    (contains also: Maria Durch Ein
    Dornwald Ging) oct DOBLINGER s.p.
    see also In Dulci Jubilo   (U9)

UNS KOMMT EIN SCHIFF GEFAHREN see Seckinger, Konrad

UN'SANEH TOKEF see Nowakowsky, David

UNSER HEILAND IST GEBORN see Miller,
Franz R.

UNSER LEBEN WAHRET SIEBZIG JAHR see
Franck, Melchior

UNSER VATER IM HIMMEL see Rohwer, Jens

UNSERE VATER HOFFTEN AUF DICH see
Brahms, Johannes

UNSERS HERZENS FREUDE see Bach, J.C.

UNSRE TRUBSAL, DIE ZEITLICH UND LEICHT
IST see Werner

UNTO THE HILLS see Purday, Charles
Henry

UNTO THE LORD IN HEAV'N see Haydn,
(Franz) Joseph, Gloria

UNTO THEE WE GIVE OUR THANKS see
Sweelinck, Jan Pieterszoon

UNTO THEE WILL I CRY see Barnes

UNTO US A BOY IS BORN see Arch, Gwyn

UNTO US A CHILD IS BORN see Handel,
George Frideric

UNTO US A CHILD IS BORN see Hyllberg,
Ruth

UNUBERWINDLICH STARKER HELD
SATB DOBLINGER S 209-210 s.p.
contains also: Cruger, Johann, Nun
Danket All   (U10)

UNVOLLENDETE MESSE ES-DUR (KYRIE,
CREDO, AGNUS DEI) see Janacek, Leos

UP AND GET US GONE see Red

UP WITH A SHOUT see Bass, Claude L.

UPHAUS
If You Love Me *hymn
SATB oct LILLENAS AN-2421 $.30
                                    (U11)

UPON EASTER DAY see Roff, Joseph

UPON MY LAP MY SOVEREIGN SITS see
Simkins, C.F.

UPON THE HIGH MIDNIGHT see Mc Cabe,
John

UPPER ROOM, THE see Wilson

UPPSTANDEN AR VAR HERRE CHRIST see
Bjarnegard, Gustaf

UPPSTANDEN AR VAR HERRE KRIST see
Vulpius, Melchior

UR SAKARIAS LOVSANG see Ritter,
Christian

URBS BEATA see Joubert, John

USHER IN THE SEASON see Track

USSACHEVSKY, VLADIMIR (1911-   )
Missa Brevis
cor,inst AM.COMP.AL.   (U12)

UT FLOS, UT ROSA see Crivelli, Giovanni
Battista

UT OMNES UNUM SINT see Hunecke, Wilhelm

UTI DIN NAD, O FADER BLID
(Angerdahl, Lars) 4pt mix cor ERIKS
99 s.p.   (U13)

UTRECHT JUBILATE, THE see Handel,
George Frideric

UTRECHT TE DEUM see Handel, George
Frideric

UTRENJA see Penderecki, Krzysztof

UTRPENI A VZKRISENI see Burghauser,
Jarmil

UVNUCHO YOMAR see Meyerbeer, Giacomo

V

V GETSEMANE see Suchy, Frantisek

VAD I BEDJEN FADERN OM see Olson,
Daniel

V'AHAVTA see Berman, Judith M.

VAIL, SILAS J.
Close To Thee *Gen,anthem/gospel
(Mickelson, Paul) SATB oct SINGSPIR
ZJP-8125 $.30   (V1)
(Wilson, Roger C.) SA/SATB (easy)
oct LORENZ A561 $.30   (V2)

VALDIVIESO, ROSANNE B.
Trust In The Lord
SSA PIONEER 1021 $.40   (V3)

VALE, CHARLES
Christ's Carol *carol
SATB,acap ROBERTON 63026 s.p. (V4)

VALLEY OF ARUN see Le Fleming,
Christopher (Kaye)

V'ANACHNU see Wyner, Yehudi

VANCE, MARGARET SHELLEY
Happiness Is Inside Of You
SA/TB&opt unis BELWIN OCT 2333 $.30
                                (V5)

Holly And The Ivy, The *Xmas
SA/TB&opt unis BELWIN OCT 2335 $.30
                                (V6)

Love The Lord
SATB BELWIN OCT 2337 $.30   (V7)

VANDALL
Jesus Is Mighty *gospel
(Schubert) SATB oct LILLENAS
AN-1653 $.30   (V8)

My Sins Are Gone *anthem/gospel
(DeCou, Harold) SAB oct SINGSPIR
ZJP-8055 $.30   (V9)

VAN DER HOECK
Love Divine, All Loves Excelling
unis (easy) OXFORD 02.009 $.20
                                (V10)

My God, And Is Thy Table Spread
SATB (med easy) OXFORD 02.014 $.25
                                (V11)

VAN DER PUY, D.
I'll Trust And Never Be Afraid
*anthem/gospel
(Ferrin, P.) SATB oct SINGSPIR
ZJP-8187 $.25   (V12)

VANDERSLICE, ELLEN
If My People *anthem
SATB oct SINGSPIR ZJP 7289 $.25
                                (V13)

VANDRE, CARL W.
Come Let Us Adore Him
SATB BOURNE B223933-358 $.60   (V14)

VAN DYKE
Immortal Babe
SATB SHAWNEE A5661 $.35   (V15)

VANHAL, FR. KRITITEL (1793-1813)
Stabat Mater In F-Moll
[Lat] mix cor,org,2horn,strings (F
min) CZECH s.p.   (V16)

VAN HORN
God's Word Shall Stand *anthem
(DeCou, Harold) SATB oct SINGSPIR
ZJP-7329 $.30   (V17)

VAN HULSE, CAMIL
All The Way From Nazareth *Adv/Xmas
SATB ART MAST 199 $.40   (V18)

Be Glad And Rejoice (from Beatitudes,
The) Bibl
[Lat/Eng] SATB (diff) FITZSIMONS
2187 $.35   (V19)

Beatitudes, The *Gen/Lent,cant
mix cor,SATBar soli,orch (med easy)
FITZSIMONS voc sc $.90, sc rental
                                (V20)

Behold, Bless Ye The Lord
SATB (med) FITZSIMONS 2113 $.20
                                (V21)

Behold, The Lord's Hand *Bibl
SATB,acap (med) FITZSIMONS 2121
$.20   (V22)

Choral Responses *CC5U
SATB,acap (easy) FITZSIMONS 2107
$.25   (V23)

Christ, Our Lord, Is Risen! *Easter
SATB,Mez/Bar solo (med) FITZSIMONS
2100 $.25   (V24)

VAN HULSE, CAMIL (cont'd.)
Christmas Oratorio, The
jr cor&mix cor,narrator,MezTBar
soli FITZSIMONS voc sc $1.25, sc
rental   (V25)

Come, Ye People *Thanks
SATB (med) FITZSIMONS 2180 $.35
                                (V26)

Easter Carol
SATB (easy) FITZSIMONS 2101 $.25
                                (V27)

Far It Was To Bethlehem *Xmas
SATB ART MAST 164 $.50   (V28)

Hear My Prayer, O Lord
SATB,acap (med) FITZSIMONS 2122
$.25   (V29)

Missa Brevis In D Minor *Commun
SATB (med) FITZSIMONS 7006 $.35
                                (V30)

Noel Nouvelet *Xmas
SAATB,SATBarB soli (med)
FITZSIMONS 2106 $.20   (V31)

O God, My Heart Is Fixed
SAATTBB,acap (med) FITZSIMONS 2123
$.20   (V32)

On This Day, O Beautiful Mother
*Gen/Marriage
SA (med) FITZSIMONS 5016 $.20 (V33)

Our Glorious King *Asc/Easter/Lent/
Thanks,ora
mix cor,TBarB soli FITZSIMONS $1.00
                                (V34)

Rejoice, Salvation Now Is Near *Adv/
Xmas
SATB ART MAST 167 $.40   (V35)

Save Me, O God
SATB,Bar solo (diff) FITZSIMONS
2149 $.25   (V36)

'Twas In The Moon Of Winter-Time
*Xmas,cant
jr cor&sr cor FITZSIMONS $.75 (V37)

Ye Sons And Daughters *Easter
[Lat/Eng] SATB,TB soli (med)
FITZSIMONS 2080 $.25   (V38)

VAN IDERSTINE, A.P.
Early In The Morning *Easter/Pent
SATB,acap ART MAST 240 $.40   (V39)

Easter Fanfare *Easter
SATB ART MAST 147 $.35   (V40)

O Clap Your Hands
SATB,acap ART MAST 114 $.50   (V41)

Who Walks With God? *anthem
SATB (easy) oct BROADMAN 4561-09
$.30   (V42)

VANN
Behold How Good And Joyful A Thing
*anthem
SATB (med) OXFORD 43.473 $.35 (V43)

VANNIUS
Domine Quid Multipicavit
4pt,acap voc pt HENN 621 s.p. (V44)

Laetatus Sum
4pt,acap voc pt HENN 612 s.p. (V45)

VANOCNI see Fiser, Lubos

VANOCNI KOLEDOVA MSE see Jirim,
Frantisek

VANOCNI KOLEDY see Nejedly, Vit

VANTINE
Easter Song
SATB oct SCHMITT 1933 $.40   (V46)

VAN WORMER, G.
Alleluia, Christ Is Risen
SATB KJOS 5905 $.40   (V47)

I Shall Give Thanks Unto God
SATB KJOS 5906 $.35   (V48)

Praise To Lord God
SATB KJOS 5902 $.40   (V49)

Yuletide Fanfare
SATB KJOS 5914 $.35   (V50)

VAR STILLA MIN SJAL see Johansen, Sven-
Erik

VAREN ICKE FORSKRACKTA see Holm, Gunnar

VARLDENS FRALSARE KOM HAR see Berg,
Gottfrid

VART RIKE SOM HAR KOMMIT I STRID see
Schonberg, Stig Gustav

VAS PRETIOSUM see Villa-Lobos, Heitor

VATER UNSER *prayer,Contemp
"Lord's Prayer, The" 2-4pt mix cor,
soli,strings/rec/org (assembled
from works of Scheidt; Bach, J. S.;
Pachelbel; and others) PELIKAN
PE732   (V51)
(Pitts, Clay) "Lord's Prayer, The"
SATB VANGUARD V 577 $.35 see from
Let Trumpets Sound   (V52)

VATER UNSER see Schwarz-Schilling,
Reinhard

VATER UNSER AM 30 JULI 1968 see
Hufschmidt, Wolfgang

VATER UNSER, DER DU BIST IM HIMMEL see
Le Maistre, Mattheus

VATER UNSER, DER DU BIST IM HIMMEL see
Schutz, Heinrich

VATER UNSER, DER DU BIST IM HIMMEL see
Staden, Johann

VATER UNSER IM HIMMELREICH see Franck

VATER UNSER IM HIMMELREICH see
Gumpelzhaimer, Adam

VATER UNSER IM HIMMELREICH see Metzger,
Hans-Arnold

VATER UNSER IM HIMMELREICH see Michel,
Josep

VATER UNSER IM HIMMELREICH see Pepping,
Ernst

VATER UNSER IM HIMMELREICH see Vento,
Ivo de

VATERUNSER see Kameke, Ernst-Ulrich von

VAUGHAN WILLIAMS, RALPH (1872-1958)
At The Name Of Jesus *Adv,anthem
(Johnson, Norman) SATB oct SINGSPIR
ZJP-7317 $.30   (V53)

Fantasia On The Old One Hundred
Fourth Psalm Tune
SATB,inst (med diff) study sc
OXFORD 46.182 $9.75, cmplt ed
OXFORD rental   (V54)

Old Hundredth Psalm Tune, The
(Stone) SATB,orch sc OXFORD 42.950
$5.00, ipa   (V55)
(Washburn) SATB,band cmplt ed
OXFORD 97.837-70 $18.00   (V56)

On Christmas Night *Xmas
unis/SATB STAINER 3.0663.1 $.40
                                    (V57)
unis/SSAA STAINER 3.0839.1 $.40
                                    (V58)

Ring Out Ye Crystal Spheres (from
This Day)
SATB (med) OXFORD 42.349 $.35   (V59)

Saviours Love
unis STAINER 3.0837.1 $.30   (V60)

Three Choral Hymns *CC3U,hymn
SATB,Bar/T solo,orch voc sc CURWEN
$1.25   (V61)

Three Choral Hymns *CC3U,Xmas/
Easter/Whitsun
mix cor,T/Bar solo,2fl,2ob,2clar,
2bsn,4horn,2trp,3trom,tuba,
strings,timp,harp,cymbals voc sc
CURWEN C03685 s.p., sc CURWEN
rental   (V62)

Truth Sent From Above
unis STAINER 3.0655.1 $.40   (V63)

Wassail Song *Xmas
unis STAINER 3.0654.1 $.40   (V64)
TTBarB STAINER 3.0657.1 $.60   (V65)

V'CHACH HOYOH OMEIR see Nowakowsky,
David

VECCHI, ORAZIO (1550-1605)
Vieni O Morte
SATB&SATB LAUDINELLA LR 85 s.p.
                                    (V66)

VECNA BAJ see Zrno, Felix

VEERTIG DAGEN, VEERTIG NACHTEN see De
Koning

VEGLIA FUNEBRE see Toni, Alceo

VENDLER, BOHUMIL (1865-1948)
Psalm 126 *see Zalm 126

Zalm 126 (Psalm 126) Op.44, Bibl
[Czech] mix cor,2fl,2ob,2clar,2bsn,
4horn,2trp,3trom,tuba,timp,
strings CZECH s.p.   (V67)

VENI CREATOR see Fatscher, Richard

VENI CREATOR see Frey, Carl

VENI CREATOR see Heftrich, Wilhelm

VENI CREATOR see Hofmayer, Karl

VENI CREATOR see Ketterer, Ernst

VENI CREATOR see Muller, A.M.

VENI CREATOR see Strauss-Konig, Richard

VENI CREATOR see Wassmer, Berthold

VENI CREATOR see Zubrod, Friedrich

VENI CREATOR SPIRITUS
see Tre Latinska Hymner

VENI CREATOR SPIRITUS see Engelhart,
F.X.

VENI CREATOR SPIRITUS see Faist, Anton

VENI CREATOR SPIRITUS see Griesbacher,
Peter

VENI CREATOR SPIRITUS see Hug, Emil

VENI CREATOR SPIRITUS see Jochum, Otto

VENI CREATOR SPIRITUS see Steinert,
Bernhard

VENI CREATOR SPIRITUS see Welcker, Max

VENI ELECTA MEA see Alder

VENI SANCTE SPIRITUS see Aiblinger,
Johann Kaspar

VENI, SANCTE SPIRITUS see Gruber,
Joseph

VENI SANCTE SPIRITUS see Mozart,
Wolfgang Amadeus

VENI, SANCTE SPIRITUS see Werner

VENI, SANCTIFICATOR see Doebler, Curt

VENI SANCTIFICATOR see Krenek, Ernst

VENITE see Brandon, George

VENITE EXSULTEMUS DOMINO see Page,
Robert E.

VENITE EXSULTEMUS DOMINO see Sweelinck,
Jan Pieterszoon

VENITE, EXULTEMUS see Gibbons, Orlando

VENITE EXULTEMUS, THE see Leitz, Darwin

VENITE, FILII see Spranger, Jorg

VENTO, IVO DE (ca. 1540-1575)
Geistliche Liedsatze
SAT/SAB HANSSLER 4.018 s.p.
contains: Gott Ist Mein Trost;
Ich Ruf Zu Dir; Mein
Zuversicht; Ob Ich Schon Arm
Und Elend Bin; Obgleich Die
Welt; Vater Unser Im
Himmelreich   (V68)

Gott Ist Mein Trost
see Geistliche Liedsatze

Ich Ruf Zu Dir
see Geistliche Liedsatze

Mein Zuversicht
see Geistliche Liedsatze

Ob Ich Schon Arm Und Elend Bin
see Geistliche Liedsatze

Obgleich Die Welt
see Geistliche Liedsatze

Vater Unser Im Himmelreich
see Geistliche Liedsatze

VERAX IPSE DEUS see Lassus, Roland de
(Orlandus)

VERBUM CARO FACTUS EST see Hassler,
Hans Leo

VERBUM SUPERNAM see Govert, Willibald

VERBUM SUPERNUM see Benkert, Lorenz

VERBUM SUPERNUM see Dantonello, Josef

VERBUM SUPERNUM see Erhard, Karl

VERBUM SUPERNUM see Kromolicki, Joseph

VERBUM SUPERNUM see Kutzer, Ernst

VERBUM SUPERNUM see Lemacher, Heinrich

VERBUM SUPERNUM see Lipp, Alban

VERBUM SUPERNUM see Messner, Joseph

VERBUM SUPERNUM see Schroeder, Hermann

VERBUM SUPERNUM see Welcker, Max

VERDI, GIUSEPPE (1813-1901)
Laudi Alla Vergine Maria *BVM
[It] SSAA EGTVED MS13A8 s.p.   (V69)

Lord's Prayer, The *see Pater Noster

Messa Da Requiem *Req
SATB,SATB soli,3fl,2ob,2clar,4bsn,
4horn,4trp,3trom,tuba,strings,
perc,timp (diff) min sc SCHOTTS
ETP 975 s.p.   (V70)

Pater Noster *prayer
"Lord's Prayer, The" [It] SSATB
EGTVED MS14B8 s.p.   (V71)

Quattro Pezzi Sacri *CC4U
[Lat] SATB,acap min sc EULENBURG
1000 s.p.   (V72)

Requiem
cor,soli,orch HENN s.p.   (V73)

Sanctus (from Requiem)
[Lat/Eng] SATB (diff) FITZSIMONS
2031 $.40   (V74)

VERDI, RALPH C.
Let Us Go To God's House (Psalm 121)
anthem
cong,cantor,org (easy) GIA G1793
$.25   (V75)

Psalm 121 *see Let Us Go To God's
House

Send Forth Your Light
SATB,acap FOSTER MF158 $.35   (V76)

VERE LANGUORES see Lotti, Antonio

VERE LANGUORES see Victoria, Tomas Luis
de

VERETTI, ANTONIO (1900-   )
Due Motetti *CC2U,mot
mix cor RICORDI-ENG 131283 s.p.
                                    (V77)

Priere Pour Demander Une Etoile
*prayer
cor,acap RICORDI-ENG 131224 s.p.
                                    (V78)

Sette Canti Penitenziali *CC7U
mix cor RICORDI-ENG 131334 s.p.
                                    (V79)

VERGISS MEIN NICHT see Kaminski,
Heinrich

VERGISS MEIN NICHT, MEIN ALLERLIEBSTER
GOTT see Kaminski, Heinrich

VERHERRLICH GOTT IN EUREM LEIBE see
Grunauer, I.

VERILY, VERILY see Mc Granahan

VERILY, VERILY I SAY UNTO YOU see
Kvandal, Johan, Sandelig, Sandelig
Sier Jeg Dig

VERKOUTEREN, ADRIAN
Three Kings Are Here *Epiph
unis,pno GRAY CMR 3315 $.30   (V80)

VERLEIH UND FRIEDEN see Crappius,
Andreas

VERLEIH UNS FRIEDEN GENADIGLICH see
Schutz, Heinrich

VERLEIH UNS FRIEDEN GNADIGLICH see
Eccard, Johannes

VERLEIH UNS FRIEDEN GNADIGLICH see
Hammerschmidt, Andreas

VERLIEH UNS FRIEDEN GNADIGLICH see
Antoniou, Theodor

VERRALL, PAMELA
Christmas Journey, The
SA EMI   (V81)

Johnny Appleseed *cant
cor,narrator, dancers and mimers
EMI   (V82)

King Of Love Is On His Way, The
*Xmas
SSA EMI   (V83)

Little King's Carol, The *Xmas
SS EMI   (V84)

VERRALL, PAMELA (cont'd.)

Peace On Earth
SSA EMI s.p.   (V85)

Rose Of Bethlehem *Xmas
SSA EMI   (V86)

Sing A Lullaby For Jesus
SA EMI   (V87)

Son Of Assisi
cor EMI   (V88)

Song Of The Bells *Xmas
unis EMI   (V89)

Stable Bare, A *Xmas
SS EMI   (V90)

Star Carol, The
SSA EMI   (V91)

Star For Maria, A *Xmas
2pt EMI   (V92)

VERSES FROM PSALM 118 see Gottlieb,
Jack

VERSICLES, RESPONSES AND LORD'S PRAYER
see Bevan, Gwilym

VERTRAUEN see Lemacher, Heinrich

VERY FIRST CHRISTMAS, THE
see Sunshine And Snowflakes

VERY FRIEND I NEED, THE see Parks

VERY LAST DAY see Stookey

VERY SAVIOR, HAIL THEE! see Mozart,
Wolfgang Amadeus, Ave Verum [1]

VERY SPECIAL see Allen

VESPER HYMN see Bortniansky, Dimitri
Stepanovitch

VESPER HYMN see Gevaert, Francois
Auguste, Hymne De L'Office Du Soir

VESPER HYMN see Hamilton, H.C.

VESPERAE DE DOMINICA see Mozart,
Wolfgang Amadeus, Vesperae Solennes
De Dominica

VESPERAE SOLENNES DE DOMINICA see
Mozart, Wolfgang Amadeus

VESPERS see Monteverdi, Claudio

VESPERS see Zimmermann, Heinz Werner

VETTER, P. PIRMIN
Missa In Honorem Sanctae Crucis
*Mass
[Lat] 4-8pt mix cor,org (without
Credo) sc,cor pts BOHM s.p. (V93)

VEXILLA REGIS see Bruckner, Anton

VEXILLA REGIS see Herrmann, Hugo

VEXILLA REGIS see Ireland, John

VEXILLA REGIS see Kromolicki, Joseph

VEXILLA REGIS see Lassus, Roland de
(Orlandus)

VEXILLA REGIS see Welcker, Max

VEXILLA REGIS PRODUENT see Wuensch

VI MISTE TRON PA TINGEN see Soderholm,
Valdemar

VIA CRUCIS see Liszt, Franz

VIA CRUCIS (DER KREUZWEG) see Liszt,
Franz

VIA SACRA see Monnikendam, Marius

VIADANA, LODOVICO GROSSI DA (1564-1645)
Adoramus Te
see HYMNEN UND MOTETTEN ALTER
MEISTER HEFT 2

VICK
Awake My Soul *anthem
unis,opt org&brass FINE ARTS
CM 1071 $.35   (V94)

Break Thou The Bread Of Life *see
Lathbury

Come, Says Jesus' Sacred Voice *see
Barbauld

Forgiveness *see Whittier

VICK (cont'd.)

God So Loved The World *Xmas,anthem
SATB (easy) oct BROADMAN 4551-02
$.30   (V95)

God's Gift *Xmas
SA BENSON S4119 $.25   (V96)

Great And Mighty Wonder, A *anthem
SATB oct BROADMAN 4551-74 $.30
(V97)

I Sing The Mighty Power Of God
*anthem
2pt oct BROADMAN 4558-59 $.28 (V98)

O Bless The Lord, My Soul! *see
Montgomery

O God Of Love, O King Of Peace
*anthem
SATB FINE ARTS CM 1118 $.35 (V99)

Psalm 121
SATB WALTON 2980 $.40   (V100)

Rejoice, The Lord Is King *anthem
SATB FINE ARTS CM 1104 $.30 (V101)

Sky Can Still Remember, The *see
Brooks

Wonderful News Of A Savior *Xmas,
anthem
1-2pt (easy) oct BROADMAN 4550-07
$.30   (V102)

VICK, BERYL, JR.
Mark Well, My Heart *Xmas
SABar&camb,pno CAMBIATA C117209
$.35   (V103)

VICTIMAE PASCHALI LAUDES see Calvi,
Lorenzo

VICTIMAE PASCHALI LAUDES see Victoria,
Tomas Luis de

VICTORIA, TOMAS LUIS DE (ca. 1549-1611)
Agnus Dei
(Ehret) "Lamb Of God" [Eng/It]
SSATBB SCHIRM.G 12039 $.45 (V104)

Ave Maria
4pt,acap voc pt HENN 321 s.p.
(V105)

Ave Regina
dbl cor/8pt mix cor LIENAU
MUSICA SACRA, NR. 57 sc s.p., cor
pts s.p.   (V106)

Beatus Vir
see Three Motets
see Three Motets

Darkness Was O'er The Earth *see
Tenebrae Factae Sunt

Domine, Non Sum Dignus
see HYMNEN UND MOTETTEN ALTER
MEISTER HEFT 3
(Herter, Joseph A.) [Eng/Lat] SATB
GIA G1957 $.30   (V107)

Ecce Nunc Benedicite Dominum
see Three Motets
see Three Motets

Eighteen Lenten Motets (Tenebrae
Responsoria) *CC18U
SATB WHITE,ERN $1.25   (V108)

In Veniste Enim Gratiam
(Klein) "You Have Been Acclaimed
The Chosen One" SATB SCHIRM.G
11966 $.30   (V109)

Is It Nothing To You? *see O Vos
Omnes?

Jesu Dulcis Memoria
4pt,acap voc pt HENN 334 s.p.
(V110)
Jesus Dulcis Memoria *Commun,mot
[Lat] 4pt mix cor,acap sc,cor pts
BOHM s.p.   (V111)

Judas, Mercator Pessimus
(Plott) TTBB BRODT DC 3 $.30 (V112)

Lamb Of God *see Agnus Dei

O Crux Ave
(Young, Percy) "O Hail! Sacred
Cross" [Eng/Lat] SATB,acap BROUDE
BR. $.40 see from MUSIC OF THE
GREAT CHURCHES VOL. VII: ST.
PETER'S BASILICA, ROME   (V113)

O Domine Jesu Christe
see Three Motets
see Three Motets

O Hail! Sacred Cross *see O Crux Ave

VICTORIA, TOMAS LUIS DE (cont'd.)

O Joyous Assembled Ones *see O
Sacrum Convivium

O Regem Coeli *Xmas,mot
(Fellerer, K.G.) men cor sc SCHOTTS
C 34 488 s.p.   (V114)

O Sacrum Convivium *mot
(Gronquist, Robert) "O Joyous
Assembled Ones" [Eng/Lat] SSAA,
acap BOONIN B 157 $.50   (V115)

O Vos Omnes?
(Klein, Maynard) "Is It Nothing To
You?" [Eng/Lat] SATB GIA G1525
$.40   (V116)

Passion According To St. John, The
*Psntd
(Lovelace, Austin C.) SATB,narrator
CONCORDIA 97-5271 $1.00   (V117)

Popule Meus *Gd.Fri./Lent
[Lat] 4pt mix cor,acap sc,cor pts
BOHM s.p.   (V118)
"Sage Mein Volk" 4pt mix cor LIENAU
MUSICA SACRA, NR. 38 sc s.p., cor
pts s.p.   (V119)

Praise To The Victim Of Easter *see
Victimae Paschali Laudes

Quem Vidistis Pastores? *Xmas
(Klein) "Whom Did You See, Kind
Shepherds?" SSATBB SCHIRM.G 11974
$.30   (V120)

Sage Mein Volk *see Popule Meus

Tantum Ergo
SATB,acap EGTVED KB69 s.p. (V121)
4pt,acap voc pt HENN 320 s.p.
(V122)

Tenebrae Factae Sunt
(Klein) "Darkness Was O'er The
Earth" SSAA SCHIRM.G 11965 $.30
(V123)
Thomas Ludovici Victoria Abulensis
Opera Omnia (Complete Works)
*sac/sec,CCU
(Pedrell, Felipe) [Lat] microfiche
UNION ESP. $30.00 8 volumes
(V124)

Three Motets *mot
(Jorkov, J.) [Lat] KERBY 5 $2.00
contains: Beatus Vir (SATB); Ecce
Nunc Benedicite Dominum (SATB);
O Domine Jesu Christe (SAATTB)
(V125)

Three Motets *mot
[Lat] cmplt ed EGTVED OCV s.p.
contains: Beatus Vir (SATB&SATB,
acap); Ecce Nunc Benedicite
Dominum (SATB&SATB,acap); O
Domine Jesu Christe (SAATTB)
(V126)

To The Paschal Victim *Easter/Lent
SSAATTBB WHITE,ERN $.50   (V127)

Truly Our Savior Suffered *see Vere
Languores

Two Angels
(Wienandt) SSAA SCHIRM.G LG51785
$.45   (V128)

Vere Languores
(Klein) "Truly Our Savior Suffered"
SATB SCHIRM.G 12004 $.35   (V129)

Victimae Paschali Laudes *Easter
(Schmeltekopf, Gary) "Praise To The
Victim Of Easter" [Eng/Lat] SATB,
org,2trp&2trom/4trom (med) GIA
G1820 $.45, ipa   (V130)

Vier Tantum Ergo (composed with
Palestrina, Giovanni) *CC4U
[Lat] 4pt mix cor,acap sc,cor pts
BOHM s.p.   (V131)

Whom Did You See, Kind Shepherds?
*see Quem Vidistis Pastores?

You Have Been Acclaimed The Chosen
One *see In Veniste Enim Gratiam

VICTORY AHEAD! see Grum

VICTORY IN JESUS *CC12L,gospel
SATB TRIUNE TUO 108 $2.95
see also: Power In The Blood (V132)

VIDAL, D. DE
Rejoice, The Lord Is King!
SAB,pno GENTRY G-281 $.30   (V133)

VIDERUNT OMNES see Lemacher, Heinrich

VIDITQUE QUOD ESSET BONUM see Pezzati,
Romano

VIEL SUSSER CHRIST see Zipp, Friedrich

VIENI O MORTE see Vecchi, Orazio

VIER CHORALMOTETTEN see Herzogenberg,
Heinrich von

VIER EUCHARISTISCHE GESANGE see
Schmider, Karl

VIER GEISTLICHE CHORE see Lendvai,
Erwin

VIER GEISTLICHE LIEDER DURCH DIE
TAGESZEITEN see Hessenberg, Kurt

VIER GESANGE UND "PANGE LINGUA" ZUR
FRONLEICHNAMSPROZESSION see Lipp,
Alban

VIER HYMNEN FUR DIE
FRONLEICHNAMSPROZESSION see
Welcker, Max

VIER KLEINE MOTETTEN see Fussan, Werner

VIER KLEINE WEIHNACHTSLIEDER see Weber,
Bernhard

VIER LATEINISCHE HYMNEN see Herrmann,
Hugo

VIER MARIANISCHE ANTIPHONEN see Faist,
Anton

VIER NEGRO-SPIRITUALS *spir
(Fackler, Edgar) [Eng] mix cor,acap/
pno BOHM sc s.p., cor pts s.p.
contains: Every Time I Feel The
Spirit; He's Got The Whole World;
Kum Ba Yah!; Somebody's Knocking
(V134)

VIER PANGE LINGUA see Mayer, Alfonso

VIER PANGE LINGUA see Sorger, Franz

VIER PANGE LINGUA see Gruber, Joseph

VIER PANGE LINGUA see Welcker, Max

VIER PASSIONSMOTETTEN see Berghorn,
Alfred

VIER TANTUM ERGO see Welcker, Max

VIER TANTUM ERGO see Victoria, Tomas
Luis de

VIER VENI CREATOR see Lemacher,
Heinrich

VIER WEIHNACHTSLIEDER see Lang, Hans

VIER WEIHNACHTSLIEDLEIN see Schroeter

VIERDANCK, JOHANN (ca. 1610-1646)
Lobe Den Herren *concerto
3S/3T,cont (easy) BAREN. BA453
(V135)

Mein Herz Ist Bereit *concerto
SAB,strings,cont sc,cor pts EGTVED
MS16B1 s.p., ipa   (V136)

VIERGE SAINTE see Missa, [Edmond Jean
Louis]

VIERZEHN PANGE LINGUA see Grau, P.
Theodor

VIERZEHN PANGE LINGUA see Grau, P.
Theodor

VIGILATE see Byrd, William

VIJF KORALEN EN SLOTKOOR UIT DE
MATTHAUS PASSION see Bach, Johann
Sebastian

VIL DU MOT MALET RENNA see Karlsen,
Kjell Mork

VIL DU MOT MALET RENNA see Schein,
Johann Hermann

VILLA-LOBOS, HEITOR (1887-1959)
Beatus Homo Invenit
see Bendita Sabedoria

Bendita Sabedoria *Bibl
SAATBB,acap (med/med diff) sc
SCHOTTS ME 6996 s.p.
contains: Beatus Homo Invenit;
Dexteram Tuam; Principium
Sapientiae; Sapientia Foris
Predicat; Vas Pretiosum; Vir
Sapiens   (V137)

Dexteram Tuam
see Bendita Sabedoria

Principium Sapientiae
see Bendita Sabedoria

Sapientia Foris Predicat
see Bendita Sabedoria

VILLA-LOBOS, HEITOR (cont'd.)

Vas Pretiosum
see Bendita Sabedoria

Vir Sapiens
see Bendita Sabedoria

VINE MOST SURELY I AM, THE see Schutz,
Heinrich

VIR SAPIENS see Villa-Lobos, Heitor

VIRGA JESSE see Bruckner, Anton

VIRGA JESSE FLORUIT see Bruckner, Anton

VIRGIN AND THE CHILD, THE see Brumby,
Colin

VIRGIN MARY HAD A BABY BOY *Xmas
(Trant) SATB (med) OXFORD 84.239 $.45
(V138)

VIRGIN MOST PURE, A see Widdicombe,
Trevor

VIRGINE MATRE SATUS see Lassus, Roland
de (Orlandus)

VIRGINIS AETERNUM see Lassus, Roland de
(Orlandus)

VIRGIN'S CRADLE SONG
see At The Manger

VIRGIN'S CRADLE SONG see Hill, Harry

VIRGO MARIA BEATA ES see Diabelli,
Anton

VIRGO MATER see Lemacher, Heinrich

VIRTUTE MAGNA see Gabrieli, Giovanni

VISION *CC10L
cor WORD 37642 $1.00   (V139)

VISION, THE see Munger, Oren

VISION OF ST. AUGUSTINE, THE see
Tippett, Michael

VISIONS OF CHRISTMAS see Kunz, Jack

VITALE, GARY
Lord Of Life *see Mitchell, David L.

VITTADINI
Le Piu Belle Melodie Religiose
*CC23U
cor,pno RICORDI-ENG 127150 s.p.
(V140)

VITTORIA, LUDOVICO
see VICTORIA, TOMAS LUIS DE

VIVALDI, ANTONIO (1678-1741)
Beatus Vir (Psalm 112)
(Picchieri) SATB SCHIRM.G LG51741
$.75   (V141)

Come, Thou Spirit Everlasting *Gen,
anthem
SATB oct SACRED S-153 $.35   (V142)

Credo *Credo
SATB,cont,strings CARUS CV 40.004
sc s.p., cor pts s.p., ipa (V143)

Domine, Ad Adiuvandum Me Festina
SATB&SATB,S solo,2cont,orch CARUS
CV 40.003 sc s.p., cor pts s.p.,
ipa   (V144)

Esurientes Implevit
(Harris) "He Hath Filled The
Hungry" SA SCHIRM.G LG51708 $.30
(V145)

Gloria (from Gloria Mass) Gloria
SATB,SSA soli,cont,ob,trp,strings
sc,cor pts CARUS CV 40.001 s.p.,
ipa   (V146)
[Lat/Eng] 4pt mix cor,soli,pno/orch
voc sc RICORDI-ENG 131415 s.p.
(V147)

(Collins) SSBar&camb CAMBIATA
M117207 $.40   (V148)
(Herrmann) SATB SCHIRM.G 2922 $2.00
(V149)

Gloria In Excelsis (from Gloria)
SATB,synthesizer MCAFEE M1074 $.45,
ipa   (V150)
(Martens) SAB WALTON 4005 $.35
(V151)

He Hath Filled The Hungry *see
Esurientes Implevit

In Memoria
(Dawson, E.) [Lat] STB/ATB,org oct
NATIONAL WHC-36 $.35   (V152)

Introduzione Al Gloria (from Gloria)
SATB,SAT soli,pno/orch JOBERT voc
sc s.p., cor pts s.p.   (V153)

VIVALDI, ANTONIO (cont'd.)

Kyrie
(Braun, Jurgen) 4pt mix cor&4pt mix
cor,SSAA soli,org/cembalo,2vln,
vla,vcl,bvl (med) min sc SCHOTTS
ETP 1090 s.p., ipa   (V154)

Lauda Jerusalem (Psalm 147)
(Braun, Jurgen) [Lat] SATB&SATB,SS
soli,org/cembalo,2vln,vla,vcl,bvl
(med easy) min sc SCHOTTS
ETP 1081 s.p., ipa   (V155)

Laudamus Te (from Gloria)
(Bevan, G.) SA (med) WATERLOO $.40
(V156)

Let All The World Praise The Lord
(Dunsmore) SATB oct SCHMITT 1446
$.40   (V157)

Magnificat *Magnif
SATB,SA/SAT soli,cont,strings,opt
2ob sc,cor pts CARUS CV 40.002
s.p., ipa   (V158)

Psalm 112 *see Beatus Vir

Psalm 147 *see Lauda Jerusalem

VIVAT FLAMAND see Housieaux, G.

VIVO SIN VIVIR see Brindle, [Reginald
Smith]

VLACH-VRUTICKY, JOSEF (1897-   )
Hospodine, Pomiluj Ny *Op.78,No.2
"Love Us, Oh Lord" [Czech] mix cor,
acap CZECH s.p.   (V159)

Love Us, Oh Lord *see Hospodine,
Pomiluj Ny

VLEUGEL, CORNELIUS
Song Of Praise And Thanksgiving
*Thanks,anthem
SATB oct SINGSPIR ZCS-4752 $.35
(V160)

VOBIS DATUM EST see Porta, Costanzo

A VOCAL COMPANION TO BACH'S
ORGELBUCHLEIN, BOOK THREE see Bach,
Johann Sebastian

VOCE MEA AD DOMINUM CLAMAVI see Croce,
Giovanni

VOGELSANGER
Wohl Denen, Die Da Wandeln
SAT/SAB/SA,opt treb inst (two
settings) HANSSLER 14.190 s.p.
(V161)

VOGLER
Hosianna
(Schonberg, Stig Gustav) mix cor,
opt org&2trp&2trom (no. 81 in A-
major; no. 82 in B-flat) ERIKS 81
s.p., ipa, ERIKS 82 s.p., ipa
(V162)

VOGT, HANS (1911-   )
Historie Der Verkundigung
SATB,SSA soli,orch ALKOR AE287
rental   (V163)

VOICE OF MY BELOVED see Wood, James

VOICE OF TRIUMPH see Ford, Faith Dell

VOICE WAS HEARD IN RAMAH, A see Bender,
Jan

VOICES UNITED TO SING GOD'S PRAISE
*anthem
1-2pt jr cor,trp,bells BROADMAN
4560-26 $.35 see from Four Festive
Anthems For Children's Voices
(V164)

VOICES UNITED TO SING GOD'S PRAISE see
Burroughs, Bob

VOILA
Kind Van Bethlehem
(Wesselink) mix cor HEER 1528
(V165)

VOLGYFY, HANS
Tantum Ergo
[Lat] 4pt mix cor,org,strings,2trp,
timp,opt 2fl&2bsn&2horn&trom&2ob/
2clar sc,cor pts BOHM s.p., ipa
(V166)

VOLLENDUNG see Philipp, Franz, Domino
Canticum Novum

VOM HIMMEL HOCH *Xmas,cant/carol/folk
2-4pt mix cor,soli,strings/rec/org
(assembled from works of Bach, J.
S.; Hassler; Cruger; and others)
PELIKAN PE731   (V167)
(Biebl, F.) [Ger] 4pt men cor
MERSEBURG EM9043   (V168)

VOM HIMMEL HOCH see Brandt, Jobst vom

VOM HIMMEL HOCH see Schelle, Johann
Hermann

VOM HIMMEL HOCH, DA KOMM ICH HER   *Xmas
(Herrmann, H.) men cor,acap TONOS
5638 s.p.   (V169)

VOM HIMMEL HOCH, DA KOMM ICH HER see
Bach, Johann Sebastian

VOM HIMMEL HOCH, DA KOMM ICH HER see
Haas, Joseph

VOM HIMMEL HOCH DA KOMM ICH HER see
Hjelmborg, Bjorn

VOM HIMMEL HOCH, DA KOMM ICH HER see
Praetorius, Michael

VOM HIMMEL HOCH, O ENGEL KOMMT see
Schroeder, Hermann

VOM OLBERGE ZEUCHT DAHER see Burck,
Joachim

VON DEN HEILIGEN WUNDEN
"Lament And Weep" see Four Easter
Chorales

VON SEINEM EW'GEN FESTEN THRON see
Spranger, Jorg

VOORMOLEN, ALEXANDER NICOLAS
(1895-   )
Ave Maria
mix cor,strings,harp DONEMUS (V170)

VOORWAARTS, CHRISTENSTRIJDERS
mix cor sc HEER 2106 s.p.   (V171)

VOUCHSAFE, O LORD see Gretchaninov,
Alexander Tikhonovitch

VOX IN RAMA see Jenni, Donald

VREDE ZIJ ULIEDEN see Schubert

VRIEND, JAN (1938-   )
Introitus (Homage To Ton De Leeuw)
mix cor,8clar,4trom DONEMUS (V172)

VRKRISENI see Folprecht, Zdenek

V'SHAMRU see Adler, Samuel

VUATAZ
Abraham *ora
cor,soli,orch HENN s.p.   (V173)

Trois Motets *CC3U,mot
4pt,acap voc pt HENN 786 s.p.
(V174)

VULPIUS, MELCHIOR (ca. 1560-1615)
Ach Bleib Mit Deiner Gnade
men cor,acap TONOS 5609 s.p. (V175)

Av Helig Langtan Hjartat Slar
4pt mix cor ERIKS 11 s.p.   (V176)

Christe, Du Bist Der Helle Tag
see Musikbeilage Zum "Evangelischen
Kirchenchor 1952"

Christus Der Ist Mein Leben
men cor,acap TONOS 5616 s.p. (V177)
(Schaefers, H.) men cor,acap TONOS
5619 s.p. contains also: Wenn
Mein Stundlein Vorhanden Ist
(V178)

Das Neugeborne Kindelein
SATB (contains also: Herr, Fur Dein
Wort Sei Hoch Gepreist)
SCHWEIZER. SK 57.05 s.p. see also
MUSIKBEILAGE ZUM "EVANGELISCHEN
KIRCHENCHOR 1957"   (V179)

Die Helle Sonn
see Vulpius, Melchior, Gelobt Sei
Gott Im Hochsten Thron

Die Stund Ist Uns Verborgn
see DREI BEERDIGUNGSGESANGE

Es Ist Das Heil Uns Kommen Her
see Musikbeilage Zum "Evangelischen
Kirchenchor 1952"

Es Ist Ein Ros Entsprungen
see Praetorius, Michael, Es Ist Ein
Ros Entsprungen

Gelobt Sei Gott Im Hochsten Thron
SATB DOBLINGER S 211-212 s.p.
contains also: Die Helle Sonn
(V180)

Good Christian Men, Rejoice And Sing
*Easter
SATB,opt brass (med) oct CONCORDIA
98-2203 $.30   (V181)

Herr Gott Vater, Wir Preisen Dich
see Musikbeilage Zum "Evangelischen
Kirchenchor 1952"

Hinunter Ist Der Sonne Schein
SATB DOBLINGER 219-220 s.p.
contains also: Braun, J.G., Ave
Maria Zart   (V182)

VULPIUS, MELCHIOR (cont'd.)

Ich Freu Mich Des
see Musikbeilage Zum "Evangelischen
Kirchenchor 1952"

Jesus Said To The Blind Man *see
Jesus Sprach Zu Dem Blinden

Jesus Sprach Zu Dem Blinden
(McCullough) "Jesus Said To The
Blind Man" SATB SCHIRM.G LG 51702
$.35   (V183)

Lob Sei Dem Allmachtigen Gott
see Musikbeilage Zum "Evangelischen
Kirchenchor 1952"

Musikbeilage Zum "Evangelischen
Kirchenchor 1952"
SATB SCHWEIZER. SK 52.01-2 s.p.
contains: Christe, Du Bist Der
Helle Tag; Es Ist Das Heil Uns
Kommen Her; Herr Gott Vater,
Wir Preisen Dich; Ich Freu Mich
Des; Lob Sei Dem Allmachtigen
Gott   (V184)

Nimm Von Uns, Herr, Du Treuer Gott
see MUSIKBEILAGE ZUM "EVANGELISCHEN
KIRCHENCHOR 1960

O Jesu Krist, Dig Till Oss Vand
4pt mix cor ERIKS 8 s.p.   (V185)

O My Dear Heart *Xmas
SA (easy) WATERLOO $.30   (V186)

On The Wood His Arms Outstretched
*Easter/Lent
SATB WHITE,ERN $.50   (V187)

Praise Ye The Lord
(Klein) SATB SCHIRM.G 11900 $.35
(V188)

Trachtet Am Ersten Nach Dem Reich
Gottes
SSAT/SSAB SCHWEIZER. SK 66.07-8
s.p. see also MUSIKBEILAGE ZUM
"EVANGELISCHEN KIRCHENCHOR 1966"
(V189)

Uns Ist Ein Kind Geboren
SSATB SCHWEIZER. SK 54.03 s.p. see
also MUSIKBEILAGE ZUM
"EVANGELISCHEN KIRCHENCHOR 1954"
(V190)

Uppstanden Ar Var Herre Krist
4pt mix cor ERIKS 320 s.p.   (V191)

Wer Mich Liebet, Der Wird Mein Wort
Halten
(Pizarro) "Whoso Loveth Me Will All
My Words Treasure" mix cor BRODT
546 $.26   (V192)

Whoso Loveth Me Will All My Words
Treasure *see Wer Mich Liebet,
Der Wird Mein Wort Halten

VYCPALEK, LADISLAV (1882-1969)
Blessed Is The Man *Op.23, cant
[Czech] mix cor,STBar soli,3fl,3ob,
3clar,3bsn,4horn,3trp,3trom,tuba,
timp,perc,strings, celeste
SUPRAPHON s.p.   (V193)

Czech Requiem *Op.24, Bibl/cant
[Czech] mix cor,soli,3fl,3ob,2clar,
3bsn,4horn,4trp,3trom,tuba,timp,
perc,strings SUPRAPHON s.p.
(V194)

Saint Luke *see Svaty Lukas

Svaty Lukas *Op.36
"Saint Luke" [Czech] wom cor,fl,
2ob,clar,bsn,horn,trp,pno,strings
CZECH s.p.   (V195)

W

WA-EDA MAH see Foss, Lukas

WACH AUF, MEIN HERZ UND SINGE see Bach,
Johann Sebastian

WACH AUF, WACH AUF, DU CHRISTLICH LAND
see Walter (Walther), Johann

WACH, NACHTIGALL, WACH AUF!
see Alte Frankische Weihnachtslieder

WACHET AUF, RUFT UNS DIE STIMME see
Bach, Johann Christoph Friedrich

WACHET AUF, RUFT UNS DIE STIMME see
Bach, Johann Sebastian

WACHET AUF, RUFT UNS DIE STIMME see
Buxtehude, Dietrich

WACHET AUF, RUFT UNS DIE STIMME see
Heer, Emil

WACHET AUF, RUFT UNS DIE STIMME see
Oertzen, Rudolf von

WACHET AUF, RUFT UNS DIE STIMME see
Praetorius, Jakob

WADE
O Come, All Ye Faithful *Xmas,anthem
(Peterson, John W.) SATB oct
SINGSPIR ZJP-3009 $.30   (W1)

WADELY, F.W. (1883-1970)
Holy Birth, The
SATB,STBar/SAT soli,fl,clar,bsn,
2horn,2trp,timp,strings voc sc
NOVELLO rental   (W2)

WAGNER
Kleiner Liedpsalter *CC10L,Psalm
SATB/SSATB HANSSLER 2.053 s.p. (W3)

Nun Danket Alle Gott
see Poser, Hans, Nun Danket Alle
Gott

WAGNER, RICHARD (1813-1883)
O Joyful Morn *Xmas/Easter/Gen
(Ganschow) SATB (med) FITZSIMONS
2043 $.20   (W4)

Pilgrims' Chorus (from Tannhauser)
TTBB,acap (med) FITZSIMONS 4021
$.20   (W5)

WAHRLICH, ER TRUG UNSRE QUAL see
Handel, George Frideric, Surely, He
Hath Borne Our Griefs

WAHRLICH, HIER IST DAS HAUS GOTTES see
Kronberg, G.

WAHRLICH, ICH SAGE EUCH see
Hammerschmidt, Andreas

WAHRLICH, ICH SAGE EUCH:ICH BIN DIE TUR
see Leisring, Volkmar

WAHRLICH, ICH SAGE EUCH: IHR WERDET
WEINEN UND HEULEN see David, Thomas
[Christian]

WAIT ON THE LORD see Zilch, Margot

WAITE
Jesu, Son Of God
see Two Carols

Let Us Gather
see Two Carols

Two Carols *Xmas,carol
SA (med easy) OXFORD 82.102 $.50
contains: Jesu, Son Of God; Let
Us Gather   (W6)

WAITS see Murray, Margaret

WAKE, AWAKE see Carlson, Gordon

WAKE EV'RY BREATH AND EV'RY STRING see
Billings, William

WALCHA, HELMUT (1907-   )
Nimm Von Uns, Herr, Du Treuer Gott
see MUSIKBEILAGE ZUM "EVANGELISCHEN
KIRCHENCHOR 1960

WALDBROEL, WILHELM (1896-1952)
Pange Lingua
[Lat] 4pt mix cor,org BOHM s.p.
contains also: Tantum Ergo   (W7)

Tantum Ergo
see Waldbroel, Wilhelm, Pange
Lingua

WALDBROEL, WILHELM (cont'd.)

Tu Es Petrus
[Lat] 4-6pt mix cor,acap BOHM s.p.
(W8)

WALK IN SUNLIGHT see Wright, Alberta
Childs

WALK SOFTLY see Horman, John D.

WALK SOFTLY IN SPRINGTIME see Lovelace,
Austin C.

WALK TO BETHLEHEM, THE see Bryson

WALK WITH ME see Langdon

WALKER, JACK
Christ's Advent
SATB&jr cor,pno (med easy) oct
GENTRY G-263 $.45   (W9)

It Was A Cold And Lonely Night
SA&unis,opt gtr, bongos (med easy)
GENTRY G-266 $.45   (W10)

WALKER, M.
Gate Of The Year, The
mix cor BRODT 604 $.24   (W11)

Let Us Now Praise Famous Men
unis BRODT 579 $.24   (W12)

Psalm 121
mix cor BRODT 588 $.25   (W13)

Song Of Life
mix cor BRODT 598 $.20   (W14)

WALKER, ROBERT
Communion Service In E
cong NOVELLO MW 40 s.p.   (W15)

Thou Wilt Keep Him In Perfect Peace
*anthem
SATB,acap NOVELLO MT 1584 s.p.
(W16)

WALKER, WILLIAM
Evening Shade
see Three Frontier Hymns

Holy Manna
see Three Frontier Hymns

Jerusalem
see Three Frontier Hymns

Three Frontier Hymns *folk
(Boyd, Jack) 3pt mix cor,acap
CANYON 6404 $.30
contains: Evening Shade; Holy
Manna; Jerusalem   (W17)

WALKING MEDLEY
see Church Is Singing Again, The

WALKING WITH THE MASTER see Protheroe,
Daniel

WALLACE, AL
As The Hart Pants
(Smith, Herb) SATB oct GOSPEL
05 TM 0141 $.20   (W18)

WALLISER, CHRISTOPH THOMAS (1568-1648)
Nun Lob, Mein Seel, Den Herren
SSATB LAUDINELLA LR 29-30 s.p.
(W19)

WALMISLEY, THOMAS ATTWOOD (1814-1856)
Father Of Heaven
mix cor BANKS MUS YS 354 $.25 (W20)

WALTER
Rise Up, O Men Of God *see Merrill

WALTER (WALTHER), JOHANN (1496-1570)
Come, Holy Ghost, Creator Blest
(Reuning, Daniel G.) [Eng/Ger] SATB
GIA G1913 $.50   (W21)

The Complete Works Of Johann Walter
Vol. I: Geistliches
Gesangbuchlein Part I *CCU
(Schroeder, D.) [Ger] cor sc,pap
CONCORDIA 97-2001 $8.00   (W22)

The Complete Works Of Johann Walter
Vol. II: Geistliches
Gesangbuchlein Part II *CCU
(Schroeder, D.) [Ger] cor sc,pap
CONCORDIA 97-2003 $8.50   (W23)

The Complete Works Of Johann Walter
Vol. III: Geistliches
Gesangbuchlein Part III *CCU
(Schroeder, D.) [Ger] cor sc,cloth
CONCORDIA 97-2006 $9.00   (W24)

The Complete Works Of Johann Walter
Vol. IV: Cantiones Septem Vocum
And Magnificat Octo Tonorum *CCU
(Schroeder, D.) [Ger] cor sc,cloth
CONCORDIA 97-2010 $9.20   (W25)

WALTER (WALTHER), JOHANN (cont'd.)

Mit Fried Und Freud Ich Fahr Dahin
*mot
(Holle, Hugo) mix cor (easy) sc
SCHOTTS C 32 829-33 s.p. (W26)

Mitten Wir Im Leben Sind *mot
(Holle, Hugo) mix cor (med) sc
SCHOTTS C 32 829 s.p.   (W27)

O Lux Beata Trinitas
SATB,acap EGTVED MK5, 11 s.p. (W28)

Wach Auf, Wach Auf, Du Christlich
Land
SATB SCHWEIZER. SK 61.06 s.p. see
also MUSIKBEILAGE ZUM
"EVANGELISCHEN KIRCHENCHOR 1961"
(W29)

Wir Glauben All An Einen Gott *mot
SSATBB HANSSLER 1.487 s.p. (W30)

WALTERS, JOHN
Hear My Prayer *anthem
SATB,acap/pno/org SHATTINGER 405
$.25   (W31)

WALTHER, JOHANN (1496-1570)
see WALTER (WALTHER), JOHANN

WALTON
All This Time
SATB,acap (easy) OXFORD 84.201 $.30
(W32)

Jubilate Deo
SSAATTBB (med) OXFORD 42.373 $.75
(W33)

WALTON, K.
Bells Of Christmas *Xmas
SA BRODT 618 $.25   (W34)

Four Anthems For Children *CC4U,Adv/
Xmas,anthem
SA BRODT 619 $.30   (W35)

Two Anthems For Children *CC2U,
Easter/Gen/Lent,anthem
SA BRODT 620 $.25   (W36)

WALVOORD, JOHN
Now Sounds *see Wyrtzen, Don

WANN MEIN SCHIFFLEIN SICH WILL WEDEN
see Lederer, F.

WAPEN, FRANCIS A.
Give Thanks To The Lord
cor,2trp,2trom,timp CONCORDIA
97-5309 $.80, ipa   (W37)

WAR GOTT NICHT MIT UNS DIESE ZEIT see
Baudach, Ulrich

WAR GOTT NICHT MIT UNS DIESE ZEIT see
Neubert, Gottfried

WARD, ARTHUR
Two Easter Carols *CC2U,Easter,carol
SATB oct THOMP.G G-539 s.p. (W38)

WARD, SAMUEL A.
America The Beautiful *Thanks,anthem
(DeCou, Harold) SA oct SINGSPIR
ZJP-2002 $.25   (W39)
(Johnson, N.) SATB oct SINGSPIR
ZJP-8214 $.35   (W40)

O For A Thousand Tongues *anthem
SATB oct SACRED S-157 $.40 (W41)

WARFORD
Alas, And Did My Savior Bleed *see
Watts

Bringing In The Sheaves *anthem
SATB oct BROADMAN 4540-79 $.30
(W42)
Master Hath Come, The *see Doudney

WARKENTIN
Ten Worship Responses *CC10U,cor-
resp
SATB PRO ART 2764 $.35   (W43)

WARMNESS OF JOY, THE see Frey, Richard

WARNER
Christ The Lord (composed with
Leinbach, E.W.)
see Warner, Softly The Night Is
Sleeping

Softly The Night Is Sleeping
(composed with Leinbach, E.W.)
(Pfohl) mix cor BRODT 105 $.24
contains also: Christ The Lord
(W44)

WARNER, P.
Noel *Xmas
SSA,bells (med) FITZSIMONS 3075
$.20   (W45)

WARREN
God Of Our Fathers *anthem
(Ferguson) SATB,trp oct LILLENAS
AN-2403 $.30   (W46)

WARREN ANGELL CHORAL COLLECTION see
Angell, Warren M.

WARREN, ELINOR REMICK (1905-   )
Let The Heavens Praise Thy Wonders!
SATB,org GRAY CMR 3313 $.30 (W47)

WARREN, GEORGE WILLIAM (1828-1902)
God Of Our Fathers *anthem
(Johnson, Norman) SATB oct SINGSPIR
ZJP-7288 $.25   (W48)

WARREN, RAYMOND (1928-   )
Passion, The *Psntd
SATB,TBar soli,fl,ob,clar,bsn,horn,
timp,perc,pno,strings, English
horn, xylophone, glockenspiel voc
sc NOVELLO rental   (W49)

WARUM IST DAS LICHT GEGEBEN DEN
MUHSELIGEN see Brahms, Johannes

WARUM IST DAS LICHT GEGEBEN DEN
MUHSELIGEN see Brahms, Johannes,
Warum Ist Das Licht Gegeben Den
Muhseligen

WARUM RETTET' DENN GOTT NUR DANIEL see
Petersen, Rolf, Didn't My Lord
Deliver Daniel

WARUM SOLLT ICH MICH DENN GRAMEN see
Ebeling, Johann Georg

WAS BETRUBST DU DICH, MEINE SEELE see
Fussan, Werner

WAS BETRUBST DU DICH, MEINE SEELE? see
Schutz, Heinrich

WAS EVER GRIEF LIKE THINE see Latrobe,
Christian I.

WAS GOTT TUT see Backer, Hans

WAS GOTT TUT, DAS IST WOHLGETAN see
Gastorius, Severius

WAS MEIN GOTT WILL see Berghorn, Alfred

WAS MEIN GOTT WILL, DAS GSCHEH ALLZEIT
see Distler, Hugo

WAS MEIN GOTT WILL, DAS GSCHEH ALLZEIT
see Franck

WAS MEIN GOTT WILL, DAS G'SCHEH'
ALLZEIT see Schutz, Heinrich

WAS MEIN GOTT WILL, DAS GSCHEH ALLZEIT
see Sermisy, Claude de

WASH ME THOROUGHLY FROM MY WICKEDNESS
see Handel, George Frideric

WASH ME THOROUGHLY FROM MY WICKEDNESS
see Wesley, S.S.

WASH YOUR HANDS YOU SINNERS see Lamb

WASHBURN
Gloria *Gloria
SATB,inst (easy) OXFORD 94.210
$.70, ipa   (W50)

WASN'T THAT A MIGHTY DAY! see
Thygerson, Robert J.

WASSAIL SONG see Vaughan Williams,
Ralph

WASSMER, BERTHOLD
Benedictus *Easter
[Lat] SA&opt TB/men cor BOHM s.p.
(W51)

In Te Speravi, Domine *Op.85, Mass
[Lat] 2-4pt mix cor,org,opt vln sc,
cor pts BOHM s.p., ipa   (W52)

Mass For Christmas *see
Weihnachtsmesse

Missa Solemnis "Laudate Dominum"
*Op.50, Mass
[Lat] 4pt mix cor,org,opt strings&
2horn&2trp sc,cor pts BOHM s.p.,
ipa   (W53)

O Engel Rein *Op.48, Mass
[Lat] 1-2pt,org/harmonium sc,cor
pts BOHM s.p.   (W54)
[Lat] SA&opt TB,acap sc,cor pts
BOHM s.p.   (W55)

Pange Lingua *Op.22
[Lat] 4pt mix cor,org/2trp,2horn,
trom,tuba, baritone horn sc,cor
pts BOHM s.p., ipa   (W56)
[Lat] 4pt mix cor,org/2clar,2trp,
2horn,trom,tuba, baritone horn
sc,cor pts BOHM s.p., ipa

WASSMER, BERTHOLD (cont'd.)

contains also: Tantum Ergo,
Op.101,No.2
[Lat] 4pt mix cor,acap sc,cor pts
BOHM s.p.   (W58)

Requiem *Op.97
[Lat] 1-3pt,org sc,cor pts BOHM
s.p.   (W59)
[Lat] SA&opt Bar,org sc,cor pts
BOHM s.p.   (W60)

St. Blasius-Messe *Op.7, Mass
[Lat] 4pt mix cor,acap sc,cor pts
BOHM s.p.   (W61)

St. Franziskus-Messe *Op.52, Mass
[Lat] 4pt mix cor,acap sc,cor pts
BOHM s.p.   (W62)

St. Meinradsmesse *Op.81, Mass
[Lat] 4pt mix cor,acap sc,cor pts
BOHM s.p.   (W63)

St. Michaelsmesse *Op.82a, Mass
[Lat] SABar,opt org/harmonium
(without Credo) sc,cor pts BOHM
s.p.   (W64)
[Lat] SAB,opt org,harmonium
(without Credo) sc,cor pts BOHM
s.p.   (W65)

Sanctae Dei Genitrix *Op.40, Mass
[Lat] SA&opt Bar,org sc,cor pts
BOHM s.p.   (W66)

Stabat Mater Dolorosa *Op.58s, Psntd
[Lat/Ger] 4pt mix cor,acap BOHM
s.p.   (W67)

Tantum Ergo *Op.101,No.2
see Wassmer, Berthold, Pange Lingua

Veni Creator *Op.21a
see Hofmayer, Karl, Veni Creator
[Lat] SA&opt TB,opt org BOHM s.p.   (W68)

Weihnachtsmesse *Op.60, Mass
"Mass For Christmas" [Lat] 4pt mix
cor,org/strings&org/org&fl&clar&
2horn&strings sc,cor pts BOHM
s.p., ipa   (W69)

WATER IS WIDE, THE *Gen,anthem/folk,
Scot
(Martin, Gilbert M.) SATB,opt S solo
(med diff) oct LORENZ C361 $.35   (W70)

WATER IS WIDE, THE see Martin, Gilbert
M.

WATERLOO ANTHEM COLLECTION NO. 1 *CCU,
anthem
(Hill, Harry) cor WATERLOO $1.25   (W71)

WATERLOO BOOK OF HYMNS WITH DESCANTS
*CCU,hymn
(MacNutt) cor WATERLOO $1.75   (W72)

WATERMAN, FRANCES
Twenty-Third Psalm - An
Interpretation *Gen/Thanks,Psalm
unis CHORISTERS A-144 $.35   (W73)

WATERS
Psalm 31
SATB SCHIRM.G 12006 $.40   (W74)

WATERS, DEANNA
All God's Children Are Singing
Tonight *see Wild, Eric

Am I Like Peter *see Wild, Eric

Christmas Is A Time For Loving *see
Wild, Eric

Come Rest In Me *see Wild, Eric

Day You Meet The Lord, The *see
Wild, Eric

Father The Hour Is Come *see Wild,
Eric

Forgive My Little Faith *see Wild,
Eric

Gather Round And Praise The Lord
*see Wild, Eric

Give Your Life To The Lord *see
Wild, Eric

God Is In Every Tomorrow *see Wild,
Eric

He Gives Light *see Wild, Eric

His Loving Kindness Lasts Forever
*see Wild, Eric

How Can I Thank The Lord *see Wild,
Eric

WATERS, DEANNA (cont'd.)

I'm Reaching Out *see Wild, Eric

In The Beginning *see Wild, Eric

Let God Be At Home In Your Heart
*see Wild, Eric

Lord Open My Eyes *see Wild, Eric

O God Of Love And Kindness *see
Wild, Eric

Oh, Perfect Teacher *see Wild, Eric

Peace To All Who Enter Here *see
Wild, Eric

To Know God Is To Love Again *see
Wild, Eric

Who Were These Men *see Wild, Eric

With Jesus Alive In My Heart *see
Wild, Eric

WATERS, CHARLES F.
Creator Spirit
SATB,org ROBERTON 85030 s.p. (W75)

WATSON, L.W.
Light Of The World
(Copes) mix cor BRODT 529 $.24
(W76)
(Copes; Pfohl) mix cor BRODT 501
$.20   (W77)

WATSON, RUTH
God Be Merciful Unto Us
SATB (med diff) WATERLOO $.40 (W78)

I Will Extol Thee
unis (med easy) WATERLOO $.35 (W79)

O King Of Kings
SATB (med easy) WATERLOO $.40 (W80)

WATSON, WALTER
Festival Psalm, A
SATB, bongos LUDWIG L1160 $.40
(W81)

Praise The Lord, Alleluia! *Gen/
Thanks
unis CHORISTERS A-133 $.45   (W82)

Rejoice *Gen/Thanks
unis CHORISTERS A-102 $.30   (W83)

Sing A New Song
unis jr cor,kbd,fl,ob LUDWIG C1163
$.40   (W84)

WATT, FATHER LEO
Altar Of God *CCU,hymn
cong,org/gtr EMI   (W85)

WATTERS, BOB
Little Touch Of Heaven, A *Contemp
(Krogstad, Bob) jr cor oct GOSPEL
05 TM 0157 $.35   (W86)

Shepherd Song, The (composed with
Watters, Lilian) *Xmas
(Walters, Bob) SATB oct GOSPEL
05 TM 0315 $.35   (W87)

There's A Difference (composed with
Watters, Lilian)
(Walters, Bob) SATB oct GOSPEL
05 TM 0316 $.35   (W88)

WATTERS, LILIAN
Shepherd Song, The *see Watters, Bob

There's A Difference *see Watters,
Bob

WATTERS, WILLIAM T.
God Is Just A Prayer Away
(Smith, Wesley) SATB oct GOSPEL
(W89)

I Can Feel The Saviour's Hand
(Smith, Wesley) SATB oct GOSPEL
(W90)

Jesus Goes With Me Wherever I Go
(Smith, Wesley) SATB oct GOSPEL
(W91)

WATTS
Alas, And Did My Savior Bleed
(composed with Wilson; Warford)
*anthem
SATB (easy) oct BROADMAN 4545-70
$.30   (W92)

At The Cross (composed with Hudson,
Richard) *Easter/Gen
(Huff, Ronn) SSATB oct BENSON S4019
$.30   (W93)

Come, Holy Spirit, Heavenly Dove
(composed with Simpson; Turner)
*anthem
unis (easy) oct BROADMAN 4554-71
$.30   (W94)

WATTS (cont'd.)

Jesus Shall Reign (composed with
Hatton) *Easter/Gen
(Marsh) SATB,brass oct BENSON S4164
$.35, ipa   (W95)

When I Survey The Wondrous Cross
(composed with Burroughs, Bob)
*Easter,anthem
SATB (easy) oct BROADMAN 4554-28
$.30   (W96)
SATB (easy) oct BROADMAN 4554-28
$.30   (W97)

WATT'S CRADLE SONG
(Simpson, John) unis EMI   (W98)

WAY OF JESUS, THE see Hovhaness, Alan

WAY OF THE CROSS MEDLEY, THE
see Mini-Musicals

WAY THAT HE LOVES, THE see Mercer

WAY THAT HE LOVES, THE see Mercer, W.
Elmo

WAYFARING STRANGER, THE *anthem/gospel
(Johnson, Norman) SATB oct SINGSPIR
ZJP-8066 $.30   (W99)

WE ADORE THEE see Ayers, Jacob S.

WE ADORE THEE see Benjamin, Thomas E.,
Adoramus Te

WE ADORE THEE see Brahms, Johannes,
Adoramus Te

WE ADORE THEE see Perti, Giacomo
Antonio, Adoramus Te

WE ADORE THEE, O CHRIST see Roff,
Joseph

WE ADORE YOU see Lotti, Antonio,
Adoramus Te [1]

WE ADORE YOU see Lotti, Antonio,
Adoramus Te [2]

WE ADORE YOU, JESUS CHRIST see Andrews,
C.T.

WE ADORE YOU, O CHRIST see Palestrina,
Giovanni

WE ADORE YOU, O JESUS see Perti,
Giacomo Antonio

WE ADORE YOU, O LORD JESUS CHRIST see
Remondi, R.

WE ARE CHILDREN OF THE KING see Wills

WE ARE CLIMBING *spir
(Zimmergren) 4pt mix cor ERIKS 316
s.p.   (W100)

WE ARE NOT ALONE see Sanders

WE ARE THE CHURCH see Avery, Richard

WE COME TO MEET THEE LORD see Dunford,
Benjamin

WE GREET YOU, JESUS see Lefebvre,
Channing

WE HAD A SHARE see Sleeth, Natalie

WE HAVE A KING see Whitecotton, Shirley

WE HAVE AN ANCHOR see Kirkpatrick

WE HAVE HEARD THE JOYFUL SOUND *anthem
(Starks) SATB,opt trp (easy) oct
BROADMAN 4540-53 $.30   (W101)

WE HAVE SEEN THE LORD see Wetzler,
Robert

WE HAVE TO FIND A WAY see Reynolds,
William Jensen

WE, HIS CHILDREN see Hafso

WE HURRY WITH TIRED, UNFALTERING
FOOTSTEPS see Bach, Johann
Sebastian

WE KNOW THAT CHRIST IS RAISED see
Nelson, Ronald A.

WE LIFT OUR HEARTS IN PRAISE
(Harris) SATB PRO ART 2791 $.40
(W102)

WE LOOK TO THEE see Burroughs, Bob

WE MAGNIFY OUR FATHER GOD see Peterson,
John W.

WE NEED MORE LOVE see Skillings, Otis

WE PLOW THE FIELDS *anthem
  (Mann, Johnny) SATB LEXICON   (W103)

WE PRAISE THEE, O GOD see Croft,
  William

WE PRAISE THEE, O GOD! see Latrobe,
  Christian I.

WE PRAISE THEE, O GOD, OUR REDEEMER
  *Thanks,anthem
  (Shepard, Bob) SATB oct SINGSPIR
  ZJP-7232 $.25   (W104)

WE PRAISE YOU FOR THE SUN see Mahnke,
  Allan

WE SEEK ONLY JESUS see Ramquist, Grace

WE SING EXCELSIS DEO see Englert,
  Eugene

WE SING NOW AT CHRISTMAS see Track,
  Gerhard

WE SING TO THEE see Schvedov,
  Constantine

WE SING WITH GRACE IN OUR HEARTS see
  Collins

WE THANK THEE see Peterson, John W.

WE THANK THEE FATHER see Horman, John
  D.

WE THANK THEE, LORD see Schutz,
  Heinrich, Wir Danken, Herr Gott

WE, THE PEOPLE! see Yahres, Samuel C.

WE WAIT FOR THY LOVING KINDNESS see
  Elvey, George Job

WE WILL CAROL JOYFULLY see Grieb,
  Herbert [C.]

WE WILL FOLLOW see Billingsley

WE WILL REJOICE see Croft, William

WE WOULD BE BUILDING see Ayers, Jacob
  S.

WE WOULD REMEMBER see Young, Phillip M.

WEARY MARCHING UP THE CALVARY ROAD see
  Colom

WEARY OF ALL TRUMPETING see Bender, Jan

WEATHERSEED, JOHN .J.
  Communion Service In E-Flat
    SATB HARRIS $.35   (W105)

  They Shall Mount Up With Wings
    SATB HARRIS $.35   (W106)

WEAVER
  Epiphany Alleluias *CCU
    SATB,org oct BOOSEY 5683 $.40
                                 (W107)

WEBB, E.
  Sing Aloud Unto God Our Strength
    SATB,3trp,3trom,timp cmplt ed
    SCHOTT 11137 s.p., voc sc SCHOTT
    11138 s.p.   (W108)

WEBB, GEORGE JAMES (1803-1830)
  Stand Up For Jesus *anthem/gospel
    (Slauson, Lloyd N.) SATB,opt 3trp
    oct SINGSPIR ZJP-8036 $.30 (W109)

WEBBE, SAMUEL (1740-1816)
  Come, Ye Disconsolate *anthem
    (DeCou, Harold) SATB oct SINGSPIR
    ZJP-7303 $.30   (W110)
    (Krogstad, Bob) SAT/SSATB oct
    GOSPEL 05 TM 0365 $.35   (W111)

WEBBER, ANDREW LLOYD
  Joseph And The Amazing Technicolor
    Dreamcoat (composed with Rice,
    Tim) *cant/pop
    unis,2fl,ob,2clar,bsn,2horn,2trp,
    trom,perc,pno,org,strings,
    xylophone, glockenspiel,
    vibrophone, guitars: lead,
    rhythm, and bass voc sc NOVELLO
    rental   (W112)

WEBER
  In Seiner Ordnung *Op.36, hymn
    mix cor,pno LIENAU cor pts s.p., sc
    s.p.   (W113)

  Juda, Hochgelobtes Land *Op.80,No.2,
    Xmas
    8pt mix cor LIENAU sc s.p., cor pts
    s.p.   (W114)

WEBER, BERNHARD (1912-1974)
  An Gott "Sieh, Wie Mein Lacheln"
    *hymn
    TTBB voc pt SCHOTTS C 39 728 01-02
    s.p. see from Drei Hymnische

WEBER, BERNHARD (cont'd.)

    Gesange   (W115)

  Ave Maria Zart *Xmas
    see Weber, Bernhard, O Kind, O
    Wahrer Gottessohn
    wom cor/jr cor (easy, contains
    also: O Jesulein Zart) sc SCHOTTS
    CHBL 582A-B s.p. see from Vier
    Kleine Weihnachtslieder   (W116)

  Den Gefallenen "Unter Den Kreuzen"
    mix cor (easy) sc SCHOTTS CHBL 340
    s.p.   (W117)

  Drei Hymnische Gesange *see An Gott
    "Sieh, Wie Mein Lacheln"; Ekstase
    "Gott, Deine Himmel";
    Lautespielender Engel "Sprich
    Mich Nicht An!"   (W118)

  Ekstase "Gott, Deine Himmel" *hymn
    TTBB voc pt SCHOTTS C 39 730 01-02
    s.p. see from Drei Hymnische
    Gesange   (W119)

  Es Ward Ein Stern Entzundet *Xmas,
    cant
    3pt treb cor&unis men cor,strings
    sc,cor pts SCHOTTS ED. 5381 s.p.,
    ipa   (W120)

  Jubilate Deo (Psalm 90)
    [Lat/Ger] 4pt mix cor,acap BOHM
    s.p.   (W121)

  Krippenlied *Xmas
    wom cor/jr cor (easy, contains
    also: Schweigt Fein Still) sc
    SCHOTTS CHBL 581A-B s.p. see from
    Vier Kleine Weihnachtslieder
                                 (W122)

  Krippenlied "Kommt Herbei Zur Krippe"
    *Xmas
    mix cor (easy) sc SCHOTTS CHBL 318
    s.p.   (W123)

  Lautespielender Engel "Sprich Mich
    Nicht An!" *hymn
    TTBB voc pt SCHOTTS C 39 729 01-02
    s.p. see from Drei Hymnische
    Gesange   (W124)

  O Jesulein Zart *Xmas
    wom cor/jr cor (easy, contains
    also: Ave Maria Zart) sc SCHOTTS
    CHBL 582A-B s.p. see from Vier
    Kleine Weihnachtslieder   (W125)

  O Kind, O Wahrer Gottessohn *Xmas
    men cor sc SCHOTTS CHBL 128A-B s.p.
    contains also: Ave Maria Zart
                                 (W126)

  Psalm 90 *see Jubilate Deo

  Schweigt Fein Still *Xmas
    wom cor/jr cor (easy, contains
    also: Krippenlied) sc SCHOTTS
    CHBL 581A-B s.p. see from Vier
    Kleine Weihnachtslieder   (W127)
    mix cor (easy) sc SCHOTTS CHBL 317
    s.p.   (W128)

  Vier Kleine Weihnachtslieder *see
    Ave Maria Zart; Krippenlied; O
    Jesulein Zart; Schweigt Fein
    Still   (W129)

WEBER, DENNIS
  Christ The Lord Is Risen Today
    *Easter,anthem
    SATB oct SINGSPIR ZJP-3529 $.30
                                 (W130)

WEBER, LUDWIG (1891-1947)
  Aus Hartem Weh *Adv
    SATBB,acap (med) sc SCHOTTS
    C 32 903 s.p.   (W131)

  Herr Christe, Komm In Unsre Not
    *Adv,mot
    men cor sc SCHOTTS CHBL 6 s.p.
                                 (W132)
    2-4pt mix cor,acap (easy) sc
    SCHOTTS C 33 472 s.p.   (W133)

WEBER, NORBERT
  O Salutaris Hostia
    [Lat] 4pt mix cor,opt org,strings
    BOHM s.p.   (W134)

WEBSTER
  In The Sweet By And By *anthem
    (Brown, Charles F.) SB WORD CS-2579
    $.30 see from OLD RUGGED CROSS,
    THE   (W135)

WEDDING BANQUET, THE see Winter, Sister
  Miriam Therese

WEDDING PSALM, A see Bryant

WEDDING RESPONSES (FOR THE MARRIAGE OF
  H.R.H. THE PRINCESS ANNE AND
  CAPTAIN MARK PHILLIPS IN
  WESTMINSTER ABBEY, 14 NOVEMBER,

1973) see Guest, Douglas

WEEDEN
  Sunlight *anthem/gospel
    (DeCou, Harold) SATB oct SINGSPIR
    ZJP-8112 $.30   (W136)

WEEK BEFORE, THE see Burroughs, Bob

WEELKES
  Magnificat And Nunc Dimittis
    *Magnif/Nunc
    SATB,acap OXFORD OCM S605   (W137)

WEELKES, THOMAS (ca. 1575-1623)
  Boy Was Born, A *Adv/Xmas
    (Fettke) SSATB,acap oct LILLENAS
    AN-6044 $.25   (W138)

  Collected Anthems *CCU
    cor STAINER 3.8923.8 $20.00 (W139)

  Let Thy Merciful Ears
    SATB,acap EGTVED KB30 s.p. contains
    also: Tye, Christopher, How Still
    And Peaceful; Hilton, John (The
    Younger), Lord, For Thy Tender
    Mercy's Sake   (W140)

  Let Thy Merciful Ears, O Lord
    (Talmadge) SSAA BRODT HC 8 $.25
                                 (W141)

  Lord Arise
    SSAATBB STAINER 3.0840.1 $.50
                                 (W142)

  Lord, To Thee I Make My Moan
    (Gronquist, Robert) SAATB,acap
    KERBY 10379-904 $.45   (W143)

WEERBECKE, GASPAR VAN (ca. 1445- ?)
  O Lord, Our God *Gen
    (Ehret, Walter) SATB,acap (med)
    PRESSER 312-41070 $.40   (W144)

WEHLE, GERHARD FURCHTEGOTT (1884-1974)
  Angelico Da Fiesole *Op.33
    men cor,S solo,pno,fl,2horn,
    strings,timp,opt harp RIES (W145)

  De Profundis *Op.17
    4pt wom cor,S/T solo,pno,2horn,
    strings,harp RIES   (W146)

WEHR, DAVID A. (1934-   )
  Lord Of All Being, Throned Afar
    SATB,hndbl GRAY HCS 21 $.30 (W147)

WEIB, WAS WEINEST DU? see Schutz,
  Heinrich

WEIGL, KARL (1881-1949)
  Early Easter Morning *Easter
    SATB BELWIN 2306 $.30   (W148)

  Two Religious Choruses Of Our Time
    *CC2U
    SATB,pno AM.COMP.AL. $4.40   (W149)

WEIGL, VALLY
  Benediction
    SATB,acap AM.COMP.AL. $1.38 (W150)

  Christchild's Lullaby
    2pt wom cor AM.COMP.AL. $.83 (W151)

  Christmas In The Holy Land *Xmas
    SATB,acap AM.COMP.AL. $1.10 (W152)

  Easter Morning *see Soli Deo Gloria

  Hear Ye, All Ye Peoples
    SATB,SATB soli,pno AM.COMP.AL.
    $4.40   (W153)

  Let Down The Bars, O Death
    TTBB,pno AM.COMP.AL. $.83   (W154)

  O Seed Of God In Humankind
    SATB,acap AM.COMP.AL. $1.38 (W155)

  Psalm 130
    SSA,T solo,pno AM.COMP.AL. $3.30
                                 (W156)

  Soli Deo Gloria
    "Easter Morning" SATB,org
    AM.COMP.AL. $1.38   (W157)

  Thou Art The Way
    SATB,acap AM.COMP.AL. $3.30 (W158)
    SATB,org AM.COMP.AL. $4.40   (W159)

  To Zion
    SSA,Bar solo,pno AM.COMP.AL. $4.40
                                 (W160)

  When The Song Of The Angels Is
    Stilled
    SATB,acap AM.COMP.AL. $.83   (W161)

WEIGLE
  I Have Found A Hiding Place (composed
    with Muller)
    SSATB oct BENSON S4140 $.30 (W162)

  I Sing Of Thee (composed with Muller)
    (Young) 2pt oct BENSON S4144 $.35
                                 (W163)

WEIHE DES TAGES see Kronberg, G.

WEIHNACHT see Genzmer, Harald

WEIHNACHT see Mullich, Hermann

WEIHNACHTEN see Kuhnhold

WEIHNACHTEN see Mendelssohn-Bartholdy, Felix

WEIHNACHTEN "DU DARFST ES WIEDER SPUREN HEUT" see Zipp, Friedrich

WEIHNACHTEN I *CCU
   4-5pt mix cor DOBLINGER TH 14 sc
   s.p., voc pt s.p. contains works
   by: Aldenburger, M.; Vulpius, M.;
   Helder, B.   (W164)

WEIHNACHTEN II *CCU
   5pt mix cor DOBLINGER TH 24 sc s.p.,
   voc pt s.p. contains works by:
   Aldenburger, M.; Vulpius, M. and
   others   (W165)

WEIHNACHTEN MIT JOHANN SEBASTIAN BACH
   see Bach, Johann Sebastian

WEIHNACHTLICHE LIED-MESSE *Xmas,Mass
   (Biebl, Franz) 4pt mix cor,solo BOHM
   sc s.p., cor pts s.p.   (W166)

WEIHNACHTS-ANTHEM "SIEHE, ICH
   VERKUNDIGE EUCH GROSSE FREUDE" see
   Purcell, Henry

WEIHNACHTS-KANTILENE see Reutter,
   Hermann

WEIHNACHTS-SINGEBUCH, PART I *CCU,Xmas
   (Lohmann, A., Diewald, J.) unis/SATD,
   opt inst CHRIS 5083-32 s.p.   (W167)

WEIHNACHTS-SINGEBUCH, PART II *CCU,
   Xmas
   (Lohmann, A.; Diewald, J.) unis/SATD,
   opt inst CHRIS 50834-35 s.p. (W168)

WEIHNACHTSCHORALE AUS DEM
   WEIHNACHTSORATORIUM see Bach,
   Johann Sebastian

WEIHNACHTSGESCHICHTE see Hessenberg,
   Kurt

WEIHNACHTSKANTATE see Briner

WEIHNACHTSKANTATE see Hessenberg, Kurt

WEIHNACHTSKANTATE see Hoffer, Paul Marx

WEIHNACHTSKANTATE see Knab, Armin

WEIHNACHTSKANTATE FUR JUNGE LEUTE see
   Wusthoff, Klaus

WEIHNACHTSKANTATEN see Esterhazy, Pal

WEIHNACHTSLICHT "NUN WARD ZU TROST UNS
   ALLEN" see Lang, Hans

WEIHNACHTSLIED see Kuhnhold

WEIHNACHTSLIED see Schultz

WEIHNACHTSLIED V.J. 1557 see Calvisius,
   Sethus

WEIHNACHTSLIED "WIR SEYND GEG'N EUCH
   WAHRHAFTE FREUND" see Werner,
   Gregor Joseph

WEIHNACHTSLIEDER *CCU,Xmas,carol/folk
   (Dite, Louis) mix cor,org,opt
   5strings&fl2horn WEINBERGER s.p.,
   ipa voc sc, cor pts includes Bach
   chorales   (W169)

WEIHNACHTSLIEDER see Brautigam, Helmut

WEIHNACHTSLIEDER *CC39U
   [Ger] unis,acap (very easy) NAGELS
   EN 1705 s.p.   (W170)

WEIHNACHTSLIEDER NACH OSTDEUTSCHEN
   WEISEN see Kuntz, Michael

WEIHNACHTSMESSE see Krieg, Franz

WEIHNACHTSMESSE see Wassmer, Berthold

WEIHNACHTSMESSE IN G see Kagerer, Chr.
   Lor.

WEIHNACHTSMOTETTE see Silcher,
   Friedrich

WEIHNACHTSMUSIK see Deutschmann,
   Gerhard

WEIHNACHTSZEIT see Kutzer, Ernst

WEIL
   No Tears Have We To Shed
   (Boyd) SATB SCHIRM.G LG51795 $.40
                        (W171)
WEIL DU MEIN GOTT UND VATER BIST see
   Scheidt, Samuel

WEIL UNSER TROST, DER HERRE CHRIST see
   Zentner, Johannes

WEINBERG, JACOB (1883-1956)
   Life Of Moses, The *Bibl/ora
   cor,soli,orch SAC.MUS.PR. voc sc
   $6.00, sc,cor pts rental, ipr
                        (W172)

   Prayer Of Thanksgiving
   mix cor oct SAC.MUS.PR. 314 $.45
                        (W173)

WEINER, LAZAR (1897-   )
   Zecher L'maaseh
   [Heb] cor (Friday Evening Service)
   TRANSCON. TCL 890 $4.00   (W174)

WEINREICH, WALTRAUT
   Drei Adventslieder *CC3U,Adv
   3-4pt mix cor MERSEBURG EM494
                        (W175)

WEINTRAUB, HIRSCH A. (1811-1882)
   Schire Beth Adonai *CCU,Fest/Rosh
   Ha-Shanah/Sab-Morn/Yom Kippur
   mix cor,cantor SAC.MUS.PR.
   S.M.P. 19-21 $20.00 three
   volumes, bound in three books
                        (W176)

WEIRICH, AUGUST
   Ave Maria
   [Lat] 4pt mix cor,acap sc,cor pts
   BOHM s.p.   (W177)

   Ecce Sacerdos
   [Lat] 4pt mix cor,acap BOHM s.p.
                        (W178)
   Missa Solemnis In Honorem Purissimi
   Cordis Beatae Mariae Virginis
   *Mass
   [Lat] 4pt mix cor,org,strings,
   2horn,trom,2ob/2clar (E flat maj)
   sc,cor pts BOHM s.p., ipa   (W179)

   Zwei Asperges Me *CC2U
   [Lat] 4pt mix cor,acap sc,cor pts
   BOHM s.p.   (W180)

   Zwei Vidi Aquam *CC2U,Easter
   [Lat] 4pt mix cor,acap sc,cor pts
   BOHM s.p.   (W181)

WEIS, FLEMMING (1898-   )
   Beatus Homo (from Liber Proverbiorum)
   see Three Motets

   Conserva, Fili Mi (from Liber
   Proverbiorum)
   see Three Motets

   Fili Me (from Liber Proverbiorum)
   see Three Motets

   Laudate Dominum
   SATB EGTVED MK14, 15 s.p.   (W182)

   Levavi Oculos Meos Ad Montes
   SATB EGTVED KB216 s.p.   (W183)

   Three Motets (from Liber
   Proverbiorum) Bibl/mot
   SATB,acap cmplt ed EGTVED KB116
   s.p.
      contains: Beatus Homo; Conserva,
      Fili Mi; Fili Me   (W184)

WEISMANN, WILHELM (1900-   )
   Hoch Vom Himmel Komm Ich Her
   SATB,high solo,org,treb inst
   SCHWEIZER. SK 63.03-4 s.p. see
   also MUSIKBEILAGE ZUM
   "EVANGELISCHEN KIRCHENCHOR 1963"
                        (W185)

WEIS-OSTBORN, RUDOLF VON
   Ecce Sacerdos
   mix cor,org,horn KRENN 1.52 (W186)

WEISS
   Psalm 116
   mix cor s.p. sc HEER 351, cor pts
   HEER 351A   (W187)

   Psalm 118
   mix cor s.p. sc HEER 350, cor pts
   HEER 350A   (W188)

WEISS, EWALD
   O Dass Doch Bald Dein Feuer Brennte
   SAT/SAB/2pt,S solo,opt treb inst
   HANSSLER 14.219 s.p.   (W189)

   Wo Gott Der Herr Nicht Bei Uns Halt
   SAT/SAB/SA,treb inst,opt bass inst
   HANSSLER 14.193 s.p.   (W190)

WEISS, MANFRED (1935-   )
   Drei Psalmen *CC3U,Psalm
   mix cor,acap HOFMEISTER DVFM7630
   s.p.   (W191)

WEISS MIR EIN BLUMLEIN BLAUE
   see Der Morgenstern Ist Aufgegangen

WEISSE
   Resurrection Fanfare (composed with
   Coggin) *Easter,anthem
   SATB (easy) oct BROADMAN 4545-44
   $.30   (W192)

WEISSEL
   Lift Up Your Heads (composed with
   Newbury, Kent A.) *anthem
   unis (easy) oct BROADMAN 4554-69
   $.30   (W193)

WELCH, RAY
   Be Still, My Soul, And Listen
   *anthem
   SSATBB oct SINGSPIR ZJP-7299 $.30
                        (W194)

WELCKER, MAX
   Aeterne Rex
   see Vier Hymnen Fur Die
   Fronleichnamsprozession

   Caligaverunt *Op.162a,No.4, Holywk
   [Lat] 4pt mix cor,acap sc,cor pts
   BOHM s.p.   (W195)

   Deutsche Seelenmesse *see Herr, Lass
   Sie Ruhn Im Frieden

   Die Vier Choral-Credo *CC4U,Greg
   [Lat] 4pt mix cor,org sc,cor pts
   BOHM s.p.   (W196)

   Gloria Tibi Domine *Op.183, Mass
   [Lat] 4pt mix cor,org,opt 5strings
   sc,cor pts BOHM s.p., ipr   (W197)

   Herr, Lass Sie Ruhn Im Frieden
   *Op.134, Req
   "Deutsche Seelenmesse" [Ger] 1-2pt,
   org sc,cor pts BOHM s.p.   (W198)

   Inimicitias Ponam *Op.204a
   [Lat] 4pt mix cor,org/harmonium sc,
   cor pts BOHM s.p.   (W199)

   Ite Ad Joseph *Op.199, Mass
   [Lat] 2-4pt mix cor,org sc,cor pts
   BOHM s.p.   (W200)

   Magnificat
   see Zwei Magnificat

   Magnificat
   see Zwei Magnificat

   Requiem *Op.106
   [Lat] unis jr cor/unis wom cor,org
   sc,cor pts BOHM s.p.   (W201)

   Requiem Mit Libera *Op.200
   [Lat] SA&opt Bar,org sc,cor pts
   BOHM s.p.   (W202)

   Sacris Solemniis
   see Vier Hymnen Fur Die
   Fronleichnamsprozession

   Salutis Humanae Sator
   see Vier Hymnen Fur Die
   Fronleichnamsprozession

   Sursum Corda *Op.140, Mass
   [Lat] 4pt mix cor,acap sc,cor pts
   BOHM s.p.   (W203)

   Veni Creator Spiritus
   see Faist, Anton, Veni Creator
   Spiritus

   Verbum Supernum
   see Vier Hymnen Fur Die
   Fronleichnamsprozession

   Vexilla Regis *Op.162a,No.3, hymn
   [Lat] 4pt mix cor,acap sc,cor pts
   BOHM s.p.   (W204)

   Vier Hymnen Fur Die
   Fronleichnamsprozession
   [Lat] 4pt mix cor,opt 5brass sc,cor
   pts BOHM s.p.
      contains: Aeterne Rex, Op.163a,
      No.4; Sacris Solemniis,
      Op.163a,No.1; Salutis Humanae
      Sator, Op.163a,No.3; Verbum
      Supernum, Op.163a,No.2   (W205)

   Vier Pange Lingua *Op.194,No.1-4,
   CC4U
   [Lat] SA/SAT/SAB,org sc,cor pts
   BOHM s.p.   (W206)

   Vier Tantum Ergo *Op.181,No.1-4,
   CC4U
   [Lat] 4pt mix cor,acap sc,cor pts
   BOHM s.p.   (W207)

   Zwei Magnificat
   [Lat] sc,cor pts BOHM s.p.
      contains: Magnificat (4pt mix
      cor,org); Magnificat (2pt mix
      cor,org)   (W208)

WELCKER, MAX (cont'd.)

Zwei Pange Lingua Und Tantum Ergo
*Op.219a, CC3U
[Lat] 4pt mix cor,opt org sc,cor
pts BOHM s.p.   (W209)

WELCOME see Nno

WELCOME ALL WONDERS IN ONE SIGHT see
Roff, Joseph

WELCOME, DEAREST JESUS see Kemp, Helen

WELCOME, HAPPY MORNING see Bowie,
William

WELCOME, HAPPY MORNING! see Havergal

WELCOME HOME CHILDREN see King

WELCOME THE CHRIST CHILD see Bennett,
F. Roy

WELCOME TO THE TABLE see Wetzler,
Robert

WELCOME YULE see Bissell, Keith W.

WELCOME YULE see Gritton, Eric

WELCOME, YULE see Owen

WELCOME YULE see Paviour, Paul

WE'LL ALL SHOUT TOGETHER see McNair,
Jacqueline Hanna

WELL DONE, THOU GOOD AND FAITHFUL
SERVANT see Fox, Baynard

WE'LL MEET THE DAWN WITH A SONG see
Wink

WE'LL TALK IT OVER see Stanphill, Ira
F.

WE'LL WORK TILL JESUS COMES *anthem
(Finley) SATB oct BROADMAN 4554-95
$.30   (W210)

WELLSPRING OF BOUNTY see Hooper, Edmund

WELSEY, BURROUGH
Behold The Savior Of Mankind
(composed with Burroughs, Bob)
*anthem
SATB (easy) oct BROADMAN 4554-63
$.30   (W211)

WELTENHOFFNUNG, MILDE, SUSSE see
Piechler, Arthur

WEM ZEIT WIE EWIGZEIT see Zoll, Paul

WENN ABER DER TROSTER KOMMEN WIRD see
Wenzel, Eberhard

WENN CHRISTUS, DER HERR see Handel,
George Frideric

WENN DER HERR DIE GEFANGENEN ZIONS
ERLOSEN WIRD see Graap, Lothar

WENN DER HERR DIE GEFANGENEN ZIONS
ERLOSEN WIRD see Hessenberg, Kurt

WENN EIN STARKER GEWAPPNETER see
Brahms, Johannes

WENN EUCH, SCHONE MADONNA, MEIN SCHMERZ
NICHT BETRUBET see Arcadelt, Jacob

WENN ICH EINMAL DER HERRGOTT see Binder

WENN ICH EINMAL SOLL SCHEIDEN see Bach,
Johann Sebastian

WENN ICH EINMAL SOLL SCHEIDEN see
Hassler, Hans Leo

WENN ICH IN TODESNOTEN BIN see Franck,
Melchior

WENN ICH NUR DICH HAB, HERR, ALLEIN see
Lange, Gregor

WENN MEIN STUNDLEIN VORHANDEN IST
see Vulpius, Melchior, Christus Der
Ist Mein Leben
men cor,acap TONOS 5632 s.p.   (W212)

WENN MEIN STUNDLEIN VORHANDEN IST see
Gumpelzhaimer, Adam

WENN MEIN STUNDLEIN VORHANDEN IST see
Hassler, Hans Leo

WENN MICH DIE SUNDEN KRANKEN see
Telemann, Georg Philipp

WENN WIR IN HOCHSTEN NOTEN
see Tod Und Ewigkeit

WENN WIR IN HOCHSTEN NOTEN SEIN see
Brahms, Johannes

WENN WIR IN HOCHSTEN NOTEN SEIN see
Schein, Johann Hermann

WENN WIR IN HOCHSTEN NOTEN SEIN see
Serranus, Johann Baptista

WENNERBERG, GUNNAR (1817-1901)
Let Us Now Our Voices Raise
(Hokanson) SSA (easy) FITZSIMONS
3078 $.20   (W213)

WENZEL, EBERHARD (1896-   )
Chorale Cantata *cant,Contemp
unis&mix cor,inst CHANTRY COC 611
$.50, ipa   (W214)

Das Gottesjahr *see Wir Haben Seinen
Stern Gesehen "Trittst Du Wieder
Vor Die Nacht"   (W215)

Deutsche Messe *Mass
[Ger] 4pt mix cor,acap MERSEBURG
EM239   (W216)

Die Geschichte Von Daniel Und Den
Lowen In Der Grube
treb cor,narrator,fl,perc,pno
MERSEBURG EM534   (W217)

Komm Her, Mit Fleiss Zu Schauen
SAT/SAB,opt treb inst HANSSLER
14.170 s.p.   (W218)

Lobe Den Herren, Meine Seele (from
Psalmtriptychon)
SA&unis men cor,2trp&trom/org/inst
(med) BAREN. BA6315   (W219)

O Konig Jesu Christe
SAT/SAB/SA,opt bass inst HANSSLER
14.203 s.p.   (W220)

Psalm 67
see Psalmtriptychon

Psalm 103
see Psalmtriptychon

Psalm 130
see Psalmtriptychon

Psalmtriptychon
SATB,org/2trp&2trom (med diff) sc,
cor pts BAREN. BA5433 s.p., ipa
contains: Psalm 67; Psalm 103;
Psalm 130   (W221)

Responsories For The Church Year
*CCU,liturg
mix cor CHANTRY LIT 714 $1.25
                                 (W222)

Responsory For Lent, "He Was Brought
As A Lamb" *anthem,Contemp
cor oct CHANTRY LIT 737 $.15 (W223)

Responsory For Reformation *liturg
mix cor CHANTRY LIT 672 $.25 (W224)

Responsory For Reformation Day
*anthem,Contemp
cor oct CHANTRY LIT 673 $.25 (W225)

Wenn Aber Der Troster Kommen Wird
SATB sc HANSSLER HE 7.146 s.p.
                                 (W226)

Wir Haben Seinen Stern Gesehen
"Trittst Du Wieder Vor Die Nacht"
mix cor sc SCHOTTS C 36 177 s.p.
see from Das Gottesjahr   (W227)

WER GOTT ZUM FREUND NICHT HAT see Zipp,
Friedrich

WER KANN DIR, HERRE see Pepping, Ernst

WER MAG DICH, HERRE GOTT see Pepping,
Ernst

WER MICH LIEBET, DER WIRD MEIN WORT
HALTEN see Vulpius, Melchior

WER NUN DEN LIEBEN GOTT LASST WALTEN
see Bach, Johann Sebastian

WER NUR DEN LIEBEN GOTT LASST WALTEN
see Berghorn, Alfred

WER NUR DEN LIEBEN GOTT LASST WALTEN
see Neumark, Georg

WER UNTER DEM SCHIRM DES ALLERHOCHSTEN
SITZT see Bergholz

WER UNTER DEM SCHIRM DES HOCHSTEN SITZT
see Eglin, Arthur

WER WALZET UNS DEN STEIN see
Hammerschmidt, Andreas

WER WEISS, WIE NAHE MIR MEIN ENDE
men cor,acap TONOS 5617 s.p.   (W228)

WE'RE GOING TO SING see Mayfield, Larry

WE'RE MARCHING TO ZION *anthem
(Cram, James D.) SATB FINE ARTS
CM 1004 $.35   (W229)

WE'RE MARCHING TO ZION see Lowry,
Robert

WERE YOU THERE? *Easter/Gd.Fri.,
anthem/spir
(DeCou, Harold) SATB oct SINGSPIR
ZJP-3518 $.30   (W230)
(Dorfmuller, Joachim) SSA/SAB MUSIKK
                                 (W231)
(Lovan) SATB (easy) oct BROADMAN
4531-61 $.30   (W232)
(Welch, John) SATB STUDIO V753 $.30
                                 (W233)

WERE YOU THERE! see Grant, Don

WERKTAG "WIR WANDERN NUN SCHON VIEL
HUNDERT JAHR" see Burkhard Willy

WERLE, FLOYD EDWARDS (1929-   )
Aldersgate Prayer
SATB BOURNE B231092-358 $.50 (W234)

Introits And Responses *CCU,cor-
resp/Introit
SATB BOURNE B217778-358 $1.00
                                 (W235)

Reverse Paternoster
2pt BOURNE B210963-352 $.50 (W236)

WERNER
Dir, Dir Jehova, Will Ich Singen
SAT/SAB/2pt,opt 2treb inst HANSSLER
14.237 s.p.   (W237)

Drei Paulus-Motetten
HANSSLER 7.171 s.p.
contains: Irret Euch Nicht, Gott
Lasst Sich Nicht Spotten,
Op.51,No.3 (SSAATTBB); Lieben
Bruder, Schicket Euch In Die
Zeit, Op.51,No.2 (SAATTBB);
Unsre Trubsal, Die Zeitlich Und
Leicht Ist, Op.51,No.1 (SATB)
                                 (W238)

Herr Jesu Christ, Du Hochstes Gut
SAT/SAB,treb inst,opt bass inst
HANSSLER 14.158 s.p.   (W239)

Irret Euch Nicht, Gott Lasst Sich
Nicht Spotten
see Drei Paulus-Motetten

Komm, Heiliger Geist, Erfull Die
Herzen
SA&opt TB HANSSLER 14.124 s.p.
                                 (W240)

Lieben Bruder, Schicket Euch In Die
Zeit
see Drei Paulus-Motetten

Psalmentriptychon *Op.50, CC3U
SATB,SB soli,2fl,3ob,2bsn,2horn,
2trp HANSSLER 10, 317 rental
                                 (W241)

Unsre Trubsal, Die Zeitlich Und
Leicht Ist
see Drei Paulus-Motetten

Veni, Sancte Spiritus *Op.44, Pent/
Whitsun,ora
SATB,SB soli,2fl,3ob,2bsn,2horn,
2trp,strings HANSSLER 10.316
rental   (W242)

WERNER, FRITZ (1898-   )
Lobet Den Herren, Alle, Die Ihn Ehren
unis&SAT/SAB (contains also: Allein
Gott In Der Hoh Sei Ehr)
SCHWEIZER. SK 67.01 s.p. see also
MUSIKBEILAGE ZUM "EVANGELISCHEN
KIRCHENCHOR 1967"   (W243)

Nun Danket Alle Gott
unis&SAT/SAB SCHWEIZER. SK 70.08
s.p. see also MUSIKBEILAGE ZUM
"EVANGELISCHEN KIRCHENCHOR 1970"
                                 (W244)

Zeuch An Die Macht, Du Arm Des Herrn
SAT/SAB/SATB SCHWEIZER. SK 61.05
s.p. see also MUSIKBEILAGE ZUM
"EVANGELISCHEN KIRCHENCHOR 1961"
                                 (W245)

WERNER, GREGOR JOSEPH (1695-1766)
Weihnachtslied "Wir Seynd Geg'n Euch
Wahrhafte Freund" *Xmas,cant
(Falvy, Zoltan) SATB,SATB soli,org,
strings (easy) min sc SCHOTTS
ETP 1084 s.p., ipa   (W246)

WESCOTT, STEVE
Gift Of Light, A *anthem
SATB,org AUGSBURG 11-1668 $.30
                                 (W247)

WESLEY
Give To The Winds Thy Fears (composed
with Powell) *anthem
SATB (easy) oct BROADMAN 4545-62
$.30   (W248)

WESLEY (cont'd.)

It Came Upon The Midnight Clear
*Xmas,carol
(Tostevin) SATB,acap (easy) OXFORD
84.240 $.30   (W249)

Jesus, Lover Of My Soul
(March; Loes, H.D.) SATB oct GOSPEL
05 TM 0104 $.20   (W250)

O How Happy Are They (composed with
Peninger) *anthem
SATB (easy) oct BROADMAN 4545-68
$.30   (W251)

WESLEY, CHARLES (1757-1834)
Christ, The Lord Is Risen Today
*Easter,anthem
SATB oct BROADMAN 4562-36 $.35   (W252)

SATB (easy) oct BROADMAN 4551-67
$.30   (W253)

(Carmichael, Ralph) SATB,brass
LEXICON CS-2505 $.40, ipa see
from NOW HEAR THIS   (W254)

WESLEY, S.S.
Blessed Be The God And Father
mix cor BANKS MUS YS 159 $.30   (W255)

Lead Me Lord
mix cor BANKS MUS YS 510 $.20   (W256)

Thou Wilt Keep Him In Perfect Peace
(Comley) mix cor BANKS MUS YS 1536
$.30   (W257)

Wash Me Thoroughly From My Wickedness
mix cor BANKS MUS YS 681 $.25   (W258)

WESLEY, SAMUEL SEBASTIAN JR.
(1810-1878)
Church's One Foundation, The *anthem
(Rasley, John M.) SATB oct SINGSPIR
ZJP-7256 $.30   (W259)

WESLEY, SAMUEL SR. (1766-1837)
Church's One Foundation, The *anthem
(Owens) SATB oct LILLENAS AN-2382
$.30   (W260)

Love Divine (composed with Zundel,
[John])
(Hall) TB,pno/org oct BENSON S4195
$.30   (W261)

WESLEY'S PSALM 150 see Lovelace, Austin
C.

WESTBROOK
Don't Knock (Just Walk Right In)
*see Staples

WESTON, DAVID
It Shall Flow Like A River *Bibl/
cant
SATB,S solo,opt 3trp&2-3trom&timp&
harp voc sc GOSPEL 05 TM 0473
$1.50, sc GOSPEL 05 TM 0385
$18.00   (W262)

WESTRA, EVERT
Be Welcome, O Emanuel *anthem,
Contemp
cor oct CHANTRY COA 7349 $.35   (W263)

Lift Up Your Heads, O Ye Gates
*anthem,Contemp
SSATTB oct CHANTRY COA 6521 $.35   (W264)

Lord Is My Shepherd, The *anthem,
Contemp
SATB oct CHANTRY COA 7144 $.30   (W265)

Lord, Your God, Will Come, The
*anthem,Contemp
SATB oct CHANTRY COA 6523 $.30   (W266)

Rejoice In The Lord Alway *anthem,
Contemp
SATB oct CHANTRY COA 6522 $.25   (W267)

WETHERILL
Be Still And Know That I Am God
SATB SHAWNEE A5693 $.30   (W268)

WETZEL, L.
Ave Maria
[Lat] SSAATTBB,acap (med)
FITZSIMONS 2020 $.20   (W269)

WETZLER
Trilogy Of Praise
SATB SCHIRM.G 11977 $.55   (W270)

WETZLER, ROBERT
All Things Are Thine
2pt mix cor TRIUNE TUM 109 $.35 see
also LET THE WORLD SING   (W271)

And Darkness Fell *Lent
SATB ART MAST 266 $.40   (W272)

WETZLER, ROBERT (cont'd.)

Carol Of Thanksgiving *Thanks
SATB,acap ART MAST 269 $.40 (W273)

Christ Is Risen, Risen Indeed
*Easter/Pent
SATB&unis,3trp ART MAST 161 $.50   (W274)

Come, Jesus, Come
2pt/SAB ART MAST 237 $.35   (W275)

Come, Take My Yoke *anthem
SATB,org AUGSBURG 11-1655 $.35   (W276)

For The Blessings Of The Field
*Thanks
SATB/unis ART MAST 165 $.35   (W277)

He Comes! He Comes! *Adv/Xmas
SATB,bvl ART MAST 198 $.35   (W278)

Jesus
2pt (easy) FISCHER,C CM 7825 (W279)

Let The Heavens Rejoice *Adv/Xmas
SATB,acap ART MAST 154 $.35 (W280)

Lord, We Are Glad For Those Who Laugh
*anthem
unis,kbd AUGSBURG 11-1663 $.30   (W281)

Love Came Down At Christmas *anthem
SATB AUGSBURG 11-1669 $.30   (W282)

Man Of Mercy *Easter/Pent
SATB ART MAST 209 $.40   (W283)

Mary *anthem
SATB,org,opt fl,bvl AUGSBURG
11-1681 $.25   (W284)

O Brother Man
SATB ART MAST 101 $.40   (W285)

O Perfect Life Of Love *Lent
SATB ART MAST 106 $.30   (W286)

Peace Be With You *Easter/Pent
SATB ART MAST 178 $.35   (W287)

Peace On Earth
SATB ART MAST 214 $.40   (W288)

Praise For This Day
2pt ART MAST 220 $.35   (W289)

Psalm 128 *anthem
SATB,kbd AUGSBURG 11-0646 $.35   (W290)

Rejoice! The Savior Is Born *Adv/
Xmas
SATB,acap ART MAST 246 $.30 (W291)

Shepherds Come A-Running *anthem
unis/SA,kbd AUGSBURG 11-1709 $.30   (W292)

Sing We With A Merry Heart *Easter/
Pent
SATB,acap ART MAST 120 $.40 (W293)
1-2pt,hndbl ART MAST 193 $.35, ipa (W294)

Sing Ye, Sing Noel *Adv/Xmas
SATB,acap ART MAST 124 $.40 (W295)
unis,hndbl ART MAST 243 $.40 (W296)

Take, Believe *Commun
SATB&unis/2pt,fl ART MAST 183 $.40   (W297)

Thy Praise We Sing
1-2pt ART MAST 207 $.30   (W298)

We Have Seen The Lord *anthem
SATB,org AUGSBURG 11-1705 $.35   (W299)

Welcome To The Table *Commun
SATB/unis/2pt ART MAST 184 $.30   (W300)

Wondrous Nativity *Xmas
SATB,acap ART MAST 273 $.50 (W301)

WE'VE A STORY TO TELL TO THE NATIONS
see Nichol, H. Ernest

WE'VE GOT A LOT TO LIVE FOR see Roesch

WEYSE
Christmas Brings Joy *Xmas
(Russell) SATB,opt hndbl&tamb PRO
ART 2790 $.35   (W302)

WHAT A FRIEND *anthem
(Bass) SATB,med solo FINE ARTS
CM 1072 $.35   (W303)

WHAT A FRIEND WE HAVE IN JESUS
see He Lives!

WHAT A FRIEND WE HAVE IN JESUS see
Converse, Charles Crozat

WHAT A FRIEND WE HAVE IN JESUS see
Peninger

WHAT A JOY see Morrison, Kenneth L.

WHAT A WONDERFUL SAVIOR! see Hoffman

WHAT ARE THOSE BELLS? see Russell,
Olive Nelson

WHAT CAN I GIVE HIM? see Elder, Dorothy
Kosanke

WHAT CAN I GIVE HIM? see Jones,
Marjorie

WHAT CHILD IS THIS *Xmas,anthem/carol
see Christmas Choir Melodies
(Fenstermaker, John) mix cor,acap/fl/
org MCAFEE M1085 $.40   (W304)
(Johnson, Norman) SATB,opt harp oct
SINGSPIR ZJP-3002 $.30   (W305)
(Krogstad, Bob) SATB,opt 2fl&ob&
2horn&3trp&3trom&3vln&vla&vcl&bvl&
timp&perc&harp voc sc GOSPEL
05 TM 0345 $.35, sc GOSPEL
05 TM 0346 $15.00   (W306)

WHAT CHILD IS THIS see Cole, William

WHAT CHILD IS THIS? see Swenson, Warren

WHAT CHILD IS THIS see Young, Carlton
R.

WHAT CHRISTMAS MEANS TO ME see
Plunkett, Bonnie

WHAT COLOR IS GOD'S SKIN?
SATB UP WITH 6507 $.40   (W307)

WHAT DO ALL OF THESE THINGS MEAN? see
Kirby, Charles

WHAT GIVES YOU THE RIGHT see
Carmichael, Ralph

WHAT GOD IS LIKE TO HIM I SERVE? see
Sims, Ezra

WHAT GRACE IS THIS! see Peterson, John
W.

WHAT IF THE FAINT MUST DIE? see
Billings, William

WHAT IS A MAN? see Jeppesen, Knud

WHAT IS EASTER? see Wood, Marilyn

WHAT IS MAN? see Holde, Arthur

WHAT IS MAN'S CHIEF PURPOSE? see Burke,
John

WHAT IS THIS FRAGRANCE *Xmas
(Hill, Harry) SSA (med easy) WATERLOO
$.30   (W308)

WHAT IS THIS FRAGRANCE see Terry,
Richard Runciman

WHAT IS THIS WONDROUS, FRAGRANT AIR?
*Adv/Xmas
(Sateren, Leland) SATB,acap ART MAST
143 $.40   (W309)

WHAT LOVE IS THIS see Parks

WHAT OFFERING SHALL I BRING? see
Elmore, Robert [Hall]

WHAT RETURN SHALL I MAKE? see Cromie,
Marguerite Biggs, Quid Retribuam

WHAT SHALL I GIVE THEE, MASTER? see
Grimes

WHAT SHALL I RENDER TO THE LORD see
Jones, Robert

WHAT SHALL WE RENDER UNTO THE LORD see
Latrobe, Christian I.

WHAT STAR IS THIS? *Xmas,anthem
(Johnson, Norman) SATB oct SINGSPIR
ZJP-3022 $.30   (W310)

WHAT SWEETER MUSIC CAN WE BRING see
Drayton, Paul

WHAT THE WORLD NEEDS see Peninger

WHAT THINK YE OF CHRIST? see Rasley

WHAT TIDINGS, MESSENGER? *Adv/Xmas
(Boody, Charles) 3pt,bells,tamb,
drums, 2 Drone Instruments ART MAST
141 $.30   (W311)

WHAT TONGUE CAN TELL see Angell

WHAT TONGUE CAN TELL see Angell, Warren
M.

WHAT WILL YOUR ANSWER BE? see Hayford

WHAT WONDROUS LOVE see Tyler

WHAT WONDROUS LOVE IS THIS
  SATB,Bar solo,acap GIA G1940 $.50
                                    (W312)

WHAT WONDROUS LOVE IS THIS see
  Williams, David H.

WHAT WONDROUS SACRED LOVE see Fairchild

WHAT YOU GONNA CALL YOUR PRETTY LITTLE
  BABY? *Xmas,spir
  (Biebl, Franz) [Eng/Ger] mix cor
  (easy) sc SCHOTTS C 43 218 s.p. see
  from Zwei Weihnachtliche Spirituals
                                    (W313)

WHAT'S THE MATTER? see Burroughs, Bob

WHEAR, PAUL WILLIAM (1925-   )
  Three Christmas Carols *CC3U,Xmas,
  carol
  SATB LUDWIG L-1106 $.35   (W314)

WHEN ALL THE WORLD see Hannahs, Roger

WHEN CHRIST WAS BORN see Pears

WHEN CHRIST WAS BORN see Pears, James
  R.

WHEN CHRIST WAS BORN see Pike, Harry
  Hale

WHEN CHRIST WAS BORN see Rickard,
  Jeffrey

WHEN CHRIST WAS BORN OF MARY FREE see
  Hooper

WHEN DAILY LIVING SINFULLY see Byrd,
  William, Peccantem Me Quotidie

WHEN DAVID HEARD THAT HIS SON WAS SLAIN
  see Chorbajian, John

WHEN GOD CAME A-VISITING see Rowley,
  Alec

WHEN GOD IS THE HONORED GUEST see
  Denton, James

WHEN GOD THE LORD see Peeters, Flor, In
  Convertendo Dominus

WHEN HE SHALL COME see Pearce

WHEN, HIS SALVATION BRINGING *Palm,
  anthem
  (Peterson, John W.) SA oct SINGSPIR
  ZJP-3501 $.30   (W315)

WHEN I CAN READ MY TITLE CLEAR see
  Lowry

WHEN I CAN READ MY TITLE CLEAR see
  Lowry, Robert

WHEN I MET MY SAVIOR see Allem

WHEN I REMEMBER see Peterson, John W.

WHEN I SEE THE FACE OF JESUS see Pearce

WHEN I SURVEY THE WONDROUS CROSS
  *Easter/Lent,anthem/medley
  (Johnson, Norman) SATB oct SINGSPIR
  ZA-4343 $.30   (W316)
  (Schubert) SATB oct LILLENAS AN-2394
  $.35   (W317)

WHEN I SURVEY THE WONDROUS CROSS see
  Miller

WHEN I SURVEY THE WONDROUS CROSS see
  Peninger

WHEN I SURVEY THE WONDROUS CROSS see
  Watts

WHEN I SURVEY THE WONDROUS CROSS see
  Williams, G.

WHEN I SURVEY THE WONDROUS CROSS see
  Work, John [Wesley]

WHEN I SURVEY THE WONDROUS CROSS see
  Young, Robert H.

WHEN I THINK OF THE CROSS see
  Carmichael, Ralph

WHEN I TRUST THE SAVIOR see Johnson,
  Paul

WHEN IN EVERY SEASON see Theophane,
  Sister M. (Hytrek)

WHEN JESUS CAME TO BIRMINGHAM see
  Kalnins, Janis

WHEN JESUS COMES see Landgrave, Phillip

WHEN JESUS INTO SION RODE see Pasquet,
  Jean

WHEN JESUS SAT AT MEAT see Nicolson

WHEN JESUS WAS A TINY BABE see Traver,
  James Ferris

WHEN JESUS WEPT see Billings, William

WHEN LIGHTS ARE LIT ON CHRISTMAS EVE
  see Knudsen

WHEN LOVE SHINES IN see Hughes

WHEN LOVE SHINES IN see Kirkpatrick

WHEN LOVE WAS BORN *Xmas,anthem
  (Rasley, John M.) SATB oct SINGSPIR
  ZJP-3036 $.30   (W318)

WHEN MARY MAGDALENE see Schein, Johann
  Hermann, Maria Magdalena Et Altera
  Maria

WHEN MORNING GILDS THE SKY see Pike,
  Harry Hale

WHEN MOTHERS OF SALEM
  (Hill, Harry) SATB (med easy)
  WATERLOO $.40   (W319)

WHEN THE CHILD OF MARY CAME see McCabe,
  Michael

WHEN THE COUNSELOR COMES see Bender,
  Jan

WHEN THE CRIMSON SUN HAD SET see
  Pettman, Edgar

WHEN THE LORD CRY HOLY see Hardwicke

WHEN THE LORD DREW NIGH see Goodman,
  Joseph

WHEN THE LORD TURNED AGAIN see
  Billings, William

WHEN THE ROLL IS CALLED UP YONDER
  (Wild, Eric) SATB (med easy) WATERLOO
  $.60   (W320)

WHEN THE ROLL IS CALLED UP YONDER see
  Black

WHEN THE ROLL IS CALLED UP YONDER see
  Black, James M.

WHEN THE SAINTS GO MARCHING IN
  (Wild, Eric) SATB,pno BERANDOL
  BER1679 $.50   (W321)

WHEN THE SAVIOUR CHRIST IS BORN
  see Polish Christmas Carols

WHEN THE SONG OF THE ANGELS IS STILLED
  see Weigl, Vally

WHEN THE SUN RISES *anthem
  (Beckham) SATB oct BROADMAN 4551-93
  $.30   (W322)

WHEN THE TERMS OF PEACE ARE MADE see
  Boyd

WHEN THE WHOLE HEART OF MAN see Rowley,
  Alec

WHEN THERE'S LOVE AT HOME see Denton,
  James

WHEN THERE'S LOVE AT HOME see
  McNaughton, J.

WHEN TO THE TEMPLE MARY WENT see
  Eccard, Johannes

WHEN WAS JESUS BORN? *Xmas
  (Ehret) SATB SCHIRM.G LG51765 $.35
                                    (W323)
  (Ehret) SA SCHIRM.G LG51766 $.35
                                    (W324)

WHEN WE ALL GET TO HEAVEN see Allen,
  Lanny

WHEN WE ALL GET TO HEAVEN see Hewitt

WHEN WE ALL GET TO HEAVEN see Wilson

WHEN WE SEE CHRIST see Rusthoi

WHEN WOE ASSAILS US THROUGH AND THROUGH
  see Brahms, Johannes, Wenn Wir In
  Hochsten Noten Sein

WHENCE ART THOU, MY MAIDEN? *Xmas,
  anthem
  (Track, Gerhard) SATB,org (easy) GIA
  G1875 $.40   (W325)

WHENCE IS THAT GOODLY FRAGRANCE *Xmas
  (Morgan, Hilda) SAB (easy) WATERLOO
  $.30   (W326)

WHENCE O SHEPHERD MAIDEN see Hill,
  Harry

WHERE HE LEADS I'LL FOLLOW see Ogden,
  W.A.

WHERE IN THE WORLD see Meilstrup, David
  G.

WHERE IS HE? see Peterson, John W.

WHERE IS IT? see Carmichael, Ralph

WHERE IS LOVE TODAY? see Meilstrup,
  David G.

WHERE IS NOW ABEL? see Aichinger,
  Gregor, Ubi Est Abel?

WHERE IS THIS OLD WORLD A-GOIN'? see
  Peterson, Pamela

WHERE IS THIS STUPENDOUS STRANGER?
  *Adv/Xmas
  (Lovelace, Austin) SATB ART MAST 265
  $.35   (W327)

WHERE NO ONE STANDS ALONE see Lister,
  Mosie

WHERE OUR LORD MAY GO see Heins

WHERE THE SPIRIT OF THE LORD IS see
  Adams, Steven R.

WHERE THERE IS LOVE see Ellis

WHEREFORE THIS GREAT JOY see Pettman,
  Edgar

WHERE'S CHRISTMAS
  see Sunshine And Snowflakes

WHEREVER HE LEADS *CC8U,hymn
  (Red, Buryl) 2pt,narrator BROADMAN
  4520-34 $2.25   (W328)

WHETHER YOUNG OR OLD see Moe, Daniel

WHIKEHART
  Love Came Down At Christmas
  SSAATTBB,acap (med) oct CONCORDIA
  98-1564 $.50   (W329)

WHILE AGES ROLL see Lister, Mosie

WHILE BY MY SHEEP see Jungst

WHILE BY OUR SHEEP *Xmas,anthem
  (Johnson, Norman) SATB oct SINGSPIR
  ZJP-3011 $.25   (W330)

WHILE I AM A CHILD see McGlohan

WHILE SHEPHERDS
  see Six Carols For SAB And Piano

WHILE SHEPHERDS WATCHED see Kent

WHILE SHEPHERDS WATCHED THEIR FLOCKS
  see Belcher, Supply

WHILE SHEPHERDS WATCHED THEIR FLOCKS BY
  NIGHT
  see Six Christmas Hymns

WHITAKER
  Old Gaelic Prayer
  SATB oct BENSON S4240 $.20   (W331)

  Our Father
  SATB oct BENSON S4250 $.35   (W332)

WHITAKER, P.
  King Of Love My Shepherd Is, The
  mix cor BRODT 615 $.25   (W333)

WHITCOMB
  Great Is The Lord
  SATB AMP A-699 $.45   (W334)

WHITE
  Glory To God In The Highest, Glory
  *Xmas,anthem
  SATB oct MCAFEE M1094 $.40   (W335)

  Morning Trumpet, The *anthem
  (Watkins, George) SSATB oct
  SINGSPIR ZJP-7226 $.25   (W336)

  Prayer
  SATB SCHIRM.G LG51834 $.40   (W337)

  Two Junior Choir Anthems *CC2U,
  Easter,anthem
  unis/SA oct SACRED S-8631 $.35
                                    (W338)

WHITE, CALVIN
  O Holy Spirit
  SATB oct GOSPEL 05 TM 0358 $.30
                                    (W339)

WHITE, EDWARD L.
  Glory To God In The Highest, Glory
  *Xmas,anthem
  (Martens, Mason) dbl cor,inst/acap
  MCAFEE M1094 $.40   (W340)

WHITE, ERNIE
Face To Face - Saved By Grace
*medley
SATB oct GOSPEL   (W341)

Tell The Whole World Now
SATB oct GOSPEL 05 TM 0319 $.35
                               (W342)

WHITE, HERBERT D.
Let Us With A Gladsome Mind
SATB (med easy) WATERLOO $.35
                               (W343)

Night Was Still *Xmas
SATB (easy) WATERLOO $.30   (W344)

WHITE, LOUIE L.
Gloria In Excelsis - Praise The Lord
*Xmas
unis,kbd,fl,strings,bells sc
CONCORDIA 97-5259 $2.75, ipa, cor
pts CONCORDIA 97-5260 $.15 (W345)

WHITE, P.
His Love Is Wonderful To Me *anthem/
gospel
(Johnson, Norman) SATB oct SINGSPIR
ZJP-8107 $.30   (W346)

Jesus, Wonderful Lord! *anthem/
gospel
(Rasley, J.) SATB oct SINGSPIR
ZJP-8205 $.35   (W347)

WHITE, REX
Two Responses For Beginning And
Ending Worship (composed with
Bock, Fred) *CC2U
unis/SATB,acap/org oct GENTRY G-262
$.30   (W348)

WHITE, RICHARD
Three Psalms *CC3U,anthem/Psalm
cor,acap oct SACRED S-173 $.40
                               (W349)

WHITECOTTON, SHIRLEY
Afternoon On A Hill
see Four Pastoral Songs

Alleluia
see Fanfare And Alleluia For Easter

Because He Loves Us All
2pt WORD CS-2643 $.30   (W350)

Call, The *Gen,anthem
SATB/SA oct SACRED S-171 $.35
                               (W351)

Carol For All Seasons *anthem/carol
SATB WORD CS-2645 $.30   (W352)

Children Of The Heavenly King
*anthem
SATB WORD CS-2646 $.30   (W353)

Fanfare
see Fanfare And Alleluia For Easter

Fanfare And Alleluia For Easter
*Easter
SATB,opt org oct HOPE A 476 $.35
contains: Alleluia; Fanfare
                               (W354)

Four Pastoral Songs
SSA,acap oct SOMERSET SP 725 $.40
contains: Afternoon On A Hill; I
Meant To Do My Work Today; I
Wandered Lonely As A Cloud; Out
In The Fields With God   (W355)

Fourth Shepherd, The *Xmas
SATB oct SCHMITT 1934 $.40   (W356)

I Meant To Do My Work Today
see Four Pastoral Songs

I Wandered Lonely As A Cloud
see Four Pastoral Songs

Light *anthem
SATB (easy) oct BROADMAN 4551-63
$.30   (W357)

None Other Lamb *anthem
SATB WORD CS-2652 $.30   (W358)

Out In The Fields With God
see Four Pastoral Songs

Star, A *Xmas,anthem
cor,S solo HERITAGE H126 $.35
                               (W359)

We Have A King *Easter,cant
unis&2pt,narrator,org/pno,opt hndbl
CHORISTERS A-112 $.95   (W360)

WHITER THAN SNOW *anthem
see Great Physician, The
(Blankenship) SATB oct BROADMAN
4540-97 $.30   (W361)
(Dean) SATB (easy) oct BROADMAN
4561-89 $.30   (W362)

WHITFIELD
I Need Thee, Precious Jesus *see
Reid

WHITFORD
On A Rugged Hill *Gd.Fri.,anthem/
gospel
(DeCou, Harold) SATB oct SINGSPIR
ZJP-8082 $.25   (W363)

WHITFORD, KEITH
On A Rugged Hill *CC10L
(Owens, Jimmy) SATB LEXICON 30065
$1.95   (W364)

WHITTEMORE
From God To Everyone *gospel
(Linn) SATB,3trp,2trom,strings oct
LILLENAS AT-1113 $.35   (W365)

His Name Is Jesus *Adv/Xmas
(Linn) SATB,3trp,2trom,4vln,gtr,
perc oct LILLENAS AT-C106 $.40
                               (W366)

WHITTER
Carol For Mary *Xmas,carol
SATB,acap (easy) OXFORD 84.242 $.25
                               (W367)

WHITTIER
Forgiveness (composed with Vick)
*anthem
SATB (easy) oct BROADMAN 4545-67
$.30   (W368)

WHITTLE
Moment By Moment
(Moody; Williams, David) SATB oct
GOSPEL 05 TM 0114 $.20   (W369)

Showers Of Blessing
(McGranahan; Ferrin, Paul) SATB oct
GOSPEL 05 TM 0211 $.20   (W370)

WHO? see Roberts

WHO AM I? see Landgrave, Phillip

WHO CAN BEHOLD see Lovelace, Austin C.

WHO? GOD! see Boozer, Pat

WHO HAS BELIEVED see Beebe, Edward J.

WHO IS JESUS? see Davis, Katherine K.

WHO IS ON THE LORD'S SIDE? *anthem
(Johnson) SATB oct BENSON S4364 $.35
                               (W371)
(Johnson, Norman) SAB oct SINGSPIR
ZJP-2000 $.25   (W372)

WHO IS ON THE LORD'S SIDE? see Goss,
John

WHO IS THIS MAN? see Burnham

WHO IS THIS THAT COMES IN GLORY? see
Young

WHO MOVED? see Blanchard

WHO ROLLS AWAY THE STONE? see
Hammerschmidt, Andreas, Wer Walzet
Uns Den Stein

WHO SHALL ABIDE see Parks

WHO SHALL ASCEND see Beebe

WHO SHALL SEPARATE US? see Beck, John
Ness

WHO SHALL SEPARATE US see Schutz,
Heinrich

WHO SLEPT THAT NIGHT IN BETHLEHEM see
Copley

WHO WALKS WITH GOD? see Van Iderstine,
A.P.

WHO WAS THE MAN see Davis, Katherine K.

WHO WERE THESE MEN see Wild, Eric

WHO WILL GO? see Burroughs, Bob

WHO WOULD BE A SHEPHERD BOY? see
Cornell, Garry A.

WHO'LL BE A WITNESS *medley/spir
(Red, Buryl) SATB TRIGON TGO 107
$1.25   (W373)

WHOM DID YE SEE, YE SHEPHERDS? *Xmas
(Follett) 2pt PRO ART 2766 $.35
                               (W374)

WHOM DID YOU SEE, KIND SHEPHERDS? see
Victoria, Tomas Luis de, Quem
Vidistis Pastores?

WHOM, O SHEPHERDS see Lassus, Roland de
(Orlandus), Quem Vidistis, Pastores

WHO'S GOING TO WALK THAT ROAD WITH ME?
see Peterson, John W.

WHO'S THE LITTLE BABY see Ehret, Walter

WHOSO LOVETH ME WILL ALL MY WORDS
TREASURE see Vulpius, Melchior, Wer
Mich Liebet, Der Wird Mein Wort
Halten

WHOSOEVER DRINKETH OF THIS WATER see
Baumgartner, H. Leroy

WHY? see Moore

WHY ART THOU SO HEAVY, O MY SOUL? see
Loosemore, Henry

WHY DO I DO? see Landgrave, Phillip

WHY DO I SING? see Wyrtzen, Don

WHY NOT NOW? see Wyrtzen, Don

WHY RAGE FIERCELY THE HEATHENS see
Mendelssohn-Bartholdy, Felix

WHY SHOULD I SING ANY OTHER SONG? see
Martin, Bruce

WHY THIS HASTE, O SHEPHERD, SAY? *Xmas
(Parkinson) SATB,acap OXFORD 84.246
                               (W375)

WHY WAS I BORN? see Smith

WICHMAN
Bell Carol, The *Xmas,carol
unis&SATB,inst (easy) OXFORD 94.004
$.40, ipr   (W376)

WICKS
Communion Service (Series III) *see
Dearnley

WIDDICOMBE, TREVOR
Virgin Most Pure, A *Xmas
SATB EMI s.p.   (W377)

WIDEEN, IVAR
Jag Har Ett Blomster Kanna Lart
4pt mix cor ERIKS 14 s.p.   (W378)

WIDER DIE FALSCHEN PROPHETEN see
Telemann, Georg Philipp

WIDMER
Barmherziger, Ewiger Gott
SAT/SAB (contains also: Wie Schon
Leuchtet Der Morgenstern)
SCHWEIZER. SK 54.05-6 s.p. see
also MUSIKBEILAGE ZUM
"EVANGELISCHEN KIRCHENCHOR 1954"
                               (W379)

WIDMEYER
Come And Dine
(Mercer, W. Elmo) SATB oct BENSON
S4058 $.35   (W380)

WIE BIN ICH DOCH SO HERZLICH FROH see
Hammerschmidt, Andreas

WIE DER HIRSCH SCHREIT NACH FRISCHEM
WASSER see Leisring, Volkmar

WIE HERRLICH GIBST DU, HERR, DICH ZU
ERKENNEN see Lohr, Ina

WIE HERRLICH GIBST DU, HERR, DICH ZU
ERKENNEN see Pidoux, Pierre

WIE LIEBLICH SCHON, HERR ZEBAOTH see
Zillinger, Erwin

WIE SCHAUERVOLL see Mastioletti,
Terribilis Est

WIE SCHON LEUCHT UNS DER MORGENSTERN
see Hunecke, Wilhelm

WIE SCHON LEUCHTET see Schein, Johann
Hermann

WIE SCHON LEUCHTET DER MORGENSTERN see
Distler, Hugo

WIE SCHON LEUCHTET DER MORGENSTERN see
Heer, Emil

WIE SCHON LEUCHTET DER MORGENSTERN see
Kuhnau, Johann

WIE SCHON LEUCHTET DER MORGENSTERN see
Pepping, Ernst

WIE SELIG WER IM GLAUBEN NUR see Briner

WIE SOLL ICH DICH EMPFANGEN see
Buxtehude, Dietrich

WIE SOLL ICH DICH EMPFANGEN see
Oertzen, Rudolf von

WIE SOLL ICH DICH EMPFANGEN see
Schweizer, Rolf

WIE SOLL ICH DICH EMPFANGEN see Zipp,
    Friedrich

WIEDERMANN, BEDRICH (1883-1951)
    Befiehl Dem Herrn
        see Drei Motetten

    Danket Dem Herrn
        see Drei Motetten

    Drei Motetten *Op.7,No.3
        8pt mix cor LIENAU cor pts s.p., sc
        s.p.
        contains: Befiehl Dem Herrn;
            Danket Dem Herrn; Gott Ist Die
            Liebe   (W381)

    Gott Ist Die Liebe
        see Drei Motetten

WIEMER, WOLFGANG (1934-   )
    Sollt Ich Meinem Gott Nicht Singen
        SAT/SAB/2-3pt HANSSLER 14.232 s.p.
                                        (W382)

WIENAND, KARL
    Jubilate Deo
        "O Be Joyful In The Lord" unis,org
        DEAN CE-102 $.35   (W383)

    O Be Joyful In The Lord *see
        Jubilate Deo

WIENANDT, ELWYN A.
    Ancient Of Days *anthem
        SATB,S solo,org AUGSBURG 11-1687
        $.30   (W384)

    Carol For Our Time, A *Xmas,anthem/
        carol
        SATB (easy) oct BROADMAN 4545-59
        $.30   (W385)

WIERUSZOWSKI, LILI (1900-   )
    Wir Stehn Von Dir, O Vater
        SSA/SATB/unis,2-3treb inst,bass
        inst LAUDINELLA LR25 s.p.   (W386)

WIESER, LUKAS
    Nun Komm, Den Heiden Heiland *Adv,
        Introit
        SATB,T solo,acap (med) BAREN.
        BA2404   (W387)

WIGGLESWORTH, FRANK (1918-   )
    Alleluia
        SA,acap AM.COMP.AL. $1.38   (W388)

    Short Mass, A
        SATB,acap AM.COMP.AL. $6.60 (W389)

WIHTOL, A.A.
    Come And Gather, Little Children
        *Xmas,anthem
        SSA oct SINGSPIR ZJP-3032 $.30
                                    (W390)

    Haleluyah, Christ Is Risen *Easter,
        anthem
        SATB oct SINGSPIR ZKP-5317 $.35
                                    (W391)

    My God And I *anthem
        (Peterson, John W.) SAB oct
        SINGSPIR ZJP-7327 $.40   (W392)
        (Peterson, John W.) SATB oct
        SINGSPIR ZJP-7296 $.40   (W393)

    My Lord And I *anthem
        (Peterson, John W.) SATB oct
        SINGSPIR ZJP-7346 $.30   (W394)
        (Rasley, John M.) SA&opt TB (easy)
        oct SINGSPIR ZJP-6001 $.30 (W395)

    Night So Dark And Hour So Late
        *Xmas,anthem
        SSA oct SINGSPIR ZJP-3031 $.30
                                    (W396)

WIJ ZIEN IN DE KRIBBE HET KINDJE see
    Setten, J.W. van

WILBYE
    Homo Natus Ex Muliere *Xmas,anthem
        (Brown) SATB OXFORD   (W397)

WILCOXON
    I Will Sing The Wondrous Story *see
        Rowley

    Jesus, Name Of Wondrous Love *see
        How

WILD, ERIC
    All God's Children Are Singing
        Tonight (composed with Waters,
        Deanna)
        SATB (easy) WATERLOO $.40   (W398)

    Am I Like Peter (composed with
        Waters, Deanna)
        SATB (easy) WATERLOO $.50   (W399)

    Christmas Is A Time For Loving
        (composed with Waters, Deanna)
        *Xmas
        SATB (easy) WATERLOO $.35   (W400)

WILD, ERIC (cont'd.)
    Come Rest In Me (composed with
        Waters, Deanna)
        SATB,pno WATERLOO $.40   (W401)

    Day You Meet The Lord, The (composed
        with Waters, Deanna)
        SATB (med easy) WATERLOO $.60
                                    (W402)

    Easter Song *Easter
        SATB (med easy) WATERLOO $.40
                                    (W403)

    Father The Hour Is Come (composed
        with Waters, Deanna)
        SATB (easy) WATERLOO $.40   (W404)

    First Christmas Morning *see Hains,
        S.B.

    Forgive My Little Faith (composed
        with Waters, Deanna)
        SATB (easy) WATERLOO $.30   (W405)

    Gather Round And Praise The Lord
        (composed with Waters, Deanna)
        SATB (easy) WATERLOO $.30   (W406)

    Give Your Life To The Lord (composed
        with Waters, Deanna)
        SATB (med easy) WATERLOO $.55
                                    (W407)

    God Is In Every Tomorrow (composed
        with Waters, Deanna)
        SATB WATERLOO $.40   (W408)

    He Gives Light (composed with Waters,
        Deanna)
        SATB (med) WATERLOO $.40   (W409)

    His Loving Kindness Lasts Forever
        (composed with Waters, Deanna)
        SATB (easy) WATERLOO $.35   (W410)

    How Can I Thank The Lord (composed
        with Waters, Deanna)
        see Wild, Eric, Lord Open My Eyes

    I'm Reaching Out (composed with
        Waters, Deanna)
        SATB (med easy) WATERLOO $.40
                                    (W411)

    In The Beginning (composed with
        Waters, Deanna)
        SATB (med easy) WATERLOO $.55
                                    (W412)

    Let God Be At Home In Your Heart
        (composed with Waters, Deanna)
        SATB (med easy) WATERLOO $.40
                                    (W413)

    Lord Open My Eyes (composed with
        Waters, Deanna)
        SATB (easy) WATERLOO $.30 contains
        also: How Can I Thank The Lord
                                    (W414)

    O God Of Love And Kindness (composed
        with Waters, Deanna)
        SATB (med easy) WATERLOO $.40
                                    (W415)

    Oh, Perfect Teacher (composed with
        Waters, Deanna)
        SATB,solo,org WATERLOO $.40 (W416)

    Peace To All Who Enter Here (composed
        with Waters, Deanna)
        SATB (easy) WATERLOO $.40   (W417)

    To Know God Is To Love Again
        (composed with Waters, Deanna)
        SATB (med easy) WATERLOO $.40
                                    (W418)

    Who Were These Men (composed with
        Waters, Deanna)
        SATB (med) WATERLOO $.40   (W419)

    With Jesus Alive In My Heart
        (composed with Waters, Deanna)
        SATB (med) WATERLOO $.60   (W420)

WILHELM
    Allelu! Rejoice And Sing! *Xmas,
        anthem
        SATB oct HERITAGE H116 $.35 (W421)

    Alleluia The Angels Sang *Xmas
        SSSA,acap PRO ART 2754 $.40 (W422)

    God Gave Him Life Again! *Easter,
        anthem
        SATB oct SACRED S-164 $.35 (W423)

    Spur Us On To Do Thy Will *anthem
        SATB,3trp oct BROADMAN 4563-04 $.50
                                    (W424)

WILHELM, PATRICIA M.
    Bright The Star That Lights Your
        Pillow
        SATB BOURNE B224121-358 $.60 (W425)

    Hills Awake To Singing, The
        SATB BOURNE B223925-358 $.60 (W426)

    Look To The Cross Of Christ *Lent
        SATB,acap (easy) oct ELKAN-V
        362-03175 $.30   (W427)

WILHELM, PATRICIA M. (cont'd.)
    Sleep, Baby, Sleep *Xmas
        SATB&opt jr cor,S solo,acap oct
        ELKAN-V 362-03172 $.30   (W428)

    Spur Us On To Do Thy Will *anthem
        SATB,3trp BROADMAN 4563-04 $.50
                                    (W429)

    Wondrous Gift
        SATB BOURNE B224139-358 $.50 (W430)

WILKINSON
    Easter Episodes *Holywk,anthem
        (med) FISCHER,C ZCM 109 $.35 (W431)

WILKINSON, CHARLES A.
    Jesu, Word Of God Incarnate *mot
        SATB HARRIS $.35   (W432)

WILL IT BE SOON? see Johnson, Norman

WILL JESUS FIND US WATCHING? see Crosby

WILL OF GOD IS ALWAYS BEST, THE see
    Bach, Johann Sebastian

WILL YOU BE READY? see Peterson, John
    W.

WILLAERT, ADRIAN (ca. 1490-1562)
    Domine Jesu Christe
        [Lat] SATB OUVRIERES 6.0005.1 $.50
                                    (W433)

WILLAN, HEALEY (1880-1968)
    All Hail The Queen
        unis HARRIS $.25   (W434)
        SA HARRIS $.25   (W435)
        SATB HARRIS $.35   (W436)
        SSA HARRIS $.30   (W437)

    Ave Verum Corpus
        "Hail O God Incarnate" SATB,acap
        HARRIS $.35   (W438)

    Christ Hath A Garden
        SATB HARRIS HC 4056 $.35   (W439)

    Come, O Come Life's Delight
        SSATB STAINER 3.0782.1 $.30 (W440)

    Create In Me A Clean Heart, O God
        SATB oct CONCORDIA 98-2238 $.30
                                    (W441)

    Day Of Resurrection, The *Easter
        SATB oct CONCORDIA 98-2206 $.35
                                    (W442)

    Hail O God Incarnate *see Ave Verum
        Corpus

    Recessional
        SATB HARRIS $.35   (W443)

    Regina Coeli Laetare
        SSAA,acap HARRIS $.30   (W444)

    Responsory In Time Of War, A
        SATB HARRIS $.35   (W445)

    Say Nought The Struggle
        TTBB HARRIS $.35   (W446)

    Sing Alleluya Forth
        SATB HARRIS HC 4027 $.40   (W447)

WILLCOCKS, DAVID
    Lord At First
        SATB,acap (easy) OXFORD 84.198 $.35
                                    (W448)

    Masters In This Hall
        SATB (med easy) OXFORD 84.208 $.45
                                    (W449)

WILLCOXON, LARRY
    Namegivers, The
        jr cor (music drama) BROADMAN
        4516-04 $3.25   (W450)

WILLEMS, JOSEF
    Hymnus
        men cor,acap TONOS 4552 s.p. (W451)

WILLIAMS
    Ave Maris Stella *BVM
        TTBB,acap OXFORD   (W452)

    Break Forth Into Joy *hymn
        1-2pt oct LILLENAS AN-2423 $.30
                                    (W453)

    Choral Carillon
        SATB SHAWNEE A5666 $.30   (W454)

    Christ Is Risen! *Easter,anthem
        (Johnson, Norman) SATB oct SINGSPIR
        ZJP-3509 $.25   (W455)

    Contentment *gospel
        SATB oct LILLENAS AN-2405 $.30
                                    (W456)

    For You I Am Praying *gospel
        SATB oct LILLENAS AN-2388 $.30
                                    (W457)

    Glorious Things Of Thee Are Spoken
        *anthem
        unis FINE ARTS CM 1031 $.30 (W458)

WILLIAMS (cont'd.)

I Love Thy Kingdom, Lord *anthem
(Peterson, John W.) SATB oct
SINGSPIR ZJP-7291 $.30   (W459)

Jesus, I Long For Thy Presence
*anthem
SAB oct LILLENAS AN-2414 $.30
(W460)

Living In A Wealthy Country *gospel
(Linn) SATB,3trp,2trom oct LILLENAS
AT-1121 $.35   (W461)

My Singing Is A Prayer *see Preston

O Thou In Whose Presence *anthem
SATB oct LILLENAS AN-2411 $.30
(W462)

Praise, O Praise Our God And King
*see Baker

Ring, Ye Bells *Xmas,anthem
unis/3pt oct SACRED S-6504 $.35 (W463)

Trust And Obey *see Sammis

WILLIAMS, A.
Bells Ring Out At Christmas, The
LESLIE 4080 $.30   (W464)

WILLIAMS, AARON (ca. 1731-1776)
Come, We That Love The Lord *anthem
(DeCou, Harold) SATB oct SINGSPIR
ZJP-7318 $.30   (W465)

WILLIAMS, D.
Christ Our Sacrifice Is Born
(Collins, Hope) SATB oct GOSPEL
05 TM 0153 $.20   (W466)

WILLIAMS, DAVID
Easter Song *Easter
SATB KJOS 5912 $.35   (W467)

Stand Up And Bless The Lord
SAA/TBB KJOS 7100 $.35   (W468)

WILLIAMS, DAVID H.
Alas, My Savior Died *Lent
SATB ART MAST 169 $.30   (W469)

All My Heart This Night Rejoices
*Xmas
unis,fl,pno/org CHORISTERS A-135
$.40   (W470)

Behold! A Stranger
2pt,org/pno GRAY CMR 3326 $.30
(W471)

Child Is Born, A *Xmas,cant
jr cor,pno/org BROADMAN 4513-06
$1.25   (W472)

Come, Let Us Sing To The Lord
see Two Swinging Psalms

Come On Knees *Adv/Xmas
unis ART MAST 245 $.35   (W473)
SATB ART MAST 253 $.35   (W474)

Easter Carol *Easter
SATB ART MAST 233 $.40   (W475)

From All That Dwell Below The Skies
SATB ART MAST 176 $.35   (W476)

I Heard Two Soldiers Talking
*Easter/Pent
SATB ART MAST 187 $.35   (W477)

If You Would Hear The Angels Sing
*Xmas
SATB,S solo GRAY CMR 3333 $.30
(W478)

In Bethlehem That Wondrous Night
*Xmas
SATB,acap ART MAST 197 $.30   (W479)

Lift Up Your Heads *Palm
unis ART MAST 190 $.35   (W480)

Look, Ye Saints! The Sight Is
Glorious *Easter/Pent
SATB,org ART MAST 170 $.40   (W481)

Make A Joyful Noise
SATB,org GRAY CMR 3305 $.30   (W482)

Sing To The Lord A New Song
see Two Swinging Psalms

Two Swinging Psalms *Psalm
1-2pt oct AGAPE AG 7166 $.40
contains: Come, Let Us Sing To
The Lord; Sing To The Lord A
New Song   (W483)

What Wondrous Love Is This *Lent
2pt ART MAST 205 $.40   (W484)

WILLIAMS, G.
When I Survey The Wondrous Cross
LESLIE 4001 $.45   (W485)

WILLIAMS, J.J.
There Came A Man
mix cor BRODT 601 $.25   (W486)

WILLIAMSON
Jesus Has Lifted Me
(Pappadopoulos) SATB oct GOSPEL
05 TM 0166 $.25   (W487)

Meeting In The Air, The
(Pappadopoulos) SATB oct GOSPEL
05 TM 0178 $.25   (W488)

Our Home In Glory
(Pappadopoulos) SATB oct GOSPEL
05 TM 0168 $.30   (W489)

WILLIAMSON, MALCOLM
Agnus Dei
SATB,S solo,org oct WEINBERGER W092
$.35   (W490)
oct WEINBERGER $.35   (W491)

Carols Of King David *see I Will
Lift Up Mine Eyes (Psalm 121)
(W492)

Dawn Carol *Xmas
unis MARKS MC 4638 $.30   (W493)
SATB MARKS MC 4633 $.45   (W494)

Dignus Est Agnus
SATB MARKS MC 4634 $.45   (W495)

Genesis
audience/cor,inst WEINBERGER voc sc
$2.50, cor pts $.50, ipa   (W496)

I Will Lift Up Mine Eyes (Psalm 121)
unis,org oct WEINBERGER W001 $.35
see from Carols Of King David
(W497)

Pange Lingua
see Two Motets

Psalm 121 *see I Will Lift Up Mine
Eyes

Sixteen Hymns And Processionals
*CC16U
unis oct AGAPE AG 7187 $.90   (W498)

Tantum Ergo
see Two Motets

Two Motets
MARKS MC 4635 $.45
contains: Pange Lingua (SATB);
Tantum Ergo (SAT)   (W499)

World At The Manger
SATB,SBar soli,pno/org WEINBERGER
W095 voc sc $8.00, cor pts $.50
(W500)

WILLIAMSTOWN *hymn
(Lindsley) TTBB,acap (easy) OXFORD
94.103 see from Five Early American
Hymn Tunes   (W501)

WILLINGHAM, GLORIA
Truly The Son Of God *Easter
cor&speak cor LILLENAS ME-213 $.50
(W502)

WILLIS
Hear My Prayer *anthem
SATB WORD CS-2628 $.30   (W503)

WILLIS, KATHE
O Star Of Bethlehem *Xmas
(Eilers, Joyce) SATB LEONARD-US
08546000 $.50   (W504)

WILLIS, RICHARD STORRS (1819-1900)
O Give Thanks *anthem
SATB WORD CS-2629 $.35   (W505)

Thou Art The Way *anthem
2pt WORD CS-2627 $.25   (W506)

WILLMS, FRANZ (1893-1946)
Christus Licht Der Welt "Nacht Und
Finsternis" *Xmas
mix cor (easy) sc SCHOTTS C 33 495
s.p.   (W507)

WILLS
Magnificat And Nunc Dimittis
*Magnif/Nunc
SATB OXFORD OCMS 602   (W508)

We Are Children Of The King (composed
with Cole) *anthem
2pt oct BROADMAN 4558-43 $.30
(W509)

WILLS, ARTHUR
Ah My Dear Angry Lord
see FIVE ANTHEMS FOR TODAY

I Hunger And Thirst *anthem
SATB,org NOVELLO NCM41 s.p.   (W510)

Prayer
SATB,org NOVELLO MW 45 s.p.   (W511)

WILMINGTON see Dare, Elkanah Kelsey

WILSON
Alas, And Did My Savior Bleed *see
Watts

And Now Bless The God Of All *see
Sirach

At The Cry Of The First Bird
SATB SHAWNEE A5671 $.35   (W512)

Bells On Christmas Day, The *Xmas,
anthem
SATB oct LORENZ A540 $.35   (W513)

Comin' Back To The Lord
(Sieber; Hansen) SATB oct SCHMITT
8072 $.40   (W514)

If The Christ Should Come To Me
*anthem
SATB oct LORENZ A554 $.35   (W515)

Jesus Calls Us *anthem
SATB oct LORENZ A545 $.35   (W516)

Sweet Music *Easter,anthem
SATB oct LORENZ A538 $.35   (W517)

Upper Room, The *Easter,anthem
SATB oct LORENZ A554 $.30   (W518)

When We All Get To Heaven *gospel
(Skillings, Otis) SATB,narrator oct
LILLENAS AN-1701 $.35   (W519)

When We All Get To Heaven *see
Hewitt

WILSON, CHARLES M.
Cherry Tree Carol *Xmas
SATB (med easy) WATERLOO $.40
(W520)

WILSON, DONALD M.
Stabile III, "Ave Maria"
3 cor,perc sc AM.COMP.AL. $6.60
(W521)

WILSON, F.
He Rode On A Donkey
(D. Amor) ALLANS 849   (W522)

WILSON, JOHN F.
He Shall Be Called Wonderful
SATB,narrator,pno/org oct HOPE
CF 181 $.40   (W523)

Just To See Him
see Wilson, John F., Lead Me On

Lead Me On
SATB,pno/org oct HOPE CF 180 $.40
contains also: Just To See Him
(W524)

WILSON, JUANITA
Three-Part Songs For Women (composed
with Burroughs, Bob) *CC25UL,
hymn
3pt wom cor BROADMAN 4523-05 $.75
(W525)

WILSON, KEITH E.
God Of Compassion
SAB,acap (easy) oct GENTRY G-215
$.30   (W526)

WILSON, R. BARCLAY
Mors Janua Vitae *sac/sec
SATB CRAMER C73   (W527)

WILSON, RICHARD (1941-   )
Birth, The (from He Lived The Good
Life) Xmas,anthem
2pt,kbd,inst AUGSBURG 11-1724 $.45
(W528)

He Lived The Good Life
1-2pt/SATB,pno,inst AUGSBURG
11-9213 $2.95   (W529)

Last Trip To Jerusalem (from He Lived
The Good Life) anthem
SATB,kbd, opt C inst AUGSBURG
11-1725 $.40   (W530)

Resurrection, The (from He Lived The
Good Life) Easter,anthem
SATB,2 soli,kbd,inst AUGSBURG
11-1726 $.45   (W531)

WILSON, ROGER C. (1912-   )
Christmas Concert, A *Xmas,cant
SATB (med easy) LORENZ $1.95   (W532)

I Met My Master *anthem
SA/SATB,med solo (easy) oct LORENZ
A559 $.30   (W533)

Shepherd Of Souls *Commun,anthem
SAB oct LORENZ 7427 $.30   (W534)

WILT THOU RUN TO THE GOAL see Schein,
Johann Hermann, Vil Du Mot Malet
Renna

WIND BLOWETH WHERE IT LISTETH, THE see
Baumgartner, H. Leroy

WINDOWS OF THE MIND see Wyrtzen, Don

WINDS OF JUDEA see Lyon

WINDS THROUGH THE OLIVE TREES see Pyle,
Francis [Johnson]

WINER, GEORG (1583-1651)
Psalm 51 *see Schaffe In Mir, Gott,
Ein Reines Herze

Schaffe In Mir, Gott, Ein Reines
Herze (Psalm 51)
SATB SCHWEIZER. SK 65.07 s.p. see
also MUSIKBEILAGE ZUM
"EVANGELISCHEN KIRCHENCHOR 1965"
(W535)

WINGS OF PRAYER see Peterson, John W.

WINK
All Things
(Wink) SATB oct SCHMITT 1935 $.40
(W536)

Proverb, A *anthem
SATB oct BROADMAN 4554-99 $.30
(W537)

Sing Alleluia *Xmas,carol
SATB,pno,perc oct BENSON S4377
$1.25
(W538)

We'll Meet The Dawn With A Song
SATB oct BENSON S4378 $.35 (W539)

WINTER
see Four Folk Songs From Abroad

WINTER CAROL see Lovelace, Austin C.

WINTER, SISTER MIRIAM THERESE
Child Of Morning *Xmas,carol,Contemp
SATB VANGUARD V705 $.35 see also
Gold, Incense And Myrrh (W540)

Christmas Ballad *Xmas,carol,Contemp
SATB VANGUARD V706 $.35 see also
Gold, Incense And Myrrh (W541)

Come Down, Lord *Bibl,Contemp
SSA VANGUARD V522 $.30 see also Joy
Is Like The Rain (W542)
(Roff, Joseph) SATB VANGUARD V513
$.35 see also Joy Is Like The
Rain (W543)

God Gives His People Strength
*Contemp
SSA VANGUARD V529 $.15 see also Joy
Is Like The Rain (W544)
(Roff, Joseph) SATB VANGUARD V517
$.30 see also Joy Is Like The
Rain (W545)

Gold, Incense And Myrrh *CC12L,Xmas,
carol,Contemp
SATB VANGUARD
see also: Child Of Morning;
Christmas Ballad; He Comes; In
The Beginning; No Longer Alone;
O What A Happening; Peace Upon
Earth; Silent The Night; Sing
Of Birth; Song Of Glory; Take
Courage; Wonderful (W546)

He Comes *Xmas,carol,Contemp
SATB VANGUARD V712 $.35 see also
Gold, Incense And Myrrh (W547)

How I Have Longed *Contemp
SSA VANGUARD V527 $.25 see also Joy
Is Like The Rain (W548)

Howl, My Soul *Bibl,Contemp
SSA VANGUARD V525 $.25 see also Joy
Is Like The Rain (W549)
(Roff, Joseph) SATB VANGUARD V515
$.35 see also Joy Is Like The
Rain (W550)

I Know The Secret *CC12U,Contemp
wom cor,gtr/inst VANGUARD V538
$2.50 (W551)

In The Beginning *Xmas,carol,Contemp
SATB VANGUARD V708 $.35 see also
Gold, Incense And Myrrh (W552)

It's A Long Road To Freedom *Contemp
SSA VANGUARD V524 $.25 see also Joy
Is Like The Rain (W553)
(Roff, Joseph) SATB VANGUARD V514
$.35 see also Joy Is Like The
Rain (W554)

Joy Is Like The Rain *Contemp
SSA VANGUARD V 519 $.15 see also
Joy Is Like The Rain (W555)
(Roff, Joseph) SATB VANGUARD V511
$.30 see also Joy Is Like The
Rain (W556)

Joy Is Like The Rain *CC12U,Contemp
wom cor,gtr/inst VANGUARD V535
$2.50
see also: Come Down, Lord; God
Gives His People Strength; How
I Have Longed; Howl, My Soul;

WINTER, SISTER MIRIAM THERESE (cont'd.)

It's A Long Road To Freedom;
Joy Is Like The Rain; Pilgrim
Song; Speak To Me, Wind; Spirit
Of God; Ten Lepers; Wedding
Banquet, The; Zaccheus (W557)

Knock, Knock *CC12U,Contemp
wom cor,gtr/inst VANGUARD V543
$2.50 (W558)

No Longer Alone *Xmas,carol,Contemp
SATB VANGUARD V704 $.35 see also
Gold, Incense And Myrrh (W559)

O What A Happening *Xmas,carol,
Contemp
SATB VANGUARD V711 $.35 see also
Gold, Incense And Myrrh (W560)

Peace Upon Earth *Xmas,carol,Contemp
SATB VANGUARD V710 $.35 see also
Gold, Incense And Myrrh (W561)

Pilgrim Song *Contemp
SSA VANGUARD V526 $.20 see also Joy
Is Like The Rain (W562)

Seasons *CC12U,Contemp
wom cor,gtr/inst VANGUARD V571
$2.50 (W563)

Silent The Night *Xmas,carol,Contemp
SATB VANGUARD V709 $.35 see also
Gold, Incense And Myrrh (W564)

Sing Of Birth *Xmas,carol,Contemp
SATB VANGUARD V707 $.35 see also
Gold, Incense And Myrrh (W565)

Song Of Glory *Xmas,carol,Contemp
SATB VANGUARD V701 $.35 see also
Gold, Incense And Myrrh (W566)

Speak To Me, Wind *Contemp
SSA VANGUARD V521 $.25 see also Joy
Is Like The Rain (W567)

Spirit Of God *Contemp
SSA VANGUARD V523 $.20 see also Joy
Is Like The Rain (W568)

Take Courage *Xmas,carol,Contemp
SATB VANGUARD V703 $.35 see also
Gold, Incense And Myrrh (W569)

Ten Lepers *Bibl,Contemp
SSA VANGUARD V528 $.25 see also Joy
Is Like The Rain (W570)
(Roff, Joseph) SATB VANGUARD V516
$.35 see also Joy Is Like The
Rain (W571)

Wedding Banquet, The *Contemp
SSA VANGUARD V530 $.25 see also Joy
Is Like The Rain (W572)
(Roff, Joseph) SATB VANGUARD V518
$.35 see also Joy Is Like The
Rain (W573)

Wonderful *Xmas,carol,Contemp
SATB VANGUARD V702 $.35 see also
Gold, Incense And Myrrh (W574)

Zaccheus *Bibl,Contemp
SSA VANGUARD 520 $.25 see also Joy
Is Like The Rain (W575)
(Roff, Joseph) SATB VANGUARD V512
$.35 see also Joy Is Like The
Rain (W576)

WINTLE
Magnificat In G *Magnif
SATB WALTON 2982 $.40 (W577)

WIR CHRISTENLEUT HABN JETZUND FREUD see
Fuger

WIR CHRISTENLEUT HABN JETZUND FREUD see
Telemann, Georg Philipp

WIR DANKEN DIR, HERR GOTT VATER see
Gumpelzhaimer, Adam

WIR DANKEN DIR, HERR JESU CHRIST, DASS
DU FUR UNS GESTORBEN BIST see
Praetorius, Michael

WIR DANKEN DIR, O GOTTES LAMM see de la
Rue, Pierre

WIR DANKEN, HERR GOTT see Schutz,
Heinrich

WIR ERWARTEN UNSERN HEILAND see
Metschnabel, Paul Joseph

WIR GEHN DAHIN see Hone, Karl-Heinz

WIR GLAUBEN ALL AN EINEN GOTT see Koch,
Heinz

WIR GLAUBEN ALL AN EINEN GOTT see Le
Maistre, Mattheus

WIR GLAUBEN ALL AN EINEN GOTT see
Matthes, Rene

WIR GLAUBEN ALL AN EINEN GOTT see
Walter (Walther), Johann

WIR HABEN EIN KINDELEIN GESEH'N "DIE
LUFT IST NOCH VOLLER GETON" see
Taubert, Karl Heinz

WIR HABEN SEINEN STERN GESEHEN "TRITTST
DU WIEDER VOR DIE NACHT" see
Wenzel, Eberhard

WIR LOBEN DICH see Woll, E.

WIR RUHMEN DICH UND DANKEN DIR see
Seckinger, Konrad

WIR RUHMEN UNS ALLEIN DES KREUZES see
Gast

WIR SINGEN DIR, IMMANUEL see Hermann,
Nikolaus

WIR STEHN VON DIR, O VATER see
Wieruszowski, Lili

WIR WEIHN DER ERDE GABEN see
Planyavsky, Peter

WIR WOLLEN ALLE FROHLICH SEIN
(Wiese, G.) men cor,acap TONOS 5626
s.p. (W578)

WIR WOLLEN ALLE FROHLICH SEIN see
Praetorius, Michael

WIR WUNSCHEN HEUT see Rothschuh, Franz

WIRICK, E.
O Sing Unto The Lord *Bibl
SA (med) FITZSIMONS 5003 $.20
(W579)

WIRSEN
Summer Psalm
SATB cor pts NORDISKA NMS 6403 s.p.
(W580)

WISDOM see Hovhaness, Alan

WISDOM HATH BUILDED HER HOUSE see
Canning, Thomas

WISE
Magnificat And Nunc Dimittis
*Magnif/Nunc
(Dearney; Greening) SATBB (med
easy) OXFORD 42.382 $.70 (W581)

WISE, GERALD J.
Dost Thou In A Manger Lie *anthem,
Contemp
cor oct CHANTRY COA 7353 $.35
(W582)

WISE MEN STILL ADORE HIM
see Sunshine And Snowflakes

WISE MEN STILL SEEK HIM see Peterson,
John W.

WITH A HOLY HUSH see Peterson, John W.

WITH AWE AND CONFIDENCE *anthem
(Brandon, G.) SATB (easy) GIA G1883
$.35 (W583)

WITH HAPPY VOICES RINGING see Lovelace,
Austin C.

WITH JESUS ALIVE IN MY HEART see Wild,
Eric

WITH JOY WE COME see Gore, Richard T.

WITH JOY WE GO UP TO THE HOUSE OF THE
LORD see Clarke, F.R.C.

WITH MUSIC AND SONG see Duchesne,
Sister

WITH PRAISES ABOUNDING see Pettman,
Edgar

WITH THANKFUL HEARTS see Barcanic,
Torrey

WITH THANKFUL HEARTS see Pulsifer,
Thomas R.

WITH THEE IS PEACE see Schubert, Franz
(Peter)

WITHIN A LITTLE STABLE see Graham,
Robert

WITHIN A MANGER HARSH WITH HAY see
Delmonte, Pauline

WITTMER, EBERHARD LUDWIG (1905-)
Exaudi Nos Erhore Uns "Herr, Gib Uns
Helle Augen"
3pt wom cor/3pt jr cor&4pt men cor
sc SCHOTTS C 40 108 s.p. (W584)

WITTMER, EBERHARD LUDWIG (cont'd.)

Festliche Hymne "Singe, O Singe Dich"
*hymn
4pt men cor,pno/3trp,3trom,tuba,
timp voc sc SCHOTTS C 39 894
s.p., cor pts SCHOTTS C 39 895
s.p., ipa   (W585)

Herr, Es Ist Zeit
men cor sc SCHOTTS C 37 889 s.p.
                                    (W586)

Hymnus Creaturae "Gross Ist Der Herr"
mix cor (med easy) sc SCHOTTS
C 40 107 s.p.   (W587)

Seele, Vergiss Sie Nicht *funeral
men cor,acap TONOS 3728 s.p. (W588)

WO DER HERR NICHT DAS HAUS BAUET see
Schutz, Heinrich

WO DER HERR SEIN HAUS see Stange, Max

WO DU HINGEHST see Becker

WO GOTT DER HERR NICHT BEI UNS HALT see
Weiss, Ewald

WO GOTT ZUM HAUS NICHT GIBT SEIN GUNST
see Gadsch, Herbert

WO IST EIN SO HERRLICH VOLK see Brahms,
Johannes

WOE IS ME see Amner, John

WOEFULLY ARRAY'D see Cornysh, William

WOEHL, WALDEMAR (1902-   )
Kleine Weihnachtslieder-Kantate
*Xmas,cant/carol
3pt jr cor/3pt wom cor/3 eq voices,
2vln,cont,opt vln&vla&gtr sc,cor
pts PELIKAN PE290   (W589)

WOES, THE see Ford, Virgil T.

WOHIN SOLL ICH MICH WENDEN? see
Schubert, Franz (Peter)

WOHL DEM, DER DEN HERREN FURCHTET see
Lohr, Ina

WOHL DEM, DER DEN HERREN FURCHTET see
Schutz, Heinrich

WOHL DEM, DER NICHT DEN WEG DES
FREVLERS WAHLT see Eglin, Arthur

WOHL DEM, DER NICHT WANDELT IM RAT DER
GOTTLOSEN see Matthes, Rene

WOHL DEM, DER NICHT WANDELT IM RAT DER
GOTTLOSEN see Schutz, Heinrich

WOHL DENEN, DIE DA WANDELN see Schutz,
Heinrich

WOHL DENEN, DIE DA WANDELN see
Vogelsanger

WOHL MIR, DASS ICH JESUM HABE see Bach,
Johann Sebastian

WOHL MITTEN IN DER NACHT *Xmas,carol/
folk
(Biebl, F.) [Ger] 4pt men cor
MERSEBURG EM9053   (W590)

WOHLAUF, DIE IHR HUNGRIG SEID see
Gottschick, Friedemann

WOHLAUF, IHR CHRISTEN, FREUET EUCH see
Praetorius, Michael

WOHLAUF IN GOTTES SCHONE WELT *folk
(Desch, R.) men cor,acap TONOS 66
s.p.   (W591)

WOHLBERG, MAX
Shahar Avakeshkha
[Heb] cong (Weekday Morning
Service) TRANSCON. TCL 385 $6.00
                                    (W592)

WOLF, HUGO (1860-1903)
Sechs Geistliche Lieder Nach
Gedichten Von Eichendorff *CC6U
[Eng/Ger] SATB,pno (med diff)
BAREN. BA19310   (W593)

WOLFE
Greater Is He That Is In Me
(Johnson) SATB oct BENSON S4121
$.40   (W594)

I Love Him Too Much (To Fail Him Now)
(Mercer, W. Elmo) SATB oct BENSON
S4142 $.35   (W595)

Only Jesus Can Satisfy Your Soul
(Huff, Ronn) SSATB oct BENSON S4248
$.35   (W596)

WOLFF
Sing We All Noel *Xmas,anthem
2pt oct BROADMAN 4558-56 $.30
                                    (W597)

WOLFF, H. DE
Het Vleesgeworden Woord *Xmas,cant
unis,pno/harmonium HEER 148 s.p.
                                    (W598)

WOLFF, HARALD
Book Of Canons, A *CC21U,canon
cor/jr cor CHANTRY CHC 604 $.35
                                    (W599)

WOLFF, S. DRUMMOND
Abide, O Dearest Jesus
SATB (med) oct CONCORDIA 98-2223
$.50   (W600)

Arise, O God, And Shine
SATB,opt trp oct CONCORDIA 98-2227
$.55   (W601)

Hope Of The World
SATB (med) oct CONCORDIA 98-2163
$.40   (W602)

Hosanna, Loud Hosanna *Adv/Palm
SS (med) oct CONCORDIA 98-2204 $.35
                                    (W603)

O Blessed Holy Trinity *Gen/Trin
SAB oct CONCORDIA 98-2218 $.35
                                    (W604)

O Come, All Ye Faithful
SATB,trp (chorale concertato) oct
CONCORDIA 98-2228 $.40, ipa
                                    (W605)

Praise To The Lord
SATB,opt brass (med) oct CONCORDIA
98-2208 $.50   (W606)

This Joyful Eastertide *Easter
SATB,2trp (chorale concertato) oct
CONCORDIA 98-2221 $.50   (W607)

WOLL, E.
Wir Loben Dich
SSAA/TTBB,org cor pts CHRIS 50693
s.p.   (W608)
SATB,org cor pts CHRIS 50691 s.p.
                                    (W609)
SATB,org voc sc CHRIS 50690 s.p.,
ipa   (W610)

WOLL, ERNA (1917-   )
Choralmesse *Mass
[Lat] 3pt mix cor&cong,opt org sc,
cor pts BOHM s.p.   (W611)

Proprium Missae In Die "Puer Natus
Est" *CCU,Xmas
[Lat] 4pt mix cor,inst sc,cor pts
BOHM s.p.   (W612)

WOLTERS, KARL-HEINZ (1929-   )
Gebet Im Zwanzigste Jahrhundert
"Herr, Der Du Die Weihe Des
Lebens Schenkst" *prayer
TTBB sc SCHOTTS C 40 138 s.p., voc
pt SCHOTTS C 39 812 01-02 s.p.
                                    (W613)

WOMEN SING *CCUL
(Huff, Ronn) SSA,pno/org BENSON B0795
$1.50 stereo recording, tapes, and-
or accompaniment tape also
available; for book-record sets
available, contact publisher (W614)

WOMMACK, CHRIS
Beatitudes, The
SATB WORD CS-2700 $.40 see from
MUSIC FOR THE YOUNG CHURCH,
VOLUME II   (W615)

Christmas In Your Heart *Adv/Xmas
SATB oct LILLENAS AT-C109 $.30
                                    (W616)

WONDER OF CHRISTMAS, THE see Peterson,
John W.

WONDER OF WONDERS see Peterson, John W.

WONDER WHEN HE'S COMING see Hughes,
Miki

WONDERFUL see Winter, Sister Miriam
Therese

WONDERFUL CHRISTMASTIME see Carmony,
Bryan M.

WONDERFUL IS JESUS! see Peterson, John
W.

WONDERFUL JESUS see Sellers, R.

WONDERFUL NEWS OF A SAVIOR see Vick

WONDERFUL PEACE see Cornell

WONDERFUL PEACE -HIDDEN PEACE see Braun

WONDERFUL WORDS OF LIFE *anthem
(Vick) 2pt oct BROADMAN 4540-81 $.30
                                    (W617)
WONDERFUL WORDS OF LIFE see Bliss, Paul

WONDROUS CROSS, THE see Landgrave,
Phillip

WONDROUS GIFT see Wilhelm, Patricia M.

WONDROUS LOVE *CC14UL,US
(McCluskey, Eugene) SATB (easy)
LORENZ $1.95   (W618)

WONDROUS LOVE *Gd.Fri.,anthem/folk/
hymn
(Collins) 1-2pt (easy) oct BROADMAN
4551-11 $.30   (W619)
(DeCou, Harold) SATB oct SINGSPIR
ZJP-7290 $.30   (W620)
(Park, J.F.) TTBB BRODT UF 3 $.25
                                    (W621)
(Smith, Douglas) SATB WORD CS-2676
$.40   (W622)
(Thiman) 1-2pt (easy) oct BROADMAN
4535-93 $.30   (W623)

WONDROUS LOVE see DeMone, Richard

WONDROUS LOVE see Page, Sue Ellen

WONDROUS LOVE see Thiman, Eric Harding

WONDROUS NATIVITY see Wetzler, Robert

WOOD
O Praise Ye The Lord
SAB SHAWNEE D5222 $.40   (W624)

WOOD, CHARLES (1866-1926)
Ding! Dong! Merrily On High *Xmas
SATB EMI s.p. contains also: Past
Three O'Clock   (W625)

Past Three O'Clock
see Wood, Charles, Ding! Dong!
Merrily On High

WOOD, DALE
Advent Carol *Adv
SATB ART MAST 119 $.40   (W626)
SA ART MAST 128 $.40   (W627)

Daniel!
SATB ART MAST 1024 $.40   (W628)

David And Goliath
SATB/unis/2pt ART MAST 1003 $.40
                                    (W629)

Elijah! *Gen/Thanks
unis treb cor/mix cor,pno,opt bvl,
gtr,perc CHORISTERS A-99 $.35
                                    (W630)

Forth The Conqueror Has Gone
*Easter/Pent
SATB&unis,3trp ART MAST 136 $.50
                                    (W631)

Gift To Be Simple, The *sac/sec
1-2pt/SSA/SAB (based on Shaker
tune) FISCHER,C CM 7893 $.40
                                    (W632)

Hymn To The Trinity
SATB ART MAST 191 $.35   (W633)

Jonah
cor, any combination of voices
(easy) FISCHER,C CM 7816 $.35
                                    (W634)

O That I Had A Thousand Voices
SATB,3trp,2trom ART MAST 121 $.50,
ipa   (W635)

Thanks We Give *Gen/Thanks
2 eq voices/SATB,org,perc
CHORISTERS A-122 $.40   (W636)

Three Carols For Young Voices *CC3U,
Xmas,anthem
jr cor CHORISTERS E-1A $3.50 (W637)

Three Little Carols *CC3U,Adv/Xmas,
carol
SATB,2harp ART MAST 129 $.50, ipa,
ipr   (W638)

WOOD, JAMES
Voice Of My Beloved
SATB GALAXY 1.2378.1 $.30   (W639)

WOOD, JEFF
In The Spirit *CC9UL
(Johnson, Paul) SATB,pno oct GENTRY
G-629 $2.50   (W640)

Side By Side
(Johnson, P.) cor BRIDGE Z 213
                                    (W641)

WOOD, MARILYN
What Is Easter? *cant
jr cor,opt hndbl FINE ARTS EC 200C
$1.00   (W642)

WOODS AND EVERY SWEET-SMELLING TREE,
THE see Miles, Russell Hancock

WOOLLEN, RUSSELL
Apotheosis Of The Blessed Virgin
SSATB,acap AM.COMP.AL. $9.90 (W643)

WOOLLEN, RUSSELL (cont'd.)

Hymn On The Morning Of Christ's
Nativity *Op.33
SATB,SA soli,2fl,2ob,2clar,2bsn,
2horn,trp,trom,pno,harp,opt timp,
perc,strings AM.COMP.AL. sc
$29.15, cor pts $13.75   (W644)

Mass
SATB,ST soli,2trp,3trom,org sc
AM.COMP.AL. $9.35   (W645)

Nativitie
SATB,acap AM.COMP.AL. $3.30 (W646)

Temple
SATB,acap AM.COMP.AL. $3.30 (W647)

WORD OF GOD WHICH NE'ER SHALL CEASE,
THE see Hus-Reimann

WORD OF OUR GOD SHALL STAND FOREVER,
THE see Hovhaness, Alan

WORD WAS MADE FLESH see Hicks, Marjorie
Kisbey

WORD WAS MADE MUSIC, THE see Gassman,
Clark

WORK, JOHN [WESLEY] (1901-   )
Alas, And Did My Saviour Bleed
*anthem
see Isaac Watts Contemplates The
Cross
SATB oct BROADMAN 4561-16 $.35 (W648)

Isaac Watts Contemplates The Cross
*Easter/Gen
SATB,STBar soli BROADMAN $.35
contains: Alas, And Did My
Saviour Bleed; Now For A Tune
Of Lofty Praise; When I Survey
The Wondrous Cross   (W649)

Now For A Tune Of Lofty Praise
*anthem
see Isaac Watts Contemplates The
Cross
SATB oct BROADMAN 4561-19 $.35
(W650)

This Ol' Hammer
TTBB GALAXY 1.0629.1 $.40   (W651)

When I Survey The Wondrous Cross
see Isaac Watts Contemplates The
Cross

WORKIN' ON A BUILDIN'
(Mercer, W. Elmo) SATB,acap oct
BENSON S4369 $.25   (W652)

WORLD AT THE MANGER see Williamson,
Malcolm

WORLD IS CHARGED WITH THE GRANDEUR OF
GOD, THE see Bliss, Sir Arthur

WORLD IS FILLED WITH GOD'S MUSIC, THE
see Long, B.

WORLD ITSELF KEEPS EASTER DAY, THE see
Lovelace, Austin C.

WORLD REJOICE see Phillips, John C.

WORSHIP see Brown, Allanson G.Y.

WORSHIP NOW OUR GOD see Oldenburg, Bob

WORTHY IS THE LAMB see Handel, George
Frideric

WORTHY IS THE LAMB see Littleton, Bill
J.

WORTHY IS THE LAMB see Wyrtzen, Don

WORTHY THE LAMB see Black, Charles

WOSS, JOSEF VENANTIUS VON (1863-1943)
Ein Danklied Sei Dem Herrn
mix cor,acap BOHM s.p.   (W653)

Messe Zu Ehren Der Heiligen Cacilia
*Mass
[Lat] 4pt mix cor,org,opt 2trp&
2trom sc,cor pts BOHM s.p., ipa
(W654)

WOUNDED FOR ME see Ovens

WRIGHT, ALBERTA CHILDS
God Is Now *anthem
unis WORD CS-2632 $.30   (W655)

Noah *anthem
unis WORD CS-2633 $.30   (W656)

Walk In Sunlight *Xmas,cant
2pt&jr cor WORD 37664 $1.50 (W657)

WRITTEN IN THE BOOK OF LOVE see
Kirschke, D.

WUENSCH
Vexilla Regis Produent *cant
mix cor,solo,org WESTERN WIM25
$1.75   (W658)

WULZ, HELMUT
Sei Gegrusst, Maria
SATB DOBLINGER G 716 s.p.   (W659)

WUNDERBARER GNADENTHRON see Praetorius,
Michael

WUNDERBARER KONIG see Ruppel, Paul
Ernst

WUORINEN, CHARLES
Prayer Of Jonah, The
SATB,2vln,vla,vcl,bvl AM.COMP.AL.
sc $13.75, ipa, voc pt $4.95 (W660)

Symphonia Sacra
cor,TBB soli,2ob,org sc AM.COMP.AL.
$19.25   (W661)

WUSTHOFF, KLAUS
Weihnachtskantate Fur Junge Leute
*Xmas,cant
cor,soli,2fl/rec,perc,pno,electric/
rec/strings, electric guitar and
electric bass guitar voc sc
MERSEBURG EM1650 s.p., ipa (W662)

WYATT
Let Us Sing The New Song
SSA PRO ART 2826 $.40   (W663)
SAB PRO ART 2822 $.40   (W664)

WYETH, JOHN
Come, Thou Fount *anthem
(DeCou, Harold) SATB oct SINGSPIR
ZJP-7270 $.30   (W665)

Come, Thou Fount Of Every Blessing
*folk
(Burroughs, Bob) SATB/jr cor,brass
oct LILLENAS AN-5081 $.35   (W666)

WYETH'S REPOSITORY OF SACRED MUSIC
*CCU,anthem/fugue/Psalm
(Wyeth, John) DA CAPO
ISBN 0-306-77001-6 LC 74-4515
$15.00 contains works by: Billings;
Holden; Holyoke; Read;and others
(W667)

WYNER, YEHUDI (1929-   )
Behold, I Build A House
SATB,cantor,pno/org AM.COMP.AL.
$7.70   (W668)

Psalm 143
SATB AMP A-675 $.45   (W669)

V'anachnu
SATB,acap AM.COMP.AL. $.28 (W670)

WYRTZEN, DON
Celebrate! *folk
SATB oct SINGSPIR ZJP-5012 $.30
(W671)

Celebration Songs For Choir *CCU
cor SINGSPIR 5858 $1.95   (W672)

Come, Let Us Sing To The Lord
*anthem/folk
SATB oct SINGSPIR ZJP-5070 $.35
(W673)

Dark-Light *folk
SATB oct SINGSPIR ZJP-5032 $.25
(W674)

Discovery *anthem/gospel
SATB oct SINGSPIR ZJP-8163 $.30
(W675)

Divine Priority, The *anthem
SATB oct SINGSPIR ZJP-8215 $.35
(W676)

For By Grace *anthem
SATB oct SINGSPIR ZJP-7352 $.30
(W677)

God-Man, The *Xmas,cant
SATB SINGSPIR 4520 $1.50   (W678)

God That Was Real *folk
SATB oct SINGSPIR ZJP-5021 $.25
(W679)

He Loves You, My Friend! *folk
SATB oct SINGSPIR ZJP-5037 $.30
(W680)

Heart Of Love, A *folk
SATB oct SINGSPIR ZJP-5014 $.25
(W681)

He'll Break Through The Blue
*anthem/gospel
SATB oct SINGSPIR ZJP-8177 $.25
(W682)

I Wonder If It's Happened Yet To You
*anthem/gospel
SATB oct SINGSPIR ZJP-8142 $.30
(W683)

I'll Never Be The Same Again *folk
unis oct SINGSPIR ZJP-5008 $.25
(W684)

Jesus, My Joy *anthem
SATB,opt 2fl/2vln oct SINGSPIR
ZJP-7314 $.30   (W685)

WYRTZEN, DON (cont'd.)

Jesus, The Very Thought Of Thee
*anthem
SA&opt TB (easy) oct SINGSPIR
ZJP-6010 $.25   (W686)

Let's Celebrate Easter! *Easter,
anthem
SATB oct SINGSPIR ZJP-5010 $.30
(W687)

Look! See My God! *anthem
SATB oct SINGSPIR ZJP-7267 $.30
(W688)

Look Up And See Jesus *folk
SATB oct SINGSPIR ZJP-5049 $.30
(W689)

Lord Is My Shepherd, The *anthem/
folk
SATB/SSAT oct SINGSPIR ZJP-5060
$.40   (W690)

Love Was When *folk
SATB oct SINGSPIR ZJP-5026 $.30
(W691)

Master's Touch, The *folk
SATB oct SINGSPIR ZJP-5019 $.25
(W692)

My All In All *anthem
SA&opt TB (easy) oct SINGSPIR
ZJP-6007 $.25   (W693)

No Lonely Day *folk
SATB oct SINGSPIR ZJP-5022 $.30
(W694)

No Time! *anthem/gospel
SATB oct SINGSPIR ZJP-8168 $.30
(W695)

Now Sounds (composed with Walvoord,
John) *CCU
jr cor SINGSPIR 4500 $2.95 (W696)

O Give Me A Soapbox *folk
unis oct SINGSPIR ZJP-5015 $.25
(W697)

On Belief *folk
SAB/STB oct SINGSPIR ZJP-5020 $.25
(W698)

Our Sacrifice Of Praise *anthem/
gospel
SATB oct SINGSPIR ZJP-8190 $.30
(W699)

Praise Him! *folk
SATB oct SINGSPIR ZJP-5016 $.30
(W700)

Sandals *folk
SATB oct SINGSPIR ZJP-5023 $.25
(W701)

Seasons Of Rapture *folk
SATB oct SINGSPIR ZJP-3587 $.30
(W702)

So Let Me Live *anthem
SA&opt B oct LORENZ 7845 $.35
(W703)

This World Outside *folk
SATB oct SINGSPIR ZJP-5024 $.25
(W704)

Till He Comes *anthem/gospel
SATB oct SINGSPIR ZJP-8186 $.30
(W705)

To Be What You Want Me To Be *folk
SATB oct SINGSPIR ZJP-5041 $.25
(W706)

Unbounded Grace *folk
2pt&opt SATB oct SINGSPIR ZJP-5039
$.30   (W707)

Why Do I Sing? *anthem
SATB oct SINGSPIR ZJP-8210 $.35
(W708)

Why Not Now? *folk
1-2pt oct SINGSPIR ZJP-5030 $.25
(W709)

Windows Of The Mind *folk
unis&opt SATB oct SINGSPIR ZJP-5025
$.30   (W710)

Worthy Is The Lamb *folk
SATB oct SINGSPIR ZJP-5050 $.30
(W711)

Yesterday, Today And Tomorrow
*anthem/gospel
SATB oct SINGSPIR ZJP-5006 $.30
(W712)

WYTON
Stephen
SATB SHAWNEE A5676 $.35   (W713)

WYTON, ALEC (1921-   )
Antiphon *Xmas,Introit
SATB,acap oct AGAPE AG 7178 $.30
(W714)

Hark! What Mean Those Holy Voices
*Xmas
SATB (med) FITZSIMONS 2214 $.30
(W715)

Nunc Dimittis *Nunc
SATB,B solo,acap oct AGAPE AG 7180
$.35   (W716)

Palm Sunday Procession *Bibl
SATB (diff) FITZSIMONS 2218 $.35
(W717)

Psalm 130 *anthem
SSAATTBB,Mez/A solo AUGSBURG
11-0547 $.30   (W718)

X

XXII *anthem,16th cent
(Bergsagel, John) [Eng/Dan] SATB
HANSEN-DEN WH 29213 s.p.   (X1)

Y

YAHRES, SAMUEL C.
Adelante! (Sail On!) (from Our Sacred
Honor)
"Columbus Theme" SATB,pno YAHRES
5024 $.30 contains also:
Billings, William, Chester
(Yahres, Samuel C.)   (Y1)

Columbus Theme *see Adelante! (Sail
On!)

Our Sacred Honor
mix cor&opt speak cor,2 narrators,
band (bicentennial documentary)
YAHRES s.p.   (Y2)

Psalm 23 *see Psalm Beautiful, The

Psalm Beautiful, The (Psalm 23)
SATB,pno YAHRES 1044 $.30   (Y3)
SA,pno YAHRES 1042 $.30   (Y4)

Theme (from Our Sacred Honor)
SATB,pno YAHRES 5014 $.30   (Y5)

We, The People! (from Our Sacred
Honor)
SATB,pno YAHRES 5154 $.30   (Y6)

YANCEY, THOMAS
Bless The Lord
SATB BOURNE B230995-358 $.50   (Y7)

YANTIS, DAVID
Beyond A Dream *CC10L
(Brown, Charles F.) jr cor WORD
37666 $1.95
see also: Create In Me A Clean
Heart Willing; Turn It Over To
Jesus, He Cares   (Y8)

Create In Me A Clean Heart Willing
*anthem
(Brown, Charles F.) SATB WORD
CS-2663 $.30 see also Beyond A
Dream   (Y9)

Turn It Over To Jesus, He Cares
*anthem
(Brown, Charles F.) SATB WORD
CS-2639 $.30 see also Beyond A
Dream   (Y10)

YARRINGTON, JOHN
Calls To Prayer, Praise, Benediction
*CCU,liturg
mix cor CHANTRY LIT 726 $.35 (Y11)

YARROW
Very Last Day *see Stookey

YDSTIE
Hosanna Today! *Easter/Lent
SA oct SCHMITT 362 $.30   (Y12)

Song Of The Shepherds
SSA/SSAA GENERAL WDS GC60 $.35
(Y13)
TTBB,opt solo GENERAL WDS GC62 $.35
(Y14)
SATB GENERAL WDS GC59 $.35 (Y15)

YE HOLY ANGELS BRIGHT see Bancroft, H.
Hugh

YE SELECT OF THE LORD see Kverno,
Trond, I Herrens Utvalgte

YE SERVANTS OF GOD see Billings,
William

YE SERVANTS OF GOD see Haydn, (Franz)
Joseph

YE SHALL BE WITNESSES see Kirk

YE SHALL KNOW THE TRUTH see Dunlop,
Merrill

YE SHEPHERDS, COME! *Xmas
(Ehret, Walter) 2pt jr cor,ob,
fing.cym.,bells LILLENAS AN-4036
$.30   (Y16)

YE SHEPHERDS, YE WISE MEN! *Xmas
(Hardwicke) SSA,opt fl PRO ART 2806
$.35   (Y17)

YE SONS AND DAUGHTERS see Track,
Gerhard

YE SONS AND DAUGHTERS see Van Hulse,
Camil

YE SONS AND DAUGHTERS OF THE KING
see Six Songs

YE TRIBES OF ADAM see Billings, William

YE WATCHERS AND YE HOLY ONES see Darst,
W. Glenn

YE WERE SOMETIMES DARKNESS see
Armstrong, Mimi

YE, WHO SEEK THE TRUTH see Perry, Julia

YEAKLE, THOMAS
For A Small Moment
SATB,A/Bar solo,org GRAY CMR 3310
$.30   (Y18)

YEAR OF JUBILEE HAS COME, THE *hymn,US
(Goemanne, Noel) SAB/SA&cong,org,opt
1-2trp GIA G1938 $.40   (Y19)

YEAR'S AT THE SPRING see Caldwell

YEAWORTH
Always Christmas
(Mercer, W. Elmo) SATB BENSON S4015
$.30   (Y20)

YEHALELU see Diament, Abraham

YES, HE DID! *anthem/gospel
(DeCou, Harold) SAB oct SINGSPIR
ZJP-8057 $.30   (Y21)

YES, I'LL SING THE WONDROUS STORY
*anthem
(Mickelson, P.) SATB oct SINGSPIR
ZJP-8194 $.30   (Y22)

YESTERDAY, TODAY AND FOREVER *CCUL
(Marsh, Don) cor BENSON B0281 $1.95
stereo recording, tapes, and-or
accompaniment tape also available;
for book-record sets available,
contact publisher   (Y23)

YESTERDAY, TODAY, AND TOMORROW see
Robinson

YESTERDAY, TODAY AND TOMORROW see
Wyrtzen, Don

YESTERDAY'S GONE see Stanphill, Ira F.

YIELD NOT TO TEMPTATION *anthem
(Bock) SATB oct BROADMAN 4540-83 $.30
(Y24)

YIGDAL see Halevy, [Jacques-Francois-
Fromental-Elie]

YOM HA-SHABBAT see Adler, Samuel

YOM-TOV see Diament, Abraham

YOM ZEH L'YISRAEL see Fromm, Herbert

YONDER LIES A BOY see Horman, John D.

YORK, C.
This Is Why I Want To Go *anthem/
gospel
(DeCou, Harold) SATB oct SINGSPIR
ZIP-8185 $.30   (Y25)

YORK, DANIEL STANLEY
Glory Be To God
SATB,pno/org oct NATIONAL WHC-31
$.40   (Y26)

YOU ARE GIVEN TO KNOW see Porta,
Costanzo, Vobis Datum Est

YOU ARE PETER see Tamblyn, William

YOU ARE THE TEMPLE see Hilty

YOU CAN HAVE A SONG IN YOUR HEART see
Stanphill, Ira F.

YOU GOT TO REAP JUST WHAT YOU SOW
*spir
see Two Spirituals For Chorus
(Dawson) mix cor WARNER R3172 $.30
(Y27)
(Dawson) SSAA WARNER R3173 $.30 (Y28)

YOU HAVE BEEN ACCLAIMED THE CHOSEN ONE
see Victoria, Tomas Luis de, In
Veniste Enim Gratiam

YOU MUST COME IN AT THE DOOR *spir
(Johnson) SATB oct LILLENAS AN-3858
$.30   (Y29)

YOU WICKED SERVANT see Bender, Jan

YOUNG
Brightest Songs We Sing *anthem
2pt oct BROADMAN 4558-64 $.30 (Y30)

Easter Chime *Easter,anthem
SATB (easy) oct BROADMAN 4540-62
$.30   (Y31)

Fanfare For Easter Morning *Easter
SATB SHAWNEE A 5668 $.35   (Y32)

YOUNG (cont'd.)

Fanfare With Alleluias *anthem
SATB,opt trp&trom&tuba&timp oct
BROADMAN 4565-01 $.35   (Y33)

God Is Gone Up
see Young, O Clap Your Hands

God Is My Shepherd
SATB SHAWNEE A5664 $.35   (Y34)

Gracious Spirit, Love Divine *anthem
SATB oct LORENZ C353 $.35   (Y35)

Holy, Lord Of Hosts *anthem
2pt (easy) oct BROADMAN 4558-22
$.30   (Y36)

How Lovely Is The House Of God
*anthem
unis,opt inst oct BROADMAN 4560-35
$.35   (Y37)

I Was Glad When They Said Unto Me
*anthem
SATB (easy) oct BROADMAN 4554-66
$.30   (Y38)

In My Garden *anthem
SA oct SACRED S-5399 $.35   (Y39)

In The Chill Of Wintertime *Xmas,
anthem
SATB oct BROADMAN 4540-80 $.30
(Y40)

Let Us Arise And Sing *anthem
SATB (easy) oct BROADMAN 4537-36
$.30   (Y41)

May Our Glad Songs Ascend *anthem
SATB (easy) oct BROADMAN 4545-60
$.30   (Y42)

O Clap Your Hands *anthem
SATB (easy) oct OXFORD 94.206 $.25
contains also: God Is Gone Up
(Y43)

O God, Our Help In Ages Past *anthem
SATB oct HERITAGE H114 $.40   (Y44)

Praise Ye The Lord
SATB,acap (med) OXFORD 43.470 $.30
(Y45)

Sing And Rejoice *anthem
2pt oct BROADMAN 4558-45 $.30 (Y46)

Sing To God A Joyful Song *anthem
2pt oct BROADMAN 4558-30 $.30 (Y47)

Sing To The Lord With Cheerful Voice
*anthem
SATB oct SACRED S-158 $.35   (Y48)

That We May Show Thy Love *anthem
SATB (easy) oct BROADMAN 4550-10
$.30   (Y49)

Three Anthems Of Commitment *CCU,
anthem
SATB oct SACRED S-151 $.40   (Y50)

Who Is This That Comes In Glory?
*Easter,anthem
SATB oct SACRED S-163 $.35   (Y51)

YOUNG, CARLTON R.
Christmas Collage For Sheep,
Shepherds, And Angels *Xmas
dbl cor&cong,2org oct AGAPE AG 7168
$.40   (Y52)

Let All The World In Every Corner
Sing
2pt mix cor TRIUNE TUM 112 $.35 see
also LET THE WORLD SING   (Y53)

Our Father
dbl cor&cong,org,bvl oct AGAPE
AG7158 $.40   (Y54)

What Child Is This *Xmas,anthem
SATB,tamb, triangle AUGSBURG
11-1721 $.30   (Y55)

YOUNG CHILD'S CAROL, THE see Spurgeon

YOUNG, GORDON (1919-   )
Advent Lullaby, An *Adv/Xmas
SATB,S solo,kbd,opt 2fl (easy)
PRESSER 312-41076 $.40   (Y56)

Cherubim Song
SATB (easy) FITZSIMONS 2222 $.25
(Y57)

Christ Is Risen, Alleluia! *Easter,
cant
jr cor BROADMAN 4515-04 $1.25 (Y58)

Christmas Kings, The *Xmas
SATB,pno, opt woodblock (very easy)
PRESSER 312-41075 $.40   (Y59)

Consider The Lilies
SATB,acap (med easy) oct PRESSER
312-41025 $.30   (Y60)

YOUNG, GORDON (cont'd.)

Forth In Thy Name *anthem
SATB WORD CS-2437 $.30   (Y61)

Forth To The New Year! *anthem
SATB WORD CS-678 $.25   (Y62)

Guide Me, O Thou Great Jehovah
2pt mix cor TRIUNE TUM 106 $.35 see
also LET THE WORLD SING   (Y63)

Holy Birth, The *Xmas,cant
SATB&opt cong,narrator&opt solo
BROADMAN 4512-12 $1.25   (Y64)

Is There A Parade In Bethlehem?
*Xmas
SATB,2fl,drums oct PRESSER
312-41040 $.35   (Y65)

Lamb Of God Most Lowly
SATB GALAXY 1.2215.1 $.30   (Y66)

Laudamus Te
SATB VOLKWEIN VB-744 $.30   (Y67)

Let All The World In Every Corner
Sing
SATB GALAXY 1.2342.1 $.30   (Y68)

Let Not Your Heart Be Troubled
SATB,pno/org (med easy) PRESSER
312-41024 $.35   (Y69)

Man Of Sorrows *Easter,cant
SATB&cong,narrator (easy) BROADMAN
4514-03 $1.00   (Y70)

Noel *Xmas,anthem
SATB (easy) oct BROADMAN 4545-04
$.30   (Y71)

Old Time Religion, The *anthem
SATB (easy) oct BROADMAN 4562-06
$.30   (Y72)

Shepherds, Arise And Leave Your Sheep
*Xmas
SATB,acap (easy) oct PRESSER
312-41037 $.30   (Y73)

Sing Alleluia *anthem
SATB (easy) oct BROADMAN 4561-58
$.30   (Y74)

Sing Unto The Lord A New Song
SATB (easy) FISCHER,C CM 7906 $.40
(Y75)

Tambourine Noel *Xmas
SATB,pno,tamb oct SOMERSET AD 1986
$.40   (Y76)

To God And Country Let Us Sing
1-2pt BROADMAN 4560-47 $.40   (Y77)

YOUNG, P.
Drop, Drop, Slow Tears
mix cor BRODT 589 $.22   (Y78)

I Sing The Mighty Power Of God
mix cor BRODT 590 $.30   (Y79)

YOUNG, PHILLIP M.
Fanfare With Alleluias
SATB,org,opt trp&trom&tuba&perc oct
BROADMAN 4565-01 $.35, ipa   (Y80)

God With Us! Emmanuel *Xmas,cant
cor,med solo&high solo,opt 3trp&
hndbl BROADMAN 4512-06 $1.25
(Y81)

Praise God Ye Sons Of Earth *anthem
SATB (easy) oct BROADMAN 4561-57
$.30   (Y82)

We Would Remember
1-2pt BROADMAN 4560-46 $.40   (Y83)

YOUNG, ROBERT H.
Love Came Down At Christmas *Xmas,
anthem
SATB WORD   (Y84)

When I Survey The Wondrous Cross
*anthem
SATB WORD CS-673 $.30   (Y85)

THE YOUNGER CHOIR NO. 2 *CC30U
jr cor LILLENAS MB-231 $1.25 (Y86)

THE YOUNGER CHOIR NO. 3 *CC33U
jr cor LILLENAS MB-246 $1.25 (Y87)

YOUNGER, JOHN B.
Lord Is My Strength And My Song, The
SATB HARRIS $.35   (Y88)

Now Is Christ Risen *Easter
SATB HARRIS $.35   (Y89)

O Heavenly Beauty
SATB HARRIS $.35   (Y90)

YOUNGER, JOHN B. (cont'd.)

There Is A Green Hill Far Away
SATB HARRIS $.35   (Y91)

'Twas In The Moon Of Wintertime
*Xmas
SATB HARRIS HC 4043 $.60   (Y92)

YOUR HOLY CROSS see Hruby, Delores

YOUR INVITATION see Skillings, Otis

YOUR LIFE HAS A PLAN see Turner, Lee

YOUR MAKER'S PRAISE
(Brandon, George) SATB (med) WATERLOO
$.40   (Y93)

YOUSE, GLAD ROBINSON (1898-   )
Lovely The Dawning
SSA (med) FITZSIMONS 3079 $.20
(Y94)

YOUTH
see Four Folk Songs From Abroad

YOUTH FAVORITES *CC132UL
(Peterson, John W.) jr cor cmplt ed
SINGSPIR 5794 $1.50, min sc
SINGSPIR 5790 $.95   (Y95)

YOUTH HYMN ANTHEMS NO. 2 *CCU,anthem/
hymn
SAB/SA/unis LORENZ $1.95   (Y96)

YOUTH IN UNISON *CCUL,hymn
unis jr cor,pno/org,fl/vln SINGSPIR
5033 $1.50   (Y97)

YOUTH SINGS SATB *CC15U,anthem
(Leach, Bill F.; Bobbitt, Paul) SATB
BROADMAN 4530-13 $1.25 contains
works by Bass; Young; Ehret (Y98)

YOUTH'S PRAYER see Kirby

YOU'VE GOT TO LIVE YOUR RELIGION see
Parks

YULETIDE FANFARE see Van Wormer, G.

YUN, ISANG (1917-   )
An Der Schwelle
wom cor,Bar solo,org,fl,ob,trp,
trom,perc BOTE sc s.p., cor pts
rental, ipr   (Y99)

Z

ZABEL, ALFRED
And There Were Shepherds *Xmas
unis,hndbl/pno/org CHORISTERS A-168
$.40 (Z1)

ZACCHEUS see Winter, Sister Miriam
Therese

ZACK, JUNIOR see Coleman, Jack

ZADOK THE PRIEST see Handel, George
Frideric

ZAHNER, BRUNO
Bei Der Krippe *Xmas,cant
1-2 eq voices/3pt mix cor,2perc,1-
2S rec/1-2fl,vln,vcl,opt pno cor
pts,sc PELIKAN PE922 s.p., ipa
(Z2)

ZAININGER, B.
Beruhmtes "Libera" *Op.16
[Lat] 4pt mix cor,org/4trp,trom sc,
cor pts BOHM s.p., ipa (Z3)

ZALM 57 see Blazek, Vilem

ZALM 126 see Vendler, Bohumil

ZALM ZEME PODKARPATSKEJ see Suchon,
Eugen

ZANGL, LUDWIG
St. Ludwigs-Messe *Op.59, Mass
[Lat] SAB&opt T,org/2vln&2horn&
opt fl&2clar&2trp&trom&timp sc,
cor pts BOHM s.p., ipa (Z4)

ZANINELLI, LUIGI
Covenant Of Peace
SATB SHAWNEE A5683 $.35 (Z5)

Let All The World In Every Corner
Sing *anthem
SATB LEXICON CS-2598 $.35 (Z6)

Praised Be The God Of Love *anthem
SATB LEXICON CS-2597 $.35 (Z7)

ZECHER L'MAASEH see Weiner, Lazar

ZEGEN ONS HUIS see Brahe, May H., Bless
This House

ZEHN PSALMSPRUCHE see Schweizer, Rolf

ZEHNER
Jauchzet, Alle Lande, Gott Zu Ehren
*cant
SATB/unis,org,2trp sc HANSSLER
10.302 s.p. (Z8)

ZELINKA, JAN EVANGELISTA (1893-)
Balada O Svatbe V Kanaan *Op.113,
cant
"Ballad About The Wedding In
Canaan" [Czech] mix cor,MezTBar
soli,2fl,2ob,3clar,2bsn,4horn,
2trp,2trom,timp,perc,harp,strings
CZECH s.p. (Z9)

Ballad About The Wedding In Canaan
*see Balada O Svatbe V Kanaan

Josef A Marie V Betleme
"Joseph And Mary At Bethlehem"
[Czech] mix cor,pno,org,strings
CZECH s.p. (Z10)

Joseph And Mary At Bethlehem *see
Josef A Marie V Betleme

ZELINKA, SR. JAN EVANGELISTA
(1856-1935)
Narozeni Pane *Xmas
[Czech] mix cor&jr cor,soli,fl,
2clar,2trp,2trom,harmonium,
strings CZECH s.p. (Z11)

ZELLER
Talk About Love *folk
(Skillings, Otis) SATB/jr cor oct
LILLENAS AN-5087 $.35 (Z12)

ZELLNER, HANS
Bairische Singmesse (composed with
Starnberg) *Mass
3pt wom cor,opt inst HIEBER sc
s.p., voc pt s.p. (Z13)

ZELTER, CARL FRIEDRICH (1758-1832)
Epiphanias
TTBB,acap oct BOOSEY 5915 $.45 see
from Four Songs For Male Voices
(Z14)
Epiphanias: Die Heiligen Drei Konige
*Epiph
men cor,acap TONOS 4353 s.p. (Z15)

ZELTER, CARL FRIEDRICH (cont'd.)
Four Songs For Male Voices *see
Epiphanias; St. Paul (Z16)

St. Paul
TTBB,acap oct BOOSEY 5914 $.40 see
from Four Songs For Male Voices
(Z17)

ZENDER, HANS
Canto IV *sac/sec
16pt,16inst BOTE rental (Z18)

Canto V *sac/sec
SATB,opt SATB soli,perc BOTE s.p.
(Z19)

ZENTNER, JOHANNES (1903-)
Triumph! Triumph! Es Kommt Mit Pracht
SAT/SAB (contains also: Wie Selig,
Wer Im Glauben Nur) SCHWEIZER.
SK 52.03 s.p. see also
MUSIKBEILAGE ZUM "EVANGELISCHEN
KIRCHENCHOR 1952" (Z20)

Weil Unser Trost, Der Herre Christ
SAT/SAB SCHWEIZER. SK 118 s.p.
(Z21)

ZETTERVALL, HOWARD
O Come, Let Us Sing *CCU,Gen,anthem
cor SACRED $1.95 (Z22)

Six Anthems With Brass *CC6U,anthem
SATB,brass SACRED $1.75, ipa (Z23)

ZEUCH AN DIE MACHT, DU ARM DES HERRN
see Werner, Fritz

ZEUCH EIN ZU DEINEN TOREN see Ebeling,
Johann Georg

ZEUNER, MARTIN (ca. 1600?)
Herr Jesu Christ, Wahr Mensch Und
Gott
SSATB (contains also: Furwahr, Es
Ist Ein Kostlich Ding) SCHWEIZER.
SK 65.01 s.p. see also
MUSIKBEILAGE ZUM "EVANGELISCHEN
KIRCHENCHOR 1965" (Z24)

ZEUTSCHNER
Gott, Sei Mir Gnadig *cant
SATB, SATB/T soli,cont,strings
HANSSLER 10.260 sc s.p., cor pts
s.p., ipa (Z25)

ZGODAVA, RICHARD A.
Carol Of Joy (Aleria) *anthem
SATB AUGSBURG 11-1713 $.45 (Z26)

Carol Of The Italian Pipers *carol
SATB,opt fl,perc SHAWNEE A967 $.40
(Z27)

Out Of The Orient Crystal Skies
*Xmas
SATB oct SCHMITT 1807 $.40 (Z28)

ZIEGELMEIER, M.
Sub Umbra Illius *Op.29, Mass
[Lat] 4pt mix cor,org sc,cor pts
BOHM s.p. (Z29)

ZIET GIJ DE STERRE SCHIJNEN see Pronk,
Arie

ZILCH, MARGOT
He Calls Me Son
SATB oct GOSPEL 05 TM 0118 $.25
(Z30)

I Dare Not Be Defeated
SATB oct GOSPEL 05 TM 0270 $.20
(Z31)

I Shall Be Satisfied
(Weston, Dave) SATB oct GOSPEL
05 TM 0171 $.20 (Z32)

If He Be God
(Krogstad, Bob) SATB oct GOSPEL
05 TM 0423 $.35 (Z33)

In The Ages To Come *gospel
(Collins) SATB oct LILLENAS AT-1107
$.30 (Z34)

May I Never Lose The Wonder
(Krogstad, Bob) SATB oct GOSPEL
05 TM 0309 $.35 (Z35)

Potter's Vessel, The
(Krogstad, Bob) SATB oct GOSPEL
05 TM 0366 $.35 (Z36)

Sound Of Music, The
SATB oct GOSPEL 05 TM 0117 $.25
(Z37)

Temple Unto God, A
(Smith, Herb) SATB oct GOSPEL
05 TM 0116 $.25 (Z38)

Wait On The Lord
(Walters, Bob) SATB oct GOSPEL
05 TM 0119 $.35 (Z39)

ZILLINGER, ERWIN (1893-)
Deutsche Messe
unis,org sc HANSSLER 25.027 s.p.
(Z40)
Die Finsternis Vergeht
SAT/SAB (contains also: Brich An,
Du Schones Morgenlicht)
SCHWEIZER. SK 68.03 s.p. see also
MUSIKBEILAGE ZUM "EVANGELISCHEN
KIRCHENCHOR 1968" (Z41)

Erhalt Uns, Herr, Bei Deinem Wort
SAT/SAB,opt treb inst&bass inst
HANSSLER 14.142 s.p. (Z42)

Wie Lieblich Schon, Herr Zebaoth
SAT/SAB/2pt,opt treb inst HANSSLER
14.184 s.p. (Z43)

ZIMMER, JAN (1926-)
Dispersit, Dedit Pauperibus
see Styri Moteta

In Hora Ultima
see Styri Moteta

Principes Persecuti
see Styri Moteta

Propter Veritatem
see Styri Moteta

Styri Moteta *mot
[Lat] SLOV.HUD.FOND s.p.
contains: Dispersit, Dedit
Pauperibus; In Hora Ultima;
Principes Persecuti; Propter
Veritatem (Z44)

ZIMMERMAN, JAMES
Rejoice! Rejoice! *Xmas
3AB,opt gtr MCAFEE M7003 $.40 (Z45)

ZIMMERMANN, HEINZ WERNER (1930-)
And The Word Became Flesh *Xmas
SATB,acap (med) oct CONCORDIA
98-2177 $.25 (Z46)

Ehre Sei Gott In Der Hohe (from Sechs
Neue Lieder)
unis/mix cor,org/acap/bvl/vcl (med)
BAREN. BA5418 see from Sechs Neue
Lieder (Z47)
4pt mix cor/unis,opt org BAREN.
BA 6312 (Z48)

Four Christmas Motets *CC4U,Xmas,
anthem,Contemp
SATB,bvl oct CHANTRY COA 6731 $.45
(Z49)
Gloria *Gloria,Contemp
SMezATB,soli,opt org,orch, combo of
trumpet, trombone, guitar, piano,
bass, and percussion (med diff)
BAREN. BA 6014 (Z50)

Gott Aber Kann Machen
unis/mix cor,org/acap/bvl/vcl (med)
BAREN. BA5418 see from Sechs Neue
Lieder (Z51)

Gott Ist Unsre Zuversicht
unis/mix cor,org/acap/bvl/vcl (med)
BAREN. BA5418 see from Sechs Neue
Lieder (Z52)
5pt mix cor/unis,opt org (med)
BAREN. BA6311 see from SECHS NEUE
LIEDER (Z53)

Have No Fear, Little Flock
SATB,acap (med) oct CONCORDIA
98-2175 $.25 (Z54)

Hymnus (Part 4)
[Eng] SSATB,hpsd,bvl, vibraphone
oct AGAPE AG 7174 $.50 see from
Vespers (Z55)

Ingressus (Part 1)
[Eng] SSATB,hpsd,bvl, vibraphone
oct AGAPE AG 7171 $.50 see from
Vespers (Z56)

Jauchzet Gott, Dem Herren, Alle Welt
*Psalm
SMezATB,acap (med) BAREN. BA5426
(Z57)

Lord Is My Light, The (Psalm 27)
SATB,acap (med) oct CONCORDIA
98-2174 $.30 (Z58)

Magnificat (Part 5) *Magnif
[Eng] SSATB,hpsd,bvl, vibraphone
oct AGAPE AG 7175 $1.00 see from
Vespers (Z59)

Make A Joyful Noise *anthem,Contemp
SSATB oct CHANTRY COA 6626 $.35
(Z60)

Now To The King Of All Worlds
*anthem,Contemp
SAB oct CHANTRY COA 7348 $.30 (Z61)

O Sing Unto The Lord *anthem,Contemp
SATB,bvl oct CHANTRY COA 6217 $.35
(Z62)

ZIMMERMANN, HEINZ WERNER (cont'd.)

Praise Him, O Servants Of God
see Two Motets

Praise The Lord (Psalm 113)
SATB,acap (med) oct CONCORDIA
98-2176 $.25   (Z63)

Psalm 13
cor,org,bvl (med diff) FISCHER,C
CM 7858 $.40   (Z64)

Psalm 27 *see Lord Is My Light, The

Psalm 46 *see Psalm (Part 3)

Psalm 67 *Gen/Thanks
SATB,org,bvl, opt glockenspiel
(med) FISCHER,C CM 7857 $.35
                               (Z65)

Psalm 113 *see Praise The Lord

Psalm 117
SATB,S solo,org,bvl,gtr (med)
FISCHER,C CM 7826 $.40   (Z66)

Psalm 118 *see Psalm (Part 2)

Psalm 125 *see Those Who Trust In
The Lord

Psalm 148
SATB,ST soli,org,bvl, vibraphone
(med) sc FISCHER,C O 4898 $2.50,
cor pts FISCHER,C O 4898A $.40,
ipa   (Z67)

Psalm (Part 2) (Psalm 118)
[Eng] SSATB,hpsd,bvl, vibraphone
oct AGAPE AG 7172 $1.00 see from
Vespers   (Z68)

Psalm (Part 3) (Psalm 46)
[Eng] SSATB,hpsd,bvl, vibraphone
oct AGAPE AG 7173 $1.00 see from
Vespers   (Z69)

Sechs Neue Lieder *see Ehre Sei Gott
In Der Hohe; Gott Ist Unsre
Zuversicht; Singet Dem Herrn Ein
Neues Lied; Und Das Wort Ward
Fleisch; Uns Ist Ein Kind Geboren
                               (Z70)

Singet Dem Herrn Ein Neues Lied
unis/mix cor,org/acap/bvl/vcl (med)
BAREN. BA5418 see from Sechs Neue
Lieder   (Z71)

This Day A Child Is Born
see Two Motets

Those Who Trust In The Lord (Psalm
125)
SATB,acap (med) oct CONCORDIA
98-2178 $.25   (Z72)

Two Motets *anthem,Contemp
SATB,bvl oct CHANTRY COA 6116 $.40
contains: Praise Him, O Servants
Of God; This Day A Child Is
Born   (Z73)

Und Das Wort Ward Fleisch
unis/mix cor,org/acap/bvl/vcl (med)
BAREN. BA5418 see from Sechs Neue
Lieder   (Z74)

Uns Ist Ein Kind Geboren
unis/mix cor,org/acap/bvl/vcl (med)
BAREN. BA5418 see from Sechs Neue
Lieder   (Z75)

Vespers *see Hymnus (Part 4);
Ingressus (Part 1); Magnificat
(Part 5); Psalm (Part 2) (Psalm
118); Psalm (Part 3) (Psalm 46)
                               (Z76)

ZINGARELLI, NICOLA ANTONIO (1752-1837)
Go Not Far From Me, O God
mix cor BANKS MUS YS 374 $.25 (Z77)

ZION HEARS THE WATCHMEN'S VOICES see
Bach, Johann Sebastian

ZIPP, FRIEDRICH (1914-   )
Allein Gott In Der Hoh Sei Ehr
unis&SAT/SAB (contains also: Lobet
Den Herren, Alle, Die Ihn Ehren)
SCHWEIZER. SK 67.01 s.p. see also
MUSIKBEILAGE ZUM "EVANGELISCHEN
KIRCHENCHOR 1967"   (Z78)

Anbetung Des Kindes "Als Ein Behutsam
Licht"
see Drei Weihnachtschore

Auf, Ihr Hirten
see Zwei Weihnachtslieder

Aus Meines Herzens Grunde
unis&SATB (contains also: Nun
Schlagt Die Stunde Mitternacht;
Es Ist Ein Freud Dem Herzen Mein)
SCHWEIZER. SK 64.01-2 s.p. see

ZIPP, FRIEDRICH (cont'd.)

also MUSIKBEILAGE ZUM
"EVANGELISCHEN KIRCHENCHOR 1964"
                               (Z79)

Das Will Ich Mir Zu Herzen Nehmen
SAT/SAB,org (contains also: Herr,
Deinen Tod Verkunden Wir)
SCHWEIZER. SK 72.07-8 s.p. see
also MUSIKBEILAGE ZUM
"EVANGELISCHEN KIRCHENCHOR 1972"
                               (Z80)

Der Gerechten Seelen Sind In Gottes
Hand *Rembrnc
cor BOHM s.p.   (Z81)

Der Morgenstern Ist Aufgedrungen
*Adv/Xmas,mot
4pt men cor&opt jr cor,opt S solo
sc SCHOTTS C 42 913 s.p. see from
Zwei Kleine Motetten   (Z82)

Die Toten Ruhn In Gott "Haltet Nicht
Fest Die Trauer" *Op.30
men cor sc SCHOTTS C 40 251 s.p.
                               (Z83)

Dort Oben Vom Berge
see Zwei Weihnachtslieder

Drei Weihnachtschore *Xmas
mix cor (easy) sc SCHOTTS C 37 837
s.p.
contains: Anbetung Des Kindes
"Als Ein Behutsam Licht",
Op.39,No.2; Weihnachten "Du
Darfst Es Wieder Spuren Heut",
Op.39,No.1; Zu Selger
Jahreswende "So Schliesse
Denn", Op.39,No.3   (Z84)

Es Flog Ein Taublein Weisse *Adv
4pt men cor&opt jr cor,opt S solo
sc SCHOTTS C 42 912 s.p. see from
Zwei Kleine Motetten   (Z85)

Gott Ist Liebe
SATB&cong,soli,acap (easy) BAREN.
BA6308   (Z86)

Gott Ist Unsere Zuversicht Und Starke
(Psalm 64)
SAT/SAB SCHWEIZER. SK 65.05 s.p.
see also MUSIKBEILAGE ZUM
"EVANGELISCHEN KIRCHENCHOR 1965"
                               (Z87)

Hor Auf, Mein Herz, In Deiner Hast
see Zwei Geistliche Lieder

Laufet, Ihr Hirten
1-2pt jr cor/1-2pt wom cor,2S rec,A
rec/vln,opt perc sc,cor pts
PELIKAN PE764   (Z88)

Lobe Den Herren, Den Machtigen Konig
*cant
SATB&opt cong,3trp,3trom,org (med)
sc,cor pts BAREN. BA5432 s.p.,
ipa, sc,cor pts BAREN.   (Z89)

Mein Schonste Zier *Op.40,No.2, mot
mix cor (med) sc SCHOTTS C 37 614
s.p. see from Zwei Geistliche
Choralmotetten   (Z90)

Mein Seel, O Herr, Muss Loben Dich
SAT/SAB/2pt,opt treb inst HANSSLER
14.200 s.p.   (Z91)

Mit Ernst, O Menschenkinder
see Zwei Adventslieder

Niederlandisches Dankgebet "Wir
Treten Zum Beten Vor Gott"
*prayer,Neth
4pt men cor,acap/2trp sc SCHOTTS
CHBL 167 s.p.   (Z92)

Nun Danket Alle Gott *Te Deum
(Cruger, Joh.) men cor sc SCHOTTS
CHBL 166 s.p.   (Z93)

Nun Jauchzt Dem Herren, Alle Welt
SAT/SAB/2pt,treb inst,bass inst,opt
org (two settings) HANSSLER
14.187 s.p.   (Z94)

O Heiland Reiss Die Himmel Auf
SAT/SAB (contains also: Jauchz, Erd
Und Himmel) SCHWEIZER. SK 66.02
s.p. see also MUSIKBEILAGE ZUM
"EVANGELISCHEN KIRCHENCHOR 1966"
                               (Z95)

Psalm 64 *see Gott Ist Unsere
Zuversicht Und Starke

Singet Frisch Und Wohlgemut
mix cor (easy) sc SCHOTTS CHBL 324
s.p.   (Z96)

Viel Susser Christ *Op.40,No.1, mot
mix cor (med) sc SCHOTTS C 38 172
s.p. see from Zwei Geistliche
Choralmotetten   (Z97)

ZIPP, FRIEDRICH (cont'd.)

Weihnachten "Du Darfst Es Wieder
Spuren Heut"
see Drei Weihnachtschore

Wer Gott Zum Freund Nicht Hat
see Zwei Geistliche Lieder

Wie Soll Ich Dich Empfangen
see Zwei Adventslieder

Zu Selger Jahreswende "So Schliesse
Denn"
see Drei Weihnachtschore

Zwei Adventslieder
TTBB,acap (med easy) MULLER SM 496A
s.p.
contains: Mit Ernst, O
Menschenkinder; Wie Soll Ich
Dich Empfangen   (Z98)

Zwei Geistliche Choralmotetten *see
Mein Schonste Zier, Op.40,No.2;
Viel Susser Christ, Op.40,No.1
                               (Z99)

Zwei Geistliche Lieder
mix cor,acap sc BOHM s.p.
contains: Hor Auf, Mein Herz, In
Deiner Hast; Wer Gott Zum
Freund Nicht Hat   (Z100)

Zwei Kleine Motetten *see Der
Morgenstern Ist Aufgedrungen; Es
Flog Ein Taublein Weisse   (Z101)

Zwei Weihnachtslieder *Xmas
mix cor (med easy) sc SCHOTTS
CHBL 322A-B s.p.
contains: Auf, Ihr Hirten; Dort
Oben Vom Berge   (Z102)

Z'MIROT YISRAEL see Naumbourg, Samuel

ZMITTST I DE NACHT see Baer, Walter

ZOLL, PAUL (1907-   )
Advents- Und Weihnachtsgesange *Adv/
Xmas
mix cor,acap BOHM sc s.p., cor pts
s.p.
contains: Es Bluhen Die Maien; Es
Bluhen Drei Rosen; Es Steht Ein
Lind Im Himmelreich; Inmitten
Der Nacht; Maria An Der Krippe;
O Jesulein Zart   (Z103)

Es Bluhen Die Maien
see Advents- Und Weihnachtsgesange

Es Bluhen Drei Rosen
see Advents- Und Weihnachtsgesange

Es Steht Ein Lind Im Himmelreich
see Advents- Und Weihnachtsgesange

Inmitten Der Nacht
see Advents- Und Weihnachtsgesange

Lobt Den Herrn, Ihr Wesen All *cant
mix cor&jr cor/men cor&jr cor,org/
brass (med) sc,cor pts SCHOTTS
ED. 5264 s.p., ipa   (Z104)

Maria An Der Krippe
see Advents- Und Weihnachtsgesange

O Jesulein Zart
see Advents- Und Weihnachtsgesange

Wem Zeit Wie Ewigzeit *mot
TTBB sc SCHOTTS C 39 093 s.p., voc
pt SCHOTTS C 39 094 01-02 s.p.
                               (Z105)

ZOUDEN WIJ OOK EENMAL KOMEN
mix cor sc HEER 2082 s.p.   (Z106)

ZOUHAR, ZDENEK (1927-   )
Advents Mass Songs No. 2 *see Roraty
C. 2

Roraty C. 2 *Adv
"Advents Mass Songs No. 2" [Czech]
jr cor&jr cor&jr cor,acap CZECH
s.p.   (Z107)

ZRNO, FELIX (1890-   )
Eternal Myth *see Vecna Baj

Vecna Baj *Xmas,folk/ora
"Eternal Myth" [Czech] mix cor,
narrator&SATB soli,fl,ob,clar,
bsn,2horn,2trp,timp,harp,org,
strings CZECH s.p.   (Z108)

ZU BETHLEHEM GEBOREN *Adv/Xmas
see Alte Frankische Weihnachtslieder
(Bauernfeind, Hans) wom cor,acap oct
DOBLINGER s.p. see also In Dulci
Jubilo   (Z109)

ZU BETHLEHEM GEBOREN see Monter, Josef

ZU BETHLEHEM GEBOREN see Poos, Heinrich

ZU BETHLEHEM GEBOREN see Schroeder, Hermann

ZU DIR, MARIA, KOMMEN WIR see Kuntz, Michael

ZU DIR, O GOTT, ERHEBEN WIR see Planyavsky, Peter

ZU DIR O HERR, ERHEBE ICH MEINE SEELE see Miller, Franz R.

ZU GOTT MEIN TROST ALLEIN ICH STELL see Le Maistre, Mattheus

ZU SELGER JAHRESWENDE "SO SCHLIESSE DENN" see Zipp, Friedrich

ZUBROD, FRIEDRICH
  Pange Lingua
    [Lat] 4pt mix cor,acap sc,cor pts
    BOHM s.p. contains also: Veni
      Creator   (Z110)

  Veni Creator
    see Zubrod, Friedrich, Pange Lingua

ZUFLUCHT see Lemacher, Heinrich

ZUM EINGANG "DIES IST DER TAG" see Trapp, Willy

ZUM JAHRESSCHLUSS "NUN GEHT DAS JAHR ZU ENDE" see Huther, K.

ZUM SANCTUS see Schubert, Franz (Peter)

ZUNDEL, [JOHN] (1815-1882)
  Love Divine *see Wesley, Samuel Sr.

ZUR GABENBEREITUNG "KOMMET, IHR HIRTEN" see Trapp, Willy

ZUR HAUSWEIHE "DU LIESSEST UNS DIESES WERK VOLLBRINGEN" see Rothschuh, Franz

ZWEI ADVENTLICHE MARIENLIEDER see Reusch, Fritz

ZWEI ADVENTSGESANGE see Metschnabel, Paul Joseph

ZWEI ADVENTSLIEDER see Zipp, Friedrich

ZWEI ADVENTSLIEDER see Biebl, Franz

ZWEI ADVENTSMOTETTEN see Schaper, Heinz-Christian

ZWEI ASPERGES ME see Weirich, August

ZWEI BEERDIGUNGSLIEDER see Lederer, F.

ZWEI CHRISTKONIGSGESANGE see Palestrina, Giovanni

ZWEI DER SERAPHINEN RIEFEN UND SPRACHEN see Staden, Johann

ZWEI DEUTSCHE MOTETTEN see Grosse-Schware, Hermann

ZWEI DEUTSCHE MOTETTEN see David, Thomas [Christian]

ZWEI EUCHARISTISCHE GESANGE see Schmid, Alfons

ZWEI GEISTLICHE CHORALMOTETTEN see Zipp, Friedrich

ZWEI GEISTLICHE CHORSATZE see Orff, Carl

ZWEI GEISTLICHE GESANGE see Scharf

ZWEI GEISTLICHE LIEDER see Zipp, Friedrich

ZWEI GEISTLICHE MOTETTEN see Haas, Joseph

ZWEI GESANGE FUR TRAUUNGEN see Bellermann, Sangerfahrt

ZWEI GRABLIEDER see Kutzer, Ernst

ZWEI JESUSGEBETE see Eglin, Arthur

ZWEI KLEINE MOTETTEN see Zipp, Friedrich

ZWEI LATEINISCHE MARIENGESANGE see Kromolicki, Joseph

ZWEI LIBERA see Gruber, Joseph

ZWEI LIBERA see Lipp, Alban

ZWEI LIEDER DES VERTRAUENS see Berghorn, Alfred

ZWEI LIEDER ZUM GEBURTSTAG ODER ZU NEUJAHR see Rothschuh, Franz

ZWEI MAGNIFICAT see Welcker, Max

ZWEI MARIENLIEDER see Kuntz, Michael

ZWEI MOTETTEN see Succo

ZWEI MOTETTEN see Lang, Hans

ZWEI MOTETTEN see Hessenberg, Kurt

ZWEI PANGE LINGUA see Barthelmes, Heinrich

ZWEI PANGE LINGUA see Kuntz, Michael

ZWEI PANGE LINGUA see Rehm, P. Otto

ZWEI PANGE LINGUA see Hoffmann, Bernhard

ZWEI PANGE LINGUA see Mutter, Gerbert

ZWEI PANGE LINGUA UND TANTUM ERGO see Hunecke, Wilhelm

ZWEI PANGE LINGUA UND TANTUM ERGO see Welcker, Max

ZWEI PASSIONS-MOTETTEN see Hunecke, Wilhelm

ZWEI PROPRIUMSGESANGE FUR DEN GRUNDONNERSTAG see Haydn, (Johann) Michael

ZWEI SAKRAMENTSGESANGE see Steinert, Bernhard

ZWEI TANTUM ERGO see Hoss, Franz

ZWEI TANTUM ERGO see Mozart, Wolfgang Amadeus

ZWEI TRAUUNGSCHORALE see Bach, Johann Sebastian

ZWEI VIDI AQUAM see Weirich, August

ZWEI WEIHNACHTLICHE CHORE see Kuntz, Michael

ZWEI WEIHNACHTLICHE SPIRITUALS *see Mary Had A Baby; What You Gonna Call Your Pretty Little Baby?
                                    (Z111)
ZWEI WEIHNACHTSLIEDER *see Joseph, Lieber Joseph Mein; Maria Durch Ein Dornwald Ging   (Z112)

ZWEI WEIHNACHTSLIEDER see Hessenberg, Kurt

ZWEI WEIHNACHTSLIEDER see Zipp, Friedrich

ZWEI WEIHNACHTSLIEDER see Seckinger, Konrad

ZWEI WEIHNACHTSLIEDLEIN see Erk

ZWEIG VON BETHLEHEM "O PILGERPAAR, MACH WEIT DIE TUR" see Lang, Hans

ZWEITE FESTMESSE IN D IN HONOREM ST. SOPHIAE see Kromolicki, Joseph

ZWISCHENGESANG "FREU DICH, ERD UND STERNENZELT" see Trapp, Willy

ZWISCHENGESANGE FUR DIE WEIHNACHTSZEIT see Seckinger, Konrad

ZWOLF LATEINISCHE KIRCHENGESANGE see Ett, Kaspar

SECULAR CHORAL MUSIC

A

A BAURABUBLE MAG I NET see Kuhlenthal, Fred

A BO VED EN SJO see Kvam, Oddvar S.

A CAPPELLA COLLECTION OF CELEBRATED SONGS *CCU
(Wick, Fred) SSA oct SCHMITT $.75
(A1)

A CHE TORMI IL BEN MIO see Monteverdi, Claudio

A CLAIRES VOIX see Arrieu, Claude

A-FLAT CRICKET AND A B-FLAT FROG, AN see Clarkson

A JA SOM Z ORAVY DEBNAR see Kafenda, Frico

A KIS ZEBU BOLCSODALA see Ibert, Jacques

A LA NANITA NANA see Luboff

A-ROVING
see Funf Seemanslieder

A SZEGENY EMBER NOTAI see Szabo, [Ferenc]

A TAL PERDIDA TAN TRISTE see Encina, Juan Del

A TEAM, THE
SATB CIMINO $.40   (A2)
TTBB CIMINO $.40   (A3)

A TENGER see Lorand, Istvan

A UN GIRO SOL DE' BELL' OCCHI see Monteverdi, Claudio

A-WALKIN' AND A-TALKIN' see Haufrecht, [Herbert]

ABEND AM CHIEMSEE see Langer, Hans-Klaus

ABEND AM DON see Bredow, Claus

ABEND AM STROM see Thehos, Adam

ABEND AN DER MEMEL *see An Des Haffes Anderm Strande; De Oadeboar; Et War Emoal Twee Schwestre Jung; Memel, Ach Memel; O Kam Das Morgenrot Herauf; Welch Ein Wunder   (A4)

ABEND "SCHWEIGT DER MENSCHEN LAUTE LUST" see Baumann, Max

ABENDFEIER see Gauss, Otto

ABENDFEIER "GLOCKLEIN, ABENDGLOCKLEIN" see Herrmann, Hugo

ABENDFRIEDEN see Schubert, Franz (Peter)

ABENDGLOCKE: WANDRER ZIEHT see Silcher, Friedrich

ABENDGLUCK see Zipp, Friedrich

ABENDKANTATE see Schuler, Karl

ABENDLIED see Leucht, Carl Friedrich

ABENDLIED see Reger, Max

ABENDLIED "AUGEN, MEINE LIEBEN FENSTERLEIN see Hessenberg, Kurt

ABENDLIED: DER MOND IST see Manhart, Eduard

ABENDLIED "DER MOND IST AUFGEGANGEN" see Zoll, Paul

ABENDLIED EINES REISENDEN see Distler, Hugo

ABENDLIED "NUN DER UBERMUDE TAG" see Beck, Conrad

ABENDLIED: NUN SICH DER TAG GEENDET see Kracke, Hans

ABENDMUSIK see Krietsch, Georg

ABENDRUHE see Mozart, Wolfgang Amadeus

ABENDSEGEN "DER TAG HAT SEINEN SCHMUCK" see Beck, Conrad

ABENDSTANDCHEN see Doppelbauer, Josef Friedrich

ABENDSTANDCHEN "HOR, ES KLAGT DIE FLOTE WIEDER" see Brahms, Johannes

ABENDSTIMMUNG see Hilger, Manfred

ABENDWOLKE see Burkhard Willy

ABENDWOLKE see Koenig, Franz

ABLOSUNG "KUCKUCK HAT SICH ZU TOD GEFALLEN" see Genzmer, Harald

ABRAHAM LINCOLN WALKS AT MIDNIGHT see Lora, Antonio

ABSCHEID *folk
(Lang, H.) [Ger] 4pt men cor
MERSEBURG EM9003 s.p.   (A5)

ABSCHIED *folk
(Bresgen, C.) [Ger] 4pt men cor
MERSEBURG EM9038 s.p.   (A6)

ABSCHIED see Heun, Hans

ABSCHIED AM BRUNNEN "SPANNT DIE PFERDE AUS" *folk,Slav
(Zoll, Paul) men cor sc SCHOTTS
C 41 863 s.p. see from Zwei Slawische Volksliedsatze   (A7)

ABSCHIED AM TORE "JETZT REISEN WIR ZUM TOR HINAUS" see Lang, Hans

ABSCHIED "DIE SCHNEEGANS ZIEHT" see Lang, Hans

ABSCHIED HAT DER TAG GENOMMEN see Nessler

ABSCHIED: MORGEN MUSSEN WIR VERREISEN see Silcher, Friedrich

ABSCHIED: MUSS I DEN *folk,Ger
(Scherchen, Hermann) men cor,acap
TONOS 7 s.p.   (A8)

ABSCHIED "SCHEIDEN TUT SO WEH" see Zoll, Paul

ABSCHIED VOM WALD see Mendelssohn-Bartholdy, Felix

ABSCHIED VON TEXAS *folk,US
(Rosenstengel, Albrecht) men cor,opt pno,opt gtr,opt perc TONOS 463 s.p.
(A9)

ABSCHIEDSGRUSS: ROSMARIN UND SALBEI see Silcher, Friedrich

ABSCHIEDSGRUSS "ROSMARIN UND SALBEIBLATTLEIN" see Silcher, Friedrich

ABSCHIEDSLIED see Brahms, Johannes

ABT, FRANZ (1819-1885)
Die Abendglocken Rufen
men cor,acap TONOS 6301 s.p. (A10)

Uber Den Sternen
men cor,acap TONOS 6306 s.p. (A11)

Waldandacht
men cor,acap TONOS 6341 s.p. (A12)

ACH ARME WELT see Brahms, Johannes

ACH, DU DUNKLE NACHT see Kubizek, Augustinian

ACH, DU LIEBSTE MEIN see Zoll, Paul

ACH ELSLEIN, LIEBES ELSELEIN see Senfl, Ludwig

ACH GOTT, WIE WEH TUT SCHEIDEN see Pepping, Ernst

ACH LIEB, HIER IST DAS HERZE see Hassler, Hans Leo

ACH, MEIN GOTT, NUR LEIDEN see Bartok, Bela

ACH, MEIN SCHATZ see Stein, F.R.

ACH, TY ZEM see Kolman, Peter

ACH, VERNIMM DIESEN TON see Weber, Bernhard

ACH, WARUM KOMMST DU NICHT? see Eben, Petr

ACHT CHORLIEDER see Genzmer, Harald

ACHT LIEDER AUS WIEN *see Am Montag, Da Fang Ma Vorn Wieder An; An Auflauf Gibt's Bei Uns; Das Pfeifenkramer-Lied; Die Ord'ntlichen Leut; Unfehlbar; Wann I Von Wean Weggageh; Was Uns Noch Fehlt; Wer A Geld Hat   (A13)

ACHT SPIRITUALS *see Deep River; Git On Board, Little Children; I Got A Robe; Let Us Break Bread Together; Little David, Play On Your Harp; Lord, I Want To Be A Christian; My Lord, What A Morning; Swing Low, Sweet Chariot   (A14)

ACHTET AUF DAS LICHT! see Bartok, Bela, Jatek

ACHTZEHN CHORLIEDER see Bartok, Bela

ACK, VARMELAND DU SKONA *folk,Swed
(Jehrlander, Karl-Fredrik) mix cor GEHRMANS KRB453   (A15)

AD UN DOLCE USIGNOLO see Banchieri, Adriano

ADAM SHALL RISE see Williamson, Malcolm

ADAMS
All In The Family Theme *see Those Were The Days

Beauty
(Nelson) SATB oct SCHMITT 1805 $.40
(A16)
Those Were The Days (composed with Strouse)
(Joyce, Jimmy) "All In The Family Theme" SATB STUDIO V727 $.45
(A17)

ADAMS, JOHN
Ktaadn
mix cor,opt inst, or electronic accompaniment EXPERIMENTAL s.p.
(A18)

ADAMS ERSTER SCHLAG "ES LEGT ADAM SICH IM PARADIESE SCHLAFEN" see Cadow, Paul

ADE! see Rubben, Hermannjosef

ADE, DU LIEBES STADTCHEN see Silcher, Friedrich

ADE, ZUR GUTEN NACHT *folk,Ger
(Nother, Willi) men cor,acap TONOS 97 s.p.   (A19)

ADE ZUR GUTEN NACHT see Rein, Walter

ADELANTE! (SAIL ON!) see Yancey

ADELEIN "WO STEHT DEINS VATERS HOF UND HAUS" see Rettich, Wilhelm

ADELONDA DA FRIGIA see Veccoli, Pietro

ADES
Get Happy!
SATB SHAWNEE A1276 $1.25   (A20)

ADIEU see Beauverd

ADIEU GAIS AMIS see Strimer, Joseph

ADIEU PRIVAS see Nitsche, Paul

ADIEU, SWEET AMARYLLIS see Wilbye, John

ADIEU, SWEET LOVE see Bateson, Thomas

ADIOS AU REVOIR AUF WIDERSEHN
SSA CIMINO $.40   (A21)

ADIOS AU REVOIR AUF WIEDERSEHN
SATB CIMINO $.40   (A22)
TTBB CIMINO $.40   (A23)

ADLER
Begin My Muse *CC5U
TTBB,inst (diff) OXFORD rental (A24)
Come, Join In Our Dance (from Some Laughter, Some Tears)
SA/SSAA (easy) OXFORD 95.412 $.40
(A25)
Fiddler (from Some Laughter, Some Tears)
see Adler, Once I Had A Greatcoat

Gone, Gone Is My Sunshine (from Some Laughter, Some Tears)
see Adler, Once I Had A Greatcoat

Once I Had A Greatcoat (from Some Laughter, Some Tears)
SA/SSAA (easy) OXFORD 95.409 $.35
contains also: Gone, Gone Is My Sunshine; Fiddler   (A26)

Spin, Dreidel, Spin
SA (very easy) OXFORD 95.407 $.20
(A27)
There's A Tree (from Some Laughter, Some Tears)
SA/SSAA (easy) OXFORD 95.410 $.30
(A28)
Tum Balalaika (from Some Laughter, Some Tears)
SA/SSAA (easy) OXFORD 95.411 $.35
(A29)

ADLER (cont'd.)

Who Can Retell?
SA (easy) OXFORD 95.408 $.25   (A30)

ADVANCE AUSTRALIA FAIR see McCormack,
P.D.

ADVICE TO YOUNG LADIES see Smith,
Leland

AEBY
Chanson Des Feuilles
men cor,acap HENN 784 s.p.   (A31)

AFOOT AND LIGHTHEARTED see Kent,
Richard

AFTER THE BATTLE OF THE WHITE MOUNTAIN
see Bendl, Karel, Po Bitve
Belohorske

AFTER THE GOLD RUSH see Young

AGE see Croce, Jim

AGER, LAURENCE
King Arthur
SSA EMI   (A32)

London Sparrow
unis CRAMER $.30   (A33)

Rhythm Of The Beating Wings
unis EMI   (A34)

AGNETE AND THE MERMAIDS see Gade, Niels
Wilhelm, Agnete Of Havfruerne

AGNETE OF HAVFRUERNE see Gade, Niels
Wilhelm

AGOSTINI, LODOVICO (1534-1590)
Cantava In Riva Al Fiume *madrigal
(Nielsen, R.) 6pt mix cor
BONGIOVANI 2394 s.p. see also
DODICI MADRIGALI DI SCUOLA
FERRARESE   (A35)

Picciola Verga E Bella *madrigal
(Nielsen, R.) 6pt mix cor
BONGIOVANI 2393 s.p. see also
DODICI MADRIGALI DI SCUOLA
FERRARESE   (A36)

Tra Giove In Cielo *madrigal
(Nielsen, R.) 5pt mix cor
BONGIOVANI 2392 s.p. see also
DODICI MADRIGALI DI SCUOLA
FERRARESE   (A37)

AGRICOLA
Se Je Fais Bien Ou Mal Aussi
(Brown) SATB,inst (med diff) OXFORD
87.002 $.70, ipr   (A38)

AH, DEAR HEART see Weber, Ben

AH FADING JOY, HOW QUICKLY ART THOU
PAST! see Holloway, Robin

AH, THOU GOLDEN MONTH OF MAY see Wilbye

AHI DISPIETATA MORTE see Marenzio, Luca

AHLE, JOHANN RUDOLPH (1625-1673)
Was Mag Doch Diese Welt
mix cor,4strings (easy) sc SCHOTTS
C 43 564 s.p. contains also:
Lemlin, Lorenz, Der Gutzgauch Auf
Dem Zaune Sass (mix cor,opt S
solo,opt inst); Franck, Melchior,
So Wunsch Ich Eine Gute Nacht
(mix cor,T solo,acap)   (A39)

AHLEN, WALDEMAR
Budskap *see Hjort, Fredrik

AHNFELT, O.
Life Is Now
SATB WALTON 9066 $.40   (A40)

AHOI, KAPT'N SEEBAR! "IN DER KNEIPE ZUM
WEISEN ELEFANTEN" see Merath,
Siegfried

AHREN IM STURM "O, WIE DER STURM SO
DUNKEL BRAUST!" see Mohler, Philipp

AIM FOR HEAVEN
SATB oct CHAPPELL W020842-357 $.40
(A41)

AIM, VOJTECH BORIVOJ (1886-   )
Day *see Den

Den
"Day" [Czech] mix cor&dbl cor,acap
CZECH s.p.   (A42)

AIMABLE PASTOURELLE *folk,Fr
(Blanchard, R.) 4pt mix cor,acap
JOBERT s.p.   (A43)

AIRS OR FANTASTIC SPIRITS (1608) EM
VOL. 13 see Weelkes, Thomas

AISOPEIA see Middeleer, Jean De

AJ, PADA ROSICKA see Suchy, Frantisek

AJ, STUPAJ see Martinu, Bohuslav

AKA SI MI KRASNA see Suchon, Eugen

AKO VONIA HORA see Ferenczy, Oto

AKOND OF SWAT see Thompson

AL FUGAREN see Pratella, Francesco
Balilla

ALABAMA RAIN see Croce, Jim

ALALA see Poos, Heinrich

ALAS, MY LOVE see Certon, Pierre, Las,
S'il Convient

ALAS, POOR WORLD see Brahms, Johannes,
Ach Arme Welt

ALAS, WHAT A WRETCHED LIFE see
Marenzio, Luca

ALBERT, HEINRICH (1604-1651)
Der Tag Beginnt Zu Vergehen
SATTB,acap (easy) BAREN. BCH29 s.p.
contains also: Isaac, Heinrich,
Innsbruck, Ich Muss Dich Lassen
(SATB,acap)   (A44)

ALBITZ
Hideaway Place *see Jones

New Tomorrows *see Jones

ALBUM FROM "THE BRILLIANT AND THE DARK"
see Williamson, Malcolm

ALBUM FROM "THE BRILLIANT AND THE DARK"
see Williamson, Malcolm

ALCALAY, LUNA
Una Strofa Di Dante
mix cor,4fl/2fl&2pic,4ob,5clar,
4bsn,4trp,4horn,4trom,tuba,4perc,
strings, English horn, bass
clarinet, contrabassoon
alternating with fourth and fifth
woodwinds MODERN s.p.   (A45)

ALCOCK, J.
Part Songs To Sing (composed with
Stirling, C.) *sac/sec,CC25U,
round
2-3pt,pno EMI   (A46)

ALDER TREES see Kuksa, Emanuel, Olse

ALEMANNISCHER LIEDERREIGEN see Haas,
Joseph

ALEXANDER
Top Of The Hill
(Ringwald) SAB SHAWNEE D190 $.35
(A47)

ALEXANDER'S FEAST (NEUE MOZART-AUSGABE)
see Handel, George Frideric

ALICE BLUE GOWN see Tierney, Harry

ALICE IN WONDERLAND see Boatner, John

ALL ALONE
TTBB (Barbershop Arrangement) CIMINO
$.40   (A48)

ALL AT ONCE WELL MET FAIR LADIES see
Weelkes, Thomas

ALL AT ONCE YOU LOVE HER see Rodgers,
Richard

ALL CREATURES NOW see Bennett, John

ALL DARK IS NOW NO MORE see Karlen,
Robert

ALL FOR LOVE see Young, Robert H.

ALL GOOD THINGS see Hellden, Daniel

ALL I KNOW see Webb

ALL IN LOVE IS FAIR
SATB,pno,opt bvl&drums&gtr SCREEN
3743AC7   (A49)
SSA,pno,opt bvl&drums&gtr SCREEN
3743AC8   (A50)

ALL IN THE APRIL EVENING see Harris

ALL IN THE FAMILY THEME see Adams,
Those Were The Days

ALL KINDS OF EVERYTHING
(Freed, Arnold) SA/SSA/SAB HANSEN-US
C517 $.40   (A51)

ALL LUST UND FREUD see Rauch, Andreas

ALL MEIN GEDANKEN see Kanetscheider,
Artur

ALL MEIN GEDANKEN see Koenig, Franz

ALL MEIN GEDANKEN see Oppel, Hans

ALL MEINE HERZGEDANKEN see Brahms,
Johannes

ALL MEINE HERZGEDANKEN see Brahms,
Johannes, All Meine Herzgedanken

ALL MORGEN IST GANZ FRISCH UND NEU see
Walter (Walther), Johann

ALL MY TRIALS *pop
(Averre, Richard) SATB,pno oct BIG
BELL $.50   (A52)
(Averre, Richard) SSA,pno oct BIG
BELL $.40   (A53)
(Averre, Richard) SAB,pno oct BIG
BELL $.40   (A54)
(Averre, Richard) SA,pno oct BIG BELL
$.40   (A55)

ALL THAT LOVE WENT TO WASTE see Barrie,
George

ALL THE THINGS YOU ARE
SSA CIMINO $.40   (A56)
SA CIMINO $.40   (A57)
SATB CIMINO $.40   (A58)
TTBB CIMINO $.40   (A59)
(Warnick) SATB,opt gtr&bvl&drums
CIMINO cor pts $.40, cmplt ed $1.50
(A60)

ALL THE THINGS YOU ARE see Kern, Jerome

ALL THE WAY
SSA,pno,opt bvl&drums&gtr SCREEN
3747AC8   (A61)
SATB,pno,opt bvl&drums&gtr SCREEN
3747AC7   (A62)

ALL THINGS ARE DOUBLE FAIR see Clarke,
Henry Leland

ALL THROUGH THE NIGHT *Welsh
(Anderson, W.H.) SSA LESLIE 3003 $.35
(A63)
(Snr, L. Kean) ALLANS 838   (A64)

ALL THROUGH THE NIGHT see Bateman,
Ronald

ALL THROUGH THE NIGHT see Sharpe,
Evelyn

ALL YOU THAT LOVE, AWAKEN NOW see
Crecquillon, Thomas, Reveillez-Vous
Tous Amoureux

ALLA SCHATZLA KUMMA see Lang, Hans

ALLE GUTE GABE
unis wom cor SCHOTTS C 42 532I s.p.
see also Alle Singen Heft 1   (A65)

ALLE MENSCHEN, GROSS UND KLEIN see
Zipp, Friedrich

ALLE SINGEN HEFT 1
unis wom cor cmplt ed SCHOTTS s.p.
contains & see also: Alle Gute
Gabe; Auf Hoher Fahrt; Bunt Sind
Schon Die Walder; Der Helle Tag;
Die Welt Erwacht; Ein Neues Lied;
Freut Euch Des Lebens; Hand In
Hand; Nach Dem Winter; Rundherum;
Seele, Vergiss Sie Nicht; Zur
Freude Bereit   (A66)

ALLE SINGEN HEFT 2
unis wom cor cmplt ed SCHOTTS s.p.
contains & see also: Bluhe, Junge
Sonne, Bluhe; Das Weite Land; Der
Herbst Beginnt; Gesellige Stunde;
Gloria In Excelsis Deo; Goldnes
Garbenfeld; Im Waldschatten;
Kling Fur Mein Herzgespiel; Singt
Dem Sommer; Steh Uns Bei; Wann
Wir Schreiten; Winter Weicht
(A67)

ALLE SINGEN MIT see Schneider, Willy

ALLE VOGEL SIND SCHON DA see Jage,
Rolf-Diether

ALLE VOGEL SIND SCHON DA see Pepping,
Ernst

ALLE WEGE SIND BEMESSEN see Edler,
Robert

ALLEGIANCE TO LIBERTY, AN see Collins,
Don L.

ALLEGRI BEVIAM see Verdi, Giuseppe

ALLEN
Home For The Holidays
(Ringwald) SATB SHAWNEE A1274 $.40
(A68)

ALLEN, PETER
I Honestly Love You (composed with
Barry, Jeff) *pop
(Nowak, Jerry) SATB,pno oct BIG
BELL $.45 (A69)

ALLERLEIRAUH see Erdlen, Hermann

ALLES IST LIEBE see Rein, Walter

ALLES IST SANG "ICH GING VORUBER" see
Zoll, Paul

ALLES STRAHLT UND LIEBT SICH see Biebl,
Franz

ALLES, WAS GESCHIEHT see Schroeder,
Hermann

ALLEWEIL EIN WENIG LUSTIG see
Rathgeber, Valentin

ALLEWEIL KANN MA NET LUSTIG SEIN
(Reiter, Albert) treb cor DOBLINGER
O 343 s.p. see from Sechs
Osterreichische Volkslieder (A70)

ALLHIER AUF GRUNER HEID see Lang, Hans

ALL'HORA I PASTORI TUTTI see
Monteverdi, Claudio

ALLONS AU VERT BOCCAGE see Costeley,
Guillaume

ALLONS DANS LES GRANDS BOIS see Missa,
[Edmond Jean Louis]

ALLONS, GAI, BERGERES see Costeley,
Guillaume

ALLT UNDER HIMMELENS FASTE *folk,Swed
(Jehrlander, Karl-Fredrik) mix cor
GEHRMANS KRB458 (A71)

ALMO DIVINO RAGGIO see Monteverdi,
Claudio

ALONE
see Two Ukrainian Folk Songs

ALONE AGAIN NATURALLY see O'Sullivan,
Gilbert

ALOUETTE (from Cvjy) folk,Fr
[Ger/Fr] 4 eq voices,acap BREITKOPF-W
CHB 4943 s.p. (A72)
(Sund, Robert) men cor GEHRMANS
KRB462 (A73)

ALS DU KLEIN WARST, MARIETTA see Mockl,
Franz

ALS FLIEDER JUNGST MIR IM GARTEN BLUHT
see Hindemith, Paul, When Lilacs
Last In The Door-Yard Bloom'd

ALS HIER OP ARDE
mix cor sc HEER 2319 s.p. (A74)

ALS ICH GESTERN GING GELASSEN see
Conseil, Jean

ALS ICH NOCH EIN ARMER KNECHT WAR see
Bresgen, Cesar

ALS ICK U VINDE see Waelrant, Hubert

ALS WIR JUNGST IN REG'NSBURG WAREN see
Muntzel, Herbert

ALTATODAL see Szeghy, Endre

ALTE KINDERREIME see Knab, Armin

ALTE LANDSKNECHTE "IM HIMMEL DROBEN"
see Lang, Hans

ALTE LIEBE *folk,Finn
(Zipp, F) men cor,acap TONOS 2014
s.p. (A75)

ALTE WEIBER "'SIST NICHTS MIT DEN ALTEN
WEIBERN" see Rein, Walter

ALTER JOE "FORT SIND SIE ALL" see Senn,
Karl

ALTER, LOUIS
I Had A Dream
(Simon, W.) SSA BIG3 $.45 (A76)
(Simon, W.) SATB,S solo BIG3 $.45
(A77)

ALTER SPRUCH "ICH LEB UND WEISS NIT WIE
LANG" see Zehm, Friedrich

ALTER UND NEUER WEIN "DER ALTE IST NOCH
LANG NICHT AUS" see Weber, Bernhard

ALTSERBISCHES IDYLL "TIEF AN EINEM
BERG" see Klefisch, Walter

ALVAD, CHRISTIAN
Introduction
SAB,pno EGTVED MS19B9 s.p. (A78)

Poor Widow
SAB,pno EGTVED MS19B13 s.p. (A79)

ALWAYS LOOK UP (NEVER LOOK DOWN)
SATB CIMINO $.40 (A80)

AM ADRIATISCHEN MEER "NACH DIR ICH MICH
SEHNE" see Gotovac, Jakov

AM EISENBAHNDAMM see Sutermeister,
Heinrich

AM GRABE see Seeger, Peter

AM MEER "DER WIND HAT UNTER DER KUSTE"
see Zoll, Paul

AM MONTAG, DA FANG MA VORN WIEDER AN
(Deutsch, Walter) mix cor DOBLINGER
G 675 s.p. see from Acht Lieder Aus
Wien (A81)

AM MORGEN see Kludas, Erich

AM MORGEN NACH DER HOCHZEIT "WO SEID
IHR LIEBEN GEBLIEBEN" see Zipp,
Friedrich

AM NEUJAHRSTAGE see Mendelssohn-
Bartholdy, Felix

AM SCHONEN RHEIN GEDENK' ICH DEIN see
Keler, Bela

AM SCHONEN RHEIN GEDENK' ICH DEIN
"SANFT TREIBT DER KAHN" see Keler,
Bela

AM SCHONSTEN SOMMERABEND *folk
(Miller, F. R.) [Ger] 4pt mix cor
MERSEBURG EM9222 s.p. (A82)
(Weber, Bernhard) [Ger] 4pt men cor
MERSEBURG EM9019 s.p. (A83)

AM STRANDE "AN WILDEM KLIPPENSTRANDE"
see Trunk, Richard

AM WILDBACH DIE WIEDEN see Brahms,
Johannes

AM ZIELE "DIE MUDEN SCHLAFER WECKT
KEINE KLAGE" see Zoll, Paul

AMABO, MEA DULCIS IPSITILLA see Thybo,
Leif

AMAZING GRACE *folk
(Miller, Carl) 2pt CHAPPELL
0063164-351 $.40 (A84)

AMBROS, VLADMIR (1890-1956)
Co Rok Dal
"What The Year Has Given" [Czech]
jr cor,pno CZECH s.p. (A85)

Maminka *cant
"Mummy" [Czech] jr cor,fl,ob,2clar,
bsn,2horn,trp,timp,perc,harp,
strings CZECH s.p. (A86)

Mummy *see Maminka

What The Year Has Given *see Co Rok
Dal

AMERICA *US
(Bennett, R.R.) 4pt mix cor SCHIRM.G
LG51770 $.40 (A87)
(Coates) SAB SHAWNEE D185 $.35 (A88)
(Van Camp, L.) 4pt mix cor,acap oct
SOMERSET SP 731 $.30 (A89)

AMERICA see Carey

AMERICA see Simon, Paul

AMERICA AGAIN see Wilson, D.

AMERICA FOR ME see Pease, Rollin

AMERICA MY HOME see Rocherolle

AMERICA SINGS: NEW ENGLAND see
Nelhybel, Vaclav

AMERICA THE BEAUTIFUL *US
(Bennett, R.R.) 4pt mix cor SCHIRM.G
LG51771 $.40 (A90)
(Mercer, W. Elmo) SSATB,acap BENSON
S4018 $.25 (A91)
(Prentice, Fred) SATB,acap FOSTER
MF332 $.35 (A92)

AMERICA THE BEAUTIFUL see Pottle, Sam

AMERICA, THE BEAUTIFUL see Ward, Samuel
A.

AMERICA, THE LAND OF THE PEOPLE see
Konowitz

AMERICAN FLAG, THE see Dvorak

AMERICAN HERITAGE
SATB CIMINO $.40 (A93)
SA CIMINO $.40 (A94)

AMERICAN HERITAGE, THE see Kinyon

AMERICAN MEDITATIONS see Goossen,
Frederic

AMERICAN PIE, PART I see McLean, Don

AMERICAN PIE, PART II see McLean, Don

AMERICAN TUNE see Simon, Paul

AMERICAN'S CREED, THE see Young

AMERIKA-SONG see Rosenstengel, Albrecht

AMES, WILLIAM
Dance To Your Daddy
SSA,pno AM.COMP.AL. $1.10 (A95)

Granite And Cypress
SATB,2fl,3ob,4bsn,4horn,3trp,3trom,
tuba,timp,perc,harp,strings
AM.COMP.AL. (A96)

Three Sons, The
SSA,pno AM.COMP.AL. $2.75 (A97)

AMINTA POI CH'A FILLI see Luzzaschi,
Luzzasco

AMMANN, BENNO (1904-   )
Das Madchen Von Misox
mix cor ZIMMER. 585 s.p. (A98)

Der Alte Berner Marsch "Alli Manne
Standet"
men cor sc SCHOTTS C 41 262 s.p.
(A99)

Des Matrosen Abschied
men cor,acap sc,cor pts TONOS 2032
s.p. (A100)

Die Schone Aus Dem Maggia-Tal
mix cor ZIMMER. 586 s.p. (A101)

Die Schone Von Onsernone
mix cor ZIMMER. 584 s.p. (A102)

La Bella Ninetta *folk
mix cor ZIMMER. 602 s.p. (A103)
men cor,acap ZIMMER. 594 s.p.
(A104)

AMONG THE MULTITUDE see Hall, William
D.

AMOR see Civil-Castellvi, Francisco

AMOR IST UBERALL see Rosenstengel,
Albrecht

AMOR IST UBERALL see Rosenstengel,
Albrecht

AMOR PER TUA MERCE see Monteverdi,
Claudio

AMOR S'IL TUO FERIRE see Monteverdi,
Claudio

AMOR VITTORIOSO see Gastoldi, Giovanni
Giacomo

AMOR Y DANZA see Civil-Castellvi,
Francisco

AMOUR, TU AS ETE MON MAITRE see
Crawford, John

AN AUFLAUF GIBT'S BEI UNS
(Deutsch, Walter) mix cor DOBLINGER
G 676 s.p. see from Acht Lieder Aus
Wien (A105)

AN DAS HANDWERK "ALS NOCH HANS SACHS
DEN PFRIEMEN SCHWANG" see Gerster,
Ottmar

AN DAS LIED see Desch, Rudolf

AN DAS LIED "AUS DES TAGES HETZE UND
HAST" see Zoll, Paul

AN DAS ROSENHERZE *folk,Dan
(Zschiegner, Fritz) men cor,opt pno,
opt inst,opt perc sc,voc sc TONOS
2122 s.p. (A106)

AN DAS VATERLAND see Kreutzer, Konradin

AN DEM BACH "AN DEM BACH IM WIESENRAIN"
see Zoll, Paul

AN DEN FLAMINGO "FLAMINGO, ICH KANN DIR
NICHT TRAUEN" see Genzmer, Harald

AN DEN FRUHLING see Schubert, Franz
(Peter)

AN DEN GEISTER see Erdlen, Hermann

AN DER GRENZE *folk
(Bresgen, C.) [Ger] 4pt men cor
MERSEBURG EM9037 s.p.   (A107)

AN DER HEIMAT HALTE FEST "MAGST DU
SCHON'RE LANDE SCHAUEN" see Biebl,
Franz

AN DER QUELLE "LAUFT EIN WASSERLEIN
WOHL" see Werner, Kurt

AN DES HAFFES ANDERM STRANDE *folk
(Felt, Gerhard) SATB MOSELER LB494
s.p. see from Abend An Der Memel
(A108)

AN DES HAFFES STRAND "AN DES HAFFES
ANDERM STRAND" see Zoll, Paul

AN DIE FREUNDE "WIEDER EINMAL
AUSGEFLOGEN" see Schwartz, Gerhard
von

AN DIE GROSSEN TOTEN see Berger

AN DIE JUGEND DER WELT see Vogel,
Wladimir

AN DIE KLEINEN LIEDER "O SCHLAGT NICHT
NIEDER SO SCHEU DIE AUGEN" see
Mockl, Franz

AN DIE MINNE see Schneider, Walther

AN DIE MUSIK (NUN HEBET FROHLICH AN,
DIE GUT MUSIK ZU PREISEN) see
Gneist, Verner

AN DIE NACHGEBORENEN see Fortner,
Wolfgang

AN DIE ROSE see Ketterer, Ernst

AN DIE SONNE "DIE SCHATTEN SIND VOM
BERG INS TAL GEZOGEN" see Gerster,
Ottmar

AN EINEM MAIENMORGEN *folk
(Weber, Bernhard) [Ger] 4pt men cor
MERSEBURG EM9020 s.p.   (A109)

AN EINEM MAIENTAG see Wert, Giaches de

AN EINEM SCHONEN MORGEN see Leucht,
Carl Friedrich

AN ERISKAY LOVE LILT see Gal, Hans

AN HELLEN TAGEN see Gastoldi, Giovanni
Giacomo

AN POLYHYMNIA see Desch, Rudolf

AN SCHONEN TAGEN see Orrel, Max

ANACREONTIC ODE see Campbell, Colin M.

ANBETUNG DES KINDES see Pepping, Ernst

ANCORA ODONO I COLLI see Bussotti,
Sylvano

AND ALL IN THE MORNING see Vaughan
Williams, Ralph

AND I LOVE YOU SO see McLean, Don

AND THE TIDE RUSHES IN see Thomas

ANDERS, ALFRED
Das Waldecker Lied
men cor,acap TONOS 3949 s.p. (A110)

ANDERS-STREHMEL, GERHARD
Lago Maggiore
men cor,acap TONOS 3901 s.p. (A111)

Sanger-Motto
men cor,acap TONOS 699 s.p. (A112)

ANDERSON, PAULA
Wherever You're Going
(Kysar, Michael) SSATB,opt 3vln&
vla&vcl&bvl&gtr KYSAR B101 cor
pts $.35, cmplt ed $16.00 (A113)

ANDERSON, STIG
Waterloo (composed with Andersson,
Benny; Ulvaeus, Bjorn)
(Simon, W.) SSA BIG3 $.50   (A114)
(Simon, W.) SATB BIG3 $.50 (A115)
(Simon, W.) SAB BIG3 $.50   (A116)

ANDERSON, THOMAS J.
Personals *cant
SATB,2horn,2trp,2trom,tuba sc
AM.COMP.AL. $15.40, ipa   (A117)

This House
TTBB, 4pitch pipes sc AM.COMP.AL.
$8.25   (A118)

ANDERSON, [WILLIAM H.]
Children's Friend, The
SSA LESLIE 3007 $.30   (A119)

Gaelic Croon, A *Ir
SSA LESLIE 3019 $.30   (A120)

Long, Long Ago
SSA LESLIE 3020 $.30   (A121)

Song Of Autumn
SSA LESLIE 3047   (A122)

White Dove, The
SSA LESLIE 3015 $.35   (A123)

ANDERSSON, BENNY
Waterloo *see Anderson, Stig

ANDRASOVAN, TIBOR (1917-   )
Pod Babou Horou
mix cor SLOV.HUD.FOND s.p. (A124)

ANDREAS GRYPHIUS see Sutermeister,
Heinrich

ANDRIESSEN, CAECILIA (1931-   )
Beestebende
jr cor,pno DONEMUS   (A125)

ANDRIESSEN, HENDRIK (1892-1964)
Lux Jocunda
mix cor,T solo,2fl,2ob,2clar,2bsn,
2horn,2trp,2trom,strings,timp
DONEMUS   (A126)

ANDRIESSEN, LOUIS (1939-   )
"Il Principe", Quotations From "The
Ruler" Of N. Machiavelli
dbl cor,pno,2fl,2ob,2clar,2bsn,
3horn,tuba,gtr DONEMUS   (A127)

ANDROZZO, ALMA BAZEL (1912-   )
If I Can Help Somebody *pop
SSA BELWIN UC 726 $.40   (A128)
SATB BELWIN UC 727 $.40   (A129)

ANDULKA *folk,Boh
(Schneider, Walther) men cor,acap
TONOS 2039 s.p.   (A130)

ANDULKA "O, KLOPF NICHT AN" see Binger,
Martin

ANEMOPHON see Schramm

ANGELL
Our Flag
SATB FINE ARTS CM 1110 $.35 (A131)

ANGELS, FROM THE REALMS OF GLORY
see Two Carols For The Caribbean

ANGIE see Best

ANGIE see Jagger, Mick

ANGST VORM SCHWIMMUNTERRICHT "VORHER
DENK ICH IMMER" see Hindemith, Paul

ANIMA DOLOROSA see Monteverdi, Claudio

ANIMALS! ANIMALS! see Martin

ANKA, PAUL
My Way (composed with Revaux) *pop
SSA BELWIN TC 15 $.40   (A132)
SATB BELWIN TC 16 $.40   (A133)

Puppy Love *pop
SA/TB BELWIN TC 20 $.40   (A134)

Put Your Head On My Shoulder *pop
SATB BELWIN TC 17 $.40   (A135)
SSA BELWIN TC 18 $.40   (A136)
SA/TB BELWIN TC 21 $.40   (A137)

ANN RUTLEDGE see Trubitt, Allen R.

ANNA SUSANNA see Edler, Robert

ANNAIK see Ladmirault, P.

ANNCHEN VON THARAU see Silcher,
Friedrich

ANNELEIN FEIN see Haussmann, Valentin

ANNEMIRL, MACH AUF *folk,Ger
(Geiss, Gottfried) men cor,acap TONOS
4570-1 s.p.   (A138)

ANNERLE, WO WARST DU? see Poos,
Heinrich

ANNIE see Coppier

ANNIE'S SONG see Denver, John

ANNUNCIATION OF SPRING, THE see
Zahradnik, Zdenek, Jarni Zvestovani

ANONYMOUS
Carmina Burana (from Benediktbeuern
And Florence Manuscripts) CC20U
(Whaples, Miriam K.) 1-3pt DEAN
CMC-105 $7.50   (A139)

Dear Hope, Blest Child Of The Skies
*see Espoir, Toi Fille Des Cieux!

Dindirin
see SPANISH RENAISSANCE: SIX SONGS

Dva Trohlasne Zbory
3pt SLOV.HUD.FOND s.p.
contains: Svaty Buoh; V Otce
Vsemohuciho   (A140)

Espoir, Toi Fille Des Cieux! *16th
cent
(Malin, Don) "Dear Hope, Blest
Child Of The Skies" SATB,acap
BELWIN 2322 $.30   (A141)

Ich Sag Ade *16th cent
mix cor (med easy) sc SCHOTTS
CHBL 365 s.p.   (A142)

Marionette Douce "Solaris Ardor
Romuli" *mot,Mediev
[Eng/Lat] SATB/AATB (med easy) sc
SCHOTTS SL 5596 s.p.   (A143)

Mon Mary M'a Diffamee
(Brown) ATT, lute (med diff) OXFORD
87.003 $.45, ipa   (A144)

Pase El Agoa
see SPANISH RENAISSANCE: SIX SONGS

Svaty Buoh
see Dva Trohlasne Zbory

V Otce Vsemohuciho
see Dva Trohlasne Zbory

Wacht Auf, Ihr Schonen Vogelein
*16th cent
mix cor (easy) sc SCHOTTS CHBL 386
s.p.   (A145)

ANOTHER OP'NIN' ANOTHER SHOW
SA CIMINO $.40   (A146)
SAB CIMINO $.40   (A147)
SATB CIMINO $.40   (A148)
SSA CIMINO $.40   (A149)
TTBB CIMINO $.40   (A150)

ANOTHER SOMEBODY DONE SOMEBODY WRONG
SONG see Butler

ANRUF "HERR, DEINE ZEIT IST REIF" see
Herrmann, Hugo

ANSWER JULY see Berger, Jean

ANT, THE see Berger, Jean

ANTHEM FROM THE 16TH CENTURY
(Bergsagel, John) [Eng/Dan] mix cor
HANSEN-DEN WH 29213 s.p. (A151)

ANTHOLOGIE DE LA RENAISSANCE *CCU,
Renais
(Paychere) wom cor,acap HENN 766 s.p.
(A152)

ANTICIPATION see Simon

ANTIFONA PER LUISA see Ghedini, Giorgio
Federico

ANTIPHON see Thompson, Randall

ANTIPHON FUR LUISE see Ghedini, Giorgio
Federico, Antifona Per Luisa

ANTIPHONARIUM PROFANUM see Tischhauser,
Franz

ANTIPOLY TROCH see Zemanovsky, A.

ANTONIOU, THEODOR (1935-   )
Cheironomies (Gesten)
8pt mix cor,opt orch (diff,
conductor's improvisation for 8
voices; a variety of possible
scorings) BAREN. BA6127 s.p.
(A153)

ANXIOUS I WAIT FOR MY DEAR FRIEND see
Des Prez, Josquin, Je Me Complains
De Mon Amy

APEX see Boyd, Jack

APHORISMEN UBER DIE LIEBE see Zechlin,
Ruth

APOLLO "TER AVE, TU ARBITER ARTIS" see
Novak, Jan

APOLOGIA SOKRATUS see Eben, Petr

APOLOGY OF SOCRATES, THE see Eben,
Petr, Apologia Sokratus

APOTHELOZ, JEAN
De Votre Beaute Regarder
mix cor,acap HENN 753 s.p.   (A154)

Le Pays
wom cor,pno sc HENN s.p.   (A155)
wom cor,pno voc pt HENN s.p. (A156)
men cor,pno sc HENN s.p.   (A157)
men cor,pno voc pt HENN s.p. (A158)
mix cor,orch HENN s.p.   (A159)

Les En Voulez-Vous Garder
mix cor,acap HENN 752 s.p.   (A160)

APOTHEOSE DES HANS SACHS see Wagner,
Richard

APPALACHIAN RHAPSODY, AN see Burroughs

APPLE, ALAN
Finale
SATB STANDARD B324MX1 $.50   (A161)

APPLE TREE AND A PIG, A see Hoddinott,
Alun

APPLEBY
More Firsts And Seconds (composed
with Fowler) *CCU
2pt,pno (easy) cmplt ed OXFORD
58.647 $3.60, cor pts OXFORD
58.648 $1.75   (A162)

APRIL see Washburn

APRIL COME SHE WILL see Simon, Paul

APRIL IN PARIS see Harburg

APRIL IS IN MY MISTRESS' FACE see
Morley, Thomas

APRIL SONG see Harelson, Harry B.

APRILISI UNNEP see Lorand, Istvan

ARAD see Diament, Abraham

ARCADELT, JACOB (ca. 1505-ca. 1560)
Da Bei Rami Scendea
(Malin, Don) "Down From The
Branches Falling" SATB,acap
BELWIN 2319 $.30   (A163)

Der Weisse Schwan *madrigal
(Weber, W.) men cor,acap TONOS 3301
s.p.   (A164)

Die Schonen Weissen Schwane
*madrigal,It
men cor sc SCHOTTS CHBL 68 s.p.
(A165)

Down From The Branches Falling *see
Da Bei Rami Scendea

Fair And Bright Is My Lady *see
L'Alma Mia Donna E Bella

Il Bianco E Dolce Cigno *madrigal
SATB RICORDI-ENG BA10362 s.p.
(A166)
SATB,acap EGTVED KB70 s.p.   (A167)

L'Alma Mia Donna E Bella
(Hall, Wm.D.) "Fair And Bright Is
My Lady" SATB,acap/4strings/
4winds NATIONAL CMS-110 $.50
(A168)

Margot, Labourez Les Vignes
SATB,acap EGTVED KB211 s.p.   (A169)

Nous Voyons Que Les Hommes
(Malin, Don) "We See That Men Do
Even" SSA BELWIN 2294 $.35 (A170)

We See That Men Do Even *see Nous
Voyons Que Les Hommes

ARCH, GWYN
Robert Brown, Instant Hero (composed
with Rooke, Pat)
jr cor voc sc EMI   (A171)

ARCHER, VIOLET (1913-   )
Landscapes
SATB (med diff) WATERLOO $.75
(A172)

ARDI O GELA see Monteverdi, Claudio

ARDO SI MA NON T'AMO see Monteverdi,
Claudio

ARDO SI MA NON T'AMO see Nicoletti, F.

ARDO, SOSPIRO see Pederson, Mogens

ARIA see Castiglioni, Niccolo

ARION AND THE DOLPHINE see Marshall,
Nicholas

ARIOSO "ICH WILL EUCH NICHT BETRUGEN"
see Zoll, Paul

ARISE, ALL SLAVS see Jeremias,
Bohuslav, Hej Slovane

ARISE, ARISE AMERICA see Artman

ARISE, GET UP see Morley, Thomas

ARISE, RUN, PASCUAL, ARISE, RUN see
Encina, Juan Del, Levanta, Pascual,
Levanta

ARMA, PAUL (1904-   )
Francia Bordalok *Fr
(Szekeres, Ferenc) eq voices
BUDAPEST 6737 s.p.   (A173)

ARMER, KLEINER TANZBAR see Bresgen,
Cesar

ARMS OF HUNGARY, THE see Kodaly, Zoltan

AROUND THE WORLD see Verrall, Pamela

AROUND THE YEAR IN ROUNDS see Terri

ARRIEU, CLAUDE (1903-   )
A Claires Voix *CCU
2-3 eq voices/2-3pt jr cor ENOCH
(A174)

Chanson Des Compagnons (from Les
Gueux Au Paradis)
3 eq voices ENOCH   (A175)

Complainte (from Les Gueux Au
Paradia)
4pt mix cor ENOCH   (A176)

ARRIGO, GIROLAMO (1930-   )
Chi D'Amor S'Arma
TTB RICORDI-ENG 132209 s.p. (A177)

Crudele Acerbo E Dispietato Core
SAB RICORDI-ENG 132257 s.p. (A178)

Epitaffi
cor,orch sc RICORDI-ENG 131831 s.p.
(A179)

Tre Madrigali *CC3U
SATTB RICORDI-ENG 132125 s.p.
(A180)

ARRIVEDERCI, ROMA see Rascel, R.

ARS AMATORIA see Pinos, Alois

ARS AMATORIA see Wimberger, Gerhard

ARSI E ALSI see Monteverdi, Claudio

ARTMAN
Arise, Arise America
SAT oct SCHMITT 8509 $.40   (A181)

ARTMAN, RUTH
Back-A-Rock
2pt LEONARD-US 0871300 $.50 (A182)

ARTNER, NORBERT
Drum Singet Doch
men cor,acap TONOS 5804 s.p. (A183)

AS I LAY SLEEPING see Russell, Welford

AS JIMMY WENT A HUNTING
(Johnston, Richard A.) SAB (med easy)
WATERLOO $.30   (A184)

AS THE BRANCH IS TO THE VINE see Day,
P.

AS THROUGH THE WOOD see Brahms,
Johannes, Es Geht Ein Wehen

ASCHER, KEN
You And Me Against The World
(composed with Williams, Paul)
*pop
(Nowak, Jerry) SATB,pno oct BIG
BELL $.45   (A185)
(Nowak, Jerry) SSA,pno oct BIG BELL
$.45   (A186)
(Nowak, Jerry) SAB,pno oct BIG BELL
$.45   (A187)
(Nowak, Jerry) SA,pno oct BIG BELL
$.45   (A188)

ASH GROVE, THE
(Wick, Fred) SATB oct SCHMITT W247
$.40   (A189)
(Wick, Fred) SSA oct SCHMITT W320
$.40   (A190)

ASPIRATIONS see Owen, Harold

ASRIEL, ANDRE (1922-   )
Kanon *canon
4 eq voices NEUE NM1009 s.p. (A191)

AT PIERROT'S DOOR
(Hill, Harry) SSA (easy) WATERLOO
$.30   (A192)

AT' PROCITNE DREVORUBEC see
Sedmidubsky, Milos

AT SUNDOWN see Dunham, Arthur

AT THE MARKET PLACE see Berg

AT THE MID HOUR OF NIGHT see Moore,
Thomas

AT THE WATERMILL see Binge

AT THE ZOO see Simon, Paul

ATKINSON
Santa Watches Grown Ups, Too
SA oct SCHMITT 364 $.40   (A193)

ATKINSON, CONDIT R.
Evening Star
SATB,S/T solo,opt bvl GALAXY
1.2528.1 $.35, ipa   (A194)

Four Things (A Man Must Learn To Do)
SATB,pno,opt gtr&bvl GALAXY
1.2568.1 $.40, ipa   (A195)

Gloria
SATB,opt perc GALAXY 1.2527.1 $.30
(A196)

Little Lamb
SA GALAXY 1.2526.1 $.30   (A197)

ATTA REGLOR UR BONDEPRACTICAN see
Johansen, Sven-Erik

AU CLAIR DE LA LUNE (from Cvjy) folk
"Bei Dem Mondenscheine" [Ger/Fr] 4pt
wom cor,acap BREITKOPF-W CHB 4950
s.p.   (A198)
(Ruthenberg, O.) "Beim Mondesschein"
[Ger/Fr] 4pt mix cor MERSEBURG
EM9248 s.p.   (A199)

AU CLAIRE DE LA LUNE see Marx, Karl

AU JOLY BOYS see Sermisy, Claude de

AU PORT DE DIEPPE *folk,Fr
(Blanchard, R.) 3pt men cor,acap
JOBERT s.p.   (A200)

AUBEPIN. . . . AUBEPINE see Havord de
la Montagne, joachim

AUCH WAS IN DIE QUER see Zipp,
Friedrich

AUCTION BLOCK *19th cent
(Pasch, Silvio) SATB (med diff)
WATERLOO $.50   (A201)

AUDITE NOVA see Lassus, Roland de
(Orlandus)

AUF, AUF, IHR HIRTEN *Xmas
(Bachl, Hans) treb cor DOBLINGER
O 327 s.p.   (A202)

AUF DAS TRINKGLAS EINES VERSTORBENEN
FREUNDES "DU HERRLICH GLAS, NUN
STEHST DU LEER" see Cadow, Paul

AUF DEM SEE see Loewe

AUF DEM SEE see Mendelssohn-Bartholdy,
Felix

AUF DER FAHRT "HOPP, HEI! UND WIR
FAHREN" *folk,Slav
(Zoll, Paul) men cor sc SCHOTTS
C 41 864 s.p. see from Zwei
Slawische Volksliedsatze   (A203)

AUF DER GARTENBANK see Kanetscheider,
Artur

AUF DER GARTENBANK "EI WAS MAG DENN DAS
DA SEIN" see Rein, Walter

AUF DER LUNEBURGER HEIDE see
Kanetscheider, Artur

AUF DER OFENBANK see Gorl, Willibald

AUF DER TECK see Weber, Wilhelm

AUF DER VOSCHILETZER BRUCKE see
Pappert, Walter

AUF DER WIESE see Kludas, Erich

AUF DIE SCHWAB'SCHE EISEBAHNE see
Krietsch, Georg

AUF, DU JUNGER WANDERSMANN see Welker,
Gotthard

AUF EINEM BAUM EIN KUCKUCK SASS see
Gebhard, Hans

AUF EINEM BAUM EIN KUCKUCK SASS see
Pepping, Ernst

AUF ERDEN GEHEST DU see Weber, Bernhard

AUF EUER WOHL see Frommlet, Dieter

AUF, GRUNER JUNG *folk,Eng
   (Rosenstengel, Albrecht) men cor,opt
   gtr,opt perc sc,cor pts TONOS 2101
   s.p.   (A204)

AUF, HIRTEN, AUF, ERWACHT *Xmas
   (Bachl, Hans) treb cor DOBLINGER
   O 335 s.p.   (A205)

AUF HOHER FAHRT
   unis wom cor SCHOTTS C 42 532H s.p.
   see also Alle Singen Heft 1   (A206)

AUF HOHER SEE "EIN SCHIFFLEIN KLEIN"
   see Weber, Bernhard, In Mezo Al Mar

AUF, IHR BRUDER! EHRT DIE LIEDER! see
   Fussan, Werner

AUF, IHR FREUNDE see Mockl, Franz

AUF IN DEN SATTEL see Edler, Robert

AUF KAPERFAHRT
   (Ketterer, E.) men cor,acap TONOS
   2016 s.p.   (A207)

AUF, KUJAWIAK see Burthel, Jakob

AUF MATZLBACH *folk,Ger
   (Biebl, Franz) men cor,acap TONOS 2
   s.p.   (A208)

AUF, SINGET UND TRINKET *folk,Ger
   (Michels, J.) men cor,acap TONOS 3926
   s.p.   (A209)

AUF UND AB DEN SCHONEN RHEIN see
   Seeger, Peter

AUF WIEDERSEHEN IN FROHER RUNDE *folk
   (Biebl, F.) [Ger] 4pt men cor
   MERSEBURG EM9077 s.p.   (A210)

AUF WIEDERSEHN "WIEDERSEHN IST EIN
   SCHONES WORT" see Lang, Hans

AUFHEITERUNG "WAS KANN DOCH AUF ERDEN"
   see Haas, Joseph

AUFREGUNG IM HUHNERHOF "DER TAG BRICHT
   AN" see Rein, Walter

AUFRUF "KOMM SINTFLUT DER SEELE" see
   Orff, Carl

AUFSTIEG see Fischer, Theo

AUGEN AUF IM STRASSENVERKEHR see
   Seeger, Peter

AULD LANG SYNE
   (Weber, Bernhard) "Die Schone Alte
   Zeit "Die Freunde All"" [Eng/Ger]
   men cor sc SCHOTTS CHBL 201 s.p.
                                     (A211)

AULD LANG SYNE see Weber, Bernhard

AUNT RHODY *folk,US
   (Mechem, Kirke) TTBB,pno (easy)
   FISCHER,C CM 7870 $.35   (A212)

AURA LEE
   (Hall, Wm.D.) SATB,pno,horn NATIONAL
   WHC-45 $.40   (A213)

AURA LEE see Thygerson, Robert J.

AUS DEM LAND DER HABANERA see Klefisch,
   Walter

AUS DER SONNE IN DIE TONNE see Edler,
   Robert

AUS FREMDEN LANDERN see Mendelssohn,
   Arnold

AUS IHREM GRAB DA STEHT EINE LINDE see
   Mendelssohn-Bartholdy, Felix

AUS MEINER KINDHEIT see Biebl, Franz

AUS VERGANGENEN ZEITEN "ACH, WIE
   UNGLUCKLICH UND ARM IST DER
   BAUERSMANN see Bartok, Bela

AUS WEITER FERNE *folk,Ir
   (Zoll, Paul) [Eng/Ger] men cor sc
   SCHOTTS C 40 294 s.p. see from Zwei
   Irische Volkslieder   (A214)

AUSGEWAHLTE WERKE see Widmann, Erasmus

AUSSCHUSS "IST IRGENDWO VIEL GELD
   VERTAN" see Desch, Rudolf

AUSTIN, FREDERICK (1872-1952)
   Songs In A Farmhouse
   SATB,SATB soli,2fl,2ob,2clar,2bsn,
   2horn,2trp,timp,strings, triangle
   voc sc NOVELLO rental   (A215)

AUTOMATIC PISTOL, THE see Kohs, Ellis
   B.

AUTUMN (from Czech Year, The)
   (Hanus, Jan) SATB,acap voc sc GENERAL
   741 SU $5.00   (A216)

AUTUMN CICADA see Cole

AUTUMN SONG see Holst, Gustav

AUTUMN SONG see Schulthorpe

AUTUMN SONG see Schumann, Robert
   (Alexander), Herbstlied

AUTUMN SYMPHONY see Novak, Vitezslav

AUTUNES, JORGE (1942-   )
   Proudhonia
   cor,acap ZERBONI 7534 s.p.   (A217)

AVALOS
   Have A Nice Day
   2pt treb cor&Bar,pno,perc PRO ART
   2778 $.40   (A218)

   Sing A Happy Song
   3pt&desc,perc, piano 4-hands PRO
   ART 2776 $.45   (A219)

AVE COLOR VINI CLARI see Ponce, Juan

AVEGEBET see Ketterer, Ernst

AVERRE, RICHARD
   Spread A Little Love *pop
   SATB,pno,perc,gtr oct BIG BELL $.40
                                     (A220)
   SSA,pno,perc,gtr oct BIG BELL $.40
                                     (A221)
   SAB,pno,perc,gtr oct BIG BELL $.40
                                     (A222)
   SA,pno,perc,gtr oct BIG BELL $.40
                                     (A223)

AVON, VALERIE
   Long Live Love (composed with Spiro,
   Harold)
   (Simon, W.) SSA BIG3 $.45   (A224)
   (Simon, W.) SATB BIG3 $.45   (A225)
   (Simon, W.) SAB BIG3 $.45   (A226)

AVRIL see Ladmirault, P.

AVSHALOMOV, JACOB (1919-   )
   City Upon A Hill
   SATB,narrator,2fl,2ob,2clar,2bsn,
   4horn,2trp,3trom,tuba,3perc,pno,
   bells,2vln,2vla,2vcl,3bvl,pic,
   contrabassoon sc AM.COMP.AL.
   $23.20   (A227)

   Hail The Great Land
   SATB,pno AM.COMP.AL. $.55   (A228)

   Inscriptions At The City Of Brass
   *ora
   SATB,narrator,3fl,pic,2ob,clar,bsn,
   4horn,3trp,3trom,tuba,timp,3perc,
   pno,2gtr,2bvl, English horn, e-
   flat clarinet, contrabassoon,
   2banjos AM.COMP.AL. sc $46.20,
   voc pt $22.00   (A229)

AWAKE, LUMBERJACK see Sedmidubsky,
   Milos, At' Procitne Drevorubec

AWAKE! THE MORNING DAWNS see Protheroe,
   Daniel

AWAKE, YOU ARE IN NEED see Distler,
   Hugo, Wacht Auf, Es Tut Euch Not!

AWARENESS OF YOU, AN see Collins, Don
   L.

AWAY FOR RIO see Cookson, Frank B.

AWAY MELANCHOLY! see Parker, Alice

AWAY WITH THESE SELF-LOVING LADS see
   Dowland, John

AXELROD, DAVID (1937-   )
   Living Hand In Hand (composed with
   Pottle, Sam)
   SATB TRIGON TGO 110 $.40   (A230)

AXIS see Jenni, Donald

AXMAN, EMIL (1887-1949)
   Ilonka Beniacova
   [Czech] mix cor,SBar soli,3fl,2ob,
   2clar,3bsn,6horn,3trp,3trom,tuba,
   timp,perc,harp,strings, celeste
   CZECH s.p.   (A231)

AYE LEE LOO
   (Kirk) SATB,acap,opt fing.cym. PRO
   ART 2854 $.35   (A232)

AZNAVOUR, CHARLES (1924-   )
   Les Comediens
   [Fr] SATB,pno CHAPPELL-FR s.p.
                                     (A233)

AZZAIOLO, F.
   My Dear Heart, Your Departing *see
   Ti Parti, Cor Mio Caro

   Ti Parti, Cor Mio Caro
   (Malin, Don) "My Dear Heart, Your
   Departing" TTBB,acap BELWIN 2329
   $.30   (A234)

   Villotte Del Fiore
   4pt mix cor,acap sc BONGIOVANI 1290
   s.p.   (A235)

B

BAA, BAA BLACK SHEEP see Clover, David

BABUSCH *folk
(Koringer, Franz) mix cor DOBLINGER
G 711 s.p. see from Funf Satze Nach
Kroatischen Volksliedern (B1)

BACCHUS see Schubert, Franz (Peter)

BACH, F.
Chanson
3pt wom cor,acap HENN 300 s.p. (B2)

BACH, JAN
Dirge For A Minstrel
SATB AMP A-706 $.50 (B3)

Three Choral Dances *CC3U
cor (med diff) FISCHER,C O 4952
$1.75 (B4)

BACH, JOHANN SEBASTIAN (1685-1750)
Bouree (from Lute Suite In E Minor)
(Helm-Basista, W.) 3-4pt mix cor,
bvl,perc (med easy) sc SCHOTTS
C 43 330 s.p. (B5)

Complete Works. Bach-Gesellschaft
Edition *sac/sec,CCU
(Rust, William; Rietz, J.;
Hauptmann, M; Becker, C.F.;
Kroll, F.; Doerffel, A.; Naumann,
E; Von Waldersee; Kretzchmar, H.)
microfiche UNIV.MUS.ED.
originally published as 47
volumes in 61 bindings, Leipzig,
1851-1899, and 1926. $310.00 (B6)

Contrapunctus I (from Die Kunst Der
Fuge)
(Schnebel, Dieter) SSSSS&AAAAA&
TTTTT&BBBBB (med diff) sc SCHOTTS
ED. 6420 s.p. (B7)

BACHMANN, ALFRED
Fuhrmanns Liedchen
men cor,acap TONOS 5807 s.p. (B8)

Ich Weiss Ein Altes Schenkenhaus
men cor,acap TONOS 5809 s.p. (B9)

BACI SOAVI E CARI see Monteverdi,
Claudio

BACK-A-ROCK see Artman, Ruth

BACK HOME AGAIN see Denver, John

BACK IN DAD AND MOTHER'S DAY see
Betzner, Jack

BACK YARD see Raphling, Sam

BACKEN see Johansen, Sven-Erik

BACKER, BILL
If You've Got The Time
(Metis, F.) SSA BIG3 $.40 (B10)
(Metis, F.) SATB BIG3 $.40 (B11)
(Metis, F.) SAB BIG3 $.40 (B12)

BACKERLIED "FLEISSIG IST DER
BACKERSMANN" see Bresgen, Cesar

BAD, BAD LEROY BROWN see Croce, Jim

BAD WATER see De Shannon, Jackie

BADEPL ATZ UND SPRUNGTURM LOCKEN
see Singende Jugend Nr. 16

BADINGS, HENK (1907-)
Klaagsang Uit "Die Dieper Reg"
mix cor,pno,2fl,2ob,2clar,2bsn,
3horn,3trp,3trom,strings,perc,
timp,celeste DONEMUS (B13)

BAER
Song Of Wind, A
SSA,pno RICORDI-ENG SD12 s.p. (B14)

BAJUSCHKI BAJU see Haus, Karl

BAJUSCHKI BAJU "SCHLAFE, KINDLEIN, TU
DICH LEGEN" see Haus, Karl

BAKER, D.
Shadows Of Evening
mix cor LESLIE 4021 $.30 (B15)

BALADA, LEONARDO
Voices No. 1
SATB SCHIRM.G 12023 $.75 (B16)

BALADA O KRASNE SMRTI see Furst,
Jaromir Karel

BALADA SLOVENSKYCH HOR see Prasil,
Frantisek

BALADE see Massis, Amable

BALADE DE BON CONSEYL see Taylor,
Clifford

BALADICKA KANTATA see Moyzes, Alexander

BALADY see Eben, Petr

BALASSA, SANDOR
Nyari Ej
wom cor BUDAPEST 6806 s.p. (B17)

BALAZS, ARPAD
Csufolo
(Csukas, Istvan) jr cor BUDAPEST
7611 s.p. (B18)

Harom Vegyeskar
(Juhasz, Frigyes) mix cor BUDAPEST
6774 s.p. (B19)

Huszonegy Korusdal *CCU
jr cor/wom cor/eq voices,pno
BUDAPEST 7253 s.p. (B20)

Ket Pasztellkep *CC2U
mix cor BUDAPEST 7350 s.p. (B21)

Kikeleti Napkoszonto *CCU
(Nadas, Katalin) jr cor,pno
BUDAPEST 7052 s.p. (B22)

Ropteto
(Gyarfas) jr cor,pno BUDAPEST 7078
s.p. (B23)

Szavak A Konyvhoz
(Vorosmarty, Mihaly) mix cor
BUDAPEST 7096 s.p. (B24)

Tavaszlesen
jr cor,pno BUDAPEST 7303 s.p. (B25)

Ugratos
men cor BUDAPEST 6706 s.p. (B26)

VIT 1973 *CCU
cor,pno BUDAPEST 7068 s.p. (B27)

BALAZS, FREDERIC
Casualty
see Two Poems

Christmas
see Two Poems

Evening Song, An
SATB,harp,strings sc AM.COMP.AL.
$3.85 (B28)

Two Poems
SATB,4horn,2trp,3trom,tuba,4timp,
perc AM.COMP.AL. sc $6.60, ipa,
voc sc $6.60
contains: Casualty; Christmas
(B29)

BALD GRAS ICH AM NECKAR *folk,Ger
(Biebl, Franz) men cor,acap TONOS 122
s.p. (B30)

BALD PRANGT, DEN MORGEN ZU VERKUNDEN
see Mozart, Wolfgang Amadeus

BALET PRO SOLOVOU TANECNICI see Emmert,
Frantisek

BALFE
Vocal Fantasia On Bohemian Girl
(Challinor) mix cor BANKS MUS
YS 857 $1.10 (B31)

BALI HA'I see Rodgers, Richard

BALLAD ABOUT BEAUTIFUL DEATH, THE see
Furst, Jaromir Karel, Balada O
Krasne Smrti

BALLAD OF NANCY DEE, THE see Gardner

BALLAD OF THE GREEN BERETS
SA CIMINO $.40 (B32)
SSA CIMINO $.40 (B33)
TTBB CIMINO $.40 (B34)
SATB CIMINO $.40 (B35)

BALLAD OF THE LION AND THE LAMB, THE
see Sutton, Nancy

BALLAD OF TREES AND THE MASTER see
Mills, Charles

BALLADE *folk,Eur
(Schollum, Robert) mix cor DOBLINGER
G 663-664 s.p. contains also:
Streifte Durch Den Buchenwald (B36)

BALLADE PETRICE KEREMPUHA see Kuljeric,
Igor

BALLADE VON DEN MUSICI see Klan, Theo

BALLET FOR SOLO DANCEUSE see Emmert,
Frantisek, Balet Pro Solovou
Tanecnici

BALLETTS AND MADRIGALS TO FIVE VOICES
(1598, 1608) EM VOL. 10 see
Weelkes, Thomas

BALLOONS IN THE SNOW see Boyd, Jeanne

BALLOU, ESTHER W.
O The Sun Comes Up-Up-Up In The
Opening
SSA,acap AM.COMP.AL. $2.20 (B37)

What If A Much Of A Which Of A Wind
SBB,fl,ob,clar,bsn,horn sc
AM.COMP.AL. $6.60, ipa (B38)

BALM IN GILEAD *spir
(Kubizek, Augustin) "Heilender Trost"
men cor DOBLINGER M 327 s.p. (B39)

BALOO, BALEERIE
(Bissell, Keith W.) SSA (med easy)
WATERLOO $.30 (B40)

BALOW see Castelnuovo-Tedesco, Mario

BANAT see Bartok, Bela

BANCHIERI, ADRIANO (1568-1634)
Ad Un Dolce Usignolo
(Hall, Wm.D.) "To A Sweet
Nightingale" [It/Eng] SATB,acap
NATIONAL WHC-66 $.45 (B41)

Battle, The *see La Battaglia

Canzoni Alla Francesca (Of 1596)
*CC14U
(Bartholomew, Leland) 8pt bds A-R
ED $9.95 contains 11 instrumental
canzonas and 3 vocal concertos
(B42)

Contraponto Bestiale Alle Mente
*madrigal
SSATB,acap EGTVED MS18B7 s.p. (B43)

Contrappunto Bestiale Alla Mente
[It] SAATB RICORDI-ENG BA9882 s.p.
(B44)

Il Zabaione Musicale
(Hall, Wm.D.) "Musical Zabaione, A"
[It/Eng] SSATB,acap NATIONAL
WHC-75 $.40 (B45)

La Battaglia
(Crabtree, Phillip D.) "Battle,
The" SATB&SATB,opt brass (med
diff) DEAN CMC-101 voc sc $1.25,
sc $4.10 (B46)

Madrigaletto *see Se Nel Mar Del Mio
Pianto

Musical Zabaione, A *see Il Zabaione
Musicale

Se Nel Mar Del Mio Pianto (from La
Pazzia Senile)
(Moore, Ray) "Madrigaletto" [Eng/
It] SAT,opt SAT soli,acap BOONIN
B 158 $.45 (B47)

To A Sweet Nightingale *see Ad Un
Dolce Usignolo

BANDOG, THE see Greaves

BANICKA KANTATA see Burlas, Ladislav

BANJO MAN, THE see Sanders

BANK, JACQUES (1943-)
Put Me On My Bike, Nr. 1
mix cor,Bar solo,rec DONEMUS (B48)

BANKS OF ALLAN WATER, THE see Sharpe,
Evelyn

BANKS OF SWEET PRIMROSES, THE *folk,
Eng
unis EMI (B49)

BANNER OF ST. GEORGE see Elgar, Edward

BANNER OF THE JEW, THE see Heilner,
Irwin

BANTOCK, GRANVILLE (1868-1946)
Fighting Temeraire, The
TTBB,acap ROBERTON 53013 s.p. (B50)

BAR KOCHBA see Heilner, Irwin

BARANYI LAKODALMAS see Farkas, Ferenc

BARATI, GEORGE (1913-)
Hawaiian Bird-Catching Song
jr cor,pno,perc/1winds sc
AM.COMP.AL. $2.20 (B51)

Waters Of Kane, The
SATB,2fl,2ob,3clar,2bsn,4horn,2trp,
3trom,tuba,timp,perc,strings sc

BARATI, GEORGE (cont'd.)

   AM.COMP.AL. $14.85   (B52)

BARBARA ALLEN *folk
  (Miller, Carl) 2pt CHAPPELL
  0063289-351 $.40   (B53)
  (Willcocks) SATB,acap OXFORD see from
  Five Folk Songs   (B54)

BARBAROSSA see Silcher, Friedrich

BARBEL UND ULI *folk
  (Hennig, W.) [Ger] 4pt men cor
  MERSEBURG EM9022 s.p.   (B55)

BARBERSHOP CHOIR, THE
  (Thygerson, Robert W.) TTBB HERITAGE
  H2875 $.75
    contains: Goat, The; He's Gone
    Away; Stephen Foster Medley, A;
    Joplin, Scott, Entertainer, The;
    Thygerson, Robert J., Aura Lee
                                              (B56)

BARBEY, BOB
  Christmas In Five-Four Time
  (Kraintz, Ken) SATB,pno,bvl,gtr
  (easy, jazz) KYSAR $.45   (B57)

BARBIERI, GATO
  Last Tango In Paris
  (Habash, J.M.) SATB BIG3 $.40 (B58)

BARCAROLA see Veneziani, Vittore

BARCAROLE see Brahms, Johannes

BARDENGESANG see Strauss, Richard

BARDOS, LAJOS (1899-   )
  Batorsag Ad Erot
  (Kolcsey, Ferenc) mix cor BUDAPEST
  7455 s.p.   (B59)

  Dolgozni II
  (Jozsef, Attila) mix cor BUDAPEST
  7338 s.p.   (B60)

  Enekeljetek
  (Pakolitz, Istvan) mix cor BUDAPEST
  7109 s.p.   (B61)

  Gaudeamus Igitur
  (Vargha, Karoly) mix cor BUDAPEST
  7339 s.p.   (B62)

  Himmusz A Bekerol
  (Radnoti, Miklos) mix cor BUDAPEST
  6577 s.p.   (B63)

  Szekesfehervar
  (Kornyei, Elek) mix cor BUDAPEST
  7340 s.p.   (B64)

  Uj Szovetneket
  (Garay, Janos) men cor BUDAPEST
  7135 s.p.   (B65)

BARENTANZLIED "BRAUNER TANZBAR, TANZE"
  see Klefisch, Walter

BARN DANCE see Donato, Anthony

BARNBY
  Sweet And Low
  (Hedgren) TTBB,acap (med)
  FITZSIMONS 4065 $.20   (B66)

BARNES, M.H.
  Scrapbook For Julie, A
  TTBB,pno KERBY 11766 $2.25   (B67)

  Scrapbook For Julie, A *CCU
  TTBB KERBY 11766 $2.25   (B68)

BARON MUNCHAUSEN see Cole, Hugo

BARRAQUE, JEAN (1928-   )
  La Temps Restitue
  cor,S solo,2fl,2ob,3clar,bsn,4vln,
  2vla,2vcl,bvl,4perc,gtr,harp,
  vibraphone, glockenspiel,
  celeste, claves, xylophone sc
  BRUZZI S.V060 s.p.   (B69)

BARRIE, GEORGE
  All That Love Went To Waste (from
  Touch Of Class, A)
  (Simon, W.) SAB BIG3 $.45   (B70)
  (Simon, W.) SATB BIG3 $.45   (B71)
  (Simon, W.) SSA BIG3 $.45   (B72)

  Touch Of Class, A
  (Metis, F.) SSA BIG3 $.45   (B73)
  (Metis, F.) SATB BIG3 $.45   (B74)
  (Metis, F.) SAB BIG3 $.45   (B75)

BARRY, JEFF
  I Honestly Love You *see Allen,
  Peter

BARTA, LUBOR
  Colombine *see Kolombina

BARTA, LUBOR (cont'd.)

  Hospoda
  "Inn, The" see Muzske Sbory

  Inn, The *see Hospoda

  Kolombina
  "Colombine" see Muzske Sbory

  Muzske Sbory
  [Czech] men cor,acap CZECH s.p.
    contains: Hospoda, "Inn, The";
    Kolombina, "Colombine"; Noc,
    "Night"   (B76)

  Night *see Noc

  Noc
  "Night" see Muzske Sbory

  Song Of The New Era *see Zpev Noveho
  Veku

  Zpev Noveho Veku *cant
  "Song Of The New Era" [Czech] mix
  cor,3fl,3ob,3bsn,3clar,6horn,
  3trp,3trom,tuba,timp,perc,strings
  CZECH s.p.   (B77)

BARTHEL, URSULA (1913-   )
  Ein Wandernder Gesele
  see Zwei Kinderchore Im Volkston

  Lob Auf Das Wasser
  see Zwei Kinderchore Im Volkston

  Zwei Kinderchore Im Volkston
  jr cor voc pt BOTE s.p.
    contains: Ein Wandernder Gesele;
    Lob Auf Das Wasser   (B78)

BARTHOLEMEY
  Urbs Aquensis
  (Baur, P.) men cor,pno TONOS 696
  s.p.   (B79)

BARTOK, BELA (1881-1945)
  Ach, Mein Gott, Nur Leiden
  see Ungarische Volkslieder Aus
  Siebenburgen

  Achtet Auf Das Licht! *see Jatek

  Achtzehn Chorlieder
  [Ger/Hung] (med easy/diff) cmplt
  ed,sc SCHOTTS C 43 783-01 s.p.
    contains & see also: Banat,
    "Scheiden"; Bolyongas,
    "Irrwege"; Csujogato,
    "Tanzlied"; Element A Madarka,
    "Fort Flog Das Vogelein";
    Hejja, Karahejja, "Boser
    Schwarzer Habicht"; Isten
    Veled!, "Lebe Wohl!"; Jatek,
    "Achtet Auf Das Licht!";
    Keserves, "Schmerz";
    Lanycsufolo, "Der Spiegel";
    Leanynezo, "Brautschau"; Level
    Az Othhoniakhoz, "Gluck Und
    Frieden"; Madardal,
    "Vogellied"; Meghalok
    Csurgoert, "Kanon"; Mihalynapi
    Koszonto, "Zum, Michaelitag";
    Ne Lattalak Volna, "Hatt' Es
    Gott Gegeben"; Parnas Tancdal,
    "In Der Alten Muhle"; Senkim A
    Vilagon, "In Steiler Felsen
    Hoh"; Van Egy Gyurum, Karika,
    "Hab' Ein Goldnes Ringelein"
                                              (B80)

  Aus Vergangenen Zeiten "Ach, Wie
  Unglucklich Und Arm Ist Der
  Bauersmann
  [Ger/Hung] TBarB,acap sc SCHOTTS
  EMB 05-6079 s.p.   (B81)

  Banat
  "Scheiden" [Ger/Hung] 3 eq voices,
  acap (med easy/diff) sc SCHOTTS
  C 43 795 s.p. see also Achtzehn
  Chorlieder   (B82)

  Bolyongas
  "Irrwege" [Ger/Hung] 3 eq voices,
  acap (med easy/diff) sc SCHOTTS
  C 43 793 s.p. see also Achtzehn
  Chorlieder   (B83)

  Boser Schwarzer Habicht *see Hejja,
  Karahejja

  Brautschau *see Leanynezo

  Csujogato
  "Tanzlied" [Ger/Hung] 3 eq voices,
  acap (med easy/diff) sc SCHOTTS
  C 43 798 s.p. see also Achtzehn
  Chorlieder   (B84)

  Der Spiegel *see Lanycsufolo

  Drei Ungarische Volkslieder *see
  Habt Ihr Schon Gehort Die Kunde;
  Hoch Des Richters Haus In Kanja
  Ragt; Markt Ist Heute In Der

BARTOK, BELA (cont'd.)

  Kleinen Stadt   (B85)

  Dunner Zwirn Und Harter Kern
  see Ungarische Volkslieder Aus
  Siebenburgen

  Element A Madarka
  "Fort Flog Das Vogelein" [Ger/Hung]
  3 eq voices,acap (med easy/diff)
  sc SCHOTTS C 43 787 s.p. see also
  Achtzehn Chorlieder   (B86)

  Elmult Idokbol *CC3U
  men cor BUDAPEST 6079 s.p.   (B87)

  Fa Follott
  (Bardos, Lajos) eq voices BUDAPEST
  6705 s.p.   (B88)

  Fort Flog Das Vogelein *see Element
  A Madarka

  Gluck Und Frieden *see Level Az
  Othhoniakhoz

  Hab' Ein Goldnes Ringelein *see Van
  Egy Gyurum, Karika

  Habt Ihr Schon Gehort Die Kunde
  (composed with Fischbach, Klaus)
  *folk,Hung
  men cor sc SCHOTTS CHBL 218 s.p.
  see from Drei Ungarische
  Volkslieder   (B89)

  Hatt' Es Gott Gegeben *see Ne
  Lattalak Volna

  Hejja, Karahejja
  "Boser Schwarzer Habicht" [Ger/
  Hung] 3 eq voices,acap (med easy/
  diff) sc SCHOTTS C 43 784 s.p.
  see also Achtzehn Chorlieder
                                              (B90)

  Hoch Des Richters Haus In Kanja Ragt
  (composed with Fischbach, Klaus)
  *folk,Hung
  men cor sc SCHOTTS CHBL 219 s.p.
  see from Drei Ungarische
  Volkslieder   (B91)

  Icike-Picike
  (Bardos, Lajos) eq voices BUDAPEST
  6704 s.p.   (B92)

  In Der Alten Muhle *see Parnas
  Tancdal

  In Steiler Felsen Hoh *see Senkim A
  Vilagon

  Irrwege *see Bolyongas

  Isten Veled!
  "Lebe Wohl!" [Ger/Hung] 3 eq
  voices,acap (med easy/diff) sc
  SCHOTTS C 43 794 s.p. see also
  Achtzehn Chorlieder   (B93)

  Jatek
  "Achtet Auf Das Licht!" [Ger/Hung]
  2 eq voices,acap (med easy/diff)
  sc SCHOTTS C 43 783 s.p. see also
  Achtzehn Chorlieder   (B94)

  Kanon *see Meghalok Csurgoert

  Keinen Pfennig
  see Ungarische Volkslieder Aus
  Siebenburgen

  Keserves
  "Schmerz" [Ger/Hung] 3 eq voices,
  acap (med easy/diff) sc SCHOTTS
  C 43 796 s.p. see also Achtzehn
  Chorlieder   (B95)

  Lanycsufolo
  "Der Spiegel" [Ger/Hung] 2 eq
  voices,acap (med easy/diff) sc
  SCHOTTS C 43 786 s.p. see also
  Achtzehn Chorlieder   (B96)

  Leanynezo
  "Brautschau" [Ger/Hung] 3 eq
  voices,acap (med easy/diff) sc
  SCHOTTS C 43 785 s.p. see also
  Achtzehn Chorlieder   (B97)

  Lebe Wohl! *see Isten Veled!

  Level Az Othhoniakhoz
  "Gluck Und Frieden" [Ger/Hung] 2 eq
  voices,acap (med easy/diff) sc
  SCHOTTS C 43 788 s.p. see also
  Achtzehn Chorlieder   (B98)

  Madardal
  "Vogellied" [Ger/Hung] 3 eq voices,
  acap (med easy/diff) sc SCHOTTS
  C 43 797 s.p. see also Achtzehn
  Chorlieder   (B99)

BARTOK, BELA (cont'd.)

Madchen, Hei, Wie Habt Ihr's Fein
see Ungarische Volkslieder Aus
Siebenburgen

Markt Ist Heute In Der Kleinen Stadt
(composed with Fischbach, Klaus)
*folk,Hung
men cor sc SCHOTTS CHBL 220 s.p.
see from Drei Ungarische
Volkslieder   (B100)

Meghalok Csurgoert
"Kanon" [Ger/Hung] 2 eq voices,acap
(med easy/diff, contains also:
Parnas Tancdal) sc SCHOTTS
C 43 791 s.p. see also Achtzehn
Chorlieder   (B101)

Mihalynapi Koszonto
"Zum, Michaelitag" [Ger/Hung] 3 eq
voices,acap (med easy/diff) sc
SCHOTTS C 43 799 s.p. see also
Achtzehn Chorlieder   (B102)

Ne Lattalak Volna
"Hatt' Es Gott Gegeben" [Ger/Hung]
2 eq voices,acap (med easy/diff)
sc SCHOTTS C 43 790 s.p. see also
Achtzehn Chorlieder   (B103)

Parnas Tancdal
"In Der Alten Muhle" [Ger/Hung] 3
eq voices,acap (med easy/diff,
contains also: Meghalok
Csurgoert) sc SCHOTTS C 43 791
s.p. see also Achtzehn Chorlieder
                                     (B104)

Sag, Warum Du All Dies Leid Mir
Angetan
see Ungarische Volkslieder Aus
Siebenburgen

Scheiden *see Banat

Schmerz *see Keserves

Senkim A Vilagon
"In Steiler Felsen Hoh" [Ger/Hung]
2 eq voices,acap (med easy/diff)
sc SCHOTTS C 43 792 s.p. see also
Achtzehn Chorlieder   (B105)

Tanz Doch, Pfarrer
see Ungarische Volkslieder Aus
Siebenburgen

Tanzlied *see Csujogato

Ungarische Volkslieder Aus
Siebenburgen *folk,Hung
[Ger] men cor sc SCHOTTS
EMB 05-4675 s.p.
contains: Ach, Mein Gott, Nur
Leiden; Dunner Zwirn Und Harter
Kern; Keinen Pfennig; Madchen,
Hei, Wie Habt Ihr's Fein; Sag,
Warum Du All Dies Leid Mir
Angetan; Tanz Doch, Pfarrer
                                     (B106)

Van Egy Gyurum, Karika
"Hab' Ein Goldnes Ringelein" [Ger/
Hung] 2 eq voices,acap (med easy/
diff) sc SCHOTTS C 43 789 s.p.
see also Achtzehn Chorlieder
                                     (B107)

Vogellied *see Madardal

Zum, Michaelitag *see Mihalynapi
Koszonto

BARTOS, JAN ZDENEK (1908-   )
Beautiful Country *see Prekrasna
Zeme

Beautiful Country *see Krasna Zeme

Bezec Miru *Op.47, cant
"Peace Race Runner, The" [Czech]
mix cor,Bar solo,3fl,2ob,3clar,
2bsn,4horn,3trp,3trom,tuba,timp,
perc,strings CZECH s.p.   (B108)

Bohatstvi Zeme
"Riches Of The Earth, The" [Czech]
mix cor,acap CZECH s.p.   (B109)

Krasna Zeme *Op.50, cant
"Beautiful Country " [Czech] jr
cor/wom cor,S solo,vln,harmonium,
pno CZECH s.p.   (B110)

March 1948 *see Pochod 1948

Muzikanti Co Delate *CCU,folk
[Czech] jr cor,2fl,2ob,2clar,2bsn,
4horn,2trp,3trom,tuba,timp,perc,
strings CZECH s.p.   (B111)

Peace Race Runner, The *see Bezec
Miru

Pochod 1948
"March 1948" [Czech] mix cor,acap
CZECH s.p.   (B112)

BARTOS, JAN ZDENEK (cont'd.)

Prekrasna Zeme
"Beautiful Country" [Czech] mix
cor,acap CZECH s.p.   (B113)

Psano Na List Kalendare
"Written On The Page Of A Calendar"
[Czech] men cor,acap CZECH s.p.
                                     (B114)

Riches Of The Earth, The *see
Bohatstvi Zeme

Written On The Page Of A Calendar
*see Psano Na List Kalendare

BARVIK, MIROSLAV (1919-   )
Greeting To Soviet Union *see
Prodrav Sovetskemu Svazu

Pioneer Story, The *see Pionyrska
Pohadka

Pionyrska Pohadka
"Pioneer Story, The" [Czech] jr
cor,acap CZECH s.p.   (B115)

Podekovani Sovetskemu Svazu
"Thanks To The Soviet Union"
[Czech] mix cor,2horn,4trp,2trom,
timp CZECH s.p.   (B116)

Pred Prichodem Rude Armady *CC5U
[Czech] men cor,acap CZECH s.p.
                                     (B117)

Prodrav Sovetskemu Svazu *cant
"Greeting To Soviet Union" [Czech]
mix cor,2horn,2trp,2trom,timp
CZECH s.p.   (B118)

Thanks To The Soviet Union *see
Podekovani Sovetskemu Svazu

BASSETT, LESLIE (1923-   )
Moonrise
wom cor,pno,3fl,vln,2vla,vcl,2perc,
celeste AM.COMP.AL. sc $6.60,
ipa, voc pt $1.10   (B119)

BASTELLIED "LASST UNS ALLEINE MACHEN"
see Hindemith, Paul

BATEMAN, RONALD
All Through The Night
SA CRAMER $.25   (B120)

Wild Hills Of Clare
SA CRAMER $.25   (B121)

BATESON, THOMAS (ca. 1570-1630)
Adieu, Sweet Love
SSAB STAINER 3.0777.1 $.50   (B122)

First Set Of Madrigals (1604) EM Vol.
21 *CC29L,madrigal
3-6pt mix cor STAINER 3.1921.1
$17.00   (B123)

Second Set Of Madrigals (1618) EM
Vol. 22 *CC30L,madrigal
3-6pt mix cor STAINER 3.1922.1
$17.00   (B124)

Your Shining Eyes
(Malin, Don) SSA BELWIN 2295 $.35
                                     (B125)

BATH, HUBERT (1883-1945)
Wake Of O'Connor
SATB,SATB soli,2fl,2ob,2clar,2bsn,
4horn,2trp,3trom,tuba,timp,perc,
org,strings voc sc NOVELLO rental
                                     (B126)

BATORSAG AD EROT see Bardos, Lajos

BATTLE, THE see Banchieri, Adriano, La
Battaglia

BATTLE HYMN OF THE REPUBLIC see Steffe,
William

BATTLE HYMN OF THE REPUBLIC, THE *US
(Bennett, R.R.) 4pt mix cor SCHIRM.G
LG51769 $.50   (B127)

BATTLE OF MARIGNAN, THE see Jannequin,
Clement, La Guerre

BATTLE OF STONINGTON, THE
(Brandon) TTBB SCHIRM.G LG51810 $.40
                                     (B128)

BAUD-BOVY
Cantate De La Restauration *cant
mix cor,acap HENN 744 s.p.   (B129)

BAUEN WIR DIE NEUE STADT
see Singende Jugend Nr. 15

BAUERLEIN UND ESEL see Biebl, Franz

BAUERNGARTEN see Pepping, Ernst

BAUERNHOCHZEIT see Reutter, Hermann

BAUERNHOCHZEIT: BEIM KRONENWIRT see
Krietsch, Georg

BAUERNKALENDER see Radermacher,
Friedrich

BAUERNLIED *folk
(Rosenstengel, Albrecht) men cor,opt
gtr,opt perc sc,voc sc TONOS 2104
s.p.   (B130)
(Zoll, P.) [Ger] 4pt men cor
MERSEBURG EM9034 s.p.   (B131)

BAUMANN, MAX (1917-   )
Abend "Schweigt Der Menschen Laute
Lust"
wom cor (med) SCHOTTS C 41 796 s.p.
see from Tageskreis   (B132)

Das Schifflein Auf Der Drave "Fahrt
Ein Schifflein Langsam Sacht"
wom cor (med) sc SCHOTTS C 41 798
s.p.   (B133)

Ich Armes Maidlein Klag Mich Sehr
wom cor (med) sc SCHOTTS C 41 797
s.p.   (B134)

Mittagsruh "Uber Bergen, Fluss Und
Talen"
wom cor (med) SCHOTTS C 41 795 s.p.
see from Tageskreis   (B135)

Morgenlied "Kein Stimmlein Noch
Schallt"
wom cor (med) SCHOTTS C 41 794 s.p.
see from Tageskreis   (B136)

Tageskreis *see Abend "Schweigt Der
Menschen Laute Lust"; Mittagsruh
"Uber Bergen, Fluss Und Talen";
Morgenlied "Kein Stimmlein Noch
Schallt"   (B137)

BAUSZNERN, DIETRICH VON (1928-   )
Der Pilgrim
men cor,acap TONOS 3729 s.p. (B138)

Die Beiden Flaschen
men cor,acap TONOS 3724 s.p. (B139)

BAYERISCHE VOLKSLIEDER HEFT 1 *CCU,
folk
(Bohm, Max) 4pt mix cor cor pts
HIEBER s.p.   (B140)

BAYERISCHE VOLKSLIEDER HEFT 2 *CCU,
folk
(Bohm, Max) 2-4pt wom cor/2-4pt jr
cor cor pts HIEBER s.p.   (B141)

BAYERISCHE VOLKSLIEDER HEFT 3 *CCU,
folk
(Bohm, Max) 3pt men cor cor pts
HIEBER s.p.   (B142)

BAYLEY, ROBERT CHARLTON
My Love Is Fair
unis HARRIS $.25   (B143)

BE A CLOWN
SSA CIMINO $.40   (B144)
TTBB CIMINO $.40   (B145)
SATB CIMINO $.40   (B146)

BE GLAD THEN AMERICA see La Montaine,
John

BE MERRY ALL THAT BE PRESENT see
Wuorinen, Charles

BE STILL see Fritschel, James

BEADELL, ROBERT M.
Biglow Papers
SATB AMP A-705 $.50 see from
Trilogy   (B147)

Shiloh
SATB AMP A-704 $.40 see from
Trilogy   (B148)

Trilogy *see Biglow Papers; Shiloh;
War Is Kind   (B149)

War Is Kind
SATB AMP A-703 $.50 see from
Trilogy   (B150)

BEAL, JOE
Jingle-Bell Rock (composed with
Boothe, Jim)
(Simon, W.) SSA BIG3 $.45   (B151)
(Simon, W.) SATB BIG3 $.50   (B152)
(Simon, W.) SAB BIG3 $.45   (B153)
(Simon, W.) SA/TB BIG3 $.45   (B154)

BEALE, WILLIAM (1784-1854)
Phyllis, Thy Lovely Looks *madrigal
(Young, Percy M.) [Eng] SATB,acap
oct BROUDE BR. $.45   (B155)

This Pleasant Month Of May *madrigal
(Young, Percy M.) [Eng] SATB,acap
oct BROUDE BR. $.50   (B156)

BEAN-STALK, THE see Hewitt, Thomas J.

BEANSTALK AND JACK, THE
(Strasek, M.K.) 1-2pt,pno CIMINO
$2.50   (B157)

BEARD
Look For The Light
SATB SHAWNEE A1280 $.40   (B158)

BEAUDROT
Cradle Song *Xmas
SATB,acap PRO ART 2763 $.35 (B159)

BEAUTIFUL COUNTRY see Bartos, Jan
Zdenek, Prekrasna Zeme

BEAUTIFUL COUNTRY see Bartos, Jan
Zdenek, Krasna Zeme

BEAUTIFUL SOUP see Fine

BEAUTIFUL SUNDAY see Boone, Daniel

BEAUTY see Adams

BEAUTY FROM THIS WORLD see L'Estocart,
Paschal de, Le Beau Du Monde
S'efface

BEAUVERD
Adieu
men cor,acap HENN 778 s.p.   (B160)

Chanson A Boire
men cor,acap HENN 779 s.p.   (B161)

La Vie - Ronde
mix cor,acap HENN 754 s.p.   (B162)

BECAUSE see Lennon, John

BECK, CONRAD (1901-   )
Abendlied "Nun Der Ubermude Tag"
mix cor,acap (med diff) sc SCHOTTS
C 33 643 s.p. see from Funf Chore
(B163)
Abendsegen "Der Tag Hat Seinen
Schmuck"
mix cor,acap (med diff) sc SCHOTTS
C 33 645 s.p. see from Funf Chore
(B164)
Der Schone Sommer Geht Uns Herein
wom cor (med) sc SCHOTTS C 33 639
s.p.   (B165)
Die Brunnlein, Die Da Fliessen *folk
wom cor (med diff) sc SCHOTTS
C 33 640 s.p.   (B166)
Die Zeit Geht Nicht, Sie Stehet Still
mix cor,acap (med diff) sc SCHOTTS
C 33 642 s.p. see from Funf Chore
(B167)
Funf Chore *see Abendlied "Nun Der
Ubermude Tag"; Abendsegen "Der
Tag Hat Seinen Schmuck"; Die Zeit
Geht Nicht, Sie Stehet Still;
Musiken Klang, Lieblicher Gesang;
Seit Die Sonne Ihren Lichten
Schein   (B168)
Ich Wollt Zu Land Ausreisen
wom cor (med) sc SCHOTTS C 33 637
s.p.   (B169)
Lyrische Kantate *cant
2-4pt wom cor,SA soli,pno,fl,ob,
2clar,2bsn,horn,trp,strings,
triangle, celeste, English horn
(diff) sc SCHOTTS rental, ipr
(B170)
Musiken Klang, Lieblicher Gesang
mix cor,acap (med diff) sc SCHOTTS
C 33 641 s.p. see from Funf Chore
(B171)
Sei Gern Allein
SA (med diff) sc SCHOTTS C 33 638
s.p.   (B172)
Seit Die Sonne Ihren Lichten Schein
mix cor,acap (med diff) sc SCHOTTS
C 33 644 s.p. see from Funf Chore
(B173)

BECKER, D.G.
Geloofsvertrouwen
mix cor,pno/harmonium HEER 722 s.p.
(B174)

BECKER, HANS-GUNTHER
Die Weite Welt
men cor,acap 3701 s.p.   (B175)

Heiteres Auftrittslied
men cor,acap 3702 s.p.   (B176)

Hell Erklingt Mein Lied
men cor&jr cor,pno sc,voc sc TONOS
5249 s.p.   (B177)

Sommerland
men cor,pno TONOS 2189 s.p. (B178)

Tschechisches Tanzlied
men cor,pno sc,cor pts TONOS 2185
s.p.   (B179)

BECKER, HANS-GUNTHER (cont'd.)
Vier Trinkspruche
men cor,acap 3935 s.p.   (B180)

BECKER, HORST
Wenn Es Winter Wird *CC12U
mix cor,acap BREITKOPF-L PB3957
s.p.   (B181)

BECKER, JOHN J. (1886-1961)
Out Of The Cradle Endlessly Rocking
SATB,ST,narrator,2fl,2ob,2clar,
2bsn,4horn,2trp,timp,strings
AM.COMP.AL.   (B182)

Pool, The
SSA,pno AM.COMP.AL. $.83   (B183)

Symphony No. 6, Out Of Bondage
cor,narrator,2fl,3ob,2clar,2bsn,
2horn,2trp,3trom,tuba,timp,perc,
strings AM.COMP.AL.   (B184)

BECKER, PETER (1934-   )
Interludium
see Kommt, Ihr G'spielen

Jetzt Kommt Die Froliche Sommerzeit
see Kommt, Ihr G'spielen

Kommt, Ihr G'spielen
see Kommt, Ihr G'spielen

Kommt, Ihr G'spielen
unis&opt 2 eq voices/2pt mix cor,
fl,ob,strings voc pt TONGER s.p.
contains: Interludium; Jetzt
Kommt Die Froliche Sommerzeit;
Kommt, Ihr G'spielen; Marsch;
Viel Freuden Mit Sich Bringet
(B185)
Marsch
see Kommt, Ihr G'spielen

Viel Freuden Mit Sich Bringet
see Kommt, Ihr G'spielen

BECKERATH, ALFRED VON (1901-   )
Kantate Zum Richtfest *cant
1-4pt mix cor,acap/inst (med easy)
sc SCHOTTS C 39 533 s.p.   (B186)

BEDRICH, JAN (1932-   )
February And Roses *see Unor A Ruze

Unor A Ruze *cant
"February And Roses" [Czech] mix
cor,3fl,3ob,3clar,3bsn,4horn,
3trp,3trom,2tuba,timp,perc,2harp,
strings CZECH s.p.   (B187)

BEEBE, HANK
This Is The Generation
SATB,pno (med) FISCHER,C CM 7819
$.35   (B188)

BEESON
Tides Of Miranda
SSATB,acap (med diff) OXFORD 95.306
$.40   (B189)

BEESTEBENDE see Andriessen, Caecilia

BEETHOVEN, LUDWIG VAN (1770-1827)
Choral Fantasy *see Chorfantasie

Chorfantasie *Op.80
"Choral Fantasy" [Ger] cor,pno,orch
min sc EULENBURG 1333 s.p. (B190)
"Chorfantasie "Schmeichelnd Hold""
SATB,pno,orch (med) min sc
SCHOTTS ETP 1333 s.p.   (B191)
(Klink, Waldemar) "Die Gaben
Schoner Kunst" jr cor (med easy)
sc SCHOTTS CHBL 531 s.p.   (B192)

Chorfantasie "Schmeichelnd Hold"
*see Chorfantasie

Complete Works *sac/sec,CCU
(Adler, Guido; Bagge, Selmar;
David, Ferdinand; Espagne, Franz;
Mandycewski, Eusebius; Nottebohm,
Gustav; Reinecke, Carl; Richter,
E.F.; Rietz, Julius) microfiche
UNIV.MUS.ED. $170.00 originally
published as 25 series, Leipzig,
1862-1888.   (B193)

Die Gaben Schoner Kunst *see
Chorfantasie

Die Himmel Ruhmen
men cor,acap 6304 s.p.   (B194)

Fra Tutte Le Pene
[It] SATB EGTVED KB81 s.p. contains
also: Quella Cetra   (B195)

Freundschaft *canon
3pt men cor,acap 6305 s.p.   (B196)

Giura Il Nocchier
[It] SATB EGTVED KB119 s.p. (B197)

BEETHOVEN, LUDWIG VAN (cont'd.)
Grablied
see VIER GRABLIEDER

Ma Tu Tremi
[It] SAB EGTVED KB77 s.p. contains
also: Per Te D'amico Aprile;
Quella Cetra   (B198)

Opferlied "Die Flamme Lodert"
(Lang, Hans) mix cor (med easy) sc
SCHOTTS CHBL 306 s.p.   (B199)

Per Te D'amico Aprile
see Beethoven, Ludwig van, Ma Tu
Tremi

Quella Cetra
see Beethoven, Ludwig van, Fra
Tutte Le Pene
see Beethoven, Ludwig van, Ma Tu
Tremi

BEFORE HER BARE HAND see Milhaud,
Darius, Devant Sa Main Nue

BEFORE SLEEP see Holst, Gustav

BEFORE THE ENDING OF THE DAY see
Waters, Charles F.

BEFORE THE NEXT TEARDROP FALLS see
Keith, Vivian

BEFORE THE PALING OF THE STARS see
Dale, Benjamin J.

BEFORE THE PALING OF THE STARS see
Silver

BEGIN MY MUSE see Adler

BEGRUSSUNG DER SANGER "IHR LIEBEN
SANGESBRUDER" see Desch, Rudolf

BEGUELIN
Bel Aubepin
men cor HENN 823 s.p.   (B200)

Mon Verger
men cor,acap HENN 791 s.p.   (B201)

Printemps
men cor,acap HENN 790 s.p.   (B202)

BEHANDELT DIE FRAUEN MIT NACHSICHT see
Krietsch, Georg

BEHERZIGUNG "ACH, WAS SOLL DER MENSCH
VERLANGEN" see Hessenberg, Kurt

BEHERZIGUNG "FEIGER GEDANKEN" see
Brahms, Johannes

BEHIND CLOSED DOORS
SSA SCREEN 1431BC2   (B203)
SATB SCREEN 1431BC1   (B204)

BEI DEM MONDENSCHEINE see Au Clair De
La Lune

BEI DEN FUNKERN see Weitzendorf, Heinz

BEI DEN KLANGEN DES FANDANGO see Zoll,
Paul

BEI LUZERN, DEM RIGIS ZUA see
Kuhlenthal, Fred

BEI MEINER BLONDEN "IM GARTEN DER
LORBEER BLUHT" see Othegraven,
August J. von

BEI MEINER BLONDINE *folk
(Seeger, P.) [Ger] 4pt men cor
MERSEBURG EM9013 s.p.   (B205)

BEI TAG UND NACHT see Pepping, Ernst

BEIM GUTEN WEIN see Steffens, Johann

BEIM HEILAND VON TSCHIGISSY see
Stravinsky, Igor

BEIM MONDESSCHEIN see Au Clair De La
Lune

BEIM SCHEIDEN "MIR IST'S ZU WOHL
ERGANGEN" see Trunk, Richard

BEIN' GREEN see Raposo, Joe

BEIN, WILHELM
Heideblute
men cor,acap 226 s.p.   (B206)

Heidefruhling
men cor,acap 227 s.p.   (B207)

BEKENNTNIS see Gorl, Willibald

BEKRANZT MIT LAUB see Fischer, Theo

BEL AUBEPIN see Beguelin

BELCHER, SUPPLY (1751-1836)
Welcome To Spring
(Van Camp, Leonard) SATB (easy)
FISCHER,C CM 7907 $.50 (B208)

BELIEVE *CCU
unis BELWIN $1.50 (B209)

BELL, THOMAS
You Make Me Feel Brand New (composed
with Creed, Linda) *pop
(Nowak, Jerry) SATB,pno oct BIG
BELL $.45 (B210)

BELLA BIONDA
(Frommlet, Dieter) men cor,acap TONOS
458 s.p. (B211)

BELLA, JAN LEVOSLAV (1843-1936)
Svadba Janosikova *cant
mix cor,STBar soli,orch
SLOV.HUD.FOND s.p. (B212)

BELLE JE NE L'SUIS PAS see Jelmoli,
Hans

BELLERMANN, SANGERFAHRT
Lieder Fur Die Jugend, Im Freien Zu
Singen, Teil I *Op.19, CC10U
mix cor LIENAU sc s.p., cor pts
s.p. (B213)

Lieder Fur Die Jugend, Im Freien Zu
Singen, Teil II *Op.28, CC10U
mix cor LIENAU sc s.p., cor pts
s.p. (B214)

Lieder Fur Die Jugend, Im Freien Zu
Singen, Teil III *Op.31, CC10U
mix cor LIENAU sc s.p., cor pts
s.p. (B215)

Lieder Fur Die Jugend, Im Freien Zu
Singen, Teil IV *Op.41, CC5U
mix cor LIENAU sc s.p., cor pts
s.p. (B216)

BELLMAN, CARL MIKAEL (1740-1795)
En Sommardag Med Bellman *CC8L
men cor,inst/acap cor pts ERIKS 98
s.p., ipa (B217)

Glada Bygd
(Hellden, Daniel) mix cor GEHRMANS
KRB449 (B218)

Gubben Noach
(Jehrlander, Karl-Fredrik) mix cor
GEHRMANS KRB444 (B219)

Joachim Uti Babylon
(Jehrlander, Karl-Fredrik) mix cor
GEHRMANS KRB460 (B220)

Sa Lunka Vi Sa Smaningom
(Jehrlander, Karl-Fredrik) mix cor
GEHRMANS KRB445 (B221)

Trad Fram, Du Nattens Gud
(Sund, Robert) mix cor GEHRMANS
KRB461 (B222)

BELLS see Paulus, Stephen

BELLS, THE see Sampson, Godfrey

BELLS DO RING, THE see Glarum

BELLS OF ABERDOVEY, THE *folk,Welsh
(Soderstrom, Emil) TTBB,acap (med)
FITZSIMONS 4059 $.30 (B223)

BELLS OF CHRISTMAS, THE see Stuart,
Mary

BELLS OF EASTER, THE see McAfee, Don

BELLS OF SANTA YNEZ, THE *CCU
SATB CIMINO $2.50 (B224)

BELOVED CANADA see Wilkinson, Charles
A.

BELOVED LAND see Konvalinka, Milos,
Milovana Zeme

BELOVED OF SEVEN ROBBERS see Huth,
Gustav, Mila Sedmi Loupezniku

BELSHAZZAR HAD A LETTER see Berger,
Jean

BEMESST DEN SCHRITT see Pepping, Ernst

BEN
SSA,pno,opt bvl&drums&gtr SCREEN
1443BC8 (B225)
SATB,pno,opt bvl&drums&gtr SCREEN
1443BC7 (B226)
SA,pno,opt bvl&drums&gtr SCREEN
1443BCX (B227)

BENDL, KAREL (1838-1897)
After The Battle Of The White
Mountain *see Po Bitve
Belohorske

Cikanske Melodie
"Gipsy Melodies" [Czech] mix cor,AB
soli,3fl,2ob,2clar,2bsn,4horn,
2trp,3trom,timp,perc,strings
CZECH s.p. (B228)

Death Of Prokop The Great, The *see
Smrt Prokopa Velikeho

Gipsy Melodies *see Cikanske Melodie

Po Bitve Belohorske
"After The Battle Of The White
Mountain" [Czech] mix cor,soli,
2fl,2ob,2clar,2bsn,4horn,2trp,
3trom,tuba,timp,perc,harp,strings
CZECH s.p. (B229)

Smrt Prokopa Velikeho
(Smatek, M.) "Death Of Prokop The
Great, The" [Czech] men cor,Bar
solo,2fl,ob,2clar,bsn,2horn,trp,
trom,tuba,timp,perc,strings,harp
CZECH s.p. (B230)

BENEATH THE OLD FLAG see Kricka,
Jaroslav, Pod Starym Praporem

BENEKEN, FRIEDRICH
Heil Dir Und Frieden
see VIER GRABLIEDER

BENEVENUTI, ARRIGO (1925-   )
Gymel E Corale
cor,electronic tape BRUZZI V.067
s.p. (B231)

La Bottega Delle Idee
cor,soli,orch BRUZZI L-068 s.p.
(B232)

Racconto I
cor,soli,orch BRUZZI L-031 s.p.
(B233)

BENGUEREL, XAVIER (1931-   )
Nocturno De Los Avisos
mix cor,S solo,2fl,2ob,2clar,2bsn,
2trp,4horn,3trom,tuba,2timp,
strings, vibraphone MODERN rental
(B234)

BENNETT
Drive Him Back To London
(Shipp) SATB SCHIRM.G LG51688 $.40
(B235)

BENNETT, JOHN
All Creatures Now *madrigal
SSATB,acap EGTVED KB258 s.p. (B236)

Sleep Fond Fancy, O
SATB STAINER 3.0728.1 $.50 (B237)

BENNETT, RICHARD RODNEY (1936-   )
Spells
mix cor,S solo,orch voc sc NOVELLO
s.p. (B238)

BENOY, A.W.
Two Rounds For Voices *CC2U
SS OXFORD (B239)

BERCEUSE see Ives, Charles

BERCEUSE POUR LE PETIT OURS see
Strimer, Joseph

BERG
At The Market Place *sac
(Hyde) SA/TB SHAWNEE E156 $.40
(B240)

BERG, GOTTFRID
En Ganglat
4pt mix cor ERIKS 313 s.p. see from
Tva Vandringsvisor (B241)

Tva Vandringsvisor *see En Ganglat;
Vandringsvisa (B242)

Vandringsvisa
4pt mix cor ERIKS 312 s.p. see from
Tva Vandringsvisor (B243)

BERGER
An Die Grossen Toten *Op.85
mix cor LIENAU voc sc s.p., cor pts
s.p. (B244)

Better Lose The Saddle Than The Horse
SSA SHAWNEE B301 $.35 (B245)

Different Drummer, A
SATB SHAWNEE 1271 $.40 (B246)

If I Can Stop One Heart From Breaking
SATB KJOS 5903 $.35 (B247)

BERGER, JEAN (1909-   )
Answer July
[Eng] SATB,pno BROUDE BR. $.45 see
from Three Poems By Emily
Dickinson (B248)

BERGER, JEAN (cont'd.)

Ant, The
see Who's Who In The Zoo

Belshazzar Had A Letter
[Eng] SATB,pno BROUDE BR. $.35 see
from Three Poems By Emily
Dickinson (B249)

Camel, The
see Who's Who In The Zoo

Cow, The
see Who's Who In The Zoo

Gander, The
see Who's Who In The Zoo

Hippopotamus, The
see Who's Who In The Zoo

Man's Life Is Well Compared To A
Feast
SATB,acap BOONIN B 207 $.50 (B250)

New Year Carol, A
wom cor,inst (med) FISCHER,C 0 4908
$1.25 (B251)

Three Poems By Emily Dickinson *see
Answer July; Belshazzar Had A
Letter; To Make A Prairie (B252)

Time Is Too Slow
SSAATBB BELWIN 2307 $.35 (B253)

To Make A Prairie
[Eng] SATB,pno BROUDE BR. $.35 see
from Three Poems By Emily
Dickinson (B254)

Who's Who In The Zoo
[Eng] SATB,2fl BROUDE BR. $.75
contains: Ant, The; Camel, The;
Cow, The; Gander, The;
Hippopotamus, The (B255)

BERGER, ROMAN
V Tichu Tak Draho Vykupenom
see MUZSKE ZBORY III

BERGH, ARTHUR (1882-1962)
Blow, Blow Thou Winter Wind
SATB (med) FITZSIMONS 1060 $.20
(B256)

Sweet And Twenty
SATB,acap (easy) FITZSIMONS 1059
$.25 (B257)

Tragic Story, A
SATB,acap (easy) FITZSIMONS 1070
$.25 (B258)

Under The Greenwood Tree
SATB,acap (easy) FITZSIMONS 1058
$.25 (B259)

BERGISCHES HEIMATLIED see Brambach,
Kaspar Joseph

BERGLIED "WIR WOLLEN AUF DEN BERG
STEIGEN" see Mohler, Philipp

BERGLIEDER see Langer, Hans-Klaus

BERGMAN
Summer Me, Winter Me *see Legrand,
Michel

BERGMANN, WALTER (1902-   )
Drummer Boy, The *folk,Fr
[Eng] unis jr cor,pno,rec,perc
(easy) sc,cor pts SCHOTTS
ED. 10 963 s.p., ipa (B260)

John Brown's Body
[Ger/Eng] 1-2pt jr cor,pno,strings,
rec,perc (easy) sc,voc sc SCHOTTS
RS 13 s.p., ipa (B261)

Matilda
1-2pt jr cor,pno,vcl,perc,S rec,A
rec, glockenspiel, xylophone sc
SCHOTT 10964 s.p., ipa (B262)

BERGMANNSGRUSS see Engel, H.

BERGMANNSLIED see Lang, Hans

BERGMANNSLIED: GLUCK AUF see Edler,
Robert

BERGREN, ALFRED HILES
Day Is Dark And Dreary, The
TTBB,Bar solo (med) FITZSIMONS 4046
$.25 (B263)

BERLIN, IRVING (1888-   )
White Christmas
ALLANS 839 (B264)

BERLIOZ, HECTOR (1803-1869)
Hail, All Hail To The Queen (from
Trojans, The)
SATB OXFORD   (B265)

Hector Berlioz Works *sac/sec,CCU
(Malherbe, Charles; Weingartner,
Felix) microfiche UNIV.MUS.ED.
$115.00 originally published as
20 volumes in 18 bindings.
Leipzig, 1900-1907.   (B266)

BERNARD, FELIX
Winter Wonderland *pop
(Warnick, Clay) SATB,pno oct BIG
BELL $.50   (B267)

BERNHARD
Deer Cries For Flowing Water, The
(Streetman) SATB SCHIRM.G LG51706
$.50   (B268)

BERNIER RENE (1905-   )
Sabots De La Vierge
(Careme, Maurice) mix cor,acap CBDM
(B269)

BERNSTEN, ELSE
Og Jenta Ho Wille Til Dansen Ga
unis NORSK NMO 8797 s.p.   (B270)

BERRE see Kvam, Oddvar S.

BERTHOMIEU, MARC
Douze Chansons Pour Les Jours
Heureux, Vol. 4
CHAPPELL-FR s.p.
contains: Meuh!... (cor,soli);
Quand L'Elephant Joue De La
Trompette (2pt,solo); Tom, Le
Nounours (2pt)   (B271)

Meuh!...
see Douze Chansons Pour Les Jours
Heureux, Vol. 4

Quand L'Elephant Joue De La Trompette
see Douze Chansons Pour Les Jours
Heureux, Vol. 4

Tom, Le Nounours
see Douze Chansons Pour Les Jours
Heureux, Vol. 4

BESAME MUCHO see Velazquez, Consuelo

BESCHWINGTE ILLUSIONEN VERZAUBERN see
Seeger, Peter

BESEIGED SERENITY see Radic, Dusan,
Opsednuta Vedrina

BESIG
Better World, A
SSA SHAWNEE B399 $.35   (B272)

Give A Little Love At Christmas
SATB SHAWNEE A1297 $.35   (B273)

If The World Could Only Be Happy!
2pt PRO ART 2767 $.35   (B274)

It's A Wonderful Thing To Be Me
SA/TB SHAWNEE E159 $.40   (B275)

BESINNUNG see Burkhart, Franz

BESINNUNG see Herf, Franz

BESINNUNG "FURCHTE NUR DIES" see Haas,
Joseph

BEST
Angie (composed with Craik)
SATB,pno,opt gtr&bvl&drums MCAFEE
M123 $.35   (B276)

That Men Might Know (composed with
Craik)
SATB,pno,gtr MCAFEE M143 $.35
(B277)

BEST THERE IS, THE
SSA CIMINO $.40   (B278)
TTBB CIMINO $.40   (B279)
SATB CIMINO $.40   (B280)

BETTEL-STANDCHEN "GESANG ERSCHALLE VOR
DEM HAUS" see Lang, Hans

BETTELLIED SIBIRISCHER LANDSTREICHER
see Reutter, Hermann

BETTER IS see London, Edwin

BETTER LOSE THE SADDLE THAN THE HORSE
see Berger

BETTER LOVE, A see Podest, Ludvik,
Laska Peknejsi

BETTER WORLD, A see Besig

BETTINELLI, BRUNO (1913-   )
Liriche Di Ungaretti
4pt mix cor RICORDI-ENG 131923 s.p.
(B281)

BETTIS
Saturday (composed with Carpenter)
(Lojeski, Ed) SATB LEONARD-US
08256000 $.50   (B282)
(Lojeski, Ed) SSA LEONARD-US
08256002 $.50   (B283)

BETTIS, JOHN
Goodbye To Love *see Carpenter,
Richard

Only Yesterday *see Carpenter,
Richard

Yesterday Once More *see Carpenter,
Richard

BETTLERFREUDE see Reutter, Hermann

BETTLERLIED see Cossetto, Emil

BETTLERLUST see Linke, Norbert

BETTS
Ramblin' Man *pop
(Burroughs; Sewell) SATB WARNER
WB-340 187 $.40   (B284)
(Burroughs; Sewell) TTB WARNER
WB-341 188 $.40   (B285)

BETZNER, JACK
Back In Dad And Mother's Day
(composed with Godfrey, Bob)
(Perry, L.) TTBB BOURNE B215392-355
$.35   (B286)

BEURDEN, BERNARD VAN (1933-   )
Lilith
mix cor,inst DONEMUS   (B287)

BEWAFFNETER FRIEDE see Kirsch, Winfried

BEWITCHED DAUGHTER, THE see Novak,
Vitezslav, Zakleta Dcera

BEYER
Man With The Blue Guitar, The
SATB SCHIRM.G 11941 $.40   (B288)

BEYOND THE SEA
SATB CIMINO $.40   (B289)
TTBB CIMINO $.40   (B290)

BEZ PRACE see Kuksa, Emanuel

BEZEC MIRU see Bartos, Jan Zdenek

BIANCHIERI
Intermedio Di Solfanari
[It] TTB RICORDI-ENG BA10363 s.p.
(B291)

BICENTENNIAL COLLECTION OF AMERICAN
CHORAL MUSIC, THE *CCU,US,18-19th
cent
(Martens, Mason) cor MCAFEE $3.50
(B292)

BIEBL, FRANZ (1906-   )
Alles Strahlt Und Liebt Sich
men cor,acap 4591 s.p.   (B293)

An Der Heimat Halte Fest "Magst Du
Schon're Lande Schauen"
men cor (easy) sc SCHOTTS C 39 768
s.p. see from Vier Leichte
Mannerchore   (B294)

Aus Meiner Kindheit
"Le Temps Je Regrette" mix cor
(med) sc SCHOTTS C 41 282 s.p.
see from Drei Deutsche Chansons
(B295)

Bauerlein Und Esel
see Zwei Spiele Fur Kinder

Chi Bela Non E *see Ich Sah Im
Olivenwalde

Chormusik Im Swing-Stil
men cor,acap cmplt ed 3720 s.p.
contains: Langsamer Marsch;
Liebeslied; Polka   (B296)

Der Taler "Hab' Gefunden Einen Taler"
men cor sc SCHOTTS CHBL 162 s.p.
see from Zwei Kleine Chorlieder
(B297)

Der Trunkene Dichter
men cor sc,voc pt SCHOTTS
C 41 554, C 41 555 01-02 s.p.
contains: Die Turken; Ein
Trunkner Dichter; Freunde,
Wasser Machet Stumm; Voll Von
Wein "Voll, Freunde, Macht Euch
Voll"; Weg, Weg; Wein Ist
Starker Als Das Wasser (B298)

Der Wolf Und Die Sieben Geisslein
jr cor,soli,inst,perc PELIKAN
PE 935 sc s.p., cor pts s.p., ipa
(B299)

Des Pudels Kern "Einen Beutel Mocht
Ich Haben"
men cor sc SCHOTTS C 40 396 s.p.
see from Zwei Heitere Chorlieder
(B300)

BIEBL, FRANZ (cont'd.)

Die Turken
see Der Trunkene Dichter

Die Welt Ist Immer Heiter "Die
Madchen Und Die Flaschchen Wein"
men cor sc SCHOTTS C 40 397 see
from Zwei Heitere Chorlieder
(B301)

Drei Deutsche Chansons *see Aus
Meiner Kindheit, "Le Temps Je
Regrette"; Ich Sah Im
Olivenwalde, "Chi Bela Non E"; Im
Nebelgeriesel, "Zigeunerlied"
(B302)

Ein Trunkner Dichter
see Der Trunkene Dichter

Finale
see Kleine Suite Im Alten Stil

Freunde, Wasser Machet Stumm
see Der Trunkene Dichter

Funf Chorduette Nach Volksweisen
*see Ich Ging Emol Spaziere; O Du
Schoner Rosengarten; Was Spricht
Man Denn Von Sachsen; Was Wirst
Du Mir Mitbringen; Wo Find Ich
Dann Deins Vaters Haus   (B303)

Furchtet Ihr Den Schwarzen Mann
see Zwei Spiele Fur Kinder

Gesang An Die Sonne "In Morgenrot
Gekleidet"
men cor (easy) sc SCHOTTS C 39 767
s.p. see from Vier Leichte
Mannerchore   (B304)

Guten Abend, Frau Bas
see Vier Abend- Und Schlaflieder

Hansel Und Gretel
jr cor,S solo,perc,pno,inst sc,voc
sc PELIKAN PE925 s.p., ipa (B305)

Ich Ging Emol Spaziere
mix cor (med easy) sc SCHOTTS
C 40 398 s.p. see from Funf
Chorduette Nach Volksweisen
(B306)

Ich Sah Im Olivenwalde
"Chi Bela Non E" mix cor (med) sc
SCHOTTS C 41 283 s.p. see from
Drei Deutsche Chansons   (B307)

Im Nebelgeriesel
"Zigeunerlied" mix cor (med) sc
SCHOTTS C 41 284 s.p. see from
Drei Deutsche Chansons   (B308)

Kleine Suite Im Alten Stil
men cor,acap cmplt ed 3710 s.p.
contains: Finale; Kleiner Tanz;
Kleines Lied; Vorspiel   (B309)

Kleiner Tanz
see Kleine Suite Im Alten Stil

Kleines Lied
see Kleine Suite Im Alten Stil

Komm Die Sonne Lacht
men cor,acap 4523 s.p.   (B310)

Langsamer Marsch
see Chormusik Im Swing-Stil

Le Temps Je Regrette *see Aus Meiner
Kindheit

Liebeslied
see Chormusik Im Swing-Stil

Marsch Von Turenne "Schritt Fur
Schritt" *folk
mix cor,opt drums (easy) sc SCHOTTS
CHBL 420 s.p.   (B311)
4pt men cor,opt drums sc SCHOTTS
CHBL 215 s.p.   (B312)

O Du Schoner Rosengarten
mix cor (med easy) sc SCHOTTS
C 48 400 s.p. see from Funf
Chorduette Nach Volksweisen
(B313)

Polka
see Chormusik Im Swing-Stil

Radlers Seligkeit
men cor,pno,opt gtr,opt perc,
accordion ad lib TONOS 4967 s.p.
(B314)

Rotkappchen
jr cor,S solo,perc,pno,inst sc,voc
sc PELIKAN PE934 s.p., ipa (B315)

Rundgesang "Nur Frohlich Leute"
men cor,Bar solo (easy) sc SCHOTTS
C 39 769 s.p. see from Vier
Leichte Mannerchore   (B316)

BIEBL, FRANZ (cont'd.)

Sie Sagt, Ich Konnt Nicht Singen
men cor,acap 4506 s.p.   (B317)

Singt Und Trinkt
men cor (easy) sc SCHOTTS C 39 770
s.p. see from Vier Leichte
Mannerchore   (B318)

Susse Trauben "Mein Vater Ist Ein
Winzer"
men cor sc SCHOTTS CHBL 144 s.p.
see from Zwei Heitere Mannerchore
(B319)

Tabak Ist Mein Leben
men cor sc SCHOTTS CHBL 161 s.p.
see from Zwei Kleine Chorlieder
(B320)

Tanzliedchen *CCU
mix cor,pno voc sc ZIMMER. 1869
s.p., voc pt ZIMMER. 583 s.p.
waltz   (B321)

Trinklied "Die Glaser Klingen"
men cor sc SCHOTTS CHBL 145 s.p.
see from Zwei Heitere Mannerchore
(B322)

Und Der Lebende Hat Recht
men cor,acap 3924 s.p.   (B323)

Vier Abend- Und Schlaflieder
1-2pt jr cor,acap (easy) sc SCHOTTS
CHBL 585 s.p.
contains: Guten Abend, Frau Bas;
Was Mochtest Du Heut Traumen;
Wer Nicht Schlaft Und Wer Nicht
Ruht; Wohin Ein Jedes Schlafen
Geht   (B324)

Vier Leichte Mannerchore *see An Der
Heimat Halte Fest "Magst Du
Schon're Lande Schauen"; Gesang
An Die Sonne "In Morgenrot
Gekleidet"; Rundgesang "Nur
Frohlich Leute"; Singt Und Trinkt
(B325)

Voll Von Wein "Voll, Freunde, Macht
Euch Voll"
see Der Trunkene Dichter

Vom Bauernhof
jr cor,perc,pno/inst PELIKAN PE924
s.p.   (B326)

Vorspiel
see Kleine Suite Im Alten Stil

Was Mochtest Du Heut Traumen
see Vier Abend- Und Schlaflieder

Was Spricht Man Denn Von Sachsen
mix cor (med easy) sc SCHOTTS
C 40 402 s.p. see from Funf
Chorduette Nach Volksweisen
(B327)

Was Wir Gerne Tun
2pt jr cor,perc,S rec (easy) sc
SCHOTTS B 134 s.p.   (B328)

Was Wirst Du Mir Mitbringen
mix cor (med easy) sc SCHOTTS
C 48 401 s.p. see from Funf
Chorduette Nach Volksweisen
(B329)

Weg, Weg
see Der Trunkene Dichter

Wein Ist Starker Als Das Wasser
see Der Trunkene Dichter

Weinlust
see DREI WEINSPRUCHE

Wer Nicht Schlaft Und Wer Nicht Ruht
see Vier Abend- Und Schlaflieder

Wo Find Ich Dann Deins Vaters Haus
mix cor (med easy) sc SCHOTTS
C 40 399 s.p. see from Funf
Chorduette Nach Volksweisen
(B330)

Wohin Ein Jedes Schlafen Geht
see Vier Abend- Und Schlaflieder

Zigeunerlied *see Im Nebelgeriesel

Zwei Heitere Chorlieder *see Des
Pudels Kern "Einen Beutel Mocht
Ich Haben"; Die Welt Ist Immer
Heiter "Die Madchen Und Die
Flaschchen Wein"   (B331)

Zwei Heitere Mannerchore *see Susse
Trauben "Mein Vater Ist Ein
Winzer"; Trinklied "Die Glaser
Klingen"   (B332)

Zwei Kleine Chorlieder *see Der
Taler "Hab' Gefunden Einen
Taler"; Tabak Ist Mein Leben
(B333)

Zwei Spiele Fur Kinder
unis jr cor,solo,inst (easy) sc
SCHOTTS B 146 s.p.
contains: Bauerlein Und Esel;

BIEBL, FRANZ (cont'd.)

Furchtet Ihr Den Schwarzen Mann
(B334)

BIELA BREZA, SESTRA MOJA see Hrusovsky,
Ivan

BIERGESANGEL see Rein, Walter

BIG ROCK CANDY MOUNTAIN see Trant

BIG ROCK CANDY MOUNTAIN, THE *folk
(Miller, Carl) 2pt CHAPPELL
0064238-351 $.40   (B335)

BIGGS, JOHN
Epitaph
SATB&SATB,acap FOSTER CP-1 $.30
(B336)

Paul Revere
SATB,narrator,horn,perc (med diff)
FOSTER CP-3 $1.50, ipa   (B337)

BIGLOW PAPERS see Beadell, Robert M.

BILDNIS IM SOMMER see Wittmer, Eberhard
Ludwig

BILENCKO, M.
Cuckoo Song
unis LESLIE 1064 $.30 contains
also: Little Fish, The   (B338)

Little Fish, The
see Bilencko, M., Cuckoo Song

Old Gypsy, Play Your Songs So Fine
mix cor LESLIE 5009 $.35   (B339)

BILL OF FARE, THE see Zollner, Karl
Friedrich

BILLETER, AGATHON
Die Heimatglocken
men cor,acap TONOS 6326 s.p. (B340)

BILLINGS
Consonance
SATB WALTON 2212 $.40   (B341)

BILLINGS, WILLIAM (1746-1800)
Chester (from Our Sacred Honor)
see Yancey, Adelante! (Sail On!)
(Van Camp, L.) SATB,acap/org oct
SOMERSET SP 729 $.40   (B342)

I Am Come Into My Garden *sac/sec
SATB,acap BROUDE BR. $.55   (B343)

I Am The Rose Of Sharon *sac/sec
SATB,acap BROUDE BR.   (B344)

I Charge You, O Ye Daughters Of
Jerusalem *sac/sec
SATB,acap BROUDE BR. $.50   (B345)

Jargon
(Van Camp, Leonard) SATB,narrator,
opt inst FOSTER MF331D $.35 see
from Meet America's William
Billings   (B346)

Meet America's William Billings *see
Jargon; Meet America's William
Billings; Modern Music   (B347)

Meet America's William Billings
(Van Camp, Leonard) SATB,narrator,
opt inst FOSTER MF331 $2.50 see
from Meet America's William
Billings   (B348)

Modern Music
(Van Camp, Leonard) SATB,opt inst
FOSTER MF331E $.50 see from Meet
America's William Billings (B349)

BILLY, DON'T BE A HERO see Callander,
Pete

BINCHOIS, GILLES (ca. 1400-1460)
Chansons (from Musikalische Denkmaler
Band II)
(Rehm, Wolfgang) mix cor (med)
cloth SCHOTTS s.p.   (B350)

BINET
Chanson
mix cor,acap HENN 760 s.p.   (B351)

Comptines De L'oiselier
mix cor,clar HENN 821 s.p.   (B352)

Eveille-Toi
mix cor,acap HENN 741 s.p.   (B353)

La Bergere
wom cor,acap HENN 699 s.p.   (B354)

Le Jeu Du Printemps
mix cor HENN 684 s.p.   (B355)

Le Pays
men cor,acap HENN 788 s.p.   (B356)

BINET (cont'd.)

Le Vieux Jean Louis
men cor,acap HENN 789 s.p.   (B357)

Les Quatre Heures
mix cor,acap HENN 759 s.p.   (B358)

Nos Peres Nous Ont Dit
mix cor,acap HENN 751 s.p.   (B359)

Premier Matin
mix cor,acap HENN 758 s.p.   (B360)

Sermon
wom cor,acap HENN 700 s.p.   (B361)

BINGE
At The Watermill
SSA MARKS MC 4605 $.40   (B362)

Jolly Swagman, The
SATB MARKS MC 4623 $.40   (B363)

Sailing By
SSA MARKS MC 4619 $.40   (B364)

Tune-A-Day *CCU
SSA MARKS MC 4615 $.40   (B365)

BINGE, RONALD
Watermill, The
SSA,pno WEINBERGER s.p.   (B366)

BINGER, MARTIN (1913-   )
Andulka "O, Klopf Nicht An"
mix cor, rhythm instruments (med
easy) sc SCHOTTS C 42 812 s.p.
see from Drei Chorlieder   (B367)

Drei Chorlieder *see Andulka "O,
Klopf Nicht An"; Oi, Korano "Oi,
Korano! Kleiner Fluss Mit Klarem,
Blauem Wasser"; Zecher-Song "Wer
Gut Trinkt"   (B368)

Oi, Korano "Oi, Korano! Kleiner Fluss
Mit Klarem, Blauem Wasser"
mix cor, rhythm instruments (med
easy) sc SCHOTTS C 42 811 s.p.
see from Drei Chorlieder   (B369)

Zecher-Song "Wer Gut Trinkt"
mix cor, rhythm instruments (med
easy) sc SCHOTTS C 42 813 s.p.
see from Drei Chorlieder   (B370)

BINKERD, GORDON (1916-   )
Christmas Day
SATB,acap oct BOOSEY 5838 $.35
(B371)

Conjuration, To Electra, A
SSSAATB,acap oct BOOSEY 5835 $.50
see from To Electra, Set II   (B372)

Ile Come To Thee In All Those Shapes
SATB,acap oct BOOSEY 5834 $.70 see
from To Electra, Set II   (B373)

My Soul, There Is A Country
SATB,acap oct BOOSEY 5845 $.45
(B374)

Never Weather-Beaten Sail
SATB,acap oct BOOSEY 5847 $.40
(B375)

Nocturne
mix cor,vcl cor pts BOOSEY $.75,
ipa   (B376)

Quasi Modo
SATB,acap oct BOOSEY 5844 $.70
(B377)

They Lie At Rest
TBB oct BOOSEY 5854 $.40   (B378)

To Electra, Set II *see Conjuration,
To Electra, A; Ile Come To Thee
In All Those Shapes   (B379)

BIRD IN MY BOWER, A see Peele, Dudley

BIRD OF HOPE, THE see Cole, Rossetter
Gleason

BIRD OF LOVE see Willan, Healey,
Rossignol Du Vert Bocage

BIRDS, THE see Leighton, Kenneth

BIRD'S COURTING SONG
(Siegmeister, Elie) SSA,pno
WEINBERGER s.p.   (B380)

BIRDS' LAWN PARTY, THE see Busch, Carl

BIS HIERHER HAT MICH GOTT GEBRACHT see
Burthel, Jakob

BISHOP
Home, Sweet Home
(Nyvall) SSAATTBB,acap (easy)
FITZSIMONS 1021 $.20   (B381)

BISSELL, KEITH W. (1912-   )
Bluebird In March, A
cor,inst WATERLOO $.75, ipr (B382)

Canada, Dear Home
unis (med easy) WATERLOO $.40
(B383)
unis&SSA,inst WATERLOO $.40, ipa
(B384)
unis&SATB WATERLOO $.40, ipa (B385)
SATB WATERLOO $.40
(B386)

Full Fathom Five
SA (med easy) WATERLOO $.30 (B387)

In April
SSA (med diff) WATERLOO $.35 (B388)

Old Adam The Carrion Crow
SATB (diff) WATERLOO $.40
(B389)

Requiem
SSA (easy) WATERLOO $.30
(B390)

Summer Evening
SSA (med easy) WATERLOO $.40 (B391)

Summer's Queen
SA (med easy) WATERLOO $.30 (B392)

BITGOOD
Power Of Music, The
SATB,org MCAFEE M152 $.40
(B393)

BITTER-SWEET see Thompson, Randall

BITTGEBET see Reiter, Josef

BIWAK "HABT IHR DIE HUSAREN GESEHN" see
Trunk, Richard

BIZET, GEORGES (1838-1875)
June Roses
SA CRAMER $.25
(B394)

Love The Vagrant
(Mansfield) SSA CRAMER $.50 (B395)

Selection (from Carmen)
(McNaught) SATB,SMezTB soli,2fl,
pic,3ob,2clar,2bsn,4horn,2trp,
3trom,timp,perc,harp,strings voc
sc NOVELLO rental
(B396)

Street Boy's Song (from Carmen)
(Horton) unis,pno,perc,2S rec sc
SCHOTT 11126 s.p., ipa (B397)

BIZTATAS see Sugar, Rezso

BLABARET see Johansen, Sven-Erik

BLACK BART see Hoddinott, Alun

BLACK CAT see Weigl, Karl

BLACK IS THE COLOR OF MY TRUE LOVE'S
HAIR *folk
(Newbury, Kent) SATB RICHMOND MI-92
$.25
(B398)

BLACK IS THE COLOUR OF MY TRUE LOVE'S
HAIR see Patriquin, Donald

BLACK KNIGHT, THE see Elgar, Edward

BLACK NOVEMBER TURKEY, A see
Corigliano, John

BLACK SHEEP
(Swift, R.) SA KENDOR $.30 (B399)

BLAHA, IVO (1936-   )
Co Je Krasy Na Svete
"So Much Beauty In The World"
[Czech] jr cor,fl,ob,clar,bsn,
horn,harp,strings CZECH s.p.
(B400)
So Much Beauty In The World *see Co
Je Krasy Na Svete

BLAKE'S CRADLE SONG see Roberton, Hugh
Stevenson

BLANCHARD, ROGER
Il N'est Fille D'Espagne
4pt mix cor,acap JOBERT s.p. see
from Trois Jongleries (B401)

Quand Au Bois S'en Va Jouer
4pt mix cor,acap JOBERT s.p. see
from Trois Jongleries (B402)

Que Ne Vous Plait-Il, Notre Dame?
4pt mix cor,acap JOBERT s.p. see
from Trois Jongleries (B403)

Trois Jongleries *see Il N'est Fille
D'Espagne; Quand Au Bois S'en Va
Jouer; Que Ne Vous Plait-Il,
Notre Dame?
(B404)

BLASS, HEINRICH
Hederitt
men cor,acap TONOS 220 s.p. (B405)

Verschutt
men cor,acap TONOS 221 s.p. (B406)

Weinlied
men cor,acap TONOS 222 s.p. (B407)

BLAUE BEEREN *folk
(Kammeier, H.) [Ger] 4pt mix cor
MERSEBURG EM9223 s.p. (B408)

BLAUE BLUMEN see Fleig, G.

BLAUER MONTAG see Frey, Oskar

BLAZEK, ZDENEK (1905-   )
Domov *Op.71, cant
"Home" [Czech] mix cor,SBar soli,
3fl,3ob,3clar,3bsn,4horn,2trp,
3trom,tuba,timp,perc,harp,strings
CZECH s.p.
(B409)

Dove, The *see Holubice

Holubice *cant
"Dove, The" [Czech] jr cor&mix cor,
soli,perc,strings CZECH s.p.
(B410)

Home *see Domov

BLEIB DOCH STEHN *folk,Russ
(Seeger, Peter) men cor,acap TONOS
2017 s.p.
(B411)

BLESS THE FOUR CORNERS OF THIS HOUSE
see Weigl, Vally

BLESS YOU see Lennon, John

BLESSED THE CHILDREN see Cobine, Al

BLESSING, A see Hardt, Richard

BLICKHAN, TIM
Polymorphous Canon *canon
mix cor MEDIA 6118
(B412)

BLINDER EIFER "EIN BLINDDARM SASS IM
BAUCHE TIEF" see Gebhard, Ludwig

BLISS, M.
Raven Days, The
TTBB BRODT NC 3 $.32
(B413)

BLISS, SIR ARTHUR (1891-   )
Mar Portugues
SATB,acap NOVELLO s.p. (B414)

Morning Heroes
SATB,narrator,3fl,pic,3ob,3clar,
3bsn,4horn,3trp,3trom,2tuba,timp,
perc,2harp,strings voc sc NOVELLO
rental
(B415)

Pastorale "Lie Strewn White Flocks"
SATB,Mez solo,fl,timp,strings voc
sc NOVELLO rental
(B416)

Sing, Mortals
SATB,org NOVELLO ANTH 1486 s.p.
(B417)

Song Of Welcome
SATB,SBar soli,2fl,2pic,2ob,2clar,
2bsn,4horn,2trp,3trom,timp,perc,
harp,strings, glockenspiel voc sc
NOVELLO rental
(B418)

BLONDES MADEL, ROTER WEIN see Hansen,
Werner

BLOOMING BRIGHT STAR OF BELLE ISLE
(Ridout, Godfrey) SSAATBB (diff)
WATERLOO $.35
(B419)

BLOW, BLOW THOU WINTER WIND see Bergh,
Arthur

BLOW, BLOW, THOU WINTER WIND see
Jeppesen, Knud

BLOW, BLOW THOU WINTER WIND see Ultan,
Lloyd

BLOW, JOHN (1649-1708)
Coronation And Verse Anthems *CCU,
anthem
cor STAINER 3.8907.8 $20.00 (B420)

Marriage Ode *Marriage
(Watkins Shaw; Bergman) cor,AB
soli,orch min sc SCHOTT 10305
s.p.
(B421)

Ode For St. Cecilia's Day 1691
[Eng/Ger] cor min sc EULENBURG 1073
s.p.
(B422)

Sing Ye Muses (from Amphion Anglicus)
(Mochnick, John) SATB,kbd,2vln DEAN
CC-102 $.65
(B423)

BLOW ON YOUR TRUMPET see White, R.

BLOW THE MAN DOWN
see Funf Seemanslieder

BLOW THOU WINTER WIND see Butler,
Eugene

BLOW YE WINDS see Cobine, Al

BLUE AUTUMN see Lucas, Robert

BLUE CHRISTMAS
SSA CIMINO $.40
(B424)
TTBB CIMINO $.40
(B425)
SATB CIMINO $.40
(B426)

BLUE, GREEN AND GOLD see Crombe, W.

BLUE O'YOUR EYES, THE see Goodell,
Walter

BLUE-TAIL FLY *folk,US
(Mechem, Kirke) TTBB,Bar solo,pno
(easy) FISCHER,C CM 7871 $.35
(B427)

BLUE VELVET
SSA CIMINO $.40
(B428)
SATB CIMINO $.40
(B429)
TTBB CIMINO $.40
(B430)

BLUEBIRD IN MARCH
(Bissell, Keith W.) SATB (diff)
WATERLOO $.75
(B431)

BLUEBIRD IN MARCH, A see Bissell, Keith
W.

BLUEBIRD OF HAPPINESS
SSA CIMINO $.40
(B432)
SA CIMINO $.40
(B433)
SAB CIMINO $.40
(B434)
TTBB CIMINO $.40
(B435)
SATB CIMINO $.40
(B436)

BLUESETTE see Gimbel

BLUH AUF! "BLUH AUF, BLUH AUF,
GEFRORNER CHRIST" see Rein, Walter

BLUH AUF, O TAG see Edler, Robert

BLUHE, JUNGE SONNE, BLUHE
unis wom cor SCHOTTS C 42 533E s.p.
see also Alle Singen Heft 2 (B437)

BLUM, ROBERT (1900-   )
Rhapsodische Gesange Am Meer
mix cor,T solo,fl,ob,clar,bsn,trp,
horn,trom,tuba,timp,perc,pno,
strings, accordion MODERN rental
(B438)

BLUMENBLUTE, MADCHENTREU *folk,Slav
(Zschiegner, Fritz) men cor,opt pno,
opt inst,opt perc sc TONOS 2123
s.p.
(B439)

BLUMLEIN BLAU "WEISS MIR EIN BLUMLEIN
BLAUE" see Herrmann, Hugo

BLUT UM BLUT see Thehos, Adam

BLYTON, CAREY
Ladies Only *CC5U
SSA,acap NOVELLO s.p. (B440)

BOATNER, JOHN
Alice In Wonderland *CCU
jr cor,narrator,SA soli,pno J.B.
PUB s.p.
(B441)

Alice In Wonderland *CCU
jr cor,narrator&SA soli,pno J.B.
PUB
(B442)

BOBBY SHAFTO see Wedd, Eric

BOBBY SHAFTOE
(Willcocks) SATB,acap OXFORD see from
Five Folk Songs
(B443)

BOCSKAI ISTVANHOZ see Szabo, [Ferenc]

BODENSEE-LIED *folk,Ger
(Leist, Peter M.) men cor,acap TONOS
55 s.p.
(B444)

BOECKX, JEAN
La Fleur Des Champs *CCU
[Fr] 2-3pt jr cor,acap (easy) sc
SCHOTTS SF 8770 s.p. (B445)

BOGEY MAN
(Coutts, G.) unis (easy) WATERLOO
$.30
(B446)

BOHAC, JOSEF (1929-   )
Cvrcek
"Grasshopper" see Mlada Laska

Faithless, The *see Neverny

Grasshopper *see Cvrcek

BOHAC, JOSEF (cont'd.)

Ignorant, The *see Nevedomi

Little Dog Met A Little Cat, A *see
  Potkal Pejsek Kocicku

Lullaby For Kittens *see Ukolebavka
  Pro Kotata

Mlada Laska
  [Czech] mix cor,acap CZECH s.p.
  contains: Cvrcek, "Grasshopper";
  Nevedomi, "Ignorant, The";
  Neverny, "Faithless, The"
                              (B447)

Nevedomi
  "Ignorant, The" see Mlada Laska

Neverny
  "Faithless, The" see Mlada Laska

Potkal Pejsek Kocicku
  "Little Dog Met A Little Cat, A"
  [Czech] jr cor,pno CZECH s.p.
                              (B448)

Prstynky
  "Rings" [Czech] wom cor,pno CZECH
  s.p.   (B449)

Rings *see Prstynky

Ukolebavka Pro Kotata
  "Lullaby For Kittens" [Czech] jr
  cor,pno CZECH s.p.   (B450)

BOHATSTVI ZEME see Bartos, Jan Zdenek

BOHEMIAN HYMN, THE see Goossen,
  Frederic

BOHMISCHE POLKA "EINMAL HIN UND EINMAL
  HER" see Fischer, Ernst

BOHMISCHE POLKA "LIEBCHEN FEIN" see
  Fischer, Ernst

BOIS, ROB DU (1934-   )
  Today Is To-morrows Yesterday, Alas
  No Fairy Tale *see Vandag Is Het
  Morgen Van Gisteren

  Vandag Is Het Morgen Van Gisteren
  "Today Is To-morrows Yesterday,
  Alas No Fairy Tale" jr cor,
  narrator,S solo,4pno,org,4fl,2ob,
  2clar,2bsn,horn,2trp,trom,
  strings,perc,harp, electric
  guitar DONEMUS   (B451)

BOJKA, PARTYZANKA see Vomacka, Boleslav

BOJKA THE WOMAN GUERRILLA FIGHTER see
  Vomacka, Boleslav, Bojka,
  Partyzanka

BOLD TURPIN see Sweetman, Paul

BOLYONGAS see Bartok, Bela

BON HOMME
  (Kenins, T.) SATB (French Canadian)
  HARRIS HC 4015 $.50   (B452)

BON JOUR see Lassus, Roland de
  (Orlandus)

BONA NOX see Mozart, Wolfgang Amadeus

BONDPOJKEN see Shield, William

BONNER
  Celebrate *see Gordon

BOOGIE WOOGIE BUGLE BOY see Raye

BOONE, CHARLES (1939-   )
  Luminous Tendril
    see Three Motets

  Moon Over Towns Moon
    see Three Motets

  O Round Moon
    see Three Motets

  Three Motets *mot
    SATB,acap SALABERT-US EAS 17219
    $.60
    contains: Luminous Tendril; Moon
    Over Towns Moon; O Round Moon
                              (B453)

BOONE, DANIEL
  Beautiful Sunday (composed with
    McQueen, Rod)
    (Metis, F.) SSA BIG3 $.45   (B454)
    (Metis, F.) SA/TB BIG3 $.45 (B455)
    (Metis, F.) SAB BIG3 $.45   (B456)
    (Metis, F.) SATB BIG3 $.45 (B457)

BOOTHE, JIM
  Jingle-Bell Rock *see Beal, Joe

BORDER RAID see Gerschefski, Edwin

BORKOVEC, PAVEL (1894-   )
  Lullaby *see Ukolebavka

  Ukolebavka
    "Lullaby" [Czech] jr cor,acap CZECH
    s.p.   (B458)

BORNEFELD, HELMUT (1932-   )
  Weiss Mir Ein Blumlein Blaue
    SAT,acap (easy) BAREN. BCH6 s.p.
    contains also: Marx, Karl, Wie
    Schon Bluht Uns Der Maien (SAB,
    acap)   (B459)

BORNSCHEIN, [FRANZ CARL] (1879-1948)
  Singers, The *cant
    SSA FITZSIMONS $.40   (B460)
    SAB FITZSIMONS $.40   (B461)

BORODIN, ALEXANDER PORFIRIEVITCH
  (1833-1887)
  Serenade "Die Stadt Ruht Im Dunkel"
    [Ger] men cor sc SCHOTTS CHBL 142
    s.p.   (B462)

BORTNIANSKY
  Russian Vesper Hymn
    (Soderstrom, Emil) SSAATTBB (easy)
    FITZSIMONS 1048 $.25   (B463)

BOSER SCHWARZER HABICHT see Bartok,
  Bela, Hejja, Karahejja

BOSSI, MARCO ENRICO (1861-1925)
  Il Brivido
    TTBB sc BONGIOVANI 1446 s.p., cor
    pts BONGIOVANI 1447 s.p.   (B464)

  Il Cieco. *Op.112
    6pt mix cor,Bar solo,3fl,3ob,2clar,
    2bsn,4horn,2trp,3trom,tuba,timp,
    perc,harp,cembalo CARISH rental
                              (B465)

BOSSI, RENZO (1883-1965)
  Canzone
    see Cinque Canti Popolari Sardi

  Cinque Canti Popolari Sardi *folk
    [It] mix cor sc SCHOTTS SZ 4985
    s.p. Sardinian
    contains: Canzone; Laude;
    Mottetto; Mottetto Triste;
    Ninna-Nanna   (B466)

  Laude
    see Cinque Canti Popolari Sardi

  Mottetto
    see Cinque Canti Popolari Sardi

  Mottetto Triste
    see Cinque Canti Popolari Sardi

  Ninna-Nanna
    see Cinque Canti Popolari Sardi

BOTH SIDES NOW see Mitchell, John

BOTH SIDES NOW see Mitchell, Joni

BOTTCHER, GEORG
  Sonnentage
    men cor,acap TONOS 4561 s.p. (B467)

BOTTJE, WILL GAY
  To An Eagle Forgotten
    SATB,3trp,3trom,tuba,pno,perc
    AM.COMP.AL. sc $12.10, ipa, voc
    sc $2.20   (B468)

  Wayward Pilgrim
    cor,S solo,2fl,ob,2clar,bsn,2horn,
    trp,trom,perc,pno,4vln,2vla,vcl,
    bvl AM.COMP.AL. sc $41.25, voc pt
    $7.70   (B469)

  What Is A Man
    cor,narrator,fl,2ob,clar,bsn,2horn,
    4trp,3trom,tuba,2pno,perc
    AM.COMP.AL. sc $26.40, voc pt
    $6.60   (B470)

BOUQUET, THE see Martinu, Bohuslav,
  Kytice

BOUQUET OF SPRING see D'indy

BOUREE see Bach, Johann Sebastian

BOVET, G.
  Gavotte Hivernale
    men cor,acap HENN 426 s.p. (B471)

  Premiere Violette
    men cor,acap HENN 425 s.p. (B472)

BOX
  I Feel Love
    (Hyde) SATB SHAWNEE A1299 $.45
                              (B473)

BOYD
  Mark Twain In Eruption
    TTBB,clar/trp SCHIRM.G LG51665 $.30
                              (B474)

BOYD (cont'd.)
  When The Terms Of Peace Are Made
    SATB,S solo,A rec,perc SCHIRM.G
    11963 $.35   (B475)

BOYD, JACK
  Apex
    SATB STANDARD B322MX1 $.50 (B476)

  Woodchuck, The
    SATB BOURNE B231035-357 $.50 (B477)

BOYD, JEANNE
  Balloons In The Snow
    SSA (med) FITZSIMONS 3025 $.20
                              (B478)

  Hunting Of The Snark, The *cant
    SA,inst FITZSIMONS cor pts $.75, sc
    ipr   (B479)

  Mr. Frog *folk
    SSA (med) FITZSIMONS 3074 $.25
                              (B480)

  On A Winding Way
    SSA,S solo (med) FITZSIMONS 3069
    $.25   (B481)

BOY'S GLEE CLUB BOOK *CCU
  (Wick, Fred) TBB oct SCHMITT $.85
                              (B482)

BOYS IN A PIE see Kelly, Bryan

BRACKMAN
  Haven't Got Time For The Pain *see
    Simon

  That's The Way I've Always Heard It
    Should Be *see Simon

BRAEIN, EDV. FLIFLET
  Ut Mot Havet
    SSA/SAB MUSIKK   (B483)

BRAHMS, JOHANNES (1833-1897)
  Abendstandchen "Hor, Es Klagt Die
    Flote Wieder" *Op.42,No.1
    SSATBB CARUS CV 40.206 s.p. (B484)

  Abschiedslied
    SATB,acap EGTVED KB137 s.p. (B485)

  Ach Arme Welt
    (Klein) "Alas, Poor World" SATB
    SCHIRM.G 11951 $.30   (B486)

  Alas, Poor World *see Ach Arme Welt

  All Meine Herzgedanken *Op.62,No.5
    SAATBB,acap EGTVED KB142 s.p.
                              (B487)
    "All Meine Herzgedanken" SSATBB
    CARUS CV 40.207 s.p.   (B488)

  All Meine Herzgedanken *see All
    Meine Herzgedanken

  Am Wildbach Die Wieden
    see Zwolf Lieder Und Romanzen Vol.
    II

  As Through The Wood *see Es Geht Ein
    Wehen

  Barcarole
    see Zwolf Lieder Und Romanzen Vol.
    I

  Beherzigung "Feiger Gedanken"
    *Op.93a,No.6
    mix cor (med easy) sc SCHOTTS
    CHBL 389 s.p.   (B489)
    SATB,acap EGTVED KB156 s.p. (B490)

  Brennessel Steht
    see Vier Zigeunerlieder

  Christmas Cradle Song
    (Wilkinson, S.) SATBB,S solo,acap
    NOVELLO CAROLS 714 s.p.   (B491)

  Cloistered Nun, The *see
    Klosterfraulein

  Complete Works *sac/sec,CCU
    (Gal, Hans; Mandyczewski, Eusebius)
    microfiche UNIV.MUS.ED. $185.00
    edition of the Society of the
    Friends of Music, Vienna.
    Published at Leipzig by Breitkopf
    and Haertel, 1926-1928 in 26
    volumes.   (B492)

  Cradle Song
    (Wick, Fred) 2pt oct SCHMITT W240
    $.30   (B493)

  Das Madchen *Op.93a,No.2
    SATBB,S solo,acap EGTVED KB152 s.p.
                              (B494)

  Dein Herzlein Mild *Op.62,No.4
    SATB,acap EGTVED KB141 s.p. (B495)

  Der Brautigam
    see Zwolf Lieder Und Romanzen Vol.
    I

BRAHMS, JOHANNES (cont'd.)

Der Bucklichte Fiedler *Op.93a,No.1
SATB,acap EGTVED KB151 s.p. (B496)

Der Falke *Op.93a,No.5
SATB,acap EGTVED KB155 s.p. (B497)

Der Jager *Op.22,No.4 (from
Marienlieder)
SATB,acap EGTVED KB15 s.p. (B498)

Die Berge Sind Spitz
see Zwolf Lieder Und Romanzen Vol.
II

Die Boten Der Liebe *Op.61,No.4
(Hall, Wm.D.) "Heralds Of Love,
The" [Eng/Ger] SA/TB,pno NATIONAL
WHC-62 $.45 (B499)

Die Braut
see Zwolf Lieder Und Romanzen Vol.
II

Die Meere *Op.20,No.3
"Seas, The" [Ger/Eng] SA/TB,pno
NATIONAL WHC-57 $.40 (B500)

Die Mullerin
see Zwolf Lieder Und Romanzen Vol.
I

Die Nonne
see Zwolf Lieder Und Romanzen Vol.
I

Es Geht Ein Wehen *Op.62,No.6
SATBB,acap EGTVED KB143 s.p. (B501)
(Richard, Charles) "As Through The
Wood" [Eng/Ger] SATB,acap BOONIN
B 179 $.40 (B502)

Fahr Wohl *Op.93a,No.4
SATB,acap EGTVED KB154 s.p. (B503)

Falcon, The
(Greyson, N.) SATB BOURNE
B230803-357 $.60 (B504)

Flirtation *see Neckereien

Fragen *Op.64,No.3
see Zwolf Lieder Und Romanzen Vol.
I
(Hall, Wm.D.) "Questions" [Eng/Ger]
SATB,pno NATIONAL WHC-60 $.50 (B505)

Heralds Of Love, The *see Die Boten
Der Liebe

Himmel Strahlt
see Vier Zigeunerlieder

Ich Fahr' Dahin
mix cor (easy) sc SCHOTTS CHBL 258
s.p. (B506)
(Koenig) men cor,acap TONOS 3001
s.p. (B507)

Im Herbst *Op.104,No.5
SATB,acap EGTVED KB149 s.p. (B508)

In Stiller Nacht (from Deutsche
Volkslieder)
see Brahms, Johannes, Von Alten
Liebesliedern "Spazieren Wollt
Ich Reiten"
SATB,acap EGTVED KB280 s.p. (B509)
mix cor (med easy) sc SCHOTTS
CHBL 259 s.p. (B510)
(Koenig, Franz) men cor,acap TONOS
3002 s.p. (B511)

Klosterfraulein *Op.61,No.2
(Hall, Wm.D.) "Cloistered Nun, The"
[Ger/Eng] SA,pno NATIONAL WHC-72
$.40 (B512)

Letztes Gluck *Op.104,No.3
SAATBB,acap EGTVED KB147 s.p.
(B513)

Liebe Schwalbe
see Vier Zigeunerlieder

Marznacht
see Zwolf Lieder Und Romanzen Vol.
II

May Night
(Wetzler) SATB ART MAST 1010 $.40
(B514)

Minnelied
see Zwolf Lieder Und Romanzen Vol.
I

Nachtwache I *Op.104,No.1
SAATBB,acap EGTVED KB145 s.p.
(B515)

Nachtwache II *Op.104,No.2
SAATBB,acap EGTVED KB146 s.p.
(B516)

Neckereien *Op.31,No.2
(Hall, W.D.) "Flirtation" [Eng/Ger]
SATB,pno NATIONAL WHC-48 $.45
(B517)

BRAHMS, JOHANNES (cont'd.)

Nun Stehn Die Rosen In Blute
see Zwolf Lieder Und Romanzen Vol.
II

O Susser Mai *Op.93a,No.3
SATBB,acap EGTVED KB153 s.p. (B518)

Pleasures In May, The
(McCullough) SATB SOUTHERN $.30
(B519)

Questions *see Fragen

Rapsodia *see Rhapsodie "Aber
Abseits Wer Ist's"

Rhapsodie "Aber Abseits Wer Ist's"
*Op.53
"Rapsodia" [It] men cor,A solo,2fl,
2ob,2clar,2bsn,2horn CARISH
rental (B520)
"Rhapsodie "Aber Abseits Wer
Ist's?"" men cor,A solo,orch sc
SCHOTTS ETP 1054 s.p. (B521)

Rhapsodie "Aber Abseits Wer Ist's?"
*see Rhapsodie "Aber Abseits Wer
Ist's"

Rosmarin *Op.62,No.1
SATB,acap EGTVED KB138 s.p. (B522)
"Rosmarin "Es Wollt Die Jungfrau
Fruh Aufstehn"" mix cor (easy) sc
SCHOTTS CHBL 390 s.p. (B523)

Rosmarin "Es Wollt Die Jungfrau Fruh
Aufstehn" *see Rosmarin

Rothe Rosenknospen
see Vier Zigeunerlieder

Seas, The *see Die Meere

She Walks In Beauty
(Hokanson, Margrethe) SABar&camb
CAMBIATA M117447 $.35 (B524)

Thought Like Music, A
(Hutcherson) SATB (med) FITZSIMONS
1079 $.25 (B525)

Und Gehst Du Uber Den Kirchhof
see Zwolf Lieder Und Romanzen Vol.
II

Variations For The Dance *see
Wechsellied Zum Tanz

Vergangen Ist Mir Gluck Und Heil
*Op.62,No.7
SATB,acap EGTVED KB144 s.p. (B526)

Verlorene Jugend *Op.104,No.4
SATBB,acap EGTVED KB148 s.p. (B527)

Verstohlen Geht Der Mond Auf
4pt mix cor,solo,opt pno (easy) sc
SCHOTTS CHBL 391 s.p. (B528)

Vier Zigeunerlieder
SATB,pno cmplt ed EGTVED MS6B13
s.p.
contains: Brennessel Steht;
Himmel Strahlt; Liebe Schwalbe;
Rothe Rosenknospen (B529)

Von Alten Liebesliedern *Op.62,No.2
SSAATTBB,acap EGTVED KB139 s.p.
(B530)
"Von Alten Liebesliedern "Spazieren
Wollt Ich Reiten"" SATB CARUS
CV 40.208 s.p. contains also: In
Stiller Nacht (B531)

Von Alten Liebesliedern "Spazieren
Wollt Ich Reiten" *see Von Alten
Liebesliedern

Waldesnacht *Op.62,No.3
SATB,acap EGTVED KB140 s.p. (B532)

Ways Of Love, The *see Weg Der Liebe

Wechsellied Zum Tanz *Op.31,No.1
(Hall, Wm.D.) "Variations For The
Dance" [Eng/Ger] SATB,pno
NATIONAL WHC-47 $.50 (B533)

Weg Der Liebe *Op.20,No.2
(Hall, Wm.D.) "Ways Of Love, The"
[Ger/Eng] SA/TB,pno NATIONAL
WHC-69 $.40 (B534)

Wiegenlied "Guten Abend, Gut' Nacht"
*cradle
(Klink, Waldemar) jr cor (easy) sc
SCHOTTS CHBL 516 s.p. (B535)

Zigeunerlieder *CCU
(Klein) [Ger/Eng] SATB SCHIRM.G
2948 $1.50 (B536)

Zwolf Lieder Und Romanzen *Op.44,
No.1-12, CC12L
wom cor,acap BREITKOPF-L PB 3237

BRAHMS, JOHANNES (cont'd.)

s.p. (B537)

Zwolf Lieder Und Romanzen Vol. I
cor BREITKOPF-L CHB 2617 s.p.
contains: Barcarole, Op.44,No.3;
Der Brautigam, Op.44,No.2; Die
Mullerin, Op.44,No.5; Die
Nonne, Op.44,No.6; Fragen,
Op.44,No.4; Minnelied, Op.44,
No.1 (B538)

Zwolf Lieder Und Romanzen Vol. II
BREITKOPF-L CHB 2618 s.p.
contains: Am Wildbach Die Wieden,
Op.44,No.9; Die Berge Sind
Spitz, Op.44,No.8; Die Braut,
Op.44,No.11; Marznacht, Op.44,
No.12; Nun Stehn Die Rosen In
Blute, Op.44,No.7; Und Gehst Du
Uber Den Kirchhof, Op.44,No.10
(B539)

BRAMBACH, KASPAR JOSEPH (1833-1902)
Bergisches Heimatlied
men cor,acap TONOS 234 s.p. (B540)

BRAND NEW LOVE AFFAIR
SATB,pno,opt bvl&drums&gtr SCREEN
5743BC7 (B541)
SSA,pno,opt bvl&drums&gtr SCREEN
5743FC8 (B542)

BRANDON
Harvest-Time Song
unis/SA KJOS 6135 $.35 (B543)

Winter Song
unis/SA KJOS 6138 $.35 (B544)

BRANDON, GEORGE
First Stars
SSAA STANDARD B320F1 $.50 (B545)

Old Order Changeth, The
SATB STANDARD B321MX1 $.50 (B546)

BRANDVIK
Singing, Ringing, Joyfully *Xmas
SATB oct SCHMITT 930 $.30 (B547)

Who Cut The Wood? *Xmas
SATB oct SCHMITT 933 $.35 (B548)

BRANSCOMBE, [GINA] (1881-   )
Woodwinds
SSAA,S solo (med) FITZSIMONS 3076
$.25 (B549)

BRAUN, HORST-HEINRICH
Horch, Was Kommt Von Draussen Rein?
men cor,opt pno&perc TONOS 128 s.p.
(B550)

BRAUNER WALD see Zoll, Paul

BRAUTIGAM, HELMUT (1916-1942)
Es Ist Nit Allewege Festabend
see Brautigam, Helmut, Was Wolln
Wir Auf Den Abend Tun

Mit Lust Tritt Ich An Diesen Tanz
mix cor (med) sc SCHOTTS
CHBL 283A-B s.p. contains also:
Schein Uns, Du Liebe Sonne (B551)

Schein Uns, Du Liebe Sonne
see Brautigam, Helmut, Mit Lust
Tritt Ich An Diesen Tanz

Was Wolln Wir Auf Den Abend Tun
mix cor (med easy) sc SCHOTTS
CHBL 285A-B s.p. contains also:
Es Ist Nit Allewege Festabend
(B552)

BRAUTIGAM, VOLKER (1939-   )
Freundlicher Zuruf
mix cor,acap DEUTSCHER DVFM7649
s.p. (B553)

BRAUTSCHAU see Bartok, Bela, Leanynezo

BREAD AND BIRDS see Kopelent, Marek,
Chleb A Ptaci

BREAK, BREAK, BREAK see Miles, Russell
Hancock

BREAK FAIREST DAWN see Handel, George
Frideric

BREDOW, CLAUS
Abend Am Don
men cor,acap TONOS 456 s.p. (B554)

Kosakenliedchen
men cor,opt perc TONOS 450 s.p.
(B555)

BREL
Marathon
(Metis) SATB MARKS MC 4617 $.50
(B556)

Seasons In The Sun
(Metis) SA/TB MARKS MC 4618 $.40
(B557)
(Metis) SATB (new arrangement)
MARKS MC 4622 $.50 (B558)

BREL, JACQUES
  If We Only Have Love (from Jacques
    Brel Is Alive And Well And Living
    In Paris)
    (Simon, W.) SATB BIG3 $.50   (B559)
    (Simon, W.) SSA BIG3 $.50   (B560)

BRENNAN ON THE MOOR
  (Wyatt) 2pt treb cor&Bar PRO ART 2848
  $.40   (B561)

BRENNESSEL STEHT see Brahms, Johannes

BRENT-SMITH, ALEXANDER (1889-1950)
  Elegy
    SATB,SBar soli,2fl,2ob,2clar,2bsn,
    4horn,3trp,3trom,timp,perc,
    strings voc sc NOVELLO rental
                                  (B562)
  Paradise Songs
    SSA,fl,ob,clar,bsn,harp/pno,strings
    voc sc NOVELLO rental   (B563)

BRESGEN, CESAR (1913-   )
  Als Ich Noch Ein Armer Knecht War
    *folk,Hung
    [Ger] men cor sc SCHOTTS C 42 626
    s.p. see from Sieben Ungarische
    Chore Nach Volksliedern   (B564)

  Armer, Kleiner Tanzbar *cant
    2-3pt jr cor,soli,vln,perc,rec,
    glockenspiel, xylophone (med) sc
    SCHOTTS ED. 5173 s.p., cor pts
    SCHOTTS ED. 5173 s.p., ipa (B565)

  Backerlied "Fleissig Ist Der
    Backersmann"
    TTBB sc SCHOTTS C 38 088 s.p., voc
    pt SCHOTTS C 38 089 01-04 s.p.
                                  (B566)
  Das Dreifache Gloria *sac,Xmas
    SATB&4pt jr cor,org,vln,opt timp
    (med easy) sc,cor pts SCHOTTS
    ED. 5669 s.p., ipa   (B567)

  Das Riesenspiel *cant
    jr cor,fl,perc (easy) sc SCHOTTS
    B 119 s.p.   (B568)

  Das Schlaraffenland *cant
    1-3pt jr cor,inst (easy) sc,cor pts
    SCHOTTS B 130 s.p., ipa   (B569)

  Den Letzten Beisst Der Hund
    men cor sc SCHOTTS C 38 525 s.p.
                                  (B570)
  Der Goldvogel *CCU
    jr cor (easy) SCHOTTS ED. 4875 s.p.
                                  (B571)
  Der Mann Im Mond
    2-3pt jr cor&mix cor,5 narrators,9
    soli,pno,fl,ob,clar,bsn,horn,trp,
    strings,harp,perc (med) voc sc
    SCHOTTS ED. 4980 s.p., ipr (B572)

  Der Struwwelpeter *cant
    1-2pt jr cor,pno,rec,perc (easy)
    sc,cor pts SCHOTTS ED. 4235 s.p.,
    ipa   (B573)

  Der Weizen Muss Reifen *folk,Hung
    [Ger] men cor sc SCHOTTS C 42 629
    s.p. see from Sieben Ungarische
    Chore Nach Volksliedern   (B574)

  Die Alte Lokomotive *cant
    2-3pt jr cor,cantor,soli,pno,rec,
    perc (easy) sc,cor pts SCHOTTS
    ED. 4884 s.p., ipa   (B575)

  Die Bettlerhochzeit
    jr cor,pno,fl,perc, glockenspiel,
    metallophone, xylophone (easy) sc
    SCHOTTS B 104 s.p., cor pts
    SCHOTTS ED. 5244 s.p., ipa (B576)

  Die Kummermuhle "An Der Donau Steht
    Eine Alte Muhle" *folk,Hung
    [Ger] men cor sc SCHOTTS C 42 623
    s.p. see from Sieben Ungarische
    Chore Nach Volksliedern   (B577)

  Dreimal Rief Die Amsel *folk,Hung
    [Ger] men cor sc SCHOTTS C 42 630
    s.p., voc pt SCHOTTS
    C 42 631 01-02 s.p. see from
    Sieben Ungarische Chore Nach
    Volksliedern   (B578)

  Drunten In Baranya "Spat Am Abend"
    *folk,Hung
    [Ger] men cor sc SCHOTTS C 42 624
    s.p. see from Sieben Ungarische
    Chore Nach Volksliedern   (B579)

  Europaische Volks- Und Kinderlieder
    Band I *CCU,folk,Eur
    4pt jr cor,clar,trp,vln,gtr,rec,
    vcl,perc (easy) sc,cor pts
    SCHOTTS B 177 s.p., ipa   (B580)

  Europaische Volks- Und Kinderlieder
    Band II *CCU,folk,Eur
    4pt jr cor,clar,trp,vln,gtr,rec,
    vcl,perc (easy) sc,cor pts

BRESGEN, CESAR (cont'd.)

    SCHOTTS B 178 s.p., ipa   (B581)

  Finstre Nacht "Ich Ging Wohl Bei Der
    Nacht"
    men cor,T solo sc SCHOTTS C 38 159
    s.p. see from Vier Mannerchore
    Nach Altdeutschen Texten   (B582)

  Fur Funfzehn Pfennige "Das Magdlein
    Will Ein Feier Haben"
    men cor,T solo sc SCHOTTS C 38 158
    s.p. see from Vier Mannerchore
    Nach Altdeutschen Texten   (B583)

  Havele, Havele, Hahne *cant
    1-2pt treb cor,solo,2S rec/2fl,
    3vln,vla,vcl (easy) voc sc,cor
    pts BAREN. BA1564 s.p., ipa   (B584)

  Hufeisen Und Rosen "Bauernknecht, Nun
    Pack Den Grossen Wagen An"
    *folk,Hung
    [Ger] men cor sc SCHOTTS C 42 627
    s.p., voc pt SCHOTTS
    C 42 628 01-02 s.p. see from
    Sieben Ungarische Chore Nach
    Volksliedern   (B585)

  Hum Fauler Lenz "Es Wollt Eine Frau
    Zum Weine Gahn"
    men cor sc SCHOTTS CHBL 69 s.p.
                                  (B586)
  Kantate Von Der Unruhe Des Menschen
    *cant
    mix cor,ST soli,pno,fl,clar,horn,
    2trom,strings,perc,timp (med) voc
    sc,cor pts SCHOTTS ED. 4519 s.p.,
    ipr   (B587)

  L'europe Curieuse *cant
    1-3pt jr cor,narrator,inst (easy)
    sc,cor pts SCHOTTS B 175 s.p.,
    ipa   (B588)

  Nachtlied "Nun Ruh Mit Sorgen"
    men cor sc SCHOTTS C 38 160 s.p. see
    from Vier Mannerchore Nach
    Altdeutschen Texten   (B589)

  Ruf Und Mahnung *cant
    4pt mix cor&3 cor,pno,fl,strings
    (med easy) sc,cor pts SCHOTTS
    ED. 5292 s.p., ipa   (B590)

  Sieben Ungarische Chore Nach
    Volksliedern *see Als Ich Noch
    Ein Armer Knecht War; Der Weizen
    Muss Reifen; Die Kummermuhle "An
    Der Donau Steht Eine Alte Muhle";
    Dreimal Rief Die Amsel; Drunten
    In Baranya "Spat Am Abend";
    Hufeisen Und Rosen "Bauernknecht,
    Nun Pack Den Grossen Wagen An";
    Wer Zum Teufel Wird Sich Sorgen
    "Banod, Biro Schulze"   (B591)

  Sonne, Sonne Scheine *CC33U
    jr cor,inst (easy) SCHOTTS B 115
    s.p.   (B592)

  Uns Ist Kommen Ein Liebe Zeit *cant
    1-3pt jr cor&opt mix cor,S/T solo,
    3strings,S rec,A rec,perc,opt bvl
    (med easy) sc,cor pts SCHOTTS
    B 127 s.p., ipa   (B593)

  Vier Mannerchore Nach Altdeutschen
    Texten *see Finstre Nacht "Ich
    Ging Wohl Bei Der Nacht"; Fur
    Funfzehn Pfennige "Das Magdlein
    Will Ein Feier Haben"; Nachtlied
    "Nun Ruh Mit Sorgen";
    Weinschroter, Schlag Die Trommel
                                  (B594)
  Von Mausen, Autos Und Anderen Tieren
    *CC25U
    1-2pt jr cor,gtr,rec, rhythm
    instruments sc SCHOTTS B 179 s.p.
                                  (B595)
  Wanderschaft "Im Walde Bluht Der
    Seidelbast"
    wom cor (easy) sc SCHOTTS CHBL 580
    s.p.   (B596)

  Weinschroter, Schlag Die Trommel
    men cor sc SCHOTTS C 38 157 s.p.
    see from Vier Mannerchore Nach
    Altdeutschen Texten   (B597)

  Wenn Sich Junge Herzen Heben *sac/
    sec
    SAB,acap (med easy) sc SCHOTTS
    CHBL 357 s.p.   (B598)
    men cor sc SCHOTTS CHBL 200 s.p.
                                  (B599)
  Wer Zum Teufel Wird Sich Sorgen
    "Banod, Biro Schulze" *folk,Hung
    [Ger] men cor sc SCHOTTS C 42 625
    s.p. see from Sieben Ungarische
    Chore Nach Volksliedern   (B600)

BRIC-A-BACH see Jergenson, Dale

BRICUSSE, LESLIE
  Who Can I Turn To (composed with
    Newley, Anthony)
    (Young, C.) SATB oct SOMERSET
    BR 2006 $.40   (B601)

BRIDAL CHORUS see Cowen, [Sir Frederic
  Hymen]

BRIDAL SONG see Castelnuovo-Tedesco,
  Mario

BRIDGE OVER TROUBLED WATER see Simon,
  Paul

BRIEF GLIMPSES INTO CONTEMPORARY FRENCH
  LITERATURE see Sims, Ezra

BRIEF, IN DER ERDE ZU HINTERLASSEN see
  Marckhl, Erich

BRIEF INTRODUCTION TO THE PROBLEMS OF
  PHILOSOPHY see Gross, Robert

BRIGHTEN MY SOUL WITH SUNSHINE see
  Eilers, Joyce Elaine

BRIGHTLY DAWNS OUR WEDDING DAY see
  Sullivan, Sir Arthur Seymour

BRINDLE, [REGINALD SMITH] (1917-   )
  Discoveries
    SATB,acap (med) OXFORD 84.183 $.65
                                  (B602)
BRING US BACK TOGETHER AGAIN
  SATB CIMINO $.40   (B603)

BRINGING US IN GOOD ALE see Jenkins,
  C.J.

BRINGS
  Sound Pieces
    SA/TB SHAWNEE E154 $.45   (B604)

BRITISH GRENADIERS
  (Robinson, S.) TTBarB STAINER
  3.0870.1 $.50   (B605)

BRITISH GRENADIERS, THE
  (Cobine, Al) SATB STUDIO V715 $.45
                                  (B606)
BRITTAN, ROBERT
  Measure The Valleys *see Woldin,
    Judd

BRITTEN
  Friday Afternoons *see New Year
    Carol   (B607)

  New Year Carol
    SSA,acap oct BOOSEY 5848 $.35 see
    from Friday Afternoons   (B608)

BRKANOVIC, IVAN (1906-   )
  Dalmatian Diptych
    SATB,MezT soli,pno,3fl,3ob,3clar,
    2bsn,4horn,3trp,3trom,tuba,
    strings,perc,timp,harp CROATICA
                                  (B609)
  Triptych Funeral Folk Rite
    SATB,S solo,pno,3fl,3ob,3clar,2bsn,
    4horn,2trp,3trom,tuba,strings,
    perc,timp,harp CROATICA   (B610)

BROADWOOD, L.E.
  Jolly Ploughboy, The
    unis CRAMER $.20   (B611)

BRONX RIVER PUZZLE see Cohn, James

BROOK, HARRY
  Starlit Night
    SA CRAMER $.20   (B612)

BROOKS, JOE
  Children's Song Of Hope, The
    (Simon, W.) SSA BIG3 $.45   (B613)
    (Simon, W.) SATB BIG3 $.45   (B614)
    (Simon, W.) SAB BIG3 $.45   (B615)
    (Simon, W.) SA/TB BIG3 $.45   (B616)
    (Simon, W.) TTBB BIG3 $.45   (B617)

BROT UND WEIN see Knab, Armin

BROTHER LOVE see Mana-Zucca, Mme.

BROTHERHOOD OF MAN, THE see Gatty, Art

BROTHERHOOD OF MAN, THE see Handel,
  George Frideric

BROUWER, LEO (1939-   )
  Cantigas Del Tiempo Nuevo *cant
    mix cor&jr cor,narrator,orch, or
    chamber ensemble (diff) sc
    SCHOTTS rental, ipr   (B618)

BROWN
  Call For The Robin-Redbreast
    see Four Madrigals

  Elegy
    SSATBB,SSATBB soli,acap (diff)
    OXFORD 56.586 $2.00   (B619)

BROWN (cont'd.)

Four Madrigals *madrigal
SATB,acap (med diff) OXFORD 56.129
$5.60
contains: Call For The Robin-
Redbreast; Merry Margaret;
Sound The Flute; With How Sad
Steps   (B620)

Merry Margaret
see Four Madrigals

Poor Wayfaring Stranger *see
Burroughs

Sound The Flute
see Four Madrigals

Strawberry Fair
SA OXFORD T 109   (B621)

Tie A Yellow Ribbon Round The Ole Oak
Tree *see Levine

With How Sad Steps
see Four Madrigals

BROWN, NORMAN
She's Like The Swallow
SATB (med easy) WATERLOO $.40
                              (B622)

BROZ, FRANTISEK (1896-1962)
Tri Pisne *CC3U
[Czech] jr cor,pno,3vln CZECH s.p.
                              (B623)

BRUCKE ZUR HEIMAT "ES KLINGT UNS ZU
ALLEN STUNDEN" see Desch, Rudolf

BRUCKER, HERMANN
Durst Auf Wein
men cor,acap TONOS 3912 s.p. (B624)

Land Der Lieder
men cor,acap TONOS 4568 s.p. (B625)

Singe Dein Lied In Den Tag
men cor,acap TONOS 3911 s.p. (B626)

BRUCKNER, ANTON (1824-1896)
Der Abendhimmel
men cor,acap TONOS 5371 s.p. (B627)

Noblest Of Songs, The
TTBB BRODT UF 2 $.30   (B628)

Sangerbund
men cor,acap TONOS 5373 s.p. (B629)

Sternschnuppen
men cor,acap TONOS 5372 s.p. (B630)

Traumen Und Wachen
men cor,acap TONOS 5374 s.p. (B631)

Trosterin Musik
men cor,acap TONOS 5375 s.p. (B632)

Um Mitternacht
men cor,acap TONOS 5376 s.p. (B633)

BRUDER, LASST DIE LIEDER see Edler,
Robert

BRUDER LIEDERLICH see Kanetscheider,
Artur

BRUDER LUSTIG *folk,Ger
(Schneider, Walther) men cor,acap
TONOS 130 s.p.   (B634)

BRUDER TOD see Krietsch, Georg

BRUDMARSCH FRAN JAMTLAND
(Jehrlander, Karl-Fredrik) mix cor
GEHRMANS KRB459   (B635)

BRUMBY, COLIN
Windy Beach, A
unis,narrator,3 soli,rec,perc,
piano four hands EMI   (B636)

BRUNSWICK, MARK (1902-   )
Eros And Death
SATB,3fl,3ob,3clar,5bsn,6horn,4trp,
4trom,tuba,timp,harp,pno,perc,
strings sc AM.COMP.AL. $33.00
                              (B637)

Four Madrigals And Motet *CCU
SATB,inst sc AM.COMP.AL. $9.35
                              (B638)

Lysistrata
SSAA,Mez solo,3fl,4ob,4clar,3bsn,
4horn,3trp,3trom,tuba,timp,perc,
pno,strings AM.COMP.AL.   (B639)

BRUSH UP ON YOUR SHAKESPEARE
TTBB CIMINO $.40   (B640)

BUBLITSCHKI *Russ
men cor ZIMMER. 590 s.p.   (B641)

BUCCHI, VALENTINO (1916-   )
Colloquio Corale
mix cor,narrator,S solo,orch sc
RICORDI-ENG 131011 s.p.   (B642)

Silence
mix cor,acap RICORDI-ENG 132014
s.p.   (B643)

BUCHHAUSER, ANDREW W.
Song To A Tree, A
SATB (med) FITZSIMONS 1043 $.25
                              (B644)
TTBB (med) FITZSIMONS 4049 $.25
                              (B645)

BUCHTGER, FRITZ (1903-   )
Drei Rilke Chore *sac
mix cor (med diff) sc SCHOTTS
C 41 076 s.p.
contains: Herbst "Die Blatter
Fallen"; Herr, Es Ist Zeit; Ich
Lebe Mein Leben   (B646)

Herbst "Die Blatter Fallen"
see Drei Rilke Chore

Herr, Es Ist Zeit
see Drei Rilke Chore

Ich Lebe Mein Leben
see Drei Rilke Chore

BUDAPEST see Hajdu, Mihaly

BUDICEK see Mikula, Zdenko

BUDOVATELUM OSTRAVSKA see Haba, Karel

BUDSKAP see Hjort, Fredrik

BUFFALO BILL'S see Yannatos, James

BUFFALO GALS *folk
(Field, Robert) SAB,pno oct PRESSER
312-41044 $.35   (B647)
(Miller, Carl) 2pt CHAPPELL
0062984-351 $.40   (B648)
(Parker) SATB SCHIRM.G LG 51712 $.30
                              (B649)

BUFFETT, JIMMY
Come Monday
(Metis, F.) SSA BIG3 $.45   (B650)
(Metis, F.) SATB BIG3 $.45   (B651)
(Metis, F.) SAB BIG3 $.45   (B652)

BUGATCH, SAMUEL (1898-   )
Jewish Legend, The *cant
[Eng/Heb] cor,orch TRANSCON.
TCL 375 $3.50, ipr   (B653)

BUGLE SONG see Franco, Johan

BUILD THEE MORE STATELY MANSIONS see
Holmes

BUMERANG see Krietsch, Georg

BUNDESLIED see Mozart, Wolfgang Amadeus

BUNDESLIED "BRUDER, REICHT DIE HAND ZUM
BUNDE!" see Mozart, Wolfgang
Amadeus

BUNDESLIED: HEHR UND HEILIG see
Silcher, Friedrich

BUNDESLIED "IN ALLEN GUTEN STUNDEN" see
Lang, Hans

BUNDESLIED "IN ALLEN GUTEN STUNDEN" see
Zelter, Carl Friedrich

BUNGE, SAS (1924-   )
Eskimo Songs *CCU
mix cor,pno DONEMUS   (B654)

BUNNELL
Tin Man
(Gargaro) SATB,opt perc WARNER
CH2004 $.40   (B655)

BUNT IST DAS LEBEN see Rosenstengel,
Albrecht

BUNT SIND SCHON DIE WALDER
unis wom cor SCHOTTS C 42 532J s.p.
see also Alle Singen Heft 1 (B656)

BURGHAUSER, JARMIL (1921-   )
Eternal Clouds *see Vecna Oblaka

Mysterious Trumpet Player, The *see
Tajemny Trubac

Pet Cesky Tancu *CC5U
[Czech] jr cor,clar,horn,trp,2vln,
vla,bvl CZECH s.p.   (B657)

Sekora's ABC *see Sekorova Abeceda

Sekorova Abeceda
"Sekora's ABC" [Czech] jr cor,2fl,
ob,2clar,bsn,2horn,trp,harp,8vln,
vcl,bvl CZECH s.p.   (B658)

BURGHAUSER, JARMIL (cont'd.)

Tajemny Trubac *cant
"Mysterious Trumpet Player, The"
[Czech] mix cor,soli,3fl,3ob,
3clar,3bsn,4horn,6trp,3trom,tuba,
timp,perc,2harp,strings CZECH
s.p.   (B659)

Vecna Oblaka *cant
"Eternal Clouds" [Czech] mix cor,S
solo,3fl,3ob,3clar,3bsn,4horn,
3trp,3trom,tuba,timp,perc,harp,
strings CZECH s.p.   (B660)

BURGHERS OF CALAIS see Joubert, John

BURIAN, EMIL FRANTISEK (1904-1959)
Pisen O Svazku Delniku A Rolniku
*cant
"Song About The Unity Of Labourers
In Factory And Farm" [Czech] mix
cor,SBar soli,3fl,3ob,3clar,3bsn,
4horn,4trp,4trom,tuba,timp,perc,
2harp,pno,strings,celeste,
saxophone CZECH s.p.   (B661)

Song About The Unity Of Labourers In
Factory And Farm *see Pisen O
Svazku Delniku A Rolniku

BURKHARD WILLY (1900-1955)
Abendwolke
see Chor-Duette, Op. 22, No. 2

Chor-Duette, Op. 22, No. 2
men cor&wom cor,acap/vln/fl (med)
BAREN. BA4986 s.p.
contains: Abendwolke; Der
Romische Brunnen; Fulle; Lenz;
Neujahrsglocken; Saerspruch
                              (B662)

Der Romische Brunnen
see Chor-Duette, Op. 22, No. 2

Fulle
see Chor-Duette, Op. 22, No. 2

Lenz
see Chor-Duette, Op. 22, No. 2

Neujahrsglocken
see Chor-Duette, Op. 22, No. 2

Saerspruch
see Chor-Duette, Op. 22, No. 2

BURKHART, FRANZ (1902-   )
Besinnung
mix cor DOBLINGER G 652 s.p. see
from Drei Ernste Chore   (B663)

Der Saemann
mix cor DOBLINGER G 653 s.p. see
from Drei Ernste Chore   (B664)

Die Vogerl Schlafen Schon
see Burkhart, Franz, S'diandl Von
Der Entern Zeil

Die Vogerl Schlafen Schon Im Wald
(Bachl, Hans) treb cor DOBLINGER
O 303-304 s.p. contains also: Mei
Mutter Mag Mi Net   (B665)

Drei Ernste Chore *see Besinnung;
Der Saemann; Morgenlied   (B666)

Drei Laub Auf Einer Linden
men cor DOBLINGER M 331 s.p. (B667)

Gruss Gott Dich, Schoner Maien
mix cor DOBLINGER G 660 s.p. (B668)

Je Hoher Der Kirchturm
men cor DOBLINGER M 332 s.p. (B669)

Mei Mutter Mag Mi Net
see Burkhart, Franz, Die Vogerl
Schlafen Schon Im Wald

Morgenlied
mix cor DOBLINGER G 654 s.p. see
from Drei Ernste Chore   (B670)

Nachtigall, Ich Hor Dich Singen
(Bachl, Hans) treb cor DOBLINGER
O 347 s.p.   (B671)

S'diandl Von Der Entern Zeil
men cor DOBLINGER M 256-257 s.p.
contains also: Die Vogerl
Schlafen Schon   (B672)

BURLAS, LADISLAV (1927-   )
Banicka Kantata *cant
mix cor,orch SLOV.HUD.FOND s.p.
                              (B673)

Metamorfozy Kras
mix cor SLOV.HUD.FOND s.p.   (B674)

BURNETT
Songs For Naomi *Xmas
unis,inst sc,voc pt RICORDI-ENG
s.p., ipa   (B675)

BURNHAM
Quarrel, The
SATB oct HERITAGE H112 $.40 (B676)

BURROUGHS
Appalachian Rhapsody, An
SATB,acap MCAFEE M114 $.35 (B677)

Christmas Rose, A *Xmas
SATB,pno/gtr,opt treb inst MCAFEE
M119 $.35 (B678)

Hang In There, But Hang Loose *pop
SSBar&camb/SS&camb/SSA CAMBIATA
L117323 $.40 (B679)

He Who Would Valiant Be
SATB,org,opt 2trp&2trom MCAFEE M149
$.40 (B680)

Letters To Uncle Sam
SATB,acap MCAFEE M150 $.35 (B681)

Life Is... *folk
SABar&camb,pno,opt strings (easy)
CAMBIATA L97318 $.35 (B682)

O Clap For Joy
SATB,org MCAFEE M177 $.35 (B683)

Poor Wayfaring Stranger (composed
with Brown)
SATB,pno/hpsd MCAFEE M131 $.30
(B684)

What A Grandmother Is
unis,pno MCAFEE M147 $.35 (B685)

BURROUGHS, BOB
Girl's Composition About Boys, A
SA/2pt girl cor HERITAGE H5012 $.35
(B686)

BURSCHEN AUS MYSTRINA *folk,Slav
(Adolf, Gustav) men cor,acap TONOS
2055 s.p. (B687)

BURSCHENLIED: BRUDER, LASS DAS MADCHEN
see Silcher, Friedrich

BURTHEL, JAKOB (1926-   )
Auf, Kujawiak
men cor,acap TONOS 2033 s.p. (B688)

Bis Hierher Hat Mich Gott Gebracht
men cor,acap TONOS 5154 s.p. (B689)

Das Neue Jahr
men cor,acap TONOS 5155 s.p. (B690)

He, Du Junger Wicht
mix cor ZIMMER. 600 s.p. (B691)

BURTON, RAY
I Am Woman *pop
(Nowak, Jerry) SATB,pno oct BIG
BELL $.40 (B692)
(Nowak, Jerry) SSA,pno oct BIG BELL
$.40 (B693)

BUSCH, CARL (1862-1943)
Birds' Lawn Party, The *cant
SA,inst FITZSIMONS cor pts $.40, sc
ipr (B694)

Hunter's Horn, The *cant
SSAA cor pts FITZSIMONS $.50 (B695)

Moon, The
SA (easy) FITZSIMONS 3056 $.20
(B696)

Spring
SSA (med) FITZSIMONS 3023 $.25
(B697)

Where Go The Boats
SA (easy) FITZSIMONS 3055 $.20
(B698)

BUSH, GEOFFREY (1920-   )
Cantata Piccola
SATB,Bar solo,pno,strings voc sc
NOVELLO rental (B699)

How Should I Your True Love Know
SATB STAINER 3.0836.1 $.40 (B700)

It Was A Lover And His Lass
SATB GALAXY 0.0003.1 $.40 (B701)

Orpheus
SATB GALAXY 0.0004.1 $.40 (B702)

Pan
SATB GALAXY 0.0005.1 $.40 (B703)

Spring, The Sweet Spring
SATB GALAXY 0.0006.1 $.40 (B704)

Summer Serenade
SATB,T solo,timp,strings voc sc
NOVELLO rental (B705)

Twelfth Night
SATB,T solo,fl,ob,clar,horn,timp
voc sc NOVELLO rental (B706)

BUSH, N.
Man In A Crane (composed with
Ralston, A.)
2pt jr cor EMI see from Three Two-
Part Songs For Children (B707)

Motorway (composed with Ralston, A.)
2pt jr cor EMI see from Three Two-
Part Songs For Children (B708)

Regent's Canal (composed with
Ralston, A.)
2pt jr cor EMI see from Three Two-
Part Songs For Children (B709)

Three Two-Part Songs For Children
*see Man In A Crane; Motorway;
Regent's Canal (B710)

BUSHES AND BRIARS see Woollen, Russell

BUSNOIS, ANTOINE (? -1492)
Faites De Moy
(Brown) 1-3pt (med) OXFORD 87.001
$.30 (B711)

BUSSOTTI, SYLVANO (1931-   )
Ancora Odono I Colli
16pt mix cor RICORDI-ENG 131362 see
from Cinque Frammenti All'Italia
(B712)

Cinque Frammenti All'Italia *see
Ancora Odono I Colli; La Curva
Dell'amore; Per Ventiquattro Voci
Adulte O Bianche; Rar'ancora;
Solo El Misterio (B713)

El Carbonero
SATBB RICORDI-ENG 132183 (B714)

La Curva Dell'amore
16pt mix cor RICORDI-ENG 131374 see
from Cinque Frammenti All'Italia
(B715)

Per Ventiquattro Voci Adulte O
Bianche
24pt mix cor RICORDI-ENG 131365 see
from Cinque Frammenti All'Italia
(B716)

Rar'ancora
16pt mix cor RICORDI-ENG 131375 see
from Cinque Frammenti All'Italia
(B717)

Siciliano
12pt men cor BRUZZI V-028 s.p.
(B718)

Solo El Misterio
mix cor RICORDI-ENG 131363 see from
Cinque Frammenti All'Italia
(B719)

BUSZKE VOROS ZASZLO see Vary, Ferenc

BUTLER
Another Somebody Done Somebody Wrong
Song (composed with Moman)
(Lojeski, Ed) SATB LEONARD-US
08200565 $.50 (B720)

Hunting Song
SSA oct SCHMITT 2590 $.40 (B721)

BUTLER, EUGENE
Blow Thou Winter Wind
SATB LEONARD-US 08005000 $.50
(B722)

Canto Of Aspiration
SATB oct SOMERSET CE 4331 $.50
(B723)

Hymn Of Freedom
SATB BOURNE B218065-357 $.60 (B724)

In The Highlands
SSA,pno (med easy) FISCHER,C
CM 7852 $.35 (B725)

Laura
cor (med) FISCHER,C CM 7905 $.40
(B726)

Let Down The Bars, O Death
SATB STANDARD B325MX1 $.50 (B727)

Music Here
4pt mix cor,pno (easy) FISCHER,C
CM 7854 $.35 (B728)

Music, When Soft Voices Die
SATB ART MAST 1017 $.30 (B729)

Nightingale, The
SSA HERITAGE H6012 $.35 (B730)

Pavane For Spring
SSA LEONARD-US 08050800 $.50 (B731)

Two Moods For Chorus
SATB RICHMOND MI-98 $.35 (B732)

BUTTSCHARDT, FERDINAND
Mondnacht
men cor,acap TONOS 235 s.p. (B733)

BUTZEMANN "ES TANZT EIN BUTZEMANN" see
Haas, Joseph

BUXTEHUDE, DIETRICH (ca. 1637-1707)
Fanfare And Chorus
SATBB,4trp,2trom,2horn KING,R
MFB 603 cor pts $.20, cmplt ed
$2.50 (B734)

BY AN' BY *spir
(Kubizek, Augustin) "Nach Und Nach"
men cor DOBLINGER M 326 s.p. (B735)

BY AND BYE see Protheroe, Daniel

BY THE BROOK see Zouhar, Zdenek,
Upotoka

BY THE SPRING NEAR ROSES RED see
Vasquez, Juan, En La Fuente Del
Rosel

BY THE TIME I GET TO PHOENIX see Webb,
Jimmy

BYLO JIM TISIC LET see Reiner, Karel

BY'N BYE
(Wiley) SATB,acap PRO ART 2784 $.35
(B736)

BYRD, WILLIAM (1543-1623)
I Thought That Love Had Been A Boy
SATB LEONARD-US 08574400 $.50
(B737)

Nightingale, The
(Barrie) SSA SCHIRM.G LG51700 $.35
(B738)

Salve Regina *sac,BVM
5pt mix cor EULENBURG 10107 s.p.
(B739)

This Sweet And Merry Month
SATB STAINER 3.0533.1 $.50 (B740)

BYRT, JOHN C.
Dashing Away With The Smoothing Iron
SATB,acap (easy) OXFORD 84.206 $.45
(B741)

C

CAAMANO
Fabulas
[Lat] SATB,acap oct BARRY-ARG $.75
(C1)

CADMAN, CHARLES WAKEFIELD (1881-1946)
Dawn In The Wood
SSAA,S solo (med) FITZSIMONS 3038
$.35   (C2)

O Maid Of My Hunting
SSA (med) FITZSIMONS 3059 $.25 (C3)

Snowflakes At My Window
SSA (med) FITZSIMONS 3047 $.25 (C4)

Wind Of March, The
SSAATTBB (med) FITZSIMONS 1033 $.25
(C5)

CADOW, PAUL (1908-   )
Adams Erster Schlag "Es Legt Adam
Sich Im Paradiese Schlafen"
see Drei Epigramme

Auf Das Trinkglas Eines Verstorbenen
Freundes "Du Herrlich Glas, Nun
Stehst Du Leer"
men cor sc SCHOTTS CHBL 222 s.p:
(C6)
Drei Epigramme *see Schweiget Mir
Vom Weibernehmen   (C7)

Drei Epigramme
3pt men cor,pno sc SCHOTTS C 41 862
s.p.
contains: Adams Erster Schlag "Es
Legt Adam Sich Im Paradiese
Schlafen"; Fritze "Nun Mag Ich
Auch Nicht Langer Leben";
Grabschrift Auf Den Windmuller
Jackson "Hier Liegt Der Muller
Jackson"   (C8)

Fritze "Nun Mag Ich Auch Nicht Langer
Leben"
see Drei Epigramme

Grabschrift Auf Den Windmuller
Jackson "Hier Liegt Der Muller
Jackson"
see Drei Epigramme

Schweiget Mir Vom Weibernehmen
men cor sc SCHOTTS CHBL 217 s.p.
see from Drei Epigramme   (C9)

CAKAJ MA HOREHONIE see Mikula, Zdenko

CALAMUS see Creston, Paul

CALDER, ROBERT
Pity Me Not
SATB AMP A-682 $.30   (C10)

CALDWELL, MARY [ELIZABETH] (1909-   )
Music
cor FISCHER,C CM 7875 $.30   (C11)

CALINO CUSTURAME
(MacNutt, Walter) SAB (med easy)
WATERLOO $.30   (C12)

CALL FOR THE ROBIN-REDBREAST see Brown

CALL ME see Hatch, Tony

CALLANDER, PETE
Billy, Don't Be A Hero (composed with
Murray, Mitch)
(Simon, W.) SSA BIG3 $.50   (C13)
(Simon, W.) SATB BIG3 $.50   (C14)
(Simon, W.) SAB BIG3 $.50   (C15)

CALLOWAY
Jumpin' Jive
(Cassey) SSA MARKS MC 4632 $.40
(C16)
CALVI
One Of Those Songs *see Holt

CAMEL, THE see Berger, Jean

CAMMIN, HEINZ (1923-   )
Lied Uber Die Grenze Heft I *CC11L,
folk
3pt jr cor,pno,bvl,gtr (med) sc,cor
pts SCHOTTS ED. 6393 s.p., ipa
(C17)
Lied Uber Die Grenze Heft II *CC10L,
folk
3pt jr cor,pno,bvl,gtr (med) sc,cor
pts SCHOTTS ED. 6600 s.p., ipa
(C18)
Spirituals And Songs *sac/sec,CC10L
[Ger/Eng] 3pt jr cor/3 eq voices,
opt pno&gtr&bvl sc,cor pts
SCHOTTS ED. 6083 s.p., ipa (C19)

CAMPANE A MERIGGO see Cremesini, M.

CAMPANE A VESPRO see Cremesini, M.

CAMPANE AD ALBA see Cremesini, M.

CAMPANE DI PRIMAVERA see Cremesini, M.

CAMPBELL, COLIN M.
Anacreontic Ode
SATB,MezBar soli,2fl,2ob,2clar,
2bsn,4horn,2trp,3trom,tuba,timp,
perc,harp,strings voc sc NOVELLO
rental   (C20)

CAMPHUYSEN-LIEDEREN see Masseus, Jan

CAN I FORGET YOU
SSA CIMINO $.40   (C21)
TTBB CIMINO $.40   (C22)
SATB CIMINO $.40   (C23)

CAN SERCH
"Lover's Complaint, The" see Lisa Lan

CANADA DEAR HOME see Bissell, Keith W.

CANADA IN SPRINGTIME see Dedrick, C.

CANADA IS SINGING
(Johnston, Richard A.) SATB (med
easy) WATERLOO $.50   (C24)

CANADA IS SINGING see Johnston, Richard

CANADA, OUR HOME see Cozens, John

CANADIAN SUNSET
SSA CIMINO $.40   (C25)
SATB CIMINO $.40   (C26)
TTBB CIMINO $.40   (C27)

CANCIONES A GUIOMAR see Nono, Luigi

CANINE COMMANDENTS see Smith, G. Alan

CANNING, THOMAS
Spring, A *madrigal
SSA,acap AM.COMP.AL. $2.20   (C28)

That Good Old Mountain Dew *folk
SSA,acap AM.COMP.AL. $4.95   (C29)

Troubles Of My Heart Are Enlarged,
The
SATB,org AM.COMP.AL. sc $5.50, voc
pt $3.85   (C30)

CANNON, (JACK) PHILLIP (1929-   )
Songs To Delight
SSA,strings voc sc NOVELLO rental
(C31)
CANONE NUPTIALE see Jelinek, Hanns

CAN'T HELP FALLING IN LOVE see
Creatore, Luigi

CAN'T HELP LOVIN' DAT MAN
SSA CIMINO $.40   (C32)
SATB CIMINO $.40   (C33)

CAN'T STAY AWAY *spir
(Shaw, Ruby) SATB,acap (easy)
FITZSIMONS 2072 $.25   (C34)

CANTA LA CICALA see Pratella, Francesco
Balilla

CANTATA ABOUT BLOOD AND STONE see
Pibernik, Zlatko

CANTATA ABOUT THE COMMUNIST PARTY see
Tausinger, Jan, Kanata O
Komunisticke Strane

CANTATA CONCERTANTE see Herrmann, Hugo

CANTATA DA CAMERA see Porena, Boris

CANTATA DU PREMIER AOUT see Martin,
Frank

CANTATA FUTURA see Soukup, Vladimir

CANTATA II see Rovics, Howard

CANTATA IN MEMORY OF THE YEAR 1918 see
Zelinka, Jan Evangelista, Kantata
Na Pamet Roku 1918

CANTATA PICCOLA see Bush, Geoffrey

CANTATA PRIMAVERA see Herrmann, Hugo

CANTATA PROFANA see Kelterborn, Rudolf

CANTATA RHYTHMICA see Rosenstengel,
Albrecht

CANTATE DE LA RESTAURATION see Baud-
Bovy

CANTAVA IN RIVA AL FIUME see Agostini,
Lodovico

CANTE ROMAGNOLE VOL. I (OP. 43) see
Pratella, Francesco Balilla

CANTE ROMAGNOLE VOL. II (OP. 49) see
Pratella, Francesco Balilla

CANTE ROMAGNOLE VOL. III (OP. 51) see
Pratella, Francesco Balilla

CANTERBURY, RICHARD
Ode To America
SATB,Bar solo (med) FITZSIMONS 1050
$.35   (C35)

CANTETTO "A COLOMBA IL SOLE"
mix cor,acap (diff) sc SCHOTTS
C 43 265 s.p.   (C36)

CANTI DELLA MONTAGNA see Malatesta,
Luigi

CANTI DI PRIGIONIA see Dallapiccola,
Luigi

CANTI FANCIULLESCHI E LAUDI see
Pratella, Francesco Balilla

CANTI POPOLARI ITALIANI see
Castellazzi, Luigi

CANTI POPOLARI ITALIANI DI REGIONI
DEVERSE see Pratella, Francesco
Balilla

CANTI ROMAGNOLE VOL. I (OP. 43) see
Pratella, Francesco Balilla

CANTI ROMAGNOLE VOL. II (OP. 49 see
Pratella, Francesco Balilla

CANTICA see Hemberg, Eskil

CANTICLE OF FIRE see Williamson,
Malcolm

CANTICLE OF THE SUN see Procter, Leland

CANTICO see Hiller, Wilfred

CANTICUM CANTICORUM see Weismann,
Wilhelm

CANTIGAS DEL TIEMPO NUEVO see Brouwer,
Leo

CANTO IV see Zender, Hans

CANTO OF ASPIRATION see Butler, Eugene

CANTO RESPONSORIALE see Hatrik, Juraj

CANTO V see Zender, Hans

CANZONE see Bossi, Renzo

CANZONE DEL CUCU see Gatti, C.

CANZONE DELLE ROSA see Gatti, C.

CANZONETS FOR TWO AND THREE VOICES EM
VOL. 1 see Morley, Thomas

CANZONETS TO FOUR VOICES (1598) EM VOL.
20 see Farnaby, Giles

CANZONETTEN, KOCHEL 439 see Mozart,
Wolfgang Amadeus

CANZONI ALLA FRANCESA (OF 1596) see
Banchieri, Adriano

CANZONI ALPINE *CCU,It
(Mingozzi, F.) 3-4pt mix cor
BONGIOVANI 2216 s.p.   (C37)

CAPE SAINT MARY'S
(Bissell, Keith W.) SATB (med diff)
WATERLOO $.50   (C38)

CAPLJANSKI TATARI see Slavenski, Josip

CAPRICCIO SUNG TO THE MOONLIGHT see
Ishiketa, M.

CAPRICHOS see Fiser, Lubos

CAPTIVITY see Cockshott, Gerald Wilfred

CAPTIVITY see Overton, Hall

CARA MADONNA MIA see Lassus, Roland de
(Orlandus)

CARACTACUS see Elgar, Edward

CAREFULLY TAUGHT see Rodgers, Richard

CARELESS LOVE *folk
(Miller, Carl) 2pt CHAPPELL
0063347-351 $.40   (C39)

CAREY
America
(Bennett) SATB SCHIRM.G LG51770
$.40   (C40)

CAREY, HENRY (1692-1743)
God Save The Queen
see McCormack, P.D., Advance
Australia Fair

CARILLON see Cremesini, M.

CARIOCA
SSA CIMINO $.40   (C41)
SAB CIMINO $.40   (C42)
SATB CIMINO $.40   (C43)
TTBB CIMINO $.40   (C44)

CARION, F.
Ce Que Disent Leurs Tombes
TTBB BROGNEAUX s.p.   (C45)

CARISSIMI, GIACOMO (1605?-1674)
Nisi Dominus *mot
(Beat, J.) SSATB,org NOVELLO
NECM 29 s.p.   (C46)

CARMELA *folk
(Biebl, F.) [Ger] 4pt men cor
MERSEBURG EM9063 s.p.   (C47)

CARMINA BURANA see Anonymous

CAROL see Vendler, Bohumil, Koleda

CAROL FOR ANOTHER CHRISTMAS
SSA CIMINO $.40   (C48)
SATB CIMINO $.40   (C49)

CAROLS THREE see Zaninelli, Luigi

CAROUSEL SELECTION *CCU
CIMINO SSA $1.25; SATB $1.25; TTBB
$1.25; SAB $1.25   (C50)

CARPENTER
Saturday *see Bettis

CARPENTER, RICHARD
Goodbye To Love (composed with
Bettis, John) *pop
(Averre, Richard) SATB,pno oct BIG
BELL $.40   (C51)
(Averre, Richard) SSA,pno oct BIG
BELL $.40   (C52)
(Averre, Richard) SA,pno oct BIG
BELL $.40   (C53)
(Averre, Richard) SAB,pno oct BIG
BELL $.40   (C54)

Only Yesterday (composed with Bettis,
John) *pop
(Nowak, Jerry) SATB,pno,opt fl,bvl,
gtr,perc BIG BELL oct $.50, sc
$3.00   (C55)

Yesterday Once More (composed with
Bettis, John) *pop
(Averre, Richard) SSA,pno oct BIG
BELL $.40   (C56)
(Averre, Richard) SATB,pno oct BIG
BELL $.40   (C57)
(Averre, Richard) SAB,pno oct BIG
BELL $.40   (C58)

CARR, ALBERT LEE
Golden Slumber
SATB STANDARD B401MX1 $.50   (C59)

CARRARD
Le Montagnard
men cor,acap HENN 477 s.p.   (C60)

Le Printemps Sur L'alpe
mix cor,acap HENN 787 s.p.   (C61)

Les Beaux Chemins De Mon Pays
men cor,acap HENN 783 s.p.   (C62)

Nacelle
men cor,acap HENN 793 s.p.   (C63)

Printemps Sur L'alpe
wom cor,acap HENN 798 s.p.   (C64)

Rondel De Mai
mix cor,acap HENN 678 s.p.   (C65)

CARSTE
Those Lazy-Hazy-Crazy Days Of Summer
*see Thomas

CARTER, J.
Jabberwocky
SSA BELWIN 2301 $.35   (C66)

Last Invocation, The
SSATB MARKS MC 4626 $.40   (C67)

CARTER, JOHN
My True Love Hath My Heart
SA,pno DEAN CB-803 $.40   (C68)

CASAGRADE, A. (1922-1964)
Fantasia Di Pinocchio
jr cor,2fl,pic,2ob,2clar,2bsn,
4horn,3trp,3trom,tuba,timp,perc,
harp, English horn CARISH rental
(C69)

CASHMAN, TERRY
Songman (composed with West, T.P.)
(Simon, W.) SSA BIG3 $.40   (C70)
(Simon, W.) SATB BIG3 $.40   (C71)
(Simon, W.) SAB BIG3 $.40   (C72)
(Simon, W.) SA/TB BIG3 $.40   (C73)
(Simon, W.) TTBB BIG3 $.40   (C74)

Sweet City Song (from American City
Suite) (composed with West, T.P.)
(Metis, F.) SSA BIG3 $.40   (C75)
(Metis, F.) SATB BIG3 $.40   (C76)
(Metis, F.) SAB BIG3 $.40   (C77)

CASTALDI, PAOLO (1930-   )
Dieci Discanti *CC10U
wom cor,orch/inst voc sc ZERBONI
8060 s.p.   (C78)

CASTELLAZZI, LUIGI
Canti Popolari Italiani *sac,CCU,
folk,It
[It] 4-5pt mix cor,acap (med easy)
sc SCHOTTS SZ 3875 s.p.   (C79)

CASTELNUOVO-TEDESCO, MARIO (1895-1968)
Balow
SATB,acap GENERAL 766CH $.60 see
from Six Carols On Early English
Poems   (C80)

Bridal Song
SATB,acap GENERAL 764CH $.60 see
from Six Carols On Early English
Poems   (C81)

Cherry Ripe
SATB,acap GENERAL 768CH $.60   (C82)

I Sing Of A Maiden
SATB,acap GENERAL 762CH $.50 see
from Six Carols On Early English
Poems   (C83)

Knight Of The Grail, The
SATB,acap GENERAL 763CH $.60 see
from Six Carols On Early English
Poems   (C84)

Nightingale, The
SATB,acap GENERAL 767CH $.60 see
from Six Carols On Early English
Poems   (C85)

Six Carols On Early English Poems
*see Balow; Bridal Song; I Sing
Of A Maiden; Knight Of The Grail,
The; Nightingale, The; That Ever
I Saw   (C86)

That Ever I Saw
SATB,acap GENERAL 765CH $.60 see
from Six Carols On Early English
Poems   (C87)

CASTEREDE, JACQUES
Visages
SMez,org,12vln,6bvl,5perc RIDEAU
s.p.   (C88)

CASTIGLIONI, NICCOLO (1932-   )
Aria (from Three Miracle Plays)
mix cor,ST soli,pno,harmonium,fl,
ob,clar,2horn,2trp,2trom,vln,perc
(med) sc SCHOTTS rental, ipr
(C89)
Gyro
[Lat] 32pt mix cor,4fl,4trp,drums
(diff) sc SCHOTTS rental, ipr
(C90)
CASTLE OF DROMORE, THE see Deale, E.M.

CASUALTY see Balazs, Frederic

CAT IN THE WOOD, THE see Trubitt, Allen
R.

CATULLI LIBER CARMINUM see Petrova,
Elena

CAVE. HIC TU FALLACI see Schultz, Svend
S.

CAVERN, THE see Davies, Lawrence H.

CE MOIS DE MAY see Jannequin, Clement

CE QUE DISENT LEURS TOMBES see Carion,
F.

CE QUE L'AINO see Vuataz

CEASE NOW YOUR TEARS, O LADIES see
Rore, Cipriano de, En Vos, Adieux,
Dames

CEASE THEN TO GIVE ME SORROW see
Gesualdo, Don Carlo, Resta Di Darmi
Noia

CELEBRATE see Gordon

CELEBRATION
SATB UP WITH 6513 $.40   (C91)

CELESTIAL COUNTRY, THE see Ives,
Charles

CELTIC LULLABY, A see Curwin, Clifford

CENEK, BOHUMIL (1869-1960)
Chceme Mir
"We Want Peace" [Czech] mix cor,
acap CZECH s.p.   (C92)

We Want Peace *see Chceme Mir

CEREMONY AFTER A FIRE RAID see Gerber,
Steven

CEREMUGA, JOSEF (1930-   )
Horske Macesky
"Mountain Pansies" [Czech] mix cor,
acap CZECH s.p.   (C93)

Mountain Pansies *see Horske Macesky

CERHA, FRIEDRICH (1926-   )
Zehn Rubaijat Des Omar Khajjam
mix cor,acap MODERN s.p.   (C94)

CERTON, PIERRE (ca. 1510-1572)
Alas, My Love *see Las, S'il
Convient

Comme Heureux T'estimerais, Mon Coeur
[Fr] SATB OUVRIERES 6.0008.1 $.50 (C95)

J'ay Le Rebours
TTBB SCHIRM.EC 2323 s.p.   (C96)

Las, S'il Convient
(Ehret) "Alas, My Love" SATB
SCHIRM.G LG 51579 $.25   (C97)

CERTOVICA see Mikula, Zdenko

CERVENY KVET JA see Vycpalek, Ladislav

CESKA MSE VANOCNI see Ryba, Jan Jakub
Simon

CESKA RIKADLA see Mrkos, Zdenek

CESKA ZIMA see Pinos, Alois

CESKE KRAJINE see Sykora, Vaclav Jan

CESKE PASTORELY see Trojan, Vaclav

CESKE PISNI see Jindrich, Jindrich

CESKE TANCE see Provaznik, Anatol

CESKY PRAPOR see Jeremias, Bohuslav

CESKY SEN see Horky, Karel

C'EST GRANT PAINE see Egk, Werner

C'EST L'AVIRON
(McCauley, William) SATB (easy)
WATERLOO $.30   (C98)

C'EST LE MON DOUS PLAISIR see Willan,
Healey

CEST PRACUJICIM see Harapat, Jindrich

C'EST SI BON see Seelen

CESTI, MARC' ANTONIO (1623-1669)
Four Chamber Duets *CC4U,cant
(Burrows, David L.) bds A-R ED
$8.95   (C99)

CHAGRIN, FRANCIS (1905-1972)
Mother I Cannot Mind My Wheel
SATB RICORDI-ENG LD572 s.p.   (C100)

CHALLENGE TO FREE MEN see Whitehead,
Alfred

CHAMBERS, H.A.
Miller Of The Dee, The
mix cor LESLIE 5001 $.35   (C101)

True Love's The Gift
mix cor LESLIE 4093 $.35   (C102)

CHAMBRIERE, CHAMBRIERE see Lefevre,
Jacques

CHAMPAGNE, CLAUDE (1891-1965)
Fair Wind *folk
TTBB (med easy) WATERLOO $.35
contains also: Lovely Frances
(C103)
SATB WATERLOO $.75 contains also:
Lovely Frances   (C104)

Isabel Went Walking
(England, Amy Bissett) TTBB (easy)
WATERLOO $.35   (C105)

Isobel Went Walking
see Champagne, Claude, Rosebush

Lovely Frances
see Champagne, Claude, Fair Wind
see Champagne, Claude, Fair Wind

CHAMPAGNE, CLAUDE (cont'd.)

Marianne Se'n Va-t-su Moulin
"Marianne Went To The Hill" unis
HARRIS $.25   (C106)

Marianne Went To The Hill *see
Marianne Se'n Va-t-su Moulin

Nez De Martin
SA (med diff) WATERLOO $.40   (C107)

Rosebush *folk
SATB WATERLOO $.35 contains also:
Isobel Went Walking   (C108)

Voici Le Temps Et La Saison
SA (med diff) WATERLOO $.30   (C109)

CHANGING SHOES see Gerschefski, Edwin

CHANSON see Bach, F.

CHANSON see Binet

CHANSON see Martin, Frank

CHANSON see Vuataz

CHANSON A BOIRE see Beauverd

CHANSON CANADIENNES FRANCAISES *CCU,
folk
(Johnston, Richard) cor WATERLOO
$1.95   (C110)

CHANSON D'AMOUR
SSA CIMINO $.40   (C111)
SA CIMINO $.40   (C112)
SATB CIMINO $.40   (C113)

CHANSON D'ANTAN see Combe

CHANSON DE LA NUIT D'ETE see Dalcroze,
Jacques

CHANSON DE PRINTEMPS see Ladmirault, P.

CHANSON DES COMPAGNONS see Arrieu,
Claude

CHANSON DES FEUILLES see Aeby

CHANSON DES MONTAGNARDS see Dalcroze,
Jacques

CHANSON DES SCIEURS *folk
(Ruthenberg, O.) [Ger/Fr] 4pt men cor
MERSEBURG EM9091 s.p.   (C114)
(Ruthenberg, O.) "Lied Des
Wallomschen Jagdgesellen" [Fr/Ger]
4pt mix cor MERSEBURG EM9250 s.p.
       (C115)

CHANSON DU BALEINIER *folk,Fr
(Blanchard, R.) 3pt men cor,Bar solo,
acap JOBERT s.p.   (C116)

CHANSON DU VENT DE MER see Maurice,
Pierre

CHANSONS see Binchois, Gilles

CHANSONS CANADIENNES FRANCAISES *CCU,
folk
(Johnston, Richard A.) SA WATERLOO
$1.95   (C117)

CHANSONS DE QUEBEC *CCU,folk
(Fowke, Edith; Johnston, Richard A.)
unis WATERLOO $2.50   (C118)

CHANSONS POPULAIRES RUSSE *CCU
(Kibaltchitch) wom cor,acap HENN 224
s.p.   (C119)

CHANT DE PAIX see Stekke, Leon

CHANT DU PACTE DU PREMIER AOUT see
Rehberg

CHANT POUR LE JOUR DES MORTS ET DE LA
TOUSSAINT see Gagnebin, Henri

CHANTONS NOEL see Phillips, John C.

CHAP-BOOK see Trojan, Vaclav

CHAPIN, HARRY
Circles
(Metis, F.) SATB BIG3 $.45   (C120)
(Metis, F.) SAB BIG3 $.45   (C121)
(Metis, F.) SSA BIG3 $.45   (C122)

CHAPLIN
This Is My Song *pop
SATB BELWIN UC 721 $.40   (C123)
SSA BELWIN UC 722 $.40   (C124)

CHAPPELL CHORAL BOOK, THE *CC20UL
SSA CHAPPELL 0096867-3741 $2.95; SATB
CHAPPELL 0096867-3742 $2.95 (C125)

CHARADE
SSA CIMINO $.40   (C126)
SATB CIMINO $.40   (C127)

CHARLES, DICK
May You Always *see Markes, Larry

CHARLIE CHAPLIN WALK
SATB CIMINO $.40   (C128)

CHARLIE IS MY DARLIN' *folk,Scot
(Knight) SSBar&camb CAMBIATA U17431
$.35   (C129)

CHARLIE IS MY DARLING
(Beethoven; Boyd) SAB SCHIRM.G
LG51762 $.35   (C130)

CHARM ME ASLEEP see Mozart, Wolfgang
Amadeus

CHARMS AND CEREMONIES see Hurd, Michael

CHAUN, FRANTISEK (1921-)
Spo Padesat Milionu *cant
[Czech] mix cor,narrator,3fl,2ob,
2clar,3bsn,4horn,4trp,3trom,tuba,
timp,perc,pno,harp,strings,
xylophone CZECH s.p.   (C131)

CHAVEZ, CARLOS (1899-)
Epistle To Be Left In The Earth
SATB BROUDE,A 776 $.70   (C132)

Nokwic
SATB BROUDE,A 780 $.60   (C133)

Nonantsin
SATB BROUDE,A 779 $.60   (C134)

Pastoral, A
SATB BROUDE,A 775 $.60   (C135)

Rarely
SATB BROUDE,A 778 $.60   (C136)

Waning Moon, The
SATB BROUDE,A 777 $.50   (C137)

CHCEME MIR see Cenek, Bohumil

CHCEME MY SE CHCEME see Martinu,
Bohuslav

CHE FAI? CHE PENSI? see Veneziani,
Vittore

CHE PIU D'UN GIORNO see Lechner,
Leonhard

CHEERY SONGS see Slater, David D.

CHEIRONOMIES (GESTEN) see Antoniou,
Theodor

CHELSEA MORNING see Mitchell, John

CHEN, NIRA
Seven Songs *CC7U
[Heb] cor OR-TAV $.75   (C138)

CHERISH see Kirkman, Terry

CHERRY BLOOMS see Thygerson, Robert J.

CHERRY RIPE see Castelnuovo-Tedesco,
Mario

CHESHIRE SOUL-CAKING SONG see Pitfield

CHESHIRE SOULING SONG see Pitfield,
Thomas Baron

CHESTER see Billings, William

CHEVALIERS DE LA TABLE RONDE see Weber,
Bernhard

CHEZ NOUS see Sutherland, Margaret

CHI BELA NON E see Biebl, Franz, Ich
Sah Im Olivenwalde

CHI D'AMOR S'ARMA see Arrigo, Girolamo

CHICAGO see Ultan, Lloyd

CHICKADEE SONG, THE see Doyle

CHIEF JUSTICE JOHN MARSHALL see Whear,
Paul William

CHIHARA, PAUL (1938-)
Dream Song *Contemp
SATB,acap (med diff) oct ELKAN-V
362-03176 $.40   (C139)

Slumber Did My Spirit Seal, A
*madrigal,Contemp
SATB,acap (med) oct ELKAN-V
362-03193 $.40   (C140)

CHILD IS BORN, A see Wilder

CHILD OF GOD, A
(Terri) SATB SCHIRM.G LG51822 $.45
       (C141)

CHILD WAVES GOODBYE, THE see Palmes

CHILDHOOD IS A GOOD TIME see Rasely

CHILDREN, JOY AND SONG see Slavicky,
Klement, Deti, Radost A Zpev

CHILDREN LEARN WHAT THEY LIVE see
Werner

CHILDREN OF DAVID see Mechem, Kirke

CHILDRENS BEDTIME SONGS see Karlins, M.
William

CHILDREN'S FRIEND, THE see Anderson,
[William H.]

CHILDREN'S SONG OF HOPE, THE see
Brooks, Joe

CHILDREN'S WINTER see O'Reilly, Dermott

CHILDS, BARNEY (1926-)
Glasse Of Truth, A
cor,electronic tape sc AM.COMP.AL.
$4.68   (C142)

Keet Seel
SATB,acap AM.COMP.AL. $3.85 (C143)

Quodlibet For Singers
cor,electronic tape sc AM.COMP.AL.
$1.65, ipa   (C144)

Variations
SATB,bells,electronic tape sc
AM.COMP.AL. $4.95   (C145)

Variations On Poems Of John Newlove
cor,SATB soli,electronic tape sc
AM.COMP.AL. $4.95   (C146)

When Lilacs Last In The Dooryard
Bloom'd
cor,STB soli,clar,trp,bsn,perc,band
AM.COMP.AL.   (C147)

CHILD'S YEAR, THE see Srnka, Jiri,
Detsky Rok

CHILE VERDE see Leisy

CHIM-CHIM-CHERI see Sherman

CHIMINEY SMOKE
SATB CIMINO $.40   (C148)
TTBB CIMINO $.40   (C149)

CHINESISCHE JAHRESZEITEN see Zipp,
Friedrich

CHINESISCHES TRINKLIED "DAS WASSER, DAS
FRISCHE" see Genzmer, Harald

CHING-A RING CHAW
(Wyatt) 3pt PRO ART 2850 $.40 (C150)

CH'IO AMI LA VITA MIA see Monteverdi,
Claudio

CHLEB A PTACI see Kopelent, Marek

CHLUBNA, OSWALD (1893-)
In The Name Of Life *see Ve Jmenu
Zivota

Je Krasna, Zeme Ma *Op.85, cant
"My Country So Beautiful" [Czech]
mix cor,3fl,3ob,3clar,3bsn,4horn,
3trp,3trom,tuba,timp,perc,harp,
strings, celeste CZECH s.p.
       (C151)

My Country So Beautiful *see Je
Krasna, Zeme Ma

Ve Jmenu Zivota *Op.94, cant
"In The Name Of Life" [Czech] mix
cor,soli,3fl,3ob,3clar,3bsn,
4horn,3trp,3trom,tuba,timp,perc,
harp,strings, celeste CZECH s.p.
       (C152)

CHOICE OF HERCULES, THE see Handel,
George Frideric

CHOIR INVISIBLE, THE see Joubert, John

CHOR DER BAUERN "WIR HABEN GEPLUGET,
WIR HABEN GESAT" see Rein, Walter

CHOR DER FROSCHPHILHARMONIKER see
Michael, Frank

CHOR DER KAUFLEUTE "IN ROLLENDEM WAGEN"
see Rein, Walter

CHOR DER WINTERSTURME see Ishii, Kan

CHOR DER WINZER "WIR HOKERN DIE
STEINIGEN PFADE HINAUF" see
Gerster, Ottmar

CHOR-DUETTE, OP. 22, NO. 2 see Burkhard
Willy

THE CHORAL ART, VOL. II see Leaf

CHORAL DIPTYCH see Harris

CHORAL FANTASIA ON FAUST see Gounod,
Charles Francois

CHORAL FANTASIA ON MARITANA see
Wallace, William Vincent

CHORAL FANTASIA ON NATIONAL AIRS see
Harris, Cuthbert

CHORAL FANTASIA ON TANNHAUSER see
Wagner, Richard

CHORAL FANTASY see Beethoven, Ludwig
van, Chorfantasie

CHORAL HYMNS FROM THE RIG VEDA SET 1
see Holst, Gustav

CHORAL HYMNS FROM THE RIG VEDA SET 2
see Holst, Gustav

CHORAL HYMNS FROM THE RIG VEDA SET 3
see Holst, Gustav

CHORAL MUSIC FOR TWO OR MORE VOICES
VOL. I see Schumann, Robert
(Alexander)

CHORAL MUSIC FOR TWO OR MORE VOICES
VOL. II see Schumann, Robert
(Alexander)

CHORAL MUSIC FOR TWO OR MORE VOICES
VOL. III see Schumann, Robert
(Alexander)

CHORAL NOCTURNE, A see Harris, Jerry
Weseley

THE CHORAL REPERTORY - BLUE BOOK *sac/
sec,CCU
(Bradley) SATB SCHIRM.G 2970 $4.00
(C153)
THE CHORAL REPERTORY - RED BOOK *sac/
sec,CCU
(Bradley) SATB SCHIRM.G 2969 $4.00
(C154)
CHORAL SELECTIONS FROM "CINDERELLA" see
Rodgers, Richard

CHORAL SELECTIONS FROM "FLOWER DRUM
SONG" see Rodgers, Richard

CHORAL SELECTIONS FROM "NO STRINGS" see
Rodgers, Richard

CHORAL SELECTIONS FROM "OKLAHOMA!" see
Rodgers, Richard

CHORAL SELECTIONS FROM "SOUTH PACIFIC"
see Rodgers, Richard

CHORAL SELECTIONS FROM "STATE FAIR" see
Rodgers, Richard

CHORAL SELECTIONS FROM "THE KING AND I"
see Rodgers, Richard

CHORAL SELECTIONS FROM "THE SOUND OF
MUSIC" see Rodgers, Richard

CHORAL SELECTIONS FROM "TWO BY TWO" see
Rodgers, Richard

CHORAL SETTINGS OF WESTERN PENNSYLVANIA
see Taylor, Clifford

CHORAL WARM-UPS see Van Camp, Leonard

CHORAL WORKS *sac/sec,CCU
(Lavi, Hava) [Heb] cor OR-TAV $1.00
contains works by: Haydn; Schubert;
Bartok; Stravinsky; Ibert   (C155)

CHORAL WORKS (SELECTED WORKS II) see
Lisinski, Vatroslav

CHORALE see Christiansen, Larry A.

CHORALE AND FUGUE see Dedrick, C.

CHORALIA see Wuytack, Jos

CHORBAJIAN, JOHN (1936-   )
Dark House
SATB SCHIRM.G 12010 $.35   (C156)

Silver Swan, The
SATB SCHIRM.G 11996 $.30   (C157)

CHORFANTASIE see Beethoven, Ludwig van

CHORFANTASIE see Henze, Hans Werner

CHORFANTASIE see Reutter, Hermann

CHORFANTASIE "SCHMEICHELND HOLD" see
Beethoven, Ludwig van, Chorfantasie

CHORFEIER-SUITE see Haas, Joseph

CHORHEFT *CCU
mix cor KRENN 2.1   (C158)

CHORISCHE TANZE see Rietz, Johannes

CHORLIEDER FUR KNABEN see Hindemith,
Paul

CHORLIEDERBUCH DES SCHWABISCHEN
SANGERBUNDES 1963 *CC43L
men cor SCHOTTS C 40 914 s.p.
contains works by: Lang; Brahms;
Ketterer; Loffler; Schumann and
others   (C159)

CHORMUSIK IM SWING-STIL see Biebl,
Franz

CHORSTUDIEN see Regner, Hermann

CHORUS OF THE FROGS see Turok, Paul

CHORUS OF WINTERSTORMS see Ishii, Kan,
Chor Der Wintersturme

CHRIST UND DIE LIEDER "WIR BITTEN DICH"
see Haas, Joseph

CHRISTIAN ISLAND (GEORGIAN BAY) see
Lightfoot, Gordon

CHRISTIANSEN, LARRY A.
Chorale
SATB STANDARD B323MX1 $.50   (C160)

CHRISTIANSEN, P.
Four Travel Pictures *see Mountains;
Ocean, The; Rolling Plains; Trees
(C161)
Mountains
SATB oct SCHMITT 15010 $.30 see
from Four Travel Pictures (C162)

Ocean, The
SATB oct SCHMITT 15013 $.35 see
from Four Travel Pictures (C163)

Rolling Plains
SATB oct SCHMITT 15012 $.35 see
from Four Travel Pictures (C164)

Trees
SATB oct SCHMITT 15011 $.35 see
from Four Travel Pictures (C165)

CHRISTIANSEN, R.
Portrait By A Neighbor
SATB KJOS PC809 $.40   (C166)

CHRISTKINDLEINS WIEGENLIED "O JESULEIN
ZART" see Genzmer, Harald

CHRISTMAS see Balazs, Frederic

CHRISTMAS CALYPSO see Patterson

CHRISTMAS CANDY CALENDAR, THE see
Maxwell, Robert

CHRISTMAS CANTATA FOR CHILDREN'S CHOIR
see Stephensen, Lise

CHRISTMAS CAROLER, THE *sac/sec,CC32L
(Cookson, Frank B.) FITZSIMONS $.40
(C167)
CHRISTMAS COMES BUT ONCE A YEAR see
Cobine, Al

CHRISTMAS CRADLE SONG see Brahms,
Johannes

CHRISTMAS CYCLE see Monnikendam, Marius

CHRISTMAS DAY see Binkerd, Gordon

CHRISTMAS EVE see McGlohan

CHRISTMAS EVE ROMANCE, THE see Tomasek,
Jaroslav, Romance Stedrovecerni

CHRISTMAS EVERYWHERE see Sateren,
Leland Bernhard

CHRISTMAS IN FIVE-FOUR TIME see Barbey,
Bob

CHRISTMAS IN SCANDINAVIA see Preston

CHRISTMAS IS A COMIN' see Pickell

CHRISTMAS IS COMING see De Cormier,
Robert

CHRISTMAS IS THE WARMEST TIME OF YEAR
see Semola

CHRISTMAS LOVE see Williams

CHRISTMAS MUSIC see London, Edwin

CHRISTMAS ON THE TRAIL see Rottura,
Joseph James

CHRISTMAS ROSE, A see Burroughs

CHRISTMAS SLEIGH see Irwin, Doreen

CHRISTMAS SONG see Grieg, Edvard
Hagerup

CHRISTMAS SONG, A see Dinn, Freda

CHRISTMAS WISH, A see McAfee, Don

CHURCHILL, FRANK
Snow White Revisited *see Morey,
Larry

CHVALA SVETLA see Havelka, Svatopluk

CI ORGANY HRAJU see Moyzes, Alexander

CIKANSKE MELODIE see Bendl, Karel

CIKKER, JAN (1911-   )
Pochod Povstalcov *cant
mix cor,orch SLOV.HUD.FOND s.p.
(C168)

CIKLUS see Kuljeric, Igor

CINCO ROBLES
SSA CIMINO $.40   (C169)
TTBB CIMINO $.40   (C170)
SATB CIMINO $.40   (C171)

CINDY
(Bissell, Keith W.) SATB (med easy)
WATERLOO $.40   (C172)

CINQ CHANSONS POPULAIRES DE SAVOIE
*CC5U
(Chaix) mix cor,acap HENN 601 s.p.
(C173)

CINQUE CANTI POPOLARI SARDI see Bossi,
Renzo

CINQUE FRAMMENTI ALL'ITALIA see
Bussotti, Sylvano

CIRCLE GAME, THE see Mitchell, John

CIRCLES see Chapin, Harry

CIRCUS BAND see Ives, Charles

CITACIE see Parik, Ivan

CITY LIGHTS see Putnam

CITY OF NEW ORLEANS
SATB CIMINO $.60   (C174)
SATB SCREEN 2705CC1   (C175)
SSA SCREEN 2705CC2   (C176)

CITY UPON A HILL see Avshalomov, Jacob

CIVIL-CASTELLVI, FRANCISCO
Amor
see Amor Y Danza

Amor Y Danza
men cor,acap cmplt ed,sc,cor pts
TONOS 3400 s.p.
contains: Amor; Danza   (C177)

Danza
see Amor Y Danza

CLAFLIN, AVERY (1898-   )
Design For The Atomic Age
see Two Madrigals

Quangle Wangle's Hat
see Two Madrigals

Two Madrigals *madrigal
SSATB,acap AM.COMP.AL. $7.15
contains: Design For The Atomic
Age; Quangle Wangle's Hat
(C178)

CLAIR DE LUNE see Debussy, Claude

CLAP YOUR HANDS see Moore

CLARK
Into The World Of Light
SATB SCHIRM.G LG51817 $.30   (C179)

Our Murmurs Have Their Musick Too
SATB SCHIRM.G LG51816 $.30   (C180)

CLARK, HENRY A.
Magic In The Raindrops
unis HARRIS $.30   (C181)

CLARK, R.
Six African Folk Songs *CC6U,folk,
Afr
SATB MARKS MC 4624 $.40   (C182)

CLARKE, HENRY LELAND (1907-   )
All Things Are Double Fair
SATB,org AM.COMP.AL. $2.20   (C183)
SAT,pno AM.COMP.AL. $2.20   (C184)

Deering's Woods
SATB,pno AM.COMP.AL. $4.40   (C185)

Fire Bringer, The
SATB,org AM.COMP.AL. $2.20   (C186)

CLARKE, HENRY LELAND (cont'd.)

Lo, The Winter Is Past
SATB,org AM.COMP.AL. $2.20 (C187)

New Land, The
cor,AT soli,pno AM.COMP.AL. $7.05 (C188)

O Wild West Wind
TTBB,pno AM.COMP.AL. $5.50 (C189)

Primavera
SSA,pno/strings AM.COMP.AL. sc
$3.58, voc sc $3.30 (C190)

Sanctus For St. Cecelia's Day
SSS/TBB/SSSTBB,pno/org AM.COMP.AL.
$2.20 (C191)

These Things Shall Be *canon
cor,acap AM.COMP.AL. (C192)

Three Madrigals *CC3U,madrigal
SATB,acap AM.COMP.AL. $4.95 (C193)

Time Shall Come, The
SATB,pno/org AM.COMP.AL. $2.20 (C194)

What Shall Endure?
SATB,acap AM.COMP.AL. $1.10 (C195)

Winter Is A Cold Thing
SATB,pno/org AM.COMP.AL. $2.20 (C196)

World-Tree, The
SATB,pno AM.COMP.AL. $3.30 (C197)

Young Dead Soldiers, The
SAB,solo,pno AM.COMP.AL. $2.20 (C198)

CLARKSON
A-Flat Cricket And A B-Flat Frog, An
(composed with Hale)
(Plank) SATB KENDOR $.35 (C199)
(Plank) SAB KENDOR $.35 (C200)

CLAUSETTI, P.
Due Canzoni *CC2U
5pt mix cor sc BONGIOVANI 1339 s.p. (C201)

CLAYRE
Lullabye, And Come Afloat
SATB,acap OXFORD 84.184 (med easy)
$.25 (C202)

CLEAR MIDNIGHT see Kunz, Alfred

CLEMENS, JACOBUS (ca. 1510-ca. 1556)
Es Steht Ein Lind
SAB,acap EGTVED KB208 s.p. (C203)

Ik Zeg Adieu
SAB,acap EGTVED KB67 s.p. (C204)

CLEMENTI, ALDO (1925-   )
Variante A
cor,orch ZERBONI 7358 rental (C205)

CLEMENTS
Young Man's Song, A
TTBB OXFORD (C206)

CLEMENTS, JOHN (1910-   )
Come Dark-Eyed Sleep
SSA ASHDOWN VT69 (C207)

CLEMENTS, OTIS
Irish Girl, An (from Irene)
(Metis, F.) SSA BIG3 $.45 (C208)
(Metis, F.) SATB BIG3 $.45 (C209)

CLERAMBAULT, LOUIS-NICOLAS (1676-1749)
L'Histoire De La Femme Adultere *ora
(Foster, Donald) [Lat] cor,soli,
cont,strings voc sc DEAN CMC-104
$4.50 (C210)

CLIC, CLAC, DANSEZ SABOTS see Poulenc,
Francis

CLICK, CLACK, WOODEN SHOES DANCE see
Poulenc, Francis, Clic, Clac,
Dansez Sabots

CLICK GO THE SHEARS
(Bissell, Keith W.) TTBB (med easy)
WATERLOO $.30 (C211)

CLIMB EV'RY MOUNTAIN see Rodgers,
Richard

CLOCHES see Danhieux, Georges

CLOCKS see Gerschefski, Edwin

CLOCKS AND CLOUDS see Ligeti, Gyorgy,
Uhren Und Wolken

CLOISTERED NUN, THE see Brahms,
Johannes, Klosterfraulein

CLOSE AS PAGES IN A BOOK
SSA oct CHAPPELL W892505-353 $.40 (C212)

SATB oct CHAPPELL W892505-357 $.40 (C213)

CLOSE TO ME
SATB CIMINO $.40 (C214)

CLOTHS OF HEAVEN see Dunhill, Thomas
Frederick

CLOUD APPROACHES, A see Distler, Hugo,
Es Geht Ein Dunkle Wolk Herein

CLOUDS see Healey, Derek

CLOVER, DAVID
Baa, Baa Black Sheep
SATB,acap EMI (C215)

Nonsense Psalm, A
SATB EMI (C216)

Three Modiversions *CC3U
SSA EMI (C217)

Three Modiversions *CC3U
SATB EMI (C218)

CLOWN SONG, THE see Willan, Healey

CO JE KRASY NA SVETE see Blaha, Ivo

CO JE TO? see Valek, Jiri

CO ROK DAL see Ambros, Vladimir

COATES
How Can I Keep From Singing
SATB SHAWNEE 1267 $.40 (C219)

It's Christmas Time
SATB SHAWNEE A1303 $.35 (C220)

Mother Country
TTBB SHAWNEE C242 $.40 (C221)
SAB SHAWNEE D191 $.40 (C222)

Snow Lay On The Ground, The
SA/TB SHAWNEE E143 $.35 (C223)

What Do I See?
SSA SHAWNEE B392 $.40 (C224)

COBB, DONALD
Heaven Conserve Thy Course In
Quiteness
SSA,vla/pno GALAXY 1.2524.1 $.35 (C225)

COBINE, AL
Blessed The Children *Xmas
SATB STUDIO V742 $.45 (C226)

Blow Ye Winds *folk,Eng
(Welch, John) SATB/SABar&camb
STUDIO V755 $.30 (C227)

Christmas Comes But Once A Year
SATB (med easy) FISCHER,C PC 1002
$.35 (C228)

I'm Waitin' Up For You
SATB,inst/band STUDIO V7111 $.45,
ipa (C229)

Little Christmas Star
SSAA STUDIO V744 $.45 (C230)

Little Toy Elf *Xmas
2pt jr cor STUDIO V745 $.45 (C231)

No Lov'lier Countryside *folk,Ger
(Welch, John) SATB/SABar&camb
STUDIO V751 $.30 (C232)

Over The River
(Welch, John) SATB/SABar&camb
STUDIO V754 $.30 (C233)

Sing Noel *Xmas
SATB STUDIO V743 $.45 (C234)

Snow's A Comin'
cor,opt bvl&perc, opt sleigh bells
(med) FISCHER,C CM 7771A s.p.,
ipa (C235)

Tavern Of The Loving People *gospel
cor,opt pno&bvl&drums (med)
FISCHER,C PC 1000 (C236)

There's Another Christmas Coming Soon
SATB STUDIO V734 $.45 (C237)

This Christmas Eve
SATB STUDIO V741 $.45 (C238)

Turn On The Christmas Lights
SATB STUDIO V732 $.45 (C239)

COCK-EYED OPTIMIST, A see Rodgers,
Richard

COCKSHOTT, GERALD WILFRED (1915-   )
Captivity
see Merciless Beauty

Escape
see Merciless Beauty

COCKSHOTT, GERALD WILFRED (cont'd.)

In Midwinter A Wood Was
[Eng] SATB,acap BROUDE BR. $.45 (C240)

Merciless Beauty
[Eng] SATB,acap RONGWEN $.70
contains: Captivity; Escape;
Rejection (C241)

Rejection
see Merciless Beauty

CODY
Laughter In The Rain *see Sedaka,
Neil

COENEN, HANS (1911-   )
Es Wollt Ein Schneider Wandern
3pt jr cor,2S rec,A rec/S rec,perc
PELIKAN PE915 s.p. (C242)

COHEN
Ballad Of The Lion And The Lamb, The
*see Sutton, Nancy

I Want To Talk To You *see Sutton,
Nancy

If I Should Learn
SSA,pno MCAFEE M151 $.35 (C243)

Questions (composed with Sutton,
Nancy)
SATB,pno MCAFEE M130 $.40 (C244)

COHEN, ALBAN
Vorspruch
men cor,acap TONOS 3745 s.p. (C245)

COHN, JAMES
Bronx River Puzzle (from Statues In
The Park)
FISCHER,C (C246)

Dress Parade (from Statues In The
Park)
FISCHER,C (C247)

Equable Explanation (from Statues In
The Park)
FISCHER,C (C248)

Gamut, The (from Statues In The Park)
FISCHER,C (C249)

Kind Of An Ode To Duty
FISCHER,C (C250)

Monumental Paradox (from Statues In
The Park)
FISCHER,C (C251)

One From One Leaves Two
FISCHER,C (C252)

Point Of View (from Statues In The
Park)
FISCHER,C (C253)

Technical Advice To Persons Planning
To Erect Memorial Statues Of
Themselves (from Statues In The
Park)
FISCHER,C (C254)

Terrible People, The
cor BELWIN (C255)

Who He? (from Statues In The Park)
FISCHER,C (C256)

COLE
Autumn Cicada
SSA,bells,harp oct BOOSEY 7017 $.55 (C257)

COLE, HUGO (1917-   )
Baron Munchausen
SATB,Bar solo,3fl,2ob,2clar,2bsn,
4horn,2trp,2trom,timp,perc,
strings voc sc NOVELLO rental (C258)

COLE, ROSSETTER GLEASON (1866-1952)
Bird Of Hope, The
SATB (med) FITZSIMONS 1017 $.20 (C259)

Far Away
SSAATTBB,acap (med) FITZSIMONS 1018
$.25 (C260)

Fisherman, The
TTBB,acap (easy) FITZSIMONS 4008
$.20 (C261)

COLEMAN, CY
It's Not Where You Start (from
Seesaw)
(Metis, F.) SSA BIG3 $.50 (C262)
(Metis, F.) TTBB BIG3 $.45 (C263)
(Metis, F.) SATB BIG3 $.50 (C264)
(Metis, F.) SAB BIG3 $.50 (C265)

What Are Heavy?
(Simon, W.) SSA BIG3 $.40 (C266)
(Simon, W.) SATB BIG3 $.50 (C267)
(Simon, W.) SAB BIG3 $.40 (C268)

COLEMAN, CY (cont'd.)

(Simon, W.) SA/TB BIG3 $.40 (C269)

COLEMAN, HENRY
Go From My Window, Go
mix cor CRAMER $.25 (C270)

COLINDE TRANSILVANE see Vlad, Roman

COLINDE TRANSILVANE see Vlad, Roman,
Pastorali Transilvane

COLLECTED EDITION see Mendelssohn-
Bartholdy, Felix

COLLECTED EDITION see Mozart, Wolfgang
Amadeus

COLLECTED WORKS see Liszt, Franz

COLLECTED WORKS see Schein, Johann
Hermann

COLLECTED WORKS see Schutz, Heinrich

COLLECTED WORKS see Sweelinck, Jan
Pieterszoon

COLLECTION OF SEVEN TWO-PART SONGS
*sac/sec,CC7UL
(Sturman, Paul) 2pt EMI (C271)

COLLEGE CREED, A see Gerschefski, Edwin

COLLINS, DON L.
Allegiance To Liberty, An
SSBar&camb,pno (Patriotic) CAMBIATA
P47435 $.35 see from Five Songs
Of Liberty (C272)

Awareness Of You, An
SSBar&camb CAMBIATA L17428 $.40
(C273)

Five Songs Of Liberty *see
Allegiance To Liberty, An; Give
Me Liberty, Or Give Me Death;
Liberty Tree, The; Life, Liberty,
And The Pursuit Of Happiness; On
Independence (C274)

Give Me Liberty, Or Give Me Death
SSBar&camb,pno (Patriotic) CAMBIATA
P47434 $.40 see from Five Songs
Of Liberty (C275)

Liberty Tree, The
SSBar&camb,pno (Patriotic) CAMBIATA
P47436 $.40 see from Five Songs
Of Liberty (C276)

Life Is Living Up Love
SSBar&camb,pno,drums,gtr CAMBIATA
L97202 $.40 (C277)

Life, Liberty, And The Pursuit Of
Happiness
SSBar&camb,pno (Patriotic) CAMBIATA
P47432 $.40 see from Five Songs
Of Liberty (C278)

On Independence
SSBar&camb,pno (Patriotic) CAMBIATA
P47433 $.40 see from Five Songs
Of Liberty (C279)

To Friendship-Right On Man! *pop
SSBar&camb/SS&camb/SSA,pno CAMBIATA
L17313 $.35 (C280)

COLLINS, LARRY
Delta Dawn *see Harvey, Alex

COLLOQUIA FAMILIARA see Strategier,
Herman

COLLOQUIO CORALE see Bucchi, Valentino

COLOMBINE see Barta, Lubor, Kolombina

COLONIAL SPRING see Kent

COLORADO TRAIL, THE *folk,US
(Lyle) SABar&camb,pno,opt gtr/strings
(very easy) CAMBIATA U17316 $.35
(C281)

COLOUR MY WORLD
SSA,pno,opt bvl&drums&gtr SCREEN
4780CC8 (C282)
SATB,pno,opt bvl&drums&gtr SCREEN
4780CC7 (C283)
SAB,pno,opt bvl&drums&gtr SCREEN
4780CC9 (C284)
SA,pno,opt bvl&drums&gtr SCREEN
4780CCX (C285)

COLUMBIA see Ingalls, Jeremiah

COLUMBIA, THE GEM OF THE OCEAN *US
(Bennett, R.R.) 4pt mix cor SCHIRM.G
LG51777 $.50 (C286)

COLUMBUS see Pfitzner, Hans

COLUMBUS THEME see Yancey, Adelante!
(Sail On!)

COMBE
Chanson D'antan
men cor,acap HENN 777 s.p. (C287)

Comme L'eau
men cor,acap HENN 776 s.p. (C288)

COME AGAIN? see Thygerson, Robert J.

COME AGAIN! SWEET LOVE DOTH NOW INVITE
see Dowland, John

COME, ALL MUSICIANS, COME see Hassler,
Hans Leo

COME ALL YE FRIENDS OF LYON *Xmas
(Bampton) SAB (easy) FITZSIMONS 6012
$.25 (C289)

COME AWAY, DEATH see Vaughan Williams,
Ralph

COME AWAY SWEET LOVE see Willey

COME BROTHER, COME FRIEND see Kunz,
Alfred

COME DARK-EYED SLEEP see Clements, John

COME DOWN TO THE TOWN DUMP see Kromer

COME, FILL THE CUP see Kent

COME FLY WITH ME
SATB,pno,opt bvl&drums&gtr SCREEN
4757CC7 (C290)
SSA,pno,opt bvl&drums&gtr SCREEN
4757CC8 (C291)

COME HITHER YOU THAT LOVE see Diemer,
Emma Lou

COME, JOIN IN OUR DANCE see Adler

COME LET US DRINK! see Purcell, Henry

COME LET US JOIN see Powell, Robert

COME LET US SING see Mozart, Wolfgang
Amadeus

COME, LET'S BEGIN see Weelkes

COME LOVE! 'TIS SPRING see Longmire,
John

COME LOVELY AND SOOTHING DEATH see
Goossen, Frederic

COME MONDAY see Buffett, Jimmy

COME, NIGHT! see Protheroe, Daniel

COME, QUICKLY DEATH see Jeffries

COME SING THIS ROUND WITH ME see
Martini, Padre

COME TO ME, MY LOVE see Dello Joio,
Norman

COME UNTO THESE YELLOW SANDS see
Thorpe, Raymond

COME WHERE MY LOVE LIES DREAMING see
Foster, Stephen

COME WITH ME see Lange

COME YE SONS OF ART see Purcell, Henry

COMIC DUET FOR TWO CATS see Rossini,
Gioacchino, Duetto Buffo Di Due
Gatti

COMITAT: NUN ZU GUTER LETZT see
Mendelssohn-Bartholdy, Felix

COMME HEUREUX T'ESTIMERAIS, MON COEUR
see Certon, Pierre

COMME L'EAU see Combe

COMMENCEMENT PROCESSIONAL HYMN, A see
Hoskins, William

COMMUNIST MANIFESTO, THE see Schulhoff,
Erwin, Komunisticky Manifest

COMPLAINTE see Arrieu, Claude

COMPLETE WORKS see Beethoven, Ludwig
van

COMPLETE WORKS see Brahms, Johannes

COMPLETE WORKS see Lasso, Orlando di

COMPLETE WORKS see Rameau, Jean-
Philippe

COMPLETE WORKS see Schumann, Robert
(Alexander)

COMPLETE WORKS see Glinka, Mikhail
Ivanovitch

COMPLETE WORKS see Schubert, Franz
(Peter)

COMPLETE WORKS see Dunstable, John

COMPLETE WORKS. BACH-GESELLSCHAFT
EDITION see Bach, Johann Sebastian

COMPOSITION BLUES see Sanders

COMPTINES DE L'OISELIER see Binet

CON QUE LA LAVARE? see Vasquez, Juan

CONCENTO DI VOCI see Orff, Carl

CONCERNING THE LAST THINGS OF A MAN see
Vycpalek, Ladislav

CONCORD HYMN see Kent

CONFESS JEHOVAH
see Freedom Song, 1776

CONGEDO DI GEROLAMO SAVONAROLA see
Dallapiccola, Luigi

CONJURATION, TO ELECTRA, A see Binkerd,
Gordon

CONQUERAR, AN MONEAM see Schultz, Svend
S.

CONRADI, J.G.
Herzliebchen Mein
(Thehos, A.) men cor,acap TONOS 281
s.p. (C292)

CONSEIL, JEAN (1498-1535)
Als Ich Gestern Ging Gelassen *sac,
Fr
[Fr/Ger] mix cor (med easy) sc
SCHOTTS C 39 771 s.p. (C293)

CONSONANCE see Billings

CONSTANT LOVER, THE
(Dexter, Harry) TTBB ENOCH EC348
(C294)

CONSTANT LOVER, THE see Mills, Charles

CONSTANTINO, JOSEPH
In Starlight (composed with Meredith,
George)
SATB BOURNE B224188-357 $.45 (C295)

CONSTITUTION, THE see Haba, Alois,
Ustava 9. Kvetna

CONTENT, NOT CATES see Jenkins, C.J.

CONTEST, THE see Root, George F.

CONTRAPONTO BESTIALE ALLE MENTE see
Banchieri, Adriano

CONTRAPPUNTO BESTIALE ALLA MENTE see
Banchieri, Adriano

CONTRAPUNCTUS I see Bach, Johann
Sebastian

CONTRASTS see Kunz, Alfred

COOKSON, FRANK B.
Away For Rio
2-4pt men cor (easy) FITZSIMONS
4069 $.20 (C296)

COPE, CECIL
Fire
see Two Songs From "The Wandering
Moon"

Shiny
see Two Songs From "The Wandering
Moon"

Two Songs From "The Wandering Moon"
unis,pno ROBERTON 75041 s.p.
contains: Fire; Shiny (C297)

COPLEY, IAN A.
Lilly Bright And Shine-A
2pt treb cor,pno ROBERTON 75046
s.p. (C298)

COPPIER
Annie
wom cor,pno HENN 650 s.p. (C299)

Jane
wom cor,acap HENN 649 s.p. (C300)

Mariez-Vous, Fillette Au Cresson
men cor,acap HENN 648 s.p. (C301)

CORI POPOLARI ITALIANI *CCU,pop,It
[It] 4-8pt mix cor/4-8pt men cor,acap
sc SCHOTTS ESZ 6086 s.p. (C302)

CORIGLIANO, JOHN (1938-   )
Black November Turkey, A
SATB SCHIRM.G 11979 $.45   (C303)

L'invitation Au Voyage
SATB SCHIRM.G 11978 $.45   (C304)

CORNELIUS
Monotone, The
(Boyd) SAATB,A/B solo (med)
FITZSIMONS 1061 $.25   (C305)

CORNELIUS, PETER (1824-1874)
Grablied "Pilger Auf Erden" *Op.9,
No.4
men cor sc SCHOTTS CHBL 13 s.p.
(C306)

Sonnenaufgang
men cor,acap TONOS 6327 s.p.   (C307)

CORNELL, GARRY A.
It's Love
SATB ART MAST 1031 $.40   (C308)

CORNYSH, WILLIAM
Worfully Arrayed
cor CHESTER JWC 8872 C s.p.   (C309)

CORO DEI MALAMMOGLIATI see
Dallapiccola, Luigi

CORO DELLE MALMARITATE see
Dallapiccola, Luigi

CORO DI MORTI see Petrassi, Goffredo

CORONACH see Coutts, George

CORONATION AND VERSE ANTHEMS see Blow,
John

CORRE AL SUO FIN MIA VITA see Nielsen,
Hans

COSMIC FESTIVAL see Felciano, Richard

COSSACK LULLABY *folk,Russ
(Lester, William) SSA (med)
FITZSIMONS 3012 $.20   (C310)

COSSETTO, EMIL (1918-   )
Bettlerlied
men cor,acap TONOS 3409 s.p.   (C311)

Dobri Denek
"Hei, Schoner Lado" [Ger/Czech] wom
cor (med) sc SCHOTTS C 40 037
s.p.   (C312)

Drumba Drumba "Ruhrt Die Trommeln"
*Marriage,Slav
[Ger] men cor sc SCHOTTS C 43 908
s.p. see from Jugoslawische
Hochzeitslieder   (C313)

Galgenlied
men cor,acap TONOS 3410 s.p. (C314)

Guslars Ballade "Sass Das Madchen
Einsam" *Marriage,Slav
[Ger] men cor,T solo sc SCHOTTS
C 43 910 s.p. see from
Jugoslawische Hochzeitslieder
(C315)
Hei, Schoner Lado *see Dobri Denek

Hochzeitstanz "Auf Zum Tanz"
*Marriage,Slav
[Ger] men cor sc SCHOTTS C 43 511
s.p. see from Jugoslawische
Hochzeitslieder   (C316)

Jodler "Taar I Nod E Bitzeli"
men cor sc SCHOTTS C 43 887 s.p. (C317)

Jugoslawische Hochzeitslieder *see
Drumba Drumba "Ruhrt Die
Trommeln"; Guslars Ballade "Sass
Das Madchen Einsam";
Hochzeitstanz "Auf Zum Tanz";
Trinkspruch "Liebe Leute, Horet"
(C318)
Partita Sefardica
mix cor,soli,pno CROATICA   (C319)

Poskocica
"Tanzlied" [Ger/Czech] wom cor (med
easy) sc SCHOTTS C 40 038 s.p.
(C320)
Rider, The (Cavalcade)
SATB,2pno,3fl,3clar,2bsn,3trp,bvl,
perc,timp CROATICA   (C321)

Tanzlied *see Poskocica

Trinklied Im Sommer
men cor,acap TONOS 3401 s.p. (C322)

Trinkspruch "Liebe Leute, Horet"
*Marriage,Slav
[Ger] men cor,T solo sc SCHOTTS
C 43 909 s.p. see from
Jugoslawische Hochzeitslieder
(C323)

COSTA
Quartetto A Canzone
mix cor LIENAU voc sc s.p., cor pts
s.p.   (C324)

COSTELEY, GUILLAUME (1531-1606)
Allons Au Vert Boccage
(Shipp) SSAA SCHIRM.G LG51692 $.40
(C325)
Allons, Gai, Bergeres
[Fr] SATB,acap EGTVED MS7B8 s.p.
(C326)

COTTON FIELDS *folk
(Hess, Reimund) [Eng/Ger] mix cor,
gtr,perc,opt bvl sc BREITKOPF-W
Z 23 s.p.   (C327)

COULTERS CANDY
(De Cormier) SA SCHIRM.G LG51612 $.30
(C328)

COULTHARD, JEAN (1908-   )
Flower In The Crannied Wall
SA (easy) OXFORD 02.011 $.20 (C329)

Sea Gulls
SA (easy) OXFORD 02.100 $.30 (C330)

COUNTRY BEYOND THE STARS, THE see
Jones, Daniel

COUNTRY SPEAKS, THE see Hanus, Jan,
Zeme Mluvi

COUNTRY SUNSHINE see Davis, Bill

COUSINS, M. THOMAS (1914-   )
Dreamer, The
SSA BRODT 512A $.28   (C331)

COUTTS, GEORGE
Coronach
SSA HARRIS $.25   (C332)

COVERSI, GIROLAMO
Sola Soletta
[It] SSATB EGTVED KB18 s.p.   (C333)

COVERT, MARY E.
Moon, The
unis HARRIS $.25   (C334)

COW, THE see Berger, Jean

COW CALL see Karjankutsu

COWAN
Sally And Her Lover
SATB WALTON 2260 $.40   (C335)

COWBOY SONG "COWBOYS SIND WIR" see
Fischer, Ernst

COWEN, [SIR FREDERIC HYMEN] (1852-1935)
Bridal Chorus (from Rose Maiden)
SATB (med) FITZSIMONS 1009 $.25
(C336)
COX
Soft Rain
SATB SHAWNEE A1304 $.45   (C337)

COZENS, JOHN
Canada, Our Home
SA HARRIS $.30   (C338)
SATB HARRIS $.30   (C339)
SAB HARRIS $.30   (C340)

To Canada Our Country
SA HARRIS $.30   (C341)
SAB HARRIS $.30   (C342)
SATB HARRIS $.30   (C343)

CRACKLIN ROSIE see Diamond, Neil

CRADLE SONG see Beaudrot

CRADLE SONG see Brahms, Johannes

CRADLE SONG see Fleming, Christopher le

CRADLE SONG see Jenkins, C.J.

CRADLE SONG OF THE COAST see Turner,
Olive

CRAIK
Angie *see Best

That Men Might Know *see Best

CRAM
Master Of Eager Youth
SATB,S solo,org MCAFEE M120 $.35
(C344)

CRAMBAMBULI see Muller-Blattau,
Wendelin

CRAWDAD SONG, THE
(Dexter, Harry) 2pt ASHDOWN EA381
(C345)
CRAWFORD
Mad Maid's Song
SSA (med diff) OXFORD 95.405 $.60
(C346)

To Music, To Becalm His Fever
SSAA (med diff) OXFORD 95.406 $.60
(C347)

CRAWFORD, JOHN (1931-   )
Amour, Tu As Ete Mon Maitre *see
Plus Ne Suis Ce Qui J'ai Ete, "I
Have Lost All That Once I Was";
Voici Le Pere Au Double Front,
"Here Is The God Who Looks Both
Ways"   (C348)

Here Is The God Who Looks Both Ways
*see Voici Le Pere Au Double
Front

I Have Lost All That Once I Was *see
Plus Ne Suis Ce Qui J'ai Ete

Plus Ne Suis Ce Qui J'ai Ete
"I Have Lost All That Once I Was"
TBB SCHIRM.EC 2176 s.p. see from
Amour, Tu As Ete Mon Maitre
(C349)
Voici Le Pere Au Double Front
"Here Is The God Who Looks Both
Ways" TBB SCHIRM.EC 2178 s.p. see
from Amour, Tu As Ete Mon Maitre
(C350)

CRAWFORD, THOMAS J.
Good Neighbors Then
mix cor LESLIE 4083 $.30   (C351)

Saint Nicholas At Christmas Time
*Xmas
mix cor LESLIE 4085 $.30   (C352)

CREATION: PROLOGUE, THE see
Ussachevsky, Vladimir

CREATORE, LUIGI
Can't Help Falling In Love (composed
with Peretti, Hugo; Weiss, George
David)
(Simon, W.) SSA BIG3 $.40   (C353)
(Simon, W.) SATB BIG3 $.50   (C354)

CRECQUILLON, THOMAS
All You That Love, Awaken Now *see
Reveillez-Vous Tous Amoureux

Jamais En Monde N'aurai
"Never In All This World Will I"
see Two Chansons

Never In All This World Will I *see
Jamais En Monde N'aurai

Reveillez-Vous Tous Amoureux
"All You That Love, Awaken Now" see
Two Chansons

Two Chansons
(Malin, Don) SATB,acap BELWIN 2326
$.35
contains: Jamais En Monde
N'aurai, "Never In All This
World Will I"; Reveillez-Vous
Tous Amoureux, "All You That
Love, Awaken Now"   (C355)

CREDIDI see Porpora, Nicola Antonio

CREED, LINDA
You Make Me Feel Brand New *see
Bell, Thomas

CREMESINI, M.
Campane A Meriggo
see Campane Di Primavera

Campane A Vespro
see Campane Di Primavera

Campane Ad Alba
see Campane Di Primavera

Campane Di Primavera
men cor sc BONGIOVANI 1552 s.p.
contains: Campane A Meriggo;
Campane A Vespro; Campane Ad
Alba   (C356)

Carillon
5pt mix cor sc BONGIOVANI 1606 s.p.
(C357)
La Caccia
4pt men cor,solo sc BONGIOVANI 1947
s.p., cor pts BONGIOVANI 2024
s.p.   (C358)

La Formicuzza
4pt mix cor sc BONGIOVANI 2202 s.p.
(C359)
Madonna Per Voi Canto Madrigale
4pt mix cor sc BONGIOVANI 1605 s.p.
(C360)
Momento Nostalgico
4pt men cor sc BONGIOVANI 1946 s.p.
(C361)
Ninna Nanna
4pt men cor sc BONGIOVANI 1607 s.p.
(C362)
Notturno
TTBB sc BONGIOVANI 1942 s.p. (C363)

Pastora
4pt mix cor sc BONGIOVANI 2203 s.p.
(C364)

CREMESINI, M. (cont'd.)

Primavera Veniente
4pt mix cor sc BONGIOVANI 2200 s.p.
(C365)

Serenata
4 eq voices,solo sc BONGIOVANI 1943
s.p.   (C366)

CRESPUSCOLO see Recli, Giulia

CRESTON, PAUL (1906-   )
Calamus *Op.104
SATB SCHIRM.G 2958 $1.50   (C367)

CRIERS see Pinos, Alois, Vyvolavaci

CRIQUETTE see Gagnebin, Henri

CROCE, JIM
Age
(Metis, F.) SSA BIG3 $.45   (C368)
(Metis, F.) SAB BIG3 $.45   (C369)
(Metis, F.) SATB BIG3 $.45   (C370)

Alabama Rain
(Simon, W.) SAB BIG3 $.45   (C371)
(Simon, W.) SATB BIG3 $.45   (C372)
(Simon, W.) SSA BIG3 $.45   (C373)

Bad, Bad Leroy Brown
(Metis, F.) SATB,solo BIG3 $.45
(C374)
(Metis, F.) TTBB BIG3 $.45   (C375)
(Metis, F.) SAB BIG3 $.45   (C376)

Hard Way Every Time, The
(Metis, F.) SSA BIG3 $.45   (C377)
(Metis, F.) SAB BIG3 $.45   (C378)
(Metis, F.) SATB BIG3 $.45   (C379)

Iley Tomorrow
(Simon, W.) SSA BIG3 $.50   (C380)
(Simon, W.) SATB BIG3 $.45   (C381)
(Simon, W.) SAB BIG3 $.50   (C382)

I'll Have To Say I Love You In A Song
(Metis, F.) SSA BIG3 $.45   (C383)
(Metis, F.) SATB BIG3 $.50   (C384)
(Metis, F.) SAB BIG3 $.45   (C385)

It Doesn't Have To Be That Way
(Simon, W.) SSA BIG3 $.45   (C386)
(Simon, W.) SATB BIG3 $.45   (C387)
(Simon, W.) SAB BIG3 $.45   (C388)

Lover's Cross
(Metis, F.) SSA BIG3 $.45   (C389)
(Metis, F.) SATB BIG3 $.45   (C390)
(Metis, F.) SAB BIG3 $.45   (C391)

One Less Set Of Footsteps
(Simon, W.) SSA BIG3 $.45   (C392)
(Simon, W.) SATB BIG3 $.45   (C393)
(Simon, W.) SAB BIG3 $.45   (C394)

Operator (That's Not The Way It Feels
(Simon, W.) SATB BIG3 $.50   (C395)
(Simon, W.) SAB BIG3 $.50   (C396)

Photographs And Memories
(Simon, W.) SSA BIG3 $.45   (C397)
(Simon, W.) SATB BIG3 $.45   (C398)

These Dreams
(Simon, W.) SAB BIG3 $.45   (C399)
(Simon, W.) SSA BIG3 $.45   (C400)
(Simon, W.) SATB BIG3 $.45   (C401)

Time In A Bottle
(Metis, F.) SSA BIG3 $.50   (C402)
(Metis, F.) SATB BIG3 $.50   (C403)
(Metis, F.) SAB BIG3 $.50   (C404)

Workin' At The Car Wash Blues
(Metis, F.) SATB BIG3 $.45   (C405)
(Metis, F.) TTBB BIG3 $.45   (C406)

You Don't Mess Around With Jim
(Metis, F.) SATB BIG3 $.45   (C407)
(Metis, F.) TTBB BIG3 $.45   (C408)

CROFTS
Diamond Girl *see Seals

We May Never Pass This Way Again
*see Seals

CROMBE, W.
Blue, Green And Gold (composed with
Laine, P.; Varotta, V.; Riema,
K.)
(Knight, E.) SATB BOURNE
B230730-357 $.55   (C409)

CROSSE
Demon Of Adachigahara *cant
unis,narrator,inst (med easy) sc
OXFORD 56.401 $7.35, ipr, cor pts
OXFORD 56.401-50 $.50   (C410)

Night-Wind
SATB,opt acap (diff) OXFORD 84.185
$.45   (C411)

CRUDELE ACERBO E DISPIETATO CORE see
Arrigo, Girolamo

CSODALKOZAS see Karai, Jozsef

CSUFOLO see Balazs, Arpad

CSUJOGATO see Bartok, Bela

CTYRI MUZSKE SBORY see Marsik, Emanuel

CUATRO SONETOS DE AMOR see Ficher,
Jacobo

CUCKOO SONG see Bilencko, M.

CUCU see Encina, Juan Del

CUGLEY, IAN
Make We Joy
unis EMI   (C412)

CUNNINGHAM, ARTHUR
Harlem Is My Home
SATB,S solo,pno (med diff) oct
PRESSER 312-41002 $.45   (C413)

CURLEW ISLE see Kurth, Burton L.

CURRIE, RANDOLPH
November Twenty-Second: An American
Elegy
SSA,pno DEAN CD-107 $.45   (C414)

CURRY, W. LAWRENCE
Nightingale
SATB,S solo (easy) FITZSIMONS 1041
$.25   (C415)
SSA,S solo (easy) FITZSIMONS 3050
$.20   (C416)

CURTAINS OF NIGHT
(Niles, John Jacob) TTBB,acap (very
easy) FOSTER MF 1054 $.35   (C417)

CURWIN, CLIFFORD
Celtic Lullaby, A
SSA CRAMER $.25   (C418)

Praise
unis CRAMER $.20   (C419)

Voice, The
unis CRAMER $.20   (C420)

CUSTER, ARTHUR (1923-   )
Found Objects I
SATB,2electronic tape AM.COMP.AL.
(C421)

CVRCEK see Bohac, Josef

CWYD DY GALON
"Lively Palr, The" see Gwelltyn Glas

CWYN MAM YNGHFRAITH
"Mother-In-Law, The" see Two Welsh
Folk Songs

CYNIC'S SONG, THE see Fennimore

CZAJOWSKI, MICHAEL
Happy Journey, The *CC3U
SATB STANDARD D910MX1 $.50   (C422)

CZECH DREAM, THE see Horky, Karel,
Cesky Sen

CZECH FLAG, THE see Jeremias, Bohuslav,
Cesky Prapor

CZECH SONG, THE see Jindrich, Jindrich,
Ceske Pisni

CZECH SONG, THE see Smetana, Bedrich

CZECH WINTER see Pinos, Alois, Ceska
Zima

D

DA BACCO IN TOSCANA see Zecchi, Adone

DA BEI RAMI SCENDEA see Arcadelt, Jacob

DA DROB'N AUF'N BERG
(Reiter, Albert) treb cor (contains
also: I Woass Net) DOBLINGER
O 341-342 s.p. see from Sechs
Osterreichische Volkslieder   (D1)

DA UNTEN IST FRIEDEN see Kloss

DAFFODILS see Shearer, C.M.

DAHEIM see Lehr, Gregor

DAHEIM IN WEITEN TALESGRUND *folk
(Klink, W.) [Ger] 4pt mix cor
MERSEBURG EM9218 s.p.   (D2)

DAISY A DAY, A see Strunk, Jud

DAJ MI BOZE see Martinu, Bohuslav

DAKUJEM TI see Ocenas, Andrej

DAL A VOROS CSILLAGROL see Kabalevsky,
Dmitri Borisovitch

DALBY, MARTIN (1942-   )
Orpheus
SATB,2ob,2horn,perc,hpsd,5strings
voc sc NOVELLO rental   (D3)

DALCROZE, JACQUES
Chanson De La Nuit D'ete
men cor,acap HENN 774 s.p.   (D4)

Chanson Des Montagnards
men cor,acap HENN 775 s.p.   (D5)

Le Joli Jeu Des Saisons, Rondes,
Chansons, Rythmique
mix cor&jr cor,soli,pno HENN 647
s.p.   (D6)

Les Plaisirs Du Bal
wom cor,acap HENN 680 s.p.   (D7)

DALE, BENJAMIN J. (1885-1943)
Before The Paling Of The Stars
SATB,2fl,ob,3clar,2bsn,3horn,timp,
perc,harp,strings voc sc NOVELLO
rental   (D8)

DALLAPICCOLA, LUIGI (1904-   )
Canti Di Prigionia
sc CARISH 20975 s.p., voc sc CARISH
21849 s.p.
contains: Congedo Di Gerolamo
Savonarola (mix cor,2pno,2harp,
timp,bells,perc, xylophone,
vibraphone); Invocazione Di
Boezio (wom cor,2pno,2harp,
timp,bells, xylophone,
vibraphone); Preghiera Di Maria
Stuarda (mix cor,2pno,2harp,
timp,bells,perc, xylophone,
vibraphone)   (D9)

Congedo Di Gerolamo Savonarola
see Canti Di Prigionia

Coro Dei Malammogliati
see Sei Cori Di Michaelangelo
Buonarroti Il Giovane Ia

Coro Delle Malmaritate
see Sei Cori Di Michaelangelo
Buonarroti Il Giovane Ia

I Balconi Della Rosa
see Sei Cori Di Michaelangelo
Buonarroti Il Giovane IIa

Il Coro Degli Zitti
see Sei Cori Di Michaelangelo
Buonarroti Il Giovane IIIa

Il Coro Dei Lanzi Briachi (Epilogo)
see Sei Cori Di Michaelangelo
Buonarroti Il Giovane IIIa

Il Papavero
see Sei Cori Di Michaelangelo
Buonarroti Il Giovane IIa

Invocazione Di Boezio
see Canti Di Prigionia

Preghiera Di Maria Stuarda
see Canti Di Prigionia

Sei Cori Di Michaelangelo Buonarroti
Il Giovane Ia
[It/Ger/Eng] sc CARISH 18657 s.p.,
voc pt CARISH 18657 rental, sc
CARISH 21893 s.p. Carisch

DALLAPICCOLA, LUIGI (cont'd.)

No.21893 has English text
contains: Coro Dei Malammogliati;
Coro Delle Malmaritate   (D10)

Sei Cori Di Michaelangelo Buonarroti
Il Giovane IIa
[It/Ger] SA,SSAA soli,2fl,ob,2clar,
bsn,2horn,2trp,trom,tuba,pno,
4strings sc CARISH 18743 s.p.,
cor pts CARISH 20878 rental, ipr
contains: I Balconi Della Rosa;
Il Papavero   (D11)

Sei Cori Di Michaelangelo Buonarroti
Il Giovane IIIa
[It/Ger] mix cor,3fl,3ob,4clar,
3bsn,4horn,3trp,3trom,tuba,timp,
2harp,perc,pno, xylophone, 2
saxophones sc CARISH 18735 s.p.,
cor pts CARISH 18805 rental, ipr
contains: Il Coro Degli Zitti; Il
Coro Dei Lanzi Briachi
(Epilogo)   (D12)

Tempus Destruendi - Tempus
Aedificandi *sac
[Lat] SSAATTBB,soli,acap (diff) sc
SCHOTTS SZ 7112 s.p.   (D13)

DALMATIAN CRADLE SONG *folk
(Roberton, Hugh S.) unis,pno ROBERTON
75012 s.p.   (D14)

DALMATIAN DIPTYCH see Brkanovic, Ivan

DALMATINISCHE BARKAROLE see Simoniti,
Rado

DALMATINISCHES LIEBESLIED *folk
(Becker, H.-G.) men cor,pno sc,cor
pts TONOS 2184 s.p.   (D15)

DALMATINISCHES SCHERZLIED *folk
(Becker, Hans-Gunther) men cor,acap
2037 s.p.   (D16)

DALTON, DAN
Old Betsy Goes Boing, Boing, Boing
(Metis, F.) SAB BIG3 $.40   (D17)
(Metis, F.) SATB BIG3 $.40   (D18)

DAMIGELLA TUTTA BELLA see Monteverdi,
Claudio

DAMMERUNG see Herrmann, Hugo

DANCE, THE see Ridout, Godfrey

DANCE, DANCE MY HEART see Diemer, Emma
Lou

DANCE TI' THY DADDY
(De Cormier) SATB SCHIRM.G LG51753
$.35   (D19)

DANCE TO YOUR DADDY see Ames, William

DANCING AND SPRINGING see Hassler, Hans
Leo, Tanzen Und Springen

DANCING DAY *CCU,carol
(Rutter) SSA,inst OXFORD ipa   (D20)

DANHIEUX, GEORGES
Cloches
1-2pt,pno BROGNEAUX cor pts s.p.,
voc sc s.p.   (D21)

Invitation
jr cor (easy) BROGNEAUX s.p.   (D22)

L'Escarpolette
jr cor (easy) BROGNEAUX s.p.   (D23)

Petit Village
jr cor (easy) BROGNEAUX s.p.   (D24)

Petites Hirondelles
jr cor (easy) BROGNEAUX s.p.   (D25)

Voici Les Vacances
jr cor (med, text in French and
Flemish) BROGNEAUX s.p.   (D26)

DANIEL see John, Elton

DANK DIR, MUSIK see Desch, Rudolf

DANK DIR, O LICHT see Rein, Walter

DANKLIED DES BERGMANNS see Wolters,
Karl-Heinz

DANNY'S SONG see Loggins, Dave

DANOFF
Take Me Home Country Roads (composed
with Nivert; Denver, John) *pop
(Metis) 2pt WARNER WB-382 $.35
    (D27)
(Siltman) SSA WARNER WB-351 183
$.50   (D28)
(Siltman) TTB WARNER WB-350 188
$.50   (D29)

DANS LA MAISON DE DOULEUR see
Killmayer, Wilhelm

DANTE see Kvam, Oddvar S.

DANZ, DANZ, QUIESELCHEN see Weber,
Bernhard

DANZA see Civil-Castellvi, Francisco

DAPHNE'S CHEEKS see Protheroe, Daniel

DAREST THOU NOW, O SOUL see Lockwood,
Normand

DARIMINI, LUDOVICO
Salve, Cara Deo Tellus Sanctissima
(Stevens, D.) unis,org/2vla/2bsn/
2trom NOVELLO MT 1580 s.p., ipa
    (D30)

DARION
Lollipop Tree, The (composed with
Kleinsinger)
(Ehret) 2pt WARNER W-3819 $.35
    (D31)

DARK EYED SAILOR see Vaughan Williams,
Ralph

DARK HOUSE see Chorbajian, John

DARK SCHERZO see Williamson, Malcolm

DARKEST HOUR, THE see Moore, Harold S.

DAS ABC see Pepping, Ernst

DAS ALTER "DAS ALTER IST EIN HOFLICH
MANN" see Hessenberg, Kurt

DAS BACHLEIN see Gauss, Otto

DAS BAUERLEIN *folk
(Lang, H.) [Ger] 4pt men cor
MERSEBURG EM9001 s.p.   (D32)
(Miller, F.R.) [Ger] 4pt mix cor
MERSEBURG EM9235 s.p.   (D33)

DAS BAUERNJAHR see Klein, Richard
Rudolf

DAS BESTE IN DER WELT see Gerster,
Ottmar

DAS BESTE "WENN DIR'S IN KOPF UND
HERZEN SCHWIRRT" see Hessenberg,
Kurt

DAS BLUMENGARTLEIN see Edler, Robert

DAS BOCKLEIN *folk
(Haus, K.) [Ger] 4pt mix cor
MERSEBURG EM9217 s.p.   (D34)

DAS DACH see Pepping, Ernst

DAS DEUTSCHE WUNSCHKONZERT see
Kiesewetter, Peter

DAS DORFCHEN see Schubert, Franz
(Peter)

DAS DREIFACHE GLORIA see Bresgen, Cesar

DAS DRITTE DT 64 LIEDERBUCH *CCU
HOFMEISTER W115 s.p.   (D35)

DAS ECHO "WENN IN DEM TIEFEN WALD" see
Rein, Walter

DAS EISENBAHNGLEICHNIS see Hoffding,
Finn

DAS EISENBAHNSPIEL see Dessau, Paul

DAS ERDEBEN "BRUDER, BRUDER, HALTE
MICH!" see Gottschalk, Wolfgang

DAS EWIGE IST STILLE see Mohler,
Philipp

DAS FLOSS DER MEDUSA see Henze, Hans
Werner

DAS FRAUENZIMMER "SABINCHEN WAR EIN
FRAUENZIMMER" see Desch, Rudolf

DAS FRUHJAHR IST GEKOMMEN see Erdlen,
Hermann

DAS GEBIRGE "NOCH IST DIE ERDE" see
Siegl, Otto

DAS GEDENKEN: MAG AUCH HEISS see
Silcher, Friedrich

DAS GELAUT ZU SPEYER "NUN KUMBT HIERHER
ALL" see Senfl, Ludwig

DAS GESTOHLENE MANTELCHEN "DAFINA, AM
FEURIGEN ROTWEIN" see Gotovac,
Jakov

DAS GLOCKCHEN "WO DAS GLOCKCHEN ERTONT
SO VERSCHWEIGEN" see Zoll, Paul

DAS GLUCK "WILL DAS GLUCK NACH SEINEM
SINN" see Rettich, Wilhelm

DAS GLUCKLICHE JAHR see Fischer, Theo

DAS GOLDENE RINGELEIN *folk,Ger
(Erdlen, Hermann) men cor,acap TONOS
37 s.p.   (D36)

DAS GOLDNE RINGELEIN *folk,Ger
(Jansen, Peter) men cor,acap TONOS
107 s.p.   (D37)

DAS GUTE LEBEN see Pepping, Ernst

DAS HASENSPIEL see Maasz, Gerhard

DAS HERZ POCHT see Edler, Robert

DAS HIMMLISCHE ORCHESTER "IHR MORSER,
ERKNALLET" see Haas, Joseph

DAS HOHE TOR see Erdlen, Hermann

DAS HOHELIED see Sutermeister, Heinrich

DAS HUHN "IN DER BAHNHOFHALLE" see
Nitsche, Paul

DAS IMPROVISIERTE CHORLIED *sac,CC20L,
folk,Eur
(Bresgen, Cesar) 3-5pt mix cor,inst
(easy) SCHOTTS B 138 s.p.   (D38)

DAS JAGEN "DAS JAGEN, DAS IST UNSER
LEBEN" *folk,Ger
(Zoll, Paul) men cor sc SCHOTTS
C 41 385 s.p. see from Drei
Deutsche Volkslieder   (D39)

DAS JAGRISCHE LEBEN *folk,Aus
(Schnurl, Karl) men cor,acap TONOS
813 s.p.   (D40)

DAS JAHR see Pepping, Ernst

DAS JAHR see Wittmer, Eberhard Ludwig

DAS JAHR IM LIED see Haas, Joseph

DAS KLEINE HERZ see Knab, Armin

DAS KOHLERWEIB IST TRUNKEN see Edler,
Robert

DAS KOSTBARE WASSER "UNS BEUDEN, CHUR
UND FURSTEN" see Werner, Kurt

DAS KRIAG'N MA NIMMERMEHR
(Lessky, Fr.) mix cor DOBLINGER G 686
s.p. see from Sechs Lieder Aus Wien
    (D41)

DAS KROKODIL "IM HEIL'GEN TEICH ZU
SINGAPUR" see Fussan, Werner

DAS LACHENDE PARADIES see Desch, Rudolf

DAS LAUB FALLT VON DEN BAUMEN see
Schroeder, Hermann

DAS LEBEN-EIN WANDERN see Zentner,
Johannes

DAS LEBENSLICHT see Knab, Armin

DAS LICHT see Pepping, Ernst

DAS LIEBEN BRINGT GROSS FREUD see
Silcher, Friedrich

DAS LIEBEN BRINGT GROSS FREUD (1) see
Edler, Robert

DAS LIEBEN BRINGT GROSS FREUD (2) see
Edler, Robert

DAS LIEBEN BRINGT SICH GROSS FREUD
*folk
(Biebl, Franz) men cor,acap TONOS 169
s.p.   (D42)

DAS LIED DER SEELE see Desch, Rudolf

DAS LIED VOM BECHERLEIN see Zanzi, G.

DAS LIED VON BLONDEN KORKEN see Hilger,
Manfred

DAS LIED VON BURLALA see Linke, Norbert

DAS LIEDCHEN VON LIEBE see Edler,
Robert

DAS LOB DER HEIMAT see Philipp, Franz

DAS MADCHEN see Brahms, Johannes

DAS MADCHEN AUS SCHEVENINGEN see
Strohbach, Siegfried, Het Meisje
Van Scheveningen

DAS MADCHEN MIT DEN HELLEN AUGEN see
Edler, Robert

DAS MADCHEN VOM LANDE "EI, MADCHEN VOM LANDE" see Erdlen, Hermann

DAS MADCHEN VON MISOX see Ammann, Benno

DAS MADCHEN WOLLT' EIN FREIER HABEN see Zipp, Friedrich

DAS MAIDLEIN WOLLT EIN LIEBSTEN HAN see Zoll, Paul

DAS MANNLEIN IM WEINBERG "WENN DIE REBEN BLUHN" see Lang, Hans

DAS MANNSBACKELIED VON DER SCHONEN MARIENKA see Zehm, Friedrich

DAS MARCHEN HIESS TAHITI "ES WAR EINMAL EIN MARCHEN" see Merath, Siegfried

DAS MARCHEN VON DEN TANZENDEN SCHWEINEN see Werdin, Eberhard

DAS MUSIKATNUSSCHEN *folk,Ger
   (Geiss, Gottfried) men cor,acap TONOS
   4570-2 s.p.   (D43)

DAS NASCHHAFTE KATZCHEN *folk
   (Deutschmann, G.) [Ger] 4pt mix cor
   MERSEBURG EM9202 s.p.   (D44)

DAS NASOBEM see Tischhauser, Franz

DAS NEUE HAUS see Desch, Rudolf

DAS NEUE JAHR see Burthel, Jakob

DAS NEUE KURRENDEHEFT *CCU
   2-3pt wom cor/2-3pt treb cor,acap/
   inst MERSEBURG EM774 s.p.   (D45)

DAS PFEIFENKRAMER-LIED
   (Deutsch, Walter) mix cor DOBLINGER
   G 677 s.p. see from Acht Lieder Aus
   Wien   (D46)

DAS REH IM WINTER see Zentner, Johannes

DAS RIESENSPIEL see Bresgen, Cesar

DAS RINGLEIN *folk
   (Seeger, P.) [Ger] 4pt men cor
   MERSEBURG EM9039 s.p.   (D47)

DAS SAMENKORN see Fegers, Karl

DAS SCHIFFLEIN AUF DER DRAVE "FAHRT EIN SCHIFFLEIN LANGSAM SACHT" see Baumann, Max

DAS SCHIFFLEIN: EIN SCHIFFLEIN ZIEHET see Silcher, Friedrich

DAS SCHLARAFFENLAND see Bresgen, Cesar

DAS SCHONSTE LAND *folk,Ger
   (Nother, Willi) men cor,acap TONOS
   113 s.p.   (D48)

DAS SILBERNE HORNLEIN see Rein, Walter

DAS TAGEWERK see Piechler, Arthur

DAS TRUNKENE LIED see Heun, Hans

DAS TUCHLEIN see Limpiate Con Mi Panuelo

DAS UNAUFHORLICHE see Hindemith, Paul

DAS VERLASSENE MAGDELEIN "TREU UND HERZINNIGLICH" see Zoll, Paul

DAS VERLASSENE MAGDLEIN "FRUH, WANN DIE HAHNE KRAHN see Schroeder, Hermann

DAS VIELVERLIEBTE HERZ see Edler, Robert

DAS VOLKSLIED see Sibille, Josef

DAS WALDECKER LIED see Anders, Alfred

DAS WALDHORN see Lang, Hans

DAS WALDKONZERT "KONZERT IST HEUTE ANGESAGT" see Zoll, Paul

DAS WEISSE ENTLEIN see Lucic, Franjo, Raca Plava Po Dravi

DAS WEITE LAND
   unis wom cor SCHOTTS C 42 533F s.p.
   see also Alle Singen Heft 2   (D49)

DAS WERMELANDER LIED "O WERMELAND, DU SCHONES" see Mendelssohn, Arnold

DAS WESSOBRUNNER GEBET see Krietsch, Georg

DAS ZWEITE DT 64 LIEDERBUCH *CCU
   HOFMEISTER W114 s.p.   (D50)

DASHING AWAY WITH THE SMOOTHING IRON see Byrt, John C.

DASS DU MICH MEIDEST see Nitsche, Paul, Greensleeves

DASS UNSRE LIEBE EINE HEIMAT HAT see Kohler, Siegfried

DASS ZWEI SICH HERZLICH LIEBEN see Weber, Bernhard

DAVE TONI ARTHUR SONG BOOK, THE *CC21U
   (Arthur, D.; Arthur, T.) cor GALLIARD
   2.2025:7 $1.75   (D51)

DAVENPORT, G.
   This Canada
     unis HARRIS $.25   (D52)

DAVID AND GOLIATH see Detweiler, Alan

DAVID AND GOLIATH see Pottle, Sam

DAVID, SWING YOUR SLING see North, Jack

DAVIDSON
   Banjo Man, The *see Sanders

   Composition Blues *see Sanders

   I Love Snow *see Sanders

   It's A Big Christmas World *see Sanders

   Man In The Red Suit, The *see Sanders

DAVIDSON, LYLE
   Voices Of The Dark
     SATB,electronic tape sc SCHIRM.EC
     2943 s.p., ipa   (D53)

DAVIES, EVAN T.
   Winds, The *see Y Gwyntoedd

   Y Gwyntoedd
     "Winds, The" [Eng/Welsh] TTBB,acap
     CURWEN 50535 s.p.   (D54)

DAVIES, HENRY WALFORD (1869-1941)
   Everyman
     SATB,SATB soli,3fl,2ob,3clar,2bsn,
     4horn,2trp,3trom,tuba,timp,perc,
     harp,org,strings voc sc NOVELLO
     rental   (D55)

DAVIES, LAWRENCE H.
   Cavern, The
     unis ASHDOWN U97   (D56)

   Rock Him Gently
     SA CRAMER $.20   (D57)

DAVIS
   Rainbow Girl
     SATB,pno/gtr MCAFEE M145 $.35   (D58)

   Two Hundred Years Ago
     unis, opt piccolo, hand bells, tom-
     tom, snare drum WARNER WB-361
     $.45   (D59)

DAVIS, BILL
   Country Sunshine (composed with West,
     Dottie)
     (Metis, F.) SSA BIG3 $.45   (D60)
     (Metis, F.) SATB BIG3 $.50   (D61)
     (Metis, F.) SAB BIG3 $.45   (D62)

DAVIS, KATHERINE K. (1892-   )
   Lamb, The
     SA GALAXY 1.2442.1 $.30   (D63)

   Shot Heard Round The World, The
     SATB,org,opt trp WARNER WB-356 187
     $.40   (D64)

   Swedish Dance Carol *Xmas
     SSA GALAXY 1.1187.1 $.40   (D65)

DAVIS, SCOTT
   Memories *see Strange, Billy

DAWN IN THE WOOD see Cadman, Charles Wakefield

DAWSON, WILLIAM LEVI (1898-   )
   Go To Sleep
     SSA (easy) FITZSIMONS 3010 $.20
                                           (D66)
     SA (easy) FITZSIMONS 3026 $.20
                                           (D67)
     TTBB (easy) FITZSIMONS 4010 $.20
                                           (D68)
     SATB (easy) FITZSIMONS 1006 $.20
                                           (D69)
   Slumber Song
     SA TUSKEGEE T136 $.35   (D70)
     SSA TUSKEGEE T137 $.40   (D71)
     SATB TUSKEGEE T138 $.40   (D72)
     TTBB TUSKEGEE T139 $.40   (D73)

DAY see Aim, Vojtech Borivoj, Den

DAY see Nejedly, Vit, Den

DAY AFTER DAY THEY ALL SAY "SING" see Lassus, Roland de (Orlandus), Tutto Lo Di Mi Dici "Canta"

DAY AND NIGHT see Weigl, Vally

DAY COLUMBUS LANDED HERE
   (Johnston, Richard A.) TTBB (med
   diff) WATERLOO $.50   (D74)

DAY DREAMING
   SA CIMINO $.40   (D75)
   SAB CIMINO $.40   (D76)
   SSA CIMINO $.40   (D77)
   SATB CIMINO $.40   (D78)
   TTBB CIMINO $.40   (D79)

DAY HAS COME, THE see Leeds

DAY IN THE LIFE OF. . . , A see Epen de Groot, Else van, "Een Dag Uit Het Leven Van. . . "

DAY IS DARK AND DREARY, THE see Bergren, Alfred Hiles

DAY, P.
   As The Branch Is To The Vine
     (Martindale) SA LESLIE 2048 $.40
                                           (D80)

DAY TRIPPER see Lennon, John

DE BLAUWE SCHUUR see Middeleer, Jean De

DE GLANS VAN HELLAS see Maessen, Antoon

DE HAMBORGER VEERMASTER "ICK HEFF MOL EN HAMBORGER VEERMASTER SEHN" see Erdlen, Hermann

DE HEABENLY CHOIR see Mana-Zucca, Mme.

DE LOS ALAMOS VENGO see Vasquez, Juan

DE OADEBOAR *folk
   (Felt, Gerhard) SSA MOSELER LB1007
   s.p. see from Abend An Der Memel
                                           (D81)

DE PROFUNDIS
   (Pohl, Frederick) SSAATTBB (diff)
   WATERLOO $.75   (D82)

DE SUTTER, J.TOUSSAINT
   L'Idylle Des Voix
     mix cor sc BROGNEAUX s.p.   (D83)

   Printemps
     mix cor sc BROGNEAUX s.p.   (D84)

DE VIERDE KRAAI OFTEWEL DE KRAAIENDE VIER (TRIJNTJE FOP) see Kox, Hans

DE VOTRE BEAUTE REGARDER see Apotheloz, Jean

DEALE, E.M.
   Castle Of Dromore, The
     SSA CRAMER $.25   (D85)

DEAR DARK HEAD see Maw

DEAR HARP OF MY COUNTRY
   (Hill, Harry) SAB (easy) WATERLOO
   $.30   (D86)

DEAR HEART
   SSA CIMINO $.40   (D87)
   SAB CIMINO $.40   (D88)
   TTBB CIMINO $.40   (D89)
   SATB CIMINO $.40   (D90)

DEAR HOPE, BLEST CHILD OF THE SKIES see Anonymous, Espoir, Toi Fille Des Cieux!

DEAR, IF YOU CHANGE see Dowland, John

DEAR LOVE, OF THEE ALONE see Hassler, Hans Leo

DEARLY BELOVED
   SA CIMINO $.40   (D91)
   SATB CIMINO $.40   (D92)
   TTBB CIMINO $.40   (D93)

DEATH see Foerster, Josef Bohuslav, Skon

DEATH, BE NOT PROUD see Goossen, Frederic

DEATH BE NOT PROUD see Jenni

DEATH, BE NOT PROUD see Russell

DEATH OF PROKOP THE GREAT, THE see Bendl, Karel, Smrt Prokopa Velikeho

DEBOUT FAUCHEURS see Goffin, A.

DEBRECEN DICSERETE see Sarai, Tibor

DEBUSSY, CLAUDE (1862-1918)
  Clair De Lune
    (Elkan, Henri) [Fr/Eng] 3 eq
    voices,acap JOBERT sc s.p., cor
    pts s.p.   (D94)

  Harom Korusdal *CCU
    (Forrai, Miklos; Szabo, Ferenc) mix
    cor BUDAPEST 6707 s.p.   (D95)

  La Damoiselle Elue
    mix cor,solo,orch HENN s.p.   (D96)

  Mandoline
    (Lethbridge) unis/SA (easy) OXFORD
    82.101 $.45   (D97)

  Sirenes (from Trois Nocturnes)
    2pt wom cor,pno/orch JOBERT voc sc
    s.p., cor pts s.p.   (D98)

DECAMP, CARROLL
  Portrait Of Christmas
    SATB STUDIO V7110 $.45   (D99)

DECEMBER CHILD see Moline

DECK THE HALL *Xmas,carol
  (Willcocks) SATB,acap (med easy)
  OXFORD 84.200 $.40   (D100)

DECK THE HALLS see Kirk

DECOLLAGE, MUSIK ZU LIGHT-SOUND see
  Holler, York

DE CORMIER, ROBERT (1922-   )
  Christmas Is Coming *Xmas
    SATB SCHIRM.G LG51752 $.30   (D101)

DEDRICK
  Like To Love, Like To Sing About
    Sunshine
    (Coates) TTBB SHAWNEE C239 $.40
                                     (D102)
DEDRICK, C.
  Canada In Springtime
    SATB,opt inst KENDOR $.45, ipa
                                     (D103)
  Chorale And Fugue
    SATB,acap KENDOR $.35   (D104)
    SAB,acap KENDOR $.35   (D105)

  Goin' Back *pop
    SATB,opt perc KENDOR $.30   (D106)
    SAB,opt perc KENDOR $.30   (D107)

  I Wanna Be There
    SATB,opt inst KENDOR $.45, ipa
                                     (D108)
  Kum Ba Yah
    SATB,opt perc KENDOR $.35, ipa
                                     (D109)
  Like To Love *pop
    SATB,opt perc KENDOR $.40   (D110)
    SAB,opt perc KENDOR $.40   (D111)

  Love Does Not Die
    SATB,opt drums, electric bass
    KENDOR $.45   (D112)

  Peter, Paul, And Mary
    SATB,opt perc KENDOR $.45, ipa
                                     (D113)
  Pineapple, Crabapple
    SATB,acap KENDOR $.45   (D114)
    SAB,acap KENDOR $.45   (D115)

  Spring Fever *pop
    SATB,SAT soli,opt perc KENDOR $.40
                                     (D116)
  Stay
    SATB,opt inst KENDOR $.45, ipa
                                     (D117)
  Symbols Ring, The
    SATB,opt inst KENDOR $.45, ipa
                                     (D118)
  There Is A Song
    SATB,opt inst KENDOR $.35   (D119)

DEE
  End Of The World, The *see Kent

DEEP BLUE SEA
  (De Cormier) SATB SCHIRM.G LG51754
  $.35   (D120)

DEEP RIVER *spir
  "Tiefe Fluten" see Spirtuals For All
    Heft II
  (Biebl, Franz) treb cor DOBLINGER
    O 312 s.p. see from Acht Spirituals
                                     (D121)
  (Hall, Wm.D.) SAATTBB,Bar solo,acap
    NATIONAL WHC-8 $.35   (D122)
  (Kubizek, Augustin) "Hinuber" men cor
    DOBLINGER M 325 s.p.   (D123)
  (Roberton, Hugh S.) SATBB,acap (easy)
    FITZSIMONS 1035 $.20   (D124)

DEER CRIES FOR FLOWING WATER, THE see
  Bernhard

DEERING'S WOODS see Clarke, Henry
  Leland

DEFEAT OF SENNACHERIB see Mussorgsky,
  Modest

DE GRANDIS, RENATO (1927-   )
  Invocazione Della Terra
    cor,acap ZERBONI 7908 s.p.   (D125)

  La Comedia Veneziana
    SSAATTBB,SB soli,pno,bvl,harp,perc,
    harmonica, mandolin (diff) sc
    SCHOTTS rental, ipr contains
    also: Un Veneto Cantar (SSAATTBB,
    acap)   (D126)

  Un Veneto Cantar
    see De Grandis, Renato, La Comedia
    Veneziana

DEIN HERZLEIN MILD see Brahms, Johannes

DEKUJI TI, PRAHO see Novak, Jiri F.

DELACHER, HERMANN
  Grablied
    men cor,acap TONOS 5813 s.p. (D127)

  Mutterlied
    men cor,acap TONOS 5814 s.p. (D128)

DELLO JOIO, NORMAN (1913-   )
  Come To Me, My Love
    SATB MARKS MC 4609 $.45   (D129)

  Leisure
    SATB AMP A-716 $.45   (D130)

  Poet's Song, The
    SATB AMP A-709 $.45   (D131)

DELNIKOVA RUKA see Kanak, Zdenek

DELTA DAWN see Harvey, Alex

DEM NEUEN JAHRE "NUN KOMMST DU
  HERGEGANGEN" see Zipp, Friedrich

DEMON OF ADACHIGAHARA see Crosse

DEN see Aim, Vojtech Borivoj

DEN see Nejedly, Vit

DEN BLOMSTERTID NU KOMMER see Kvam,
  Oddvar S.

DEN GEFALLENEN "UNTER DEN KREUZEN" see
  Weber, Bernhard

DEN LETZTEN BEISST DER HUND see
  Bresgen, Cesar

DEN ODE DNE SE SIRI see Haba, Alois

DEN SOMMEREN see Mostad, Jon

DEN TOTEN "FREI VON MENSCHLICHEN
  GEBOTEN" see Knab, Armin

DEN WEIN SCHENKT EIN see Heinrichs,
  Hans L.

DENIS, DIDIER (1947-   )
  La Vieille Danse
    cor,S solo,pno,vln,vla,vcl,fl,clar,
    perc RIDEAU s.p.   (D132)

  Le Coq
    12pt mix cor RIDEAU s.p.   (D133)

DENKEN DIE HIMMLISCHEN see Reutter,
  Hermann

DENKMAELER DER TONKUNST IN OESTERREICH
    *sac/sec,CCU
  microfiche UNIV.MUS.ED. editors
  include: Haber; Rietsch; Bezecny;
  Wolf, Johannes; Nettl, Paul;
  Webern, Albert Von and others.
  Originally published as 83 volumes
  in 79 bindings. $495.00   (D134)

DENKMAELER DEUTSCHER TONKUNST *sac/
    sec,CCU
  (Musikgeschichtlichen Kommission;
  Moser, Hans Joachim; Crosby Jr., C.
  Russel) microfiche UNIV.MUS.ED. 65
  volumes, includes original
  Breitkopf and Haertel edition of
  1892-1931 with critical revisions
  by Akademische Druckund
  Verlagsantalt, Graz, 1957-1961.
  $425.00   (D135)

DENVER, JOHN
  Annie's Song
    (Metis) 2pt,opt bvl&gtr WARNER
    WB-376 $.40   (D136)
    (Metis) SSA,opt bvl&gtr WARNER
    WB-375 $.50   (D137)
    (Metis) SATB,opt bvl&gtr WARNER
    WB-373 $.50   (D138)
    (Metis) SAB,opt bvl&gtr WARNER
    WB-374 $.50   (D139)

DENVER, JOHN (cont'd.)

    (Siltman) TBB WARNER CT0770 $.40
                                     (D140)
  Back Home Again
    (Metis) SATB WARNER CH0786 $.40
                                     (D141)
  Eagle And The Hawk, The (composed
    with Taylor) *pop
    (Bretton; Fox) SSA,opt perc WARNER
    WB-355 183 $.50   (D142)
    (Bretton; Fox) SATB,opt perc WARNER
    WB-354 187 $.50   (D143)

  Farewell Andromeda *pop
    (Bune) "Welcome To My Morning"
    SATB,pno/gtr WARNER WB-346 187
    $.50   (D144)

  I'd Rather Be A Cowboy (Lady's
    Chains) *pop
    (Bune) SATB,pno/bvl,gtr, harmonica
    WARNER WB-325 187 $.75   (D145)

  Sunshine On My Shoulders (composed
    with Kniss; Taylor) *pop
    (Bune) SATB,pno/gtr WARNER
    WB-356 187 $.40   (D146)
    (Bune) SATB,opt fl&bvl&gtr WARNER
    WB-372 $.50   (D147)
    (Ehret) SAB WARNER WB-368 $.50
                                     (D148)
    (Ehret) SA/SSA WARNER WB-367 $.35
                                     (D149)

  Take Me Home, Country Roads *see
    Danoff

  Welcome To My Morning *see Farewell
    Andromeda

DER ABEND IST DA *folk
  (Lang, H.) [Ger] 4pt men cor
    MERSEBURG EM9004 s.p.   (D150)
  (Zipp, F.) [Ger] 4pt mix cor
    MERSEBURG EM9230 s.p.   (D151)

DER ABEND "SENKE, STRAHLENDER GOTT" see
  Reutter, Hermann

DER ABENDHIMMEL see Bruckner, Anton

DER ALTE BERNER MARSCH "ALLI MANNE
  STANDET" see Ammann, Benno

DER ALTE FORSTER PUSTERICH see Rein,
  Walter

DER ALTE HERR PROFESSOR see Francaix,
  Jean

DER APFEL "ICH GEB' MEINEM LIEB EINEN
  APFEL" see Zoll, Paul, I Will Give
  My Love An Apple

DER AUSBRUCH DES BAUERNKRIEGES see
  Kunad, Rainer

DER BACH "INMITTEN DES RAUSCHENDEN
  HERBSTREGENS" see Zipp, Friedrich

DER BAUER see Schertzer, Daniel, Le
  Bouvier

DER BAUER "HINTERM PFLUG, IN GLEICHEM
  SCHRITT" see Fussan, Werner

DER BEREDSAMKEIT "FREUNDE, WASSER
  MACHET STUMM" see Haydn, (Franz)
  Joseph

DER BETRUNKENE SEEMANN "WAS SOLLN WIR
  TUN" see Kubizek, Augustinian

DER BIGAMIST see Hollfelder, Waldram

DER BLUMEN RACHE see Pfitzner, Hans

DER BOHMISCHE WIND *folk,Ger
  (Erdlen, Hermann) men cor,acap TONOS
    33 s.p.   (D152)

DER BRAUTIGAM see Brahms, Johannes

DER BREITE FLUSS *folk
  (Schrey, W.) [Ger] 4pt men cor
    MERSEBURG EM9032 s.p.   (D153)

DER BROTCHENVERKAUFER *folk
  (Biebl, F.) [Ger] 4pt men cor
    MERSEBURG EM9079 s.p.   (D154)

DER BUCKLICHTE FIEDLER see Brahms,
  Johannes

DER BUCKLIGTE FIEDLER see Erdlen,
  Hermann

DER BUHLE IM KELLER "DEN LIEBSTEN
  BULEN" see Werdin, Eberhard

DER BUTZEMANN "ES TANZT EIN BUTZEMANN"
  see Haas, Joseph

DER D-ZUG KOMMT *folk,US
  (Rosenstengel, Albrecht) men cor,opt
    gtr,opt perc sc,cor pts TONOS 2301

s.p. (D155)

DER DU DIE ZEIT IN HANDEN HAST see Zipp, Friedrich

DER EDELSTE BRUNNEN "MAN SAGT WOL" see Werdin, Eberhard

DER EDLE DUKE OF YORK see Noble Duke Of York, The

DER ENTFERNTEN see Schubert, Franz (Peter)

DER ESEL see Leist, Peter Marzellin

DER ESEL see Schmid, A.

DER ESEL "ES STAND VOR EINES HAUSES TOR" see Klein, Richard Rudolf

DER EWIGE STROM see Maler, Wilhelm

DER FAHRMANN "BEIM SCHEIN DES MONDENLICHTS" see Rettich, Wilhelm

DER FALKE see Brahms, Johannes

DER FAULE SCHAFER see Sturmer, Bruno

DER FISCHER UND DAS MADCHEN *folk
(Beckerath, A. Von) [Ger] 4pt mix cor MERSEBURG EM9204 s.p. (D156)

DER FLOH see Fegers, Karl

DER FREIER *folk
(Dietsch, F.) [Ger] 4pt men cor MERSEBURG EM9067 s.p. (D157)

DER FREISCHUTZ ALS THEATERZETTEL see Kassmayer

DER FROHE WANDERSMANN see Mendelssohn-Bartholdy, Felix

DER FROHLICHE SCHIFFER "SCHIMOTZUI IST EIN GUTER HAFEN" see Sakamoto, Yoshitaka, Shimotzui Bushi

DER FROHLICHKEIT LASST IHREN LAUF see Fresen, Heinrich

DER FROSCH SITZT IN DEM ROHRE see Lang, Hans

DER FUNFTON *CCU
(Jode, Fritz; Kraus, Egon) jr cor (easy) sc SCHOTTS B 123 s.p. (D158)

DER FUNKE see Fegers, Karl

DER GANG ZUR WIEGE see Erdlen, Hermann

DER GARTNER see Ketterer, Ernst

DER GECK "EIN BURSCH IST IM STADTCHEN" see Lang, Hans

DER GEFALLIGE NACHBAR see Haag, Heinz

DER GELIEBTEN: WAS, TRAUTE BRUDER see Silcher, Friedrich

DER GESCHEITE HANSEL "HANSEL AM BACH" see Haas, Joseph

DER GLUCKLICHE see Mendelssohn-Bartholdy, Felix

DER GLUCKLICHE BAUER see Reutter, Hermann

DER GLUCKLICHE FARMER see Happy Farmer, The

DER GOLDVOGEL see Bresgen, Cesar

DER GONDELFAHRER "ES TANZEN MOND UND STERNE" see Schubert, Franz (Peter)

DER GREIS "HIN IST ALLE MEINE KRAFT" see Haydn, (Franz) Joseph

DER GRIMASSENTANZ "WIR TANZEN UND SCHNEIDEN FRATZEN" see Klefisch, Walter

DER GROSSE KALENDER see Reutter, Hermann

DER GUTE KAMERAD: ICH HATT EINEN KAMERAD see Silcher, Friedrich

DER GUTZGAUCH AUF DEM ZAUNE SASS see Lemlin, Lorenz

DER HAHN "ZORNKAMM. GOCKEL, KORNERSCHLINGER" see Sutermeister, Heinrich

DER HECHT "HECHTFISCH KAM DAHER" see Stravinsky, Igor

DER HELD "DEN WIR ZUM SCHATZ ERKOREN" see Lang, Hans

DER HELLE TAG
unis wom cor SCHOTTS C 42 532F s.p. see also Alle Singen Heft 1 (D159)

DER HERBST BEGINNT
unis wom cor SCHOTTS C 42 533J s.p. see also Alle Singen Heft 2 (D160)

DER HERBST DES EINSAMEN see Moeschinger, Albert

DER HERD see Pepping, Ernst

DER HERR ROUSSELLE *folk
(Biebl, F.) [Ger] 4pt mix cor MERSEBURG EM9226 s.p. (D161)

DER HERZENSDIEB *folk
(Fischbach, Klaus) wom cor,pno,opt fl sc BREITKOPF-W CHB 4918 s.p. see from Sieben Europaische Volkslieder (D162)

DER HEUSCHRECK *folk
(Rietz, Johannes) men cor,acap TONOS 4201 s.p. (D163)

DER HEUSCHRECK see Rietz, Johannes

DER HIRT see Fredrich, Gunter

DER HOFFNUNGSLOSE "ICH SCHAUTE IN DEN NEBEL" see Genzmer, Harald

DER HUFSCHMIED "SCHWARZBRAUNER HUFSCHMIED" see Rein, Walter

DER HUHNERDIEB "IHR WISST, WAS IN DER ZEITUNG STAND" see Desch, Rudolf

DER JAGER *folk,Ger
(Kracke, H.) men cor,acap TONOS 124 s.p. (D164)
(Lang, H.) [Ger] 4pt men cor MERSEBURG EM9005 s.p. (D165)

DER JAGER see Brahms, Johannes

DER JAGER see Rasch, Hugo

DER JAGER ABSCHIED see Mendelssohn-Bartholdy, Felix

DER JAGER AUS KURPFALZ see Lang, Hans

DER JAGER UND SEIN LIEBCHEN "ES JAGT EIN JAGER WOHLGEMUT" see Zipp, Friedrich

DER JODELPLATZ: Z'NACHST BIN I HALT see Silcher, Friedrich

DER JUGEND MORGENGESANG see Seeger, Peter

DER JUNGBRUNNEN see Linke, Norbert

DER JUNGGESELLE *folk,Slav
(Zschiegner, Fritz) men cor,opt pno, opt inst,opt perc sc,voc sc TONOS 2117 s.p. (D166)

DER KAISER VON CHINA "IN DER MITTE ALLER DINGE" see Sutermeister, Heinrich

DER KEHRAUS see Weber, Bernhard

DER KIEBITZ "DER HERGOTT HANGT DIE SONN' HERAUS" see Haas, Joseph

DER KLEINE TSCHING "DER KLEINE TSCHING SUCHT EINEN RING" see Merath, Siegfried

DER KLEINEN KATZE TOD see Francaix, Jean

DER KOBOLD "DAS HAUS HAB ICH ERBAUT" see Lang, Hans

DER KONIG IN THULE "ES WAR EIN KONIG IN THULE" see Lang, Hans

DER KOSAK " IN DEM GRUNEN WALDE" see Zipp, Friedrich

DER KRAKAUER *folk
(Doppelbauer, J. F.) [Ger] 4pt men cor MERSEBURG EM9035 s.p. (D167)

DER KRIEG IST AUS see Krietsch, Georg

DER KUCKUCK see Steffens, Johann

DER KUCKUCK AUF DEM TURME SASS see Marx, Karl

DER KUCKUCK AUF DEM ZAUNE see Lemacher, Heinrich

DER KUCKUCK AUF DEM ZAUNE SASS see Stephani, Johann

DER KUCKUCK "AUF EINEM BAUM EIN KUCKUCK SASS" see Lang, Hans

DER KUCKUCK RUFT IM GRUNEN WALD see Zoll, Paul

DER KUHLE MAIEN see Schein, Johann Hermann

DER LERCHE "HORT DIE ERSTE LERCHE SINGEN" see Zoll, Paul

DER LIEBE EWIGKEIT "DIE LIEBE HEMMET NICHTS" see Rein, Walter

DER LIEBE LANGE TAG see Edler, Robert

DER LIEBESBRUNNEN *folk
(Klink, W.) [Ger] 4pt mix cor MERSEBURG EM9220 s.p. (D168)

DER LIEBSTE BUHLE "DEN LIEBSTEN BUHLEN, DEN ICH HAN" see Rein, Walter

DER LINDENBAUM see Loewe

DER LINDENBAUM: AM BRUNNEN see Silcher, Friedrich

DER MAI IST GEKOMMEN see Jage, Rolf-Diether

DER MAIE see Knab, Armin

DER MAIEN, DER MAIEN BRINGT UNS DER BLUMLEIN VIEL
(Nehrkorn, Alex) SATB MOSELER LB540 (D169)

DER MANN IM MOND see Bresgen, Cesar

DER MARSCH DER KONIGE "DES MORGENS FRUH IM DAMMER" see Zoll, Paul

DER MAYEN, DER PRINGT UNS PLUEMELEIN VIL see Wimberger, Gerhard

DER MENSCH LEBT UND BESTEHET see Doppelbauer, Josef Friedrich

DER MINNEBOTE: ES FLOG EIN see Weber, Bernhard

DER MOND see Orrel, Max

DER MOND DER STEHT AM HOCHSTEN see Othmayr, Kaspar

DER MOND IST AUFGEGANGEN see Fussan, Werner

DER MOND IST AUFGEGANGEN see Kuhlenthal, Fred

DER MOND IST AUFGEGANGEN see Lang, Hans

DER MOND IST AUFGEGANGEN see Schulz

DER MOND IST AUFGEGANGEN see Thehos, Adam

DER MOND SOLL IM KALENDAR STEHN see Zipp, Friedrich

DER MORGEN see Pepping, Ernst

DER MORGEN see Seib, Valentin

DER MORGEN HEBT DIE FLUGEL see Heinrichs, Hans L.

DER MORGEN IST ERWACHT "NUN GILT'S! DIE TAGELANGEN" see Ophoven, Hermann

DER MORGENSTERN "HORCH AUS DER GESTORBNEN DAMMERWELT" see Lang, Hans

DER MORGENSTERN IST AUFGEGANGEN see Knab, Armin

DER MUSIKALISCHE DRACHE "IHR LEUTE, HORT" see Haus, Karl

DER MUSIKANT see Wallas, Herbert

DER MUSIKATELLER *folk
(Krietsch, G.) men cor,acap TONOS 25 s.p. (D170)

DER MUTIGE JAGER "JETZT NEHM ICH MEINE FLINTE" see Zoll, Paul

DER NEUE JAHRGANG see Edler, Robert

DER OPTIMIST see Hollfelder, Waldram

DER OZEAN see Edler, Robert

DER PAPAGEI AUS KUBA see Sutermeister, Heinrich

DER PESSIMIST see Hollfelder, Waldram

DER PFERDEMIST see Hollfelder, Waldram

DER PFIFFIGE PAL   *folk
   (Gramss, K.) [Ger] 4pt mix cor
   MERSEBURG EM9213 s.p.   (D171)

DER PFLAUMENBAUM "IM HOFE STEHT EIN
   PFLAUMENBAUM" see Poos, Heinrich

DER PILGRIM see Bausznern, Dietrich von

DER POSTILLON   *folk
   (Geiss, Gottfried) men cor,opt trp
   TONOS 4231 s.p.   (D172)

DER POSTILLON "WAS WILLST DU AUF DIESER
   STATION" see Mohler, Philipp

DER PRINZ "WIR WOLLTEN ZUSAMMEN BAUEN"
   see Schubert, Heino

DER RATTENFANGER see Krietsch, Georg

DER REGEN see Schnitzler, Heinrich

DER REGENBOGEN see Rein, Walter

DER REGENBOGEN see Rein, Walter

DER REIF UND AUCH DER KALTE SCHNEE see
   Lendvai, Erwin

DER REITER   *folk
   (Biebl, F.) [Ger] 4pt men cor
   MERSEBURG EM9072 s.p.   (D173)

DER REITER UND DAS MADCHEN "WOHLAN DIE
   ZEIT IST KOMMEN" see Lang, Hans

DER RODENSTEINER see Klingler, Ludwig

DER ROMISCHE BRUNNEN see Burkhard Willy

DER ROMISCHE BRUNNEN "AUFSTEIGT DER
   STRAHL" see Schroeder, Hermann

DER ROSENGARTEN see Thehos, Adam

DER ROSENGARTEN "ICH WEISS EIN GARTEN"
   see Rein, Walter

DER ROTE PLATZ see Spies, Leo

DER ROTE SARAFAN   *Russ
   (Warlamoff; Karpowitsch) men cor
   ZIMMER. 592 s.p.   (D174)

DER RUF DER FREIHEIT see Lendvai, Erwin

DER SAEMANN see Burkhart, Franz

DER SAMANN see Leist, Peter Marzellin

DER SANDWIRT   *folk,Aus
   (Kanetscheider, Artur) men cor,acap
   TONOS 808 s.p.   (D175)

DER SCHLITTEN EILT see Zoll, Paul

DER SCHMIED "BEGRUSS DEN MORGENFRISCHEN
   TAG" see Koelble, Fritz

DER SCHNEIDER AUF DER WANDERSCHAFT "ES
   WOLLT' EIN SCHNEIDER WANDERN" see
   Lang, Hans

DER SCHNEIDER VON ULM "BISCHOF, ICH
   KANN FLIEGEN" see Poos, Heinrich

DER SCHNUPFEN "FIN SCHNUPFEN HOCKT AUF
   DER TERASSE" see Nitsche, Paul

DER SCHONE SOMMER GEHT UNS HEREIN see
   Beck, Conrad

DER SCHULCHOR BAND I   *CC82L
   mix cor SCHOTTS ED. 5401 s.p.
      contains works by: Albert;
      Bornefeld; Franck; Knab; Mohler;
      Reger; Walter and others   (D176)

DER SCHULCHOR BAND V: MADRIGALE UND
   CHANSONS   *CC42L,Eng/Fr/Ger/It
   mix cor SCHOTTS ED. 5405 s.p.
      contains works by: Verdelot;
      Vecchi; Debussy; Poulenc; Gibbons;
      Morley; Widmann; Haussmann and
      others   (D177)

DER SCHWARZE MOND "IN DIE MONDLOSE
   NACHT" see Genzmer, Harald

DER SEUFZER "EIN SEUFZER LIEF
   SCHLITTSCHUH" see Nitsche, Paul

DER SICH EIN FAULES GRETCHEN see
   Michels, Josef

DER SINGKREISEL   *CCU,canon
   (Jode, Fritz) jr cor (med easy) sc
   SCHOTTS B 101 s.p.   (D178)

DER SOMMER "SOMMER, ACH SOMMER" see
   Zoll, Paul

DER SPIEGEL see Bartok, Bela,
   Lanycsufolo

DER STEIN see Fegers, Karl

DER STRUWWELPETER see Bresgen, Cesar

DER STRUWWELPETER see Hessenberg, Kurt

DER TAG BEGINNT ZU VERGEHEN see Albert,
   Heinrich

DER TAG BRICHT AN see Edler, Robert

DER TAG, ER ENDET see Edler, Robert

DER TAG VERTREIBT DIE DUNKLE NACHT see
   Praetorius, Michael

DER TAG VERTREIBT DIE FINSTRE NACHT see
   Metzler, Friedrich

DER TALER "HAB' GEFUNDEN EINEN TALER"
   see Biebl, Franz

DER TAMBOUR "WENN MEINE MUTTER HEXEN
   KONNT" see Rein, Walter

DER TANZ "WO IM FROHEN ZECHERKREISE"
   see Rossini, Gioacchino

DER TOD "GESTERN, BRUDER, KONNT IHRS
   GLAUBEN" see Genzmer, Harald

DER TOD IST HERGEKOMMEN see Edler,
   Robert

DER TOD VON FLANDERN "DER TOD REIT' AUF
   EINEM KOHLSCHWARZEN RAPPEN" see
   Mohler, Philipp

DER TRAUMENDE SEE see Schumann, Robert
   (Alexander)

DER TRAUMENDE SEE "DER SEE RUHT TIEF IM
   BLAUEN TRAUM" see Schumann, Robert
   (Alexander)

DER TREUE KNABE   *folk,Ger
   (Biebl, Franz) men cor,acap TONOS 65
   s.p.   (D179)

DER TRUNKENE DICHTER see Biebl, Franz

DER VERLIEBTE   *folk
   (Seeger, P.) [Ger] 4pt men cor
   MERSEBURG EM9040 s.p.   (D180)

DER VERSCHWUNDENE STERN "ES STAND EIN
   STERNLEIN AM HIMMEL" see Genzmer,
   Harald

DER VOGEL ABSCHIED "ADE, IHR
   FELSENHALLEN" see Hessenberg, Kurt

DER WAGEN see Pepping, Ernst

DER WAGEN HEFT 1: BAUERNGARTEN see
   Pepping, Ernst

DER WAGEN HEFT 2: DAS LICHT see
   Pepping, Ernst

DER WAGEN HEFT 3: DER HERD see Pepping,
   Ernst

DER WAGEN HEFT 4: JAHRAUS-JAHREIN see
   Pepping, Ernst

DER WAGEN HEFT 5: IM WEINLAND see
   Pepping, Ernst

DER WAGEN HEFT 6: HERR WALTHER VON DER
   VOGELWEIDE see Pepping, Ernst

DER WANDERER: EIN STRAUSSCHEN see
   Silcher, Friedrich

DER WEANER GEHT NET UNTER
   (Lessky, Fr.) mix cor DOBLINGER G 684
   s.p. see from Sechs Lieder Aus Wien
                                 (D181)

DER WECKRUF HALLT see Lendvai, Erwin

DER WEG DER TOTEN see Krietsch, Georg

DER WEINFUHRMANN "ES WOLLT EIN FUHRMANN
   FAHREN" see Rein, Walter

DER WEINSCHWELG "NUN OHNE LUGEN" see
   Genzmer, Harald

DER WEISSE HIRSCH see Kreutzer,
   Konradin

DER WEISSE HIRSCH "ES GINGEN DREI JAGER
   WOHL AUF DIE BIRSCH" see Kreutzer,
   Konradin

DER WEISSE SCHWAN see Arcadelt, Jacob

DER WEIZEN MUSS REIFEN see Bresgen,
   Cesar

DER WETTSTREIT "MEIN MADCHEN UND MEIN
   WEIN" see Rein, Walter

DER WILDBACH see Leist, Peter Marzellin

DER WINTER see Rein, Walter

DER WINTER HAT VERLOREN   *folk
   (Biebl, F.) [Ger] 4pt mix cor
   MERSEBURG EM9232 s.p.   (D182)

DER WINTER IST VERGANGEN   *folk,Ger
   (Krietsch, .G) men cor,acap TONOS 5
   s.p.   (D183)

DER WINTER IST VERGANGEN see Jage,
   Rolf-Diether

DER WINTER IST VERGANGEN see Marx, Karl

DER WINTER IST VERGANGEN see Non Papa,
   Jacobus Clemens

DER WINTER IST VERGANGEN see Simon,
   Hermann

DER WINTER KALT see Eccard, Johannes

DER WIRTIN TOCHTERLEIN: ES ZOGEN see
   Silcher, Friedrich

DER WOLF UND DIE SIEBEN GEISSLEIN see
   Biebl, Franz

DER ZAUBERLEHRLING "HAT DER ALTE
   HEXENMEISTER" see Weber, Bernhard

DER ZECHER "BRUDER IHR AN DER
   TAFELRUNDE" see Weber, Bernhard,
   Chevaliers De La Table Ronde

DERBY RAM see Marx, Karl

DES GESANGES MACHT see Gauss, Otto

DES LEBENS SONNENSCHEIN see Haas,
   Joseph

DES MATROSEN ABSCHIED see Ammann, Benno

DES PUDELS KERN "EINEN BEUTEL MOCHT ICH
   HABEN" see Biebl, Franz

DES TEUFELS RITT "REITET DER TEUFEL MIT
   KLAPPERNDEM HUF" see Kubizek,
   Augustinian

DESCH, RUDOLF (1911-   )
   An Das Lied
      men cor,acap TONOS 4548 s.p. (D184)

   An Polyhymnia
      men cor,acap TONOS 3747 s.p. (D185)

   Ausschuss "Ist Irgendwo Viel Geld
      Vertan"
      men cor sc SCHOTTS CHBL 175 s.p.
      see from Vier Heitere Mannerchore
                                 (D186)
   Begrussung Der Sanger "Ihr Lieben
      Sangesbruder"
      see Desch, Rudolf, Sangerspruch Des
      Sangerbundes Rheinland-Pfalz "Du
      Land Der Burgen"
      see Desch, Rudolf, Sangerspruch Des
      SB. Rheinland-Pfalz "Du Land Der
      Burgen"

   Brucke Zur Heimat "Es Klingt Uns Zu
      Allen Stunden"   *sac/sec
      mix cor (med) sc SCHOTTS CHBL 360
      s.p.   (D187)
      men cor sc SCHOTTS CHBL 138 s.p.
                                 (D188)
   Dank Dir, Musik
      men cor,acap TONOS 4547 s.p. (D189)

   Das Frauenzimmer "Sabinchen War Ein
      Frauenzimmer"
      men cor sc SCHOTTS C 41 382 s.p.
                                 (D190)
   Das Lachende Paradies
      men cor,pno (song cycle) sc,cor pts
      SCHOTTS ED. 5259 s.p.   (D191)

   Das Lied Der Seele
      men cor,acap TONOS 3738 s.p. (D192)

   Das Neue Haus
      men cor,acap TONOS 4528 s.p. (D193)

   Der Huhnerdieb "Ihr Wisst, Was In Der
      Zeitung Stand"
      men cor/wom cor/jr cor,pno sc
      SCHOTTS C 40 387 s.p., cor pts
      SCHOTTS C 40 388 01-02 s.p.
                                 (D194)
   Die Heirat "Ratsam Ist Und Bleibt Es
      Immer"
      men cor sc SCHOTTS CHBL 177 s.p.
      see from Vier Heitere Mannerchore
                                 (D195)
   Die Schnupftabakdose "Es War Eine
      Schnupftabakdose"
      men cor sc SCHOTTS CHBL 178 s.p.
      see from Vier Heitere Mannerchore
                                 (D196)

DESCH, RUDOLF (cont'd.)

Dort Nieden An Dem Rheine
men cor,acap TONOS 78 s.p.   (D197)

Ei Du Mein Lieber Goldschmied
men cor sc SCHOTTS C 41 680 s.p.
(D198)

Ein Lied Muss Sein
men cor,acap TONOS 4539 s.p. (D199)

Ein Mensch, Der Einen Andern Traf
men cor sc SCHOTTS C 39 194 s.p.,
cor pts SCHOTTS C 39 195 01-02
s.p.   (D200)

Es Ging Ein Jungfrau Zarte
men cor,acap TONOS 51 s.p.   (D201)

Fahnenweihe
men cor,acap TONOS 4527 s.p. (D202)

Fruhling Am Bodensee *CC7L
4pt men cor,T solo,pno sc,cor pts
SCHOTTS C 41 521 s.p.   (D203)

He-Uchla!
[Ger/Russ] men cor sc SCHOTTS
CHBL 207 s.p.   (D204)

Heimatland
men cor,acap TONOS 4559 s.p. (D205)

Herzland Der Liebe
men cor,TBar soli,2fl,2ob,2clar,
2bsn,4horn,2trp,3trom,tuba,timp,
strings TONOS 4963 voc sc,cor pts
s.p., sc rental, ipr   (D206)

Himmelwarts Und Heimatwarts
men cor,acap TONOS 5692 s.p. (D207)

Hunsrucklied
men cor,acap TONOS 3992 s.p. (D208)

Ich Hab Mir Einen Garten Geplanzet
*folk
mix cor (med easy) sc SCHOTTS
C 41 913 s.p. see from Zwei
Volkslied-Variationen   (D209)

Im Fruhtau Zu Berge "Wir Wandern Ohne
Sorgen" *sac
mix cor (easy) sc SCHOTTS CHBL 381
s.p.   (D210)

In Dem Tal, Im Kustenland
"Nelly Gray" [Ger/Eng] men cor sc
SCHOTTS C 43 507 s.p.   (D211)

In Feuers Hitz Ergluht Mein Herz
*madrigal
men cor sc SCHOTTS CHBL 173 s.p.
(D212)

Ins Heu "Es Hatte Ein Bauer" *sac
SSAA&TTBB,acap (med) sc SCHOTTS
C 38 750 s.p., voc pt SCHOTTS
C 38 751A-H s.p.   (D213)

Jetzt Kommt Die Zeit, Dass Ich
Wandern Muss
men cor sc SCHOTTS CHBL 174 s.p.
(D214)

Junitage
men cor,pno,fl sc,cor pts TONOS
4211 s.p.   (D215)

Klinge Lieblich Und Sacht
men cor&jr cor,acap TONOS 1304 s.p.
(D216)

Lied, Du Herrliche Gabe
men cor,acap sc,cor pts TONOS 4018
s.p.   (D217)

Lob Der Faulheit "Faulheit, Jetzt
Will Ich Dir"
men cor sc SCHOTTS CHBL 176 s.p.
see from Vier Heitere Mannerchore
(D218)

Lobegesang
men cor,acap TONOS 5693 s.p. (D219)

Lustig Ist Das Hirtenleben
men cor&jr cor,acap TONOS 1306 s.p.
(D220)

Madel, Kamm Dich, Putz Dich *sac/
sec,folk
mix cor (easy) sc SCHOTTS CHBL 382
s.p.   (D221)
4pt men cor&2pt jr cor,acap sc
SCHOTTS CHBL 205 s.p.   (D222)

Nachtlicher Jazz "Die Nacht, Ein
Fremder, Schwarzer Geiger"
TTBB sc SCHOTTS C 41 386 s.p., cor
pts SCHOTTS C 41 387 01-03 s.p.
(D223)

Naheland-Heimatland
men cor,acap TONOS 4558 s.p. (D224)

Nelly Gray *see In Dem Tal, Im
Kustenland

O Wie So Schon Und Gut *sac
mix cor (easy) sc SCHOTTS CHBL 407
s.p.   (D225)

DESCH, RUDOLF (cont'd.)

Sanger Heraus
men cor,acap TONOS 4529 s.p. (D226)

Sangerspruch Des Sangerbundes
Rheinland-Pfalz "Du Land Der
Burgen"
4pt mix cor,acap/brass (easy) sc
SCHOTTS CHBL 331A-B s.p., ipa
contains also: Begrussung Der
Sanger "Ihr Lieben Sangesbruder"
(mix cor)   (D227)

Sangerspruch Des SB. Rheinland-Pfalz
"Du Land Der Burgen"
4pt mix cor,acap/3trp,3horn,2trom,
tuba,timp sc SCHOTTS CHBL 129A-B
s.p., ipa contains also:
Begrussung Der Sanger "Ihr Lieben
Sangesbruder" (men cor)   (D228)

Schenk Ein
men cor,acap TONOS 3732 s.p. (D229)

Schone Zeit Der Nachtigallen
men cor,acap TONOS 3968 s.p. (D230)

Vaganten-Trinklied
men cor,acap TONOS 4578 s.p. (D231)

Vier Heitere Mannerchore *see
Ausschuss "Ist Irgendwo Viel Geld
Vertan"; Die Heirat "Ratsam Ist
Und Bleibt Es Immer"; Die
Schnupftabakdose "Es War Eine
Schnupftabakdose"; Lob Der
Faulheit "Faulheit, Jetzt Will
Ich Dir"   (D232)

Von Allerlei Hunden *cant
1-3pt jr cor,pno,perc,bvl,
glockenspiel (med easy) sc,cor
pts SCHOTTS B 182 s.p., ipa
(D233)

Waldhymne
men cor,acap sc,cor pts TONOS 4075
s.p.   (D234)

Wie Schon Ist Der Mai
men cor,acap TONOS 3965 s.p. (D235)

Wir Tanzen Im Maien
men cor&jr cor,acap TONOS 1305 s.p.
(D236)

Wir Wollen Zu Land Ausfahren
4pt men cor BRATFISCH GB3257 s.p.
(D237)

Wohl Ist Die Welt So Gross Und Weit
men cor sc SCHOTTS C 39 445 s.p.,
voc pt SCHOTTS C 39 446 01-02
s.p.   (D238)

Zogen Einst Funf Wilde Schwane
men cor&1-2pt jr cor,acap sc
SCHOTTS CHBL 214 s.p.   (D239)

Zu Meinem Schatzchen Muss Ich Gehn
"Ich Kann Nicht Sitzen" *folk
mix cor (med easy) sc SCHOTTS
C 41 911 s.p., voc pt SCHOTTS
C 41 912A-B s.p. see from Zwei
Volkslied-Variationen   (D240)

Zwei Volkslied-Variationen *see Ich
Hab Mir Einen Garten Geplanzet;
Zu Meinem Schatzchen Muss Ich
Gehn "Ich Kann Nicht Sitzen"
(D241)

DE SEVERAC, DEODAT
Mignonne, Allons Voir Si La Rose
men cor JOBERT sc s.p., cor pts
s.p.   (D242)

DE SHANNON, JACKIE
Bad Water (composed with Holiday,
Jimmy; Myers Randy)
(Sanford, W.) SAB BIG3 $.40 (D243)
(Sanford, W.) TTBB BIG3 $.40 (D244)
(Sanford, W.) SATB,solo BIG3 $.40
(D245)

DESIGN FOR THE ATOMIC AGE see Claflin,
Avery

DES PREZ, JOSQUIN (ca. 1450-1521)
Anxious I Wait For My Dear Friend
*see Je Me Complains De Mon Amy

Je Me Complains De Mon Amy
(Couraud, Marcel) "Anxious I Wait
For My Dear Friend" [Fr/Eng]
SSAAT,acap SALABERT-US EAS 17037
$.65   (D246)

DESSAU, PAUL (1894-   )
Das Eisenbahnspiel
jr cor,soli,pno/2vln BOTE cor pts
s.p., sc s.p.   (D247)

Die Erziehung Der Hirse
cor&treb cor,narrator,Bar solo,orch
NEUE NM206 s.p.   (D248)

Geschaftsbericht
8pt mix cor&wom cor,soli,3pno,6bvl,
perc,trom NEUE NM249 s.p. (D249)

DESSAU, PAUL (cont'd.)

Marburger Bericht
4pt mix cor&jr cor,TB soli,orch
NEUE NM232 s.p.   (D250)

DESTRUCTION'S OUR DELIGHT see Purcell,
Henry

DET AR VACKRAST NAR DET SKYMMER see
Hagg, Torsten

DET GALLER ATT KLIPPA TILL FORST see
Hemberg, Eskil

DET VACKRASTE LANDET see Hagg, Torsten

DETI, RADOST A ZPEV see Slavicky,
Klement

DETONI, DUBRAVKO (1937-   )
Notturni
SATB&jr cor,TB soli,5fl,5ob,5clar,
4horn,3trp,3trom,5perc,2harp,
2gtr,cembalo,org,electronic tape,
4 saxophones, celesta MUSIC INFO
rental   (D251)

DETSKE TANECNE PIESNE see Wick, Vojtech

DETSKE ZBORY see Letnan, Julius

DETSKY ROK see Pinos, Alois

DETSKY ROK see Srnka, Jiri

DETSKY ZBORY see Ocenas, Andrej

DETSKY ZBORY see Prasil, Frantisek

DETWEILER, ALAN
David And Goliath
SATB,soli,inst voc sc NOVELLO s.p.,
ipr   (D252)

DEUTSCHE HEIMAT, DEINE LAND see
Krietsch, Georg

DEUTSCHE LIEBESLIEDER see Walcha,
Helmut

DEUTSCHLANDS KLAGE see Severin, W.

DEUX BERCEUSES see Thiriet, [Maurice]

DEUX FABLES DE JEAN DE LA FONTAINE see
Jongen, Leon

DEVANT SA MAIN NUE see Milhaud, Darius

DEVATY, ANTONIN (1903-   )
Moravskym Krajem *CCU,folk
[Czech] mix cor,SATB soli,2fl,2ob,
2clar,bsn,3horn,2trp,trom,timp,
perc,harp,strings CZECH s.p.
(D253)

DEVCIC, NATKO (1914-   )
Igra Rijeci
"Wordplay" mix cor,2 narrators,vln,
vla,vcl,bvl,pno,perc,electronic
tape MUSIC INFO rental   (D254)

Wordplay *see Igra Rijeci

DEW IS FALLING, THE see Suchy,
Frantisek, Aj, Pada Rosicka

DE WERT
Fantasia No. 1 (from Fantasias A 4)
DEAN CMC-102 $6.85 contains also:
Fantasia No. 3   (D255)

Fantasia No. 3 (from Fantasias A 4)
see De Wert, Fantasia No. 1

DEXTER, HARRY
Snowy, Snowy Mountains
2pt EMI   (D256)

DEY CAN'T COTCH ME TO BURY ME see
Rider-Meyer, L.

D'HAENE, RAFAEL LODEWIJK (1943-   )
Klage Der Ariadne *cant
cor,ABar soli ANDEL s.p.   (D257)

Miroir Des Vanites
cor,acap ANDEL s.p.   (D258)

DIALOGO A DIECI see Varotto, Michele

DIAMENT, ABRAHAM
Arad
SA,pno ISR.PUB.AG. s.p.   (D259)

Song Of The Valley
SATB,pno ISR.PUB.AG. s.p.   (D260)

DIAMOND DEW, THE see Protheroe, Daniel

DIAMOND GIRL see Seals

DIAMOND, NEIL
  Cracklin Rosie
    (Carubia) SATB/SAB,opt band ALFRED
    6534 $.50   (D261)

DIAPHANA see Ruzdjak, Marko

DICH SOLL MEIN LIED see Loewe

DICHTERWORT see Leist, Peter Marzellin

DICKINSON, PETER (1934-   )
  Outcry
    SATB,A solo,2fl,pic,2ob,2clar,2bsn,
    2horn,2trp,3trom,timp,perc,pno,
    strings voc sc NOVELLO rental
                                (D262)

DICKS, ERNEST A.
  May I Paint A Kiss
    SATB HARRIS $.30   (D263)

DIDN'T MY LORD DELIVER DANIEL
  "Warum Rettet' Denn Gott Nur Daniel"
  see Spirituals For All Heft I

DIDO see Novak, Jan

DIE ABENDGLOCKEN RUFEN see Abt, Franz

DIE ABREISE "MORGEN WILL MEIN SCHATZ
  VERREISEN" see Schauss, Karl

DIE ALMHUTTE *folk,Ger
  (Geiss, Gottfried) men cor,acap TONOS
  4570-3 s.p.   (D264)

DIE ALTE LOKOMOTIVE see Bresgen, Cesar

DIE ALTE UHR "IN MEINEM VATERHAUSE" see
  Lang, Hans

DIE AMEISEN see Krietsch, Georg

DIE AMSEL "IM BLUTENBAUM SASS EINE
  AMSEL" see Gebhard, Ludwig

DIE AUSERWAHLTE: MADELE RUCK see
  Silcher, Friedrich

DIE BALLADE VON DES CORTEZ LEUTEN see
  Suter, Robert

DIE BAUERN see Knab, Armin

DIE BEIDEN FLASCHEN see Bausznern,
  Dietrich von

DIE BEIDEN VOGEL "ZWEI VERLIEBTE KLEINE
  VOGEL" see Zoll, Paul

DIE BEREDSAMKEIT "FREUNDE, WASSER
  MACHET STUMM" see Haydn, (Franz)
  Joseph

DIE BERGE SIND SPITZ see Brahms,
  Johannes

DIE BESCHWERLICHKEITEN DES EHESTANDES
  "WENN ICH WILL DEN EHSTAND" see
  Rathgeber, Valentin

DIE BESTE ZEIT IM JAHR IST MAI'N see
  Gwinner, Volker

DIE BESTE ZEIT IM JAHR IST MEIN see
  Pepping, Ernst

DIE BESTE ZEIT IM JAHR IST MEIN see
  Willms, Franz

DIE BETTLERHOCHZEIT see Bresgen, Cesar

DIE BLUMELEIN, SIE SCHLAFEN see
  Kuhlenthal, Fred

DIE BOTEN DER LIEBE see Brahms,
  Johannes

DIE BRAUT see Brahms, Johannes

DIE BRUCKE VON AVIGNON *folk,Fr
  (Zschiegner, Fritz) men cor,opt pno,
  opt inst,opt perc sc,voc sc TONOS
  2115 s.p.   (D265)

DIE BRUCKE VON AVIGNON "KENNT IHR
  SCHON, KENNT IHR SCHON AVIGNON" see
  Lang, Hans

DIE BRUCKE VON VINHACA see Klefisch,
  Walter

DIE BRUNNLEIN, DIE DA FLIESSEN see
  Beck, Conrad

DIE DREI PRINZESSINEN see Les Trois
  Princesses

DIE DREI ROSELEIN: JETZT GANG I ANS
  BRUNNELE see Silcher, Friedrich

DIE DUMME ALTE "IN PARIS KENN ICH'NE
  ALTE" see Pappert, Walter

DIE EICHE see Schertzer, Daniel

DIE ERZIEHUNG DER HIRSE see Dessau,
  Paul

DIE FEDER see Fegers, Karl

DIE FEDER IM WIND *folk,Belg
  (Zschiegner, Fritz) men cor,opt pno,
  opt inst,opt perc sc,voc sc TONOS
  2116 s.p.   (D266)

DIE FROHLICHE SOMMERZEIT see Metzger,
  Fritz B.

DIE FUNF HUHNERCHEN "ICH WAR MAL IN DEM
  DORFE" see Erdlen, Hermann

DIE GABEN SCHONER KUNST see Beethoven,
  Ludwig van, Chorfantasie

DIE GASTE DER BUCHE "MIETGASTE VIER IM
  HAUS" see Erdlen, Hermann

DIE GEDANKEN SIND FREI *folk
  (Edler, Rudolf) men cor,acap TONOS 98
  s.p.   (D267)

DIE GEDANKEN SIND FREI see Keldorfer

DIE GEDANKEN SIND FREI see Lang, Hans

DIE GEDANKEN SIND FREI see Mohler,
  Philipp

DIE GEDANKEN SIND FREI see Zipp,
  Friedrich

DIE GELBE ROSE VON TEXAS *folk,US
  (Rosenstengel, Albrecht) men cor,opt
  pno,opt gtr,opt perc TONOS 462 s.p.
                                (D268)

DIE GESTIRNE see Schubert, Franz
  (Peter)

DIE GEWISSHEIT "OB ICH MORGEN LEBEN
  WERDE" see Genzmer, Harald

DIE GEZEITEN "WAS GEBOREN WARD, MUSS
  STERBEN" see Rein, Walter

DIE GLOCKE see Krietsch, Georg

DIE GLOCKEN VON NANTES "IM KERKERTURM
  VON NANTES" see Motte, Diether de
  la

DIE GULDENE SONNE see Metzler,
  Friedrich

DIE GULDENE SONNE see Metzler,
  Friedrich

DIE GULDENE SONNE see Simon, Hermann

DIE GULDNE SONNE see Metzler, Friedrich

DIE GULDNE SONNE see Metzler, Friedrich

DIE HARMONIE IN DER EHE "O WUNDERBARE
  HARMONIE" see Haydn, (Franz) Joseph

DIE HEILIGE ELISABETH see Haas, Joseph

DIE HEILIGEN DREI KONIGE see Marx, Karl

DIE HEIMAT see Erdlen, Hermann

DIE HEIMAT: DIE WINDE RAUSCHEN see
  Fischer, Karl Ludwig

DIE HEIMATGLOCKEN see Billeter, Agathon

DIE HEINZELMANNCHEN see Werdin,
  Eberhard

DIE HEINZELMANNCHEN ZU KOLN see Weber,
  Bernhard

DIE HEIRAT "RATSAM IST UND BLEIBT ES
  IMMER" see Desch, Rudolf

DIE HELLE SONN LEUCHT JETZT HERFUR see
  Kuhlenthal, Fred

DIE HELLE SONN LEUCHT JETZT HERFUR see
  Metzler, Friedrich

DIE HIMMEL RUHMEN see Beethoven, Ludwig
  van

DIE HIRTEN VON CANIGO *folk
  (Biebl, F.) [Ger] 4pt mix cor
  MERSEBURG EM9231 s.p.   (D269)

DIE HUTTEN see Langer, Hans-Klaus

DIE JAGD GEHORT IHR! "UND DER BLICK,
  DER GEHT WEIT" see Seeger, Peter

DIE JAHRE "DIE JAHRE SIND ALLERLIEBSTE
  LEUT" see Hessenberg, Kurt

DIE JUNGE SCHAFERIN see Schertzer,
  Daniel, La Jeune Bergere

DIE KEMENATE see Willms, Franz

DIE KONKURRENTEN see Rosenstengel,
  Albrecht

DIE KUMMERMUHLE "AN DER DONAU STEHT
  EINE ALTE MUHLE" see Bresgen, Cesar

DIE KUSSE "ALS ICH AUS EIGENNUTZ ELISE"
  see Weber, Bernhard

DIE LANDSCHAFT SINGT see Krietsch,
  Georg

DIE LANDSKNECHTE "WACHT AUF, HERR WIRT"
  see Sutermeister, Heinrich

DIE LANGE NASE see Sutermeister,
  Heinrich

DIE LEINEWEBER *folk
  (Krietsch, G.) men cor,acap TONOS 23
  s.p.   (D270)

DIE LEINEWEBERZUNFT *folk
  (Welker, Gotthard) men cor&jr cor,
  acap sc,cor pts TONOS 3847 s.p.
                                (D271)

DIE LIEBE see Doppelbauer, Josef
  Friedrich

DIE LIEBE HORET NIMMER AUF see Geiss,
  Gottfried

DIE LIEBE MEIN see Strohbach,
  Siegfried, L'amour De Moy

DIE LINIEN DES LEBENS SIND VERSCHIEDEN
  see Pepping, Ernst

DIE LORE: VON ALLEN DEN MADCHEN see
  Silcher, Friedrich

DIE LOTOSBLUME see Schumann, Robert
  (Alexander)

DIE LUSTIGEN SPOTTER see Schilling,
  Otto-Erich

DIE MADCHEN VON BATAVIA "RUHIG UBER
  SANFTE WOGEN" see Erdlen, Hermann

DIE MASCHINEN see Lendvai, Erwin

DIE MEERE see Brahms, Johannes

DIE MEINEN ZU HAUS "WEIT, WEIT VON HIER
  AM SWANEE RIBBER" see Swanee Ribber

DIE MINNESANGER see Schumann, Robert
  (Alexander)

DIE MOTTE "EIN PELZTIERMANTEL HING IM
  SCHRANK" see Gebhard, Ludwig

DIE MULLERIN see Brahms, Johannes

DIE MUSIK ALLEIN see Weber, Bernhard

DIE MUSIKANTENFIBEL see Jode, Fritz

DIE NACHT WAR VOLLER TRAUME see
  Gutesha, M.

DIE NACHT "WIE SCHON BIST DU" see
  Schubert, Franz (Peter)

DIE NACHTIGALL *folk,Russ
  (Erbelding, Dietrich) men cor,acap
  sc,cor pts TONOS 455 s.p.   (D272)

DIE NACHTIGALL see Mendelssohn-
  Bartholdy, Felix

DIE NACHTIGALL see Schertzer, Daniel,
  Rossignol Du Bois

DIE NACHTIGALL "BESCHEIDEN VERBORGEN"
  *Op.11,No.2 (from Fv)
  (Gotze-Kohler) TTBB,pno sc SCHOTTS
  C 39 508 s.p., voc pt SCHOTTS
  C 39 509, 01-04 s.p.   (D273)

DIE NACHTTROMMLER see Seeger, Peter

DIE NAHE see Fischer, Theo

DIE NONNE see Brahms, Johannes

DIE NUDELN see Maccheroni

DIE OFFENTLICHEN VERLEUMDER "EIN
  UNGEZIEFER RUHT IN STAUB" see
  Hessenberg, Kurt

DIE OHREN see Knab, Armin

DIE ORD'NTLICHEN LEUT
  (Deutsch, Walter) mix cor DOBLINGER
  G 678 s.p. see from Acht Lieder Aus
  Wien   (D274)

DIE PETERSBURGER LANDSTRASSE ENTLANG
  see Fleig, G.

DIE PRIMEL see Mendelssohn-Bartholdy, Felix

DIE PRINZESSIN UND DER TROMMLER see Zoll, Paul

DIE QUELLE "STEHE STILL, WANDRER see Wedig, Hans Josef

DIE RATSEL DER ELFEN "DIE ELFEN SITZEN IM FELSENSCHACHT" see Mockl, Franz

DIE ROSE STAND IM TAU see Schumann, Robert (Alexander)

DIE ROSEN VON LIDICE see Stolte, Siegfried

DIE SCHAUKEL see Reda, Siegfried

DIE SCHLAFENDE SCHAFERIN *folk
   (Gramss, K.) [Ger] 4pt mix cor
   MERSEBURG EM9203 s.p.   (D275)

DIE SCHMIEDE *folk
   (Desch, R.) [Ger] 4pt men cor
   MERSEBURG EM9068 s.p.   (D276)

DIE SCHNITTERIN "VOR EINEM GRUNEN WALDE" see Lang, Hans

DIE SCHNUPFTABAKDOSE "ES WAR EINE SCHNUPFTABAKDOSE" see Desch, Rudolf

DIE SCHONE ALTE ZEIT see Weber, Bernhard, Auld Lang Syne

DIE SCHONE ALTE ZEIT "DIE FREUNDE ALL" see Auld Lang Syne

DIE SCHONE AUS DEM MAGGIA-TAL see Ammann, Benno

DIE SCHONE PREDI' "DER ALTE PFARRER VON WAXELMOOS" see Poos, Heinrich

DIE SCHONE VOM LANDE *folk
   (Beckerath, A. Von) [Ger] 4pt mix cor
   MERSEBURG EM9205 s.p.   (D277)

DIE SCHONE VON ONSERNONE see Ammann, Benno

DIE SCHONEN WEISSEN SCHWANE see Arcadelt, Jacob

DIE SCHONSTE VON ALLEN *folk
   (Fischer, Theo) men cor,acap TONOS 45
   s.p.   (D278)

DIE SEEFAHRT NACH RIO see Geese, Heinz

DIE SEELEUTE see Edler, Robert

DIE SEIFENBLASE see Fegers, Karl

DIE SICHEL see Edler, Robert

DIE SINGENDE STADT see Lendvai, Erwin

DIE SONN' ERWACHT see Weber, Carl Maria von

DIE SONNE SINKT see Edler, Robert

DIE SONNE SINKT VON HINNEN see Distler, Hugo

DIE SPIELZEUGTRUHE see Gebhard, Ludwig

DIE SPRODE see Knab, Armin

DIE STADT "AM GRAUEN STRAND, AM GRAUEN MEER" see Rein, Walter

DIE STEIRISCHE ROAS
   see Ich Weiss Einen Lindenbaum Stehen

DIE STIMMEN DER TIERE see Lischka, Rainer

DIE STRASSBURGER MUNSTER-ENGELCHEN "GIB DIR WEITER KEINE MUH'" see Wolters, Karl-Heinz

DIE TANZWEISE see Rosenstengel, Albrecht

DIE TRAUBEN VOM PARADIES see Edler, Robert

DIE TRAUERNDE: MEI MUTTER MAG MI NET see Silcher, Friedrich

DIE TRAUERWEIDE see Edler, Robert

DIE TRAURIGE BALLADE VOM REISEN SCHLUCK UND FRISS "HORT DIE TRAURIGE GESCHICHTE" see Haus, Karl

DIE TRENNUNG *folk
   (Zoll, P.) [Ger] 4pt men cor
   MERSEBURG EM9007 s.p.   (D279)

DIE TROMMEL see Krietsch, Georg

DIE TURKEN see Biebl, Franz

DIE UNENDLICHE STRASSE see Krietsch, Georg

DIE VIER JAHRESZEITENELEMENTE see Eckert, Alex

DIE VIER VERHALTNISSE "EIN JUNGGESELL MUSS TRINKEN" see Fussan, Werner

DIE VOGEL WARTEN IM WINTER VOR DEM FENSTER "ICH BIN DER SPERLING" see Poos, Heinrich

DIE VOGELHOCHZEIT see Goller, Fritz

DIE VOGERL SCHLAFEN SCHON see Burkhart, Franz

DIE VOGERL SCHLAFEN SCHON IM WALD see Burkhart, Franz

DIE VOGLEIN IN DEM WALDE *folk,Ger
   (Zoll, Paul) men cor sc SCHOTTS
   C 41 383 s.p. see from Drei
   Deutsche Volkslieder   (D280)

DIE VOGLEIN IN DEM WALDE see Pepping, Ernst

DIE WEIBER VON ARLON *folk
   (Zschiegner, Fritz) men cor,opt pno,
   opt inst,opt perc sc TONOS 2119
   s.p.   (D281)

DIE WEIHE DER NACHT "NACHTLICHE STILLE" see Genzmer, Harald

DIE WEIHNACHTSNACHTIGALL see Engel, H.

DIE WEITE WELT see Becker, Hans-Gunther

DIE WELT ERWACHT
   unis wom cor SCHOTTS C 42 532D s.p.
   see also Alle Singen Heft 1   (D282)

DIE WELT IST IMMER HEITER "DIE MADCHEN UND DIE FLASCHCHEN WEIN" see Biebl, Franz

DIE WILDGANSE see Schwaen, Kurt

DIE WINZER see Edler, Robert

DIE WINZERIN *folk,Ger
   (Wittmer, Eberhard L.) men cor,acap
   TONOS 123 s.p.   (D283)

DIE ZEIT GEHT NICHT, SIE STEHET STILL see Beck, Conrad

DIE ZEIT "SEID MIR NUR NICHT GAR SO TRAURIG" see Rettich, Wilhelm

DIE ZWEI HASEN see Lang, Hans

DIE ZWEI TUGENDWEGE "ZWEI SIND DER WEGE" see Schubert, Franz (Peter)

DIE ZWIEBELHANDLER "HOPHEJ! ZWIEBELHANDLER DA, VOR DEM HAUS" see Kubizek, Augustinian

DIECI DISCANTI see Castaldi, Paolo

DIECKMANN, JOHANNES (1893-1969)
   Kinder- Und Weihnachtslieder *CCU,
   Xmas
   jr cor,acap BREITKOPF-L PB3959 s.p.
                                  (D284)

DIEFFENBACHER, EUGEN
   Harmonie Fuhrt Uns Zusammen
   men cor,acap TONOS 6343 s.p.   (D285)

DIEMER
   Laughing Song
   SATB SHAWNEE A1275 $.45   (D286)

DIEMER, EMMA LOU (1927-   )
   Come Hither You That Love
   SSA MARKS MC 4614 $.45   (D287)

   Dance, Dance My Heart
   SATB,opt pno/org,opt 3perc (med)
   FISCHER,C CM 7831 $.35   (D288)

   Romance
   mix cor,pno, opt triangle (med)
   FISCHER,C CM 7859 $.35   (D289)

DIES FUGENLOSE GESCHMEIDE see Rein, Walter

DIETERLEIN "WOHLAUF, IHR NARR'N, ZIEHT ALL MIT MIR" see Zipp, Friedrich

DIETRICH, FRITZ (1905-1945)
   Wenn Alle Brunnlein Fliessen
   SATB,acap BAREN. BCH163 s.p.
   contains also: Neumeyer, Fritz,
   Viel Freuden Mit Sich Bringet
                                  (D290)

DIETRICH, KARL
   Winterlied
   3pt jr cor,pno NEUE NM1017 s.p.
                                  (D291)

DIFFERENT DRUMMER, A see Berger

DIFFICILE LECTU MIHI MARS see Mozart, Wolfgang Amadeus

DIGO GIANETTA see Nitsche, Paul, Sag Mir, Gianetta

DIGO GIANNETTA (from Cvjy) folk
   4pt wom cor,acap BREITKOPF-W CHB 4947
   s.p. contains also: Sag Doch,
   Giannetta   (D292)

DIJK, JAN VAN (1918-   )
   Pros Romaious *cant
   mix cor,narrator,TB soli,2fl,2ob,
   2clar,2bsn,2horn,2trp,trom,
   strings,perc DONEMUS   (D293)

DI LASSO, ORLANDO
   see LASSUS, ROLAND DE (ORLANDUS)

DILBERKA see Slavenski, Josip

DINA OGON *folk
   (Hellden, Daniel) mix cor GEHRMANS
   KRB441   (D294)

DINDIRIN see Anonymous

D'INDY
   Bouquet Of Spring
   SSA,acap SALABERT-US $.40   (D295)

DING, DONG, SING A SONG see Muhr, Nessy

DINN, FREDA (1910-   )
   Christmas Song, A *Ger
   [Eng] jr cor,pno,2S rec,A rec,opt
   strings&perc (easy) sc SCHOTTS
   RS 33 s.p., ipa contains also:
   Virgin Mary's Lullaby, The   (D296)

   Virgin Mary's Lullaby, The
   see Dinn, Freda, Christmas Song, A

DIPPING IN THE MILKY WAY see Protheroe, Daniel

DIRGE FOR A MINSTREL see Bach, Jan

DIRNDAL, MERK DIR DEN BAM *folk,Aus
   (Schollum, Robert) mix cor DOBLINGER
   G 657-658 s.p. contains also: Ei,
   Ei, Ei, Sagt Mein Wei   (D297)

DIRRIWACHTER, WIM (1937-   )
   Todesfuge
   4pt,B solo,pno,2fl,2ob,3clar,2bsn,
   4horn,2trp,2trom,strings,2perc,
   timp DONEMUS   (D298)

DIS-MOI, JEANNETTE see Passani, Emile

DISCOVERIES see Brindle, [Reginald Smith]

DISPUTE see Massis, Amable

DISTLER, HUGO (1908-1942)
   Abendlied Eines Reisenden
   (Richter, Clifford G.) "Evening
   Song Of A Traveller" [Eng/Ger]
   TTBB,acap BOONIN B 238 $.40
                                  (D299)
   Awake, You Are In Need *see Wacht
   Auf, Es Tut Euch Not!

   Cloud Approaches, A *see Es Geht Ein
   Dunkle Wolk Herein

   Die Sonne Sinkt Von Hinnen
   (Richter, Clifford G.) "Sun Is
   Slowly Sinking, The" [Eng/Ger]
   SATB BOONIN B 237 $.40   (D300)

   Ein Stundlein Wohl Vor Tag
   (Richter, Clifford G.) "Moment Ere
   The Dawn, A" [Eng/Ger] SATB
   BOONIN B 240 $.40 see from
   Morike-Chorliederbuch, Op. 19
                                  (D301)
   Er Ist's
   "Spring Has Come" see Songs From
   The Morikelieder

   Es Geht Ein Dunkle Wolk Herein
   (Richter, Clifford G.) "Cloud
   Approaches, A" [Eng/Ger] SATB
   BOONIN B 236 $.40   (D302)

   Evening Song Of A Traveller *see
   Abendlied Eines Reisenden

   Fare Thee Well *see Lebewohl

   Hunter's Song *see Jagerlied

   I Know A Lovely Rose *Op.5b,No.1
   (Richter, Clifford G.) [Eng/Ger]
   SAB,acap BOONIN B 235 $.30 (D303)

DISTLER, HUGO (cont'd.)

Jagerlied
"Hunter's Song" see Songs From The Morikelieder

Lebewohl
(Richter, Clifford G.) "Fare Thee Well" [Eng/Ger] SSATTBB BOONIN B 242 $.40 see from Morike-Chorliederbuch, Op. 19   (D304)

Lied Vom Winde
(Richter, Clifford G.) "Song Of The Winds" [Eng/Ger] SSA,S solo BOONIN B 241 $.75 see from Morike-Chorliederbuch, Op. 19   (D305)

Lob Auf Die Musik
(Richter, Clifford G.) "Praise To Music" [Eng/Ger] SATB,acap BOONIN B 233 $.40   (D306)

Moment Ere The Dawn, A *see Ein Stundlein Wohl Vor Tag

Morike-Chorliederbuch, Op. 19 *see Ein Stundlein Wohl Vor Tag, "Moment Ere The Dawn, A"; Lebewohl, "Fare Thee Well"; Lied Vom Winde, "Song Of The Winds"; Vorspruch, "Preamble"   (D307)

Praise To Music *see Lob Auf Die Musik

Preamble *see Vorspruch

Song Of The Winds *see Lied Vom Winde

Songs From The Morikelieder *Op.19 SA/TB,acap NATIONAL WHC-19 $.35
contains: Er Ist's, "Spring Has Come"; Jagerlied, "Hunter's Song"   (D308)

Spring Has Come *see Er Ist's

Sun Is Slowly Sinking, The *see Die Sonne Sinkt Von Hinnen

Vorspruch
(Richter, Clifford G.) "Preamble" [Eng/Ger] SATBB BOONIN B 239 $.40 see from Morike-Chorliederbuch, Op. 19   (D309)

Wacht Auf, Es Tut Euch Not!
(Richter, Clifford G.) "Awake, You Are In Need" [Eng/Ger] SATB BOONIN B 234 $.40   (D310)

DITES-MOI see Rodgers, Richard

DIVERSI LINGUAGGI see Marenzio, Luca

DIX CHANSONS AMBASSADE DU VIN see Samson

DIXIE see Emmett, Daniel Decatur

DIXIE "ICH WOLLT', ICH WAR IM BAUMWOLLAND" see Senn, Karl

DIXIE LAND *folk
(Biebl, F.) [Ger] 4pt mix cor MERSEBURG EM9236 s.p.   (D311)

DNES see Mikula, Zdenko

DNES see Mikula, Zdenko

DO I LOVE YOU BECAUSE YOU'RE BEAUTIFUL? see Rodgers, Richard

DO KOLECKA DO KOLA see Novak, Milan

DO-RE-MI see Rodgers, Richard

DO RUZOVA see Eben, Petr

DO SKOLY see Prasil, Frantisek

DO YOU SEE THAT THERE BIRD
(Farrell, Dennis) SAA WATERLOO $.40   (D312)

DOBER DANEK TOMU DOMU see Lucic, Franjo

DOBIAS, VACLAV (1909-   )
Festival Song *see Festivalova Pisen

Festivalova Pisen
"Festival Song" [Czech] mix cor, 3fl,2ob,2clar,2bsn,4horn,3trp, 3trom,tuba,timp,perc,harp,strings CZECH s.p.   (D313)

Order No. 368 *see Rozkaz C. 368

Pisen O Strane
"Song Of The Party" [Czech] jr cor& mix cor,ABar soli,2fl,ob,2clar, bsn,4horn,3trp,2trom,tuba,timp, perc,strings CZECH s.p.   (D314)

DOBIAS, VACLAV (cont'd.)

Red Army *see Ruda Armada

Rozkaz C. 368 *cant
"Order No. 368" [Czech] men cor,Bar solo,3fl,3ob,3clar,3bsn,4horn, 3trp,3trom,tuba,timp,perc,2harp, pno,strings CZECH s.p.   (D315)

Ruda Armada
"Red Army" [Czech] men cor,2fl,ob, 2clar,bsn,3horn,3trp,3trom,tuba, timp,perc,strings CZECH s.p.   (D316)

Song Of The Party *see Pisen O Strane

DOBRI DENEK see Cossetto, Emil

DOBRONIC, ANTUN (1878-1955)
Gubec's Peasant Fighters cor CROATICA   (D317)

DOBRY DEN see Prasil, Frantisek

DOCTOR AND THE PATIENT, THE see Jeffries

DODDS
N.R.G. Song (composed with Richelson)
(Burden, James) SSA CHARTER CO30214   (D318)
(Burden, James) SA CHARTER CO30216   (D319)
(Burden, James) SATB CHARTER CO30213   (D320)
(Burden, James) SAB CHARTER CO30215   (D321)
Something For Tomorrow (composed with Richelson)
(Burden, James) SATB CHARTER CO30217   (D322)

DODICI MADRIGALI DI SCUOLA FERRARESE *madrigal
(Nielsen, R.) 5pt mix cor cmplt ed BONGIOVANI 2395 s.p.
contains & see also: Agostini, Lodovico, Cantava In Riva Al Fiume; Agostini, Lodovico, Picciola Verga E Bella; Agostini, Lodovico, Tra Giove In Cielo; Luzzaschi, Luzzasco, Aminta Poi Ch'a Filli; Luzzaschi, Luzzasco, Dolce Mia Fiamma; Luzzaschi, Luzzasco, Geloso Amante; Luzzaschi, Luzzasco, Itene A Volo; Nicoletti, F., Ardo Si Ma Non T'amo; Virchi, P., Dovea La Fredda Neve; Virchi, P., Non Fonte O Fiume; Virchi, P., Qual Cervo Errando   (D323)

DOESN'T ANYTHING WHERETO? see Radulescu, Horatiu

DOG SUITE - SINGING DOGS IN THE MOONLIGHT see Valek, Jiri, Psi Suita - Zpivajici Psici Pri Mesici

DR. ZIPRABOM see Kuhlenthal, Fred

DOLCE MIA FIAMMA see Luzzaschi, Luzzasco

DOLGOZNI II see Bardos, Lajos

DOMINE, SALVE FAC see Willan, Healey

DOMOV see Blazek, Zdenek

DOMOVE see Vlach-Vruticky, Josef

DOMOVINA MOJA see Mikula, Zdenko

DOMOVO see Hanus, Jan

DONALDSON, WALTER (1893-1947)
Yes Sir, That's My Baby (composed with Kahn, Gus)
TTBB BOURNE B215061-355 $.40 (D324)

DONATI, BALDASSARE (ca. 1530-1603)
Villanella Alla Napolitana [It] SATB,acap EGTVED KB95 s.p.   (D325)

Wenn Wir Hinausziehn
mix cor (med) sc SCHOTTS CHBL 370 s.p.   (D326)

DONATO, ANTHONY (1909-   )
Barn Dance
SATB,acap (med) FITZSIMONS 1075 $.25   (D327)

DONAUSTRUDEL ALS WIR JUNGST IN REGENSBURG see Lang

DONNA S'IO MIRO VOI see Monteverdi, Claudio

DON'T EVER LEAVE ME
SA CIMINO $.40   (D328)
SAB CIMINO $.40   (D329)
SSA CIMINO $.40   (D330)

SATB CIMINO $.40   (D331)

DON'T LET IT GET YOU DOWN see Nestico, G.

DON'T LET THE SUN GO DOWN ON ME see John

DON'T MARRY ME see Rodgers, Richard

D'ONT VIENT CE SOULEIL see Egk, Werner

DON'T YOU FORGET IT
SSA CIMINO $.40   (D332)
SATB CIMINO $.40   (D333)

DOPPELBAUER, JOSEF FRIEDRICH (1918-   )
Abendstandchen
eq voices,opt rec/fl DOBLINGER O 325 s.p. see from Sechs Chore Fur Gleiche Stimmen Nach Texten Verschiedner Dichter   (D334)

Der Mensch Lebt Und Bestehet
eq voices DOBLINGER O 322 s.p. see from Sechs Chore Fur Gleiche Stimmen Nach Texten Verschiedner Dichter   (D335)

Die Liebe
eq voices DOBLINGER O 321 s.p. see from Sechs Chore Fur Gleiche Stimmen Nach Texten Verschiedner Dichter   (D336)

Erntedank
eq voices DOBLINGER O 323 s.p. see from Sechs Chore Fur Gleiche Stimmen Nach Texten Verschiedner Dichter   (D337)

Sechs Chore Fur Gleiche Stimmen Nach Texten Verschiedner Dichter *see Abendstandchen; Der Mensch Lebt Und Bestehet; Die Liebe; Erntedank; Stilles Reifen; Wer Sich Die Musik Erkeist   (D338)

Stilles Reifen
eq voices DOBLINGER O 324 s.p. see from Sechs Chore Fur Gleiche Stimmen Nach Texten Verschiedner Dichter   (D339)

Wer Sich Die Musik Erkeist
eq voices DOBLINGER O 320 s.p. see from Sechs Chore Fur Gleiche Stimmen Nach Texten Verschiedner Dichter   (D340)

DORET
Pauvre Pierre
men cor,acap HENN 013 s.p.   (D341)

DORFABEND "DER SCHAFER MIT DEN SCHAFEN" see Rothschuh, Franz

DORFMUSIK see Heuken, Hans Jakob

DORT AM FLUSSCHEN *folk
(Haus, K.) [Ger] 4pt men cor MERSEBURG EM 9030 s.p.   (D342)

DORT BIN ICH DAHEIM *folk
(Biebl, F.) [Ger] 4pt men cor MERSEBURG EM9061 s.p.   (D343)

DORT IM DORFE *folk,Hung
(Krietsch, G.) men cor,acap TONOS 2055 s.p.   (D344)

DORT JENES BRUNNLEIN see Zoll, Paul

DORT NIEDEN AN DEM RHEINE see Desch, Rudolf

DORT UNTER DER LINDE see Lang, Hans

D'OTTOBRE see Zecchi, Adone

DOUBLE OR NOTHING see Jeffries

DOULCE MEMOIRE see Sandrin, Pierre

DOUZE CHANSONS CANADIENNES *CC12U,folk
(Coutts, George) cor WATERLOO $2.50   (D345)

DOUZE CHANSONS POUR LES JOURS HEUREUX, VOL. 4 see Berthomieu, Marc

DOVE, THE see Blazek, Zdenek, Holubice

DOVE, THE see Sveceny, Ladislav, Holoubek

DOVEA LA FREDDA NEVE see Virchi, P.

DOWLAND, JOHN (1563-1626)
Away With These Self-Loving Lads SATB,acap EGTVED MS13B14 s.p.   (D346)

Come Again! Sweet Love Doth Now Invite
"Susses Lieb" [Eng/Ger] mix cor (med easy) sc SCHOTTS C 39 920

DOWLAND, JOHN (cont'd.)

s.p.   (D347)
(Weber, W.) "Susses Lieb" men cor,
acap TONOS 3319 s.p.   (D348)

Dear, If You Change
(Brandvik; Sahlen) SATB oct SCHMITT
1209 $.35   (D349)

Eight Airs *CC8L
(Alvad, Th.) SATB,acap cmplt ed
EGTVED MS10B6 s.p.   (D350)

Me, Me, And None But Me
SATB,acap EGTVED MS12B4 s.p. (D351)

Sag, Amor
(Weber, W.) men cor,acap TONOS 3308
s.p.   (D352)

Scheiden Muss Ich Jetzt
(Weber, W.) men cor,acap TONOS 3315
s.p.   (D353)

Shall I Sue
SATB,acap EGTVED KB86 s.p.   (D354)

Shepherd In A Shade, A
SATB,acap EGTVED KB66 s.p.   (D355)

Susses Lieb *see Come Again! Sweet
Love Doth Now Invite

DOWN BY THE FAIR RIVER
(Johnston, Richard A.) SATB (med
easy) WATERLOO $.30   (D356)

DOWN BY THE RIVERSIDE
(Scheider, Werner) SATB MOSELER LB739
s.p.   (D357)

DOWN BY THE SALLEY GARDENS see Kennedy

DOWN BY THE SALLY GARDENS
(Deale, Edgar) SATB (med easy)
WATERLOO $.40   (D358)
(Mitchell, Helen) SATB (med easy)
WATERLOO $.35   (D359)

DOWN BY THE SALLY GARDENS see Turner,
Olive

DOWN FROM THE BRANCHES FALLING see
Arcadelt, Jacob, Da Bei Rami
Scendea

DOWN IN YON FOREST
see Eight Christmas Carols, Set 2

DOWN IN YON FOREST see Vaughan
Williams, Ralph

DOWNTOWN see Hatch, Tony

DOYLE
Chickadee Song, The
SA KENDOR $.35   (D360)

DOZEN ROUNDS, A see Mason, Lowell

DOZINKY see Kuksa, Emanuel

DOZSA see Sugar, Rezso

DOZSA see Sugar, Rezso

DOZSA SIRATOJA see Lendvay, Kamillo

DR. HARINGTON'S COMPLIMENT see Haydn,
(Franz) Joseph

DRAHTS, WILLI (1911-   )
Frohliche Weihnacht Uberall *CC37U,
Xmas
1-2pt jr cor,opt gtr sc SCHOTTS
ED. 5400 s.p.   (D361)

DRATH, WALTER
Hunsrucklied
men cor,acap TONOS 243 s.p.   (D362)

DRAUSSA EM WALD
see Ich Weiss Einen Lindenbaum Stehen

DRAZAN, JOSEF (1909-   )
To My Native Land *see Zemi Rodne

Zemi Rodne *cant
"To My Native Land" [Czech] mix
cor,Bar solo,3fl,3ob,3clar,2bsn,
4horn,4trp,3trom,tuba,timp,perc,
harp,pno,org,strings, celeste
CZECH s.p.   (D363)

DREAM see Mellnas, Arne

DREAM see Mercer

DREAM OF GERONTIUS see Elgar, Edward

DREAM ON see Lambert, Dennis

DREAM SONG see Chihara, Paul

DREAMER, THE see Cousins, M. Thomas

DREAMLAND CITY see Kurth, Burton L.

DREAMS see Tiffault

DREAMS OF SPRING see Saar, Louis Victor

DREAMS OF SPRING see Strauss

DREH DICH, RADCHEN see Solter, Heinz

DREI ALTE LANDSKNECHTSLIEDER see Knab,
Armin

DREI ALTE VOLKSLIEDER-NEU DARGEBOTEN
*folk
(Rosenstengel, Albrecht) men cor/men
cor&jr cor,pno,opt bvl,opt gtr,opt
perc sc,voc sc TONOS 1210 s.p.
contains: Im Rosengartelien; Wach
Auf, Meins Herzens Schone; Weiss
Mir Ein Schones Roselein   (D364)

DREI AMERIKANISCHE VOLKSLIEDER *folk,
US
(Putz, Eduard) men cor,acap cmplt ed
TONOS 2380 s.p.
contains: Jeannie With The Light
Brown Hair; My Old Kentucky Home;
Swanee River   (D365)

DREI ANTIKE GESANGE see Genzmer, Harald

DREI BAUERNLIEDER see Knab, Armin

DREI BERG UND DREI TAL
(Reiter, Albert) treb cor DOBLINGER
O 344 s.p. see from Sechs
Osterreichische Volkslieder (D366)

DREI BITT- UND LOBGESANGE see Weber,
Bernhard

DREI BITTEN see Haas, Joseph

DREI CHOR-DUETTE *see Lang, Hans, Es
Gingen Drei Gesellen   (D367)

DREI CHOR-DUETTE see Lang, Hans

DREI CHORE see Genzmer, Harald

DREI CHORE see Schroeder, Hermann

DREI CHORE see Reger, Max

DREI CHORE NACH MITTELHOCHDEUTSCHEN
TEXTEN see Werdin, Eberhard

DREI CHORE NACH RUSSISCHEN TEXTEN see
Zoll, Paul

DREI CHORLIEDER see Binger, Martin

DREI CHORLIEDER see Sutermeister,
Heinrich

DREI CHORLIEDER see Rettich, Wilhelm

DREI CHORLIEDER NACH GEDICHTEN VON
BERTOLT BRECHT see Poos, Heinrich

DREI CHORLIEDER VOM WEIN see Genzmer,
Harald

DREI CHORLIEDER VOM WEIN see Genzmer,
Harald

DREI CHORSATZE see Orff, Carl

DREI DEUTSCHE CHANSONS see Biebl, Franz

DREI DEUTSCHE VOLKSLIEDER *see Das
Jagen "Das Jagen, Das Ist Unser
Leben"; Die Voglein In Dem Walde;
Fruhmorgens Auf Der Jagd
"Fruhmorgens, Wenn Das Jagdhorn
Schallt"   (D368)

DREI EPIGRAMME see Cadow, Paul

DREI EPIGRAMME see Cadow, Paul

DREI ERNSTE CHORE see Burkhart, Franz

DREI ERNSTE GESANGE see Rein, Walter

DREI FRAGMENTE see Tsouyopoulos,
Georges S.

DREI FRANZOSISCHE CHORE see Egk, Werner

DREI FRAUENCHORE see Sturmer, Bruno

DREI GEDICHTE VON GOTTFRIED KELLER see
Hessenberg, Kurt

DREI GESANGE see Sturmer, Bruno

DREI GESANGE FUR MANNERCHOR *see
Mohler, Philipp, Heimkehr "Weint
Nicht Mehr, Ihr Mutter"   (D369)

DREI GESANGE FUR MANNERCHOR see Mohler,
Philipp

DREI GUTE DINGE "WIR LIEBEN SEHR IM
HERZEN" see Friderici, Daniel

DREI HEITERE VOLKSLIEDER see Zipp,
Friedrich

DREI HUBSCHE MADCHEN see Rohwer, Jens

DREI JAHRESWENDLIEDER see Taubert, Karl
Heinz

DREI JUGOSLAWISCHE VOLKSLIEDER see
Klefisch, Walter

DREI LANDSKNECHTS-LIEDER see Zipp,
Friedrich

DREI LAUB AUF EINER LINDEN see
Burkhart, Franz

DREI LIEDER see Sutermeister, Heinrich

DREI MADRIGALE see Reutter, Hermann

DREI MADRIGALE NACH SLOWAKISCHEN
LIEBESLIEDERN see Poos, Heinrich

DREI MAHRISCHE VOLKSLIEDER see Poos,
Heinrich

DREI MANNERCHORE see Trunk, Richard

DREI MANNERCHORE MIT HORNERBEGLEITUNG
see Schlemm, Gustav Adolf

DREI RILKE CHORE see Buchtger, Fritz

DREI RUSSISCHE VOLKSLIEDER see Zipp,
Friedrich

DREI RUSSISCHE VOLKSLIEDER see Zoll,
Paul

DREI SHANTIES UND SEEMANNSLIEDER see
Erdlen, Hermann

DREI SOLDATENLIEDER see Mohler, Philipp

DREI-SPRACHEN-LIEDERBUCH *CCU
(Strube, A.) MERSEBURG EM369   (D370)

DREI SPRUCHE IN KANONISCHER FORM UND
DREI KANONS see Schwarz-Schilling,
Reinhard

DREI UNGARISCHE VOLKSLIEDER see Bartok,
Bela

DREI VOLKSLIEDER see Zoll, Paul

DREI VOLKSLIEDSATZE see Lang, Hans

DREI VOLKSLIEDSATZE see Zoll, Paul

DREI VOLKSWEISEN see Lang, Hans

DREI WEINSPRUCHE
men cor,acap cmplt ed TONOS 3982 s.p.
contains: Biebl, Franz, Weinlust;
Papandopulo, Boris, Ich Bin Durch
Liebe; Wittmer, Eberhard Ludwig,
Schenkst Du Guten Ein   (D371)

DREI ZIGEUNER see Schertzer, Daniel,
Three Gypsies

DREIDEL see McLean, Don

DREIKONIG *Xmas
(Bachl, Hans) treb cor DOBLINGER
O 329-330 s.p. contains also: Im
Wald Is' So Stand   (D372)

DREIMAL RIEF DIE AMSEL see Bresgen,
Cesar

DREIMAL WEIN "WER KEIN MADCHEN HAT" see
Weber, Bernhard

DREIMOL OMS STADELE see Rein, Walter

DREISSIG KANONS NACH GLOCKENINSCHRIFTEN
see Hartl, Rudolf

DREIZEHN LIEDER FUR FRAUENCHOR see
Linke, Norbert

DREJSL, RADIM (1923-1953)
Jdem A Jdem A Nic Nas Nezastavi
"We Shall March And March And
Nothing Shall Stop Us" [Czech]
mix cor,narrator,3fl,2ob,3clar,
2bsn,4horn,3trp,3trom,tuba,timp,
perc,strings CZECH s.p.   (D373)

We Shall March And March And Nothing
Shall Stop Us *see Jdem A Jdem A
Nic Nas Nezastavi

DRESCHERLIED "IM DREITAKT DER DRESCHER"
see Gerster, Ottmar

DRESS PARADE see Cohn, James

DRINK TO ME ONLY
(Willcocks) SATB,acap OXFORD see from
Five Folk Songs   (D374)

DRINKING SONG
(Deale, Edgar) SATB (med easy)
WATERLOO $.35   (D375)

DRINKING SONG see Holst, Gustav

DRINKING SONG see Mendelssohn-
Bartholdy, Felix, Trinklied

DRIVE HIM BACK TO LONDON see Bennett

DROP, SLOW TEARS see Kechley, [Gerald]

DRUBEN IM FLUSTERNEN WALDE see Orrel,
Max

DRUM SINGET DOCH see Artner, Norbert

DRUMBA DRUMBA "RUHRT DIE TROMMELN" see
Cossetto, Emil

DRUMMER BOY, THE see Bergmann, Walter

DRUNTEN IM UNTERLAND *folk,Ger
(Scherchen, Hermann) men cor,acap
TONOS 10 s.p.   (D376)

DRUNTEN IM UNTERLAND see Rein, Walter

DRUNTEN IN BARANYA "SPAT AM ABEND" see
Bresgen, Cesar

DRUSHBA-FREUNDSCHAFT *CCU
mix cor,soli,pno HOFMEISTER G2209
s.p.   (D377)

DU BIST MIN see Genzmer, Harald

DU BIST MIN see Werdin, Eberhard

DU GRUNES TAL see Edler, Robert

DU LIEBE FLUR IM SEENGRUND see Gal,
Hans, Ye Banks And Braes

DU SKA ITTE TRO I GRASET see
Storbekken, Egil

DU SOLLST MEIN EIGEN SEIN *folk,Ger
(Zipp, F.) men cor,acap TONOS 120
s.p.   (D378)

DU SONNIGE, WONNIGE WELT see
Rheinberger, Josef

DU VERKLAGEST DAS WEIB see Koenig,
Franz

DUAS LENDAS AMERINDIAS EM NHEENGATU see
Villa-Lobos, Heitor

DUBBELKANON VID KRAFTSKIVA see
Johansen, Sven-Erik

DUBUQUE, A.
Sei Nicht Traurig, Liebe Mutter
wom cor ZIMMER. 596 s.p.   (D379)

DUCKWORTH, ARTHUR (? -1974)
Heave-Yo-Ho
unis,opt solo,pno/orch ROBERTON
75017 s.p.   (D380)

DUE CANZONI see Clausetti, P.

DUE CANZONI VERONESI see Girotto,
Almerigo

DUE MADRIGALI see Veretti, Antonio

DUE MADRIGALI see Piva, Franco

DUE PUPILLE AMABILE see Mozart,
Wolfgang Amadeus

DUETTO BUFFO DI DUE GATTI see Rossini,
Gioacchino

DUIS, ERNST (1896-1967)
Europa Singt *CC8L,folk,Eur
2-4pt mix cor,acap sc SCHOTTS
C 40 119 s.p.   (D381)

DUIZEND FRAGEN see Pronk, Arie

DUKE
April In Paris *see Harburg

DUKELSKA DUMBA see Kvapil, Jaroslav

DUKLA REVERIE see Kvapil, Jaroslav,
Dukelska Dumba

DULCIS AMICA see Handl, Jacob

DUMB, DUMB, DUMB *folk,Eng
(Osborne, Chester G.) SSAA,pno (med)
oct ELKAN-V 362-03161 $.40   (D382)

DUNCAN, CHESTER
Then And Now
unis (easy) WATERLOO $.75 (D383)

DUNDAI *folk,Isr
(Garfinkle, Sonya) SATB,pno/acap
FOSTER MF329 $.30   (D384)

DUNHAM, ARTHUR
At Sundown
TTBB (med) FITZSIMONS 4043 $.20
                            (D385)

DUNHILL, THOMAS FREDERICK (1877-1946)
Cloths Of Heaven
(Davis) SSA GALAXY 1.1386.1 $.30
                            (D386)

Frog, The
mix cor BANKS MUS YS 1486 $.20
                            (D387)

Harp That Once Thro' Tara's Halls,
The
SA LESLIE 2801 $.20   (D388)

Tubal Cain *Op.15
SATB,2fl,2ob,2clar,2bsn,4horn,2trp,
3trom,tuba,timp,perc,strings voc
sc NOVELLO rental   (D389)

DUNJA *folk
(Koringer, Franz) mix cor DOBLINGER
G 710 s.p. see from Funf Satze Nach
Kroatischen Volksliedern   (D390)

DUNKLE WOLKEN "ES GEHT EIN DUNKLE
WOLKEN REIN" see Rein, Walter

DUNKLER LICHTGLANZ see Schumann, Robert
(Alexander)

DUNNER ZWIRN UND HARTER KERN see
Bartok, Bela

DUNSTABLE, JOHN (ca. 1385-1453)
Complete Works *sac/sec,CCU
cor GALAXY AMS 9.0002.08 $27.50
                            (D391)

DUR UND MOLL see Fischer, Erich

DURCH DIE BLUME see Edler, Robert

DURCH FELD UND BUCHENHALLEN see Zelter,
Carl Friedrich

DURCH NACHT ZUM LICHT see Kiesewetter,
Peter

DURKO, ZSOLT
Het Dallamrajz *CC7U
mix cor,pno BUDAPEST 7516 s.p.
                            (D392)

DURST AUF WEIN see Brucker, Hermann

DUSCHKAS LIED "SPRINGE PFERDCHEN" see
Wedig, Hans Josef

DUSON, DEDE
Mist, The
SATB oct HERITAGE H109 $.35 (D393)

DUSTY FEET see Vantine

DUT-GER-FR see Sweelinck, Jan
Pieterszoon

DVA DETSKE SBORY see Podesva, Jaromir

DVA DETSKE SBORY see Svobodo, Jiri

DVA DETSKE SBORY see Smatek, Milos

DVA MAJE see Tomasek, Jaroslav

DVA TROHLASNE ZBORY see Anonymous

DVACATERO DIKU see Kricka, Jaroslav

DVE SLAVNOSTNICH SBORU see Vlach-
Vruticky, Josef

DVE UKOLEBAVKY see Matej, Jozka

DVORACEK, JIRI (1928-   )
From The Diary Of A Prisoner *see Z
Deniku Vezne

Nove Jaro *CC4U
[Czech/Ger] wom cor,S solo,acap
CZECH s.p.   (D394)

Z Deniku Vezne
"From The Diary Of A Prisoner"
[Czech] mix cor,acap CZECH s.p.
                            (D395)

DVORAK
American Flag, The
SATB SCHIRM.G 402 $2.00   (D396)

DVORAK, ANTONIN (1841-1904)
Festival Song *see Slavnostni Zpev

Heirs Of The White Mountains *see
Hymnus

Hymn Of Czech Peasants *see Rolnicka

DVORAK, ANTONIN (cont'd.)

Hymnus *Op.30
"Heirs Of The White Mountains"
[Czech/Eng/Ger] mix cor,2fl,2ob,
2clar,2bsn,4horn,2trp,3trom,tuba,
harp,strings SUPRAPHON s.p.,
rental   (D397)

Rolnicka *Op.28
"Hymn Of Czech Peasants" [Czech/
Eng/Ger] mix cor,2fl,2ob,2clar,
2bsn,4horn,3trom,timp,strings
SUPRAPHON s.p.   (D398)

Slavnostni Zpev *Op.113
"Festival Song" [Czech] mix cor,
3fl,2ob,2clar,2bsn,4horn,2trp,
3trom,tuba,timp,perc,strings
CZECH s.p.   (D399)
"Festival Song" [Czech/Eng/Ger] mix
cor,3fl,2ob,2clar,2bsn,4horn,
2trp,3trom,tuba,timp,perc,strings
SUPRAPHON s.p.   (D400)

Spectre's Bride, The *Op.69
[Czech/Eng/Ger] mix cor,STB soli,
2fl,2ob,2clar,2bsn,4horn,2trp,
3trom,tuba,timp,perc,harp,strings
SUPRAPHON s.p., rental   (D401)

DYER, D.
Who Do You Think You Are? *see
Scott, C.

DYLAN, ROBERT (BOB) (1941-   )
Forever Young
(O'Reilly) SATB ALFRED 6812 $.50
                            (D402)
(O'Reilly) SATB/SAB ALFRED 6801
$.50   (D403)

Going, Going, Gone
(O'Reilly) SATB ALFRED 6813 $.50
                            (D404)
(O'Reilly) SATB/SAB ALFRED 6802
$.50   (D405)

DYLAN THOMAS SETTINGS see Gerber,
Steven

DYSON, GEORGE (1883-1964)
Four Songs For Sailors *CC4U
SATB,2trp,3trom,timp,strings voc sc
NOVELLO rental   (D406)

Quo Vadis
SATB,SATB soli,3fl,3ob,3clar,3bsn,
4horn,3trp,3trom,tuba,timp,perc,
harp,org,strings voc sc NOVELLO
rental   (D407)

Sweet Thames Run Softly
SATB,Bar solo,2fl,2ob,2clar,2bsn,
4horn,2trp,3trom,tuba,timp,perc,
harp,strings voc sc NOVELLO
rental   (D408)

Three Songs Of Courage *CC3U
SATB,SATB soli,2trp,3trom,timp,
strings voc sc NOVELLO rental
                            (D409)

D'ZIT ISCHT DO *folk
(Kanetscheider, Artur) men cor,acap
TONOS 804 s.p.   (D410)

E

E' BAL D' LA VINIZIENA see Pratella, Francesco Balilla

E TRISCON see Pratella, Francesco Balilla

EAGLE AND THE HAWK, THE see Denver, John

EARLY ONE MORNING
(Willcocks) SATB,acap OXFORD see from Five Folk Songs (E1)

EARLY ONE MORNING see Gal, Hans

EARLY SPRING
(Bissell, Keith W.) SATB (med diff) WATERLOO $.50 (E2)

EARLY SPRING see Jenni

EARTH SONG see Washburn

EAST, MICHAEL (ca. 1580-ca. 1648)
First Set Of Madrigals EM Vol. 29 *CC24L,madrigal
3-6pt mix cor STAINER 3.1929.1 $11.50 (E3)

Fourth Set Of Books (1618) EM Vol. 31b *CC24L
4-6pt mix cor STAINER 3.1937.1 $13.00 (E4)

Second Set Of Madrigals (1606) EM Vol. 30 *CC21L
3-6pt mix cor STAINER 3.1930.1 $11.50 (E5)

Third Set Of Books (1610) EM Vol. 31a *CC23L
4-6pt mix cor,soli,inst STAINER 3.1931.1 $11.50 (E6)

Your Shining Eyes
SSATBarB STAINER 3.0723.1 $.50 (E7)

EBEL, E.
Leise Rieselt Der Schnee
(Dedekind, A.) 4pt men cor BRATFISCH s.p. (E8)
(Erdlen, Hermann) 4pt men cor&jr cor,opt fl&vln BRATFISCH GB3250 s.p. (E9)
(Hanssler, F.) 3pt mix cor BRATFISCH s.p. (E10)
(Hanssler, F.) 3pt jr cor/3pt wom cor BRATFISCH GB3055 s.p. (E11)
(Koenig, Franz) men cor,acap TONOS 152 s.p. (E12)

EBEL, F.
Uz Zraje Podzim
jr cor SLOV.HUD.FOND EZS 6 s.p. (E13)

EBEN, PETR (1929-   )
Ach, Warum Kommst Du Nicht?
SATB MOSELER LB741 s.p. (E14)

Apologia Sokratus *ora
"Apology Of Socrates, The" [Greek] mix cor&jr cor,ABar soli,3fl,3ob, 3clar,3bsn,4horn,3trp,3trom,tuba, timp,perc,harp,pno,strings SUPRAPHON s.p. (E15)

Apology Of Socrates, The *see Apologia Sokratus

Balady *CCU
[Czech] mix cor,soli,3fl,2ob,2clar, 2bsn,4horn,2trp,3trom,tuba,timp, perc,harp,pno,strings CZECH s.p. (E16)

Do Ruzova
"In Pink" [Czech] jr cor,solo,pno SUPRAPHON s.p. (E17)

Green In The Branch
[Czech/Ger] jr cor,pno,winds,vla SUPRAPHON s.p. (E18)

In Pink *see Do Ruzova

Jarni Popevky *CCU
[Czech] jr cor,3trp,2trom,perc,pno, bvl CZECH s.p. (E19)

Trag Mich, Pferdchen
SATB MOSELER LB740 s.p. (E20)

ECCARD, JOHANNES (1553-1611)
Der Winter Kalt
SSAB,acap EGTVED KB96 s.p. (E21)

Now Come And Join The Song
(Harris) SSA SCHIRM.G 12031 $.40 (E22)

ECCARD, JOHANNES (cont'd.)
Nun Schurz Dich, Gretlein
mix cor (med easy) sc SCHOTTS CHBL 367 s.p. (E23)

Zanni Et Magnifico
see MADRIGALI A DIVERSI LINGUAGGI

ECCHO see Lassus, Roland de (Orlandus)

ECCO MORMORAR L'ONDE see Monteverdi, Claudio

ECCO QUEL FIERO ISTANTE see Mozart, Wolfgang Amadeus

ECHO "IMITARI MELICOS DOCTA MODOS" see Novak, Jan

ECHO-LIED "WIE HEISST DER BURGERMEISTER VON WESEL?" see Zoll, Paul

ECHO VOM HIMMEL "OH FREUDENHIMMEL" see Genzmer, Harald

ECHOING GREEN, THE see Fleming, Christopher le

ECHOLIEDER-SUITE see Haas, Joseph

ECKERT, ALEX (1946-   )
Die Vier Jahreszeitenelemente
jr cor,4 narrators,inst (med) sc SCHOTTS WKS 10 s.p. (E24)

Galgenlieder
jr cor&cor,narrator,brass,strings, perc (med) sc SCHOTTS WKS 1 s.p. (E25)

ECLOGA VIII see Penderecki, Krzysztof

ECUATORIAL see Varese, Edgar

EDELWEISS see Rodgers, Richard

EDIT NONNA see Schubert, Franz (Peter)

EDLE, SCHONE KUNST MUSIK see Lehr, Gregor

EDLER, ROBERT
Alle Wege Sind Bemessen
men cor,acap TONOS 3999 s.p. (E26)

Anna Susanna
see Vier Heitere Gesange

Auf In Den Sattel
men cor,acap TONOS 3998 s.p. (E27)

Aus Der Sonne In Die Tonne
see Das Vielverliebte Herz

Bergmannslied: Gluck Auf
men cor,acap TONOS 79 s.p. (E28)

Bluh Auf, O Tag
men cor,acap TONOS 4573 s.p. (E29)

Bruder, Lasst Die Lieder
men cor&jr cor,4horn,2trom,2trp, timp, triangle voc sc TONOS 4931 s.p., ipa (E30)

Das Blumengartlein
men cor,acap TONOS 4085 s.p. (E31)

Das Herz Pocht
see Das Vielverliebte Herz

Das Kohlerweib Ist Trunken
men cor,acap TONOS 4089 s.p. (E32)

Das Lieben Bringt Gross Freud (1)
men cor,acap TONOS 1 s.p. (E33)

Das Lieben Bringt Gross Freud (2)
men cor,acap TONOS 24 s.p. (E34)

Das Liedchen Von Liebe
men cor,acap TONOS 3945 s.p. (E35)

Das Madchen Mit Den Hellen Augen
men cor,acap TONOS 4068 s.p. (E36)

Das Vielverliebte Herz
men cor,acap cmplt ed TONOS 4510 s.p.
contains: Aus Der Sonne In Die Tonne; Das Herz Pocht; Durch Die Blume; In Den Rosen; Noah (E37)

Der Liebe Lange Tag
see Vier Heitere Gesange

Der Neue Jahrgang
men cor,acap TONOS 3955 s.p. (E38)

Der Ozean
see Seefahrt Tut Not

Der Tag Bricht An
men cor,acap TONOS 4598 s.p. (E39)

EDLER, ROBERT (cont'd.)
Der Tag, Er Endet
see Lieder Am Grabe

Der Tod Ist Hergekommen
see Totenfeier

Die Seeleute
see Seefahrt Tut Not

Die Sichel
men cor,acap TONOS 4071 s.p. (E40)

Die Sonne Sinkt
men cor,acap cmplt ed,sc,cor pts TONOS 4083 s.p.
contains: Heiterkeit, Guldne; Nicht Lange Durstest Du; Tag, Meines Lebens (E41)

Die Trauben Vom Paradies
see Erlenbacher Weinlieder

Die Trauerweide
men cor,acap TONOS 4072 s.p. (E42)

Die Winzer *cant
men cor,SBar soli,2fl,2ob,2clar, 2bsn,2horn,2trp,trom,perc,strings sc,cor pts TONOS 4960 rental (E43)

Du Grunes Tal
men cor,acap TONOS 3947 s.p. (E44)

Durch Die Blume
see Das Vielverliebte Herz

Ein Guter Trunk
see Erlenbacher Weinlieder

Einmal Wird Das Heil Erscheinen
men cor,2trp,2horn,2trom,tuba voc sc,cor pts TONOS 4922 s.p., ipa (E45)

Erlenbacher Weinlieder
men cor,acap cmplt ed TONOS 4560 s.p.
contains: Die Trauben Vom Paradies; Ein Guter Trunk; Wein Vom Alten Fass (E46)

Erntelied
see Lope-De-Vega-Lieder

Es Mahlen Die Muhlen
men cor,winds TONOS 4228 s.p. (E47)

Es Ruhen Die Toten
men cor,acap TONOS 4549 s.p. (E48)

Feierspruch Und Fahnenlied
men cor,acap TONOS 4518 s.p. (E49)

Fiedellieder
men cor,acap/clar&bsn&2horn&perc cmplt ed TONOS 3990 s.p.
contains: In Den Garten Eingestiegen (men cor,acap); Lang Und Breit (men cor,acap); Musikanten Wollen Wandern (men cor,acap); Musikus Und Musika; Wenn Mir Unterm Fiedelbogen (men cor,acap) (E50)

Freier Geist, Gesang, Und Wein
men cor,acap TONOS 3989 s.p. (E51)

Freude Hebt Die L. Schwingen
men cor,acap TONOS 4599 s.p. (E52)

Friede Sei Der Flamme Licht
men cor,acap TONOS 3963 s.p. (E53)

Froh Hinaus
men cor,acap TONOS 3967 s.p. (E54)

Ganz Allein Fur Mich
see Vier Heitere Gesange

Gib Uns Sanften Tod
see Lieder Am Grabe

Grune Saat
men cor,acap TONOS 4503 s.p. (E55)

Hausrecht
men cor,acap TONOS 4522 s.p. (E56)

Heiliges Land
men cor,2trp&2horn&2trom&tuba voc sc,cor pts TONOS 4923, AUSGABE A s.p., ipa (E57)
men cor/men cor&jr cor,2fl,4clar, 5horn,2trp,2trom,tuba, 2 flugelhorns, baritone horn, tenor horn voc sc,cor pts TONOS 4923, AUSGABE B s.p., ipa (E58)
men cor, trombone choir voc sc,cor pts TONOS 4923, AUSGABE C s.p., ipa (E59)
men cor,strings voc sc,cor pts TONOS 4923, AUSGABE D s.p., ipa (E60)

EDLER, ROBERT (cont'd.)

Heiterkeit, Guldne
see Die Sonne Sinkt

Hymne An Das Lied
men cor,acap TONOS 4924 s.p.   (E61)
men cor,2trp,2horn,2trom,tuba voc
sc,cor pts TONOS 4924, AUSGABE A
s.p., ipa   (E62)
men cor,2fl,4clar,2horn,2trp,3trom,
tuba,timp, 2 flugelhorns, 2 tenor
horns, baritone horn, 2 bass
trombones voc sc,cor pts TONOS
4924, AUSGABE B s.p., ipa   (E63)
men cor,4trom voc sc,cor pts TONOS
4924, AUSGABE C s.p., ipa   (E64)

Hymne Auf Den Kraichgau
men cor/men cor&jr cor,2trp,2trom,
tuba voc sc,cor pts TONOS 4933
s.p., ipa   (E65)

Ich Reit Auf Einem Rosselein
men cor,acap TONOS 77 s.p.   (E66)

Im Takte Der Hammer
men cor,acap TONOS 4076 s.p.   (E67)

Im Weine Spiegelt Sich
men cor,acap TONOS 4532 s.p.   (E68)

In Dem Wald
men cor,acap TONOS 4063 s.p.   (E69)

In Den Garten Eingestiegen
see Fiedellieder

In Den Rosen
see Das Vielverliebte Herz

In Veritas
men cor,acap TONOS 4565 s.p.   (E70)

Jetzt Singt Der Tod
see Totenfeier

Jugendflucht
men cor,acap TONOS 4074 s.p.   (E71)

Kein Schoner Land
men cor,acap, piano part by G.
Monreal, ad lib. TONOS 67 s.p.
                                (E72)

Kellerprobe
men cor,acap TONOS 4531 s.p.   (E73)

Komm Mit
men cor,acap TONOS 4502 s.p.   (E74)

Land
men cor,acap TONOS 4554 s.p.   (E75)

Lang Und Breit
see Fiedellieder

Leuchte, Scheine, Goldne Sonne
men cor&jr cor,2trp,2horn,2trom,
tuba voc sc,cor pts TONOS 4921
s.p., ipa   (E76)

Liebe
men cor,acap TONOS 4519 s.p.   (E77)

Liebe, Gottliche Harmonie
men cor,acap TONOS 4084 s.p.   (E78)

Liebe, Lied, Und Wein
men cor,acap TONOS 4065 s.p.   (E79)

Liebe Und Treue
see Vier Heitere Gesange

Lied Der Kohlenhauer
men cor,2clar,2horn,2trp,trom,perc,
vcl,bvl TONOS 4939 s.p.   (E80)

Lied Des Einsiedels
men cor,acap TONOS 4087 s.p.   (E81)

Lieder Am Grabe
men cor,acap cmplt ed TONOS 4030
s.p.
contains: Der Tag, Er Endet; Gib
Uns Sanften Tod; Troste, Herr;
Vor Dem Grabe   (E82)

Lieder Am Grabe
men cor,acap TONOS 4030 s.p.   (E83)

Linos *cant
men cor,Bar solo,2fl,2ob,2clar,
2bsn,2trp,2horn,3trom,tuba,harp,
pno,perc,strings sc,cor pts TONOS
rental   (E84)

Lope-De-Vega-Lieder
men cor,acap cmplt ed TONOS 4550
s.p.
contains: Erntelied; Tagelied;
Wachterlied   (E85)

Madel, Musst Den Weissen Trinken
men cor,acap TONOS 3969 s.p.   (E86)

EDLER, ROBERT (cont'd.)

Maiengrun
men cor,acap TONOS 4504 s.p.   (E87)

Metzelsuppenlied
men cor,acap TONOS 4088 s.p.   (E88)

Morgenlicht
men cor,acap TONOS 4925 s.p.   (E89)
men cor/men cor&jr cor,2trp,2horn,
3trom,tuba voc sc,cor pts TONOS
4925, AUSGABE A s.p., ipa   (E90)
men cor/men cor&jr cor,2fl,2ob,
2clar,2bsn,4horn,2trp,3trom,tuba
voc sc,cor pts TONOS
4925, AUSGABE B s.p., ipa   (E91)

Musikanten Wollen Wandern
see Fiedellieder

Musikus Und Musika
see Fiedellieder

Nicht Lange Durstest Du
see Die Sonne Sinkt

Niederrheinische Landschaft
men cor,acap TONOS 4069 s.p.   (E92)

Noah
see Das Vielverliebte Herz

O Welche Tiefe Des Reichtums
men cor&jr cor,opt org,2trp,2horn,
2trom,tuba,timp TONOS 4927 s.p.,
ipa   (E93)

Puer Falerni
men cor,acap TONOS 4576 s.p.   (E94)

Rebenland
men cor,acap TONOS 3988 s.p.   (E95)

Schlussgesang
see Trauungsgesange

Schwebe, Wonnige Melodie
men cor,acap TONOS 3962 s.p.   (E96)

Seefahrt Tut Not
men cor,acap/fl&2clar&2trp&timp&
perc&strings, or accordion alone
or with combo cmplt ed,sc,cor pts
TONOS 4520 s.p.
contains: Der Ozean (men cor,
acap); Die Seeleute (men cor,
acap); Seefahrt Tut Not (men
cor,acap); Und Wir Fahren (men
cor,acap)   (E97)

Seefahrt Tut Not
see Seefahrt Tut Not

Stahl
men cor,acap,opt 3timp TONOS 4232
s.p.   (E98)

Tag, Meines Lebens
see Die Sonne Sinkt

Tagelied
see Lope-De-Vega-Lieder

Totenfeier *funeral
men cor/men cor&jr cor,acap/2horn&
2trp&2trom&tuba cmplt ed,sc,voc
sc TONOS 4932 s.p., ipa
contains: Der Tod Ist
Hergekommen; Jetzt Singt Der
Tod   (E99)

Trauungsgesange
men cor,acap cmplt ed TONOS 4081
s.p.
contains: Schlussgesang; Vor Dem
Altar; Zum Anfang   (E100)

Troste, Herr
see Lieder Am Grabe

Und Wir Fahren
see Seefahrt Tut Not

Verschwunden Ist Die Finstre Nacht
men cor,acap TONOS 3975 s.p.   (E101)

Vier Heitere Gesange
men cor,acap cmplt ed TONOS 4530
s.p.
contains: Anna Susanna; Der Liebe
Lange Tag; Ganz Allein Fur
Mich; Liebe Und Treue   (E102)

Vom Wein
men cor,acap TONOS 4064 s.p.   (E103)

Von Den Heimlichen Rosen
men cor,acap TONOS 4575 s.p.   (E104)

Vor Dem Altar
see Trauungsgesange

Vor Dem Grabe
see Lieder Am Grabe

EDLER, ROBERT (cont'd.)

Wachterlied
see Lope-De-Vega-Lieder

Wanderer, Kommst Du Nach Sparta
men cor,acap TONOS 3974 s.p.   (E105)

Weihe Der Halle
men cor&jr cor,2trp TONOS 4934
s.p., ipa   (E106)

Wein Vom Alten Fass
see Erlenbacher Weinlieder

Weizenlied
men cor,acap TONOS 4038 s.p.   (E107)

Weltschopfung
men cor,2trp,2horn,3trom voc sc,cor
pts TONOS 4929 s.p., ipa   (E108)

Wenn Der Zeiten Kreis Sich Fullt
men cor,SBar soli,2fl,2ob,2clar,
2bsn,3trp,4horn,3trom,tuba,pno,
harp,strings sc,cor pts TONOS
4962 rental   (E109)

Wenn Ich Deinen Namen
men cor,acap TONOS 3948 s.p.   (E110)

Wenn Mir Unterm Fiedelbogen
see Fiedellieder

Wir Brauchen Frieden
men cor&jr cor,2trp,2horn,2trom,
tuba voc sc,cor pts TONOS 4935
s.p., ipa   (E111)

Zum Anfang
see Trauungsgesange

EDLUND, LARS (1922-   )
Triad (composed with Hammarskjold)
cor,band NORDISKA NMS 6466 s.p.
                                (E112)

EDWARDS
Flute Players
SATB SCHIRM.G LG51726 $.45   (E113)

EDWIN HAWKINS CHORAL COLLECTION, THE
*CCU
CIMINO SSA $1.75; SATB $1.75   (E114)

"EEN DAG UIT HET LEVEN VAN. . ." see
Epen de Groot, Else van

EENS ZAL OP DE GROTE MORGEN see Pronk,
Arie

EFFINGER
Let Your Mind Wander Over America
SATB SCHIRM.G 11959 $.40   (E115)

EG SER DEG UTFOR GLUGGEN see Strohbach,
Siegfried

EGK, WERNER (1901-   )
C'est Grant Paine (from Joan Von
Zarissa)
see Drei Franzosische Chore

D'ont Vient Ce Souleil (from Joan Von
Zarissa)
see Drei Franzosische Chore

Drei Franzosische Chore (from Joan
Von Zarissa) Fr
5pt wom cor&5pt men cor,acap (diff)
sc SCHOTTS ED. 5846 s.p.
contains: C'est Grant Paine;
D'ont Vient Ce Souleil; Vous Y
Fiez Vous   (E116)

Furchtlosigkeit Und Wohlwollen *cant
mix cor,T solo,pno,2fl,2ob,2bsn,
2horn,2trp,2trom,strings,harp,
perc,timp (diff) min sc SCHOTTS
ED. 5020 s.p., sc SCHOTTS rental,
ipr   (E117)

Mein Vaterland "Dir Ist Dein Haupt
Umkranzt"
unis men cor,org/2fl&2ob&2clar&
2bsn&4horn&3trp&3trom&
strings&timp voc sc SCHOTTS
C 35 275 s.p., voc pt SCHOTTS
C 35 276 s.p., ipr   (E118)

Vous Y Fiez Vous (from Joan Von
Zarissa)
see Drei Franzosische Chore

EGLIN, ARTHUR (1932-   )
Ein Silbern ABC *CCU,canon
2-8pt LAUDINELLA LR 17 s.p.   (E119)

Funfzehn Kanons *CC15U,canon
2-8pt LAUDINELLA LR 55 s.p.   (E120)

Neun Kanons *CC9U,canon
2-4pt LAUDINELLA LR 67 s.p.   (E121)

EH ICH MICH NIEDERLEGE see Zipp,
Friedrich

EHEMANN'S LEIDEN *folk,Ger
(Brucker, Hermann) men cor,acap TONOS
57 s.p.   (E122)

EHESPRUCH "WER SICH MIT EINEM WEIB
VERBINDT" see Weber, Bernhard

EHRET, WALTER (1918-   )
Hear The Bells! See The Star! *Xmas,
carol,Pol
SA/TB MCAFEE M8018 $.40   (E123)

High Hangs The Holly *Xmas,anthem
SA oct HERITAGE H5009 $.35   (E124)

Love Brings All People Riches Untold
SATB SCHIRM.G LG51658 $.40   (E125)

One Night So Long Ago *Xmas
SA/TB MCAFEE M8008 $.35   (E126)

Sweet Lamb
SSA SHAWNEE B388 $.35   (E127)

Therefore Be Merry
SATB SHAWNEE 1272 $.35   (E128)
SA/TB SHAWNEE E147 $.35   (E129)

EI DU MEIN LIEBER GOLDSCHMIED see
Desch, Rudolf

EI, EI, EI, SAGT MEIN WEI
see Dirndal, Merk Dir Den Bam

EI, MADCHEN VOM LANDE *folk,Ger
(Frey, Oscar) men cor,acap TONOS 89
s.p.   (E130)

EI, STEIG AUF see Martinu, Bohuslav,
Aj, Stupaj

EI, WIE GEHTS IM HIMMEL ZU *folk,Ger
(Fischer, Theo) men cor,acap TONOS 48
s.p.   (E131)

EI, WOHL EINE SCHONE ZEIT see Marx,
Karl

EIA BEIA WIEGENSTROH see Weber,
Bernhard

EIA, MEIN KINDCHEN see Zoll, Paul

EIDSVOOG
Gift, The *Xmas
SAB oct SCHMITT 5546 $.40   (E132)
SATB oct SCHMITT 6104 $.40   (E133)

Let The Year Begin
SSA oct SCHMITT 2138 $.40   (E134)

EIGHT AIRS see Dowland, John

EIGHT CHORAL SONGS see Nielsen, Tage

EIGHT CHRISTMAS CAROLS, SET 2
(Rutter) SATB,inst (easy) OXFORD
48.009 $1.20, ipr
contains: Down In Yon Forest; I Saw
Three Ships; Quelle Est Cette
Odeur?; Twelve Days Of Christmas
(E135)

EIGHT ENGLISH NURSERY SONGS *CC8U
(Orff; Murray) cor, Orff inst SCHOTT
10842 s.p.   (E136)

EIGHT FOR CHRISTMAS *sac/sec,CC8U,
Xmas,carol,Fr
(Ratcliffe, D.) SATB NOVELLO s.p.
(E137)

EIGHT IMPRESSIONS see Kunz, Alfred

EIGHTS see Parker, Alice

EILERS, JOYCE ELAINE
Brighten My Soul With Sunshine
3pt LEONARD-US 08541000 $.50 (E138)

Jose, The Temporary Reindeer *Xmas
2pt,pno (easy) oct GENTRY G-223
$.35   (E139)

Takin' A Ride On Your Mind
SATB LEONARD-US 08547000 $.50
(E140)

Wildflower
SSA LEONARD-US 08549000 $.50 (E141)

EIN ALTER WIENER-BITZ
(Lessky, Fr.) mix cor DOBLINGER G 685
s.p. see from Sechs Lieder Aus Wien
(E142)

EIN BROTLAIB "EIN BROTLAIB AUF DEM
TISCHE RUHT" see Knab, Armin

EIN ERGOTZLICH LIEDERSINGEN see
Gebhard, Hans

EIN FREIER MUT "O WIE SO SCHON UND GUT"
see Mohler, Philipp

EIN GETREUES HERZ see Sutermeister,
Heinrich

EIN GETREUES HERZE WISSEN see Grell,
Eduard August

EIN GUTER TRUNK see Edler, Robert

EIN HELLER TAG BRICHT AN see Klein,
Richard Rudolf

EIN HENNLEIN WEISS see Scandello,
Antonio

EIN HERING LIEBT EINE AUSTER see
Fussan, Werner

EIN HOHES TOR see Erdlen, Hermann

EIN JAGER AUS KURPFALZ see Ketterer,
Ernst

EIN JAGER LANGS DEM WEIHER GING see
Poos, Heinrich

EIN JAGER WOLLT' ZUM JAGEN GEHN see
Zoll, Paul

EIN JEDER MEINT, ER SEI DER BEST see
Lechner, Konrad

EIN JEGLICHES HAT SEINE ZEIT see Poos,
Heinrich

EIN KINDERTAG see Kludas, Erich

EIN KLAGEGESANG "RAUHER WIND" see
Genzmer, Harald

EIN KLEINER HUND MIT NAMEN FIPS see
Rein, Walter

EIN KLEINER HUND MIT NAMEN FIPS see
Schmid, A.

EIN KLEINES LIED see Grote, Hermann

EIN KLEINES LIED see Jansen, Peter

EIN LAMMLEIN, DAS GEGANGEN see Mockl,
Franz

EIN LICHT WILL SICH ENTZUNDEN "DIE
STADT ERGLANZT IM TALE" see
Rothschuh, Franz

EIN LIED MUSS SEIN see Desch, Rudolf

EIN LIED MUSS SEIN see Zipp, Friedrich

EIN LIED ZUR NACHT see Lang, Hans

EIN LIED ZUR NACHT see Zschiecha, Alf

EIN MADCHEN UND EIN GLASCHEN WEIN see
Rein, Walter

EIN MANNLEIN STEHT IM WALDE see Lang,
Hans

EIN MENSCH, DER EINEN ANDERN TRAF see
Desch, Rudolf

EIN MUSIKANT WOLLT FROHLICH SEIN see
Zelter, Carl Friedrich

EIN NEUES LIED
unis wom cor SCHOTTS C 42 532A s.p.
see also Alle Singen Heft 1 (E143)

EIN SCHONER VOGEL FIEL see Zoll, Paul

EIN SILBERN ABC see Eglin, Arthur

EIN SOMMERLIED see Wilbrandt, Jurgen

EIN STUNDLEIN WOHL VOR TAG see Distler,
Hugo

EIN STUNDLEIN WOHL VOR TAG "DERWEIL ICH
SCHLAFEND LAG" see Schroeder,
Hermann

EIN TRAUM IST UNSER LEBEN see Mohler,
Philipp

EIN TRUNK AUS BURGUND see Miller, Franz
R.

EIN TRUNKNER DICHTER see Biebl, Franz

EIN UBERLEBENDER VON WARSCHAU see
Schoenberg, Arnold

EIN WANDERNDER GESELLE see Barthel,
Ursula

EIN WINTERABEND "WENN DER SCHNEE ANS
FENSTER FALLT" see Knab, Armin

EINBILDUNG "IN EINEM SCHREBERGARTEN
TRAUMTE" see Gebhard, Ludwig

EINE BLUME AM HUT *folk
(Seeger, P.) [Ger] 4pt men cor
MERSEBURG EM9014 s.p.   (E144)

EINE SUITE VOM WIND see Karkoschka,
Erhard

EINEM WIRTSHAUS GEGENUBER "EINER
MANDOLINE ZITTERN" see
Sutermeister, Heinrich

EINEN SOMMER LANG see Siegl, Otto

EINES MENSCHEN SEELE see Rosenstengel,
Albrecht

EINFACHE SINGSATZE see Rohwer, Jens

EINKEHR see Zollner, Karl Friedrich

EINKLANG "EINKLANG! GLORIA DER WELT"
see Lendvai, Erwin

EINMAL WIRD DAS HEIL ERSCHEINEN see
Edler, Robert

EINSAM SINGT EIN WELKER BAUM see Ishii,
Kan

EINST LIEBT ICH EIN MADCHEN SEHR see
Schroeder, Hermann

EINST STAND ICH see Michels, Josef

EINTONIG KLINGT DAS GLOCKCHEN *Russ
mix cor ZIMMER. 574 s.p.   (E145)

EISENSTEIN, JUDITH KAPLAN
Shir Hashahar *cant
"Song Of The Dawn" [Eng/Heb] wom
cor/jr cor,SBar soli TRANSCON.
TCL 377 $2.50   (E146)

Song Of The Dawn *see Shir Hashahar

EISLER, HANNS (1898-1962)
Woodbury-Liederbuchlein *CCU
wom cor,acap DEUTSCHER DVFM7653
s.p.   (E147)

EISMA, WILL (1929-   )
Pages From Albion Moonlight
mix cor,soli,org,2fl,ob,3clar,2bsn,
2horn,2trp,trom,tuba,strings,
timp,harp, alto saxophone DONEMUS
(E148)

EJ, HOR SA SVETA PROLETARI see Letnan,
Julius

EJSZAKA II see Lendvay, Kamillo

EKLOF, EINAR (1886-1954)
Morgon (Sverige)
men cor ERIKS 340 s.p.   (E149)
4pt mix cor ERIKS 339 s.p.   (E150)

EKLUND, STIG
En Dod
men cor GEHRMANS KVB353   (E151)

Hemkomsten
men cor GEHRMANS KVB352   (E152)

Stilla Sova De Nu
mix cor GEHRMANS KRB448   (E153)

EL CARBONERO see Bussotti, Sylvano

EL CONDOR PASA *pop
(Reed, W.; Milchberg, J.; Robles, D.)
"If I Could" SATB,pno,opt fl oct
BIG BELL $.40   (E154)
(Reed, W.; Milchberg, J.; Robles, D.)
"If I Could" SSA,pno,opt fl oct BIG
BELL $.40   (E155)
(Reed, W.; Milchberg, J.; Robles, D.)
"If I Could" SAB,pno,opt fl oct BIG
BELL $.40   (E156)
(Reed, W.; Milchberg, J.; Robles, D.)
"If I Could" SA,pno,opt fl oct BIG
BELL $.40   (E157)

ELCKERLYC-EVERYMAN see Monnikendam,
Marius

ELDRIDGE, GUY H. (1904-   )
Fortune Seeker, The
SA CRAMER $.20   (E158)

ELEGIE see Glinka, H.

ELEGIEN see Strobl, Otto

ELEGY see Brent-Smith, Alexander

ELEGY see Brown

ELEMENT A MADARKA see Bartok, Bela

ELERGY see Zimmer, Jan

ELFENSANG "UM MITTERNACHT" see Sturmer,
Bruno

ELGAR
I'll Always Remember
(Lojeski; Cofield) SATB LEONARD-US
08231000 $.50   (E159)
(Lojeski; Cofield) SSA LEONARD-US
08231002 $.50   (E160)

ELGAR, EDWARD (1857-1934)
  Banner Of St. George
    SATB,opt S solo,2fl,pic,2ob,2clar,
    2bsn,4horn,3trp,3trom,tuba,timp,
    perc,org,strings voc sc NOVELLO
    rental   (E161)

  Black Knight, The *Op.25
    SATB,SATB soli,3fl,2ob,3clar,2bsn,
    4horn,2trp,3trom,tuba,timp,perc,
    org,strings voc sc NOVELLO rental
                                      (E162)

  Caractacus *Op.35
    SATB,STBarB soli,2fl,pic,2ob,3trp,
    3trom,4horn,4trp,3trom,tuba,timp,
    perc,harp,org,strings,
    glockenspiel voc sc NOVELLO
    rental   (E163)

  Dream Of Gerontius *Op.38
    SATB,MezTB soli,3fl,3ob,3clar,3bsn,
    4horn,3trp,3trom,tuba,timp,perc,
    1-2harp,org,strings voc sc
    NOVELLO rental   (E164)

  For The Fallen (from Spirit Of
    England, The)
    SATB,T/S solo,3fl,3ob,3clar,3bsn,
    4horn,3trp,3trom,tuba,timp,perc,
    2harp,org,strings voc sc NOVELLO
    rental   (E165)

  It Comes From The Misty Ages (from
    Banner Of St. George)
    SATB,2fl,2ob,2clar,2bsn,4horn,3trp,
    3trom,tuba,timp,perc,org,strings
    voc sc NOVELLO rental   (E166)

  King Olaf *Op.30
    SATB&STB,2fl,pic,2ob,3clar,2bsn,
    4horn,3trp,3trom,tuba,timp,perc,
    harp,org,strings, English horn
    voc sc NOVELLO rental   (E167)

  Kingdom, The *Op.51
    SATB,SATB soli,3fl,pic,3ob,3clar,
    3bsn,4horn,3trp,3trom,tuba,timp,
    perc,harp,org,strings voc sc
    NOVELLO rental   (E168)

  Light Of Life *Op.29
    SATB,SATBar soli,2fl,pic,2ob,2clar,
    3bsn,4horn,2trp,3trom,tuba,timp,
    perc,harp,org,strings voc sc
    NOVELLO rental   (E169)

  Lullaby
    SATB STAINER 3.0797.1 $.50   (E170)

  Music Makers, The *Op.69
    SATB,A solo,3fl,3ob,3clar,3bsn,
    4horn,3trp,3trom,tuba,timp,perc,
    2harp,org,strings voc sc NOVELLO
    rental   (E171)

  Nederland En Oranje (from Pomp And
    Circumstance, No.1)
    (De Wolff) mix cor sc HEER 482 s.p.
                                      (E172)
    (De Wolff) mix cor cor pts HEER
    482A s.p.   (E173)
    (De Wolff) men cor sc HEER 485 s.p.
                                      (E174)
    (De Wolff) men cor cor pts HEER
    485A s.p.   (E175)

  Prelude And Angel's Farewell (from
    Dream Of Gerontius)
    SATB,T solo,2fl,3ob,3clar,3bsn,
    4horn,3trp,3trom,tuba,timp,perc,
    harp,org,strings voc sc NOVELLO
    rental   (E176)

  Spirit Of England, The *Op.80
    SATB,T/S solo,3fl,3ob,3clar,3bsn,
    4horn,3trp,3trom,tuba,timp,perc,
    2harp,org,strings voc sc NOVELLO
    rental   (E177)

ELIZABETHAN TWO-PART SONGS *CCU
  (Fellowes, E.H.) 2pt STAINER 3.0557.1
  $3.00   (E178)

ELIZABETHAN TWO-PART SONGS *CCU
  (Fellowes, E.H.) SA STAINER 3.0557.1
  $3.00   (E179)

ELLIOTT, CARLETON
  Three Carols *CC3U
    SSA,acap HARRIS $.25   (E180)

ELMULT IDOKBOL see Bartok, Bela

ELOHIM HASHIVAYNU see Rossi, Salomone

ELOTTED A KUZDES see Szonyi, Erzsebet

ELYSIAN FIELDS see Kurtz, Eugene

EM FRUELIG ZUE see Stern, Alfred

EMELEUS, JOHN
  Huntsmen, The
    girl cor,pno WEINBERGER s.p. (E181)

EMIGRANTVISA *folk,Swed
  (Jehrlander, Karl-Fredrik) mix cor
  GEHRMANS KRB451   (E182)

EMMERT, FRANTISEK (1940-   )
  Balet Pro Solovou Tanecnici
    "Ballet For Solo Danceuse" [Czech]
    mix cor,fl,3perc,2gtr CZECH s.p.
                                      (E183)
  Ballet For Solo Danceuse *see Balet
    Pro Solovou Tanecnici

EMMETT, DANIEL DECATUR (1815-1904)
  Dixie
    (Snyder, J.A.) SATB,acap oct
    SOMERSET BR 2010 $.30   (E184)

EN BRODER MER see Johansen, Sven-Erik

EN DOD see Eklund, Stig

EN EGO CAMPANA see Handl, Jacob

EN GANG see Kvam, Oddvar S.

EN GANGLAT see Berg, Gottfrid

EN LA FUENTE DEL ROSEL see Vasquez,
  Juan

EN MER see Filleul

EN PARADIS see Ladmirault, P.

EN SOMMARDAG MED BELLMAN see Bellman,
  Carl Mikael

EN SORTANT DE L'ECOLE see Kosma, J.

EN VOS, ADIEUX, DAMES see Rore,
  Cipriano de

ENCHANTED VALLEY, THE *folk,Ir
  (Nelson, Havelock) SSA,S solo,acap
  ROBERTON 75039 s.p.   (E185)

ENCINA, JUAN DEL (1468-1529)
  A Tal Perdida Tan Triste
    "For A Loss So Bleak, Oh So Sad"
    see Encina, Juan Del, Triste
    Espana, Sin Ventura!

  Arise, Run, Pascual, Arise, Run *see
    Levanta, Pascual, Levanta

  Cucu
    see SPANISH RENAISSANCE: SIX SONGS

  Fata La Parte
    see SPANISH RENAISSANCE: SIX SONGS

  For A Loss So Bleak, Oh So Sad *see
    A Tal Perdida Tan Triste

  Let Us Eat, Drink And Be Merry *see
    Oy Comamos Y Bebamos

  Levanta, Pascual, Levanta
    "Arise, Run, Pascual, Arise, Run"
    see Encina, Juan Del, Qu'es De
    Ti, Desconsolado?

  Oy Comamos Y Bebamos
    (Malin, Don) "Let Us Eat, Drink And
    Be Merry" TTBB,acap BELWIN 2328
    $.35   (E186)

  Pues Que Jamais Olvidaros
    see SPANISH RENAISSANCE: SIX SONGS

  Qu'es De Ti, Desconsolado? *Span
    (Nin-Culmell, Joaquin) "What Of
    Thee, Disconsolate One?" [Eng/
    Span] STB,acap/inst BROUDE BR.
    $.55 contains also: Levanta,
    Pascual, Levanta, "Arise, Run,
    Pascual, Arise, Run" (STB,trp,
    2trom,tamb)   (E187)

  Quien Te Trajo, Caballero?
    "Who Did Bring Thee, Knight So
    Lonely?" see Ribera, Antonio de,
    Por Unos Puertos Arriba

  Spain, Sad Spain, Misfortunate One
    *see Triste Espana, Sin Ventura!

  Triste Espana
    see SPANISH RENAISSANCE: SIX SONGS

  Triste Espana, Sin Ventura! *Span
    (Nin-Culmell, Joaquin) "Spain, Sad
    Spain, Misfortunate One" [Eng/
    Span] SATB,acap/inst BROUDE BR.
    $.40 contains also: A Tal Perdida
    Tan Triste, "For A Loss So Bleak,
    Oh So Sad"   (E188)

  What Of Thee, Disconsolate One? *see
    Qu'es De Ti, Desconsolado?

  Who Did Bring Thee, Knight So Lonely?
    *see Quien Te Trajo, Caballero?

ENCORE, THREE TEMPERANCE SONGS see
  Hunter

END OF THE WORLD
  SATB CIMINO $.40   (E189)

END OF THE WORLD, THE see Kent

ENE MENE see Holm, Peder

ENE MENE TINTENFASS see Thiel, Jorn

ENEKELJETEK see Bardos, Lajos

ENFIELD, PATRICK
  Girls In The Garden
    SA,pno WEINBERGER s.p.   (E190)

ENGEL, H.
  Bergmannsgruss
    men cor,acap ERDMANN 123 s.p.
                                      (E191)
  Die Weihnachtsnachtigall *Xmas
    men cor,acap ERDMANN 124 s.p.
                                      (E192)
  Frohliche Weihnacht Uberall *Xmas
    men cor,acap ERDMANN 125 s.p.
                                      (E193)
  Gluck Auf, Der Steiger Kommt
    men cor,acap ERDMANN 127 s.p.
                                      (E194)

ENGLAND, MY ENGLAND see Willan, Healey,
  Pro Rege Nostra

ENGLISCH HORN see Genzmer, Harald

ENGLISH AND FRENCH FOLK SONGS *CCU,
  folk,Eng/Fr
  (Clausen, Karl) cor,solo,pno HANSEN-
  DEN WH 29244 s.p.   (E195)

ENGLISH GIRLS see Mechem, Kirke

ENGVICK
  While We're Young *see Wilder

ENOCH see Gyring, Elizabeth

ENTER THE YOUNG see Kirkman, Terry

ENTERTAINER, THE see Joplin, Scott

ENTERTAINERS, THE see Joplin, Scott

ENTFLIEH' MIT MIR see Mendelssohn-
  Bartholdy, Felix

ENTLAUBET IST DER WALDE see Senfl,
  Ludwig

ENTSCHULDIGUNG: UND SITZ ICH see
  Silcher, Friedrich

ENTSCHULDIGUNG "UND SITZ ICH IN DER
  SCHENKE" see Silcher, Friedrich

ENTTAUSCHTE LIEBE *folk
  (Witt, G. De) [Ger] 4pt men cor
  MERSEBURG EM9027 s.p.   (E196)

EPEN DE GROOT, ELSE VAN (1919-   )
  Day In The Life Of. . ., A *see
    "Een Dag Uit Het Leven Van. . . "

  "Een Dag Uit Het Leven Van. . . "
    "Day In The Life Of. . . ., A" mix
    cor,TBar soli,2fl,ob,3clar,bsn,
    2horn,3trp,3trom,strings,perc,
    harp DONEMUS   (E197)

EPIGRAMMA see Kounadis, Arghyris

EPISTLE TO BE LEFT IN THE EARTH see
  Chavez, Carlos

EPITAFFI see Arrigo, Girolamo

EPITAPH see Biggs, John

EPITAPH FOR PRUDENCE PRINGLE see Silver

EPITAPHE POUR EVARISTE GALOIS see
  Wildberger, Jacques

EPITAPHS see McAfee, Don

EPPERSON, EMERY G.
  Our Dear Old High School
    unis (easy) FITZSIMONS 3019 $.20
                                      (E198)

EPSTEIN
  Fancy
    SATB SCHIRM.G LG51759 $.45   (E199)

EQUABLE EXPLANATION see Cohn, James

ER IST'S see Distler, Hugo

ER WAS EREIS see Linden, N. v.d.

ERATO "EGO TE VOCE HIANTI NIMIS ORO"
  see Novak, Jan

ERBELDING, DIETRICH
Wir Wandern Im Sonnenschein
men cor,acap TONOS 2043 s.p. (E200)

ERCOLANO, T.
Io Tacero
cor BONGIOVANI 2367 s.p. (E201)

Occhi Leggiadri
cor BONGIOVANI 2366 s.p. (E202)

Quell'augellin Che Canta
cor BONGIOVANI 2369 s.p. (E203)

Villanella
cor BONGIOVANI 2368 s.p. (E204)

ERDLEN, HERMANN (1893-1972)
Allerleirauh
see Das Hohe Tor

An Den Geister
see Das Hohe Tor

Das Fruhjahr Ist Gekommen
men cor sc SCHOTTS C 38 074 s.p.
(E205)

Das Hohe Tor
men cor,acap cmplt ed TONOS 4080
s.p.
contains: Allerleirauh (contains
also: Wintersonnenwende); An
Den Geister (contains also:
Wandernder Winterwind); Der
Gang Zur Wiege (contains also:
O Tanne Grun); Ein Hohes Tor
(contains also: Es Grunt Ein
Reis); Es Grunt Ein Reis
(contains also: Ein Hohes Tor);
Knecht Ruprechts Erzahlung; O
Tanne Grun (contains also: Der
Gang Zur Wiege); Schlachtefest;
Wandernder Winterwind (contains
also: An Den Geister);
Winterlied; Wintersonnenwende
(contains also: Allerleirauh)
(E206)

Das Madchen Vom Lande "Ei, Madchen
Vom Lande"
men cor sc SCHOTTS CHBL 153 s.p.
see from Vier Leichte Mannerchore
(E207)

De Hamborger Veermaster "Ick Heff Mol
En Hamborger Veermaster Sehn"
4pt men cor,solo, opt accordion sc,
cor pts SCHOTTS
C 38 637, C 38 638 s.p. see from
Drei Shanties Und Seemannslieder
(E208)

Der Buckligte Fiedler
men cor sc SCHOTTS C 38 518 s.p.
(E209)

Der Gang Zur Wiege
see Das Hohe Tor

Die Funf Huhnerchen "Ich War Mal In
Dem Dorfe"
jr cor (easy) sc SCHOTTS CHBL 536
s.p. (E210)

Die Gaste Der Buche "Mietgaste Vier
Im Haus"
jr cor (easy) sc SCHOTTS CHBL 534
s.p. (E211)

Die Heimat
see Lieder Von Leid Und Licht

Die Madchen Von Batavia "Ruhig Uber
Sanfte Wogen"
4pt men cor,solo, opt accordion sc,
cor pts SCHOTTS
C 38 641, C 38 642 s.p. see from
Drei Shanties Und Seemannslieder
(E212)

Drei Shanties Und Seemannslieder
*see De Hamborger Veermaster "Ick
Heff Mol En Hamborger Veermaster
Sehn"; Die Madchen Von Batavia
"Ruhig Uber Sanfte Wogen";
Magelhan-Song "Doar Fohr Von
Hamborg Mol So'n Oolen Kassen"
(E213)

Ein Hohes Tor
see Das Hohe Tor

Es Blies Ein Jager Wohl In Sein Horn
men cor&jr cor,acap TONOS 1312 s.p.
(E214)

Es Grunt Ein Reis
see Das Hohe Tor

Es Naht Die Polizei "Wehe Dem, Der
Boses Tut"
men cor sc SCHOTTS C 38 273 s.p.
(E215)

Fruhstuck "Alle Unsre Tauben"
jr cor (easy) sc SCHOTTS CHBL 535
s.p. (E216)

Gesegnete Not
see Lieder Von Leid Und Licht

Guten Morgen, Spielmann
see Erdlen, Hermann, Will Ich In
Mein Gartlein Gehn

ERDLEN, HERMANN (cont'd.)

Heilige Arbeit
see Lieder Von Leid Und Licht

Hochzeitslied "Aus Meinem Brunnlein
Fliesst"
men cor sc SCHOTTS CHBL 152 s.p.
see from Vier Leichte Mannerchore
(E217)

Knecht Ruprechts Erzahlung
see Das Hohe Tor

Lied Vor Tag "Was Bewegt Dich"
see Erdlen, Hermann, Lied Zur Nacht
"Eh Ich Mich Niederlege"

Lied Zur Nacht "Eh Ich Mich
Niederlege"
4pt wom cor (easy) sc SCHOTTS
CHBL 540A;B s.p. contains also:
Lied Vor Tag "Was Bewegt Dich"
(E218)

Lieder Des Lebens
men cor,acap TONOS 3970 s.p. (E219)

Lieder Von Leid Und Licht
men cor,acap cmplt ed TONOS 4010
s.p.
contains: Die Heimat; Gesegnete
Not; Heilige Arbeit; Wach Auf!
(E220)

Lob Des Lebens, Preis Der Erde "Lasst
Die Goldnen Becher Kreisen"
men cor sc SCHOTTS C 38 517 s.p.
(E221)

Magelhan-Song "Doar Fohr Von Hamborg
Mol So'n Oolen Kassen"
4pt men cor,solo, opt accordion sc,
cor pts SCHOTTS C 38 639, 38 640
s.p. see from Drei Shanties Und
Seemannslieder (E222)

Maienlied
men cor,acap TONOS 4541 s.p. (E223)

Morgenlied "Bald Ist Der Nacht Ein
End' Gemacht"
4pt men cor,2trp sc SCHOTTS
CHBL 104 s.p. (E224)

Morgenlied "Verschwunden Ist Die
Finstre Nacht"
men cor sc SCHOTTS CHBL 150 s.p.
see from Vier Leichte Mannerchore
(E225)

Neues Leben "Es Schlief Die Gute
Mutter Erde" (from Die Schone
Lilofee")
wom cor (easy) sc SCHOTTS CHBL 518
s.p. (E226)

O Tanne Grun
see Das Hohe Tor

Pflugerlied
men cor,acap sc,cor pts TONOS 4005
s.p. (E227)

Schlachtefest
see Das Hohe Tor

Schneckenlied "Schneck, Schneck,
Mauschen"
jr cor (easy) sc SCHOTTS CHBL 532
s.p. (E228)

Schwefelholzle
men cor&jr cor,acap TONOS 1314 s.p.
(E229)

So Treiben Wir Den Winter Aus *cant
mix cor&jr cor/wom cor,Bar solo,fl,
ob,2clar,bsn,horn,2trp,strings,
timp (med easy) voc sc,cor pts
SCHOTTS ED. 5166 s.p., ipa (E230)

Tageslied "Wenn Durch Die Nebelfruhe"
men cor sc SCHOTTS CHBL 151 s.p.
see from Vier Leichte Mannerchore
(E231)

Trara! So Blasen Die Jager *canon/
folk
mix cor (med easy, all 3 versions
may be performed together) sc
SCHOTTS CHBL 400 s.p. (E232)
men cor (med easy, all 3 versions
may be performed together) sc
SCHOTTS CHBL 204 s.p. (E233)
3pt wom cor (med easy, all 3
versions may be performed
together) sc SCHOTTS CHBL 599
s.p. (E234)

Treue Liebe
men cor,acap TONOS 36 s.p. (E235)

Trinklied "Freunde, Das Ist Unsre
Zeit"
men cor sc SCHOTTS C 37 947 s.p.
(E236)

Vier Leichte Mannerchore *see Das
Madchen Vom Lande "Ei, Madchen
Vom Lande"; Hochzeitslied "Aus
Meinem Brunnlein Fliesst";
Morgenlied "Verschwunden Ist Die
Finstre Nacht"; Tageslied "Wenn

ERDLEN, HERMANN (cont'd.)

Durch Die Nebelfruhe" (E237)

Wach Auf!
see Lieder Von Leid Und Licht

Wandernder Winterwind
see Das Hohe Tor

Will Ich In Mein Gartlein Gehn
wom cor (easy) sc SCHOTTS
CHBL 572A;B s.p. contains also:
Guten Morgen, Spielmann (E238)

Winterlied
see Das Hohe Tor

Wintersonnenwende
see Das Hohe Tor

ERDMANN, DIETRICH
Liebes Pferd
4pt mix cor,acap NEUE NM1012 s.p.
(E239)

EREIGNIS see Werdin, Eberhard

ERES ALTA
(De Cormier) TBB SCHIRM.G LG51620
$.30 (E240)

ERES TU
"Touch The Wind" SAB CIMINO $.40
(E241)
"Touch The Wind" SSA CIMINO $.40
(E242)
"Touch The Wind" SATB CIMINO $.40
(E243)

ERFAHRUNG see Gerster, Ottmar

ERFAHRUNGEN see Steffen, Wolfgang

ERGO BIBAMUS see Fichtner, Christian

ERHABEN, O HERR see Grell, Eduard
August

ERINNERUNG see Strecke, Gerhard

ERKALTETER LANDGENDARM IM SCHNEE "ES
SCHNEIT" see Zehm, Friedrich

ERKEL, FRANZ (FERENC) (1810-1893)
Gyaszkar
(Matyas, Janos; Raics, Istvan) mix
cor BUDAPEST 6708 s.p. (E244)
(Matyas, Janos; Raics, Istvan) men
cor BUDAPEST 6709 s.p. (E245)

ERKENNEN UND SCHAFFEN see Sutermeister,
Heinrich

ERLENBACHER WEINLIEDER see Edler,
Robert

ERNTEDANK see Doppelbauer, Josef
Friedrich

ERNTEDANK "HERR, DIE FELDER SIND NUN
LEER" see Poos, Heinrich

ERNTEDANKLIED "WIR BRINGEN MIT GESAND
UND TANZ" see Schulz, Joh. Abraham
Peter

ERNTEKANTATE see Schuler, Karl

ERNTELIED see Edler, Robert

ERNTEREIGEN "WIR BRINGEN MIT GESANG"
see Lang, Hans

ERNTETAG see Siegl, Otto

ERNTETANZLIED *folk
(Zoll, P.) [Ger] 4pt men cor
MERSEBURG EM9009 s.p. (E246)

EROS AND DEATH see Brunswick, Mark

ERSTES MUSIKALISCHES STRAUSSLEIN, 1617
see Friderici, Daniel

ERZSIKEHEZ see Szabo, Csaba

ES BEGAB SICH see Gebhard, Ludwig

ES BLIES EIN JAGER WOHL IN SEIN HORN
(Wangenheim, Volker) men cor
HOFMEISTER G2205 s.p. (E247)

ES BLIES EIN JAGER WOHL IN SEIN HORN
see Erdlen, Hermann

ES BLINKEN SO LUSTIG DIE STERNE see
Weber, Carl Maria von

ES BLUHEN DIE MAIEN see Haas, Joseph

ES BLUS EIN JAGER WOHL IN SEIN HORN see
Fussan, Werner

ES DUNKELT SCHON IN DER HEIDE see Lang,
Hans

ES, ES, ES UND ES see Knab, Armin

ES, ES, ES UND ES see Zipp, Friedrich

ES FIEL EIN REIF IN DER FRUHLINGSNACHT
see Hessenberg, Kurt

ES FIEL EIN REIF IN DER FRUHLINGSNACHT
see Mendelssohn-Bartholdy, Felix

ES FOLGT MIR AUS DER JUGENDZEIT see
Gauss, Otto

ES FUHR EIN BAU'R INS HOLZ
see Offenes Singen Nr. 89

ES GEHT EIN DUNKLE WOLK HEREIN see
Distler, Hugo

ES GEHT EIN PFLUGER UBERS LAND see
Fussan, Werner

ES GEHT EIN WEHEN see Brahms, Johannes

ES GEHT WOHL ANDERS ALS DU MEINST see
Mohler, Philipp

ES GEHT WOHL ANDERS ALS DU MEINST see
Pepping, Ernst

ES GEHT WOHL ZU DER SOMMERZEIT see
Zipp, Friedrich

ES GING EIN BAUERLEIN
(Reiter, Albert) treb cor DOBLINGER
O 346 s.p. see from Sechs
Osterreichische Volkslieder (E248)

ES GING EIN JUNGFRAU ZARTE see Desch,
Rudolf

ES GING EIN MADCHEN see Michels, Josef

ES GING EINE JUNGFRAU ZARTE see Zoll,
Paul

ES GINGEN DREI GESELLEN see Lang, Hans

ES GIT NIT LUSTIGERS UF DER WALD see
Zahner, Bruno

ES GRABT DER BERGMANN see Michels,
Josef

ES GRUNT EIN REIS see Erdlen, Hermann

ES HAT JA SCHON DREI G'SCHLAGN *folk
(Wulz, Helmut) mix cor DOBLINGER
G 714-715 s.p. contains also: Gelt,
Diandle, Dei Bua Tuat Nix Schean
(E249)

ES IST EIN SCHNEE GEFALLEN *folk,Ger
(Lendvai, E.) men cor,acap TONOS 14
s.p. (E250)

ES IST EIN SCHNEE GEFALLEN see Othmayr,
Kaspar

ES IST EIN SCHNITTER
see Sichers Teutschland, Schlafst Du
Noch?

ES IST NIT ALLEWEGE FESTABEND see
Brautigam, Helmut

ES IST SO STILL GEWORDEN see Haas,
Joseph

ES IST SO STILL GEWORDEN see Spitta,
Heinrich

ES KOMMT EIN HEIMLICH FREUEN see
Kanetscheider, Artur

ES LEBEN DIE SOLDATEN see Mohler,
Philipp

ES LOHNT SICH see Krietsch, Georg

ES MAHLEN DIE MUHLEN see Edler, Robert

ES NAHT DIE POLIZEI "WEHE DEM, DER
BOSES TUT" see Erdlen, Hermann

ES QUELLEN ALLE BRONNEN see Leist,
Peter Marzellin

ES RUHEN DIE TOTEN see Edler, Robert

ES SASS EIN KAFER AUF'M BAUMEL see
Gebhard, Hans

ES SCHEINEN DIE STERNLEIN *folk
(Koenig, F.) men cor,acap TONOS 43
s.p. (E251)

ES SCHLAFT IN ALLEM DING EIN KLANG see
Rein, Walter

ES SITZT EIN VOGEL see Kirsch, Winfried

ES SOLL EIN WEIN SEIN see Seib,
Valentin

ES STEHN DREI STERNLEIN see Michels,
Josef

ES STEHT EIN LIND *folk,Ger
(Lendvai, E.) men cor,acap TONOS 15
s.p. (E252)

ES STEHT EIN LIND see Clemens, Jacobus

ES STEHT EIN LIND IN JENEM TAL see
Hessenberg, Kurt

ES STUND EIN FROWE ALLEINE see Werdin,
Eberhard

ES TAGET VOR DEM WALDE *folk
(Nehrkorn, Alex) SSATB MOSELER LB538
(E253)

ES TAGET VOR DEM WALDE see Hessenberg,
Kurt

ES TONEN DIE LIEDER see Jage, Rolf-
Diether

ES WANDELN SICH DIE REICHE see Zipp,
Friedrich

ES WAR EINMAL EIN GARTNER *folk,Ger
(Schneider, Walther) men cor,acap
TONOS 84 s.p. (E254)

ES WAREN ZWEI KONIGSKINDER see Zipp,
Friedrich

ES WERDE LICHT! see Haas, Joseph

ES WOHNT EIN MULLER AN JENEM TEICH see
Fussan, Werner

ES WOLLT EIN JAGER JAGEN see Greitter,
Matthaeus

ES WOLLT EIN JAGERLEIN JAGEN see Rein,
Walter

ES WOLLT EIN SCHNEIDER WANDERN see
Coenen, Hans

ESCAPE see Cockshott, Gerald Wilfred

ESCE JEDNU see Martinu, Bohuslav

ESCONDIDO *folk,So Am
see Singende Jugend Nr. 16
(Edler, Rudolf) men cor,acap TONOS
2052 s.p. (E255)

ESEL, ESEL, MULLERSKNECHT see Rein,
Walter

ESELREIGEN see Werdin, Eberhard

ESKIMO SONGS see Bunge, Sas

ESKYMACKA UKOLEBAVKA see Hurnik, Ilja

ESKYMO LULLABY see Hurnik, Ilja,
Eskymacka Ukolebavka

ESPANA EN EL CORAZON see Nono, Luigi

ESPOIR, TOI FILLE DES CIEUX! see
Anonymous

ESSEN, TRINKEN see Mozart, Wolfgang
Amadeus

ESSEN-TRINKEN see Orrel, Max

ESTINGUERAI LA MUSA see Lorenzini,
Danzio

L'ESTOCART, PASCHAL DE (1539-1584)
Beauty From This World *see Le Beau
Du Monde S'efface

Le Beau Du Monde S'efface
(Malin, Don) "Beauty From This
World" SSA BELWIN 2292 $.35
(E256)

ESTRANGED RETURN see In Der Fremde

ET LA LA LA see Ninot le Petit

ET WAR EMOAL TWEE SCHWESTRE JUNG *folk
(Felt, Gerhard) SSA MOSELER LB1008
s.p. see from Abend An Der Memel
(E257)

ETERNAL CLOUDS see Burghauser, Jarmil,
Vecna Oblaka

ETLER, ALVIN [DERALD] (1913-1973)
Slogan For An Artist
SA,acap BOONIN B 159 $.30 (E258)

ETON CHOIRBOOK 1 *CCU
(Harrison) STAINER 3.8910.8 $22.50
(E259)

ETON CHOIRBOOK 2 *CCU
(Harrison) cor STAINER 3.8911.8
$22.50 (E260)

ETON CHOIRBOOK 3 *CCU
(Harrison) cor STAINER 3.8912.8
$22.50 (E261)

ETTI, KARL (1912-)
Mich Wundert, Dass Ich Frohlich Bin
men cor DOBLINGER M 263 s.p. (E262)

Schieb Den Riegel Vor *folk
mix cor DOBLINGER 673 s.p. (E263)

Wer Im Werk Den Lohn Gefunden
(Wildgans, A.) men cor DOBLINGER
M 264 s.p. (E264)

EUROPA SINGT *CC10L,folk,Eur
(Duis, Ernst) 2-4pt mix cor SCHOTTS
C 40 119 s.p. (E265)

EUROPA SINGT see Duis, Ernst

EUROPAISCHE MADRIGALE, HEFT 1 *CCU,
madrigal
3-5pt mix cor,acap bds PELIKAN PE802
s.p. (E266)

EUROPAISCHE MADRIGALE, HEFT 2 *CCU,
madrigal
2-4 eq voices,acap bds PELIKAN PE803
s.p. (E267)

EUROPAISCHE MADRIGALE, HEFT 3 *CCU,
madrigal
3-5pt mix cor,acap PELIKAN PE821 bds
s.p., cloth s.p. (E268)

EUROPAISCHE MADRIGALE, HEFT 4 *CCU,
madrigal
2-4 eq voices,acap PELIKAN PE821 bds
s.p., cloth s.p. (E269)

EUROPAISCHE VOLKS- UND KINDERLIEDER
BAND I see Bresgen, Cesar

EUROPAISCHE VOLKS- UND KINDERLIEDER
BAND II see Bresgen, Cesar

EVANS
Man In A Rowboat, The
cor,pno MCAFEE M1049 $.40 (E270)

Tongue Twister
SSA MARKS MC 4639 $.40 (E271)

EVANS, PAUL
That's What Lovin' You Is All About
(composed with Hatcher, Edger;
Michlin, Spencer)
(Simon, W.) SATB BIG3 $.45 (E272)
(Simon, W.) SAB BIG3 $.45 (E273)
(Simon, W.) SSA BIG3 $.45 (E274)

EVE AND MORN OF CHRISTMAS, THE see
Hagemann, P.

EVE, MY SWEET see Kodaly, Zoltan

EVEILLE-TOI see Binet

EVEILLEZ-VOUS *folk
(Osburg, R.) "Fruhlingslied" [Ger/Fr]
4pt mix cor MERSEBURG EM9247 s.p.
(E275)

EVENING SHADOWS GENTLY FALLING see
Track, Gerhard

EVENING SONG, AN see Balazs, Frederic

EVENING SONG OF A TRAVELLER see
Distler, Hugo, Abendlied Eines
Reisenden

EVENING STAR see Atkinson, Condit R.

EVENTIDE see Lockwood, Normand

EVER HOMEWARD
SA CIMINO $.40 (E276)

EVERGREEN see Pinkham, Daniel

EVERY MAN WANTS TO BE FREE
SSA CIMINO $.40 (E277)
SATB CIMINO $.40 (E278)

EVERY NIGHT WHEN THE SUN GOES IN *folk
(Newbury, Kent) SSA RICHMOND F-28
$.35 (E279)

EVERYBODY GETS TO GO TO THE MOON see
Webb

EVERYBODY LOVES SOMEBODY
SATB,pno,opt bvl&drums&gtr SCREEN
7034EC7 (E280)
SSA,pno,opt bvl&drums&gtr SCREEN
7034EC8 (E281)

EVERYBODY NEEDS A RAINBOW
SATB,pno,opt bvl&drums&gtr SCREEN
7039EC7 (E282)

EVERYBODY NEEDS A RAINBOW see Martine

EVERYBODY'S GOT A HOME BUT ME see
Rodgers, Richard

EVERYMAN see Davies, Henry Walford

EVERYTHING IS BEAUTFUL
   SATB,pno,opt bvl&drums&gtr SCREEN
   7033EC7   (E283)

EVERYTHING IS BEAUTIFUL
   SSA,pno,opt bvl&drums&gtr SCREEN
   7033EC8   (E284)
   SAB,pno,opt bvl&drums&gtr SCREEN
   7033EC9   (E285)
   SA,pno,opt bvl&drums&gtr SCREEN
   7033ECX   (E286)

EVERYTHING THAT TOUCHES YOU see
   Kirkman, Terry

EVETT, ROBERT (1922-   )
   Five Boons Of Life, The
   SBB,hpsd AM.COMP.AL. $7.70   (E287)

   Prime
   SATB,acap AM.COMP.AL. $3.85   (E288)

EVILLE
   Last Song
   (Simon, W.) SAB BIG3 $.50   (E289)
   (Simon, W.) SSA BIG3 $.50   (E290)
   (Simon, W.) SATB BIG3 $.45   (E291)

EV'RY TIME I FEEL THE SPIRIT *spir
   (Scheider, Werner) SSATB MOSELER
   LB612 s.p. contains also: Go Down,
   Moses (SATB)   (E292)

EWIGE LIEBE see Schubert, Franz (Peter)

EWIGER STREIT see Fischer, Ernst

EXEMPLARY SOLDIER, AN see Sedlacek,
   Bohuslav, Vzorny Vojak

EXERCITIA MYTHOLOGICA see Novak, Jan

EYES OF BEAUTY, EYES FLASHING BRIGHT
   see Mozart, Wolfgang Amadeus, Luci
   Care Belle

F

FA FOLLOTT see Bartok, Bela

FABULAS see Caamano

FACE OF THE NIGHT see Johnston, Richard

FAHNENWEIHE see Desch, Rudolf

FAHR HIN, GUTS LIEDELEIN see Hassler,
   Hans Leo

FAHR WOHL see Brahms, Johannes

FAHRENDE GESELLEN see Miller, Franz R.

FAIR, THE see McAfee, Don

FAIR AND BRIGHT IS MY LADY see
   Arcadelt, Jacob, L'Alma Mia Donna E
   Bella

FAIR DAFFODILS see Parry, Charles
   Hubert Hastings

FAIR IS FAIR
   2pt oct CHAPPELL W422500-351 $.40
                                 (F1)
   SSA oct CHAPPELL W422500-353 $.40
                                 (F2)
   SAB oct CHAPPELL W422500-356 $.40
                                 (F3)
   SATB oct CHAPPELL W422500-357 $.40
                                 (F4)

FAIR LOVE see Peaslee, Richard

FAIR PHYLLIS see Farmer, John

FAIR WIND see Champagne, Claude

FAIREST ISLE see Purcell, Henry

FAIREST ROSE IN ALL THE GARDEN
   (Deale, Edgar) SA (med easy) WATERLOO
   $.35   (F5)

FAIRY BALL see Fox, George

FAIRY FLUTE see Kurth, Burton L.

FAIRY SONG see Peaslee, Richard

FAIRY SONG see Weigl, Vally

FAITES DE MOY see Busnois, Antoine

FAITH
   Somewhere In Your Heart *pop
   (Kehner) SATB BELWIN UC 728 $.40
                                 (F6)

FAITH OF OUR FATHERS
   (Johnson, Derric) SATB (various tapes
   and recording also available)
   BENSON B0985 $.75   (F7)

FAITHFUL AND TRUE see Lassus, Roland de
   (Orlandus)

FAITHLESS, THE see Bohac, Josef,
   Neverny

FALCON, THE see Brahms, Johannes

FALLING OF THE LEAVES, THE see Kennedy

FALSCHE ZUNGEN "MEIN SCHATZ DER IST AUF
   WANDER SCHAFT" see Lang, Hans

FALSE FACE LEGEND
   (Sweetman, Paul W.) SA,narrator,pno
   (med easy) WATERLOO $.75   (F8)

FALSE SPRING see Kodaly, Zoltan

FALTUS, L.
   Nursery Rhymes II *CCU
   jr cor sc SLOV.HUD.FOND s.p. (F9)

FAMILIES OF SON MY, THE see Tanenbaum,
   Elias

FAMOUS SONGS OF ISRAEL *CCU
   (Hadar, Joseph) [Heb] 2 eq voices/3
   eq voices OR-TAV $2.00   (F10)

FANCIES see Rutter

FANCY see Epstein

FANDANGO "AM HEISSEN TAGE MIT SEINER
   PLAGE" see Zoll, Paul

FANFARE AND CHORUS see Buxtehude,
   Dietrich

FANFAREN-INTRADE see Mohler, Philipp

FANFAREN-RUF see Mohler, Philipp,
   Fanfaren-Intrade

FANGARNAS KOR see Verdi, Giuseppe

FANING, EATON (1850-1927)
   Song Of The Vikings
   (Protheroe, Daniel) SA (med)
   FITZSIMONS 3005 $.25   (F11)

FANTASIA DI PINOCCHIO see Casagrade, A.

FANTASIA NO. 1 see De Wert

FANTASIA NO. 3 see De Wert

FAR AWAY see Cole, Rossetter Gleason

FAR, FAR AWAY *Finn
   (Wick, Fred) TTBB oct SCHMITT W147
   $.30   (F12)

FARE THEE WELL see Distler, Hugo,
   Lebewohl

FARE WELL see Thompson, Randall

FARE YOU WELL
   (Follett) SSA PRO ART 2770 $.35 (F13)

FAREWELL ANDROMEDA see Denver, John

FAREWELL, CRUEL AND UNKIND see
   Marenzio, Luca

FAREWELL SONG, THE see Kalanzi

FAREWELL TO THE FARM see Shearer, C.M.

FARJEON, ELEANOR
   Morning Has Broken (composed with
   Stevens, Cat) *pop
   (Averre, Richard) SATB,pno oct BIG
   BELL $.40   (F14)
   (Averre, Richard) SSA,pno oct BIG
   BELL $.40   (F15)
   (Averre, Richard) SAB,pno oct BIG
   BELL $.40   (F16)
   (Averre, Richard) SA,pno oct BIG
   BELL $.40   (F17)

FARKAS, FERENC (1905-   )
   Baranyi Lakodalmas
   mix cor BUDAPEST 7502 s.p.   (F18)

   Szivarvany
   (Erdelyi, Jozsef) men cor BUDAPEST
   7511 s.p.   (F19)

   Vallon Szerenad
   (Dalos, Laszlo) eq voices BUDAPEST
   7140 s.p.   (F20)
   (Dalos, Laszlo) mix cor BUDAPEST
   7199 s.p.   (F21)

FARLEG FERD see Kvam, Oddvar S.

FARMER AND THE COWMAN, THE see Rodgers,
   Richard

FARMER, JOHN (fl. 1591-1601)
   Fair Phyllis
   SATB,acap EGTVED KB25 s.p.   (F22)

   Stay Sweet Love
   SATB GALAXY 1.5071.1 $.30   (F23)

FARMERS BOY see Vaughan Williams, Ralph

FARMERS SON SO SWEET see Vaughan
   Williams, Ralph

FARMER'S SONG *folk,Chin
   (Lum, Maryette) SATB (easy)
   FITZSIMONS 1052 $.25   (F24)

FARNABY, GILES (ca. 1560-1640)
   Canzonets To Four Voices (1598) EM
   Vol. 20 *CC21L
   4pt STAINER 3.1920.1 $8.50   (F25)

FARRAR
   Have You Never Been Mellow
   (Gargaro) SATB,opt perc WARNER
   CH0797 $.50   (F26)

FARRELL, DENNIS
   May Flower
   see Two Poems

   Pines Of The Northwest Arm, The
   see Two Poems

   Shinum Place
   SATB (med) WATERLOO $.60   (F27)

   Two Poems
   SATB (easy) WATERLOO $.35
   contains: May Flower; Pines Of
   The Northwest Arm, The   (F28)

FATA LA PARTE see Encina, Juan Del

FATEFUL WEDDING, THE see Zich, Otakor,
   Osudna Svatba

FAULE MUSIKANTEN *folk
 (Mockl, F.) [Ger] 4pt mix cor
  MERSEBURG EM9209 s.p.   (F29)

FAUN, THE see Matz, Rudolf

FAY, V.
 Song Of The Old Mother, The
  TTBB BRODT 592 $.26   (F30)

FEARIS, JOHN S.
 On The Shore Of The Zuider Zee
  SA (med) FITZSIMONS 3027 $.20 (F31)

FEBRUARY AND ROSES see Bedrich, Jan,
 Unor A Ruze

FEELINGS
 SA,pno,opt bvl&drums&gtr SCREEN
  1415FCX   (F32)
 SAB,pno,opt bvl&drums&gtr SCREEN
  1415FC9   (F33)
 SSA,pno,opt bvl&drums&gtr SCREEN
  1415FC8   (F34)
 SATB,pno,opt bvl&drums&gtr SCREEN
  1415FC7   (F35)

FEGERS, KARL (1926-   )
 Das Samenkorn
  see Sechs Kleine Weisen

 Der Floh
  see Sechs Kleine Weisen

 Der Funke
  see Sechs Kleine Weisen

 Der Stein
  see Sechs Kleine Weisen

 Die Feder
  see Sechs Kleine Weisen

 Die Seifenblase
  see Sechs Kleine Weisen

 Sechs Kleine Weisen
  jr cor,2A rec,perc (easy) sc,cor
   pts SCHOTTS B 142 s.p., ipa
   contains: Das Samenkorn; Der
    Floh; Der Funke; Der Stein; Die
    Feder; Die Seifenblase   (F36)

FEHER, ANDRAS
 Homo Sapiens No. 2
  mix cor BUDAPEST 7442 s.p.   (F37)

FEHLT DIR, O MENSCH, DIE HARMONIE see
 Seeger, Peter

FEIERSPRUCH UND FAHNENLIED see Edler,
 Robert

FEIERTAG IN DIXIELAND "HEUT IST EIN
 FEST" see Fischer, Ernst

FEIFEL, HERMANN
 Lob Der Musik
  men cor,acap TONOS 4569 s.p. (F38)

 Mein Paradies Ist Oberschwaben
  men cor,acap TONOS 257 s.p. (F39)

FEIN SEIN, BEINANDER BLEIBN see
 Kanetscheider, Artur

FEINSLIEB, DU HAST MICH G'FANGEN see
 Hassler, Hans Leo

FEINSLIEBCHEN, DU SOLLST MIR NICHT
 BARFUSS GEHN see Wimberger, Gerhard

FELCIANO, RICHARD (1930-   )
 Cosmic Festival
  unis,electronic tape sc SCHIRM.EC
   2938 s.p., ipa see from Two
   Public Pieces   (F40)

 Fye On Sinful Fantasy!
  see Three Madrigals From William
   Shakespeare

 Not-Yet Flower, The
  unis,electronic tape sc SCHIRM.EC
   2937 s.p., ipa see from Two
   Public Pieces   (F41)

 O He Did Whistle And She Did Sing
  unis jr cor,3strings SCHIRM.EC 2810
   sc s.p., ipa, cor pts s.p. (F42)

 Somerset Wassail
  SATB SCHIRM.EC 2912 s.p.   (F43)
  SSA SCHIRM.EC 2809 s.p.   (F44)

 Take, O Take Those Lips Away
  see Three Madrigals From William
   Shakespeare

 Tell Me Where Is Fancy Bred?
  see Three Madrigals From William
   Shakespeare

 Three Madrigals From William
  Shakespeare
  SATB SCHIRM.EC 2917 s.p.

FELCIANO, RICHARD (cont'd.)

  contains: Fye On Sinful Fantasy!;
   Take, O Take Those Lips Away;
   Tell Me Where Is Fancy Bred?
                                 (F45)

 Two Public Pieces *see Cosmic
  Festival; Not-Yet Flower, The (F46)

FELD, JINDRICH (1925-   )
 Inventionen
  SATB,acap (med diff) BAREN. BA4987
   s.p.   (F47)

 Pam Pim Pam
  SATB,acap BOONIN B 152 $.35 see
   from Three Inventions   (F48)

 Pidy Bidy Bim Pim
  SATB,acap BOONIN B 151 $.50 see
   from Three Inventions   (F49)

 Tam Tam Ta Dam
  SATB,acap BOONIN B 153 $.55 see
   from Three Inventions   (F50)

 Three Inventions *see Pam Pim Pam;
  Pidy Bidy Bim Pim; Tam Tam Ta Dam
                                 (F51)

FELDEINSAMKEIT "ICH RUHE STILL" see
 Rein, Walter

FELDSHER, HOWARD M.
 My Love Is Like A Red, Red Rose
  SATB,acap AULOS   (F52)

FELEGYHAZI-STRASSE see Stein, F.R.

FELICE CHI VI MIRA see Nielsen, Hans

FELIX, VACLAV (1928-   )
 Legend About Lenin, The *see Povest
  O Leninovi

 Pat Zvonkoyvych Hlasov
  jr cor sc SLOV.HUD.FOND s.p. (F53)

 Povest O Leninovi *ora
  "Legend About Lenin, The" [Czech]
   mix cor,TB soli,3fl,3ob,3clar,
   3bsn,6horn,3trp,3trom,tuba,timp,
   perc,strings CZECH s.p.   (F54)

 Tri Balady *Op.6, CC3U
  [Czech] mix cor,solo,acap CZECH
   s.p.   (F55)

FELLOW NEEDS A GIRL, A see Rodgers,
 Richard

FEM KORSANGE see Holm, Peder

FEMALE CHORUS ALBUM see Nakada, Y.

FENNIMORE
 Cynic's Song, The
  MARKS MC 4607 $.40   (F56)

FENYBEN FURDIK A FOLD see Ranki, Gyorgy

FERENCZY, OTO (1921-   )
 Ako Vonia Hora
  see Tri Miesane Zbory
  mix cor SLOV.HUD.FOND s.p.   (F57)

 Hviezda Severu *cant
  mix cor,Bar solo,orch SLOV.HUD.FOND
   s.p.   (F58)

 Maje
  see Tri Muzske Zbory

 Oda
  see Tri Miesane Zbory

 Tri Miesane Zbory
  mix cor SLOV.HUD.FOND s.p.
   contains: Ako Vonia Hora; Oda;
   Zimna Piesen   (F59)

 Tri Muzske Zbory
  men cor SLOV.HUD.FOND s.p.
   contains: Maje; Verbunk; Volanie
                                 (F60)
 Verbunk
  see Tri Muzske Zbory

 Volanie
  see Tri Muzske Zbory

 Vyzka
  men cor SLOV.HUD.FOND s.p.   (F61)

 Vyzva
  see MUZSKE ZBORY II

 Zimna Piesen
  see Tri Miesane Zbory

FERFIKAROK see Kodaly, Zoltan

FERGUSON
 Joshua Fit The Battle Of Jericho
  SATB oct HERITAGE H120 $.35   (F62)

FERN NACH SUD KOSAKEN *folk,Russ
 (Schmid, Alfons) men cor,acap TONOS
  2009 s.p.   (F63)

FERRARI, GIORGIO
 Se Mi Vuoi Bene
  4pt mix cor sc ZANIBON 5362 s.p.
                                 (F64)

 Sentenze (Da Qohelet)
  SATB,perc sc ZANIBON 5369 s.p.
                                 (F65)

FERRYMAN, THE see Wilkinson, Philip G.

FEST DER JUGEND "ZUM TANZ, ZUM TANZ"
 see Marx, Karl

FEST-KANTATE "UNSER SIND DIE STUNDEN"
 see Fussan, Werner

FEST UND FEIER see Zipp, Friedrich

FESTGESANG see Mendelssohn, Arnold

FESTGESANG AN DIE KUNSTLER see
 Mendelssohn-Bartholdy, Felix

FESTGESANG "FREUDENKLANGE, FROHE
 FESTGESANGE" see Gluck, Christoph
 Willibald Ritter von

FESTIVAL FOR AUTUMN, A see Mendoza,
 Anne

FESTIVAL OF SOUND see Rottura, Joseph
 James

FESTIVAL SONG see Dobias, Vaclav,
 Festivalova Pisen

FESTIVAL SONG see Dvorak, Antonin,
 Slavnostni Zpev

FESTIVAL SONGS FOR SAB *CCU
 (Bissell, Keith W.) cor WATERLOO
  $1.00   (F66)

FESTIVALOVA PISEN see Dobias, Vaclav

FESTIVE CHORUS see Janacek, Leos

FESTLICHE KANTATE see Motte, Diether de
 la

FESTLICHE LIED-KANTATE see Mohler,
 Philipp

FESTSPRUCH see Koch, Adolf

FETTKE, TOM
 Love Is Merely A Madness *canon
  SATB,acap (med) oct GENTRY G-285
   $.40   (F67)

FEUILLES D'AUTOMNE see Missa, [Edmond
 Jean Louis]

FIALA, JAROMIR (1941-   )
 Vsetci Sme Jedno
  wom cor SLOV.HUD.FOND s.p.   (F68)

FIALA, JIRI JULIUS (1928-   )
 Maj
  "May" [Czech] mix cor,soli,3fl,3ob,
   3clar,3bsn,4horn,3trp,3trom,tuba,
   timp,perc,harp,strings, celeste
   CZECH s.p.   (F69)

 May *see Maj

FIALA, PETR (1943-   )
 Navraty *cant
  "Returns" [Czech] mix cor,Bar&
   narrator,org,pno,horn,5strings
   CZECH s.p.   (F70)

 Returns *see Navraty

FIBICH, ZDENKO (1850-1900)
 Melusine *see Meluzina

 Meluzina *Op.55
  "Melusine" [Czech/Ger] mix cor,SB
   soli,3fl,2ob,2clar,2bsn,4horn,
   3trp,3trom,tuba,timp,perc,harp,
   strings CZECH s.p.   (F71)

FICHER, JACOBO (1896-   )
 Cuatro Sonetos De Amor *CC4U
  mix cor PEER $1.25   (F72)

 Tres Coros A Capella *CC3U
  mix cor,acap PEER $.75   (F73)

FICHTELGEBIRGSLIED see Reichardt

FICHTNER, CHRISTIAN
 Ergo Bibamus
  men cor,acap TONOS 131 s.p.   (F74)

 Freude Am Gesang
  men cor,acap sc,cor pts TONOS 3703
   s.p.   (F75)

 Rhythmischer Auftakt
  men cor, combo ad lib TONOS 2205
   s.p.   (F76)

FIDDLE-DEE see Kodaly, Zoltan

FIDDLER see Adler

FIDELIUS, CORNELIUS
Sechse, Sieben, Oder Acht
men cor,pno,opt 2trp sc,cor pts
TONOS 291 s.p. (F77)

Umkehr
men cor,pno,opt 2trp sc,cor pts
TONOS 292 s.p. (F78)

FIEDELHANS *folk,Boh
(Rosenstengel, Albrecht) men cor,opt
pno,opt gtr,opt perc sc,cor pts
TONOS 2111 s.p. (F79)

FIEDELLIEDER see Edler, Robert

FIELDS
Pick Yourself Up *see Kern, Jerome

FIESTA see Vogt, Paul G.

FIFTEEN ROUNDS FOR READING, RECREATION,
AND CONCERT *CC15U
(Van Camp, Leonard) SATB oct SCHMITT
1314 $.50 (F80)

FIFTY-NINTH STREET BRIDGE SONG, THE
(FEELIN' GROOVY) see Simon, Paul

FIGHTING TEMERAIRE, THE see Bantock,
Granville

FILL EVERY GLASS see Pinkham, Daniel

FILLETTES DE CHAMPAGNE *folk,Fr
(Blanchard, R.) 4pt mix cor,acap
JOBERT s.p. (F81)

FILLEUL
En Mer
4pt mix cor GRAS s.p. (F82)

FILLI CARA E AMATA see Monteverdi,
Claudio

FINALE see Apple, Alan

FINALE see Biebl, Franz

FINALE see Ocenas, Andrej

FINALE FROM SYMPHONY NO. 2 see Mahler,
Gustav

FINE
Beautiful Soup (from Alice In
Wonderland)
SSA WARNER W-3495 $.50 (F83)

Knave's Letter, The (from Alice In
Wonderland)
SSA WARNER W-3493 $.40 (F84)

White Knight's Song, The (from Alice
In Wonderland)
SA WARNER W-3494 $.35 (F85)

FINE AND MELLOW see Holiday

FINITURUS ERAM see Schultz, Svend S.

FINNEGIN'S FUGUE see Silver

FINNISCHE LIED "UBER DEN BERG" see
Genzmer, Harald

FINNISSY, MICHAEL (1946-   )
Tsuru-Kame
wom cor,S/A solo,fl,vla,2perc
MODERN rental (F86)

FINSTRE NACHT "ICH GING WOHL BEI DER
NACHT" see Bresgen, Cesar

FIRE see Cope, Cecil

FIRE BRINGER, THE see Clarke, Henry
Leland

FIRE, FIRE see Morley, Thomas

FIRE, FLOOD AND OLIVE TREE see
Nierenberg

FIREFLIES, THE see Trojan, Vaclav

FIREMAN'S BRIDE, THE
TTBB oct CHAPPELL W485002-355 $.40
(F87)
SATB oct CHAPPELL W485002-357 $.40
(F88)

FIRES FOR THE SAINTS see Williamson,
Malcolm

FIRES OF TROY, THE see Pooler

FIRST BOOK OF BALLETTS (1595) EM VOL. 4
see Morley, Thomas

FIRST BOOK OF MADRIGALS, THE see
Monteverdi, Claudio

FIRST BOOK OF MADRIGALS, THE see
Monteverdi, Claudio

FIRST BOOK OF MADRIGALS (1594) EM VOL.
2 see Morley, Thomas

FIRST CHORAL SYMPHONY see Holst, Gustav

FIRST CRITICAL EDITION see Palestrina,
Giovanni

FIRST LOVE, THE see Y Cariad Cyntaf

FIRST SET OF MADRIGALS (1597) EM VOL.
24 see Kirbye, George

FIRST SET OF MADRIGALS (1598) EM VOL. 6
see Wilbye, John

FIRST SET OF MADRIGALS (1604) EM VOL.
21 see Bateson, Thomas

FIRST SET OF MADRIGALS (1607) EM VOL.
35A see Jones, Robert

FIRST SET OF MADRIGALS (1613) EM VOL.
19 see Ward, John

FIRST SET OF MADRIGALS AND MOTETS
(1612) EM VOL. 5 see Gibbons,
Orlando

FIRST SET OF MADRIGALS AND PASTORALS OF
THREE, FOUR, AND FIVE PARTS (1613)
EM VOL. 25 see Pilkington, Francis

FIRST SET OF MADRIGALS EM VOL. 29 see
East, Michael

FIRST STARS see Brandon, George

FISCHBACH, KLAUS (1935-   )
Drei Ungarische Volkslieder *see
Bartok, Bela

Habt Ihr Schon Gehort Die Kunde *see
Bartok, Bela

Hoch Des Richters Haus In Kanja Ragt
*see Bartok, Bela

Markt Ist Heute In Der Kleinen Stadt
*see Bartok, Bela

FISCHE see Strobl, Otto

FISCHER, ERICH (1887-   )
Dur Und Moll
2 eq voices,pno/3vln PELIKAN PE255
sc s.p., cor pts s.p., ipa (F89)

FISCHER, ERNST (1900-   )
Bohmische Polka "Einmal Hin Und
Einmal Her"
mix cor (med easy) sc SCHOTTS
C 40 540 s.p. see from Tanzlieder
(F90)
Bohmische Polka "Liebchen Fein" *Boh
men cor sc SCHOTTS C 40 127 s.p.
see from Funf Neue Tanzlieder
(F91)
Cowboy Song "Cowboys Sind Wir"
men cor sc SCHOTTS C 39 367 s.p.
see from Funf Tanzweisen (F92)

Ewiger Streit
see O, Diese Frauen! - Nein, Diese
Manner!

Feiertag In Dixieland "Heut Ist Ein
Fest"
men cor sc SCHOTTS C 39 370 s.p.
see from Funf Tanzweisen (F93)

Funf Neue Tanzlieder *see Bohmische
Polka "Liebchen Fein"; Landler
"Am Sonntag Ist Kirchweih";
Schottische Hirtenweise "Heut
Spielt Der Dudelsack"; Serenata
Cubana "Spielt Die Habanera";
Tarantelle Siziliana "Signorina
Aus Messina" (F94)

Funf Tanzweisen *see Cowboy Song
"Cowboys Sind Wir"; Feiertag In
Dixieland "Heut Ist Ein Fest";
Lied Des Meeres "Ewiges Meer";
Spanische Nachte "Das Ist Der
Zauber"; Wanderliedchen "O Wie
Schon Ist Die Welt" (F95)

Hobbies
men cor,soli,pno/perc,bvl,gtr (song
cycle) sc,cor pts SCHOTTS
ED. 5282 s.p., ipa (F96)

Ich Hab' Nichts Anzuziehn
see O, Diese Frauen! - Nein, Diese
Manner!

Landler "Am Sonntag Ist Kirchweih"
men cor sc SCHOTTS C 40 130 s.p.
see from Funf Neue Tanzlieder
(F97)

FISCHER, ERNST (cont'd.)

Lied Des Meeres "Ewiges Meer"
men cor sc SCHOTTS C 39 369 s.p.
see from Funf Tanzweisen (F98)
mix cor (med easy) sc SCHOTTS
C 40 538 s.p. see from Tanzlieder
(F99)

Lob Des Rheins "Stimmt An, Lasst Uns
Singen"
mix cor,orch (med easy) sc SCHOTTS
C 39 139 s.p., voc pt SCHOTTS
C 39 140A-D s.p., ipa (F100)
men cor,TBar soli,pno/orch voc sc
SCHOTTS C 39 137 s.p., cor pts
SCHOTTS C 39 138 01-04 s.p., ipa
(F101)

O, Diese Frauen! - Nein, Diese
Manner!
mix cor,pno,bvl,gtr,perc (med) sc,
cor pts SCHOTTS ED. 6104 s.p.,
ipa
contains: Ewiger Streit; Ich Hab'
Nichts Anzuziehn; Schonheit
Muss Leiden; Wo Bleibt Das
Geld?; Zum Guten Ende (F102)

Schonheit Muss Leiden
see O, Diese Frauen! - Nein, Diese
Manner!

Schottische Hirtenweise "Heut Spielt
Der Dudelsack" *Scot
men cor sc SCHOTTS C 40 129 s.p.
see from Funf Neue Tanzlieder
(F103)

Serenata Cubana "Spielt Die Habanera"
*So Am
men cor,T solo sc SCHOTTS C 40 128
s.p. see from Funf Neue
Tanzlieder (F104)

Spanische Nachte "Das Ist Der Zauber"
men cor sc SCHOTTS C 39 368 s.p.
see from Funf Tanzweisen (F105)

Spanische Nachte "Das Ist Der Zauber
Der Spanischen Nachte"
mix cor (med easy) sc SCHOTTS
C 40 539 s.p. see from Tanzlieder
(F106)

Tanzlieder *see Bohmische Polka
"Einmal Hin Und Einmal Her"; Lied
Des Meeres "Ewiges Meer";
Spanische Nachte "Das Ist Der
Zauber Der Spanischen Nachte";
Wanderliedchen "O, Wie Schon Ist
Die Welt" (F107)

Tarantelle Siziliana "Signorina Aus
Messina" *It
men cor sc SCHOTTS C 40 131 s.p.
see from Funf Neue Tanzlieder
(F108)

Wanderliedchen "O, Wie Schon Ist Die
Welt"
wom cor sc SCHOTTS C 42 161 s.p.
(F109)
men cor sc SCHOTTS C 39 371 s.p.
see from Funf Tanzweisen (F110)
SSATTBB (med easy) sc SCHOTTS
C 40 537 s.p. see from Tanzlieder
(F111)

Wo Bleibt Das Geld?
see O, Diese Frauen! - Nein, Diese
Manner!

Zum Guten Ende
see O, Diese Frauen! - Nein, Diese
Manner!

FISCHER, HANS
Kleine Bauerliche Kantate *cant
1-3pt jr cor,pno/2vln,vcl (easy) sc
SCHOTTS C 43 754 s.p., cor pts
SCHOTTS C 43 755A s.p., ipa
(F112)

FISCHER, KARL LUDWIG
Die Heimat: Die Winde Rauschen
men cor,acap TONOS 6328 s.p. (F113)

FISCHER, OTTO
Wo Alle Reben Grussen
men cor,acap TONOS 228 s.p. (F114)

FISCHER, THEO
Aufstieg
men cor,acap sc,cor pts TONOS 4514
s.p. (F115)

Bekranzt Mit Laub
men cor&jr cor,pno sc,voc sc TONOS
1301-K s.p. (F116)
men cor&jr cor,acap/4horn/2trp&
horn&2trom&tuba&timp sc,voc sc
TONOS 1301 s.p., ipa (F117)

Das Gluckliche Jahr
men cor,acap TONOS 3914 s.p. (F118)

Die Nahe
men cor,fl,ob,2clar,bsn,2horn,timp,
strings TONOS 4961 voc sc,cor pts
s.p., sc rental (F119)

FISCHER, THEO (cont'd.)

Goldner Herbst
men cor,opt 2trp&horn&trom&tuba&
timp sc,cor pts TONOS 3931 s.p.,
ipa   (F120)

Herbei, Ihr Freunde
men cor,acap TONOS 3913 s.p. (F121)

Hort Der Glaser Kling Und Klang
men cor,opt 2trp&horn&trom&tuba&
timp sc,cor pts TONOS s.p., ipa
(F122)

Im Krug Zum Grunen Kranze
men cor&jr cor,pno sc,voc sc TONOS
1311-K s.p.   (F123)
men cor&jr cor,acap/4horn/2trp&
horn&trom&tuba&perc sc,voc sc
TONOS 1311 s.p., ipa   (F124)

Kein Schoner Land
men cor&jr cor,acap TONOS 1302 s.p.
(F125)

Lob Der Heimat
men cor,2trp,horn,trom sc,cor pts
TONOS 3739 s.p., ipa   (F126)

Optimisten
men cor,acap TONOS 4513 s.p. (F127)

Schoner Bei Dir
men cor,acap TONOS 3956 s.p. (F128)

Schones Land
men cor,opt 2trp&horn&trom sc,cor
pts TONOS 3957 s.p., ipa   (F129)

Sonniges Rebenland
men cor,acap TONOS 3733 s.p. (F130)

Tausend Flugel
men cor&jr cor,fl,ob,2clar,bsn,
2trp,2horn,trom,tuba,timp,strings
sc,voc sc TONOS 4936
s.p., ipr   (F131)

Tausend Flugel Sollen Tragen
men cor&jr cor,pno sc,cor pts TONOS
4936 s.p.   (F132)

Zag Nicht!
men cor,acap sc,cor pts TONOS 4515
s.p.   (F133)

FISCHERLIED *folk
(Zoll, P.) [Ger] 4pt men cor
MERSEBURG EM9089 s.p.   (F134)

FISER, LUBOS (1935-   )
Caprichos
[Span] dbl cor, chamber chorus and
mixed chorus SUPRAPHON s.p.
(F135)

FISHER
Come, Quickly Death *see Jeffries

Doctor And The Patient, The *see
Jeffries

Double Or Nothing *see Jeffries

Grasshopper And The Ant, The *see
Jeffries

How To Flatter A Raven *see Jeffries

Little Red Fox, The *see Jeffries

Mis-Matched *see Jeffries

Nobody's Ever Satisfied *see
Jeffries

Putting It Off *see Jeffries

Tell Me, Nightingale *see Jeffries

Tortoise And The Hare, The *see
Jeffries

We Are The Music Makers
SATB MCAFEE M1059 $.40   (F136)

Where It's At *see Jeffries

FISHER, FRED
They Go Wild, Simply Wild, Over Me
(Simon, W.) SATB BIG3 $.45   (F137)

FISHERMAN, THE see Cole, Rossetter
Gleason

FISHERMAN'S SONG *folk,Chin
(Lum, Maryette) SATB (med) FITZSIMONS
1053 $.25   (F138)

FITTIG
Gruss An's Ober Inntal *Op.139
men cor cor pts FORBERG s.p. (F139)
mix cor cor pts FORBERG s.p. (F140)

FIVE BOONS OF LIFE, THE see Evett,
Robert

FIVE CHILDHOOD LYRICS see Rutter

FIVE CHINESE PROVERBS see Johnson

FIVE ENGLISH FOLK SONGS see Vaughan
Williams, Ralph

FIVE ENGLISH GIRLS see Mechem, Kirke

FIVE FOLK SONGS *see Barbara Allen;
Bobby Shaftoe; Drink To Me Only;
Early One Morning; Lass Of Richmond
Hill   (F141)

FIVE IRISH SONGS see Maw

FIVE SONGS see Purcell, Henry

FIVE SONGS OF EXPERIENCE see Harbison,
John

FIVE SONGS OF EXPERIENCE see Harbison,
John

FIVE SONGS OF LIBERTY see Collins, Don
L.

FJARRAN HAN DROJER *folk,Finn
(Jehrlander, Karl-Fredrik) mix cor
GEHRMANS KRB443   (F142)

FLAG OF PEACE ABOVE DUKLA, THE see
Vomacka, Boleslav, Prapor Miru Nad
Duklou

FLEIG, G.
Blaue Blumen *folk,Eng
wom cor ZIMMER. 595 s.p.   (F143)

Die Petersburger Landstrasse Entlang
*folk,Russ
wom cor ZIMMER. 597 s.p.   (F144)

FLEMING
Soft Shadows Falling, And When You
Were My Sweetheart
(Wick, Fred) SATB oct SCHMITT W406
$.30   (F145)

FLEMING, CHRISTOPHER LE
Cradle Song (from Echoing Green, The)
[Eng] SA/jr cor,S solo,pno CHESTER
s.p.   (F146)

Echoing Green, The *cant
[Eng] SA,SA soli,pno,opt strings
CHESTER N9734 $2.15   (F147)

FLEMING, R.
Kangaroo Sat On An Oak, A
mix cor LESLIE 5029 $.30   (F148)

FLEMING, ROBERT
Madrigal *madrigal
SA (med diff) WATERLOO $.30 (F149)

FLICK'RING CANDLES see Milidantri

FLIEG DAHIN, LIED see Zoll, Paul

FLIEHENDER SOMMER "MARGUERITE" see
Zoll, Paul

FLIRT, THE see Kunz, Alfred

FLIRTATION see Brahms, Johannes,
Neckereien

FLOGEN EINST DREI WILDE TAUBEN *folk
(Doppelbauer, Josef Friedrich) mix
cor DOBLINGER G 697 s.p.   (F150)

FLORA NOW CALLETH FORTH EACH FLOWER see
Smith, John Stafford

FLORIDANS NACHTKLAGE "O DUNKLE NACHT"
see Sutermeister, Heinrich

FLORILEGIUM CANTIONUM LATINARUM,
FASCICULE II *CCU,Lat
(Novak, Jan) cor,kbd ZANIBON 5421
s.p.   (F151)

FLOSMAN, OLDRICH (1925-   )
Pet Magrigalu *CC5U,madrigal
[Czech] mix cor,acap CZECH s.p.
(F152)

Tri Zastaveni *CC3U
[Czech] jr cor,3 soli,2fl,ob,2clar,
2bsn,2horn,2trp,2trom,tuba,timp,
perc,harp,pno,strings, xylophone
CZECH s.p.   (F153)

FLOW MY TEARS see Willey

FLOWER IN THE CRANNIED WALL see
Coulthard, Jean

FLOWER SONGS see Hurd, Michael

FLOWERS NEVER BEND WITH THE RAINFALL
see Simon, Paul

FLOWERS O' THE FOREST, THE *folk
(Roberton, Hugh S.) SSA,acap (easy)
FITZSIMONS 3052 $.20   (F154)

FLUCHT see Schubert, Franz (Peter)

FLUGEL INS LICHT see Schmid, A.

FLUGEL, UM ZU FLIEGEN see Mockl, Franz

FLUSS IM SCHNEE "DER VOGEL FLUG" see
Zipp, Friedrich

FLUTE PLAYERS see Edwards

FLUTERS BALL
SATB CIMINO $.40   (F155)

FLUTTERING BIRDS see Mana-Zucca, Mme.

FLY LITTLE WHITE DOVE FLY
SSA CIMINO $.40   (F156)
SATB CIMINO $.40   (F157)

FLY NOT SO FAST see Ward, Samuel A.

FLY NOT SO SWIFT see Wilbye, John

FLYING DOWN TO RIO *CCU
SATB CIMINO $.85   (F158)

FLYING DOWN TO RIO
SATB CIMINO $.40   (F159)

FODELSEDAGSVISA see Johansen, Sven-Erik

FOERSTER, JOSEF BOHUSLAV (1859-1951)
Death *see Skon

Jarni Noc *Op.77,No.2
"Spring Night" [Czech] mix cor,2fl,
2ob,2clar,2bsn,4horn,2trp,3trom,
timp,harp,strings CZECH s.p.
(F160)

Life *see Zivot

Pisen Bratra Slunce *Op.173, cant
"Song Of Brother Sun, The" [Czech]
men cor,Bar solo,2fl,3ob,3clar,
3bsn,4horn,2trp,3trom,tuba,timp,
perc,harp,strings CZECH s.p.
(F161)

St. Wenceslas *see Svaty Vaclav

Skon *Op.77,No.1
"Death" [Czech] mix cor,2fl,2ob,
2clar,2bsn,4horn,3trom,timp,harp,
strings CZECH s.p.   (F162)

Song Of Brother Sun, The *see Pisen
Bratra Slunce

Spring Night *see Jarni Noc

Svaty Vaclav *cant
"St. Wenceslas" [Czech] mix cor,
soli,3fl,3ob,3clar,3bsn,4horn,
3trp,3trom,tuba,timp,perc,2harp,
org,strings, celeste CZECH s.p.
(F163)

Tri Zenske Sbory, Op. 178 *CC3U
[Czech] wom cor,2fl,2ob,2clar,2bsn,
4horn,timp,perc,harp,strings
CZECH s.p.   (F164)

Zivot *Op.112, cant
"Life" [Czech] mix cor,2fl,2ob,
2clar,2bsn,4horn,2trp,3trom,tuba,
timp,perc,harp,strings CZECH s.p.
(F165)

FOG see Paynter, John P.

FOLK SONGS NO. 1 *CCU
(Ben-Porat, Zvi) [Heb] eq voices OR-
TAV $1.00   (F166)

FOLK SONGS NO. 2 *CCU
(Netzer, Effi) [Heb] eq voices OR-TAV
$1.00   (F167)

FOLK SONGS OF CANADA *CCU,folk
(Fowke, Edith; Johnston, Richard) cor
WATERLOO cloth $7.50, cor pts $2.50
(F168)

FOLK SONGS OF QUEBEC *CCU,folk
(Fowke, Edith; Johnston, Richard) cor
WATERLOO cloth $4.95, voc pt $2.50
(F169)

FOLLOW, FOLLOW ME see Karlin, Fred

FOLLOW ME UP TO CARLOW
(Deale, Edgar) SATB (med) WATERLOO
$.40   (F170)

FOLLOW MY LEADER see Greaves

FOLLOW YOUR HEART see Lucas, Robert

FOLTZ, KARL (1918-   )
Freunde, Euch Grusst Unser Lied
men cor sc SCHOTTS CHBL 113 s.p.
(F171)

Hymne An Die Musik "Aus Tonen Baust
Du Eine Neue Welt"
4-11pt mix cor,acap (med) sc
SCHOTTS C 39 196 s.p.   (F172)

FOOL ON THE HILL, THE see Lennon, John

FOR A LOSS SO BLEAK, OH SO SAD see
Encina, Juan Del, A Tal Perdida Tan
Triste

FOR ALL BLASPHEMERS see Simons, Netty

FOR ALL CHILDREN see Kohoutek, Ctirad,
Za Vsechny Deti

FOR HER LOVE see Lora, Antonio

FOR ONCE IN MY LIFE
SATB SCREEN 4717FC1C   (F173)
SSA SCREEN 4717FC2C   (F174)

FOR PEACE see Haba, Alois, Za Mir

FOR THE FALLEN see Elgar, Edward

FOR THE TRAGIC ANNIVERSARY OF MUNICH
see Svobodo, Jiri, K Tragickemu
Vyroci Mniochova

FOR THEE, THE FUTURE see Nowak, Jerry

FOR WHAT IT'S WORTH see Stills

FORD, THOMAS (ca. 1580-1648)
There Is A Lady Sweet And Kind
SATB STAINER 3.0729.1 $.30   (F175)

FOREVER YOUNG see Dylan, Robert (Bob)

FORSAKEN MERMAN, THE see Somervell,
Arthur

FORT FLOG DAS VOGELEIN see Bartok,
Bela, Element A Madarka

FORTNER, WOLFGANG (1907-   )
An Die Nachgeborenen *cant
mix cor,narrator,T solo,2fl,3ob,
3clar,3bsn,3trp,2trom,tuba,
strings,perc,timp,harp,celeste
(diff) sc SCHOTTS rental, ipr
(F176)
Glaubenslied "Wie Stein Mit Meissel
Ficht"
men cor sc SCHOTTS C 33 747 s.p.
(F177)
Grenzen Der Menschheit *cant
5pt mix cor,Bar solo,2fl,2ob,2bsn,
horn,2trp,trom,strings,timp
(diff) sc SCHOTTS rental, ipr
(F178)
Lied Der Welt "Flieg Hin, Zeit"
men cor sc SCHOTTS C 39 780 s.p.
(F179)
FORTUNE SEEKER, THE see Eldridge, Guy
H.

FORWARD see Grieg, Edvard Hagerup

FORWARDS see Kalas, Julius, Jen Dal

FORWARDS see Zrno, Felix, Jen Dal

FOSS, LUKAS (1922-   )
Fragments Of Archilochos, The
4 cor&opt cor,narrator,T solo,gtr,
perc, mandolin (diff, (joint
edition with Carl Fischer, Inc.))
sc SCHOTTS rental, ipr   (F180)

FOSTER
I Need Not Your Needles
see Two More Tongue-Twisters

Jonah And The Whale
unis/SA,narrator,inst (easy) sc
OXFORD 50.121 $4.95, ipa, cor pts
OXFORD 50.121-55   (F181)

Leith Police
see Two More Tongue-Twisters

Two More Tongue-Twisters
unis (easy) OXFORD 81.139 $.45
contains: I Need Not Your
Needles; Leith Police   (F182)

FOSTER, ARNOLD (1898-1963)
There Was A Pig Went Out To Dig
SSA CRAMER $.25   (F183)

FOSTER, STEPHEN (1826-1864)
Come Where My Love Lies Dreaming
(Smith) SATB SCHIRM.G 12014 $.50
(F184)
I Dream Of Jeanie
(Soderstrom) SATB (med) FITZSIMONS
1047 $.25   (F185)
(Soderstrom, Emil) TTBB (med)
FITZSIMONS 4052 $.25   (F186)

My Old Kentucky Home
(Rosenbecker) SSAA (easy)
FITZSIMONS 3018 $.20   (F187)

Some Folks
(Smith) SATB SCHIRM.G 12017 $.40
(F188)
FOUND OBJECTS I see Custer, Arthur

FOUR CHAMBER DUETS see Cesti, Marc'
Antonio

FOUR CHICAGO POEMS BY CARL SANDBURG see
Raphling, Sam

FOUR CHORAL SONGS ON DEATH AND MAN see
Weigl, Vally

FOUR ELIZABETHAN SONGS see Mollicone,
Henry

FOUR LATIN MADRIGALS 1974 see Schultz,
Svend S.

FOUR LITTLE FOXES see Furman

FOUR MADRIGALS see Brown

FOUR MADRIGALS AND MOTET see Brunswick,
Mark

FOUR POEMS BY MAO TSE-TUNG see
Lorentzen, Bent

FOUR SEASONS, THE see Weigl, Vally

FOUR SHAKESPEARE SONGS see Jeppesen,
Knud

FOUR SISTERS, THE see Hogben, Dorothy

FOUR SONGS see Weigl, Vally

FOUR SONGS FOR MALE VOICES see Zelter

FOUR SONGS FOR MEN'S VOICES see
Washburn

FOUR SONGS FOR SAILORS see Dyson,
George

FOUR SONGS FROM "THE BEGGAR'S OPERA"
(Medinger) SATB,acap (easy) OXFORD
95.310 $.40
contains: If The Heart Of A Man;
Man May Escape; Over The Hills;
Turtle Thus, The   (F189)

FOUR SONNETS see Ridout, Godfrey

FOUR STATIONS ON THE ROAD TO FREEDOM
see Joubert, John

FOUR THINGS (A MAN MUST LEARN TO DO)
see Atkinson, Condit R.

FOUR TRAVEL PICTURES see Christiansen,
P.

FOUR WILLIAM BLAKE SONGS see Kirk

FOUR WINDS see Jakes

FOURTEEN FOLK TUNES FOR YOUNG MEN
*CC15L,folk
(Lefebvre, C.) TBB GALAXY 1.1625.1
$1.25   (F190)

FOURTH SET OF BOOKS (1618) EM VOL. 31B
see East, Michael

FOWLER
More Firsts And Seconds *see Appleby

FOX, CHARLES
I Got A Name *pop
(Lowden, Jeff) SATB,pno oct BIG
BELL $.40   (F191)

FOX, GEORGE
Fairy Ball
unis HARRIS HC 1003 $.25   (F192)

FOXX, CHARLES
Killing Me Softly With His Song
(Metis, F.) SSA BIG3 $.50   (F193)
(Metis, F.) SATB BIG3 $.45   (F194)
(Metis, F.) SAB BIG3 $.45   (F195)

Mockingbird (composed with Foxx,
Inez)
(Sanford, W.) SSA BIG3 $.45 (F196)
(Sanford, W.) SATB BIG3 $.45 (F197)
(Sanford, W.) SAB BIG3 $.45 (F198)

FOXX, INEZ
Mockingbird *see Foxx, Charles

FRA TUTTE LE PENE see Beethoven, Ludwig
van

FRACKENPOHL, ARTHUR (1924-   )
Man Is For The Woman Made
SAB MARKS MC 4628 $.40   (F199)
TBB MARKS MC 4629 $.40   (F200)

Marriage Of True Minds, The
SATB STANDARD D911MX1 $.50   (F201)

Three Recent Rulings
SATB STANDARD D909MX1 $.50   (F202)

FRAGEN see Brahms, Johannes

FRAGMENTS OF ARCHILOCHOS, THE see Foss,
Lukas

FRAJT, LUDMILA (1919-   )
Pesme Noci *CCU
wom cor,strings,harp,pno MUSIC INFO
rental   (F203)

FRANCAIX, JEAN (1912-   )
Der Alte Herr Professor
see Funf Chansons Fur Kinder

Der Kleinen Katze Tod
see Funf Chansons Fur Kinder

Funf Chansons Fur Kinder
[Ger/Fr] 1-2pt jr cor,pno (easy) sc
SCHOTTS ME 28-0189 s.p.
contains: Der Alte Herr
Professor; Der Kleinen Katze
Tod; Mickey; Papa Und Mama;
Walzer   (F204)

Mickey
see Funf Chansons Fur Kinder

Papa Und Mama
see Funf Chansons Fur Kinder

Walzer
see Funf Chansons Fur Kinder

FRANCIA BORDALOK see Arma, Paul

FRANCK, MELCHIOR (ca. 1579-1639)
Kommt, Ihr G'spielen
men cor,acap TONOS 3329 s.p. (F205)

Lasst Uns Ein Stundlein Lustig Sein
(Mockl, Franz) men cor sc SCHOTTS
CHBL 211 s.p.   (F206)

Lustig, Ihr Herren, Allzumal (from
Newes Teutsches Musicalisches
Froliches Convivium)
(Gramss, Knut) mix cor (easy) sc
SCHOTTS CHBL 410 s.p.   (F207)

Mich Erfreut, Schons Lieb, Dein
Uneblick
(Malin, Don) "Rapt Am I, Dear Love,
With Your Sweet Glance" SATB,acap
BELWIN 2325 $.35   (F208)

Rapt Am I, Dear Love, With Your Sweet
Glance *see Mich Erfreut, Schons
Lieb, Dein Uneblick

Schon Singen Ist Ein Feine Kunst
SSATB,acap (alternate version
provided with editorial
embellishments) MOSELER MOR43
s.p.   (F209)

So Wunsch Ich Eine Gute Nacht
see Ahle, Johann Rudolph, Was Mag
Doch Diese Welt

Wie Weh Tut Mir Mein Scheiden
mix cor (easy) sc SCHOTTS CHBL 384
s.p.   (F210)

FRANCO, JOHAN (1908-   )
Bugle Song
SATB,acap AM.COMP.AL. $3.30 (F211)

Hail, Coming Age!
SATB,acap AM.COMP.AL. $1.10 (F212)

Hail The Dawning Day
SATB,acap AM.COMP.AL. $.55   (F213)

Hold Fast To The Spirit
SATB,acap AM.COMP.AL. $2.75 (F214)

Let Our Heart Be Open
SATB,acap AM.COMP.AL. $2.20 (F215)

Marching Song
SATB,acap AM.COMP.AL. $1.10 (F216)

Ode
TTBB,fl,2ob,2clar,bsn,4horn,4trp,
4trom,tuba,timp,harp,3perc,bvl,
3cornets, 2 baritone horns
AM.COMP.AL. sc $8.25, voc sc
$3.85   (F217)

Seven Songlets *CC7U
SSA,pno AM.COMP.AL. $.44   (F218)

Song Of Life, The
SATB,pno/clar, English horn, bass
clarinet sc AM.COMP.AL. $3.30,
ipa   (F219)

Spirit Quickeneth, The
SATB,Mez solo,acap AM.COMP.AL.
$1.38   (F220)

Till The Old Cat Dies
2pt,acap AM.COMP.AL. $.55   (F221)

Two Duets For Children *CC2U
SA,acap AM.COMP.AL. $.55   (F222)

FRANK, MARCEL [GUSTAVE] (1909-   )
  Jingle Bells *Xmas
    SATB GALAXY 1.1891.1 $.30   (F223)

FRANKISCHE VOLKSLIEDER see Lang, Hans

FRANKISCHER LIEDERREIGEN see Haas,
  Joseph

FRANZ
  Mother, O Sing Me To Sleep
    (Hines) SSA SCHIRM.G LG51819 $.40
                     (F224)

FRANZEN, BENGT
  Mulet Vader
    men cor ERIKS 329 s.p.   (F225)

FRAU LILLY MILLY PUTTY see Haus, Karl

FRAU MUSICA see Hindemith, Paul

FRAU MUSIKA
  see Vier Alte Volkslieder-Im Neuen
  Gewand

FRAU NACHTIGALL *folk,Belg
  (Zschiegner, Fritz) men cor,opt pno,
  opt inst,opt perc sc,voc sc TONOS
  2121 s.p.   (F226)

FRAU NACHTIGALL "ES STEHT EIN LIND IN
  JENEM TAL" see Herrmann, Hugo

FRAU NACHTIGALL, MACH DICH BEREIT see
  Rosthius, Nicolaus

FRAU NACHTIGALL "NACHTIGALL, ICH HOR
  DICH SINGEN" see Genzmer, Harald

FRAUENSTROPHE
  (Kunz, Alfred) "O Love Sweep Into My
  Heart" SATB (med easy) WATERLOO
  $.30   (F227)

FREDRICH, GUNTER
  Der Hirt
    mix cor HOFMEISTER G2201 s.p.
                    (F228)

FREE see Suchy, Frantisek, Svobodni

FREE AS THE WIND see Shaper

FREE AT LAST
  (Hairston, J.; Wilson, H.R.) SATB
    BOURNE B230680-357 $.45   (F229)

FREE LUNCH CADETS, THE see Sousa, John
  Philip

FREE, MY LORD, FREE AT LAS'
  (De Cormier) SATB SCHIRM.G LG 51743
  $.45   (F230)

FREE SPIRIT
  SATB UP WITH 6503 $.40   (F231)
  SA/TB UP WITH 6504 $.40   (F232)

FREEDOM see Merman

FREEDOM see Tillis, Frederick

FREEDOM PROCLAMATION see La Montaine,
  John

FREEDOM SONG, 1776 *US
  (Kirk) SATB,narrator,pno,opt fl,drums
  PRO ART 1443 $1.50
    contains: Confess Jehovah; Hail
    Columbia; Liberty Song; My Days
    Have Been So Wondrous Free; On
    Far Away Hill; Yankee Doodle
                   (F233)

FREEDOM TRAIL
  (Boody, Charles) SATB,acap ART MAST
  1016 $.30   (F234)

FREEDOM TREE, THE see Harris, Edward

FREIER GEIST, GESANG, UND WEIN see
  Edler, Robert

FREIHEIT, DIE ICH MEINE see Groos, Karl

FREIHEIT, DIE ICH MEINE see Rein,
  Walter

FRERE JACQUES
  (Tate) SATB,bvl,perc (easy) OXFORD
  84.171 $.45, ipa   (F235)

FRESEN, HEINRICH
  Der Frohlichkeit Lasst Ihren Lauf
    men cor,acap TONOS 4093 s.p. (F236)

FREU DICH, ERD UND STERNENZELT *CCU
  2-4pt mix cor,opt inst PELIKAN PE800
  s.p.   (F237)

FREUDE AM GESANG see Fichtner,
  Christian

FREUDE HEBT DIE L. SCHWINGEN see Edler,
  Robert

FREUDE HEBT DIE LICHTEN SCHWINGEN see
  Gwinner, Volker

FREUND DICKSACK "EINSTMALS TRABTE" see
  Stravinsky, Igor

FREUND HUSCH "HUSCH, ICH SCHLUPFE AUS
  DEM BUSCH" see Haas, Joseph

FREUNDE, EUCH GRUSST UNSER LIED see
  Foltz, Karl

FREUNDE, WASSER MACHET STUMM see Biebl,
  Franz

FREUNDLICHER ZURUF see Brautigam,
  Volker

FREUNDSCHAFT see Beethoven, Ludwig van

FREUNDSCHAFT, JUGEND DER WELT!
  mix cor HOFMEISTER V1612 s.p. (F238)

FREUNDSCHAFT SCHAFFT FRIEDEN see Orrel,
  Max

FREUT EUCH DES LEBENS
  unis wom cor SCHOTTS C 42 532L s.p.
    see also Alle Singen Heft 1 (F239)

FREUT EUCH, IHR SCHAFERSLEUT see Marx,
  Karl

FREY, OSKAR
  Blauer Montag
    men cor,acap TONOS 4095 s.p. (F240)

  Herrliches Land Vor Der Haardt
    men cor,acap TONOS 3942 s.p. (F241)
    men cor&jr cor,acap TONOS 261 s.p.
                  (F242)

  Sang Und Wein
    men cor,acap TONOS 4097 s.p. (F243)

  Wenn Kuhl Der Morgen Atmet
    men cor,acap TONOS 86 s.p. (F244)

  Wenn Mein Madel Tanzen Mag
    men cor,acap TONOS 90 s.p. (F245)

FRIBEC, KRESIMIR (1908-   )
  Mother Stojanka Of Knezpolje
    cor CROATICA   (F246)

FRIDAY AFTERNOONS see Britten

FRIDERICI, DANIEL (1584-1638)
  Drei Gute Dinge "Wir Lieben Sehr Im
    Herzen"
    mix cor (med) sc SCHOTTS CHBL 274
    s.p.   (F247)

  Erstes Musikalisches Strausslein,
    1617 *see Wir Lieben Sehr Im
    Herzen   (F248)

  Wir Lieben Sehr Im Herzen
    see Gastoldi, Giovanni Giacomo, An
      Hellen Tagen
    (Lendvai, Erwin) 4pt wom cor (easy)
      sc SCHOTTS C 37 589 s.p. see from
      Erstes Musikalisches Strausslein,
      1617   (F249)
    (Malin, Don) "Within Our Hearts We
      Cherish" TTBB,acap BELWIN 2332
      $.35   (F250)

  Within Our Hearts We Cherish *see
    Wir Lieben Sehr Im Herzen

FRIEDE ANNO 48 see Hartmann, Karl
  Amadeus

FRIEDE SEI DER FLAMME LICHT see Edler,
  Robert

FRIENDS
  SAB CIMINO $.40   (F251)
  SSA CIMINO $.40   (F252)

FRIENDSHIP AND FREEDOM see Grant, W.
  Parks

FRISCH ANGEPACKET DEN TAG see Langer,
  Hans-Klaus

FRISCH AUF, IHR BERGLEUT *folk,Ger
  (Wolters, Karl-Heinz) men cor,acap
  TONOS 74 s.p.   (F253)

FRISCH AUF, IHR MUSIKANTEN see Haas,
  Joseph

FRISCH AUF UND LASST UNS SINGEN see
  Peuerl, Paul

FRISCH AUF ZUM FROHLICHEN JAGEN see
  Poos, Heinrich

FRISCH AUF, ZUM JAGEN *folk
  (Desch, Rudolf) men cor,acap TONOS
  119 s.p.   (F254)

FRISCH FROHLICH WOLLN WIR SINGEN see
  Steffens, Johann

FRISCH GESUNGEN: HAB OFT IM KREISE see
  Silcher, Friedrich

FRITSCHEL, JAMES
  Be Still
    SATB WALTON 2920 $.40   (F255)

FRITZE "NUN MAG ICH AUCH NICHT LANGER
  LEBEN" see Cadow, Paul

FRIVOLOUS FRAULEINS see Krone

FROG, THE see Dunhill, Thomas Frederick

FROH HINAUS see Edler, Robert

FROH ZU SEIN, BEDARF ES WENIG see
  Gebhard, Hans

FROHBOTSCHAFT see Siegl, Otto

FROHER AUSKLANG "FREUDE SOLL IN DEINEN
  WERKEN SEIN" see Haas, Joseph

FROHES LEBEN see Zentner, Johannes

FROHLICH FANGT ALLE AN ZU SINGEN see
  Jeep, Johann

FROHLICHE FREITE see Lang, Hans

FROHLICHE TIERGESCHICHTEN see Lang,
  Hans

FROHLICHE WANDERKANTATE see Hoffer,
  Paul Marx

FROHLICHE WEIHNACHT UBERALL see Drahts,
  Willi

FROHLICHE WEIHNACHT UBERALL see Engel,
  H.

FROHLICHER JAHRMARKT see Zipp,
  Friedrich

FROHLICHES HANDWERK see Lang, Hans

FROHLOCKET, IHR MENSCHEN *Xmas
  (Bachl, Hans) treb cor DOBLINGER
  O 334 s.p.   (F256)

FROM CRADLE TO ALTAR see Smetacek,
  Vaclav, Ode Kolebky K Oltari

FROM THE DIARY OF A PRISONER see
  Dvoracek, Jiri, Z Deniku Vezne

FROM THE POPLAR TREES I COME see
  Vasquez, Juan, De Los Alamos Vengo

FROM THE PROVERBS OF THE SLAVONIC
  NATIONS see Haba, Alois, Z
  Mudroslovi Narodu Slovanskych

FROM THIS HOUR, FREEDOM see Whitman

FROM TIME AND ETERNITY see Weigl, Vally

FROMM, HERBERT (1905-   )
  Memorial Cantata
    cor,T solo,org/pno/orch TRANSCON.
    TCL 380 $3.00, ipr   (F257)

FROMMER WUNSCH "HARTE TALER MUSST ES
  REGNEN" see Seeger, Peter

FROMMLET, DIETER
  Auf Euer Wohl
    men cor,acap TONOS 4574 s.p. (F258)

  In Jedem Vollen Glase Wein
    men cor,acap TONOS 4562 s.p. (F259)

FROMMLET, FRANZ (1901-   )
  Fur Trauerfeiern
    men cor,acap TONOS 435 s.p. (F260)

  Gebet
    men cor,acap TONOS 4542 s.p. (F261)

  Gleichnis
    men cor,acap TONOS 4563 s.p. (F262)

  Lob Der Heimat "Wir Gehen Uber Unsre
    Erde"
    4pt men cor&2pt jr cor,2fl,3clar,
    2horn,2trp,3trom,2tuba,perc,timp,
    2flugelhorn, 2tenor horn,
    baritone horn sc,cor pts SCHOTTS
    ED. 4515 s.p., ipa   (F263)

  Oberschwaben
    men cor,acap TONOS 258 s.p. (F264)

  Vagabundenlied
    men cor,acap TONOS 3987 s.p. (F265)

FROSTY THE SNOW MAN see Nelson, Steve

FRUH, DES MORGENS FRUH see Lang, Hans

FRUH NOCH AM TAGE see Gal, Hans, Early
  One Morning

FRUHER, DA ICH UNERFAHREN see Kirsch, Winfried

FRUHLING AM BODENSEE see Desch, Rudolf

FRUHLING IST KOMMEN *folk,Swed
(Seib, Valentin) men cor,acap TONOS
2044 s.p.   (F266)

FRUHLING UND SOMMERBEGINN see Orff, Carl

FRUHLING - WINTER "WENN PRIMELN GELB"
see Genzmer, Harald

FRUHLINGS- UND WANDERLIEDER HEFT 2
*CCU
2-4 eq voices PELIKAN PE286 s.p.
contains works by: Distler; Marx;
Knab and others   (F267)

FRUHLINGS- UND WANDERLIEDER HEFT 3
*CCU
2-5pt mix cor PELIKAN PE287 s.p.
contains works by: Lahusen;
Brunner; Wolters and others (F268)

FRUHLINGSAHNUNG see Mendelssohn-
Bartholdy, Felix

FRUHLINGSERWARTEN see Seeger, Peter

FRUHLINGSFEIER see Mendelssohn-
Bartholdy, Felix

FRUHLINGSGLAUBE: DIE LINDEN LUFTE see
Silcher, Friedrich

FRUHLINGSGLAUBE "ES WANDERT EINE SCHONE
SAGE" see Hessenberg, Kurt

FRUHLINGSGRUSS see Schumann, Robert
(Alexander)

FRUHLINGSGRUSS "SO SEI GEGRUSST VIEL
TAUSENDMAL" see Schumann, Robert
(Alexander)

FRUHLINGSLIED see Eveillez-Vous

FRUHLINGSLIED: O SIEH, WIE RINGS DER
LENZ SICH REGT see Klefisch, Walter

FRUHLINGSLIEDER-POTPOURRI see Jage,
Rolf-Diether

FRUHLINGSZEIT see Wilhelm, Karl

FRUHMORGENS AUF DER JAGD "FRUHMORGENS,
WENN DAS JAGDHORN SCHALLT" *folk,
Ger
(Zoll, Paul) men cor sc SCHOTTS
C 41 380 s.p. see from Drei
Deutsche Volkslieder   (F269)

FRUHMORGENS "DER RAUCH DER DAMMERNDEN
FRUHE" see Sutermeister, Heinrich

FRUHSTUCK "ALLE UNSRE TAUBEN" see
Erdlen, Hermann

FRUHZEITIGER FRUHLING see Mendelssohn-
Bartholdy, Felix

FRYRA LEKTIONER see Johansen, Sven-Erik

FUHRMANNS LIEDCHEN see Bachmann, Alfred

FUHRMANNSLIED: HAB MEIN WAGEN see
Krietsch, Georg

FUJIWARA, Y.
Hokke-Senpo
men cor (based on theme of cabda-
vidya in Tendai-Jimon sect Onjo-
Ji temple) ONGAKU s.p.   (F270)

FUJIYAMA see Hirai, Kozaburo

FUKUSHIMA, KAZUO
Shizu
[It/Jap] wom cor,S solo,2fl,harp
(med diff) sc SCHOTTS ESZ 6249
s.p., ipr contains also: Uta
(F271)
Uta
see Fukushima, Kazuo, Shizu

FULL FATHOM FIVE see Bissell, Keith W.

FULL FATHOM FIVE see Swayne

FULLE see Burkhard Willy

FULLET MIT SCHALLE see Gluck, Christoph
Willibald Ritter von

FUM, FUM, FUM *Xmas,folk,Span
(Springfield) SS&camb&opt Bar,acap/
pno/bvl&gtr CAMBIATA U117211 $.30
(F272)

FUMIA LA PASTORELLA see Monteverdi,
Claudio

FUNERAL MARCH OF THE DEATH OF HEROES
see McElheran

FUNERAL ON KANK see Klicka, Josef,
Pohreb Na Kanku

FUNF ALTE VOLKSLIEDER see Hessenberg,
Kurt

FUNF CHANSONS FUR KINDER see Francaix,
Jean

FUNF CHORDUETTE NACH VOLKSWEISEN see
Biebl, Franz

FUNF CHORE see Beck, Conrad

FUNF CHORE see Genzmer, Harald

FUNF CHORLIEDER see Genzmer, Harald

FUNF JUGOSLAWISCHE CHORE see Lucic,
Franjo

FUNF MANNERCHORE see Rein, Walter

FUNF NEUE TANZLIEDER see Fischer, Ernst

FUNF OSTPREUSSISCHE VOLKSLIEDER see
Zoll, Paul

FUNF SATZE NACH KROATISCHEN
VOLKSLIEDERN *see Babusch; Dunja;
Jovo; Regen; Ziganka   (F273)

FUNF SEEMANSLIEDER *folk
(Biebl, Franz) men cor,acap cmplt ed
TONOS 2010 s.p.
contains: A-Roving (Eng), Blow The
Man Down (US); Rio Grande (US);
Sacramento (US); Shenandoah (US)
(F274)

FUNF TANZLIEDER see Lang, Hans

FUNF TANZLIEDER see Lang, Hans

FUNF TANZWEISEN see Fischer, Ernst

FUNFZEHN KANONS see Eglin, Arthur

FUR FUNFZEHN PFENNIGE "DAS MAGDLEIN
WILL EIN FEIER HABEN" see Bresgen,
Cesar

FUR KLEIN UND GROSS see Horler, Ernst

FUR TRAUERFEIERN see Frommlet, Franz

FURCHTET IHR DEN SCHWARZEN MANN see
Biebl, Franz

FURCHTLOSIGKEIT UND WOHLWOLLEN see Egk,
Werner

FURER, ARTHUR (1924-   )
Jahreszeitenlieder *Op.23
3 eq voices/3pt wom cor,opt 3vln
PELIKAN PE927 s.p.   (F275)

Portum Inveni *cant
mix cor,pno/pno,strings/fl,ob,trp,
horn,trom,strings,timp (med easy)
sc,cor pts SCHOTTS ED. 5291 s.p.,
ipa   (F276)

FURIANT see Smetana, Bedrich

FURMAN
Four Little Foxes
SATB,acap (med diff) OXFORD 95.309
$.60
contains: Go Lightly; Speak
Gently; Step Softly; Walk
Softly   (F277)

Go Lightly
see Four Little Foxes

Speak Gently
see Four Little Foxes

Step Softly
see Four Little Foxes

Walk Softly
see Four Little Foxes

FURST, JAROMIR KAREL (1895-   )
Balada O Krasne Smrti *cant
"Ballad About Beautiful Death, The"
[Czech] mix cor,SA soli,2fl,2ob,
2clar,2bsn,4horn,2trp,3trom,tuba,
timp,perc,harp,strings CZECH s.p.
(F278)
Ballad About Beautiful Death, The
*see Balada O Krasne Smrti

FURTHER WE REACH OUT, THE
SATB UP WITH 6505 $.40   (F279)

FUSSAN, WERNER (1913-   )
Auf, Ihr Bruder! Ehrt Die Lieder!
4pt men cor,acap/pno/3trp&2horn&
3trom&tuba voc sc SCHOTTS
C 39 177 s.p., cor pts SCHOTTS
CHBL 93 s.p., ipa   (F280)

FUSSAN, WERNER (cont'd.)

Das Krokodil "Im Heil'gen Teich Zu
Singapur"
4-7pt mix cor,acap (med diff) sc
SCHOTTS C 38 885 s.p. see from
Heiteres Aquarium   (F281)

Der Bauer "Hinterm Pflug, In Gleichem
Schritt"
men cor sc SCHOTTS C 39 435 s.p.
(F282)

Der Mond Ist Aufgegangen *folk
2pt jr cor&4pt men cor,acap (easy)
sc SCHOTTS C 38 532 s.p. see from
Vier Volkslieder   (F283)

Die Vier Verhaltnisse "Ein Junggesell
Muss Trinken"
TTBB sc SCHOTTS C 41 969 s.p., voc
pt SCHOTTS C 41 970 01-02 s.p.
(F284)

Ein Hering Liebt Eine Auster
mix cor (med diff) sc SCHOTTS
C 38 886 s.p. see from Heiteres
Aquarium   (F285)

Es Blus Ein Jager Wohl In Sein Horn
*folk
2pt jr cor&4pt men cor,acap (easy)
sc SCHOTTS C 38 531 s.p. see from
Vier Volkslieder   (F286)

Es Geht Ein Pfluger Ubers Land
TTBB sc SCHOTTS C 40 170 s.p., voc
pt SCHOTTS C 40 171 01-02 s.p.
(F287)

Es Wohnt Ein Muller An Jenem Teich
*folk
2pt jr cor&4pt men cor,acap (easy)
sc SCHOTTS C 38 529 s.p. see from
Vier Volkslieder   (F288)

Fest-Kantate "Unser Sind Die Stunden"
*Fest,cant
4pt men cor/2pt jr cor/2pt wom cor,
trp,strings,timp sc,cor pts
SCHOTTS ED. 6228 s.p., ipa (F289)

Halunkenlied "Mein Gaul Ist Alt Und
Will Nicht Mehr"
men cor,acap/perc sc SCHOTTS
C 43 609 s.p.   (F290)

Heiteres Aquarium *see Das Krokodil
"Im Heil'gen Teich Zu Singapur";
Ein Hering Liebt Eine Auster;
Plumps "Der Frosch Und Eine
Krote"   (F291)

Ich Fahr Dahin
men cor sc SCHOTTS CHBL 105 s.p.
(F292)

Kommt Herr Mond Zu Guter Nacht
men cor sc SCHOTTS C 38 263 s.p.
(F293)

Lob Der Schneider "Ich Bin Der
Meister Schneider" *folk
2pt jr cor&4pt men cor,acap (easy)
sc SCHOTTS C 38 530 s.p. see from
Vier Volkslieder   (F294)

Morgenlied "Noch Ahnt Man Kaum Der
Sonne Licht"
men cor sc SCHOTTS C 39 845 s.p.
(F295)

Plumps "Der Frosch Und Eine Krote"
4-5pt mix cor,acap (med diff) sc
SCHOTTS C 38 887 s.p. see from
Heiteres Aquarium   (F296)

Sangerruf
see LIEDPROGRAMM DES DEUTSCHEN
SANGERBUNDES FOLGE 3: "ESSENER
LIEDERBLATT" - "CHORFEIER"

Schenk Ein Den Wein Geselle Mein
men cor sc SCHOTTS C 38 264 s.p.
(F297)

Swing And Sing *CC10L
4pt mix cor, rhythmic group (med)
sc,cor pts SCHOTTS ED. 6572 s.p.,
ipa dance suite   (F298)

Tanzlieder-Kantate *cant
mix cor,ST soli,fl,ob,2clar,bsn,
horn,trp,strings (med) sc,cor pts
SCHOTTS ED. 5906 s.p., ipa (F299)

Verratene Liebe "Da Nachts Wir Uns
Kussten"
TTBB sc SCHOTTS C 38 635 s.p., voc
pt SCHOTTS C 38 636 01-04 s.p.
(F300)

Vier Volkslieder *see Der Mond Ist
Aufgegangen; Es Blus Ein Jager
Wohl In Sein Horn; Es Wohnt Ein
Muller An Jenem Teich; Lob Der
Schneider "Ich Bin Der Meister
Schneider"   (F301)

Wein Her, Es Lebe Die Welt! "Stimmt
Eure Seelen"
men cor sc SCHOTTS C 42 732 s.p.
(F302)

FUSSAN, WERNER (cont'd.)

Winzerchor "Wir Hockern Die Steinigen
Pfade Hinauf"
mix cor (med easy) sc SCHOTTS
C 40 680 s.p.   (F303)

FYE ON SINFUL FANTASY! see Felciano,
Richard

G

GABOLD, INGOLF (1942-   )
I Nattens Midte
"In The Middle Of Night" SATB
HANSEN-DEN WH 29265 s.p.   (G1)

In The Middle Of Night *see I
Nattens Midte

Written In Sand
wom cor&men cor HANSEN-DEN WH 29195
s.p.   (G2)

Your Sister's Drown'd
[Eng] TTBB,S solo HANSEN-DEN s.p.
                                (G3)

GABRIEL, SR., CHARLES H. (1856-1932)
Little Teetotalers
(Davis, Michael) SATB,acap FOSTER
MF333 $.45   (G4)

GABRIELI
Ten Madrigals *CC10L,madrigal
(Arnold) [It] SATB,acap (med)
OXFORD 58.649 $5.00   (G5)

GADE, NIELS WILHELM (1817-1890)
Agnete And The Mermaids *see Agnete
Of Havfruerne

Agnete Of Havfruerne *Op.3
"Agnete And The Mermaids" [Eng/Ger/
Dan] wom cor,Mez solo,orch
HANSEN-DEN s.p.   (G6)

Morgengesang
(Koenig, F.) men cor&jr cor,acap
TONOS 1351 s.p.   (G7)

Morgenwanderung
[Ger] SATB EGTVED MS13B3 s.p.   (G8)

O Du, Der Du Die Liebe Bist
[Ger] SATB EGTVED MS13B1 s.p.   (G9)

Ritter Fruhling
[Ger] SATB EGTVED MS13B2 s.p.   (G10)

GAELIC CROON, A see Anderson, [William
H.]

GAGLIARDI, GEORGE
My Favorite Time To Cry
SATB,fl,gtr FINE ARTS EP 21 $.35
                                (G11)

GAGNEBIN, HENRI (1886-   )
Chant Pour Le Jour Des Morts Et De La
Toussaint
mix cor,soli,orch HENN 187 s.p.
                                (G12)

Criquette
wom cor,acap HENN 462 s.p.   (G13)

Si Notre Vie
mix cor,acap HENN 590 s.p.   (G14)

Trois Chansons Othon De Grand Son
*CC3U
mix cor,acap HENN 764 s.p.   (G15)

GAL, HANS (1890-   )
An Eriskay Love Lilt *sac,folk
"Liebesruf Aus Eriskay" [Eng/Ger]
mix cor (med) sc SCHOTTS C 42 311
s.p. see from Vier Britische
Volkslieder   (G16)

Du Liebe Flur Im Seengrund *see Ye
Banks And Braes

Early One Morning *sac,folk
"Fruh Noch Am Tage" [Eng/Ger] mix
cor (med) sc SCHOTTS C 42 310
s.p. see from Vier Britische
Volkslieder   (G17)

Fruh Noch Am Tage *see Early One
Morning

Lebenskreise *cant
SATB&treb cor,SATB soli,orch ALKOR
AE297 rental   (G18)

Liebesruf Aus Eriskay *see An
Eriskay Love Lilt

O Can Ye Sew Chushions *sac,folk
"Wiegenlied" [Eng/Ger] mix cor
(med) sc SCHOTTS C 42 312 s.p.
see from Vier Britische
Volkslieder   (G19)

Vier Britische Volkslieder *see An
Eriskay Love Lilt, "Liebesruf Aus
Eriskay"; Early One Morning,
"Fruh Noch Am Tage"; O Can Ye Sew
Chushions, "Wiegenlied"; Ye Banks
And Braes, "Du Liebe Flur Im
Seengrund"   (G20)

GAL, HANS (cont'd.)

Wiegenlied *see O Can Ye Sew
Chushions

Ye Banks And Braes *sac,folk
"Du Liebe Flur Im Seengrund" [Eng/
Ger] mix cor (med) sc SCHOTTS
C 42 313 s.p. see from Vier
Britische Volkslieder   (G21)

GALGENLIED see Cossetto, Emil

GALGENLIEDER see Eckert, Alex

GALLIARD CAROL, THE see Monelle,
Raymond

GAMBLE, KENNY
Love Train (composed with Huff, Leon)
*pop
(Nowak, Jerry) SATB,pno oct BIG
BELL $.40   (G22)

GAMUT, THE see Cohn, James

GANDER, THE see Berger, Jean

GANNON
Under Paris Skies *pop
(Drejac; Giraud) SSA BELWIN UC 705
$.40   (G23)
(Drejac; Giraud) SATB BELWIN UC 706
$.40   (G24)

GANZ ALLEIN FUR MICH see Edler, Robert

GAR LIEBLICH HAT SICH GESELLET see
Kanetscheider, Artur

GARDEZ LE TRAIT DE LA FENETRE see Hahn

GARDNER
Ballad Of Nancy Dee, The
SSAA (med) OXFORD 83.089 $.75 see
from Three Amorous Airs   (G25)

German Flute, The
SSA (med) OXFORD 83.088 $.45 see
from Three Amorous Airs   (G26)

Three Amorous Airs *see Ballad Of
Nancy Dee, The; German Flute,
The; Waly, Waly   (G27)

Waly, Waly
SSA (med) OXFORD 83.087 $.45 see
from Three Amorous Airs   (G28)

Who Is Sylvia?
SSAA (med diff) OXFORD 83.094 $.50
                                (G29)

GARFUNKEL, ART
Scarborough Fair-Canticle *see
Simon, Paul

GARVARENTZ, GEORGES
Un Enfant Est Ne
[Fr] 3pt,pno CHAPPELL-FR s.p. (G30)

GASTOLDI, GIOVANNI GIACOMO (? -1622)
Amor Vittorioso
[It] SSATB,acap EGTVED KB121 s.p.
contains also: Il Bell' Humore
                                (G31)

An Hellen Tagen *sac/sec
mix cor (easy) sc SCHOTTS CHBL 369
s.p.   (G32)
SSATB CARUS CV 40.204 s.p. contains
also: Hassler, Hans Leo,
Feinslieb, Du Hast Mich Gfangen
(SATB); Hassler, Hans Leo, Tanzen
Und Springen (SSATB); Friderici,
Daniel, Wir Lieben Sehr Im Herzen
(SATB)   (G33)

Il Bell' Humore
see Gastoldi, Giovanni Giacomo,
Amor Vittorioso

Im Maienhellen Tagen
(Mittergradnegger, G.) men cor,acap
TONOS 3332 s.p.   (G34)

Lo Schernito
(Ehret) "When I See You Dear, So
Pleasing" SATB SCHIRM.G LG 51601
$.25   (G35)

Speme Amorosa
[It] SSATB,acap EGTVED KB205 s.p.
                                (G36)
When I See You Dear, So Pleasing
*see Lo Schernito

GASTRONOMISCHE KANTATE see Haug, [Hans]

GATATUMBA see Klefisch, Walter

GATHER YE ROSEBUDS see Sanderson W.

GATTERMAYER, HEINRICH (1923-   )
Spruch
men cor,acap TONOS 5815 s.p.   (G37)

GATTERMAYER, HEINRICH (cont'd.)

Und Alle Welt Vergeht
  men cor,acap TONOS 5816 s.p.   (G38)

GATTI, C. (1876-1965)
Canzone Del Cucu
  4pt mix cor,3fl,2ob,2clar,3bsn,
  4horn,3trp,4trom,timp CARISH
  rental   (G39)

Canzone Delle Rosa
  2pt wom cor,2fl,2ob,2clar,2bsn,
  3horn,2trp,2trom,tuba,timp,harp,
  pno CARISH rental   (G40)

I Falciatori
  4pt men cor,2fl,2ob,2clar,2bsn,
  4horn,3trp,3trom,timp,perc CARISH
  rental   (G41)

Piccola Cantata
  jr cor&3pt wom cor,harp,pno,strings
  CARISH rental   (G42)

GATTY, ART
Brotherhood Of Man, The
  SATB,pno YAHRES 1574 $.35   (G43)

GAUDEAMUS IGITUR
  see Two Traditional Songs
  (Mammel, Rolf) men cor,opt 2trp&2trom
  TONOS 4227 s.p.   (G44)

GAUDEAMUS IGITUR see Bardos, Lajos

GAUSS, OTTO
Abendfeier
  see Zehn Lyrische Gesange

Das Bachlein
  see Zehn Lyrische Gesange

Des Gesanges Macht
  see Zehn Lyrische Gesange

Es Folgt Mir Aus Der Jugendzeit
  see Zehn Lyrische Gesange

Gute Nacht
  see Zehn Lyrische Gesange

Hab Sonne Im Herzen
  see Zehn Lyrische Gesange

Hymnus
  see Zehn Lyrische Gesange

Meine Welt
  see Zehn Lyrische Gesange

Mondnacht
  see Zehn Lyrische Gesange

Sonntagsfeier
  see Zehn Lyrische Gesange

Zehn Lyrische Gesange
  men cor,acap cmplt ed TONOS 4070
  s p
    contains: Abendfeier; Das
    Bachlein; Des Gesanges Macht;
    Es Folgt Mir Aus Der
    Jugendzeit; Gute Nacht; Hab
    Sonne Im Herzen; Hymnus; Meine
    Welt; Mondnacht; Sonntagsfeier
                                  (G45)

GAVIN, KEVIN
We're Together (composed with
  Waloshin, Sid)
  (Metis, F.) SA/TB BIG3 $.50   (G46)
  (Metis, F.) SATB BIG3 $.50   (G47)
  (Metis, F.) SAB BIG3 $.50   (G48)
  (Metis, F.) SSA BIG3 $.50   (G49)

GAVOTTE HIVERNALE see Bovet, G.

GAYLORD, RONNIE
I Will Never Pass This Way Again
  (Simon, W.) SAB BIG3 $.45   (G50)
  (Simon, W.) SSA BIG3 $.45   (G51)
  (Simon, W.) SATB BIG3 $.40   (G52)

GEAH, DIANDLE, BIST LAUNIG
  see In Da Molltalleiten

GEBED VOOR HET VADERLAND see Spoel, A.

GEBET see Frommlet, Franz

GEBET DER SCHIFFER "DIE STUNDEN EILEN"
  see Pestalozzi, Heinrich

GEBET DES WELKEN BAUMES ZUR SONNE see
  Ishii, Kan

GEBET "LEIH AUS DEINES HIMMELS HOHEN"
  see Gluck, Christoph Willibald
  Ritter von

GEBET "MARIA, MUTTER ICH FLEH' ZU DIR"
  see Klefisch, Walter

GEBHARD, HANS
Auf Einem Baum Ein Kuckuck Sass
  1-2pt wom cor&4pt men cor,acap
  (contains also: Froh Zu Sein,
  Bedarf Es Wenig) sc SCHOTTS
  C 38 539 s.p. see from Ein
  Ergotzlich Liedersingen   (G53)

Ein Ergotzlich Liedersingen *see Auf
  Einem Baum Ein Kuckuck Sass; Es
  Sass Ein Kafer Auf'm Baumel; Froh
  Zu Sein, Bedarf Es Wenig; Lustig,
  Ihr Bruder   (G54)

Es Sass Ein Kafer Auf'm Baumel
  1-2pt wom cor&4pt men cor,acap sc
  SCHOTTS C 38 540 s.p. see from
  Ein Ergotzlich Liedersingen   (G55)

Froh Zu Sein, Bedarf Es Wenig
  1-2pt wom cor&4pt men cor,acap
  (contains also: Auf Einem Baum
  Ein Kuckuck Sass) sc SCHOTTS
  C 38 540 s.p. see from Ein
  Ergotzlich Liedersingen   (G56)
  1-2pt wom cor&4pt men cor,acap
  (contains also: Lustig, Ihr
  Bruder) sc SCHOTTS C 38 538 s.p.
  see from Ein Ergotzlich
  Liedersingen   (G57)

In Die Hoh! "Viel Essen Macht Viel
  Breiter"
  men cor sc SCHOTTS CHBL 58 s.p.
                                  (G58)

Lustig, Ihr Bruder
  1-2pt wom cor&4pt men cor,acap
  (contains also: Froh Zu Sein,
  Bedarf Es Wenig) sc SCHOTTS
  C 38 538 s.p. see from Ein
  Ergotzlich Liedersingen   (G59)

Wachterlied
  men cor,opt fl,ob,gtr TONOS 4202
  s.p.   (G60)

Wenn Alle Brunnlein Fliessen *Op.29
  mix cor,fl,2clar,bsn,2horn,strings
  (med easy) voc pt SCHOTTS
  ED. 3192 s.p., ipa   (G61)

GEBHARD, LUDWIG (1907-   )
Blinder Eifer "Ein Blinddarm Sass Im
  Bauche Tief"
  see Humoritaten

Die Amsel "Im Blutenbaum Sass Eine
  Amsel"
  see Humoritaten

Die Motte "Ein Pelztiermantel Hing Im
  Schrank"
  see Humoritaten

Die Spielzeugtruhe *Op.20, cant
  1-3pt jr cor,soli,treb inst,pno,opt
  perc (easy) sc,cor pts SCHOTTS
  ED. 4522 s.p., ipa   (G62)

Einbildung "In Einem Schrebergarten
  Traumte"
  see Humoritaten

Es Begab Sich *Op.35, Xmas,cant
  wom cor,soli,narrator,inst (med)
  sc,cor pts SCHOTTS ED. 5767 s.p.,
  ipa   (G63)

Humoritaten *Op.42
  TTBB,opt perc sc SCHOTTS C 42 566
  s.p., voc pt SCHOTTS
  C 42 567 01-02 s.p., ipa
  contains: Blinder Eifer "Ein
    Blinddarm Sass Im Bauche Tief";
    Die Amsel "Im Blutenbaum Sass
    Eine Amsel"; Die Motte "Ein
    Pelztiermantel Hing Im
    Schrank"; Einbildung "In Einem
    Schrebergarten Traumte"   (G64)

GEBURTSTAG see Kludas, Erich

GEBURTSTAG "DEIN LEBEN IST EIN
  FRUHLINGSLIED" see Herrmann, Hugo

GEDANKENREISE see Rubben, Hermannjosef

GEDICHTE "GEDICHTE SIND GEMALTE
  FENSTERSCHEIBEN" see Hessenberg,
  Kurt

GEELEN, MATHIEU (1933-   )
Kind Of Existence, A
  cor,3fl,3ob,2clar,3bsn,4horn,3trp,
  3trom,tuba,strings,perc,timp
  DONEMUS   (G65)

GEESE, HEINZ (1930-   )
Die Seefahrt Nach Rio *cant
  (Cammin, Heinz) 3pt jr cor,
  narrator,opt inst,pno, or
  accordion (easy) sc SCHOTTS s.p.,
  voc sc SCHOTTS ED. 6585 s.p.,
  pts SCHOTTS ED. 6585-6 s.p., ipa
                                  (G66)

GEGENWART "ALLES KUNDET DICH AN" see
  Rein, Walter

GEH AUS, MEIN HERZ see Lang, Hans

GEH HIN, MOSES see Go Down, Moses

GEHN TAGLICH VIEL LEUTE see Marx, Karl

GEHRECKE
Nobody Else Like You (composed with
  Richardson; Hale) *pop
  (Plank) SATB,opt perc KENDOR $.40
                                  (G67)
  (Plank) SAB,opt perc KENDOR $.40
                                  (G68)
  (Plank) SSA,opt perc KENDOR $.40
                                  (G69)

GEHRING, PHILIP (1925-   )
Shenandoah
  (Plott) TTBB BRODT DC 6 $.24   (G70)

GEHT ALLES UM UND UM see Zipp,
  Friedrich

GEHT'S, BUAMA *Xmas
  (Bachl, Hans) treb cor DOBLINGER
  O 336-337 s.p. contains also:
  Still, Still   (G71)

GEIGE UND KLARINETT' see Mockl, Franz

GEISLER
Orchestra, The
  (Hosier) 5pt (med easy) sc OXFORD
  50.116 $2.00, cor pts OXFORD
  50.117 $.55   (G72)

GEISS, GOTTFRIED
Die Liebe Horet Nimmer Auf
  men cor,acap sc,cor pts TONOS 4008
  s.p.   (G73)

GELOBNIS see Herrmann, Hugo

GELOOFSVERTROUWEN see Becker, D.G.

GELOSO AMANTE see Luzzaschi, Luzzasco

GELT, DIANDLE, DEI BUA TUAT NIX SCHEAN
  see Es Hat Ja Schon Drei G'schlagn

GENERATION OF PEACE, A see Wolf,
  Richard

GENIALISCH TREIBEN "SO WALZ ICH OHNE
  UNTERLASS" see Hessenberg, Kurt

GENIALISCH TREIBEN "SO WALZ ICH OHNE
  UNTERLASS" see Zelter, Carl
  Friedrich

GENIALISCHES TREIBEN "SO WALZ ICH OHNE
  UNTERLASS" see Rein, Walter

GENTLE CARPENTER OF BETHLEHEM
  SSA CIMINO $.40   (G74)
  TB CIMINO $.40   (G75)
  SAB CIMINO $.40   (G76)
  SA CIMINO $.40   (G77)

GENTLE MAINDEN, THE see Sharpe, Evelyn

GENTLE WIND see Roff

GENTLY, JOHNNY, MY JINGALO
  (Hall, Wm.D.) TB,pno NATIONAL WHC-5
  $.30   (G78)

GENZMER, HARALD (1909-   )
Ablosung "Kuckuck Hat Sich Zu Tod
  Gefallen" (from Des Knaben
  Wunderhorn)
  4pt wom cor (med, contains also:
  Frau Nachtigall "Nachtigall, Ich
  Hor Dich Singen") sc SCHOTTS
  C 39 372 s.p. see from Acht
  Chorlieder   (G79)

Acht Chorlieder *see Ablosung
  "Kuckuck Hat Sich Zu Tod
  Gefallen" (from Des Knaben
  Wunderhorn); Christkindleins
  Wiegenlied "O Jesulein Zart"
  (from Des Knaben Wunderhorn); Der
  Verschwundene Stern "Es Stand Ein
  Sternlein Am Himmel" (from Des
  Knaben Wunderhorn); Frau
  Nachtigall "Nachtigall, Ich Hor
  Dich Singen" (from Des Knaben
  Wunderhorn); Kauzlein "Ich Armes
  Kauzlein" (from Des Knaben
  Wunderhorn); Kinderpredigt "Ein
  Huhn Und Ein Hahn" (from Des
  Knaben Wunderhorn); Urlicht "O
  Roschen Rot" (from Des Knaben
  Wunderhorn); Wacht Auf Ihr
  Schonen Vogelein (from Des Knaben
  Wunderhorn)   (G80)

An Den Flamingo "Flamingo, Ich Kann
  Dir Nicht Trauen"
  [Ger] men cor sc SCHOTTS C 41 553
  s.p. see from Vier Indische
  Lieder   (G81)

GENZMER, HARALD (cont'd.)

Chinesisches Trinklied "Das Wasser,
   Das Frische"
   see Zwei Lieder Beim Wein

Christkindleins Wiegenlied "O
   Jesulein Zart" (from Des Knaben
   Wunderhorn)
   4pt wom cor sc SCHOTTS C 39 376
   s.p. see from Acht Chorlieder
                                    (G82)

Der Hoffnungslose "Ich Schaute In Den
   Nebel"
   [Ger/Slav] SATB,Bar solo (med,
   contains also: Tanzliedchen "Tanz
   Doch, Pfarrer") sc SCHOTTS
   C 40 992 s.p. see from Lieder Der
   Welt   (G83)

Der Schwarze Mond "In Die Mondlose
   Nacht" *So Am
   4-5pt mix cor (med diff) sc SCHOTTS
   C 39 935 s.p. see from
   Sudamerikanische Gesange   (G84)

Der Tod "Gestern, Bruder, Konnt Ihrs
   Glauben"
   see Zwei Lieder Beim Wein

Der Verschwundene Stern "Es Stand Ein
   Sternlein Am Himmel" (from
   Knaben Wunderhorn)
   4pt wom cor (med, contains also:
   Wacht Auf Ihr Schonen Vogelein)
   sc SCHOTTS C 39 374 s.p. see from
   Acht Chorlieder   (G85)

Der Weinschwelg "Nun Ohne Lugen"
   [Ger] TTBB sc SCHOTTS C 39 973 s.p.
   see from Drei Chorlieder Vom Wein
                                    (G86)

Die Gewissheit "Ob Ich Morgen Leben
   Werde"
   [Ger] TTBB sc SCHOTTS C 39 972 s.p.
   see from Drei Chorlieder Vom Wein
                                    (G87)

Die Weihe Der Nacht "Nachtliche
   Stille"
   men cor sc SCHOTTS C 41 389 s.p.
   see from Lieder Der Nacht   (G88)

Drei Antike Gesange
   mix cor,3trp&2trom, or piano four
   hands (med) sc,voc pt SCHOTTS
   ED. 6570 s.p., ipa
   contains: Orphische Hymne "An Die
   Nacht"; Rechnung; Wechsellied
   Beim Weine   (G89)

Drei Chore *see Haus-Segen "Nun Ist
   Ein Haus Neu Aufgerichtet"; Herz,
   Werde Wach Und Singe; Wiegenlied
   An Der Bergstrasse "Tropf, Tropf
   Tau"   (G90)

Drei Chorlieder Vom Wein *see Der
   Weinschwelg "Nun Ohne Lugen"; Die
   Gewissheit "Ob Ich Morgen Leben
   Werde"; Romische Weinspruche
   "Pete Me Imple"   (G91)

Drei Chorlieder Vom Wein *see
   Romische Weinspruche "Pete Me
   Imple"   (G92)

Du Bist Min *sac
   [Ger] mix cor (med easy, contains
   also: Klageliche Not) sc SCHOTTS
   C 39 666 s.p. see from Funf
   Chorlieder   (G93)

Echo Vom Himmel "Oh Freudenhimmel"
   [Ger] 6pt men cor,TB soli sc
   SCHOTTS C 42 486 s.p. see from
   Englisch Horn   (G94)

Ein Klagegesang "Rauher Wind"
   [Ger] 6pt men cor,TB soli sc
   SCHOTTS C 42 487 s.p. see from
   Englisch Horn   (G95)

Englisch Horn *see Echo Vom Himmel
   "Oh Freudenhimmel"; Ein
   Klagegesang "Rauher Wind";
   Fruhling - Winter "Wenn Primeln
   Gelb"; Oft In Der Stillen Nacht;
   Rondell "Eur Augenpaar";
   Seemannslied "Der Meister, Der
   Schiffsjung"; Sonett "So Lieblich
   Kusst Die Sonne Nicht"; Sturm, Du
   Winterwind   (G96)

Finnische Lied "Uber Den Berg"
   [Ger] SSATBB (med, contains also:
   Tagelied "Die Hahne Krahen") sc
   SCHOTTS C 40 991 s.p. see from
   Lieder Der Welt   (G97)

Frau Nachtigall "Nachtigall, Ich Hor
   Dich Singen" (from Des Knaben
   Wunderhorn)
   4pt wom cor (med, contains also:
   Ablosung "Kuckuck Hat Sich Zu Tod
   Gefallen") sc SCHOTTS C 39 372
   s.p. see from Acht Chorlieder

GENZMER, HARALD (cont'd.)

                                    (G98)
Fruhling - Winter "Wenn Primeln Gelb"
   [Ger] men cor sc SCHOTTS C 42 492
   s.p. see from Englisch Horn
                                    (G99)

Funf Chore *see Lied Des
   Vogelstellers "Der Vogel, Der Im
   Fluge Ruht"; Rechenstunde "Zwei
   Und Zwei Sind Vier"; Stadturlaub
   "Ich Hab Mein Kappi In Den Spind
   Getan"; Ungeheuer Und Rot
   Erscheint Die Wintersonne; Wie
   Man Ein Vogel Malt "Male Zuerst
   Einen Kafig"   (G100)

Funf Chorlieder *see Du Bist Min;
   Ich Will Truren Fahren Lan;
   Klageliche Not; Swel Man Ein Guot
   Wip Hat; Wurze Des Waldes   (G101)

Haus-Segen "Nun Ist Ein Haus Neu
   Aufgerichtet"
   men cor sc SCHOTTS CHBL 158 s.p.
   see from Drei Chore   (G102)

Herz, Werde Wach Und Singe
   men cor sc SCHOTTS CHBL 160 s.p.
   see from Drei Chore   (G103)

Herz, Wo Warst Du In Der Nacht
   [Ger] SSATBB (med, contains also:
   Tanzende "Dunkelaugige, Du";
   Mistral Uber Den Grabern "Sei
   Still") sc SCHOTTS C 40 993 s.p.
   see from Lieder Der Welt   (G104)

Ich Will Truren Fahren Lan *sac
   [Ger] mix cor (med easy, contains
   also: Wurze Des Waldes) sc
   SCHOTTS C 39 665 s.p. see from
   Funf Chorlieder   (G105)

In Der Nacht Gesungen "Hohe,
   Feierliche Nacht"
   mix cor (med) sc SCHOTTS CHBL 339
   s.p.   (G106)

Kauzlein "Ich Armes Kauzlein" (from
   Des Knaben Wunderhorn)
   wom cor,SSA soli sc SCHOTTS
   C 39 375 s.p. see from Acht
   Chorlieder   (G107)

Kinderpredigt "Ein Huhn Und Ein Hahn"
   (from Des Knaben Wunderhorn)
   4pt wom cor (med, contains also:
   Urlicht "O Roschen Rot") sc
   SCHOTTS C 39 373 s.p. see from
   Acht Chorlieder   (G108)

Klageliche Not *sac
   [Ger] mix cor (med easy, contains
   also: Du Bist Min) sc SCHOTTS
   C 39 666 s.p. see from Funf
   Chorlieder   (G109)

Lied Des Vogelstellers "Der Vogel,
   Der Im Fluge Ruht"
   [Ger] 4-8pt mix cor (med diff) sc
   SCHOTTS C 41 580 s.p. see from
   Funf Chore   (G110)

Lieder Der Nacht *see Die Weihe Der
   Nacht "Nachtliche Stille";
   Nachtlied "Quellende, Schwellende
   Nacht"; Stille Quellen "Flieht
   Auch Der Jugend Glanz"   (G111)

Lieder Der Welt *see Der
   Hoffnungslose "Ich Schaute In Den
   Nebel"; Finnische Lied "Uber Den
   Berg"; Herz, Wo Warst Du In Der
   Nacht; Mandalay "Wo Der Alte
   Moulmeintempel"; Mistral Uber Den
   Grabern "Sei Still"; Tagelied
   "Die Hahne Krahen"; Tanzende
   "Dunkelaugige, Du"; Tanzliedchen
   "Tanz Doch, Pfarrer"   (G112)

Mandalay "Wo Der Alte Moulmeintempel"
   [Ger] SSATBB (med) sc SCHOTTS
   C 40 994 s.p. see from Lieder Der
   Welt   (G113)

Manfreds Bannfluch "Wenn Der Mond Ist
   Auf Der Welle"
   4-8pt mix cor (med) sc SCHOTTS
   C 38 672 s.p., voc pt SCHOTTS
   C 39 673A-B s.p.   (G114)

Mistral Uber Den Grabern "Sei Still"
   [Ger] SATB (med, contains also:
   Herz, Wo Warst Du In Der Nacht;
   Tanzende "Dunkelaugige, Du") sc
   SCHOTTS C 40 993 s.p. see from
   Lieder Der Welt   (G115)

Mondaufgang "Die Erde Ist Gehullt"
   [Ger] men cor sc SCHOTTS C 41 552
   s.p. see from Vier Indische
   Lieder   (G116)

GENZMER, HARALD (cont'd.)

Moosburger Graduale
   cor,soli,2vln,vla,vcl/bvl,opt
   brass,perc,timp (med) sc,cor pts
   SCHOTTS ED. 6505 s.p., ipa (G117)

Nachtlied "Quellende, Schwellende
   Nacht"
   men cor sc SCHOTTS C 41 388 s.p.
   see from Lieder Der Nacht   (G118)

Oft In Der Stillen Nacht
   [Ger] men cor sc SCHOTTS C 42 485
   s.p. see from Englisch Horn
                                    (G119)

Oktober-Narr "Oktoberlicht,
   Oktoberbrand"
   see Vier Gedichte

Orphische Hymne "An Die Nacht"
   see Drei Antike Gesange

Racine Kantate *cant
   [Ger] mix cor,Bar solo,2fl,ob,2bsn,
   2horn,2trp,strings,timp, English
   horn (med) sc SCHOTTS rental, ipr
                                    (G120)

Rechenstunde "Zwei Und Zwei Sind
   Vier"
   [Ger] 4-7pt mix cor (med diff) sc
   SCHOTTS C 39 971 s.p. see from
   Funf Chore   (G121)

Rechnung
   see Drei Antike Gesange

Romische Weinspruche "Pete Me Imple"
   TTBB voc pt SCHOTTS C 39 975-01, 02
   s.p. see from Drei Chorlieder Vom
   Wein   (G122)
   [Lat] TTBB sc SCHOTTS C 39 974 s.p.
   see from Drei Chorlieder Vom Wein
                                    (G123)

Rondell "Eur Augenpaar"
   [Ger] men cor sc SCHOTTS C 42 488
   s.p. see from Englisch Horn
                                    (G124)

Schweigen Der Liebe "So Ihr Nun
   Stimmen Hort"
   see Vier Gedichte

Seemannslied "Der Meister, Der
   Schiffsjung"
   [Ger] men cor sc SCHOTTS C 42 491
   s.p. see from Englisch Horn
                                    (G125)

Sehnsucht "Schweift Auch Mein Blick"
   [Ger] men cor (contains also:
   Warnung "Mein Tochterlein, Ich
   Warne Dich") sc SCHOTTS C 41 551
   s.p. see from VIER INDISCHE
   LIEDER   (G126)

Sensemaya "Die Kulebra Hat Augen Aus
   Glas" *So Am
   8pt mix cor (med diff) sc SCHOTTS
   C 39 937 s.p. see from
   Sudamerikanische Gesange   (G127)

Singe, Mein Herz
   men cor sc SCHOTTS C 43 937 s.p.
                                    (G128)

Solche, Die In Schenken Sitzen
   see Vier Gedichte

Sonett "So Lieblich Kusst Die Sonne
   Nicht"
   [Ger] men cor sc SCHOTTS C 42 490
   s.p. see from Englisch Horn
                                    (G129)

Sonett Vom Goldenen Herbst "O
   Goldener Herbst
   see Vier Gedichte

Stadturlaub "Ich Hab Mein Kappi In
   Den Spind Getan"
   [Ger] 6pt mix cor (med diff) sc
   SCHOTTS C 39 970 s.p. see from
   Funf Chore   (G130)

Stille Quellen "Flieht Auch Der
   Jugend Glanz"
   men cor sc SCHOTTS C 41 390 s.p.
   see from Lieder Der Nacht   (G131)

Sturm, Du Winterwind
   [Ger] men cor sc SCHOTTS C 42 489
   s.p. see from Englisch Horn
                                    (G132)

Sudamerikanische Gesange *see Der
   Schwarze Mond "In Die Mondlose
   Nacht"; Sensemaya "Die Kulebra
   Hat Augen Aus Glas"; Tristissima
   Nox "Stunde Unermesslichen
   Friedens"; Weisse Verlassenheit
   "In Der Stille Des Traumes"
                                    (G133)

Swel Man Ein Guot Wip Hat *sac
   [Ger] mix cor (med easy) sc SCHOTTS
   C 39 667 s.p. see from Funf
   Chorlieder   (G134)

Tagelied "Die Hahne Krahen"
   [Ger/Slav] SSATTBB (med, contains
   also: Finnische Lied "Uber Den

GENZMER, HARALD (cont'd.)

Berg") sc SCHOTTS C 40 991 s.p.
see from Lieder Der Welt   (G135)

Tanzende "Dunkelaugige, Du"
[Ger] SATB (med, contains also:
Mistral Uber Den Grabern "Sei
Still"; Herz, Wo Warst Du In Der
Nacht) sc SCHOTTS C 40 993 s.p.
see from Lieder Der Welt   (G136)

Tanzliedchen "Tanz Doch, Pfarrer"
[Ger/Hung] SATTBB (med, contains
also: Der Hoffnungslose "Ich
Schaute In Den Nebel") sc SCHOTTS
C 40 992 s.p. see from Lieder Der
Welt   (G137)

Tristissima Nox "Stunde
Unermesslichen Friedens" *So Am
5-9pt mix cor (med diff) sc SCHOTTS
C 39 936 s.p. see from
Sudamerikanische Gesange   (G138)

Ungeheuer Und Rot Erscheint Die
Wintersonne
[Ger] 4-8pt mix cor (med diff) sc
SCHOTTS C 41 579 s.p. see from
Funf Chore   (G139)

Urlicht "O Roschen Rot" (from Des
Knaben Wunderhorn)
3-4pt wom cor (med, contains also:
Kinderpredigt "Ein Huhn Und Ein
Hahn") sc SCHOTTS C 39 373 s.p.
see from Acht Chorlieder   (G140)

Vier Gedichte
men cor, piano four hands sc,cor
pts SCHOTTS ED. 5179 s.p.
contains: Oktober-Narr
"Oktoberlicht, Oktoberbrand";
Schweigen Der Liebe "So Ihr Nun
Stimmen Hort"; Solche, Die In
Schenken Sitzen; Sonett Vom
Goldenen Herbst "O Goldener
Herbst   (G141)

Vier Indische Lieder *see An Den
Flamingo "Flamingo, Ich Kann Dir
Nicht Trauen"; Mondaufgang "Die
Erde Ist Gehullt"   (G142)

Vom Abenteuer Der Freude
men cor/wom cor/mix cor,4horn,3trp,
3trom,tuba,5strings,perc (med)
sc,cor pts SCHOTTS ED. 5168 s.p.,
ipa   (G143)

Wacht Auf Ihr Schonen Vogelein (from
Des Knaben Wunderhorn)
4pt wom cor (med, contains also:
Der Verschwundene Stern "Es Stand
Ein Sternlein Am Himmel") sc
SCHOTTS C 39 374 s.p. see from
Acht Chorlieder   (G144)

Warnung "Mein Tochterlein, Ich Warne
Dich"
[Ger] men cor (contains also:
Sehnsucht "Schweift Auch Mein
Blick") sc SCHOTTS C 41 551 s.p.
see from VIER INDISCHE LIEDER
     (G145)

Wechsellied Beim Weine
see Drei Antike Gesange

Weisse Verlassenheit "In Der Stille
Des Traumes" *So Am
7pt mix cor (med diff) sc SCHOTTS
C 39 934 s.p. see from
Sudamerikanische Gesange   (G146)

Wie Man Einen Vogel Malt "Male Zuerst
Einen Kafig" *sac
[Ger] 4-10pt mix cor (med diff) sc
SCHOTTS C 39 670 s.p., voc pt
SCHOTTS C 39 671A-B s.p. see from
Funf Chore   (G147)

Wiegenlied An Der Bergstrasse "Tropf,
Tropf Tau"
men cor,T solo sc SCHOTTS CHBL 159
s.p. see from Drei Chore   (G148)

Wurze Des Waldes *sac
[Ger] mix cor (med easy, contains
also: Ich Will Truren Fahren Lan)
sc SCHOTTS C 39 665 s.p. see from
Funf Chorlieder   (G149)

Zwei Lieder Beim Wein
men cor sc SCHOTTS C 43 577 s.p.
contains: Chinesisches Trinklied
"Das Wasser, Das Frische"; Der
Tod "Gestern, Bruder, Konnt
Ihrs Glauben"   (G150)

GEOGRAPHY ISN'T HARD see Shearer, C.M.

GEORG FRIEDRICH HANDEL'S WORKS see
Handel, George Frideric

GEORGE
Love Song, A *see Loggins, Dave

GEORGE, EARL (1924-   )
Infant Joy
see Songs Of Innocence

Introduction
see Songs Of Innocence

Lamb, The
see Songs Of Innocence

Laughing Song
see Songs Of Innocence

Shepherd, The
see Songs Of Innocence

Songs Of Innocence *sac/sec
SATB SUMMY $2.50
contains: Infant Joy;
Introduction; Lamb, The;
Laughing Song; Shepherd, The
     (G151)

GERANIUMS ROUGES see Yvoire

GERBER, STEVEN
Ceremony After A Fire Raid
SATB,acap AM.COMP.AL. $3.85   (G152)

Dylan Thomas Settings
SATB,acap AM.COMP.AL. $5.50   (G153)

Illuminations
SATB,acap AM.COMP.AL. $3.85   (G154)

GERLITZ, EUGENE
We Are The Sons
SATB,TBar soli,acap NATIONAL WHC-26
$.40   (G155)

GERMAN, EDWARD (1862-1936)
Just So Songs
(Jacob) SATB,2fl,pic,2ob,2clar,
2bsn,4horn,2trp,3trom,tuba,timp,
perc,harp,strings voc sc NOVELLO
rental   (G156)

GERMAN FLUTE, THE see Gardner

GERSCHEFSKI, EDWIN (1909-   )
Border Raid *Op.57,No.1
SATB,pno AM.COMP.AL. $9.90   (G157)

Changing Shoes
wom cor/jr cor,pno AM.COMP.AL.
$3.30 see also Six Songs   (G158)

Clocks
wom cor/jr cor,pno AM.COMP.AL.
$3.30 see also Six Songs   (G159)

College Creed, A *Op.42,No.1
wom cor,pno AM.COMP.AL. $3.30
     (G160)

October *Op.36,No.4
SSA,org AM.COMP.AL. $2.20   (G161)

Salutation Of The Dawn *Op.37
mix cor,3fl,2ob,2clar,4horn,3trp,
3trom,tuba,perc,strings
AM.COMP.AL. sc $13.20, voc pt
$11.00   (G162)

Six Songs *Op.39
wom cor/jr cor,pno AM.COMP.AL.
$8.80
contains & see also: Changing
Shoes; Clocks; Sky And Stars;
Snow; Think About Wheels (G163)

Six Songs *CC6U
SATB,pno,perc sc AM.COMP.AL. $9.90
     (G164)

Sky And Stars
wom cor/jr cor,pno AM.COMP.AL.
$2.75 see also Six Songs   (G165)

Snow
wom cor/jr cor,pno AM.COMP.AL.
$2.75 see also Six Songs   (G166)

Think About Wheels
wom cor/jr cor,pno AM.COMP.AL.
$3.30 see also Six Songs   (G167)

GERSHWIN AND PORTER ON LOVE
(Hayward) SATB SHAWNEE A1279 $1.25
     (G168)

GERSHWIN, GEORGE (1898-1937)
Gershwin Revisted
(Slater) SATB, stage band WARNER
CH2012 $.35, ipa   (G169)

GERSHWIN REVISTED see Gershwin, George

GERSTER, OTTMAR (1897-1969)
An Das Handwerk "Als Noch Hans Sachs
Den Pfriemen Schwang"
voc pt SCHOTTS C 33 731, 01-04 s.p.
see from STANDELIEDER   (G170)
men cor sc SCHOTTS C 33 730 s.p.
see from Standelieder   (G171)

GERSTER, OTTMAR (cont'd.)

An Die Sonne "Die Schatten Sind Vom
Berg Ins Tal Gezogen" *cant
men cor&jr cor,S solo,2fl,2ob,
2clar,2bsn,4horn,2trp,3trom,
strings,perc,timp sc SCHOTTS
rental, ipr   (G172)

Chor Der Winzer "Wir Hokern Die
Steinigen Pfade Hinauf"
voc pt SCHOTTS C 33 990, 01-03 s.p.
see from STANDELIEDER   (G173)
men cor sc SCHOTTS C 33 989 s.p.
see from Standelieder   (G174)

Das Beste In Der Welt
men cor,acap TONOS 4056 s.p. (G175)

Drescherlied "Im Dreitakt Der
Drescher"
men cor sc SCHOTTS C 33 987 s.p.
see from Standelieder   (G176)

Erfahrung
see Vier Sinngedichte

Guten Morgen, Jungfer
see Zwei Tanzlieder

Himmel Und Erde
see Vier Sinngedichte

"In Den Rheinbergen Bluht Schon Der
Wein"
"Vini Boni Veritas" men cor sc
SCHOTTS C 39 384 s.p.   (G177)

Preis Des Schopfers "Tausendfaltig,
Vielgestaltig"
men cor sc SCHOTTS C 33 995 s.p.
     (G178)

Seemannschor "Wir Lichten Die Anker"
men cor sc SCHOTTS C 33 993 s.p.
see from Standelieder   (G179)

Standelieder *see An Das Handwerk
"Als Noch Hans Sachs Den Pfriemen
Schwang"; Drescherlied "Im
Dreitakt Der Drescher";
Seemannschor "Wir Lichten Die
Anker"   (G180)

Taglicher Wunsch
see Vier Sinngedichte

Vier Sinngedichte
3-5pt wom cor,acap (med) sc SCHOTTS
C 34 562 s.p.
contains: Erfahrung; Himmel Und
Erde; Taglicher Wunsch;
Zweierlei Nacht Und Zweierlei
Tag   (G181)

Vini Boni Veritas *see "In Den
Rheinbergen Bluht Schon Der Wein"

Was Hilft Mir Ein Roter Apfel
see Zwei Tanzlieder

Zwei Tanzlieder
men cor,acap cmplt ed TONOS 4058
s.p.
contains: Guten Morgen, Jungfer;
Was Hilft Mir Ein Roter Apfel
     (G182)
Zweierlei Nacht Und Zweierlei Tag
see Vier Sinngedichte

GERUSALEM! GERUSALEM! see Verdi,
Giuseppe

GESANG AN DIE SONNE "IN MORGENROT
GEKLEIDET" see Biebl, Franz

GESANG DER GEISTER UBER DEN WASSERN see
Koetsier, Jan

GESANG DES DEUTSCHEN see Reutter,
Hermann

GESANG EINES WELKEN BAUMES UND DER
SONNE see Ishii, Kan

GESANG IN DER FRUHE see Wittmer,
Eberhard Ludwig

GESANGE see Mohler, Philipp

GESCHAFTSBERICHT see Dessau, Paul

GESEGN DICH LAUB see Wimberger, Gerhard

GESEGNETE NOT see Erdlen, Hermann

GESELLEN DER NACHT see Rein, Walter

GESELLENLIEBE "WACH AUF, DU LUSTIGER
SANGER" see Zoll, Paul

GESELLIGE STUNDE
unis wom cor SCHOTTS C 42 533B s.p.
see also Alle Singen Heft 2 (G183)

GESELLSCHAFTSLIED see Hirth, Hermann

GESPRACH ZWISCHEN BLUMEN UND SONNE see
Ishii, Kan

GESUALDO, DON CARLO (ca. 1560-1613)
Cease Then To Give Me Sorrow *see
Resta Di Darmi Noia

Non T'amo O Voce Ingrata *madrigal
SAATB RICORDI-ENG BA9830 s.p.
(G184)

Resta Di Darmi Noia
"Cease Then To Give Me Sorrow"
SSATB STAINER 3.0795.1 $.50
(G185)

GET DOWN see O'Sullivan, Gilbert

GET HAPPY! see Ades

GET INTO HEAV'N see Mc Kay, David
Phares

GETTING IT TOGETHER *medley
(Red, Buryl) SATB (Gay Nineties
Ragtime Melodies) TRIGON TGO 108
$1.25   (G186)

GETTING TO KNOW YOU see Rodgers,
Richard

GETTYSBURG ADDRESS, THE see Pease,
Rollin

GETTYSBURG ADDRESS, THE see Thall,
Peter Morgan

GETTYSBURG ADDRESS, THE see Walker

GETTYSBURG ADDRESS, THE see Walker,
William

GHEDINI, GIORGIO FEDERICO (1892-1965)
Antifona Per Luisa
"Antiphon Fur Luise" [Lat] wom cor&
jr cor,org/3vln&vcl&bvl (easy) sc
SCHOTTS ESZ 4401 s.p.   (G187)

Antiphon Fur Luise *see Antifona Per
Luisa

GHOSTS, FIRE, WATER see Mews

GIACHETTI, ENRICO (1890-1954)
Silentium
cor,soli,2fl,3ob,2clar,2bsn,4horn,
3trp,3trom,tuba,timp,harp CARISH
rental   (G188)

GIARDINI, FELICE DE' (1716-1796)
Viva Tutte Le Vezzose
[It] SAB EGTVED MS13B6 s.p.   (G189)

GIB UNS SANFTEN TOD see Edler, Robert

GIBBONS, ORLANDO (1583-1625)
First Set Of Madrigals And Motets
(1612) EM Vol. 5 *CC21L
5-6pt mix cor STAINER 3.1905.1
$11.50   (G190)

Silver Swan, The
(Deller) SATTB SCHIRM.G 12043 $.40
(G191)

GIDEON, MIRIAM (1906-   )
Sweet Western Wind
SATB,acap AM.COMP.AL. $2.20   (G192)

GIFT, THE see Eidsvoog

A GIFT OF MADRIGALS AND MOTETS VOL. II
*sac/sec,CC30U,madrigal/mot,16th
cent
(Slim, H. Colin) cor, cantus, tenor,
bassus, and quintus et VI pap
UNIV.CH ISBN: 0-226-76272-6 $7.50
(G193)
A GIFT OF MADRIGALS AND MOTETS VOLS. I
& II *sac/sec,CC30U,madrigal/mot,
16th cent
(Slim, H. Colin) cor cmplt ed,cloth
UNIV.CH ISBN:0-226-76271-8 $37.50
Vol. I Contains Artistic And
Historical Background   (G194)

GIFT TO BE SIMPLE, THE see Wood, Dale

GIFTS see Weigl, Vally

GIMBEL
Bluesette *pop
(Thielemans) SSA BELWIN UC 708 $.40
(G195)
GIPPS, RUTH (1921-   )
Goblin Market
SSA,2S,strings voc sc NOVELLO
rental   (G196)

GIPSY MELODIES see Bendl, Karel,
Cikanske Melodie

GIRL, A see Van Wormer, G.

GIRL FROM IPANEMA see Jobim, Antonio
Carlos

GIRL I LEFT BEHIND ME see Simpson, John

GIRL WITH THE BUCKLES ON HER SHOES, THE
*folk,Ir
(Nelson, Havelock) unis,pno CURWEN
72694 s.p.   (G197)

GIRL'S COMPOSITION ABOUT BOYS, A see
Burroughs, Bob

GIRLS IN THE GARDEN see Enfield,
Patrick

GIROMETA see Pratella, Francesco
Balilla

GIROTTO, ALMERIGO
Due Canzoni Veronesi *CC2U
cor sc ZANIBON 5464 s.p.   (G198)

Quattro Suites (I & II) *CC2U
cor,pno sc ZANIBON 5462 s.p.   (G199)

Quattro Suites (III & IV) *CC2U
cor,pno sc ZANIBON 5463 s.p.   (G200)

GIT ON BOARD, LITTLE CHILDREN
(Biebl, Franz) treb cor DOBLINGER
O 313 s.p. see from Acht Spirituals
(G201)

GIURA IL NOCCHIER see Beethoven, Ludwig
van

GIVE A LITTLE LOVE AT CHRISTMAS see
Besig

GIVE ME LIBERTY, OR GIVE ME DEATH see
Collins, Don L.

GIVE ME THE SPLENDID SILENT SUN see
Lockwood, Normand

GIVE US MEN TO MATCH OUR MOUNTAINS see
Krone

GJENDEM, JOHAN J.
Samspill Og Sang
SSA/SAB MUSIKK   (G202)

GLADA BYGD see Bellman, Carl Mikael

GLADE JUL see Gruber, Nyhus, Rolf

GLAGOLITICA see Laburda, Jiri

GLARUM
Bells Do Ring, The
SATB,opt hndbl SCHIRM.G 12008 $.40
(G203)
GLASSE OF TRUTH, A see Childs, Barney

GLAUBENSLIED see Krietsch, Georg

GLAUBENSLIED "WIE STEIN MIT MEISSEL
FICHT" see Fortner, Wolfgang

GLEICHGEWINN "GEHT EINER MIT DEM
ANDEREN HIN" see Pepping, Ernst

GLEICHNIS see Frommlet, Franz

GLI SCARIOLANTI see Pratella, Francesco
Balilla

GLINKA, H.
Elegie
men cor,acap ZIMMER. 577 s.p.
(G204)
GLINKA, MIKHAIL IVANOVITCH (1804-1857)
Complete Works *sac/sec,CCU
(Schwartz, Boris) [Russ/Eng]
microfiche UNIV.MUS.ED. 18
volumes in 23 bindings $250.00
(G205)

GLOCKEN see Trunk, Richard

GLOCKEN see Zschiegner, Fritz

GLOCKEN, DIE NICHT KLINGEN see
Rosenstengel, Albrecht

GLOCKENLIED "GLOCKEN MIT DEM
SILBERMUND" see Lendvai, Erwin

GLOCKENSEGEN "KOMM IN DIESEM
GLOCKENSEGEN" see Mohler, Philipp

GLORIA see Atkinson, Condit R.

GLORIA see Knab, Armin

GLORIA IM HIMMEL *folk
(Seeger, P.) [Ger] 4pt mix cor
MERSEBURG EM9241 s.p.   (G206)

GLORIA IN EXCELSIS DEO
unis wom cor SCHOTTS C 42 533L s.p.
see also Alle Singen Heft 2   (G207)

GLORY BE TO WORK see Riha, Oldrich,
Praci Cest

GLORY OF CHRISTMAS
SSA CIMINO $.40   (G208)
SATB CIMINO $.40   (G209)

GLORY OF HELLAS, THE see Maessen,
Antoon, De Glans Van Hellas

GLORY OF THE DOVE, THE see Stoker,
Richard

GLOVE - FULL OF LOVE, A see Kricka,
Jaroslav, Oblazky Z Lasky

GLUCK AUF, DER STEIGER KOMMT see Engel,
H.

GLUCK AUF, IHR BERGLEUT *folk,Ger
(Desch, Rudolf) men cor,acap TONOS 30
s.p.   (G210)

GLUCK, CHRISTOPH WILLIBALD RITTER VON
(1714-1787)
Festgesang "Freudenklange, Frohe
Festgesange" (from Iphigenie In
Aulis)
(Gerster, Ottmar) jr cor (easy) sc
SCHOTTS CHBL 544 s.p.   (G211)

Fullet Mit Schalle
(Rietz, Johannes) men cor,acap
TONOS 3005 s.p.   (G212)

Gebet "Leih Aus Deines Himmels Hohen"
(from Iphigenie In Tauris)
(Klink, Waldemar) mix cor (easy) sc
SCHOTTS CHBL 277 s.p.   (G213)

GLUCK DES SOMMERS see Zoll, Paul

GLUCK "GLUCK IST WIE EIN SONNENBLICK"
see Lang, Hans

GLUCK UND FRIEDEN see Bartok, Bela,
Level Az Otthoniakhoz

GLUCKLICHES LEBEN see Lang, Hans

GLUCKSELIG MUSS MAN PREISEN, DIE
GLEICHE LIEB UND TREU see Rein,
Walter

GLUCKWUNSCH-KANTATE see Lang, Hans

GLYCERA see Schultz, Svend S.

GNEIST, VERNER (1898-   )
An Die Musik (Nun Hebet Frohlich An,
Die Gut Musik Zu Preisen)
see Marx, Karl, Sine Musica Nulla
Vita

GO DOWN, MOSES *spir
see Ev'ry Time I Feel The Spirit
"Geh Hin, Moses" see Spirtuals For
All Heft II
(Kubizek, Augustin) "Geh Hin, Moses"
men cor DOBLINGER M 299 s.p. (G214)

GO DOWN MOSES see Weber, Bernhard

GO FROM MY WINDOW, GO see Coleman,
Henry

GO LIGHTLY see Furman

GO MY WAY see Lightfoot, Gordon

GO, TELL IT ON THE MOUNTAINS *sac/sec,
Xmas,spir
(Huntley, Fred H.) TTBB,acap (easy)
FITZSIMONS 4067 $.20   (G215)
(Soderstrom, Emil) SATB (med)
FITZSIMONS 2114 $.25   (G216)

GO TO SLEEP see Dawson, William Levi

GOAT, THE
see Barbershop Choir, The

GOBLIN MARKET see Gipps, Ruth

GOD BLESS AMERICA MEDLEY
(Mercer, W. Elmo) SATB BENSON S4115
$.30   (G217)

GOD BLESS CANADA see Roff, Joseph

GOD SAVE THE QUEEN
(Bissell, Keith W.) SAB (med)
WATERLOO $.30   (G218)

GOD SAVE THE QUEEN see Carey, Henry

GODDEN, REGINALD
Linda Rose
unis HARRIS $.25   (G219)

Little Hans
unis HARRIS $.25   (G220)

GODFREY, BOB
Back In Dad And Mother's Day *see
Betzner, Jack

GOD'S LARK AT MORNING see Jordan, Alice

GOFFIN, A.
  Debout Faucheurs
    TTBB sc BROGNEAUX s.p.   (G221)

GOHRE, WERNER
  Westfalenlied
    men cor,opt pic&2fl&ob&3clar&bsn&
    3horn&4trp&3trom&2tuba&perc, 2
    flugelhorns, 2 tenor horns,
    baritone horn voc sc TONOS 3979
    s.p., ipa   (G222)

GOIN' BACK see Dedrick, C.

GOIN' TO BOSTON
  (Parker) SATB SCHIRM.G LG51738 $.40
                                    (G223)

GOING BAROQUE
  (Atkinson) SAB,inst oct SCHMITT 8070
    $.40   (G224)

GOING, GOING, GONE see Thygerson,
  Robert J.

GOING, GOING, GONE see Dylan, Robert
  (Bob)

GOING OUT MY HEAD
  SAB CIMINO $.40   (G225)

GOING OUT OF MY HEAD
  SA CIMINO $.40   (G226)
  SSA CIMINO $.40   (G227)
  SATB CIMINO $.40   (G228)
  TTBB CIMINO $.40   (G229)

GOING TO THE ZOO see Paxton

GOLD, ERNEST (1921-   )
  Night Has A Thousand Eyes, The
    [Eng] SATB,acap BROUDE BR. $.50
                                    (G230)

  White Rose, A
    [Eng] SATB,acap BROUDE BR. $.50
                                    (G231)

GOLDEN ODER ROT DER WEIN see Mockl,
  Franz

GOLDEN SLUMBER see Carr, Albert Lee

GOLDEN SLUMBERS see Mozart, Wolfgang
  Amadeus

GOLDEN SLUMBERS see Roberton

GOLDEN SPINNING-WHEEL, THE see Kricka,
  Jaroslav, Zlaty Kolovrat

GOLDNER HERBST see Fischer, Theo

GOLDNES GARBENFELD
  unis wom cor SCHOTTS C 42 533H s.p.
    see also Alle Singen Heft 2 (G232)

GOLDSMITH
  Free As The Wind *see Shaper

GOLDWURFELSPIEL *folk
  (Haus, K.) [Ger] 4pt mix cor
    MERSEBURG EM9212 s.p.   (G233)

GOLLER, FRITZ (1914-   )
  Die Vogelhochzeit *cant
    jr cor,pno,opt fl&vln&vcl (easy)
    sc,cor pts SCHOTTS ED. 4231 s.p.,
    ipa   (G234)

GOMBERT, NICOLAS (ca. 1490-1550)
  Votre Beaute Plaisante Et Lie
    (Malin, Don) "Your Beauty Binds Me
    Pleasantly" SATB,acap BELWIN 2327
    $.30   (G235)

  Your Beauty Binds Me Pleasantly *see
    Votre Beaute Plaisante Et Lie

GONDOLIER'S EVENING SONG see
  Mendelssohn-Bartholdy, Felix

GONE, GONE IS MY SUNSHINE see Adler

GONNA GET ALONG WITHOUT YA NOW
  SA CIMINO $.40   (G236)
  SSA CIMINO $.40   (G237)
  TTBB CIMINO $.40   (G238)
  SATB CIMINO $.40   (G239)

GONNA GET ALONG WITHOUT YOU NOW see
  Kellem

GOOD COMPANY see Hewitt-Jones, Tony

GOOD DAY, HERR BEETHOVEN see White,
  Herbert D.

GOOD HOUSEWIFE, THE see Kodaly, Zoltan

GOOD KING WENCESLAUS *sac/sec,Xmas
  (Bergman) unis,pno,strings,perc,rec
    SCHOTT RS23 cmplt ed s.p., sc s.p.,
    ipa   (G240)

GOOD LIFE, THE
  SSA CIMINO $.40   (G241)
  SAB CIMINO $.40   (G242)

GOOD MAN, YOU ARE COMPLAINING see
  Lange, Gregor, Gut G'sell, Du
  Machst Dein Klagen

GOOD MORNING see Grieg, Edvard Hagerup

GOOD MORNING, FATHER CHRISTMAS see
  Niles, John Jacob

GOOD MORNING SKY see Shearer, C.M.

GOOD MORROW, TIS ST. VALENTINE'S DAY
  see Spencer, Williametta

GOOD NEIGHBORS THEN see Crawford,
  Thomas J.

GOOD NIGHT see Klein, Lothar

GOOD WIVES OF PIONEERS see Sly, Allan

GOODBYE LOVE see Kraintz, Ken

GOODBYE TO LOVE see Carpenter, Richard

GOODBYE YELLOW BRICK ROAD see John,
  Elton

GOODELL, WALTER
  Blue O'Your Eyes, The
    SATB (med) FITZSIMONS 1056 $.25
                                    (G243)

GOODLY HERITAGE, A *CC12L
  (Jacob, G.) SSA voc sc STAINER
    3.0799.1 $3.25   (G244)

GOODNIGHT BELOVED see Protheroe, Daniel

GOOSSEN, FREDERIC
  American Meditations *see Bohemian
    Hymn, The; Come Lovely And
    Soothing Death; It Is No Dream Of
    Mine; Man's Life Is Like A Rose;
    Only God   (G245)

  Bohemian Hymn, The *sac/sec
    SA,acap PEER $.40 see from American
    Meditations   (G246)

  Come Lovely And Soothing Death *sac/
    sec
    SSA,acap PEER $.60 see from
    American Meditations   (G247)

  Death, Be Not Proud
    TTBB,acap PEER $.45   (G248)

  It Is No Dream Of Mine *sac/sec
    SSA,acap PEER $.40 see from
    American Meditations   (G249)

  Man's Life Is Like A Rose *sac/sec
    SSA,acap PEER $.40 see from
    American Meditations   (G250)

  Only God *sac/sec
    SSA,acap PEER $.40 see from
    American Meditations   (G251)

GORDON
  Celebrate (composed with Bonner)
    (Lojeski, Ed) SATB LEONARD-US
    08206500 $.50   (G252)
    (Lojeski, Ed) SSA LEONARD-US
    08206502 $.50   (G253)

GORDON, JOHN
  Gulf Country, The
    SAB EMI see from Two Choral Songs
                                    (G254)

  Magpies At Morning
    SAB EMI see from Two Choral Songs
                                    (G255)

  Two Choral Songs *see Gulf Country,
    The; Magpies At Morning (G256)

GORDON, PHILIP (1894-   )
  Tyrlee, Tyrlo
    SATB BOURNE B216895-357 $.40 (G257)

GOREAU, LAURRAINE
  Shrimp Boy
    SATB BOURNE B224550-357 $.40 (G258)

GORL, WILLIBALD
  Auf Der Ofenbank
    men cor,acap TONOS 4534 s.p. (G259)

  Bekenntnis
    men cor,acap TONOS 231 s.p. (G260)

  Schneeflockenlied
    men cor,acap TONOS 4535 s.p. (G261)

  Sommerdorfchen
    men cor,acap TONOS 4571 s.p. (G262)

GORM GRYMM see Maurice, Pierre

GOSPEL BOOGIE
  SSA CIMINO $.40   (G263)
  SATB CIMINO $.40   (G264)

GOSPELS, SHANTIES, AND FOLKLORE
  *CC122U,folk/pop/spir
  (Senft, Joche) [Ger] unis,opt gtr

MOSELER s.p.   (G265)

GOT TO GET YOU INTO MY LIFE see Lennon,
  John

GOTOVAC, JAKOV (1895-   )
  Am Adriatischen Meer "Nach Dir Ich
    Mich Sehne"
    [Ger] TTBB sc SCHOTTS C 37 833
    s.p., voc pt SCHOTTS
    C 37 834, 01-04 s.p.   (G266)

  Das Gestohlene Mantelchen "Dafina, Am
    Feurigen Rotwein" *Op.15,No.3
    [Ger] TTBB sc SCHOTTS C 37 835
    s.p., voc pt SCHOTTS
    C 37 836, 01-04 s.p.   (G267)

  Koleda *Op.11, Slav
    [Ger/Czech] men cor,3clar,bsn,timp
    (song cycle) sc,cor pts SCHOTTS
    ED. 5189 s.p., ipa   (G268)

  Koleda-Folk Rite In Five Parts
    TB,3clar,2bsn,tamb/timp CROATICA
                                    (G269)

  Liebeswerbung "Warum Bist Du
    Brunnenwasser" *Op.15,No.1
    men cor sc SCHOTTS C 39 203 s.p.
                                    (G270)

GOTT B'HUTE DICH see Lechner, Leonhard

GOTT GSEGN DICH, LAUB see Pepping,
  Ernst

GOTT IST GEWALTIG see Schaefers

GOTT, LASS SONNE SCHEINEN *CC16U,folk
  3-4 eq voices MOSELER HEFT35 s.p.
                                    (G271)

GOTT SEGNE DEN REBENSAFT see Heun, Hans

GOTTHARDT, PETER (1941-   )
  Hor, Angela!
    4pt mix cor,opt solo NEUE NM1007
    s.p.   (G272)

GOTTSCHALK, LOUIS MOREAU (1829-1869)
  Tournament Galop (composed with
    Jeffries)
    (McAfee, Don) cor,synthesizer/pno
    MCAFEE M1075 $.40, ipa   (G273)

GOTTSCHALK, WOLFGANG (1929-   )
  Das Erdeben "Bruder, Bruder, Halte
    Mich!"
    men cor sc SCHOTTS C 40 739 s.p.
                                    (G274)

GOULD, MORTON (1913-   )
  Two For Chorus *CCU
    2pt oct CHAPPELL 0093609-351 $.50
                                    (G275)

GOUNOD, CHARLES FRANCOIS (1818-1893)
  Choral Fantasia On Faust
    (Challinor) mix cor BANKS MUS
    YS 823 $1.10   (G276)

GOW, DAVID (1924-   )
  Music For Chorus (composed with
    Nielsen, Carl) *CCU
    SATB CHESTER JWC 8893 s.p.   (G277)

GRAB UND MOND see Schubert, Franz
  (Peter)

GRABE TAG UM TAG *folk,Russ
  (Seeger, Peter) men cor,acap TONOS
    2018 s.p.   (G278)

GRABLIED see Beethoven, Ludwig van

GRABLIED see Delacher, Hermann

GRABLIED see Thehos, Adam

GRABLIED "PILGER AUF ERDEN" see
  Cornelius, Peter

GRABLIED "SO STILL DIE LUFT" see
  Wittmer, Eberhard Ludwig

GRABNER, HERMANN (1886-1969)
  Hymne An Deutschland (Land Des
    Glaubens, Deutsches Land)
    4pt men cor,opt orch sc,cor pts
    MERSEBURG EM654 s.p., ipa (G279)
    4pt mix cor,strings sc,cor pts
    MERSEBURG EM655 s.p., ipa (G280)
    4pt men cor,strings sc,cor pts
    MERSEBURG EM656 s.p., ipa (G281)
    4pt men cor,band sc,cor pts
    MERSEBURG EM657 s.p., ipa (G282)
    3pt wom cor/3pt treb cor,opt 2vln&
    vcl sc,cor pts MERSEBURG
    EM651 s.p., ipa   (G283)
    3pt men cor,opt 2vln&vcl&pno sc,cor
    pts MERSEBURG EM652 s.p., ipa
                                    (G284)
    4pt mix cor,opt orch sc,cor pts
    MERSEBURG EM653 s.p., ipa (G285)

GRABSCHRIFT "ALS KNABE VERSCHLOSSEN UND
  TRUTZIG" see Hessenberg, Kurt

GRABSCHRIFT AUF DEN WINDMULLER JACKSON
    "HIER LIEGT DER MULLER JACKSON" see
    Cadow, Paul

GRADY
    Same Old Monday
        (Littleton, Bill J.) SATB FINE ARTS
        EP 33 $.35   (G286)

GRAFFITI see McAfee, Don

GRAHAM
    Hawaiian Anthem, A *US
        SATB oct HERITAGE H115 $.35   (G287)

GRAINGER, PERCY ALDRIDGE (1882-1961)
    Hunter In His Career, The
        [Eng] unis,2pno (med) sc SCHOTTS
        SL 4477 s.p., ipa   (G288)

    I'm Seventeen Come Sunday
        SATB SCHOTT 11339 s.p.   (G289)

    Sea-Wife, The
        [Eng] mix cor, piano four hands
        (med) sc SCHOTTS SL 5401 s.p.
                                         (G290)
GRAM ZERNAGT MEIN HERZCHEN see Martinu,
    Bohuslav, Hlavenka Me Boli

GRANADA see Stanislav, Josef

GRAND IS THE SEEN see Stearns, Peter
    Pindar

GRANDMA'S ADVICE *folk
    (Brandon, George) SATB STANDARD
    C606MX1 $.50   (G291)

GRANITE AND CYPRESS see Ames, William

GRANT, W. PARKS
    Friendship And Freedom *Op.32,No.1
        SATB,acap AM.COMP.AL. $2.20   (G292)

    Prayer For Philadelphia *Op.32,No.2
        SATB,acap AM.COMP.AL. $3.30   (G293)

    There Is A Santa Claus *Op.52,No.2
        SATB,pno AM.COMP.AL. $3.30   (G294)

GRAPE GROWIN' MAN see Nestico, G.

GRASS ROOTS BOOK 1 *CCU
    (Bacon, Ernst) 1-2pt,pno/org,opt
        winds&brass&perc BELWIN $1.50 based
        on American Folk Tunes   (G295)

GRASS ROOTS BOOK 2 *CCU
    (Bacon, Ernst) 1-2pt,pno/org,opt
        winds&brass&perc BELWIN $1.50 based
        on American Folk Tunes   (G296)

GRASSHOFFIADE see Zehm, Friedrich

GRASSHOFFIADE see Zehm, Friedrich

GRASSHOPPER see Bohac, Josef, Cvrcek

GRASSHOPPER AND THE ANT, THE see
    Jeffries

GRATIFACTION see Sherman, Richard M.

GRATITUDE TO MOTHER EARTH see Roff,
    Joseph

GRAUER TAUBER see Nitsche, Paul

GRAVE AND THE MOON, THE see Schubert,
    Franz (Peter)

GREAT BUDDAH see Hirai, Kozaburo

GREAT DAY see Youmans

GREAVES
    Bandog, The
        see Three Children's Songs

    Follow My Leader *CC4U,canon
        SA/TB (easy) OXFORD 50.114 $.65
                                         (G297)
    Old Tailor, The
        see Three Children's Songs

    Please To Remember
        see Three Children's Songs

    Three Children's Songs
        unis (med) OXFORD 81.113 $.30
            contains: Bandog, The; Old
            Tailor, The; Please To Remember
                                         (G298)
    Tinker, Tailor *CC8U
        unis (med easy) OXFORD 68.054 $.65
                                         (G299)

GREEN
    Happy To Know You
        (Lojeski, Ed) SATB LEONARD-US
            08221650 $.50   (G300)
        (Lojeski, Ed) SSA LEONARD-US
            08221652 $.50   (G301)
        (Lojeski, Ed) SAB LEONARD-US
            08221654 $.50   (G302)
        (Lojeski, Ed) 2pt LEONARD-US

GREEN (cont'd.)

        08221656 $.50   (G303)

GREEN BROOM see Simpson, John

GREEN, DOROTHY M.
    I Pledge Allegiance To The Flag
        SATB,pno (easy) oct GENTRY G-227
        $.35   (G304)

GREEN GRASS see Gwelltyn Glas

GREEN GROW THE RUSHES-O
    (Kirk) 3pt PRO ART 2775 $.40   (G305)

GREEN GROW THE RUSHES, OH *Eng
    (Suerte) SSBar&camb CAMBIATA U97206
    $.40   (G306)

GREEN IN THE BRANCH see Eben, Petr

GREEN IS THE MAY see Lechner, Leonhard,
    Grun Ist Der Mai

GREEN, RAY (1909-   )
    Westron Wind
        SATB,high solo,pno/acap AM.MUS.ED.
        $.25   (G307)

GREENSLEEVES *folk,Ir
    (Erbelding, Dietrich) men cor,opt gtr
        TONOS 451 s.p.   (G308)
    (Lefebvre, C.) SATB GALAXY 1.1968.1
        $.25   (G309)
    (Lefebvre, C.) SSA GALAXY 1.1969.1
        $.35   (G310)
    (Lefebvre, C.) TTBB GALAXY 1.1961.1
        $.30   (G311)
    (Miller, Carl) 2pt CHAPPELL
        0064170-351 $.40   (G312)
    (Stenlund, D.O.) men cor GEHRMANS
        KVB356   (G313)
    (Stenlund, Dan-Olof) mix cor GEHRMANS
        KRB450   (G314)

GREENSLEEVES see Nitsche, Paul

GREENWOOD TREE see Patriquin, Donald

GREETING - PROMISE see Simek, Miroslav,
    Pozdrav - Prisaha

GREETING TO SOVIET UNION see Barvik,
    Miroslav, Prodrav Sovetskemu Svazu

GREETINGS TO MOSCOW see Vignati, Milos,
    Pozdrav Moskve

GREETINGS TO THE PRESIDENT see Sauer,
    Frantisek, Zdravice Panu
    Presidentovi

GREGHESCHE, LIBRO I (1564) *CC39U
    (Cisilino, Siro) 4-5pt mix cor
        ZANIBON 5459 s.p. modern
        transcriptions   (G315)

GREGOR *Russ
    (Biebl) men cor ZIMMER. 598 s.p.
                                         (G316)
GREIFT ZUM BECHLER see Seeger, Peter

GREITTER, MATTHAEUS (ca. 1490-1550)
    Es Wollt Ein Jager Jagen
        (Weber, W.) men cor,acap TONOS 3309
        s.p.   (G317)

GREIZER HOCHZEITS-CARMINA see Rein,
    Walter

GRELL, EDUARD AUGUST (1800-1886)
    Ein Getreues Herze Wissen
        mix cor,S/A solo LIENAU sc s.p.,
        cor pts s.p.   (G318)

    Erhaben, O Herr
        (Koenig, F.) men cor,acap TONOS
        3004 s.p.   (G319)

    Urfinsternis "Hans Sachse Sang"
        men cor&TTBB,opt TTBB soli,acap sc
        SCHOTTS C 39 056 s.p., cor pts
        SCHOTTS C 39 057-58   (G320)
        (Noack, Friedrich) SSAATTBB (med)
        sc SCHOTTS C 39 059 s.p., voc pt
        SCHOTTS C 39 060A-D s.p.   (G321)

GREMLICH, WILLI
    Heiter Und Unbeschwert
        3pt mix cor,acap PELIKAN PE824 s.p.
                                         (G322)
GRENZEN DER MENSCHHEIT see Fortner,
    Wolfgang

GRESAK, JOZEF (1907-   )
    Madrigal
        men cor SLOV.HUD.FOND s.p.   (G323)

    Nove Slovensko
        see MUZSKE ZBORY III

    Vystahovalecka
        men cor&men cor SLOV.HUD.FOND s.p.
                                         (G324)

GRIEG, EDVARD HAGERUP (1843-1907)
    Christmas Song
        (Hansen) SATB oct SCHMITT 5909 $.40
                                         (G325)
    Forward
        (Wick, Fred) TTBB oct SCHMITT W193
        $.40   (G326)

    Good Morning
        (Wick, Fred) TTBB oct SCHMITT W188
        $.30   (G327)

    Land-Sighting
        TTBB,Bar solo (med) FITZSIMONS 4019
        $.30   (G328)

    Last Spring
        (Boyd) SSAATTBB,acap (med)
        FITZSIMONS 1054 $.25   (G329)

    When Summits Pierce The Blue
        (Sateren) SATB ART MAST 1028 $.30
                                         (G330)
GROOS, KARL
    Freiheit, Die Ich Meine
        men cor,acap TONOS 6342 s.p. (G331)
        mix cor (easy) sc SCHOTTS CHBL 361
        s.p.   (G332)

GROOTVADER'S KLOK
    mix cor s.p. sc HEER 478, cor pts
        HEER 478A   (G333)

GROSS, ROBERT
    Brief Introduction To The Problems Of
        Philosophy
        SATB,acap AM.COMP.AL. $6.60 (G334)

GROSSSTADT see Wehle, Gerhard
    Furchtegott

GROTE, HERMANN
    Ein Kleines Lied
        men cor,acap TONOS 246 s.p. (G335)

GROUCH, THE see Protheroe, Daniel

GROW, TRESSES see Kodaly, Zoltan

GRUBER
    Glade Jul *see Nyhus, Rolf

    Nyhus, Rolf *Xmas
        "Glade Jul" SSA/SAB MUSIKK   (G336)

GRUN IST DER MAI see Lechner, Leonhard

GRUNDMAN
    Zoo Illogical
        unis,opt pno,inst oct BOOSEY 5855
        $.45, ipa   (G337)

GRUNDUBUNGEN see Orff, Carl

GRUNE SAAT see Edler, Robert

GRUNET DIE HOFFNUNG see Lang, Hans

GRUNET, FELDER, GRUNET, WIESEN *Xmas
    (Bachl, Hans) treb cor DOBLINGER
    O 332 s.p.   (G338)

GRUNET FELDER, GRUNET WIESEN see Lang,
    Hans

GRUNET FELDER, GRUNET WIESEN see
    Nitsche, Paul

GRUSS AN'S OBER INNTAL see Fittig

GRUSS GOTT DICH, SCHONER MAIEN see
    Burkhart, Franz

GRUSS GOTT, DU SCHONER MAIE see Knab,
    Armin

GRUSS GOTT, DU SCHONER MAIEN see Lang,
    Hans

GUANTANAMERA *folk,So Am
    (Hess, Reimund) mix cor,fl,gtr,ob,
        pno, or accordion sc BREITKOPF-W
        Z18 s.p.   (G339)
    (Hess, Reimund) 4pt men cor,fl,gtr,
        bvl,pno, or accordion sc BREITKOPF-
        W Z 34 s.p.   (G340)

GUBBEN NOACH see Bellman, Carl Mikael

GUBEC'S PEASANT FIGHTERS see Dobronic,
    Antun

GUBITOSI, E. (1887-1972)
    Sonata In Bianco Minore
        4pt wom cor,2fl,ob,clar,bsn,horn,
        harp,pno,cembalo CARISH rental
                                         (G341)
GUERRERO, FRANCISCO (1528-1599)
    Villanesca
        [Span] TTB RICORDI-ENG BA10089 s.p.
                                         (G342)
GUESS WHAT'S BEHIND YOU
    SAB CIMINO $.50   (G343)

GULF COUNTRY, THE see Gordon, John

GURNEY
    Severn Meadows
        (Graves) SSA (easy) OXFORD 83.083
        $.25   (G344)

GUSLARS BALLADE "SASS DAS MADCHEN
    EINSAM" see Cossetto, Emil

GUT G'SELL, DU MACHST DEIN KLAGEN see
    Lange, Gregor

GUT IST'S, EIN WEIB ZU HABEN see
    Seeger, Peter

GUT NACHT, LADIES *folk,Eng
    (Rosenstengel, Albrecht) men cor,opt
    gtr,opt perc sc,cor pts TONOS 2106
    s.p.   (G345)

GUT NACHT, MEIN FEINES LIEB see
    Silcher, Friedrich

GUT SINGER UND EIN ORGANIST see
    Lechner, Leonhard

GUTE NACHT *folk,Aus
    (Schnurl, Karl) men cor,acap TONOS
    814 s.p.   (G346)

GUTE NACHT see Gauss, Otto

GUTE NACHT, KAMMERADEN see Wolters,
    Gottfried

GUTE NACHT, O WELT see Rein, Walter

GUTEN ABEND, EUCH ALLEIN see Wolters,
    Karl-Heinz

GUTEN ABEND, FRAU BAS see Biebl, Franz

GUTEN ABEND, LIEBE HIRTEN *Xmas
    (Bachl, Hans) treb cor DOBLINGER
    O 333 s.p.   (G347)

GUTEN MORGEN, AMERIKA "NUN STEHT ONKEL
    SAM NOCH AN DER SPITZE DER WELT"
    see Krenek, Ernst

GUTEN MORGEN, JUNGFER see Gerster,
    Ottmar

GUTEN MORGEN, SPIELMANN see Erdlen,
    Hermann

GUTEN TAG see Lucic, Franjo, Dober
    Danek Tomu Domu

GUTER RAT "BIST DU JUNGE FRAU GEWORDEN"
    see Lang, Hans

GUTESHA, M.
    Die Nacht War Voller Traume
        8pt mix cor,strings sc ZIMMER. 575
        s.p., ipa   (G348)

GUTHRIE, WOODY
    This Land Is Your Land
        (Lojeski, Ed) SATB&SSA,strings
        (includes 14 choral parts) cmplt
        ed LEONARD-US $14.95   (G349)
        (Lojeski, Ed) SATB&SSA,strings
        LEONARD-US $14.50   (G350)

GWELLTYN GLAS *folk,Welsh
    (Holst, Gustav) "Green Grass" [Eng/
    Welsh] SATB,acap CURWEN 61588 s.p.
    contains also: Cwyd Dy Galon,
    "Lively Pair, The"   (G351)

GWILT, DAVID (1932-   )
    Song Of Good Life, A *cant
        SATB,TB soli,2fl,2horn,2trp,pno voc
        sc NOVELLO rental   (G352)

GWINNER, VOLKER (1916-   )
    Die Beste Zeit Im Jahr Ist Mai'n
        mix cor (med) sc SCHOTTS CHBL 304
        s.p.   (G353)

    Freude Hebt Die Lichten Schwingen
        men cor sc SCHOTTS CHBL 165 s.p.
                                         (G354)

    Wir Sind Die Jungen
        4-5pt mix cor,acap (med) sc SCHOTTS
        C 39 686 s.p., voc pt SCHOTTS
        C 39 752A-B s.p.   (G355)

GYASZKAR see Erkel, Franz (Ferenc)

GYERMEK- ES NOIKAROK see Kodaly, Zoltan

GYMEL E CORALE see Benevenuti, Arrigo

GYRING, ELIZABETH
    Enoch
        SSA,org AM.COMP.AL. $3.85   (G356)

    Heresy For A Classroom
        SSA,acap AM.COMP.AL. $3.30   (G357)

    New York
        SATB,pno AM.COMP.AL. $1.38   (G358)

GYRING, ELIZABETH (cont'd.)

    Secret Of Liberty, The
        cor,4 soli,2fl,ob,2clar,horn,trp,
        trom,tuba,strings AM.COMP.AL. sc
        $13.75, voc pt $7.15   (G359)

GYRO see Castiglioni, Niccolo

H

HA HA! THE WORLD DOTH PASS see Weelkes

HA MAJD A BOSEG KOSARABOL see Juhasz,
    Frigyes

HAAG, HEINZ (1909-   )
    Der Gefallige Nachbar *cant
        jr cor,2-3rec (easy) sc SCHOTTS
        ED. 3913 s.p.   (H1)

HAAS, JOSEPH (1879-1960)
    Alemannischer Liederreigen *Op.89,
        No.1, CCU
        1-2pt jr cor/1-2pt wom cor,pno
        (easy) sc,cor pts SCHOTTS
        ED. 4296 s.p.   (H2)

    Aufheiterung "Was Kann Doch Auf
        Erden" *Op.98,No.3
        men cor sc SCHOTTS C 37 738 s.p.
        see from Chorfeier-Suite   (H3)

    Besinnung "Furchte Nur Dies" *Op.98,
        No.2
        men cor sc SCHOTTS C 37 737 s.p.
        see from Chorfeier-Suite   (H4)

    Butzemann "Es Tanzt Ein Butzemann"
        see Sechs Kanons Heft 2

    Chorfeier-Suite *see Aufheiterung
        "Was Kann Doch Auf Erden", Op.98,
        No.3; Besinnung "Furchte Nur
        Dies", Op.98,No.2; Drei Bitten,
        Op.98,No.1; Froher Ausklang
        "Freude Soll In Deinen Werken
        Sein", Op.98,No.4   (H5)

    Christ Und Die Lieder "Wir Bitten
        Dich" *Op.44
        3pt jr cor/3pt wom cor (easy) sc
        SCHOTTS C 35 149 s.p. see from
        Sechs Lieder   (H6)

    Das Himmlische Orchester "Ihr Morser,
        Erknallet"
        mix cor (easy) sc SCHOTTS CHBL 291
        s.p.   (H7)

    Das Jahr Im Lied *Op.103, ora
        mix cor,narrator,SATB soli,pno,fl,
        clar,horn,2trp,strings,perc,timp
        (med) voc sc,voc pt SCHOTTS
        ED. 4340 s.p., ipa, sc SCHOTTS
        rental   (H8)

    Der Butzemann "Es Tanzt Ein
        Butzemann"
        see Haas, Joseph, Heissa,
        Kathreinerle

    Der Gescheite Hansel "Hansel Am Bach"
        see Sechs Kanons Heft 2

    Der Kiebitz "Der Hergott Hangt Die
        Sonn' Heraus" *Op.44
        3pt jr cor/3pt wom cor (easy) sc
        SCHOTTS C 35 147 s.p. see from
        Sechs Lieder   (H9)

    Des Lebens Sonnenschein *Op.73,No.1
        (from Hymnen An Den Frohsinn)
        3pt jr cor/3pt wom cor,pno (med)
        sc,cor pts SCHOTTS ED. 2153 s.p.
                                         (H10)

    Die Heilige Elisabeth *Op.84, ora
        mix cor&men cor&jr cor,narrator,S
        solo,org,2fl,2ob,2clar,2bsn,
        4horn,2trp,3trom,strings,perc,
        2timp (med) sc SCHOTTS rental,
        ipr, voc sc SCHOTTS ED. 3260 s.p.
                                         (H11)

    Drei Bitten *Op.98,No.1
        men cor,Bar solo sc SCHOTTS
        C 37 436 s.p. see from Chorfeier-
        Suite   (H12)

    Echolieder-Suite *see Morgengloria
        "Dunkel, Uber Der Erde Noch",
        Op.110,No.4; Nur "Ein Ton Ist's,
        Nur Ein Ton", Op.110,No.2;
        Wachtelschlag "Am Kirchturm Steht
        Der Abendstern", Op.110,No.3;
        Zueignung "Im Widerhall Wird Hier
        Zum Dort", Op.110,No.1   (H13)

    Es Bluhen Die Maien
        wom cor (easy) sc SCHOTTS CHBL 591
        s.p.   (H14)

    Es Ist So Still Geworden
        mix cor (easy) sc SCHOTTS CHBL 327
        s.p.   (H15)

    Es Werde Licht! *Op.82
        6pt wom cor/6pt men cor (med) sc
        SCHOTTS C 32 818 s.p., voc pt
        SCHOTTS C 32 818-01-06   (H16)

HAAS, JOSEPH (cont'd.)

Frankischer Liederreigen *Op.89,
  No.2, CCU
  1-2pt jr cor/1-2pt wom cor,pno
  (easy) sc,cor pts SCHOTTS
  ED. 4297 s.p.   (H17)

Freund Husch "Husch, Ich Schlupfe Aus
  Dem Busch" *Op.44
  3pt jr cor/3pt wom cor (easy) sc
  SCHOTTS C 35 150 s.p. see from
  Sechs Lieder   (H18)

Frisch Auf, Ihr Musikanten (from Das
  Jahr Im Lied)
  4pt mix cor,4 soli,acap (med easy)
  sc SCHOTTS CHBL 302 s.p.   (H19)

Froher Ausklang "Freude Soll In
  Deinen Werken Sein" *Op.98,No.4
  men cor,Bar solo sc SCHOTTS
  C 37 739 s.p. see from Chorfeier-
  Suite   (H20)

Heissa, Kathreinerle
  jr cor (easy) sc SCHOTTS
  CHBL 530A-B s.p. contains also:
  Der Butzemann "Es Tanzt Ein
  Butzemann"   (H21)

Hinter Der Donaubrucke
  see Sechs Kanons Heft 2

Ich Bin Schon Siebenhundert Jahr
  jr cor/wom cor (med easy) sc
  SCHOTTS CHBL 553 s.p.   (H22)

Jetzt Woll'mer
  see Sechs Kanons Heft 1

Kleiner Morgenwanderer "Frisch Auf!"
  *Op.44
  3pt jr cor/3pt wom cor (easy) sc
  SCHOTTS C 35 148 s.p. see from
  Sechs Lieder   (H23)

Kommt, Lasst Uns Allesamt *Op.73,
  No.2 (from Hymnen An Den
  Frohsinn)
  3pt jr cor/3pt wom cor,pno (med)
  sc,cor pts SCHOTTS ED. 2154 s.p.
                                       (H24)

Madel Kamm Dich, Putz Dich *folk
  jr cor/wom cor (med easy) sc
  SCHOTTS CHBL 501 s.p.   (H25)

Mailied "Dudeldumdei!" *Op.44
  3pt jr cor/3pt wom cor (easy) sc
  SCHOTTS C 35 145 s.p. see from
  Sechs Lieder   (H26)

Morgengloria "Dunkel, Uber Der Erde
  Noch" *Op.110,No.4
  men cor sc SCHOTTS C 40 056 s.p.
  see from Echolieder-Suite   (H27)

Nachtwandler "Trommler, Lass Dein
  Kalbfell Klingen" *Op.102
  4pt men cor,T solo,pno/fl&clar&
  horn&perc&timp&3vln&vla&bvl
  sc,voc pt SCHOTTS ED. 4295 s.p.,
  ipa   (H28)

Naschmaulchen "Der Fritz, Der Kleine
  Butzel"
  see Sechs Kanons Heft 1

Nur "Ein Ton Ist's, Nur Ein Ton"
  *Op.110,No.2
  men cor sc SCHOTTS C 40 054 s.p.
  see from Echolieder-Suite   (H29)

Sechs Kanons Heft 1 *canon
  jr cor (easy) sc SCHOTTS C 35 143
  s.p.
  contains: Jetzt Woll'mer;
    Naschmaulchen "Der Fritz, Der
    Kleine Butzel"; Teuerung "Und
    Die Eier Und's Feuer"   (H30)

Sechs Kanons Heft 2 *canon
  jr cor (easy) sc SCHOTTS C 35 144
  s.p.
  contains: Butzemann "Es Tanzt Ein
    Butzemann"; Der Gescheite
    Hansel "Hansel Am Bach"; Hinter
    Der Donaubrucke   (H31)

Sechs Lieder *see Christ Und Die
  Lieder "Wir Bitten Dich", Op.44;
  Der Kiebitz "Der Hergott Hangt
  Die Sonn' Heraus", Op.44; Freund
  Husch "Husch, Ich Schlupfe Aus
  Dem Busch", Op.44; Kleiner
  Morgenwanderer "Frisch Auf!",
  Op.44; Mailied "Dudeldumdei!",
  Op.44; Weigenlied "Vor Der Ture",
  Op.44   (H32)

Steh Auf, Nordwind! *Op.66,No.1
  TTBB sc SCHOTTS C 35 154 s.p., voc
  pt SCHOTTS C 35 155, 01-04 s.p.
                                       (H33)

HAAS, JOSEPH (cont'd.)

Still, O Himmel
  4pt wom cor (med) sc SCHOTTS
  CHBL 590 s.p.   (H34)

Teuerung "Und Die Eier Und's Feuer"
  see Sechs Kanons Heft 1

Wachtelschlag "Am Kirchturm Steht Der
  Abendstern" *Op.110,No.3
  men cor sc SCHOTTS C 40 055 s.p.
  see from Echolieder-Suite   (H35)
  men cor voc pt SCHOTTS
  C 40 103, 01-02 s.p. see from
  Echolieder-Suite   (H36)

Weigenlied "Vor Der Ture" *Op.44
  3pt jr cor/3pt wom cor (easy) sc
  SCHOTTS C 35 146 s.p. see from
  Sechs Lieder   (H37)

Wiegenlied "Sumsala, Sumsala"
  *cradle
  4pt mix cor&3pt men cor&unis jr cor
  (med) sc SCHOTTS C 38 985 s.p.,
  cor pts SCHOTTS C 38 986-987-988
  s.p.   (H38)

Zueignung "Im Widerhall Wird Hier Zum
  Dort" *Op.110,No.1
  men cor voc pt SCHOTTS
  C 40 102, 01-02 s.p. see from
  Echolieder-Suite   (H39)
  men cor sc SCHOTTS C 40 053 s.p.
  see from Echolieder-Suite   (H40)

Zum Lob Der Arbeit *Op.81,No.4, cant
  1-3pt jr cor,org&strings/pno (med
  easy) sc,cor pts SCHOTTS ED. 2857
  s.p., ipa   (H41)

Zum Lob Der Musik *Op.81, cant
  mix cor&1-3pt jr cor,pno/org/
  strings/brass (easy) voc sc,voc
  pt SCHOTTS ED. 2151 s.p., ipa   (H42)

Zum Lob Der Natur *Op.81,No.2, cant
  1-3pt jr cor,org&strings/pno (med
  easy) sc,cor pts SCHOTTS ED. 2152
  s.p., ipa   (H43)

HAB' EIN GOLDNES RINGELEIN see Bartok,
  Bela, Van Egy Gyurum, Karika

HAB MEIN WAGE VOLLGELADE see Lang, Hans

HAB MEINE LIEBE WOHL VERBORGEN see
  Motte, Diether de la

HAB SONNE IM HERZEN see Gauss, Otto

HABA, ALOIS (1893-   )
  Constitution, The *see Ustava 9.
  Kvetna

  Den Ode Dne Se Siri
    "Spreading Day By Day" [Czech] men
    cor,acap CZECH s.p.   (H44)

  For Peace *see Za Mir

  From The Proverbs Of The Slavonic
    Nations *see Z Mudroslovi Narodu
    Slovanskych

  Kosa A Rosa *Op.65b
    "Sythe And The Dew, The" [Czech]
    men cor,acap CZECH s.p.   (H45)

  Meditace *Op.66, CCU
    [Czech] men cor,acap CZECH s.p.
                                       (H46)
  Mir
    "Peace" [Czech] men cor,acap CZECH
    s.p.   (H47)

  Mnichov *Op.65c
    "Munich" [Czech] men cor,acap CZECH
    s.p.   (H48)

  Munich *see Mnichov

  Peace *see Mir

  Spreading Day By Day *see Den Ode
    Dne Se Siri

  Sythe And The Dew, The *see Kosa A
    Rosa

  Ustava 9. Kvetna *Op.77
    "Constitution, The" [Czech] men
    cor,acap CZECH s.p.   (H49)

  Z Mudroslovi Narodu Slovanskych
    "From The Proverbs Of The Slavonic
    Nations" [Czech] jr cor/wom cor,
    pno CZECH s.p.   (H50)

  Za Mir *Op.68, cant
    "For Peace" [Czech] mix cor,3fl,
    3ob,3clar,3bsn,4horn,3trp,3trom,
    tuba,timp,perc,2harp,strings
    CZECH s.p.   (H51)

HABA, KAREL (1898-1972)
  Budovatelum Ostravska *Op.34, cant
    "To The Builders Of Ostrava"
    [Czech] mix cor,3fl,3ob,3clar,
    3bsn,4horn,3trp,3trom,timp,perc,
    harp,strings CZECH s.p.   (H52)

  To The Builders Of Ostrava *see
    Budovatelum Ostravska

HABICHT UND KROTE see Schmid, A.

HABT IHR SCHON GEHORT DIE KUNDE see
  Bartok, Bela

HACKADY, HAL
  Shake Me I Rattle (composed with
    Naylor, Charles)
    (Newman , Richard) 2pt,pno oct
    REGENT R-503 $.30   (H53)

HADLEY
  My Beloved Spake
    SATB SCHIRM.G C11983 $.40   (H54)

HAENNI, G.
  Les Vendangeuses
    wom cor,acap HENN 696 s.p.   (H55)

HAGEMANN, P.
  Eve And Morn Of Christmas, The
    SATB,acap/inst MCAFEE M1083 $.50   (H56)

  How Revolting!
    SAB,fl/pic,drums,pno MCAFEE M7004
    $.45   (H57)

HAGG, TORSTEN
  Det Ar Vackrast Nar Det Skymmer
    men cor GEHRMANS KVB358   (H58)

  Det Vackraste Landet
    men cor GEHRMANS KVB357   (H59)

HAHN
  Gardez Le Trait De La Fenetre
    (Boyd) SATB SCHIRM.G 51724 $.35
                                       (H60)

  La Jour
    (Boyd) SATB SCHIRM.G LG51723 $.40 (H61)

  La Nuit
    (Boyd) SATB SCHIRM.G LG51725 $.35
                                       (H62)

HAIL, ALL HAIL TO THE QUEEN see
  Berlioz, Hector

HAIL! BRIGHT ABODE see Wagner, Richard

HAIL COLUMBIA
  see Freedom Song, 1776

HAIL, COMING AGE! see Franco, Johan

HAIL THE DAWNING DAY see Franco, Johan

HAIL THE GREAT LAND see Avshalomov,
  Jacob

HAIRSTON, JESTER (1901-   )
  Rise Up Shepherd And Foller
    SATB BOURNE B224170-357 $.40   (H63)

HAJDU, MIHALY
  Budapest
    (Dutka, Akos) mix cor BUDAPEST 7512
    s.p.   (H64)

HAJEK, MAXMILIAN (1909-1969)
  Oh Land Of Bohemia *see Ty Zeme
    Ceska

  Ty Zeme Ceska *Op.63
    "Oh Land Of Bohemia" [Czech] mix
    cor,3fl,3ob,3clar,3bsn,4horn,
    3trp,3trom,tuba,timp,perc,harp,
    strings, vibraphone CZECH s.p.
                                       (H65)

HAKEL-PAKEL see Orrel, Max

HALE
  A-Flat Cricket And A B-Flat Frog, An
    *see Clarkson

  Nobody Else Like You *see Gehrecke

HALF A FORTNIGHT see Kelly, Bryan

HALF AN ALPHABET see Thompson

HALL, WILLIAM D.
  Among The Multitude
    see Leaves Of Grass

  Here The Frailest Leaves Of Me
    see Leaves Of Grass

  Leaves Of Grass
    NATIONAL WHC-51 $.45
    contains: Among The Multitude
      (SATB,Bar solo,acap); Here The
      Frailest Leaves Of Me (SATB,A
      solo,acap); Sometimes With One
      I Love (SATB,T solo,acap) (H66)

HALL, WILLIAM D. (cont'd.)

Sometimes With One I Love
see Leaves Of Grass

When I Am Dead, My Dearest
SSATTB,S/T solo,acap NATIONAL WHC-7
$.35   (H67)

HALLO! WELCH SCHONES ECHO! see Lasso,
Orlando di

HALLODRIO see Orrel, Max

HALSTEAD STREET CAR see Raphling, Sam

HALUNKENLIED "MEIN GAUL IST ALT UND
WILL NICHT MEHR" see Fussan, Werner

HAMBLEN
It Is No Secret *pop
SSA BELWIN UC 719 $.40   (H68)
SATB BELWIN UC 720 $.40   (H69)
(Kerr) cor BELWIN UC 736 $.40   (H70)

HAME, DEARIE, HAME *folk,Scot
(Bartholomew, M.) SSATB GALAXY
1.0513.1 $.25   (H71)

HAMMARSKJOLD
Triad *see Edlund, Lars

HAMMOND
Little Arrows *pop
(Hazelwood) SAB BELWIN UC 732 $.40
(H72)

HAMMOND, ALBERT
It Never Rains In Southern California
*see Hazelwood, Mike

HAMMOND, HAROLD
Sunrise
SATB (med) FITZSIMONS 1042 $.30   (H73)

HAND IN HAND
unis wom cor SCHOTTS C 42 532G s.p.
see also Alle Singen Heft 1   (H74)

HANDEL, GEORGE FRIDERIC (1685-1759)
Alexander's Feast (Neue Mozart-
Ausgabe) *cant
(Mozart, Wolfgang Amadeus) SATB,SAB
soli,orch (med diff) cmplt ed
BAREN. BA4527 rental, cloth
BAREN. s.p.   (H75)

Break Fairest Dawn
(Orchs, S.) SATB EMI   (H76)

Brotherhood Of Man, The
(Wiley) 2pt PRO ART 2821 $.35 (H77)

Choice Of Hercules, The
(Stone) SATB,4 soli,2fl,2ob,2horn,
2trp,timp,strings voc sc NOVELLO
rental   (H78)

Georg Friedrich Handel's Works *sac/
sec,CCU
microfiche UNIV.MUS.ED. edition of
the Deutschen
Haendelgesellschaft. Edited By:
Friedrich Chrysander, 1858-1894.
96 volumes and 6 supplements.
$375.00   (H79)

Music From "Semele"
(Blower) SSA,opt T solo,strings voc
sc NOVELLO rental   (H80)

O Happy Indeed
(Brahms, Johannes) [Eng/It] SA,pno
NATIONAL WHC-41 $.40   (H81)

HANDL, JACOB
Dulcis Amica *madrigal
(Crabtree, Phillip D.) [Lat] SATB,
acap (med easy) DEAN CA-103 $.45
(H82)

En Ego Campana *madrigal
(Crabtree, Phillip D.) [Lat] SATB,
acap (med easy) DEAN CA-102 $.50
(H83)

The Moralia (Of 1596): Part I *CCU
(Skei, Allen B.) bds A-R ED $9.95
(H84)

The Moralia (Of 1596): Part II *CCU
(Skei, Allen B.) bds A-R ED $9.95
(H85)

HANDS OF TIME, THE
TTBB SCREEN 0011HC4   (H86)

HANDWERKSBURCHENPENNE see Krietsch,
Georg

HANDWERKSBURSCHEN-ABSCHIED "ES, ES, ES
UND ES" see Lang, Hans

HANDWERKSBURSCHEN ABSCHIED "ES, ES, ES
UND ES" see Rein, Walter

HANDWERKSBURSCHEN-WANDERLIED "AUF DU
JUNGER WANDERSMANN" see Lang, Hans

HANG IN THERE, BUT HANG LOOSE see
Burroughs

HANNAY, ROGER
Leaf, A
mix cor MEDIA 6120   (H87)

HANNELE UND STEFFELE *folk,Boh
(Rosenstengel, Albrecht) men cor,opt
pno,opt gtr,opt perc sc,cor pts
TONOS 2113 s.p.   (H88)

HANNIBAL MO-(ZOUREE)! see Sherman,
Richard M.

HANOUSEK, VLADIMIR (1907-   )
Heroic Oratorio *see Heroicke
Oratorium

Heroicke Oratorium *ora
"Heroic Oratorio" [Czech] mix cor&
speak cor,5 narrators&SATB soli,
3fl,3ob,3clar,3bsn,4horn,4trp,
3trom,tuba,timp,perc,harp,pno,
strings, celeste CZECH s.p. (H89)

HANS BEUTLER DER WOLLT REITEN AUS see
Senfl, Ludwig

HANSEL UND GRETEL see Biebl, Franz

HANSEN, WERNER (1913-   )
Blondes Madel, Roter Wein *Czech
men cor sc SCHOTTS CHBL 118 s.p.
(H90)

Heidschi Bumbeidschi "Aber Heidschi
Bumbeidschi, Schlaf Lange"
3pt jr cor/3pt wom cor,pno,opt inst
(easy) sc SCHOTTS CHBL 569 s.p.
(H91)

Kehr Ich Abends Heim *Czech
men cor sc SCHOTTS CHBL 117 s.p.
(H92)

HANUS, JAN (1915-   )
Country Speaks, The *see Zeme Mluvi

Domovo *Op.47, CC3U
[Czech] mix cor,acap CZECH s.p.
(H93)

Maminka
"Mummy" [Czech] girl cor,acap CZECH
s.p.   (H94)

Mummy *see Maminka

Once Upon A Time *see Povidam,
Povidam Pohadku

Povidam, Povidam Pohadku
"Once Upon A Time" [Czech] jr cor,A
solo,fl,ob,clar,bsn,perc,pno,
strings CZECH s.p.   (H95)

Zeme Mluvi *cant
"Country Speaks, The" [Czech] mix
cor&wom cor&men cor,S solo,3fl,
3ob,2clar,2bsn,4horn,3trp,3trom,
tuba,timp,perc,strings CZECH s.p.
(H96)

HAPPINESS IS YOU AND ME see O'Sullivan,
Gilbert

HAPPY BIRTHDAY DEAR CHRIST CHILD
SATB CIMINO $.40   (H97)

HAPPY CHRISTMAS, LITTLE FRIEND see
Rodgers, Richard

HAPPY FARMER,THE *folk
(Seeger, P.) [Eng/Ger] 4pt mix cor
MERSEBURG EM9256 s.p.   (H98)
(Seeger, P.) "Der Gluckliche Farmer"
[Eng/Ger] 4pt men cor MERSEBURG
EM9085 s.p.   (H99)

HAPPY JOURNEY, THE see Czajowski,
Michael

HAPPY LITTLE CHRISTMAS PEOPLE see
Tiffault

HAPPY TALK see Rodgers, Richard

HAPPY TO KNOW YOU see Green

HAR AR DEN SKONA SOMMER see Taube,
Evert

HARAPAT, JINDRICH (1895-   )
Cest Pracujicim
"Honours To The Working Class"
[Czech] men cor,acap CZECH s.p.
(H100)
Honours To The Working Class *see
Cest Pracujicim

HARBISON, JOHN (1938-   )
Five Songs Of Experience *CC5U
SATB,SATB soli,4strings sc
AM.COMP.AL. $13.20, ipa   (H101)

Five Songs Of Experience *CC5U
4pt mix cor,4 soli,4strings,perc
AMP A-710 $3.00   (H102)

HARBISON, JOHN (cont'd.)

Music When Soft Voices Die
SATB AMP A-707 $.40   (H103)

HARBURG
April In Paris (composed with Duke)
(Barduhn, Dave) SATB,pno,inst
(jazz, includes recording and 14
choral octavos) LEONARD-US
07250100 $14.95   (H104)

HARCJATEK see Kompanyejec

HARD WAY EVERY TIME, THE see Croce, Jim

HARDI LES GARS!
(Blanchard, R.) 3pt men cor,acap
JOBERT s.p.   (H105)

HARDT, RICHARD
Blessing, A
SATB GENERAL 758CH $.45   (H106)
SSA GENERAL 757CH $.45   (H107)

Mouse And The Lion, The
SSA GENERAL 755CH $.45   (H108)
SATB GENERAL 756CH $.45   (H109)

HARELSON, HARRY B.
April Song
SSA (med) FITZSIMONS 3042 $.20
(H110)

HARK, HARK, THE LARK see Swayne

HARK, THE BIRDS MELODIOUS SING see
Linley, Jr, Thomas

HARLEM IS MY HOME see Cunningham,
Arthur

HARMONIE FUHRT UNS ZUSAMMEN see
Dieffenbacher, Eugen

HARMONY see Kaplan

HARMONY see Simon

HAROM GOMORI NEPDAL see Kodaly, Zoltan

HAROM KINAI DAL see Szervanszky, Endre

HAROM KORUSDAL see Debussy, Claude

HAROM VEGYESKAR see Balazs, Arpad

HARP THAT ONCE THRO' TARA'S HALLS, THE
see Dunhill, Thomas Frederick

HARRIES
Little Cantata *cant
SA (easy) OXFORD 56.123 $1.80
(H111)

HARRIS
All In The April Evening *Easter
SATB PRO ART 2833 $.35   (H112)

Choral Diptych
SATB,acap PRO ART 2812 $.35 (H113)

O Food Of Men Wayfaring *Commun/Gen
SATB PRO ART 2813 $.35   (H114)

HARRIS, CUTHBERT
Choral Fantasia On National Airs
mix cor BANKS MUS YS 983 $1.10
(H115)

HARRIS, EDWARD
Freedom Tree, The
2pt LEONARD-US 08574000 $.50 (H116)

HARRIS, JERRY WESELEY (1933-   )
Choral Nocturne, A
HERITAGE H6013 $.35   (H117)

HARRISON, A.F.
In The Gloaming
SA CRAMER $.25   (H118)

HARROWING OF HELL see Milner, Anthony

HART, BOBBY
Keep On Singing (composed with
Janssen, Danny)
(Simon, W.) SATB BIG3 $.50   (H119)
(Simon, W.) SAB BIG3 $.50   (H120)
(Simon, W.) SSA BIG3 $.50   (H121)

HARTL, RUDOLF (1927-   )
Dreissig Kanons Nach
Glockeninschriften *CC30L,canon
jr cor/wom cor/3 eq voices (easy)
min sc SCHOTTS B 169 s.p.   (H122)

HARTMANN, KARL AMADEUS (1905-1963)
Friede Anno 48
mix cor,S solo,pno (diff) sc,cor
pts SCHOTTS ED. 6006 s.p.   (H123)

HARTMANN, ROBERT
Oh, I Love You
SAB LEONARD-US 08575700 $.50 (H124)

HARTY, SIR HAMILTON (1879-1941)
Mystic Trumpeter, The
SATB,Bar solo,3fl,pic,3ob,2clar,
2bsn,4horn,3trp,3trom,tuba,timp,
perc,harp,opt org,strings voc sc
NOVELLO rental   (H125)

HARVEST FESTIVITIES see Kuksa, Emanuel,
Dozinky

HARVEST MARCH, THE see Stanislav,
Josef, Pochod Urody

HARVEST-TIME SONG see Brandon

HARVEY, ALEX
Delta Dawn (composed with Collins,
Larry)
(Metis, F.) SSA BIG3 $.50   (H126)
(Metis, F.) SATB BIG3 $.50   (H127)
(Metis, F.) SAB BIG3 $.50   (H128)

Someone Who Cares
(Foust, Alan) SATB STUDIO V713 $.35
(H129)

HARVEY, JONATHAN (1939-   )
Cantata 1
SATB,SBar soli,org,strings voc sc
NOVELLO rental   (H130)

Cantata 4 *see Ludus Amoris

Cantata 7 *see On Vision

Love
[Eng] SSATB,acap (med) sc SCHOTTS
ED. 10 946 s.p.   (H131)

Ludus Amoris (Cantata 4)
SATB,ST soli,2fl,2ob,2clar,2bsn,
4horn,3trp,3trom,tuba,timp,perc,
pno,strings, glockenspiel,
vibraphone voc sc NOVELLO rental
(H132)

On Vision (Cantata 7)
SATB,ST soli,3fl,2pic,3ob,3clar,
3bsn,4horn,3trp,3trom,tuba,perc,
harp,pno,strings,electronic tape,
English horn, bass clarinet,
contrabassoon, vibraphone,
glockenspiel voc sc NOVELLO
rental   (H133)

HARWOOD, BASIL (1859-1949)
Song On May Morning
SATB,soli,2fl,pic,2ob,2clar,2bsn,
4horn,2trp,3trom,tuba,timp,perc,
strings voc sc NOVELLO rental
(H134)

HAS SORROW THY YOUNG DAYS SHADED? see
Parke, Dorothy

HASKINS, WILLIAM
My Heart's In The Highlands
SATB,acap AM.COMP.AL. $3.30 (H135)

HASSLER, HANS LEO (1564-1612)
Ach Lieb, Hier Ist Das Herze
mix cor (med easy) sc SCHOTTS
C 38 070A s.p. contains also:
Rosthius, Nicolaus, Frau
Nachtigall, Mach Dich Bereit
(H136)

SSAA (med easy) sc SCHOTTS
C 38 070-01 s.p. contains also:
Rosthius, Nicolaus, Frau
Nachtigall, Mach Dich Bereit
(H137)

Come, All Musicians, Come
(Harris) SSATBB SCHIRM.G 12032 $.40
(H138)

Dancing And Springing *see Tanzen
Und Springen

Dear Love, Of Thee Alone
(Kirk) SSATB KJOS 5918 $.35   (H139)

Fahr Hin, Guts Liedelein
SSATTB MOSELER LB492 s.p.   (H140)

Feinslieb, Du Hast Mich Gfangen
see Gastoldi, Giovanni Giacomo, An
Hellen Tagen
mix cor (easy) sc SCHOTTS CHBL 366
s.p.   (H141)
(Weber, W.) men cor,acap TONOS 3311
s.p.   (H142)

I Part From You With Sorrow *see Ich
Scheid Von Dir Mit Leide

Ich Scheid Von Dir Mit Leide
(Field, Robert) "I Part From You
With Sorrow" [Eng/Ger] SSATBB,
acap (med) oct PRESSER 312-41032
$.40   (H143)

Ihr Musici, Frisch Auf!
SSATTB MOSELER LB610 s.p.   (H144)

Im Kuhlen Maien Tun Sich All Ding
Erfreuen
SATB&SATB (med easy) sc SCHOTTS
C 43 536 s.p.   (H145)

HASSLER, HANS LEO (cont'd.)
Jungfrau, Dein Schon Gestalt
(Weber, W.) men cor,acap TONOS 3310
s.p.   (H146)

Mein Gmut Ist Mir
(Weber, W.) men cor,acap TONOS 3320
s.p.   (H147)

Nun Fanget An!
mix cor (med) sc SCHOTTS CHBL 288
s.p.   (H148)

Oh, The Good Life Gives Me Pleasure
(Field, Robert) SSATB,acap (med
easy) oct PRESSER 312-41031 $.35
(H149)

Tanzen Und Springen
see Gastoldi, Giovanni Giacomo, An
Hellen Tagen
SSATB (easy) sc SCHOTTS CHBL 368
s.p.   (H150)
(Harris) "Dancing And Springing"
2pt treb cor&Bar PRO ART 2779
$.35   (H151)

HAST DU MICH UBERWUNDEN see Zoll, Paul

HAT DICH DIE LIEBE see Schlemm, Gustav
Adolf

HAT KORISMU see Rauch, Andreas

HAT MEIN LIEB EIN SCHLEHLEIN see Poos,
Heinrich

HAT ZWEI FENSTER MEINE SEELE see Zoll,
Paul

HATCH, TONY
Call Me *pop
SAB BELWIN UC 733 $.40   (H152)

Downtown *pop
SAB BELWIN UC 734 $.40   (H153)

HATCHER, EDGER
That's What Lovin' You Is All About
*see Evans, Paul

HATRIK, JURAJ (1941-   )
Canto Responsoriale
dbl cor,timp SLOV.HUD.FOND s.p.
(H154)

HATT' ES GOTT GEGEBEN see Bartok, Bela,
Ne Tallalak Volna

HATTE KONIG HEINRICH see Si Le Roy
M'avait Donne

HATTEN MICH SCHON AUFGEGEBEN see
Mendelssohn, Arnold

HAUFRECHT, [HERBERT] (1909-   )
A-Walkin' And A-Talkin' *folk
SATB,acap AM.COMP.AL. $1.10   (H155)

Life
SATB,pno AM.COMP.AL. $1.10   (H156)

Riding To Town
SATB,Bar solo,acap AM.COMP.AL.
$5.50   (H157)

Strange Lullaby
SATB/SSAATTB,pno AM.COMP.AL. $3.58
(H158)

Viva! *round
3pt,acap AM.COMP.AL. $.28   (H159)

We Build A Land
cor,soli&narrator,pno AM.COMP.AL.
$8.25   (H160)

HAUG, [HANS] (1900-   )
Gastronomische Kantate *cant
mix cor,narrator&SATB soli,2fl/fl&
pic,2ob,2clar,2bsn,2trp,2horn,
2trom,timp,harp,perc,hpsd,
strings, English horn and bass
clarinet alternate with second
oboe and clarinet; celeste MODERN
rental   (H161)

HAUG, LUKAS
Morgenlied An Die Sonne
men cor,acap TONOS 4505 s.p. (H162)

HAUS, KARL (1928-   )
Bajuschki Baju *cradle,Russ
jr cor (easy) sc SCHOTTS CHBL 602
s.p.   (H163)

Bajuschki Baju "Schlafe, Kindlein, Tu
Dich Legen" *cradle,Russ
mix cor (easy) sc SCHOTTS CHBL 414
s.p.   (H164)

Der Musikalische Drache "Ihr Leute,
Hort"
see Vier Kuriose Geschichten

Die Traurige Ballade Vom Reisen
Schluck Und Friss "Hort Die
Traurige Geschichte"

HAUS, KARL (cont'd.)
see Vier Kuriose Geschichten

Frau Lilly Milly Putty
see Vier Kuriose Geschichten

Hochzeitslied
men cor,acap TONOS 3964 s.p. (H165)

Jahrein-Jahraus *CC4U
1-2pt jr cor/3-4pt mix cor,opt inst
cmplt ed PELIKAN PE936 s.p.
available separately   (H166)

Nachtliches Standchen
men cor,acap TONOS 3958 s.p. (H167)

Vier Kuriose Geschichten
men cor&opt jr cor/wom cor,perc sc,
cor pts SCHOTTS B 168 s.p., ipa
contains: Der Musikalische Drache
"Ihr Leute, Hort"; Die Traurige
Ballade Vom Reisen Schluck Und
Friss "Hort Die Traurige
Geschichte"; Frau Lilly Milly
Putty; Wann Zwitschern Die
Elefanten   (H168)

Wann Zwitschern Die Elefanten
see Vier Kuriose Geschichten

Wer Frohlich Sein Will
men cor/mix cor sc SCHOTTS C 43 309
s.p.   (H169)

Zigeunertanz "Burschen, Madchen
Schnell Herbei" *folk
[Ger] men cor,opt winds/vln,gtr sc
SCHOTTS CHBL 221 s.p.   (H170)

HAUS-SEGEN "NUN IST EIN HAUS NEU
AUFGERICHTET" see Genzmer, Harald

HAUS-SPRUCH "WASSER RAUSCHT VORBEI AM
HAUS" see Rein, Walter

HAUSRECHT see Edler, Robert

HAUSSMANN, VALENTIN
Annelein Fein *madrigal
SSAA/SSAT (med easy) sc SCHOTTS
C 38 070B s.p.   (H171)

Mit Seufzen Und Mit Klag
(Malin, Don) "With Sighing And
Lament" TTBB,acap BELWIN 2331
$.35   (H172)

With Sighing And Lament *see Mit
Seufzen Und Mit Klag

HAUSSPRUCH see Pepping, Ernst

HAUSSPRUCH "DAS IST DAS BESTE AUF DER
WELT" see Mohler, Philipp

HAVE A NICE DAY see Avalos

HAVE A PARTY see Milidantri

HAVE YOU NEVER BEEN MELLOW see Farrar

HAVE YOU SEEN BUT A WHITE LILY GROW?
see Southam

HAVELE, HAVELE, HAHNE see Bresgen,
Cesar

HAVELKA, SVATOPLUK (1925-   )
Chvala Svetla *cant
"In Praise Of Light" [Czech/Eng/
Ger] mix cor,soli,3fl,3ob,6clar,
3bsn,4horn,4trp,3trom,tuba,timp,
perc,harp,pno,strings, saxophone,
celeste PANTON s.p.   (H173)

In Praise Of Light *see Chvala
Svetla

HAVEN'T GOT TIME FOR THE PAIN see Simon

HAVIRI see Strniste, Jiri

HAVORD DE LA MONTAGNE, JOACHIM
Aubepin. . . . Aubepine
[Fr] SATB,acap CHAPPELL-FR s.p.
(H174)

Le P'Tit Homme
[Fr] SATB,acap CHAPPELL-FR s.p.
(H175)

HAWAIIAN ANTHEM, A see Graham

HAWAIIAN BIRD-CATCHING SONG see Barati,
George

HAWAIIAN WEDDING SONG see Hoffman

HAWTHORNE
Listen To The Mocking Bird
(Smith) SATB SCHIRM.G 12013 $.40
(H176)

HAWTHORNE, GRACE
America The Beautiful *see Pottle,
Sam

David And Goliath *see Pottle, Sam

If We Don't Make It Work, Who Will?
*see Red, Buryl

Jonah And The Whale *see Pottle, Sam

Noah And The Ark *see Pottle, Sam

Revolutionary Ideas *see Red, Buryl

Samson And Delilah *see Pottle, Sam

Sea Of Liberty *see Red, Buryl

Summer Soldier *see Red, Buryl

HAYDN, (FRANZ) JOSEPH (1732-1809)
Der Beredsamkeit "Freunde, Wasser
Machet Stumm"
mix cor (med) sc SCHOTTS C 37 674
s.p. (H177)

Der Greis "Hin Ist Alle Meine Kraft"
mix cor (med) sc SCHOTTS CHBL 271
s.p. (H178)
SATB,pno EGTVED KB80 s.p. (H179)

Die Beredsamkeit "Freunde, Wasser
Machet Stumm"
(Bohm, F.) TTBB sc SCHOTTS C 39 401
s.p., voc pt SCHOTTS
C 39 402, 01-04 s.p. (H180)

Die Harmonie In Der Ehe "O Wunderbare
Harmonie"
mix cor (med) sc SCHOTTS C 38 152
s.p. (H181)

Dr. Harington's Compliment
[Eng/Ger] SSTB,S solo,pno BROUDE
BR. $.40 (H182)

Nachtigallenkanon "Alles Schweiget"
mix cor (easy) sc SCHOTTS
CHBL 298A-B s.p. contains also:
Lang, Hans, Kein Schoner Land
(H183)

Seasons, The
(Shaw) SATB SCHIRM.G LG51747 $2.25
(H184)

Three Canons *CC3U,canon
(Bird; Van Camp) TTBB SCHIRM.G
LG51812 $.35 (H185)

HAYES, ISAAC
John Shaft (composed with Krutcher,
Betty) *pop
(Averre, Richard) SATB,pno,bvl,gtr,
drums,tamb oct BIG BELL $.40
(H186)

HAYS
Put The Right Man At The Wheel
(Smith) SATB SCHIRM.G 12015 $.40
(H187)

HAZELWOOD
I'm A Train *pop
(Hamilton) SATB BELWIN UC 712 $.40
(H188)
(Hamilton) SA BELWIN UC 713 $.40
(H189)

HAZELWOOD, MIKE
It Never Rains In Southern California
(composed with Hammond, Albert)
(Metis, F.) SAB BIG3 $.40 ('H190)
(Metis, F.) SATB BIG3 $.50 (H191)
(Metis, F.) SSA BIG3 $.40 (H192)

HAZY SHADE OF WINTER *pop
SATB,pno oct BIG BELL $.40 (H193)

HE, DU JUNGER WICHT see Burthel, Jakob

HE MARCHED
SSA CIMINO $.40 (H194)
SATB CIMINO $.40 (H195)

HE-UCHLA! see Desch, Rudolf

HE UCHLA! see Mendelssohn, Arnold

HE WHO WOULD VALIANT BE see Burroughs

HEADING, ROGER
Mill Wheel, The
SAB EMI (H196)

HEADLESS HORSEMAN, THE
TTBB CIMINO $.40 (H197)

HEALEY, DEREK
Clouds
SATB (diff) WATERLOO $.60 (H198)

HEAR THE BELLS! SEE THE STAR! see
Ehret, Walter

HEAR THE SOUND OF THE MODES see Van
Slyck, Nicholas

HEATH
Love-Song
SATB SCHIRM.G 11940 $.30 (H199)

HEAVE-YO-HO see Duckworth, Arthur

HEAVEN CONSERVE THY COURSE IN QUITENESS
see Cobb, Donald

HECKENKIND see Thehos, Adam

HECTOR BERLIOZ WORKS see Berlioz,
Hector

HEDERITT see Blass, Heinrich

HEI! ALLE KOMMT HERBEI see Martinu,
Bohuslav, Hej! Mame Na Prodej

HEI, MEIN SCHATZLEIN *CC18U,folk
SATB MOSELER HEFT 24 s.p. (H200)

HEI, SCHONER LADO see Cossetto, Emil,
Dobri Denek

HEIDEBLUTE see Bein, Wilhelm

HEIDEFRUHLING see Bein, Wilhelm

HEIDSCHI BUMBEIDSCHI "ABER HEIDSCHI
BUMBEIDSCHI, SCHLAF LANGE" see
Hansen, Werner

HEIJA, IM FRISCHEN MAI see Rein, Walter

HEIL DIR UND FRIEDEN see Beneken,
Friedrich

HEILENDER TROST see Balm In Gilead

HEILIGE ARBEIT see Erdlen, Hermann

HEILIGE FLAMME see Wittmer, Eberhard
Ludwig

HEILIGE NACHT "HEILIGE NACHT DER
UNENDLICHEN LIEBE" see Reichardt,
Johann Friedrich

HEILIGES LAND see Edler, Robert

HEILMANN, HARALD (1924-   )
Maienkantate Nach Alten Volksweisen
2 eq voices/wom cor/jr cor,S rec,A
rec,vln PELIKAN PE917 s.p. (H201)

HEILNER, IRWIN
Banner Of The Jew, The
SATB,pno AM.COMP.AL. sc $3.58, voc
pt $1.93 (H202)

Bar Kochba
SATB,pno AM.COMP.AL. sc $4.95, voc
pt $1.93 (H203)

I Have A Dream
SATB,pno AM.COMP.AL. $3.58 (H204)

Jewish Cemetery At Newport, The
SATB,pno AM.COMP.AL. sc $8.25, voc
pt $3.85 (H205)

Sonnet 76
SATB,acap AM.COMP.AL. $2.75 (H206)

HEIMAT see Ketterer, Ernst

HEIMAT see Rein, Walter

HEIMAT "HEIMAT, WIR SIND ALLE DEIN" see
Wittmer, Eberhard Ludwig

HEIMAT, MEIN REBENLAND see Orrel, Max

HEIMAT UND JUGENDZEIT see Orrel, Max

HEIMATERDE see Hermanns, Willy

HEIMATLAND see Desch, Rudolf

HEIMATLIED: WO AUF DES TALES see Orrel,
Max

HEIMGEGANGEN "HEIMGEGANGEN BIST DU" see
Zoll, Paul

HEIMKEHR *folk
(Seib, V.) [Ger] 4pt men cor
MERSEBURG EM9075 s.p. (H207)

HEIMKEHR see Trunk, Richard

HEIMKEHR "O BRICH NICHT, STEG" see
Knab, Armin

HEIMKEHR "WEINT NICHT MEHR, IHR MUTTER"
see Mohler, Philipp

HEIMLICHE LIEBE see Vignau, Hans von

HEIMLICHE LIEBE: WENN ALLE BRUNNLEIN
see Silcher, Friedrich

HEIMWEH "ANDERS WIRD DIE WELT" see
Schroeder, Hermann

HEINRICHS, HANS L.
Den Wein 'Schenkt Ein
men cor,acap TONOS 3981 s.p. (H208)

Der Morgen Hebt Die Flugel
men cor,acap TONOS 3966 s.p. (H209)

HEIPPATIRALLA
"Hey Tralala" see Tyttoset

HEIRATSPOST-KANTATE see Wimberger,
Gerhard

HEIRLOOMS
(Smith) SATB (med diff) WATERLOO $.40
(H210)

HEIRS OF THE WHITE MOUNTAINS see
Dvorak, Antonin, Hymnus

HEISSA, KATHREINERLE *folk,Ger
(Biebl, Franz) men cor,acap TONOS 121
s.p. (H211)

HEISSA, KATHREINERLE see Haas, Joseph

HEISSA KATHREINERLE see Lang, Hans

HEISSE HERZEN, KUHLER WEIN see Kelling,
Hajo

HEISSISCHER SANGERSPRUCH "VON DER
ARBEIT, VON DER FREIHEIT" see Zoll,
Paul

HEITER IST DES LEBENS KUNST "KOMMT ES
MAL, WIE DU'S NICHT DENKST" see
Wolters, Karl-Heinz

HEITER UND UNBESCHWERT see Gremlich,
Willi

HEITERER SANGERGRUSS see Heun, Hans

HEITERES AQUARIUM see Fussan, Werner

HEITERES AUFTRITTSLIED see Becker,
Hans-Gunther

HEITERES TIERSPIEL see Zipp, Friedrich

HEITERKEIT, GULDNE see Edler, Robert

HEJ! MAME NA PRODEJ see Martinu,
Bohuslav

HEJ SLOVANE see Jeremias, Bohuslav

HEJ, UZ SA NA TEL HORE see Mikula,
Zdenko

HEJJA, KARAHEJJA see Bartok, Bela

HELDENGEDENKEN see Koenig, Franz

HELFRITZ, HANS (1902-   )
Neun Mexikanische Volkslieder *CC9L,
folk,Mex
[Ger/Span] jr cor,rec,perc,timp
(easy) sc,cor pts SCHOTTS B 176
s.p. (H212)

HELL ERKLINGT MEIN LIED see Becker,
Hans-Gunther

HELLDEN, DANIEL
All Good Things
SATB WALTON 2714 $.40 (H213)

I Var Tid
men cor GEHRMANS KRB463 see from
Tva Lyriska Korer (H214)

Rosemary
SATB,acap EGTVED MS19B15 s.p.
(H215)

Sommarens Gras
men cor GEHRMANS KRB463 see from
Tva Lyriska Korer (H216)

Tva Lyriska Korer *see I Var Tid;
Sommarens Gras (H217)

HELLEMAN
Het Graf Onder De Meidoorn
wom cor s.p. sc HEER 490, cor pts
HEER 490A (H218)

HELLO, YOUNG LOVERS see Rodgers,
Richard

HELLOW MR. SANTA CLAUS
SA CIMINO $.50 (H219)

HELP ME see Mitchell

HEMBERG, ESKIL
Cantica *Op.27
cor,soli,orch NORDISKA NMS 6406
s.p. (H220)

Det Galler Att Klippa Till Forst
mix cor,acap NORDISKA NMS 6583 s.p.
(H221)

HEMEL, OSCAR VAN (1892-   )
  Memorial Hymn
    mix cor,2fl,3ob,3clar,2bsn,4horn,
    3trp,3trom,tuba,strings,perc,timp
    DONEMUS   (H222)

HEMKOMSTEN see Eklund, Stig

HENDERSON
  Sing A Song (composed with
    Stoutamire)
    SAB,opt 2pno,bvl,drums PRO ART 2824
    $.40   (H223)
    SSA,opt 2pno,bvl,drums PRO ART 2828
    $.40   (H224)

HENZE, HANS WERNER (1926-   )
  Chorfantasie
    mix cor,trom,2vcl,bvl,perc,timp,org
    (diff) sc SCHOTTS rental,ipr
                                       (H225)
  Das Floss Der Medusa *ora
    16pt mix cor&jr cor,narrator,SBar
    soli,orch (diff) min sc SCHOTTS
    ED. 6326 s.p., voc sc SCHOTTS
    ED. 6103 s.p., cor pts SCHOTTS
    rental, ipr   (H226)
  Moralitaten *cant
    mix cor,narrator,AB soli,pno&fl&ob&
    clar&bsn&horn&trp&trom&strings&
    perc&timp/2pno (diff) sc,cor
    pts SCHOTTS ED. 6033 s.p., ipr
                                       (H227)
  Musen Siziliens
    4pt mix cor,2pno,2fl,2ob,2clar,
    2bsn,4horn,2trp,2trom,timp (diff)
    min sc SCHOTTS ED. 5515 s.p., cor
    pts SCHOTTS rental, ipr   (H228)
  Wiegenlied Der Mutter Gottes
    unis jr cor,opt solo,fl,clar,horn,
    trp,trom,vln,vcl,bvl,harp (diff)
    sc SCHOTTS rental, ipr   (H229)

HER HAIR THE NET OF GOLDEN WIRE see
  Wilbye, John

HER MIT DEM WEIN! see Schrey, Wilhelm

HERALDS OF LOVE, THE see Brahms,
  Johannes, Die Boten Der Liebe

HERBEI, IHR FREUNDE see Fischer, Theo

HERBEI, WER LUSTIG SEIN WILL HIER see
  Schein, Johann Hermann

HERBER ABSCHIED: WIE DIE BLUMLEIN see
  Silcher, Friedrich

HERBST see Stravinsky, Igor

HERBST "DIE BLATTER FALLEN" see
  Buchtger, Fritz

HERBSTLIED see Mendelssohn-Bartholdy,
  Felix

HERBSTLIED see Rein, Walter

HERBSTLIED see Schumann, Robert
  (Alexander)

HERBSTLIED "SCHON IM GOLDNEN
  AHRENKRANZ" see Mockl, Franz

HERBSTNACHTE "O IHR HERBSTLICH LANGEN
  NACHTE" see Slavenski, Josip,
  Jesenske Noci

HERDMAN'S SONG, A see Lindgren, Kurt

HERE COMES THE AVANT-GARDE see
  McElheran

HERE IS THE GOD WHO LOOKS BOTH WAYS see
  Crawford, John, Voici Le Pere Au
  Double Front

HERE THE FRAILEST LEAVES OF ME see
  Hall, William D.

HERE, THERE AND EVERYWHERE see Lennon,
  John

HERE WE COME A-WASSAILING *Xmas
  (Lefebvre, C.) SSA GALAXY 1.1219.1
  $.35   (H230)

HERE'S THAT RAINY DAY
  (Shaw, Kirby) SATB,pno,inst (jazz,
  includes recording and 14 choral
  octavos) LEONARD-US 07853800 $14.95
                                       (H231)

HERE'S TO AMERICA see North, Jack

HERESY FOR A CLASSROOM see Gyring,
  Elizabeth

HERF, FRANZ
  Besinnung
    men cor,acap TONOS 5817 s.p. (H232)

HERITAGE see Ringwald, [Roy]

HERMAN, WOODY
  Woodchoppers' Ball
    (Brooks, Harvey) SATB,pno,inst
    (jazz, includes recording and 14
    choral octavos) LEONARD-US
    07259075 $14.95   (H233)

HERMANNS, WILLY
  Heimaterde
    men cor,acap sc,cor pts TONOS 421
    s.p.   (H234)
  Wanderlust
    men cor,acap TONOS 239 s.p. (H235)
  Wandrers Nachtlied
    men cor,acap TONOS 225 s.p. (H236)

HEROIC ORATORIO see Hanousek, Vladmir,
  Heroicke Oratorium

HEROICKE ORATORIUM see Hanousek,
  Vladmir

HERO'S SONG, THE see Podesva, Jaromir,
  Zpev Hrdinov

HERR ANDERSSON... ELLER DEN SKULLE NI
  HA HORT! see Holmdahl

HERR, ES IST ZEIT see Buchtger, Fritz

HERR, SCHICKE, WAS DU WILT see Rein,
  Walter

HERR WALTHER VON DER VOGELWEIDE see
  Pepping, Ernst

HERRAN RUKOUS see Rautavaara,
  Einojuhani

HERRLICHES LAND VOR DER HAARDT see
  Frey, Oskar

HERRMANN, BERNARD (1911-   )
  Moby Dick *cant
    TTBB,TTBarB soli,3fl,3ob,3clar,
    3bsn,4horn,3trp,3trom,tuba,perc,
    harp,strings voc sc NOVELLO
    rental   (H237)

HERRMANN, HUGO (1896-1967)
  Abendfeier "Glocklein,
    Abendglocklein"
    2pt wom cor/2pt jr cor&4pt men cor,
    acap (med) sc SCHOTTS C 38 281
    s.p.   (H238)
  Anruf "Herr, Deine Zeit Ist Reif"
    men cor sc SCHOTTS CHBL 134 s.p.
                                       (H239)
  Blumlein Blau "Weiss Mir Ein Blumlein
    Blaue"
    see Zwei Volkslieder
  Cantata Concertante
    mix cor,SBar soli,pno,2fl,2ob,
    2clar,2bsn,4horn,2trp,3trom,tuba,
    strings,harp,perc,timp,celeste
    (med) voc sc,cor pts SCHOTTS
    ED. 5527 s.p., ipr   (H240)
  Cantata Primavera *cant
    men cor&wom cor&mix cor&jr cor,2fl,
    2ob,2clar,2bsn,2trp,2trom,
    tuba,strings,perc,3timp,harp/pno
    voc sc,cor pts SCHOTTS ED. 4628
    s.p., ipr   (H241)
  Dammerung
    men cor,acap TONOS 4059 s.p. (H242)
  Frau Nachtigall "Es Steht Ein Lind In
    Jenem Tal"
    mix cor (med) sc SCHOTTS C 40 459
    s.p., voc pt SCHOTTS C 40 460A-B
    s.p.   (H243)
  Geburtstag "Dein Leben Ist Ein
    Fruhlingslied"
    see Herrmann, Hugo, Nachruf "Du
    Gabst Mit Gottes Handen
  Gelobnis
    men cor,acap TONOS 4567 s.p. (H244)
  Hymne An Das Meer
    men cor,acap sc,cor pts TONOS 4001
    s.p.   (H245)
  Hymne An Frau Musica "Was Mag Doch
    Diese Welt"
    4pt mix cor,pno/4strings/2trp&
    2horn&trom&tuba (med easy) sc
    SCHOTTS CHBL 316 s.p., ipa   (H246)
  Lichtgesant "Gottes Gewaltigster Flug
    Ist Das Licht"
    men cor sc SCHOTTS C 38 031 s.p.
                                       (H247)
  Nachruf "Du Gabst Mit Gottes Handen
    mix cor (med easy) sc SCHOTTS
    CHBL 325A-B s.p. contains also:
    Geburtstag "Dein Leben Ist Ein

HERRMANN, HUGO (cont'd.)
  Fruhlingslied"   (H248)
  Roslein Auf Der Heiden "Sie Gleicht
    Wohl Einem Rosenstock"
    see Zwei Volkslieder
  Rosmarienbaum
    jr cor/wom cor (med easy) sc
    SCHOTTS CHBL 583 s.p.   (H249)
  Triumph Der Liebe
    mix cor&wom cor&men cor,2trp,2horn,
    2trom,tuba,timp (med) sc SCHOTTS
    rental, ipr   (H250)
  Zwei Volkslieder *folk
    men cor sc SCHOTTS CHBL 189A-B s.p.
    contains: Blumlein Blau "Weiss
      Mir Ein Blumlein Blaue";
      Roslein Auf Der Heiden "Sie
      Gleicht Wohl Einem Rosenstock"
                                       (H251)

HERTS, CHARLES LEE
  Look Off, Dear Love
    SSA (diff) FITZSIMONS 3067 $.25
                                       (H252)
  When All The World Is Young
    TTBB,acap (med) FITZSIMONS 4060
    $.25   (H253)

HERZ, SEI BEREIT see Zipp, Friedrich

HERZ, WERDE WACH see Wolters, Karl-
  Heinz

HERZ, WERDE WACH UND SING see Lissmann,
  Kurt

HERZ, WERDE WACH UND SINGE see Genzmer,
  Harald

HERZ, WO WARST DU IN DER NACHT see
  Genzmer, Harald

HERZENSWEH: MEIN HERZLEIN TUT see
  Silcher, Friedrich

HERZERL, WAS KRANKT DICH see Silcher,
  Friedrich

HERZLAND DER LIEBE see Desch, Rudolf

HERZLIEBCHEN MEIN see Conradi, J.G.

HE'S GONE AWAY
  see Barbershop Choir, The

HESSENBERG, KURT (1908-   )
  Abendlied "Augen, Meine Lieben
    Fensterlein
    see Vier Gedichte
  Beherzigung "Ach, Was Soll Der Mensch
    Verlangen"
    see Lieder Und Epigramme Heft II
  Das Alter "Das Alter Ist Ein Hoflich
    Mann"
    see Lieder Und Epigramme Heft II
  Das Beste "Wenn Dir's In Kopf Und
    Herzen Schwirrt"
    see Lieder Und Epigramme Heft I
  Der Struwwelpeter *cant
    "Petrulus Hirrutus" [Ger/Lat] 1-3pt
    jr cor,pno,2fl,strings,perc (med)
    sc SCHOTTS rental, voc sc,cor pts
    SCHOTTS ED. 6082 s.p., ipa   (H254)
  Der Vogel Abschied "Ade, Ihr
    Felsenhallen" *Op.31,No.4
    5-8pt mix cor (med diff) sc SCHOTTS
    C 37 937 s.p. see from Vier
    Chorlieder   (H255)
  Die Jahre "Die Jahre Sind
    Allerliebste Leut"
    see Lieder Und Epigramme Heft II
  Die Offentlichen Verleumder "Ein
    Ungeziefer Ruht In Staub"
    *Op.59,No.2
    men cor sc SCHOTTS C 39 020 s.p.
    see from Drei Gedichte Von
    Gottfried Keller   (H256)
    men cor voc pt SCHOTTS
    C 39 021, 01-02 s.p. see from
    DREI GEDICHTE VON GOTTFRIED
    KELLER   (H257)
  Drei Gedichte Von Gottfried Keller
    *see Die Offentlichen Verleumder
    "Ein Ungeziefer Ruht In Staub",
    Op.59,No.2; Fruhlingsglaube "Es
    Wandert Eine Schone Sage", Op.59,
    No.1; Morgen "Sooft Die Sonne
    Aufersteht", Op.59,No.3   (H258)
  Es Fiel Ein Reif In Der
    Fruhlingsnacht *folk
    men cor sc SCHOTTS C 40 457 s.p.
    see from Zwei Volksliedsatze
                                       (H259)

HESSENBERG, KURT (cont'd.)

Es Steht Ein Lind In Jenem Tal
SATB (med easy, contains also:
Lieblich Hat Sich Gesellet) sc
SCHOTTS C 41 287 s.p. see from
Funf Alte Volkslieder   (H260)

Es Taget Vor Dem Walde
SATB (med easy) sc SCHOTTS C 41 286
s.p. see from Funf Alte
Volkslieder   (H261)

Fruhlingsglaube "Es Wandert Eine
Schone Sage" *Op.59,No.1
men cor sc SCHOTTS C 38 765 s.p.
see from Drei Gedichte Von
Gottfried Keller   (H262)

Funf Alte Volkslieder *see Es Steht
Ein Lind In Jenem Tal; Es Taget
Vor Dem Walde; Lieblich Hat Sich
Gesellet; Maienzeit Bannet Leid;
Mit Lust Tret Ich In Diesen Tanz
                               (H263)

Gedichte "Gedichte Sind Gemalte
Fensterscheiben"
see Lieder Und Epigramme Heft I

Genialisch Treiben "So Walz Ich Ohne
Unterlass"
see Lieder Und Epigramme Heft I

Grabschrift "Als Knabe Verschlossen
Und Trutzig"
see Lieder Und Epigramme Heft II

Lieblich Hat Sich Gesellet
SATB (med easy, contains also: Es
Steht Ein Lind In Jenem Tal) sc
SCHOTTS C 41 287 s.p. see from
Funf Alte Volkslieder   (H264)

Lieder Und Epigramme Heft I
men cor sc SCHOTTS C 37 581 s.p.
contains: Das Beste "Wenn Dir's
In Kopf Und Herzen Schwirrt";
Gedichte "Gedichte Sind Gemalte
Fensterscheiben"; Genialisch
Treiben "So Walz Ich Ohne
Unterlass"; Meine Wahl "Ich
Liebe Den Heitern Mann";
Totalitat "Ein Kavalier Von
Kopf Und Herz"   (H265)

Lieder Und Epigramme Heft II
men cor sc SCHOTTS C 37 582 s.p.
contains: Beherzigung "Ach, Was
Soll Der Mensch Verlangen"; Das
Alter "Das Alter Ist Ein
Hoflich Mann"; Die Jahre "Die
Jahre Sind Allerliebste Leut";
Grabschrift "Als Knabe
Verschlossen Und Trutzig"   (H266)

Maienzeit Bannet Leid
SATBB (med easy) sc SCHOTTS
C 41 285 s.p. see from Funf Alte
Volkslieder   (H267)

Mein Madel Hat Einen Rosenmund *folk
men cor sc SCHOTTS C 40 458 s.p.
see from Zwei Volksliedsatze
                               (H268)

Meine Wahl "Ich Liebe Den Heitern
Mann"
see Lieder Und Epigramme Heft I

Mit Lust Tret Ich In Diesen Tanz
SATB (med easy) sc SCHOTTS C 41 288
s.p. see from Funf Alte
Volkslieder   (H269)

Morgen "Sooft Die Sonne Aufersteht"
*Op.59,No.3
men cor sc SCHOTTS C 38 766 s.p.
see from Drei Gedichte Von
Gottfried Keller   (H270)

Morgenlied "Die Sterne Sind
Erblichen" *Op.31
men cor sc SCHOTTS C 38 164 s.p.
                               (H271)
mix cor (med) sc SCHOTTS C 37 933
s.p. see from Vier Chorlieder
                               (H272)

Nachtmusikanten "Hier Sind Wir Arme
Narrn" *Op.31,No.3
4-6pt mix cor,T solo (med) sc
SCHOTTS C 37 935 s.p., voc pt
SCHOTTS C 37 936A-D s.p. see from
Vier Chorlieder   (H273)

Nicht Wiedersehn "Nun Ade, Mein
Herzliebster Schatz" *Op.31,No.2
4-6pt mix cor,T solo (med) sc
SCHOTTS C 37 934 s.p. see from
Vier Chorlieder   (H274)

Petrulus Hirrutus *see Der
Struwwelpeter

Regen-Sommer "Nasser Staub Auf Allen
Wegen
see Vier Gedichte

HESSENBERG, KURT (cont'd.)

Siehst Du Den Stern
see Vier Gedichte

Totalitat "Ein Kavalier Von Kopf Und
Herz"
see Lieder Und Epigramme Heft I

Vier Chorlieder *see Der Vogel
Abschied "Ade, Ihr Felsenhallen",
Op.31,No.4; Morgenlied "Die
Sterne Sind Erblichen", Op.31,
No.1; Nachtmusikanten "Hier Sind
Wir Arme Narrn", Op.31,No.3;
Nicht Wiedersehn "Nun Ade, Mein
Herzliebster Schatz", Op.31,No.2
                               (H275)

Vier Gedichte
(med) SCHOTTS s.p.
contains: Abendlied "Augen, Meine
Lieben Fensterlein, Op.81,No.4
(SSATBB); Regen-Sommer "Nasser
Staub Auf Allen Wegen, Op.81,
No.3 (SSATBB); Siehst Du Den
Stern, Op.81,No.2 (SAATBB); Wir
Wahnten Lange Recht Zu Leben,
Op.81,No.1 (SAATB)   (H276)

Vom Wesen Und Vergehen *Op.45, cant
mix cor,SBar soli,2fl,2ob,2clar,
2bsn,strings (med) voc sc,cor pts
SCHOTTS ED. 4341 s.p., ipr   (H277)

Weinlein, Nun Gang Ein! *Op.72, cant
men cor,T solo,2fl,ob,2clar,bsn,
3horn,trp,trom,strings,perc,timp
voc sc,voc pt SCHOTTS ED. 4994
s.p., ipr, sc SCHOTTS rental
                               (H278)

Wenn Die Bettelleute Tanzen
men cor sc SCHOTTS C 39 849 s.p.
                               (H279)

Wir Wahnten Lange Recht Zu Leben
see Vier Gedichte

Zwei Volksliedsatze *see Es Fiel Ein
Reif In Der Fruhlingsnacht; Mein
Madel Hat Einen Rosenmund   (H280)

HESSISCHE HEIMATHYMNE see Stege, Fritz

HET DALLAMRAJZ see Durko, Zsolt

HET GRAF ONDER DE MEIDOORN see Helleman

HET MEISJE VAN SCHEVENINGEN see
Strohbach, Siegfried

HET VERLOREN ACCOORD see Sullivan, Sir
Arthur Seymour, Lost Chord, The

HEUKEN, HANS JAKOB (1904-   )
Dorfmusik
men cor,acap TONOS 3736 s.p. (H281)

Uber Nacht
men cor,acap TONOS 4015 s.p. (H282)

Wein Is Liebe Und Gesang
men cor,acap TONOS 3735 s.p. (H283)

HEUN, HANS
Abschied
men cor,acap TONOS 233 s.p. (H284)

Das Trunkene Lied
men cor,acap sc,cor pts TONOS 419
s.p.   (H285)

Gott Segne Den Hebensaft
men cor,acap sc,cor pts TONOS 427
s.p.   (H286)

Heiterer Sangergruss
men cor,acap TONOS 238 s.p. (H287)

Humulus Lupulus
men cor,acap sc,cor pts TONOS 423
s.p.   (H288)

Komm Zum Tanz
men cor,acap TONOS 241 s.p. (H289)

Kosackenhockzeit
men cor,acap TONOS 425 s.p. (H290)

Punschlied
men cor,acap sc,cor pts TONOS 428
s.p.   (H291)

Wanderlied: Frohes Wandern
men cor,acap sc,cor pts TONOS 422
s.p.   (H292)

HEUREIGEN "WENN KUHL DER MORGEN ATMET"
see Lang, Hans

HEUSER
Romanze
men cor cor pts FORBERG s.p. (H293)

HEUT KOMMT DER HANS *folk,Ger
(Ophoven, Hermann) men cor,acap TONOS
112 s.p.   (H294)

HEUT SCHEINT DER MOND *folk,Ger
(Biebl, Franz) men cor,acap TONOS 3
s.p.   (H295)

HEUT SOLL DAS GROSSE FLACHSERNTEN SEIN
see Werdin, Eberhard

HEUTE HIER - MORGEN DORT see Weber,
Bernhard

HEUTE TUT SICH AUF DAS TOR see Zipp,
Friedrich

HEWITT, THOMAS J.
Bean-Stalk, The
unis EMI   (H296)

HEWITT-JONES, TONY (1926-   )
Good Company
SATB,Bar solo,2fl,2ob,2clar,2bsn,
2horn,2trp,timp,strings voc sc
NOVELLO rental   (H297)

Seven Sea Poems *CC7U
SATB,A,opt Bar soli,ob,strings voc
sc NOVELLO rental   (H298)

HEY TOMORROW see Croce, Jim

HEY TRALALA see Heippatiralla

HEYMAN
When I Fall In Love (composed with
Young)
(Azelton, Phil) SATB,acap (jazz,
includes recording and 14 choral
octavos) LEONARD-US 07259000
$14 95   (H299)

HICKS, VAL
Showboat Came To Town, The
SSAA BOURNE B230623-353 $.40 (H300)

Women's Lib March
SSA BOURNE B223750-353 $.50 (H301)

HIDE AND SEEK see Williamson, Malcolm

HIDEAWAY PLACE see Jones

HIE KANN NIT SEIN EIN BOSER MUT see
Hindemith, Paul

HIGH BARBARY see Manley, Dorothy

HIGH GERMANY see Vaughan Williams,
Ralph

HIGH HANGS THE HOLLY see Ehret, Walter

HIGH IS THE MOON ABOVE US see Othmayr,
Kaspar, Der Mond Der Steht Am
Hochsten

HIGH LEVEL RANTERS SONG AND TUNE BOOK
*CC15U
(Handle, J.) cor GALLIARD 2.8151.7
$2.50   (H302)

HIGH SCHOOL BAND, THE see Paynter, John
P.

HIGH TIDE, THE see Thiman, Eric Harding

HIGHLAND HYMN see Silver

HILGER, MANFRED
Abendstimmung
men cor,acap TONOS 436 s.p. (H303)

Das Lied Von Blonden Korken
men cor,pno,opt perc sc,cor pts
TONOS 2203 s.p.   (H304)

HILL "JESTED", THE see Huth, Gustav,
Jested

HILLER, WILFRED (1941-   )
Cantico
see Muspilli

Muspilli
mix cor,acap cor pts ORLANDO s.p.
contains: Cantico; Muspilli;
Wessobrunner Gebet   (H305)

Muspilli
see Muspilli

Wessobrunner Gebet
see Muspilli

HILLIARD
Our Day Will Come *pop
(Garson) SSA BELWIN UC 670 $.40
                               (H306)
(Garson) SATB BELWIN UC 671 $.40
                               (H307)
(Garson) SA/TB BELWIN UC 718 $.40
                               (H308)

HILLS, THE see Ireland, John

HILMERA, OLDRICH (1891-1948)
Zahrajte Mne, Mizikanti *CC4U
[Czech] jr cor,fl,ob,2clar,2horn,
2trp,perc,strings CZECH s.p.
(H309)

HILS BORGE see Holm, Peder

HILTON
My Mistress Frowns
(Ehret) SSA SCHIRM.G LG51694 $.30
(H310)

HILTON, JOHN
When Flora Frowns
SSA STAINER 3.0730.1 $.30   (H311)

HILTON, JOHN (THE YOUNGER) (1599-1657)
Now Is The Summer Springing
(Malin, Don) SSA BELWIN 2300 $.35
(H312)

HIMMEL STRAHLT see Brahms, Johannes

HIMMEL UND ERDE see Gerster, Ottmar

HIMMELSAUEN, WOLKENFLUH see Zipp,
Friedrich

HIMMELWARTS UND HEIMATWARTS see Desch,
Rudolf

HIMMUSZ A BEKEROL see Bardos, Lajos

HIMNUSZ A BEKEROL see Ribari, Antal

HINDEMITH, PAUL (1895-1963)
Als Flieder Jungst Mir Im Garten
Bluht *see When Lilacs Last In
The Door-Yard Bloom'd

Angst Vorm Schwimmunterricht "Vorher
Denk Ich Immer"
jr cor (med) sc SCHOTTS C 32 759
s.p. see from Chorlieder Fur
Knaben   (H313)

Bastellied "Lasst Uns Alleine Machen"
jr cor (med) sc SCHOTTS C 32 757
s.p. see from Chorlieder Fur
Knaben   (H314)

Chorlieder Fur Knaben *see Angst
Vorm Schwimmunterricht "Vorher
Denk Ich Immer"; Bastellied
"Lasst Uns Alleine Machen"; Lied
Des Musterknaben "Meine Eltern
Zeigen"; Schundromane Lesen "Das
Ist Das Schonste"   (H315)

Das Unaufhorliche *ora
[Eng/Ger] mix cor&jr cor,STBarB
soli,3fl,2ob,2clar,2bsn,3horn,
2trp,2trom,tuba,strings,perc,
timp,opt org (diff) SCHOTTS
ED. 3258 cor pts s.p., voc sc
s.p., sc rental   (H316)

Frau Musica *Op.45,No.1, CCU
1-2pt mix cor,fl,strings (med) sc,
cor pts SCHOTTS ED. 1460 s.p.,
ipa   (H317)

Hie Kann Nit Sein Ein Boser Mut
see Vier Kanons

Kanon "Musica Divinas Laudes"
see Hindemith, Paul, Spruch Eines
Fahrenden "Dass Gott Die Berate"

Lied Des Musterknaben "Meine Eltern
Zeigen"
jr cor (med) sc SCHOTTS C 32 758
s.p. see from Chorlieder Fur
Knaben   (H318)

Mahnung An Die Jugend, Sich Der Musik
Zu Befliessigen *cant
3pt jr cor,narrator,solo,strings,
brass,opt perc (med) sc,cor pts
SCHOTTS ED. 1624 s.p., ipa (H319)

Mainzer Umzug
SAB&cor&speak cor,STBar soli,2fl,
2ob,2clar,2bsn,2horn,2trp,2trom,
strings,perc (med diff) sc
SCHOTTS rental, ipr   (H320)

Martinslied "Was Haben Doch Die Ganse
Getan"
unis wom cor,fl,ob,clar,bsn,
strings,opt bvl (med) sc,voc pt
SCHOTTS ED. 1570 s.p., ipa (H321)

Martinslied "Was Haben Uns Die Gans
Getan"
unis,3inst (med) sc,cor pts SCHOTTS
ED. 1570 s.p.   (H322)

Musica Divina Laudes
see Vier Kanons

Schundromane Lesen "Das Ist Das
Schonste"
jr cor (med) sc SCHOTTS C 32 760
s.p. see from Chorlieder Fur
Knaben   (H323)

HINDEMITH, PAUL (cont'd.)
Sine Musica Nulla Disciplina
see Vier Kanons

Spruch Eines Fahrenden "Dass Gott Die
Berate"
3pt wom cor/3pt jr cor,acap (med
diff) sc SCHOTTS C 37 729 s.p.
contains also: Kanon "Musica
Divinas Laudes" (3pt wom cor,
acap)   (H324)

Vier Kanons *canon
2-3pt jr cor (med) sc SCHOTTS
CHBL 515 s.p.
contains: Hie Kann Nit Sein Ein
Boser Mut; Musica Divina
Laudes; Sine Musica Nulla
Disciplina; Wer Sich Die Musik
Erkiest   (H325)

Wer Sich Die Musik Erkiest
(Jode, Fritz) jr cor,4inst (med)
sc,cor pts SCHOTTS B 107 s.p.,
ipa   (H326)

Wer Sich Die Musik Erkiest
see Vier Kanons
jr cor,strings (med) sc,cor pts
SCHOTTS B 107 s.p., ipa   (H327)

When Lilacs Last In The Door-Yard
Bloom'd *Req
"Als Flieder Jungst Im Garten
Bluht" mix cor,MezBar soli,org,
2fl,2ob,2clar,2bsn,3horn,2trp,
2trom,tuba,perc,timp (med diff)
voc sc,cor pts SCHOTTS ED. 3800
s.p., ipr   (H328)

Wir Bauen Eine Stadt
jr cor,inst (easy) sc,cor pts
SCHOTTS ED. 5424 s.p., ipa (H329)

HINDERMANN, WALTER FELIX (1931-   )
Sie Wollen Es Nicht Wahrhaben
SAT/SAB,inst LAUDINELLA LR 89 s.p.
(H330)

HINTER DER DONAUBRUCKE see Haas, Joseph

HINUBER see Deep River

HIOB 19 see Huber, Klaus

HIP-HIP HORATIO see Hurd, Michael

HIPPOPOTAMUS, THE see Berger, Jean

HIRAI, KOZABURO (1910-   )
Fujiyama *cant
cor ONGAKU s.p.   (H331)

Great Buddah *cant
cor ONGAKU s.p.   (H332)

HIRNER, TEODOR (1910-   )
Na Tvoju Slavu Piesen Zvoni *cant
mix cor,T solo,orch SLOV.HUD.FOND
s.p.   (H333)

Pozdrav Do Moskvy *cant
mix cor,T solo,orch sc
SLOV.HUD.FOND s.p.   (H334)

HIROSHIMA see Tanenbaum, Elias

HIROSIMA see Hrusovsky, Ivan

HIRSCHHORN, JOEL
Morning After, The *see Kasha, Al

HIRTENLIEBE: KOMM MIT MIR INS TALE see
Silcher, Friedrich

HIRTENWEIHNACHT *CCU
(Abel-Struth, Sigrid; Bialas, Gunter)
1-3pt jr cor,opt inst (med easy) sc
SCHOTTS B 135 s.p.   (H335)

HIRTH, HERMANN
Gesellschaftslied
men cor,acap TONOS 230 s.p. (H336)

HISTOIRE see Massis, Amable

HISTORIA see Johansen, Sven-Erik

HJORT, FREDRIK
Budskap (composed with Ahlen,
Waldemar)
"Message" unis,solo,org NORDISKA
NMS 6527 s.p.   (H337)

Message *see Budskap

HLAVENKA ME BOLI see Martinu, Bohuslav

HOBBIES see Fischer, Ernst

HOCH AM BERG "HOCH AM BERG, IN DEM
WALD" see Zoll, Paul

HOCH DES RICHTERS HAUS IN KANJA RAGT
see Bartok, Bela

HOCH IM GEREUTE *folk,Slav
(Marolt, France) men cor,acap TONOS
2902 s.p.   (H338)

HOCHZEIT HIELT DAS MUCKELEIN see Poos,
Heinrich

HOCHZEITS-MADRIGAL "LIEBE FUHRT DURCH
NACHT UND DUNKEL" see Rein, Walter

HOCHZEITSLIED see Haus, Karl

HOCHZEITSLIED "AUS MEINEM BRUNNLEIN
FLIESST" see Erdlen, Hermann

HOCHZEITSLIED "HAHNENFUSS UND
FRAUENSCHUH" see Weber, Bernhard

HOCHZEITSLIED "HEUT IST DER LIEBSTE
TAG" see Wittmer, Eberhard Ludwig

HOCHZEITSLIED "KOMM MIR IN DEN SINN"
see Slavenski, Josip, Svatovska

HOCHZEITSLIEDER see Reutter, Hermann

HOCHZEITSTANZ "AUF ZUM TANZ" see
Cossetto, Emil

HODDINOTT, ALUN (1929-   )
Apple Tree And A Pig, A
SATB,acap (med diff) OXFORD 56.589
$1.50   (H339)

Black Bart
SATB,inst (med diff) voc sc OXFORD
56.588 $3.00, ipr   (H340)

HOEDOWN! see Thygerson, Robert J.

HOFERS ABSCHIED VOM LEBEN see Poll,
Joseph

HOFFDING, FINN (1899-   )
Das Eisenbahngleichnis
"Railway Parable, The" mix cor,pno,
opt inst HANSEN-DEN WH 29221 s.p.
(H341)

Railway Parable, The *see Das
Eisenbahngleichnis

HOFFER, PAUL MARX (1895-1949)
Frohliche Wanderkantate *cant
mix cor,ABar soli,fl,3vln,vcl,perc,
opt pno (med easy) voc sc,voc pt
SCHOTTS ED. 4856 s.p., ipa (H342)

HOFFMAN
Hawaiian Wedding Song
(Manning; King) SATB BELWIN UC 680
$.40   (H343)
(Manning; King) SSA BELWIN UC 681
$.40   (H344)

HOFFNUNG see Lendvai, Erwin

HOGBEN, DOROTHY
Four Sisters, The
SSA,pno NOVELLO TRIOS 675 s.p.
(H345)

HOHN UND SPOTT see Thehos, Adam

HOKKE-SENPO see Fujiwara, Y.

HOL MICH NACH HAUS see Swing Low, Sweet
Chariot

HOL UBER, FAHRMANN MORGENROT see
Schwaen, Kurt

HOLD FAST TO THE SPIRIT see Franco,
Johan

HOLDERLIN see Manzoni, Giacomo

HOLIDAY
Fine And Mellow
(Grean) MARKS MC 4612 $.40   (H346)

HOLIDAY CAROL see Silver

HOLIDAY IN SPAIN see Reaks

HOLIDAY, JIMMY
Bad Water *see De Shannon, Jackie

HOLLANDE, J. DE
Le Rossignol Daus Son Nid Chante
(Malin, Don) "Nightingale At Rest
Is Singing, The" TTBB,acap BELWIN
2330 $.30   (H347)

Nightingale At Rest Is Singing, The
*see Le Rossignol Daus Son Nid
Chante

HOLLER, YORK (1944-   )
Decollage, Musik Zu Light-Sound
2 speak cor,org, electric guitar
and violoncello; with lighting
effects (diff) sc SCHOTTS rental,
ipr   (H348)

HOLLFELDER, WALDRAM (1924-   )
Der Bigamist
see Von Allerlei Mist

Der Optimist
see Von Allerlei Mist

Der Pessimist
see Von Allerlei Mist

Der Pferdemist
see Von Allerlei Mist

Lausige Zeiten
men cor,acap TONOS 3746 s.p. (H349)

Von Allerlei Mist
TB,acap cmplt ed,sc,cor pts TONOS
3950 s.p.
contains: Der Bigamist; Der
Optimist; Der Pessimist; Der
Pferdemist   (H350)

HOLLINS, ALFRED (1865-1942)
Life's A Dream Worth Dreaming
SSATTB,acap (med) FITZSIMONS 1045
$.25   (H351)

HOLLOWAY, ROBIN
Ah Fading Joy, How Quickly Art Thou
Past! *madrigal
SATB NOVELLO MT 1578 s.p.   (H352)

HOLLY AND THE IVY
(Lefebvre, C.) SSA GALAXY 1.0584.1
$.35   (H353)

HOLLY AND THE IVY, THE *Xmas,carol
(Graves) SATB,acap (med easy) OXFORD
84.190 $.25   (H354)

HOLLY JOLLY CHRISTMAS see Marks

HOLLY TREE CAROL, THE see Ritchie, Jean

HOLM, PEDER (1926-   )
Ene Mene
see Fem Korsange

Fem Korsange *folk
SATB cmplt ed HANSEN-DEN WH 29178
s.p.
contains: Ene Mene; Hils Borge,
"Regards To Borge"; Indskrift,
"Inscription"; Mobile;
Septemberaften, "September
Evening"   (H355)

Hils Borge
"Regards To Borge" see Fem Korsange

Indskrift
"Inscription" see Fem Korsange

Inscription *see Indskrift

Mobile
see Fem Korsange

Regards To Borge *see Hils Borge

September Evening *see
Septemberaften

Septemberaften
"September Evening" see Fem
Korsange

HOLMDAHL
Herr Andersson... Eller Den Skulle Ni
Ha Hort!
(Johanson) men cor ERIKS 360 s.p.
(H356)

HOLMES
Build Thee More Stately Mansions
SATB LEONARD-US 08005270 $.50
(H357)

Rock The Boat
(Davis) SATB,opt perc WARNER WB-377
$.50   (H358)

HOLMES, H. REUBEN
Mallow Fling, The
SA CRAMER $.20   (H359)

HOLOUBEK see Sveceny, Ladislav

HOLOUBEK, LADISLAV (1913-   )
Jarna
see Pesnicky Pre Male Skolske Deti

Maciatko A Husky
see Pesnicky Pre Male Skolske Deti

Moj Kraj
see MUZSKE ZBORY III
men cor SLOV.HUD.FOND s.p.   (H360)

Pesnicky Pre Male Skolske Deti
mix cor SLOV.HUD.FOND s.p.
contains: Jarna; Maciatko A
Husky; Raz A Dva; Taborak; V
Detske Izbe; Zberatel   (H361)

HOLOUBEK, LADISLAV (cont'd.)
Raz A Dva
see Pesnicky Pre Male Skolske Deti

Taborak
see Pesnicky Pre Male Skolske Deti

V Detske Izbe
see Pesnicky Pre Male Skolske Deti

Zberatel
see Pesnicky Pre Male Skolske Deti

HOLST, GUSTAV (1874-1934)
Autumn Song
SATB GALAXY 1.5079.1 $.40   (H362)

Before Sleep
TB,pno/org oct BOOSEY 5928 $.35 see
from Six Choruses For Male Voices
(H363)

Choral Hymns From The Rig Veda Set 1
*CCU
SATB,pno/orch GALAXY 1.5089.1
$1.25, ipr   (H364)

Choral Hymns From The Rig Veda Set 2
*CCU
SSA,orch/pno GALAXY 1.5090.1 $1.25
(H365)

Choral Hymns From The Rig Veda Set 3
*CCU
SSA,pno/harp GALAXY 1.5091.1 $1.25
(H366)

Drinking Song
TTBB oct BOOSEY 5927 $.40 see from
Six Choruses For Male Voices
(H367)

First Choral Symphony *Op.41
SATB,S solo,3fl,3ob,3clar,3bsn,
4horn,3trp,3trom,tuba,timp,perc,
2harp,org,strings, glockenspiel,
xylophone, celeste voc sc NOVELLO
rental   (H368)

I Love Thee
SATB GALAXY 1.5082.1 $.35   (H369)

In Youth Is Pleasure
SATB STAINER 3.0582.1 $.30   (H370)

King Estmere *Op.17
SATB,2fl,2ob,2clar,2bsn,4horn,2trp,
3trom,timp,perc,harp,strings voc
sc NOVELLO rental   (H371)

Love Song, A
TB oct BOOSEY 5926 $.40 see from
Six Choruses For Male Voices
(H372)

Ode To Death *Op.38
SATB,2fl,3ob,2clar,2bsn,4horn,2trp,
3trom,timp,harp,org,strings,
celeste voc sc NOVELLO rental
(H373)
SATB,orch NOVELLO study sc s.p.,
voc sc s.p.   (H374)

Pastoral
SSA GALAXY 1.5084.1 $.30   (H375)

Seven Part-Songs *CC7U
wom cor,strings NOVELLO sc s.p.,
voc sc s.p.   (H376)

Six Choruses For Male Voices *see
Before Sleep; Drinking Song; Love
Song, A   (H377)

Terly Terlow
SATB,ob/vcl GALAXY 1.5081.1 $.40
(H378)

This Have I Done For My True Love
SATB GALAXY 1.5080.1 $.50   (H379)

Two Eastern Pictures *CC2U
SA,harp/pno GALAXY 1.5078.1 $.50
(H380)

HOLT
One Of Those Songs (composed with
Calvi) *pop
SATB BELWIN UC 735 $.40   (H381)
(Calvi) SSA BELWIN UC 702 $.40
(H382)
(Calvi) SATB BELWIN UC 701 $.40
(H383)
(Calvi) SA/TB BELWIN UC 717 $.40
(H384)

HOLUBICE see Blazek, Zdenek

HOLZL, PETER
Sudtiroler Lied: Heiliges Land Im
Gebirge
men cor,acap TONOS 5808 s.p. (H385)

HOMBE *folk,Afr
(Ekwueme) SATB SCHIRM.G LG51807 $.45
(H386)

HOME see Blazek, Zdenek, Domov

HOME see Vlach-Vruticky, Josef, Domove

HOME FOR THE HOLIDAYS see Allen

HOME, SWEET HOME see Bishop

HOMECOMING QUEEN
SATB CIMINO $.40   (H387)

HOMEWARD BOUND see Simon, Paul

HOMEWARD WITH A SONG see Noble, Harold

HOMO SAPIENS NO. 2 see Feher, Andras

HONEYBAGS, THE see Peaslee, Richard

HONOURS TO THE WORKING CLASS see
Harapat, Jindrich, Cest Pracujicim

HOP-POLKA see Smetana, Bedrich

HOPE IS THE THING WITH FEATHERS see
Rasely

HOPLOPOIA see Ruiter, Wim de

HOR, ANGELA! see Gotthardt, Peter

HOR, LIEBCHEN *folk,Ger
(Burthel, Jakob) men cor,acap TONOS
2051 s.p.   (H388)

HORACKE BALADY PRO DETSKY SBOR see
Istvan, Miloslav

HORAH NITSACHON see Kessler, Minuetta

HORCH, DIE GLOCKE RUFT see Kling,
Klang, Klockan Slar

HORCH, DIE WELLEN *folk,Russ
(Fischer, Otto) men cor,acap
TONOS 319 s.p.   (H389)

HORCH, WAS KOMMT VON DRAUSSEN REIN? see
Braun, Horst-Heinrich

HORCH, WAS KOMMT VON DRAUSSEN REIN? see
Lang, Hans

HORCH, WAS KOMMT VON DRAUSSEN REIN see
Linke, Norbert

HORCH, WIE UBERS WASSER HALLEND see
Ketterer, Ernst

HORE HU! see Rajter, Ludovit

HORE ICH GITARRENKLANG *folk,Russ
(Erbelding, Dietrich) men cor,acap
sc,cor pts TONOS 454 s.p.   (H390)

HORKY, KAREL (1909-   )
Cesky Sen *cant
"Czech Dream, The" [Czech] mix cor,
3fl,3ob,3clar,3bsn,4horn,3trp,
3trom,tuba,timp,perc,harp,strings
CZECH s.p.   (H391)

Czech Dream, The *see Cesky Sen

HORLER, ERNST
Fur Klein Und Gross
1-4pt mix cor,pno PELIKAN PE329
s.p.   (H392)

HOROVITZ, JOSEPH
Horrortorio
mix cor,SATB soli,orch voc sc
NOVELLO s.p., ipr   (H393)

HORRORTORIO see Horovitz, Joseph

HORSKE MACESKY see Ceremuga, Josef

HORSLEY, WILLIAM (1774-1858)
See The Chariot *madrigal
(Young, Percy M.) [Eng] SATB,acap
oct BROUDE BR. $.50   (H394)

HORT DER GLASER KLING UND KLANG see
Fischer, Theo

HORTICULTURAL WIFE, THE see Hutchinsons

HORTON
Weep You No More, Sad Fountains
TTBB oct SCHMITT 3028 $.35   (H395)

HORTON, JOHN
Old Mountain Tunes From Sweden *CCU,
Swed
[Eng/Swed] unis jr cor,S rec,A rec,
T rec (easy) sc SCHOTTS
ED. 10 967 s.p.   (H396)

HOSEA! see Powell, Robert

HOSKINS, WILLIAM
Commencement Processional Hymn, A
SATB,pno/org AM.COMP.AL. $.55
(H397)

Jacksonville University Processional
SATB,org,fl,clar,2trp,2trom,2tuba,
perc, 2 saxophones, baritone horn
AM.COMP.AL.   (H398)

HOSPODA see Barta, Lubor

HOSTLOVET see Johansen, Sven-Erik

HOUSE IS NOT A HOME
  SATB CIMINO $.50   (H399)

HOUSE THAT JACK BUILT, THE see
  Wilkinson, Philip G.

HOUSEHOLD MAGIC see Kubik, Gail

HOVHANESS, ALAN (1911-   )
  My Sorrow Is My Love *Op.258
    [Eng] SATB,acap RONGWEN $.35 see
      from Three Madrigals   (H400)

  Pencil Of The Holy Ghost, The
    *Op.258
    [Eng] SATB,acap RONGWEN $.30 see
      from Three Madrigals   (H401)

  Rose Tree Blossoms, A *Op.246,No.4
    SSATBB,opt org PETERS P66515 (H402)

  They All Laugh *Op.258
    [Eng] SATB,acap RONGWEN $.35 see
      from Three Madrigals   (H403)

  Though Night Is Dark
    SATB,acap BELWIN OCT 2313 $.30
                                (H404)
  Three Madrigals *see My Sorrow Is My
    Love, Op.258; Pencil Of The Holy
    Ghost, The, Op.258; They All
    Laugh, Op.258   (H405)

HOVOR MI TISKO see Nemeth-Samorinsky,
  Stefan

HOW BEAUTIFUL IS NIGHT see Kunz, Alfred

HOW CAN I KEEP FROM SINGING see Coates

HOW COME see Murray

HOW COME? see Sherman, Richard M.

HOW GOOD IT IS
  (Goldman) SATB SCHIRM.G LG51821 $.50
                                (H406)

HOW LIKE A BRIEF DAY OUR LIFE PASSES
  see Lechner, Leonhard, Che Piu D'un
  Giorno

HOW MANY SUNS see Valek, Jiri, Kolik
  Slunicek

HOW REVOLTING! see Hagemann, P.

HOW SHOULD I YOUR TRUE LOVE KNOW see
  Bush, Geoffrey

HOW TO FLATTER A RAVEN see Jeffries

HOWELLS, HERBERT NORMAN (1892-   )
  Kent Yeoman's Wooing Song, A
    SATB,SBar soli,2fl,pic,2ob,2clar,
    2bsn,4horn,3trp,3trom,tuba,timp,
    perc,pno,harp,strings, celeste
    voc sc NOVELLO rental   (H407)

HRUSOVSKY, IVAN (1927-   )
  Biela Breza, Sestra Moja *cant
    wom cor SLOV.HUD.FOND s.p.   (H408)

  Hirosima *cant
    mix cor,narrator,orch SLOV.HUD.FOND
    s.p.   (H409)

  Sen Nesmrtelny
    see Tri Madrigalove Impresie

  Sen O Cloveku *cant
    mix cor,S&narrator,orch
    SLOV.HUD.FOND s.p.   (H410)

  Sen O Dialke
    see Tri Madrigalove Impresie

  Sen O Hlase
    see Tri Madrigalove Impresie

  Tri Madrigalove Impresie
    mix cor SLOV.HUD.FOND s.p.
    contains: Sen Nesmrtelny; Sen O
      Dialke; Sen O Hlase   (H411)

HUBER, KLAUS (1924-   )
  Hiob 19
    SATB,horn,trp,trom,3vcl,bvl,perc
    (diff) sc SCHOTTS rental, ipr
                                (H412)

  . . . Inwendig Voller Figur
    mix cor,soli,5fl,4ob,4clar,4bsn,
    4horn,5trp,5trom,4tuba,10vla,
    8bvl,2harp,perc,4timp,electronic
    tape (diff) min sc SCHOTTS AV 312
    s.p., sc SCHOTTS rental, ipr
                                (H413)

HUDBA see Zeljenka, Ilja

HUDSON
  Understanding
    (Burden, James) SATB CHARTER
    CO30204   (H414)
    (Burden, James) SSA CHARTER CO30209
                                (H415)

HUFEISEN UND ROSEN "BAUERNKNECHT, NUN
  PACK DEN GROSSEN WAGEN AN" see
  Bresgen, Cesar

HUFF, LEON
  Love Train *see Gamble, Kenny

HUGHES
  Tambourines To Glory (composed with
    Moore) *sac/sec
    SATB,acap WARNER WB-321 187 $.35
                                (H416)
  When Susanna Jones Wears Red
    (composed with Undine)
    (Moore) SATB WARNER CH0795 $.35
                                (H417)

HUM FAULER LENZ "ES WOLLT EINE FRAU ZUM
  WEINE GAHN" see Bresgen, Cesar

HUMORITATEN see Gebhard, Ludwig

HUMULUS LUPULUS see Heun, Hans

HUNNICUTT, JUDY
  Song Of Christmas, A *Xmas,anti
    1-2pt,inst (easy) FISCHER,C CM 7881
    $.35   (H418)

HUNSRUCKLIED see Desch, Rudolf

HUNSRUCKLIED see Drath, Walter

HUNT, FRANK
  Stay In Touch With The World
    (composed with Mac Gillivary,
    John; Simon, Norman)
    (Simon, W.) SAB BIG3 $.50   (H419)
    (Simon, W.) SA/TB BIG3 $.50 (H420)
    (Simon, W.) SSA BIG3 $.50   (H421)
    (Simon, W.) SATB BIG3 $.50   (H422)

HUNT, REGINALD (1891-   )
  O Good Ale
    cor,inst ASHDOWN SGMS.10   (H423)

HUNTER
  Encore, Three Temperance Songs *CC3U
    TTBB MARKS MC 4603 $.35   (H424)

HUNTER, THE see Jenkins, C.J.

HUNTER IN HIS CAREER, THE see Grainger,
  Percy Aldridge

HUNTER'S HORN, THE see Busch, Carl

HUNTER'S SONG see Distler, Hugo,
  Jagerlied

HUNTING OF THE SNARK, THE see Boyd,
  Jeanne

HUNTING SONG see Butler

HUNTING SONG see Mendelssohn-Bartholdy,
  Felix

HUNTLEY, FRED H.
  Protest, A
    TTBB,acap (med) FITZSIMONS 4014
    $.20   (H425)

  Robin's Egg, The
    TTBB,acap (med) FITZSIMONS 4015
    $.20   (H426)

HUNTSMEN, THE see Emeleus, John

HURD, MICHAEL (1928-   )
  Charms And Ceremonies
    unis&SS&opt A,strings voc sc
    NOVELLO rental   (H427)

  Flower Songs *CCU
    SA/SSA,strings/pno NOVELLO s.p.
                                (H428)

  Hip-Hip Horatio *ora/pop
    cor,T solo,pno voc sc NOVELLO s.p.
                                (H429)

  Music's Praise
    SATB,strings voc sc NOVELLO rental
                                (H430)

  Song For St.Cecilia
    SATB,2fl,ob,2clar,bsn,2horn,2trp,
    timp,perc,strings voc sc NOVELLO
    rental   (H431)
    SATB,2fl,ob,2clar,bsn,2horn,3trp,
    trom,tuba,timp,perc,pno,
    xylophone, glockenspiel voc sc
    NOVELLO rental   (H432)

HURNIK, ILJA (1922-   )
  Eskymacka Ukolebavka
    "Eskymo Lullaby" [Czech] mix cor,
    acap CZECH s.p.   (H433)

  Eskymo Lullaby *see Eskymacka
    Ukolebavka

HURNIK, ILJA (cont'd.)
  Maryka *cant
    [Czech/Ger] mix cor,S solo,2fl,2ob,
    2clar,2bsn,4horn,2trp,3trom,timp,
    perc,harp,pno,strings PANTON s.p.
                                (H434)

  Pisnicky O Zviratech *CCU
    [Czech] wom cor,fl,bsn,horn,trp,vln
    CZECH s.p.   (H435)

  Three Daughters *see Tri Dcery

  Tri Dcery
    "Three Daughters" [Czech] mix cor,
    acap CZECH s.p.   (H436)

HURRY MARTHA see Lora, Antonio

HURT SO BAD
  SSA CIMINO $.40   (H437)

HURTS SO BAD
  TTBB CIMINO $.40   (H438)

HUSZONEGY KORUSDAL see Balazs, Arpad

HUTCHENS, F.
  Paddy's Market
    3pt ALLANS 848   (H439)

HUTCHERSON, RITA
  Night Will Never Stay, The
    SATB,acap (med) FITZSIMONS 1078
    $.20   (H440)

HUTCHESON, FRANCIS (1721-1780)
  Return, Return, My Lovely Maid
    *madrigal
    (Young, Percy M.) [Eng] SSTB,acap
    oct BROUDE BR. $.50   (H441)

HUTCHINSONS
  Horticultural Wife, The
    (Smith) SATB SCHIRM.G 12018 $.45
                                (H442)

HUTH, GUSTAV (1902-1968)
  Beloved Of Seven Robbers *see Mila
    Sedmi Loupezniku

  Hill "Jested", The *see Jested

  Jested
    "Hill "Jested", The" [Czech] mix
    cor,acap CZECH s.p.   (H443)

  King Lavra *see Kral Lavra

  Kral Lavra *cant/folk
    "King Lavra" [Czech] mix cor,soli,
    2fl,2ob,2clar,2bsn,3horn,2trp,
    2trom,timp,perc,strings CZECH
    s.p.   (H444)

  Mila Sedmi Loupezniku *cant
    "Beloved Of Seven Robbers" [Czech]
    mix cor,3 soli,3fl,2ob,2clar,
    2bsn,4horn,2trp,3trom,tuba,timp,
    perc,harp,strings CZECH s.p.
                                (H445)

  Nas Zivot *cant
    "Our Life" [Czech] cor,2fl,2ob,
    2clar,2bsn,3horn,trp,trom,timp,
    perc,strings CZECH s.p.   (H446)

  Our Life *see Nas Zivot

  Tri Zenske Sbory *CC3U
    [Czech] wom cor,2fl,2ob,2clar,2bsn,
    2horn,strings CZECH s.p.   (H447)

HUTSCHI HEILI
  (Reiter, Albert) treb cor DOBLINGER
  O 345 s.p. see from Sechs
  Osterreichische Volkslieder (H448)

HVA VILDE KAN see Kvam, Oddvar S.

HVEM EIER --? see Kvam, Oddvar S.

HVIEZDA SEVERU see Ferenczy, Oto

HYBLER, JINDRICH (1891-1966)
  Me Vlasti *cant
    "My Country" [Czech] mix cor,soli,
    2fl,2ob,2clar,2bsn,4horn,3trp,
    3trom,tuba,timp,perc,2harp,
    strings CZECH s.p.   (H449)

  My Country *see Me Vlasti

HYDE, HERBERT E.
  Quest Of The Queer Prince, The *cant
    SA,inst FITZSIMONS cor pts $.75, sc
    ipr   (H450)

HYMN see Zimmer, Jan

HYMN FOR SCHOLARS AND PUPILS see
  Thompson, Randall

HYMN OF CZECH PEASANTS see Dvorak,
  Antonin, Rolnicka

HYMN OF FREEDOM see Butler, Eugene

HYMN OF PEACE
(Kent, Ada Twohey) SATB (med)
WATERLOO $.30   (H451)

HYMN TO THE MORNING see Wagner, Richard

HYMN TO THE NIGHT see Wood, Joseph

HYMNE see Jacob, Dom Clement

HYMNE see Schubert, Franz (Peter)

HYMNE AN DAS LIED see Edler, Robert

HYMNE AN DAS MEER see Herrmann, Hugo

HYMNE AN DEUTSCHLAND (LAND DES
GLAUBENS, DEUTSCHES LAND) see
Grabner, Hermann

HYMNE AN DEUTSCHLAND "LAND DES
GLAUBENS, DEUTSCHES LAND" see
Reutter, Hermann

HYMNE AN DIE KUNST see Lorenz

HYMNE AN DIE MUSIK "AUS TONEN BAUST DU
EINE NEUE WELT" see Foltz, Karl

HYMNE AN FRAU MUSICA "WAS MAG DOCH
DIESE WELT" see Herrmann, Hugo

HYMNE AUF DEN KRAICHGAU see Edler,
Robert

HYMNEN DER NATIONEN *CCU
(Czernik, W.) 4pt mix cor ZIMMER.
1310 s.p.   (H452)

HYMNUS see Dvorak, Antonin

HYMNUS see Gauss, Otto

I

I AM COME INTO MY GARDEN see Billings,
William

I AM THE ROSE OF SHARON see Billings,
William

I AM WOMAN see Burton, Ray

I BALCONI DELLA ROSA see Dallapiccola,
Luigi

I BELIEVE IN SUNSHINE see Miller

I CAN HELP see Swan, Billy

I CAN SEE CLEARLY NOW see Nash, Johnny

I CAN'T BELIEVE I'M LOSING YOU
SSA CIMINO $.40   (I1)
TTBB CIMINO $.40   (I2)
SATB CIMINO $.40   (I3)

I CANTI DEI TROVATORI see Korte,
Oldrich Frantisek, Trobadorske
Zpevy

I CARRY YOUR HEART see Mathew

I CHARGE YOU, O YE DAUGHTERS OF
JERUSALEM see Billings, William

I DO NOT LIKE THEE, DR. FELL see
Nelhybel, Vaclav

I DREAM OF JEANIE see Foster, Stephen

I DYED MY PETTICOAT RED
(Johnston, Richard A.) SSA (med diff)
WATERLOO $.35   (I4)

I ENJOY BEING A GIRL see Rodgers,
Richard

I FALCIATORI see Gatti, C.

I FEEL LOVE see Box

I FORARSSOL see Mostad, Jon

I GAVE HER CAKES see Purcell, Henry

I GAVE MY LOVE A CHERRY *folk
(McCarthy, John) SATB,opt gtr&bvl&
drums MCAFEE M1087 $.40   (I5)

I GOT A NAME see Fox, Charles

I GOT A ROBE
(Biebl, Franz) treb cor DOBLINGER
O 314 s.p. see from Acht Spirituals
                                  (I6)

I HAB A HERZELE *folk
(Edler, Rudolf) men cor,acap TONOS 40
s.p.   (I7)

I HAB A SCHONS HAUS *folk,Ger
(Eisenbart, Karl M.) men cor,acap
TONOS 63 s.p.   (I8)

I HAD A DREAM see Alter, Louis

I HAVE A DREAM see Heilner, Irwin

I HAVE A DREAM see Reed, Phyllis
Luidens

I HAVE A NEW GARDEN see Searle,
Humphrey

I HAVE LOST ALL THAT ONCE I WAS see
Crawford, John, Plus Ne Suis Ce Qui
J'ai Ete

I HEARD THE BELLS ON CHRISTMAS DAY see
Marks, John

I HONESTLY LOVE YOU see Allen, Peter

I JUST WANTED TO TALK TO YOU see Shaw,
Kirby

I KNOW A FAIR MAIDEN see Lassus, Roland
de (Orlandus), Ich Waiss Mir Ein
Miedlein

I KNOW A LOVELY ROSE see Distler, Hugo

I KNOW WHERE I'M GOIN'
(Hall, Wm.D.) SA,pno,fl NATIONAL
WHC-1 $.40   (I9)

I LIKE THE SOUND OF AMERICA see Price,
Florence B.

I LOVE AMERICA *Fest
(Boyce; Wilhousky) cor (med) FISCHER,
C CM 7850 $.40   (I10)

I LOVE MY LADY see Zonn, Paul

I LOVE MY LOVE IN THE MORNING *folk,Ir
(Olden, G. Ronald C.) SATB (med)
FITZSIMONS 1044 $.25   (I11)

I LOVE SNOW see Sanders

I LOVE THEE see Holst, Gustav

I LOVE YOU see Stiby, Tue, Jar Alskar
Dig

I LOVE YOU SO see Mana-Zucca, Mme.

I MUST GO BACK TO THE SOUTH see
Miessner, W. Otto

I NATTENS MIDTE see Gabold, Ingolf

I NEED NOT YOUR NEEDLES see Foster

I NEVER SAW A MOOR see Monaco, Richard
A.

I PART FROM YOU WITH SORROW see
Hassler, Hans Leo, Ich Scheid Von
Dir Mit Leide

I PLEDGE ALLEGIANCE TO THE FLAG see
Green, Dorothy M.

I SAW LOVELY PHILLIS see Pearsall,
Robert Lucas de

I SAW THREE SHIPS
see Eight Christmas Carols, Set 2

I SEE THE MOON
(Osborne, Chester G.) SSAA,acap
(easy) oct ELKAN-V 362-01329 $.35
                                  (I12)

I SEE YOU PASSING see Shaw, Kirby

I SEE YOU THROUGH THE WINDOW
(Johnston, Richard A.) SA (med diff)
WATERLOO $.35   (I13)

I SEE YOU THROUGH THE WINDOW see
Johnston, Richard

I SHALL NOT DIE FOR THEE see Maw

I SHALL SING see Morrison

I SING OF A MAIDEN see Castelnuovo-
Tedesco, Mario

I SING OF A MAIDEN see MacMillan,
Ernest Campbell

I STILL BELIEVE IN TOMORROW see Wild

I, THE RED BLOSSOM see Vycpalek,
Ladislav, Cerveny Kvet Ja

I THOUGHT THAT LOVE HAD BEEN A BOY see
Byrd, William

I VAR TID see Hellden, Daniel

I WALK A STRANGER ON THIS LAND see
Wood, Dale

I WANNA BE THERE see Dedrick, C.

I WANT A GIRL
SSA CIMINO $.40   (I14)
SATB CIMINO $.40   (I15)
TTBB CIMINO $.40   (I16)
TTBB (Barbershop Arrangement) CIMINO
$.40   (I17)

I WANT TO BE FREE see Staton, Merrill

I WANT TO HOLD YOUR HAND see Lennon,
John

I WANT TO TALK TO YOU see Sutton, Nancy

I WANT YOU FOR CHRISTMAS see Schroeder

I WHISTLE A HAPPY TUNE see Rodgers,
Richard

I WILL GIVE MY LOVE AN APPLE see Marx,
Karl, Nimm, Liebste, Diesen Apfel

I WILL GIVE MY LOVE AN APPLE see Zoll,
Paul

I WILL NEVER PASS THIS WAY AGAIN see
Gaylord, Ronnie

I WILL WAIT FOR YOU
SSA CIMINO $.40   (I18)
SA CIMINO $.40   (I19)
SAB CIMINO $.40   (I20)
TTBB CIMINO $.40   (I21)

I WILL WALK WITH MY LOVE
(Deale, Edgar) SATB (easy) WATERLOO
$.50   (I22)

I WOASS NET
   (Reiter, Albert) treb cor (contains
   also: Da Drob'n Auf'n Berg)
   DOBLINGER O 341-342 s.p. see from
   Sechs Osterreichische Volkslieder
                                    (I23)

I WONDER WHEN I SHALL BE MARRIED *folk
   (Nelson, Havelock) SSA,pno ROBERTON
   75037 s.p.   (I24)

I WON'T LAST A DAY WITHOUT YOU see
   Nichols, Roger

IBERISCHES LIEDERSPIEL see Zoll, Paul

IBERT, JACQUES (1890-1962)
   A Kis Zebu Bolcsodala
   wom cor BUDAPEST 6798 s.p.   (I25)

ICH ARMES MAIDLEIN KLAG MICH SEHR see
   Baumann, Max

ICH ARMES MAIDLEIN KLAG MICH SEHR see
   Pepping, Ernst

ICH BIN DEIN *folk
   (Doppelbauer, J. F.) [Ger] 4pt men
   cor MERSEBURG EM9025 s.p.   (I26)

ICH BIN DURCH LIEBE see Papandopulo,
   Boris

ICH BIN SCHON SIEBENHUNDERT JAHR see
   Haas, Joseph

ICH FAHR DAHIN see Brahms, Johannes

ICH FAHR DAHIN see Fussan, Werner

ICH GING EMOL SPAZIERE see Biebl, Franz

ICH GING VORUBER see Zoll, Paul

ICH HAB MEIN SACH see Zelter, Carl
   Friedrich

ICH HAB MEIN SACH AUF NICHTS GESTELLT
   see Lang, Hans

ICH HAB MIR EINEN GARTEN GEPLANZET see
   Desch, Rudolf

ICH HAB' NICHTS ANZUZIEHN see Fischer,
   Ernst

ICH HABE DEN FRUHLING GESEHEN *folk,
   Ger
   (Hermanns, Willy) men cor,acap TONOS
   224 s.p.   (I27)

ICH HABE MEIN FEINSLIEBCHEN see Lang,
   Hans

ICH HALTE DICH IM HERZEN FEST see Jag
   Unnar Dig Anda Allt Gott

ICH HORE HORNER BLASEN see Rettich,
   Wilhelm

ICH HORT EIN SICHLEIN RAUSCHEN see
   Ketterer, Ernst

ICH HORT EIN SICHLEIN RAUSCHEN see
   Trunk, Richard

ICH KOMM VON ALABAMA *folk,US
   (Rosenstengel, Albrecht) men cor,opt
   pno,opt gtr,opt perc TONOS 461 s.p.
                                    (I28)

ICH LAG EINST UNTE LINDEN see Michels,
   Josef

ICH LEB UND WEISS NIT WIE LANG see
   Pepping, Ernst

ICH LEBE MEIN LEBEN see Buchtger, Fritz

ICH LIEBTE EINST EIN MADCHEN *folk,Ger
   (Schneider, Walther) men cor,acap
   TONOS 96 s.p.   (I29)

ICH REIT AUF EINEM ROSSELEIN see Edler,
   Robert

ICH SAG ADE *folk
   (Desch, R.) [Ger] 4pt men cor
   MERSEBURG EM9081 s.p.   (I30)
   (Desch, R.) [Ger] 4pt mix cor
   MERSEBURG EM9251 s.p.   (I31)

ICH SAG ADE see Anonymous

ICH SAG ADE see Strohbach, Siegfried,
   Ik Zeg Adieu

ICH SAH IM OLIVENWALDE see Biebl, Franz

ICH SAH MIR EINEN BLAUEN STORCHEN see
   Pepping, Ernst

ICH SCHEID VON DIR MIT LEIDE see
   Hassler, Hans Leo

ICH SEH DICH VOR DEM FENSTER see
   Strohbach, Siegfried, Eg Ser Deg
   Utfor Gluggen

ICH SEH IN EINEM GARTEN see Jeep,
   Johann

ICH SINGE WIEDER, WENN ES TAGT "DIE
   ZWEIFLER SAGEN" see Krenek, Ernst

ICH SPRING IN DIESEM RINGE see Lang,
   Hans

ICH TRAG EIN GOLDNES RINGELEIN *folk,
   Ger
   (Jung, Max) men cor,acap TONOS 56
   s.p.   (I32)

ICH TRAG EIN GOLDNES RINGELEIN see
   Zipp, Friedrich

ICH WAISS MIR EIN MIEDLEIN see Lassus,
   Roland de (Orlandus)

ICH WEISS EIN ALTES SCHENKENHAUS see
   Bachmann, Alfred

ICH WEISS EIN JAGER, DER BLAST SEIN
   HORN see Zoll, Paul

ICH WEISS EINEN LINDENBAUM see Thehos,
   Adam

ICH WEISS EINEN LINDENBAUM STEHEN
   (Kuhlenthal, Fred) SSAA/TTBB CARUS
   CV 40.210 s.p. contains also: O
   Tannenbaum (SSA/TTB); Die
   Steirische Roas (SSAA/TTBB);
   Draussa Em Wald (SSAA/TTBB)   (I33)

ICH WEISS, WO ROTE ROSEN STEHN see
   Silcher, Friedrich

ICH WILL TRUREN FAHREN LAN see Genzmer,
   Harald

ICH WILL TRUREN FAHREN LAN see Poos,
   Heinrich

ICH WILL TRUREN VAREN LAN see Werdin,
   Eberhard

ICH WOLLT, DASS ICH DAHEIME WAR see
   Rein, Walter

ICH WOLLT ZU LAND AUSREISEN see Beck,
   Conrad

ICIKE-PICIKE see Bartok, Bela

ICIRI-PICIRI see Kosa, Gyorgy

I'D RATHER BE A COWBOY (LADY'S CHAINS)
   see Denver, John

IDENTITY see Mathew

IF I CAN HELP SOMEBODY see Androzzo,
   Alma Bazel

IF I CAN STOP ONE HEART FROM BREAKING
   see Berger

IF I COULD see El Condor Pasa

IF I HAD A RIBBON BOW
   (De Cormier) SA SCHIRM.G LG51756 $.30
                                    (I34)

IF I HAD WINGS TO FLY *folk,Ger
   (Brown, F.E.) 2pt ALLANS 831   (I35)
   (Brown, F.E.) 3pt ALLANS 835   (I36)

IF I LOVED YOU
   SAB CIMINO $.40   (I37)
   SA CIMINO $.40   (I38)
   SSA CIMINO $.40   (I39)
   TTBB CIMINO $.40   (I40)
   SATB CIMINO $.40   (I41)

IF I SHOULD LEARN see Cohen

IF I'M DREAMING
   TTBB CIMINO $.40   (I42)

IF IN THE WORLD THERE BE MORE WOE see
   Russell, Welford

IF LOVE, LIKE SPRING, CAN COME AND GO
   see Weil

IF THE GOOD LORD ONLY LETS YOU LOVE ME
   see Shuman

IF THE HEART OF A MAN
   see Four Songs From "The Beggar's
   Opera"

IF THE WORLD COULD ONLY BE HAPPY! see
   Besig

IF THERE'S A SONG see Ydstie

IF WE DON'T MAKE IT WORK, WHO WILL? see
   Red, Buryl

IF WE ONLY HAVE LOVE see Brel, Jacques

IF YOU'RE HAPPY NOTIFY YOUR FACE see
   Paxton

IF YOU'VE GOT THE TIME see Backer, Bill

IF'N I WAS GOD see Sherman, Richard M.

IGNORANT, THE see Bohac, Josef,
   Nevedomi

IGRA RIJECI see Devcic, Natko

IHR MEINT, DAS LEBEN SEI KURZ see
   Wildberger, Jacques

IHR MUSICI, FRISCH AUF! see Hassler,
   Hans Leo

IHR SEID UNSER see Krietsch, Georg

IHRKE, WALTER
   Wind Is Tapping, The
   SSA (med) FITZSIMONS 3070 $.20
                                    (I43)

IK ZEG ADIEU see Clemens, Jacobus

IK ZEG ADIEU see Strohbach, Siegfried

IL BALLO DELLA VENEZIANA see Pratella,
   Francesco Balilla, E' Bal D' La
   Viniziena

IL BELL' HUMORE see Gastoldi, Giovanni
   Giacomo

IL BIANCO E DOLCE CIGNO see Arcadelt,
   Jacob

IL BIANCO E DOLCE CIGNO see Vecchi,
   Orazio

IL BRIVIDO see Bossi, Marco Enrico

IL CIECO see Bossi, Marco Enrico

IL CORO DEGLI ZITTI see Dallapiccola,
   Luigi

IL CORO DEI LANZI BRIACHI (EPILOGO) see
   Dallapiccola, Luigi

IL DAMONE see Stradella, Alessandro

IL EST BEL ET BON see Passereau

IL N'EST FILLE D'ESPAGNE see Blanchard,
   Roger

IL PAPAVERO see Dallapiccola, Luigi

IL PRIMO LIBRO DE MADRIGALI see
   Monteverdi, Claudio

"IL PRINCIPE", QUOTATIONS FROM "THE
   RULER" OF N. MACHIAVELLI see
   Andriessen, Louis

IL SETTIMO LIBRO DE MADRIGALI BOOK I
   see Marenzio, Luca

IL SETTIMO LIBRO DE MADRIGALI BOOK II
   see Marenzio, Luca

IL SETTIMO LIBRO DE MADRIGALI BOOK III
   see Marenzio, Luca

IL SOLDATO PRIGIONIERO see Pratella,
   Francesco Balilla

IL TRESCONE see Pratella, Francesco
   Balilla, E Triscon

IL ZABAIONE MUSICALE see Banchieri,
   Adriano

ILE COME TO THEE IN ALL THOSE SHAPES
   see Binkerd, Gordon

I'LL ALWAYS REMEMBER see Elgar

I'LL BE ON THE ROAD AGAIN
   (Chasson; Stecher; Horowitz; Gordon)
   SATB oct SCHMITT 1206 $.35   (I44)

I'LL BE SEEING YOU
   SSA oct CHAPPELL W655512-353 $.40
                                    (I45)
   TTBB oct CHAPPELL W65512-355 $.40
                                    (I46)
   SATB oct CHAPPELL W655512-357 $.40
                                    (I47)

I'LL HAVE TO SAY I LOVE YOU IN A SONG
   see Croce, Jim

I'LL NEVER SMILE AGAIN see Lowe, R.

I'LL REMEMBER APRIL see Raye

I'LL TAKE ROMANCE
   mix cor CHAPPELL W659027-361 $.40
                                    (I48)

ILLO, MARIA
   Revolution Come The Spring *CC16U
   unis,gtr GALLIARD 2.2026.7 $2.50
                                    (I49)

ILLUMINATIONS see Gerber, Steven

J

J.A. COMENIUS' TESTAMENT see Macha,
Otmar

JA, CHARLIE IST MEIN LIEBLING *folk
(Biebl, F.) [Ger] 4pt mix cor
MERSEBURG EM9224 s.p.   (J1)

JA JEDNORUKY JOZEF JASO see Kardos,
Dezider

JA NOCH EINMAL see Martinu, Bohuslav,
Esce Jednu

JA SOM BACA VELMI STARY see Kafenda,
Frico

JA, WENN DER JAGER IN DEN WALD HINEIN
GEHT see Linke, Norbert

JABBERWOCKY see Carter, J.

JABBERWOCKY see Pottle, Sam

JABLONE see Mikula, Zdenko

JACK IN THE PULPIT see Lester, William

JACK WAS EVERY INCH A SAILOR
(Johnston, Richard A.) TTBB (med
diff) WATERLOO $.50   (J2)

JACKIE AND BRIDIES SONG BOOK, BOOK 1
*CCU
(Mc Donald, J.; Mc Donald, Bridie)
cor GALLIARD 2.2030.7 $1.75   (J3)

JACKIE AND BRIDIES SONG BOOK, BOOK 2
*CCU
(Mc Donald, J.; Mc Donald, Bridie)
cor GALLIARD 2.2027.7 $1.75   (J4)

JACKSON
Tangents V
SATB SHAWNEE A1277 $.35   (J5)

JACKSONVILLE UNIVERSITY PROCESSIONAL
see Hoskins, William

JACOB, DOM CLEMENT
Hymne
3 eq voices,acap JOBERT cor pts
s.p., sc s.p.   (J6)

JACOB, GORDON (1895-   )
Nun's Priest Tale, The
SATB,SATB soli,2fl,pic,2ob,2clar,
2bsn,4horn,2trp,3trom,tuba,timp,
perc,strings, xylophone,
glockenspiel voc sc NOVELLO
rental   (J7)

Under The Greenwood Tree
SSA STAINER 3.0825.1 $.40   (J8)

Winter Rain
SSA STAINER 3.0828.1 $.50   (J9)

JACOT, ANDRE (1906-   )
Tag Des Kindes
jr cor,vln,vln/fl sc,cor pts
PELIKAN PE737 s.p.   (J10)

JAG UNNAR DIG ANDA ALLT GOTT (from
Cvjy) folk
"Ich Halte Dich Im Herzen Fest" [Ger/
Swed] 4pt wom cor,acap BREITKOPF-W
CHB 4941 s.p.   (J11)

JAGDGLUCK: ES RITT EIN JAGER see
Silcher, Friedrich

JAGDLIED see Mendelssohn-Bartholdy,
Felix

JAGE, ROLF-DIETHER (1927-   )
Alle Vogel Sind Schon Da
see Fruhlingslieder-Potpourri

Der Mai Ist Gekommen
see Fruhlingslieder-Potpourri

Der Winter Ist Vergangen
see Fruhlingslieder-Potpourri

Es Tonen Die Lieder
see Fruhlingslieder-Potpourri

Fruhlingslieder-Potpourri
mix cor,pno,bvl,gtr,perc (med easy)
sc,cor pts SCHOTTS ED. 6091 s.p.
contains: Alle Vogel Sind Schon
Da; Der Mai Ist Gekommen; Der
Winter Ist Vergangen; Es Tonen
Die Lieder; Kuckuck Ruft's Aus
Dem Wald; Wie Schon Bluht Uns
Der Maien   (J12)

JAGE, ROLF-DIETHER (cont'd.)

Keinen Tropfen Im Becher Mehr
see Trinklieder-Potpourri

Kuckuck Ruft's Aus Dem Wald
see Fruhlingslieder-Potpourri

Lustig Ihr Bruder
see Trinklieder-Potpourri

Lustig Ist Das Zigeunerleben
see Trinklieder-Potpourri

Trinklieder-Potpourri
men cor,pno/pno&bvl&gtr&perc sc,cor
pts SCHOTTS ED. 6092 s.p.; ipa
contains: Keinen Tropfen Im
Becher Mehr; Lustig Ihr Bruder;
Lustig Ist Das Zigeunerleben;
Wenn Alle Brunnlein Fliessen;
Wohlauf Noch Getrunken   (J13)

Wenn Alle Brunnlein Fliessen
see Trinklieder-Potpourri

Wie Schon Bluht Uns Der Maien
see Fruhlingslieder-Potpourri

Wohlauf Noch Getrunken
see Trinklieder-Potpourri

JAGEN, HETZEN UND FEDERSPIEL see
Lechner, Leonhard

JAGERCHOR see Weber, Carl Maria von

JAGERCHOR: DIE TALE DAMPFEN see Weber,
Carl Maria von

JAGERCHOR "WAS GLEICHT WOHL AUF ERDEN"
see Weber, Carl Maria von

JAGERLIED see Distler, Hugo

JAGERLIED see Kanetscheider, Artur

JAGERLIED "AUF, IHR WILDEN MANNER" see
Rein, Walter

JAGERLIED: ES STIESS EIN JUNGER JAGER
see Silcher, Friedrich

JAGERLIED "ZIERLICH IST DES VOGELS
TRITT IM SCHNEE" see Schroeder,
Hermann

JAGGER, MICK
Angie (composed with Richard) *pop
(Sanford) SATB,opt perc WARNER
WB-332 187 $.75   (J14)

JAHR, DEIN HAUPT NEIG! see Zipp,
Friedrich

JAHRAUS-JAHREIN see Pepping, Ernst

JAHREIN-JAHRAUS see Haus, Karl

JAHRESZEITEN-KANTATE see Zentner,
Johannes

JAHRESZEITENLIEDER see Furer, Arthur

J'AI PRIS LA CLEF DE MON JARDIN *folk,
Fr
(Blanchard, R.) 4pt mix cor,acap
JOBERT s.p.   (J15)

J'AI VU LE LOUP *folk,Fr
(Blanchard, R.) 4pt mix cor,acap
JOBERT s.p.   (J16)

JAK JE MNE see Martinu, Bohuslav

JAKES
Four Winds (composed with Martin)
*Xmas
SATB MCAFEE M1054 $.35   (J17)

JALKAISIN SAIN KULKEA see Tuominen,
Harri

JAMAICAN DONKEY see Sanfilippo

JAMAIS EN MONDE N'AURAI see
Crecquillon, Thomas

JAMES, WILL (1896-   )
Roadways
TTBB (easy) FITZSIMONS 4063 $.25
                              (J18)
Who's That Tapping At My Door?
SSA (easy) FITZSIMONS 3073 $.25
                              (J19)
SATB (easy) FITZSIMONS 1072 $.25
                              (J20)
TTBB (easy) FITZSIMONS 4051 $.25
                              (J21)

JANACEK, KAREL (1903-   )
Joy And Work *see Radost A Prace

Radost A Prace
"Joy And Work" [Czech] jr cor,
3winds CZECH s.p.   (J22)

JANACEK, LEOS (1854-1928)
Festive Chorus
[Czech/Ger] mix cor,soli,acap
SUPRAPHON s.p.   (J23)

Octenas
mix cor,pno/harp SUPRAPHON s.p.
                              (J24)

There Upon The Mountains *cant
[Czech] men cor,3fl,3ob,2clar,2bsn,
4horn,timp,perc,harp,strings
SUPRAPHON s.p.   (J25)

JANE see Coppier

JANKOVIC, SLAVKO (1897-1971)
Slavonian Dirge
cor CROATICA   (J26)

JANNEQUIN, CLEMENT (ca. 1475-ca. 1560)
Battle Of Marignan, The *see La
Guerre

Ce Mois De May
(Contino, Fiora) "This Month Of
May" SATB,acap DEAN CA-106 $.45
                              (J27)

Je Ne Fus Jamais Si Aise
SSAB,acap EGTVED KB212 s.p.   (J28)

La Guerre
"Battle Of Marignan, The" [Fr/Eng]
SATB,acap SALABERT-US $2.50 (J29)

This Month Of May *see Ce Mois De
May

JANOS SPIELT see Stein, F.R.

JANSE
Sad The Day, Long The Night
SATB oct SCHMITT 1806 $.45   (J30)

JANSEN, PETER
Ein Kleines Lied
men cor,acap TONOS 3726 s.p. (J31)

JANSSEN, DANNY
Keep On Singing *see Hart, Bobby

JAPANISCHES ABENDLIED see
Mittergradnegger, Gunther

JAPANISCHES MADCHENLIED "DIE ERDE
GLANZT" see Sturmer, Bruno

JAPO, MAMO HOTE GLEDET see Lucic,
Franjo

JAR see Moyzes, Alexander

JAR ALSKAR DIG see Stiby, Tue

JARGON see Billings, William

JARNA see Holoubek, Ladislav

JARNI NOC see Foerster, Josef Bohuslav

JARNI POPEVKY see Eben, Petr

JARNI ZVESTOVANI see Zahradnik, Zdenek

JASCHA LIEBT KATJUSCHKA *folk,Russ
(Seib, Valentin) men cor,acap TONOS
2045 s.p.   (J32)

JASCHA SPIELT AUF *folk
(Heinrichs, W.) [Ger] 4pt mix cor
MERSEBURG EM9255 s.p.   (J33)
(Heinrichs, W.) [Ger] 4pt men cor
MERSEBURG EM9029 s.p.   (J34)

JATEK see Bartok, Bela

J'AY LE REBOURS see Certon, Pierre

JDEM A JDEM A NIC NAS NEZASTAVI see
Drejsl, Radim

JE HOHER DER KIRCHTURM see Burkhart,
Franz

JE KRASNA, ZEME MA see Chlubna, Oswald

JE ME COMPLAINS DE MON AMY see Des
Prez, Josquin

JE NE FUS JAMAIS SI AISE see Jannequin,
Clement

JE SAIS BIEN QUELQUE CHOSE
(McCauley, William) SSA (med easy)
WATERLOO $.50   (J35)

JEANNIE WITH THE LIGHT BROWN HAIR
see Drei Amerikanische Volkslieder

JEDE BITTERSTE NOT see Zoll, Paul

JEDE SCHONHEIT, GELIEBTE see
Palestrina, Giovanni

JEEP, JOHANN (1581-1644)
Frohlich Fangt Alle An Zu Singen
(from Studentgartlein)
SSAT,acap MOSELER MOR46 s.p.
contains also: Nur Ein Figur Hat
Die Natur   (J36)

Ich Seh In Einem Garten
(Weber, W.) men cor,acap TONOS 3324
s.p.   (J37)

Musika, Die Ganz Liebliche Kunst
(Oppel, Hans) men cor,acap TONOS
3323 s.p.   (J38)

Nur Ein Figur Hat Die Natur (from
Studentgartlein)
see Jeep, Johann, Frohlich Fangt
Alle An Zu Singen

JEFFRIES
Come, Quickly Death (composed with
Fisher)
unis,pno/gtr MCAFEE M167 $.35 (J39)

Doctor And The Patient, The (composed
with Fisher)
unis,pno/gtr MCAFEE M171 $.35 (J40)

Double Or Nothing (composed with
Fisher)
unis,pno/gtr MCAFEE M168 $.35 (J41)

Grasshopper And The Ant, The
(composed with Fisher)
unis,pno,gtr MCAFEE M174 $.35 (J42)

How To Flatter A Raven (composed with
Fisher)
unis,pno,gtr MCAFEE M164 $.35 (J43)

Little Red Fox, The (composed with
Fisher)
unis,pno,gtr MCAFEE M170 $.35 (J44)

Mis-Matched (composed with Fisher)
SATB,pno MCAFEE M148 $.40   (J45)

Nobody's Ever Satisfied (composed
with Fisher)
unis,pno,gtr MCAFEE M172 $.35 (J46)

Peppermint Fugue (composed with
McAfee, Don)
SATB MCAFEE M1058 $.45   (J47)

Putting It Off (composed with Fisher)
unis,pno,gtr MCAFEE M173 $.35 (J48)

Tell Me, Nightingale (composed with
Fisher)
unis,pno,gtr MCAFEE M165 $.30 (J49)

Tortoise And The Hare, The (composed
with Fisher)
unis,pno,opt gtr&bvl&drums MCAFEE
M175 $.35   (J50)

Tournament Galop *see Gottschalk,
Louis Moreau

Where It's At (composed with Fisher)
unis,pno,gtr MCAFEE M166 $.30 (J51)

JELINEK, HANNS (1901-1969)
Canone Nuptiale *Marriage,canon
mix cor,acap MODERN s.p.   (J52)

JELMOLI, HANS (1877-1936)
Belle Je Ne L'suis Pas
wom cor,acap HENN 447 s.p.   (J53)

JEN DAL see Kalas, Julius

JEN DAL see Zrno, Felix

JENKINS, C.
Old King Cole
SA LESLIE 2024 $.30   (J54)

Summer Is Icumen In
SSAA LESLIE 3041 $.30   (J55)

JENKINS, C.J.
Bringing Us In Good Ale
ALLANS 840 see from Three Feasting
Songs   (J56)

Content, Not Cates
ALLANS 840 see from Three Feasting
Songs   (J57)

Cradle Song
2pt ALLANS 836   (J58)

Hunter, The
2pt ALLANS 837   (J59)

Let Every Man Be Jolly
ALLANS 840 see from Three Feasting
Songs   (J60)

Three Feasting Songs *see Bringing
Us In Good Ale; Content; Let Every
Man Be Jolly
Cates; Let Every Man Be Jolly
(J61)

JENKINS, MARSHAL
"Perfect Man", The
SATB PARAGON 1001 $.25   (J62)

JENNI
Death Be Not Proud.
SATB AMP A-701 $.40   (J63)

Early Spring
SATB AMP A-711 $.40   (J64)

JENNI, DONALD
Axis
SATB,2horn,2trp,trom,2perc,pno sc
AM.COMP.AL. $6.60   (J65)

JENNY KISSED ME see Mechem, Kirke

JENSEITS DES GRUNEN MEERES see Reda,
Siegfried

JENSEITS DES TALES STANDEN IHRE ZEIT
see Zoll, Paul

J'ENTENDS LE MOULIN
(Ridout, Godfrey) SATB (med diff)
WATERLOO $.40   (J66)

JEPPESEN, KNUD (1892-1974)
Blow, Blow, Thou Winter Wind
see Four Shakespeare Songs

Four Shakespeare Songs
SATB,acap cmplt ed EGTVED KB229
s.p.
contains: Blow, Blow, Thou Winter
Wind; Spring; Under The
Greenwood Tree; Winter (J67)

Spring
see Four Shakespeare Songs

Under The Greenwood Tree
see Four Shakespeare Songs

Winter
see Four Shakespeare Songs

JEREMIAS, BOHUSLAV (1859-1918)
Arise, All Slavs *see Hej Slovane

Cesky Prapor *Op.23
"Czech Flag, The" [Czech] mix cor,
3fl,2ob,2clar,2bsn,4horn,2trp,
3trom,tuba,timp,strings CZECH
s.p.   (J68)

Czech Flag, The *see Cesky Prapor

Hej Slovane
"Arise, All Slavs" [Czech] men cor,
2fl,2ob,2clar,bsn,4horn,2trp,
3trom,tuba,timp,strings CZECH
s.p.   (J69)

JEREMIAS, OTAKAR (1892-1962)
Pisen O Rodne Zemi *cant
"Song Of The Native Land" [Czech]
mix cor,SBar soli,3fl,3ob,3clar,
3bsn,6horn,4trp,3trom,tuba,timp,
perc,2harp,pno,org,strings,
celeste CZECH s.p.   (J70)

Song Of The Native Land *see Pisen O
Rodne Zemi

JERGENSON, DALE
Bric-A-Bach
SATB SCHIRM.G 2978 $1.50   (J71)

JEROME
Singing A Happy Song *see Randl

JEROME KERN MEDLEY see Kern, Jerome

JESEN LESY PREFUKUJE see Rosinsky,
Jozef

JESENSKE NOCI see Slavenski, Josip

JESSIE MUNRO
(Johnston, Richard A.) SSA (easy)
WATERLOO $.35   (J72)

JESTED see Huth, Gustav

JESUS ON THE WATERSIDE *sac/sec,spir
(Aschenbrenner, Walter) TTTTBBBB,acap
(med) FITZSIMONS 4044 $.25   (J73)

JETZT FANGT DAS NEUE FRUHJAHR AN see
Rische, Quirin

JETZT FANGT DAS SCHONE FRUHJAHR AN see
Werdin, Eberhard

JETZT KOMMEN DIE LUSTIGE TAGE see Marx,
Karl

JETZT KOMMEN DIE LUSTIGEN TAGE see
Marx, Karl

JETZT KOMMT DIE FROHLICHE SOMMERZEIT
see Marx, Karl

JETZT KOMMT DIE FROHLICHE SOMMERZEIT
see Zipp, Friedrich

JETZT KOMMT DIE FROLICHE SOMMERZEIT see
Becker, Peter

JETZT KOMMT DIE ZEIT, DASS ICH WANDERN
MUSS see Desch, Rudolf

JETZT REISEN WIR ZUM TOR HINAUS see
Michels, Josef

JETZT SCHWINGEN WIR see Schneider,
Walther

JETZT SCHWINGEN WIR DEN HUT see
Schneider, Walther

JETZT SINGT DER TOD see Edler, Robert

JETZT WOLL'MER see Haas, Joseph

JEUX see Massis, Amable

JEWELL, KENNETH W.
Leavetaking
SATB,S solo,acap FISCHER,J
FEC 10113 $.30   (J74)

JEWISH CEMETERY AT NEWPORT, THE see
Heilner, Irwin

JEWISH LEGEND, THE see Bugatch, Samuel

JINDRICH, JINDRICH (1876-1967)
Ceske Pisni
(Devaty, A.) "Czech Song, The"
[Czech] mix cor,2fl,2ob,2clar,
2bsn,4horn,2trp,3trom,tuba,timp,
harp,strings CZECH s.p.   (J75)

Czech Song, The *see Ceske Pisni

JINGLE-BELL ROCK see Beal, Joe

JINGLE BELLS *folk
(Biebl, F.) [Ger] 4pt mix cor
MERSEBURG EM9237 s.p.   (J76)

JINGLE BELLS see Frank, Marcel
[Gustave]

JINGLE BELLS FANTASY *CCU
SATB CIMINO $1.00   (J77)

JIRA, MILAN (1935-   )
Pet Mardigalu *CC5U,madrigal
[Czech] mix cor,acap CZECH s.p.
(J78)

JIRASEK, IVO (1920-   )
Laska *cant
"Love" [Czech] wom cor,SB soli,fl,
ob,clar,bsn,horn,trp,trom,timp,
perc,pno,bvl CZECH s.p.   (J79)

Love *see Laska

Rikadla *CCU
[Czech] jr cor,5winds,perc CZECH
s.p. nursery rhymes   (J80)

JIRKO, IVO (1926-   )
Zpevy Stare Ciny *CCU
[Czech] mix cor,acap CZECH s.p.
(J81)

JOACHIM UTI BABYLON see Bellman, Carl
Mikael

JOBIM, ANTONIO CARLOS
Girl From Ipanema *pop
(Gimbel; De Moraes) SATB BELWIN
UC 684 $.40   (J82)
(Gimbel; De Moraes) SSA BELWIN
UC 685 $.40   (J83)

Meditation
(Gimbel; Mendonca) SATB BELWIN
UC 683 $.40   (J84)
(Gimbel; Mendonca) SSA BELWIN
UC 682 $.40   (J85)

JODE, FRITZ
Die Musikantenfibel *CCU
jr cor (easy) sc SCHOTTS B 109 s.p.
(J86)

JODLER "TAAR I NOD E BITZELI" see
Cossetto, Emil

JOEL, BILLY
Piano Man *pop
(Nowak, Jerry) SATB,pno oct BIG
BELL $.50   (J87)

JOHANSEN, SVEN-ERIK
Atta Reglor Ur Bondepractican *CC8L
4pt mix cor ERIKS 51 s.p.   (J88)

Backen
3pt mix cor ERIKS 306 s.p. see also
Manniska Pa Jorden   (J89)

Blabaret
3pt mix cor ERIKS 305 s.p. see also
Manniska Pa Jorden   (J90)

JOHANSEN, SVEN-ERIK (cont'd.)

Dubbelkanon Vid Kraftskiva *canon
4pt mix cor ERIKS 325 s.p.   (J91)

En Broder Mer
3pt mix cor ERIKS 74 s.p.   (J92)

Fodelsedagsvisa
men cor ERIKS 326 s.p.   (J93)

Fryra Lektioner
3-4pt mix cor ERIKS 50 s.p.
    contains: Historia; Kemi;
    Sockerkakan; Varldens Stader
                                    (J94)

Historia
see Fryra Lektioner

Hostlovet
4pt mix cor ERIKS 307 s.p. see also
    Manniska Pa Jorden   (J95)

Kemi
see Fryra Lektioner

Madrigal
mix cor GEHRMANS KRB457   (J96)

Manniska Pa Jorden
4pt mix cor ERIKS
    contains & see also: Backen;
    Blabaret; Hostlovet; Manniskan
    Pa Jorden; Regndroppen;
    Snoflingen; Tanken; Vita
    Flingor   (J97)

Manniskan Pa Jorden
3pt mix cor ERIKS 304 s.p. see also
    Manniska Pa Jorden   (J98)

Regndroppen
4pt mix cor ERIKS 308 s.p. see also
    Manniska Pa Jorden   (J99)

Snabbt Jagar Stormen Vara Ar (from
Psaltare Och Lyra)
4pt mix cor ERIKS 344 s.p.   (J100)

Snapsvisa
men cor ERIKS 327 s.p.   (J101)

Snoflingen
3pt mix cor ERIKS 309 s.p. see also
    Manniska Pa Jorden   (J102)

Sockerkakan
see Fryra Lektioner

Tanken
4pt mix cor ERIKS 310 s.p. see also
    Manniska Pa Jorden   (J103)

Varldens Stader
see Fryra Lektioner

Visa Vid Brollopsmiddan
men cor ERIKS 328 s.p.   (J104)

Vita Flingor
4pt mix cor ERIKS 311 s.p. see also
    Manniska Pa Jorden   (J105)

JOHANSSON, BENGT (1914-   )
Venus And Adonis: Epilogue *madrigal
[Eng] mix cor,acap FAZER 46 s.p.
                                    (J106)
Venus And Adonis: Fourth Encounter
*madrigal
[Eng] mix cor,acap FAZER 45 s.p.
                                    (J107)
Venus And Adonis: Third Encounter
*madrigal
[Eng] mix cor,acap FAZER 44 s.p.
                                    (J108)

JOHN
Don't Let The Sun Go Down On Me *pop
(Taupin) SATB BELWIN TTC 101 $.40
                                    (J109)

JOHN BROWN'S BODY see Bergmann, Walter

JOHN, ELTON
Daniel (composed with Taupin) *pop
SATB,opt perc WARNER WB-310 187
$.40   (J110)

Goodbye Yellow Brick Road *pop
(Taupin) WARNER WB-343 187 $.50
                                    (J111)

JOHN GILPIN see Waddington, Sidney
Peine

JOHN HENRY *folk
(Miller, Carl) 2pt CHAPPELL
0063040-351 $.40   (J112)

JOHN PEEL *folk
(Kracke, H.) [Ger] 4pt mix cor
MERSEBURG EM9225 s.p.   (J113)
(Weber, Bernhard) [Ger] 4pt men cor
MERSEBURG EM9017 s.p.   (J114)

JOHN SHAFT see Hayes, Isaac

JOHNNY JOHN see Putz, Eduard

JOHNNY, JOHNNY, JOHN see Schaefers,
Anton

JOHNS, SIDNEY
Sea Gypsy, The
TTBB (easy) FITZSIMONS 4058 $.20
                                    (J115)

JOHNSON
Five Chinese Proverbs *CC5U
SSA MARKS MC 4613 $.50   (J116)

Resurrection Of Feng-Huang, The
SATB,S solo,acap (diff) OXFORD
56.597 $4.00   (J117)

Why Not You? (Give Away)
SATB BENSON S4370 $.40   (J118)

JOHNSON, D.
Prayer For America, A
SATB oct SCHMITT 5912 $.50   (J119)

JOHNSON, DERRIC
We Pledge Allegiance
SATB (various tapes and recording
also available) BENSON B0984
$1.00   (J120)

What Price Freedom?
SSAATTBB,orch (accompaniment tape
and 5-screen multi-slide
presentation available) BENSON
S4387 $1.00, ipa   (J121)

JOHNSON, G.
Letters To Santa Claus
SATB MARKS MC 4625 $.50   (J122)

JOHNSON, HOWARD
What Do You Want To Make Those Eyes
At Me For? (from Irene) (composed
with McCarthy, Joe; Monaco, James
V.)
(Simon, W.) SATB BIG3 $.45   (J123)
(Simon, W.) TTBB BIG3 $.45   (J124)

JOHNSTON, RICHARD
Canada Is Singing
SATB,orch WATERLOO $.50, ipr (J125)

Face Of The Night
SATB (med diff) WATERLOO $.60
                                    (J126)

I See You Through The Window
SATB (med diff) WATERLOO $.40
                                    (J127)

Nocturne
SATB (med diff) WATERLOO $.35
                                    (J128)

Owl And The Pussy-Cat
unis (med easy) WATERLOO $.30
                                    (J129)

JOLLY PLOUGHBOY, THE see Broadwood,
L.E.

JOLLY SWAGMAN, THE see Binge

JON A TAVASZ see Lorand, Istvan

JONAH AND THE WHALE see Foster

JONAH AND THE WHALE see Pottle, Sam

JONES
Hideaway Place (composed with Albitz)
*CC3U
(Drake, Jim) SATB TRIGON TGO 105
$1.25   (J130)

I'm Nobody
SATB WALTON 2984 $.45   (J131)

New Tomorrows (composed with Albitz)
*CC3U
(Drake, Jim) SATB TRIGON TGO 106
$1.25   (J132)

JONES, DANIEL (1912-   )
Country Beyond The Stars, The *cant
SATB,2fl,pic,2ob,2clar,2bsn,4horn,
2trp,3trom,timp,perc,strings,
glockenspiel voc sc NOVELLO
rental   (J133)

JONES, ROBERT
First Set Of Madrigals (1607) EM Vol.
35a *CC16L,madrigal
3-6pt mix cor STAINER 3.1935.1
$10.25   (J134)

JONES, ROBERT GOMER
Song Of The North Wind
SAATB,S solo (med) FITZSIMONS 1020
$.30   (J135)

JONES, THAD
Child Is Born, A *see Wilder

JONGEN, LEON (1885-   )
Deux Fables De Jean De La Fontaine
wom cor/jr cor,pno BROGNEAUX cor
pts s.p., voc sc s.p.
contains: Le Loup Et L'Agneau;
L'Huitre Et Les Plaideurs

JONGEN, LEON (cont'd.)
                                    (J136)
La Grenouille Qui Veut Se Faire Aussi
Grosse Que Le Boeuf
see Six Fables De La Fontaine

La Laitiere Et Le Pot Au Lait
see Six Fables De La Fontaine

Le Chat, La Belette Et Le Petit Lapin
see Six Fables De La Fontaine

Le Corbeau Et Le Renard
see Six Fables De La Fontaine

Le Loup Et L'Agneau
see Deux Fables De Jean De La
Fontaine
see Six Fables De La Fontaine

L'Huitre Et Les Plaideurs
see Deux Fables De Jean De La
Fontaine
see Six Fables De La Fontaine

Six Fables De La Fontaine
wom cor/jr cor cor pts,voc sc,sc
BROGNEAUX ipr
contains: La Grenouille Qui Veut
Se Faire Aussi Grosse Que Le
Boeuf; La Laitiere Et Le Pot Au
Lait; Le Chat, La Belette Et Le
Petit Lapin; Le Corbeau Et Le
Renard; Le Loup Et L'Agneau;
L'Huitre Et Les Plaideurs
                                    (J137)

JONI MITCHELL MEDLEY see Mitchell, John

JOPLIN, SCOTT (1868-1917)
Entertainer, The
see BARBERSHOP CHOIR, THE
(Cacavas) SATB BELWIN 64390 $.45
                                    (J138)
(Gladstone, Jerry; Bock, Fred) SA/
TB,pno (easy) oct GENTRY G-276
$.50   (J139)
(Roberts, D.L.) SATB,pno FOX
XCX 300 $.35   (J140)

Entertainers, The *sac/sec
(Frackenpohl) SA/TB SHAWNEE E148
$.35   (J141)
(Frackenpohl) SATB SHAWNEE $.35
                                    (J142)

JORDAHL
Songs From Shakespeare
SATB SHAWNEE A1269 $.35   (J143)

JORDAN, ALICE
God's Lark At Morning
SSA,acap (med) FITZSIMONS 3082 $.20
                                    (J144)

JORDAN, HELLMUT
So Nimm Denn Meine Hande
(Silcher, Friedrich) men cor,acap
TONOS 3009 s.p.   (J145)

JOSE, THE TEMPORARY REINDEER see
Eilers, Joyce Elaine

JOSEPHS, WILFRED (1927-   )
So She Went Into The Garden
3 eq voices,pno,opt rec NOVELLO
TRIOS 677 s.p.   (J146)

Songs Of Innocence
SATB&opt jr cor,2fl,2ob,2clar,2bsn,
2horn,2trp,2trom,timp,perc,
strings, xylophone, optional
vibraphone voc sc NOVELLO rental
                                    (J147)

JOSH'A FIT DE BATTLE OB JERICHO *sac/
sec,spir
(Enders, Harvey) TTBB,acap (med)
FITZSIMONS 4057 $.25   (J148)

JOSHUA FIT DE BATTLE OB JERICHO *folk/
spir
(Heinrichs, W.) [Eng] 4pt mix cor
MERSEBURG EM9260 s.p.   (J149)
(Heinrichs, W.) [Eng] 4pt men cor
MERSEBURG EM9092 s.p.   (J150)

JOSHUA FIT DE BATTLE OF JERICO
"Josua Schlug Die Schlacht Von
Jerico" see Spirtuals For All Heft
II

JOSHUA FIT THE BATTLE OF JERICHO see
Ferguson

JOSUA SCHLUG DIE SCHLACHT VON JERICO
see Joshua Fit De Battle Of Jerico

JOUBERT, JOHN (1927-   )
Burghers Of Calais *cant
SATB,SATTBarB soli,fl,ob,clar,bsn,
horn,trp,trom,timp,perc,pno,
strings voc sc NOVELLO rental
                                    (J151)

Choir Invisible, The
SATB,Bar solo,3fl,pic,3ob,3clar,
3bsn,4horn,3trp,3trom,tuba,timp,
perc,pno,harp,org,strings,
xylophone voc sc NOVELLO rental

JOUBERT, JOHN (cont'd.)
(J152)
   Four Stations On The Road To Freedom
   SSAATTBB,acap NOVELLO s.p.   (J153)

JOVO *folk
  (Koringer, Franz) mix cor DOBLINGER
  G 707 s.p. see from Funf Satze Nach
  Kroatischen Volksliedern   (J154)

JOY AND WORK see Janacek, Karel, Radost
  A Prace

JUCHHE, TIROLERBUA
  (Kubizek, Augustin) men cor DOBLINGER
  M 328 s.p.   (J155)

JUCHHEI, DICH MUSS: ICH GING EMOL see
  Silcher, Friedrich

JUGENDFLUCHT see Edler, Robert

JUGOSLAWISCHE HOCHZEITSLIEDER see
  Cossetto, Emil

JUHASZ, FRIGYES
  Ha Majd A Boseg Kosarabol *canon
  (Petofi, Sandor) mix cor BUDAPEST
  6871 s.p.   (J156)

JULIA'S VOICE see Mechem, Kirke

JULY see Washburn

JUMBLIES, THE see Thompson

JUMPIN' JIVE see Calloway

JUNE IS BUSTIN' OUT ALL OVER
  SA CIMINO $.40   (J157)
  SAB CIMINO $.40   (J158)
  SSA CIMINO $.40   (J159)
  TTBB CIMINO $.40   (J160)
  SATB CIMINO $.40   (J161)

JUNE ROSES see Bizet, Georges

JUNG WOLLN WIR SEIN see Seeger, Peter

JUNGE SONNE "UBER SCHNEEBEDECKTE ERDE"
  see Wittmer, Eberhard Ludwig

JUNGE TSCHAPAJEWER
  see Singende Jugend Nr. 16

JUNGER BAUM IN MENSCHENHAND see Zipp,
  Friedrich

JUNGER TAMBOUR *folk,Fr
  (Strobl, Otto) men cor,acap TONOS
  2071 s.p.   (J162)

JUNGFER CATHLEEN *folk
  (Weber, Bernhard) [Ger] 4pt men cor
  MERSEBURG EM9018 s.p.   (J163)

JUNGFRAU see Strobl, Otto

JUNGFRAU, DEIN SCHON GESTALT see
  Hassler, Hans Leo

JUNGGESELLEN "FISCHEN, JAGEN,
  VOGELSTELLEN" see Rein, Walter

JUNGGESELLENLIED *folk
  (Haus, K.) [Ger] 4pt men cor
  MERSEBURG EM9031 s.p.   (J164)

JUNGGESELLENLIED "BURSCHE GING INS TAL"
  see Zipp, Friedrich

JUNITAGE see Desch, Rudolf

JUNKER UBERMUT see Kanetscheider, Artur

JUNKMAN, THE see Talmadge, Charles L.

JUROVSKY, SIMON (1912-1963)
  Slovenska *cant
  mix cor,orch sc SLOV.HUD.FOND s.p.
       (J165)

JUST AS THE TIDE WAS FLOWING see
  Vaughan Williams, Ralph

JUST AS YOUR MOTHER WAS
  TTBB (Barbershop Arrangement) CIMINO
  $.40   (J166)

JUST DO YOUR THING see Muccigrosso

JUST FOR TODAY
  SATB CIMINO $.40   (J167)

JUST ONE SONG
  SATB oct CHAPPELL 0097600-357 $.50
       (J168)

JUST SO SONGS see German, Edward

JUST THE WAY YOU ARE
  SSA CIMINO $.40   (J169)
  SATB CIMINO $.40   (J170)
  TTBB CIMINO $.40   (J171)

K

K TRAGICKEMU VYROCI MNIOCHOVA see
  Svobodo, Jiri

KABALEVSKY, DMITRI BORISOVITCH
  (1904-)
  Dal A Voros Csillagrol
  (Sebestyen, Andras; Nadas, Katalin)
  jr cor,pno BUDAPEST 7288 s.p.
       (K1)

KABELAC, MILOSLAV (1908-)
  Love Song *see Milostna

  Milostna *Op.40,No.1
  "Love Song" [Czech] mix cor,3fl,
  2ob,3clar,2bsn,2horn,trp,strings
  CZECH s.p.   (K2)

  We Are Singing *see Zpivame

  Zpivame *Op.43
  "We Are Singing" [Czech] jr cor,pno
  CZECH s.p.   (K3)

KAD SI BILA MALA MARE see Mockl, Franz,
  Als Du Klein Warst, Marietta

KAFENDA, FRICO (1883-1963)
  A Ja Som Z Oravy Debnar
  see Okienko Do Minulosti

  Ja Som Baca Velmi Stary
  see Okienko Do Minulosti

  L'udova Veselica
  see Okienko Do Minulosti

  Okienko Do Minulosti
  men cor SLOV.HUD.FOND s.p.
   contains: A Ja Som Z Oravy
   Debnar; Ja Som Baca Velmi
   Stary; L'udova Veselica   (K4)

  Tri Muzske Zbory *CC3U
  men cor SLOV.HUD.FOND s.p.   (K5)

KAHN, ERICH ITOR (1905-1956)
  Rhapsodie Hassidique
  TTBB,acap AM.COMP.AL. $6.60   (K6)

  Three Madrigals *CC3U,madrigal
  SATB,acap AM.COMP.AL. $6.60   (K7)

  Vocalise
  5pt,acap AM.COMP.AL. $2.75   (K8)

KAHN, GUS (1886-1941)
  Yes Sir, That's My Baby *see
  Donaldson, Walter

KAIHAN, M.
  Now Is The Hour (composed with Scott;
  Stewart) *pop
  SATB BELWIN UC 731 $.40   (K9)
  SA/TB BELWIN UC 730 $.40   (K10)

KAISERSTUHL-LIED see Philipp, Franz

KALANZI
  Farewell Song, The
  SA/TB MCAFEE M8005 $.40   (K11)

  Potato Song, The
  SA/TB MCAFEE M8006 $.35   (K12)

KALAS, JULIUS (1902-1967)
  Forwards *see Jen Dal

  Jen Dal *Op.70, cant
  "Forwards" [Czech] mix cor,2fl,2ob,
  2clar,2bsn,4horn,3trp,3trom,tuba,
  timp,perc,strings CZECH s.p.
       (K13)
  Song About The Land Of Bohemia *see
  Zpev O Zemi Ceske

  Zpev O Zemi Ceske
  "Song About The Land Of Bohemia"
  [Czech] mix cor,3fl,3ob,3clar,
  3bsn,4horn,3trp,3trom,tuba,timp,
  perc,harp,strings, celeste CZECH
  s.p.   (K14)

KALCIC, JOSIP (1912-)
  Nokturno
  mix cor,pno,org,gtr,perc MUSIC INFO
  rental   (K15)

KALEENKA
  (Goldman) SATB SCHIRM.G LG 51713 $.40
       (K16)

KALENDERSPRUCH see Ketterer, Ernst

KALINKA
  (Pitfield) TTBB,inst (easy) OXFORD
  85.016 $.45, ipa, ipr   (K17)

KALJINKA *folk,Russ
  (Becker, Hans-Gunther) men cor,acap/
  pno 2062 s.p.   (K18)
  (Schmid, Alfons) men cor,acap TONOS
  2008 s.p.   (K19)

KAM, DENNIS
  Most Of The Time
  mix cor MEDIA 6121   (K20)

KANAK, ZDENEK (1910-)
  Delnikova Ruka
  "Labourer's Hand, The" [Czech] cor,
  acap CZECH s.p.   (K21)

  Labourer's Hand, The *see Delnikova
  Ruka

  Ladeni
  jr cor SLOV.HUD.FOND EZS 7 s.p.
       (K22)

KANATA O KOMUNISTICKE STRANE see
  Tausinger, Jan

KANETSCHEIDER, ARTUR
  All Mein Gedanken
  men cor,acap TONOS 87 s.p.   (K23)

  Auf Der Gartenbank
  men cor,acap TONOS 3906 s.p.   (K24)

  Auf Der Luneburger Heide
  men cor,acap TONOS 812 s.p.   (K25)

  Bruder Liederlich
  men cor,acap TONOS 3922 s.p.   (K26)

  Es Kommt Ein Heimlich Freuen
  men cor,acap TONOS 815 s.p.   (K27)

  Fein Sein, Beinander Bleibn
  men cor,acap TONOS 805 s.p.   (K28)

  Gar Lieblich Hat Sich Gesellet
  men cor,acap TONOS 88 s.p.   (K29)

  Jagerlied
  men cor,acap TONOS 806 s.p.   (K30)

  Junker Ubermut
  men cor,acap TONOS 3921 s.p.   (K31)

  O Landle, Du Mi Hoamatland
  men cor,acap TONOS 5811 s.p.   (K32)

  Unsere Berge
  men cor,acap TONOS 5805 s.p.   (K33)

  Unsere Heimat
  men cor,acap TONOS 5812 s.p.   (K34)

KANGAROO SAT ON AN OAK, A see Fleming,
  R.

KANON see Asriel, Andre

KANON see Bartok, Bela, Meghalok
  Csurgoert

KANON "MUSICA DIVINAS LAUDES" see
  Hindemith, Paul

KANSAS CITY see Rodgers, Richard

KANTATA NA PAMET ROKU 1918 see Zelinka,
  Jan Evangelista

KANTATE see Maler, Wilhelm

KANTATE DER FREUNDSCHAFT see Kurzbach,
  Paul

KANTATE NO. 2 see Sutermeister,
  Heinrich

KANTATE VOM FROHLICHEN MUSIKANTEN see
  Lang, Hans

KANTATE VON DER UNRUHE DES MENSCHEN see
  Bresgen, Cesar

KANTATE ZUM ERNTEFEST see Klein,
  Richard Rudolf

KANTATE ZUM RICHTFEST see Beckerath,
  Alfred von

KAPLAN
  Harmony
  (Ades) TTBB SHAWNEE C236 $.40 (K35)
  (Ades) SA/TB SHAWNEE E141 $.40
       (K36)
  (Ades) SAB SHAWNEE D181 $.40 (K37)

  Harmony *see Simon

KAPR, JAN (1914-)
  Pisen Rodne Zemi *cant
  "Song To The Native Land" [Czech]
  mix cor,3fl,2ob,2clar,3bsn,4horn,
  3trp,3trom,tuba,timp,perc,pno,
  strings CZECH s.p.   (K38)

  Sny A Plany *CCU
  [Czech] mix cor,acap CZECH s.p. (K39)

KAPR, JAN (cont'd.)

Song To The Native Land *see Pisen
Rodne Zemi

Symphony No. 7 "Region Of Childhood"
[Czech] jr cor,3fl,ob,3clar,4horn,
3trp,3trom,tuba,timp,perc,2harp,
strings, cimbalon CZECH s.p.
(K40)

KARAI, JOZSEF
Csodalkozas
(Jozsef, Attila) mix cor BUDAPEST
7119 s.p.   (K41)

Neha Ugy Erzem
mix cor BUDAPEST 7317 s.p.   (K42)

Rog A Roghoz
(Jozsef, Attila) men cor BUDAPEST
7316 s.p.   (K43)

Szabadsag, Szallj Kozenk
(Rossa, Erno) eq voices BUDAPEST
7393 s.p.   (K44)

KARDOS, DEZIDER (1914-   )
Ja Jednoruky Jozef Jaso
see MUZSKE ZBORY II

Mierova Kantata *cant
mix cor,Bar solo,orch SLOV.HUD.FOND
s.p.   (K45)

Pomozeme Slavikovi *CCU
jr cor,pno SLOV.HUD.FOND s.p. (K46)

Pozdrav Velkej Zemi *cant
mix cor,S solo,orch SLOV.HUD.FOND
s.p.   (K47)

3pev O Laske
wom cor SLOV.HUD.FOND s.p.   (K48)

KARJANKUTSU
"Cow Call" see Tyttoset

KARKOSCHKA, ERHARD (1923-   )
Eine Suite Vom Wind *CC9L
SSAATBB,S solo,acap (diff) sc
SCHOTTS rental   (K49)

KARL UND ROSA, ODER LOB DER PARTEI see
Schwaen, Kurt

KARLEN, ROBERT (1923-   )
All Dark Is Now No More
SATB,opt electronic tape cmplt ed
SCHMITT 668A $7.50   (K50)
SATB oct SCHMITT 668 $.40   (K51)

KARLIN, FRED
Follow, Follow Me (composed with
Kymry, Tylwyth)
(Klimes, Bob) 2pt jr cor STUDIO
V725 $.45   (K52)

KARLINS, M. WILLIAM
Childrens Bedtime Songs *CCU
SATB,acap AM.COMP.AL. $7.70   (K53)

Three Love Songs *CC3U
men cor,acap AM.COMP.AL. $3.58
(K54)

Three Poems For Chorus *CC3U
SSATBB,acap AM.COMP.AL. $3.85 (K55)

KAROLINCHEN *folk
(Desch, R.) [Ger] 4pt men cor
MERSEBURG EM9069 s.p.   (K56)

KAROLYI, PAL
Incanto
mix cor&mix cor BUDAPEST 7351 s.p.
(K57)

KARPOWITSCH, A.
Kosakisches Wiegenlied *folk,Russ
wom cor ZIMMER. 578 s.p.   (K58)

KASHA, AL
Morning After, The (composed with
Hirschhorn, Joel) *pop
SATB,pno,bvl,perc,gtr oct BIG BELL
$.45   (K59)
SSA,pno,bvl,perc,gtr oct BIG BELL
$.45   (K60)

KASKA see Ocenas, Andrej

KASSMAYER
Der Freischutz Als Theaterzettel
*Op.10
mix cor LIENAU voc sc s.p., cor pts
s.p.   (K61)

KATJUSCHA *Russ
(Karpowitsch, A.) men cor ZIMMER. 591
s.p.   (K62)

KATJUSCHKA see Schertzer, Daniel

KATT, LEOPOLD (1917-1965)
Viele Kunst Kann Der Teufel
see Marx, Karl, Sine Musica Nulla
Vita

KAUFMANN, DIETER (1941-   )
PAX
18pt, requires amplification system
(diff) sc SCHOTTS AV 522LC s.p.
(K63)

KAUZLEIN "ICH ARMES KAUZLEIN" see
Genzmer, Harald

KEBY VSETKY DETI SVETA see Novak, Milan

KECHLEY, [GERALD] (1919-   )
Drop, Slow Tears
SATB,pno/ob&2vln&vcl&hpsd GALAXY
1.2547.1 $.35, ipa   (K64)

KEEL, FREDERICK
Lullaby
(Hales) SSA GALAXY 1.2440.1 $.30
(K65)

KEEP A LITTLE SUNSHINE
TTBB CIMINO $.40   (K66)

KEEP A LITTLE SUNSHINE IN YOUR HEART
SATB CIMINO $.40   (K67)

KEEP IT GAY see Rodgers, Richard

KEEP ON SINGING see Hart, Bobby

KEEP THE BELL OF FREEDOM RINGING
SATB CIMINO $.50   (K68)

KEEPER, THE
(Wetzler, Robert) SATB ART MAST 1002
$.40   (K69)

KEET SEEL see Childs, Barney

KEHR ICH ABENDS HEIM see Hansen, Werner

KEIN FEUER, KEINE KOHLE see Rein,
Walter

KEIN SCHONER LAND see Edler, Robert

KEIN SCHONER LAND see Fischer, Theo

KEIN SCHONER LAND see Lang, Hans

KEIN SCHONER LAND see Zipp, Friedrich

KEIN SCHONER LAND IN DIESER ZEIT see
Kuhlenthal, Fred

KEINEN PFENNIG see Bartok, Bela

KEINEN TROPFEN IM BECHER MEHR see Jage,
Rolf-Diether

KEINER KANN MEINEN KUMMER VERSTEHN see
Nobody Knows De Trouble, I've Seen

KEITH, VIVIAN
Before The Next Teardrop Falls
(composed with Peters, Ben)
(Metis, F.) SSA BIG3 $.45   (K70)
(Metis, F.) SAB BIG3 $.45   (K71)
(Metis, F.) SATB BIG3 $.45   (K72)

KELDORFER
Die Gedanken Sind Frei
see LIEDPROGRAMM DES DEUTSCHEN
SANGERBUNDES FOLGE 3: "ESSENER
LIEDERBLATT" - "CHORFEIER"

KELER, BELA (1820-1882)
Am Schonen Rhein Gedenk' Ich Dein
*Op.83
(Willms, Franz) 4pt men cor,pno/
orch (waltzes) sc SCHOTTS
C 33 500 s.p., voc pt SCHOTTS
C 33 501, 01-02 s.p., ipa   (K73)

Am Schonen Rhein Gedenk' Ich Dein
"Sanft Treibt Der Kahn" *CCU
(Willms, Franz) 4pt mix cor,pno/
orch (med easy) sc SCHOTTS
C 33 647 s.p., voc pt SCHOTTS
C 33 648A-D s.p., ipa   (K74)

KELLEM
Gonna Get Along Without You Now
(Gold) SATB ALFRED 6799 $.50 (K75)
(Gold) SATB/SAB ALFRED 6811 $.50
(K76)

KELLER, WILHELM
Quibus, Quabus *CC45U
jr cor/sr cor,opt inst (easy) sc
SCHOTTS B 124 s.p.   (K77)

KELLERPROBE see Edler, Robert

KELLING, HAJO (1907-   )
Heisse Herzen, Kuhler Wein
men cor,acap TONOS 3995 s.p. (K78)

Im Laube Die Traube
men cor,acap TONOS 3973 s.p. (K79)

Lerche Oder Hahn "Sie Sagt, Ich Konnt
Nicht Singen"
men cor sc SCHOTTS CHBL 149 s.p.
(K80)

O Musica "O Musica, Du Edle Kunst"
men cor sc SCHOTTS CHBL 137 s.p.
(K81)

KELLING, HAJO (cont'd.)

Wie Schon Bluht Uns Der Maien *cant
2-4 eq voices/2-4pt mix cor,fl,
strings sc PELIKAN PE931
s.p., ipa   (K82)

KELLY, BRYAN (1934-   )
Boys In A Pie
2pt treb cor,pno ROBERTON 75042
s.p.   (K83)

Half A Fortnight *CC7U
cor,pno,opt perc NOVELLO sc s.p.,
cor pts s.p., ipa   (K84)

KELTERBORN, RUDOLF (1931-   )
Cantata Profana *cant
mix cor,Bar solo,fl,ob,2clar,bsn,
trp,perc,2vln,vla, bass clarinet
MODERN rental   (K85)

KELTERSPRUCH see Pepping, Ernst

KEMI see Johansen, Sven-Erik

KEMP, WALTER
Latvian Boat Song
SATB (med diff) WATERLOO $.40 (K86)

KENNEDY
Down By The Salley Gardens
TTB oct BOOSEY 5840 $.40   (K87)

Falling Of The Leaves, The
SATB oct BOOSEY 5839 $.40   (K88)

Lizzie Borden
SATB MCAFEE M1050 $.40   (K89)

Look, The Kiss And Joy, The
SSA,acap oct BOOSEY 5819 $.40 (K90)

Travel Notes
2pt,acap (easy) FISCHER,C CM 7885
$.35   (K91)

Two Reflections *CC2U
SSA,acap oct BOOSEY 5811 $.40 (K92)

What A Lovely Day!
1-3pt jr cor,pno,opt vcl,
glockenspiel FISCHER,C CM 7893
$.40   (K93)

KENNEDY, JOHN BRODBIN
Limericks Anon An'On *CC3U
SATB,pno,opt perc (easy) FISCHER,C
CM 7835 $.35   (K94)

One Flower
SATB,pno,opt fl&bvl&perc&gtr (easy)
FISCHER,C CM 7845 $.35   (K95)

Sweet Thoughts Of You
SATB,pno (easy) FISCHER,C CM 7827
$.35   (K96)

KENNT IHR DAS LAND *folk
(Edler, Rudolf) men cor,acap TONOS 99
s.p.   (K97)

KENT
Colonial Spring
"March" SATB SCHIRM.G LG51867 $.30
(K98)

Come, Fill The Cup
SATB SCHIRM.G LG51631 $.35   (K99)

Concord Hymn
SATB,2trp SCHIRM.G LG51701 $.35
(K100)

End Of The World, The (composed with
Dee)
(Lojeski, Ed) SATB LEONARD-US
08213500 $.50   (K101)
(Lojeski, Ed) SSA LEONARD-US
08213502 $.50   (K102)

March *see Colonial Spring

KENT, RICHARD
Afoot And Lighthearted
see Three Whitman Choruses

Listen! I Will Be Honest
see Three Whitman Choruses

Three Whitman Choruses
SATB,acap/inst BELWIN 2317 $.40
contains: Afoot And Lighthearted;
Listen! I Will Be Honest; When
I Heard The Learn'd Astronomer
(K103)
When I Heard The Learn'd Astronomer
see Three Whitman Choruses

KENT, TWOHY A.
When Love's Afar
SSAA,acap HARRIS $.30   (K104)

KENT YEOMAN'S WOOING SONG, A see
Howells, Herbert Norman

KENTUCKY-HEIMAT "DIE SONNE SCHEINT" see
   Old Kentucky Home

KEREMPUH'S SONG see Lhotka-Kalinski,
   Ivo

KERN, JEROME (1885-1945)
   All The Things You Are
      (Gold) SATB/SAB,opt band ALFRED
      6809 $.50   (K105)
      (Gold) SSA/SATB,opt band ALFRED
      6797 $.50   (K106)

   Jerome Kern Medley
      (O'Reilly) SATB/SAB ALFRED 6810
      $.75   (K107)
      (O'Reilly) SATB ALFRED 6798 $.75
                                     (K108)

   Pick Yourself Up (composed with
      Fields)
      (Gold) SATB/SAB ALFRED 6803 $.50
                                     (K109)
      (Gold) SATB ALFRED 6822 $.50   (K110)

KESERVES see Bartok, Bela

KESSLER, MINUETTA
   Horah Nitsachon
      "Victory Hora" [Heb] mix cor
      TRANSCON. TCL 150 $.60   (K111)

   Victory Hora *see Horah Nitsachon

KET KIS KORUS see Kovacs, Matyas

KET KORUSMU see Soproni, Jozsef

KET OLASZ MADRIGAL see Schutz, Heinrich

KET PASZTELLKEP see Balazs, Arpad

KET PETOFI TOREDEK see Ribari, Antal

KETTERER, ERNST
   An Die Rose
      see Zyklus Sommerbilder

   Avegebet
      men cor,acap TONOS 3979 s.p. (K112)

   Der Gartner
      see Zyklus Sommerbilder

   Ein Jager Aus Kurpfalz
      men cor,acap TONOS 64 s.p.   (K113)

   Heimat
      men cor,acap TONOS 3933 s.p. (K114)

   Horch, Wie Ubers Wasser Hallend
      men cor,acap TONOS 2006 s.p. (K115)

   Ich Hort Ein Sichlein Rauschen
      men cor,acap TONOS 54 s.p.   (K116)

   Kalenderspruch
      men cor,acap TONOS 698 s.p.   (K117)

   Mit Lust Tat Ich Ausreiten
      men cor,acap TONOS 70 s.p.   (K118)

   Sommerbild
      see Zyklus Sommerbilder

   Stiller Waldwinkel
      see Zyklus Sommerbilder

   Zyklus Sommerbilder
      men cor,acap cmplt ed TONOS 4090
      s.p.
         contains: An Die Rose; Der
         Gartner; Sommerbild; Stiller
         Waldwinkel   (K119)

KEY, FRANCIS SCOTT (1779-1843)
   Star Spangled Banner, The *anthem
      (Mann, Johnny) SATB LEXICON   (K120)

KIENZL, WILHELM (1857-1941)
   Wanderers Nachtlied *Op.17,No.1
      men cor RIES sc s.p., voc pt s.p.
                                     (K121)

KIESEWETTER, PETER (1945-   )
   Das Deutsche Wunschkonzert
      men cor,TTBB soli,org,2pno,fl,clar,
      horn,trp,trom,2harp,strings,
      4perc, saxophone cor pts ORLANDO
      s.p.   (K122)

   Durch Nacht Zum Licht
      men cor,TTBB soli,org,pno,fl,ob,
      clar,bsn,2horn,2trp,strings,
      4perc, Zither cor pts ORLANDO
      rental   (K123)

KIKELETI NAPKOSZONTO see Balazs, Arpad

KILLING ME SOFTLY WITH HIS SONG see
   Foxx, Charles

KILLMAYER, WILHELM (1927-   )
   Dans La Maison De Douleur
      SSSAAA,acap (diff) sc SCHOTTS
      C 42 182 s.p. see from Sept
      Rondeaux   (K124)

KILLMAYER, WILHELM (cont'd.)
   La Vraie Histoire De Douleur
      SSSAAA,acap (diff) sc SCHOTTS
      C 42 178 s.p. see from Sept
      Rondeaux   (K125)

   Lauda "Amore, Amore Che Si M'hai
      Ferito"
      SSAATTBB,acap/orch (diff) sc
      SCHOTTS C 42 263 s.p., ipr   (K126)

   Le Temps A Laissie Son Manteau
      SSSAAA,acap (diff) sc SCHOTTS
      C 42 181 s.p. see from Sept
      Rondeaux   (K127)

   Le Tourment Cache
      SSSAAA,acap (diff) sc SCHOTTS
      C 42 180 s.p. see from Sept
      Rondeaux   (K128)

   Les Fourriers D'Este Sont Venus
      SSSAAA,acap (diff) sc SCHOTTS
      C 42 179 s.p. see from Sept
      Rondeaux   (K129)

   Les Petits Enfanconnets
      SSSAAA,acap (diff) sc SCHOTTS
      C 42 183 s.p. see from Sept
      Rondeaux   (K130)

   Lieder, Oden Und Szenen *CC9L
      mix cor (diff) sc SCHOTTS ED. 5148
      s.p.   (K131)

   Retour De Melancolie
      SSSAAA,acap (diff) sc SCHOTTS
      C 42 184 s.p. see from Sept
      Rondeaux   (K132)

   Romantische Chorlieder *CC7L
      2-3pt men cor,opt horn sc SCHOTTS
      C 41 644 s.p.   (K133)

   Sept Rondeaux *see Dans La Maison De
      Douleur; La Vraie Histoire De
      Douleur; Le Temps A Laissie Son
      Manteau; Le Tourment Cache; Les
      Fourriers D'Este Sont Venus; Les
      Petits Enfanconnets; Retour De
      Melancolie   (K134)

KIM, ANDY
   Rock Me Gently
      (Metis, F.) SSA BIG3 $.50   (K135)
      (Metis, F.) SATB BIG3 $.50   (K136)
      (Metis, F.) SAB BIG3 $.50   (K137)

KIND OF AN ODE TO DUTY see Cohn, James

KIND OF EXISTENCE, A see Geelen,
   Mathieu

KINDER- UND WEIHNACHTSLIEDER see
   Dieckmann, Johannes

KINDERKUCHE see Weber, Bernhard

KINDERPREDIGT "EIN HUHN UND EIN HAHN"
   see Genzmer, Harald

KINDERREIGEN IM FRUHLING "KOMMT, WIR
   WOLLEN TANZEN" see Knab, Armin

KINDHEIT see Knab, Armin

KING ARTHUR *folk,Eng
   (Whitehead, A.) SSA LESLIE 1002 $.30
                                     (K138)

KING ARTHUR see Ager, Laurence

KING ESTMERE see Holst, Gustav

KING JESUS IS A-LISTENING *sac/sec,
   spir
   (Dawson, William L.) SSA (med)
      FITZSIMONS 3061 $.25   (K139)
   (Dawson, William L.) SATB (med)
      FITZSIMONS 2004 $.25   (K140)
   (Dawson, William L.) TTBB,acap (med)
      FITZSIMONS $.25   (K141)

KING LAVRA see Huth, Gustav, Kral Lavra

KING OLAF see Elgar, Edward

KING STREET PARADE see Kunz, Alfred

KINGDOM, THE see Elgar, Edward

KINYON
   American Heritage, The
      SA,band ALFRED 6815 $.60   (K142)

KIRBYE, GEORGE
   First Set Of Madrigals (1597) EM Vol.
      24 *CC25L,madrigal
      3-6pt mix cor STAINER 3.1924.1
      $13.00   (K143)

   Sorrow Consumes Me
      (Hall, Wm.D.) SSATB,inst NATIONAL
      CMS-105 $.45   (K144)

KIRBYE, GEORGE (cont'd.)
   Sorrow Consumes Me (First Part)
      SSATB STAINER 3.0734.1 $.40   (K145)

   Sweet Love, O Cease Thy Flying
      (Hall, Wm.D.) SSATB,fl&ob&clar&
      horn&bsn/2vln&vla&vcl&bvl,opt
      hpsd NATIONAL CMS-113 $.50   (K146)

KIRCHLEIN MIT MELONENTURM see Klefisch,
   Walter

KIRK
   Deck The Halls
      SATB KJOS 5919 $.35   (K147)

   Four William Blake Songs *CC4U
      SATB PARKS PC808 $.35   (K148)

   Sun Don't Set In The Mornin'
      SATB,acap PRO ART 2758 $.40   (K149)

KIRK, THERON W. (1919-   )
   Lady Who Ran Up A Tree, The
      SATB BOURNE B231028-357 $.50   (K150)

KIRKMAN, TERRY
   Cherish
      (Foust, Alan) SATB STUDIO V711 $.90
      see from Songs Of The Association
                                     (K151)
   Enter The Young
      (Cobine, Al) SATB STUDIO V722 $.45
                                     (K152)
   Everything That Touches You
      (Foust, Alan) SATB STUDIO V711 $.90
      see from Songs Of The Association
                                     (K153)
   Requiem For The Masses
      (Foust, Alan) SATB STUDIO V711 $.90
      see from Songs Of The Association
                                     (K154)
   Songs Of The Association *see
      Cherish; Everything That Touches
      You; Requiem For The Masses
                                     (K155)

KIRMES MUSIK see Schuler, Karl

KIRSCH, WINFRIED
   Bewaffneter Friede
      men cor,acap TONOS 3730-1 s.p.
                                     (K156)
   Es Sitzt Ein Vogel
      men cor,acap TONOS 3730-2 s.p.
                                     (K157)
   Fruher, Da Ich Unerfahren
      men cor,acap TONOS 3730-3 s.p.
                                     (K158)

KIRTENLUST see Schein, Johann Hermann

KISS ME KATE SELECTION *CCU
   CIMINO SSA $.85; SATB $.85   (K159)

KITTREDGE, WALTER
   Tenting On The Old Campground
      (Van Camp, Leonard) TBB FOSTER
      MF1055 $.45   (K160)

KITTRIDGE
   Tenting On The Old Camp Ground
      (Smith) SATB SCHIRM.G 12013 $.40
                                     (K161)

KJERULF, [HALFDAN] (1815-1868)
   Synmove's Song
      2pt ALLANS 830   (K162)

KLAAGSANG UIT "DIE DIEPER REG" see
   Badings, Henk

KLAGE DER ARIADNE see D'Haene, Rafael
   Lodewijk

KLAGE: ICH HABE DEN FRUHLING see
   Silcher, Friedrich

KLAGELICHE NOT see Genzmer, Harald

KLAGELIED see Vecchi, Orazio

KLAGLIED DES BLINDEN "ACH, BESCHENKT
   MICH, LIEBEN LEUTE" see Slavenski,
   Josip, Slepacka

KLAGT NICHT MEHR "KLAGT NICHT, IHR
   FRAUEN" see Sturmer, Bruno

KLAN, THEO
   Ballade Von Den Musici
      men cor,acap sc,cor pts TONOS 4016
      s.p.   (K163)

KLANG, KLANG, GLOCKENSCHLAG *folk
   (Tiedemann, H.-J.) [Ger] 4pt mix cor
   MERSEBURG EM9214 s.p.   (K164)

KLASSEBESOK I KUNSTGALLERIET see Kvam,
   Oddvar S.

KLATOVSKA POLKA see Spilka, Frantisek

KLATSCHMON *folk,Fr
   (Zipp, F.) [Fr] men cor,acap TONOS
   2049A s.p.   (K165)
   (Zipp, F.) [Ger] men cor,acap TONOS
   2049 s.p.   (K166)

KLEFISCH, WALTER (1910-   )
   Altserbisches Idyll "Tief An Einem
      Berg" *folk,Slav
      [Ger] men cor (contains also: Gebet
      "Maria, Mutter Ich Fleh' Zu Dir")
      sc SCHOTTS C 41 684 s.p. see from
      Drei Jugoslawische Volkslieder
                                      (K167)
   Aus Dem Land Der Habanera *see Der
      Grimassentanz "Wir Tanzen Und
      Schneiden Fratzen"; Die Brucke
      Von Vinhaca; Kirchlein Mit
      Melonenturm   (K168)
   Barentanzlied "Brauner Tanzbar,
      Tanze"
      [Ger] men cor sc SCHOTTS C 41 685
      s.p. see from Drei Jugoslawische
      Volkslieder   (K169)
   Der Grimassentanz "Wir Tanzen Und
      Schneiden Fratzen"
      [Ger] men cor sc SCHOTTS C 41 965
      s.p. see from Aus Dem Land Der
      Habanera   (K170)
   Die Brucke Von Vinhaca
      [Ger] men cor (contains also:
      Kirchlein Mit Melonenturm) sc
      SCHOTTS C 41 964 s.p. see from
      Aus Dem Land Der Habanera   (K171)
   Drei Jugoslawische Volkslieder *see
      Altserbisches Idyll "Tief An
      Einem Berg"; Barentanzlied
      "Brauner Tanzbar, Tanze"; Gebet
      "Maria, Mutter Ich Fleh' Zu Dir"
                                      (K172)
   Fruhlingslied: O Sieh, Wie Rings Der
      Lenz Sich Regt
      mix cor voc pt BOTE s.p.   (K173)
   Gatatumba *folk,Span
      3pt jr cor/3pt wom cor,acap/gtr&
      perc (easy) sc SCHOTTS CHBL 603
      s.p.   (K174)
   Gebet "Maria, Mutter Ich Fleh' Zu
      Dir" *folk,Slav
      [Ger] men cor (contains also:
      Altserbisches Idyll "Tief An
      Einem Berg") sc SCHOTTS C 41 684
      s.p. see from Drei Jugoslawische
      Volkslieder   (K175)
   Kirchlein Mit Melonenturm
      [Ger] men cor (contains also: Die
      Brucke Von Vinhaca) sc SCHOTTS
      C 41 964 s.p. see from Aus Dem
      Land Der Habanera   (K176)
   Mlada Aga "Seht, Wie Die Sonne Lacht"
      *folk,Slav
      mix cor (easy) sc SCHOTTS C 42 621
      s.p.   (K177)
      men cor sc SCHOTTS C 39 027 s.p.
                                      (K178)

KLEIN
   Old Faithful
      SSAATTBB,band BOOSEY 5222 sc,cmplt
      ed $24.00, cor pts $.40 see from
      Yellowstone Suite   (K179)
   Yellowstone Suite *see Old Faithful
                                      (K180)

KLEIN, LOTHAR (1932-   )
   Good Night
      SSA (easy) WATERLOO $.40   (K181)
   Three Laments *CC3U
      SATB,acap oct PRESSER 312-41048
      $.40   (K182)
   Three Pastoral Songs *CC3U
      SSA (med) WATERLOO $.50   (K183)

KLEIN, RICHARD RUDOLF
   Das Bauernjahr *CC12U
      1-2pt jr cor,1-2vln (easy) sc
      SCHOTTS B 112 s.p.   (K184)
   Der Esel "Es Stand Vor Eines Hauses
      Tor"
      TTB,acap sc SCHOTTS CHBL 135 s.p.
                                      (K185)
   Ein Heller Tag Bricht An *cant
      3pt jr cor/SSA,2vln,vcl,A rec (med
      easy) sc,cor pts SCHOTTS ED. 4239
      s.p., ipa   (K186)
   Kantate Zum Erntefest *cant
      2pt jr cor,2vln,A rec (easy) sc,cor
      pts SCHOTTS ED. 4518 s.p., ipa
                                      (K187)
   Lob Des Sommers *cant
      3pt mix cor,soli,2fl,2vln,vcl (med)
      sc,voc pt SCHOTTS ED. 4249 s.p.,
      ipa   (K188)

KLEINE ABZAHLVERSGESCHICHTE "EHLE,
   MEHLE" see Zehm, Friedrich

KLEINE BANDITENBALLADE see Schneider,
   Walther

KLEINE BARKE *folk
   (Witt, G. De) [Ger] 4pt men cor
      MERSEBURG EM9028 s.p.   (K189)

KLEINE BAUERLICHE KANTATE see Fischer,
   Hans

KLEINE, BRAUNE SCHONE! "WIR TESSINER
   SIND TAPF'RE SOLDATEN" see Zoll,
   Paul

KLEINE SENORITA *folk,Mex
   (Seib, Valentin) men cor,acap TONOS
      2047 s.p.   (K190)

KLEINE STROPHEN DER UNSTERBLICHKEIT see
   Krietsch, Georg

KLEINE SUITE IM ALTEN STIL see Biebl,
   Franz

KLEINE SUITE NACH UNGARISCHEN
   VOLKSLIEDERN see Stein, F.R.

KLEINE TANZBALLADE "JUNG ELSBETH LIEBTE
   MICH NICHT SO SEHR" see Weber,
   Bernhard

KLEINE TOREN - GROSSE TOREN see Seeger,
   Peter

KLEINE WASSERMUSIK see Werner, Kurt

KLEINER MARSCH see Owen

KLEINER MARSCH see Welker, Gotthard

KLEINER MORGENWANDERER "FRISCH AUF!"
   see Haas, Joseph

KLEINER TANZ see Biebl, Franz

KLEINES CHORHEFT 1974 *CCU
   4pt mix cor,acap MERSEBURG EM793 s.p.
                                      (K191)
KLEINES LIEBESLIED "WO SIND DIE STUNDEN
   DER SUSSEN ZEIT" see Rein, Walter

KLEINES LIED see Biebl, Franz

KLEINSINGER
   Lollipop Tree, The *see Darion

KLICKA, JOSEF (1855-1937)
   Funeral On Kank *see Pohreb Na Kanku

   Pohreb Na Kanku *Op.31
      "Funeral On Kank" [Czech] mix cor,
      SSATBar soli,3fl,3ob,3clar,2bsn,
      4horn,3trp,3trom,tuba,timp,perc,
      harp,strings CZECH s.p.   (K192)

KLING AUF, MEIN LIED see Weber,
   Bernhard

KLING FUR MEIN HERZGESPIEL
   unis wom cor SCHOTTS C 42 533K s.p.
      see also Alle Singen Heft 2   (K193)

KLING, KLANG, KLOCKAN SLAR (from Cvjy)
   folk
   "Horch, Die Glocke Ruft" [Ger/Swed]
      5pt wom cor,acap BREITKOPF-W
      CHB 4940 s.p.   (K194)

KLINGE LIEBLICH UND SACHT see Desch,
   Rudolf

KLINGENDE JAHRESZEITEN see Maasz,
   Gerhard

KLINGENDES LAND-LIEDER AN DER SAAR see
   Michels, Josef

KLINGLER, LUDWIG
   Der Rodensteiner
      men cor,acap TONOS 247 s.p.   (K195)

KLIRR, SENSE, KLIRR see Lendvai, Erwin

KLOESSING, D.D.
   Kloessing's Rounds *CC25U,round
      [Ger/Eng] cor EMI   (K196)

KLOESSING'S ROUNDS see Kloessing, D.D.

KLOSS
   Da Unten Ist Frieden
      see VIER GRABLIEDER

KLOSTERFRAULEIN see Brahms, Johannes

KLUDAS, ERICH
   Am Morgen (composed with Schreiter,
      Heinz)
      mix cor,orch,perc,harp,timp RIES
      see from Ein Kindertag   (K197)
   Auf Der Wiese (composed with
      Schreiter, Heinz)
      mix cor,orch,perc,harp,timp RIES
      see from Ein Kindertag   (K198)
   Ein Kindertag *see Am Morgen; Auf
      Der Wiese; Geburtstag; Laterne;
      Rummelplatz   (K199)

KLUDAS, ERICH (cont'd.)
   Geburtstag (composed with Schreiter,
      Heinz)
      mix cor,orch,perc,harp,timp RIES
      see from Ein Kindertag   (K200)
   Laterne (composed with Schreiter,
      Heinz)
      mix cor,orch,perc,harp,timp RIES
      see from Ein Kindertag   (K201)
   Rummelplatz (composed with Schreiter,
      Heinz)
      mix cor,orch,perc,harp,timp RIES
      see from Ein Kindertag   (K202)

KNAB, ARMIN (1881-1951)
   Alte Kinderreime *CC14L
      1-2pt jr cor,1-2inst (easy) sc,cor
      pts SCHOTTS ED. 1698 s.p.   (K203)
   Brot Und Wein *see Ein Winterabend
      "Wenn Der Schnee Ans Fenster
      Fallt"; Mittagsstille "Klangmude
      Zeit Im Mittaglichen Feld";
      Verklarter Herbst "Gewaltig Endet
      So Das Jahr"   (K204)
   Das Kleine Herz
      see Kindheit
   Das Lebenslicht
      jr cor,narrator,SSSSSSSABarBBB
      soli,fl,ob,2clar,bsn,2horn,
      strings (med easy) voc sc SCHOTTS
      ED. 4443 s.p., ipr   (K205)
   Den Toten "Frei Von Menschlichen
      Geboten"
      1-3pt mix cor,opt brass&strings
      (med easy) cor pts SCHOTTS
      C 37 859 s.p.   (K206)
   Der Maie
      see Lang, Hans, Abschied "Die
      Schneegans Zieht"
   Der Morgenstern Ist Aufgegangen
      wom cor (med easy) sc SCHOTTS
      CHBL 550A-B s.p. contains also:
      Weiss Mir Ein Blumlein Blaue
                                      (K207)
   Die Bauern
      cmplt ed SCHOTTS C 32 821 s.p.
      contains & see also: Ein Brotlaib
      "Ein Brotlaib Auf Dem Tische
      Ruht"; Pfingsten "Wir Halten
      Unsere Haupter Still; Spruch
      Auf Einem Friedhofstore "O
      Wecke Nicht Mit Zahren"; Wir
      Bauern "Wir Bauern Dulden
      Keinen Spott"   (K208)
   Die Ohren
      see Kindheit
   Die Sprode
      (Klink, Waldemar) wom cor (easy) sc
      SCHOTTS CHBL 577 s.p.   (K209)
   Drei Alte Landsknechtslieder *see
      Schenkenbachs Reiterlied "Von
      Erst So Wolln Wir Loben";
      Trinklied "Frisch Auf, Gut
      G'sell"; Wir Zogen In Das Feld
                                      (K210)
   Drei Bauernlieder *see Ein Brotlaib
      "Ein Brotlaib Auf Dem Tische
      Ruht"; Pfingsten "Wir Halten
      Unsere Haupter Still"; Spruch Auf
      Einem Friedhofstore "O Wecke
      Nicht Mit Zahren"   (K211)
   Ein Brotlaib "Ein Brotlaib Auf Dem
      Tische Ruht"
      men cor cor pts SCHOTTS CHBL 1 s.p.
      see also Die Bauern   (K212)
      SATB (med easy) voc pt cmplt ed
      SCHOTTS C 35 476A-D C 35 473 s.p.
      s.p. see from Drei Bauernlieder
                                      (K213)
   Ein Winterabend "Wenn Der Schnee Ans
      Fenster Fallt"
      4pt wom cor,acap (med diff) sc
      SCHOTTS C 37 932 see from Brot
      Und Wein   (K214)
   Es, Es, Es Und Es
      1-2pt jr cor/1-2pt wom cor (med
      easy) sc SCHOTTS CHBL 598A-B s.p.
      contains also: Rosa Mystica
                                      (K215)
   Gloria
      see Kindheit
   Gruss Gott, Du Schoner Maie *cant
      1-2pt jr cor,soli,narrator,vln,rec
      (easy) sc,cor pts SCHOTTS
      ED. 2444 s.p.   (K216)
   Heimkehr "O Brich Nicht, Steg"
      mix cor (med) sc SCHOTTS C 34 551
      s.p.   (K217)

KNAB, ARMIN (cont'd.)

Kinderreigen Im Fruhling "Kommt, Wir
　Wollen Tanzen"
　jr cor (med easy) sc SCHOTTS
　C 34 226 s.p.　　　　　　　(K218)

Kindheit
　unis jr cor/unis wom cor,2vln
　(easy) sc SCHOTTS ED. 1568 s.p.
　contains: Das Kleine Herz; Die
　Ohren; Gloria　　　　　　(K219)

Maisang "Noch Einmal Nun Das Schone
　Lied"
　mix cor (med easy) sc SCHOTTS
　CHBL 254 s.p.　　　　　　(K220)

Mariae Geburt
　2pt wom cor,A solo,fl,ob,clar,
　strings (med easy) sc SCHOTTS
　C 34 188 s.p., voc sc SCHOTTS
　C 34 190 s.p., cor pts SCHOTTS
　C 34 191 s.p., ipa　　　(K221)

Mild Und Machtiges Erbarmen
　[Ger] men cor sc SCHOTTS C 33 997
　s.p.　　　　　　　　　　(K222)

Mittagsstille "Klangmude Zeit Im
　Mittaglichen Feld"
　4pt wom cor,acap (med diff) sc
　SCHOTTS C 37 930 s.p. see from
　Brot Und Wein　　　　　(K223)

Mitten Wir Im Leben Sind
　jr cor/wom cor (med easy) sc
　SCHOTTS CHBL 502 s.p.　　(K224)

Pfingsten "Wir Halten Unsere Haupter
　Still
　TBB voc pt SCHOTTS C 32 821, 01-03
　s.p. see also Die Bauern　(K225)
　SATB (med easy) voc pt SCHOTTS
　C 35 474A-D s.p. see from Drei
　Bauernlieder　　　　　　(K226)

Rosa Mystica
　see Knab, Armin, Es, Es, Es Und Es

St. Michael Am Meer "Sankt Michael,
　Du Starker Held"
　wom cor (med) sc SCHOTTS CHBL 549
　s.p.　　　　　　　　　　(K227)

Schenkenbachs Reiterlied "Von Erst So
　Wolln Wir Loben"
　TBB,acap sc SCHOTTS C 34 250 s.p.
　see from Drei Alte
　Landsknechtslieder　　　(K228)

So Treiben Wir Den Winter Aus
　jr cor/wom cor (easy) sc SCHOTTS
　CHBL 505A-B s.p. contains also:
　Rein, Walter, O Tannenbaum, Du
　Tragst, Ein' Grunen Zweig　(K229)

Spruch Auf Einem Friedhofstore "O
　Wecke Nicht Mit Zahren"
　TTBB voc pt SCHOTTS C 32 823, 01-04
　s.p. see also Die Bauern　(K230)
　SATB (med easy) voc pt SCHOTTS
　C 35 475 s.p. see from Drei
　Bauernlieder　　　　　　(K231)

Streitlied Zwischen Leben Und Tod "So
　Spricht Das Leben"
　4-8pt mix cor,acap (med) sc SCHOTTS
　C 34 003 s.p., voc pt SCHOTTS
　C 34 004A-D s.p.　　　　(K232)

Trinklied "Frisch Auf, Gut G'sell"
　TBB,acap sc SCHOTTS C 34 251 s.p.
　see from Drei Alte
　Landsknechtslieder　　　(K233)

Verklarter Herbst "Gewaltig Endet So
　Das Jahr"
　4pt wom cor,acap (med diff) sc
　SCHOTTS C 37 931 s.p. see from
　Brot Und Wein　　　　　(K234)

Weiss Mir Ein Blumlein Blaue
　see Knab, Armin, Der Morgenstern
　Ist Aufgegangen

Wer Je Gelebt In Liebesarmen
　mix cor (med easy) sc SCHOTTS
　C 34 553 s.p.　　　　　(K235)

Wir Bauern "Wir Bauern Dulden Keinen
　Spott"
　TTBB voc pt SCHOTTS C 32 822, 01-04
　s.p. see also Die Bauern　(K236)

Wir Zogen In Das Feld
　TBB,acap sc SCHOTTS C 34 249 s.p.
　see from Drei Alte
　Landsknechtslieder　　　(K237)

Zeitkranz　*CC10L
　mix cor (med) sc,voc pt SCHOTTS
　ED. 2930 s.p.　　　　　(K238)

KNAP, ROLF (1937-　)
　Liederen Van Doofstommen (Songs Of
　Deaf-Mutes), First Cycle　*CCU
　cor,S solo,4fl,4ob,4clar,4bsn,
　4horn,4trp,4trom,4tuba,strings,
　3perc DONEMUS　　　　　(K239)

KNAVE'S LETTER, THE see Fine

KNECHT, DU SOLLST NICHT NACH DEN MAGDEN
　SCHAUN　*folk
　(Fischbach, Klaus) wom cor,pno,fl sc
　BREITKOPF-W CHB 4920 s.p. see from
　Sieben Europaische Volkslieder
　　　　　　　　　　　　(K240)

KNECHT RUPRECHTS ERZAHLUNG see Erdlen,
　Hermann

KNIGHT OF THE GRAIL, THE see
　Castelnuovo-Tedesco, Mario

KNIGHTS IN SHINING ARMOR see
　Williamson, Malcolm

KNISS
　Sunshine On My Shoulders　*see
　Denver, John

KOCH, ADOLF
　Festspruch
　men cor,acap TONOS 3704 s.p. (K241)

　Trinklied: Wer Trinkt
　men cor,acap TONOS 282 s.p.　(K242)

KOCH, KARL
　Sudtirol
　men cor,acap TONOS 5806 s.p. (K243)

KOCSAR, MIKLOS
　Tuz, Te Gyonyoru
　(Nagy, Laszlo) mix cor BUDAPEST
　7305 s.p.　　　　　　　(K244)

　Tuzciterak
　wom cor BUDAPEST 7352 s.p.　(K245)

KODACHROME see Simon, Paul

KODALY EMLEKEZETE see Ranki, Gyorgy

KODALY, ZOLTAN (1882-1967)
　Arms Of Hungary, The
　(Russell-Smith) SATB,acap oct
　BOOSEY 5871 $.35　　　　(K246)

　Eve, My Sweet
　SA,acap oct BOOSEY 5873 $.35 (K247)

　False Spring
　SSA,acap oct BOOSEY 5869 $.35
　　　　　　　　　　　　(K248)

　Ferfikarok　*CCU
　men cor BUDAPEST 6726 s.p.　(K249)

　Fiddle-Dee
　SSAA,acap oct BOOSEY 5868 $.35
　　　　　　　　　　　　(K250)

　Good Housewife, The
　(Russell-Smith) SS,acap oct BOOSEY
　5872 $.35　　　　　　　(K251)

　Grow, Tresses
　(Russell-Smith) SSA,acap oct BOOSEY
　5875 $.35　　　　　　　(K252)

　Gyermek- Es Noikarok　*CCU
　jr cor&wom cor BUDAPEST 6724 s.p.
　　　　　　　　　　　　(K253)

　Harom Gomori Nepdal
　jr cor&wom cor BUDAPEST 6836 s.p.
　　　　　　　　　　　　(K254)

　'Mid The Oak Trees
　(Russell-Smith) SSA,acap oct BOOSEY
　5870 $.35　　　　　　　(K255)

　Vegyeskarok　*CCU
　mix cor BUDAPEST 6725 s.p.　(K256)

　Wine, Sweet Wine
　(Russell-Smith) SSSAAA,acap oct
　BOOSEY 5865 $.40　　　　(K257)

KOELBLE, FRITZ
　Der Schmied "Begruss Den
　Morgenfrischen Tag"
　men cor sc SCHOTTS C 39 169 s.p.
　　　　　　　　　　　　(K258)

　Rausch "Rausch, Mein Riesiger"
　men cor sc SCHOTTS C 39 170 s.p.
　　　　　　　　　　　　(K259)

　Standchen "Gute Nacht! Madchen"
　TTBB sc SCHOTTS C 39 167 s.p., voc
　pt SCHOTTS C 39 168, 01-02 s.p.
　　　　　　　　　　　　(K260)

KOENIG, FRANZ
　Abendwolke
　men cor,acap TONOS 3937 s.p. (K261)

　All Mein Gedanken
　men cor,acap TONOS 132 s.p.　(K262)

　Du Verklagest Das Weib
　men cor,acap TONOS 4049 s.p. (K263)

KOENIG, FRANZ (cont'd.)

　Heldengedenken
　men cor,acap TONOS 4544 s.p. (K264)

　Im Wein Birgt Sich Viel
　men cor,acap TONOS 4545 s.p. (K265)

　Kommet, Ihr Hirten
　men cor,acap TONOS 150 s.p.　(K266)

　Nachtgerausche
　men cor,acap TONOS 3939 s.p. (K267)

　Soldatenbrot
　men cor,acap TONOS 4096 s.p. (K268)

　Sucht Die Besten Weine Aus
　men cor,acap TONOS 4566 s.p. (K269)

　Wankelmut
　men cor,acap TONOS 3991 s.p. (K270)

　Weihelied Und Hochgesang
　men cor,acap TONOS 4543 s.p. (K271)

　Weiss Ich Ein Schones Roselein
　men cor,acap TONOS 31 s.p.　(K272)

KOETSIER, JAN (1911-　)
　Gesang Der Geister Uber Den Wassern
　mix cor,inst DONEMUS　　(K273)

　Von Gottes Und Des Menschen Wesen
　*CC7U,madrigal
　mix cor,7inst DONEMUS　　(K274)

KOHLENGRABERLIED "MOND SCHIMMERT AUF"
　see Sakamoto, Yoshitaka, Kyushu
　Tanko Bushi

KOHLER, SIEGFRIED (1927-　)
　Dass Unsre Liebe Eine Heimat Hat
　mix cor,acap DEUTSCHER DVFM7645
　s.p.　　　　　　　　　(K275)

KOHOUTEK, CTIRAD (1929-　)
　For All Children　*see Za Vsechny
　Deti

　Podvecerni Koncert U Chaty
　3pt jr cor,acap/treb inst&bass inst
　SLOV.HUD.FOND s.p.　　　(K276)

　Za Vsechny Deti　*cant
　"For All Children" [Czech] mix cor,
　S solo,3fl,3ob,3clar,3bsn,4horn,
　3trp,3trom,tuba,timp,perc,harp,
　strings CZECH s.p.　　　(K277)

KOHS, ELLIS B. (1916-　)
　Automatic Pistol, The
　TB,acap AM.COMP.AL. $2.75　(K278)

　Symphony No. 2
　cor,2fl,2ob,2clar,2bsn,2horn,2trp,
　2trom,tuba,3timp,perc,harp,
　strings sc AM.COMP.AL. $18.15
　　　　　　　　　　　　(K279)

　Three Medieval Latin Student Songs
　*CC3U
　TTBB,TB soli,acap AM.COMP.AL. $3.30
　　　　　　　　　　　　(K280)

KOLEDA see Gotovac, Jakov

KOLEDA see Vendler, Bohumil

KOLEDA-FOLK RITE IN FIVE PARTS see
　Gotovac, Jakov

KOLIK SLUNICEK see Valek, Jiri

KOLMAN, PETER (1937-　)
　Ach, Ty Zem　*cant
　cor,orch SLOV.HUD.FOND s.p. (K281)

KOLO see Slavenski, Josip

KOLOMBINA see Barta, Lubor

KOMITAT "NUN ZU GUTER LETZT" see
　Mendelssohn-Bartholdy, Felix

KOMM DIE SONNE LACHT see Biebl, Franz

KOMM GEIST AUS HEILIGER FERN! "HORCH
　AUF, BRUDER" see Weber, Ludwig

KOMM, HERZENS FREUD　*folk
　(Weber, Bernhard) [Ger] 4pt men cor
　MERSEBURG EM9016 s.p.　　(K282)

KOMM MIT see Edler, Robert

KOMM, TRINK UND LACH AM RHEIN! "ICH
　LIEBTE VOR JAHREN EIN MADCHEN" see
　Raymond, Fred

KOMM, TROST DER NACHT, O NACHTIGALL see
　Rein, Walter

KOMM TROST DER WELT, DU STILLE NACHT
　see Rein, Walter

KOMM UNTER MEIN PLAIDIE *folk,Scot
(Mittergradnegger) [Ger] men cor,acap
TONOS 2809 s.p.   (K283)

KOMM, WIR WOLLEN TANZEN see Kukuck,
Felicitas

KOMM ZU MIR ZURUCK *folk
(Fischbach, Klaus) wom cor,pno,fl sc
BREITKOPF-W CHB 4923 s.p. see from
Sieben Europaische Volkslieder
(K284)

KOMM ZUM TANZ see Heun, Hans

KOMMET, IHR HIRTEN see Koenig, Franz

KOMMT HERR MOND ZU GUTER NACHT see
Fussan, Werner

KOMMT, IHR GESPIELEN see Lang, Hans

KOMMT, IHR G'SPIELEN see Werdin,
Eberhard

KOMMT, IHR G'SPIELEN see Becker, Peter

KOMMT, IHR G'SPIELEN see Franck,
Melchior

KOMMT, IHR GSPIELEN see Lang, Hans

KOMMT IHR G'SPIELEN see Werdin,
Eberhard

KOMMT, IHR G'SPIELEN see Becker, Peter

KOMMT, IHR G'SPIELEN *CC10L,folk
(Stadlmair, Hans) unls jr cor/unis
wom cor,2vln,vcl,rec,timp,
glockenspiel, triangle, xylophone
cmplt ed BREITKOPF-W MSP 11 s.p.
(K285)

KOMMT, IHR LIEBLICHEN STIMMEN ALLE see
Marenzio, Luca

KOMMT, LASST UNS ALLESAMT see Haas,
Joseph

KOMMT VON DER ARBEIT see Lassus, Roland
de (Orlandus)

KOMMT, WIR GEHN AUF SCHMALEM WEGE see
Poos, Heinrich

KOMMT ZEIT, KOMMT RAT "WER WILL DENN
ALLES GLEICH" see Pepping, Ernst

KOMPANYEJEC
Harcjatek
(Szadovszkij; Nadas, Katalin) jr
cor,pno BUDAPEST 6888 s.p. (K286)

KOMUNISTICKY MANIFEST see Schulhoff,
Erwin

KONIG DAGOBERT *folk,Fr
(Kracke, H.) [Ger] 4pt mix cor
MERSEBURG EM9228 s.p.   (K287)
(Zschiegner, Fritz) men cor,opt pno,
opt inst,opt perc sc,voc sc TONOS
2118 s.p.   (K288)

KONIG MIDAS see Werdin, Eberhard

KONOWITZ
America, The Land Of The People
2pt/SSA/SATB, opt vocal
improvisation ALFRED $.60 (K289)

KONTRASZTOS TAJKEP see Marton, Lajos

KONVALINKA, MILOS (1919-   )
Beloved Land *see Milovana Zeme

Milovana Zeme *cant
"Beloved Land" [Czech] mix cor,S
solo,2fl,2ob,2clar,2bsn,4horn,
3trp,3trom,tuba,timp,perc,harp,
strings CZECH s.p.   (K290)

KOPELENT, MAREK (1932-   )
Bread And Birds *see Chleb A Ptaci

Chleb A Ptaci *cant
"Bread And Birds" [Czech] mix cor,
A&narrator,3fl,ob,3clar,3bsn,
4trp,3trom,timp,perc,pno,vln,bvl,
vibraphone, celeste CZECH s.p.
(K291)

Nenie S Fletnou
"Nenie With Flute" [Czech] 9pt wom
cor,fl,ob,2clar,bsn,2trp,3trom,
timp,perc,pno,electronic tape
PANTON s.p.   (K292)

Nenie With Flute *see Nenie S
Fletnou

KORF "KORF ERFINDET EINE ART VON
WITZEN" see Nitsche, Paul

KORINEK, MILOSLAV (1925-   )
Krajina Mieru
see MUZSKE ZBORY I

KORINEK, MILOSLAV (cont'd.)

Pozdrav Krajine Vitazstva
mix cor SLOV.HUD.FOND s.p.   (K293)

KORN IST GEMAHT see Strohbach,
Siegfried, Marken Er Mejet

KORN, PETER JONA
Zwei Edle Brauer
men cor,acap TONOS 3737 s.p. (K294)

KORNDIEBE see Rein, Walter

KORTE, OLDRICH FRANTISEK (1926-   )
I Canti Dei Trovatori *see
Trobadorske Zpevy

Trobadorske Zpevy
"I Canti Dei Trovatori" [Czech]
cor,soli,inst PANTON s.p.   (K295)

KORUS-SZVIT see Vary, Ferenc

KOSA A ROSA see Haba, Alois

KOSA, GYORGY (1897-   )
Iciri-Piciri *CC5U
(Moricz) jr cor BUDAPEST 6808 s.p.
(K296)

KOSACKENHOCKZEIT see Heun, Hans

KOSAKENLIEDCHEN see Bredow, Claus

KOSAKENRITT see Mardi, Hans-Jurgen

KOSAKISCHES WIEGENLIED see Karpowitsch,
A.

KOSMA, J.
En Sortant De L'Ecole
4pt mix cor ENOCH   (K297)

Les Femmes
4pt mix cor ENOCH   (K298)

Traquenard
4pt mix cor ENOCH   (K299)

Un, Deux, Trois
4pt mix cor ENOCH   (K300)

KOSMOGONIA see Penderecki, Krzysztof

KOUNADIS, ARGHYRIS (1924-   )
Epigramma
dbl cor,harp,pno,perc, vibraphone,
celesta MODERN s.p., rental
(K301)

KOVACS, MATYAS
Ket Kis Korus *CC2U
(Rab, Zsuzsa) jr cor BUDAPEST 7108
s.p.   (K302)

KOX, HANS (1930-   )
De Vierde Kraai Oftewel De Kraaiende
Vier (Trijntje Fop)
men cor,4brass,perc DONEMUS (K303)

Requiem For Europa
4 cor,2org,4horn,3trp,3trom,
strings,perc DONEMUS   (K304)

KRACKE, HANS
Abendlied: Nun Sich Der Tag Geendet
men cor,acap TONOS 58 s.p.   (K305)

Minnelied: Es Flog Ein
men cor,acap TONOS 60 s.p.   (K306)

Schonster Tag
men cor,acap TONOS 4589 s.p. (K307)

KRAINTZ, KEN
Goodbye Love
SSATBB,acap (med, jazz) KYSAR A105
$.35   (K308)

I'm Feelin' Right
SATB,pno,bvl,gtr (jazz) KYSAR A104
$.45   (K309)

We're Goin' Uptown (composed with
Walthall, Bennie)
SSATB,pno,bvl,gtr (med easy, jazz)
KYSAR A101 $.45   (K310)

KRAJINA MIERU see Korinek, Miloslav

KRAKOWIAK
see Singende Jugend Nr. 16

KRAKOWIAK see Rosenstengel, Albrecht

KRAL LAVRA see Huth, Gustav

KRALZEK
Viney Flower And Rosemary Tree
SATB SCHIRM.G LG51669 $.40   (K311)

KRASNA ZEME see Bartos, Jan Zdenek

KRATOCHVIL, JIRI (1924-   )
Ostrava *cant
[Czech] mix cor,Mez solo,3fl,3ob,
2clar,2bsn,4horn,3trp,3trom,tuba,
timp,strings CZECH s.p.   (K312)

KRCEK, JAROSLAV (1939-   )
Specta Et Audi *CC3U
[Lat] jr cor/girl cor,Mez solo,trp,
timp,perc,harp,strings CZECH s.p.
(K313)

KREBS see Strobl, Otto

KREJCI see Strebl, Alois

KREMBERG, JACOB
Trunet Die Hoffnung
see LIEDPROGRAMM DES DEUTSCHEN
SANGERBUNDES FOLGE 3: "ESSENER
LIEDERBLATT" - "CHORFEIER"

KRENEK, ERNST (1900-   )
Guten Morgen, Amerika "Nun Steht
Onkel Sam Noch An Der Spitze Der
Welt"
mix cor (med) sc SCHOTTS C 39 551
s.p.   (K314)

Ich Singe Wieder, Wenn Es Tagt "Die
Zweifler Sagen"
4pt mix cor,strings (med diff) sc,
cor pts SCHOTTS ED. 4981 s.p.,
ipa   (K315)

Mitternacht Und Tag *Op.95
[Eng/Ger] wom cor,orch sc SCHOTTS
rental, ipr   (K316)

KREUTZ
Trees, Horizons And Memories
SSAA SHAWNEE B390 $.50   (K317)

KREUTZ, ROBERT E.
Silverheels
SATB,acap oct SOMERSET BR 2009 $.50
(K318)

KREUTZER, KONRADIN
An Das Vaterland
men cor,acap TONOS 6339 s.p. (K319)

Der Weisse Hirsch
men cor,acap TONOS 6309 s.p. (K320)

Der Weisse Hirsch "Es Gingen Drei
Jager Wohl Auf Die Birsch"
men cor sc SCHOTTS CHBL 103 s.p.
(K321)

Schafers Sonntagslied
men cor,acap TONOS 6311 s.p. (K322)

Trinklied "Tres Faciunt Collegium"
TTB,acap sc SCHOTTS CHBL 102 s.p.
(K323)

KRICKA, JAROSLAV (1882-1969)
Beneath The Old Flag *see Pod Starym
Praporem

Dvacatero Diku *cant
"Thank You Twenty Times" [Lat/It]
mix cor,Bar solo,2fl,2ob,2clar,
2bsn,2horn,2trp,perc,harp,strings
CZECH s.p.   (K324)

Glove - Full Of Love, A *see Oblazky
Z Lasky

Golden Spinning-Wheel, The *see
Zlaty Kolovrat

Oblazky Z Lasky
"Glove - Full Of Love, A" [Czech]
jr cor,pno PANTON s.p.   (K325)

Pisen Lidu *CCU,folk
(Lucky, Stepan) [Czech] mix cor,AT
soli,2fl,2ob,3clar,2bsn,2horn,
2trp,trom,timp,perc,strings CZECH
s.p.   (K326)

Pod Starym Praporem
"Beneath The Old Flag" [Czech]
unis,2fl,2ob,2clar,2bsn,4horn,
3trp,3trom,tuba,timp,perc,strings
CZECH s.p.   (K327)

Praze *Op.123, cant
"To Prague" [Czech] mix cor,2fl,
2ob,2clar,2bsn,4horn,3trp,3trom,
tuba,timp,perc,harp,strings CZECH
s.p.   (K328)

Thank You Twenty Times *see
Dvacatero Diku

To Prague *see Praze

Tyrolean Elegies *see Tyrolske
Elegie

Tyrolske Elegie *cant
"Tyrolean Elegies" [Czech] men cor,
T solo,3fl,2ob,2clar,2bsn,4horn,
2trp,3trom,tuba,timp,perc,harp,
strings CZECH s.p.   (K329)

KRICKA, JAROSLAV (cont'd.)

Zlaty Kolovrat *cant
"Golden Spinning-Wheel, The"
[Czech] mix cor,6 soli,2fl,3ob,
3clar,2bsn,4horn,3trp,3trom,tuba,
timp,perc,harp,strings CZECH s.p.
(K330)

KRIEGSLIEDER see Victory, Gerard

KRIETSCH, GEORG (1904-1969)
Abendmusik
men cor,A solo,acap sc,cor pts
TONOS 4007 s.p.   (K331)

Auf Die Schwab'sche Eisebahne
men cor,acap sc,cor pts TONOS 4014
s.p.   (K332)

Bauernhochzeit: Beim Kronenwirt
men cor,acap TONOS 26 s.p.   (K333)

Behandelt Die Frauen Mit Nachsicht
men cor,acap TONOS 4048 s.p. (K334)

Bruder Tod
men cor,acap TONOS 4047 s.p. (K335)

Bumerang
see Wunderland-Zyklus

Das Wessobrunner Gebet
men cor&opt wom cor,opt A solo,acap
sc,cor pts TONOS 4012 s.p. (K336)

Der Krieg Ist Aus
see Wer Ruft?

Der Rattenfanger
men cor,acap TONOS 4011 s.p. (K337)

Der Weg Der Toten
see Wer Ruft?

Deutsche Heimat, Deine Land
men cor,acap TONOS 4098 s.p. (K338)

Die Ameisen
see Wunderland-Zyklus

Die Glocke
men cor,acap TONOS 4511 s.p. (K339)

Die Landschaft Singt
men cor,acap TONOS 4002 s.p. (K340)

Die Trommel
men cor,acap TONOS 4512 s.p. (K341)

Die Unendliche Strasse
men cor,acap TONOS 4043 s.p. (K342)

Es Lohnt Sich
see Lieder Fur Die Freunde

Fuhrmannslied: Hab Mein Wagen
men cor,acap TONOS 32 s.p.   (K343)

Glaubenslied
see Zuckmayer-Chorzyklus

Handwerksburchenpenne
men cor,acap TONOS 4041 s.p. (K344)

Ihr Seid Unser
see Wer Ruft?

Im Park
see Wunderland-Zyklus

Kleine Strophen Der Unsterblichkeit
see Zuckmayer-Chorzyklus

Leb Wohl, Frau Welt
men cor,acap TONOS 4045 s.p. (K345)

Lebensabschnitt
see Lieder Fur Die Freunde

Liebesscherz: Wo E Kleins Huttle
men cor,acap TONOS 9 s.p.   (K346)

Lieder Fur Die Freunde
men cor,acap cmplt ed TONOS 4590
s.p.
contains: Es Lohnt Sich;
Lebensabschnitt; Melodie (K347)

Madel Wink: Wenn Wir Marschieren
men cor,acap TONOS 11 s.p.   (K348)

Marschlied
see Zuckmayer-Chorzyklus

Melodie
see Lieder Fur Die Freunde

Mond Und Trinker
men cor,acap TONOS 4092 s.p. (K349)

Morituri
see Zuckmayer-Chorzyklus

Schenke Im Fruhling
men cor,acap sc,cor pts TONOS 4046
s.p.   (K350)

KRIETSCH, GEORG (cont'd.)

Sonnengesang
men cor,A solo,acap sc,cor pts
TONOS 4009 s.p.   (K351)

Sturmsang Der Taufer
see Zuckmayer-Chorzyklus

Totengedenken
men cor,acap TONOS 4099 s.p. (K352)

Uberall Ist Wunderland
see Wunderland-Zyklus

Vision
see Wer Ruft?

Vogelzug
men cor,acap TONOS 4066 s.p. (K353)

Weihnachtslied
see Zuckmayer-Chorzyklus

Weltenfriede
men cor,acap TONOS 4044 s.p. (K354)

Wer Ruft?
men cor,acap cmplt ed TONOS 4540
s.p.
contains: Der Krieg Ist Aus; Der
Weg Der Toten; Ihr Seid Unser;
Vision   (K355)

Wiegenlied An Der Bergstrasse
see Zuckmayer-Chorzyklus

Wunderland-Zyklus
men cor,acap cmplt ed TONOS 4050
s.p.
contains: Bumerang; Die Ameisen;
Im Park; Uberall Ist Wunderland
(K356)

Zuckmayer-Chorzyklus
men cor,acap cmplt ed TONOS 4020
s.p.
contains: Glaubenslied; Kleine
Strophen Der Unsterblichkeit;
Marschlied; Morituri; Sturmsang
Der Taufer; Weihnachtslied;
Wiegenlied An Der Bergstrasse
(K357)

KRISTALLE, DIE FEINEN *folk,Norw
(Langer, Hans-Klaus) men cor,acap
TONOS 2002 s.p.   (K358)

KRISTALLEN DEN FINA see Strohbach,
Siegfried

KROMER
Come Down To The Town Dump (composed
with Silver)
unis,pno,opt gtr&bvl&drums MCAFEE
M162 $.35   (K359)

KRONE
Frivolous Frauleins
SA KJOS 6139 $.35   (K360)

Give Us Men To Match Our Mountains
SATB KJOS 5921 $.35   (K361)

Silversmith, The
SAB KJOS 5744 $.35   (K362)

KRUSNE HORY MTS. CANTATA, THE see
Sehnal, Frantisek, Krusnohorsha
Kantata

KRUSNOHORSHA KANTATA see Sehnal,
Frantisek

KRUTCHER, BETTY
John Shaft *see Hayes, Isaac

KTAADN see Adams, John

KUBIK, GAIL (1914-   )
Household Magic
SATB,perc STANDARD B402MX1EN $.50
(K363)

KUBIN, RUDOLF (1909-   )
In The Mountains Beskydy *see V
Beskydach

Lesni Veselice
"Summer Festivities" [Czech] jr
cor,soli,S solo,5winds CZECH s.p.
(K364)

Summer Festivities *see Lesni
Veselice

V Beskydach (from Ostrava)
"In The Mountains Beskydy" [Czech]
mix cor,acap CZECH s.p.   (K365)

KUBIZEK, AUGUSTINIAN (1918-   )
Ach, Du Dunkle Nacht
mix cor (easy) sc SCHOTTS CHBL 411
s.p.   (K366)

Der Betrunkene Seemann "Was Solln Wir
Tun"
[Eng/Ger] men cor sc SCHOTTS
CHBL 212 s.p.   (K367)

KUBIZEK, AUGUSTINIAN (cont'd.)

Des Teufels Ritt "Reitet Der Teufel
Mit Klapperndem Huf"
men cor sc SCHOTTS C 43 261 s.p.
(K368)

Die Zwiebelhandler "Hophej!
Zwiebelhandler Da, Vor Dem Haus"
mix cor (easy) sc SCHOTTS C 43 259
s.p.   (K369)

Makkaroni *folk
mix cor,soli DOBLINGER G 656 s.p.
(K370)

(Kubizek, Augustin) men cor,soli
DOBLINGER M 329 s.p.   (K371)

KUCHARI see Ocenas, Andrej

KUCKUCK RUFT IM TANNENWALD *folk,Finn
(Miller, Franz R.) men cor,acap TONOS
2012 s.p.   (K372)

KUCKUCK RUFT'S AUS DEM WALD see Jage,
Rolf-Diether

KUHLAU, FRIEDERICH (1786-1832)
Mailied
men cor,acap TONOS 6313 s.p. (K373)

Uber Allen Gipfeln Ist Ruh
men cor,acap TONOS 6314 s.p. (K374)

KUHLENTHAL, FRED (1908-1943)
A Baurabuble Mag I Net
see Kuhlenthal, Fred, Kein Schoner
Land In Dieser Zeit

Bei Luzern, Dem Rigis Zua
see Kuhlenthal, Fred, Kein Schoner
Land In Dieser Zeit

Der Mond Ist Aufgegangen
see Kuhlenthal, Fred, Die Helle
Sonn Leucht Jetzt Herfur

Die Blumelein, Sie Schlafen
see Kuhlenthal, Fred, Die Helle
Sonn Leucht Jetzt Herfur

Die Helle Sonn Leucht Jetzt Herfur
SSA/SAT CARUS CV 40.209 s.p.
contains also: Steht Auf, Ihr
Lieben Kinderlein (SSA/SAT); Die
Blumelein, Sie Schlafen (SSA/
TTB); Der Mond Ist Aufgegangen
(SSA/TTB)   (K375)

Dr. Ziprabom
see Kuhlenthal, Fred, Wenn I Au
Kein Schatz Net Hab

Kein Schoner Land In Dieser Zeit
SAT/SAB CARUS CV 40.402 s.p.
contains also: Bei Luzern, Dem
Rigis Zua (SATB); Weiss Mir Ein
Blumlein Blaue (SSA/TBB); A
Baurabuble Mag I Net (SATB)
(K376)

'S Sitzt A Kleins Vogele Im Tannawald
see Kuhlenthal, Fred, Wenn I Au
Kein Schatz Net Hab

Schwabisches Quodlibet
SATB CARUS 40.203 s.p.   (K377)

Steht Auf, Ihr Lieben Kinderlein
see Kuhlenthal, Fred, Die Helle
Sonn Leucht Jetzt Herfur

Weiss Mir Ein Blumlein Blaue
see Kuhlenthal, Fred, Kein Schoner
Land In Dieser Zeit

Wenn I Au Kein Schatz Net Hab
SATB CARUS CV 40.201 s.p. contains
also: Dr. Ziprabom (SSA/TTB,2
soli); 'S Sitzt A Kleins Vogele
Im Tannawald (SAT/SAB,opt fl)
(K378)

KUHN, RUDOLF
Trinklied
men cor,acap TONOS 4067 s.p. (K379)

KUHNHOLD
Sternengrusse *Op.22,No.6
mix cor LIENAU sc s.p., cor pts
s.p.   (K380)

KUKSA, EMANUEL (1923-   )
Alder Trees *see Olse

Bez Prace
"Without Work" [Czech] men cor,acap
CZECH s.p.   (K381)

Dozinky
"Harvest Festivities" [Czech] wom
cor,acap CZECH s.p.   (K382)

Harvest Festivities *see Dozinky

Olse
"Alder Trees" [Czech] men cor,acap
CZECH s.p.   (K383)

KUKSA, EMANUEL (cont'd.)

Promise, The *see Slib

Slib
  "Promise, The" [Czech] men cor,acap
  CZECH s.p.   (K384)

Without Work *see Bez Prace

KUKUCK, FELICITAS (1914-   )
Komm, Wir Wollen Tanzen *CC8L
  jr cor,inst (easy) sc SCHOTTS B 114
  s.p.   (K385)

KULJERIC, IGOR (1938-   )
Ballade Petrice Kerempuha *CCU
  mix cor&wom cor&jr cor,narrator,
  orch MUSIC INFO rental   (K386)

Ciklus *CCU
  cor,pno,electric,2harp,perc MUSIC
  INFO rental   (K387)

Omaggio A Lukacic
  SATB,electric,perc MUSIC INFO
  rental   (K388)

KULJESKELLEN see Tuominen, Harri

KULMBACHER-GREGORIUS-MARSCH see
  Matthes, Rene

KUM BA YAH see Dedrick, C.

KUM, GESELLE MIN see Mittergradnegger,
  Gunther

KUNAD, RAINER
Der Ausbruch Des Bauernkrieges
  jr cor,narrator,solo HOFMEISTER
  G2208 s.p.   (K389)

KUNDE JAG FOLJA DIG see Wieslander,
  Ingvar

KUNST, JOS (1936-   )
Trajectoire
  16pt,fl,ob,clar,bsn,horn,vln,vla,
  vcl,timp,harp DONEMUS   (K390)

KUNZ, ALFRED
Clear Midnight
  SATB (med diff) WATERLOO $.30
                                (K391)
Come Brother, Come Friend
  SATB (med) WATERLOO $.30   (K392)

Contrasts
  SATB (med easy) WATERLOO $.40
  contains: How Beautiful Is Night;
    Roses And Thorns   (K393)

Eight Impressions
  SATB (med diff) WATERLOO $.75
                                (K394)
Flirt, The
  see Three Works For Male Chorus

How Beautiful Is Night
  see Contrasts

King Street Parade (from Sketches Of
    Waterloo County)
  cor,narrator THOMP.G $.75   (K395)

Leisure
  see Three Works For Male Chorus

O Cool Is The Valley Now
  see Three Works For Male Chorus

Plain Folk Buggy Song (from Sketches
    Of Waterloo County)
  SATB THOMP.G $.50   (K396)

Rhinoceros
  SATB (med) WATERLOO $.40   (K397)

Roses And Thorns
  see Contrasts

Sleeping Giant (composed with Reaney,
    James)
  SA (med easy) WATERLOO $.50   (K398)

Slow Slow Fresh Fount
  SATB (med easy) WATERLOO $.35
                                (K399)
Three Works For Male Chorus
  TTBB (med easy) WATERLOO $.50
  contains: Flirt, The; Leisure; O
    Cool Is The Valley Now   (K400)

To Hear An Oriole Sing
  SSA (med diff) WATERLOO $.30 (K401)

Will You Come
  cor (med) WATERLOO $1.50   (K402)

KUNZ, JACK
On An English Proverb
  SATB,acap ART MAST 1020 $.40 (K403)

KUPKA, KAREL (1927-   )
Poklady Se Otviraji *cant
  "Treasures Are Opening, The"
  [Czech] mix cor,4fl,3ob,3clar,
  3bsn,6horn,4trp,4trom,tuba,timp,
  perc,harp,pno,strings,celeste,
  xylophone CZECH s.p.   (K404)

Treasures Are Opening, The *see
  Poklady Se Otviraji

KUROSHIO see Loudova, Ivana, Kurosio

KUROSIO see Loudova, Ivana

KURTH, BURTON L.
Curlew Isle
  see Three More Festival Songs

Dreamland City
  see Three More Festival Songs

Fairy Flute
  see Three Festival Songs

Little Dreamer
  see Two Songs For Juniors

Lullabe Ship
  see Three More Festival Songs

My Ginger Kitty
  see Three Festival Songs

Picture Gallery
  see Three Festival Songs

Three Festival Songs
  unis LESLIE 1099 $.90
  contains: Fairy Flute; My Ginger
    Kitty; Picture Gallery   (K405)

Three More Festival Songs
  unis LESLIE 1117 $.90
  contains: Curlew Isle; Dreamland
    City; Lullabe Ship   (K406)

Two Kites And A Rain Cloud
  see Two Songs For Juniors

Two Songs For Juniors
  unis jr cor LESLIE 1118 $.60
  contains: Little Dreamer; Two
    Kites And A Rain Cloud   (K407)

KURTZ, EUGENE (1923-   )
Elysian Fields
  men cor,T solo,pno sc JOBERT s.p.
                                (K408)
KURZBACH, PAUL
Kantate Der Freundschaft *cant
  cor,high solo,SBar soli,orch NEUE
  NM223 s.p.   (K409)

KUZMICH, NATALIE
When Icicles Hang By The Wall
  SSA (med diff) WATERLOO $.30 (K410)

KVAM, ODDVAR S.
A Bo Ved En Sjo
  SSA/SAB MUSIKK   (K411)

Berre
  SSA/SAB MUSIKK   (K412)

Dante
  SSA/SAB MUSIKK   (K413)

Den Blomstertid Nu Kommer *folk,Swed
  (Nyhus, Rolf) SSA/SAB MUSIKK (K414)

En Gang
  SSA/SAB MUSIKK   (K415)

Farleg Ferd
  SSA/SAB MUSIKK   (K416)

Hva Vilde Kan
  SSA/SAB MUSIKK   (K417)

Hvem Eier --?
  SSA/SAB MUSIKK   (K418)

Klassebesok I Kunstgalleriet
  SSA/SAB MUSIKK   (K419)

Nirvana
  SSA/SAB MUSIKK   (K420)

Olav Liljukrans *13th cent
  (Groven, Eivind) mix cor MUSIKK
                                (K421)
Varregn
  SSA/SAB MUSIKK   (K422)

KVAPIL, JAROSLAV (1892-1958)
Dukelska Dumba
  "Dukla Reverie" [Czech] mix cor,
  acap CZECH s.p.   (K423)

Dukla Reverie *see Dukelska Dumba

KYMRY, TYLWYTH
Follow, Follow Me *see Karlin, Fred

KYPTA, F.A. (1906-   )
Pisen Vitezna
  "Song Of Victory" [Czech] mix cor,
  3fl,2ob,2clar,3bsn,4horn,2trp,
  3trom,tuba,perc,strings CZECH
  s.p.   (K424)

Song Of Victory *see Pisen Vitezna

KYTICE see Martinu, Bohuslav

KYUSHU TANKO BUSHI see Sakamoto,
  Yoshitaka

L

LA BARQUE D'AZENOR *folk,Fr
   (Blanchard, R.) 4pt mix cor,acap
   JOBERT s.p.   (L1)

LA BATTAGLIA see Banchieri, Adriano

LA BELLA NINETTA see Ammann, Benno

LA BELLE SE SIED AU PIED DE LA TOUR see
   Poulenc, Francis

LA BERGERE see Binet

LA BOTTEGA DELLE IDEE see Benevenuti,
   Arrigo

LA CACCIA see Cremesini, M.

LA CANTA DELLA PIPITA see Pratella,
   Francesco Balilla, La Canta Dla
   Puvida

LA CANTA D'IMOLA see Pratella,
   Francesco Balilla, La Chenta 'D
   Iomla

LA CANTA DLA PUVIDA see Pratella,
   Francesco Balilla

LA CANZONE DEL SONNO see Pratella,
   Francesco Balilla

LA CARITA see Rossini, Gioacchino

LA CASINA BIANCA see Pratella,
   Francesco Balilla, La Casteina
   Bienca

LA CASTEINA BIENCA see Pratella,
   Francesco Balilla

LA CHENTA 'D IOMLA see Pratella,
   Francesco Balilla

LA COLPA, IL PENTIMENTO E LA GRAZIA see
   Scarlatti, Alessandro

LA COMEDIA VENEZIANA see De Grandis,
   Renato

LA CURVA DELL'AMORE see Bussotti,
   Sylvano

LA DAMOISELLE ELUE see Debussy, Claude

LA DANSE *folk,Fr
   (Blanchard, R.) 4pt mix cor,acap
   JOBERT s.p.   (L2)

LA FAGIOLATA see Pratella, Francesco
   Balilla, La Fasulera

LA FASULERA see Pratella, Francesco
   Balilla

LA FEDE see Rossini, Gioacchino

LA FIALAIRA *folk,Fr
   (Blanchard, R.) 3pt wom cor,acap
   JOBERT s.p.   (L3)

LA FLEUR DES CHAMPS see Boeckx, Jean

LA FORMICUZZA see Cremesini, M.

LA GNOT DAI MUARZ see Liani, Davide

LA GRANGE BLEUE see Middeleer, Jean De

LA GRENOUILLE QUI VEUT SE FAIRE AUSSI
   GROSSE QUE LE BOEUF see Jongen,
   Leon

LA GUERRE see Jannequin, Clement

LA JEUNE BERGERE see Schertzer, Daniel

LA JOUR see Hahn

LA LA LOVE YOU see McLean, Don

LA, LA, MAISTRE PIERRE see Non Papa,
   Jacobus Clemens

LA LAITIERE ET LE POT AU LAIT see
   Jongen, Leon

LA LEZIONE DELLO SPIANTATOIO see
   Pratella, Francesco Balilla

LA MIA CRUDA BRUNETTA see Pederson,
   Mogens

LA NIQUE A SATAN see Martin, Frank

LA NUIT see Hahn

LA PESTA DI ATENE DA "DE RERUM NATURA"
   see Procaccini, T.

LA PIAGA CH'HO NEL CORE see Monteverdi,
   Claudio

LA PIAGA C'HO NEL CORE see Monteverdi,
   Claudio

LA RONDINELLA D'AMORE see Pratella,
   Francesco Balilla

LA ROSE AU BOUE *folk,Fr
   (Blanchard, R.) 3pt wom cor,acap
   JOBERT s.p.   (L4)

LA SISA see Pratella, Francesco Balilla

LA SPERANZA see Rossini, Gioacchino

LA TEMPS RESTITUE see Barraque, Jean

LA VAGA PASTORELLA see Monteverdi,
   Claudio

LA VIE - RONDE see Beauverd

LA VIEILLE DANSE see Denis, Didier

LA VIOLETTE see Ladmirault, P.

LA VRAIE HISTOIRE DE DOULEUR see
   Killmayer, Wilhelm

LABOURER'S HAND, THE see Kanak, Zdenek,
   Delnikova Ruka

LABURDA, JIRI (1931-   )
   Glagolitica *cant
   [Czech] mix cor,4 soli,4horn,4trp,
   3trom,tuba,timp,perc,pno CZECH
   s.p.   (L5)

   Metamorphoses *cant
   [Czech/Ger] mix cor,narrator&SATB
   soli,4fl,2ob,2clar,2bsn,4horn,
   4trp,3trom,tuba,timp,perc,harp,
   pno,strings, xylophone, celeste
   CZECH s.p.   (L6)

LABUTI PERICKO see Tausinger, Jan

LACHEUR, REX
   Three Shakespearian Trios *CC3U
   SSA HARRIS $.75   (L7)

LACHNER, FRANZ (1803-1890)
   Wann Ich Weiss, Was Du Weisst
   *Op.114,No.1, canon
   mix cor (easy) sc SCHOTTS C 24 409
   s.p.   (L8)

LADENI see Kanak, Zdenek

LADIES ONLY see Blyton, Carey

LADMIRAULT, P.
   Annaik
   3 eq voices,acap JOBERT s.p.   (L9)

   Avril
   4pt mix cor,acap JOBERT s.p.   (L10)

   Chanson De Printemps
   3 eq voices,acap JOBERT s.p.   (L11)

   En Paradis
   4pt mix cor,acap JOBERT s.p.   (L12)

   La Violette
   4pt mix cor,acap JOBERT s.p.   (L13)

   Le Reveil Du Village
   3 eq voices,acap JOBERT s.p.   (L14)

   Le Tambourinaire
   3 eq voices,acap JOBERT s.p.   (L15)

   Reminiscences
   3 eq voices,acap JOBERT s.p.   (L16)

   Voici Le Mai
   4pt mix cor,acap JOBERT s.p.   (L17)

LADY MADONNA see Lennon, John

LADY WHO RAN UP A TREE, THE see Kirk,
   Theron W.

LAETARE see Mohler, Philipp

LAETARE see Wolters, Karl-Heinz

LAGO MAGGIORE see Anders-Strehmel,
   Gerhard

LAHAINA see Messina

LAINE, P.
   Blue, Green And Gold *see Crombe, W.

LAKSIN MINA KESAYONA KAYMAAN
   "On A Summer Night" see Tyttoset

L'ALMA MIA DONNA E BELLA see Arcadelt,
   Jacob

L'AMARA DIPARTITA see Pederson, Mogens

LAMB
   Fair, The *see McAfee, Don

   Where Will You Spend Christmas Eve?
   *see McAfee, Don

LAMB, THE see Davis, Katherine K.

LAMB, THE see George, Earl

LAMB, THE see Wood, Joseph

LAMBERT, DENNIS
   Dream On (composed with Potter,
   Brian)
   (Simon, W.) SATB BIG3 $.50   (L18)
   (Simon, W.) SAB BIG3 $.50   (L19)
   (Simon, W.) SSA BIG3 $.50   (L20)

   Look In My Eyes, Pretty Woman
   (composed with Potter, Brian)
   (Metis, F.) SSA BIG3 $.50   (L21)
   (Metis, F.) SATB BIG3 $.50   (L22)
   (Metis, F.) SAB BIG3 $.50   (L23)

   Put A Little Love Away (composed with
   Potter, Brian) *pop
   (Metis, F.) SSA BIG3 $.50   (L24)
   (Metis, F.) SATB BIG3 $.50   (L25)
   (Metis, F.) SAB BIG3 $.45   (L26)
   (Nowak, Jerry) SATB,pno oct BIG
   BELL $.45   (L27)

   This Heart (composed with Potter,
   Brian)
   (Metis, F.) SSA BIG3 $.45   (L28)
   (Metis, F.) SATB BIG3 $.45   (L29)
   (Metis, F.) SAB BIG3 $.45   (L30)

L'AME DES FORGERONS see Stekke, Leon

LAMENT FOR A CHORAL CONDUCTOR see
   Mechem, Kirke

LAMENT OF ELEKTRA, THE see Sydeman,
   William

LAMENTATION see Ingalls, Jeremiah

LAMENTO PACIS see Leeuw, Ton de

LA MONTAINE, JOHN (1920-   )
   Be Glad Then America *Op.43, sac/sec
   cor,4 soli,orch FREDONIA   (L31)

   Freedom Proclamation *anthem
   mix cor,2 soli,org,hndbl FREDONIA
                                    (L32)

   Nonsense Songs From Mother Goose
   *Op.19, CC7L
   mix cor,pno FREDONIA   (L33)

L'AMOUR DE MOY see Strohbach, Siegfried

LAMPELL
   Lonesome Train, The
   (Robinson) SATB SHAWNEE A1298 $2.50
                                    (L34)

LAND see Edler, Robert

LAND DER LIEDER see Brucker, Hermann

LAND OF DREAMS
   SSA CIMINO $.40   (L35)
   TTBB CIMINO $.40   (L36)
   SATB CIMINO $.40   (L37)

LAND OF LIBERTY (AMERICA)
   (Jurey; Graham) SAB,opt band/orch
   HIGHLAND 4134 $.30   (L38)
   (Jurey; Graham) SATB,opt band/orch
   HIGHLAND 4135 $.30   (L39)
   (Jurey; Graham) SA,opt band/orch
   HIGHLAND 5105 $.30   (L40)
   (Jurey; Graham) SSA,opt band/orch
   HIGHLAND 5106 $.30   (L41)

LAND OF LOST CONTENT
   SATB CIMINO $.40   (L42)

LAND OF SLEEP see Wilkinson, Philip G.

LAND OF THE SILVER BIRCH see Muskoka

LAND-SIGHTING see Grieg, Edvard Hagerup

LAND THAT I LOVE! see Yahres, Samuel C.

LANDLER "AM SONNTAG IST KIRCHWEIH" see
   Fischer, Ernst

LANDLICHES LIED see Schumann, Robert
   (Alexander)

LANDLORD, FILL THE FLOWING BOWL
   (Watson, J.P.) TTBB BRODT NC 4 $.32
                                    (L43)

LANDSCAPE see Williamson, Malcolm

LANDSCAPES see Archer, Violet

LANDSCAPES see Paynter, John P.

LANDSKNECHTSTANDCHEN see Lasso, Orlando
  di

LANG
  Donaustrudel Als Wir Jungst In
    Regensburg
  men cor,acap TONOS 18 s.p.   (L44)

LANG, HANS (1897-1968)
  Abschied Am Tore "Jetzt Reisen Wir
    Zum Tor Hinaus"
  men cor sc SCHOTTS CHBL 2 s.p. see
    from Frankische Volkslieder (L45)

  Abschied "Die Schneegans Zieht"
    jr cor/wom cor (easy) sc SCHOTTS
    CHBL 552A-B s.p. contains also:
    Knab, Armin, Der Maie   (L46)

  Alla Schatzla Kumma
    4pt mix cor&4pt men cor,acap sc
    SCHOTTS C 40 061 s.p. see from
    Drei Chor-Duette   (L47)

  Allhier Auf Gruner Heid *see Der
    Jager Aus Kurpfalz; Der Kuckuck
    "Auf Einem Baum Ein Kuckuck
    Sass"; Im Walde, Da Wachsen Die
    Beer'n   (L48)

  Alte Landsknechte "Im Himmel Droben"
    TTBB sc SCHOTTS C 38 343 s.p., voc
    pt SCHOTTS C 38 344, 01-04 s.p.
                              (L49)
  Auf Wiedersehn "Wiedersehn Ist Ein
    Schones Wort"
    see Lang, Hans, Willkommen "Seid
    Willkommen, Liebe Bruder"
    men cor sc SCHOTTS CHBL 198 A-B
    s.p. contains also: Willkommen
    "Seid Willkommen, Liebe Bruder"
                              (L50)
  Bergmannslied
    see LIEDPROGRAMM DES DEUTSCHEN
    SANGERBUNDES FOLGE 3: "ESSENER
    LIEDERBLATT" - "CHORFEIER"

  Bettel-Standchen "Gesang Erschalle
    Vor Dem Haus"
    men cor sc SCHOTTS CHBL 111 s.p.
    see from Zwei Standchen   (L51)

  Bundeslied "In Allen Guten Stunden"
    4pt men cor,4horn,3trp,3trom,tuba
    voc sc SCHOTTS C 37 787 s.p., cor
    pts SCHOTTS C 37 788 s.p., ipa
                              (L52)
  Das Mannlein Im Weinberg "Wenn Die
    Reben Bluhn"
    men cor sc SCHOTTS C 40 407 s.p.
    see from Gluckliches Leben (L53)

  Das Waldhorn
    see Im Grunen Wald

  Der Frosch Sitzt In Dem Rohre
    see Frohliche Tiergeschichten

  Der Geck "Ein Bursch Ist Im
    Stadtchen" *Op.49
    wom cor (med easy) sc SCHOTTS
    C 35 110 s.p. see from Frohliche
    Freite   (L54)

  Der Held "Den Wir Zum Schatz Erkoren"
    *Op.49
    wom cor (med easy) sc SCHOTTS
    C 35 109 s.p. see from Frohliche
    Freite   (L55)

  Der Jager Aus Kurpfalz
    see Im Grunen Wald
    4pt mix cor&1-2pt jr cor (med easy)
    sc SCHOTTS C 38 578 s.p. see from
    Allhier Auf Gruner Heid   (L56)
    men cor,Bar solo sc SCHOTTS
    C 37 697 s.p. see from Drei
    Volksliedsatze   (L57)

  Der Kobold "Das Haus Hab Ich Erbaut"
    men cor sc SCHOTTS C 39 275 s.p.
    see from Zwei Mannerchore (L58)

  Der Konig In Thule "Es War Ein Konig
    In Thule"
    (Zelter, C. Fr.) men cor sc SCHOTTS
    CHBL 3 s.p.   (L59)

  Der Kuckuck "Auf Einem Baum Ein
    Kuckuck Sass"
    4pt mix cor&1-2pt jr cor (med easy)
    sc SCHOTTS C 38 515 s.p. see from
    Allhier Auf Gruner Heid   (L60)

  Der Mond Ist Aufgegangen *Op.50,
    Eve,cant
    3pt wom cor&unis jr cor&opt men
    cor,cantor,pno,ob,2rec/2clar,trp,
    horn,2vln,vcl,opt bvl sc
    SCHOTTS ED. 2967 s.p., voc sc
    SCHOTTS ED. 3747 s.p., ipa (L61)

LANG, HANS (cont'd.)
  Der Morgenstern "Horch Aus Der
    Gestorbnen Dammerwelt"
    men cor sc SCHOTTS C 38 274 s.p.
    see from Zwei Mannerchore   (L62)

  Der Reiter Und Das Madchen "Wohlan
    Die Zeit Ist Kommen"
    men cor sc SCHOTTS C 33 613 s.p.
    see from Frankische Volkslieder
                              (L63)
  Der Schneider Auf Der Wanderschaft
    "Es Wollt' Ein Schneider Wandern"
    men cor sc SCHOTTS C 33 623 s.p.
    see from Frankische Volkslieder
                              (L64)
  Die Alte Uhr "In Meinem Vaterhause"
    men cor sc SCHOTTS C 40 406 s.p.
    see from Gluckliches Leben (L65)

  Die Brucke Von Avignon "Kennt Ihr
    Schon, Kennt Ihr Schon Avignon"
    4pt men cor&4pt mix cor,T solo,acap
    sc SCHOTTS C 41 289 s.p., cor pts
    SCHOTTS C 41 290, 291 s.p. (L66)

  Die Gedanken Sind Frei
    men cor sc SCHOTTS C 37 698 s.p.
    see from Drei Volksliedsatze
                              (L67)
  Die Schnitterin "Vor Einem Grunen
    Walde"
    men cor sc SCHOTTS C 40 405 s.p.
    see from Gluckliches Leben (L68)

  Die Zwei Hasen
    see Frohliche Tiergeschichten

  Dort Unter Der Linde
    mix cor (easy) sc SCHOTTS C 34 282
    s.p. see from Funf Tanzlieder
                              (L69)
    men cor sc SCHOTTS C 35 924 s.p.
    see from Funf Tanzlieder   (L70)

  Drei Chor-Duette *see Alla Schatzla
    Kumma; Schwesterlein, Wann Gehn
    Wir Nach Haus?   (L71)

  Drei Volksliedsatze *see Der Jager
    Aus Kurpfalz; Die Gedanken Sind
    Frei; Hab Mein Wage Vollgelade
                              (L72)
  Drei Volksweisen *see Falsche Zungen
    "Mein Schatz Der Ist Auf Wander
    Schaft"; Guter Rat "Bist Du Junge
    Frau Geworden"; Im Rosengarten
    "Gestern Bei Mondenschein Ging
    Ich Spaziern"   (L73)

  Ein Lied Zur Nacht
    see Lang, Hans, Wenn Die Bunten
    Fahnen Wehen

  Ein Mannlein Steht Im Walde
    see Im Grunen Wald

  Erntereigen "Wir Bringen Mit Gesang"
    men cor sc SCHOTTS C 35 922 s p
    see from Funf Tanzlieder   (L74)
    mix cor (easy) sc SCHOTTS C 34 280
    s.p. see from Funf Tanzlieder
                              (L75)
  Es Dunkelt Schon In Der Heide
    men cor sc SCHOTTS CHBL 41 s.p.
                              (L76)
  Es Gingen Drei Gesellen
    cor pts SCHOTTS C 40 059-060 s.p.
    see from DREI CHOR-DUETTE (L77)
    4pt mix cor&4pt men cor,acap sc
    SCHOTTS C 40 058 s.p. see from
    Drei Chor-Duette   (L78)

  Falsche Zungen "Mein Schatz Der Ist
    Auf Wander Schaft" *folk
    wom cor (med easy) sc SCHOTTS
    C 34 734 s.p. see from Drei
    Volksweisen   (L79)

  Frankische Volkslieder *see Abschied
    Am Tore "Jetzt Reisen Wir Zum Tor
    Hinaus"; Der Reiter Und Das
    Madchen "Wohlan Die Zeit Ist
    Kommen"; Der Schneider Auf Der
    Wanderschaft "Es Wollt' Ein
    Schneider Wandern";
    Handwerksburschen-Abschied "Es,
    Es, Es Und Es";
    Handwerksburschen-Wanderlied "Auf
    Du Junger Wandersmann"; Unser
    Vetter Veitl; Verkehrte Welt "Wie
    Sind Mir Meine Stiefel
    Geschwoll'n   (L80)

  Frohliche Freite *see Der Geck "Ein
    Bursch Ist Im Stadtchen", Op.49;
    Der Held "Den Wir Zum Schatz
    Erkoren", Op.49; Neun Freier "Im
    Herbst Beim Apfelschalen", Op.49
                              (L81)
  Frohliche Tiergeschichten
    1-2pt jr cor,pno/fl&ob&clar&bsn&
    horn&2vln&vla&vcl&bvl, voc
    pt SCHOTTS ED. 4507 s.p., ipa
    contains: Der Frosch Sitzt In Dem

LANG, HANS (cont'd.)
    Rohre; Die Zwei Hasen; Suse,
    Liebe Suse; Widewidewenne (L82)

  Frohliches Handwerk *cant
    3pt mix cor,pno/2vln&vcl&rec (easy)
    sc,cor pts SCHOTTS ED. 4036 s.p.,
    ipa   (L83)

  Fruh, Des Morgens Fruh
    see Im Grunen Wald

  Funf Tanzlieder *see Dort Unter Der
    Linde; Erntereigen "Wir Bringen
    Mit Gesang"; Heissa Kathreinerle;
    Ich Spring In Diesem Ringe;
    Kommt, Ihr Gspielen   (L84)

  Funf Tanzlieder *see Dort Unter Der
    Linde; Erntereigen "Wir Bringen
    Mit Gesang"; Heissa Kathreinerle;
    Ich Spring In Diesem Ringe;
    Kommt, Ihr Gespielen   (L85)

  Geh Aus, Mein Herz
    mix cor (easy) sc SCHOTTS CHBL 328
    s.p.   (L86)

  Gluck "Gluck Ist Wie Ein Sonnenblick"
    men cor sc SCHOTTS C 40 408 s.p.
    see from Gluckliches Leben (L87)

  Gluckliches Leben *see Das Mannlein
    Im Weinberg "Wenn Die Reben
    Bluhn"; Die Alte Uhr "In Meinem
    Vaterhause"; Die Schnitterin "Vor
    Einem Grunen Walde"; Gluck "Gluck
    Ist Wie Ein Sonnenblick";
    Turmchoral "Die Stadt Liegt Noch"
                              (L88)
  Gluckwunsch-Kantate *Op.44, cant
    4pt mix cor,S solo,fl,ob,clar,trp,
    2vln,vla (med easy) sc,cor pts
    SCHOTTS ED. 4238 s.p., ipa (L89)
    men cor,S solo,fl,ob,clar,trp,2vln,
    vla sc SCHOTTS C 35 422 s.p., voc
    pt SCHOTTS C 36 388, 01-02 s.p.,
    ipa   (L90)
  Grunet Die Hoffnung
    wom cor (easy) sc SCHOTTS CHBL 556
    s.p.   (L91)

  Grunet Felder, Grunet Wiesen
    unis jr cor&4pt men cor,acap (easy)
    sc SCHOTTS C 40 656 s.p.   (L92)

  Gruss Gott, Du Schoner Maien
    men cor sc SCHOTTS CHBL 21 s.p.
                              (L93)
  Guter Rat "Bist Du Junge Frau
    Geworden" *folk
    wom cor (med easy) sc SCHOTTS
    C 34 735 s.p. see from Drei
    Volksweisen   (L94)

  Hab Mein Wage Vollgelade
    men cor sc SCHOTTS C 37 696 s.p.
    see from Drei Volksliedsatze
                              (L95)
  Handwerksburschen-Abschied "Es, Es,
    Es Und Es"
    men cor sc SCHOTTS C 33 619 s.p.
    see from Frankische Volkslieder
                              (L96)
  Handwerksburschen-Wanderlied "Auf Du
    Junger Wandersmann"
    men cor sc SCHOTTS C 33 621 s.p.
    see from Frankische Volkslieder
                              (L97)
  Heissa Kathreinerle
    men cor sc SCHOTTS C 35 926 s.p.
    see from Funf Tanzlieder   (L98)
    mix cor (easy) sc SCHOTTS C 34 284
    s.p. see from Funf Tanzlieder
                              (L99)
  Heureigen "Wenn Kuhl Der Morgen
    Atmet"
    mix cor (easy) sc SCHOTTS CHBL 255
    s.p.   (L100)

  Horch, Was Kommt Von Draussen Rein?
    men cor sc SCHOTTS CHBL 28 s.p.
                              (L101)
  Ich Hab Mein Sach Auf Nichts Gestellt
    men cor sc SCHOTTS CHBL 7 s.p.
                              (L102)
  Ich Habe Mein Feinsliebchen
    men cor sc SCHOTTS CHBL 99 s.p.
                              (L103)
  Ich Spring In Diesem Ringe
    mix cor (easy) sc SCHOTTS C 34 276
    s.p. see from Funf Tanzlieder
                              (L104)
    men cor sc SCHOTTS C 35 918 s.p.
    see from Funf Tanzlieder   (L105)

  Im Fruhtau Zu Berge
    wom cor (easy) sc SCHOTTS CHBL 526
    s.p.   (L106)

  Im Grunen Wald
    1-2pt jr cor,pno,fl,clar,bsn,horn,
    2vln,vla,vcl,bvl (easy) sc,voc pt
    SCHOTTS ED. 4506 s.p., ipa

LANG, HANS (cont'd.)

contains: Das Waldhorn; Der Jager
Aus Kurpfalz; Ein Mannlein
Steht Im Walde; Fruh, Des
Morgens Fruh; Im Walde, Da
Wachsen Die Beer'n   (L107)

Im Rosengarten "Gestern Bei
Mondenschein Ging Ich Spazieren"
*folk
wom cor (med easy) sc SCHOTTS
C 34 733 s.p. see from Drei
Volksweisen   (L108)

Im Walde, Da Wachsen Die Beer'n
see Im Grunen Wald
4pt mix cor&1-2pt jr cor (med easy)
sc SCHOTTS C 38 516 see from
Allhier Auf Gruner Heid   (L109)

Kantate Vom Frohlichen Musikanten
*Op.46, cant
mix cor/wom cor,fl,ob,vln&vla/2vln
(easy) sc,cor pts SCHOTTS
ED. 4037 s.p., ipa   (L110)

Kein Schoner Land *folk
see Haydn, (Franz) Joseph,
Nachtigallenkanon "Alles
Schweiget"
2pt jr cor,2 narrators,pno/inst
(easy) sc,voc pt SCHOTTS ED. 3748
s.p., ipa   (L111)

Kommt, Ihr Gespielen
men cor sc SCHOTTS C 35 920 s.p.
see from Funf Tanzlieder   (L112)

Kommt, Ihr Gspielen
mix cor (easy) sc SCHOTTS C 34 278
s.p. see from Funf Tanzlieder
                            (L113)

Lustig, Ihr Bruder (from Der Mond Ist
Aufgegangen)
2-3pt jr cor/2-3pt wom cor,trp,
strings,2rec (easy) sc SCHOTTS
CHBL 592 s.p.   (L114)

Lustige Leut *folk
3pt jr cor,pno/fl&ob&clar&bsn&horn
(easy) sc,cor pts SCHOTTS
ED. 4508 s.p.
contains: Unser Hans Hat Hosen
An; Wenn Die Betteleute Tanzen;
Wir Sind Mir Meine Stiefel
Geschwolln   (L115)

Neun Freier "Im Herbst Beim
Apfelschalen" *Op.49
wom cor (med easy) sc SCHOTTS
C 35 111 s.p. see from Frohliche
Freite   (L116)

Nun Will Der Lenz Uns Grussen
(Battke, M.) men cor sc SCHOTTS
CHBL 36 s.p.   (L117)

Plaudertasche "Du Liebes
Pappelmaulchen"
men cor sc SCHOTTS C 38 337 s.p.
see from Wilhelm Busch-Zyklus (L118)

Schone Welt "Wie Liegt Die Welt So
Frisch Und Tauig"
men cor sc SCHOTTS C 39 007 s.p.
see from Wilhelm Busch-Zyklus (L119)

Schwesterlein, Wann Gehn Wir Nach
Haus?
4pt mix cor&4pt men cor,acap sc
SCHOTTS C 40 057 s.p. see from
Drei Chor-Duette   (L120)

Standchen "Wir Haben Uns Als Musici"
men cor sc SCHOTTS CHBL 112 s.p.
see from Zwei Standchen   (L121)

Suse, Liebe Suse
see Frohliche Tiergeschichten

Turmchoral "Die Stadt Liegt Noch"
men cor sc SCHOTTS C 40 404 s.p.
see from Gluckliches Leben (L122)

Unser Hans Hat Hosen An
see Lustige Leut

Unser Vetter Veitl
men cor sc SCHOTTS C 33 625 s.p.
see from Frankische Volkslieder
                            (L123)

Verkehrte Welt "Wie Sind Mir Meine
Stiefel Geschwoll'n
men cor sc SCHOTTS C 33 627 s.p.
see from Frankische Volkslieder
                            (L124)

Vom Baumelein "Es Ist Ein Baumlein
Gestanden"
4pt wom cor,S solo,acap (med) sc
SCHOTTS C 40 697 s.p., cor pts
SCHOTTS C 40 697-01:02 s.p.
                            (L125)

Waldwege "So Viel Wege Laufen Durch
Den Wald"
men cor sc SCHOTTS CHBL 67 s.p.

LANG, HANS (cont'd.)
                            (L126)
Wanderschaft "Im Walde Bluht Der
Seidelbast"
men cor sc SCHOTTS CHBL 157 s.p.
                            (L127)
Wenn Alle Brunnlein Fliessen
mix cor (easy) sc SCHOTTS
CHBL 300A-B s.p. contains also:
Mozart, Wolfgang Amadeus, Bona
Nox   (L128)
men cor sc SCHOTTS CHBL 23 s.p.
                            (L129)
Wenn Die Betteleute Tanzen
see Lustige Leut

Wenn Die Bunten Fahnen Wehen
3pt jr cor,solo,acap (easy) sc
SCHOTTS CHBL 529A-B s.p. contains
also: Ein Lied Zur Nacht   (L130)

Wenn Mer Sonntags
men cor sc SCHOTTS CHBL 48 s.p.
                            (L131)
Widewidewenne
see Frohliche Tiergeschichten

Wilhelm Busch-Zyklus *see
Plaudertasche "Du Liebes
Pappelmaulchen"; Schone Welt "Wie
Liegt Die Welt So Frisch Und
Tauig"   (L132)

Willkommen "Seid Willkommen, Liebe
Bruder"
see Lang, Hans, Auf Wiedersehn
"Wiedersehn Ist Ein Schones Wort"
mix cor (easy) sc SCHOTTS
CHBL 397A-B s.p. contains also:
Auf Wiedersehn "Wiedersehn Ist
Ein Schones Wort"   (L133)

Wir Sind Mir Meine Stiefel Geschwolln
see Lustige Leut

Zogen Einst Funf Wilde Schwane
men cor sc SCHOTTS CHBL 38 s.p.
                            (L134)
Zur Trauung "Ewge Liebe, Ewge Liebe"
jr cor/wom cor (med easy) sc
SCHOTTS CHBL 547 s.p.   (L135)

Zwei Mannerchore *see Der Kobold
"Das Haus Hab Ich Erbaut"; Der
Morgenstern "Horch Aus Der
Gestorbnen Dammerwelt"   (L136)

Zwei Standchen *see Bettel-Standchen
"Gesang Erschalle Vor Dem Haus";
Standchen "Wir Haben Uns Als
Musici"   (L137)

LANG, ISTVAN
Oktober Emleke
eq voices,pno BUDAPEST 7527 s.p.
                            (L138)
Tuz
(Nagy, Laszlo) eq voices BUDAPEST
7510 s.p.   (L139)

LANG UND BREIT see Edler, Robert

LANGE
Come With Me
(Muller; Wick) SATB oct SCHMITT
W248 $.40   (L140)

LANGE, GREGOR (ca. 1540-1587)
Good Man, You Are Complaining *see
Gut G'sell, Du Machst Dein Klagen

Gut G'sell, Du Machst Dein Klagen
(Malin, Don) "Good Man, You Are
Complaining" SSA BELWIN 2296 $.35
                            (L141)
Lenz Kommt Herbei
(Malin, Don) "Spring Now Is Near"
SSA BELWIN 2293 $.35   (L142)

Spring Now Is Near *see Lenz Kommt
Herbei

LANGER, HANS-KLAUS
Abend Am Chiemsee
see Berg_lieder

Berglieder
men cor,acap cmplt ed TONOS 4500
s.p.
contains: Abend Am Chiemsee; Die
Hutten; Frisch Angepacket Den
Tag   (L143)

Die Hutten
see Berglieder

Frisch Angepacket Den Tag
see Berglieder

Such, Herz, Nun
men cor,acap TONOS 4509 s.p. (L144)

LANGSAMER MARSCH see Biebl, Franz

LANYCSUFOLO see Bartok, Bela

LARGO see Mule, Giuseppe

LARIDAH "ACH, MEIN SCHATZ IST
DURCHGEGANGEN" see Zoll, Paul

LARK IN THE CLEAR AIR
(Deale, Edgar) SSA (med easy)
WATERLOO $.40   (L145)

L'ARTE MUSICALE IN ITALIA *sac/sec,
CCU,14-18th cent
(Torchi, Luigi) microfiche
UNIV.MUS.ED. $55.00 7 volumes
                            (L146)
L'ARTE MUSICALE IN ITALIA, VOL. I see
Torchi

L'ARTE MUSICALE IN ITALIA, VOL. II see
Torchi

L'ARTE MUSICALE IN ITALIA, VOL.IV see
Torchi

L'ARTE MUSICALE IN ITALIA, VOL. V see
Torchi

LAS, S'IL CONVIENT see Certon, Pierre

LASKA see Jirasek, Ivo

LASKA, BOZE, LASKA see Mikula, Zdenko

LASKA PEKNEJSI see Podest, Ludvik

LASKA ZA LASKU see Podest, Ludvik

LASKER
Schlaf, Freund
see VIER GRABLIEDER

LASS OF RICHMOND HILL
(Willcocks) SATB,acap OXFORD see from
Five Folk Songs   (L147)

LASSEN, EDUARD (1830-1904)
When Thy Blue Eyes
SA CRAMER $.25   (L148)

LASSET UNS TRINKEN see Michels, Josef

LASSO, ORLANDO DI
Complete Works *sac/sec,CCU
(Haberl, F.X.; Sandberger, Adolf)
microfiche UNIV.MUS.ED. $100.00
Breitkopf and Haertel, 1894-1927
in 21 volumes.   (L149)

Hallo! Welch Schones Echo!
[Ger/It] mix cor (med easy) sc
SCHOTTS CHBL 268 s.p.   (L150)

Landsknechtstandchen
(Hirsch) men cor FORBERG sc s.p.,
voc pt s.p.   (L151)
(Hirsch) mix cor FORBERG sc s.p.,
voc pt s.p.   (L152)

Matona Mia Cara "Lanzknecht-
Standchen"
[Ger/It] mix cor (med easy) sc
SCHOTTS C 42 741 s.p.   (L153)

Wenn Das Gluck Dich Heut Veracht
[Fr/Ger] mix cor (easy) sc SCHOTTS
C 39 773 s.p.   (L154)

LASST MICH ALLEIN see Sermisy, Claude
de

LASST SICH AMOR BEI EUCH SCHAUEN see Se
Amor Mai Da Vu Se Vede

LASST UNS ALL' NACH HAUSE GEHEN see
Linke, Norbert

LASST UNS EIN STUNDLEIN LUSTIG SEIN see
Franck, Melchior

LASST UNS GLAUBEN see Rein, Walter

LASST UNS WANDERN, LASST UNS REISEN see
Zoll, Paul

LASST UNS ZUSAMMEN IN GOTTES NAMEN
SINGEN see Steffens, Johann

LASSU TANCNOTA see Petrovics, Emil

LASSUS, ROLAND DE (ORLANDUS)
(1532-1594)
Audite Nova
(Weber, W.) men cor,acap TONOS 3306
s.p.   (L155)

Bon Jour
(Biggs, John) SATB,acap (med)
FOSTER CP-2 $.50   (L156)

Cara Madonna Mia
(Desch, Rudolf) "Matona Mia Cara"
[Ger/It] men cor sc SCHOTTS
C 39 718 s.p.   (L157)

LASSUS, ROLAND DE (ORLANDUS) (cont'd.)

Day After Day They All Say "Sing"
*see Tutto Lo Di Mi Dici "Canta"

Eccho *madrigal
[It] SSAATTBB RICORDI-ENG BA9884
s.p.   (L158)

Faithful And True
(Ehret) SATB SCHIRM.G LG 51840 $.40
(L159)

I Know A Fair Maiden *see Ich Waiss
Mir Ein Miedlein

Ich Waiss Mir Ein Miedlein
(Klein) "I Know A Fair Maiden" SATB
SCHIRM.G 11962 $.30   (L160)

Kommt Von Der Arbeit
(Weber, W.) men cor,acap TONOS 3317
s.p.   (L161)

Matona Mia Cara *madrigal
[It] SATB RICORDI-ENG BA9885 s.p.
(L162)
[It] SATB,acap EGTVED MS6B14 s.p.
(L163)

Matona Mia Cara *see Cara Madonna
Mia

My Heart Is Yours
(McCullough) SATB SOUTHERN $.30
(L164)

My Heart Leaps Up
(McCullough) SATB SOUTHERN $.30
(L165)

My Little Sweetheart
(Holgate) SATB SCHIRM.G LG51837
$.40   (L166)

S'io Fusse Ciaul
(Klein) "Were I A Tiny Bird" SATB
SCHIRM.G 11960 $.30   (L167)

Super Flumina Babylonis
SATB MCAFEE M1065 $.35   (L168)

Ten Madrigals *CC10U,madrigal
(Arnold) cor OXFORD   (L169)

Tutto Lo Di Mi Dici "Canta"
(Klein) "Day After Day They All Say
"Sing"" SATB SCHIRM.G 11961 $.30
(L170)
Were I A Tiny Bird *see S'io Fusse
Ciaul

Who Sleepeth Here?
(Field, Robert) [Eng/Fr] SATB,acap
(med) oct PRESSER 312-40943 $.35
(L171)
LAST INVOCATION, THE see Carter, J.

LAST, JAMES
When The Snow Is On The Roses
(Metis, F.) SSA BIG3 $.40   (L172)
(Metis, F.) SATB BIG3 $.40   (L173)

LAST OF THE JUST, THE see Tanenbaum,
Elias

LAST ORGAN GRINDER see Tate

LAST ROSE OF SUMMER, THE *folk
(Lester, William) SATB (med)
FITZSIMONS 1031 $.25   (L174)

LAST ROSE OF SUMMER, THE see Moore,
Thomas

LAST ROSE OF SUMMER, THE see Sharpe,
Evelyn

LAST SONG see Eville

LAST SPRING see Grieg, Edvard Hagerup

LAST TANGO IN PARIS see Barbieri, Gato

LAST THING ON MY MIND, THE see Paxton,
Tom

LAST TIME I SAW PARIS
SSA CIMINO $.40   (L175)
SAB CIMINO $.40   (L176)
SA CIMINO $.40   (L177)
SATB CIMINO $.40   (L178)

LATE NITE NURSERY RHYMES see Tiffault

LATERNE see Kludas, Erich

LATT OCH BLANDAT FOR BLANDAT KOR see
Lindahl, Allan

LATVIAN BOAT SONG see Kemp, Walter

LAUDA "AMORE, AMORE CHE SI M'HAI
FERITO" see Killmayer, Wilhelm

LAUDE see Bossi, Renzo

LAUGHING ON THE OUTSIDE (CRYING ON THE
INSIDE) see Raleigh

LAUGHING SONG see Diemer

LAUGHING SONG see George, Earl

LAUGHTER IN THE RAIN see Sedaka, Neil

LAURA see Butler, Eugene

LAWSON, MALCOLM
Proud Maisie
SSA,acap CRAMER U49   (L179)

LAY DOWN (CANDLES IN THE RAIN)
SSA CIMINO $.40   (L180)
SATB CIMINO $.40   (L181)

LAZICKI
Song Of The Storm
(Wood) SATB,fl,gtr ART MAST 1023
$.40   (L182)

LAZY JUNE see Washburn

LE BEAU DU MONDE S'EFFACE see
L'Estocart, Paschal de

LE BERGER see Monteverdi, Claudio

LE BOUVIER see Schertzer, Daniel

LE CHARBONNIER see Passani, Emile

LE CHAT, LA BELETTE ET LE PETIT LAPIN
see Jongen, Leon

LE CHAT QUI DORT see Strimer, Joseph

LE COQ see Denis, Didier

LE CORBEAU ET LE RENARD see Jongen,
Leon

LE CRUCIFIX see Passani, Emile

LE CYGNE *folk,Fr
(Blanchard, R.) 4pt mix cor,acap
JOBERT s.p.   (L183)

LE FAINEANT see Strimer, Joseph

LE FOCARINE see Pratella, Francesco
Balilla, Al Fugaren

LE GRILLON see Pileur

LE GROS MOINE *folk,Fr
(Blanchard, R.) 4pt mix cor,acap
JOBERT s.p.   (L184)

LE JALOUX see Passani, Emile

LE JEU DU PRINTEMPS see Binet

LE JOLI JEU DES SAISONS, RONDES,
CHANSONS, RYTHMIQUE see Dalcroze,
Jacques

LE JOUR DES MORTS see Martin, Ch.

LE LOUP ET L'AGNEAU see Jongen, Leon

LE MECHANTE HORLOGE see Strimer, Joseph

LE MENAGE DE LA SAINTE FAMILLE *folk,
Fr
(Blanchard, R.) 4pt mix cor,acap
JOBERT s.p.   (L185)

LE MIROIR see Willan, Healey

LE MONDE, NOUS VOULONS LE CONNAITRE see
Stekke, Leon

LE MONTAGNARD see Carrard

LE NAVIRE DE BAYONNE see Willan, Healey

LE PAYS see Apotheloz, Jean

LE PAYS see Binet

LE PRINTEMPS SUR L'ALPE see Carrard

LE P'TIT HOMME see Havord de la
Montagne, joachim

LE RETOUR DES HIRONDELLES see Puget, P.

LE REVEIL DU VILLAGE see Ladmirault, P.

LE ROSSIGNOL DAUS SON NID CHANTE see
Hollande, J. de

LE ROY A FAIT BATTRE TAMBOUR *folk,Fr
(Blanchard, R.) 4pt mix cor,acap
JOBERT s.p.   (L186)

LE TAMBOURINAIRE see Ladmirault, P.

LE TEMPS A LAISSIE SON MANTEAU see
Killmayer, Wilhelm

LE TEMPS JE REGRETTE see Biebl, Franz,
Aus Meiner Kindheit

LE TIC-TAC DU MOULIN *folk,Fr
(Blanchard, R.) 4pt mix cor,acap
JOBERT s.p.   (L187)

LE TOURMENT CACHE see Killmayer,
Wilhelm

LE VENT see Strimer, Joseph

LE VIEUX JEAN LOUIS see Binet

LEAF
The Choral Art, Vol. II *CCU
SATB SCHIRM.G LG51732 $3.50   (L188)

LEAF, A see Hannay, Roger

LEAF, ROBERT
One Starry Night
unis,pno/org NATIONAL WHC-58 $.30
(L189)

LEANYNEZO see Bartok, Bela

LEAVES IN AUTUMN FADE AND FALL see
Sullivan, Sir Arthur Seymour

LEAVES OF GRASS see Hall, William D.

LEAVETAKING see Jewell, Kenneth W.

LEB WOHL, DU SCHONER WALD *folk,Ger
(Edler, Rudolf) men cor,acap TONOS 68
s.p.   (L190)

LEB' WOHL DU SCHONES STADTCHEN see
Nitsche, Paul, Adieu Privas

LEB WOHL, FRAU WELT see Krietsch, Georg

LEBE WOHL! see Bartok, Bela, Isten
Veled!

LEBEN UND BESTEHEN see Schroeder,
Hermann

LEBENSABSCHNITT see Krietsch, Georg

LEBENSKREISE see Gal, Hans

LEBEWOHL see Distler, Hugo

LECHNER, KONRAD (1911-   )
Ein Jeder Meint, Er Sei Der Best
see Rosthius, Nicolaus, Lieblich
Wohl Kommt Der Mai

LECHNER, LEONHARD (ca. 1550-1606)
Che Piu D'un Giorno
(Malin, Don) "How Like A Brief Day
Our Life Passes" SATB BELWIN 2318
$.30   (L191)

Gott B'hute Dich
SATB,acap BAREN. BCH70 s.p.   (L192)
(Koenig, F.) men cor,acap TONOS
3328 s.p.   (L193)

Green Is The May *see Grun Ist Der
Mai

Grun Ist Der Mai
(Malin, Don) "Green Is The May"
SSAA BELWIN 2298 $.35   (L194)

Gut Singer Und Ein Organist
men cor sc SCHOTTS C 38 813 s.p.
contains also: Lechner, Leonhard,
Jagen, Hetzen Und Federspiel;
Rauch, Andreas, All Lust Und
Freud   (L195)

How Like A Brief Day Our Life Passes
*see Che Piu D'un Giorno

Jagen, Hetzen Und Federspiel
see Lechner, Leonhard, Gut Singer
Und Ein Organist

LEEDS
Day Has Come, The (composed with
McAfee, Don)
1-2pt,pno/gtr MCAFEE M109 $.30
(L196)
Wintertime (composed with Silver)
unis,pno MCAFEE M127 $.30   (L197)

LEEUW, TON DE (1926-   )
Lamento Pacis
mix cor,fl,2vln,2vla,2bvl,2perc
DONEMUS   (L198)

Litany Of Our Time
men cor,S solo,pno,fl,bvl,perc,
harp,electronic tape (television
play) DONEMUS   (L199)

LEFANU, NICOLA (1947-   )
Let The Valleys Sing
SATB,2bsn,2trp,3trom voc sc NOVELLO
rental   (L200)

LEFEVRE, JACQUES
Chambriere, Chambriere
(Tunley, D.) SAT,acap NOVELLO
MT 1575 s.p.   (L201)

Tu Ne L'Entends Pas
(Tunley, D.) "You're Not List'ning
To Me" SAT NOVELLO MT 1582 s.p. (L202)

You're Not List'ning To Me *see Tu
Ne L'Entends Pas

LE FLEMING, CHRISTOPHER (KAYE)
(1908-   )
Six Country Songs *Op.34, CC6U
SATB,2fl,2ob,2clar,2bsn,4horn,2trp,
3trom,timp,perc,strings voc sc
NOVELLO rental   (L203)

LEGEND, A see Tchaikovsky, Piotr
Ilyitch

LEGEND ABOUT LENIN, THE see Felix,
Vaclav, Povest O Leninovi

LEGEND FROM THE SMOKE OF POTATO FIRES
see Martinu, Bohuslav

LEGEND OF THE FROGS see Sousa, John
Philip

LEGRAND, MICHEL (1932-   )
Summer Me, Winter Me (composed with
Bergman) *pop
(Slater) "Theme From Picasso
Summer" SSA,opt perc WARNER
WB-307 183 $.40   (L204)
(Slater) "Theme From Picasso
Summer" SATB,opt perc WARNER
WB-306 187 $.40   (L205)

Theme From Picasso Summer *see
Summer Me, Winter Me

LEHR, GREGOR
Daheim
men cor,acap TONOS 229 s.p.   (L206)

Edle, Schone Kunst Musik
men cor,acap TONOS 3983 s.p.   (L207)

LEHRER LAMPEL see Sutermeister,
Heinrich

LEICHTER SINN see Weber, Bernhard

LEIGHTON, KENNETH (1929-   )
Birds, The *Op.28
SATB,S/T solo,pno,strings,opt timp,
optional cymbals voc sc NOVELLO
rental   (L208)
SATB,S/T solo,2pno,opt timp,
optional cymbals voc sc NOVELLO
rental   (L209)

Light Invisible *Op.16
SATB,T solo,2fl,pic,2ob,2clar,3bsn,
4horn,3trp,3trom,timp,perc,harp,
strings voc sc NOVELLO rental   (L210)

LEISE RIESELT DER SCHNEE see Ebel, E.

LEIST, PETER MARZELLIN
Der Esel
men cor,acap TONOS 4091 s.p.   (L211)

Der Samann
men cor,acap TONOS 3971 s.p.   (L212)

Der Wildbach
men cor,acap sc,cor pts TONOS 4521
s.p.   (L213)

Dichterwort
men cor,acap TONOS 252 s.p.   (L214)

Es Quellen Alle Bronnen
men cor,acap TONOS 4557 s.p.   (L215)

Mein Deutsches Lied
men cor,acap TONOS 253 s.p.   (L216)

'S Ist Weihnacht
men cor,acap TONOS 254 s.p.   (L217)

Taglich Zu Singen
men cor,acap TONOS 4556 s.p.   (L218)

LEISURE see Dello Joio, Norman

LEISURE see Kunz, Alfred

LEISY
Chile Verde
SATB ALFRED 6818 $.50   (L219)

LEITH POLICE see Foster

LEITSPRUCH see Strobl, Otto

LE JEUNE, CLAUDE (1528-1600)
That Joyous Season Spring *see Voicy
Du Gay Printems

LE JEUNE, CLAUDE (cont'd.)
Voicy Du Gay Printems
"That Joyous Season Spring" [Fr/
Eng] SATB,acap SALABERT-US $.60 (L220)

Weep Now
(Ehret) SATB SCHIRM.G LG 51580 $.30 (L221)

LEKBERG, SVEN (1899-   )
Years Prophetical
SATB,S/T solo,pno STANDARD B400MX1
$1.35   (L222)

LEMACHER, HEINRICH (1891-1966)
Der Kuckuck Auf Dem Zaune
men cor,acap TONOS 38 s.p.   (L223)

Mit Lust Tat Ich Ausreiten
men cor,acap TONOS s.p.   (L224)

LEMLIN, LORENZ (1485-1540)
Der Gutzgauch Auf Dem Zaune Sass
see Ahle, Johann Rudolph, Was Mag
Doch Diese Welt

LENDVAI, ERWIN (1882-1949)
Der Reif Und Auch Der Kalte Schnee
men cor,acap TONOS 13 s.p.   (L225)

Der Ruf Der Freiheit
men cor,acap TONOS 4039 s.p.   (L226)

Der Weckruf Hallt
men cor,acap TONOS 4017 s.p.   (L227)

Die Maschinen
men cor,acap TONOS 4027 s.p.   (L228)

Die Singende Stadt
men cor,acap TONOS 4024 s.p.   (L229)

Einklang "Einklang! Gloria Der Welt"
4-6pt men cor,acap sc SCHOTTS
C 31 497D s.p.   (L230)

Glockenlied "Glocken Mit Dem
Silbermund"
SATBB,acap (med diff) sc SCHOTTS
C 32 910 s.p., voc pt SCHOTTS
C 32 910A-E s.p.   (L231)

Hoffnung
men cor,acap TONOS 4029 s.p.   (L232)

Klirr, Sense, Klirr
men cor,acap TONOS 4025 s.p.   (L233)

Licht Muss Wieder Werden
4-8pt men cor&2pt jr cor,acap sc
SCHOTTS C 31 497 s.p.   (L234)

Lied Der Arbeit
men cor,acap TONOS 4023 s.p.   (L235)

Lied Der Kohlenhauer
men cor,acap TONOS 4028 s.p.   (L236)

Schmiede Der Zeit
men cor,acap TONOS 4022 s.p.   (L237)

Sommermadrigal "Singe, Meine Liebe
Seele" *madrigal
TBarB,acap sc SCHOTTS C 33 759 s.p.
(L238)

Wahlspruch: Strebe Empor
men cor,acap TONOS 4021 s.p.   (L239)

LENDVAY, KAMILLO
Dozsa Siratoja
(Kovesdy, Janos) mix cor BUDAPEST
6834 s.p.   (L240)

Ejszaka II
(Vaci, Mihaly) mix cor BUDAPEST
7509 s.p.   (L241)

Mig Az Ember
(Kovesdy) mix cor BUDAPEST 7155
s.p.   (L242)

LENGENDE VOM WEISEN UND ZOLLNER see
Schilling, Hans Ludwig

LENINS EWIGE STIMME see Lukowsky, Rolf

LENNON, JOHN (1940-   )
Because (composed with McCartney,
John Paul)
(Holcombe, Bill) SSA CHARTER
CO30211   (L243)
(Holcombe, Bill) SATB CHARTER
CO30202   (L244)

Bless You
(Metis, F.) SSA BIG3 $.50   (L245)
(Metis, F.) SAB BIG3 $.50   (L246)
(Metis, F.) SATB BIG3 $.50   (L247)

Day Tripper (composed with McCartney,
John Paul) *pop
(Lojeski, Ed) SAB LEONARD-US
08211004 $.50   (L248)
(Lojeski, Ed) SATB LEONARD-US
08211000 $.50   (L249)
(Lojeski, Ed) SSA LEONARD-US

LENNON, JOHN (cont'd.)
08211002 $.50   (L250)

Fool On The Hill, The (composed with
McCartney, John Paul) *pop
(Slater) SSA,opt perc WARNER
WB-315 183 $.50   (L251)
(Slater) SATB,opt perc WARNER
WB-314 187 $.50   (L252)

Got To Get You Into My Life (composed
with McCartney, John Paul)
(Strommen) SATB/SSA (opt. stage
band) ALFRED 6179 $.50   (L253)
(Strommen) SATB/SAB (opt. stage
band) ALFRED 6822 $.50   (L254)

Here, There And Everywhere (composed
with McCartney, John Paul) *pop
(Wahlstrom, Jim) SATB,acap (jazz,
includes recording and 14 choral
octavos) LEONARD-US 07253000
$14.95   (L255)
(Wilson) SATB,acap WARNER
WB-335 187 $.35   (L256)

I Want To Hold Your Hand (composed
with McCartney, John Paul) *pop
SA/TB BELWIN UC 715 $.40   (L257)

Lady Madonna (composed with
McCartney, John Paul)
(Azelton, Phil) SATB,pno,inst
(jazz, includes recording and 14
choral octavos) LEONARD-US
07254000 $14.95   (L258)

Lucy In The Sky With Diamonds
(composed with McCartney, John
Paul)
(Gargaro) SATB,opt 2gtr WARNER
CH0794 $.50   (L259)

Mother Natures Son (composed with
McCartney, John Paul)
(Holcombe, Bill) SATB CHARTER
CO30201   (L260)
(Holcombe, Bill) SSA CHARTER
CO30212   (L261)

Ninth Dream
(Metis, F.) SAB BIG3 $.50   (L262)
(Metis, F.) SSA BIG3 $.50   (L263)
(Metis, F.) SATB BIG3 $.50   (L264)

Whatever Gets You Thru The Night
(Metis, F.) SSA BIG3 $.50   (L265)
(Metis, F.) SATB BIG3 $.50   (L266)
(Metis, F.) SAB BIG3 $.50   (L267)

LENZ see Burkhard Willy

LENZ see Wittmer, Eberhard Ludwig

LENZ KOMMT HERBEI see Lange, Gregor

LEPA ROZA see Lucic, Franjo

LEPI JURO see Lucic, Franjo

LERCHE ODER HAHN "SIE SAGT, ICH KONNT
NICHT SINGEN" see Kelling, Hajo

LERCHENGESANG see Mendelssohn-
Bartholdy, Felix

LES BEAUX CHEMINS DE MON PAYS see
Carrard

LES COMEDIENS see Aznavour, Charles

LES DITHYRAMBES see Martin, Frank

LES EN VOULEZ-VOUS GARDER see
Apotheloz, Jean

LES FEMMES see Kosma, J.

LES FILLES DE LA ROCHELLE *folk,Fr
(Blanchard, R.) 4pt mix cor,acap
JOBERT s.p.   (L268)

LES FOURRIERS D'ESTE SONT VENUS see
Killmayer, Wilhelm

LES LIBELLULES see Pierne, Gabriel

LES MAITRES MUSICIENS DE LA RENAISSANCE
FRANCAISE *sac/sec,CCU,16th cent
(Expert, Henry) microfiche
UNIV.MUS.ED. $70.00 contains 23
volumes and the Bibliographie
Thematique.   (L269)

LES MONTAGNARDS *folk,Fr
(Ammann, Benno) men cor,acap sc,cor
pts TONOS 2031 s.p.   (L270)

LES NEVEUX DE JEAN-BART
(Blanchard, R.) 3pt men cor,acap
JOBERT s.p.   (L271)

LES PETITS ENFANCONNETS see Killmayer,
Wilhelm

LES PLAISIRS DU BAL see Dalcroze,
Jacques

LES QUATRE HEURES see Binet

LES RAFTSMEN *Nor Am
(Watson, Ruth) SATB THOMP.G $.50
(L272)

LES TROIS PRINCESSES *folk,Fr
(Zipp, F.) "Die Drei Prinzessinen"
[Ger] men cor,acap TONOS 2048 s.p.
(L273)
(Zipp, F.) "Die Drei Prinzessinen"
[Fr] men cor,acap TONOS 2048A s.p.
(L274)

LES VENDANGEUSES see Haenni, G.

L'ESCARPOLETTE see Danhieux, Georges

LESLIE
Lullaby Of Life
(Thomas) SAA,acap (med) FITZSIMONS
3037 $.25   (L275)

LESNI VESELICE see Kubin, Rudolf

LESSARD, JOHN [AYRES] (1920-   )
Two Madrigals *CC2U,madrigal
SATB,opt fl&vln&bvl sc AM.COMP.AL.
$8.25   (L276)

LESTER, WILLIAM
Jack In The Pulpit
SSA (med) FITZSIMONS 3021 $.30
(L277)

Little Red Lark, The
SSA (med) FITZSIMONS 3004 $.25
(L278)

LET ALL MY LIFE BE MUSIC see Track

LET DOWN THE BARS, O DEATH see Butler,
Eugene

LET EVERY MAN BE JOLLY see Jenkins,
C.J.

LET IT BE FORGOTTEN see Merrill

LET IT BE ME
(Shaw, Kirby) SATB,pno,inst (jazz,
includes recording and 14 choral
octavos) LEONARD-US 07855000 $14.95
(L279)

LET IT SNOW see Styne, [Jule]

LET ME, CARELESS AND UNTHOUGHTFUL LYING
see Linley, Thomas

LET OUR HEART BE OPEN see Franco, Johan

LET THE VALLEYS SING see LeFanu, Nicola

LET THE YEAR BEGIN see Eidsvoog

LET THERE BE LOVE
(Shaw, Kirby) SATB,pno,inst (jazz,
includes recording and 14 choral
octavos) LEONARD-US 07855120 $14.95
(L280)

LET US BREAK BREAD TOGETHER
(Biebl, Franz) treb cor DOBLINGER
O 315 s.p. see from Acht Spirituals
(L281)

LET US EAT, DRINK AND BE MERRY see
Encina, Juan Del, Oy Comamos Y
Bebamos

LET US GIVE THANKS TO AMERICA
SSA CIMINO $.40   (L282)
SATB CIMINO $.40   (L283)

LET YOUR MIND WANDER OVER AMERICA see
Effinger

LETNAN, JULIUS (1914-   )
Detske Zbory
jr cor SLOV.HUD.FOND s.p.
contains: Vitaj, Prvy Maj!; Vola
Hora   (L284)

Ej, Hor Sa Sveta Proletari
mix cor SLOV.HUD.FOND s.p.   (L285)

Vitaj, Prvy Maj!
see Detske Zbory

Vitaj, Sokoliku
wom cor SLOV.HUD.FOND s.p.   (L286)

Vola Hora
see Detske Zbory

LET'S GET TOGETHER see Powers

LET'S MAKE AMERICA WHAT IT USED TO
SSA CIMINO $.40   (L287)
SATB CIMINO $.40   (L288)
TTBB CIMINO $.40   (L289)

LET'S PUT IT ALL TOGETHER see Weiss,
George David

LETTERS TO SANTA CLAUS see Johnson, G.

LETTERS TO UNCLE SAM see Burroughs

LETTURA DI MICHELANGELO see Vlad, Roman

LETZTER STREICH see Sutermeister,
Heinrich

LETZTES GLUCK see Brahms, Johannes

LEUCHT, CARL FRIEDRICH
Abendlied
men cor,acap TONOS 34 s.p.   (L290)

An Einem Schonen Morgen
see Zwei Sinnspruche

Licht Und Schatten
see Zwei Sinnspruche

Zwei Sinnspruche
men cor,acap cmplt ed TONOS 4551
s.p.
contains: An Einem Schonen
Morgen; Licht Und Schatten
(L291)

LEUCHTE, SCHEINE, GOLDNE SONNE see
Edler, Robert

L'EUROPE CURIEUSE see Bresgen, Cesar

LEVANTA, PASCUAL, LEVANTA see Encina,
Juan Del

LEVEL AZ OTTHHONIAKHOZ see Bartok, Bela

LEVINE
Tie A Yellow Ribbon Round The Ole Oak
Tree (composed with Brown) *pop
(Metis) SATB,opt perc WARNER
WB-302 187 $.40   (L292)
(Metis) SSA,opt perc WARNER
WB-303 183 $ 40   (L293)

LEWIS
Sing Happy Child
(Simpson) SATB EMI   (L294)

Song Of The Refuge Children
(Simpson) SATB EMI   (L295)

LEWIS, PETER T.
Three For Jazzchoir *CC3U
SATB,acap AM.COMP.AL. $3.85   (L296)

Three Insignificant Tragedies
SATB,acap AM.COMP.AL. $6.60   (L297)

We Stood On The Wall
SATB,acap AM.COMP.AL. $.55   (L298)

When I Was Born
SATB,pno/org AM.COMP.AL. $3.30   (L299)

L'HISTOIRE DE LA FEMME ADULTERE see
Clerambault, Louis-Nicolas

L'HOMME DESARME see Mul, Jan

LHOTKA-KALINSKI, IVO (1913-   )
Kerempuh's Song *cant
SATB,TTABar soli,pno,3fl,3ob,3clar,
3bsn,4horn,3trp,3trom,tuba,
strings,timp,harp CROATICA (L300)

L'HUITRE ET LES PLAIDEURS see Jongen,
Leon

LIANI, DAVIDE
La Gnot Dai Muarz
cor,narrator&SBar soli,pno cor pts
ZANIBON 5232 s.p.   (L301)

LIBERTY BELL, THE see Sousa, John
Philip

LIBERTY SONG
see Freedom Song, 1776

LIBERTY TREE, THE see Collins, Don L.

LICHFIELD, HENRY
Madrigals Of Five Parts (1612) EM
Vol. 17 *CC19L
5pt STAINER 3.1917.1 $11.50 (L302)

LICHT MUSS WIEDER WERDEN see Lendvai,
Erwin

LICHT UND SCHATTEN see Leucht, Carl
Friedrich

LICHTGESANT "GOTTES GEWALTIGSTER FLUG
IST DAS LICHT" see Herrmann, Hugo

LICHTMESS see Pepping, Ernst

L'IDYLLE DES VOIX see De Sutter,
J.Toussaint

LIEB HEIMATLAND, ADE *folk,Ger
(Edler, Robert) men cor&jr cor,acap
TONOS 1307 s.p.   (L303)

LIEBE see Edler, Robert

LIEBE, GOTTLICHE HARMONIE see Edler,
Robert

LIEBE IN DIESER ZEIT *folk,Slav
(Marolt, France) men cor,acap TONOS
2903 s.p.   (L304)

LIEBE "LASS DIE WURZEL UNSERES HANDELNS
LIEBE SEIN" see Weber, Ludwig

LIEBE LEUT, ICH BIN NUN SO see
Rathgeber, Valentin

LIEBE "LIEBE RAUSCHT DER SILBERBACH"
see Schubert, Franz (Peter)

LIEBE, LIED, UND WEIN see Edler, Robert

LIEBE SCHWALBE see Brahms, Johannes

LIEBE UND TREUE see Edler, Robert

LIEBE UND WEIN see Mendelssohn-
Bartholdy, Felix

LIEBER FREISTADTLER see Mozart,
Wolfgang Amadeus

LIEBER NACHBAR *folk
(Miller, Franz R.) men cor,acap TONOS
12 s.p.   (L305)

LIEBERMANN, ROLF (1910-   )
Song Of Life And Death, The *see
Streitlied Zwischen Leben Und Tod

Streitlied Zwischen Leben Und Tod
"Song Of Life And Death, The" [Eng/
Ger] mix cor,SMezTB soli,pno,2fl,
2ob,3clar,2bsn,3trp,3trom,tuba,
strings,harp,perc,timp (diff) min
sc SCHOTTS AV 57 s.p., voc sc
SCHOTTS AV 3 s.p., ipr (L306)

LIEBERT
Why I Love Her
(Lojeski, Ed) SATB LEONARD-US
08208000 $.60   (L307)

LIEBES MADCHEN HOR MIR ZU see Mozart,
Wolfgang Amadeus

LIEBES PFERD see Erdmann, Dietrich

LIEBESFREUD, LIEBESLIED see Rein,
Walter

LIEBESGEWITTER "AUCH DIE LIEBE BRAUCHT
GEWITTER" see Ophoven, Hermann

LIEBESGEWITTER "AUCH DIE LIEBE BRAUCHT
GEWITTER" see Wolters, Karl-Heinz

LIEBESHANDEL *folk,Russ
(Seeger, Peter) men cor,acap TONOS
2019 s.p.   (L308)

LIEBESLIED *folk
(Dietsch, F.) [Ger] 4pt men cor
MERSEBURG EM9066 s.p.   (L309)

LIEBESLIED see Biebl, Franz

LIEBESLIED "GESTERN ICH UND MEIN
GESPIEL" see Slavenski, Josip,
Dilberka

LIEBESLIEDCHEN
HOFMEISTER V1618 s.p. contains also:
Marupolka; O Musica, Liebliche
Kunst   (L310)

LIEBESRUF AUS ERISKAY see Gal, Hans, An
Eriskay Love Lilt

LIEBESSCHERZ: WO E KLEINS HUTTLE see
Krietsch, Georg

LIEBESWEH see Thehos, Adam

LIEBESWERBUNG "WARUM BIST DU
BRUNNENWASSER" see Gotovac, Jakov

LIEBESZAUBER *folk
(Mockl, F.) [Ger] 4pt mix cor
MERSEBURG EM9207 s.p.   (L311)

LIEBLICH HAT SICH GESELLET see
Hessenberg, Kurt

LIEBLICH HAT SICH GESLLET
(Weber, Wilhelm) men cor,acap TONOS
3303 s.p.   (L312)

LIEBLICH WOHL KOMMT DER MAI see
Rosthius, Nicolaus

LIEBLICHE BLUMEN see Palestrina,
Giovanni

LIEBSTE, ICH MUSS NUN SCHEIDEN see
Zoll, Paul

LIEBSTER, ADE *folk
(Fischbach, Klaus) wom cor,pno,2fl sc
BREITKOPF-W CHB 4919 s.p. see from

Sieben Europaische Volkslieder
(L313)
LIED
  (Kunz, Alfred) "Song" TTBB (med easy)
  WATERLOO $.30   (L314)

LIED DER ARBEIT see Lendvai, Erwin

LIED DER HIRTEN *folk,Eur
  (Schollum, Robert) mix cor DOBLINGER
  G 666 s.p.   (L315)

LIED DER KOHLENHAUER see Edler, Robert

LIED DER KOHLENHAUER see Lendvai, Erwin

LIED DER NACHTIGALL "DIE NACHTIGALL,
  DIE SANG EIN LIED" see Rettich,
  Wilhelm

LIED DER PLASSENBURG see Matthes, Rene

LIED DER REPUBLIK
  mix cor,pno HOFMEISTER V1617 s.p.
  (L316)
LIED DER SONNE see Rein, Walter

LIED DER WELT "FLIEG HIN, ZEIT" see
  Fortner, Wolfgang

LIED DES EINSIEDELS see Edler, Robert

LIED DES FISCHERS "WENN ICH EIN MOVCHEN
  FRAGE" see Sakamoto, Yoshitaka,
  Soran Bushi

LIED DES MEERES "EWIGES MEER" see
  Fischer, Ernst

LIED DES MUSTERKNABEN "MEINE ELTERN
  ZEIGEN" see Hindemith, Paul

LIED DES VOGELSTELLERS "DER VOGEL, DER
  IM FLUGE RUHT" see Genzmer, Harald

LIED DES WALLOMSCHEN JAGDGESELLEN see
  Chanson Des Scieurs

LIED, DU HERRLICHE GABE see Desch,
  Rudolf

LIED IN DEN ROSEN "LASST UNS SINGEN UND
  FROHLICH SEIN" see Zoll, Paul

LIED IST UBER DEM WORT see Zipp,
  Friedrich

LIED UBER DIE GRENZE HEFT I see Cammin,
  Heinz

LIED UBER DIE GRENZE HEFT II see
  Cammin, Heinz

LIED VOM HASELNUSSSTRAUCH "ES SOLLTE
  EIN MAGDLEIN" see Rettich, Wilhelm

LIED VOM REGEN see Rein, Walter

LIED VOM WINDE see Distler, Hugo

LIED VOR TAG "WAS BEWEGT DICH" see
  Erdlen, Hermann

LIED ZUR NACHT "EH ICH MICH NIEDERLEGE"
  see Erdlen, Hermann

LIEDER AM GRABE see Edler, Robert

LIEDER AM GRABE see Edler, Robert

LIEDER AUS DEM KLEINEN ROSENGARTEN see
  Thehos, Adam

LIEDER DER KLEINSTEN see Simon, Hermann

LIEDER DER NACHT see Genzmer, Harald

LIEDER DER VAGANTEN see Miller, Franz
  R.

LIEDER DER WELT see Genzmer, Harald

LIEDER DES LEBENS see Erdlen, Hermann

LIEDER FUR DIE FREUNDE see Krietsch,
  Georg

LIEDER FUR DIE JUGEND, IM FREIEN ZU
  SINGEN, TEIL I see Bellermann,
  Sangerfahrt

LIEDER FUR DIE JUGEND, IM FREIEN ZU
  SINGEN, TEIL II see Bellermann,
  Sangerfahrt

LIEDER FUR DIE JUGEND, IM FREIEN ZU
  SINGEN, TEIL III see Bellermann,
  Sangerfahrt

LIEDER FUR DIE JUGEND, IM FREIEN ZU
  SINGEN, TEIL IV see Bellermann,
  Sangerfahrt

LIEDER FUR DIE SCHULE HEFT I see Orff,
  Carl

LIEDER FUR DIE SCHULE HEFT II see Orff,
  Carl

LIEDER FUR DIE SCHULE HEFT III see
  Orff, Carl

LIEDER FUR DIE SCHULE HEFT IV see Orff,
  Carl

LIEDER FUR DIE SCHULE HEFT V see Orff,
  Carl

LIEDER FUR DIE SCHULE HEFT VI see Orff,
  Carl

LIEDER FUR DIE SCHULE HEFT VII see
  Orff, Carl

LIEDER, GOLDNE BRUCKEN see Seeger,
  Peter

LIEDER, ODEN UND SZENEN see Killmayer,
  Wilhelm

LIEDER UND EPIGRAMME HEFT I see
  Hessenberg, Kurt

LIEDER UND EPIGRAMME HEFT II see
  Hessenberg, Kurt

LIEDER VON LEID UND LICHT see Erdlen,
  Hermann

LIEDER VOR TAG see Watkinson, Percy
  Gerd

LIEDERBUCH DES DEUTSCHEN SANGERBUNDES
  *sac/sec,CC107L
  mix cor SCHOTTS s.p. contains works
  by: Ahle; Cruger; Hindemith;
  Morley; Schulz; Senfl and others
  (L317)

LIEDERBUCH GRADE 1 see Orff, Carl

LIEDERBUCH GRADE 2 see Orff, Carl

LIEDERBUCH GRADE 3 see Orff, Carl

LIEDEREN VAN DOOFSTOMMEN (SONGS OF
  DEAF-MUTES), FIRST CYCLE see Knap,
  Rolf

LIEDPROGRAMM DES DEUTSCHEN SANGERBUNDES
  FOLGE 1: STUTTGARTER LIEDERBLATT
  *CC12U
  mix cor/wom cor/men cor/eq voices/jr
  cor SCHOTTS C 43 566 s.p. contains
  works by: Friderici; Haas; Knab;
  Lau; Rein and others   (L318)

LIEDPROGRAMM DES DEUTSCHEN SANGERBUNDES
  FOLGE 2: ZWANZIG MANNERCHORE
  *CC20U
  men cor SCHOTTS C 39 950 s.p.
  contains works by: Bresgen;
  Hassler; Lang; Sehlbach; Zelter and
  others   (L319)

LIEDPROGRAMM DES DEUTSCHEN SANGERBUNDES
  FOLGE 3: "ESSENER LIEDERBLATT" -
  "CHORFEIER"
  sc SCHOTTS C 43 567 s.p., ipa
  contains: Fussan, Werner, Sangerruf
  (men cor); Keldorfer, Die
  Gedanken Sind Frei (men cor);
  Kremberg, Jacob, Trunet Die
  Hoffnung (cor); Lang, Hans,
  Bergmannslied (men cor); Mozart,
  Wolfgang Amadeus, Bundeslied (men
  cor); Schaefers, Gott Ist
  Gewaltig (mix cor)   (L320)

LIFE see Foerster, Josef Bohuslav,
  Zivot

LIFE see Haufrecht, [Herbert]

LIFE see Luboff

LIFE IS... see Burroughs

LIFE IS LIVING UP LOVE see Collins, Don
  L.

LIFE IS NOW see Ahnfelt, O.

LIFE, LIBERTY, AND THE PURSUIT OF
  HAPPINESS see Collins, Don L.

LIFE SONGS see Rasely

LIFE'S A DREAM WORTH DREAMING see
  Hollins, Alfred

LIGEIA, OR THE SHADOW OUT OF TIME see
  Strietman, Willem

LIGETI, GYORGY (1923-   )
  Clocks And Clouds *see Uhren Und
  Wolken

  Nacht Und Morgen *CC2U
  [Ger/Eng/Hung] mix cor,acap (med
  diff) sc SCHOTTS ED. 6415 s.p.
  (L321)

LIGETI, GYORGY (cont'd.)

  Uhren Und Wolken
  "Clocks And Clouds" 12pt wom cor,
  5fl,3ob,5clar,4bsn,2trp,strings,
  2harp, glockspiel, vibraphone,
  celeste (diff) sc SCHOTTS rental
  (L322)

LIGHT INVISIBLE see Leighton, Kenneth

LIGHT OF LIFE see Elgar, Edward

LIGHT THE MENORAH see Milidantri

LIGHT UP THE WORLD see Nestico, G.

LIGHTFOOT, GORDON
  Christian Island (Georgian Bay) *pop
  (Bune) SATB,pno/gtr WARNER
  WB-342 187 $.50   (L323)

  Go My Way *pop
  (Bune) SATB,pno/bvl&gtr WARNER
  WB-329 $.50   (L324)
  (Bune) SATB,pno/gtr WARNER
  WB-329 187 $.50   (L325)

  Sundown
  (Shay) 2pt,opt gtr WARNER WB-366
  $.50   (L326)
  (Shay) SATB,opt gtr WARNER WB-365
  $.50   (L327)

LIGHTS OF HANUKKAH
  SATB CIMINO $.50   (L328)

LIKE TO LOVE see Dedrick, C.

LIKE TO LOVE, LIKE TO SING ABOUT
  SUNSHINE see Dedrick

LI'L ELSA'S TUNE see Wunsch, Frank,
  Unter Verwendung Des Liedes "Ach
  Elslein, Liebes Elselein"

LILIEDAHL
  Mother Country *sac/sec
  (Coates) SA/TB SHAWNEE E153 $.40
  (L329)
  (Coates) SSA SHAWNEE B393 $.40
  (L330)

LILITH see Beurden, Bernard van

LILLY BRIGHT AND SHINE-A see Copley,
  Ian A.

LIMERICKS ANON AN'ON see Kennedy, John
  Brodbin

LIMPIATE CON MI PANUELO *folk
  (Desch, R.) "Das Tuchlein" [Span/Ger]
  4pt mix cor MERSEBURG EM9244 s.p.
  (L331)

LINDA ROSE see Godden, Reginald

LINDAHL, ALLAN
  Latt Och Blandat For Blandat Kor
  *CCU
  mix cor (easy) NORDISKA NMS 6423
  s.p.   (L332)

LINDEN, N. V.D.
  Er Was Ereis
  men cor s.p. sc HEER 480, cor pts
  HEER 480A   (L333)

LINDGREN, KURT
  Herdman's Song, A
  4pt mix cor cor pts NORDISKA
  NMS 6531 s.p.   (L334)

LINKE, NORBERT (1933-   )
  Bettlerlust
  wom cor BREITKOPF-W CHB 4965 s.p.
  see from Dreizehn Lieder Fur
  Frauenchor   (L335)

  Das Lied Von Burlala
  wom cor BREITKOPF-W CHB 4964 s.p.
  see from Dreizehn Lieder Fur
  Frauenchor   (L336)

  Der Jungbrunnen
  wom cor BREITKOPF-W CHB 4970 s.p.
  see from Dreizehn Lieder Fur
  Frauenchor   (L337)

  Dreizehn Lieder Fur Frauenchor *see
  Bettlerlust; Das Lied Von
  Burlala; Der Jungbrunnen; Horch,
  Was Kommt Von Draussen Rein; Ja,
  Wenn Der Jager In Den Wald Hinein
  Geht; Lasst Uns All' Nach Hause
  Gehen; Mein Lieb Ist Wie Der
  Morgenstein; Nun Ruhen Alle
  Walder; Scherzlied; Schon Ist Die
  Welt; Stehn Zwei Stern Am Hohen
  Himmel; Stehst So Still Mein
  Pferdchen; Suse, Leewe Suse
  (L338)
  Horch, Was Kommt Von Draussen Rein
  wom cor BREITKOPF-W CHB 4967 s.p.
  see from Dreizehn Lieder Fur
  Frauenchor   (L339)

LINKE, NORBERT (cont'd.)

Ja, Wenn Der Jager In Den Wald Hinein
Geht
wom cor BREITKOPF-W CHB 4972 s.p.
see from Dreizehn Lieder Fur
Frauenchor   (L340)

Lasst Uns All' Nach Hause Gehen
wom cor BREITKOPF-W CHB 4966 s.p.
see from Dreizehn Lieder Fur
Frauenchor   (L341)

Mein Lieb Ist Wie Der Morgenstein
wom cor BREITKOPF-W CHB 4969 s.p.
see from Dreizehn Lieder Fur
Frauenchor   (L342)

Nun Ruhen Alle Walder
wom cor BREITKOPF-W CHB 4973 s.p.
see from Dreizehn Lieder Fur
Frauenchor   (L343)

Scherzlied
wom cor BREITKOPF-W CHB 4962 s.p.
see from Dreizehn Lieder Fur
Frauenchor   (L344)

Schon Ist Die Welt
wom cor BREITKOPF-W CHB 4963 s.p.
see from Dreizehn Lieder Fur
Frauenchor   (L345)

Stehn Zwei Stern Am Hohen Himmel
wom cor BREITKOPF-W CHB 4968 s.p.
see from Dreizehn Lieder Fur
Frauenchor   (L346)

Stehst So Still Mein Pferdchen
wom cor BREITKOPF-W CHB 4974 s.p.
see from Dreizehn Lieder Fur
Frauenchor   (L347)

Suse, Leewe Suse
wom cor BREITKOPF-W CHB 4971 s.p.
see from Dreizehn Lieder Fur
Frauenchor   (L348)

LINLEY, JR, THOMAS (1756-1778)
Hark, The Birds Melodious Sing
*madrigal
(Young, Percy M.) [Eng] SSATB,acap
oct BROUDE BR. $.50   (L349)

LINLEY, THOMAS (1733-1795)
Let Me, Careless And Unthoughtful
Lying *madrigal
(Young, Percy M.) [Eng] SATBB,acap
oct BROUDE BR. $.50   (L350)

LINOS see Edler, Robert

L'INVITATION AU VOYAGE see Corigliano,
John

LIRICHE DI UNGARETTI see Bettinelli,
Bruno

LIRUM, BILILIRUM see Ninot le Petit

LISA LAN *folk,Welsh
(Holst, Gustav) [Eng/Welsh] SATB,acap
CURWEN 61584 s.p. contains also:
Can Serch, "Lover's Complaint, The"
-                               (L351)

LISCHKA, RAINER
Die Stimmen Der Tiere
4pt jr cor,acap NEUE 1015 s.p.
                                (L352)

LISINSKI, VATROSLAV (1819-1854)
Choral Works (Selected Works II)
*CCU
cor CROATICA   (L353)

LISSMANN, KURT (1902-   )
Herz, Werde Wach Und Sing
TTBB sc SCHOTTS C 39 061 s.p., voc
pt SCHOTTS C 39 062, 01-02 s.p.
                                (L354)

Mondnacht "Es War Als Hatt Der
Himmel"
men cor sc SCHOTTS CHBL 95 s.p.
                                (L355)

LISTEN! I WILL BE HONEST see Kent,
Richard

LISTEN TO THE MOCKING BIRD see
Hawthorne

LISZT, FRANZ (1811-1886)
Collected Works *sac/sec,CCU
(D'Albert; Busoni; Raabe, Peter;
Stradel, August; V. Da Motta, J.;
Kellermann, B.; Bartok, Bela;
Taubmann, Otto; Wolfrum, Philipp;
Stavenhagen, B.) microfiche
UNIV.MUS.ED. $150.00 originally
published as 34 volumes in 33
bindings by Breitkopf and
Haertal, Leipzig, 1907-1936
                                (L356)
Peace Be With You
(Hines) TTBB SCHIRM.G LG51820 $.40
                                (L357)

LITANY OF OUR TIME see Leeuw, Ton de

LITTLE ARROWS see Hammond

LITTLE BIRD, LITTLE BIRD
(Coutts, G.) unis (easy) WATERLOO
$.30   (L358)

LITTLE BOY ALONE see Lora, Antonio

LITTLE BOY LOST, THE see Sapp, Allen
Dwight

LITTLE CANTATA see Harries

LITTLE CHORAL SUITE see Warren, Elinor
Remick

LITTLE CHRISTMAS STAR see Cobine, Al

LITTLE CHRISTOPHER see McAfee, Don

LITTLE CLOUD, THE see Simek, Miroslav,
Oblacek

LITTLE DAVID, PLAY ON YOUR HARP *folk
(Biebl, Franz) treb cor DOBLINGER
O 316 s.p. see from Acht Spirituals
                                (L359)
(Heinrichs, W.) [Eng] 4pt mix cor
MERSEBURG EM9258 s.p.   (L360)
(Heinrichs, W.) [Eng] 4pt men cor
MERSEBURG EM9087 s.p.   (L361)

LITTLE DOG MET A LITTLE CAT, A see
Bohac, Josef, Potkal Pejsek Kocicku

LITTLE DREAMER see Kurth, Burton L.

LITTLE FISH, THE see Bilencko, M.

LITTLE GREEN FOREST see Turner, Olive

LITTLE HANS see Godden, Reginald

LITTLE LAMB see Atkinson, Condit R.

LITTLE LAMBS WHERE DO YOU SLEEP see
Morgan, Hilda

LITTLE MAN YOU'VE HAD A BUSY DAY
SATB CIMINO $.40   (L362)
TTBB CIMINO $.40   (L363)

LITTLE MOTHER see Willan, Healey

LITTLE PRINCE, THE see Loudova, Ivana,
Maly Princ

LITTLE RED DRUM, THE
(Wetzler, Robert) TTBB,drums ART MAST
1033 $.40   (L364)

LITTLE RED FOX, THE see Jeffries

LITTLE RED LARK, THE see Lester,
William

LITTLE SONG OF LIFE, A see Warren,
Elinor Remick

LITTLE TEETOTALERS see Gabriel, Sr.,
Charles H.

LITTLE TOY ELF see Cobine, Al

LIVE AND LET DIE see McCartney, John
Paul

LIVELY PAIR, THE see Cwyd Dy Galon

LIVING HAND IN HAND see Axelrod, David

LIVING TODAY see Moore

LIVINGSTON
Tammy *pop
(Evans) SA/TB BELWIN UC 729 $.40
                                (L365)

LIZZIE BORDEN see Kennedy

LO SCHERNITO see Gastoldi, Giovanni
Giacomo

LO SGRICCIOLO see Sinigaglia, Leone

LO, THE WINTER IS PAST see Clarke,
Henry Leland

LOB AUF DAS WASSER see Barthel, Ursula

LOB AUF DIE MUSIK see Distler, Hugo

LOB AUF DIE MUSIKA see Taubert, Karl
Heinz

LOB DER EINSAMKEIT see Schubert, Franz
(Peter)

LOB DER FAULHEIT "FAULHEIT, JETZT WILL
ICH DIR" see Desch, Rudolf

LOB DER GELIEBTEN "SEHT MEINER LIEBSTEN
BRAUNE AUGEN" see Weber, Bernhard

LOB DER HEIMAT see Fischer, Theo

LOB DER HEIMAT "WIR GEHEN UBER UNSRE
ERDE" see Frommlet, Franz

LOB DER LEINEWEBER *folk,Ger
(Welker, Gotthard) men cor,acap TONOS
167 s.p.   (L366)

LOB DER MUSIK see Feifel, Hermann

LOB DER SCHNEIDER "ICH BIN DER MEISTER
SCHNEIDER" see Fussan, Werner

LOB DER TORHEIT see Zimmermann, Bernd
Alois

LOB DES HERINGS "DER HERING IST EIN
SALZIG TIER" see Rein, Walter

LOB DES LEBENS, PREIS DER ERDE "LASST
DIE GOLDNEN BECHER KREISEN" see
Erdlen, Hermann

LOB DES RHEINS "STIMMT AN, LASST UNS
SINGEN" see Fischer, Ernst

LOB DES SOMMERS see Klein, Richard
Rudolf

LOBEGESANG see Desch, Rudolf

LOBGESANG see Siegl, Otto

LOCAL BAND see Tate

LOCH LOMOND *folk,Scot
(Biebl, F.) [Ger] 4pt men cor
MERSEBURG EM9065 s.p.   (L367)
(Gietz, Bernd Hans) [Eng/Ger] mix
cor,acap cor pts BREITKOPF-W Z 65
s.p.   (L368)

LOCH LOMOND "WOHL AM TRAUTEN STRAND"
see Othegraven, August J. von

LOCHLAINN, COLM O.
Mrs. McGrath
(Feldsher, Howard M.) SATB,pno,
drums AULOS   (L369)

LOCKWOOD, NORMAND (1906-   )
Darest Thou Now, O Soul
SSAATTBB,pno AM.COMP.AL. $7.15
                                (L370)

Eventide
SATB STANDARD B327MX1 $.50   (L371)

Give Me The Splendid Silent Sun
SATB,2fl,2ob,2clar,2bsn,2horn,2trp,
tuba,timp,perc,strings
AM.COMP.AL.   (L372)

Sweet And Low
SSAATTBB,acap GALAXY 1.0747.1 $.40
                                (L373)

LODGE
Minstrel's Song *pop
(Myrow) SSA MCA UC 667 $.40   (L374)
(Myrow) SATB MCA UC 668 $.40   (L375)

Tortoise And The Hare, The *pop
(Myrow) SATB MCA UC 666 $.40   (L376)
(Myrow) SATB MCA UC 654 $.40   (L377)

LOEWE
Auf Dem See *Op.80
see Loewe, Der Lindenbaum

Der Lindenbaum *Op.80
mix cor LIENAU sc s.p., cor pts
s.p. contains also: Auf Dem See;
Dich Soll Mein Lied   (L378)

Dich Soll Mein Lied *Op.80
see Loewe, Der Lindenbaum

LOEWE, CARL
In Der Marienkirche "Unzerstorbare
Liebe" *Op.81,No.4, folk
mix cor (med easy) sc SCHOTTS
CHBL 260 s.p.   (L379)

L'OFFICE DES ORACLES see Ohana, Maurice

LOGGINS
Please Come To Boston *pop
SATB BELWIN UC 711 $.50   (L380)

LOGGINS, DAVE
Danny's Song (composed with Messina)
see Sounds Of Loggins And Messina

Love Song, A (composed with George)
(Shay) 2pt/SSA,opt perc WARNER
WB-381 $.35   (L381)
(Shay) SAB/SATB,opt perc WARNER
WB-380 $.35   (L382)

Sounds Of Loggins And Messina
(composed with Messina) *pop
(Cassey) SSA,opt perc WARNER
WB-337 183 $.75; SATB,opt perc
WARNER WB-336 187 $.75
contains: Danny's Song; Thinking
Of You; Your Mama Don't Dance

LOGGINS, DAVE (cont'd.)

Thinking Of You (composed with
Messina)
see Sounds Of Loggins And Messina (L383)

Your Mama Don't Dance (composed with
Messina)
see Sounds Of Loggins And Messina

LOLLIPOP TREE, THE see Darion

LONDON, EDWIN
Better Is
SSSSSSAAA,opt 9 soli,acap BOONIN
B 178 $.60   (L384)

Christmas Music *Xmas
mix cor,T solo,Hamm,bells oct
SOMERSET AG 7161 $1.00   (L385)

Polonius Platitudes, The
men cor, balloons (in graphic
notation) BOONIN B 132 $.60   (L386)

LONDON SPARROW see Ager, Laurence

LONDONDERRY AIR *folk
(Lester, William) "O Irish Hills" SSA
(easy) FITZSIMONS 3011 $.20   (L387)
(Lester, William) "O Irish Hills" SAB
(easy) FITZSIMONS 6001 $.25   (L388)

LONELINESS see Wood

LONELY GOATHERD, THE see Rodgers,
Richard

LONESOME DOVE, THE
(Hall, Wm.D.) SATB,rec NATIONAL
WHC-24 $.35   (L389)

LONESOME TRAIN, THE see Lampell

LONG AGO (AND FAR AWAY)
SAB CIMINO $.40   (L390)
SSA CIMINO $.40   (L391)
TTBB CIMINO $.40   (L392)
SATB CIMINO $.40   (L393)

LONG LIVE LOVE see Avon, Valerie

LONG, LONG AGO see Anderson, [William
H.]

LONGING FOR VIRGINNY see Protheroe,
Daniel

LONGMIRE, JOHN
Come Love! 'Tis Spring
SSA EMI   (L394)

LOOK FOR THE LIGHT see Beard

LOOK FOR THE LIGHT see Moore, Daniel

LOOK FOR THE SILVER LINING
SSA CIMINO $.40   (L395)
SAB CIMINO $.40   (L396)
TTBB CIMINO $.40   (L397)
SA CIMINO $.40   (L398)
SATB CIMINO $.40   (L399)

LOOK IN MY EYES, PRETTY WOMAN see
Lambert, Dennis

LOOK NO FURTHER see Rodgers, Richard

LOOK OFF, DEAR LOVE see Herts, Charles
Lee

LOOK, THE KISS AND JOY, THE see Kennedy

LOPE-DE-VEGA-LIEDER see Edler, Robert

LORA, ANTONIO
Abraham Lincoln Walks At Midnight
SATB,3fl,2ob,2clar,2bsn,4horn,2trp,
3trom,tuba,2timp,strings
AM.COMP.AL. $16.50   (L400)

For Her Love
SSA,pno AM.COMP.AL. $3.58   (L401)

Hurry Martha
SSA,pno AM.COMP.AL. $2.75   (L402)

Little Boy Alone
TTBB,acap AM.COMP.AL. $1.10   (L403)

Storm
TTBB,pno AM.COMP.AL. $2.75   (L404)

LORAND, ISTVAN
A Tenger
(Vaci, Mihaly) eq voices/mix cor,
pno BUDAPEST 6899 s.p.   (L405)

Aprilisi Unnep
(Nadas, Katalin) jr cor,pno
BUDAPEST 7683 s.p.   (L406)

Jon A Tavasz *CCU
(Weores, Sandor) jr cor (easy)
BUDAPEST 7095 s.p.   (L407)

LORAND, ISTVAN (cont'd.)
Majusi Kanon
(Nadas, Katalin) jr cor BUDAPEST
7684 s.p.   (L408)

LORD, I WANT TO BE A CHRISTIAN
(Biebl, Franz) treb cor DOBLINGER
O 317 s.p. see from Acht Spirituals
(L409)

LORD'S GONNA RAIN DOWN FIRE, THE *spir
(Jaeger, Richard) SSATTBB (easy)
FITZSIMONS 2177 $.25   (L410)

LORELEI: ICH WEISS NICHT, WAS SOLL ES
see Silcher, Friedrich

LORENTZEN, BENT (1935-   )
Four Poems By Mao Tse-Tung *CC4U
4pt mix cor,acap HANSEN-DEN
WH 29212 s.p.   (L411)

Three Poems By Mao Tse-Tung *CC3U
unis HANSEN-DEN WH 29211 s.p.
(L412)

LORENZ
Hymne An Die Kunst *Op.25
mix cor LIENAU voc sc s.p., cor pts
s.p.   (L413)

LORENZINI, DANZIO (1952-   )
Estinguerai La Musa
wom cor,acap ZERBONI 7909 s.p.
(L414)

LORTZING, (GUSTAV) ALBERT (1801-1851)
Trinklied "Viel Schone Gaben
Vaterlich" (from Undine)
(Klink, Waldemar) men cor sc
SCHOTTS C 38 277 s.p.   (L415)

LOST CHORD, THE see Sullivan, Sir
Arthur Seymour

LOTHAR, MARK
Nachtmusikanten *Op.13
men cor RIES sc s.p., voc pt s.p.
(L416)

Wanderspruche
mix cor RIES sc s.p., voc pt s.p.
(L417)

LOTHRINGER LIEDERKREIS see Michels,
Josef

LOUCHHEIM, STUART F.
Spirit Of Christmas, The *Xmas
(Ehret, Walter) SATB,pno oct REGENT
R-101 $.25   (L418)

LOUDOVA, IVANA (1941-   )
Kuroshio *see Kurosio

Kurosio
"Kuroshio" [Czech] mix cor,S solo,
acap CZECH s.p.   (L419)

Little Prince, The *see Maly Princ

Maly Princ *cant
"Little Prince, The" [Czech] jr
cor,narrator&SA soli,fl,clar,trp,
perc,pno CZECH s.p.   (L420)

LOVE see Harvey, Jonathan

LOVE see Jirasek, Ivo, Laska

LOVE AND WINE see Mendelssohn-
Bartholdy, Felix, Liebe Und Wein

LOVE BRINGS ALL PEOPLE RICHES UNTOLD
see Ehret, Walter

LOVE DOES NOT DIE see Dedrick, C.

LOVE IN A VILLAGE see Spencer,
Williametta

LOVE IN EXCHANGE see Podest, Ludvik,
Laska Za Lasku

LOVE IS A SICKNESS see Vaughan
Williams, Ralph

LOVE IS ALL AROUND see Roberts, David
Lee

LOVE IS MERELY A MADNESS see Fettke,
Tom

LOVE IS THE ANSWER see Weiss, George
David

LOVE IS THE ONLY REPLY see Lovelace

LOVE, LOOK AWAY see Rodgers, Richard

LOVE-SONG see Heath

LOVE SONG see Kabelac, Miloslav,
Milostna

LOVE SONG, A see Holst, Gustav

LOVE SONG, A see Loggins, Dave

LOVE THAT IS HOARDED see Lovelace,
Austin C.

LOVE THE VAGRANT see Bizet, Georges

LOVE TRAIN see Gamble, Kenny

LOVELACE
Love Is The Only Reply
SATB MCAFEE M1068 $.40   (L421)

LOVELACE, AUSTIN C. (1919-   )
Love That Is Hoarded
SATB,acap KERBY 7978-004 $.40
(L422)

Stamp And Shout *sac/sec
jr cor KERBY 10771 $.30   (L423)

LOVELINESS OF CHRISTMAS, THE see
Wheeler

LOVELOCK
Vocalise
SATB WALTON 2977 $.40   (L424)

LOVELOCK, WILLIAM
Island Heart
SATB EMI   (L425)

Old Peter Groom
SSAATTBB EMI   (L426)

LOVELY FLOWER see Schumann, Robert
(Alexander), Schon Blumelein

LOVELY FRANCES see Champagne, Claude

LOVELY MOLLY
(Johnston, Richard A.) SA (med easy)
WATERLOO $.30   (L427)

LOVELY NIGHT, A see Rodgers, Richard

LOVELY THE DAWNING see Youse, Glad
Robinson

LOVELY TO LOOK AT
SA CIMINO $.40   (L428)
SAB CIMINO $.40   (L429)
SSA CIMINO $.40   (L430)
TTBB CIMINO $.40   (L431)
SATB CIMINO $.40   (L432)

LOVELY WAY TO SPEND AN EVENING, A
SATB CIMINO $.40   (L433)

LOVER'S COMPLAINT, THE see Can Serch

LOVER'S CROSS see Croce, Jim

LOVER'S GHOST see Vaughan Williams,
Ralph

LOVE'S LINES ANGLES AND RHYMES
SSA CIMINO $.40   (L434)
SATB CIMINO $.40   (L435)

LOVES ME LIKE A ROCK see Simon, Paul

LOVE'S THE REASON WHY see Nelson, Jerry

LOVE'S THEME
SSA CIMINO $.50   (L436)
SAB CIMINO $.50   (L437)
SATB CIMINO $.50   (L438)

LOWE see Strobl, Otto

LOWE, R.
I'll Never Smile Again *pop
SATB BELWIN UC 725 $.40   (L439)
SSA BELWIN UC 724 $.40   (L440)

LUBOFF
A La Nanita Nana
TTBB WALTON 1016 $.40   (L441)

Life
SATB WALTON 3059 $.40   (L442)

Ring The Bell
SATB WALTON 3071 $.40   (L443)

L'UBOST see Ocenas, Andrej

L'UBOSTNA SONATINA see Novak, Milan

LUCAS, ROBERT
Blue Autumn
(Letson, Roger) SATB,pno,inst
(jazz, includes recording and 14
choral octavos) LEONARD-US
07250600 $14.95   (L444)

Follow Your Heart
(Letson, Roger) SATB,pno,inst
(jazz, includes recording and 14
choral octavos) LEONARD-US
07252000 $14.95   (L445)

LUCI CARE BELLE see Mozart, Wolfgang
Amadeus

LUCI CARE, LUCI BELLE see Mozart,
Wolfgang Amadeus

LUCIC, FRANJO (1889-   )
  Das Weisse Entlein *see Raca Plava
    Po Dravi

  Dober Danek Tomu Domu *Slav
    "Guten Tag" mix cor sc SCHOTTS
    C 40 467 s.p. see from Funf
    Jugoslawische Chore   (L446)

  Funf Jugoslawische Chore *see Dober
    Danek Tomu Domu, "Guten Tag";
    Japo, Mamo Hote Gledet, "Vater,
    Mutter, Eilt Herbei"; Lepa Roza,
    "Schone Rose"; Lepi Juro,
    "Schoner Georg"; Raca Plava Po
    Dravi, "Das Weisse Entlein"   (L447)

  Guten Tag *see Dober Danek Tomu Domu

  Japo, Mamo Hote Gledet *Slav
    "Vater, Mutter, Eilt Herbei" mix
    cor sc SCHOTTS C 40 469 s.p. see
    from Funf Jugoslawische Chore
                                           (L448)

  Lepa Roza *Slav
    "Schone Rose" mix cor sc SCHOTTS
    C 40 465 s.p. see from Funf
    Jugoslawische Chore   (L449)

  Lepi Juro *Slav
    "Schoner Georg" mix cor sc SCHOTTS
    C 40 468 s.p. see from Funf
    Jugoslawische Chore   (L450)

  Raca Plava Po Dravi *Slav
    "Das Weisse Entlein" mix cor sc
    SCHOTTS C 40 466 s.p. see from
    Funf Jugoslawische Chore (L451)

  Schone Rose *see Lepa Roza

  Schoner Georg *see Lepi Juro

  Vater, Mutter, Eilt Herbei *see
    Japo, Mamo Hote Gledet

LUCNE HRY PRE MIESANY ZBOR see Mikula,
  Zdenko

LUCY IN THE SKY WITH DIAMONDS see
  Lennon, John

LUDERITZ, WOLFGANG
  So Im Ubermut
    men cor,acap TONOS 3976 s.p. (L452)

L'UDOVA VESELICA see Kafenda, Frico

LUDUS AMORIS see Harvey, Jonathan

LUENING, OTTO (1900-   )
  Vocalise
    SSAA,acap HIGHGATE 7.0034.1 $.40
                                           (L453)

LUGENMARCHEN "SO GEHT ES IM
  SCHNUTZELPUTZHAUSEL" see Zoll, Paul

LUKAS, ZDENEK (1928-   )
  Symphony No. 3
    [Czech/Eng] mix cor,2fl,2ob,3clar,
    2bsn,4horn,2trp,3trom,tuba,timp,
    perc SUPRAPHON s.p.   (L454)

LUKOWSKY, ROLF (1926-   )
  Lenins Ewige Stimme
    mix cor,acap DEUTSCHER DVFM7611
    s.p.   (L455)

  Republik, Mein Vaterland
    men cor,pno HOFMEISTER G2215 s.p.
                                           (L456)

LULLABE SHIP see Kurth, Burton L.

LULLABY see Borkovec, Pavel, Ukolebavka

LULLABY see Elgar, Edward

LULLABY see Keel, Frederick

LULLABY see Sweetman, Paul

LULLABY see Vick

LULLABY FOR KITTENS see Bohac, Josef,
  Ukolebavka Pro Kotata

LULLABY OF LIFE see Leslie

LULLABY OF THE LITTLE HORSES
  (Johnson, Mark) SATB,acap ART MAST
    1029 $.30   (L457)

LULLABYE, AND COME AFLOAT see Clayre

LULLAY, THOU LITTLE TINY CHILD
  see Two Carols For The Caribbean

LUMIERE see Wissmer, Pierre

LUMINOUS TENDRIL see Boone, Charles

LUMPENLIED "ICH BIN EIN ARMER
  BETTELMUSIKANT" see Zoll, Paul

LUSTIG, IHR BRUDER *folk,Ger
  (Schneider, Walther) men cor,acap
    TONOS 80 s.p.   (L458)
  (Zipp, F.) men cor,acap TONOS 20 s.p.
                                           (L459)

LUSTIG, IHR BRUDER see Gebhard, Hans

LUSTIG IHR BRUDER see Jage, Rolf-
  Diether

LUSTIG, IHR BRUDER see Lang, Hans

LUSTIG, IHR BRUDER see Schneider,
  Walther

LUSTIG, IHR BRUDER see Schroeder,
  Hermann

LUSTIG, IHR HERREN, ALLZUMAL see
  Franck, Melchior

LUSTIG IST DAS HIRTENLEBEN see Desch,
  Rudolf

LUSTIG IST DAS ZIGEUNERLEBEN see Jage,
  Rolf-Diether

LUSTIGE LEUT see Lang, Hans

LUSTIGE TIERFABELN PART I see Schmid,
  A.

LUSTIGE TIERFABELN PART II see Schmid,
  A.

LUSTIGES HANDWERKLIED *folk
  (Hennig, W.) [Ger] 4pt men cor
    MERSEBURG EM9021 s.p.   (L460)

LUTTENBERGER, GOTTFRIED
  Tod Und Ewigkeit
    men cor,acap TONOS 255 s.p.   (L461)

LUTZ, OSWALD (1908-   )
  Sieben Gedanken Uber: Es Ist Ein
    Schnitter
    cor,strings MODERN rental   (L462)

  Trauermusik *funeral
    cor,strings MODERN rental   (L463)

LUTZOWS WILDE VERWEGENE JAGD see Weber

LUX JOCUNDA see Andriessen, Hendrik

LUZZASCHI, LUZZASCO (1545-1607)
  Aminta Poi Ch'a Filli *madrigal
    (Nielsen, R.) 5pt mix cor
    BONGIOVANI 2388 s.p. see also
    DODICI MADRIGALI DI SCUOLA
    FERRARESE   (L464)

  Dolce Mia Fiamma *madrigal
    (Nielsen, R.) 5pt mix cor
    BONGIOVANI 2391 s.p. see also
    DODICI MADRIGALI DI SCUOLA
    FERRARESE   (L465)

  Geloso Amante *madrigal
    (Nielsen, R.) 5pt mix cor
    BONGIOVANI 2390 s.p. see also
    DODICI MADRIGALI DI SCUOLA
    FERRARESE   (L466)

  Itene A Volo *madrigal
    (Nielsen, R.) 5pt mix cor
    BONGIOVANI 2389 s.p. see also
    DODICI MADRIGALI DI SCUOLA
    FERRARESE   (L467)

LYRISCHE KANTATE see Beck, Conrad

LYSISTRATA see Brunswick, Mark

M

MA CHATTE DANSE see Strimer, Joseph

MA LASKA see Matys, Jiri

MA TU TREMI see Beethoven, Ludwig van

MAASZ, GERHARD (1906-   )
  Das Hasenspiel *cant
    1-2pt jr cor,2vln,vcl,2rec,perc
    (easy) sc,voc pt SCHOTTS B 163
    s.p., ipa   (M1)

  Klingende Jahreszeiten *CCU
    jr cor,fl,vln (easy) sc SCHOTTS
    B 106 s.p.   (M2)

MCAFEE, DON
  Bells Of Easter, The *Easter
    unis MCAFEE M8001 $.40   (M3)

  Christmas Wish, A *Xmas
    SATB,opt soli MCAFEE M1078 $.40
                                           (M4)

  Day Has Come, The *see Leeds

  Epitaphs
    SATB,pno MCAFEE M144 $.40   (M5)

  Fair, The (composed with Lamb)
    SATB,pno,opt gtr&bvl&drums MCAFEE
    M122 $.40   (M6)

  Graffiti
    SATB,acap MCAFEE M135 $.30   (M7)

  Little Christopher *Xmas
    SA/SATB,pno,opt fl&tamb&gtr&drums
    MCAFEE M163 $.40   (M8)

  Morning Times, The
    SATB,acap MCAFEE M125 $.30   (M9)

  Parting Round, A
    unis&SATB&audience (easy) MCAFEE
    M8020 $.40   (M10)

  Peppermint Fugue *see Jeffries

  Where Will You Spend Christmas Eve?
    (composed with Lamb) *Xmas
    SATB,pno MCAFEE M140 $.35   (M11)

MACARTHUR PARK see Webb

MC BRIDE, ROBERT GUYN (1911-   )
  Vocalise Waltz -Warm-Up On Nonsense
    Syllables
    SATB,pno AM.COMP.AL. $5.50   (M12)

MC CABE, JOHN (1939-   )
  This Town's A Corporation Full Of
    Crooked Streets
    mix cor&jr cor,T&narrator,trp,perc,
    pno,org,strings, xylophone,
    vibraphone, glockenspiel voc sc
    NOVELLO rental   (M13)

  Upon The High Midnight *sac/sec,
    CC3U,Xmas
    SATB,SATB soli NOVELLO s.p.   (M14)

  Voyage
    mix cor&boy cor,SMezATBarB soli,
    3fl,pic,3ob,3clar,3bsn,4horn,
    4trp,3trom,tuba,timp,perc,harp,
    org,strings, English horn,
    vibraphone, glockenspiel, celeste
    voc sc NOVELLO rental   (M15)

MCCARTHY, JOE
  What Do You Want To Make Those Eyes
    At Me For? *see Johnson, Howard

MCCARTNEY, JOHN PAUL (1942-   )
  Because *see Lennon, John

  Day Tripper *see Lennon, John

  Fool On The Hill, The *see Lennon,
    John

  Got To Get You Into My Life *see
    Lennon, John

  Here, There And Everywhere *see
    Lennon, John

  I Want To Hold Your Hand *see
    Lennon, John

  Lady Madonna *see Lennon, John

  Live And Let Die (composed with
    McCartney, Linda)
    (Metis F.) SAB BIG3 $.50   (M16)
    (Metis F.) SSA BIG3 $.45   (M17)
    (Metis F.) SATB BIG3 $.45   (M18)

MCCARTNEY, JOHN PAUL (cont'd.)

Lucy In The Sky With Diamonds *see
Lennon, John

Mother Natures Son *see Lennon, John

MCCARTNEY, LINDA
Live And Let Die *see McCartney,
John Paul

MACCHERONI *folk
(Desch, R.) "Die Nudeln" [Ger/It] 4pt
men cor MERSEBURG EM9082 s.p. (M19)
(Desch, R.) "Die Nudeln" [Ger/It] 4pt
mix cor MERSEBURG EM9242 s.p. (M20)

MACCHI, EGISTO
Voci
mix cor sc BRUZZI V-040 s.p. (M21)

MCCORMACK, P.D.
Advance Australia Fair *anthem
ALLANS 475 contains also: Carey,
Henry, God Save The Queen (M22)

MC CRAY, JAMES
Rise Up, My Love, My Fair One
SSA,S solo,pno,fl NATIONAL WHC-44
$.35 (M23)

MCELFRESH, CLAIR T.
Very Merry Christmas, A
SATB,acap LUDWIG L1164 $.30 (M24)

MCELHERAN
Funeral March Of The Death Of Heroes
any voices (easy) OXFORD 95.004
$.25 (M25)

Here Comes The Avant-Garde
any voices (med) OXFORD 95.005 $.60
(M26)

Patterns In Sound: Coda (Canon And
Coda)
SSAATBB,acap (med) OXFORD 95.314
$.75 (M27)

Patterns In Sound: Section A (Etude
And Sounds)
SSAATBB,acap (med) OXFORD 95.313
$.50 (M28)

Patterns In Sound: Section C (Etude
And Scherzo)
SSAATBB,acap (med) OXFORD 95.307
$.50 (M29)

MAC GILLIVARY, JOHN
Stay In Touch With The World *see
Hunt, Frank

MCGLOHAN
Christmas Eve *Xmas
(Fote) SSA KENDOR $.35 (M30)
(Fote) SAB KENDOR $.35 (M31)
(Fote) SATB KENDOR $.35 (M32)

It's Christmas Time *Xmas
(Fote) SATB KENDOR $.40 (M33)
(Fote) SA KENDOR $.40 (M34)

MACHA, OTMAR (1922-)
J.A. Comenius' Testament *ora
[Czech/Ger] mix cor,Mez solo,2fl,
3ob,3bsn,4trp,3trom,tuba,timp,
perc,org,strings SUPRAPHON s.p.,
rental (M35)

MACIATKO A HUSKY see Holoubek, Ladislav

MC KAY, DAVID PHARES
Get Into Heav'n
SATB SUMMY 5953 $.85 (M36)

MCLAUGHLIN, MARIAN
New Settings Of Old Catches *CCU
SATB,pno FISCHER,J FEC 10120 $.40
(M37)

MCLEAN, DON
American Pie, Part I
(Habash, J.M.) SATB,soli,opt gtr
BIG3 $.75 (M38)

American Pie, Part II
(Habash, J.M.) SATB,soli,opt gtr
BIG3 $.75 (M39)

And I Love You So
(Simon, W.) SSA BIG3 $.50 (M40)
(Simon, W.) SAB BIG3 $.50 (M41)
(Simon, W.) SATB BIG3 $.50 (M42)
(Simon, W.) TTBB BIG3 $.50 (M43)

Dreidel
(Metis, F.) SSA BIG3 $.50 (M44)
(Metis, F.) SAB BIG3 $.50 (M45)
(Metis, F.) SATB BIG3 $.50 (M46)

La La Love You
(Metis, F.) SAB BIG3 $.50 (M47)
(Metis, F.) SATB BIG3 $.50 (M48)
(Metis, F.) SSA BIG3 $.50 (M49)

MCLEAN, DON (cont'd.)

Vincent
(Metis, F.) SSA BIG3 $.50 (M50)
(Metis, F.) SATB BIG3 $.50 (M51)

Winter Has Me In Its Grip
(Simon, W.) SSA BIG3 $.50 (M52)
(Simon, W.) SATB BIG3 $.50 (M53)
(Simon, W.) SAB BIG3 $.50 (M54)

Wonderful Baby
(Metis, F.) SAB BIG3 $.50 (M55)
(Metis, F.) SSA BIG3 $.50 (M56)
(Metis, F.) SATB BIG3 $.50 (M57)

You Have Lived
(Simon, W.) SSA BIG3 $.50 (M58)
(Simon, W.) SATB BIG3 $.50 (M59)
(Simon, W.) SAB BIG3 $.50 (M60)

MAC LELLAN, GENE
Put Your Hand In The Hand
(Cobine, Al) SSA STUDIO V7112 $.45
(M61)
(Cobine, Al) SAB STUDIO V7113 $.45
(M62)
(Foust, Alan) SATB STUDIO V714 $.45
(M63)

MCLEOD, ROBERT
Snow, The
SSA (med) FITZSIMONS 3049 $.25
(M64)

MCLIN
Winter, Spring, Summer, Autumn
SATB KJOS 5899 $.40 (M65)

MACMILLAN, ERNEST CAMPBELL (1893-1973)
I Sing Of A Maiden
see Two Christmas Carols

Storke, The
see Two Christmas Carols

Two Christmas Carols *Xmas,carol
unis,3strings HARRIS $.30
contains: I Sing Of A Maiden;
Storke, The (M66)

MCQUEEN, ROD
Beautiful Sunday *see Boone, Daniel

MAD MADRIGALS *CCU
SATB WALTON 2922 (M67)

MAD MAID'S SONG see Crawford

MADAM, MADAM YOU CAME COURTING
(Johnston, Richard A.) SSA (med easy)
WATERLOO $.30 (M68)

MADARDAL see Bartok, Bela

MADCHEN AM BRUNNEN "DANA GING AUS" see
Zoll, Paul

MADCHEN, HEI, WIE HABT IHR'S FEIN see
Bartok, Bela

MADEL, KAMM DICH, PUTZ DICH see Desch,
Rudolf

MADEL KAMM DICH, PUTZ DICH see Haas,
Joseph

MADEL, MUSST DEN WEISSEN TRINKEN see
Edler, Robert

MADEL WINK: WENN WIR MARSCHIEREN see
Krietsch, Georg

MADELE MEIN *folk
(Biebl, F.) [Ger] 4pt men cor
MERSEBURG EM9071 s.p. (M69)

MADELE RUCK, RUCK, RUCK *folk,Ger
(Braun, Horst-Heinrich) men cor,acap
TONOS 127 s.p. (M70)
(Krietsch, G.) men cor,acap TONOS 8
s.p. (M71)

MADERNA, BRUNO (1920-1973)
Tre Liriche Greche *cant
[It] 4pt mix cor,S solo,pno,2fl,
2clar,perc,4timp, bass clarinet
(diff) sc SCHOTTS rental, ipr
(M72)

MADONN' IO NON LO SO PERCHE LO FAI see
Willaert, Adrian

MADONNA MIA GENTIL RINGRATIO AMORE see
Marenzio, Luca

MADONNA PER VOI CANTO MADRIGALE see
Cremesini, M.

MADRIGAL see Fleming, Robert

MADRIGAL see Gresak, Jozef

MADRIGAL see Johansen, Sven-Erik

MADRIGAL see Nowak, Lionel

MADRIGAL see Weigl, Vally

MADRIGAL see Wilson, Donald M.

MADRIGALETTO see Banchieri, Adriano, Se
Nel Mar Del Mio Pianto

MADRIGALI A CINQUE VOCI, LIBRO I see
India, Sigismondo d'

MADRIGALI A DIVERSI LINGUAGGI
*madrigal
MOSELER DAS CHORWERK 125 s.p.
contains: Eccard, Johannes, Zanni
Et Magnifico (SATTB); Marenzio,
Luca, Diversi Linguaggi (composed
with Vecchi, Orazio) (SSATB&
STTT); Varotto, Michele, Dialogo
A Dieci (SATTB&SATTB) (M73)

MADRIGALS OF FIVE AND SIX PARTS (1600)
EM 11 & 12 see Weelkes, Thomas

MADRIGALS OF FIVE PARTS (1612) EM VOL.
17 see Lichfield, Henry

MADRIGALS TO THREE, FOUR, FIVE AND SIX
VOICES (1597) EM VOL. 9 see
Weelkes, Thomas

MADRIGALY see Slavicky, Klement

MAESSEN, ANTOON (1919-)
De Glans Van Hellas
"Glory Of Hellas, The" mix cor,2fl,
2ob,2clar,2bsn,4horn,3trp,2trom,
strings,perc,timp DONEMUS (M74)

Glory Of Hellas, The *see De Glans
Van Hellas

Spotlights
2pt jr cor,pno,strings DONEMUS
(M75)

MAG AUCH DIE LIEBE WEINEN
see Vier Grablieder

MAG IMMER AUCH GESCHEHEN see Rein,
Walter

MAGASCHAN *folk,Hung
(Becker, Hans-Gunther) men cor,acap
2035 s.p. (M76)

MAGELHAN-SONG "DOAR FOHR VON HAMBORG
MOL SO'N OOLEN KASSEN" see Erdlen,
Hermann

MAGIC CARPET, THE see Mozart, Wolfgang
Amadeus

MAGIC IN THE RAINDROPS see Clark, Henry
A.

MAGIC TO DO see Schwartz, Stephen

MAGPIES AT MORNING see Gordon, John

MAGST DU ZU DEM ALTEN HALTEN see
Pepping, Ernst

MAHLER, GUSTAV (1860-1911)
Finale From Symphony No. 2
(Neuman) SATB,SA soli,org/inst/orch
(med diff) FISCHER,C CM 7832
$.40, ipr (M77)

MAHNSPRUCH "FREUND, SO DO ETWAS BIST"
see Schwarz-Schilling, Reinhard

MAHNUNG AN DIE JUGEND, SICH DER MUSIK
ZU BEFLEISSIGEN see Hindemith, Paul

MAHRISCHE VOLKSLIEDER see Poos,
Heinrich

MAIANDACHT "MARIA STEHT IN ROSEN" see
Sturmer, Bruno

MAID OF BUNCLODY, THE *folk,Ir
(Nelson, Havelock) TTBB,acap ROBERTON
53002 s.p. (M78)

MAIDEN BY THE TOWER, THE see Poulenc,
Francis, La Belle Se Sied Au Pied
De La Tour

MAIDEN SO BEAUTIFUL see Monteverdi,
Claudio, Damigella Tutta Bella

MAIENFAHRT see Taubert, Karl Heinz

MAIENFAHRT see Zipp, Friedrich

MAIENGRUN see Edler, Robert

MAIENKANTATE NACH ALTEN VOLKSWEISEN see
Heilmann, Harald

MAIENKANTATE UBER EIN ALTES TANZLIED
AUS DEM RHEINLAND see Marx, Karl

MAIENLIED *folk
(Seeger, P.) [Ger] 4pt men cor
MERSEBURG EM9062 s.p. (M79)

MAIENLIED see Erdlen, Hermann

MAIENZEIT BANNET LEID see Hessenberg, Kurt

MAILIED see Kuhlau, Friederich

MAILIED see Mendelssohn-Bartholdy, Felix

MAILIED see Schubert, Franz (Peter)

MAILIED "DUDELDUMDEI!" see Haas, Joseph

MAINE see Rodgers, Richard

MAINZER UMZUG see Hindemith, Paul

MAIR, WIE DIE WILDE ROS' IM WALD
  mix cor LIENAU LIEDERHARFE NR. 5 sc
  s.p., cor pts s.p.   (M80)

MAISANG "NOCH EINMAL NUN DAS SCHONE
  LIED" see Knab, Armin

MAJ see Fiala, Jiri Julius

MAJE see Ferenczy, Oto

MAJUSI KANON see Lorand, Istvan

MAKE BELIEVE
  SAB CIMINO $.40   (M81)
  SA CIMINO $.40   (M82)
  SSA CIMINO $.40   (M83)
  TTB CIMINO $.40   (M84)
  SSAA CIMINO $.40   (M85)
  SATB CIMINO $.40   (M86)
  TTBB CIMINO $.40   (M87)

MAKE WAY FOR MAN see Sateren, Leland
  Bernhard

MAKE WE JOY see Cugley, Ian

MAKE WE MERRY see Simpson, John

MAKE YOUR OWN KIND OF MUSIC
  SA,pno,opt bvl&drums&gtr SCREEN
    0004MCX   (M88)
  SATB,pno opt bvl&drums&gtr SCREEN
    0004MC7   (M89)
  SSA,pno,opt bvl&drums&gtr SCREEN
    004MC8   (M90)

MAKE YOUR OWN WORLD see Ydstie

MAKIN' MUSIC
  SATB UP WITH 6509 $.40   (M91)

MAKKARONI see Kubizek, Augustinian

MAKSIMOVIC, RAJKO (1935-   )
  Three Haiku *CC3U
  SA&SA,pno,4fl,12vln,2harp,4timp,
    perc MUSIC INFO rental   (M92)

MALA KANTATA see Pauer, Jiri

MALATESTA, LUIGI (1900-   )
  Canti Della Montagna *CCU
  [It] 3-4pt men cor/3-4pt mix cor,
    acap/pno (easy) sc SCHOTTS
    SZ 3726 s.p.   (M93)

  Inno Di Teodulfo
    mix cor,org,strings sc CARISH 21790
    s.p., cor pts CARISH 21792
    rental, ipr   (M94)

MALER, WILHELM (1902-   )
  Der Ewige Strom *ora
  mix cor,STB soli,2fl,2ob,2clar,
    2bsn,4horn,2trp,3trom,tuba,
    strings,harp,perc,timp,celeste
    (med diff) sc SCHOTTS rental, ipr
                                        (M95)
  Kantate *cant
    mix cor,B solo,2fl,2ob,2trp,3trom,
    strings,timp (med) sc SCHOTTS
    rental, ipr   (M96)

MALLOW FLING, THE see Holmes, H. Reuben

MALY PRINC see Loudova, Ivana

MAMIE see Raphling, Sam

MAMINKA see Ambros, Vladimir

MAMINKA see Hanus, Jan

MAMLOCK, URSULA
  Mosaics
    SATB,acap AM.COMP.AL. $3.85   (M97)

MAN IN A CRANE see Bush, N.

MAN IN A ROWBOAT, THE see Evans

MAN IN THE RED SUIT, THE see Sanders

MAN IS FOR THE WOMAN MADE see
  Frackenpohl, Arthur

MAN IS FOR THE WOMAN MADE see Purcell,
  Henry

MAN MAY ESCAPE
  see Four Songs From "The Beggar's
  Opera"

MAN MUST BE FREE see Rinehart, C.

MAN OF LIFE UPRIGHT see Sweetman, Paul

MAN WITH A HOE, THE see Ultan, Lloyd

MAN WITH THE BLUE GUITAR, THE see Beyer

MANA-ZUCCA, MME. (1894-   )
  Brother Love
    TTBB CONGRESS 1201 $.35   (M98)
    SATB CONGRESS 1201 $.35   (M99)

  De Heabenly Choir
    TTBB CONGRESS 1753 $.35   (M100)
    SATB CONGRESS 1754 $.35   (M101)

  Fluttering Birds
    SSA CONGRESS 1104 $.35   (M102)

  I Love You So
    SSA CONGRESS 2628 $.35   (M103)

  It Matters Not
    SA/TB CONGRESS 1006 $.35   (M104)

  Nichevo
    "Nothing Matters" SSA CONGRESS $.35
                                        (M105)
  Nothing Matters *see Nichevo

  Ode To Music
    SATB CONGRESS 1004 $.50   (M106)

  Old Mill's Grist, The
    SSA CONGRESS 2659 $.35   (M107)

  Sleep, My Darling
    SSA CONGRESS 1414 $.35   (M108)

  Those Days Gone By
    SSA CONGRESS 1101 $.35   (M109)

  Top O' The Morning
    SSA CONGRESS 1107 $.35   (M110)
    TTBB CONGRESS $.35   (M111)

  Two Little Shoes
    SATB CONGRESS 1005 $.35   (M112)
    SSA CONGRESS 1102 $.35   (M113)

  Unless
    SSA CONGRESS 1103 $.35   (M114)

MANCHICOURT, PIERRE DE (1510-1586)
  Twenty-Nine Chansons *CC29U
  (Baird, Margery Anthea) bds A-R ED
    $9.95   (M115)

MANCHMAL see Sometimes I Feel

MANDALAY "WO DER ALTE MOULMEINTEMPEL"
  see Genzmer, Harald

MANDEL
  Songs To Laugh By *CCU
    SAB MARKS MC 4608 $.40   (M116)

MANDOLINE see Debussy, Claude

MANDY
  TTBB SCREEN 0086MC4   (M117)

MANFREDS BANNFLUCH "WENN DER MOND IST
  AUF DER WELLE" see Genzmer, Harald

MANHART, EDUARD
  Abendlied: Der Mond Ist
    men cor,acap TONOS 803 s.p.   (M118)

MANIFEST see Schulhoff, Erwin

MANIFESTO see Schulhoff, Erwin,
  Manifest

MANLEY, DOROTHY (1908-   )
  High Barbary *folk,Eng
    unis jr cor,pno,strings,perc,2S
    rec,A rec (easy) sc,voc pt
    SCHOTTS RS 32 s.p., ipa   (M119)

MANN IM MONDE "LIEBER MANN IM MONDE"
  see Radermacher, Friedrich

MANNECKE, DANIEL (1939-   )
  Qui Iustus Est, Lustificatur Adhuc
    *cant
  mix cor,clar,trom,perc,gtr DONEMUS
                                        (M120)
MANNING
  Morningside Of The Mountain, The
    (composed with Stock)
  (Metis) SATB,opt bvl&gtr WARNER
    CH0798 $.40   (M121)

MANNISKA PA JORDEN see Johansen, Sven-
  Erik

MANNISKAN PA JORDEN see Johansen, Sven-
  Erik

MAN'S GOTTA BE, A see Sherman, Richard
  M.

MAN'S LIFE IS LIKE A ROSE see Goossen,
  Frederic

MAN'S LIFE IS WELL COMPARED TO A FEAST
  see Berger, Jean

MANY A NEW DAY see Rodgers, Richard

MANY WAYS TO LOOK AT A WOMAN see
  Yannatos, James

MANY YEARS AGO see Sharpe, Evelyn

MANZONI, GIACOMO (1932-   )
  Holderlin
    cor,orch sc RICORDI-ENG 132006 s.p.
                                        (M122)
MAR PORTUGUES see Bliss, Sir Arthur

MARATHON see Brel

MARBURGER BERICHT see Dessau, Paul

MARCH see Kent, Colonial Spring

MARCH 1948 see Bartos, Jan Zdenek,
  Pochod 1948

MARCHE DES CORNEMUSEAUX see Pahnke

MARCHING ON
  (Wick, Fred) TTBB oct SCHMITT W195
    $.40   (M123)

MARCHING SONG see Franco, Johan

MARCKHL, ERICH (1902-   )
  Brief, In Der Erde Zu Hinterlassen
    [Ger] mix cor,acap MODERN s.p.
                                        (M124)
MARDI, HANS-JURGEN
  Kosakenritt
    men cor,acap TONOS 429 s.p. (M125)

MARENZIO, LUCA (1553-1599)
  Ahi Dispietata Morte *madrigal
    4pt mix cor BONGIOVANI 2374 s.p.
                                        (M126)
  Alas, What A Wretched Life
    SATB STAINER 3.0784.1 $.40   (M127)

  Diversi Linguaggi (composed with
    Vecchi, Orazio)
    see MADRIGALI A DIVERSI LINGUAGGI

  Farewell, Cruel And Unkind
    SATB STAINER 3.0786.1 $.30   (M128)

  Il Settimo Libro De Madrigali Book I
    *CCU,madrigal
    (Steele, John) 5pt REN LM-573 $5.00
                                        (M129)
  Il Settimo Libro De Madrigali Book II
    *CCU,madrigal
    (Steele, John) 5pt REN LM-572 $5.00
                                        (M130)
  Il Settimo Libro De Madrigali Book
    III *CCU,madrigal
    (Steele, John) 5pt REN LM-571 $5.00
                                        (M131)
  Kommt, Ihr Lieblichen Stimmen Alle
    see Widmann, Erasmus, Wer Lieb Und
    Lust Zu Musik Hat

  Madonna Mia Gentil Ringratio Amore
    (Malin, Don) "To Love, My Lady, I
    Now Offer Praises" SSATB,acap
    BELWIN 2324 $.30   (M132)

  Scaldava Il Sol
    (Hall, Wm.D.) "Sun's Warm Rays,
    The" SSATB,fl,ob&clar&horn&bsn/
    ob&clar&horn&vcl/S rec&2T rec&B
    rec,opt hpsd NATIONAL CMS-109
    $.50   (M133)

  Schau Ich Dir In Die Augen
    (Weber, W.) men cor,acap TONOS 3305
    s.p.   (M134)

  Sun's Warm Rays, The *see Scaldava
    Il Sol

  Sweet Singing Amaryllis
    SSATB STAINER 3.0785.1 $.40 (M135)

  Thine Eyes I Would Be Seeing
    (Ehret) SATB SCHIRM.G LG51663 $.35
                                        (M136)
  Thirsis That Heat Refrained
    see Marenzio, Luca, Thirsis To Die
    Desired

  Thirsis To Die Desired
    SATTB STAINER 3.0844.1 $.40
    contains also: Thirsis That Heat
    Refrained   (M137)

MARX, KARL (cont'd.)

I Will Give My Love An Apple *see
   Nimm, Liebste, Diesen Apfel

Jetzt Kommen Die Lustige Tage
   SATB,acap BAREN. BCH157 s.p.
   contains also: Ei, Wohl Eine
   Schone Zeit   (M192)

Jetzt Kommen Die Lustigen Tage *cant
   SATB,2S rec,A rec,strings (easy)
   sc,cor pts BAREN. BA3153 s.p.,
   ipa   (M193)

Jetzt Kommt Die Frohliche Sommerzeit
   *cant
   SATB,2S rec,ob/T rec,strings (easy)
   sc,cor pts BAREN. BA3158 s.p.,
   ipa   (M194)

Maienkantate Uber Ein Altes Tanzlied
   Aus Dem Rheinland *cant
   SATB,ob/fl/A rec/clar,strings,opt
   bsn,opt bvl, and glockenspiel and
   triangle (med easy) sc,cor pts
   BAREN. BA748 s.p., ipa   (M195)

Musik, Du Edle Trosterin *cant
   SATB,2rec,ob/A rec/vln,strings
   (med) sc,cor pts BAREN. BA3151
   s.p., ipa   (M196)

Nimm, Liebste, Diesen Apfel *cant
   "I Will Give My Love An Apple"
   [Ger/Eng] SA&unis men cor,2rec,
   ob/A rec/vln,strings (easy) sc,
   cor pts BAREN. BA3942 s.p., ipa
                        (M197)

O Tannenbaum, O Tannenbaum, Du Tragst
   Ein Grunen Zweig *cant
   SATB,ob/T rec,3vln (easy) sc,cor
   pts BAREN. BA 3157 s.p., ipa
                        (M198)

Sine Musica Nulla Vita *canon
   4pt (easy) BAREN. BCH165 s.p.
   contains also: Gneist, Verner, An
   Die Musik (Nun Hebet Frohlich An,
   Die Gut Musik Zu Preisen) (4pt);
   Katt, Leopold, Viele Kunst Kann
   Der Teufel (3pt)   (M199)

Und In Dem Schneegebirge *cant
   SAB,S rec,A rec,ob/T rec,strings
   (easy) sc,cor pts BAREN. BA3155
   s.p., ipa   (M200)

Wenn Alle Brunnlein Fliessen *cant
   SATB,S rec,ob/vln,strings (easy)
   voc sc,cor pts BAREN. BA3156
   s.p., ipa   (M201)

Widewidewenne
   see Zwei Kindercantaten

Wie Schon Bluht Uns Der Maien
   see Bornefeld, Helmut, Weiss Mir
   Ein Blumlein Blaue

Winterlied "Der Sommer Ist
   Verstrichen" *Op.13,No.4
   SAT,acap (med easy) sc SCHOTTS
   CHBL 319 s.p.   (M202)

Zwei Kindercantaten *cant
   1-2pt treb cor,S rec,S rec/A rec,
   2vln (easy) sc,cor pts BAREN.
   BA3160 s.p., ipa
   contains: Freut Euch, Ihr
      Schafersleut; Widewidewenne
                        (M203)

MARY ANN *folk,Ir
   (Watson, Ruth) mix cor THOMP.G $.45
                        (M204)

MARY ANN-JAMAICA FAREWELL
   (Hudson, Hazel) 2pt ASHDOWN EA375
                        (M205)

MARYKA see Hurnik, Ilja

MARZIALS, THEO.
   Twickenham Ferry
   (Soderstrom, Emil) TTBB (med)
   FITZSIMONS 4042 $.25   (M206)

MARZNACHT see Brahms, Johannes

MASON, LOWELL (1792-1872)
   Dozen Rounds, A (composed with Webb,
   George James) *CC12U
   (Van Camp, Leonard) cor (easy)
   FISCHER,C CM 7927 $.40   (M207)

MASSEUS, JAN (1913-   )
   Camphuysen-Liederen
   mix cor,3trp,3trom,tuba DONEMUS
                        (M208)

MASSIS, AMABLE
   Balade
   2pt,pno JOBERT voc sc s.p., cor pts
   s.p. see from Six Enfantines
                        (M209)

Dispute
   2pt,pno JOBERT voc sc s.p., cor pts
   s.p. see from Six Enfantines
                        (M210)

MASSIS, AMABLE (cont'd.)

Histoire
   2pt,pno JOBERT voc sc s.p., cor pts
   s.p. see from Six Enfantines
                        (M211)

Jeux
   2pt,pno JOBERT voc sc s.p., cor pts
   s.p. see from Six Enfantines
                        (M212)

Promenade En Foret
   2pt,pno JOBERT voc sc s.p., cor pts
   s.p. see from Six Enfantines
                        (M213)

Ronde
   2pt,pno JOBERT voc sc s.p., cor pts
   s.p. see from Six Enfantines
                        (M214)

Six Enfantines *see Balade; Dispute;
   Histoire; Jeux; Promenade En
   Foret; Ronde   (M215)

MASTER AND JOURNEYMAN see Zelter

MASTER OF EAGER YOUTH see Cram

MASTERPIECE, THE
   (Christopher, John) SAB,pno MCAFEE
   M7006 $.40   (M216)

MASTERPIECE, THE see Mouret

MATEJ, JOZKA (1922-   )
   Dve Ukolebavky *CC2U
   [Heb] men cor,S solo,gtr CZECH s.p.
                        (M217)

Iniciаly
   "Initials" [Czech] mix cor,T&
   narrator,2fl,3ob,3clar,2bsn,3trp,
   4trom,timp,perc,pno,strings CZECH
   s.p.   (M218)

Initials *see Iniciаly

MATER ET FILIA see Orff, Carl

MATETIC-RONJGOV, IVAN (1880-1960)
   Morning Song On The Waterfront In
   Rijeka
   cor CROATICA   (M219)

Morning Song To The Homeland
   mix cor,narrator,soli CROATICA
                        (M220)
MATHEW
   I Carry Your Heart
   SATB MARKS MC 4621 $.40   (M221)

Identity
   4 speak cor (easy) OXFORD 95.312
   $.60   (M222)

MATILDA see Bergmann, Walter

MATKA A JABLON see Svobodo, Jiri

MATKA ZEME see Stanislav, Josef

MATONA MIA CARA see Lassus, Roland de
   (Orlandus)

MATONA MIA CARA see Lassus, Roland de
   (Orlandus), Cara Madonna Mia

MATONA MIA CARA "LANZKNECHT-STANDCHEN"
   see Lasso, Orlando di

MATROSENLEBEN *folk,Ger
   (Weber, Bernhard) men cor,acap TONOS
   125 s.p.   (M223)

MATTHES, RENE (1891-   )
   Kulmbacher-Gregorius-Marsch
   unis jr cor/unis wom cor,gtr
   BRATFISCH GB3272 s.p.   (M224)

Lied Der Plassenburg
   mix cor BRATFISCH s.p.   (M225)
   men cor BRATFISCH s.p.   (M226)

Weihelied: In Dieser Feierstunde
   mix cor BRATFISCH s.p.   (M227)
   unis jr cor/unis wom cor BRATFISCH
   s.p.   (M228)

MATTHEW, MARK, LUKE, AND JOHN see
   Rutter

MATTHEWS
   Meanwhile, The Rain
   SSA PARKS PC658 $.35   (M229)

MATTHUS, SIEGFRIED (1934-   )
   Wie Die Saiten Der Gitarre *CC3U
   jr cor/wom cor,acap DEUTSCHER
   DVFM 7647 s.p.   (M230)

MATTSON
   Sing Lullaby *Xmas
   SATB oct SCHMITT 8510 $.40   (M231)

MATYS, JIRI (1927-   )
   In The Nature *see Prirode

MATYS, JIRI (cont'd.)

Ma Laska *cant
   "My Love" [Czech] mix cor,Bar solo,
   3fl,2ob,3clar,3bsn,4horn,3trp,
   3trom,tuba,timp,perc,strings
   CZECH s.p.   (M232)

My Love *see Ma Laska

Prirode
   "In The Nature" [Czech] 4 cor/jr
   cor&girl cor,acap CZECH s.p.
                        (M233)
MATZ, RUDOLF (1901-   )
   Faun, The *CCU
   mix cor,ST soli CROATICA   (M234)

Im Alten Dom
   men cor,acap sc,cor pts TONOS 3407
   s.p.   (M235)

MAURICE, PIERRE (1868-1936)
   Chanson Du Vent De Mer
   wom cor,pno HENN 440 s.p.   (M236)

Gorm Grymm
   mix cor,Bar solo,pno HENN 505 s.p.
                        (M237)
MAW
   Dear Dark Head
   SATB,acap oct BOOSEY 5908 $.40 see
   from Five Irish Songs   (M238)

Five Irish Songs *see Dear Dark
   Head; I Shall Not Die For Thee;
   Popular Song; Ringleted Youth Of
   My Love   (M239)

I Shall Not Die For Thee
   SATB,acap oct BOOSEY 5907 $.40 see
   from Five Irish Songs   (M240)

Popular Song
   SATB,acap oct BOOSEY 5909 $.40 see
   from Five Irish Songs   (M241)

Ringleted Youth Of My Love
   SATB,acap oct BOOSEY 5910 $.40 see
   from Five Irish Songs   (M242)

MAX UND MORITZ see Sutermeister,
   Heinrich

MAXWELL, ROBERT
   Christmas Candy Calendar, The
   (Simon, W.) SSA BIG3 $.50   (M243)
   (Simon, W.) SAB BIG3 $.50   (M244)
   (Simon, W.) SATB BIG3 $.50 (M245)
   (Simon, W.) SA/TB BIG3 $.50 (M246)

This Is My America
   (Simon, W.) SATB,perc ROBBINS
   SH5013 $.50   (M247)

MAY see Fiala, Jiri Julius, Maj

MAY see Washburn

MAY DEW see Thorpe, Raymond

MAY FLOWER see Farrell, Dennis

MAY I PAINT A KISS see Dicks, Ernest A.

MAY NIGHT see Brahms, Johannes

MAY THE GOOD LORD BLESS AND KEEP YOU
   see Willson, Meredith

MAY YOU ALWAYS see Markes, Larry

MAYER, OTTO
   Zum Volkstrauertag
   (Koenig, F.) men cor,acap TONOS
   3006 s.p.   (M248)

MAZURKA "DIE MAZURKA LOCKT" see
   Schroeder, Hermann

ME AND JULIO DOWN BY THE SCHOOLYARD see
   Simon, Paul

ME, ME, AND NONE BUT ME see Dowland,
   John

M'E PIU DOLCE IL PENAR see Monteverdi,
   Claudio

ME VLASTI see Hybler, Jindrich

MEADOWLANDS *folk,Russ
   (Cobine, Al) SATB STUDIO V723 $.45
                        (M249)
MEANWHILE, THE RAIN see Matthews

MEASURE THE VALLEYS see Woldin, Judd

MECHEM, KIRKE (1925-   )
   Children Of David *see Pied Beauty
                        (M250)

English Girls *see Jenny Kissed Me;
   Julia's Voice   (M251)

MECHEM, KIRKE (cont'd.)

Five English Girls *see To Celia
                            (M252)

Jenny Kissed Me
   TBB oct BOOSEY 5856 $.45 see from
     English Girls   (M253)

Julia's Voice
   TBB oct BOOSEY 5857 $.40 see from
     English Girls   (M254)

Lament For A Choral Conductor
   3pt wom cor&3pt men cor,pic,trp,vcl
   NATIONAL WHC-28 $.25   (M255)

Pied Beauty
   SATB oct BOOSEY 5887 $.70 see from
     Children Of David   (M256)

Speech To A Crowd *Op.44
   SATB,Bar solo,2pno&2fl&2ob&
    3clar&2bsn&4horn&3trp&3trom&tuba&
    timp&harp&strings&4perc, bass
    clarinet, celeste voc sc NATIONAL
    MW-101 $1.85, ipr   (M257)

Spirit Of '76, The
   SSA,opt drums&pic (med) FISCHER,C
    CM 7932 $.45, ipa   (M258)
   TBB,opt drums,opt pic (med)
    FISCHER,C 7933 $.45, ipa   (M259)
   SATB,opt drums,opt pic (med)
    FISCHER,C CM 7931 $.45, ipa
                           (M260)

To Celia
   TBB oct BOOSEY 5858 $.70 see from
    Five English Girls   (M261)

MEDIEVAL CAROLS *sac/sec,CCU
  (Weelkes) cor (med) STAINER 3.8904.8
  $20.00   (M262)

MEDIN, N. (1904-1969)
  Tufo Ardeatino
    cor,soli,orch CARISH rental (M263)

MEDITACE see Haba, Alois

MEDITATION see Jobim, Antonio Carlos

MEDITATION ON THE SYLLABLE OM see
  Nelson, R.

MEEK, KENNETH
  Song Of The Fathers, The
    mix cor LESLIE 4092 $.30   (M264)

MEET AMERICA'S WILLIAM BILLINGS see
  Billings, William

MEET AMERICA'S WILLIAM BILLINGS see
  Billings, William

MEGHALOK CSURGOERT see Bartok, Bela

MEHR, SHELDON
  No, My Darling Daughter
    SSATBB SUMMY 5957 $.45   (M265)

MEHR VOM LEBEN see Rosenstengel,
  Albrecht

MEHRSTIMMIGE LAMENTATIONEN *sac,CCU,
  Holywk,16th cent
  mix cor (med) cloth SCHOTTS
    MUSIKALISCHE DENKMALER, BAND 3VI
    s.p.   (M266)

MEI MAIDLE HOT E GSICHTLE see Silcher,
  Friedrich

MEI MUTTER MAG MI NET see Burkhart,
  Franz

MEIN BONNIE see My Bonnie

MEIN DEUTSCHES LIED see Leist, Peter
  Marzellin

MEIN FEINSLIEBCHEN *folk,Ger
  (Frey, Oscar) men cor,acap TONOS 44
    s.p.   (M267)

MEIN GMUT IST MIR see Hassler, Hans Leo

MEIN LIEB IST WIE DER MORGENSTEIN see
  Linke, Norbert

MEIN LIEBSTER FUHR UBER DEN OZEAN see
  My Bonnie Lies Over The Ocean

MEIN MADEL HAT EINEN ROSENMUND *folk,
  Ger
  (Becker, Hans-Gunther) men cor,acap
    114 s.p.   (M268)
  (Heinrichs, Hans) men cor,acap TONOS
    27 s.p.   (M269)

MEIN MADEL HAT EINEN ROSENMUND see
  Hessenberg, Kurt

MEIN PARADIES IST OBERSCHWABEN see
  Feifel, Hermann

MEIN SCHATZ, DER IST AUF DIE
  WANDERSCHAFT HIN see Wimberger,
  Gerhard

MEIN SCHATZ IST EIN SCHREINER see
  Seeger, Peter

MEIN SCHATZELEIN *folk
  (Schrey, W.) [Ger] 4pt men cor
    MERSEBURG EM9036 s.p.   (M270)

MEIN SINNEN BRINGT ZU IHR MICH HIN see
  Rein, Walter

MEIN VATERLAND "DIR IST DEIN HAUPT
  UMKRANZT" see Egk, Werner

MEINE HEIMAT see Rische, Quirin

MEINE HEIMAT "NIRGENDS IST DER HIMMEL
  SO HOCH" see Zoll, Paul

MEINE WAHL "ICH LIEBE DEN HEITERN MANN"
  see Hessenberg, Kurt

MEINE WELT see Gauss, Otto

MEISTER ANTON PILGRAM see Pepping,
  Ernst

MEISTER UND GESELL "A SCHLOSSER HOT AN
  GSELLEN GHABT" see Zelter, Carl
  Friedrich

MELANCHOLY MAN see Pinder

MELLNAS, ARNE (1933-   )
  Dream
    SATB NORDISKA s.p.   (M271)

MELODIE see Krietsch, Georg

MELUSINE see Fibich, Zdenko, Meluzina

MELUZINA see Fibich, Zdenko

MEMEL, ACH MEMEL *folk
  (Felt, Gerhard) SATB,2 soli MOSELER
    LB493 s.p. see from Abend An Der
    Memel   (M272)

MEMENTO see Nono, Luigi

MEMENTO MORI see Sturmer, Bruno

MEMORIAL CANTATA see Fromm, Herbert

MEMORIAL HYMN see Hemel, Oscar van

MEMORIES see Strange, Billy

MEN ARE FOOLS THAT WISH TO DIE *folk
  (Diemer, Emma Lou) SATB STANDARD
    C620MX1 $.50   (M273)

MEN OF HARLECH *Welsh
  (Rice, M.R.) TTBB,inst BRODT 594
    $.26, ipa   (M274)
  (Snr, L. Kean) ALLANS 841   (M275)

MEN OF THE DEEPS *CCU
  (O'Donnell) men cor WATERLOO $1.95
                          (M276)

MENDELSSOHN, ARNOLD (1855-1933)
  Aus Fremden Landern *see Das
    Wermelander Lied "O Wermeland, Du
    Schones"; Hatten Mich Schon
    Aufgegeben; He Uchla!; Tanzlied
    "Hei! Wir Beginnen Einen Lustigen
    Tanz"   (M277)

  Das Wermelander Lied "O Wermeland, Du
    Schones" *Swed
    men cor sc SCHOTTS C 32 683 s.p.
    see from Aus Fremden Landern
                          (M278)

  Festgesang
    men cor,pno/orch FORBERG sc s.p.,
    voc pt s.p., ipr   (M279)

  Hatten Mich Schon Aufgegeben *Czech
    men cor sc SCHOTTS C 32 691 s.p.
    see from Aus Fremden Landern
                          (M280)

  He Uchla! *Russ
    men cor sc SCHOTTS C 32 686 s.p.
    see from Aus Fremden Landern
                          (M281)

  Tanzlied "Hei! Wir Beginnen Einen
    Lustigen Tanz" *Swed
    men cor sc SCHOTTS C 32 684 s.p.
    see from Aus Fremden Landern
                          (M282)

MENDELSSOHN-BARTHOLDY, FELIX
  (1809-1847)
  Abschied Vom Wald *Op.59,No.3
    mix cor,acap BREITKOPF-W CHB 4777
    s.p. see from Mit Der Freude
    Zieht Der Schmerz   (M283)

  Am Neujahrstage
    "On New Year's Day" SATB WALTON
    2257 $.40   (M284)

MENDELSSOHN-BARTHOLDY, FELIX (cont'd.)

  Auf Dem See *Op.41,No.6
    mix cor,acap BREITKOPF-W CHB 4768
    s.p. see from Mit Der Freude
    Zieht Der Schmerz   (M285)

  Aus Ihrem Grab Da Steht Eine Linde
    *Op.41,No.4
    mix cor,acap BREITKOPF-W CHB 4766
    s.p. see from Mit Der Freude
    Zieht Der Schmerz   (M286)

  Collected Edition *sac/sec,CCU
    (Rietz, Julius) microfiche
    UNIV.MUS.ED. $175.00 originally
    published as 19 series in 36
    bindings, Leipzig, 1874-1877.
                          (M287)

  Comitat: Nun Zu Guter Letzt
    men cor,acap TONOS 6315 s.p. (M288)

  Der Frohe Wandersmann
    men cor,acap TONOS 6335 s.p. (M289)

  Der Gluckliche *Op.88,No.2
    mix cor,acap BREITKOPF-W CHB 4782
    s.p. see from Mit Der Freude
    Zieht Der Schmerz   (M290)

  Der Jager Abschied
    men cor,acap TONOS 6316 s.p. (M291)

  Die Nachtigall *Op.59,No.4
    mix cor (easy) sc SCHOTTS CHBL 392
    s.p.   (M292)
    mix cor,acap BREITKOPF-W CHB 4778
    s.p. see from Mit Der Freude
    Zieht Der Schmerz   (M293)

  Die Primel *Op.48,No.2
    mix cor,acap BREITKOPF-W CHB 4770
    s.p. see from Mit Der Freude
    Zieht Der Schmerz   (M294)

  Drinking Song *see Trinklied

  Entflieh' Mit Mir *Op.41,No.2
    mix cor,acap BREITKOPF-W CHB 4764
    s.p. see from Mit Der Freude
    Zieht Der Schmerz   (M295)

  Es Fiel Ein Reif In Der
    Fruhlingsnacht *Op.41,No.3
    mix cor,acap BREITKOPF-W CHB 4765
    s.p. see from Mit Der Freude
    Zieht Der Schmerz   (M296)

  Festgesang An Die Kunstler
    TTBB,4trp,3trom,4horn, Baritone
    Horn KING,R MFB 615 cor pts $.50,
    cmplt ed $7.00   (M297)

  Fruhlingsahnung *Op.48,No.1
    mix cor,acap BREITKOPF-W CHB 4769
    s.p. see from Mit Der Freude
    Zieht Der Schmerz   (M298)

  Fruhlingsfeier *Op.48,No.3
    mix cor,acap BREITKOPF-W CHB 4771
    s.p. see from Mit Der Freude
    Zieht Der Schmerz   (M299)

  Fruhzeitiger Fruhling *Op.59,No.2
    mix cor,acap BREITKOPF-W CHB 4776
    s.p. see from Mit Der Freude
    Zieht Der Schmerz   (M300)

  Gondolier's Evening Song (from Songs
    Without Words)
    (Gingrich) SATB (easy) FITZSIMONS
    1007 $.25   (M301)

  Herbstlied *Op.48,No.6
    mix cor,acap BREITKOPF-W CHB 4774
    s.p. see from Mit Der Freude
    Zieht Der Schmerz   (M302)

  Hunting Song (from Songs Without
    Words)
    (Gingrich) SATB (med) FITZSIMONS
    1008 $.25   (M303)

  Im Grunen *Op.59,No.1
    mix cor,acap BREITKOPF-W CHB 4775
    s.p. see from Mit Der Freude
    Zieht Der Schmerz   (M304)

  Im Walde *Op.41,No.1
    mix cor,acap BREITKOPF-W CHB 4763
    s.p. see from Mit Der Freude
    Zieht Der Schmerz   (M305)

  Jagdlied *Op.59,No.6
    mix cor,acap BREITKOPF-W CHB 4780
    s.p. see from Mit Der Freude
    Zieht Der Schmerz   (M306)

  Komitat "Nun Zu Guter Letzt" *Op.76,
    No.4
    men cor sc SCHOTTS CHBL 25 s.p.
                          (M307)

  Lerchengesang *Op.48,No.4
    mix cor,acap BREITKOPF-W CHB 4772
    s.p. see from Mit Der Freude
    Zieht Der Schmerz   (M308)

MENDELSSOHN-BARTHOLDY, FELIX (cont'd.)

Liebe Und Wein
(Mueller) "Love And Wine" [Eng/Ger]
TTBB AMP 12033 $.50   (M309)

Love And Wine *see Liebe Und Wein

Mailied *Op.41,No.5
mix cor,acap BREITKOPF-W CHB 4767
s.p. see from Mit Der Freude
Zieht Der Schmerz   (M310)

Mit Der Freude Zieht Der Schmerz
*see Abschied Vom Wald, Op.59,
No.3; Auf Dem See, Op.41,No.6;
Aus Ihrem Grab Da Steht Eine
Linde, Op.41,No.4; Der
Gluckliche, Op.88,No.2; Die
Nachtigall, Op.59,No.4; Die
Primel, Op.48,No.2; Entflieh' Mit
Mir, Op.41,No.2; Es Fiel Ein Reif
In Der Fruhlingsnacht, Op.41,
No.3; Fruhlingsahnung, Op.48,
No.1; Fruhlingsfeier, Op.48,No.3;
Fruhzeitiger Fruhling, Op.59,
No.2; Herbstlied, Op.48,No.6; Im
Grunen, Op.59,No.1; Im Walde,
Op.41,No.1; Jagdlied, Op.59,No.6;
Lerchengesang, Op.48,No.4;
Mailied, Op.41,No.5; Morgengebet,
Op.48,No.5; Neujahrslied, Op.88,
No.1; Ruhetal, Op.59,No.5 (M311)

Morgengebet *Op.48,No.5
mix cor,acap BREITKOPF-W CHB 4773
s.p. see from Mit Der Freude
Zieht Der Schmerz   (M312)

Neujahrslied *Op.88,No.1
mix cor,acap BREITKOPF-W CHB 4781
s.p. see from Mit Der Freude
Zieht Der Schmerz   (M313)

O Taler Weit, O Hohen
mix cor (easy) sc SCHOTTS CHBL 385
s.p.   (M314)

O Wunderbares, Tiefes Schweigen
mix cor (easy) sc SCHOTTS CHBL 393
s.p.   (M315)

On New Year's Day *see Am
Neujahrstage

Ruhetal *Op.59,No.5
mix cor,acap BREITKOPF-W CHB 4779
s.p. see from Mit Der Freude
Zieht Der Schmerz   (M316)

Trinklied
men cor,acap TONOS 6336 s.p. (M317)
(Mueller) "Drinking Song" [Eng/Ger]
TTBB AMP 12034 $.45   (M318)

MENDOZA, ANNE
Festival For Autumn, A
cor NOVELLO sc s.p., cor pts s.p.,
ipa   (M319)

MERATH, SIEGFRIED (1923-   )
Ahoi, Kapt'n Seebar! "In Der Kneipe
Zum Weisen Elefanten"
men cor sc SCHOTTS C 39 928 s.p.
see from Musikalische Weltreise
                             (M320)
Das Marchen Hiess Tahiti "Es War
Einmal Ein Marchen"
men cor sc SCHOTTS C 39 932 s.p.
see from Musikalische Weltreise
                             (M321)
Der Kleine Tsching "Der Kleine
Tsching Sucht Einen Ring"
men cor sc SCHOTTS C 39 931 s.p.
see from Musikalische Weltreise
                             (M322)
Musikalische Weltreise *see Ahoi,
Kapt'n Seebar! "In Der Kneipe Zum
Weisen Elefanten"; Das Marchen
Hiess Tahiti "Es War Einmal Ein
Marchen"; Der Kleine Tsching "Der
Kleine Tsching Sucht Einen Ring";
So Sind Die Madchen Von Trinidad
"Stell Dir Vor, Du Gehst Einfach
Spazieren"; Wenn Der Donald
Macdonald "Es Lebte In
Schottland"; Wumba-Wumba "Wenn
Owambo Schmerzen Plagen"   (M323)

So Sind Die Madchen Von Trinidad
"Stell Dir Vor, Du Gehst Einfach
Spazieren"
men cor sc SCHOTTS C 39 930 s.p.
see from Musikalische Weltreise
                             (M324)
Wenn Der Donald Macdonald "Es Lebte
In Schottland"
men cor sc SCHOTTS C 39 929 s.p.
see from Musikalische Weltreise
                             (M325)
Wumba-Wumba "Wenn Owambo Schmerzen
Plagen"
men cor sc SCHOTTS C 39 933 s.p.
see from Musikalische Weltreise
                             (M326)

MERCER
Dream
SATB WALTON 9067 $.40   (M327)

Once Upon A Summertime *pop
(Marnay; Basclay; Legrand) SSA
BELWIN UC 707 $.40   (M328)

MERCILESS BEAUTY see Cockshott, Gerald
Wilfred

MEREDITH, GEORGE
In Starlight *see Constantino,
Joseph

MERKSPRUCH "WER IMMER STREBEND SICH
BEMUHT" see Schwarz-Schilling,
Reinhard

MERMAN
Freedom
SA/TB SHAWNEE E161 $.50   (M329)

MERRILL
Let It Be Forgotten
SSAA/SSAATB,acap (med) OXFORD
95.205 $.35   (M330)

MERRY CHRISTMAS SONG, A *Xmas
(Goldman) SATB SCHIRM.G LG51831 $.40
                             (M331)

MERRY MADRIGAL, A see Read, Gardner

MERRY MARGARET see Brown

MESICE see Schneeweiss, Jan

MESICEK SVITI see Spilka, Frantisek

MESSAGE see Hjort, Fredrik, Budskap

MESSAGE TO THE LIVING see Seidel, Jan,
Vzkaz Zivym

MESSINA
Danny's Song *see Loggins, Dave

Lahaina
(Rocherolle) unis/SA/SSA WARNER
WB-378 $.50   (M332)

Sounds Of Loggins And Messina *see
Loggins, Dave

Thinking Of You *see Loggins, Dave

Your Mama Don't Dance *see Loggins,
Dave

MESSZESEGEK see Maros, Rudolf

METAMORFOZY KRAS see Burlas, Ladislav

METAMORPHOSES see Laburda, Jiri

METYELITSA *folk,Russ
(Hopkins, Ewart) SATB,acap ROBERTON
63029 s.p.   (M333)

METZELSUPPENLIED see Edler, Robert

METZGER, FRITZ B. (1908-   )
Die Frohliche Sommerzeit *cant
1-3pt jr cor,2S rec,2A rec,perc
(easy) cor pts SCHOTTS ED. 4247
s.p., ipa   (M334)

METZLER, FRIEDRICH (1910-   )
Der Tag Vertreibt Die Finstre Nacht
see Die Guldene Sonne
see Die Guldne Sonne

Die Guldene Sonne
mix cor&jr cor,inst (med easy) sc,
cor pts SCHOTTS B 117 s.p., ipa
contains: Der Tag Vertreibt Die
Finstre Nacht; Die Guldene
Sonne; Die Helle Sonn Leucht
Jetzt Herfur   (M335)

Die Guldene Sonne
see Die Guldene Sonne

Die Guldne Sonne *cant
SABar,inst (med easy) sc,cor pts
SCHOTTS B 117 s.p., ipa
contains: Der Tag Vertreibt Die
Finstre Nacht; Die Guldne
Sonne; Die Helle Sonn Leucht
Jetzt Herfur   (M336)

Die Guldne Sonne
see Die Guldene Sonne

Die Helle Sonn Leucht Jetzt Herfur
see Die Guldene Sonne
see Die Guldne Sonne

MEUH!... see Berthomieu, Marc

MEWS
Ghosts, Fire, Water
SATB,A solo,acap (diff) OXFORD
56.130 $1.45   (M337)

MEXICO-LIEDCHEN see Rosenstengel,
Albrecht

MEYER
Nicolas De Flue *ora
mix cor,soli,orch HENN 373 s.p.
                             (M338)

MEYER, W.
Schmoll-Lieschen "Lieschen, Wass
Fallt Dir Ein"
3pt mix cor BRATFISCH s.p. (M339)

MEZZETTI
Morning Train
(Siltman) TTB WARNER P1021 188 $.35
                             (M340)

MI LAGNERO TACENDO see Mozart, Wolfgang
Amadeus

MICH ERFREUT, SCHONS LIEB, DEIN
UNEBLICK see Franck, Melchior

MICH WUNDERT, DASS ICH FROHLICH BIN see
Etti, Karl

MICHAEL, FRANK (1943-   )
Chor Der Froschphilharmoniker
4pt,acap cor pts BREITKOPF-W
CHB 4819 s.p.   (M341)

MICHEL, PAUL-BAUDOUIN
Petit Zodiaque Sentimental, Part I
(Broussier, Jacques) mix cor,acap
CBDM   (M342)

Petit Zodiaque Sentimental, Part II
(Broussier, Jacques) mix cor,acap
CBDM   (M343)

Petit Zodiaque Sentimental, Part III
(Broussier, Jacques) mix cor,acap
CBDM   (M344)

MICHELS, JOSEF
Der Sich Ein Faules Gretchen
see Lothringer Liederkreis

Einst Stand Ich
see Lothringer Liederkreis

Es Ging Ein Madchen
see Klingendes Land-Lieder An Der
Saar

Es Grabt Der Bergmann
see Klingendes Land-Lieder An Der
Saar

Es Stehn Drei Sternlein
see Lothringer Liederkreis

Ich Lag Einst Unte Linden
see Klingendes Land-Lieder An Der
Saar

Jetzt Reisen Wir Zum Tor Hinaus
see Klingendes Land-Lieder An Der
Saar

Klingendes Land-Lieder An Der Saar
men cor,acap TONOS s.p.
contains: Es Ging Ein Madchen; Es
Grabt Der Bergmann; Ich Lag
Einst Unte Linden; Jetzt Reisen
Wir Zum Tor Hinaus; Wo Ist Denn
Das Madchen   (M345)

Lasset Uns Trinken
men cor,acap TONOS 3927 s.p. (M346)

Lothringer Liederkreis
men cor,acap TONOS s.p.
contains: Der Sich Ein Faules
Gretchen; Einst Stand Ich; Es
Stehn Drei Sternlein; Nach
Gross Trauer; Schafersmann
                             (M347)

Nach Gross Trauer
see Lothringer Liederkreis

Schafersmann
see Lothringer Liederkreis

Trage Uns Zum Licht Empor
men cor,acap TONOS 3928 s.p. (M348)

Wo Ist Denn Das Madchen
see Klingendes Land-Lieder An Der
Saar

MICHIGAN, MY MICHIGAN see Miessner, W.
Otto

MICHLIN, SPENCER
That's What Lovin' You Is All About
*see Evans, Paul

MICHNA, ADAM VACLAV (ca. 1600-1676)
Missa Sancti Wenceslai *Xmas
[Lat] mix cor,2trp,org,strings
SUPRAPHON s.p., rental   (M349)

MICKEY see Francaix, Jean

MOHLER, PHILIPP (cont'd.)

    C 38 058-57 s.p., ipa   (M450)
    men cor,pno/3trp,4horn,3trom,tuba,
    timp sc SCHOTTS C 43 594 s.p.,
    cor pts SCHOTTS C 43 840 s.p.,
    ipa   (M451)

    Wer Jetzig Zeiten Leben Will" *Op.9,
    No.2
    TTBB sc SCHOTTS C 34 199 s.p., voc
    pt SCHOTTS C 34 200, 01-04 s.p.
    see from Drei Soldatenlieder
                                   (M452)

    Zum Abschied "Fort Mit Den Grillen"
    jr cor/wom cor (easy) sc SCHOTTS
    CHBL 537 s.p.   (M453)

MOJ KRAJ see Holoubek, Ladislav

MOJA RODNA see Mikula, Zdenko

MOJE ZEME see Mrkos, Zdenek

MOLINE
    December Child
    (Hayward) SATB SHAWNEE A1273 $.40
                                   (M454)

MOLLICONE, HENRY
    Four Elizabethan Songs *CC4U
    SSA,S solo,2vln,vla,opt perc sc
    AM.COMP.AL. $7.70   (M455)

    Iola's Epitaph
    SATB,acap AM.COMP.AL. $2.75 (M456)

    Out Of Lucretius
    SSA,2vln,vla,vcl sc AM.COMP.AL.
    $5.50   (M457)

    Three Christmas Songs *CC3U,Xmas
    SSAA,acap AM.COMP.AL. $1.10 (M458)

    Three Christmas Songs *CC3U,Xmas
    SSA,ob/vln,vla, or English horn sc
    AM.COMP.AL. $1.10   (M459)

MOLLY MALONE *folk
    (Seeger, P.) [Ger] 4pt men cor
    MERSEBURG EM9064 s.p.   (M460)

MOLN see Wieslander, Ingvar

MOMAN
    Another Somebody Done Somebody Wrong
    Song *see Butler

MOMENT ERE THE DAWN, A see Distler,
    Hugo, Ein Stundlein Wohl Vor Tag

MOMENTO NOSTALGICO see Cremesini, M.

MOMENTS TO REMEMBER
    SSA CIMINO $.40   (M461)
    SATB CIMINO $.40   (M462)

MON MARY M'A DIFFAMEE see Anonymous

MON VERGER see Beguelin

MONACO, JAMES V.
    What Do You Want To Make Those Eyes
    At Me For? *see Johnson, Howard

    You Made Me Love You (from Irene)
    (Metis, F.) SSA BIG3 $.45   (M463)
    (Metis, F.) SATB BIG3 $.50   (M464)
    (Metis, F.) SAB BIG3 $.45   (M465)

MONACO, RICHARD A.
    I Never Saw A Moor
    SA,org,perc FISCHER,J FEC 10108
    $.35   (M466)

MOND UND TRINKER see Krietsch, Georg

MONDAUFGANG "DIE ERDE IST GEHULLT" see
    Genzmer, Harald

MONDAY'S CHILD see Rutter

MONDNACHT see Buttschardt, Ferdinand

MONDNACHT see Gauss, Otto

MONDNACHT "ES WAR ALS HATT DER HIMMEL"
    see Lissmann, Kurt

MONELLE, RAYMOND
    Galliard Carol, The
    SSA oct BOOSEY 5876 $.50   (M467)

    Nowell Sing We, Both All And Some
    SSA oct BOOSEY 5874 $.45   (M468)

MONNIKENDAM, MARIUS (1896-   )
    Christmas Cycle *sac/sec,CC6U,carol
    mix cor,org DONEMUS   (M469)

    Elckerlyc-Everyman
    mix cor&boy cor,org,fl,ob,clar,bsn,
    opt 2trp&2trom,strings,perc
    DONEMUS s.p.   (M470)
    men cor&boy cor,org,fl,ob,clar,bsn,
    2trp,2trom,strings,perc DONEMUS
    s.p.   (M471)

MONNIKENDAM, MARIUS (cont'd.)

    Trois Psaumes, Pour Le Temps Present
    *sac/sec,CC3U,Psalm
    mix cor,4 soli,2fl,2ob,2clar,2bsn,
    3horn,strings,perc,timp,
    xylophone DONEMUS   (M472)

MONOTONE, THE see Cornelius

MONSIEUR ROUSSELLE *folk
    (Seeger, P.) [Ger] 4pt men cor
    MERSEBURG EM 9011 s.p.   (M473)

MONSTER SONG, THE see Muccigrosso

MONTEVERDI, CLAUDIO (ca. 1567-1643)
    A Che Tormi Il Ben Mio *madrigal
    (De Surcy, Bernard Bailly) [Eng/Fr/
    Ger/It] cor,kbd (contains also:
    Amor Per Tua Merce) REN ER 2 $.50
    see from Il Primo Libro De
    Madrigali   (M474)

    A Un Giro Sol De' Bell' Occhi
    *madrigal
    SSATB,acap EGTVED KB218 s.p. (M475)

    All'hora I Pastori Tutti *madrigal
    (De Surcy, Bernard Bailly) [Eng/Fr/
    Ger/It] cor,kbd (contains also:
    Fumia La Pastorella; Almo Divino
    Raggio) REN ER 5 $.75 see from Il
    Primo Libro De Madrigali   (M476)

    Almo Divino Raggio *madrigal
    (De Surcy, Bernard Bailly) [Eng/Fr/
    Ger/It] cor,kbd (contains also:
    Fumia La Pastorella; All'hora I
    Pastori Tutti) REN ER 5 $.75 see
    from Il Primo Libro De Madrigali
                                   (M477)

    Amor Per Tua Merce *madrigal
    (De Surcy, Bernard Bailly) [Eng/Fr/
    Ger/It] cor,kbd (contains also: A
    Che Tormi Il Ben Mio) REN ER 2
    $.50 see from Il Primo Libro De
    Madrigali   (M478)

    Amor S'il Tuo Ferire *madrigal
    (De Surcy, Bernard Bailly) [Eng/Fr/
    Ger/It] cor,kbd (contains also:
    Donna S'io Miro Voi) REN ER 8
    $.50 see from Il Primo Libro De
    Madrigali   (M479)

    Anima Dolorosa *madrigal
    SSATB,acap EGTVED OCIV, 3 s.p. see
    also Six Madrigals   (M480)

    Ardi O Gela *madrigal
    (De Surcy, Bernard Bailly) [Eng/Fr/
    Ger/It] cor,kbd (contains also:
    Ardo Si Ma Non T'amo; Arsi E
    Alsi) REN ER 9 $.75 see from Il
    Primo Libro De Madrigali   (M481)

    Ardo Si Ma Non T'amo *madrigal
    (De Surcy, Bernard Bailly) [Eng/Fr/
    Ger/It] cor,kbd (contains also:
    Ardi O Gela; Arsi E Alsi) REN
    ER 9 $.75 see from Il Primo Libro
    De Madrigali   (M482)

    Arsi E Alsi *madrigal
    (De Surcy, Bernard Bailly) [Eng/Fr/
    Ger/It] cor,kbd (contains also:
    Ardo Si Ma Non T'amo; Ardi O
    Gela) REN ER 9 $.75 see from Il
    Primo Libro De Madrigali   (M483)

    Baci Soavi E Cari *madrigal
    (De Surcy, Bernard Bailly) [Eng/Fr/
    Ger/It] cor,kbd (contains also:
    Se Por Non Mi Consenti) REN ER 3
    $.50 see from Il Primo Libro De
    Madrigali   (M484)

    Ch'io Ami La Vita Mia *madrigal
    (De Surcy, Bernard Bailly) [Eng/Fr/
    Ger/It] cor,kbd (contains also:
    Se Per Havervi, Oime) REN ER 1
    $.50 see from Il Primo Libro De
    Madrigali   (M485)

    Damigella Tutta Bella
    (Contino, Fiora) "Maiden So
    Beautiful" [It/Eng] SAB/TTB,kbd,
    2vln DEAN CC-101 $.45 see from
    Scherzi Musicali   (M486)

    Donna S'io Miro Voi *madrigal
    (De Surcy, Bernard Bailly) [Eng/Fr/
    Ger/It] cor,kbd (contains also:
    Amor S'il Tuo Ferire) REN ER 9
    $.50 see from Il Primo Libro De
    Madrigali   (M487)

    Ecco Mormorar L'onde *madrigal
    (Helmborg, Bjorn) SSATB,acap EGTVED
    OCIV, 1 s.p. see also Six
    Madrigals   (M488)

    Filli Cara E Amata *madrigal
    (De Surcy, Bernard Bailly) [Eng/Fr/
    Ger/It] cor,kbd (contains also:

MONTEVERDI, CLAUDIO (cont'd.)

    Poi Che Del Mio Dolore) REN ER 4
    $.50 see from Il Primo Libro De
    Madrigali   (M489)

    First Book Of Madrigals, The *CCU
    (De Surcy, Bernard Bailly) cor REN
    $15.00   (M490)

    First Book Of Madrigals, The *CCU
    cor REN $16.00 facsimile of the
    1621 edition   (M491)

    Fumia La Pastorella *madrigal
    (De Surcy, Bernard Bailly) [Eng/Fr/
    Ger/It] cor,kbd (contains also:
    Almo Divino Raggio; All'hora I
    Pastori Tutti) REN ER 5 $.75 see
    from Il Primo Libro De Madrigali
                                   (M492)

    Il Primo Libro De Madrigali *see A
    Che Tormi Il Ben Mio; All'hora I
    Pastori Tutti; Almo Divino
    Raggio; Amor Per Tua Merce; Amor
    S'il Tuo Ferire; Ardi O Gela;
    Ardo Si Ma Non T'amo; Arsi E
    Alsi; Baci Soavi E Cari; Ch'io
    Ami La Vita Mia; Donna S'io Miro
    Voi; Filli Cara E Amata; Fumia La
    Pastorella; La Vaga Pastorella;
    Poi Che Del Mio Dolore; Questa
    Ordi Il Laccio; Se Nel Partir Da
    Voi; Se Per Havervi, Oime; Se Por
    Non Mi Consenti; Tra Mille
    Fiamme; Vsciam Ninfe Homai (M493)

    La Piaga Ch'ho Nel Core *madrigal
    SSATB,acap EGTVED OCIV, 4 s.p. see
    also Six Madrigals   (M494)

    La Piaga C'ho Nel Core
    (Malin, Don) "Pain Within My Heart,
    The" SSATB,acap BELWIN 2323 $.30
                                   (M495)

    La Vaga Pastorella *madrigal
    (De Surcy, Bernard Bailly) [Eng/Fr/
    Ger/It] cor,kbd (contains also:
    Vsciam Ninfe Homai; Questa Ordi
    Il Laccio) REN ER 7 $.75 see from
    Il Primo Libro De Madrigali
                                   (M496)

    Le Berger
    eq voices HENN 805 s.p.   (M497)

    Maiden So Beautiful *see Damigella
    Tutta Bella

    M'e Piu Dolce Il Penar *madrigal
    SSATB,acap EGTVED OCIV, 5 s.p. see
    also Six Madrigals   (M498)

    O Come E' Gran Martire *madrigal
    SSATB,acap EGTVED OCIV, 2 s.p. see
    also Six Madrigals   (M499)

    Pain Within My Heart, The *see La
    Piaga C'ho Nel Core

    Petit Madrigal
    eq voices HENN 804 s.p.   (M500)

    Poi Che Del Mio Dolore *madrigal
    (De Surcy, Bernard Bailly) [Eng/Fr/
    Ger/It] cor,kbd (contains also:
    Filli Cara E Amata) REN ER 4 $.50
    see from Il Primo Libro De
    Madrigali   (M501)

    Questa Ordi Il Laccio *madrigal
    (De Surcy, Bernard Bailly) [Eng/Fr/
    Ger/It] cor,kbd (contains also:
    Vsciam Ninfe Homai; La Vaga
    Pastorella) REN ER 7 $.75 see
    from Il Primo Libro De Madrigali
                                   (M502)

    Scherzi Musicali *see Damigella
    Tutta Bella, "Maiden So
    Beautiful"   (M503)

    Se Nel Partir Da Voi *madrigal
    (De Surcy, Bernard Bailly) [Eng/Fr/
    Ger/It] cor,kbd (contains also:
    Tra Mille Fiamme) REN ER 6 $.50
    see from Il Primo Libro De
    Madrigali   (M504)

    Se Per Havervi, Oime *madrigal
    (De Surcy, Bernard Bailly) [Eng/Fr/
    Ger/It] cor,kbd (contains also:
    Ch'io Ami La Vita Mia) REN ER 1
    $.50 see from Il Primo Libro De
    Madrigali   (M505)

    Se Por Non Mi Consenti *madrigal
    (De Surcy, Bernard Bailly) [Eng/Fr/
    Ger/It] cor,kbd (contains also:
    Baci Soavi E Cari) REN ER 3 $.50
    see from Il Primo Libro De
    Madrigali   (M506)

    Six Madrigals *madrigal
    cmplt ed EGTVED OCIV s.p.
    contains & see also: Anima
    Dolorosa; Ecco Mormorar L'onde;
    La Piaga Ch'ho Nel Core; M'e

MIT HJERTE ALTID VANKER see Stenlev,
Leif

MIT LUST TAT ICH AUSREITEN see
Ketterer, Ernst

MIT LUST TAT ICH AUSREITEN see
Lemacher, Heinrich

MIT LUST TAT ICH AUSREITEN see Zipp,
Friedrich

MIT LUST TAT ICH SPAZIEREN see
Steffens, Johann

MIT LUST TRET ICH IN DIESEN TANZ see
Hessenberg, Kurt

MIT LUST TRITT ICH AN DIESEN TANZ see
Brautigam, Helmut

MIT MADCHEN SICH VERTRAGEN see Rein,
Walter

MIT SEUFZEN UND MIT KLAG see Haussmann,
Valentin

MITCHELL
Help Me
(Gargaro) SSA WARNER CQ0788 $.40
(M398)

MITCHELL, JOHN
Both Sides Now
see Joni Mitchell Medley

Chelsea Morning
see Joni Mitchell Medley

Circle Game, The
see Joni Mitchell Medley

Joni Mitchell Medley *pop
(Burroughs; Sewell) SSA WARNER
WB-345 183 $.50; SATB WARNER
WB-344 187 $.50
contains: Both Sides Now; Chelsea
Morning; Circle Game, The
(M399)

MITCHELL, JONI
Both Sides Now *pop
(Burroughs) SSA,opt perc WARNER
WB-319 183 $.40 (M400)
(Burroughs) SATB,opt perc WARNER
WB-318 187 $.40 (M401)

MITCHELL, RANDY
We Are Americans
SATB PARAGON 510 $.30 (M402)

MITTAGSRUH "UBER BERGEN, FLUSS UND
TALEN" see Baumann, Max

MITTAGSSTILLE "KLANGMUDE ZEIT IM
MITTAGLICHEN FELD" see Knab, Armin

MITTELBACH, OTTO
Standchen
men cor,acap TONOS 3972 s.p. (M403)

MITTEN WIR IM LEBEN SIND see Knab,
Armin

MITTERGRADNEGGER, GUNTHER
Japanisches Abendlied
men cor,acap TONOS 2027 s.p. (M404)

Kum, Geselle Min
men cor,acap TONOS 802 s.p. (M405)

Trinklied
men cor,acap TONOS 3919 s.p. (M406)

Vorspruch: Wer Sich Die Musik
men cor,acap TONOS 5801 s.p. (M407)

MITTERNACHT UND TAG see Krenek, Ernst

MLADA AGA "SEHT, WIE DIE SONNE LACHT"
see Klefisch, Walter

MLADA LASKA see Bohac, Josef

MLADEZI see Mikula, Zdenko

MLADYM KOMUNISTUM see Strniste, Jiri

MNICHOV see Haba, Alois

MOBILE see Holm, Peder

MOBY DICK see Herrmann, Bernard

MOCKINGBIRD see Foxx, Charles

MOCKL, FRANZ (1925-)
Als Du Klein Warst, Marietta *Slav
"Kad Si Bila Mala Mare" mix cor
(easy) sc SCHOTTS C 43 438 s.p.
(M408)
"Kad Si Bila Mala Mare" jr cor/wom
cor (easy) sc SCHOTTS CHBL 604
s.p. (M409)

An Die Kleinen Lieder "O Schlagt
Nicht Nieder So Scheu Die Augen"
3-5pt wom cor (contains also:

MOCKL, FRANZ (cont'd.)
Flugel, Um Zu Fliegen; Herbstlied
"Schon Im Goldnen Ahrenkranz") sc
SCHOTTS C 41 721-01 s.p. see from
Sechs Chorlieder (M410)

Auf, Ihr Freunde
men cor,acap TONOS 3961 s.p. (M411)

Die Ratsel Der Elfen "Die Elfen
Sitzen Im Felsenschacht"
3-5pt wom cor (contains also: In
Der Kirche "Auf Der Bank, Wie Sie
Sonst Sitzet") sc SCHOTTS
C 41 721-02 s.p. see from Sechs
Chorlieder (M412)

Ein Lammlein, Das Gegangen
3-5pt wom cor sc SCHOTTS
C 41 721-03 s.p. see from Sechs
Chorlieder (M413)

Flugel, Um Zu Fliegen
3-5pt wom cor (contains also: An
Die Kleinen Lieder "O Schlagt
Nicht Nieder So Scheu Die Augen";
Herbstlied "Schon Im Goldnen
Ahrenkranz") sc SCHOTTS
C 41 721-01 s.p. see from Sechs
Chorlieder (M414)

Geige Und Klarinett'
see Mockl, Franz, Golden Oder Rot
Der Wein

Golden Oder Rot Der Wein
mix cor/eq voices (easy) sc SCHOTTS
C 43 429 s.p. contains also:
Geige Und Klarinett' (mix cor)
(M415)

Herbstlied "Schon Im Goldnen
Ahrenkranz"
3-5pt wom cor (contains also: An
Die Kleinen Lieder "O Schlagt
Nicht Nieder So Scheu Die Augen";
Flugel, Um Zu Fliegen) sc SCHOTTS
C 41 721-01 s.p. see from Sechs
Chorlieder (M416)

In Der Kirche "Auf Der Bank, Wie Sie
Sonst Sitzet"
3-5pt wom cor (contains also: Die
Ratsel Der Elfen "Die Elfen
Sitzen Im Felsenschacht") sc
SCHOTTS C 41 721-02 s.p. see from
Sechs Chorlieder (M417)
3-5pt wom cor (contains also: Die
Ratsel Der Elfen "Die Elfen
Sitzen Im Felsenschacht") sc
SCHOTTS C 41 721-02 s.p. see from
Sechs Chorlieder (M418)

Kad Si Bila Mala Mare *see Als Du
Klein Warst, Marietta

Sechs Chorlieder *see An Die Kleinen
Lieder "O Schlagt Nicht Nieder So
Scheu Die Augen"; Die Ratsel Der
Elfen "Die Elfen Sitzen Im
Felsenschacht"; Ein Lammlein, Das
Gegangen; Flugel, Um Zu Fliegen;
Herbstlied "Schon Im Goldnen
Ahrenkranz"; In Der Kirche "Auf
Der Bank, Wie Sie Sonst Sitzet"
(M419)

Sinn- Und Unsinn-Spruche *CC5U
mix cor (med) sc SCHOTTS C 43 538
s.p. (M420)

MODERN MUSIC see Billings, William

MOESCHINGER, ALBERT (1897-)
Der Herbst Des Einsamen *Op.69,
CC12U
wom cor,acap MODERN s.p. (M421)

MOHLER, PHILIPP (1908-)
Ahren Im Sturm "O, Wie Der Sturm So
Dunkel Braust!"
men cor sc SCHOTTS C 38 056 s.p.
(M422)

Berglied "Wir Wollen Auf Den Berg
Steigen" *Op.32,No.2
TTBB sc SCHOTTS C 38 520 s.p. see
from Drei Gesange Fur Mannerchor
(M423)
TTBB voc pt SCHOTTS 38 521, 01-04
s.p. see from DREI GESANGE FUR
MANNERCHOR (M424)

Das Ewige Ist Stille *Op.42,No.3
men cor sc SCHOTTS C 40 947 (M425)

Der Postillon "Was Willst Du Auf
Dieser Station" (from
Wandspruchen, Op. 33)
mix cor (med) sc SCHOTTS C 40 262
s.p. see from Gesange (M426)

Der Tod Von Flandern "Der Tod Reit'
Auf Einem Kohlschwarzen Rappen"
*Op.9,No.1
TTBB sc SCHOTTS C 34 197 s.p., voc
pt SCHOTTS C 34 198, 01-04 s.p.
see from Drei Soldatenlieder

MOHLER, PHILIPP (cont'd.)
(M427)

Die Gedanken Sind Frei
jr cor/wom cor (easy) sc SCHOTTS
CHBL 503 s.p. (M428)

Drei Gesange Fur Mannerchor *see
Berglied "Wir Wollen Auf Den Berg
Steigen", Op.32,No.2; Trost "Wenn
Wir Auch Durftig Hausen", Op.32,
No.1 (M429)

Drei Soldatenlieder *see Der Tod Von
Flandern "Der Tod Reit' Auf Einem
Kohlschwarzen Rappen", Op.9,No.1;
Es Leben Die Soldaten, Op.9,No.3;
Wer Jetzig Zeiten Leben Will",
Op.9,No.2 (M430)

Ein Freier Mut "O Wie So Schon Und
Gut"
jr cor/wom cor (easy) sc SCHOTTS
CHBL 538 s.p. (M431)

Ein Traum Ist Unser Leben
men cor sc SCHOTTS C 37 838 (M432)

Es Geht Wohl Anders Als Du Meinst
(from Wandspruchen, Op. 33)
mix cor (med) sc SCHOTTS C 40 261
s.p. see from Gesange (M433)

Es Leben Die Soldaten *Op.9,No.3
TTBB sc SCHOTTS C 34 201 s.p., voc
pt SCHOTTS C 34 202, 01-04 s.p.
see from Drei Soldatenlieder
(M434)

Fanfaren-Intrade *Op.38
men cor,4horn,3trp,3trom,tuba,timp
sc SCHOTTS FG 21 s.p. (M435)
"Fanfaren-Ruf" men cor,3trp,3trom
(short version of Fanfaren-
Intrade) sc SCHOTTS FG 21A s.p.
(M436)

Fanfaren-Ruf *see Fanfaren-Intrade

Festliche Lied-Kantate *Op.37, Fest,
cant
men cor&mix cor,4horn,3trp,3trom,
tuba,timp voc sc SCHOTTS C 39 527
s.p., ipa (M437)

Gesange *see Der Postillon "Was
Willst Du Auf Dieser Station"
(from Wandspruchen, Op. 33); Es
Geht Wohl Anders Als Du Meinst
(from Wandspruchen, Op. 33)
(M438)

Glockensegen "Komm In Diesem
Glockensegen" *Op.39,No.2
men cor sc SCHOTTS C 40 035 (M439)

Hausspruch "Das Ist Das Beste Auf Der
Welt" *Op.42,No.1
men cor sc SCHOTTS C 40 036 (M440)

Heimkehr "Weint Nicht Mehr, Ihr
Mutter" *Op.32,No.3
TTBB voc pt SCHOTTS C 38 523, 01-04
s.p. see from DREI GESANGE FUR
MANNERCHOR (M441)
TTBB sc SCHOTTS C 38 522 s.p. see
from Drei Gesange Fur Mannerchor
(M442)

Im Fruhtau Zu Berge
2-3pt jr cor/2-3pt wom cor,acap
(easy) sc SCHOTTS CHBL 584 s.p.
(M443)

Laetare *Op.43, cant
men cor,solo,2fl,2ob,2clar,2bsn,
4horn,3trp,3trom,perc,timp,
strings,opt tuba,harp voc sc,cor
pts SCHOTTS ED. 6015 s.p., ipr,
sc SCHOTTS rental (M444)

Nachtmusikanten *Op.24
mix cor,T solo,fl,clar,bsn,horn,
trp,strings,perc,timp (med diff)
voc sc,cor pts SCHOTTS ED. 3898
s.p., sc SCHOTTS rental, ipr
(M445)

Singend Sei Dein Tag Begonnen
*Op.29,No.1
men cor sc SCHOTTS CHBL 78 (M446)

Trost "Wenn Wir Auch Durftig Hausen"
*Op.32,No.1
men cor sc SCHOTTS C 38 519 s.p.
see from Drei Gesange Fur
Mannerchor (M447)

Vergangen Ist Die Nacht *cant
jr cor/wom cor,fl,strings (med
easy) sc,cor pts SCHOTTS ED. 3740
s.p., ipa (M448)

Viva La Musica *Op.41, cant
men cor,solo,strings&opt 3trp/orch
sc,cor pts SCHOTTS ED. 5260 s.p.,
ipa, ipr (M449)

Wandspruch-Kantate *Op.29, cant
mix cor,pno/4horn,3trp,3trom,tuba,
timp (med easy) sc SCHOTTS
C 40 740 s.p., cor pts SCHOTTS

MONTEVERDI, CLAUDIO (cont'd.)

Piu Dolce Il Penar; O Come E'
Gran Martire; T'amo Mia Vita
(M507)

T'amo Mia Vita *madrigal
SSATB,cont EGTVED OCIV, 6 s.p. see
also Six Madrigals   (M508)

Tra Mille Fiamme *madrigal
(De Surcy, Bernard Bailly) [Eng/Fr/
Ger/It] cor,kbd (contains also:
Se Nel Partir Da Voi) REN ER 6
$.50 see from Il Primo Libro De
Madrigali   (M509)

Vsciam Ninfe Homai *madrigal
(De Surcy, Bernard Bailly) [Eng/Fr/
Ger/It] cor,kbd (contains also:
Questa Ordi Il Laccio; La Vaga
Pastorella) REN ER 7 $.75 see
from Il Primo Libro De Madrigali
(M510)

MONTGOMERY, BRUCE (1921-   )
Venus's Praise *CC7U
SATB,strings voc sc NOVELLO rental,
ipr   (M511)

MONUMENTAL PARADOX see Cohn, James

MOOD INDIGO
see Portrait Of Duke Ellington

MOOLENAAR, FR.
Naar Die Groote Stad *cant
cmplt ed HEER 44 s.p.   (M512)

MOON, THE see Busch, Carl

MOON, THE see Covert, Mary E.

MOON IS SHINING, THE see Spilka,
Frantisek, Mesicek Sviti

MOON OVER TOWNS MOON see Boone, Charles

MOONRAKERS see Williamson, Malcolm

MOONRISE see Bassett, Leslie

MOORE
Clap Your Hands
2pt oct HERITAGE H5700 $.40 (M513)

Living Today
SATB oct HERITAGE H107 $.35 (M514)

Tambourines To Glory *see Hughes

MOORE, DANIEL
Look For The Light
(Metis, F.) SAB BIG3 $.45   (M515)
(Metis, F.) SATB BIG3 $.45   (M516)
(Metis, F.) SSA BIG3 $.45   (M517)

MOORE, EARL VINCENT (1890-   )
Voyage Of Arion, The *cant
jr cor,Bar solo,inst FITZSIMONS cor
pts $.75, sc ipr   (M518)

MOORE, HAROLD S.
Darkest Hour, The
SATB,STBarB soli,2fl,2ob,2clar,
2bsn,4horn,2trp,3trom,tuba,timp,
perc,org,strings, English horn
voc sc NOVELLO rental, ipr (M519)

MOORE, THOMAS
At The Mid Hour Of Night
2pt ASHDOWN EA373   (M520)

Last Rose Of Summer, The
2pt ASHDOWN EA372   (M521)

Young May Moon, The
2pt ASHDOWN EA374   (M522)

MOOSBURGER GRADUALE see Genzmer, Harald

THE MORALIA (OF 1596): PART I see
Handl, Jacob

THE MORALIA (OF 1596): PART II see
Handl, Jacob

MORALITATEN see Henze, Hans Werner

MORAVSKYM KRAJEM see Devaty, Antonin

MORE see Sokola, Milos

MORE AND MORE
TTBB CIMINO $.40   (M523)
SSA CIMINO $.40   (M524)
SATB CIMINO $.40   (M525)

MORE FIRSTS AND SECONDS see Appleby

MORE LITTLE THINGS THAT CREEP AND CRAWL
AND SOMETIMES FLY see Peninger

MORE LOVE OR MORE DISDAIN I CRAVE see
Purcell, Henry

MOREY, LARRY (1905-   )
Snow White Revisited (composed with
Churchill, Frank)
(King, P.) SSA BOURNE B230987-353
$.65   (M526)
(King, P.) SATB BOURNE B230987-357
$.65   (M527)

MORGAN, HILDA
Little Lambs Where Do You Sleep
unis (easy) WATERLOO $.30 (M528)

Snowdrop And Lamb
unis (med easy) WATERLOO $.30
(M529)

MORGEN see Sturmer, Bruno

MORGEN "SOOFT DIE SONNE AUFERSTEHT" see
Hessenberg, Kurt

MORGENBAD see Rein, Walter

MORGENGEBET see Mendelssohn-Bartholdy,
Felix

MORGENGESANG see Gade, Niels Wilhelm

MORGENGLORIA "DUNKEL, UBER DER ERDE
NOCH" see Haas, Joseph

MORGENLICHT see Edler, Robert

MORGENLIED see Burkhart, Franz

MORGENLIED see Schaefers, Anton

MORGENLIED see Schneider, Walther

MORGENLIED see Werdin, Eberhard

MORGENLIED AN DIE SONNE see Haug, Lukas

MORGENLIED "BALD IST DER NACHT EIN END'
GEMACHT" see Erdlen, Hermann

MORGENLIED "DIE STERNE SIND ERBLICHEN"
see Hessenberg, Kurt

MORGENLIED "KEIN STIMMLEIN NOCH
SCHALLT" see Baumann, Max

MORGENLIED "NOCH AHNT MAN KAUM DER
SONNE LICHT" see Fussan, Werner

MORGENLIED "VERSCHWUNDEN IST DIE
FINSTRE NACHT" see Erdlen, Hermann

MORGENLIED "VERSCHWUNDEN IST DIE
FINSTRE NACHT" see Seeger, Peter

MORGENMUSIK "ES LEUCHTEN ALLE MORGEN"
see Wolters, Karl-Heinz

MORGENWANDERUNG see Gade, Niels Wilhelm

MORGON (SVERIGE) see Eklof, Einar

MORIKE-CHORLIEDERBUCH, OP. 19 see
Distler, Hugo

MORIKE - ZYKLUS see Rein, Walter

MORITURI see Krietsch, Georg

MORLEY, THOMAS (1557-1602)
April Is In My Mistress' Face
(Churchill, Kenneth) SATB BOURNE
B200573-358 $.50   (M530)

Arise, Get Up
SAB,acap EGTVED MS9B4 s.p. (M531)

Canzonets For Two And Three Voices EM
Vol. 1 *CC12L
2-3pt STAINER 3.1901.1 $10.25
(M532)

Fire, Fire *madrigal
SSATB,acap EGTVED KB248 s.p. (M533)

First Book Of Balletts (1595) EM Vol.
4 *CC22L
5-6pt mix cor STAINER 3.1904.1
$10.50   (M534)

First Book Of Madrigals (1594) EM
Vol. 2 *CC25L,madrigal
4-6pt mix cor STAINER 3.1902.1
$10.50   (M535)

It Was A Lover And His Lass
SA CRAMER $.25   (M536)
SATB,acap EGTVED MS14B5 s.p. (M537)

Now Is The Gentle Season
SATB,acap EGTVED KB72 s.p. (M538)

Now Is The Month Of Maying
SSATB CARUS CV 40.205 s.p. contains
also: Sing We And Chant It (M539)

Nun Strahlt Der Mai Den Herzen
SAATB,acap (easy) sc SCHOTTS
CHBL 362 s.p.   (M540)

MORLEY, THOMAS (cont'd.)

Sing We And Chant It
see Morley, Thomas, Now Is The
Month Of Maying

MORNING AFTER, THE see Kasha, Al

MORNING HAS BROKEN see Farjeon, Eleanor

MORNING HEROES see Bliss, Sir Arthur

MORNING SONG see Thiman, Eric Harding

MORNING SONG ON THE WATERFRONT IN
RIJEKA see Matetic-Ronjgov, Ivan

MORNING SONG TO THE HOMELAND see
Matetic-Ronjgov, Ivan

MORNING TIMES, THE see McAfee, Don

MORNING TRAIN see Mezzetti

MORNINGSIDE OF THE MOUNTAIN, THE see
Manning

MORRISON
I Shall Sing *pop
(Rocherolle) SSA WARNER WB-349 183
$.50   (M541)
(Rocherolle) SATB WARNER WB-348 187
$.50   (M542)

MORS JANUA VITAE see Wilson, R. Barclay

MORTARI, VIRGILIO (1902-   )
Trittico
wom cor,SMez soli,3fl,3ob,3clar,
2bsn,4horn,3trp,3trom,tuba,timp,
perc,harp,pno CARISH rental
(M543)

MOSAICS see Mamlock, Ursula

MOSELWEIN "REBEN, REBEN, SO WEIT MAN
SCHAUT" see Weber, Bernhard

MOST BEAUTIFUL GIRL, THE
SATB SCREEN 4722MCIC   (M544)
SSA SCREEN 4722MC2C   (M545)

MOST BEAUTIFUL GIRL IN THE WORLD
SSA CIMINO $.40   (M546)
TTBB CIMINO $.40   (M547)
SATB CIMINO $.40   (M548)

MOST BEAUTIFUL SONG, THE
(Sjoberg, Per-Anders) SATB NORDISKA
NMS 6419 s.p.   (M549)

MOST OF THE TIME see Kam, Dennis

MOSTAD, JON
Den Sommeren
SSA/SAB MUSIKK   (M550)

I Forarssol
SSA/SAB MUSIKK   (M551)

MOTETTE see Nageli, Johann (Hans) Georg

MOTHER AND CHILD REUNION see Simon,
Paul

MOTHER AND THE APPLE TREE see Svobodo,
Jiri, Matka A Jablon

MOTHER COUNTRY see Coates

MOTHER COUNTRY see Liliedahl

MOTHER EARTH see Stanislav, Josef,
Matka Zeme

MOTHER I CANNOT MIND MY WHEEL see
Chagrin, Francis

MOTHER-IN-LAW, THE see Cwyn Mam
Ynghfraith

MOTHER NATURES SON see Lennon, John

MOTHER, O SING ME TO SLEEP see Franz

MOTHER STOJANKA OF KNEZPOLJE see
Fribec, Kresimir

MOTORWAY see Bush, N.

MOTTE, DIETHER DE LA (1928-   )
Die Glocken Von Nantes "Im Kerkerturm
Von Nantes"
see Zwei Franzosische Volkslieder

Festliche Kantate *cant
mix cor,pno,2fl,clar,2trp,strings,
perc,timp (med) sc,cor pts
SCHOTTS ED. 4972 s.p., ipa (M552)

Hab Meine Liebe Wohl Verborgen
see Zwei Franzosische Volkslieder

Standchen Fur Don Quixote "Damit Euer
Gnaden"
4-6pt men cor,3 narrators,T solo
sc,cor pts SCHOTTS ED. 5134 s.p.

MOTTE, DIETHER DE LA (cont'd.)

(M553)
Zwei Franzosische Volkslieder *folk,
Fr
[Ger] men cor sc SCHOTTS C 40 298
s.p.
contains: Die Glocken Von Nantes
"Im Kerkerturm Von Nantes"; Hab
Meine Liebe Wohl Verborgen
(M554)

MOTTETTO see Bossi, Renzo

MOTTETTO TRISTE see Bossi, Renzo

MOUNTAIN PANSIES see Ceremuga, Josef,
Horske Macesky

MOUNTAINS see Christiansen, P.

MOURANT, WALTER
Winter Elegy
SATB,harp sc AM.COMP.AL. $2.75
(M555)
SATB,pno AM.COMP.AL. $2.75   (M556)

MOURET
Masterpiece, The (composed with
Parnes)
cor,pno MCAFEE M1048 $.40   (M557)

MOUSE AND THE LION, THE see Hardt,
Richard

MOVE THE MOUNTAIN
(Singer, Henry A.) SATB (med easy)
WATERLOO $.50   (M558)

MOVIN' *spir
(Rodby, W.) SATB,solo,pno oct
SOMERSET WR 1019 $.45   (M559)

MOYZES, ALEXANDER (1906-   )
Baladicka Kantata *cant
mix cor,T solo,orch SLOV.HUD.FOND
s.p.   (M560)

Ci Organy Hraju *CCU
jr cor SLOV.HUD.FOND s.p.   (M561)

Jar
mix cor SLOV.HUD.FOND s.p.   (M562)

My L'udia V Modrych Bluzach *cant
mix cor,orch SLOV.HUD.FOND s.p.
(M563)

Piesen Pracujucich *cant
cor,orch SLOV.HUD.FOND s.p.   (M564)

Travnice
jr cor SLOV.HUD.FOND EZS 12 s.p.
(M565)

Ty Krasna Zem
mix cor SLOV.HUD.FOND s.p.   (M566)

MOZART, WOLFGANG AMADEUS (1756-1791)
Abendruhe
men cor,acap TONOS 6344 s.p. (M567)

Bald Prangt, Den Morgen Zu Verkunden
(from Die Zauberflote)
jr cor/wom cor (easy) sc SCHOTTS
CHBL 511 s.p.   (M568)

Bona Nox
see Lang, Hans, Wenn Alle Brunnlein
Fliessen

Bundeslied
see LIEDPROGRAMM DES DEUTSCHEN
SANGERBUNDES FOLGE 3: "ESSENER
LIEDERBLATT" - "CHORFEIER"
men cor,acap TONOS 6318 s.p. (M569)

Bundeslied "Bruder, Reicht Die Hand
Zum Bunde!" *K.623
men cor sc SCHOTTS CHBL 20 s.p.
(M570)

Canzonetten, Kochel 439 *see Due
Pupille Amabile; Ecco Quel Fiero
Istante; Luci Care, Luci Belle;
Mi Lagnero Tacendo; Piu Non Si
Trovano; Se Lontan Ben Mio Tu Sei
(M571)

Charm Me Asleep
(Leupold, U.S.) SAB (med diff)
WATERLOO $.40   (M572)

Collected Edition *sac/sec,CCU
microfiche UNIV.MUS.ED. editors
include: Brahms, Johannes;
Espagne, Franz; Goldschmidt,
Otto; Joachim, Joseph and others.
Originally published as 24 series
in 67 bindings, Leipzig, 1876-
1907. $290.00   (M573)

Come Let Us Sing
(Leupold, U.S.) SAB (med diff)
WATERLOO $.30   (M574)

Difficile Lectu Mihi Mars
see Vier Weltliche Kanons

MOZART, WOLFGANG AMADEUS (cont'd.)

Due Pupille Amabile *K.439
[It] SSB,3winds/pno (contains also:
Ecco Quel Fiero Istante) EGTVED
MS8B13 s.p. see from Canzonetten,
Kochel 439   (M575)
(Carl, Robert) "Two Starry Beams"
[It/Eng] SAB,3clar NATIONAL
CMS-103 $.40   (M576)

Ecco Quel Fiero Istante *K.436
[It] SSB,3winds/pno (contains also:
Due Pupille Amabile) EGTVED
MS8B13 s.p. see from Canzonetten,
Kochel 439   (M577)
(Carl, Robert) "Time's Most Cruel
Moment" [It/Eng] SAB,3clar
NATIONAL CMS-102 $.45   (M578)

Essen, Trinken
see Vier Weltliche Kanons

Eyes Of Beauty, Eyes Flashing Bright
*see Luci Care Belle

Golden Slumbers
(Leupold, U.S.) SAB (med easy)
WATERLOO $.30   (M579)

In The Starlight
(Leupold, U.S.) SAB (med easy)
WATERLOO $.30   (M580)

Lieber Freistadtler
see Vier Weltliche Kanons

Liebes Madchen Hor Mir Zu *K.441c
(Klink, Waldemar) men cor sc
SCHOTTS CHBL 24 s.p.   (M581)

Luci Care Belle
(Klein) "Eyes Of Beauty, Eyes
Flashing Bright" SSA SCHIRM.G
11947 $.25   (M582)

Luci Care, Luci Belle
[It] SSB,3winds/pno (contains also:
Piu Non Si Trovano; Se Lontan Ben
Mio Tu Sei) EGTVED MS9B1 s.p. see
from Canzonetten, Kochel 439
(M583)

Magic Carpet, The
(Jennings; Spiegl) SATB,acap (med)
OXFORD 53.095 $.75   (M584)

Mi Lagnero Tacendo
[It] SSB,3winds/pno EGTVED MS9B6
see from Canzonetten, Kochel 439
(M585)

O Du Eselhafter Martin *K.560b,
canon
TTBB SCHIRM.EC 2328 s.p.   (M586)

O Schutzgeist (from Die Zauberflote)
men cor,pno sc,cor pts TONOS 6317
s.p.   (M587)

Piu Non Si Trovano *K.549
[It] SSB,3winds/pno (contains also:
Luci Care, Luci Belle; Se Lontan
Ben Mio Tu Sei) EGTVED MS9B1 s.p.
see from Canzonetten, Kochel 439
(M588)
(Carl, Robert) "Seek Not For
Constancy" [It/Eng] SAB,3clar
NATIONAL CMS-101 $.45   (M589)

Se Lontan Ben Mio Tu Sei *K.438
[It] SSB,3winds/pno (contains also:
Piu Non Si Trovano; Luci Care,
Luci Belle) EGTVED MS9B1 s.p. see
from Canzonetten, Kochel 439
(M590)
(Carl, Robert) "Whenever, Love,
You're Far From Me" [It/Eng] SAB,
3clar NATIONAL CMS-104 $.40 (M591)

Seek Not For Constancy *see Piu Non
Si Trovano

Sing Care Away
(Leupold, U.S.) SAB (med easy)
WATERLOO $.30   (M592)

Time's Most Cruel Moment *see Ecco
Quel Fiero Istante

Trinkkanon
see Vier Weltliche Kanons

Two Starry Beams *see Due Pupille
Amabile

Vier Weltliche Kanons *canon
3-4pt jr cor (med easy) sc SCHOTTS
CHBL 571 s.p.
contains: Difficile Lectu Mihi
Mars, K.559; Essen, Trinken,
K.234; Lieber Freistadtler,
K.232; Trinkkanon, K.560 (M593)

Warnung
mix cor BRATFISCH GB2968 s.p.
(M594)

MOZART, WOLFGANG AMADEUS (cont'd.)

Weep You No More Sad Fountains
(Leupold, U.S.) SAB (med easy)
WATERLOO $.40   (M595)

Whenever, Love, You're Far From Me
*see Se Lontan, Ben Mio, Tu Sei

Where Shall The Lover Rest
(Leupold, U.S.) SAB (med easy)
WATERLOO $.40   (M596)

Wiegenlied "Schlafe Prinzchen, Schlaf
Ein"
(Zipp, Friedrich) 3pt jr cor/3pt
wom cor,solo,opt vln (easy) sc
SCHOTTS CHBL 507 s.p.   (M597)

MR. FROG see Boyd, Jeanne

MRKOS, ZDENEK (1919-   )
Ceska Rikadla *CCU
jr cor SLOV.HUD.FOND EZS 8 s.p.
(M598)

Moje Zeme
mix cor,acap SUPRAPHON s.p. (M599)

Sonnet
[Czech] wom cor,pno CZECH s.p.
(M600)

MRS. MCGRATH see Lochlainn, Colm O.

MRS. ROBINSON see Simon, Paul

MUCCIGROSSO
Just Do Your Thing
(Bove) SAB KENDOR $.35   (M601)

Monster Song, The
(Bove) SA KENDOR $.30   (M602)

MUCHOS VAN DE AMOR
(Merrill) cor OXFORD 95.003 (M603)

MUCZYNSKI, ROBERT (1929-   )
Synonym For Life
SATB SCHIRM.G 11982 $.45   (M604)

MUFFIN MAN, THE see Tiffault

MUHR, NESSY
Ding, Dong, Sing A Song *CC30U,canon
2-4pt jr cor RICORDI-ENG BA 12934
s.p.   (M605)

MUL, JAN (1911-   )
L'Homme Desarme *cant
cor,soli,2fl,2ob,2clar,2bsn,2horn,
2trp,2trom,strings,perc,timp,harp
DONEMUS   (M606)

MULE, GIUSEPPE (1885-1951)
Largo
4pt mix cor sc BONGIOVANI 2199 s.p.
(M607)

MULET VADER see Franzen, Bengt

MULLER, PETER (1791-1877)
Rheinland
men cor,acap sc,cor pts TONOS 432
s.p.   (M608)

MULLER, SIEGFRIED (1926-   )
Wir Haben In Uns Einen Sommer
mix cor,acap HOFMEISTER G2198 s.p.
(M609)

MULLER-BLATTAU, WENDELIN
Crambambuli
men cor,acap TONOS 690-1 s.p.
(M610)

MUMBLIN' WORD see Wood, Joseph

MUMMY see Ambros, Vladmir, Maminka

MUMMY see Hanus, Jan, Maminka

MUNDUS CANTAT, HEFT 2 *folk
(Kubizek, A.) mix cor DOBLINGER
42 847 s.p.   (M611)

MUNICH see Haba, Alois, Mnichov

MUNTZEL, HERBERT (1909-   )
Als Wir Jungst In Reg'nsburg Waren
SATB,acap (easy) BAREN. BCH173 s.p.
contains also: Zum Tanze, Da Geht
Ein Madel   (M612)

Zum Tanze, Da Geht Ein Madel
see Muntzel, Herbert, Als Wir
Jungst In Reg'nsburg Waren

MURRAY
How Come
cor oct SCHMITT 2137 $.40   (M613)

On The Devide
SATB SCHIRM.G LG51742 $.40   (M614)

We're A Family Tree
SATB oct SCHMITT 4014 $.40   (M615)
cor oct SCHMITT 2588 $.40   (M616)

MURRAY, BAIN
Ode To Peace
SATB,acap STUDIO V719 $.40 (M617)

MURRAY, MITCH
Billy, Don't Be A Hero *see Callander, Pete

Night Chicago Died, The
(Simon, W.) SAB BIG3 $.50 (M618)
(Simon, W.) SSA BIG3 $.50 (M619)
(Simon, W.) SATB BIG3 $.50 (M620)

MUSEN SIZILIENS see Henze, Hans Werner

MUSIC see Caldwell, Mary [Elizabeth]

MUSIC FOR "A MIDSUMMER NIGHT'S DREAM"
see Peaslee, Richard

MUSIC FOR CHORUS see Gow, David

MUSIC FOR QUEEN MARY II see Purcell, Henry

MUSIC FOR SOPHOCLES' "ANTIGONE" see Sollberger, Harvey

MUSIC FOR WINDS, PERCUSSION, CELLO, AND VOICES see Yttrehus, Rolv

MUSIC FROM "SEMELE" see Handel, George Frideric

MUSIC HERE see Butler, Eugene

MUSIC MAKERS, THE see Elgar, Edward

MUSIC, WHEN SOFT VOICES DIE see Butler, Eugene

MUSIC WHEN SOFT VOICES DIE see Harbison, John

MUSIC WORKSHOP, BOOK 1 see Pont

MUSIC WORKSHOP, BOOK 2 see Pont

MUSICA DIVINA LAUDES see Hindemith, Paul

MUSICAL ZABAIONE, A see Banchieri, Adriano, Il Zabaione Musicale

MUSICK'S EMPIRE see Platts, Kenneth

MUSIC'S PRAISE see Hurd, Michael

MUSIK, DU EDLE TROSTERIN see Marx, Karl

MUSIK ERFULLT DIE WELT *folk,Eng
(Schneider, Walther) men cor,acap TONOS 2038 s.p. (M621)

MUSIK FUR DIE JUGEND
2-3pt jr cor,inst sc NEUE NM226 s.p., voc pt NEUE NM226A s.p., ipa (M622)

MUSIK UND JAGEREI "ICH SETZ EIN STREIT: MUSIK UND JAGEREI" see Rein, Walter

MUSIK VON ALTERS IST GEEHRT see Steffens, Johann

MUSIKA, DIE GANZ LIEBLICHE KUNST see Jeep, Johann

MUSIKALISCHE WELTREISE see Merath, Siegfried

MUSIKANTEN-KANTATE see Rosenstengel, Albrecht

MUSIKANTEN, SPIELET AUF see Rein, Walter

MUSIKANTEN, WARUM SCHWEIGT IHR see Poos, Heinrich

MUSIKANTEN WOLLEN WANDERN see Edler, Robert

MUSIKEN KLANG, LIEBLICHER GESANG see Beck, Conrad

MUSIKUS UND MUSIKA see Edler, Robert

MUSIQUE POUR "OEDIPE A COLONE DE SOPHOCLE" see Stroe, Aurel

MUSKOKA
(Pasch, Silvio) "Land Of The Silver Birch" SATB,perc WATERLOO $.40 (M623)

MUSPILLI see Hiller, Wilfred

MUSPILLI see Hiller, Wilfred

MUSS I DENN *folk,Ger
(Boyd) "Must I Now" SATB WARNER WB-326 187 $.40 (M624)
(Braun, Horst-Heinrich) men cor,acap TONOS 129 s.p. (M625)
(Lang, Hans) cor (med easy) sc SCHOTTS CHBL 266 s.p. (M626)

MUSS I DENN see Rein, Walter

MUSS I DENN ZUM STADTELE HINAUS see Silcher, Friedrich

MUSSORGSKY, MODEST (1839-1881)
Defeat Of Sennacherib
mix cor,pno/orch BOOSEY cor pts $1.00, sc rental (M627)

Wiegenlied Lullaby
(Track) SSA KJOS 6140 $.35 (M628)

MUST I NOW see Muss I Denn

MUTTERLIED see Delacher, Hermann

MUZIKANTI CO DELATE see Bartos, Jan Zdenek

MUZSKE SBORY see Barta, Lubor

MUZSKE ZBORY I
men cor SLOV.HUD.FOND s.p.
contains: Korinek, Miloslav, Krajina Mieru; Mikula, Zdenko, Jablone; Prasil, Frantisek, Slovensko (M629)

MUZSKE ZBORY II
men cor SLOV.HUD.FOND s.p.
contains: Ferenczy, Oto, Vyzva; Kardos, Dezider, Ja Jednoruky Jozef Jaso; Ocenas, Andrej, Dakujem Ti (M630)

MUZSKE ZBORY III
men cor SLOV.HUD.FOND s.p.
contains: Berger, Roman, V Tichu Tak Draho Vykupenom; Gresak, Jozef, Nove Slovensko; Holoubek, Ladislav, Moj Kraj; Zimmer, Jan, Na Slavu Banilov (M631)

MY BELOVED SPAKE see Hadley

MY BELOVED SPAKE see Purcell, Henry

MY BONNIE *folk,Eng
(Langer, Hans-Klaus) "Mein Bonnie" [Ger] men cor,acap sc,cor pts TONOS 2001 s.p. (M632)

MY BONNIE IS OVER THE OCEAN
(Scheider, Werner) SATB MOSELER LB742 s.p. contains also: Wir Fahren Ubers Weite Meer (M633)

MY BONNIE LIES OVER THE OCEAN *folk
(Poos, H.) "Mein Liebster Fuhr Uber Den Ozean" [Eng/Ger] 4pt mix cor MERSEBURG FM9252 s.p. (M634)

MY BOY
SATB,pno,opt bvl&drums&gtr SCREEN 8006MC7 (M635)

MY CHERIE AMOUR
SSA,pno,opt bvl&drums&gtr SCREEN 8043MC8 (M636)

MY COUNTRY see Hybler, Jindrich, Me Vlasti

MY COUNTRY SO BEAUTIFUL see Chlubna, Oswald, Je Krasna, Zeme Ma

MY DAYS HAVE BEEN SO WONDROUS FREE see Freedom Song, 1776

MY DEAR HEART, YOUR DEPARTING see Azzaiolo, F., Ti Parti, Cor Mio Caro

MY ELUSIVE DREAMS
SSA,pno,opt bvl&drums&gtr SCREEN 80022MC8 (M637)
SATB,pno,opt bvl&drums&gtr SCREEN 8002MC7 (M638)

MY ELUSIVE DREAMS see Putman, Curly

MY FAVORITE THINGS see Rodgers, Richard

MY FAVORITE TIME TO CRY see Gagliardi, George

MY GINGER KITTY see Kurth, Burton L.

MY HEART IS INDITING see Purcell, Henry

MY HEART IS YOURS see Lassus, Roland de (Orlandus)

MY HEART LEAPS UP see Lassus, Roland de (Orlandus)

MY HEART'S IN THE HIGHLANDS see Haskins, William

MY LADY CELIA
(Deale, Edgar) SATB (med easy) WATERLOO $.35 (M639)

MY LITTLE SWEETHEART see Lassus, Roland de (Orlandus)

MY LORD, WHAT A MORNING
(Biebl, Franz) treb cor DOBLINGER O 318 s.p. see from Acht Spirituals (M640)

MY LORD, WHAT A MOURNING *spir
(Dawson, William L.) SATTB,acap (med) FITZSIMONS 2009 $.25 (M641)

MY LOVE see Matys, Jiri, Ma Laska

MY LOVE IS FAIR see Bayley, Robert Charlton

MY LOVE IS LIKE A RED, RED ROSE see Feldsher, Howard M.

MY L'UDIA V MODRYCH BLUZACH see Moyzes, Alexander

MY MELODY OF LOVE
SA SCREEN 8062MC5 (M642)
SAB SCREEN 8062MC3 (M643)

MY MISTRESS FROWNS see Hilton

MY OLD KENTUCKY HOME
see Drei Amerikanische Volkslieder

MY OLD KENTUCKY HOME see Foster, Stephen

MY ROMANCE
SSA CIMINO $.40 (M644)
SA CIMINO $.40 (M645)
SAB CIMINO $.40 (M646)
SATB CIMINO $.40 (M647)
TTBB CIMINO $.40 (M648)

MY SORROW IS MY LOVE see Hovhaness, Alan

MY SOUL, THERE IS A COUNTRY see Binkerd, Gordon

MY TRUE LOVE HATH MY HEART see Carter, John

MY WAY see Anka, Paul

MYERS RANDY
Bad Water *see De Shannon, Jackie

MYGGEDANS see Nyhus, Rolf

MYSTERIOUS TRUMPET PLAYER, THE see Burghauser, Jarmil, Tajemny Trubac

MYSTIC ODE see Scott, Cyril Meir

MYSTIC TRUMPETER, THE see Harty, Sir Hamilton

MYSTIC TRUMPETER, THE see Spencer, Williametta

N

N. C. R. V. LIED
mix cor,pno/harmonium HEER 681 s.p.
(N1)

N.R.G. SONG see Dodds

NA BAHIA TEM see Villa-Lobos, Heitor

NA, DA HAB'N MA'S G'FANGT
(Lessky, Fr.) mix cor DOBLINGER G 688
s.p. see from Sechs Lieder Aus Wien
(N2)

NA KAZDEM ZALEZI see Martinek, Stepan

NA PERONE see Simai, Pavol

NA SLAVU BANILOV see Zimmer, Jan

NA TVOJU SLAVU PIESEN ZVONI see Hirner,
Teodor

NAAR DIE GROOTE STAD see Moolenaar, Fr.

NACELLE see Carrard

NACH DEM WINTER
unis wom cor SCHOTTS C 42 532C s.p.
see also Alle Singen Heft 1   (N3)

NACH GROSS TRAUER see Michels, Josef

NACH GRUNER FARB MEIN HERZ VERLANGT see
Rein, Walter

NACH HAUS *folk,Eng
(Kuhn, Rudolf) [Ger] men cor,acap
TONOS 2028 s.p.   (N4)

NACH SUDEN NUN SICH LENKEN
(Zoll, Paul) men cor sc SCHOTTS
C 38 916 s.p.   (N5)

NACH UND NACH see By An' By

NACHRUF "DU GABST MIT GOTTES HANDEN see
Herrmann, Hugo

NACHT see Schubert, Franz (Peter)

NACHT UND MORGEN see Ligeti, Gyorgy

NACHTGERAUSCHE see Koenig, Franz

NACHTHELLE see Schubert, Franz (Peter)

NACHTIGALL, ICH HOR DICH SINGEN see
Burkhart, Franz

NACHTIGALLENKANON "ALLES SCHWEIGET" see
Haydn, (Franz) Joseph

NACHTLICHER JAZZ "DIE NACHT, EIN
FREMDER, SCHWARZER GEIGER" see
Desch, Rudolf

NACHTLICHES STANDCHEN see Haus, Karl

NACHTLICHES STANDCHEN "LEISE, LEISE,
LASS UNS SINGEN" see Schubert,
Franz (Peter)

NACHTLIED "NUN RUH MIT SORGEN" see
Bresgen, Cesar

NACHTLIED "QUELLENDE, SCHWELLENDE
NACHT" see Genzmer, Harald

NACHTMUSIK see Schubert, Franz (Peter)

NACHTMUSIKANTEN see Lothar, Mark

NACHTMUSIKANTEN see Mohler, Philipp

NACHTMUSIKANTEN "HIER SIND WIR ARME
NARRN" see Hessenberg, Kurt

NACHTWACHE I see Brahms, Johannes

NACHTWACHE II see Brahms, Johannes

NACHTWANDLER "TROMMLER, LASS DEIN
KALBFELL KLINGEN" see Haas, Joseph

NACUVAJ DUSI see Mikula, Zdenko

NADESEL CAS see Podest, Ludvik

NAGELI, JOHANN (HANS) GEORG (1773-1836)
Motette
men cor,acap TONOS 6330 s.p.   (N6)

NAH IST UND SCHWER ZU FASSEN DER GOTT
see Reutter, Hermann

NAHELAND-HEIMATLAND see Desch, Rudolf

NAISSEZ DONS DE FLORE see Rameau, Jean-
Philippe

NAKADA, Y.
Female Chorus Album *CCU
treb cor ONGAKU s.p.   (N7)

NARREN UBERALL "NARREN, NARREN" see
Sturmer, Bruno

NARREN UBERALL "NARREN SIND AN ALLEN
ECKEN" see Sturmer, Bruno

NARRENS SISTA VISA see Soderlundh,
Lille Bror

NAS ZIVOT see Huth, Gustav

NASCHMAULCHEN "DER FRITZ, DER KLEINE
BUTZEL" see Haas, Joseph

NASH, GRAHAM
Nowadays Clancy Can't Even Sing
(composed with Young, Neil)
see Sounds Of Neil Young And Graham
Nash

Sounds Of Neil Young And Graham Nash
(composed with Young, Neil) *pop
(Metis) SSA,opt perc WARNER
WB-339 183 $.75; SATB,opt perc
WARNER WB-338 187 $.75
contains: Nowadays Clancy Can't
Even Sing; Teach Your Children;
There's A World   (N8)

Teach Your Children (composed with
Young, Neil)
see Sounds Of Neil Young And Graham
Nash

There's A World (composed with Young,
Neil)
see Sounds Of Neil Young And Graham
Nash

NASH, JOHNNY
I Can See Clearly Now
(Metis, F.) SSA BIG3 $.50   (N9)
(Metis, F.) SAB BIG3 $.50   (N10)
(Metis, F.) SATB BIG3 $.50   (N11)

NATALE see Tesoriero, Gaetano

NATION OF BROTHERHOOD, A see Sullivan,
Leon

NATURE'S HARMONY see Schubert, Franz
(Peter)

NATURE'S WAY see Ives, Charles

NAUTICAL PRELUDES see Werle, Lars-Johan

NAVRATY see Fiala, Petr

NAVRATY KE STUDANCE see Vacek, Milos

NAYLOR, CHARLES
Shake Me I Rattle *see Hackady, Hal

NE LATTALAK VOLNA see Bartok, Bela

NECKEREIEN see Brahms, Johannes

NEDERLAND EN ORANJE see Elgar, Edward

NEED TO BE, THE see Weatherly

NEED YOU
SSA CIMINO $.40   (N12)
SATB CIMINO $.40   (N13)

NEHA UGY ERZEM see Karai, Jozsef

NEHMT ABSCHIED, BRUDER *folk,Scot
(Hollfelder, W.) men cor,acap TONOS
2025 s.p.   (N14)

NEJEDLY, VIT (1912-1945)
Day *see Den

Den *cant
"Day" [Czech] mix cor,Bar&narrator,
fl,clar,trp,trom,perc,pno,strings
CZECH s.p.   (N15)

To You, Red Army *see Tobe, Ruda
Armado

Tobe, Ruda Armado *cant
"To You, Red Army" [Czech] men cor,
soli,3fl,3ob,3clar,3bsn,4horn,
3trp,3trom,tuba,timp,perc,harp,
strings,celeste CZECH s.p. (N16)

NELHYBEL, VACLAV (1919-   )
America Sings: New England
cor,band cmplt ed KERBY 10534
$35.00, sc KERBY 10533 $11.50,
ipa, cor pts KERBY 10578 $.75
(N17)
I Do Not Like Thee, Dr. Fell *CC7U
2pt,opt winds&perc KERBY 9772 (N18)

NELLY GRAY see Desch, Rudolf, In Dem
Tal, Im Kustenland

NELSON, JERRY
Love's The Reason Why
SABar&camb CAMBIATA L117448 $.40
(N19)

NELSON, R.
Meditation On The Syllable OM
men cor,acap oct BOOSEY 5809 $.40
(N20)

NELSON, STEVE
Frosty The Snow Man (composed with
Rollins, Jack)
(Simon, W.) SSA BIG3 $.45   (N21)
(Simon, W.) SA/TB BIG3 $.45   (N22)
(Simon, W.) SATB BIG3 $.45   (N23)
(Simon, W.) SAB BIG3 $.40   (N24)

NEMETH-SAMORINSKY, STEFAN (1896-   )
Hovor Mi Tisko
wom cor SLOV.HUD.FOND s.p.   (N25)

Piesen O Vlasti
wom cor SLOV.HUD.FOND s.p.   (N26)

V Mene Mieru *cant
mix cor,orch SLOV.HUD.FOND s.p.
(N27)

NENIE S FLETNOU see Kopelent, Marek

NENIE WITH FLUTE see Kopelent, Marek,
Nenie S Fletnou

NESSLER
Abschied Hat Der Tag Genommen
men cor FORBERG sc s.p., voc pt
s.p.   (N28)

NESTASTNY JANO see Simek, Miroslav

NESTICO, G.
Don't Let It Get You Down (composed
with Nestico, S.) *pop
(Fote) SSAATB,opt perc KENDOR $.40
(N29)

Grape Growin' Man (composed with
Nestico, S.) *pop
(Petersen) SATB,opt perc KENDOR
$.40   (N30)
(Petersen) SSA,opt perc KENDOR $.40
(N31)
(Petersen) SAB,opt perc KENDOR $.40
(N32)

Light Up The World (composed with
Nestico, S.) *Xmas,pop
(Plank, D.) SATB,opt gtr&bvl KENDOR
$.40   (N33)
(Plank, D.) SA,opt gtr&bvl KENDOR
$.40   (N34)
(Plank, D.) SAB,opt gtr&bvl KENDOR
$.40   (N35)
(Plank, D.) SSA,opt gtr&bvl KENDOR
$.40   (N36)

NESTICO, S.
Don't Let It Get You Down *see
Nestico, G.

Grape Growin' Man *see Nestico, G.

Light Up The World *see Nestico, G.

NETHERCLIFT, JOSEPH (1792-1863)
Thou, Fatal Love *madrigal
(Young, Percy M.) [Eng] SATB,acap
oct BROUDE BR. $.50   (N37)

NEUE HOFFNUNG "LEISE SCHWINDEN DIE
LANGEN SCHATTEN" see Pantillon,
Francois

NEUE LIEDER, HEFT 2 *CCU
2-4 eq voices,acap PELIKAN PE 286
s.p. contains works by: Distler;
Marx; Knab and others   (N38)

NEUE LIEDER, HEFT 3 *CCU
3-5pt mix cor,acap PELIKAN PE287 s.p.
contains works by Lahusen; Brunner;
Wolters; and others   (N39)

NEUE TEUTSCHE WELTLICHE MADRIGALE see
Stephani, Johann

NEUES LEBEN "ES SCHLIEF DIE GUTE MUTTER
ERDE" see Erdlen, Hermann

NEUJAHRSGLOCKEN see Burkhard Willy

NEUJAHRSLIED *folk
(Wulz, Helmut) mix cor DOBLINGER
G 717-718 s.p. contains also: Wo,
Wo Ist Doch Mein Schafelein   (N40)

NEUJAHRSLIED see Mendelssohn-Bartholdy,
Felix

NEUMEYER, FRITZ (1900-   )
Viel Freuden Mit Sich Bringet
see Dietrich, Fritz, Wenn Alle
Brunnlein Fliessen

NEUN FREIER "IM HERBST BEIM
APFELSCHALEN" see Lang, Hans

NEUN KANONS see Eglin, Arthur

NEUN MEXIKANISCHE VOLKSLIEDER see
  Helfritz, Hans

NEUWEINLIED see Wittmer, Eberhard
  Ludwig

NEVEDOMI see Bohac, Josef

NEVER IN ALL THIS WORLD WILL I see
  Crecquillon, Thomas, Jamais En
  Monde N'aurai

NEVER WEATHER-BEATEN SAIL see Binkerd,
  Gordon

NEVERNY see Bohac, Josef

NEVYDAM SA ZA SLIMAKA see Prasil,
  Frantisek

NEW LAND, THE see Clarke, Henry Leland

NEW PRINCE, NEW POMP see Ireland, John

NEW SETTINGS OF OLD CATCHES see
  McLaughlin, Marian

NEW SPRING see Sommer, Vladimir, Nove
  Jaro

NEW TOMORROWS see Jones

NEW YEAR CAROL see Britten

NEW YEAR CAROL, A see Berger, Jean

NEW YORK see Gyring, Elizabeth

NEWBURY
  Sepulcher Of Famous Men, The *Fest
    SATB SCHIRM.G 11957 $.30   (N41)

  Shout For Joy
    SATB oct HERITAGE H123 $.40   (N42)

  Watcher, The
    SA/SSA SCHIRM.G LG51845 $.40 (N43)

NEWBURY, KENT A.
  Shendoah
    TTBB STANDARD D904M1 $.50   (N44)

NEWER WORLD, A see Whear, Paul William

NEWLEY, ANTHONY
  Who Can I Turn To *see Bricusse,
    Leslie

NEZ DE MARTIN see Champagne, Claude

NICE YOUNG MAIDENS see Rutter

NICHEVO see Mana-Zucca, Mme.

NICHOLS, ROGER
  I Won't Last A Day Without You *pop
    (Nowak, Jerry) SSA,pno oct BIG BELL
      $.45   (N45)
    (Nowak, Jerry) SATB,pno oct BIG
      BELL $.45   (N46)
    (Nowak, Jerry) SA,pno oct BIG BELL
      $.45   (N47)
    (Nowak, Jerry) SAB,pno oct BIG BELL
      $.40   (N48)

NICHT LANGE DURSTEST DU see Edler,
  Robert

NICHT WIEDERSEHN "NUN ADE, MEIN
  HERZLIEBSTER SCHATZ" see
  Hessenberg, Kurt

NICOLAS DE FLUE see Meyer

NICOLETTI, F.
  Ardo Si Ma Non T'amo *madrigal
    (Nielsen, R.) 5pt mix cor
      BONGIOVANI 2384 s.p. see also
      DODICI MADRIGALI DI SCUOLA
      FERRARESE   (N49)

NIEDERLANDISCHE VOLKSLIEDKANTATE see
  Rettich, Wilhelm

NIEDERRHEINISCHE LANDSCHAFT see Edler,
  Robert

NIELSEN, CARL (1865-1931)
  Music For Chorus *see Gow, David

NIELSEN, HANS (ca. 1585- ?)
  Corre Al Suo Fin Mia Vita
    SSATB,acap EGTVED OCI, 5 s.p. (N50)

  Felice Chi Vi Mira
    SSATB,acap EGTVED OCI, 6 s.p. (N51)

NIELSEN, S.
  Imperia
    SATB HANSEN-DEN s.p.   (N52)

NIELSEN, TAGE
  Eight Choral Songs *CC8U
    1-4pt HANSEN-DEN WH 29277 s.p. also
      available as separate sheets
                                  (N53)

NIEMALS VERGESS ICH DEN TAG see Ride
  The Chariot

NIEMAN, ALFRED (1913-   )
  Three Expressions
    SATB STAINER 3.0787.1 $1.50   (N54)

NIEMAND ERFAHRT DAS LIED see Nobody
  Knows

NIERENBERG
  Fire, Flood And Olive Tree
    SATB SHAWNEE A1300 $.40   (N55)

NIGHT see Barta, Lubor, Noc

NIGHT see Watson, Helen

NIGHT, THE see Schubert, Franz (Peter)

NIGHT CHICAGO DIED, THE see Murray,
  Mitch

NIGHT HAS A THOUSAND EYES, THE see
  Gold, Ernest

NIGHT OF PRAYER see Weigl, Vally

NIGHT OF SNOW see Poulenc, Francis, Un
  Soir De Neige

NIGHT RIDER see Warren

NIGHT SHE CRIED IN MY BEER
  TTBB CIMINO $.40   (N56)

NIGHT SPEECH FOR SPEECH-CHORUS AND TWO
  PLAYERS OF INSTRUMENTS see
  Roussakis, Nicolas

NIGHT WAS MADE FOR LOVE
  SSA CIMINO $.40   (N57)
  SAB CIMINO $.40   (N58)
  SA CIMINO $.40   (N59)
  TTBB CIMINO $.40   (N60)
  SATB CIMINO $.40   (N61)

NIGHT WILL NEVER STAY, THE see
  Hutcherson, Rita

NIGHT-WIND see Crosse

NIGHTINGALE see Curry, W. Lawrence

NIGHTINGALE, THE see Butler, Eugene

NIGHTINGALE, THE see Byrd, William

NIGHTINGALE, THE see Castelnuovo-
  Tedesco, Mario

NIGHTINGALE AND LINNET, THE *folk,
  Welsh
  (Holst, Gustav) SATB,acap CURWEN
    61292 s.p.   (N62)

NIGHTINGALE AT REST IS SINGING, THE see
  Hollande, J. de, Le Rossignol Daus
  Son Nid Chante

NIGHTS see Petrova, Elena, Noci

NILES, JOHN JACOB (1892-   )
  Good Morning, Father Christmas *Xmas
    cor (med easy) FISCHER,C CM 7904
    $.40   (N63)

NILSSON, HARRY
  Remember *pop
    (Nowak, Jerry) SATB,pno oct BIG
      BELL $.45   (N64)

NILSSON, TORSTEN (1920-   )
  Stora Har Ju Skor Och Tycker Man
    Skall Skratta
    4pt mix cor ERIKS 333 s.p.   (N65)

NIMM, LIEBSTE, DIESEN APFEL see Marx,
  Karl

NIMM VON UNS, HERRE *folk
  (Seeger, Peter) men cor,acap TONOS
    3734 s.p.   (N66)

NINA NANA see Pratella, Francesco
  Balilla

NINE HUNDRED MILES see Sturman, Paul

NINE HUNDRED MILES FROM HOME
  (Schillio) SATB AMP A712 $.45   (N67)

NINNA- NANNA see Bossi, Renzo

NINNA NANNA see Cremesini, M.

NINNA NANNA see Pratella, Francesco
  Balilla, Nina Nana

NINNA NONNA see Tesoriero, Gaetano

NINOSCHKA see Schneider, Walther

NINOT LE PETIT
  Et La La La *Renais
    (Echols, Paul) SATB MCAFEE M1069
    $.40   (N68)

  Lirum, Bililirum *Renais
    (Echols, Paul) SATB MCAFEE M1070
    $.45   (N69)

NINTH DREAM see Lennon, John

NIRVANA see Kvam, Oddvar S.

NISI DOMINUS see Carissimi, Giacomo

NITSCHE, PAUL (1909-   )
  Adieu Privas
    "Leb' Wohl Du Schones Stadtchen"
    [Ger/Fr] mix cor (easy) sc
    SCHOTTS CHBL 403 s.p.   (N70)

  Das Huhn "In Der Bahnhofhalle"
    mix cor (med) sc SCHOTTS C 38 053
    s.p. see from Vier
    Morgensternlieder   (N71)

  Dass Du Mich Meidest *see
    Greensleeves

  Der Schnupfen "Fin Schnupfen Hockt
    Auf Der Terasse"
    mix cor (med) sc SCHOTTS C 38 054
    s.p. see from Vier
    Morgensternlieder   (N72)

  Der Seufzer "Ein Seufzer Lief
    Schlittschuh"
    mix cor (med) sc SCHOTTS C 38 052
    s.p. see from Vier
    Morgensternlieder   (N73)

  Digo Gianetta *see Sag Mir, Gianetta

  Grauer Tauber
    see Nitsche, Paul, Wo Pole Berjosa

  Greensleeves
    "Dass Du Mich Meidest" [Eng/Ger]
    mix cor,opt gtr,treb inst, or
    accordion (easy) sc SCHOTTS
    CHBL 404 s.p.   (N74)

  Grunet Felder, Grunet Wiesen
    3pt jr cor,acap,opt inst (easy) sc
    SCHOTTS CHBL 597 s.p.   (N75)

  Korf "Korf Erfindet Eine Art Von
    Witzen"
    mix cor (med) sc SCHOTTS C 38 055
    s.p. see from Vier
    Morgensternlieder   (N76)

  Leb' Wohl Du Schones Stadtchen *see
    Adieu Privas

  Sag Mir, Gianetta
    "Digo Gianetta" [Ger/It] mix cor,
    opt drums,gtr (easy) sc SCHOTTS
    CHBL 402 s.p.   (N77)

  Stand Ein Birkenbaum
    "Wo Pole Berjosa" [Ger/Russ] mix
    cor (easy) sc SCHOTTS CHBL 405A-B
    s.p. contains also: Grauer Tauber
    [Ger] (mix cor)   (N78)

  Vier Morgensternlieder *see Das Huhn
    "In Der Bahnhofhalle"; Der
    Schnupfen "Fin Schnupfen Hockt
    Auf Der Terasse"; Der Seufzer
    "Ein Seufzer Lief Schlittschuh";
    Korf "Korf Erfindet Eine Art Von
    Witzen"   (N79)

  Wo Pole Berjosa *see Stand Ein
    Birkenbaum

NIVERT
  Take Me Home Country Roads *see
    Danoff

NO LOV'LIER COUNTRYSIDE see Cobine, Al

NO, MY DARLING DAUGHTER see Mehr,
  Sheldon

NO OTHER LOVE see Rodgers, Richard

NO STRINGS see Rodgers, Richard

NO TEARS HAVE WE TO SHED see Weil

NOAH see Edler, Robert

NOAH AND THE ARK see Pottle, Sam

NOBISKRUG see Rietz, Johannes

NOBLE DUKE OF YORK, THE *folk,Eng
  (Hennig, Walter) "Der Edle Duke Of
    York" [Ger] men cor,acap TONOS 2024
    s.p.   (N80)

NOBLE, HAROLD (1903-   )
  Homeward With A Song
  SA EMI   (N81)

NOBLEST OF SONGS, THE see Bruckner,
  Anton

NOBODY ELSE LIKE YOU see Gehrecke

NOBODY HOME
  (Huntley, Fred H.) TTBB,acap (easy)
  FITZSIMONS 4016 $.20   (N82)

NOBODY KNOWS *folk,US
  (Zoll, Paul) "Niemand Erfahrt Das
  Lied" men cor sc SCHOTTS C 40 110
  s.p. see from Vier Amerikanische
  Volkslieder   (N83)

NOBODY KNOWS DE TROUBLE, I'VE SEEN
  "Keiner Kann Meinen Kummer Verstehn"
  see Spirituals For All Heft I

NOBODY KNOWS THE TROUBLE I'VE SEEN
  *spir
  SATB WALTON 3036 $.30   (N84)

NOBODY TOLD ME see Rodgers, Richard

NOBODY'S EVER SATISFIED see Jeffries

NOC see Barta, Lubor

NOCH BIN ICH NICHT DEIN see Zoll, Paul

NOCI see Petrova, Elena

NOCTURNAL see Varese, Edgar

NOCTURNAL SERENADE see Schubert

NOCTURNE see Binkerd, Gordon

NOCTURNE see Johnston, Richard

NOCTURNE see Taube, Evert

NOCTURNO see Zimmer, Jan

NOCTURNO DE LOS AVISOS see Benguerel,
  Xavier

NOCTURNO "NACHT IST ES" see Weber,
  Bernhard

NOKTURNO see Kalcic, Josip

NOKWIC see Chavez, Carlos

NON FONTE O FIUME see Virchi, P.

NON PAPA, JACOBUS CLEMENS
  Der Winter Ist Vergangen *folk
  TTB sc SCHOTTS C 38 818 s.p. (N85)

  La, La, Maistre Pierre
  SATB MCAFEE M1063 $.35   (N86)

NON T'AMO O VOCE INGRATA see Gesualdo,
  Don Carlo

NONANTSIN see Chavez, Carlos

NONO, LUIGI (1924-   )
  Canciones A Guiomar *Span
  [Span] 6pt wom cor,S solo,vla,vcl,
  bvl,gtr,perc,celeste (diff) sc
  SCHOTTS rental, ipr   (N87)

  Espana En El Corazon *CC3U
  [Span] mix cor,SBar soli,pno,2fl,
  2clar,vln,vla,vcl,harp,perc, bass
  clarinet, celeste (diff) sc
  SCHOTTS AV 42 rental, ipr   (N88)

  Memento
  [Span] mix cor&speak cor,narrator,
  3fl,2ob,4clar,2bsn,4horn,4trp,
  3trom,tuba,strings,2harp,perc,
  timp, celeste (diff) sc SCHOTTS
  AV 49 rental, ipr   (N89)

NONSENSE see Petrassi, Goffredo

NONSENSE PSALM, A see Clover, David

NONSENSE SONGS FROM MOTHER GOOSE see La
  Montaine, John

NONSTOP-SONGS see Zehm, Friedrich

NORDHALM, IB
  Offer, Op. 34 *CC6U
  mix cor HANSEN-DEN WH 29010 s.p.
                                            (N90)

NORTH, JACK
  David, Swing Your Sling
  2pt LEONARD-US 08572800 $.50   (N91)

  Here's To America
  3pt LEONARD-US 08574220 $.50   (N92)

NORTHERN LIGHTS
  (Bennett) TTBB (med) SCHIRM.G LG51776
  $.50   (N93)

NOS PERES NOUS ONT DIT see Binet

NOT AVALON IN APRIL see Weigl, Vally

NOT-YET FLOWER, THE see Felciano,
  Richard

NOTE OF GOLDEN SONG, A see Saar, Louis
  Victor

NOTHING MATTERS see Mana-Zucca, Mme.,
  Nichevo

NOTTURNI see Detoni, Dubravko

NOTTURNO see Cremesini, M.

NOUS ETIONS DIX DEDANS UN PRE *folk,Fr
  (Blanchard, R.) 3pt wom cor,acap
  JOBERT s.p.   (N94)

NOUS VOYONS QUE LES HOMMES see
  Arcadelt, Jacob

NOVAK, JAN (1921-   )
  Apollo "Ter Ave, Tu Arbiter Artis"
  [Lat] SSATBB,acap (med) sc SCHOTTS
  C 42 848 s.p. see from Exercitia
  Mythologica   (N95)

  Dido *cant
  [Lat] men cor,3fl,3ob,3clar,3bsn,
  4horn,3trp,3trom,tuba,timp,perc,
  harp,strings CZECH s.p.   (N96)

  Echo "Imitari Melicos Docta Modos"
  [Lat] SSSATTTB (med) sc SCHOTTS
  C 42 852 s.p. see from Exercitia
  Mythologica   (N97)

  Erato "Ego Te Voce Hianti Nimis Oro"
  [Lat] SATB (med) sc SCHOTTS
  C 42 850 s.p. see from Exercitia
  Mythologica   (N98)

  Exercitia Mythologica *see Apollo
  "Ter Ave, Tu Arbiter Artis"; Echo
  "Imitari Melicos Docta Modos";
  Erato "Ego Te Voce Hianti Nimis
  Oro"; Midas "Criticos Artis
  Inertes Superus"; Minerva "Rogito
  Num Tumeat Bucca Tibi An Mamma
  Magis"; Orpheus "Fide Tu
  Suavisonanti Canis"; Terpsichore
  "Hilaris Terpsichore Ter Pede
  Terram"; Tityrus "Amarylli,
  Strepit Et Tota Sonat Silva"
                                            (N99)

  Midas "Criticos Artis Inertes
  Superus"
  [Lat] SATB (med) sc SCHOTTS
  C 42 851 s.p. see from Exercitia
  Mythologica   (N100)

  Minerva "Rogito Num Tumeat Bucca Tibi
  An Mamma Magis"
  [Lat] SSAATTB (med) sc SCHOTTS
  C 42 853 s.p. see from Exercitia
  Mythologica   (N101)

  Orpheus "Fide Tu Suavisonanti Canis"
  [Lat] SAATTB (med) sc SCHOTTS
  C 42 849 s.p. see from Exercitia
  Mythologica   (N102)

  Terpsichore "Hilaris Terpsichore Ter
  Pede Terram"
  [Lat] SATB&SATB (med) sc SCHOTTS
  C 42 855 s.p. see from Exercitia
  Mythologica   (N103)

  Tityrus "Amarylli, Strepit Et Tota
  Sonat Silva"
  [Lat] SATB (med) sc SCHOTTS
  C 42 854 s.p. see from Exercitia
  Mythologica   (N104)

NOVAK, JIRI F. (1913-   )
  Dekuji Ti, Praho *Op.20, cant
  "Thank You - Prague" [Czech] mix
  cor,T solo,3fl,3ob,3clar,3bsn,
  6horn,3trom,3trp,tuba,timp,perc,
  harp,strings, celeste CZECH s.p.
                                            (N105)
  Thank You - Prague *see Dekuji Ti,
  Praho

NOVAK, MILAN (1927-   )
  Do Kolecka Do Kola
  jr cor,pno SLOV.HUD.FOND s.p.
                                            (N106)
  Keby Vsetky Deti Sveta
  jr cor,pno SLOV.HUD.FOND s.p.
                                            (N107)
  L'ubostna Sonatina
  wom cor SLOV.HUD.FOND s.p.   (N108)

  Optimisticka Piesen
  mix cor SLOV.HUD.FOND s.p.   (N109)

  Spev O Povstani
  mix cor SLOV.HUD.FOND s.p.   (N110)

  Styri Slovenske Narodne Piesne *CC4U
  mix cor SLOV.HUD.FOND s.p.   (N111)

NOVAK, VITEZSLAV (1870-1949)
  Autumn Symphony *Op.62
  [Czech/Fr] men cor&wom cor,3fl,3ob,
  3clar,3bsn,6horn,3trp,3trom,timp,
  perc,harp,pno,org,strings,gtr,
  celeste, cymbal, mandolin
  SUPRAPHON s.p.   (N112)

  Bewitched Daughter, The *see Zakleta
  Dcera

  Zakleta Dcera *Op.19
  "Bewitched Daughter, The" [Czech]
  mix cor,2fl,2ob,2clar,2bsn,5horn,
  3trom,strings CZECH s.p.   (N113)

NOVE JARO see Dvoracek, Jiri

NOVE JARO see Sommer, Vladimir

NOVE SLOVENSKO see Gresak, Jozef

NOVEMBER TWENTY-SECOND: AN AMERICAN
  ELEGY see Currie, Randolph

NOVEMU OBCIANKOVI see Vilec, Michal

NOW AM I FREE see Regnard, Jacob, Nun
  Bin Ich Einmal Frei

NOW COME AND JOIN THE SONG see Eccard,
  Johannes

NOW IS THE CAROLLING SEASON see
  Priesing

NOW IS THE GENTLE SEASON see Morley,
  Thomas

NOW IS THE HOUR see Kaihan, M.

NOW IS THE MONTH OF MAYING see Morley,
  Thomas

NOW IS THE SUMMER SPRINGING see Hilton,
  John (The Younger)

NOW MUST I FLEE ALL EARTHLY CREATURES
  see Spruch

NOW PHOEBUS SINKETH IN THE WEST see
  Thorpe, Raymond

NOW SING NOW *sac/sec,CCU,gospel
  (MacKenzie) cor,gtr BENSON B0488
  $1.95   (N114)

NOW THE TIME HAS COME see Schneeweiss,
  Jan, Ted' Prisel Cas

NOWADAYS CLANCY CAN'T EVEN SING see
  Nash, Graham

NOWAK, JERRY
  For Thee, The Future *pop
  SATB,pno oct BIG BELL $.35   (N115)

NOWAK, LIONEL (1911-   )
  Madrigal
  SATB,acap AM.COMP.AL. $2.20   (N116)

NOWELL SING WE, BOTH ALL AND SOME see
  Monelle, Raymond

NU SKALL VI SKORDA LINET
  (Ohrwall) 4pt mix cor ERIKS 70 s.p.
                                            (N117)

NUN BIN ICH EINMAL FREI see Regnard,
  Jacob

NUN FANGET AN! see Hassler, Hans Leo

NUN GEHT DER MOND see Stolte, Siegfried

NUN IST DIE SCHONE FRUHLINGZEIT *folk
  (Desch, Rudolf) men cor,acap TONOS
  111 s.p.   (N118)

NUN IST VORBEI DIE FINSTRE NACHT see
  Woll, Erna

NUN RUHEN ALLE WALDER see Linke,
  Norbert

NUN RUHEN ALLE WALDER see Zoll, Paul

NUN SCHURZ DICH, GRETLEIN see Eccard,
  Johannes

NUN STEHN DIE ROSEN IN BLUTE see
  Brahms, Johannes

NUN STRAHLT DER MAI DEN HERZEN see
  Morley, Thomas

NUN WILL DER LENZ UNS GRUSSEN see Lang,
  Hans

NUN WOHLAN, IHR WAIDLEUT' ALL see Zoll,
  Paul

NUN WOLLN WIR ABER HEBEN AN see Werner,
  Kurt

NUN ZU DIESEN ZEITEN *CC7U
    SATB/SSATB,acap MOSELER HEFT 25 s.p.
    contains works by Friderici,
    Daniel; Forster, Georg; Franck,
    Melchior; di Lasso, Orlando;
    Steuccius, Heinrich   (N119)

NUNES, EMMANUEL (1941-   )
    Voyage Du Corps
    mix cor, 2synthesizers sc JOBERT
    s.p.   (N120)

NUN'S PRIEST TALE, THE see Jacob,
    Gordon

NUR DICH ALLEIN *folk,Slav
    (Marolt, France) men cor,acap TONOS
    2901 s.p.   (N121)

NUR EIN FIGUR HAT DIE NATUR see Jeep,
    Johann

NUR "EIN TON IST'S, NUR EIN TON" see
    Haas, Joseph

NUR FROHLICH IN DEN TAG HINEIN see
    Wolters, Karl-Heinz

NURSERY RHYMES II see Faltus, L.

NURSERY RYHME see Schneeweiss, Jan,
    Rikanka

NYARI EJ see Balassa, Sandor

NYHUS, ROLF
    Myggedans
    SSA/SAB MUSIKK   (N122)

NYHUS, ROLF see Gruber

NYMPHS AND SHEPHERDS DANCED see Marson,
    George

NYMPHS ARE SPORTING see Pearsall,
    Robert Lucas de

NYOLC KORUSMU see Rauch, Andreas

NYSTEDT, KNUT (1915-   )
    Shells
    SSAA AMP A-715 $.45   (N123)

    Suoni *Op.62
    SA,fl, marimba AMP $.30   (N124)

O

O AMENDOEIRA (from Cvjy) folk
    "O Du Mandelbaum" [Ger/Port] 3pt wom
    cor,acap BREITKOPF-W CHB 4944 s.p.
                                  (O1)

O BRUADER *Xmas
    (Bachl, Hans) treb cor DOBLINGER
    O 328 s.p.   (O2)

O CAN YE SEW CHUSHIONS see Gal, Hans

O CANADA
    (LaCheur, Rex) [Fr/Eng] SATB HARRIS
    HC 4055 $.35   (O3)
    (Roy, Fred) TTBB HARRIS HC 5001 $.30
                                  (O4)
    (Willan, Healey) unis HARRIS $.25
                                  (O5)
    (Willan, Healey) SSA HARRIS $.30 (O6)
    (Willan, Healey) SATB HARRIS $.35
                                  (O7)
    (Willan, Healey) TTBB HARRIS $.35
                                  (O8)

O CLAP FOR JOY see Burroughs

O CLOVEKU see Suchon, Eugen

O COME E' GRAN MARTIRE see Monteverdi,
    Claudio

O COOL IS THE VALLEY NOW see Kunz,
    Alfred

O DEAR WHAT CAN THE MATTER BE
    (MacNutt, Walter) SAB (easy) WATERLOO
    $.35   (O9)

O DEPTH OF WEALTH see Pinkham, Daniel

O, DIESE FRAUEN! - NEIN, DIESE MANNER!
    see Fischer, Ernst

O DU, DER DU DIE LIEBE BIST see Gade,
    Niels Wilhelm

O DU ESELHAFTER MARTIN see Mozart,
    Wolfgang Amadeus

O DU MANDELBAUM see O Amendoeira

O DU SCHONER ROSENGARTEN see Biebl,
    Franz

O FILIA PULCHRA "DER TAG IST NUN
    VERBLICHEN" see Zoll, Paul

O FOOD OF MEN WAYFARING see Harris

O GOOD ALE see Hunt, Reginald

O HAPPY INDEED see Handel, George
    Frideric

O HE DID WHISTLE AND SHE DID SING see
    Felciano, Richard

O HEIN! *folk,Eng
    (Rosenstengel, Albrecht) men cor,opt
    gtr,opt perc TONOS 2103 s.p. (O10)

O HERR, GIB JEDEM SEINEN EIGNEN TOD see
    Pepping, Ernst

O HORACH see Suchon, Eugen

O IRISH HILLS see Londonderry Air

O IT'S GOOD-BYE LIZA JANE *US
    (Ehret, Walter) SABar&opt camb,pno
    (med easy) CAMBIATA U97321 $.40
                                  (O11)

O JUANA *folk
    (Osburg, R.) [Ger] 4pt mix cor
    MERSEBURG EM9245 s.p.   (O12)
    (Osburg, R.) [Ger] 4pt men cor
    MERSEBURG EM9090 s.p.   (O13)

O KAM DAS MORGENROT HERAUF *folk
    (Felt, Gerhard) SATB MOSELER LB611
    s.p. see from Abend An Der Memel
                                  (O14)

O KAM DAS MORGENROT HERAUF see Zoll,
    Paul

O LAMENTATIONE! "ALTE KUHE, FAULE
    FISCH" see Rein, Walter

O LANDLE, DU MI HOAMATLAND see
    Kanetscheider, Artur

O LIEBE, LIEBE see Poos, Heinrich

O LIED "O LIED, DU MACHST DEN ARMEN
    STARK UND REICH" see Zoll, Paul

O LORD, SAVE THY SERVANT ELIZABETH see
    Willan, Healey, Domine, Salve Fac

O LOVE SWEEP INTO MY HEART see
    Frauenstrophe

O MAID OF MY HUNTING see Cadman,
    Charles Wakefield

O MUSIC, SWEET MUSIC
    (Krone, B.) SAB KJOS 5740 $.35   (O15)

O MUSICA see Seeger, Peter

O MUSICA, DU EDLE KINST see Peuerl,
    Paul

O MUSICA, DU EDLE KUNST see Peuerl,
    Paul

O MUSICA, LIEBLICHE KUNST
    see Liebesliedchen

O MUSICA, LIEBLICHE KUNST see Widmann,
    Erasmus

O MUSICA "O MUSICA, DU EDLE KUNST" see
    Kelling, Hajo

O MUSICA' THOU NOBLE ART see Peuerl,
    Paul

O NIGHT, O JEALOUS NIGHT see Russell,
    Welford

O RHEIN, DU HEILIGER STROM see Weber,
    Bernhard

O ROUND MOON see Boone, Charles

O SAIMA-SEE *folk
    (Mockl, F.) [Ger] 4pt mix cor
    MERSEBURG EM9216 s.p.   (O16)

O SCHONE HEIMAT *folk
    (Zoll, P.) [Ger] 4pt men cor
    MERSEBURG EM9033 s.p.   (O17)

O SCHONSTER ROSENGARTEN see Rein,
    Walter

O SCHUTZGEIST see Mozart, Wolfgang
    Amadeus

O SIGNORE, DAL TETTO NATIO see Verdi,
    Giuseppe

O SLUNECNIKU, MESICNIKU A VETRNIKU see
    Pinos, Alois

O SOAVE CONFORTO see Scarlatti,
    Alessandro

O SUSSER MAI see Brahms, Johannes

O TALER WEIT, O HOHEN see Mendelssohn-
    Bartholdy, Felix

O TANNE GRUN see Erdlen, Hermann

O TANNENBAUM
    see Ich Weiss Einen Lindenbaum Stehen

O TANNENBAUM, DU TRAGST, EIN' GRUNEN
    ZWEIG see Rein, Walter

O TANNENBAUM, O TANNENBAUM, DU TRAGST
    EIN GRUNEN ZWEIG see Marx, Karl

O THE SUN COMES UP-UP-UP IN THE OPENING
    see Ballou, Esther W.

O WEARY NIGHT see Peaslee, Richard

O WELCHE TIEFE DES REICHTUMS see Edler,
    Robert

O WIE HERBE IST DAS SCHEIDEN see
    Silcher, Friedrich

O WIE SO SCHON UND GUT see Desch,
    Rudolf

O WILD WEST WIND see Clarke, Henry
    Leland

O WUNDERBARES, TIEFES SCHWEIGEN see
    Mendelssohn-Bartholdy, Felix

O WUNNA UBER WUNNA *Xmas
    (Bachl, Hans) treb cor DOBLINGER
    O 331 s.p.   (O18)

O ZIVOTE see Ocenas, Andrej

OAK AND THE ASH, THE see Sturman, Paul

OAN WIDL GARN
    (Schollum, Robert) mix cor DOBLINGER
    G 659 s.p.   (O19)

OB DIE SONNE SCHEINT
    see Offenes Singen Nr. 89

OBERSCHWABEN see Frommlet, Franz

OBLACEK see Simek, Miroslav

ON A SUMMER NIGHT see Laksin Mina
  Kesayona Kaymaan

ON A WINDING WAY see Boyd, Jeanne

ON AN ENGLISH PROVERB see Kunz, Jack

ON CHRISTMAS EVE see Weigl, Vally

ON FAR AWAY HILL
  see Freedom Song, 1776

ON INDEPENDENCE see Collins, Don L.

ON MEADOW AND HILLSIDE see Weil

ON MOTHER'S DAY see Innes, Gertrude

ON NEW YEAR'S DAY see Mendelssohn-
  Bartholdy, Felix, Am Neujahrstage

ON SOMMAREN SKONA
  (Aldenbjork, Herbert) "In The
  Beautiful Summer" 2pt mix cor
  NORDISKA NMS 6493 s.p.   (O62)

ON THE DEVIDE see Murray

ON THE DISPUTE ABOUT IMAGES see
  Pinkham, Daniel

ON THE PLAINS, FAIRY TRAINS see Weelkes

ON THE SHORE OF THE ZUIDER ZEE see
  Fearis, John S.

ON THE WAY HOME see Robinson, Betty
  Jean

ON TOP OF OLD SMOKEY *folk
  (Miller, Carl) 2pt CHAPPELL
  0063222-351 $.40   (O63)

ON VISION see Harvey, Jonathan

ONCE A CUCKOO BIRD *folk
  (Bilencko, M.) SSA LESLIE 3033 $.30
                                  (O64)

ONCE I HAD A GREATCOAT see Adler

ONCE, TWICE, THRICE I JULIA TRIED see
  Purcell, Henry

ONCE UPON A MYSTERY see Williams, Paul

ONCE UPON A SUMMERTIME see Mercer

ONCE UPON A TIME see Hanus, Jan,
  Povidam, Povidam Pohadku

ONE FLOWER see Kennedy, John Brodbin

ONE FROM ONE LEAVES TWO see Cohn, James

ONE LESS SET OF FOOTSTEPS see Croce,
  Jim

ONE MAY MORNING *folk,Eng
  (Archibeque, Charlene) SATB,pno
  NATIONAL WHC-12 $.40   (O65)

ONE NIGHT SO LONG AGO see Ehret, Walter

ONE OF THOSE SONGS see Holt

ONE SMALL PLANET
  SATB UP WITH 6506 $.40   (O66)

ONE STARRY NIGHT see Leaf, Robert

ONE STRING MELODY see Silver

ONE SUMMER MORN see Tchaikovsky, Piotr
  Ilyitch

ONKEL MOND see Rein, Walter

ONKEL MOND STEHT AM TOR see Zipp,
  Friedrich

ONLY GOD see Goossen, Frederic

ONLY YESTERDAY see Carpenter, Richard

ONWARD THROUGH PASSES HIGH ABOVE see
  Ribera, Antonio de, Por Unos
  Puertos Arriba

OP 'T KERKHOF see Spoel, A.

OPEN UP YOUR HEART see Miller

OPENING THE WELLS see Martinu, Bohuslav

OPERATOR (THAT'S NOT THE WAY IT FEELS
  see Croce, Jim

OPFERLIED "DIE FLAMME LODERT" see
  Beethoven, Ludwig van

OPHOVEN, HERMANN (1914-   )
  Der Morgen Ist Erwacht "Nun Gilt's!
  Die Tagelangen"
  men cor sc SCHOTTS CHBL 193 s.p.
                                  (O67)

OPHOVEN, HERMANN (cont'd.)

  Liebesgewitter "Auch Die Liebe
  Braucht Gewitter"
  men cor sc SCHOTTS CHBL 146 s.p.
                                  (O68)

  Sing Mit!
  men cor,acap TONOS 3909 s.p.   (O69)

  Wer Frohlich Will Singen
  men cor,acap TONOS 3918 s.p.   (O70)

  Zollt Dank Der Edlen Musika
  men cor,acap TONOS 3917 s.p.   (O71)

OPPEL, HANS
  All Mein Gedanken
  men cor,acap TONOS 116 s.p.   (O72)

OPSEDNUTA VEDRINA see Radic, Dusan

OPTIMISTEN see Fischer, Theo

OPTIMISTICKA PIESEN see Novak, Milan

ORANGE CAROL BOOK *CCU
  (Horder, Mervyn) mix cor SCHOTT 11235
  s.p.   (O73)

ORCHESTRA, THE see Geisler

ORCHIDS IN THE MOONLIGHT
  SSA CIMINO $.40   (O74)
  SAB CIMINO $.40   (O75)
  SA CIMINO $.40   (O76)
  TTBB CIMINO $.40   (O77)
  SATB CIMINO $.40   (O78)

ORDER NO. 368 see Dobias, Vaclav,
  Rozkaz C. 368

O'REILLY, DERMOTT
  Children's Winter *folk,Ir
  (Cable, Howard) 2pt THOMP.G $.35
                                  (O79)

ORFF, CARL (1895-   )
  Aufruf "Komm Sintflut Der Seele"
  see Orff, Carl, Von Der
  Freundlichkeit Der Welt "Auf Die
  Erde Voller Kaltem Wind"

  Concento Di Voci *see Sunt Lacrimae
  Rerum   (O80)

  Drei Chorsatze (from Orff Schul-Werk)
  (med) sc SCHOTTS C 42 618 s.p.
  contains: Mater Et Filia; Te
  Lucis Ante Terminum; Tres Magi
                                  (O81)
  Fruhling Und Sommerbeginn (from Orff
  Schul-Werk) CCU
  jr cor SCHOTTS ED. 4893 s.p.   (O82)

  Grundubungen (from Orff Schul-Werk)
  CCU
  (Werdin, Eberhard) jr cor sc
  SCHOTTS ED. 4455 s.p.   (O83)

  Lieder Fur Die Schule Heft I *CCUL
  (Keetman, Gunild) 1-3pt jr cor,
  Orff instruments sc SCHOTTS
  ED. 5140 s.p.   (O84)

  Lieder Fur Die Schule Heft II *CCUL
  (Willert, Gertrud) 1-3pt jr cor,
  Orff instruments sc SCHOTTS
  ED. 5141 s.p.   (O85)

  Lieder Fur Die Schule Heft III *CCUL
  (Keetman, Gunild) 1-3pt jr cor,
  Orff instruments sc SCHOTTS
  ED. 5142 s.p.   (O86)

  Lieder Fur Die Schule Heft IV *CCUL
  (Willert, Gertrud) 1-3pt jr cor,
  Orff instruments sc SCHOTTS
  ED. 5245 s.p.   (O87)

  Lieder Fur Die Schule Heft V *CCUL
  (Keetman, Gunild) 1-3pt jr cor,
  Orff instruments sc SCHOTTS
  ED. 5246 s.p.   (O88)

  Lieder Fur Die Schule Heft VI *CCUL
  (Orff, Carl; Willert, Gertrud) 1-
  3pt jr cor, Orff instruments sc
  SCHOTTS ED. 5247 s.p.   (O89)

  Lieder Fur Die Schule Heft VII *CCU
  (Keetman, Gunild) 1-3pt jr cor,
  Orff instruments sc SCHOTTS
  ED. 5589 s.p.   (O90)

  Liederbuch Grade 1 *CCU
  (Keller, Wilhelm) jr cor SCHOTTS
  ED. 5232 s.p.   (O91)

  Liederbuch Grade 2 *CCU
  (Keller, Wilhelm) jr cor SCHOTTS
  ED. 5233 s.p.   (O92)

  Liederbuch Grade 3 *CCU
  (Keller, Wilhelm) jr cor SCHOTTS
  ED. 5234 s.p.   (O93)

ORFF, CARL (cont'd.)

  Mater Et Filia (from Orff Schul-Werk)
  see Drei Chorsatze

  Odi Et Amo (from Catulli Carmina)
  [Lat] mix cor (med easy) sc SCHOTTS
  CHBL 398 s.p.   (O94)

  Reime Und Spiellieder (from Orff
  Schul-Werk Vol.1: Pentatonic) CCU
  jr cor sc SCHOTTS ED. 3574 s.p.
                                  (O95)
  Rota "Summer Is Icumen In"
  cor,inst sc,cor pts SCHOTTS
  ED. 6412 s.p., ipa   (O96)

  Sonnengesang Des Heiligen Franziskus
  [It] 4pt jr cor/4pt wom cor,acap
  (med) sc SCHOTTS C 42 186 s.p.
                                  (O97)
  Stucke Fur Sprechchor *CC12L
  mix cor/jr cor (med) sc SCHOTTS
  ED 5583 s.p.   (O98)

  Sunt Lacrimae Rerum
  [Lat] 6pt men cor,TBarB soli,acap
  (Schott Score No. C39 534-02
  Revised In 1957) sc SCHOTTS
  C 39 534-01 s.p., sc SCHOTTS
  C 39 534-02 s.p. see from
  Concento Di Voci   (O99)

  Te Lucis Ante Terminum (from Orff
  Schul-Werk)
  see Drei Chorsatze

  Tres Magi (from Orff Schul-Werk)
  see Drei Chorsatze

  Vom Fruhjahr, Oltank Und Vom Fliegen
  [Eng/Ger] 4-6pt mix cor&5pt men
  cor,2pno,6-9perc,opt 3clar sc,cor
  pts SCHOTTS ED. 6023 s.p., ipa
                                  (O100)
  Von Der Freundlichkeit Der Welt
  *cant
  [Eng/Ger] mix cor,3pno,8perc (med)
  sc,cor pts SCHOTTS ED. 5706 s.p.,
  ipa   (O101)

  Von Der Freundlichkeit Der Welt "Auf
  Die Erde Voller Kaltem Wind"
  men cor sc SCHOTTS C 41 921 s.p.
  contains also: Aufruf "Komm
  Sintflut Der Seele" (TTB)   (O102)

ORPHEUS see Bush, Geoffrey

ORPHEUS see Dalby, Martin

ORPHEUS AND HIS LUTE *folk
  (Frackenpohl, Arthur) SATB STANDARD
  C622MX1 $.50   (O103)

ORPHEUS "FIDE TU SUAVISONANTI CANIS"
  see Novak, Jan

ORPHISCHE HYMNE "AN DIE NACHT" see
  Genzmer, Harald

ORREL, MAX
  An Schonen Tagen
  men cor,acap TONOS 209 s.p.   (O104)

  Der Mond
  men cor,acap TONOS 214 s.p.   (O105)

  Druben Im Flusternen Walde
  men cor,acap TONOS 204 s.p.   (O106)

  Essen-Trinken
  men cor,acap TONOS 213 s.p.   (O107)

  Freundschaft Schafft Frieden
  men cor,acap TONOS 215 s.p.   (O108)

  Hakel-Pakel
  men cor,acap TONOS 206 s.p.   (O109)

  Hallodrio
  men cor,acap TONOS 216 s.p.   (O110)

  Heimat, Mein Rebenland
  men cor,acap TONOS 211 s.p.   (O111)

  Heimat Und Jugendzeit
  men cor,acap TONOS 205 s.p.   (O112)

  Heimatlied: Wo Auf Des Tales
  men cor,acap TONOS 202 s.p.   (O113)

  Im Mondenschein
  men cor,acap TONOS 212 s.p.   (O114)

  In Der Heimat
  men cor,acap TONOS 207 s.p.   (O115)

  Irgendwo
  men cor,acap TONOS 201 s.p.   (O116)

  Susse Ruhe, Stille Der Nacht
  men cor,acap TONOS 203 s.p.   (O117)

ORREL, MAX (cont'd.)

Um Die Tafelrunde
men cor,acap TONOS 210 s.p.   (O118)

Wer Andern Eine Grube Grabt
men cor,acap TONOS 208 s.p.   (O119)

OSEM PODDUKELSKYCH UKRAJINSKYCH
L'UDOVYCH PIESNI see Mikula, Zdenko

OSLOBODENA ZEM see Ocenas, Andrej

OSM PISNI see Skvor, Frantisek

OSM ZENSKYCH SBORU see Provaznik,
Anatol

OSTERN, PER RHOAR
Singing Is So Good A Thing
mix cor MUSIKK   (O120)

OSTRAVA see Kratochvil, Jiri

OSUDNA SVATBA see Zich, Otakor

O'SULLIVAN, GILBERT
Alone Again Naturally *pop
SAB BELWIN TC 22 $.40   (O121)

Get Down
SATB BELWIN TC 13 $.40   (O122)
SSA BELWIN TC 12 $.40   (O123)

Happiness Is You And Me *pop
SATB BELWIN TC 19 $.40   (O124)

OTHEGRAVEN, AUGUST J. VON (1864-1946)
Bei Meiner Blonden "Im Garten Der
Lorbeer Bluht" *Op.74,No.2
men cor sc SCHOTTS C 32 444 s.p.
                                (O125)
Loch Lomond "Wohl Am Trauten Strand"
*Op.74,No.1
[Ger] men cor sc SCHOTTS C 32 443
s.p.   (O126)

OTHMAYR, KASPAR (1515-1553)
Der Mond Der Steht Am Hochsten
(Malin, Don) "High Is The Moon
Above Us" SATB,acap BELWIN 2320
$.30   (O127)

Es Ist Ein Schnee Gefallen
PELIKAN PE398 s.p.   (O128)
(Weber, W.) men cor,acap TONOS 3318
s.p.   (O129)

High Is The Moon Above Us *see Der
Mond Der Steht Am Hochsten

Mir Ist Ein Feins Brauns Maidelein
mix cor (med easy) sc SCHOTTS
CHBL 401 s.p.   (O130)
(Weber, W.) men cor,acap TONOS 3304
s.p.   (O131)

OTTHON see Marton, Lajos

OU COURS-TU, CHEVRETTE see Strimer,
Joseph

OUR DAY WILL COME see Hilliard

OUR DEAR OLD HIGH SCHOOL see Epperson,
Emery G.

OUR FLAG see Angell

OUR LIFE see Huth, Gustav, Nas Zivot

OUR MURMURS HAVE THEIR MUSICK TOO see
Clark

OUR SACRED HONOR see Yahres, Samuel C.

OUR STATE FAIR see Rodgers, Richard

OUR WORLD IS ONE see Weigl, Vally

OUT IN THE FIELDS see Protheroe, Daniel

OUT OF LUCRETIUS see Mollicone, Henry

OUT OF MY DREAMS see Rodgers, Richard

OUT OF THE CRADLE ENDLESSLY ROCKING see
Becker, John J.

OUTCRY see Dickinson, Peter

OVER HERE *folk,Ir
(Roberton, Hugh S.) TTBB,acap
ROBERTON 53007 s.p.   (O132)

OVER HILL, OVER DALE see Shaw, Martin

OVER THE HILLS
see Four Songs From "The Beggar's
Opera"

OVER THE RIVER see Cobine, Al

OVERTON, HALL (1920-   )
Captivity
TBB,acap AM.COMP.AL. $1.38   (O133)

OVERTURE FOR VOICES see Rottura, Joseph
James

OWEN
Kleiner Marsch
(Welker, Gotthard) men cor,acap
TONOS 3946 s.p.   (O134)

OWEN, HAROLD
Aspirations
(Warland, Dale) 6 speak cor ART
MAST 1025 $.40   (O135)

OWENS, BUCK
Together Again
(Cobine, Al) SATB (easy) STUDIO
V718 $.40   (O136)

OWL, THE see Shearer, C.M.

OWL AND THE PUSSY-CAT see Johnston,
Richard

OWL AND THE PUSSY-CAT, THE see Rutter

OXFORD SCOTTISH SONG BOOK
(Davie; McVicar) unis (med) bds
OXFORD 58.644 $6.20   (O137)

OY COMAMOS Y BEBAMOS see Encina, Juan
Del

P

PA BROLLOP "E LITTA VISE VILL JAG
FRAMSTECKE" *folk
(Olson, Daniel) men cor ERIKS 87 s.p.
                                (P1)

PADDY'S MARKET see Hutchens, F.

PAGE
Stairway To Heaven (composed with
Plant)
(Gargaro) SATB WARNER WB-371 $.60
                                (P2)

PAGEANT OF CHARACTERS FROM WILLIAM
SHAKESPEARE see Taylor, Clifford

PAGES FROM ALBION MOONLIGHT see Eisma,
Will

PAHLEN, KURT (1907-   )
Sechszehn Kinderlieder Nach Texten
Von James Kruss *CC16U
jr cor,pno,opt perc BOTE sc s.p.,
voc pt s.p.   (P3)

PAHNKE
Marche Des Cornemuseaux
wom cor,acap HENN 463 s.p.   (P4)

PAIN WITHIN MY HEART, THE see
Monteverdi, Claudio, La Piaga C'ho
Nel Core

PALENICEK, JOSEF (1914-   )
Poem About Man *see Poema O Cloveku

Poema O Cloveku *cant
"Poem About Man" [Czech] dbl cor&jr
cor,4fl,5ob,4clar,5bsn,6horn,
4trp,3trom,tuba,timp,perc,2harp,
pno,2org,strings CZECH s.p.   (P5)

PALESTRINA, GIOVANNI (1525-1594)
First Critical Edition *sac/sec,CCU
(De Witt, Theodor; Rauch, J.N.;
Espagne, Franz; Commer, Fr.;
Haberl, Fr. X.) microfiche
UNIV.MUS.ED. $240.00 33 volumes
published at Leipzig, 1862-1907.
                                (P6)
Jede Schonheit, Geliebte
(Koenig, F.) men cor,acap TONOS
3326 s.p.   (P7)

Liebliche Blumen
(Weber, W.) men cor,acap sc,cor pts
TONOS 3312 s.p.   (P8)

Selig Ist Es Zu Sterben
(Koenig, F.) men cor,acap TONOS
3313 s.p.   (P9)

PALITZ
While We're Young *see Wilder

PALKOVSKY, OLDRICH (1907-   )
Pioneer, The *see Pionyr

Pionyr
"Pioneer, The" [Czech] jr cor,3fl,
2ob,2clar,2bsn,4horn,2trp,3trom,
tuba,timp,perc,strings CZECH s.p.
                                (P10)

PALMER, G.
Slumber Song , The
unis HARRIS $.30   (P11)

PALMES
Child Waves Goodbye, The
SAB SHAWNEE D192 $.35   (P12)

PAM PIM PAM see Feld, Jindrich

PAN see Bush, Geoffrey

PANDORA see Reutter, Hermann

PANTILLON, FRANCOIS (1928-   )
Neue Hoffnung "Leise Schwinden Die
Langen Schatten"
men cor sc SCHOTTS C 43 264 s.p.
                                (P13)

PANYCHIDA see Picha, Frantisek

PANYCHIDE see Picha, Frantisek,
Panychida

PAPA UND MAMA see Francaix, Jean

PAPANDOPULO, BORIS (1906-   )
Ich Bin Durch Liebe
see DREI WEINSPRUCHE

Istarske Freske *CCU
mix cor,orch MUSIC INFO rental
                                (P14)
Stojanka Majka Knezpoljka
mix cor,S solo,orch MUSIC INFO
rental   (P15)

PAPANDOPULO, BORIS (cont'd.)

Winzer-Trinklied
men cor,acap TONOS 3403 s.p.   (P16)

PAPER CUP see Webb, Jimmy

PAPPERT, WALTER (1936-   )
Auf Der Voschiletzer Brucke
men cor sc SCHOTTS CHBL 224 s.p.
(P17)

Die Dumme Alte "In Paris Kenn Ich'ne
Alte"
men cor,TB soli sc SCHOTTS CHBL 223
s.p.   (P18)

Slowenischer Weinstrauss "Sussen Wein
Wir Trinken"
men cor,Bar solo sc SCHOTTS
CHBL 216 s.p.   (P19)

PARADISE LOST see Steel, Christopher
[Charles]

PARADISE SONGS see Brent-Smith,
Alexander

PARIK, IVAN (1936-   )
Citacie *CCU
mix cor SLOV.HUD.FOND s.p.   (P20)

PARKE, DOROTHY
Has Sorrow Thy Young Days Shaded?
SA CRAMER C76   (P21)

PARKER, ALICE (1925-   )
Away Melancholy!
SA/SSAA,tamb SCHIRM.EC 2816 s.p.
(P22)

Eights
see Play On Numbers, A

Play On Numbers, A
SS,pno SCHIRM.EC 2817 s.p.
contains: Eights; Twos And Fours;
Twos And Threes   (P23)

Twos And Fours
see Play On Numbers, A

Twos And Threes
see Play On Numbers, A

PARNAS TANCDAL see Bartok, Bela

PARNES
Masterpiece, The *see Mouret

PAROBSKE SPEVY PRE MUZSKY ZBOR see
Mikula, Zdenko

PAROBSKY see Mikula, Zdenko

PARRIS, ROBERT (1924-   )
Walking Around
men cor,clar,vln,2perc,pno sc
AM.COMP.AL. $9.90, ipa   (P24)

PARRY, CHARLES HUBERT HASTINGS
(1848-1918)
Fair Daffodils *madrigal
(Young, Percy M.) [Eng] SSATB,acap
oct BROUDE BR. $.60   (P25)

PARSLEY, SAGE, ROSEMARY AND THYME
*folk
(Miller, Carl) 2pt CHAPPELL
0063404-351 $.40   (P26)

PART SONGS TO SING see Alcock, J.

PARTING ROUND, A see McAfee, Don

PARTITA SEFARDICA see Cossetto, Emil

PARTOMI DONNA E TECO LASC'IL CORE see
Piccioli, G.

PARTON
Sad Sweet Dreamer
(Kerr) SATB,opt perc BELWIN UC 737
$.40   (P27)

PASCI ANGIONEDDA *folk,It
(Crestani, Marco) 4pt men cor ZANIBON
5211 s.p.   (P28)
(Crestani, Marco) 4pt mix cor ZANIBON
5214 s.p.   (P29)

PASE EL AGOA see Anonymous

PASEL JANEK SIVE VOLKY see Mikula,
Zdenko

PASSANI, EMILE
Dis-Moi, Jeannette
3 eq voices,acap JOBERT s.p.   (P30)

Le Charbonnier
3 eq voices,acap JOBERT s.p.   (P31)

Le Crucifix
3 eq voices,acap JOBERT s.p.   (P32)

PASSANI, EMILE (cont'd.)

Le Jaloux
3 eq voices,acap JOBERT s.p.   (P33)

PASSEREAU
Il Est Bel Et Bon
SATB,acap EGTVED MS12B3 s.p.   (P34)

PASSING BY see Purcell, Henry

PASSING BY see Willan, Healey

PASTORA see Cremesini, M.

PASTORAL see Holst, Gustav

PASTORAL, A see Chavez, Carlos

PASTORALE "LIE STREWN WHITE FLOCKS" see
Bliss, Sir Arthur

PASTORALI TRANSILVANE see Vlad, Roman

PAT ZVONKOYVYCH HLASOV see Felix,
Vaclav

PATRIA OPPRESSA! see Verdi, Giuseppe

PATRIOTIC MEDLEY
(Huff, Ronn) SSATB BENSON S4247 $.35
(P35)

PATRIOT'S DREAM, THE see Red, Buryl

PATRIQUIN, DONALD
Black Is The Colour Of My True Love's
Hair
SSATB (easy) WATERLOO $.30   (P36)

Greenwood Tree
SATB (diff) WATERLOO $.35   (P37)

PATTERNS see Simon, Paul

PATTERNS IN SOUND: CODA (CANON AND
CODA) see McElheran

PATTERNS IN SOUND: SECTION A (ETUDE AND
SOUNDS) see McElheran

PATTERNS IN SOUND: SECTION C (ETUDE AND
SCHERZO) see McElheran

PATTERSON
Christmas Calypso
cor oct SCHMITT 8073 $.40   (P38)

PAUER, JIRI (1919-   )
Mala Kantata *cant
"Small Cantata" [Czech] men cor,
SBar soli,3fl,3ob,3clar,3bsn,
4horn,3trp,3trom,tuba,timp,perc,
harp,org,strings CZECH s.p.   (P39)

Small Cantata *see Mala Kantata

PAUL, HEINZ OTTO
Sangerwort
men cor,acap TONOS 3721 s.p.   (P40)

Unser Lied
men cor,acap TONOS 3722 s.p.   (P41)

PAUL ON THE HILL
(Johnston, Richard A.) SATB (med
easy) WATERLOO $.50   (P42)

PAUL REVERE see Biggs, John

PAULUS, STEPHEN
Bells
3pt,pno/fl/rec,fing.cym., wood
block, suspended cymbal (med)
FISCHER,C CM 7909 $.45   (P43)

PAUVRE PIERRE see Doret

PAVANE FOR SPRING see Butler, Eugene

PAX see Kaufmann, Dieter

PAXTON
Going To The Zoo
(Bune) SATB,bvl,gtr, or banjo
WARNER CH0787 $.60   (P44)

If You're Happy Notify Your Face
(Burroughs; Sewell) 2pt/SSA WARNER
CQ0801 $.40   (P45)

PAXTON, GARY
Too Busy
(Metis, F.) SAB BIG3 $.50   (P46)
(Metis, F.) SSA BIG3 $.50   (P47)
(Metis, F.) SATB BIG3 $.50   (P48)

PAXTON, TOM
Last Thing On My Mind, The
(Simon, W.) SSA BIG3 $.50   (P49)
(Simon, W.) SAB BIG3 $.50   (P50)
(Simon, W.) SATB BIG3 $.50   (P51)

PAYNE, WARREN
Questions
(Kysar, Michael) SSATB,SSST soli,
kbd,bvl,gtr (med diff, jazz-rock
chart, contrapuntal chants) KYSAR
A102 $.60   (P52)

PAYNTER, JOHN P.
Fog
jr cor,inst oct PRESSER UE 15477
$.90   (P53)

High School Band, The
SATB,acap (med diff) OXFORD 84.238
$.65   (P54)

Landscapes
SATB,acap,opt ob (diff) OXFORD
56.595 $2.55, ipa   (P55)

Windhover, The
SATB,acap (diff) OXFORD 84.205 $.70
(P56)

PEACE see Haba, Alois, Mir

PEACE BE WITH YOU see Liszt, Franz

PEACE HYMN see Weigl, Vally

PEACE RACE RUNNER, THE see Bartos, Jan
Zdenek, Bezec Miru

PEANUT SONG, THE
(Dexter, Harry) 2pt ASHDOWN EA380
(P57)

PEARSALL, ROBERT LUCAS DE (1795-1856)
I Saw Lovely Phillis *madrigal
(Young, Percy M.) [Eng] SATB,acap
oct BROUDE BR. $.35   (P58)

Nymphs Are Sporting *madrigal
(Young, Percy M.) [Eng] SATB,acap
oct BROUDE BR. $.35   (P59)

Sing We And Chant It *madrigal
(Young, Percy M.) [Eng] SATB/SATB&
SATB,acap oct BROUDE BR. $.45
(P60)

Why Weeps, Alas! My Lady Love
(Opheim) SSATB oct SCHMITT 1213
$.45   (P61)

PEASE, ROLLIN
America For Me
(Wilson) TTBB (med) FITZSIMONS 4002
$.25   (P62)

Gettysburg Address, The
SSAATTBB,acap (easy) FITZSIMONS
1055 $.25   (P63)

PEASLEE, RICHARD
Fair Love
SATBarB,bvl,gtr,perc BOONIN B 222
$.60, ipa see from Music For "A
Midsummer Night's Dream"   (P64)

Fairy Song
SATB,ST soli,bvl,gtr,perc BOONIN
B 224 $.60, ipa see from Music
For "A Midsummer Night's Dream"
(P65)

Honeybags, The
SATB,solo,bvl,gtr,perc BOONIN B 225
$.60, ipa see from Music For "A
Midsummer Night's Dream"   (P66)

Music For "A Midsummer Night's Dream"
*see Fair Love; Fairy Song;
Honeybags, The; O Weary Night;
Tide Life, Tide Death; Titania
(P67)

O Weary Night
SATB,bvl,gtr BOONIN B 223 $.40, ipa
see from Music For "A Midsummer
Night's Dream"   (P68)

Tide Life, Tide Death
SATB,TB soli,bvl,gtr BOONIN B 226
$.40, ipa see from Music For "A
Midsummer Night's Dream"   (P69)

Titania
SATB,bvl,perc,gtr BOONIN B 227
$.45, ipa see from Music For "A
Midsummer Night's Dream"   (P70)

PEDERSON, MOGENS (ca. 1580-1623)
Ardo, Sospiro *madrigal
[It] SATTB,acap EGTVED OCI, 3 s.p.
(P71)

La Mia Cruda Brunetta *madrigal
[It] SSATB,acap EGTVED OCI, 2 s.p.
(P72)

L'amara Dipartita *madrigal
[It] SSB,acap EGTVED OCI, 4 s.p.
(P73)

Udite, Amanti *madrigal
[It] SATTB,acap EGTVED OCI, 1 s.p.
(P74)

PEELE, DUDLEY
Bird In My Bower, A
SSA (easy) FITZSIMONS 3058 $.25
(P75)

PEELE, DUDLEY (cont'd.)

Indian Serenade, The
TTBB (diff) FITZSIMONS 4028 $.25
(P76)

Psalm Of Life, A
SATB (easy) FITZSIMONS 1027 $.30
(P77)

PEJ, SESTRA see Rosinsky, Jozef

PENCIL OF THE HOLY GHOST, THE see
Hovhaness, Alan

PENDERECKI, KRZYSZTOF (1933-   )
Ecloga VIII
6pt men cor study sc SCHOTTS
ED. 6341 s.p.   (P78)

Kosmogonia
20pt mix cor,STB soli,orch (diff)
min sc SCHOTTS ED. 6324 s.p., sc
SCHOTTS rental, ipr   (P79)

PENINGER
More Little Things That Creep And
Crawl And Sometimes Fly
SA oct HERITAGE H5010 $.45   (P80)

PENN, ROBERT
Wit And Wisdom Of Benjamin Franklin,
The
SATB,acap DEAN CD-101 $1.00   (P81)

PENNY, THE
(Johnson) SATB,narrator BENSON S4313
$.35   (P82)

PEOPLE WILL SAY WE'RE IN LOVE see
Rodgers, Richard

PEP SONG, A see Protheroe, Daniel

PEPPERMINT FUGUE see Jeffries

PEPPING, ERNST (1901-   )
Ach Gott, Wie Weh Tut Scheiden
see Der Morgen

Alle Vogel Sind Schon Da *folk
jr cor/wom cor (med easy) sc
SCHOTTS CHBL 557A-B s.p. contains
also: Schlaf, Kindchen, Schlaf
(cradle)   (P83)

Anbetung Des Kindes
see Der Wagen Heft 2: Das Licht

Auf Einem Baum Ein Kuckuck Sass
jr cor/wom cor (med easy) sc
SCHOTTS CHBL 558 s.p.   (P84)

Bauerngarten
see Der Wagen Heft 1: Bauerngarten

Bei Tag Und Nacht *folk
SSATB,acap (med) sc SCHOTTS
ED. 3910 s.p.
contains: Die Beste Zeit Im Jahr
Ist Mein; Die Voglein In Dem
Walde; Schwefelhelzle Muss Ma
Ha
see also: Die Beste Zeit Im Jahr
Ist Mein   (P85)

Bemesst Den Schritt
see Das Gute Leben

Das ABC
SATB,acap (med) BAREN. BA2275 s.p.
(P86)

Das Dach
see Der Wagen Heft 3: Der Herd

Das Gute Leben
mix cor (med) sc SCHOTTS C 34 769
s.p.
contains: Bemesst Den Schritt;
Die Linien Des Lebens Sind
Verschieden; Ich Leb Und Weiss
Nit Wie Lang   (P87)

Das Jahr *CC12U
mix cor (med) sc SCHOTTS ED. 2913
s.p.   (P88)

Das Licht
see Der Wagen Heft 2: Das Licht

Der Herd
see Der Wagen Heft 3: Der Herd

Der Morgen *folk
4-6pt mix cor,acap (med) sc SCHOTTS
ED. 3909 s.p.
contains: Ach Gott, Wie Weh Tut
Scheiden; Ich Sah Mir Einen
Blauen Storchen; Wann Ich Des
Morgens Fruh Aufsteh; Wann Ich
Des Morgens Fruh Aufsteh;
Zwischen Berg Und Tiefem Tal
(P89)

Der Wagen
see Der Wagen Heft 4: Jahraus-
Jahrein

PEPPING, ERNST (cont'd.)

Der Wagen Heft 1: Bauerngarten
4-5pt mix cor,acap (med) sc SCHOTTS
ED. 3902 s.p.
contains: Bauerngarten; Marterl;
Stiefelknecht Und Wetterhahn
(P90)

Der Wagen Heft 2: Das Licht
4-5pt mix cor,acap (med diff) sc
SCHOTTS ED. 3903 s.p.
contains: Anbetung Des Kindes;
Das Licht; Lichtmess   (P91)

Der Wagen Heft 3: Der Herd
4-5pt mix cor,acap (med diff) sc
SCHOTTS ED. 3904 s.p.
contains: Das Dach; Der Herd;
Hausspruch   (P92)

Der Wagen Heft 4: Jahraus-Jahrein
4-5pt mix cor,acap (med) sc SCHOTTS
ED. 3905 s.p.
contains: Der Wagen; Jahraus-
Jahrein; Sankt Laurentius (P93)

Der Wagen Heft 5: Im Weinland
4-5pt mix cor,acap (med diff) sc
SCHOTTS ED. 3906 s.p.
contains: Im Weinland;
Kelterspruch; Sieveringer
Oktoberlied   (P94)

Der Wagen Heft 6: Herr Walther Von
Der Vogelweide
4-5pt mix cor,acap (med diff) sc
SCHOTTS ED. 3907 s.p.
contains: Herr Walther Von Der
Vogelweide; Meister Anton
Pilgram; Schnitzwerk An Einem
Hochaltar   (P95)

Die Beste Zeit Im Jahr Ist Mein
mix cor (med) sc SCHOTTS C 36 679
s.p. see also Bei Tag Und Nacht
(P96)

Die Linien Des Lebens Sind
Verschieden
see Das Gute Leben

Die Voglein In Dem Walde
see Bei Tag Und Nacht

Es Geht Wohl Anders Als Du Meinst
see Spruche Und Lieder Nach
Gedichten Von Goethe, Rilke Und
Eichendorff

Gleichgewinn "Geht Einer Mit Dem
Anderen Hin"
see Spruche Und Lieder Nach
Gedichten Von Goethe, Rilke Und
Eichendorff

Gott Gsegn Dich, Laub
SATBB,acap (med) BAREN. BA2273 s.p.
(P97)

Hausspruch
see Der Wagen Heft 3: Der Herd

Herr Walther Von Der Vogelweide
see Der Wagen Heft 6: Herr Walther
Von Der Vogelweide

Ich Armes Maidlein Klag Mich Sehr
3 eq voices,acap BAREN. BA2274 s.p.
(P98)

Ich Leb Und Weiss Nit Wie Lang
see Das Gute Leben

Ich Sah Mir Einen Blauen Storchen
see Der Morgen

Im Weinland
see Der Wagen Heft 5: Im Weinland

Jahraus-Jahrein
see Der Wagen Heft 4: Jahraus-
Jahrein

Kelterspruch
see Der Wagen Heft 5: Im Weinland

Kommt Zeit, Kommt Rat "Wer Will Denn
Alles Gleich"
see Spruche Und Lieder Nach
Gedichten Von Goethe, Rilke Und
Eichendorff

Lichtmess
see Der Wagen Heft 2: Das Licht

Magst Du Zu Dem Alten Halten
see Spruche Und Lieder Nach
Gedichten Von Goethe, Rilke Und
Eichendorff

Marterl
see Der Wagen Heft 1: Bauerngarten

Meister Anton Pilgram
see Der Wagen Heft 6: Herr Walther
Von Der Vogelweide

PEPPING, ERNST (cont'd.)

O Herr, Gib Jedem Seinen Eignen Tod
see Spruche Und Lieder Nach
Gedichten Von Goethe, Rilke Und
Eichendorff

Sankt Laurentius
see Der Wagen Heft 4: Jahraus-
Jahrein

Schlaf, Kindchen, Schlaf
see Pepping, Ernst, Alle Vogel Sind
Schon Da

Schnitzwerk An Einem Hochaltar
see Der Wagen Heft 6: Herr Walther
Von Der Vogelweide

Schwefelhelzle Muss Ma Ha
see Bei Tag Und Nacht

Sieveringer Oktoberlied
see Der Wagen Heft 5: Im Weinland

Spruche Und Lieder Nach Gedichten Von
Goethe, Rilke Und Eichendorff
3-5pt mix cor,acap (med diff) sc
SCHOTTS C 32 679 s.p.
contains: Es Geht Wohl Anders Als
Du Meinst; Gleichgewinn "Geht
Einer Mit Dem Anderen Hin";
Kommt Zeit, Kommt Rat "Wer Will
Denn Alles Gleich"; Magst Du Zu
Dem Alten Halten; O Herr, Gib
Jedem Seinen Eignen Tod; Wenn
Was Irgend Ist Geschehen" (P99)

Stiefelknecht Und Wetterhahn
see Der Wagen Heft 1: Bauerngarten

Volkslieder *CC32L,folk
2-3pt jr cor/2-3pt wom cor,acap sc
SCHOTTS ED. 3899 s.p.   (P100)

Wann Ich Des Morgens Fruh Aufsteh
see Der Morgen

Wenn Was Irgend Ist Geschehen"
see Spruche Und Lieder Nach
Gedichten Von Goethe, Rilke Und
Eichendorff

Wohlan, Die Zeit Ist Kommen
jr cor/wom cor (med easy) sc
SCHOTTS CHBL 559 s.p.   (P101)

Zwischen Berg Und Tiefem Tal
see Der Morgen

PER TE D'AMICO APRILE see Beethoven,
Ludwig van

PER VENTIQUATTRO VOCI ADULTE O BIANCHE
see Bussotti, Sylvano

PERETTI, HUGO
Can't Help Falling In Love *see
Creatore, Luigi

"PERFECT MAN", THE see Jenkins, Marshal

PERGAMENT, MOSES (1893-   )
Sub Luna
3pt mix cor,Bar solo ERIKS s.p.
(P102)

PERSONALS see Anderson, Thomas J.

PERVIGILIUM VENERIS see Schultz, Svend
S.

PESME NOCI see Frajt, Ludmila

PESNICKY PRE MALE SKOLSKE DETI see
Holoubek, Ladislav

PESTALOZZI, HEINRICH (1878-1940)
Gebet Der Schiffer "Die Stunden
Eilen"
TTBB sc,voc pt SCHOTTS
C 31 276, 01-04 s.p.   (P103)

PET CESKY TANCU see Burghauser, Jarmil

PET MAGRIGALU see Flosman, Oldrich

PET MARDIGALU see Jira, Milan

PETER, PAUL, AND MARY see Dedrick, C.

PETERS, BEN
Before The Next Teardrop Falls *see
Keith, Vivian

PETIT MADRIGAL see Monteverdi, Claudio

PETIT VILLAGE see Danhieux, Georges

PETIT ZODIAQUE SENTIMENTAL, PART I see
Michel, Paul-Baudouin

PETIT ZODIAQUE SENTIMENTAL, PART II see
Michel, Paul-Baudouin

PETIT ZODIAQUE SENTIMENTAL, PART III
see Michel, Paul-Baudouin

PETITES HIRONDELLES see Danhieux,
Georges

PETOFI KORUSOK I *CCU
eq voices BUDAPEST 6679 s.p.   (P104)

PETOFI KORUSOK II *CCU
men cor BUDAPEST 6680 s.p.   (P105)

PETOFI KORUSOK III *CCU
mix cor BUDAPEST 6681 s.p.   (P106)

PETRASSI, GOFFREDO (1904-   )
Coro Di Morti
men cor,3pno,4horn,4trp,3trom,tuba,
bvl,perc min sc SCHOTTS ESZ 4976
s.p., voc sc SCHOTTS ESZ 3942
s.p., ipr, sc SCHOTTS rental
(P107)

Nonsense
[Eng/It] 4pt mix cor,acap (diff) sc
SCHOTTS SZ 4924 s.p.   (P108)

Sesto Non-Sense
[Eng/It] SSATTBB,acap (diff) sc
SCHOTTS SZ 6531 s.p.   (P109)

PETROVA, ELENA (1929-   )
Catulli Liber Carminum *CCU,madrigal
[Lat] mix cor,acap CZECH s.p.
(P110)

Nights *see Noci

Noci
"Nights" [Czech] mix cor,T solo,
3fl,2ob,3clar,2bsn,4horn,3trp,
3trom,tuba,timp,perc,harp,
strings, celeste, xylophone CZECH
s.p.   (P111)

PETROVICS, EMIL
Lassu Tancnota
mix cor BUDAPEST 7375 s.p.   (P112)

PETRULUS HIRRUTUS see Hessenberg, Kurt,
Der Struwwelpeter

PETRVALD see Simek, Miroslav

PEUERL, PAUL (ca. 1570-ca. 1624)
Frisch Auf Und Lasst Uns Singen
SSATB,acap (med) sc SCHOTTS
C 38 126B s.p.   (P113)

O Musica, Du Edle Kinst
SSATB (med easy) sc SCHOTTS
CHBL 308 s.p.   (P114)

O Musica, Du Edle Kunst
(Desch, Rudolf) men cor sc SCHOTTS
CHBL 94 s.p.   (P115)

O Musica' Thou Noble Art
(Van Camp) SATB SCHIRM.G LG51774
$.30   (P116)

PFALZER HEIMATLIED see Wolfgarten, Hans

PFALZISCHE LIEDKANTATE see Seeger,
Peter

PFAUENART "LEUCHT HELLER DENN DIE
SONNE" see Trunk, Richard

PFAUTSCH, LLOYD (1921-   )
Omnis Spiritus Laudet Dominum
SATB SCHIRM.G LG51802 $.45   (P117)

This Is My Own, My Native Land *Fest
SATB,band (med) FISCHER,C CM 7887
$.35   (P118)

PFERDE ZU VIEREN TRABEN see Zoll, Paul

PFINGSTEN "WIR HALTEN UNSERE HAUPTER
STILL see Knab, Armin

PFIRISCHBLUTE see Reda, Siegfried

PFIRSICH ESS ICH GERNE "SIND DIE
PFIRSICH RUND UND REIF" see Seeger,
Peter

PFITZNER, HANS (1869-1949)
Columbus *Op.16
8pt RIES sc s.p., voc pt s.p.
(P119)

Der Blumen Rache
wom cor,A solo,orch RIES voc pt
s.p., voc sc rental, ipr   (P120)

PFLUGERLIED see Erdlen, Hermann

PHENOMINAL TENOR, THE see Skolnik,
Walter

PHILIPP, FRANZ (1890-   )
Das Lob Der Heimat
men cor,acap TONOS 3941 s.p.   (P121)

Kaiserstuhl-Lied
men cor,acap TONOS 696 s.p.   (P122)

PHILIPP, FRANZ (cont'd.)

Vorspruch
men cor,acap TONOS 3936 s.p.   (P123)

PHILIPS, PETER (1561-1628)
Select Madrigals *CCU,madrigal
(Harrison) cor STAINER 3.8929.8
$28.75   (P124)

PHILLIPS, JOHN C. (1921-   )
Chantons Noel *CC3U,carol,Fr
SSA,pno,4strings/orch voc sc
NOVELLO rental, ipr   (P125)

PHOTOGRAPHS AND MEMORIES see Croce, Jim

PHYLLIS, THY LOVELY LOOKS see Beale,
William

PHYLLIS UND PHILANDER see Reutter,
Hermann

PIANO MAN see Joel, Billy

PIANTONI
Quatre Poemes *CC4U
wom cor,acap HENN 682 s.p.   (P126)

PIBERNIK, ZLATKO (1926-   )
Cantata About Blood And Stone
SATB&SATB,10 narrators,pno,3fl,2ob,
3clar,bsn,4horn,3trp,3trom,tuba,
strings,timp CROATICA   (P127)

PICCIOLA VERGA E BELLA see Agostini,
Lodovico

PICCIOLI, G.
Partomi Donna E Teco Lasc'il Core
see Piccioli, G., Sia Benedetta
L'hor

Sia Benedetta L'hor'
SAT/SAB LAUDINELLA LR 131 s.p.
contains also: Partomi Donna E
Teco Lasc'il Core   (P128)

Voci Che Amavi
(Negri, A.) 2pt sc BONGIOVANI 1804
s.p.   (P129)

PICCOLA CANTATA see Gatti, C.

PICCOLA SUITE CORALE see Veneziani,
Vittore

PICHA, FRANTISEK (1893-1946)
Panychida *Op.34, cant
"Panychide" [Czech] mix cor,3fl,
3ob,3clar,3bsn,6horn,3trp,3trom,
tuba,timp,perc,harp,strings CZECH
s.p.   (P130)

Panychide *see Panychida

PICK OCH PACK (KITKAT KITKAT) see
Tornudd, Axel

PICK YOURSELF UP see Kern, Jerome

PICKELL
Christmas Is A Comin' *Xmas
SAB PRO ART 2843 $.35   (P131)

Through The Eyes Of A Child *Xmas
SAB PRO ART 2772 $.35   (P132)

PICTURE GALLERY see Kurth, Burton L.

PIDY DIDY DIM DIM see Feld, Jindrich

PIE IN THE SKY
SATB UP WITH 6510 $.40   (P133)

PIECHLER, ARTHUR (1896-1974)
Das Tagewerk *Op.43, CCU
mix cor&opt jr cor,SBar soli,2fl,
2ob,2clar,bsn,2horn,3trp,2trom,
tuba,strings,perc,timp, celeste
(med) sc SCHOTTS rental, ipr
(P134)

PIED BEAUTY see Mechem, Kirke

PIED PIPER OF HAMELIN see Walthew,
[Richard Henry]

PIERCE
Solitude Of Space
SATB WALTON 2978 $.45   (P135)

With Joyful Mirth
SATB WALTON 2988 $.40   (P136)

PIERNE, GABRIEL (1863-1937)
Les Libellules
2pt,pno JOBERT voc sc s.p., cor pts
s.p.   (P137)

PIERNE, PAUL (1874-1950)
Train, The
SSA,acap SALABERT-US $.45   (P138)
SATB,pno SALABERT-US $.45   (P139)
(Frank, Marcel) 2pt treb cor,pno
SALABERT-US   (P140)

PIESEN see Ocenas, Andrej

PIESEN NASHO L'UDU see Szelepcsenyi,
Jan

PIESEN O HRDINOVI see Mikula, Zdenko

PIESEN O JAVORE see Mikula, Zdenko

PIESEN O RODNEJ RIEKE see Mikula,
Zdenko

PIESEN O SLAVICKOVI see Urbanec,
Bartolomej

PIESEN O SPOLOCNEJ VLASTI! see Suchon,
Eugen

PIESEN O VLASTI see Nemeth-Samorinsky,
Stefan

PIESEN PRACUJUCICH see Moyzes,
Alexander

PILEUR
Le Grillon
men cor,acap HENN 780 s.p.   (P141)

Sultan Achmet
mix cor,acap HENN 677 s.p.   (P142)

Triolet
mix cor,acap HENN 676 s.p.   (P143)
men cor,acap HENN 792 s.p.   (P144)

PILGRIM'S CHORUS see Wagner, Richard

PILKINGTON, FRANCIS (ca. 1562-1638)
First Set Of Madrigals And Pastorals
Of Three, Four, And Five Parts
(1613) EM Vol. 25 *CC22L,
madrigal
3-5pt STAINER 3.1925.1 $13.00
(P145)

Rest, Sweet Nymphs
SATB,acap EGTVED MS14B3 s.p. (P146)

Second Set Of Madrigals And Pastorals
Of Three Four, And Five Parts
(1613) EM Vol. 25 *CC22L,
madrigal
3-5pt STAINER 3.1925.2 $13.00
(P147)

Second Set Of Madrigals And Pastorals
Of Three, Four, And Five Parts
(1624) EM Vol. 26 *CC26L
3-5pt STAINER 3.1926.1 $19.00
(P148)

PINDER
Melancholy Man
(Myrow) SATB MCA UC 698 $.40 (P149)

PINEAPPLE, CRABAPPLE see Dedrick, C.

PINES OF THE NORTHWEST ARM, THE see
Farrell, Dennis

PINEY, THE LONELY CHRISTMAS TREE see
Sivanich

PINKHAM, DANIEL (1923-   )
Evergreen
unis SCHIRM.EC 2962 s.p.   (P150)

Fill Every Glass (from The Beggar's
Opera)
SATB,T solo,pno AM.COMP.AL. (P151)

In Youth Is Pleasure
unis,pno/gtr SCHIRM.EC 2814 s.p.
(P152)

O Depth Of Wealth
SATB SCHIRM.EC 2951 s.p.   (P153)

On The Dispute About Images
SATB,SATB soli SCHIRM.EC 2923 s.p.
(P154)

Pleasure It Is
1-2pt SCHIRM.EC 2830 s.p.   (P155)

To Troubled Friends
SATB,strings,electronic tape voc sc
SCHIRM.EC 2942 s.p., ipa   (P156)

PINOS, ALOIS (1925-   )
Ars Amatoria *cant
[Lat] men cor,SBar soli,orch CZECH
s.p.   (P157)

Ceska Zima
"Czech Winter" [Czech] men cor,acap
CZECH s.p.   (P158)

Criers *see Vyvolavaci

Czech Winter *see Ceska Zima

Detsky Rok *CC4U
[Czech] jr cor,pno CZECH s.p.
(P159)

O Slunecniku, Mesicniku A Vetrniku
*CC3U
[Czech] jr cor,acap CZECH s.p.
(P160)

PINOS, ALOIS (cont'd.)

Vyvolavaci
  "Criers" [Czech] 2pt girl cor&mix
    cor,fl,clar,trp,tuba,perc,vln,bvl
    CZECH s.p.   (P161)

PIONEER, THE see Palkovsky, Oldrich,
  Pionyr

PIONEER STORY, THE see Barvik,
  Miroslav, Pionyrska Pohadka

PIONEER WALTZ, THE see Smatek, Milos,
  Pionyrsky Valcik

PIONEERS *folk
  (Brandon, George) SATB STANDARD
    C607MX1 $.50   (P162)

PIONEER'S SING, THE see Strniste, Jiri,
  Pionyrska

PIONYR see Palkovsky, Oldrich

PIONYRSKA see Strniste, Jiri

PIONYRSKA POHADKA see Barvik, Miroslav

PIONYRSKY VALCIK see Smatek, Milos

PIPER O' DUNDEE, THE *folk
  (Seton) SA (easy) OXFORD 84.091 $.45
                                      (P163)
PIPER O' DUNDEE, THE see Simpson, John

PIPERS ANSWER, THE see Reakes, Brian

PIPER'S SONG see Innes, Gertrude

PIPING TIM OF GALWAY
  (Wick, Fred) 2pt oct SCHMITT W238
    $.30   (P164)

PIPPIN see Schwartz, Stephen

PIQUE LA BALEINE
  (Blanchard, R.) 3pt men cor,Bar solo,
    acap JOBERT s.p.   (P165)

PIRATES, THE see Protheroe, Daniel

PIROSKAHOZ see Szabo, Csaba

PISEN BRATRA SLUNCE see Foerster, Josef
  Bohuslav

PISEN LIDU see Kricka, Jaroslav

PISEN MIRU see Schneeweiss, Jan

PISEN O RODNE ZEMI see Jeremias, Otakar

PISEN O STRANE see Dobias, Vaclav

PISEN O STRANE see Seidel, Jan

PISEN O SVAZKU DELNIKU A ROLNIKU see
  Burian, Emil Frantisek

PISEN PISNI see Vackar, Dalibor C.

PISEN RODNE ZEMI see Kapr, Jan

PISEN VITEZNA see Kypta, F.A.

PISK, PAUL AMADEUS (1893-   )
  In Memoriam Carl Sandburg
    SATB,acap AM.COMP.AL. $5.50 (P166)

  Song From Shakespeare's "Much Ado
    About Nothing"
    SATB,acap AM.COMP.AL. $2.75 (P167)

  Sunset *Op.81
    SSAA,acap AM.COMP.AL. $1.38 (P168)

  Trail Of Life, The *Op.88, cant
    cor,2 soli,narrator,2fl,2ob,2clar,
    2bsn,2horn,2trp,2trom,timp,perc,
    strings AM.COMP.AL.   (P169)

PISNE PRO ZENSKY SBOR see Skvor,
  Frantisek

PISNICKY O ZVIRATECH see Hurnik, Ilja

PISTOL PACKIN' MAMA
  TTBB CIMINO $.40   (P170)

PITFIELD
  Cheshire Soul-Caking Song
    2pt (easy) OXFORD 82.104 $.30
                                      (P171)
PITFIELD, THOMAS BARON (1903-   )
  Cheshire Souling Song
    SSA CRAMER $.30   (P172)

PITY ME NOT see Calder, Robert

PIU NON SI TROVANO see Mozart, Wolfgang
  Amadeus

PIVA, FRANCO
  Due Madrigali *CC2U,madrigal
    ZANIBON 5422 s.p.   (P173)

PLACE I COME FROM, THE
  SATB UP WITH 6514 $.40   (P174)

PLAGUE 1665 see Williamson, Malcolm

PLAIN FOLK BUGGY SONG see Kunz, Alfred

PLAINT OF THE CAMEL see Innes, Gertrude

PLAISIR D'AMOUR see Martini, Jean Paul
  Egide

PLAISIR D'AMOUR see Martinu

PLANK
  Man Must Be Free *see Rinehart, C.

PLANT
  Stairway To Heaven *see Page

PLATTS, KENNETH
  Musick's Empire
    SATB,orch ENOCH EC351 s.p., ipr
                                      (P175)
  Three Bird Songs *CC3U
    cor,inst ASHDOWN SGMS.11   (P176)

PLAUDERTASCHE "DU LIEBES
  PAPPELMAULCHEN" see Lang, Hans

PLAY ON NUMBERS, A see Parker, Alice

PLAYGROUND IN MY MIND see Vance, Paul

PLEASE COME TO BOSTON see Loggins

PLEASE TO REMEMBER see Greaves

PLEASURE IT IS
  (Kirk) SATB KJOS 5909 $.35   (P177)

PLEASURE IT IS see Pinkham, Daniel

PLEASURES IN MAY, THE see Brahms,
  Johannes

PLEDGE OF ALLEGIANCE, THE
  (Liebert, Billy; Svarda, Bill) cor,
    narrator,band STUDIO V731 $.45, ipa
                                      (P178)
PLUMPS "DER FROSCH UND EINE KROTE" see
  Fussan, Werner

PLUS NE SUIS CE QUI J'AI ETE see
  Crawford, John

PO BITVE BELOHORSKE see Bendl, Karel

PO DESTI see Zouhar, Zdenek

POCHOD 1948 see Bartos, Jan Zdenek

POCHOD POVSTALCOV see Cikker, Jan

POCHOD URODY see Stanislav, Josef

POCKRISS, LEO
  Playground In My Mind *see Vance,
    Paul

POCUVAJ, POCUVAJ see Mikula, Zdenko

POCUVAJ, POCUVAJ see Mikula, Zdenko

POCUVAJ, POCUVAJ see Mikula, Zdenko

POD BABOU HOROU see Andrasovan, Tibor

POD PRAPOREM KOMUNISMU see Vomacka,
  Boleslav

POD STARYM PRAPOREM see Kricka,
  Jaroslav

POD ZVICINOU see Simek, Miroslav

PODEKOVANI SOVETSKEMU SVAZU see Barvik,
  Miroslav

PODEST, LUDVIK (1921-1968)
  Better Love, A *see Laska Peknejsi

  Laska Peknejsi *cant
    "Better Love, A" [Czech] wom cor,
    SATB soli,2fl,2ob,2clar,2bsn,
    3horn,trp,strings, cymbal,
    accordion CZECH s.p.   (P179)

  Laska Za Lasku *cant
    "Love In Exchange" [Czech] mix cor,
    2fl,2ob,2clar,2bsn,4horn,3trp,
    3trom,tuba,timp,perc,harp,
    harmonium,strings CZECH s.p.
                                      (P180)
  Love In Exchange *see Laska Za Lasku

  Nadesel Cas
    "Time Has Come, The" [Czech] unis,
    acap CZECH s.p.   (P181)

PODEST, LUDVIK (cont'd.)

  Time Has Come, The *see Nadesel Cas

  Vsedni Den
    "Workday" [Czech] unis,acap CZECH
    s.p.   (P182)

  Workday *see Vsedni Den

PODESVA, JAROMIR (1927-   )
  Dva Detske Sbory *CC2U
    [Czech] jr cor,acap CZECH s.p.
                                      (P183)
  Hero's Song, The *see Zpev Hrdinov

  Tri Detske Sbory *CC3U
    [Czech] jr cor,acap CZECH s.p.
                                      (P184)
  Zpev Hrdinov
    "Hero's Song, The" [Czech] men cor,
    acap CZECH s.p.   (P185)

PODVECERNI KONCERT U CHATY see
  Kohoutek, Ctirad

POEM ABOUT MAN see Palenicek, Josef,
  Poema O Cloveku

POEMA O CLOVEKU see Palenicek, Josef

POEMS OF WAR RESISTANCE see Rovics,
  Howard

POET'S SONG, THE see Dello Joio, Norman

POHREB NA KANKU see Klicka, Josef

POI CHE DEL MIO DOLORE see Monteverdi,
  Claudio

POINT OF VIEW see Cohn, James

POKLADY SE OTVIRAJI see Kupka, Karel

POLKA see Biebl, Franz

POLKA see Smetana, Bedrich

POLKA IS OFF, THE see Zich, Otakor,
  Polka Jede

POLKA JEDE see Zich, Otakor

POLKA OF KLATOVY TOWN see Spilka,
  Frantisek, Klatovska Polka

POLL, JOSEPH
  Hofers Abschied Vom Leben
    men cor,acap TONOS 807 s.p. (P186)

  Tiroler Krippenlied
    men cor,acap TONOS 809 s.p. (P187)

POLLA TA DINA see Xenakis, Yannis
  (Iannis)

POLLY-WOLLY-DOODLE *folk
  (Biebl, F.) [Ger] 4pt mix cor
    MERSEBURG EM9240 s.p.   (P188)
  (Olson) SATB oct SCHMITT 7048 $.45
                                      (P189)
POLNISCH *Pol
  (Kremser) mix cor LIENAU
    LIEDERHARFE NR. 7, 1 sc s.p., cor
    pts s.p.   (P190)

POLOLANIK, ZDENEK (1935-   )
  Song Of Dead Children, The *see Zpev
    Mrtvych Deti

  Zpev Mrtvych Deti
    "Song Of Dead Children, The"
    [Czech/Lat] mix cor,narrator,
    3trp,perc CZECH s.p.   (P191)

POLONIUS PLATITUDES, THE see London,
  Edwin

POLYFONIA STARYCH MAJSTROV NA LATINSKE
  TEXTY *CCU
  (Schleicher, L.) [Lat] jr cor
    SLOV.HUD.FOND s.p.   (P192)

POLYMORPHOUS CANON see Blickhan, Tim

POMOZEME SLAVIKOVI see Kardos, Dezider

PONCE, JUAN
  Ave Color Vini Clari
    [Lat] SATB,acap EGTVED KB89 s.p.
                                      (P193)
PONT
  Music Workshop, Book 1 *CCU
    unis,2vln,vcl,perc,rec sc OXFORD
    50.118 $4.75, ipa, cor pts OXFORD
    $1.60   (P194)

  Music Workshop, Book 2 *CCU
    unis,2vln,vcl,perc,rec sc OXFORD
    50.119 $4.75, ipa, cor pts OXFORD
    $1.60   (P195)

POOL, THE see Becker, John J.

POOLER
 Fires Of Troy, The
  SATB WALTON 2986 $.40   (P196)

 Who Are You
  SATB WALTON 2976 $.45   (P197)

POOR LONESOME COWBOY *US
 (Giles) BarBar&2camb CAMBIATA U97446
                                 (P198)
POOR OLD HORSE see Wilkinson, Philip G.

POOR PIERROT
 SAB CIMINO $.40   (P199)
 SSA CIMINO $.40   (P200)
 TTBB CIMINO $.40   (P201)
 SATB CIMINO $.40   (P202)

POOR WAYFARING STRANGER *folk
 (Fred, Herbert W.) SSATTBB (med)
 FITZSIMONS 1063 $.25   (P203)

POOR WAYFARING STRANGER see Burroughs

POOR WIDOW see Alvad, Christian

POOS, HEINRICH (1928-   )
 Alala *folk,Span
  3-4pt wom cor,acap (med, song
  cycle) sc SCHOTTS C 43 462 s.p.
                                 (P204)
 Annerle, Wo Warst Du? *madrigal,Slav
  SSAATTBB (med) sc SCHOTTS C 41 867
  s.p. see from Drei Madrigale Nach
  Slowakischen Liebesliedern (P205)

 Der Pflaumenbaum "Im Hofe Steht Ein
  Pflaumenbaum"
  see Drei Chorlieder Nach Gedichten
  Von Bertolt Brecht

 Der Schneider Von Ulm "Bischof, Ich
  Kann Fliegen"
  see Drei Chorlieder Nach Gedichten
  Von Bertolt Brecht

 Die Schone Predi' "Der Alte Pfarrer
  Von Waxelmoos"
  men cor sc SCHOTTS CHBL 203 s.p.
                                 (P206)
 Die Vogel Warten Im Winter Vor Dem
  Fenster "Ich Bin Der Sperling"
  see Drei Chorlieder Nach Gedichten
  Von Bertolt Brecht

 Drei Chorlieder Nach Gedichten Von
  Bertolt Brecht
  mix cor (med) sc SCHOTTS C 41 525
  s.p.
  contains: Der Pflaumenbaum "Im
   Hofe Steht Ein Pflaumenbaum";
   Der Schneider Von Ulm "Bischof,
   Ich Kann Fliegen"; Die Vogel
   Warten Im Winter Vor Dem
   Fenster "Ich Bin Der Sperling"
                                 (P207)
 Drei Madrigale Nach Slowakischen
  Liebesliedern *see Annerle, Wo
  Warst Du?; Kommt, Wir Gehn Auf
  Schmalem Wege; Um Jaroschau
  Fliessen Zwei Der Bache   (P208)

 Drei Mahrische Volkslieder *see
  Musikanten, Warum Schweigt Ihr;
  Sing Mir, O Nachtigall; Wenn Ich
  Durch Die Berge Meiner Heimat
  Fahre   (P209)

 Ein Jager Langs Dem Weiher Ging
  TTBB,Bar solo sc,voc pt SCHOTTS
  C 42 564, C 42 565 01-02 o.p. see
  from Vom Edlen Jagerleben (P210)

 Ein Jegliches Hat Seine Zeit
  men cor,narrator,S solo,2clar,bsn,
  3horn,2trom,strings,perc sc,cor
  pts SCHOTTS ED. 6548 s.p., ipr
                                 (P211)
 Erntedank "Herr, Die Felder Sind Nun
  Leer"
  men cor&2pt jr cor/2pt wom cor,
  acap/pno/2trp&3trom sc SCHOTTS
  C 42 729 s.p., cor pts SCHOTTS
  C 42 730 s.p., ipa   (P212)

 Frisch Auf Zum Frohlichen Jagen
  TTBB sc,voc pt SCHOTTS
  C 42 561, C 42 562, 01-02 s.p.
  see from Vom Edlen Jagerleben
                                 (P213)
 Hat Mein Lieb Ein Schlehlein *Czech
  men cor sc SCHOTTS C 41 956 s.p.
                                 (P214)
 Hochzeit Hielt Das Muckelein
  men cor sc SCHOTTS C 40 819 s.p.,
  voc pt SCHOTTS C 40 820, 01-02
  s.p. see from Mahrische
  Volkslieder   (P215)
  mix cor (med) sc SCHOTTS C 43 584
  s.p.   (P216)

 Ich Will Truren Fahren Lan *cant
  mix cor,pno,fl,bvl (med) sc,voc sc,
  cor pts SCHOTTS ED. 6255 s.p.,
  ipa   (P217)

POOS, HEINRICH (cont'd.)

 Kommt, Wir Gehn Auf Schmalem Wege
  *madrigal,Slav
  SSATBB (med) sc SCHOTTS C 41 869
  s.p. see from Drei Madrigale Nach
  Slowakischen Liebesliedern (P218)

 Mahrische Volkslieder *see Hochzeit
  Hielt Das Muckelein; Mir Entfloh
  Die Wachtel; O Liebe, Liebe;
  Spiele Mir, Geigerlein   (P219)

 Mir Entfloh Die Wachtel
  [Ger] men cor sc SCHOTTS C 40 816
  s.p. see from Mahrische
  Volkslieder   (P220)

 Musikanten, Warum Schweigt Ihr *folk
  5-8pt mix cor,acap (med) sc SCHOTTS
  C 40 561 s.p. see from Drei
  Mahrische Volkslieder   (P221)

 O Liebe, Liebe
  [Ger] men cor (contains also:
  Spiele Mir, Geigerlein) sc
  SCHOTTS C 40 817 s.p. see from
  Mahrische Volkslieder   (P222)

 Schneider-Courage "Es Ist Ein Schuss
  Gefallen"
  men cor sc SCHOTTS CHBL 202 s.p.
                                 (P223)
 Seht Es Regnen, Seht Es Giessen
  *Czech
  mix cor (med) sc SCHOTTS C 43 585
  s.p.   (P224)
  men cor sc SCHOTTS C 41 952 s.p.
                                 (P225)
 Sing Mir, O Nachtigall *folk
  5-8pt mix cor,acap (med, contains
  also: Wenn Ich Durch Die Berge
  Meiner Heimat Fahre) sc SCHOTTS
  C 40 562 s.p. see from Drei
  Mahrische Volkslieder   (P226)

 Spiele Mir, Geigerlein
  [Ger] men cor (contains also: O
  Liebe, Liebe) sc SCHOTTS C 40 817
  s.p. see from Mahrische
  Volkslieder   (P227)

 Totenklage Um Samogonski "Bruder,
  Samogonski Ist Gestorben"
  men cor,narrator sc SCHOTTS
  C 43 490 s.p.   (P228)

 Um Jaroschau Fliessen Zwei Der Bache
  *madrigal,Slav
  SSATBB (med) sc SCHOTTS C 41 868
  s.p. see from Drei Madrigale Nach
  Slowakischen Liebesliedern (P229)

 Vom Edlen Jagerleben *see Ein Jager
  Langs Dem Weiher Ging; Frisch Auf
  Zum Frohlichen Jagen; Wie
  Lieblich Schallt Durch Busch Und
  Wald   (P230)

 Von Der Bruderlichkeit "Die Arzenei
  Fur Aller Welten"
  men cor sc SCHOTTS CHBL 208 s.p.
                                 (P231)
 Wenn Ich Durch Die Berge Meiner
  Heimat Fahre *folk
  5-8pt mix cor,acap (med, contains
  also: Sing Mir, O Nachtigall) sc
  SCHOTTS C 40 562 s.p. see from
  Drei Mahrische Volkslieder (P232)

 Wie Lieblich Schallt Durch Busch Und
  Wald
  men cor sc SCHOTTS C 42 563 s.p.
  see from Vom Edlen Jagerleben
                                 (P233)
POPEVKY NA DVORE see Sauer, Frantisek

POPULAR ITALIAN MADRIGALS OF THE
 SIXTEENTH CENTURY *CCU,madrigal
 (Harman) cor OXFORD   (P234)

POPULAR SONG see Maw

POR UNOS PUERTOS ARRIBA see Ribera,
 Antonio de

PORE JUD see Rodgers, Richard

PORENA, BORIS (1927-   )
 Cantata Da Camera *cant
  men cor,B solo,3trom,6vcl,timp sc
  SCHOTTS ESZ 6463 s.p., ipr (P235)
  wom cor,S solo,clar,6vln, mandolin
  (diff) sc SCHOTTS ESZ 6460 s.p.,
  ipr   (P236)

PORPORA, NICOLA ANTONIO (1686-1768)
 Credidi
  SSAA,org,strings voc sc NOVELLO
  rental, ipr   (P237)

PORTRAIT BY A NEIGHBOR see
 Christiansen, R.

PORTRAIT OF CHRISTMAS see DeCamp,
 Carroll

PORTRAIT OF DUKE ELLINGTON
 (Cacavas, John) SATB,pno,opt bvl&
 drums&gtr BELWIN $1.00
 contains: It Don't Mean A Thing;
  Mood Indigo; Satin Doll;
  Solitude; Sophisticated Lady
                                 (P238)
PORTUM INVENI see Furer, Arthur

POSKOCICA see Cossetto, Emil

POSTREMA VERBA see Roos, Robert de

POTATO SONG, THE see Kalanzi

POTKAL PEJSEK KOCICKU see Bohac, Josef

POTTER, BRIAN
 Dream On *see Lambert, Dennis

 Look In My Eyes, Pretty Woman *see
  Lambert, Dennis

 Put A Little Love Away *see Lambert,
  Dennis

 This Heart *see Lambert, Dennis

POTTLE, SAM (1934-   )
 America The Beautiful (composed with
  Hawthorne, Grace)
  (Red, Buryl) SATB TRIGON TUM 115
  $.35   (P239)
 David And Goliath (composed with
  Hawthorne, Grace)
  SATB,pno,2trp,2trom,bvl,perc,gtr,
  drums, banjo, harmonica TRIGON
  TGO 104 $1.25, ipr   (P240)
 Jabberwocky
  SATB oct TRIGON TGM 103 $.35 (P241)

 Jonah And The Whale (composed with
  Hawthorne, Grace)
  SATB,pno,bsn, trp,trom,pic,drums,
  timp, xylophone, ship bell,
  suspended cymbal TRIGON TGO 102
  $1.25, ipr   (P242)
 Living Hand In Hand *see Axelrod,
  David

 Noah And The Ark (composed with
  Hawthorne, Grace)
  SATB,pno,trp,trom,bvl,drums,timp,
  gtr, accordion, xylophone, anvil,
  vibes TRIGON TGO 101 $1.25, ipr
                                 (P243)
 Samson And Delilah (composed with
  Hawthorne, Grace)
  SATB,pno,2trp,trom,bvl,perc,drums,
  gtr, 3 saxophones TRIGON TGO 103
  $1.25, ipr   (P244)
 Shaker Patchwork *cant
  SATB,perc, pno four hands,
  especially suitable for madrigal
  groups TRIGON TGO 112 $1.50
                                 (P245)
 We'll Find America
  SATB,pno,fl/pic,2trp,2trom,bvl,
  perc,drums,gtr TRIGON TGM 101
  $.35   (P246)

POULENC, FRANCIS (1899-1963)
 Clic, Clac, Dansez Sabots
  "Click, Clack, Wooden Shoes Dance"
  [Fr/Eng] TBB,acap SALABERT-US
  $.65   (P247)

 Click, Clack, Wooden Shoes Dance
  *see Clic, Clac, Dansez Sabots

 La Belle Se Sied Au Pied De La Tour
  "Maiden By The Tower, The" [Fr/Eng]
  SATBB,acap SALABERT-US $.45
                                 (P248)
  (Frank, Marcel) "Maiden By The
  Tower, The" 2pt treb cor
  SALABERT-US   (P249)

 Maiden By The Tower, The *see La
  Belle Se Sied Au Pied De La Tour

 Margoton *see Margoton Va T'A L'Iau

 Margoton Va T'A L'Iau
  "Margoton" [Fr/Eng] SATB,acap
  SALABERT-US $.65   (P250)

 Marianita
  (Chailley) SSAA,acap SALABERT-US
  $.35   (P251)
  (Chailley) SATB,acap SALABERT-US
  $.35   (P252)

 Night Of Snow *see Un Soir De Neige

 Troyak
  (Chailley) SATB,acap SALABERT-US
  $.60   (P253)

POULENC, FRANCIS (cont'd.)

Un Soir De Neige *cant
"Night Of Snow" [Fr/Eng] SSATBB,
acap SALABERT-US $2.50   (P254)

POVEST O LENINOVI see Felix, Vaclav

POVIDAM, POVIDAM POHADKU see Hanus, Jan

POVSTANIE see Zimmer, Jan

POWELL, ROBERT
Come Let Us Join
SATB (easy) FISCHER,C CM 7823 $.30
(P255)

Hosea!
cor (easy) FISCHER,C CM 7833 $.35
(P256)

POWER OF MUSIC, THE see Bitgood

POWERS
Let's Get Together
(Lojeski, Ed) SSA LEONARD-US
08237302 $.50   (P257)
(Lojeski, Ed) SATB LEONARD-US
08237300 $.50   (P258)

POWERS, ANTHONY
This Enders Night *carol
SATB,acap NOVELLO MT 1579 s.p.
(P259)

POZDRAV see Urbanec, Bartolomej

POZDRAV DO MOSKVY see Hirner, Teodor

POZDRAV KRAJINE VITAZSTVA see Korinek,
Miloslav

POZDRAV MOSKVE see Vignati, Milos

POZDRAV - PRISAHA see Simek, Miroslav

POZDRAV STRANE see Stanislav, Josef

POZDRAV VELKEJ ZEMI see Kardos, Dezider

PRACI CEST see Riha, Oldrich

PRACTICAL EARTH SATELLITES see Weigl,
Vally

PRAETORIUS, MICHAEL (1571-1621)
Der Tag Vertreibt Die Dunkle Nacht
SATB,acap BAREN. BCH45 s.p.
contains also: Walter (Walther),
Johann, All Morgen Ist Ganz
Frisch Und Neu (SA&unis men cor,
acap)   (P260)

PRAIRIE SONG
(Sateren, Leland) SATB,acap ART MAST
1034 $.30   (P261)

PRAISE see Curwin, Clifford

PRAISE TO MUSIC see Distler, Hugo, Lob
Auf Die Musik

PRAPOR MIRU NAD DUKLOU see Vomacka,
Boleslav

PRASIL, FRANTISEK (1902-   )
Balada Slovenskych Hor
see Detsky Zbory

Detsky Zbory
wom cor SLOV.HUD.FOND s.p.
contains: Balada Slovenskych Hor;
Do Skoly; Dobry Den; Nevydam Sa
Za Slimaka; Pri Tabourku (P262)

Do Skoly
see Detsky Zbory

Dobry Den
see Detsky Zbory

Nevydam Sa Za Slimaka
see Detsky Zbory

Pri Tabourku
see Detsky Zbory

Slovensko
see MUZSKE ZBORY I

PRATELLA, FRANCESCO BALILLA (1880-1955)
Al Fugaren
(Negri, A.) "Le Focarine" 2pt
BONGIOVANI 1656 s.p. see from
Canti Romagnole Vol. I (Op. 43)
(P263)

Canta La Cicala
STB voc pt BONGIOVANI 2011 s.p.
(P264)

Cante Romagnole Vol. I (Op. 43)
*CC9L
(Negri, A.) 2pt BONGIOVANI 300 s.p.
text in Romagnese dilect with the
Italian version also   (P265)

Cante Romagnole Vol. II (Op. 49)
*CC9L
(Negri, A.) 2pt BONGIOVANI 1516
s.p. text in Romagnese dialect

PRATELLA, FRANCESCO BALILLA (cont'd.)

with the Italian also   (P266)

Cante Romagnole Vol. III (Op. 51)
*CC7L
(Negri, A.) 2pt BONGIOVANI 1671
s.p. text in Romagnese dialect
with the Italian also
see also: E' Bal D' La Viniziena,
"Il Ballo Della Veneziana"; La
Chenta 'D Iomla, "La Canta
D'Imola"; La Lezione Dello
Spiantatoio; La Sisa   (P267)

Canti Fanciulleschi E Laudi *CCU
cor,pno/harmonium voc pt BONGIOVANI
2158 s.p.   (P268)

Canti Popolari Italiani Di Regioni
Deverse *CCU
cor voc pt BONGIOVANI 1929 s.p.
(P269)

Canti Romagnole Vol. I (Op. 43) *see
Al Fugaren, "Le Focarine"; La
Fasulera, "La Fagiolata"; Nina
Nana, "Ninna Nanna"   (P270)

Canti Romagnole Vol. II (Op. 49 *see
E Triscon, "Il Trescone"; La
Canta Dla Puvida, "La Canta Della
Pipita"; La Casteina Bienca, "La
Casina Bianca"; Premavera,
"Primavera"   (P271)

E' Bal D' La Viniziena
(Negri, A.) "Il Ballo Della
Veneziana" STB voc pt BONGIOVANI
1959 s.p. see also Cante
Romagnole Vol. III (Op. 51)
(P272)

E Triscon
(Negri, A.) "Il Trescone" 2pt voc
pt BONGIOVANI 2138 s.p. see from
Canti Romagnole Vol. II (Op. 49
(P273)

Girometa
STTB voc pt BONGIOVANI 1929 s.p.
(P274)

Gli Scariolanti
STB voc pt BONGIOVANI 1964 s.p.
(P275)

Il Ballo Della Veneziana *see E' Bal
D' La Viniziena

Il Soldato Prigioniero
STB voc pt BONGIOVANI 2009 s.p.
(P276)

Il Trescone *see E Triscon

La Canta Della Pipita *see La Canta
Dla Puvida

La Canta D'Imola *see La Chenta 'D
Iomla

La Canta Dla Puvida
(Negri, A.) "La Canta Della Pipita"
2pt BONGIOVANI 1669 s.p. see from
Canti Romagnole Vol. II (Op. 49
(P277)

La Canzone Del Sonno
STB voc pt BONGIOVANI 2164 s.p.
(P278)

La Casina Bianca *see La Casteina
Bienca

La Casteina Bienca
(Negri, A.) "La Casina Bianca" 2pt
BONGIOVANI 1667 s.p. see from
Canti Romagnole Vol. II (Op. 49
(P279)

La Chenta 'D Iomla
(Negri, A.) "La Canta D'Imola" TB
voc pt BONGIOVANI 2006 s.p. see
also Cante Romagnole Vol. III
(Op. 51)   (P280)

La Fagiolata *see La Fasulera

La Fasulera
(Negri, A.) "La Fagiolata" 2pt
BONGIOVANI 1655 s.p. see from
Canti Romagnole Vol. I (Op. 43)
(P281)

La Lezione Dello Spiantatoio
(Negri, A.) STB voc pt BONGIOVANI
2008 s.p. see also Cante
Romagnole Vol. III (Op. 51)
(P282)

La Rondinella D'amore
STB voc pt BONGIOVANI 1958 s.p.
(P283)

La Sisa
(Negri, A.) STB voc pt BONGIOVANI
2007 s.p. see also Cante
Romagnole Vol. III (Op. 51)
(P284)

Le Focarine *see Al Fugaren

Nina Nana
(Negri, A.) "Ninna Nanna" 2pt
BONGIOVANI 1660 s.p. see from
Canti Romagnole Vol. I (Op. 43)
(P285)

PRATELLA, FRANCESCO BALILLA (cont'd.)

Ninna Nanna *see Nina Nana

Premavera
(Negri, A.) "Primavera" 2pt
BONGIOVANI 1664 s.p. see from
Canti Romagnole Vol. II (Op. 49
(P286)

Primavera *see Premavera

Serenata
STB voc pt BONGIOVANI 2010 s.p.
(P287)

PRAYER FOR AMERICA, A see Johnson, D.

PRAYER FOR PEACE
SSA CIMINO $.40   (P288)

PRAYER FOR PHILADELPHIA see Grant, W.
Parks

PRAZE see Kricka, Jaroslav

PREAMBLE see Distler, Hugo, Vorspruch

PREAMBLE TO THE CHARTER OF UNITED
NATIONS, THE see Vackar, Dalibor C.

PRED PRICHODEM RUDE ARMADY see Barvik,
Miroslav

PREGHIERA DI MARIA STUARDA see
Dallapiccola, Luigi

PREHRADA see Odstrcil, Karel

PREIS DES SCHOPFERS "TAUSENDFALTIG,
VIELGESTALTIG" see Gerster, Ottmar

PREKRASNA ZEME see Bartos, Jan Zdenek

PRELUDE AND ANGEL'S FAREWELL see Elgar,
Edward

PRELUDE AND FUGUE (FOR TONGUE-IN-CHEEK)
see Van Slyck, Nicholas

PRELUDIUM see Rodgers, Richard

PREMAVERA see Pratella, Francesco
Balilla

PREMIER MATIN see Binet

PREMIERE VIOLETTE see Bovet, G.

PRESTON
Christmas In Scandinavia *sac
SA/TB SHAWNEE E142 $.45   (P289)

PRETTY LITTLE BABY see Martin

PRETTY SARO *folk,Nor Am
(Vance, Margaret Shelley) SATB BELWIN
OCT 2336 $.30   (P290)

PRI TABOURKU see Prasil, Frantisek

PRICE, FLORENCE B. (1888-1953)
I Like The Sound Of America *cant
jr cor LEXICON 37669 $1.95   (P291)

PRIDDY
Sea Of Forever
(Albam) SATB WALTON 9080 $.45
(P292)

PRIESING
Now Is The Carolling Season
(Coates) TTBB SHAWNEE 237 $.35
(P293)
(Coates) SSA,acap SHAWNEE B389 $.35
(P294)
(Coates) SAB SHAWNEE D184 $.35
(P295)

PRILRETELA POD OKENKO see Svobodo, Jiri

PRIMA TUAE MENTI VENIAT see Schultz,
Svend S.

PRIMAVERA see Clarke, Henry Leland

PRIMAVERA see Pratella, Francesco
Balilla, Premavera

PRIMAVERA VENIENTE see Cremesini, M.

PRIME see Evett, Robert

PRINTEMPS see Beguelin

PRINTEMPS see De Sutter, J.Toussaint

PRINTEMPS SUR L'ALPE see Carrard

PRINZ EUGEN, DER EDLE RITTER see
Silcher, Friedrich

PRIPITOK see Mikula, Zdenko

PRIRODE see Matys, Jiri

PRISMA see St. Fauth, Ulrich

PRO REGE NOSTRA see Willan, Healey

PROCACCINI, T. (1934-   )
La Pesta Di Atene Da "De Rerum
Natura"
cor,3fl,2ob,3clar,2bsn,4horn,3trp,
3trom,tuba,timp,perc CARISH
rental   (P296)

PROCTER, LELAND
Canticle Of The Sun *cant
SATB,org AM.COMP.AL. $12.10 (P297)

PRODRAV SOVETSKEMU SVAZU see Barvik,
Miroslav

PROKOFIEV, SERGE (1891-1953)
Midnight Sleigh Bells
(Hebble) SATB SHAWNEE A1296 $.35
(P298)

PROLOGUE "SOOMER IS I-COOMEN IN" see
Tippett, Michael

PROMENADE EN FORET see Massis, Amable

PROMISE, THE see Kuksa, Emanuel, Slib

PROMISED LAND, THE *folk/medley,US
(Red, Buryl) SATB TRIGON TGO 109
$1.25   (P299)

PRONK, ARIE
Duizend Fragen
mix cor sc HEER 1523 s.p. (P300)

Eens Zal Op De Grote Morgen
mix cor sc HEER 1516 s.p. (P301)

Waarom Toch?
mix cor s.p. sc HEER 1515, cor pts
HEER 1515A   (P302)

PROS ROMAIOUS see Dijk, Jan van

PROSPECTS see Trifunovic, Vitomir,
Vidici

PROTEST, A see Huntley, Fred H.

PROTHEROE, DANIEL (1866-1934)
Awake! The Morning Dawns
SAB (med) FITZSIMONS 6003 $.20
(P303)

By And Bye *sac/sec
TTBB,acap (med) FITZSIMONS 4039
$.25   (P304)

Come, Night!
SSA (med) FITZSIMONS 3043 $.25
(P305)

Daphne's Cheeks
TTBB,acap (med) FITZSIMONS 4018
$.25   (P306)

Diamond Dew, The
SA (easy) FITZSIMONS 3006 $.20
(P307)

Dipping In The Milky Way
SSA (easy) FITZSIMONS 3008 $.15
(P308)

Goodnight Beloved
SATB (med) FITZSIMONS 1030 $.25
(P309)
SSA (med) FITZSIMONS 3041 $.20
(P310)

Grouch, The
TTBB (med) FITZSIMONS 4024 $.25
(P311)

Longing For Virginny
TTBB (easy) FITZSIMONS 4009 $.20
(P312)

Out In The Fields *sac/sec,Xmas
TTBB,acap (easy) FITZSIMONS 4013
$.25   (P313)
SAB (easy) FITZSIMONS 6004 $.20
(P314)

Pep Song, A
TTBB (easy) FITZSIMONS 4023 $.25
(P315)

Pirates, The
unis (med) FITZSIMONS 3007 $.20
(P316)
TB (easy) FITZSIMONS 4032 $.20
(P317)

Sea Maidens, The
SA (easy) FITZSIMONS 3002 $.20
(P318)

Seascape, A
SSAATTBB (med) FITZSIMONS 1026 $.20
(P319)

Song Of The Adventurers
TTBB (easy) FITZSIMONS 4041 $.25
(P320)

Song Of The Marching Men
SATB (med) FITZSIMONS 1016 $.25
(P321)
TTBB (med) FITZSIMONS 4004 $.25
(P322)

Song Of The Road, A
TTBB,acap (easy) FITZSIMONS 4006
$.20   (P323)

Song Of The Waves, The
TTBB (med) FITZSIMONS 4012 $.25
(P324)

PROTHEROE, DANIEL (cont'd.)
Song Of The Western Men
TTBB (easy) FITZSIMONS 4001 $.20
(P325)

Spider And The Fly, The *cant
SA,inst FITZSIMONS cor pts $.40, sc
ipr   (P326)

Springtime Is Calling
SSA (med) FITZSIMONS 3016 $.20
(P327)

Strawberry Fair
SSA (med) FITZSIMONS 3009 $.25
(P328)

PROUD MAISIE see Lawson, Malcolm

PROUDHONIA see Autunes, Jorge

PROVAZNIK, ANATOL (1887-1950)
Ceske Tance *CCU
[Czech] mix cor,2fl,2ob,2clar,2bsn,
4horn,2trp,3trom,tuba,timp,perc,
strings CZECH s.p.   (P329)

Osm Zenskych Sboru *CC8U
[Czech] wom cor,acap CZECH s.p.
(P330)

Sedm Muzskych Sboru *CC7U
[Czech] men cor,acap CZECH s.p.
(P331)

PROVERBIAL MUSIC see Russell

PROVERBS see Stoker, Richard

PRSTYNKY see Bohac, Josef

PRUNE SONG, THE *folk,US
(Archibeque, Charlene) SATB,acap
NATIONAL WHC-17 $.25   (P332)

PSALM OF LIFE, A see Peele, Dudley

PSANO NA LIST KALENDARE see Bartos, Jan
Zdenek

PSI SUITA - ZPIVAJICI PSICI PRI MESICI
see Valek, Jiri

PUBLICATIONS OF THE MUSICAL ANTIQUARIAN
SOCIETY *sac/sec,CCU
microfiche UNIV.MUS.ED. $80.00 (1840-
1848) 19 volumes. Editors include:
Rimbault, Edward F.; Smart, Sir
George; McFarren, G. Alex; Hopkins,
Edward J. and others   (P333)

PUBLIKATIONEN AELTERER PRAKTISCHER UND
THEORETISCHER MUSIKWERKE *sac/sec,
CCU,16-17th cent
(Eitner, Robert) microfiche
UNIV.MUS.ED. $150.00 (1873-1905) 29
volumes   (P334)

PUER FALERNI see Edler, Robert

PUER NATUS EST *sac/sec,CCU,Xmas,carol
(Kox, Hans) cor,2fl,2ob,2bsn,4horn,
2trp,strings,harp DONEMUS   (P335)

PUES QUE JAMAIS OLVIDAROS see Encina,
Juan Del

PUGET, P.
Le Retour Des Hirondelles
2 eq voices,pno JOBERT voc sc s.p.,
cor pts s.p.   (P336)

PUISQU'EN AMOUR see Sermisy, Claude de

PUJDME see Martinu, Bohuslav

PUNSCHLIED see Heun, Hans

PUNSCHLIED "VIER ELEMENTE" see Reutter,
Hermann

PUPPY LOVE see Anka, Paul

PURCELL, HENRY (ca. 1659-1695)
Come Let Us Drink! *CC57U,round
cor GALLIARD 2.9020.1 $2.95 (P337)

Come Ye Sons Of Art
(Blower) SSA,pno,4strings/orch voc
sc NOVELLO rental, ipr   (P338)
(Herrmann) SATB SCHIRM.G 2944 $2.50
(P339)
(Tippett; Bergman) "Ode For The
Birthday Of Queen Mary" cor,SAAB
soli,orch s.p. min sc SCHOTT
11080, min sc SCHOTT   (P340)

Destruction's Our Delight (from Dido
And Aeneas)
SATB EGTVED KB63 s.p.   (P341)

Fairest Isle
(Mansfield) SA CRAMER $.20 (P342)

Five Songs *CC5U
(Cooper) SATB,ST soli,strings,
cembalo voc sc NOVELLO rental,
ipr   (P343)

PURCELL, HENRY (cont'd.)
I Gave Her Cakes
see Two Carnal Catches

In These Delightful, Pleasant Groves
SATB EGTVED MS18B9 s.p.   (P344)

Man Is For The Woman Made (from Mock
Marriage, The)
(Cumming) SATB oct BOOSEY 5805 $.45
(P345)
(Ehret, Walter) SATB,pno oct ELKAN-
V 362-03194 $.40   (P346)

More Love Or More Disdain I Crave
(Rice) BRODT 593 $.22   (P347)

Music For Queen Mary II
SATB,2trp,2trom,2horn, Baritone
Horn KING,R MFB 608 cor pts $.20,
cmplt ed $1.50   (P348)

My Beloved Spake
(Dent) SATB,org,strings voc sc
NOVELLO rental, ipr   (P349)

My Heart Is Inditing
(Simkins) dbl cor,8 soli,kbd,
strings min sc SCHOTT 10304 s.p.
(P350)

Ode For St. Cecelia's Day (1692):
Hail Bright Cecilia
(Tippett; Bergman) cor,SAATBB soli,
orch min sc SCHOTT 10296 s.p.
(P351)

Ode For The Birthday Of Queen Mary
*see Come Ye Sons Of Art

Once, Twice, Thrice I Julia Tried
see Two Carnal Catches

Passing By
(Gulbrandsen) SATB,acap (easy)
FITZSIMONS 1062 $.25   (P352)

Two Carnal Catches
TTBB SCHIRM.EC 2322 s.p.
contains: I Gave Her Cakes; Once,
Twice, Thrice I Julia Tried
(P353)

Welcome To All The Pleasures
(Cooper) SATB,ATB soli,strings,cont
voc sc NOVELLO rental, ipr (P354)

With Drooping Wings (from Dido And
Aeneas)
SATB EGTVED KB64 s.p.   (P355)

PURDUE CHORAL COLLECTION *CCU
(Stewart; Luhman) SSA/SSAA SHAWNEE
GB62 $2.50   (P356)

PUT A LITTLE LOVE AWAY see Lambert,
Dennis

PUT ME ON MY BIKE, NR. 1 see Bank,
Jacques

PUT THE RIGHT MAN AT THE WHEEL see Hays

PUT YOUR HAND IN THE HAND see Mac
Lellan, Gene

PUT YOUR HEAD ON MY SHOULDER see Anka,
Paul

PUTMAN, CURLY
My Elusive Dreams (composed with
Sherrill, Billy)
(Simon, W.) SAB BIG3 $.60 (P357)
(Simon, W.) SATB BIG3 $.50 (P358)
(Simon, W.) SSA BIG3 $.50 (P359)

PUTNAM
City Lights
(Plank) SSAATTBB,acap KENDOR $.35
(P360)

PUTTING IT OFF see Jeffries

PUTZ, EDUARD
Johnny John
men cor,acap TONOS 426 s.p. (P361)

PYGOTT
Quid Petis O Fili
(Deller) SSA SCHIRM.G 12045 $.60
(P362)

PYLE, FRANCIS [JOHNSON] (1901-   )
Sail Forth
SATB,acap DEAN CB-804 $.55 (P363)

Q

QUAL CERVO ERRANDO see Virchi, P.

QUAND AU BOIS S'EN VA JOUER see
  Blanchard, Roger

QUAND J'ETAIS JEUNE *folk,Fr
  (Blanchard, R.) 4pt mix cor,acap
  JOBERT s.p.   (Q1)

QUAND LE MUGUET FLEURIRA see Strimer,
  Joseph

QUAND L'ELEPHANT JOUE DE LA TROMPETTE
  see Berthomieu, Marc

QUANDO V'ODO PARLAR SI DOLCEMENTE see
  Veneziani, Vittore

QUANGLE WANGLE'S HAT see Claflin, Avery

QUARREL, THE see Burnham

QUARTAR see Ronnefeld, Peter

QUARTETT see Villa-Lobos, Heitor

QUARTETTO A CANZONE see Costa

QUASI MODO see Binkerd, Gordon

QUATRE POEMES see Piantoni

QUATTORDICI CANTI INTERNAZIONALI
  *CC14U
  (Casagrande, Efrem) men cor ZANIBON
  5293 s.p.   (Q2)

QUATTRO CORI PER FANCIULLI see Veretti,
  Antonio

QUATTRO SUITES (I & II) see Girotto,
  Almerigo

QUATTRO SUITES (III & IV) see Girotto,
  Almerigo

QUATTUOR FRAGMENTA EX OVIDII ARS AMANDI
  see Schultz, Svend S.

QUE NE VOUS PLAIT-IL, NOTRE DAME? see
  Blanchard, Roger

QUELLA CETRA see Beethoven, Ludwig van

QUELL'AUGELLIN CHE CANTA see Ercolano,
  T.

QUELLE EST CETTE ODEUR?
  see Eight Christmas Carols, Set 2

QU'ES DE TI, DESCONSOLADO? see Encina,
  Juan Del

QUEST OF THE QUEER PRINCE, THE see
  Hyde, Herbert E.

QUESTA ORDI IL LACCIO see Monteverdi,
  Claudio

QUESTIONS see Brahms, Johannes, Fragen

QUESTIONS see Cohen

QUESTIONS see Payne, Warren

QUI IUSTUS EST, LUSTIFICATUR ADHUC see
  Mannecke, Daniel

QUIBUS, QUABUS see Keller, Wilhelm

QUICK TO THE DEAD, THE see Vomacka,
  Boleslav

QUID PETIS O FILI see Pygott

QUIEN TE TRAJO, CABALLERO? see Encina,
  Juan Del

QUIET SOUNDS see Milidantri

QUO PINUS see Schultz, Svend S.

QUO VADIS see Dyson, George

QUODLIBET FOR SINGERS see Childs,
  Barney

R

RACA PLAVA PO DRAVI see Lucic, Franjo

RACCOLTA CORALE LIBRO V: CANTE IN CORO
  DELLA VECCHIA ROMAGNA *CC15L
  4pt mix cor BONGIOVANI 1567 s.p.   (R1)

RACCONTO I see Benevenuti, Arrigo

RACHMANINOFF, SERGEY VASSILIEVITCH
  (1873-1943)
  Soft Hills And Soothing Wind *Op.34,
  No.14
  (Sateren, Leland B.) SATB,pno ART
  MAST 1022 $.40   (R2)

RACINE KANTATE see Genzmer, Harald

RADERMACHER, FRIEDRICH (1924-   )
  Bauernkalender
  4pt men cor,A solo,orch cor pts
  GERIG AV 110 s.p., sc GERIG
  rental, ipr   (R3)

  Mann Im Monde "Lieber Mann Im Monde"
  men cor sc SCHOTTS CHBL 143 s.p.
                                     (R4)

  Von Den Wolken *CCU
  4pt men cor,horn,trp,trom GERIG
  AV 111 rental   (R5)

RADIC, DUSAN (1929-   )
  Beseiged Serenity *see Opsednuta
  Vedrina

  Opsednuta Vedrina
  "Beseiged Serenity" SAT,2pno,
  strings,4timp,perc, vibraphone
  MUSIC INFO rental   (R6)

RADICA, RUBEN (1931-   )
  Interferentions For Elocutionist,
  Choir And Orchestra
  cor,narrator,pno,3fl,3ob,3clar,
  3bsn,2horn,2trp,trom,tuba,
  strings,perc,timp,harp, 2
  saxophones, celeste, xylophone,
  vibraphone CROATICA   (R7)

RADIOLAND *gospel/medley
  (Red, Buryl) SATB TRIGON TGO 106
  $1.25   (R8)

RADLERS SELIGKEIT see Biebl, Franz

RADOST A PRACE see Janacek, Karel

RADULESCU, HORATIU (1942-   )
  Doesn't Anything Whereto?
  cor, composer and 23 children
  MODERN s.p., rental   (R9)

RAFFMAN, RELLY
  Three Ravens, The
  [Eng] SATB,acap BROUDE BR. $.50
                                     (R10)

  Virtue
  [Eng] SATB,acap BROUDE BR. $.40
                                     (R11)

RAICHL, MIROSLAV (1930-   )
  Verse Psane Na Vodu
  "Verses Written For Water" [Czech]
  wom cor,pno CZECH s.p.   (R12)

  Verses Written For Water *see Verse
  Psane Na Vodu

RAILWAY PARABLE, THE see Hoffding,
  Finn, Das Eisenbahngleichnis

RAIN SLIPPERS see Warren, Elinor Remick

RAINBOW GIRL see Davis

RAINBOW 'ROUND MY SHOULDER
  (De Cormier) TTBB SCHIRM.G LG51757
  $.40   (R13)

RAISE A RUCKUS
  (Van Wyatt) 2pt treb cor&Bar,pno,tamb
  PRO ART 2780 $.40   (R14)

RAJTER, LUDOVIT (1906-   )
  Hore Hu!
  men cor SLOV.HUD.FOND s.p.   (R15)

RALEIGH
  Laughing On The Outside (Crying On
  The Inside) (composed with Wayne)
  (Slater) SATB,opt perc WARNER
  CH0789 $.50   (R16)
  (Slater) SSA,opt perc WARNER CQ0789
  $.50   (R17)

RALSTON, A.
  Man In A Crane *see Bush, N.

RALSTON, A. (cont'd.)
  Motorway *see Bush, N.

  Regent's Canal *see Bush, N.

  Three Two-Part Songs For Children
  *see Bush, N.

RAMBLIN' MAN see Betts

RAMEAU, JEAN-PHILIPPE (1683-1764)
  Complete Works *sac/sec,CCU
  (Saint-Saens, Camille; Malherbe,
  Ch.; Emmanuel, M.; Teneo, M.)
  microfiche UNIV.MUS.ED. $220.00
  originally published in 18
  volumes, A. Durand, Paris 1895-
  1913.   (R18)

  Naissez Dons De Flore
  wom cor,acap HENN 414 s.p.   (R19)

RANDL
  Singing A Happy Song (composed with
  Jerome)
  (Ades) SATB SHAWNEE A1306 $.45
                                     (R20)
  (Ades) SA/TB SHAWNEE E162 $.45
                                     (R21)
  (Ades) SAB SHAWNEE D193 $.45   (R22)
  (Ades) SSA SHAWNEE B401 $.45   (R23)

RANKI, GYORGY (1907-   )
  Fenyben Furdik A Fold
  (Raics, Istvan) mix cor BUDAPEST
  7513 s.p.   (R24)

  Kodaly Emlekezete
  (Szabolcsi) wom cor&mix cor, cymbal
  BUDAPEST 6966 s.p.   (R25)

RAPHLING, SAM (1910-   )
  Back Yard
  SATB,acap GENERAL 774CH $.50 see
  from Four Chicago Poems By Carl
  Sandburg   (R26)

  Four Chicago Poems By Carl Sandburg
  *see Back Yard; Halstead Street
  Car; Mamie; Under A Telephone
  Pole   (R27)

  Halstead Street Car
  SATB,acap GENERAL 773CH $.50 see
  from Four Chicago Poems By Carl
  Sandburg   (R28)

  Mamie
  SATB,acap GENERAL 772CH $.60 see
  from Four Chicago Poems By Carl
  Sandburg   (R29)

  Under A Telephone Pole
  SATB,acap GENERAL 775CH $.50 see
  from Four Chicago Poems By Carl
  Sandburg   (R30)

RAPOSO, JOE
  Bein' Green
  (Barduhn, Dave) SATB,pno,inst
  (jazz, includes recording and 14
  choral octavos) LEONARD-US
  07250440 $14.95   (R31)

  Sing (from Sesame Street) pop
  (Cleveland) TTBB/TB/TTB WARNER
  WB-313 188 $.35   (R32)
  (Cleveland) SSA,opt fl WARNER
  WB-312 183 $.35   (R33)
  (Lee) SAB WARNER CG0339 $.40   (R34)

  You Will Be My Music
  (Shay) SATB WARNER WB-379 $.35
                                     (R35)

RAPSODIA see Brahms, Johannes,
  Rhapsodie "Aber Abseits Wer Ist's"

RAPT AM I, DEAR LOVE, WITH YOUR SWEET
  GLANCE see Franck, Melchior, Mich
  Erfreut, Schons Lieb, Dein Uneblick

RAR'ANCORA see Bussotti, Sylvano

RARELY see Chavez, Carlos

RASCEL, R.
  Arrivederci, Roma
  (Simon, W.) SATB BIG3 $.40   (R36)
  (Simon, W.) SSA BIG3 $.40   (R37)

RASCH, HUGO
  Der Jager
  men cor cor pts RIES s.p. contains
  also: Verschmolzene Herzen   (R38)

  Verschmolzene Herzen
  see Rasch, Hugo, Der Jager

RASELY
  Childhood Is A Good Time
  SATB KENDOR $.35   (R39)

  Hope Is The Thing With Feathers
  see Two Songs Of Hope

RASELY (cont'd.)

    Life Songs (from Choral Symphony No.
      1)
      SATB,opt fl,drums&strings, or
      electric bass KENDOR $.40   (R40)

    Silver Bird
      see Two Songs Of Hope

    Skipping Stones
      SATB KENDOR $.30   (R41)
      SA KENDOR $.30   (R42)
      SA KENDOR $.30   (R43)

    Two Songs Of Hope
      SATB,acap KENDOR $.30
      contains: Hope Is The Thing With
      Feathers; Silver Bird   (R44)

RATAPLAN see Verdi, Giuseppe

RATHGEBER

    Singer's Creed, A
      (Trant) TTBB/ATTB,acap (easy)
      OXFORD 85.017 $.30   (R45)

RATHGEBER, VALENTIN (1682-1750)
    Alleweil Ein Wenig Lustig
      (Klink, Waldemar) mix cor (med
      easy) sc SCHOTTS C 41 391 s.p.
                           (R46)

    Die Beschwerlichkeiten Des Ehestandes
      "Wenn Ich Will Den Ehstand"
      (Klink, Waldemar) men cor sc
      SCHOTTS CHBL 192 s.p.   (R47)

    Liebe Leut, Ich Bin Nun So
      (Klink, Waldemar) SSAA,acap (med
      easy) sc SCHOTTS CHBL 387 s.p.
                           (R48)

    Ohrenvergnugendes Und
      Gemuthergotzendes Tafelkonfekt
      *CCU
      jr cor (med) cloth SCHOTTS
      BSS 36 781 L s.p.   (R49)

    Von Der Edlen Musik "Der Hat
      Vergeben"
      (Klink, Waldemar) mix cor (med
      easy) sc SCHOTTS CHBL 270 s.p.
                           (R50)
      (Lang, Hans) mix cor (med easy) sc
      SCHOTTS CHBL 330 s.p.   (R51)

    Wir Haben Drei Katzen
      (Klink, Waldemar) mix cor (med
      easy) sc SCHOTTS CHBL 388 s.p.
                           (R52)

RAUCH, ANDREAS
    All Lust Und Freud
      see Lechner, Leonhard, Gut Singer
      Und Ein Organist

    Hat Korismu *CCU
      (Jancsovics, Antal; Kistetenyi,
      Melinda) men cor BUDAPEST 7319
      s.p.   (R53)

    Nyolc Korusmu
      (Jancsovics, Antal; Kistetenyi,
      Melinda) eq voices BUDAPEST 6923
      s.p.   (R54)

RAULSTON
    Spirit And Celebration
      (Burden, James) SATB CHARTER
      CO30205   (R55)

    Time Is My Friend
      (Burden, James) SATB CHARTER
      CO30203   (R56)
      (Burden, James) SSA CHARTER CO30210
                           (R57)

RAUSCH "RAUSCH, MEIN RIESIGER" see
    Koelble, Fritz

RAUTAVAARA, EINOJUHANI (1928-   )
    Herran Rukous *Op.79
      [Finn] SATB,acap FAZER 42 s.p.
                           (R58)

RAVEN DAYS, THE see Bliss, M.

RAVOSA
    Mister Snow's Shoes *sac
      (Coates) SA/TB SHAWNEE E150 $.35
                           (R59)

    Story Songs *CCU
      unis SHAWNEE GF63 $3.00   (R60)

RAXACH, ENRIQUE (1932-   )
    Interface (from Esoteric Garden, The)
      mix cor,pno,2Hamm,3fl,3ob,4clar,
      3bsn,4horn,3trp,3trom,tuba,4perc,
      electronic tape, electric guitar
      and electric double bass DONEMUS
                           (R61)

RAYE
    Boogie Woogie Bugle Boy
      (Prince; Metis) SATB MCA UC 658
      $.40   (R62)
      (Prince; Metis) SSA MCA UC 657 $.40
                           (R63)

    I'll Remember April
      (De Paul; Johnston) SSA BELWIN
      UC 700 $.40   (R64)

RAYE (cont'd.)

    (De Paul; Johnston) SATB BELWIN
      UC 699 $.40   (R65)

RAYMOND, FRED (1900-1954)
    Komm, Trink Und Lach Am Rhein! "Ich
      Liebte Vor Jahren Ein Madchen"
      (Esdorf, Peter) men cor sc SCHOTTS
      C 33 722 s.p.   (R66)

RAZ A DVA see Holoubek, Ladislav

REACH OUT AND TOUCH (SOMEBODY'S HAND)
    SAB SCREEN 1420RC3   (R67)
    SA SCREEN 1420RC5   (R68)
    SATB,pno,opt bvl&drums&gtr SCREEN
      1420RC7   (R69)
    SSA,pno,opt bvl&drums&gtr SCREEN
      1420RC8   (R70)

READ, GARDNER (1913-   )
    Merry Madrigal, A
      SSSSAA,acap (med) FITZSIMONS 3057
      $.25   (R71)
      SSATB (med) FITZSIMONS 1080 $.25
                           (R72)

REAKES, BRIAN
    Pipers Answer, The
      unis EMI   (R73)

REAKS
    Holiday In Spain
      see Time For Travel

    Sea Cruise
      see Time For Travel

    Time For Travel
      unis (easy) OXFORD 81.142 $.50
      contains: Holiday In Spain; Sea
      Cruise   (R74)

REAL NICE CLAMBAKE, A
    SATB CIMINO $.40   (R75)
    SSA CIMINO $.40   (R76)
    SAB CIMINO $.40   (R77)
    SA CIMINO $.40   (R78)
    TTBB CIMINO $.40   (R79)

REANEY, JAMES
    Sleeping Giant *see Kunz, Alfred

REBENLAND see Edler, Robert

RECHENSTUNDE "ZWEI UND ZWEI SIND VIER"
    see Genzmer, Harald

RECHNUNG see Genzmer, Harald

RECLI, GIULIA
    Crespuscolo
      4pt mix cor sc BONGIOVANI 1820 s.p.
                           (R80)

    Voci Di Laguna
      4pt mix cor sc BONGIOVANI 1821 s.p.
                           (R81)
RED ARMY see Dobias, Vaclav, Ruda
    Armada

RED, BURYL
    If We Don't Make It Work, Who Will?
      (from Revolutionary Times)
      (composed with Hawthorne, Grace)
      SAB/SA oct TRIGON TGM 108 $.40
                           (R82)

    Patriot's Dream, The
      SATB oct TRIGON TGM 104 $.35   (R83)

    Revolutionary Ideas (composed with
      Hawthorne, Grace)
      SAB/SA,narrator,kbd,fl,opt pic,ob,
      clar,bsn/vcl,trp,trom,opt bvl,
      perc,opt drums,opt gtr, opt tenor
      sax (concert musical) TRIGON
      TGO 111 $2.50, ipr   (R84)

    Sea Of Liberty (from Revolutionary
      Ideas) (composed with Hawthorne,
      Grace)
      SAB/SA oct TRIGON TGM 106 $.40
                           (R85)

    Summer Soldier (from Revolutionary
      Ideas) (composed with Hawthorne,
      Grace)
      SAB/SA oct TRIGON TGM 107 $.40
                           (R86)
RED FLAG, THE see Seidel, Jan, Rudy
    Prapor

RED SARAFAN, THE see Warlamoff

REDA, SIEGFRIED (1916-1968)
    Die Schaukel
      SATB,acap BAREN. BA3854 s.p.
      contains also: Pfirischblute
                           (R87)

    Jenseits Des Grunen Meeres
      SATB,acap BAREN. BA3855 s.p.   (R88)

    Pfirischblute
      see Reda, Siegfried, Die Schaukel

REDDING, OTIS
    Sittin' On The Dock Of The Bay *pop
      (Lojeski, Ed) SATB LEONARD-US
      08256700 $.50   (R89)
      (Lojeski, Ed) SSA LEONARD-US
      08256702 $.50   (R90)

REDMAN, REGINALD
    Three Country West Idylls *CC3U
      SATB,timp,pno,strings voc sc
      NOVELLO rental, ipr   (R91)

REED, ALFRED (1921-   )
    Testament Of An American
      SATB,pno/org,band/orch BELWIN 2311
      $.40, ipa   (R92)

REED, PHYLLIS LUIDENS
    I Have A Dream
      SATB GALAXY 1.2549.1 $.30   (R93)

REGARDS TO BORGE see Holm, Peder, Hils
    Borge

REGEN *folk
    (Koringer, Franz) mix cor DOBLINGER
      G 708 s.p. see from Funf Satze Nach
      Kroatischen Volksliedern   (R94)

REGEN-SOMMER "NASSER STAUB AUF ALLEN
    WEGEN see Hessenberg, Kurt

REGENT'S CANAL see Bush, N.

REGER, MAX (1873-1916)
    Abendlied
      see Drei Chore

    Drei Chore
      mix cor,pno (med) sc,voc pt SCHOTTS
      ED 4233 s.p.
      contains: Abendlied, Op.6,No.3;
      Trost, Op.6,No.1; Zur Nacht,
      Op.6,No.2   (R95)

    Trost
      see Drei Chore

    Zur Nacht
      see Drei Chore

REGI MESTEREK EGYNEMUKARAI VII see
    Szekeres, Ferenc

REGI MESTEREK VEGYESKARAI XVII see
    Szekeres, Ferenc

REGI MESTEREK VEGYESKARAI XVIII see
    Szekeres, Ferenc

REGI MESTERK VEGYESKARAI XIX see
    Szekeres, Ferenc

REGI MESTERK VEGYESKARAI XX see
    Szekeres, Ferenc

REGI MESTERK VEGYESKARAI XXI see
    Szekeres, Ferenc

REGNARD, JACOB (ca. 1540-1599)
    Now Am I Free *see Nun Bin Ich
      Einmal Frei

    Nun Bin Ich Einmal Frei
      (Malin, Don) "Now Am I Free" SSA
      BELWIN 2297 $.35   (R96)

    Wenn Ich Gedenk
      (Weber, W.) men cor,acap TONOS 3321
      s.p.   (R97)

REGNDROPPEN see Johansen, Sven-Erik

REGNER, HERMANN (1928-   )
    Chorstudien *CCU
      mix cor/eq voices (med) sc SCHOTTS
      WKS 11 s.p.   (R98)

REGNEY, NOEL
    Sweet, Sweet, Sweet Little Jesus
      (composed with Shayne, Gloria)
      (Ehret, Walter) SATB,pno oct REGENT
      R-108 $.25   (R99)

REGRUTSKY see Mikula, Zdenko

REHBERG
    Chant Du Pacte Du Premier Aout
      men cor,acap HENN 355 s.p.   (R100)

REICHARDT
    Fichtelgebirgslied
      (Schonauer, Heinrich) men cor,acap
      TONOS 256 s.p.   (R101)

REICHARDT, JOHANN FRIEDRICH (1752-1814)
    Heilige Nacht "Heilige Nacht Der
      Unendlichen Liebe" *Xmas
      (Klink, Waldemar) jr cor/wom cor
      (easy) sc SCHOTTS CHBL 508 s.p.
                           (R102)

REIGEN DER VERSCHMAHTEN MADCHEN "SWAZ
    HIE GAT UMBE" see Werdin, Eberhard

REIM DICH OD'R ICH FRESS DICH see
Schneider, Walther

REIME UND SPIELLIEDER see Orff, Carl

REIN, WALTER (1893-1955)
Ade Zur Guten Nacht
men cor sc SCHOTTS CHBL 16 s.p.
(R103)

Alles Ist Liebe *cant
1-3pt jr cor&3pt wom cor&6pt mix
cor,fl,ob,clar,bsn,horn,trp,
strings, opt glockenspiel,
triangel (med) sc,cor pts SCHOTTS
ED. 4527 s.p.   (R104)

Alte Weiber "'Sist Nichts Mit Den
Alten Weibern"
men cor sc SCHOTTS C 37 695 s.p.
(R105)

Auf Der Gartenbank "Ei Was Mag Denn
Das Da Sein"
men cor sc SCHOTTS C 39 617 s.p.
see from Funf Mannerchore (R106)

Aufregung Im Huhnerhof "Der Tag
Bricht An"
jr cor (med easy) sc SCHOTTS
CHBL 560 s.p. see from Spassige
Geschichten   (R107)

Biergesangel
men cor (rondo) sc SCHOTTS C 38 623
s.p.   (R108)

Bluh Auf! "Bluh Auf, Bluh Auf,
Gefrorner Christ"
wom cor (med) sc SCHOTTS C 32 627
s.p. see from Drei Ernste Gesange (R109)

Chor Der Bauern "Wir Haben Gepfluget,
Wir Haben Gesat"
TBarB sc SCHOTTS CHBL 42 s.p. (R110)

Chor Der Kaufleute "In Rollendem
Wagen"
men cor sc SCHOTTS C 37 172 s.p.
(R111)

Dank Dir, O Licht
4pt mix cor,acap PELIKAN PE171 s.p.
(R112)

Das Echo "Wenn In Dem Tiefen Wald"
men cor,4 soli sc SCHOTTS C 38 176
s.p.   (R113)

Das Silberne Hornlein
see Der Regenbogen

Der Alte Forster Pusterich
men cor sc SCHOTTS C 38 791 s.p.
contains also: Ein Kleiner Hund
Mit Namen Fips   (R114)

Der Hufschmied "Schwarzbrauner
Hufschmied"
3pt men cor&3pt wom cor (med) sc
SCHOTTS C 37 983 s.p., cor pts
SCHOTTS C 37 984-985 s.p. (R115)

Der Liebe Ewigkeit "Die Liebe Hemmet
Nichts"
men cor sc SCHOTTS C 32 268 s.p.
(R116)

Der Liebste Buhle "Den Liebsten
Buhlen, Den Ich Han"
men cor sc SCHOTTS CHBL 4 s.p.
(R117)

Der Regenbogen
1-3pt jr cor,fl,2vln,vcl (med easy)
sc,cor pts SCHOTTS ED. 4523 s.p.,
ipa
contains: Das Silberne Hornlein;
Der Regenbogen; Esel, Esel,
Mullersknecht; Korndiebe;
Morgenbad   (R118)

Der Regenbogen
see Der Regenbogen

Der Rosengarten "Ich Weiss Ein
Garten"
men cor sc SCHOTTS C 39 616 s.p.
see from Funf Mannerchore (R119)

Der Tambour "Wenn Meine Mutter Hexen
Konnt"
men cor sc SCHOTTS C 38 477 s.p.
(R120)

Der Weinfuhrmann "Es Wollt Ein
Fuhrmann Fahren"
men cor sc SCHOTTS CHBL 130A-B s.p.
contains also: Zelter, Carl
Friedrich, Bundeslied "In Allen
Guten Stunden"   (R121)

Der Wettstreit "Mein Madchen Und Mein
Wein"
men cor&cor,opt narrator sc SCHOTTS
CHBL 62 s.p.   (R122)

Der Winter *cant
4pt mix cor&unis jr cor,ABar soli,
clar,horn,2vln,vla,vcl,bvl (med)
sc,cor pts SCHOTTS ED. 4366 s.p.,
ipa   (R123)

REIN, WALTER (cont'd.)
Die Gezeiten "Was Geboren Ward, Muss
Sterben"
wom cor (med) sc SCHOTTS C 32 626
s.p. see from Drei Ernste Gesange (R124)

Die Stadt "Am Grauen Strand, Am
Grauen Meer"
men cor sc SCHOTTS CHBL 89 s.p.
(R125)

Dies Fugenlose Geschmeide
SSATB (med easy) sc SCHOTTS
C 39 077 s.p. see from Greizer
Hochzeits-Carmina   (R126)

Drei Ernste Gesange *see Bluh Auf!
"Bluh Auf, Bluh Auf, Gefrorner
Christ"; Die Gezeiten "Was
Geboren Ward, Muss Sterben";
Herr, Schicke, Was Du Wilt (R127)

Dreimol Oms Stadele
men cor sc SCHOTTS C 39 592 s.p.
(R128)

Drunten Im Unterland
mix cor (easy) sc SCHOTTS C 39 630
s.p.   (R129)

Dunkle Wolken "Es Geht Ein Dunkle
Wolken Rein"
men cor sc SCHOTTS CHBL 17 s.p.
(R130)

Ein Kleiner Hund Mit Namen Fips
see Rein, Walter, Der Alte Forster
Pusterich

Ein Madchen Und Ein Glaschen Wein
men cor sc SCHOTTS CHBL 22 s.p.
(R131)

Es Schlaft In Allem Ding Ein Klang
men cor sc SCHOTTS C 37 891 s.p.
(R132)

Es Wollt Ein Jagerlein Jagen
3-4pt jr cor/3-4pt wom cor (med
easy) sc SCHOTTS C 39 589 s.p.
(R133)
TBarB sc SCHOTTS CHBL 5 s.p. (R134)

Esel, Esel, Mullersknecht
see Der Regenbogen

Feldeinsamkeit "Ich Ruhe Still"
men cor sc SCHOTTS CHBL 98 s.p.
(R135)

Freiheit, Die Ich Meine
4pt men cor,acap/brass sc SCHOTTS
CHBL 101 s.p.   (R136)

Funf Mannerchore *see Auf Der
Gartenbank "Ei Was Mag Denn Das
Da Sein"; Der Rosengarten "Ich
Weiss Ein Garten"; Rose Weiss,
Rose Rot; Schab Ab "Jetzt Kommt
Der Sommer In Das Land "; Warnung
"Du Hast Gesagt"   (R137)

Gegenwart "Alles Kundet Dich An"
SAT,acap (med) sc SCHOTTS C 32 752
s.p.   (R138)

Genialisches Treiben "So Walz Ich
Ohne Unterlass"
mix cor (med easy) sc SCHOTTS
C 32 751 s.p.   (R139)

Gesellen Der Nacht
1-3pt jr cor,fl,2vln,vcl (med easy)
sc,cor pts SCHOTTS ED.4510 s.p.,
ipa see from Sonne, Mond Und
Sterne   (R140)

Gluckselig Muss Man Preisen, Die
Gleiche Lieb Und Treu
mix cor (med easy) sc SCHOTTS
C 37 942 s.p. see from Greizer
Hochzeits-Carmina   (R141)

Greizer Hochzeits-Carmina *see Dies
Fugenlose Geschmeide; Gluckselig
Muss Man Preisen, Die Gleiche
Lieb Und Treu; O Schonster
Rosengarten   (R142)

Gute Nacht, O Welt
see Rein, Walter, Mag Immer Auch
Geschehen

Handwerksburschen Abschied "Es, Es,
Es Und Es"
men cor sc SCHOTTS C 39 623 s.p.
(R143)

Haus-Spruch "Wasser Rauscht Vorbei Am
Haus"
wom cor (med) sc SCHOTTS CHBL 554
s.p.   (R144)

Heija, Im Frischen Mai
men cor sc SCHOTTS C 37 694 s.p.
(R145)

Heimat *cant
men cor&jr cor/wom cor,brass/
strings sc,cor pts SCHOTTS
ED. 4512 s.p., ipa   (R146)

REIN, WALTER (cont'd.)
Herbstlied
wom cor/jr cor (med easy) sc
SCHOTTS C 39 633 s.p.   (R147)

Herr, Schicke, Was Du Wilt
wom cor (med) sc SCHOTTS C 32 628
s.p. see from Drei Ernste Gesange (R148)

Hochzeits-Madrigal "Liebe Fuhrt Durch
Nacht Und Dunkel" *Marriage,
madrigal
men cor sc SCHOTTS CHBL 63 s.p.
(R149)

Ich Wollt, Dass Ich Daheime War *mot
mix cor (med) sc SCHOTTS C 38 417
s.p.   (R150)

Jagerlied "Auf, Ihr Wilden Manner"
men cor sc SCHOTTS CHBL 18 s.p.
(R151)

Junggesellen "Fischen, Jagen,
Vogelstellen"
men cor sc SCHOTTS C 37 622 s.p.
(R152)

Kein Feuer, Keine Kohle
jr cor/wom cor (med easy) sc
SCHOTTS CHBL 517 s.p.   (R153)

Kleines Liebeslied "Wo Sind Die
Stunden Der Sussen Zeit"
men cor sc SCHOTTS CHBL 114 s.p.
(R154)

Komm, Trost Der Nacht, O Nachtigall
unis jr cor&3pt wom cor&4pt men
cor,acap/2trp,3trom,tuba (med) sc
SCHOTTS C 39 346 s.p., cor pts
SCHOTTS C 39 347-8 s.p., ipa
(R155)

Komm Trost Der Welt, Du Stille Nacht
unis jr cor&4pt men cor,acap (med
easy) sc SCHOTTS C 38 297 s.p.
(R156)

Korndiebe
see Der Regenbogen

Lasst Uns Glauben *cant
4pt mix cor&2pt jr cor,2fl,2ob,
2clar,2bsn,2horn,2trp,3trom,
strings,timp (med) sc,cor pts
SCHOTTS ED. 4232 s.p., ipr (R157)

Liebesfreud, Liebeslied (from Alles
Ist Liebe)
SSATB,acap (med easy) sc SCHOTTS
C 40 864 s.p.   (R158)

Lied Der Sonne
1-3pt jr cor,fl,2vln,vcl (med easy)
sc,cor pts SCHOTTS ED. 4509 s.p.,
ipa see from Sonne, Mond Und
Sterne   (R159)

Lied Vom Regen
3pt jr cor/3pt wom cor,acap (med
easy) sc SCHOTTS C 39 634 s.p.
(R160)

Lob Des Herings "Der Hering Ist Ein
Salzig Tier"
men cor sc SCHOTTS C 38 790 s.p.
(R161)

Mag Immer Auch Geschehen
mix cor (easy) sc SCHOTTS C 39 629
s.p. contains also: Gute Nacht, O
Welt   (R162)

Mein Sinnen Bringt Zu Ihr Mich Hin
mix cor (easy) sc SCHOTTS CHBL 264
s.p.   (R163)

Minnelied "Schon Bist Du Vor Allen"
*madrigal
men cor sc SCHOTTS CHBL 76 s.p.
(R164)

Mit Madchen Sich Vertragen
men cor (rondo) sc SCHOTTS CHBL 96
s.p.   (R165)

Morgenbad
see Der Regenbogen

Morike - Zyklus
4pt men cor,3horn (song cycle) sc,
voc pt SCHOTTS ED. 4236 s.p., ipa
(R166)

Musik Und Jagerei "Ich Setz Ein
Streit: Musik Und Jagerei"
TTBB,fl,horn,trp,2vln,vcl,opt bvl
sc,voc pt SCHOTTS ED. 4263 s.p.,
ipa   (R167)

Musikanten, Spielet Auf
3pt jr cor,pno/2vln&vcl&winds sc,
voc sc PELIKAN PE736 s.p., ipa (R168)

Muss I Denn
men cor sc SCHOTTS CHBL 8 s.p.
(R169)

Nach Gruner Farb Mein Herz Verlangt
*folk
unis jr cor&4pt men cor,acap (med
easy) sc SCHOTTS C 39 067 s.p.
(R170)
2pt jr cor&mix cor,acap (med) sc
SCHOTTS C 39 066 s.p.   (R171)

REIN, WALTER (cont'd.)

O Lamentatione! "Alte Kuhe, Faule
    Fisch"
    men cor sc SCHOTTS CHBL 19 s.p.
                                        (R172)

O Schonster Rosengarten
    mix cor (med easy) sc SCHOTTS
    C 37 943 s.p. see from Greizer
    Hochzeits-Carmina   (R173)

O Tannenbaum, Du Tragst, Ein' Grunen
    Zweig
    see Knab, Armin, So Treiben Wir Den
    Winter Aus

Onkel Mond
    1-3pt jr cor,fl,2vln,vcl (med easy)
    sc,cor pts SCHOTTS ED. 4511 s.p.
    see from Sonne, Mond Und Sterne
                                        (R174)

Rose Weiss, Rose Rot
    men cor sc SCHOTTS C 39 614 s.p.
    see from Funf Mannerchore   (R175)

Sandmannchen "Der Abendwind, Der
    Tragt Ein Kleines Reiterlein"
    jr cor (med easy) sc SCHOTTS
    CHBL 563 s.p. see from Spassige
    Geschichten   (R176)

Sangerwettstreit "Freunde, Horet
    Unser Musizieren"
    4pt men cor,4 soli,acap sc SCHOTTS
    C 39 101 s.p., cor pts SCHOTTS
    C 39 102-103 s.p.   (R177)

Schab Ab "Jetzt Kommt Der Sommer In
    Das Land "
    men cor sc SCHOTTS C 39 613 s.p.
    ooo from Funf Mannerchore   (R178)

Schwabisches Tanzlied "Rosenstock,
    Holderbluh" *folk
    men cor sc SCHOTTS C 39 593 s.p.
                                        (R179)

Sommerdorfchen "Ich Weiss Ein
    Dorfchen Voll Sonnenschein"
    men cor sc SCHOTTS C 37 890 s.p.
                                        (R180)

Sonne, Mond Und Sterne *see Gesellen
    Der Nacht; Lied Der Sonne; Onkel
    Mond   (R181)

Spassige Geschichte "Eins, Zwei,
    Drei, Hicke Hacke Heu"
    jr cor (med easy) sc SCHOTTS
    CHBL 562 s.p. see from Spassige
    Geschichten   (R182)

Spassige Geschichten *see Aufregung
    Im Huhnerhof "Der Tag Bricht An";
    Sandmannchen "Der Abendwind, Der
    Tragt Ein Kleines Reiterlein";
    Spassige Geschichte "Eins, Zwei,
    Drei, Hicke Hacke Heu"; Streit
    Zwischen Loffel Und Gabel "Herr
    Loffel Und Frau Gabel"   (R183)

Stehn Zwei Stern Am Hohen Himmel
    men cor sc SCHOTTS CHBL 15 s.p.
                                        (R184)

Streit Zwischen Loffel Und Gabel
    "Herr Loffel Und Frau Gabel"
    jr cor (med easy) sc SCHOTTS
    CHBL 561 s.p. see from Spassige
    Geschichten   (R185)

Stundenruf Des Wachters "Hort, Ihr
    Herrn" *folk
    2pt jr cor&4pt men cor,Bar solo,
    acap (easy) sc SCHOTTS CHBL 55
    s.p.   (R186)

Tanz Ruber, Tanz Nuber
    jr cor,2rec/inst (easy) sc SCHOTTS
    CHBL 504 s.p.   (R187)

Trinklied "Bruder, Lasst Uns Lustig
    Sein"
    men cor sc SCHOTTS CHBL 77 s.p.
                                        (R188)

Tu Mir Auf, Meine Taube
    men cor sc SCHOTTS C 38 742 s.p.
                                        (R189)

Turmerlied "Zum Sehen Geboren, Zum
    Schauen Bestellt"
    TTBB,3trp,3trom sc SCHOTTS C 33 559
    s.p., voc pt SCHOTTS
    C 33 560, 01-04 s.p., ipa   (R190)

Uber Die Heide Hallet Mein Schritt
    men cor sc SCHOTTS CHBL 97 s.p.
                                        (R191)

Und In Dem Schneegebirge
    TTBar/TTB,acap sc SCHOTTS CHBL 37
    s.p.
    jr cor/wom cor (easy) sc SCHOTTS
    CHBL 524 s.p.   (R193)

Wach Auf Mein Herzens Schone
    (Reichardt, J. Fr.) men cor sc
    SCHOTTS C 39 591 s.p.   (R194)

REIN, WALTER (cont'd.)

Warnung "Du Hast Gesagt"
    men cor sc SCHOTTS C 39 615 s.p.
    see from Funf Mannerchore   (R195)

Weihe Der Nacht "Nachtliche Stille,
    Heilige Fulle" *cant
    4pt mix cor&3pt jr cor,fl,4clar,
    4horn,2trp,2trom,2tuba,
    2tenorhorns, baritone horn voc
    sc,cor pts SCHOTTS ED. 4448 s.p.,
    ipa   (R196)

Wer Sich Die Musik Erkiest
    3pt jr cor/3pt wom cor&4pt men cor,
    acap (med) sc SCHOTTS 37 918
    s.p., voc pt SCHOTTS
    C 37 919A-D, 920 s.p.   (R197)

Wunderlichstes Buch Der Bucher
    men cor sc SCHOTTS C 38 480 s.p.
                                        (R198)

Zum Tanze Da Geht Ein Madel
    mix cor (easy) sc SCHOTTS CHBL 278
    s.p.   (R199)
    jr cor/wom cor (easy) sc SCHOTTS
    CHBL 523 s.p.   (R200)

Zur Ernte "Das Feld Ist Weiss"
    men cor sc SCHOTTS CHBL 39 s.p.
                                        (R201)

REINER, KAREL (1910-   )
    Bylo Jim Tisic Let *cant
    "They Were A Thousand Years Old"
    [Czech] mix cor,narrator&TBar
    soli,3fl,2ob,2clar,2bsn,4horn,
    3trp,3trom,tuba,timp,perc,harp,
    strings,celeste CZECH s.p.
                                        (R202)

They Were A Thousand Years Old *see
    Bylo Jim Tisic Let

REISELIED see Schaefers, Anton

REISERUF see Werdin, Eberhard

REITER, JOSEF (1862-1939)
    Bittgebet
    men cor,acap TONOS 5818 s.p. (R203)

REITER, SCHMUCK UND FEIN see Zoll, Paul

REITERGLUCK see Siegler, Winfried

REITERLIED see Steiner, Heinrich

REIZENDE DROHUNG *folk
    (Deutschmann, G.) [Ger] 4pt mix cor
    MERSEBURG EM9210 s.p.   (R204)

REIZENSTEIN, FRANZ (1911-1968)
    Voices Of Night *cant
    SATB,SBar soli,3fl,pic,3ob,3clar,
    3bsn,4horn,3trp,3trom,tuba,timp,
    perc,pno,strings, English horn,
    bass clarinet, contrabassoon,
    xylophone, glockenspiel, celeste
    voc sc NOVELLO rental, ipr (R205)

REJECTION see Cockshott, Gerald Wilfred

REMEMBER see Nilsson, Harry

REMEMBER ME see Stevens, Halsey

REMINISCENCES see Ladmirault, P.

REPUBLIK, MEIN VATERLAND see Lukowsky,
    Rolf

REQUIEM see Bissell, Keith W.

REQUIEM FOR EUROPE see Kox, Hans

REQUIEM FOR THE MASSES see Kirkman,
    Terry

REQUIEM FUR DIE OPFER DES KRIEGES see
    Rudzinski, Zbigniew

REQUIEM FUR EINEN JUNGEN DICHTER see
    Zimmermann, Bernd Alois

REQUIESCAT see Stoker, Richard

REST, SWEET NYMPHS see Pilkington,
    Francis

RESTA DI DARMI NOIA see Gesualdo, Don
    Carlo

RESURRECTION OF FENG-HUANG, THE see
    Johnson

RETOUR DE MELANCOLIE see Killmayer,
    Wilhelm

RETTICH, WILHELM (1892-   )
    Adelein "Wo Steht Deins Vaters Hof
    Und Haus"
    see Vier Niederlandische
    Volkslieder

RETTICH, WILHELM (cont'd.)

Das Gluck "Will Das Gluck Nach Seinem
    Sinn" *Op.118
    TTBB sc SCHOTTS C 42 091 s.p. see
    from Drei Chorlieder   (R206)

Der Fahrmann "Beim Schein Des
    Mondenlichts" *Op.118
    TTB sc SCHOTTS C 42 089 s.p. see
    from Drei Chorlieder   (R207)

Die Zeit "Seid Mir Nur Nicht Gar So
    Traurig" *Op.118
    TTB sc SCHOTTS C 42 090 s.p. see
    from Drei Chorlieder   (R208)

Drei Chorlieder *see Das Gluck "Will
    Das Gluck Nach Seinem Sinn",
    Op.118; Der Fahrmann "Beim Schein
    Des Mondenlichts", Op.118; Die
    Zeit "Seid Mir Nur Nicht Gar So
    Traurig", Op.118   (R209)

Ich Hore Horner Blasen
    men cor RIES sc s.p., voc pt s.p.
                                        (R210)

Lied Der Nachtigall "Die Nachtigall,
    Die Sang Ein Lied"
    see Vier Niederlandische
    Volkslieder

Lied Vom Haselnussstrauch "Es Sollte
    Ein Magdlein"
    see Vier Niederlandische
    Volkslieder

Minnelied "Vom Minne Bin Ich So
    Verwundt"
    see Vier Niederlandische
    Volkslieder

Niederlandische Volksliedkantate
    *cant,Dut
    men cor,ST soli,fl,clar,strings sc,
    cor pts,voc sc TONOS 4969 rental
                                        (R211)

Vier Niederlandische Volkslieder
    *folk,Neth
    SATB (med) sc,voc pt SCHOTTS
    C 40 773, C40 774A-B s.p.
    contains: Adelein "Wo Steht Deins
    Vaters Hof Und Haus", Op.116,
    No.3; Lied Der Nachtigall "Die
    Nachtigall, Die Sang Ein Lied",
    Op.116,No.2; Lied Vom
    Haselnussstrauch "Es Sollte Ein
    Magdlein", Op.116,No.4;
    Minnelied "Vom Minne Bin Ich So
    Verwundt", Op.116,No.1   (R212)

Zwei Bulgarische Volkslieder

RETURN, RETURN, MY LOVELY MAID see
    Hutcheson, Francis

RETURNS see Fiala, Petr, Navraty

RETURNS TO THE WELL see Vacek, Milos,
    Navraty Ke Studance

REUBEN AND RACHEL see Schroth, Gerhard

REUTTER, HERMANN (1900-   )
    Bauernhochzeit *CC8U
    mix cor,2fl,2ob,2clar,2bsn,2horn,
    strings,harp,perc (med) sc
    SCHOTTS rental, ipr   (R213)

Bettellied Sibirischer Landstreicher
    see Vier Bettellieder

Bettlerfreude
    see Vier Bettellieder

Chorfantasie *Op.52, cant
    mix cor,SBar soli,pno,2fl,2ob,
    2clar,2bsn,4horn,2trp,3trom,tuba,
    strings,harp,perc,timp, celeste
    (med) voc sc SCHOTTS ED. 2915
    s.p., cor pts SCHOTTS rental, ipr
                                        (R214)

Denken Die Himmlischen
    see Drei Madrigale

Der Abend "Senke, Strahlender Gott"
    see Triptychon

Der Gluckliche Bauer *Op.44, cant
    1-2pt mix cor&men cor,pno,2fl,
    2clar,bsn,horn,2trp,strings,perc,
    timp sc,cor pts SCHOTTS ED. 3315
    s.p., ipa   (R215)

Der Grosse Kalender *Op.43, ora
    mix cor&jr cor,SBar soli,org,2fl,
    2ob,2clar,3bsn,2horn,2trp,2trom,
    tuba,strings,2perc,5timp (med
    diff) sc SCHOTTS rental, ipr
                                        (R216)

Drei Madrigale *madrigal
    mix cor (med diff) sc SCHOTTS
    C 37 733 s.p.
    contains: Denken Die Himmlischen,
    Op.71,No.3; Nah Ist Und Schwer

RIVER SONG see Sherman, Richard M.

ROAD TO PEACE, THE see Weigl, Vally

ROAD TO VAUX see Van Grove

ROADWAYS see James, Will

ROBERT BROWN, INSTANT HERO see Arch, Gwyn

ROBERTA LEE see Whalum

ROBERTA SELECTION *CCU
  SATB CIMINO $.85   (R263)

ROBERTON
  Golden Slumbers
    SATB SCHIRM.G LG51778 $.45   (R264)

  Sing My Fair Love Good Morrow
    SATB SCHIRM.G LG51779 $.40   (R265)

ROBERTON, HUGH STEVENSON (1874-1952)
  Blake's Cradle Song *cradle
    unis,pno ROBERTON 75040 s.p. (R266)

  Serenade
    TTBB,acap ROBERTON 53015 s.p.
                        (R267)

ROBERTS, DAVID LEE
  Love Is All Around
    SATB,pno FOX XCX 302 $.40   (R268)

ROBIN ADAIR
  (Beethoven; Boyd) SATB SCHIRM.G
    LG51763 $.35   (R269)

ROBIN ADAIR see Silcher, Friedrich

ROBIN'S EGG, THE see Huntley, Fred H.

ROBINSON, BETTY JEAN
  On The Way Home
    (Metis, F.) SSA BIG3 $.50   (R270)
    (Metis, F.) SAB BIG3 $.50   (R271)
    (Metis, F.) SATB BIG3 $.50   (R272)

ROCHEROLLE
  America My Home
    SA/SAB,opt fl/band WARNER CE0800
      $.45, ipa   (R273)

ROCK HIM GENTLY see Davies, Lawrence H.

ROCK ME GENTLY see Kim, Andy

ROCK THE BOAT see Holmes

RODACI see Ocenas, Andrej

RODGERS AND HAMMERSTEIN see Rodgers, Richard

RODGERS AND HAMMERSTEIN SINGTIME see Rodgers, Richard

RODGERS, RICHARD (1902-   )
  All At Once You Love Her
    2pt oct CHAPPELL W132506-351 $.40
                       (R274)
    TTBB oct CHAPPELL W132506-355 $.40
                       (R275)
    SSA oct CHAPPELL W132506-353 $.40
                       (R276)
    SATB oct CHAPPELL W132506-357 $.40
                       (R277)
    SAB oct CHAPPELL W132506-356 $.40
                       (R278)
  Bali Ha'i (from South Pacific)
    SSA oct CHAPPELL W367508-353 $.40
                       (R279)
    2pt oct CHAPPELL W367508-351 $.40
                       (R280)
    SATB oct CHAPPELL W367508-357 $.40
                       (R281)
    SAB oct CHAPPELL W367508-356 $.40
                       (R282)
    TTBB oct CHAPPELL W367508-355 $.40
                       (R283)
  Carefully Taught (from South Pacific)
    SSA oct CHAPPELL W725002-353 $.40
                       (R284)
    SATB oct CHAPPELL W725002-357 $.40
                       (R285)
    TTBB oct CHAPPELL W725002-355 $.40
                       (R286)
  Choral Selections From "Cinderella"
    *CCU
    SATB CHAPPELL W865006-357 $1.25
                       (R287)
  Choral Selections From "Flower Drum
    Song" *CCU
    SSA CHAPPELL W507508-353 $1.25;
      TTBB CHAPPELL W507508-355 $1.25;
      SAB CHAPPELL W507508-356 $1.25;
      SATB CHAPPELL W507508-357 $1.25
                       (R288)
  Choral Selections From "No Strings"
    *CCU
    SSA CHAPPELL W137501-353 $1.25;
      SATB CHAPPELL W137501-357 $1.25
                       (R289)
  Choral Selections From "Oklahoma!"
    *CCU
    SSA CHAPPELL W290003-353 $1.25;

RODGERS, RICHARD (cont'd.)
    TTBB CHAPPELL W290003-355 $1.25;
    TTBB CHAPPELL W290003-357 $1.25
                       (R290)
  Choral Selections From "South
    Pacific" *CCU
    SSA CHAPPELL W407507-353 $1.25;
      TTBB CHAPPELL W407507-355 $1.25;
      SATB CHAPPELL W407507-357 $1.25
                       (R291)
  Choral Selections From "State Fair"
    *CCU
    SSA CHAPPELL W472501-353 $1.25;
      SATB CHAPPELL W472501-357 $1.25
                       (R292)
  Choral Selections From "The King And
    I" *CCU
    SSA CHAPPELL W075009-353 $1.25;
      TTBB CHAPPELL W075009-355 $1.25;
      SATB CHAPPELL W075009-357 $1.25
                       (R293)
  Choral Selections From "The Sound Of
    Music" *CCU
    2pt CHAPPELL W400015-351 $1.25; SSA
      CHAPPELL W400015-353 $1.25; TTBB
      CHAPPELL W400015-355 $1.25; SAB
      CHAPPELL W400015-356 $1.25; SATB
      CHAPPELL W400015-357 $1.25 (R294)
  Choral Selections From "Two By Two"
    *CCU
    SATB CHAPPELL W013243-357 $1.25
                       (R295)
  Climb Ev'ry Mountain (from Sound Of
    Music, The)
    SSA oct CHAPPELL W887505-353 $.40
                       (R296)
    2pt oct CHAPPELL W887505-351 $.40
                       (R297)
    SATB oct CHAPPELL W887505-357 $.40
                       (R298)
    SAB oct CHAPPELL W887505-356 $.40
                       (R299)
    TTBB oct CHAPPELL W887505-355 $.40
                       (R300)
  Cock-Eyed Optimist, A (from South
    Pacific)
    TTBB oct CHAPPELL W900001-355 $.40
                       (R301)
    SATB oct CHAPPELL W900001-357 $.40
                       (R302)
  Dites-Moi (from South Pacific)
    2pt oct CHAPPELL W187509-351 $.40
                       (R303)
    SATB oct CHAPPELL W187509-357 $.40
                       (R304)
    SSA oct CHAPPELL W187509-353 (R305)
  Do I Love You Because You're
    Beautiful? (from Cinderella)
    SATB oct CHAPPELL W197870-357 $.40
                       (R306)
    TTBB oct CHAPPELL W197870-355 $.40
                       (R307)
    SSA oct CHAPPELL W197870-353 $.40
                       (R308)
  Do-Re-Mi (from Sound Of Music, The)
    2pt oct CHAPPELL W205004-351 $.40
                       (R309)
    SATB oct CHAPPELL W205004-357 $.40
                       (R310)
    SAB oct CHAPPELL W205004-356 $.40
                       (R311)
    TTBB oct CHAPPELL W205004-355 $.40
                       (R312)
    SSA oct CHAPPELL W205004-353 $.40
                       (R313)
  Don't Marry Me
    TTBB oct CHAPPELL W227503-355 $.40
                       (R314)
  Edelweiss (from Sound Of Music, The)
    2pt oct CHAPPELL W325000-351 $.40
                       (R315)
    SAB oct CHAPPELL W325000-356 $.40
                       (R316)
    SSA oct CHAPPELL W325000-353 $.40
                       (R317)
    SATB oct CHAPPELL W325000-357 $.40
                       (R318)
  Everybody's Got A Home But Me
    SATB oct CHAPPELL W375005-357 $.40
                       (R319)
    SSA oct CHAPPELL W375005-353 $.40
                       (R320)
    2pt oct CHAPPELL W375005-351 $.40
                       (R321)
    SAB oct CHAPPELL W375005-356 $.40
                       (R322)
    TTBB oct CHAPPELL W375005-355 $.40
                       (R323)
  Farmer And The Cowman, The (from
    Oklahoma)
    SATB oct CHAPPELL W452515-357 $.40
                       (R324)
  Fellow Needs A Girl, A
    2pt oct CHAPPELL W461250-351 $.40
                       (R325)
    SAB oct CHAPPELL W461250-356 $.40
                       (R326)
    TTBB oct CHAPPELL W461250-355 $.40
                       (R327)
    SATB oct CHAPPELL W461250-357 $.40
                       (R328)
    SSA oct CHAPPELL W461250-353 $.40
                       (R329)

RODGERS, RICHARD (cont'd.)
  Getting To Know You (from King And I,
    The)
    SAB oct CHAPPELL W677509-356 $.40
                       (R330)
    TTBB oct CHAPPELL W677509-355 $.40
                       (R331)
    SSA oct CHAPPELL W677509-353 $.40
                       (R332)
    2pt oct CHAPPELL W677509-351 $.40
                       (R333)
    SATB oct CHAPPELL W677509-357 $.40
                       (R334)
  Happy Christmas, Little Friend
    2pt oct CHAPPELL W890003-351 $.40
                       (R335)
    TTBB oct CHAPPELL W89003-355 $.40
                       (R336)
    SSA oct CHAPPELL W890003-353 $.40
                       (R337)
    SAB oct CHAPPELL W890003-356 $.40
                       (R338)
    SATB oct CHAPPELL W890003-357
                       (R339)
  Happy Talk (from South Pacific)
    SATB oct CHAPPELL W897503-357 $.40
                       (R340)
    SSA oct CHAPPELL W897503-353 $.40
                       (R341)
  Hello, Young Lovers (from King And I,
    The)
    SATB oct CHAPPELL W957505-357 $.40
                       (R342)
    SAB oct CHAPPELL W957505-356 $.40
                       (R343)
    TTBB oct CHAPPELL W957505-355 $.40
                       (R344)
    SSA oct CHAPPELL W957505-353 $.40
                       (R345)
    2pt oct CHAPPELL W957505-351 $.40
                       (R346)
  I Enjoy Being A Girl (from South
    Pacific)
    2pt oct CHAPPELL W207504-351 $.40
                       (R347)
    SSA oct CHAPPELL W207504-353 $.40
                       (R348)
  I Whistle A Happy Tune (from King And
    I, The)
    2pt oct CHAPPELL W525004-351 $.40
                       (R349)
    SAB oct CHAPPELL W525004-356 $.40
                       (R350)
    TTBB oct CHAPPELL W525004-355 $.40
                       (R351)
    SATB oct CHAPPELL W525004-357 $.40
                       (R352)
    mix cor,opt bvl&drums&gtr cor pts
      CHAPPELL W525004-373 $.30, sc
      CHAPPELL W525004-372 $1.50 (R353)
    SSA oct CHAPPELL W525004-353 $.40
                       (R354)
  I'm Gonna Wash That Man Right Outa My
    Hair (from South Pacific)
    SSA oct CHAPPELL W665602-353 (R355)
  I'm Your Girl
    SAB oct CHAPPELL W677409-356 $.40
                       (R356)
    SSA oct CHAPPELL W677409-353 $.40
                       (R357)
    SATB oct CHAPPELL W677409-357 $.40
                       (R358)
  In My Own Little Corner (from
    Cinderella)
    2pt oct CHAPPELL W700003-351 $.40
                       (R359)
    SSA oct CHAPPELL W700003-353 $.40
                       (R360)
  It Might As Well Be Spring (from
    State Fair)
    SSA oct CHAPPELL W777506-353 $.40
                       (R361)
    SATB oct CHAPPELL W777506-357 $.40
                       (R362)
    TTBB oct CHAPPELL W777506-355 $.40
                       (R363)
  It's The Little Things In Texas (from
    State Fair)
    SSA oct CHAPPELL W860252-353 $.40
                       (R364)
    2pt oct CHAPPELL W860252-351 $.40
                       (R365)
    SATB oct CHAPPELL W860252-357 $.40
                       (R366)
    SAB oct CHAPPELL W860252-356 $.40
                       (R367)
    TTBB oct CHAPPELL W860252-355 $.40
                       (R368)
  Kansas City (from Oklahoma)
    TTBB oct CHAPPELL W050002-355 $.40
                       (R369)
  Keep It Gay
    SAB oct CHAPPELL W062502-356 $.40
                       (R370)
    TTBB oct CHAPPELL WO62502-355 $.40
                       (R371)
    SSA oct CHAPPELL W062502-353 $.40
                       (R372)
    2pt oct CHAPPELL W062502-351 $.40
                       (R373)
    SATB oct CHAPPELL W062502-357 $.40
                       (R374)

RODGERS, RICHARD (cont'd.)

Lonely Goatherd, The (from Sound Of
Music, The)
SSA oct CHAPPELL W387503-353 $.40
(R375)
SATB oct CHAPPELL W387503-357 $.40
(R376)
Look No Further
2pt oct CHAPPELL W430006-351 $.40
(R377)
SATB oct CHAPPELL W430006-357 $.40
(R378)
SAB oct CHAPPELL W430006 $.40
(R379)
TTBB oct CHAPPELL W430006-355 $.40
(R380)
SSA oct CHAPPELL W430006-353 $.40
(R381)
Love, Look Away (from Flower Drum
Song)
SATB oct CHAPPELL W487501-357 $.40
(R382)
SAB oct CHAPPELL W487501-356 $.40
(R383)
TTBB oct CHAPPELL W487501-355 $.40
(R384)
SSA oct CHAPPELL W487501-353 $.40
(R385)
2pt oct CHAPPELL W487501 $.40
(R386)
Lovely Night, A (from Cinderella)
SSA oct CHAPPELL W523750-351 $.40
(R387)
SATB oct CHAPPELL W523750-357 $.40
(R388)
TTBB oct CHAPPELL W523750-351 $.40
(R389)
Maine
SATB oct CHAPPELL W020412-357 $.40
(R390)
SAB oct CHAPPELL W020412-356 $.40
(R391)
TTBB oct CHAPPELL W020412-355 $.40
(R392)
SSA oct CHAPPELL W020412-353 $.40
(R393)
2pt oct CHAPPELL W020412-351 $.40
(R394)
Many A New Day (from Oklahoma)
2pt oct CHAPPELL W645009-351 $.40
(R395)
TTBB oct CHAPPELL W645009-355 $.40
(R396)
SSA oct CHAPPELL 645009-353 $.40
(R397)
SAB oct CHAPPELL W645009-356 $.40
(R398)
SATB oct CHAPPELL W645009-357 $.40
(R399)
Maria (from Sound Of Music, The)
SSA oct CHAPPELL W672508-353 $.40
(R400)
2pt oct CHAPPELL W672508-351 $.40
(R401)
SATB oct CHAPPELL W672508-357 $.40
(R402)
SAB oct CHAPPELL W672508-356 $.40
(R403)
My Favorite Things (from Sound Of
Music, The)
SSA oct CHAPPELL W087536-353 $.40
(R404)
2pt oct CHAPPELL W087536-351 $.40
(R405)
SATB oct CHAPPELL W087536-357 $.40
(R406)
SAB oct CHAPPELL W087536-356 $.40
(R407)
TTBB oct CHAPPELL W087536-355 $.40
(R408)
No Other Love
2pt oct CHAPPELL W127502-351 $.40
(R409)
SATB oct CHAPPELL W127502-357 $.40
(R410)
SAB oct CHAPPELL W127502-356 $.40
(R411)
TTBB oct CHAPPELL W127502-355 $.40
(R412)
SSA oct CHAPPELL W127502-353 $.40
(R413)
No Strings
SATB oct CHAPPELL W137519-357 $.40
(R414)
SAB oct CHAPPELL W137519-356 $.40
(R415)
TTBB oct CHAPPELL W137519-355 $.40
(R416)
SSA oct CHAPPELL W137519-353 $.40
(R417)
2pt oct CHAPPELL W137519-351 $.40
(R418)
Nobody Told Me
2pt oct CHAPPELL W157509-351 $.40
(R419)
TTBB oct CHAPPELL W157509-355 $.40
(R420)
SSA oct CHAPPELL W157509-353 $.40
(R421)
SAB oct CHAPPELL W157509-356
W157509-357 $.40 $.40   (R422)
Oh, What A Beautiful Mornin' (from
Oklahoma)
2pt oct CHAPPELL W235016-351 $.40

(R423)
TTBB oct CHAPPELL W235016-355 $.40
(R424)
SSA oct CHAPPELL W235016-353 $.40
(R425)
SATB oct CHAPPELL W235016-357 $.40
(R426)
SAB oct CHAPPELL W235016-356 $.40
(R427)
Oklahoma (from Oklahoma)
SSA oct CHAPPELL W285003-353 $.40
(R428)
2pt oct CHAPPELL W285003-351 $.40
(R429)
SATB oct CHAPPELL W285003-357 $.40
(R430)
SAB oct CHAPPELL W285003-356 $.40
(R431)
TTBB oct CHAPPELL W285003-355 $.40
(R432)
Our State Fair (from State Fair)
2pt oct CHAPPELL W447504-351 $.40
(R433)
SATB oct CHAPPELL W447504-357 $.40
(R434)
SAB oct CHAPPELL W447504-356 $.40
(R435)
TTBB oct CHAPPELL W447504-355 $.40
(R436)
SSA oct CHAPPELL W447504-353 $.40
(R437)
Out Of My Dreams (from Oklahoma)
SATB oct CHAPPELL W452504-357 $.40
(R438)
SAB oct CHAPPELL W452504-356 $.40
(R439)
TTBB oct CHAPPELL W452504-355 $.40
(R440)
SSA oct CHAPPELL W452504-353 $.40
(R441)
2pt oct CHAPPELL W452504-351 $.40
(R442)
People Will Say We're In Love (from
Oklahoma)
2pt oct CHAPPELL W567517-351 $.40
(R443)
TTBB oct CHAPPELL W567517-355 $.40
(R444)
SSA oct CHAPPELL W567517-353 $.40
(R445)
SATB oct CHAPPELL W567517-357 $.40
(R446)
SAB oct CHAPPELL W567517-356 $.40
(R447)
Pore Jud (from Oklahoma)
TTBB oct CHAPPELL W667507-355 $.40
(R448)
Preludium
SSA oct CHAPPELL W710000-353 $.40
(R449)
SATB oct CHAPPELL W710000-357 $.40
(R450)
Rodgers And Hammerstein *CCU
(Miller, Carl) $.40 2pt CHAPPELL
020685-3741; SSA CHAPPELL
020685-3742; TTBB CHAPPELL
020685-3743; SAB CHAPPELL
020685-3744; SATB CHAPPELL
020685-3745   (R451)

Rodgers And Hammerstein Singtime
*CCU
(Miller, Carl) unis CHAPPELL
020768-3742 $1.50   (R452)
Sixteen Going On Seventeen (from
Sound Of Music, The)
SSA oct CHAPPELL W202502-353 $.40
(R453)
TTBB oct CHAPPELL W202502-355 $.40
(R454)
SATB oct CHAPPELL W202502-357
(R455)
So Far
2pt oct CHAPPELL W260005-351 $.40
(R456)
SSA oct CHAPPELL W260005-353 $.40
(R457)
TTBB oct CHAPPELL W260005-355 $.40
(R458)
SAB oct CHAPPELL W260005-356 $.40
(R459)
SATB oct CHAPPELL W260005-357 $.40
(R460)
So Long, Farewell (from Sound Of
Music, The)
2pt oct CHAPPELL W265004-351 $.40
(R461)
SSA oct CHAPPELL W265004-353 $.40
SAB oct CHAPPELL W265004-356 $.40
(R462)
(R463)
SATB oct CHAPPELL W265004-357 $.40
(R464)
Sound Of Music, The (from Sound Of
Music, The)
2pt oct CHAPPELL W400007-351 $.40
(R465)
SSA oct CHAPPELL W400007-353 $.40
(R466)
TTBB oct CHAPPELL W400007-355 $.40
(R467)
SAB oct CHAPPELL W400007-356 $.40
(R468)
SATB oct CHAPPELL W400007-357 $.40

(R469)
Surrey With The Fringe On Top, The
(from Oklahoma)
2pt oct CHAPPELL W592514-351 $.40
(R470)
SSA oct CHAPPELL W592514-353 $.40
(R471)
TTBB oct CHAPPELL W592514-355 $.40
(R472)
SAB oct CHAPPELL W592514-356 $.40
(R473)
SATB oct CHAPPELL W592514-357 $.40
(R474)
Ten Minutes Ago (from Cinderella)
SSA oct CHAPPELL W727508-353 $.40
(R475)
TTBB oct CHAPPELL W727508-355 $.40
(R476)
SATB oct CHAPPELL W727508-357 $.40
(R477)
There Is Nothing Like A Dame (from
South Pacific)
TTBB oct CHAPPELL W895008-355 $.40
(R478)
SATB oct CHAPPELL 895008-357 $.40
(R479)
This Nearly Was Mine (from South
Pacific)
SSA oct CHAPPELL W992508-353 $.40
(R480)
TTBB oct CHAPPELL W992508-355 $.40
(R481)
SATB oct CHAPPELL W992508-357 $.40
(R482)
Two By Two (from Two By Two)
SATB oct CHAPPELL W025601-357 $.40
(R483)
We Kiss In A Shadow (from King And I,
The)
2pt oct CHAPPELL W397509-351 $.40
(R484)
SSA oct CHAPPELL W397509-353 $.40
(R485)
TTBB oct CHAPPELL W397509-355 $.40
(R486)
SAB oct CHAPPELL W397509-356 $.40
(R487)
SATB oct CHAPPELL W397509-357 $.40
(R488)
Wonderful Guy, A
SSA oct CHAPPELL W740005-353 $.40
(R489)
SATB oct CHAPPELL W740005-357 $.40
(R490)
You Are Beautiful
2pt oct CHAPPELL W800007-351 $.40
(R491)
SSA oct CHAPPELL W800007-353 $.40
(R492)
TTBB oct CHAPPELL W800007-355 $.40
(R493)
SAB oct CHAPPELL W800007-356 $.40
(R494)
SATB oct CHAPPELL W800007-357 $.40
(R495)
Younger Than Springtime (from South
Pacific)
SATB oct CHAPPELL W925002-357 $.40
(R496)
2pt oct CHAPPELL W925002-351 $.40
(R497)
SSA oct CHAPPELL W925002-353 $.40
(R498)
TTBB oct CHAPPELL W925002-355 $.40
(R499)
SAB oct CHAPPELL W925002-356 $.40
(R500)
RODRIGO MARTINEZ
(Merrill) SA/TB OXFORD 95.002 (R501)
ROFF
Gentle Wind
SATB SHAWNEE A1307 $.35   (R502)
ROFF, JOSEPH
God Bless Canada
unis (med easy) WATERLOO $.30
(R503)
Gratitude To Mother Earth
(Snyder) SATB BELWIN 2305 $.35
(R504)
ROG A ROGHOZ see Karai, Jozsef
ROGERS
Sing We Noel
2pt,opt tamb/perc oct SCHMITT 2905
$.40   (R505)
ROHAN, JOY
Song For Human Rights
unis EMI   (R506)
ROHDE
Tolling Bells
SATB SCHIRM.G LG51721 $.40   (R507)
ROHWER, JENS (1914-   )
Drei Hubsche Madchen *CC15L
jr cor&opt T (med) sc SCHOTTS B 136
s.p.   (R508)
Einfache Singsatze *CC18L
jr cor,opt inst (med) sc SCHOTTS
B 125 s.p.   (R509)

ROHWER, JENS (cont'd.)

Sieben Madchenlieder Nach
Slowakischen Volksliedtexten
*CC7L,folk,Slav
SABar,acap (med) sc SCHOTTS
ED. 5149 s.p. (R510)

ROI RENAUD-NOEL SAVOYSIEN see Thiriet,
[Maurice]

ROLLIN' DOWN TO JORDAN *spir
(Bjorkland) TTBB oct SCHMITT W192
$.30 (R511)

ROLLING PLAINS see Christiansen, P.

ROLLINS, JACK
Frosty The Snow Man *see Nelson,
Steve

ROLNICKA see Dvorak, Antonin

ROMANCE see Diemer, Emma Lou

ROMANCE ABOUT KING JECMINEK, THE see
Sveceny, Ladislav, Romance O Krali
Jecminkovi

ROMANCE FROM THE DANDELIONS see
Martinu, Bohuslav

ROMANCE O KRALI JECMINKOVI see Sveceny,
Ladislav

ROMANCE STEDROVECERNI see Tomasek,
Jaroslav

ROMANTISCHE CHORLIEDER see Killmayer,
Wilhelm

ROMANZE see Heuser

ROMISCHE BRUNNEN see Schroeder, Hermann

ROMISCHE FONTANE "ZWEI BECKEN, EINS DAS
ANDRE UBERSTEIGEND" see Schroeder,
Hermann

ROMISCHE WEINSPRUCHE "PETE ME IMPLE"
see Genzmer, Harald

RONDE see Massis, Amable

RONDEL see Turchi, Guido

RONDEL DE MAI see Carrard

RONDELL "EUR AUGENPAAR" see Genzmer,
Harald

RONNEFELD, PETER (1935-1965)
Quartar *Op.5, cant
mix cor&speak cor,narrator,S solo,
3fl,3ob,3clar,3bsn,3trp,4horn,
3trom,tuba,timp,4perc,harp,pno,
strings, piccolo, English horn,
bass clarinet, and contrabassoon
alternate with third woodwinds
MODERN s.p. (R512)

ROOKE, PAT
Robert Brown, Instant Hero *see
Arch, Gwyn

ROOM FULL OF ROSES see Spencer, Tim

ROOS, ROBERT DE (1907-)
Postrema Verba *cant
mix cor,Bar solo,fl,clar,2horn,
3trp,3trom,strings,perc,timp
DONEMUS (R513)

ROOT, GEORGE F. (1820-1895)
Contest, The
(Brandon, George) mix cor
(bicentennial) HERITAGE H128 $.35
(R514)

ROPTETO see Balazs, Arpad

RORE, CIPRIANO DE (1516-1565)
Cease Now Your Tears, O Ladies *see
En Vos, Adieux, Dames

En Vos, Adieux, Dames
(Malin, Don) "Cease Now Your Tears,
O Ladies" SATB,acap BELWIN 2321
$.30 (R515)

ROSA *folk,Fr
(Blanchard, R.) 4pt mix cor,acap
JOBERT s.p. (R516)

ROSA MYSTICA see Knab, Armin

ROSALINDA "AN DAS TOR DES PALASTES" see
Zoll, Paul

ROSE, THE see Tomlins, Greta

ROSE, THE see Yannatos, James

ROSE, MICHAEL (1916-)
Summer Music
SATB,T solo,timp,perc,strings,pno,
4-hands voc sc NOVELLO rental,
ipr (R517)

Winter Music
SATB,opt perc,pno, 4-hands voc sc
NOVELLO rental, ipr (R518)

ROSE TREE BLOSSOMS, A see Hovhaness,
Alan

ROSE WEISS, ROSE ROT see Rein, Walter

ROSEBUSH see Champagne, Claude

ROSEMARIE see Thehos, Adam

ROSEMARY see Hellden, Daniel

ROSENBERG, HILDING (1892-)
Skordesang (from Lycksalighetens O)
4pt mix cor ERIKS 27 s.p. (R519)

ROSENFELD, GERHARD
Singen Will Ich Frohe Lieder
4pt mix cor,acap NEUE NM1010 s.p.
(R520)

ROSENSTENGEL, ALBRECHT
Amerika-Song
men cor,opt gtr,opt perc TONOS 465
s.p. (R521)

Amor Ist Uberall *CC5U
men cor,pno,perc cmplt ed,sc,cor
pts TONOS 2200 s.p. (R522)

Amor Ist Uberall *CC5U
men cor&jr cor,pno cmplt ed,sc,cor
pts TONOS 2280 s.p. (R523)

Bunt Ist Das Leben
men cor,pno,gtr,bvl,perc sc TONOS
s.p. see also Tanz-Suite (R524)

Cantata Rhythmica
mix cor,pno,opt bvl&perc ipa sc
BREITKOPF-W Z 67, cor pts
BREITKOPF-W Z 68 (R525)

Die Konkurrenten
men cor,opt gtr,opt perc TONOS 449
s.p. (R526)

Die Tanzweise *CCU
men cor&jr cor,perc,pno cmplt ed,
sc,cor pts TONOS 4964 s.p. (R527)

Eines Menschen Seele
men cor,pno sc,cor pts TONOS 4205
s.p. (R528)

Glocken, Die Nicht Klingen
men cor,pno,gtr,bvl,perc sc TONOS
s.p. see also Tanz-Suite (R529)

Krakowiak
men cor,pno,gtr,perc sc,cor pts
TONOS 2105 s.p. (R530)

Mehr Vom Leben
men cor&jr cor,pno,opt perc cmplt
ed,sc,cor pts TONOS 2290 s.p.
(R531)

Mexico-Liedchen
men cor,opt gtr,opt perc TONOS 466
s.p. (R532)

Musikanten-Kantate *cant
men cor&jr cor,solo,pno,opt strings
sc,voc sc TONOS 2270 s.p. (R533)

Sambaliedchen
men cor,pno,perc sc,cor pts TONOS
1622 s.p. (R534)

Sechs Tanz-Kanons *CC6U,canon
men cor/men cor&jr cor,pno sc,voc
sc TONOS 1200 s.p. (R535)

Tag Der Freude
men cor,pno sc,cor pts TONOS 5750
s.p. (R536)

Tanz-Suite
men cor,pno,gtr,bvl,perc cmplt ed,
cor pts TONOS 1620 s.p.
contains & see also: Bunt Ist Das
Leben; Glocken, Die Nicht
Klingen; Tanzen, Immer Tanzen
(R537)

Tanzen, Immer Tanzen
men cor,pno,gtr,bvl,perc sc TONOS
s.p. see also Tanz-Suite (R538)

Tanzende Herzen *CC3U
men cor,pno,gtr,bvl,perc cmplt ed,
sc,cor pts TONOS 2210 s.p. (R539)

Tanzvergnugen
men cor,pno sc,cor pts TONOS 2191
s.p. (R540)

ROSENSTENGEL, ALBRECHT (cont'd.)

Zum Ausklang
men cor,acap TONOS 407 s.p. (R541)

ROSENTHAL, MANUEL (1904-)
Sonnet
4pt mix cor,pno JOBERT cor pts
s.p., sc s.p. see from Trois
Burlesques (R542)

Stances
4pt mix cor,pno JOBERT sc s.p., cor
pts s.p. see from Trois
Burlesques (R543)

Tableau De Paris
4pt mix cor,pno JOBERT sc s.p., cor
pts s.p. see from Trois
Burlesques (R544)

Trois Burlesques *see Sonnet;
Stances; Tableau De Paris (R545)

ROSENZEIT see Schroeder, Hermann

ROSENZEIT see Thehos, Adam

ROSES AND THORNS see Kunz, Alfred

ROSESTOCK, HOLDERBLUT see Silcher,
Friedrich

ROSINSKY, JOZEF (1897-)
Jesen Lesy Prefukuje *cant
mix cor,solo,orch SLOV.HUD.FOND
s.p. (R546)

Pej, Sestra *cant
wom cor,S solo,orch SLOV.HUD.FOND
s.p. (R547)

Zbor Mnichov Z Opery Matus Cak
Trenciansky *cant
cor,orch SLOV.HUD.FOND s.p. (R548)

ROSLEIN AUF DER HEIDEN "SIE GLEICHT
WOHL EINEM ROSENSTOCK" see
Herrmann, Hugo

ROSMARIENBAUM see Herrmann, Hugo

ROSMARIN see Brahms, Johannes

ROSMARIN "ES WOLLT DIE JUNGFRAU FRUH
AUFSTEHN" see Brahms, Johannes,
Rosmarin

ROSMARIN "ES WOLLT DIE JUNGFRAU FRUH
AUFSTEHN" see Trunk, Richard

ROSSI, SALOMONE (ca. 1570-ca. 1630)
Elohim Hashivaynu
(Isaacson) SATB SCHIRM.G LG51883
$.40 (R549)

Riede La Primavera
see Two Madrigals

Temer Donna Non Dei
see Two Madrigals

Two Madrigals *madrigal
(Luce) SA BRODT WC 3 $.28
contains: Riede La Primavera;
Temer Donna Non Dei (R550)

ROSSIGNOL DU BOIS see Schertzer, Daniel

ROSSIGNOL DU VERT BOCAGE see Willan,
Healey

ROSSINI, GIOACCHINO (1792-1868)
Comic Duet For Two Cats *see Duetto
Buffo Di Due Gatti

Der Tanz "Wo Im Frohen Zecherkreise"
*It
(Fischer, Jakob) [Ger] 4pt men cor,
T solo,pno/orch voc sc SCHOTTS
C 39 098 s.p., cor pts SCHOTTS
C 39 099 s.p., ipa (R551)

Duetto Buffo Di Due Gatti
(Feline, A.) "Comic Duet For Two
Cats" 2pt men cor/2pt wom cor,pno
NATIONAL WHC-52 $.35 (R552)

La Carita
[It/Fr] SSA,S solo,pno RICORDI-ENG
122237 s.p. (R553)

La Fede
[Fr/It] SSA,pno RICORDI-ENG 122235
s.p. (R554)

La Speranza
[Fr/It] SSA,pno RICORDI-ENG 122236
s.p. (R555)

ROSTHIUS, NICOLAUS
Frau Nachtigall, Mach Dich Bereit
see Hassler, Hans Leo, Ach Lieb,
Hier Ist Das Herze
see Hassler, Hans Leo, Ach Lieb,
Hier Ist Das Herze

ROSTHIUS, NICOLAUS (cont'd.)

   Lieblich Wohl Kommt Der Mai
     SSSA,acap MOSELER LB1005 s.p.
       contains also: Lechner, Konrad,
       Ein Jeder Meint, Er Sei Der Best
                       (R556)

ROSZKOWSZKY, PANTALEON
   Vesperae Bacchanales *cant
     cor,solo,cembalo,orch SLOV.HUD.FOND
     s.p.   (R557)

ROTA see Ruzdjak, Marko

ROTA "SUMMER IS ICUMEN IN" see Orff,
   Carl

ROTER WEIN *folk
   (Doppelbauer, Josef Friedrich) mix
   cor DOBLINGER G 698 s.p.   (R558)

ROTHE ROSENKNOSPEN see Brahms, Johannes

ROTHSCHUH, FRANZ (1921-   )
   Dorfabend "Der Schafer Mit Den
     Schafen"
     see Zwei Chorlieder

   Ein Licht Will Sich Entzunden "Die
     Stadt Erglanzt Im Tale"
     see Zwei Chorlieder

   Zwei Chorlieder *Op.32
     wom cor (easy) sc SCHOTTS
     CHBL 578A-B s.p.
       contains: Dorfabend "Der Schafer
       Mit Den Schafen"; Ein Licht
       Will Sich Entzunden "Die Stadt
       Erglanzt Im Tale"   (R559)

ROTKAPPCHEN see Biebl, Franz

ROTTURA, JOSEPH JAMES (1929-   )
   Christmas On The Trail
     SATB ALFRED A-100 s.p.   (R560)

   Festival Of Sound
     SATB (vocalise) ALFRED A-108 s.p.
                       (R561)

   Overture For Voices
     SATB ALFRED 1-101 s.p.   (R562)
     SSA ALFRED 1-101 s.p.   (R563)

ROUSSAKIS, NICOLAS
   Night Speech For Speech-Chorus And
     Two Players Of Instruments
     speak cor, 2pails of water, 2
     lengths of rubber hose (ea. 2 ft
     long), sandpaper (coarse and
     fine), 2blocks of wood, 2 large
     sheets of paper (1 thick, 1
     thin), high and low shell wind
     chimes, very high brass wind
     chimes, high brass wind chimes
     high and low bamboo wind chimes
     high gong, (a. soft mallet, b.
     metal object), low gong, (a. soft
     mallet b. wood object),
     harmonicas or circular chromatic
     pitch pipes for each member of
     the chorus sc BROUDE,A $2.50
                       (R564)

ROVICS, HOWARD
   Cantata II
     SATB,pno,ob, oboe d'amore sc
     AM.COMP.AL. $8.80   (R565)

   Poems Of War Resistance *sac/sec,
     cant
     cor,S,narrator,2ob,2trp,vcl,2-
     3perc,pno, tenor saxophone sc
     AM.COMP.AL. $12.10   (R566)

ROW ROW ROW
     SSA CIMINO $.40   (R567)
     TTBB CIMINO $.40   (R568)
     SATB CIMINO $.40   (R569)

ROXBURY, RONALD
   That Yonge Child
     SATB WALTON 2253 $.30   (R570)

ROZHRO SA, VATRA
   (Francisci, O.) jr cor,acap
     SLOV.HUD.FOND s.p.   (R571)

ROZKAZ C. 368 see Dobias, Vaclav

RUBBEN, HERMANNJOSEF (1928-   )
   Ade!
     men cor,acap TONOS 3952 s.p. (R572)

   Gedankenreise
     men cor,acap TONOS 3953 s.p. (R573)

RUDA ARMADA see Dobias, Vaclav

RUDOLPH THE RED-NOSED REINDEER see
   Marks

RUDOLPH'S CHRISTMAS MEDLEY see Marks,
   John

RUDY PRAPOR see Seidel, Jan

RUDZINSKI, ZBIGNIEW (1935-   )
   Requiem Fur Die Opfer Des Krieges
     SSAATTBB,narrator,pno,3fl,3ob,
     3clar,3bsn,4horn,3trp,3trom,tuba,
     strings,4perc,timp (diff) sc
     SCHOTTS rental; ipr   (R574)

RUF UND MAHNUNG see Bresgen, Cesar

RUGALICA see Slavenski, Josip

RUH' IN FRIEDEN
   see Vier Grablieder

RUHE SANFT
   see Vier Grablieder

RUHE, SCHONSTES GLUCK DER ERDE see
   Schubert, Franz (Peter)

RUHETAL see Mendelssohn-Bartholdy,
   Felix

RUITER, WIM DE (1943-   )
   Hoplopoia
     SATB,2fl,2ob,2clar,bsn,2horn,2trp,
     trom,strings,2perc DONEMUS (R575)

RUMMELPLATZ see Kludas, Erich

RUNDADINELLA "HOLLA, GUT G'SELL" see
   Schein, Johann Hermann

RUNDGESANG "NUR FROHLICH LEUTE" see
   Biebl, Franz

RUNDHERUM
   unis wom cor SCHOTTS C 42 532B s.p.
     see also Alle Singen Heft 1 (R576)

RURAL SONG see Schumann, Robert
   (Alexander), Landliches Lied

RUSCH, MILTON
   Vagabond Song, A
     SSA (diff) FITZSIMONS 3022 $.25
                       (R577)

RUSLA, WENN DU MEINE WARST *folk
   (Doppelbauer, Josef Friedrich) mix
     cor DOBLINGER G 696 s.p.   (R578)

RUSSELL
   Death, Be Not Proud
     SSA SCHIRM.G 12049 $.40   (R579)

   Proverbial Music
     SATB SCHIRM.G 12040 $.75   (R580)

RUSSELL, WELFORD
   As I Lay Sleeping
     SATB (med easy) WATERLOO $.40
                       (R581)

   If In The World There Be More Woe
     SATB (med easy) WATERLOO $.40
                       (R582)

   O Night, O Jealous Night
     SATB (med easy) WATERLOO $.50
                       (R583)

   Shall I Come Sweet Love To Thee
     SATB (med easy) WATERLOO $.35
                       (R584)

   Weep Not My Wanton
     SATB (med easy) WATERLOO $.35
                       (R585)

   When Will The Fountain Of My Tears Be
     Dry
     SATB (med easy) WATERLOO $.40
                       (R586)

RUSSIAN VESPER HYMN see Bortniansky

RUSSINISH *Russ
   (Kremser) mix cor LIENAU
     LIEDERHARFE NR. 7, 2 sc s.p., cor
     pts s.p.   (R587)

RUTHENBERG, OTTO (1936-   )
   Slawka *CC5U,folk,Slav
     4pt mix cor,pno,gtr,bvl sc,voc sc
     MERSEBURG EM9301 s.p., ipa (R588)

RUTTER
   Fancies
     SATB,inst (med diff) voc sc OXFORD
     56.596 $4.00, ipr   (R589)

   Five Childhood Lyrics *see Matthew,
     Mark, Luke, And John; Monday's
     Child; Owl And The Pussy-Cat,
     The; Sing A Song Of Sixpence;
     Windy Nights   (R590)

   Matthew, Mark, Luke, And John
     SATB,acap OXFORD see from Five
     Childhood Lyrics   (R591)

   Monday's Child
     SATB,acap OXFORD see from Five
     Childhood Lyrics   (R592)

   Nice Young Maidens
     SATB (med easy) OXFORD 84.182
     $.55   (R593)

   Owl And The Pussy-Cat, The
     SATB,acap OXFORD see from Five
     Childhood Lyrics   (R594)

RUTTER (cont'd.)

   Riddle Song, The (from Fancies)
     SATB (med) OXFORD 84.230 $.55
                       (R595)

   Sing A Song Of Sixpence
     SATB,acap OXFORD see from Five
     Childhood Lyrics   (R596)

   Windy Nights
     SATB,acap OXFORD see from Five
     Childhood Lyrics   (R597)

RUZDJAK, MARKO (1946-   )
   Diaphana
     SA,strings,perc MUSIC INFO rental
                       (R598)

   Rota
     cor,4vln,4vla,4vcl,4bvl,4trp,perc,
     cembalo,gtr,harp, mandolin MUSIC
     INFO rental   (R599)

RYBA, JAN JAKUB SIMON (1765-1815)
   Ceska Mse Vanocni
     cor SUPRAPHON s.p.   (R600)

RYCHLIK, JAN (1916-1964)
   Rise, Oh You Shepherds... *see
     Vstavejte, Pastusci...

   Sibenicni Madrigaly *CCU,madrigal
     [Czech/Lat/Ger] mix cor,acap CZECH
     s.p.   (R601)

   Vstavejte, Pastusci... *cant
     "Rise, Oh You Shepherds..." [Czech]
     mix cor,soli,3horn,3trp,3trom,
     strings CZECH s.p.   (R602)

RYMA RYMA REJ *CCU
   mix cor,acap HOFMEISTER G2199 s.p.
                       (R603)

S

'S DIRNDL VON DER ALM *folk,Ger
  (Geiss, Gottfried) men cor,acap TONOS
  4570-4 s.p.   (S1)

'S HERZ "MAIDLE, LASS DIR WAS VERZAHLE"
  see Silcher, Friedrich

'S IST WEIHNACHT see Leist, Peter
  Marzellin

'S SITZT A KLEINS VOGELE IM TANNAWALD
  see Kuhlenthal, Fred

'S WASCHERMADL VON LICHTENTHAL
  (Lessky, Fr.) mix cor DOBLINGER G 683
  s.p. see from Sechs Lieder Aus Wien
                                     (S2)

SA LUNKA VI SA SMANINGOM see Bellman,
  Carl Mikael

SAAR, LOUIS VICTOR (1868-1937)
  Dreams Of Spring
    SSA (med) FITZSIMONS 3029 $.30 (S3)

  Note Of Golden Song, A *sac/sec
    SSSSAA (med) FITZSIMONS 3020 $.25
                                     (S4)
    SATB,acap (med) FITZSIMONS 1038
    $.25   (S5)
    SATB (med) FITZSIMONS 1011 $.25
                                     (S6)
    TTTTBBBB (med) FITZSIMONS 4022 $.25
                                     (S7)

  To Music
    TTBB,acap (med) FITZSIMONS 4027
    $.25   (S8)

SABOTS DE LA VIERGE see Bernier Rene

SACHA *Russ
  (Biebl) men cor ZIMMER. 599 s.p. (S9)

SACRAMENTO
  see Funf Seemanslieder

SACRED AND SECULAR SONGS FOR THREE
  VOICES, VOL. I see Turnhout, Gerard
  de

SACRED AND SECULAR SONGS FOR THREE
  VOICES, VOL. II see Turnhout,
  Gerard de

SAD SWEET DREAMER see Parton

SAD THE DAY, LONG THE NIGHT see Janse

SAERLIED see Strecke, Gerhard

SAERSPRUCH see Burkhard Willy

SAG, AMOR see Dowland, John

SAG DOCH, GIANNETTA (from Cvjy)
  see Digo Giannetta

SAG MIR, GIANETTA see Nitsche, Paul

SAG MIR, GOTT see Martinu, Bohuslav,
  Daj Mi Boze

SAG, WARUM DU ALL DIES LEID MIR ANGETAN
  see Bartok, Bela

SAIL FORTH see Pyle, Francis [Johnson]

SAILING BY see Binge

SAILING IN see Tate

SAILOR SHANTIES, SECOND SELECTION
  *CC9L,folk,Eng
  (Terry, Richard Runciman) TTBB,Bar
  solo,pno CURWEN 50572 s.p.   (S10)

SAILOR'S GREETING, A
  (Wick, Fred) TTBB oct SCHMITT W170
  $.30   (S11)

ST. FAUTH, ULRICH (1940-   )
  Prisma
    men cor,narrator,5perc sc SCHOTTS
    WKS 9 s.p., cor pts SCHOTTS
    WKS 9-01 s.p.   (S12)

SAINT-GILLES *folk,Fr
  (Blanchard, R.) 4pt mix cor,acap
  JOBERT s.p.   (S13)

SAINT-MARIE, BUFFY
  Until It's Time For You To Go *pop
  (Wilson) SSA WARNER WB-353 183 $.50
                                   (S14)
  (Wilson) SATB WARNER WB-352 187
  $.50   (S15)

ST. MICHAEL AM MEER "SANKT MICHAEL, DU
  STARKER HELD" see Knab, Armin

SAINT NICHOLAS AT CHRISTMAS TIME see
  Crawford, Thomas J.

SAINT NICHOLAS, COME ON IN see Sint
  Niklaasje Kom Maar

ST. WENCESLAS see Foerster, Josef
  Bohuslav, Svaty Vaclav

SAINTE MARGUERITE
  see Two French Folk Songs
  (Ridout, Godfrey) SATB (med diff)
  WATERLOO $.35   (S16)

SAINTE MARGUERITE see Willan, Healey

SAKAC, BRANIMIR
  Omaggio-Canto Dalla Commedia
  SATB,vln,perc CROATICA   (S17)

SAKAMOTO, YOSHITAKA (1898-1968)
  Der Frohliche Schiffer "Schimotzui
    Ist Ein Guter Hafen" *see
    Shimotzui Bushi

  Kohlengraberlied "Mond Schimmert Auf"
    *see Kyushu Tanko Bushi

  Kyushu Tanko Bushi *Jap
    "Kohlengraberlied "Mond Schimmert
    Auf"" [Jap/Ger] men cor sc
    SCHOTTS C 41 731 s.p. see from
    Vier Japanische Chorlieder   (S18)

  Lied Des Fischers "Wenn Ich Ein
    Movchen Frage" *see Soran Bushi

  Sansa Sigure *Jap
    "Tanzlied "O Sansa, Aus Grauem
    Himmel"" [Jap/Ger] men cor sc
    SCHOTTS C 41 730 s.p. see from
    Vier Japanische Chorlieder   (S19)

  Shimotzui Bushi *Jap
    "Der Frohliche Schiffer "Schimotzui
    Ist Ein Guter Hafen"" [Jap/Ger]
    men cor sc SCHOTTS C 41 732 s.p.
    see from Vier Japanische
    Chorlieder   (S20)

  Soran Bushi *Jap
    "Lied Des Fischers "Wenn Ich Ein
    Movchen Frage"" [Jap/Ger] men cor
    sc SCHOTTS C 41 729 s.p. see from
    Vier Japanische Chorlieder   (S21)

  Tanzlied "O Sansa, Aus Grauem Himmel"
    *see Sansa Sigure

  Vier Japanische Chorlieder *see
    Kyushu Tanko Bushi,
    "Kohlengraberlied "Mond Schimmert
    Auf""; Sansa Sigure, "Tanzlied "O
    Sansa, Aus Grauem Himmel"";
    Shimotzui Bushi, "Der Frohliche
    Schiffer "Schimotzui Ist Ein
    Guter Hafen""; Soran Bushi, "Lied
    Des Fischers "Wenn Ich Ein
    Movchen Frage""   (S22)

SALJIVKA see Slavenski, Josip

SALLY
  SSA CIMINO $.40   (S23)
  SATB CIMINO $.40   (S24)
  TTBB CIMINO $.40   (S25)

SALLY AND HER LOVER see Cowan

SALLY GARDENS
  (Ericson, Christopher) SATB,pno,horn
  NATIONAL WHC-59 $.40   (S26)

SALUTATION OF THE DAWN see Gerschefski,
  Edwin

SALUTATIONS TO THE PARTY see Stanislav,
  Josef, Pozdrav Strane

SALVE, CARA DEO TELLUS SANCTISSIMA see
  DaRimini, Ludovico

SALVE REGINA see Byrd, William

SAMBALIEDCHEN see Rosenstengel,
  Albrecht

SAME OLD MONDAY see Grady

SAMPSON, GODFREY (1902-   )
  Bells, The
    dbl cor,3fl,pic,3ob,3clar,3bsn,
    4horn,3trp,3trom,tuba,timp,perc,
    harp,pno,strings, glockenspiel,
    celeste voc sc NOVELLO rental,
    ipr   (S27)

SAMSON
  Dix Chansons Ambassade Du Vin *CC10U
  mix cor,acap HENN 679 s.p.   (S28)

SAMSON AND DELILAH see Pottle, Sam

SAMSPILL OG SANG see Gjendem, Johan J.

SANCTUS FOR ST. CECELIA'S DAY see
  Clarke, Henry Leland

SANDERS
  Banjo Man, The (composed with
    Davidson)
    (Strommen) 2pt/SSA (jazz-rock)
    ALFRED 6817 $.50   (S29)
    (Strommen) SAB (jazz-rock) ALFRED
    6821 $.50   (S30)

  Composition Blues (composed with
    Davidson)
    (Strommen) SAB/SATB (jazz-rock)
    ALFRED 6820 $.60   (S31)
    (Strommen) 2pt/SSA (jazz-rock)
    ALFRED 6816 $.60   (S32)

  I Love Snow (composed with Davidson)
    *Xmas
    SA ALFRED 6806 $.50   (S33)

  It's A Big Christmas World (composed
    with Davidson)
    SA ALFRED 6807 $.50   (S34)

  Man In The Red Suit, The (composed
    with Davidson) *Xmas
    SA ALFRED 6808 $.50   (S35)

SANDERSON W.
  Gather Ye Rosebuds
  SA CRAMER $.25   (S36)

SANDMANNCHEN "DER ABENDWIND, DER TRAGT
  EIN KLEINES REITERLEIN" see Rein,
  Walter

SANDRIN, PIERRE (? -ca. 1561)
  Doulce Memoire
  (Echols, Paul) SATB MCAFEE M1071
  $.40   (S37)

SANFILIPPO
  Jamaican Donkey
  2pt,opt drums PRO ART 2852 $.35
                                   (S38)

SANFILIPPO, JOSEPHINE
  Spotted Duckling, The (composed with
    Sanfilippo, Morghuita)
  2pt BOURNE B224196-351 $.40   (S39)

SANFILIPPO, MORGHUITA
  Spotted Duckling, The *see
    Sanfilippo, Josephine

SANG UND WEIN see Frey, Oskar

SANGEN see Stenhammar, Wilhelm

SANGER HERAUS see Desch, Rudolf

SANGER-MOTTO see Anders-Strehmel,
  Gerhard

SANGERBUND see Bruckner, Anton

SANGERGRUSS "SEID WILLKOMMEN" see Zoll,
  Paul

SANGERRUF see Fussan, Werner

SANGERSPRUCH DES SANGERBUNDES
  RHEINLAND-PFALZ "DU LAND DER
  BURGEN" see Desch, Rudolf

SANGERSPRUCH DES SB. RHEINLAND-PFALZ
  "DU LAND DER BURGEN" see Desch,
  Rudolf

SANGERSPRUCH "STIMMET AN DEN GESANG"
  see Zoll, Paul

SANGERWETTSTREIT "FREUNDE, HORET UNSER
  MUSIZIEREN" see Rein, Walter

SANGERWORT see Paul, Heinz Otto

SANGESMUT see Schaefers, Anton

SANKT LAURENTIUS see Pepping, Ernst

SANKT PAULUS "SANKT PAULUS WAR EIN
  MEDIKUS" see Zelter, Carl Friedrich

SANKT URBAN, LIEBER HERRE see Seeger,
  Peter

SANSA SIGURE see Sakamoto, Yoshitaka

SANTA WATCHES GROWN UPS, TOO see
  Atkinson

SAPP, ALLEN DWIGHT (1922-   )
  Little Boy Lost, The *cant
  SATB,opt orch AM.COMP.AL.   (S40)

SARAI, TIBOR
  Debrecen Dicserete
  (Jokai, Mor) jr cor&jr cor&jr cor
  BUDAPEST 7349 s.p.   (S41)

SARIE MARAIS *folk
  (Biebl, F.) [Ger] 4pt men cor
  MERSEBURG EM9076 s.p.   (S42)

SARTORIUS, THOMAS
    Wohlauf, Ihr Lieben Gaste
        (Weber, W.) men cor,acap TONOS 3307
        s.p.   (S43)

SAT THERE A-ROCKIN' ALL NIGHT see
    Thygerson, Robert J.

SATEREN, LELAND BERNHARD (1913-   )
    Christmas Everywhere
        SATB oct SCHMITT 15022 $.35   (S44)

    Make Way For Man
        TTBB oct SCHMITT 418 $.30   (S45)

SATIN DOLL
    see Portrait Of Duke Ellington

SATURDAY see Bettis

SAUER, FRANTISEK (1938-   )
    Greetings To The President *see
        Zdravice Panu Presidentovi

    Popevky Na Dvore *CCU
        [Czech] jr cor,pno/5winds CZECH
        s.p.   (S46)

    Sest Detskych Pisni *CC6U
        [Czech] jr cor,pno/5winds CZECH
        s.p.   (S47)

    Zdravice Panu Presidentovi
        "Greetings To The President"
        [Czech] mix cor,acap CZECH s.p.
                                          (S48)

SAVE ME FROM THE GRAVE AND WISE
    (Beethoven; Boyd) SATB SCHIRM.G
    LG51760 $.35   (S49)

SAVOYARD SONG see Thorpe, Raymond

SAY A PRAYER FOR THE BOYS
    SATB CIMINO $.40   (S50)

SCALDAVA IL SOL see Marenzio, Luca

SCANDELLO, ANTONIO (1517-1580)
    Ein Hennlein Weiss
        (Lendvai, Erwin) 4pt wom cor (med)
        sc SCHOTTS C 37 599 s.p.   (S51)

SCARBOROUGH FAIR
    (Archibeque, Charlene) SSA,pno,gtr,
    glockenspiel NATIONAL WHC-10 $.40
                                          (S52)

SCARBOROUGH FAIR-CANTICLE see Simon,
    Paul

SCARLATTI, ALESSANDRO (1660-1725)
    La Colpa, Il Pentimento E La Grazia
        (Gubitosi, E.) wom cor,ob,horn
        (Recitative And Duet) CARISH
        rental contains also: O Soave
        Conforto   (S53)

    O Soave Conforto
        see Scarlatti, Alessandro, La
        Colpa, Il Pentimento E La Grazia

SCARLET SARAFAN, THE *folk,Russ
    (Bilencko, M.) SSA LESLIE 3032 $.30
                                          (S54)

SCENARIO, A see Tanenbaum, Elias

SCHAB AB see Thehos, Adam

SCHAB AB "JETZT KOMMT DER SOMMER IN DAS
    LAND " see Rein, Walter

SCHAEFERS
    Gott Ist Gewaltig
        see LIEDPROGRAMM DES DEUTSCHEN
        SANGERBUNDES FOLGE 3: "ESSENER
        LIEDERBLATT" - "CHORFEIER"

SCHAEFERS, ANTON
    Johnny, Johnny, John
        men cor,acap TONOS 2020-1 s.p.
                                          (S55)

    Morgenlied
        see Vier Eichendorff-Lieder

    Reiselied
        see Vier Eichendorff-Lieder

    Sangesmut
        see Vier Eichendorff-Lieder

    Trost
        see Vier Eichendorff-Lieder

    Vier Eichendorff-Lieder
        men cor,acap cmplt ed TONOS 3980
        s.p.
        contains: Morgenlied; Reiselied;
        Sangesmut; Trost   (S56)

    Whisky
        men cor,acap TONOS 2020-2 s.p.
                                          (S57)

SCHAFERIN UND KONIGSSOHN *folk,Fr
    (Seeger, Peter) men cor,acap TONOS
    2013 s.p.   (S58)

SCHAFERLEBEN: NICHTS KANN AUF ERDEN see
    Silcher, Friedrich

SCHAFERS SONNTAGSLIED see Kreutzer,
    Konradin

SCHAFERSMANN see Michels, Josef

SCHAFFHAUSER-LIEDERBUCH *CCU
    3pt mix cor PELIKAN PE804 s.p.   (S59)

SCHATZ, WENN DU UBER DIE GASSE see
    Schneider, Walther

SCHAU ICH DIR IN DIE AUGEN see
    Marenzio, Luca

SCHAUSS, KARL (1856-1929)
    Die Abreise "Morgen Will Mein Schatz
        Verreisen" *folk
        men cor sc SCHOTTS C 33 203 s.p.
                                          (S60)

SCHECHER, FRED
    Schlaf Wohl, Du Himmelsknabe
        men cor,acap TONOS 154 s.p.   (S61)

SCHEIDEN see Bartok, Bela, Banat

SCHEIDEN MUSS ICH JETZT see Dowland,
    John

SCHEIN, JOHANN HERMANN (1586-1630)
    Collected Works *sac/sec,CCU
        (Pruefer, Arthur) microfiche
        UNIV.MUS.ED. $65.00 7 volumes,
        originally published at Leipzig,
        1901-1923.   (S62)

    Der Kuhle Maien
        3pt wom cor/3pt mix cor (easy) sc
        SCHOTTS C 38 126-03 s.p.   (S63)

    Herbei, Wer Lustig Sein Will Hier
        SSATB (med easy) sc SCHOTTS
        CHBL 372 s.p.   (S64)

    Kirtenlust *CC5U,madrigal
        5pt mix cor,cont (med) BAREN.
        BA4400 s.p.   (S65)

    Rundadinella "Holla, Gut G'sell"
        SSATB (med easy) sc SCHOTTS
        CHBL 371 s.p.   (S66)

    Trinklieder (from Studentenschmaus;
        Venuskranzlein) CC7U,madrigal
        SSATB/SATTB,cont/acap (med) BAREN.
        BA6227 s.p.   (S67)

    Viel Schoner Blumelien
        men cor,acap TONOS 3331 s.p. (S68)

SCHEIN UNS, DU LIEBE SONNE see
    Brautigam, Helmut

SCHEINE, SONNE, SCHEINE see Zoll, Paul

SCHELMENLIEDCHEN "AUF DEM WASE GRAST
    DER HASE" see Zoll, Paul

SCHELTWORTE EINER GRIESGRAMENDEN MUTTER
    "KANNST DU NICHT, WENN'S FINSTER
    IST, NACH HAUSE GEHN?" see
    Sutermeister, Heinrich

SCHENK EIN see Desch, Rudolf

SCHENK EIN DEN WEIN GESELLE MEIN see
    Fussan, Werner

SCHENKE IM FRUHLING see Krietsch, Georg

SCHENKENBACHS REITERLIED see Zipp,
    Friedrich

SCHENKENBACHS REITERLIED "VON ERST SO
    WOLLN WIR LOBEN" see Knab, Armin

SCHENKST DU GUTEN EIN see Wittmer,
    Eberhard Ludwig

SCHERTZER, DANIEL (1928-   )
    Der Bauer *see Le Bouvier

    Die Eiche *folk,Russ
        [Ger/Russ] mix cor (med easy) sc
        SCHOTTS CHBL 419 s.p. see from
        Vier Russische Volkslieder   (S69)

    Die Junge Schaferin *see La Jeune
        Bergere

    Die Nachtigall *see Rossignol Du
        Bois

    Drei Zigeuner *see Three Gypsies

    Katjuschka *folk,Russ
        [Ger/Russ] SSATTBB,acap (med easy)
        sc SCHOTTS CHBL 418 s.p. see from
        Vier Russische Volkslieder   (S70)

    La Jeune Bergere *folk,Eur
        "Die Junge Schaferin" [Ger/Fr] mix
        cor (easy, contains also: Le
        Bouvier) sc SCHOTTS CHBL 408A-B

SCHERTZER, DANIEL (cont'd.)
        s.p. see from Vier Europaische
        Volkslieder   (S71)

    Le Bouvier *folk,Eur
        "Der Bauer" [Ger/Fr] mix cor (easy,
        contains also: La Jeune Bergere)
        sc SCHOTTS CHBL 408A-B s.p. see
        from Vier Europaische Volkslieder
                                          (S72)

    Rossignol Du Bois *folk,Eur
        "Die Nachtigall" [Ger/Fr] mix cor
        (easy, contains also: Three
        Gypsies) sc SCHOTTS CHBL 409A-B
        s.p. see from Vier Europaische
        Volkslieder   (S73)

    Three Gypsies *folk,Eur
        "Drei Zigeuner" [Ger/Eng] mix cor
        (easy, contains also: Rossignol
        Du Bois) sc SCHOTTS CHBL 409A-B
        s.p. see from Vier Europaische
        Volkslieder   (S74)

    Troika *folk,Russ
        [Ger/Russ] SATTBB,Bar solo,acap
        (med easy) sc SCHOTTS CHBL 417
        s.p. see from Vier Russische
        Volkslieder   (S75)

    Verchovino *folk,Russ
        [Ger/Russ] 4pt mix cor,S solo,acap
        (med easy) sc SCHOTTS CHBL 416
        s.p. see from Vier Russische
        Volkslieder   (S76)

    Vier Europaische Volkslieder *see La
        Jeune Bergere, "Die Junge
        Schaferin"; Le Bouvier, "Der
        Bauer"; Rossignol Du Bois, "Die
        Nachtigall"; Three Gypsies, "Drei
        Zigeuner"   (S77)

    Vier Russische Volkslieder *see Die
        Eiche; Katjuschka; Troika;
        Verchovino   (S78)

SCHERZI MUSICALI see Monteverdi,
    Claudio

SCHERZLIED *folk,Ger
    (Fischer, Theo) men cor,acap TONOS 49
    s.p.   (S79)

SCHERZLIED see Linke, Norbert

SCHERZLIED "KAUFE NICHT, TOLLE NICHT"
    see Slavenski, Josip, Saljivka

SCHICKELE, PETER (1935-   )
    Seasonings, The *cant
        SATB,orch (med) oct PRESSER
        411-41054 $2.25, ipr   (S80)

SCHIEB DEN RIEGEL VOR see Etti, Karl

SCHIFFERLIED: ES LOSCHT DAS MEER see
    Silcher, Friedrich

SCHILFLIEDER "DRUBEN GEHT DIE SONNE
    SCHEIDEN" see Sutermeister,
    Heinrich

SCHILLING, HANS LUDWIG (1927-   )
    Lengende Vom Weisen Und Zollner
        mix cor&speak cor,narrator,pno/
        cembalo,3fl,ob,2clar,2horn,3trp,
        3trom,strings,perc,gtr, celeste,
        saxophone (med) sc,cor pts
        SCHOTTS ED. 5528 s.p., ipr   (S81)

SCHILLING, OTTO-ERICH (1910-1967)
    Die Lustigen Spotter
        men cor,acap TONOS 4572 s.p. (S82)

SCHLACHTEFEST see Erdlen, Hermann

SCHLAF, FREUND see Lasker

SCHLAF, KINDCHEN, SCHLAF see Pepping,
    Ernst

SCHLAF WOHL, DU HIMMELSKNABE see
    Schecher, Fred

SCHLECTWETTER-KANTATE see Wilhelm,
    Heinz

SCHLEMM, GUSTAV ADOLF
    Drei Mannerchore Mit Hornerbegleitung
        men cor,4horn sc,cor pts TONOS 4230
        s.p., ipa
        contains: Hat Dich Die Liebe;
        Waldgruss; Wenn Der Fruhling
                                          (S83)

    Hat Dich Die Liebe
        see Drei Mannerchore Mit
        Hornerbegleitung

    In Allem Zur Hohe
        men cor,acap TONOS 4055 s.p. (S84)

    Waldgruss
        see Drei Mannerchore Mit
        Hornerbegleitung

SCHLEMM, GUSTAV ADOLF (cont'd.)

Wenn Der Fruhling
see Drei Mannerchore Mit
Hornerbegleitung

Wir Heissen Euch Hoffen
men cor,acap TONOS 4053 s.p. (S85)

SCHLUSSGESANG see Edler, Robert

SCHMERZ see Bartok, Bela, Keserves

SCHMID, A.
Der Esel
see Lustige Tierfabeln Part II

Ein Kleiner Hund Mit Namen Fips
see Lustige Tierfabeln Part I

Flugel Ins Licht
men cor,acap/pno ZIMMER. 581 sc
s.p., voc pt s.p. (S86)

Habicht Und Krote
see Lustige Tierfabeln Part I

Lustige Tierfabeln Part I
men cor,acap ZIMMER. 579 s.p.
contains: Ein Kleiner Hund Mit
Namen Fips; Habicht Und Krote
(S87)

Lustige Tierfabeln Part II
men cor,acap ZIMMER. 580 s.p.
contains: Der Esel; Sie War Ein
Blumelein (S88)

Sie War Ein Blumelein
see Lustige Tierfabeln Part II

SCHMID, HEINRICH KASPAR (1874-1953)
Weihnachtslied *Op.22, Xmas
4pt jr cor,pno,harmonium,vln (med)
sc SCHOTTS C 30 754 s.p., voc pt
SCHOTTS C 30 754A-B s.p., ipa
(S89)

SCHMIEDE DER ZEIT see Lendvai, Erwin

SCHMOLL-LIESCHEN *folk
(Meyer, W.) 3pt mix cor BRATFISCH
s.p. (S90)

SCHMOLL-LIESCHEN "LIESCHEN, WASS FALLT
DIR EIN" see Meyer, W.

SCHMUCK DICH, MADCHEN see Sutermeister,
Heinrich

SCHNECKENLIED "SCHNECK, SCHNECK,
MAUSCHEN" see Erdlen, Hermann

SCHNEEBALLSTRAUCH AM MEER *folk
(Klink, W.) [Ger] 4pt mix cor
MERSEBURG EM9219 s.p. (S91)

SCHNEEFLOCKENLIED see Gorl, Willibald

SCHNEEWEISS, JAN (1904-   )
Mesice *CC14U
[Czech] jr cor,5winds CZECH s.p.
(S92)

Now The Time Has Come *see Ted'
Prisel Cas

Nursery Ryhme *see Rikanka

Pisen Miru
"Song Of Peace, The" [Czech] jr
cor/wom cor,opt pno CZECH s.p.
(S93)

Rikanka
"Nursery Ryhme" [Czech] jr cor,acap
CZECH s.p. (S94)

Song Of Peace, The *see Pisen Miru

Ted' Prisel Cas
"Now The Time Has Come" [Czech]
unis,pno CZECH s.p. (S95)

SCHNEIDER, WILLY
Alle Singen Mit (from Lied Und
Blaserspiel) CCU
wom cor,brass SCHOTTS BSS 39 651
s.p., ipa (S96)

SCHNEIDER BOCK see Sutermeister,
Heinrich

SCHNEIDER-COURAGE "ES IST EIN SCHUSS
GEFALLEN" see Poos, Heinrich

SCHNEIDER-TRNAVSKY, MIKULAS (1881-1958)
Miesane Zbory *CCU
mix cor SLOV.HUD.FOND s.p. (S97)

Slovenske L'udove Piesne *CCU
men cor SLOV.HUD.FOND s.p. (S98)

Sl'ub Vlasti
mix cor SLOV.HUD.FOND s.p. (S99)

Vokalnej Tvorby *CCU
mix cor SLOV.HUD.FOND EZS 5 s.p.
(S100)

SCHNEIDER-TRNAVSKY, MIKULAS (cont'd.)

Vyber Zo Sovietskej
mix cor SLOV.HUD.FOND s.p. (S101)

SCHNEIDER, WALTHER
An Die Minne
men cor,acap sc,cor pts TONOS 3932
s.p. (S102)

Jetzt Schwingen Wir
see Vom Singen, Trinken, Und
Frohlichsein

Jetzt Schwingen Wir Den Hut
men cor,acap TONOS 3923 s.p. (S103)

Kleine Banditenballade
men cor,pno sc,voc sc TONOS 2221
s.p. see from Zwei Chansons
(S104)

Lustig, Ihr Bruder
see Vom Singen, Trinken, Und
Frohlichsein

Morgenlied
men cor,acap TONOS 3985 s.p. (S105)

Ninoschka
men cor,pno sc,voc sc TONOS 2222
s.p. see from Zwei Chansons
(S106)

Reim Dich Od'r Ich Fress Dich
men cor,acap TONOS 126 s.p. (S107)

Schatz, Wenn Du Uber Die Gasse
men cor,acap TONOS 85 s.p. (S108)

Vom Singen, Trinken, Und Frohlichsein
men cor,opt 2trp&2horn&2trom&2tuba,
2 tenor horns sc,cor pts TONOS
4930 s.p., ipa
contains: Jetzt Schwingen Wir;
Lustig, Ihr Bruder; Wer Hier
Mit Uns (S109)

Wer Hier Mit Uns
see Vom Singen, Trinken, Und
Frohlichsein
men cor,acap TONOS 3978 s.p. (S110)

Zwei Chansons *see Kleine
Banditenballade; Ninoschka (S111)

SCHNITZLER, HEINRICH (1908-   )
Der Regen
see Zwei Chorlieder

Sommerlied "Mir Ist Der Helle Sommer"
see Zwei Chorlieder

Zwei Chorlieder
mix cor (med easy) sc SCHOTTS
CHBL 379A-B s.p.
contains: Der Regen; Sommerlied
"Mir Ist Der Helle Sommer"
(S112)

SCHNITZWERK AN EINEM HOCHALTAR see
Pepping, Ernst

SCHOENBERG, ARNOLD (1874-1951)
Ein Uberlebender Von Warschau
*Op.46, cant
"Survivor From Warsaw, A" [Ger/Fr/
Eng] men cor,narrator,2fl,2ob,
2clar,2bsn,4horn,3trp,3trom,tuba,
strings,perc,timp,harp sc SCHOTTS
rental, ipr (S113)

Survivor From Warsaw, A *see Ein
Uberlebender Von Warschau

SCHOLA CANTANS *CCU,Lat
(Novak, Jan) cor cor pts ZANIBON 5413
s.p. (S114)

SCHOLA CANTORUM, VOL. I *sac/sec,CCU,
chorale/mot,15-16th cent
[Eng/Fr/Ger/Lat/It] BOOSEY $1.75
contains works by: Agricola; Di
Lasso; Friedrich; Morley; Fux,
J.J.; Obrecht, J. and others (S115)

SCHOLA CANTORUM, VOL. II *sac/sec,CCU,
chorale/mot,15-16th cent
[Eng/Fr/Ger/Lat/It] BOOSEY $1.75
contains works by: Agricola; Di
Lasso; Friedrich; Morley; Fux,
J.J.; Obrecht, J. and others (S116)

SCHOLA CANTORUM, VOL. III *sac/sec,
CCU,chorale/mot,15-16th cent
[Eng/Fr/Ger/Lat/It] BOOSEY $1.75
contains works by: Agricola; Di
Lasso; Friedrich; Morley; Fux,
J.J.; Obrecht, J. and others (S117)

SCHOLA CANTORUM, VOL. IV *sac/sec,CCU,
chorale/mot,15-16th cent
[Eng/Fr/Ger/Lat/It] BOOSEY $1.75
contains works by: Agricola; Di
Lasso; Friedrich; Morley; Fux,
J.J.; Obrecht, J. and others (S118)

SCHON BLUMELEIN see Schumann, Robert
(Alexander)

SCHON IST DIE WELT see Linke, Norbert

SCHON IST DIE WELT see Schroeder,
Hermann

SCHON ROTRAUT "WIE HEISST KONIG
RINGANGS TOCHTERLEIN?" see
Schumann, Robert (Alexander)

SCHON SINGEN IST EIN FEINE KUNST see
Franck, Melchior

SCHONE JUNGFRAU "SCHONE JUNGFRAU, WILL
DIR KLAGEN" see Weber, Bernhard

SCHONE MINKA *folk,Russ
(Dallinger, Fridolin) men cor,acap
TONOS 811 s.p. (S119)

SCHONE ROSE see Lucic, Franjo, Lepa
Roza

SCHONE WELT "WIE LIEGT DIE WELT SO
FRISCH UND TAUIG" see Lang, Hans

SCHONE ZEIT DER NACHTIGALLEN see Desch,
Rudolf

SCHONER BEI DIR see Fischer, Theo

SCHONER GEORG see Lucic, Franjo, Lepi
Juro

SCHONER SUMMER *folk
(Seeger, P.) [Ger] 4pt mix cor
MERSEBURG EM9246 s.p. (S120)

SCHONES LAND see Fischer, Theo

SCHONHEIT MUSS LEIDEN see Fischer,
Ernst

SCHONSTER ABENDSTERN *folk,Swiss
(Nehrkorn, Alex) SAATB MOSELER LB537
(S121)
(Weber, Bernhard) [Ger] 4pt men cor
MERSEBURG EM9023 s.p. (S122)
(Zoll, Paul) men cor,acap TONOS 117
s.p. (S123)

SCHONSTER TAG see Kracke, Hans

SCHOTTISCHE BARDENCHOR: STUMM SCHLAFT
see Silcher, Friedrich

SCHOTTISCHE HIRTENWEISE "HEUT SPIELT
DER DUDELSACK" see Fischer, Ernst

SCHOTT'S CHORBUCH BAND II *sac/sec,
CC27L
(Lang, Hans) 4pt men cor SCHOTTS
ED. 4052 s.p. contains works by:
Isaac; Caldara; Praetorius; Knab;
Schutz and others (S124)

SCHOTT'S CHORBUCH BAND III *CC35L
(Lang, Hans) 3 eq voices SCHOTTS
ED. 4053 s.p. contains works by:
Knab; Lang; Rein; Haas; Willms;
Lendvai; Simon; Mohler (S125)

SCHRAMM
Anemophon
SATB,acap (aleatory) MCAFEE M146
$.30 (S126)

SCHREITER, HEINZ
Am Morgen *see Kludas, Erich

Auf Der Wiese *see Kludas, Erich

Ein Kindertag *see Kludas, Erich

Geburtstag *see Kludas, Erich

Laterne *see Kludas, Erich

Rummelplatz *see Kludas, Erich

SCHREY, WILHELM (1915-1967)
Her Mit Dem Wein!
men cor,acap TONOS 4564 s.p. (S127)

SCHROEDER
I Want You For Christmas
SA oct SCHMITT 361 $.40 (S128)

SCHROEDER, HERMANN (1904-   )
Alles, Was Geschieht
men cor sc SCHOTTS C 40 356 s.p.
(S129)

Das Laub Fallt Von Den Baumen
2pt jr cor&4pt men cor,acap sc
SCHOTTS C 42 467 s.p. see from
Drei Chore (S130)

Das Verlassene Magdlein "Fruh, Wann
Die Hahne Krahn
see Sechs Morike-Chore

Der Romische Brunnen "Aufsteigt Der
Strahl"
mix cor (med diff) sc SCHOTTS

SCHROEDER, HERMANN (cont'd.)

C 37 990 s.p. see from Romische
Brunnen   (S131)

Drei Chore *see Das Laub Fallt Von
Den Baumen; Lustig, Ihr Bruder;
Schon Ist Die Welt   (S132)

Ein Stundlein Wohl Vor Tag "Derweil
Ich Schlafend Lag"
see Sechs Morike-Chore

Einst Liebt Ich Ein Madchen Sehr
*folk
mix cor (med easy) sc SCHOTTS
C 42 413 s.p. see from Zwei
Volkslieder   (S133)

Heimweh "Anders Wird Die Welt"
see Sechs Morike-Chore

Jagerlied "Zierlich Ist Des Vogels
Tritt Im Schnee"
see Sechs Morike-Chore

Leben Und Bestehen *cant
mix cor/wom cor,3vln/2vln&vla,2A
rec/2fl,pno,opt vcl/bvl,
glockenspiel, xylophone (med
easy) sc,cor pts SCHOTTS ED. 5200
s.p., ipa   (S134)

Lustig, Ihr Bruder
2pt jr cor&4pt men cor,acap sc
SCHOTTS C 42 465 s.p. see from
Drei Chore   (S135)

Mazurka "Die Mazurka Lockt" *folk
mix cor (med easy) sc SCHOTTS
C 42 414 s.p. see from Zwei
Volkslieder   (S136)

Romische Brunnen *see Der Romische
Brunnen "Aufsteigt Der Strahl";
Romische Fontane "Zwei Becken,
Eins Das Andre Ubersteigend";
Spruch "In Dem Grossen Strom Des
Lebens"   (S137)

Romische Fontane "Zwei Becken, Eins
Das Andre Ubersteigend"
mix cor (med diff) sc SCHOTTS
C 37 991 s.p. see from Romische
Brunnen   (S138)

Rosenzeit
see Sechs Morike-Chore

Schon Ist Die Welt
2pt jr cor&4pt men cor,acap sc
SCHOTTS C 42 466 s.p. see from
Drei Chore   (S139)

Sechs Morike-Chore
4-6pt mix cor,acap (med) sc SCHOTTS
C 40 995 s.p.
contains: Das Verlassene Magdlein
"Fruh, Wann Die Hahne Krahn;
Ein Stundlein Wohl Vor Tag
"Derweil Ich Schlafend Lag";
Heimweh "Anders Wird Die Welt";
Jagerlied "Zierlich Ist Des
Vogels Tritt Im Schnee";
Rosenzeit; Verborgenheit "Lass,
O Welt, O Lass Mich Sein"
                                 (S140)

Spruch "In Dem Grossen Strom Des
Lebens"
mix cor (med diff) sc SCHOTTS
C 37 992 s.p. see from Romische
Brunnen   (S141)

Verborgenheit "Lass, O Welt, O Lass
Mich Sein"
see Sechs Morike-Chore

Zwei Volkslieder *see Einst Liebt
Ich Ein Madchen Sehr; Mazurka
"Die Mazurka Lockt"   (S142)

SCHROTH, GERHARD
Reuben And Rachel
SATB WINGERT s.p.   (S143)

SCHUBERT
Nocturnal Serenade
TTBB WALTON 7500 $.35   (S144)
SATB WALTON 7023 $.35   (S145)

SCHUBERT, FRANZ (PETER) (1797-1828)
Abendfrieden
men cor,acap TONOS 4370 s.p. (S146)

An Den Fruhling
men cor,acap TONOS 4361 s.p. (S147)

Bacchus
men cor,acap TONOS 4384 s.p. (S148)

Complete Works *sac/sec,CCU
(Brahms, Johannes; Bruell, Ignaz;
Door, Anton; Epstein, Julius;
Fuchs, J.N.; Gaensbacher, J.;
Hellmesberger, J.; Mandyczewski,
Eusebius) microfiche UNIV.MUS.ED.

SCHUBERT, FRANZ (PETER) (cont'd.)

$185.00 21 series in 33 bindings,
Leipzig, 1884-1897.   (S149)

Das Dorfchen
men cor,pno sc,cor pts TONOS 4262
s.p.   (S150)

Der Entfernten
men cor,acap sc,cor pts TONOS 4382
s.p.   (S151)

Der Gondelfahrer "Es Tanzen Mond Und
Sterne" *Op.28
men cor,pno sc,cor pts TONOS 4250
s.p.   (S152)
(Kohler-Gotze) TTBB,pno voc sc
SCHOTTS C 39 510 s.p., voc pt
SCHOTTS C 39 511, 01-04 s.p.
                               (S153)

Die Gestirne
mix cor,pno BRATFISCH GB2744 s.p.
                               (S154)

Die Nacht "Wie Schon Bist Du"
*Op.17,No.4
men cor sc SCHOTTS CHBL 11 s.p.
                               (S155)

Die Zwei Tugendwege "Zwei Sind Der
Wege"
men cor sc SCHOTTS CHBL 141 s.p.
                               (S156)
men cor,acap TONOS 4364 s.p. (S157)

Edit Nonna
[Lat/Eng] TTBB,acap FOSTER MF1053
$.30   (S158)

Ewige Liebe
men cor,acap TONOS 4365 s.p. (S159)

Flucht
men cor,acap TONOS 4366 s.p. (S160)

Grab Und Mond
men cor,acap TONOS 4367 s.p. (S161)

Grave And The Moon, The
(Plott) TTBB BRODT DC 1 $.20 (S162)

Hymne
men cor,acap TONOS 4255 s.p. (S163)

Liebe "Liebe Rauscht Der Silberbach"
men cor sc SCHOTTS CHBL 140 s.p.
                               (S164)
men cor,acap TONOS 4368 s.p. (S165)

Lob Der Einsamkeit
men cor,acap TONOS 4377 s.p. (S166)

Mailied
men cor,acap TONOS 4369 s.p. (S167)

Nacht
men cor,acap TONOS 4373 s.p. (S168)

Nachthelle
men cor,pno sc,cor pts TONOS 4257
s.p.   (S169)

Nachtliches Standchen "Leise, Leise,
Lass Uns Singen"
see Schubert, Franz (Peter), Zum
Rundetanz "Auf, Es Dunkelt"
men cor,acap TONOS 4385 s.p. (S170)

Nachtmusik
men cor,acap TONOS 4360 s.p. (S171)

Nature's Harmony
(Lethbridge) SSA (med easy) OXFORD
54.951 $1.30   (S172)

Night, The
(Plott) TTBB BRODT DC 5 $.24 (S173)

Ruhe, Schonstes Gluck Der Erde
men cor,acap TONOS 4371 s.p. (S174)

Sehnsucht
5pt men cor BREITKOPF-W CHB 4857
s.p.   (S175)

Selig Durch Die Liebe
men cor sc SCHOTTS CHBL 80 s.p.
                               (S176)

Serenade
(McCarthy, John) [Eng] SATB MCAFEE
M1088 $.40   (S177)

Shepherdess, The
TTBB BRODT UF 1 $.25   (S178)

To Spring
(McCullough) SATB SOUTHERN $.30
                               (S179)

Wand'ring Miller
(Brown, F.E.) 3pt ALLANS 829 (S180)

Wehmut
men cor,acap TONOS 4381 s.p. (S181)

Weihegesang
men cor,acap TONOS 4383 s.p. (S182)

SCHUBERT, FRANZ (PETER) (cont'd.)

Wohin Soll Ich Mich Wenden?
men cor,acap TONOS 4376 s.p. (S183)

Zum Rundetanz "Auf, Es Dunkelt"
men cor sc SCHOTTS CHBL 155A-B s.p.
contains also: Nachtliches
Standchen "Leise, Leise, Lass Uns
Singen"   (S184)
men cor,acap TONOS 4372 s.p. (S185)

SCHUBERT, HEINO (1928-)
Der Prinz "Wir Wollten Zusammen
Bauen"
SAB,acap (med easy) sc SCHOTTS
CHBL 337 s.p.   (S186)

Wanderschaft "Im Walde Bluht Der
Seidelbast"
SAB,acap (med easy) sc SCHOTTS
CHBL 336 s.p.   (S187)

SCHULER, KARL (1894-1945)
Abendkantate *cant
3pt wom cor/3pt jr cor,pno/fl&vln&
vla (med easy) sc,voc pt SCHOTTS
ED. 5417 s.p., ipa   (S188)

Erntekantate *Op.31, cant
3 eq voices,2rec/vln&vla&vcl/3vln/
3clar (med) sc,cor pts SCHOTTS
ED. 5418 s.p., ipa   (S189)

Kirmes Musik *CCU
1-3pt jr cor/1-3pt mix cor/1-3 eq
voices,2inst (med easy) sc
SCHOTTS C 39 494 s.p., cor pts
SCHOTTS C 39 595 s.p., ipa (S190)

SCHULHOFF, ERWIN (1894-1942)
Communist Manifesto, The *see
Komunisticky Manifest

Komunisticky Manifest *ora
(Havelka, Sv.) "Communist
Manifesto, The" [Czech/Ger] boy
cor&mix cor,SATB soli,3fl,3ob,
3clar,3bsn,4horn,4trp,3trom,tuba,
timp,perc,strings PANTON s.p.
                               (S191)

Manifest *cant
"Manifesto" [Czech/Ger] dbl cor&jr
cor,4 soli,2fl,2clar,4horn,7trp,
3trom,timp,perc, 5 bugle horns, 3
bass euhponiums CZECH s.p. (S192)

Manifesto *see Manifest

SCHULTHORPE
Autumn Song
SATBB SCHIRM.G F11980 $.30 (S193)

SCHULTZ, SVEND S. (1913-   )
Cave. Hic Tu Fallaci
[Lat] SSAATB,opt fl EGTVED KB220
s.p. see from Quattuor Fragmenta
Ex Ovidii Ars Amandi   (S194)

Conquerar, An Moneam
[Lat] SSAATB,opt fl EGTVED KB221
s.p. see from Quattuor Fragmenta
Ex Ovidii Ars Amandi   (S195)

Finiturus Eram
[Lat] SSAATB,opt fl EGTVED KB222
s.p. see from Quattuor Fragmenta
Ex Ovidii Ars Amandi   (S196)

Four Latin Madrigals 1974 *see
Glycera; Pervigilium Veneris; Quo
Pinus; Ver Redit Optatum   (S197)

Glycera *madrigal
[Lat] SSATB,acap EGTVED KB252 s.p.
see from Four Latin Madrigals
1974   (S198)

Pervigilium Veneris *madrigal
[Lat] SSATB,acap EGTVED KB250 s.p.
see from Four Latin Madrigals
1974   (S199)

Prima Tuae Menti Veniat
[Lat] SSAATB,opt fl EGTVED KB219
s.p. see from Quattuor Fragmenta
Ex Ovidii Ars Amandi   (S200)

Quattuor Fragmenta Ex Ovidii Ars
Amandi *see Cave. Hic Tu
Fallaci; Conquerar, An Moneam;
Finiturus Eram; Prima Tuae Menti
Veniat   (S201)

Quo Pinus *madrigal
[Lat] SSATB,acap EGTVED KB251 s.p.
see from Four Latin Madrigals
1974   (S202)

Ver Redit Optatum *madrigal
[Lat] SSATB,acap EGTVED KB249 s.p.
see from Four Latin Madrigals
1974   (S203)

SCHULZ
Der Mond Ist Aufgegangen
(Nother, Willi) men cor&jr cor,acap
TONOS 1303 s.p.   (S204)

SCHULZ, JOH. ABRAHAM PETER (1747-1800)
Erntedanklied "Wir Bringen Mit Gesand
Und Tanz"
(Rein, Walter) mix cor (easy) sc
SCHOTTS CHBL 265 s.p.   (S205)

SCHUMANN, ROBERT (ALEXANDER)
(1810-1856)
Autumn Song *see Herbstlied

Choral Music For Two Or More Voices
Vol. I *CCU
cor min sc KALMUS 1137 $1.50
contains: Op. 24, 43, 78, 106,
26, 69   (S206)

Choral Music For Two Or More Voices
Vol. II *CCU
cor min sc KALMUS 1138 $1.50
contains: Op. 91, 74, 101 (S207)

Choral Music For Two Or More Voices
Vol. III *CCU
cor min sc KALMUS 1139 $1.50
contains: Op. 114, 138   (S208)

Complete Works *sac/sec,CCU
(Schumann, Clara; Brahms, Johannes)
microfiche UNIV.MUS.ED. published
in 14 series, Leipzig, 1879-1893.
(S209)

Der Traumende See
men cor,acap TONOS 6322 s.p. (S210)

Der Traumende See "Der See Ruht Tief
Im Blauen Traum" *Op.33,No.1
men cor sc SCHOTTS CHBL 30 s.p.
(S211)

Die Lotosblume
men cor,acap TONOS 6333 s.p. (S212)

Die Minnesanger
men cor,acap TONOS 6325 s.p. (S213)

Die Rose Stand Im Tau *Op.65,No.1
men cor,acap TONOS 6323 s.p. (S214)
men cor sc SCHOTTS CHBL 12 s.p.
(S215)

Dunkler Lichtglanz *Op.138,No.10
(Hall, Wm.D.) "In The Twilight"
[Eng/Ger] SATB,pno, 4 hands
NATIONAL WHC-65 $.45   (S216)

Fruhlingsgruss
men cor,acap TONOS 6332 s.p. (S217)

Fruhlingsgruss "So Sei Gegrusst Viel
Tausendmal" *Op.79,No.4
(Klink, Waldemar) wom cor/jr cor
(easy) sc SCHOTTS CHBL 510 s.p. (S218)

Herbstlied
(Hall, Wm.D.) "Autumn Song" [Eng/
Ger] SATB,pno NATIONAL WHC-55
$.40   (S219)
(Hall, Wm.D.) "Autumn Song" [Eng/
Ger] SA/TB,pno NATIONAL WHC-54
$.40   (S220)

Im Walde "Es Zog Eine Hochzeit"
2pt mix cor (easy) sc SCHOTTS
CHBL 394 s.p.   (S221)

In The Twilight *see Dunkler
Lichtglanz

Landliches Lied *Op.29,No.1
(Hall, Wm.D.) "Rural Song" [Eng/
Ger] SA/TB,pno NATIONAL WHC-56
$.40   (S222)

Lovely Flower *see Schon Blumelein

Rural Song *see Landliches Lied

Schon Blumelein *Op.43,No.3
(Hall, Wm.D.) "Lovely Flower" [Eng/
Ger] SA/TB,pno NATIONAL WHC-61
$.40   (S223)
(Hall, Wm.D.) "Lovely Flower" [Eng/
Ger] SATB,pno NATIONAL WHC-68
$.45   (S224)

Schon Rotraut "Wie Heisst Konig
Ringangs Tochterlein?"
mix cor (easy) sc SCHOTTS CHBL 395
s.p.   (S225)

Sommerlied "Seinen Traum Lind Wob"
*Op.146,No.4
mix cor (easy) sc SCHOTTS CHBL
396 s.p.   (S226)

Song Of The Wanderer
(Christiansen, P.) SATB oct SCHMITT
1211 $.35   (S227)

Zigeunerleben
SATB,pno sc EGTVED KB125 s.p.
(S228)

SCHUMANN, ROBERT (ALEXANDER) (cont'd.)
Zum Anfang "Mache Deinem Meister
Ehre"
men cor sc SCHOTTS CHBL 199 s.p.
(S229)

Zur Hohen Jagd
men cor,4horn sc,cor pts TONOS 4271
s.p., ipa   (S230)

Zurne Nicht Des Herbstes Wind
men cor,acap TONOS 6324 s.p. (S231)

SCHUMANN, WILLIAM HOWARD (1910-   )
To Thy Love
SSA,acap (choral fantasy) oct
PRESSER 342-40100 $.35   (S232)

SCHUNDROMANE LESEN "DAS IST DAS
SCHONSTE" see Hindemith, Paul

SCHUTZ, HEINRICH (1585-1672)
Collected Works *sac/sec,CCU
(Spitta, Philipp; Schering, Arnold;
Spitta, Heinrich) [Ger/Lat/It]
microfiche UNIV.MUS.ED. $90.00
originally published as 18
volumes, Leipzig, Breitkopf and
Haertel, 1885-1927.   (S233)

Ket Olasz Madrigal *CC2U,madrigal,It
(Szekeres) mix cor BUDAPEST 6831
s.p.   (S234)

Wie Nun, Ihr Herren?
see Sichers Teutschland, Schlafst
Du Noch?

SCHUTZE see Strobl, Otto

SCHUYT, NICO (1922-   )
To The Moon
wom cor&mix cor,4fl,2ob,2clar,2bsn,
2horn,2trp,strings,6perc,3timp,
piano 4-hands DONEMUS   (S235)

SCHWABISCHE LIEBESLIEDCHEN: E BISSELE
LIEB see Silcher, Friedrich

SCHWABISCHE TANZLIED: BIN I NET see
Silcher, Friedrich

SCHWABISCHES LIEBESLIEDCHEN see Rische,
Quirin

SCHWABISCHES QUODLIBET see Kuhlenthal,
Fred

SCHWABISCHES TANZLIED "ROSENSTOCK,
HOLDERBLUH" see Rein, Walter

SCHWABISCHES TANZLIEDCHEN: MEI SCHATZLE
see Silcher, Friedrich

SCHWAEN, KURT (1909-   )
Die Wildganse
wom cor/jr cor,acap HOFMEISTER
G2214 s.p.   (S236)

Hol Uber, Fahrmann Morgenrot
4pt mix cor,pno NEUE NM1001 s.p.
(S237)

Karl Und Rosa, Oder Lob Der Partei
4pt mix cor,4 narrators,MezBar
soli,orch NEUE NM218 s.p. (S238)

SCHWARTZ, GERHARD VON (1902-   )
An Die Freunde "Wieder Einmal
Ausgeflogen"
SATB,acap (med easy) BAREN. BCH42
s.p.   (S239)

SCHWARTZ, PAUL (1907-   )
Survey Of Literature
[Eng] SATB,SBar soli,pno RONGWEN
$.50   (S240)

SCHWARTZ, STEPHEN
Magic To Do (from Pippin)
(Fischer) SATB BELWIN 2302 $.45
(S241)

Pippin *medley
(Cassey, Chuck) BELWIN $1.50 (S242)

SCHWARZ IST DAS HAAR *folk,Eng
(Erbelding, Dietrich) men cor,acap
TONOS 2041 s.p.   (S243)

SCHWARZ-SCHILLING, REINHARD (1904-   )
Drei Spruche In Kanonischer Form Und
Drei Kanons *canon
2-3pt (med easy) cmplt ed BAREN.
BCH 86 s.p.
contains: Mahnspruch "Freund, So
Do Etwas Bist"; Merkspruch "Wer
Immer Strebend Sich Bemuht";
Trostspruch "Die Musik Allein";
Wahlspruch "Andre Haben Andre
Schwingen"; Weckruf "Wach Auf,
Es Kommt Der Tag Herauf"; Wer
Freudig Tut   (S244)

Mahnspruch "Freund, So Do Etwas Bist"
see Drei Spruche In Kanonischer
Form Und Drei Kanons

SCHWARZ-SCHILLING, REINHARD (cont'd.)
Merkspruch "Wer Immer Strebend Sich
Bemuht"
see Drei Spruche In Kanonischer
Form Und Drei Kanons

Trostspruch "Die Musik Allein"
see Drei Spruche In Kanonischer
Form Und Drei Kanons

Wahlspruch "Andre Haben Andre
Schwingen"
see Drei Spruche In Kanonischer
Form Und Drei Kanons

Weckruf "Wach Auf, Es Kommt Der Tag
Herauf"
see Drei Spruche In Kanonischer
Form Und Drei Kanons

Wer Freudig Tut
see Drei Spruche In Kanonischer
Form Und Drei Kanons

SCHWARZBRAUNES MADCHEN *folk
(Mockl, Franz) men cor,acap TONOS 133
s.p.   (S245)

SCHWARZE KIRSCHEN *folk
(Biebl, F.) [Ger] 4pt men cor
MERSEBURG EM9074 s.p.   (S246)

SCHWEBE, WONNIGE MELODIE see Edler,
Robert

SCHWEFELHELZLE MUSS MA HA see Pepping,
Ernst

SCHWEFELHOLZLE see Erdlen, Hermann

SCHWEFELHOLZLE see Zoll, Paul

SCHWEIGEN DER LIEBE "SO IHR NUN STIMMEN
HORT" see Genzmer, Harald

SCHWEIGET MIR VOM WEIBERNEHMEN see
Cadow, Paul

SCHWERER ABSCHIED *folk,Norw
(Schwind, Gunter) men cor,acap TONOS
2011 s.p.   (S247)

SCHWESTERLEIN, WANN GEHN WIR NACH HAUS?
see Lang, Hans

SCHWING SANFT, MEIN GUT GEFAHRT see
Swing Low, Sweet Chariot

SCOTT
Now Is The Hour *see Kaihan, M.

This Is My Own, My Native Land
(Butler) SATB WILLIS 9786 $.30
(S248)
(Butler) TTBB WILLIS 9787 $.30
(S249)

SCOTT, ALICIA ANN
Think On Me
SA GALAXY 1.707.1 $.30   (S250)
(Bartholomew) SATB GALAXY 1.0964.1
$.30   (S251)
(Bartholomew) SSAA GALAXY 1.0965.1
$.30   (S252)
(Bartholomew) TTBB GALAXY 1.0951.1
$.30   (S253)
(Perrenot) SSA GALAXY 1.1381.1 $.30
(S254)

SCOTT, C.
Who Do You Think You Are? (composed
with Dyer, D.)
(Metis, F.) SSA BIG3 $.45 (S255)
(Metis, F.) SAB BIG3 $.45 (S256)
(Metis, F.) SATB BIG3 $.45 (S257)

SCOTT, CYRIL MEIR (1879-1970)
Mystic Ode
men cor,2bsn,4horn,2trp,3trom,tuba,
timp,perc,harp,org,vcl,bvl voc sc
NOVELLO rental, ipr   (S258)

Ode To Great Men
AAA,T/narrator,3fl,3ob,3clar,3bsn,
4horn,3trp,3trom,tuba,perc,pno,
harp,org,strings, celeste voc sc
NOVELLO rental, ipr   (S259)

SCRAPBOOK FOR JULIE, A see Barnes, M.H.

SCRAPBOOK FOR JULIE, A see Barnes, M.H.

S'DIANDL VON DER ENTERN ZEIL see
Burkhart, Franz

SE AMOR MAI DA VU SE VEDE *folk
(Weber, Bernhard) "Lasst Sich Amor
Bei Euch Schauen" [Ger/It] 4pt mix
cor MERSEBURG EM9243 s.p. (S260)

SE JE FAIS BIEN OU MAL AUSSI see
Agricola

SE LONTAN BEN MIO TU SEI see Mozart,
Wolfgang Amadeus

SE MI VUOI BENE see Ferrari, Giorgio

SE NEL MAR DEL MIO PIANTO see
Banchieri, Adriano

SE NEL PARTIR DA VOI see Monteverdi,
Claudio

SE PER HAVERVI, OIME see Monteverdi,
Claudio

SE POR NON MI CONSENTI see Monteverdi,
Claudio

SEA, THE see Sokola, Milos, More

SEA CRUISE see Reaks

SEA GULLS see Coulthard, Jean

SEA GYPSY, THE see Johns, Sidney

SEA MAIDENS, THE see Protheroe, Daniel

SEA OF FOREVER see Priddy

SEA OF LIBERTY see Red, Buryl

SEA-WIFE, THE see Grainger, Percy
Aldridge

SEAL LULLABY see Shearer, C.M.

SEALS
Diamond Girl (composed with Crofts)
*pop
(Shay) SATB WARNER WB-322 187 $.50
(S261)
We May Never Pass This Way Again
(composed with Crofts) *pop
(Frank) SSA,opt perc WARNER
WB-334 183 $.40   (S262)
(Frank) SATB,opt perc WARNER
WB-333 187 $.40   (S263)

SEARCH-SONGS OF THE SUN *CC23U
(Campbell, D.) cor GALLIARD 2.9021.7
$2.25   (S264)

SEARLE, HUMPHREY (1915-   )
I Have A New Garden
SSABarB,acap NOVELLO MT 1576 s.p.
(S265)

SEAS, THE see Brahms, Johannes, Die
Meere

SEASCAPE see Williamson, Malcolm

SEASCAPE, A see Protheroe, Daniel

SEASONINGS, THE see Schickele, Peter

SEASONS see Sturman, Paul

SEASONS, THE see Haydn, (Franz) Joseph

SEASONS IN THE SUN see Brel

SEBESKY, GERALD
She Walks In Beauty
SATB STUDIO V726 $.45   (S266)

SECHS CHORE see Reutter, Hermann

SECHS CHORE FUR GLEICHE STIMMEN NACH
TEXTEN VERSCHIEDNER DICHTER see
Doppelbauer, Josef Friedrich

SECHS CHORLIEDER see Mockl, Franz

SECHS KANONS HEFT 1 see Haas, Joseph

SECHS KANONS HEFT 2 see Haas, Joseph

SECHS KLEINE WEISEN see Fegers, Karl

SECHS LIEDER see Haas, Joseph

SECHS LIEDER AUS WIEN *see Das Kriag'n
Ma Nimmermehr; Der Weaner Geht Net
Unter; Ein Alter Wiener-Bitz; Na,
Da Hab'n Ma's G'fangt; 'S
Waschermadl Von Lichtenthal; Wann I
Anmal Stirb   (S267)

SECHS MORIKE-CHORE see Schroeder,
Hermann

SECHS OSTERREICHISCHE VOLKSLIEDER *see
Alleweil Kann Ma Net Lustig Sein;
Da Drob'n Auf'n Berg; Drei Berg Und
Drei Tal; Es Ging Ein Bauerlein;
Hutschi Heili; I Woass Net   (S268)

SECHS SERBISCHE VOLKSLIEDER see
Slavenski, Josip

SECHS TANZ-KANONS see Rosenstengel,
Albrecht

SECHSE, SIEBEN, ODER ACHT see Fidelius,
Cornelius

SECHSZEHN KINDERLIEDER NACH TEXTEN VON
JAMES KRUSS see Pahlen, Kurt

SECOND SET OF MADRIGALS (1606) EM VOL.
30 see East, Michael

SECOND SET OF MADRIGALS (1609) EM VOL.
7 see Wilbye, John

SECOND SET OF MADRIGALS (1618) EM VOL.
22 see Bateson, Thomas

SECOND SET OF MADRIGALS AND PASTORALS
OF THREE FOUR, AND FIVE PARTS
(1613) EM VOL. 25 see Pilkington,
Francis

SECOND SET OF MADRIGALS AND PASTORALS
OF THREE, FOUR, AND FIVE PARTS
(1624) EM VOL. 26 see Pilkington,
Francis

SECOND TRIO BOOK OF THE SINGING PERIOD
SERIES *CCU
(Hill, Harry) cor WATERLOO $.75
(S269)

SECOND YOUTH SONG BOOK *CC10U
(Hughes) SAB,inst (easy) OXFORD
58.633 $1.00, ipa   (S270)

SECRET see Smiley, Pril

SECRET OF LIBERTY, THE see Gyring,
Elizabeth

SECULAR REQUIEM, A see Tate

SEDAKA, NEIL
Laughter In The Rain (composed with
Cody)
(Cassey) SATB,opt bvl&drums&2gtr
WARNER CH0791 $.40   (S271)

SEDLACEK, BOHUSLAV (1879-1944)
Exemplary Soldier, An *see Vzorny
Vojak

Vzorny Vojak
"Exemplary Soldier, An" [Czech] men
cor,acap CZECH s.p.   (S272)

SEDM MUZSKYCH SBORU see Provaznik,
Anatol

SEDMIDUBSKY, MILOS (1924-   )
At' Procitne Drevorubec *cant
"Awake, Lumberjack" [Czech] mix
cor,Bar solo,3fl,3ob,3clar,3bsn,
6horn,3trp,3trom,tuba,timp,perc,
harp,strings CZECH s.p.   (S273)

Awake, Lumberjack *see At' Procitne
Drevorubec

SEE THE CHARIOT see Horsley, William

SEEDS OF LOVE see Vaughan Williams,
Ralph

SEEFAHRER-SONG see Siegler, Winfried

SEEFAHRT TUT NOT see Edler, Robert

SEEFAHRT TUT NOT see Edler, Robert

SEEGER, PETER
Am Grabe
men cor,opt org/harmonium TONOS
3997 s.p.   (S274)

Auf Und Ab Den Schonen Rhein
men cor,acap TONOS 3743 s.p. (S275)

Augen Auf Im Strassenverkehr
2pt jr cor,soli,inst (easy) sc,cor
pts SCHOTTS ED. 4854 s.p., ipa
(S276)
Beschwingte Illusionen Verzaubern
men cor sc SCHOTTS C 41 966 s.p.
see from Illusionen   (S277)

Der Jugend Morgengesang
men cor,acap TONOS 4586 s.p. (S278)

Die Jagd Gehort Ihr! "Und Der Blick,
Der Geht Weit"
TTB,acap sc SCHOTTS CHBL 108 s.p.
see from Vier Lustige Lieder
(S279)
Die Nachttrommler
men cor,acap TONOS 4004 s.p. (S280)

Fehlt Dir, O Mensch, Die Harmonie
men cor sc SCHOTTS CHBL 190 s.p.
see from Zwei Zeitglossen (S281)

Frommer Wunsch "Harte Taler Musst Es
Regnen"
TTB,acap sc SCHOTTS CHBL 109 s.p.
see from Vier Lustige Lieder
(S282)
Fruhlingserwarten *cant
3pt wom cor,T solo,strings (med)
sc,cor pts SCHOTTS ED. 4724 s.p.,
ipa   (S283)

Greift Zum Bechler
men cor,acap TONOS 4587 s.p. (S284)

SEEGER, PETER (cont'd.)

Gut Ist's, Ein Weib Zu Haben
men cor sc SCHOTTS C 41 967 s.p.
see from Illusionen   (S285)

Illusionen *see Beschwingte
Illusionen Verzaubern; Gut Ist's,
Ein Weib Zu Haben; Kleine Toren -
Grosse Toren   (S286)

Jung Wolln Wir Sein
men cor,acap TONOS 4595 s.p. (S287)

Kleine Toren - Grosse Toren
men cor sc SCHOTTS C 41 968 s.p.
see from Illusionen   (S288)

Lieder, Goldne Brucken
men cor,acap TONOS 3954 s.p. (S289)

Mein Schatz Ist Ein Schreiner
mix cor (med easy) sc SCHOTTS
CHBL 334 s.p.   (S290)

Morgenlied "Verschwunden Ist Die
Finstre Nacht"
mix cor (med easy) sc SCHOTTS
CHBL 335 s.p.   (S291)

O Musica
men cor,S solo,strings voc sc,cor
pts TONOS 4966 s.p., ipa, ipr
(S292)
Pfalzische Liedkantate
men cor,brass sc,cor pts SCHOTTS
ED. 5455 s.p., ipa   (S293)

Pfirsich Ess Ich Gerne "Sind Die
Pfirsich Rund Und Reif"
TTB,acap sc SCHOTTS CHBL 107 s.p.
see from Vier Lustige Lieder
(S294)
Sankt Urban, Lieber Herre
men cor,acap TONOS 3993 s.p. (S295)

Sieben Madchen Nah Und Fern
TTB,acap sc SCHOTTS CHBL 106 s.p.
see from Vier Lustige Lieder
(S296)
Singe, Mein Herz
men cor,acap TONOS 4585 s.p. (S297)

Vier Lustige Lieder *see Die Jagd
Gehort Ihr! "Und Der Blick, Der
Geht Weit"; Frommer Wunsch "Harte
Taler Musst Es Regnen"; Pfirsich
Ess Ich Gerne "Sind Die Pfirsich
Rund Und Reif"; Sieben Madchen
Nah Und Fern   (S298)

Warehouse-Life *CC10L
mix cor,narrator,soli,trp,trom,bvl,
perc,gtr, alto saxophone (med
easy) sc,cor pts SCHOTTS ED. 6524
s.p., ipa   (S299)

Weinlied
men cor,acap TONOS 3994 s.p. (S300)

Wer Hat Zeit? Niemand Hat Zeit?
men cor sc SCHOTTS CHBL 191 s.p.
see from Zwei Zeitglossen (S301)

Zum Begrabnis "Wer Weiss, Wie Nahe
Mir Mein Ende"
wom cor (easy, contains two
settings) sc SCHOTTS CHBL 600A;B
s.p.   (S302)

Zwei Zeitglossen *see Fehlt Dir, O
Mensch, Die Harmonie; Wer Hat
Zeit? Niemand Hat Zeit?   (S303)

SEEK NOT FOR CONSTANCY see Mozart,
Wolfgang Amadeus, Piu Non Si
Trovano

SEELE, VERGISS SIE NICHT
unis wom cor SCHOTTS C 42 532K s.p.
see also Alle Singen Heft 1 (S304)

SEELEN
C'Est Si Bon *pop
(Hornez; Betti) SATB BELWIN UC 710
$.40   (S305)
(Hornez; Betti) SSA BELWIN UC 709
$.40   (S306)

SEEMANNS HEIMKEHR *folk
(Zoll, P.) [Ger] 4pt men cor
MERSEBURG EM9010 s.p.   (S307)

SEEMANNSCHOR "WIR LICHTEN DIE ANKER"
see Gerster, Ottmar

SEEMANNSLIED "DER MEISTER, DER
SCHIFFSJUNG" see Genzmer, Harald

SEERAUBERLIED *folk
(Heinrichs, W.) [Ger] 4pt men cor
MERSEBURG EM9026 s.p.   (S308)

SEHNAL, FRANTISEK (1902-   )
Krusne Hory Mts. Cantata, The *see
Krusnohorsha Kantata

Krusnohorsha Kantata *cant
"Krusne Hory Mts. Cantata, The"
[Czech] mix cor,Bar solo,2fl,2ob,
2clar,2bsn,4horn,2trp,2trom,tuba,
timp,perc,strings CZECH s.p.
(S309)

SEHNSUCHT *folk
(Tiedemann, H.-J.) [Ger] 4pt mix cor
MERSEBURG EM9215 s.p.   (S310)

SEHNSUCHT see Schubert, Franz (Peter)

SEHNSUCHT: DER SUSSE SCHLAF see
Silcher, Friedrich

SEHNSUCHT "SCHWEIFT AUCH MEIN BLICK"
see Genzmer, Harald

SEHNSUCHTSLIED see Siegl, Otto

SEHT ES REGNEN, SEHT ES GIESSEN see
Poos, Heinrich

SEHT, KONIG DAGOBERT *folk
(Seeger, P.) [Ger] 4pt men cor
MERSEBURG EM9015 s.p.   (S311)

SEI CORI DI MICHAELANGELO BUONARROTI IL
GIOVANE IA see Dallapiccola, Luigi

SEI CORI DI MICHAELANGELO BUONARROTI IL
GIOVANE IIA see Dallapiccola, Luigi

SEI CORI DI MICHAELANGELO BUONARROTI IL
GIOVANE IIIA see Dallapiccola,
Luigi

SEI GERN ALLEIN see Beck, Conrad

SEI NICHT TRAURIG, LIEBE MUTTER see
Dubuque, A.

SEIB, VALENTIN
Der Morgen
men cor,acap sc,cor pts TONOS 4042
s.p.   (S312)

Es Soll Ein Wein Sein
men cor,acap TONOS 3742 s.p. (S313)

Slawisches Tanzlied
men cor,acap TONOS 434 s.p. (S314)

Wacht Auf!
men cor,acap TONOS 3741 s.p. (S315)

Wanderlied
men cor,acap TONOS 433 s.p. (S316)

SEID NICHT BOSE *folk,Boh
(Langer, Hans-Klaus) men cor,acap
TONOS 2003 s.p.   (S317)

SEIDEL, JAN (1908-   )
Message To The Living *see Vzkaz
Zivym

Pisen O Strane
"Song Of The Party" [Czech] mix
cor,2fl,2ob,2clar,2bsn,4horn,
2trp,3trom,timp,perc,harp,strings
CZECH s.p.   (S318)

Red Flag, The *see Rudy Prapor

Rudy Prapor *cant
"Red Flag, The" [Czech] mix cor,
2fl,2ob,2clar,2bsn,4horn,4trp,
3trom,tuba,timp,perc,strings
CZECH s.p.   (S319)

Song Of The Party *see Pisen O
Strane

Vzkaz Zivym
"Message To The Living" [Czech] mix
cor,2fl,2ob,3clar,2bsn,4horn,
3trp,3trom,tuba,timp,perc,strings
PANTON s.p.   (S320)

SEIT DIE SONNE IHREN LICHTEN SCHEIN see
Beck, Conrad

SEKORA'S ABC see Burghauser, Jarmil,
Sekorova Abeceda

SEKOROVA ABECEDA see Burghauser, Jarmil

SEKS SANGER see Olsen, Sparre

SELECT MADRIGALS see Philips, Peter

SELECTED CHORUSES FOR SATB *sac/sec,
CCU
SATB SCHIRM.G LG51496 $3.00   (S321)

SELECTION see Bizet, Georges

SELIG DURCH DIE LIEBE see Schubert,
Franz (Peter)

SELIG IST ES ZU STERBEN see Palestrina,
Giovanni

SELIG SIND DIE TOTEN see Willems, Josef

SEMOLA
Christmas Is The Warmest Time Of Year
(Ades) SATB SHAWNEE A1305 $.45
(S322)

SEN A RANO see Simai, Pavol

SEN A RANO see Simai, Pavol

SEN NESMRTELNY see Hrusovsky, Ivan

SEN O CLOVEKU see Hrusovsky, Ivan

SEN O DIALKE see Hrusovsky, Ivan

SEN O HLASE see Hrusovsky, Ivan

SENFL, LUDWIG (ca. 1490-1543)
Ach Elslein, Liebes Elselein
mix cor (med easy) sc SCHOTTS
CHBL 363 s.p.   (S323)

Das Gelaut Zu Speyer "Nun Kumbt
Hierher All"
SAATBB,acap (med easy) sc SCHOTTS
C 37 870 s.p., voc pt SCHOTTS
C 37 871A-D s.p.   (S324)

Entlaubet Ist Der Walde
mix cor (med easy) sc SCHOTTS
CHBL 311 s.p.   (S325)

Hans Beutler Der Wollt Reiten Aus
men cor sc SCHOTTS C 38 815 s.p.
contains also: Widmann, Erasmus,
O Musica, Liebliche Kunst   (S326)

In Maytime
(Kirk) SATB KJOS 5908 $.40   (S327)

SENKIM A VILAGON see Bartok, Bela

SENN, KARL (1878-   )
Alter Joe "Fort Sind Sie All"
men cor sc SCHOTTS C 32 396 s.p.
(S328)
Dixie "Ich Wollt', Ich War Im
Baumwolland"
men cor sc SCHOTTS C 32 395 s.p.
(S329)

SENSEMAYA "DIE KULEBRA HAT AUGEN AUS
GLAS" see Genzmer, Harald

SENTENZE (DA QOHELET) see Ferrari,
Giorgio

SEPT RONDEAUX see Killmayer, Wilhelm

SEPTEMBER EVENING see Holm, Peder,
Septemberaften

SEPTEMBERAFTEN see Holm, Peder

SEPULCHER OF FAMOUS MEN, THE see
Newbury

SERBISCHE VOLKSLIEDER see Slavenski,
Josip

SERENADE see Roberton, Hugh Stevenson

SERENADE see Schubert, Franz (Peter)

SERENADE see Zentner, Johannes

SERENADE "DIE STADT RUHT IM DUNKEL" see
Borodin, Alexander Porfirievitch

SERENADE "MADCHEN, MEIN BRAUNES" see
Zoll, Paul

SERENADE TO SPRING *medley
SATB,opt band/orch CHAPPELL
W065008-3601 $.85   (S330)
SSA,opt band/orch CHAPPELL
2065008-3602 $.85   (S331)

SERENATA see Cremesini, M.

SERENATA see Pratella, Francesco
Balilla

SERENATA CUBANA "SPIELT DIE HABANERA"
see Fischer, Ernst

SERF HAS RISEN, THE see Markovic,
Adalbert

SERMISY, CLAUDE DE (ca. 1490-1562)
Au Joly Boys
"Im Grunen Wald" [Ger/Fr] mix cor
(easy) sc SCHOTTS C 39 772 s.p.
(S332)
Im Grunen Wald *see Au Joly Boys

Lasst Mich Allein
(Weber, W.) men cor,acap TONOS 3316
s.p.   (S333)

Puisqu'en Amour
(Ehret) "Since When One Loves" SATB
SCHIRM.G LG 51551 $.25   (S334)

SERMISY, CLAUDE DE (cont'd.)
Since When One Loves *see Puisqu'en
Amour

SERMON see Binet

SEST DETSKYCH PISNI see Sauer,
Frantisek

SEST MADRIGALU see Vrana, Frantisek

SEST SMISENYCH SBORU see Skvor,
Frantisek

SESTAK, ZDENEK (1925-   )
Spain Keeps Silent *see Spanelsko
Mlci

Spanelsko Mlci
"Spain Keeps Silent" [Czech] mix
cor,acap CZECH s.p.   (S335)

Zeme Dvojjedina *cant
mix cor,2pno SLOV.HUD.FOND s.p.
(S336)

SESTO NON-SENSE see Petrassi, Goffredo

SEVEN CONTRASTED SATB SONGS *CC7UL
(Thorpe, Raymond) SATB EMI   (S337)

SEVEN PART-SONGS see Holst, Gustav

SEVEN ROUNDS IN VARIOUS MOODS see
Weigl, Vally

SEVEN SEA POEMS see Hewitt-Jones, Tony

SEVEN SONGLETS see Franco, Johan

SEVEN SONGS see Chen, Nira

SEVERIN, W.
Deutschlands Klage
men cor BRATFISCH GB2482 s.p.
(S338)

SEVERN MEADOWS see Gurney

SHADOWS OF EVENING see Baker, D.

SHAKE ME I RATTLE see Hackady, Hal

SHAKER PATCHWORK see Pottle, Sam

SHAKESPEARE SYMPHONY, A see Steel,
Christopher [Charles]

SHALL I COME SWEET LOVE TO THEE see
Russell, Welford

SHALL I SUE see Dowland, John

SHANTY SEQUENCE, A *medley
(Bailey, Leon) SATB,acap CURWEN 61582
s.p.   (S339)

SHAPER
Free As The Wind (composed with
Goldsmith)
(Lojeski, Ed) SSA LEONARD-US
08217502 $.50   (S340)
(Lojeski, Ed) SATB LEONARD-US
08217500 $.50   (S341)

SHARE THE LAND
SSA CIMINO $.40   (S342)
SATB CIMINO $.40   (S343)

SHARPE, EVELYN
All Through The Night
SA CRAMER $.20   (S344)

Banks Of Allan Water, The
SA CRAMER $.25   (S345)

Gentle Mainden, The
SA CRAMER $.20   (S346)

Last Rose Of Summer, The
SA CRAMER $.20   (S347)

Many Years Ago
unis CRAMER $.30   (S348)

Skye Boat Song
SA CRAMER $.50   (S349)

Skye Boat Song (Descant)
SA CRAMER $.30   (S350)

Stars All Dotted Over The Sky
unis CRAMER $.20   (S351)

SHAW, KIRBY
I Just Wanted To Talk To You
SATB,pno,inst (jazz, includes
recording and 14 choral octavos)
LEONARD-US 07853900 $14.95   (S352)

I See You Passing
SATB,pno,inst (jazz, includes
recording and 14 choral octavos)
LEONARD-US 07853950 $14.95   (S353)

SHAW, MARTIN (1875-1958)
Over Hill, Over Dale
SA CRAMER $.20   (S354)

Song Of The Music Makers, The
SA CRAMER $.25   (S355)

SHAYNE, GLORIA
Sweet, Sweet, Sweet Little Jesus
*see Regney, Noel

SHE DIDN'T SAY YES
SSA CIMINO $.40   (S356)
TTBB CIMINO $.40   (S357)

SHE WALKS IN BEAUTY see Brahms,
Johannes

SHE WALKS IN BEAUTY see Sebesky, Gerald

SHEARER, C.M.
Daffodils
SATB,acap SOUTHERN SC 47 $.30
(S358)

Farewell To The Farm
SSA,acap SOUTHERN SC 46 $.30 (S359)

Geography Isn't Hard
TTBB SOUTHERN $.25   (S360)

Good Morning Sky
SSA SOUTHERN $.25   (S361)

Oh! Remember Me
SSA,acap SOUTHERN SC 44 $.35 (S362)

Owl, The
SSA,acap SOUTHERN SC 36 $.25 (S363)

Seal Lullaby
SATB,acap SOUTHERN SC 48 $.35
(S364)

There Was A Roaring In The Wind
TTBB SOUTHERN $.25   (S365)

Weary Lot Is Thine, A
TTBB,acap SOUTHERN SC 45 $.35
(S366)

Who Has Seen The Wind?
SATB SOUTHERN $.30   (S367)

SHE'LL BE COMING *folk
(Poos, H.) [Eng/Ger] 4pt mix cor
MERSEBURG EM9253 s.p.   (S368)
(Poos, H.) "Wenn Sie Kommt" [Eng/Ger]
4pt men cor MERSEBURG EM9086 s.p.
(S369)

SHELLS see Nystedt, Knut

SHELTERS see Spilka, Frantisek, Tisiny

SHENANDOAH *folk
see Funf Seemanslieder
(Erb) SATB SCHIRM.G LG51846 $.40
(S370)
(Miller, Carl) 2pt CHAPPELL
0063107-351 $.40   (S371)
(Olson) TTBB oct SCHMITT 419 $.35
(S372)

SHENANDOAH see Gehring, Philip

SHENDOAH see Newbury, Kent A.

SHENK
Shepherd's Nativity Song, The *Xmas
SATB MCAFEE M1056 $.40   (S373)

SHEPHERD
(Bissell, Keith W.) SSA (med easy)
WATERLOO $.30   (S374)

SHEPHERD, THE see George, Earl

SHEPHERD IN A SHADE, A see Dowland,
John

SHEPHERD KEPT SHEEP see Wildman, Wesley

SHEPHERDESS, THE see Schubert, Franz
(Peter)

SHEPHERD'S NATIVITY SONG, THE see Shenk

SHERMAN
Chim-Chim-Cheri
(Desch, Rudolf) men cor,acap TONOS
3748 s.p.   (S375)

You're Sixteen *pop
(Metis) SATB WARNER WB 347 187 $.40
(S376)

SHERMAN, RICHARD M.
Gratifaction (from Tom Saywer)
(composed with Sherman, Robert
B.)
(Metis, F.) SSA BIG3 $.40   (S377)
(Metis, F.) SAB BIG3 $.40   (S378)
(Metis, F.) SA/TB BIG3 $.45   (S379)
(Metis, F.) SATB BIG3 $.40   (S380)

Hannibal Mo-(Zouree)! (from Tom
Sawyer) (composed with Sherman,
Robert B.)
(Habash, J.M.) SAB BIG3 $.50 (S381)
(Habash, J.M.) SATB BIG3 $.40
(S382)

SHERMAN, RICHARD M. (cont'd.)
How Come? (from Tom Sawyer) (composed
with Sherman, Robert B.)
(Metis, F.) SA/TB BIG3 $.40   (S383)
(Metis, F.) SAB BIG3 $.40   (S384)
(Metis, F.) SSA BIG3 $.40   (S385)
(Metis, F.) SATB BIG3 $.40   (S386)

If'n I Was God (from Tom Sawyer)
(composed with Sherman, Robert
B.)
(Simon, W.) SATB BIG3 $.45   (S387)
(Simon, W.) SATB BIG3 $.40   (S388)
(Simon, W.) SA/TB BIG3 $.50   (S389)
(Simon, W.) SAB BIG3 $.40   (S390)

Man's Gotta Be, A (composed with
Sherman, Robert B.)
(Habash, J.M.) SATB BIG3 $.50
(S391)

River Song (composed with Sherman,
Robert B.)
(Simon, W.) SSA BIG3 $.45   (S392)
(Simon, W.) SATB BIG3 $.40   (S393)
(Simon, W.) SA/TB BIG3 $.45   (S394)
(Simon, W.) 3AB BIG3 $.50   (S395)

SHERMAN, ROBERT B.
Gratifaction *see Sherman, Richard
M.

Hannibal Mo-(Zouree)! *see Sherman,
Richard M.

How Come? *see Sherman, Richard M.

If'n I Was God *see Sherman, Richard
M.

Man's Gotta Be, A *see Sherman,
Richard M.

River Song *see Sherman, Richard M.

SHERRILL, BILLY
My Elusive Dreams *see Putman, Curly

SHE'S LIKE THE SWALLOW see Brown,
Norman

SHIELD, WILLIAM (1748-1829)
Bondpojken
(Jehrlander, Karl-Fredrik) mix cor
GEHRMANS KRB452   (S396)

SHILOH see Beadell, Robert M.

SHIMOTZUI BUSHI see Sakamoto, Yoshitaka

SHINUM PLACE see Farrell, Dennis

SHINY see Cope, Cecil

SHIPS IN THE WIND see Wilkinson, Philip
G.

SHIR HASHAHAR see Eisenstein, Judith
Kaplan

SHIZU see Fukushima, Kazuo

SHORE TO SHORE
see Two Welsh Love Songs

SHORT, MICHAEL
Song's Eternity
SSA,pno ROBERTON 75043 s.p.   (S397)

SHORTNIN' BREAD
(Arch, Gwyn) SSA EMI   (S398)

SHOT HEARD ROUND THE WORLD, THE see
Davis, Katherine K.

SHOUT FOR JOY see Newbury

SHOW BOAT (MEDLEY)
SSA CIMINO $1.00   (S399)
SATB CIMINO $1.00   (S400)
TTBB CIMINO $1.00   (S401)

SHOWBOAT CAME TO TOWN, THE see Hicks,
Val

SHOWTIME CHORAL COLLECTION VOL. 2 *CCU
CIMINO SA $1.75; SSA $1.75; SAB
$1.75; SATB $1.75; TTBB $1.75
(S402)

SHRIMP BOY see Goreau, Laurraine

SHUMAN
If The Good Lord Only Lets You Love
Me
(Straigis) SATB MARKS MC 4620 $.50
(S403)

SHUTTERS AND BOARDS
SSA CIMINO $.40   (S404)
SATB CIMINO $.40   (S405)

SI J'ETAIN PETITE MERE see Willan,
Healey, Little Mother

SI LE ROY M'AVAIT DONNE (from Cvjy)
folk
"Hatte Konig Heinrich" [Ger/Fr] 4pt

men cor,acap BREITKOPF-W CHB 4952
s.p.   (S406)

SI NOTRE VIE see Gagnebin, Henri

SIA BENEDETTA L'HOR' see Piccioli, G.

SIBELIUS, JEAN (1865-1957)
Vainamoinen's Song *Op.110
mix cor,orch PEER

SIBENICNI MADRIGALY see Rychlik, Jan

SIBILLE, JOSEF
Das Volkslied
men cor,acap TONOS 242 s.p. (S407)

SICHERS TEUTSCHLAND, SCHLAFST DU NOCH?
*folk,17th cent
4pt mix cor,acap HOFMEISTER V1110
s.p. contains also: Weber, Lutzows
Wilde Verwegene Jagd (Quaegber);
Schutz, Heinrich, Wie Nun, Ihr
Herren?; Es Ist Ein Schnitter
(Koch) (folk)   (S408)

SICILIANO see Bussotti, Sylvano

SIDE SHOW, THE see Ives, Charles

SIE SAGT, ICH KONNT NICHT SINGEN see
Biebl, Franz

SIE WAR EIN BLUMELEIN see Schmid, A.

SIE WOLLEN ES NICHT WAHRHABEN see
Hindermann, Walter Felix

SIEBEN DEUTSCHE VOLKSLIEDER *CC7U,
folk,16-17th cent
(Reznicek, E.N.) BIRNBACH men cor,pno
sc s.p.; men cor,pno voc pt s.p.;
mix cor,opt pno

SIEBEN EUROPAISCHE VOLKSLIEDER *see
Der Herzensdieb; Knecht, Du Sollst
Nicht Nach Den Magden Schaun; Komm
Zu Mir Zuruck; Liebster, Ade;
Tanzlied Aus Schweden;
Tschechisches Wiegenlied;
Wiegenlied Aus Portugal   (S409)

SIEBEN GEDANKEN UBER: ES IST EIN
SCHNITTER see Lutz, Oswald

SIEBEN MADCHEN NAH UND FERN see Seeger,
Peter

SIEBEN MADCHENLIEDER NACH SLOWAKISCHEN
VOLKSLIEDTEXTEN see Rohwer, Jens

SIEBEN UNGARISCHE CHORE NACH
VOLKSLIEDERN see Bresgen, Cesar

SIEBZG SCHLICHTE VOLKSLIEDSATZE
*CC70U,folk
(Kuhlenthal, Fred) eq voices/mix cor,
acap/inst cmplt ed CARUS MO 1 s.p.
(S410)
SIEBZIG SCHLICHTE VOLKSLIEDSATZE, HEFT
1 *CC17L,folk
(Kuhlenthal, Fred) eq voices/mix cor,
acap/inst CARUS MO 11 s.p.   (S411)

SIEBZIG SCHLICHTE VOLKSLIEDSATZE, HEFT
2 *CC11L,folk
(Kuhlenthal, Fred) eq voices/mix cor,
acap/inst CARUS MO 12 s.p.   (S412)

SIEBZIG SCHLICHTE VOLKSLIEDSATZE, HEFT
3 *CC7L,folk
(Kuhlenthal, Fred) eq voices/mix cor,
acap/inst CARUS MO 13 s.p.   (S413)

SIEBZIG SCHLICHTE VOLKSLIEDSATZE, HEFT
4 *CC9L,folk
(Kuhlenthal, Fred) eq voices/mix cor,
acap/inst CARUS MO 14 s.p.   (S414)

SIEBZIG SCHLICHTE VOLKSLIEDSATZE, HEFT
5 *CC9L,folk
(Kuhlenthal, Fred) eq voices/mix cor,
acap/inst CARUS MO 15 s.p.   (S415)

SIEBZIG SCHLICHTE VOLKSLIEDSATZE, HEFT
6 *CC10L,folk
(Kuhlenthal, Fred) eq voices/mix cor,
acap/inst CARUS MO 16 s.p.   (S416)

SIEBZIG SCHLICHTE VOLKSLIEDSATZE, HEFT
7 *CC9L,folk
(Kuhlenthal, Fred) eq voices/mix cor,
acap/inst CARUS MO 17 s.p.   (S417)

SIEGL, OTTO (1896-   )
Das Gebirge "Noch Ist Die Erde"
*cant
TTBB,2fl,2ob,2clar,2bsn,4horn,2trp,
3trom,tuba,strings,perc,timp,opt
harp voc sc SCHOTTS rental, voc
pt SCHOTTS ED. 4216 s.p., sc
SCHOTTS rental, ipr   (S418)

Einen Sommer Lang
men cor,acap TONOS 4061 s.p. (S419)

SIEGL, OTTO (cont'd.)

Erntetag
men cor,acap TONOS 4062 s.p. (S420)

Frohbotschaft
men cor,acap ZIMMER. 588 s.p.
(S421)

Lobgesang
men cor,acap ZIMMER. 572 s.p.
(S422)

Sehnsuchtslied
men cor,acap ZIMMER. 589 s.p.
(S423)

Trink Aus, Kamerad
men cor,acap ZIMMER. 573 s.p.
(S424)

SIEGLER, WINFRIED
Reitergluck
men cor,acap TONOS 3744 s.p. (S425)

Seefahrer-Song
men cor,acap sc,cor pts TONOS 431
s.p.   (S426)

SIEHST DU DEN MOND DORT AM HIMMEL
STEHN?
see Offenes Singen Nr. 89

SIEHST DU DEN STERN see Hessenberg,
Kurt

SIEVERINGER OKTOBERLIED see Pepping,
Ernst

SIGH NO MORE LADIES see Willan, Healey

SIGN OF THE ORIENT, THE see Zupanovic,
Lovro

SIKORSKI, TOMASZ (1939-   )
Vox Humana
cor,4trp,4horn,4trom,2pno, 4 gongs,
4 tam-tams MODERN s.p.   (S427)

SILCHER, FRIEDRICH (1789-1860)
Abendglocke: Wandrer Zieht
men cor,acap TONOS 5310 s.p. (S428)

Abschied: Morgen Mussen Wir Verreisen
men cor,acap TONOS 4305 s.p. (S429)

Abschiedsgruss: Rosmarin Und Salbei
men cor,acap TONOS 4328 s.p. (S430)

Abschiedsgruss "Rosmarin Und
Salbeiblattlein"
men cor sc SCHOTTS CHBL 194A-B s.p.
contains also: Untreue "Durch's
Wiesetal Gang I Jetzt Na" (S431)

Ade, Du Liebes Stadtchen
men cor,acap TONOS 4320 s.p. (S432)

Annchen Von Tharau
men cor,acap TONOS 5314 s.p. (S433)

Barbarossa
men cor,acap TONOS 4334 s.p. (S434)

Bundeslied: Hehr Und Heilig
men cor,acap TONOS 4333 s.p. (S435)

Burschenlied: Bruder, Lass Das
Madchen
men cor,acap TONOS 4326 s.p. (S436)

Das Gedenken: Mag Auch Heiss
men cor,acap TONOS 4327 s.p. (S437)

Das Lieben Bringt Gross Freud
men cor,acap TONOS 5316 s.p. (S438)

Das Schifflein: Ein Schifflein Ziehet
men cor,acap TONOS 5349 s.p. (S439)

Der Geliebten: Was, Traute Bruder
men cor,acap TONOS 5308 s.p. (S440)
men cor,acap TONOS 5308 s.p. (S441)

Der Gute Kamerad: Ich Hatt Einen
Kamerad
men cor,acap TONOS 5323 s.p. (S442)

Der Jodelplatz: Z'nachst Bin I Halt
men cor,acap TONOS 5347 s.p. (S443)

Der Lindenbaum: Am Brunnen
men cor,acap TONOS 5339 s.p. (S444)

Der Wanderer: Ein Strausschen
men cor,acap TONOS 5330 s.p. (S445)

Der Wirtin Tochterlein: Es Zogen
men cor,acap TONOS 5335 s.p. (S446)

Die Auserwahlte: Madele Ruck
men cor,acap TONOS 5332 s.p. (S447)

Die Drei Roselein: Jetzt Gang I Ans
Brunnele
men cor,acap TONOS 4339 s.p. (S448)

Die Lore: Von Allen Den Madchen
men cor,acap TONOS 5307 s.p. (S449)

SILCHER, FRIEDRICH (cont'd.)

Die Trauernde: Mei Mutter Mag Mi Net
men cor,acap TONOS 4315 s.p. (S450)

Entschuldigung: Und Sitz Ich
men cor,acap TONOS 5304 s.p. (S451)

Entschuldigung "Und Sitz Ich In Der
Schenke"
men cor sc SCHOTTS CHBL 133 s.p.
(S452)

Frisch Gesungen: Hab Oft Im Kreise
men cor,acap TONOS 4317 s.p. (S453)

Fruhlingsglaube: Die Linden Lufte
men cor,acap TONOS 5313 s.p. (S454)

Gut Nacht, Mein Feines Lieb
men cor,acap TONOS 5311 s.p. (S455)

Heimliche Liebe: Wenn Alle Brunnlein
men cor,acap TONOS 5309 s.p. (S456)

Herber Abschied: Wie Die Blumlein
men cor,acap TONOS 5306 s.p. (S457)

Herzensweh: Mein Herzlein Tut
men cor,acap TONOS 4325 s.p. (S458)

Herzerl, Was Krankt Dich
men cor,acap TONOS 4309 s.p. (S459)

Hirtenliebe: Komm Mit Mir Ins Tale
men cor,acap TONOS 5303 s.p. (S460)

Ich Weiss, Wo Rote Rosen Stehn
men cor,acap TONOS 4312 s.p. (S461)

Im Mai: Drauss Ist Alles So Prachtig
men cor,acap TONOS 4329 s.p. (S462)

In Der Ferne: Nun Leb Wohl
men cor,acap TONOS 5329 s.p. (S463)

Jagdgluck: Es Ritt Ein Jager
men cor,acap TONOS 5343 s.p. (S464)

Jagerlied: Es Stiess Ein Junger Jager
men cor,acap TONOS 5302 s.p. (S465)

Juchhei, Dich Muss: Ich Ging Emol
men cor,acap TONOS 5336 s.p. (S466)

Klage: Ich Habe Den Fruhling
men cor,acap TONOS 5337 s.p. (S467)

Lorelei: Ich Weiss Nicht, Was Soll Es
men cor,acap TONOS 4306 s.p. (S468)

Mei Maidle Hot E Gsichtle
men cor,acap TONOS 4311 s.p. (S469)

Muss I Denn Zum Stadtele Hinaus
men cor,acap TONOS 4331 s.p. (S470)

O Wie Herbe Ist Das Scheiden
men cor,acap TONOS 4319 s.p. (S471)

Prinz Eugen, Der Edle Ritter
men cor,acap TONOS 4308 s.p. (S472)

Robin Adair
men cor,acap TONOS 5348 s.p. (S473)

Rosestock, Holderblut
men cor,acap TONOS 4314 s.p. (S474)

'S Herz "Maidle, Lass Dir Was
Verzahle"
men cor sc SCHOTTS CHBL 195 s.p.
(S475)
men cor,acap TONOS 4318 s.p. (S476)

Schaferleben: Nichts Kann Auf Erden
men cor,acap TONOS 5315 s.p. (S477)

Schifferlied: Es Loscht Das Meer
men cor,acap TONOS 5319 s.p. (S478)

Schottische Bardenchor: Stumm Schlaft
men cor,acap TONOS 5318 s.p. (S479)

Schwabische Liebesliedchen: E Bissele
Lieb
men cor,acap TONOS 4332 s.p. (S480)

Schwabische Tanzlied: Bin I Net
men cor,acap TONOS 4313 s.p. (S481)

Schwabisches Tanzliedchen: Mei
Schatzle
men cor,acap TONOS 4303 s.p. (S482)

Sehnsucht: Der Susse Schlaf
men cor,acap TONOS 4307 s.p. (S483)

So Nimm Denn Meine Hande
men cor,acap TONOS 5341 s.p. (S484)

Suss' Liebe Liebt Den Mai "Ein Bursch
Und Magdlein Flink Und Schon"
men cor sc SCHOTTS CHBL 196 s.p.
(S485)
men cor,acap TONOS 4316 s.p. (S486)

SILCHER, FRIEDRICH (cont'd.)

Trinklied: Bruder, Zu Den Festlichen
men cor,acap TONOS 5345 s.p. (S487)

Untreue "Durch's Wiesetal Gang I
Jetzt Na"
see Silcher, Friedrich,
Abschiedsgruss "Rosmarin Und
Salbeiblattlein"
men cor,acap TONOS 4304 s.p. (S488)

Untreue: In Einem Kuhlen Grunde
men cor,acap TONOS 5338 s.p. (S489)

Waldlied: Waldnacht! Waldlust!
men cor,opt 4horn TONOS 5346 s.p.
(S490)

Waldlust: Wie Herrlich Ist's Im Wald
men cor,acap TONOS 4335 s.p. (S491)

Weinlied: Ein Konig Ist Der Wein
men cor,acap TONOS 4310 s.p. (S492)

Werbung: O Maidle, Du Bist
men cor,acap TONOS 4321 s.p. (S493)

Wie Lieblich Schallt
(Erdlen, Hermann) men cor&jr cor,
acap TONOS 1313 s.p.   (S494)

Wir Sind Konige Der Welt
men cor,acap TONOS 4336 s.p. (S495)

Wo E Kleins Huttle Steht
men cor,acap TONOS 5301 s.p. (S496)

Wohin Mit Der Freud: Ach Du
men cor,acap TONOS 4322 s.p. (S497)

Zu Augsburg Steht Ein Hohes Haus
men cor,acap TONOS 4323 s.p. (S498)

Zu End: Mir Ist's Zu Wohl Ergangen
men cor,acap TONOS 4330 s.p. (S499)

SILENCE see Bucchi, Valentino

SILENTIUM see Giachetti, Enrico

SILHOUETTES *CCU
CIMINO SSA $.85; SATB $.85   (S500)

SILVER
Before The Paling Of The Stars
SATB,pno MCAFEE M115 $.35   (S501)

Come Down To The Town Dump *see
Kromer

Epitaph For Prudence Pringle
cor,pno MCAFEE M1034 $.40   (S502)

Finnegin's Fugue
SA/TB MCAFEE M8011 $.40   (S503)

Highland Hymn
1-2pt,pno MCAFEE M8003 $.40 (S504)

Holiday Carol *Xmas
1-2pt MCAFEE M8014 $.35   (S505)

Old Ark Rock
unis MCAFEE M8013 $.35   (S506)

Old Maid's Prayer, The
unis,pno MCAFEE M136 $.40   (S507)

One String Melody
unis/SA/TB MCAFEE M8012 $.40 (S508)

Something To Sing About
SA/TB MCAFEE M8010 $.35   (S509)

Twelve Days After Christmas, The
*Xmas
SATB,pno,opt winds MCAFEE M138
$.50, ipa   (S510)
SA/SSA,pno,opt winds MCAFEE M137
$.50, ipa   (S511)
unis,pno,opt winds MCAFEE M110
$.50, ipa   (S512)

Twelve Days Before Christmas, The
*Xmas
1-2pt MCAFEE M8004 $.40   (S513)

Wintertime *see Leeds

SILVER BIRD see Rasely

SILVER, FREDERICK
Something To Sing About *CCU
1-2pt/1-2pt jr cor MCAFEE $2.00
(S514)

We're Talented Musicians
unis,opt soli MCAFEE M8016 $.40
(S515)

SILVER SWAN, THE see Chorbajian, John

SILVER SWAN, THE see Gibbons, Orlando

SILVERHEELS see Kreutz, Robert E.

SILVERSMITH, THE see Krone

SIMAI, PAVOL (1930-)
  Na Perone
    see Sen A Rano

  Sen A Rano
    mix cor SLOV.HUD.FOND s.p.
      contains: Na Perone; Sen A Rano;
      Stred Zeme; Vecer Cintoriny
                          (S516)

  Sen A Rano
    see Sen A Rano

  Stred Zeme
    see Sen A Rano

  Vecer Cintoriny
    see Sen A Rano

SIMEK, MIROSLAV (1891-1967)
  Greeting - Promise *see Pozdrav -
    Prisaha

  Little Cloud, The *see Oblacek

  Nestastny Jano
    "Unhappy Jano" [Czech] men cor,Bar
    solo,acap CZECH s.p.   (S517)

  Oblacek
    "Little Cloud, The" [Czech] wom
    cor,acap CZECH s.p.   (S518)

  Petrvald
    [Czech] men cor,acap CZECH s.p.
                          (S519)

  Pod Zvicinou *CCU,folk
    [Czech] mix cor,STB soli,2fl,2ob,
    2clar,2bsn,4horn,2trp,3trom,timp,
    perc,harp,strings, celeste CZECH
    s.p.   (S520)

  Pozdrav - Prisaha
    "Greeting - Promise" [Czech] men
    cor,acap CZECH s.p.   (S521)

  Unhappy Jano *see Nestastny Jano

SIMON
  Anticipation
    (Gargaro) SATB,opt perc WARNER
    CH0792 $.40   (S522)

  Harmony (composed with Kaplan)
    (Ades) SSA SHAWNEE B386 $.40 (S523)
    (Lojeski, Ed) SATB LEONARD-US
    08222500 $.50   (S524)
    (Lojeski, Ed) SAB LEONARD-US
    08222504 $.50   (S525)

  Haven't Got Time For The Pain
    (composed with Brackman)
    (Shay) SAB/SATB WARNER WB-362 $.50
                         (S526)
    (Shay) 2pt,opt perc WARNER WB-364
    $.50   (S527)
    (Shay) SSA/SA WARNER WB-363 $.50
                         (S528)

  That's The Way I've Always Heard It
    Should Be (composed with
    Brackman)
    (Slater) SSA,opt perc WARNER CQ2006
    $.40   (S529)

SIMON, HERMANN
  Der Winter Ist Vergangen
    jr cor/wom cor (easy) sc SCHOTTS
    CHBL 506A-B s.p. contains also:
    Die Guldene Sonne   (S530)

  Die Guldene Sonne
    see Simon, Hermann, Der Winter Ist
    Vergangen

  Lieder Der Kleinsten *CC10L
    jr cor (easy) sc SCHOTTS ED. 3749
    s.p.   (S531)

SIMON, NORMAN
  Stay In Touch With The World *see
    Hunt, Frank

SIMON, PAUL
  America *pop
    (Metis, Frank) SATB,pno oct BIG
    BELL $.40   (S532)

  American Tune *pop
    (Averre, Richard) SATB,pno oct BIG
    BELL $.40   (S533)
    (Averre, Richard) SAB,pno oct BIG
    BELL $.40   (S534)
    (Averre, Richard) SSA,pno oct BIG
    BELL $.40   (S535)

  April Come She Will *pop
    (Ehret, Walter) SSA,pno oct BIG
    BELL $.40   (S536)
    (Ehret, Walter) SATB,pno oct BIG
    BELL $.40   (S537)

  At The Zoo *pop
    SAB,pno oct BIG BELL $.40 (S538)
    SSA,pno oct BIG BELL $.40 (S539)

SIMON, PAUL (cont'd.)
  Bridge Over Troubled Water *pop
    (Sechler, Clyde) SSA,pno oct BIG
    BELL $.40   (S540)
    (Sechler, Clyde) SATB,pno oct BIG
    BELL $.40   (S541)
    (Sechler, Clyde) SA,pno oct BIG
    BELL $.40   (S542)
    (Sechler, Clyde) SAB,pno oct BIG
    BELL $.40   (S543)

  Fifty-Ninth Street Bridge Song, The
    (Feelin' Groovy) *pop
    (Metis, Frank) SSA,pno oct BIG BELL
    $.40   (S544)
    (Metis, Frank) SA,pno oct BIG BELL
    $.40   (S545)
    (Metis, Frank) SATB,pno oct BIG
    BELL $.40   (S546)
    (Metis, Frank) SAB,pno oct BIG BELL
    $.40   (S547)

  Flowers Never Bend With The Rainfall
    *pop
    SATB,pno oct BIG BELL $.40   (S548)

  Homeward Bound *pop
    SATB,pno oct BIG BELL $.40   (S549)
    SSA,pno oct BIG BELL $.40   (S550)

  Kodachrome *pop
    (Nowak, Jerry) SATB,pno oct BIG
    BELL $.40   (S551)

  Loves Me Like A Rock *pop
    (Nowak, Jerry) SATB,pno oct BIG
    BELL $.40   (S552)

  Me And Julio Down By The Schoolyard
    *pop
    (Averre, Richard) SATB,pno oct BIG
    BELL $.45   (S553)

  Mother And Child Reunion *pop
    (Apple, Allan) SATB,pno oct BIG
    BELL $.40   (S554)

  Mrs. Robinson *pop
    (Ehret, Walter) SATB,pno oct BIG
    BELL $.40   (S555)

  Patterns *pop
    SATB,pno oct BIG BELL $.40   (S556)

  Scarborough Fair-Canticle (composed
    with Garfunkel, Art) *pop
    (Ehret, Walter) SATB,pno oct BIG
    BELL $.40   (S557)
    (Ehret, Walter) SSA,pno oct BIG
    BELL $.40   (S558)
    (Ehret, Walter) SAB,pno oct BIG
    BELL $.40   (S559)
    (Ehret, Walter) SA,pno oct BIG BELL
    $.40   (S560)

  Song For The Asking *pop
    (Metis, Frank) SATB,pno,gtr oct BIG
    BELL $.40   (S561)
    (Metis, Frank) SSA,pno,gtr oct BIG
    BELL $.40   (S562)

  Sound Of Silence, The *pop
    (Metis, Frank) SATB,pno oct BIG
    BELL $.40   (S563)
    (Metis, Frank) SSA,pno oct BIG BELL
    $.40   (S564)
    (Metis, Frank) SAB,pno oct BIG BELL
    $.40   (S565)
    (Metis, Frank) SA,pno oct BIG BELL
    $.40   (S566)

  Sounds Of Simon And Garfunkel
    *medley/pop
    (Nowak, Jerry) SATB,pno,bvl,drums
    oct BIG BELL $.95   (S567)

SIMONITI, RADO
  Dalmatinische Barkarole
    men cor,acap TONOS 457 s.p. (S568)

SIMONS, NETTY
  For All Blasphemers
    TTBB,acap AM.COMP.AL. $6.60 (S569)

SIMPSON, JOHN
  Girl I Left Behind Me
    SAB EMI   (S570)

  Green Broom
    unis treb cor EMI   (S571)

  Make We Merry
    unis EMI   (S572)

  Piper O' Dundee, The
    SAB EMI   (S573)

  Wi' A Hundred Pipers An' A'
    SAB EMI   (S574)

  Will Ye Not Come Back Again
    SAB EMI   (S575)

SIMS, EZRA (1928-)
  Brief Glimpses Into Contemporary
    French Literature *CCU,round
    cor,acap AM.COMP.AL. $3.58 (S576)

SINCE ROBIN HOOD see Weelkes, Thomas

SINCE WHEN ONE LOVES see Sermisy,
  Claude de, Puisqu'en Amour

SINE MUSICA NULLA DISCIPLINA see
  Hindemith, Paul

SINE MUSICA NULLA VITA see Marx, Karl

SINE NOMINE see Vogt, Hans

SING see Raposo, Joe

SING A HAPPY SONG see Avalos

SING A SONG see Henderson

SING A SONG OF SIXPENCE see Rutter

SING, AFRICA! *CC12U,folk,Afr
  (Sephula, M.) [Eng/Afr] unis,pno
  GALLIARD 2.9055.1 $2.00   (S577)

SING AGAIN, AFRICA! *CC12U,folk,Afr
  (Sephula, M.) [Eng/Afr] unis,pno
  GALLIARD 2.9056.1 $2.00   (S578)

SING AMERICA FIRST! see Yahres, Samuel
  C.

SING CARE AWAY see Mozart, Wolfgang
  Amadeus

SING DEIN LIED *CCU
  (Abel; Rothenberg; Schreiber)
  MERSEBURG EM356   (S579)

SING HAPPY CHILD see Lewis

SING, KLEINE NACHTIGALL "EIN WINZER
  HATT' EIN TOCHTERLEIN" see Zoll,
  Paul

SING LULLABY see Mattson

SING ME A SILLY SONG see Young

SING MIR, O NACHTIGALL see Poos,
  Heinrich

SING MIT! see Ophoven, Hermann

SING MIT, PIONIER! *CCU
  mix cor,acap HOFMEISTER W89 s.p.
                        (S580)

SING, MORTALS see Bliss, Sir Arthur

SING MY FAIR LOVE GOOD MORROW see
  Roberton

SING NOEL see Cobine, Al

SING WE AND CHANT IT see Morley, Thomas

SING WE AND CHANT IT see Pearsall,
  Robert Lucas de

SING WE NOEL see Rogers

SING YE MUSES see Blow, John

SING YE! TENORS AND BASSES *sac/sec,
  CC24U
  (Cookson, Frank B.) TTBB FITZSIMONS
  $.75   (S581)

SINGE! see Wehle, Gerhard Furchtegott

SINGE DEIN LIED IN DEN TAG see Brucker,
  Hermann

SINGE, MEIN HERZ see Genzmer, Harald

SINGE, MEIN HERZ see Seeger, Peter

SINGEN WILL ICH FROHE LIEDER see
  Rosenfeld, Gerhard

SINGEND SEI DEIN TAG BEGONNEN see
  Mohler, Philipp

SINGENDE JUGEND NR. 15
  mix cor,pno HOFMEISTER G2203 s.p.
    contains: Bauen Wir Die Neue Stadt;
    Unsere Strassen   (S582)

SINGENDE JUGEND NR. 16
  mix cor,pno HOFMEISTER G2217 s.p.
    contains: Badepl Atz Und Sprungturm
    Locken; Escondido; Junge
    Tschapajewer; Krakowiak (S583)

SINGENDEN JAHR see Wolters, Gottfried

SINGERS, THE see Bornschein, [Franz
  Carl]

SINGERS ALL *CC10L,folk
  (Cooper) 4-part songs for unchanged
    and changing voices (easy) OXFORD

SLOWENISCHES LIEBESLIED *folk
(Becker, Hans-Gunther) [Ger] men cor,
acap 2036 s.p. (S624)

SL'UB VLASTI see Schneider-Trnavsky,
Mikulas

SLUKA, LUBOS (1928-   )
In The Name Of Life *see Ve Jmenu
Zivota

Ve Jmenu Zivota
"In The Name Of Life" [Czech] men
cor,narrator,2fl,2ob,2clar,2bsn,
4horn,3trp,2trom,timp,strings
CZECH s.p. (S625)

SLUMBER DID MY SPIRIT SEAL, A see
Chihara, Paul

SLUMBER SONG
(Hill, Harry) SSA (easy) WATERLOO
$.30 (S626)

SLUMBER SONG see Dawson, William Levi

SLUMBER SONG , THE see Palmer, G.

SLUTSANG *Ir
(Hellden, Daniel) men cor GEHRMANS
KVB354 (S627)

SLY, ALLAN
Good Wives Of Pioneers
mix cor,pno/orch BOOSEY cor pts
$1.00, sc rental (S628)

SMALL CANTATA see Pauer, Jiri, Mala
Kantata

SMALL HOUR, THE see Wood, Joseph

SMATEK, MILOS (1895-   )
Dva Detske Sbory *CC2U
[Czech] jr cor,fl,ob,2clar,bsn,
3horn,timp,perc,strings CZECH
s.p. (S629)

Pioneer Waltz, The *see Pionyrsky
Valcik

Pionyrsky Valcik
"Pioneer Waltz, The" [Czech] jr
cor,2fl,2ob,2clar,2bsn,4horn,
2trp,3trom,timp,perc,strings
CZECH s.p. (S630)

SMES NARODNICH PISNI *CCU
(Jeremias, Otakar) [Czech] jr cor,
soli,2fl,2ob,2clar,2bsn,3horn,2trp,
timp,perc,strings CZECH s.p. (S631)

SMETACEK, VACLAV (1906-   )
From Cradle To Altar *see Ode
Kolebky K Oltari

Ode Kolebky K Oltari *folk
"From Cradle To Altar" [Czech] mix
cor,2fl,2ob,2clar,2bsn,3horn,
2trp,3trom,timp,org/harmonium,
strings CZECH s.p. (S632)

SMETANA, BEDRICH (1824-1884)
Czech Song, The *cant
[Czech/Ger] mix cor,2fl,2ob,2clar,
2bsn,4horn,2trp,3trom,timp,perc,
strings SUPRAPHON s.p. (S633)

Furiant (from Bartered Bride, The)
see Smetana, Bedrich, Polka

Hop-Polka (from Bartered Bride, The)
see Smetana, Bedrich, Polka

Polka (from Bartered Bride, The)
[Czech] mix cor,3fl,2ob,2clar,2bsn,
4horn,2trp,3trom,timp,perc,
strings SUPRAPHON s.p., rental
contains also: Furiant; Hop-Polka
(S634)

Slavnostni Sbor *CCU
cor SUPRAPHON s.p. (S635)

SMILE A LITTLE SMILE FOR ME
SSA CIMINO $.40 (S636)
SATB CIMINO $.40 (S637)

SMILEY, PRIL
Secret
jr cor,2vln,vla,vcl sc AM.COMP.AL.
$3.30 (S638)

SMITH
I'm Coming Home
SATB MARKS MC 4616 $.40 (S639)

Wonder What Kind Of A Day It Will Be
(Nelson) SATB oct SCHMITT 7049 $.40
(S640)
(Nelson) SAT oct SCHMITT 8508 $.40
(S641)

SMITH, G. ALAN
Canine Commandments
SSATB,acap (med diff) oct GENTRY
G-256 $.40 (S642)

SMITH, G. ALAN (cont'd.)
Revelation Revolution
SATB (med) FISCHER,C CM 7895 $.40
(S643)

SMITH, JOHN STAFFORD (1750-1836)
Flora Now Calleth Forth Each Flower
*madrigal
(Young, Percy M.) [Eng] SSATB,acap
oct BROUDE BR. $.60 (S644)

SMITH, LELAND (1925-   )
Advice To Young Ladies
wom cor,clar&vln&vcl/pno sc
AM.COMP.AL. $6.60 (S645)
wom cor,pno AM.COMP.AL. $3.30
(S646)

SMITHERY BOX *Ir
(Anderson, W.H.) unis LESLIE 1055
$.30 (S647)

SMOKE GETS IN YOUR EYES
SA CIMINO $.40 (S648)
SATB CIMINO $.40 (S649)
SATB CIMINO $.40 (S650)
SSA CIMINO $.40 (S651)
TTBB CIMINO $.40 (S652)
(Metis) SAB CIMINO $.40 (S653)
(Metis) SSA CIMINO $.40 (S654)
(Metis) TTBB CIMINO $.40 (S655)
(Metis) SATB CIMINO $.40 (S656)

SMRT PROKOPA VELIKEHO see Bendl, Karel

SNABBT JAGAR STORMEN VARA AR see
Johansen, Sven-Erik

SNAPSVISA see Johansen, Sven-Erik

SNOFLINGEN see Johansen, Sven-Erik

SNOW see Gerschefski, Edwin

SNOW, THE see McLeod, Robert

SNOW LAY ON THE GROUND, THE see Coates

SNOW WHITE REVISITED see Morey, Larry

SNOW WOLF see Williamson, Malcolm

SNOWDROP AND LAMB see Morgan, Hilda

SNOWFLAKES AT MY WINDOW see Cadman,
Charles Wakefield

SNOW'S A COMIN' see Cobine, Al

SNOWY, SNOWY MOUNTAINS see Dexter,
Harry

SNY A PLANY see Kapr, Jan

SO FAR see Rodgers, Richard

SO GEHT ES IM SCHNUTZELPUTZHAUSEL see
Wolters, Karl-Heinz

SO I HAVE SEEN A SILVER SWAN *folk
(Diemer, Emma Lou) SATB STANDARD
C619MX1 $.50 (S657)

SO IM UBERMUT see Luderitz, Wolfgang

SO IN LOVE
TTBB CIMINO $.40 (S658)
SSA CIMINO $.40 (S659)
SAB CIMINO $.40 (S660)
SA CIMINO $.40 (S661)
SATB CIMINO $.40 (S662)

SO LONG, FAREWELL see Rodgers, Richard

SO MUCH BEAUTY IN THE WORLD see Blaha,
Ivo, Co Je Krasy Na Svete

SO NIMM DENN MEINE HANDE see Jordan,
Hellmut

SO NIMM DENN MEINE HANDE see Silcher,
Friedrich

SO SHE WENT INTO THE GARDEN see
Josephs, Wilfred

SO SIND DIE MADCHEN VON TRINIDAD "STELL
DIR VOR, DU GEHST EINFACH
SPAZIEREN" see Merath, Siegfried

SO TREIBEN WIR DEN WINTER AUS see
Erdlen, Hermann

SO TREIBEN WIR DEN WINTER AUS see Knab,
Armin

SO TREIBEN WIR DEN WINTER AUS see
Werdin, Eberhard

SO WUNSCH ICH EINE GUTE NACHT see
Franck, Melchior

SOCKERKAKAN see Johansen, Sven-Erik

SODERHOLM, VALDEMAR (1909-   )
Minnas (from Strykfagel)
see Tre Korsanger

Om Vintern (from Strykfagel)
see Tre Korsanger

Tre Korsanger (from Strykfagel)
4pt mix cor ERIKS 79 s.p.
contains: Minnas; Om Vintern;
Vinterstycke (S663)

Vinterstycke (from Strykfagel)
see Tre Korsanger

SODERLUNDH, LILLE BROR
Narrens Sista Visa (from
Trettondagsafton)
men cor ERIKS 1 s.p. (S664)

SOFT HILLS AND SOOTHING WIND see
Rachmaninoff, Sergey Vassilievitch

SOFT RAIN see Cox

SOFT SHADOWS FALLING, AND WHEN YOU WERE
MY SWEETHEART see Fleming

SOFTLY THE WINDS BLEW *Xmas
(Coggin) SATB PRO ART 2841 (S665)
(Coggin) SSA PRO ART 2835 (S666)
(Coggin) 2pt PRO ART 2838 (S667)

SOHAL NARESH
Surya
SATB,fl,perc voc sc NOVELLO rental,
ipr (S668)

SOKOLA, MILOS (1913-   )
More
"Sea, The" [Czech] mix cor,Bar
solo,3fl,3ob,3clar,3bsn,6horn,
4trp,3trom,tuba,timp,perc,pno,
harp,org,strings, celeste,
xylophone CZECH s.p. (S669)

Sea, The *see More

Stastnemu Devceti
"To The Happy Girl" [Czech] men
cor,acap CZECH s.p. (S670)

To The Happy Girl *see Stastnemu
Devceti

SOLA SOLETTA see Coversi, Girolamo

SOLANG MAN NUCHTERN IST see Zelter,
Carl Friedrich

SOLCHE, DIE IN SCHENKEN SITZEN see
Genzmer, Harald

SOLDATENBROT see Koenig, Franz

SOLDIER, SOLDIER, WON'T YOU MARRY ME?
(Parker) SATB SCHIRM.G LG 51711 $.40
(S671)

SOLITUDE
see Portrait Of Duke Ellington

SOLITUDE OF SPACE see Pierce

SOLLBERGER, HARVEY
Music For Sophocles' "Antigone"
speak cor,electronic tape
AM.COMP.AL. (S672)

SOLO EL MISTERIO see Bussotti, Sylvano

SOLTER, HEINZ
Dreh Dich, Radchen *cant
3 eq voices/jr cor/wom cor,2vln,
vcl,pno sc,voc sc PELIKAN PE932
s.p. (S673)

SOLVEIG'S SONG see Thorpe, Raymond

SOME FOLKS see Foster, Stephen

SOME KIND OF WONDERFUL
(Shaw, Kirby) SATB,pno,inst (jazz,
includes recording and 14 choral
octavos) LEONARD-US 07857500 $14.95
(S674)

SOMEBODY'S KNOCKIN' AT YOUR DOOR
(Barthelson) SSA SCHIRM.G LG51727
$.35 (S675)

SOMEBODY'S KNOCKING *CCU,folk/spir
(Schibler, A.) jr cor,orch voc sc
EULENBURG EES504 s.p. (S676)

SOMEONE
see Two Welsh Love Songs

SOMEONE WHO CARES see Harvey, Alex

SOMERSET WASSAIL see Felciano, Richard

SOMERVELL, ARTHUR (1863-1937)
Forsaken Merman, The
SATB,B solo,2fl,2ob,2clar,2bsn,
4horn,2trp,3trom,tuba,timp,harp,
strings voc sc NOVELLO rental,
ipr (S677)

SOMETHING FOR EVERYBODY see Strilko, Anthony

SOMETHING FOR TOMORROW see Dodds

SOMETHING TO SING ABOUT see Silver, Frederick

SOMETHING TO SING ABOUT see Silver

SOMETIMES
SATB CIMINO $.40 (S678)

SOMETIMES I FEEL *spir
(Kubizek, Augustin) "Manchmal" men cor DOBLINGER M 323 s.p. (S679)

SOMETIMES I FEEL LIKE A MOTHERLESS CHILD *spir
see When The Saints Go Marchin' In (Thygerson, Robert) SA RICHMOND SA-9 $.35 (S680)

SOMETIMES WITH ONE I LOVE see Hall, William D.

SOMEWHERE IN YOUR HEART see Faith

SOMMARENS GRAS see Hellden, Daniel

SOMMARVISA FRAN DALARNA
(Jehrlander, Karl-Fredrik) mix cor GEHRMANS KRB442 (S681)

SOMMER "AM ABEND SCHWEIGT DIE KLAGE" see Zoll, Paul

SOMMER, VLADIMIR (1921-   )
New Spring *see Nove Jaro

Nove Jaro
"New Spring" [Czech] mix cor,acap CZECH s.p. (S682)

Tri Zenske Sbory *CC3U
[Czech] wom cor,acap CZECH s.p. (S683)

SOMMERBILD see Ketterer, Ernst

SOMMERDORFCHEN see Gorl, Willibald

SOMMERDORFCHEN "ICH WEISS EIN DORFCHEN VOLL SONNENSCHEIN" see Rein, Walter

SOMMERGLUCK *folk,It
(Becker, Hans-Gunther) men cor,pno sc,cor pts TONOS 2183 s.p. (S684)

SOMMERLAND see Becker, Hans-Gunther

SOMMERLIED "MIR IST DER HELLE SOMMER" see Schnitzler, Heinrich

SOMMERLIED "SEINEN TRAUM LIND WOB" see Schumann, Robert (Alexander)

SOMMERMADRIGAL "SINGE, MEINE LIEBE SEELE" see Lendvai, Erwin

SOMMERNACHT "DIE SOMMERNACHT HAT MIR'S ANGETAN" see Trunk, Richard

SOMMERREIGEN *folk,Ger
(Desch, Rudolf) men cor,acap TONOS 19 s.p. (S685)

SONATA IN BIANCO MINORE see Gubitosi, E.

SONETT "SO LIEBLICH KUSST DIE SONNE NICHT" see Genzmer, Harald

SONETT VOM GOLDENEN HERBST "O GOLDENER HERBST see Genzmer, Harald

SONG see Lied

SONG ABOUT THE LAND OF BOHEMIA see Kalas, Julius, Zpev O Zemi Ceske

SONG ABOUT THE UNITY OF LABOURERS IN FACTORY AND FARM see Burian, Emil Frantisek, Pisen O Svazku Delniku A Rolniku

SONG FOR HUMAN RIGHTS see Rohan, Joy

SONG FOR ST.CECILIA see Hurd, Michael

SONG FOR THE ASKING see Simon, Paul

SONG FROM SHAKESPEARE'S "MUCH ADO ABOUT NOTHING" see Pisk, Paul Amadeus

SONG IS YOU
SA CIMINO $.40 (S686)
SAB CIMINO $.40 (S687)
SSA CIMINO $.40 (S688)
SATB CIMINO $.40 (S689)
TTBB CIMINO $.40 (S690)

SONG OF AUTUMN see Anderson, [William H.]

SONG OF BROTHER SUN, THE see Foerster, Josef Bohuslav, Pisen Bratra Slunce

SONG OF CHRISTMAS see Ringwald, [Roy]

SONG OF CHRISTMAS, A see Hunnicutt, Judy

SONG OF DEAD CHILDREN, THE see Pololanik, Zdenek, Zpev Mrtvych Deti

SONG OF GOOD LIFE, A see Gwilt, David

SONG OF HOPE, A see Weigl, Vally

SONG OF LIFE, THE see Franco, Johan

SONG OF LIFE AND DEATH, THE see Liebermann, Rolf, Streitlied Zwischen Leben Und Tod

SONG OF PEACE, THE see Schneeweiss, Jan, Pisen Miru

SONG OF REJOICING, A see Verrall, John

SONG OF SLUMBER see Weber, Carl Maria von

SONG OF SONGS, THE see Vackar, Dalibor C., Pisen Pisni

SONG OF THE ADVENTURERS see Protheroe, Daniel

SONG OF THE DAWN see Eisenstein, Judith Kaplan, Shir Hashahar

SONG OF THE FATHERS, THE see Meek, Kenneth

SONG OF THE FLEA see Zelter

SONG OF THE LITTLE FAIRIES see Verdi, Giuseppe

SONG OF THE MARCHING MEN see Protheroe, Daniel

SONG OF THE MUSIC MAKERS, THE see Shaw, Martin

SONG OF THE NATIVE LAND see Jeremias, Otakar, Pisen O Rodne Zemi

SONG OF THE NEW ERA see Barta, Lubor, Zpev Noveho Veku

SONG OF THE NORTH WIND see Jones, Robert Gomer

SONG OF THE OLD MOTHER, THE see Fay, V.

SONG OF THE PARTY see Dobias, Vaclav, Pisen O Strane

SONG OF THE PARTY see Seidel, Jan, Pisen O Strane

SONG OF THE REFUGE CHILDREN see Lewis

SONG OF THE ROAD, A see Protheroe, Daniel

SONG OF THE SHADOWS, THE see Weigl, Vally

SONG OF THE STORM see Lazicki

SONG OF THE TINKER, THE see Olds, [William Benjamin]

SONG OF THE VALLEY see Diament, Abraham

SONG OF THE VIKINGS see Faning, Eaton

SONG OF THE WANDERER see Schumann, Robert (Alexander)

SONG OF THE WAVES, THE see Protheroe, Daniel

SONG OF THE WESTERN MEN see Protheroe, Daniel

SONG OF THE WINDS see Distler, Hugo, Lied Vom Winde

SONG OF THE WINDS see Vanderbilt, Adriaan

SONG OF VICTORY see Kypta, F.A., Pisen Vitezna

SONG OF WELCOME see Bliss, Sir Arthur

SONG OF WIND, A see Baer

SONG ON MAY MORNING see Harwood, Basil

SONG TO A TREE, A see Buchhauser, Andrew W.

SONG TO THE NATIVE LAND see Kapr, Jan, Pisen Rodne Zemi

SONGBOOK ONE *CCU
(Taylor, J.) cor GALLIARD 2.0400.7 $2.25 (S691)

SONGBOOK TWO *CCU
(Taylor, J.) cor GALLIARD 2.0401.7 $2.25 (S692)

SONGMAN see Cashman, Terry

SONGS *CC18U
(Campbell, A.) cor GALLIARD 2.9022.7 $2.25 (S693)

SONGS BY MANCINI *CCU
SATB CIMINO $3.25 (S694)

SONG'S ETERNITY see Short, Michael

SONGS FOR CHOIRS *CC18U
(Appleby; Fowler) SATB,opt acap (easy/med) OXFORD $3.00 (S695)

SONGS FOR NAOMI see Burnett

SONGS FROM SHAKESPEARE see Jordahl

SONGS FROM THE MORIKELIEDER see Distler, Hugo

SONGS FROM "THE TEMPEST" see Spencer, Williametta

SONGS IN A FARMHOUSE see Austin, Frederick

SONGS OF DIVERS AIRS AND NATURES (1619) EM VOL. 34 see Vautor, Thomas

SONGS OF ENGLAND see Thiman, Eric Harding

SONGS OF INNOCENCE see George, Earl

SONGS OF INNOCENCE see Josephs, Wilfred

SONGS OF JIM WEBB see Webb, Jimmy

SONGS OF SAILORS AND OF THE SEA see Thiman, Eric Harding

SONGS OF THE ASSOCIATION see Kirkman, Terry

SONGS OF THE NIGHT see Stein, Leon

SONGS OF THREE, FOUR, FIVE AND SIX PARTS (1622) EM VOL. 18 see Tomkins, Thomas

SONGS TO DELIGHT see Cannon, (Jack) Phillip

SONGS TO LAUGH BY see Mandel

SONNE, MOND UND STERNE see Rein, Walter

SONNE, SONNE SCHEINE see Bresgen, Cesar

SONNENAUFGANG see Cornelius, Peter

SONNENGESANG see Krietsch, Georg

SONNENGESANG DES HEILIGEN FRANZISKUS see Orff, Carl

SONNENLEUCHTEN see Wittmer, Eberhard Ludwig

SONNENTAGE see Bottcher, Georg

SONNENWENDE see Steffen, Wolfgang

SONNET see Mrkos, Zdenek

SONNET see Rosenthal, Manuel

SONNET see Zimmer, Jan

SONNET 76 see Heilner, Irwin

SONNET EIGHTEEN
SATB oct CHAPPELL W020917-357 $.40 (S696)

SONNET TWENTY-NINE see Slater

SONNIGES REBENLAND see Fischer, Theo

SONNTAGSFEIER see Gauss, Otto

SOPHISTICATED LADY
see Portrait Of Duke Ellington

SOPRONI, JOZSEF
Ket Korusmu *CC2U
(Juhasz, Gyula) mix cor BUDAPEST 7083 s.p. (S697)

SORAN BUSHI see Sakamoto, Yoshitaka

SORROW CONSUMES ME see Kirbye, George

SORROW CONSUMES ME (FIRST PART) see
   Kirbye, George

SOUKUP, VLADIMIR (1930-   )
   Cantata Futura
      [Czech] mix cor,narrator,3fl,2ob,
      3clar,3bsn,4horn,3trp,3trom,tuba,
      timp,perc,pno,strings CZECH s.p.
                                    (S698)

SOUND see Tanenbaum, Elias

SOUND OF MUSIC, THE see Rodgers,
   Richard

SOUND OF SILENCE, THE see Simon, Paul

SOUND PIECES see Brings

SOUND THE FLUTE see Brown

SOUNDS OF LOGGINS AND MESSINA see
   Loggins, Dave

SOUNDS OF NEIL YOUNG AND GRAHAM NASH
   see Nash, Graham

SOUNDS OF SIMON AND GARFUNKEL see
   Simon, Paul

SOURWOOD MOUNTAIN *folk
   SSA CIMINO $.40   (S699)

SOUSA, JOHN PHILIP (1854-1932)
   Free Lunch Cadets, The
      (Hunter) SATB MARKS MC 4630 $.50
                                    (S700)
   Legend Of The Frogs
      (Hunter) SATB MARKS MC 4631 $.50
                                    (S701)
   Liberty Bell, The
      (Carleton, Bruce) SATB,pno (easy)
      oct PRESSER 322-40043 $.35 (S702)

SOUTHAM
   Have You Seen But A White Lily Grow?
      SA (med easy) OXFORD 82.103 $.30
                                    (S703)
SOUTHERN COMFORT *medley
   (Bennett) TTBB SCHIRM.G LG51775 $.60
                                    (S704)
SPAIN KEEPS SILENT see Sestak, Zdenek,
   Spanelsko Mlci

SPAIN, SAD SPAIN, MISFORTUNATE ONE see
   Encina, Juan Del, Triste Espana,
   Sin Ventura!

SPANELSKO MLCI see Sestak, Zdenek

SPANISCHE NACHTE "DAS IST DER ZAUBER"
   see Fischer, Ernst

SPANISCHE NACHTE "DAS IST DER ZAUBER
   DER SPANISCHEN NACHTE" see Fischer,
   Ernst

SPANISCHES LIEDERSPIEL see Zoll, Paul

SPANISH EYES
   SSA SCREEN 5002SC2   (S705)
   SA SCREEN 6002SC5   (S706)
   SAB SCREEN 5002SC3   (S707)

SPANISH RENAISSANCE: SIX SONGS *Renais
   [Span] SATB,acap cmplt ed EGTVED
   MS10B9 s.p.
      contains: Anonymous, Dindirin;
      Anonymous, Pase El Agoa; Encina,
      Juan Del, Cucu; Encina, Juan Del,
      Fata La Parte; Encina, Juan Del,
      Pues Que Jamais Olvidaros;
      Encina, Juan Del, Triste Espana
                                    (S708)
SPASSIGE GESCHICHTE "EINS, ZWEI, DREI,
   HICKE HACKE HEU" see Rein, Walter

SPASSIGE GESCHICHTEN see Rein, Walter

SPEAK GENTLY see Furman

SPECTA ET AUDI see Krcek, Jaroslav

SPECTRE'S BRIDE, THE see Dvorak,
   Antonin

SPEECH TO A CROWD see Mechem, Kirke

SPELL OF CREATION, THE see Ussachevsky,
   Vladimir

SPELLS see Bennett, Richard Rodney

SPEME AMOROSA see Gastoldi, Giovanni
   Giacomo

SPENCER, M.
   Who Seeketh Beauty
      unis HARRIS $.25   (S709)

SPENCER, TIM
   Room Full Of Roses
      (Metis, F.) SATB BIG3 $.45 (S710)
      (Metis, F.) SSA BIG3 $.45   (S711)
      (Metis, F.) SAB BIG3 $.45   (S712)

SPENCER, WILLIAMETTA
   Good Morrow, Tis St. Valentine's Day
      see Two Glees

   Love In A Village
      see Two Glees

   Mystic Trumpeter, The
      SATB,acap NATIONAL WHC-15 $.45
                                    (S713)
   Songs From "The Tempest" *CC3U
      SSA,acap NATIONAL WHC-11 $.35
                                    (S714)
   Two Glees
      SSA,acap NATIONAL WHC-16 $.40
      contains: Good Morrow, Tis St.
      Valentine's Day; Love In A
      Village   (S715)

SPEV NA KSS see Ocenas, Andrej

SPEV O LASKE see Kardos, Dezider

SPEV O POVSTANI see Novak, Milan

SPIDER AND THE FLY, THE see Protheroe,
   Daniel

SPIELE MIR, GEIGERLEIN see Poos,
   Heinrich

SPIELMANNS MAIENFAHRT see Welcker, Max

SPIES, LEO
   Der Rote Platz *cant
      4pt mix cor,Bar solo,orch NEUE
      NM216 s.p.   (S716)

SPILKA, FRANTISEK (1877-1960)
   Klatovska Polka
      "Polka Of Klatovy Town" [Czech] men
      cor,acap CZECH s.p.   (S717)

   Mesicek Sviti
      "Moon Is Shining, The" [Czech] men
      cor,acap CZECH s.p.   (S718)

   Moon Is Shining, The *see Mesicek
      Sviti

   Polka Of Klatovy Town *see Klatovska
      Polka

   Shelters *see Tisiny

   Tisiny
      "Shelters" [Czech] wom cor&wom cor,
      acap CZECH s.p.   (S719)

SPIN, DREIDEL, SPIN see Adler

SPINNING SONG *folk
   (Lester, William) SA (easy)
      FITZSIMONS 3017 $.20   (S720)

SPINNING WHEEL
   SSA CIMINO $.40   (S721)
   SATB CIMINO $.40   (S722)

SPIRIT AND CELEBRATION see Raulston

SPIRIT OF '76, THE see Mechem, Kirke

SPIRIT OF CHRISTMAS, THE see Louchheim,
   Stuart F.

SPIRIT OF CHRISTMAS, THE *sac/sec,
   CC8UL,Xmas,pop
      WARNER $1.50   (S723)

SPIRIT OF ENGLAND, THE see Elgar,
   Edward

SPIRIT QUICKENETH, THE see Franco,
   Johan

SPIRITUALS AND SONGS see Cammin, Heinz

SPIRITUALS FOR ALL HEFT I *spir
   (Petersen, Ralf) [Eng/Ger] men cor,
   pno,opt bvl,gtr sc,cor pts SCHOTTS
   ED. 5928 s.p., ipa
      contains: Didn't My Lord Deliver
      Daniel, "Warum Rettet' Denn Gott
      Nur Daniel"; Nobody Knows De
      Trouble, I've Seen, "Keiner Kann
      Meinen Kummer Verstehn"; Swing
      Low, Sweet Chariot, "Trag Mich
      Auf Sanften Schwingen"   (S724)

SPIRO, HAROLD
   Long Live Love *see Avon, Valerie

SPIRTUALS FOR ALL HEFT II *spir
   (Petersen, Ralf) [Eng/Ger] men cor,
   pno,opt bvl,gtr sc,cor pts SCHOTTS
   ED. 5929 s.p., ipa
      contains: Deep River, "Tiefe
      Fluten"; Go Down, Moses, "Geh
      Hin, Moses"; Joshua Fit De Battle
      Of Jerico, "Josua Schlug Die
      Schlacht Von Jerico"   (S725)

SPITTA, HEINRICH (1902-   )
   Es Ist So Still Geworden
      mix cor (med easy) sc SCHOTTS
      CHBL 303A-B s.p. contains also:
      Wenn Ich Ein Klein Waldvogelein
      War   (S726)

   Immer Strebe Ich Zum Ganzen *Op.80
      SSATB,acap (med diff) sc SCHOTTS
      C 39 176 s.p.   (S727)

   Wenn Ich Ein Klein Waldvogelein War
      see Spitta, Heinrich, Es Ist So
      Still Geworden

SPO PADESAT MILIONU see Chaun,
   Frantisek

SPOEL, A.
   Gebed Voor Het Vaderland
      mix cor s.p. sc HEER 495, cor pts
      HEER 495A   (S728)

   Op 'T Kerkhof *Op.14a
      mix cor s.p. sc HEER 497, cor pts
      HEER 497A   (S729)

   Van Een Koningsvrouwe *Op.5
      men cor s.p. sc HEER 491, cor pts
      HEER 491A   (S730)

SPOTLIGHTS see Maessen, Antoon

SPOTTED DUCKLING, THE see Sanfilippo,
   Josephine

SPOTTLIED *folk,Eur
   (Schollum, Robert) mix cor DOBLINGER
   G 667 s.p.   (S731)

SPOTTLIED "SASSEN UNSRER FUNF IM
   KELLER" see Slavenski, Josip,
   Rugalica

SPRAVNA VEC see Tausinger, Jan

SPREAD A LITTLE LOVE see Averre,
   Richard

SPREADING DAY BY DAY see Haba, Alois,
   Den Ode Dne Se Siri

SPRING (from Czech Year, The)
   (Hanus, Jan) SATB,acap voc sc GENERAL
   s.p.   (S732)

SPRING see Busch, Carl

SPRING see Jeppesen, Knud

SPRING see White, Herbert D.

SPRING, A see Canning, Thomas

SPRING CAROL, A see Wetzler, Robert

SPRING FEVER see Dedrick, C.

SPRING GARLAND, A see Thiman, Eric
   Harding

SPRING HAS COME see Distler, Hugo, Er
   Ist's

SPRING IS CROWNED see Williamson,
   Malcolm

SPRING NIGHT see Foerster, Josef
   Bohuslav, Jarni Noc

SPRING NOW IS NEAR see Lange, Gregor,
   Lenz Kommt Herbei

SPRING, THE SWEET SPRING see Bush,
   Geoffrey

SPRING TIME OF THE YEAR see Vaughan
   Williams, Ralph

SPRINGTIME IS CALLING see Protheroe,
   Daniel

SPRUCH
   (Kunz, Alfred) "Now Must I Flee All
   Earthly Creatures" SATB (med easy)
   WATERLOO $.30   (S733)

SPRUCH see Gattermayer, Heinrich

SPRUCH AUF EINEM FRIEDHOFSTORE "O WECKE
   NICHT MIT ZAHREN" see Knab, Armin

SPRUCH DES KONFUZIUS "DREIFACH IST DES
   RAUMES MASS" see Reutter, Hermann

SPRUCH "EIN MADCHEN UND EIN GLASCHEN
   WEIN" see Zehm, Friedrich

SPRUCH EINES FAHRENDEN "DASS GOTT DIE
   BERATE" see Hindemith, Paul

SPRUCH "IN DEM GROSSEN STROM DES
   LEBENS" see Schroeder, Hermann

SPRUCH WANDERNDER TOTENGRABER see
    Reutter, Hermann

SPRUCHE UND LIEDER NACH GEDICHTEN VON
    GOETHE, RILKE UND EICHENDORFF see
    Pepping, Ernst

SRNKA, JIRI (1907-   )
    Child's Year, The *see Detsky Rok

    Detsky Rok
        "Child's Year, The" [Czech] jr cor,
        fl,ob,2clar,bsn,horn,pno CZECH
        s.p.   (S734)

STADE
    Vor Jena
        men cor FORBERG sc s.p., voc pt
        s.p.   (S735)

STADEN, JOHANN (1581-1634)
    Wer Musicam Verachten Tut
        see Widmann, Erasmus, O Musica,
        Liebliche Kunst

STADTURLAUB "ICH HAB MEIN KAPPI IN DEN
    SPIND GETAN" see Genzmer, Harald

STAHL see Edler, Robert

STAIRWAY TO HEAVEN see Page

STAMP AND SHOUT see Lovelace, Austin C.

STAN' STILL, JORDAN *spir
    (Kubizek, Augustin) "Steh Still,
    Jordan" men cor DOBLINGER M 324
    s.p.   (S736)

STANCES see Rosenthal, Manuel

STAND EIN BIRKENBAUM *folk,Russ
    (Kracke, Hans) men cor,acap TONOS
    2021 s.p.   (S737)

STAND EIN BIRKENBAUM see Nitsche, Paul

STANDCHEN see Mittelbach, Otto

STANDCHEN FUR DON QUIXOTE "DAMIT EUER
    GNADEN" see Motte, Diether de la

STANDCHEN "GUTE NACHT! MADCHEN" see
    Koelble, Fritz

STANDCHEN "WIR HABEN UNS ALS MUSICI"
    see Lang, Hans

STANDELIEDER *see Gerster, Ottmar,
    Chor Der Winzer "Wir Hokern Die
    Steinigen Pfade Hinauf"   (S738)

STANDELIEDER see Gerster, Ottmar

STANISLAV, JOSEF (1897-   )
    Granada *cant
        [Czech] mix cor,2fl,2ob,2clar,2bsn,
        3horn,2trp,3trom,tuba,timp,perc,
        harp,strings PANTON s.p.   (S739)

    Harvest March, The *see Pochod Urody

    Matka Zeme *cant
        "Mother Earth" [Czech] mix cor,3fl,
        2ob,2clar,3bsn,4horn,3trp,3trom,
        timp,perc,harp,strings CZECH s.p.
                                          (S740)
    Mother Earth *see Matka Zeme

    Pochod Urody
        "Harvest March, The" [Czech] mix
        cor,3fl,3ob,4clar,3bsn,4horn,
        3trp,3trom,tuba,timp,perc,harp,
        strings CZECH s.p.   (S741)

    Pozdrav Strane *cant
        "Salutations To The Party" [Czech]
        mix cor,3fl,2ob,2clar,2bsn,4horn,
        3trp,3trom,tuba,timp,perc,strings
        CZECH s.p.   (S742)

    Salutations To The Party *see
        Pozdrav Strane

STAPLETON, ERIC
    In Praise Of Essex
        SAB EMI   (S743)

STAR BRIGHT, STARLIGHT see Verrall,
    Pamela

STAR SPANGLED BANNER, THE
    (McKelvy, James) SATB,acap FOSTER
    MF335 $.35   (S744)
    (White; Bennett) SATB SCHIRM.G
    LG51772 $.40   (S745)

STAR SPANGLED BANNER, THE see Key,
    Francis Scott

STAR-SPANGLED BANNER THROUGH HISTORY,
    THE (1814-1942)
    (Van Camp, Leonard) mix cor,pno DEAN
    CD-104 $.55   (S746)

STARLIT NIGHT see Brook, Harry

STARS ALL DOTTED OVER THE SKY see
    Sharpe, Evelyn

STARS LOOK DOWN, THE see Miles, Russell
    Hancock

STARS SHININ' BY N' BY
    (De Cormier) SATB SCHIRM.G LG51751
    $.30   (S747)

STASTNEMU DEVCETI see Sokola, Milos

STATON, MERRILL
    I Want To Be Free
        3pt,pno oct REGENT R-113 $.30
                                          (S748)

STAY see Dedrick, C.

STAY IN TOUCH WITH THE WORLD see Hunt,
    Frank

STAY SWEET LOVE see Farmer, John

STEARNS, PETER PINDAR
    Grand Is The Seen
        SATB,acap AM.COMP.AL. $2.20 (S749)

STEEL, CHRISTOPHER [CHARLES]
    (1939-   )
    Paradise Lost *Op.34
        SATB,STBar soli,2fl,2ob,2clar,2bsn,
        4horn,2trp,3trom,tuba,timp,perc,
        harp,org,strings, vibraphone,
        xylophone, celeste voc sc NOVELLO
        rental, ipr   (S750)

    Shakespeare Symphony, A *Op.25
        SATB,Bar solo,2fl,pic,2ob,2clar,
        2bsn,4horn,2trp,3trom,tuba,timp,
        perc,harp,strings, vibraphone,
        celeste voc sc NOVELLO rental,
        ipr   (S751)

STEFFE, WILLIAM
    Battle Hymn Of The Republic
        (Bennett) SATB SCHIRM.G LG51769
        $.50   (S752)

STEFFEN, WOLFGANG (1923-   )
    Erfahrungen *Op.40
        cor,6 narrators,inst BOTE rental
                                          (S753)

    Sonnenwende
        men cor voc sc RIES s.p.   (S754)

    Volksweise
        men cor voc sc RIES s.p.   (S755)

STEFFENS, JOHANN (? -1616)
    Beim Guten Wein (from Newe Teutsche
        Weltliche Madrigalia Und
        Balleten)
        [Ger] SSATB/SATTB MOSELER MOR48
        s.p. contains also: Musik Von
        Alters Ist Geehrt   (S756)

    Der Kuckuck (from Newe Teutsche
        Weltliche Madrigalia Und
        Balletten)
        see Steffens, Johann, Frisch
        Frohlich Wolln Wir Singen

    Frisch Frohlich Wolln Wir Singen
        (from Newe Teutsche Weltliche
        Madrigalia Und Balletten)
        [Ger] SSATB MOSELER MOR50 s.p.
        contains also: Der Kuckuck (S757)

    Im Maien (from Newe Teutsche
        Weltliche Madrigalia Und
        Balletten)
        see Steffens, Johann, Mit Lust Tat
        Ich Spazieren

    Lasst Uns Zusammen In Gottes Namen
        Singen (from Newe Teutsche
        Weltliche Madrigalia Und
        Balletten)
        [Ger] SSATB,acap MOSELER MOR47 s.p.
                                          (S758)
    Mit Lust Tat Ich Spazieren (from Newe
        Teutsche Weltliche Madrigalia Und
        Balletten)
        [Ger] SSATB MOSELER MOR49 s.p.
        contains also: Im Maien   (S759)

    Musik Von Alters Ist Geehrt (from
        Newe Teutsche Weltliche
        Madrigalia Und Balleten)
        see Steffens, Johann, Beim Guten
        Wein

STEGE, FRITZ
    Hessische Heimathymne
        men cor&jr cor,acap TONOS 232 s.p.
                                          (S760)

STEH AUF, NORDWIND! see Haas, Joseph

STEH STILL, JORDAN see Stan' Still,
    Jordan

STEH UNS BEI
    unis wom cor SCHOTTS C 42 533A s.p.
        see also Alle Singen Heft 2 (S761)

STEHN ZWEI STERN *folk,Ger
    (Weber, Bernhard) men cor,acap TONOS
    21 s.p.   (S762)

STEHN ZWEI STERN AM HOHEN HIMMEL see
    Linke, Norbert

STEHN ZWEI STERN AM HOHEN HIMMEL see
    Rein, Walter

STEHST SO STILL MEIN PFERDCHEN see
    Linke, Norbert

STEHT AUF, IHR LIEBEN KINDERLEIN see
    Kuhlenthal, Fred

STEIN, F.R.
    Ach, Mein Schatz
        see Kleine Suite Nach Ungarischen
        Volksliedern

    Felegyhazi-Strasse
        see Kleine Suite Nach Ungarischen
        Volksliedern

    Janos Spielt
        see Kleine Suite Nach Ungarischen
        Volksliedern

    Kleine Suite Nach Ungarischen
        Volksliedern
        men cor,pno ZIMMER. 601 s.p.
        contains: Ach, Mein Schatz;
        Felegyhazi-Strasse; Janos
        Spielt; Ware, Ach Der
        Morgenstern So Gerne   (S763)

    Ware, Ach Der Morgenstern So Gerne
        see Kleine Suite Nach Ungarischen
        Volksliedern

STEIN, LEON
    Songs Of The Night
        SATB,pno AM.COMP.AL. $8.80   (S764)

STEINBOCK see Strobl, Otto

STEINER, HEINRICH
    Reiterlied
        men cor RIES sc s.p., voc pt s.p.
                                          (S765)

STEKKE, LEON
    Chant De Paix *Op.27
        jr cor (easy) BROGNEAUX s.p. (S766)

    In Memoriam *Op.14
        TTBB sc BROGNEAUX s.p.   (S767)

    L'Ame Des Forgerons
        TTBB sc BROGNEAUX s.p.   (S768)

    Le Monde, Nous Voulons Le Connaitre
        2 eq voices (med) BROGNEAUX s.p.
                                          (S769)
    Ode Orpheonique
        TTBB (med) sc BROGNEAUX s.p. (S770)

STENHAMMAR
    Three Choral Ballads *CC3U
        SATB WALTON 2720 $.60   (S771)

STENHAMMAR, WILHELM (1871-1927)
    Sangen *Op.44, cant
        4pt mix cor voc sc ERIKS 115 s.p.
                                          (S772)

STENLEV, LEIF
    Mit Hjerte Altid Vanker *Xmas,cant
        cor,soli,orch sc HANSEN-DEN
        WH 29273 s.p.   (S773)

STENT, KEITH (1934-   )
    Two Carols In Modern Vein *CC2U,
        carol
        SATB,2fl,2ob,2clar,2bsn,2horn,2trp,
        3trom,tuba,timp,perc,pno,strings
        voc sc NOVELLO rental, ipr (S774)

STEP SOFTLY see Furman

STEPHANI, JOHANN
    Der Kuckuck Auf Dem Zaune Sass
        *madrigal
        (Lendvai, Erwin) 4pt wom cor/4pt jr
        cor,solo (med) sc SCHOTTS
        C 37 597 s.p. see from Neue
        Teutsche Weltliche Madrigale
                                          (S775)

    Neue Teutsche Weltliche Madrigale
        *see Der Kuckuck Auf Dem Zaune
        Sass   (S776)

STEPHEN FOSTER MEDLEY, A
    see Barbershop Choir, The

STEPHENSEN, LISE
    Christmas Cantata For Children's
        Choir *Xmas,cant
        jr cor,inst HANSEN-DEN WH 29210
        s.p.   (S777)

STERN, ALFRED (1901-   )
    Em Fruelig Zue (composed with Stern,
        Klara)
        1-4 eq voices,inst/S rec,
        glockenspiel PELIKAN PE704 s.p.
                                          (S778)

STERN, KLARA
  Em Fruelig Zue *see Stern, Alfred

STERNBILDER see Strobl, Otto

STERNENGRUSSE see Kuhnhold

STERNSCHNUPPEN see Bruckner, Anton

STEVENS, CAT
  Morning Has Broken *see Farjeon,
    Eleanor

STEVENS, HALSEY (1908-   )
  Remember Me
    TBB,acap FOSTER EH10 $.40   (S779)

STEVENS, [RICHARD JOHN SAMUEL]
    (1757-1837)
  It Was A Lover And His Lass
    *madrigal
    (Young, Percy M.) [Eng] SSATB,acap
    oct BROUDE BR. $.50   (S780)

STEWART
  Now Is The Hour *see Kaihan, M.

STIBY, TUE
  I Love You *see Jar Alskar Dig

  Jar Alskar Dig
    (Sjoberg, P.A.) "I Love You" mix
    cor,acap NORDISKA NMS 6529 s.p.
                                   (S781)

STIEFELKNECHT UND WETTERHAHN see
  Pepping, Ernst

STIER see Strobl, Otto

STILL, O HIMMEL see Haas, Joseph

STILL, STILL
  see Geht's, Buama

STILL WILL BE see Weigl, Vally

STILLA SOVA DE NU see Eklund, Stig

STILLE HUGEL, SANFTE TALE see Woll,
  Erna

STILLE NACHT
  2-4pt mix cor,opt inst PELIKAN PE928
  s.p.   (S782)

STILLE QUELLEN "FLIEHT AUCH DER JUGEND
  GLANZ" see Genzmer, Harald

STILLER WALDWINKEL see Ketterer, Ernst

STILLES REIFEN see Doppelbauer, Josef
  Friedrich

STILLS
  For What It's Worth *pop
    (Metis) SATB,opt perc WARNER
    WB-300 187 $.40   (S783)

  Isn't It About Time *pop
    (Cassey) SATB WARNER WB-308 187
    $.40   (S784)

STIMMUNG IM FRUHLING "WIE DICHT DAS
  GRAS HIER WACHST" see Zipp,
  Friedrich

STIRLING, C.
  Part Songs To Sing *see Alcock, J.

STOCK
  Morningside Of The Mountain, The
    *see Manning

  To A Firefly
    (Noelte) SSA (diff) FITZSIMONS 3040
    $.25   (S785)

STODOLA PUMPA *folk,Czech
  (Barrie) SAB SCHIRM.G LG51790 $.40
                                   (S786)
  (Barrie) SA SCHIRM.G LG51789 $.35
                                   (S787)
  (Field, Robert) SSA,pno,opt bvl oct
    PRESSER 312-41045 $.35   (S788)

STOJANKA MAJKA KNEZPOLJKA see
  Papandopulo, Boris

STOKER, RICHARD (1938-   )
  Glory Of The Dove, The
    SATB ENOCH EC350   (S789)

  Proverbs
    SATB ENOCH EC354 s.p., ipr   (S790)

  Requiescat
    2pt ASHDOWN EA370   (S791)

  Supplication, A
    SAB ASHDOWN VT70   (S792)

STOLTE, SIEGFRIED
  Die Rosen Von Lidice
    wom cor/jr cor,Mez solo,acap
    HOFMEISTER G2213 s.p.   (S793)

STOLTE, SIEGFRIED (cont'd.)

  Nun Geht Der Mond *Eve,cant
    wom cor,pno HOFMEISTER G2204 s.p.
                                   (S794)

STONE WALL see Williamson, Malcolm

STORA HAR JU SKOR OCH TYCKER MAN SKALL
  SKRATTA see Nilsson, Torsten

STORBEKKEN, EGIL
  Du Ska Itte Tro I Graset
    mix cor MUSIKK   (S795)

STORKE, THE see MacMillan, Ernest
  Campbell

STORM see Lora, Antonio

STORM'S ENDING see Sweetman, Paul

STORY SONGS see Ravosa

STOUTAMIRE
  Sing A Song *see Henderson

STRADELLA, ALESSANDRO (1645-1682)
  Il Damone
    (Martinotti) cor,SSSSATB soli,
    strings,cont ZERBONI 7355 s.p.
                                   (S796)

STRANGE, BILLY
  Memories (composed with Davis, Scott)
    (Metis, F.) SAB BIG3 $.45   (S797)
    (Metis, F.) SSA BIG3 $.45   (S798)
    (Metis, F.) SATB BIG3 $.45   (S799)

STRANGE LULLABY see Haufrecht,
  [Herbert]

STRATEGIER, HERMAN (1912-   )
  Colloquia Familiara
    mix cor,S solo,strings DONEMUS
                                   (S800)

  Zoo, Buddingh'zoo
    mix cor,Bar solo,2fl,2ob,2clar,
    2bsn,2horn,2trp,strings,perc,timp
    DONEMUS   (S801)

STRAUSS
  Dreams Of Spring (from Die
    Fledermaus)
    (Saar) SATB (med) FITZSIMONS 1022
    $.35   (S802)

STRAUSS, RICHARD (1864-1949)
  Bardengesang *Op.55
    [Eng/Ger] men cor,orch sc SCHOTTS
    rental, ipr   (S803)

  Olympische Hymne
    mix cor,3fl,3ob,3clar,3bsn,4horn,
    6trp,6trom,2tuba,strings,perc,
    timp (med) sc SCHOTTS rental, ipr
                                   (S804)
  Taillefer *Op.52
    mix cor,STB soli,6fl,6ob,7clar,
    5bsn,8horn,6trp,4trom,2tuba,
    strings,perc,timp (med diff) sc
    SCHOTTS rental, ipr   (S805)

STRAVINSKY, IGOR (1882-1972)
  Beim Heiland Von Tschigissy
    see Unterschale

  Der Hecht "Hechtfisch Kam Daher"
    see Unterschale

  Freund Dicksack "Einstmals Trabte"
    see Unterschale

  Herbst
    see Unterschale

  Unterschale *Russ
    men cor/wom cor,solo,4horn sc
    SCHOTTS C 39 491 s.p., cor pts
    SCHOTTS C 32 640 s.p., ipa
    contains: Beim Heiland Von
    Tschigissy; Der Hecht
    "Hechtfisch Kam Daher"; Freund
    Dicksack "Einstmals Trabte";
    Herbst   (S806)

STRAW BULL, THE see Zelinka, Jan
  Evangelista, Slameny Bycek

STRAWBERRY FAIR see Brown

STRAWBERRY FAIR see Protheroe, Daniel

STREBL, ALOIS (1837-1906)
  Krejci
    "Tailor, The" [Czech] mix cor,fl,
    ob,2clar,2horn,trp,trom,timp,
    strings CZECH s.p.   (S807)

  Tailor, The *see Krejci

STRECKE, GERHARD
  Erinnerung
    men cor,acap TONOS 4507 s.p. (S808)

  Saerlied
    men cor,acap TONOS 4052 s.p. (S809)

STRECKE, GERHARD (cont'd.)

  Werbung
    men cor,acap TONOS 4051 s.p. (S810)

STRECNO see Mikula, Zdenko

STRED ZEME see Simai, Pavol

STREET BOY'S SONG see Bizet, Georges

STREET SOUNDS see Tate

STREETS OF LAREDO
  (MacNutt, Walter) SAB (med easy)
    WATERLOO $.30   (S811)

STREIFTE DURCH DEN BUCHENWALD
  see Ballade

STREIT ZWISCHEN LOFFEL UND GABEL "HERR
  LOFFEL UND FRAU GABEL" see Rein,
  Walter

STREITLIED ZWISCHEN LEBEN UND TOD see
  Liebermann, Rolf

STREITLIED ZWISCHEN LEBEN UND TOD "SO
  SPRICHT DAS LEBEN" see Knab, Armin

STREITLIED ZWISCHEN LEBEN UND TOD "SO
  SPRICHT DAS LEBEN" see Weber,
  Bernhard

STRIETMAN, WILLEM (1918-   )
  Ligeia, Or The Shadow Out Of Time
    cor,org,fl,6perc,harp DONEMUS
                                   (S812)

STRILKO, ANTHONY (1931-   )
  Something For Everybody
    STB SCHIRM.G LG51825 $.45   (S813)

STRIMER, JOSEPH (1881-   )
  Adieu Gais Amis
    2pt,pno JOBERT voc sc s.p., cor pts
    s.p.   (S814)

  Berceuse Pour Le Petit Ours
    3 eq voices,acap JOBERT s.p. (S815)

  Le Chat Qui Dort
    3 eq voices,acap JOBERT s.p. (S816)

  Le Faineant
    2pt,pno JOBERT voc sc s.p., cor pts
    s.p.   (S817)

  Le Mechante Horloge
    2pt,pno JOBERT voc sc s.p., cor pts
    s.p.   (S818)

  Le Vent
    3 eq voices,acap JOBERT s.p. (S819)

  Ma Chatte Danse
    3 eq voices,acap JOBERT s.p. (S820)

  Ou Cours-Tu, Chevrette
    3 eq voices,acap JOBERT s.p. (S821)

  Quand Le Muguet Fleurira
    2pt,pno JOBERT voc sc s.p., cor pts
    s.p.   (S822)

STRNISTE, JIRI (1914-   )
  Haviri
    "Miners" [Czech] jr cor,acap CZECH
    s.p.   (S823)

  Miners *see Haviri

  Mladym Komunistum *cant
    "To Young Communists" [Czech] mix
    cor,Bar solo,3fl,3ob,3clar,3bsn,
    4horn,3trp,3trom,tuba,timp,perc,
    harp,strings CZECH s.p.   (S824)

  Pioneer's Sing, The *see Pionyrska

  Pionyrska
    "Pioneer's Sing, The" [Czech] jr
    cor,acap CZECH s.p.   (S825)

  To Young Communists *see Mladym
    Komunistum

STROBL, OTTO (1927-   )
  Elegien
    men cor,acap TONOS 3705 s.p. (S826)

  Fische
    (Weinheber, J.) mix cor DOBLINGER
    G 721 s.p. see from Sternbilder
                                   (S827)

  Jungfrau
    (Weinheber, J.) mix cor DOBLINGER
    G 727 s.p. see from Sternbilder
                                   (S828)

  Krebs
    (Weinheber, J.) mix cor DOBLINGER
    G 725 s.p. see from Sternbilder
                                   (S829)

  Leitspruch
    men cor,acap TONOS 697 s.p. (S830)

STROBL, OTTO (cont'd.)

   Lowe
     (Weinheber, J.) mix cor DOBLINGER
     G 726 s.p. see from Sternbilder
                         (S831)

   Schutze
     (Weinheber, J.) mix cor DOBLINGER
     G 730 s.p. see from Sternbilder
                         (S832)

   Skorpion
     (Weinheber, J.) mix cor DOBLINGER
     G 729 s.p. see from Sternbilder
                         (S833)

   Steinbock
     (Weinheber, J.) mix cor DOBLINGER
     G 719 s.p. see from Sternbilder
                         (S834)

   Sternbilder *see Fische; Jungfrau;
     Krebs; Lowe; Schutze; Skorpion;
     Steinbock; Stier; Waage;
     Wassermann; Widder; Zwillinge
                         (S835)

   Stier
     (Weinheber, J.) mix cor DOBLINGER
     G 723 s.p. see from Sternbilder
                         (S836)

   Waage
     (Weinheber, J.) mix cor DOBLINGER
     G 728 s.p. see from Sternbilder
                         (S837)

   Wassermann
     (Weinheber, J.) mix cor DOBLINGER
     G 720 s.p. see from Sternbilder
                         (S838)

   Widder
     (Weinheber, J.) mix cor DOBLINGER
     G 722 s.p. see from Sternbilder
                         (S839)

   Zwillinge
     (Weinheber, J.) mix cor DOBLINGER
     G 724 s.p. see from Sternbilder
                         (S840)

STROE, AUREL (1932-   )
   Musique Pour "Oedipe A Colone De
     Sophocle"
     men cor,Mez solo,2fl,2ob,2clar,
     4horn,3trp,3trom,perc sc SCHOTTS
     rental, ipr   (S841)

STROHBACH, SIEGFRIED (1929-   )
   Das Madchen Aus Scheveningen *see
     Het Meisje Van Scheveningen

   Die Liebe Mein *see L'amour De Moy

   Eg Ser Deg Utfor Gluggen *folk
     "Ich Seh Dich Vor Dem Fenster"
     [Ger/Norw] 4-5pt mix cor,acap
     BREITKOPF-W CHB 4951 s.p. (S842)

   Het Meisje Van Scheveningen *folk
     "Das Madchen Aus Scheveningen"
     [Ger/Neth] 4pt mix cor,acap
     BREITKOPF-W CHB 4945 s.p. (S843)

   Ich Sag Ade *see Ik Zeg Adieu

   Ich Seh Dich Vor Dem Fenster *see Eg
     Ser Deg Utfor Gluggen

   Ik Zeg Adieu *folk
     "Ich Sag Ade" [Ger/Neth] 3pt mix
     cor,acap BREITKOPF-W CHB 4946
     s.p.   (S844)

   Korn Ist Gemaht *see Marken Er Mejet

   Kristallen Den Fina *folk
     "Wie Kristallener Schimmer" [Ger/
     Swed] 4pt men cor,acap BREITKOPF-
     W CHB 4942 s.p.   (S845)

   L'amour De Moy *folk
     "Die Liebe Mein" [Ger/Fr] 4-5pt mix
     cor,acap BREITKOPF-W CHB 4949
     s.p.   (S846)

   Marken Er Mejet *folk
     "Korn Ist Gemaht" [Ger/Dan] 3pt mix
     cor,acap BREITKOPF-W s.p. (S847)

   Wie Kristallener Schimmer *see
     Kristallen Den Fina

STROUSE
   Those Were The Days *see Adams

STRUNK, JUD
   Daisy A Day, A
     (Metis, F.) SATB BIG3 $.50 (S848)
     (Metis, F.) SSA BIG3 $.45 (S849)
     (Metis, F.) SA/TB BIG3 $.50 (S850)
     (Metis, F.) SAB BIG3 $.45 (S851)

STUART, MARY
   Bells Of Christmas, The
     (Simon, W.) SAB BIG3 $.50 (S852)
     (Simon, W.) SATB BIG3 $.50 (S853)
     (Simon, W.) SSA BIG3 $.50 (S854)

STUCKE FUR SPRECHCHOR see Orff, Carl

STUDENT'S CHORUS see Offenbach, Jacques

STUDNICKA see Ocenas, Andrej

STUNDENRUF DES WACHTERS "HORT, IHR
  HERRN" see Rein, Walter

STURM, DU WINTERWIND see Genzmer,
  Harald

STURM "HOJEHO! DER NORDSTURM SETZT DAS
  BLANKE HORN" see Wittmer, Eberhard
  Ludwig

STURM IM HERBST see Wittmer, Eberhard
  Ludwig

STURMAN, PAUL
   Nine Hundred Miles
     2pt EMI   (S855)

   Oak And The Ash, The
     2pt EMI   (S856)

   Seasons
     unis voc sc ASHDOWN U96 s.p., cor
     pts ASHDOWN U96A s.p.   (S857)

STURMER, BRUNO (1892-1958)
   Der Faule Schafer
     men cor,acap TONOS 4033 s.p. (S858)

   Drei Frauenchore *see Klagt Nicht
     Mehr "Klagt Nicht, Ihr Frauen",
     Op.94; Trost Im Winkel "Lass Es
     Gehn, Herz", Op.94; Wiegenlied
     "Kleine Lieder Wiegen Leise",
     Op.94   (S859)

   Drei Gesange *Op.5
     4pt wom cor,S solo sc SCHOTTS
     C 30 924 s.p.
     contains: Elfensang "Um
     Mitternacht"; Japanisches
     Madchenlied "Die Erde Glanzt";
     Maiandacht "Maria Steht In
     Rosen"   (S860)

   Elfensang "Um Mitternacht"
     see Drei Gesange

   Japanisches Madchenlied "Die Erde
     Glanzt"
     see Drei Gesange

   Klagt Nicht Mehr "Klagt Nicht, Ihr
     Frauen" *Op.94
     wom cor (med easy) sc SCHOTTS
     C 34 877 s.p. see from Drei
     Frauenchore   (S861)

   Maiandacht "Maria Steht In Rosen"
     see Drei Gesange

   Memento Mori
     men cor,acap TONOS 4035 s.p. (S862)

   Morgen
     men cor,acap TONOS 4034 s.p. (S863)

   Narren Uberall "Narren, Narren"
     see Von Liebe Und Narren

   Narren Uberall "Narren Sind An Allen
     Ecken" *Op.90,No.3
     men cor sc SCHOTTS C 38 411 s.p.
                         (S864)

   Tanzlied "Lasset Uns Scherzen"
     see Von Liebe Und Narren

   Trost Im Winkel "Lass Es Gehn, Herz"
     *Op.94
     wom cor (med easy) sc SCHOTTS
     C 34 874 s.p. see from Drei
     Frauenchore   (S865)

   Vergebliches Standchen "Ich Wunschte,
     Es Ware Nacht"
     men cor sc SCHOTTS C 38 005 s.p.
                         (S866)

   Verlassen
     men cor,acap TONOS 4031 s.p. (S867)

   Von Liebe Und Narren
     mix cor (med easy) SCHOTTS s.p.
     contains: Narren Uberall "Narren,
     Narren", Op.90,No.3; Tanzlied
     "Lasset Uns Scherzen", Op.90,
     No.1; Zweene "Zweene Schlafen
     Sichrer Ein", Op.90,No.2 (S868)

   Weite Aussicht
     men cor,acap TONOS 4032 s.p. (S869)

   Wiegenlied "Kleine Lieder Wiegen
     Leise" *Op.94
     wom cor (med easy) sc SCHOTTS
     C 34 876 s.p. see from Drei
     Frauenchore   (S870)

   Zweene "Zweene Schlafen Sichrer Ein"
     see Von Liebe Und Narren

STURMSANG DER TAUFER see Krietsch,
  Georg

STYNE, [JULE] (1905-   )
   Let It Snow *sac
     (Ades) SA/TB SHAWNEE E145 $.40
                         (S871)

STYRI MADRIGALY see Zimmer, Jan

STYRI SLOVENSKE NARODNE PIESNE see
  Novak, Milan

SUB LUNA see Pergament, Moses

SUCCESSION OF THE FOUR SWEET MONTHS see
  Washburn

SUCH, HERZ, NUN see Langer, Hans-Klaus

SUCHON, EUGEN (1908-   )
   Aka Si Mi Krasna
     mix cor SLOV.HUD.FOND s.p. (S872)

   O Cloveku *CCUL
     mix cor SLOV.HUD.FOND s.p. in three
     parts   (S873)

   O Horach
     men cor SLOV.HUD.FOND s.p. (S874)

   Piesen O Spolocnej Vlasti!
     wom cor SLOV.HUD.FOND s.p. (S875)
     mix cor SLOV.HUD.FOND s.p. (S876)

SUCHT DIE BESTEN WEINE AUS see Koenig,
  Franz

SUCHY, FRANTISEK (1902-   )
   Aj, Pada Rosicka
     "Dew Is Falling, The" [Czech] mix
     cor,acap CZECH s.p.   (S877)

   Dew Is Falling, The *see Aj, Pada
     Rosicka

   Free *see Svobodni

   Svobodni *Op.20, cant
     "Free" [Czech] mix cor,ABarB soli,
     3fl,3ob,3clar,3bsn,4horn,3trp,
     3trom,tuba,timp,perc,harp,strings
     CZECH s.p.   (S878)

SUDAMERIKANISCHE GESANGE see Genzmer,
  Harald

SUDTIROL see Koch, Karl

SUDTIROLER LIED: HEILIGES LAND IM
  GEBIRGE see Holzl, Peter

SUGAR, REZSO (1919-   )
   Biztatas
     (Batsanyi, Janos) mix cor BUDAPEST
     7105 s.p.   (S879)

   Dozsa *CCU
     (Kovesdy, Janos) mix cor&jr cor
     BUDAPEST 6837 s.p.   (S880)

   Dozsa
     (Kovesdy, Janos) jr cor BUDAPEST
     6911 s.p.   (S881)

   Tavaszi Zsoltar
     (Hars, Gyorgy) mix cor BUDAPEST
     6727 s.p.   (S882)

   Tavaszodnik
     (Aprily, Lajos) mix cor BUDAPEST
     7268 s.p.   (S883)

SUITE DALL'OPERA "PENTEO" see
  Valdambrini, Francesco

SUK, JOSEF (1874-1935)
   Ripening *Op.34
     wom cor,3fl,3ob,3clar,3bsn,6horn,
     9trp,3trom,tuba,timp,perc,2harp,
     pno,strings, celeste SUPRAPHON
     s.p.   (S884)

SULIKO *folk,Russ
   (Langer, Hans-Klaus) men cor,acap
   TONOS 2005 s.p.   (S885)

SULIRAM
   (De Cormier) SATB SCHIRM.G LG51755
   $.30   (S886)

SULLIVAN, LEON
   Nation Of Brotherhood, A
     (Fisher, Sydney) SATB,A solo,pno
     (easy) oct PRESSER 312-41074 $.40
                         (S887)

SULLIVAN, SIR ARTHUR SEYMOUR
  (1842-1900)
   Brightly Dawns Our Wedding Day
     SATB EGTVED MS16B16 s.p.   (S888)

   Het Verloren Accoord *see Lost
     Chord, The

   Leaves In Autumn Fade And Fall
     SATB EGTVED MS16B17 s.p.   (S889)

   Lost Chord, The
     (De Wolff) "Het Verloren Accoord"
     mix cor,acap s.p. sc HEER 483,

SULLIVAN, SIR ARTHUR SEYMOUR (cont'd.)

cor pts HEER 483A　　　　(S890)

When Love And Beauty *madrigal
(Young, Percy M.) [Eng] SSATB,acap
oct BROUDE BR. $.65　　　(S891)

SULTAN ACHMET see Pileur

SUMMER (from Czech Year, The)
(Hanus, Jan) SATB,acap voc sc GENERAL
s.p.　　　　　　　　　　(S892)

SUMMER DANCE OF OLD AND YOUNG see
Williamson, Malcolm

SUMMER DANCE OF THE YOUNG see
Williamson, Malcolm

SUMMER EVENING see Bissell, Keith W.

SUMMER FESTIVITIES see Kubin, Rudolf,
Lesni Veselice

SUMMER IS ICUMEN IN see Jenkins, C.

SUMMER ME, WINTER ME see Legrand,
Michel

SUMMER MUSIC see Rose, Michael

SUMMER SERENADE see Bush, Geoffrey

SUMMER SOLDIER see Red, Buryl

SUMMERLIN
Three Western Songs *CC3U
TTBB SOUTHERN $.30　　　(S893)

SUMMER'S QUEEN see Bissell, Keith W.

SUN DON'T SET IN THE MORNIN' see Kirk

SUN IS SLOWLY SINKING, THE see Distler,
Hugo, Die Sonne Sinkt Von Hinnen

SUNDAY
SATB oct CHAPPELL W57007-357 $.40
(S894)
2pt oct CHAPPELL W570007-351 $.40
(S895)
SSA oct CHAPPELL W570007-353 $.40
(S896)
TTBB oct CHAPPELL W570007-355 $.40
(S897)
SAB oct CHAPPELL W570007-356 $.40
(S898)

SUNDAY SUNDAY
(Bissell, Keith W.) TTBB (med diff)
WATERLOO $.40　　　　　(S899)

SUNDOWN see Lightfoot, Gordon

SUNRISE see Hammond, Harold

SUN'S WARM RAYS, THE see Marenzio,
Luca, Scaldava Il Sol

SUNSET see Pisk, Paul Amadeus

SUNSHINE ON MY SHOULDERS see Denver,
John

SUNSHINE SMILE see Swanson, Brad

SUNT LACRIMAE RERUM see Orff, Carl

SUONI see Nystedt, Knut

SUPER FLUMINA BABYLONIS see Lassus,
Roland de (Orlandus)

SUPPLICATION, A see Stoker, Richard

SUR LE PONT D'AVIGNON *folk,Fr
see Two French Folk Songs
(Becker, Hans-Gunther) men cor,opt
pno, combo ad lib 2061 s.p.　(S900)
(Weber, Bernhard) [Fr] 4pt men cor
MERSEBURG EM9083 s.p.　　(S901)
(Weber, Ernhard) [Fr] 4pt mix cor
MERSEBURG EM9249 s.p.　　(S902)

SURREY WITH THE FRINGE ON TOP, THE see
Rodgers, Richard

SURVEY OF LITERATURE see Schwartz, Paul

SURVIVOR FROM WARSAW, A see Schoenberg,
Arnold, Ein Uberlebender Von
Warschau

SURYA see Sohal Naresh

SUSE, LEEWE SUSE see Linke, Norbert

SUSE, LIEBE SUSE see Lang, Hans

SUSS' LIEBE LIEBT DEN MAI "EIN BURSCH
UND MAGDLEIN FLINK UND SCHON" see
Silcher, Friedrich

SUSSE RUHE, STILLE DER NACHT see Orrel,
Max

SUSSE TRAUBEN "MEIN VATER IST EIN
WINZER" see Biebl, Franz

SUSSES LIEB see Dowland, John, Come
Again! Sweet Love Doth Now Invite

SUTER, ROBERT (1919-　　)
Die Ballade Von Des Cortez Leuten
mix cor,narrator,fl/pic,ob,clar,
trp,horn,trom,tuba,pno,3perc,
strings MODERN rental　　(S903)

SUTERMEISTER, HEINRICH (1910-　　　)
Am Eisenbahndamm
see Drei Chorlieder

Andreas Gryphius *CC7L
4pt mix cor,acap (med diff) sc
SCHOTTS C 34 999 s.p.　　(S904)

Cantata 4　*see Das Hohelied

Cantata 5　*see Der Papagei Aus Kuba

Cantata 6　*see Erkennen Und Schaffen

Cantata 8　*see Omnia Ad Unum

Das Hohelied (Cantata 4) cant
mix cor,SBar soli,2fl,2ob,2clar,
2bsn,4horn,3trp,3trom,tuba,
strings,harp,perc,timp, celeste
(med easy) voc sc,cor pts SCHOTTS
ED. 5161 s.p., ipr　　　(S905)

Der Hahn "Zornkamm. Gockel,
Kornerschlinger"
see Drei Lieder

Der Kaiser Von China "In Der Mitte
Aller Dinge"
TTBB sc SCHOTTS C 42 733 s.p., voc
pt SCHOTTS C 42 734, 01-02 s.p.
(S906)

Der Papagei Aus Kuba (Cantata 5)
mix cor,fl,ob,clar,bsn,horn,trp,
strings,perc,timp,pno, or celeste
(med) voc sc,cor pts SCHOTTS
ED. 5293 s.p., ipr　　　(S907)

Die Landsknechte "Wacht Auf, Herr
Wirt"
TTBB sc SCHOTTS C 42 329 s.p. see
from Zwei Mannerchore　　(S908)

Die Lange Nase
see Drei Chorlieder

Drei Chorlieder
3pt jr cor,pno (med) sc,cor pts
SCHOTTS ED. 6444 s.p.
contains: Am Eisenbahndamm; Die
Lange Nase; Im Park　　(S909)

Drei Lieder
TTBB sc SCHOTTS C 40 699 s.p., voc
pt SCHOTTS 40 700, 01-02 s.p.
contains: Der Hahn "Zornkamm.
Gockel, Kornerschlinger"; Einem
Wirtshaus Gegenuber "Einer
Mandoline Zittern"; Fruhmorgens
"Der Rauch Der Dammernden
Fruhe"　　　　　　　　(S910)

Ein Getreues Herz (from Der Rote
Stiefel)
see Zwei Madrigale

Einem Wirtshaus Gegenuber "Einer
Mandoline Zittern"
see Drei Lieder

Erkennen Und Schaffen (Cantata 6)
mix cor,SBar soli,pno,2fl,2ob,
2clar,2bsn,2horn,3trp,2trom,
strings,harp,perc, celeste (med)
voc sc,cor pts SCHOTTS ED. 5294
s.p., ipr　　　　　　　(S911)

Floridans Nachtklage "O Dunkle Nacht"
see Zwei Barocklieder

Fruhmorgens "Der Rauch Der Dammernden
Fruhe"
see Drei Lieder

Im Park
see Drei Chorlieder

Kantate No. 2　*cant
mix cor,A solo,2pno (med) sc,cor
pts SCHOTTS ED. 2560 s.p. (S912)

Lehrer Lampel
see Max Und Moritz

Letzter Streich
see Max Und Moritz

Max Und Moritz
4pt mix cor, piano four hands (med)
sc,cor pts SCHOTTS ED. 4211 s.p.
contains: Lehrer Lampel; Letzter
Streich; Schneider Bock;
Vorwort; Witwe Bolte　　(S913)

SUTERMEISTER, HEINRICH (cont'd.)

Omnia Ad Unum (Cantata 8)
4pt mix cor,Bar solo,pno,3fl,3ob,
3clar,3bsn,4horn,3trp,3trom,tuba,
strings,harp,perc,timp, celeste
(med) voc sc,cor pts SCHOTTS
ED. 5762 s.p., ipr　　　(S914)

Scheltworte Einer Griesgramenden
Mutter "Kannst Du Nicht, Wenn's
Finster Ist, Nach Hause Gehn?"
see Zwei Barocklieder

Schilflieder "Druben Geht Die Sonne
Scheiden"
TTBB sc,voc pt SCHOTTS
C 42 327, C 42 328, 01-02 s.p.
see from Zwei Mannerchore　(S915)

Schmuck Dich, Madchen (from Der Rote
Stiefel)
see Zwei Madrigale

Schneider Bock
see Max Und Moritz

Vorwort
see Max Und Moritz

Witwe Bolte
see Max Und Moritz

Zwei Barocklieder
4pt mix cor,SATB soli,acap (med
diff) sc SCHOTTS C 39 028 s.p.
contains: Floridans Nachtklage "O
Dunkle Nacht"; Scheltworte
Einer Griesgramenden Mutter
"Kannst Du Nicht, Wenn's
Finster Ist, Nach Hause Gehn?"
(S916)

Zwei Madrigale (from Der Rote
Stiefel) madrigal
[Ger/Fr] mix cor (diff) sc SCHOTTS
C 40 980 s.p.
contains: Ein Getreues Herz;
Schmuck Dich, Madchen　　(S917)

Zwei Mannerchore　*see Die
Landsknechte "Wacht Auf, Herr
Wirt"; Schilflieder "Druben Geht
Die Sonne Scheiden"　　　(S918)

SUTHERLAND, MARGARET
Chez Nous
SA EMI　　　　　　　　　(S919)

SUTIL UND LAAR see Wyttenbach, Jurg

SUTTON, NANCY
Ballad Of The Lion And The Lamb, The
(composed with Cohen)
1-2pt,pno MCAFEE M118 $.30　(S920)

I Want To Talk To You (composed with
Cohen)
SATB,pno,opt perc MCAFEE M1093 $.50
(S921)

Questions　*see Cohen

SUZIE'S LOVE SONG see Tiffault

SVADBA JANOSIKOVA see Bella, Jan
Levoslav

SVATOVSKA see Slavenski, Josip

SVATY BUOH see Anonymous

SVATY VACLAV see Foerster, Josef
Bohuslav

SVECENY, LADISLAV (1881-　　)
Dove, The　*see Holoubek

Holoubek　*cant
"Dove, The" [Czech] mix cor,soli,
2fl,2ob,2clar,2bsn,4horn,2trp,
2trom,tuba,timp,perc,harp,strings
CZECH s.p.　　　　　　(S922)

Romance About King Jecminek, The
*see Romance O Krali Jecminkovi

Romance O Krali Jecminkovi　*cant
"Romance About King Jecminek, The"
[Czech] mix cor,3 soli,3fl,2ob,
2clar,2bsn,4horn,2trp,2trom,tuba,
timp,perc,pno,strings CZECH s.p.
(S923)

SVOBODNI see Suchy, Frantisek

SVOBODO, JIRI (1897-　　)
Dva Detske Sbory
[Czech] jr cor,acap CZECH s.p.
contains: Matka A Jablon, "Mother
And The Apple Tree"; Prilretela
Pod Okenko, "It Came Flying To
My Window"　　　　　　(S924)

For The Tragic Anniversary Of Munich
*see K Tragickemu Vyroci
Mniochova

SVOBODO, JIRI (cont'd.)

It Came Flying To My Window *see Prilretela Pod Okenko

K Tragickemu Vyroci Mniochova *Op.31, cant "For The Tragic Anniversary Of Munich" [Czech] men cor,3fl,3ob, 2clar,3bsn,4horn,3trp,3trom,tuba, timp,perc,harp,strings CZECH s.p. (S925)

Matka A Jablon "Mother And The Apple Tree" see Dva Detske Sbory

Mother And The Apple Tree *see Matka A Jablon

Prilretela Pod Okenko "It Came Flying To My Window" see Dva Detske Sbory

Tri Narodni Pisne *Op.38, CC3U,folk [Czech] jr cor/wom cor,acap CZECH s.p. (S926)

SWAN, BILLY
I Can Help
(Simon, W.) SATB,Bar solo BIG3 $.50 (S927)
(Simon, W.) SSA BIG3 $.50 (S928)
(Simon, W.) SAB BIG3 $.50 (S929)

SWANEE RIBBER *folk,US
(Zoll, Paul) "Die Meinen Zu Haus "Weit, Weit Von Hier Am Swanee Ribber"" men cor sc SCHOTTS C 40 112 s.p. see from Vier Amerikanische Volkslieder (S930)

SWANEE RIVER
see Drei Amerikanische Volkslieder

SWANSON, BRAD
Sunshine Smile
(Fabre, Rene; Kysar, Michael) SATB, pno,brass (med diff, jazz) KYSAR A106 $.60 (S931)

SWAYNE
Full Fathom Five
see Three Shakespeare Songs

Hark, Hark, The Lark
see Three Shakespeare Songs

Three Shakespeare Songs
SATB,acap (diff) OXFORD 56.598 $2.55
contains: Full Fathom Five; Hark, Hark, The Lark; Where The Bee Sucks (S932)

Where The Bee Sucks
see Three Shakespeare Songs

SWEDISH DANCE CAROL see Davis, Katherine K.

SWEELINCK, JAN PIETERSZOON (1562-1621)
Dut-Ger-Fr

SWEET AND LOW see Barnby

SWEET AND LOW see Lockwood, Normand

SWEET AND LOW see Williamson, Malcolm

SWEET AND TWENTY see Bergh, Arthur

SWEET CITY SONG see Cashman, Terry

SWEET FREEDOM'S SONG see Ward, Robert

SWEET LAMB see Ehret, Walter

SWEET LOVE, O CEASE THY FLYING see Kirbye, George

SWEET NIGHTINGALE
(Bissell, Keith W.) SAAB (med) WATERLOO $.50 (S933)
(Bissell, Keith W.) SAB (med) WATERLOO $.50 (S934)

SWEET SINGING AMARYLLIS see Marenzio, Luca

SWEET SUFFOLK OWL see Sweetman, Paul

SWEET, SWEET, SWEET LITTLE JESUS see Regney, Noel

SWEET THAMES RUN SOFTLY see Dyson, George

SWEET THOUGHTS OF YOU see Kennedy, John Brodbin

SWEET WESTERN WIND see Gideon, Miriam

SWEETEST SOUNDS, THE
mix cor,opt bvl&drums&gtr cor pts CHAPPELL W612502-373 $.30, sc CHAPPELL W612502-372 $1.50 (S935)

SATB oct CHAPPELL W612502-357 $.40 (S936)
TTBB oct CHAPPELL W612502-355 $.40 (S937)
SAB oct CHAPPELL W612502-356 $.40 (S938)
2pt oct CHAPPELL W612502-351 $.40 (S939)
SSA oct CHAPPELL W612502-353 $.40 (S940)

SWEETHEART TREE
SSA CIMINO $.40 (S941)
SAB CIMINO $.40 (S942)
SATB CIMINO $.40 (S943)
TTBB CIMINO $.40 (S944)

SWEETMAN, PAUL
Bold Turpin
unis men cor/unis boy cor (easy) WATERLOO $.30 (S945)

Lullaby
SSA (med easy) WATERLOO $.30 (S946)

Man Of Life Upright
unis (easy) WATERLOO $.30 (S947)

Slow Slow Fresh Fount
SSA (med easy) WATERLOO $.30 (S948)

Storm's Ending
SSA (easy) WATERLOO $.30 (S949)

Sweet Suffolk Owl
SATB (med easy) WATERLOO $.40 (S950)

Widow Bird
SSA (easy) WATERLOO $.30 (S951)

SWEL MAN EIN GUOT WIP HAT see Genzmer, Harald

SWING AND SING see Fussan, Werner

SWING LOW, SWEET CHARIOT *folk/spir,US
"Trag Mich Auf Sanften Schwingen" see Spirituals For All Heft I
(Biebl, Franz) treb cor DOBLINGER O 319 s.p. see from Acht Spirituals (S952)
(Cain, Noble) SATB,acap (med) FITZSIMONS 1012 $.25 (S953)
(Kubizek, Augustin) "Schwing Sanft, Mein Gut Gefahrt" men cor DOBLINGER M 322 s.p. (S954)
(Zoll, Paul) "Hol Mich Nach Haus" men cor sc SCHOTTS C 40 109 s.p. see from Vier Amerikanische Volkslieder (S955)

SWINGLE NOVAE see Zbar, Michel

SYDEMAN, WILLIAM (1928-   )
Lament Of Elektra, The
SATB,A solo,orch sc SCHIRM.EC 2690 s.p., ipr (S956)

SYKORA, VACLAV JAN (1918-   )
Ceske Krajine
"To The Czech Country" [Czech] mix cor,acap CZECH s.p. (S957)

To The Czech Country *see Ceske Krajine

SYMBOLS RING, THE see Dedrick, C.

SYMPHONIE IMMAGINAIRE see Sinopoli, Giuseppe

SYMPHONY NO. 2 see Kohs, Ellis B.

SYMPHONY NO. 3 see Lukas, Zdenek

SYMPHONY NO. 6, OUT OF BONDAGE see Becker, John J.

SYMPHONY NO. 7 "REGION OF CHILDHOOD" see Kapr, Jan

SYNCOPATED LULLABY see Sinn, Clarence E.

SYNMOVE'S SONG see Kjerulf, [Halfdan]

SYNONYM FOR LIFE see Muczynski, Robert

SYTHE AND THE DEW, THE see Haba, Alois, Kosa A Rosa

SZABADSAG, SZALLJ KOZENK see Karai, Jozsef

SZABO, CSABA
Erzsikehez
(Toth, Istvan) men cor BUDAPEST 7284 s.p. (S958)

Piroskahoz
(Toth, Istvan) mix cor BUDAPEST 7283 s.p. (S959)

SZABO, [FERENC] (1902-1969)
A Szegeny Ember Notai
(Jozsef, Attila) men cor BUDAPEST 6889 s.p. (S960)

SZABO, [FERENC] (cont'd.)

Bocskai Istvanhoz
mix cor BUDAPEST 7286 s.p. (S961)

Sirato Jannus Pannoniusrol
mix cor BUDAPEST 7285 s.p. (S962)

SZAVAK A KONYVHOZ see Balazs, Arpad

SZEGHY, ENDRE
Altatodal
(Mora, Ferenc) mix cor BUDAPEST 6892 s.p. (S963)

SZEKERES, FERENC
Regi Mesterek Egynemukarai VII
eq voices BUDAPEST 7310 s.p. (S964)

Regi Mesterek Vegyeskarai XVII
mix cor BUDAPEST 6609 s.p. (S965)

Regi Mesterek Vegyeskarai XVIII
mix cor BUDAPEST 6883 s.p. (S966)

Regi Mesterk Vegyeskarai XIX
mix cor BUDAPEST 6884 s.p. (S967)

Regi Mesterk Vegyeskarai XX
mix cor BUDAPEST 7102 s.p. (S968)

Regi Mesterk Vegyeskarai XXI
mix cor BUDAPEST 7309 s.p. (S969)

SZEKESFEHERVAR see Bardos, Lajos

SZELEPCSENYI, JAN (1937-   )
Piesen Nasho L'udu
mix cor SLOV.HUD.FOND s.p. (S970)

SZERVANSZKY, ENDRE (1912-   )
Harom Kinai Dal
men cor BUDAPEST 6807 s.p. (S971)

SZIVARVANY see Farkas, Ferenc

SZOKOLAY, SANDOR
Ven Epulet Mar A Vilag
(Petofi, Sandor) mix cor BUDAPEST 7515 s.p. (S972)

SZONYI, ERZSEBET
Elotted A Kuzdes *canon
(Arany, Janos) eq voices BUDAPEST 6895 s.p. (S973)

SZOVJET KORUSMUVEK I *CCU
wom cor BUDAPEST 7063 s.p. (S974)

SZOVJET KORUSMUVEK II *CCU
men cor BUDAPEST 7065 s.p. (S975)

SZOVJET KORUSMUVEK III *CCU
mix cor BUDAPEST 7066 s.p. (S976)

SZOVJET KORUSMUVEK IV *CCU
wom cor BUDAPEST 7067 s.p. (S977)

T

'T WAS NOT SO LONG AGO
SSA CIMINO $.40   (T1)
TTBB CIMINO $.40   (T2)
SATB CIMINO $.40   (T3)

'T ZIJ VREUGDE MIJN DEEL IS
mix cor sc HEER 2264 s.p.   (T4)

TA SLOVENSKA PIESEN! see Mikula, Zdenko

TABAK IST MEIN LEBEN see Biebl, Franz

TABLEAU DE PARIS see Rosenthal, Manuel

TABORAK see Holoubek, Ladislav

TACE IL VENTO see Verdi, Giuseppe

TAFELLIED "WIE HEHR IM GLASE BLINKET"
see Zelter, Carl Friedrich

TAG DER FREUDE see Rosenstengel,
Albrecht

TAG DES KINDES see Jacot, Andre

TAG, MEINES LEBENS see Edler, Robert

TAGELIED see Edler, Robert

TAGELIED "DIE HAHNE KRAHEN" see
Genzmer, Harald

TAGESKREIS see Baumann, Max

TAGESLIED "WENN DURCH DIE NEBELFRUHE"
see Erdlen, Hermann

TAGLICH ZU SINGEN see Leist, Peter
Marzellin

TAGLICHER WUNSCH see Gerster, Ottmar

TAILLEFER see Strauss, Richard

TAILOR, THE see Strebl, Alois, Krejci

TAILOR OF CAMBERWELL GREEN, THE see
Winters

TAJEMNY TRUBAC see Burghauser, Jarmil

TAKE HERE MY HEART see Weelkes

TAKE ME HOME, COUNTRY ROADS see Danoff

TAKE, O TAKE THOSE LIPS AWAY see
Felciano, Richard

TAKE TIME IN LIFE *folk,Afr
(Vance, Margaret Shelley) SA/TB,pno,
perc BELWIN OCT 2334 $.30   (T5)

TAKE YOUR FINGER OUT OF YOUR MOUTH
TTBB CIMINO $.40   (T6)

TAKIN' A RIDE ON YOUR MIND see Eilers,
Joyce Elaine

TALK ABOUT A CHILD THAT DO LOVE JESUS
*spir
(Dawson, William L.) SATTBB,S solo
(med) FITZSIMONS 2015 $.25   (T7)

TALK OF FLOWERS AND THE SUN see Ishii,
Kan, Gesprach Zwischen Blumen Und
Sonne

TALMADGE, CHARLES L.
Junkman, The
TTBB,pno FISCHER,J FEC 10109 $.35
(T8)

TAM TAM TA DAM see Feld, Jindrich

TAMBOURINES TO GLORY see Hughes

TAMMY see Livingston

T'AMO MIA VITA see Monteverdi, Claudio

TAN TA RA CRIES MARS see Weelkes,
Thomas

TANECNY see Mikula, Zdenko

TANENBAUM, ELIAS
Families Of Son My, The
SATB/SSAA,electronic tape
AM.COMP.AL.   (T9)

Hiroshima
2pt jr cor,pno,perc,band
AM.COMP.AL. sc $7.98, voc sc
$8.80   (T10)

Last Of The Just, The
SATB&SATB,2fl,3ob,3clar,3bsn,4horn,
3trp,3trom,tuba,timp,perc,harp,

TANENBAUM, ELIAS (cont'd.)

strings sc AM.COMP.AL. $48.40
(T11)
Scenario, A
jr cor,band,pno,electronic tape
AM.COMP.AL. sc $7.70, voc pt
$1.38   (T12)
Sound
8pt,2trp,3trom,electric,pno,2perc,
electronic tape, alto saxophone
sc AM.COMP.AL. $20.35   (T13)

TANGENTS V see Jackson

TANKEN see Johansen, Sven-Erik

TANZ DOCH, PFARRER see Bartok, Bela

TANZ MIR NICHT MIT MEINER JUNGFER
KATHEN *folk
(Nehrkorn, Alex) SAATB MOSELER LB539
(T14)

TANZ MIT DER DORDL *folk,Ger
(Ophoven, Hermann) men cor,acap TONOS
110 s p   (T15)

TANZ RUBER, TANZ NUBER see Rein, Walter

TANZ-SUITE see Rosenstengel, Albrecht

TANZEN, IMMER TANZEN see Rosenstengel,
Albrecht

TANZEN SOLL DIE DANITZA *folk
(Heinrichs, W.,) [Ger] 4pt men cor
MERSEBURG EM9070 s.p.   (T16)

TANZEN UND SPRINGEN see Hassler, Hans
Leo

TANZENDE "DUNKELAUGIGE, DU" see
Genzmer, Harald

TANZENDE HERZEN see Rosenstengel,
Albrecht

TANZLIED *folk
(Seib, V.) [Ger] 4pt men cor
MERSEBURG EM9073 s.p.   (T17)
(Zoll, P.) [Ger] 4pt men cor
MERSEBURG EM9008 s.p.   (T18)

TANZLIED see Bartok, Bela, Csujogato

TANZLIED see Cossetto, Emil, Poskocica

TANZLIED AUS SCHWEDEN *folk
(Fischbach, Klaus) wom cor,pno sc
BREITKOPF-W CHB 4921 s.p. see from
Sieben Europaische Volkslieder
(T19)
TANZLIED "HEI! WIR BEGINNEN EINEN
LUSTIGEN TANZ" see Mendelssohn,
Arnold

TANZLIED "LASSET UNS SCHERZEN" see
Sturmer, Bruno

TANZLIED "O SANSA, AUS GRAUEM HIMMEL"
see Sakamoto, Yoshitaka, Sansa
Sigure

TANZLIEDCHEN see Biebl, Franz

TANZLIEDCHEN "TANZ DOCH, PFARRER" see
Genzmer, Harald

TANZLIEDER see Fischer, Ernst

TANZLIEDER-KANTATE see Fussan, Werner

TANZVERGNUGEN see Rosenstengel,
Albrecht

TARABA, BOHUSLAV (1894-   )
Slovensku
"To Slovakia" [Czech] mix cor,4fl,
3ob,4clar,3bsn,4horn,4trp,3trom,
tuba,timp,perc,strings CZECH s.p.
(T20)
To Slovakia *see Slovensku

TARANTELLA see Verdi, Giuseppe

TARANTELLE SIZILIANA "SIGNORINA AUS
MESSINA" see Fischer, Ernst

TATE
Last Organ Grinder
SATB,perc (med easy) cor pts OXFORD
$.50 see also Street Sounds (T21)

Local Band
SATB,perc (med easy) cor pts OXFORD
$.50 see also Street Sounds (T22)

Ring Out, Sing Out
unis,inst (easy) sc OXFORD 50.120
$5.10, ipa, cor pts OXFORD $.35
(T23)
Sailing In
SATB (med) OXFORD 84.220 $.70 (T24)

TATE (cont'd.)

Secular Requiem, A
SATB,inst (med diff) OXFORD 56.590
$2.40   (T25)

Street Sounds
SATB,perc (med easy) sc OXFORD
56.124 $3.85, ipa
contains & see also: Last Organ
Grinder; Local Band; Village
Interlude   (T26)

To Words By Joseph Beaumont
SSA OXFORD   (T27)

Village Interlude
SATB,perc (med easy) cor pts OXFORD
$.50 see also Street Sounds (T28)

Wassail All Over The Town *Xmas
SATB (med easy) OXFORD 84.189 $.35
(T29)

TAUBE, EVERT
Har Ar Den Skona Sommer
(Eklund, Stig) mix cor GEHRMANS
KRB440   (T30)

Nocturne
(Jehrlander, Karl-Fredrik) mix cor
GEHRMANS KRB454   (T31)

TAUBERT, KARL HEINZ
Drei Jahreswendlieder *CC3U
men cor voc sc RIES s.p.   (T32)

Lob Auf Die Musika
mix cor,vcl/vla,kbd/3treb inst cor
pts RIES s.p., ipa   (T33)

Maienfahrt *CCU
3pt,treb inst, or four-hand piano
voc pt RIES s.p., ipa   (T34)

TAUPIN
Daniel *see John, Elton

TAUSEND FLUGEL see Fischer, Theo

TAUSEND FLUGEL SOLLEN TRAGEN see
Fischer, Theo

TAUSINGER, JAN (1921-   )
Cantata About The Communist Party
*see Kanata O Komunisticke Strane

Kanata O Komunisticke Strane *cant
"Cantata About The Communist Party"
[Czech] mix cor,A solo,3fl,2ob,
2clar,3bsn,4horn,3trp,3trom,tuba,
timp,harp,strings CZECH s.p.
(T35)

Labuti Pericko *CCU
[Czech] mix cor,soli,fl,ob,clar,
bsn,trp,perc,strings, xylophone,
vibraphone, claves CZECH s.p.
(T36)

Right Thing, The *see Spravna Vec

Spravna Vec
"Right Thing, The" [Czech] mix cor,
T solo,3fl,2ob,3clar,3bsn,4horn,
3trp,3trom,tuba,timp,perc,harp,
pno,strings, xylophone CZECH s.p.
(T37)

Vertigo *see Zavrat

Zavrat *cant
"Vertigo" [Czech] cor,2fl,2ob,
2clar,2bsn,3horn,2trp,2trom,timp,
perc,strings, saxophone CZECH
s.p.   (T38)

TAVASZI ZSOLTAR see Sugar, Rezso

TAVASZLESEN see Balazs, Arpad

TAVASZODNIK see Sugar, Rezso

TAVERN OF THE LOVING PEOPLE see Cobine,
Al

TAYLOR
Eagle And The Hawk, The *see Denver,
John

Sunshine On My Shoulders *see
Denver, John

TAYLOR, CLIFFORD
Balade De Bon Conseyl (from
Commencement Suite)
SSA/TTB,2fl,2ob,2clar,2bsn,4horn,
2trp,2trom,tuba,timp,perc,
strings,opt harp AM.COMP.AL. sc
$8.25, voc sc $3.85   (T39)

Choral Settings Of Western
Pennsylvania *CCU
SATB,soli,pno AM.COMP.AL. $9.35
(T40)
Pageant Of Characters From William
Shakespeare
SATB,soli,acap AM.COMP.AL. $11.00
(T41)

TAYLOR, CLIFFORD (cont'd.)

Two Folk Madrigals *Op.9
SATB,acap AM.COMP.AL. $6.60   (T42)

TCHAIKOVSKY, PIOTR ILYITCH (1840-1893)
Legend, A
(Brown, F.E.) 2pt ALLANS 833   (T43)
(Brown, F.E.) 3pt ALLANS 832   (T44)

One Summer Morn
(Dicks) mix cor BANKS MUS YS 392
$.20   (T45)

TE KIELDRESHT see Van Streel, R.

TE LUCIS ANTE TERMINUM see Orff, Carl

TEACH YOUR CHILDREN see Nash, Graham

TEAR AGO, A
SATB CIMINO $.40   (T46)

TEARS ARE IDLE AND SAID THE SWALLOW see
Weil

TECHNICAL ADVICE TO PERSONS PLANNING TO
ERECT MEMORIAL STATUES OF
THEMSELVES see Cohn, James

TED' PRISEL CAS see Schneeweiss, Jan

TEGENZANGEN see Vries, Klaas de

TEIRLINCK, GEO (1922-   )
Viva Musica *CC12U,canon
2-5pt jr cor (easy) sc SCHOTTS
SF 9063 s.p.   (T47)

TEL UW ZEGENINGEN
mix cor sc HEER 2256 s.p.   (T48)

TELL ME, NIGHTINGALE see Jeffries

TELL ME, OH MISTRESS MINE see Willaert,
Adrian, Madonn' Io Non Lo So Perche
Lo Fai

TELL ME THAT YOU LOVE ME
SSA CIMINO $.40   (T49)
SAB CIMINO $.40   (T50)
SA CIMINO $.40`   (T51)
TTBB CIMINO $.40   (T52)
SATB CIMINO $.40   (T53)

TELL ME WHAT MONTH *Xmas,folk,US
(Bune) SATB,bvl,gtr,2rec WARNER
CH0799 $.50   (T54)

TELL ME WHERE IS FANCY BRED? see
Felciano, Richard

TEMER DONNA NON DEI see Rossi, Salomone

TEMPUS DESTRUENDI - TEMPUS AEDIFICANDI
see Dallapiccola, Luigi

TEN MADRIGALS see Gabrieli

TEN MADRIGALS see Lassus, Roland de
(Orlandus)

TEN MINUTES AGO see Rodgers, Richard

TENDER LOVE
(Luboff, Norman) SATB CHARTER 3070
(T55)

TENTING ON THE OLD CAMP GROUND see
Kittridge

TENTING ON THE OLD CAMPGROUND see
Kittredge, Walter

TERLY TERLOW see Holst, Gustav

TERPSICHORE "HILARIS TERPSICHORE TER
PEDE TERRAM" see Novak, Jan

TERRI
Around The Year In Rounds *sac/sec,
CCU,round
cor SCHIRM.G LG51746 $2.00   (T56)

TERRIBLE PEOPLE, THE see Cohn, James

TESORIERO, GAETANO
Natale
unis EMI   (T57)

Ninna Nonna
2pt EMI   (T58)

TESTAMENT OF AN AMERICAN see Reed,
Alfred

TEUERUNG "UND DIE EIER UND'S FEUER" see
Haas, Joseph

TEXASLIED *folk,US
(Rosenstengel, A.) men cor,pno,gtr,
perc sc,cor pts TONOS 1621 s.p.
(T59)

THALL, PETER MORGAN
Gettysburg Address, The
TTBB BIG3 $.45   (T60)
SATB BIG3 $.45   (T61)

THANK GOD FOR CHRISTMAS
SATB CIMINO $.40   (T62)

THANK THE LORD FOR THIS THANKSGIVING
DAY
SSA CIMINO $.40   (T63)
SATB CIMINO $.40   (T64)
TTBB CIMINO $.40   (T65)

THANK YOU - PRAGUE see Novak, Jiri F.,
Dekuji Ti, Praho

THANK YOU TWENTY TIMES see Kricka,
Jaroslav, Dvacatero Diku

THANKS TO THE SOVIET UNION see Barvik,
Miroslav, Podekovani Sovetskemu
Svazu

THANKSGIVING SUITE
(Rizzo, J.) SATB BOURNE B231142-352
$.45   (T66)

THAT EVER I SAW see Castelnuovo-
Tedesco, Mario

THAT GOOD OLD MOUNTAIN DEW see Canning,
Thomas

THAT JOYOUS SEASON SPRING see Le Jeune,
Claude, Voicy Du Gay Printems

THAT MEN MIGHT KNOW see Best

THAT YONGE CHILD see Roxbury, Ronald

THAT'S ENTERTAINMENT *medley
(Simon, W.) SATB BIG3 $1.50   (T67)
(Simon, W.) SSA BIG3 $1.50   (T68)

THAT'S FOR ME
SATB oct CHAPPELL W780804-357 $.40
(T69)
SSA oct CHAPPELL W780804-353 $.40
(T70)
TTBB oct CHAPPELL W780804-355 $.40
(T71)

THAT'S MORE TO MY MIND! *folk
(Cookson, Frank B.) SSA (med)
FITZSIMONS 3068 $.25   (T72)

THAT'S THE WAY I'VE ALWAYS HEARD IT
SHOULD BE see Simon

THAT'S WHAT LOVIN' YOU IS ALL ABOUT see
Evans, Paul

ENGLISH MADRIGALISTS SERIES, VOL. 36
cor STAINER 3.1938.1 $11.50 contains
works by: Holborne, William;
Cavendish, Michael; Greaves,
Thomas; Edwards, Richard   (T73)

THEHOS, ADAM
Abend Am Strom
men cor,acap TONOS 4078 s.p. (T74)

Blut Um Blut
see Lieder Aus Dem Kleinen
Rosengarten

Der Mond Ist Aufgegangen
men cor,acap TONOS 53 s.p.   (T75)

Der Rosengarten
see Lieder Aus Dem Kleinen
Rosengarten

Grablied
men cor,acap TONOS 3708 s.p. (T76)

Heckenkind
see Lieder Aus Dem Kleinen
Rosengarten

Hohn Und Spott
see Lieder Aus Dem Kleinen
Rosengarten

Ich Weiss Einen Lindenbaum
see Lieder Aus Dem Kleinen
Rosengarten

Liebesweh
see Lieder Aus Dem Kleinen
Rosengarten

Lieder Aus Dem Kleinen Rosengarten
men cor,acap cmplt ed TONOS 4060
s.p.
contains: Blut Um Blut; Der
Rosengarten; Heckenkind; Hohn
Und Spott; Ich Weiss Einen
Lindenbaum; Liebesweh;
Rosemarie; Uber Die Heide;
Warnung: Du Hast Gesagt   (T77)

Rosemarie
see Lieder Aus Dem Kleinen
Rosengarten

THEHOS, ADAM (cont'd.)

Rosenzeit
men cor,acap TONOS 4079 s.p. (T78)

Schab Ab
men cor,acap TONOS 3709 s.p. (T79)

Uber Die Heide
see Lieder Aus Dem Kleinen
Rosengarten

Warnung: Du Hast Gesagt
see Lieder Aus Dem Kleinen
Rosengarten

Weinfahrt
men cor,acap TONOS 284 s.p.   (T80)

THEME see Yahres, Samuel C.

THEME FROM PICASSO SUMMER see Legrand,
Michel, Summer Me, Winter Me

THEN AND NOW
(Duncan, Chester) SSA (easy) WATERLOO
$.75   (T81)

THEN AND NOW see Duncan, Chester

THERE IS A JEWEL see Wilbye, John

THERE IS A LADY SWEET AND KIND see
Ford, Thomas

THERE IS A LADY SWEET AND KIND see
Whicher, James

THERE IS A LANE see Ives, Charles

THERE IS A SANTA CLAUS see Grant, W.
Parke

THERE IS A SONG see Dedrick, C.

THERE IS LOVE see Wedding Song

THERE IS NO HOLDING ME
TTBB CIMINO $.40   (T82)

THERE IS NOTHING LIKE A DAME see
Rodgers, Richard

THERE IS THIS NEED
SSA CIMINO $.40   (T83)
TTBB CIMINO $.40   (T84)
SATB CIMINO $.40   (T85)

THERE UPON THE MOUNTAINS see Janacek,
Leos

THERE WAS A PIG WENT OUT TO DIG see
Foster, Arnold

THERE WAS A ROARING IN THE WIND see
Shearer, C.M.

THEREFORE BE MERRY see Ehret, Walter

THERE'S A TREE see Adler

THERE'S A WORLD see Nash, Graham

THERE'S ANOTHER CHRISTMAS COMING SOON
see Cobine, Al

THERE'S NO HIDIN' PLACE see Wood,
Joseph

THESE DREAMS see Croce, Jim

THESE THINGS SHALL BE see Clarke, Henry
Leland

THEY ALL LAUGH see Hovhaness, Alan

THEY ARE COMING see Wah Gee Tee Bee

THEY DIDN'T BELIEVE ME
TTBB CIMINO $.40   (T86)
SSA CIMINO $.40   (T87)
SAB CIMINO $.40   (T88)
SA CIMINO $.40   (T89)
SATB CIMINO $.40   (T90)

THEY GO WILD, SIMPLY WILD, OVER ME see
Fisher, Fred

THEY LIE AT REST see Binkerd, Gordon

THEY SHALL NEVER THIRST see Verrall,
John

THEY WERE A THOUSAND YEARS OLD see
Reiner, Karel, Bylo Jim Tisic Let

THIEL, JORN
Ene Mene Tintenfass
1-3pt jr cor,pno,2S rec,drums, 3
xylophones, glockenspiel,
triangel, cymbals (easy) sc,cor
pts SCHOTTS B 131 s.p., ipa (T91)

THIMAN, ERIC HARDING (1900-   )
High Tide, The
SATB,2fl,2ob,2clar,2bsn,2horn,timp,
pno,strings voc sc NOVELLO
rental, ipr   (T92)

Morning Song
SA (med easy) WATERLOO $.35   (T93)

Six Hymns Of Courage And Praise
*CC6U
unis oct WEINBERGER W079 $.75 (T94)

Songs Of England
SATB,2fl,2ob,2clar,2bsn,2horn,2trp,
2trom,timp,perc,strings voc sc
NOVELLO rental, ipr   (T95)

Songs Of Sailors And Of The Sea *CCU
SATB,fl,ob,clar,bsn,2horn,2trp,
timp,strings,drums voc sc NOVELLO
rental, ipr   (T96)

Spring Garland, A
SATB,fl,pno,strings voc sc NOVELLO
rental, ipr   (T97)

Thrush In Spring, The
2pt treb cor,pno ROBERTON 75035
s.p.   (T98)

Voices Of Children
SA (med easy) WATERLOO $.40   (T99)

When I Was A Little Boy
SA (med easy) WATERLOO $.30   (T100)

You Spotted Snakes
2 eq voices (easy) WATERLOO $.40
                              (T101)

THINE EYES I WOULD BE SEEING see
Marenzio, Luca

THINK ABOUT WHEELS see Gerschefski,
Edwin

THINK ON ME see Scott, Alicia Ann

THINKING OF YOU see Loggins, Dave

THIRD SET OF BOOKS (1610) EM VOL. 31A
see East, Michael

THIRIET, [MAURICE] (1906-   )
Deux Berceuses *CC2U
mix cor,acap HENN 755 s.p.   (T102)

Roi Renaud-Noel Savoysien
mix cor,acap HENN 756 s.p.   (T103)

THIRSIS THAT HEAT REFRAINED see
Marenzio, Luca

THIRSIS TO DIE DESIRED see Marenzio,
Luca

THIRTY CHANSONS FOR THREE AND FOUR
VOICES FROM ATTAINGNANT'S
COLLECTIONS *CCU
(Seay, Albert) 3-4pt bds A-R ED $8.95
                              (T104)
THIRTY NEGRO SPIRITUALS, BOOK 1 *CCU,
spir
(Brown) 2pt,inst (easy) cmplt ed
OXFORD 58.655 $2.50, ipa, cor pts
OXFORD 58.656 $1.25   (T105)

THIRTY NEGRO SPIRITUALS, BOOK 1 *CCU,
spir
(Brown) unis,inst (easy) cmplt ed
OXFORD 58.651 $2.50, ipa, cor pts
OXFORD 58.652 $1.00   (T106)

THIRTY NEGRO SPIRITUALS, BOOK 2 *CCU,
spir
(Brown) 2pt,inst (easy) cmplt ed
OXFORD 58.657 $2.50, ipa, cor pts
OXFORD 58.658 $1.25   (T107)

THIRTY NEGRO SPIRITUALS, BOOK 2 *CCU,
spir
(Brown) unis,inst (easy) cmplt ed
OXFORD 58.653 $2.50, ipa, cor pts
OXFORD 58.654 $1.00   (T108)

THIS CANADA see Davenport, G.

THIS CHRISTMAS EVE see Cobine, Al

THIS ENDERS NIGHT see Powers, Anthony

THIS HAVE I DONE FOR MY TRUE LOVE see
Holst, Gustav

THIS HEART see Lambert, Dennis

THIS HOUSE see Anderson, Thomas J.

THIS IS MY AMERICA see Maxwell, Robert

THIS IS MY OWN, MY NATIVE LAND see
Pfautsch, Lloyd

THIS IS MY OWN, MY NATIVE LAND see
Scott

THIS IS MY SONG see Chaplin

THIS IS THE GENERATION see Beebe, Hank

THIS LAND IS YOUR LAND see Guthrie,
Woody

THIS MONTH OF MAY see Jannequin,
Clement, Ce Mois De May

THIS NEARLY WAS MINE see Rodgers,
Richard

THIS OL' HAMMER
(Work, J.W.) SATB GALAXY 1.0629.1
$.40   (T109)

THIS PLEASANT MONTH OF MAY see Beale,
William

THIS SWEET AND MERRY MONTH see Byrd,
William

THIS TOWN'S A CORPORATION FULL OF
CROOKED STREETS see Mc Cabe, John

THIS WORLD occ Track

THOMAS
And The Tide Rushes In *pop
(Myrow) SATB MCA UC 655 $.40 (T110)
(Myrow) SSA MCA UC 656 $.40 (T111)

Those Lazy-Hazy-Crazy Days Of Summer
(composed with Carste)
(Gold) SATB ALFRED 6735 $.50 (T112)
(Gold) SATB/SAB ALFRED 6791 $.50
                             (T113)
THOMAS LUDOVICI VICTORIA ABULENSIS
OPERA OMNIA (COMPLETE WORKS) see
Victoria, Tomas Luis de

THOMPSON
Akond Of Swat (from Cantata On Poems
Of Edward Lear)
SATB SCHIRM.G 12037 $.75   (T114)

Half An Alphabet (from Cantata On
Poems Of Edward Lear)
SATB SCHIRM.G 12036 $.75   (T115)

Jumblies, The (from Cantata On Poems
Of Edward Lear)
SATB SCHIRM.G 12035 $.75   (T116)

THOMPSON, RANDALL (1899-   )
Antiphon
SATB SCHIRM.EC 2915 s.p. see from
Two Herbert Settings   (T117)

Bitter-Sweet
SATB SCHIRM.EC 2904 s.p. see from
Two Herbert Settings   (T118)

Fare Well
SATB SCHIRM.EC 2957 s.p.   (T119)

Hymn For Scholars And Pupils
SATB,orch SCHIRM.EC 2958 s.p., ipr
                             (T120)
SSAA,orch SCHIRM.EC 2829 s.p., ipr
                             (T121)
Two Herbert Settings *see Antiphon;
Bitter-Sweet   (T122)

THOMSEN-MUCHOVA, GERALDINA (1917-   )
Zenske Sbory *CCU
[Czech] wom cor,acap CZECH s.p.
                             (T123)
THORPE, RAYMOND
Come Unto These Yellow Sands
SSA EMI   (T124)

May Dew
SA EMI   (T125)

Now Phoebus Sinketh In The West
SSA EMI   (T126)

Savoyard Song
SS EMI   (T127)

Solveig's Song
SA EMI   (T128)

Weep Ye No More Sad Fountains
SSA EMI   (T129)

THOSE DAYS GONE BY see Mana-Zucca, Mme.

THOSE LAZY-HAZY-CRAZY DAYS OF SUMMER
see Thomas

THOSE SPOTS UPON MY LADY'S FACE see
Weelkes, Thomas

THOSE WERE THE DAYS see Adams

THOU, FATAL LOVE see Netherclift,
Joseph

THOUGH NIGHT IS DARK see Hovhaness,
Alan

THOUGHT LIKE MUSIC, A see Brahms,
Johannes

THREE AMOROUS AIRS see Gardner

THREE BIRD SONGS see Platts, Kenneth

THREE BLIND MICE
(Shaw, Ruby) SATB (diff) FITZSIMONS
1071 $.25   (T130)

THREE CANONS see Haydn, (Franz) Joseph

THREE CAROLS see Elliott, Carleton

THREE CHILDREN'S SONGS see Greaves

THREE CHORAL BALLADS see Stenhammar

THREE CHORAL DANCES see Bach, Jan

THREE CHRISTMAS SONGS see Mollicone,
Henry

THREE CHRISTMAS SONGS see Mollicone,
Henry

THREE COUNTRY WEST IDYLLS see Redman,
Reginald

THREE DAUGHTERS see Hurnik, Ilja, Tri
Dcery

THREE EARLY ENGLISH LYRICS see Walker,
Robert

THREE ENGLISH LYRICS see Reznick, D.

THREE EXPRESSIONS see Nieman, Alfred

THREE FEASTING SONGS see Jenkins, C.J.

THREE FESTIVAL SONGS see Kurth, Burton
L.

THREE FOR JAZZCHOIR see Lewis, Peter T.

THREE FRENCH CAROLS *CC3U,folk
(Apple, Alan) SATB STANDARD C618MX1
$.50   (T131)

THREE FRENCH SONGS see Rhodes, Phillip

THREE GYPSIES see Schertzer, Daniel

THREE HAIKU see Maksimovic, Rajko

THREE HALLOWED WORDS
TTBB CIMINO $.40   (T132)
SATB CIMINO $.40   (T133)

THREE HUNGARIAN FOLKSONGS *CC3U
SATB FOSTER MF316 $.40   (T134)

THREE INSIGNIFICANT TRAGEDIES see
Lewis, Peter T.

THREE INVENTIONS see Feld, Jindrich

THREE JAMAICAN FOLK SONGS *CC3U
(Murray) cor OXFORD   (T135)

THREE LAMENTS see Klein, Lothar

THREE LOVE SONGS see Karlins, M.
William

THREE MADRIGALS see Hovhaness, Alan

THREE MADRIGALS see Clarke, Henry
Leland

THREE MADRIGALS see Kahn, Erich Itor

THREE MADRIGALS see Woollen, Russell

THREE MADRIGALS FOR MIXED CHORUS see
White

THREE MADRIGALS FROM WILLIAM
SHAKESPEARE see Felciano, Richard

THREE MEDIEVAL LATIN STUDENT SONGS see
Kohs, Ellis B.

THREE MODIVERSIONS see Clover, David

THREE MODIVERSIONS see Clover, David

THREE MORE FESTIVAL SONGS see Kurth,
Burton L.

THREE MOTETS see Boone, Charles

THREE NOVA SCOTIA FOLK SONGS *CC3U,
folk,Nor Am
(Fleming, Robert) SSA (med) WATERLOO
$.90   (T136)

THREE PASTORAL SONGS see Klein, Lothar

THREE POEMS BY EMILY DICKINSON see
Berger, Jean

THREE POEMS BY MAO TSE-TUNG see
  Lorentzen, Bent

THREE POEMS FOR CHORUS see Karlins, M.
  William

THREE RAVENS, THE see Raffman, Relly

THREE RECENT RULINGS see Frackenpohl,
  Arthur

THREE SCOTTISH SONGS *CC3U
  (Whitecotton) SATB oct HERITAGE H111
  $.40   (T137)

THREE SETTINGS OF E.E. CUMMINGS see
  Yannatos, James

THREE SHAKER SONGS *CC3U
  (Czajkowski, Michael) SATB STANDARD
  B326MX1 $.50   (T138)

THREE SHAKESPEARE SONGS see Swayne

THREE SHAKESPEARIAN TRIOS see LaCheur,
  Rex

THREE SONGS OF COURAGE see Dyson,
  George

THREE SONGS ON THE SHORTNESS OF LIFE
  see Trubitt, Allen R.

THREE SONS, THE see Ames, William

THREE TWO-PART SONGS FOR CHILDREN see
  Bush, N.

THREE WESTERN SONGS see Summerlin

THREE WHITMAN CHORUSES see Kent,
  Richard

THREE WORKS FOR MALE CHORUS see Kunz,
  Alfred

THROUGH THE EYES OF A CHILD see Pickell

THROUGH THE SOUND BARRIER *CC24U
  (Coleby, Geoffrey) cor, for low and
  breaking voices with piano EMI voc
  sc s.p., cor pts s.p.   (T139)

THRUSH IN SPRING, THE see Thiman, Eric
  Harding

THYBO, LEIF
  Amabo, Mea Dulcis Ipsitilla
    [Lat] SATB,acap EGTVED KB120 s.p.
                                      (T140)

THYGERSON, ROBERT J.
  Aura Lee
    see BARBERSHOP CHOIR, THE
    SAT/SSA oct HERITAGE H6506 $.35
                                      (T141)

  Cherry Blooms
    SAT oct HERITAGE H6505 $.35   (T142)

  Come Again? *CCU,folk/spir
    SSA/SAT/SA&camb HERITAGE $1.95
                                      (T143)

  Going, Going, Gone *CCU
    SSA/SAT/3pt jr cor HERITAGE $1.95
                                      (T144)

  Hoedown!
    SATB oct HERITAGE H118 $.35   (T145)

  Sat There A-Rockin' All Night *Xmas,
    anthem
    SATB oct HERITAGE H113 $.40   (T146)

TI PARTI, COR MIO CARO see Azzaiolo, F.

TIC E TIC E TOC *folk,Finn
  (Rosenstengel, Albrecht) men cor,opt
  gtr,opt perc TONOS 2102 s.p. (T147)

TIC E TIC E TOC, MEIN SCHWARZER KNABE
  *folk
  (Beckerath, A. Von) [Ger] 4pt mix cor
  MERSEBURG EM9206 s.p.   (T148)

TIDE LIFE, TIDE DEATH see Peaslee,
  Richard

TIDES OF MIRANDA see Beeson

TIE A YELLOW RIBBON ROUND THE OLE OAK
  TREE see Levine

TIEFE FLUTEN see Deep River

TIERNEY, HARRY (1895-1965)
  Alice Blue Gown (from Irene)
    (Simon, W.) SAB BIG3 $.45   (T149)
    (Simon, W.) SATB BIG3 $.45   (T150)
    (Simon, W.) SSA BIG3 $.50   (T151)

  Irene (from Irene)
    (Simon, W.) SAB BIG3 $.45   (T152)
    (Simon, W.) SATB BIG3 $.45   (T153)

TIFFAULT
  Dreams
    SA,opt vln KENDOR $.30   (T154)

  Happy Little Christmas People
    2pt,opt gtr PRO ART 2797 $.35
                                      (T155)

  Late Nite Nursery Rhymes
    SATB PRO ART 2798 $.40   (T156)
    SSA PRO ART 2800 $.40   (T157)

  Muffin Man, The
    SATB,gtr PRO ART 2796 $.35   (T158)

  Suzie's Love Song
    SA KENDOR $.30   (T159)

TIGER, THE see Wood, Joseph

TILL THE OLD CAT DIES see Franco, Johan

TILLIS, FREDERICK
  Freedom
    SATB,acap PEER $1.25   (T160)

TIME FOR TRAVEL see Reaks

TIME HAS COME, THE see Podest, Ludvik,
  Nadesel Cas

TIME IN A BOTTLE see Croce, Jim

TIME IS MY FRIEND see Raulston

TIME IS TOO SLOW see Berger, Jean

TIME SHALL COME, THE see Clarke, Henry
  Leland

TIME'S MOST CRUEL MOMENT see Mozart,
  Wolfgang Amadeus, Ecco, Quel Fiero
  Istante

TIME'S PASSING, A see Woolf, Gregory

TIMOKWEIN *folk,Slav
  (Zschiegner, Fritz) men cor,opt pno,
  opt inst,opt perc sc,voc sc TONOS
  2114 s.p.   (T161)

TIN MAN see Bunnell

TINKER, TAILOR see Greaves

TIPPETT, MICHAEL (1905-   )
  Prologue "Soomer Is I-Coomen In"
    4pt mix cor,pno (med diff) sc
    SCHOTTS ED. 10 911 s.p.   (T162)

TIROLER KRIPPENLIED see Poll, Joseph

'TIS THE GIFT TO BE SIMPLE *folk
  (Newbury, Kent) SATB RICHMOND MI-89
  $.35   (T163)

TISCHHAUSER, FRANZ (1921-   )
  Antiphonarium Profanum *CC50UL
    men cor&men cor,acap sc,cor pts
    SCHOTTS ED. 5908 s.p.   (T164)

  Das Nasobem *CC7L
    mix cor (med) sc SCHOTTS ED. 4229
    s.p.   (T165)

TISINY see Spilka, Frantisek

TITANIA see Peaslee, Richard

TITYRUS "AMARYLLI, STREPIT ET TOTA
  SONAT SILVA" see Novak, Jan

TO A CHILD DANCING IN THE WIND see
  Wood, Hugh

TO A FIREFLY see Stock

TO A SWEET NIGHTINGALE see Banchieri,
  Adriano, Ad Un Dolce Usignolo

TO AMERICA WITH LOVE
  SATB CIMINO $.40   (T166)
  TTBB CIMINO $.40   (T167)

TO AN EAGLE FORGOTTEN see Bottje, Will
  Gay

TO BE OR NOT TO BE see Ydstie

TO CANADA OUR COUNTRY see Cozens, John

TO CELIA see Mechem, Kirke

TO DAISIES NOT TO SHUT SO SOON
  (Broadhead, G.) SATB,opt acap CRAMER
                                      (T168)

TO ELECTRA, SET II see Binkerd, Gordon

TO FRIENDSHIP-RIGHT ON MAN! see
  Collins, Don L.

TO HEAR AN ORIOLE SING see Kunz, Alfred

TO KNOW YOU IS TO LOVE YOU
  TTBB CIMINO $.40   (T169)
  SATB CIMINO $.40   (T170)

TO LOVE, MY LADY, I NOW OFFER PRAISES
  see Marenzio, Luca, Madonna Mia
  Gentil Ringratio Amore

TO MAKE A PRAIRIE see Berger, Jean

TO MUSIC see Saar, Louis Victor

TO MUSIC, TO BECALM HIS FEVER see
  Crawford

TO MY NATIVE LAND see Drazan, Josef,
  Zemi Rodne

TO PRAGUE see Kricka, Jaroslav, Praze

TO SEAL OUR LOVE FOREVER
  SATB oct CHAPPELL W020925-357 $.40
                                      (T171)

TO SLOVAKIA see Taraba, Bohuslav,
  Slovensku

TO SPRING see Schubert, Franz (Peter)

TO THE BUILDERS OF OSTRAVA see Haba,
  Karel, Budovatelum Ostravska

TO THE CZECH COUNTRY see Sykora, Vaclav
  Jan, Ceske Krajine

TO THE HAPPY GIRL see Sokola, Milos,
  Stastnemu Devceti

TO THE LABRADOR
  (Johnston, Richard A.) SAB (med easy)
  WATERLOO $.30   (T172)

TO THE MOON see Schuyt, Nico

TO THY LOVE see Schumann, William
  Howard

TO TROUBLED FRIENDS see Pinkham, Daniel

TO VIOLETS see Willan, Healey

TO WORDS BY JOSEPH BEAUMONT see Tate

TO YOU, RED ARMY see Nejedly, Vit,
  Tobe, Ruda Armado

TO YOUNG COMMUNISTS see Strniste, Jiri,
  Mladym Komunistum

TOBACCO IS LIKE LOVE see Willey

TOBE, RUDA ARMADO see Nejedly, Vit

TOD UND EWIGKEIT see Luttenberger,
  Gottfried

TODAY IS TO-MORROWS YESTERDAY, ALAS NO
  FAIRY TALE see Bois, Rob du, Vandag
  Is Het Morgen Van Gisteren

TODESFUGE see Dirriwachter, Wim

TOGETHER
  SSA CIMINO $.40   (T173)
  SATB CIMINO $.40   (T174)
  TTBB CIMINO $.40   (T175)

TOGETHER AGAIN see Owens, Buck

TOGNI, CAMILLO (1922-   )
  Tre Pezzi *CC3U
    cor,orch sc ZERBONI 7510 s.p.
                                      (T176)

TOLLING BELLS see Rohde

TOM, LE NOUNOURS see Berthomieu, Marc

TOM SAWYER, AMERICAN BOY
  (Strasek, M.K.) 1-2pt,pno CIMINO
  $2.50   (T177)

TOMASEK, JAROSLAV (1896-   )
  Christmas Eve Romance, The *see
    Romance Stedrovecerni

  Dva Maje
    "Two Mays" [Czech] mix cor,3fl,2ob,
    2clar,2bsn,4horn,3trp,3trom,tuba,
    timp,perc,strings CZECH s.p.
                                      (T178)
  Romance Stedrovecerni *cant
    "Christmas Eve Romance, The"
    [Czech] mix cor,2fl,2ob,2clar,
    2bsn,4horn,trp,trom,timp,harp,
    strings CZECH s.p.   (T179)

  Two Mays *see Dva Maje

TOMKINS, THOMAS (ca. 1572-1656)
  Songs Of Three, Four, Five And Six
    Parts (1622) EM Vol. 18 *CC26L
    3-6pt STAINER 3.1918.1 $17.00
                                      (T180)

TOMLINS, GRETA
  Rose, The
    SSA CRAMER C74   (T181)

TOMORROW'S GONNA BE A FRESH NEW DAY
  SATB UP WITH 6508 $.40   (T182)

TONGUE TWISTER see Evans

TOO BUSY see Paxton, Gary

TOP O' THE MORNING see Mana-Zucca, Mme.

TOP OF THE HILL see Alexander

TORCHI
　　L'arte Musicale In Italia, Vol. I
　　　*sac/sec,CCU,14-16th cent
　　　mix cor RICORDI-ENG 101366 s.p.
　　　　　　　　　　　　　　　　　　　(T183)
　　L'arte Musicale In Italia, Vol. II
　　　*sac/sec,CCU,16th cent
　　　mix cor RICORDI-ENG 101409 s.p.
　　　　　　　　　　　　　　　　　　　(T184)
　　L'arte Musicale In Italia, Vol.IV
　　　*CCU,17th cent
　　　cor RICORDI-ENG 104297 s.p. (T185)

　　L'arte Musicale In Italia, Vol. V
　　　*CCU,17th cent
　　　cor RICORDI-ENG 104327 s.p. (T186)

TORNUDD, AXEL
　　Pick Och Pack (Kitkat Kitkat)
　　　men cor ERIKS 53 s.p.　　　　(T187)

TORTOISE AND THE HARE, THE see Jeffries

TORTOISE AND THE HARE, THE see Lodge

TOTALITAT "EIN KAVALIER VON KOPF UND
　　HERZ" see Hessenberg, Kurt

TOTENFEIER see Edler, Robert

TOTENGEDENKEN see Krietsch, Georg

TOTENKLAGE UM SAMOGONSKI "BRUDER,
　　SAMOGONSKI IST GESTORBEN" see Poos,
　　Heinrich

TOU NASOU DOLINECKOU see Mikula, Zdenko

TOUCH OF CLASS, A see Barrie, George

TOUCH OF YOUR HAND
　　SAB CIMINO $.40　　　　　　　　(T188)
　　SA CIMINO $.40　　　　　　　　　(T189)
　　TTBB CIMINO $.40　　　　　　　　(T190)
　　SATB CIMINO $.40　　　　　　　　(T191)

TOUCH OF YOUR HAND, THE
　　SSA CIMINO $.40　　　　　　　　　(T192)

TOUCH THE WIND see Eres Tu

TOURNAMENT GALOP see Gottschalk, Louis
　　Moreau

TOWN AND COUNTRY see Williamson,
　　Malcolm

TRA GIOVE IN CIELO see Agostini,
　　Lodovico

TRA MILLE FIAMME see Monteverdi,
　　Claudio

TRACK
　　Let All My Life Be Music
　　　SATB SCHIRM.G LG51833 $.40 (T193)

　　This World
　　　SATB oct SCHMITT 1311 $.45 (T194)

TRACK, GERHARD (1934-　　)
　　Evening Shadows Gently Falling
　　　SSAA LEONARD-US 08553500 $.50
　　　　　　　　　　　　　　　　　　　(T195)

TRAD FRAM, DU NATTENS GUD see Bellman,
　　Carl Mikael

TRADER, WILLI (1920-　　)
　　Uber Jahr Und Tag　*CC25L
　　　3-4 eq voices/3-4pt mix cor,acap/
　　　2vln,vcl,opt fl (easy) sc SCHOTTS
　　　B 128 s.p., ipa　　　　　　　(T196)

TRAG MICH AUF SANFTEN SCHWINGEN see
　　Swing Low, Sweet Chariot

TRAG MICH, PFERDCHEN see Eben, Petr

TRAGE UNS ZUM LICHT EMPOR see Michels,
　　Josef

TRAGIC STORY, A see Bergh, Arthur

TRAIL OF LIFE, THE see Pisk, Paul
　　Amadeus

TRAIN, THE see Pierne, Paul

TRAIN OF THOUGHT see O'Day

TRAJECTOIRE see Kunst, Jos

TRANT
　　Big Rock Candy Mountain
　　　SSA (med) OXFORD 83.084 $.30 (T197)

TRANT (cont'd.)

　　Riddle Song, The
　　　SSA,acap (med easy) OXFORD 83.095
　　　$.30　　　　　　　　　　　　　(T198)

TRAQUENARD see Kosma, J.

TRARA, DIE POST IST DA　*folk
　　(Thehos, A.) men cor,acap TONOS 69
　　s.p.　　　　　　　　　　　　　　(T199)

TRARA! SO BLASEN DIE JAGER see Erdlen,
　　Hermann

TRAUE NIMMER DEINEM GLUCKE see Zoll,
　　Paul

TRAUERMUSIK see Lutz, Oswald

TRAUMEN UND WACHEN see Bruckner, Anton

TRAUUNGSGESANGE see Edler, Robert

TRAVEL NOTES see Kennedy

TRAVNICE see Moyzes, Alexander

TRAVNICE A LUCNE SPEVY Z CICMIAN A
　　TERCHOVEJ see Zemanovsky, A.

TRE GOTLANDSKA FOLKVISOR　*CC3U,folk
　　(Edlund, Lars) mix cor,acap NORDISKA
　　NMS 6479 s.p.　　　　　　　　　(T200)

TRE KORSANGER see Soderholm, Valdemar

TRE LIRICHE GRECHE see Maderna, Bruno

TRE MADRIGALI see Arrigo, Girolamo

TRE PEZZI see Togni, Camillo

TREASURES ARE OPENING, THE see Kupka,
　　Karel, Poklady Se Otviraji

TREES see Christiansen, P.

TREES, HORIZONS AND MEMORIES see Kreutz

TRES COROS A CAPELLA see Ficher, Jacobo

TRES MAGI see Orff, Carl

TREUE LIEBE see Erdlen, Hermann

TRI BALADY see Felix, Vaclav

TRI DCERY see Hurnik, Ilja

TRI DETSKE SBORY see Podesva, Jaromir

TRI DETSKE ZBORY see Mikula, Zdenko

TRI MADRIGALOVE IMPRESIE see Hrusovsky,
　　Ivan

TRI MIESANE ZBORY see Ferenczy, Oto

TRI MUZSKE ZBORY see Ferenczy, Oto

TRI MUZSKE ZBORY see Kafenda, Frico

TRI NARODNI PISNE see Svobodo, Jiri

TRI ODPOVEDE see Zemanovsky, A.

TRI PISNE see Broz, Frantisek

TRI ZASTAVENI see Flosman, Oldrich

TRI ZENSKE SBORY see Sommer, Vladimir

TRI ZENSKE SBORY see Huth, Gustav

TRI ZENSKE SBORY, OP. 178 see Foerster,
　　Josef Bohuslav

TRIAD see Edlund, Lars

TRIFUNOVIC, VITOMIR (1916-　　)
　　Prospects　*see Vidici

　　Vidici　*cant
　　　"Prospects" mix cor,orch MUSIC INFO
　　　rental　　　　　　　　　　　　(T201)

TRILOGY see Beadell, Robert M.

TRINK AUS, KAMERAD see Siegl, Otto

TRINK MIR MIT DEINEN AUGEN ZU see
　　Weber, Bernhard

TRINKKANON see Mozart, Wolfgang Amadeus

TRINKLIED see Kuhn, Rudolf

TRINKLIED see Mendelssohn-Bartholdy,
　　Felix

TRINKLIED see Mittergradnegger, Gunther

TRINKLIED see Wittmer, Eberhard Ludwig

TRINKLIED "BRUDER, LASST UNS LUSTIG
　　SEIN" see Rein, Walter

TRINKLIED: BRUDER, ZU DEN FESTLICHEN
　　see Silcher, Friedrich

TRINKLIED "DIE GLASER KLINGEN" see
　　Biebl, Franz

TRINKLIED "FREUNDE, DAS IST UNSRE ZEIT"
　　see Erdlen, Hermann

TRINKLIED "FRISCH AUF, GUT G'SELL" see
　　Knab, Armin

TRINKLIED "ICH WEISS ES WOHL, DER WEIN
　　IST GIFT" see Weber, Bernhard

TRINKLIED IM SOMMER see Cossetto, Emil

TRINKLIED IM SOMMER see Zipp, Friedrich

TRINKLIED "TRES FACIUNT COLLEGIUM" see
　　Kreutzer, Konradin

TRINKLIED "VIEL SCHONE GABEN VATERLICH"
　　see Lortzing, (Gustav) Albert

TRINKLIED: WER TRINKT see Koch, Adolf

TRINKLIEDER see Schein, Johann Hermann

TRINKLIEDER-POTPOURRI see Jage, Rolf-
　　Diether

TRINKSPRUCH "LIEBE LEUTE, HORET" see
　　Cossetto, Emil

TRIOLET see Pileur

TRIPTYCH FUNERAL FOLK RITE see
　　Brkanovic, Ivan

TRIPTYCHON see Reutter, Hermann

TRISTE ESPANA see Encina, Juan Del

TRISTE ESPANA, SIN VENTURA! see Encina,
　　Juan Del

TRISTISSIMA NOX "STUNDE UNERMESSLICHEN
　　FRIEDENS" see Genzmer, Harald

TRITTICO see Mortari, Virgilio

TRIUMFATOR see Weiss, Karel

TRIUMPH DER LIEBE see Herrmann, Hugo

TRIUMPHANT see Weiss, Karel, Triumfator

TRIUMPHS OF ORIANA (1601) EM VOL. 32
　　*CC23L,madrigal
　　5-6pt mix cor STAINER 3.1932.1 $17.00
　　contains works by: Moreley;
　　Weelkes; Kirbye and others　(T202)

TROBADORSKE ZPEVY see Korte, Oldrich
　　Frantisek

TROIKA see Schertzer, Daniel

TROIS BELLES PRINCESSES　*folk,Fr
　　(Blanchard, R.) 4pt mix cor,acap
　　JOBERT s.p.　　　　　　　　　　(T203)

TROIS BURLESQUES see Rosenthal, Manuel

TROIS CHANSONS OTHON DE GRAND SON see
　　Gagnebin, Henri

TROIS CHANTS SAVOYSIENS　*CC3U
　　(Marescotti) mix cor,acap HENN 493
　　s.p.　　　　　　　　　　　　　(T204)

TROIS JONGLERIES see Blanchard, Roger

TROIS PSAUMES, POUR LE TEMPS PRESENT
　　see Monnikendam, Marius

TROJAN, VACLAV (1907-　　)
　　Ceske Pastorely　*CCU
　　　[Czech] jr cor/wom cor,soli,pno/
　　　perc, and two accordions CZECH
　　　s.p.　　　　　　　　　　　　　(T205)

　　Chap-Book　*CCU
　　　[Czech/Ger] jr cor,soli,3fl,3ob,
　　　3clar,3bsn,4horn,3trp,3trom,tuba,
　　　timp,perc,pno,harp,strings
　　　SUPRAPHON s.p.　　　　　　　(T206)

　　Fireflies, The
　　　[Czech] jr cor,fl,pic,clar,pno,vla,
　　　vcl SUPRAPHON s.p.　　　　　(T207)

　　Midsummer Night's Dream　*CCU
　　　[Czech] jr cor&girl cor,3fl,3ob,
　　　4clar,3bsn,4horn,3trp,3trom,tuba,
　　　timp,perc,harp,pno,strings,
　　　cembalo, vibraphone, cymbal,
　　　saxophone, xylophone SUPRAPHON
　　　s.p.　　　　　　　　　　　　　(T208)

TROST see Reger, Max

TROST see Schaefers, Anton

TROST IM LEID "WENN DU IN NOTEJAHREN" see Zipp, Friedrich

TROST IM WINKEL "LASS ES GEHN, HERZ" see Sturmer, Bruno

TROST "WENN WIR AUCH DURFTIG HAUSEN" see Mohler, Philipp

TROSTE, HERR see Edler, Robert

TROSTERIN MUSIK see Bruckner, Anton

TROSTSPRUCH "DIE MUSIK ALLEIN" see Schwarz-Schilling, Reinhard

TROUBLES OF MY HEART ARE ENLARGED, THE see Canning, Thomas

TROYAK see Poulenc, Francis

TRUBITT, ALLEN R.
Ann Rutledge
SATB,acap DEAN CD-108 $.45 (T209)

Cat In The Wood, The
TTBB (med) DEAN CB-802 $.30 (T210)

Three Songs On The Shortness Of Life *CC3U
SATB,acap (med diff) DEAN CB-801 $.60 (T211)

TRUE LOVE'S THE GIFT see Chambers, H.A.

TRUNET DIE HOFFNUNG see Kremberg, Jacob

TRUNK, RICHARD (1879-1968)
Am Strande "An Wildem Klippenstrande" *Op.56
men cor sc SCHOTTS C 40 517 s.p. see from Drei Mannerchore (T212)

Beim Scheiden "Mir Ist's Zu Wohl Ergangen" *Op.56
men cor sc SCHOTTS C 40 516 s.p. see from Drei Mannerchore (T213)

Biwak "Habt Ihr Die Husaren Gesehn" (from Des Knaben Wunderhorn, Op. 30)
men cor (contains also: Weine Nur Nicht) sc SCHOTTS CHBL 172A-B s.p. (T214)

Drei Mannerchore *see Am Strande "An Wildem Klippenstrande", Op.56; Beim Scheiden "Mir Ist's Zu Wohl Ergangen", Op.56; Sommernacht "Die Sommernacht Hat Mir's Angetan", Op.56 (T215)

Glocken
see Vier Lieder

Heimkehr
see Vier Lieder

Ich Hort Ein Sichlein Rauschen (from Des Knaben Wunderhorn, Op. 30)
men cor (contains also: Zierlichkeit Des Schaferlebens "Nichts Kann Auf Erden") sc SCHOTTS CHBL 171 A-B s.p. (T216)

Pfauenart "Leucht Heller Denn Die Sonne" (from Des Knaben Wunderhorn, Op. 30)
men cor (contains also: Rosmarin "Es Wollt Die Jungfrau Fruh Aufstehn") sc SCHOTTS CHBL 170A-B s.p. (T217)

Rosmarin "Es Wollt Die Jungfrau Fruh Aufstehn" (from Des Knaben Wunderhorn, Op. 30)
men cor (contains also: Pfauenart "Leucht Heller Denn Die Sonne") sc SCHOTTS CHBL 170A-B s.p. (T218)

Sommernacht "Die Sommernacht Hat Mir's Angetan" *Op.56
men cor sc SCHOTTS C 40 518 s.p. see from Drei Mannerchore (T219)

Verirrt
see Vier Lieder

Vier Lieder *Op.93
TTBB sc SCHOTTS C 40 695 s.p., voc pt SCHOTTS C 40 696, 01-02 s.p.
contains: Glocken; Heimkehr; Verirrt; Zweisamkeit (T220)

Weine Nur Nicht (from Des Knaben Wunderhorn, Op. 30)
men cor (contains also: Biwak "Habt Ihr Die Husaren Gesehn") sc SCHOTTS CHBL 172A-B s.p. (T221)

TRUNK, RICHARD (cont'd.)
Zierlichkeit Des Schaferlebens "Nichts Kann Auf Erden" (from Des Knaben Wunderhorn, Op. 30)
men cor (contains also: Ich Hort Ein Sichlein Rauschen) sc SCHOTTS CHBL 171A-B s.p. (T222)

Zweisamkeit
see Vier Lieder

TSCHAPLJANER TATAREN see Slavenski, Josip, Capljanski Tatari

TSCHECHISCHE MADRIGALE see Martinu, Bohuslav

TSCHECHISCHES TANZLIED see Becker, Hans-Gunther

TSCHECHISCHES WIEGENLIED *folk
(Fischbach, Klaus) wom cor,pno sc BREITKOPF-W CHB 4922 s.p. see from Sieben Europaische Volkslieder (T223)

TSCHUBTSCHIK *Russ
(Karpowitsch, A.) men cor ZIMMER. 593 s.p. (T224)

TSOUYOPOULOS, GEORGES S. (1930-   )
Drei Fragmente
mix cor,3fl/2fl&pic,2ob,3clar, 4horn,2trp,2trom,timp,4perc, English horn; bass clarinet alternating with third clarinet MODERN rental (T225)

TSURU-KAME see Finnissy, Michael

TU MIR AUF, MEINE TAUBE see Rein, Walter

TU NE L'ENTENDS PAS see Lefevre, Jacques

TUBAL CAIN see Dunhill, Thomas Frederick

TUFO ARDEATINO see Medin, N.

TULL, FISHER
Winter Bells *Xmas
SSAA BELWIN 2291 $.35 (T226)

TUM BALALAIKA see Adler

TUMBA CANA
(Roberts) SATB SCHIRM.G LG 51685 $.35 (T227)

TUMBLING TUMBLEWEEDS
2pt oct CHAPPELL W187512-351 $.40 (T228)
SSA oct CHAPPELL W187512-353 $.40 (T229)
TTBB oct CHAPPELL W187512-355 $.40 (T230)
SAB oct CHAPPELL W187512-356 $.40 (T231)
SATB oct CHAPPELL W187512-357 $.40 (T232)

TUNE-A-DAY see Binge

TUOMINEN, HARRI
Jalkaisin Sain Kulkea
[Finn] SATB,solo,acap FAZER 37 s.p. (T233)
Kuljeskellen
[Finn] SATB,acap FAZER 43 s.p. (T234)

TURCHI, GUIDO (1916-   )
Rondel
cor,acap ZERBONI 7545 s.p. (T235)

TURMCHORAL "DIE STADT LIEGT NOCH" see Lang, Hans

TURMERLIED see Rietz, Johannes

TURMERLIED "ZUM SEHEN GEBOREN, ZUM SCHAUEN BESTELLT" see Rein, Walter

TURN AROUND *pop
(Nowak, Jerry) SATB,pno oct BIG BELL $.45 (T236)
(Nowak, Jerry) SSA,pno oct BIG BELL $.45 (T237)
(Nowak, Jerry) SAB,pno oct BIG BELL $.45 (T238)
(Nowak, Jerry) SA,pno oct BIG BELL $.45 (T239)

TURN BACK O MAN see Ringwald, [Roy]

TURN BACK THE HANDS OF TIME
SSA CIMINO $.40 (T240)
SATB CIMINO $.40 (T241)

TURN ON THE CHRISTMAS LIGHTS see Cobine, Al

TURN YE TO ME *folk
(Hutcheson) SATB,acap (med) FITZSIMONS 1077 $.20 (T242)

TURNER, OLIVE
Cradle Song Of The Coast
SA CRAMER $.25 (T243)

Down By The Sally Gardens
SA CRAMER $.25 (T244)

Little Green Forest
SA CRAMER $.25 (T245)

TURNHOUT, GERARD DE (1520-1580)
Sacred And Secular Songs For Three Voices, Vol. I *sac/sec,CCU
(Wagner, Lavern J.) bds A-R ED $9.95 (T246)

Sacred And Secular Songs For Three Voices, Vol. II *sac/sec,CCU
(Wagner, Lavern J.) bds A-R ED $9.95 (T247)

TUROK, PAUL
Chorus Of The Frogs
SATB SCHIRM.G 12041 $.60 (T248)

TURTLE DOVE
(Bissell, Keith W.) SAAB (med) WATERLOO $.40 (T249)
(Bissell, Keith W.) SAB (med) WATERLOO $.40 (T250)

TURTLE THUS, THE
see Four Songs From "The Beggar's Opera"

TUTOR WHO TOOTED THE FLUTE see Skolnik, Walter

TUTTO LO DI MI DICI "CANTA" see Lassus, Roland de (Orlandus)

TUZ see Lang, Istvan

TUZ, TE GYONYORU see Kocsar, Miklos

TUZBY PO KRASE see Ocenas, Andrej

TUZCITERAK see Kocsar, Miklos

TVA LYRISKA KORER see Hellden, Daniel

TVA VANDRINGSVISOR see Berg, Gottfrid

TWELFTH NIGHT see Bush, Geoffrey

TWELVE DAYS AFTER CHRISTMAS, THE see Silver

TWELVE DAYS BEFORE CHRISTMAS, THE see Silver

TWELVE DAYS OF CHRISTMAS
see Eight Christmas Carols, Set 2
(Grimes, G.) unis EMI (T251)

TWELVE FOLKSONGS *CC12U
(Omer, Benjamin) [Heb] 2 eq voices/3 eq voices OR-TAV $1.00 (T252)

TWENTY-NINE CHANSONS see Manchicourt, Pierre De

TWENTY-ONE LINCOLNSHIRE FOLK SONGS *CC21U
(Grainger; O'Shaughnessy) unis (easy) OXFORD 68.233 $2.55 (T253)

TWICKENHAM FERRY see Marzials, Theo.

TWO BY TWO see Rodgers, Richard

TWO CARNAL CATCHES see Purcell, Henry

TWO CAROLS FOR THE CARIBBEAN *Xmas, carol
(Stent, K.) SATB,pno,perc voc sc NOVELLO s.p.
contains: Angels, From The Realms Of Glory; Lullay, Thou Little Tiny Child (T254)

TWO CAROLS IN MODERN VEIN see Stent, Keith

TWO CHANSONS see Crecquillon, Thomas

TWO CHORAL SONGS see Gordon, John

TWO CHRISTMAS CAROLS see MacMillan, Ernest Campbell

TWO DUETS FOR CHILDREN see Franco, Johan

TWO EASTERN PICTURES see Holst, Gustav

TWO FOLK MADRIGALS see Taylor, Clifford

TWO FOR CHORUS see Gould, Morton

TWO FRENCH FOLK SONGS *folk,Fr
(Anderson, W.H.) unis LESLIE 1074 $.30
contains: Sainte Marguerite; Sur Le Pont D'Avignon (T255)

TWO GLEES see Spencer, Williametta

TWO HERBERT SETTINGS see Thompson, Randall

TWO HUNDRED YEARS see Irwin, Doreen

TWO HUNDRED YEARS AGO see Davis

TWO IDYLLS see Whitecotton, Shirley

TWO IS BETTER THAN ONE see Milidantri

TWO KITES AND A RAIN CLOUD see Kurth, Burton L.

TWO LITTLE SHOES see Mana-Zucca, Mme.

TWO MADRIGALS see Rossi, Salomone

TWO MADRIGALS see Claflin, Avery

TWO MADRIGALS see Lessard, John [Ayres]

TWO MAYS see Tomasek, Jaroslav, Dva Maje

TWO MOODS FOR CHORUS see Butler, Eugene

TWO MORE TONGUE-TWISTERS see Foster

TWO MOTETS see Wesley, Samuel

TWO POEMS see Farrell, Dennis

TWO POEMS see Balazs, Frederic

TWO PUBLIC PIECES see Felciano, Richard

TWO REFLECTIONS see Kennedy

TWO ROMAN ELEGIES BY GOETHE (DEUX ELEGIES ROMAINES DE GOETHE) see Milhaud, Darius

TWO ROUNDS FOR VOICES see Benoy, A.W.

TWO SHORT ROUNDS see Weigl, Vally

TWO SONGS FOR JUNIORS see Kurth, Burton L.

TWO SONGS FROM "THE WANDERING MOON" see Cope, Cecil

TWO SONGS OF HOPE see Rasely

TWO SONGS OF MOURNING see Ingalls, Jeremiah

TWO STARRY BEAMS see Mozart, Wolfgang Amadeus, Due Pupille Amabile

TWO TRADITIONAL SONGS
TTBB SCHIRM.EC 2321 s.p.
contains: Gaudeamus Igitur; Integer Vitae   (T256)

TWO TWO-PART SONGS see Willan, Healey

TWO UKRAINIAN FOLK SONGS *folk
(Anderson, W.H.) unis LESLIE 1063 $.30
contains: Alone; In The Garden Flowers Are Growing   (T257)

TWO WELSH FOLK SONGS *folk,Welsh
(Holst, Gustav) CURWEN 61583 s.p.
contains: Cwyn Mam Ynghfraith, "Mother-In-Law, The" (SAB,acap); Y Cariad Cyntaf, "First Love, The" (SATB,acap)   (T258)

TWO WELSH LOVE SONGS
(Thomas) SATB,acap (med easy) OXFORD 84.231 $.50
contains: Shore To Shore; Someone   (T259)

TWO WHITE HORSES
(Prussing) SATB oct SCHMITT 666 $.45
                                       (T260)

TWOS AND FOURS see Parker, Alice

TWOS AND THREES see Parker, Alice

TY KRASNA ZEM see Moyzes, Alexander

TY ZEME CESKA see Hajek, Maxmilian

TYRLEE, TYRLO see Gordon, Philip

TYROLEAN ELEGIES see Kricka, Jaroslav, Tyrolske Elegie

TYROLSKE ELEGIE see Kricka, Jaroslav

TYTTOSET *folk,Finn
(Bergman, E.) [Finn/Eng] FAZER 41 s.p.
contains: Heippatiralla, "Hey Tralala" (SATB,acap); Karjankutsu, "Cow Call" (SMezA,S solo,acap); Laksin Mina Kesayona Kaymaan, "On A Summer Night" (SMezA,MezBar soli,acap)   (T261)

U

UBER ALLEN GIPFELN IST RUH see Kuhlau, Friedrich

UBER DEN STERNEN see Abt, Franz

UBER DIE HEIDE see Thehos, Adam

UBER DIE HEIDE HALLET MEIN SCHRITT see Rein, Walter

UBER JAHR UND TAG see Trader, Willi

UBER NACHT see Heuken, Hans Jakob

UBERALL IST WUNDERLAND see Krietsch, Georg

UBERMUT: ALLEWEIL EIN WENIG LUSTIG see Rioohc, Quirin

UDITE, AMANTI see Pederson, Mogens

UGRATOS see Balazs, Arpad

UHREN UND WOLKEN see Ligeti, Gyorgy

UJ SZOVETNEKET see Bardos, Lajos

UKOLEBAVKA see Borkovec, Pavel

UKOLEBAVKA PRO KOTATA see Bohac, Josef

ULTAN, LLOYD
Blow, Blow Thou Winter Wind
SATB,acap AM.COMP.AL. $3.30   (U1)

Chicago
SATB,pno AM.COMP.AL. $8.80   (U2)

Man With A Hoe, The *cant
SATB,soli,4fl,3ob,3clar,2bsn,4horn, 3trp,3trom,tuba,3perc,4timp,harp, strings AM.COMP.AL. sc $52.25, voc pt $14.30   (U3)

ULVAEUS, BJORN
Waterloo *see Anderson, Stig

UM DIE TAFELRUNDE see Orrel, Max

UM JAROSCHAU FLIESSEN ZWEI DER BACHE see Poos, Heinrich

UM MITTERNACHT see Bruckner, Anton

UMBRELLAS OF CHERBOURG, THE (SELECTION) *CCU
CIMINO SSA $.85; SATB $.85; TTBB $.85   (U4)

UMKEHR see Fidelius, Cornelius

UMRAUSCHEN AUCH FREUDEN *folk,Scot
(Abt, Franz) men cor,acap TONOS 6302 s.p.   (U5)

UN, DEUX, TROIS see Kosma, J.

UN ENFANT EST NE see Garvarentz, Georges

UN SOIR DE NEIGE see Poulenc, Francis

UN VENETO CANTAR see De Grandis, Renato

UNA BHAN "O UNA BHAN, DU SCHLANKE" *folk,Ir
(Zoll, Paul) [Ger] men cor sc SCHOTTS C 40 295 s.p. see from Zwei Irische Volkslieder   (U6)

UNA STROFA DI DANTE see Alcalay, Luna

UND ALLE WELT VERGEHT see Gattermayer, Heinrich

UND DER LEBENDE HAT RECHT see Biebl, Franz

UND GEHST DU UBER DEN KIRCHHOF see Brahms, Johannes

UND IN DEM SCHNEEGEBIRGE *folk
(Edler, Rudolf) men cor,acap TONOS 35 s.p.   (U7)

UND IN DEM SCHNEEGEBIRGE see Marx, Karl

UND IN DEM SCHNEEGEBIRGE see Rein, Walter

UND JETZO KOMMT DIE NACHT HEREIN see Zoll, Paul

UND WIR FAHREN see Edler, Robert

UNDER A TELEPHONE POLE see Raphling, Sam

UNDER PARIS SKIES see Gannon

UNDER THE FLAG OF COMMUNISM see Vomacka, Boleslav, Pod Praporem Komunismu

UNDER THE GREENWOOD TREE see Bergh, Arthur

UNDER THE GREENWOOD TREE see Jacob, Gordon

UNDER THE GREENWOOD TREE see Jeppesen, Knud

UNDERSTANDING see Hudson

UNDINE
When Susanna Jones Wears Red   *see Hughes

UNFEHLBAR
(Deutsch, Walter) mix cor DOBLINGER G 679 s.p. see from Acht Lieder Aus Wien   (U8)

UNGARISCHE VOLKSLIEDER AUS SIEBENBURGEN see Bartok, Bela

UNGARISCHES FEST *folk,Hung
(Rosenstengel, A.) men cor,pno,perc sc,cor pts TONOS 2188 s.p.   (U9)

UNGARMADEL, SEI MEIN *folk,Hung
(Fischer, Theo) men cor,acap TONOS 2004 s.p.   (U10)

UNGEHEUER UND ROT ERSCHEINT DIE WINTERSONNE see Genzmer, Harald

UNHAPPY JANO see Simek, Miroslav, Nestastny Jano

UNLESS see Mana-Zucca, Mme.

UNOR A RUZE see Bedrich, Jan

UNRETURNING HOSTS, THE see Mills, Charles

UNS IST KOMMEN EIN LIEBE ZEIT see Bresgen, Cesar

UNSER HANS HAT HOSEN AN see Lang, Hans

UNSER LIED *CCU
(Schiegl; Staatl) jr cor cloth HIEBER s.p.   (U11)

UNSER LIED see Paul, Heinz Otto

UNSER VETTER VEITL see Lang, Hans

UNSERE BERGE see Kanetscheider, Artur

UNSERE HEIMAT see Kanetscheider, Artur

UNSERE STRASSEN
see Singende Jugend Nr. 15

UNSRE FREUNDSCHAFT-UNSER SIEG
mix cor HOFMEISTER V1614 s.p.   (U12)

UNSRER LIEBE GLUCK see Martinu, Bohuslav, Chceme My Se Chceme

UNTER VERWENDUNG DES LIEDES "ACH ELSLEIN, LIEBES ELSELEIN" see Wunsch, Frank

UNTERSCHALE see Stravinsky, Igor

UNTIL IT'S TIME FOR YOU TO GO see Saint-Marie, Buffy

UNTREUE "DURCH'S WIESETAL GANG I JETZT NA" see Silcher, Friedrich

UNTREUE: IN EINEM KUHLEN GRUNDE see Silcher, Friedrich

UP, UP AND AWAY see Webb, Jimmy

UPON THE HIGH MIDNIGHT see Mc Cabe, John

UPOTOKA see Zouhar, Zdenek

URBANEC, BARTOLOMEJ (1925-   )
Piesen O Slavickovi
mix cor,S solo SLOV.HUD.FOND s.p.   (U13)

Pozdrav *cant
cor,orch SLOV.HUD.FOND s.p.   (U14)

URBS AQUENSIS see Bartholemey

URFINSTERNIS "HANS SACHSE SANG" see Grell, Eduard August

URLICHT "O ROSCHEN ROT" see Genzmer, Harald

USPAVANKA see Ocenas, Andrej

USSACHEVSKY, VLADIMIR (1911-   )
    Creation: Prologue, The
        4 cor,electronic tape AM.COMP.AL.
                                              (U15)
    Spell Of Creation, The
        SATB,electronic tape AM.COMP.AL.
                                              (U16)

USTAVA 9. KVETNA see Haba, Alois

UT MOT HAVET see Braein, Edv. Fliflet

UTA see Fukushima, Kazuo

UZ ZRAJE PODZIM see Eben, F.

V

V BESKYDACH see Kubin, Rudolf

V DETSKE IZBE see Holoubek, Ladislav

V MENE MIERU see Nemeth-Samorinsky,
    Stefan

V OTCE VSEMOHUCIHO see Anonymous

V TICHU TAK DRAHO VYKUPENOM see Berger,
    Roman

VA, PENSIERO, SULL'ALI DORATE see
    Verdi, Giuseppe

VACEK, MILOS (1928-   )
    Navraty Ke Studance
        "Returns To The Well" [Czech] wom
        cor&wom cor&wom cor,acap CZECH
        s.p.   (V1)

    Returns To The Well *see Navraty Ke
        Studance

VACKAR, DALIBOR C. (1906-   )
    Pisen Pisni
        "Song Of Songs, The" [Czech] mix
        cor,acap CZECH s.p.   (V2)

    Preamble To The Charter Of United
        Nations, The
        [Eng] mix cor,perc CZECH s.p.   (V3)

    Song Of Songs, The *see Pisen Pisni

VAGABOND SONG, A see Rusch, Milton

VAGABUNDENLIED see Frommlet, Franz

VAGANTEN-TRINKLIED see Desch, Rudolf

VAINAMOINEN'S SONG see Sibelius, Jean

VALDAMBRINI, FRANCESCO (1933-   )
    Suite Dall'opera "Penteo" *CCU
        cor,MezTBar soli,orch ZERBONI 8016
        rental   (V4)

VALEK, JIRI (1923-   )
    Co Je To? *CCU
        [Czech] jr cor,gtr, children's
        carillon CZECH s.p.   (V5)

    Dog Suite - Singing Dogs In The
        Moonlight *see Psi Suita -
        Zpivajici Psici Pri Mesici

    How Many Suns *see Kolik Slunicek

    Kolik Slunicek *cant
        "How Many Suns" [Czech] jr cor,fl,
        ob,clar,bsn,3horn,trp,timp,perc,
        pno,strings, celeste CZECH s.p.
                                          (V6)
    Psi Suita - Zpivajici Psici Pri
        Mesici
        "Dog Suite - Singing Dogs In The
        Moonlight" [Czech] jr cor,pno&fl&
        2trp/clar&gtr&fl CZECH s.p.   (V7)

VALENTINA *folk,Mex
    (Klepisch, Walter) men cor,acap TONOS
    2026 s.p.   (V8)

VALLON SZERENAD see Farkas, Ferenc

VAN EEN KONINGSVROUWE see Spoel, A.

VAN EGY GYURUM, KARIKA see Bartok, Bela

VAN CAMP, LEONARD
    Choral Warm-Ups *CCU
        SATB SCHIRM.G LG 51720 $1.00   (V9)

VANCE, PAUL
    Playground In My Mind (composed with
        Pockriss, Leo)
        (Metis, F.) SAB BIG3 $.45   (V10)
        (Metis, F.) SA/TB BIG3 $.45   (V11)
        (Metis, F.) SSA BIG3 $.45   (V12)
        (Metis, F.) SATB BIG3 $.45   (V13)

VANDAG IS HET MORGEN VAN GISTEREN see
    Bois, Rob du

VANDERBILT, ADRIAAN
    Song Of The Winds
        TTBB (diff) FITZSIMONS 4035 $.30
                                         (V14)

VANDRINGSVISA see Berg, Gottfrid

VAN GROVE
    Road To Vaux
        (Soderstrom, Emil) TTBB (med)
        FITZSIMONS 4026 $.25   (V15)

VAN SLYCK, NICHOLAS
    Hear The Sound Of The Modes
        SATB,fl GENERAL 795CH $.60   (V16)

    Prelude And Fugue (For Tongue-in-
        Cheek)
        SATB,timp, vibes GENERAL 780CH $.75
                                         (V17)

VAN STREEL, R.
    Te Kieldresht
        TTBB (easy) sc BROGNEAUX s.p.   (V18)

VANTINE
    Dusty Feet
        SATB oct SCHMITT 1310 $.30   (V19)

VAN WORMER, G.
    Girl, A
        SATB KJOS 5901 $.35   (V20)

    Immortality, An
        SATB KJOS 5900 $.35   (V21)

VARESE, EDGAR (1883-1965)
    Ecuatorial
        B,pno,org,4trp,4trom,perc, ondes
        martenot COLFRANC COL5 $9.00
                                         (V22)
    Nocturnal
        (Wen-Chung, Chou) B,S solo,orch
        COLFRANC COL9 $12.00   (V23)

VARIANTE A see Clementi, Aldo

VARIATIONS see Childs, Barney

VARIATIONS FOR THE DANCE see Brahms,
    Johannes, Wechsellied Zum Tanz

VARIATIONS ON A CAMP SONG
    (Wetzler, Robert) SATB,acap ART MAST
    1019 $.35   (V24)

VARIATIONS ON POEMS OF JOHN NEWLOVE see
    Childs, Barney

VARLDENS STADER see Johansen, Sven-Erik

VAROTTA, V.
    Blue, Green And Gold *see Crombe, W.

VAROTTO, MICHELE
    Dialogo A Dieci
        see MADRIGALI A DIVERSI LINGUAGGI

VARREGN see Kvam, Oddvar S.

VARY, FERENC
    Buszke Voros Zaszlo
        (Nadas, Katalin) eq voices/mix cor,
        pno BUDAPEST 6885 s.p.   (V25)

    Korus-Szvit
        (Demeny, Otto) eq voices BUDAPEST
        6866 s.p.   (V26)

VASQUEZ, JUAN
    By The Spring Near Roses Red *see En
        La Fuente Del Rosel

    Con Que La Lavare? *Span
        (Nin-Culmell, Joaquin) "With What,
        How Shall I Cleanse?" [Eng/Span]
        SATB,acap BROUDE BR. $.65   (V27)

    De Los Alamos Vengo *Span
        (Nin-Culmell, Joaquin) "From The
        Poplar Trees I Come" [Eng/Span]
        SATB,acap BROUDE BR. $.65   (V28)

    En La Fuente Del Rosel *Span
        (Nin-Culmell, Joaquin) "By The
        Spring Near Roses Red" [Eng/Span]
        SATB,acap BROUDE BR. $.55   (V29)

    From The Poplar Trees I Come *see De
        Los Alamos Vengo

    Vos Me Matastes *Span
        (Nin-Culmell, Joaquin) "You Have
        Wounded Me" [Eng/Span] SSATB,acap
        BROUDE BR. $.45   (V30)

    With What, How Shall I Cleanse? *see
        Con Que La Lavare?

    You Have Wounded Me *see Vos Me
        Matastes

VATER, MUTTER, EILT HERBEI see Lucic,
    Franjo, Japo, Mamo Hote Gledet

VAUGHAN WILLIAMS, RALPH (1872-1958)
    And All In The Morning
        unis STAINER 3.0656.1 $.40   (V31)

    Come Away, Death
        SSATB STAINER 3.0652.1 $.50   (V32)

    Dark Eyed Sailor *folk,Eng
        SATB,acap GALAXY see from Five
        English Folk Songs   (V33)

    Down In Yon Forest
        unis STAINER 3.0662.1 $.50   (V34)
        SSAA STAINER 3.0648.1 $.50   (V35)

VAUGHAN WILLIAMS, RALPH (cont'd.)

Farmers Boy
TTBB STAINER 3.0658.1 $.50   (V36)

Farmers Son So Sweet
TBarB STAINER 3.0832.1 $.30   (V37)
SSATBarB STAINER 3.0838.1 $.40
(V38)

Five English Folk Songs *see Dark
Eyed Sailor; Just As The Tide Was
Flowing; Lover's Ghost; Spring
Time Of The Year; Wassail Song
(V39)

High Germany
TBarB STAINER 3.0660.1 $.40   (V40)

Just As The Tide Was Flowing *folk,
Eng
SATB,acap GALAXY see from Five
English Folk Songs   (V41)

Love Is A Sickness
SATB STAINER 3.0653.1 $.40   (V42)

Lover's Ghost *folk,Eng
SATB,acap GALAXY see from Five
English Folk Songs   (V43)
SATB STAINER 3.0651.1 $.40   (V44)

Rich Old Lady, The
(Sharp; Karpeles) unis (very easy)
OXFORD 81.135 $.30   (V45)

Seeds Of Love
TBarB STAINER 3.0661.1 $.40   (V46)

Spring Time Of The Year *folk,Eng
SATB,acap GALAXY see from Five
English Folk Songs   (V47)

Wassail Song *folk,Eng
SATB,acap GALAXY see from Five
English Folk Songs   (V48)
TBarB STAINER 3.0657.1 $.60   (V49)

VAUTOR, THOMAS (ca. 1590- ?)
Songs Of Divers Airs And Natures
(1619) EM Vol. 34 *CC22L
cor STAINER 3.1934.1 $19.00   (V50)

VE JMENU ZIVOTA see Chlubna, Oswald

VE JMENU ZIVOTA see Sluka, Lubos

VEAL
Irish Fiddler, The
unis (easy) OXFORD 81.146 $.45
(V51)

VECCHI, ORAZIO (1550-1605)
Diversi Linguaggi *see Marenzio,
Luca

Il Bianco E Dolce Cigno *madrigal
[It] SSATB,acap EGTVED KB257 s.p.
(V52)

Klagelied
(Lendvai) men cor,acap TONOS 3330
s.p.   (V53)

VECCOLI, PIETRO
Adelonda Da Frigia
(Goitre) cor,acap voc sc ZERBONI
7416 s.p.   (V54)

VECER CINTORINY see Simai, Pavol

VECNA OBLAKA see Burghauser, Jarmil

VEGYESKAROK see Kodaly, Zoltan

VELAZQUEZ, CONSUELO
Besame Mucho
(Azelton, Phil) SATB,pno,inst
(jazz, includes recording and 14
choral octavos) LEONARD-US
07250500 $14.95   (V55)

VEN EPULET MAR A VILAG see Szokolay,
Sandor

VENDLER, BOHUMIL (1865-1948)
Carol *see Koleda

Koleda
"Carol" [Czech] mix cor,3fl,2ob,
2clar,2bsn,4horn,2trp,3trom,timp,
perc,strings CZECH s.p.   (V56)

VENEZIANI, VITTORE
Barcarola
4pt men cor s.p. sc BONGIOVANI 93,
voc pt BONGIOVANI 93A   (V57)

Che Fai? Che Pensi?
4pt men cor s.p. sc BONGIOVANI 94,
voc pt BONGIOVANI 94A   (V58)

Piccola Suite Corale *CC7L
4pt mix cor BONGIOVANI 2405 s.p.
(V59)

Quando V'odo Parlar Si Dolcemente
3pt men cor s.p. sc BONGIOVANI 95,
voc pt BONGIOVANI 95A   (V60)

VENOVANIE see Ocenas, Andrej

VENUS AND ADONIS: EPILOGUE see
Johansson, Bengt

VENUS AND ADONIS: FOURTH ENCOUNTER see
Johansson, Bengt

VENUS AND ADONIS: THIRD ENCOUNTER see
Johansson, Bengt

VENUS'S PRAISE see Montgomery, Bruce

VER REDIT OPTATUM see Schultz, Svend S.

VERBORGENHEIT "LASS, O WELT, O LASS
MICH SEIN" see Schroeder, Hermann

VERBUNK see Ferenczy, Oto

VERCHOVINO see Schertzer, Daniel

VERDI, GIUSEPPE (1813-1901)
Allegri Beviam (from Ernani)
cor s.p. sc RICORDI-ENG 128482, voc
pt RICORDI-ENG 125133T;125133B
(V61)

Fangarnas Kor (from Nebukadnessar)
4pt mix cor ERIKS 19 s.p.   (V62)

Gerusalem! Gerusalem! (from I
Lombardi)
cor s.p. voc sc RICORDI-ENG 32121,
cor pts RICORDI-ENG
125339D;125339U   (V63)

O Signore, Dal Tetto Natio (from I
Lombardi)
cor s.p. voc sc RICORDI-ENG 32127,
voc pt RICORDI-ENG
125261D; 125261U   (V64)

Patria Oppressa! (from Macbeth)
cor voc pt RICORDI-ENG
128260; 128261 s.p.   (V65)

Rataplan (from La Forza Del Destino)
cor cor pts RICORDI-ENG
125122D;125122U s.p.   (V66)

Song Of The Little Fairies
(Goldman) SSA SCHIRM.G LG51813 $.50
(V67)

Tace Il Vento (from I Due Foscari)
SA RICORDI-ENG 128288 s.p.   (V68)
TB RICORDI-ENG 128289 s.p.   (V69)

Tarantella (from La Forza Del
Destino)
cor cor pts RICORDI-ENG
127774D;127774U s.p.   (V70)

Va, Pensiero, Sull'ali Dorate (from
Nabucco)
mix cor voc sc RICORDI-ENG 103924
s.p., voc pt RICORDI-ENG
8295;8296 s.p.   (V71)

Viva Augusta (from Ernani)
TB RICORDI-ENG 15160 s.p.   (V72)

VERETTI, ANTONIO (1900-   )
Due Madrigali *CC2U
mix cor RICORDI-ENG 131284 s.p.
(V73)

Quattro Cori Per Fanciulli *CC4U
2pt RICORDI-ENG 128531 s.p.   (V74)

VERGANGEN IST DIE NACHT see Mohler,
Philipp

VERGANGEN IST MIR GLUCK UND HEIL see
Brahms, Johannes

VERGANGLICHES GLUCK *folk
(Deutschmann, G.) [Ger] 4pt mix cor
MERSEBURG EM9211 s.p.   (V75)

VERGANGLICHKEIT *folk
(Mockl, F.) [Ger] 4pt mix cor
MERSEBURG EM9208 s.p.   (V76)

VERGEBLICHES STANDCHEN "ICH WUNSCHTE,
ES WARE NACHT" see Sturmer, Bruno

VERGISSMEINNICH "O DU LEISES WEH" see
Zoll, Paul

VERIRRT see Trunk, Richard

VERKEHRTE WELT "WIE SIND MIR MEINE
STIEFEL GESCHWOLL'N see Lang, Hans

VERKLARTER HERBST "GEWALTIG ENDET SO
DAS JAHR" see Knab, Armin

VERLASSEN see Sturmer, Bruno

VERLING
Wenn Ostern Wird Am Tiberstrom
*Op.38
6pt mix cor LIENAU sc s.p., cor pts
s.p.   (V77)

VERLORENE JUGEND see Brahms, Johannes

VERONA CANTA *CC16U
cor sc,cor pts ZANIBON 5400 s.p.
contains works by: Muraro; Giusti;
Garzoni   (V78)

VERRALL, JOHN (1908-   )
Song Of Rejoicing, A
jr cor,bells sc AM.COMP.AL. $.28
(V79)

They Shall Never Thirst
SATB,acap AM.COMP.AL. $2.20   (V80)

VERRALL, PAMELA
Around The World *CC6U
cor,perc,rec EMI   (V81)

Ring-A-Ding Bells
SA EMI   (V82)

Star Bright, Starlight
SA EMI   (V83)

VERRATENE LIEBE "DA NACHTS WIR UNS
KUSSTEN" see Fussan, Werner

VERSCHMOLZENE HERZEN see Rasch, Hugo

VERSCHNEIT see Zoll, Paul

VERSCHUTT see Blass, Heinrich

VERSCHWUNDEN IST DIE FINSTRE NACHT see
Edler, Robert

VERSE PSANE NA VODU see Raichl,
Miroslav

VERSES WRITTEN FOR WATER see Raichl,
Miroslav, Verse Psane Na Vodu

VERSTOHLEN GEHT DER MOND AUF see
Brahms, Johannes

VERTIGO see Tausinger, Jan, Zavrat

VERY MERRY CHRISTMAS, A see McElfresh,
Clair T.

VERZIERTE VOLKSLIEDSATZE see Werdin,
Eberhard

VESPERAE BACCHANALES see Roszkowszky,
Pantaleon

VESTENVINDEN
(Jacobsen; Bertelsen; Bergman;
Hemberg; Kvam) "West Wind, The" mix
cor,acap NORDISKA NMS 6428 s.p.
(V84)

VICK
Lullaby
SATB WALTON 2983 $.40   (V85)

VICTORIA, TOMAS LUIS DE (ca. 1549-1611)
Thomas Ludovici Victoria Abulensis
Opera Omnia (Complete Works)
*sac/sec,CCU
(Pedrell, Felipe) [Lat] microfiche
UNIV.MUS.ED. $30.00 8 volumes
(V86)

VICTORY, GERARD (1921-   )
Kriegslieder
SATB,T solo,perc,trp, xylophone
vibraphone voc sc NOVELLO rental,
ipr   (V87)

VICTORY HORA see Kessler, Minuetta,
Horah Nitsachon

VIDICI see Trifunovic, Vitomir

VIDOSIC, TIHOMIL (1902-   )
Istrian Scherzo
mix cor,2ob,2bsn CROATICA   (V88)

VIEL FREUDEN MIT SICH BRINGET see
Becker, Peter

VIEL FREUDEN MIT SICH BRINGET see
Neumeyer, Fritz

VIEL SCHONER BLUMELIEN see Schein,
Johann Hermann

VIELE KUNST KANN DER TEUFEL see Katt,
Leopold

VIER ABEND- UND SCHLAFLIEDER see Biebl,
Franz

VIER ALTE VOLKSLIEDER-IM NEUEN GEWAND
*folk
(Rosenstengel, Albrecht) men cor/men
cor&jr cor,pno,opt gtr,opt bvl,opt
perc sc,voc sc TONOS 1230 s.p.
contains: Frau Musika; Weiss Mir
Ein Blumlein Blaue; Wenn Alle
Brunnlein Fliessen; Wenn Ich Ein
Voglein War   (V89)

VIER AMERIKANISCHE VOLKSLIEDER *see
Nobody Knows, "Niemand Erfahrt Das
Lied"; Old Kentucky Home,
"Kentucky-Heimat "Die Sonne

Scheint""; Swanee Ribber, "Die
Meinen Zu Haus "Weit, Weit Von Hier
Am Swanee Ribber""; Swing Low,
Sweet Chariot, "Hol Mich Nach Haus"
(V90)

VIER BETTELLIEDER see Reutter, Hermann

VIER BRITISCHE VOLKSLIEDER see Gal,
Hans

VIER CHORLIEDER see Hessenberg, Kurt

VIER EDLE ROSSE *folk
(Biebl, F.) [Ger] 4pt mix cor
MERSEBURG EM9233 s.p. (V91)

VIER EICHENDORFF-LIEDER see Schaefers,
Anton

VIER EUROPAISCHE VOLKSLIEDER see
Schertzer, Daniel

VIER GEDICHTE see Genzmer, Harald

VIER GEDICHTE see Hessenberg, Kurt

VIER GRABLIEDER
mix cor,acap cor pts ERDMANN 554 s.p.
contains: Mag Auch Die Liebe
Weinen; Ruh' In Frieden; Ruhe
Sanft; Wie Sie So Sanftruh'n
(V92)

VIER GRABLIEDER
(Gluck, Fr.) men cor,acap cor pts
ERDMANN 148 s.p.
contains: Beethoven, Ludwig van,
Grablied; Beneken, Friedrich,
Heil Dir Und Frieden; Kloss, Da
Unten Ist Frieden; Lasker,
Schlaf, Freund (V93)

VIER HEITERE CHORLIEDER see Zehm,
Friedrich

VIER HEITERE CHORLIEDER see Zoll, Paul

VIER HEITERE GESANGE see Edler, Robert

VIER HEITERE MANNERCHORE see Desch,
Rudolf

VIER INDISCHE LIEDER *see Genzmer,
Harald, Sehnsucht "Schweift Auch
Mein Blick"; Genzmer, Harald,
Warnung "Mein Tochterlein, Ich
Warne Dich" (V94)

VIER INDISCHE LIEDER see Genzmer,
Harald

VIER JAPANISCHE CHORLIEDER see
Sakamoto, Yoshitaka

VIER KANONS see Hindemith, Paul

VIER KINDERLIEDER see Werdin, Eberhard

VIER KURIOSE GESCHICHTEN see Haus, Karl

VIER LEICHTE MANNERCHORE see Biebl,
Franz

VIER LEICHTE MANNERCHORE see Erdlen,
Hermann

VIER LIEDER see Trunk, Richard

VIER LUSTIGE LIEDER see Seeger, Peter

VIER MANNERCHORE NACH ALTDEUTSCHEN
TEXTEN see Bresgen, Cesar

VIER MORGENSTERNLIEDER see Nitsche,
Paul

VIER NIEDERLANDISCHE VOLKSLIEDER see
Rettich, Wilhelm

VIER RUSSISCHE VOLKSLIEDER see
Schertzer, Daniel

VIER SATZE NACH DEUTSCHEN VOLKSLIEDERN
see Wimberger, Gerhard

VIER SINNGEDICHTE see Gerster, Ottmar

VIER TRINKSPRUCHE see Becker, Hans-
Gunther

VIER VOLKSLIED-DUETTE see Zoll, Paul

VIER VOLKSLIEDER see Fussan, Werner

VIER WELTLICHE KANONS see Mozart,
Wolfgang Amadeus

VIER ZIGEUNERLIEDER see Brahms,
Johannes

VIGNATI, MILOS (1897-1966)
Greetings To Moscow *see Pozdrav
Moskve

Pozdrav Moskve
"Greetings To Moscow" [Czech] men
cor,acap CZECH s.p. (V95)

VIGNAU, HANS VON
Heimliche Liebe
men cor RIES sc s.p., cor pts s.p.
(V96)

VILEC, MICHAL (1902-   )
Novemu Obciankovi
wom cor SLOV.HUD.FOND s.p. (V97)

VILLA-LOBOS, HEITOR (1887-1959)
Duas Lendas Amerindias Em Nheengatu
*CC2U
4pt mix cor,acap (med) sc SCHOTTS
ME 6902 s.p. (V98)

Na Bahia Tem
men cor sc SCHOTTS ME 90-2312 s.p.
(V99)

Quartett
wom cor,fl,harp,celeste,alto
saxophone (diff) sc SCHOTTS
rental, ipr (V100)

VILLAGE INTERLUDE see Tate

VILLANELLA see Ercolano, T.

VILLANELLA ALLA NAPOLITANA see Donati,
Baldassare

VILLANELLE see Martin, Ch.

VILLANESCA see Guerrero, Francisco

VILLE DE SARLAT *folk,Fr
(Blanchard, R.) 4pt mix cor,acap
JOBERT s.p. (V101)

VILLOTTE DEL FIORE see Azzaiolo, F.

VINCENT see McLean, Don

VINEY FLOWER AND ROSEMARY TREE see
Kralzek

VINI BONI VERITAS see Gerster, Ottmar,
"In Den Rheinbergen Bluht Schon Der
Wein"

VINI BONI VERITAS see Zoller, Anton

VINO UND AMORE *folk,It
(Burthel, Jacob) men cor,pno, also
peformable with combo sc,cor pts
TONOS 2204 s.p. (V102)

VINTERSTYCKE see Soderholm, Valdemar

VINUM SCHENK EIN see Widmann, Erasmus

VIRCHI, P.
Dovea La Fredda Neve *madrigal
(Nielsen, R.) 5pt mix cor
BONGIOVANI 2385 s.p. see also
DODICI MADRIGALI DI SCUOLA
FERRARESE (V103)

Non Fonte O Fiume *madrigal
(Nielsen, R.) 5pt mix cor
BONGIOVANI 2387 s.p. see also
DODICI MADRIGALI DI SCUOLA
FERRARESE (V104)

Qual Cervo Errando *madrigal
(Nielsen, R.) 5pt mix cor
BONGIOVANI 2386 s.p. see also
DODICI MADRIGALI DI SCUOLA
FERRARESE (V105)

VIRGIN MARY'S LULLABY, THE see Dinn,
Freda

VIRTUE see Raffman, Relly

VISA VID BROLLOPSMIDDAN see Johansen,
Sven-Erik

VISAGES see Casterede, Jacques

VISION see Krietsch, Georg

VIT 1973 see Balazs, Arpad

VITA FLINGOR see Johansen, Sven-Erik

VITAJ, LUCKA see Mikula, Zdenko

VITAJ, PRVY MAJ! see Letnan, Julius

VITAJ, SOKOLIKU see Letnan, Julius

VIVA! see Haufrecht, [Herbert]

VIVA AUGUSTA see Verdi, Giuseppe

VIVA LA MUSICA see Mohler, Philipp

VIVA MUSICA see Teirlinck, Geo

VIVA TUTTE LE VEZZOSE see Giardini,
Felice de'

VIVA TUTTI *folk,It
TTB SCHIRM.EC 2326 s.p. (V106)

VIVE LA COOKERY MAID see Rice, M.R.

VIVE L'AMOUR *folk
(Biebl, F.) [Ger] 4pt men cor
MERSEBURG EM9080 s.p. (V107)

VLACH-VRUTICKY, JOSEF (1897-   )
Domove *Op.144
"Home" [Czech] mix cor,acap CZECH
s.p. (V108)

Dve Slavnostnich Sboru *Op.23, CC2U
[Czech] mix cor,acap CZECH s.p.
(V109)

Home *see Domove

VLAD, ROMAN (1919-   )
Colinde Transilvane *CCU
mix cor (med) sc SCHOTTS SZ 5413
s.p. (V110)

Colinde Transilvane *see Pastorali
Transilvane

Lettura Di Michelangelo
SATB RICORDI-ENG 131025 s.p. (V111)

Pastorali Transilvane
"Colinde Transilvane" [It/Rum] 3pt
wom cor,acap (med diff) sc
SCHOTTS ESZ 5417 s.p. (V112)

VOCAL FANTASIA ON BOHEMIAN GIRL see
Balfe

VOCALISE see Kahn, Erich Itor

VOCALISE see Lovelock

VOCALISE see Luening, Otto

VOCALISE see Young

VOCALISE WALTZ -WARM-UP ON NONSENSE
SYLLABLES see Mc Bride, Robert Guyn

VOCI see Macchi, Egisto

VOCI CHE AMAVI see Piccioli, G.

VOCI DI LAGUNA see Recli, Giulia

VOGEL, WLADIMIR
An Die Jugend Der Welt
4-5pt mix cor,fl,2clar,bsn,2trp,
trom,strings,perc,timp (med diff)
min sc SCHOTTS AV 67 s.p., ipr
(V113)

VOGELLIED see Bartok, Bela, Madardal

VOGELZUG see Krietsch, Georg

VOGLEIN IM KAFIG "ARMES VOGLEIN, BIST
DU KRANK" see Zoll, Paul

VOGLEIN SCHWERMUT "EIN SCHWARZES
VOGLEIN FLIEGT UBER DIE WELT" see
Weber, Bernhard

VOGT, HANS (1911-   )
Sine Nomine *cant
SATB,T solo,orch ALKOR AE326 rental
(V114)

VOGT, PAUL G. (1927-   )
Fiesta
mix cor,7 narrators,MezBarB soli,
clar,2trp,electric,2vln,vcl,pno,
perc, 3 electric guitars (med
easy) voc sc,cor pts SCHOTTS
ED. 6516 s.p., ipa (V115)

VOICE, THE see Curwin, Clifford

VOICES NO. 1 see Balada, Leonardo

VOICES OF CHILDREN see Thiman, Eric
Harding

VOICES OF NIGHT see Reizenstein, Franz

VOICES OF THE DARK see Davidson, Lyle

VOICI LA PENTECOTE *folk,Fr
(Blanchard, R.) 4pt mix cor,acap
JOBERT s.p. (V116)

VOICI LE MAI see Ladmirault, P.

VOICI LE PERE AU DOUBLE FRONT see
Crawford, John

VOICI LE TEMPS ET LA SAISON see
Champagne, Claude

VOICI LES VACANCES see Danhieux,
Georges

VOICY DU GAY PRINTEMS see Le Jeune,
Claude

VOKALNEJ TVORBY see Schneider-Trnavsky,
Mikulas

VOLA HORA see Letnan, Julius

VOLANIE see Ferenczy, Oto

VOLKSLIEDBEARBEITUNGEN FUR FRAUENCHOR
*CCU,folk
(Brahms, Johannes) SSAA,acap (med)
BAREN. BA3175 s.p.   (V117)

VOLKSLIEDER see Pepping, Ernst

VOLKSLIEDER FREMDER VOLKER see Zoll,
Paul

VOLKSWEISE see Steffen, Wolfgang

VOLL VON WEIN "VOLL, FREUNDE, MACHT
EUCH VOLL" see Biebl, Franz

VOM ABENTEUER DER FREUDE see Genzmer,
Harald

VOM BAUERNHOF see Biebl, Franz

VOM BAUMELEIN "ES IST EIN BAUMLEIN
GESTANDEN" see Lang, Hans

VOM EDLEN JAGERLEBEN see Poos, Heinrich

VOM FRUHJAHR, OLTANK UND VOM FLIEGEN
see Orff, Carl

VOM SINGEN, TRINKEN, UND FROHLICHSEIN
see Schneider, Walther

VOM WEIN see Edler, Robert

VOM WESEN UND VERGEHEN see Hessenberg,
Kurt

VOMACKA, BOLESLAV (1887-1965)
Bojka, Partyzanka *Op.56, cant
"Bojka The Woman Guerrilla Fighter"
[Czech] mix cor,3fl,2ob,2clar,
2bsn,4horn,2trp,3trom,tuba,perc,
timp,harp,strings CZECH s.p.
(V118)

Bojka The Woman Guerrilla Fighter
*see Bojka, Partyzanka

Flag Of Peace Above Dukla, The *see
Prapor Miru Nad Duklou

Pod Praporem Komunismu *Op.67, cant
"Under The Flag Of Communism"
[Czech] mix cor,3fl,2ob,2clar,
2bsn,4horn,4trp,3trom,tuba,timp,
perc,harp,strings CZECH s.p.
(V119)

Prapor Miru Nad Duklou *Op.55, cant
"Flag Of Peace Above Dukla, The"
[Czech] men cor,B solo,fl,ob,
clar,bsn,3horn,trp,trom,tuba,
timp,perc,harp,strings CZECH s.p.
(V120)

Quick To The Dead, The *Op.16
[Czech/Ger] mix cor,3fl,3ob,2clar,
3bsn,4horn,2trp,3trom,tuba,harp,
strings,timp,perc, celeste
SUPRAPHON s.p.   (V121)

Under The Flag Of Communism *see Pod
Praporem Komunismu

Youth *Op.20
[Czech/Ger] mix cor,4fl,3ob,4clar,
3bsn,6horn,4trp,4trom,tuba,timp,
perc,2harp,org,strings,celeste,
cymbal SUPRAPHON s.p.   (V122)

VON ALLEN BLAUEN HUGELN see Wolters,
Gottfried

VON ALLERLEI HUNDEN see Desch, Rudolf

VON ALLERLEI MIST see Hollfelder,
Waldram

VON ALTEN LIEBESLIEDERN see Brahms,
Johannes

VON ALTEN LIEBESLIEDERN "SPAZIEREN
WOLLT ICH REITEN" see Brahms,
Johannes, Von Alten Liebesliedern

VON DEN HEIMLICHEN ROSEN see Edler,
Robert

VON DEN WOLKEN see Radermacher,
Friedrich

VON DER BRUDERLICHKEIT "DIE ARZENEI FUR
ALLER WELTEN" see Poos, Heinrich

VON DER EDLEN MUSIK "DER HAT VERGEBEN"
see Rathgeber, Valentin

VON DER FREUNDLICHKEIT DER WELT see
Orff, Carl

VON DER FREUNDLICHKEIT DER WELT "AUF
DIE ERDE VOLLER KALTEM WIND" see
Orff, Carl

VON GOTTES UND DES MENSCHEN WESEN see
Koetsier, Jan

VON LIEBE UND NARREN see Sturmer, Bruno

VON MAUSEN, AUTOS UND ANDEREN TIEREN
see Bresgen, Cesar

VOR DEM ALTAR see Edler, Robert

VOR DEM GRABE see Edler, Robert

VOR DEM WEIN see Rische, Quirin

VOR JENA see Stade

VORSPIEL see Biebl, Franz

VORSPRUCH see Cohen, Alban

VORSPRUCH see Distler, Hugo

VORSPRUCH see Philipp, Franz

VORSPRUCH: WER SICH DIE MUSIK see
Mittergradnegger, Gunther

VORWARTS, PFERDCHEN *folk,Russ
(Erbelding, Dietrich) men cor,acap
TONOS 463 o.p.   (V123)

VORWORT see Sutermeister, Heinrich

VOS ME MATASTES see Vasquez, Juan

VOTRE BEAUTE PLAISANTE ET LIE see
Gombert, Nicolas

VOUS Y FIEZ VOUS see Egk, Werner

VOX HUMANA see Sikorski, Tomasz

VOYAGE see Mc Cabe, John

VOYAGE DU CORPS see Nunes, Emmanuel

VOYAGE OF ARION, THE see Moore, Earl
Vincent

VRANA, FRANTISEK (1914-   )
Sest Madrigalu *Op.40, CC6U
[Czech] cor,acap CZECH s.p.   (V124)

VRBY PRI VAHU see Mikula, Zdenko

VRIES, KLAAS DE
Tegenzangen
mix cor&speak cor,2fl,2ob,2clar,
2bsn,2horn,trp,2trom,tuba,
strings,perc,timp DONEMUS (V125)

VSCIAM NINFE HOMAI see Monteverdi,
Claudio

VSEDNI DEN see Podest, Ludvik

VSETCI SME JEDNO see Fiala, Jaromir

VSTAN, PANNA ODKLIATA see Mikula,
Zdenko

VSTAVEJTE, PASTUSCI... see Rychlik, Jan

VUATAZ
Ce Que L'aino
mix cor,acap HENN 757 s.p.   (V126)

Chanson
wom cor,acap HENN 685 s.p.   (V127)

VYBER ZO SOVIETSKEJ see Schneider-
Trnavsky, Mikulas

VYCPALEK, LADISLAV (1882-1969)
Cerveny Kvet Ja
"I, The Red Blossom" [Czech] mix
cor,acap CZECH s.p.   (V128)

Concerning The Last Things Of A Man
*Op.16, cant
[Czech] mix cor,SBar soli,3fl,3ob,
3clar,2bsn,4horn,2trp,3trom,timp,
perc,strings, xylophone SUPRAPHON
s.p.   (V129)

I, The Red Blossom *see Cerveny Kvet
Ja

VYSTAHOVALECKA see Gresak, Jozef

VYVOLAVACI see Pinos, Alois

VYZKA see Ferenczy, Oto

VYZVA see Ferenczy, Oto

VZKAZ ZIVYM see Seidel, Jan

VZORNY VOJAK see Sedlacek, Bohuslav

W

WAAGE see Strobl, Otto

WAAROM TOCH? see Pronk, Arie

WACH AUF! see Erdlen, Hermann

WACH AUF, DU DEUTSCHES LAND see
Walther, Johann Gottfried

WACH AUF! ES NAHET GEN DEN TAG see
Wagner, Richard

WACH AUF MEIN HERZENS SCHONE see Rein,
Walter

WACH AUF, MEINS HERZENS SCHONE *folk,
Ger
see Drei Alte Volkslieder-Neu
Dargeboten
mix cor,acap HOFMEISTER G2197 s.p.
(W1)

WACH AUF, MEIN'S HERZENS SCHONE see
Zipp, Friedrich

WACHT AUF! see Seib, Valentin

WACHT AUF, ES TUT EUCH NOT! see
Distler, Hugo

WACHT AUF, IHR SCHONEN VOGELEIN see
Anonymous

WACHT AUF IHR SCHONEN VOGELEIN see
Genzmer, Harald

WACHTELSCHLAG "AM KIRCHTURM STEHT DER
ABENDSTERN" see Haas, Joseph

WACHTERLIED see Edler, Robert

WACHTERLIED see Gebhard, Hans

WADDINGTON, SIDNEY PEINE (1869-1953)
John Gilpin
SATB,2fl,2ob,2clar,2bsn,2horn,2trp,
3trom,timp,strings voc sc NOVELLO
rental, ipr   (W2)

WADELY, F.W. (1883-1970)
Old English Suite *CCU
SATB,2fl,pic,2ob,2clar,2bsn,4horn,
2trp,3trom,timp,perc,strings voc
sc NOVELLO rental, ipr   (W3)

WAELRANT, HUBERT (ca. 1517-1595)
Als Ick U Vinde
SATB,acap EGTVED KB210 s.p.   (W4)

WAGNER, FRANZ
Weihegesang
men cor BRATFISCH GB2536 s.p.   (W5)

WAGNER, RICHARD (1813-1883)
Apotheose Des Hans Sachs (from Die
Meistersinger Von Nurnberg)
(Kistler, Cyrill) TTBB/TTTBBB,pno/
2fl,2ob,2clar,2bsn,4horn,3trp,
3trom,tuba,strings,perc,timp sc
SCHOTTS C 24 061 s.p., voc sc
SCHOTTS C 26 545 s.p., voc pt
SCHOTTS C 26 545, 01-04 s.p., ipa
(W6)

Choral Fantasia On Tannhauser
(Challinor) mix cor BANKS MUS
YS 872 $.80   (W7)

Hail! Bright Abode (from Tannhauser)
SSAATTBB (med) FITZSIMONS 1019 $.25
(W8)

Hymn To The Morning (from Die
Meistersinger)
(Martin) SATB,acap (med) FITZSIMONS
1074 $.20   (W9)
(Wilson) SSAA,acap (med) FITZSIMONS
3045 $.20   (W10)
(Wilson) TTTTBBBB,acap (med)
FITZSIMONS 4048 $.20   (W11)

Pilgrim's Chorus (from Tannhauser)
TTBB,acap (med) FITZSIMONS 4021
$.20   (W12)

Wach Auf! Es Nahet Gen Den Tag (from
Die Meistersinger Von Nurnberg)
(Haas, Joseph) jr cor/wom cor (med
easy) sc SCHOTTS CHBL 545 s.p.
(W13)

WAH GEE TEE BEE *Afr
(Nebo) "They Are Coming" SATB
SCHIRM.G LG51509 $.40   (W14)

WAHLSPRUCH "ANDRE HABEN ANDRE
SCHWINGEN" see Schwarz-Schilling,
Reinhard

WAHLSPRUCH: STREBE EMPOR see Lendvai,
Erwin

WAHRE FREUNDSCHAFT *folk,Ger
(Koenig, Franz) men cor,acap TONOS 28
s.p. (W15)

WAKE OF O'CONNOR see Bath, Hubert

WALCHA, HELMUT (1907-)
Deutsche Liebeslieder *CC23L
2 eq voices,acap (easy) SCHOTTS
ED. 3596 s.p. (W16)

WALDANDACHT see Abt, Franz

WALDESNACHT see Brahms, Johannes

WALDGRUSS see Schlemm, Gustav Adolf

WALDHYMNE see Desch, Rudolf

WALDLIED: WALDNACHT! WALDLUST! see
Silcher, Friedrich

WALDLUST: WIE HERRLICH IST'S IM WALD
see Silcher, Friedrich

WALDWEGE "SO VIEL WEGE LAUFEN DURCH DEN
WALD" see Lang, Hans

WALK SOFTLY see Furman

WALK WITH FAITH IN YOUR HEART
SATB CIMINO $.40 (W17)

WALK WITH ME
SA CIMINO $.40 (W18)
SSA CIMINO $.40 (W19)
SATB CIMINO $.40 (W20)
TTBB CIMINO $.40 (W21)

WALKER
Gettysburg Address, The
SATB MCAFEE M1066 $.45 (W22)

WALKER, ERNEST (1870-1949)
Ode To A Nightingale *Op.14
SATB, Bar solo,2fl,2clar,2bsn,4horn,
strings voc sc NOVELLO rental,
ipr (W23)

WALKER, ROBERT
Three Early English Lyrics *CC3U
SSAA,acap WEINBERGER s.p. (W24)

WALKER, WILLIAM
Gettysburg Address, The
1-2pt,narrator MCAFEE M8019 $.40
(W25)

WALKING AROUND see Parris, Robert

WALLACE, WILLIAM VINCENT (1812-1865)
Choral Fantasia On Maritana
(Challinor) mix cor BANKS MUS
YS 811 $1.10 (W26)

WALLAS, HERBERT
Der Musikant
men cor,acap TONOS 283 s.p. (W27)

WALOSHIN, SID
We're Together *see Gavin, Kevin

WALTER (WALTHER), JOHANN (1496-1570)
All Morgen Ist Ganz Frisch Und Neu
see Praetorius, Michael, Der Tag
Vertreibt Die Dunkle Nacht

WALTHALL, BENNIE
We're Goin' Uptown *see Kraintz, Ken

WALTHER, GEORG
Wie Ist Doch Die Erde So Schon
men cor,acap TONOS 250 s.p. (W28)

WALTHER, JOHANN GOTTFRIED (1684-1748)
Wach Auf, Du Deutsches Land
(Weber, W.) men cor,acap TONOS 3322
s.p. (W29)

WALTHEW, [RICHARD HENRY] (1872-1951)
Pied Piper Of Hamelin
SATB,TBar soli,2fl,2ob,2clar,2bsn,
2horn,2trp,3trom,timp,strings voc
sc NOVELLO rental,ipr (W30)

WALTZING MATILDA *folk,Austral
(Cooper, Gwyneth) S&camb&opt Bar
(easy) CAMBIATA U117451 $.30 (W31)

WALY, WALY see Gardner

WALZER see Francaix, Jean

WANDERER, KOMMST DU NACH SPARTA see
Edler, Robert

WANDERER UND BRUNNEN "JA BRUNNLEIN, DU
HAST WASSERS DIE FULL" see Werner,
Kurt

WANDERERS NACHTLIED
men cor,acap TONOS 6346 s.p. (W32)

WANDERERS NACHTLIED see Kienzl, Wilhelm

WANDERLIED *folk
(Biebl, F.) [Ger] 4pt mix cor
MERSEBURG EM9229 s.p. (W33)

WANDERLIED see Seib, Valentin

WANDERLIED "DIE SONN' ERWACHT, MIT
IHRER PRACHT" see Weber, Carl Maria
von

WANDERLIED: FROHES WANDERN see Heun,
Hans

WANDERLIEDCHEN "O, WIE SCHON IST DIE
WELT" see Fischer, Ernst

WANDERLUST see Hermanns, Willy

WANDERN MUSSEN WIR see Martinu,
Bohuslav, Pujdme

WANDERNDER WINTERWIND see Erdlen,
Hermann

WANDERSCHAFT see Zollner, Karl
Friedrich

WANDERSCHAFT "IM WALDE BLUHT DER
SEIDELBAST" see Bresgen, Cesar

WANDERSCHAFT "IM WALDE BLUHT DER
SEIDELBAST" see Lang, Hans

WANDERSCHAFT "IM WALDE BLUHT DER
SEIDELBAST" see Schubert, Heino

WANDERSCHAFT "IM WALDE BLUHT DER
SEIDELBAST" see Zoll, Paul

WANDERSPRUCHE see Lothar, Mark

WAND'RERS NACHTGEBET see Weber,
Bernhard Anselm

WANDRERS NACHTLIED see Hermanns, Willy

WAND'RING MILLER see Schubert, Franz
(Peter)

WANDSPRUCH-KANTATE see Mohler, Philipp

WANING MOON, THE see Chavez, Carlos

WANKELMUT see Koenig, Franz

WANN I ANMAL STIRB
(Lessky, Fr.) mix cor DOBLINGER G 687
s.p. see from Sechs Lieder Aus Wien
(W34)

WANN I VON WEAN WEGGAGEH
(Deutsch, Walter) mix cor DOBLINGER
G 680 s.p. see from Acht Lieder Aus
Wien (W35)

WANN ICH DES MORGENS FRUH AUFSTEH see
Pepping, Ernst

WANN ICH WEISS, WAS DU WEISST see
Lachner, Franz

WANN WIR SCHREITEN
unis wom cor SCHOTTS C 42 533D s.p.
see also Alle Singen Heft 2 (W36)

WANN ZWITSCHERN DIE ELEFANTEN see Haus,
Karl

WAR ICH MADCHEN OHNE MANN GEBLIEBEN see
Zoll, Paul

WAR IS KIND see Beadell, Robert M.

WARD, JOHN (1571?-1641)
First Set Of Madrigals (1613) EM Vol.
19 *CC21L,madrigal
3-6pt STAINER 3.1919.1 $17.00 (W37)

WARD, ROBERT (1917-)
Sweet Freedom's Song *cant
cor,SBar soli,orch HIGHGATE
7.0039.1 $4.50, ipr (W38)

WARD, SAMUEL A.
America, The Beautiful
(Bennett) SATB SCHIRM.G LG51771
$.40 (W39)
(Wick, Fred) TTBB oct SCHMITT W182
$.40 (W40)
(Wick, Fred) cor,4 soli oct SCHMITT
W259 $.40 (W41)

Fly Not So Fast
(Shipp) SSA SCHIRM.G LG51659 $.40
(W42)

WARE, ACH DER MORGENSTERN SO GERNE see
Stein, F.R.

WAREHOUSE-LIFE see Seeger, Peter

WARLAMOFF
Red Sarafan, The
(Aschenbrenner) SSAATTBB,acap (med)
FITZSIMONS 1036 $.25 (W43)

WARNUNG see Mozart, Wolfgang Amadeus

WARNUNG "DU HAST GESAGT" see Rein,
Walter

WARNUNG: DU HAST GESAGT see Thehos,
Adam

WARNUNG "MEIN TOCHTERLEIN, ICH WARNE
DICH" see Genzmer, Harald

WARREN
Night Rider
SATB SCHIRM.G LG51878 $.45 (W44)

WARREN, ELINOR REMICK (1905-)
Little Choral Suite
SSA, opt fl&strings (easy) FISCHER,C
CM 7814 $.40
contains: Little Song Of Life, A;
Rain Slippers; Sleep Walks Over
The Hill (W45)

Little Song Of Life, A
see Little Choral Suite

Rain Slippers
see Little Choral Suite

Sleep Walks Over The Hill
see Little Choral Suite

WARUM NICHT LUSTIG? *CC9U
3-4pt men cor,acap MOSELER HEFT 44
s.p. contains works by: Jeep,
Johann; Lechner, Leonhard; Gosswin,
Anton; Zangius, Nikolaus; Morley,
Thomas; Eccard, Johann; Steuccius,
Heinrich; Hausmann, Valentin (W46)

WARUM RETTET' DENN GOTT NUR DANIEL see
Didn't My Lord Deliver Daniel

WAS DER ALTE DACHTE, ALS ER ZU HEIRATEN
GEDACHTE see Zehm, Friedrich

WAS HILFT MIR EIN ROTER APFEL see
Gerster, Ottmar

WAS MAG DOCH DIESE WELT see Ahle,
Johann Rudolph

WAS MOCHTEST DU HEUT TRAUMEN see Biebl,
Franz

WAS SPRICHT MAN DENN VON SACHSEN see
Biebl, Franz

WAS UNS NOCH FEHLT
(Deutsch, Walter) mix cor DOBLINGER
G 681 s.p. see from Acht Lieder Aus
Wien (W47)

WAS WIR GERNE TUN see Biebl, Franz

WAS WIRST DU MIR MITBRINGEN see Biebl,
Franz

WAS WOLLN WIR AUF DEN ABEND TUN?
see Im Maien, Im Maien, Hort Man Die
Hahnen Schreien

WAS WOLLN WIR AUF DEN ABEND TUN see
Brautigam, Helmut

WASHBURN
April (from Spring Cantata)
SATB,acap oct BOOSEY 5896 $.35
(W48)
Earth Song
SATB,pno/org oct BOOSEY 5900 $.45
(W49)
Four Songs For Men's Voices *CC4U
men cor SCHIRM.G 2983 $1.25 (W50)

July (from Spring Cantata)
SATB,acap oct BOOSEY 5899 $.40
(W51)
Lazy June (from Spring Cantata)
SATB,acap oct BOOSEY 5898 $.40
(W52)
May (from Spring Cantata)
SATB,acap oct BOOSEY 5897 $.40
(W53)
Succession Of The Four Sweet Months
(from Spring Cantata)
SATB,acap oct BOOSEY 5895 $.40
(W54)

WASSAIL ALL OVER THE TOWN see Tate

WASSAIL SONG see Vaughan Williams,
Ralph

WASSERMANN see Strobl, Otto

WAT DE TOEKOMST BRENGE MOGE
(De Wolff) mix cor/unis,org HEER 1512
s.p. (W55)

WATCH WHAT HAPPENS
SSA CIMINO $.40 (W56)
SA CIMINO $.40 (W57)
TTBB CIMINO $.40 (W58)
SATB CIMINO $.40 (W59)

WATCHER, THE see Newbury

WATER AND THE FIRE, THE see Milner,
  Anthony

WATERLOO see Anderson, Stig

WATERMILL, THE see Binge, Ronald

WATERS, CHARLES F.
  Before The Ending Of The Day
    SATB STAINER 3.0761.1 $.40   (W60)

WATERS OF KANE, THE see Barati, George

WATKINSON, PERCY GERD (1918-   )
  Lieder Vor Tag *CC7L
    mix cor (med) sc SCHOTTS C 40 753
    s.p.   (W61)

WATSON, HELEN
  Night
    SSA (med) FITZSIMONS 3036 $.25
                                  (W62)

WAY YOU LOOK TONIGHT
  SSA CIMINO $.40   (W63)
  SATB CIMINO $.40   (W64)
  TTBB CIMINO $.40   (W65)

WAYFARING STRANGER *folk,US
  (Mechem, Kirke) TBB FISCHER,C CM 7872
  $.35   (W66)

WAYNE
  Laughing On The Outside (Crying On
    The Inside) *see Raleigh

WAYS OF LOVE, THE see Brahms, Johannes,
  Weg Der Liebe

WAYWARD PILGRIM see Bottje, Will Gay

WAYWARD WIND
  SSA CIMINO $.40   (W67)
  SA CIMINO $.40   (W68)
  TTBB CIMINO $.40   (W69)

WAYWARD WIND, THE
  SATB CIMINO $.40   (W70)

WE ARE AMERICANS see Mitchell, Randy

WE ARE SINGING see Kabelac, Miloslav,
  Zpivame

WE ARE THE MUSIC MAKERS see Fisher

WE ARE THE SONS see Gerlitz, Eugene

WE BUILD A LAND see Haufrecht,
  [Herbert]

WE KISS IN A SHADOW see Rodgers,
  Richard

WE MAY NEVER PASS THIS WAY AGAIN see
  Seals

WE PLEDGE ALLEGIANCE see Johnson,
  Derric

WE SEE THAT MEN DO EVEN see Arcadelt,
  Jacob, Nous Voyons Que Les Hommes

WE SHALL MARCH AND MARCH AND NOTHING
  SHALL STOP US see Drejsl, Radim,
  Jdem A Jdem A Nic Nas Nezastavi

WE SING AMERICA
  SATB CIMINO $.40   (W71)

WE SING OF IDAHO
  SATB CIMINO $.50   (W72)

WE STOOD ON THE WALL see Lewis, Peter
  T.

WE, THE PEOPLE! see Yahres, Samuel C.

WE WANT PEACE see Cenek, Bohumil,
  Chceme Mir

WE WISH YOU A MERRY CHRISTMAS *Xmas
  (Kirk) 3pt PRO ART 2777 $.40   (W73)

WEARY LOT IS THINE, A see Shearer, C.M.

WEATHERLY
  Need To Be, The
    (Boyd) SATB WARNER CH0790 $.40
                                  (W74)
    (Boyd) SSA WARNER CQ0790 $.40 (W75)

WEBB
  All I Know *pop
    (Boyd) SSA,opt perc WARNER
    WB-331 183 $.40   (W76)
    (Boyd) SATB,opt perc WARNER
    WB-330 187 $.40   (W77)

  Everybody Gets To Go To The Moon
    *pop
    (Slater) SATB WARNER WB-316 187
    $.50   (W78)
    (Slater) SSA WARNER WB-317 183 $.50
                                  (W79)

WEBB (cont'd.)
  MacArthur Park *pop
    (Burroughs; Sewell) SATB,opt brass
    WARNER WB-327 187   (W80)
    (Burroughs; Sewell) SSA,opt 4brass
    WARNER WB-328 183   (W81)

WEBB, GEORGE JAMES (1803-1830)
  Dozen Rounds, A *see Mason, Lowell

WEBB, JIMMY
  By The Time I Get To Phoenix
    (Joyce, Jimmy) SATB STUDIO V724
    $.90 see from Songs Of Jim Webb
                                  (W82)
  Paper Cup
    (Joyce, Jimmy) SATB STUDIO V724
    $.90 see from Songs Of Jim Webb
                                  (W83)
  Songs Of Jim Webb *see By The Time I
    Get To Phoenix; Paper Cup; Up, Up
    And Away   (W84)

  Up, Up And Away
    (Azelton, Phil) SATB,pno,inst
    (jazz, includes recording and 14
    choral octavos) LEONARD-US
    07258500 $14.95   (W85)
    (Joyce, Jimmy) SATB STUDIO V724
    $.90 see from Songs Of Jim Webb
                                  (W86)

WEBER
  Lutzows Wilde Verwegene Jagd
    see Sichers Teutschland, Schlafst
    Du Noch?

WEBER, BEN (1916-   )
  Ah, Dear Heart *Op.43,No.1
    SATB,acap AM.COMP.AL. $2.20   (W87)

WEBER, BERNHARD (1912-1974)
  Ach, Vernimm Diesen Ton
    men cor sc SCHOTTS C 42 221 s.p.
    see from Drei Bitt- Und
    Lobgesange   (W88)

  Alter Und Neuer Wein "Der Alte Ist
    Noch Lang Nicht Aus"
    men cor sc SCHOTTS C 41 279 s.p.
                                  (W89)

  Auf Erden Gehest Du
    men cor sc SCHOTTS C 42 222 s.p.,
    voc pt SCHOTTS C 42 223, 01-02
    s.p. see from Drei Bitt- Und
    Lobgesange   (W90)

  Auf Hoher See "Ein Schifflein Klein"
    *see In Mezo Al Mar

  Auld Lang Syne *folk,Scot
    "Die Schone Alte Zeit" [Eng/Ger]
    mix cor (easy) sc SCHOTTS
    CHBL 380 s.p.   (W91)

  Chevaliers De La Table Ronde *folk,
    Fr
    "Der Zecher "Bruder Ihr An Der
    Tafelrunde"" [Ger/Fr] TTBB sc
    SCHOTTS C 38 974 s.p., voc pt
    SCHOTTS C 38 975, 01-02 s.p.
                                  (W92)

  Danz, Danz, Quieselchen
    jr cor sc SCHOTTS CHBL 586 s.p.
                                  (W93)

  Dass Zwei Sich Herzlich Lieben
    men cor sc SCHOTTS CHBL 86 s.p.
                                  (W94)

  Den Gefallenen "Unter Den Kreuzen"
    men cor sc SCHOTTS CHBL 124 s.p.
                                  (W95)

  Der Kehraus
    mix cor sc SCHOTTS C 43 439 s.p.
                                  (W96)

  Der Minnebote: Es Flog Ein
    men cor,acap TONOS 22 s.p.   (W97)

  Der Zauberlehrling "Hat Der Alte
    Hexenmeister"
    TTBB sc SCHOTTS C 39 668 s.p., voc
    pt SCHOTTS C 39 669, 01-02 s.p.
                                  (W98)

  Der Zecher "Bruder Ihr An Der
    Tafelrunde" *see Chevaliers De
    La Table Ronde

  Die Heinzelmannchen Zu Koln (from
    Cvjy) folk
    mix cor,pno s.p. sc BREITKOPF-W
    PB 4983, cor pts BREITKOPF-W
    CHB 4938   (W99)

  Die Kusse "Als Ich Aus Eigennutz
    Elise"
    men cor sc SCHOTTS C 39 257 s.p.
                                  (W100)

  Die Musik Allein
    men cor&jr cor,acap sc,cor pts
    TONOS 3815 s.p.   (W101)
    men cor,acap TONOS 3915 s.p. (W102)

  Die Schone Alte Zeit *see Auld Lang
    Syne

WEBER, BERNHARD (cont'd.)
  Drei Bitt- Und Lobgesange *see Ach,
    Vernimm Diesen Ton; Auf Erden
    Gehest Du; Zeitchoral "Gross Ist
    Aller Menschheit Not"   (W103)

  Dreimal Wein "Wer Kein Madchen Hat"
    men cor sc SCHOTTS C 41 682 s.p.
                                  (W104)

  Ehespruch "Wer Sich Mit Einem Weib
    Verbindt"
    men cor sc SCHOTTS C 38 347 s.p.
                                  (W105)

  Eia Beia Wiegenstroh
    4pt jr cor,acap sc SCHOTTS CHBL 587
    s.p.   (W106)

  Go Down Moses *spir
    [Eng] men cor sc SCHOTTS CHBL 213
    s.p.   (W107)

  Heute Hier - Morgen Dort
    mix cor (med easy) sc SCHOTTS
    C 40 073 s.p.   (W108)

  Hochzeitslied "Hahnenfuss Und
    Frauenschuh"
    mix cor (med) sc SCHOTTS CHBL 287 s.p.
                                  (W109)

  In Mezo Al Mar
    "Auf Hoher See "Ein Schifflein
    Klein"" [Ger/It] TTB&men cor,opt
    soli sc SCHOTTS C 40 846 s.p.,
    cor pts SCHOTTS C 40 847, 01-02
    s.p.   (W110)

  Kinderkuche
    jr cor sc SCHOTTS CHBL 588 s.p.
                                  (W111)

  Kleine Tanzballade "Jung Elsbeth
    Liebte Mich Nicht So Sehr"
    SATB (med) sc SCHOTTS C 40 483
    s.p., voc pt SCHOTTS C 40 484A-B
    s.p.   (W112)

  Kling Auf, Mein Lied
    4pt men cor,acap/pno/2horn&3trp&
    3trom&tuba sc SCHOTTS C 38 777
    s.p., cor pts SCHOTTS CHBL 74
    s.p., ipa   (W113)
    mix cor (med) sc SCHOTTS CHBL 359
    s.p.   (W114)

  Leichter Sinn
    men cor,acap TONOS 3916 s.p. (W115)

  Lob Der Geliebten "Seht Meiner
    Liebsten Braune Augen"
    see Zwei Flamische Volksweisen

  Moselwein "Reben, Reben, So Weit Man
    Schaut"
    men cor sc SCHOTTS C 40 564 s.p.
                                  (W116)

  Nocturno "Nacht Ist Es"
    men cor sc SCHOTTS C 38 759 s.p.
                                  (W117)

  O Rhein, Du Heiliger Strom
    4pt men cor,acap/3horn&3trp&3trom&
    tuba&timp voc sc SCHOTTS C 40 751
    s.p., cor pts SCHOTTS C 39 258
    s.p., ipa   (W118)

  Schone Jungfrau "Schone Jungfrau,
    Will Dir Klagen"
    see Zwei Flamische Volksweisen

  Streitlied Zwischen Leben Und Tod "So
    Spricht Das Leben"
    TTBB sc SCHOTTS C 40 199 s.p., voc
    pt SCHOTTS C 40 200, 01-02 s.p.
                                  (W119)

  Trink Mir Mit Deinen Augen Zu
    [Eng/Ger] men cor sc SCHOTTS
    CHBL 169 s.p.   (W120)

  Trinklied "Ich Weiss Es Wohl, Der
    Wein Ist Gift"
    men cor sc SCHOTTS CHBL 53 s.p.
                                  (W121)

  Voglein Schwermut "Ein Schwarzes
    Voglein Fliegt Uber Die Welt"
    men cor sc SCHOTTS CHBL 81 s.p.
                                  (W122)

  Wieviel Schonheit Ist Auf Erden
    men cor sc SCHOTTS C 38 202 s.p.
                                  (W123)

  Zeitchoral "Gross Ist Aller
    Menschheit Not"
    men cor sc SCHOTTS C 42 220 s.p.
    see from Drei Bitt- Und
    Lobgesange   (W124)

  Zu Frankfurt An Der Oder
    mix cor (med easy) sc SCHOTTS
    C 40 485 s.p.   (W125)

  Zwei Flamische Volksweisen *folk
    [Ger] men cor sc SCHOTTS
    CHBL 154A-B s.p.
    contains: Lob Der Geliebten "Seht
    Meiner Liebsten Braune Augen";
    Schone Jungfrau "Schone
    Jungfrau, Will Dir Klagen"
                                  (W126)

WEBER, BERNHARD ANSELM (1766-1821)
Wand'rers Nachtgebet
men cor,acap TONOS 6329 s.p. (W127)

WEBER, CARL MARIA VON (1786-1826)
Die Sonn' Erwacht
men cor,acap TONOS 6319 s.p. (W128)

Es Blinken So Lustig Die Sterne (from
Preziosa)
4pt mix cor,pno/fl,3vln,vcl (med
easy) sc SCHOTTS C 39 499 s.p.,
cor pts SCHOTTS C 39 500 s.p.,
voc pt SCHOTTS C 39 504A-E s.p.
(W129)
(Hecht, Gustav) 4pt men cor,pno,
3vln,vcl,opt fl cor pts SCHOTTS
C 39 503 s.p., ipa (W130)
(Hecht, Gustav) SSA,pno/fl&3vln&vcl
(med easy) sc SCHOTTS C 42 402
s.p., cor pts SCHOTTS C 42 402-01
s.p., ipa (W131)

Im Wald (from Preziosa)
(Klink, Waldemar) mix cor (easy) sc
SCHOTTS CHBL 276 s.p. (W132)

Jagerchor (from Der Freischutz)
men cor,pno sc,cor pts TONOS 4270
s.p. (W133)

Jagerchor: Die Tale Dampfen
men cor,acap TONOS 6320 s.p. (W134)

Jagerchor "Was Gleicht Wohl Auf
Erden" (from Der Freischutz)
men cor sc SCHOTTS CHBL 10 s.p.
(W135)

Song Of Slumber
(Plott) TTBB BRODT DC 2 $.24 (W136)

Wanderlied "Die Sonn' Erwacht, Mit
Ihrer Pracht" (from Preziosa)
(Heim, Ignaz) men cor sc SCHOTTS
CHBL 31 s.p. (W137)

WEBER, LUDWIG (1891-1947)
Komm Geist Aus Heiliger Fern! "Horch
Auf, Bruder"
mix cor (med easy) sc SCHOTTS
CHBL 256 s.p. (W138)

Liebe "Lass Die Wurzel Unseres
Handelns Liebe Sein"
SSATTBB,org/4horn,2trp,3trom,tuba
(med) sc SCHOTTS C 33 470 s.p.,
voc pt SCHOTTS C 33 471A-C s.p.,
ipa (W139)

WEBER, WILHELM (1859-1918)
Auf Der Teck
men cor,acap TONOS 245 s.p. (W140)

WECHSELLIED BEIM WEINE see Genzmer,
Harald

WECHSELLIED ZUM TANZ see Brahms,
Johannes

WECKRUF "WACH AUF, ES KOMMT DER TAG
HERAUF" see Schwarz-Schilling,
Reinhard

WEDD, ERIC (1905-   )
Bobby Shafto
unis jr cor,pno,strings,perc,rec,
opt. 3 harmonicas (easy) sc,voc
sc,voc pt SCHOTTS RS 31 s.p., ipa
(W141)

WEDDING SONG *Marriage,pop
(Cassey) "There Is Love" SSA WARNER
WB-305 183 $.40 (W142)
(Cassey) "There Is Love" SATB WARNER
WB-304 187 $.40 (W143)

WEDDING SONG, THE see Willan, Healey,
C'est Le Mon Dous Plaisir

WEDIG, HANS JOSEF (1898-   )
Die Quelle "Stehe Still, Wandrer
men cor sc SCHOTTS C 39 807 s.p.
(W144)
Duschkas Lied "Springe Pferdchen"
TTBB sc SCHOTTS C 41 292 s.p., voc
pt SCHOTTS C 41 293, 01-02 s.p.
(W145)

WEE COOPER O' FIFE, THE *folk,Scot
(Roberton, Hugh S.) SATB,acap
ROBERTON 61089 s.p. (W146)

WEE WILLIE WINKIE *folk,Scot
(Roberton, Hugh S.) unis,pno ROBERTON
75022 s.p. (W147)

WEELKES
Come, Let's Begin
(Shipp) SSA SCHIRM.G LG51662 $.30
(W148)
Ha Ha! The World Doth Pass
(Shipp) SSA SCHIRM.G LG51644 $.30
(W149)
On The Plains, Fairy Trains
(Deller) SSATB SCHIRM.G 12044 $.40
(W150)

WEELKES (cont'd.)

Take Here My Heart
(Barrie) SSATB SCHIRM.G LG51736
$.45 (W151)

WEELKES, THOMAS (ca. 1575-1623)
Airs Or Fantastic Spirits (1608) EM
Vol. 13 *CC25L
3-6pt mix cor/3-6pt men cor STAINER
3.1913.1 $8.50 (W152)

All At Once Well Met Fair Ladies
(Hall, Wm.D.) SSATB,2trp&horn&
2trom/fl&S rec&2T rec&bsn/fl&ob&
clar&horn&bsn,opt hpsd NATIONAL
CMS-106 $.50 (W153)

Balletts And Madrigals To Five Voices
(1598, 1608) EM Vol. 10 *CC24L
5pt STAINER 3.1910.1 $8.50 (W154)

Madrigals Of Five And Six Parts
(1600) EM 11 & 12 *CC20L
5-6pt STAINER 3.1911.1 $11.50
(W155)

Madrigals To Three, Four, Five And
Six Voices (1597) EM Vol. 9
*CC23L,madrigal
3-6pt STAINER 3.1909.1 $10.25
(W156)

Since Robin Hood
SAB,acap EGTVED MS7B11 s.p.
contains also: Tan Ta Ra Cries
Mars (W157)

Tan Ta Ra Cries Mars
see Weelkes, Thomas, Since Robin
Hood

Those Spots Upon My Lady's Face
SSAAB STAINER 3.0733.1 $.50 (W158)

WEEP NOT MY WANTON see Russell, Welford

WEEP NOW see Le Jeune, Claude

WEEP YE NO MORE SAD FOUNTAINS see
Thorpe, Raymond

WEEP YOU NO MORE, SAD FOUNTAINS see
Horton

WEEP YOU NO MORE SAD FOUNTAINS see
Mozart, Wolfgang Amadeus

WEG DER LIEBE see Brahms, Johannes

WEG, WEG see Biebl, Franz

WEHLE, GERHARD FURCHTEGOTT (1884-1974)
Grossstadt
men cor,Bar solo,orch voc sc RIES
rental, ipr (W159)

Singe! *Op.61,No.1
men cor RIES sc s.p., voc pt s.p.
(W160)

WEHMUT see Schubert, Franz (Peter)

WEIB, KOMM NACH HAUS *folk
(Kammeier, H.) [Ger] 4pt mix cor
MERSEBURG EM9234 s.p. (W161)

WEIGENLIED "VOR DER TURE" see Haas,
Joseph

WEIGL, KARL (1881-1949)
Black Cat
SATB,pno AM.COMP.AL. $1.38 (W162)

Four Seasons, The *see Weigl, Vally

Six Children's Songs *Op.11, CC6U
2pt wom cor/2pt jr cor,pno
AM.COMP.AL. $3.85 (W163)

WEIGL, VALLY
Bless The Four Corners Of This House
SATB,pno AM.COMP.AL. $.83 (W164)

Day And Night
SATB,Mez solo,acap AM.COMP.AL.
$1.38 (W165)

Fairy Song
3pt wom cor,acap AM.COMP.AL. $1.38
(W166)

Four Choral Songs On Death And Man
*CC4U
SATB,acap AM.COMP.AL. $4.68 (W167)

Four Seasons, The (composed with
Weigl, Karl)
jr cor/SSA,pno AM.COMP.AL. sc
$9.90, cor pts $4.40 (W168)

Four Songs *CC4U
jr cor/wom cor,pno AM.COMP.AL.
$1.10 (W169)

From Time And Eternity
SATB/SSATB,pno AM.COMP.AL. $1.38
(W170)

WEIGL, VALLY (cont'd.)

Gifts
SATB,pno AM.COMP.AL. $1.10 (W171)

In Just Spring
4pt mix cor,soli,acap AM.COMP.AL.
$1.38 (W172)

Madrigal
SSATB,acap AM.COMP.AL. $1.38 (W173)

Night Of Prayer
SATB,opt ST soli,acap AM.COMP.AL.
$3.58 (W174)

Not Avalon In April
SSA,acap AM.COMP.AL. $.55 (W175)

Ode To Beauty
SATB,horn,pno/strings sc
AM.COMP.AL. $3.30, ipa (W176)

Oh, Fair To See
SATB,acap AM.COMP.AL. $.83 (W177)

On Christmas Eve *Xmas
SATB,pno AM.COMP.AL. $.55 (W178)

Our World Is One
SATB,pno AM.COMP.AL. $.83 (W179)

Peace Hymn
SSA,pno AM.COMP.AL. $1.38 (W180)

Practical Earth Satellites
SATB,acap AM.COMP.AL. $3.30 (W181)

Road To Peace, The
unis,pno AM.COMP.AL. $.55 (W182)

Seven Rounds In Various Moods *CC7U,
round
3-4pt mix cor,acap AM.COMP.AL. $.83
(W183)

Song Of Hope, A
SSA,pno AM.COMP.AL. $1.38 (W184)

Song Of The Shadows, The
SATB,pno AM.COMP.AL. $1.38 (W185)

Still Will Be
SSATB,acap AM.COMP.AL. $.55 (W186)

Two Short Rounds *CC2U,canon
SSATB,acap AM.COMP.AL. $.55 (W187)

What Once The Heart Has Loved
SSA,acap AM.COMP.AL. $1.38 (W188)

Who Goes There Through The Night?
SATB,acap AM.COMP.AL. $.55 (W189)

Who Has Seen The Wind
SSA,fl/vln,pno sc AM.COMP.AL. $.55
(W190)

WEIHE DER HALLE see Edler, Robert

WEIHE DER NACHT "NACHTLICHE STILLE,
HEILIGE FULLE" see Rein, Walter

WEIHEGESANG see Schubert, Franz (Peter)

WEIHEGESANG see Wagner, Franz

WEIHELIED "FAHNE, DICH WEIHEN WIR" see
Zoll, Paul

WEIHELIED: IN DIESER FEIERSTUNDE see
Matthes, Rene

WEIHELIED UND HOCHGESANG see Koenig,
Franz

WEIHNACHTSLIED see Krietsch, Georg

WEIHNACHTSLIED see Schmid, Heinrich
Kaspar

WEIL
If Love, Like Spring, Can Come And Go
*Op.35,No.6 (from In Maytime)
(Boyd) SATB SCHIRM.G 51797 $.40
(W191)

No Tears Have We To Shed (from In
Maytime)
(Boyd) SATB SCHIRM.G LG51795 $.45
(W192)

On Meadow And Hillside
(Boyd) SATB SCHIRM.G LG51794 $.40
(W193)

Tears Are Idle And Said The Swallow
(from In Maytime)
(Boyd) SATB SCHIRM.G LG51796 $.40
(W194)

Ye Winds Of Winter
(Boyde) SATB SCHIRM.G LG51793 $.40
(W195)

WEIN HER, ES LEBE DIE WELT! "STIMMT
EURE SEELEN" see Fussan, Werner

WEIN IS LIEBE UND GESANG see Heuken,
Hans Jakob

WEIN IST STARKER ALS DAS WASSER see
    Biebl, Franz

WEIN UND WEIBER *folk
    (Zoll, P.) [Ger] 4pt men cor
    MERSEBURG EM9006 s.p.   (W196)

WEIN VOM ALTEN FASS see Edler, Robert

WEINE NUR NICHT see Trunk, Richard

WEINFAHRT see Thehos, Adam

WEINLEIN, NUN GANG EIN! see Hessenberg,
    Kurt

WEINLIED see Blass, Heinrich

WEINLIED see Seeger, Peter

WEINLIED: EIN KONIG IST DER WEIN see
    Silcher, Friedrich

WEINLUST see Biebl, Franz

WEINSCHROTER, SCHLAG DIE TROMMEL see
    Bresgen, Cesar

WEISMANN, WILHELM (1900-   )
    Canticum Canticorum *CCU
    5-6pt DEUTSCHER DVFM7640 s.p.
                                  (W197)

WEISS, GEORGE DAVID
    Can't Help Falling In Love *see
        Creatore, Luigi

    Let's Put It All Together
        (Metls, F.) SAB BIG3 $.45   (W198)
        (Metls, F.) SATB BIG3 $.45 (W199)
        (Metls, F.) SSA BIG3 $.45   (W200)

    Love Is The Answer
        (Simon, W.) SAB BIG3 $.50   (W201)
        (Simon, W.) SATB BIG3 $.50 (W202)
        (Simon, W.) SSA BIG3 $.50   (W203)
        (Simon, W.) SA/TB BIG3 $.50 (W204)

WEISS ICH EIN SCHONES ROSELEIN see
    Koenig, Franz

WEISS, KAREL (1862-1944)
    Triumfator *Op.20
    "Triumphant" [Czech] men cor,soli,
    3fl,2ob,2clar,2bsn,4horn,2trp,
    3trom,tuba,timp,perc,org,harp,
    strings CZECH s.p.   (W205)

    Triumphant *see Triumfator

WEISS MIR EIN BLUMLEIN BLAUE
    see Vier Alte Volkslieder-Im Neuen
        Gewand

WEISS MIR EIN BLUMLEIN BLAUE see
    Bornefeld, Helmut

WEISS MIR EIN BLUMLEIN BLAUE see Knab,
    Armin

WEISS MIR EIN BLUMLEIN BLAUE see
    Kuhlenthal, Fred

WEISS MIR EIN SCHONES ROSELEIN
    see Drei Alte Volkslieder-Neu
        Dargeboten

WEISS MIR EIN SCHONES ROSELEIN see
    Zipp, Friedrich

WEISSE VERLASSENHEIT "IN DER STILLE DES
    TRAUMES" see Genzmer, Harald

WEITE AUSSICHT see Sturmer, Bruno

WEITZENDORF, HEINZ
    Bei Den Funkern (from Alarm Fur Den
        Frieden)
    2pt jr cor,pno NEUE 1016 s.p.
                                  (W206)

WEIZENLIED see Edler, Robert

WELCH EIN WUNDER *folk
    (Felt, Gerhard) TTBB MOSELER M80 s.p.
    see from Abend An Der Memel (W207)

WELCKER, MAX
    Spielmanns Maienfahrt
    men cor,acap TONOS 237 s.p. (W208)

WELCOME TO ALL THE PLEASURES see
    Purcell, Henry

WELCOME TO MY MORNING see Denver, John,
    Farewell Andromeda

WELCOME TO SPRING see Belcher, Supply

WELKER, GOTTHARD
    Auf, Du Junger Wandersmann
    men cor&jr cor,acap sc,cor pts
        TONOS 568 s.p.   (W209)

    Kleiner Marsch
    men cor&jr cor,acap sc,cor pts
        TONOS 1846 s.p.   (W210)

WE'LL FIND AMERICA see Pottle, Sam

WE'LL RANT AND WE'LL ROAR
    (Kunz, Alfred) TTBB (med easy)
    WATERLOO $.40   (W211)

WE'LL RANT AND WE'LL ROAR see Ridout,
    Godfrey

WELTENFRIEDE see Krietsch, Georg

WELTSCHOPFUNG see Edler, Robert

WENN A ALT FRAU SCHNUBBT *folk,Ger
    (Fischer, Theo) men cor,acap TONOS
    144 s.p.   (W212)

WENN ALLE BRUNNLEIN *folk,Ger
    (Biebl, Franz) men cor,acap TONOS 170
    s.p.   (W213)

WENN ALLE BRUNNLEIN FLIESSEN
    see Vier Alte Volkslieder-Im Neuen
        Gewand
    see Wenn Ich Ein Voglein War

WENN ALLE BRUNNLEIN FLIESSEN see
    Dietrich, Fritz

WENN ALLE BRUNNLEIN FLIESSEN see
    Gebhard, Hans

WENN ALLE BRUNNLEIN FLIESSEN see Jage,
    Rolf-Diether

WENN ALLE BRUNNLEIN FLIESSEN see Lang,
    Hans

WENN ALLE BRUNNLEIN FLIESSEN see Marx,
    Karl

WENN DAS GLUCK DICH HEUT VERACHT see
    Lasso, Orlando di

WENN DER DONALD MACDONALD "ES LEBTE IN
    SCHOTTLAND" see Merath, Siegfried

WENN DER FRUHLING see Schlemm, Gustav
    Adolf

WENN DER ZEITEN KREIS SICH FULLT see
    Edler, Robert

WENN DIE BETTELEUTE TANZEN see Lang,
    Hans

WENN DIE BETTELLEUTE TANZEN see
    Hessenberg, Kurt

WENN DIE BUNTEN FAHNEN WEHEN see Lang,
    Hans

WENN DIE BUNTEN FAHNEN WEHEN see
    Zschiecha, Alf

WENN DU MICH LIEBTEST, GEVATTERIN "O,
    EUER HAHN, GEWATTERIN" see Zoll,
    Paul

WENN ES WINTER WIRD see Becker, Horst

WENN I AU KEIN SCHATZ NET HAB see
    Kuhlenthal, Fred

WENN ICH DEINEN NAMEN see Edler, Robert

WENN ICH DURCH DIE BERGE MEINER HEIMAT
    FAHRE see Poos, Heinrich

WENN ICH EIN KLEIN WALDVOGELEIN WAR see
    Spitta, Heinrich

WENN ICH EIN VOGLEIN WAR
    see Vier Alte Volkslieder-Im Neuen
        Gewand
    (Wangenheim, Volker) mix cor
    HOFMEISTER G2206 s.p. contains
    also: Wenn Alle Brunnlein Fliessen
                                  (W214)

WENN ICH GEDENK see Regnard, Jacob

WENN KUHL DER MORGEN ATMET see Frey,
    Oskar

WENN MEIN MADEL TANZEN MAG see Frey,
    Oskar

WENN MER SONNTAGS see Lang, Hans

WENN MIR UNTERM FIEDELBOGEN see Edler,
    Robert

WENN OSTERN WIRD AM TIBERSTROM see
    Verling

WENN SICH JUNGE HERZEN HEBEN see
    Bresgen, Cesar

WENN SIE KOMMT see She'll Be Coming

WENN WAS IRGEND IST GESCHEHEN" see
    Pepping, Ernst

WENN WIR HINAUSZIEHN see Donati,
    Baldassare

WER A GELD HAT
    (Deutsch, Walter) mix cor DOBLINGER
    G 682 s.p. see from Acht Lieder Aus
    Wien   (W215)

WER ANDERN EINE GRUBE GRABT see Orrel,
    Max

WER FREUDIG TUT see Schwarz-Schilling,
    Reinhard

WER FROHLICH SEIN WILL see Haus, Karl

WER FROHLICH WILL SINGEN see Ophoven,
    Hermann

WER GEHT MIT, JUCHHE, UBER SEE? *folk,
    Dut
    (Brune, W.) men cor,acap TONOS 52
    s.p.   (W216)

WER HAT ZEIT see Zoll, Paul

WER HAT ZEIT? NIEMAND HAT ZEIT? see
    Seeger, Peter

WER HIER MIT UNS see Schneider, Walther

WER IM WERK DEN LOHN GEFUNDEN see Etti,
    Karl

WER JE GELEBT IN LIEBESARMEN see Knab,
    Armin

WER JETZIG ZEITEN LEBEN WILL *folk
    (Fischer, Theo) men cor,acap TONOS 50
    s.p.   (W217)

WER JETZIG ZEITEN LEBEN WILL" see
    Mohler, Philipp

WER LIEB UND LUST ZU MUSIK HAT see
    Widmann, Erasmus

WER LUST UND LIEB ZUR MUSIK HAT see
    Widmann, Erasmus

WER MUSICAM VERACHTEN TUT see Staden,
    Johann

WER NICHT SCHLAFT UND WER NICHT RUHT
    see Biebl, Franz

WER RUFT? see Krietsch, Georg

WER SICH DIE MUSIK ERKEIST see
    Doppelbauer, Josef Friedrich

WER SICH DIE MUSIK ERKIEST see
    Hindemith, Paul

WER SICH DIE MUSIK ERKIEST see
    Hindemith, Paul

WER SICH DIE MUSIK ERKIEST see Rein,
    Walter

WER SO EIN FAULES GRETCHEN HAT see
    Zipp, Friedrich

WER STEIGT FUR MICH ZU HIMMEL see Wert,
    Giaches de

WER ZUM TEUFEL WIRD SICH SORGEN "BANOD,
    BIRO SCHULZE" see Bresgen, Cesar

WERBUNG see Strecke, Gerhard

WERBUNG: O MAIDLE, DU BIST see Silcher,
    Friedrich

WERDIN, EBERHARD (1911-   )
    Das Marchen Von Den Tanzenden
        Schweinen
    1-3pt jr cor,11 narrators,3treb
    inst,bvl, xylophone (easy) sc,cor
    pts SCHOTTS B 158 s.p., ipa
                                  (W218)
    Der Buhle Im Keller "Den Liebsten
        Bulen"
    see Zwei Trinklieder

    Der Edelste Brunnen "Man Sagt Wol"
    see Zwei Trinklieder

    Die Heinzelmannchen
    jr cor,treb inst,perc (med easy)
    sc,cor pts SCHOTTS B 126 s.p.,
    ipa   (W219)

    Drei Chore Nach Mittelhochdeutschen
        Texten *see Es Stund Ein Frowe
        Alleine; Ich Will Truren Varen
        Lan; Reigen Der Verschmahten
        Madchen "Swaz Hie Gat Umbe"
                                  (W220)
    Du Bist Min
    4-6pt mix cor,acap (med easy) sc
    SCHOTTS C 38 034 s.p.   (W221)

    Ereignis
    see Vier Kinderlieder

    Es Stund Ein Frowe Alleine
    4pt wom cor,acap (med) sc SCHOTTS
    C 38 038 s.p. see from Drei Chore

WHICHER, JAMES
There Is A Lady Sweet And Kind
  SATB (med easy) WATERLOO $.40
                    (W261)

WHILE WE'RE YOUNG see Wilder

WHIP-POOR-WILL
  TTBB CIMINO $.40   (W262)

WHISKY see Schaefers, Anton

WHISTLE, DAUGHTER, WHISTLE
  (Olson) SSAA oct SCHMITT 2591 $.45
                    (W263)

WHITE
  Three Madrigals For Mixed Chorus
    *CC3U,madrigal
    mix cor SCHIRM.G 2924 $1.50 (W264)

WHITE CHRISTMAS see Berlin, Irving

WHITE DOVE, THE see Anderson, [William H.]

WHITE, HERBERT D.
  Good Day, Herr Beethoven
    SA (med easy) WATERLOO $.35 (W265)

  Indian Lullaby
    unis (easy) WATERLOO $.30   (W266)

  Spring
    unis (med easy) WATERLOO $.30
                    (W267)

WHITE KNIGHT'S SONG, THE see Fine

WHITE LENT *folk
  (Czajkowski, Michael) SATB STANDARD
  C623MX4 $.50   (W268)

WHITE, R.
  Blow On Your Trumpet
    unis oct SCHMITT 366 $.35   (W269)

WHITE ROSE, A see Gold, Ernest

WHITECOTTON, SHIRLEY
  Two Idylls *CC2U
    SSA GALAXY 1.2530.1 $.25   (W270)

WHITEHEAD, ALFRED
  Challenge To Free Men
    unis GALAXY 1.1831.1 $.30   (W271)

WHITMAN
  From This Hour, Freedom
    SATB LEONARD-US 08016800 $.50
                    (W272)

WHO
  SSA CIMINO $.40   (W273)
  SAB CIMINO $.40   (W274)
  SSAA CIMINO $.40   (W275)
  SA CIMINO $.40   (W276)
  TTBB CIMINO $.40   (W277)
  SATB CIMINO $.40   (W278)

WHO ARE YOU see Pooler

WHO CAN I TURN TO see Bricusse, Leslie

WHO CAN RETELL? see Adler

WHO CUT THE WOOD? see Brandvik

WHO DID BRING THEE, KNIGHT SO LONELY?
  see Encina, Juan Del, Quien Te
  Trajo, Caballero?

WHO DO YOU THINK YOU ARE? see Scott, C.

WHO GOES THERE THROUGH THE NIGHT? see
  Weigl, Vally

WHO HAS SEEN THE WIND? see Shearer,
  C.M.

WHO HAS SEEN THE WIND see Weigl, Vally

WHO HE? see Cohn, James

WHO IS SYLVIA? see Gardner

WHO KILLED COCK ROBIN?
  (De Cormier) SATB SCHIRM.G LG 51710
  $.35   (W279)

WHO SEEKETH BEAUTY see Spencer, M.

WHO SLEEPETH HERE? see Lassus, Roland
  de (Orlandus)

WHO WILL ANSWER
  SATB CIMINO $.40   (W280)
  TTBB CIMINO $.40   (W281)

WHO'S THAT TAPPING AT MY DOOR? see
  James, Will

WHO'S WHO IN THE ZOO see Berger, Jean

WHY DO I LOVE YOU
  SA CIMINO $.40   (W282)
  SSAA CIMINO $.40   (W283)
  SAB CIMINO $.40   (W284)
  SSA CIMINO $.40   (W285)
  TTBB CIMINO $.40   (W286)

SATB CIMINO $.40   (W287)

WHY I LOVE HER see Liebert

WHY NOT YOU? (GIVE AWAY) see Johnson

WHY SO PALE AND WAN? see Mills, Charles

WHY WAS I BORN
  SSA CIMINO $.40   (W288)
  SAB CIMINO $.40   (W289)
  SA CIMINO $.40   (W290)
  TTBB CIMINO $.40   (W291)

WHY WEEPS, ALAS! MY LADY LOVE see
  Pearsall, Robert Lucas de

WI' A HUNDRED PIPERS AN' A' see
  Simpson, John

WICK, FRED
  Old Jonah Had A "Whale Of A Time" In
    A Whale
    TTBB oct SCHMITT W144 $.30 (W292)

WICK, VOJTECH (1908-)
  Detske Tanecne Piesne *CCU
    wom cor,pno SLOV.HUD.FOND s.p.
                    (W293)

WICK'S CHORUS BOOK FOR BOY'S GLEE CLUB
  *CCU
  boy cor oct SCHMITT $.85   (W294)

WIDDECOMBE FAIR *folk
  (McCarthy, John) SAB,soli (easy)
  MCAFEE M7002 $.40   (W295)

WIDDER see Strobl, Otto

WIDEWIDEWENNE see Lang, Hans

WIDEWIDEWENNE see Marx, Karl

WIDMANN, ERASMUS (1572-1634)
  Ausgewahlte Werke *CCU
    (Reichart, Georg) mix cor (med)
    cloth SCHOTTS
    DAS ERBE DEUTSCHER MUSIK, SONDERREIHE BAND 3
    s.p.   (W296)

  O Musica, Liebliche Kunst *canon
    see Senfl, Ludwig, Hans Beutler Der
    Wollt Reiten Aus
    SAA&unis men cor,acap MOSELER LB491
    s.p. contains also: Staden,
    Johann, Wer Musicam Verachten Tut
    (3-8pt)   (W297)

  Vinum Schenk Ein
    (Paul) men cor,acap TONOS 3333 s.p.
                    (W298)

  Wer Lieb Und Lust Zu Musik Hat
    SSSA,acap MOSELER LB1006 s.p.
    contains also: Marenzio, Luca,
    Kommt, Ihr Lieblichen Stimmen
    Alle (SSA,acap)   (W299)

  Wer Lust Und Lieb Zur Musik Hat
    men cor sc SCHOTTS C 38 814 s.p.
                    (W300)

  Zu Miltenberg Am Maine
    mix cor (easy) sc SCHOTTS CHBL 281
    s.p.   (W301)
    (Klink, Waldemar) men cor sc
    SCHOTTS CHBL 40 s.p.   (W302)

WIDOW BIRD see Sweetman, Paul

WIE BENEID ICH DEN MANN see Reutter,
  Hermann

WIE DIE SAITEN DER GITARRE see Matthus,
  Siegfried

WIE IST DOCH DIE ERDE SO SCHON see
  Walther, Georg

WIE KRISTALLENER SCHIMMER see
  Strohbach, Siegfried, Kristallen
  Den Fina

WIE LIEBLICH SCHALLT see Silcher,
  Friedrich

WIE LIEBLICH SCHALLT DURCH BUSCH UND
  WALD see Poos, Heinrich

WIE MAN EINEN VOGEL MALT "MALE ZUERST
  EINEN KAFIG" see Genzmer, Harald

WIE MIR IST see Martinu, Bohuslav, Jak
  Je Mne

WIE NUN, IHR HERREN? see Schutz,
  Heinrich

WIE SCHON BLUHT UNS DER MAIEN see Jage,
  Rolf-Diether

WIE SCHON BLUHT UNS DER MAIEN see
  Kelling, Hajo

WIE SCHON BLUHT UNS DER MAIEN see Marx,
  Karl

WIE SCHON IST DER MAI see Desch, Rudolf

WIE SCHON IST'S DRAUSSEN *folk
  (Doppelbauer, Josef Friedrich) mix
  cor DOBLINGER G 699 s.p.   (W303)

WIE SIE SO SANFTRUH'N
  see Vier Grablieder

WIE WEH TUT MIR MEIN SCHEIDEN see
  Franck, Melchior

WIEGENLIED *folk
  (Weber, Bernhard) [Ger] 4pt mix cor
  MERSEBURG EM9254 s.p.   (W304)

WIEGENLIED see Gal, Hans, O Can Ye Sew
  Chushions

WIEGENLIED see Reutter, Hermann

WIEGENLIED AN DER BERGSTRASSE see
  Krietsch, Georg

WIEGENLIED AN DER BERGSTRASSE "TROPF,
  TROPF TAU" see Genzmer, Harald

WIEGENLIED AUS PORTUGAL *folk
  (Fischbach, Klaus) wom cor,acap sc
  BREITKOPF-W CHB 4917 s.p. see from
  Sieben Europaische Volkslieder
                    (W305)

WIEGENLIED DER MUTTER GOTTES see Henze,
  Hans Werner

WIEGENLIED "GUTEN ABEND, GUT' NACHT"
  see Brahms, Johannes

WIEGENLIED "KLEINE LIEDER WIEGEN LEISE"
  see Sturmer, Bruno

WIEGENLIED LULLABY see Mussorgsky,
  Modest

WIEGENLIED "SCHLAFE PRINZCHEN, SCHLAF
  EIN" see Mozart, Wolfgang Amadeus

WIEGENLIED "SUMSALA, SUMSALA" see Haas,
  Joseph

WIEGENLIED "WASCH DIE FUSSCHEN MEINEM
  KIND" see Zoll, Paul

WIESLANDER, INGVAR
  Kunde Jag Folja Dig
    mix cor GEHRMANS KRB447   (W306)

  Moln
    mix cor GEHRMANS KRB446   (W307)

WIEVIEL SCHONHEIT IST AUF ERDEN see
  Weber, Bernhard

WIGGLESWORTH, FRANK (1918-)
  Sleep Becalmed
    SATB,2fl,2ob,2clar,2horn,2trp,trom,
    perc,strings AM.COMP.AL. (W308)

WILBRANDT, JURGEN (1922-)
  Ein Sommerlied
    4pt mix cor,acap NEUE NM1005 s.p.
                    (W309)

WILBYE
  Ah, Thou Golden Month Of May
    (Kaplan) SATB SCHIRM.G LG51798 $.40
                    (W310)

WILBYE, JOHN (1574-1638)
  Adieu, Sweet Amaryllis *madrigal
    SATB,acap EGTVED MS14B4 s.p. (W311)

  First Set Of Madrigals (1598) EM Vol.
    6 *CC31L,madrigal
    cor STAINER 3.1906.1 $14.25 (W312)

  Fly Not So Swift
    SATB STAINER 3.0780.1 $.60 (W313)

  Her Hair The Net Of Golden Wire
    SSATTB STAINER 3.0726.1 $.50 (W314)

  Second Set Of Madrigals (1609) EM
    Vol. 7 *CCU
    cor STAINER 3.1907.1 $19.00 (W315)

  There Is A Jewel
    SAB,acap EGTVED MS7B10 s.p. (W316)

WILD
  I Still Believe In Tomorrow *pop
    (Scott) SA/TB BELWIN UC 716 $.40
                    (W317)

WILD HILLS OF CLARE see Bateman, Ronald

WILDBERGER, JACQUES (1922-)
  Epitaphe Pour Evariste Galois
    [Ger] speak cor,SBar,narrator,2fl,
    pic,2ob,2clar,bsn,3trp,4horn,
    3trom,tuba,6perc,pno,strings,
    electronic tape, English horn,
    bass clarinet, contrabassoon
    MODERN rental   (W318)

  Ihr Meint, Das Leben Sei Kurz
    mix cor,fl,clar,perc,harp,pno,2vln,
    vla,bvl, bass clarinet,
    contrabassoon MODERN rental

WILDBERGER, JACQUES (cont'd.)

(W319)

WILDER
Child Is Born, A (composed with
Jones, Thad) *pop
(Dedric, A.) SATB,opt perc KENDOR
$.35   (W320)
(Dedrick, A.) SSA,opt perc KENDOR
$.35   (W321)
(Dedrick, A.) SAB,opt perc KENDOR
$.35   (W322)

While We're Young (composed with
Palitz; Engvick) *pop
(Dedrick, A.) SSA,gtr KENDOR $.35 (W323)
(Dedrick, A.) SAB,gtr KENDOR $.30
(W324)

WILDFLOWER see Eilers, Joyce Elaine

WILDMAN, WESLEY
Shepherd Kept Sheep
unis (med easy) WATERLOO $.30
(W325)

WILHELM BUSCH-ZYKLUS see Lang, Hans

WILHELM, HEINZ (1912-   )
Schlectwetter-Kantate *cant
4pt mix cor,STB soli,2vln,vla,vcl,
bvl (med easy) sc,cor pts SCHOTTS
ED. 4244 s.p., ipa   (W326)

WILHELM, KARL
Fruhlingszeit
men cor,acap TONOS 6321 s.p. (W327)

WILKINSON, CHARLES A.
Beloved Canada
SATB HARRIS $.35   (W328)

WILKINSON, PHILIP G.
Ferryman, The
see Wilkinson, Philip G., Ships In
The Wind

House That Jack Built, The
unis EMI   (W329)

Land Of Sleep
unis EMI   (W330)

Poor Old Horse
unis EMI   (W331)

Ships In The Wind
unis EMI contains also: Ferryman,
The   (W332)

West Sussex Drinking Song
TBB EMI   (W333)

WILL ICH IN MEIN GARTLEIN GEHN see
Erdlen, Hermann

WILL YE NOT COME BACK AGAIN see
Simpson, John

WILL YOU COME see Kunz, Alfred

WILLAERT, ADRIAN (ca. 1490-1562)
Madonn' Io Non Lo So Perche Lo Fai
(Hall, Wm.D.) "Tell Me, Oh Mistress
Mine" SATB,acap/2trp&horn&trom/S
rec&2T rec&bsn/S rec&2T rec&vcl/
fl&ob&clar&bsn,opt hpsd NATIONAL
CMS 107 $.50   (W334)

Tell Me, Oh Mistress Mine *see
Madonn' Io Non Lo So Perche Lo
Fai

WILLAN, HEALEY (1880-1968)
Bird Of Love *see Rossignol Du Vert
Bocage

C'est Le Mon Dous Plaisir
"Wedding Song, The" SSA HARRIS $.25
(W335)

Clown Song, The
see Two Two-Part Songs

Domine, Salve Fac
"O Lord, Save Thy Servant
Elizabeth" SATB HARRIS $.35
(W336)

England, My England *see Pro Rege
Nostra

Le Miroir
"Mirror, The" SSA HARRIS $.25
(W337)

Le Navire De Bayonne
SSA HARRIS $.30   (W338)

Little Mother
"Si J'etain Petite Mere" SSA HARRIS
$.30   (W339)

Mirror, The *see Le Miroir

O Lord, Save Thy Servant Elizabeth
*see Domine, Salve Fac

WILLAN, HEALEY (cont'd.)
Passing By
SA HARRIS $.25   (W340)
SATB HARRIS $.35   (W341)
TTBB HARRIS $.35   (W342)

Pro Rege Nostra
"England, My England" SATB HARRIS
$.30   (W343)

Rossignol Du Vert Bocage
"Bird Of Love" SSA HARRIS $.25
(W344)

Sainte Marguerite
SATB HARRIS $.35   (W345)
SSA HARRIS $.30   (W346)

Si J'etain Petite Mere *see Little
Mother

Sigh No More Ladies
SSA HARRIS $.35   (W347)

To Violets
SSA HARRIS $.25   (W348)

Two Two-Part Songs
SA HARRIS $.30
contains: Clown Song, The; When
Belinda Sings   (W349)

Wedding Song, The *see C'est Le Mon
Dous Plaisir

When Belinda Sings
see Two Two-Part Songs

WILLEMS, JOSEF
Selig Sind Die Toten
men cor&jr cor,acap TONOS 1352 s.p.
(W350)

WILLEY
Come Away Sweet Love
SATB SCHIRM.G LG51650 $.40   (W351)

Flow My Tears
SATB SCHIRM.G LG51649 $.40   (W352)

Tobacco Is Like Love
SATB SCHIRM.G LG51648 $.35   (W353)

WILLIAMS
Christmas Love
(Prin) SATB oct SCHMITT 1312 $.40
(W354)

WILLIAMS, PAUL
Once Upon A Mystery
(Simon, W.) SA/TB BIG3 $.50 (W355)
(Simon, W.) SAB BIG3 $.50   (W356)
(Simon, W.) SATB BIG3 $.50   (W357)
(Simon, W.) SSA BIG3 $.50   (W358)

You And Me Against The World *see
Ascher, Ken

WILLIAMSON, MALCOLM
Adam Shall Rise (from Brilliant And
The Dark, The)
SA,pno WEINBERGER s.p.   (W359)

Album From "The Brilliant And The
Dark" (from The Brilliant And The
Dark, The) CCU
unis/SA,pno WEINBERGER s.p. (W360)

Album From "The Brilliant And The
Dark" (from The Brilliant And The
Dark, The) CCU
SSA/SSAA,pno WEINBERGER s.p. (W361)

Canticle Of Fire
SATB,org WEINBERGER cor pts $.40,
voc sc $7.00   (W362)

Dark Scherzo (from Brilliant And The
Dark, The)
SA,pno WEINBERGER s.p.   (W363)

Fires For The Saints (from Brilliant
And The Dark, The)
SA,pno WEINBERGER s.p.   (W364)

Hide And Seek (from Brilliant And The
Dark, The)
SA,pno WEINBERGER s.p.   (W365)

Knights In Shining Armor
audience/cor,pno WEINBERGER voc sc
$1.25, cor pts $.35   (W366)

Landscape (from Brilliant And The
Dark, The)
unis,pno WEINBERGER s.p.   (W367)

Moonrakers
audience/cor,pno/orch WEINBERGER
voc sc $2.00, cor pts $.60 (W368)

Ode To Music
mix cor&cor,orch/pno WEINBERGER
s.p. voc sc, cor pts   (W369)
anti cor,pno/orch WEINBERGER voc sc
$2.00, cor pts $.40, ipr   (W370)

WILLIAMSON, MALCOLM (cont'd.)
Plague 1665 (from Brilliant And The
Dark, The)
SA,pno WEINBERGER s.p.   (W371)

Seascape (from Brilliant And The
Dark, The)
SSA,pno WEINBERGER s.p.   (W372)
unis,pno WEINBERGER s.p.   (W373)

Snow Wolf
audience/cor,pno WEINBERGER voc sc
$2.50, cor pts $.60   (W374)

Spring Is Crowned (from Brilliant And
The Dark, The)
SA,pno WEINBERGER s.p.   (W375)

Stone Wall
audience/cor,pno/orch WEINBERGER
voc sc $2.00, cor pts $.40, ipr
(W376)

Summer Dance Of Old And Young (from
Brilliant And The Dark, The)
unis,pno WEINBERGER s.p.   (W377)

Summer Dance Of The Young (from
Brilliant And The Dark, The)
SSA,pno WEINBERGER s.p.   (W378)

Sweet And Low
SSA,pno WEINBERGER s.p.   (W379)

Town And Country (from Brilliant And
The Dark, The)
SA,pno WEINBERGER s.p.   (W380)

Winter Star
audience/cor,inst WEINBERGER voc sc
$4.50, cor pts $.40, ipa   (W381)

WILLIE, TAKE YOUR LITTLE DRUM
(Hall, Wm.D.) SATB,pno,2rec,perc
NATIONAL WHC-63 $.35   (W382)

WILLKOMMEN "SEID WILLKOMMEN, LIEBE
BRUDER" see Lang, Hans

WILLMS, FRANZ (1893-1946)
Die Beste Zeit Im Jahr Ist Mein
wom cor (easy) sc SCHOTTS CHBL 574
s.p.   (W383)

Die Kemenate *CC15L,folk,Ger
3-4pt wom cor/3-4pt jr cor,acap
SCHOTTS ED. 3592 s.p.   (W384)

WILLSON, MEREDITH (1902-   )
May The Good Lord Bless And Keep You
*pop
SATB BELWIN UC 660 $.40   (W385)
SA/TB BELWIN UC 723 $.40   (W386)
SSA BELWIN UC 659 $.40   (W387)

WILSON, D.
America Again
SA,inst oct SCHMITT 365 $.40 (W388)

WILSON, DONALD M.
Madrigal
TTB,acap AM.COMP.AL. $1.10   (W389)

WILSON, R. BARCLAY
Mors Janua Vitae *sac/sec
SATB CRAMER C73   (W390)

WIMBERGER, GERHARD (1923-   )
Ars Amatoria *cant
8pt mix cor,SBar soli,fl,clar,trp,
perc,harp,bvl,6vla, alto
saxophone, celeste, vibraphone,
electric guitar (diff) sc SCHOTTS
rental, ipr   (W391)

Der Mayen, Der Pringt Uns Pluemelein
Vil
see Vier Satze Nach Deutschen
Volksliedern

Feinsliebchen, Du Sollst Mir Nicht
Barfuss Gehn
see Vier Satze Nach Deutschen
Volksliedern

Gesegn Dich Laub
see Vier Satze Nach Deutschen
Volksliedern

Heiratspost-Kantate
mix cor,bvl,cembalo (med diff) sc,
cor pts SCHOTTS ED. 4773 s.p.
(W392)

Mein Schatz, Der Ist Auf Die
Wanderschaft Hin
see Vier Satze Nach Deutschen
Volksliedern

Vier Satze Nach Deutschen
Volksliedern
mix cor,S solo,pno,bvl,perc,clar,
or vibraphone (med) sc,cor pts
SCHOTTS ED. 5841 s.p., ipa
contains: Der Mayen, Der Pringt
Uns Pluemelein Vil;
Feinsliebchen, Du Sollst Mir

WIMBERGER, GERHARD (cont'd.)

    Nicht Barfuss Gehn; Gesegn Dich
    Laub; Mein Schatz, Der Ist Auf
    Die Wanderschaft Hin   (W393)

WIND IS TAPPING, THE see Ihrke, Walter

WIND OF MARCH, THE see Cadman, Charles
    Wakefield

WINDE WEHN *folk,Finn
    (Zipp, F.) men cor,acap TONOS 2015
    s.p.   (W394)

WINDFREUDE "WENN DER WIND UBER WIESEN
    UND FELDER RENNT" see Zoll, Paul

WINDHOVER, THE see Paynter, John P.

WINDS, THE see Davies, Evan T., Y
    Gwyntoedd

WINDY BEACH, A see Brumby, Colin

WINDY NIGHTS see Rutter

WINE, SWEET WINE see Kodaly, Zoltan

WINTER (from Czech Year, The)
    (Hanus, Jan) SATB,acap voc sc GENERAL
    742 SU $5.00   (W395)

WINTER see Jeppesen, Knud

WINTER BELLS see Tull, Fisher

WINTER ELEGY see Mourant, Walter

WINTER HAS ME IN ITS GRIP see McLean,
    Don

WINTER IS A COLD THING see Clarke,
    Henry Leland

WINTER MUSIC see Rose, Michael

WINTER RAIN see Jacob, Gordon

WINTER SONG see Brandon

WINTER, SPRING, SUMMER, AUTUMN see
    McLin

WINTER STAR see Williamson, Malcolm

WINTER WEICHT
    unis wom cor SCHOTTS C 42 533C s.p.
    see also Alle Singen Heft 2 (W396)

WINTER WONDERLAND see Bernard, Felix

WINTERLIED see Dietrich, Karl

WINTERLIED see Erdlen, Hermann

WINTERLIED "DER SOMMER IST VERSTRICHEN"
    see Marx, Karl

WINTERNACHT see Wittmer, Eberhard
    Ludwig

WINTERS
    Tailor Of Camberwell Green, The
    unis,inst (easy) OXFORD 81.140
    $.30, ipa   (W397)

WINTERSONNENWENDE see Erdlen, Hermann

WINTERTIME see Leeds

WINZER-TRINKLIED see Papandopulo, Boris

WINZERCHOR "WIR HOCKERN DIE STEINIGEN
    PFADE HINAUF" see Fussan, Werner

WIR BAUEN EINE STADT see Hindemith,
    Paul

WIR BAUERN "WIR BAUERN DULDEN KEINEN
    SPOTT" see Knab, Armin

WIR BRAUCHEN FRIEDEN see Edler, Robert

WIR FAHREN UBERS WEITE MEER
    see My Bonnie Is Over The Ocean

WIR HABEN DREI KATZEN see Rathgeber,
    Valentin

WIR HABEN IN UNS EINEN SOMMER see
    Muller, Siegfried

WIR HEISSEN EUCH HOFFEN see Schlemm,
    Gustav Adolf

WIR LIEBEN SEHR IM HERZEN see
    Friderici, Daniel

WIR SIND DIE JUNGEN see Gwinner, Volker

WIR SIND JUNG see Wittmer, Eberhard
    Ludwig

WIR SIND KONIGE DER WELT see Silcher,
    Friedrich

WIR SIND MIR MEINE STIEFEL GESCHWOLLN
    see Lang, Hans

WIR SINGEN BAND 4: JUNGERE VOLKSLIEDER
    IN NEUEN SATZEN *CCU
    eq voices HOFMEISTER W113 s.p. (W398)

WIR TANZEN IM MAIEN *folk
    (Rische, Quirin) men cor,acap TONOS
    17 s.p.   (W399)

WIR TANZEN IM MAIEN see Desch, Rudolf

WIR WAHNTEN LANGE RECHT ZU LEBEN see
    Hessenberg, Kurt

WIR WANDERN IM SONNENSCHEIN see
    Erbelding, Dietrich

WIR WOLLEN ZU LAND AUSFAHREN see Desch,
    Rudolf

WIR ZOGEN IN DAS FELD
    (Weber, Wilhelm) men cor,acap TONOS
    3302 s.p.   (W400)

WIR ZOGEN IN DAS FELD see Knab, Armin

WISSMER, PIERRE (1915-   )
    Lumiere
    wom cor,acap HENN 812 s.p. (W401)

WIT AND WISDOM OF BENJAMIN FRANKLIN,
    THE see Penn, Robert

WITH DROOPING WINGS see Purcell, Henry

WITH HOW SAD STEPS see Brown

WITH JOYFUL MIRTH see Pierce

WITH SIGHING AND LAMENT see Haussmann,
    Valentin, Mit Seufzen Und Mit Klag

WITH WHAT, HOW SHALL I CLEANSE? see
    Vasquez, Juan, Con Que La Lavare?

WITHERED TREE SINGS ALONE, A see Ishii,
    Kan, Einsam Singt Ein Welker Baum

WITHERED TREE'S PRAYER TO THE SUN, THE
    see Ishii, Kan, Gebet Des Welken
    Baumes Zur Sonne

WITHIN OUR HEARTS WE CHERISH see
    Friderici, Daniel, Wir Lieben Sehr
    Im Herzen

WITHOUT WORK see Kuksa, Emanuel, Bez
    Prace

WITTMER, EBERHARD LUDWIG (1905-   )
    Bildnis Im Sommer
    see Das Jahr

    Das Jahr
    men cor,acap cmplt ed TONOS 4000
    s.p.
      contains: Bildnis Im Sommer;
      Lenz; Sturm Im Herbst;
      Winternacht   (W402)

    Gesang In Der Fruhe
    men cor,acap sc,cor pts TONOS 4013
    s.p.   (W403)

    Grablied "So Still Die Luft"
    see Wittmer, Eberhard Ludwig,
    Hochzeitslied "Heut Ist Der
    Liebste Tag"

    Heilige Flamme
    men cor,acap TONOS 4581 s.p. (W404)

    Heimat "Heimat, Wir Sind Alle Dein"
    men cor sc SCHOTTS C 37 941 s.p.
    (W405)

    Hochzeitslied "Heut Ist Der Liebste
    Tag"
    men cor SCHOTTS CHBL 60A-B s.p.
      contains also: Grablied "So Still
      Die Luft"   (W406)

    Im Schonen Monat Mai
    men cor,acap TONOS 4583 s.p. (W407)

    Junge Sonne "Uber Schneebedeckte
    Erde"
    men cor sc SCHOTTS C 39 444 s.p.
    (W408)

    Lenz
    see Das Jahr

    Margaret
    men cor,acap TONOS 3984 s.p. (W409)

    Neuweinlied
    men cor,acap TONOS 4579 s.p. (W410)

    Schenkst Du Guten Ein
    see DREI WEINSPRUCHE

WITTMER, EBERHARD LUDWIG (cont'd.)

    Sonnenleuchten
    men cor,acap TONOS 4584 s.p. (W411)

    Sturm "Hojeho! Der Nordsturm Setzt
    Das Blanke Horn"
    TTBB sc SCHOTTS C 39 811 s.p., voc
    pt SCHOTTS C 39 812, 01 -02 s.p.
    (W412)

    Sturm Im Herbst
    see Das Jahr

    Trinklied
    men cor,acap TONOS 3731 s.p. (W413)

    Winternacht
    see Das Jahr

    Wir Sind Jung
    men cor,acap TONOS 4582 s.p. (W414)

WITWE BOLTE see Sutermeister, Heinrich

WO ALLE REBEN GRUSSEN see Fischer, Otto

WO BLEIBT DAS GELD? see Fischer, Ernst

WO DIE WOLGA FLIESST *folk,Russ
    (Erbelding, Dietrich) men cor,acap
    TONOS 452 s.p.   (W415)

WO E KLEINS HUTTLE *folk,Ger
    (Rische, Quirin) men cor,acap TONOS
    109 s.p.   (W416)

WO E KLEINS HUTTLE STEHT see Silcher,
    Friedrich

WO FIND ICH DANN DEINS VATERS HAUS see
    Biebl, Franz

WO IST DENN DAS MADCHEN see Michels,
    Josef

WO POLE BERJOSA see Nitsche, Paul,
    Stand Ein Birkenbaum

WO, WO IST DOCH MEIN SCHAFELEIN
    see Neujahrslied

WOHIN EIN JEDES SCHLAFEN GEHT see
    Biebl, Franz

WOHIN MIT DER FREUD: ACH DU see
    Silcher, Friedrich

WOHIN SOLL ICH MICH WENDEN? see
    Schubert, Franz (Peter)

WOHL HEUTE NOCH UND MORGEN *folk
    (Zoll, Paul) men cor,acap TONOS 118
    s.p.   (W417)

WOHL IST DIE WELT SO GROSS UND WEIT see
    Desch, Rudolf

WOHLAN, DIE ZEIT IST KOMMEN see
    Pepping, Ernst

WOHLAUF, GESELLEN, SEID FROH UND MUNTER
    see Zoll, Paul

WOHLAUF, IHR LIEBEN GASTE see
    Sartorius, Thomas

WOHLAUF, IHR WANDERSLEUT *folk,Ger
    (Kracke, Hans) men cor,acap TONOS 59
    s.p.   (W418)

WOHLAUF, IN GOTTES SCHONE WELT see
    Zoll, Paul

WOHLAUF NOCH GETRUNKEN see Jage, Rolf-
    Diether

WOLDIN, JUDD
    Measure The Valleys (from Raisin)
    (composed with Brittan, Robert)
    pop
    (Nowak, Jerry) SATB,solo,pno oct
    BIG BELL $.45   (W419)

WOLF, RICHARD
    Generation Of Peace, A
    (Habash, J.M.) SA/TB BIG3 $.40
    (W420)
    (Habash, J.M.) SATB BIG3 $.40
    (W421)
    (Habash, J.M.) SSS BIG3 $.40 (W422)
    (Habash, J.M.) SAB BIG3 $.40 (W423)

WOLFGARTEN, HANS
    Pfalzer Heimatlied
    men cor,acap TONOS 244 s.p. (W424)

WOLL, ERNA (1917-   )
    Nun Ist Vorbei Die Finstre Nacht
    2 eq voices/2pt mix cor,fl/rec,
    2vln,vcl PELIKAN PE738 s.p.
    (W425)

    Stille Hugel, Sanfte Tale
    3 eq voices,fl/S rec,2vln,vcl,
    glockenspiel PELIKAN PE739 s.p.
    (W426)

WOLLT IHR WISSEN? *folk,Boh
(Rosenstengel, Albrecht) men cor,opt
pno,opt gtr,opt perc TONOS 2112
s.p. (W427)

WOLLT ZUM WEIB DICH NEHMEN see Zoll,
Paul

WOLTERS, GOTTFRIED (1910-   )
Gute Nacht, Kammeraden *canon
(contains also: Von Allen Blauen
Hugeln) oct MOSELER s.p. see from
Singenden Jahr (W428)

Singenden Jahr *see Gute Nacht,
Kammeraden; Von Allen Blauen
Hugeln (W429)

Von Allen Blauen Hugeln *canon
(contains also: Gute Nacht,
Kammeraden) oct MOSELER s.p. see
from Singenden Jahr (W430)

WOLTERS, KARL-HEINZ (1929-   )
Danklied Des Bergmanns
men cor,acap TONOS 75 s.p. (W431)

Die Strassburger Munster-Engelchen
"Gib Dir Weiter Keine Muh'"
TTBB sc SCHOTTS C 41 318 s.p., voc
pt SCHOTTS C 41 319, 01-02 s.p.
(W432)

Guten Abend, Euch Allein
men cor&jr cor,acap TONOS 1321 s.p.
(W433)

Heiter Ist Des Lebens Kunst "Kommt Es
Mal, Wie Du's Nicht Denkst"
men cor sc SCHOTTS CHBL 180 s.p.
see from Zwei Kleine Chore (W434)

Herz, Werde Wach
men cor,acap sc,cor pts TONOS 4003
s.p. (W435)

Laetare
men cor, piano 4-hands sc,cor pts
TONOS 4204 s.p. (W436)

Liebesgewitter "Auch Die Liebe
Braucht Gewitter"
men cor sc SCHOTTS CHBL 147 s.p.
(W437)

Marsch Vom Kleinen Mann
men cor,acap TONOS 4006 s.p. (W438)

Morgenmusik "Es Leuchten Alle Morgen"
men cor sc SCHOTTS CHBL 179 s.p.
see from Zwei Kleine Chore (W439)

Nur Frohlich In Den Tag Hinein
men cor sc SCHOTTS CHBL 139 s.p.
(W440)

So Geht Es Im Schnutzelputzhausel
men cor&jr cor,acap TONOS 1322 s.p.
(W441)

Zum Tanze, Da Geht Ein Madel
men cor&jr cor,acap/pno TONOS 1323
s.p. (W442)

Zwei Kleine Chore *see Heiter Ist
Des Lebens Kunst "Kommt Es Mal,
Wie Du's Nicht Denkst";
Morgenmusik "Es Leuchten Alle
Morgen" (W443)

WOMEN ARE WANTING THE VOTE
(Van Camp, Leonard) SATB FOSTER MF334
$.45 (W444)

WOMEN FROM DOVER
(Johnston, Richard A.) SSA (med easy)
WATERLOO $.30 (W445)

WOMEN'S INSTITUTE SONG BOOK *CCU
cor WATERLOO $1.50 (W446)

WOMEN'S LIB MARCH see Hicks, Val

WONDER WHAT KIND OF A DAY IT WILL BE
see Smith

WONDERFUL BABY see McLean, Don

WONDERFUL GUY, A see Rodgers, Richard

WOOD
Loneliness
SATB,opt gtr FINE ARTS EP 50 $.35
(W447)

WOOD, DALE
Gift To Be Simple, The *sac/sec
1-2pt/SSA/SAB (based on Shaker
tune) FISCHER,C CM 7893 $.40
(W448)
I Walk A Stranger On This Land
SATB/unis ART MAST 1021 $.40 (W449)

WOOD, HUGH (1932-   )
To A Child Dancing In The Wind
SATB,acap NOVELLO MT 1572 s.p.
(W450)

WOOD, JOSEPH (1915-   )
Hymn To The Night
TTBB,acap AM.COMP.AL. $2.75 (W451)

WOOD, JOSEPH (cont'd.)

Lamb, The
SATB,acap AM.COMP.AL. $1.38 (W452)

Mumblin' Word *spir
SATB,acap AM.COMP.AL. $2.75 (W453)

Small Hour, The
treb cor,pno AM.COMP.AL. $6.60
(W454)

There's No Hidin' Place *spir
SATB,acap AM.COMP.AL. $3.30 (W455)

Tiger, The
SATB,acap AM.COMP.AL. $1.38 (W456)

WOODBURY-LIEDERBUCHLEIN see Eisler,
Hanns

WOODCHOPPERS' BALL see Herman, Woody

WOODCHUCK, THE see Boyd, Jack

WOODWINDS see Branscombe, [Gina]

WOOLF, GREGORY
Time's Passing, A
SATB AMP A-659 $.30 (W457)

WOOLLEN, RUSSELL
Bushes And Briars *folk
SSA,acap AM.COMP.AL. $3.30 (W458)

Three Madrigals *CC3U,madrigal
SATB,acap AM.COMP.AL. $6.60 (W459)

WORDPLAY see Devcic, Natko, Igra Rijeci

WORFULLY ARRAYED see Cornysh, William

WORKDAY see Podest, Ludvik, Vsedni Den

WORKIN' AT THE CAR WASH BLUES see
Croce, Jim

WORLD IS A GHETTO, THE
(Metis, F.) SSA (words and music by:
Allen, Sylvester; Brown, Harold R.;
Dickerson, Morris; Jordan, Leroy;
Miller, Charles W.; Oskar, Lee;
Scott, Howard) BIG3 $.40 (W460)
(Metis, F.) SATB (words and music by:
Allen, Sylvester; Brown, Harold R.;
Dickerson, Morris; Jordan, Leroy;
Miller, Charles W.; Oskar, Lee;
Scott, Howard) BIG3 $.40 (W461)
(Metis, F.) SAB (words and music by:
Allen, Sylvester; Brown, Harold R.;
Dickerson, Morris; Jordan, Leroy;
Miller, Charles W.; Oskar, Lee;
Scott, Howard) BIG3 $.40 (W462)

WORLD-TREE, THE see Clarke, Henry
Leland

WRITTEN IN SAND see Gabold, Ingolf

WRITTEN ON THE PAGE OF A CALENDAR see
Bartos, Jan Zdenek, Psano Na List
Kalendare

WRUBEL, ALLIE
Zip-A-Dee Doo-Dah
(Simon, W.) SSA BIG3 $.50 (W463)
(Simon, W.) SATB BIG3 $.50 (W464)
(Simon, W.) SA/TB BIG3 $.50 (W465)
(Simon, W.) SAB BIG3 $.50 (W466)

WUMBA-WUMBA "WENN OWAMBO SCHMERZEN
PLAGEN" see Merath, Siegfried

WUNDERBAR
SA CIMINO $.40 (W467)
SAB CIMINO $.40 (W468)
SSA CIMINO $.40 (W469)
TTBB CIMINO $.40 (W470)
SSA CIMINO $.40 (W471)
SATB CIMINO $.40 (W472)
SATB CIMINO $.40 (W473)

WUNDERLAND-ZYKLUS see Krietsch, Georg

WUNDERLICHSTES BUCH DER BUCHER see
Rein, Walter

WUNSCH, FRANK (1945-   )
Li'l Elsa's Tune *see Unter
Verwendung Des Liedes "Ach
Elslein, Liebes Elselein"

Unter Verwendung Des Liedes "Ach
Elslein, Liebes Elselein"
"Li'l Elsa's Tune" 4pt mix cor,
jazz combo (med easy) sc SCHOTTS
C 43 284 s.p., cor pts SCHOTTS
C 43 285 s.p., ipa (W474)

WUORINEN, CHARLES
Be Merry All That Be Present
SATB,org AM.COMP.AL. $2.20 (W475)

WURZE DES WALDES see Genzmer, Harald

WUYTACK, JOS
Choralia *CC55U
mix cor (easy) cor pts SCHOTTS
SF 9283 s.p. (W476)

WYTTENBACH, JURG (1935-   )
Sutil Und Laar *CC10L
SABarB, piano four hands (med) sc,
cor pts SCHOTTS ED. 5675 s.p.
(W477)

X

XENAKIS, YANNIS (IANNIS) (1922-   )
   Polla Ta Dina
      [Greek/Eng] jr cor,pic,fl,2ob,clar,
      bsn,2trp,2horn,2trom,timp,perc,
      strings, bass clarinet,
      contrabassoon MODERN rental   (X1)

Y

Y CARIAD CYNTAF
   "First Love, The" see Two Welsh Folk
   Songs

Y GWYNTOEDD see Davies, Evan T.

YA BA BOM
   (Goldman) SATB SCHIRM.G LG51814 $.40
                                        (Y1)
YAHRES, SAMUEL C.
   Land That I Love!
      SA,pno YAHRES 1542 $.25   (Y2)

   Our Sacred Honor
      mix cor&opt speak cor,2 narrators,
      band (bicentennial documentary)
      YAHRES s.p.   (Y3)

   Sing America First!
      SATB,opt band YAHRES 1124 $.30, ipa
                                        (Y4)
      SAB,opt band YAHRES 1125 $.30, ipa
                                        (Y5)
      SSA,opt band YAHRES 1123 $.30, ipa
                                        (Y6)
      TTBB,opt band YAHRES 1126 $.30, ipa
                                        (Y7)
   Theme (from Our Sacred Honor)
      SATB,pno YAHRES 5014 $.30   (Y8)
      SAAB YAHRES 5005 $.30   (Y9)
      SSA YAHRES 5003 $.30   (Y10)
      TTBB YAHRES 5006 $.30   (Y11)

   We, The People! (from Our Sacred
      Honor)
      SATB,pno YAHRES 5154 $.30   (Y12)
      SAB YAHRES 5155 $.30   (Y13)
      SSA YAHRES 5153 $.30   (Y14)
      TTBB YAHRES 5156 $.30   (Y15)

YANCEY
   Adelante! (Sail On!) (from Our Sacred
      Honor)
      "Columbus Theme" SATB,pno YAHRES
      5024 $.30 contains also:
      Billings,William, Chester
      (Yahres, Samuel C.)   (Y16)

   Columbus Theme *see Adelante! (Sail
      On!)

YANKEE DOODLE
   see Freedom Song, 1776
   (Kirk) SATB PRO ART 2858 $.45   (Y17)

YANNATOS, JAMES
   Buffalo Bill's *No.1
      TTBB AMP A-646 $.30 see from Three
      Settings Of E.E. Cummings   (Y18)

   In Just *No.3
      SSATB AMP A-648 $.30 see from Three
      Settings Of E.E. Cummings   (Y19)

   Many Ways To Look At A Woman *cant
      cor,acap AM.COMP.AL. $5.50   (Y20)

   Rose, The *No.2
      SSAA AMP A-647 $.30 see from Three
      Settings Of E.E. Cummings   (Y21)

   Three Settings Of E.E. Cummings *see
      Buffalo Bill's, No.1; In Just,
      No.3; Rose, The, No.2   (Y22)

YDSTIE
   If There's A Song
      SATB oct SCHMITT 1313 $.45   (Y23)

   Make Your Own World
      cor oct SCHMITT 2136 $.40   (Y24)

   To Be Or Not To Be
      TTBB GENERAL WDS GC 58 $.35   (Y25)

YE BANKS AND BRAES *folk,Scot
   (Soderstrom, Emil) SSATTBB,acap (med)
      FITZSIMONS 1076 $.25   (Y26)

YE BANKS AND BRAES see Gal, Hans

YE WINDS OF WINTER see Weil

YEARS PROPHETICAL see Lekberg, Sven

YELLOWSTONE SUITE see Klein

YES SIR, THAT'S MY BABY see Donaldson,
   Walter

YESTERDAY ONCE MORE see Carpenter,
   Richard

YESTERDAYS
   SSA CIMINO $.40   (Y27)
   SA CIMINO $.40   (Y28)
   SATB CIMINO $.40   (Y29)
   TTBB CIMINO $.40   (Y30)

   (Warnick) SATB,opt gtr&bvl&drums
      CIMINO cor pts $.40, cmplt ed $1.50
                                        (Y31)
YOU AND ME AGAINST THE WORLD see
   Ascher, Ken

YOU ARE BEAUTIFUL see Rodgers, Richard

YOU ARE LOVE
   SA CIMINO $.40   (Y32)
   SSA CIMINO $.40   (Y33)
   SAB CIMINO $.40   (Y34)
   TTBB CIMINO $.40   (Y35)
   SATB CIMINO $.40   (Y36)

YOU ARE THE SUNSHINE OF MY LIFE
   SAB,pno,opt bvl&drums&gtr SCREEN
      4777YC3   (Y37)
   TTBB SCREEN 477YC4   (Y38)
   SSA,pno,opt bvl&drums&gtr SCREEN
      4777YC8   (Y39)
   SATB,pno,opt bvl&drums&gtr SCREEN
      477YC7   (Y40)

YOU CAN'T SEE THE SUN WHEN YOU'RE
   CRYING
   SSAA (Barbershop Arrangement) CIMINO
      $.40   (Y41)

YOU DON'T MESS AROUND WITH JIM see
   Croce, Jim

YOU HAVE LIVED see McLean, Don

YOU HAVE WOUNDED ME see Vasquez, Juan,
   Vos Me Matastes

YOU MADE ME LOVE YOU see Monaco, James
   V.

YOU MAKE ME FEEL BRAND NEW see Bell,
   Thomas

YOU SPOTTED SNAKES see Thiman, Eric
   Harding

YOU WILL BE MY MUSIC see Raposo, Joe

YOULL, HENRY (ca. 1600- ?)
   In The Merry Month Of May
      (Malin, Don) SSA BELWIN 2299 $.35
                                        (Y42)
YOU'LL NEVER WALK ALONE
   SAB CIMINO $.40   (Y43)
   SSA CIMINO $.40   (Y44)
   SA CIMINO $.40   (Y45)
   TTBB CIMINO $.40   (Y46)
   SSA CIMINO $.40   (Y47)
   SATB CIMINO $.40   (Y48)
   (Stickles) SATB CIMINO $.40   (Y49)
   (Warnick) SATB CIMINO $.40   (Y50)

YOUMANS
   Great Day
      (Ringwald) SATB SHAWNEE A1302 $.50
                                        (Y51)
YOUNG
   After The Gold Rush
      (Shay) SATB WARNER CH2001 $.35
                                        (Y52)
   American's Creed, The
      SATB oct HERITAGE H108 $.35   (Y53)

   Sing Me A Silly Song
      SATB oct HERITAGE H121 $.35   (Y54)

   Vocalise
      SATB WALTON 2716 $.35   (Y55)

   When I Fall In Love *pop
      (Hayman) SA/TB BELWIN UC 714 $.40
                                        (Y56)
   When I Fall In Love *see Heyman

YOUNG DEAD SOLDIERS, THE see Clarke,
   Henry Leland

YOUNG, GORDON (1919-   )
   It's The Birthday Of Our Country
      *CCU
      cor,pno,pic,drums HERITAGE H130
      $.35 bicentennial   (Y57)

YOUNG MAN WHO WOULDN'T HOE CORN
   (Bailey, Terrence) SSA (med easy)
      WATERLOO $.40   (Y58)

YOUNG MAN'S SONG, A see Clements

YOUNG MAY MOON, THE see Moore, Thomas

YOUNG, NEIL
   Nowadays Clancy Can't Even Sing *see
      Nash, Graham

   Sounds Of Neil Young And Graham Nash
      *see Nash, Graham

   Teach Your Children *see Nash,
      Graham

   There's A World *see Nash, Graham

YOUNG, ROBERT H.
All For Love
SATB,acap (med) FISCHER,C CM 7812
$.30 (Y59)

When I Am Dead, My Dearest
SATB,acap (med easy) FOSTER MF327
$.30 (Y60)

YOUNGER THAN SPRINGTIME see Rodgers,
Richard

YOUR BEAUTY BINDS ME PLEASANTLY see
Gombert, Nicolas, Votre Beaute
Plaisante Et Lie

YOUR MAMA DON'T DANCE see Loggins, Dave

YOUR SHINING EYES see Bateson, Thomas

YOUR SHINING EYES see East, Michael

YOUR SISTER'S DROWN'D see Gabold,
Ingolf

YOU'RE NOT LIST'NING TO ME see Lefevre,
Jacques, Tu Ne L'Entends Pas

YOU'RE SIXTEEN see Sherman

YOU'RE THE FIRST, THE LAST, MY
EVERYTHING
SSA CIMINO $.50 (Y61)
SAB CIMINO $.40 (Y62)
SATB CIMINO $.50 (Y63)

YOUSE, GLAD ROBINSON (1898-)
Lovely The Dawning
SSA (easy) FITZSIMONS 3079 $.20
(Y64)

YOUTH see Vomacka, Boleslav

YTTREHUS, ROLV
Music For Winds, Percussion, Cello,
And Voices
cor,fl,horn,trp,trom,perc,vcl,pic,
bass clarinet, bass trombone
AM.COMP.AL. sc $17.60, ipa, voc
pt $1.10 (Y65)

YVOIRE
Geraniums Rouges
mix cor HENN 800 s.p. (Y66)

Z

Z DENIKU VEZNE see Dvoracek, Jiri

Z MUDROSLOVI NARODU SLOVANSKYCH see
Haba, Alois

ZA MIR see Haba, Alois

ZA VSECHNY DETI see Kohoutek, Ctirad

ZAG NICHT! see Fischer, Theo

ZAHNER, BRUNO
Es Git Nit Lustigers Uf Der Wald
*cant
2-4 eq voices/2-4pt mix cor,2vln/
strings,fl,timp,pno sc,voc sc
PELIKAN PE918 s.p., ipa (Z1)

ZAHRADNIK, ZDENEK (1936-)
Annunciation Of Spring, The *see
Jarni Zvestovani

Jarni Zvestovani *cant
"Annunciation Of Spring, The"
[Czech] mix cor,S&narrator,fl,ob,
2clar,bsn,2horn,2trp,trom,timp,
perc,harp,strings CZECH s.p. (Z2)

ZAHRAJTE MNE, MIZIKANTI see Hilmera,
Oldrich

ZAKLETA DCERA see Novak, Vitezslav

ZANINELLI, LUIGI
Carols Three
SATB SHAWNEE A1270 $.40 (Z3)

ZANNI ET MAGNIFICO see Eccard, Johannes

ZANZI, G.
Das Lied Vom Becherlein
(Ammann, Benno) mix cor ZIMMER. 587
s.p. (Z4)
(Ammann, Benno) men cor,acap
ZIMMER. 576 s.p. (Z5)

ZASVIETILO SLUNEKO see Mikula, Zdenko

ZAVRAT see Tausinger, Jan

ZBAR, MICHEL (1942-)
Swingle Novae
8pt mix cor,narrator,Hamm,pno,fl,
pic,ob,clar,bsn,horn,2trp,trom,
tuba,vln,vla,vcl,bvl,harp,gtr,
5perc, English horn, bass
clarinet, contrabassoon RIDEAU
s.p. (Z6)

ZBERATEL see Holoubek, Ladislav

ZBOR MNICHOV Z OPERY MATUS CAK
TRENCIANSKY see Rosinsky, Jozef

ZDRAVICE PANU PRESIDENTOVI see Sauer,
Frantisek

ZECCHI, ADONE (1904-)
Da Bacco In Toscana
4pt mix cor sc BONGIOVANI 1997 s.p.
(Z7)
D'Ottobre
4pt men cor s.p. sc BONGIOVANI
1900, voc pt BONGIOVANI 2141 (Z8)

ZECHER-SONG "WER GUT TRINKT" see
Binger, Martin

ZECHERWEISHEIT *folk
(Weber, Bernhard) [Ger] 4pt men cor
MERSEBURG EM9024 s.p. (Z9)

ZECHLIN, RUTH (1926-)
Aphorismen Uber Die Liebe
mix cor,acap DEUTSCHER DVFM7643
s.p. (Z10)

ZEHM, FRIEDRICH (1923-)
Alter Spruch "Ich Leb Und Weiss Nit
Wie Lang"
SSAATTBB,acap (med diff) sc SCHOTTS
C 42 464 s.p. see from Vier
Heitere Chorlieder (Z11)

Das Mannsbackelied Von Der Schonen
Marienka
see Grasshoffiade

Erkalteter Landgendarm Im Schnee "Es
Schneit"
see Grasshoffiade

Grasshoffiade
TTBB,pno sc SCHOTTS C 42 338 s.p.,
voc pt SCHOTTS C 42 339, 01-02
s.p.
contains: Erkalteter Landgendarm
Im Schnee "Es Schneit"; Kleine

ZEHM, FRIEDRICH (cont'd.)

Abzahlversgeschichte "Ehle,
Mehle" (Z12)

Grasshoffiade
sc SCHOTTS C 42 340 s.p., voc pt
SCHOTTS C 42 341, 01-02 s.p.
contains: Das Mannsbackelied Von
Der Schonen Marienka (TTBB,
acap); Was Der Alte Dachte, Als
Er Zu Heiraten Gedachte (TTBB,B
solo,acap) (Z13)

Inserat "Die Verehrlichen Jungen"
mix cor (med diff, contains also:
Spruch "Ein Madchen Und Ein
Glaschen Wein") sc SCHOTTS
C 42 462 s.p. see from Vier
Heitere Chorlieder (Z14)

Kleine Abzahlversgeschichte "Ehle,
Mehle"
see Grasshoffiade

Nonstop-Songs *cant
jr cor,narrator,inst (med) voc sc,
cor pts SCHOTTS ED. 6257 s.p.,
ipa (Z15)

Spruch "Ein Madchen Und Ein Glaschen
Wein"
mix cor (med diff, contains also:
Inserat "Die Verehrlichen
Jungen") sc SCHOTTS C 42 462 s.p.
see from Vier Heitere Chorlieder
(Z16)

Vier Heitere Chorlieder *see Alter
Spruch "Ich Leb Und Weiss Nit Wie
Lang"; Inserat "Die Verehrlichen
Jungen"; Spruch "Ein Madchen Und
Ein Glaschen Wein"; Zur Verlobung
"Sie Hat Nichts" (Z17)

Was Der Alte Dachte, Als Er Zu
Heiraten Gedachte
see Grasshoffiade

Zur Verlobung "Sie Hat Nichts"
mix cor (med diff) sc SCHOTTS
C 42 463 s.p. see from Vier
Heitere Chorlieder (Z18)

ZEHN LYRISCHE GESANGE see Gauss, Otto

ZEHN RUBAIJAT DES OMAR KHAJJAM see
Cerha, Friedrich

ZEITCHORAL "GROSS IST ALLER MENSCHHEIT
NOT" see Weber, Bernhard

ZEITGENOSSISCHE KOMPOSITIONEN FUR
FRAUENCHOR *CCU
2-4pt wom cor,acap PELIKAN PE801 s.p.
(Z19)

ZEITKRANZ see Knab, Armin

ZELINKA, JAN EVANGELISTA (1893-)
Cantata In Memory Of The Year 1918
*see Kantata Na Pamet Roku 1918

Kantata Na Pamet Roku 1918 *cant
"Cantata In Memory Of The Year
1918" [Czech] mix cor,T solo,2fl,
2ob,2clar,2bsn,4horn,2trp,2trom,
tuba,timp,perc,pno,strings CZECH
s.p. (Z20)

Slameny Bycek *cant
"Straw Bull, The" [Czech] mix cor,
soli,clar,bsn,horn,trp,timp,pno,
harp,strings CZECH s.p. (Z21)

Straw Bull, The *see Slameny Bycek

ZELJENKA, ILJA (1932-)
Hudba *cant
cor,orch SLOV.HUD.FOND s.p. (Z22)

ZELTER
Four Songs For Male Voices *see
Master And Journeyman; Song Of
The Flea (Z23)

Master And Journeyman
TTBB,acap (contains also: Song Of
The Flea) oct BOOSEY 5913 $.40
see from Four Songs For Male
Voices (Z24)

Song Of The Flea
TTBB,acap (contains also: Master
And Journeyman) oct BOOSEY 5913
$.40 see from Four Songs For Male
Voices (Z25)

ZELTER, CARL FRIEDRICH (1758-1832)
Bundeslied "In Allen Guten Stunden"
see Rein, Walter, Der Weinfuhrmann
"Es Wollt Ein Fuhrmann Fahren"
men cor,acap TONOS 4347 s.p. (Z26)

Durch Feld Und Buchenhallen
(Grohe) men cor,acap TONOS 4355
s.p. (Z27)

ZELTER, CARL FRIEDRICH (cont'd.)

Ein Musikant Wollt Frohlich Sein
men cor sc SCHOTTS CHBL 35 s.p.
(Z28)

men cor,acap TONOS 4350 s.p. (Z29)

Genialisch Treiben "So Walz Ich Ohne
Unterlass"
BBB sc SCHOTTS CHBL 115 s.p. (Z30)
men cor,acap TONOS 4351 s.p. (Z31)

Ich Hab Mein Sach
(Krietsch) men cor,acap TONOS 4349
s.p. (Z32)

Meister Und Gesell "A Schlosser Hot
An Gsellen Ghabt"
men cor,acap TONOS 4348 s.p. (Z33)
men cor sc SCHOTTS CHBL 121 s.p. (Z34)

Sankt Paulus "Sankt Paulus War Ein
Medikus"
men cor sc SCHOTTS C 39 846 s.p. (Z35)

Solang Man Nuchtern Ist
men cor sc SCHOTTS CHBL 116 s.p.
(Z36)
men cor,acap TONOS 4352 s.p. (Z37)

Tafellied "Wie Hehr Im Glase Blinket"
men cor sc SCHOTTS CHBL 132 s.p.
(Z38)

ZEMANOVSKY, A.
Antipoly Troch
3pt jr cor,acap SLOV.HUD.FOND s.p.
(Z39)

Travnice A Lucne Spevy Z Cicmian A
Terchovej
jr cor SLOV.HUD.FOND EZS 9 s.p.
(Z40)

Tri Odpovede *CC3U
jr cor,acap SLOV.HUD.FOND s.p.
(Z41)

ZEME DVOJJEDINA see Sestak, Zdenek

ZEME MLUVI see Hanus, Jan

ZEMI RODNE see Drazan, Josef

ZEMIROT *CCU
[Heb] cor OR-TAV $1.75 (Z42)

ZENDER, HANS
Canto IV *sac/sec
16pt,16inst BOTE rental (Z43)

Canto V *sac/sec
[Greek] SATB,opt SATB soli,perc min
sc BOTE s.p. (Z44)

ZENSKE SBORY see Thomsen-Muchova,
Geraldina

ZENTNER, JOHANNES (1903-)
Das Leben-Ein Wandern *cant
4-7pt mix cor,pno/orch voc sc
PELIKAN PE920 s.p. (Z45)

Das Reh Im Winter
2 eq voices,pno/org/orch sc,voc sc
PELIKAN PE923 s.p., ipa (Z46)

Frohes Leben *cant
4pt mix cor,pno/org/strings/winds
PELIKAN PE175 s.p. (Z47)

Jahreszeiten-Kantate *cant
2 eq voices,2S rec,2vln,bvl PELIKAN
PE314 sc s.p., cor pts s.p., ipa
(Z48)

Serenade
wom cor,fl,vla,pno voc sc PELIKAN
PE919 s.p. (Z49)

Zwischen Heute Und Morgen *cant
wom cor,B solo,2pno/orch voc sc
PELIKAN PE921 s.p. (Z50)

ZICH, OTAKOR (1879-1934)
Fateful Wedding, The *see Osudna
Svatba

Osudna Svatba *Op.1
"Fateful Wedding, The" [Czech] mix
cor,3fl,3ob,3clar,2bsn,4horn,
4trp,3trom,tuba,timp,perc,harp,
strings CZECH s.p. (Z51)
"Fateful Wedding, The" [Czech] mix
cor,2fl,2ob,2clar,2bsn,3horn,
2trp,3trom,timp,perc,harp,strings
CZECH s.p. (Z52)

Polka Is Off, The *see Polka Jede

Polka Jede *Op.5, cant
"Polka Is Off, The" [Czech] mix
cor,soli,3fl,2ob,2clar,2bsn,
4horn,2trp,3trom,tuba,timp,perc,
strings CZECH s.p. (Z53)

ZIERLICHKEIT DES SCHAFERLEBENS "NICHTS
KANN AUF ERDEN" see Trunk, Richard

ZIGANKA *folk
(Koringer, Franz) mix cor DOBLINGER
G 709 s.p. see from Funf Satze Nach
Kroatischen Volksliedern (Z54)

ZIGEUNERLEBEN see Schumann, Robert
(Alexander)

ZIGEUNERLIED see Biebl, Franz, Im
Nebelgeriesel

ZIGEUNERLIEDER see Brahms, Johannes

ZIGEUNERLIEDER see Ohse, Reinhard

ZIGEUNERTANZ "BURSCHEN, MADCHEN SCHNELL
HERBEI" see Haus, Karl

ZIMMER, JAN (1926-)
Elergy
see Styri Madrigaly

Hymn
see Styri Madrigaly

Na Slavu Banilov
see MUZSKE ZBORY III

Nocturno
see Styri Madrigaly

Povstanie *cant
mix cor,orch SLOV.HUD.FOND s.p.
(Z55)

Sonnet
see Styri Madrigaly

Styri Madrigaly
[Eng] mix cor SLOV.HUD.FOND s.p.
contains: Elergy; Hymn; Nocturno;
Sonnet (Z56)

ZIMMERMANN, BERND ALOIS (1918-)
Lob Der Torheit *cant
SSAATTBB,STB soli,2pno,3fl,3ob,
3clar,3bsn,4horn,3trp,3trom,tuba,
strings,perc,timp,harp,celeste
(diff) sc SCHOTTS rental, ipr
(Z57)

Requiem Fur Einen Jungen Dichter
3 cor,narrator,SBar soli,org,orch,
jazz combo (diff) sc SCHOTTS
rental, ipr (Z58)

ZIMNA PIESEN see Ferenczy, Oto

ZIP-A-DEE DOO-DAH see Wrubel, Allie

ZIPP, FRIEDRICH (1914-)
Abendgluck
men cor,acap TONOS 4526 s.p. (Z59)

Alle Menschen, Gross Und Klein
see Geht Alles Um Und Um

Am Morgen Nach Der Hochzeit "Wo Seid
Ihr Lieben Geblieben" *folk,Russ
mix cor (med) sc SCHOTTS C 40 167
s.p. see from Drei Russische
Volkslieder (Z60)

Auch Was In Die Quer
see Geht Alles Um Und Um
see Geht Alles Um Und Um

Chinesische Jahreszeiten *see Der
Bach "Inmitten Des Rauschenden
Herbstregens", Op.19,No.2; Fluss
Im Schnee "Der Vogel Flug",
Op.19,No.3; Stimmung Im Fruhling
"Wie Dicht Das Gras Hier Wachst",
Op.19,No.1 (Z61)

Das Madchen Wollt' Ein Freier Haben
men cor sc SCHOTTS CHBL 44 s.p. see
from Drei Heitere Volkslieder
(Z62)

Dem Neuen Jahre "Nun Kommst Du
Hergegangen"
mix cor (easy) cor pts SCHOTTS
CHBL 383 s.p. see from Fest Und
Feier (Z63)

Der Bach "Inmitten Des Rauschenden
Herbstregens" *Op.19,No.2
mix cor (med) sc SCHOTTS C 37 896
s.p. see from Chinesische
Jahreszeiten (Z64)

Der Du Die Zeit In Handen Hast
see Zwei Lieder Zum Jahreswechsel

Der Jager Und Sein Liebchen "Es Jagt
Ein Jager Wohlgemut"
men cor sc SCHOTTS CHBL 43 s.p. see
from Drei Heitere Volkslieder (Z65)

Der Kosak " In Dem Grunen Walde"
*folk,Russ
mix cor (med) sc SCHOTTS C 40 168
s.p. see from Drei Russische
Volkslieder (Z66)

Der Mond Soll Im Kalendar Stehn
see Geht Alles Um Und Um

ZIPP, FRIEDRICH (cont'd.)

Die Gedanken Sind Frei
men cor,acap TONOS 62 s.p. (Z67)

Dieterlein "Wohlauf, Ihr Narr'n,
Zieht All Mit Mir"
TTBB,solo sc SCHOTTS C 38 556 s.p.,
voc pt SCHOTTS C 38 591, 01-04
s.p. (Z68)

Drei Heitere Volkslieder *see Das
Madchen Wollt' Ein Freier Haben;
Der Jager Und Sein Liebchen "Es
Jagt Ein Jager Wohlgemut"; Wer So
Ein Faules Gretchen Hat (Z69)

Drei Landsknechts-Lieder *see Es
Geht Wohl Zu Der Sommerzeit; Mit
Lust Tat Ich Ausreiten;
Schenkenbachs Reiterlied (Z70)

Drei Russische Volkslieder *see Am
Morgen Nach Der Hochzeit "Wo Seid
Ihr Lieben Geblieben"; Der Kosak
" In Dem Grunen Walde";
Junggesellenlied "Bursche Ging
Ins Tal" (Z71)

Eh Ich Mich Niederlege *Op.49,No.2
see Zipp, Friedrich, Es Wandeln
Sich Die Reiche
wom cor (easy) sc SCHOTTS
CHBL 575A-B s.p. contains also:
Es Wandeln Sich Die Reiche (Z72)

Ein Lied Muss Sein
men cor,acap TONOS 4525 s.p. (Z73)

Es, Es, Es Und Es
see Zwei Volkslieder

Es Geht Wohl Zu Der Sommerzeit
men cor,acap TONOS 81 s.p. see from
Drei Landsknechts-Lieder (Z74)

Es Wandeln Sich Die Reiche *Op.49,
No.1
see Zipp, Friedrich, Eh Ich Mich
Niederlege
mix cor (med) sc SCHOTTS
CHBL 289A-B s.p. contains also:
Eh Ich Mich Niederlege, Op.49,
No.2 (Z75)

Es Waren Zwei Konigskinder *CC5U
1-2 eq voices/jr cor/wom cor,S rec,
A rec,vln/gtr,perc sc,voc sc
PELIKAN PE933 s.p., ipa (Z76)

Fest Und Feier *see Dem Neuen Jahre
"Nun Kommst Du Hergegangen" (Z77)

Fluss Im Schnee "Der Vogel Flug"
*Op.19,No.3
SAATB (med) sc SCHOTTS C 37 744
s.p. see from Chinesische
Jahreszeiten (Z78)

Frohlicher Jahrmarkt *cant
1-2pt jr cor,inst (easy) sc,cor pts
SCHOTTS B 141 s.p., ipa (Z79)

Geht Alles Um Und Um
men cor sc SCHOTTS C 40 478 s.p.
contains: Alle Menschen, Gross
Und Klein; Auch Was In Die
Quer; Auch Was In Die Quer; Der
Mond Soll Im Kalendar Stehn;
Zum Kessel Sprach Der Neue Topf
(Z80)

Heiteres Tierspiel
1-2pt jr cor,inst (easy) sc,cor pts
SCHOTTS B 129 s.p., ipa (Z81)

Herz, Sei Bereit
4 eq voices/4pt mix cor,2trp,opt
timp,strings,pno sc,voc sc
PELIKAN PE937 s.p., ipa (Z82)

Heute Tut Sich Auf Das Tor *Op.41,
cant
3pt mix cor/2pt jr cor/2pt wom cor,
narrator,solo,6strings/6winds,opt
pno (med easy) sc,cor pts SCHOTTS
ED. 4496 s.p., ipa (Z83)
SAB (easy) sc SCHOTTS CHBL 332 s.p.
(Z84)

Himmelsauen, Wolkenfluh *Op.21,
cradle
wom cor (med) sc SCHOTTS C 37 893
s.p. see from Zwei Wiegenlieder
(Z85)

Ich Trag Ein Goldnes Ringelein
see Zwei Volkslieder

Jahr, Dein Haupt Neig!
see Zwei Lieder Zum Jahreswechsel

Jetzt Kommt Die Frohliche Sommerzeit
mix cor sc SCHOTTS CHBL 282 s.p.
(Z86)

Junger Baum In Menschenhand *cant
1-2pt jr cor/wom cor/3pt mix cor/
4pt men cor,acap/inst sc,cor pts
SCHOTTS ED. 4852 s.p., ipa (Z87)

ZIPP, FRIEDRICH (cont'd.)

Junggesellenlied "Bursche Ging Ins
Tal" *folk,Russ
mix cor (med) sc SCHOTTS C 40 166
s.p. see from Drei Russische
Volkslieder (Z88)

Kein Schoner Land *cant/folk
1-2pt jr cor,rec,strings,perc
(easy) sc SCHOTTS B 102 s.p.
(Z89)

Lied Ist Uber Dem Wort
men cor sc SCHOTTS CHBL 188 s.p.
(Z90)

Maienfahrt *Op.6,No.1, cant
2pt jr cor,fl,strings (easy) sc,cor
pts SCHOTTS ED. 2919 s.p., ipa
(Z91)

Mit Lust Tat Ich Ausreiten
men cor,acap TONOS 83 s.p. see from
Drei Landsknechts-Lieder (Z92)

Onkel Mond Steht Am Tor *Op.21,
cradle
wom cor (med) sc SCHOTTS C 37 892
s.p. see from Zwei Wiegenlieder
(Z93)

Schenkenbachs Reiterlied
men cor,acap TONOS 82 s.p. see from
Drei Landsknechts-Lieder (Z94)

Stimmung Im Fruhling "Wie Dicht Das
Gras Hier Wachst" *Op.19,No.1
SSAATB (med) sc SCHOTTS C 37 894
s.p., voc pt SCHOTTS C 37 895A-D
s.p. see from Chinesische
Jahreszeiten (Z95)

Trinklied Im Sommer
men cor,acap TONOS 4597 s.p. (Z96)

Trost Im Leid "Wenn Du In Notejahren"
men cor sc SCHOTTS CHBL 131 s.p.
(Z97)

Wach Auf, Mein's Herzens Schone
men cor,acap TONOS 4 s.p. (Z98)

Weiss Mir Ein Schones Roselein *cant
3pt wom cor,solo,fl,clar,strings
(med easy) sc,cor pts SCHOTTS
ED. 2918 s.p., ipa (Z99)

Wer So Ein Faules Gretchen Hat
men cor sc SCHOTTS CHBL 45 s.p. see
from Drei Heitere Volkslieder
(Z100)

Zum Kessel Sprach Der Neue Topf
see Geht Alles Um Und Um

Zwei Lieder Zum Jahreswechsel
SAT/SAB,acap (med) sc SCHOTTS
CHBL 374A-B s.p.
contains: Der Du Die Zeit In
Handen Hast; Jahr, Dein Haupt
Neig! (Z101)

Zwei Volkslieder *Op.43, folk
4pt men cor&unis jr cor,acap, or
piano four hands (easy) sc,cor
pts SCHOTTS ED. 5449 s.p.
contains: Es, Es, Es Und Es; Ich
Trag Ein Goldnes Ringelein
(Z102)

Zwei Wiegenlieder *see Himmelsauen,
Wolkenfluh, Op.21; Onkel Mond
Steht Am Tor, Op.21 (Z103)

ZIRKUS TROLL see Werdin, Eberhard

ZIVOT see Foerster, Josef Bohuslav

ZLATY KOLOVRAT see Kricka, Jaroslav

ZOG EINST DURCH PARIS *folk
(Seeger, P.) [Ger] 4pt men cor
MERSEBURG EM9012 s.p. (Z104)

ZOGEN EINST FUNF WILDE SCHWANE see
Desch, Rudolf

ZOGEN EINST FUNF WILDE SCHWANE see
Lang, Hans

ZOLL, PAUL (1907-   )
Abendlied "Der Mond Ist Aufgegangen"
men cor sc SCHOTTS CHBL 65A-B s.p.
contains also: Nun Ruhen Alle
Walder (Z105)

Abschied "Scheiden Tut So Weh"
mix cor (easy) sc SCHOTTS CHBL 279
s.p. (Z106)

Ach, Du Liebste Mein
men cor sc SCHOTTS C 43 313 s.p.
see from Vier Heitere Chorlieder
(Z107)

Alles Ist Sang "Ich Ging Voruber"
SAATBB,acap (med) sc,voc pt SCHOTTS
C 39 008, C 39 009A-D s.p.
contains: Brauner Wald; Ein
Schoner Vogel Fiel; Ich Ging
Voruber; Jede Bitterste Not;
Wer Hat Zeit (Z108)

ZOLL, PAUL (cont'd.)

Am Meer "Der Wind Hat Unter Der
Kuste"
men cor sc SCHOTTS CHBL 66 s.p.
(Z109)

Am Ziele "Die Muden Schlafer Weckt
Keine Klage"
men cor sc SCHOTTS CHBL 87A-B s.p.
contains also: Heimgegangen
"Heimgegangen Bist Du" (Z110)

An Das Lied "Aus Des Tages Hetze Und
Hast"
mix cor (med) sc SCHOTTS CHBL 358
s.p. (Z111)
men cor sc SCHOTTS CHBL 163 s.p.
(Z112)

An Dem Bach "An Dem Bach Im
Wiesenrain"
mix cor sc SCHOTTS C 38 664 s.p.
see from Volkslieder Fremder
Volker (Z113)

An Des Haffes Strand "An Des Haffes
Anderm Strand" *folk
mix cor (med easy, contains also:
Dort Jenes Brunnlein) sc SCHOTTS
CHBL 353A-B s.p. see from Funf
Ostpreussische Volkslieder (Z114)

Arioso "Ich Will Euch Nicht Betrugen"
men cor sc SCHOTTS CHBL 186 s.p.
(Z115)

Bei Den Klangen Des Fandango *Span
[Ger] TTBB,pno sc,voc pt SCHOTTS
ED. 4986 s.p.
contains: Fandango "Am Heissen
Tage Mit Seiner Plage"; In All
Den Dunkelen Nachten "Gross Und
Schlank"; Rosalinda "An Das Tor
Des Palastes"; Traue Nimmer
Deinem Glucke; Wenn Du Mich
Liebtest, Gevatterin "O, Euer
Hahn, Gewatterin" (Z116)

Brauner Wald
see Alles Ist Sang "Ich Ging
Voruber"

Das Glockchen "Wo Das Glockchen
Ertont So Verschweigen"
men cor sc SCHOTTS C 37 857 s.p.
see from Drei Russische
Volkslieder (Z117)

Das Maidlein Wollt Ein Liebsten Han
see Drei Volkslieder

Das Verlassene Magdelein "Treu Und
Herzinniglich"
4pt jr cor/4pt wom cor (easy) sc
SCHOTTS CHBL 525 s.p. (Z118)

Das Waldkonzert "Konzert Ist Heute
Angesagt"
TTBB sc SCHOTTS C 38 104 s.p., voc
pt SCHOTTS C 38 105, 01-04 s.p.
(Z119)

Der Apfel "Ich Geb' Meinem Lieb Einen
Apfel" *see I Will Give My Love
An Apple

Der Kuckuck Ruft Im Grunen Wald
3pt wom cor/3pt jr cor,2 soli
(easy) sc SCHOTTS CHBL 539 s.p.
(Z120)

Der Lerche "Hort Die Erste Lerche
Singen"
4pt wom cor,acap (easy) sc SCHOTTS
CHBL 570A-B s.p. contains also:
Eia, Mein Kindchen (Z121)

Der Marsch Der Konige "Des Morgens
Fruh Im Dammer"
TTBB sc SCHOTTS C 39 501 s.p., voc
pt SCHOTTS C 39 502, 01-02 s.p.
(Z122)

Der Mutige Jager "Jetzt Nehm Ich
Meine Flinte"
men cor sc SCHOTTS CHBL 182 s.p.
(Z123)

Der Schlitten Eilt
SATTBB sc SCHOTTS C 38 665 s.p. see
from Volkslieder Fremder Volker
(Z124)

Der Sommer "Sommer, Ach Sommer"
see In Freuden Froh

Die Beiden Vogel "Zwei Verliebte
Kleine Vogel"
[Ger] men cor sc SCHOTTS C 40 772
s.p. (Z125)

Die Prinzessin Und Der Trommler
TTBB (rondo) sc SCHOTTS C 38 658
s.p., voc pt SCHOTTS
C 38 659, 01-04 s.p. (Z126)

Dort Jenes Brunnlein *folk
mix cor (easy, contains also: An
Des Haffes Strand "An Des Haffes
Anderm Strand") sc SCHOTTS
CHBL 353A-B s.p. see from Funf
Ostpreussische Volkslieder (Z127)

ZOLL, PAUL (cont'd.)

Drei Chore Nach Russischen Texten
*see Hat Zwei Fenster Meine
Seele; War Ich Madchen Ohne Mann
Geblieben; Wiegenlied "Wasch Die
Fusschen Meinem Kind" (Z128)

Drei Russische Volkslieder *see Das
Glockchen "Wo Das Glockchen
Ertont So Verschweigen"; "Im
Garten Die Beere, Die Rote";
Ringsum Leuchten Apfelbluten
(Z129)

Drei Volkslieder
4pt mix cor,pno (med easy) voc sc,
cor pts SCHOTTS ED. 4782 s.p.
contains: Das Maidlein Wollt Ein
Liebsten Han; Lugenmarchen "So
Geht Es Im
Schnutzelputzhausel";
Schwefelholzle (Z130)

Drei Volksliedsatze *see Es Ging
Eine Jungfrau Zarte; I Will Give
My Love An Apple, "Der Apfel "Ich
Geb' Meinem Lieb Einen Apfel"";
Ich Weiss Ein Jager, Der Blast
Sein Horn (Z131)

Echo-Lied "Wie Heisst Der
Burgermeister Von Wesel?"
3pt jr cor&4pt men cor,acap (easy)
sc SCHOTTS C 38 348 s.p. (Z132)

Eia, Mein Kindchen
see Zoll, Paul, Der Lerche "Hort
Die Erste Lerche Singen"

Ein Jager Wollt' Zum Jagen Gehn
SATTBB (med easy) sc SCHOTTS
CHBL 71 s.p. (Z133)
men cor&4pt wom cor/4pt jr cor
(easy) sc SCHOTTS CHBL 71 s.p.
(Z134)

Ein Schoner Vogel Fiel
see Alles Ist Sang "Ich Ging
Voruber"

Es Ging Eine Jungfrau Zarte *folk
mix cor (med easy) sc SCHOTTS
CHBL 375 s.p. see from Drei
Volksliedsatze (Z135)

Fandango "Am Heissen Tage Mit Seiner
Plage"
see Bei Den Klangen Des Fandango

Flieg Dahin, Lied
men cor sc SCHOTTS C 40 950 s.p.
see from Zwei Mannerchore (Z136)

Fliehender Sommer "Marguerite"
see Gluck Des Sommers

Funf Ostpreussische Volkslieder *see
An Des Haffes Strand "An Des
Haffes Anderm Strand"; Dort Jenes
Brunnlein; In Der Sonntagsfruhe;
O Kam Das Morgenrot Herauf;
Reiter, Schmuck Und Fein (Z137)

Gesellenliebe "Wach Auf, Du Lustiger
Sanger"
4pt men cor&4pt wom cor,acap (med
easy) sc SCHOTTS C 38 350 s.p.
see from Zwei Frohliche Lieder
(Z138)

Gluck Des Sommers
SATB (med) sc,voc pt SCHOTTS
C 40 479, C 40 480A-B s.p.
contains: Fliehender Sommer
"Marguerite"; Hoch Am Berg
"Hoch Am Berg, In Dem Wald"; Im
Grase "Glocken Und Zyanen"; Im
Korn "Durch Das Kornfeld";
Sommer "Am Abend Schweigt Die
Klage"; Vergissmeinnich "O Du
Leises Weh" (Z139)

Hast Du Mich Uberwunden
see In Freuden Froh

Hat Zwei Fenster Meine Seele
wom cor (med easy, contains also:
Wiegenlied "Wasch Die Fusschen
Meinem Kind") sc SCHOTTS C 41 865
s.p. see from Drei Chore Nach
Russischen Texten (Z140)

Heimgegangen "Heimgegangen Bist Du"
see Zoll, Paul, Am Ziele "Die Muden
Schlafer Weckt Keine Klage"

Heissischer Sangerspruch "Von Der
Arbeit, Von Der Freiheit"
mix cor (easy) sc SCHOTTS CHBL 378
s.p. (Z141)

Hoch Am Berg "Hoch Am Berg, In Dem
Wald"
see Gluck Des Sommers

I Will Give My Love An Apple *folk
"Der Apfel "Ich Geb' Meinem Lieb
Einen Apfel"" mix cor (easy/med

ZOLL, PAUL (cont'd.)

    easy) sc SCHOTTS CHBL 376 s.p.
    see from Drei Volksliedsatze
                       (Z142)

Iberisches Liederspiel
    wom cor,pno,opt perc (med) sc,cor
    pts SCHOTTS ED. 5297 s.p. (Z143)

Ich Ging Voruber
    see Alles Ist Sang "Ich Ging
    Voruber"

Ich Weiss Ein Jager, Der Blast Sein
    Horn *folk
    mix cor (med easy) sc SCHOTTS
    CHBL 377 s.p. see from Drei
    Volksliedsatze   (Z144)

Im Fruhlingsregen "Regen Rieselt,
    Fallt Ganz Leise"
    men cor sc SCHOTTS C 40 771 s.p.
                       (Z145)

"Im Garten Die Beere, Die Rote"
    men cor sc SCHOTTS C 37 858 s.p.
    see from Drei Russische
    Volkslieder   (Z146)

Im Grase "Glocken Und Zyanen"
    see Gluck Des Sommers

Im Korn "Durch Das Kornfeld"
    see Gluck Des Sommers

In All Den Dunkelen Nachten "Gross
    Und Schlank"
    see Bei Den Klangen Des Fandango

In Der Sonntagsfruhe
    mix cor (med easy) sc SCHOTTS
    CHBL 355 s.p. see from Funf
    Ostpreussische Volkslieder (Z147)

In Freuden Froh
    mix cor (med easy) sc SCHOTTS
    CHBL 297A-B s.p.
      contains: Der Sommer "Sommer, Ach
      Sommer"; Hast Du Mich
      Uberwunden   (Z148)

Irgendwo "Bluht Wohl Ein Wein: Fern
    Irgendwo"
    men cor sc SCHOTTS C 40 951 s.p.
    see from Zwei Mannerchore (Z149)

Jede Bitterste Not
    see Alles Ist Sang "Ich Ging
    Voruber"

Jenseits Des Tales Standen Ihre Zeit
    (Gotz, Robert) men cor sc SCHOTTS
    C 42 582 s.p.   (Z150)

Kleine, Braune Schone! "Wir Tessiner
    Sind Tapf're Soldaten"
    [Ger/It] men cor sc SCHOTTS
    C 39 278 s.p.   (Z151)

Laridah "Ach, Mein Schatz Ist
    Durchgegangen"
    men cor sc SCHOTTS C 43 316 s.p.
    see from Vier Heitere Chorlieder
                       (Z152)

Lasst Uns Wandern, Lasst Uns Reisen
    4pt men cor&4pt wom cor,acap (med)
    sc SCHOTTS C 38 349 s.p. see from
    Zwei Frohliche Lieder   (Z153)

Liebste, Ich Muss Nun Scheiden
    men cor sc SCHOTTS CHBL 206 s.p.
                       (Z154)

Lied In Den Rosen "Lasst Uns Singen
    Und Frohlich Sein"
    men cor sc SCHOTTS CHBL 61 s.p.
                       (Z155)

Lugenmarchen "So Geht Es Im
    Schnutzelputzhausel"
    see Drei Volkslieder

Lumpenlied "Ich Bin Ein Armer
    Bettelmusikant"
    men cor sc SCHOTTS C 43 314 s.p.
    see from Vier Heitere Chorlieder
                       (Z156)

Madchen Am Brunnen "Dana Ging Aus"
    mix cor sc SCHOTTS C 38 663 s.p.
    see from Volkslieder Fremder
    Volker   (Z157)

Meine Heimat "Nirgends Ist Der Himmel
    So Hoch"
    men cor sc SCHOTTS C 41 379 s.p.
                       (Z158)

Noch Bin Ich Nicht Dein
    mix cor sc SCHOTTS C 38 661 s.p.
    see from Volkslieder Fremder
    Volker   (Z159)

Nun Ruhen Alle Walder
    see Zoll, Paul, Abendlied "Der Mond
    Ist Aufgegangen"

Nun Wohlan, Ihr Waidleut' All
    3pt wom cor/3pt jr cor&men cor
    (easy) sc SCHOTTS CHBL 136 s.p.
                       (Z160)

ZOLL, PAUL (cont'd.)

O Filia Pulchra "Der Tag Ist Nun
    Verblichen"
    men cor sc SCHOTTS C 38 913 s.p.
                       (Z161)

O Kam Das Morgenrot Herauf
    mix cor (easy) sc SCHOTTS CHBL 354
    s.p. see from Funf Ostpreussische
    Volkslieder   (Z162)

O Lied "O Lied, Du Machst Den Armen
    Stark Und Reich"
    mix cor (med easy) sc SCHOTTS
    CHBL 290 s.p.   (Z163)
    4pt men cor,acap/pno/2horn,2trp,
    3trom,tuba voc sc SCHOTTS
    C 38 779 s.p., cor pts SCHOTTS
    CHBL 57 s.p., ipa   (Z164)

Pferde Zu Vieren Traben
    men cor sc SCHOTTS CNBL 56 s.p.
                       (Z165)

Reiter, Schmuck Und Fein
    mix cor (easy) sc SCHOTTS
    CHBL 356 s.p. see from Funf
    Ostpreussische Volkslieder (Z166)

Rheinisches Fuhrmanns Lied "Gibt Es
    Denn Ein Schoner Leben"
    men cor sc SCHOTTS C 39 350 s.p.
                       (Z167)

Ringsum Leuchten Apfelbluten
    TTBB sc SCHOTTS C 37 866 s.p., voc
    pt SCHOTTS C 37 867, 01-04 s.p.
    see from Drei Russische
    Volkslieder   (Z168)

Rosalinda "An Das Tor Des Palastes"
    see Bei Den Klangen Des Fandango

Sangergruss "Seid Willkommen"
    men cor,acap/brass sc SCHOTTS
    CHBL 120 s.p., ipa   (Z169)

Sangerspruch "Stimmet An Den Gesang"
    men cor,acap/brass sc SCHOTTS
    CHBL 119 s.p.   (Z170)

Scheine, Sonne, Scheine
    4pt jr cor (easy) sc SCHOTTS
    CHBL 564 s.p.   (Z171)

Schelmenliedchen "Auf Dem Wase Grast
    Der Hase"
    men cor sc SCHOTTS C 38 201 s.p.
                       (Z172)

Schwefelholzle
    see Drei Volkslieder

Serenade "Madchen, Mein Braunes"
    men cor,T solo sc SCHOTTS C 38 662
    s.p.   (Z173)

Sing, Kleine Nachtigall "Ein Winzer
    Hatt' Ein Tochterlein"
    men cor sc SCHOTTS C 40 481 s.p.
                       (Z174)

Sommer "Am Abend Schweigt Die Klage"
    see Gluck Des Sommers

Spanisches Liederspiel *CC7L,Span
    mix cor,pno,opt tamb, triangle,
    castanets (med) sc,cor pts
    SCHOTTS ED. 5073 s.p.   (Z175)

Traue Nimmer Deinem Glucke
    see Bei Den Klangen Des Fandango

Und Jetzo Kommt Die Nacht Herein
    men cor sc SCHOTTS CHBL 183 s.p.
                       (Z176)

Vergissmeinnich "O Du Leises Weh"
    see Gluck Des Sommers

Verschneit
    men cor,acap TONOS 3943 s.p. (Z177)

Vier Heitere Chorlieder *see Ach, Du
    Liebste Mein; Laridah "Ach, Mein
    Schatz Ist Durchgegangen";
    Lumpenlied "Ich Bin Ein Armer
    Bettelmusikant"; Zwei Spielleut
    "Es Zogen Zwei Spielleut" (Z178)

Vier Volkslied-Duette *CC4U,folk
    2 eq voices/2pt mix cor,pno PELIKAN
    PE805 s.p.   (Z179)

Voglein Im Kafig "Armes Voglein, Bist
    Du Krank"
    mix cor sc SCHOTTS C 38 660 s.p.
    see from Volkslieder Fremder
    Volker   (Z180)

Volkslieder Fremder Volker *see An
    Dem Bach "An Dem Bach Im
    Wiesenrain"; Der Schlitten Eilt;
    Madchen Am Brunnen "Dana Ging
    Aus"; Noch Bin Ich Nicht Dein;
    Voglein Im Kafig "Armes Voglein,
    Bist Du Krank"   (Z181)

Wanderschaft "Im Walde Bluht Der
    Seidelbast"
    men cor sc SCHOTTS CHBL 156 s.p.

ZOLL, PAUL (cont'd.)

                       (Z182)
War Ich Madchen Ohne Mann Geblieben
    wom cor (med easy) sc SCHOTTS
    C 41 866 s.p. see from Drei Chore
    Nach Russischen Texten   (Z183)

Weihelied "Fahne, Dich Weihen Wir"
    men cor sc SCHOTTS CHBL 88A-B s.p.
    contains also: Zur Hochzeit
    "Lieber Morgenstern"   (Z184)

Wenn Du Mich Liebtest, Gevatterin "O,
    Euer Hahn, Gewatterin"
    see Bei Den Klangen Des Fandango

Wer Hat Zeit
    see Alles Ist Sang "Ich Ging
    Voruber"

Wiegenlied "Wasch Die Fusschen Meinem
    Kind"
    wom cor (med easy, contains also:
    Hat Zwei Fenster Meine Seele) sc
    SCHOTTS C 41 865 s.p. see from
    Drei Chore Nach Russischen Texten
                       (Z185)

Windfreude "Wenn Der Wind Uber Wiesen
    Und Felder Rennt"
    4pt jr cor (med easy) sc SCHOTTS
    CHBL 565 s.p.   (Z186)

Wohlauf, Gesellen, Seid Froh Und
    Munter
    men cor sc SCHOTTS CHBL 181 s.p.
                       (Z187)

Wohlauf, In Gottes Schone Welt
    men cor sc SCHOTTS CHBL 72 s.p.
                       (Z188)

Wollt Zum Weib Dich Nehmen
    mix cor (easy) sc SCHOTTS CHBL 280
    s.p.   (Z189)

Zu Regensburg "Zu Regensburg Auf Der
    Kirchturmspitz"
    TTBB sc SCHOTTS C 40 249 s.p., voc
    pt SCHOTTS C 40 250, 01-02 s.p.
                       (Z190)

Zur Hochzeit "Lieber Morgenstern"
    see Zoll, Paul, Weihelied "Fahne,
    Dich Weihen Wir"
    mix cor (easy) sc SCHOTTS CHBL 299
    s.p.   (Z191)

Zur Stillen Nacht
    SSATTB,solo,acap (easy) sc SCHOTTS
    C 40 949 s.p.   (Z192)

Zwei Frohliche Lieder *see
    Gesellenliebe "Wach Auf, Du
    Lustiger Sanger"; Lasst Uns
    Wandern, Lasst Uns Reisen (Z193)

Zwei Mannerchore *see Flieg Dahin,
    Lied; Irgendwo "Bluht Wohl Ein
    Wein: Fern Irgendwo"   (Z194)

Zwei Spielleut "Es Zogen Zwei
    Spielleut"
    men cor sc SCHOTTS C 43 315 s.p.
    see from Vier Heitere Chorlieder
                       (Z195)

ZOLLER, ANTON
    Vini Boni Veritas
    men cor,acap TONOS 3977 s.p. (Z196)

ZOLLNER, KARL FRIEDRICH (1800-1860)
    Bill Of Fare, The
    (Leslie, C.E.) mix cor,acap (easy)
    oct PRESSER 332-06860 $.12 (Z197)

Einkehr
    men cor,acap TONOS 6308 s.p. (Z198)

Im Krug Zum Grunen Kranze
    men cor sc SCHOTTS CHBL 51 s.p.
                       (Z199)

Wanderschaft
    men cor,acap TONOS 6307 s.p. (Z200)

ZOLLT DANK DER EDLEN MUSIKA see
    Ophoven, Hermann

ZONN, PAUL
    I Love My Lady *madrigal
    3pt men cor,3clar sc AM.COMP.AL.
    $3.85, ipa   (Z201)

ZOO, BUDDINGH'ZOO see Strategier,
    Herman

ZOO ILLOGICAL see Grundman

ZOUHAR, ZDENEK (1927-   )
    By The Brook *see Upotoka

Po Desti
    jr cor SLOV.HUD.FOND EZS 10 s.p.
                       (Z202)

Upotoka
    "By The Brook" [Czech] jr cor,acap
    CZECH s.p.   (Z203)

ZPEV HRDINOV see Podesva, Jaromir

ZPEV MRTVYCH DETI see Pololanik, Zdenek

ZPEV NOVEHO VEKU see Barta, Lubor

ZPEV O ZEMI CESKE see Kalas, Julius

ZPEVY STARE CINY see Jirko, Ivo

ZPIVAME see Kabelac, Miloslav

ZRNO, FELIX (1890-   )
  Forwards *see Jen Dal

  Jen Dal
    "Forwards" [Czech] mix cor,acap
    CZECH s.p.   (Z204)

ZSCHIECHA, ALF (1908-   )
  Ein Lied Zur Nacht
    see Zschiecha, Alf, Wenn Die Bunten
    Fahnen Wehen

  Wenn Die Bunten Fahnen Wehen
    (Lang, Hans) jr cor (easy) sc
    SCHOTTS CHBL 529A-B s.p. contains
    also: Ein Lied Zur Nacht   (Z205)

ZSCHIEGNER, FRITZ
  Glocken
    men cor,acap TONOS 259 s.p.   (Z206)

ZU AUGSBURG STEHT EIN HOHES HAUS see
  Silcher, Friedrich

ZU END: MIR IST'S ZU WOHL ERGANGEN see
  Silcher, Friedrich

ZU FRANKFURT AN DER ODER see Weber,
  Bernhard

ZU KOBLENZ AUF DER BRUCKEN see Werner,
  Kurt

ZU MEINEM SCHATZCHEN MUSS ICH GEHN "ICH
  KANN NICHT SITZEN" see Desch,
  Rudolf

ZU MILTENBERG AM MAINE see Widmann,
  Erasmus

ZU REGENSBURG "ZU REGENSBURG AUF DER
  KIRCHTURMSPITZ" see Zoll, Paul

ZUCKMAYER-CHORZYKLUS see Krietsch,
  Georg

ZUEIGNUNG "IM WIDERHALL WIRD HIER ZUM
  DORT" see Haas, Joseph

ZUM ABSCHIED "FORT MIT DEN GRILLEN" see
  Mohler, Philipp

ZUM ANFANG see Edler, Robert

ZUM ANFANG "MACHE DEINEM MEISTER EHRE"
  see Schumann, Robert (Alexander)

ZUM AUSKLANG see Rosenstengel, Albrecht

ZUM BEGRABNIS "WER WEISS, WIE NAHE MIR
  MEIN ENDE" see Seeger, Peter

ZUM GUTEN ENDE see Fischer, Ernst

ZUM KESSEL SPRACH DER NEUE TOPF see
  Zipp, Friedrich

ZUM LOB DER ARBEIT see Haas, Joseph

ZUM LOB DER MUSIK see Haas, Joseph

ZUM LOB DER NATUR see Haas, Joseph

ZUM, MICHAELITAG see Bartok, Bela,
  Mihalynapi Koszonto

ZUM RIO GRANDE *folk,Eng
  (Cadow, Paul) men cor,pno sc,voc sc
  TONOS 2186 s.p.   (Z207)

ZUM RUNDETANZ "AUF, ES DUNKELT" see
  Schubert, Franz (Peter)

ZUM TANZE, DA GEHT EIN MADEL *folk
  (Biebl, F.) [Ger] 4pt mix cor
  MERSEBURG EM9221 s.p.   (Z208)

ZUM TANZE, DA GEHT EIN MADEL see
  Muntzel, Herbert

ZUM TANZE, DA GEHT EIN MADEL see Rein,
  Walter

ZUM TANZE, DA GEHT EIN MADEL see
  Rische, Quirin

ZUM TANZE, DA GEHT EIN MADEL see
  Werdin, Eberhard

ZUM TANZE, DA GEHT EIN MADEL see
  Wolters, Karl-Heinz

ZUM VOLKSTRAUERTAG see Mayer, Otto

ZUPANOVIC, LOVRO (1925-   )
  Sign Of The Orient, The
    cor CROATICA   (Z209)

ZUR ERNTE "DAS FELD IST WEISS" see
  Rein, Walter

ZUR FREUDE BEREIT
  unis wom cor SCHOTTS C 42 532E s.p.
  see also Alle Singen Heft 1   (Z210)

ZUR HOCHZEIT "LIEBER MORGENSTERN" see
  Zoll, Paul

ZUR HOHEN JAGD see Schumann, Robert
  (Alexander)

ZUR NACHT see Reger, Max

ZUR STILLEN NACHT see Zoll, Paul

ZUR TRAUUNG "EWGE LIEBE, EWGE LIEBE"
  see Lang, Hans

ZUR VERLOBUNG "SIE HAT NICHTS" see
  Zehm, Friedrich

ZURNE NICHT DES HERBSTES WIND see
  Schumann, Robert (Alexander)

ZVITANIE see Ocenas, Andrej

ZWA STERNDLAN *CC2U
  (Kremser) mix cor LIENAU
  LIEDERHARFE NR.9 sc s.p., cor pts
  s.p.   (Z211)

ZWEENE "ZWEENE SCHLAFEN SICHRER EIN"
  see Sturmer, Bruno

ZWEI BAROCKLIEDER see Sutermeister,
  Heinrich

ZWEI BULGARISCHE VOLKSLIEDER see
  Rettich, Wilhelm

ZWEI CHANSONS see Schneider, Walther

ZWEI CHORLIEDER see Schnitzler,
  Heinrich

ZWEI CHORLIEDER see Rothschuh, Franz

ZWEI-DREIMAL UMS HAUS *folk
  (Kracke, Hans) men cor,acap TONOS 71
  s.p.   (Z212)

ZWEI EDLE BRAUER see Korn, Peter Jona

ZWEI FLAMISCHE VOLKSWEISEN see Weber,
  Bernhard

ZWEI FRANZOSISCHE VOLKSLIEDER see
  Motte, Diether de la

ZWEI FROHLICHE LIEDER see Zoll, Paul

ZWEI GITARREN--RASPOSCHOL *folk,Russ
  (Seib, Valentin) men cor,acap sc,cor
  pts TONOS 2034 s.p.   (Z213)

ZWEI HEITERE CHORLIEDER see Biebl,
  Franz

ZWEI HEITERE MANNERCHORE see Biebl,
  Franz

ZWEI IRISCHE VOLKSLIEDER *see Aus
  Weiter Ferne; Una Bhan "O Una Bhan,
  Du Schlanke"   (Z214)

ZWEI KINDERCANTATEN see Marx, Karl

ZWEI KINDERCHORE IM VOLKSTON see
  Barthel, Ursula

ZWEI KLEINE CHORE see Wolters, Karl-
  Heinz

ZWEI KLEINE CHORLIEDER see Biebl, Franz

ZWEI LIEDER BEIM WEIN see Genzmer,
  Harald

ZWEI LIEDER ZUM JAHRESWECHSEL see Zipp,
  Friedrich

ZWEI MADRIGALE see Sutermeister,
  Heinrich

ZWEI MANNERCHORE see Lang, Hans

ZWEI MANNERCHORE see Sutermeister,
  Heinrich

ZWEI MANNERCHORE see Zoll, Paul

ZWEI SINNSPRUCHE see Leucht, Carl
  Friedrich

ZWEI SLAWISCHE VOLKSLIEDSATZE *see
  Abschied Am Brunnen "Spannt Die
  Pferde Aus"; Auf Der Fahrt "Hopp,
  Hei! Und Wir Fahren"   (Z215)

ZWEI SPIELE FUR KINDER see Biebl, Franz

ZWEI SPIELLEUT "ES ZOGEN ZWEI
  SPIELLEUT" see Zoll, Paul

ZWEI STANDCHEN see Lang, Hans

ZWEI TANZLIEDER see Gerster, Ottmar

ZWEI TRINKLIEDER see Werdin, Eberhard

ZWEI VOLKSLIED-VARIATIONEN see Desch,
  Rudolf

ZWEI VOLKSLIEDER see Zipp, Friedrich

ZWEI VOLKSLIEDER see Herrmann, Hugo

ZWEI VOLKSLIEDER see Schroeder, Hermann

ZWEI VOLKSLIEDSATZE see Hessenberg,
  Kurt

ZWEI WIEGENLIEDER see Zipp, Friedrich

ZWEI ZEITGLOSSEN see Seeger, Peter

ZWEIERLEI NACHT UND ZWEIERLEI TAG see
  Gerster, Ottmar

ZWEISAMKEIT see Trunk, Richard

ZWEIUNDZWANZIG VOLKSLIEDER *CC22U,
  folk,Ger
  cor,brass/strings SCHOTTS C 40 494-01
  s.p., ipa   (Z216)

ZWILLINGE see Strobl, Otto

ZWISCHEN BERG UND TIEFEM TAL see
  Pepping, Ernst

ZWISCHEN HEUTE UND MORGEN see Zentner,
  Johannes

ZWOLF LIEDER UND ROMANZEN see Brahms,
  Johannes

ZWOLF LIEDER UND ROMANZEN VOL. I see
  Brahms, Johannes

ZWOLF LIEDER UND ROMANZEN VOL. II see
  Brahms, Johannes

ZYKLUS SOMMERBILDER see Ketterer, Ernst

Publishers and Addresses

The list of publishers which follows contains the code assigned for each publisher, the name and address of the publisher, and agents who distribute their publications. This is the master list used for the Music-In-Print series and represents those publishers included in all volumes thus far published. Therefore, all of the publishers do not necessarily occur in the present volume.

Code	Publisher	Agent
ABC	ABC Music Co.	BIG 3
ABER	The Aberbach Group	BIG 3
ABINGDON	Abingdon Press 201 Eighth Ave. S. Nashville, TN 37202	
AGAPE	Agape	HOPE
ALBERSEN	Muziekhandel Albersen & Co.	DONEMUS
ALBERT	J. Albert & Son Pty. Ltd.	EMI
ALCOVE	Alcove Music	WESTERN
ALFRED	Alfred Publishing Co., Inc. 75 Channel Drive Port Washington, NY 11050	
ALKOR	Alkor Edition	BAREN.
ALLANS	Allans Music Pty. Ltd. 276 Collins Street Melbourne, Australia	
ALLOWAY	Alloway Publications Box 25 Santa Monica, CA 90406	
ALPHENAAR	W. Alphenaar	DONEMUS
ALSBACH	G. Alsbach & Co.	PETERS
ALSBACH & D	Alsbach & Doyer	PETERS
AM. COMP. AL.	American Composers Alliance 170 West 74th Street New York, NY 10023	
AM. INST. MUS.	American Institute of Musicology	HANSSLER
AM. MUS. ED.	American Music Edition	FISCHER, C
	American Musicological Society	GALAXY
AMP	AMP	SCHIRM. G
AMICI	Gli Amici della Musica da Camera Via Bocca di Leone 25 Rome, Italy	
AMPHION	Editions Amphion	KERBY
ANDEL	Edition Andel Madeliefjeslaan, 26 8400 Oostende Belgium	
APOGEE	Apogee Press, Inc.	WORLD
A-R ED	A-R Editions, Inc. 152 West Johnson St. Madison, WI 53703	
ARCO	Arco Music Publishers	WESTERN
ARION	Coleccion Arion	MEXICANAS
ARNOLD	Edward Arnold Series	NOVELLO
ARS NOVA	Ars Nova	DONEMUS PRESSER
ART MAST	Art Masters 2614 Nicollet Ave. Minneapolis, MN 55408	
ARTIA	Artia	BOOSEY
ARTRANSA	Artransa Music	WESTERN
ASHDOWN	Edwin Ashdown Ltd.	BOOSEY-CAN
ASHLEY	Ashley Publications, Inc.	CENTURY
	Associated Music Publishers see AMP	
AUGSBURG	Augsburg Publishing House 426 S. Fifth Street Minneapolis, MN 55415	
AULOS	Aulos Music Publishers P.O. Box 411 Montgomery, NY 12547	
AUTRY	Gene Autry's Publishing Companies	BIG 3
AVANT	Avant Music	WESTERN
BANK	Annie Bank	PETERS
BANKS MUS	Banks Music Co.	BRODT
BAREN.	Bärenreiter Verlag Heinrich Schütz Allee 29-37 3500 Kassel-Wilhelmshöhe Germany	BOONIN MAGNAMUSIC
BARON, M	M. Baron Co. Box 149 Oyster Bay, NY 11771	
BARRY-ARG	Barry & Cia	BOOSEY
BASART	Les Editions Internationales Basart	GENERAL
BEACON HILL	Beacon Hill Press	LILLENAS
BECKEN	Beckenhorst	PRESSER
BEECHWD	Beechwood Music Corp.	BIG 3
BELAIEFF	M.P. Belaieff	PETERS
BELMONT	Belmont Music Publishers P.O. Box 49961 Los Angeles, CA 90049	
BELWIN	Belwin-Mills Publishing Corp. Melville, NY 11746	
BENSON	John T. Benson 1625 Broadway Nashville, TN 37202	
BERANDOL	Berandol Music Ltd. 11 St. Joseph Street Toronto, Ontario Canada	

Code	Publisher	Agent
BERBEN	Edizioni Musicali Berben	PRESSER
BERGMANS	W. Bergmans	PETERS
BERLIN	Irving Berlin Music Corp. 1290 Avenue of the Americas New York, NY 10019	
BERNOUILLI	Ed. Bernouilli	DONEMUS
BEZIGE BIJ	De Bezige Bij	DONEMUS
BIELER	Edmund Bieler Musikverlag Zulpicher Strasse 85 5 Cologne-Sulz, West Germany	
BIG 3	Big 3 Music Corp. 729 Seventh Avenue New York, NY 10019	
BIG BELL	Big Bells, Inc. 33 Hovey Ave. Trenton, NJ 08610	
BILLAUDOT	Editions Billaudot	PRESSER
BIRNBACH	Richard Birnbach Dürerstrasse 28a 1 Berlin-Lichterfelde-West Germany	
BOHM	Anton Böhm & Sohn Postfach 11036 g Lange Gasse 26 D-89 Augsburg 11, West Germany	
BOMART	Bomart Music Publications	AMP
BONGIOVANI	Casa Musicale Francesco Bongiovani	BELWIN
BOONIN	Joseph Boonin, Inc. P.O. Box 2124 S. Hackensack, NJ 07606	
BOOSEY	Boosey & Hawkes, Inc. Oceanside, NY 11572	
BOOSEY-CAN	Boosey & Hawkes Ltd. 279 Yorkland Blvd. Willowdale, Ontario Canada	BOOSEY
BOOSEY-ENG	Boosey & Hawkes	BOOSEY
BOSSE	Gustav Bosse Verlag	MAGNAMUSIC BOONIN
BORNEMANN	Editions Bornemann	BELWIN
BOSTON	Boston Music Company	FRANK
BOSWORTH	Bosworth & Company, Ltd. 14/18 Heddon Street Regent Street London, W.1, England	
BOTE	Bote & Bock	AMP
BOURNE	Bourne Co. 1212 Avenue of the Americas New York, NY 10036	
BRANDON	Brandon Press, Inc. 221 Columbus Avenue Boston, MA 02116	
BRATFISCH	Musikverlag Georg Bratfisch Trendelstrasse 5 865 Kulmbach, West Germany	
BRAUER	Editions Musicales Herman Brauer 30, Rue Saint Christophe, 30 Bruxelles, Belgium	

Code	Publisher	Agent
BREITKOPF-L	Breitkopf & Härtel, Leipzig	BROUDE, A
BREITKOPF-W	Breitkopf & Härtel, Wiesbaden	AMP
BRIDGE	Bridge Music Publishing Co. 1350 Villa St. Mountain View, CA 94042	
BRIGHT STAR	Bright Star Music Pubications	WESTERN
BR. CONT. MUS.	British and Continental Music Agencies, Ltd.	EMI
BROADMAN	Broadman Press 127 Ninth Avenue North Nashville, TN 37203	
BRODT	Brodt Music Co. P.O. Box 1207 Charlotte, NC 28201	
BROEKMANS	Broekmans & Van Poppel	PETERS
BROGNEAUX	Editions Musicales Brogneaux	ELKAN, H
BROUDE, A	Alexander Broude, Inc. 225 West 57 Street New York, NY 10019	
BROUDE BR.	Broude Brothers Ltd. 56 West 45 Street New York, NY 10036	
BROWN	Brown University Choral Series	BOOSEY
BRUZZI	Aldo Bruzzichelli, Editore	AMP
BUDAPEST	Editio Musica Budapest P.O.B. 322 Budapest, Hungary	BOOSEY
CAILLET	Lucien Caillet	SOUTHERN
CAMBIATA	Cambiata Press P.O. Box 1151 Conway, AR 72032	
CANAAN	Canaanland Publications	WORD
CANYON	Canyon Press, Inc.	KERBY
CAPELLA	Capella Music, Inc.	BOURNE
CARISH	Carisch S.p.A. Via General Fara, 39 20124 Milan, Italy	
CARLTON	Carlton Musikverlag	GERIG
CARUS	Carus-Verlag	HANSSLER
CBDM	Centre Belge De Documentation Musicale	ELKAN, H
CENTURY	Century Music Publishing Co. 263 Veterans Boulevard Carlstadt, NJ 07072	
CENTURY PR	Century Press Publishers 412 North Hudson Oklahoma City, OK 73102	
CHANT	Editions Le Chant Du Monde 64, rue Ampere Paris, France	
CHANTRY	Chantry Music Press, Inc. Wittenberg University Box 1101 Springfield, OH 45501	
CHAPLET	Chaplet Music Corp.	PARAGON

Code	Publisher	Agent	Code	Publisher	Agent
CHAPPELL	Chappell & Co., Inc. 810 Seventh Avenue New York, NY 10019		CROATICA	Croation Music Institute	DRUS. HRVAT. SKLAD.
CHAPPELL-ENG	Chappell & Co., Ltd. Classical Music Division 50 New Bond St. London, W1, England		CURCI	Edizioni Curci Galleria del Corso 4 20122 Milan, Italy	
CHAPPELL-FR	Chappell S.A. 25, rue d'Hauteville Paris, France		CURWEN	J. Curwen & Sons	SCHIRM. G
			CZECH	Czechoslovak Music Information Centre Besedni 3 Prague 1, Czechoslovakia	
CHAPUIS	Editions Henn-Chapuis	HENN			
CHAR CROS	Charing Cross Music, Inc.	BIG BELL	DA CAPO	Da Capo Press, Inc. 227 West 17 Street New York, NY 10011	
CHARTER	Charter Publications, Inc. Valley Forge, PA 19481				
CHESTER	J. & W. Chester, Ltd.	BROUDE, A MAGNAMUSIC	DEAN	Roger Dean Publishing Co. 324 W. Jackson Macomb, IL 61455	
CHORISTERS	Choristers Guild 440 Northlake Center P.O. Box 38188 Dallas, TX 75238		DEIRO	Pietro Deiro Publications 133 Seventh Ave. South New York, NY 10014	
CHOUDENS	Choudens	PETERS	DELRIEU	Georges Delrieu & Cie	GALAXY
CHRIS	Christophorus-Verlag Herder Hermann-Herder-Strasse 4 D-7800 Freiburg/Breisgau, West Germany		DEUTSCHER	Deutscher Verlag für Musik	BROUDE, A
			DITSON	Oliver Ditson Co.	PRESSER
			DOBLINGER	Ludwig Doblinger Verlag	AMP
CHURCH	John Church Co.	PRESSER	DONEMUS	Stichting Donemus	PETERS
CIMINO	Cimino Publications P.O. Box 75 1646 New Highway Farmingdale, L.I., NY 11735		DOVER	Dover Publications, Inc. 180 Varick Street New York, NY 10014	
CLARK	Clark and Cruickshank Music Publishers	BERANDOL	DRUS. HRVAT. SKLAD.	Drustvo Hrvatskih Skladatelja Berislaviceva 9 Zagreb, Yugoslavia	
COLE	M. M. Cole Publishing Co. 251 East Grand Avenue Chicago, IL 60611		DRUSTVO	Drustvo Slovenskih Skladateljev Trg Francoske Revolucije 6 61000 Ljubljana, Yugoslavia	
COLFRANC	Colfranc Music Publishing Corp.	KERBY	DRZAVNA	Drzavna Zalozba Slovenije	DRUSTVO
COLOMBO	Franco Colombo Publications	BELWIN	DURAND	Durand & Cie	ELKAN-V
COMP/PERF	Composer/Performer Edition 2101 22 Street Sacramento, CA 95818		ECK	Van Eck & Zn.	DONEMUS
			EGTVED	Edition Egtved Musikhojskolens Forlag ApS DK-6040 Egtved, Denmark	
CONCERT	Concert Music Publishing Co.	BOURNE	EIGEN UITGAVE	Eigen Uitgave van de Componist (Self-published by the composer)	DONEMUS
CONCORD	Concord Music Publishing Co.	ELKAN, H			
CONCORDIA	Concordia Publishing House 3558 S. Jefferson Avenue St. Louis, MO 63118		ELKAN, H	Henri Elkan Music Publisher 1316 Walnut Street Philadelphia, PA 19107	
CONGRESS	Congress Music Publications 501 Fagler Federal Bldg. 111 N.E. 1 St. Miami, FL 33132		ELKAN-V	Elkan-Vogel, Inc.	PRESSER
			ELKIN	Elkin & Co. Ltd.	NOVELLO
			EMI	EMI Music Publishing Ltd. 21 Denmark St. London, WC2H 8NE, England	
CONSORTIUM	Consortium Musical	ELKAN-V			
CRAMER	J.B. Cramer & Co., Ltd.	BRODT	ENGSTROEM	Engstroem & Soedering	PETERS
CRES.-NETH	Uitg. Crescendo	DONEMUS	ENOCH	Enoch & Cie	AMP
CRESCENDO	Crescendo Music Sales Co. Box 395 Naperville, IL 60540		ERDMANN	Rudolf Erdmann, Musikverlag Adolfsallee 34 62 Wiesbaden, Germany	
CRITERION	Criterion Music Corp. 17 W. 60th Street New York, NY 10028		ERIKS	Eriks Musikhandel & Förlag AB Karlavägen 40 Stockholm Ö, Sweden	

Code	Publisher	Agent
ESCHIG	Editions Max Eschig	AMP
ESSO	Van Esso & Co.	DONEMUS
EULENBURG	Edition Eulenburg	PETERS
EXPERIMENTAL	Experimental Music Catalogue 208 Ladbroke Grove London, W.10, England	
FABER	Faber Music Ltd.	SCHIRM. G
FAR WEST	Far West Music	WESTERN
FARRELL	The Wes Farrell Organization	BIG 3
FAZER	Musik Fazer Aleksanterinkatu 11 Helsinki 11, Finland	
FELDMAN, B	B. Feldman & Co., Ltd.	EMI
FEMA	Fema Music Publications	CRESCENDO
FINE ARTS	Fine Arts Music Press P.O. Box 45144 Tulsa, OK 74145	
FISCHER, C	Carl Fischer 62 Cooper Square New York, NY 10003	
FISCHER, J	J. Fischer & Bro.	BELWIN
FISHER	Fisher Music Co.	PLYMOUTH
FITZSIMONS	H. T. Fitzsimons Co. 615 North LaSalle St. Chicago, IL 60610	
FLAMMER	Harold Flammer, Inc.	SHAWNEE
FOETISCH	Foetisch Freres	SCHIRM. EC
FOG	Dan Fog Musikforlag	PETERS
FORBERG	Rob. Forberg-P. Jurgenson, Musikverlag	PETERS
FORLIVESI	A. Forlivesi & C. Via Roma 4 Florence, Italy	
FORNI	Arnaldo Forni Editore Via Triumvirato 7 40132 Bologna, Italy	
FORTRESS PR	Fortress Press 2900 Queen Lane Philadelphia, PA 19129	
FOSTER	Mark Foster Music Co. Box 4012 Champaign, IL 61820	
FOSTER-HALL	Foster-Hall Publications	PRESSER
FOUR ST	Four Star Publishing Co.	BIG 3
FOX	Sam Fox Music Sales Corp.	PEPPER
FRANCIS	Francis, Day & Hunter, Ltd.	EMI
FRANK	Frank Distributing Corp. 116 Boylston Street Boston, MA 02116	
FRANTON	Franton Music 4620 Sea Isle Memphis, TN 38117	
FREDONIA	Fredonia Press c/o Paul J. Sifler 3947 Fredonia Dr. Hollywood, CA 90028	

Code	Publisher	Agent
FREEMAN, H	H. Freeman & Co., Ltd.	EMI
GALAXY	Galaxy Music Corp. 2121 Broadway New York, NY 10023	
GALLEON	Galleon Press 94 Greenwich Ave. New York, NY 10011	
GALLIARD	Galliard, Ltd.	GALAXY
GEHRMANS	Carl Gehrmans Musikförlag Postbox 505 10126 Stockholm, Sweden	
GENERAL	General Music Publishing Co.	FRANK
GENERAL WDS	General Words and Music Co.	KJOS
GENTRY	Gentry Publications	PRESSER
GERIG	Musikverlage Hans Gerig Drususgasse 7-11 5 Köln, Germany	
GIA	GIA Publications 7404 S. Mason Avenue Chicago, IL 60638	
GILLMAN	Gillman Publications	PRESSER
GORNSTON	David Gornston	FOX
GOSPEL	Gospel Publishing House 1445 Boonville Ave. Springfield, MO 65802	
GRAS	Editions Gras	BARON, M
GRAY	H. W. Gray Co., Inc.	BELWIN
GREENWOOD	Greenwood Press	WORLD
GREGG	Gregg International Publishers, Ltd. 1 Westmead, Farnborough, Hants England	
	Gregorian Institute of America see GIA	
HAMELLE	Hamelle & Cie	ELKAN-V
HANSEN-DEN	Wilhelm Hansen Edition	BROUDE, A MAGNAMUSIC
HANSEN-ENG	Hansen, London	ALBERT
HANSEN-US	Hansen Press 1842 West Avenue Miami Beach, FL 33139	
HANSSLER	Hänssler-Verlag	PETERS
HARMONIA	Harmonia Uitgave	PETERS
HARRIS	Frederick Harris Music Co., Ltd. P.O. Box 670 Oakville, Ontario Canada	
HART	F. Pitman Hart & Co., Ltd.	BRODT
HASTINGS	Hastings Music Corp.	BIG 3
HATIKVAH	Hatikvah Publications	TRANSCON.
HEER	Joh. de Heer & Zn.	PETERS
HEIDELBERGER	Heidelberger	BAREN.
HEINRICH.	Heinrichshofen's Verlag	PETERS
HELIOS	Editio Helios	FOSTER

Code	Publisher	Agent
HENLE	G. Henle Verlag Schongauerstrasse 24 8 Munich 55, Germany	
HENN	Editions Henn 8 rue de Hesse Geneve, Switzerland	
	Editions Henn-Chapuis	HENN
HENREES	Henrees Music Ltd.	EMI
HERITAGE	Heritage Music Press	LORENZ
HERITAGE PUB	Heritage Publications	CENTURY
HEUGEL	Heugel & Cie	PRESSER
HEUWEKE.	Edition Heuwekemeijer	PRESSER
HIEBER	Musikverlag Max Hieber Kaufingerstrasse 23 8000 Munich 33, Germany	
HIGHGATE	Highgate Press	GALAXY
HIGHLAND	Highland Music Co. 1311 N. Highland Avenue Hollywood, CA 90028	
HINRICHSEN	Hinrichsen Edition, Ltd.	PETERS
HOFMEISTER	Veb Friedrich Hofmeister, Musikverlag, Leipzig	BROUDE, A
HOLLY-PIX	Holly-Pix Music Publishing Co.	WESTERN
HONOUR	Honour Publications	WESTERN
HOPE	Hope Publishing Co. 380 S. Main Place Carol Stream, IL 60187	
HUG	Hug & Company	PETERS
HUNTZINGER	R. L. Huntzinger Publications	WILLIS
ICELAND	Iceland Music Information Centre	ELKAN, H
INTERNAT.	International Music Co. 511 Fifth Avenue New York, NY 10017	
INTERNAT. S.	International Music Service Box 66, Ansonia Station New York, NY 10023	
ISR. MUS. INST.	Israel Music Institute	BOOSEY
ISR. PUB. AG.	Israel Publishers Agency	SESAC
ISRAELI	Israeli Music Publications	BROUDE, A
JAPAN	Japan Federation of Composers Ohminato Building 14, Suga-Cho Shinjuku-ku Tokyo, Japan	
J.B. PUB	J.B. Publications P.O. Box 3 Interlochen, MI 49643	
JEANNETTE	Ed. Jeannette	DONEMUS
JEHLE	Jehle	HANSSLER
JOBERT	Editions Jean Jobert	PRESSER
JOHNSON	Johnson Reprint Corp. 111 Fifth Avenue New York, NY 10003	
JRB	JRB Music Education Materials Distributor	PRESSER

Code	Publisher	Agent
JUSKO	Jusko Publications	WILLIS
KALMUS	Edwin F. Kalmus Miami-Dade Industrial Park P.O. Box 1007 Opa-Locka, FL 33054	
KAMMEN	J. & J. Kammen Co., Inc. 351 West 52 St. New York, NY 10019	
KANE	Walter Kane & Son, Inc. 351 West 52 St. New York, NY 10019	
KENDOR	Kendor Music, Inc. Delevan, NY 14042	
KENYON	Kenyon Publications	PLYMOUTH
KERBY	E. C. Kerby, Ltd.	BOONIN
KING	King Music Publishing Co.	KANE
KING, R	Robert King Music Co. 112 A. Main St. North Easton, MA 02356	
KISTNER	Kistner & Siegel	TONGER
KJOS	Neil A. Kjos Music Co. 525 Busse Hwy. Park Ridge, IL 60068	
KON BOND	Kon Bond van Chr. Zang-en Oratoriumverenigingen	DONEMUS
KONINKLIJK	Koninklijk Nederlands Zangersverbond	DONEMUS
KRENN	Ludwig Krenn Reindorfgasse 42 1150 Wien 45, Austria	
KROMPHOLZ	Krompholz & Co. Spitalgasse 28 3001 Bern, Switzerland	
KRUSEMAN	Ed. Philip Kruseman	DONEMUS
KYSAR	Michael Kysar 1250 S. 211th Place Seattle, WA 98148	
LAND	A. Land Ezn, Muziekuitgevers	DONEMUS
LANDES	Landesverbands Evangliche Kirchenchöre in Bayern	HANSSLER
LAUDINELLA	Laudinella Reihe	HANSSLER
LAWSON	Lawson-Gould	SCHIRM. G
LEDUC	Alphonse Leduc	BARON, M PRESSER
LEMOINE	Henry Lemoine & Cie	ELKAN-V
LENGNICK	Alfred Lengnick & Co., Ltd.	HARRIS
LEONARD-ENG	Leonard, Gould & Bolttler	LESLIE
LEONARD-US	Hal Leonard Music 960 East Mark St. Winona, MN 55987	
LESLIE	Leslie Music Supply	BRODT
LEUCKART	F.E.C. Leuckart	AMP
LEXICON	Lexicon Music, Inc.	WORD
LICHTENAUER	W. F. Lichtenauer	DONEMUS
LIENAU	Robert Lienau, Musikverlag	PETERS

Code	Publisher	Agent
LILLENAS	Lillenas Publishing Co.	BELWIN
LITURGICAL	Liturgical Press St. Johns Abbey Collegeville, MN 56321	
LOOP	Loop Music Co.	KJOS
LORENZ	Lorenz Industries 501 E. Third Street Dayton, OH 45401	
LUDWIG	Ludwig Music Publishing Co. 557-67 E. 140 Street Cleveland, OH 44110	
LUNDQUIST	Abr. Lundquist AB, Musikforlag Katarina Bangata 17 116 25 Stockholm, Sweden	
LYCHE	Harald Lyche	PETERS
MAGNAMUSIC	Magnamusic-Baton, Inc. 10370 Page Industrial Blvd. St. Louis, MO 63132	
MARCHAND	Marchand, Paap en Strooker	DONEMUS
MARKS	Edward B. Marks Music Corp.	BELWIN
MCA	Mills/MCA Joint Venture	BELWIN
MCAFEE	McAfee Music Corp.	LORENZ
MCGIN-MARX	McGinnis & Marx	DEIRO
MEDIA	Media Press Box 895 Champaign, IL 61820	
MEL BAY	Mel Bay Publications, Inc. 107 West Jefferson Ave. Kirkwood, MO 63122	
MERCURY	Mercury Music Corp.	PRESSER
MERION	Merion Music, Inc.	PRESSER
MERSEBURG	Verlag Merseburger Berlin	BAREN. PETERS
MERRYMOUNT	Merrymount Music, Inc.	PRESSER
METROPOLIS	Editions Metropolis	ELKAN, H
MEXICANAS	Ediciones Mexicanas De Musica Avenida Juarez 18 Mexico City, Mexico	
MILLER	Miller Music Corp.	BIG 3
MINKOFF	Minkoff Reprints Chemin de la Mousse 46 1225 Chêne-Bourg Geneva, Switzerland	
MJQ	MJQ Music, Inc.	FOX
MODERN	Edition Modern Musikverlag Hans Wewerka Franz-Joseph-Strasse 2 8 München 13, Germany	
MOECK	Hermann Moeck Verlag	BELWIN
MORAVIAN	Moravian Music Foundation	ABINGDON BELWIN BOOSEY BRODT PETERS
MOSELER	Möseler Verlag Postfach 460 3340 Wolfenbüttel Germany	

Code	Publisher	Agent
MOWBRAY	A. R. Mowbray & Co., Ltd.	PRESSER
MULLER	Willy Müller	PETERS
MUNSTER	Van Munster Editie	DONEMUS
MURPHY	Spud Murphy Publications	WESTERN
MUS. ANT. BOH.	Musica Antiqua Bohemia	BOOSEY
MUS. VIVA. HIST.	Musica Viva Historica	BOOSEY
MUSIC	Music Sales Corp. 33 West 60 Street New York, NY 10023	
MUSIC INFO	Muzichi Informationi Centar	GERIG
MUSICO	Musico Muziekuitgeverij	DONEMUS
MUSICUS	Edition Musicus P.O. Box 1341 Stamford, CT 06904	
MUSIKAL.	Musikaliska Konstföreningen	NORDISKA
MUSIKHOJ	Musikhojskolens Forlag	BOONIN
MUSIKK	Musikk-Huset A/S	PETERS
MUSIKWISS.	Musikwissenschaftlicher Verlag	AMP BAREN.
NAGELS	Nagels Verlag	MAGNAMUSIC BOONIN
NATIONAL	National Music Publishers P.O. Box 868 Tustin, CA 92680	
NEUE	Verlag Neue Musik	BAREN.
NEW VALLEY	New Valley Music Press of Smith College Sage Hall 3 Northampton, MA 01060	
NIEUWE	De Nieuwe Musiekhandel	DONEMUS
NOORDHOFF	P. Noordhoff	DONEMUS
NORDISKA	AB Nordiska Musikförlaget	BROUDE, A MAGNAMUSIC
NORSK	Norsk Musikforlag A/S	MAGNAMUSIC
NORTON	W. W. Norton & Co., Inc. 500 Fifth Avenue New York, NY 10003	
NOSKE	A. A. Noske	DONEMUS
NOVELLO	Novello & Co., Ltd.	BIG BELL (Sales) BELWIN (Rental)
OLSCHKI	Casa Editrice, Leo S. Olschki Viuzzo Del Pozzetto Firenze Firenze, 50126, Italy	
ONGAKU	Ongaku-No-Tomo Sha Co., Ltd. Kagurazaka 6-30, Shinjuku-ku Tokyo, Japan	
OPUS	Opus Music Publishers, Inc. 612 N. Michigan Ave. Chicago, IL 60611	
OR-TAV	Or-Tav Music Publications P.O. Box 3200 Tel-Aviv, Israel	
ORGAN	Organ Music Co.	WESTERN
ORLANDO	Orlando-Musikverlag Kaprunerstrasse 1 D-8000 Munich 21 Germany	

Code	Publisher	Agent	Code	Publisher	Agent
OSTARA	Ostara Press, Inc.	WESTERN	RICHMOND	Richmond Music Press, Inc. P.O. Box 465 P.P. Sta. Richmond, IN 47374	
OSTER	Österreichischer Bundesverlag	AMP	RICORDI-ARG	Ricordi Americana S.A.	BELWIN
OUVRIERES	Les Editions Ouvrieres	GALAXY	RICORDI-ENG	G. Ricordi & Company, Ltd.	BELWIN
OXFORD	Oxford University Press 200 Madison Avenue New York, NY 10016		RICORDI-FR	Societe Anonyme des Editions Ricordi	BELWIN
PALLMA	Pallma Music Co.	KJOS	RIDEAU	Les Editions Rideau Rouge	ELKAN-V
PANTON	Panton	GENERAL	RIES	Ries & Erler	PETERS
PARAGON	Paragon Music Publishers 71 Fourth Avenue New York, NY 10003		ROBBINS	Robbins Music Corp.	BIG 3
			ROBERTON	Roberton Publications	SCHIRM. G
PARIS	Uitgeverij H.J. Paris	DONEMUS	ROCHESTER	Rochester Music Publishers, Inc. 358 Aldrich Road Fairport, NY 14450	
PARKS	Parks Music Corp.	KJOS			
PATERSON	Paterson's Publications, Ltd.	FISCHER, C	RODEHEAVER	Rodeheaver Publications	WORD
PAXTON	Paxton Publications	NOVELLO	RONGWEN	Rongwen Music, Inc.	BROUDE BR.
PEER	Peer-Southern Organization 1740 Broadway New York, NY 10019		ROSSUM	Wed. J. R. van Rossum	PETERS
			ROUART	Rouart-Lerolle & Cie	SALABERT-US
PELIKAN	Musikverlag Pelikan	BAREN.	ROYAL	Royal School of Church Music Addington Place Croydon, Surrey England	
PENN STATE	Pennsylvania State University Press 215 Wagner Building University Park, PA 16802				
PEPPER	J. & W. Pepper Co. P.O. Box 850 Valley Forge, PA 19482		ROZSAVO	Rozsavölgyi & Co.	DONEMUS
			RUBANK	Rubank, Inc. 16215 N.W. 15 Avenue Miami, FL 33169	
PETERS	C. F. Peters Corp. 373 Park Avenue South New York, NY 10016		SAC. MUS. PR.	Sacred Music Press of Hebrew Union College	PRESSER
PHILIPPO	Editions Philippo	ELKAN-V			
PILLIN	Pillin Music	WESTERN	SACRED	Sacred Music Press	LORENZ
PIONEER	Pioneer Music Press 975 SW Temple Street Salt Lake City, UT 84101		SACRED SNGS	Sacred Songs, Inc.	WORD
			SALABERT-FR	Francis Salabert Editions	SALABERT-US
PLENUM	Plenum Publishing Corp.	DA CAPO	SALABERT-US	Edition Salabert, Inc. 575 Madison Avenue New York, NY 10022	
PLYMOUTH	Plymouth Music Co., Inc. 17 West 60 Street New York, NY 10023		SAMFUNDET	Samfundet til udgivelse af dansk Musik	PETERS
POLSKIE	Polskie Wydawnictwo Muzyczne	BELWIN			
POLYPHON	Polyphon Musikverlag	GERIG	SANTIS	Edizioni de Santis Via Cassia 13 00191 Rome, Italy	
PORT. MUS.	Portugaliae Musicae	BAREN.			
PRESSER	Theodore Presser Co. Presser Place Bryn Mawr, PA 19010		SCHIRM. EC	E. C. Schirmer Music Co. 112 South Street Boston, MA 02111	
PRIMAVERA	Editions Primavera	GENERAL	SCHIRM. G	G. Schirmer, Inc. 866 Third Avenue New York, NY 10022	
PRO ART	Pro Art Publications, Inc. 469 Union Avenue Westbury, NY 11590				
			SCHMITT	Schmitt Music Centers 110 N. Fifth Street Minneapolis, MN 55403	
PROSVETNI	Prosvetni Servis	DRUSTVO			
PROWSE	Keith Prowse Music Publishing Co.	EMI	SCHOLA	Editions Musicales de la Schola Cantorium Paris	PRESSER
PRUETT	Pruett Pub. Co. P.O. Box 1560 Boulder, CO 80302		SCHOTT	Schott & Co., Ltd.	BELWIN
			SCHOTT-FRER	Schott Frères	BELWIN
REGENT	Regent Music Corp.	BIG BELL	SCHOTTS	B. Schotts Söhne	BELWIN
REN	Les Editions Renaissantes	BOONIN	SCHUBERTH	Edward Schuberth & Co., Inc.	ASHLEY

Code	Publisher	Agent
SCHWANN	Musikverlag Schwann	PETERS
SCHWEIZER.	Schweizerischen Kirchengesangsbundes	HANSSLER
SCOTT	G. Scott Music Publishing Co.	WESTERN
SCREEN	Screen Gems-Columbia Publications 16333 N.W. 54th Ave. Miami, FL 33014	
SEESAW	Seesaw Music Corporation 177 East 87 Street New York, NY 10028	
SENART	Ed. Maurice Senart	SALABERT-US
SESAC	Sesac, Inc. 10 Columbus Circle New York, NY 10019	
SHAPIRO	Shapiro, Bernstein & Co.	PLYMOUTH
SHATTINGER	Shattinger Music Co. 252 Paul Brown Bldg. St. Louis, MO 63101	
SHAWNEE	Shawnee Press Delaware Water Gap, PA 18327	
SHEPPARD	John Sheppard Music Press	BOONIN
SIDEMTON	Sidemton-Verlag	GERIG
SIFLER	Paul J. Sifler	FREDONIA
SIKORSKI	Hans Sikorski Verlag	BELWIN
SIMROCK	N. Simrock, A. Benjamin, D. Rahter	AMP
SINGSPIR	Singspiration Music The Zondervan Corp. 1415 Lake Dr. S.E. Grand Rapids, MI 49506	
SIRIUS	Sirius-Verlag	PETERS
SKAND.	Skandinavisk Musikforlag	MAGNAMUSIC
SLOV. AKA.	Slovenska akademija znanosti in umetnosti	DRUSTVO
SLOV. HUD. FOND.	Slovensky Hudobny Fond Gorkeho 19 Bratislava, Czechoslovakia	
SLOV. MAT.	Slovenska Matica	DRUSTVO
SOMERSET	Somerset Press	HOPE
SOUTHERN	Southern Music Co. 1100 Broadway San Antonio, TX 78292	
SPIRE	Spire Editions	FISCHER, C WORLD
SPRATT	Spratt Music Company	PLYMOUTH
ST. GREG.	St. Gregory Publishing Co. 4 West Hill Road Hoddesdon, Hertfordshire England	
ST. MARTIN	St. Martin Music Co., Inc.	ROYAL
STAFF	Staff Music Publishing Co., Inc.	PLYMOUTH
STAINER	Stainer & Bell, Ltd.	GALAXY
STANDARD	Standard Music Publishing, Inc. P.O. Box 1043 Whitman Square Turnersville, NJ 08012	

Code	Publisher	Agent
STEIN	Edition Steingräber Offenbach/M. 62 Wiesbaden, Postfach 471 Germany	
STUDIO	Studio Publications 224 S. Lebanon St. Lebanon, IN 46052	
SUMMY	Summy-Birchard Co. 1834 Ridge Avenue Evanston, IL 60204	
SUPRAPHON	Editio Supraphon	BOOSEY
THOMP.	Thompson Music House P.O. Box 12463 Nashville, TN 37212	
THOMP. G	Gordon V. Thompson, Ltd. 29 Birch Avenue Toronto, Ontario Canada	
TIEROLFF	Tierolff Muziek Centrale Markt 90-92 Roosendaal, Netherlands	
TONGER	P. J. Tonger, Musikverlag	PETERS
TONOS	Edition Tonos Ahastrasse 7 6100 Darmstadt, Germany	
TOORTS	Uit. De Toorts	DONEMUS
TRANSAT.	Editions Transatlantiques	PRESSER
TRANSCON.	Transcontinental Music Publications 1674 Broadway New York, NY 10019	
TRIGON	Trigon Music Inc.	TRIUNE
TRIUNE	Triune Music Inc. 1710 Hayes Street Nashville, TN 37203	
TRO	Tro Songways Service, Inc.	PLYMOUTH
TUSKEGEE	Tuskegee Music Institute Press	KJOS
UNION ESP.	Union Musical Espanola	AMP
UNITED ART	United Artists Group	BIG 3
UNIV. MUS. ED.	University Music Editions P.O. Box 192—Ft. George Station New York, NY 10040	
UNIV. CAL	University of California Press 2223 Fulton Street Berkeley, CA 94720	
UNIV. CH	University of Chicago Press 5801 S. Ellis Avenue Chicago, IL 60637	
UNIV. NC	University of North Carolina Press Box 2288 Chapel Hill, NC 27514	
UNIVER.	Universal Edition	BOONIN
UP WITH	Up With People Music	LORENZ
VALANDO	Valando Music, Inc.	PLYMOUTH
VANGUARD	Vanguard Music Corp. 250 W. 57th St. New York, NY 10019	
VIEWEG	Chr. Friedrich Vieweg	PETERS
VOLK	Arno Volk Verlag	GERIG

Code	Publisher	Agent
VOLKWEIN	Volkwein Brothers, Inc. 117 Sandusky Street Pittsburgh, PA 15212	
WAGENAAR	J. A. H. Wagenaar	ELKAN, H
WALTON	Walton Music Corp.	PLYMOUTH
WARNER	Warner Brothers Publications, Inc. 265 Secaucus Rd. Secaucus, NJ 07094	
WATERLOO	Waterloo Music Co., Ltd.	AMP
WEINBERGER	Josef Weinberger, Ltd.	BOOSEY
WESTERN	Western International Music 2859 Holt Avenue Los Angeles, CA 90034	
WESTWOOD	Westwood Press	WORLD
WHITE HARV.	White Harvest Publications Box 87 Stewartsville, MO 64490	
WHITE, ERN	Ernest White Editions 755 Clinton Ave. Bridgeport, CT 06604	
WILHELM.	Wilhelmiana Musikverlag	MAGNAMUSIC

Code	Publisher	Agent
WILLIS	Willis Music Company 7380 Industrial Highway Florence, KY 41042	
WILLSHIRE	Willshire Press Music Foundation, Inc.	WESTERN
WINGERT	Wingert-Jones Music, Inc. 2026 Broadway Box 1878 Kansas City, MO 64141	
WOLF	Wolf-Mills Music	WESTERN
WORD	Word, Incorporated 4800 W. Waco Drive Waco, TX 76703	
WORLD	World Library Publications, Inc. 2145 Central Parkway Cincinnati, OH 45214	
YAHRES	Yahres Publications 1315 Vance Ave. Coreopolis, PA 15108	
YORKE	Yorke Edition	GALAXY
ZANIBON	G. Zanibon Edition Company	PETERS
ZENEM.	Zenemükiado Vallalat	GENERAL
ZENGERINK	Herman Zengerink, Amsterdam	PETERS
ZERBONI	Suvini Zerboni	BELWIN
ZIMMER.	Wilhelm Zimmermann, Musikverlag	PETERS

Publishers' Advertisements

Quality Music and Supplies

CONTEMPORARY COMPOSERS
REPRESENTED IN OUR
CATALOG

Gerald Bales

John Ness Beck

Bruce Bednarchuk

Curt Blake

David Blakeley

Charles Boody

George Brandon

Herbert Brokering

Bob Burroughs

Eugene Butler

J. Bert Carlson

John Carter	Peter Wm. Holbrook	Robert Powell
Larry Christiansen	David N. Johnson	Richard Proulx
Paul J. Christiansen	Mark Johnson	Richard Purvis
Garry Cornell	Robert Karlén	Jeffrey Rickard
Katherine K. Davis	Robert Leaf	Leland B. Sateren
Walter Ehret	Austin C. Lovelace	Mark Sedio
Dorothy Elder	Katherine Lyon	Natalie Sleeth
Robert Elmore	Don McAfee	Camil Van Hulse
John Erickson	Michael McCabe	A. P. Van Iderstine
Paul Fetler	Allan Mahnke	Douglas E. Wagner
Richard Frey	Jane Marshall	Robert Wetzler
Arthur Goetze	Harold Owen	David H. Williams
Robert Graham	Stephen Paulus	Dale Wood
Raymond Haan	Walter Pelz	Linda Wood

AMSI

ART MASTERS STUDIOS INC. Phone (612) 822-2551
2614 Nicollet Avenue, Minneapolis, Minnesota 55408

Musical Highlights from Singspiration

God's Love Gift (SATB)
by Harold De Cou, 4369
Christ Is Born
by John W. Peterson, 4451
Last Week, The (SATB)
by John W. Peterson, 5884
Happiness (SATB)
by Bob Krogstad and
David Kirschke, 4366
There'll Always Be a Christmas
(SATB) by John M. Rasley, 4291
I Love America
by John W. Peterson and
Don Wyrtzen, 4385
Rock On The Head (SA)
by Don Wyrtzen, 4365
Miracle, The (SATB)
by Paul Mickelson, 4312
Glory To The Lamb (SATB)
by Norman Johnson, 4269

Singspiration MUSIC

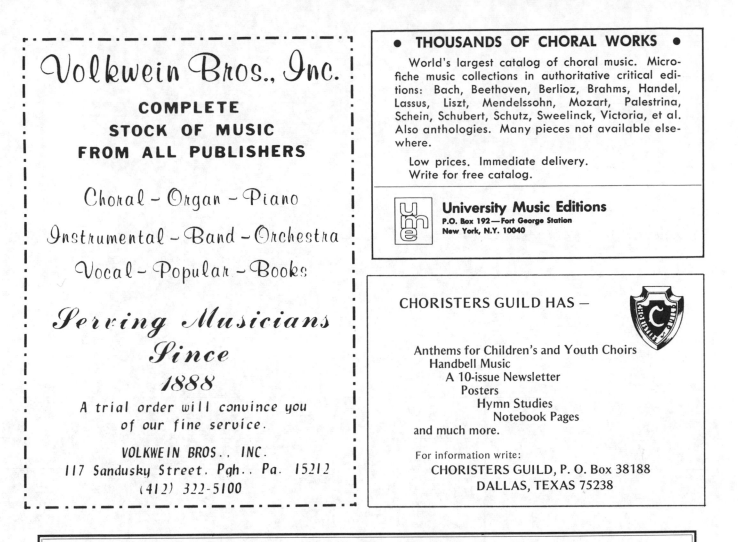